OTHER PMIC TITLES OF INTEREST

CODING AND REIMBURSEMENT

Codelink® Guides to CPT and ICD-9-CM Code Linkages
Collections Made Easy!
CPT Coders Choice®, Thumb Indexed
CPT TimeSaver®, Ring Binder, Tab Indexed
CPT & HCPCS Coding Made Easy!
E/M Coding Made Easy!
4-in-1 Master Coder
HCPCS Coders Choice®, Color Coded, Thumb Indexed
Health Insurance Carrier Directory
ICD-9-CM, Coders Choice®, Thumb Indexed
ICD-9-CM, TimeSaver®, Ring Binder, Tab Indexed
ICD-9-CM Coding For Physicians Offices
ICD-9-CM Coding Made Easy!
Medicare Rules & Regulations
Medical Fees Guide
Reimbursement Manual for the Medical Office
Working with Insurance and Managed Care Plans

PRACTICE MANAGEMENT

365 Ways to Manage the Business Called Private Practice
Achieving Profitability with a Medical Office System
Choosing and Using a Medical Office Computer
Computerizing Your Medical Office
Designing and Building Your Professional Office
Doctor Business
Encyclopedia of Practice and Financial Management
Getting Paid for What You Do
Health Information Management
Managing Medical Office Personnel
Managing the Physician's Office Laboratory
Marketing Strategies for Physicians
Medical Marketing Handbook
Medical Practice Handbook
Medical Software, Systems & Services Directory
Medical Staff Privileges
Negotiating Managed Care Contracts
New Practice Handbook
Patient Satisfaction
Patients Build Your Practice
Physician's Office Laboratory
Professional and Practice Development
Promoting Your Medical Practice
Starting in Medical Practice

**AVAILABLE FROM YOUR LOCAL MEDICAL
BOOKSTORE OR CALL 1-800-MED-SHOP
INTERNET ORDERS:** *http://medicalbookstore.com*

OTHER PMIC TITLES OF INTEREST

FINANCIAL MANAGEMENT

Accounts Receivable Management for the Medical Practice
Business Ventures for Physicians
Financial Planning Workbook for Physicians
Financial Valuation of Your Practice
Pension Plan Strategies
Physician Financial Planning in a Changing Environment
Securing Your Assets
Selling or Buying a Medical Practice

RISK MANAGEMENT

Behavioral Types and the Art of Patient Management
Law, Liability and Ethics for Medical Office Personnel
Malpractice Depositions
Malpractice: Managing Your Defense
Medical Malpractice: A Physician's Guide
Medical Risk Management
Testifying in Court

DICTIONARIES AND OTHER REFERENCE

Drug Interactions Index
Health and Medicine on the Internet
Medical Acronyms, Eponyms and Abbreviations
Medical Phrase Index
Medical Word Building
Medico-Legal Glossary
Medico Mnemonica
Spanish/English Handbook for Medical Professionals

MEDICAL REFERENCE AND CLINICAL

Anesthesiology: Problems in Primary Care
Cardiology: Problems in Primary Care
Drugs of Abuse
Gastroenterology: Problems in Primary Care
Medical Care of the Adolescent Athlete
Medical Procedures for Referral
Neurology: Problems in Primary Care
Orthopaedics: Problems in Primary Care
Patient Care Emergency Handbook
Patient Care Flowchart Manual
Patient Care Procedures for Your Practice
Pulmonary Medicine: Problems in Primary Care
Questions & Answers on AIDS
Sexually Transmitted Diseases
Urology: Problems in Primary Care

ICD·9·CM

MILLENNIUM EDITION

International Classification of Diseases
9th Revision

Clinical Modification
Sixth Edition

Color Coded
2001

Volumes 1 & 2

ISBN 1-57066-176-6 (Soft cover)
ISBN 1-57066-179-0 (Hard cover)

Volumes 1, 2, & 3

ISBN 1-57066-177-4 (Soft cover)
ISBN 1-57066-178-2 (Timesaver Binder)

Non-indexed versions

ISBN 1-57066-181-2 (Volumes 1 & 2)
ISBN 1-57066-182-0 (Volumes 1, 2, & 3)

Practice Management Information Corporation [PMIC]
4727 Wilshire Boulevard, Suite 300
Los Angeles, California 90010
1-800-MED-SHOP
http://www.medicalbookstore.com

Printed in the United States of America

Preface

Health care professionals have long used coding systems to describe procedures, services, and supplies. However, most described the reason for the procedure, service or supply with a diagnostic statement. Of those health care professionals who do code the diagnosis, either due to a requirement for a computer billing system and/or electronic claims filing, many do not code completely or accurately. With the passage of the Medicare Catastrophic Coverage Act of 1988, diagnostic coding using *ICD-9-CM* became mandatory for Medicare claims. In the area of health care reimbursement rules and regulations, the typical progression is that changes required for Medicare are followed shortly by similar changes for Medicaid and private insurance carriers.

To some professionals, the requirement to use diagnostic coding may have seemed like a burden or simply another excuse for Medicare intermediaries to delay or deny payment. However, it is important to understand that the proper use of coding systems for both procedures and diagnoses gives the professional absolute control over his or her billing and reimbursement. Accurate diagnosis coding is not easy. It requires a good working knowledge of medical terminology and a fundamental understanding of *ICD-9-CM*. In addition, the coder must know the rules and regulations required to comply with Medicare requirements for coding.

This edition of the *International Classification of Diseases, 9th Revision, Clinical Modification (ICD-9-CM)* is published by Practice Management Information Corporation in recognition of its responsibility to promulgate this classification throughout the United States for morbidity coding and billing purposes. The *International Classification of Diseases, 9th Revision*, originally published by the World Health Organization (WHO) is the foundation of the *ICD-9-CM* and continues to be the classification employed in cause-of-death coding in the United States.

The *ICD-9-CM* is recommended for use in all clinical settings, but is required for reporting diagnoses and diseases to all U.S. Public Health Service and Health Care Financing Administration programs. This version faithfully follows and contains the same information found in the U.S. Public Health Service and Health Care Financing Administration version of the *ICD-9-CM*.

All official authorized addenda effective October 1, 2000 have been included in this edition. A new revision will be available approximately September 15th of each year. Revised editions may be purchased from:

Practice Management Information Corporation
4727 Wilshire Boulevard, Suite 300
Los Angeles, California 90010
1-800-MED-SHOP

Or by contacting our web site at http://www.medicalbookstore.com.

Disclaimer

This publication is identical in content to U.S. Department of Health and Human Services Publication No. (PHS) 91-1260 with the exception that this publication includes special symbols to indicate additions and revisions from the previous edition and special symbols to facilitate identification of diagnostic codes that require 4th or 5th digit specificity, the use of color coding to alert the user to special coding considerations, and thumb indexing to make locating codes easier. This publication is revised annually so that we may present the most current information possible. Though all of the information is carefully researched and checked for accuracy and completeness, the publisher accepts no responsibility with regard to errors, omissions, misuse or misinterpretation.

Table of Contents

Table of Contents

Table of Contents

Table of Contents

(1) These listings appear only in the three volume edition

Introduction to ICD-9-CM

ICD-9-CM is an acronym for *International Classification of Diseases, 9th Revision, Clinical Modification*, published under different names since 1900. *ICD-9-CM* is a statistical classification system that arranges diseases and injuries into groups according to established criteria. Most *ICD-9-CM* codes are numeric and consist of three, four or five numbers and a description. The codes are revised approximately every 10 years by the World Health Organization and annual updates are published by HCFA.

HISTORICAL PERSPECTIVE

The *International Classification of Diseases, 9th Revision, Clinical Modification (ICD-9-CM)* is based on the official version of the *World Health Organization's (WHO) 9th Revision, International Classification of Diseases (ICD-9)*. *ICD-9* is designed for the classification of morbidity and mortality information for statistical purposes, and for the indexing of medical records by disease and operations, and for data storage and retrieval. *ICD-9-CM* replaced the Eighth Revision International Classification of Diseases, Adapted for Use in the United States commonly referred to as *ICDA*.

The concept of extending the International Classification of Diseases for use in hospital indexing was originally developed in response to a need for a more efficient basis for storage and retrieval of diagnostic data. In 1950, the U.S. Public Health Service and the Veterans Administration began independent tests of the International Classification of Diseases for hospital indexing purposes. In the following year, the Columbia Presbyterian Medical Center in New York City adopted the International Classification of Diseases, 6th Revision for use in its medical record department. A few years later, the Commission on Professional and Hospital Activities adopted the International Classification of Diseases for use in hospitals participating in the Professional Activity Study (PAS).

In view of the growing interest in the use of the International Classification of Diseases for hospital indexing, a study was undertaken in 1956 by the American Medical Association and the American Medical Record Association of the relative efficiencies of coding systems for diagnostic indexing. Following this study, the major uses of the International Classification of Diseases for hospital indexing purposes consolidated their experiences and an adaptation was published in December 1959. A revision containing the first "Classification of Operations and Treatments" was published in 1962.

In 1968, following a study by the American Hospital Association, the United States Public Health Service published the Eighth Revision International Classification of Diseases, Adapted for Use in the United States. This publication became commonly known as ICDA, and served as the basis for coding diagnostic data for official morbidity and mortality statistics in the United States.

ICD-9-CM Background

In February 1977, a committee was convened by the National Center for Health Statistics to provide advice and counsel for the development of clinical modification of the ICD-9. The organizations represented on the committee included:

American Association of Health Data Systems
American Hospital Association
American Medical Record Association
Association for Health Records
Council on Clinical Classifications, sponsored by:

American Academy of Pediatrics
American College of Obstetricians and Gynecologists
American College of Physicians
American College of Surgeons
American Psychiatric Association

Commission on Professional and Hospital Activities
Health Care Financing Administration
WHO Center for Classification of Diseases

The resulting *ICD-9-CM* is a clinical modification of the *World Health Organization's International Classification of Diseases, 9th Revision (ICD-9)*. The term "clinical" is used to emphasize the modifications intent; namely, to serve as a useful tool in the area of classification of morbidity data for indexing of medical records, medical care review, ambulatory and other medical care programs, as well as for basic health statistics.

In use since January 1979, *ICD-9-CM* provides a diagnostic coding system that is more precise than those needed only for statistical groupings and trend analysis. Official addenda (updates) to *ICD-9-CM* are issued in October each year by the Health Care Financing Administration.

Use of ICD-9-CM Codes for Professional Billing

Until passage of the Medicare Catastrophic Coverage Act of 1988, health care professionals were not required to report *ICD-9-CM* codes when billing government or private insurance carriers for reimbursement. The exception to this requirement was for those health care professionals who filed insurance claims electronically and those who used "code driven" computer billing services or computer systems.

Most health care professionals simply included the text or description of the injury, illness, sign or symptom that was the reason for the encounter. Insurance carriers who used *ICD-9-CM* coding had to code the diagnostic statements prior to input into their computer systems for reimbursement processing.

A specific requirement of the Medicare Catastrophic Coverage Act of 1988 required health care professionals to include *ICD-9-CM* codes on their Medicare claim forms effective April 1, 1989. A two-month grace period, to June 1, 1989, was allowed at the request of the American Medical Association, to allow health care professionals additional time to develop the knowledge and systems necessary to implement the requirement.

TERMINOLOGY

There are terms used throughout this publication that are important for a proper understanding of *ICD-9-CM*. The following terms are defined specifically as they are used for *ICD-9-CM* with the knowledge that some terms may have other definitions and meanings.

acute	refers to the condition that is the primary reason for the current encounter.
addenda	official updates to *ICD-9-CM* published continuously since 1986, that become effective on October 1st of each year.
adverse	any response to a drug that is noxious and unintended and occurs with proper dosage.
aftercare	an encounter for something planned in advance, for example, cast removal.
AHFS	American Hospital Formulary Service.
alphabetic	the portion of *ICD-9-CM* that lists definitions and codes in alphabetic order. Also called Volume 2.
category	refers to diagnoses codes listed within a specific three-digit category, for example category 250, Diabetes Mellitus.
cause	that which brings about any condition or produces any effect.
chronic	continuing over a long period of time or recurring frequently.
coding	the process of transferring written or verbal descriptions of diseases, injuries and procedures into numerical designations.
combination	a code that combines a diagnosis with an associated secondary process or complication.
complication	the occurrence of two or more diseases in the same patient at the same time.
concurrent	when a patient is being treated by more than one provider for different care conditions at the same time.
conventions	refers to the use of certain abbreviations, punctuation, symbols, type faces, and other instructions that must be clearly understood in order to use *ICD-9-CM*.
CPT	Current Procedural Terminology. Listing of codes and descriptions for procedures, services and supplies published by the American Medical Association. Used to bill insurance carriers.
diagnosis	a written description of the reason(s) for the procedure, service, supply or encounter.
down coding	the process where insurance carriers reduce the value of a procedure, and the resulting reimbursement, due to either 1) a mismatch of CPT code and description or 2) ICD-9-CM code does not justify the procedure or level of service.
E codes	specific ICD-9-CM codes used to identify the cause of injury, poisoning and other adverse effects.
eponyms	medical procedures or conditions named after a person or a place.
etiology	the cause(s) or origin of a disease.
HCFA	Health Care Financing Administration. The government agency that administers the Medicare and Medicaid programs.

HCFA1500	Uniform Health Insurance Claim Form used for billing services to Medicare and other insurance carriers.
hierarchy	a system that ranks items one above another.
ICD-9-CM	International Classification of Diseases, 9th Revision, Clinical Modification.
ICD-10	International Classification of Diseases, 10th Revision
late effect	a residual effect (condition produced) after the acute phase of an illness or injury has ended.
main term	refers to listings in the Alphabetic Index appearing BOLDFACE type.
manifestation	characteristic signs or symptoms of an illness.
multiple	refers to the need to use more than one ICD-9-CM code to fully identify coding a condition.
primary code	the ICD-9-CM code that defines the main reason for the current encounter.
residual	the long-term condition(s) resulting from a previous acute illness or injury.
rule out	refers to a method used to indicate that a condition is probable, suspected, or questionable but unconfirmed. ICD-9-CM has no provisions for the use of this term.
secondary	code(s) listed after the primary code that further indicate the cause(s) codefor the current encounter or define the need for higher levels of care.
sections	refers to portions of the Tabular List that are organized in groups of three-digit code numbers. For example, Malignant Neoplasm of Lip, Oral Cavity and Pharynx (140-149).
sequencing	the process of listing ICD-9-CM codes in the proper order.
specificity	refers to the requirement to code to the highest number of digits possible, 3, 4 or 5, when choosing an ICD-9-CM code.
sub term	refers to listings appearing in the Alphabetic Index under MAIN TERMS and always indented two spaces to the right.
subcategories	refers to groupings of four-digit codes listed under three-digit categories.
tabular list	the portion of ICD-9-CM that lists codes and definitions in numeric order. Also referred to as Volume 1.
V codes	specific ICD-9-CM codes used to identify encounters for reasons other than illness or injury, for example, immunization.
Volume 1	see TABULAR LIST
Volume 2	see ALPHABETIC INDEX
Volume 3	procedure codes used only for hospital coding. Volume 3 contains both a numeric listing and alphabetic index.

FORMAT OF ICD-9-CM

The *International Classification of Diseases, 9th Revision, Clinical Modification* was originally published as a three volume set (2nd edition). Newer versions of ICD-9-CM, Sixth Edition, are available as two separate books (Volume 1 and Volume 2) and as a single book containing Volume 1 and Volume 2, or Volumes 1, 2 and 3 depending on the publisher. It is also now available on CD-ROM from the U.S. Government.

The Third Edition of ICD-9-CM includes all official addenda from October 1986 through October 1988. The Fourth Edition of ICD-9-CM includes all official addenda from October 1986 through October 1994. The Fifth Edition of ICD-9-CM includes all official addenda from October 1986 through October 1998.

The Tabular List (Volume 1)

The Tabular List (Volume 1) is a <u>numeric</u> listing of diagnosis codes and descriptions consisting of 17 chapters that classify diseases and injuries, two sections containing supplementary codes (V codes and E codes) and six appendices.

Classification of Diseases and Injuries

The Classification of Diseases and Injuries includes the following 17 chapters:

Chapter 1	Infectious and Parasitic Diseases (001-139)
Chapter 2	Neoplasms (140-239)
Chapter 3	Endocrine, Nutritional and Metabolic Diseases, and Immunity Disorders (240-279)
Chapter 4	Diseases of the Blood and Blood-Forming Organs (280-289)
Chapter 5	Mental Disorders (290-319)
Chapter 6	Diseases of the Nervous System and Sense Organs
Chapter 7	Diseases of the Circulatory System (390-459)
Chapter 8	Diseases of the Respiratory System (460-519)
Chapter 9	Diseases of the Digestive System (520-579)
Chapter 10	Diseases of the Genitourinary System (580-629)
Chapter 11	Complications of Pregnancy, Childbirth, and the Puerperium (630-676)
Chapter 12	Diseases of the Skin and Subcutaneous Tissue (680-709)
Chapter 13	Diseases of the Musculoskeletal System and Connective Tissue (710-739)
Chapter 14	Congenital Anomalies (740-759)
Chapter 15	Certain Conditions Originating in the Perinatal Period (760-779)
Chapter 16	Symptoms, Signs and Ill-defined Conditions (780-799)
Chapter 17	Injury and Poisoning (800-999)

Each chapter of the Tabular List (Volume 1) is structured into four components; namely:

Sections: groups of three-digit code numbers

Categories: three-digit code numbers

Subcategories: four-digit code numbers

Fifth-Digit Subclassifications: five-digit code numbers

Supplementary Classifications

There are two supplementary classifications included in the Tabular List (Volume 1). These are:

V Codes   Supplementary Classification of Factors Influencing Health Status and Contact with Health Services (V01-V82)

E Codes   Supplementary Classification of External Causes of Injury and Poisoning (E800-E999)

Appendices

The Tabular List (Volume 1) includes six appendices. These are:

Appendix 1   Morphology of Neoplasms

Appendix 2   Glossary of Mental Disorders

Appendix 3   Classification of Drugs by American Hospital Formulary Service List Number and their ICD-9-CM Equivalents

Appendix 4   Classification of Industrial Accidents According to Agency

Appendix 5   List of Three-Digit Categories

Appendix 6   Supplementary Classification of External Causes of Injury and Poisoning (E codes)

Specifications for the Tabular List

1. Three-digit rubrics and their contents are unchanged from *ICD-9*.

2. The sequence of three-digit rubrics is unchanged from *ICD-9*.

3. Three-digit rubrics are not added to the main body of the classification.

4. Unsubdivided three-digit rubrics are subdivided where necessary to:

    a) Add clinical detail

    b) Isolate terms for clinical accuracy

5. The modification in *ICD-9-CM* is accomplished by the addition of a fifth digit to existing *ICD-9* rubrics, except as noted under #7 below.

6. Four-digit rubrics are added to subdivided three-digit codes only when there is no other means of achieving desired detail. These codes, unique to *ICD-9-CM* (28 three-digit categories) are marked with the symbol in the Tabular List.

7. The optional dual classification in *ICD-9* is modified.

    a) Duplicate rubrics are deleted:

        1) Four-digit manifestation categories duplicating etiology entries.

        2) Manifestation inclusion terms duplicating etiology entries.

    b) Manifestations of diseases are identified, to the extent possible, by creating five digit codes in the etiology rubrics.

    c) When the manifestation of a disease cannot be included in the etiology rubrics, provision for its identification is made by retaining the *ICD-9* rubrics used for classifying manifestations of disease.

8. The format of *ICD-9-CM* is revised from that used in *ICD-9*.

    a) American spelling of medical terms is used.

    b) Inclusion terms are indented beneath the titles of codes.

    c) Codes not to be used for primary tabulation of disease are printed in italics with the notation, "code also underlying disease."

The Alphabetical Index (Volume 2)

The Alphabetic Index (Volume 2) of ICD-9-CM consists of an alphabetic list of terms and codes, two supplementary Sections following the alphabetic listing, plus two special tables found within the alphabetic listing. The Alphabetic Index (Volume 2) is structured as follows:

MAIN TERMS: appear in **BOLDFACE** type

SUBTERMS: are always indented two spaces to the right under main terms

CARRY-OVER   are always indented more than two spaces from the level of the
LINES: preceding line

Supplementary Sections

The supplementary sections following the Alphabetic Index are:

TABLE OF DRUGS AND CHEMICALS

This table contains a classification of drugs and other chemical substances to identify poisoning states and external causes of adverse effects.

INDEX TO EXTERNAL CAUSES OF INJURIES & POISONINGS (E-CODES)

This section contains the index to the codes that classify environmental events, circumstances, and other conditions as the cause of injury and other adverse effects.

Special Tables

The two special tables, located within the Alphabetic Index, and found under the main terms as underlined below, are:

HYPERTENSION TABLE

NEOPLASM TABLE

Specifications for the Alphabetic Index

1.   Format of the Alphabetic Index follows the format of the *ICD-9*.

2.   Main terms in the Alphabetic Index are printed in bold face type.

3.   When two codes are required to indicate etiology and manifestation, the optional manifestation code appears in brackets, e.g., diabetic cataract 250.5 *[366.41]*.

Procedures: Tabular List and Alphabetic Index (Volume 3)

Volume 3 consists of two sections, a tabular list of codes and an alphabetic index. These codes define procedures instead of diagnoses. Frequently used incorrectly by health care professionals, codes from Volume 3 are intended only for use by hospitals. The Fourth Edition of ICD-9-CM printed by the U.S. Government Printing Office did not include Volume 3. The Fifth Edition of ICD-9-CM issued by the U.S. Government included Volume 3 on a CD-ROM.

The ICD-9-CM Procedure Classification is a modification of WHO's "Fascicle V, Surgical Procedures," and is published as Volume 3 of ICD-9-CM. It contains both a Tabular List and an Alphabetic Index. Greater detail has been added to the ICD-9-CM Procedure Classification necessitating expansion of the codes from three to four digits. Approximately 90% of the rubrics refer to surgical procedures with the remaining 10% accounting for other investigative and therapeutic procedures.

Tabular List of Procedures

The Tabular List includes 16 chapters containing codes and descriptions for surgical procedures and miscellaneous diagnostic and therapeutic procedures.

Alphabetic Index to Procedures

The Alphabetic Index provides an alphabetic index to the Tabular List of Volume 3

Specifications for the Procedure Classification

1. The *ICD-9-CM* Procedure Classification is published in its own volume containing both a Tabular List and an Alphabetic Index.

2. The classification is a modification of Fascicle V "Surgical Procedures" of the *ICD-9* Classification of Procedures in Medicine, working from the draft dated Geneva, 30 September-6 October 1975, and labeled WHO/ICD-9/Rev. Conf. 75.4.

3. All three-digit rubrics in the range 01-86 are maintained as they appear in Fascicle V, whenever feasible.

4. Nonsurgical procedures are segregated from the surgical procedures and confined to the rubrics 87-99, whenever feasible.

5. Selected detail contained in the remaining fascicles of the *ICD-9 Classification of Procedures in Medicine* is accommodated where possible.

6. The structure of the classification is based on anatomy rather than surgical specialty.

7. The *ICD-9-CM* Procedure Classification is numeric only, i.e., no alphabetic characters are used.

8. The classification is based on a two-digit structure with two decimal digits where necessary.

9. Compatibility with the *ICD-9 Classification of Procedures in Medicine* was not maintained when a different axis was deemed more clinically appropriate.

CONVENTIONS USED IN THE TABULAR LIST

The ICD-9-CM Tabular List (Volume 1) makes use of certain abbreviations, punctuation, symbols, and other conventions that must be clearly understood. The purpose of these conventions is to first, provide special coding instructions, and second, to conserve space.

Abbreviations

NOS   Not Otherwise Specified. Equivalent to Unspecified. This abbreviation refers to a lack of sufficient detail in the statement of diagnosis to be able to assign it to a more specific sub division within the classification.

NEC   Not Elsewhere Classified. Used with ill-defined terms to alert the coder that a specified form of the condition is classified differently. The category number for the term including NEC is to be used only when the coder lacks the information necessary to code the term to a more specific category.

Punctuation

( )   PARENTHESIS are used to enclose supplementary words that may be present or absent in a statement of disease without effecting the code assignment.

[ ]   SQUARE BRACKETS are used to enclose synonyms, alternate wordings or explanatory phrases.

:   COLONS are used after an incomplete phrase or term that requires one or more of the modifiers indented under it to make it assignable to a given category. EXCEPTION to this rule pertains to the abbreviation NOS.

{ }   BRACES are used to connect a series of terms to a common stem. Each term on the left of the brace is incomplete and must be completed by a term to the right of the brace.

Symbols

●   A filled BLACK CIRCLE preceding a code indicates that the code is new to this revision of *ICD-9-CM*. A symbol key appears on all left-hand pages of the Tabular List, Volume 1.

▲   A filled BLACK TRIANGLE preceding a code indicates that there is a revision to the text or notes of an existing code. A symbol key appears on all left-hand pages of the Tabular List, Volume 1.

④ ⑤   A circle containing the number 4 or the number 5 preceding a code indicates that a fourth or fifth digit is required for coding to the highest level of specificity. Valid digits are in [brackets] under each code. Definitions of valid fifth digits are found under the major category.

Other conventions

Type Face:

BOLD: Bold type face is used for all codes and titles in the Tabular List.

Italics: Italicized type face is used for all exclusion notes and to identify those rubrics that are not to be used for primary tabulations of disease.

Format: *ICD-9-CM* uses an indented format for ease in reference.

Instructional Notations

Instructional terms define what is, or what is not, included in a given subdivision. This is accomplished by using both inclusion and exclusion terms.

INCLUDES:

Indicates separate terms, such as, modifying adjectives, sites and conditions, entered under a subdivision, such as a category, to further define or give examples of, the content of the category.

Excludes:

Exclusion terms are enclosed in a box and are printed in italics to draw attention to their presence. The importance of this instructional term is its use as a guideline to direct the coder to the proper code assignment. In other words, all terms following the word EXCLUDES: are to be coded elsewhere as indicated in each instance.

NOTES

These are used to define terms and give coding instructions. Often used to list the fifth-digit subclassifications for certain categories.

SEE

Acts as a cross reference and, is an explicit direction to look elsewhere. This instructional term must always be followed. (Cross references provide the user with other possible modifiers for a term, or, its synonyms.)

SEE CATEGORY

A variation of the instructional term SEE. This refers the coder to a specific category. You must *always* follow this instructional term.

SEE ALSO

A direction given to look elsewhere if the main term or subterm(s) are not sufficient to code the information you have.

CODE FIRST

This instructional note is used for those codes not intended to be used as a principal diagnosis, or not to be sequenced before the underlying disease. The note requires that the underlying disease (etiology) be coded first with the code the note is applied to being coded second. This note appears only in the tabular list (Vol. 1).

USE ADDITIONAL CODE

This instruction is placed in the Tabular List in those categories where the coder may wish to add further information, by using an additional code, to give a more complete picture of the diagnosis or procedure.

Related terms

AND

Whenever this term appears in a title, it should be interpreted as "and/or."

WITH

When this term is used in a title it indicates a requirement that both parts of the title must be present in the diagnostic statement.

COLOR CODING

All PMIC versions of *ICD-9-CM* include color-coding to alert the user to special coding situations or conditions that require additional attention. The use of color-coding is found in the Tabular List of Volume 1 and the Tabular List of Volume 3. The color is applied as solid rectangular bars over the codes only so that the descriptions remain clear and legible. The color codes and definitions are printed at the bottom of all right-sided pages of Volume 1 and Volume 3.

Volume 1

Three digit codes. Coding to fourth or fifth digit specificity is required.

Unspecified code. Descriptions include the term "unspecified". Use only if a more specific diagnosis is not known or available.

Nonspecific code. Descriptions include the term "nonspecific, unspecified, other specified or other". A report *may* be required by insurance carriers.

Manifestation codes. Used only to code the manifestation of an underlying disease. Code the underlying disease first.

Medicare secondary payer (MSP) alert. Diagnoses that may trigger a post-payment review by Medicare. Medicare is usually the secondary payer for these diagnoses.

Volume 3[*]

Noncovered operating room procedure. An operating room procedure that is not covered by Medicare.

Non-operating room procedure. A procedure that is not performed in the operating room that affects DRG assignment.

Bilateral procedure.

Valid operating room procedure. Prompts a change in DRG assignment.

Nonspecific operating room procedure. Choose a more precise code if possible.

*These colors appear only in the three-volume edition

MEDICARE REQUIREMENTS FOR ICD-9-CM CODING

The Medicare Catastrophic Coverage Act of 1988 (PL 100-330) requires that health care professionals submit an appropriate diagnosis code, using the *International Classification of Diseases, 9th Revision, Clinical Modification (ICD-9-CM)* for each procedure, service, or supply billed under Medicare Part B.

To comply with the regulations, health care professionals must convert the reason(s) for the procedures, services or supplies, performed or issued, from written diagnostic statements that may include specific diagnoses, signs, symptoms and/or complaints, into ICD-9-CM diagnosis codes. The Health Care Financing Administration originally set the implementation date for this requirement as April 1, 1989, however, it was subsequently delayed until June 1, 1989, at the request of the American Medical Association, to give health care providers additional time to prepare for the change.

HCFA Guidelines for Using ICD-9-CM Codes

The Health Care Financing Administration (HCFA) has prepared guidelines for using ICD-9-CM codes and instructions on how to report them on claim forms. In addition, HCFA has directed your medicare intermediary to provide you with a written copy of these instructions. The basic HCFA guidelines are summarized below, however, it is very important that you obtain a copy of the guidelines from your Medicare intermediary as implementation of HCFA requirements varies from one intermediary to another.

1. Indicate on the claim form or itemized statement the appropriate code(s) from the ICD-9-CM code range 001.0 through V82.9 to identify diagnoses, symptoms, conditions, problems, complaints or other reason(s) for the procedure, service or supply provided.

    A. In choosing codes to describe the reason for the encounter, the health care professional will frequently be using codes within the range from 001.0 through 999.9, the section of ICD-9-CM for the classification of diseases and injuries (e.g. infectious and parasitic diseases; neoplasms; signs, symptoms and ill-defined conditions). Codes that describe symptoms as opposed to diagnoses are acceptable if this is the highest level of certainty documented by the physician.

    B. ICD-9-CM also provides codes to deal with visits for circumstances other than a disease or injury, such as an encounter for a laboratory test only. These codes are found in the V-code section and range from V01.0 through V82.9.

2. The ICD-9-CM code for the diagnosis, condition, problem, or other reason for the encounter documented in the medical record as the main reason for the procedure, service or supply provided should be listed first. Additional ICD-9-CM codes that describe any current coexisting conditions are then listed. Do not include codes for conditions that were previously treated and no longer exist.

3.   ICD-9-CM codes should be used at their highest level of specificity.

    A.   Assign three digit codes only if there are no four digit codes within the coding category.

    B.   Assign four digit codes only if there is no fifth digit subclassification for that category.

    C.   Assign the fifth digit subclassification code for those categories where it exists.

Claims submitted with three or four digit codes where four and five digit codes are available may be returned to you by the Medicare intermediary for proper coding. It is recognized that a very specific diagnosis may not be known at the time of the initial encounter. However, that is not an acceptable reason to submit a three digit code when four or five digits are available.

For example, if the patient has chronic bronchitis, ICD-9-CM code 491, and the physician has not yet documented whether the bronchitis is simple, mucopurulent, or obstructive, the code for unspecified chronic bronchitis, ICD-9-CM code 491.9, should be listed.

4.   Diagnoses documented as "probable," "suspected," "questionable," or "rule out" should not be coded as if the diagnosis is confirmed. The condition(s) should be coded to the highest degree of certainty for the encounter, such as describing symptoms, signs, abnormal test results, or other reasons for the encounter.

5.   Chronic disease(s) treated on an ongoing basis may be coded and reported as many times as the patient receives treatment and care for the condition(s).

6.   When patients receive ancillary diagnostic services only during an encounter, the appropriate "V code" for the service should be listed first, and the diagnosis or problem for which the diagnostic procedures are being performed should be listed second.

    A.   V codes will be used frequently by radiologists who perform radiological examinations on referrals. For example, ICD-9-CM code V72.5, Radiological examination, not elsewhere classified, describes the reason for the encounter and should be listed first on the claim form or statement. If the reason for the referral is known, a second ICD-9-CM code that describes the signs or symptoms for which the examination was ordered should be listed.

    B.   Failure to list a second ICD-9-CM code in addition to the V code may result in claim delays or denials. The ICD-9-CM code V72.5, Radio-logical examination, not elsewhere classified, includes referrals for routine chest x-rays that are not covered by the Medicare program. Medicare intermediaries may establish screening programs to verify that the referrals were not for routine chest x-rays.
By supplying a second ICD-9-CM code to describe the reason for the referral, these claims can be clearly identified by the Medicare intermediary as referrals to evaluate symptoms, signs or diagnoses. The mission of a second ICD-9-CM code may lead to requests for additional information from Medicare intermediaries prior to processing the claim.

7.   For patients receiving only ancillary therapeutic services during an encounter, list the appropriate V code first, followed by the ICD-9-CM code for the diagnosis or problem for which the services are being performed. For example, a patient with multiple sclerosis presenting for rehabilitation services would be coded using code V57.1, Other physical therapy, or code V57.89, Other care involving use of rehabilitation procedures, followed by code 340, multiple sclerosis.

8.   For surgical procedures, use the ICD-9-CM code for the diagnosis for which the surgery was performed. If the postoperative diagnosis is known to be different at the time the claim is filed, use the ICD-9-CM code for the post-operative diagnosis.

9.   Code all documented conditions that coexist at the time of the visit that require or affect patient care, treatment or management. Do not code conditions that were previously treated and no longer exist.

Completing the HCFA1500 Claim Form

Health care professionals using the Uniform Health Insurance Claim Form, HCFA1500, to file claims for services provided to Medicare beneficiaries must list a minimum of one ICD-9-CM code and may list up to four total ICD-9-CM codes on the claim form.

The ICD-9-CM code for the diagnosis, condition, problem or other reason for the encounter is listed first, followed by up to three additional codes that describe any coexisting conditions. At times, there may be several conditions that equally resulted in the encounter. In these cases, the health care professional is free to select the one that will be listed first.

The ICD-9-CM codes are listed in Box 23 of the "old" HCFA1500 (10/84) claim form and Box 21 of the "new" HCFA1500 (12/90) claim form (sce example). In addition, in Box 24 D of both versions of the form, you must indicate by a number from 1 to 4, or combination of numbers, which diagnoses from Box 23 support the procedure, service or supply listed in Box 24 C.

Due to space limitations on the claim form you may use only up to four ICD-9-CM codes for diagnoses, conditions, or signs and symptoms. Frequently the patient may have more than four conditions present at the time of the encounter, however, you must choose only four codes to be listed on the claim form.

If you strongly believe that additional diagnostic information is needed by the Medicare intermediary for proper claim processing you may attach additional supporting documentation to your manual claim. Keep in mind that in most cases the additional documentation will be ignored by the claims examiners, and, in other cases will result in reimbursement delay while someone reviews your documentation.

Medicare Penalties for Non-compliance

The Medicare Catastrophic Coverage Act of 1988 mandates submission of an appropriate ICD-9-CM diagnosis code or codes for each procedure, service, or supply furnished by the health care professional to Medicare Part B beneficiaries. The Act further specifies that compliance is mandatory and that penalties may be assessed for noncompliance.

The penalties for noncompliance differ depending upon whether or not the health care professional has agreed to accept assignment or not.

1.   For health care professionals who accept assignment on a Medicare claim and who fail to include ICD-9-CM codes as required will have their claim(s) returned for proper coding and may be subject to post-payment review by the Medicare intermediary, as well as payment denials.

2.   For health care professionals who do not accept assignment, the penalties are more severe.

   A.   If the original claim form does not include ICD-9-CM codes as required, and the health care professional refuses to provide the codes promptly on request to the Medicare intermediary, the professional may be subject to a civil monetary penalty in an amount not to exceed $2,000, per claim.

   B.   If the health care professional continuously fails to provide ICD-9-CM codes as requested, the professional may be subject to the sanction process described in section 1842 (j) (2) (A), that mandates that the professional may be barred from participation in the Medicare program for a period not to exceed five years.

CODING AND BILLING ISSUES

Diagnosis Codes Must Support Procedure Codes

Each service or procedure performed for a patient should be represented by a diagnosis that would substantiate those particular services or procedures as necessary in the investigation or treatment of their condition based on currently accepted standards of practice by the medical profession.

Place (Location) of Service

The actual setting that the services are rendered in for particular diagnoses plays an important part in reimbursement. Many people became accustomed to using Emergency Rooms for any type of illness or injury. By utilizing highly specialized places of service for conditions that were not true emergencies, third party payer were being billed with CPT codes indicating emergency services were rendered. Since the cost of services rendered on an emergency basis is considerably more expensive than those services in an non-emergency situation, third party payers began watching for those claims with diagnoses that did not indicate that a true emergency existed. Payment then was based on what the cost would have been had the patient been treated in the proper setting.

Level of Service Provided

The patient's condition and the treatment of that condition must be billed according to the criteria, as published by the AMA, for each level of service (i.e., minimal, brief, limited, intermediate, extended, comprehensive). Many practices bill the office visit level that they know will pay better rather than to consider the criteria that must be met to use a particular level of service. Again, the patient's diagnosis enters into this concept as well as it is often the diagnosis that indicates the complexity of the level of service to be used.

Frequency of Services

Many times claims are submitted for a patient with the same diagnosis and the same procedure(s) time after time. When the diagnosis indicates a chronic condition and the claims do not indicate any change in the patient's treatment or, give any indication that the patient's condition has been altered (i.e., exacerbated, other symptomology) the third party payer may deny payment based on the frequency of services for the reported condition.

Down Coding

Down coding is the process of reducing a code from one of a higher value to one of a lower value that results in lowered reimbursement. In the area of procedure coding, this process results in the loss of millions of dollars annually by health care professionals and their patients.

With procedure coding, down coding claims is easily resolved by either providing a procedure description that matches that of Current Procedural Terminology (CPT) exactly, or, even better, by eliminating all procedure descriptions from your claim forms, that forces the insurance carrier to allow full value for your procedure, service, or supply. With diagnosis coding, the issue is not mismatch of description to code, as the description is not required, but that the ICD-9-CM code(s) provide justification for the procedure, service or supply or the level of service provided.

A key point to remember is that if there are any current coexisting conditions that may complicate the treatment for the primary condition, it is very important to include the ICD-9-CM codes for the coexisting conditions that will help to justify the level of service provided.

Concurrent Care

Reimbursement problems often arise when a patient is being treated by different professionals, within the same billing entity (medical group or clinic), for different problems at the same time. This is known as concurrent care. For example, a patient may be hospitalized by a clinic's general surgeon for an operation and may also be seen while hospitalized by the group's cardiologist for an unrelated cardiac condition.

If you submit claims for daily hospital visits by both of the above professionals without explanation, most insurance carriers would reject one daily visit as an apparent "duplication" of service. Prior to publication of the 1992 edition of CPT, the key to obtaining proper reimbursement for concurrent care was first, to use the procedure modifier - 75, Concurrent Care, Services Rendered by More than One Physician, and second, to submit a different *ICD-9-CM* code for the services provided by each physician, that support and justify the need for those services.

Note that modifier -75 was deleted in the 1992 edition of CPT, therefore, when using the new CPT Evaluation and Management codes to bill Medicare, the *ICD-9-CM* code becomes the key factor for proper reimbursement of concurrent care.

ICD-10

Since 1948, the World Health Organization has revised the *International Classification of Diseases* approximately every 10 years, with a modified version appearing in the United States about one to three years following the WHO publication. Based on the regular schedule, *ICD-10* should have been released in 1987. However, due to difficulties in coordinating the international committees, the first volume of *ICD-10*, the Tabular List, was not published until June of 1992.

Implementation of ICD-10 in the United States

Prior to being implemented in the United States, *ICD-10* must be converted to "American" English and pass through a variety of private and government committees, agencies, associations and organizations. As of this printing, the official position of the Health Care Financing Administration (HCFA) is that *ICD-10* will not be mandated for Medicare claims until 2003 or later.

WHERE TO GET ANSWERS TO QUESTIONS ABOUT ICD-9-CM

Questions regarding the use and interpretation of the *International Classification of Diseases, 9th Revision, Clinical Modification* should be directed in writing to any of the organizations listed below.

Coding Advice/Central Office on ICD-9-CM
American Hospital Association
One North Franklin
Chicago, Illinois 60606

World Health Organization Collaborating Center
for Classification of Diseases in North America
National Center for Health Statistics
Department of Health and Human Services
6525 Belcrest Road
Hyattsville, Maryland 20782

Morbidity Classification Branch
National Center for Health Statistics
Department of Health and Human Services
6525 Belcrest Road, Room 1100
Hyattsville, Maryland 20782

Health Care Financing Administration (HCFA)
Division of Prospective Payment
Mail Stop C5-06-27
7500 Security Blvd.
Baltimore, MD 21244-1850

Comments, questions or suggestions regarding the PMIC version of *ICD-9-CM* should be directed in writing to:

Managing Editor
Practice Management Information Corporation
4727 Wilshire Boulevard, Suite 300
Los Angeles, California 90010
http://www.medicalbookstore.com

ICD-9-CM CODING FUNDAMENTALS

Learning and following the basic steps of coding will increase your chances of better and faster reimbursement from third party payers, as well as establish meaningful profiles for future reimbursement rates. To become a proficient coder, two basic principles always must be considered.

First, it is imperative that you use both the Alphabetic Index (Volume 2) and the Tabular List (Volume 1) when locating and assigning codes. Coding only from the Alphabetic Index will cause you to miss any additional information provided only in the Tabular List....such as, exclusions, instructions to use additional codes or the need for a fifth-digit.

Second, the level of specificity is important in all coding situations. A three-digit code that has subdivisions indicates you must use the appropriate subdivision code. Also, any time a fifth-digit subclassification is provided, you must use the fifth-digit code.

NINE STEPS FOR ACCURATE ICD-9-CM CODING

1. Locate the main term within the diagnostic statement.

2. Locate that main term in the Alphabetic Index (Volume 2). Keep in mind that the primary arrangement for main terms is by condition in the Alphabetic Index (Volume 2); main terms can be referred to in outmoded, ill-defined and lay terms as well as proper medical terms; main terms can be expressed in broad or specific terms, as nouns, adjectives or eponyms and can be with or without modifiers. Certain conditions may be listed under more than one main term.

3. Remember to refer to all notes under the main term. Be guided by the instructions in any notes appearing in a box immediately after the main term.

4. Examine any modifiers appearing in parentheses next to the main term. See if any of these modifiers apply to any of the qualifying terms used in the diagnostic statement.

5. Take note of the subterms indented beneath the main term. Subterms differ from main terms in that they provide greater specificity, becoming more specific the further they are indented to the right of the main term in 2-space increments; also, they provide the anatomical sites affected by the disease or injury.

6. Be sure to follow any cross reference instructions. These instructional terms ("see" or "see also") must be followed to locate the correct code.

7. Confirm the code selection in the Tabular List (Volume 1). make certain you have selected the appropriate classification in accordance with the diagnosis.

8. Follow instructional terms in the Tabular List (Volume 1). Watch for exclusion terms, notes and fifth-digit instructions that apply to the code number you are verifying. It is necessary to search not only the selected code number for instructions but also the category, section and chapter in which the code number is collapsible. Many times the instructional information is located one or more pages preceding the actual page you find the code number on.

9. Finally, assign the code number you have determined to be correct.

ITALICIZED ENTRIES

During the process of designating a code to identify a principal diagnosis it is important to remember that italicized entries or codes in slanted brackets cannot be used. In these instances, it is required that the etiology code be sequenced first and the manifestation code be listed second even if the physician recorded them in the opposite order.

OTHER AND UNSPECIFIED CODES

Subcategories for diagnoses listed as "Other" and "Unspecified" are referred to as residual subcategories. Remember, the subdivisions are arranged in a hierarchy starting with the more specific and ending with the least specific. In the Tabular List (Volume 1), in most instances, the four-digit subcategory ".8" has been reserved for "Other" specified conditions not classifiable elsewhere and the four-digit subcategory ".9" has been reserved for "Unspecified" conditions. Following is an example demonstrating this principle.

005 Other food poisoning (bacterial)

Excludes:	salmonella infections (003.0-003.9)
	toxic effect of:
	food contaminants (989.7)
	noxious foodstuffs (988-0-988.9)

005.0 Staphylococcal food poisoning
Staphylococcal toxemia specified as due to food

005.1 Botulism
Food poisoning due to Clostridium botulinum

005.2 Food poisoning due to Clostridium perfringens [C. welchii]
Enteritis necroticans

005.3 Food poisoning due to other Clostridia

005.4 Food poisoning due to Vibrio parahaemolyticus

005.8 Other bacterial food poisoning

Excludes: salmonella food poisoning (003.0-003.9)

005.81 Food poisoning due to Vibrio vulnificus

005.89 Other bacterial food poisoning
Food poisoning due to Bacillus cereus

005.9 Food poisoning, unspecified

As you look at Category 005, note that codes 005.0-005.4 indicate that the food poisoning is related to specific types of organisms. Therefore, subcategories 005.0-005.4 are regarded as more specific than subcategory 005.9. Fifth-digit subclassification 005.89 *Other bacterial food poisoning* would include other specific types of <u>bacterial</u> food poisoning not classified elsewhere, as well as <u>bacterial</u> food poisoning NOS. Whereas subcategory 005.9 *Food poisoning unspecified* would be used for a diagnostic statement of "Food poisoning NOS" where the causative organism is not mentioned.

The hierarchy from more specific to less specific is not consistently maintained at the fifth-digit level. The level of specificity at the fifth-digit level is usually (not always) indicated by the use of 0 and 9. The digit 9 identifies the entry for "Other specified" while the digit 0 identifies the "Unspecified" entry. Below is an example.

279 Disorders involving the immune mechanism

    279.0 Deficiency of humoral immunity

        279.00 Hypogammaglobulinemia, unspecified
                  Agammaglobulinemia NOS

        279.01 Selective IgA immunodeficiency

        279.02 Selective IgM immunodeficiency

        279.03 Other selective immunoglobulin deficiencies
                  Selective deficiency of IgG

        279.04 Congenital hypogammaglobulinemia
                  Agammaglobulinemia:
                      Bruton's type
                      X-linked

        279.05 Immunodeficiency with increased IgM
                  Immunodeficiency with hyper-IgM:
                      autosomal recessive
                      X-linked

        279.06 Common variable immunodeficiency
                  Dysgammaglobulinemia (acquired)
                      (congenital) (primary)
                  Hypogammaglobulinemia:
                      acquired primary
                      congenital non-sex-linked
                      sporadic

        279.09 Other
                  Transient hypogammaglobulinemia of infancy

Notice that the fifth-digit 0 identifies "Unspecified" and the fifth-digit 9 identifies "Other specified."

ACUTE AND CHRONIC CODING

Whenever a particular condition is described as both acute and chronic, code according to the subentries in the Alphabetic Index (Volume 2) for the stated condition. The following directions should be considered.

1.   If there are separate subentries listed for acute, subacute and chronic, then use both codes, sequencing the code for the acute condition first.

2.   If there are no subentries to identify acute, subacute or chronic, ignore these adjectives when selecting the code for the particular condition.

3.   If a certain condition is described as a subacute condition and the index does not provide a subentry designating subacute, then code the condition as if it were acute.

CODING SUSPECTED CONDITIONS

Whenever the diagnosis is stated as "questionable," "probable," "likely," or "rule out," it is advisable to code documented symptoms or complaints by the patient. The reason for this is that you do not want an insurance carrier to include a disease code in the patient's history if in fact the "suspected" condition is never proven.

Keep in mind that there are no "rule out" codes per se in the ICD-9-CM coding system. If your diagnostic statement is "Rule out Breast Carcinoma" and you use code 174.9 *Malignant neoplasm of female breast, unspecified*, the code definition does not state "rule out." Therefore, the insurance carrier processes the code 174.9 as is, which results in the patient having an insurance history of breast cancer.

To avoid what could become a problem for you and your patient (including the potential of litigation), you should use codes for signs and symptoms in these cases. For example, use code 611.72 *Lump or mass in breast*, or 611.71 *Mastodynia (breast pain)* if these symptoms exist and this is the highest degree of certainty you can code to.

If the patient is asymptomatic but there is a family history of breast cancer then you should consider using a V-code, such as V16.3 *Family history of malignant neoplasm, breast* as your diagnosis code. There are also V-codes to indicate screening for a particular illness or disease. In the above example, code V76.1 *Special screening for malignant neoplasm, breast* could also have been used.

It is important to note that when you use a screening code from the V-code section you should also code signs or symptoms. The reason for doing so is because most health insurance carriers do not provide coverage for routine screening procedures or preventive medicine.

COMBINATION CODES

A combination code is used to fully identify an instance where two diagnoses or a diagnosis with an associated secondary process (manifestation) or complication is included in the description of a single code number. These combination codes are identified by referring to the subterms in the Alphabetic Index (Volume 2) and the inclusion and exclusion terms in the Tabular List (Volume 1).

Examples of commonly used combination codes include 034.0 *Streptococcal sore throat* and 404 *Hypertensive heart and renal disease*. Code 034.0 exists because the throat is often infected with Streptococcus and code 404 must be used whenever a patient has both heart and renal disease instead of assigning codes from categories 402 and 403.

Two main terms may be joined together by combination terms listed in the Alphabetic Index (Volume 2) as subterms such as:

associated with   *in*
complicated (by)   *secondary to*
due to   *with*
during   *without*
following

The listing for the above terms advises the coder to use one or two codes depending on the condition.

MULTIPLE CODING

The concept of multiple coding is encouraged when the use of more than one code number will fully identify a given condition. Thus, use of multiple codes allows all the components of a complex diagnosis to be identified. However, the statement of diagnosis must mention the presence of all the elements for each code number used.

When is multiple coding mandatory? Only if the instructional term "Code Also" appears in italics under an italicized subdivision in the Tabular List (Volume 1). In this instance, you should interpret mandatory as....requires the use of both codes, and that these codes must be sequenced with the code for the etiology being listed first and the code identifying the manifestation listed second. You will recognize mandatory multiple coding situations by instructional terms used in the Tabular List (Volume 1). Terms to watch for are: "Code also....," "Use additional code...," and "Note:..."

If you turn to Category 330 in the Tabular List (Volume 1), you will notice the instructional term cited: "Use additional code if desired, to identify associated mental retardation." The phrase "...identify associated mental retardation..." should be interpreted as "...identify associated mental retardation, if stated to be present in the diagnostic statement." With this understood, these diagnostic statements would be coded as below.

Coding Examples

Cerebral degeneration in childhood with mental retardation

> **330.9**   Unspecified cerebral degeneration in childhood

> **319**   Unspecified mental retardation

Cerebral degeneration in childhood

> **330.9**   Unspecified cerebral degeneration in childhood

In the Alphabetic Index (Volume 2), if two codes are listed, the first should be sequenced first with the code in italicized brackets listed second to indicate the additional code. However, the fact that two codes appear after a subterm in the Alphabetic Index does not automatically indicate mandatory multiple coding. It is necessary to verify both code numbers in the Tabular List. If, in the Tabular List, the code number is also in italics as in the Alphabetical Index and, the instructional term "Code also" appears in italics, then both criteria have been met for mandatory multiple coding.

Coding Example

Diabetic neuropathy

> **250.60** Diabetes with neurological manifestations
>
> **[357.2]** Polyneuropathy in diabetes
>
> In the Alphabetic Index (Volume 2) under "Diabetes," you will find "Neuropathy" listed followed by the codes 250.6 and [357.2] in brackets.

It should also be noted at this point, that even though mandatory multiple coding is always indicated by the presence of the instructional term "Code first" in italics beneath the italicized code number and title for the manifestation, this does not always hold true under the code number for the etiology. Multiple coding is not to be used in those instances when a combination code accurately identifies all of the elements within the diagnostic statement.

CODING LATE EFFECTS

You use late effects coding when coding diagnostic statements that identify a residual effect (condition produced) after the acute phase of an illness or injury has ended. The proper coding sequence is to list the code number identifying the residual (the current condition) first, with the code number identifying the cause (original illness/injury no longer present in its acute phase but which was the cause of the long term residual condition) listed second.

Coding Example

Hemiplegia due to previous cerebral vascular accident

> **342.90** Hemiplegia, unspecified, affecting unspecified side
>
> **438.20** Late effects of cerebrovascular disease, Hemiplegia affecting unspecified side
>
> The <u>residual</u> for this statement is "Hemiplegia" as it is the long term condition that resulted from a previous acute illness. The <u>cause</u> for this statement is "Cerebral vascular accident" as it is the original illness no longer in its acute phase but which did cause the long term residual condition now present.

How do you recognize when to use late effects coding and when not to? Often, the diagnostic statement will contain key words to help identify a late effects situation. Key words used in defining late effects include:

> *late*
> *due to an old injury*
> *due to a previous illness/injury*
> *due to an illness/injury occurring one year or more ago*

In cases where these key words (phrases) are not included within the diagnostic statement, an effect is considered to be late if sufficient time has elapsed between the occurrence of the acute illness/injury and the development of the residual effect.

Coding Example

Excessive scar tissue due to third degree burn, right leg

709.2   Scar conditions and fibrosis of skin

906.7   Late effect of burn of other extremities

The previous diagnostic statement does not indicate the time element with any modifying terms as "old" or "previous." The fact that enough time has elapsed for the development of scar tissue indicates that the acute phase of the injury has subsided and the scarring should be coded as a late effect.

If a diagnostic statement only specifies the cause of the late effect and does not indicate the residual, then use the code number for the cause.

Coding Example

Residuals of tuberculosis

137   Late effects of tuberculosis

The above statement does not identify the actual residuals, so you would use the code for the cause.

To find the code for such a statement in the Alphabetic Index (Volume 2), refer to the main term "LATE" and the subterm "EFFECTS OF." The only codes available for causes of late effects are:

137   Late effects of tuberculosis

138   Late effects of acute poliomyelitis

139   Late effects of other infectious and parasitic diseases

268.1   Rickets, late effects

326   Late effects of intracranial abscess or pyogenic infection

438   Late effects of cerebrovascular disease

677   Late effects of complication of pregnancy, childbirth and the puerperium

905   Late effects of musculoskeletal and connective tissue injuries

906   Late effects of injuries to skin and subcutaneous tissues

907   Late effects of injuries to the nervous system

908   Late effects of other and unspecified injuries

909   Late effects of other and unspecified external causes

Be sure to distinguish between a late effect and a historical statement in a diagnosis. Whenever the statement uses the terms "effects of old...," "sequela of...," or "residuals of...," then code as late effects. If the diagnosis is expressed in terms as "history of...," these are coded to personal history of the illness or injury and are coded to the V-Codes (V-10 to V-15).

CODING INJURIES

Injuries comprise a major section of ICD-9-CM. Categories 800-959 include fractures, dislocations, sprains and various other types of injuries. Injuries are classified first according to the general type of injury and within each type there is a further breakdown by anatomical site.

In cases where a patient has multiple injuries, the most severe injury is the principal diagnosis. Where multiple sites of injury are specified in the diagnosis, you should interpret the term "with" as indicating involvement of both sites, and interpret the term "and" as indicating involvement of either or both sites. You will also note that fifth-digits are commonly used when coding injuries to provide information regarding level of consciousness, specific anatomical sites and severity of injuries.

Some general rules to apply when coding fractures follow. Fractures can either be "open" or "closed." An "open" fracture is when the skin has been broken and there is communication with the bone and the outside of the body. Whereas, with a "closed" fracture the bone does not have contact with the outside of the body.

Note the following descriptions as set forth in the ICD-9-CM at the four-digit subdivision level to help distinguish between an "open" and "closed" fracture.

Closed Fractures

comminuted	*simple*
linear	*greenstick*
fissured	*depressed*
spiral	*march*
impacted	*fractured nos*
elevated	*slipped epiphysis*

Open Fractures

compound	*with foreign body*
missile	*infected*
puncture	

Anytime that it is not indicated whether a fracture is open or closed, code it as if it were closed. Fracture-dislocations are classified as fractures. Pathological fractures are classified to the condition causing the fracture (i.e. osteoporosis) with the use of an additional code to identify the *Pathological fracture* (733.1).

When coding burns, code only the most severe degree of burns when the burns are of the same site but of different degrees. In cases of burns where it is noted that there is an infection, assign the code for the burn and also the code for the infection (958.3 *Posttraumatic wound infection NEC*).

The percentage of the body surface involved with burns is specified by using Category 948. This code may be used as a solo code when the site of the burn is unspecified. There is also a fifth-digit subclassification included in Category 948 to identify the percentage of the total body surface involved with third degree burns. Use Category 949 only when neither the site nor the percentage of the body surface involved is specified in the diagnosis.

POISONING AND ADVERSE EFFECTS OF DRUGS

There are two different sets of code numbers to use to differentiate between poisoning and adverse reactions to the correct substances properly administered. First, you must make the distinction between poisoning and adverse reaction. Poisoning by drugs includes:

Poisoning

Accidental

1.   Given in error during diagnostic or therapeutic procedures.

2.   Given in error by one person to another (for example, mother to child).

3.   Taken in error by self.

Purposeful

1.   Suicide attempt.

2.   Homicide attempt.

Adverse Reaction in Spite of Proper Administration of Correct Substance

1.   In therapeutic of diagnostic procedure.

2.   Taken by self or given to another as prescribed.

3.   Accumulative effect (intoxication due to....).

4.   Interaction of prescribed drugs.

5.   Synergistic reaction (enhancing the effect of another drug).

6.   Allergic reaction.

7.   Hypersensitivity.

To code poisoning by drugs, use the Alphabetic Index (Volume 2) which contains the Table of Drugs and Chemicals. This table includes one column to identify the poisoning code (960-989) and four columns of External Cause Codes to classify whether the poisoning was an accident, suicide, assault or undetermined.

The column labeled "Therapeutic Use" is not used for poisonings but in coding adverse reactions to correct substances properly administered. The External Cause Codes are optional but may be used if a facility's coding policy requires their use.

Note that in the Alphabetic Index (Volume 2) that the subterm entry "Drug" under the main term of "Poisoning" refers the coder to the Table of Drugs and Chemicals for the code assignment. Because the Table of Drugs and Chemicals is so extensive, it is acceptable to code directly from the Table without verifying the code obtained in Volume 1.

What if the drug which caused the poisoning is not listed in the Table of Drugs and Chemicals?

1.   Refer to Appendix C in Volume 1 (American Hospital Formulary Service) and locate the name of the drug.

2.   Note the AHFS category number listed.

3.   Turn to the Table of Drugs and Chemicals in the Alphabetic Index (Volume 2) of ICD-9-CM.

4.   Locate the term "Drug."

5.   Refer to the subterm "AHFS List."

6.   Look through the list until you find the AHFS Category Number determined in step 2 above. The AHFS Category Numbers are listed in numeric order.

7.   Assign the code.

How Do You Identify Poisoning by Drugs?

The statement of diagnosis will usually have descriptive terms that would indicate poisoning. Look for terms such as:

Intoxication	*Toxic effect*
Overdose	*Wrong drug given/taken in error*
Poisoning	*Wrong dosage given/taken in error*

Adverse effects of a medicine taken in combination with alcohol or from taking a prescribed drug in combination with a drug the patient took on his/her own initiative (for example antihistamines) are coded as poisonings. If you wish to code a manifestation of the poisoning as well, this code is always listed second, after listing the code identifying the poison first.

Adverse Effects of Drugs

The World Health Organization (WHO) defines adverse drug reaction as any response to a drug "which is noxious and unintended and which occurs at doses used in man for prophylaxis, diagnosis or therapy." Notice that this definition does not include the terms "overdose" or "poisoning."

Why does ICD-9-CM differentiate between poisoning and adverse drug reaction? Tabulation of statistical data indicates how often a drug reaction occurred because of the drug itself versus how often the drug was either not given or taken properly.

Two codes are required when coding adverse drug reactions to the correct substance properly administered. One code is used to identify the manifestation or the nature of the adverse reaction such as urticaria, vertigo, gastritis, etc. This code is assigned from Categories 001-799 in Volume 1.

Refer to the main term identifying the manifestation in the Alphabetic Index (Volume 2). But remember that the Table of Drugs and Chemicals is not used to locate the code for the manifestation, and the code used to identify the manifestation does not identify the drug responsible for the adverse reaction.

A second code is required to identify the drug causing the adverse reaction. In ICD-9-CM, the only codes provided to identify the drug causing an adverse reaction to a substance properly administered are E930 through E949. Anytime a code is selected from the E930-E949 range, it can never be sequenced first or stand as a solo code.

Locating the Proper E Code

How do you locate the proper E code to identify the drug which was responsible for causing an adverse reaction to a correct substance properly administered? Turn to the Table of Drugs and Chemicals in the Alphabetic Index (Volume 2). Earlier we noted that the column labeled "Therapeutic Use" was not used for coding instances involving poisoning. However, for adverse drug reactions to a correct substance properly administered, the "Therapeutic Use" column is used to find the proper code within the range E930 through E949 to identify the drug.

Drug Interactions Between Two or More Drugs

Drug interactions between two or more prescribed drugs are classified as adverse drug reactions to a correct substance properly administered. This holds true regardless of whether the drugs were prescribed by the same physician or different physicians.

Two types of drug interactions should be noted:

1. Synergistic interaction. One drug enhances the action of another drug so that the combined effect is greater than the sum of the effects of each used alone.

2. Antagonistic interaction. One drug represses the action of another drug.

To properly code drug interactions, first code the manifestation. Then code each drug involved in the interaction using the E codes from the column labeled "Therapeutic Use" from the Table of Drugs and Chemicals.

Coding Example

Gastritis due to interaction between Motrin and Procainamide

> **535.50** Unspecified gastritis and gastroduodenitis
> *List the manifestation first*
>
> **E935.8** Other specified analgesics and antipyretics
>
> **E942.0** Cardiac rhythm regulators

Coding Example

When a diagnostic statement does not state specifically the manifestation or nature of the adverse reaction, you should use the code provided to identify an adverse drug reaction of unspecified nature, 995.2 *Unspecified adverse effect of drug, medicinal and biological substance*. For example:

Allergic reaction to Motrin, proper dose

995.2 Unspecified adverse effect of drug medicinal and biological substance

E935.8 Other specified analgesics and antipyretics

Note in the above example that the code indicating the manifestation, although unspecified as to the nature, is listed first followed by the E code to identify the drug. When the drug causing an adverse effect is unknown or unspecified, use code E947.9 *Unspecified drug or medicinal substance*.

It is very important to remember that codes in the range 960 through 979 are never used in combination with codes in the range E930 through E949 because codes in the range 960-979 identify poisonings and codes in the range E930-E949 identify the external cause of adverse reactions to the correct substance properly administered.

CODING COMPLICATIONS OF MEDICAL AND SURGICAL CARE

A complication is when you have the occurrence of two or more diseases in the same patient. Recent studies have revealed serious deficiencies in properly coding complications for insurance claims processing. Often the complication is never mentioned. Complications are responsible for many of the procedures that are ordered for patients, therefore the complication should be coded and submitted on your insurance claims.

Postoperative complications that affect a specific anatomical site or body system are classified to the appropriate chapter 1 through 16 of the Tabular Index (Volume 1). Postoperative complications affecting more than one anatomical site or body system are classified in the chapter on injury and poisoning (Chapter 17, Categories 996-999). If the Alphabetic Index (Volume 2) does not provide a specific main term and subterm to identify a postoperative complication, classify the complication to categories 996-999.

Coding Example

Postcholecystectomy syndrome

576.0 Postcholecystectomy syndrome

The Alphabetic Index (Volume 2) specifically classifies the postoperative condition to one of the categories from 001 through 799. See main term "Complication," subterms "surgical procedure" and "postcholecystectomy syndrome."

Coding Examples

Postoperative wound infection

> **998.5**   Postoperative infection

The Alphabetic Index (Volume 2) has a main term "Infection" and subterms "wound, postoperative" for this condition. Note that this code appears in Chapter 17 within categories 996-999.

Postoperative atelectasis

> **997.3**   Respiratory complications

Refer to the main term "Atelectasis" in the Alphabetic Index (Volume 2). Note there is no subterm for postoperative beneath this main term. Therefore, you must presume this complication is classified to one of the categories in the range 969-999. You may also code 518.0 *Pulmonary collapse*, to identify the nature of the respiratory complication for statistical purposes; however, the code for the complication must be listed first.

COMPLICATIONS FROM MECHANICAL DEVICES

Subcategories in the range 996.0 through 996.5 are used to identify mechanical complications of devices. Mechanical complications are the result of a malfunction on the part of the internal prosthetic implant or device. What indicates a mechanical complication? Breakdown or obstruction, displacement, leakage, perforation or protrusion of the devices are all forms of mechanical complications.

Coding Examples

Displacement of cardiac pacemaker electrode

> **996.01**   Mechanical complication of cardiac device, implant, and graft due to cardiac pacemaker (electrode)

Protrusion of nail into acetabulum

> **996.4**   Mechanical complication of internal orthopedic device, implant, and graft

Other complications of devices, such as infection or hemorrhage, are due to an abnormal reaction of the body to an otherwise properly functioning device. All complications involving infection are coded to category 996.7 Other complications of internal prosthetic device, implant and graft.

Coding Examples

Infected arteriovenous shunt

> **996.6**   Infection and inflammatory reaction due to internal prosthetic device, implant, and graft

Anterior chamber hemorrhage due to displaced prosthetic lens

> **996.7** Other complications of internal (biologic) (synthetic) prosthetic device, implant, and graft

CARDIAC COMPLICATIONS

In the case of cardiac complications, ICD-9-CM defines the "immediate postoperative period" as "the period between surgery and the time of discharge from the hospital." This definition is the basis of whether to code cardiac complications under subcategory 997.1 *Cardiac complications affecting specified body systems, not elsewhere classified*, or under subcategory 429.4 *Functional disturbances following cardiac surgery.*

Use 997.1 for a cardiac complication that occurs anytime between surgery and hospital discharge from any type of procedure performed. Use subcategory 429.4 to code long-term cardiac complications resulting from cardiac surgery.

It is important to distinguish between complications and aftercare. Aftercare is usually an encounter for something planned in advance (example, removal of Kirshner wire). Aftercare is classified using codes in the range of V51-V58. An encounter for a complication occurs from unforeseen circumstances, such as wound infection, resulting in complication of the patient's condition.

SPECIAL CODING SITUATIONS

As you become an experienced coder you will encounter situations where the standard rules do not seem to apply, or which require a special understanding in order to code properly. These situations include coding of circulatory diseases, diabetes, mental disorders, infectious diseases, manifestations, neoplasms, and pregnancy and childbirth. The following sections address these specific special coding situations.

CODING CIRCULATORY DISEASES

Because of the variety of terms and phrases used by physicians to identify diseases of the circulatory system, you will often experience difficulty in coding. To accurately code disorders of the circulatory system, it is imperative that the coder carefully read all inclusion, exclusion and "use additional code" notations contained in the Tabular List (Volume 1).

Fifth digit subclassifications are also frequently used to code combination disorders or to provide further specificity in this section. Even those in specialties other than cardiology will frequently find themselves coding circulatory system diagnoses due to the prevalence of circulatory disorders in this country.

Chapter 7 of the Tabular List (Volume 1), titled Diseases of the Circulatory System, contains the following major sections:

Acute Rheumatic Fever (390-392)

Chronic Rheumatic Heart Disease (393-398)

Hypertensive Disease (401-405)

Ischemic Heart Disease (410-414)

Diseases of Pulmonary Circulation (415-417)

Other Forms of Heart Disease (420-429)

Cerebrovascular Disease (430-438)

Diseases of Arteries, Arterioles, and Capillaries (440-448)

Diseases of Veins, Lymphatics, and Ohter Diseases of the Circulatory System (451-459)

Diseases of Mitral and Aortic Valves

Certain diseases of the mitral valve of unspecified etiology are presumed to be of rheumatic origin and others are not. None of the disorders of the aortic valve of unspecified etiology are presumed to be of rheumatic origin. When you have disorders involving both the mitral and aortic valves of unspecified etiology, then they are presumed to be of rheumatic origin.

Coding Examples

Mitral valve insufficiency

> **424.0**   Mitral valve disorders

> Refer to the main term "Insufficiency" in the Alphabetic Index (Volume 2). Note the subterm "mitral (valve)."

Mitral valve stenosis

> **394.0**   Mitral stenosis

> Refer to the main term "Stenosis" and the sub-term "mitral (valve)" in the Alphabetic Index (Volume 2).

Aortic valve insufficiency

> **424.1**   Aortic valve disorders

Aortic valve stenosis

> **424.1**   Aortic valve disorders

Look up the main term "Stenosis" and the subterm "aortic" in the Alphabetic Index (Volume 2). Remember that aortic valve disorders of unspecified etiology are not considered rheumatic in nature or origin.

Insufficiency of mitral and aortic valves

> **396.3**   Mitral valve insufficiency and aortic valve insufficiency

Under the main term "Insufficiency" in the Alphabetic Index (Volume 2) you will find the subterm "aortic." Further review will locate "with," "mitral valve disease," "insufficiency, incompetence or regurgitation" which directs you to code 396.3

Ischemic Heart Disease

In ischemic heart disease, the manifestations are due to a lack of blood flow to the heart rather than to the anatomical lesion of the coronary arteries. The most common cause of coronary heart disease is coronary atherosclerosis. However, ischemic heart disease can be due to non-coronary disease, such as aortic valvular stenosis, as well. There are many synonyms used to indicate ischemic heart disease such as: coronary artery heart disease, ASHD, and coronary ischemia. Categories in the range 410-414, Ischemic Heart Disease, includes that with mention of hypertension. Use an additional code to identify the presence of hypertension.

Coding Examples

Angina pectoris

> **413.9**   Other and unspecified angina pectoris

As no mention of hypertension is made in the diagnostic statement, a single code is all that is required.

Angina pectoris with essential hypertension

> **413.9**   Other and unspecified angina pectoris

> **401.9**   Essential hypertension, unspecified

In this example, the mention of hypertension in the diagnostic statement requires the use of a second code.

Myocardial Infarction

A myocardial infarction is classified as acute if it is either specified as "acute" in the diagnostic statement or with a stated duration of eight weeks or less. When a myocardial infarction is specified as "chronic" or with symptoms after eight weeks from the date of the onset, it should be coded to subcategory 414.8 *Other specified forms of chronic ischemic heart disease.* If a myocardial infarction is specified as old or healed or has been diagnosed by special investigation (EKG) but is currently not presenting any symptoms, code using category 412 *Old myocardial infarction.*

Coding Examples

Myocardial infarction three weeks ago

> **410.9**   Acute myocardial infarction, unspecified site

Chronic myocardial infarction with angina

>**414.8**   Other specified forms of chronic ischemic heart disease
>
>**413.9**   Other and unspecified angina pectoris

Myocardial infarction diagnoses by EKG, symptomatic

>**412**   Old myocardial infarction

Arteriosclerotic Cardiovascular Disease (ASCVD)

Arteriosclerotic cardiovascular disease (ASCVD) is classified to subcategory 429.2 *Cardiovascular disease, unspecified.* You should use an additional code to identify the presence of arteriosclerosis when coding ASCVD. For example, the diagnostic statement "generalized arteriosclerotic cardiovascular disease" should be coded using 429.2 followed by 440.9 *Generalized and unspecified atherosclerosis.*

"Other forms of heart disease", categories 420-429, are used for multiple coding purposes to fully identify a stated diagnosis. The exception to this rule is if the Alphabetic Index (Volume 2) or Tabular List (Volume 1) specifically instructs you otherwise.

Coding Examples

Arteriosclerotic heart disease with acute pulmonary edema

>**428.1**   Left heart failure
>
>**414.0**   Coronary atherosclerosis

Note that the code for ASHD (414.0) is listed second as a possible underlying cause of the acute situation.

Arteriosclerotic heart disease with congestive heart failure

>**428.0**   Congestive heart failure
>
>**414.0**   Coronary atherosclerosis

Cerebrovascular Disease

When coding cerebrovascular disease (codes 430-438), you should code the component parts of the diagnostic statement identifying the cerebrovascular disease, unless specifically instructed to do otherwise in the Alphabetic Index (Volume 2) or Tabular List (Volume 1).

Coding Examples

Cerebrovascular arteriosclerosis with subarachnoid hemorrhage

>**430**   Subarachnoid hemorrhage
>
>**437.0**   Cerebral atherosclerosis

Cerebrovascular accident secondary to thrombosis

> **434.00**   Cerebral thrombosis, without mention of cerebral infarction

> In this example, you use only one code because of the instructions in the Alphabetic Index (Volume 2). When you look up the main term "Accident" with subterm "cerebrovascular," you are instructed to "(*see also* Disease, cerebrovascular, acute) 436". When you locate the main term "Disease" and subterms "cerebrovascular," "acute" and "thrombotic," you are further instructed to "*see* Thrombosis, brain". This is where you finally locate the single code for this diagnosis, 434.0. When you look up the code in the Tabular List (Volume 1), you are instructed to add a fifth digit "0" if it is without mention of cerebral infarction, and "1" if it is with cerebral infarction.

Whenever there are conditions resulting from the acute cerebrovascular disease, code them if they are stated to be residual(s). If the resulting condition is stated to be transient, do not code them.

Coding Examples

Cerebrovascular accident with residual aphasia

> **436**   Acute, but ill-defined, cerebrovascular disease

> **784.3**   Aphasia

Cerebrovascular accident with transient hemiparesis

> **436**   Acute, but ill-defined, cerebrovascular disease

Hypertensive Disease

As demonstrated earlier with ischemic heart disease, conditions that are classified to cerebrovascular disease (codes 430-438) include that with mention of hypertension, but you must identify the hypertension with another code (401-405) and list it second.

Hypertensive disease is classified to the categories 401-405. The Table of Hypertension is located in the Alphabetic Index (Volume 2) under the main term "Hypertension." This Table contains subterms to identify types of hypertension and complications as well as three columns labeled "malignant," "benign," and "unspecified."

Hypertension is frequently the cause of various forms of heart and vascular disease. However, the mention of hypertension with some heart conditions should not be interpreted as a combination resulting in hypertensive heart disease. The combination is only to be made if there is a cause-and-effect relationship between hypertension and a heart condition classified to subcategories 425.8, 428.0-428.9, 429.0-429.3 and 429.8-429.9.

First you need to be able to make a distinction between conditions specified as "due to" or "with" hypertension. Keep in mind that the phrase "due to hypertension" and the word "hypertensive" are considered synonymous.

Coding Examples

Hypertensive heart disease

> **402.90** Hypertensive heart disease, unspecified, without congestive heart failure

Heart disease due to hypertension

> **402.90** Hypertensive heart disease, unspecified, without congestive heart failure

> Each of the above diagnostic statements indicate clearly a cause-and-effect relationship between hypertension and the condition by specifying that the condition is "due to." Therefore, both statements are coded using 402.90.

If the phrase "with hypertension" is stated or, the diagnostic statement mentions the conditions separately, then you code the conditions separately.

Coding Example

Myocarditis with hypertension

> **429.0** Myocarditis, unspecified

> **401.9** Essential hypertension, unspecified

> As a cause-and-effect relationship is not indicated in the diagnostic statement, the conditions are coded separately.

High Blood Pressure Versus Elevated Blood Pressure

With the ICD-9-CM coding system there is a differentiation made between high blood pressure (hypertension) and elevated blood pressure without a diagnosis of hypertension. If the diagnostic statement indicates elevated blood pressure without the diagnosis of hypertension, it is coded to subcategory 796.2 *Elevated blood pressure reading without diagnosis of hypertension*. If the diagnostic statement indicates high blood pressure or hypertension, it is coded to category 401 *Essential hypertension*.

DIABETES MELLITUS CODING (250)

In 1980, the American Diabetic Association reclassified the types of diabetes mellitus to signify whether or not the patient is dependent on insulin for survival of life. In 1994, additional classifications were added. Note the revisions (bracketed portions) of the statements below for the fifth-digit subclassification.

0 type II [non-insulin dependent type] [NIDDM type] [adult-onset type] or unspecified type, not stated as uncontrolled

> Fifth digit 0 is for use with type II, adult onset diabetic patients, even if the patient requires insulin

1 type I [insulin dependent type] [IDDM] [juvenile type], not stated as uncontrolled

2   type II [non-insulin dependent type] [NIDDM] [adult-onset type] or unspecified type, uncontrolled

Fifth digit 2 is for use with type II, adult onset diabetic patients, even if the patient requires insulin

3   type I [insulin dependent type][IDDM][juvenile type], uncontrolled

Do not assume a patient has insulin-dependent diabetes simply because the patient is receiving insulin, as some non-dependent diabetics may require temporary use when they encounter stressful situations such as surgery or physical or mental illness.

Anytime diabetes is described as "brittle" or "uncontrolled" you should interpret it as diabetes mellitus complicated and assign code 250.9 with the appropriate fifth-digit, 0, 1, 2 or 3. However, if there is also a specific complication present, then assign the code identifying that specific complication, for example, Diabetes mellitus, brittle, with ketoacidosis would be 250.13.

CODING MENTAL DISORDERS

You should be aware of the existence of the glossary of mental disorders in Appendix B of the Tabular List (Volume 1). This glossary is not used for coding purposes but rather as a guide to provide a common frame of reference for statistical comparisons. It is simply an alphabetized listing of mental disorders with definitions.

The coder should choose code assignments based on the terminology used by the physician or psychiatrist and not by the coder's impression of the content of the categories and subcategories. The chapter on mental disorders has many fifth digit subclassifications to watch for when selecting your code.

INFECTIOUS AND PARASITIC DISEASES

There are two categories for identifying the organism causing diseases classified elsewhere. These codes may be used as either additional codes, or as solo codes depending on the diagnostic statement.

041   Bacterial infection in conditions classified elsewhere and of unspecified site

079   Viral and chlamydial infection in conditions classified elsewhere and of unspecified site

Coding Examples

Acute UTI due to Escherchia coli

599.0   Urinary tract infection, site not specified

041.4   Escherchia coli

Staphylococcus infection

041.11   Staphylococcus aureus

Bacterial infection

> **041.9**   Bacterial infection, unspecified

The basic coding principles regarding combination codes (one code accurately identifies the components of the condition) applies throughout the chapter on Infectious and Parasitic Diseases.

In the Alphabetic Index (Volume 2), a subterm that identifies an infectious organism takes precedence in code assignment over a subterm at the same indentation level that identifies a site or other descriptive term.

Coding Example

Chronic syphilitic cystitis

> **095.8**   Other specified forms of late symptomatic syphilis

> Using the Alphabetic Index (Volume 2) to look up the main term "Cystitis (bacillary)," you will note the subterms "chronic 595.2" and "syphilitic 095.8" at the same indentation level under the main term. Therefore, code 095.8 is assigned to this diagnostic statement, as the organism has precedence over other descriptive terms or anatomical sites.

MANIFESTATIONS

Manifestations are characteristic signs or symptoms of an illness. Signs and symptoms that point rather definitely to a given diagnosis are assigned to the appropriate chapter of ICD-9-CM. For example, hematuria is assigned to the Genitourinary System chapter. However, Chapter 16 *Symptoms, Signs and Ill-Defined Conditions* (780-799), includes ill-defined conditions and symptoms that may suggest two or more diseases or may point to two or more systems of the body, and are used in cases lacking the necessary study to make a final diagnosis.

Conditions allocated to Chapter 16 include:

1.   Cases for which no more specific diagnosis can be made even after all facts bearing on the case have been investigated; for example code 784.0 *Headache.*

2.   Signs or symptoms existing at the time of initial encounter that proved to be transient and whose cause could not be determined; for example code 780.2 *Syncope and collapse.*

3.   Provisional diagnoses in a patient who failed to return for further investigation or care; for example code 782.4 *Jaundice, unspecified, not of newborn.*

4.   Cases referred elsewhere for investigation or treatment before the diagnosis was made; for example code 782.5 *Cyanosis.*

5.   Cases in which a more precise diagnosis was not available for any other reason; for example code 780.4 *Dizziness and giddiness.*

6.   Certain symptoms which represent important problems in medical care and which it might be desired to classify in addition to a known cause; for example, code 780.01 *Coma.*

In the last case, if the cause of a symptom or sign is stated in the diagnosis, assign the code identifying the cause. An additional code may be assigned to further identify this symptom or sign if there is a need to further identify the symptom or sign. In such cases, the code identifying the cause will ordinarily be listed as the principal diagnosis.

CODING OF NEOPLASMS

The coding of neoplasms requires a good understanding of medical terminology. All neoplasms are classified in the Tabular List (Volume 1) in Chapter 2 *Neoplasms* 140-239 which contains the following broad groups:

140-195	Malignant neoplasms, stated or presumed to be primary, of specified sites, except of lymphatic and hematopoietic tissue
196-198	Malignant neoplasms, stated or presumed to be secondary, of specified sites
199	Malignant neoplasms, without specification of site
200-208	Malignant neoplasms, stated or presumed to be primary of lymphatic and hematopoietic tissue
210-229	Benign neoplasms
230-234	Carcinoma in situ
235-238	Neoplasms of uncertain behavior
239	Neoplasms of unspecified nature

Table of Neoplasms

The Table of Neoplasms appears in the Alphabetic Index (Volume 2) under the main term "Neoplasms." This table gives the code numbers for neoplasms of anatomical site. For each anatomical site there are six possible code numbers according to whether the neoplasm in questions is either:

Malignant:
 Primary
 Secondary
 Ca in situ
Benign
Of uncertain behavior
Of unspecified nature

Definitions of Site and Behaviors of Neoplasms

Primary	Identifies the stated or presumed site of origin.
Secondary	Identifies site(s) to which the primary site has spread (direct extension) or metastasized by lymphatic spread, invading local blood vessels, or by implantation as tumor cells shed into body cavities.

In-situ
: Tumor cells that are undergoing malignant changes but are still confined to the point of origin without invasion of surrounding normal tissue (non-infiltrating, non-invasive or pre-invasive carcinoma).

Benign
: Tumor does not invade adjacent structures or spread to distant sites but may displace or exert pressure on adjacent structures.

Of Uncertain Behavior
: The pathologist is not able to determine whether the tumor is benign or malignant because some features of each are present.

Of Unspecified Nature
: Neither the behavior nor the histological type of tumors are specified in the diagnostic statement. This type of diagnosis may be encountered when the patient has been treated elsewhere and comes in terminally ill without accompanying information, is referred elsewhere for work-up, or no work-up is performed because of advanced age or poor condition of the patient.

Steps to Coding Neoplasms

1. ICD-9-CM disregards classification of neoplasms by histological type (according to tissue origin) with the exception of lymphatic and hematopoietic neoplasms, malignant melanoma of skin, lipoma, and a few common tumors of bone, uterus, ovary, etc. All other tumors are classified by system, organ or site. The existence of these exceptions makes it necessary to first consult the Alphabetic Index (Volume 2) to determine whether a specific code has been assigned to a specified histological type. For example, *Malignant melanoma of skin of scalp* is coded 172.4 although the code specified in the "Malignant: Primary Column" of the Neoplasm Table for skin of scalp is 173.4.

2. The General Alphabetical Index (Volume 2) also provides guidance to the appropriate column for neoplasms which are not assigned a specific code by histological type. For example, if you look up *Lipomyoma, specified site* in the Alphabetic Index (Volume 2), you will find "*see* Neoplasm, connective tissue, benign."

   The guidance in the Alphabetic Index (Volume 2) can be over-ridden if a descriptor is present. For example, *Malignant adenoma of colon* is coded as 153.9 and not as 211.3 because the adjective "malignant" overrides the entry "adenoma — *see also* Neoplasm, benign."

3. The Neoplasm Table may be consulted directly if a specific neoplasm diagnosis indicates which column of the table is appropriate but does not delineate a specific type of tumor.

4. Sites marked with an asterisk (*), such as buttock NEC* or calf*, should be classified to malignant neoplasm of skin of these sites if the variety of neoplasm is a squamous cell carcinoma or an epidermoid carcinoma and to benign neoplasm of skin of these sites if the variety of neoplasm is a papilloma (of any type).

5. Primary malignant neoplasms are classified to the site of origin of the neoplasm. In some cases, it may not be possible to identify the site of origin, such as malignant neoplasms originating from contiguous sites.

    Neoplasms with overlapping site boundaries are classified to the fourth-digit subcategory .8 "other." For example, code 151.8 *Malignant neoplasm of contiguous or overlapping sites of stomach* whose point of origin cannot be determined.

6. Neoplasms which demonstrate functional activity require an additional code to identify the functional activity.

    Coding Example

    Cushing's syndrome due to malignant pheochromocytoma

    > **194.0**   Malignant neoplasm of adrenal gland

    > **255.0**   Disorders of adrenal glands; Cushing's syndrome

    Code sequencing depends on the circumstances of the encounter.

7. Two categories in the malignant neoplasm section represent departures from the usual principles of classification in that the fourth-digit subdivisions in each case are not mutually exclusive. These categories are 150 *Malignant neoplasm of esophagus* and 201 *Hodgkin's disease*. The dual axis is provided to account for differing terminology, for there is no uniform international agreement on the use of these terms.

    Coding Example

    Malignant neoplasm of the esophagus

    > **150.0**   Cervical esophagus

    > **150.1**   Thoracic esophagus

    > **150.2**   Abdominal esophagus

    or using alternate coding

    > **150.3**   Upper third of esophagus

    > **150.4**   Middle third of esophagus

    > **150.5**   Lower third of esophagus

8. When the treatment is directed at the primary site of the malignancy, designate the primary site as the principal diagnosis, except when the encounter or hospital admission is solely for *Radiotherapy* (V58.0) or, for *Chemotherapy* (V58.1).

9. When surgical intervention for removal of a primary site or secondary site malignancy is followed by adjunct chemotherapy or radiotherapy, code the malignancy using codes in the 140-198 series, or, where appropriate, in the

200-203 series as long as chemotherapy or radiotherapy is being actively administered. If the admission is for chemotherapy or radiotherapy, the malignancy code is listed second.

10. When the primary malignancy has been previously excised or eradicated from its site and there is no adjunct treatment directed to that site, and there is no evidence of any remaining malignancy at the primary site, use the appropriate code from the V10 series to indicate the site of the primary malignancy. Any mention of extension, invasion or metastasis to a nearby structure or organ, or to a distant site, is coded as a secondary malignant neoplasm to that site and may be the principal diagnosis in the absence of the primary site.

11. If the patient has no secondary malignancy and if the reason for admission or for the visit is follow-up of the malignancy, two codes are used and sequenced.

Coding Example

Follow-up of breast cancer treated with chemotherapy. No evidence of recurrence.

> **V67.2**   Follow-up examination following chemotherapy
>
> **V10.3**   Personal history of carcinoma of breast

12. Malignancies of hematopoietic and lymphatic tissue are always coded to the 200.0-208.9 series unless specified as "in remission." If they are in remission, they are coded as V10.60-V10.79.

13. If the primary malignant neoplasm previously excised or eradicated has recurred, code it as primary malignancy of the stated site unless the Alphabetic Index (Volume 2) directs you to do otherwise.

Coding Examples

Recurrence of prostate carcinoma

> **185**   Malignant neoplasm of prostate

Recurrence of breast carcinoma in mastectomy site

> **198.2**   Secondary malignant neoplasm of other specified sites, skin of breast

Make sure to code any mention of secondary site(s).

14. Terminology referring to metastatic cancer is often ambiguous, so when there is doubt as to the meaning intended, the following rules should be used:

A. Cancer described as metastatic "from" a site should be interpreted as primary of that site.

B. Cancer described as metastatic "to" a site should be interpreted as secondary of that site.

Coding Examples

Carcinoma in axillary lymph nodes and lungs metastatic from breast

174.9   Malignant neoplasm of female breast, unspecified

196.3   Secondary and unspecified malignant neoplasm of lymph nodes of axilla and upper limb

197.0   Secondary malignant neoplasm of lung

Adenocarcinoma of colon with extension to peritoneum

153.9   Malignant neoplasm of colon, unspecified

197.6   Secondary malignant neoplasm of retroperitoneum and peritoneum

15. Diagnostic statements when only one site is identified as metastatic:

A. Code to the category for "primary of unspecified site" for the morphological type concerned UNLESS the code thus obtained is either 199.0 or 199.1.

B. If the code obtained in the above step is 199.0 or 199.1, then code the site qualified as "metastatic" as for a primary malignant neoplasm of the stated site EXCEPT for the sites listed below, which should always be coded as secondary neoplasm of the state site:

Bone	Mediastinum
Brain	Meninges
Diaphragm	Peritoneum
Heart	Pleura
Liver	Retroperitoneum
Lymph nodes	Spinal cord

Sites classifiable to 195

C. Also assign the appropriate code for primary or secondary malignant neoplasm of specified or unspecified site, depending on the diagnostic statement you are coding.

Coding Examples

Metastatic renal cell carcinoma of lung

189.0   Malignant neoplasm of kidney, except pelvis

197.0   Secondary malignant neoplasm of lung

Metastatic carcinoma of lung

162.9 Malignant neoplasm of bronchus and lung, unspecified

199.1 Malignant neoplasm without specification of site, other

This code is assigned to identify "secondary neoplasm of unspecified site" per the instructions in step C above.

Metastatic carcinoma of brain

198.3 Secondary malignant neoplasm of other specified sites, brain and spinal cord

199.1 Malignant neoplasm without specification of site, other

In this case, the brain is one of the sites listed in Step B as an exception. So for this diagnostic statement, the code assignment is for secondary neoplasm of the brain and primary malignant neoplasm of unspecified site.

16. When two or more sites are stated in the diagnostic statement and all are qualified to be "metastatic," you should code as for "primary site unknown" and code the stated sites as secondary neoplasms of those sites.

Coding Example

Metastatic melanoma of lung and liver

172.9 Malignant melanoma of skin, site unspecified

197.0 Secondary malignant neoplasm of lung

197.7 Secondary malignant neoplasm of liver, specified as secondary

17. When there is no site specified in the diagnostic statement, but the morphological type is qualified as "metastatic," code as for "primary site unknown." Then assign the code for secondary neoplasms of unspecified site.

Coding Example

Metastatic apocrine adenocarcinoma

173.9 Other malignant neoplasms of skin, site unspecified

199.1 Malignant neoplasm without specification of site, other

18. When two or more sites are stated in the diagnosis and only some are qualified as "metastatic" while others are not, code as for "primary site unknown." However, you should interpret the following sites as secondary neoplasms:

Bone	*Meninges*
Brain	*Peritoneum*
Diaphragm	*Pleura*
Heart	*Retroperitoneum*
Liver	*Spinal Cord*

Sites classifiable to category 195

Coding Example

Carcinoma of lung, metastatic, and brain

198.3   Secondary malignant neoplasm of brain and spinal cord

197.0   Secondary malignant neoplasm of lung

199.1   Malignant neoplasm without specification of site, other

Pregnancy, Childbirth, and the Puerperium

Chapter 11 of the Tabular List (Volume 1) uses fifth-digit subclassifications extensively. In general, the fifth digit is not given in the Alphabetic Index (Volume 2), so each code must be verified in the Tabular List (Volume 1).

The codes for Ectopic and Molar Pregnancy (630-633), do not require the fifth digit. Note also that for the codes 634-638, there is a "common" set of fourth-digit subcategory codes to include complications. Be aware of the use of section marks with categories 634-637 to indicate the need for a fifth digit. All other codes, 640-676 require the use of a fifth digit with the single exception of code 650 *Normal delivery*.

Coding Example

Pregnancy, 3 months gestation complicated by benign essential hypertension

642.03   Benign essential hypertension complicating pregnancy, childbirth, and the puerperium, antepartum condition or complication

Categories 647 and 648 are used for conditions that are usually classified elsewhere, but which have been classified here because they are complications of pregnancy. The interaction of certain conditions with the pregnant state complicates the pregnancy and/or aggravates the non-obstetrical condition (i.e., diabetes mellitus, drug dependence, thyroid dysfunction) and are the main reasons for the obstetrical care provided.

Coding Examples

Rubella in woman, 7 months gestation

647.53   Infectious and parasitic conditions in the mother classifiable elsewhere, but complicating pregnancy, childbirth or the puerperium, rubella, antepartum condition or complication

Pregnancy with diabetes mellitus

648.03   Other current conditions in the mother classifiable elsewhere, but complicating pregnancy, childbirth or the puerperium, diabetes mellitus, antepartum condition or complication

If greater detail is needed for the complication, use an additional code to identify the complication more completely.

Coding Example

Pregnancy with pernicious anemia

> **648.23** Other current conditions in the mother classifiable elsewhere, but complicating pregnancy, childbirth or the puerperium, anemia, antepartum condition or complication
>
> **281.0** Pernicious anemia

Using V Codes

V-codes are used to identify encounters with the health care setting for reasons other than an illness or injury, for example, immunization. V-codes are also used to identify encounters of persons who are injured or ill and whose injury or illness is influenced by some circumstance or problem classified to the V-codes, for example, a person with a functioning pacemaker who requires emergency gastrointestinal surgery. V-codes fall into one of three categories: problems, services or factual.

Problem
: These v-codes identify a circumstance or problem that could affect a patient's overall health status but is not itself a current illness or injury. In other words, you may note that a patient has a drug allergy to sulfonamides by using code V14.2 *Personal history of allergy to sulfonamides.* Although this allergy is not considered an illness or a problem in a healthy person, it may affect how the physician will actually care for the patient. You would only use a problem V-code when the problem has a potential effect on the patient's current diagnosis and the physician's treatment plan for management of the illness or injury.

Service
: These v-codes describe circumstances other than an illness or injury which prompt the patient's visit. This type of visit often occurs when the patient has a chronic disease but is not acutely ill. An example would be a patient with a known neoplasm that has sought care to receive chemotherapy. In this instance, you would assign V58.1 *Maintenance chemotherapy* as the primary code on your claim and list the code to identify the known neoplasm second.

Factual
: These v-codes are used to describe certain facts that do not fall into the "problem" or "service" categories. For example, coding the type of birth using code V30.1 *Single liveborn, born before admission to hospital.*

V-codes can be used as a solo code, a principal code or as a secondary code. It is important to use V-codes properly. If a complication is present, the complication should be coded to categories 001-799 instead of to a V-code.

Coding Example

Colostomy status with colostomy malfunction

> **569.60** Colostomy and enterostomy complications, unspecified

> Code V44.3 *Artificial opening status, colostomy* would not be used in this case because of the complication.

Key words found in diagnostic statements which may result in selection of a V code include:

Admission for	*Health or healthy*
Aftercare	*History (of)*
Attention to	*Maintenance*
Care (of)	*Maladjustment*
Carrier	*Observation*
Checking/checkup	*Problem (with)*
Contact	*Prophylactic*
Contraception	*Replacement (by)(of)*
Counseling	*Screening*
Dialysis	*Status*
Donor	*Supervision (of)*
Examination	*Test*
Fitting of	*Transplant*
Follow up	*Vaccination*

Using E Codes

E-codes permit the classification of environmental events, circumstances and conditions as the cause of injury, poisoning and other adverse effects. The use of E-codes together with the code identifying the injury or condition provides additional information of particular concern to industrial medicine, insurance carriers, national safety programs and public health agencies.

The E-codes may be assigned with any of the codes in the main classification 001-999 to identify the external cause of an injury or condition. E-codes are *never* used as solo codes or as principal diagnostic codes.

When using E-codes, search the Alphabetic Index (Volume 2) for the main term identifying the cause such as "accident," "fire," "shooting," "fall," or "collision." To find the E-code for an adverse reaction to surgical or medical treatment, use the main term "reaction."

Coding Example

Burns to right arm, occurred while burning trash

> **943.00** Burn of upper limb, except wrist and hand, unspecified degree

> **E897** Accident caused by controlled fire not in building or structure

E-codes are important for providing the details of an accident to an insurance carrier to enable them to issue faster and more accurate reimbursement. Most insurance carriers want to be sure they reimburse only for services covered under their policy and not for services covered under worker's compensation, automobile or homeowner's insurance. A clear understanding of the circumstances will eliminate questions from the insurance carrier which cause delays in reimbursements.

Coding Example

Fractured ribs due to fall from ladder at home

> **807.00** Fracture of ribs, closed, unspecified
>
> **E881.0** Fall from ladder
>
> **E849.0** Place of occurrence, home

Using the above E-codes to provide important information regarding the circumstances of the injury to the insurance carrier eliminates any doubt about the insurer's responsibility for coverage.

When using E-codes always list the E-codes as secondary or supplemental to the code(s) describing the injury.

Anatomical Illustrations

A fundamental knowledge and understanding of basic human anatomy and physiology is a prerequisite for accurate diagnosis coding. While a comprehensive treatment of anatomy and physiology is beyond the scope of this text, the large scale, full color anatomical illustrations on the following pages are designed to facilitate the diagnosis coding process for both beginning and experienced coders.

The illustrations provide an anatomical perspective of diagnosis coding by providing a side-by-side view of the major systems of the human body and a corresponding list of the most common diagnoses categories used to support medical, surgical and diagnostic services performed on the illustrated system.

The diagnostic categories listed on the left facing page of each anatomical illustration are three-digit categories and may not be used for coding. These categories are provided as "pointers" to the appropriate section of the ICD-9-CM Volume 1 where the complete listings, including 4th and 5th digits if appropriate, may be found.

PLATE 1. SKIN AND SUBCUTANEOUS TISSUE - MALE

Viral diseases accompanied by exanthem	050-057

Neoplasms

Malignant melanoma of skin	172
Other malignant neoplasm of skin	173
Malignant neoplasm of male breast	175
Kaposi's sarcoma	176
Benign neoplasm of skin	216
Carcinoma in situ of skin	232

Infections of skin and subcutaneous tissue

Carbuncle and furuncle	680
Cellulitis and abscess of finger and toe	681
Other cellulitis and abscess	682
Acute lymphadenitis	683
Impetigo	684
Pilonidal cyst	685
Other local infections of skin and subcutaneous tissue	686

Other inflammatory conditions of skin and subcutaneous tissue

Erythematosquamous dermatosis	690
Atopic dermatitis and related conditions	691
Contact dermatitis and other eczema	692
Dermatitis due to substances taken internally	693
Bullous dermatoses	694
Erythematous conditions	695
Psoriasis and similar disorders	696
Lichen	697
Pruritus and related conditions	698

Other diseases of skin and subcutaneous tissue

Corns and callosities	700
Other hypertrophic and atrophic conditions of skin	701
Diseases of nail	703
Diseases of hair and hair follicles	704
Disorders of sweat glands	705
Diseases of sebaceous glands	706
Chronic ulcer of skin	707
Urticaria	708
Other disorders of skin and subcutaneous tissue	709
Symptoms involving skin and other integumentary tissue	782

Symptoms, signs and ill-defined conditions	780-799

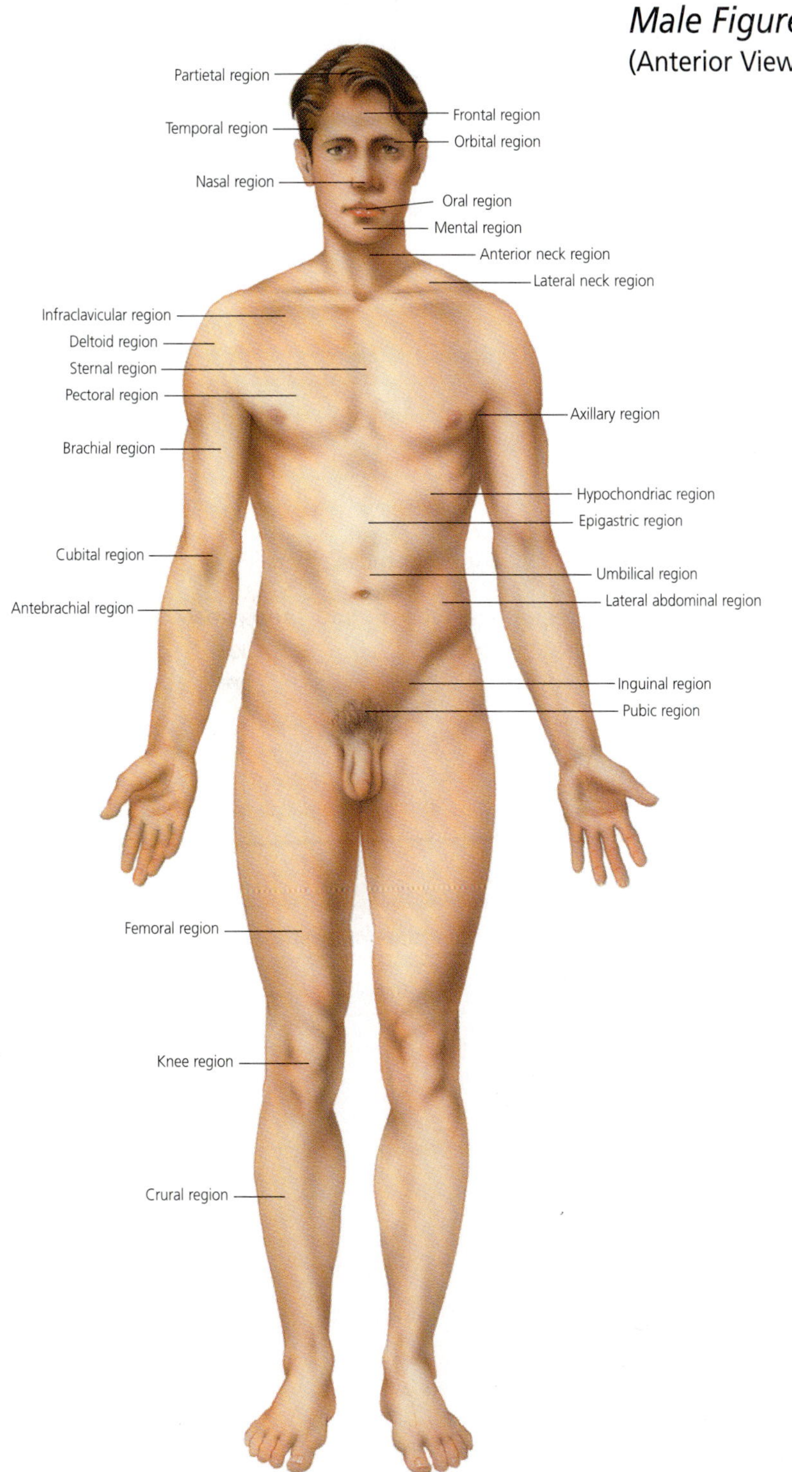

Male Figure
(Anterior View)
Partietal region
Temporal region
Frontal region
Orbital region
Nasal region
Oral region
Mental region
Anterior neck region
Lateral neck region
Infraclavicular region
Deltoid region
Sternal region
Pectoral region
Axillary region
Brachial region
Hypochondriac region
Epigastric region
Cubital region
Umbilical region
Antebrachial region
Lateral abdominal region
Inguinal region
Pubic region
Femoral region
Knee region
Crural region

PLATE 2. SKIN AND SUBCUTANEOUS TISSUE - FEMALE

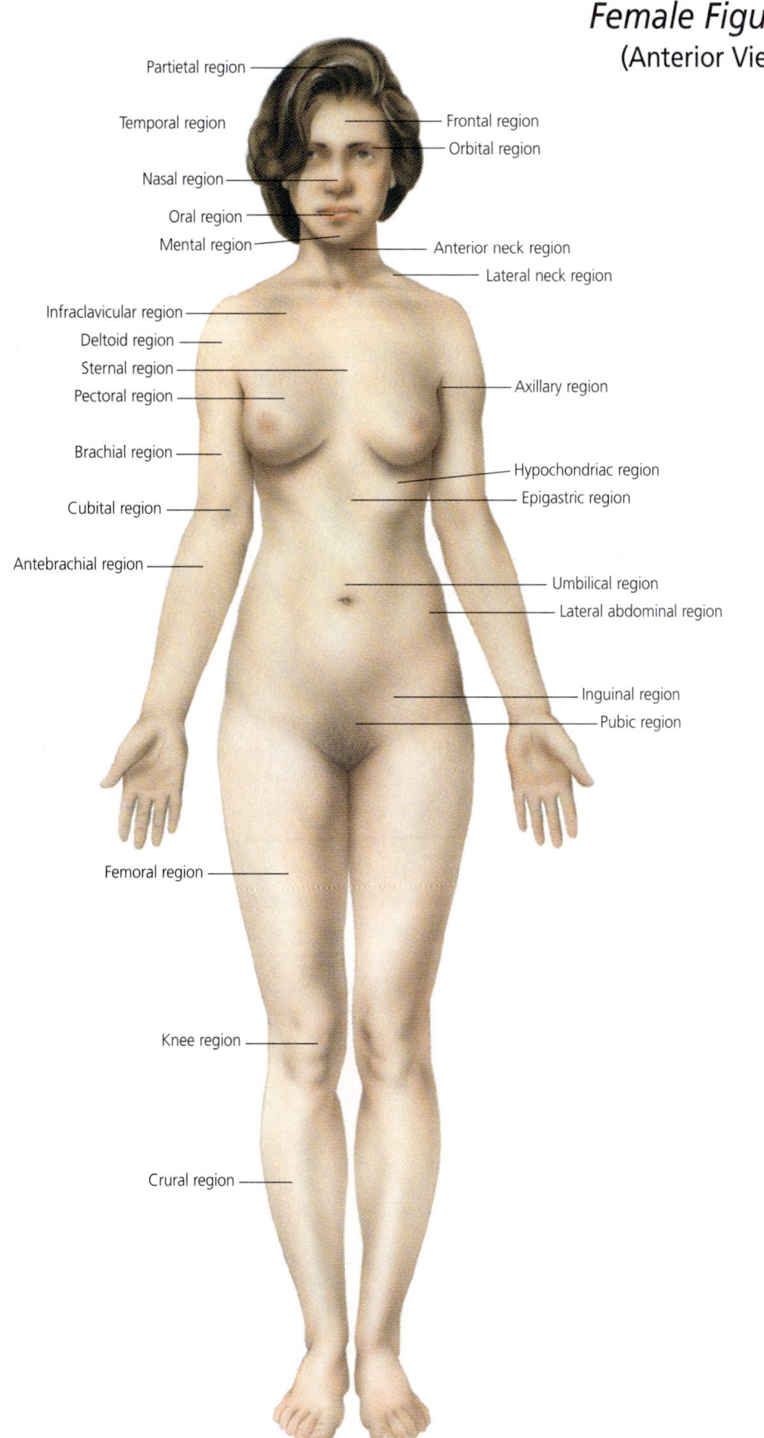

Female Figure
(Anterior View)
Partietal region
Temporal region
Frontal region
Orbital region
Nasal region
Oral region
Mental region
Anterior neck region
Lateral neck region
Infraclavicular region
Deltoid region
Sternal region
Pectoral region
Axillary region
Brachial region
Hypochondriac region
Epigastric region
Cubital region
Antebrachial region
Umbilical region
Lateral abdominal region
Inguinal region
Pubic region
Femoral region
Knee region
Crural region
©Practice Management Information Corp., Los Angeles, CA

PLATE 3. FEMALE BREAST

Female Breast

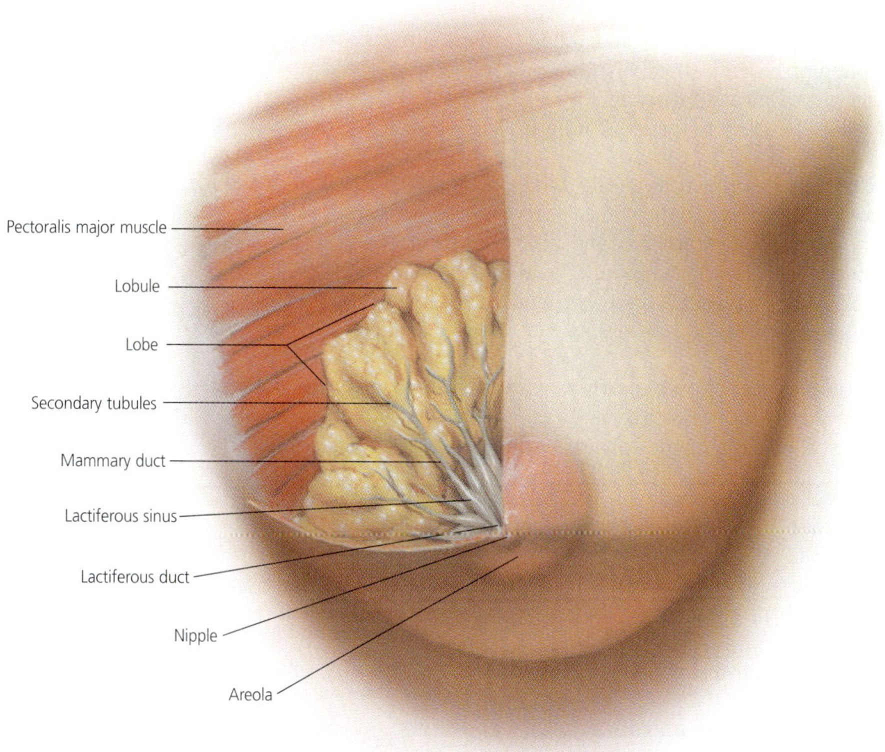

PLATE 4. MUSCULAR SYSTEM AND CONNECTIVE TISSUE - ANTERIOR VIEW

Arthropathies and related disorders	
Diffuse diseases of connective tissue	710
Arthropathy associated with infections	711
Crystal arthropathies	712
Arthropathy associated with other disorders classified elsewhere	713
Rheumatoid arthritis and other inflammatory polyarthropathies	714
Osteoarthrosis and allied disorders	715
Internal derangement of knee	717
Other derangement of joint	718
Dorsopathies	
Ankylosing spondylitis and other inflammatory spondylopathies	720
Spondylosis and allied disorders	721
Intervertebral disc disorders	722
Other disorders of cervical region	723
Rheumatism, excluding the back	
Polymyalgia rheumatica	725
Peripheral enthesopathies and allied syndromes	726
Other disorders of synovium, tendon, and bursa	727
Disorders of muscle, ligament, and fascia	728
Other disorders of soft tissues	729
Osteopathies, chondropathies, and acquired musculoskeletal deformities	
Osteomyelitis, periostitis, and other infections involving bone	730
Osteitis deformans and osteopathies associated with other disorders classified elsewhere	731
Osteochondropathies	732
Flat foot	734
Acquired deformities of toe	735
Other acquired deformities of limbs	736
Curvature of spine	737
Other acquired deformity	738
Nonallopathic lesions, not elsewhere classified	739
Symptoms, signs and ill-defined conditions	780-799

Muscular System
(Anterior View)

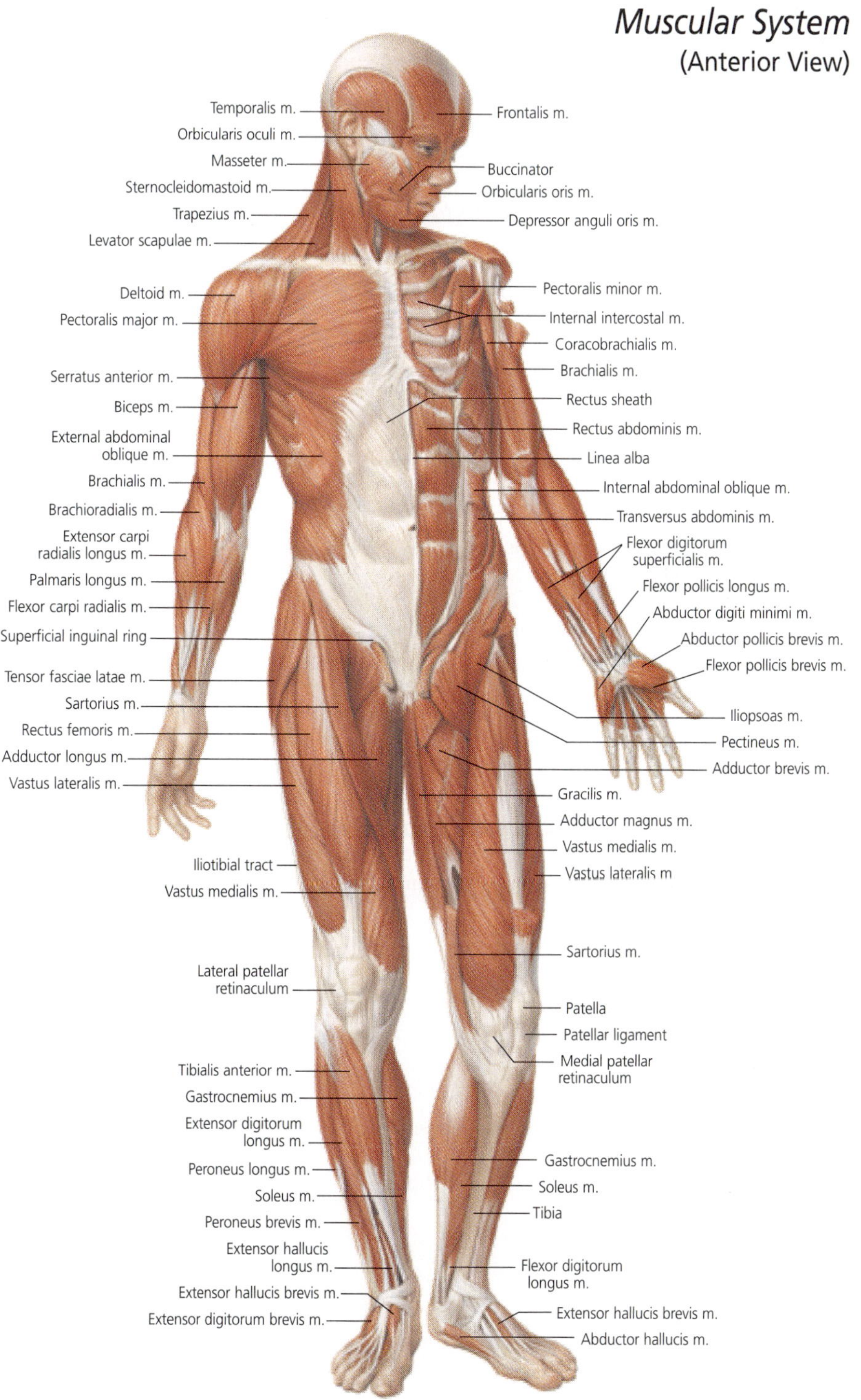

PLATE 5. MUSCULAR SYSTEM AND CONNECTIVE TISSUE - POSTERIOR VIEW

Arthropathies and related disorders	
Diffuse diseases of connective tissue	710
Arthropathy associated with infections	711
Crystal arthropathies	712
Arthropathy associated with other disorders classified elsewhere	713
Rheumatoid arthritis and other inflammatory polyarthropathies	714
Osteoarthrosis and allied disorders	715
Other and unspecified arthropathies	716
Internal derangement of knee	717
Other derangement of joint	718
Other and unspecified disorders of joint	719
Dorsopathies	
Ankylosing spondylitis and other inflammatory spondylopathies	720
Spondylosis and allied disorders	721
Intervertebral disc disorders	722
Other disorders of cervical region	723
Other and unspecified disorders of back	724
Rheumatism, excluding the back	
Polymyalgia rheumatica	725
Peripheral enthesopathies and allied syndromes	726
Other disorders of synovium, tendon, and bursa	727
Disorders of muscle, ligament, and fascia	728
Other disorders of soft tissues	729
Osteopathies, chondropathies, and acquired musculoskeletal deformities	
Osteomyelitis, periostitis, and other infections involving bone	730
Osteitis deformans and osteopathies associated with other disorders classified elsewhere	731
Osteochondropathies	732
Other disorders of bone and cartilage	733
Flat foot	734
Acquired deformities of toe	735
Other acquired deformities of limbs	736
Curvature of spine	737
Other acquired deformity	738
Nonallopathic lesions, not elsewhere classified	739
Symptoms, signs and ill-defined conditions	780-799

Muscular System
(Posterior View)

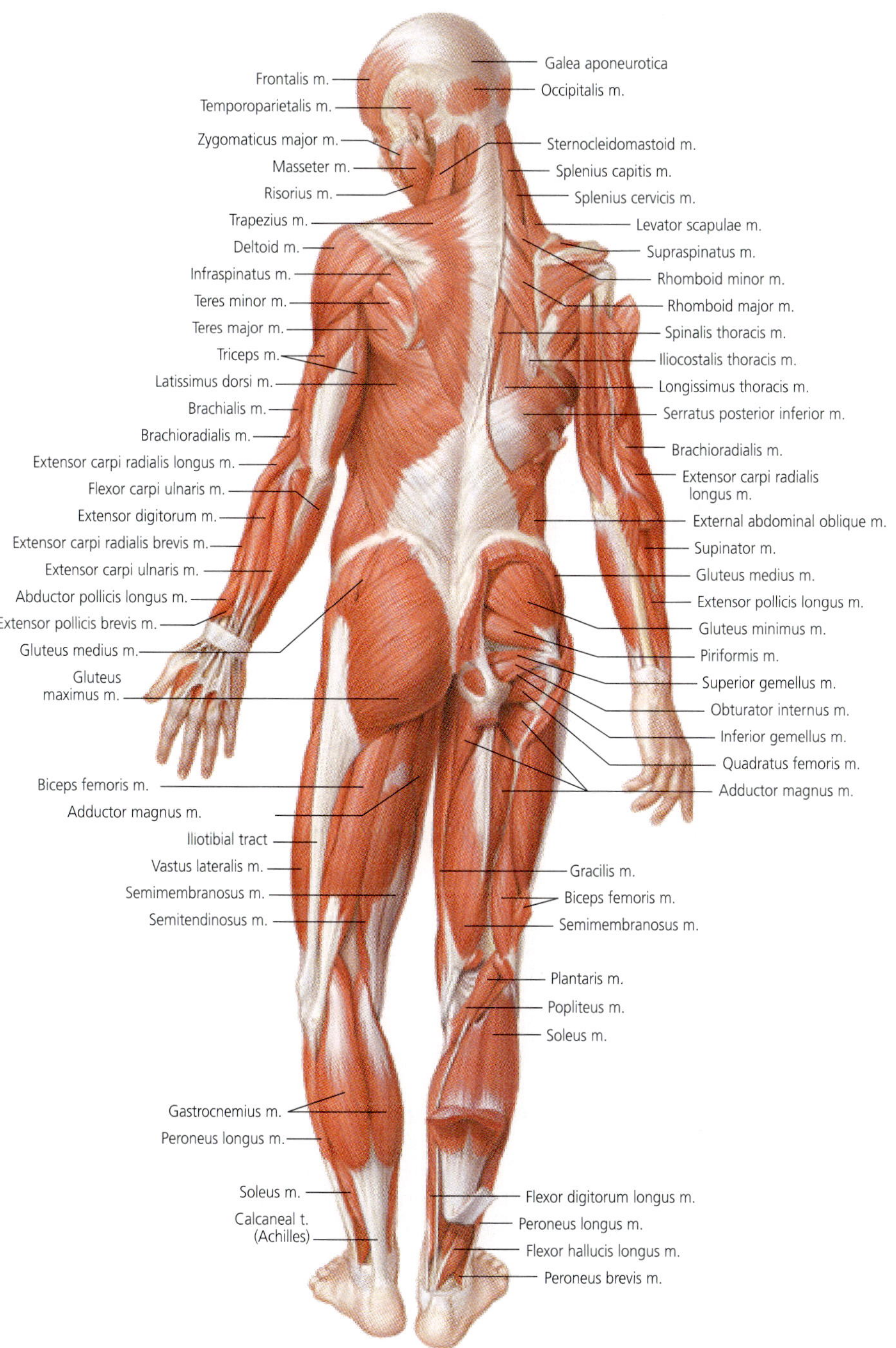

PLATE 6. MUSCULAR SYSTEM - SHOULDER AND ELBOW

Arthropathies and related disorders	
Diffuse diseases of connective tissue	710
Arthropathy associated with infections	711
Crystal arthropathies	712
Arthropathy associated with other disorders classified elsewhere	713
Rheumatoid arthritis and other inflammatory polyarthropathies	714
Osteoarthrosis and allied disorders	715
Other and unspecified arthropathies	716
Internal derangement of knee	717
Other derangement of joint	718
Other and unspecified disorders of joint	719
Dorsopathies	
Ankylosing spondylitis and other inflammatory spondylopathies	720
Spondylosis and allied disorders	721
Intervertebral disc disorders	722
Other disorders of cervical region	723
Other and unspecified disorders of back	724
Rheumatism, excluding the back	
Polymyalgia rheumatica	725
Peripheral enthesopathies and allied syndromes	726
Other disorders of synovium, tendon, and bursa	727
Disorders of muscle, ligament, and fascia	728
Other disorders of soft tissues	729
Osteopathies, chondropathies, and acquired musculoskeletal deformities	
Osteomyelitis, periostitis, and other infections involving bone	730
Osteitis deformans and osteopathies associated with other disorders classified elsewhere	731
Osteochondropathies	732
Other disorders of bone and cartilage	733
Flat foot	734
Acquired deformities of toe	735
Other acquired deformities of limbs	736
Curvature of spine	737
Other acquired deformity	738
Nonallopathic lesions, not elsewhere classified	739
Symptoms, signs and ill-defined conditions	780-799
Sprains and strains of joints and adjacent muscles	
Sprains and strains of shoulder and upper arm	840
Sprains and strains of elbow and forearm	841
Other and ill-defined sprains and strains	848

Shoulder and Elbow
(Anterior View)

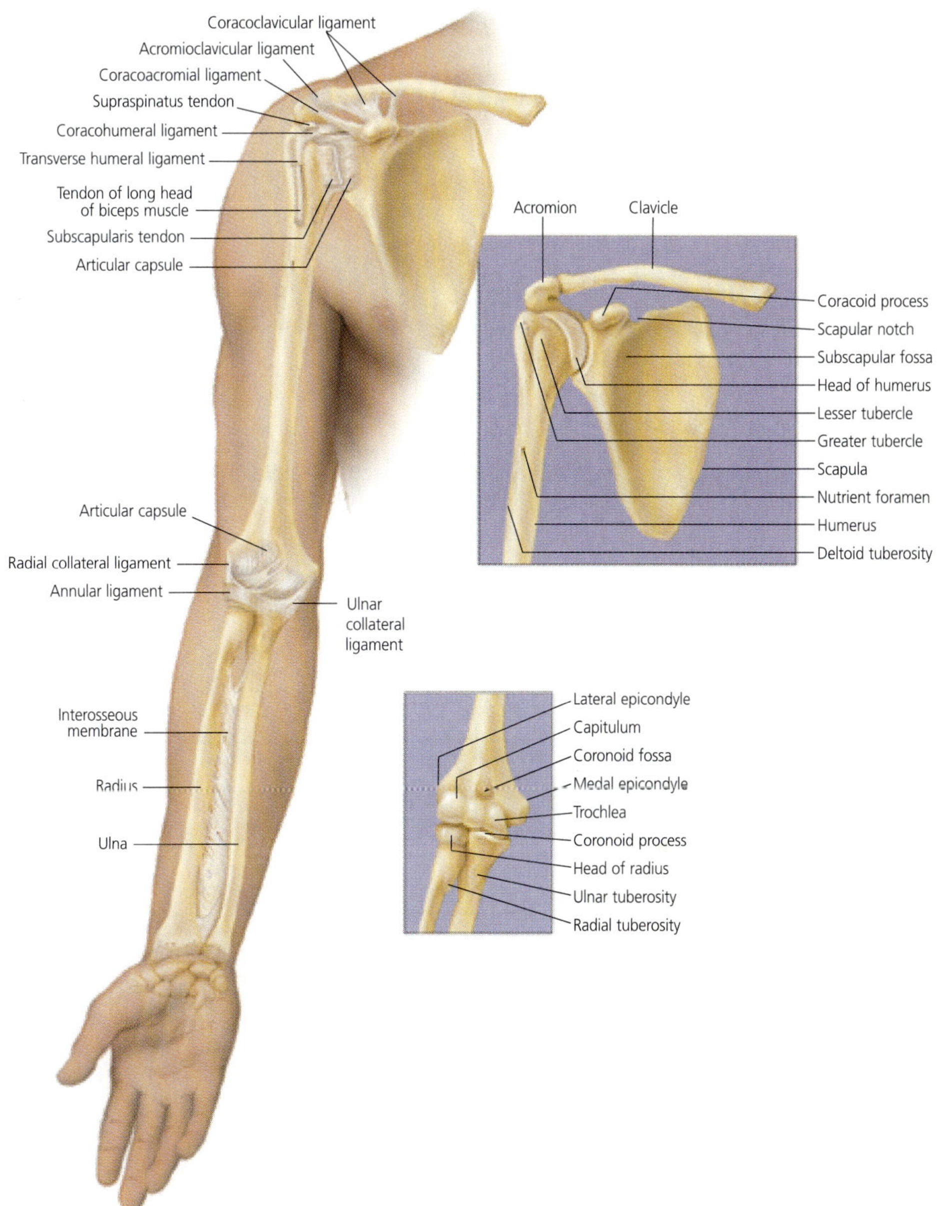

PLATE 7. MUSCULAR SYSTEM - HAND AND WRIST

Arthropathies and related disorders	
Diffuse diseases of connective tissue	710
Arthropathy associated with infections	711
Crystal arthropathies	712
Arthropathy associated with other disorders classified elsewhere	713
Rheumatoid arthritis and other inflammatory polyarthropathies	714
Osteoarthrosis and allied disorders	715
Other and unspecified arthropathies	716
Other derangement of joint	718
Other and unspecified disorders of joint	719
Rheumatism, excluding the back	
Polymyalgia rheumatica	725
Peripheral enthesopathies and allied syndromes	726
Other disorders of synovium, tendon, and bursa	727
Disorders of muscle, ligament, and fascia	728
Other disorders of soft tissues	729
Osteopathies, chondropathies, and acquired musculoskeletal deformities	
Osteomyelitis, periostitis, and other infections involving bone	730
Osteitis deformans and osteopathies associated with other disorders classified elsewhere	731
Osteochondropathies	732
Other disorders of bone and cartilage	733
Other acquired deformities of limbs	736
Other acquired deformity	738
Nonallopathic lesions, not elsewhere classified	739
Symptoms, signs and ill-defined conditions	780-799
Sprains and strains of joints and adjacent muscles	
Sprains and strains of wrist and hand	842
Other and ill-defined sprains and strains	848

Hand and Wrist

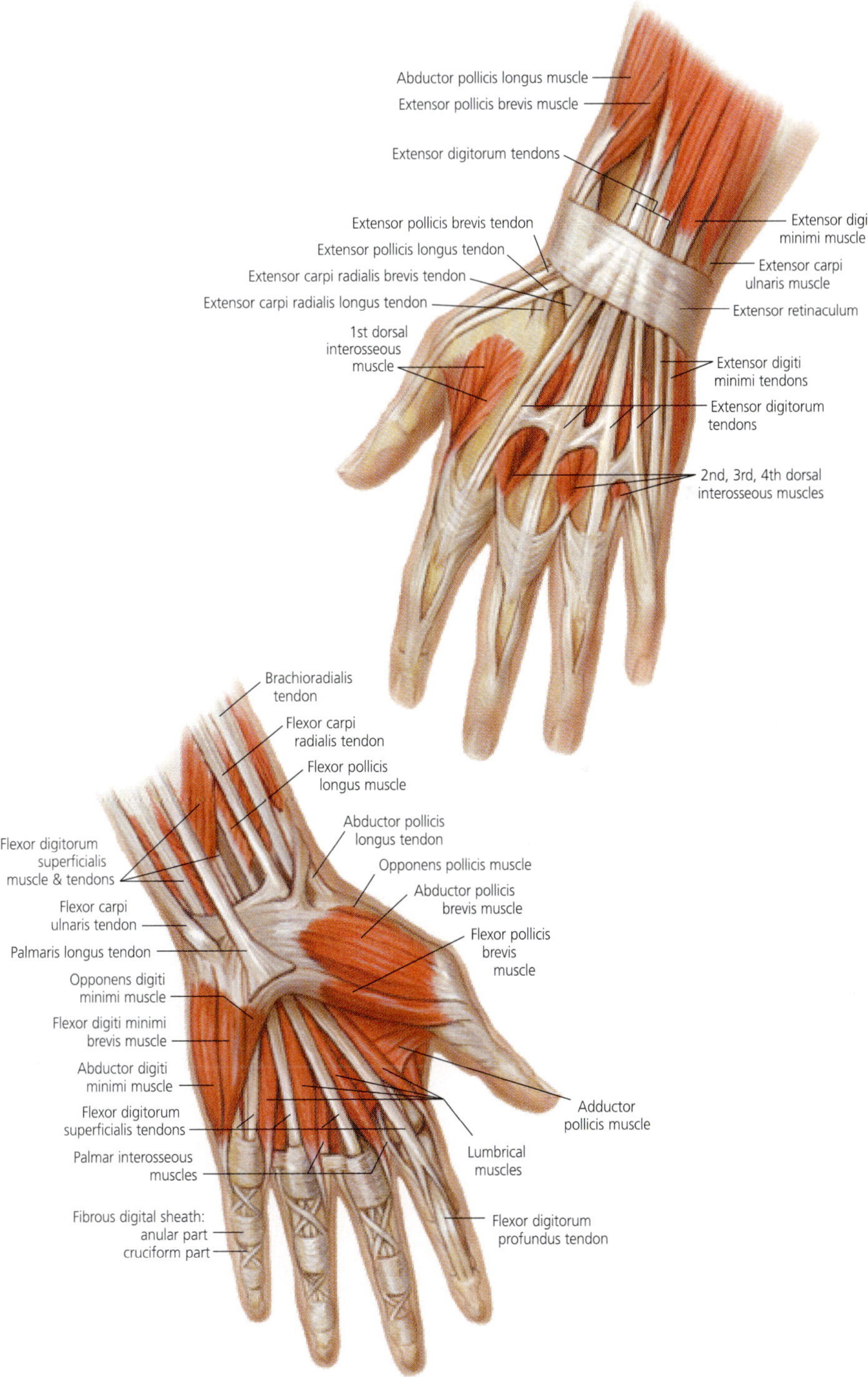

PLATE 8. MUSCULOSKELETAL SYSTEM - HIP AND KNEE

Arthropathies and related disorders	
Diffuse diseases of connective tissue	710
Arthropathy associated with infections	711
Crystal arthropathies	712
Arthropathy associated with other disorders classified elsewhere	713
Rheumatoid arthritis and other inflammatory polyarthropathies	714
Osteoarthrosis and allied disorders	715
Other and unspecified arthropathies	716
Internal derangement of knee	717
Other derangement of joint	718
Other and unspecified disorders of joint	719
Rheumatism, excluding the back	
Polymyalgia rheumatica	725
Peripheral enthesopathies and allied syndromes	726
Other disorders of synovium, tendon, and bursa	727
Disorders of muscle, ligament, and fascia	728
Other disorders of soft tissues	729
Osteopathies, chondropathies, and acquired musculoskeletal deformities	
Osteomyelitis, periostitis, and other infections involving bone	730
Osteitis deformans and osteopathies associated with other disorders classified elsewhere	731
Osteochondropathies	732
Other disorders of bone and cartilage	733
Other acquired deformities of limbs	736
Curvature of spine	737
Other acquired deformity	738
Nonallopathic lesions, not elsewhere classified	739
Symptoms, signs and ill-defined conditions	780-799
Sprains and strains of joints and adjacent muscles	
Sprains and strains of hip and thigh	843
Sprains and strains of knee and leg	844
Other and ill-defined sprains and strains	848

Hip and Knee
(Anterior View)

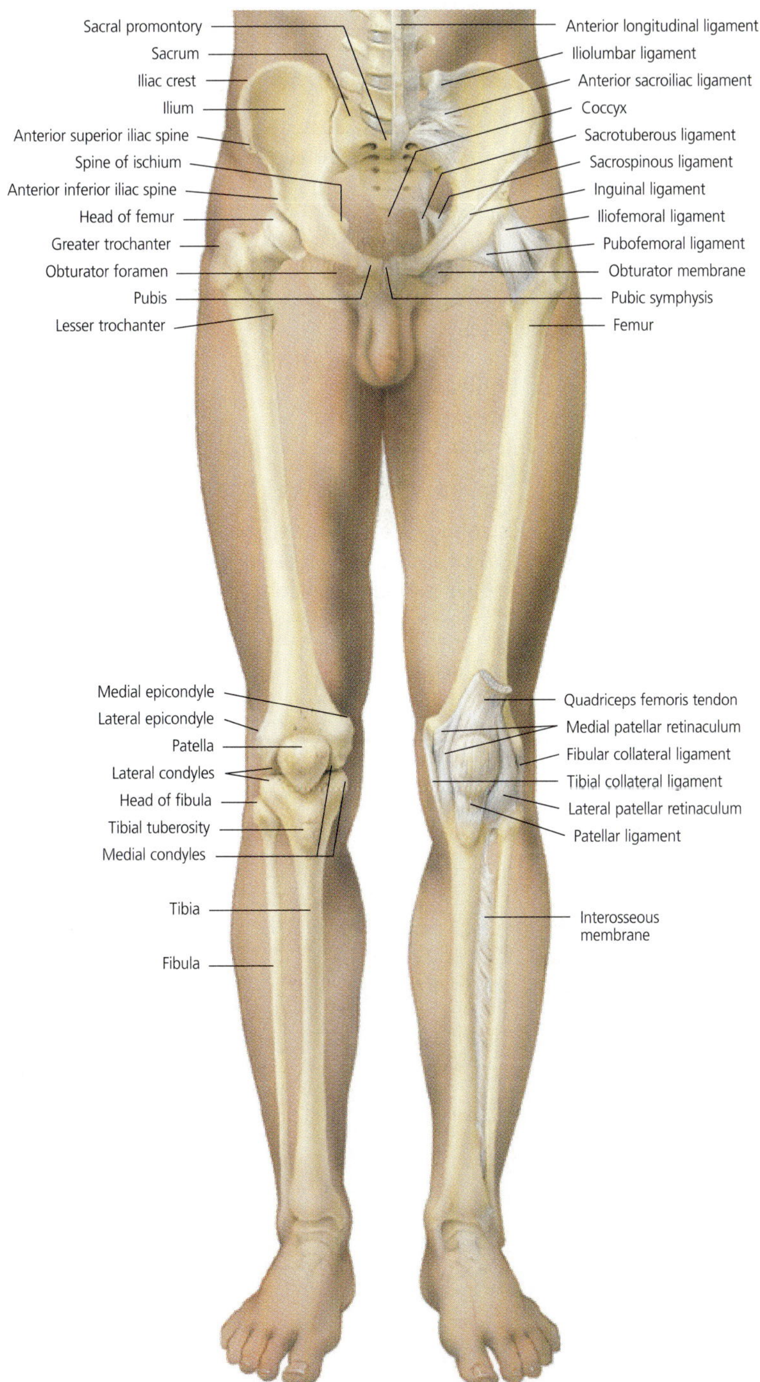

©Scientific Publishing Ltd., Rolling Meadows, IL

PLATE 9. MUSCULOSKELETAL SYSTEM - FOOT AND ANKLE

Arthropathies and related disorders	
Diffuse diseases of connective tissue	710
Arthropathy associated with infections	711
Crystal arthropathies	712
Arthropathy associated with other disorders classified elsewhere	713
Rheumatoid arthritis and other inflammatory polyarthropathies	714
Osteoarthrosis and allied disorders	715
Other and unspecified arthropathies	716
Other derangement of joint	718
Other and unspecified disorders of joint	719
Rheumatism, excluding the back	
Polymyalgia rheumatica	725
Peripheral enthesopathies and allied syndromes	726
Other disorders of synovium, tendon, and bursa	727
Disorders of muscle, ligament, and fascia	728
Other disorders of soft tissues	729
Osteopathies, chondropathies, and acquired musculoskeletal deformities	
Osteomyelitis, periostitis, and other infections involving bone	730
Osteitis deformans and osteopathies associated with other disorders classified elsewhere	731
Osteochondropathies	732
Other disorders of bone and cartilage	733
Flat foot	734
Acquired deformities of toe	735
Other acquired deformities of limbs	736
Other acquired deformity	738
Nonallopathic lesions, not elsewhere classified	739
Symptoms, signs and ill-defined conditions	780-799
Sprains and strains of joints and adjacent muscles	
Sprains and strains of ankle and foot	845
Other and ill-defined sprains and strains	848

Foot and Ankle

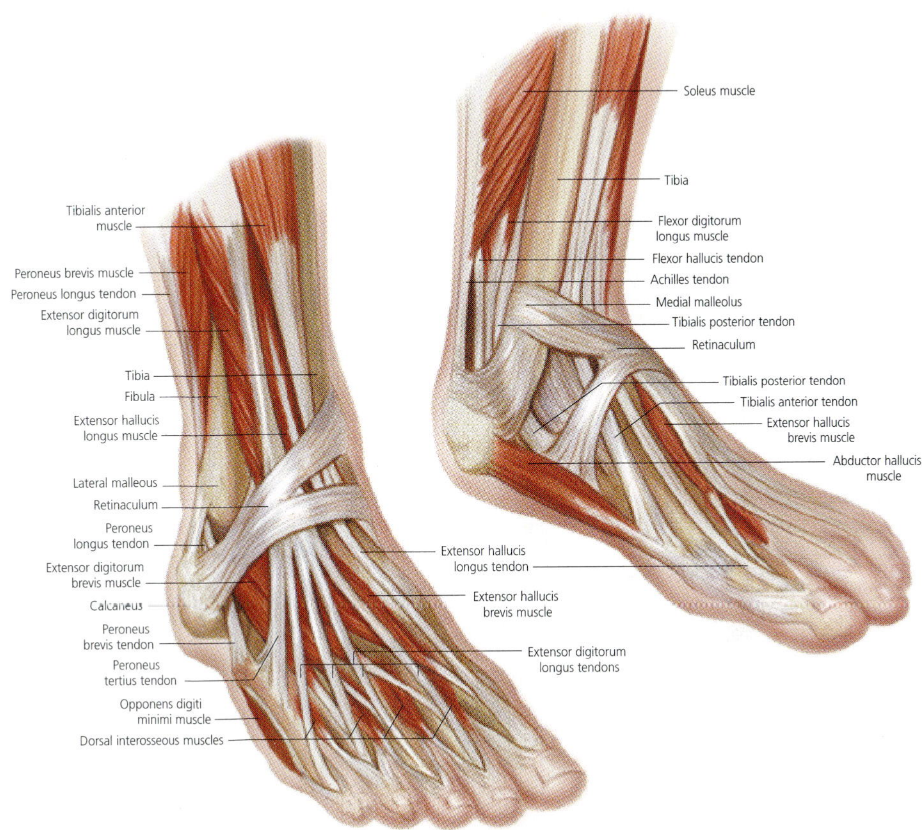

PLATE 10. SKELETAL SYSTEM - ANTERIOR VIEW

Symptoms, signs and ill-defined conditions 780-799

Fracture of skull

Fracture of vault of skull	800
Fracture of base of skull	801
Fracture of face bones	802
Multiple fractures involving skull or face with other bones	804

Fracture of neck and trunk

Fracture of vertebral column without mention of spinal cord injury	805
Fracture of vertebral column with spinal cord injury	806
Fracture of rib(s), sternum, larynx and trachea	807
Fracture of pelvis	808

Fracture of upper limb

Fracture of clavicle	810
Fracture of scapula	811
Fracture of humerus	812
Fracture of radius and ulna	813
Fracture of carpal bone(s)	814
Fracture of metacarpal bone(s)	815
Fracture of one or more phalanges of hand	816
Multiple fractures of hand bones	817

Fracture of lower limb

Fracture of neck of femur	820
Fracture of other and unspecified parts of femur	821
Fracture of patella	822
Fracture of tibia and fibula	823
Fracture of ankle	824
Fracture of one or more tarsal and metatarsal bones	825
Fracture of one or more phalanges of foot	826

Dislocation

Dislocation of jaw	830
Dislocation of shoulder	831
Dislocation of elbow	832
Dislocation of wrist	833
Dislocation of finger	834
Dislocation of hip	835
Dislocation of knee	836
Dislocation of ankle	837
Dislocation of foot	838

Skeletal System
(Anterior View)

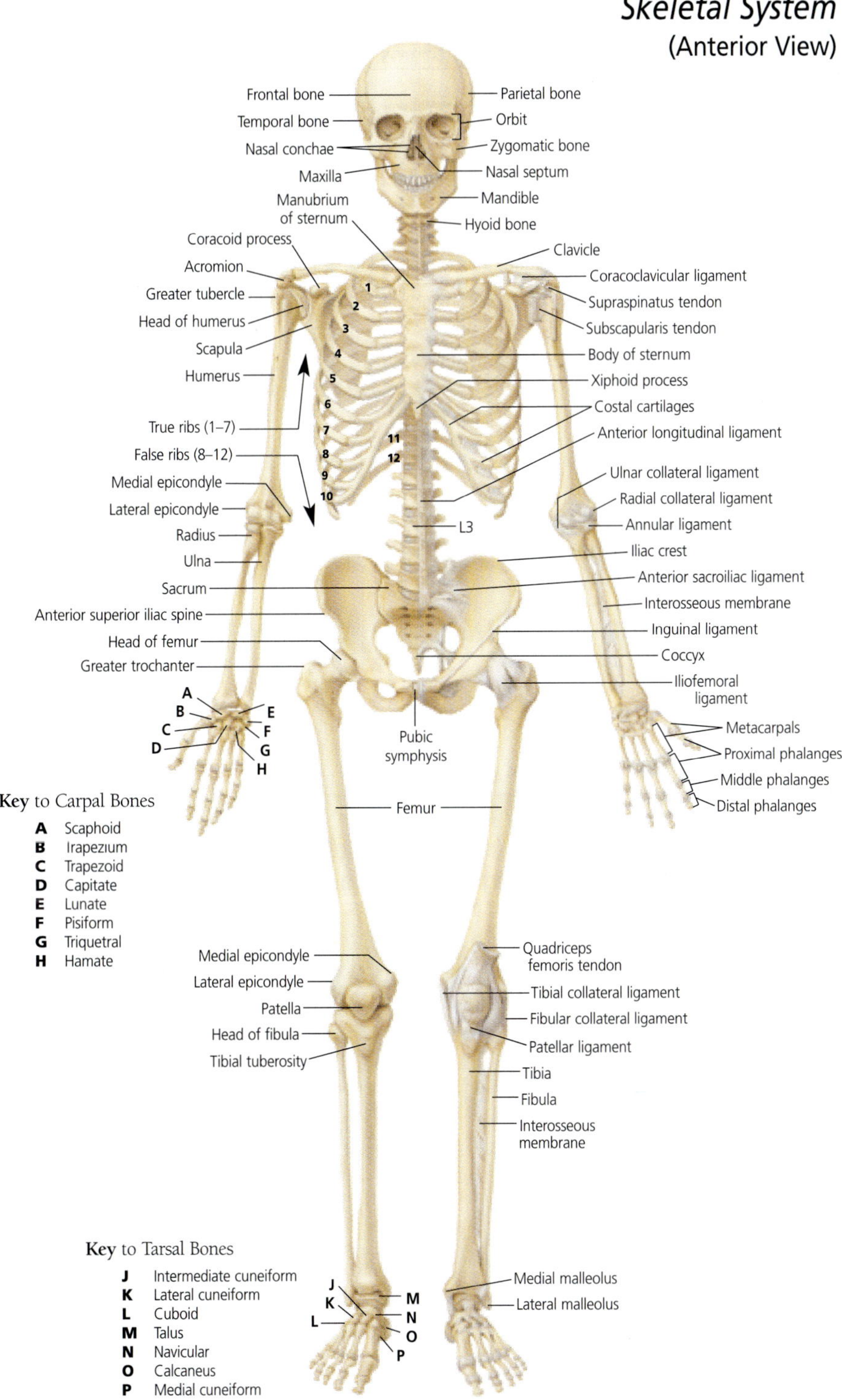

Key to Carpal Bones

A	Scaphoid
B	Trapezium
C	Trapezoid
D	Capitate
E	Lunate
F	Pisiform
G	Triquetral
H	Hamate

Key to Tarsal Bones

J	Intermediate cuneiform
K	Lateral cuneiform
L	Cuboid
M	Talus
N	Navicular
O	Calcaneus
P	Medial cuneiform

PLATE 11. SKELETAL SYSTEM - POSTERIOR VIEW

Skeletal System
(Posterior View)

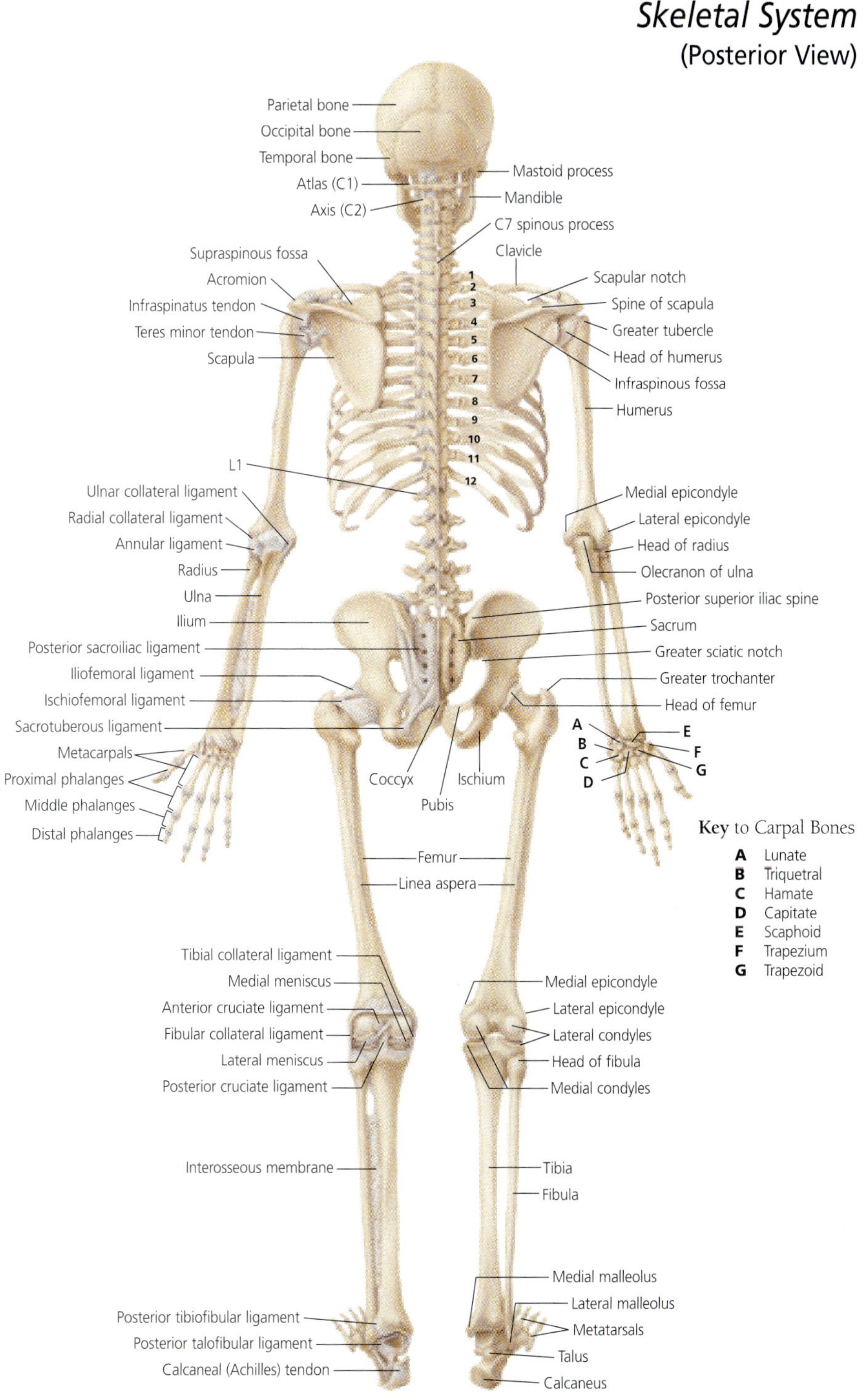

PLATE 12. SKELETAL SYSTEM - VERTEBRAL COLUMN

Arthropathies and related disorders	
Diffuse diseases of connective tissue	710
Arthropathy associated with infections	711
Crystal arthropathies	712
Arthropathy associated with other disorders classified elsewhere	713
Rheumatoid arthritis and other inflammatory polyarthropathies	714
Osteoarthrosis and allied disorders	715
Dorsopathies	
Ankylosing spondylitis and other inflammatory spondylopathies	720
Spondylosis and allied disorders	721
Intervertebral disc disorders	722
Other disorders of cervical region	723
Other and unspecified disorders of back	724
Osteopathies, chondropathies, and acquired musculoskeletal deformities	
Osteomyelitis, periostitis, and other infections involving bone	730
Osteitis deformans and osteopathies associated with other disorders classified elsewhere	731
Osteochondropathies	732
Other disorders of bone and cartilage	733
Curvature of spine	737
Other acquired deformity	738
Nonallopathic lesions, not elsewhere classified	739
Symptoms, signs and ill-defined conditions	780-799
Fracture of neck and trunk	
Fracture of vertebral column without mention of spinal cord injury	805
Fracture of vertebral column with spinal cord injury	806

Vertebral Column
(Lateral View)

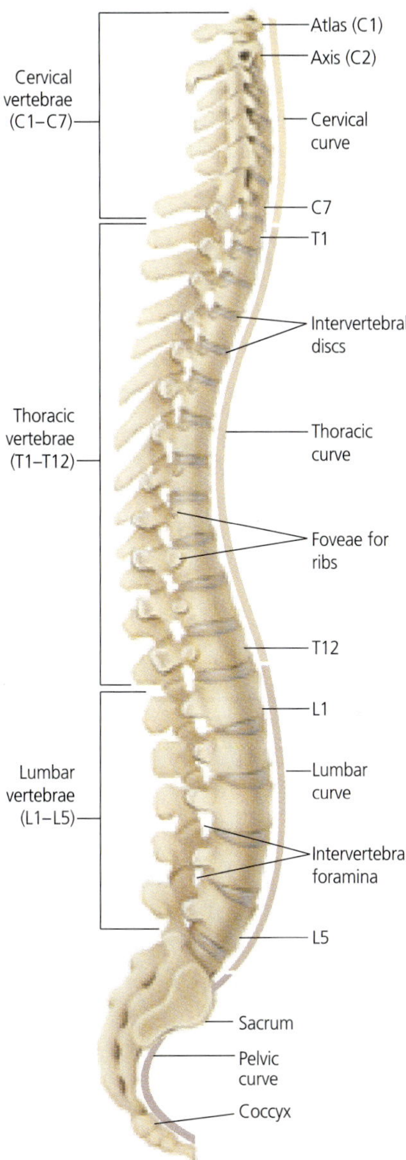

PLATE 13. RESPIRATORY SYSTEM

Respiratory System

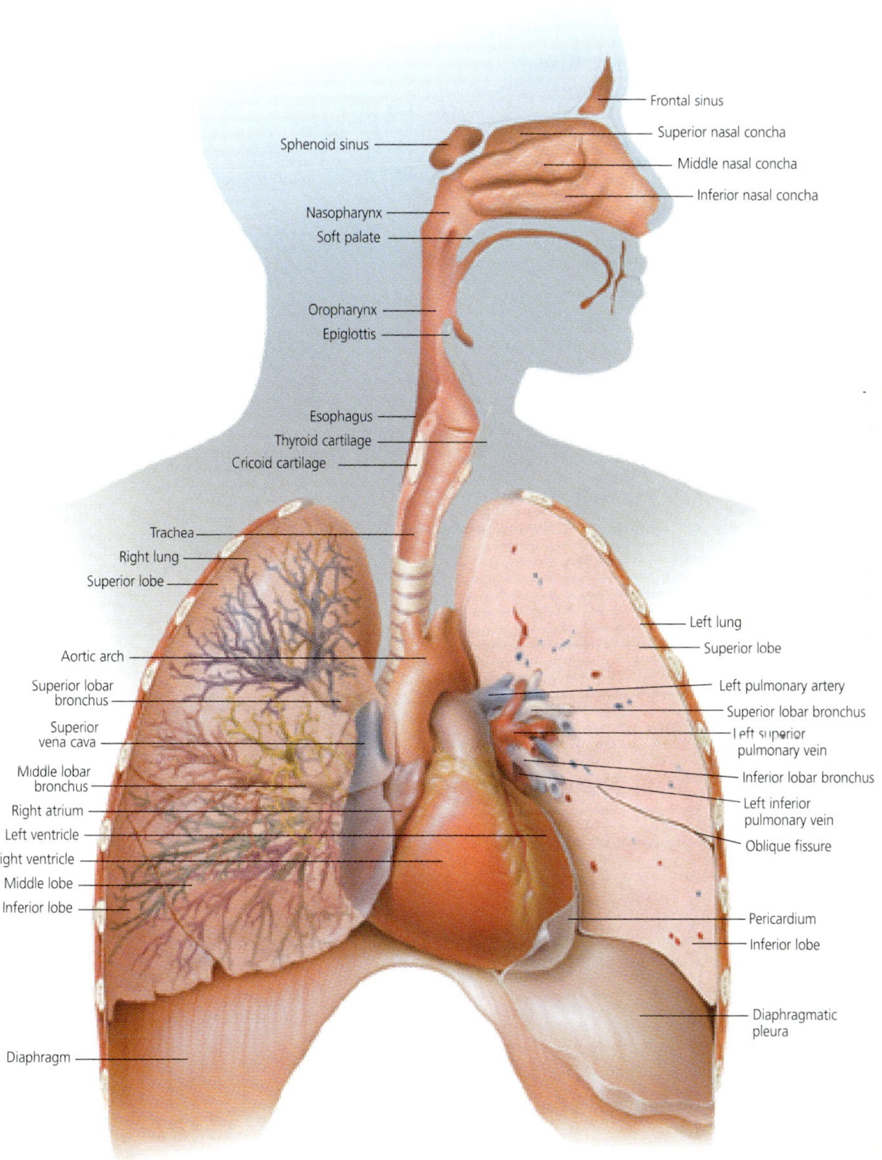

PLATE 14. HEART AND PERICARDIUM

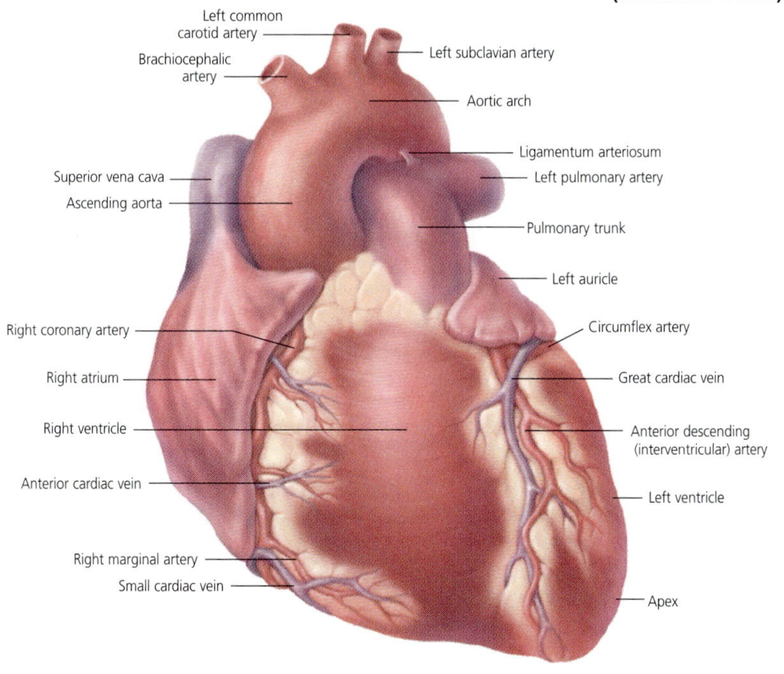

Heart
(External View)
Left common carotid artery
Brachiocephalic artery
Left subclavian artery
Aortic arch
Ligamentum arteriosum
Left pulmonary artery
Superior vena cava
Ascending aorta
Pulmonary trunk
Left auricle
Right coronary artery
Circumflex artery
Right atrium
Great cardiac vein
Right ventricle
Anterior descending (interventricular) artery
Anterior cardiac vein
Left ventricle
Right marginal artery
Small cardiac vein
Apex

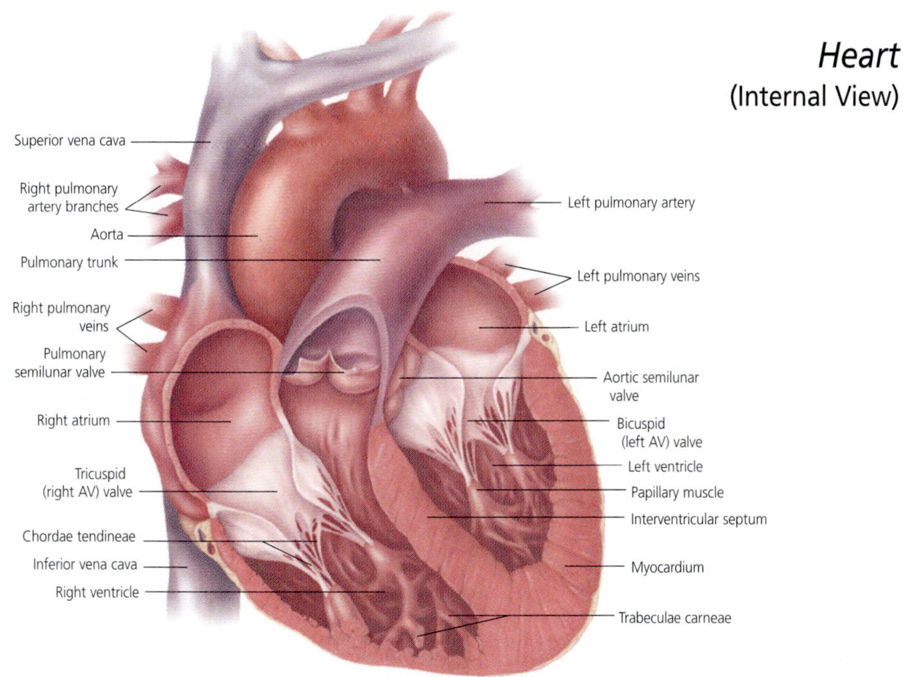

Heart
(Internal View)
Superior vena cava
Right pulmonary artery branches
Left pulmonary artery
Aorta
Pulmonary trunk
Left pulmonary veins
Right pulmonary veins
Left atrium
Pulmonary semilunar valve
Aortic semilunar valve
Right atrium
Bicuspid (left AV) valve
Left ventricle
Tricuspid (right AV) valve
Papillary muscle
Interventricular septum
Chordae tendineae
Inferior vena cava
Myocardium
Right ventricle
Trabeculae carneae

PLATE 15. CIRCULATORY SYSTEM

Vascular System

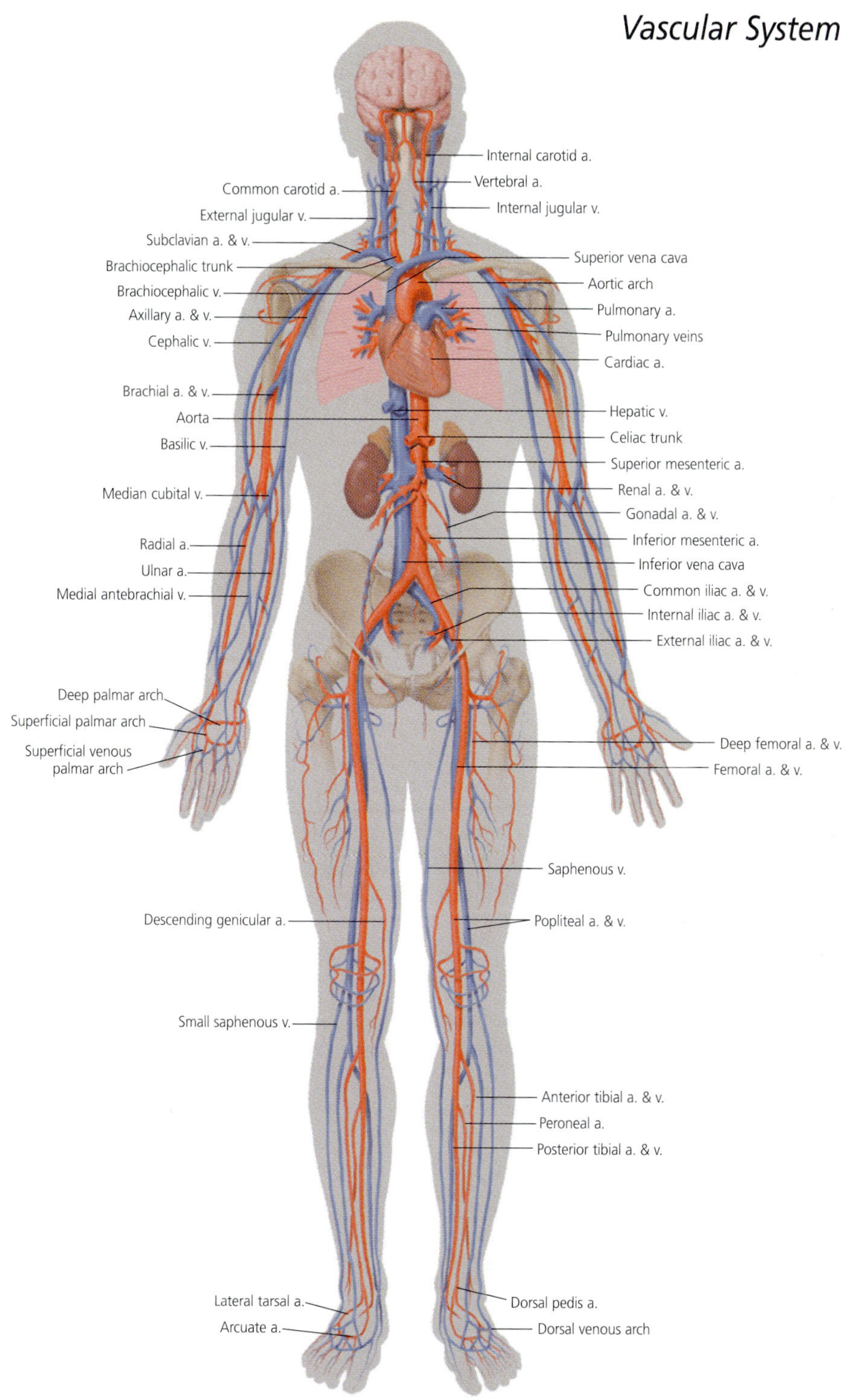

PLATE 16. DIGESTIVE SYSTEM

Digestive System

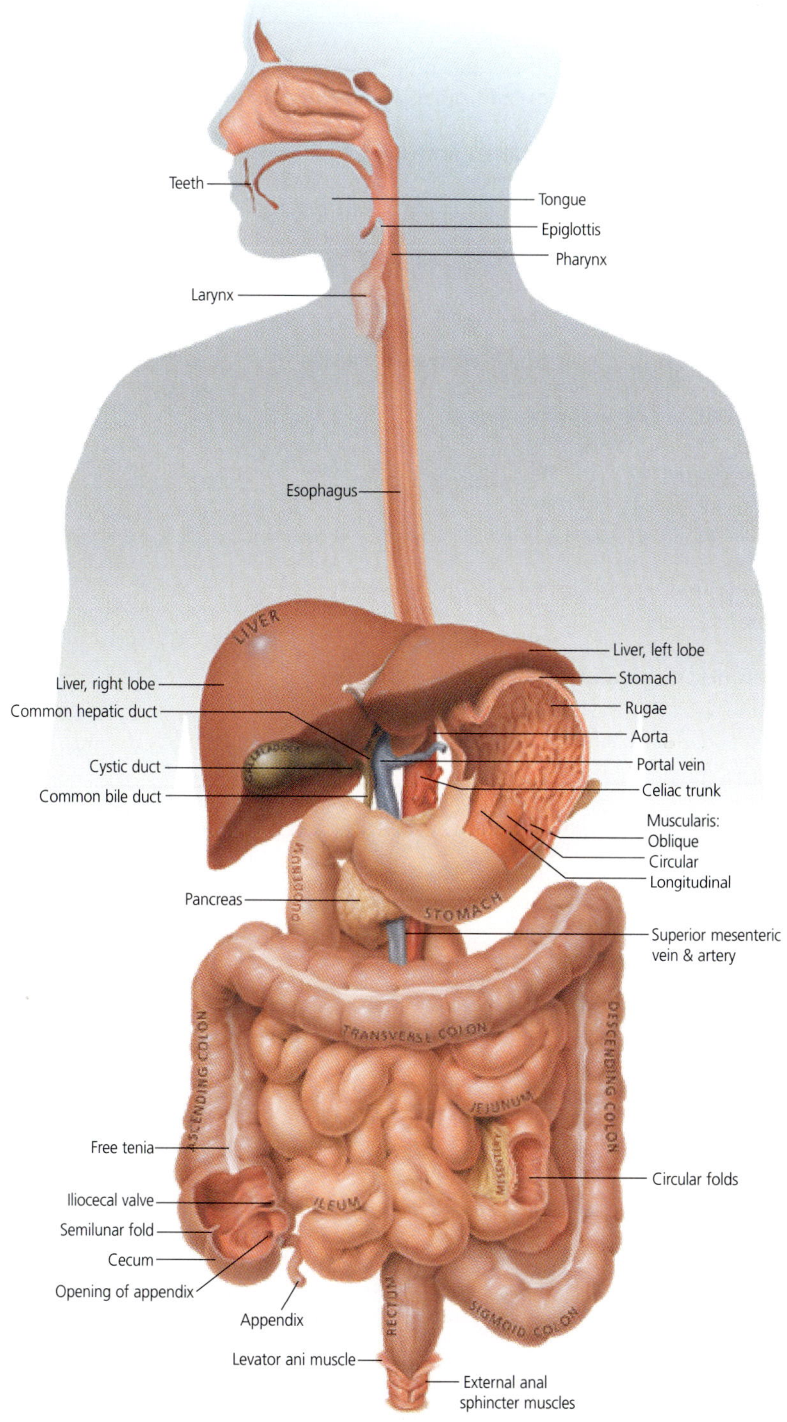

PLATE 17. GENITOURINARY SYSTEM

Urinary System

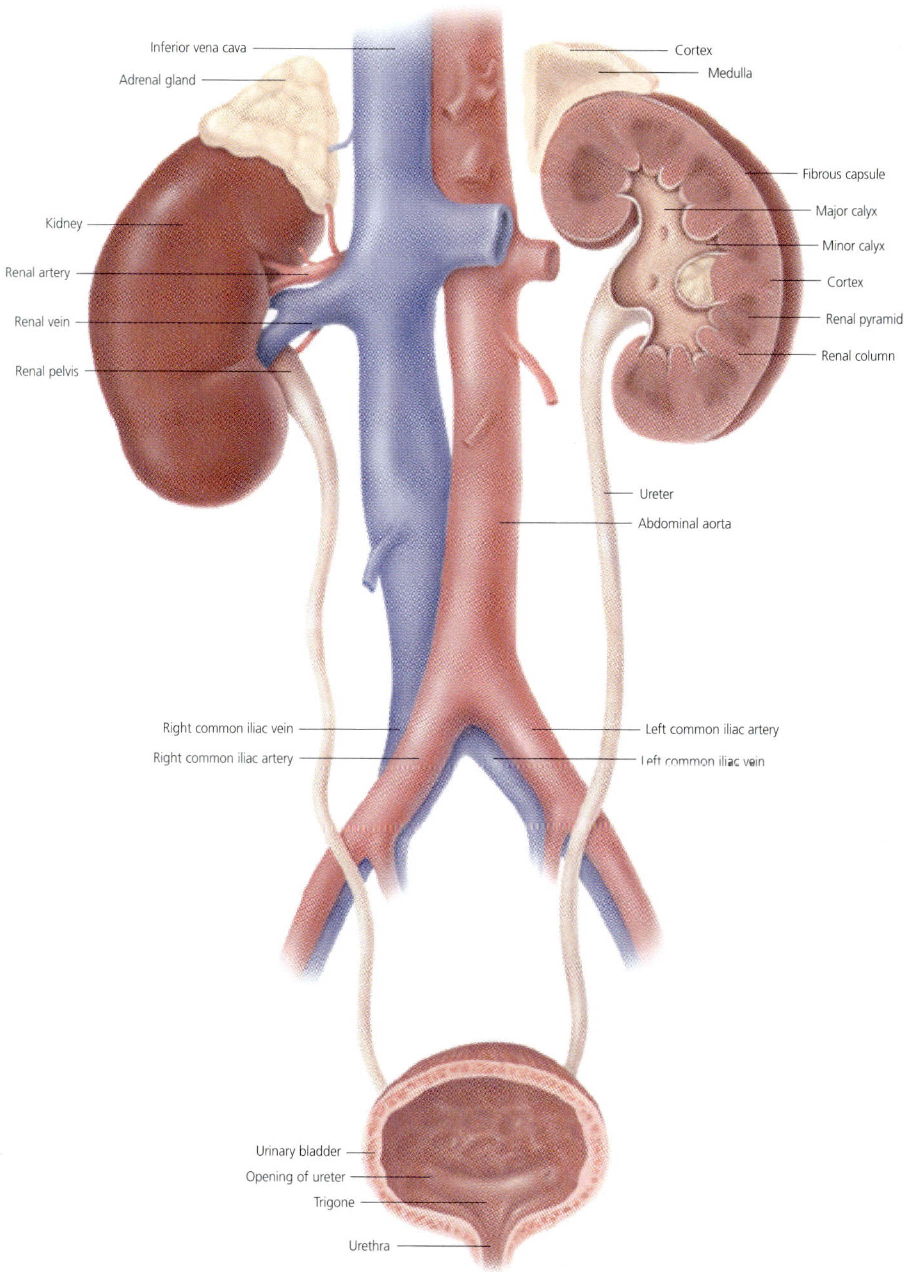

PLATE 18. MALE GENITAL ORGANS

Male Reproductive System

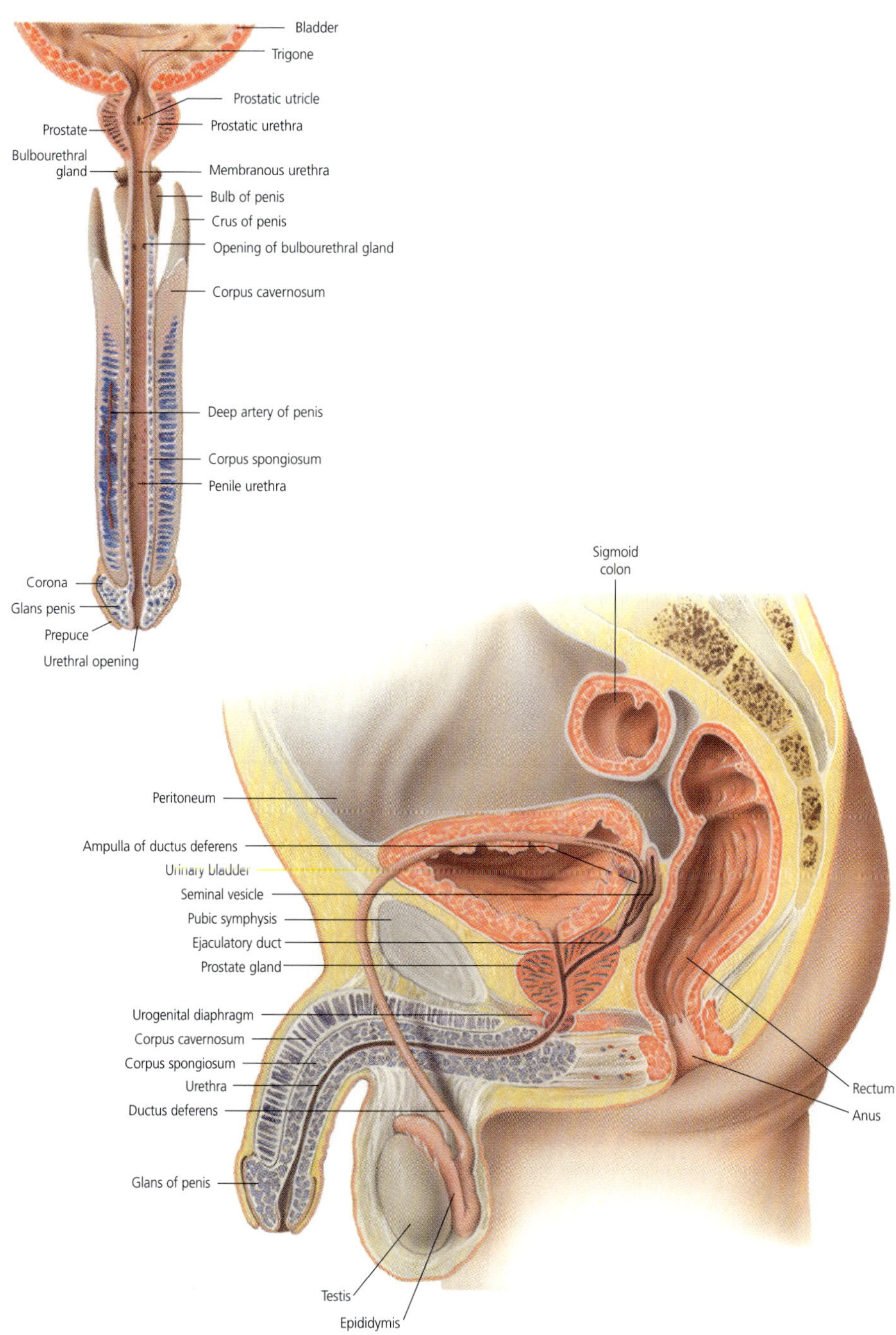

PLATE 19. FEMALE GENITAL ORGANS

Female Reproductive System

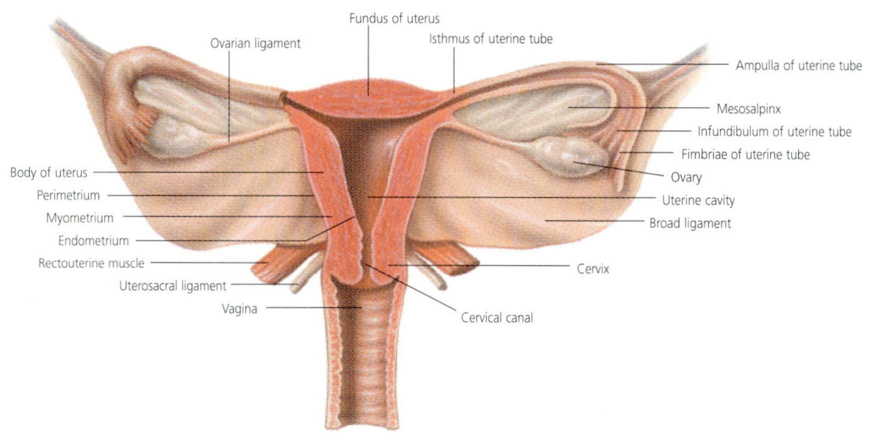

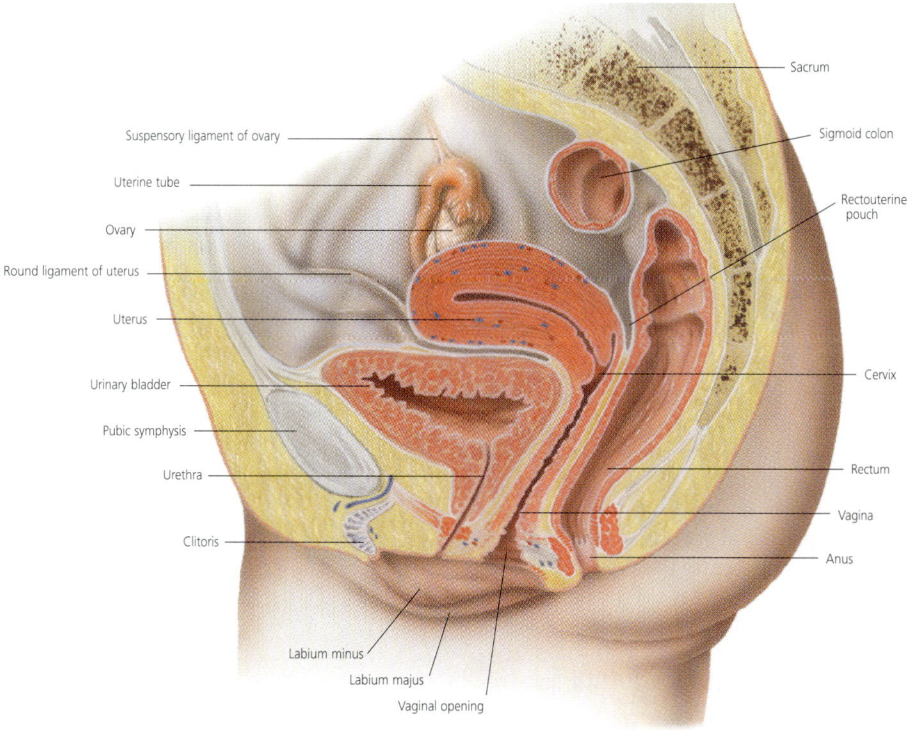

PLATE 20. PREGNANCY, CHILDBIRTH AND THE PUERPERIUM

Ectopic and molar pregnancy	
Hydatidiform mole	630
Other abnormal product of conception	631
Missed abortion	632
Ectopic pregnancy	633
Other pregnancy with abortive outcome	
Abortion	634
Legally induced abortion	635
Complications following abortion and ectopic and molar pregnancies	639
Complications mainly related to pregnancy	
Hemorrhage in early pregnancy	640
Antepartum hemorrhage, abruptio placentae, and placenta previa	641
Hypertension complicating pregnancy, childbirth, and the puerperium	642
Excessive vomiting in pregnancy	643
Early or threatened labor	644
Late pregnancy	645
Normal delivery, other indications for care in pregnancy and delivery	
Normal delivery	650
Multiple gestation	651
Malposition and malpresentation of fetus	652
Disproportion	653
Polyhydramnios	657
Complications occurring mainly in the course of labor and delivery	
Obstructed labor	660
Abnormality of forces of labor	661
Long labor	662
Umbilical cord complications	663
Trauma to perineum and vulva during delivery	664
Postpartum hemorrhage	666
Retained placenta or membranes, without hemorrhage	667
Complications of the puerperium	
Major puerperal infection	670
Venous complications in pregnancy and the puerperium	671
Pyrexia of unknown origin during the puerperium	672
Obstetrical pulmonary embolism	673
Persons encountering health services in circumstances related to reproduction	
Normal pregnancy	V22
Supervision of high-risk pregnancy	V23
Postpartum care and examination	V24
Encounter for contraceptive management	V25
Procreative management	V26

Female Reproductive System: Pregnancy
(Lateral View)

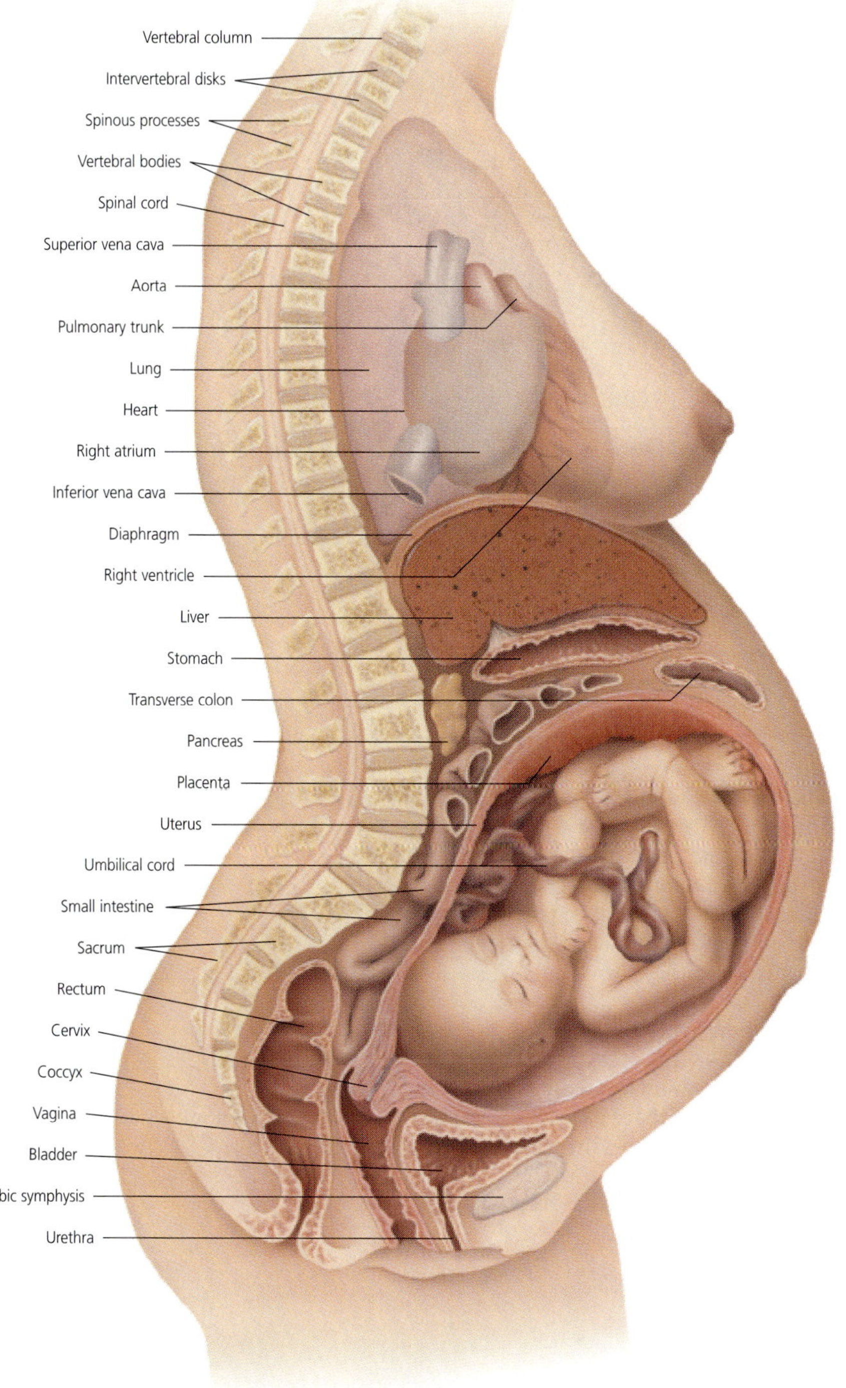

PLATE 21. NERVOUS SYSTEM - BRAIN

Brain
(Base View)

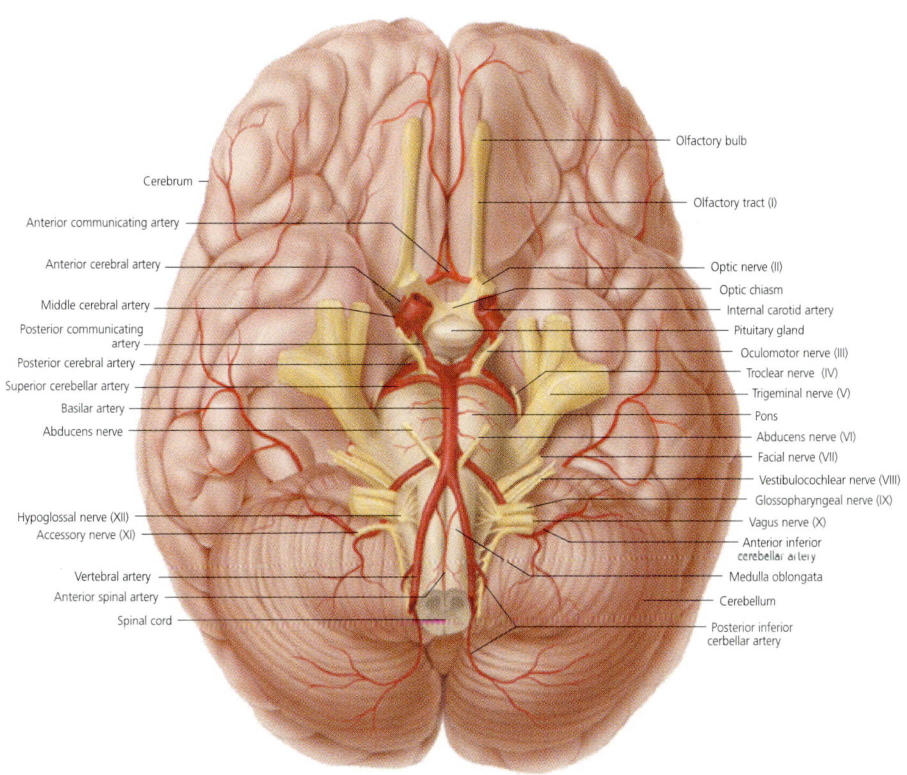

PLATE 22. NERVOUS SYSTEM

Nervous System

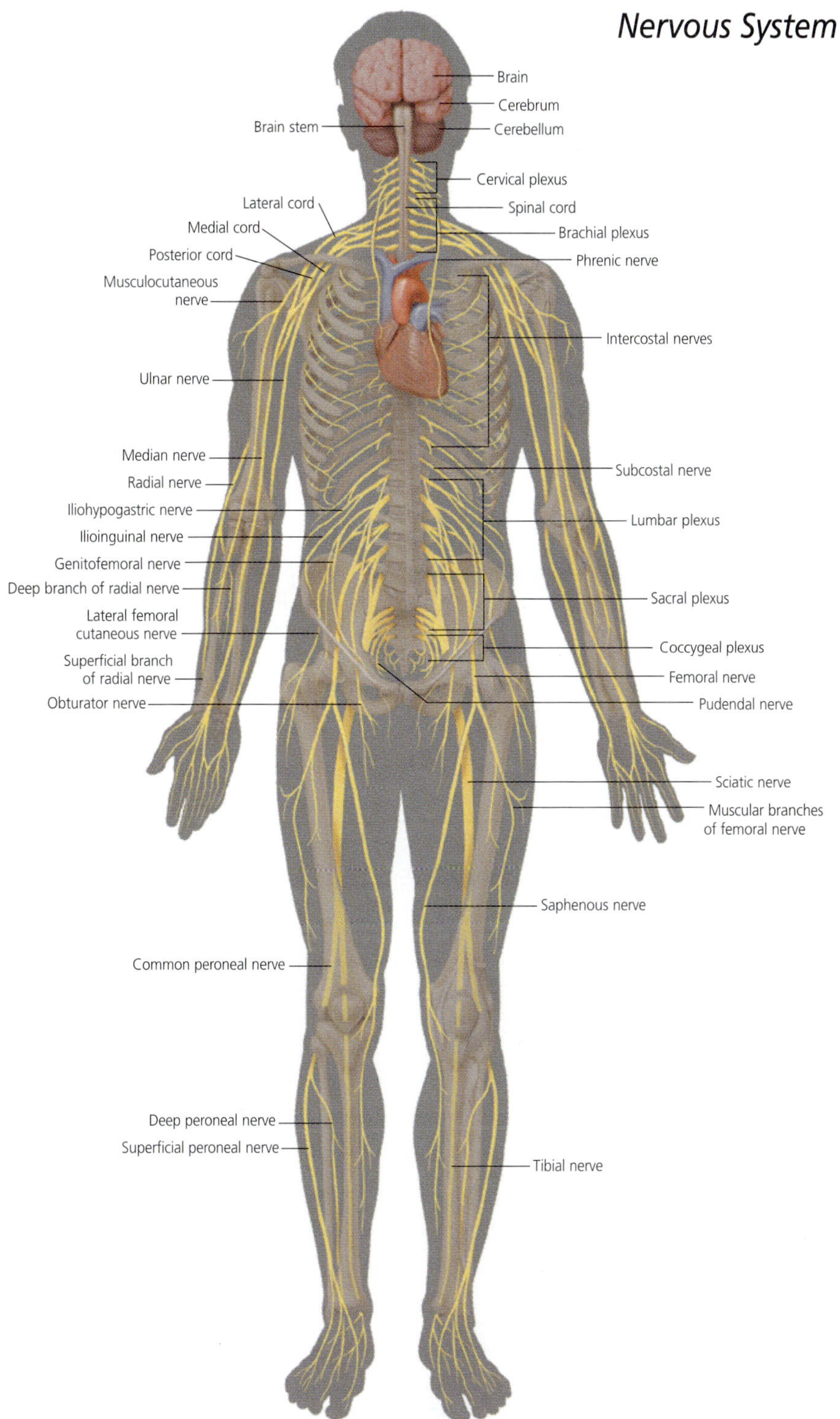

PLATE 23. EYE AND OCULAR ADNEXA

Right Eye
(Horizontal Section)

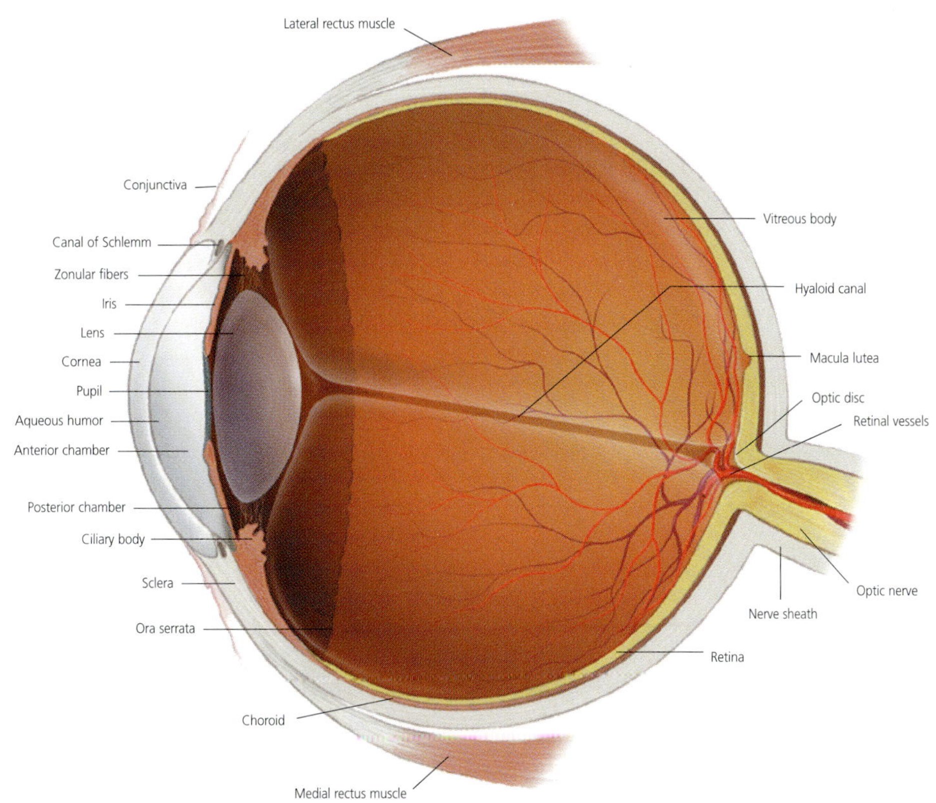

PLATE 24. AUDITORY SYSTEM

Diseases of the ear and mastoid process	
Disorders of external ear	380
Nonsuppurative otitis media and Eustachian tube disorders	381
Suppurative and unspecified otitis media	382
Mastoiditis and related conditions	383
Other disorders of tympanic membrane	384
Other disorders of middle ear and mastoid	385
Vertiginous syndromes and other disorders of vestibular system	386
Otosclerosis	387
Hearing loss	389
Symptoms, signs and ill-defined conditions	780-799

The Ear

Temporalis bone
Temporalis muscle
Cartilage
Auricle
External auditory canal
Middle ear
Semicircular canals
Cochlea
Cochlear nerve
Eustachian tube
Cartilage
Nasopharynx
Ossicles:
Stapes
Incus
Malleus
Tympanic membrane

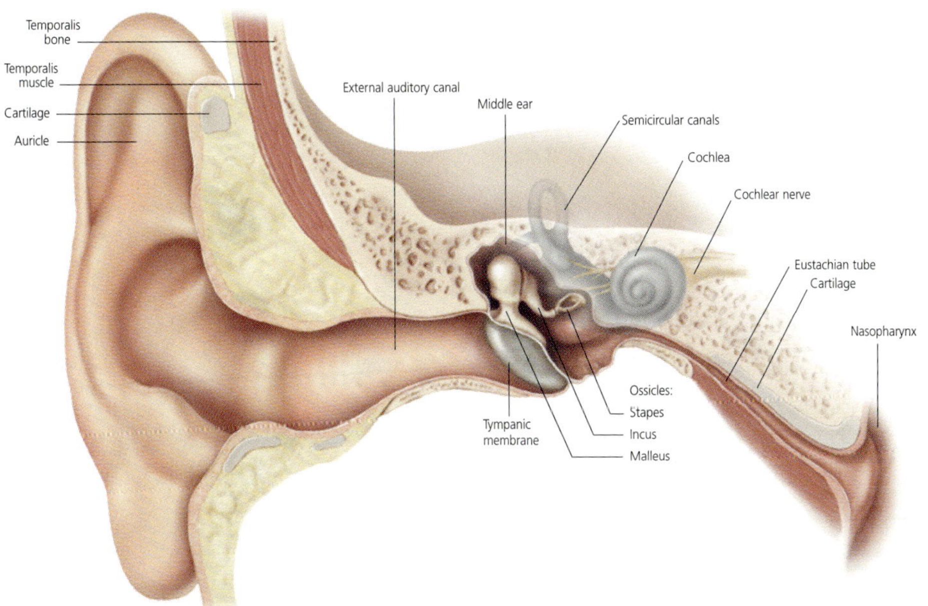

DISEASES: TABULAR LIST
VOLUME 1

1. INFECTIOUS AND PARASITIC DISEASES (001-139)

Note: Categories for "late effects" of infectious and parasitic diseases are to be found at 137-139.
Includes: diseases generally recognized as communicable or transmissible as well as a few diseases of unknown but possibly infectious origin

> Excludes: acute respiratory infections (460-466)
> carrier or suspected carrier of infectious organism (V02.0-V02.9)
> certain localized infections
> influenza (487.0-487.8)

INTESTINAL INFECTIOUS DISEASES (001-009)

> Excludes: helminthiases (120.0-129)

001 **Cholera**

    001.0 Due to Vibrio cholerae

    001.1 Due to Vibrio cholerae el tor

    001.9 Cholera, unspecified

002 **Typhoid and paratyphoid fevers**

    002.0 Typhoid fever
        Typhoid (fever) (infection) [any site]

    002.1 Paratyphoid fever A

    002.2 Paratyphoid fever B

    002.3 Paratyphoid fever C

    002.9 Paratyphoid fever, unspecified

003 **Other salmonella infections**
    Includes: infection or food poisoning by Salmonella [any serotype]

    003.0 Salmonella gastroenteritis
        Salmonellosis

    003.1 Salmonella septicemia

   ⑤ **003.2 Localized salmonella infections**

        003.20 Localized salmonella infection, unspecified

        003.21 Salmonella meningitis

        003.22 Salmonella pneumonia

        003.23 Salmonella arthritis

        003.24 Salmonella osteomyelitis

        003.29 Other

    003.8 Other specified salmonella infections

    003.9 Salmonella infection, unspecified

004 **Shigellosis**
    Includes: bacillary dysentery

    004.0 Shigella dysenteriae
        Infection by group A Shigella (Schmitz) (Shiga)

    004.1 Shigella flexneri
        Infection by group B Shigella

    004.2 Shigella boydii
        Infection by group C Shigella

    004.3 Shigella sonnei
        Infection by group D Shigella

    004.8 Other specified shigella infections

    004.9 Shigellosis, unspecified

005 **Other food poisoning (bacterial)**

> Excludes: salmonella infections (003.0-003.9)
> toxic effect of:
>   food contaminants (989.7)
>   noxious foodstuffs (988.0-988.9)

    005.0 Staphylococcal food poisoning
        Staphylococcal toxemia specified as due to food

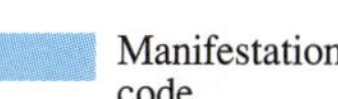

005.1 Botulism
Food poisoning due to Clostridium botulinum

005.2 Food poisoning due to Clostridium perfringens [C. welchii]
Enteritis necroticans

005.3 Food poisoning due to other Clostridia

005.4 Food poisoning due to Vibrio parahaemolyticus

⑤ **005.8 Other bacterial food poisoning**

Excludes: salmonella food poisoning (003.0-003.9)

    005.81 Food poisoning due to Vibrio vulnificus

    005.89 Other bacterial food poisoning
Food poisoning due to Bacillus cereus

005.9 Food poisoning, unspecified

006 Amebiasis
Includes: infection due to Entamoeba histolytica

Excludes: amebiasis due to organisms other than Entamoeba histolytica (007.8)

006.0 Acute amebic dysentery without mention of abscess
Acute amebiasis

006.1 Chronic intestinal amebiasis without mention of abscess
Chronic:
  amebiasis
  amebic dysentery

006.2 Amebic nondysenteric colitis

006.3 Amebic liver abscess
Hepatic amebiasis

006.4 Amebic lung abscess
Amebic abscess of lung (and liver)

006.5 Amebic brain abscess
Amebic abscess of brain (and liver) (and lung)

006.6 Amebic skin ulceration
Cutaneous amebiasis

006.8 Amebic infection of other sites
Amebic: Ameboma
  appendicitis
  balanitis

Excludes: specific infections by free-living amebae (136.2)

006.9 Amebiasis, unspecified
Amebiasis NOS

007 Other protozoal intestinal diseases
Includes: protozoal:
        colitis
        diarrhea
        dysentery

007.0 Balantidiasis
Infection by Balantidium coli

007.1 Giardiasis
Infection by Giardia lamblia
Lambliasis

007.2 Coccidiosis
Infection by Isospora belli and Isospora hominis
Isosporiasis

007.3 Intestinal trichomoniasis

007.4 Cryptosporidiosis

● **007.5 Cyclosporiasis**

007.8 Other specified protozoal intestinal diseases
Amebiasis due to organisms other than Entamoeba histolytica

007.9 Unspecified protozoal intestinal disease
Flagellate diarrhea   Protozoal dysentery NOS

● Code new   ▲ Revision of   ④ ⑤ Fourth or fifth
  to this edition   existing code   digit required

008 Intestinal infections due to other organisms
Includes: any condition classifiable to 009.0-009.3 with mention of the responsible organisms

Excludes: *food poisoning by these organisms (005.0-005.9)*

⑤ **008.0 Escherichia coli [E. coli]**

008.00 E. coli, unspecified
E. coli enteritis NOS

008.01 Enteropathogenic E. coli

008.02 Enterotoxigenic E. coli

008.03 Enteroinvasive E. coli

008.04 Enterohemorrhagic E. coli

008.09 Other intestinal E. coli infections

008.1 Arizona group of paracolon bacilli

008.2 Aerobacter aerogenes
Enterobacter aerogenes

008.3 Proteus (mirabilis) (morganii)

⑤ **008.4 Other specified bacteria**

008.41 Staphylococcus
Staphylococcal enterocolitis

008.42 Pseudomonas

008.43 Campylobacter

008.44 Yersinia enterocolitica

008.45 Clostridium difficile
Pseudomembranous colitis

008.46 Other anaerobes
Anaerobic enteritis NOS
Gram-negative anaerobes
Bacteroides (fragilis)

008.47 Other Gram-negative bacteria
Gram-negative enteritis NOS

Excludes: *Gram-negative anaerobes (008.46)*

008.49 Other

008.5 Bacterial enteritis, unspecified

⑤ **008.6 Enteritis due to specified virus**

008.61 Rotavirus

008.62 Adenovirus

008.63 Norwalk virus
Norwalk-like agent

008.64 Other small round viruses [SRV's]
Small round virus NOS

008.65 Calcivirus

008.66 Astrovirus

008.67 Enterovirus NEC
Coxsackie virus
Echovirus

Excludes: *poliovirus (045.0-045.9)*

008.69 Other viral enteritis
Torovirus

008.8 Other organism, not elsewhere classified
Viral:
enteritis NOS
gastroenteritis

Excludes: *influenza with involvement of gastrointestinal tract (487.8)*

■ Add 4th or 5th digit	■ Nonspecific code	■ Unspecified code	■ Manifestation code

009   Ill-defined intestinal infections

> *Excludes:* *diarrheal disease or intestinal infection due to specified organism (001.0-008.8)*
> *diarrhea following gastrointestinal surgery (564.4)*
> *intestinal malabsorption (579.0-579.9)*
> *ischemic enteritis (557.0-557.9)*
> *other noninfectious gastroenteritis and colitis (558.1-558.9)*
> *regional enteritis (555.0-555.9)*
> *ulcerative colitis (556)*

009.0   Infectious colitis, enteritis, and gastroenteritis

Colitis		Dysentery:
Enteritis	septic	NOS
Gastroenteritis		catarrhal
		hemorrhagic

009.1   Colitis, enteritis, and gastroenteritis of presumed infectious origin

> *Excludes:* *colitis NOS (558.9)*
> *enteritis NOS (558.9)*
> *gastroenteritis NOS (558.9)*

009.2   Infectious diarrhea

Diarrhea: Infectious diarrheal disease NOS
  dysenteric
  epidemic

009.3   Diarrhea of presumed infectious origin

> *Excludes:* *diarrhea NOS (787.91)*

TUBERCULOSIS (010-018)

Includes: infection by Mycobacterium tuberculosis (human) (bovine)

> *Excludes:* *congenital tuberculosis (771.2)*
> *late effects of tuberculosis (137.0-137.4)*

The following fifth-digit subclassification is for use with categories 010-018:

0   unspecified

1   bacteriological or histological examination not done

2   bacteriological or histological examination unknown (at present)

3   tubercle bacilli found (in sputum) by microscopy

4   tubercle bacilli not found (in sputum) by microscopy, but found by bacterial culture

5   tubercle bacilli not found by bacteriological examination, but tuberculosis confirmed histologically

6   tubercle bacilli not found by bacteriological or histological examination but tuberculosis confirmed by other methods [inoculation of animals]

⑤ **010   Primary tuberculous infection**

> *Excludes:* *nonspecific reaction to tuberculin skin test without active tuberculosis (795.5)*
> *positive PPD (795.5)*
> *positive tuberculin skin test without active tuberculosis (795.5)*

⑤ **010.0   Primary tuberculous complex**

⑤ **010.1   Tuberculous pleurisy in primary progressive tuberculosis**

⑤ **010.8   Other primary progressive tuberculosis**

> *Excludes:* *tuberculous erythema nodosum (017.1)*

⑤ **010.9   Primary tuberculous infection, unspecified**

⑤ **011   Pulmonary tuberculosis**

Use additional code, if desired, to identify any associated silicosis (502)

⑤ **011.0   Tuberculosis of lung, infiltrative**

⑤ **011.1   Tuberculosis of lung, nodular**

⑤ **011.2   Tuberculosis of lung with cavitation**

⑤ **011.3   Tuberculosis of bronchus**

> *Excludes:* *isolated bronchial tuberculosis (012.2)*

⑤ **011.4   Tuberculous fibrosis of lung**

⑤ **011.5   Tuberculous bronchiectasis**

● Code new to this edition   ▲ Revision of existing code   ④ ⑤ Fourth or fifth digit required

⑤ **011.6 Tuberculous pneumonia [any form]**

⑤ **011.7 Tuberculous pneumothorax**

⑤ **011.8 Other specified pulmonary tuberculosis**

⑤ **011.9 Pulmonary tuberculosis, unspecified**
Respiratory tuberculosis NOS
Tuberculosis of lung NOS

⑤ **012 Other respiratory tuberculosis**

> Excludes: *respiratory tuberculosis, unspecified (011.9)*

⑤ **012.0 Tuberculous pleurisy**
Tuberculosis of pleura   Tuberculous hydrothorax
Tuberculous empyema

> Excludes: *pleurisy with effusion without mention of cause (511.9)*
> *tuberculous pleurisy in primary progressive tuberculosis (010.1)*

⑤ **012.1 Tuberculosis of intrathoracic lymph nodes**
Tuberculosis of lymph nodes:
  hilar
  mediastinal
  tracheobronchial
Tuberculous tracheobronchial adenopathy

> Excludes: *that specified as primary (010.0-010.9)*

⑤ **012.2 Isolated tracheal or bronchial tuberculosis**

⑤ **012.3 Tuberculous laryngitis**
Tuberculosis of glottis

⑤ **012.8 Other specified respiratory tuberculosis**
Tuberculosis of: Tuberculosis of:
  mediastinum   nose (septum)
  nasopharynx   sinus [any nasal]

⑤ **013 Tuberculosis of meninges and central nervous system**

⑤ **013.0 Tuberculous meningitis**
Tuberculosis of meninges   Tuberculous:
  (cerebral) (spinal)   leptomeningitis
                                 meningoencephalitis

> Excludes: *tuberculoma of meninges (013.1)*

⑤ **013.1 Tuberculoma of meninges**

⑤ **013.2 Tuberculoma of brain**
Tuberculosis of brain (current disease)

⑤ **013.3 Tuberculous abscess of brain**

⑤ **013.4 Tuberculoma of spinal cord**

⑤ **013.5 Tuberculous abscess of spinal cord**

⑤ **013.6 Tuberculous encephalitis or myelitis**

⑤ **013.8 Other specified tuberculosis of central nervous system**

⑤ **013.9 Unspecified tuberculosis of central nervous system**
Tuberculosis of central nervous system NOS

⑤ **014 Tuberculosis of intestines, peritoneum, and mesenteric glands**

⑤ **014.0 Tuberculous peritonitis**
Tuberculous ascites

⑤ **014.8 Other**
Tuberculosis (of):   Tuberculous enteritis
  anus
  intestine (large) (small)
  mesenteric glands
  rectum
  retroperitoneal (lymph nodes)

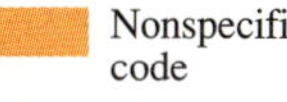

⑤ **015 Tuberculosis of bones and joints**

Use additional code, if desired, to identify manifestation, as:
  tuberculous:
    arthropathy (711.4)
    necrosis of bone (730.8)
    osteitis (730.8)
    osteomyelitis (730.8)
    synovitis (727.01)
    tenosynovitis (727.01)

⑤ **015.0 Vertebral column**
        Pott's disease

Use additional code, if desired, to identify manifestation, as:
          curvature of spine [Pott's] (737.4)
          kyphosis (737.4)
          spondylitis (720.81)

⑤ **015.1 Hip**

⑤ **015.2 Knee**

⑤ **015.5 Limb bones**
        Tuberculous dactylitis

⑤ **015.6 Mastoid**
        Tuberculous mastoiditis

⑤ **015.7 Other specified bone**

⑤ **015.8 Other specified joint**

⑤ **015.9 Tuberculosis of unspecified bones and joints**

⑤ **016 Tuberculosis of genitourinary system**

⑤ **016.0 Kidney**
        Renal tuberculosis

Use additional code, if desired, to identify manifestation, as:
          tuberculous:
            nephropathy (583.81)
            pyelitis (590.81)
            pyelonephritis (590.81)

⑤ **016.1 Bladder**

⑤ **016.2 Ureter**

⑤ **016.3 Other urinary organs**

⑤ **016.4 Epididymis**

⑤ **016.5 Other male genital organs**

Use additional code, if desired, to identify manifestation, as:
          tuberculosis of:
            prostate (601.4)
            seminal vesicle (608.81)
            testis (608.81)

⑤ **016.6 Tuberculous oophoritis and salpingitis**

⑤ **016.7 Other female genital organs**
        Tuberculous:
          cervicitis
          endometritis

⑤ **016.9 Genitourinary tuberculosis, unspecified**

⑤ **017 Tuberculosis of other organs**

⑤ **017.0 Skin and subcutaneous cellular tissue**

Lupus:	Tuberculosis:
exedens	colliquativa
vulgaris	cutis
Scrofuloderma	lichenoides
	papulonecrotica
	verrucosa cutis

Excludes: *lupus erythematosus (695.4)*
          disseminated (710.0)
          lupus NOS (710.0)
          nonspecific reaction to tuberculin skin test without active tuberculosis (795.5)
          positive PPD (795.5)
          positive tuberculin skin test without active tuberculosis (795.5)

● Code new to this edition   ▲ Revision of existing code   ④ ⑤ Fourth or fifth digit required

⑤ **017.1 Erythema nodosum with hypersensitivity reaction in tuberculosis**

    Bazin's disease   Tuberculosis indurativa
    Erythema:
      induratum
      nodosum, tuberculous

> *Excludes:* erythema nodosum NOS (695.2)

⑤ **017.2 Peripheral lymph nodes**

    Scrofula   Tuberculous adenitis
    Scrofulous abscess

> *Excludes:* tuberculosis of lymph nodes:
>   bronchial and mediastinal (012.1)
>   mesenteric and retroperitoneal (014.8)
>   tuberculous tracheobronchial adenopathy (012.1)

⑤ **017.3 Eye**

Use additional code, if desired, to identify manifestation, as:
    tuberculous:
      chorioretinitis, disseminated (363.13)
      episcleritis (379.09)
      interstitial keratitis (370.59)
      iridocyclitis, chronic (364.11)
      keratoconjunctivitis (phlyctenular) (370.31)

⑤ **017.4 Ear**

    Tuberculosis of ear
    Tuberculous otitis media

> *Excludes:* tuberculous mastoiditis (015.6)

⑤ **017.5 Thyroid gland**

⑤ **017.6 Adrenal glands**

    Addison's disease, tuberculous

⑤ **017.7 Spleen**

⑤ **017.8 Esophagus**

⑤ **017.9 Other specified organs**

Use additional code, if desired, to identify manifestation, as:
    tuberculosis of:
      endocardium [any valve] (424.91)
      myocardium (422.0)
      pericardium (420.0)

⑤ **018 Miliary tuberculosis**

    Includes: tuberculosis:
      disseminated
      generalized
      miliary, whether of a single specified site, multiple sites, or unspecified site
      polyserositis

⑤ **018.0 Acute miliary tuberculosis**

⑤ **018.8 Other specified miliary tuberculosis**

⑤ **018.9 Miliary tuberculosis, unspecified**

ZOONOTIC BACTERIAL DISEASES (020-027)

020 Plague

    Includes: infection by Yersinia [Pasteurella] pestis

020.0 Bubonic

020.1 Cellulocutaneous

020.2 Septicemic

020.3 Primary pneumonic

020.4 Secondary pneumonic

020.5 Pneumonic, unspecified

020.8 Other specified types of plague

    Abortive plague   Pestis minor
    Ambulatory plague

020.9 Plague, unspecified

021 Tularemia
    Includes: deerfly fever
               infection by Francisella [Pasteurella] tularensis
               rabbit fever

021.0 Ulceroglandular tularemia

021.1 Enteric tularemia
    Tularemia:
      cryptogenic
      intestinal
      typhoidal

021.2 Pulmonary tularemia
    Bronchopneumonic tularemia

021.3 Oculoglandular tularemia

021.8 Other specified tularemia
    Tularemia:
      generalized or disseminated
      glandular

021.9 Unspecified tularemia

022 Anthrax

022.0 Cutaneous anthrax
    Malignant pustule

022.1 Pulmonary anthrax
    Respiratory anthrax   Wool-sorters' disease

022.2 Gastrointestinal anthrax

022.3 Anthrax septicemia

022.8 Other specified manifestations of anthrax

022.9 Anthrax, unspecified

023 Brucellosis
    Includes: fever:
                 Malta
                 Mediterranean
                 undulant

023.0 Brucella melitensis

023.1 Brucella abortus

023.2 Brucella suis

023.3 Brucella canis

023.8 Other brucellosis
    Infection by more than one organism

023.9 Brucellosis, unspecified

024 Glanders
    Infection by: Farcy
      Actinobacillus mallei   Malleus
      Malleomyces mallei
      Pseudomonas mallei

025 Melioidosis
    Infection by:
      Malleomyces pseudomallei
      Pseudomonas pseudomallei
      Whitmore's bacillus
    Pseudoglanders

026 Rat-bite fever

026.0 Spirillary fever
    Rat-bite fever due to Spirillum minor [S. minus]
    Sodoku

026.1 Streptobacillary fever
    Epidemic arthritic erythema
    Haverhill fever
    Rat-bite fever due to Streptobacillus moniliformis

026.9 Unspecified rat-bite fever

027 Other zoonotic bacterial diseases

● Code new   ▲ Revision of   ④ ⑤ Fourth or fifth
  to this edition   existing code   digit required

027.0 Listeriosis

Infection
Septicemia } by Listeria monocytogenes

Use additional code, if desired, to identify manifestation, as meningitis (320.7)

Excludes: *congenital listeriosis (771.2)*

027.1 Erysipelothrix infection

Erysipeloid (of Rosenbach)
Infection
Septicemia } by Erysipelothrix insidiosa [E. rhusiopathiae]

027.2 Pasteurellosis

Pasteurella pseudotuberculosis infection
Mesenteric adenitis
Septic infection (cat bite) (dog bite) } by Pasteurella multocida [P. septica]

Excludes: *infection by:*

Francisella [Pasteurella] tularensis (021.0-021.9)
Yersinia [Pasteurella] pestis (020.0-020.9)

027.8 Other specified zoonotic bacterial diseases

027.9 Unspecified zoonotic bacterial disease

OTHER BACTERIAL DISEASES (030-041)

Excludes: *bacterial venereal diseases (098.0-099.9)*
bartonellosis (088.0)

030 Leprosy

Includes: Hansen's disease
infection by Mycobacterium leprae

030.0 Lepromatous [type L]

Lepromatous leprosy (macular) (diffuse) (infiltrated) (nodular) (neuritic)

030.1 Tuberculoid [type T]

Tuberculoid leprosy (macular) (maculoanesthetic) (major) (minor) (neuritic)

030.2 Indeterminate [group I]

Indeterminate [uncharacteristic] leprosy (macular) (neuritic)

030.3 Borderline [group B]

Borderline or dimorphous leprosy (infiltrated) (neuritic)

030.8 Other specified leprosy

030.9 Leprosy, unspecified

031 Diseases due to other mycobacteria

031.0 Pulmonary

Infection by Mycobacterium:
avium
intracellulare [Battey bacillus]
kansasii
Battey disease

031.1 Cutaneous

Buruli ulcer
Infection by Mycobacterium:
marinum [M. balnei]
ulcerans

031.2 Disseminated

Disseminated mycobacterium avium-intracellulare complex (DMAC)
Mycobacterium avium-intracellulare complex (MAC) bacteremia

031.8 Other specified mycobacterial diseases

031.9 Unspecified diseases due to mycobacteria

Atypical mycobacterium infection NOS

032 Diphtheria

Includes: infection by Corynebacterium diphtheriae

032.0 Faucial diphtheria

Membranous angina, diphtheritic

032.1 Nasopharyngeal diphtheria

032.2 Anterior nasal diphtheria

032.3 Laryngeal diphtheria

Laryngotracheitis, diphtheritic

⑤ **032.8 Other specified diphtheria**

    032.81 Conjunctival diphtheria
       Pseudomembranous diphtheritic conjunctivitis

    032.82 Diphtheritic myocarditis

    032.83 Diphtheritic peritonitis

    032.84 Diphtheritic cystitis

    032.85 Cutaneous diphtheria

    032.89 Other

032.9 Diphtheria, unspecified

033 Whooping cough
    Includes: pertussis

Use additional code, if desired, to identify any associated pneumonia (484.3)

033.0 Bordetella pertussis [B. pertussis]

033.1 Bordetella parapertussis [B. parapertussis]

033.8 Whooping cough due to other specified organism
    Bordetella bronchiseptica [B. bronchiseptica]

033.9 Whooping cough, unspecified organism

034 Streptococcal sore throat and scarlet fever

034.0 Streptococcal sore throat

Septic:	Streptococcal:
angina	angina
sore throat	laryngitis
	pharyngitis
	tonsillitis

034.1 Scarlet fever
    Scarlatina

    Excludes: *parascarlatina (057.8)*

035 Erysipelas

    Excludes: *postpartum or puerperal erysipelas (670)*

036 Meningococcal infection

036.0 Meningococcal meningitis

Cerebrospinal fever	Meningitis:
(meningococcal)	cerebrospinal
	epidemic

036.1 Meningococcal encephalitis

036.2 Meningococcemia
    Meningococcal septicemia

036.3 Waterhouse-Friderichsen syndrome, meningococcal
    Meningococcal hemorrhagic adrenalitis
    Meningococcic adrenal syndrome
    Waterhouse-Friderichsen syndrome NOS

⑤ **036.4 Meningococcal carditis**

    036.40 Meningococcal carditis, unspecified

    036.41 Meningococcal pericarditis

    036.42 Meningococcal endocarditis

    036.43 Meningococcal myocarditis

⑤ **036.8 Other specified meningococcal infections**

    036.81 Meningococcal optic neuritis

    036.82 Meningococcal arthropathy

    036.89 Other

036.9 Meningococcal infection, unspecified
    Meningococcal infection NOS

● Code new
to this edition
    ▲ Revision of
existing code
    ④ ⑤ Fourth or fifth
digit required

037 Tetanus

> *Excludes:* *tetanus:*
>
> > *complicating:*
> > *abortion (634-638 with .0, 639.0)*
> > *ectopic or molar pregnancy (639.0)*
> > *neonatorum (771.3)*
> > *puerperal (670)*

038 Septicemia

> *Excludes:* *bacteremia (790.7)*
>
> > *during labor (659.3)*
> > *following ectopic or molar pregnancy (639.0)*
> > *following infusion, injection, transfusion, or vaccination (999.3)*
> > *postpartum, puerperal (670)*
> > *that complicating abortion (634-638 with .0, 639.0)*

038.0 Streptococcal septicemia

⑤ **038.1 Staphylococcal septicemia**

    038.10 Staphylococcal septicemia, unspecified

    038.11 Staphylococcus aureus septicemia

    038.19 Other staphylococcal septicemia

038.2 Pneumococcal septicemia

038.3 Septicemia due to anaerobes
Septicemia due to bacteroides

> *Excludes:* *gas gangrene (040.0)*
>
> > *that due to anaerobic streptococci (038.0)*

⑤ **038.4 Septicemia due to other gram-negative organisms**

    038.40 Gram-negative organism, unspecified
       Gram-negative septicemia NOS

    038.41 Hemophilus influenzae [H. influenzae]

    038.42 Escherichia coli [E. coli]

    038.43 Pseudomonas

    038.44 Serratia

    038.49 Other

038.8 Other specified septicemias

> *Excludes:* *septicemia (due to):*
>
> > *anthrax (022.3)*
> > *gonococcal (098.89)*
> > *herpetic (054.5)*
> > *meningococcal (036.2)*
> > *septicemic plague (020.2)*

038.9 Unspecified septicemia
Septicemia NOS

> *Excludes:* *bacteremia NOS (790.7)*

039 Actinomycotic infections
Includes: actinomycotic mycetoma
infection by Actinomycetales, such as species of Actinomyces, Actinomadura,
  Nocardia, Streptomyces
maduromycosis (actinomycotic)
schizomycetoma (actinomycotic)

039.0 Cutaneous
Erythrasma   Trichomycosis axillaris

039.1 Pulmonary
Thoracic actinomycosis

039.2 Abdominal

039.3 Cervicofacial

039.4 Madura foot

> *Excludes:* *madura foot due to mycotic infection (117.4)*

039.8 Of other specified sites

<table>
<tr><td>Add 4th or 5th digit</td><td>Nonspecific code</td><td>Unspecified code</td><td>Manifestation code</td></tr>
</table>

039.9 Of unspecified site
Actinomycosis NOS   Nocardiosis NOS
Maduromycosis NOS

040 Other bacterial diseases

> *Excludes:* *bacteremia NOS (790.7)*
> *bacterial infection NOS (041.9)*

040.0 Gas gangrene
Gas bacillus infection   Malignant edema
    or gangrene   Myonecrosis, clostridial
Infection by Clostridium: Myositis, clostridial
    histolyticum
    oedematiens
    perfringens [welchii]
    septicum
    sordellii

040.1 Rhinoscleroma

040.2 Whipple's disease
Intestinal lipodystrophy

040.3 Necrobacillosis

⑤ **040.8 Other specified bacterial diseases**

040.81 Tropical pyomyositis

040.89 Other

041 Bacterial infection in conditions classified elsewhere and of unspecified site
Note: This category is provided to be used as an additional code where it is desired to identify
    the bacterial agent in diseases classified elsewhere. This category will also be used to
    classify bacterial infections of unspecified nature or site.

> *Excludes:* *bacteremia NOS (790.7)*
> *septicemia (038.0-038.9)*

⑤ **041.0 Streptococcus**

041.00 Streptococcus, unspecified

041.01 Group A

041.02 Group B

041.03 Group C

041.04 Group D [Enterococcus]

041.05 Group G

041.09 Other Streptococcus

⑤ **041.1 Staphylococcus**

041.10 Staphylococcus, unspecified

041.11 Staphylococcus aureus

041.19 Other Staphylococcus

041.2 Pneumococcus

041.3 Friedländer's bacillus
Infection by Klebsiella pneumoniae

041.4 Escherichia coli [E. coli]

041.5 Hemophilus influenzae [H. influenzae]

041.6 Proteus (mirabilis) (morganii)

041.7 Pseudomonas

⑤ **041.8 Other specified bacterial infections**

041.81 Mycoplasma
Eaton's agent
Pleuropneumonia-like organisms [PPLO]

041.82 Bacillus fragilis

041.83 Clostridium perfringens

041.84 Other anaerobes
Gram-negative anaerobes
Bacteroides (fragilis)

> *Excludes:* *Helicobacter pylori (041.86)*

● Code new   ▲ Revision of   ④ ⑤ Fourth or fifth
    to this edition   existing code   digit required

041.85 **Other Gram-negative organisms**
Aerobacter aerogenes
Gram-negative bacteria NOS
Mima polymorpha
Serratia

Excludes: Gram-negative anaerobes (041.84)

041.86 **Helicobacter pylori (H. pylori)**

041.89 **Other specified bacteria**

041.9 **Bacterial infection, unspecified**

HUMAN IMMUNODEFICIENCY VIRUS (HIV) INFECTION (042)

042 **Human immunodeficiency virus [HIV] disease**
Acquired immune deficiency syndrome
Acquired immunodeficiency syndrome
AIDS
AIDS-like syndrome
AIDS-related complex
ARC
HIV infection, symptomatic

Use additional code(s) to identify all manifestations of HIV

Use additional code, if desired, to identify HIV-2 infection (079.53)

Excludes: asymptomatic HIV infection status (V08)
exposre to HIV virus (V01.7)
nonspecific serologic evidence of HIV (795.71)

POLIOMYELITIS AND OTHER NON-ARTHROPOD-BORNE VIRAL DISEASES OF CENTRAL NERVOUS SYSTEM (045-049)

⑤ **045** **Acute poliomyelitis**

Excludes: late effects of acute poliomyelitis (138)

The following fifth-digit subclassification is for use with category 045:

0 **poliovirus, unspecified type**

1 **poliovirus type I**

2 **poliovirus type II**

3 **poliovirus type III**

⑤ **045.0** **Acute paralytic poliomyelitis specified as bulbar**
Infantile paralysis (acute)
Poliomyelitis (acute) (anterior) } specified as bulbar
Polioencephalitis (acute) (bulbar)
Polioencephalomyelitis (acute) (anterior) (bulbar)

⑤ **045.1** **Acute poliomyelitis with other paralysis**
Paralysis:
acute atrophic, spinal infantile, paralytic
Poliomyelitis (acute) }
anterior   with paralysis except bulbar
epidemic

⑤ **045.2** **Acute nonparalytic poliomyelitis**
Poliomyelitis (acute) }
anterior   specified as nonparalytic
epidemic

⑤ **045.9** **Acute poliomyelitis, unspecified**
Infantile paralysis }
Poliomyelitis (acute)   unspecified whether paralytic or nonparalytic
anterior
epidemic

046 **Slow virus infection of central nervous system**

046.0 **Kuru**

046.1 **Jakob-Creutzfeldt disease**
Subacute spongiform encephalopathy

046.2 **Subacute sclerosing panencephalitis**
Dawson's inclusion body encephalitis
Van Bogaert's sclerosing leukoencephalitis

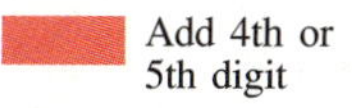

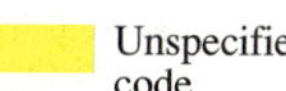

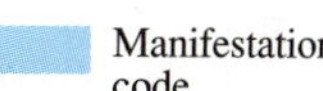

046.3 Progressive multifocal leukoencephalopathy
Multifocal leukoencephalopathy NOS

046.8 Other specified slow virus infection of central nervous system

046.9 Unspecified slow virus infection of central nervous system

047 Meningitis due to enterovirus
Includes: meningitis:
abacterial
aseptic
viral

Excludes: *meningitis due to:*
adenovirus (049.1)
arthropod-borne virus (060.0-066.9)
leptospira (100.81)
virus of:
herpes simplex (054.72)
herpes zoster (053.0)
lymphocytic choriomeningitis (049.0)
mumps (072.1)
poliomyelitis (045.0-045.9)
any other infection specifically classified elsewhere

047.0 Coxsackie virus

047.1 ECHO virus
Meningo-eruptive syndrome

047.8 Other specified viral meningitis

047.9 Unspecified viral meningitis
Viral meningitis NOS

048 Other enterovirus diseases of central nervous system
Boston exanthem

049 Other non-arthropod-borne viral diseases of central nervous system

Excludes: *late effects of viral encephalitis (139.0)*

049.0 Lymphocytic choriomeningitis
Lymphocytic:
meningitis (serous) (benign)
meningoencephalitis (serous) (benign)

049.1 Meningitis due to adenovirus

049.8 Other specified non-arthropod-borne viral diseases of central nervous system

Encephalitis:	Encephalitis:
acute:	lethargica
inclusion body	Rio Bravo
necrotizing	von Economo's disease
epidemic	

049.9 Unspecified non-arthropod-borne viral diseases of central nervous system
Viral encephalitis NOS

VIRAL DISEASES ACCOMPANIED BY EXANTHEM (050-057)

Excludes: *arthropod-borne viral diseases (060.0-066.9)*
Boston exanthem (048)

050 Smallpox

050.0 Variola major

Hemorrhagic (pustular)	Malignant smallpox
smallpox	Purpura variolosa

050.1 Alastrim
Variola minor

050.2 Modified smallpox
Varioloid

050.9 Smallpox, unspecified

051 Cowpox and paravaccinia

051.0 Cowpox
Vaccinia not from vaccination

Excludes: *vaccinia (generalized) (from vaccination) (999.0)*

● Code new to this edition   ▲ Revision of existing code   ④ ⑤ Fourth or fifth digit required

051.1 Pseudocowpox
Milkers' node

051.2 Contagious pustular dermatitis
Ecthyma contagiosum   Orf

051.9 Paravaccinia, unspecified

052 Chickenpox

052.0 Postvaricella encephalitis
Postchickenpox encephalitis

052.1 Varicella (hemorrhagic) pneumonitis

052.7 With other specified complications

052.8 With unspecified complication

052.9 Varicella without mention of complication
Chickenpox NOS
Varicella NOS

053 Herpes zoster
Includes: shingles
zona

053.0 With meningitis

⑤ **053.1 With other nervous system complications**

053.10 With unspecified nervous system complication

053.11 Geniculate herpes zoster
Herpetic geniculate ganglionitis

053.12 Postherpetic trigeminal neuralgia

053.13 Postherpetic polyneuropathy

053.19 Other

⑤ **053.2 With ophthalmic complications**

053.20 Herpes zoster dermatitis of eyelid
Herpes zoster ophthalmicus

053.21 Herpes zoster keratoconjunctivitis

053.22 Herpes zoster iridocyclitis

053.29 Other

⑤ **053.7 With other specified complications**

053.71 Otitis externa due to herpes zoster

053.79 Other

053.8 With unspecified complication

053.9 Herpes zoster without mention of complication
Herpes zoster NOS

054 Herpes simplex

Excludes: congenital herpes simplex (771.2)

054.0 Eczema herpeticum
Kaposi's varicelliform eruption

⑤ **054.1 Genital herpes**

054.10 Genital herpes, unspecified
Herpes progenitalis

054.11 Herpetic vulvovaginitis

054.12 Herpetic ulceration of vulva

054.13 Herpetic infection of penis

054.19 Other

054.2 Herpetic gingivostomatitis

054.3 Herpetic meningoencephalitis
Herpes encephalitis   Simian B disease

⑤ **054.4 With ophthalmic complications**

054.40 With unspecified ophthalmic complication

054.41 Herpes simplex dermatitis of eyelid

054.42 Dendritic keratitis

054.43 Herpes simplex disciform keratitis

054.44 Herpes simplex iridocyclitis

054.49 Other

054.5 Herpetic septicemia

054.6 Herpetic whitlow
Herpetic felon

⑤ **054.7 With other specified complications**

054.71 Visceral herpes simplex

054.72 Herpes simplex meningitis

054.73 Herpes simplex otitis externa

054.79 Other

054.8 With unspecified complication

054.9 Herpes simplex without mention of complication

055 Measles
Includes: morbilli
rubeola

055.0 Postmeasles encephalitis

055.1 Postmeasles pneumonia

055.2 Postmeasles otitis media

⑤ **055.7 With other specified complications**

055.71 Measles keratoconjunctivitis
Measles keratitis

055.79 Other

055.8 With unspecified complication

055.9 Measles without mention of complication

056 Rubella
Includes: German measles

Excludes: *congenital rubella (771.0)*

⑤ **056.0 With neurological complications**

056.00 With unspecified neurological complication

056.01 Encephalomyelitis due to rubella
Encephalitis
Meningoencephalitis ⎫ due to rubella

056.09 Other

⑤ **056.7 With other specified complications**

056.71 Arthritis due to rubella

056.79 Other

056.8 With unspecified complications

056.9 Rubella without mention of complication

057 Other viral exanthemata

057.0 Erythema infectiosum [fifth disease]

057.8 Other specified viral exanthemata
Dukes (-Filatow) disease   Parascarlatina
Exanthema subitum   Pseudoscarlatina
[sixth disease]   Roseola infantum
Fourth disease

057.9 Viral exanthem, unspecified

ARTHROPOD-BORNE VIRAL DISEASES (060-066)

Use additional code, if desired, to identify any associated meningitis (321.2)

Excludes: *late effects of viral encephalitis (139.0)*

060 Yellow fever

● Code new   ▲ Revision of   ④ ⑤ Fourth or fifth
to this edition   existing code   digit required

060.0 Sylvatic
Yellow fever:
  jungle
  sylvan

060.1 Urban

060.9 Yellow fever, unspecified

061 Dengue
Breakbone fever

Excludes: hemorrhagic fever caused by dengue virus (065.4)

062 Mosquito-borne viral encephalitis

062.0 Japanese encephalitis
Japanese B encephalitis

062.1 Western equine encephalitis

062.2 Eastern equine encephalitis

Excludes: Venezuelan equine encephalitis (066.2)

062.3 St. Louis encephalitis

062.4 Australian encephalitis
Australian arboencephalitis
Australian X disease
Murray Valley encephalitis

062.5 California virus encephalitis
Encephalitis: Tahyna fever
  California
  La Crosse

062.8 Other specified mosquito-borne viral encephalitis
Encephalitis by Ilheus virus

062.9 Mosquito-borne viral encephalitis, unspecified

063 Tick-borne viral encephalitis
Includes: diphasic meningoencephalitis

063.0 Russian spring-summer [taiga] encephalitis

063.1 Louping ill

063.2 Central European encephalitis

063.8 Other specified tick-borne viral encephalitis
Langat encephalitis   Powassan encephalitis

063.9 Tick-borne viral encephalitis, unspecified

064 Viral encephalitis transmitted by other and unspecified arthropods
Arthropod-borne viral encephalitis, vector unknown
Negishi virus encephalitis

Excludes: viral encephalitis NOS (049.9)

065 Arthropod-borne hemorrhagic fever

065.0 Crimean hemorrhagic fever [CHF Congo virus]
Central Asian hemorrhagic fever

065.1 Omsk hemorrhagic fever

065.2 Kyasanur Forest disease

065.3 Other tick-borne hemorrhagic fever

065.4 Mosquito-borne hemorrhagic fever
Chikungunya hemorrhagic fever
Dengue hemorrhagic fever

Excludes: Chikungunya fever (066.3)
       dengue (061)
       yellow fever (060.0-060.9)

065.8 Other specified arthropod-borne hemorrhagic fever
Mite-borne hemorrhagic fever

065.9 Arthropod-borne hemorrhagic fever, unspecified
Arbovirus hemorrhagic fever NOS

066 Other arthropod-borne viral diseases

066.0 Phlebotomus fever
Changuinola fever   Sandfly fever

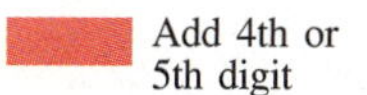

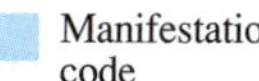

066.1 Tick-borne fever
Nairobi sheep disease
Tick fever:
  American mountain
  Colorado
Tick fever:
  Kemerovo
  Quaranfil

066.2 Venezuelan equine fever
Venezuelan equine encephalitis

066.3 Other mosquito-borne fever
Fever (viral):
  Bunyamwera
  Bwamba
  Chikungunya
  GuamaR Mayaro
  Mucambo
  O'nyong-nyong
Fever (viral):
  Oropouche
  Pixuna
  Rift valley
  Ross river
  Wesselsbron
  West Nile
  Zika

Excludes: *dengue (061)*
        yellow fever (060.0-060.9)

066.8 Other specified arthropod-borne viral diseases
Chandipura fever   Piry fever

066.9 Arthropod-borne viral disease, unspecified
Arbovirus infection NOS

OTHER DISEASES DUE TO VIRUSES AND CHLAMYDIAE (070-079)

070 Viral hepatitis
Includes: viral hepatitis (acute) (chronic)
Excludes: *cytomegalic inclusion virus hepatitis (078.5)*
The following fifth-digit subclassification is for use with categories 070.2 and 070.3:

  0 **acute or unspecified, without mention of hepatitis delta**

  1 **acute or unspecified, with hepatitis delta**

  2 **chronic, without mention of hepatitis delta**

  3 **chronic, with hepatitis delta**

070.0 Viral hepatitis A with hepatic coma

070.1 Viral hepatitis A without mention of hepatic coma
Infectious hepatitis

⑤ **070.2 Viral hepatitis B with hepatic coma**

⑤ **070.3 Viral hepatitis B without mention of hepatic coma**
Serum hepatitis

⑤ **070.4 Other specified viral hepatitis with hepatic coma**

  070.41 Acute or unspecified hepatitis C with hepatic coma

  070.42 Hepatitis delta without mention of active hepatitis B disease with hepatic coma
    Hepatitis delta with hepatitis B carrier state

  070.43 Hepatitis E with hepatic coma

  070.44 Chronic hepatitis C with hepatic coma

  070.49 Other specified viral hepatitis with hepatic coma

⑤ **070.5 Other specified viral hepatitis without mention of hepatic coma**

  070.51 Acute or unspecified hepatitis C without mention of hepatic coma

  070.52 Hepatitis delta without mention of active hepatitis B disease or hepatic coma

  070.53 Hepatitis E without mention of hepatic coma

  070.54 Chronic hepatitis C without mention of hepatic coma

  070.59 Other specified viral hepatitis without mention of hepatic coma

070.6 Unspecified viral hepatitis with hepatic coma

070.9 Unspecified viral hepatitis without mention of hepatic coma
Viral hepatitis NOS

071 Rabies
Hydrophobia   Lyssa

072 Mumps

072.0 Mumps orchitis

● Code new
  to this edition
▲ Revision of
  existing code
④ ⑤ Fourth or fifth
  digit required

072.1 Mumps meningitis

072.2 Mumps encephalitis
Mumps meningoencephalitis

072.3 Mumps pancreatitis

⑤ **072.7 Mumps with other specified complications**

    072.71 Mumps hepatitis

    072.72 Mumps polyneuropathy

    072.79 Other

072.8 Mumps with unspecified complication

072.9 Mumps without mention of complication
Epidemic parotitis   Infectious parotitis

073 Ornithosis
Includes: parrot fever
         psittacosis

073.0 With pneumonia
Lobular pneumonitis due to ornithosis

073.7 With other specified complications

073.8 With unspecified complication

073.9 Ornithosis, unspecified

074 Specific diseases due to Coxsackie virus

> *Excludes:* *Coxsackie virus:*
> *infection NOS (079.2)*
> *meningitis (047.0)*

074.0 Herpangina
Vesicular pharyngitis

074.1 Epidemic pleurodynia
Bornholm disease   Epidemic:
Devil's grip   myalgia
                myositis

⑤ **074.2 Coxsackie carditis**

    074.20 Coxsackie carditis, unspecified

    074.21 Coxsackie pericarditis

    074.22 Coxsackie endocarditis

    074.23 Coxsackie myocarditis
    Aseptic myocarditis of newborn

074.3 Hand, foot, and mouth disease
Vesicular stomatitis and exanthem

074.8 Other specified diseases due to Coxsackie virus
Acute lymphonodular pharyngitis

075 Infectious mononucleosis
Glandular fever   Pfeiffer's disease
Monocytic angina

076 Trachoma

> *Excludes:* *late effect of trachoma (139.1)*

076.0 Initial stage
Trachoma dubium

076.1 Active stage
Granular conjunctivitis (trachomatous)
Trachomatous:
  follicular conjunctivitis
  pannus

076.9 Trachoma, unspecified
Trachoma NOS

077 Other diseases of conjunctiva due to viruses and Chlamydiae

> *Excludes:* *ophthalmic complications of viral diseases classified elsewhere*

Add 4th or
5th digit

Nonspecific
code

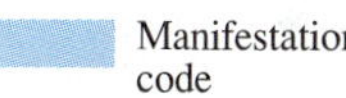
Unspecified
code

Manifestation
code

077.0 Inclusion conjunctivitis
Paratrachoma
Swimming pool conjunctivitis

> Excludes: *inclusion blennorrhea (neonatal) (771.6)*

077.1 Epidemic keratoconjunctivitis
Shipyard eye

077.2 Pharyngoconjunctival fever
Viral pharyngoconjunctivitis

077.3 Other adenoviral conjunctivitis
Acute adenoviral follicular conjunctivitis

077.4 Epidemic hemorrhagic conjunctivitis
Apollo:
  conjunctivitis
  disease
Conjunctivitis due to enterovirus type 70
Hemorrhagic conjunctivitis (acute) (epidemic)

077.8 Other viral conjunctivitis
Newcastle conjunctivitis

⑤ **077.9 Unspecified diseases of conjunctiva due to viruses and Chlamydiae**

  077.98 Due to Chlamydiae

  077.99 Due to viruses
  Viral conjunctivitis NOS

078 Other diseases due to viruses and Chlamydiae

> Excludes: *viral infection NOS (079.0-079.9)*
> *viremia NOS (790.8)*

078.0 Molluscum contagiosum

⑤ **078.1 Viral warts**
Viral warts due to Human papillomavirus

  078.10 Viral warts, unspecified
  Condyloma NOS
  Verruca:
    NOS
    vulgaris
  Warts (infectious)

  078.11 Condyloma acuminatum

  078.19 Other specified viral warts
  Genital warts NOS
  Verruca:
    plana
    plantaris

078.2 Sweating fever
Miliary fever   Sweating disease

078.3 Cat-scratch disease
Benign lymphoreticulosis (of inoculation)
Cat-scratch fever

078.4 Foot and mouth disease
Aphthous fever
Epizootic:
  aphthae
  stomatitis

078.5 Cytomegaloviral disease
Cytomegalic inclusion disease
Salivary gland virus disease
Use additional code, if desired, to identify manifestation, as:
        cytomegalic inclusion virus:
          hepatitis (573.1)
          pneumonia (484.1)

> Excludes: *congenital cytomegalovirus infection (771.1)*

078.6 Hemorrhagic nephrosonephritis
Hemorrhagic fever: Hemorrhagic fever:
  epidemic   Russian
  Korean   with renal syndrome

● Code new   ▲ Revision of   ④ ⑤ Fourth or fifth
to this edition   existing code   digit required

078.7 Arenaviral hemorrhagic fever
Hemorrhagic fever: Hemorrhagic fever:
   Argentine   Junin virus
   Bolivian   Machupo virus

⑤ **078.8 Other specified diseases due to viruses and Chlamydiae**

Excludes: *epidemic diarrhea (009.2)*
        lymphogranuloma venereum (099.1)

078.81 Epidemic vertigo

078.82 Epidemic vomiting syndrome
Winter vomiting disease

078.88 Other specified diseases due to Chlamydiae

078.89 Other specified diseases due to viruses
Epidemic cervical myalgia
Marburg disease
Tanapox

079 Viral and chlamydial infection in conditions classified elsewhere and of unspecified site

Note: This category is provided to be used as an additional code where it is desired to identify the viral agent in diseases classifiable elsewhere. This category will also be used to classify virus infection of unspecified nature or site.

079.0 Adenovirus

079.1 ECHO virus

079.2 Coxsackievirus

079.3 Rhinovirus

▲ **079.4 Human papillomavirus**

⑤ **079.5 Retrovirus**

Excludes: *human immunodeficiency virus, type 1 [HIV-1] (042)*
        human T-cell lymphotrophic virus, type III [HTLV-III] (042)
        lymphadenopathy-associated virus [LAV] (042)

079.50 Retrovirus, unspecified

079.51 Human T-cell lymphotrophic virus, type I [HTLV-I]

079.52 Human T-cell lymphotrophic virus, type II [HTLV-II]

079.53 Human immunodeficiency virus, type 2 [HIV-2]

079.59 Other specified retrovirus

079.6 Respiratory syncytial virus (RSV)

⑤ **079.8 Other specified viral and chlamydial infections**

079.81 Hantavirus

079.88 Other specified chlamydial infection

079.89 Other specified viral infection

⑤ **079.9 Unspecified viral and chlamydial infections**

Excludes: *viremia NOS (790.8)*

079.98 Unspecified chlamydial infection
Chlamydial infection NOS

079.99 Unspecified viral infection
Viral infection NOS

RICKETTSIOSES AND OTHER ARTHROPOD-BORNE DISEASES (080-088)

Excludes: *arthropod-borne viral diseases (060.0-066.9)*

080 Louse-borne [epidemic] typhus
Typhus (fever):   Typhus (fever):
   classical   exanthematic NOS
   epidemic   louse-borne

081 Other typhus

081.0 Murine [endemic] typhus
Typhus (fever):
   endemic
   flea-borne

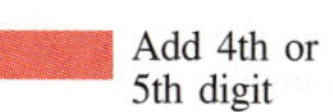

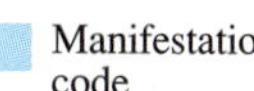

081.1 Brill's disease
    Brill-Zinsser disease
    Recrudescent typhus (fever)

081.2 Scrub typhus

Japanese river fever	Mite-borne typhus
Kedani fever	Tsutsugamushi

081.9 Typhus, unspecified
    Typhus (fever) NOS

082 Tick-borne rickettsioses

082.0 Spotted fevers
    Rocky mountain spotted fever
    São Paulo fever

082.1 Boutonneuse fever

African tick typhus	Marseilles fever
India tick typhus	Mediterranean tick fever
Kenya tick typhus	

082.2 North Asian tick fever
    Siberian tick typhus

082.3 Queensland tick typhus

● **082.4 Ehrlichiosis**

  ● **082.40 Ehrlichiosis, unspecified**

  ● **082.41 Ehrlichiosis chafeensis (*E. chafeensis*)**

  ● **082.49 Other ehrlichiosis**

082.8 Other specified tick-borne rickettsioses
    Lone star fever

082.9 Tick-borne rickettsiosis, unspecified
    Tick-borne typhus NOS

083 Other rickettsioses

083.0 Q fever

083.1 Trench fever

Quintan fever	Wolhynian fever

083.2 Rickettsialpox
    Vesicular rickettsiosis

083.8 Other specified rickettsioses

083.9 Rickettsiosis, unspecified

084 Malaria

Note: Subcategories 084.0-084.6 exclude the listed conditions with mention of pernicious complications (084.8-084.9).

    Excludes: *congenital malaria (771.2)*

084.0 Falciparum malaria [malignant tertian]
    Malaria (fever):
      by Plasmodium falciparum
      subtertian

084.1 Vivax malaria [benign tertian]
    Malaria (fever) by Plasmodium vivax

084.2 Quartan malaria
    Malaria (fever) by Plasmodium malariae
    Malariae malaria

084.3 Ovale malaria
    Malaria (fever) by Plasmodium ovale

084.4 Other malaria
    Monkey malaria

084.5 Mixed malaria
    Malaria (fever) by more than one parasite

084.6 Malaria, unspecified
    Malaria (fever) NOS

● Code new to this edition	▲ Revision of existing code	④ ⑤ Fourth or fifth digit required

084.7 Induced malaria
Therapeutically induced malaria

Excludes: accidental infection from syringe, blood transfusion, etc. (084.0-084.6, above, according to parasite species)
transmission from mother to child during delivery (771.2)

084.8 Blackwater fever
Hemoglobinuric: Malarial hemoglobinuria
  fever (bilious)
  malaria

084.9 Other pernicious complications of malaria
Algid malaria
Cerebral malaria

Use additional code, if desired, to identify complication, as:
  malarial:
    hepatitis (573.2)
    nephrosis (581.81)

085 Leishmaniasis

085.0 Visceral [kala-azar]
Dumdum fever   Leishmaniasis:
Infection by Leishmania: dermal, post-kala-azar
  donovani   Mediterranean
  infantum   visceral (Indian)

085.1 Cutaneous, urban
Aleppo boil   Leishmaniasis, cutaneous:
Baghdad boil   dry form
Delhi boil   late
Infection by Leishmania   recurrent
  tropica (minor)   ulcerating
                        Oriental sore

085.2 Cutaneous, Asian desert
Infection by Leishmania tropica major
Leishmaniasis, cutaneous:
  acute necrotizing
  rural
  wet form
  zoonotic form

085.3 Cutaneous, Ethiopian
Infection by Leishmania ethiopica
Leishmaniasis, cutaneous:
  diffuse
  lepromatous

085.4 Cutaneous, American
Chiclero ulcer
Infection by Leishmania mexicana
Leishmaniasis tegumentaria diffusa

085.5 Mucocutaneous (American)
Espundia
Infection by Leishmania braziliensis
Uta

085.9 Leishmaniasis, unspecified

086 Trypanosomiasis

Use additional code, if desired, to identify manifestations, as:
  trypanosomiasis:
    encephalitis (323.2)
    meningitis (321.3)

086.0 Chagas' disease with heart involvement
American trypanosomiasis   }
Infection by Trypanosoma cruzi   } with heart involvement
Any condition classifiable to 086.2   }

086.1 Chagas' disease with other organ involvement
American trypanosomiasis   } with involvement of organ other
Infection by Trypanosoma cruzi   } than heart
Any condition classifiable to 086.2

086.2 Chagas' disease without mention of organ involvement
American trypanosomiasis
Infection by Trypanosoma cruzi

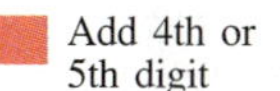

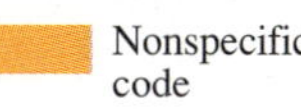

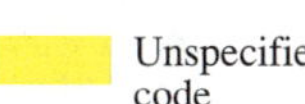

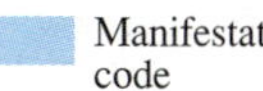

086.3 Gambian trypanosomiasis
Gambian sleeping sickness
Infection by Trypanosoma gambiense

086.4 Rhodesian trypanosomiasis
Infection by Trypanosoma rhodesiense
Rhodesian sleeping sickness

086.5 African trypanosomiasis, unspecified
Sleeping sickness NOS

086.9 Trypanosomiasis, unspecified

087 Relapsing fever
Includes: recurrent fever

087.0 Louse-borne

087.1 Tick-borne

087.9 Relapsing fever, unspecified

088 Other arthropod-borne diseases

088.0 Bartonellosis
Carrión's disease   Verruga peruana
Oroya fever

⑤ **088.8 Other specified arthropod-borne diseases**

088.81 Lyme Disease
Erythema chronicum migrans

088.82 Babesiosis
Babesiasis

088.89 Other

088.9 Arthropod-borne disease, unspecified

SYPHILIS AND OTHER VENEREAL DISEASES (090-099)

Excludes: *nonvenereal endemic syphilis (104.0)*
urogenital trichomoniasis (131.0)

090 Congenital syphilis

090.0 Early congenital syphilis, symptomatic
Congenital syphilitic: Syphilitic (congenital):
  choroiditis   epiphysitis
  coryza (chronic)   osteochondritis
  hepatomegaly   pemphigus
  mucous patches   Any congenital syphilitic condition specified as early
  periostitis   or manifest less than two years after birth
  splenomegaly

090.1 Early congenital syphilis, latent
Congenital syphilis without clinical manifestations, with positive serological reaction
and negative spinal fluid test, less than two years after birth

090.2 Early congenital syphilis, unspecified
Congenital syphilis NOS, less than two years after birth

090.3 Syphilitic interstitial keratitis
Syphilitic keratitis:
  parenchymatous
  punctata profunda

Excludes: *interstitial keratitis NOS (370.50)*

⑤ **090.4 Juvenile neurosyphilis**
Use additional code, if desired, to identify any associated mental disorder

090.40 Juvenile neurosyphilis, unspecified
Congenital neurosyphilis
Dementia paralytica juvenilis
Juvenile:
  general paresis
  tabes
  taboparesis

090.41 Congenital syphilitic encephalitis

090.42 Congenital syphilitic meningitis

090.49 Other

● Code new
  to this edition   ▲ Revision of
                              existing code   ④ ⑤ Fourth or fifth
                                                          digit required

090.5 Other late congenital syphilis, symptomatic
Gumma due to congenital syphilis
Hutchinson's teeth
Syphilitic saddle nose
Any congenital syphilitic condition specified as late or manifest two years or more after birth

090.6 Late congenital syphilis, latent
Congenital syphilis without clinical manifestations, with positive serological reaction and negative spinal fluid test, two years or more after birth

090.7 Late congenital syphilis, unspecified
Congenital syphilis NOS, two years or more after birth

090.9 Congenital syphilis, unspecified

091 Early syphilis, symptomatic

> Excludes: *early cardiovascular syphilis (093.0-093.9)*
> *early neurosyphilis (094.0-094.9)*

091.0 Genital syphilis (primary)
Genital chancre

091.1 Primary anal syphilis

091.2 Other primary syphilis
Primary syphilis of: Primary syphilis of:
  breast   lip
  fingers   tonsils

091.3 Secondary syphilis of skin or mucous membranes
Condyloma latum   Secondary syphilis of:
Secondary syphilis of: skin
  anus   tonsils
  mouth   vulva
  pharynx

091.4 Adenopathy due to secondary syphilis
Syphilitic adenopathy (secondary)
Syphilitic lymphadenitis (secondary)

⑤ **091.5 Uveitis due to secondary syphilis**

    091.50 Syphilitic uveitis, unspecified

    091.51 Syphilitic chorioretinitis (secondary)

    091.52 Syphilitic iridocyclitis (secondary)

⑤ **091.6 Secondary syphilis of viscera and bone**

    091.61 Secondary syphilitic periostitis

    091.62 Secondary syphilitic hepatitis
Secondary syphilis of liver

    091.69 Other viscera

091.7 Secondary syphilis, relapse
Secondary syphilis, relapse (treated) (untreated)

⑤ **091.8 Other forms of secondary syphilis**

    091.81 Acute syphilitic meningitis (secondary)

    091.82 Syphilitic alopecia

    091.89 Other

091.9 Unspecified secondary syphilis

092 Early syphilis, latent
Includes: syphilis (acquired) without clinical manifestations, with positive serological reaction and negative spinal fluid test, less than two years after infection

092.0 Early syphilis, latent, serological relapse after treatment

092.9 Early syphilis, latent, unspecified

093 Cardiovascular syphilis

093.0 Aneurysm of aorta, specified as syphilitic
Dilatation of aorta, specified as syphilitic

093.1 Syphilitic aortitis

⑤ **093.2 Syphilitic endocarditis**

    093.20 Valve, unspecified
Syphilitic ostial coronary disease

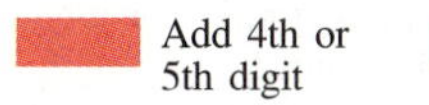

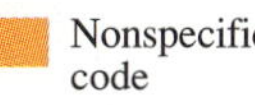

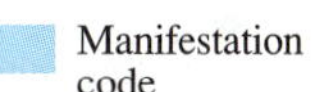

093.21 Mitral valve

093.22 Aortic valve
 Syphilitic aortic incompetence or stenosis

093.23 Tricuspid valve

093.24 Pulmonary valve

⑤ **093.8 Other specified cardiovascular syphilis**

093.81 Syphilitic pericarditis

093.82 Syphilitic myocarditis

093.89 Other

093.9 Cardiovascular syphilis, unspecified

094 Neurosyphilis
Use additional code, if desired, to identify any associated mental disorder

094.0 Tabes dorsalis
 Locomotor ataxia (progressive)
 Posterior spinal sclerosis (syphilitic)
 Tabetic neurosyphilis
Use additional code, if desired, to identify manifestation, as:
 neurogenic arthropathy [Charcot's joint disease] (713.5)

094.1 General paresis
 Dementia paralytica   Paretic neurosyphilis
 General paralysis (of the   Taboparesis
  insane) (progressive)

094.2 Syphilitic meningitis
 Meningovascular syphilis

 Excludes: *acute syphilitic meningitis (secondary) (091.81)*

094.3 Asymptomatic neurosyphilis

⑤ **094.8 Other specified neurosyphilis**

094.81 Syphilitic encephalitis

094.82 Syphilitic Parkinsonism

094.83 Syphilitic disseminated retinochoroiditis

094.84 Syphilitic optic atrophy

094.85 Syphilitic retrobulbar neuritis

094.86 Syphilitic acoustic neuritis

094.87 Syphilitic ruptured cerebral aneurysm

094.89 Other

094.9 Neurosyphilis, unspecified
 Gumma (syphilitic)
 Syphilis (early) (late) } of central nervous system NOS
 Syphiloma

095 Other forms of late syphilis, with symptoms
 Includes: gumma (syphilitic)
   syphilis, late, tertiary, or unspecified stage

095.0 Syphilitic episcleritis

095.1 Syphilis of lung

095.2 Syphilitic peritonitis

095.3 Syphilis of liver

095.4 Syphilis of kidney

095.5 Syphilis of bone

095.6 Syphilis of muscle
 Syphilitic myositis

095.7 Syphilis of synovium, tendon, and bursa
 Syphilitic:
  bursitis
  synovitis

095.8 Other specified forms of late symptomatic syphilis

 Excludes: *cardiovascular syphilis (093.0-093.9)*
   neurosyphilis (094.0-094.9)

● Code new   ▲ Revision of   ④ ⑤ Fourth or fifth
 to this edition   existing code   digit required

095.9 **Late symptomatic syphilis, unspecified**

096 **Late syphilis, latent**
>   Syphilis (acquired) without clinical manifestations, with positive serological reaction and negative spinal fluid test, two years or more after infection

097 **Other and unspecified syphilis**

097.0 **Late syphilis, unspecified**

097.1 **Latent syphilis, unspecified**
>   Positive serological reaction for syphilis

097.9 **Syphilis, unspecified**
>   Syphilis (acquired) NOS

>   *Excludes:* *syphilis NOS causing death under two years of age (090.9)*

098 **Gonococcal infections**

098.0 **Acute, of lower genitourinary tract**

Gonococcal:	Gonorrhea (acute):
Bartholinitis (acute)	NOS
urethritis (acute)	genitourinary (tract) NOS
vulvovaginitis (acute)	

⑤ **098.1** **Acute, of upper genitourinary tract**

098.10 **Gonococcal infection (acute) of upper genitourinary tract, site unspecified**

098.11 **Gonococcal cystitis (acute)**
>   Gonorrhea (acute) of bladder

098.12 **Gonococcal prostatitis (acute)**

098.13 **Gonococcal epididymo-orchitis (acute)**
>   Gonococcal orchitis (acute)

098.14 **Gonococcal seminal vesiculitis (acute)**
>   Gonorrhea (acute) of seminal vesicle

098.15 **Gonococcal cervicitis (acute)**
>   Gonorrhea (acute) of cervix

098.16 **Gonococcal endometritis (acute)**
>   Gonorrhea (acute) of uterus

098.17 **Gonococcal salpingitis, specified as acute**

098.19 **Other**

098.2 **Chronic, of lower genitourinary tract**
>   Gonococcal:
>   Bartholinitis
>   urethritis
>   vulvovaginitis   } specified as chronic or with
>   Gonorrhea: duration of two months or more
>   NOS
>   genitourinary (tract)
>   Any condition classifiable
>   to 098.0

⑤ **098.3** **Chronic, of upper genitourinary tract**
>   Includes: any condition classifiable to 098.1 stated as chronic or with a duration of two months or more

098.30 **Chronic gonococcal infection of upper genitourinary tract, site unspecified**

098.31 **Gonococcal cystitis, chronic**
>   Any condition classifiable to 098.11, specified as chronic
>   Gonorrhea of bladder, chronic

098.32 **Gonococcal prostatitis, chronic**
>   Any condition classifiable to 098.12, specified as chronic

098.33 **Gonococcal epididymo-orchitis, chronic**
>   Any condition classifiable to 098.13, specified as chronic
>   Chronic gonococcal orchitis

098.34 **Gonococcal seminal vesiculitis, chronic**
>   Any condition classifiable to 098.14, specified as chronic
>   Gonorrhea of seminal vesicle, chronic

098.35 **Gonococcal cervicitis, chronic**
>   Any condition classifiable to 098.15, specified as chronic
>   Gonorrhea of cervix, chronic

Add 4th or 5th digit

Nonspecific code

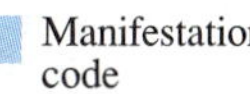
Unspecified code

Manifestation code

098.36 Gonococcal endometritis, chronic
Any condition classifiable to 098.16, specified as chronic

098.37 Gonococcal salpingitis (chronic)

098.39 Other

⑤ **098.4 Gonococcal infection of eye**

098.40 Gonococcal conjunctivitis (neonatorum)
Gonococcal ophthalmia (neonatorum)

098.41 Gonococcal iridocyclitis

098.42 Gonococcal endophthalmia

098.43 Gonococcal keratitis

098.49 Other

098.5 Gonococcal infection of joint

098.50 Gonococcal arthritis
Gonococcal infection of joint NOS

098.51 Gonococcal synovitis and tenosynovitis

098.52 Gonococcal bursitis

098.53 Gonococcal spondylitis

098.59 Other
Gonococcal rheumatism

098.6 Gonococcal infection of pharynx

098.7 Gonococcal infection of anus and rectum
Gonococcal proctitis

⑤ **098.8 Gonococcal infection of other specified sites**

098.81 Gonococcal keratosis (blennorrhagica)

098.82 Gonococcal meningitis

098.83 Gonococcal pericarditis

098.84 Gonococcal endocarditis

098.85 Other gonococcal heart disease

098.86 Gonococcal peritonitis

098.89 Other
Gonococcemia

099 Other venereal diseases

099.0 Chancroid

Bubo (inguinal):	Chancre:
chancroidal	Ducrey's
due to Hemophilus ducreyi	simple
	soft
	Ulcus molle (cutis) (skin)

099.1 Lymphogranuloma venereum

Climatic or tropical bubo	Esthiomene
(Durand-) Nicolas- Favre	Lymphogranuloma inguinale
disease	

099.2 Granuloma inguinale

Donovanosis	Granuloma venereum
Granuloma pudendi	Pudendal ulcer
(ulcerating)	

099.3 Reiter's disease
Reiter's syndrome
Use additional code for associated:
arthropathy (711.1)
conjunctivitis (372.33)

⑤ **099.4 Other nongonococcal urethritis [NGU]**

099.40 Unspecified
Nonspecific urethritis

099.41 Chlamydia trachomatis

099.49 Other specified organism

● Code new
to this edition

▲ Revision of
existing code

④ ⑤ Fourth or fifth
digit required

⑤ **099.5 Other venereal diseases due to Chlamydia trachomatis**

> *Excludes:* *Chlamydia trachomatis infection of conjunctiva (076.0-076.9, 077.0, 077.9)*
> *Lymphogranuloma venereum (099.1)*

099.50 Unspecified site

099.51 Pharynx

099.52 Anus and rectum

099.53 Lower genitourinary sites

> *Excludes:* *urethra (099.41)*

Use additional code, if desired, to specify site of infection, such as:
    bladder (595.4)
    cervix (616.0)
    vagina and vulva (616.11)

099.54 Other genitourinary sites
Use additional code, if desired, to specify site of infection, such as:
    pelvic inflammatory disease NOS (614.9)
    testis and epididymis (604.91)

099.55 Unspecified genitourinary site

099.56 Peritoneum
    Perihepatitis

099.59 Other specified site

099.8 Other specified venereal diseases

099.9 Venereal disease, unspecified

OTHER SPIROCHETAL DISEASES (100-104)

100 Leptospirosis

100.0 Leptospirosis icterohemorrhagica
    Leptospiral or spirochetal jaundice (hemorrhagic)
    Weil's disease

⑤ **100.8 Other specified leptospiral infections**

100.81 Leptospiral meningitis (aseptic)

100.89 Other

Fever:	Infection by Leptospira:
Fort Bragg	australis
pretibial	bataviae
swamp	pyrogenes

100.9 Leptospirosis, unspecified

101 Vincent's angina

Acute necrotizing ulcerative:	Spirochetal stomatitis
gingivitis	Trench mouth
stomatitis	Vincent's:
Fusospirochetal pharyngitis	gingivitis
	infection [any site]

102 Yaws

Includes: frambesia
            pian

102.0 Initial lesions

Chancre of yaws	Initial frambesial ulcer
Frambesia, initial or primary	Mother yaw

102.1 Multiple papillomata and wet crab yaws

Butter yaws	Planter or palmer papilloma of yaws
Frambesioma	
Pianoma	

102.2 Other early skin lesions
    Early yaws (cutaneous) (macular) (papular) (maculopapular) (micropapular)
    Frambeside of early yaws
    Cutaneous yaws, less than five years after infection

102.3 Hyperkeratosis
    Ghoul hand
    Hyperkeratosis, palmer or plantar (early) (late) due to yaws
    Worm-eaten soles

	Add 4th or 5th digit		Nonspecific code		Unspecified code		Manifestation code

102.4 Gummata and ulcers
Nodular late yaws (ulcerated)
Gummatous frambeside

102.5 Gangosa
Rhinopharyngitis mutilans

102.6 Bone and joint lesions
Goundou
Gumma, bone } of yaws (late)
Gummatous osteitis or periostitis

Hydrarthrosis
Osteitis } of yaws (early) (late)
Periostitis (hypertrophic)

102.7 Other manifestations
Juxta-articular nodules of yaws
Mucosal yaws

102.8 Latent yaws
Yaws without clinical manifestations, with positive serology

102.9 Yaws, unspecified

103 Pinta

103.0 Primary lesions
Chancre (primary)
Papule (primary) } of pinta [carate]
Pintid

103.1 Intermediate lesions
Erythematous plaques
Hyperchromic lesions } of pinta [carate]
Hyperkeratosis

103.2 Late lesions
Cardiovascular lesions
Skin lesions:
  achromic
  cicatricial } of pinta [carate]
  dyschromic
Vitiligo

103.3 Mixed lesions
Achromic and hyperchromic skin lesions of pinta [carate]

103.9 Pinta, unspecified

104 Other spirochetal infection

104.0 Nonvenereal endemic syphilis
Bejel   Njovera

104.8 Other specified spirochetal infections
Excludes: *relapsing fever (087.0-087.9)*
            syphilis (090.0-097.9)

104.9 Spirochetal infection, unspecified

MYCOSES (110-118)

Use additional code, if desired, to identify manifestation, as:
arthropathy (711.6)
meningitis (321.0-321.1)
otitis externa (380.15)

Excludes: *infection by Actinomycetales, such as species of Actinomyces, Actinomadura,*
            Nocardia, Streptomyces (039.0-039.9)

110 Dermatophytosis
Includes:
        infection by species of Epidermophyton, Microsporum, and Trichophyton
        tinea, any type except those in 111

110.0 Of scalp and beard
Kerion
Sycosis, mycotic
Trichophytic tinea [black dot tinea], scalp

● Code new   ▲ Revision of   ④ ⑤ Fourth or fifth
  to this edition   existing code   digit required

110.1 Of nail
Dermatophytic onychia   Tinea unguium
Onychomycosis

110.2 Of hand
Tinea manuum

110.3 Of groin and perianal area
Dhobie itch   Tinea cruris
Eczema marginatum

110.4 Of foot
Athlete's foot   Tinea pedis

110.5 Of the body
Herpes circinatus
Tinea imbricata [Tokelau]

110.6 Deep seated dermatophytosis
Granuloma trichophyticum
Majocchi's granuloma

110.8 Of other specified sites

110.9 Of unspecified site
Favus NOS   Ringworm NOS
Microsporic tinea NOS

111 Dermatomycosis, other and unspecified

111.0 Pityriasis versicolor
Infection by Malassezia [Pityrosporum] furfur
Tinea flava
Tinea versicolor

111.1 Tinea nigra
Infection by   Microsporosis nigra
   Cladosporium species   Pityriasis nigra
Keratomycosis nigricans   Tinea palmaris nigra

111.2 Tinea blanca
Infection by Trichosporon (beigelii) cutaneum
White piedra

111.3 Black piedra
Infection by Piedraia hortai

111.8 Other specified dermatomycoses

111.9 Dermatomycosis, unspecified

112 Candidiasis
Includes: infection by Candida species
          moniliasi

Excludes: neonatal monilial infection (771.7)

112.0 Of mouth
Thrush (oral)

112.1 Of vulva and vagina
Candidal vulvovaginitis   Monilial vulvovaginitis

112.2 Of other urogenital sites
Candidal balanitis

112.3 Of skin and nails
Candidal intertrigo   Candidal perionyxis [paronychia]
Candidal onychia

112.4 Of lung
Candidal pneumonia

112.5 Disseminated
Systemic candidiasis

⑤ **112.8 Of other specified sites**

    112.81 Candidal endocarditis

    112.82 Candidal otitis externa
        Otomycosis in moniliasis

    112.83 Candidal meningitis

    112.84 Candidal esophagitis

    112.85 Candidal enteritis

    112.89 Other

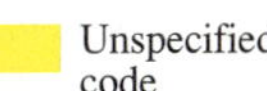

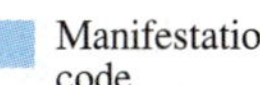

Manifestation
code

112.9 Of unspecified site

114 Coccidioidomycosis
Includes: infection by Coccidioides (immitis)
Posada-Wernicke disease

114.0 Primary coccidioidomycosis (pulmonary)
Acute pulmonary coccidioidomycosis
Coccidioidomycotic pneumonitis
Desert rheumatism
Pulmonary coccidioidomycosis
San Joaquin Valley fever

114.1 Primary extrapulmonary coccidioidomycosis
Chancriform syndrome
Primary cutaneous coccidioidomycosis

114.2 Coccidioidal meningitis

114.3 Other forms of progressive coccidioidomycosis
Coccidioidal granuloma
Disseminated coccidioidomycosis

114.4 Chronic pulmonary coccidioidomycosis

114.5 Pulmonary coccidioidomycosis, unspecified

114.9 Coccidioidomycosis, unspecified

⑤ **115 Histoplasmosis**
The following fifth-digit subclassification is for use with category 115:

0   without mention of manifestation

1   meningitis

2   retinitis

3   pericarditis

4   endocarditis

5   pneumonia

9   other

⑤ **115.0 Infection by Histoplasma capsulatum**
American histoplasmosis
Darling's disease
Reticuloendothelial cytomycosis
Small form histoplasmosis

⑤ **115.1 Infection by Histoplasma duboisii**
African histoplasmosis
Large form histoplasmosis

⑤ **115.9 Histoplasmosis, unspecified**
Histoplasmosis NOS

116 Blastomycotic infection

116.0 Blastomycosis
Blastomycotic dermatitis
Chicago disease
Cutaneous blastomycosis
Disseminated blastomycosis
Gilchrist's disease
Infection by Blastomyces [Ajellomyces] dermatitidis
North American blastomycosis
Primary pulmonary blastomycosis

116.1 Paracoccidioidomycosis
Brazilian blastomycosis
Infection by Paracoccidioides [Blastomyces] brasiliensis
Lutz-Splendore-Almeida disease
Mucocutaneous-lymphangitic paracoccidioidomycosis
Pulmonary paracoccidioidomycosis
South American blastomycosis
Visceral paracoccidioidomycosis

116.2 Lobomycosis
Infections by Loboa [Blastomyces] loboi
Keloidal blastomycosis
Lobo's disease

117 Other mycoses

● Code new to this edition   ▲ Revision of existing code   ④ ⑤ Fourth or fifth digit required

117.0 Rhinosporidiosis
Infection by Rhinosporidium seeberi

117.1 Sporotrichosis
Cutaneous sporotrichosis
Disseminated sporotrichosis
Infection by Sporothrix [Sporotrichum] schenckii
Lymphocutaneous sporotrichosis
Pulmonary sporotrichosis
Sporotrichosis of the bones

117.2 Chromoblastomycosis
Chromomycosis
Infection by Cladosporidium carrionii, Fonsecaea compactum, Fonsecaea pedrosoi, Phialophora verrucosa

117.3 Aspergillosis
Infection by Aspergillus species, mainly A. fumigatus, A. flavus group, A. terreus group

117.4 Mycotic mycetomas
Infection by various genera and species of Ascomycetes and Deuteromycetes, such as Acremonium [Cephalosporium] falciforme, Neotestudina rosatii, Madurella grisea, Madurella mycetomii, Pyrenochaeta romeroi, Zopfia [Leptosphaeria] senegalensis
Madura foot, mycotic
Maduromycosis, mycotic

| Excludes: | actinomycotic mycetomas (039.0-039.9) |

117.5 Cryptococcosis

Busse-Buschke's disease	Pulmonary cryptococcosis
European cryptococcosis	Systemic cryptococcosis
Infection by Cryptococcus neoformans	Torula

117.6 Allescheriosis [Petriellidosis]
Infections by Allescheria [Petriellidium] boydii [Monosporium apiospermum]

| Excludes: | mycotic mycetoma (117.4) |

117.7 Zygomycosis [Phycomycosis or Mucormycosis]
Infection by species of Absidia, Basidiobolus, Conidiobolus, Cunninghamella, Entomophthora, Mucor, Rhizopus, Saksenaea

117.8 Infection by dematiacious fungi, [Phaehyphomycosis]
Infection by dematiacious fungi, such as Cladosporium trichoides [bantianum], Dreschlera hawaiiensis, Phialophora gougerotii, Phialophora jeanselmi

117.9 Other and unspecified mycoses

118 Opportunistic mycoses
Infection of skin, subcutaneous tissues, and/or organs by a wide variety of fungi generally considered to be pathogenic to compromised hosts only (e.g., infection by species of Alternaria, Dreschlera, Fusarium)

HELMINTHIASES (120-129)

120 Schistosomiasis [bilharziasis]

120.0 Schistosoma haematobium
Vesical schistosomiasis NOS

120.1 Schistosoma mansoni
Intestinal schistosomiasis NOS

120.2 Schistosoma japonicum
Asiatic schistosomiasis NOS
Katayama disease or fever

120.3 Cutaneous

Cercarial dermatitis	Schistosome dermatitis
Infection by cercariae of Schistosoma	Swimmers' itch

120.8 Other specified schistosomiasis

Infection by Schistosoma:	Infection by Schistosoma spindale
bovis	Schistosomiasis chestermani
intercalatum	
mattheii	

120.9 Schistosomiasis, unspecified

Blood flukes NOS	Hemic distomiasis

121 Other trematode infections

	Add 4th or 5th digit		Nonspecific code		Unspecified code		Manifestation code

121.0 Opisthorchiasis
Infection by:
cat liver fluke
Opisthorchis (felineus) (tenuicollis) (viverrini)

121.1 Clonorchiasis
Biliary cirrhosis due to clonorchiasis
Chinese liver fluke disease
Hepatic distomiasis due to Clonorchis sinensis
Oriental liver fluke disease

121.2 Paragonimiasis
Infection by Paragonimus   Pulmonary distomiasis
Lung fluke disease (oriental)

121.3 Fascioliasis
Infection by Fasciola: Liver flukes NOS
gigantica   Sheep liver fluke infection
hepatica

121.4 Fasciolopsiasis
Infection by Fasciolopsis [buski]
Intestinal distomiasis

121.5 Metagonimiasis
Infection by Metagonimus yokogawai

121.6 Heterophyiasis
Infection by:
Heterophyes heterophyes
Stellantchasmus falcatus

121.8 Other specified trematode infections
Infection by:
Dicrocoelium dendriticum
Echinostoma ilocanum
Gastrodiscoides hominis

121.9 Trematode infection, unspecified
Distomiasis NOS   Fluke disease NOS

122 Echinococcosis
Includes: echinococciasis
hydatid disease
hydatidosis

122.0 Echinococcus granulosus infection of liver

122.1 Echinococcus granulosus infection of lung

122.2 Echinococcus granulosus infection of thyroid

122.3 Echinococcus granulosus infection, other

122.4 Echinococcus granulosus infection, unspecified

122.5 Echinococcus multilocularis infection of liver

122.6 Echinococcus multilocularis infection, other

122.7 Echinococcus multilocularis infection, unspecified

122.8 Echinococcosis, unspecified, of liver

122.9 Echinococcosis, other and unspecified

123 Other cestode infection

123.0 Taenia solium infection, intestinal form
Pork tapeworm (adult) (infection)

123.1 Cysticercosis
Cysticerciasis
Infection by Cysticercus cellulosae [larval form of Taenia solium]

123.2 Taenia saginata infection
Beef tapeworm (infection)
Infection by Taeniarhynchus saginatus

123.3 Taeniasis, unspecified

123.4 Diphyllobothriasis, intestinal
Diphyllobothrium (adult) (latum) (pacificum) infection
Fish tapeworm (infection)

● Code new   ▲ Revision of   ④ ⑤ Fourth or fifth
to this edition   existing code   digit required

123.5 Sparganosis [larval diphyllobothriasis]
Infection by:
Diphyllobothrium larvae
Sparganum (mansoni) (proliferum)
Spirometra larvae

123.6 Hymenolepiasis
Dwarf tapeworm (infection)
Hymenolepis (diminuta) (nana) infection
Rat tapeworm (infection)

123.8 Other specified cestode infection
Diplogonoporus (grandis)
Dipylidium (caninum) } infection
Dog tapeworm (infection)

123.9 Cestode infection, unspecified
Tapeworm (infection) NOS

124 Trichinosis
Trichinella spiralis infection   Trichinellosis
Trichiniasis

125 Filarial infection and dracontiasis

125.0 Bancroftian filariasis
Chyluria
Elephantiasis
Infection } due to Wuchereria bancrofti
Lymphadenitis
Lymphangitis
Wuchereriasis

125.1 Malayan filariasis
Brugia filariasis
Chyluria
Elephantiasis } due to Brugia [Wuchereria] malayi
Infection
Lymphadenitis
Lymphangitis

125.2 Loiasis
Eyeworm disease of Africa
Loa loa infection

125.3 Onchocerciasis
Onchocerca volvulus infection
Onchocercosis

125.4 Dipetalonemiasis
Infection by:
Acanthocheilonema perstans
Dipetalonema perstans

125.5 Mansonella ozzardi infection
Filariasis ozzardi

125.6 Other specified filariasis
Dirofilaria infection
Infection by:
Acanthocheilonema streptocerca
Dipetalonema streptocerca

125.7 Dracontiasis
Guinea-worm infection
Infection by Dracunculus medinensis

125.9 Unspecified filariasis

126 Ancylostomiasis and necatoriasis
Includes: cutaneous larva migrans due to Ancylostoma
hookworm (disease) (infection)
uncinariasis

126.0 Ancylostoma duodenale

126.1 Necator americanus

126.2 Ancylostoma braziliense

126.3 Ancylostoma ceylanicum

126.8 Other specified Ancylostoma

126.9 Ancylostomiasis and necatoriasis, unspecified
　　　Creeping eruption NOS
　　　Cutaneous larva migrans NOS

127 Other intestinal helminthiases

127.0 Ascariasis
　　　Ascaridiasis
　　　Infection by Ascaris lumbricoides
　　　Roundworm infection

127.1 Anisakiasis
　　　Infection by Anisakis larva

127.2 Strongyloidiasis
　　　Infection by Strongyloides stercoralis

　　　Excludes: *trichostrongyliasis (127.6)*

127.3 Trichuriasis
　　　Infection by Trichuris trichiuria
　　　Trichocephaliasis
　　　Whipworm (disease) (infection)

127.4 Enterobiasis
　　　Infection by Enterobius vermicularis
　　　Oxyuriasis
　　　Oxyuris vermicularis infection
　　　Pinworn (disease) (infection)
　　　Threadworm infection

127.5 Capillariasis
　　　Infection by Capillaria philippinensis

　　　Excludes: *infection by Capillaria hepatica (128.8)*

127.6 Trichostrongyliasis
　　　Infection by Trichostrongylus species

127.7 Other specified intestinal helminthiasis
　　　Infection by:
　　　　　Oesophagostomum apiostomum and related species
　　　　　Ternidens diminutus
　　　　　other specified intestinal helminth
　　　Physalopteriasis

127.8 Mixed intestinal helminthiasis
　　　Infection by intestinal helminths classified to more than one of the categories
　　　　　120.0-127.7
　　　Mixed helminthiasis NOS

127.9 Intestinal helminthiasis, unspecified

128 Other and unspecified helminthiases

128.0 Toxocariasis
　　　Larva migrans visceralis
　　　Toxocara (canis) (cati) infection
　　　Visceral larva migrans syndrome

128.1 Gnathostomiasis
　　　Infection by Gnathostoma spinigerum and related species

128.8 Other specified helminthiasis
　　　Infection by:
　　　　　Angiostrongylus cantonensis
　　　　　Capillaria hepatica
　　　　　other specified helminth

128.9 Helminth infection, unspecified
　　　Helminthiasis NOS　　　　　　　Worms NOS

129 Intestinal parasitism, unspecified

OTHER INFECTIOUS AND PARASITIC DISEASES (130-136)

130 Toxoplasmosis
　　　Includes: infection by toxoplasma gondii
　　　　　　　　toxoplasmosis (acquired)

　　　Excludes: *congenital toxoplasmosis (771.2)*

130.0 Meningoencephalitis due to toxoplasmosis
　　　Encephalitis due to acquired toxoplasmosis

● Code new　　　　　▲ Revision of　　　　④ ⑤ Fourth or fifth
　to this edition　　　　　existing code　　　　　　digit required

130.1 Conjunctivitis due to toxoplasmosis

130.2 Chorioretinitis due to toxoplasmosis
Focal retinochoroiditis due to acquired toxoplasmosis

130.3 Myocarditis due to toxoplasmosis

130.4 Pneumonitis due to toxoplasmosis

130.5 Hepatitis due to toxoplasmosis

130.7 Toxoplasmosis of other specified sites

130.8 Multisystemic disseminated toxoplasmosis
Toxoplasmosis of multiple sites

130.9 Toxoplasmosis, unspecified

131 Trichomoniasis
Includes: infection due to Trichomonas (vaginalis)

⑤ **131.0 Urogenital trichomoniasis**

131.00 Urogenital trichomoniasis, unspecified
Fluor (vaginalis) ⎫ trichomonal or due to Trichomonas
Leukorrhea (vaginalis) ⎬ (vaginalis)

131.01 Trichomonal vulvovaginitis
Vaginitis, trichomonal or due to Trichomonas (vaginalis)

131.02 Trichomonal urethritis

131.03 Trichomonal prostatitis

131.09 Other

131.8 Other specified sites

Excludes: intestinal (007.3)

131.9 Trichomoniasis, unspecified

132 Pediculosis and phthirus infestation

132.0 Pediculus capitis [head louse]

132.1 Pediculus corporis [body louse]

132.2 Phthirus pubis [pubic louse]
Pediculus pubis

132.3 Mixed infestation
Infestation classifiable to more than one of the categories 132.0-132.2

132.9 Pediculosis, unspecified

133 Acariasis

133.0 Scabies
Infestation by Sarcoptes Norwegian scabies
scabiei Sarcoptic itch

133.8 Other acariasis
Chiggers
Infestation by:
Demodex folliculorum
Trombicula

133.9 Acariasis, unspecified
Infestation by mites NOS

134 Other infestation

134.0 Myiasis
Infestation by: Infestation by:
Dermatobia (hominis) maggots
fly larvae Oestrus ovis
Gasterophilus (intestinalis)

134.1 Other arthropod infestation
Infestation by: Jigger disease
chigoe Scarabiasis
sand flea Tungiasis
Tunga penetrans

134.2 Hirudiniasis
Hirudiniasis (external) (internal)
Leeches (aquatic) (land)

134.8 Other specified infestations

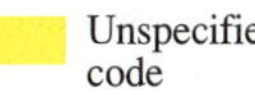

134.9 Infestation, unspecified
 Infestation (skin) NOS   Skin parasites NOS

135 Sarcoidosis
 Besnier-Boeck- Schaumann disease   Sarcoid (any site):
 Lupoid (miliary) of Boeck   NOS
 Lupus pernio (Besnier)   Boeck
 Lymphogranulomatosis, benign   Darier-Roussy
  (Schaumann's)   Uveoparotid fever

136 Other and unspecified infectious and parasitic diseases

136.0 Ainhum
 Dactylolysis spontanea

136.1 Behçet's syndrome

136.2 Specific infections by free-living amebae
 Meningoencephalitis due to Naegleria

136.3 Pneumocystosis
 Pneumonia due to Pneumocystis carinii

136.4 Psorospermiasis

136.5 Sarcosporidiosis
 Infection by Sarcocystis lindemanni

136.8 Other specified infectious and parasitic diseases
 Candiru infestation

136.9 Unspecified infectious and parasitic diseases
 Infectious disease NOS
 Parasitic disease NOS

LATE EFFECTS OF INFECTIOUS AND PARASITIC DISEASES (137-139)

137 Late effects of tuberculosis
 Note: This category is to be used to indicate conditions classifiable to 010-018 as the cause of
 late effects, which are themselves classified elsewhere. The "late effects" include those
 specified as such, as sequelae, or as due to old or inactive tuberculosis, without evidence
 of active disease.

137.0 Late effects of respiratory or unspecified tuberculosis

137.1 Late effects of central nervous system tuberculosis

137.2 Late effects of genitourinary tuberculosis

137.3 Late effects of tuberculosis of bones and joints

137.4 Late effects of tuberculosis of other specified organs

138 Late effects of acute poliomyelitis
 Note: This category is to be used to indicate conditions classifiable to 045 as the cause of late
 effects, which are themselves classified elsewhere. The "late effects" include conditions
 specified as such, or as sequelae, or as due to old or inactive poliomyelitis, without
 evidence of active disease.

139 Late effects of other infectious and parasitic diseases
 Note: This category is to be used to indicate conditions classifiable to categories 001-009,
 020-041, 046-136 as the cause of late effects, which are themselves classified elsewhere.
 The "late effects" include conditions specified as such; they also include sequela of
 diseases classifiable to the above categories if there is evidence that the disease itself is
 no longer present.

139.0 Late effects of viral encephalitis
 Late effects of conditions classifiable to 049.8-049.9, 062-064

139.1 Late effects of trachoma
 Late effects of conditions classifiable to 076

139.8 Late effects of other and unspecified infectious and parasitic diseases

● Code new   ▲ Revision of   ④ ⑤ Fourth or fifth
  to this edition   existing code   digit required

2.   NEOPLASMS (140-239)

Notes:

1.   Content
This chapter contains the following broad groups:

140-195	**Malignant neoplasms, stated or presumed to be primary, of specified sites, except of lymphatic and hematopoietic tissue**
196-198	**Malignant neoplasms, stated or presumed to be secondary, of specified sites**
199	**Malignant neoplasms, without specification of site**
200-208	**Malignant neoplasms, stated or presumed to be primary, of lymphatic and hematopoietic tissue**
210-229	**Benign neoplasms**
230-234	**Carcinoma in situ**
235-238	**Neoplasms of uncertain behavior [see Note, page 92]**
239	**Neoplasms of unspecified nature**

2.   Functional activity
All neoplasms are classified in this chapter, whether or not functionally active. An additional code from Chapter 3 may be used, if desired, to identify such functional activity associated with any neoplasm, e.g.:

catecholamine-producing malignant pheochromocytoma of adrenal:
   code 194.0, additional code 255.6
basophil adenoma of pituitary with Cushing's syndrome:
   code 227.3, additional code 255.0

3.   Morphology [Histology]
For those wishing to identify the histological type of neoplasms, a comprehensive coded nomenclature, which comprises the morphology rubrics of the ICD-Oncology, is given on pages 529-542.

4.   Malignant neoplasms overlapping site boundaries
Categories 140-195 are for the classification of primary malignant neoplasms according to their point of origin. A malignant neoplasm that overlaps two or more subcategories within a three-digit rubric and whose point of origin cannot be determined should be classified to the subcategory .8 "Other." For example, "carcinoma involving tip and ventral surface of tongue" should be assigned to 141.8. On the other hand, "carcinoma of tip of tongue, extending to involve the ventral surface" should be coded to 141.2, as the point of origin, the tip, is known. Three subcategories (149.8, 159.8, 165.8) have been provided for malignant neoplasms that overlap the boundaries of three-digit rubrics within certain systems. Overlapping malignant neoplasms that cannot be classified as indicated above should be assigned to the appropriate subdivision of category 195 (Malignant neoplasm of other and ill-defined sites).

MALIGNANT NEOPLASM OF LIP, ORAL CAVITY, AND PHARYNX (140-149)

Excludes: carcinoma in situ (230.0)

140 **Malignant neoplasm of lip**

Excludes: skin of lip (173.0)

140.0 Upper lip, vermilion border
Upper lip:
  NOS
  external
  lipstick area

140.1 Lower lip, vermilion border
Lower lip:
  NOS
  external
  lipstick area

140.3 Upper lip, inner aspect

Upper lip:	Upper lip:
buccal aspect	mucosa
frenulum	oral aspect

140.4 Lower lip, inner aspect

Lower lip:	Lower lip:
buccal aspect	mucosa
frenulum	oral aspect

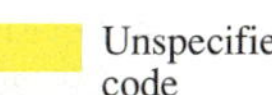

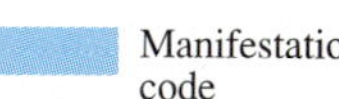

Manifestation
code

140.5 Lip, unspecified, inner aspect
Lip, not specified whether upper or lower:
buccal aspect
frenulum
mucosa
oral aspect

140.6 Commissure of lip
Labial commissure

140.8 Other sites of lip
Malignant neoplasm of contiguous or overlapping sites of lip whose point of origin
cannot be determined

140.9 Lip, unspecified, vermilion border
Lip, not specified as upper or lower:
NOS
external
lipstick area

141 Malignant neoplasm of tongue

141.0 Base of tongue
Dorsal surface of base of tongue
Fixed part of tongue NOS

141.1 Dorsal surface of tongue
Anterior two-thirds of tongue, dorsal surface
Dorsal tongue NOS
Midline of tongue

> *Excludes:* dorsal surface of base of tongue (141.0)

141.2 Tip and lateral border of tongue

141.3 Ventral surface of tongue
Anterior two-thirds of tongue, ventral surface
Frenulum linguae

141.4 Anterior two-thirds of tongue, part unspecified
Mobile part of tongue NOS

141.5 Junctional zone
Border of tongue at junction of fixed and mobile parts at insertion of anterior tonsillar
pillar

141.6 Lingual tonsil

141.8 Other sites of tongue
Malignant neoplasm of contiguous or overlapping sites of tongue whose point of origin
cannot be determined

141.9 Tongue, unspecified
Tongue NOS

142 Malignant neoplasm of major salivary glands
Includes: salivary ducts

> *Excludes:* malignant neoplasm of minor salivary glands:
> NOS (145.9)
> buccal mucosa (145.0)
> soft palate (145.3)
> tongue (141.0-141.9)
> tonsil, palatine (146.0)

142.0 Parotid gland

142.1 Submandibular gland
Submaxillary gland

142.2 Sublingual gland

142.8 Other major salivary glands
Malignant neoplasm of contiguous or overlapping sites of salivary glands and ducts
whose point of origin cannot be determined

142.9 Salivary gland, unspecified
Salivary gland (major) NOS

● Code new
to this edition   ▲ Revision of
existing code   ④ ⑤ Fourth or fifth
digit required

143 **Malignant neoplasm of gum**
    Includes: alveolar (ridge) mucosa
                 gingiva (alveolar) (marginal)
                 interdental papillae

       Excludes: *malignant odontogenic neoplasms (170.0-170.1)*

143.0 **Upper gum**

143.1 **Lower gum**

143.8 **Other sites of gum**
    Malignant neoplasm of contiguous or overlapping sites of gum whose point of origin cannot be determined

143.9 **Gum, unspecified**

144 **Malignant neoplasm of floor of mouth**

144.0 **Anterior portion**
    Anterior to the premolar-canine junction

144.1 **Lateral portion**

144.8 **Other sites of floor of mouth**
    Malignant neoplasm of contiguous or overlapping sites of floor of mouth whose point of origin cannot be determined

144.9 **Floor of mouth, part unspecified**

145 **Malignant neoplasm of other and unspecified parts of mouth**

       Excludes: *mucosa of lips (140.0-140.9)*

145.0 **Cheek mucosa**
    Buccal mucosa   Cheek, inner aspect

145.1 **Vestibule of mouth**
    Buccal sulcus (upper) (lower)
    Labial sulcus (upper) (lower)

145.2 **Hard palate**

145.3 **Soft palate**

       Excludes: *nasopharyngeal [posterior] [superior] surface of soft palate (147.3)*

145.4 **Uvula**

145.5 **Palate, unspecified**
    Junction of hard and soft palate
    Roof of mouth

145.6 **Retromolar area**

145.8 **Other specified parts of mouth**
    Malignant neoplasm of contiguous or overlapping sites of mouth whose point of origin cannot be determined

145.9 **Mouth, unspecified**
    Buccal cavity NOS
    Minor salivary gland, unspecified site
    Oral cavity NOS

146 **Malignant neoplasm of oropharynx**

146.0 **Tonsil**
    Tonsil:
      NOS
      faucial
      palatine

       Excludes: *lingual tonsil (141.6)*
                 pharyngeal tonsil (147.1)

146.1 **Tonsillar fossa**

146.2 **Tonsillar pillars (anterior) (posterior)**
    Faucial pillar   Palatoglossal arch
    Glossopalatine fold   Palatopharyngeal arch

146.3 **Vallecula**
    Anterior and medial surface of the pharyngoepiglottic fold

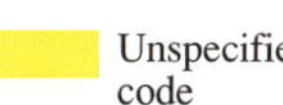

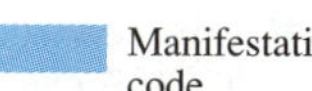

Manifestation
code

146.4 Anterior aspect of epiglottis
Epiglottis, free border [margin] Glossoepiglottic fold(s)

Excludes: *epiglottis:*
    NOS (161.1)
    suprahyoid portion (161.1)

146.5 Junctional region
Junction of the free margin of the epiglottis, the aryepiglottic fold, and the
    pharyngoepiglottic fold

146.6 Lateral wall of oropharynx

146.7 Posterior wall of oropharynx

146.8 Other specified sites of oropharynx
Branchial cleft
Malignant neoplasm of contiguous or overlapping sites of oropharynx whose point of
    origin cannot be determined

146.9 Oropharynx, unspecified

147 Malignant neoplasm of nasopharynx

147.0 Superior wall
Roof of nasopharynx

147.1 Posterior wall
Adenoid   Pharyngeal tonsil

147.2 Lateral wall
Fossa of Rosenmüller   Pharyngeal recess
Opening of auditory tube

147.3 Anterior wall
Floor of nasopharynx
Nasopharyngeal [posterior] [superior] surface of soft palate
Posterior margin of nasal septum and choanae

147.8 Other specified sites of nasopharynx
Malignant neoplasm of contiguous or overlapping sites of nasopharynx whose point of
    origin cannot be determined

147.9 Nasopharynx, unspecified
Nasopharyngeal wall NOS

148 Malignant neoplasm of hypopharynx

148.0 Postcricoid region

148.1 Pyriform sinus
Pyriform fossa

148.2 Aryepiglottic fold, hypopharyngeal aspect
Aryepiglottic fold or interarytenoid fold:
    NOS
    marginal zone

Excludes: *aryepiglottic fold or interarytenoid fold, laryngeal aspect (161.1)*

148.3 Posterior hypopharyngeal wall

148.8 Other specified sites of hypopharynx
Malignant neoplasm of contiguous or overlapping sites of hypopharynx whose point of
    origin cannot be determined

148.9 Hypopharynx, unspecified
Hypopharyngeal wall NOS   Hypopharynx NOS

149 Malignant neoplasm of other and ill-defined sites within the lip, oral cavity, and pharynx

149.0 Pharynx, unspecified

149.1 Waldeyer's ring

149.8 Other
Malignant neoplasms of lip, oral cavity, and pharynx whose point of origin cannot be
    assigned to any one of the categories 140-148

Excludes: *"book leaf" neoplasm [ventral surface of tongue and floor of mouth] (145.8)*

149.9 Ill-defined

   ● Code new
    to this edition   ▲ Revision of
            existing code   ④ ⑤ Fourth or fifth
                  digit required

MALIGNANT NEOPLASM OF DIGESTIVE ORGANS AND PERITONEUM (150-159)

Excludes: carcinoma in situ (230.1-230.9)

150 Malignant neoplasm of esophagus

150.0 Cervical esophagus

150.1 Thoracic esophagus

150.2 Abdominal esophagus

Excludes: adenocarcinoma (151.0)
cardio-esophageal junction (151.0)

150.3 Upper third of esophagus
Proximal third of esophagus

150.4 Middle third of esophagus

150.5 Lower third of esophagus
Distal third of esophagus

Excludes: adenocarcinoma (151.0)
cardio-esophageal junction (151.0)

150.8 Other specified part
Malignant neoplasm of contiguous or overlapping sites of esophagus whose point of origin cannot be determined

150.9 Esophagus, unspecified

151 Malignant neoplasm of stomach

151.0 Cardia
Cardiac orifice   Cardio-esophageal junction

Excludes: squamous cell carcinoma (150.2, 150.5)

151.1 Pylorus
Prepylorus   Pyloric canal

151.2 Pyloric antrum
Antrum of stomach NOS

151.3 Fundus of stomach

151.4 Body of stomach

151.5 Lesser curvature, unspecified
Lesser curvature, not classifiable to 151.1-151.4

151.6 Greater curvature, unspecified
Greater curvature, not classifiable to 151.0-151.4

151.8 Other specified sites of stomach
Anterior wall, not classifiable to 151.0-151.4
Posterior wall, not classifiable to 151.0-151.4
Malignant neoplasm of contiguous or overlapping sites of stomach whose point of origin cannot be determined

151.9 Stomach, unspecified
Carcinoma ventriculi   Gastric cancer

152 Malignant neoplasm of small intestine, including duodenum

152.0 Duodenum

152.1 Jejunum

152.2 Ileum

Excludes: ileocecal valve (153.4)

152.3 Meckel's diverticulum

152.8 Other specified sites of small intestine
Duodenojejunal junction
Malignant neoplasm of contiguous or overlapping sites of small intestine whose point of origin cannot be determined

152.9 Small intestine, unspecified

153 Malignant neoplasm of colon

153.0 Hepatic flexure

153.1 Transverse colon

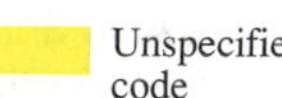

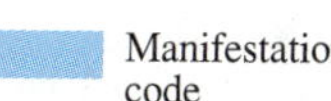

153.2 Descending colon
Left colon

153.3 Sigmoid colon
Sigmoid (flexure)

Excludes: rectosigmoid junction (154.0)

153.4 Cecum
Ileocecal valve

153.5 Appendix

153.6 Ascending colon
Right colon

153.7 Splenic flexure

153.8 Other specified sites of large intestine
Malignant neoplasm of contiguous or overlapping sites of colon whose point of origin cannot be determined

Excludes: ileocecal valve (153.4)
rectosigmoid junction (154.0)

153.9 Colon, unspecified
Large intestine NOS

154 Malignant neoplasm of rectum, rectosigmoid junction, and anus

154.0 Rectosigmoid junction
Colon with rectum   Rectosigmoid (colon)

154.1 Rectum
Rectal ampulla

154.2 Anal canal
Anal sphincter

Excludes: skin of anus (172.5, 173.5)

154.3 Anus, unspecified

Excludes: anus:
margin (172.5, 173.5)
skin (172.5, 173.5)
perianal skin (172.5, 173.5)

154.8 Other
Anorectum
Cloacogenic zone
Malignant neoplasm of contiguous or overlapping sites of rectum, rectosigmoid junction, and anus whose point of origin cannot be determined

155 Malignant neoplasm of liver and intrahepatic bile ducts

155.0 Liver, primary
Carcinoma:
liver, specified as primary
hepatocellular
liver cell
Hepatoblastoma

155.1 Intrahepatic bile ducts
Canaliculi biliferi   Intrahepatic:
Interlobular: biliary passages
bile ducts   canaliculi
biliary canals   gall duct

Excludes: hepatic duct (156.1)

155.2 Liver, not specified as primary or secondary

156 Malignant neoplasm of gallbladder and extrahepatic bile ducts

156.0 Gallbladder

156.1 Extrahepatic bile ducts
Biliary duct or passage NOS   Cystic duct
Common bile duct   Hepatic duct
Sphincter of Oddi

156.2 Ampulla of Vater

● Code new to this edition   ▲ Revision of existing code   ④ ⑤ Fourth or fifth digit required

156.8 Other specified sites of gallbladder and extrahepatic bile ducts
Malignant neoplasm of contiguous or overlapping sites of gallbladder and extrahepatic bile ducts whose point of origin cannot be determined

156.9 Biliary tract, part unspecified
Malignant neoplasm involving both intrahepatic and extrahepatic bile ducts

157 Malignant neoplasm of pancreas

157.0 Head of pancreas

157.1 Body of pancreas

157.2 Tail of pancreas

157.3 Pancreatic duct
Duct of:
Santorini
Wirsung

157.4 Islets of Langerhans
Islets of Langerhans, any part of pancreas

Use additional code, if desired, to identify any functional activity

157.8 Other specified sites of pancreas
Ectopic pancreatic tissue
Malignant neoplasm of contiguous or overlapping sites of pancreas whose point of origin cannot be determined

157.9 Pancreas, part unspecified

158 Malignant neoplasm of retroperitoneum and peritoneum

158.0 Retroperitoneum

Periadrenal tissue	Perirenal tissue
Perinephric tissue	Retrocecal tissue

158.8 Specified parts of peritoneum

Cul-de-sac (of Douglas)	Peritoneum:
Mesentery	parietal
Mesocolon	pelvic
Omentum	Rectouterine pouch

Malignant neoplasm of contiguous or overlapping sites of retroperitoneum and peritoneum whose point of origin cannot be determined

158.9 Peritoneum, unspecified

159 Malignant neoplasm of other and ill-defined sites within the digestive organs and peritoneum

159.0 Intestinal tract, part unspecified
Intestine NOS

159.1 Spleen, not elsewhere classified
Angiosarcoma
Fibrosarcoma } of spleen

Excludes: *Hodgkin's disease (201.0-201.9)*
lymphosarcoma (200.1)
reticulosarcoma (200.0)

159.8 Other sites of digestive system and intra-abdominal organs
Malignant neoplasm of digestive organs and peritoneum whose point of origin cannot be assigned to any one of the categories 150-158

Excludes: *anus and rectum (154.8)*
cardio-esophageal junction (151.0)
colon and rectum ORANGE (154.0)

159.9 Ill-defined
Alimentary canal or tract NOS
Gastrointestinal tract NOS

Excludes: *abdominal NOS (195.2)*
intra-abdominal NOS (195.2)

Add 4th or 5th digit	Nonspecific code	Unspecified code	Manifestation code

MALIGNANT NEOPLASM OF RESPIRATORY AND INTRATHORACIC ORGANS (160-165)

Excludes: carcinoma in situ (231.0-231.9)

160 Malignant neoplasm of nasal cavities, middle ear, and accessory sinuses

160.0 Nasal cavities

Cartilage of nose
Conchae, nasal
Internal nose

Septum of nose
Vestibule of nose

Excludes: nasal bone (170.0)
nose NOS (195.0)
olfactory bulb (192.0)
posterior margin of septum and choanae (147.3)
skin of nose (172.3, 173.3)
turbinates (170.0)

160.1 Auditory tube, middle ear, and mastoid air cells

Antrum tympanicum
Eustachian tube

Tympanic cavity

Excludes: auditory canal (external) (172.2, 173.2)
bone of ear (meatus) (170.0)
cartilage of ear (171.0)
ear (external) (skin) (172.2, 173.2)

160.2 Maxillary sinus

Antrum (Highmore) (maxillary)

160.3 Ethmoidal sinus

160.4 Frontal sinus

160.5 Sphenoidal sinus

160.8 Other

Malignant neoplasm of contiguous or overlapping sites of nasal cavities, middle ear, and accessory sinuses whose point of origin cannot be determined

160.9 Accessory sinus, unspecified

161 Malignant neoplasm of larynx

161.0 Glottis

Intrinsic larynx
Laryngeal commissure
(anterior) (posterior)

True vocal cord
Vocal cord NOS

161.1 Supraglottis

Aryepiglottic fold or interarytenoid fold, laryngeal aspect
Epiglottis (suprahyoid portion) NOS
Extrinsic larynx
False vocal cords
Posterior (laryngeal) surface of epiglottis
Ventricular bands

Excludes: anterior aspect of epiglottis (146.4)
aryepiglottic fold or interarytenoid fold:
NOS (148.2)
hypopharyngeal aspect (148.2)
marginal zone (148.2)

161.2 Subglottis

161.3 Laryngeal cartilages

Cartilage:
arytenoid
cricoid

Cartilage:
cuneiform
thyroid

161.8 Other specified sites of larynx

Malignant neoplasm of contiguous or overlapping sites of larynx whose point of origin cannot be determined

161.9 Larynx, unspecified

162 Malignant neoplasm of trachea, bronchus, and lung

162.0 Trachea

Cartilage } of trachea
Mucosa

● Code new
   to this edition

▲ Revision of
   existing code

④ ⑤ Fourth or fifth
   digit required

162.2 Main bronchus
Carina   Hilus of lung

162.3 Upper lobe, bronchus or lung

162.4 Middle lobe, bronchus or lung

162.5 Lower lobe, bronchus or lung

162.8 Other parts of bronchus or lung
Malignant neoplasm of contiguous or overlapping sites of bronchus or lung whose point of origin cannot be determined

162.9 Bronchus and lung, unspecified

163 Malignant neoplasm of pleura

163.0 Parietal pleura

163.1 Visceral pleura

163.8 Other specified sites of pleura
Malignant neoplasm of contiguous or overlapping sites of pleura whose point of origin cannot be determined

163.9 Pleura, unspecified

164 Malignant neoplasm of thymus, heart, and mediastinum

164.0 Thymus

164.1 Heart
Endocardium   Myocardium
Epicardium   Pericardium

Excludes: *great vessels (171.4)*

164.2 Anterior mediastinum

164.3 Posterior mediastinum

164.8 Other
Malignant neoplasm of contiguous or overlapping sites of thymus, heart, and mediastinum whose point of origin cannot be determined

164.9 Mediastinum, part unspecified

165 Malignant neoplasm of other and ill-defined sites within the respiratory system and intrathoracic organs

165.0 Upper respiratory trace, part unspecified

165.8 Other
Malignant neoplasm of respiratory and intrathoracic organs whose point of origin cannot be assigned to any one of the categories 160-164

165.9 Ill-defined sites within the respiratory system
Respiratory tract NOS

Excludes: *intrathoracic NOS (195.1)*
thoracic NOS (195.1)

MALIGNANT NEOPLASM OF BONE, CONNECTIVE TISSUE, SKIN, AND BREAST (170-176)

Excludes: *carcinoma in situ:*
breast (233.0)
skin (232.0-232.9)

170 Malignant neoplasm of bone and articular cartilage
Includes: cartilage (articular) (joint)
periosteum

Excludes: *bone marrow NOS (202.9)*

cartilage:
ear (171.0)
eyelid (171.0)
larynx (161.3)
nose (160.0)
synovia (171.0-171.9)

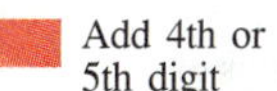

170.0 Bones of skull and face, except mandible

Bone:
ethmoid
frontal
malar
nasal
occipital
orbital
parietal

Bone:
sphenoid
temporal
zygomatic
Maxilla (superior)
Turbinate
Upper jaw bone
Vomer

Excludes: *carcinoma, any type except intraosseous or odontogenic:*
maxilla, maxillary (sinus) (160.2)
upper jaw bone (143.0)
jaw bone (lower) (170.1)

170.1 Mandible

Inferior maxilla
Jaw bone NOS

Lower jaw bone

Excludes: *carcinoma, any type except intraosseous or odontogenic:*
jaw bone NOS (143.9)
lower (143.1)
upper jaw bone (170.0)

170.2 Vertebral column, excluding sacrum and coccyx

Spinal column
Spine

Vertebra

Excludes: *sacrum and coccyx (170.6)*

170.3 Ribs, sternum, and clavicle

Costal cartilage
Costovertebral joint

Xiphoid process

170.4 Scapula and long bones of upper limb

Acromion
Bones NOS of upper limb
Humerus

Radius
Ulna

170.5 Short bones of upper limb

Carpal
Cuneiform, wrist
Metacarpal
Navicular, of hand
Phalanges of hand
Pisiform

Scaphoid (of hand)
Semilunar or lunate
Trapezium
Trapezoid
Unciform

170.6 Pelvic bones, sacrum, and coccyx

Coccygeal vertebra
Ilium
Ischium

Pubic bone
Sacral vertebra

170.7 Long bones of lower limb

Bones NOS of lower limb
Femur

Fibula
Tibia

170.8 Short bones of lower limb

Astragalus [talus]
Calcaneus
Cuboid
Cuneiform, ankle
Metatarsal

Navicular (of ankle)
Patella
Phalanges of foot
Tarsal

170.9 Bone and articular cartilage, site unspecified

● Code new
to this edition

▲ Revision of
existing code

④ ⑤ Fourth or fifth
digit required

171 **Malignant neoplasm of connective and other soft tissue**

Includes: blood vessel
bursa
fascia
fat
ligament, except uterine
muscle
peripheral, sympathetic, and parasympathetic nerves and ganglia
synovia
tendon (sheath)

Excludes: *cartilage (of):*
articular (170.0-170.9)
larynx (161.3)
nose (160.0)
connective tissue:
breast (174.0-175.9)
internal organs—code to malignant neoplasm of the site [e.g., leiomyosarcoma of stomach, 151.9]
heart (164.1)
uterine ligament (183.4)

171.0 **Head, face, and neck**
Cartilage of:
ear
eyelid

171.2 **Upper limb, including shoulder**
Arm   Forearm
Finger   Hand

171.3 **Lower limb, including hip**
Foot   Thigh
Leg   Toe
Popliteal space

171.4 **Thorax**
Axilla   Great vessels
Diaphragm

Excludes: *heart (164.1)*
mediastinum (164.2-164.9)
thymus (164.0)

171.5 **Abdomen**
Abdominal wall   Hypochondrium

Excludes: *peritoneum (158.8)*
retroperitoneum (158.0)

171.6 **Pelvis**
Buttock   Inguinal region
Groin   Perineum

Excludes: *pelvic peritoneum (158.8)*
retroperitoneum (158.0)
uterine ligament, any (183.3-183.5)

171.7 **Trunk, unspecified**
Back NOS   Flank NOS

171.8 **Other specified sites of connective and other soft tissue**
Malignant neoplasm of contiguous or overlapping sites of connective tissue whose point of origin cannot be determined

171.9 **Connective and other soft tissue, site unspecified**

172 **Malignant melanoma of skin**

Includes: melanocarcinoma
melanoma (skin) NOS

Excludes: *skin of genital organs (184.0-184.9, 187.1-187.9)*
sites other than skin—code to malignant neoplasm of the site

172.0 **Lip**

Excludes: *vermilion border of lip (140.0-140.1, 140.9)*

172.1 **Eyelid, including canthus**

	Add 4th or 5th digit		Nonspecific code		Unspecified code		Manifestation code

172.2 Ear and external auditory canal
  Auricle (ear)
  Auricular canal, external
  External [acoustic] meatus
  Pinna

172.3 Other and unspecified parts of face
Cheek (external)	Forehead
Chin	Nose, external
Eyebrow	Temple

172.4 Scalp and neck

172.5 Trunk, except scrotum
Axilla	Perianal skin
Breast	Perineum
Buttock	Umbilicus
Groin	

> *Excludes:* anal canal (154.2)
> anus NOS (154.3)
> scrotum (187.7)

172.6 Upper limb, including shoulder
Arm	Forearm
Finger	Hand

172.7 Lower limb, including hip
Ankle	Leg
Foot	Popliteal area
Heel	Thigh
Knee	Toe

172.8 Other specified sites of skin
  Malignant melanoma of contiguous or overlapping sites of skin whose point of origin
  cannot be determined

172.9 Melanoma of skin, site unspecified

173 Other malignant neoplasm of skin
  Includes: malignant neoplasm of:
  sebaceous glands
  sudoriferous, sudoriparous glands
  sweat glands

> *Excludes:* Kaposi's sarcoma (176.0-176.9)
> malignant melanoma of skin (172.0-172.9)
> skin of genital organs (184.0-184.9, 187.1-187.9)

173.0 Skin of lip

> *Excludes:* vermilion border of lip (140.0-140.1, 140.9)

173.1 Eyelid, including canthus

> *Excludes:* cartilage of eyelid (171.0)

173.2 Skin of ear and external auditory canal
Auricle (ear)	External meatus
Auricular canal, external	Pinna

> *Excludes:* cartilage of ear (171.0)

173.3 Skin of other and unspecified parts of face
Cheek, external	Forehead
Chin	Nose, external
Eyebrow	Temple

173.4 Scalp and skin of neck

● Code new
  to this edition

▲ Revision of
  existing code

④ ⑤ Fourth or fifth
  digit required

173.5 Skin of trunk, except scrotum
Axillary fold
Perianal skin
Skin of:
  abdominal wall
  anus
  back
  breast
Skin of:
  buttock
  chest wall
  groin
  perineum
Umbilicus

Excludes: *anal canal (154.2)*
anus NOS (154.3)
skin of scrotum (187.7)

173.6 Skin of upper limb, including shoulder
Arm
Finger
Forearm
Hand

173.7 Skin of lower limb, including hip
Ankle
Foot
Heel
Knee
Leg
Popliteal area
Thigh
Toe

173.8 Other specified sites of skin
Malignant neoplasm of contiguous or overlapping sites of skin whose point of origin
cannot be determined

173.9 Skin, site unspecified

174 Malignant neoplasm of female breast
Includes:
breast (female)
connective tissue
soft parts
Paget's disease of:
breast
nipple

Excludes: *skin of breast (172.5, 173.5)*

174.0 Nipple and areola

174.1 Central portion

174.2 Upper-inner quadrant

174.3 Lower-inner quadrant

174.4 Upper-outer quadrant

174.5 Lower-outer quadrant

174.6 Axillary tail

174.8 Other specified sites of female breast
Ectopic sites
Inner breast
Lower breast
Malignant neoplasm of
  contiguous or overlapping
  sites of breast whose point of
  origin cannot be determined
Midline of breast
Outer breast
Upper breast

174.9 Breast (female), unspecified

175 Malignant neoplasm of male breast

Excludes: *skin of breast (172.5, 173.5)*

175.0 Nipple and areola

175.9 Other and unspecified sites of male breast
Ectopic breast tissue, male

176 Kaposi's sarcoma

176.0 Skin

176.1 Soft Tissue
Includes:
blood vessel
connective tissue
fascia
ligament
lymphatic(s) NEC
muscle

Excludes: *lymph glands and nodes (176.5)*

176.2 Palate

176.3 Gastrointestinal sites

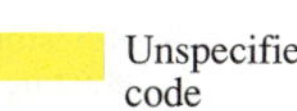

Manifestation
code

176.4 Lung

176.5 Lymph nodes

176.8 Other specified sites
Includes: oral cavity NEC

176.9 Unspecified
Viscera NOS

MALIGNANT NEOPLASM OF GENITOURINARY ORGANS (179-189)

Excludes: carcinoma in situ (233.1-233.9)

179 Malignant neoplasm of uterus, part unspecified

180 Malignant neoplasm of cervix uteri
Includes: invasive malignancy [carcinoma]

Excludes: carcinoma in situ (233.1)

180.0 Endocervix
Cervical canal NOS   Endocervical gland
Endocervical canal

180.1 Exocervix

180.8 Other specified sites of cervix
Cervical stump
Squamocolumnar junction of cervix
Malignant neoplasm of contiguous or overlapping sites of cervix uteri whose point of
origin cannot be determined

180.9 Cervix uteri, unspecified

181 Malignant neoplasm of placenta
Choriocarcinoma NOS   Chorioepithelioma NOS

Excludes: chorioadenoma (destruens) (236.1)
hydatidiform mole (630)
malignant (236.1)
invasive mole (236.1)
male choriocarcinoma NOS (186.0-186.9)

182 Malignant neoplasm of body of uterus

Excludes: carcinoma in situ (233.2)

182.0 Corpus uteri, except isthmus
Cornu   Fundus
Endometrium   Myometrium

182.1 Isthmus
Lower uterine segment

182.8 Other specified sites of body of uterus
Malignant neoplasm of contiguous or overlapping sites of body of uterus whose point
of origin cannot be determined

Excludes: uterus NOS (179)

183 Malignant neoplasm of ovary and other uterine adnexa

Excludes: Douglas' cul-de-sac (158.8)

183.0 Ovary
Use additional code, if desired, to identify any functional activity

183.2 Fallopian tube
Oviduct   Uterine tube

183.3 Broad ligament
Mesovarium   Parovarian region

183.4 Parametrium
Uterine ligament NOS   Uterosacral ligament

183.5 Round ligament

183.8 Other specified sites of uterine adnexa
Tubo-ovarian
Utero-ovarian
Malignant neoplasm of contiguous or overlapping sites of ovary and other uterine
adnexa whose point of origin cannot be determined

183.9 Uterine adnexa, unspecified

● Code new   ▲ Revision of   ④ ⑤ Fourth or fifth
to this edition   existing code   digit required

184 Malignant neoplasm of other and unspecified female genital organs

> *Excludes:* carcinoma in situ (233.3)

184.0 Vagina
Gartner's duct   Vaginal vault

184.1 Labia majora
Greater vestibular [Bartholin's] gland

184.2 Labia minora

184.3 Clitoris

184.4 Vulva, unspecified
External female genitalia NOS
Pudendum

184.8 Other specified sites of female genital organs
Malignant neoplasm of contiguous or overlapping sites of female genital organs whose point of origin cannot be determined

184.9 Female genital organ, site unspecified
Female genitourinary tract NOS

185 Malignant neoplasm of prostate

> *Excludes:* seminal vesicles (187.8)

186 Malignant neoplasm of testis
Use additional code, if desired, to identify any functional activity

186.0 Undescended testis
Ectopic testis   Retained testis

186.9 Other and unspecified testis
Testis:
NOS
descended
scrotal

187 Malignant neoplasm of penis and other male genital organs

187.1 Prepuce
Foreskin

187.2 Glans penis

187.3 Body of penis
Corpus cavernosum

187.4 Penis, part unspecified
Skin of penis NOS

187.5 Epididymis

187.6 Spermatic cord
Vas deferens

187.7 Scrotum
Skin of scrotum

187.8 Other specified sites of male genital organs
Seminal vesicle
Tunica vaginalis
Malignant neoplasm of contiguous or overlapping sites of penis and other male genital organs whose point of origin cannot be determined

187.9 Male genital organ, site unspecified
Male genital organ or tract NOS

188 Malignant neoplasm of bladder

> *Excludes:* carcinoma in situ (233.7)

188.0 Trigone of urinary bladder

188.1 Dome of urinary bladder

188.2 Lateral wall of urinary bladder

188.3 Anterior wall of urinary bladder

188.4 Posterior wall of urinary bladder

188.5 Bladder neck
Internal urethral orifice

188.6 Ureteric orifice

188.7 Urachus

Add 4th or 5th digit | Nonspecific code | Unspecified code | Manifestation code

188.8 Other specified sites of bladder
Malignant neoplasm of contiguous or overlapping sites of bladder whose point of origin cannot be determined

188.9 Bladder, part unspecified
Bladder wall NOS

189 Malignant neoplasm of kidney and other and unspecified urinary organs

189.0 Kidney, except pelvis
Kidney NOS   Kidney parenchyma

189.1 Renal pelvis
Renal calyces   Ureteropelvic junction

189.2 Ureter

Excludes: *ureteric orifice of bladder (188.6)*

189.3 Urethra

Excludes: *urethral orifice of bladder (188.5)*

189.4 Paraurethral glands

189.8 Other specified sites of urinary organs
Malignant neoplasm of contiguous or overlapping sites of kidney and other urinary organs whose point of origin cannot be determined

189.9 Urinary organ, site unspecified
Urinary system NOS

MALIGNANT NEOPLASM OF OTHER AND UNSPECIFIED SITES (190-199)

Excludes: *carcinoma in situ (234.0-234.9)*

190 Malignant neoplasm of eye

Excludes: *carcinoma in situ (234.0)*
eyelid (skin) (172.1, 173.1)
cartilage (171.0)
optic nerve (192.0)
orbital bone (170.0)

190.0 Eyeball, except conjunctiva, cornea, retina, and choroid
Ciliary body   Sclera
Crystalline lens   Uveal tract
Iris

190.1 Orbit
Connective tissue of orbit
Extraocular muscle
Retrobulbar

Excludes: *bone of orbit (170.0)*

190.2 Lacrimal gland

190.3 Conjunctiva

190.4 Cornea

190.5 Retina

190.6 Choroid

190.7 Lacrimal duct
Lacrimal sac   Nasolacrimal duct

190.8 Other specified sites of eye
Malignant neoplasm of contiguous or overlapping sites of eye whose point of origin cannot be determined

190.9 Eye, part unspecified

191 Malignant neoplasm of brain

Excludes: *cranial nerves (192.0)*
retrobulbar area (190.1)

191.0 Cerebrum, except lobes and ventricles
Basal ganglia   Globus pallidus
Cerebral cortex   Hypothalamus
Corpus striatum   Thalamus

191.1 Frontal lobe

● Code new to this edition   ▲ Revision of existing code   ④ ⑤ Fourth or fifth digit required

191.2 Temporal lobe
Hippocampus — Uncus

191.3 Parietal lobe

191.4 Occipital lobe

191.5 Ventricles
Choroid plexus — Floor of ventricle

191.6 Cerebellum NOS
Cerebellopontine angle

191.7 Brain stem
Cerebral peduncle — Midbrain
Medulla oblongata — Pons

191.8 Other parts of brain
Corpus callosum
Tapetum
Malignant neoplasm of contiguous or overlapping sites of brain whose point of origin cannot be determined

191.9 Brain, unspecified
Cranial fossa NOS

192 Malignant neoplasm of other and unspecified parts of nervous system

> *Excludes:* *peripheral, sympathetic, and parasympathetic nerves and ganglia (171.0-171.9)*

192.0 Cranial nerves
Olfactory bulb

192.1 Cerebral meninges
Dura (mater) — Meninges NOS
Falx (cerebelli) (cerebri) — Tentorium

192.2 Spinal cord
Cauda equina

192.3 Spinal meninges

192.8 Other specified sites of nervous system
Malignant neoplasm of contiguous or overlapping sites of other parts of nervous system whose point of origin cannot be determined

192.9 Nervous system, part unspecified
Nervous system (central) NOS

> *Excludes:* *meninges NOS (192.1)*

193 Malignant neoplasm of thyroid gland
Sipple's syndrome — Thyroglossal duct
Use additional code, if desired, to identify any functional activity

194 Malignant neoplasm of other endocrine glands and related structures
Use additional code, if desired, to identify any functional activity

> *Excludes:* *islets of Langerhans (157.4)*
> *ovary (183.0)*
> *testis (186.0-186.9)*
> *thymus (164.0)*

194.0 Adrenal gland
Adrenal cortex — Suprarenal gland
Adrenal medulla

194.1 Parathyroid gland

194.3 Pituitary gland and craniopharyngeal duct
Craniobuccal pouch — Rathke's pouch
Hypophysis — Sella turcica

194.4 Pineal gland

194.5 Carotid body

194.6 Aortic body and other paraganglia
Coccygeal body — Para-aortic body
Glomus jugulare

194.8 Other
Pluriglandular involvement NOS

Note: If the sites of multiple involvements are known, they should be coded separately.

194.9 Endocrine gland, site unspecified

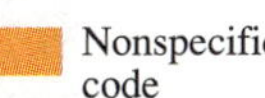

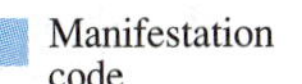

195 Malignant neoplasm of other and ill-defined sites

Includes: malignant neoplasms of contiguous sites, not elsewhere classified, whose point of origin cannot be determined

Excludes: *malignant neoplasm:*
lymphatic and hematopoietic tissue (200.0-208.9)
secondary sites (196.0-198.8)
unspecified site (199.0-199.1)

195.0 Head, face, and neck

Cheek NOS
Jaw NOS
Nose NOS
Supraclavicular region NOS

195.1 Thorax

Axilla
Chest (wall) NOS
Intrathoracic NOS

195.2 Abdomen

Intra-abdominal NOS

195.3 Pelvis

Groin
Inguinal region NOS
Presacral region
Sacrococcygeal region
Sites overlapping systems within pelvis, as:
  rectovaginal (septum)
  rectovesical (septum)

195.4 Upper limb

195.5 Lower limb

195.8 Other specified sites

Back NOS
Flank NOS
Trunk NOS

196 Secondary and unspecified malignant neoplasm of lymph nodes

Excludes: *any malignant neoplasm of lymph nodes, specified as primary (200.0-202.9)*
Hodgkin's disease (201.0-201.9)
lymphosarcoma (200.1)
reticulosarcoma (200.0)
other forms of lymphoma (202.0-202.9)

196.0 Lymph nodes of head, face, and neck

Cervical
Cervicofacial
Scalene
Supraclavicular

196.1 Intrathoracic lymph nodes

Bronchopulmonary
Intercostal
Mediastinal
Tracheobronchial

196.2 Intra-abdominal lymph nodes

Intestinal
Mesenteric
Retroperitoneal

196.3 Lymph nodes of axilla and upper limb

Brachial
Epitrochlear
Infraclavicular
Pectoral

196.5 Lymph nodes of inguinal region and lower limb

Femoral
Groin
Popliteal
Tibial

196.6 Intrapelvic lymph nodes

Hypogastric
Iliac
Obturator
Parametrial

196.8 Lymph nodes of multiple sites

196.9 Site unspecified

Lymph nodes NOS

197 Secondary malignant neoplasm of respiratory and digestive systems

Excludes: *lymph node metastasis (196.0-196.9)*

197.0 Lung

Bronchus

197.1 Mediastinum

197.2 Pleura

● Code new to this edition   ▲ Revision of existing code   ④ ⑤ Fourth or fifth digit required

197.3 Other respiratory organs
Trachea

197.4 Small intestine, including duodenum

197.5 Large intestine and rectum

197.6 Retroperitoneum and peritoneum

197.7 Liver, specified as secondary

197.8 Other digestive organs and spleen

198 Secondary malignant neoplasm of other specified sites

$Excludes:$ *lymph node metastasis (196.0-196.9)*

198.0 Kidney

198.1 Other urinary organs

198.2 Skin
Skin of breast

198.3 Brain and spinal cord

198.4 Other parts of nervous system
Meninges (cerebral) (spinal)

198.5 Bone and bone marrow

198.6 Ovary

198.7 Adrenal gland
Suprarenal gland

⑤ **198.8 Other specified sites**

198.81 Breast

$Excludes:$ *skin of breast (198.2)*

198.82 Genital organs

198.89 Other

$Excludes:$ *retroperitoneal lymph nodes (196.2)*

199 Malignant neoplasm without specification of site

199.0 Disseminated
Carcinomatosis
Generalized:
  cancer
  malignancy
Multiple cancer
} unspecified site (primary) (secondary)

199.1 Other
Cancer
Carcinoma
Malignancy
} unspecified site (primary) (secondary)

MALIGNANT NEOPLASM OF LYMPHATIC AND HEMATOPOIETIC TISSUE (200-208)

$Excludes:$ *secondary neoplasm of:*
bone marrow (198.5)
spleen (197.8)
secondary and unspecified neoplasm of lymph nodes (196.0-196.9)

The following fifth-digit subclassification is for use with categories 200-202:

0 unspecified site, extranodal and solid organ sites

1 lymph nodes of head, face, and neck

2 intrathoracic lymph nodes

3 intra-abdominal lymph nodes

4 lymph nodes of axilla and upper limb

5 lymph nodes of inguinal region and lower limb

6 intrapelvic lymph nodes

7 spleen

8 lymph nodes of multiple sites

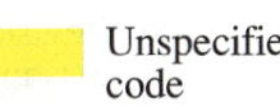

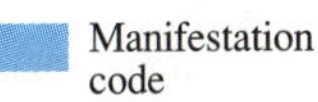

Manifestation
code

⑤ **200** **Lymphosarcoma and reticulosarcoma**

⑤ **200.0** **Reticulosarcoma**
Lymphoma (malignant):
  histiocytic (diffuse):
    nodular
    pleomorphic cell type
  reticulum cell type
Reticulum cell sarcoma:
  NOS
  pleomorphic cell type

⑤ **200.1** **Lymphosarcoma**
Lymphoblastoma (diffuse)
Lymphoma (malignant):
  lymphoblastic (diffuse)
  lymphocytic (cell type)
    (diffuse)
  lymphosarcoma type

Lymphosarcoma:
  NOS
  diffuse NOS
  lymphoblastic (diffuse)
  lymphocytic (diffuse)
  prolymphocytic

Excludes: lymphosarcoma:
  follicular or nodular (202.0)
  mixed cell type (200.8)
  lymphosarcoma cell leukemia (207.8)

⑤ **200.2** **Burkitt's tumor or lymphoma**
Malignant lymphoma, Burkitt's type

⑤ **200.8** **Other named variants**
Lymphoma (malignant):
  lymphoplasmacytoid type
  mixed lymphocytic-histiocytic (diffuse)
Lymphosarcoma, mixed cell type (diffuse)
Reticulolymphosarcoma (diffuse)

⑤ **201** **Hodgkin's disease**

⑤ **201.0** **Hodgkin's paragranuloma**

⑤ **201.1** **Hodgkin's granuloma**

⑤ **201.2** **Hodgkin's sarcoma**

⑤ **201.4** **Lymphocytic-histiocytic predominance**

⑤ **201.5** **Nodular sclerosis**
Hodgkin's disease, nodular sclerosis:
  NOS
  cellular phase

⑤ **201.6** **Mixed cellularity**

⑤ **201.7** **Lymphocytic depletion**
Hodgkin's disease, lymphocytic depletion:
  NOS
  diffuse fibrosis
  reticular type

⑤ **201.9** **Hodgkin's disease, unspecified**
Hodgkin's:
  disease NOS
  lymphoma NOS

Malignant:
  lymphogranuloma
  lymphogranulomatosis

⑤ **202** **Other malignant neoplasms of lymphoid and histiocytic tissue**

⑤ **202.0** **Nodular lymphoma**
Brill-Symmers disease
Lymphoma:
  follicular (giant)
  lymphocytic, nodular

Lymphosarcoma:
  follicular (giant)
  nodular
Reticulosarcoma, follicular or nodular

⑤ **202.1** **Mycosis fungoides**

⑤ **202.2** **Sézary's disease**

⑤ **202.3** **Malignant histiocytosis**
Histiocytic medullary reticulosis
Malignant:
  reticuloendotheliosis
  reticulosis

⑤ **202.4** **Leukemic reticuloendotheliosis**
Hairy-cell leukemia

● Code new
to this edition

▲ Revision of
existing code

④ ⑤ Fourth or fifth
digit required

⑤ **202.5 Letterer-Siwe disease**
Acute:
  differentiated progressive histiocytosis
  histiocytosis X (progressive)
  infantile reticuloendotheliosis
  reticulosis of infancy

Excludes: *Hand-Schüller-Christian disease (277.8)*
  histiocytosis (acute) (chronic) (277.8)
  histiocytosis X (chronic) (277.8)

⑤ **202.6 Malignant mast cell tumors**
Malignant: Mast cell sarcoma
  mastocytoma   Systemic tissue mast cell disease
  mastocytosis

Excludes: *mast cell leukemia (207.8)*

⑤ **202.8 Other lymphomas**
Lymphoma (malignant):
  NOS
  diffuse

Excludes: *benign lymphoma (229.0)*

⑤ **202.9 Other and unspecified malignant neoplasms of lymphoid and histiocytic tissue**
Malignant neoplasm of bone marrow NOS

⑤ **203 Multiple myeloma and immunoproliferative neoplasms**
The following fifth-digit subclassification is for use with category 203

  0 without mention of remission

  1 in remission

⑤ **203.0 Multiple myeloma**
Kahler's disease   Myelomatosis

Excludes: *solitary myeloma (238.6)*

⑤ **203.1 Plasma cell leukemia**
Plasmacytic leukemia

⑤ **203.8 Other immunoproliferative neoplasms**

⑤ **204 Lymphoid leukemia**
Includes:
            leukemia: leukemia:
              lymphatic   lymphocytic
              lymphoblastic   lymphogenous
The following fifth-digit subclassification is for use with category 204

  0 without mention of remission

  1 in remission

⑤ **204.0 Acute**

Excludes: *acute exacerbation of chronic lymphoid leukemia (204.1)*

⑤ **204.1 Chronic**

⑤ **204.2 Subacute**

⑤ **204.8 Other lymphoid leukemia**
Aleukemic leukemia:
  lymphatic
  lymphocytic
  lymphoid

⑤ **204.9 Unspecified lymphoid leukemia**

⑤ **205 Myeloid leukemia**
Includes:
            leukemia: leukemia:
              granulocytic   myelomonocytic
              myeloblastic   myelosclerotic
              myelocytic   myelosis
              Tmyelogenous
The following fifth-digit subclassification is for use with category 205

  0 without mention of remission

  1 in remission

Manifestation
code

⑤ **205.0   Acute**
Acute promyelocytic leukemia

Excludes: acute exacerbation of chronic myeloid leukemia (205.1)

⑤ **205.1   Chronic**
Eosinophilic leukemia   Neutrophilic leukemia

⑤ **205.2   Subacute**

⑤ **205.3   Myeloid sarcoma**
Chloroma
Granulocytic sarcoma

⑤ **205.8   Other myeloid leukemia**
Aleukemic leukemia:
  granulocytic
  myelogenous
  myeloid
Aleukemic myelosis

⑤ **205.9   Unspecified myeloid leukemia**

⑤ **206   Monocytic leukemia**
Includes: leukemia:
  histiocytic
  monoblastic
  monocytoid

The following fifth-digit subclassification is for use with category 206

0   **without mention of remission**

1   **in remission**

⑤ **206.0   Acute**

Excludes: acute exacerbation of chronic monocytic leukemia (206.1)

⑤ **206.1   Chronic**

⑤ **206.2   Subacute**

⑤ **206.8   Other monocytic leukemia**
Aleukemic:
  monocytic leukemia
  monocytoid leukemia

⑤ **206.9   Unspecified monocytic leukemia**

⑤ **207   Other specified leukemia**

Excludes: leukemic reticuloendotheliosis (202.4)
  plasma cell leukemia (203.1)

The following fifth-digit subclassification is for use with category 207

0   **without mention of remission**

1   **in remission**

⑤ **207.0   Acute erythremia and erythroleukemia**
Acute erythremic myelosis   Erythremic myelosis
Di Guglielmo's disease

⑤ **207.1   Chronic erythremia**
Heilmeyer-Schöner disease

⑤ **207.2   Megakaryocytic leukemia**
Megakaryocytic myelosis   Thrombocytic leukemia

⑤ **207.8   Other specified leukemia**
Lymphosarcoma cell leukemia

⑤ **208   Leukemia of unspecified cell type**
The following fifth-digit subclassification is for use with category 208

0   **without mention of remission**

1   **in remission**

⑤ **208.0   Acute**
Acute leukemia NOS   Stem cell leukemia
Blast cell leukemia

Excludes: acute exacerbation of chronic unspecified leukemia (208.1)

⑤ **208.1   Chronic**
Chronic leukemia NOS

● Code new   ▲ Revision of   ④ ⑤ Fourth or fifth
  to this edition   existing code   digit required

⑤ **208.2 Subacute**
Subacute leukemia NOS

⑤ **208.8 Other leukemia of unspecified cell type**

⑤ **208.9 Unspecified leukemia**
Leukemia NOS

BENIGN NEOPLASMS (210-229)

210 Benign neoplasm of lip, oral cavity, and pharynx

Excludes: *cyst (of):*
  jaw (526.0-526.2, 526.89)
  oral soft tissue (528.4)
  radicular (522.8)

210.0 Lip
Frenulum labii
Lip (inner aspect) (mucosa) (vermilion border)

Excludes: *labial commissure (210.4)*
  skin of lip (216.0)

210.1 Tongue
Lingual tonsil

210.2 Major salivary glands
Gland:
 parotid
 sublingual
 submandibular

Excludes: *benign neoplasms of minor salivary glands:*
  NOS (210.4)
  buccal mucosa (210.4)
  lips (210.0)
  palate (hard) (soft) (210.4)
  tongue (210.1)
  tonsil, palatine (210.5)

210.3 Floor of mouth

210.4 Other and unspecified parts of mouth

Gingiva	Oral mucosa
Gum (upper) (lower)	Palate (hard) (soft)
Labial commissure	Uvula
Oral cavity NOS	

Excludes: *benign odontogenic neoplasms of bone (213.0-213.1)*
  developmental odontogenic cysts (526.0)
  mucosa of lips (210.0)
  nasopharyngeal [posterior] [superior] surface of soft palate (210.7)

210.5 Tonsil
Tonsil (faucial) (palatine)

Excludes: *lingual tonsil (210.1)*
  pharyngeal tonsil (210.7)
  tonsillar:
   fossa (210.6)
   pillars (210.6)

210.6 Other parts of oropharynx
Branchial cleft or vestiges
Epiglottis, anterior aspect
Fauces NOS
Mesopharynx NOS
Tonsillar:
 fossa
 pillars
Vallecula

Excludes: *epiglottis:*
  NOS (212.1)
  suprahyoid portion (212.1)

210.7 Nasopharynx

Adenoid tissue	Pharyngeal tonsil
Lymphadenoid tissue	Posterior nasal septum

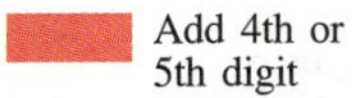

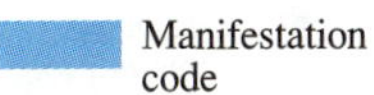

210.8 Hypopharynx
Arytenoid fold   Postcricoid region
Laryngopharynx   Pyriform fossa

210.9 Pharynx, unspecified
Throat NOS

211 **Benign neoplasm of other parts of digestive system**

211.0 Esophagus

211.1 Stomach
Body   Cardiac orifice
Cardia   } stomach   Pylorus
Fundus

211.2 Duodenum, jejunum, and ileum
Small intestine NOS

> *Excludes:* *ampulla of Vater (211.5)*
> *ileocecal valve (211.3)*

211.3 Colon
Appendix   Ileocecal valve
Cecum   Large intestine NOS

> *Excludes:* *rectosigmoid junction (211.4)*

211.4 Rectum and anal canal
Anal canal or sphincter   Rectosigmoid junction
Anus NOS

> *Excludes:* *anus:*
> *margin (216.5)*
> *skin (216.5)*
> *perianal skin (216.5)*

211.5 Liver and biliary passages
Ampulla of Vater   Gallbladder
Common bile duct   Hepatic duct
Cystic duct   Sphincter of Oddi

211.6 Pancreas, except islets of Langerhans

211.7 Islets of Langerhans
Islet cell tumor

Use additional code, if desired, to identify any functional activity

211.8 Retroperitoneum and peritoneum
Mesentery   Omentum
Mesocolon   Retroperitoneal tissue

211.9 Other and unspecified site
Alimentary tract NOS   Intestinal tract NOS
Digestive system NOS   Intestine NOS
Gastrointestinal tract NOS   Spleen, not elsewhere classified

212 **Benign neoplasm of respiratory and intrathoracic organs**

212.0 Nasal cavities, middle ear, and accessory sinuses
Cartilage of nose   Sinus:
Eustachian tube   ethmoidal
Nares   frontal
Septum of nose   maxillary
                              sphenoidal

> *Excludes:* *auditory canal (external) (216.2)*
> *bone of:*
> *ear (213.0)*
> *nose [turbinates] (213.0)*
> *cartilage of ear (215.0)*
> *ear (external) (skin) (216.2)*
> *nose NOS (229.8)*
> *skin (216.3)*
> *olfactory bulb (225.1)*
> *polyp of:*
> *accessory sinus (471.8)*
> *ear (385.30-385.35)*
> *nasal cavity (471.0)*
> *posterior margin of septum and choanae (210.7)*

● Code new to this edition   ▲ Revision of existing code   ④ ⑤ Fourth or fifth digit required

212.1 Larynx
Cartilage: Epiglottis (suprahyoid portion) NOS
  arytenoid   Glottis
  cricoid   Vocal cords (false) (true)
  cuneiform
  thyroid

Excludes: *epiglottis, anterior aspect (210.6)*
          polyp of vocal cord or larynx (478.4)

212.2 Trachea

212.3 Bronchus and lung
Carina   Hilus of lung

212.4 Pleura

212.5 Mediastinum

212.6 Thymus

212.7 Heart

Excludes: *great vessels (215.4)*

212.8 Other specified sites

212.9 Site unspecified
Respiratory organ NOS
Upper respiratory tract NOS

Excludes: *intrathoracic NOS (229.8)*
          thoracic NOS (229.8)

213 Benign neoplasm of bone and articular cartilage
Includes: cartilage (articular) (joint)
         periosteum

Excludes: *cartilage of:*
     ear (215.0)
     eyelid (215.0)
     larynx (212.1)
     nose (212.0)
  exostosis NOS (726.91)
  synovia (215.0-215.9)

213.0 Bones of skull and face

Excludes: *lower jaw bone (213.1)*

213.1 Lower jaw bone

213.2 Vertebral column, excluding sacrum and coccyx

213.3 Ribs, sternum, and clavicle

213.4 Scapula and long bones of upper limb

213.5 Short bones of upper limb

213.6 Pelvic bones, sacrum, and coccyx

213.7 Long bones of lower limb

213.8 Short bones of lower limb

213.9 Bone and articular cartilage, site unspecified

214 Lipoma
Includes: angiolipoma
         fibrolipoma
         hibernoma
         lipoma (fetal) (infiltrating) (intramuscular)
         myelolipoma
         myxolipoma

214.0 Skin and subcutaneous tissue of face

214.1 Other skin and subcutaneous tissue

214.2 Intrathoracic organs

214.3 Intra-abdominal organs

214.4 Spermatic cord

214.8 Other specified sites

214.9 Lipoma, unspecified site

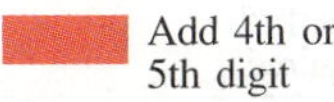

Manifestation
code

215 Other benign neoplasm of connective and other soft tissue
Includes:

blood vessel	peripheral, sympathetic, and parasympathetic nerves
bursa	and ganglia
fascia	synovia
ligament	tendon (sheath)
muscle	

> *Excludes:* *cartilage:*
> *articular (213.0-213.9)*
> *larynx (212.1)*
> *nose (212.0)*
> *connective tissue of:*
> *breast (217)*
> *internal organ, except lipoma and hemangioma — code to benign neoplasm of the site*
> *lipoma (214.0-214.9)*

215.0 Head, face, and neck

215.2 Upper limb, including shoulder

215.3 Lower limb, including hip

215.4 Thorax

> *Excludes:* *heart (212.7)*
> *mediastinum (212.5)*
> *thymus (212.6)*

215.5 Abdomen

Abdominal wall	Hypochondrium

215.6 Pelvis

Buttock	Inguinal region
Groin	Perineum

> *Excludes:* *uterine:*
> *leiomyoma (218.0-218.9)*
> *ligament, any (221.0)*

215.7 Trunk, unspecified

Back NOS	Flank NOS

215.8 Other specified sites

215.9 Site unspecified

216 Benign neoplasm of skin
Includes:

blue nevus	pigmented nevus
dermatofibroma	syringoadenoma
hydrocystoma	syringoma

> *Excludes:* *skin of genital organs (221.0-222.9)*

216.0 Skin of lip

> *Excludes:* *vermilion border of lip (210.0)*

216.1 Eyelid, including canthus

> *Excludes:* *cartilage of eyelid (215.0)*

216.2 Ear and external auditory canal

Auricle (ear)	External meatus
Auricular canal, external	Pinna

> *Excludes:* *cartilage of ear (215.0)*

216.3 Skin of other and unspecified parts of face

Cheek, external	Nose, external
Eyebrow	Temple

216.4 Scalp and skin of neck

● Code new to this edition   ▲ Revision of existing code   ④ ⑤ Fourth or fifth digit required

216.5 Skin of trunk, except scrotum
Axillary fold
Perianal skin
Skin of:
abdominal wall
anus
back
breast
Skin of:
buttock
chest wall
groin
perineum
Umbilicus

> *Excludes:* *anal canal (211.4)*
> *anus NOS (211.4)*
> *skin of scrotum (222.4)*

216.6 Skin of upper limb, including shoulder

216.7 Skin of lower limb, including hip

216.8 Other specified sites of skin

216.9 Skin, site unspecified

217 Benign neoplasm of breast
Breast (male) (female)
connective tissue
glandular tissue
soft parts

> *Excludes:* *adenofibrosis (610.2)*
> *benign cyst of breast (610.0)*
> *fibrocystic disease (610.1)*
> *skin of breast (216.5)*

218 Uterine leiomyoma
Includes: fibroid (bleeding) (uterine)
uterine:
fibromyoma
myoma

218.0 Submucous leiomyoma of uterus

218.1 Intramural leiomyoma of uterus
Interstitial leiomyoma of uterus

218.2 Subserous leiomyoma of uterus
Subperitoneal leiomyoma of uterus

218.9 Leiomyoma of uterus, unspecified

219 Other benign neoplasm of uterus

219.0 Cervix uteri

219.1 Corpus uteri
Endometrium   Myometrium
Fundus

219.8 Other specified parts of uterus

219.9 Uterus, part unspecified

220 Benign neoplasm of ovary
Use additional code, if desired, to identify any functional activity (256.0-256.1)

> *Excludes:* *cyst:*
> *corpus albicans (620.2)*
> *corpus luteum (620.1)*
> *endometrial (617.1)*
> *follicular (atretic) (620.0)*
> *graafian follicle (620.0)*
> *ovarian NOS (620.2)*
> *retention (620.2)*

221 Benign neoplasm of other female genital organs
Includes: adenomatous polyp
benign teratoma

> *Excludes:* *cyst:*
> *epoophoron (752.11)*
> *fimbrial (752.11)*
> *Gartner's duct (752.11)*
> *parovarian (752.11)*

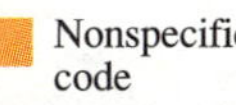

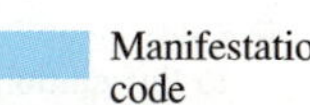

221.0 Fallopian tube and uterine ligaments
Oviduct
Parametrium

Uterine ligament (broad) (round) (uterosacral)
Uterine tube

221.1 Vagina

221.2 Vulva
Clitoris
External female genitalia NOS
Greater vestibular [Bartholin's] gland
Labia (majora) (minora)
Pudendum

| Excludes: | *Bartholin's (duct) (gland) cyst (616.2)* |

221.8 Other specified sites of female genital organs

221.9 Female genital organ, site unspecified
Female genitourinary tract NOS

222 Benign neoplasm of male genital organs

222.0 Testis

Use additional code, if desired, to identify any functional activity

222.1 Penis
Corpus cavernosum
Glans penis

Prepuce

222.2 Prostate

| Excludes: | *adenomatous hyperplasia of prostate (600.2)* |

prostatic:
adenoma (600.2)
enlargement (600.0)
hypertrophy (600.0)

222.3 Epididymis

222.4 Scrotum
Skin of scrotum

222.8 Other specified sites of male genital organs
Seminal vesicle
Spermatic cord

222.9 Male genital organ, site unspecified
Male genitourinary tract NOS

223 Benign neoplasm of kidney and other urinary organs

223.0 Kidney, except pelvis
Kidney NOS

| Excludes: | *renal:* |

calyces (223.1)
pelvis (223.1)

223.1 Renal pelvis

223.2 Ureter

| Excludes: | *ureteric orifice of bladder (223.3)* |

223.3 Bladder

⑤ **223.8 Other specified sites of urinary organs**

    223.81 Urethra

| Excludes: | *urethral orifice of bladder (223.3)* |

    223.89 Other
Paraurethral glands

223.9 Urinary organ, site unspecified
Urinary system NOS

224 Benign neoplasm of eye

| Excludes: | *cartilage of eyelid (215.0)* |

eyelid (skin) (216.1)
optic nerve (225.1)
orbital bone (213.0)

224.0 Eyeball, except conjunctiva, cornea, retina, and choroid
Ciliary body
Iris

Sclera
Uveal tract

● Code new
to this edition

▲ Revision of
existing code

④ ⑤ Fourth or fifth
digit required

224.1 Orbit
Excludes: *bone of orbit (213.0)*

224.2 Lacrimal gland

224.3 Conjunctiva

224.4 Cornea

224.5 Retina
Excludes: *hemangioma of retina (228.03)*

224.6 Choroid

224.7 Lacrimal duct
Lacrimal sac   Nasolacrimal duct

224.8 Other specified parts of eye

224.9 Eye, part unspecified

225 Benign neoplasm of brain and other parts of nervous system
Excludes: *hemangioma (228.02)*
neurofibromatosis (237.7)
peripheral, sympathetic, and parasympathetic nerves and ganglia (215.0-215.9)
retrobulbar (224.1)

225.0 Brain

225.1 Cranial nerves

225.2 Cerebral meninges
Meninges NOS   Meningioma (cerebral)

225.3 Spinal cord
Cauda equina

225.4 Spinal meninges
Spinal meningioma

225.8 Other specified sites of nervous system

225.9 Nervous system, part unspecified
Nervous system (central) NOS
Excludes: *meninges NOS (225.2)*

226 Benign neoplasm of thyroid glands
Use additional code, if desired, to identify any functional activity

227 Benign neoplasm of other endocrine glands and related structures
Use additional code, if desired, to identify any functional activity
Excludes: *ovary (220)*
pancreas (211.6)
testis (222.0)

227.0 Adrenal gland
Suprarenal gland

227.1 Parathyroid gland

227.3 Pituitary gland and craniopharyngeal duct (pouch)
Craniobuccal pouch   Rathke's pouch
Hypophysis   Sella turcica

227.4 Pineal gland
Pineal body

227.5 Carotid body

227.6 Aortic body and other paraganglia
Coccygeal body   Para-aortic body
Glomus jugulare

227.8 Other

227.9 Endocrine gland, site unspecified

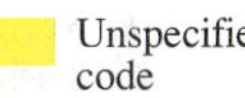

228 Hemangioma and lymphangioma, any site

Includes: angioma (benign) (cavernous) (congenital) NOS
cavernous nevus
glomus tumor
hemangioma (benign) (congenital)

Excludes: *benign neoplasm of spleen, except hemangioma and lymphangioma (211.9)*
glomus jugulare (227.6)
nevus:
NOS (216.0-216.9)
blue or pigmented (216.0-216.9)
vascular (757.32)

⑤ **228.0 Hemangioma, any site**

228.00 Of unspecified site

228.01 Of skin and subcutaneous tissue

228.02 Of intracranial structures

228.03 Of retina

228.04 Of intra-abdominal structures
Peritoneum   Retroperitoneal tissue

228.09 Of other sites
Systemic angiomatosis

228.1 Lymphangioma, any site
Congenital lymphangioma   Lymphatic nevus

229 Benign neoplasm of other and unspecified sites

229.0 Lymph nodes

Excludes: *lymphangioma (228.1)*

229.8 Other specified sites
Intrathoracic NOS   Thoracic NOS

229.9 Site unspecified

CARCINOMA IN SITU (230-234)

Includes: Bowen's disease
erythroplasia
Queyrat's erythroplasia

Excludes: *leukoplakia—see Alphabetic Index*

230 Carcinoma in situ of digestive organs

230.0 Lip, oral cavity, and pharynx
Gingiva   Oropharynx
Hypopharynx   Salivary gland or duct
Mouth [any part]   Tongue
Nasopharynx

Excludes: *aryepiglottic fold or interarytenoid fold, laryngeal aspect (231.0)*
epiglottis:
NOS (231.0)
suprahyoid portion (231.0)
skin of lip (232.0)

230.1 Esophagus

230.2 Stomach
Body
Cardia   } of stomach
Fundus

Cardiac orifice
Pylorus

230.3 Colon
Appendix   Ileocecal valve
Cecum   Large intestine NOS

Excludes: *rectosigmoid junction (230.4)*

230.4 Rectum
Rectosigmoid junction

230.5 Anal canal
Anal sphincter

● Code new
to this edition

▲ Revision of
existing code

④ ⑤ Fourth or fifth
digit required

230.6 Anus, unspecified

> *Excludes:* *anus:*
> *margin (232.5)*
> *skin (232.5)*
> *perianal skin (232.5)*

230.7 Other and unspecified parts of intestine

Duodenum	Jejunum
Ileum	Small intestine NOS

> *Excludes:* *ampulla of Vater (230.8)*

230.8 Liver and biliary system

Ampulla of Vater	Gallbladder
Common bile duct	Hepatic duct
Cystic duct	Sphincter of Oddi

230.9 Other and unspecified digestive organs

Digestive organ NOS	Pancreas
Gastrointestinal tract NOS	Spleen

231 Carcinoma in situ of respiratory system

231.0 Larynx

Cartilage:	Epiglottis:
arytenoid	NOS
cricoid	posterior surface
cuneiform	suprahyoid portion
thyroid	Vocal cords (false) (true)

> *Excludes:* *aryepiglottic fold or interarytenoid fold:*
> *NOS (230.0)*
> *hypopharyngeal aspect (230.0)*
> *marginal zone (230.0)*

231.1 Trachea

231.2 Bronchus and lung

Carina	Hilus of lung

231.8 Other specified parts of respiratory system

Accessory sinuses	Nasal cavities
Middle ear	Pleura

> *Excludes:* *ear (external) (skin) (232.2)*
> *nose NOS (234.8)*
> *skin (232.3)*

231.9 Respiratory system, part unspecified
Respiratory organ NOS

232 Carcinoma in situ of skin
Includes: pigment cells

232.0 Skin of lip

> *Excludes:* *vermilion border of lip (230.0)*

232.1 Eyelid, including canthus

232.2 Ear and external auditory canal

232.3 Skin of other and unspecified parts of face

232.4 Scalp and skin of neck

232.5 Skin of trunk, except scrotum

Anus, margin	Skin of:
Axillary fold	breast
Perianal skin	buttock
Skin of:	chest wall
abdominal wall	groin
anus	perineum
back	Umbilicus

> *Excludes:* *anal canal (230.5)*
> *anus NOS (230.6)*
> *skin of genital organs (233.3, 233.5-233.6)*

232.6 Skin of upper limb, including shoulder

232.7 Skin of lower limb, including hip

232.8 Other specified sites of skin

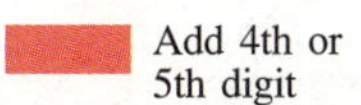

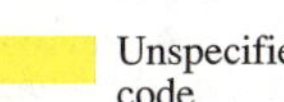

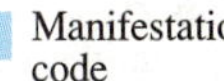

232.9 Skin, site unspecified

233 Carcinoma in situ of breast and genitourinary system

233.0 Breast

> Excludes: *Paget's disease (174.0-174.9)*
> *skin of breast (232.5)*

233.1 Cervix uteri

233.2 Other and unspecified parts of uterus

233.3 Other and unspecified female genital organs

233.4 Prostate

233.5 Penis

233.6 Other and unspecified male genital organs

233.7 Bladder

233.9 Other and unspecified urinary organs

234 Carcinoma in situ of other and unspecified sites

234.0 Eye

> Excludes: *cartilage of eyelid (234.8)*
> *eyelid (skin) (232.1)*
> *optic nerve (234.8)*
> *orbital bone (234.8)*

234.8 Other specified sites
Endocrine gland [any]

234.9 Site unspecified
Carcinoma in situ NOS

NEOPLASMS OF UNCERTAIN BEHAVIOR (235-238)

Note: Categories 235-238 classify by site certain histo-morphologically well-defined neoplasms, the subsequent behavior of which cannot be predicted from the present appearance.

235 Neoplasm of uncertain behavior of digestive and respiratory systems

235.0 Major salivary glands
Gland:
parotid
sublingual
submandibular

> Excludes: *minor salivary glands (235.1)*

235.1 Lip, oral cavity, and pharynx

Gingiva   Nasopharynx
Hypopharynx   Oropharynx
Minor salivary glands   Tongue
Mouth

> Excludes: *aryepiglottic fold or interarytenoid fold, laryngeal aspect (235.6)*
> *epiglottis:*
> *NOS (235.6)*
> *suprahyoid portion (235.6)*
> *skin of lip (238.2)*

235.2 Stomach, intestines, and rectum

235.3 Liver and biliary passages

Ampulla of Vater   Gallbladder
Bile ducts [any]   Liver

235.4 Retroperitoneum and peritoneum

235.5 Other and unspecified digestive organs

Anal: Esophagus
canal   Pancreas
sphincter   Spleen
Anus NOS

> Excludes: *anus:*
> *margin (238.2)*
> *skin (238.2)*
> *perianal skin (238.2)*

● Code new to this edition   ▲ Revision of existing code   ④ ⑤ Fourth or fifth digit required

235.6 Larynx

> *Excludes:* *aryepiglottic fold or interarytenoid fold:*
> *NOS (235.1)*
> *hypopharyngeal aspect (235.1)*
> *marginal zone (235.1)*

235.7 Trachea, bronchus, and lung

235.8 Pleura, thymus, and mediastinum

235.9 Other and unspecified respiratory organs

Accessory sinuses   Nasal cavities
Middle ear   Respiratory organ NOS

> *Excludes:* *ear (external) (skin) (238.2)*
> *nose (238.8)*
> *skin (238.2)*

236 Neoplasm of uncertain behavior of genitourinary organs

236.0 Uterus

236.1 Placenta

Chorioadenoma (destruens)
Invasive mole
Malignant hydatid(iform) mole

236.2 Ovary

Use additional code, if desired, to identify any functional activity

236.3 Other and unspecified female genital organs

236.4 Testis

Use additional code, if desired, to identify any functional activity

236.5 Prostate

236.6 Other and unspecified male genital organs

236.7 Bladder

⑤ **236.9 Other and unspecified urinary organs**

  236.90 Urinary organ, unspecified

  236.91 Kidney and ureter

  236.99 Other

237 Neoplasm of uncertain behavior of endocrine glands and nervous system

237.0 Pituitary gland and craniopharyngeal duct

Use additional code, if desired, to identify any functional activity

237.1 Pineal gland

237.2 Adrenal gland

Suprarenal gland

Use additional code, if desired, to identify any functional activity

237.3 Paraganglia

Aortic body   Coccygeal body
Carotid body   Glomus jugulare

237.4 Other and unspecified endocrine glands

Parathyroid gland   Thyroid gland

237.5 Brain and spinal cord

237.6 Meninges

Meninges:
 NOS
 cerebral
 spinal

⑤ **237.7 Neurofibromatosis**

von Recklinghausen's disease

  237.70 Neurofibromatosis, unspecified

  237.71 Neurofibromatosis, Type I [von Recklinghausen's disease]

  237.72 Neurofibromatosis, Type II [acoustic neurofibromatosis]

237.9 Other and unspecified parts of nervous system

Cranial nerves

> *Excludes:* *peripheral, sympathetic, and parasympathetic nerves and ganglia (238.1)*

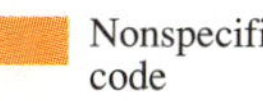

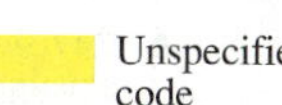

Manifestation
code

238 **Neoplasm of uncertain behavior of other and unspecified sites and tissues**

238.0 **Bone and articular cartilage**

Excludes: *cartilage:*

ear (238.1)
eyelid (238.1)
larynx (235.6)
nose (235.9)
synovia (238.1)

238.1 **Connective and other soft tissue**

Peripheral, sympathetic, and parasympathetic nerves and ganglia

Excludes: *cartilage (of):*

articular (238.0)
larynx (235.6)
nose (235.9)
connective tissue of breast (238.3)

238.2 **Skin**

Excludes: *anus NOS (235.5)*

skin of genital organs (236.3, 236.6)
vermilion border of lip (235.1)

238.3 **Breast**

Excludes: *skin of breast (238.2)*

238.4 **Polycythemia vera**

238.5 **Histiocytic and mast cells**

Mast cell tumor NOS   Mastocytoma NOS

238.6 **Plasma cells**

Plasmacytoma NOS   Solitary myeloma

238.7 **Other lymphatic and hematopoietic tissues**

Disease:
  lymphoproliferative (chronic) NOS
  myeloproliferative (chronic) NOS
Idiopathic thrombocythemia
Megakaryocytic myelosclerosis
Myelodysplastic syndrome
Myelosclerosis with myeloid metaplasia
Panmyelosis (acute)

Excludes: *myelofibrosis (289.8)*

myelosclerosis NOS (289.8)
myelosis:
  NOS (205.9)
  megakaryocytic (207.2)

238.8 **Other specified sites**

Eye   Heart

Excludes: *eyelid (skin) (238.2)*

cartilage (238.1)

238.9 **Site unspecified**

NEOPLASMS OF UNSPECIFIED NATURE (239)

239 **Neoplasms of unspecified nature**

Note: Category 239 classifies by site neoplasms of unspecified morphology and behavior. The
     term "mass," unless otherwise stated, is not to be regarded as a neoplastic growth.
Includes: "growth" NOS
          neoplasm NOS
          new growth NOS
          tumor NOS

239.0 **Digestive system**

Excludes: *anus:*

margin (239.2)
skin (239.2)
perianal skin (239.2)

239.1 **Respiratory system**

● Code new
   to this edition

▲ Revision of
   existing code

④ ⑤ Fourth or fifth
      digit required

239.2 **Bone, soft tissue, and skin**

Excludes: *anal canal (239.0)*
anus NOS (239.0)
bone marrow (202.9)
cartilage:
  larynx (239.1)
  nose (239.1)
connective tissue of breast (239.3)
skin of genital organs (239.5)
vermilion border of lip (239.0)

239.3 **Breast**

Excludes: *skin of breast (239.2)*

239.4 **Bladder**

239.5 **Other genitourinary organs**

239.6 **Brain**

Excludes: *cerebral meninges (239.7)*
cranial nerves (239.7)

239.7 **Endocrine glands and other parts of nervous system**

Excludes: *peripheral, sympathetic, and parasympathetic nerves and ganglia (239.2)*

239.8 **Other specified sites**

Excludes: *eyelids (skin) (239.2)*
  cartilage (239.2)
great vessels (239.2)
optic nerve (239.7)

239.9 **Site unspecified**

Add 4th or
5th digit

Nonspecific
code

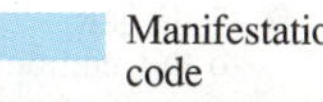
Unspecified
code

Manifestation
code

● Code new
to this edition

▲ Revision of
existing code

④ ⑤ Fourth or fifth
digit required

3. ENDOCRINE, NUTRITIONAL AND METABOLIC DISEASES, AND IMMUNITY DISORDERS (240-279)

> *Excludes:* *endocrine and metabolic disturbances specific to the fetus and newborn (775.0-775.9)*

Note: All neoplasms, whether functionally active or not, are classified in Chapter 2. Codes in Chapter 3 (i.e., 242.8, 246.0, 251-253, 255-259) may be used, if desired, to identify such functional activity associated with any neoplasm, or by ectopic endocrine tissue.

DISORDERS OF THYROID GLAND (240-246)

240 Simple and unspecified goiter

240.0 Goiter, specified as simple
Any condition classifiable to 240.9, specified as simple

240.9 Goiter, unspecified

Enlargement of thyroid
Goiter or struma:
  NOS
  diffuse colloid
  endemic

Goiter or struma:
  hyperplastic
  nontoxic (diffuse)
  parenchymatous
  sporadic

> *Excludes:* *congenital (dyshormonogenic) goiter (246.1)*

241 Nontoxic nodular goiter

> *Excludes:* *adenoma of thyroid (226)*
> *cystadenoma of thyroid (226)*

241.0 Nontoxic uninodular goiter
Thyroid nodule
Uninodular goiter (nontoxic)

241.1 Nontoxic multinodular goiter
Multinodular goiter (nontoxic)

241.9 Unspecified nontoxic nodular goiter
Adenomatous goiter
Nodular goiter (nontoxic) NOS
Struma nodosa (simplex)

⑤ 242 Thyrotoxicosis with or without goiter

> *Excludes:* *neonatal thyrotoxicosis (775.3)*

The following fifth-digit subclassification is for use with category 242:

  0 without mention of thyrotoxic crisis or storm

  1 with mention of thyrotoxic crisis or storm

⑤ 242.0 Toxic diffuse goiter
Basedow's disease
Exophthalmic or toxic goiter NOS
Graves' disease
Primary thyroid hyperplasia

⑤ 242.1 Toxic uninodular goiter
Thyroid nodule
Uninodular goiter } toxic or with hyperthyroidism

⑤ 242.2 Toxic multinodular goiter
Secondary thyroid hyperplasia

⑤ 242.3 Toxic nodular goiter, unspecified
Adenomatous goiter
Nodular goiter } toxic or with hyperthyroidism
Struma nodosa
Any condition classifiable to 241.9 specified as toxic or with hyperthyroidism

⑤ 242.4 Thyrotoxicosis from ectopic thyroid nodule

⑤ 242.8 Thyrotoxicosis of other specified origin
Overproduction of thyroid-stimulating hormone [TSH]
Thyrotoxicosis:
  factitia
  from ingestion of excessive thyroid material

Use additional E code to identify cause, if drug-induced

⑤ 242.9 Thyrotoxicosis without mention of goiter or other cause
Hyperthyroidism NOS   Thyrotoxicosis NOS

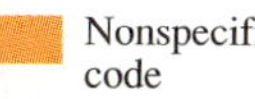

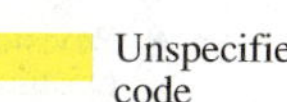

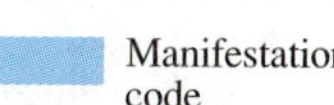

Manifestation
code

243 Congenital hypothyroidism
  Congenital thyroid insufficiency
  Cretinism (athyrotic) (endemic)
Use additional code to identify associated mental retardation

> *Excludes:* congenital (dyshormonogenic) goiter (246.1)

244 Acquired hypothyroidism
  Includes: athyroidism (acquired)
         hypothyroidism (acquired)
         myxedema (adult) (juvenile)
         thyroid (gland) insufficiency (acquired)

244.0 Postsurgical hypothyroidism

244.1 Other postablative hypothyroidism
  Hypothyroidism following therapy, such as irradiation

244.2 Iodine hypothyroidism
  Hypothyroidism resulting from administration or ingestion of iodide
Use additional E code to identify drug

244.3 Other iatrogenic hypothyroidism
  Hypothyroidism resulting from:
    P-aminosalicylic acid [PAS]
    Phenylbutazone
    Resorcinol
  Iatrogenic hypothyroidism NOS
Use additional E code to identify drug

244.8 Other specified acquired hypothyroidism
  Secondary hypothyroidism NEC

244.9 Unspecified hypothyroidism
  Hypothyroidism ⎫
  Myxedema   ⎬ primary or NOS

245 Thyroiditis

245.0 Acute thyroiditis
  Abscess of thyroid
  Thyroiditis:
    nonsuppurative, acute
    pyogenic
    suppurative
Use additional code to identify organism

245.1 Subacute thyroiditis
  Thyroiditis: Thyroiditis:
    de Quervain's   granulomatous
    giant cell   viral

245.2 Chronic lymphocytic thyroiditis
  Hashimoto's disease   Thyroiditis:
  Struma lymphomatosa   autoimmune
                             lymphocytic (chronic)

245.3 Chronic fibrous thyroiditis
  Struma fibrosa
  Thyroiditis:
    invasive (fibrous)
    ligneous
    Riedel's

245.4 Iatrogenic thyroiditis
Use additional code to identify cause

245.8 Other and unspecified chronic thyroiditis
  Chronic thyroiditis:
    NOS
    nonspecific

245.9 Thyroiditis, unspecified
  Thyroiditis NOS

246 Other disorders of thyroid

246.0 Disorders of thyrocalcitonin secretion
  Hypersecretion of calcitonin or thyrocalcitonin

● Code new   ▲ Revision of   ④ ⑤ Fourth or fifth
  to this edition   existing code   digit required

246.1 Dyshormonogenic goiter
Congenital (dyshormonogenic) goiter
Goiter due to enzyme defect in synthesis of thyroid hormone
Goitrous cretinism (sporadic)

246.2 Cyst of thyroid

Excludes: *cystadenoma of thyroid (226)*

246.3 Hemorrhage and infarction of thyroid

246.8 Other specified disorders of thyroid
Abnormality of   Hyper-TBG-nemia
  thyroid-binding globulin   Hypo-TBG-nemia
Atrophy of thyroid

246.9 Unspecified disorder of thyroid

DISEASES OF OTHER ENDOCRINE GLANDS (250-259)

⑤ **250 Diabetes mellitus**

Excludes: *gestational diabetes (648.8)*

hyperglycemia NOS (790.6)
neonatal diabetes mellitus (775.1)
nonclinical diabetes (790.2)

The following fifth-digit subclassification is for use with category 250:

0 type II [non-insulin dependent type] [NIDDM type] [adult-onset type] or unspecified type, not stated as uncontrolled

Fifth-digit 0 is for use with type II, adult-onset diabetic patients, even if the patient requires insulin

1 type I [insulin dependent type] [IDDM] [juvenile type], not stated as uncontrolled

2 type II [non-insulin dependent type] [NIDDM type] [adult-onset type] or unspecified type, uncontrolled

Fifth-digit 2 is for use with type II, adult-onset diabetic patients, even if the patient requires insulin

3 type I [insulin dependent type] [IDDM] [juvenile type], uncontrolled

⑤ **250.0 Diabetes mellitus without mention of complication**
Diabetes mellitus without mention of complication or manifestation classifiable to
  250.1-250.9
Diabetes (mellitus) NOS

⑤ **250.1 Diabetes with ketoacidosis**
Diabetic:
  acidosis
  ketosis } without mention of coma

⑤ **250.2 Diabetes with hyperosmolarity**
Hyperosmolar (nonketotic) coma

⑤ **250.3 Diabetes with other coma**
Diabetic coma (with ketoacidosis)
Diabetic hypoglycemic coma
Insulin coma NOS

Excludes: *diabetes with hyperosmolar coma (250.2)*

⑤ **250.4 Diabetes with renal manifestations**
Use additional code to identify manifestation, as:
  diabetic:
    nephropathy NOS (583.81)
    nephrosis (581.81)
    intercapillary glomerulosclerosis (581.81)
    Kimmelstiel-Wilson syndrome (581.81)

⑤ **250.5 Diabetes with ophthalmic manifestations**
Use additional code to identify manifestation, as:
  diabetic:
    blindness (369.00-369.9)
    cataract (366.41)
    glaucoma (365.44)
    retinal edema (362.83)
    retinopathy (362.01-362.02)

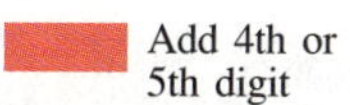

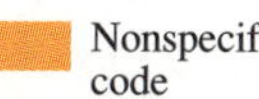

⑤ **250.6 Diabetes with neurological manifestations**
Use additional code to identify manifestation, as:
       diabetic:
          amyotrophy (358.1)
          mononeuropathy (354.0-355.9)
          neurogenic arthropathy (713.5)
          peripheral autonomic neuropathy (337.1)
          polyneuropathy (357.2)

⑤ **250.7 Diabetes with peripheral circulatory disorders**
Use additional code to identify manifestation, as:
       diabetic:
          gangrene (785.4)
          peripheral angiopathy (443.81)

⑤ **250.8 Diabetes with other specified manifestations**
       Diabetic hypoglycemia
       Hypoglycemic shock

Use additional code to identify manifestation, as:
          any associated ulceration (707.10-707.9)
          diabetic bone changes (731.8)

Use additional E code to identify cause, if drug-induced

⑤ **250.9 Diabetes with unspecified complication**

251 Other disorders of pancreatic internal secretion

251.0 Hypoglycemic coma
       Iatrogenic hyperinsulinism   Non-diabetic insulin coma
Use additional E code to identify cause, if drug-induced

> *Excludes:* *hypoglycemic coma in diabetes mellitus (250.3)*

251.1 Other specified hypoglycemia
Use additional E code to identify cause, if drug-induced
       Hyperinsulinism:
        NOS
        ectopic
        functional
       Hyperplasia of pancreatic islet beta cells NOS

> *Excludes:* *hypoglycemia in diabetes mellitus (250.8)*
> *hypoglycemia in infant of diabetic mother (775.0)*
> *hypoglycemic coma (251.0)*
> *neonatal hypoglycemia (775.6)*

251.2 Hypoglycemia, unspecified
       Hypoglycemia:
        NOS
        reactive
        spontaneous

> *Excludes:* *hypoglycemia:*
> *with coma (251.0)*
> *in diabetes mellitus (250.8)*
> *leucine-induced (270.3)*

251.3 Postsurgical hypoinsulinemia
       Hypoinsulinemia following complete or partial pancreatectomy
       Postpancreatectomy hyperglycemia

251.4 Abnormality of secretion of glucagon
       Hyperplasia of pancreatic islet alpha cells with glucagon excess

251.5 Abnormality of secretion of gastrin
       Hyperplasia of pancreatic alpha cells with gastrin excess
       Zollinger-Ellison syndrome

251.8 Other specified disorders of pancreatic internal secretion

251.9 Unspecified disorder of pancreatic internal secretion
       Islet cell hyperplasia NOS

● Code new to this edition   ▲ Revision of existing code   ④ ⑤ Fourth or fifth digit required

252 **Disorders of parathyroid gland**

252.0 Hyperparathyroidism
Hyperplasia of parathyroid
Osteitis fibrosa cystica generalisata
von Recklinghausen's disease of bone

Excludes: *ectopic hyperparathyroidism (259.3)*
secondary hyperparathyroidism (of renal origin) (588.8)

252.1 Hypoparathyroidism
Parathyroiditis (autoimmune)
Tetany:
 parathyroid
 parathyroprival

Excludes: *pseudohypoparathyroidism (275.4)*
pseudo-pseudohypoparathyroidism (275.4)
tetany NOS (781.7)
transitory neonatal hypoparathyroidism (775.4)

252.8 Other specified disorders of parathyroid gland
Cyst
Hemorrhage } of parathyroid gland

252.9 Unspecified disorder of parathyroid gland

253 Disorders of the pituitary gland and its hypothalamic control
Includes: the listed conditions whether the disorder is in the pituitary or the hypothalamus

Excludes: *Cushing's syndrome (255.0)*

253.0 Acromegaly and gigantism
Overproduction of growth hormone

253.1 Other and unspecified anterior pituitary hyperfunction
Forbes-Albright syndrome

Excludes: *overproduction of:*
ACTH (255.3)
thyroid-stimulating hormone [TSH] (242.8)

253.2 Panhypopituitarism
Cachexia, pituitary   Sheehan's syndrome
Necrosis of pituitary   Simmonds' disease
 (postpartum)
Pituitary insufficiency NOS

Excludes: *iatrogenic hypopituitarism (253.7)*

253.3 Pituitary dwarfism
Isolated deficiency of (human) growth hormone [HGH]
Lorain-Levi dwarfism

253.4 Other anterior pituitary disorders
Isolated or partial deficiency of an anterior pituitary hormone, other than growth hormone
Prolactin deficiency

253.5 Diabetes insipidus
Vasopressin deficiency

Excludes: *nephrogenic diabetes insipidus (588.1)*

253.6 Other disorders of neurohypophysis
Syndrome of inappropriate secretion of antidiuretic hormone [ADH]

Excludes: *ectopic antidiuretic hormone secretion (259.3)*

253.7 Iatrogenic pituitary disorders
Hypopituitarism:
 hormone-induced
 hypophysectomy-induced
 postablative
 radiotherapy-induced
Use additional E code to identify cause

253.8 Other disorders of the pituitary and other syndromes of diencephalohypophyseal origin
Abscess of pituitary   Cyst of Rathke's pouch
Adiposogenital dystrophy   Fröhlich's syndrome

Excludes: *craniopharyngioma (237.0)*

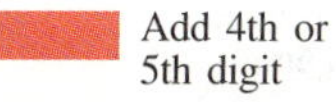

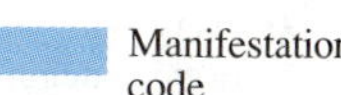

253.9 Unspecified
Dyspituitarism

254 Diseases of thymus gland

> *Excludes:* *aplasia or dysplasia with immunodeficiency (279.2)*
> *hypoplasia with immunodeficiency (279.2)*
> *myasthenia gravis (358.0)*

254.0 Persistent hyperplasia of thymus
Hypertrophy of thymus

254.1 Abscess of thymus

254.8 Other specified diseases of thymus gland
Atrophy ⎫
Cyst   ⎬ of thymus

> *Excludes* *thymoma (212.6)*

254.9 Unspecified disease of thymus gland

255 Disorders of adrenal glands
Includes: the listed conditions whether the basic disorder is in the adrenals or is pituitary-induced

255.0 Cushing's syndrome

Adrenal hyperplasia due to excess ACTH	Ectopic ACTH syndrome
Cushing's syndrome:	Iatrogenic syndrome of excess cortisol
NOS	Overproduction of cortisol
iatrogenic	
idiopathic	
pituitary-dependent	

Use additional E code to identify cause, if drug-induced

> *Excludes:* *congenital adrenal hyperplasia (255.2)*

255.1 Hyperaldosteronism

Aldosteronism (primary)	Bartter's syndrome
(secondary)	Conn's syndrome

255.2 Adrenogenital disorders
Adrenogenital syndromes, virilizing or feminizing, whether acquired or associated with congenital adrenal hyperplasia consequent on inborn enzyme defects in hormone synthesis
Achard-Thiers syndrome
Congenital adrenal hyperplasia
Female adrenal pseudohermaphroditism
Male:
    macrogenitosomia praecox
    sexual precocity with adrenal hyperplasia
Virilization (female) (suprarenal)

> *Excludes:* *adrenal hyperplasia due to excess ACTH (255.0)*
> *isosexual virilization (256.4)*

255.3 Other corticoadrenal overactivity
Acquired benign adrenal androgenic overactivity
Overproduction of ACTH

255.4 Corticoadrenal insufficiency

Addisonian crisis	Adrenal:
Addison's disease NOS	crisis
Adrenal:	hemorrhage
atrophy (autoimmune)	infarction
calcification	insufficiency NOS

> *Excludes:* *tuberculous Addison's disease (017.6)*

255.5 Other adrenal hypofunction
Adrenal medullary insufficiency

> *Excludes:* *Waterhouse-Friderichsen syndrome (meningococcal) (036.3)*

255.6 Medulloadrenal hyperfunction
Catecholamine secretion by pheochromocytoma

255.8 Other specified disorders of adrenal glands
Abnormality of cortisol-binding globulin

255.9 Unspecified disorder of adrenal glands

● Code new to this edition   ▲ Revision of existing code   ④ ⑤ Fourth or fifth digit required

256 Ovarian dysfunction

256.0 Hyperestrogenism

256.1 Other ovarian hyperfunction
Hypersecretion of ovarian androgens

256.2 Postablative ovarian failure
Ovarian failure:
  iatrogenic
  postirradiation
  postsurgical

> Excludes: asymptomatic age-related (natural) postmenopausal status (V49.81)

256.3 Other ovarian failure
Premature menopause NOS
Primary ovarian failure

> Excludes: asymptomatic age-related (natural) postmenopausal status (V49.81)

256.4 Polycystic ovaries
Isosexual virilization   Stein-Leventhal syndrome

256.8 Other ovarian dysfunction

256.9 Unspecified ovarian dysfunction

257 Testicular dysfunction

257.0 Testicular hyperfunction
Hypersecretion of testicular hormones

257.1 Postablative testicular hypofunction
Testicular hypofunction:
  iatrogenic
  postirradiation
  postsurgical

257.2 Other testicular hypofunction
Defective biosynthesis of testicular androgen
Eunuchoidism:
  NOS
  hypogonadotropic
Failure:
  Leydig's cell, adult
  seminiferous tubule, adult
Testicular hypogonadism

> Excludes: azoospermia (606.0)

257.8 Other testicular dysfunction
Goldberg-Maxwell syndrome
Male pseudohermaphroditism with testicular feminization
Testicular feminization

257.9 Unspecified testicular dysfunction

258 Polyglandular dysfunction and related disorders

258.0 Polyglandular activity in multiple endocrine adenomatosis
Wermer's syndrome

258.1 Other combinations of endocrine dysfunction
Lloyd's syndrome   Schmidt's syndrome

258.8 Other specified polyglandular dysfunction

258.9 Polyglandular dysfunction, unspecified

259 Other endocrine disorders

259.0 Delay in sexual development and puberty, not elsewhere classified
Delayed puberty

259.1 Precocious sexual development and puberty, not elsewhere classified
Sexual precocity:
  NOS
  constitutional
  cryptogenic
  idiopathic

259.2 Carcinoid syndrome
Hormone secretion by carcinoid tumors

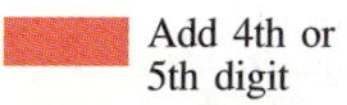
Add 4th or
5th digit

Nonspecific
code

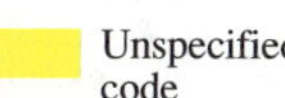
Unspecified
code

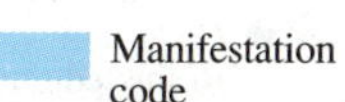
Manifestation
code

259.3 Ectopic hormone secretion, not elsewhere classified
Ectopic:
antidiuretic hormone secretion [ADH]
hyperparathyroidism

| *Excludes:* | *ectopic ACTH syndrome (255.0)* |

259.4 Dwarfism, not elsewhere classified
Dwarfism:
NOS
constitutional

| *Excludes:* | *dwarfism:* |

> *achondroplastic (756.4)*
> *intrauterine (759.7)*
> *nutritional (263.2)*
> *pituitary (253.3)*
> *renal (588.0)*
> *progeria (259.8)*

259.8 Other specified endocrine disorders
Pineal gland dysfunction   Werner's syndrome
Progeria

259.9 Unspecified endocrine disorder
Disturbance: Infantilism NOS
endocrine NOS
hormone NOS

NUTRITIONAL DEFICIENCIES (260-269)

| *Excludes:* | *deficiency anemias (280.0-281.9)* |

260 Kwashiorkor
Nutritional edema with dyspigmentation of skin and hair

261 Nutritional marasmus
Nutritional atrophy   Severe malnutrition NOS
Severe calorie deficiency

262 Other severe protein-calorie malnutrition
Nutritional edema without mention of dyspigmentation of skin and hair

263 Other and unspecified protein-calorie malnutrition

263.0 Malnutrition of moderate degree

263.1 Malnutrition of mild degree

263.2 Arrested development following protein-calorie malnutrition
Nutritional dwarfism
Physical retardation due to malnutrition

263.8 Other protein-calorie malnutrition

263.9 Unspecified protein-calorie malnutrition
Dystrophy due to malnutrition
Malnutrition (calorie) NOS

| *Excludes:* | *nutritional deficiency NOS (269.9)* |

264 Vitamin A deficiency

264.0 With conjunctival xerosis

264.1 With conjunctival xerosis and Bitot's spot
Bitot's spot in the young child

264.2 With corneal xerosis

264.3 With corneal ulceration and xerosis

264.4 With keratomalacia

264.5 With night blindness

264.6 With xerophthalmic scars of cornea

264.7 Other ocular manifestations of vitamin A deficiency
Xerophthalmia due to vitamin A deficiency

264.8 Other manifestations of vitamin A deficiency
Follicular keratosis } due to vitamin A deficiency
Xeroderma

264.9 Unspecified vitamin A deficiency
Hypovitaminosis A NOS

● Code new to this edition   ▲ Revision of existing code   ④ ⑤ Fourth or fifth digit required

265 **Thiamine and niacin deficiency states**

265.0 **Beriberi**

265.1 **Other and unspecified manifestations of thiamine deficiency**
Other vitamin B_1 deficiency states

265.2 **Pellagra**
Deficiency:
  niacin (-tryptophan)
  nicotinamide
  nicotinic acid
  vitamin PP
Pellagra (alcoholic)

266 **Deficiency of B-complex components**

266.0 **Ariboflavinosis**
Riboflavin [vitamin B_2] deficiency

266.1 **Vitamin B_6 deficiency**
Deficiency: Vitamin B_6 deficiency syndrome
  pyridoxal
  pyridoxamine
  pyridoxine

| Excludes: | vitamin B_6-responsive sideroblastic anemia (285.0) |

266.2 **Other B-complex deficiencies**
Deficiency:
  cyanocobalamin
  folic acid
  vitamin B_{12}

Excludes:	combined system disease with anemia (281.0-281.1)
	deficiency anemias (281.0-281.9)
	subacute degeneration of spinal cord with anemia (281.0-281.1)

266.9 **Unspecified vitamin B deficiency**

267 **Ascorbic acid deficiency**
Deficiency of vitamin C   Scurvy

| Excludes: | scorbutic anemia (281.8) |

268 **Vitamin D deficiency**

Excludes:	vitamin D-resistant:
	osteomalacia (275.3)
	rickets (275.3)

268.0 **Rickets, active**

| Excludes: | celiac rickets (579.0) |
| | renal rickets (588.0) |

268.1 **Rickets, late effect**
Any condition specified as due to rickets and stated to be a late effect or sequela of rickets

Use additional code to identify the nature of late effect

268.2 **Osteomalacia, unspecified**

268.9 **Unspecified vitamin D deficiency**
Avitaminosis D

269 **Other nutritional deficiencies**

269.0 **Deficiency of vitamin K**

| Excludes: | deficiency of coagulation factor due to vitamin K deficiency (286.7) |
| | vitamin K deficiency of newborn (776.0) |

269.1 **Deficiency of other vitamins**
Deficiency:
  vitamin E
  vitamin P

269.2 **Unspecified vitamin deficiency**
Multiple vitamin deficiency NOS

Add 4th or 5th digit

Nonspecific code

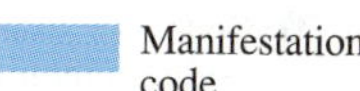
Unspecified code

Manifestation code

269.3 Mineral deficiency, not elsewhere classified
Deficiency:
calcium, dietary
iodine

Excludes: *deficiency:*
calcium NOS (275.4)
potassium (276.8)
sodium (276.1)

269.8 Other nutritional deficiency

Excludes: *adult failure to thrive (783.7)*
failure to thrive in childhood (783.41)
feeding problems (783.3)
newborn (779.3)

269.9 Unspecified nutritional deficiency

OTHER METABOLIC AND IMMUNITY DISORDERS (270-279)

Use additional code to identify any associated mental retardation

270 Disorders of amino-acid transport and metabolism

Excludes: *abnormal findings without manifest disease (790.0-796.9)*
disorders of purine and pyrimidine metabolism (277.1-277.2)
gout (274.0-274.9)

270.0 Disturbances of amino-acid transport
Cystinosis
Cystinuria
Fanconi (-de Toni) (-Debré) syndrome
Glycinuria (renal)
Hartnup disease

270.1 Phenylketonuria [PKU]
Hyperphenylalaninemia

270.2 Other disturbances of aromatic amino-acid metabolism
Albinism
Alkaptonuria
Alkaptonuric ochronosis
Disturbances of metabolism
of tyrosine and tryptophan
Homogentisic acid defects
Hydroxykynureninuria
Hypertyrosinemia
Indicanuria
Kynureninase defects
Oasthouse urine disease
Ochronosis
Tyrosinosis
Tyrosinuria
Waardenburg syndrome

Excludes: *vitamin B$_6$-deficiency syndrome (266.1)*

270.3 Disturbances of branched-chain amino-acid metabolism
Disturbances of metabolism of leucine, isoleucine, and valine
Hypervalinemia
Intermittent branched-chain ketonuria
Leucine-induced hypoglycemia
Leucinosis
Maple syrup urine disease

270.4 Disturbances of sulphur-bearing amino-acid metabolism
Cystathioninemia
Cystathioninuria
Disturbances of metabolism of methionine, homocystine, and cystathionine
Homocystinuria
Hypermethioninemia
Methioninemia

270.5 Disturbances of histidine metabolism
Carnosinemia
Histidinemia
Hyperhistidinemia
Imidazole aminoaciduria

270.6 Disorders of urea cycle metabolism
Argininosuccinic aciduria
Citrullinemia
Disorders of metabolism of ornithine, citrulline, argininosuccinic acid, arginine, and ammonia
Hyperammonemia
Hyperornithinemia

● Code new
to this edition

▲ Revision of
existing code

④ ⑤ Fourth or fifth
digit required

270.7 Other disturbances of straight-chain amino-acid metabolism

Glucoglycinuria
Glycinemia (with methyl-
   malonic acidemia)
Hyperglycinemia
Hyperlysinemia
Pipecolic acidemia

Saccharopinuria
Other disturbances of metabolism of glycine, threonine,
   serine, glutamine, and lysine

270.8 Other specified disorders of amino-acid metabolism

Alaninemia
Ethanolaminuria
Glycoprolinuria
Hydroxyprolinemia
Hyperprolinemia

Iminoacidopathy
Prolinemia
Prolinuria
Sarcosinemia

270.9 Unspecified disorder of amino-acid metabolism

271 Disorders of carbohydrate transport and metabolism

> *Excludes:* *abnormality of secretion of glucagon (251.4)*
> *diabetes mellitus (250.0-250.9)*
> *hypoglycemia NOS (251.2)*
> *mucopolysaccharidosis (277.5)*

271.0 Glycogenosis

Amylopectinosis
Glucose-6-phosphatase
   deficiency
Glycogen storage disease

McArdle's disease
Pompe's disease
von Gierke's disease

271.1 Galactosemia

Galactose-1-phosphate uridyl transferase deficiency
Galactosuria

271.2 Hereditary fructose intolerance

Essential benign fructosuria
Fructosemia

271.3 Intestinal disaccharidase deficiencies and disaccharide malabsorption

Intolerance or malabsorption (congenital) (of):
   glucose-galactose
   lactose
   sucrose-isomaltose

271.4 Renal glycosuria

Renal diabetes

271.8 Other specified disorders of carbohydrate transport and metabolism

Essential benign pentosuria
Fucosidosis
Glycolic aciduria
Hyperoxaluria (primary)

Mannosidosis
Oxalosis
Xylosuria
Xylulosuria

271.9 Unspecified disorder of carbohydrate transport and metabolism

272 Disorders of lipoid metabolism

> *Excludes:* *localized cerebral lipidoses (330.1)*

272.0 Pure hypercholesterolemia

Familial hypercholesterolemia
Fredrickson Type IIa hyperlipoproteinemia
Hyperbetalipoproteinemia
Hyperlipidemia, Group A
Low-density-lipoid-type [LDL] hyperlipoproteinemia

272.1 Pure hyperglyceridemia

Endogenous hyperglyceridemia
Frederickson Type IV hyperlipoproteinemia
Hyperlipidemia, Group B
Hyperprebetalipoproteinemia
Hypertriglyceridemia, essential
Very-low-density-lipoid-type [VLDL] hyperlipoproteinemia

272.2 Mixed hyperlipidemia

Broad- or floating-betalipoproteinemia
Fredrickson Type IIb or III hyperlipoproteinemia
Hypercholesterolemia with endogenous hyperglyceridemia
Hyperbetalipoproteinemia with prebetalipoproteinemia
Tubo-eruptive xanthoma
Xanthoma tuberosum

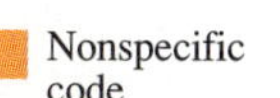

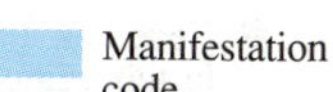

272.3 Hyperchylomicronemia
Bürger-Grütz syndrome
Fredrickson type I or V
hyperlipoproteinemia
Hyperlipidemia, Group D
Mixed hyperglyceridemia

272.4 Other and unspecified hyperlipidemia
Alpha-lipoproteinemia
Combined hyperlipidemia
Hyperlipidemia NOS
Hyperlipoproteinemia NOS

272.5 Lipoprotein deficiencies
Abetalipoproteinemia
Bassen-Kornzweig syndrome
High-density lipoid deficiency
Hypoalphalipoproteinemia
Hypobetalipoproteinemia (familial)

272.6 Lipodystrophy
Barraquer-Simons disease
Progressive lipodystrophy

Use additional E code to identify cause, if iatrogenic

> *Excludes:* intestinal lipodystrophy (040.2)

272.7 Lipidoses
Chemically-induced lipidosis
Disease:
  Anderson's
  Fabry's
  Gaucher's
  I cell [mucolipidosis I]
  lipoid storage NOS
  Neimann-Pick
  pseudo-Hurler's or
  mucolipidosis III
Disease:
  triglyceride storage, Type I or II
  Wolman's or triglyceride storage, Type III
Mucolipidosis II
Primary familial xanthomatosis

> *Excludes:* cerebral lipidoses (330.1)
> Tay-Sachs disease (330.1)

272.8 Other disorders of lipoid metabolism
Hoffa's disease or liposynovitis prepatellaris
Launois-Bensaude's lipomatosis
Lipoid dermatoarthritis

272.9 Unspecified disorder of lipoid metabolism

273 Disorders of plasma protein metabolism

> *Excludes:* agammaglobulinemia and hypogammaglobulinemia (279.0 -279.2)
> coagulation defects (286.0-286.9)
> hereditary hemolytic anemias (282.0-282.9)

273.0 Polyclonal hypergammaglobulinemia
Hypergammaglobulinemic purpura:
  benign primary
  Waldenström's

273.1 Monoclonal paraproteinemia
Benign monoclonal hypergammaglobulinemia [BMH]
Monoclonal gammopathy:
  NOS
  associated with lymphoplasmacytic dyscrasias
  benign
Paraproteinemia:
  benign (familial)
  secondary to malignant or inflammatory disease

273.2 Other paraproteinemias
Cryoglobulinemic:
  purpura
  vasculitis
Mixed cryoglobulinemia

273.3 Macroglobulinemia
Macroglobulinemia (idiopathic) (primary)
Waldenström's macroglobulinemia

273.8 Other disorders of plasma protein metabolism
Abnormality of transport protein
Bisalbuminemia

273.9 Unspecified disorder of plasma protein metabolism

● Code new
to this edition
▲ Revision of
existing code
④ ⑤ Fourth or fifth
digit required

274 Gout

> *Excludes:* *lead gout (984.0-984.9)*

274.0 Gouty arthropathy

⑤ **274.1 Gouty nephropathy**

274.10 Gouty nephropathy, unspecified

274.11 Uric acid nephrolithiasis

274.19 Other

⑤ **274.8 Gout with other specified manifestations**

274.81 Gouty tophi of ear

274.82 Gouty tophi of other sites
Gouty tophi of heart

274.89 Other
Use additional code to identify manifestations, as:
gouty:
iritis (364.11)
neuritis (357.4)

274.9 Gout, unspecified

275 Disorders of mineral metabolism

> *Excludes:* *abnormal findings without manifest disease (790.0-796.9)*

275.0 Disorders of iron metabolism
Bronzed diabetes   Pigmentary cirrhosis (of liver)
Hemochromatosis

> *Excludes:* *anemia:*
> *iron deficiency (280.0-280.9)*
> *sideroblastic (285.0)*

275.1 Disorders of copper metabolism
Hepatolenticular degeneration
Wilson's disease

275.2 Disorders of magnesium metabolism
Hypermagnesemia   Hypomagnesemia

275.3 Disorders of phosphorus metabolism
Familial hypophosphatemia
Hypophosphatasia
Vitamin D-resistant:
osteomalacia
rickets

⑤ **275.4 Disorders of calcium metabolism**

> *Excludes:* *parathyroid disorders (252.0-252.9)*
> *vitamin D deficiency (268.0-268.9)*

275.40 Unspecified disorder of calcium metabolism

275.41 Hypocalcemia

275.42 Hypercalcemia

275.49 Other disorders of calcium metabolism
Nephrocalcinosis
Pseudohypoparathyroidism
Pseudopseudohypoparathyroidism

275.8 Other specified disorders of mineral metabolism

275.9 Unspecified disorder of mineral metabolism

276 Disorders of fluid, electrolyte, and acid-base balance

> *Excludes:* *diabetes insipidus (253.5)*
> *familial periodic paralysis (359.3)*

276.0 Hyperosmolality and/or hypernatremia
Sodium [Na] excess   Sodium [Na] overload

276.1 Hyposmolality and/or hyponatremia
Sodium [Na] deficiency

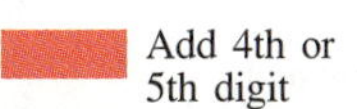

276.2 Acidosis
    Acidosis:
     NOS
     lactic
     metabolic
     respiratory

 Excludes: *diabetic acidosis (250.1)*

276.3 Alkalosis
    Alkalosis:
     NOS
     metabolic
     respiratory

276.4 Mixed acid-base balance disorder
    Hypercapnia with mixed acid-base disorder

276.5 Volume depletion
    Dehydration
    Depletion of volume of plasma or extracellular fluid
    Hypovolemia

 Excludes: *hypovolemic shock:*
       postoperative (998.0)
       traumatic (958.4)

276.6 Fluid overload
    Fluid retention

 Excludes: *ascites (789.5)*
       localized edema (782.3)

276.7 Hyperpotassemia
    Hyperkalemia
    Potassium [K]:
      excess
      intoxication
      overload

276.8 Hypopotassemia
    Hypokalemia   Potassium [K] deficiency

276.9 Electrolyte and fluid disorders not elsewhere classified
    Electrolyte imbalance   Hypochloremia
    Hyperchloremia

 Excludes: *electrolyte imbalance:*
       associated with hyperemesis gravidarum (643.1)
       complicating labor and delivery (669.0)
       following abortion and ectopic or molar pregnancy (634-638 with .4, 639.4)

277 Other and unspecified disorders of metabolism

⑤ **277.0 Cystic fibrosis**
    Fibrocystic disease of the pancreas
    Mucoviscidosis

     277.00   Without mention of meconium ileus

     277.01   With meconium ileus
            Meconium:
             ileus (of newborn)
             obstruction of intestine in mucoviscidosis

277.1 Disorders of porphyrin metabolism
    Hematoporphyria   Porphyrinuria
    Hematoporphyrinuria   Protocoproporphyria
    Hereditary coproporphyria   Protoporphyria
    Porphyria   Pyrroloporphyria

277.2 Other disorders of purine and pyrimidine metabolism
    Hypoxanthine-guanine-phosphoribosyltransferase deficiency [HG-PRT deficiency]
    Lesch-Nyhan syndrome
    Xanthinuria

 Excludes: *gout (274.0-274.9)*
       orotic aciduric anemia (281.4)

● Code new   ▲ Revision of   ④ ⑤ Fourth or fifth
  to this edition   existing code   digit required

277.3 **Amyloidosis**
   Amyloidosis:
     NOS
     inherited systemic
     nephropathic
     neuropathic (Portuguese) (Swiss)
     secondary
   Benign paroxysmal peritonitis
   Familial Mediterranean fever
   Hereditary cardiac amyloidosis

277.4 **Disorders of bilirubin excretion**
   Hyperbilirubinemia: Syndrome:
     congenital   Crigler-Najjar
     constitutional   Dubin-Johnson
                   Gilbert's
                   Rotor's

> *Excludes:* *hyperbilirubinemias specific to the perinatal period (774.0-774.7)*

277.5 **Mucopolysaccharidosis**
   Gargoylism   Morquio-Brailsford disease
   Hunter's syndrome   Osteochondrodystrophy
   Hurler's syndrome   Sanfilippo's syndrome
   Lipochondrodystrophy   Scheie's syndrome
   Maroteaux-Lamy syndrome

277.6 **Other deficiencies of circulating enzymes**
   Alpha 1-antitrypsin deficiency
   Hereditary angioedema

277.8 **Other specified disorders of metabolism**
   Hand-Schüller-Christian disease
   Histiocytosis (acute) (chronic)
   Histiocytosis X (chronic)

> *Excludes:* *histiocytosis:*
>   *acute differentiated progressive (202.5)*
>   *X, acute (progressive) (202.5)*

277.9 **Unspecified disorder of metabolism**
   Enzymopathy NOS

278 **Obesity and other hyperalimentation**

> *Excludes:* *hyperalimentation NOS (783.6)*
>   *poisoning by vitamins NOS (963.5)*
>   *polyphagia (783.6)*

⑤ **278.0** **Obesity**

> *Excludes:* *adiposogenital dystrophy (253.8)*
>   *obesity of endocrine origin NOS (259.9)*

   278.00 **Obesity, unspecified**
     Obesity NOS

   278.01 **Morbid obesity**

278.1 **Localized adiposity**
   Fat pad

278.2 **Hypervitaminosis A**

278.3 **Hypercarotinemia**

278.4 **Hypervitaminosis D**

278.8 **Other hyperalimentation**

279 **Disorders involving the immune mechanism**

⑤ **279.0** **Deficiency of humoral immunity**

   279.00 **Hypogammaglobulinemia, unspecified**
     Agammaglobulinemia NOS

   279.01 **Selective IgA immunodeficiency**

   279.02 **Selective IgM immunodeficiency**

   279.03 **Other selective immunoglobulin deficiencies**
     Selective deficiency of IgG

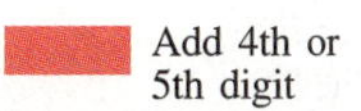

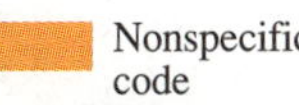

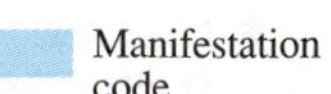

279.04 Congenital hypogammaglobulinemia
Agammaglobulinemia:
  Bruton's type
  X-linked

279.05 Immunodeficiency with increased IgM
Immunodeficiency with hyper-IgM:
  autosomal recessive
  X-linked

279.06 Common variable immunodeficiency
Dysgammaglobulinemia (acquired) (congenital) (primary)
Hypogammaglobulinemia:
  acquired primary
  congenital non-sex-linked
  sporadic

279.09 Other
Transient hypogammaglobulinemia of infancy

⑤ **279.1 Deficiency of cell-mediated immunity**

279.10 Immunodeficiency with predominant T-cell defect, unspecified

279.11 DiGeorge's syndrome
Pharyngeal pouch syndrome
Thymic hypoplasia

279.12 Wiskott-Aldrich syndrome

279.13 Nezelof's syndrome
Cellular immunodeficiency with abnormal immunoglobulin deficiency

279.19 Other

Excludes: *ataxia-telangiectasia (334.8)*

279.2 Combined immunity deficiency
Agammaglobulinemia:
  autosomal recessive
  Swiss-type
  x-linked recessive
Severe combined immunodeficiency [SCID]
Thymic:
  alymphoplasia
  aplasia or dysplasia with immunodeficiency

Excludes: *thymic hypoplasia (279.11)*

279.3 Unspecified immunity deficiency

279.4 Autoimmune disease, not elsewhere classified
Autoimmune disease NOS

Excludes: *transplant failure or rejection (996.80-996.89)*

279.8 Other specified disorders involving the immune mechanism
Single complement [C$_1$-C$_9$] deficiency or dysfunction

279.9 Unspecified disorder of immune mechanism

● Code new
to this edition

▲ Revision of
existing code

④ ⑤ Fourth or fifth
digit required

4.   DISEASES OF THE BLOOD AND BLOOD-FORMING ORGANS (280-289)

> *Excludes:* *anemia complicating pregnancy or the puerperium (648.2)*

280 Iron deficiency anemias

Includes: anemia:
        asiderotic
        hypochromic-microcytic
        sideropenic

> *Excludes:* *familial microcytic anemia (282.4)*

280.0 Secondary to blood loss (chronic)
Normocytic anemia due to blood loss

> *Excludes:* *acute posthemorrhagic anemia (285.1)*

280.1 Secondary to inadequate dietary iron intake

280.8 Other specified iron deficiency anemias
Paterson-Kelly syndrome
Plummer-Vinson syndrome
Sideropenic dysphagia

280.9 Iron deficiency anemia, unspecified
Anemia:
    achlorhydric
    chlorotic
    idiopathic hypochromic
    iron [Fe] deficiency NOS

281 Other deficiency anemias

281.0 Pernicious anemia
Anemia: Congenital intrinsic factor [Castle's] deficiency
    Addison's
    Biermer's
    congenital pernicious

> *Excludes:* *combined system disease without mention of anemia (266.2)*
> *subacute degeneration of spinal cord without mention of anemia (266.2)*

281.1 Other vitamin B_{12} deficiency anemia
Anemia:
    vegan's
    vitamin B_{12} deficiency (dietary)
    due to selective vitamin B_{12} malabsorption with proteinuria
Syndrome:
    Imerslund's
    Imerslund-Gräsbeck

> *Excludes:* *combined system disease without mention of anemia (266.2)*
> *subacute degeneration of spinal cord without mention of anemia (266.2)*

281.2 Folate-deficiency anemia
Congenital folate malabsorption
Folate or folic acid deficiency anemia:
    NOS
    dietary
    drug-induced
Goat's milk anemia
Nutritional megaloblastic anemia (of infancy)
Use additional E code, if desired, to identify drug

281.3 Other specified megaloblastic anemias not elsewhere classified
Combined B_{12} and folate-deficiency anemia
Refractory megaloblastic anemia

281.4 Protein-deficiency anemia
Amino-acid-deficiency anemia

281.8 Anemia associated with other specified nutritional deficiency
Scorbutic anemia

281.9 Unspecified deficiency anemia
Anemia: Anemia:
    dimorphic   nutritional NOS
    macrocytic   simple chronic
    megaloblastic NOS

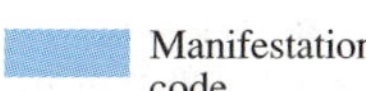

	Add 4th or 5th digit		Nonspecific code		Unspecified code		Manifestation code

282 Hereditary hemolytic anemias

282.0 Hereditary spherocytosis
   Acholuric (familial) jaundice
   Congenital hemolytic anemia (spherocytic)
   Congenital spherocytosis
   Minkowski-Chauffard syndrome
   Spherocytosis (familial)

   Excludes: *hemolytic anemia of newborn (773.0-773.5)*

282.1 Hereditary elliptocytosis
   Elliptocytosis (congenital)
   Ovalocytosis (congenital) (hereditary)

282.2 Anemias due to disorders of glutathione metabolism
   Anemia:
      6-phosphogluconic dehydrogenase deficiency
      enzyme deficiency, drug-induced
      erythrocytic glutathione deficiency
      glucose-6-phosphate dehydrogenase [G-6-PD] deficiency
      glutathione-reductase deficiency
      hemolytic nonspherocytic (hereditary), type I
   Disorder of pentose phosphate pathway
   Favism

282.3 Other hemolytic anemias due to enzyme deficiency
   Anemia:
      hemolytic nonspherocytic (hereditary), type II
      hexokinase deficiency
      pyruvate kinase [PK] deficiency
      triosephosphate isomerase deficiency

282.4 Thalassemias
   Cooley's anemia
   Hereditary leptocytosis
   Mediterranean anemia (with other hemoglobinopathy)
   Microdrepanocytosis
   Sickle-cell thalassemia
   Thalassemia (alpha) (beta) (intermedia) (major) (minima) (minor) (mixed) (trait) (with other hemoglobinopathy)
   Thalassemia-Hb-S disease

   Excludes: *sickle-cell:*
      anemia (282.60-282.69)
      trait (282.5)

282.5 Sickle-cell trait
   Hb-AS genotype   Heterozygous:
   Hemoglobin S [Hb-S] trait   hemoglobin S
                                        Hb-S

   Excludes: *that with other hemoglobinopathy (282.60-282.69)*
      that with thalassemia (282.4)

⑤ **282.6 Sickle-cell anemia**

   Excludes: *sickle-cell thalassemia (282.4)*
      sickle-cell trait (282.5)

   282.60 Sickle-cell anemia, unspecified

   282.61 Hb-S disease without mention of crisis

   282.62 Hb-S disease with mention of crisis
      Sickle-cell crisis NOS

   282.63 Sickle-cell/Hb-C disease
      Hb-S/Hb-C disease

   282.69 Other
      Disease: Disease:
         Hb-S/Hb-D   sickle-cell/Hb-D
         Hb-S/Hb-E   sickle-cell/Hb-E

● Code new
   to this edition

▲ Revision of
   existing code

④ ⑤ Fourth or fifth
   digit required

282.7 **Other hemoglobinopathies**
Abnormal hemoglobin NOS
Congenital Heinz-body anemia
Disease:
  Hb-Bart's
  hemoglobin C [Hb-C]
  hemoglobin D [Hb-D]
  hemoglobin E [Hb-E]
  hemoglobin Zurich [Hb-Zurich]
Hemoglobinopathy NOS
Hereditary persistence of fetal hemoglobin [HPFH]
Unstable hemoglobin hemolytic disease

Excludes: *familial polycythemia (289.6)*
hemoglobin M [Hb-M] disease (289.7)
high-oxygen-affinity hemoglobin (289.0)

282.8 **Other specified hereditary hemolytic anemias**
Stomatocytosis

282.9 **Hereditary hemolytic anemia, unspecified**
Hereditary hemolytic anemia NOS

283 **Acquired hemolytic anemias**

283.0 **Autoimmune hemolytic anemias**
Autoimmune hemolytic anemias (cold type) (warm type)
Chronic cold hemagglutinin disease
Cold agglutinin disease or hemoglobinuria
Hemolytic anemia:
  cold type (secondary) (symptomatic)
  drug-induced
  warm type (secondary) (symptomatic)
Use additional E code, if desired, to identify cause, if drug-induced

Excludes: *Evans' syndrome (287.3)*
hemolytic disease of newborn (773.0-773.5)

⑤ **283.1** **Non-autoimmune hemolytic anemias**

283.10 **Non-autoimmune hemolytic anemia, unspecified**

283.11 **Hemolytic-uremic syndrome**

283.19 **Other non-autoimmune hemolytic anemias**
Hemolytic anemia:
  mechanical
  microangiopathic
  toxic
Use additional E code, if desired, to identify cause

283.2 **Hemoglobinuria due to hemolysis from external causes**
Acute intravascular hemolysis
Hemoglobinuria:
  from exertion
  march
  paroxysmal (cold) (nocturnal)
  due to other hemolysis
Marchiafava-Micheli syndrome
Use additional E code, if desired, to identify cause

283.9 **Acquired hemolytic anemia, unspecified**
Acquired hemolytic anemia NOS
Chronic idiopathic hemolytic anemia

284 **Aplastic anemia**

284.0 **Constitutional aplastic anemia**
Aplasia, (pure) red cell: Familial hypoplastic anemia
  congenital   Fanconi's anemia
  of infants   Pancytopenia with malformations
  primary
Blackfan-Diamond syndrome

	Add 4th or 5th digit		Nonspecific code		Unspecified code		Manifestation code

284.8 Other specified aplastic anemias

Aplastic anemia (due to): Pancytopenia (acquired)
chronic systemic disease Red cell aplasia (acquired) (adult) (pure) (with
drugs thymoma)
infection
radiation
toxic (paralytic)

Use additional E code, if desired, to identify cause

284.9 Aplastic anemia, unspecified

Anemia: Anemia:
aplastic (idiopathic) NOS nonregenerative
aregenerative refractory
hypoplastic NOS Medullary hypoplasia

285 Other and unspecified anemias

285.0 Sideroblastic anemia

Anemia:
hypochromic with iron loading
sideroachrestic
sideroblastic
acquired
congenital
hereditary
primary
refractory
secondary (drug-induced) (due to disease)
sex-linked hypochromic
vitamin B_6-responsive
Pyridoxine-responsive (hypochromic) anemia

Use additional E code, if desired, to identify cause, if drug induced

285.1 Acute posthemorrhagic anemia

Anemia due to acute blood loss

Excludes: *anemia due to chronic blood loss (280.0)*
blood loss anemia NOS (280.0)

● **285.2 Anemia in chronic illness**

● **285.21 Anemia in end-stage renal disease**

● **285.22 Anemia in neoplastic disease**

● **285.29 Anemia of other chronic illness**

285.8 Other specified anemias

Anemia:
dyserythropoietic (congenital)
dyshematopoietic (congenital)
leukoerythroblastic
von Jaksch's
Infantile pseudoleukemia

285.9 Anemia, unspecified

Anemia: Anemia:
NOS profound
essential progressive
normocytic, not due to blood secondary
loss Oligocythemia

Excludes: *anemia (due to):*
blood loss:
acute (285.1)
chronic or unspecified (280.0)
iron deficiency (280.0-280.9)

● Code new
to this edition

▲ Revision of
existing code

④ ⑤ Fourth or fifth
digit required

286 Coagulation defects

286.0 Congenital factor VIII disorder

Antihemophilic globulin
   [AHG]
   deficiency
Factor VIII (functional)
   deficiency

Hemophilia:
   NOS
   A
   classical
   familial
   hereditary
Subhemophilia

Excludes: *factor VIII deficiency with vascular defect (286.4)*

286.1 Congenital factor IX disorder

Christmas disease
Deficiency:
   factor IX (functional)
   plasma thromboplastin component [PTC]
Hemophilia B

286.2 Congenital factor XI deficiency

Hemophilia C
Plasma thromboplastin antecedent [PTA] deficiency
Rosenthal's disease

286.3 Congenital deficiency of other clotting factors

Congenital afibrinogenemia
Deficiency:
   AC globulin factor:
   I [fibrinogen]
   II [prothrombin]
   V [labile]
   VII [stable]
   X [Stuart-Prower]
   XII [Hageman]
   XIII [fibrin stabilizing]

Deficiency:
   Laki-Lorand factor
   proaccelerin
Disease:
   Owren's
   Stuart-Prower
Dysfibrinogenemia (congenital)
Dysprothrombinemia (constitutional)
Hypoproconvertinemia
Hypoprothrombinemia (hereditary)
Parahemophilia

286.4 von Willebrand's disease

Angiohemophilia (A) (B)
Constitutional thrombopathy
Factor VIII deficiency with vascular defect
Pseudohemophilia type B
Vascular hemophilia
von Willebrand's (-Jürgens') disease

Excludes: *factor VIII deficiency:*
   NOS (286.0)
   with functional defect (286.0)
   hereditary capillary fragility (287.8)

286.5 Hemorrhagic disorder due to circulating anticoagulants

Antithrombinemia
Antithromboplastinemia
Antithromboplastinogenemia
Hyperheparinemia

Increase in:
   anti-VIIIa
   anti-IXa
   anti-Xa
   anti-XIa
   antithrombin
Systemic lupus erythematosus [SLE] inhibitor

Use additional E code, if desired, to identify cause, if drug induced

286.6 Defibrination syndrome

Afibrinogenemia, acquired
Consumption coagulopathy
Diffuse or disseminated intravascular coagulation [DIC syndrome]
Fibrinolytic hemorrhage, acquired
Hemorrhagic fibrinogenolysis
Pathologic fibrinolysis
Purpura:
   fibrinolytic
   fulminans

Excludes: *that complicating:*
   abortion (634-638 with .1, 639.1)
   pregnancy or the puerperium (641.3, 666.3)
   disseminated intravascular coagulation in newborn (776.2)

 Add 4th or 5th digit   Nonspecific code   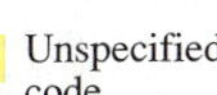 Unspecified code   Manifestation code

286.7 Acquired coagulation factor deficiency
Deficiency of coagulation factor due to:
  liver disease
  vitamin K deficiency
Hypoprothrombinemia, acquired

> *Excludes:* *vitamin K deficiency of newborn (776.0)*

Use additional E-code, if desired, to identify cause, if drug induced

286.9 Other and unspecified coagulation defects
Defective coagulation NOS
Deficiency, coagulation factor NOS
Delay, coagulation
Disorder:
  coagulation
  hemostasis

> *Excludes:* *abnormal coagulation profile (790.92)*
> *hemorrhagic disease of newborn (776.0)*
> *that complicating:*
>   *abortion (634-638 with .1, 639.1)*
>   *pregnancy or the puerperium (641.3, 666.3)*

287 Purpura and other hemorrhagic conditions

> *Excludes:* *hemorrhagic thrombocythemia (238.7)*
> *purpura fulminans (286.6)*

287.0 Allergic purpura
Peliosis rheumatica
Purpura:
  anaphylactoid
  autoimmune
  Henoch's
Purpura:
  nonthrombocytopenic:
    hemorrhagic
    idiopathic
    rheumatica
    Schönlein-Henoch
    vascular
Vasculitis, allergic

> *Excludes:* *hemorrhagic purpura (287.3)*
> *purpura annularis telangiectodes (709.1)*

287.1 Qualitative platelet defects
Thrombasthenia (hemorrhagic) (hereditary)
Thrombocytasthenia
Thrombocytopathy (dystrophic)
Thrombopathy (Bernard-Soulier)

> *Excludes:* *von Willebrand's disease (286.4)*

287.2 Other nonthrombocytopenic purpuras
Purpura:
  NOS
  senile
  simplex

287.3 Primary thrombocytopenia
Evans' syndrome
Megakaryocytic hypoplasia
Purpura, thrombocytopenic
  congenital
  hereditary
  idiopathic
Thrombocytopenia:
  congenital
  hereditary
  primary
Tidal platelet dysgenesis

> *Excludes:* *thrombotic thrombocytopenic purpura (446.6)*
> *transient thrombocytopenia of newborn (776.1)*

287.4 Secondary thrombocytopenia
Posttransfusion purpura
Thrombocytopenia (due to):
  dilutional
  drugs
  extracorporeal circulation of blood
  massive blood transfusion
  platelet alloimmunization

Use additional E code, if desired, to identify cause

> *Excludes:* *transient thrombocytopenia of newborn (776.1)*

● Code new
  to this edition
▲ Revision of
  existing code
④ ⑤ Fourth or fifth
  digit required

287.5 Thrombocytopenia, unspecified

287.8 Other specified hemorrhagic conditions
Capillary fragility (hereditary)
Vascular pseudohemophilia

287.9 Unspecified hemorrhagic conditions
Hemorrhagic diathesis (familial)

288 Diseases of white blood cells

> Excludes: *leukemia (204.0-208.9)*

288.0 Agranulocytosis

Infantile genetic agranulo-
  cytosis
Kostmann's syndrome
Neutropenia:
  NOS
  cyclic

Neutropenia:
  drug-induced
  immune
  periodic
  toxic
Neutropenic splenomegaly

Use additional E code, if desired, to identify drug or other cause

> Excludes: *transitory neonatal neutropenia (776.7)*

288.1 Functional disorders of polymorphonuclear neutrophils
Chronic (childhood) granulomatous disease
Congenital dysphagocytosis
Job's syndrome
Lipochrome histiocytosis (familial)
Progressive septic granulomatosis

288.2 Genetic anomalies of leukocytes
Anomaly (granulation) (granulocyte) or syndrome:
  Alder's (-Reilly)
  Chédiak-Steinbrinck (-Higashi)
  Jordan's
  May-Hegglin
  Pelger-Huet
Hereditary:
  hypersegmentation
  hyposegmentation
  leukomelanopathy

288.3 Eosinophilia
Eosinophilia
  allergic
  hereditary
  idiopathic
  secondary
Eosinophilic leukocytosis

> Excludes: *Löffler's syndrome (518.3)*
> *pulmonary eosinophilia (518.3)*

288.8 Other specified disease of white blood cells
Leukemoid reaction
  lymphocytic
  monocytic
  myelocytic
Leukocytosis
Lymphocytopenia

Lymphocytosis (symptomatic)
Lymphopenia
Monocytosis (symptomatic)
Plasmacytosis

> Excludes: *immunity disorders (279.0-279.9)*

288.9 Unspecified disease of white blood cells

Add 4th or
5th digit

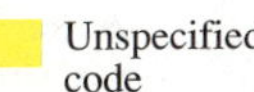
Nonspecific
code

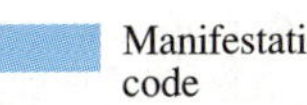
Unspecified
code

Manifestation
code

289 **Other diseases of blood and blood-forming organs**

289.0 **Polycythemia, secondary**

High-oxygen-affinity
   hemoglobin
Polycythemia:
   acquired
   benign
   due to:
      fall in plasma volume
      high altitude
Polycythemia:
   emotional
   erythropoietin
   hypoxemic
   nephrogenous
   relative
   spurious
   stress

Excludes: polycythemia:
   neonatal (776.4)
   primary (238.4)
   vera (238.4)

289.1 **Chronic lymphadenitis**

Chronic:
   adenitis
   lymphadenitis } any lymph node, except mesenteric

Excludes: acute lymphadenitis (683)
      mesenteric (289.2)
   enlarged glands NOS (785.6)

289.2 **Nonspecific mesenteric lymphadenitis**
Mesenteric lymphadenitis (acute) (chronic)

289.3 **Lymphadenitis, unspecified, except mesenteric**

289.4 **Hypersplenism**
"Big spleen" syndrome   Hypersplenia
Dyssplenism

Excludes: primary splenic neutropenia (288.0)

⑤ **289.5** **Other diseases of spleen**

   289.50 **Disease of spleen, unspecified**

   289.51 **Chronic congestive splenomegaly**

   289.59 **Other**

Lien migrans
Perisplenitis
Splenic:
   abscess
   atrophy
   cyst
Splenic:
   fibrosis
   infarction
   rupture, nontraumatic
Splenitis
Wandering spleen

Excludes: bilharzial splenic fibrosis (120.0-120.9)
   hepatolienal fibrosis (571.5)
   splenomegaly NOS (789.2)

289.6 **Familial polycythemia**
Familial:
   benign polycythemia
   erythrocytosis

289.7 **Methemoglobinemia**
Congenital NADH [DPNH]-methemoglobin-reductase deficiency
Hemoglobin M [Hb-M] disease
Methemoglobinemia:
   NOS
   acquired (with sulfhemoglobinemia)
   hereditary
   toxic
Stokvis' disease
Sulfhemoglobinemia

Use additional E code, if desired, to identify cause

289.8 **Other specified diseases of blood and blood-forming organs**
Hypergammaglobulinemia   Pseudocholinesterase deficiency
Myelofibrosis

289.9 **Unspecified diseases of blood and blood-forming organs**
Blood dyscrasia NOS   Erythroid hyperplasia

● Code new
   to this edition
▲ Revision of
   existing code
④ ⑤ Fourth or fifth
   digit required

5.   MENTAL DISORDERS (290-319)

In the International Classification of Diseases, 9th Revision (*ICD-9*), the corresponding Chapter V, "Mental Disorders," includes a glossary which defines the contents of each category. The introduction to Chapter V in *ICD-9* indicates that the glossary is intended so that psychiatrists can make the diagnosis based on the descriptions provided rather than from the category titles. Lay coders are instructed to code whatever diagnosis the physician records.

Chapter 5, "Mental Disorders," in *ICD-9-CM* uses the standard classification format with inclusion and exclusion terms, omitting the glossary as part of the main text.

The mental disorders section of *ICD-9-CM* has been expanded to incorporate additional psychiatric disorders not listed in *ICD-9*. The glossary from *ICD-9* does not contain all these terms. It now appears in Appendix B, pages 543-564 which also contains descriptions and definitions for the terms added in *ICD-9-CM*. Some of these were provided by the American Psychiatric Association's Task Force on Nomenclature and Statistics who are preparing the *Diagnostic and Statistical Manual*, Third Edition (DSM-III), and others from *A Psychiatric Glossary*.

The American Psychiatric Association provided invaluable assistance in modifying Chapter 5 of *ICD-9-CM* to incorporate detail useful to American clinicians and gave permission to use material from the aforementioned sources.

1. **Manual of the *International Statistical Classification of Diseases, Injuries, and Causes of Death*, 9th Revision, World Health Organization, Geneva, Switzerland, 1975.**

2. **American Psychiatric Association, Task Force on Nomenclature and Statistics, Robert L. Spitzer, M.D., Chairman.**

3. ***A Psychiatric Glossary*, Fourth Edition, American Psychiatric Association, Washington, D.C., 1975.**

PSYCHOSES (290-299)

> Excludes: *mental retardation (317-319)*

ORGANIC PSYCHOTIC CONDITIONS (290-294)

Includes: psychotic organic brain syndrome

> Excludes: *nonpsychotic syndromes of organic etiology (310.0-310.9)*
>
> *psychoses classifiable to 295-298 and without impairment of orientation, comprehension, calculation, learning capacity, and judgement, but associated with physical disease, injury, or condition affecting the brain [e.g., following childbirth] (295.0-298.8)*

290   Senile and presenile organic psychotic conditions
Code first the associated neurological condition

> Excludes: *dementia not classified as senile, presenile, or arteriosclerotic (294.10-294.11)*
>
> *psychoses classifiable to 295-298 occurring in the senium without dementia or delirium (295.0-298.8)*
> *senility with mental changes of nonpsychotic severity (310.1)*
> *transient organic psychotic conditions (293.0-293.9)*

290.0   Senile dementia, uncomplicated
Senile dementia:
  NOS
  simple type

> Excludes: *mild memory disturbances, not amounting to dementia, associated with senile brain disease (310.1)*
> *senile dementia with:*
>   *delirium or confusion (290.3)*
>   *delusional [paranoid] features (290.20)*
>   *depressive features (290.21)*

⑤ **290.1   Presenile dementia**
Brain syndrome with presenile brain disease

> Excludes: *arteriosclerotic dementia (290.40-290.43)*
>
> *dementia associated with other cerebral conditions (294.10-294.11)*

290.10   Presenile dementia, uncomplicated
Presenile dementia:
  NOS
  simple type

290.11   Presenile dementia with delirium
Presenile dementia with acute confusional state

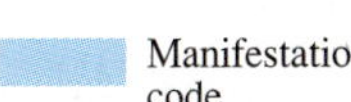

290.12 Presenile dementia with delusional features
Presenile dementia, paranoid type

290.13 Presenile dementia with depressive features
Presenile dementia, depressed type

⑤ **290.2 Senile dementia with delusional or depressive features**

Excludes: *senile dementia:*
NOS (290.0)
with delirium and/or confusion (290.3)

290.20 Senile dementia with delusional features
Senile dementia, paranoid type
Senile psychosis NOS

290.21 Senile dementia with depressive features

290.3 Senile dementia with delirium
Senile dementia with acute confusional state

Excludes: *senile:*
dementia NOS (290.0)
psychosis NOS (290.20)

⑤ **290.4 Arteriosclerotic dementia**
Multi-infarct dementia or psychosis
Use additional code to identify cerebral atherosclerosis (437.0)

Excludes: *suspected cases with no clear evidence of arteriosclerosis (290.9)*

290.40 Arteriosclerotic dementia, uncomplicated
Arteriosclerotic dementia:
NOS
simple type

290.41 Arteriosclerotic dementia with delirium
Arteriosclerotic dementia with acute confusional state

290.42 Arteriosclerotic dementia with delusional features
Arteriosclerotic dementia, paranoid type

290.43 Arteriosclerotic dementia with depressive features
Arteriosclerotic dementia, depressed type

290.8 Other specified senile psychotic conditions
Presbyophrenic psychosis

290.9 Unspecified senile psychotic condition

291 Alcoholic psychoses

Excludes: *alcoholism without psychosis (303.0-303.9)*

291.0 Alcohol withdrawal delirium
Alcoholic delirium   Delirium tremens

Excludes: *alcohol withdrawal (291.81)*

291.1 Alcohol amnestic syndrome
Alcoholic polyneuritic psychosis
Korsakoff's psychosis, alcoholic
Wernicke-Korsakoff syndrome (alcoholic)

291.2 Other alcoholic dementia
Alcoholic dementia NOS
Alcoholism associated with dementia NOS
Chronic alcoholic brain syndrome

291.3 Alcohol withdrawal hallucinosis
Alcoholic:
hallucinosis (acute)
psychosis with hallucinosis

Excludes: *alcohol withdrawal with delirium (291.0)*
schizophrenia (295.0-295.9) and paranoid states (297.0-297.9) taking the form of
chronic hallucinosis with clear consciousness in an alcoholic

● Code new
to this edition

▲ Revision of
existing code

④ ⑤ Fourth or fifth
digit required

291.4 Idiosyncratic alcohol intoxication
　　　Pathologic:
　　　　alcohol intoxication
　　　　drunkenness

　　Excludes: *acute alcohol intoxication (305.0)*
　　　　　　　in alcoholism (303.0)
　　　　　simple drunkenness (305.0)

291.5 Alcoholic jealousy
　　　Alcoholic:
　　　　paranoia
　　　　psychosis, paranoid type

　　Excludes: *nonalcoholic paranoid states (297.0-297.9)*
　　　　　schizophrenia, paranoid type (295.3)

⑤ **291.8 Other specified alcoholic psychosis**

　　　291.81 Alcohol withdrawal
　　　　　Alcohol:
　　　　　　withdrawal syndrome or symptoms
　　　　　　abstinence syndrome or symptoms

　　　Excludes: *alcohol withdrawal:*
　　　　　　delirium (291.0)
　　　　　　hallucinosis (291.3)
　　　　　delirium tremens (291.0)

　　　291.89 Other

291.9 Unspecified alcoholic psychosis
　　　Alcoholic:
　　　　mania NOS
　　　　psychosis NOS
　　　Alcoholism (chronic) with psychosis

292 Drug psychoses
　　　Includes: drug-induced mental disorders
　　　　　　organic brain syndrome associated with consumption of drugs

Use additional code for any associated drug dependence (304.0-304.9)

Use additional E code, if desired, to identify drug

292.0 Drug withdrawal syndrome
　　　Drug:
　　　　abstinence syndrome or symptoms
　　　　withdrawal syndrome or symptoms

⑤ **292.1 Paranoid and/or hallucinatory states induced by drugs**

　　　292.11 Drug-induced organic delusional syndrome
　　　　　Paranoid state induced by drugs

　　　292.12 Drug-induced hallucinosis
　　　　　Hallucinatory state induced by drugs

　　　Excludes: *states following LSD or other hallucinogens, lasting only a few days or less ["bad trips"] (305.3)*

292.2 Pathological drug intoxication
　　　Drug reaction:
　　　　NOS
　　　　idiosyncratic　　} resulting in brief psychotic states
　　　　pathologic

　　Excludes: *expected brief psychotic reactions to hallucinogens ["bad trips"] (305.3)*
　　　　physiological side-effects of drugs (e.g., dystonias)

⑤ **292.8 Other specified drug-induced mental disorders**

　　　292.81 Drug-induced delirium

　　　292.82 Drug-induced dementia

　　　292.83 Drug-induced amnestic syndrome

　　　292.84 Drug-induced organic affective syndrome
　　　　　Depressive state induced by drugs

　　　292.89 Other
　　　　　Drug-induced organic personality syndrome

292.9 Unspecified drug-induced mental disorder
　　　Organic psychosis NOS due to or associated with drugs

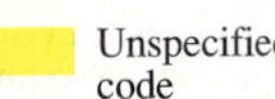

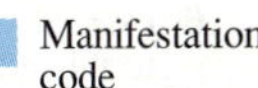

293 Transient organic psychotic conditions
Includes: transient organic mental disorders not associated with alcohol or drugs
Code first the associated physical or neurological condition

Excludes: *confusional state or delirium superimposed on senile dementia (290.3)*
dementia due to:
alcohol (291.0-291.9)
arteriosclerosis (290.40-290.43)
drugs (292.82)
senility (290.0)

293.0 *Acute delirium*
Acute:
confusional state
infective psychosis
organic reaction
posttraumatic organic
psychosis
psycho-organic syndrome

Acute psychosis associated with endocrine, metabolic,
or cerebrovascular disorder
Epileptic:
confusional state
twilight state

293.1 *Subacute delirium*
Subacute:
confusional state
infective psychosis
organic reaction
posttraumatic organic
psychosis

Subacute:
psycho-organic syndrome
psychosis associated with endocrine or metabolic
disorder

⑤ **293.8 *Other specified transient organic mental disorders***

293.81 *Organic delusional syndrome*
Transient organic psychotic condition, paranoid type

293.82 *Organic hallucinosis syndrome*
Transient organic psychotic condition, hallucinatory type

293.83 *Organic affective syndrome*
Transient organic psychotic condition, depressive type

293.84 *Organic anxiety syndrome*

293.89 *Other*

293.9 *Unspecified transient organic mental disorder*
Organic psychosis:
infective NOS
posttraumatic NOS
transient NOS

Psycho-organic syndrome

294 Other organic psychotic conditions (chronic)
Includes: organic psychotic brain syndromes (chronic), not elsewhere classified

294.0 Amnestic syndrome
Korsakoff's psychosis or syndrome (nonalcoholic)

Excludes: *alcoholic:*
amnestic syndrome (291.1)
Korsakoff's psychosis (291.1)

⑤ **294.1 *Dementia in conditions classified elsewhere***
Code first any underlying physical condition, as:
dementia in:
Alzheimer's disease (331.0)
cerebral lipidoses (330.1)
epilepsy (345.0-345.9)
general paresis [syphilis] (094.1)
hepatolenticular degeneration (275.1)
Huntington's chorea (333.4)
Jakob-Creutzfeldt disease (046.1)
multiple sclerosis (340)
Pick's disease of the brain (331.1)
polyarteritis nodosa (446.0)
syphilis (094.1)

Excludes: *dementia:*
arteriosclerotic (290.40-290.43)
presenile (290.10-290.13)
senile (290.0)
epileptic psychosis NOS (294.8)

● Code new
to this edition

▲ Revision of
existing code

④ ⑤ Fourth or fifth
digit required

- *294.10* ***Dementia in conditions classified elsewhere without behavioral disturbance***
  Dementia in conditions classified elsewhere NOS

- *294.11* ***Dementia in conditions classified elsewhere with behavioral disturbance***
  Aggressive behavior
  Combative behavior
  Violent behavior
  Wandering off

294.8 **Other specified organic brain syndromes (chronic)**
Epileptic psychosis NOS
Mixed paranoid and affective organic psychotic states

Use additional code for associated epilepsy (345.0-345.9)

Excludes: *mild memory disturbances, not amounting to dementia (310.1)*

294.9 **Unspecified organic brain syndrome (chronic)**
Organic psychosis (chronic)

OTHER PSYCHOSES (295-299)

Use additional code to identify any associated physical disease, injury, or condition affecting the brain with psychoses classifiable to 295-298

⑤ **295** **Schizophrenic disorders**
Includes: schizophrenia of the types described in 295.0-295.9 occurring in children

Excludes: *childhood type schizophrenia (299.9)*

infantile autism (299.0)

The following fifth-digit subclassification is for use with category 295:

0 **unspecified**

1 **subchronic**

2 **chronic**

3 **subchronic with acute exacerbation**

4 **chronic with acute exacerbation**

5 **in remission**

⑤ **295.0** **Simple type**
Schizophrenia simplex

Excludes: *latent schizophrenia (295.5)*

⑤ **295.1** **Disorganized type**
Hebephrenia
Hebephrenic type schizophrenia

⑤ **295.2** **Catatonic type**

Catatonic (schizophrenia):	Schizophrenic:
agitation	catalepsy
excitation	catatonia
excited type	flexibilitas cerea
stupor	
withdrawn type	

⑤ **295.3** **Paranoid type**
Paraphrenic schizophrenia

Excludes: *involutional paranoid state (297.2)*

paranoia (297.1)
paraphrenia (297.2)

⑤ **295.4** **Acute schizophrenic episode**
Oneirophrenia
Schizophreniform:
  attack
  disorder
  psychosis, confusional type

Excludes: *acute forms of schizophrenia of:*

catatonic type (295.2)
hebephrenic type (295.1)
paranoid type (295.3)
simple type (295.0)
undifferentiated type (295.8)

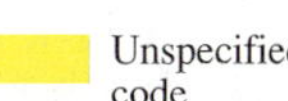

⑤ **295.5 Latent schizophrenia**
Latent schizophrenic reaction   Schizophrenia:
Schizophrenia: prepsychotic
  borderline   prodromal
  incipient   pseudoneurotic
                                            pseudopsychopathic

| *Excludes:* | *schizoid personality (301.20-301.22)* |

⑤ **295.6 Residual schizophrenia**
Chronic undifferentiated schizophrenia
Restzustand (schizophrenic)
Schizophrenic residual state

⑤ **295.7 Schizo-affective type**
Cyclic schizophrenia
Mixed schizophrenic and affective psychosis
Schizo-affective psychosis
Schizophreniform psychosis, affective type

⑤ **295.8 Other specified types of schizophrenia**
Acute (undifferentiated) schizophrenia
Atypical schizophrenia
Cenesthopathic schizophrenia

| *Excludes:* | *infantile autism (299.0)* |

⑤ **295.9 Unspecified schizophrenia**
Schizophrenia: Schizophrenic reaction NOS
  NOS   Schizophreniform psychosis NOS
  mixed NOS
  undifferentiated NOS

296 Affective psychoses
Includes: episodic affective disorders

Excludes:	*neurotic depression (300.4)*
	reactive depressive psychosis (298.0)
	reactive excitation (298.1)

The following fifth-digit subclassification is for use with categories 296.0-296.6:

0 unspecified

1 mild

2 moderate

3 severe, without mention of psychotic behavior

4 severe, specified as with psychotic behavior

5 in partial or unspecified remission

6 in full remission

⑤ **296.0 Manic disorder, single episode**
Hypomania (mild) NOS
Hypomanic psychosis
Mania (monopolar) NOS   } single episode or unspecified
Manic-depressive psychosis or reaction:
  hypomanic
  manic

| *Excludes:* | *circular type, if there was a previous attack of depression (296.4)* |

⑤ **296.1 Manic disorder, recurrent episode**
Any condition classifiable to 296.0, stated to be recurrent

| *Excludes:* | *circular type, if there was a previous attack of depression (296.4)* |

⑤ **296.2 Major depressive disorder, single episode**
Depressive psychosis
Endogenous depression
Involutional melancholia
Manic-depressive psychosis or reaction,   } single episode or unspecified
  depressed type
Monopolar depression
Psychotic depression

● Code new   ▲ Revision of   ④ ⑤ Fourth or fifth
  to this edition   existing code   digit required

⑤ **296.3 Major depressive disorder, recurrent episode**
Any condition classifiable to 296.2, stated to be recurrent

⑤ **296.4 Bipolar affective disorder, manic**
Bipolar disorder, now manic
Manic-depressive psychosis, circular type but currently manic

⑤ **296.5 Bipolar affective disorder, depressed**
Bipolar disorder, now depressed
Manic-depressive psychosis, circular type but currently depressed

⑤ **296.6 Bipolar affective disorder, mixed**
Manic-depressive psychosis, circular type, mixed

296.7 Bipolar affective disorder, unspecified
Atypical bipolar affective disorder NOS
Manic-depressive psychosis, circular type, current condition not specified as either manic
or depressive

⑤ **296.8 Manic-depressive psychosis, other and unspecified**

296.80 Manic-depressive psychosis, unspecified
Manic-depressive:
reaction NOS
syndrome NOS

296.81 Atypical manic disorder

296.82 Atypical depressive disorder

296.89 Other
Manic-depressive psychosis, mixed type

⑤ **296.9 Other and unspecified affective psychoses**

296.90 Unspecified affective psychosis
Affective psychosis NOS
Melancholia NOS

296.99 Other specified affective psychoses
Mood swings:
brief compensatory
rebound

297 Paranoid states (Delusional disorders)
Includes: paranoid disorders

297.0 Paranoid state, simple

297.1 Paranoia
Chronic paranoid psychosis
Sander's disease
Systematized delusions

297.2 Paraphrenia
Involutional paranoid state
Late paraphrenia
Paraphrenia (involutional)

297.3 Shared paranoid disorder
Folie à deux
Induced psychosis or paranoid disorder

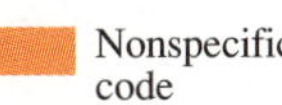

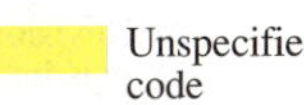

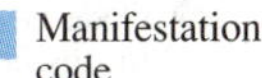

Manifestation
code

297.8 Other specified paranoid states
Paranoia querulans
Sensitiver Beziehungswahn

Excludes: *acute paranoid reaction or state (298.3)*
senile paranoid state (290.20)

297.9 Unspecified paranoid state
Paranoid: Paranoid:
  disorder NOS   reaction NOS
  psychosis   state NOS

298 Other nonorganic psychoses
Includes: psychotic conditions due to or provoked by:
      emotional stress
      environmental factors as major part of etiology

298.0 Depressive type psychosis
Psychogenic depressive psychosis
Psychotic reactive depression
Reactive depressive psychosis

Excludes: *manic-depressive psychosis, depressed type (296.2-296.3)*
neurotic depression (300.4)
reactive depression NOS (300.4)

298.1 Excitative type psychosis
Acute hysterical psychosis   Reactive excitation
Psychogenic excitation

Excludes: *manic-depressive psychosis, manic type (296.0-296.1)*

298.2 Reactive confusion
Psychogenic confusion
Psychogenic twilight state

Excludes: *acute confusional state (293.0)*

298.3 Acute paranoid reaction
Acute psychogenic paranoid psychosis
Bouffée délirante

Excludes: *paranoid states (297.0-297.9)*

298.4 Psychogenic paranoid psychosis
Protracted reactive paranoid psychosis

298.8 Other and unspecified reactive psychosis
Brief reactive psychosis NOS
Hysterical psychosis
Psychogenic psychosis NOS
Psychogenic stupor

Excludes: *acute hysterical psychosis (298.1)*

298.9 Unspecified psychosis
Atypical psychosis   Psychosis NOS

⑤ **299 Psychoses with origin specific to childhood**
Includes: pervasive developmental disorders

Excludes: *adult type psychoses occurring in childhood, as:*
affective disorders (296.0-296.9)
manic-depressive disorders (296.0-296.9)
schizophrenia (295.0-295.9)

The following fifth-digit subclassification is for use with category 299:

0 current or active state

1 residual state

⑤ **299.0 Infantile autism**
Childhood autism   Kanner's syndrome
Infantile psychosis

Excludes: *disintegrative psychosis (299.1)*
Heller's syndrome (299.1)
schizophrenic syndrome of childhood (299.9)

● Code new   ▲ Revision of   ④ ⑤ Fourth or fifth
  to this edition   existing code   digit required

⑤ **299.1 Disintegrative psychosis**
Heller's syndrome

Use additional code to identify any associated neurological disorder

Excludes: *infantile autism (299.0)*
schizophrenic syndrome of childhood (299.9)

⑤ **299.8 Other specified early childhood psychoses**
Atypical childhood psychosis
Borderline psychosis of childhood

Excludes: *simple stereotypies without psychotic disturbance (307.3)*

⑤ **299.9 Unspecified**
Child psychosis NOS
Schizophrenia, childhood type NOS
Schizophrenic syndrome of childhood NOS

Excludes: *schizophrenia of adult type occurring in childhood (295.0-295.9)*

NEUROTIC DISORDERS, PERSONALITY DISORDERS, AND OTHER NONPSYCHOTIC MENTAL DISORDERS (300-316)

300 Neurotic disorders

⑤ **300.0 Anxiety states**

Excludes: *anxiety in:*
acute stress reaction (308.0)
transient adjustment reaction (309.24)
neurasthenia (300.5)
psychophysiological disorders (306.0-306.9)
separation anxiety (309.21)

300.00 Anxiety state, unspecified
Anxiety:
neurosis
reaction
state (neurotic)
Atypical anxiety disorder

300.01 Panic disorder
Panic:
attack
state

300.02 Generalized anxiety disorder

300.09 Other

⑤ **300.1 Hysteria**

Excludes: *adjustment reaction (309.0-309.9)*
anorexia nervosa (307.1)
gross stress reaction (308.0-308.9)
hysterical personality (301.50-301.59)
psychophysiologic disorders (306.0-306.9)

300.10 Hysteria, unspecified

300.11 Conversion disorder
Astasia-abasia, hysterical
Conversion hysteria or reaction
Hysterical:
blindness
deafness
paralysis

300.12 Psychogenic amnesia
Hysterical amnesia

300.13 Psychogenic fugue
Hysterical fugue

300.14 Multiple personality
Dissociative identity disorder

300.15 Dissociative disorder or reaction, unspecified

300.16 Factitious illness with psychological symptoms
Compensation neurosis
Ganser's syndrome, hysterical

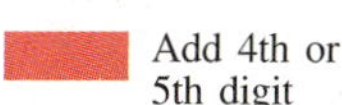
Add 4th or 5th digit

Nonspecific code

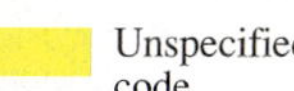
Unspecified code

Manifestation code

300.19 Other and unspecified factitious illness
Factitious illness (with physical symptoms) NOS

Excludes: *multiple operations or hospital addiction syndrome (301.51)*

⑤ **300.2 Phobic disorders**

Excludes: *anxiety state not associated with a specific situation or object (300.0-300.09)*
obsessional phobias (300.3)

300.20 Phobia, unspecified
Anxiety-hysteria NOS
Phobia NOS

300.21 Agoraphobia with panic attacks
Fear of:
open spaces
streets } with panic attacks
travel

300.22 Agoraphobia without mention of panic attacks
Any condition classifiable to 300.21 without mention of panic attacks

300.23 Social phobia
Fear of:
eating in public
public speaking
washing in public

300.29 Other isolated or simple phobias
Acrophobia   Claustrophobia
Animal phobias   Fear of crowds

300.3 Obsessive-compulsive disorders
Anancastic neurosis   Obsessional phobia [any]
Compulsive neurosis

Excludes: *obsessive-compulsive symptoms occurring in:*
endogenous depression (296.2-296.3)
organic states (e.g., encephalitis)
schizophrenia (295.0-295.9)

300.4 Neurotic depression
Anxiety depression   Dysthymic disorder
Depression with anxiety   Neurotic depressive state
Depressive reaction   Reactive depression

Excludes: *adjustment reaction with depressive symptoms (309.0-309.1)*
depression NOS (311)
manic-depressive psychosis, depressed type (296.2-296.3)
reactive depressive psychosis (298.0)

300.5 Neurasthenia
Fatigue neurosis   Psychogenic:
Nervous debility   asthenia
                             general fatigue

Use additional code to identify any associated physical disorder

Excludes: *anxiety state (300.00-300.09)*
neurotic depression (300.4)
psychophysiological disorders (306.0-306.9)
specific nonpsychotic mental disorders following organic brain damage
(310.0-310.9)

300.6 Depersonalization syndrome
Depersonalization disorder
Derealization (neurotic)
Neurotic state with depersonalization episode

Excludes: *depersonalization associated with:*
anxiety (300.00-300.09)
depression (300.4)
manic-depressive disorder or psychosis (296.0-296.9)
schizophrenia (295.0-295.9)

● Code new   ▲ Revision of   ④ ⑤ Fourth or fifth
to this edition   existing code   digit required

300.7 Hypochondriasis
Body dysmorphic disorder

Excludes: *hypochondriasis in:*
hysteria (300.10-300.19)
manic-depressive psychosis, depressed type (296.2-296.3)
neurasthenia (300.5)
obsessional disorder (300.3)
schizophrenia (295.0-295.9)

⑤ **300.8 Other neurotic disorders**

300.81 Somatization disorder
Briquet's disorder
Severe somatoform disorder

300.82 Undifferentiated somatoform disorder
Atypical somatoform disorder
Somatoform disorder NOS

300.89 Other
Occupational neurosis, including writers' cramp
Psychasthenia
Psychasthenic neurosis

300.9 Unspecified neurotic disorder
Neurosis NOS   Psychoneurosis NOS

301 Personality disorders
Includes: character neurosis

Use additional code to identify any associated neurosis or psychosis, or physical condition

Excludes: *nonpsychotic personality disorder associated with organic brain syndromes*
(310.0-310.9)

301.0 Paranoid personality disorder
Fanatic personality
Paranoid personality (disorder)
Paranoid traits

Excludes: *acute paranoid reaction (298.3)*
alcoholic paranoia (291.5)
paranoid schizophrenia (295.3)
paranoid states (297.0-297.9)

⑤ **301.1 Affective personality disorder**

Excludes: *affective psychotic disorders (296.0-296.9)*
neurasthenia (300.5)
neurotic depression (300.4)

301.10 Affective personality disorder, unspecified

301.11 Chronic hypomanic personality disorder
Chronic hypomanic disorder
Hypomanic personality

301.12 Chronic depressive personality disorder
Chronic depressive disorder
Depressive character or personality

301.13 Cyclothymic disorder
Cycloid personality
Cyclothymia
Cyclothymic personality

⑤ **301.2 Schizoid personality disorder**

Excludes: *schizophrenia (295.0-295.9)*

301.20 Schizoid personality disorder, unspecified

301.21 Introverted personality

301.22 Schizotypal personality

301.3 Explosive personality disorder
Aggressive: Emotional instability (excessive)
  personality   Pathological emotionality
  reaction   Quarrelsomeness
Aggressiveness

Excludes: *dyssocial personality (301.7)*
hysterical neurosis (300.10-300.19)

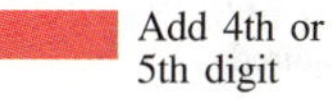

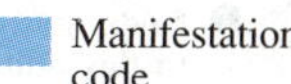

301.4 Compulsive personality disorder
Anancastic personality
Obsessional personality

Excludes: *obsessive-compulsive disorder (300.3)*
phobic state (300.20-300.29)

⑤ **301.5 Histrionic personality disorder**

Excludes: *hysterical neurosis (300.10-300.19)*

301.50 Histrionic personality disorder, unspecified
Hysterical personality NOS

301.51 Chronic factitious illness with physical symptoms
Hospital addiction syndrome
Multiple operations syndrome
Munchausen syndrome

301.59 Other histrionic personality disorder
Personality:
emotionally unstable
labile
psychoinfantile

301.6 Dependent personality disorder
Asthenic personality   Passive personality
Inadequate personality

Excludes: *neurasthenia (300.5)*
passive-aggressive personality (301.84)

301.7 Antisocial personality disorder
Amoral personality
Asocial personality
Dyssocial personality
Personality disorder with predominantly sociopathic or asocial manifestation

Excludes: *disturbance of conduct without specifiable personality disorder (312.0-312.9)*
explosive personality (301.3)

⑤ **301.8 Other personality disorders**

301.81 Narcissistic personality

301.82 Avoidant personality

301.83 Borderline personality

301.84 Passive-aggressive personality

301.89 Other
Personality: Personality:
eccentric   masochistic
"haltlose" type   psychoneurotic
immature

Excludes: *psychoinfantile personality (301.59)*

301.9 Unspecified personality disorder
Pathological personality   Psychopathic:
NOS   constitutional state
Personality disorder NOS   personality (disorder)

302 Sexual deviations and disorders

Excludes: *sexual disorder manifest in:*
organic brain syndrome (290.0-294.9, 310.0-310.9)
psychosis (295.0-298.9)

302.0 Ego-dystonic homosexuality
Ego-dystonic lesbianism
Homosexual conflict disorder

Excludes: *homosexual pedophilia (302.2)*

302.1 Zoophilia
Bestiality

302.2 Pedophilia

302.3 Transvestism

Excludes: *trans-sexualism (302.5)*

302.4 Exhibitionism

● Code new to this edition   ▲ Revision of existing code   ④ ⑤ Fourth or fifth digit required

⑤ **302.5 Trans-sexualism**

> *Excludes:* *transvestism (302.3)*

 302.50 With unspecified sexual history

 302.51 With asexual history

 302.52 With homosexual history

 302.53 With heterosexual history

302.6 Disorders of psychosexual identity
Feminism in boys
Gender identity disorder of childhood

> *Excludes:* *gender identity disorder in adult (302.85)*
> *homosexuality (302.0)*
> *trans-sexualism (302.50-302.53)*
> *transvestism (302.3)*

⑤ **302.7 Psychosexual dysfunction**

> *Excludes:* *impotence of organic origin (607.84)*
> *normal transient symptoms from ruptured hymen*
> *transient or occasional failures of erection due to fatigue, anxiety, alcohol, or drugs*

 302.70 Psychosexual dysfunction, unspecified

 302.71 With inhibited sexual desire

 302.72 With inhibited sexual excitement
  Frigidity   Impotence

 302.73 With inhibited female orgasm

 302.74 With inhibited male orgasm

 302.75 With premature ejaculation

 302.76 With functional dyspareunia
  Dyspareunia, psychogenic

 302.79 With other specified psychosexual dysfunctions

⑤ **302.8 Other specified psychosexual disorders**

 302.81 Fetishism

 302.82 Voyeurism

 302.83 Sexual masochism

 302.84 Sexual sadism

 302.85 Gender identity disorder of adolescent or adult life

 302.89 Other
  Nymphomania   Satyriasis

302.9 Unspecified psychosexual disorder
Pathologic sexuality NOS   Sexual deviation NOS

⑤ **303 Alcohol dependence syndrome**
Use additional code to identify any associated condition, as:
 alcoholic psychoses (291.0-291.9)
 drug dependence (304.0-304.9)
 physical complications of alcohol, such as:
  cerebral degeneration (331.7)
  cirrhosis of liver (571.2)
  epilepsy (345.0-345.9)
  gastritis (535.3)
  hepatitis (571.1)
  liver damage NOS (571.3)

> *Excludes:* *drunkenness NOS (305.0)*

The following fifth-digit subclassification is for use with category 303:

 0 unspecified

 1 continuous

 2 episodic

 3 in remission

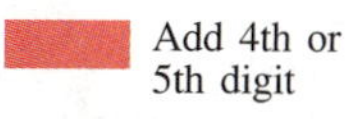 Add 4th or 5th digit

 Nonspecific code

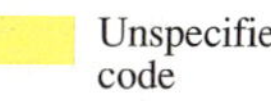 Unspecified code

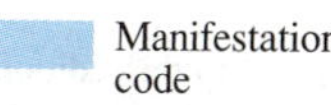 Manifestation code

⑤ **303.0 Acute alcoholic intoxication**
  Acute drunkenness in alcoholism

⑤ **303.9 Other and unspecified alcohol dependence**
  Chronic alcoholism   Dipsomania

⑤ **304 Drug dependence**

  Excludes: *nondependent abuse of drugs (305.1-305.9)*

  The following fifth-digit subclassification is for use with category 304:

  0 unspecified

  1 continuous

  2 episodic

  3 in remission

⑤ **304.0 Opioid type dependence**
  Heroin   Opium alkaloids and their derivatives
  Meperidine   Synthetics with morphine-like effects
  Methadone
  Morphine
  Opium

⑤ **304.1 Barbiturate and similarly acting sedative or hypnotic dependence**
  Barbiturates
  Nonbarbiturate sedatives and tranquilizers with a similar effect:
    chlordiazepoxide
    diazepam
    glutethimide
    meprobamate
    methaqualone

⑤ **304.2 Cocaine dependence**
  Coca leaves and derivatives

⑤ **304.3 Cannabis dependence**
  Hashish   Marihuana
  Hemp

⑤ **304.4 Amphetamine and other psychostimulant dependence**
  Methylphenidate   Phenmetrazine

⑤ **304.5 Hallucinogen dependence**
  Dimethyltryptamine [DMT]
  Lysergic acid diethylamide [LSD] and derivatives
  Mescaline
  Psilocybin

⑤ **304.6 Other specified drug dependence**
  Absinthe addiction   Glue sniffing

  Excludes: *tobacco dependence (305.1)*

⑤ **304.7 Combinations of opioid type drug with any other**

⑤ **304.8 Combinations of drug dependence excluding opioid type drug**

⑤ **304.9 Unspecified drug dependence**
  Drug addiction NOS   Drug dependence NOS

⑤ **305 Nondependent abuse of drugs**

  Note: Includes cases where a person, for whom no other diagnosis is possible, has come under
    medical care because of the maladaptive effect of a drug on which he is not dependent
    and that he has taken on his own initiative to the detriment of his health or social
    functioning.

  Excludes: *alcohol dependence syndrome (303.0-303.9)*
        drug dependence (304.0-304.9)
        drug withdrawal syndrome (292.0)
        poisoning by drugs or medicinal substances (960.0-979.9)

  The following fifth-digit subclassification is for use with codes 305.0, 305.2-305.9:

  0 unspecified

  1 continuous

  2 episodic

  3 in remission

   ● Code new   ▲ Revision of   ④ ⑤ Fourth or fifth
     to this edition   existing code   digit required

⑤ **305.0 Alcohol abuse**
Drunkenness NOS
Excessive drinking of alcohol NOS
"Hangover" (alcohol)
Inebriety NOS

Excludes: *acute alcohol intoxication in alcoholism (303.0)*
alcoholic psychoses (291.0-291.9)

305.1 Tobacco use disorder
Tobacco dependence

Excludes: *history of tobacco use (V15.82)*

⑤ **305.2 Cannabis abuse**

⑤ **305.3 Hallucinogen abuse**
Acute intoxication from hallucinogens ["bad trips"]
LSD reaction

⑤ **305.4 Barbiturate and similarly acting sedative or hypnotic abuse**

⑤ **305.5 Opioid abuse**

⑤ **305.6 Cocaine abuse**

⑤ **305.7 Amphetamine or related acting sympathomimetic abuse**

⑤ **305.8 Antidepressant type abuse**

⑤ **305.9 Other, mixed, or unspecified drug abuse**
"Laxative habit"
Misuse of drugs NOS
Nonprescribed use of drugs or patent medicinals

306 Physiological malfunction arising from mental factors
Includes: psychogenic:
physical symptoms
physiological manifestations   } not involving tissue damage

Excludes: *hysteria (300.11-300.19)*

physical symptoms secondary to a psychiatric disorder classified elsewhere
psychic factors associated with physical conditions involving tissue damage
classified elsewhere (316)
specific nonpsychotic mental disorders following organic brain damage (310.0-310.9)

306.0 Musculoskeletal
Psychogenic paralysis   Psychogenic torticollis

Excludes: *Gilles de la Tourette's syndrome (307.23)*

paralysis as hysterical or conversion reaction (300.11)
tics (307.20-307.22)

306.1 Respiratory
Psychogenic: Psychogenic:
air hunger   hyperventilation
cough   yawning
hiccough

Excludes: *psychogenic asthma (316 and 493.9)*

306.2 Cardiovascular
Cardiac neurosis
Cardiovascular neurosis
Neurocirculatory asthenia
Psychogenic cardiovascular disorder

Excludes: *psychogenic paroxysmal tachycardia (316 and 427.2)*

306.3 Skin
Psychogenic pruritus

Excludes: *psychogenic:*

alopecia (316 and 704.00)
dermatitis (316 and 692.9)
eczema (316 and 691.8 or 692.9)
urticaria (316 and 708.0-708.9)

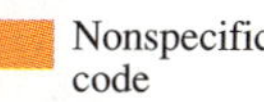

Add 4th or
5th digit

Nonspecific
code

Unspecified
code

Manifestation
code

306.4 Gastrointestinal

Aerophagy

Cyclical vomiting,
  psychogenic

Diarrhea, psychogenic

Nervous gastritis

Psychogenic dyspepsia

Excludes: *cyclical vomiting NOS (536.2)*

globus hystericus (300.11)
mucous colitis (316 and 564.9)
psychogenic:
  cardiospasm (316 and 530.0)
  duodenal ulcer (316 and 532.0-532.9)
  gastric ulcer (316 and 531.0-531.9)
  peptic ulcer NOS (316 and 533.0-533.9)
  vomiting NOS (307.54)

⑤ **306.5 Genitourinary**

Excludes: *enuresis, psychogenic (307.6)*

frigidity (302.72)
impotence (302.72)
psychogenic dyspareunia (302.76)

306.50 Psychogenic genitourinary malfunction, unspecified

306.51 Psychogenic vaginismus

Functional vaginismus

306.52 Psychogenic dysmenorrhea

306.53 Psychogenic dysuria

306.59 Other

306.6 Endocrine

306.7 Organs of special sense

Excludes: *hysterical blindness or deafness (300.11)*

psychophysical visual disturbances (368.16)

306.8 Other specified psychophysiological malfunction

Bruxism

Teeth grinding

306.9 Unspecified psychophysiological malfunction

Psychophysiologic disorder NOS

Psychosomatic disorder NOS

307 Special symptoms or syndromes, not elsewhere classified

Note: This category is intended for use if the psychopathology is manifested by a single specific
symptom or group of symptoms which is not part of an organic illness or other mental
disorder classifiable elsewhere.

Excludes: *those due to mental disorders classified elsewhere*

those of organic origin

307.0 Stammering and stuttering

Excludes: *dysphasia (784.5)*

lisping or lalling (307.9)
retarded development of speech (315.31-315.39)

307.1 Anorexia nervosa

Excludes: *eating disturbance NOS (307.50)*

feeding problem (783.3)
  of nonorganic origin (307.59)
loss of appetite (783.0)
  of nonorganic origin (307.59)

⑤ **307.2 Tics**

Excludes: *nail-biting or thumb-sucking (307.9)*

stereotypies occurring in isolation (307.3)
tics of organic origin (333.3)

307.20 Tic disorder, unspecified

307.21 Transient tic disorder of childhood

307.22 Chronic motor tic disorder

307.23 Gilles de la Tourette's disorder

Motor-verbal tic disorder

● Code new
  to this edition

▲ Revision of
  existing code

④ ⑤ Fourth or fifth
  digit required

307.3 Stereotyped repetitive movements

Body-rocking   Spasmus nutans
Head banging   Stereotypies NOS

Excludes: *tics (307.20-307.23)*
            of organic origin (333.3)

⑤ **307.4 Specific disorders of sleep of nonorganic origin**

Excludes: *narcolepsy (347)*
            those of unspecified cause (780.50-780.59)

307.40 **Nonorganic sleep disorder, unspecified**

307.41 **Transient disorder of initiating or maintaining sleep**

Hyposomnia ⎤
Insomnia   ⎬ associated with acute or intermittent emotional reactions
Sleeplessness ⎦ or conflicts

307.42 **Persistent disorder of initiating or maintaining sleep**

Hyposomnia, insomnia, or sleeplessness associated with:
  anxiety
  conditioned arousal
  depression (major) (minor)
  psychosis

307.43 **Transient disorder of initiating or maintaining wakefulness**

Hypersomnia associated with acute or intermittent emotional reactions or
  conflicts

307.44 **Persistent disorder of initiating or maintaining wakefulness**

Hypersomnia associated with depression (major) (minor)

307.45 **Phase-shift disruption of 24-hour sleep-wake cycle**

Irregular sleep-wake rhythm, nonorganic origin
Jet lag syndrome
Rapid time-zone change
Shifting sleep-work schedule

307.46 **Somnambulism or night terrors**

307.47 **Other dysfunctions of sleep stages or arousal from sleep**

Nightmares: Sleep drunkenness
  NOS
  REM-sleep type

307.48 **Repetitive intrusions of sleep**

Repetitive intrusion of sleep with:
  atypical polysomnographic features
  environmental disturbances
  repeated REM-sleep interruptions

307.49 **Other**

"Short-sleeper"
Subjective insomnia complaint

⑤ **307.5 Other and unspecified disorders of eating**

Excludes: *anorexia:*

        nervosa (307.1)
        of unspecified cause (783.0)
      overeating, of unspecified cause (783.6)
      vomiting:
        NOS (787.0)
        cyclical (536.2)
        psychogenic (306.4)

307.50 **Eating disorder, unspecified**

307.51 **Bulimia**

Overeating of nonorganic origin

307.52 **Pica**

Perverted appetite of nonorganic origin

307.53 **Psychogenic rumination**

Regurgitation, of nonorganic origin, of food with reswallowing

Excludes: *obsessional rumination (300.3)*

307.54 **Psychogenic vomiting**

	Add 4th or 5th digit		Nonspecific code		Unspecified code		Manifestation code

307.59 Other

Infantile feeding disturbances
Loss of appetite } of nonorganic origin

307.6 Enuresis

Enuresis (primary) (secondary) of nonorganic origin

Excludes: *enuresis of unspecified cause (788.3)*

307.7 Encopresis

Encopresis (continuous) (discontinuous) of nonorganic origin

Excludes: *encopresis of unspecified cause (787.6)*

⑤ **307.8 Psychalgia**

307.80 Psychogenic pain, site unspecified

307.81 Tension headache

Excludes: *headache:*
NOS (784.0)
migraine (346.0-346.9)

307.89 Other

Psychogenic backache

Excludes: *pains not specifically attributable to a psychological cause (in):*
back (724.5)
joint (719.4)
limb (729.5)
lumbago (724.2)
rheumatic (729.0)

307.9 Other and unspecified special symptoms or syndromes, not elsewhere classified

Hair plucking	Masturbation
Lalling	Nail-biting
Lisping	Thumb-sucking

308 Acute reaction to stress

Includes: catastrophic stress
combat fatigue
gross stress reaction (acute)
transient disorders in response to exceptional physical or mental stress which
usually subside within hours or days

Excludes: *adjustment reaction or disorder (309.0-309.9)*
chronic stress reaction (309.1-309.9)

308.0 Predominant disturbance of emotions

Anxiety
Emotional crisis } as acute reaction to exceptional [gross] stress
Panic state

308.1 Predominant disturbance of consciousness

Fugues as acute reaction to exceptional [gross] stress

308.2 Predominant psychomotor disturbance

Agitation states } as acute reaction to exceptional [gross] stress
Stupor

308.3 Other acute reactions to stress

Acute situational disturbance
Brief or acute posttraumatic stress disorder

Excludes: *prolonged posttraumatic emotional disturbance (309.81)*

308.4 Mixed disorders as reaction to stress

308.9 Unspecified acute reaction to stress

309 Adjustment reaction

Includes: adjustment disorders
reaction (adjustment) to chronic stress

Excludes: *acute reaction to major stress (308.0-308.9)*
neurotic disorders (300.0-300.9)

● Code new
to this edition

▲ Revision of
existing code

④ ⑤ Fourth or fifth
digit required

309.0 Brief depressive reaction
Adjustment disorder with depressed mood
Grief reaction

Excludes: *affective psychoses (296.0-296.9)*
neurotic depression (300.4)
prolonged depressive reaction (309.1)
psychogenic depressive psychosis (298.0)

309.1 Prolonged depressive reaction

Excludes: *affective psychoses (296.0-296.9)*
brief depressive reaction (309.0)
neurotic depression (300.4)
psychogenic depressive psychosis (298.0)

⑤ **309.2 With predominant disturbance of other emotions**

309.21 Separation anxiety disorder

309.22 Emancipation disorder of adolescence and early adult life

309.23 Specific academic or work inhibition

309.24 Adjustment reaction with anxious mood

309.28 Adjustment reaction with mixed emotional features
Adjustment reaction with anxiety and depression

309.29 Other
Culture shock

309.3 With predominant disturbance of conduct
Conduct disturbance ⎫
Destructiveness ⎭ as adjustment reaction

Excludes: *destructiveness in child (312.9)*
disturbance of conduct NOS (312.9)
dyssocial behavior without manifest psychiatric disorder (V71.01-V71.02)
personality disorder with predominantly sociopathic or asocial manifestations (301.7)

309.4 With mixed disturbance of emotions and conduct

⑤ **309.8 Other specified adjustment reactions**

309.81 Prolonged posttraumatic stress disorder
Chronic posttraumatic stress disorder
Concentration camp syndrome

Excludes: *posttraumatic brain syndrome:*
nonpsychotic (310.2)
psychotic (293.0-293.9)

309.82 Adjustment reaction with physical symptoms

309.83 Adjustment reaction with withdrawal
Elective mutism as adjustment reaction
Hospitalism (in children) NOS

309.89 Other

309.9 Unspecified adjustment reaction
Adaptation reaction NOS   Adjustment reaction NOS

310 Specific nonpsychotic mental disorders due to organic brain damage

Excludes: *neuroses, personality disorders, or other nonpsychotic conditions occurring in a*
form similar to that seen with functional disorders but in association with a
physical condition (300.0-300.9, 301.0-301.9)

310.0 Frontal lobe syndrome
Lobotomy syndrome
Postleucotomy syndrome [state]

Excludes: *postcontusion syndrome (310.2)*

310.1 Organic personality syndrome
Cognitive or personality change of other type, of nonpsychotic severity
Mild memory disturbance
Organic psychosyndrome of nonpsychotic severity
Presbyophrenia NOS
Senility with mental changes of nonpsychotic severity

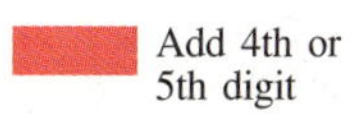

310.2 Postconcussion syndrome
Postcontusion syndrome or encephalopathy
Posttraumatic brain syndrome, nonpsychotic
Status postcommotio cerebri

Excludes: *frontal lobe syndrome (310.0)*
postencephalitic syndrome (310.8)
any organic psychotic conditions following head injury (293.0—294.0)

310.8 Other specified nonpsychotic mental disorders following organic brain damage
Postencephalitic syndrome
Other focal (partial) organic psychosyndromes

310.9 Unspecified nonpsychotic mental disorder following organic brain damage

311 Depressive disorder, not elsewhere classified
Depressive disorder NOS
Depressive state NOS   Depression NOS

Excludes: *acute reaction to major stress with depressive symptoms (308.0)*
affective personality disorder (301.10-301.13)
affective psychoses (296.0-296.9)
brief depressive reaction (309.0)
depressive states associated with stressful events (309.0-309.1)
disturbance of emotions specific to childhood and adolescence, with misery and
*   unhappiness (313.1)*
mixed adjustment reaction with depressive symptoms (309.4)
neurotic depression (300.4)
prolonged depressive adjustment reaction (309.1)
psychogenic depressive psychosis (298.0)

312 Disturbance of conduct, not elsewhere classified

Excludes: *adjustment reaction with disturbance of conduct (309.3)*
drug dependence (304.0-304.9)
dyssocial behavior without manifest psychiatric disorder (V71.01-V71.02)
personality disorder with predominantly sociopathic or asocial manifestations
*   (301.7)*
sexual deviations (302.0-302.9)

The following fifth-digit subclassification is for use with categories 312.0-312.2:

0 unspecified

1 mild

2 moderate

3 severe

⑤ **312.0 Undersocialized conduct disorder, aggressive type**
Aggressive outburst   Unsocialized aggressive disorder
Anger reaction

⑤ **312.1 Undersocialized conduct disorder, unaggressive type**
Childhood truancy,   Solitary stealing
    unsocialized   Tantrums

⑤ **312.2 Socialized conduct disorder**
Childhood truancy, socialized
Group delinquency

Excludes: *gang activity without manifest psychiatric disorder (V71.01)*

⑤ **312.3 Disorders of impulse control, not elsewhere classified**

312.30 Impulse control disorder, unspecified

312.31 Pathological gambling

312.32 Kleptomania

312.33 Pyromania

312.34 Intermittent explosive disorder

312.35 Isolated explosive disorder

312.39 Other

312.4 Mixed disturbance of conduct and emotions
Neurotic delinquency

Excludes: *compulsive conduct disorder (312.3)*

⑤ **312.8 Other specified disturbances of conduct, not elsewhere classified**

   ● Code new   ▲ Revision of   ④ ⑤ Fourth or fifth
     to this edition   existing code   digit required

312.81   **Conduct disorder, childhood onset type**

312.82   **Conduct disorder, adolescent onset type**

312.89   **Other conduct disorder**

312.9 **Unspecified disturbance of conduct**
Delinquency (juvenile)

313 **Disturbance of emotions specific to childhood and adolescence**

Excludes: *adjustment reaction (309.0-309.9)*
emotional disorder of neurotic type (300.0-300.9)
masturbation, nail-biting, thumb-sucking, and other isolated symptoms (307.0-307.9)

313.0 **Overanxious disorder**
Anxiety and fearfulness
Overanxious disorder   } of childhood and adolescence

Excludes: *abnormal separation anxiety (309.21)*
anxiety states (300.00-300.09)
hospitalism in children (309.83)
phobic state (300.20-300.29)

313.1 **Misery and unhappiness disorder**

Excludes: *depressive neurosis (300.4)*

⑤ **313.2** **Sensitivity, shyness, and social withdrawal disorder**

Excludes: *infantile autism (299.0)*
schizoid personality (301.20-301.22)
schizophrenia (295.0-295.9)

313.21   **Shyness disorder of childhood**
Sensitivity reaction of childhood or adolescence

313.22   **Introverted disorder of childhood**
Social withdrawal
Withdrawal reaction   } of childhood or adolescence

313.23   **Elective mutism**

Excludes: *elective mutism as adjustment reaction (309.83)*

313.3 **Relationship problems**
Sibling jealousy

Excludes: *relationship problems associated with aggression, destruction, or other forms of*
conduct disturbance (312.0-312.9)

⑤ **313.8** **Other or mixed emotional disturbances of childhood or adolescence**

313.81   **Oppositional disorder**

313.82   **Identity disorder**

313.83   **Academic underachievement disorder**

313.89   **Other**

313.9 **Unspecified emotional disturbance of childhood or adolescence**

314 **Hyperkinetic syndrome of childhood**

Excludes: *hyperkinesis as symptom of underlying disorder—code the underlying disorder*

⑤ **314.0** **Attention deficit disorder**
Adult
Child

314.00   **Without mention of hyperactivity**
Predominantly inattentive type

314.01   **With hyperactivity**
Combined type
Overactivity NOS
Predominantly hyperactive/impulsive type
Simple disturbance of attention with overactivity

314.1 **Hyperkinesis with developmental delay**
Developmental disorder of hyperkinesis
Use additional code to identify any associated neurological disorder

314.2 **Hyperkinetic conduct disorder**
Hyperkinetic conduct disorder without developmental delay

Excludes: *hyperkinesis with significant delays in specific skills (314.1)*

Add 4th or 5th digit	Nonspecific code	Unspecified code	Manifestation code

314.8 Other specified manifestations of hyperkinetic syndrome

314.9 Unspecified hyperkinetic syndrome
Hyperkinetic reaction of childhood or adolescence NOS
Hyperkinetic syndrome NOS

315 Specific delays in development

Excludes: *that due to a neurological disorder (320.0-389.9)*

⑤ **315.0 Specific reading disorder**

315.00 Reading disorder, unspecified

315.01 Alexia

315.02 Developmental dyslexia

315.09 Other
Specific spelling difficulty

315.1 Specific arithmetical disorder
Dyscalculia

315.2 Other specific learning difficulties

Excludes: *specific arithmetical disorder (315.1)*
specific reading disorder (315.00-315.09)

⑤ **315.3 Developmental speech or language disorder**

315.31 Developmental language disorder
Developmental aphasia
Expressive language disorder
Word deafness

Excludes: *acquired aphasia (784.3)*
elective mutism (309.83, 313.0, 313.23)

315.32 Receptive language disorder (mixed)
Receptive expressive language disorder

315.39 Other
Developmental articulation disorder
Dyslalia

Excludes: *lisping and lalling (307.9)*
stammering and stuttering (307.0)

315.4 Coordination disorder
Clumsiness syndrome
Dyspraxia syndrome
Specific motor development disorder

315.5 Mixed development disorder

315.8 Other specified delays in development

315.9 Unspecified delay in development
Developmental disorder NOS

316 Psychic factors associated with diseases classified elsewhere
Psychologic factors in physical conditions classified elsewhere
Use additional code to identify the associated physical condition, as:
psychogenic:
asthma (493.9)
dermatitis (692.9)
duodenal ulcer (532.0-532.9)
eczema (691.8, 692.9)
gastric ulcer (531.0-531.9)
mucous colitis (564.9)
paroxysmal tachycardia (427.2)
ulcerative colitis (556)
urticaria (708.0-708.9)
psychosocial dwarfism (259.4)

Excludes: *physical symptoms and physiological malfunctions, not involving tissue damage, of*
mental origin (306.0-306.9)

● Code new
to this edition

▲ Revision of
existing code

④ ⑤ Fourth or fifth
digit required

MENTAL RETARDATION (317-319)

Use additional code(s) to identify any associated psychiatric or physical condition(s)

317 Mild mental retardation
High-grade defect
IQ 50-70

Mild mental subnormality

318 Other specified mental retardation

318.0 Moderate mental retardation
IQ 35-49

Moderate mental subnormality

318.1 Severe mental retardation
IQ 20-34
Severe mental subnormality

318.2 Profound mental retardation
IQ under 20

Profound mental subnormality

319 Unspecified mental retardation
Mental deficiency NOS

Mental subnormality NOS

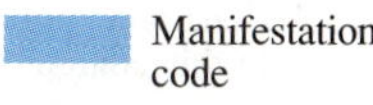

Manifestation
code

● Code new
to this edition

▲ Revision of
existing code

④ ⑤ Fourth or fifth
digit required

6. DISEASES OF THE NERVOUS SYSTEM AND SENSE ORGANS (320-389)

INFLAMMATORY DISEASES OF THE CENTRAL NERVOUS SYSTEM (320-326)

320 Bacterial meningitis

Includes:

arachnoiditis
leptomeningitis
meningitis
meningoencephalitis } bacterial
meningomyelitis
pachymeningitis

320.0 Hemophilus meningitis

Meningitis due to Hemophilus influenzae [H. influenzae]

320.1 Pneumococcal meningitis

320.2 Streptococcal meningitis

320.3 Staphylococcal meningitis

320.7 *Meningitis in other bacterial diseases classified elsewhere*

Code first underlying disease, as:
actinomycosis (039.8)
listeriosis (027.0)
typhoid fever (002.0)
whooping cough (033.0-033.9)

Excludes: *meningitis (in):*

epidemic (036.0)
gonococcal (098.82)
meningococcal (036.0)
salmonellosis (003.21)
syphilis:
NOS (094.2)
congenital (090.42)
meningovascular (094.2)
secondary (091.81)
tuberculous (013.0)

⑤ **320.8 Meningitis due to other specified bacteria**

320.81 Anaerobic meningitis

Bacteroides (fragilis)
Gram-negative anaerobes

320.82 Meningitis due to Gram-negative bacteria, not elsewhere classified

Aerobacter aerogenes
Escherichia coli [E. coli]
Friedlander bacillus
Klebsiella pneumoniae
Proteus morganii
Pseudomonas

Excludes: *Gram-negative anaerobes (320.81)*

320.89 Meningitis due to other specified bacteria

Bacillus pyocyaneus

320.9 Meningitis due to unspecified bacterium

Meningitis:　　　　　　　　　Meningitis:
bacterial NOS　　　　　　　　pyogenic NOS
purulent NOS　　　　　　　　suppurative NOS

321 Meningitis due to other organisms

Includes:

arachnoiditis
leptomeningitis } due to organisms other than bacteria
meningitis
pachymeningitis

321.0 *Cryptococcal meningitis*

Code first underlying disease (117.5)

321.1 *Meningitis in other fungal diseases*

Code first underlying disease (110.0-118)

Excludes: *meningitis in:*

Manifestation
code

candidiasis (112.83)
coccidioidomycosis (114.2)
histoplasmosis (115.01, 115.11, 115.91)

321.2 **Meningitis due to viruses not elsewhere classified**
Code first underlying disease, as:
meningitis due to arbovirus (060.0-066.9)

Excludes: *meningitis (due to):*
abacterial (047.0-047.9)
adenovirus (049.1)
aseptic NOS (047.9)
Coxsackie (virus) (047.0)
ECHO virus (047.1)
enterovirus (047.0-047.9)
herpes simplex virus (054.72)
herpes zoster virus (053.0)
lymphocytic choriomeningitis virus (049.0)
mumps (072.1)
viral NOS (047.9)
meningo-eruptive syndrome (047.1)

321.3 **Meningitis due to trypanosomiasis**
Code first underlying disease (086.0-086.9)

321.4 **Meningitis in sarcoidosis**
Code first underlying disease (135)

321.8 **Meningitis due to other nonbacterial organisms classified elsewhere**
Code first underlying disease

Excludes: *leptospiral meningitis (100.81)*

322 **Meningitis of unspecified cause**
Includes:

arachnoiditis
leptomeningitis   } with no organism specified as cause
meningitis
pachymeningitis

322.0 **Nonpyogenic meningitis**
Meningitis with clear cerebrospinal fluid

322.1 **Eosinophilic meningitis**

322.2 **Chronic meningitis**

322.9 **Meningitis, unspecified**

323 **Encephalitis, myelitis, and encephalomyelitis**
Includes: acute disseminated encephalomyelitis
meningoencephalitis, except bacterial
meningomyelitis, except bacterial
myelitis (acute):
ascending
transverse

Excludes: *bacterial:*
meningoencephalitis (320.0-320.9)
meningomyelitis (320.0-320.9)

323.0 **Encephalitis in viral diseases classified elsewhere**
Code first underlying disease, as:
cat-scratch disease (078.3)
infectious mononucleosis (075)
ornithosis (073.7)

Excludes: *encephalitis (in):*
arthropod-borne viral (062.0-064)
herpes simplex (054.3)
mumps (072.2)
poliomyelitis (045.0-045.9)
rubella (056.01)
slow virus infections of central nervous system (046.0-046.9)
other viral diseases of central nervous system (049.8-049.9)
viral NOS (049.9)

323.1 **Encephalitis in rickettsial diseases classified elsewhere**
Code first underlying disease (080-083.9)

● Code new   ▲ Revision of   ④ ⑤ Fourth or fifth
  to this edition   existing code   digit required

323.2 *Encephalitis in protozoal diseases classified elsewhere*
Code first underlying disease, as:
malaria (084.0-084.9)
trypanosomiasis (086.0-086.9)

323.4 *Other encephalitis due to infection classified elsewhere*
Code first underlying disease

Excludes: *encephalitis (in):*

meningococcal (036.1)
syphilis:
NOS (094.81)
congenital (090.41)
toxoplasmosis (130.0)
tuberculosis (013.6)
meningoencephalitis due to free-living ameba [Naegleria] (136.2)

323.5 **Encephalitis following immunization procedures**
Encephalitis
Encephalomyelitis } postimmunization or postvaccinal

Use additional E code, if desired, to identify vaccine

323.6 *Postinfectious encephalitis*
Code first underlying disease

Excludes: *encephalitis:*

postchickenpox (052.0)
postmeasles (055.0)

323.7 *Toxic encephalitis*
Code first underlying cause, as:
carbon tetrachloride (982.1)
hydroxyquinoline derivatives (961.3)
lead (984.0-984.9)
mercury (985.0)
thallium (985.8)

323.8 **Other causes of encephalitis**

323.9 **Unspecified cause of encephalitis**

324 **Intracranial and intraspinal abscess**

324.0 **Intracranial abscess**

Abscess (embolic):
cerebellar
cerebral

Abscess (embolic) of brain [any part]:
epidural
extradural
otogenic
subdural

Excludes: *tuberculous (013.3)*

324.1 **Intraspinal abscess**
Abscess (embolic) of spinal cord [any part]:
epidural
extradural
subdural

Excludes: *tuberculous (013.5)*

324.9 **Of unspecified site**
Extradural or subdural abscess NOS

325 **Phlebitis and thrombophlebitis of intracranial venous sinuses**
Embolism
Endophlebitis
Phlebitis, septic or suppurative
Thrombophlebitis
Thrombosis } of cavernous, lateral, or other intracranial or unspecified intracranial venous sinus

Excludes: *that specified as:*

complicating pregnancy, childbirth, or the puerperium (671.5)
of nonpyogenic origin (437.6)

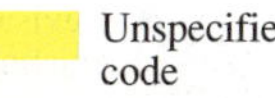

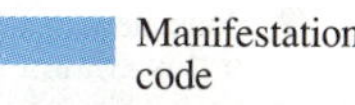

Manifestation
code

326 Late effects of intracranial abscess or pyogenic infection

Note: This category is to be used to indicate conditions whose primary classification is to 320-325 [excluding 320.7, 321.0-321.8, 323.0-323.4, 323.6-323.7] as the cause of late effects, themselves classifiable elsewhere. The "late effects" include conditions specified as such, or as sequelae, which may occur at any time after the resolution of the causal condition.

Use additional code, if desired, to identify condition, as:
hydrocephalus (331.4)
paralysis (342.0-342.9, 344.0-344.9)

HEREDITARY AND DEGENERATIVE DISEASES OF THE CENTRAL NERVOUS SYSTEM (330-337)

Excludes: *hepatolenticular degeneration (275.1)*

multiple sclerosis (340)
other demyelinating diseases of central nervous system (341.0-341.9)

330 Cerebral degenerations usually manifest in childhood

Use additional code, if desired, to identify associated mental retardation

330.0 Leukodystrophy

Krabbe's disease
Leukodystrophy:
  NOS
  globoid cell

Leukodystrophy:
  metachromatic
  sudanophilic
Pelizaeus-Merzbacher disease
Sulfatide lipidosis

330.1 Cerebral lipidoses

Amaurotic (familial) idiocy
Disease:
  Batten
  Jansky-Bielschowsky

Disease:
  Kufs'
  Spielmeyer-Vogt
  Tay-Sachs
Gangliosidosis

330.2 *Cerebral degeneration in generalized lipidoses*
Code first underlying disease, as:
Fabry's disease (272.7)
Gaucher's disease (272.7)
Neimann-Pick disease (272.7)
sphingolipidosis (272.7)

330.3 *Cerebral degeneration of childhood in other diseases classified elsewhere*
Code first underlying disease, as:
Hunter's disease (277.5)
mucopolysaccharidosis (277.5)

330.8 Other specified cerebral degenerations in childhood
Alpers' disease or gray-matter degeneration
Infantile necrotizing encephalomyelopathy
Leigh's disease
Subacute necrotizing encephalopathy or encephalomyelopathy

330.9 Unspecified cerebral degeneration in childhood

331 Other cerebral degenerations

331.0 Alzheimer's disease

331.1 Pick's disease

331.2 Senile degeneration of brain

Excludes: *senility NOS (797)*

331.3 Communicating hydrocephalus

Excludes: *congenital hydrocephalus (741.0, 742.3)*

331.4 Obstructive hydrocephalus
Acquired hydrocephalus NOS

Excludes: *congenital hydrocephalus (741.0, 742.3)*

● Code new
to this edition

▲ Revision of
existing code

④ ⑤ Fourth or fifth
digit required

331.7   Cerebral degeneration in diseases classified elsewhere
Code first underlying disease, as:
alcoholism (303.0-303.9)
beriberi (265.0)
cerebrovascular disease (430-438)
congenital hydrocephalus (741.0, 742.3)
neoplastic disease (140.0-239.9)
myxedema (244.0-244.9)
vitamin B_{12} deficiency (266.2)

Excludes: *cerebral degeneration in:*

Jakob-Creutzfeldt disease (046.1)
progressive multifocal leukoencephalopathy (046.3)
subacute spongiform encephalopathy (046.1)

⑤ **331.8   Other cerebral degeneration**

331.81   Reye's syndrome

331.89   Other
Cerebral ataxia

331.9   Cerebral degeneration, unspecified

332   Parkinson's disease

332.0   Paralysis agitans
Parkinsonism or Parkinson's disease:
NOS
idiopathic
primary

332.1   Secondary Parkinsonism
Parkinsonism due to drugs

Use additional E code, if desired, to identify drug, if drug-induced

Excludes: *Parkinsonism (in):*

Huntington's disease (333.4)
progressive supranuclear palsy (333.0)
Shy-Drager syndrome (333.0)
syphilitic (094.82)

333   Other extrapyramidal disease and abnormal movement disorders
Includes: other forms of extrapyramidal, basal ganglia, or striatopallidal disease

Excludes: *abnormal movements of head NOS (781.0)*

333.0   Other degenerative diseases of the basal ganglia
Atrophy or degeneration:
olivopontocerebellar [Déjérine-Thomas syndrome]
pigmentary pallidal [Hallervorden-Spatz disease]
striatonigral
Parkinsonian syndrome associated with:
idiopathic orthostatic hypotension
symptomatic orthostatic hypotension
Progressive supranuclear ophthalmoplegia
Shy-Drager syndrome

333.1   Essential and other specified forms of tremor
Benign essential tremor   Familial tremor

Use additional E code, if desired, to identify drug, if drug-induced

Excludes: *tremor NOS (781.0)*

333.2   Myoclonus
Familial essential myoclonus
Progressive myoclonic epilepsy
Unverricht-Lundborg disease

Use additional E code, if desired, to identify drug, if drug-induced

333.3   Tics of organic origin

Excludes: *Gilles de la Tourette's syndrome (307.23)*

habit spasm (307.22)
tic NOS (307.20)

Use additional E code, if desired, to identify drug, if drug-induced

333.4   Huntington's chorea

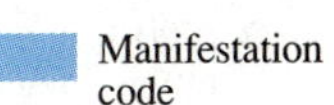

333.5 **Other choreas**
    Hemiballism(us)
    Paroxysmal choreo-athetosis

    Excludes: *Sydenham's or rheumatic chorea (392.0-392.9)*

Use additional E code, if desired, to identify drug, if drug-induced

333.6 **Idiopathic torsion dystonia**
    Dystonia:
      deformans progressiva
      musculorum deformans
    (Schwalbe-) Ziehen-Oppenheim disease

333.7 **Symptomatic torsion dystonia**
    Athetoid cerebral palsy [Vogt's disease]
    Double athetosis (syndrome)

Use additional E code, if desired, to identify drug, if drug-induced

⑤ **333.8** **Fragments of torsion dystonia**

Use additional E code, if desired, to identify drug, if drug-induced

    333.81 **Blepharospasm**

    333.82 **Orofacial dyskinesia**

    333.83 **Spasmodic torticollis**

    Excludes: *torticollis:*
        NOS (723.5)
        hysterical (300.11)
        psychogenic (306.0)

    333.84 **Organic writers' cramp**

    Excludes: *psychogenic (300.89)*

    333.89 **Other**

⑤ **333.9** **Other and unspecified extrapyramidal diseases and abnormal movement disorders**

    333.90 **Unspecified extrapyramidal disease and abnormal movement disorder**

    333.91 **Stiff-man syndrome**

    333.92 **Neuroleptic malignant syndrome**
      Use additional E code to identify drug

    333.93 **Benign shuddering attacks**

    333.99 **Other**
      Restless legs

334 **Spinocerebellar disease**

    Excludes: *olivopontocerebellar degeneration (333.0)*
        peroneal muscular atrophy (356.1)

334.0 **Friedreich's ataxia**

334.1 **Hereditary spastic paraplegia**

334.2 **Primary cerebellar degeneration**
    Cerebellar ataxia:
      Marie's
      Sanger-Brown
    Dyssynergia cerebellaris myoclonica
    Primary cerebellar degeneration:
      NOS
      hereditary
      sporadic

334.3 **Other cerebellar ataxia**
    Cerebellar ataxia NOS

Use additional E code, if desired, to identify drug, if drug-induced

334.4 *Cerebellar ataxia in diseases classified elsewhere*
    Code first underlying disease, as:
      alcoholism (303.0-303.9)
      myxedema (244.0-244.9)
      neoplastic disease (140.0-239.9)

334.8 **Other spinocerebellar diseases**
    Ataxia-telangiectasia [Louis-Bar syndrome]
    Corticostriatal-spinal degeneration

334.9 **Spinocerebellar disease, unspecified**

● Code new to this edition   ▲ Revision of existing code   ④ ⑤ Fourth or fifth digit required

335 **Anterior horn cell disease**

335.0 **Werdnig-Hoffmann disease**
Infantile spinal muscular atrophy
Progressive muscular atrophy of infancy

⑤ **335.1** **Spinal muscular atrophy**

335.10 **Spinal muscular atrophy, unspecified**

335.11 **Kugelberg-Welander disease**
Spinal muscular atrophy:
familial
juvenile

335.19 **Other**
Adult spinal muscular atrophy

⑤ **335.2** **Motor neuron disease**

335.20 **Amyotrophic lateral sclerosis**
Motor neuron disease (bulbar) (mixed type)

335.21 **Progressive muscular atrophy**
Duchenne-Aran muscular atrophy
Progressive muscular atrophy (pure)

335.22 **Progressive bulbar palsy**

335.23 **Pseudobulbar palsy**

335.24 **Primary lateral sclerosis**

335.29 **Other**

335.8 **Other anterior horn cell diseases**

335.9 **Anterior horn cell disease, unspecified**

336 **Other diseases of spinal cord**

336.0 **Syringomyelia and syringobulbia**

336.1 **Vascular myelopathies**
Acute infarction of spinal cord (embolic) (nonembolic)
Arterial thrombosis of spinal cord
Edema of spinal cord
Hematomyelia
Subacute necrotic myelopathy

336.2 *Subacute combined degeneration of spinal cord in diseases classified elsewhere*
Code first underlying disease, as:
pernicious anemia (281.0)
other vitamin B_{12} deficiency anemia (281.1)
vitamin B_{12} deficiency (266.2)

336.3 *Myelopathy in other diseases classified elsewhere*
Code first underlying disease, as:
myelopathy in neoplastic disease (140.0-239.9)

| Excludes: | *myelopathy in:* |
intervertebral disc disorder (722.70-722.73)
spondylosis (721.1, 721.41-721.42, 721.91)

336.8 **Other myelopathy**
Myelopathy:
drug-induced
radiation-induced
Use additional E code, if desired, to identify cause

336.9 **Unspecified disease of spinal cord**
Cord compression NOS   Myelopathy NOS

| Excludes: | *myelitis (323.0-323.9)* |
spinal (canal) stenosis (723.0, 724.00-724.09)

337 **Disorders of the autonomic nervous system**
Includes: disorders of peripheral autonomic, sympathetic, parasympathetic, or vegetative system

| Excludes: | *familial dysautonomia [Riley-Day syndrome] (742.8)* |

337.0 **Idiopathic peripheral autonomic neuropathy**
Carotid sinus syncope or syndrome
Cervical sympathetic dystrophy or paralysis

| Add 4th or 5th digit | Nonspecific code | Unspecified code | Manifestation code |

337.1 *Peripheral autonomic neuropathy in disorders classified elsewhere*
Code first underlying disease, as:
amyloidosis (277.3)
diabetes (250.6)

⑤ **337.2 Reflex sympathetic dystrophy**

337.20 **Reflex sympathetic dystrophy, unspecified**

337.21 **Reflex sympathetic dystrophy of the upper limb**

337.22 **Reflex sympathetic dystrophy of the lower limb**

337.29 **Reflex sympathetic dystrophy of other specified site**

337.3 Autonomic dysreflexia

Use additional code to identify the underlying cause, such as:
decubitus ulcer (707.0)
fecal impaction (560.39)
urinary tract infection (599.0)

337.9 Unspecified disorder of autonomic nervous system

OTHER DISORDERS OF THE CENTRAL NERVOUS SYSTEM (340-349)

340 Multiple sclerosis
Disseminated or multiple sclerosis:
NOS
brain stem
cord
generalized

341 Other demyelinating diseases of central nervous system

341.0 Neuromyelitis optica

341.1 Schilder's disease
Baló's concentric sclerosis
Encephalitis periaxialis:
concentrica [Baló's]
diffusa [Schilder's]

341.8 Other demyelinating diseases of central nervous system
Central demyelination of corpus callosum
Central pontine myelinosis
Marchiafava (-Bignami) disease

341.9 Demyelinating disease of central nervous system, unspecified

⑤ **342 Hemiplegia and hemiparesis**

Excludes: *congenital (343.1)*
hemiplegia due to late effect of cerebrovascular accident (438.20-438.22)
infantile NOS (343.4)

Note: This category is to be used when hemiplegia (complete) (incomplete) is reported without further specification, or is stated to be old or long-standing but of unspecified cause. The category is also for use in multiple coding to identify these types of hemiplegia resulting from any cause.

The following fifth-digits are for use with codes 342.0-342.9

0 **affecting unspecified site**

1 **affecting dominant site**

2 **affecting nondominant site**

⑤ **342.0 Flaccid hemiplegia**

⑤ **342.1 Spastic hemiplegia**

⑤ **342.8 Other specified hemiplegia**

⑤ **342.9 Hemiplegia, unspecified**

● Code new
to this edition

▲ Revision of
existing code

④ ⑤ Fourth or fifth
digit required

343 Infantile cerebral palsy
Includes: cerebral:
palsy NOS
spastic infantile paralysis
congenital spastic paralysis (cerebral)
Little's disease
paralysis (spastic) due to birth injury:
intracranial
spinal

Excludes: *hereditary cerebral paralysis, such as:*
hereditary spastic paraplegia (334.1)
Vogt's disease (333.7)
spastic paralysis specified as noncongenital or noninfantile (344.0-344.9)

343.0 Diplegic
Congenital diplegia   Congenital paraplegia

343.1 Hemiplegic
Congenital hemiplegia

Excludes: *infantile hemiplegia NOS (343.4)*

343.2 Quadriplegic
Tetraplegic

343.3 Monoplegic

343.4 Infantile hemiplegia
Infantile hemiplegia (postnatal) NOS

343.8 Other specified infantile cerebral palsy

343.9 Infantile cerebral palsy, unspecified
Cerebral palsy NOS

344 Other paralytic syndromes
Note: This category is to be used when the listed conditions are reported without further
specification or are stated to be old or long-standing but of unspecified cause. The category
is also for use in multiple coding to identify these conditions resulting from any cause.
Includes: paralysis (complete) (incomplete), except as classifiable to 342 and 343

Excludes: *congenital or infantile cerebral palsy (343.0-343.9)*
hemiplegia (342.0-342.9)
congenital or infantile (343.1, 343.4)

⑤ **344.0 Quadriplegia and quadriparesis**

344.00 Quadriplegia, unspecified

344.01 C1-C4, complete

344.02 C1-C4, incomplete

344.03 C5-C7, complete

344.04 C5-C7, incomplete

344.09 Other

344.1 Paraplegia
Paralysis of both lower limbs
Paraplegia (lower)

344.2 Diplegia of upper limbs
Diplegia (upper)
Paralysis of both upper limbs

⑤ **344.3 Monoplegia of lower limb**
Paralysis of lower limb

Excludes: *monoplegia of lower limb due to late effect of cerebrovascular accident*
(438.40-438.42)

344.30 affecting unspecified side

344.31 affecting dominant side

344.32 affecting nondominant side

⑤ **344.4 Monoplegia of upper limb**
Paralysis of upper limb

Excludes: *monoplegia of upper limb due to late effect of cerebrovascular accident*
(438.30-438.32)

344.40 affecting unspecified side

Add 4th or 5th digit   Nonspecific code   Unspecified code   Manifestation code

344.41 **affecting dominant side**

344.42 **affecting nondominant side**

344.5 **Unspecified monoplegia**

⑤ **344.6** **Cauda equina syndrome**

344.60 **Without mention of neurogenic bladder**

344.61 **With neurogenic bladder**
Acontractile bladder
Autonomic hyperreflexia of bladder
Cord bladder
Detrusor hyperreflexia

⑤ **344.8** **Other specified paralytic syndromes**

344.81 **Locked-in state**

344.89 **Other specified paralytic syndrome**

344.9 **Paralysis, unspecified**

345 **Epilepsy**

The following fifth-digit subclassification is for use with categories 345.0, 345.1, 345.4-345.9:

0 **without mention of intractable epilepsy**

1 **with intractable epilepsy**

Excludes: *progressive myoclonic epilepsy (333.2)*

⑤ **345.0** **Generalized nonconvulsive epilepsy**
Absences: Pykno-epilepsy
  atonic   Seizures:
  typical   akinetic
Minor epilepsy   atonic
Petit mal

⑤ **345.1** **Generalized convulsive epilepsy**
Epileptic seizures: Grand mal
  clonic   Major epilepsy
  myoclonic
  tonic
  tonic-clonic

Excludes: *convulsions:*

NOS (780.3)
infantile (780.3)
newborn (779.0)
infantile spasms (345.6)

345.2 **Petit mal status**
Epileptic absence status

345.3 **Grand mal status**
Status epilepticus NOS

Excludes: *epilepsia partialis continua (345.7)*

status:
psychomotor (345.7)
temporal lobe (345.7)

⑤ **345.4** **Partial epilepsy, with impairment of consciousness**
Epilepsy:
  limbic system
  partial:
    secondarily generalized
    with memory and ideational disturbances
  psychomotor
  psychosensory
  temporal lobe
Epileptic automatism

⑤ **345.5** **Partial epilepsy, without mention of impairment of consciousness**
Epilepsy: Epilepsy:
  Bravais-Jacksonian NOS sensory-induced
  focal (motor) NOS   somatomotor
  Jacksonian NOS   somatosensory
  motor partial   visceral
  partial NOS   visual

● Code new to this edition   ▲ Revision of existing code   ④ ⑤ Fourth or fifth digit required

⑤ **345.6 Infantile spasms**
    Hypsarrhythmia   Salaam attacks
    Lightning spasms

Excludes: salaam tic (781.0)

⑤ **345.7 Epilepsia partialis continua**
    Kojevnikov's epilepsy

⑤ **345.8 Other forms of epilepsy**
    Epilepsy:
      cursive [running]
      gelastic

⑤ **345.9 Epilepsy, unspecified**
    Epileptic convulsions, fits, or seizures NOS

Excludes: convulsive seizure or fit NOS (780.3)

⑤ **346 Migraine**

The following fifth-digit subclassification is for use with category 346:

    0 without mention of intractable migraine

    1 with intractable migraine, so stated

⑤ **346.0 Classical migraine**
    Migraine preceded or accompanied by transient focal neurological phenomena
    Migraine with aura

⑤ **346.1 Common migraine**
    Atypical migraine   Sick headache

⑤ **346.2 Variants of migraine**
    Cluster headache   Migraine:
    Histamine cephalgia   lower half
    Horton's neuralgia   retinal
    Migraine: Neuralgia:
      abdominal   ciliary
      basilar   migrainous

⑤ **346.8 Other forms of migraine**
    Migraine:
      hemiplegic
      ophthalmoplegic

⑤ **346.9 Migraine, unspecified**

347 Cataplexy and narcolepsy

348 Other conditions of brain

348.0 Cerebral cysts
    Arachnoid cyst   Porencephaly, acquired
    Porencephalic cyst   Pseudoporencephaly

Excludes: porencephaly (congenital) (742.4)

348.1 Anoxic brain damage

Excludes: that occurring in:
        abortion (634-638 with .7, 639.8)
        ectopic or molar pregnancy (639.8)
        labor or delivery (668.2, 669.4)
        that of newborn (767.0, 768.0-768.9, 772.1-772.2)

Use additional E code, if desired, to identify cause

348.2 Benign intracranial hypertension
    Pseudotumor cerebri

Excludes: hypertensive encephalopathy (437.2)

348.3 Encephalopathy, unspecified

348.4 Compression of brain
    Compression ⎫
    Herniation   ⎬ brain (stem)
    Posterior fossa compression syndrome

348.5 Cerebral edema

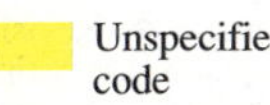

348.8 Other conditions of brain
  Cerebral:
   calcification
   fungus

348.9 Unspecified condition of brain

349 Other and unspecified disorders of the nervous system

 349.0 Reaction to spinal or lumbar puncture
   Headache following lumbar puncture

 349.1 Nervous system complications from surgically implanted device

   Excludes: *immediate postoperative complications (997.00-997.09)*
      mechanical complications of nervous system device (996.2)

 349.2 Disorders of meninges, not elsewhere classified
   Adhesions, meningeal (cerebral) (spinal)
   Cyst, spinal meninges
   Meningocele, acquired
   Pseudomeningocele, acquired

 ⑤ **349.8 Other specified disorders of nervous system**

  349.81 Cerebrospinal fluid rhinorrhea

   Excludes: *cerebrospinal fluid otorrhea (388.61)*

  349.82 Toxic encephalopathy
   Use additional E code, if desired, to identify cause

  349.89 Other

 349.9 Unspecified disorders of nervous system
   Disorder of nervous system (central) NOS

DISORDERS OF THE PERIPHERAL NERVOUS SYSTEM (350-359)

   Excludes: *diseases of:*
     acoustic [8th] nerve (388.5)
     oculomotor [3rd, 4th, 6th] nerves (378.0-378.9)
     optic [2nd] nerve (377.0-377.9)
     peripheral autonomic nerves (337.0-337.9)
     neuralgia
     neuritis } *NOS or "rheumatic" (729.2)*
     radiculitis
     peripheral neuritis in pregnancy (646.4)

350 Trigeminal nerve disorders
   Includes: disorders of 5th cranial nerve

 350.1 Trigeminal neuralgia
   Tic douloureux   Trigeminal neuralgia NOS
   Trifacial neuralgia

   Excludes: *postherpetic (053.12)*

 350.2 Atypical face pain

 350.8 Other specified trigeminal nerve disorders

 350.9 Trigeminal nerve disorder, unspecified

351 Facial nerve disorders
   Includes: disorders of 7th cranial nerve

   Excludes: *that in newborn (767.5)*

 351.0 Bell's palsy
   Facial palsy

 351.1 Geniculate ganglionitis
   Geniculate ganglionitis NOS

   Excludes: *herpetic (053.11)*

 351.8 Other facial nerve disorders
   Facial myokymia   Melkersson's syndrome

 351.9 Facial nerve disorder, unspecified

352 Disorders of other cranial nerves

 352.0 Disorders of olfactory [1st] nerve

 352.1 Glossopharyngeal neuralgia

 ● Code new   ▲ Revision of   ④ ⑤ Fourth or fifth
  to this edition   existing code   digit required

352.2 Other disorders of glossopharyngeal [9th] nerve

352.3 Disorders of pneumogastric [10th] nerve
Disorders of vagal nerve

Excludes: *paralysis of vocal cords or larynx (478.30-478.34)*

352.4 Disorders of accessory [11th] nerve

352.5 Disorders of hypoglossal [12th] nerve

352.6 Multiple cranial nerve palsies
Collet-Sicard syndrome   Polyneuritis cranialis

352.9 Unspecified disorder of cranial nerves

353 Nerve root and plexus disorders

Excludes: *conditions due to:*
intervertebral disc disorders (722.0-722.9)
spondylosis (720.0-721.9)
vertebrogenic disorders (723.0-724.9)

353.0 Brachial plexus lesions
Cervical rib syndrome   Thoracic outlet syndrome
Costoclavicular syndrome
Scalenus anticus syndrome

Excludes: *brachial neuritis or radiculitis NOS (723.4)*
that in newborn (767.6)

353.1 Lumbosacral plexus lesions

353.2 Cervical root lesions, not elsewhere classified

353.3 Thoracic root lesions, not elsewhere classified

353.4 Lumbosacral root lesions, not elsewhere classified

353.5 Neuralgic amyotrophy
Parsonage-Aldren-Turner syndrome

353.6 Phantom limb (syndrome)

353.8 Other nerve root and plexus disorders

353.9 Unspecified nerve root and plexus disorder

354 Mononeuritis of upper limb and mononeuritis multiplex

354.0 Carpal tunnel syndrome
Median nerve entrapment   Partial thenar atrophy

354.1 Other lesion of median nerve
Median nerve neuritis

354.2 Lesion of ulnar nerve
Cubital tunnel syndrome   Tardy ulnar nerve palsy

354.3 Lesion of radial nerve
Acute radial nerve palsy

354.4 Causalgia of upper limb

Excludes: *causalgia:*
NOS (355.9)
lower limb (355.71)

354.5 Mononeuritis multiplex
Combinations of single conditions classifiable to 354 or 355

354.8 Other mononeuritis of upper limb

354.9 Mononeuritis of upper limb, unspecified

355 Mononeuritis of lower limb and unspecified site

355.0 Lesion of sciatic nerve

Excludes: *sciatica NOS (724.3)*

355.1 Meralgia paresthetica
Lateral cutaneous femoral nerve of thigh compression or syndrome

355.2 Other lesion of femoral nerve

355.3 Lesion of lateral popliteal nerve
Lesion of common peroneal nerve

355.4 Lesion of medial popliteal nerve

355.5 Tarsal tunnel syndrome

| Add 4th or 5th digit | Nonspecific code | Unspecified code | Manifestation code |

355.6 Lesion of plantar nerve
Morton's metatarsalgia, neuralgia, or neuroma

⑤ **355.7 Other mononeuritis of lower limb**

355.71 Causalgia of lower limb

Excludes: *causalgia:*
NOS (355.9)
upper limb (354.4)

`355.79` **Other mononeuritis of lower limb**

`355.8` **Mononeuritis of lower limb, unspecified**

`355.9` **Mononeuritis of unspecified site**
Causalgia NOS

Excludes: *causalgia:*
lower limb (355.71)
upper limb (354.4)

`356` **Hereditary and idiopathic peripheral neuropathy**

356.0 Hereditary peripheral neuropathy
Déjérine-Sottas disease

356.1 Peroneal muscular atrophy
Charcot-Marie-Tooth disease
Neuropathic muscular atrophy

356.2 Hereditary sensory neuropathy

356.3 Refsum's disease
Heredopathia atactica polyneuritiformis

356.4 Idiopathic progressive polyneuropathy

`356.8` **Other specified idiopathic peripheral neuropathy**
Supranuclear paralysis

`356.9` **Unspecified**

`357` **Inflammatory and toxic neuropathy**

357.0 Acute infective polyneuritis
Guillain-Barré syndrome
Postinfectious polyneuritis

`357.1` *Polyneuropathy in collagen vascular disease*
Code first underlying disease, as:
disseminated lupus erythematosus (710.0)
polyarteritis nodosa (446.0)
rheumatoid arthritis (714.0)

`357.2` *Polyneuropathy in diabetes*
Code first underlying disease (250.6)

`357.3` *Polyneuropathy in malignant disease*
Code first underlying disease (140.0-208.9)

`357.4` *Polyneuropathy in other diseases classified elsewhere*
Code first underlying disease, as:
amyloidosis (277.3)
beriberi (265.0)
deficiency of B vitamins (266.0-266.9)
diphtheria (032.0-032.9)
hypoglycemia (251.2)
pellagra (265.2)
porphyria (277.1)
sarcoidosis (135)
uremia (585)

Excludes: *polyneuropathy in:*
herpes zoster (053.13)
mumps (072.72)

357.5 Alcoholic polyneuropathy

357.6 Polyneuropathy due to drugs
Use additional E code, if desired, to identify drug

`357.7` **Polyneuropathy due to other toxic agents**
Use additional E code, if desired, to identify toxic agent

  ● Code new
to this edition   ▲ Revision of
existing code   ④ ⑤ Fourth or fifth
digit required

357.8 Other
Chronic inflammatory demyelinating polyneuritis

357.9 Unspecified

358 Myoneural disorders

358.0 Myasthenia gravis

358.1 Myasthenic syndromes in diseases classified elsewhere
Amyotrophy
Eaton-Lambert syndrome   } from stated cause classified elsewhere
Code first underlying disease, as:
  botulism (005.1)
  diabetes mellitus (250.6)
  hypothyroidism (244.0-244.9)
  malignant neoplasm (140.0-208.9)
  pernicious anemia (281.0)
  thyrotoxicosis (242.0-242.9)

358.2 Toxic myoneural disorders
Use additional E code, if desired, to identify toxic agent

358.8 Other specified myoneural disorders

358.9 Myoneural disorders, unspecified

359 Muscular dystrophies and other myopathies

Excludes: *idiopathic polymyositis (710.4)*

359.0 Congenital hereditary muscular dystrophy
Benign congenital myopathy
Central core disease
Centronuclear myopathy
Myotubular myopathy
Nemaline body disease

Excludes: *arthrogryposis multiplex congenita (754.89)*

359.1 Hereditary progressive muscular dystrophy
Muscular dystrophy: Muscular dystrophy:
  NOS   Gower's
  distal   Landouzy-Déjérine
  Duchenne   limb-girdle
  Erb's   ocular
  fascioscapulohumeral   oculopharyngeal

359.2 Myotonic disorders
Dystrophia myotonica   Paramyotonia congenita
Eulenburg's disease   Steinert's disease
Myotonia congenita   Thomsen's disease

359.3 Familial periodic paralysis
Hypokalemic familial periodic paralysis

359.4 Toxic myopathy
Use additional E code, if desired, to identify toxic agent

359.5 Myopathy in endocrine diseases classified elsewhere
Code first underlying disease, as:
  Addison's disease (255.4)
  Cushing's syndrome (255.0)
  hypopituitarism (253.2)
  myxedema (244.0-244.9)
  thyrotoxicosis (242.0-242.9)

359.6 Symptomatic inflammatory myopathy in diseases classified elsewhere
Code first underlying disease, as:
  amyloidosis (277.3)
  disseminated lupus erythematosus (710.0)
  malignant neoplasm (140.0-208.9)
  polyarteritis nodosa (446.0)
  rheumatoid arthritis (714.0)
  sarcoidosis (135)
  scleroderma (710.1)
  Sjögren's disease (710.2)

359.8 Other myopathies

359.9 Myopathy, unspecified

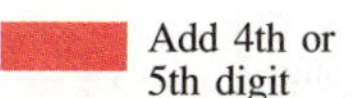

DISORDERS OF THE EYE AND ADNEXA (360-379)

360 Disorders of the globe
Includes: disorders affecting multiple structures of eye

⑤ **360.0 Purulent endophthalmitis**

360.00 Purulent endophthalmitis, unspecified

360.01 **Acute endophthalmitis**

360.02 **Panophthalmitis**

360.03 **Chronic endophthalmitis**

360.04 **Vitreous abscess**

⑤ **360.1 Other endophthalmitis**

360.11 **Sympathetic uveitis**

360.12 **Panuveitis**

360.13 **Parasitic endophthalmitis NOS**

360.14 **Ophthalmia nodosa**

360.19 Other
Phacoanaphylactic endophthalmitis

⑤ **360.2 Degenerative disorders of globe**

360.20 Degenerative disorder of globe, unspecified

360.21 **Progressive high (degenerative) myopia**
Malignant myopia

360.23 **Siderosis**

360.24 Other metallosis
Chalcosis

360.29 Other

Excludes: xerophthalmia (264.7)

⑤ **360.3 Hypotony of eye**

360.30 Hypotony, unspecified

360.31 **Primary hypotony**

360.32 **Ocular fistula causing hypotony**

360.33 Hypotony associated with other ocular disorders

360.34 **Flat anterior chamber**

⑤ **360.4 Degenerated conditions of globe**

360.40 Degenerated globe or eye, unspecified

360.41 **Blind hypotensive eye**
Atrophy of globe   Phthisis bulbi

360.42 **Blind hypertensive eye**
Absolute glaucoma

360.43 **Hemophthalmos, except current injury**

Excludes: traumatic (871.0-871.9, 921.0-921.9)

360.44 **Leucocoria**

⑤ **360.5 Retained (old) intraocular foreign body, magnetic**

Excludes: current penetrating injury with magnetic foreign body (871.5)
retained (old) foreign body of orbit (376.6)

360.50 Foreign body, magnetic, intraocular, unspecified

360.51 **Foreign body, magnetic, in anterior chamber**

360.52 **Foreign body, magnetic, in iris or ciliary body**

360.53 **Foreign body, magnetic, in lens**

360.54 **Foreign body, magnetic, in vitreous**

360.55 **Foreign body, magnetic, in posterior wall**

360.59 Foreign body, magnetic, in other or multiple sites

● Code new
to this edition
▲ Revision of
existing code
④ ⑤ Fourth or fifth
digit required

⑤ **360.6 Retained (old) intraocular foreign body, nonmagnetic**
Retained (old) foreign body:
  NOS
  nonmagnetic

Excludes: *current penetrating injury with (nonmagnetic) foreign body (871.6)*
retained (old) foreign body in orbit (376.6)

360.60 Foreign body, intraocular, unspecified

360.61 Foreign body in anterior chamber

360.62 Foreign body in iris or ciliary body

360.63 Foreign body in lens

360.64 Foreign body in vitreous

360.65 Foreign body in posterior wall

360.69 Foreign body in other or multiple sites

⑤ **360.8 Other disorders of globe**

360.81 Luxation of globe

360.89 Other

360.9 Unspecified disorder of globe

361 Retinal detachments and defects

⑤ **361.0 Retinal detachment with retinal defect**
Rhegmatogenous retinal detachment

Excludes: *detachment of retinal pigment epithelium (362.42-362.43)*
retinal detachment (serous) (without defect) (361.2)

361.00 Retinal detachment with retinal defect, unspecified

361.01 Recent detachment, partial, with single defect

361.02 Recent detachment, partial, with multiple defects

361.03 Recent detachment, partial, with giant tear

361.04 Recent detachment, partial, with retinal dialysis
Dialysis (juvenile) of retina (with detachment)

361.05 Recent detachment, total or subtotal

361.06 Old detachment, partial
Delimited old retinal detachment

361.07 Old detachment, total or subtotal

⑤ **361.1 Retinoschisis and retinal cysts**

Excludes: *juvenile retinoschisis (362.73)*
microcystoid degeneration of retina (362.62)
parasitic cyst of retina (360.13)

361.10 Retinoschisis, unspecified

361.11 Flat retinoschisis

361.12 Bullous retinoschisis

361.13 Primary retinal cysts

361.14 Secondary retinal cysts

361.19 Other
Pseudocyst of retina

361.2 Serous retinal detachment
Retinal detachment without retinal defect

Excludes: *central serous retinopathy (362.41)*
retinal pigment epithelium detachment (362.42-362.43)

⑤ **361.3 Retinal defects without detachment**

Excludes: *chorioretinal scars after surgery for detachment (363.30-363.35)*
peripheral retinal degeneration without defect (362.60-362.66)

361.30 Retinal defect, unspecified
Retinal break(s) NOS

361.31 Round hole of retina without detachment

361.32 Horseshoe tear of retina without detachment
Operculum of retina without mention of detachment

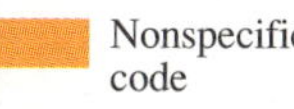

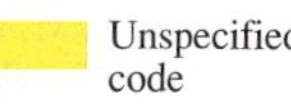

Manifestation
code

361.33 **Multiple defects of retina without detachment**

⑤ 361.8 **Other forms of retinal detachment**

361.81 **Traction detachment of retina**
Traction detachment with vitreoretinal organization

361.89 **Other**

361.9 **Unspecified retinal detachment**

362 **Other retinal disorders**

Excludes: *chorioretinal scars (363.30-363.35)*
chorioretinitis (363.0-363.2)

⑤ *362.0* *Diabetic retinopathy*
Code first diabetes (250.5)

362.01 *Background diabetic retinopathy*
Diabetic retinal microaneurysms
Diabetic retinopathy NOS

362.02 *Proliferative diabetic retinopathy*

⑤ 362.1 **Other background retinopathy and retinal vascular changes**

362.10 **Background retinopathy, unspecified**

362.11 **Hypertensive retinopathy**

362.12 **Exudative retinopathy**
Coats' syndrome

362.13 **Changes in vascular appearance**
Vascular sheathing of retina
Use additional code for any associated atherosclerosis (440.8)

362.14 **Retinal microaneurysms NOS**

362.15 **Retinal telangiectasia**

362.16 **Retinal neovascularization NOS**
Neovascularization:
choroidal
subretinal

362.17 **Other intraretinal microvascular abnormalities**
Retinal varices

362.18 **Retinal vasculitis**
Eales' disease   Retinal:
Retinal: perivasculitis
arteritis   phlebitis
endarteritis

⑤ 362.2 **Other proliferative retinopathy**

362.21 **Retrolental fibroplasia**

362.29 **Other nondiabetic proliferative retinopathy**

⑤ 362.3 **Retinal vascular occlusion**

362.30 **Retinal vascular occlusion, unspecified**

362.31 **Central retinal artery occlusion**

362.32 **Arterial branch occlusion**

362.33 **Partial arterial occlusion**
Hollenhorst plaque   Retinal microembolism

362.34 **Transient arterial occlusion**
Amaurosis fugax

362.35 **Central retinal vein occlusion**

362.36 **Venous tributary (branch) occlusion**

362.37 **Venous engorgement**
Occlusion:
incipient   ⎫
partial   ⎬ of retinal vein

● Code new
to this edition

▲ Revision of
existing code

④ ⑤ Fourth or fifth
digit required

⑤ **362.4 Separation of retinal layers**

> *Excludes:* *retinal detachment (serous) (361.2)*
> *rhegmatogenous (361.00-361.07)*

362.40 Retinal layer separation, unspecified

362.41 Central serous retinopathy

362.42 Serous detachment of retinal pigment epithelium
Exudative detachment of retinal pigment epithelium

362.43 Hemorrhagic detachment of retinal pigment epithelium

⑤ **362.5 Degeneration of macula and posterior pole**

> *Excludes:* *degeneration of optic disc (377.21-377.24)*
> *hereditary retinal degeneration [dystrophy] (362.70-362.77)*

362.50 Macular degeneration (senile), unspecified

362.51 Nonexudative senile macular degeneration
Senile macular degeneration:
   atrophic
   dry

362.52 Exudative senile macular degeneration
Kuhnt-Junius degeneration
Senile macular degeneration:
   disciform
   wet

362.53 Cystoid macular degeneration
Cystoid macular edema

362.54 Macular cyst, hole, or pseudohole

362.55 Toxic maculopathy
Use additional E code, if desired, to identify drug, if drug induced

362.56 Macular puckering
Preretinal fibrosis

362.57 Drusen (degenerative)

⑤ **362.6 Peripheral retinal degenerations**

> *Excludes:* *hereditary retinal degeneration [dystrophy] (362.70-362.77)*
> *retinal degeneration with retinal defect (361.00-361.07)*

362.60 Peripheral retinal degeneration, unspecified

362.61 Paving stone degeneration

362.62 Microcystoid degeneration
Blessig's cysts   Iwanoff's cysts

362.63 Lattice degeneration
Palisade degeneration of retina

362.64 Senile reticular degeneration

362.65 Secondary pigmentary degeneration
Pseudoretinitis pigmentosa

362.66 Secondary vitreoretinal degenerations

⑤ **362.7 Hereditary retinal dystrophies**

362.70 Hereditary retinal dystrophy, unspecified

362.71 *Retinal dystrophy in systemic or cerebroretinal lipidoses*
Code first underlying disease, as:
   cerebroretinal lipidoses (330.1)
   systemic lipidoses (272.7)

362.72 *Retinal dystrophy in other systemic disorders and syndromes*
Code first underlying disease, as:
   Bassen-Kornzweig syndrome (272.5)
   Refsum's disease (356.3)

362.73 Vitreoretinal dystrophies
Juvenile retinoschisis

362.74 Pigmentary retinal dystrophy
Retinal dystrophy, albipunctate
Retinitis pigmentosa

362.75 Other dystrophies primarily involving the sensory retina
Progressive cone (-rod) dystrophy
Stargardt's disease

362.76 Dystrophies primarily involving the retinal pigment epithelium
Fundus flavimaculatus
Vitelliform dystrophy

362.77 Dystrophies primarily involving Bruch's membrane
Dystrophy:
hyaline
pseudoinflammatory foveal
Hereditary drusen

⑤ **362.8 Other retinal disorders**

Excludes: *chorioretinal inflammations (363.0-363.2)*
chorioretinal scars (363.30-363.35)

362.81 Retinal hemorrhage
Hemorrhage:
preretinal
retinal (deep) (superficial)
subretinal

362.82 Retinal exudates and deposits

362.83 Retinal edema
Retinal:
cotton wool spots
edema (localized) (macular) (peripheral)

362.84 Retinal ischemia

362.85 Retinal nerve fiber bundle defects

362.89 Other retinal disorders

362.9 Unspecified retinal disorder

363 Chorioretinal inflammations, scars, and other disorders of choroid

⑤ **363.0 Focal chorioretinitis and focal retinochoroiditis**

Excludes: *focal chorioretinitis or retinochoroiditis in:*
histoplasmosis (115.02, 115.12, 115.92)
toxoplasmosis (130.2)
congenital infection (771.2)

363.00 Focal chorioretinitis, unspecified
Focal:
choroiditis or chorioretinitis NOS
retinitis or retinochoroiditis NOS

363.01 Focal choroiditis and chorioretinitis, juxtapapillary

363.03 Focal choroiditis and chorioretinitis of other posterior pole

363.04 Focal choroiditis and chorioretinitis, peripheral

363.05 Focal retinitis and retinochoroiditis, juxtapapillary
Neuroretinitis

363.06 Focal retinitis and retinochoroiditis, macular or paramacular

363.07 Focal retinitis and retinochoroiditis of other posterior pole

363.08 Focal retinitis and retinochoroiditis, peripheral

⑤ **363.1 Disseminated chorioretinitis and disseminated retinochoroiditis**

Excludes: *disseminated choroiditis or chorioretinitis in secondary syphilis (091.51)*
neurosyphilitic disseminated retinitis or retinochoroiditis (094.83)
retinal (peri)vasculitis (362.18)

363.10 Disseminated chorioretinitis, unspecified
Disseminated:
choroiditis or chorioretinitis NOS
retinitis or retinochoroiditis NOS

363.11 Disseminated choroiditis and chorioretinitis, posterior pole

363.12 Disseminated choroiditis and chorioretinitis, peripheral

363.13 *Disseminated choroiditis and chorioretinitis, generalized*
Code first any underlying disease, as:
tuberculosis (017.3)

363.14 Disseminated retinitis and retinochoroiditis, metastatic

---

● Code new
to this edition   ▲ Revision of
existing code   ④ ⑤ Fourth or fifth
digit required

363.15 Disseminated retinitis and retinochoroiditis, pigment epitheliopathy
Acute posterior multifocal placoid pigment epitheliopathy

⑤ **363.2 Other and unspecified forms of chorioretinitis and retinochoroiditis**

Excludes: *panophthalmitis (360.02)*
sympathetic uveitis (360.11)
uveitis NOS (364.3)

363.20 Chorioretinitis, unspecified
Choroiditis NOS
Retinitis NOS
Uveitis, posterior NOS

363.21 Pars planitis
Posterior cyclitis

363.22 Harada's disease

⑤ **363.3 Chorioretinal scars**
Scar (postinflammatory) (postsurgical) (posttraumatic):
choroid
retina

363.30 Chorioretinal scar, unspecified

363.31 Solar retinopathy

363.32 Other macular scars

363.33 Other scars of posterior pole

363.34 Peripheral scars

363.35 Disseminated scars

⑤ **363.4 Choroidal degenerations**

363.40 Choroidal degeneration, unspecified
Choroidal sclerosis NOS

363.41 Senile atrophy of choroid

363.42 Diffuse secondary atrophy of choroid

363.43 Angioid streaks of choroid

⑤ **363.5 Hereditary choroidal dystrophies**
Hereditary choroidal atrophy:
partial [choriocapillaris]
total [all vessels]

363.50 Hereditary choroidal dystrophy or atrophy, unspecified

363.51 Circumpapillary dystrophy of choroid, partial

363.52 Circumpapillary dystrophy of choroid, total
Helicoid dystrophy of choroid

363.53 Central dystrophy of choroid, partial
Dystrophy, choroidal:
central areolar
circinate

363.54 Central choroidal atrophy, total
Dystrophy, choroidal:
central gyrate
serpiginous

363.55 Choroideremia

363.56 Other diffuse or generalized dystrophy, partial
Diffuse choroidal sclerosis

363.57 Other diffuse or generalized dystrophy, total
Generalized gyrate atrophy, choroid

⑤ **363.6 Choroidal hemorrhage and rupture**

363.61 Choroidal hemorrhage, unspecified

363.62 Expulsive choroidal hemorrhage

363.63 Choroidal rupture

⑤ **363.7 Choroidal detachment**

363.70 Choroidal detachment, unspecified

363.71 Serous choroidal detachment

363.72 Hemorrhagic choroidal detachment

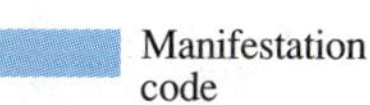

Add 4th or 5th digit	Nonspecific code	Unspecified code	Manifestation code

363.8 **Other disorders of choroid**

363.9 **Unspecified disorder of choroid**

364 **Disorders of iris and ciliary body**

⑤ **364.0** **Acute and subacute iridocyclitis**

Anterior uveitis
Cyclitis
Iridocyclitis
Iritis

acute
subacute

Excludes: *gonococcal (098.41)*
herpes simplex (054.44)
herpes zoster (053.22)

364.00 **Acute and subacute iridocyclitis, unspecified**

364.01 **Primary iridocyclitis**

364.02 **Recurrent iridocyclitis**

364.03 **Secondary iridocyclitis, infectious**

364.04 **Secondary iridocyclitis, noninfectious**
Aqueous:
cells
fibrin
flare

364.05 **Hypopyon**

⑤ **364.1** **Chronic iridocyclitis**

Excludes: *posterior cyclitis (363.21)*

364.10 **Chronic iridocyclitis, unspecified**

364.11 *Chronic iridocyclitis in diseases classified elsewhere*
Code first underlying disease, as:
sarcoidosis (135)
tuberculosis (017.3)

Excludes: *syphilitic iridocyclitis (091.52)*

⑤ **364.2** **Certain types of iridocyclitis**

Excludes: *posterior cyclitis (363.21)*
sympathetic uveitis (360.11)

364.21 **Fuchs' heterochromic cyclitis**

364.22 **Glaucomatocyclitic crises**

364.23 **Lens-induced iridocyclitis**

364.24 **Vogt-Koyanagi syndrome**

364.3 **Unspecified iridocyclitis**
Uveitis NOS

⑤ **364.4** **Vascular disorders of iris and ciliary body**

364.41 **Hyphema**
Hemorrhage of iris or ciliary body

364.42 **Rubeosis iridis**
Neovascularization of iris or ciliary body

⑤ **364.5** **Degenerations of iris and ciliary body**

364.51 **Essential or progressive iris atrophy**

364.52 **Iridoschisis**

364.53 **Pigmentary iris degeneration**
Acquired heterochromia
Pigment dispersion syndrome
Translucency

of iris

364.54 **Degeneration of pupillary margin**
Atrophy of sphincter
Ectropion of pigment epithelium

of iris

364.55 **Miotic cysts of pupillary margin**

364.56 **Degenerative changes of chamber angle**

364.57 **Degenerative changes of ciliary body**

● Code new
to this edition

▲ Revision of
existing code

④ ⑤ Fourth or fifth
digit required

364.59 Other iris atrophy
Iris atrophy (generalized) (sector shaped)

⑤ **364.6 Cysts of iris, ciliary body, and anterior chamber**

Excludes: *miotic pupillary cyst (364.55)*
parasitic cyst (360.13)

364.60 Idiopathic cysts

364.61 Implantation cysts
Epithelial down-growth, anterior chamber
Implantation cysts (surgical) (traumatic)

364.62 Exudative cysts of iris or anterior chamber

364.63 Primary cyst of pars plana

364.64 Exudative cyst of pars plana

⑤ **364.7 Adhesions and disruptions of iris and ciliary body**

Excludes: *flat anterior chamber (360.34)*

364.70 Adhesions of iris, unspecified
Synechiae (iris) NOS

364.71 Posterior synechiae

364.72 Anterior synechiae

364.73 Goniosynechiae
Peripheral anterior synechiae

364.74 Pupillary membranes
Iris bombé
Pupillary:
occlusion
seclusion

364.75 Pupillary abnormalities
Deformed pupil   Rupture of sphincter, pupil
Ectopic pupil

364.76 Iridodialysis

364.77 Recession of chamber angle

364.8 Other disorders of iris and ciliary body
Prolapse of iris NOS

Excludes: *prolapse of iris in recent wound (871.1)*

364.9 Unspecified disorder of iris and ciliary body

365 Glaucoma

Excludes: *blind hypertensive eye [absolute glaucoma] (360.42)*
congenital glaucoma (743.20-743.22)

⑤ **365.0 Borderline glaucoma [glaucoma suspect]**

365.00 Preglaucoma, unspecified

365.01 Open angle with borderline findings
Open angle with:
borderline intraocular pressure
cupping of optic discs

365.02 Anatomical narrow angle

365.03 Steroid responders

365.04 Ocular hypertension

⑤ **365.1 Open-angle glaucoma**

365.10 Open-angle glaucoma, unspecified
Wide-angle glaucoma NOS

365.11 Primary open angle glaucoma
Chronic simple glaucoma

365.12 Low tension glaucoma

365.13 Pigmentary glaucoma

365.14 Glaucoma of childhood
Infantile or juvenile glaucoma

365.15 Residual stage of open angle glaucoma

⑤ **365.2 Primary angle-closure glaucoma**

Add 4th or 5th digit   Nonspecific code   Unspecified code   Manifestation code

365.20   **Primary angle-closure glaucoma, unspecified**

365.21   **Intermittent angle-closure glaucoma**
> Angle-closure glaucoma:
>> interval
>> subacute

365.22   **Acute angle-closure glaucoma**

365.23   **Chronic angle-closure glaucoma**

365.24   **Residual stage of angle-closure glaucoma**

⑤ **365.3**   **Corticosteroid-induced glaucoma**

365.31   **Glaucomatous stage**

365.32   **Residual stage**

⑤ **365.4**   **Glaucoma associated with congenital anomalies, dystrophies, and systemic syndromes**

365.41   *Glaucoma associated with chamber angle anomalies*
> *Code first associated disorder, as:*
>> Axenfeld's anomaly (743.44)
>> Rieger's anomaly or syndrome (743.44)

365.42   *Glaucoma associated with anomalies of iris*
> *Code first associated disorder, as:*
>> aniridia (743.45)
>> essential iris atrophy (364.51)

365.43   *Glaucoma associated with other anterior segment anomalies*
> *Code first associated disorder, as:*
>> microcornea (743.41)

365.44   *Glaucoma associated with systemic syndromes*
> *Code first associated disease, as:*
>> neurofibromatosis (237.7)
>> Sturge-Weber (-Dimitri) syndrome (759.6)

⑤ **365.5**   **Glaucoma associated with disorders of the lens**

365.51   **Phacolytic glaucoma**
> Use additional code for associated hypermature cataract (366.18)

365.52   **Pseudoexfoliation glaucoma**
> Use additional code for associated pseudoexfoliation of capsule (366.11)

365.59   **Glaucoma associated with other lens disorders**
> Use additional code for associated disorder, as:
>> dislocation of lens (379.33-379.34)
>> spherophakia (743.36)

⑤ **365.6**   **Glaucoma associated with other ocular disorders**

365.60   **Glaucoma associated with unspecified ocular disorder**

365.61   **Glaucoma associated with pupillary block**
> Use additional code for associated disorder, as:
>> seclusion of pupil [iris bombé] (364.74)

365.62   **Glaucoma associated with ocular inflammations**
> Use additional code for associated disorder, as:
>> glaucomatocyclitic crises (364.22)
>> iridocyclitis (364.0-364.3)

365.63   **Glaucoma associated with vascular disorders**
> Use additional code for associated disorder, as:
>> central retinal vein occlusion (362.35)
>> hyphema (364.41)

365.64   **Glaucoma associated with tumors or cysts**
> Use additional code for associated disorder, as:
>> benign neoplasm (224.0-224.9)
>> epithelial down-growth (364.61)
>> malignant neoplasm (190.0-190.9)

365.65   **Glaucoma associated with ocular trauma**
> Use additional code for associated condition, as:
>> contusion of globe (921.3)
>> recession of chamber angle (364.77)

⑤ **365.8**   **Other specified forms of glaucoma**

365.81   **Hypersecretion glaucoma**

365.82   **Glaucoma with increased episcleral venous pressure**

● Code new to this edition   ▲ Revision of existing code   ④ ⑤ Fourth or fifth digit required

365.89 Other specified glaucoma

365.9 Unspecified glaucoma

366 **Cataract**

> Excludes: congenital cataract (743.30-743.34)

⑤ **366.0** Infantile, juvenile, and presenile cataract

    366.00 Nonsenile cataract, unspecified

    366.01 Anterior subcapsular polar cataract

    366.02 Posterior subcapsular polar cataract

    366.03 Cortical, lamellar, or zonular cataract

    366.04 Nuclear cataract

    366.09 Other and combined forms of nonsenile cataract

⑤ **366.1** Senile cataract

    366.10 Senile cataract, unspecified

    366.11 Pseudoexfoliation of lens capsule

    366.12 Incipient cataract
        Cataract: Water clefts
          coronary
          immature NOS
          punctate

    366.13 Anterior subcapsular polar senile cataract

    366.14 Posterior subcapsular polar senile cataract

    366.15 Cortical senile cataract

    366.16 Nuclear sclerosis
        Cataracta brunescens
        Nuclear cataract

    366.17 Total or mature cataract

    366.18 Hypermature cataract
        Morgagni cataract

    366.19 Other and combined forms of senile cataract

⑤ **366.2** Traumatic cataract

    366.20 Traumatic cataract, unspecified

    366.21 Localized traumatic opacities
        Vossius' ring

    366.22 Total traumatic cataract

    366.23 Partially resolved traumatic cataract

⑤ **366.3** Cataract secondary to ocular disorders

    366.30 Cataracts complicata, unspecified

    366.31 *Glaucomatous flecks (subcapsular)*
        Code first underlying glaucoma (365.0-365.9)

    366.32 *Cataract in inflammatory disorders*
        Code first underlying condition, as:
        chronic choroiditis (363.0-363.2)

    366.33 *Cataract with neovascularization*
        Code first underlying condition, as:
        chronic iridocyclitis (364.10)

    366.34 *Cataract in degenerative disorders*
        Sunflower cataract
        Code first underlying condition, as:
        chalcosis (360.24)
          degenerative myopia (360.21)
          pigmentary retinal dystrophy (362.74)

⑤ **366.4** Cataract associated with other disorders

    366.41 *Diabetic cataract*
        Code first diabetes (250.5)

    366.42 *Tetanic cataract*
        Code first underlying disease, as:
        calcinosis (275.4)
        hypoparathyroidism (252.1)

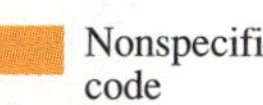

366.43 Myotonic cataract
Code first underlying disorder (359.2)

366.44 Cataract associated with other syndromes
Code first underlying condition, as:
craniofacial dysostosis (756.0)
galactosemia (271.1)

366.45 Toxic cataract
Drug-induced cataract
Use additional E code, if desired, to identify drug or other toxic substance

366.46 Cataract associated with radiation and other physical influences
Use additional E code, if desired, to identify cause

⑤ **366.5 After-cataract**

366.50 After-cataract, unspecified
Secondary cataract NOS

366.51 Soemmering's ring

366.52 Other after-cataract, not obscuring vision

366.53 After-cataract, obscuring vision

366.8 Other cataract
Calcification of lens

366.9 Unspecified cataract

367 Disorders of refraction and accommodation

367.0 Hypermetropia
Far-sightedness   Hyperopia

367.1 Myopia
Near-sightedness

⑤ **367.2 Astigmatism**

367.20 Astigmatism, unspecified

367.21 Regular astigmatism

367.22 Irregular astigmatism

⑤ **367.3 Anisometropia and aniseikonia**

367.31 Anisometropia

367.32 Aniseikonia

367.4 Presbyopia

⑤ **367.5 Disorders of accommodation**

367.51 Paresis of accommodation
Cycloplegia

367.52 Total or complete internal ophthalmoplegia

367.53 Spasm of accommodation

⑤ **367.8 Other disorders of refraction and accommodation**

367.81 Transient refractive change

367.89 Other
Drug-induced ⎫
Toxic   ⎬ disorders of refraction and accommodation
             ⎭

367.9 Unspecified disorder of refraction and accommodation

368 Visual disturbances

Excludes: electrophysiological disturbances (794.11-794.14)

⑤ **368.0 Amblyopia ex anopsia**

368.00 Amblyopia, unspecified

368.01 Strabismic amblyopia
Suppression amblyopia

368.02 Deprivation amblyopia

368.03 Refractive amblyopia

⑤ **368.1 Subjective visual disturbances**

368.10 Subjective visual disturbance, unspecified

368.11 Sudden visual loss

● Code new   ▲ Revision of   ④ ⑤ Fourth or fifth
to this edition   existing code   digit required

368.12 **Transient visual loss**
    Concentric fading   Scintillating scotoma

368.13 **Visual discomfort**
    Asthenopia   Photophobia
    Eye strain

368.14 **Visual distortions of shape and size**
    Macropsia   Micropsia
    Metamorphopsia

368.15 **Other visual distortions and entoptic phenomena**
    Photopsia   Visual halos
    Refractive:
      diplopia
      polyopia

368.16 **Psychophysical visual disturbances**
    Visual:
      agnosia
      disorientation syndrome
      hallucinations

368.2 **Diplopia**
    Double vision

⑤ **368.3** **Other disorders of binocular vision**

368.30 **Binocular vision disorder, unspecified**

368.31 **Suppression of binocular vision**

368.32 **Simultaneous visual perception without fusion**

368.33 **Fusion with defective stereopsis**

368.34 **Abnormal retinal correspondence**

⑤ **368.4** **Visual field defects**

368.40 **Visual field defect, unspecified**

368.41 **Scotoma involving central area**
    Scotoma:
      central
      centrocecal
      paracentral

368.42 **Scotoma of blind spot area**
    Enlarged: Paracecal scotoma
      angioscotoma
      blind spot

368.43 **Sector or arcuate defects**
    Scotoma:
      arcuate
      Bjerrum
      Seidel

368.44 **Other localized visual field defect**
    Scotoma: Visual field defect:
      NOS   nasal step
      ring   peripheral

368.45 **Generalized contraction or constriction**

368.46 **Homonymous bilateral field defects**
    Hemianopsia (altitudinal) (homonymous)
    Quadrant anopia

368.47 **Heteronymous bilateral field defects**
    Hemianopsia:
      binasal
      bitemporal

⑤ **368.5** **Color vision deficiencies**
    Color blindness

368.51 **Protan defect**
    Protanomaly   Protanopia

368.52 **Deutan defect**
    Deuteranomaly   Deuteranopia

368.53 **Tritan defect**
    Tritanomaly   Tritanopia

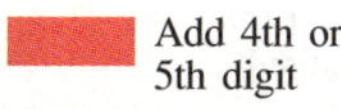

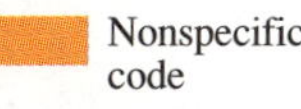

368.54 Achromatopsia
    Monochromatism (cone) (rod)

368.55 Acquired color vision deficiencies

368.59 Other color vision deficiencies

⑤ **368.6 Night blindness**
    Hemeralopia   Nyctalopia

368.60 Night blindness, unspecified

368.61 Congenital night blindness
    Hereditary night blindness
    Oguchi's disease

368.62 Acquired night blindness

Excludes: *that due to vitamin A deficiency (264.5)*

368.63 Abnormal dark adaptation curve
    Abnormal threshold
    Delayed adaptation   } of cones or rods

368.69 Other night blindness

368.8 Other specified visual disturbances
    Blurred vision NOS

368.9 Unspecified visual disturbance

369 Blindness and low vision

Note: Visual impairment refers to a functional limitation of the eye (e.g., limited visual acuity or visual field). It should be distinguished from visual disability, indicating a limitation of the abilities of the individual (e.g., limited reading skills, vocational skills), and from visual handicap, indicating a limitation of personal and socioeconomic independence (e.g., limited mobility, limited employability.)

The levels of impairment defined in the table on page 174 are based on the recommendations of the WHO Study Group on Prevention of Blindness (Geneva, November 6-10, 1972; WHO Technical Report Series 518), and of the International Council of Ophthalmology (1976).

Note that definitions of blindness vary in different settings.

For international reporting WHO defines blindness as profound impairment. This definition can be applied to blindness of one eye (369.1, 369.6) and to blindness of the individual (369.0).

For determination of benefits in the U.S.A., the definition of legal blindness as severe impairment is often used. This definition applies to blindness of the individual only.

Excludes: *correctable impaired vision due to refractive errors (367.0-367.9)*

⑤ **369.0 Profound impairment, both eyes**

369.00 Impairment level not further specified
    Blindness:
      NOS according to WHO definition
      both eyes

369.01 Better eye: total impairment;
      lesser eye: total impairment

369.02 Better eye: near-total impairment;
      lesser eye: not further specified

369.03 Better eye: near-total impairment;
      lesser eye: total impairment

369.04 Better eye: near-total impairment;
      lesser eye: near-total impairment

369.05 Better eye: profound impairment;
      lesser eye: not further specified

369.06 Better eye: profound impairment;
      lesser eye: total impairment

369.07 Better eye: profound impairment;
      lesser eye: near-total impairment

369.08 Better eye: profound impairment;
      lesser eye: profound impairment

⑤ **369.1 Moderate or severe impairment, better eye, profound impairment lesser eye**

● Code new to this edition   ▲ Revision of existing code   ④ ⑤ Fourth or fifth digit required

369.10   Impairment level not further specified
  Blindness, one eye, low vision other eye

369.11   Better eye: severe impairment;
    lesser eye: blind, not further specified

369.12   Better eye: severe impairment;
    lesser eye: total impairment

369.13   Better eye: severe impairment;
    lesser eye: near-total impairment

369.14   Better eye: severe impairment;
    lesser eye: profound impairment

369.15   Better eye: moderate impairment;
    lesser eye: blind, not further specified

369.16   Better eye: moderate impairment;
    lesser eye: total impairment

369.17   Better eye: moderate impairment;
    lesser eye: near-total impairment

369.18   Better eye: moderate impairment;
    lesser eye: profound impairment

⑤ **369.2**   Moderate or severe impairment, both eyes

369.20   Impairment level not further specified
  Low vision, both eyes NOS

369.21   Better eye: severe impairment;
    lesser eye: not further specified

369.22   Better eye: severe impairment;
    lesser eye: severe impairment

369.23   Better eye: moderate impairment;
    lesser eye: not further specified

369.24   Better eye: moderate impairment;
    lesser eye: severe impairment

369.25   Better eye: moderate impairment;
    lesser eye: moderate impairment

369.3   Unqualified visual loss, both eyes

Excludes:	blindness NOS:
	legal [U.S.A. definition] (369.4)
	WHO definition (369.00)

369.4   Legal blindness, as defined in U.S.A.
  Blindness NOS according to U.S.A. definition

Excludes:	legal blindness with specification of impairment level (369.01-369.08, 369.11-369.14, 369.21-369.22)

⑤ **369.6**   Profound impairment, one eye

369.60   Impairment level not further specified
  Blindness, one eye

369.61   One eye: total impairment; other eye: not specified

369.62   One eye: total impairment; other eye: near-normal vision

369.63   One eye: total impairment; other eye: normal vision

369.64   One eye: near-total impairment; other eye: not specified

369.65   One eye: near-total impairment; other eye: near-normal vision

369.66   One eye: near-total impairment; other eye: normal vision

369.67   One eye: profound impairment; other eye: not specified

369.68   One eye: profound impairment; other eye: near-normal vision

369.69   One eye: profound impairment; other eye: normal vision

⑤ **369.7**   Moderate or severe impairment, one eye

369.70   Impairment level not further specified
  Low vision, one eye

369.71   One eye: severe impairment; other eye: not specified

369.72   One eye: severe impairment; other eye: near-normal vision

369.73   One eye: severe impairment; other eye: normal vision

369.74   One eye: moderate impairment; other eye: not specified

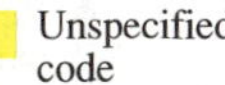

■	Add 4th or 5th digit	■	Nonspecific code	■	Unspecified code	■	Manifestation code

Classification		LEVELS OF VISUAL IMPAIRMENT					Additional Descriptors which may be encountered
"legal"	WHO	Visual Acuity and/or Visual Field Limitation (*whichever is worse*)					
	(NEAR-) NORMAL VISION	**RANGE OF NORMAL VISION**					
		20/10	20/13	20/16	20/20	20/25	
		2.0	1.6	1.25	1.0	0.8	
		NEAR-NORMAL VISION					
			20/30	20/40	20/50	20/60	
		0.7	0.6	0.5	0.4	0.3	
	LOW VISION	**MODERATE VISUAL IMPAIRMENT**					Moderate low vision
		20/70	20/80	20/100	20/125	20/160	
			0.25	0.20	0.16	0.12	
		SEVERE VISUAL IMPAIRMENT					Severe low vision, "legal" blindness
			20/200	20/250	20/320	20/400	
			0.10	0.08	0.06	0.05	
		Visual Field: 20 degrees or less					
LEGAL BLINDNESS	BLINDNESS	**PROFOUND VISUAL IMPAIRMENT**					Profound low vision, moderate blindness
			20/500	20/630	20/800	20/1000	
			0.04	0.03	0.025	0.02	
		Count Fingers at: less than 3m (10 ft)					
		Visual Field: 10 degrees or less					
		NEAR-TOTAL VISUAL IMPAIRMENT					Severe blindness
		Visual Acuity: less than 0.02 (20/1000)					
		Count Fingers at: 1m (3 ft) or less					
(USA) both eyes	(WHO) one or both eyes	Hand Movements: 5m (15 ft) or less					Near-total blindness
		Light projection, light perception					
		Visual Field: 5 degrees or less					
		TOTAL VISUAL IMPAIRMENT					Total blindness
		No light perception (NLP)					

Visual acuity refers to best achievable acuity with correction
Non-listed Snellen fractions may be classified by converting to the nearest decimal equivalent, e.g., 10/200=0.05, 6/30=0.20
CF (count fingers) without designation of distance, may be classified to profound impairment.
HM (hand motion) without designation of distance, may be classified to near-total impairment.
Visual field measurements refer to the largest field diameter for a 1/100 white test object.

369.75   One eye: moderate impairment; other eye: near-normal vision

369.76   One eye: moderate impairment; other eye: normal vision

369.8   Unqualified visual loss, one eye

369.9   Unspecified visual loss

370   Keratitis

⑤ 370.0   Corneal ulcer

Excludes: *that due to vitamin A deficiency (264.3)*

370.00   **Corneal ulcer, unspecified**

370.01   **Marginal corneal ulcer**

370.02   **Ring corneal ulcer**

370.03   **Central corneal ulcer**

370.04   **Hypopyon ulcer**
Serpiginous ulcer

370.05   **Mycotic corneal ulcer**

370.06   **Perforated corneal ulcer**

370.07   **Mooren's ulcer**

⑤ 370.2   **Superficial keratitis without conjunctivitis**

Excludes: *dendritic [herpes simplex] keratitis (054.42)*

370.20   **Superficial keratitis, unspecified**

● Code new to this edition   ▲ Revision of existing code   ④ ⑤ Fourth or fifth digit required

370.21 Punctate keratitis
Thygeson's superficial punctate keratitis

370.22 Macular keratitis
Keratitis: Keratitis:
  areolar   stellate
  nummular   striate

370.23 Filamentary keratitis

370.24 Photokeratitis
Snow blindness   Welders' keratitis

⑤ **370.3 Certain types of keratoconjunctivitis**

370.31 Phlyctenular keratoconjunctivitis
Phlyctenulosis
Use additional code for any associated tuberculosis (017.3)

370.32 Limbar and corneal involvement in vernal conjunctivitis
Use additional code for vernal conjunctivitis (372.13)

370.33 Keratoconjunctivitis sicca, not specified as Sjögren's

Excludes:	*Sjögren's syndrome (710.2)*

370.34 Exposure keratoconjunctivitis

370.35 Neurotrophic keratoconjunctivitis

⑤ **370.4 Other and unspecified keratoconjunctivitis**

370.40 Keratoconjunctivitis, unspecified
Superficial keratitis with conjunctivitis NOS

370.44 Keratitis or keratoconjunctivitis in exanthema
Code first underlying condition (050.0-052.9)

Excludes:	*herpes simplex (054.43)*
	herpes zoster (053.21)
	measles (055.71)

370.49 Other

Excludes:	*epidemic keratoconjunctivitis (077.1)*

⑤ **370.5 Interstitial and deep keratitis**

370.50 Interstitial keratitis, unspecified

370.52 Diffuse interstitial keratitis
Cogan's syndrome

370.54 Sclerosing keratitis

370.55 Corneal abscess

370.59 Other

Excludes:	*disciform herpes simplex keratitis (054.43)*
	syphilitic keratitis (090.3)

⑤ **370.6 Corneal neovascularization**

370.60 Corneal neovascularization, unspecified

370.61 Localized vascularization of cornea

370.62 Pannus (corneal)

370.63 Deep vascularization of cornea

370.64 Ghost vessels (corneal)

370.8 Other forms of keratitis

370.9 Unspecified keratitis

371 Corneal opacity and other disorders of cornea

⑤ **371.0 Corneal scars and opacities**

Excludes:	*that due to vitamin A deficiency (264.6)*

371.00 Corneal opacity, unspecified
Corneal scar NOS

371.01 Minor opacity of cornea
Corneal nebula

371.02 Peripheral opacity of cornea
Corneal macula not interfering with central vision

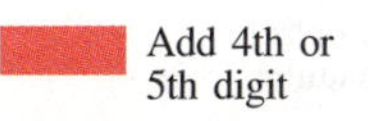

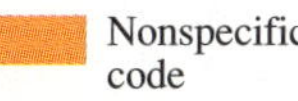

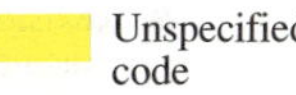

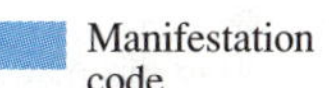

371.03 Central opacity of cornea
  Corneal: ⎫
    leucoma ⎬ interfering with central vision
    macula ⎭

371.04 Adherent leucoma

371.05 *Phthisical cornea*
  Code first underlying tuberculosis (017.3)

⑤ **371.1 Corneal pigmentations and deposits**

371.10 Corneal deposit, unspecified

371.11 Anterior pigmentations
  Stähli's lines

371.12 Stromal pigmentations
  Hematocornea

371.13 Posterior pigmentations
  Krukenberg spindle

371.14 Kayser-Fleischer ring

371.15 Other deposits associated with metabolic disorders

371.16 Argentous deposits

⑤ **371.2 Corneal edema**

371.20 Corneal edema, unspecified

371.21 Idiopathic corneal edema

371.22 Secondary corneal edema

371.23 Bullous keratopathy

371.24 Corneal edema due to wearing of contact lenses

⑤ **371.3 Changes of corneal membranes**

371.30 Corneal membrane change, unspecified

371.31 Folds and rupture of Bowman's membrane

371.32 Folds in Descemet's membrane

371.33 Rupture in Descemet's membrane

⑤ **371.4 Corneal degenerations**

371.40 Corneal degeneration, unspecified

371.41 Senile corneal changes
  Arcus senilis   Hassall-Henle bodies

371.42 Recurrent erosion of cornea

Excludes: *Mooren's ulcer (370.07)*

371.43 Band-shaped keratopathy

371.44 Other calcerous degenerations of cornea

371.45 Keratomalacia NOS

Excludes: *that due to vitamin A deficiency (264.4)*

371.46 Nodular degeneration of cornea
  Salzmann's nodular dystrophy

371.48 Peripheral degenerations of cornea
  Marginal degeneration of cornea [Terrien's]

371.49 Other
  Discrete colliquative keratopathy

⑤ **371.5 Hereditary corneal dystrophies**

371.50 Corneal dystrophy, unspecified

371.51 Juvenile epithelial corneal dystrophy

371.52 Other anterior corneal dystrophies
  Corneal dystrophy:
    microscopic cystic
    ring-like

371.53 Granular corneal dystrophy

371.54 Lattice corneal dystrophy

371.55 Macular corneal dystrophy

● Code new   ▲ Revision of   ④ ⑤ Fourth or fifth
  to this edition   existing code   digit required

371.56 **Other stromal corneal dystrophies**
Crystalline corneal dystrophy

371.57 **Endothelial corneal dystrophy**
Combined corneal dystrophy
Cornea guttata
Fuchs' endothelial dystrophy

371.58 **Other posterior corneal dystrophies**
Polymorphous corneal dystrophy

⑤ **371.6** **Keratoconus**

371.60 **Keratoconus, unspecified**

371.61 **Keratoconus, stable condition**

371.62 **Keratoconus, acute hydrops**

⑤ **371.7** **Other corneal deformities**

371.70 **Corneal deformity, unspecified**

371.71 **Corneal ectasia**

371.72 **Descemetocele**

371.73 **Corneal staphyloma**

⑤ **371.8** **Other corneal disorders**

371.81 **Corneal anesthesia and hypoesthesia**

371.82 **Corneal disorder due to contact lens**

Excludes: *corneal edema due to contact lens (371.24)*

371.89 **Other**

371.9 **Unspecified corneal disorder**

372 **Disorders of conjunctiva**

Excludes: *keratoconjunctivitis (370.3-370.4)*

⑤ **372.0** **Acute conjunctivitis**

372.00 **Acute conjunctivitis, unspecified**

372.01 **Serous conjunctivitis, except viral**

Excludes. *viral conjunctivitis NOS (077.9)*

372.02 **Acute follicular conjunctivitis**
Conjunctival folliculosis NOS

Excludes: *conjunctivitis:*
  adenoviral (acute follicular) (077.3)
  epidemic hemorrhagic (077.4)
  inclusion (077.0)
  Newcastle (077.8)
  epidemic keratoconjunctivitis (077.1)
  pharyngoconjunctival fever (077.2)

372.03 **Other mucopurulent conjunctivitis**
Catarrhal conjunctivitis

Excludes: *blennorrhea neonatorum (gonococcal) (098.40)*
  neonatal conjunctivitis (771.6)
  ophthalmia neonatorum NOS (771.6)

372.04 **Pseudomembranous conjunctivitis**
Membranous conjunctivitis

Excludes: *diphtheritic conjunctivitis (032.81)*

372.05 **Acute atopic conjunctivitis**

⑤ **372.1** **Chronic conjunctivitis**

372.10 **Chronic conjunctivitis, unspecified**

372.11 **Simple chronic conjunctivitis**

372.12 **Chronic follicular conjunctivitis**

372.13 **Vernal conjunctivitis**

372.14 **Other chronic allergic conjunctivitis**

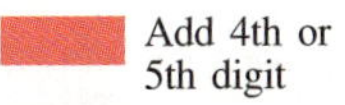 Add 4th or 5th digit    Nonspecific code    Unspecified code    Manifestation code

372.15 *Parasitic conjunctivitis*
Code first underlying disease, as:
filariasis (125.0-125.9)
mucocutaneous leishmaniasis (085.5)

⑤ **372.2 Blepharoconjunctivitis**

372.20 Blepharoconjunctivitis, unspecified

372.21 Angular blepharoconjunctivitis

372.22 Contact blepharoconjunctivitis

⑤ **372.3 Other and unspecified conjunctivitis**

372.30 Conjunctivitis, unspecified

372.31 *Rosacea conjunctivitis*
Code first underlying rosacea dermatitis (695.3)

372.33 *Conjunctivitis in mucocutaneous disease*
Code first underlying disease, as:
erythema multiforme (695.1)
Reiter's disease (099.3)

Excludes: ocular pemphigoid (694.61)

372.39 Other

⑤ **372.4 Pterygium**

Excludes: pseudopterygium (372.52)

372.40 Pterygium, unspecified

372.41 Peripheral pterygium, stationary

372.42 Peripheral pterygium, progressive

372.43 Central pterygium

372.44 Double pterygium

372.45 Recurrent pterygium

⑤ **372.5 Conjunctival degenerations and deposits**

372.50 Conjunctival degeneration, unspecified

372.51 Pinguecula

372.52 Pseudopterygium

372.53 Conjunctival xerosis

Excludes: conjunctival xerosis due to vitamin A deficiency (264.0, 264.1, 264.7)

372.54 Conjunctival concretions

372.55 Conjunctival pigmentations
Conjunctival argyrosis

372.56 Conjunctival deposits

⑤ **372.6 Conjunctival scars**

372.61 Granuloma of conjunctiva

372.62 Localized adhesions and strands of conjunctiva

372.63 Symblepharon
Extensive adhesions of conjunctiva

372.64 Scarring of conjunctiva
Contraction of eye socket (after enucleation)

⑤ **372.7 Conjunctival vascular disorders and cysts**

372.71 Hyperemia of conjunctiva

372.72 Conjunctival hemorrhage
Hyposphagma
Subconjunctival hemorrhage

372.73 Conjunctival edema
Chemosis of conjunctiva
Subconjunctival edema

372.74 Vascular abnormalities of conjunctiva
Aneurysm(ata) of conjunctiva

372.75 Conjunctival cysts

⑤ **372.8 Other disorders of conjunctiva**

● Code new to this edition   ▲ Revision of existing code   ④ ⑤ Fourth or fifth digit required

● **372.81 Conjunctivochalasis**

● **372.89 Other disorders of conjunctiva**

372.9 Unspecified disorder of conjunctiva

373 Inflammation of eyelids

⑤ **373.0 Blepharitis**

> |Excludes:| *blepharoconjunctivitis (372.20-372.22)*

373.00 Blepharitis, unspecified

373.01 Ulcerative blepharitis

373.02 Squamous blepharitis

⑤ **373.1 Hordeolum and other deep inflammation of eyelid**

373.11 Hordeolum externum
Hordeolum NOS
Stye

373.12 Hordeolum internum
Infection of meibomian gland

373.13 Abscess of eyelid
Furuncle of eyelid

373.2 Chalazion
Meibomian (gland) cyst

> |Excludes:| *infected meibomian gland (373.12)*

⑤ **373.3 Noninfectious dermatoses of eyelid**

373.31 Eczematous dermatitis of eyelid

373.32 Contact and allergic dermatitis of eyelid

373.33 Xeroderma of eyelid

373.34 Discoid lupus erythematosus of eyelid

373.4 *Infective dermatitis of eyelid of types resulting in deformity*
Code first underlying disease, as:
leprosy (030.0-030.9)
lupus vulgaris (tuberculous) (017.0)
yaws (102.0-102.9)

373.5 *Other infective dermatitis of eyelid*
Code first underlying disease, as:
actinomycosis (039.3)
impetigo (684)
mycotic dermatitis (110.0-111.9)
vaccinia (051.0)
postvaccination (999.0)

> |Excludes:| *herpes:*
> *simplex (054.41)*
> *zoster (053.20)*

373.6 *Parasitic infestation of eyelid*
Code first underlying disease, as:
leishmaniasis (085.0-085.9)
loiasis (125.2)
onchocerciasis (125.3)
pediculosis (132.0)

373.8 Other inflammations of eyelids

373.9 Unspecified inflammation of eyelid

374 Other disorders of eyelids

⑤ **374.0 Entropion and trichiasis of eyelid**

374.00 Entropion, unspecified

374.01 Senile entropion

374.02 Mechanical entropion

374.03 Spastic entropion

374.04 Cicatricial entropion

374.05 Trichiasis without entropion

⑤ **374.1 Ectropion**

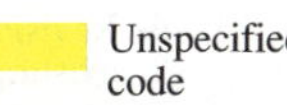

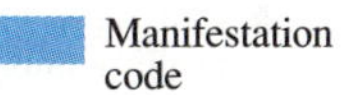

Manifestation
code

374.10 **Ectropion, unspecified**

374.11 **Senile ectropion**

374.12 **Mechanical ectropion**

374.13 **Spastic ectropion**

374.14 **Cicatricial ectropion**

⑤ 374.2 **Lagophthalmos**

374.20 **Lagophthalmos, unspecified**

374.21 **Paralytic lagophthalmos**

374.22 **Mechanical lagophthalmos**

374.23 **Cicatricial lagophthalmos**

⑤ 374.3 **Ptosis of eyelid**

374.30 **Ptosis of eyelid, unspecified**

374.31 **Paralytic ptosis**

374.32 **Myogenic ptosis**

374.33 **Mechanical ptosis**

374.34 **Blepharochalasis**
Pseudoptosis

⑤ 374.4 **Other disorders affecting eyelid function**

Excludes:	blepharoclonus (333.81)

blepharospasm (333.81)
facial nerve palsy (351.0)
third nerve palsy or paralysis (378.51-378.52)
tic (psychogenic) (307.20-307.23)
  organic (333.3)

374.41 **Lid retraction or lag**

374.43 **Abnormal innervation syndrome**
Jaw-blinking
Paradoxical facial movements

374.44 **Sensory disorders**

374.45 **Other sensorimotor disorders**
Deficient blink reflex

374.46 **Blepharophimosis**
Ankyloblepharon

⑤ 374.5 **Degenerative disorders of eyelid and periocular area**

374.50 **Degenerative disorder of eyelid, unspecified**

374.51 ***Xanthelasma***
Xanthoma (planum) (tuberosum) of eyelid
Code first underlying condition (272.0-272.9)

374.52 **Hyperpigmentation of eyelid**
Chloasma   Dyspigmentation

374.53 **Hypopigmentation of eyelid**
Vitiligo of eyelid

374.54 **Hypertrichosis of eyelid**

374.55 **Hypotrichosis of eyelid**
Madarosis of eyelid

374.56 **Other degenerative disorders of skin affecting eyelid**

⑤ 374.8 **Other disorders of eyelid**

374.81 **Hemorrhage of eyelid**

Excludes:	black eye (921.0)

374.82 **Edema of eyelid**
Hyperemia of eyelid

374.83 **Elephantiasis of eyelid**

374.84 **Cysts of eyelids**
Sebaceous cyst of eyelid

374.85 **Vascular anomalies of eyelid**

374.86 **Retained foreign body of eyelid**

● Code new
to this edition

▲ Revision of
existing code

④ ⑤ Fourth or fifth
digit required

374.87   **Dermatochalasis**

374.89   **Other disorders of eyelid**

374.9   **Unspecified disorder of eyelid**

375   **Disorders of lacrimal system**

⑤ **375.0**   **Dacryoadenitis**

375.00   **Dacryoadenitis, unspecified**

375.01   **Acute dacryoadenitis**

375.02   **Chronic dacryoadenitis**

375.03   **Chronic enlargement of lacrimal gland**

⑤ **375.1**   **Other disorders of lacrimal gland**

375.11   **Dacryops**

375.12   **Other lacrimal cysts and cystic degeneration**

375.13   **Primary lacrimal atrophy**

375.14   **Secondary lacrimal atrophy**

375.15   **Tear film insufficiency, unspecified**
     Dry eye syndrome

375.16   **Dislocation of lacrimal gland**

⑤ **375.2**   **Epiphora**

375.20   **Epiphora, unspecified as to cause**

375.21   **Epiphora due to excess lacrimation**

375.22   **Epiphora due to insufficient drainage**

⑤ **375.3**   **Acute and unspecified inflammation of lacrimal passages**

Excludes: *neonatal dacryocystitis (771.6)*

375.30   **Dacryocystitis, unspecified**

375.31   **Acute canaliculitis, lacrimal**

375.32   **Acute dacryocystitis**
     Acute peridacryocystitis

375.33   **Phlegmonous dacryocystitis**

⑤ **375.4**   **Chronic inflammation of lacrimal passages**

375.41   **Chronic canaliculitis**

375.42   **Chronic dacryocystitis**

375.43   **Lacrimal mucocele**

⑤ **375.5**   **Stenosis and insufficiency of lacrimal passages**

375.51   **Eversion of lacrimal punctum**

375.52   **Stenosis of lacrimal punctum**

375.53   **Stenosis of lacrimal canaliculi**

375.54   **Stenosis of lacrimal sac**

375.55   **Obstruction of nasolacrimal duct, neonatal**

Excludes: *congenital anomaly of nasolacrimal duct (743.65)*

375.56   **Stenosis of nasolacrimal duct, acquired**

375.57   **Dacryolith**

⑤ **375.6**   **Other changes of lacrimal passages**

375.61   **Lacrimal fistula**

375.69   **Other**

⑤ **375.8**   **Other disorders of lacrimal system**

375.81   **Granuloma of lacrimal passages**

375.89   **Other**

375.9   **Unspecified disorder of lacrimal system**

376   **Disorders of the orbit**

⑤ **376.0**   **Acute inflammation of orbit**

376.00   **Acute inflammation of orbit, unspecified**

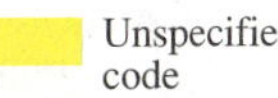

376.01   **Orbital cellulitis**
Abscess of orbit

376.02   **Orbital periostitis**

376.03   **Orbital osteomyelitis**

376.04   **Tenonitis**

⑤ **376.1**   **Chronic inflammatory disorders of orbit**

376.10   **Chronic inflammation of orbit, unspecified**

376.11   **Orbital granuloma**
Pseudotumor (inflammatory) of orbit

376.12   **Orbital myositis**

376.13   *Parasitic infestation of orbit*
Code first underlying disease, as:
hydatid infestation of orbit (122.3, 122.6, 122.9)
myiasis of orbit (134.0)

⑤ *376.2*   *Endocrine exophthalmos*
Code first underlying thyroid disorder (242.0-242.9)

376.21   *Thyrotoxic exophthalmos*

376.22   *Exophthalmic ophthalmoplegia*

⑤ **376.3**   **Other exophthalmic conditions**

376.30   **Exophthalmos, unspecified**

376.31   **Constant exophthalmos**

376.32   **Orbital hemorrhage**

376.33   **Orbital edema or congestion**

376.34   **Intermittent exophthalmos**

376.35   **Pulsating exophthalmos**

376.36   **Lateral displacement of globe**

⑤ **376.4**   **Deformity of orbit**

376.40   **Deformity of orbit, unspecified**

376.41   **Hypertelorism of orbit**

376.42   **Exostosis of orbit**

376.43   **Local deformities due to bone disease**

376.44   **Orbital deformities associated with craniofacial deformities**

376.45   **Atrophy of orbit**

376.46   **Enlargement of orbit**

376.47   **Deformity due to trauma or surgery**

⑤ **376.5**   **Enophthalmos**

376.50   **Enophthalmos, unspecified as to cause**

376.51   **Enophthalmos due to atrophy of orbital tissue**

376.52   **Enophthalmos due to trauma or surgery**

376.6   **Retained (old) foreign body following penetrating wound of orbit**
Retrobulbar foreign body

⑤ **376.8**   **Other orbital disorders**

376.81   **Orbital cysts**
Encephalocele of orbit

376.82   **Myopathy of extraocular muscles**

376.89   **Other**

376.9   **Unspecified disorder of orbit**

377   **Disorders of optic nerve and visual pathways**

⑤ **377.0**   **Papilledema**

377.00   **Papilledema, unspecified**

377.01   **Papilledema associated with increased intracranial pressure**

377.02   **Papilledema associated with decreased ocular pressure**

377.03   **Papilledema associated with retinal disorder**

377.04   **Foster-Kennedy syndrome**

● Code new to this edition   ▲ Revision of existing code   ④ ⑤ Fourth or fifth digit required

⑤ **377.1 Optic atrophy**

377.10 Optic atrophy, unspecified

377.11 Primary optic atrophy

Excludes: neurosyphilitic optic atrophy (094.84)

377.12 Postinflammatory optic atrophy

377.13 Optic atrophy associated with retinal dystrophies

377.14 Glaucomatous atrophy [cupping] of optic disc

377.15 Partial optic atrophy
Temporal pallor of optic disc

377.16 Hereditary optic atrophy
Optic atrophy:
dominant hereditary
Leber's

⑤ **377.2 Other disorders of optic disc**

377.21 Drusen of optic disc

377.22 Crater-like holes of optic disc

377.23 Coloboma of optic disc

377.24 Pseudopapilledema

⑤ **377.3 Optic neuritis**

Excludes: meningococcal optic neuritis (036.81)

377.30 Optic neuritis, unspecified

377.31 Optic papillitis

377.32 Retrobulbar neuritis (acute)

Excludes: syphilitic retrobulbar neuritis (094.85)

377.33 Nutritional optic neuropathy

377.34 Toxic optic neuropathy
Toxic amblyopia

377.39 Other

Excludes: ischemic optic neuropathy (377.41)

⑤ **377.4 Other disorders of optic nerve**

377.41 Ischemic optic neuropathy

377.42 Hemorrhage in optic nerve sheaths

377.49 Other
Compression of optic nerve

⑤ **377.5 Disorders of optic chiasm**

377.51 Associated with pituitary neoplasms and disorders

377.52 Associated with other neoplasms

377.53 Associated with vascular disorders

377.54 Associated with inflammatory disorders

⑤ **377.6 Disorders of other visual pathways**

377.61 Associated with neoplasms

377.62 Associated with vascular disorders

377.63 Associated with inflammatory disorders

⑤ **377.7 Disorders of visual cortex**

Excludes: visual:
agnosia (368.16)
hallucinations (368.16)
halos (368.15)

377.71 Associated with neoplasms

377.72 Associated with vascular disorders

377.73 Associated with inflammatory disorders

377.75 Cortical blindness

377.9 Unspecified disorder of optic nerve and visual pathways

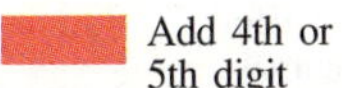
Add 4th or 5th digit

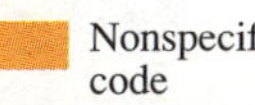
Nonspecific code

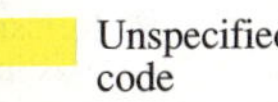
Unspecified code

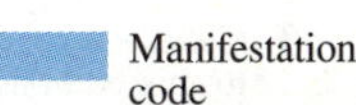
Manifestation code

378 **Strabismus and other disorders of binocular eye movements**

> *Excludes:* *nystagmus and other irregular eye movements (379.50-379.59)*

⑤ **378.0** **Esotropia**
Convergent concomitant strabismus

> *Excludes:* *intermittent esotropia (378.20-378.22)*

378.00 **Esotropia, unspecified**

378.01 **Monocular esotropia**

378.02 **Monocular esotropia with A pattern**

378.03 **Monocular esotropia with V pattern**

378.04 **Monocular esotropia with other noncomitancies**
Monocular esotropia with X or Y pattern

378.05 **Alternating esotropia**

378.06 **Alternating esotropia with A pattern**

378.07 **Alternating esotropia with V pattern**

378.08 **Alternating esotropia with other noncomitancies**
Alternating esotropia with X or Y pattern

⑤ **378.1** **Exotropia**
Divergent concomitant strabismus

> *Excludes:* *intermittent exotropia (378.20, 378.23-378.24)*

378.10 **Exotropia, unspecified**

378.11 **Monocular exotropia**

378.12 **Monocular exotropia with A pattern**

378.13 **Monocular exotropia with V pattern**

378.14 **Monocular exotropia with other noncomitancies**
Monocular exotropia with X or Y pattern

378.15 **Alternating exotropia**

378.16 **Alternating exotropia with A pattern**

378.17 **Alternating exotropia with V pattern**

378.18 **Alternating exotropia with other noncomitancies**
Alternating exotropia with X or Y pattern

⑤ **378.2** **Intermittent heterotropia**

> *Excludes:* *vertical heterotropia (intermittent) (378.31)*

378.20 **Intermittent heterotropia, unspecified**
Intermittent:
  esotropia NOS
  exotropia NOS

378.21 **Intermittent esotropia, monocular**

378.22 **Intermittent esotropia, alternating**

378.23 **Intermittent exotropia, monocular**

378.24 **Intermittent exotropia, alternating**

⑤ **378.3** **Other and unspecified heterotropia**

378.30 **Heterotropia, unspecified**

378.31 **Hypertropia**
Vertical heterotropia (constant) (intermittent)

378.32 **Hypotropia**

378.33 **Cyclotropia**

378.34 **Monofixation syndrome**
Microtropia

378.35 **Accommodative component in esotropia**

⑤ **378.4** **Heterophoria**

378.40 **Heterophoria, unspecified**

378.41 **Esophoria**

378.42 **Exophoria**

378.43 **Vertical heterophoria**

● Code new
  to this edition

▲ Revision of
  existing code

④ ⑤ Fourth or fifth
    digit required

378.44   Cyclophoria

378.45   Alternating hyperphoria

⑤ **378.5**   **Paralytic strabismus**

     `378.50`   Paralytic strabismus, unspecified

     378.51   Third or oculomotor nerve palsy, partial

     378.52   Third or oculomotor nerve palsy, total

     378.53   Fourth or trochlear nerve palsy

     378.54   Sixth or abducens nerve palsy

     378.55   External ophthalmoplegia

     378.56   Total ophthalmoplegia

⑤ **378.6**   **Mechanical strabismus**

     `378.60`   Mechanical strabismus, unspecified

     378.61   Brown's (tendon) sheath syndrome

     `378.62`   Mechanical strabismus from other musculofascial disorders

     `378.63`   Limited duction associated with other conditions

⑤ **378.7**   **Other specified strabismus**

     378.71   Duane's syndrome

     378.72   Progressive external ophthalmoplegia

     `378.73`   Strabismus in other neuromuscular disorders

⑤ **378.8**   **Other disorders of binocular eye movements**

     | Excludes: | nystagmus (379.50-379.56)

     378.81   Palsy of conjugate gaze

     378.82   Spasm of conjugate gaze

     378.83   Convergence insufficiency or palsy

     378.84   Convergence excess or spasm

     378.85   Anomalies of divergence

     378.86   Internuclear ophthalmoplegia

     `378.87`   Other dissociated deviation of eye movements
           Skew deviation

`378.9`   **Unspecified disorder of eye movements**
     Ophthalmoplegia NOS   Strabismus NOS

`379`   **Other disorders of eye**

⑤ **379.0**   **Scleritis and episcleritis**

     | Excludes: | syphilitic episcleritis (095.0)

     `379.00`   Scleritis, unspecified
           Episcleritis NOS

     379.01   Episcleritis periodica fugax

     379.02   Nodular episcleritis

     379.03   Anterior scleritis

     379.04   Scleromalacia perforans

     379.05   Scleritis with corneal involvement
           Scleroperikeratitis

     379.06   Brawny scleritis

     379.07   Posterior scleritis
           Sclerotenonitis

     `379.09`   Other
           Scleral abscess

⑤ **379.1**   **Other disorders of sclera**

     | Excludes: | blue sclera (743.47)

     379.11   Scleral ectasia
           Scleral staphyloma NOS

     379.12   Staphyloma posticum

     379.13   Equatorial staphyloma

379.14 **Anterior staphyloma, localized**

379.15 **Ring staphyloma**

379.16 **Other degenerative disorders of sclera**

379.19 **Other**

⑤ 379.2 **Disorders of vitreous body**

379.21 **Vitreous degeneration**
Vitreous:
cavitation
detachment
liquefaction

379.22 **Crystalline deposits in vitreous**
Asteroid hyalitis   Synchysis scintillans

379.23 **Vitreous hemorrhage**

379.24 **Other vitreous opacities**
Vitreous floaters

379.25 **Vitreous membranes and strands**

379.26 **Vitreous prolapse**

379.29 **Other disorders of vitreous**

Excludes: *vitreous abscess (360.04)*

⑤ 379.3 **Aphakia and other disorders of lens**

Excludes: *after-cataract (366.50-366.53)*

379.31 **Aphakia**

Excludes: *cataract extraction status (V45.61)*

379.32 **Subluxation of lens**

379.33 **Anterior dislocation of lens**

379.34 **Posterior dislocation of lens**

379.39 **Other disorders of lens**

⑤ 379.4 **Anomalies of pupillary function**

379.40 **Abnormal pupillary function, unspecified**

379.41 **Anisocoria**

379.42 **Miosis (persistent), not due to miotics**

379.43 **Mydriasis (persistent) not due to mydriatics**

379.45 **Argyll Robertson pupil, atypical**
Argyll Robertson phenomenon or pupil, nonsyphilitic

Excludes: *Argyll Robertson pupil (syphilitic) (094.89)*

379.46 **Tonic pupillary reaction**
Adie's pupil or syndrome

379.49 **Other**
Hippus
Pupillary paralysis

⑤ 379.5 **Nystagmus and other irregular eye movements**

379.50 **Nystagmus, unspecified**

379.51 **Congenital nystagmus**

379.52 **Latent nystagmus**

379.53 **Visual deprivation nystagmus**

379.54 **Nystagmus associated with disorders of the vestibular system**

379.55 **Dissociated nystagmus**

379.56 **Other forms of nystagmus**

379.57 **Deficiencies of saccadic eye movements**
Abnormal optokinetic response

379.58 **Deficiencies of smooth pursuit movements**

379.59 **Other irregularities of eye movements**
Opsoclonus

379.8 **Other specified disorders of eye and adnexa**

● Code new   ▲ Revision of   ④ ⑤ Fourth or fifth
to this edition   existing code   digit required

⑤ **379.9 Unspecified disorder of eye and adnexa**

379.90 Disorder of eye, unspecified

379.91 Pain in or around eye

379.92 Swelling or mass of eye

379.93 Redness or discharge of eye

379.99 Other ill-defined disorders of eye

Excludes: *blurred vision NOS (368.8)*

DISEASES OF THE EAR AND MASTOID PROCESS (380-389)

380 Disorders of external ear

⑤ **380.0 Perichondritis of pinna**
Perichondritis of auricle

380.00 Perichondritis of pinna, unspecified

380.01 Acute perichondritis of pinna

380.02 Chronic perichondritis of pinna

⑤ **380.1 Infective otitis externa**

380.10 Infective otitis externa, unspecified
Otitis externa (acute):
NOS
circumscribed
diffuse
hemorrhagica
infective NOS

380.11 Acute infection of pinna

Excludes: *furuncular otitis externa (680.0)*

380.12 Acute swimmers' ear
Beach ear   Tank ear

380.13 Other acute infections of external ear
Code first underlying disease, as:
erysipelas (035)
impetigo (684)
seborrheic dermatitis (690.10-690.18)

Excludes: *herpes simplex (054.73)*

herpes zoster (053.71)

380.14 Malignant otitis externa

380.15 Chronic mycotic otitis externa
Code first underlying disease, as:
aspergillosis (117.3)
otomycosis NOS (111.9)

Excludes: *candidal otitis externa (112.82)*

380.16 Other chronic infective otitis externa
Chronic infective otitis externa NOS

⑤ **380.2 Other otitis externa**

380.21 Cholesteatoma of external ear
Keratosis obturans of external ear (canal)

Excludes: *cholesteatoma NOS (385.30-385.35)*

postmastoidectomy (383.32)

380.22 Other acute otitis externa
Acute otitis externa:
actinic
chemical
contact
eczematoid
reactive

380.23 Other chronic otitis externa
Chronic otitis externa NOS

⑤ **380.3 Noninfectious disorders of pinna**

380.30 Disorder of pinna, unspecified

380.31 Hematoma of auricle or pinna

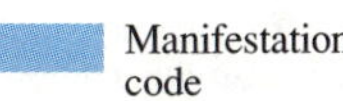

380.32 Acquired deformities of auricle or pinna

Excludes: *cauliflower ear (738.7)*

380.39 Other

Excludes: *gouty tophi of ear (274.81)*

380.4 Impacted cerumen
Wax in ear

⑤ **380.5 Acquired stenosis of external ear canal**
Collapse of external ear canal

380.50 Acquired stenosis of external ear canal, unspecified as to cause

380.51 Secondary to trauma

380.52 Secondary to surgery

380.53 Secondary to inflammation

⑤ **380.8 Other disorders of external ear**

380.81 Exostosis of external ear canal

380.89 Other

380.9 Unspecified disorder of external ear

381 Nonsuppurative otitis media and Eustachian tube disorders

⑤ **381.0 Acute nonsuppurative otitis media**
Acute tubotympanic catarrh
Otitis media, acute or subacute:
catarrhal
exudative
transudative
with effusion

Excludes: *otitic barotrauma (993.0)*

381.00 Acute nonsuppurative otitis media, unspecified

381.01 Acute serous otitis media
Acute or subacute secretory otitis media

381.02 Acute mucoid otitis media
Acute or subacute seromucinous otitis media
Blue drum syndrome

381.03 Acute sanguinous otitis media

381.04 Acute allergic serous otitis media

381.05 Acute allergic mucoid otitis media

381.06 Acute allergic sanguinous otitis media

⑤ **381.1 Chronic serous otitis media**
Chronic tubotympanic catarrh

381.10 Chronic serous otitis media, simple or unspecified

381.19 Other
Serosanguinous chronic otitis media

⑤ **381.2 Chronic mucoid otitis media**
Glue ear

Excludes: *adhesive middle ear disease (385.10-385.19)*

381.20 Chronic mucoid otitis media, simple or unspecified

381.29 Other
Mucosanguinous chronic otitis media

381.3 Other and unspecified chronic nonsuppurative otitis media

Otitis media, chronic:	Otitis media, chronic:
allergic	seromucinous
exudative	transudative
secretory	with effusion

381.4 Nonsuppurative otitis media, not specified as acute or chronic

Otitis media:	Otitis media:
allergic	secretory
catarrhal	seromucinous
exudative	serous
mucoid	transudative
	with effusion

● Code new
to this edition
▲ Revision of
existing code
④ ⑤ Fourth or fifth
digit required

⑤ **381.5 Eustachian salpingitis**

    381.50 Eustachian salpingitis, unspecified

    381.51 Acute Eustachian salpingitis

    381.52 Chronic Eustachian salpingitis

⑤ **381.6 Obstruction of Eustachian tube**

    Stenosis
    Stricture   } of Eustachian tube

    381.60 Obstruction of Eustachian tube, unspecified

    381.61 Osseous obstruction of Eustachian tube
        Obstruction of Eustachian tube from cholesteatoma, polyp, or other osseous lesion

    381.62 Intrinsic cartilagenous obstruction of Eustachian tube

    381.63 Extrinsic cartilagenous obstruction of Eustachian tube
        Compression of Eustachian tube

381.7 Patulous Eustachian tube

⑤ **381.8 Other disorders of Eustachian tube**

    381.81 Dysfunction of Eustachian tube

    381.89 Other

381.9 Unspecified Eustachian tube disorder

382 Suppurative and unspecified otitis media

⑤ **382.0 Acute suppurative otitis media**
    Otitis media, acute:
      necrotizing NOS
      purulent

    382.00 Acute suppurative otitis media without spontaneous rupture of ear drum

    382.01 Acute suppurative otitis media with spontaneous rupture of ear drum

    382.02 *Acute suppurative otitis media in diseases classified elsewhere*
      Code first underlying disease, as:
        influenza (487.8)
        scarlet fever (034.1)

    Excludes: *postmeasles otitis (055.2)*

382.1 Chronic tubotympanic suppurative otitis media
    Benign chronic suppurative otitis media   } (with anterior perforation of ear
    Chronic tubotympanic disease   drum)

382.2 Chronic atticoantral suppurative otitis media
    Chronic atticoantral disease   } (with posterior or superior
    Persistent mucosal disease   marginal perforation of ear drum)

382.3 Unspecified chronic suppurative otitis media
    Chronic purulent otitis media

    Excludes: *tuberculous otitis media (017.4)*

382.4 Unspecified suppurative otitis media
    Purulent otitis media NOS

382.9 Unspecified otitis media
    Otitis media:
      NOS
      acute NOS
      chronic NOS

383 Mastoiditis and related conditions

⑤ **383.0 Acute mastoiditis**
    Abscess of mastoid   Empyema of mastoid

    383.00 Acute mastoiditis without complications

    383.01 Subperiosteal abscess of mastoid

    383.02 Acute mastoiditis with other complications
      Gradenigo's syndrome

383.1 Chronic mastoiditis
    Caries of mastoid   Fistula of mastoid

    Excludes: *tuberculous mastoiditis (015.6)*

Add 4th or 5th digit	Nonspecific code	Unspecified code	Manifestation code

⑤ **383.2 Petrositis**
Coalescing osteitis
Inflammation
Osteomyelitis } of petrous bone

383.20 Petrositis, unspecified

383.21 Acute petrositis

383.22 Chronic petrositis

⑤ **383.3 Complications following mastoidectomy**

383.30 Postmastoidectomy complication, unspecified

383.31 Mucosal cyst of postmastoidectomy cavity

383.32 Recurrent cholesteatoma of postmastoidectomy cavity

383.33 Granulations of postmastoidectomy cavity
Chronic inflammation of postmastoidectomy cavity

⑤ **383.8 Other disorders of mastoid**

383.81 Postauricular fistula

383.89 Other

383.9 Unspecified mastoiditis

384 Other disorders of tympanic membrane

⑤ **384.0 Acute myringitis without mention of otitis media**

384.00 Acute myringitis, unspecified
Acute tympanitis NOS

384.01 Bullous myringitis
Myringitis bullosa hemorrhagica

384.09 Other

384.1 Chronic myringitis without mention of otitis media
Chronic tympanitis

⑤ **384.2 Perforation of tympanic membrane**
Perforation of ear drum:
NOS
persistent posttraumatic
postinflammatory

Excludes: *otitis media with perforation of tympanic membrane (382.00-382.9)*
traumatic perforation [current injury] (872.61)

384.20 Perforation of tympanic membrane, unspecified

384.21 Central perforation of tympanic membrane

384.22 Attic perforation of tympanic membrane
Pars flaccida

384.23 Other marginal perforation of tympanic membrane

384.24 Multiple perforations of tympanic membrane

384.25 Total perforation of tympanic membrane

⑤ **384.8 Other specified disorders of tympanic membrane**

384.81 Atrophic flaccid tympanic membrane
Healed perforation of ear drum

384.82 Atrophic nonflaccid tympanic membrane

384.9 Unspecified disorder of tympanic membrane

385 Other disorders of middle ear and mastoid

Excludes: *mastoiditis (383.0-383.9)*

⑤ **385.0 Tympanosclerosis**

385.00 Tympanosclerosis, unspecified as to involvement

385.01 Tympanosclerosis involving tympanic membrane only

385.02 Tympanosclerosis involving tympanic membrane and ear ossicles

385.03 Tympanosclerosis involving tympanic membrane, ear ossicles, and middle ear

385.09 Tympanosclerosis involving other combination of structures

● Code new to this edition   ▲ Revision of existing code   ④ ⑤ Fourth or fifth digit required

⑤ **385.1 Adhesive middle ear disease**
Adhesive otitis

Otitis media:
chronic adhesive
fibrotic

Excludes: *glue ear (381.20-381.29)*

385.10 Adhesive middle ear disease, unspecified as to involvement

385.11 Adhesions of drum head to incus

385.12 Adhesions of drum head to stapes

385.13 Adhesions of drum head to promontorium

385.19 Other adhesions and combinations

⑤ **385.2 Other acquired abnormality of ear ossicles**

385.21 Impaired mobility of malleus
Ankylosis of malleus

385.22 Impaired mobility of other ear ossicles
Ankylosis of ear ossicles, except malleus

385.23 Discontinuity or dislocation of ear ossicles

385.24 Partial loss or necrosis of ear ossicles

⑤ **385.3 Cholesteatoma of middle ear and mastoid**
Cholesterosis
Epidermosis
Keratosis
Polyp

} of (middle) ear

Excludes: *cholesteatoma:*
external ear canal (380.21)
recurrent of postmastoidectomy cavity (383.32)

385.30 Cholesteatoma, unspecified

385.31 Cholesteatoma of attic

385.32 Cholesteatoma of middle ear

385.33 Cholesteatoma of middle ear and mastoid

385.35 Diffuse cholesteatosis

⑤ **385.8 Other disorders of middle ear and mastoid**

385.82 Cholesterin granuloma

385.83 Retained foreign body of middle ear

385.89 Other

385.9 Unspecified disorder of middle ear and mastoid

386 Vertiginous syndromes and other disorders of vestibular system

Excludes: *vertigo NOS (780.4)*

⑤ **386.0 Ménière's disease**
Endolymphatic hydrops
Lermoyez's syndrome

Ménière's syndrome or vertigo

386.00 Ménière's disease, unspecified
Ménière's disease (active)

386.01 Active Ménière's disease, cochleovestibular

386.02 Active Ménière's disease, cochlear

386.03 Active Ménière's disease, vestibular

386.04 Inactive Ménière's disease
Ménière's disease in remission

⑤ **386.1 Other and unspecified peripheral vertigo**

Excludes: *epidemic vertigo (078.81)*

386.10 Peripheral vertigo, unspecified

386.11 Benign paroxysmal positional vertigo
Benign paroxysmal positional nystagmus

386.12 Vestibular neuronitis
Acute (and recurrent) peripheral vestibulopathy

386.19 Other
Aural vertigo　　　　　Otogenic vertigo

Manifestation
code

386.2 Vertigo of central origin
Central positional nystagmus
Malignant positional vertigo

⑤ **386.3 Labyrinthitis**

386.30 Labyrinthitis, unspecified

386.31 Serous labyrinthitis
Diffuse labyrinthitis

386.32 Circumscribed labyrinthitis
Focal labyrinthitis

386.33 Suppurative labyrinthitis
Purulent labyrinthitis

386.34 Toxic labyrinthitis

386.35 Viral labyrinthitis

⑤ **386.4 Labyrinthine fistula**

386.40 Labyrinthine fistula, unspecified

386.41 Round window fistula

386.42 Oval window fistula

386.43 Semicircular canal fistula

386.48 Labyrinthine fistula of combined sites

⑤ **386.5 Labyrinthine dysfunction**

386.50 Labyrinthine dysfunction, unspecified

386.51 Hyperactive labyrinth, unilateral

386.52 Hyperactive labyrinth, bilateral

386.53 Hypoactive labyrinth, unilateral

386.54 Hypoactive labyrinth, bilateral

386.55 Loss of labyrinthine reactivity, unilateral

386.56 Loss of labyrinthine reactivity, bilateral

386.58 Other forms and combinations

386.8 Other disorders of labyrinth

386.9 Unspecified vertiginous syndromes and labyrinthine disorders

387 Otosclerosis
Includes: otospongiosis

387.0 Otosclerosis involving oval window, nonobliterative

387.1 Otosclerosis involving oval window, obliterative

387.2 Cochlear otosclerosis
Otosclerosis involving:
otic capsule
round window

387.8 Other otosclerosis

387.9 Otosclerosis, unspecified

388 Other disorders of ear

⑤ **388.0 Degenerative and vascular disorders of ear**

388.00 Degenerative and vascular disorders, unspecified

388.01 Presbyacusis

388.02 Transient ischemic deafness

⑤ **388.1 Noise effects on inner ear**

388.10 Noise effects on inner ear, unspecified

388.11 Acoustic trauma (explosive) to ear
Otitic blast injury

388.12 Noise-induced hearing loss

388.2 Sudden hearing loss, unspecified

⑤ **388.3 Tinnitus**

388.30 Tinnitus, unspecified

388.31 Subjective tinnitus

388.32 Objective tinnitus

● Code new   ▲ Revision of   ④ ⑤ Fourth or fifth
to this edition   existing code   digit required

⑤ **388.4 Other abnormal auditory perception**

388.40 Abnormal auditory perception, unspecified

388.41 **Diplacusis**

388.42 **Hyperacusis**

388.43 **Impairment of auditory discrimination**

388.44 **Recruitment**

388.5 **Disorders of acoustic nerve**
Acoustic neuritis
Degeneration
Disorder } of acoustic or eighth nerve

Excludes: *acoustic neuroma (225.1)*
syphilitic acoustic neuritis (094.86)

⑤ **388.6 Otorrhea**

388.60 Otorrhea, unspecified
Discharging ear NOS

388.61 **Cerebrospinal fluid otorrhea**

Excludes: *cerebrospinal fluid rhinorrhea (349.81)*

388.69 Other
Otorrhagia

⑤ **388.7 Otalgia**

388.70 Otalgia, unspecified
Earache NOS

388.71 **Otogenic pain**

388.72 **Referred pain**

388.8 Other disorders of ear

388.9 Unspecified disorder of ear

389 Hearing loss

⑤ **389.0 Conductive hearing loss**
Conductive deafness

389.00 Conductive hearing loss, unspecified

389.01 **Conductive hearing loss, external ear**

389.02 **Conductive hearing loss, tympanic membrane**

389.03 **Conductive hearing loss, middle ear**

389.04 **Conductive hearing loss, inner ear**

389.08 **Conductive hearing loss of combined types**

⑤ **389.1 Sensorineural hearing loss**
Perceptive hearing loss or deafness

Excludes: *abnormal auditory perception (388.40-388.44)*
psychogenic deafness (306.7)

389.10 Sensorineural hearing loss, unspecified

389.11 **Sensory hearing loss**

389.12 **Neural hearing loss**

389.14 **Central hearing loss**

389.18 **Sensorineural hearing loss of combined types**

389.2 **Mixed conductive and sensorineural hearing loss**
Deafness or hearing loss of type classifiable to 389.0 with type classifiable to 389.1

389.7 **Deaf mutism, not elsewhere classifiable**
Deaf, nonspeaking

389.8 Other specified forms of hearing loss

389.9 Unspecified hearing loss
Deafness NOS

Add 4th or
5th digit

Nonspecific
code

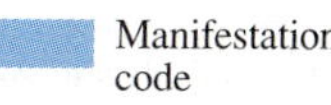
Unspecified
code

Manifestation
code

● Code new
to this edition

▲ Revision of
existing code

④ ⑤ Fourth or fifth
digit required

7. DISEASES OF THE CIRCULATORY SYSTEM (390-459)

ACUTE RHEUMATIC FEVER (390-392)

390 Rheumatic fever without mention of heart involvement
Arthritis, rheumatic, acute or subacute
Rheumatic fever (active) (acute)
Rheumatism, articular, acute or subacute

Excludes: *that with heart involvement (391.0-391.9)*

391 Rheumatic fever with heart involvement

Excludes: *chronic heart diseases of rheumatic origin (393.0-398.9) unless rheumatic fever is also present or there is evidence of recrudescence or activity of the rheumatic process*

391.0 Acute rheumatic pericarditis
Rheumatic:
fever (active) (acute) with pericarditis
pericarditis (acute)
Any condition classifiable to 390 with pericarditis

Excludes: *that not specified as rheumatic (420.0-420.9)*

391.1 Acute rheumatic endocarditis
Rheumatic:
endocarditis, acute
fever (active) (acute) with endocarditis or valvulitis
valvulitis acute
Any condition classifiable to 390 with endocarditis or valvulitis

391.2 Acute rheumatic myocarditis
Rheumatic fever (active) (acute) with myocarditis
Any condition classifiable to 390 with myocarditis

391.8 Other acute rheumatic heart disease
Rheumatic:
fever (active) (acute) with other or multiple types of heart involvement
pancarditis, acute
Any condition classifiable to 390 with other or multiple types of heart involvement

391.9 Acute rheumatic heart disease, unspecified
Rheumatic:
carditis, acute
fever (active) (acute) with unspecified type of heart involvement
heart disease, active or acute
Any condition classifiable to 390 with unspecified type of heart involvement

392 Rheumatic chorea
Includes: Sydenham's chorea

Excludes: *chorea:*
NOS (333.5)
Huntington's (333.4)

392.0 With heart involvement
Rheumatic chorea with heart involvement of any type classifiable to 391

392.9 Without mention of heart involvement

CHRONIC RHEUMATIC HEART DISEASE (393-398)

393 Chronic rheumatic pericarditis
Adherent pericardium, rheumatic
Chronic rheumatic:
mediastinopericarditis
myopericarditis

Excludes: *pericarditis NOS or not specified as rheumatic (423.0-423.9)*

394 Diseases of mitral valve

Excludes: *that with aortic valve involvement (396.0-396.9)*

394.0 Mitral stenosis
Mitral (valve):
obstruction (rheumatic)
stenosis NOS

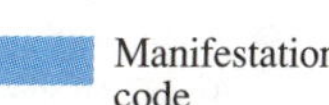

	Add 4th or 5th digit		Nonspecific code		Unspecified code		Manifestation code

394.1 Rheumatic mitral insufficiency
  Rheumatic mitral:
    incompetence
    regurgitation

  Excludes: *that not specified as rheumatic (424.0)*

394.2 Mitral stenosis with insufficiency
  Mitral stenosis with incompetence or regurgitation

394.9 Other and unspecified mitral valve diseases
  Mitral (valve):
    disease (chronic)
    failure

395 Diseases of aortic valve

  Excludes: *that not specified as rheumatic (424.1)*
         that with mitral valve involvement (396.0-396.9)

395.0 Rheumatic aortic stenosis
  Rheumatic aortic (valve) obstruction

395.1 Rheumatic aortic insufficiency
  Rheumatic aortic:
    incompetence
    regurgitation

395.2 Rheumatic aortic stenosis with insufficiency
  Rheumatic aortic stenosis with incompetence or regurgitation

395.9 Other and unspecified rheumatic aortic diseases
  Rheumatic aortic (valve) disease

396 Diseases of mitral and aortic valves
  Includes: involvement of both mitral and aortic valves, whether specified as rheumatic or not

396.0 Mitral valve stenosis and aortic valve stenosis
  Atypical aortic (valve) stenosis
  Mitral and aortic (valve) obstruction (rheumatic)

396.1 Mitral valve stenosis and aortic valve insufficiency

396.2 Mitral valve insufficiency and aortic valve stenosis

396.3 Mitral valve insufficiency and aortic valve insufficiency
  Mitral and aortic (valve):
    incompetence
    regurgitation

396.8 Multiple involvement of mitral and aortic valves
  Stenosis and insufficiency of mitral or aortic valve with stenosis or insufficiency, or
     both, of the other valve

396.9 Mitral and aortic valve diseases, unspecified

397 Diseases of other endocardial structures

397.0 Diseases of tricuspid valve
  Tricuspid (valve) (rheumatic):
    disease
    insufficiency
    obstruction
    regurgitation
    stenosis

397.1 Rheumatic diseases of pulmonary valve

  Excludes: *that not specified as rheumatic (424.3)*

397.9 Rheumatic diseases of endocardium, valve unspecified
  Rheumatic:
    endocarditis (chronic)
    valvulitis (chronic)

  Excludes: *that not specified as rheumatic (424.90-424.99)*

398 Other rheumatic heart disease

398.0 Rheumatic myocarditis
  Rheumatic degeneration of myocardium

  Excludes: *myocarditis not specified as rheumatic (429.0)*

⑤ **398.9 Other and unspecified rheumatic heart diseases**

● Code new   ▲ Revision of   ④ ⑤ Fourth or fifth
  to this edition   existing code   digit required

398.90 **Rheumatic heart disease, unspecified**
    Rheumatic:
      carditis
      heart disease NOS

Excludes: *carditis not specified as rheumatic (429.89)*
    heart disease NOS not specified as rheumatic (429.9)

398.91 **Rheumatic heart failure (congestive)**
    Rheumatic left ventricular failure

398.99 **Other**

HYPERTENSIVE DISEASE (401-405)

Excludes: *that complicating pregnancy, childbirth, or the puerperium (642.0-642.9)*
    that involving coronary vessels (410.00-414.9)

401 **Essential hypertension**
    Includes: high blood pressure
              hyperpiesia
              hyperpiesis
              hypertension (arterial) (essential) (primary) (systemic)
              hypertensive vascular:
                degeneration
                disease

Excludes: *elevated blood pressure without diagnosis of hypertension (796.2)*
    pulmonary hypertension (416.0-416.9)
    that involving vessels of:
      brain (430-438)
      eye (362.11)

401.0 **Malignant**

401.1 **Benign**

401.9 **Unspecified**

402 **Hypertensive heart disease**
    Includes: hypertensive:
              cardiomegaly
              cardiopathy
              cardiovascular disease
              heart (disease) (failure)
        any condition classifiable to 428, 429.0-429.3, 429.8, 429.9 due to hypertension

⑤ **402.0** **Malignant**

402.00 **Without congestive heart failure**

402.01 **With congestive heart failure**

⑤ **402.1** **Benign**

402.10 **Without congestive heart failure**

402.11 **With congestive heart failure**

⑤ **402.9** **Unspecified**

402.90 **Without congestive heart failure**

402.91 **With congestive heart failure**

⑤ **403** **Hypertensive renal disease**

The following fifth-digit subclassification is for use with category 403:

    0   **without mention of renal failure**

    1   **with renal failure**
    Includes: arteriolar nephritis
              arteriosclerosis of:
                kidney
                renal arterioles
              arteriosclerotic nephritis (chronic) (interstitial)
              hypertensive:
                nephropathy
                renal failure
                uremia (chronic)
              nephrosclerosis
              renal sclerosis with hypertension
        any condition classifiable to 585, 586, or 587 with any condition classifiable to 401

Excludes: *acute renal failure (584.5-584.9)*

continued

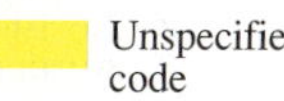

renal disease stated as not due to hypertension
renovascular hypertension (405.0-405.9 with fifth-digit 1)

⑤ **403.0 Malignant**

⑤ **403.1 Benign**

⑤ **403.9 Unspecified**

⑤ **404 Hypertensive heart and renal disease**

The following fifth-digit subclassification is for use with category 404:

    **0 without mention of congestive heart failure
or renal failure**

    1 with congestive heart failure

    2 with renal failure

    3 with congestive heart failure and renal failure
Includes: disease:
      cardiornal
      cardiovascular renal
    any condition classifiable to 402 with any condition classifiable to 403

⑤ **404.0 Malignant**

⑤ **404.1 Benign**

⑤ **404.9 Unspecified**

405 Secondary hypertension

⑤ **405.0 Malignant**

    405.01 Renovascular

    405.09 Other

⑤ **405.1 Benign**

    405.11 Renovascular

    405.19 Other

⑤ **405.9 Unspecified**

    405.91 Renovascular

    405.99 Other

ISCHEMIC HEART DISEASE (410-414)

Includes: that with mention of hypertension

Use additional code, if desired, to identify presence of hypertension (401.0-405.9)

⑤ **410 Acute myocardial infarction**
Includes: cardiac infarction
coronary (artery):
    embolism
    occlusion
    rupture
    thrombosis
infarction of heart, myocardium, or ventricle
rupture of heart, myocardium, or ventricle
any condition classifiable to 414.1-414.9 specified as acute or with a stated
    duration of 8 weeks or less

The following fifth-digit subclassification is for use with category 410:

    0 episode of care unspecified
Use when the source document does not contain sufficient information for the
assignment of fifth digit 1 or 2.

    1 initial episode of care
Use fifth digit 1 to designate the first episode of care (regardless of facility site) for
a newly diagnosed myocardial infarction. The fifth digit 1 is assigned regardless
of the number of times a patient may be transferred during the initial episode of
care

    2 subsequent episode of care
Use fifth digit 2 to designate an episode of care following the initial episode when
the patient is admitted for further observation, evaluation, or treatment for a
myocardial infarction that has received initial treatment, but is still less than 8
weeks old.

⑤ **410.0 Of anterolateral wall**

    ● Code new   ▲ Revision of   ④ ⑤ Fourth or fifth
      to this edition   existing code   digit required

⑤ **410.1 Of other anterior wall**
Infarction:
anterior (wall) NOS ⎫
anteroapical ⎬ (with contiguous portion of intraventricular septum)
anteroseptal ⎭

⑤ **410.2 Of inferolateral wall**

⑤ **410.3 Of inferoposterior wall**

⑤ **410.4 Of other inferior wall**
Infarction:
diaphragmatic wall ⎫
inferior (wall) NOS ⎬ (with contiguous portion of intraventricular septum)

⑤ **410.5 Of other lateral wall**
Infarction: Infarction:
apical-lateral   high lateral
basal-lateral   posterolateral

⑤ **410.6 True posterior wall infarction**
Infarction:
posterobasal
strictly posterior

⑤ **410.7 Subendocardial infarction**
Nontransmural infarction

⑤ **410.8 Of other specified sites**
Infarction of:
atrium
papillary muscle
septum alone

⑤ **410.9 Unspecified site**
Acute myocardial infarction NOS
Coronary occlusion NOS

411 Other acute and subacute forms of ischemic heart disease

411.0 Postmyocardial infarction syndrome
Dressler's syndrome

411.1 Intermediate coronary syndrome
Impending infarction   Preinfarction syndrome
Preinfarction angina   Unstable angina

Excludes: *angina (pectoris) (413.9)*
decubitus (413.0)

⑤ **411.8 Other**

411.81 Coronary occlusion without myocardial infarction
Coronary (artery): ⎫
embolism ⎬ without or not resulting in myocardial infarction
occlusion ⎪
thrombosis ⎭

Excludes: *occlusion without infarction due to atherosclerosis (414.00-414.05)*

411.89 Other
Coronary insufficiency (acute)
Subendocardial ischemia

412 Old myocardial infarction
Healed myocardial infarction
Past myocardial infarction diagnosed on ECG [EKG] or other special investigation, but currently presenting no symptoms

413 Angina pectoris

413.0 Angina decubitus
Nocturnal angina

413.1 Prinzmetal angina
Variant angina pectoris

413.9 Other and unspecified angina pectoris
Angina: Anginal syndrome
NOS   Status anginosus
cardiac   Stenocardia
of effort   Syncope anginosa

Excludes: *preinfarction angina (411.1)*

▮	Add 4th or 5th digit	▮	Nonspecific code	▮	Unspecified code	▮	Manifestation code

414 **Other forms of chronic ischemic heart disease**

> *Excludes:* *arteriosclerotic cardiovascular disease [ASCVD] (429.2)*
> *cardiovascular:*
> *arteriosclerosis or sclerosis (429.2)*
> *degeneration or disease (429.2)*

⑤ **414.0** **Coronary atherosclerosis**
Arteriosclerotic heart disease [ASHD]
Atherosclerotic heart disease
Coronary (artery):
arteriosclerosis
arteritis or endarteritis
atheroma
sclerosis
stricture

> *Excludes:* *embolism of graft (996.72)*
> *occlusion NOS of graft (996.72)*
> *thrombus of graft (996.72)*

414.00 **Of unspecified type of vessel, native or graft**

414.01 **Of native coronary artery**

414.02 **Of autologous vein bypass graft**

414.03 **Of nonautologous biological bypass graft**

414.04 **Of artery bypass graft**
Internal mammary artery

414.05 **Of unspecified type of bypass graft**
Bypass graft NOS

⑤ **414.1** **Aneurysm of heart**

414.10 **Of heart (wall)**
Aneurysm (arteriovenous):
mural
ventricular

414.11 **Of coronary vessels**
Aneurysm (arteriovenous) of coronary vessels

414.19 **Other**
Arteriovenous fistula, acquired, of heart

414.8 **Other specified forms of chronic ischemic heart disease**
Chronic coronary insufficiency
Ischemia, myocardial (chronic)
Any condition classifiable to 410 specified as chronic, or presenting with symptoms
after 8 weeks from date of infarction

> *Excludes:* *coronary insufficiency (acute) (411.89)*

414.9 **Chronic ischemic heart disease, unspecified**
Ischemic heart disease NOS

DISEASES OF PULMONARY CIRCULATION (415-417)

415 **Acute pulmonary heart disease**

415.0 **Acute cor pulmonale**

> *Excludes:* *cor pulmonale NOS (416.9)*

⑤ **415.1** **Pulmonary embolism and infarction**
Pulmonary (artery) (vein):
apoplexy
embolism
infarction (hemorrhagic)
thrombosis

> *Excludes:* *that complicating:*
> *abortion (634-638 with .6, 639.6)*
> *ectopic or molar pregnancy (639.6)*
> *pregnancy, childbirth, or the puerperium (673.0-673.8)*

415.11 **Iatrogenic pulmonary embolism and infarction**

415.19 **Other**

416 **Chronic pulmonary heart disease**

● Code new to this edition   ▲ Revision of existing code   ④ ⑤ Fourth or fifth digit required

416.0 Primary pulmonary hypertension
Idiopathic pulmonary arteriosclerosis
Pulmonary hypertension (essential) (idiopathic) (primary)

416.1 Kyphoscoliotic heart disease

416.8 Other chronic pulmonary heart diseases
Pulmonary hypertension, secondary

416.9 Chronic pulmonary heart disease, unspecified
Chronic cardiopulmonary disease
Cor pulmonale (chronic) NOS

417 Other diseases of pulmonary circulation

417.0 Arteriovenous fistula of pulmonary vessels

Excludes: congenital arteriovenous fistula (747.3)

417.1 Aneurysm of pulmonary artery

Excludes: congenital aneurysm (747.3)

417.8 Other specified diseases of pulmonary circulation
Pulmonary:
  arteritis
  endarteritis
Rupture ⎫
Stricture ⎭ of pulmonary vessel

417.9 Unspecified disease of pulmonary circulation

OTHER FORMS OF HEART DISEASE (420-429)

420 Acute pericarditis
Includes: acute:
  mediastinopericarditis
  myopericarditis
  pericardial effusion
  pleuropericarditis
  pneumopericarditis

Excludes: acute rheumatic pericarditis (391.0)

postmyocardial infarction syndrome [Dressler's] (411.0)

420.0 Acute pericarditis in diseases classified elsewhere
Code first underlying disease, as:
  actinomycosis (039.8)
  amebiasis (006.8)
  nocardiosis (039.8)
  tuberculosis (017.9)
  uremia (585)

Excludes: pericarditis (acute) (in):
  Coxsackie (virus) (074.21)
  gonococcal (098.83)
  histoplasmosis (115.0-115.9 with fifth-digit 3)
  meningococcal infection (036.41)
  syphilitic (093.81)

⑤ **420.9 Other and unspecified acute pericarditis**

420.90 Acute pericarditis, unspecified
Pericarditis (acute):
  NOS
  infective NOS
  sicca

420.91 Acute idiopathic pericarditis
Pericarditis, acute:
  benign
  nonspecific
  viral

420.99 Other

Pericarditis (acute):	Pericarditis (acute):
pneumococcal	streptococcal
purulent	suppurative
staphylococcal	Pneumopyopericardium
	Pyopericardium

Excludes: pericarditis in diseases classified elsewhere (420.0)

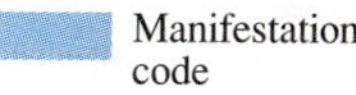

Manifestation
code

421   Acute and subacute endocarditis

421.0   Acute and subacute bacterial endocarditis

Endocarditis (acute)
  (chronic) (subacute):
   bacterial
   infective NOS
   lenta
   malignant
   purulent

Endocarditis (acute) (chronic) (subacute):
  septic
  ulcerative
  vegetative
Infective aneurysm
Subacute bacterial endocarditis [SBE]

Use additional code, if desired, to identify infectious organism [e.g., Streptococcus 041.0, Staphylococcus 041.1]

421.1   *Acute and subacute infective endocarditis in diseases classified elsewhere*

Code first underlying disease, as:
  blastomycosis (116.0)
  Q fever (083.0)
  typhoid (fever) (002.0)

Excludes: *endocarditis (in):*

> *Coxsackie (virus) (074.22)*
> *gonococcal (098.84)*
> *histoplasmosis (115.0-115.9 with fifth-digit 4)*
> *meningococcal infection (036.42)*
> *monilial (112.81)*

421.9   Acute endocarditis, unspecified

Endocarditis
Myoendocarditis } acute or subacute
Periendocarditis

Excludes: *acute rheumatic endocarditis (391.1)*

422   Acute myocarditis

Excludes: *acute rheumatic myocarditis (391.2)*

422.0   *Acute myocarditis in diseases classified elsewhere*

Code first underlying disease, as:
  myocarditis (acute):
   influenzal (487.8)
   tuberculous (017.9)

Excludes: *myocarditis (acute) (due to):*

> *aseptic, of newborn (074.23)*
> *Coxsackie (virus) (074.23)*
> *diphtheritic (032.82)*
> *meningococcal infection (036.43)*
> *syphilitic (093.82)*
> *toxoplasmosis (130.3)*

⑤ **422.9   Other and unspecified acute myocarditis**

422.90   Acute myocarditis, unspecified

Acute or subacute (interstitial) myocarditis

422.91   Idiopathic myocarditis

Myocarditis (acute or subacute):
  Fiedler's
  giant cell
  isolated (diffuse) (granulomatous)
  nonspecific granulomatous

422.92   Septic myocarditis

Myocarditis, acute or subacute:
  pneumococcal
  staphylococcal

Use additional code, if desired, to identify infectious organism [e.g., Staphylococcus 041.1]

Excludes: *myocarditis, acute or subacute:*

> *in bacterial diseases classified elsewhere (422.0)*
> *streptococcal (391.2)*

422.93   Toxic myocarditis

422.99   Other

● Code new   ▲ Revision of   ④ ⑤ Fourth or fifth
  to this edition   existing code   digit required

423 **Other diseases of pericardium**

> *Excludes:* that specified as rheumatic (393)

423.0 **Hemopericardium**

423.1 **Adhesive pericarditis**

Adherent pericardium
Fibrosis of pericardium
Milk spots

Pericarditis:
  adhesive
  obliterative
Soldiers' patches

423.2 **Constrictive pericarditis**

Concato's disease
Pick's disease of heart (and liver)

423.8 **Other specified diseases of pericardium**

Calcification
Fistula
} of pericardium

423.9 **Unspecified disease of pericardium**

424 **Other diseases of endocardium**

> *Excludes:* bacterial endocarditis (421.0-421.9)
>   rheumatic endocarditis (391.1, 394.0-397.9)
>   syphilitic endocarditis (093.20-093.24)

424.0 **Mitral valve disorders**

Mitral (valve):
  incompetence
  insufficiency
  regurgitation
} NOS of specified cause, except rheumatic

> *Excludes:* mitral (valve):
>   disease (394.9)
>   failure (394.9)
>   stenosis (394.0)
>   the listed conditions:
>   specified as rheumatic (394.1)
>   unspecified as to cause but with mention of:
>   diseases of aortic valve (396.0-396.9)
>   mitral stenosis or obstruction (394.2)

424.1 **Aortic valve disorders**

Aortic (valve):
  incompetence
  insufficiency
  regurgitation
  stenosis
} NOS of specified cause, except rheumatic

> *Excludes:* hypertrophic subaortic stenosis (425.1)
>   that specified as rheumatic (395.0-395.9)
>   that of unspecified cause but with mention of diseases of mitral valve (396.0-396.9)

424.2 **Tricuspid valve disorders, specified as nonrheumatic**

Tricuspid valve:
  incompetence
  insufficiency
  regurgitation
  stenosis
} of specified cause, except rheumatic

> *Excludes:* rheumatic or of unspecified cause (397.0)

424.3 **Pulmonary valve disorders**

Pulmonic:
  incompetence NOS
  insufficiency NOS

Pulmonic:
  regurgitation NOS
  stenosis NOS

> *Excludes:* that specified as rheumatic (397.1)

⑤ **424.9** **Endocarditis, valve unspecified**

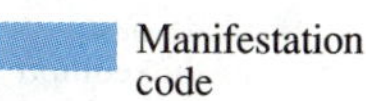

■ Add 4th or 5th digit	■ Nonspecific code	■ Unspecified code	■ Manifestation code

424.90 Endocarditis, valve unspecified, unspecified cause
Endocarditis (chronic):
   NOS
   nonbacterial thrombotic
Valvular:
   incompetence
   insufficiency
   regurgitation } of unspecified valve, unspecified cause
   stenosis
Valvulitis (chronic)

424.91 *Endocarditis in diseases classified elsewhere*
Code first underlying disease, as:
   atypical verrucous endocarditis [Libman-Sacks] (710.0)
   disseminated lupus erythematosus (710.0)
   tuberculosis (017.9)

|Excludes:| *syphilitic (093.20-093.24)*

424.99 Other
Any condition classifiable to 424.90 with specified cause, except rheumatic

|Excludes:| *endocardial fibroelastosis (425.3)*
that specified as rheumatic (397.9)

425 Cardiomyopathy
Includes: myocardiopathy

425.0 Endomyocardial fibrosis

425.1 Hypertrophic obstructive cardiomyopathy
Hypertrophic subaortic stenosis (idiopathic)

425.2 Obscure cardiomyopathy of Africa
Becker's disease
Idiopathic mural endomyocardial disease

425.3 Endocardial fibroelastosis
Elastomyofibrosis

425.4 Other primary cardiomyopathies

Cardiomyopathy:	Cardiomyopathy:
NOS	idiopathic
congestive	nonobstructive
constrictive	obstructive
familial	restrictive
hypertrophic	Cardiovascular collagenosis

425.5 Alcoholic cardiomyopathy

425.7 *Nutritional and metabolic cardiomyopathy*
Code first underlying disease, as:
   amyloidosis (277.3)
   beriberi (265.0)
   cardiac glycogenosis (271.0)
   mucopolysaccharidosis (277.5)
   thyrotoxicosis (242.0-242.9)

|Excludes:| *gouty tophi of heart (274.82)*

425.8 *Cardiomyopathy in other diseases classified elsewhere*
Code first underlying disease, as:
   Friedreich's ataxia (334.0)
   myotonia atrophica (359.2)
   progressive muscular dystrophy (359.1)
   sarcoidosis (135)

|Excludes:| *cardiomyopathy in Chagas' disease (086.0)*

425.9 Secondary cardiomyopathy, unspecified

426 Conduction disorders

426.0 Atrioventricular block, complete
Third degree atrioventricular block

⑤ **426.1 Atrioventricular block, other and unspecified**

426.10 Atrioventricular block, unspecified
Atrioventricular [AV] block (incomplete) (partial)

● Code new   ▲ Revision of   ④ ⑤ Fourth or fifth
   to this edition   existing code   digit required

426.11   First degree atrioventricular block
Incomplete atrioventricular block, first degree
Prolonged P-R interval NOS

426.12   Mobitz (type) II atrioventricular block
Incomplete atrioventricular block:
   Mobitz (type) II
   second degree, Mobitz (type) II

426.13   Other second degree atrioventricular block
Incomplete atrioventricular block:
   Mobitz (type) I [Wenckebach's]
   second degree:
      NOS
      Mobitz (type) I
   with 2:1 atrioventricular response [block]
Wenckebach's phenomenon

426.2   Left bundle branch hemiblock
Block:
   left anterior fascicular
   left posterior fascicular

426.3   Other left bundle branch block
Left bundle branch block:
   NOS
   anterior fascicular with posterior fascicular
   complete
   main stem

426.4   Right bundle branch block

⑤ **426.5   Bundle branch block, other and unspecified**

426.50   Bundle branch block, unspecified

426.51   Right bundle branch block and left posterior fascicular block

426.52   Right bundle branch block and left anterior fascicular block

426.53   Other bilateral bundle branch block
Bifascicular block NOS
Bilateral bundle branch block NOS
Right bundle branch with left bundle branch block (incomplete) (main stem)

426.54   Trifascicular block

426.6   Other heart block
Intraventricular block: Sinoatrial block
   NOS   Sinoauricular block
   diffuse
   myofibrillar

426.7   Anomalous atrioventricular excitation
Atrioventricular conduction:
   accelerated
   accessory
   pre-excitation
Ventricular pre-excitation
Wolff-Parkinson-White syndrome

⑤ **426.8   Other specified conduction disorders**

426.81   Lown-Ganong-Levine syndrome
Syndrome of short P-R interval, normal QRS complexes, and supraventricular
   tachycardias

426.89   Other
Dissociation:
   atrioventricular [AV]
   interference
   isorhythmic
Nonparoxysmal AV nodal tachycardia

426.9   Conduction disorder, unspecified
Heart block NOS   Stokes-Adams syndrome

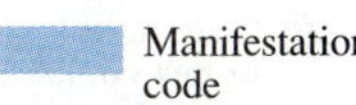

Manifestation
code

427 Cardiac dysrhythmias

> Excludes: *that complicating:*
>> *abortion (634-638 with .7, 639.8)*
>> *ectopic or molar pregnancy (639.8)*
>> *labor or delivery (668.1, 669.4)*

427.0 Paroxysmal supraventricular tachycardia
Paroxysmal tachycardia:
atrial [PAT]
atrioventricular [AV]
junctional
nodal

427.1 Paroxysmal ventricular tachycardia
Ventricular tachycardia (paroxysmal)

427.2 Paroxysmal tachycardia, unspecified
Bouveret-Hoffmann syndrome
Paroxysmal tachycardia:
NOS
essential

⑤ **427.3 Atrial fibrillation and flutter**

  427.31 Atrial fibrillation

  427.32 Atrial flutter

⑤ **427.4 Ventricular fibrillation and flutter**

  427.41 Ventricular fibrillation

  427.42 Ventricular flutter

427.5 Cardiac arrest
Cardiorespiratory arrest

⑤ **427.6 Premature beats**

  427.60 Premature beats, unspecified
  Ectopic beats
  Extrasystoles
  Extrasystolic arrhythmia
  Premature contractions or systoles NOS

  427.61 Supraventricular premature beats
  Atrial premature beats, contractions, or systoles

  427.69 Other
  Ventricular premature beats, contractions, or systoles

⑤ **427.8 Other specified cardiac dysrhythmias**

  427.81 Sinoatrial node dysfunction
  Sinus bradycardia: Syndrome:
  persistent   sick sinus
  severe   tachycardia-bradycardia

  > Excludes: *sinus bradycardia NOS (427.89)*

  427.89 Other
  Rhythm disorder: Wandering (atrial) pacemaker
  coronary sinus
  ectopic
  nodal

  > Excludes: *carotid sinus syncope (337.0)*
  >> *reflex bradycardia (337.0)*
  >> *tachycardia (785.0)*

427.9 Cardiac dysrhythmia, unspecified
Arrhythmia (cardiac) NOS

428 Heart failure

> Excludes: *following cardiac surgery (429.4)*
>> *rheumatic (398.91)*
>> *that complicating:*
>>> *abortion (634-638 with .7, 639.8)*
>>> *ectopic or molar pregnancy (639.8)*
>>> *labor or delivery (668.1, 669.4)*
>> *that due to hypertension (402.0-402.9 with fifth-digit 1)*

● Code new to this edition   ▲ Revision of existing code   ④ ⑤ Fourth or fifth digit required

428.0 Congestive heart failure
Congestive heart disease
Right heart failure (secondary to left heart failure)

428.1 Left heart failure
Acute edema of lung
Acute pulmonary edema } with heart disease NOS or heart failure
Cardiac asthma
Left ventricular failure

428.9 Heart failure, unspecified
Cardiac failure NOS   Myocardial failure NOS
Heart failure NOS   Weak heart

429 Ill-defined descriptions and complications of heart disease

429.0 Myocarditis, unspecified
Myocarditis:
  NOS
  chronic (interstitial) } (with mention of arteriosclerosis)
  fibroid
  senile

Use additional code, if desired, to identify presence of arteriosclerosis

Excludes: *acute or subacute (422.0-422.9)*
rheumatic (398.0)
acute (391.2)
that due to hypertension (402.0-402.9)

429.1 Myocardial degeneration
Degeneration of heart or myocardium:
  fatty
  mural
  muscular } (with mention of arteriosclerosis)
Myocardial:
  degeneration disease

Use additional code, if desired, to identify presence of arteriosclerosis

Excludes: *that due to hypertension (402.0-402.9)*

429.2 Cardiovascular disease, unspecified
Arteriosclerotic cardiovascular disease [ASCVD]
Cardiovascular arteriosclerosis
Cardiovascular:
  degeneration
  disease } (with mention of arteriosclerosis)
  sclerosis

Use additional code, if desired, to identify presence of arteriosclerosis

Excludes: *that due to hypertension (402.0-402.9)*

429.3 Cardiomegaly
Cardiac: Ventricular dilatation
  dilatation
  hypertrophy

Excludes: *that due to hypertension (402.0-402.9)*

429.4 Functional disturbances following cardiac surgery
Cardiac insufficiency
Heart failure } following cardiac surgery or due to prosthesis
Postcardiotomy syndrome
Postvalvulotomy syndrome

Excludes: *cardiac failure in the immediate postoperative period (997.1)*

429.5 Rupture of chordae tendineae

429.6 Rupture of papillary muscle

Manifestation
code

⑤ **429.7 Certain sequelae of myocardial infarction, not elsewhere classified**
Use additional code to identify the associated myocardial infarction:
with onset of 8 weeks or less (410.00-410.92)
with onset of more than 8 weeks (414.8)

Excludes: *congenital defects of heart (745, 746)*
coronary aneurysm (414.11)
disorders of papillary muscle (429.6, 429.81)
postmyocardial infarction syndrome (411.0)
rupture of chordae tendineae (429.5)

429.71   Acquired cardiac septal defect

Excludes: *acute septal infarction (410.00-410.92)*

429.79   Other
Mural thrombus (atrial) (ventricular), acquired, following myocardial infarction

⑤ **429.8 Other ill-defined heart diseases**

429.81   Other disorders of papillary muscle
Papillary muscle: Papillary muscle:
  atrophy   incompetence
  degeneration   incoordination
  dysfunction   scarring

429.82   Hyperkinetic heart disease

429.89   Other
Carditis

Excludes: *that due to hypertension (402.0-402.9)*

429.9 Heart disease, unspecified
Heart disease (organic) NOS
Morbus cordis NOS

Excludes: *that due to hypertension (402.0-402.9)*

CEREBROVASCULAR DISEASE (430-438)

Includes: with mention of hypertension (conditions classifiable to 401-405)
Use additional code, if desired, to identify presence of hypertension

Excludes: *any condition classifiable to 430-434, 436, 437 occurring during pregnancy,*
childbirth, or the puerperium, or specified as puerperal (674.0)

430 Subarachnoid hemorrhage
Meningeal hemorrhage
Ruptured:
berry aneurysm
(congenital) cerebral aneurysm NOS

Excludes: *syphilitic ruptured cerebral aneurysm (094.87)*

431 Intracerebral hemorrhage
Hemorrhage (of):   Hemorrhage (of):
  basilar   intrapontine
  bulbar   pontine
  cerebellar   subcortical
  cerebral   ventricular
  cerebromeningeal   Rupture of blood vessel in brain
  cortical
  internal capsule

432 Other and unspecified intracranial hemorrhage

432.0 Nontraumatic extradural hemorrhage
Nontraumatic epidural hemorrhage

432.1 Subdural hemorrhage
Subdural hematoma, nontraumatic

432.9 Unspecified intracranial hemorrhage
Intracranial hemorrhage NOS

● Code new
  to this edition

▲ Revision of
  existing code

④ ⑤ Fourth or fifth
  digit required

⑤ **433** **Occlusion and stenosis of precerebral arteries**

The following fifth-digit subclassification is for use with category 433:

    0 **without mention of cerebral infarction**

    1 **with cerebral infarction**

Includes:

    embolism
    narrowing
    obstruction   } of basilar, carotid, and vertebral arteries
    thrombosis

Excludes: *insufficiency NOS of precerebral arteries (435.0-435.9)*

⑤ **433.0** **Basilar artery**

⑤ **433.1** **Carotid artery**

⑤ **433.2** **Vertebral artery**

⑤ **433.3** **Multiple and bilateral**

⑤ **433.8** **Other specified precerebral artery**

⑤ **433.9** **Unspecified precerebral artery**
    Precerebral artery NOS

⑤ **434** **Occlusion of cerebral arteries**

The following fifth-digit subclassification is for use with category 434:

    0 **without mention of cerebral infarction**

    1 **with cerebral infarction**

⑤ **434.0** **Cerebral thrombosis**
    Thrombosis of cerebral arteries

⑤ **434.1** **Cerebral embolism**

⑤ **434.9** **Cerebral artery occlusion, unspecified**

435 **Transient cerebral ischemia**
    Includes: cerebrovascular insufficiency (acute) with transient focal neurological signs and
            symptoms
           insufficiency of basilar, carotid, and vertebral arteries
           spasm of cerebral arteries

Excludes: *acute cerebrovascular insufficiency NOS (437.1)*
          that due to any condition classifiable to 433 (433.0-433.9)

435.0 **Basilar artery syndrome**

435.1 **Vertebral artery syndrome**

435.2 **Subclavian steal syndrome**

435.3 **Vertebrobasilar artery syndrome**

435.8 **Other specified transient cerebral ischemias**

435.9 **Unspecified transient cerebral ischemia**
    Impending cerebrovascular accident
    Intermittent cerebral ischemia
    Transient ischemic attack [TIA]

436 **Acute, but ill-defined, cerebrovascular disease**
    Apoplexy, apoplectic: Cerebral seizure
      NOS   Cerebrovascular accident [CVA] NOS
      attack   Stroke
      cerebral
      seizure

Excludes: *any condition classifiable to categories 430-435*

437 **Other and ill-defined cerebrovascular disease**

437.0 **Cerebral atherosclerosis**
    Atheroma of cerebral arteries
    Cerebral arteriosclerosis

437.1 **Other generalized ischemic cerebrovascular disease**
    Acute cerebrovascular insufficiency NOS
    Cerebral ischemia (chronic)

437.2 **Hypertensive encephalopathy**

437.3 Cerebral aneurysm, nonruptured
Internal carotid artery, intracranial portion
Internal carotid artery NOS

Excludes: *congenital cerebral aneurysm, nonruptured (747.81)*
internal carotid artery, extracranial portion (442.81)

437.4 Cerebral arteritis

437.5 Moyamoya disease

437.6 Nonpyogenic thrombosis of intracranial venous sinus

Excludes: *pyogenic (325)*

437.7 Transient global amnesia

437.8 Other

437.9 Unspecified
Cerebrovascular disease or lesion NOS

438 Late effects of cerebrovascular disease
Note: This category is to be used to indicate conditions in 430-437 as the cause of late effects. The "late effects" include conditions specified as such, as sequelae, which may occur at any time after the onset of the causal condition.

438.0 Cognitive deficits

⑤ **438.1 Speech and language deficits**

    438.10 Speech and language deficit, unspecified

    438.11 Aphasia

    438.12 Dysphasia

    438.19 Other speech and language deficits

⑤ **438.2 Hemiplegia/hemiparesis**

    438.20 Hemiplegia affecting unspecified side

    438.21 Hemiplegia affecting dominant side

    438.22 Hemiplegia affecting nondominant side

⑤ **438.3 Monoplegia of upper limb**

    438.30 Monoplegia of upper limb affecting unspecified side

    438.31 Monoplegia of upper limb affecting dominant side

    438.32 Monoplegia of upper limb affecting nondominant side

⑤ **438.4 Monoplegia of lower limb**

    438.40 Monoplegia of lower limb affecting unspecified side

    438.41 Monoplegia of lower limb affecting dominant side

    438.42 Monoplegia of lower limb affecting nondominant side

⑤ **438.5 Other paralytic syndrome**
Use additional code to identify type of paralytic syndrome, such as:
locked-in state (344.81)
quadriplegia (344.00-344.09)

Excludes: *late effects of cerebrovascular accident with:*
hemiplegia/hemiparesis (438.20-438.22)
monoplegia of lower limb (438.40-438.42)
monoplegia of upper limb (438.30-438.32)

    438.50 Other paralytic syndrome affecting unspecified side

    438.51 Other paralytic syndrome affecting dominant side

    438.52 Other paralytic syndrome affecting nondominant side

    438.53 Other paralytic syndrome, bilateral

⑤ **438.8 Other late effects of cerebrovascular disease**

    438.81 Apraxia

    438.82 Dysphagia

    438.89 Other late effects of cerebrovascular disease
    Use additional code to identify the late effect

438.9 Unspecified late effects of cerebrovascular disease

● Code new to this edition   ▲ Revision of existing code   ④ ⑤ Fourth or fifth digit required

DISEASES OF ARTERIES, ARTERIOLES, AND CAPILLARIES (440-448)

440 **Atherosclerosis**

Includes: arteriolosclerosis
arteriosclerosis (obliterans) (senile)
arteriosclerotic vascular disease
atheroma
degeneration:
arterial
arteriovascular
vascular
endarteritis deformans or obliterans
senile arteritis
senile endarteritis

Excludes: *atherosclerosis of bypass graft of the extremities (440.30-440.32)*

440.0 Of aorta

440.1 Of renal artery

Excludes: *atherosclerosis of renal arterioles (403.00-403.91)*

⑤ **440.2 Of native arteries of the extremities**

Excludes: *atherosclerosis of bypass graft of the extremities (440.30-440.32)*

440.20 **Atherosclerosis of the extremities, unspecified**

440.21 **Atherosclerosis of the extremities with intermittent claudication**

440.22 **Atherosclerosis of the extremities with rest pain**
Includes: any condition classifiable to 440.21

440.23 **Atherosclerosis of the extremities with ulceration**
Includes: any condition classifiable to 440.21 and 440.22
Use additional code for any associated ulceration (707.10-707.9)

440.24 **Atherosclerosis of the extremities with gangrene**
Includes: any condition classifiable to 440.21, 440.22, and 440.23
with ischemic gangrene 785.4

Excludes: *gas gangrene 040.0*

440.29 **Other**

⑤ **440.3 Of bypass graft of the extremities**

Excludes: *atherosclerosis of native artery of the extremity (440.21-440.24)*
embolism [occlusion NOS] [thrombus]
of graft (996.74)

440.30 **Of unspecified graft**

440.31 **Of autologous vein bypass graft**

440.32 **Of nonautologous biological bypass graft**

440.8 Of other specified arteries

Excludes: *basilar (433.0)*

carotid (433.1)
cerebral (437.0)
coronary (414.00-414.05)
mesenteric (557.1)
precerebral (433.0-433.9)
pulmonary (416.0)
vertebral (433.2)

440.9 Generalized and unspecified atherosclerosis
Arteriosclerotic vascular disease NOS

Excludes: *arteriosclerotic cardiovascular disease [ASCVD] (429.2)*

441 **Aortic aneurysm and dissection**

Excludes: *syphilitic aortic aneurysm (093.0)*

traumatic aortic aneurysm (901.0, 902.0)

⑤ **441.0 Dissection of aorta**
Dissecting aneurysm of aorta (ruptured)

441.00 **Unspecified site**

441.01 **Thoracic**

441.02 **Abdominal**

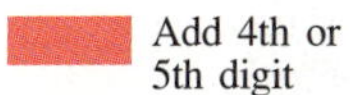

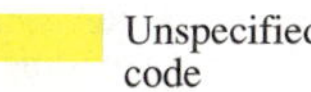

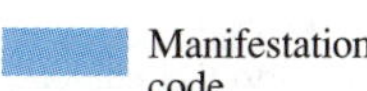

441.03   Thoracoabdominal

441.1   Thoracic aneurysm, ruptured

441.2   Thoracic aneurysm without mention of rupture

441.3   Abdominal aneurysm, ruptured

441.4   Abdominal aneurysm without mention of rupture

441.5   Aortic aneurysm of unspecified site, ruptured
  Rupture of aorta NOS

441.6   Thoracoabdominal aneurysm, ruptured

441.7   Thoracoabdominal aneurysm, without mention of rupture

441.9   Aortic aneurysm of unspecified site without mention of rupture
  Aneurysm
  Dilatation   } of aorta
  Hyaline necrosis

442   Other aneurysm
  Includes: aneurysm (ruptured) (cirsoid) (false) (varicose)
        aneurysmal varix

  Excludes: *arteriovenous aneurysm or fistula:*
        acquired (447.0)
        congenital (747.60-747.69)
        traumatic (900.0-904.9)

442.0   Of artery of upper extremity

442.1   Of renal artery

442.2   Of iliac artery

442.3   Of artery of lower extremity
  Aneurysm:
    femoral   } artery
    popliteal

⑤ **442.8   Of other specified artery**

  442.81   Artery of neck
      Aneurysm of carotid artery (common) (external) (internal, extracranial portion)

  Excludes: *internal carotid artery, intracranial portion (437.3)*

  442.82   Subclavian artery

  442.83   Splenic artery

  442.84   Other visceral artery
      Aneurysm:
        celiac
        gastroduodenal
        gastroepiploic
        hepatic   } artery
        pancreaticoduodenal
        superior mesenteric

  442.89   Other
      Aneurysm:
        mediastinal   } artery
        spinal

  Excludes: *cerebral (nonruptured) (437.3)*
        congenital (747.81)
        ruptured (430)
        coronary (414.11)
        heart (414.10)
        pulmonary (417.1)

442.9   Of unspecified site

443   Other peripheral vascular disease

443.0   Raynaud's syndrome
  Raynaud's:
    disease
    phenomenon (secondary)
  Use additional code, if desired, to identify gangrene (785.4)

443.1   Thromboangiitis obliterans [Buerger's disease]
  Presenile gangrene

● Code new   ▲ Revision of   ④ ⑤ Fourth or fifth
  to this edition   existing code   digit required

⑤ **443.8 Other specified peripheral vascular diseases**

443.81 *Peripheral angiopathy in diseases classified elsewhere*
Code first underlying disease, as:
diabetes mellitus (250.7)

443.89 Other
Acrocyanosis
Acroparesthesia:
simple [Schultze's type]
vasomotor [Nothnagel's type]
Erythrocyanosis
Erythromelalgia

Excludes: *chilblains (991.5)*
frostbite (991.0-991.3)
immersion foot (991.4)

443.9 Peripheral vascular disease, unspecified
Intermittent claudication NOS
Peripheral:
angiopathy NOS
vascular disease NOS
Spasm of artery

Excludes: *atherosclerosis of the arteries of the extremities (440.20-440.22)*
spasm of cerebral artery (435.0-435.9)

444 Arterial embolism and thrombosis
Includes: infarction:
embolic
thrombotic
occlusion

Excludes: *that complicating:*
abortion (634-638 with .6, 639.6)
ectopic or molar pregnancy (639.6)
pregnancy, childbirth, or the puerperium (673.0-673.8)

444.0 Of abdominal aorta
Aortic bifurcation syndrome   Leriche's syndrome
Aortoiliac obstruction   Saddle embolus

444.1 Of thoracic aorta
Embolism or thrombosis of aorta (thoracic)

⑤ **444.2 Of arteries of the extremities**

444.21 Upper extremity

444.22 Lower extremity
Arterial embolism or thrombosis:
femoral
peripheral NOS
popliteal

Excludes: *iliofemoral (444.81)*

⑤ **444.8 Of other specified artery**

444.81 Iliac artery

444.89 Other

Excludes: *basilar (433.0)*
carotid (433.1)
cerebral (434.0-434.9)
coronary (410.00-410.92)
mesenteric (557.0)
ophthalmic (362.30-362.34)
precerebral (433.0-433.9)
pulmonary (415.19)
renal (593.81)
retinal (362.30-362.34)
vertebral (433.2)

444.9 Of unspecified artery

446 Polyarteritis nodosa and allied conditions

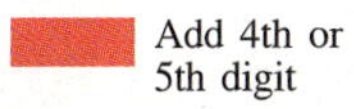

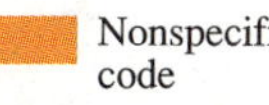

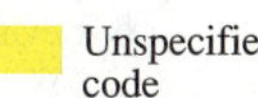

446.0 Polyarteritis nodosa
Disseminated necrotizing   Panarteritis (nodosa)
periarteritis   Periarteritis (nodosa)
Necrotizing angiitis

446.1 Acute febrile mucocutaneous lymph node syndrome [MCLS]
Kawasaki disease

⑤ **446.2 Hypersensitivity angiitis**

| Excludes: | antiglomerular basement membrane disease without pulmonary hemorrhage (583.89) |

446.20 Hypersensitivity angiitis, unspecified

446.21 Goodpasture's syndrome
Antiglomerular basement membrane antibody-mediated nephritis with
pulmonary hemorrhage
Use additional code, if desired, to identify renal disease (583.81)

446.29 Other specified hypersensitivity angiitis

446.3 Lethal midline granuloma
Malignant granuloma of face

446.4 Wegener's granulomatosis
Necrotizing respiratory granulomatosis
Wegener's syndrome

446.5 Giant cell arteritis
Cranial arteritis   Temporal arteritis
Horton's disease

446.6 Thrombotic microangiopathy
Moschcowitz's syndrome
Thrombotic thrombocytopenic purpura

446.7 Takayasu's disease
Aortic arch arteritis   Pulseless disease

447 Other disorders of arteries and arterioles

447.0 Arteriovenous fistula, acquired
Arteriovenous aneurysm, acquired

| Excludes: | cerebrovascular (437.3) |

coronary (414.19)
pulmonary (417.0)
surgically created arteriovenous shunt or fistula:
complication (996.1, 996.61-996.62)
status or presence (V45.1)
traumatic (900.0-904.9)

447.1 Stricture of artery

447.2 Rupture of artery
Erosion
Fistula, except arteriovenous   } of artery
Ulcer

| Excludes: | traumatic rupture of artery (900.0-904.9) |

447.3 Hyperplasia of renal artery
Fibromuscular hyperplasia of renal artery

447.4 Celiac artery compression syndrome
Celiac axis syndrome   Marable's syndrome

447.5 Necrosis of artery

447.6 Arteritis, unspecified
Aortitis NOS
Endarteritis NOS

| Excludes: | arteritis, endarteritis: |

aortic arch (446.7)
cerebral (437.4)
coronary (414.00-414.05)
deformans (440.0-440.9)
obliterans (440.0-440.9)
pulmonary (417.8)
senile (440.0-440.9)
polyarteritis NOS (446.0)
syphilitic aortitis (093.1)

● Code new   ▲ Revision of   ④ ⑤ Fourth or fifth
to this edition   existing code   digit required

447.8 **Other specified disorders of arteries and arterioles**
Fibromuscular hyperplasia of arteries, except renal

447.9 **Unspecified disorders of arteries and arterioles**

448 **Disease of capillaries**

448.0 **Hereditary hemorrhagic telangiectasia**
Rendu-Osler-Weber disease

448.1 **Nevus, non-neoplastic**

Nevus: Nevus:
   araneus   spider
   senile   stellar

Excludes: *neoplastic (216.0-216.9)*
port wine (757.32)
strawberry (757.32)

448.9 **Other and unspecified capillary diseases**
Capillary:
   hemorrhage
   hyperpermeability
   thrombosis

Excludes: *capillary fragility (hereditary) (287.8)*

DISEASES OF VEINS AND LYMPHATICS, AND OTHER DISEASES OF CIRCULATORY SYSTEM (451-459)

451 **Phlebitis and thrombophlebitis**
Includes: endophlebitis
           inflammation, vein
           periphlebitis
           suppurative phlebitis

Use additional E Code, if desired, to identify drug, if drug-induced

Excludes: *that complicating:*
abortion (634-638 with .7, 639.8)
ectopic or molar pregnancy (639.8)
pregnancy, childbirth, or the puerperium (671.0-671.9)
that due to or following:
implant or catheter device (996.61-996.62)
infusion, perfusion, or transfusion (999.2)

451.0 **Of superficial vessels of lower extremities**
Saphenous vein (greater) (lesser)

⑤ **451.1** **Of deep vessels of lower extremities**

451.11 **Femoral vein (deep) (superficial)**

451.19 **Other**
Femoropopliteal vein
Popliteal vein
Tibial vein

451.2 **Of lower extremities, unspecified**

⑤ **451.8** **Of other sites**

Excludes: *intracranial venous sinus (325)*
nonpyogenic (437.6)
portal (vein) (572.1)

451.81 **Iliac vein**

451.82 **Of superficial veins of upper extremities**
Antecubital vein
Basilic vein
Cephalic vein

451.83 **Of deep veins of upper extremities**
Brachial vein
Radial vein
Ulnar vein

451.84 **Of upper extremities, unspecified**

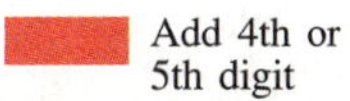

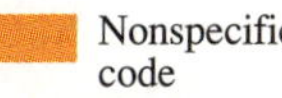

Manifestation
code

451.89 Other
Axillary vein
Jugular vein
Subclavian vein
Thrombophlebitis of breast (Mondor's disease)

451.9 Of unspecified site

452 Portal vein thrombosis
Portal (vein) obstruction

Excludes: *hepatic vein thrombosis (453.0)*
phlebitis of portal vein (572.1)

453 Other venous embolism and thrombosis

Excludes: *that complicating:*
abortion (634-638 with .7, 639.8)
ectopic or molar pregnancy (639.8)
pregnancy, childbirth, or the puerperium (671.0-671.9)
that with inflammation, phlebitis, and thrombophlebitis (451.0-451.9)

453.0 Budd-Chiari syndrome
Hepatic vein thrombosis

453.1 Thrombophlebitis migrans

453.2 Of vena cava

453.3 Of renal vein

453.8 Of other specified veins

Excludes: *cerebral (434.0-434.9)*
coronary (410.00-410.92)
intracranial venous sinus (325)
  nonpyogenic (437.6)
mesenteric (557.0)
portal (452)
precerebral (433.0-433.9)
pulmonary (415.19)

453.9 Of unspecified site
Embolism of vein   Thrombosis (vein)

454 Varicose veins of lower extremities

Excludes: *that complicating pregnancy, childbirth, or the puerperium (671.0)*

454.0 With ulcer
Varicose ulcer (lower extremity, any part)
Varicose veins with ulcer of lower extremity [any part] or of unspecified site
Any condition classifiable to 454.9 with ulcer or specified as ulcerated

454.1 With inflammation
Stasis dermatitis
Varicose veins with inflammation of lower extremity [any part] or of unspecified site
Any condition classifiable to 454.9 with inflammation or specified as inflamed

454.2 With ulcer and inflammation
Varicose veins with ulcer and inflammation of lower extremity [any part] or of
  unspecified site
Any condition classifiable to 454.9 with ulcer and inflammation

454.9 Without mention of ulcer or inflammation
Phlebectasia
Varicose veins   } of lower extremity [any part] or of unspecified site
Varix

455 Hemorrhoids
Includes: hemorrhoids (anus) (rectum)
piles
varicose veins, anus or rectum

Excludes: *that complicating pregnancy, childbirth or the puerperium (671.8)*

455.0 Internal hemorrhoids without mention of complication

455.1 Internal thrombosed hemorrhoids

455.2 Internal hemorrhoids with other complication
Internal hemorrhoids: Internal hemorrhoids:
  bleeding   strangulated
  prolapsed   ulcerated

● Code new   ▲ Revision of   ④ ⑤ Fourth or fifth
  to this edition   existing code   digit required

455.3   External hemorrhoids without mention of complication

455.4   External thrombosed hemorrhoids

455.5   External hemorrhoids with other complication
External hemorrhoids: External hemorrhoids:
  bleeding   strangulated
  prolapsed   ulcerated

455.6   Unspecified hemorrhoids without mention of complication
Hemorrhoids NOS

455.7   Unspecified thrombosed hemorrhoids
Thrombosed hemorrhoids, unspecified whether internal or external

455.8   Unspecified hemorrhoids with other complication
Hemorrhoids, unspecified whether internal or external:
  bleeding
  prolapsed
  strangulated
  ulcerated

455.9   Residual hemorrhoidal skin tags
Skin tags, anus or rectum

456   Varicose veins of other sites

456.0   Esophageal varices with bleeding

456.1   Esophageal varices without mention of bleeding

⑤ *456.2   Esophageal varices in diseases classified elsewhere*
Code first underlying cause, as:
  cirrhosis of liver (571.0-571.9)
  portal hypertension (572.3)

456.20   *With bleeding*

456.21   *Without mention of bleeding*

456.3   Sublingual varices

456.4   Scrotal varices
Varicocele

456.5   Pelvic varices
Varices of broad ligament

456.6   Vulval varices
Varices of perineum

| Excludes: | *that complicating pregnancy, childbirth, or the puerperium (671.1)* |

456.8   Varices of other sites
Varicose veins of nasal septum (with ulcer)

| Excludes: | *placental varices (656.7)* |

retinal varices (362.17)
varicose ulcer of unspecified site (454.0)
varicose veins of unspecified site (454.9)

457   Noninfectious disorders of lymphatic channels

457.0   Postmastectomy lymphedema syndrome
Elephantiasis
Obliteration of lymphatic vessel   } due to mastectomy

457.1   Other lymphedema
Elephantiasis (nonfilarial) NOS
Lymphangiectasis
Lymphedema:
  acquired (chronic)
  praecox
  secondary
Obliteration, lymphatic vessel

| Excludes: | *elephantiasis (nonfilarial):* |

congenital (757.0)
eyelid (374.83)
vulva (624.8)

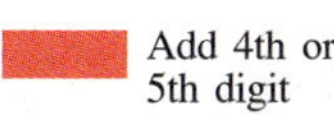

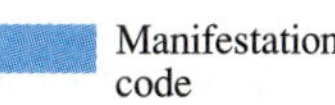

457.2 Lymphangitis
Lymphangitis:
  NOS
  chronic
  subacute

Excludes: *acute lymphangitis (682.0-682.9)*

457.8 Other noninfectious disorders of lymphatic channels
Chylocele (nonfilarial)   Lymph node or vessel:
Chylous: fistula
  ascites   infarction
  cyst   rupture

Excludes: *chylocele:*
            filarial (125.0-125.9)
            tunica vaginalis (nonfilarial) (608.84)

457.9 Unspecified noninfectious disorder of lymphatic channels

458 Hypotension
Includes: hypopiesis

Excludes: *cardiovascular collapse (785.50)*
            maternal hypotension syndrome (669.2)
            shock (785.50-785.59)
            Shy-Drager syndrome (333.0)

458.0 Orthostatic hypotension
Hypotension:
  orthostatic (chronic)
  postural

458.1 Chronic hypotension
Permanent idiopathic hypotension

458.2 Iatrogenic hypotension
Postoperative hypotension

458.8 Other specified hypotension

458.9 Hypotension, unspecified
Hypotension (arterial) NOS

459 Other disorders of circulatory system

459.0 Hemorrhage, unspecified
Rupture of blood vessel NOS
Spontaneous hemorrhage NEC

Excludes: *hemorrhage:*
            gastrointestinal NOS (578.9)
            in newborn NOS (772.9)
            secondary or recurrent following trauma (958.2)
            traumatic rupture of blood vessel (900.0-904.9)

459.1 Postphlebitic syndrome

459.2 Compression of vein
Stricture of vein
Vena cava syndrome (inferior) (superior)

⑤ **459.8 Other specified disorders of circulatory system**

  459.81 Venous (peripheral) insufficiency, unspecified
Chronic venous insufficiency NOS
Use additional code for any associated ulceration (707.10-707.9)

  459.89 Other
Collateral circulation (venous), any site
Phlebosclerosis
Venofibrosis

459.9 Unspecified circulatory system disorder

● Code new   ▲ Revision of   ④ ⑤ Fourth or fifth
  to this edition   existing code   digit required

8. DISEASES OF THE RESPIRATORY SYSTEM (460-519)

Use additional code, if desired, to identify infectious organism

ACUTE RESPIRATORY INFECTIONS (460-466)

Excludes: *pneumonia and influenza (480.0-487.8)*

460 Acute nasopharyngitis [common cold]

Coryza (acute)
Nasal catarrh, acute
Nasopharyngitis:
  NOS
  acute
  infective NOS

Rhinitis:
  acute
  infective

Excludes: *nasopharyngitis, chronic (472.2)*
  pharyngitis:
    acute or unspecified (462)
    chronic (472.1)
  rhinitis:
    allergic (477.0-477.9)
    chronic or unspecified (472.0)
  sore throat:
    acute or unspecified (462)
    chronic (472.1)

461 Acute sinusitis

Includes: abscess
  empyema
  infection   } acute, of sinus (accessory) (nasal)
  inflammation
  suppuration

Excludes: *chronic or unspecified sinusitis (473.0-473.9)*

461.0 Maxillary
Acute antritis

461.1 Frontal

461.2 Ethmoidal

461.3 Sphcnoidal

461.8 Other acute sinusitis
Acute pansinusitis

461.9 Acute sinusitis, unspecified
Acute sinusitis NOS

462 Acute pharyngitis

Acute sore throat NOS
Pharyngitis (acute):
  NOS
  gangrenous
  infective
  phlegmonous
  pneumococcal

Pharyngitis (acute):
  staphylococcal
  suppurative
  ulcerative
Sore throat (viral) NOS
Viral pharyngitis

Excludes: *abscess:*
      peritonsillar [quinsy] (475)
      pharyngeal NOS (478.29)
      retropharyngeal (478.24)
    chronic pharyngitis (472.1)
    infectious mononucleosis (075)
    that specified as (due to):
      Coxsackie (virus) (074.0)
      gonococcus (098.6)
      herpes simplex (054.79)
      influenza (487.1)
      septic (034.0)
      streptococcal (034.0)

	Add 4th or 5th digit		Nonspecific code		Unspecified code		Manifestation code

463 Acute tonsillitis

Tonsillitis (acute):
  NOS
  follicular
  gangrenous
  infective
  pneumococcal

Tonsillitis (acute):
  septic
  staphylococcal
  suppurative
  ulcerative
  viral

Excludes: *chronic tonsillitis (474.0)*
  hypertrophy of tonsils (474.1)
  peritonsillar abscess [quinsy] (475)
  sore throat:
    acute or NOS (462)
    septic (034.0)
  streptococcal tonsillitis (034.0)

464 Acute laryngitis and tracheitis

Excludes: *that associated with influenza (487.1)*
  that due to Streptococcus (034.0)

464.0 Acute laryngitis

Laryngitis (acute):
  NOS
  edematous
  Hemophilus influenza
    [H. influenzae]

Laryngitis (acute):
  pneumococcal
  septic
  suppurative
  ulcerative

Excludes: *chronic laryngitis (476.0-476.1)*
  influenzal laryngitis (487.1)

⑤ **464.1 Acute tracheitis**

Tracheitis (acute):
  NOS
  catarrhal
  viral

Excludes: *chronic tracheitis (491.8)*

  464.10 Without mention of obstruction

  464.11 With obstruction

⑤ **464.2 Acute laryngotracheitis**

Laryngotracheitis (acute)
Tracheitis (acute) with laryngitis (acute)

Excludes: *chronic laryngotracheitis (476.1)*

  464.20 Without mention of obstruction

  464.21 With obstruction

⑤ **464.3 Acute epiglottitis**

Viral epiglottitis

Excludes: *epiglottitis, chronic (476.1)*

  464.30 Without mention of obstruction

  464.31 With obstruction

464.4 Croup

Croup syndrome

465 Acute upper respiratory infections of multiple or unspecified sites

Excludes: *upper respiratory infection due to:*
  influenza (487.1)
  Streptococcus (034.0)

465.0 Acute laryngopharyngitis

465.8 Other multiple sites

Multiple URI

465.9 Unspecified site

Acute URI NOS
Upper respiratory infection (acute)

● Code new to this edition   ▲ Revision of existing code   ④ ⑤ Fourth or fifth digit required

466 **Acute bronchitis and bronchiolitis**
    Includes: that with:
            bronchospasm
            obstruction

466.0 **Acute bronchitis**
    Bronchitis, acute or subacute:
      fibrinous
      membranous
      pneumococcal
      purulent
      septic
      viral
      with tracheitis
    Croupous bronchitis
    Tracheobronchitis, acute

    Excludes: *acute bronchitis with:*
        asthma (493.0-493.9 with fifth digit 2)
        bronchiectasis (494.1)
        chronic obstructive pulmonary disease (491.21)

⑤ **466.1** **Acute bronchiolitis**
    Bronchiolitis (acute)
    Capillary pneumonia

    466.11   **Acute bronchiolitis due to respiratory syncytial virus (RSV)**

    466.19   **Acute bronchiolitis due to other infectious organisms**
      Use additional code to identify organism

OTHER DISEASES OF THE UPPER RESPIRATORY TRACT (470-478)

470 **Deviated nasal septum**
    Deflected septum (nasal) (acquired)

    Excludes: *congenital (754.0)*

471 **Nasal polyps**

    Excludes: *adenomatous polyps (212.0)*

471.0 **Polyp of nasal cavity**
    Polyp:
      choanal
      nasopharyngeal

471.1 **Polypoid sinus degeneration**
    Woakes' syndrome or ethmoiditis

471.8 **Other polyp of sinus**

Polyp of sinus:	Polyp of sinus:
accessory	maxillary
ethmoidal	sphenoidal

471.9 **Unspecified nasal polyp**
    Nasal polyp NOS

472 **Chronic pharyngitis and nasopharyngitis**

472.0 **Chronic rhinitis**

Ozena	Rhinitis:
Rhinitis:	hypertrophic
NOS	obstructive
atrophic	purulent
granulomatous	ulcerative

    Excludes: *allergic rhinitis (477.0-477.9)*

472.1 **Chronic pharyngitis**
    Chronic sore throat
    Pharyngitis:
      atrophic
      granular (chronic)
      hypertrophic

472.2 **Chronic nasopharyngitis**

    Excludes: *acute or unspecified nasopharyngitis (460)*

Add 4th or 5th digit

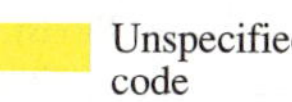
Nonspecific code

Unspecified code

Manifestation code

473 **Chronic sinusitis**
Includes:

abscess
empyema
infection
suppuration
} (chronic) of sinus (accessory) (nasal)

Excludes: *acute sinusitis (461.0-461.9)*

473.0 Maxillary
Antritis (chronic)

473.1 Frontal

473.2 Ethmoidal

Excludes: *Woakes' ethmoiditis (471.1)*

473.3 Sphenoidal

473.8 Other chronic sinusitis
Pansinusitis (chronic)

473.9 Unspecified sinusitis (chronic)
Sinusitis (chronic) NOS

474 **Chronic disease of tonsils and adenoids**

⑤ **474.0 Chronic tonsillitis and adenoiditis**

Excludes: *acute or unspecified tonsillitis (463)*

474.00 Chronic tonsillitis

474.01 Chronic adenoiditis

474.02 Chronic tonsillitis and adenoiditis

⑤ **474.1 Hypertrophy of tonsils and adenoids**
Enlargement
Hyperplasia
Hypertrophy
} of tonsils or adenoids

Excludes: *that with adenoiditis (474.01)*
that with adenoiditis and tonsillitis (474.02)
that with tonsillitis (474.00)

474.10 Tonsils with adenoids

474.11 Tonsils alone

474.12 Adenoids alone

474.2 Adenoid vegetations

474.8 Other chronic disease of tonsils and adenoids
Amygdalolith
Calculus, tonsil
Cicatrix of tonsil (and adenoid)
Tonsillar tag
Ulcer, tonsil

474.9 Unspecified chronic disease of tonsils and adenoids
Disease (chronic) of tonsils (and adenoids)

475 Peritonsillar abscess
Abscess of tonsil   Quinsy
Peritonsillar cellulitis

Excludes: *tonsillitis:*

acute or NOS (463)
chronic (474.0)

476 **Chronic laryngitis and laryngotracheitis**

476.0 Chronic laryngitis
Laryngitis:
catarrhal
hypertrophic
sicca

● Code new
  to this edition   ▲ Revision of
                               existing code   ④ ⑤ Fourth or fifth
                                                            digit required

476.1 Chronic laryngotracheitis
Laryngitis, chronic, with tracheitis (chronic)
Tracheitis, chronic, with laryngitis

Excludes: *chronic tracheitis (491.8)*

laryngitis and tracheitis, acute or unspecified (464.0-464.4)

477 Allergic rhinitis
Includes: allergic rhinitis (nonseasonal) (seasonal)
hay fever
spasmodic rhinorrhea

Excludes: *allergic rhinitis with asthma (bronchial) (493.0)*

477.0 Due to pollen
Pollinosis

● **477.1 Due to food**

477.8 Due to other allergen

477.9 Cause unspecified

478 Other diseases of upper respiratory tract

478.0 Hypertrophy of nasal turbinates

478.1 Other diseases of nasal cavity and sinuses
Abscess
Necrosis ⎫ of nose (septum)
Ulcer ⎭
Cyst or mucocele of sinus (nasal)
Rhinolith

Excludes: *varicose ulcer of nasal septum (456.8)*

⑤ **478.2 Other diseases of pharynx, not elsewhere classified**

478.20 Unspecified disease of pharynx

478.21 Cellulitis of pharynx or nasopharynx

478.22 Parapharyngeal abscess

478.24 Retropharyngeal abscess

478.25 Edema of pharynx or nasopharynx

478.26 Cyst of pharynx or nasopharynx

478.29 Other
Abscess of pharynx or nasopharynx

Excludes: *ulcerative pharyngitis (462)*

⑤ **478.3 Paralysis of vocal cords or larynx**

478.30 Paralysis, unspecified
Laryngoplegia   Paralysis of glottis

478.31 Unilateral, partial

478.32 Unilateral, complete

478.33 Bilateral, partial

478.34 Bilateral, complete

478.4 Polyp of vocal cord or larynx

Excludes: *adenomatous polyps (212.1)*

478.5 Other diseases of vocal cords
Abscess
Cellulitis ⎫ of vocal cords
Granuloma ⎬
Leukoplakia ⎭
Chorditis (fibrinous) (nodosa) (tuberosa)
Singers' nodes

478.6 Edema of larynx
Edema (of):
glottis
subglottic
supraglottic

⑤ **478.7 Other diseases of larynx, not elsewhere classified**

478.70 Unspecified disease of larynx

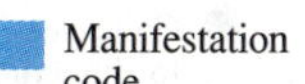

Add 4th or 5th digit	Nonspecific code	Unspecified code	Manifestation code

478.71 Cellulitis and perichondritis of larynx

478.74 Stenosis of larynx

478.75 Laryngeal spasm
Laryngismus (stridulus)

478.79 Other
Abscess
Necrosis
Obstruction } of larynx
Pachyderma
Ulcer

Excludes: *ulcerative laryngitis (464.0)*

478.8 Upper respiratory tract hypersensitivity reaction, site unspecified

Excludes: *hypersensitivity reaction of lower respiratory tract, as:*
extrinsic allergic alveolitis (495.0-495.9)
pneumoconiosis (500-505)

478.9 Other and unspecified diseases of upper respiratory tract
Abscess
Cicatrix } of trachea

PNEUMONIA AND INFLUENZA (480-487)

Excludes: *pneumonia:*
allergic or eosinophilic (518.3)
aspiration:
NOS (507.0)
newborn (770.1)
solids and liquids (507.0-507.8)
congenital (770.0)
lipoid (507.1)
passive (514)
rheumatic (390)

480 Viral pneumonia

480.0 Pneumonia due to adenovirus

480.1 Pneumonia due to respiratory syncytial virus

480.2 Pneumonia due to parainfluenza virus

480.8 Pneumonia due to other virus not elsewhere classified

Excludes: *congenital rubella pneumonitis (771.0)*
influenza with pneumonia, any form (487.0)
pneumonia complicating viral diseases classified elsewhere (484.1-484.8)

480.9 Viral pneumonia, unspecified

481 Pneumococcal pneumonia [Streptococcus pneumoniae pneumonia]
Lobar pneumonia, organism unspecified

482 Other bacterial pneumonia

482.0 Pneumonia due to Klebsiella pneumoniae

482.1 Pneumonia due to Pseudomonas

482.2 Pneumonia due to Hemophilus influenzae [H. influenzae]

⑤ **482.3 Pneumonia due to Streptococcus**

Excludes: *Streptococcus pneumoniae pneumonia (481)*

482.30 Streptococcus, unspecified

482.31 Group A

482.32 Group B

482.39 Other Streptococcus

⑤ **482.4 Pneumonia due to Staphylococcus**

482.40 Pneumonia due to Staphylococcus, unspecified

482.41 Pneumonia due to Staphylococcus aureus

482.49 Other Staphylococcus pneumonia

⑤ **482.8 Pneumonia due to other specified bacteria**

Excludes: *pneumonia complicating infectious disease classified elsewhere (484.1-484.8)*

● Code new
  to this edition

▲ Revision of
  existing code

④ ⑤ Fourth or fifth
    digit required

482.81 Anaerobes
Bacteroides (melaninogenicus)
Gram-negative anaerobes

482.82 Escherichia coli [E. coli]

482.83 Other gram-negative bacteria
Gram-negative pneumonia NOS
Proteus
Serratia marcescens

Excludes: *Gram-negative anaerobes (482.81)*
Legionnaires' disease (482.84)

482.84 Legionnaires' disease

482.89 Other specified bacteria

482.9 Bacterial pneumonia unspecified

483 Pneumonia due to other specified organism

483.0 Mycoplasma pneumoniae
Eaton's agent
Pleuropneumonia-like organism [PPLO]

483.1 Chlamydia

483.8 Other specified organism

484 Pneumonia in infectious diseases classified elsewhere

Excludes: *influenza with pneumonia, any form (487.0)*

484.1 Pneumonia in cytomegalic inclusion disease
Code first underlying disease (078.5)

484.3 Pneumonia in whooping cough
Code first underlying disease (033.0-033.9)

484.5 Pneumonia in anthrax
Code first underlying disease (022.1)

484.6 Pneumonia in aspergillosis
Code first underlying disease (117.3)

484.7 Pneumonia in other systemic mycoses
Code first underlying disease

Excludes: *pneumonia in:*
candidiasis (112.4)
coccidioidomycosis (114.0)
histoplasmosis (115.0-115.9 with fifth-digit 5)

484.8 Pneumonia in other infectious diseases classified elsewhere
Code first underlying disease, as:
Q fever (083.0)
typhoid fever (002.0)

Excludes: *pneumonia in:*
actinomycosis (039.1)
measles (055.1)
nocardiosis (039.1)
ornithosis (073.0)
Pneumocystis carinii (136.3)
salmonellosis (003.22)
toxoplasmosis (130.4)
tuberculosis (011.6)
tularemia (021.2)
varicella (052.1)

485 Bronchopneumonia, organism unspecified

Bronchopneumonia:	Pneumonia:
hemorrhagic	lobular
terminal	segmental
Pleurobronchopneumonia	

Excludes: *bronchiolitis (acute) (466.11-466.19)*
chronic (491.8)
lipoid pneumonia (507.1)

486 Pneumonia, organism unspecified

Excludes: *hypostatic or passive pneumonia (514)*
influenza with pneumonia, any form (487.0)
inhalation or aspiration pneumonia due to foreign materials (507.0-507.8)
pneumonitis due to fumes and vapors (506.0)

487 Influenza

Excludes: *Hemophilus influenzae [H. influenzae]:*
infection NOS (041.5)
laryngitis (464.0)
meningitis (320.0)
pneumonia (482.2)

487.0 With pneumonia
Influenza with pneumonia, any form
Influenzal:
  bronchopneumonia
  pneumonia

487.1 With other respiratory manifestations
Influenza NOS
Influenzal:
  laryngitis
  pharyngitis
  respiratory infection (upper) (acute)

487.8 With other manifestations
Encephalopathy due to influenza
Influenza with involvement of gastrointestinal tract

Excludes: *"intestinal flu" [viral gastroenteritis] (008.8)*

CHRONIC OBSTRUCTIVE PULMONARY DISEASE AND ALLIED CONDITIONS (490-496)

490 Bronchitis, not specified as acute or chronic
Bronchitis NOS: Tracheobronchitis NOS
  catarrhal
  with tracheitis NOS

Excludes: *bronchitis:*
allergic NOS (493.9)
asthmatic NOS (493.9)
due to fumes and vapors (506.0)

491 Chronic bronchitis

Excludes: *chronic obstructive asthma (493.2)*

491.0 Simple chronic bronchitis
Catarrhal bronchitis, chronic
Smokers' cough

491.1 Mucopurulent chronic bronchitis
Bronchitis (chronic) (recurrent):
  fetid
  mucopurulent
  purulent

⑤ **491.2 Obstructive chronic bronchitis**
Bronchitis: Bronchitis with:
  asthmatic, chronic   chronic airway obstruction
  emphysematous   emphysema
  obstructive (chronic) (diffuse)

Excludes: *asthmatic bronchitis (acute) NOS (493.9)*
chronic obstructive asthma (493.2)

491.20 Without mention of acute exacerbation
Chronic asthmatic bronchitis
Emphysema with chronic bronchitis

491.21 With acute exacerbation
Acute bronchitis with chronic obstructive pulmonary disease [COPD]
Acute and chronic obstructive bronchitis
Acute exacerbation of chronic obstructive pulmonary disease [COPD]
Chronic asthmatic bronchitis with acute exacerbation
Emphysema with both acute and chronic bronchitis

● Code new to this edition   ▲ Revision of existing code   ④ ⑤ Fourth or fifth digit required

491.8 Other chronic bronchitis
Chronic:
tracheitis
tracheobronchitis

491.9 Unspecified chronic bronchitis

492 Emphysema

492.0 Emphysematous bleb
Giant bullous emphysema
Ruptured emphysematous bleb
Tension pneumatocele
Vanishing lung

492.8 Other emphysema

Emphysema (lung or
pulmonary):
NOS
centriacinar
centrilobular
obstructive
panacinar

Emphysema (lung or pulmonary):
panlobular
unilateral
vesicular
MacLeod's syndrome
Swyer-James syndrome
Unilateral hyperlucent lung

Excludes: emphysema:

compensatory (518.2)
due to fumes and vapors (506.4)
interstitial (518.1)
newborn (770.2)
mediastinal (518.1)
surgical (subcutaneous) (998.81)
traumatic (958.7)
with chronic bronchitis (491.20)
with both acute and chronic bronchitis (491.21)

493 Asthma

Excludes: wheezing NOS (786.07)

The following fifth-digit subclassification is for use with category 493:

0 without mention of status asthmaticus

1 with status asthmaticus

2 with acute exacerbation

493.0 extrinsic asthma
Asthma:
allergic with stated cause
atopic
childhood
hay
platinum
Hay fever with asthma

Excludes: asthma:

allergic NOS (493.9)
detergent (507.8)
miners' (500)
wood (495.8)

493.1 Intrinsic asthma
Late-onset asthma

493.2 Chronic obstructive asthma
Asthma with chronic obstructive pulmonary disease [COPD]

Excludes: chronic asthmatic bronchitis (491.2)
chronic obstructive bronchitis (491.2)

493.9 Asthma, unspecified
Asthma (bronchial) (allergic NOS)
Bronchitis:
allergic
asthmatic

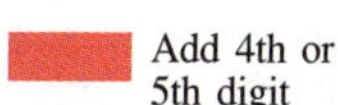

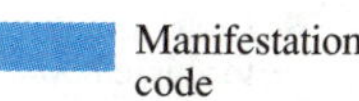

494 Bronchiectasis
Bronchiectasis (fusiform) (postinfectious) (recurrent)
Bronchiolectasis

> *Excludes:* *congenital (748.61)*
>
> *tuberculous bronchiectasis (current disease) (011.5)*

● **494.0 Bronchiectasis without acute exacerbation**

● **494.1 Bronchiectasis with acute exacerbation**
Acute bronchitis with bronchiectasis

495 Extrinsic allergic alveolitis
Includes: allergic alveolitis and pneumonitis due to inhaled organic dust particles of fungal, thermophilic actinomycete, or other origin

495.0 Farmers' lung

495.1 Bagassosis

495.2 Bird-fanciers' lung
Budgerigar-fanciers' disease or lung
Pigeon-fanciers' disease or lung

495.3 Suberosis
Cork-handlers' disease or lung

495.4 Malt workers' lung
Alveolitis due to Aspergillus clavatus

495.5 Mushroom workers' lung

495.6 Maple bark-strippers' lung
Alveolitis due to Cryptostroma corticale

495.7 "Ventilation" pneumonitis
Allergic alveolitis due to fungal, thermophilic actinomycete, and other organisms growing in ventilation [air conditioning] systems

495.8 Other specified allergic alveolitis and pneumonitis

Cheese-washers' lung	Pituitary snuff-takers' disease
Coffee workers' lung	Sequoiosis or red-cedar asthma
Fish-meal workers' lung	Wood asthma
Furriers' lung	
Grain-handlers' disease or lung	

495.9 Unspecified allergic alveolitis and pneumonitis
Alveolitis, allergic (extrinsic)
Hypersensitivity pneumonitis

496 Chronic airway obstruction, not elsewhere classified
Note: This code is not to be used with any code from categories 491-493
Chronic:
nonspecific lung disease
obstructive lung disease
obstructive pulmonary disease [COPD] NOS

> *Excludes:* *chronic obstructive lung disease [COPD] specified (as) (with):*
>
> > *allergic alveolitis (495.0-495.9)*
> > *asthma (493.2)*
> > *bronchiectasis (494.0-494.1)*
> > *bronchitis (491.20-491.21)*
> > > *with emphysema (491.20-491.21)*
> > *emphysema (492.0-492.8)*

PNEUMOCONIOSES AND OTHER LUNG DISEASES DUE TO EXTERNAL AGENTS (500-508)

500 Coal workers' pneumoconiosis

Anthracosilicosis	Coal workers' lung
Anthracosis	Miner's asthma
Black lung disease	

501 Asbestosis

502 Pneumoconiosis due to other silica or silicates
Pneumoconiosis due to talc
Silicotic fibrosis (massive) of lung
Silicosis (simple) (complicated)

● Code new to this edition	▲ Revision of existing code	④ ⑤ Fourth or fifth digit required

503 Pneumoconiosis due to other inorganic dust

Aluminosis (of lung)

Bauxite fibrosis (of lung)

Berylliosis

Graphite fibrosis (of lung)

Siderosis

Stannosis

504 Pneumonopathy due to inhalation of other dust

Byssinosis

Cannabinosis

Flax-dressers' disease

> *Excludes:* *allergic alveolitis (495.0-495.9)*
>
> *asbestosis (501)*
>
> *bagassosis (495.1)*
>
> *farmers' lung (495.0)*

505 Pneumoconiosis, unspecified

506 Respiratory conditions due to chemical fumes and vapors

Use additional E code, if desired, to identify cause

506.0 Bronchitis and pneumonitis due to fumes and vapors

Chemical bronchitis (acute)

506.1 Acute pulmonary edema due to fumes and vapors

Chemical pulmonary edema (acute)

> *Excludes:* *acute pulmonary edema NOS (518.4)*
>
> *chronic or unspecified pulmonary edema (514)*

506.2 Upper respiratory inflammation due to fumes and vapors

506.3 Other acute and subacute respiratory conditions due to fumes and vapors

506.4 Chronic respiratory conditions due to fumes and vapors

Emphysema (diffuse) (chronic)

Obliterative bronchiolitis (chronic) (subacute)   } due to inhalation of chemical

Pulmonary fibrosis (chronic)   fumes and vapors

506.9 Unspecified respiratory conditions due to fumes and vapors

Silo-fillers' disease

507 Pneumonitis due to solids and liquids

> *Excludes:* *fetal aspiration pneumonitis (770.1)*

507.0 Due to inhalation of food or vomitus

Aspiration pneumonia (due to):

NOS

food (regurgitated)

gastric secretions

milk

saliva

vomitus

507.1 Due to inhalation of oils and essences

Lipoid pneumonia (exogenous)

> *Excludes:* *endogenous lipoid pneumonia (516.8)*

507.8 Due to other solids and liquids

Detergent asthma

508 Respiratory conditions due to other and unspecified external agents

Use additional E code, if desired, to identify cause

508.0 Acute pulmonary manifestations due to radiation

Radiation pneumonitis

508.1 Chronic and other pulmonary manifestations due to radiation

Fibrosis of lung following radiation

508.8 Respiratory conditions due to other specified external agents

508.9 Respiratory conditions due to unspecified external agent

OTHER DISEASES OF RESPIRATORY SYSTEM (510-519)

510 Empyema

Use additional code, if desired, to identify infectious organism (041.0-041.9)

> *Excludes:* *abscess of lung (513.0)*

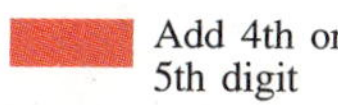

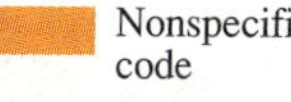

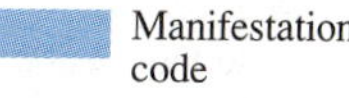

510.0 **With fistula**

Fistula:	Fistula:
bronchocutaneous	mediastinal
bronchopleural	pleural
hepatopleural	thoracic

Any condition classifiable to 510.9 with fistula

510.9 **Without mention of fistula**

Abscess:	Pleurisy:
pleura	purulent
thorax	septic
Empyema (chest) (lung)	seropurulent
(pleura)	suppurative
Fibrinopurulent pleurisy	Pyopneumothorax
	Pyothorax

511 **Pleurisy**

Excludes: *malignant pleural effusion (197.2)*

        pleurisy with mention of tuberculosis, current disease (012.0)

511.0 **Without mention of effusion or current tuberculosis**

Adhesion, lung or pleura	Pleurisy:
Calcification of pleura	NOS
Pleurisy (acute) (sterile):	pneumococcal
diaphragmatic	staphylococcal
fibrinous	streptococcal
interlobar	Thickening of pleura

511.1 **With effusion, with mention of a bacterial cause other than tuberculosis**

Pleurisy with effusion (exudative) (serous):
  pneumococcal
  staphylococcal
  streptococcal
  other specified nontuberculous bacterial cause

511.8 **Other specified forms of effusion, except tuberculous**

Encysted pleurisy	Hydropneumothorax
Hemopneumothorax	Hydrothorax
Hemothorax	

Excludes: *traumatic (860.2-860.5, 862.29, 862.39)*

511.9 **Unspecified pleural effusion**

Pleural effusion NOS	Pleurisy:
Pleurisy:	serous
exudative	with effusion NOS
serofibrinous	

512 **Pneumothorax**

512.0 **Spontaneous tension pneumothorax**

512.1 **Iatrogenic pneumothorax**

Postoperative pneumothorax

512.8 **Other spontaneous pneumothorax**

Pneumothorax:
  NOS
  acute
  chronic

Excludes: *pneumothorax:*

      congenital (770.2)
      traumatic (860.0-860.1, 860.4-860.5)
      tuberculous, current disease (011.7)

513 **Abscess of lung and mediastinum**

513.0 **Abscess of lung**

Abscess (multiple) of lung
Gangrenous or necrotic pneumonia
Pulmonary gangrene or necrosis

513.1 **Abscess of mediastinum**

● Code new to this edition   ▲ Revision of existing code   ④ ⑤ Fourth or fifth digit required

514 Pulmonary congestion and hypostasis
   Hypostatic:
      bronchopneumonia
      pneumonia
   Passive pneumonia
   Pulmonary congestion (chronic) (passive)
   Pulmonary edema:
      NOS
      chronic

   Excludes: *acute pulmonary edema:*
           NOS (518.4)
           with mention of heart disease or failure (428.1)

515 Postinflammatory pulmonary fibrosis
   Cirrhosis of lung
   Fibrosis of lung (atrophic)
      (confluent) (massive) } chronic or unspecified
      (perialveolar) (peribronchial)
   Induration of lung

516 Other alveolar and parietoalveolar pneumonopathy

   516.0 Pulmonary alveolar proteinosis

   516.1 *Idiopathic pulmonary hemosiderosis*
      Essential brown induration of lung
      Code first underlying disease (275.0)

   516.2 Pulmonary alveolar microlithiasis

   516.3 Idiopathic fibrosing alveolitis
      Alveolar capillary block
      Diffuse (idiopathic) (interstitial) pulmonary fibrosis
      Hamman-Rich syndrome

   516.8 Other specified alveolar and parietoalveolar pneumonopathies
      Endogenous lipoid pneumonia
      Interstitial pneumonia (desquamative) (lymphoid)

   Excludes: *lipoid pneumonia, exogenous or unspecified (507.1)*

   516.9 Unspecified alveolar and parietoalveolar pneumonopathy

517 Lung involvement in conditions classified elsewhere

   Excludes: *rheumatoid lung (714.81)*

   517.1 *Rheumatic pneumonia*
      Code first underlying disease (390)

   517.2 *Lung involvement in systemic sclerosis*
      Code first underlying disease (710.1)

   517.8 *Lung involvement in other diseases classified elsewhere*
      Code first underlying disease, as:
         amyloidosis (277.3)
         polymyositis (710.4)
         sarcoidosis (135)
         Sjögren's disease (710.2)
         systemic lupus erythematosus (710.0)

   Excludes: *syphilis (095.1)*

518 Other diseases of lung

   518.0 Pulmonary collapse
      Atelectasis
      Collapse of lung
      Middle lobe syndrome

   Excludes: *atelectasis:*
         congenital (partial) (770.5)
           primary (770.4)
         tuberculous, current disease (011.8)

   518.1 Interstitial emphysema
      Mediastinal emphysema

   Excludes: *surgical (subcutaneous) emphysema (998.81)*
         that in fetus or newborn (770.2)
         traumatic emphysema (958.7)

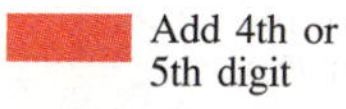

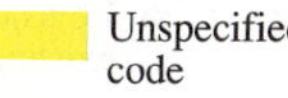

518.2 Compensatory emphysema

518.3 Pulmonary eosinophilia
Eosinophilic asthma   Tropical eosinophilia
Löffler's syndrome
Pneumonia:
  allergic
  eosinophilic

518.4 Acute edema of lung, unspecified
Acute pulmonary edema NOS
Pulmonary edema, postoperative

Excludes: *pulmonary edema:*
  acute, with mention of heart disease or failure (428.1)
  chronic or unspecified (514)
  due to external agents (506.0-508.9)

518.5 Pulmonary insufficiency following trauma and surgery
Adult respiratory distress syndrome
Pulmonary insufficiency following:
  shock
  surgery
  trauma
Shock lung

Excludes: *adult respiratory distress syndrome associated with other conditions (518.82)*
  pneumonia:
    aspiration (507.0)
    hypostatic (514)
  respiratory failure in other conditions (518.81, 518.83-518.84)

518.6 Allergic bronchopulmonary aspergillosis

⑤ **518.8 Other diseases of lung**

518.81 Acute respiratory failure
Respiratory failure NOS

Excludes: *acute and chronic respiratory failure (518.84)*
  acute respiratory distress (518.82)
  chronic respiratory failure (518.83)
  respiratory arrest (799.1)
  respiratory failure, newborn (770.8)

518.82 Other pulmonary insufficiency, not elsewhere classified
Acute respiratory distress
Acute respiratory insufficiency
Adult respiratory distress syndrome NEC

Excludes: *adult respiratory distress syndrome associated with trauma and surgery (518.5)*
  pulmonary insufficiency following trauma and surgery (518.5)
  respiratory distress:
    NOS (786.09)
    newborn (770.8)
    syndrome, newborn (769)
  shock lung (518.5)

518.83 Chronic respiratory failure

518.84 Acute and chronic respiratory failure
Acute or chronic respiratory failure

518.89 Other diseases of lung, not elsewhere classified
Broncholithiasis   Lung disease NOS
Calcification of lung   Pulmolithiasis

519 Other diseases of respiratory system

⑤ **519.0 Tracheostomy complications**

519.00 Tracheostomy complication, unspecified

519.01 Infection of tracheostomy
Use additional code to identify type of infection, such as:
  abscess or cellulitis of neck (682.1)
  septicemia (038.0-038.9)
Use additional code to identify organism (041.00-041.9)

519.02 Mechanical complication of tracheostomy
Tracheal stenosis due to tracheostomy

   ● Code new   ▲ Revision of   ④ ⑤ Fourth or fifth
     to this edition   existing code   digit required

519.09 **Other tracheostomy complications**
Hemorrhage due to tracheostomy
Tracheoesophageal fistula due to tracheostomy

519.1 **Other diseases of trachea and bronchus, not elsewhere classified**
Calcification of bronchus or trachea
Stenosis of bronchus or trachea
Ulcer of bronchus or trachea

519.2 **Mediastinitis**

519.3 **Other diseases of mediastinum, not elsewhere classified**
Fibrosis of mediastinum
Hernia of mediastinum
Retraction of mediastinum

519.4 **Disorders of diaphragm**
Diaphragmitis
Paralysis of diaphragm
Relaxation of diaphragm

Excludes: *congenital defect of diaphragm (756.6)*
diaphragmatic hernia (551-553 with .3)
congenital (756.6)

519.8 **Other diseases of respiratory system, not elsewhere classified**

519.9 **Unspecified disease of respiratory system**
Respiratory disease (chronic) NOS

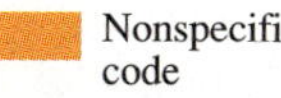

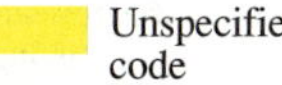

● Code new
to this edition

▲ Revision of
existing code

④ ⑤ Fourth or fifth
digit required

9.   DISEASES OF THE DIGESTIVE SYSTEM (520-579)

DISEASES OF ORAL CAVITY, SALIVARY GLANDS, AND JAWS (520-529)

520 **Disorders of tooth development and eruption**

520.0 Anodontia
Absence of teeth (complete) (congenital) (partial)
Hypodontia
Oligodontia

Excludes: acquired absence of teeth (525.1)

520.1 Supernumerary teeth
Distomolar	Paramolar
Fourth molar	Supplemental teeth
Mesiodens	

Excludes: supernumerary roots (520.2)

520.2 Abnormalities of size and form
Concrescence		Macrodontia
Fusion		Microdontia
Gemination	of teeth	Peg-shaped [conical] teeth
Dens evaginatus		Supernumerary roots
Dens in dente		Taurodontism
Dens invaginatus		Tuberculum paramolare
Enamel pearls		

Excludes: that due to congenital syphilis (090.5)
tuberculum Carabelli, which is regarded as a normal variation

520.3 Mottled teeth
Dental fluorosis
Mottling of enamel
Nonfluoride enamel opacities

520.4 Disturbances of tooth formation
Aplasia and hypoplasia of cementum	Horner's teeth
Dilaceration of tooth	Hypocalcification of teeth
Enamel hypoplasia (neonatal) (postnatal) (prenatal)	Regional odontodysplasia
	Turner's tooth

Excludes: Hutchinson's teeth and mulberry molars in congenital syphilis (090.5)
mottled teeth (520.3)

520.5 Hereditary disturbances in tooth structure, not elsewhere classified
Amelogenesis
Dentinogenesis imperfecta
Odontogenesis
Dentinal dysplasia
Shell teeth

520.6 Disturbances in tooth eruption
Teeth:	Tooth eruption:
embedded	late
impacted	obstructed
natal	premature
neonatal	
primary [deciduous]:	
persistent	
shedding, premature	

Excludes: exfoliation of teeth (attributable to disease of surrounding tissues) (525.0-525.1)
impacted or embedded teeth with abnormal position of such teeth or adjacent teeth (524.3)

520.7 Teething syndrome

520.8 Other specified disorders of tooth development and eruption
Color changes during tooth formation
Pre-eruptive color changes

Excludes: posteruptive color changes (521.7)

520.9 Unspecified disorder of tooth development and eruption

Add 4th or 5th digit	Nonspecific code	Unspecified code	Manifestation code

521 **Diseases of hard tissues of teeth**

521.0 **Dental caries**
Caries (of):
arrested
cementum
dentin (acute) (chronic)
enamel (acute) (chronic) (incipient)
Infantile melanodontia
Odontoclasia
White spot lesions of teeth

521.1 **Excessive attrition**
Approximal wear   Occlusal wear

521.2 **Abrasion**
Abrasion:
dentifrice
habitual
occupational   } of teeth
ritual
traditional
Wedge defect NOS

521.3 **Erosion**
Erosion of teeth: Erosion of teeth:
NOS   idiopathic
due to: occupational
medicine
persistent vomiting

521.4 **Pathological resorption**
Internal granuloma of pulp
Resorption of tooth or root (external) (internal)

521.5 **Hypercementosis**
Cementation hyperplasia

521.6 **Ankylosis of teeth**

521.7 **Posteruptive color changes**
Staining [discoloration] of teeth:
NOS
due to:
drugs
metals
pulpal bleeding

Excludes: accretions [deposits] on teeth (523.6)
pre-eruptive color changes (520.8)

521.8 **Other specified diseases of hard tissues of teeth**
Irradiated enamel   Sensitive dentin

521.9 **Unspecified disease of hard tissues of teeth**

522 **Diseases of pulp and periapical tissues**

522.0 **Pulpitis**
Pulpal: Pulpitis:
abscess   acute
polyp   chronic (hyperplastic) (ulcerative)
                                   suppurative

522.1 **Necrosis of the pulp**
Pulp gangrene

522.2 **Pulp degeneration**
Denticles   Pulp stones
Pulp calcifications

522.3 **Abnormal hard tissue formation in pulp**
Secondary or irregular dentin

522.4 **Acute apical periodontitis of pulpal origin**

522.5 **Periapical abscess without sinus**
Abscess:
dental
dentoalveolar

Excludes: periapical abscess with sinus (522.7)

● Code new   ▲ Revision of   ④ ⑤ Fourth or fifth
to this edition   existing code   digit required

522.6 **Chronic apical periodontitis**
Apical or periapical granuloma
Apical periodontitis NOS

522.7 **Periapical abscess with sinus**
Fistula:
alveolar process
dental

522.8 **Radicular cyst**
Cyst:
apical (periodontal)
periapical
radiculodental
residual radicular

Excludes: *lateral developmental or lateral periodontal cyst (526.0)*

522.9 **Other and unspecified diseases of pulp and periapical tissues**

523 **Gingival and periodontal diseases**

523.0 **Acute gingivitis**

Excludes: *acute necrotizing ulcerative gingivitis (101)*
herpetic gingivostomatitis (054.2)

523.1 **Chronic gingivitis**
Gingivitis (chronic):   Gingivitis (chronic):
NOS   simple marginal
desquamative   ulcerative
hyperplastic   Gingivostomatitis

Excludes: *herpetic gingivostomatitis (054.2)*

523.2 **Gingival recession**
Gingival recession (generalized) (localized) (postinfective) (postoperative)

523.3 **Acute periodontitis**
Acute: Paradontal abscess
pericementitis   Periodontal abscess
pericoronitis

Excludes: *acute apical periodontitis (522.4)*
periapical abscess (522.5, 522.7)

523.4 **Chronic periodontitis**
Alveolar pyorrhea   Periodontitis:
Chronic pericoronitis   NOS
Pericementitis (chronic)   complex
    simplex

Excludes: *chronic apical periodontitis (522.6)*

523.5 **Periodontosis**

523.6 **Accretions on teeth**
Dental calculus: Deposits on teeth:
subgingival   betel
supragingival   materia alba
    soft
    tartar
    tobacco

523.8 **Other specified periodontal diseases**
Giant cell: Gingival polyp
epulis   Periodontal lesions due to traumatic occlusion
peripheral granuloma   Peripheral giant cell granuloma
Gingival:
cysts
enlargement NOS
fibromatosis

Excludes: *leukoplakia of gingiva (528.6)*

523.9 **Unspecified gingival and periodontal disease**

524 **Dentofacial anomalies, including malocclusion**

⑤ **524.0** **Major anomalies of jaw size**

Excludes: *hemifacial atrophy or hypertrophy (754.0)*
unilateral condylar hyperplasia or hypoplasia of mandible (526.89)

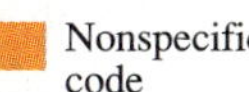

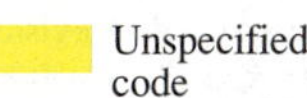

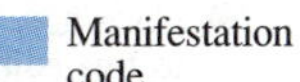

Manifestation
code

524.00 Unspecified anomaly

524.01 Maxillary hyperplasia

524.02 Mandibular hyperplasia

524.03 Maxillary hypoplasia

524.04 Mandibular hypoplasia

524.05 Macrogenia

524.06 Microgenia

524.09 Other specified anomaly

⑤ **524.1 Anomalies of relationship of jaw to cranial base**

524.10 Unspecified anomaly
   prognathism
   retrognathism

524.11 Maxillary asymmetry

524.12 Other jaw asymmetry

524.19 Other specified anomaly

524.2 Anomalies of dental arch relationship
   Crossbite (anterior) (posterior)   Overbite (excessive)
   Disto-occlusion   deep
   Mesio-occlusion   horizontal
   Midline deviation   vertical
   Open bite (anterior) (posterior)   Overjet
                                           Posterior lingual occlusion of mandibular teeth
                                           Soft tissue impingement

   Excludes: *hemifacial atrophy or hypertrophy (754.0)*
               unilateral condylar hyperplasia or hypoplasia of mandible (526.89)

524.3 Anomalies of tooth position
   Crowding
   Diastema
   Displacement   } of tooth, teeth
   Rotation
   Spacing, abnormal
   Transposition
   Impacted or embedded teeth with abnormal position of such teeth or adjacent teeth

524.4 Malocclusion, unspecified

524.5 Dentofacial functional abnormalities
   Abnormal jaw closure
   Malocclusion due to:
      abnormal swallowing
      mouth breathing
      tongue, lip, or finger habits

⑤ **524.6 Temporomandibular joint disorders**

   Excludes: *current temporomandibular joint:*
               dislocation (830.0-830.1)
               strain (848.1)

524.60 Temporomandibular joint disorders, unspecified
   Temporomandibular joint-pain-dysfunction syndrome [TMJ]

524.61 Adhesions and ankylosis (bony or fibrous)

524.62 Arthralgia of temporomandibular joint

524.63 Articular disc disorder (reducing or non-reducing)

524.69 Other specified temporomandibular joint disorders

⑤ **524.7 Dental alveolar anomalies**

524.70 Unspecified alveolar anomaly

524.71 Alveolar maxillary hyperplasia

524.72 Alveolar mandibular hyperplasia

524.73 Alveolar maxillary hypoplasia

524.74 Alveolar mandibular hypoplasia

524.79 Other specified alveolar anomaly

524.8 Other specified dentofacial anomalies

● Code new   ▲ Revision of   ④ ⑤ Fourth or fifth
   to this edition   existing code   digit required

524.9 **Unspecified dentofacial anomalies**

525 **Other diseases and conditions of the teeth and supporting structures**

525.0 **Exfoliation of teeth due to systemic causes**

525.1 **Loss of teeth due to accident, extraction, or local periodontal disease**
Acquired absence of teeth

525.2 **Atrophy of edentulous alveolar ridge**

525.3 **Retained dental root**

525.8 **Other specified disorders of the teeth and supporting structures**
Enlargement of alveolar ridge NOS
Irregular alveolar process

525.9 **Unspecified disorder of the teeth and supporting structures**

526 **Diseases of the jaws**

526.0 **Developmental odontogenic cysts**
Cyst: Cyst:
  dentigerous   lateral periodontal
  eruption   primordial
  follicular   Keratocyst
  lateral developmental

Excludes: radicular cyst (522.8)

526.1 **Fissural cysts of jaw**
Cyst:
  globulomaxillary
  incisor canal
  median anterior maxillary
  median palatal
  nasopalatine
  palatine of papilla

Excludes: cysts of oral soft tissues (528.4)

526.2 **Other cysts of jaws**
Cyst of jaw: Cyst of jaw:
  NOS   hemorrhagic
  aneurysmal   traumatic

526.3 **Central giant cell (reparative) granuloma**

Excludes: peripheral giant cell granuloma (523.8)

526.4 **Inflammatory conditions**
Abscess
Osteitis
Osteomyelitis (neonatal)   } of jaw (acute) (chronic) (suppurative)
Periostitis
Sequestrum of jaw bone

Excludes: alveolar osteitis (526.5)

526.5 **Alveolitis of jaw**
Alveolar osteitis
Dry socket

⑤ **526.8** **Other specified diseases of the jaws**

    526.81 **Exostosis of jaw**
        Torus mandibularis
        Torus palatinus

    526.89 **Other**
        Cherubism
        Fibrous dysplasia   } of jaw(s)
        Latent bone cyst
        Osteoradionecrosis of jaw(s)
        Unilateral condylar hyperplasia or hypoplasia of mandible

526.9 **Unspecified disease of the jaws**

527 **Diseases of the salivary glands**

527.0 **Atrophy**

527.1 **Hypertrophy**

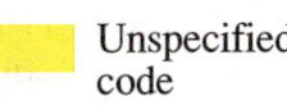

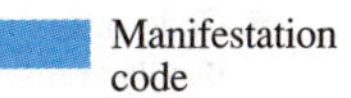

527.2 Sialoadenitis

Parotitis: Sialoangitis
  NOS Sialodochitis
  allergic
  toxic

Excludes: *epidemic or infectious parotitis (072.0-072.9)*
  uveoparotid fever (135)

527.3 Abscess

527.4 Fistula

Excludes: *congenital fistula of salivary glands (750.24)*

527.5 Sialolithiasis

Calculus
Stone } *of salivary gland or duct*
Sialodocholithiasis

527.6 Mucocele

Mucous:
  extravasation cyst of salivary gland
  retention cyst of salivary gland
Ranula

527.7 Disturbance of salivary secretion

Hyposecretion Sialorrhea
Ptyalism Xerostomia

527.8 Other specified diseases of the salivary glands

Benign lymphoepithelial lesion of salivary gland
Sialectasia
Sialosis
Stenosis
Stricture } of salivary duct

527.9 Unspecified disease of the salivary glands

528 Diseases of the oral soft tissues, excluding lesions specific for gingiva and tongue

528.0 Stomatitis

Stomatitis: Vesicular stomatitis
  NOS
  ulcerative

Excludes: *stomatitis:*
  acute necrotizing ulcerative (101)
  aphthous (528.2)
  gangrenous (528.1)
  herpetic (054.2)
  Vincent's (101)

528.1 Cancrum oris

Gangrenous stomatitis Noma

528.2 Oral aphthae

Aphthous stomatitis Recurrent aphthous ulcer
Canker sore Stomatitis herpetiformis
Periadenitis mucosa necrotica recurrens

Excludes: *herpetic stomatitis (054.2)*

528.3 Cellulitis and abscess

Cellulitis of mouth (floor)
Ludwig's angina
Oral fistula

Excludes: *abscess of tongue (529.0)*
  cellulitis or abscess of lip (528.5)
  fistula (of):
    dental (522.7)
    lip (528.5)
  gingivitis (523.0-523.1)

● Code new
  to this edition

▲ Revision of
  existing code

④ ⑤ Fourth or fifth
  digit required

528.4 Cysts
Dermoid cyst
Epidermoid cyst
Epstein's pearl } of mouth
Lymphoepithelial cyst
Nasoalveolar cyst
Nasolabial cyst

Excludes: cyst:
    gingiva (523.8)
    tongue (529.8)

528.5 Diseases of lips
Abscess
Cellulitis
Fistula } of lip(s)
Hypertrophy

Cheilitis:
  NOS
  angular
Cheilodynia
Cheilosis

Excludes: *actinic cheilitis (692.79)*
    congenital fistula of lip (750.25)
    leukoplakia of lips (528.6)

528.6 Leukoplakia of oral mucosa, including tongue
Leukokeratosis of oral mucosa
Leukoplakia of:
  gingiva
  lips
  tongue

Excludes: *carcinoma in situ (230.0, 232.0)*
    leukokeratosis nicotina palati (528.7)

528.7 Other disturbances of oral epithelium, including tongue
Erythroplakia
Focal epithelial
  hyperplasia
Leukoedema } of mouth or tongue
Leukokeratosis
  nicotina palati

Excludes: *carcinoma in situ (230.0, 232.0)*
    leukokeratosis NOS (702)

528.8 Oral submucosal fibrosis, including of tongue

528.9 Other and unspecified diseases of the oral soft tissues
Cheek and lip biting
Denture sore mouth
Denture stomatitis
Melanoplakia
Papillary hyperplasia of palate
Eosinophilic granuloma
Irritative hyperplasia } of oral mucosa
Pyogenic granuloma
Ulcer (traumatic)

529 Diseases and other conditions of the tongue

529.0 Glossitis
Abscess
Ulceration (traumatic) } of tongue

Excludes: *glossitis:*
    benign migratory (529.1)
    Hunter's (529.4)
    median rhomboid (529.2)
    Moeller's (529.4)

529.1 Geographic tongue
Benign migratory glossitis
Glossitis areata exfoliativa

529.2 Median rhomboid glossitis

Unspecified
code

Manifestation
code

529.3 Hypertrophy of tongue papillae
Black hairy tongue
Coated tongue
Hypertrophy of foliate papillae
Lingua villosa nigra

529.4 Atrophy of tongue papillae
Bald tongue   Glossodynia exfoliativa
Glazed tongue   Smooth atrophic tongue
Glossitis:
  Hunter's
  Moeller's

529.5 Plicated tongue
Fissured
Furrowed   } tongue
Scrotal

Excludes: fissure of tongue, congenital (750.13)

529.6 Glossodynia
Glossopyrosis   Painful tongue

Excludes: glossodynia exfoliativa (529.4)

529.8 Other specified conditions of the tongue
Atrophy
Crenated
Enlargement   } (of) tongue
Hypertrophy
Glossocele
Glossoptosis

Excludes: erythroplasia of tongue (528.7)
          leukoplakia of tongue (528.6)
          macroglossia (congenital) (750.15)
          microglossia (congenital) (750.16)
          oral submucosal fibrosis (528.8)

529.9 Unspecified condition of the tongue

DISEASES OF ESOPHAGUS, STOMACH, AND DUODENUM (530-537)

530 Diseases of esophagus

Excludes: esophageal varices (456.0-456.2)

530.0 Achalasia and cardiospasm
Achalasia (of cardia)
Aperistalsis of esophagus
Megaesophagus

Excludes: congenital cardiospasm (750.7)

⑤ **530.1 Esophagitis**
Abscess of esophagus   Esophagitis:
Esophagitis: postoperative
  NOS   regurgitant
  chemical
  peptic

Use additional E code, if desired, to identify cause, if induced by chemical

Excludes: tuberculous esophagitis (017.8)

530.10 Esophagitis, unspecified

530.11 Reflux esophagitis

530.19 Other esophagitis

530.2 Ulcer of esophagus
Ulcer of esophagus   Ulcer of esophagus due to ingestion of:
  fungal   aspirin
  peptic   chemicals
                                 medicines

Use additional E code, if desired, to identify cause, if induced by chemical or drug

---

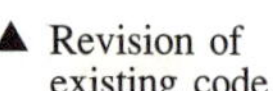

▲ Revision of
existing code

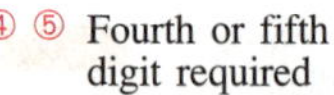

530.3 Stricture and stenosis of esophagus
Compression of esophagus
Obstruction of esophagus

Excludes: congenital stricture of esophagus (750.3)

530.4 Perforation of esophagus
Rupture of esophagus

Excludes: traumatic perforation of esophagus (862.22, 862.32, 874.4-874.5)

530.5 Dyskinesia of esophagus
Corkscrew esophagus   Esophagospasm
Curling esophagus   Spasm of esophagus

Excludes: cardiospasm (530.0)

530.6 Diverticulum of esophagus, acquired
Diverticulum, acquired:
epiphrenic
pharyngoesophageal
pulsion
subdiaphragmatic
traction
Zenker's (hypopharyngeal)
Esophageal pouch, acquired
Esophagocele, acquired

Excludes: congenital diverticulum of esophagus (750.4)

530.7 Gastroesophageal laceration-hemorrhage syndrome
Mallory-Weiss syndrome

⑤ **530.8 Other specified disorders of esophagus**

530.81 Esophageal reflux
Gastroesophageal reflux

Excludes: reflux esophagitis (530.11)

530.82 Esophageal hemorrhage

Excludes: hemorrhage due to esophageal varices (456.0-456.2)

530.83 Esophageal leukoplakia

530.84 Tracheoesophageal fistula

Excludes: congenital tracheoesophageal fistula (750.3)

530.89 Other

Excludes: Paterson-Kelly syndrome (280.8)

530.9 Unspecified disorder of esophagus

⑤ **531 Gastric ulcer**
Includes: ulcer (peptic):
prepyloric
pylorus
stomach

Use additional E code, if desired, to identify drug, if drug-induced

Excludes: peptic ulcer NOS (533.0-533.9)

The following fifth-digit subclassification is for use with category 531:

0   without mention of obstruction

1   with obstruction

⑤ **531.0 Acute with hemorrhage**

⑤ **531.1 Acute with perforation**

⑤ **531.2 Acute with hemorrhage and perforation**

⑤ **531.3 Acute without mention of hemorrhage or perforation**

⑤ **531.4 Chronic or unspecified with hemorrhage**

⑤ **531.5 Chronic or unspecified with perforation**

⑤ **531.6 Chronic or unspecified with hemorrhage and perforation**

⑤ **531.7 Chronic without mention of hemorrhage or perforation**

⑤ **531.9 Unspecified as acute or chronic, without mention of hemorrhage or perforation**

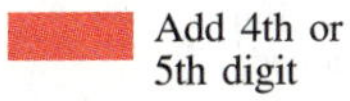
Add 4th or
5th digit

Nonspecific
code

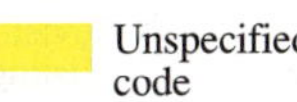
Unspecified
code

Manifestation
code

⑤ **532** **Duodenal ulcer**
    Includes: erosion (acute) of duodenum
                ulcer (peptic):
                    duodenum
                    postpyloric
    Use additional E code, if desired, to identify drug, if drug-induced
       Excludes: *peptic ulcer NOS (533.0-533.9)*
    The following fifth-digit subclassification is for use with category 532:
        0 **without mention of obstruction**
        1 **with obstruction**

⑤ **532.0** **Acute with hemorrhage**

⑤ **532.1** **Acute with perforation**

⑤ **532.2** **Acute with hemorrhage and perforation**

⑤ **532.3** **Acute without mention of hemorrhage or perforation**

⑤ **532.4** **Chronic or unspecified with hemorrhage**

⑤ **532.5** **Chronic or unspecified with perforation**

⑤ **532.6** **Chronic or unspecified with hemorrhage and perforation**

⑤ **532.7** **Chronic without mention of hemorrhage or perforation**

⑤ **532.9** **Unspecified as acute or chronic, without mention of hemorrhage or perforation**

⑤ **533** **Peptic ulcer, site unspecified**
    Includes: gastroduodenal ulcer NOS
                peptic ulcer NOS
                stress ulcer NOS
    Use additional E code, if desired, to identify drug, if drug-induced
       Excludes: *peptic ulcer:*
               duodenal (532.0-532.9)
               gastric (531.0-531.9)
    The following fifth-digit subclassification is for use with category 533:
        0 **without mention of obstruction**
        1 **with obstruction**

⑤ **533.0** **Acute with hemorrhage**

⑤ **533.1** **Acute with perforation**

⑤ **533.2** **Acute with hemorrhage and perforation**

⑤ **533.3** **Acute without mention of hemorrhage and perforation**

⑤ **533.4** **Chronic or unspecified with hemorrhage**

⑤ **533.5** **Chronic or unspecified with perforation**

⑤ **533.6** **Chronic or unspecified with hemorrhage and perforation**

⑤ **533.7** **Chronic without mention of hemorrhage or perforation**

⑤ **533.9** **Unspecified as acute or chronic, without mention of hemorrhage or perforation**

⑤ **534** **Gastrojejunal ulcer**
    Includes: ulcer (peptic) or erosion:
                anastomotic
                gastrocolic
                gastrointestinal
                gastrojejunal
                jejunal
                marginal
                stomal
       Excludes: *primary ulcer of small intestine (569.82)*
    The following fifth-digit subclassification is for use with category 534:
        0 **without mention of obstruction**
        1 **with obstruction**

⑤ **534.0** **Acute with hemorrhage**

⑤ **534.1** **Acute with perforation**

⑤ **534.2** **Acute with hemorrhage and perforation**

⑤ **534.3** **Acute without mention of hemorrhage or perforation**

⑤ **534.4** **Chronic or unspecified with hemorrhage**

● Code new   ▲ Revision of   ④ ⑤ Fourth or fifth
   to this edition   existing code   digit required

⑤ **534.5 Chronic or unspecified with perforation**

⑤ **534.6 Chronic or unspecified with hemorrhage and perforation**

⑤ **534.7 Chronic without mention of hemorrhage or perforation**

⑤ **534.9 Unspecified as acute or chronic, without mention of hemorrhage or perforation**

⑤ **535 Gastritis and duodenitis**

The following fifth-digit subclassification is for use with category 535

    0 without mention of hemorrhage

    1 with hemorrhage

⑤ **535.0 Acute gastritis**

⑤ **535.1 Atrophic gastritis**
Gastritis:
  atrophic-hyperplastic
  chronic (atrophic)

⑤ **535.2 Gastric mucosal hypertrophy**
Hypertrophic gastritis

⑤ **535.3 Alcoholic gastritis**

⑤ **535.4 Other specified gastritis**

Gastritis:	Gastritis:
allergic	superficial
bile induced	toxic
irritant	

⑤ **535.5 Unspecified gastritis and gastroduodenitis**

⑤ **535.6 Duodenitis**

536 Disorders of function of stomach

Excludes: functional disorders of stomach specified as psychogenic (306.4)

536.0 Achlorhydria

536.1 Acute dilatation of stomach
Acute distention of stomach

536.2 Persistent vomiting
Habit vomiting
Persistent vomiting [not of pregnancy]
Uncontrollable vomiting

Excludes: excessive vomiting in pregnancy (643.0-643.9)
  vomiting NOS (787.0)

536.3 Gastroparesis

⑤ **536.4 Gastrostomy complications**

536.40 Gastrostomy complications, unspecified

536.41 Infection of gastrostomy
Use additional code to specify type of infection, such as:
  abscess or cellulitis of abdomen (682.2)
  septicemia (038.0-038.9)
Use additional code to identify organism (041.00-041.9)

536.42 Mechanical complication of gastrostomy

536.49 Other gastrostomy complications

536.8 Dyspepsia and other specified disorders of function of stomach

Achylia gastrica	Hyperchlorhydria
Hourglass contraction of stomach	Hypochlorhydria
Hyperacidity	Indigestion

Excludes: achlorhydria (536.0)
  heartburn (787.1)

536.9 Unspecified functional disorder of stomach
Functional gastrointestinal:
  disorder
  disturbance
  irritation

537 Other disorders of stomach and duodenum

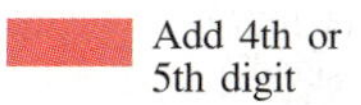

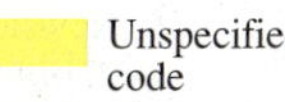

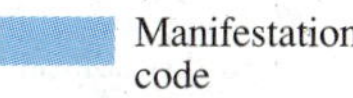

537.0 Acquired hypertrophic pyloric stenosis
Constriction
Obstruction } of pylorus, acquired or adult
Stricture

Excludes: *congenital or infantile pyloric stenosis (750.5)*

537.1 Gastric diverticulum

Excludes: *congenital diverticulum of stomach (750.7)*

537.2 Chronic duodenal ileus

537.3 Other obstruction of duodenum
Cicatrix
Stenosis } of duodenum
Stricture
Volvulus

Excludes: *congenital obstruction of duodenum (751.1)*

537.4 Fistula of stomach or duodenum
Gastrocolic fistula
Gastrojejunocolic fistula

537.5 Gastroptosis

537.6 Hourglass stricture or stenosis of stomach
Cascade stomach

Excludes: *congenital hourglass stomach (750.7)*
hourglass contraction of stomach (536.8)

⑤ **537.8 Other specified disorders of stomach and duodenum**

537.81 Pylorospasm

Excludes: *congenital pylorospasm (750.5)*

537.82 Angiodysplasia of stomach and duodenum without mention of hemorrhage

537.83 Angiodysplasia of stomach and duodenum with hemorrhage

537.89 Other
Gastric or duodenal:
prolapse
rupture
Intestinal metaplasia of gastric mucosa
Passive congestion of stomach

Excludes: *diverticula of duodenum (562.00-562.01)*
gastrointestinal hemorrhage (578.0-578.9)

537.9 Unspecified disorder of stomach and duodenum

APPENDICITIS (540-543)

540 Acute appendicitis

540.0 With generalized peritonitis
Appendicitis (acute):
fulminating
gangrenous } with: perforation peritonitis (generalized) rupture
obstructive
Cecitis (acute)
Rupture of appendix

Excludes: *acute appendicitis with peritoneal abscess (540.1)*

540.1 With peritoneal abscess
Abscess of appendix
With generalized peritonitis

540.9 Without mention of peritonitis
Acute:
appendicitis:
fulminating
gangrenous } without mention of perforation, peritonitis, or rupture
inflamed
obstructive
cecitis

541 Appendicitis, unqualified

● Code new
to this edition

▲ Revision of
existing code

④ ⑤ Fourth or fifth
digit required

542 Other appendicitis

Appendicitis: Appendicitis:
  chronic   relapsing
  recurrent   subacute

Excludes: hyperplasia (lymphoid) of appendix (543.0)

543 Other diseases of appendix

543.0 Hyperplasia of appendix (lymphoid)

543.9 Other and unspecified diseases of appendix
Appendicular or appendiceal:
  colic
  concretion
  fistula
Diverticulum ⎫
Fecalith   ⎬ of appendix
Intussusception
Mucocele
Stercolith

HERNIA OF ABDOMINAL CAVITY (550-553)

Includes: hernia:
  acquired
  congenital, except diaphragmatic or hiatal

⑤ 550 Inguinal hernia
Includes: bubonocele
  inguinal hernia (direct) (double) (indirect) (oblique) (sliding)
  scrotal hernia

The following fifth-digit subclassification is for use with category 550:

0 unilateral or unspecified (not specified as recurrent)
Unilateral NOS

1 unilateral or unspecified, recurrent

2 bilateral (not specified as recurrent)
Bilateral NOS

3 bilateral, recurrent

⑤ 550.0 Inguinal hernia, with gangrene
Inguinal hernia with gangrene (and obstruction)

⑤ 550.1 Inguinal hernia, with obstruction, without mention of gangrene
Inguinal hernia with mention of incarceration, irreducibility, or strangulation

⑤ 550.9 Inguinal hernia, without mention of obstruction or gangrene
Inguinal hernia NOS

551 Other hernia of abdominal cavity, with gangrene
Includes: that with gangrene (and obstruction)

⑤ 551.0 Femoral hernia with gangrene

551.00 Unilateral or unspecified (not specified as recurrent)
Femoral hernia NOS with gangrene

551.01 Unilateral or unspecified, recurrent

551.02 Bilateral (not specified as recurrent)

551.03 Bilateral, recurrent

551.1 Umbilical hernia with gangrene
Parumbilical hernia specified as gangrenous

⑤ 551.2 Ventral hernia with gangrene

551.20 Ventral, unspecified, with gangrene

551.21 Incisional, with gangrene
Hernia: ⎫
  postoperative   ⎬ specified as gangrenous
  recurrent, ventral

551.29 Other
Epigastric hernia specified as gangrenous

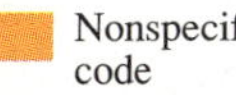

551.3 Diaphragmatic hernia with gangrene
Hernia:
   hiatal (esophageal) (sliding)   }
   paraesophageal   specified as gangrenous
   Thoracic stomach

> *Excludes:* *congenital diaphragmatic hernia (756.6)*

551.8 Hernia of other specified sites, with gangrene
Any condition classifiable to 553.8 if specified as gangrenous

551.9 Hernia of unspecified site, with gangrene
Any condition classifiable to 553.9 if specified as gangrenous

552 Other hernia of abdominal cavity, with obstruction, but without mention of gangrene

> *Excludes:* *that with mention of gangrene (551.0-551.9)*

⑤ **552.0 Femoral hernia with obstruction**
Femoral hernia specified as incarcerated, irreducible, strangulated, or causing obstruction

    552.00 Unilateral or unspecified (not specified as recurrent)

    552.01 Unilateral or unspecified, recurrent

    552.02 Bilateral (not specified as recurrent)

    552.03 Bilateral, recurrent

552.1 Umbilical hernia with obstruction
Parumbilical hernia specified as incarcerated, irreducible, strangulated, or causing
   obstruction

⑤ **552.2 Ventral hernia with obstruction**
Ventral hernia specified as incarcerated, irreducible, strangulated, or causing obstruction

    552.20 Ventral, unspecified, with obstruction

    552.21 Incisional, with obstruction
       Hernia:
          postoperative   } specified as incarcerated, irreducible, strangulated, or
          recurrent, ventral }   causing obstruction

    552.29 Other
       Epigastric hernia specified as incarcerated, irreducible, strangulated, or causing
       obstruction

552.3 Diaphragmatic hernia with obstruction
Hernia:
   hiatal (esophageal) (sliding)   } specified as incarcerated,
   paraesophageal   irreducible, strangulated, or
   Thoracic stomach   causing obstruction

> *Excludes:* *congenital diaphragmatic hernia (756.6)*

552.8 Hernia of other specified sites, with obstruction
Any condition classifiable to 553.8 if specified as incarcerated, irreducible, strangulated,
   or causing obstruction

552.9 Hernia of unspecified site, with obstruction
Any condition classifiable to 553.9 if specified as incarcerated, irreducible, strangulated,
   or causing obstruction

553 Other hernia of abdominal cavity without mention of obstruction or gangrene

> *Excludes:* *the listed conditions with mention of:*
>   *gangrene (and obstruction) (551.0-551.9)*
>   *obstruction (552.0-552.9)*

⑤ **553.0 Femoral hernia**

    553.00 Unilateral or unspecified (not specified as recurrent)
       Femoral hernia NOS

    553.01 Unilateral or unspecified, recurrent

    553.02 Bilateral (not specified as recurrent)

    553.03 Bilateral, recurrent

553.1 Umbilical hernia
Parumbilical hernia

⑤ **553.2 Ventral hernia**

    553.20 Ventral, unspecified

● Code new to this edition   ▲ Revision of existing code   ④ ⑤ Fourth or fifth digit required

553.21 Incisional
    Hernia:
      postoperative
      recurrent, ventral

553.29 Other
    Hernia:
      epigastric
      spigelian

553.3 Diaphragmatic hernia
    Hernia:
      hiatal (esophageal) (sliding)
      paraesophageal
    Thoracic stomach

Excludes: *congenital:*

      diaphragmatic hernia (756.6)
      hiatal hernia (750.6)
      esophagocele (530.6)

553.8 Hernia of other specified sites

Hernia:
  ischiatic
  ischiorectal
  lumbar
  obturator
  pudendal

Hernia:
  retroperitoneal
  sciatic
Other abdominal hernia of specified site

Excludes: *vaginal enterocele (618.6)*

553.9 Hernia of unspecified site

Enterocele
Epiplocele
Hernia:
  NOS
  interstitial

Hernia:
  intestinal
  intra-abdominal
Rupture (nontraumatic)
Sarcoepiplocele

NONINFECTIOUS ENTERITIS AND COLITIS (555-558)

555 Regional enteritis
    Includes: Crohn's disease
             Granulomatous enteritis

    Excludes: *ulcerative colitis (556)*

555.0 Small intestine

Ileitis:
  regional
  segmental
  terminal

Regional enteritis or Crohn's disease of:
  duodenum
  ileum
  jejunum

555.1 Large intestine

Colitis:
  granulomatous
  regional
  transmural

Regional enteritis or Crohn's disease of:
  colon
  large bowel
  rectum

555.2 Small intestine with large intestine
    Regional ileocolitis

555.9 Unspecified site
    Crohn's disease NOS
    Regional enteritis NOS

556 Ulcerative colitis

556.0 Ulcerative (chronic) enterocolitis

556.1 Ulcerative (chronic) ileocolitis

556.2 Ulcerative (chronic) proctitis

556.3 Ulcerative (chronic) proctosigmoiditis

556.4 Pseudopolyposis of colon

556.5 Left-sided ulcerative (chronic) colitis

556.6 Universal ulcerative (chronic) colitis
    Pancolitis

556.8 Other ulcerative colitis

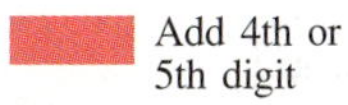
Add 4th or 5th digit

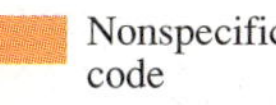
Nonspecific code

Unspecified code

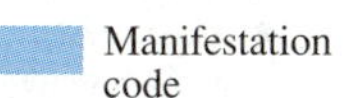
Manifestation code

556.9 Ulcerative colitis, unspecified
Ulcerative enteritis NOS

557 Vascular insufficiency of intestine

[Excludes:] *necrotizing enterocolitis of the newborn (777.5)*

557.0 Acute vascular insufficiency of intestine
Acute:
hemorrhagic enterocolitis
ischemic colitis, enteritis, or enterocolitis
massive necrosis of intestine
Bowel infarction
Embolism of mesenteric artery
Fulminant enterocolitis
Hemorrhagic necrosis of intestine
Infarction of appendices epiploicae
Intestinal gangrene
Intestinal infarction (acute) (agnogenic) (hemorrhagic) (nonocclusive)
Mesenteric infarction (embolic) (thrombotic)
Necrosis of intestine
Terminal hemorrhagic enteropathy
Thrombosis of mesenteric artery

557.1 Chronic vascular insufficiency of intestine
Angina, abdominal
Chronic ischemic colitis, enteritis, or enterocolitis
Ischemic stricture of intestine
Mesenteric:
angina
artery syndrome (superior)
vascular insufficiency

557.9 Unspecified vascular insufficiency of intestine
Alimentary pain due to vascular insufficiency
Ischemic colitis, enteritis, or enterocolitis NOS

558 Other noninfectious gastroenteritis and colitis

[Excludes:] *infectious:*

colitis, enteritis, or gastroenteritis (009.0-009.1)
diarrhea (009.2-009.3)

558.1 Gastroenteritis and colitis due to radiation
Radiation enterocolitis

558.2 Toxic gastroenteritis and colitis
Use additional E code, if desired, to identify cause

● **558.3 Allergic gastroenteritis and colitis**

558.9 Other and unspecified noninfectious gastroenteritis and colitis
Colitis
Diarrhea
Enteritis
Gastroenteritis ⎬ NOS, dietetic, or noninfectious
Ileitis
Jejunitis
Sigmoiditis

OTHER DISEASES OF INTESTINES AND PERITONEUM (560-569)

560 Intestinal obstruction without mention of hernia

[Excludes:] *duodenum (537.2-537.3)*

inguinal hernia with obstruction (550.1)
intestinal obstruction complicating hernia (552.0-552.9)
mesenteric:
embolism (557.0)
infarction (557.0)
thrombosis (557.0)
neonatal intestinal obstruction (277.01, 777.1-777.2, 777.4)

560.0 Intussusception
Intussusception (colon) (intestine) (rectum)
Invagination of intestine or colon

[Excludes:] *intussusception of appendix (543.9)*

● Code new   ▲ Revision of   ④ ⑤ Fourth or fifth
to this edition   existing code   digit required

560.1 Paralytic ileus
Adynamic ileus
Ileus (of intestine) (of bowel) (of colon)
Paralysis of intestine or colon

Excludes: *gallstone ileus (560.31)*

560.2 Volvulus
Knotting
Strangulation
Torsion
Twist
} of intestine, bowel, or colon

⑤ **560.3 Impaction of intestine**

560.30 Impaction of intestine, unspecified
Impaction of colon

560.31 Gallstone ileus
Obstruction of intestine by gallstone

560.39 Other
Concretion of intestine
Enterolith
Fecal impaction

⑤ **560.8 Other specified intestinal obstruction**

560.81 Intestinal or peritoneal adhesions with obstruction (postoperative) (postinfection)

Excludes: *adhesions without obstruction (568.0)*

560.89 Other
Mural thickening causing obstruction

Excludes: *ischemic stricture of intestine (557.1)*

560.9 Unspecified intestinal obstruction
Enterostenosis
Obstruction
Occlusion
Stenosis
Stricture
} of intestine or colon

Excludes: *congenital stricture or stenosis of intestine (751.1-751.2)*

562 Diverticula of intestine
Use additional code, if desired, to identify any associated:
peritonitis (567.0-567.9)

Excludes: *congenital diverticulum of colon (751.5)*
diverticulum of appendix (543.9)
Meckel's diverticulum (751.0)

⑤ **562.0 Small intestine**

562.00 Diverticulosis of small intestine (without mention of hemorrhage)
Diverticulosis:
duodenum
ileum
jejunum
} without mention of diverticulitis

562.01 Diverticulitis of small intestine (without mention of hemorrhage)
Diverticulitis (with diverticulosis):
duodenum
ileum
jejunum
small intestine

562.02 Diverticulosis of small intestine with hemorrhage

562.03 Diverticulitis of small intestine with hemorrhage

⑤ **562.1 Colon**

562.10 Diverticulosis of colon (without mention of hemorrhage)
Diverticulosis:
NOS
intestine (large)
Diverticular disease (colon)
} without mention of diverticulitis

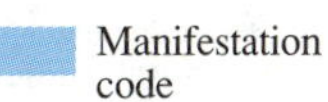

562.11 Diverticulitis of colon (without mention of hemorrhage)
Diverticulitis (with diverticulosis):
NOS
colon
intestine (large)

562.12 Diverticulosis of colon with hemorrhage

562.13 Diverticulitis of colon with hemorrhage

564 Functional digestive disorders, not elsewhere classified

Excludes: *functional disorders of stomach (536.0-536.9)*
those specified as psychogenic (306.4)

564.0 Constipation

▲ **564.1 Irritable bowel syndrome**
Irritable colon   Spastic colon

564.2 Postgastric surgery syndromes
Dumping syndrome   Postgastrectomy syndrome
Jejunal syndrome   Postvagotomy syndrome

Excludes: *malnutrition following gastrointestinal surgery (579.3)*
postgastrojejunostomy ulcer (534.0-534.9)

564.3 Vomiting following gastrointestinal surgery
Vomiting (bilious) following gastrointestinal surgery

564.4 Other postoperative functional disorders
Diarrhea following gastrointestinal surgery

Excludes: *colostomy and enterostomy complications (569.60-569.69)*

564.5 Functional diarrhea

Excludes: *diarrhea:*
NOS (787.91)
psychogenic (306.4)

564.6 Anal spasm
Proctalgia fugax

564.7 Megacolon, other than Hirschsprung's
Dilatation of colon

Excludes: *megacolon:*
congenital [Hirschsprung's] (751.3)
toxic (556)

⑤ **564.8 Other specified functional disorders of intestine**

Excludes: *malabsorption (579.0-579.9)*

564.81 Neurogenic bowel

564.89 Other functional disorders of intestine
Atony of colon

564.9 Unspecified functional disorder of intestine

565 Anal fissure and fistula

565.0 Anal fissure
Tear of anus, nontraumatic

Excludes: *traumatic (863.89, 863.99)*

565.1 Anal fistula
Fistula:
anorectal
rectal
rectum to skin

Excludes: *fistula of rectum to internal organs—see Alphabetic Index*
ischiorectal fistula (566)
rectovaginal fistula (619.1)

● Code new to this edition   ▲ Revision of existing code   ④ ⑤ Fourth or fifth digit required

566 Abscess of anal and rectal regions

Abscess:
  ischiorectal
  perianal
  perirectal

Cellulitis:
  anal
  perirectal
  rectal
Ischiorectal fistula

567 Peritonitis

Excludes: *peritonitis:*

benign paroxysmal (277.3)
pelvic, female (614.5, 614.7)
periodic familial (277.3)
puerperal (670)
with or following:
  abortion (634-638 with .0, 639.0)
  appendicitis (540.0-540.1)
  ectopic or molar pregnancy (639.0)

567.0 *Peritonitis in infectious diseases classified elsewhere*
Code first underlying disease

Excludes: *peritonitis:*

gonococcal (098.86)
syphilitic (095.2)
tuberculous (014.0)

567.1 Pneumococcal peritonitis

567.2 Other suppurative peritonitis

Abscess (of):
  abdominopelvic
  mesenteric
  omentum
  peritoneum
  retrocecal
  retroperitoneal
  subdiaphragmatic

Abscess (of):
  subhepatic
  subphrenic
Peritonitis (acute):
  general
  pelvic, male
  subphrenic
  suppurative

567.8 Other specified peritonitis
Chronic proliferative peritonitis
Fat necrosis of peritoneum
Mesenteric saponification
Peritonitis due to:
  bile
  urine

567.9 Unspecified peritonitis
Peritonitis:
  NOS
  of unspecified cause

568 Other disorders of peritoneum

568.0 Peritoneal adhesions (postoperative) (postinfection)
Adhesions (of):
  abdominal (wall)
  diaphragm
  intestine
  male pelvis

Adhesions (of):
  mesenteric
  omentum
  stomach
Adhesive bands

Excludes: *adhesions:*

pelvic, female (614.6)
with obstruction:
  duodenum (537.3)
  intestine (560.81)

⑤ **568.8 Other specified disorders of peritoneum**

568.81 Hemoperitoneum (nontraumatic)

568.82 Peritoneal effusion (chronic)

Excludes: *ascites NOS (789.5)*

568.89 Other
Peritoneal:
  cyst
  granuloma

568.9 Unspecified disorder of peritoneum

569 **Other disorders of intestine**

569.0 **Anal and rectal polyp**
Anal and rectal polyp NOS

Excludes: *adenomatous anal and rectal polyp (211.4)*

569.1 **Rectal prolapse**

Procidentia:	Prolapse:
anus (sphincter)	anal canal
rectum (sphincter)	rectal mucosa
Proctoptosis	

Excludes: *prolapsed hemorrhoids (455.2, 455.5)*

569.2 **Stenosis of rectum and anus**
Stricture of anus (sphincter)

569.3 **Hemorrhage of rectum and anus**

Excludes: *gastrointestinal bleeding NOS (578.9)*
melena (578.1)

⑤ **569.4** **Other specified disorders of rectum and anus**

569.41 **Ulcer of anus and rectum**
Solitary ulcer ⎫
Stercoral ulcer ⎭ of anus (sphincter) or rectum (sphincter)

569.42 **Anal or rectal pain**

569.49 **Other**
Granuloma ⎫
Rupture ⎭ of rectum (sphincter)

Hypertrophy of anal papillae
Proctitis NOS

Excludes: *fistula of rectum to:*
internal organs—see Alphabetic Index
skin (565.1)
hemorrhoids (455.0-455.9)
incontinence of sphincter ani (787.6)

569.5 **Abscess of intestine**

Excludes: *appendiceal abscess (540.1)*

⑤ **569.6** **Colostomy and enterostomy complications**

569.60 **Colostomy and enterostomy complication, unspecified**

569.61 **Infection of colostomy or enterostomy**
Use additional code to specify type of infection, such as:
abscess or cellulitis of abdomen (682.2)
septicemia (038.0-038.9)
Use additional code to identify organism (041.00-041.9)

569.62 **Mechanical complication of colostomy and enterostomy**
Malfunction of colostomy and enterostomy

569.69 **Other complication**
Fistula
Hernia
Prolapse

⑤ **569.8** **Other specified disorders of intestine**

569.81 **Fistula of intestine, excluding rectum and anus**

Fistula:	Fistula:
abdominal wall	enteroenteric
enterocolic	ileorectal

Excludes: *fistula of intestine to internal organs —see Alphabetic Index*
persistent postoperative fistula (998.6)

569.82 **Ulceration of intestine**
Primary ulcer of intestine
Ulceration of colon

Excludes: *that with perforation (569.83)*

569.83 **Perforation of intestine**

569.84 **Angiodysplasia of intestine (without mention of hemorrhage)**

● Code new
to this edition
▲ Revision of
existing code
④ ⑤ Fourth or fifth
digit required

569.85 Angiodysplasia of intestine with hemorrhage

569.89 Other
Enteroptosis
Granuloma
Prolapse $\Big\}$ of intestine
Pericolitis
Perisigmoiditis
Visceroptosis

Excludes: *gangrene of intestine, mesentery, or omentum (557.0)*
hemorrhage of intestine NOS (578.9)
obstruction of intestine (560.0-560.9)

569.9 Unspecified disorder of intestine

OTHER DISEASES OF DIGESTIVE SYSTEM (570-579)

570 Acute and subacute necrosis of liver
Acute hepatic failure
Acute or subacute hepatitis, not specified as infective
Necrosis of liver (acute) (diffuse) (massive) (subacute)
Parenchymatous degeneration of liver
Yellow atrophy (liver) (acute) (subacute)

Excludes: *icterus gravis of newborn (773.0-773.2)*
serum hepatitis (070.2-070.3)
that with:
abortion (634-638 with .7, 639.8)
ectopic or molar pregnancy (639.8)
pregnancy, childbirth, or the puerperium (646.7)
viral hepatitis (070.0-070.9)

571 Chronic liver disease and cirrhosis

571.0 Alcoholic fatty liver

571.1 Acute alcoholic hepatitis
Acute alcoholic liver disease

571.2 Alcoholic cirrhosis of liver
Florid cirrhosis
Laennec's cirrhosis (alcoholic)

571.3 Alcoholic liver damage, unspecified

⑤ **571.4 Chronic hepatitis**

Excludes: *viral hepatitis (acute) (chronic) (070.0-070.9)*

571.40 Chronic hepatitis, unspecified

571.41 Chronic persistent hepatitis

571.49 Other
Chronic hepatitis:
active
aggressive
Recurrent hepatitis

571.5 Cirrhosis of liver without mention of alcohol
Cirrhosis of liver:
NOS
cryptogenic
macronodular
micronodular

Cirrhosis of liver:
posthepatitic
postnecrotic
Healed yellow atrophy (liver)
Portal cirrhosis

571.6 Biliary cirrhosis
Chronic nonsuppurative destructive cholangitis
Cirrhosis:
cholangitic
cholestatic

571.8 Other chronic nonalcoholic liver disease
Chronic yellow atrophy (liver)
Fatty liver, without mention of alcohol

571.9 Unspecified chronic liver disease without mention of alcohol

572 Liver abscess and sequelae of chronic liver disease

572.0 Abscess of liver

Excludes: *amebic liver abscess (006.3)*

Add 4th or 5th digit   Nonspecific code   Unspecified code   Manifestation code

572.1 Portal pyemia
Phlebitis of portal vein   Pylephlebitis
Portal thrombophlebitis   Pylethrombophlebitis

572.2 Hepatic coma
Hepatic encephalopathy
Hepatocerebral intoxication
Portal-systemic encephalopathy

572.3 Portal hypertension

572.4 Hepatorenal syndrome

> *Excludes:* *that following delivery (674.8)*

572.8 Other sequelae of chronic liver disease

573 Other disorders of liver

> *Excludes:* *amyloid or lardaceous degeneration of liver (277.3)*
> *congenital cystic disease of liver (751.62)*
> *glycogen infiltration of liver (271.0)*
> *hepatomegaly NOS (789.1)*
> *portal vein obstruction (452)*

573.0 Chronic passive congestion of liver

573.1 *Hepatitis in viral diseases classified elsewhere*
Code first underlying disease as:
Coxsackie virus disease (074.8)
cytomegalic inclusion virus disease (078.5)
infectious mononucleosis (075)

> *Excludes:* *hepatitis (in):*
> *mumps (072.71)*
> *viral (070.0-070.9)*
> *yellow fever (060.0-060.9)*

573.2 *Hepatitis in other infectious diseases classified elsewhere*
Code first underlying disease, as:
malaria (084.9)

> *Excludes:* *hepatitis in:*
> *late syphilis (095.3)*
> *secondary syphilis (091.62)*
> *toxoplasmosis (130.5)*

573.3 Hepatitis, unspecified
Toxic (noninfectious) hepatitis
Use additional E code, if desired, to identify cause

573.4 Hepatic infarction

573.8 Other specified disorders of liver
Hepatoptosis

573.9 Unspecified disorder of liver

⑤ 574 Cholelithiasis

The following fifth-digit subclassification is for use with category 574:

    0 without mention of obstruction

    1 with obstruction

⑤ 574.0 Calculus of gallbladder with acute cholecystitis
Biliary calculus
Calculus of cystic   } with acute cholecystitis
  duct
Cholelithiasis
Any condition classifiable to 574.2 with acute cholecystitis

⑤ 574.1 Calculus of gallbladder with other cholecystitis
Biliary calculus
Calculus of cystic   } with cholecystitis
  duct
Cholelithiasis
Cholecystitis with cholelithiasis NOS
Any condition classifiable to 574.2 with cholecystitis (chronic)

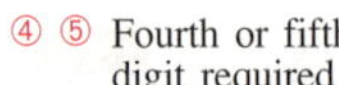

● Code new   ▲ Revision of   ④ ⑤ Fourth or fifth
   to this edition   existing code   digit required

⑤ **574.2 Calculus of gallbladder without mention of cholecystitis**

Biliary:
  calculus NOS
  colic NOS
Calculus of cystic duct
Cholelithiasis NOS
Colic (recurrent) of gallbladder
Gallstone (impacted)

⑤ **574.3 Calculus of bile duct with acute cholecystitis**

Calculus of bile duct [any] } with acute cholecystitis
Choledocholithiasis
Any condition classifiable to 574.5 with acute cholecystitis

⑤ **574.4 Calculus of bile duct with other cholecystitis**

Calculus of bile duct [any] } with cholecystitis (chronic)
Choledocholithiasis
Any condition classifiable to 574.5 with cholecystitis (chronic)

⑤ **574.5 Calculus of bile duct without mention of cholecystitis**

Calculus of:
  bile duct [any]
  common duct
  hepatic duct
Choledocholithiasis
Hepatic:
  colic (recurrent)
  lithiasis

⑤ **574.6 Calculus of gallbladder and bile duct with acute cholecystitis**

Any condition classifiable to 574.0 and 574.3

⑤ **574.7 Calculus of gallbladder and bile duct with other cholecystitis**

Any condition classifiable to 574.1 and 574.4

⑤ **574.8 Calculus of gallbladder and bile duct with acute and chronic cholecystitis**

Any condition classifiable to 574.6 and 574.7

⑤ **574.9 Calculus of gallbladder and bile duct without cholecystitis**

Any condition classifiable to 574.2 and 574.5

575 Other disorders of gallbladder

575.0 Acute cholecystitis

Abscess of gallbladder
Angiocholecystitis
Cholecystitis:
  emphysematous (acute)
  gangrenous
  suppurative
Empyema of gallbladder
Gangrene of gallbladder
} without mention of calculus

Excludes: *that with:*

  acute and chronic cholecystitis (575.12)
  choledocholithiasis (574.3)
  choledocholithiasis and cholelithiasis (574.6)
  cholelithiasis (574.0)

⑤ **575.1 Other cholecystitis**

Cholecystitis:
  NOS
  chronic
} without mention of calculus

Excludes: *that with:*

  choledocholithiasis (574.4)
  choledocholithiasis and cholelithiasis (574.8)
  cholelithiasis (574.1)

575.10 Cholecystitis, unspecified
Cholecystitis NOS

575.11 Chronic cholecystitis

575.12 Acute and chronic cholecystits

575.2 Obstruction of gallbladder

Occlusion
Stenosis
Stricture
} of cystic duct or gallbladder without mention of calculus

Excludes: *that with calculus (574.0-574.2 with fifth-digit 1)*

575.3 Hydrops of gallbladder
Mucocele of gallbladder

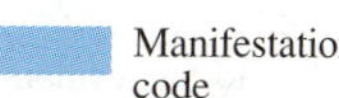

575.4 Perforation of gallbladder
    Rupture of cystic duct or gallbladder

575.5 Fistula of gallbladder
    Fistula:
        cholecystoduodenal
        cholecystoenteric

575.6 Cholesterolosis of gallbladder
    Strawberry gallbladder

575.8 Other specified disorders of gallbladder

Adhesions
Atrophy
Cyst
Hypertrophy   (of)   cystic duct
Nonfunctioning   gallbladder
Ulcer
Biliary dyskinesia

    Excludes: *nonvisualization of gallbladder (793.3)*

575.9 Unspecified disorder of gallbladder

576 Other disorders of biliary tract

    Excludes: *that involving the:*
        cystic duct (575.0-575.9)
        gallbladder (575.0-575.9)

576.0 Postcholecystectomy syndrome

576.1 Cholangitis

Cholangitis: Cholangitis:
  NOS   recurrent
  acute   sclerosing
  ascending   secondary
  chronic   stenosing
  primary   suppurative

576.2 Obstruction of bile duct

Occlusion
Stenosis   of bile duct, except cystic duct, without mention of calculus
Stricture

    Excludes: *congenital (751.61)*
        that with calculus (574.3-574.5 with fifth-digit 1)

576.3 Perforation of bile duct
    Rupture of bile duct, except cystic duct

576.4 Fistula of bile duct
    Choledochoduodenal fistula

576.5 Spasm of sphincter of Oddi

576.8 Other specified disorders of biliary tract

Adhesions
Atrophy
Cyst
Hypertrophy   of bile duct [any]
Stasis
Ulcer

    Excludes: *congenital choledochal cyst (751.69)*

576.9 Unspecified disorder of biliary tract

577 Diseases of pancreas

577.0 Acute pancreatitis

Abscess of pancreas   Pancreatitis:
Necrosis of pancreas: NOS
  acute   acute (recurrent)
  infective   apoplectic
                       hemorrhagic
                       subacute
                       suppurative

    Excludes: *mumps pancreatitis (072.3)*

● Code new to this edition   ▲ Revision of existing code   ④ ⑤ Fourth or fifth digit required

577.1 Chronic pancreatitis

Chronic pancreatitis: Pancreatitis:
  NOS painless
  infectious recurrent
  interstitial relapsing

577.2 Cyst and pseudocyst of pancreas

577.8 Other specified diseases of pancreas

Atrophy Pancreatic:
Calculus infantilism
Cirrhosis } of pancreas necrosis:
Fibrosis NOS
  aseptic
  fat
Pancreatolithiasis

Excludes: *fibrocystic disease of pancreas (277.00-277.01)*
  islet cell tumor of pancreas (211.7)
  pancreatic steatorrhea (579.4)

577.9 Unspecified disease of pancreas

578 Gastrointestinal hemorrhage

Excludes: *that with mention of :*
  angiodysplasia of stomach and duodenum (537.83)
  angiodysplasia of intestine (569.85)
  diverticulitis, intestine:
    large (562.13)
    small (562.03)
  diverticulosis, intestine:
    large (562.12)
    small (562.02)
  gastritis and duodenitis (535.0-535.6)
  ulcer:
    duodenal (532.0-532.9)
    gastric (531.0-531.9)
    gastrojejunal (534.0-534.9)
    peptic (533.0-533.9)

578.0 Hematemesis

Vomiting of blood

578.1 Blood in stool

Melena

Excludes: *occult blood (792.1)*

578.9 Hemorrhage of gastrointestinal tract, unspecified

Gastric hemorrhage Intestinal hemorrhage

579 Intestinal malabsorption

579.0 Celiac disease

Celiac: Gee (-Herter) disease
  crisis Gluten enteropathy
  infantilism Idiopathic steatorrhea
  rickets Nontropical sprue

579.1 Tropical sprue

Sprue: Tropical steatorrhea
  NOS
  tropical

579.2 Blind loop syndrome

Postoperative blind loop syndrome

579.3 Other and unspecified postsurgical nonabsorption

Hypoglycemia
Malnutrition } following gastrointestinal surgery

579.4 Pancreatic steatorrhea

579.8 Other specified intestinal malabsorption

Enteropathy: Steatorrhea (chronic)
  exudative
  protein-losing

579.9 Unspecified intestinal malabsorption

Malabsorption syndrome NOS

Add 4th or 5th digit	Nonspecific code	Unspecified code	Manifestation code

● Code new
to this edition

▲ Revision of
existing code

④ ⑤ Fourth or fifth
digit required

10. DISEASES OF THE GENITOURINARY SYSTEM (580-629)

NEPHRITIS, NEPHROTIC SYNDROME, AND NEPHROSIS (580-589)

Excludes: *hypertensive renal disease (403.00-403.91)*

580 Acute glomerulonephritis
Includes: acute nephritis

580.0 With lesion of proliferative glomerulonephritis
Acute (diffuse) proliferative glomerulonephritis
Acute poststreptococcal glomerulonephritis

580.4 With lesion of rapidly progressive glomerulonephritis
Acute nephritis with lesion of necrotizing glomerulitis

⑤ **580.8 With other specified pathological lesion in kidney**

580.81 *Acute glomerulonephritis in diseases classified elsewhere*
Code first underlying disease, as:
infectious hepatitis (070.0-070.9)
mumps (072.79)
subacute bacterial endocarditis (421.0)
typhoid fever (002.0)

580.89 Other
Glomerulonephritis, acute, with lesion of:
exudative nephritis
interstitial (diffuse) (focal) nephritis

580.9 Acute glomerulonephritis with unspecified pathological lesion in kidney
Glomerulonephritis:
NOS
hemorrhagic } specified as acute
Nephritis
Nephropathy

581 Nephrotic syndrome

581.0 With lesion of proliferative glomerulonephritis

581.1 With lesion of membranous glomerulonephritis
Epimembranous nephritis
Idiopathic membranous glomerular disease
Nephrotic syndrome with lesion of:
focal glomerulosclerosis
sclerosing membranous glomerulonephritis
segmental hyalinosis

581.2 With lesion of membranoproliferative glomerulonephritis
Nephrotic syndrome with lesion (of):
endothelial
hypocomplementemic persistent
lobular } glomerulonephritis
mesangiocapillary
mixed membranous and proliferative

581.3 With lesion of minimal change glomerulonephritis
Foot process disease   Minimal change:
Lipoid nephrosis   glomerular disease
                                    glomerulitis
                                    nephrotic syndrome

⑤ **581.8 With other specified pathological lesion in kidney**

581.81 *Nephrotic syndrome in diseases classified elsewhere*
Code first underlying disease, as:
amyloidosis (277.3)
diabetes mellitus (250.4)
malaria (084.9)
polyarteritis (446.0)
systemic lupus erythematosus (710.0)

Excludes: *nephrosis in epidemic hemorrhagic fever (078.6)*

581.89 Other
Glomerulonephritis with edema and lesion of:
exudative nephritis
interstitial (diffuse) (focal) nephritis

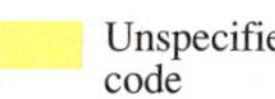
Add 4th or 5th digit | Nonspecific code

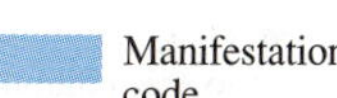
Unspecified code | Manifestation code

581.9 Nephrotic syndrome with unspecified pathological lesion in kidney
Glomerulonephritis with edema NOS
Nephritis:
nephrotic NOS
with edema NOS
Nephrosis NOS
Renal disease with edema NOS

582 Chronic glomerulonephritis
Includes: chronic nephritis

582.0 With lesion of proliferative glomerulonephritis
Chronic (diffuse) proliferative glomerulonephritis

582.1 With lesion of membranous glomerulonephritis
Chronic glomerulonephritis:
membranous
sclerosing
Focal glomerulosclerosis
Segmental hyalinosis

582.2 With lesion of membranoproliferative glomerulonephritis
Chronic glomerulonephritis:
endothelial
hypocomplementemic persistent
lobular
membranoproliferative
mesangiocapillary
mixed membranous and proliferative

582.4 With lesion of rapidly progressive glomerulonephritis
Chronic nephritis with lesion of necrotizing glomerulitis

⑤ **582.8 With other specified pathological lesion in kidney**

582.81 *Chronic glomerulonephritis in diseases classified elsewhere*
Code first underlying disease, as:
amyloidosis (277.3)
systemic lupus erythematosus (710.0)

582.89 **Other**
Chronic glomerulonephritis with lesion of:
exudative nephritis
interstitial (diffuse) (focal) nephritis

582.9 Chronic glomerulonephritis with unspecified pathological lesion in kidney
Glomerulonephritis:
NOS
hemorrhagic   } specified as chronic
Nephritis
Nephropathy

583 Nephritis and nephropathy, not specified as acute or chronic
Includes: "renal disease" so stated, not specified as acute or chronic but with stated pathology
or cause

583.0 With lesion of proliferative glomerulonephritis
Proliferative:
glomerulonephritis (diffuse) NOS
nephritis NOS
nephropathy NOS

583.1 With lesion of membranous glomerulonephritis
Membranous: Membranous nephropathy NOS
glomerulonephritis NOS
nephritis NOS

583.2 With lesion of membranoproliferative glomerulonephritis
Membranoproliferative:
glomerulonephritis NOS
nephritis NOS
nephropathy NOS
Nephritis NOS, with lesion of:
hypocomplementemic persistent
lobular   } glomerulonephritis
mesangiocapillary
mixed membranous and proliferative

● Code new   ▲ Revision of   ④ ⑤ Fourth or fifth
to this edition   existing code   digit required

583.4 With lesion of rapidly progressive glomerulonephritis
Necrotizing or rapidly progressive:
  glomerulitis NOS
  glomerulonephritis NOS
  nephritis NOS
  nephropathy NOS
Nephritis, unspecified, with lesion of necrotizing glomerulitis

583.6 With lesion of renal cortical necrosis
Nephritis NOS
Nephropathy NOS } with (renal) cortical necrosis
Renal cortical necrosis NOS

583.7 With lesion of renal medullary necrosis
Nephritis NOS
Nephropathy NOS } with (renal) medullary [papillary] necrosis

⑤ **583.8 With other specified pathological lesion in kidney**

583.81 *Nephritis and nephropathy, not specified as acute or chronic, in diseases classified elsewhere*
Code first underlying disease, as:
  amyloidosis (277.3)
  diabetes mellitus (250.4)
  gonococcal infection (098.19)
  Goodpasture's syndrome (446.21)
  systemic lupus erythematosus (710.0)
  tuberculosis (016.0)

Excludes: *gouty nephropathy (274.10)*
syphilitic nephritis (095.4)

583.89 Other
Glomerulitis
Glomerulo-
  nephritis
Nephritis } with lesion of:
Nephropathy   exudative nephritis
Renal disease   interstitial nephritis

583.9 With unspecified pathological lesion in kidney
Glomerulitis
Glomerulonephritis } NOS
Nephritis
Nephropathy

Excludes: *nephropathy complicating pregnancy, labor, or the puerperium (642.0-642.9, 646.2)*
renal disease NOS with no stated cause (593.9)

584 Acute renal failure

Excludes: *following labor and delivery (669.3)*
posttraumatic (958.5)
that complicating:
  abortion (634-638 with .3, 639.3)
  ectopic or molar pregnancy (639.3)

584.5 With lesion of tubular necrosis
Lower nephron nephrosis
Renal failure with (acute) tubular necrosis
Tubular necrosis:
  NOS
  acute

584.6 With lesion of renal cortical necrosis

584.7 With lesion of renal medullary [papillary] necrosis
Necrotizing renal papillitis

584.8 With other specified pathological lesion in kidney

584.9 Acute renal failure, unspecified

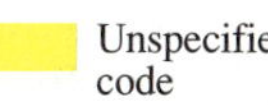

Manifestation
code

585 Chronic renal failure
Chronic uremia

Use additional code, if desired, to identify manifestation as:
uremic:
neuropathy (357.4)
pericarditis (420.0)

Excludes: *that with any condition classifiable to 401 (403.0-403.9 with fifth-digit 1)*

586 Renal failure, unspecified
Uremia NOS

Excludes: *following labor and delivery (669.3)*
posttraumatic renal failure (958.5)
that complicating:
abortion (634-638 with .3, 639.3)
ectopic or molar pregnancy (639.3)
uremia:
extrarenal (788.9)
prerenal (788.9)
with any condition classifiable to 401 (403.0-403.9 with fifth-digit 1)

587 Renal sclerosis, unspecified

Atrophy of kidney
Contracted kidney

Renal:
cirrhosis
fibrosis

Excludes: *nephrosclerosis (arteriolar) (arteriosclerotic) (403.00-403.92)*
with hypertension (403.00-403.92)

588 Disorders resulting from impaired renal function

588.0 Renal osteodystrophy

Azotemic osteodystrophy
Phosphate-losing tubular
disorders

Renal:
dwarfism
infantilism
rickets

588.1 Nephrogenic diabetes insipidus

Excludes: *diabetes insipidus NOS (253.5)*

588.8 Other specified disorders resulting from impaired renal function
Hypokalemic nephropathy
Secondary hyperparathyroidism (of renal origin)

Excludes: *secondary hypertension (405.0-405.9)*

588.9 Unspecified disorder resulting from impaired renal function

589 Small kidney of unknown cause

589.0 Unilateral small kidney

589.1 Bilateral small kidneys

589.9 Small kidney, unspecified

OTHER DISEASES OF URINARY SYSTEM (590-599)

590 Infections of kidney

Use additional code, if desired, to identify organism, such as Escherichia coli [E. coli] (041.4)

⑤ *590.0 Chronic pyelonephritis*
Chronic pyelitis   Chronic pyonephrosis
Code first any associated vesicoureteral reflux (593.70-593.73)

590.00 Without lesion of renal medullary necrosis

590.01 With lesion of renal medullary necrosis

⑤ **590.1 Acute pyelonephritis**
Acute pyelitis   Acute pyonephrosis

590.10 Without lesion of renal medullary necrosis

590.11 With lesion of renal medullary necrosis

● Code new
to this edition

▲ Revision of
existing code

④ ⑤ Fourth or fifth
digit required

590.2 Renal and perinephric abscess
Abscess: Carbuncle of kidney
  kidney
  nephritic
  perirenal

590.3 Pyeloureteritis cystica
Infection of renal pelvis and ureter
Ureteritis cystica

⑤ **590.8 Other pyelonephritis or pyonephrosis, not specified as acute or chronic**

590.80 Pyelonephritis, unspecified
Pyelitis NOS   Pyelonephritis NOS

590.81 ***Pyelitis or pyelonephritis in diseases classified elsewhere***
Code first underlying disease, as:
  tuberculosis (016.0)

590.9 Infection of kidney, unspecified

Excludes: *urinary tract infection NOS (599.0)*

591 Hydronephrosis
Hydrocalycosis   Hydroureteronephrosis
Hydronephrosis

Excludes: *congenital hydronephrosis (753.29)*
hydroureter (593.5)

592 Calculus of kidney and ureter

Excludes: *nephrocalcinosis (275.4)*

592.0 Calculus of kidney
Nephrolithiasis NOS   Staghorn calculus
Renal calculus or stone   Stone in kidney

Excludes: *uric acid nephrolithiasis (274.11)*

592.1 Calculus of ureter
Ureteric stone   Ureterolithiasis

592.9 Urinary calculus, unspecified

593 Other disorders of kidney and ureter

593.0 Nephroptosis
Floating kidney   Mobile kidney

593.1 Hypertrophy of kidney

593.2 Cyst of kidney, acquired
Cyst (multiple) (solitary) of kidney, not congenital
Peripelvic (lymphatic) cyst

Excludes: *calyceal or pyelogenic cyst of kidney (591)*
congenital cyst of kidney (753.1)
polycystic (disease of) kidney (753.1)

593.3 Stricture or kinking of ureter
Angulation
Constriction   } of ureter (postoperative)
Stricture of pelviureteric junction

593.4 Other ureteric obstruction
Idiopathic retroperitoneal fibrosis
Occlusion NOS of ureter

Excludes: *that due to calculus (592.1)*

593.5 Hydroureter

Excludes: *congenital hydroureter (753.22)*
hydroureteronephrosis (591)

593.6 Postural proteinuria
Benign postural proteinuria
Orthostatic proteinuria

Excludes: *proteinuria NOS (791.0)*

⑤ **593.7   Vesicoureteral reflux**
Use additional code to identify:
      chronic pyelonephritis (590.00-590.01)
      renal agenesis (753.0)
      renal dysplasia (753.15)

    593.70   Unspecified or without reflux nephropathy

    593.71   With reflux nephropathy, unilateral

    593.72   With reflux nephropathy, bilateral

    593.73   With reflux nephropathy NOS

⑤ **593.8   Other specified disorders of kidney and ureter**

    593.81   Vascular disorders of kidney
        Renal (artery):   Renal infarction
          embolism
          hemorrhage
          thrombosis

    593.82   Ureteral fistula
        Intestinoureteral fistula

> *Excludes:* *fistula between ureter and female genital tract (619.0)*

    593.89   Other
        Adhesions, kidney or Polyp of ureter
          ureter   Pyelectasia
        Periureteritis   Ureterocele

> *Excludes:* *tuberculosis of ureter (016.2)*
>   *ureteritis cystica (590.3)*

593.9   Unspecified disorder of kidney and ureter
    Renal disease NOS
    Salt-losing nephritis or syndrome

> *Excludes:* *cystic kidney disease (753.1)*
>   *nephropathy, so stated (583.0-583.9)*
>   *renal disease:*
>   *acute (580.0-580.9)*
>   *arising in pregnancy or the puerperium (642.1-642.2, 642.4-642.7, 646.2)*
>   *chronic (582.0-582.9)*
>   *not specified as acute or chronic, but with stated pathology or cause*
>   *(583.0-583.9)*

594   Calculus of lower urinary tract

  594.0   Calculus in diverticulum of bladder

  594.1   Other calculus in bladder
    Urinary bladder stone

> *Excludes:* *staghorn calculus (592.0)*

  594.2   Calculus in urethra

  594.8   Other lower urinary tract calculus

  594.9   Calculus of lower urinary tract, unspecified

> *Excludes:* *calculus of urinary tract NOS (592.9)*

595   Cystitis

> *Excludes:* *prostatocystitis (601.3)*

Use additional code, if desired, to identify organism, such as Escherichia coli [E. coli] (041.4)

  595.0   Acute cystitis

> *Excludes:* *trigonitis (595.3)*

  595.1   Chronic interstitial cystitis
    Hunner's ulcer   Submucous cystitis
    Panmural fibrosis of bladder

  595.2   Other chronic cystitis
    Chronic cystitis NOS   Subacute cystitis

> *Excludes:* *trigonitis (595.3)*

● Code new to this edition   ▲ Revision of existing code   ④ ⑤ Fourth or fifth digit required

595.3 Trigonitis
Follicular cystitis
Trigonitis (acute) (chronic)
Urethrotrigonitis

595.4 *Cystitis in diseases classified elsewhere*
Code first underlying disease, as:
actinomycosis (039.8)
amebiasis (006.8)
bilharziasis (120.0-120.9)
Echinococcus infestation (122.3, 122.6)

Excludes: *cystitis:*

diphtheritic (032.84)
gonococcal (098.11, 098.31)
monilial (112.2)
trichomonal (131.09)
tuberculous (016.1)

⑤ **595.8 Other specified types of cystitis**

595.81 Cystitis cystica

595.82 Irradiation cystitis
Use additional E code, if desired, to identify cause

595.89 Other
Abscess of bladder
Cystitis:
bullous
emphysematous
glandularis

595.9 Cystitis, unspecified

596 Other disorders of bladder
Use additional code, if desired, to identify urinary incontinence (625.6, 788.30-788.39)

596.0 Bladder neck obstruction
Contracture (acquired)
Obstruction (acquired) } of bladder neck or vesicourethral orifice
Stenosis (acquired)

Excludes: *congenital (753.6)*

596.1 Intestinovesical fistula

Fistula:	Fistula:
enterovesical	vesicoenteric
vesicocolic	vesicorectal

596.2 Vesical fistula, not elsewhere classified

Fistula:	Fistula:
bladder NOS	vesicocutaneous
urethrovesical	vesicoperineal

Excludes: *fistula between bladder and female genital tract (619.0)*

596.3 Diverticulum of bladder
Diverticulitis
Diverticulum (acquired) } of bladder
(false)

Excludes: *that with calculus in diverticulum of bladder (594.0)*

596.4 Atony of bladder
High compliance bladder
Hypotonicity } of bladder
Inertia

Excludes: *neurogenic bladder (596.54)*

⑤ **596.5 Other functional disorders of bladder**

Excludes: *cauda equina syndrome*
with neurogenic bladder (344.61)

596.51 Hypertonicity of bladder
Hyperactivity
Overactive bladder

596.52 Low bladder compliance

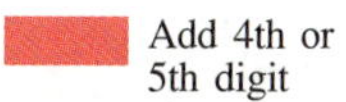

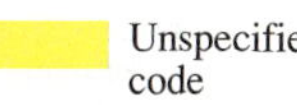

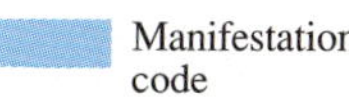

596.53 Paralysis of bladder

596.54 Neurogenic bladder NOS

596.55 Detrusor sphincter dyssynergia

596.59 Other functional disorder of bladder
Detrusor instability

596.6 Rupture of bladder, nontraumatic

596.7 Hemorrhage into bladder wall
Hyperemia of bladder

Excludes: *acute hemorrhagic cystitis (595.0)*

596.8 Other specified disorders of bladder

Bladder:	Bladder:
calcified	hemorrhage
contracted	hypertrophy

Excludes: *cystocele, female (618.0, 618.2-618.4)*
        hernia or prolapse of bladder, female (618.0, 618.2-618.4)

596.9 Unspecified disorder of bladder

597 Urethritis, not sexually transmitted, and urethral syndrome

Excludes: *nonspecific urethritis, so stated (099.4)*

597.0 Urethral abscess

Abscess of:	Abscess:
bulbourethral gland	periurethral
Cowper's gland	urethral (gland)
Littré's gland	Periurethral cellulitis

Excludes: *urethral caruncle (599.3)*

⑤ **597.8 Other urethritis**

597.80 Urethritis, unspecified

597.81 Urethral syndrome NOS

597.89 Other

Adenitis, Skene's	Meatitis, urethral
glands	Ulcer, urethra (meatus)
Cowperitis	Verumontanitis

Excludes: *trichomonal (131.02)*

598 Urethral stricture
Includes: pinhole meatus
        stricture of urinary meatus

Excludes: *congenital stricture of urethra and urinary meatus (753.6)*
Use additional code to identify urinary incontinence (625.6, 788.30-788.39)

⑤ **598.0 Urethral stricture due to infection**

598.00 Due to unspecified infection

598.01 *Due to infective diseases classified elsewhere*
        Code first underlying disease, as:
        gonococcal infection (098.2)
        schistosomiasis (120.0-120.9)
        syphilis (095.8)

598.1 Traumatic urethral stricture
Stricture of urethra:
        late effect of injury
        postobstetric

Excludes: *postoperative following surgery on genitourinary tract (598.2)*

598.2 Postoperative urethral stricture
Postcatheterization stricture of urethra

598.8 Other specified causes of urethral stricture

598.9 Urethral stricture, unspecified

599 Other disorders of urethra and urinary tract

● Code new
to this edition

▲ Revision of
existing code

④ ⑤ Fourth or fifth
digit required

599.0 Urinary tract infection, site not specified
Pyuria

Excludes: *Candidiasis of urinary tract (112.2)*

Use additional code to identify organism, such as Escherichia coli [*E. coli*] (041.4)

599.1 Urethral fistula
Fistula: Urinary fistula NOS
   urethroperineal
   urethrorectal

Excludes: *fistula:*

urethroscrotal (608.89)
urethrovaginal (619.0)
urethrovesicovaginal (619.0)

599.2 Urethral diverticulum

599.3 Urethral caruncle
Polyp of urethra

599.4 Urethral false passage

599.5 Prolapsed urethral mucosa
Prolapse of urethra   Urethrocele

Excludes: *urethrocele, female (618.0, 618.2-618.4)*

599.6 Urinary obstruction, unspecified
Obstructive uropathy NOS
Urinary (tract) obstruction NOS

Excludes: *obstructive nephropathy NOS (593.89)*

Use additional code, if desired, to identify urinary incontinence (625.6, 788.30-788.39)

599.7 Hematuria
Hematuria (benign) (essential)

Excludes: *hemoglobinuria (791.2)*

⑤ **599.8 Other specified disorders of urethra and urinary tract**

Excludes: *symptoms and other conditions classifiable to 788.0-788.9, 791.0-791.9*

Use additional code, if desired, to identify urinary incontinence (625.6, 788.30-788.39)

    599.81 Urethral hypermobility

    599.82 Intrinsic (urethral) sphincter deficiency [ISD]

    599.83 Urethral instability

    599.84 Other specified disorders of urethra
       Rupture of urethra (nontraumatic)
       Urethral:
          cyst
          granuloma

    599.89 Other specified disorders of urinary tract

599.9 Unspecified disorder of urethra and urinary tract

DISEASES OF MALE GENITAL ORGANS (600-608)

600 Hyperplasia of prostate
Use additional code, if desired, to identify urinary incontinence (788.30-788.39)

● **600.0 Hypertrophy (benign) of prostate**
Benign prostatic hypertrophy
Enlargement of prostate
Smooth enlarged prostate
Soft enlarged prostate

● **600.1 Nodular prostate**
Hard, firm prostate
Multinodular prostate

Excludes: *malignant neoplasm of prostate (185)*

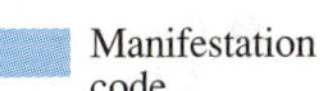

Manifestation
code

● **600.2 Benign localized hyperplasia of prostate**
  Adenofibromatous hypertrophy of prostate
  Adenoma of prostate
  Fibroadenoma of prostate
  Fibroma of prostate
  Myoma of prostate
  Polyp of prostate

  Excludes: *benign neoplasm of prostate (222.2)*
     hypertrophy of prostate (600.0)
     malignant neoplasm of prostate (185)

● **600.3 Cyst of prostate**
● **600.9 Hyperplasia of prostate, unspecified**
  Median bar
  Prostatic obstruction NOS

601 Inflammatory diseases of prostate
  Use additional code, if desired, to identify organism, such as Staphylococcus (041.1), or
     Streptococcus (041.0)

  601.0 Acute prostatitis

  601.1 Chronic prostatitis

  601.2 Abscess of prostate

  601.3 Prostatocystitis

  601.4 Prostatitis in diseases classified elsewhere
     Code first underlying disease, as:
        actinomycosis (039.8)
        blastomycosis (116.0)
        syphilis (095.8)
        tuberculosis (016.5)

     Excludes: *prostatitis:*
        gonococcal (098.12, 098.32)
        monilial (112.2)
        trichomonal (131.03)

  601.8 Other specified inflammatory diseases of prostate
     Prostatitis:
        cavitary
        diverticular
        granulomatous

  601.9 Prostatitis, unspecified
     Prostatitis NOS

602 Other disorders of prostate

  602.0 Calculus of prostate
     Prostatic stone

  602.1 Congestion or hemorrhage of prostate

  602.2 Atrophy of prostate

  602.8 Other specified disorders of prostate
     Fistula   Periprostatic adhesions
     Infarction } of prostate
     Stricture

  602.9 Unspecified disorder of prostate

603 Hydrocele
     Includes: hydrocele of spermatic cord, testis, or tunica vaginalis

     Excludes: *congenital (778.6)*

  603.0 Encysted hydrocele

  603.1 Infected hydrocele
  Use additional code, if desired, to identify organism

  603.8 Other specified types of hydrocele

  603.9 Hydrocele, unspecified

604 Orchitis and epididymitis
  Use additional code, if desired, to identify organism, such as Escherichia coli [E. coli] (041.4),
     Staphylococcus (041.1), or Streptococcus (041.0)

     ● Code new   ▲ Revision of   ④ ⑤ Fourth or fifth
        to this edition   existing code   digit required

604.0 Orchitis, epididymitis, and epididymo-orchitis, with abscess
Abscess of epididymis or testis

⑤ **604.9 Other orchitis, epididymitis, and epididymo-orchitis, without mention of abscess**

604.90 Orchitis and epididymitis, unspecified

604.91 *Orchitis and epididymitis in diseases classified elsewhere*
Code first underlying disease, as:
diphtheria (032.89)
filariasis (125.0-125.9)
syphilis (095.8)

Excludes: *orchitis:*
gonococcal (098.13, 098.33)
mumps (072.0)
tuberculous (016.5)
tuberculous epididymitis (016.4)

604.99 Other

605 Redundant prepuce and phimosis
Adherent prepuce   Phimosis (congenital)
Paraphimosis   Tight foreskin

606 Infertility, male

606.0 Azoospermia
Absolute infertility
Infertility due to:
germinal (cell) aplasia
spermatogenic arrest (complete)

606.1 Oligospermia
Infertility due to:
germinal cell desquamation
hypospermatogenesis
incomplete spermatogenic arrest

606.8 Infertility due to extratesticular causes
Infertility due to:
drug therapy
infection
obstruction of efferent ducts
radiation
systemic disease

606.9 Male infertility, unspecified

607 Disorders of penis

Excludes: *phimosis (605)*

607.0 Leukoplakia of penis
Kraurosis of penis

Excludes: *carcinoma in situ of penis (233.5)*
erythroplasia of Queyrat (233.5)

607.1 Balanoposthitis
Balanitis

Use additional code, if desired, to identify organism

607.2 Other inflammatory disorders of penis
Abscess
Boil
Carbuncle } of corpus cavernosum or penis
Cellulitis
Cavernitis (penis)

Use additional code, if desired, to identify organism

Excludes: *herpetic infection (054.13)*

607.3 Priapism
Painful erection

⑤ **607.8 Other specified disorders of penis**

607.81 Balanitis xerotica obliterans
Induratio penis plastica

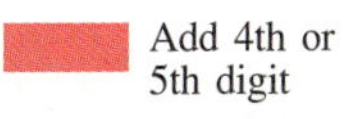

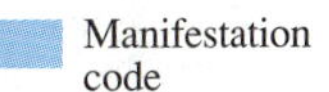

607.82　Vascular disorders of penis

Embolism
Hematoma
　(nontraumatic)　⎫ of corpus cavernosum or penis
Hemorrhage
Thrombosis

607.83　Edema of penis

607.84　Impotence of organic origin

Excludes: *nonorganic or unspecified (302.72)*

607.89　Other

Atrophy
Fibrosis　⎫ of corpus cavernosum or penis
Hypertrophy
Ulcer (chronic)

607.9　Unspecified disorder of penis

608　Other disorders of male genital organs

608.0　Seminal vesiculitis

Abscess
Cellulitis　⎫ of seminal vesicle
Vesiculitis (seminal)

Use additional code, if desired, to identify organism

Excludes: *gonococcal infection (098.14, 098.34)*

608.1　Spermatocele

608.2　Torsion of testis

Torsion of:
　epididymis
　spermatic cord
　testicle

608.3　Atrophy of testis

608.4　Other inflammatory disorders of male genital organs

Abscess
Boil
Carbuncle　⎫ of scrotum, spermatic cord, testis [except abscess],
Cellulitis　　　 tunica vaginalis, or vas deferens
Vasitis

Use additional code, if desired, to identify organism

Excludes: *abscess of testis (604.0)*

⑤ **608.8　Other specified disorders of male genital organs**

608.81　*Disorders of male genital organs in diseases classified elsewhere*

Code first underlying disease, as:
　filariasis (125.0-125.9)
　tuberculosis (016.5)

608.83　Vascular disorders

Hematoma (nontraumatic)　⎫ of seminal vesicle, spermatic
Hemorrhage　　　　　　　　 cord, testis, scrotum, tunica
Thrombosis　　　　　　　　 vaginalis, or vas deferens

Hematocele NOS, male

608.84　Chylocele of tunica vaginalis

608.85　Stricture

Stricture of:
　spermatic cord
　tunica vaginalis
　vas deferens

608.86　Edema

608.89　Other

Atrophy　⎫ of seminal vesicle, spermatic cord, testis, scrotum,
Fibrosis　　 tunica vaginalis, or vas deferens
Hypertrophy
Ulcer

Excludes: *atrophy of testis (608.3)*

● Code new　　　　▲ Revision of　　　　④ ⑤ Fourth or fifth
　to this edition　　　 existing code　　　　　 digit required

608.9 Unspecified disorder of male genital organs

DISORDERS OF BREAST (610-611)

610 Benign mammary dysplasias

610.0 **Solitary cyst of breast**
Cyst (solitary) of breast

610.1 **Diffuse cystic mastopathy**
Chronic cystic mastitis
Cystic breast
Fibrocystic disease of breast

610.2 **Fibroadenosis of breast**
Fibroadenosis of breast:
  NOS
  chronic
  cystic
Fibroadenosis of breast:
  diffuse
  periodic
  segmental

610.3 **Fibrosclerosis of breast**

610.4 **Mammary duct ectasia**
Comedomastitis
Dust ectasia
Mastitis:
  periductal
  plasma cell

610.8 **Other specified benign mammary dysplasias**
Mazoplasia
Sebaceous cyst of breast

610.9 **Benign mammary dysplasia, unspecified**

611 Other disorders of breast

Excludes: *that associated with lactation or the puerperium (675.0-676.9)*

611.0 **Inflammatory disease of breast**
Abscess (acute) (chronic) (nonpuerperal) of:
  areola
  breast
Mammillary fistula
Mastitis (acute) (subacute) (nonpuerperal):
  NOS
  infective
  retromammary
  submammary

Excludes: *carbuncle of breast (680.2)*
chronic cystic mastitis (610.1)
neonatal infective mastitis (771.5)
thrombophlebitis of breast [Mondor's disease] (451.89)

611.1 **Hypertrophy of breast**
Gynecomastia
Hypertrophy of breast:
  NOS
  massive pubertal

611.2 **Fissure of nipple**

611.3 **Fat necrosis of breast**
Fat necrosis (segmental) of breast

611.4 **Atrophy of breast**

611.5 **Galactocele**

611.6 **Galactorrhea not associated with childbirth**

⑤ **611.7** **Signs and symptoms in breast**

  611.71 **Mastodynia**
    Pain in breast

  611.72 **Lump or mass in breast**

  611.79 **Other**
    Induration of breast
    Inversion of nipple
    Nipple discharge
    Retraction of nipple

611.8 **Other specified disorders of breast**
Hematoma (nontraumatic)
Infarction } of breast
Occlusion of breast duct
Subinvolution of breast (postlactational) (postpartum)

611.9 **Unspecified breast disorder**

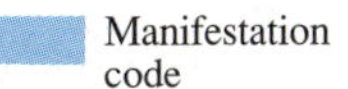

Manifestation
code

INFLAMMATORY DISEASE OF FEMALE PELVIC ORGANS (614-616)

Use additional code, if desired, to identify organism, such as Staphylococcus (041.1), or Streptococcus (041.0)

| *Excludes:* | *that associated with pregnancy, abortion, childbirth, or the puerperium (630-676.9)* |

614 Inflammatory disease of ovary, fallopian tube, pelvic cellular tissue, and peritoneum

| *Excludes:* | *endometritis (615.0-615.9)* |

major infection following delivery (670)
that complicating:
abortion (634-638 with .0, 639.0)
ectopic or molar pregnancy (639.0)
pregnancy or labor (646.6)

614.0 Acute salpingitis and oophoritis
Any condition classifiable to 614.2, specified as acute or subacute

614.1 Chronic salpingitis and oophoritis
Hydrosalpinx
Salpingitis:
follicularis
isthmica nodosa
Any condition classifiable to 614.2, specified as chronic

614.2 Salpingitis and oophoritis not specified as acute, subacute, or chronic
Abscess (of):   Perisalpingitis
fallopian tube   Pyosalpinx
ovary   Salpingitis
tubo-ovarian   Salpingo-oophoritis R Tubo-ovarian inflammatory disease
Oophoritis
Perioophoritis

| *Excludes:* | *gonococcal infection (chronic) (098.37)* |

acute (098.17)
tuberculous (016.6)

614.3 Acute parametritis and pelvic cellulitis
Acute inflammatory pelvic disease
Any condition classifiable to 614.4, specified as acute

614.4 Chronic or unspecified parametritis and pelvic cellulitis
Abscess (of):
broad ligament
parametrium
pelvis, female   } chronic or NOS
pouch of Douglas
Chronic inflammatory pelvic disease
Pelvic cellulitis, female

| *Excludes:* | *tuberculous (016.7)* |

614.5 Acute or unspecified pelvic peritonitis, female

614.6 Pelvic peritoneal adhesions, female (postoperative) (postinfection)
Adhesions:
peritubal
tubo-ovarian

Use additional code, if desired, to identify any associated infertility (628.2)

614.7 Other chronic pelvic peritonitis, female

| *Excludes:* | *tuberculous (016.7)* |

614.8 Other specified inflammatory disease of female pelvic organs and tissues

614.9 Unspecified inflammatory disease of female pelvic organs and tissues
Pelvic infection or inflammation, female NOS
Pelvic inflammatory disease [PID]

615 Inflammatory diseases of uterus, except cervix

| *Excludes:* | *following delivery (670)* |

hyperplastic endometritis (621.3)
that complicating:
abortion (634-638 with .0, 639.0)
ectopic or molar pregnancy (639.0)
pregnancy or labor (646.6)

615.0 Acute
Any condition classifiable to 615.9, specified as acute or subacute

● Code new to this edition   ▲ Revision of existing code   ④ ⑤ Fourth or fifth digit required

615.1 Chronic
Any condition classifiable to 615.9, specified as chronic

615.9 Unspecified inflammatory disease of uterus
Endometritis   Perimetritis
Endomyometritis   Pyometra
Metritis   Uterine abscess
Myometritis

616 Inflammatory disease of cervix, vagina, and vulva

Excludes: *that complicating:*

abortion (634-638 with .0, 639.0)
ectopic or molar pregnancy (639.0)
pregnancy, childbirth, or the puerperium (646.6)

616.0 Cervicitis and endocervicitis
Cervicitis
Endocervicitis   } with or without mention of erosion or ectropion
Nabothian (gland) cyst or follicle

Excludes: *erosion or ectropion without mention of cervicitis (622.0)*

616.1 Vaginitis and vulvovaginitis

616.10 Vaginitis and vulvovaginitis, unspecified
Vaginitis: Vulvitis NOS
  NOS   Vulvovaginitis NOS
  postirradiation
Use additional code, if desired, to identify organism, such as Escherichia coli [E. coli] (041.4), Staphylococcus (041.1), or Streptococcus (041.0)

Excludes: *noninfective leukorrhea (623.5)*

postmenopausal or senile vaginitis (627.3)

616.11 Vaginitis and vulvovaginitis in diseases classified elsewhere
Code first underlying disease, as:
pinworm vaginitis (127.4)

Excludes: *herpetic vulvovaginitis (054.11)*

monilial vulvovaginitis (112.1)
trichomonal vaginitis or vulvovaginitis (131.01)

616.2 Cyst of Bartholin's gland
Bartholin's duct cyst

616.3 Abscess of Bartholin's gland
Vulvovaginal gland abscess

616.4 Other abscess of vulva
Abscess
Carbuncle   } of vulva
Furuncle

616.5 Ulceration of vulva

616.50 Ulceration of vulva, unspecified
Ulcer NOS of vulva

616.51 Ulceration of vulva in diseases classified elsewhere
Code first underlying disease, as:
Behçet's syndrome (136.1)
tuberculosis (016.7)

Excludes: *vulvar ulcer (in):*

gonococcal (098.0)
herpes simplex (054.12)
syphilitic (091.0)

616.8 Other specified inflammatory diseases of cervix, vagina, and vulva
Caruncle, vagina or labium
Ulcer, vagina

Excludes: *noninflammatory disorders of:*

cervix (622.0-622.9)
vagina (623.0-623.9)
vulva (624.0-624.9)

616.9 Unspecified inflammatory disease of cervix, vagina, and vulva

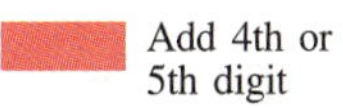

OTHER DISORDERS OF FEMALE GENITAL TRACT (617-629)

617 Endometriosis

617.0 Endometriosis of uterus

Adenomyosis

Endometriosis:
cervix
internal
myometrium

Excludes: stromal endometriosis (236.0)

617.1 Endometriosis of ovary
Chocolate cyst of ovary
Endometrial cystoma of ovary

617.2 Endometriosis of fallopian tube

617.3 Endometriosis of pelvic peritoneum

Endometriosis:
broad ligament
cul-de-sac (Douglas')

Endometriosis:
parametrium
round ligament

617.4 Endometriosis of rectovaginal septum and vagina

617.5 Endometriosis of intestine
Endometriosis:
appendix
colon
rectum

617.6 Endometriosis in scar of skin

617.8 Endometriosis of other specified sites

Endometriosis:
bladder
lung

Endometriosis:
umbilicus
vulva

617.9 Endometriosis, site unspecified

618 Genital prolapse

Use additional code, if desired, to identify urinary incontinence (625.6, 788.31, 788.33-788.39)

Excludes: that complicating pregnancy, labor, or delivery (654.4)

618.0 Prolapse of vaginal walls without mention of uterine prolapse

Cystocele
Cystourethrocele
Proctocele, female } without mention of uterine prolapse
Rectocele
Urethrocele, female
Vaginal prolapse

Excludes: that with uterine prolapse (618.2-618.4)
enterocele (618.6)
vaginal vault prolapse following hysterectomy (618.5)

618.1 Uterine prolapse without mention of vaginal wall prolapse

Descensus uteri
Uterine prolapse:
NOS
complete

Uterine prolapse:
first degree
second degree
third degree

Excludes: that with mention of cystocele, urethrocele, or rectocele (618.2-618.4)

618.2 Uterovaginal prolapse, incomplete

618.3 Uterovaginal prolapse, complete

618.4 Uterovaginal prolapse, unspecified

618.5 Prolapse of vaginal vault after hysterectomy

618.6 Vaginal enterocele, congenital or acquired
Pelvic enterocele, congenital or acquired

618.7 Old laceration of muscles of pelvic floor

618.8 Other specified genital prolapse
Incompetence or weakening of pelvic fundus
Relaxation of vaginal outlet or pelvis

618.9 Unspecified genital prolapse

● Code new
to this edition

▲ Revision of
existing code

④ ⑤ Fourth or fifth
digit required

619 Fistula involving female genital tract

> *Excludes:* vesicorectal and intestinovesical fistula (596.1)

619.0 Urinary-genital tract fistula, female
Fistula:
  cervicovesical
  ureterovaginal
  urethrovaginal
  urethrovesicovaginal
Fistula:
  uteroureteric
  uterovesical
  vesicocervicovaginal
  vesicovaginal

619.1 Digestive-genital tract fistula, female
Fistula:
  intestinouterine
  intestinovaginal
  rectovaginal
Fistula:
  rectovulval
  sigmoidovaginal
  uterorectal

619.2 Genital tract-skin fistula, female
Fistula:
  uterus to abdominal wall
  vaginoperineal

619.8 Other specified fistulas involving female genital tract
Fistula:
  cervix
  cul-de-sac (Douglas')
Fistula:
  uterus
  vagina

619.9 Unspecified fistula involving female genital tract

620 Noninflammatory disorders of ovary, fallopian tube, and broad ligament

> *Excludes:* hydrosalpinx (614.1)

620.0 Follicular cyst of ovary
Cyst of graafian follicle

620.1 Corpus luteum cyst or hematoma
Corpus luteum hemorrhage or rupture
Lutein cyst

620.2 Other and unspecified ovarian cyst
Cyst:
  NOS
  corpus albicans
  retention NOS   } of ovary
  serous
  theca-lutein
Simple cystoma of ovary

> *Excludes:* cystadenoma (benign) (serous) (220)
>   developmental cysts (752.0)
>   neoplastic cysts (220)
>   polycystic ovaries (256.4)
>   Stein-Leventhal syndrome (256.4)

620.3 Acquired atrophy of ovary and fallopian tube
Senile involution of ovary

620.4 Prolapse or hernia of ovary and fallopian tube
Displacement of ovary and fallopian tube
Salpingocele

620.5 Torsion of ovary, ovarian pedicle, or fallopian tube
Torsion:
  accessory tube
  hydatid of Morgagni

620.6 Broad ligament laceration syndrome
Masters-Allen syndrome

620.7 Hematoma of broad ligament
Hematocele, broad ligament

620.8 Other noninflammatory disorders of ovary, fallopian tube, and broad ligament

Cyst
Polyp } of broad ligament or fallopian tube

Infarction
Rupture
Hematosalpinx } of ovary or fallopian tube

Excludes: *hematosalpinx in ectopic pregnancy (639.2)*
peritubal adhesions (614.6)
torsion of ovary, ovarian pedicle, or fallopian tube (620.5)

620.9 Unspecified noninflammatory disorder of ovary, fallopian tube, and broad ligament

621 Disorders of uterus, not elsewhere classified

621.0 Polyp of corpus uteri
Polyp:
endometrium
uterus NOS

Excludes: *cervical polyp NOS (622.7)*

621.1 Chronic subinvolution of uterus

Excludes: *puerperal (674.8)*

621.2 Hypertrophy of uterus
Bulky or enlarged uterus

Excludes: *puerperal (674.8)*

621.3 Endometrial cystic hyperplasia
Hyperplasia (adenomatous) (cystic) (glandular) of endometrium
Hyperplastic endometritis

621.4 Hematometra
Hemometra

Excludes: *that in congenital anomaly (752.2-752.3)*

621.5 Intrauterine synechiae
Adhesions of uterus   Band(s) of uterus

621.6 Malposition of uterus
Anteversion
Retroflexion } of uterus
Retroversion

Excludes: *malposition complicating pregnancy, labor, or delivery (654.3-654.4)*
prolapse of uterus (618.1-618.4)

621.7 Chronic inversion of uterus

Excludes: *current obstetrical trauma (665.2)*
prolapse of uterus (618.1-618.4)

621.8 Other specified disorders of uterus, not elsewhere classified
Atrophy, acquired
Cyst
Fibrosis NOS } of uterus
Old laceration (postpartum)
Ulcer

Excludes: *bilharzial fibrosis (120.0-120.9)*
endometriosis (617.0)
fistulas (619.0-619.8)
inflammatory diseases (615.0-615.9)

621.9 Unspecified disorder of uterus

622 Noninflammatory disorders of cervix

Excludes: *abnormality of cervix complicating pregnancy, labor, or delivery (654.5-654.6)*
fistula (619.0-619.8)

622.0 Erosion and ectropion of cervix
Eversion
Ulcer } of cervix

Excludes: *that in chronic cervicitis (616.0)*

● Code new
to this edition
▲ Revision of
existing code
④ ⑤ Fourth or fifth
digit required

622.1 Dysplasia of cervix (uteri)
Anaplasia of cervix
Cervical atypism

Excludes: *carcinoma in situ of cervix (233.1)*
cervical intraepithelial neoplasia III [CIN III] (233.1)

622.2 Leukoplakia of cervix (uteri)

Excludes: *carcinoma in situ of cervix (233.1)*

622.3 Old laceration of cervix
Adhesions
Band(s) } of cervix
Cicatrix (postpartum)

Excludes: *current obstetrical trauma (665.3)*

622.4 Stricture and stenosis of cervix
Atresia (acquired)
Contracture } of cervix
Occlusion
Pinpoint os uteri

Excludes: *congenital (752.49)*
that complicating labor (654.6)

622.5 Incompetence of cervix

Excludes: *complicating pregnancy (654.5)*
that affecting fetus or newborn (761.0)

622.6 Hypertrophic elongation of cervix

622.7 Mucous polyp of cervix
Polyp NOS of cervix

Excludes: *adenomatous polyp of cervix (219.0)*

622.8 Other specified noninflammatory disorders of cervix
Atrophy (senile)
Cyst } of cervix
Fibrosis
Hemorrhage

Excludes: *endometriosis (617.0)*
fistula (619.0-619.8)
inflammatory diseases (616.0)

622.9 Unspecified noninflammatory disorder of cervix

623 Noninflammatory disorders of vagina

Excludes: *abnormality of vagina complicating pregnancy, labor, or delivery (654.7)*
congenital absence of vagina (752.49)
congenital diaphragm or bands (752.49)
fistulas involving vagina (619.0-619.8)

623.0 Dysplasia of vagina

Excludes: *carcinoma in situ of vagina (233.3)*

623.1 Leukoplakia of vagina

623.2 Stricture or atresia of vagina
Adhesions (postoperative) (postradiation) of vagina
Occlusion of vagina
Stenosis, vagina

Use additional E code, if desired, to identify any external cause

Excludes: *congenital atresia or stricture (752.49)*

623.3 Tight hymenal ring
Rigid hymen
Tight hymenal ring } acquired or congenital
Tight introitus

Excludes: *imperforate hymen (752.42)*

623.4 Old vaginal laceration

Excludes: *old laceration involving muscles of pelvic floor (618.7)*

Add 4th or 5th digit	Nonspecific code	Unspecified code	Manifestation code

623.5 Leukorrhea, not specified as infective
Leukorrhea NOS of vagina   Vaginal discharge NOS

Excludes: trichomonal (131.00)

623.6 Vaginal hematoma

Excludes: current obstetrical trauma (665.7)

623.7 Polyp of vagina

623.8 Other specified noninflammatory disorders of vagina
Cyst
Hemorrhage } of vagina

623.9 Unspecified noninflammatory disorder of vagina

624 Noninflammatory disorders of vulva and perineum

Excludes: abnormality of vulva and perineum complicating pregnancy, labor, or delivery
(654.8)
condyloma acuminatum (078.1)
fistulas involving:
perineum—see Alphabetic Index
vulva (619.0-619.8)
vulval varices (456.6)
vulvar involvement in skin conditions (690-709.9)

624.0 Dystrophy of vulva
Kraurosis
Leukoplakia } of vulva

Excludes: carcinoma in situ of vulva (233.3)

624.1 Atrophy of vulva

624.2 Hypertrophy of clitoris

Excludes: that in endocrine disorders (255.2, 256.1)

624.3 Hypertrophy of labia
Hypertrophy of vulva NOS

624.4 Old laceration or scarring of vulva

624.5 Hematoma of vulva

Excludes: that complicating delivery (664.5)

624.6 Polyp of labia and vulva

624.8 Other specified noninflammatory disorders of vulva and perineum
Cyst
Edema
Stricture } of vulva

624.9 Unspecified noninflammatory disorder of vulva and perineum

625 Pain and other symptoms associated with female genital organs

625.0 Dyspareunia

Excludes: psychogenic dyspareunia (302.76)

625.1 Vaginismus
Colpospasm   Vulvismus

Excludes: psychogenic vaginismus (306.51)

625.2 Mittelschmerz
Intermenstrual pain   Ovulation pain

625.3 Dysmenorrhea
Painful menstruation

Excludes: psychogenic dysmenorrhea (306.52)

625.4 Premenstrual tension syndromes
Menstrual: Premenstrual syndrome
migraine   Premenstrual tension NOS
molimen

625.5 Pelvic congestion syndrome
Congestion-fibrosis syndrome
Taylor's syndrome

● Code new
to this edition   ▲ Revision of
existing code   ④ ⑤ Fourth or fifth
digit required

625.6 Stress incontinence, female

> *Excludes:* *mixed incontinence (788.33)*
> *stress incontinence, male (788.32)*

625.8 Other specified symptoms associated with female genital organs

625.9 Unspecified symptom associated with female genital organs

626 Disorders of menstruation and other abnormal bleeding from female genital tract

> *Excludes:* *menopausal and premenopausal bleeding (627.0)*
> *pain and other symptoms associated with menstrual cycle (625.2-625.4)*
> *postmenopausal bleeding (627.1)*

626.0 Absence of menstruation
Amenorrhea (primary) (secondary)

626.1 Scanty or infrequent menstruation
Hypomenorrhea   Oligomenorrhea

626.2 Excessive or frequent menstruation
Heavy periods   Menorrhagia
Menometrorrhagia   Polymenorrhea

> *Excludes:* *premenopausal (627.0)*
> *that in puberty (626.3)*

626.3 Puberty bleeding
Excessive bleeding associated with onset of menstrual periods
Pubertal menorrhagia

626.4 Irregular menstrual cycle
Irregular:
  bleeding NOS
  menstruation
  periods

626.5 Ovulation bleeding
Regular intermenstrual bleeding

626.6 Metrorrhagia
Bleeding unrelated to menstrual cycle
Irregular intermenstrual bleeding

626.7 Postcoital bleeding

626.8 Other
Dysfunctional or functional uterine hemorrhage NOS
Menstruation:
  retained
  suppression of

626.9 Unspecified

627 Menopausal and postmenopausal disorders

> *Excludes:* *asymptomatic age-related (natural) postmenopausal status (V49.81)*

627.0 Premenopausal menorrhagia
Excessive bleeding associated   Menorrhagia:
  with onset of menopause   climacteric
                                menopausal
                                preclimacteric

627.1 Postmenopausal bleeding

627.2 Menopausal or female climacteric states
Symptoms, such as flushing, sleeplessness, headache, lack of concentration, associated
  with the menopause

627.3 Postmenopausal atrophic vaginitis
Senile (atrophic) vaginitis

627.4 States associated with artificial menopause
Postartificial menopause syndromes
Any condition classifiable to 627.1, 627.2, or 627.3 which follows induced menopause

627.8 Other specified menopausal and postmenopausal disorders

> *Excludes:* *premature menopause NOS (256.3)*

627.9 Unspecified menopausal and postmenopausal disorder

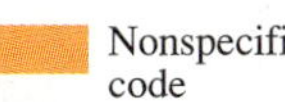
Add 4th or 5th digit

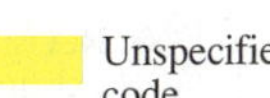
Nonspecific code

Unspecified code

Manifestation code

628 **Infertility, female**
Includes: primary and secondary sterility

628.0 Associated with anovulation
Anovulatory cycle

Use additional code for any associated Stein-Leventhal syndrome (256.4)

628.1 *Of pituitary-hypothalamic origin*
Code first underlying cause, as:
adiposogenital dystrophy (253.8)
anterior pituitary disorder (253.0-253.4)

628.2 Of tubal origin
Infertility associated with congenital anomaly of tube
Tubal:
block
occlusion
stenosis

Use additional code for any associated peritubal adhesions (614.6)

628.3 Of uterine origin
Infertility associated with congenital anomaly of uterus
Nonimplantation

Use additional code for any associated tuberculous endometritis (016.7)

628.4 Of cervical or vaginal origin
Infertility associated with:
anomaly of cervical mucus
congenital structural anomaly
dysmucorrhea

628.8 Of other specified origin

628.9 Of unspecified origin

629 **Other disorders of female genital organs**

629.0 Hematocele, female, not elsewhere classified

Excludes: *hematocele or hematoma:*
broad ligament (620.7)
fallopian tube (620.8)
that associated with ectopic pregnancy (633.0-633.9)
uterus (621.4)
vagina (623.6)
vulva (624.5)

629.1 Hydrocele, canal of Nuck
Cyst of canal of Nuck (acquired)

Excludes: *congenital (752.41)*

629.8 Other specified disorders of female genital organs

629.9 Unspecified disorder of female genital organs
Habitual aborter without current pregnancy

● Code new
to this edition   ▲ Revision of
existing code   ④ ⑤ Fourth or fifth
digit required

11. COMPLICATIONS OF PREGNANCY, CHILDBIRTH, AND THE PUERPERIUM (630-677)

ECTOPIC AND MOLAR PREGNANCY (630-633)

Use additional code from category 639 to identify any complications

630 Hydatidiform mole
Trophoblastic disease NOS
Vesicular mole

> *Excludes:* *chorioadenoma (destruens) (236.1)*
> *chorionepithelioma (181)*
> *malignant hydatidiform mole (236.1)*

631 Other abnormal product of conception

Blighted ovum
Mole:
  NOS
  carneous

Mole:
  fleshy
  stone

632 Missed abortion
Early fetal death before completion of 22 weeks' gestation with retention of dead fetus
Retained products of conception, not following spontaneous or induced abortion or delivery

> *Excludes:* *failed induced abortion (638.0-638.9)*
> *fetal death (intrauterine) (late) (656.4)*
> *missed delivery (656.4)*
> *that with abnormal product of conception (630, 631)*

633 Ectopic pregnancy
Includes: ruptured ectopic pregnancy

633.0 Abdominal pregnancy
Intraperitoneal pregnancy

633.1 Tubal pregnancy
Fallopian pregnancy
Rupture of (fallopian) tube due to pregnancy
Tubal abortion

633.2 Ovarian pregnancy

633.8 Other ectopic pregnancy

Pregnancy:
  cervical
  combined
  cornual

Pregnancy:
  intraligamentous
  mesometric
  mural

633.9 Unspecified ectopic pregnancy

OTHER PREGNANCY WITH ABORTIVE OUTCOME (634-639)

Note: Use the following fifth-digit subclassification with categories 634-637:

0 Unspecified

1 Incomplete

2 Complete

The following fourth-digit subdivisions are for use with categories 634-638:

.0 Complicated by genital tract and pelvic infection
Endometritis
Salpingo-oophoritis
Sepsis NOS
Septicemia NOS
Any condition classifiable to 639.0, with condition classifiable to 634-638

> *Excludes:* *urinary tract infection (634-638 with .7)*

.1 Complicated by delayed or excessive hemorrhage
Afibrinogenemia
Defibrination syndrome
Intravascular hemolysis
Any condition classifiable to 639.1, with condition classifiable to 634-638

.2 Complicated by damage to pelvic organs and tissues
Laceration, perforation, or tear of:
  bladder
  uterus
Any condition classifiable to 639.2, with condition classifiable to 634-638

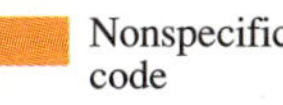
Add 4th or 5th digit

Nonspecific code

Unspecified code

Manifestation code

.3 Complicated by renal failure
    Oliguria
    Uremia
    Any condition classifiable to 639.3, with condition classifiable to 634-638

.4 Complicated by metabolic disorder
    Electrolyte imbalance with conditions classifiable to 634-638

.5 Complicated by shock
    Circulatory collapse
    Shock (postoperative) (septic)
    Any condition classifiable to 639.5, with condition classifiable to 634-638

.6 Complicated by embolism
    Embolism:
      NOS
      amniotic fluid
      pulmonary
    Any condition classifiable to 639.6, with condition classifiable to 634-638

.7 With other specified complications
    Cardiac arrest or failure
    Urinary tract infection
    Any condition classifiable to 639.8, with condition classifiable to 634-638

.8 With unspecified complication

.9 Without mention of complication

⑤ **634 Abortion**
    Includes: miscarriage
              spontaneous abortion

⑤ **634.0 Complicated by genital tract and pelvic infection**

⑤ **634.1 Complicated by delayed or excessive hemorrhage**

⑤ **634.2 Complicated by damage to pelvic organs or tissues**

⑤ **634.3 Complicated by renal failure**

⑤ **634.4 Complicated by metabolic disorder**

⑤ **634.5 Complicated by shock**

⑤ **634.6 Complicated by embolism**

⑤ **634.7 With other specified complications**

⑤ **634.8 With unspecified complication**

⑤ **634.9 Without mention of complication**

⑤ **635 Legally induced abortion**
    Includes: abortion or termination of pregnancy:
              elective
              legal
              therapeutic

    Excludes: *menstrual extraction or regulation (V25.3)*

⑤ **635.0 Complicated by genital tract and pelvic infection**

⑤ **635.1 Complicated by delayed or excessive hemorrhage**

⑤ **635.2 Complicated by damage to pelvic organs or tissues**

⑤ **635.3 Complicated by renal failure**

⑤ **635.4 Complicated by metabolic disorder**

⑤ **635.5 Complicated by shock**

⑤ **635.6 Complicated by embolism**

⑤ **635.7 With other specified complications**

⑤ **635.8 With unspecified complication**

⑤ **635.9 Without mention of complication**

⑤ **636 Illegally induced abortion**
    Includes: abortion:
              criminal
              illegal
              self-induced

⑤ **636.0 Complicated by genital tract and pelvic infection**

⑤ **636.1 Complicated by delayed or excessive hemorrhage**

⑤ **636.2 Complicated by damage to pelvic organs or tissues**

● Code new
to this edition
    ▲ Revision of
existing code
    ④ ⑤ Fourth or fifth
digit required

⑤ **636.3** Complicated by renal failure

⑤ **636.4** Complicated by metabolic disorder

⑤ **636.5** Complicated by shock

⑤ **636.6** Complicated by embolism

⑤ **636.7** With other specified complications

⑤ **636.8** With unspecified complication

⑤ **636.9** Without mention of complication

⑤ **637** Unspecified abortion

> Includes: abortion NOS
> retained products of conception following abortion, not classifiable elsewhere

⑤ **637.0** Complicated by genital tract and pelvic infection

⑤ **637.1** Complicated by delayed or excessive hemorrhage

⑤ **637.2** Complicated by damage to pelvic organs or tissues

⑤ **637.3** Complicated by renal failure

⑤ **637.4** Complicated by metabolic disorder

⑤ **637.5** Complicated by shock

⑤ **637.6** Complicated by embolism

⑤ **637.7** With other specified complications

⑤ **637.8** With unspecified complication

⑤ **637.9** Without mention of complication

638 Failed attempted abortion

> Includes: failure of attempted induction of (legal) abortion

> *Excludes:* *incomplete abortion (634.0-637.9)*

638.0 Complicated by genital tract and pelvic infection

638.1 Complicated by delayed or excessive hemorrhage

638.2 Complicated by damage to pelvic organs or tissues

638.3 Complicated by renal failure

638.4 Complicated by metabolic disorder

638.5 Complicated by shock

638.6 Complicated by embolism

638.7 With other specified complications

638.8 With unspecified complication

638.9 Without mention of complication

639 Complications following abortion and ectopic and molar pregnancies

> Note: This category is provided for use when it is required to classify separately the complications classifiable to the fourth-digit level in categories 634-638; for example:
> a) when the complication itself was responsible for an episode of medical care, the abortion, ectopic or molar pregnancy itself having been dealt with at a previous episode
> b) when these conditions are immediate complications of ectopic or molar pregnancies classifiable to 630-633 where they cannot be identified at fourth-digit level.

639.0 Genital tract and pelvic infection

> Endometritis
> Parametritis
> Pelvic peritonitis
> Salpingitis } following conditions classifiable to 630-638
> Salpingo-oophoritis
> Sepsis NOS
> Septicemia NOS

> *Excludes:* *urinary tract infection (639.8)*

639.1 Delayed or excessive hemorrhage

> Afibrinogenemia
> Defibrination syndrome } following conditions classifiable to 630-638
> Intravascular hemolysis

639.2 Damage to pelvic organs and tissues
Laceration, perforation, or tear of:
bladder
bowel
broad ligament
cervix
periurethral tissue
uterus
vagina
} following conditions classifiable to 630-638

639.3 Renal failure
Oliguria
Renal:
failure (acute)
shutdown
tubular necrosis
Uremia
} following conditions classifiable to 630-638

639.4 Metabolic disorders
Electrolyte imbalance following conditions classifiable to 630-638

639.5 Shock
Circulatory collapse
Shock (postoperative) (septic)
} following conditions classifiable to 630-638

639.6 Embolism
Embolism:
NOS
air
amniotic fluid
blood-clot
fat
pulmonary
pyemic
septic
soap
} following conditions classifiable to 630-638

639.8 Other specified complications following abortion or ectopic and molar pregnancy
Acute yellow atrophy or necrosis of liver
Cardiac arrest or failure
Cerebral anoxia
Urinary tract infection
} following conditions classifiable to 630-638

639.9 Unspecified complication following abortion or ectopic and molar pregnancy
Complication(s) not further specified following conditions classifiable to 630-638

COMPLICATIONS MAINLY RELATED TO PREGNANCY (640-648)

Includes: the listed conditions even if they arose or were present during labor, delivery, or the puerperium

The following fifth-digit subclassification is for use with categories 640-648 to denote the current episode of care:

0 unspecified as to episode of care or not applicable

1 delivered, with or without mention of antepartum condition
Antepartum condition with delivery
Delivery NOS
Intrapartum obstetric condition
Pregnancy, delivered
} (with mention of antepartum complication during current episode of care)

2 delivered, with mention of postpartum complication
Delivery with mention of puerperal complication during current episode of care

3 antepartum condition or complication
Antepartum obstetric condition, not delivered during the current episode of care

4 postpartum condition or complication
Postpartum or puerperal obstetric condition or complication following delivery that occurred:
during previous episode of care
outside hospital, with subsequent admission for observation or care

⑤ **640 Hemorrhage in early pregnancy**
Includes: hemorrhage before completion of 22 weeks' gestation

⑤ **640.0 Threatened abortion**
[0,1,3]

● Code new to this edition   ▲ Revision of existing code   ④ ⑤ Fourth or fifth digit required

⑤ **640.8 Other specified hemorrhage in early pregnancy**
[0,1,3]

⑤ **640.9 Unspecified hemorrhage in early pregnancy**
[0,1,3]

⑤ **641 Antepartum hemorrhage, abruptio placentae, and placenta previa**

⑤ **641.0 Placenta previa without hemorrhage**
[0,1,3] Low implantation of placenta
Placenta previa noted:
during pregnancy
before labor (and delivered by cesarean delivery) } without hemorrhage

⑤ **641.1 Hemorrhage from placenta previa**
[0,1,3] Low-lying placenta
Placenta previa
incomplete
marginal } NOS or with hemorrhage (intrapartum)
partial
total

> *Excludes:* hemorrhage from vasa previa (663.5)

⑤ **641.2 Premature separation of placenta**
[0,1,3] Ablatio placentae
Abruptio placentae
Accidental antepartum hemorrhage
Couvelaire uterus
Detachment of placenta (premature)
Premature separation of normally implanted placenta

⑤ **641.3 Antepartum hemorrhage associated with coagulation defects**
[0,1,3] Antepartum or intrapartum hemorrhage associated with:
afibrinogenemia
hyperfibrinolysis
hypofibrinogenemia

⑤ **641.8 Other antepartum hemorrhage**
[0,1,3] Antepartum or intrapartum hemorrhage associated with:
trauma
uterine leiomyoma

⑤ **641.9 Unspecified antepartum hemorrhage**
[0,1,3] Hemorrhage:
antepartum NOS
intrapartum NOS
of pregnancy NOS

⑤ **642 Hypertension complicating pregnancy, childbirth, and the puerperium**

⑤ **642.0 Benign essential hypertension complicating pregnancy, childbirth, and the puerperium**
[0-4] Hypertension:
benign essential
chronic NOS } specified as complicating, or as a reason for obstetric
essential care during pregnancy, childbirth, or the puerperium
pre-existing NOS

⑤ **642.1 Hypertension secondary to renal disease, complicating pregnancy, childbirth, and the puerperium**
[0-4] Hypertension secondary to renal disease, specified as complicating, or as a reason for obstetric care during pregnancy, childbirth, or the puerperium

⑤ **642.2 Other pre-existing hypertension complicating pregnancy, childbirth, and the puerperium**
[0-4] Hypertensive:
heart and renal disease } specified as complicating, as a reason for obstetric care
heart disease during pregnancy, childbirth, or the puerperium
renal disease
Malignant hypertension

⑤ **642.3 Transient hypertension of pregnancy**
[0-4] Gestational hypertension
Transient hypertension, so described, in pregnancy, childbirth, or the puerperium

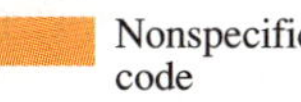

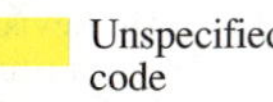

⑤ **642.4 Mild or unspecified pre-eclampsia**
[0-4]   Hypertension in pregnancy, childbirth, or the puerperium, not specified as pre-existing,
         with either albuminuria or edema, or both; mild or unspecified
         Pre-eclampsia: Toxemia (pre-eclamptic):
         NOS   NOS
         mild   mild

> Excludes: albuminuria in pregnancy, without mention of hypertension (646.2)
>   edema in pregnancy, without mention of hypertension (646.1)

⑤ **642.5 Severe pre-eclampsia**
[0-4]   Hypertension in pregnancy, childbirth, or the puerperium, not specified as pre-existing,
         with either albuminuria or edema, or both; specified as severe
         Pre-eclampsia, severe
         Toxemia (pre-eclamptic), severe

⑤ **642.6 Eclampsia**
[0-4]   Toxemia:
           eclamptic
           with convulsions

⑤ **642.7 Pre-eclampsia or eclampsia superimposed on pre-existing hypertension**
[0-4]   Conditions classifiable to 642.4-642.6, with conditions classifiable to 642.0-642.2

⑤ **642.9 Unspecified hypertension complicating pregnancy, childbirth, or the puerperium**
[0-4]   Hypertension NOS, without mention of albuminuria or edema, complicating pregnancy,
         childbirth, or the puerperium

⑤ **643 Excessive vomiting in pregnancy**
         Includes:
                   hyperemesis   ⎫
                   vomiting: ⎬ arising during pregnancy
                     persistent   ⎪
                     vicious   ⎭
                   hyperemesis gravidarum

⑤ **643.0 Mild hyperemesis gravidarum**
[0,1,3] Hyperemesis gravidarum, mild or unspecified, starting before the end of the 22nd week
         of gestation

⑤ **643.1 Hyperemesis gravidarum with metabolic disturbance**
[0,1,3] Hyperemesis gravidarum, starting before the end of the 22nd week of gestation, with
         metabolic disturbance, such as:
           carbohydrate depletion
           dehydration
           electrolyte imbalance

⑤ **643.2 Late vomiting of pregnancy**
[0,1,3] Excessive vomiting starting after 22 completed weeks of gestation

⑤ **643.8 Other vomiting complicating pregnancy**
[0,1,3] Vomiting due to organic disease or other cause, specified as complicating pregnancy, or
         as a reason for obstetric care during pregnancy

         Use additional code, if desired, to specify cause

⑤ **643.9 Unspecified vomiting of pregnancy**
[0,1,3] Vomiting as a reason for care during pregnancy, length of gestation unspecified

⑤ **644 Early or threatened labor**

⑤ **644.0 Threatened premature labor**
[0,3]   Premature labor after 22 weeks, but before 37 completed weeks of gestation without
         delivery

> Excludes: that occurring before 22 completed weeks of gestation (640.0)

⑤ **644.1 Other threatened labor**
[0,3]   False labor: ⎫
           NOS   ⎬
           after 37 completed weeks of gestation   ⎬ without delivery
         Threatened labor NOS   ⎭

⑤ **644.2 Early onset of delivery**
[0,1]   Onset (spontaneous) of delivery   ⎫ before 37 completed weeks of
         Premature labor with onset of delivery   ⎬ gestation

▲ **645 Late pregnancy**

● **645.1 Post term pregnancy**
[0,1,3] Pregnancy over 40 weeks to 42 weeks gestation

● Code new   ▲ Revision of   ④ ⑤ Fourth or fifth
  to this edition   existing code   digit required

● **645.2 Prolonged pregnancy**
[0,1,3] Pregnancy which has advanced beyond 42 weeks gestation

⑤ **646 Other complications of pregnancy, not elsewhere classified**
Use additional code(s) to further specify complication

⑤ **646.0 Papyraceous fetus**
[0,1,3]

⑤ **646.1 Edema or excessive weight gain in pregnancy, without mention of hypertension**
[0-4] Gestational edema
Maternal obesity syndrome

Excludes: *that with mention of hypertension (642.0-642.9)*

⑤ **646.2 Unspecified renal disease in pregnancy, without mention of hypertension**
[0-4] Albuminuria
Nephropathy NOS
Renal disease NOS } in pregnancy or the puerperium, without mention of hypertension
Uremia
Gestational proteinuria

Excludes: *that with mention of hypertension (642.0-642.9)*

⑤ **646.3 Habitual aborter**
[0,1,3]

Excludes: *with current abortion (634.0-634.9)*
without current pregnancy (629.9)

⑤ **646.4 Peripheral neuritis in pregnancy**
[0-4]

⑤ **646.5 Asymptomatic bacteriuria in pregnancy**
[0-4]

⑤ **646.6 Infections of genitourinary tract in pregnancy**
[0-4] Conditions classifiable to 590, 595, 597, 599.0, 616 complicating pregnancy, childbirth, or the puerperium
Conditions classifiable to 614-615 complicating pregnancy or labor

Excludes: *major puerperal infection (670)*

⑤ **646.7 Liver disorders in pregnancy**
[0,1,3] Acute yellow atrophy of liver (obstetric) (true) }
Icterus gravis } of pregnancy
Necrosis of liver }

Excludes: *hepatorenal syndrome following delivery (674.8)*
viral hepatitis (647.6)

⑤ **646.8 Other specified complications of pregnancy**
[0-4] Fatigue during pregnancy   Insufficient weight gain of pregnancy
Herpes gestationis   Uterine size-date discrepancy

⑤ **646.9 Unspecified complication of pregnancy**
[0,1,3]

⑤ **647 Infectious and parasitic conditions in the mother classifiable elsewhere, but complicating pregnancy, childbirth, or the puerperium**
Includes: the listed conditions when complicating the pregnant state, aggravated by the pregnancy, or when a main reason for obstetric care

Excludes: *those conditions in the mother known or suspected to have affected the fetus (655.0-655.9)*

Use additional code(s) to further specify complication

⑤ **647.0 Syphilis**
[0-4] Conditions classifiable to 090-097

⑤ **647.1 Gonorrhea**
[0-4] Conditions classifiable to 098

⑤ **647.2 Other venereal diseases**
[0-4] Conditions classifiable to 099

⑤ **647.3 Tuberculosis**
[0-4] Conditions classifiable to 010-018

⑤ **647.4 Malaria**
[0-4] Conditions classifiable to 084

⑤ **647.5 Rubella**
[0-4] Conditions classifiable to 056

Add 4th or 5th digit	Nonspecific code	Unspecified code	Manifestation code

⑤ **647.6 Other viral diseases**
[0-4]   Conditions classifiable to 042 and 050-079, except 056

⑤ **647.8 Other specified infectious and parasitic diseases**
[0-4]

⑤ **647.9 Unspecified infection or infestation**
[0-4]

⑤ **648 Other current conditions in the mother classifiable elsewhere, but complicating pregnancy, childbirth, or the puerperium**
    Includes: the listed conditions when complicating the pregnant state, aggravated by the pregnancy, or when a main reason for obstetric care

    Excludes: *those conditions in the mother known or suspected to have affected the fetus (655.0-655.9)*

Use additional code(s) to identify the condition

⑤ **648.0 Diabetes mellitus**
[0-4]   Conditions classifiable to 250

    Excludes: *gestational diabetes (648.8)*

⑤ **648.1 Thyroid dysfunction**
[0-4]   Conditions classifiable to 240-246

⑤ **648.2 Anemia**
[0-4]   Conditions classifiable to 280-285

⑤ **648.3 Drug dependence**
[0-4]   Conditions classifiable to 304

⑤ **648.4 Mental disorders**
[0-4]   Conditions classifiable to 290-303, 305-316, 317-319

⑤ **648.5 Congenital cardiovascular disorders**
[0-4]   Conditions classifiable to 745-747

⑤ **648.6 Other cardiovascular diseases**
[0-4]   Conditions classifiable to 390-398, 410-429

    Excludes: *cerebrovascular disorders in the puerperium (674.0)*
        venous complications (671.0-671.9)

⑤ **648.7 Bone and joint disorders of back, pelvis, and lower limbs**
[0-4]   Conditions classifiable to 720-724, and those classifiable to 711-719 or 725-738, specified as affecting the lower limbs

⑤ **648.8 Abnormal glucose tolerance**
[0-4]   Conditions classifiable to 790.2
    Gestational diabetes

⑤ **648.9 Other current conditions classifiable elsewhere**
[0-4]   Conditions classifiable to 440-459
    Nutritional deficiencies [conditions classifiable to 260-269]

NORMAL DELIVERY, AND OTHER INDICATIONS FOR CARE IN PREGNANCY, LABOR, AND DELIVERY (650-659)

650 Normal delivery
    Delivery requiring minimal or no assistance, with or without episiotomy, without fetal manipulation [e.g., rotation version] or instrumentation [forceps] of spontaneous, cephalic, vaginal, full-term, single, live born infant. This code is for use as a single diagnosis code and is not to be used with any other code in the range 630-676.

    Excludes: *breech delivery (assisted) (spontaneous) NOS (652.2)*
        delivery by vacuum extractor, forceps, cesarean section, or breech extraction, without specified complication (669.5-669.7)

Use additional code to indicate outcome of delivery (V27.0)

The following fifth-digit subclassification is for use with categories 651-659 to denote the current episode of care:

    0 unspecified as to episode of care or not applicable

    1 delivered, with or without mention of antepartum condition

    2 delivered, with mention of postpartum complication

    3 antepartum condition or complication

    4 postpartum condition or complication

● Code new to this edition   ▲ Revision of existing code   ④ ⑤ Fourth or fifth digit required

⑤ **651** Multiple gestation

  ⑤ **651.0** Twin pregnancy
    [0,1,3]

  ⑤ **651.1** Triplet pregnancy
    [0,1,3]

  ⑤ **651.2** Quadruplet pregnancy
    [0,1,3]

  ⑤ **651.3** Twin pregnancy with fetal loss and retention of one fetus
    [0,1,3]

  ⑤ **651.4** Triplet pregnancy with fetal loss and retention of one or more fetus(es)
    [0,1,3]

  ⑤ **651.5** Quadruplet pregnancy with fetal loss and retention of one or more fetus(es)
    [0,1,3]

  ⑤ **651.6** Other multiple pregnancy with fetal loss and retention of one or more fetus(es)
    [0,1,3]

  ⑤ **651.8** Other specified multiple gestation
    [0,1,3]

  ⑤ **651.9** Unspecified multiple gestation
    [0,1,3]

⑤ **652** Malposition and malpresentation of fetus
    Code first any associated obstructed labor (660.0)

  ⑤ **652.0** Unstable lie
    [0,1,3]

  ⑤ **652.1** Breech or other malpresentation successfully converted to cephalic presentation
    [0,1,3]   Cephalic version NOS

  ⑤ **652.2** Breech presentation without mention of version
    [0,1,3]   Breech delivery (assisted) (spontaneous) NOS
            Buttocks presentation
            Complete breech
            Frank breech

        Excludes: footling presentation (652.8)
                    incomplete breech (652.8)

  ⑤ **652.3** Transverse or oblique presentation
    [0,1,3]   Oblique lie   Transverse lie

        Excludes: transverse arrest of fetal head (660.3)

  ⑤ **652.4** Face or brow presentation
    [0,1,3]   Mentum presentation

  ⑤ **652.5** High head at term
    [0,1,3]   Failure of head to enter pelvic brim

  ⑤ **652.6** Multiple gestation with malpresentation of one fetus or more
    [0,1,3]

  ⑤ **652.7** Prolapsed arm
    [0,1,3]

  ⑤ **652.8** Other specified malposition or malpresentation
    [0,1,3]   Compound presentation

  ⑤ **652.9** Unspecified malposition or malpresentation
    [0,1,3]

⑤ **653** Disproportion
    Code first any associated obstructed labor (660.1)

  ⑤ **653.0** Major abnormality of bony pelvis, not further specified
    [0,1,3]   Pelvic deformity NOS

  ⑤ **653.1** Generally contracted pelvis
    [0,1,3]   Contracted pelvis NOS

  ⑤ **653.2** Inlet contraction of pelvis
    [0,1,3]   Inlet contraction (pelvis)

  ⑤ **653.3** Outlet contraction of pelvis
    [0,1,3]   Outlet contraction (pelvis)

  ⑤ **653.4** Fetopelvic disproportion
    [0,1,3]   Cephalopelvic disproportion NOS
            Disproportion of mixed maternal and fetal origin, with normally formed fetus

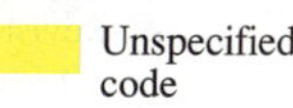

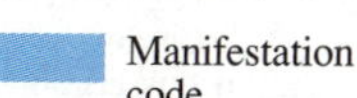

⑤ **653.5 Unusually large fetus causing disproportion**
[0,1,3]   Disproportion of fetal origin with normally formed fetus
           Fetal disproportion NOS

  Excludes: *that when the reason for medical care was concern for the fetus (656.6)*

⑤ **653.6 Hydrocephalic fetus causing disproportion**
[0,1,3]

  Excludes: *that when the reason for medical care was concern for the fetus (655.0)*

⑤ **653.7 Other fetal abnormality causing disproportion**
[0,1,3]   Conjoined twins   Fetal:
           Fetal: myelomeningocele
             ascites   sacral teratoma
             hydrops   tumor

⑤ **653.8 Disproportion of other origin**
[0,1,3]

  Excludes: *shoulder (girdle) dystocia (660.4)*

⑤ **653.9 Unspecified disproportion**
[0,1,3]

⑤ **654 Abnormality of organs and soft tissues of pelvis**
           Includes: the listed conditions during pregnancy, childbirth, or the puerperium
           Code first any associated obstructed labor (660.2)

⑤ **654.0 Congenital abnormalities of uterus**
[0-4]   Double uterus   Uterus bicornis

⑤ **654.1 Tumors of body of uterus**
[0-4]   Uterine fibroids

⑤ **654.2 Previous cesarean delivery NOS**
[0,1,3]   Uterine scar from previous cesarean delivery

⑤ **654.3 Retroverted and incarcerated gravid uterus**
[0-4]

⑤ **654.4 Other abnormalities in shape or position of gravid uterus and of neighboring structures**
[0-4]   Cystocele   Prolapse of gravid uterus
           Pelvic floor repair   Rectocele
           Pendulous abdomen   Rigid pelvic floor

⑤ **654.5 Cervical incompetence**
[0-4]   Presence of Shirodkar suture with or without mention of cervical incompetence

⑤ **654.6 Other congenital or acquired abnormality of cervix**
[0-4]   Cicatricial cervix   Stenosis or stricture of cervix
           Polyp of cervix   Tumor of cervix
           Previous surgery to cervix
           Rigid cervix (uteri)

⑤ **654.7 Congenital or acquired abnormality of vagina**
[0-4]   Previous surgery to vagina   Stricture of vagina
           Septate vagina   Tumor of vagina
           Stenosis of vagina (acquired)
             (congenital)

⑤ **654.8 Congenital or acquired abnormality of vulva**
[0-4]   Fibrosis of perineum
           Persistent hymen
           Previous surgery to perineum or vulva
           Rigid perineum
           Tumor of vulva

  Excludes: *varicose veins of vulva (671.1)*

⑤ **654.9 Other and unspecified**
[0-4]   Uterine scar NEC

      ● Code new   ▲ Revision of   ④ ⑤ Fourth or fifth
           to this edition   existing code   digit required

⑤ **655 Known or suspected fetal abnormality affecting management of mother**
Includes: the listed conditions in the fetus as a reason for observation or obstetrical care of the mother, or for termination of pregnancy

⑤ **655.0 Central nervous system malformation in fetus**
[0,1,3]   Fetal or suspected fetal:
anencephaly
hydrocephalus
spina bifida (with myelomeningocele)

⑤ **655.1 Chromosomal abnormality in fetus**
[0,1,3]

⑤ **655.2 Hereditary disease in family possibly affecting fetus**
[0,1,3]

⑤ **655.3 Suspected damage to fetus from viral disease in the mother**
[0,1,3]   Suspected damage to fetus from maternal rubella

⑤ **655.4 Suspected damage to fetus from other disease in the mother**
[0,1,3]   Suspected damage to fetus from maternal:
alcohol addiction
listeriosis
toxoplasmosis

⑤ **655.5 Suspected damage to fetus from drugs**
[0,1,3]

⑤ **655.6 Suspected damage to fetus from radiation**
[0,1,3]

⑤ **655.7 Decreased fetal movements**
[0,1,3]

⑤ **655.8 Other known or suspected fetal abnormality, not elsewhere classified**
[0,1,3]   Suspected damage to fetus from:
environmental toxins
intrauterine contraceptive device

⑤ **655.9 Unspecified**
[0,1,3]

⑤ **656 Other fetal and placental problems affecting management of mother**

⑤ **656.0 Fetal-maternal hemorrhage**
[0,1,3]   Leakage (microscopic) of fetal blood into maternal circulation

⑤ **656.1 Rhesus isoimmunization**
[0,1,3]   Anti-D [Rh] antibodies
Rh incompatibility

⑤ **656.2 Isoimmunization from other and unspecified blood-group incompatibility**
[0,1,3]   ABO isoimmunization

⑤ **656.3 Fetal distress**
[0,1,3]   Fetal metabolic acidemia

     Excludes: *abnormal fetal acid-base balance (656.8)*
abnormality in fetal heart rate or rhythm (659.7)
fetal bradycardia (659.7)
fetal tachycardia (659.7)
meconium in liquor (656.8)

⑤ **656.4 Intrauterine death**
[0,1,3]   Fetal death:
NOS
after completion of 22 weeks' gestation
late
Missed delivery

     Excludes: *missed abortion (632)*

⑤ **656.5 Poor fetal growth**
[0,1,3]   "Light-for-dates"   "Small-for-dates"
"Placental insufficiency"

⑤ **656.6 Excessive fetal growth**
[0,1,3]   "Large-for-dates"

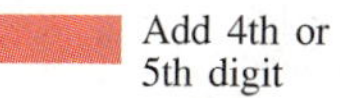

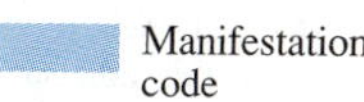

⑤ **656.7 Other placental conditions**
[0,1,3]   Abnormal placenta   Placental infarct

> *Excludes:* *placental polyp (674.4)*
> *placentitis (658.4)*

⑤ **656.8 Other specified fetal and placental problems**
[0,1,3]   Abnormal acid-base balance
Intrauterine acidosis
Lithopedian
Meconium in liquor

⑤ **656.9 Unspecified fetal and placental problem**
[0,1,3]

⑤ **657 Polyhydramnios**
[0,1,3]   Hydramnios
Use 0 as fourth-digit for this category

⑤ **658 Other problems associated with amniotic cavity and membranes**

> *Excludes:* *amniotic fluid embolism (673.1)*

⑤ **658.0 Oligohydramnios**
[0,1,3]   Oligohydramnios without mention of rupture of membranes

⑤ **658.1 Premature rupture of membranes**
[0,1,3]   Rupture of amniotic sac less than 24 hours prior to the onset of labor

⑤ **658.2 Delayed delivery after spontaneous or unspecified rupture of membranes**
[0,1,3]   Prolonged rupture of membranes NOS
Rupture of amniotic sac 24 hours or more prior to the onset of labor

⑤ **658.3 Delayed delivery after artificial rupture of membranes**
[0,1,3]

⑤ **658.4 Infection of amniotic cavity**
[0,1,3]   Amnionitis   Membranitis
Chorioamnionitis   Placentitis

⑤ **658.8 Other**
[0,1,3]   Amnion nodosum   Amniotic cyst

⑤ **658.9 Unspecified**
[0,1,3]

⑤ **659 Other indications for care or intervention related to labor and delivery, not elsewhere classified**

⑤ **659.0 Failed mechanical induction**
[0,1,3]   Failure of induction of labor by surgical or other instrumental methods

⑤ **659.1 Failed medical or unspecified induction**
[0,1,3]   Failed induction NOS
Failure of induction of labor by medical methods, such as oxytocic drugs

⑤ **659.2 Maternal pyrexia during labor, unspecified**
[0,1,3]

⑤ **659.3 Generalized infection during labor**
[0,1,3]   Septicemia during labor

⑤ **659.4 Grand multiparity**
[0,1,3]

> *Excludes:* *supervision only, in pregnancy (V23.3)*
> *without current pregnancy (V61.5)*

⑤ **659.5 Elderly primigravida**
[0,1,3]   First pregnancy in a woman who will be 35 years of age or older at expected date of delivery

> *Excludes:* *supervision only, in pregnancy (V23.81)*

⑤ **659.6 Elderly multigravida**
[0,1,3]   Second or more pregnancy in a woman who will be 35 years of age or older at expected date of delivery

> *Excludes:* *elderly primigravida 659.5*
> *supervision only, in pregnancy (V23.82)*

● Code new to this edition   ▲ Revision of existing code   ④ ⑤ Fourth or fifth digit required

⑤ **659.7** **Abnormality in fetal heart rate or rhythm**
[0,1,3]   Depressed fetal heart tones
Fetal:
  bradycardia
  tachycardia
Fetal heart rate decelerations
Non-reassuring fetal heart rate or rhythm

⑤ **659.8** **Other specified indications for care or intervention related to labor and delivery**
[0,1,3]   Pregnancy in female less than 16 years old at expected date of delivery
Very young maternal age

⑤ **659.9** **Unspecified indication for care or intervention related to labor and delivery**
[0,1,3]

COMPLICATIONS OCCURRING MAINLY IN THE COURSE OF LABOR AND DELIVERY (660-669)

The following fifth-digit subclassification is for use with categories 660-669 to denote the current episode of care:

0   unspecified as to episode of care or not applicable

1   delivered, with or without mention of antepartum condition

2   delivered, with mention of postpartum complication

3   antepartum condition or complication

4   postpartum condition or complication

⑤ **660** **Obstructed labor**

⑤ **660.0** **Obstruction caused by malposition of fetus at onset of labor**
[0,1,3]   Any condition classifiable to 652, causing obstruction during labor
Use additional code from 652.0-652.9, if desired, to identify condition

⑤ **660.1** **Obstruction by bony pelvis**
[0,1,3]   Any condition classifiable to 653, causing obstruction during labor
Use additional code from 653.0-653.9, if desired, to identify condition

⑤ **660.2** **Obstruction by abnormal pelvic soft tissues**
[0,1,3]   Prolapse of anterior lip of cervix
Any condition classifiable to 654, causing obstruction during labor
Use additional code from 654.0-654.9, if desired, to identify condition

⑤ **660.3** **Deep transverse arrest and persistent occipitoposterior position**
[0,1,3]

⑤ **660.4** **Shoulder (girdle) dystocia**
[0,1,3]   Impacted shoulders

⑤ **660.5** **Locked twins**
[0,1,3]

⑤ **660.6** **Failed trial of labor, unspecified**
[0,1,3]   Failed trial of labor, without mention of condition or suspected condition

⑤ **660.7** **Failed forceps or vacuum extractor, unspecified**
[0,1,3]   Application of ventouse or forceps, without mention of condition

⑤ **660.8** **Other causes of obstructed labor**
[0,1,3]

⑤ **660.9** **Unspecified obstructed labor**
[0,1,3]   Dystocia:
  NOS
  fetal NOS
  maternal NOS

⑤ **661** **Abnormality of forces of labor**

⑤ **661.0** **Primary uterine inertia**
[0,1,3]   Failure of cervical dilation
Hypotonic uterine dysfunction, primary
Prolonged latent phase of labor

⑤ **661.1** **Secondary uterine inertia**
[0,1,3]   Arrested active phase of labor
Hypotonic uterine dysfunction, secondary

⑤ **661.2** **Other and unspecified uterine inertia**
[0,1,3]   Desultory labor   Poor contractions
Irregular labor   Slow slope active phase of labor

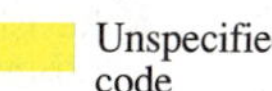

⑤ **661.3 Precipitate labor**
[0,1,3]

⑤ **661.4 Hypertonic, incoordinate, or prolonged uterine contractions**
[0,1,3]   Cervical spasm   Incoordinate uterine action
Contraction ring (dystocia)   Retraction ring (Bandl's) (pathological)
Dyscoordinate labor   Tetanic contractions
Hourglass contraction of   Uterine dystocia NOS
    uterus   Uterine spasm
Hypertonic uterine dysfunction

⑤ **661.9 Unspecified abnormality of labor**
[0,1,3]

⑤ **662 Long labor**

⑤ **662.0 Prolonged first stage**
[0,1,3]

⑤ **662.1 Prolonged labor, unspecified**
[0,1,3]

⑤ **662.2 Prolonged second stage**
[0,1,3]

⑤ **662.3 Delayed delivery of second twin, triplet, etc.**
[0,1,3]

⑤ **663 Umbilical cord complications**

⑤ **663.0 Prolapse of cord**
[0,1,3]   Presentation of cord

⑤ **663.1 Cord around neck, with compression**
[0,1,3]   Cord tightly around neck

⑤ **663.2 Other and unspecified cord entanglement, with compression**
[0,1,3]   Entanglement of cords of twins in mono-amniotic sac
Knot in cord (with compression)

⑤ **663.3 Other and unspecified cord entanglement, without mention of compression**
[0,1,3]

⑤ **663.4 Short cord**
[0,1,3]

⑤ **663.5 Vasa previa**
[0,1,3]

⑤ **663.6 Vascular lesions of cord**
[0,1,3]   Bruising of cord   Thrombosis of vessels of cord
Hematoma of cord

⑤ **663.8 Other umbilical cord complications**
[0,1,3]   Velamentous insertion of umbilical cord

⑤ **663.9 Unspecified umbilical cord complication**
[0,1,3]

⑤ **664 Trauma to perineum and vulva during delivery**
Includes: damage from instruments
           that from extension of episiotomy

⑤ **664.0 First-degree perineal laceration**
[0,1,4]   Perineal laceration, rupture, or tear involving:
fourchette
hymen
labia
skin
vagina
vulva

⑤ **664.1 Second-degree perineal laceration**
[0,1,4]   Perineal laceration, rupture, or tear (following episiotomy) involving:
pelvic floor
perineal muscles
vaginal muscles

Excludes: *that involving anal sphincter (664.2)*

● Code new   ▲ Revision of   ④ ⑤ Fourth or fifth
  to this edition   existing code   digit required

⑤ **664.2 Third-degree perineal laceration**
[0,1,4] Perineal laceration, rupture, or tear (following episiotomy) involving:
    anal sphincter
    rectovaginal septum
    sphincter NOS

    | Excludes: | *that with anal or rectal mucosal laceration (664.3)*

⑤ **664.3 Fourth-degree perineal laceration**
[0,1,4] Perineal laceration, rupture, or tear as classifiable to 664.2 and involving also:
    anal mucosa
    rectal mucosa

⑤ **664.4 Unspecified perineal laceration**
[0,1,4] Central laceration

⑤ **664.5 Vulval and perineal hematoma**
[0,1,4]

⑤ **664.8 Other specified trauma to perineum and vulva**
[0,1,4]

⑤ **664.9 Unspecified trauma to perineum and vulva**
[0,1,4]

⑤ **665 Other obstetrical trauma**
    Includes: damage from instruments

⑤ **665.0 Rupture of uterus before onset of labor**
[0,1,3]

⑤ **665.1 Rupture of uterus during labor**
[0,1] Rupture of uterus NOS

⑤ **665.2 Inversion of uterus**
[0,2,4]

⑤ **665.3 Laceration of cervix**
[0,1,4]

⑤ **665.4 High vaginal laceration**
[0,1,4] Laceration of vaginal wall or sulcus without mention of perineal laceration

⑤ **665.5 Other injury to pelvic organs**
[0,1,4] Injury to:
    bladder
    urethra

⑤ **665.6 Damage to pelvic joints and ligaments**
[0,1,4] Avulsion of inner symphyseal cartilage
    Damage to coccyx
    Separation of symphysis (pubis)

⑤ **665.7 Pelvic hematoma**
[0,1,2,4] Hematoma of vagina

⑤ **665.8 Other specified obstetrical trauma**
[0-4]

⑤ **665.9 Unspecified obstetrical trauma**
[0-4]

⑤ **666 Postpartum hemorrhage**

⑤ **666.0 Third-stage hemorrhage**
[0,2,4] Hemorrhage associated with retained, trapped, or adherent placenta
    Retained placenta NOS

⑤ **666.1 Other immediate postpartum hemorrhage**
[0,2,4] Atony of uterus
    Hemorrhage within the first 24 hours following delivery of placenta
    Postpartum hemorrhage (atonic) NOS

⑤ **666.2 Delayed and secondary postpartum hemorrhage**
[0,2,4] Hemorrhage:
    after the first 24 hours following delivery
    associated with retained portions of placenta or membranes
    Postpartum hemorrhage specified as delayed or secondary
    Retained products of conception NOS, following delivery

⑤ **666.3 Postpartum coagulation defects**
[0,2,4] Postpartum afibrinogenemia
    Postpartum fibrinolysis

⑤ **667 Retained placenta or membranes, without hemorrhage**

| Add 4th or 5th digit | Nonspecific code | Unspecified code | Manifestation code |

⑤ **667.0 Retained placenta without hemorrhage**
[0,2,4]   Placenta accreta
    Retained placenta: ⎱
      NOS   ⎰ without hemorrhage
      total

⑤ **667.1 Retained portions of placenta or membranes, without hemorrhage**
[0,2,4]   Retained products of conception following delivery, without hemorrhage

⑤ **668 Complications of the administration of anesthetic or other sedation in labor and delivery**
    Includes: complications arising from the administration of a general or local anesthetic, analgesic, or other sedation in labor and delivery

    Excludes: *reaction to spinal or lumbar puncture (349.0)*
             spinal headache (349.0)

Use additional code(s) to further specify complication

⑤ **668.0 Pulmonary complications**
[0-4]   Inhalation [aspiration] of stomach contents or
        secretions   following anesthesia or other
    Mendelson's syndrome   sedation in labor or delivery
    Pressure collapse of lung

⑤ **668.1 Cardiac complications**
[0-4]   Cardiac arrest or failure following anesthesia or other sedation in labor and delivery

⑤ **668.2 Central nervous system complications**
[0-4]   Cerebral anoxia following anesthesia or other sedation in labor and delivery

⑤ **668.8 Other complications of anesthesia or other sedation in labor and delivery**
[0-4]

⑤ **668.9 Unspecified complication of anesthesia and other sedation**
[0-4]

⑤ **669 Other complications of labor and delivery, not elsewhere classified**

⑤ **669.0 Maternal distress**
[0-4]   Metabolic disturbance in labor and delivery

⑤ **669.1 Shock during or following labor and delivery**
[0-4]   Obstetric shock

⑤ **669.2 Maternal hypotension syndrome**
[0-4]

⑤ **669.3 Acute renal failure following labor and delivery**
[0,2,4]

⑤ **669.4 Other complications of obstetrical surgery and procedures**
[0-4]   Cardiac:
      arrest   following cesarean or other obstetrical surgery or
      failure   procedure, including delivery NOS
    Cerebral anoxia

    Excludes: *complications of obstetrical surgical wounds (674.1-674.3)*

⑤ **669.5 Forceps or vacuum extractor delivery without mention of indication**
[0,1]   Delivery by ventouse, without mention of indication

⑤ **669.6 Breech extraction, without mention of indication**
[0,1]

    Excludes: *breech delivery NOS (652.2)*

⑤ **669.7 Cesarean delivery, without mention of indication**
[0,1]

⑤ **669.8 Other complications of labor and delivery**
[0-4]

⑤ **669.9 Unspecified complication of labor and delivery**
[0-4]

● Code new   ▲ Revision of   ④ ⑤ Fourth or fifth
   to this edition   existing code   digit required

COMPLICATIONS OF THE PUERPERIUM (670-677)

Note: Categories 671 and 673-676 include the listed conditions even if they occur during pregnancy or childbirth.

The following fifth-digit subclassification is for use with categories 670-676 to denote the current episode of care:

0 **unspecified as to episode of care or not applicable**

1 **delivered, with or without mention of antepartum condition**

2 **delivered, with mention of postpartum complication**

3 **antepartum condition or complication**

4 **postpartum condition or complication**

⑤ **670 Major puerperal infection**
[0,2,4]

Puerperal:	Puerperal:
endometritis	peritonitis
fever (septic)	pyemia
pelvic:	salpingitis
cellulitis	septicemia
sepsis	

Use 0 as fourth-digit for this category

Excludes: *infection following abortion (639.0)*

minor genital tract infection following delivery (646.6)
puerperal pyrexia NOS (672)
puerperal fever NOS (672)
puerperal pyrexia of unknown origin (672)
urinary tract infection following delivery (646.6)

⑤ **671 Venous complications in pregnancy and the puerperium**

⑤ **671.0 Varicose veins of legs**
[0-4]   Varicose veins NOS

⑤ **671.1 Varicose veins of vulva and perineum**
[0-4]

⑤ **671.2 Superficial thrombophlebitis**
[0-4]   Thrombophlebitis (superficial)

⑤ **671.3 Deep phlebothrombosis, antepartum**
[0,1,3]   Deep-vein thrombosis, antepartum

⑤ **671.4 Deep phlebothrombosis, postpartum**
[0,2,4]   Deep-vein thrombosis, postpartum
         Pelvic thrombophlebitis, postpartum
         Phlegmasia alba dolens (puerperal)

⑤ **671.5 Other phlebitis and thrombosis**
[0-4]   Cerebral venous thrombosis
         Thrombosis of intracranial venous sinus

⑤ **671.8 Other venous complications**
[0-4]   Hemorrhoids

⑤ **671.9 Unspecified venous complication**
[0-4]   Phlebitis NOS
         Thrombosis NOS

⑤ **672 Pyrexia of unknown origin during the puerperium**
[0,2,4]   Puerperal fever NOS
         Postpartum fever NOS

Use 0 as fourth-digit for this category

⑤ **673 Obstetrical pulmonary embolism**
Includes: pulmonary emboli in pregnancy, childbirth, or the puerperium, or specified as puerperal

Excludes: *embolism following abortion (639.6)*

⑤ **673.0 Obstetrical air embolism**
[0-4]

⑤ **673.1 Amniotic fluid embolism**
[0-4]

⑤ **673.2 Obstetrical blood-clot embolism**
[0-4]   Puerperal pulmonary embolism NOS

⑤ **673.3 Obstetrical pyemic and septic embolism**
[0-4]

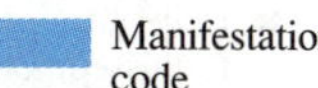

Manifestation
code

⑤ **673.8 Other pulmonary embolism**
[0-4]   Fat embolism

⑤ **674 Other and unspecified complications of the puerperium, not elsewhere classified**

⑤ **674.0 Cerebrovascular disorders in the puerperium**
[0-4]   Any condition classifiable to 430-434, 436-437 occurring during pregnancy, childbirth, or the puerperium, or specified as puerperal

Excludes: *intracranial venous sinus thrombosis (671.5)*

⑤ **674.1 Disruption of cesarean wound**
[0,2,4]   Dehiscence or disruption of uterine wound

⑤ **674.2 Disruption of perineal wound**
[0,2,4]   Breakdown of perineum   Secondary perineal tear
              Disruption of wound of:
                episiotomy
                perineal laceration

⑤ **674.3 Other complications of obstetrical surgical wounds**
[0,2,4]   Hematoma of cesarean section or perineal wound
              Hemorrhage of cesarean section or perineal wound
              Infection of cesarean section or perineal wound

Excludes: *damage from instruments in delivery (664.0-665.9)*

⑤ **674.4 Placental polyp**
[0,2,4]

⑤ **674.8 Other**
[0,2,4]   Hepatorenal syndrome, following delivery
              Postpartum:
                cardiomyopathy
                subinvolution of uterus
                uterine hypertrophy

⑤ **674.9 Unspecified**
[0,2,4]   Sudden death of unknown cause during the puerperium

⑤ **675 Infections of the breast and nipple associated with childbirth**
              Includes: the listed conditions during pregnancy, childbirth, or the puerperium

⑤ **675.0 Infections of nipple**
[0-4]   Abscess of nipple

⑤ **675.1 Abscess of breast**
[0-4]   Abscess: Mastitis:
              mammary   purulent
              subareolar   retromammary
              submammary   submammary

⑤ **675.2 Nonpurulent mastitis**
[0-4]   Lymphangitis of breast   Mastitis:
                                          NOS
                                          interstitial
                                          parenchymatous

⑤ **675.8 Other specified infections of the breast and nipple**
[0-4]

⑤ **675.9 Unspecified infection of the breast and nipple**
[0-4]

⑤ **676 Other disorders of the breast associated with childbirth and disorders of lactation**
              Includes: the listed conditions during pregnancy, the puerperium, or lactation

⑤ **676.0 Retracted nipple**
[0-4]

⑤ **676.1 Cracked nipple**
[0-4]   Fissure of nipple

⑤ **676.2 Engorgement of breasts**
[0-4]

⑤ **676.3 Other and unspecified disorder of breast**
[0-4]

⑤ **676.4 Failure of lactation**
[0-4]   Agalactia

⑤ **676.5 Suppressed lactation**
[0-4]

● Code new   ▲ Revision of   ④ ⑤ Fourth or fifth
  to this edition   existing code   digit required

⑤ **676.6 Galactorrhea**
[0-4]

> Excludes: galactorrhea not associated with childbirth (611.6)

⑤ **676.8 Other disorders of lactation**
[0-4]   Galactocele

⑤ **676.9 Unspecified disorder of lactation**
[0-4]

677 Late effect of complication of pregnancy, childbirth, and the puerperium

Note: This category is to be used to indicate conditions in 632-648.9 and 651-676.9 as the cause of the late effect, themselves classifiable elsewhere. The "late effects" include conditions specified as such, or as sequelae, which may occur at any time after the puerperium.

Code first any sequelae

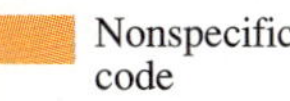

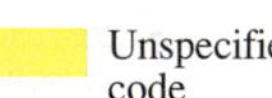

Manifestation
code

● Code new
to this edition

▲ Revision of
existing code

④ ⑤ Fourth or fifth
digit required

12. DISEASES OF THE SKIN AND SUBCUTANEOUS TISSUE (680-709)

INFECTIONS OF SKIN AND SUBCUTANEOUS TISSUE (680-686)

Excludes: *certain infections of skin classified under "Infectious and Parasitic Diseases," such as:*
erysipelas (035)
erysipeloid of Rosenbach (027.1)
herpes:
simplex (054.0-054.9)
zoster (053.0-053.9)
molluscum contagiosum (078.0)
viral warts (078.1)

680 Carbuncle and furuncle

Includes: boil
furunculosis

680.0 Face

Ear [any part]
Face [any part, except eye]
Nose (septum)
Temple (region)

Excludes: *eyelid (373.13)*
lacrimal apparatus (375.31)
orbit (376.01)

680.1 Neck

680.2 Trunk

Abdominal wall	Flank
Back [any part, except buttocks]	Groin
Breast	Pectoral region
Chest wall	Perineum
	Umbilicus

Excludes: *buttocks (680.5)*
external genital organs:
female (616.4)
male (607.2, 608.4)

680.3 Upper arm and forearm
Arm [any part, except hand]
Axilla
Shoulder

680.4 Hand
Finger [any]   Wrist
Thumb

680.5 Buttock
Anus   Gluteal region

680.6 Leg, except foot
Ankle   Knee
Hip   Thigh

680.7 Foot
Heel   Toe

680.8 Other specified sites
Head [any part, except face]
Scalp

Excludes: *external genital organs:*
female (616.4)
male (607.2, 608.4)

680.9 Unspecified site
Boil NOS   Furuncle NOS
Carbuncle NOS

681 Cellulitis and abscess of finger and toe
Includes: that with lymphangitis
Use additional code, if desired, to identify organism, such as Staphylococcus (041.1)

⑤ **681.0 Finger**

681.00 Cellulitis and abscess, unspecified

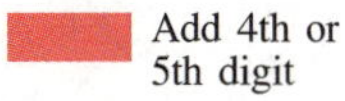

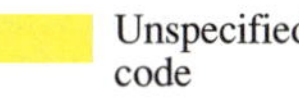

681.01 Felon
Pulp abscess   Whitlow

Excludes: *herpetic whitlow (054.6)*

681.02 Onychia and paronychia of finger
Panaritium
Perionychia } of finger

⑤ **681.1 Toe**

681.10 Cellulitis and abscess, unspecified

681.11 Onychia and paronychia of toe
Panaritium
Perionychia } of toe

681.9 Cellulitis and abscess of unspecified digit
Infection of nail NOS

682 Other cellulitis and abscess
Includes:
abscess (acute)
cellulitis (diffuse)
lymphangitis, acute } (with lymphangitis) except of finger or toe

Use additional code, if desired, to identify organism, such as Staphylococcus (041.1)

Excludes: *lymphangitis (chronic) (subacute) (457.2)*

682.0 Face
Cheek, external   Nose, external
Chin   Submandibular
Forehead   Temple (region)

Excludes: *ear [any part] (380.10-380.16)*
eyelid (373.13)
lacrimal apparatus (375.31)
lip (528.5)
mouth (528.3)
nose (internal) (478.1)
orbit (376.01)

682.1 Neck

682.2 Trunk
Abdominal wall   Groin
Back [any part, except   Pectoral region
  buttock]   Perineum
Chest wall   Umbilicus, except newborn
Flank

Excludes: *anal and rectal regions (566)*
breast:
NOS (611.0)
puerperal (675.1)
external genital organs:
female (616.3-616.4)
male (604.0, 607.2, 608.4)
umbilicus, newborn (771.4)

682.3 Upper arm and forearm
Arm [any part, except hand]
Axilla
Shoulder

Excludes: *hand (682.4)*

682.4 Hand, except fingers and thumb
Wrist

Excludes: *finger and thumb (681.00-681.02)*

682.5 Buttock
Gluteal region

Excludes: *anal and rectal regions (566)*

682.6 Leg, except foot
Ankle   Knee
Hip   Thigh

● Code new   ▲ Revision of   ④ ⑤ Fourth or fifth
  to this edition   existing code   digit required

682.7 Foot, except toes
    Heel

> *Excludes:* toe (681.10-681.11)

682.8 Other specified sites
    Head [except face]   Scalp

> *Excludes:* face (682.0)

682.9 Unspecified site
    Abscess NOS   Lymphangitis, acute NOS
    Cellulitis NOS

> *Excludes:* lymphangitis NOS (457.2)

683 Acute lymphadenitis

    Abscess (acute)
    Adenitis, acute } lymph gland or node, except mesenteric
    Lymphadenitis, acute

Use additional code, if desired, to identify organism, such as Staphylococcus (041.1)

> *Excludes:* enlarged glands NOS (785.6)
>
>   *lymphadenitis:*
>   *chronic or subacute, except mesenteric (289.1)*
>   *mesenteric (acute) (chronic) (subacute) (289.2)*
>   *unspecified (289.3)*

684 Impetigo

Impetiginization of other dermatoses
Impetigo (contagiosa) [any site] [any organism]:
    bullous
    circinate
    neonatorum
    simplex
Pemphigus neonatorum

> *Excludes:* impetigo herpetiformis (694.3)

685 Pilonidal cyst

Includes:
      fistula
      sinus } coccygeal or pilonidal

685.0 With abscess

685.1 Without mention of abscess

686 Other local infections of skin and subcutaneous tissue

Use additional code, if desired, to identify any infectious organism (041.0-041.8)

⑤ **686.0 Pyoderma**
    Dermatitis:
      purulent
      septic
      suppurative

    686.00 Pyoderma, unspecified

    686.01 Pyoderma gangrenosum

    686.09 Other pyoderma

686.1 Pyogenic granuloma
    Granuloma:
      septic
      suppurative
      telangiectaticum

> *Excludes:* pyogenic granuloma of oral mucosa (528.9)

686.8 Other specified local infections of skin and subcutaneous tissue
    Bacterid (pustular)   Ecthyma
    Dermatitis vegetans   Perlèche

> *Excludes:* dermatitis infectiosa eczematoides (690.8)
>   panniculitis (729.30-729.39)

686.9 Unspecified local infection of skin and subcutaneous tissue
    Fistula of skin NOS   Skin infection NOS

> *Excludes:* fistula to skin from internal organs—see Alphabetic Index

OTHER INFLAMMATORY CONDITIONS OF SKIN AND SUBCUTANEOUS TISSUE (690-698)

> *Excludes:* panniculitis (729.30-729.39)

690 Erythematosquamous dermatosis

> *Excludes:* eczematous dermatitis of eyelid (373.31)
> parakeratosis variegata (696.2)
> psoriasis (696.0-696.1)
> seborrheic keratosis (702)

⑤ **690.1 Seborrheic dermatitis**

690.10 Seborrheic dermatitis, unspecified
Seborrheic dermatitis NOS

690.11 Seborrhea capitis
Cradle cap

690.12 Seborrheic infantile dermatitis

690.18 Other seborrheic dermatitis

690.8 Other erythematosquamous dermatosis

691 Atopic dermatitis and related conditions

691.0 Diaper or napkin rash
Ammonia dermatitis
Diaper or napkin:
  dermatitis
  erythema
  rash
Psoriasiform napkin eruption

691.8 Other atopic dermatitis and related conditions
Atopic dermatitis   Neurodermatitis:
Besnier's prurigo   atopic
Eczema: diffuse (of Brocq)
  atopic
  flexural
  intrinsic (allergic)

692 Contact dermatitis and other eczema
Includes:

dermatitis: eczema (acute) (chronic):
  NOS   NOS
  contact   allergic
  occupational   erythematous
  venenata   occupational

> *Excludes:* allergy NOS (995.3)
> contact dermatitis of eyelids (373.32)
> dermatitis due to substances taken internally (693.0-693.9)
> eczema of external ear (380.22)
> perioral dermatitis (695.3)
> urticarial reactions (708.0-708.9, 995.1)

692.0 Due to detergents

692.1 Due to oils and greases

692.2 Due to solvents
Dermatitis due to solvents of:
  chlorocompound group
  cyclohexane group
  ester group
  glycol group
  hydrocarbon group
  ketone group

● Code new to this edition   ▲ Revision of existing code   ④ ⑤ Fourth or fifth digit required

692.3 Due to drugs and medicines in contact with skin
  Dermatitis (allergic) (contact) due to:
    arnica
    fungicides
    iodine
    keratolytics
    mercurials
    neomycin
    pediculocides
    phenols
    scabicides
    any drug applied to skin
  Dermatitis medicamentosa due to drug applied to skin
Use additional E code, if desired, to identify drug

> *Excludes:* *allergy NOS due to drugs (995.2)*
> *dermatitis due to ingested drugs (693.0)*
> *dermatitis medicamentosa NOS (693.0)*

692.4 Due to other chemical products
Dermatitis due to:	Dermatitis due to:
acids	insecticide
adhesive plaster	nylon
alkalis	plastic
caustics	rubber
dichromate	

692.5 Due to food in contact with skin
Dermatitis, contact, due to:	Dermatitis, contact, due to:
cereals	fruit
fish	meat
flour	milk

> *Excludes:* *dermatitis due to:*
> *dyes (692.89)*
> *ingested foods (693.1)*
> *preservatives (692.89)*

692.6 Due to plants [except food]
  Dermatitis due to:
    lacquer tree [Rhus verniciflua]
    poison ivy [Rhus toxicodendron]
    poison oak [Rhus diversiloba]
    poison sumac [Rhus venenata]
    poison vine [Rhus radicans]
    primrose [Primula]
    ragweed [Senecio jacobae]
    other plants in contact with the skin

> *Excludes:* *allergy NOS due to pollen (477.0)*
> *nettle rash (708.8)*

⑤ **692.7 Due to solar radiation**

  692.70 Unspecified dermatitis due to sun

  692.71 Sunburn

  692.72 Acute dermatitis due to solar radiation
      Berloque dermatitis
      Photoallergic response
      Phototoxic response
      Polymorphus light eruption
      Acute solar skin damage NOS

> *Excludes:* *sunburn (692.71)*
> Use additional E code, if desired, to identify drug, if drug induced

  692.73 Actinic reticuloid and actinic granuloma

  692.74 Other chronic dermatitis due to solar radiation
      solar elastosis
      chronic solar skin damage NOS

> *Excludes:* *actinic [solar] keratosis (702.0)*

  ● **692.75 Disseminated superficial actinic porokeratosis (DSAP)**

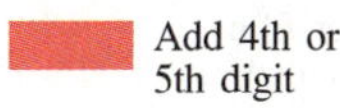

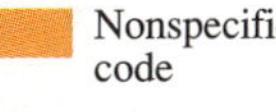

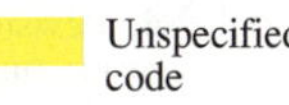

692.79 Other dermatitis due to solar radiation
    Hydroa aestivale
    Photodermatitis due to sun
    Photosensitiveness due to sun
    Solar skin damage NOS

⑤ **692.8 Due to other specified agents**

    692.81 Dermatitis due to cosmetics

    692.82 Dermatitis due to other radiation
        infrared rays
        light, except from sun
        radiation NOS
        ultraviolet rays, except from sun
        x-rays

      Excludes: *that due to solar radiation (692.70-692.79)*

    692.83 Dermatitis due to metals
        jewelry

    692.89 Other
        Dermatitis due to:
          cold weather
          dyes
          furs
          hot weather
        preservatives

      Excludes: *allergy NOS due to animal hair, dander (animal), or dust (477.8)*
          sunburn (692.71)

692.9 Unspecified cause
    Dermatitis: Eczema NOS
      NOS
      contact NOS
      venenata NOS

693 Dermatitis due to substances taken internally

      Excludes: *adverse effect NOS of drugs and medicines (995.2)*
          allergy NOS (995.3)
          contact dermatitis (692.0-692.9)
          urticarial reactions (708.0-708.9, 995.1)

693.0 Due to drugs and medicines
    Dermatitis medicamentosa NOS

Use additional E code, if desired, to identify drug

      Excludes: *that due to drugs in contact with skin (692.3)*

693.1 Due to food

693.8 Due to other specified substances taken internally

693.9 Due to unspecified substance taken internally

      Excludes: *dermatitis NOS (692.9)*

694 Bullous dermatoses

694.0 Dermatitis herpetiformis
    Dermatosis herpetiformis
    Duhring's disease
    Hydroa herpetiformis

      Excludes: *herpes gestationis (646.8)*
          dermatitis herpetiformis:
          juvenile (694.2)
          senile (694.5)

694.1 Subcorneal pustular dermatosis
    Sneddon-Wilkinson disease or syndrome

694.2 Juvenile dermatitis herpetiformis
    Juvenile pemphigoid

694.3 Impetigo herpetiformis

● Code new   ▲ Revision of   ④ ⑤ Fourth or fifth
  to this edition   existing code   digit required

694.4 Pemphigus

Pemphigus:
NOS
erythematosus
foliaceus

Pemphigus:
malignant
vegetans
vulgaris

Excludes: *pemphigus neonatorum (684)*

694.5 Pemphigoid

Benign pemphigus NOS
Bullous pemphigoid
Herpes circinatus bullosus
Senile dermatitis herpetiformis

⑤ **694.6 Benign mucous membrane pemphigoid**

Cicatricial pemphigoid
Mucosynechial atrophic bullous dermatitis

694.60 Without mention of ocular involvement

694.61 With ocular involvement
Ocular pemphigus

694.8 Other specified bullous dermatoses

Excludes: *herpes gestationis (646.8)*

694.9 Unspecified bullous dermatoses

695 Erythematous conditions

695.0 Toxic erythema
Erythema venenatum

695.1 Erythema multiforme

Erythema iris
Herpes iris
Lyell's syndrome

Scalded skin syndrome
Stevens-Johnson syndrome
Toxic epidermal necrolysis

695.2 Erythema nodosum

Excludes: *tuberculous erythema nodosum (017.1)*

695.3 Rosacea

Acne:
erythematosa
rosacea

Perioral dermatitis
Rhinophyma

695.4 Lupus erythematosus
Lupus:
erythematodes (discoid)
erythematosus (discoid), not disseminated

Excludes: *lupus (vulgaris) NOS (017.0)*
systemic [disseminated] lupus erythematosus (710.0)

⑤ **695.8 Other specified erythematous conditions**

695.81 Ritter's disease
Dermatitis exfoliativa neonatorum

695.89 Other
Erythema intertrigo
Intertrigo
Pityriasis rubra (Hebra)

Excludes: *mycotic intertrigo (111.0-111.9)*

695.9 Unspecified erythematous condition
Erythema NOS   Erythroderma (secondary)

696 Psoriasis and similar disorders

696.0 Psoriatic arthropathy

696.1 Other psoriasis
Acrodermatitis continua
Dermatitis repens
Psoriasis:
NOS
any type, except arthropathic

Excludes: *psoriatic arthropathy (696.0)*

696.2 Parapsoriasis
Parakeratosis variegata
Parapsoriasis lichenoides chronica
Pityriasis lichenoides et varioliformis

696.3 Pityriasis rosea
Pityriasis circinata (et maculata)

696.4 Pityriasis rubra pilaris
Devergie's disease
Lichen ruber acuminatus

Excludes: *pityriasis rubra (Hebra) (695.89)*

696.5 Other and unspecified pityriasis
Pityriasis:
NOS
alba
streptogenes

Excludes: *pityriasis simplex (690.18)*
pityriasis versicolor (111.0)

696.8 Other

697 Lichen

Excludes: *lichen:*

obtusus corneus (698.3)
pilaris (congenital) (757.39)
ruber acuminatus (696.4)
sclerosus et atrophicus (701.0)
scrofulosus (017.0)
simplex chronicus (698.3)
spinulosus (congenital) (757.39)
urticatus (698.2)

697.0 Lichen planus
Lichen:
planopilaris
ruber planus

697.1 Lichen nitidus
Pinkus' disease

697.8 Other lichen, not elsewhere classified
Lichen:
ruber moniliforme
striata

697.9 Lichen, unspecified

698 Pruritus and related conditions

Excludes: *pruritus specified as psychogenic (306.3)*

698.0 Pruritus ani
Perianal itch

698.1 Pruritus of genital organs

698.2 Prurigo
Lichen urticatus   Urticaria papulosa (Hebra)
Prurigo:
NOS
Hebra's
mitis
simplex

Excludes: *prurigo nodularis (698.3)*

698.3 Lichenification and lichen simplex chronicus
Hyde's disease
Neurodermatitis (circumscripta) (local)
Prurigo nodularis

Excludes: *neurodermatitis, diffuse (of Brocq) (691.8)*

698.4 Dermatitis factitia [artefacta]
Dermatitis ficta
Neurotic excoriation
Use additional code, if desired, to identify any associated mental disorder

● Code new
to this edition   ▲ Revision of
existing code   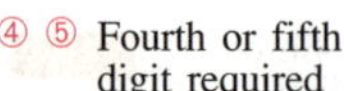 Fourth or fifth
digit required

698.8 Other specified pruritic conditions
Pruritus: Winter itch
 hiemalis
 senilis

698.9 Unspecified pruritic disorder
Itch NOS   Pruritus NOS

OTHER DISEASES OF SKIN AND SUBCUTANEOUS TISSUE (700-709)

Excludes: *conditions confined to eyelids (373.0-374.9)*
          congenital conditions of skin, hair, and nails (757.0-757.9)

700 Corns and callosities
Callus   Clavus

701 Other hypertrophic and atrophic conditions of skin

Excludes: *dermatomyositis (710.3)*
          hereditary edema of legs (757.0)
          scleroderma (generalized) (710.1)

701.0 Circumscribed scleroderma
Addison's keloid
Dermatosclerosis, localized
Lichen sclerosus et atrophicus
Morphea
Scleroderma, circumscribed or localized

701.1 Keratoderma, acquired
Acquired:
 ichthyosis
 keratoderma palmaris et plantaris
Elastosis perforans serpiginosa
Hyperkeratosis:
 NOS
 follicularis in cutem penetrans
 palmoplantaris climacterica
Keratoderma:
 climactericum
 tylodes, progressive
Keratosis (blennorrhagica)

Excludes: *Darier's disease [keratosis follicularis] (congenital) (757.39)*
          keratosis:
           arsenical (692.4)
           gonococcal (098.81)

701.2 Acquired acanthosis nigricans
Keratosis nigricans

701.3 Striae atrophicae
Atrophic spots of skin
Atrophoderma maculatum
Atrophy blanche (of Milian)
Degenerative colloid atrophy
Senile degenerative atrophy
Striae distensae

701.4 Keloid scar
Cheloid   Keloid
Hypertrophic scar

701.5 Other abnormal granulation tissue
Excessive granulation

701.8 Other specified hypertrophic and atrophic conditions of skin
Acrodermatitis atrophicans chronica
Atrophia cutis senilis
Atrophoderma neuriticum
Confluent and reticulate papillomatosis
Cutis laxa senilis
Elastosis senilis
Folliculitis ulerythematosa reticulata
Gougerot-Carteaud syndrome or disease

701.9 Unspecified hypertrophic and atrophic conditions of skin
Atrophoderma

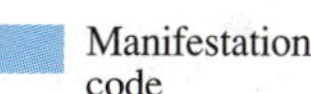

Add 4th or   Nonspecific   Unspecified   Manifestation
5th digit   code   code   code

702 Other dermatoses

> *Excludes:* carcinoma in situ (232.0-232.9)

702.0 Actinic keratosis

⑤ **702.1 Seborrheic keratosis**

702.11 Inflamed seborrheic keratosis

702.19 Other seborrheic keratosis
Seborrheic keratosis NOS

702.8 Other specified dermatoses

703 Diseases of nail

> *Excludes:* congenital anomalies (757.5)
> onychia and paronychia (681.02, 681.11)

703.0 Ingrowing nail
Ingrowing nail with infection
Unguis incarnatus

> *Excludes:* infection, nail NOS (681.9)

703.8 Other specified diseases of nail
Dystrophia unguium   Onychauxis
Hypertrophy of nail   Onychogryposis
Koilonychia   Onycholysis
Leukonychia (punctata) (striata)

703.9 Unspecified disease of nail

704 Diseases of hair and hair follicles

> *Excludes:* congenital anomalies (757.4)

⑤ **704.0 Alopecia**

> *Excludes:* madarosis (374.55)
> syphilitic alopecia (091.82)

704.00 Alopecia, unspecified
Baldness   Loss of hair

704.01 Alopecia areata
Ophiasis

704.02 Telogen effluvim

704.09 Other
Folliculitis decalvans
Hypotrichosis:
  NOS
    postinfectional NOS
Pseudopelade

704.1 Hirsutism
Hypertrichosis: Polytrichia
  NOS
  lanuginosa, acquired

> *Excludes:* hypertrichosis of eyelid (374.54)

704.2 Abnormalities of the hair
Atrophic hair   Trichiasis:
Clastothrix   NOS
Fragilitas crinium   cicatrical
                            Trichorrhexis (nodosa)

> *Excludes:* trichiasis of eyelid (374.05)

704.3 Variations in hair color
Canities (premature)   Poliosis:
Grayness, hair (premature)   NOS
Heterochromia of hair   circumscripta, acquired

● Code new   ▲ Revision of   ④ ⑤ Fourth or fifth
to this edition   existing code   digit required

704.8 Other specified diseases of hair and hair follicles
Folliculitis: Sycosis:
  NOS   NOS
  abscedens et suffodiens   barbae [not parasitic]
  pustular   lupoid
Perifolliculitis: vulgaris
  NOS
  capitis abscedens et suffodiens
  scalp

704.9 Unspecified disease of hair and hair follicles

705 Disorders of sweat glands

705.0 Anhidrosis
Hypohidrosis   Oligohidrosis

705.1 Prickly heat
Heat rash
Miliaria rubra (tropicalis)
Sudamina

⑤ **705.8 Other specified disorders of sweat glands**

    705.81 Dyshidrosis
        Cheiropompholyx   Pompholyx

    705.82 Fox-Fordyce disease

    705.83 Hidradenitis
        Hidradenitis suppurativa

    705.89 Other
        Bromhidrosis   Granulosis rubra nasi
        Chromhidrosis   Urhidrosis

Excludes: hidrocystoma (216.0-216.9)
           hyperhidrosis (780.8)

705.9 Unspecified disorder of sweat glands
Disorder of sweat glands NOS

706 Diseases of sebaceous glands

706.0 Acne varioliformis
Acne:
  frontalis
  necrotica

706.1 Other acne
Acne: Blackhead
  NOS   Comedo
  conglobata
  cystic
  pustular
  vulgaris

Excludes: acne rosacea (695.3)

706.2 Sebaceous cyst
Atheroma, skin   Wen
Keratin cyst

706.3 Seborrhea

Excludes: seborrhea:
      capitis (690.11)
      sicca (690.18)
    seborrheic keratosis (702)

706.8 Other specified diseases of sebaceous glands
Asteatosis (cutis)   Xerosis cutis

706.9 Unspecified disease of sebaceous glands

707 Chronic ulcer of skin
Includes: non-infected sinus of skin
          non-healing ulcer

Excludes: specific infections classified under "Infectious and Parasitic Diseases" (001.0-136.9)
      varicose ulcer (454.0, 454.2)

707.0 Decubitus ulcer
Bed sore   Plaster ulcer
Decubitus ulcer [any site] Pressure ulcer

⑤ **707.1 Ulcer of lower limbs, except decubitus**
Ulcer, chronic, neurogenic, of lower limb
Ulcer, chronic, trophic, of lower limb

Code first any associated underlying condition:
atherosclerosis of the extremities with ulceration (440.23)
diabetes mellitus (250.80-250.83)

● **707.10 Ulcer of lower limb, unspecified**

● **707.11 Ulcer of thigh**

● **707.12 Ulcer of calf**

● **707.13 Ulcer of ankle**

● **707.14 Ulcer of heel and midfoot**
Plantar surface of midfoot

● **707.15 Ulcer of other part of foot**
Toes

● **707.19 Ulcer of other part of lower limb**

707.8 Chronic ulcer of other specified sites
Ulcer, chronic:
neurogenic ⎫
trophic ⎭ of other specified sites

707.9 Chronic ulcer of unspecified site
Chronic ulcer NOS   Tropical ulcer NOS
Trophic ulcer NOS   Ulcer of skin NOS

708 Urticaria

Excludes: *edema:*
angioneurotic (995.1)
Quincke's (995.1)
hereditary angioedema (277.6)
urticaria:
giant (995.1)
papulosa (Hebra) (698.2)
pigmentosa (juvenile) (congenital) (757.33)

708.0 Allergic urticaria

708.1 Idiopathic urticaria

708.2 Urticaria due to cold and heat
Thermal urticaria

708.3 Dermatographic urticaria
Dermatographia   Factitial urticaria

708.4 Vibratory urticaria

708.5 Cholinergic urticaria

708.8 Other specified urticaria
Nettle rash
Urticaria:
chronic
recurrent periodic

708.9 Urticaria, unspecified
Hives NOS

709 Other disorders of skin and subcutaneous tissue

⑤ **709.0 Dyschromia**

Excludes: *albinism (270.2)*
pigmented nevus (216.0-216.9)
that of eyelid (374.52-374.53)

709.00 Dyschromia, unspecified

709.01 Vitiligo

709.09 Other

709.1 Vascular disorders of skin
Angioma serpiginosum
Purpura (primary) annularis telangiectodes

● Code new   ▲ Revision of   ④ ⑤ Fourth or fifth
to this edition   existing code   digit required

709.2 Scar conditions and fibrosis of skin
Adherent scar (skin)
Cicatrix
Disfigurement (due to scar)
Fibrosis, skin NOS
Scar NOS

Excludes: keloid scar (701.4)

709.3 Degenerative skin disorders

Calcinosis:
  circumscripta
  cutis
Colloid milium

Degeneration, skin
Deposits, skin
Senile dermatosis NOS
Subcutaneous calcification

709.4 Foreign body granuloma of skin and subcutaneous tissue

Excludes: residual foreign body without granuloma of skin and subcutaneous tissue (729.6)
that of muscle (728.82)

709.8 Other specified disorders of skin
Epithelial hyperplasia
Menstrual dermatosis

Vesicular eruption

709.9 Unspecified disorder of skin and subcutaneous tissue
Dermatosis NOS

● Code new
to this edition

▲ Revision of
existing code

④ ⑤ Fourth or fifth
digit required

13. DISEASES OF THE MUSCULOSKELETAL SYSTEM AND CONNECTIVE TISSUE (710-739)

The following fifth-digit subclassification is for use with categories 711-712, 715-716, 718-719, and 730:

0 site unspecified

1 shoulder region
Acromioclavicular
Glenohumeral   } joint(s)
Sternoclavicular
Clavicle
Scapula

2 upper arm
Elbow joint   Humerus

3 forearm
Radius   Wrist joint
Ulna

4 hand
Carpus   Phalanges [fingers]
Metacarpus

5 pelvic region and thigh
Buttock   Hip (joint)
Femur

6 lower leg
Fibula   Patella
Knee joint   Tibia

7 ankle and foot
Ankle joint   Phalanges, foot
Digits [toes]   Tarsus
Metatarsus   Other joints in foot

8 other specified sites
Head   Skull
Neck   Trunk
Ribs   Vertebral column

9 multiple sites

ARTHROPATHIES AND RELATED DISORDERS (710-719)

Excludes: *disorders of spine (720.0-724.9)*

710 Diffuse diseases of connective tissue

Includes: all collagen diseases whose effects are not mainly confined to a single system

Use additional code, if desired, to identify manifestation, as:
lung involvement (517.8)
myopathy (359.6)

Excludes: *those affecting mainly the cardiovascular system, i.e., polyarteritis nodosa and allied conditions (446.0-446.7)*

710.0 Systemic lupus erythematosus
Disseminated lupus erythematosus
Libman-Sacks disease

Use additional code, if desired, to identify manifestation, as:
endocarditis (424.91)
nephritis (583.81)
chronic (582.81)
nephrotic syndrome (581.81)

Excludes: *lupus erythematosus (discoid) NOS (695.4)*

710.1 Systemic sclerosis
Acrosclerosis
CRST syndrome
Progressive systemic sclerosis
Scleroderma

Excludes: *circumscribed scleroderma (701.0)*

710.2 Sicca syndrome
Keratoconjunctivitis sicca
Sjögren's disease

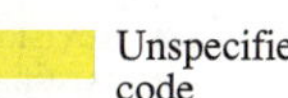

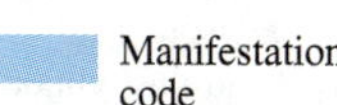

710.3 Dermatomyositis
Poikilodermatomyositis
Polymyositis with skin involvement

710.4 Polymyositis

710.5 Eosinophilia myalgia syndrome
Toxic oil syndrome

Use additional E code, if desired, to identify drug, if drug induced

710.8 Other specified diffuse diseases of connective tissue
Multifocal fibrosclerosis (idiopathic) NEC
Systemic fibrosclerosing syndrome

710.9 Unspecified diffuse connective tissue disease
Collagen disease NOS

⑤ **711 Arthropathy associated with infections**
Includes:
arthritis
arthropathy
polyarthritis
polyarthropathy
} associated with conditions classifiable below

Excludes: *rheumatic fever (390)*

The following fifth-digit subclassification is for use with category 711; valid digits are in [brackets] under each code. For definitions, see the beginning of this chapter:

0 site unspecified

1 shoulder region

2 upper arm

3 forearm

4 hand

5 pelvic region and thigh

6 lower leg

7 ankle and foot

8 other specified sites

9 multiple sites

⑤ **711.0 Pyogenic arthritis**
[0-9]   Arthritis or polyarthritis (due to):
coliform [Escherichia coli]
Hemophilus influenzae [H. influenzae]
pneumococcal
Pseudomonas
staphylococcal
streptococcal
Pyarthrosis

Use additional code, if desired, to identify infectious organism (041.0-041.8)

⑤ **711.1 *Arthropathy associated with Reiter's disease and nonspecific urethritis***
[0-9]   *Code first underlying disease, as:*
nonspecific urethritis (099.4)
Reiter's disease (099.3)

⑤ **711.2 *Arthropathy in Behçet's syndrome***
[0-9]   *Code first underlying disease (136.1)*

⑤ **711.3 *Postdysenteric arthropathy***
[0-9]   *Code first underlying disease, as:*
dysentery (009.0)
enteritis, infectious (008.0-009.3)
paratyphoid fever (002.1-002.9)
typhoid fever (002.0)

Excludes: *salmonella arthritis (003.23)*

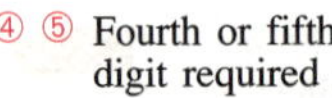

● Code new   ▲ Revision of   ④ ⑤ Fourth or fifth
  to this edition   existing code   digit required

⑤ **711.4** *Arthropathy associated with other bacterial diseases*
[0-9]   *Code first underlying disease, as:*
      diseases classifiable to 010-040, 090-099, except as in 711.1, 711.3, and 713.5
      leprosy (030.0-030.9)
      tuberculosis (015.0-015.9)

Excludes: *gonococcal arthritis (098.50)*
            meningococcal arthritis (036.82)

⑤ **711.5** *Arthropathy associated with other viral diseases*
[0-9]   *Code first underlying disease, as:*
      diseases classifiable to 045-049, 050-079, 480, 487
      O'nyong nyong (066.3)

Excludes: *that due to rubella (056.71)*

⑤ **711.6** *Arthropathy associated with mycoses*
[0-9]   *Code first underlying disease (110.0-118)*

⑤ **711.7** *Arthropathy associated with helminthiasis*
[0-9]   *Code first underlying disease, as:*
      filariasis (125.0-125.9)

⑤ **711.8** *Arthropathy associated with other infectious and parasitic diseases*
[0-9]   *Code first underlying disease, as:*
      diseases classifiable to 080-088, 100-104, 130-136

Excludes: *arthropathy associated with sarcoidosis (713.7)*

⑤ **711.9** **Unspecified infective arthritis**
[0-9]   Infective arthritis or polyarthritis (acute) (chronic) (subacute) NOS

⑤ **712** **Crystal arthropathies**
      Includes: crystal-induced arthritis and synovitis

Excludes: *gouty arthropathy (274.0)*

The following fifth-digit subclassification is for use with category 712; valid digits are in
      [brackets] under each code. See beginning of this chapter for definitions:

0   **site unspecified**
1   **shoulder region**
2   **upper arm**
3   **forearm**
4   **hand**
5   **pelvic region and thigh**
6   **lower leg**
7   **ankle and foot**
8   **other specified sites**
9   **multiple sites**

⑤ **712.1** *Chondrocalcinosis due to dicalcium phosphate crystals*
[0-9]   Chondrocalcinosis due to dicalcium phosphate crystals (with other crystals)
      Code first underlying disease (275.4)

⑤ **712.2** *Chondrocalcinosis due to pyrophosphate crystals*
[0-9]   *Code first underlying disease (275.4)*

⑤ **712.3** *Chondrocalcinosis, unspecified*
[0-9]   *Code first underlying disease (275.4)*

⑤ **712.8** **Other specified crystal arthropathies**
[0-9]

⑤ **712.9** **Unspecified crystal arthropathy**
[0-9]

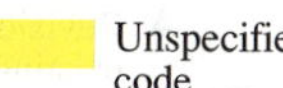

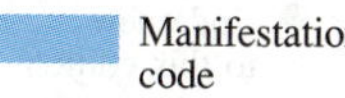

713 **Arthropathy associated with other disorders classified elsewhere**
    Includes:

        arthritis
        arthropathy
        polyarthritis } associated with conditions classifiable below
        polyarthropathy

713.0 *Arthropathy associated with other endocrine and metabolic disorders*
    Code first underlying disease, as:
        acromegaly (253.0)
        hemochromatosis (275.0)
        hyperparathyroidism (252.0)
        hypogammaglobulinemia (279.00-279.09)
        hypothyroidism (243-244.9)
        lipoid metabolism disorder (272.0-272.9)
        ochronosis (270.2)

    Excludes: *arthropathy associated with:*
        amyloidosis (713.7)
        crystal deposition disorders, except gout (712.1-712.9)
        diabetic neuropathy (713.5)
        gouty arthropathy (274.0)

713.1 *Arthropathy associated with gastrointestinal conditions other than infections*
    Code first underlying disease, as:
        regional enteritis (555.0-555.9)
        ulcerative colitis (556)

713.2 *Arthropathy associated with hematological disorders*
    Code first underlying disease, as:
        hemoglobinopathy (282.4-282.7)
        hemophilia (286.0-286.2)
        leukemia (204.0-208.9)
        malignant reticulosis (202.3)
        multiple myelomatosis (203.0)

    Excludes: *arthropathy associated with Henoch-Schönlein purpura (713.6)*

713.3 *Arthropathy associated with dermatological disorders*
    Code first underlying disease, as:
        erythema multiforme (695.1)
        erythema nodosum (695.2)

    Excludes: *psoriatic arthropathy (696.0)*

713.4 *Arthropathy associated with respiratory disorders*
    Code first underlying disease, as:
        diseases classifiable to 490-519

    Excludes: *arthropathy associated with respiratory infections (711.0, 711.4-711.8)*

713.5 *Arthropathy associated with neurological disorders*
    Charcot's arthropathy
    Neuropathic arthritis } associated with diseases classifiable elsewhere
    Code first underlying disease, as:
        neuropathic joint disease [Charcot's joints]:
            NOS (094.0)
            diabetic (250.6)
            syringomyelic (336.0)
            tabetic [syphilitic] (094.0)

713.6 *Arthropathy associated with hypersensitivity reaction*
    Code first underlying disease, as:
        Henoch (-Schönlein) purpura (287.0)
        serum sickness (999.5)

    Excludes: *allergic arthritis NOS (716.2)*

713.7 *Other general diseases with articular involvement*
    Code first underlying disease, as:
        amyloidosis (277.3)
        familial Mediterranean fever (277.3)
        sarcoidosis (135)

● Code new to this edition   ▲ Revision of existing code   ④ ⑤ Fourth or fifth digit required

713.8 *Arthropathy associated with other conditions classifiable elsewhere*
Code first underlying disease, as:
conditions classifiable elsewhere except as in 711.1-711.8, 712, and 713.0-713.7

714 Rheumatoid arthritis and other inflammatory polyarthropathies

Excludes: *rheumatic fever (390)*
rheumatoid arthritis of spine NOS (720.0)

714.0 Rheumatoid arthritis
Arthritis or polyarthritis:
atrophic
rheumatic (chronic)
Use additional code, if desired, to identify manifestation, as:
myopathy (359.6)
polyneuropathy (357.1)

Excludes: *juvenile rheumatoid arthritis NOS (714.30)*

714.1 Felty's syndrome
Rheumatoid arthritis with splenoadenomegaly and leukopenia

714.2 Other rheumatoid arthritis with visceral or systemic involvement
Rheumatoid carditis

⑤ **714.3 Juvenile chronic polyarthritis**

714.30 Polyarticular juvenile rheumatoid arthritis, chronic or unspecified
Juvenile rheumatoid arthritis NOS
Still's disease

714.31 Polyarticular juvenile rheumatoid arthritis, acute

714.32 Pauciarticular juvenile rheumatoid arthritis

714.33 Monoarticular juvenile rheumatoid arthritis

714.4 Chronic postrheumatic arthropathy
Chronic rheumatoid nodular fibrositis
Jaccoud's syndrome

⑤ **714.8 Other specified inflammatory polyarthropathies**

714.81 Rheumatoid lung
Caplan's syndrome
Diffuse interstitial rheumatoid disease of lung
Fibrosing alveolitis, rheumatoid

714.89 Other

714.9 Unspecified inflammatory polyarthropathy
Inflammatory polyarthropathy or polyarthritis NOS

Excludes: *polyarthropathy NOS (716.5)*

⑤ **715 Osteoarthrosis and allied disorders**
Note: Localized, in the subcategories below, includes bilateral involvement of the same site.
Includes: arthritis or polyarthritis:
degenerative
hypertrophic
degenerative joint disease
osteoarthritis

Excludes: *Marie-Strümpell spondylitis (720.0)*
osteoarthrosis [osteoarthritis] of spine (721.0-721.9)

The following fifth-digit subclassification is for use with category 715; valid digits are in [brackets] under each code. See beginning of this chapter for definitions:

0 site unspecified

1 shoulder region

2 upper arm

3 forearm

4 hand

5 pelvic region and thigh

6 lower leg

7 ankle and foot

8 other specified sites

9 multiple sites

⑤ **715.0 Osteoarthrosis, generalized**
[0,4,9]   Degenerative joint disease, involving multiple joints
              Primary generalized hypertrophic osteoarthrosis

⑤ **715.1 Osteoarthrosis, localized, primary**
[0-8]   Localized osteoarthropathy, idiopathic

⑤ **715.2 Osteoarthrosis, localized, secondary**
[0-8]   Coxae malum senilis

⑤ **715.3 Osteoarthrosis, localized, not specified whether primary or secondary**
[0-8]   Otto's pelvis

⑤ **715.8 Osteoarthrosis involving, or with mention of more than one site, but not specified as generalized**
[0,9]

⑤ **715.9 Osteoarthrosis, unspecified whether generalized or localized**
[0-8]

⑤ **716 Other and unspecified arthropathies**

> *Excludes:* cricoarytenoid arthropathy (478.79)

The following fifth-digit subclassification is for use with category 716; valid digits are in [brackets] under each code. See beginning of this chapter for definitions:

0 **site unspecified**
1 **shoulder region**
2 **upper arm**
3 **forearm**
4 **hand**
5 **pelvic region and thigh**
6 **lower leg**
7 **ankle and foot**
8 **other specified sites**
9 **multiple sites**

⑤ **716.0 Kaschin-Beck disease**
[0-9]   Endemic polyarthritis

⑤ **716.1 Traumatic arthropathy**
[0-9]

⑤ **716.2 Allergic arthritis**
[0-9]

> *Excludes:* arthritis associated with Henoch-Schönlein purpura or serum sickness (713.6)

⑤ **716.3 Climacteric arthritis**
[0-9]   Menopausal arthritis

⑤ **716.4 Transient arthropathy**
[0-9]

> *Excludes:* palindromic rheumatism (719.3)

⑤ **716.5 Unspecified polyarthropathy or polyarthritis**
[0-9]

⑤ **716.6 Unspecified monoarthritis**
[0-8]   Coxitis

⑤ **716.8 Other specified arthropathy**
[0-9]

⑤ **716.9 Arthropathy, unspecified**
[0-9]   Arthritis ⎫
            Arthropathy ⎬ (acute) (chronic) (subacute)
            Articular rheumatism (chronic)
            Inflammation of joint NOS

● Code new to this edition   ▲ Revision of existing code   ④ ⑤ Fourth or fifth digit required

717 Internal derangement of knee

Includes:

degeneration
rupture, old } of articular cartilage or meniscus of knee
tear, old

Excludes: *acute derangement of knee (836.0-836.6)*
ankylosis (718.5)
contracture (718.4)
current injury (836.0-836.6)
deformity (736.4-736.6)
recurrent dislocation (718.3)

717.0 Old bucket handle tear of medial meniscus
Old bucket handle tear of unspecified cartilage

717.1 Derangement of anterior horn of medial meniscus

717.2 Derangement of posterior horn of medial meniscus

717.3 Other and unspecified derangement of medial meniscus
Degeneration of internal semilunar cartilage

⑤ **717.4 Derangement of lateral meniscus**

717.40 Derangement of lateral meniscus, unspecified

717.41 Bucket handle tear of lateral meniscus

717.42 Derangement of anterior horn of lateral meniscus

717.43 Derangement of posterior horn of lateral meniscus

717.49 Other

717.5 Derangement of meniscus, not elsewhere classified
Congenital discoid meniscus
Cyst of semilunar cartilage
Derangement of semilunar cartilage NOS

717.6 Loose body in knee
Joint mice, knee
Rice bodies, knee (joint)

717.7 Chondromalacia of patella
Chondromalacia patellae
Degeneration [softening] of articular cartilage of patella

⑤ **717.8 Other internal derangement of knee**

717.81 Old disruption of lateral collateral ligament

717.82 Old disruption of medial collateral ligament

717.83 Old disruption of anterior cruciate ligament

717.84 Old disruption of posterior cruciate ligament

717.85 Old disruption of other ligaments of knee
Capsular ligament of knee

717.89 Other
Old disruption of ligaments of knee NOS

717.9 Unspecified internal derangement of knee
Derangement NOS of knee

⑤ **718 Other derangement of joint**

Excludes: *current injury (830.0-848.9)*
jaw (524.6)

The following fifth-digit subclassification is for use with category 718; valid digits are in [brackets] under each code. See beginning of this chapter for definitions:

0 site unspecified

1 shoulder region

2 upper arm

3 forearm

4 hand

5 pelvic region and thigh

6 lower leg

7 ankle and foot

continued

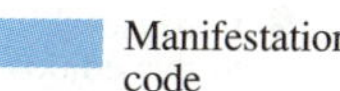

Manifestation
code

8 other specified sites

9 multiple sites

⑤ **718.0 Articular cartilage disorder**
[0-5, 7-9] Meniscus:
      disorder
      rupture, old
      tear, old
    Old rupture of ligament(s) of joint NOS

> *Excludes:* *articular cartilage disorder:*
>   *in ochronosis (270.2)*
>   *knee (717.0-717.9)*
>   *chondrocalcinosis (275.4)*
>   *metastatic calcification (275.4)*

⑤ **718.1 Loose body in joint**
[0-5, 7-9] Joint mice

> *Excludes:* *knee (717.6)*

⑤ **718.2 Pathological dislocation**
[0-9]   Dislocation or displacement of joint, not recurrent and not current injury
      Spontaneous dislocation (joint)

⑤ **718.3 Recurrent dislocation of joint**
[0-9]

⑤ **718.4 Contracture of joint**
[0-9]

⑤ **718.5 Ankylosis of joint**
[0-9]   Ankylosis of joint (fibrous) (osseous)

> *Excludes:* *spine (724.9)*
>   *stiffness of joint without mention of ankylosis (719.5)*

⑤ **718.6 Unspecified intrapelvic protrusion of acetabulum**
[0, 5]   Protrusio acetabuli, unspecified

⑤ **718.8 Other joint derangement, not elsewhere classified**
[0-9]   Flail joint (paralytic)   Instability of joint

> *Excludes:* *deformities classifiable to 736 (736.0-736.9)*

⑤ **718.9 Unspecified derangement of joint**
[0-5, 7-9]

> *Excludes:* *knee (717.9)*

⑤ **719 Other and unspecified disorders of joint**

> *Excludes:* *jaw (524.6)*

The following fifth-digit subclassification is for use with category 719; valid digits are in [brackets] under each code. See beginning of this chapter for definitions:

  0 site unspecified

  1 shoulder region

  2 upper arm

  3 forearm

  4 hand

  5 pelvic region and thigh

  6 lower leg

  7 ankle and foot

  8 other specified sites

  9 multiple sites

⑤ **719.0 Effusion of joint**
[0-9]   Hydrarthrosis
      Swelling of joint, with or without pain

> *Excludes:* *intermittent hydrarthrosis (719.3)*

● Code new to this edition   ▲ Revision of existing code   ④ ⑤ Fourth or fifth digit required

⑤ **719.1 Hemarthrosis**
[0-9]

> Excludes: current injury (840.0-848.9)

⑤ **719.2 Villonodular synovitis**
[0-9]

⑤ **719.3 Palindromic rheumatism**
[0-9] Hench-Rosenberg syndrome
Intermittent hydrarthrosis

⑤ **719.4 Pain in joint**
[0-9] Arthralgia

⑤ **719.5 Stiffness of joint, not elsewhere classified**
[0-9]

⑤ **719.6 Other symptoms referable to joint**
[0-9] Joint crepitus   Snapping hip

⑤ **719.7 Difficulty in walking**
[0, 5-9]

> Excludes: abnormality of gait (781.2)

⑤ **719.8 Other specified disorders of joint**
[0-9] Calcification of joint   Fistula of joint

> Excludes: temporomandibular joint-pain-dysfunction syndrome [Costen's syndrome] (524.6)

⑤ **719.9 Unspecified disorder of joint**
[0-9]

DORSOPATHIES (720-724)

> Excludes: curvature of spine (737.0-737.9)
> osteochondrosis of spine (juvenile) (732.0)
> adult (732.8)

720 Ankylosing spondylitis and other inflammatory spondylopathies

720.0 Ankylosing spondylitis
Rheumatoid arthritis of spine NOS
Spondylitis:
Marie-Strümpell
rheumatoid

720.1 Spinal enthesopathy
Disorder of peripheral ligamentous or muscular attachments of spine
Romanus lesion

720.2 Sacroiliitis, not elsewhere classified
Inflammation of sacroiliac joint NOS

⑤ **720.8 Other inflammatory spondylopathies**

720.81 *Inflammatory spondylopathies in diseases classified elsewhere*
Code first underlying disease, as:
tuberculosis (015.0)

720.89 Other

720.9 Unspecified inflammatory spondylopathy
Spondylitis NOS

721 Spondylosis and allied disorders

721.0 Cervical spondylosis without myelopathy
Cervical or cervicodorsal:
arthritis
osteoarthritis
spondylarthritis

721.1 Cervical spondylosis with myelopathy
Anterior spinal artery compression syndrome
Spondylogenic compression of cervical spinal cord
Vertebral artery compression syndrome

Add 4th or 5th digit	Nonspecific code	Unspecified code	Manifestation code

721.2 Thoracic spondylosis without myelopathy
Thoracic:
arthritis
osteoarthritis
spondylarthritis

721.3 Lumbosacral spondylosis without myelopathy
Lumbar or lumbosacral:
arthritis
osteoarthritis
spondylarthritis

⑤ **721.4 Thoracic or lumbar spondylosis with myelopathy**

> **721.41 Thoracic region**
> Spondylogenic compression of thoracic spinal cord

> **721.42 Lumbar region**
> Spondylogenic compression of lumbar spinal cord

721.5 Kissing spine
Baastrup's syndrome

721.6 Ankylosing vertebral hyperostosis

721.7 Traumatic spondylopathy
Kümmell's disease or spondylitis

721.8 **Other allied disorders of spine**

⑤ **721.9 Spondylosis of unspecified site**

> **721.90 Without mention of myelopathy**
> Spinal:
> arthritis (deformans) (degenerative) (hypertrophic)
> osteoarthritis NOS
> Spondylarthrosis NOS

> **721.91 With myelopathy**
> Spondylogenic compression of spinal cord NOS

722 Intervertebral disc disorders

722.0 Displacement of cervical intervertebral disc without myelopathy
Neuritis (brachial) or radiculitis due to displacement or rupture of cervical intervertebral
disc
Any condition classifiable to 722.2 of the cervical or cervicothoracic intervertebral disc

⑤ **722.1 Displacement of thoracic or lumbar intervertebral disc without myelopathy**

> **722.10 Lumbar intervertebral disc without myelopathy**
> Lumbago or sciatica due to displacement of intervertebral disc
> Neuritis or radiculitis due to displacement or rupture of lumbar intervertebral
> disc
> Any condition classifiable to 722.2 of the lumbar or lumbosacral intervertebral
> disc

> **722.11 Thoracic intervertebral disc without myelopathy**
> Any condition classifiable to 722.2 of thoracic intervertebral disc

722.2 Displacement of intervertebral disc, site unspecified, without myelopathy
Discogenic syndrome NOS
Herniation of nucleus pulposus NOS
Intervertebral disc NOS:
extrusion
prolapse
protrusion
rupture
Neuritis or radiculitis due to displacement or rupture of intervertebral disc

⑤ **722.3 Schmorl's nodes**

> **722.30 Unspecified region**

> **722.31 Thoracic region**

> **722.32 Lumbar region**

> **722.39 Other**

722.4 Degeneration of cervical intervertebral disc
Degeneration of cervicothoracic intervertebral disc

⑤ **722.5 Degeneration of thoracic or lumbar intervertebral disc**

> **722.51 Thoracic or thoracolumbar intervertebral disc**

> **722.52 Lumbar or lumbosacral intervertebral disc**

● Code new
to this edition

▲ Revision of
existing code

④ ⑤ Fourth or fifth
digit required

722.6 Degeneration of intervertebral disc, site unspecified
Degenerative disc disease NOS
Narrowing of intervertebral disc or space NOS

⑤ **722.7 Intervertebral disc disorder with myelopathy**

722.70 Unspecified region

722.71 Cervical region

722.72 Thoracic region

722.73 Lumbar region

⑤ **722.8 Postlaminectomy syndrome**

722.80 Unspecified region

722.81 Cervical region

722.82 Thoracic region

722.83 Lumbar region

⑤ **722.9 Other and unspecified disc disorder**
Calcification of intervertebral cartilage or disc
Discitis

722.90 Unspecified region

722.91 Cervical region

722.92 Thoracic region

722.93 Lumbar region

723 Other disorders of cervical region

> *Excludes:* *conditions due to:*
> *intervertebral disc disorders (722.0-722.9)*
> *spondylosis (721.0-721.9)*

723.0 Spinal stenosis in cervical region

723.1 Cervicalgia
Pain in neck

723.2 Cervicocranial syndrome
Barré-Liéou syndrome
Posterior cervical sympathetic syndrome

723.3 Cervicobrachial syndrome (diffuse)

723.4 Brachial neuritis or radiculitis NOS
Cervical radiculitis
Radicular syndrome of upper limbs

723.5 Torticollis, unspecified
Contracture of neck

> *Excludes:* *congenital (754.1)*
> *due to birth injury (767.8)*
> *hysterical (300.11)*
> *psychogenic (306.0)*
> *spasmodic (333.83)*
> *traumatic, current (847.0)*

723.6 Panniculitis specified as affecting neck

723.7 Ossification of posterior longitudinal ligament in cervical region

723.8 Other syndromes affecting cervical region
Cervical syndrome NEC
Klippel's disease
Occipital neuralgia

723.9 Unspecified musculoskeletal disorders and symptoms referable to neck
Cervical (region) disorder NOS

724 Other and unspecified disorders of back

> *Excludes:* *collapsed vertebra (code to cause, e.g., osteoporosis, 733.00-733.09)*
> *conditions due to:*
> *intervertebral disc disorders (722.0-722.9)*
> *spondylosis (721.0-721.9)*

⑤ **724.0 Spinal stenosis, other than cervical**

724.00 Spinal stenosis, unspecified region

724.01 Thoracic region

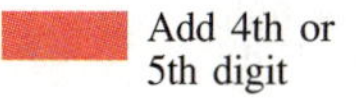

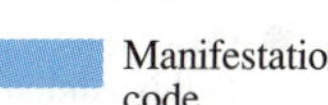

724.02 Lumbar region

724.09 Other

724.1 Pain in thoracic spine

724.2 Lumbago
Low back pain Lumbalgia
Low back syndrome

724.3 Sciatica
Neuralgia or neuritis of sciatic nerve

Excludes: specified lesion of sciatic nerve (355.0)

724.4 Thoracic or lumbosacral neuritis or radiculitis, unspecified
Radicular syndrome of lower limbs

724.5 Backache, unspecified
Vertebrogenic (pain) syndrome NOS

724.6 Disorders of sacrum
Ankylosis
Instability } lumbosacral or sacroiliac (joint)

⑤ **724.7 Disorders of coccyx**

724.70 Unspecified disorder of coccyx

724.71 Hypermobility of coccyx

724.79 Other
Coccygodynia

724.8 Other symptoms referable to back
Ossification of posterior longitudinal ligament NOS
Panniculitis specified as sacral or affecting back

724.9 Other unspecified back disorders
Ankylosis of spine NOS
Compression of spinal nerve root NEC
Spinal disorder NOS

Excludes: sacroiliitis (720.2)

RHEUMATISM, EXCLUDING THE BACK (725-729)

Includes: disorders of muscles and tendons and their attachments, and of other soft tissues

725 Polymyalgia rheumatica

726 Peripheral enthesopathies and allied syndromes
Note: Enthesopathies are disorders of peripheral ligamentous or muscular attachments.

Excludes: spinal enthesopathy (720.1)

726.0 Adhesive capsulitis of shoulder

⑤ **726.1 Rotator cuff syndrome of shoulder and allied disorders**

726.10 Disorders of bursae and tendons in shoulder region, unspecified
Rotator cuff syndrome NOS
Supraspinatus syndrome NOS

726.11 Calcifying tendinitis of shoulder

726.12 Bicipital tenosynovitis

726.19 Other specified disorders

Excludes: complete rupture of rotator cuff, nontraumatic (727.61)

726.2 Other affections of shoulder region, not elsewhere classified
Periarthritis of shoulder
Scapulohumeral fibrositis

⑤ **726.3 Enthesopathy of elbow region**

726.30 Enthesopathy of elbow, unspecified

726.31 Medial epicondylitis

726.32 Lateral epicondylitis
Epicondylitis NOS Tennis elbow
Golfers' elbow

726.33 Olecranon bursitis
Bursitis of elbow

726.39 Other

● Code new
to this edition

▲ Revision of
existing code

④ ⑤ Fourth or fifth
digit required

726.4 Enthesopathy of wrist and carpus
Bursitis of hand or wrist
Periarthritis of wrist

726.5 Enthesopathy of hip region
Bursitis of hip
Gluteal tendinitis
Iliac crest spur
Psoas tendinitis
Trochanteric tendinitis

⑤ **726.6 Enthesopathy of knee**

726.60 Enthesopathy of knee, unspecified
Bursitis of knee NOS

726.61 Pes anserinus tendinitis or bursitis

726.62 Tibial collateral ligament bursitis
Pellegrini-Stieda syndrome

726.63 Fibular collateral ligament bursitis

726.64 Patellar tendinitis

726.65 Prepatellar bursitis

726.69 Other
Bursitis:
infrapatellar
subpatellar

⑤ **726.7 Enthesopathy of ankle and tarsus**

726.70 Enthesopathy of ankle and tarsus, unspecified
Metatarsalgia NOS

Excludes:	Morton's metatarsalgia (355.6)

726.71 Achilles bursitis or tendinitis

726.72 Tibialis tendinitis
Tibialis (anterior) (posterior) tendinitis

726.73 Calcaneal spur

726.79 Other
Peroneal tendinitis

726.8 Other peripheral enthesopathies

⑤ **726.9 Unspecified enthesopathy**

726.90 Enthesopathy of unspecified site
Capsulitis NOS   Tendinitis NOS
Periarthritis NOS

726.91 Exostosis of unspecified site
Bone spur NOS

727 Other disorders of synovium, tendon, and bursa

⑤ **727.0 Synovitis and tenosynovitis**

727.00 Synovitis and tenosynovitis, unspecified
Synovitis NOS   Tenosynovitis NOS

727.01 *Synovitis and tenosynovitis in diseases classified elsewhere*
Code first underlying disease, as:
tuberculosis (015.0-015.9)

Excludes:	*crystal-induced (275.4)*
	gonococcal (098.51)
	gouty (274.0)
	syphilitic (095.7)

727.02 Giant cell tumor of tendon sheath

727.03 Trigger finger (acquired)

727.04 Radial styloid tenosynovitis
de Quervain's disease

727.05 Other tenosynovitis of hand and wrist

727.06 Tenosynovitis of foot and ankle

727.09 Other

727.1 Bunion

 Add 4th or 5th digit	Nonspecific code	Unspecified code	 Manifestation code

727.2 **Specific bursitides often of occupational origin**
    Beat: Chronic crepitant synovitis of wrist
      elbow   Miners':
      hand   elbow
      knee   knee

727.3 **Other bursitis**
    Bursitis NOS

> *Excludes:* *bursitis:*
>   *gonococcal (098.52)*
>   *subacromial (726.19)*
>   *subcoracoid (726.19)*
>   *subdeltoid (726.19)*
>   *syphilitic (095.7)*
>   *"frozen shoulder" (726.0)*

⑤ **727.4** **Ganglion and cyst of synovium, tendon, and bursa**

    727.40 **Synovial cyst, unspecified**

> *Excludes:* *that of popliteal space (727.51)*

    727.41 **Ganglion of joint**

    727.42 **Ganglion of tendon sheath**

    727.43 **Ganglion, unspecified**

    727.49 **Other**
        Cyst of bursa

⑤ **727.5** **Rupture of synovium**

    727.50 **Rupture of synovium, unspecified**

    727.51 **Synovial cyst of popliteal space**
        Baker's cyst (knee)

    727.59 **Other**

⑤ **727.6** **Rupture of tendon, nontraumatic**

    727.60 **Nontraumatic rupture of unspecified tendon**

    727.61 **Complete rupture of rotator cuff**

    727.62 **Tendons of biceps (long head)**

    727.63 **Extensor tendons of hand and wrist**

    727.64 **Flexor tendons of hand and wrist**

    727.65 **Quadriceps tendon**

    727.66 **Patellar tendon**

    727.67 **Achilles tendon**

    727.68 **Other tendons of foot and ankle**

    727.69 **Other**

⑤ **727.8** **Other disorders of synovium, tendon, and bursa**

    727.81 **Contracture of tendon (sheath)**
        Short Achilles tendon (acquired)

    727.82 **Calcium deposits in tendon and bursa**
        Calcification of tendon NOS
        Calcific tendinitis NOS

> *Excludes:* *peripheral ligamentous or muscular attachments (726.0-726.9)*

    ● **727.83** **Plica syndrome**
        Plica knee

    727.89 **Other**
        Abscess of bursa or tendon

> *Excludes:* *xanthomatosis localized to tendons (272.7)*

727.9 **Unspecified disorder of synovium, tendon, and bursa**

728 **Disorders of muscle, ligament, and fascia**

> *Excludes:* *enthesopathies (726.0-726.9)*
>   *muscular dystrophies (359.0-359.1)*
>   *myoneural disorders (358.0-358.9)*
>   *myopathies (359.2-359.9)*
>   *old disruption of ligaments of knee (717.81-717.89)*

728.0 Infective myositis
Myositis:
   purulent
   suppurative

Excludes: *myositis:*
     epidemic (074.1)
     interstitial (728.81)
     syphilitic (095.6)
     tropical (040.81)

⑤ **728.1 Muscular calcification and ossification**

  728.10 Calcification and ossification, unspecified
    Massive calcification (paraplegic)

  728.11 Progressive myositis ossificans

  728.12 Traumatic myositis ossificans
    Myositis ossificans (circumscripta)

  728.13 Postoperative heterotopic calcification

  728.19 Other
    Polymyositis ossificans

728.2 Muscular wasting and disuse atrophy, not elsewhere classified
Amyotrophia NOS   Myofibrosis

Excludes: *neuralgic amyotrophy (353.5)*
     progressive muscular atrophy (335.0-335.9)

728.3 Other specific muscle disorders
Arthrogryposis
Immobility syndrome (paraplegic)

Excludes: *arthrogryposis multiplex congenita (754.89)*
     stiff-man syndrome (333.91)

728.4 Laxity of ligament

728.5 Hypermobility syndrome

728.6 Contracture of palmar fascia
Dupuytren's contracture

⑤ **728.7 Other fibromatoses**

  728.71 Plantar fascial fibromatosis
    Contracture of plantar fascia
    Plantar fasciitis (traumatic)

  728.79 Other
    Garrod's or knuckle pads
    Nodular fasciitis
    Pseudosarcomatous fibromatosis (proliferative) (subcutaneous)

⑤ **728.8 Other disorders of muscle, ligament, and fascia**

  728.81 Interstitial myositis

  728.82 Foreign body granuloma of muscle
    Talc granuloma of muscle

  728.83 Rupture of muscle, nontraumatic

  728.84 Diastasis of muscle
    Diastasis recti (abdomen)

Excludes: *diastasis recti complicating pregnancy, labor, and delivery (665.8)*

  728.85 Spasm of muscle

  728.86 Necrotizing fasciitis
    Use additional code to identify:
     infectious organism (041.00 - 041.89)
     gangrene (785.4), if applicable

  728.89 Other
    Eosinophilic fasciitis
    Use additional E code, if desired, to identify drug, if drug induced

728.9 Unspecified disorder of muscle, ligament, and fascia

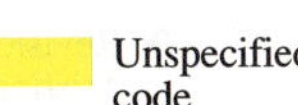

Unspecified
code

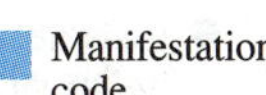

729 **Other disorders of soft tissues**

Excludes: acroparesthesia (443.89)
carpal tunnel syndrome (354.0)
disorders of the back (720.0-724.9)
entrapment syndromes (354.0-355.9)
palindromic rheumatism (719.3)
periarthritis (726.0-726.9)
psychogenic rheumatism (306.0)

729.0 **Rheumatism, unspecified and fibrositis**

729.1 **Myalgia and myositis, unspecified**
Fibromyositis NOS

729.2 **Neuralgia, neuritis, and radiculitis, unspecified**

Excludes: brachial radiculitis (723.4)
cervical radiculitis (723.4)
lumbosacral radiculitis (724.4)
mononeuritis (354.0-355.9)
radiculitis due to intervertebral disc involvement (722.0-722.2, 722.7)
sciatica (724.3)

⑤ **729.3** **Panniculitis, unspecified**

729.30 **Panniculitis, unspecified site**
Weber-Christian disease

729.31 **Hypertrophy of fat pad, knee**
Hypertrophy of infrapatellar fat pad

729.39 **Other site**

Excludes: panniculitis specified as (affecting):
back (724.8)
neck (723.6)
sacral (724.8)

729.4 **Fasciitis, unspecified**

Excludes: necrotizing fasciitis (728.86)
nodular fasciitis (728.79)

729.5 **Pain in limb**

729.6 **Residual foreign body in soft tissue**

Excludes: foreign body granuloma:
muscle (728.82)
skin and subcutaneous tissue (709.4)

⑤ **729.8** **Other musculoskeletal symptoms referable to limbs**

729.81 **Swelling of limb**

729.82 **Cramp**

729.89 **Other**

Excludes: abnormality of gait (781.2)
tetany (781.7)
transient paralysis of limb (781.4)

729.9 **Other and unspecified disorders of soft tissue**
Polyalgia

OSTEOPATHIES, CHONDROPATHIES, AND ACQUIRED MUSCULOSKELETAL DEFORMITIES (730-739)

⑤ **730** **Osteomyelitis, periostitis, and other infections involving bone**

Excludes: jaw (526.4-526.5)
petrous bone (383.2)

Use additional code, if desired, to identify organism, such as Staphylococcus (041.1)

The following fifth-digit subclassification is for use with category 730; valid digits are in [brackets] under each code. See beginning of this chapter for definitions:

0 **site unspecified**

1 **shoulder region**

2 **upper arm**

3 **forearm**

● Code new
to this edition

▲ Revision of
existing code

④ ⑤ Fourth or fifth
digit required

    4   **hand**

    5   **pelvic region and thigh**

    6   **lower leg**

    7   **ankle and foot**

    8   **other specified sites**

    9   **multiple sites**

⑤ **730.0**   **Acute osteomyelitis**
[0-9]   Abscess of any bone except accessory sinus, jaw, or mastoid
    Acute or subacute osteomyelitis, with or without mention of periostitis

⑤ **730.1**   **Chronic osteomyelitis**
[0-9]   Brodie's abscess
    Chronic or old osteomyelitis, with or without mention of periostitis
    Necrosis (acute) ⎫
    Sequestrum   ⎬ of bone
    Sclerosing osteomyelitis of Garré

    Excludes: *aseptic necrosis of bone (733.40-733.49)*

⑤ **730.2**   **Unspecified osteomyelitis**
[0-9]   Osteitis or osteomyelitis NOS, with or without mention of periostitis

⑤ **730.3**   **Periostitis without mention of osteomyelitis**
[0-9]

    Abscess of periosteum ⎫
    Periostosis   ⎬ without mention of osteomyelitis

    Excludes: *that in secondary syphilis (091.61)*

⑤ **730.7**   ***Osteopathy resulting from poliomyelitis***
[0-9]   *Code first underlying disease (045.0-045.9)*

⑤ **730.8**   ***Other infections involving bone in diseases classified elsewhere***
[0-9]   *Code first underlying disease, as:*
        tuberculosis (015.0-015.9)
        typhoid fever (002.0)

    Excludes: *syphilis of bone NOS (095.5)*

⑤ **730.9**   **Unspecified infection of bone**
[0-9]

731 **Osteitis deformans and osteopathies associated with other disorders classified elsewhere**

    731.0   **Osteitis deformans without mention of bone tumor**
        Paget's disease of bone

    731.1   ***Osteitis deformans in diseases classified elsewhere***
        Code first underlying disease, as:
            malignant neoplasm of bone (170.0-170.9)

    731.2   **Hypertrophic pulmonary osteoarthropathy**
        Bamberger-Marie disease

    731.8   ***Other bone involvement in diseases classified elsewhere***
        Code first underlying disease, as:
            diabetes mellitus (250.8)
        Use additional code to specify bone condition, such as:
            acute osteomyelitis (730.00-730.09)

732 **Osteochondropathies**

    732.0   **Juvenile osteochondrosis of spine**
        Juvenile osteochondrosis (of):
            marginal or vertebral epiphysis (of Scheuermann)
            spine NOS
        Vertebral epiphysitis

    Excludes: *adolescent postural kyphosis (737.0)*

    732.1   **Juvenile osteochondrosis of hip and pelvis**
        Coxa plana
        Ischiopubic synchondrosis (of van Neck)
        Osteochondrosis (juvenile) of:
            acetabulum
            head of femur (of Legg-Calvé-Perthes)
            iliac crest (of Buchanan)
            symphysis pubis (of Pierson)
        Pseudocoxalgia

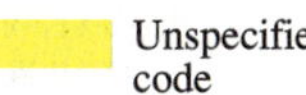

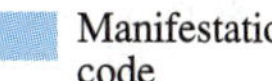

Manifestation
code

732.2 Nontraumatic slipped upper femoral epiphysis
Slipped upper femoral epiphysis NOS

732.3 Juvenile osteochondrosis of upper extremity
Osteochondrosis (juvenile) of:
capitulum of humerus (of Panner)
carpal lunate (of Kienbock)
hand NOS
head of humerus (of Haas)
heads of metacarpals (of Mauclaire)
lower ulna (of Burns)
radial head (of Brailsford)
upper extremity NOS

732.4 Juvenile osteochondrosis of lower extremity, excluding foot
Osteochondrosis (juvenile) of:
lower extremity NOS
primary patellar center (of Köhler)
proximal tibia (of Blount)
secondary patellar center (of Sinding-Larsen)
tibial tubercle (of Osgood-Schlatter)
Tibia vara

732.5 Juvenile osteochondrosis of foot
Calcaneal apophysitis
Epiphysitis, os calcis
Osteochondrosis (juvenile) of:
astragalus (of Diaz)
calcaneum (of Sever)
foot NOS
metatarsal
second (of Freiberg)
fifth (of Iselin)
os tibiale externum (Haglund)
tarsal navicular (of Köhler)

732.6 Other juvenile osteochondrosis
Apophysitis
Epiphysitis
Osteochondritis } specified as juvenile, of other site, or site NOS
Osteochondrosis

732.7 Osteochondritis dissecans

732.8 Other specified forms of osteochondropathy
Adult osteochondrosis of spine

732.9 Unspecified osteochondropathy
Apophysitis
Epiphysitis   NOS
Osteochondritis } Not specified as adult or juvenile, of unspecified site
Osteochondrosis

733 Other disorders of bone and cartilage

Excludes: *bone spur (726.91)*
cartilage of, or loose body in, joint (717.0-717.9, 718.0-718.9)
giant cell granuloma of jaw (526.3)
osteitis fibrosa cystica generalisata (252.0)
osteomalacia (268.2)
polyostotic fibrous dysplasia of bone (756.54)
prognathism, retrognathism (524.1)
xanthomatosis localized to bone (272.7)

⑤ **733.0 Osteoporosis**

733.00 Osteoporosis, unspecified
Wedging of vertebra NOS

733.01 Senile osteoporosis
Postmenopausal osteoporosis

733.02 Idiopathic osteoporosis

733.03 Disuse osteoporosis

733.09 Other
Drug-induced osteoporosis
Use additional E code, if desired, to identify drug

● Code new   ▲ Revision of   ④ ⑤ Fourth or fifth
to this edition   existing code   digit required

⑤ **733.1 Pathologic fracture**
Spontaneous fracture

Excludes: *traumatic fracture (800-829)*

733.10 Pathologic fracture, unspecified site

733.11 Pathologic fracture of humerus

733.12 Pathologic fracture of distal radius and ulna
Wrist NOS

733.13 Pathologic fracture of vertebrae
Collapse of vertebra NOS

733.14 Pathologic fracture of neck of femur
Femur NOS
Hip NOS

733.15 Pathologic fracture of other specified part of femur

733.16 Pathologic fracture of tibia or fibula
Ankle NOS

733.19 Pathologic fracture of other specified site

⑤ **733.2 Cyst of bone**

733.20 Cyst of bone (localized), unspecified

733.21 Solitary bone cyst
Unicameral bone cyst

733.22 Aneurysmal bone cyst

733.29 Other
Fibrous dysplasia (monostotic)

Excludes: *cyst of jaw (526.0-526.2, 526.89)*
osteitis fibrosa cystica (252.0)
polyostotic fibrous dysplasia of bone (756.54)

733.3 Hyperostosis of skull
Hyperostosis interna frontalis
Leontiasis ossium

⑤ **733.4 Aseptic necrosis of bone**

Excludes: *necrosis of bone NOS (730.1)*
osteochondropathies (732.0-732.9)

733.40 Aseptic necrosis of bone, site unspecified

733.41 Head of humerus

733.42 Head and neck of femur
Femur NOS

Excludes: *Legg-Calvé-Perthes disease (732.1)*

733.43 Medial femoral condyle

733.44 Talus

733.49 Other

733.5 Osteitis condensans
Piriform sclerosis of ilium

733.6 Tietze's disease
Costochondral junction syndrome
Costochondritis

733.7 Algoneurodystrophy
Disuse atrophy of bone   Sudeck's atrophy

⑤ **733.8 Malunion and nonunion of fracture**

733.81 Malunion of fracture

733.82 Nonunion of fracture
Pseudoarthrosis (bone)

⑤ **733.9 Other and unspecified disorders of bone and cartilage**

733.90 Disorder of bone and cartilage, unspecified

733.91 Arrest of bone development or growth
Epiphyseal arrest

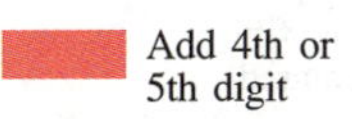 Add 4th or 5th digit
 Nonspecific code
Unspecified code
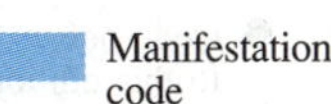 Manifestation code

733.92 Chondromalacia
Chondromalacia:
NOS
localized, except patella
systemic
tibial plateau

Excludes: *chondromalacia of patella (717.7)*

733.99 Other
Diaphysitis   Relapsing polychondritis
Hypertrophy of bone

734 Flat foot
Pes planus (acquired)
Talipes planus (acquired)

Excludes: *congenital (754.61)*
rigid flat foot (754.61)
spastic (everted) flat foot (754.61)

735 Acquired deformities of toe

Excludes: *congenital (754.60-754.69, 755.65-755.66)*

735.0 Hallux valgus (acquired)

735.1 Hallux varus (acquired)

735.2 Hallux rigidus

735.3 Hallux malleus

735.4 Other hammer toe (acquired)

735.5 Claw toe (acquired)

735.8 Other acquired deformities of toe

735.9 Unspecified acquired deformity of toe

736 Other acquired deformities of limbs

Excludes: *congenital (754.3-755.9)*

⑤ **736.0 Acquired deformities of forearm, excluding fingers**

736.00 Unspecified deformity
Deformity of elbow, forearm, hand, or wrist (acquired) NOS

736.01 Cubitus valgus (acquired)

736.02 Cubitus varus (acquired)

736.03 Valgus deformity of wrist (acquired)

736.04 Varus deformity of wrist (acquired)

736.05 Wrist drop (acquired)

736.06 Claw hand (acquired)

736.07 Club hand, acquired

736.09 Other

736.1 Mallet finger

⑤ **736.2 Other acquired deformities of finger**

736.20 Unspecified deformity
Deformity of finger (acquired) NOS

736.21 Boutonniere deformity

736.22 Swan-neck deformity

736.29 Other

Excludes: *trigger finger (727.03)*

⑤ **736.3 Acquired deformities of hip**

736.30 Unspecified deformity
Deformity of hip (acquired) NOS

736.31 Coxa valga (acquired)

736.32 Coxa vara (acquired)

736.39 Other

⑤ **736.4 Genu valgum or varum (acquired)**

736.41 Genu valgum (acquired)

● Code new
to this edition

▲ Revision of
existing code

④ ⑤ Fourth or fifth
digit required

736.42 Genu varum (acquired)

736.5 Genu recurvatum (acquired)

736.6 Other acquired deformities of knee
Deformity of knee (acquired) NOS

⑤ **736.7 Other acquired deformities of ankle and foot**

Excludes: deformities of toe (acquired) (735.0-735.9)
pes planus (acquired) (734)

736.70 Unspecified deformity of ankle and foot, acquired

736.71 Acquired equinovarus deformity
Clubfoot, acquired

Excludes: clubfoot not specified as acquired (754.5-754.7)

736.72 Equinus deformity of foot, acquired

736.73 Cavus deformity of foot

Excludes: that with claw foot (736.74)

736.74 Claw foot, acquired

736.75 Cavovarus deformity of foot, acquired

736.76 Other calcaneus deformity

736.79 Other
Acquired:
pes
talipes } not elsewhere classified

⑤ **736.8 Acquired deformities of other parts of limbs**

736.81 Unequal leg length (acquired)

736.89 Other
Deformity (acquired):
arm or leg, not elsewhere classified
shoulder

736.9 Acquired deformity of limb, site unspecified

737 Curvature of spine

Excludes: congenital (754.2)

737.0 Adolescent postural kyphosis

Excludes: osteochondrosis of spine (juvenile) (732.0)
adult (732.8)

⑤ **737.1 Kyphosis (acquired)**

737.10 Kyphosis (acquired) (postural)

737.11 Kyphosis due to radiation

737.12 Kyphosis, postlaminectomy

737.19 Other

Excludes: that associated with conditions classifiable elsewhere (737.41)

⑤ **737.2 Lordosis (acquired)**

737.20 Lordosis (acquired) (postural)

737.21 Lordosis, postlaminectomy

737.22 Other postsurgical lordosis

737.29 Other

Excludes: that associated with conditions classifiable elsewhere (737.42)

⑤ **737.3 Kyphoscoliosis and scoliosis**

737.30 Scoliosis [and kyphoscoliosis], idiopathic

737.31 Resolving infantile idiopathic scoliosis

737.32 Progressive infantile idiopathic scoliosis

737.33 Scoliosis due to radiation

737.34 Thoracogenic scoliosis

Add 4th or 5th digit	Nonspecific code	Unspecified code	Manifestation code

737.39 Other

Excludes: *that associated with conditions classifiable elsewhere (737.43)*
that in kyphoscoliotic heart disease (416.1)

⑤ **737.4 *Curvature of spine associated with other conditions***
Code first associated condition, as:
Charcot-Marie-Tooth disease (356.1)
mucopolysaccharidosis (277.5)
neurofibromatosis (237.7)
osteitis deformans (731.0)
osteitis fibrosa cystica (252.0)
osteoporosis (733.00-733.09)
poliomyelitis (138)
tuberculosis [Pott's curvature] (015.0)

737.40 *Curvature of spine, unspecified*

737.41 *Kyphosis*

737.42 *Lordosis*

737.43 *Scoliosis*

737.8 Other curvatures of spine

737.9 Unspecified curvature of spine
Curvature of spine (acquired) (idiopathic) NOS
Hunchback, acquired

Excludes: *deformity of spine NOS (738.5)*

738 Other acquired deformity

Excludes: *congenital (754.0-756.9, 758.0-759.9)*
dentofacial anomalies (524.0-524.9)

738.0 Acquired deformity of nose
Deformity of nose (acquired)
Overdevelopment of nasal bones

Excludes: *deflected or deviated nasal septum (470)*

⑤ **738.1 Other acquired deformity of head**

738.10 Unspecified deformity

738.11 Zygomatic hyperplasia

738.12 Zygomatic hypoplasia

738.19 Other specified deformity

738.2 Acquired deformity of neck

738.3 Acquired deformity of chest and rib
Deformity: Pectus:
chest (acquired)   carinatum, acquired
rib (acquired)   excavatum, acquired

738.4 Acquired spondylolisthesis
Degenerative spondylolisthesis
Spondylolysis, acquired

Excludes: *congenital (756.12)*

738.5 Other acquired deformity of back or spine
Deformity of spine NOS

Excludes: *curvature of spine (737.0-737.9)*

738.6 Acquired deformity of pelvis
Pelvic obliquity

Excludes: *intrapelvic protrusion of acetabulum (718.6)*
that in relation to labor and delivery (653.0-653.4, 653.8-653.9)

738.7 Cauliflower ear

738.8 Acquired deformity of other specified site
Deformity of clavicle

738.9 Acquired deformity of unspecified site

● Code new
to this edition   ▲ Revision of
existing code   ④ ⑤ Fourth or fifth
digit required

739 **Nonallopathic lesions, not elsewhere classified**
Includes: segmental dysfunction
somatic dysfunction

739.0 Head region
Occipitocervical region

739.1 Cervical region
Cervicothoracic region

739.2 Thoracic region
Thoracolumbar region

739.3 Lumbar region
Lumbosacral region

739.4 Sacral region
Sacrococcygeal region   Sacroiliac region

739.5 Pelvic region
Hip region   Pubic region

739.6 Lower extremities

739.7 Upper extremities
Acromioclavicular region   Sternoclavicular region

739.8 Rib cage
Costochondral region   Sternochondral region
Costovertebral region

739.9 Abdomen and other

Add 4th or   Nonspecific   Unspecified   Manifestation
5th digit   code   code   code

● Code new
to this edition

▲ Revision of
existing code

④ ⑤ Fourth or fifth
digit required

14. CONGENITAL ANOMALIES (740-759)

740 Anencephalus and similar anomalies

740.0 Anencephalus

Acrania	Hemianencephaly
Amyelencephalus	Hemicephaly

740.1 Craniorachischisis

740.2 Iniencephaly

⑤ 741 Spina bifida

| Excludes: | spina bifida occulta (756.17) |

The following fifth-digit subclassification is for use with category 741:

0 unspecified region

1 cervical region

2 dorsal [thoracic] region

3 lumbar region

⑤ 741.0 With hydrocephalus
Arnold-Chiari syndrome, type II
Any condition classifiable to 741.9 with any condition classifiable to 742.3
Chiari malformation, type II

⑤ 741.9 Without mention of hydrocephalus

Hydromeningocele (spinal)	Myelocystocele
Hydromyelocele	Rachischisis
Meningocele (spinal)	Spina bifida (aperta)
Meningomyelocele	Syringomyelocele
Myelocele	

742 Other congenital anomalies of nervous system

742.0 Encephalocele

Encephalocystocele	Meningocele, cerebral
Encephalomyelocele	Meningoencephalocele
Hydroencephalocele	
Hydromeningocele, cranial	

742.1 Microcephalus

Hydromicrocephaly	Micrencephaly

742.2 Reduction deformities of brain

Absence		Agyria
Agenesis	of part of brain	Arhinencephaly
Aplasia		Holoprosencephaly
Hypoplasia		Microgyria

742.3 Congenital hydrocephalus
Aqueduct of Sylvius:
  anomaly
  obstruction, congenital
  stenosis
Atresia of foramina of Magendie and Luschka
Hydrocephalus in newborn

| Excludes: | hydrocephalus: |

    acquired (331.3-331.4)
    due to congenital toxoplasmosis (771.2)
    with any condition classifiable to 741.9 (741.0)

742.4 Other specified anomalies of brain

Congenital cerebral cyst	Multiple anomalies of brain NOS
Macroencephaly	Porencephaly
Macrogyria	Ulegyria
Megalencephaly	

⑤ 742.5 Other specified anomalies of spinal cord

742.51 Diastematomyelia

742.53 Hydromyelia
Hydrorhachis

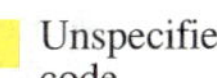

■ Add 4th or 5th digit	■ Nonspecific code	■ Unspecified code	■ Manifestation code

742.59 **Other**
Amyelia
Atelomyelia
Congenital anomaly of spinal meninges
Defective development of cauda equina
Hypoplasia of spinal cord
Myelatelia
Myelodysplasia

742.8 **Other specified anomalies of nervous system**
Agenesis of nerve
Displacement of brachial
 plexus
Familial dysautonomia
Jaw-winking syndrome
Marcus-Gunn syndrome
Riley-Day syndrome

Excludes: neurofibromatosis (237.7)

742.9 **Unspecified anomaly of brain, spinal cord, and nervous system**
Anomaly
Congenital:
 disease
 lesion
Deformity
} of {
brain
nervous system
spinal cord

743 **Congenital anomalies of eye**

⑤ **743.0** **Anophthalmos**

743.00 **Clinical anophthalmos, unspecified**
Agenesis
Congenital absence
Anophthalmos NOS
} of eye

743.03 **Cystic eyeball, congenital**

743.06 **Cryptophthalmos**

⑤ **743.1** **Microphthalmos**
Dysplasia
Hypoplasia
Rudimentary eye
} of eye

743.10 **Microphthalmos, unspecified**

743.11 **Simple microphthalmos**

743.12 **Microphthalmos associated with other anomalies of eye and adnexa**

⑤ **743.2** **Buphthalmos**
Glaucoma:
 congenital
 newborn
Hydrophthalmos

Excludes: glaucoma of childhood (365.14)
 traumatic glaucoma due to birth injury (767.8)

743.20 **Buphthalmos, unspecified**

743.21 **Simple buphthalmos**

743.22 **Buphthalmos associated with other ocular anomalies**
Keratoglobus, congenital
Megalocornea
} associated with buphthalmos

⑤ **743.3** **Congenital cataract and lens anomalies**

Excludes: infantile cataract (366.00-366.09)

743.30 **Congenital cataract, unspecified**

743.31 **Capsular and subcapsular cataract**

743.32 **Cortical and zonular cataract**

743.33 **Nuclear cataract**

743.34 **Total and subtotal cataract, congenital**

743.35 **Congenital aphakia**
Congenital absence of lens

743.36 **Anomalies of lens shape**
Microphakia
Spherophakia

743.37 **Congenital ectopic lens**

743.39 **Other**

● Code new
 to this edition
▲ Revision of
 existing code
④ ⑤ Fourth or fifth
 digit required

⑤ **743.4 Coloboma and other anomalies of anterior segment**

743.41 Anomalies of corneal size and shape
Microcornea

Excludes: *that associated with buphthalmos (743.22)*

743.42 Corneal opacities, interfering with vision, congenital

743.43 Other corneal opacities, congenital

743.44 Specified anomalies of anterior chamber, chamber angle, and related structures
Anomaly:
Axenfeld's
Peters'
Rieger's

743.45 Aniridia

743.46 Other specified anomalies of iris and ciliary body
Anisocoria, congenital
Atresia of pupil
Coloboma of iris
Corectopia

743.47 Specified anomalies of sclera

743.48 Multiple and combined anomalies of anterior segment

743.49 Other

⑤ **743.5 Congenital anomalies of posterior segment**

743.51 Vitreous anomalies
Congenital vitreous opacity

743.52 Fundus coloboma

743.53 Chorioretinal degeneration, congenital

743.54 Congenital folds and cysts of posterior segment

743.55 Congenital macular changes

743.56 Other retinal changes, congenital

743.57 Specified anomalies of optic disc
Coloboma of optic disc (congenital)

743.58 Vascular anomalies
Congenital retinal aneurysm

743.59 Other

⑤ **743.6 Congenital anomalies of eyelids, lacrimal system, and orbit**

743.61 Congenital ptosis

743.62 Congenital deformities of eyelids
Ablepharon   Congenital:
Absence of eyelid   ectropion
Accessory eyelid   entropion

743.63 Other specified congenital anomalies of eyelid
Absence, agenesis, of cilia

743.64 Specified congenital anomalies of lacrimal gland

743.65 Specified congenital anomalies of lacrimal passages
Absence, agenesis of:
lacrimal apparatus
punctum lacrimale
Accessory lacrimal canal

743.66 Specified congenital anomalies of orbit

743.69 Other
Accessory eye muscles

743.8 Other specified anomalies of eye

Excludes: *congenital nystagmus (379.51)*
ocular albinism (270.2)
retinitis pigmentosa (362.74)

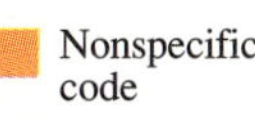

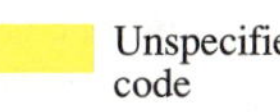

743.9 **Unspecified anomaly of eye**
Congenital:
anomaly NOS ⎤
deformity NOS ⎦ of eye [any part]

744 **Congenital anomalies of ear, face, and neck**

Excludes: *anomaly of:*

cervical spine (754.2, 756.10-756.19)
larynx (748.2-748.3)
nose (748.0-748.1)
parathyroid gland (759.2)
thyroid gland (759.2)
cleft lip (749.10-749.25)

⑤ **744.0** **Anomalies of ear causing impairment of hearing**

Excludes: *congenital deafness without mention of cause (389.0-389.9)*

744.00 **Unspecified anomaly of ear with impairment of hearing**

744.01 **Absence of external ear**
Absence of:
auditory canal (external)
auricle (ear) (with stenosis or atresia of auditory canal)

744.02 **Other anomalies of external ear with impairment of hearing**
Atresia or stricture of auditory canal (external)

744.03 **Anomaly of middle ear, except ossicles**
Atresia or stricture of osseous meatus (ear)

744.04 **Anomalies of ear ossicles**
Fusion of ear ossicles

744.05 **Anomalies of inner ear**
Congenital anomaly of:
membranous labyrinth
organ of Corti

744.09 **Other**
Absence of ear, congenital

744.1 **Accessory auricle**
Accessory tragus   Supernumerary:
Polyotia   ear
Preauricular appendage   lobule

⑤ **744.2** **Other specified anomalies of ear**

Excludes: *that with impairment of hearing (744.00-744.09)*

744.21 **Absence of ear lobe, congenital**

744.22 **Macrotia**

744.23 **Microtia**

744.24 **Specified anomalies of Eustachian tube**
Absence of Eustachian tube

744.29 **Other**
Bat ear   Prominence of auricle
Darwin's tubercle   Ridge ear
Pointed ear

Excludes: *preauricular sinus (744.46)*

744.3 **Unspecified anomaly of ear**
Congenital:
anomaly NOS ⎤
deformity NOS ⎦ of ear, not elsewhere classified

⑤ **744.4** **Branchial cleft cyst or fistula; preauricular sinus**

744.41 **Branchial cleft sinus or fistula**
Branchial:
sinus (external) (internal)
vestige

744.42 **Branchial cleft cyst**

744.43 **Cervical auricle**

744.46 **Preauricular sinus or fistula**

744.47 **Preauricular cyst**

● Code new   ▲ Revision of   ④ ⑤ Fourth or fifth
to this edition   existing code   digit required

744.49 **Other**
Fistula (of):
auricle, congenital
cervicoaural

744.5 **Webbing of neck**
Pterygium colli

⑤ **744.8** **Other specified anomalies of face and neck**

744.81 **Macrocheilia**
Hypertrophy of lip, congenital

744.82 **Microcheilia**

744.83 **Macrostomia**

744.84 **Microstomia**

744.89 **Other**

Excludes: *congenital fistula of lip (750.25)*
musculoskeletal anomalies (754.0-754.1, 756.0)

744.9 **Unspecified anomalies of face and neck**
Congenital:
anomaly NOS
deformity NOS } of face [any part] or neck [any part]

745 **Bulbus cordis anomalies and anomalies of cardiac septal closure**

745.0 **Common truncus**
Absent septum
Communication (abnormal) } between aorta and pulmonary artery
Aortic septal defect
Common aortopulmonary trunk
Persistent truncus arteriosus

⑤ **745.1** **Transposition of great vessels**

745.10 **Complete transposition of great vessels**
Transposition of great vessels:
NOS
classical

745.11 **Double outlet right ventricle**
Dextratransposition of aorta
Incomplete transposition of great vessels
Origin of both great vessels from right ventricle
Taussig-Bing syndrome or defect

745.12 **Corrected transposition of great vessels**

745.19 **Other**

745.2 **Tetralogy of Fallot**
Fallot's pentalogy
Ventricular septal defect with pulmonary stenosis or atresia, dextraposition of aorta, and
hypertrophy of right ventricle

Excludes: *Fallot's triad (746.09)*

745.3 **Common ventricle**
Cor triloculare biatriatum   Single ventricle

745.4 **Ventricular septal defect**
Eisenmenger's defect or complex
Gerbode defect
Interventricular septal defect
Left ventricular-right atrial communication
Roger's disease

Excludes: *common atrioventricular canal type (745.69)*
single ventricle (745.3)

745.5 **Ostium secundum type atrial septal defect**
Defect: Patent or persistent:
atrium secundum   foramen ovale
fossa ovalis   ostium secundum
Lutembacher's syndrome

⑤ **745.6** **Endocardial cushion defects**

745.60 **Endocardial cushion defect, unspecified type**

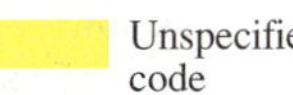

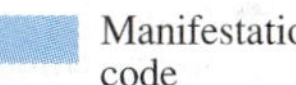

Manifestation
code

745.61 Ostium primum defect
Persistent ostium primum

745.69 Other
Absence of atrial septum
Atrioventricular canal type ventricular septal defect
Common atrioventricular canal
Common atrium

745.7 Cor biloculare
Absence of atrial and ventricular septa

745.8 Other

745.9 Unspecified defect of septal closure
Septal defect NOS

746 Other congenital anomalies of heart

    Excludes: *endocardial fibroelastosis (425.3)*

⑤ **746.0 Anomalies of pulmonary valve**

    Excludes: *infundibular or subvalvular pulmonic stenosis (746.83)*
               tetralogy of Fallot (745.2)

746.00 Pulmonary valve anomaly, unspecified

746.01 Atresia, congenital
Congenital absence of pulmonary valve

746.02 Stenosis, congenital

746.09 Other
Congenital insufficiency of pulmonary valve
Fallot's triad or trilogy

746.1 Tricuspid atresia and stenosis, congenital
Absence of tricuspid valve

746.2 Ebstein's anomaly

746.3 Congenital stenosis of aortic valve
Congenital aortic stenosis

    Excludes: *congenital:*
           subaortic stenosis (746.81)
           supravalvular aortic stenosis (747.22)

746.4 Congenital insufficiency of aortic valve
Bicuspid aortic valve
Congenital aortic insufficiency

746.5 Congenital mitral stenosis
Fused commissure
Parachute deformity   } of mitral valve
Supernumerary cusps

746.6 Congenital mitral insufficiency

746.7 Hypoplastic left heart syndrome
Atresia, or marked hypoplasia, of aortic orifice or valve, with hypoplasia of ascending
aorta and defective development of left ventricle (with mitral valve atresia)

⑤ **746.8 Other specified anomalies of heart**

746.81 Subaortic stenosis

746.82 Cor triatriatum

746.83 Infundibular pulmonic stenosis
Subvalvular pulmonic stenosis

746.84 Obstructive anomalies of heart, not elsewhere classified
Uhl's disease

746.85 Coronary artery anomaly
Anomalous origin or communication of coronary artery
Arteriovenous malformation of coronary artery
Coronary artery:
absence
arising from aorta or pulmonary trunk
single

746.86 Congenital heart block
Complete or incomplete atrioventricular [AV] block

● Code new   ▲ Revision of   ④ ⑤ Fourth or fifth
to this edition   existing code   digit required

746.87 Malposition of heart and cardiac apex
Abdominal heart   Levocardia (isolated)
Dextrocardia   Mesocardia
Ectopia cordis

Excludes: *dextrocardia with complete transposition of viscera (759.3)*

746.89 Other
Atresia
Hypoplasia } of cardiac vein
Congenital:
cardiomegaly
diverticulum, left ventricle
pericardial defect

746.9 Unspecified anomaly of heart
Congenital:
anomaly of heart NOS
heart disease NOS

747 Other congenital anomalies of circulatory system

747.0 Patent ductus arteriosus
Patent ductus Botalli
Persistent ductus arteriosus

⑤ **747.1 Coarctation of aorta**

747.10 Coarctation of aorta (preductal) (postductal)
Hypoplasia of aortic arch

747.11 Interruption of aortic arch

⑤ **747.2 Other anomalies of aorta**

747.20 Anomaly of aorta, unspecified

747.21 Anomalies of aortic arch
Anomalous origin, right subclavian artery
Dextraposition of aorta
Double aortic arch
Kommerell's diverticulum
Overriding aorta
Persistent:
convolutions, aortic arch
right aortic arch
Vascular ring

Excludes: *hypoplasia of aortic arch (747.10)*

747.22 Atresia and stenosis of aorta
Absence
Aplasia
Hypoplasia } of aorta
Stricture
Supra (valvular)-aortic stenosis

Excludes: *congenital aortic (valvular) stenosis or stricture, so stated (746.3)*
hypoplasia of aorta in hypoplastic left heart syndrome (746.7)

747.29 Other
Aneurysm of sinus of Valsalva
Congenital:
aneurysm
dilation } of aorta

747.3 Anomalies of pulmonary artery
Agenesis
Anomaly
Atresia
Coarctation } of pulmonary artery
Hypoplasia
Stenosis
Pulmonary arteriovenous aneurysm

⑤ **747.4 Anomalies of great veins**

747.40 Anomaly of great veins, unspecified
Anomaly NOS of:
pulmonary veins
vena cava

Add 4th or 5th digit	Nonspecific code	Unspecified code	Manifestation code

747.41 **Total anomalous pulmonary venous connection**
Total anomalous pulmonary venous return [TAPVR]:
  subdiaphragmatic
  supradiaphragmatic

747.42 **Partial anomalous pulmonary venous connection**
Partial anomalous pulmonary venous return

747.49 **Other anomalies of great veins**
Absence
Congenital stenosis } of vena cava (inferior) (superior)
Persistent:
  left posterior cardinal vein
  left superior vena cava
Scimitar syndrome
Transposition of pulmonary veins NOS

747.5 **Absence or hypoplasia of umbilical artery**
Single umbilical artery

⑤ **747.6** **Other anomalies of peripheral vascular system**
Absence
Anomaly } of artery or vein, not elsewhere classified
Atresia
Arteriovenous aneurysm (peripheral)
Arteriovenous malformation of the peripheral vascular system
Congenital:
  aneurysm (peripheral)
  phlebectasia
  stricture, artery
  varix
Multiple renal arteries

Excludes: *anomalies of:*
    cerebral vessels (747.81)
    pulmonary artery (747.3)
   congenital retinal aneurysm (743.58)
   hemangioma (228.00-228.09)
   lymphangioma (228.1)

747.60 **Anomaly of the peripheral vascular system, unspecified site**

747.61 **Gastrointestinal vessel anomaly**

747.62 **Renal vessel anomaly**

747.63 **Upper limb vessel anomaly**

747.64 **Lower limb vessel anomaly**

747.69 **Anomalies of other specified sites of peripheral vascular system**

⑤ **747.8** **Other specified anomalies of circulatory system**

747.81 **Anomalies of cerebrovascular system**
Arteriovenous malformation of brain
Cerebral arteriovenous aneurysm, congenital
Congenital anomalies of cerebral vessels

Excludes: *ruptured cerebral (arteriovenous) aneurysm (430)*

747.82 **Spinal vessel anomaly**
Arteriovenous malformation of spinal vessel

747.89 **Other**
Aneurysm, congenital, specified site not elsewhere classified

Excludes: *congenital aneurysm:*
   coronary (746.85)
   peripheral (747.6)
   pulmonary (747.3)
   retinal (743.58)

747.9 **Unspecified anomaly of circulatory system**

748 **Congenital anomalies of respiratory system**

Excludes: *congenital defect of diaphragm (756.6)*

748.0 **Choanal atresia**
Atresia
Congenital stenosis } of nares (anterior) (posterior)

● Code new to this edition   ▲ Revision of existing code   ④ ⑤ Fourth or fifth digit required

748.1 Other anomalies of nose

Absent nose
Accessory nose
Cleft nose
Deformity of wall of nasal
  sinus

Congenital:
  deformity of nose
  notching of tip of nose
  perforation of wall of nasal sinus

Excludes: *congenital deviation of nasal septum (754.0)*

748.2 Web of larynx

Web of larynx:
  NOS
  glottic
  subglottic

748.3 Other anomalies of larynx, trachea, and bronchus

Absence or agenesis of:
  bronchus
  larynx
  trachea
Anomaly (of):
  cricoid cartilage
  epiglottis
  thyroid cartilage
  tracheal cartilage
Atresia (of):
  epiglottis
  glottis
  larynx
  trachea
Cleft thyroid, cartilage,
  congenital

Congenital:
  dilation, trachea
  stenosis:
    larynx
    trachea
  tracheocele
Diverticulum:
  bronchus
  trachea
Fissure of epiglottis
Laryngocele
Posterior cleft of cricoid cartilage (congenital)
Rudimentary tracheal bronchus
Stridor, laryngeal, congenital

748.4 Congenital cystic lung

Disease, lung:
  cystic, congenital
  polycystic, congenital

Honeycomb lung, congenital

Excludes: *acquired or unspecified cystic lung (518.89)*

748.5 Agenesis, hypoplasia, and dysplasia of lung

Absence of lung (fissures) (lobe)
Aplasia of lung
Hypoplasia of lung (lobe)
Sequestration of lung

⑤ **748.6 Other anomalies of lung**

748.60 Anomaly of lung, unspecified

748.61 Congenital bronchiectasis

748.69 Other

Accessory lung (lobe)
Azygos lobe (fissure), lung

748.8 Other specified anomalies of respiratory system

Abnormal communication between pericardial and pleural sacs
Anomaly, pleural folds
Atresia of nasopharynx
Congenital cyst of mediastinum

748.9 Unspecified anomaly of respiratory system

Anomaly of respiratory system NOS

749 Cleft palate and cleft lip

⑤ **749.0 Cleft palate**

749.00 Cleft palate, unspecified

749.01 Unilateral, complete

749.02 Unilateral, incomplete

Cleft uvula

749.03 Bilateral, complete

749.04 Bilateral, incomplete

⑤ **749.1 Cleft lip**

Cheiloschisis
Congenital fissure of lip

Harelip
Labium leporinum

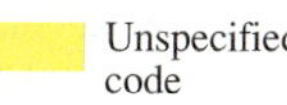

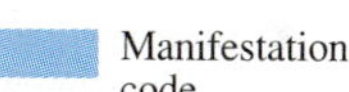

Manifestation
code

749.10 Cleft lip, unspecified

749.11 Unilateral, complete

749.12 Unilateral, incomplete

749.13 Bilateral, complete

749.14 Bilateral, incomplete

⑤ **749.2** Cleft palate with cleft lip
Cheilopalatoschisis

749.20 Cleft palate with cleft lip, unspecified

749.21 Unilateral, complete

749.22 Unilateral, incomplete

749.23 Bilateral, complete

749.24 Bilateral, incomplete

749.25 Other combinations

750 Other congenital anomalies of upper alimentary tract

Excludes: dentofacial anomalies (524.0-524.9)

750.0 Tongue tie
Ankyloglossia

⑤ **750.1** Other anomalies of tongue

750.10 Anomaly of tongue, unspecified

750.11 Aglossia

750.12 Congenital adhesions of tongue

750.13 Fissure of tongue
Bifid tongue   Double tongue

750.15 Macroglossia
Congenital hypertrophy of tongue

750.16 Microglossia
Hypoplasia of tongue

750.19 Other

⑤ **750.2** Other specified anomalies of mouth and pharynx

750.21 Absence of salivary gland

750.22 Accessory salivary gland

750.23 Atresia, salivary duct
Imperforate salivary duct

750.24 Congenital fistula of salivary gland

750.25 Congenital fistula of lip
Congenital (mucus) lip pits

750.26 Other specified anomalies of mouth
Absence of uvula

750.27 Diverticulum of pharynx
Pharyngeal pouch

750.29 Other specified anomalies of pharynx
Imperforate pharynx

750.3 Tracheoesophageal fistula, esophageal atresia and stenosis
Absent esophagus   Congenital fistula:
Atresia of esophagus   esophagobronchial
Congenital: esophagotracheal
  esophageal ring   Imperforate esophagus
  stenosis of esophagus   Webbed esophagus
  stricture of esophagus

● Code new   ▲ Revision of   ④ ⑤ Fourth or fifth
  to this edition   existing code   digit required

750.4 Other specified anomalies of esophagus
Dilatation, congenital
Displacement, congenital
Diverticulum
Duplication } (of) esophagus
Giant
Esophageal pouch

Excludes: *congenital hiatus hernia (750.6)*

750.5 Congenital hypertrophic pyloric stenosis
Congenital or infantile:
constriction
hypertrophy
spasm } of pylorus
stenosis
stricture

750.6 Congenital hiatus hernia
Displacement of cardia through esophageal hiatus

Excludes: *congenital diaphragmatic hernia (756.6)*

750.7 Other specified anomalies of stomach
Congenital: Duplication of stomach
  cardiospasm Megalogastria
  hourglass stomach Microgastria
Displacement of stomach Transposition of stomach
Diverticulum of stomach,
  congenital

750.8 Other specified anomalies of upper alimentary tract

750.9 Unspecified anomaly of upper alimentary tract
Congenital:
anomaly NOS
deformity NOS } of upper alimentary tract [any part, except tongue]

751 Other congenital anomalies of digestive system

751.0 Meckel's diverticulum
Meckel's diverticulum (displaced) (hypertrophic)
Persistent:
omphalomesenteric duct
vitelline duct

751.1 Atresia and stenosis of small intestine
Atresia of:
duodenum
ileum
intestine NOS
Congenital:
absence
obstruction
stenosis } of small intestine or intestine NOS
stricture
Imperforate jejunum

751.2 Atresia and stenosis of large intestine, rectum, and anal canal
Absence: Congenital or infantile:
  anus (congenital)   obstruction of large intestine
  appendix, congenital   occlusion of anus
  large intestine, congenital   stricture of anus
  rectum Imperforate:
Atresia of: anus
  anus   rectum
  colon Stricture of rectum, congenital
  rectum

751.3 Hirschsprung's disease and other congenital functional disorders of colon
Aganglionosis Congenital megacolon
Congenital dilation of colon Macrocolon

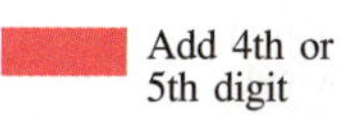

751.4 Anomalies of intestinal fixation

Congenital adhesions:
  omental, anomalous
  peritoneal
Jackson's membrane
Malrotation of colon

Rotation of cecum or colon:
  failure of
  incomplete
  insufficient
Universal mesentery

751.5 Other anomalies of intestine

Congenital diverticulum,
  colon
Dolichocolon
Duplication of:
  anus
  appendix
  cecum
  intestine
Ectopic anus

Megaloappendix
Megaloduodenum
Microcolon
Persistent cloaca
Transposition of:
  appendix
  colon
  intestine

⑤ **751.6 Anomalies of gallbladder, bile ducts, and liver**

751.60 Unspecified anomaly of gallbladder, bile ducts, and liver

751.61 Biliary atresia

Congenital:
  absence
  hypoplasia
  obstruction
  stricture
} of bile duct (common) or passage

751.62 Congenital cystic disease of liver

Congenital polycystic disease of liver
Fibrocystic disease of liver

751.69 Other anomalies of gallbladder, bile ducts, and liver

Absence of:
  gallbladder, congenital
  liver (lobe)
Accessory:
  hepatic ducts
  liver
Congenital:
  choledochal cyst
  hepatomegaly

Duplication of:
  biliary duct
  cystic duct
  gallbladder
  liver
Floating:
  gallbladder
  liver
Intrahepatic gallbladder

751.7 Anomalies of pancreas

Absence
Agenesis
Hypoplasia
} of pancreas

Accessory pancreas

Annular pancreas
Ectopic pancreatic tissue
Pancreatic heterotopia

Excludes: *diabetes mellitus:*
    congenital (250.0-250.9)
    neonatal (775.1)
  fibrocystic disease of pancreas (277.00-277.01)

751.8 Other specified anomalies of digestive system

Absence (complete) (partial) of alimentary tract NOS
Duplication
Malposition, congenital } of digestive organs NOS

Excludes: *congenital diaphragmatic hernia (756.6)*
    congenital hiatus hernia (750.6)

751.9 Unspecified anomaly of digestive system

Congenital:
  anomaly NOS
  deformity NOS } of digestive system NOS

752 Congenital anomalies of genital organs

Excludes: *syndromes associated with anomalies in the number and form of chromosomes*
    (758.0-758.9)
    testicular feminization syndrome (257.8)

● Code new
  to this edition

▲ Revision of
  existing code

④ ⑤ Fourth or fifth
  digit required

752.0 Anomalies of ovaries
Absence, congenital
Accessory
Ectopic
Streak
} (of) ovary

⑤ **752.1 Anomalies of fallopian tubes and broad ligaments**

752.10 Unspecified anomaly of fallopian tubes and broad ligaments

752.11 Embryonic cyst of fallopian tubes and broad ligaments
Cyst: Cyst:
  epoophoron   Gartner's duct
  fimbrial   parovarian

752.19 Other
Absence
Accessory
Atresia
} (of) fallopian tube or broad ligament

752.2 Doubling of uterus
Didelphic uterus
Doubling of uterus [any degree] (associated with doubling of cervix and vagina)

752.3 Other anomalies of uterus
Absence, congenital
Agenesis
Aplasia
} of uterus
Bicornuate uterus
Uterus unicornis
Uterus with only one functioning horn

⑤ **752.4 Anomalies of cervix, vagina, and external female genitalia**

752.40 Unspecified anomaly of cervix, vagina, and external female genitalia

752.41 Embryonic cyst of cervix, vagina, and external female genitalia
Cyst of:
  canal of Nuck, congenital
  vagina, embryonal
  vulva, congenital

752.42 Imperforate hymen

752.49 Other anomalies of cervix, vagina, and external female genitalia
Absence
Agenesis
} of cervix, clitoris, vagina, or vulva
Congenital stenosis or stricture of:
  cervical canal
  vagina

Excludes: double vagina associated with total duplication (752.2)

⑤ **752.5 Undescended and retractile testicle**

752.51 Undescended testis
Cryptorchism
Ectopic testis

752.52 Retractile testis

⑤ **752.6 Hypospadias and epispadias and other penile anomalies**

752.61 Hypospadias

752.62 Epispadias
Anaspadias

752.63 Congenital chordee

752.64 Micropenis

752.65 Hidden penis

752.69 Other penile anomalies

Add 4th or 5th digit	Nonspecific code	Unspecified code	Manifestation code

752.7 Indeterminate sex and pseudohermaphroditism
Gynandrism
Hermaphroditism
Ovotestis
Pseudohermaphroditism (male) (female)
Pure gonadal dysgenesis

Excludes: *pseudohermaphroditism:*

> *female, with adrenocortical disorder (255.2)*
> *male, with gonadal disorder (257.8)*
> *with specified chromosomal anomaly (758.0-758.9)*
> *testicular feminization syndrome (257.8)*

752.8 Other specified anomalies of genital organs
Absence of:
  prostate
  spermatic cord
  vas deferens
Anorchism
Aplasia (congenital) of:
  prostate
  round ligament
  testicle
Atresia of:
  ejaculatory duct
  vas deferens
Fusion of testes
Hypoplasia of testis
Monorchism
Polyorchism

Excludes: *congenital hydrocele (778.6)*

> *penile anomalies (752.61-752.69)*
> *phimosis or paraphimosis (605)*

752.9 Unspecified anomaly of genital organs
Congenital:
  anomaly NOS
  deformity NOS } of genital organ, not elsewhere classified

753 Congenital anomalies of urinary system

753.0 *Renal agenesis and dysgenesis*
Atrophy of kidney:
  congenital
  infantile
Congenital absence of kidney(s)
Hypoplasia of kidney(s)
Code first any associated vesicoureteral reflux (593.70-593.73)

⑤ **753.1 Cystic kidney disease**

Excludes: *acquired cyst of kidney (593.2)*

753.10 Cystic kidney disease, unspecified

753.11 Congenital single renal cyst

753.12 Polycystic kidney, unspecified type

753.13 Polycystic kidney, autosomal dominant

753.14 Polycystic kidney, autosomal recessive

753.15 *Renal dysplasia*
Code first any associated vesicoureteral reflux (593.70-593.73)

753.16 Medullary cystic kidney
Nephronopthisis

753.17 Medullary sponge kidney

753.19 Other specified cystic kidney disease
Multicystic kidney

⑤ **753.2 Obstructive defects of renal pelvis and ureter**

753.20 Unspecified obstructive defect of renal pelvis and ureter

753.21 Congenital obstruction of ureteropelvic junction

753.22 Congenital obstruction of ureterovesical junction
Adynamic ureter
Congenital hydroureter

753.23 Congenital ureterocele

753.29 Other

● Code new
to this edition

▲ Revision of
existing code

④ ⑤ Fourth or fifth
digit required

753.3 Other specified anomalies of kidney

Accessory kidney	Fusion of kidneys
Congenital:	Giant kidney
calculus of kidney	Horseshoe kidney
displaced kidney	Hyperplasia of kidney
Discoid kidney	Lobulation of kidney
Double kidney with double	Malrotation of kidney
pelvis	Trifid kidney (pelvis)
Ectopic kidney	

753.4 Other specified anomalies of ureter

Absent ureter	Double ureter
Accessory ureter	Ectopic ureter
Deviation of ureter	Implantation, anomalous of ureter
Displaced ureteric orifice	

753.5 Exstrophy of urinary bladder

Ectopia vesicae	Extroversion of bladder

753.6 Atresia and stenosis of urethra and bladder neck

Congenital obstruction:	Imperforate urinary meatus
bladder neck	Impervious urethra
urethra	Urethral valve formation
Congenital stricture of:	
urethra (valvular)	
urinary meatus	
vesicourethral orifice	

753.7 Anomalies of urachus

Cyst
Fistula   } (of) urachus   Persistent umbilical sinus
Patent

753.8 Other specified anomalies of bladder and urethra

Absence, congenital of:	Congenital urethrorectal fistula
bladder	Congenital prolapse of:
urethra	bladder (mucosa)
Accessory:	urethra
bladder	Double:
urethra	urethra
Congenital:	urinary meatus
diverticulum of bladder	
hernia of bladder	

753.9 Unspecified anomaly of urinary system

Congenital:
  anomaly NOS
  deformity NOS   } of urinary system [any part, except urachus]

754 Certain congenital musculoskeletal deformities

Includes: nonteratogenic deformities which are considered to be due to intrauterine malposition and pressure

754.0 Of skull, face, and jaw

Asymmetry of face	Dolichocephaly
Compression facies	Plagiocephaly
Depressions in skull	Potter's facies
Deviation of nasal	Squashed or bent nose, congenital
septum, congenital	

Excludes: dentofacial anomalies (524.0-524.9)
       syphilitic saddle nose (090.5)

754.1 Of sternocleidomastoid muscle

Congenital sternomastoid torticollis
Congenital wryneck
Contracture of sternocleidomastoid (muscle)
Sternomastoid tumor

754.2 Of spine

Congenital postural:
  lordosis
  scoliosis

⑤ **754.3 Congenital dislocation of hip**

  754.30 Congenital dislocation of hip, unilateral
    Congenital dislocation of hip NOS

  754.31 Congenital dislocation of hip, bilateral

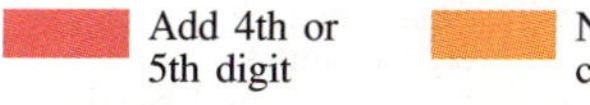

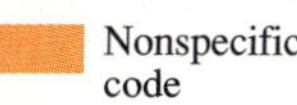

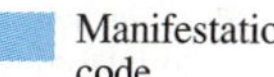

754.32 Congenital subluxation of hip, unilateral
Congenital flexion deformity, hip or thigh
Predislocation status of hip at birth
Preluxation of hip, congenital

754.33 Congenital subluxation of hip, bilateral

754.35 Congenital dislocation of one hip with subluxation of other hip

⑤ **754.4 Congenital genu recurvatum and bowing of long bones of leg**

754.40 Genu recurvatum

754.41 Congenital dislocation of knee (with genu recurvatum)

754.42 Congenital bowing of femur

754.43 Congenital bowing of tibia and fibula

754.44 Congenital bowing of unspecified long bones of leg

⑤ **754.5 Varus deformities of feet**

Excludes: *acquired (736.71, 736.75, 736.79)*

754.50 Talipes varus
Congenital varus deformity of foot, unspecified
Pes varus

754.51 Talipes equinovarus
Equinovarus (congenital)

754.52 Metatarsus primus varus

754.53 Metatarsus varus

754.59 Other
Talipes calcaneovarus

⑤ **754.6 Valgus deformities of feet**

Excludes: *valgus deformity of foot (acquired) (736.79)*

754.60 Talipes valgus
Congenital valgus deformity of foot, unspecified

754.61 Congenital pes planus
Congenital rocker bottom flat foot
Flat foot, congenital

Excludes: *pes planus (acquired) (734)*

754.62 Talipes calcaneovalgus

754.69 Other
Talipes:
equinovalgus
planovalgus

⑤ **754.7 Other deformities of feet**

Excludes: *acquired (736.70-736.79)*

754.70 Talipes, unspecified
Congenital deformity of foot NOS

754.71 Talipes cavus
Cavus foot (congenital)

754.79 Other
Asymmetric talipes
Talipes:
calcaneus
equinus

⑤ **754.8 Other specified nonteratogenic anomalies**

754.81 Pectus excavatum
Congenital funnel chest

754.82 Pectus carinatum
Congenital pigeon chest [breast]

754.89 Other
Club hand (congenital)
Congenital:
deformity of chest wall
dislocation of elbow
Generalized flexion contractures of lower limb joints, congenital
Spade-like hand (congenital)

  ● Code new
to this edition   ▲ Revision of
existing code   ④ ⑤ Fourth or fifth
digit required

755 Other congenital anomalies of limbs

> *Excludes:* those deformities classifiable to 754.0-754.8

⑤ **755.0 Polydactyly**

755.00 Polydactyly, unspecified digits
Supernumerary digits

755.01 Of fingers
Accessory fingers

755.02 Of toes
Accessory toes

⑤ **755.1 Syndactyly**
Symphalangy   Webbing of digits

755.10 Of multiple and unspecified sites

755.11 Of fingers without fusion of bone

755.12 Of fingers with fusion of bone

755.13 Of toes without fusion of bone

755.14 Of toes with fusion of bone

⑤ **755.2 Reduction deformities of upper limb**

755.20 Unspecified reduction deformity of upper limb
Ectromelia NOS ⎫
Hemimelia NOS ⎬ of upper limb
Shortening of arm, congenital

755.21 Transverse deficiency of upper limb
Amelia of upper limb
Congenital absence of:
  fingers, all (complete or partial)
  forearm, including hand and fingers
  upper limb, complete
Congenital amputation of upper limb
Transverse hemimelia of upper limb

755.22 Longitudinal deficiency of upper limb, not elsewhere classified
Phocomelia NOS of upper limb
Rudimentary arm

755.23 Longitudinal deficiency, combined, involving humerus, radius, and ulna (complete or incomplete)
Congenital absence of arm and forearm (complete or incomplete) with or
  without metacarpal deficiency and/or phalangeal deficiency, incomplete
Phocomelia, complete, of upper limb

755.24 Longitudinal deficiency, humeral, complete or partial (with or without distal deficiencies, incomplete)
Congenital absence of humerus (with or without absence of some [but not all]
  distal elements)
Proximal phocomelia of upper limb

755.25 Longitudinal deficiency, radioulnar, complete or partial (with or without distal deficiencies, incomplete)
Congenital absence of radius and ulna (with or without absence of some [but
  not all] distal elements)
Distal phocomelia of upper limb

755.26 Longitudinal deficiency, radial, complete or partial (with or without distal deficiencies, incomplete)
Agenesis of radius
Congenital absence of radius (with or without absence of some [but not all]
  distal elements)

755.27 Longitudinal deficiency, ulnar, complete or partial (with or without distal deficiencies, incomplete)
Agenesis of ulna
Congenital absence of ulna (with or without absence of some [but not all] distal
  elements)

755.28 Longitudinal deficiency, carpals or metacarpals, complete or partial (with or without incomplete phalangeal deficiency)

Add 4th or 5th digit • Nonspecific code • Unspecified code • Manifestation code

755.29 Longitudinal deficiency, phalanges, complete or partial
Absence of finger, congenital
Aphalangia of upper limb, terminal, complete or partial

Excludes: *terminal deficiency of all five digits (755.21)*
transverse deficiency of phalanges (755.21)

⑤ **755.3 Reduction deformities of lower limb**

755.30 Unspecified reduction deformity of lower limb
Ectromelia NOS ⎫
Hemimelia NOS ⎬ of lower limb
Shortening of leg, congenital

755.31 Transverse deficiency of lower limb
Amelia of lower limb
Congenital absence of:
  foot
    leg, including foot and toes
    lower limb, complete
    toes, all, complete
Transverse hemimelia of lower limb

755.32 Longitudinal deficiency of lower limb, not elsewhere classified
Phocomelia NOS of lower limb

755.33 Longitudinal deficiency, combined, involving femur, tibia, and fibula (complete or incomplete)
Congenital absence of thigh and (lower) leg (complete or incomplete) with or without metacarpal deficiency and/or phalangeal deficiency, incomplete
Phocomelia, complete, of lower limb

755.34 Longitudinal deficiency, femoral, complete or partial (with or without distal deficiencies, incomplete)
Congenital absence of femur (with or without absence of some [but not all] distal elements)
Proximal phocomelia of lower limb

755.35 Longitudinal deficiency, tibiofibular, complete or partial (with or without distal deficiencies, incomplete)
Congenital absence of tibia and fibula (with or without absence of some [but not all] distal elements)
Distal phocomelia of lower limb

755.36 Longitudinal deficiency, tibia, complete or partial (with or without distal deficiencies, incomplete)
Agenesis of tibia
Congenital absence of tibia (with or without absence of some [but not all] distal elements)

755.37 Longitudinal deficiency, fibular, complete or partial (with or without distal deficiencies, incomplete)
Agenesis of fibula
Congenital absence of fibula (with or without absence of some [but not all] distal elements)

755.38 Longitudinal deficiency, tarsals or metatarsals, complete or partial (with or without incomplete phalangeal deficiency)

755.39 Longitudinal deficiency, phalanges, complete or partial
Absence of toe, congenital
Aphalangia of lower limb, terminal, complete or partial

Excludes: *terminal deficiency of all five digits (755.31)*
transverse deficiency of phalanges (755.31)

755.4 Reduction deformities, unspecified limb
Absence, congenital (complete or partial) of limb NOS
Amelia ⎫
Ectromelia ⎬ of unspecified limb
Hemimelia ⎪
Phocomelia ⎭

⑤ **755.5 Other anomalies of upper limb, including shoulder girdle**

755.50 Unspecified anomaly of upper limb

755.51 Congenital deformity of clavicle

755.52 Congenital elevation of scapula
Sprengel's deformity

755.53 Radioulnar synostosis

● Code new
to this edition

▲ Revision of
existing code

④ ⑤ Fourth or fifth
digit required

755.54 **Madelung's deformity**

755.55 **Acrocephalosyndactyly**
Apert's syndrome

755.56 **Accessory carpal bones**

755.57 **Macrodactylia (fingers)**

755.58 **Cleft hand, congenital**
Lobster-claw hand

755.59 **Other**
Cleidocranial dysostosis
Cubitus:
  valgus, congenital
  varus, congenital

Excludes: club hand (congenital) (754.89)
congenital dislocation of elbow (754.89)

⑤ **755.6** **Other anomalies of lower limb, including pelvic girdle**

755.60 **Unspecified anomaly of lower limb**

755.61 **Coxa valga, congenital**

755.62 **Coxa vara, congenital**

755.63 **Other congenital deformity of hip (joint)**
Congenital anteversion of femur (neck)

Excludes: congenital dislocation of hip (754.30-754.35)

755.64 **Congenital deformity of knee (joint)**
Congenital:
  absence of patella
  genu valgum [knock-knee]
  genu varum [bowleg]
Rudimentary patella

755.65 **Macrodactylia of toes**

755.66 **Other anomalies of toes**
Congenital:
  hallux valgus
  hallux varus
  hammer toe

755.67 **Anomalies of foot, not elsewhere classified**
Astragaloscaphoid synostosis
Calcaneonavicular bar
Coalition of calcaneus
Talonavicular synostosis
Tarsal coalitions

755.69 **Other**
Congenital:
  angulation of tibia
  deformity (of):
    ankle (joint)
    sacroiliac (joint)
  fusion of sacroiliac joint

755.8 **Other specified anomalies of unspecified limb**

755.9 **Unspecified anomaly of unspecified limb**
Congenital:
  anomaly NOS
  deformity NOS } of unspecified limb

Excludes: reduction deformity of unspecified limb (755.4)

756 **Other congenital musculoskeletal anomalies**

Excludes: those deformities classifiable to 754.0-754.8

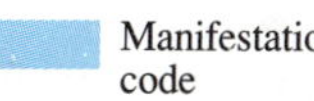

756.0 Anomalies of skull and face bones
Absence of skull bones
Acrocephaly
Congenital deformity of
  forehead
Craniosynostosis
Crouzon's disease
Hypertelorism
Imperfect fusion of skull
Oxycephaly
Platybasia
Premature closure of cranial sutures
Tower skull
Trigonocephaly

Excludes: *acrocephalosyndactyly [Apert's syndrome] (755.55)*
   dentofacial anomalies (524.0-524.9)
   skull defects associated with brain anomalies, such as:
     anencephalus (740.0)
     encephalocele (742.0)
     hydrocephalus (742.3)
     microcephalus (742.1)

⑤ **756.1 Anomalies of spine**

756.10 Anomaly of spine, unspecified

756.11 Spondylolysis, lumbosacral region
Prespondylolisthesis (lumbosacral)

756.12 Spondylolisthesis

756.13 Absence of vertebra, congenital

756.14 Hemivertebra

756.15 Fusion of spine [vertebra], congenital

756.16 Klippel-Feil syndrome

756.17 Spina bifida occulta

Excludes: *spina bifida (aperta) (741.0-741.9)*

756.19 Other
Platyspondylia
Supernumerary vertebra

756.2 Cervical rib
Supernumerary rib in the cervical region

756.3 Other anomalies of ribs and sternum
Congenital absence of:
  rib
  sternum
Congenital:
  fissure of sternum
  fusion of ribs
Sternum bifidum

Excludes: *nonteratogenic deformity of chest wall (754.81-754.89)*

756.4 Chondrodystrophy
Achondroplasia
Chondrodystrophia (fetalis)
Dyschondroplasia
Enchondromatosis
Ollier's disease

Excludes: *lipochondrodystrophy [Hurler's syndrome] (277.5)*
   Morquio's disease (277.5)

⑤ **756.5 Osteodystrophies**

756.50 Osteodystrophy, unspecified

756.51 Osteogenesis imperfecta
Fragilitas ossium
Osteopsathyrosis

756.52 Osteopetrosis

756.53 Osteopoikilosis

756.54 Polyostotic fibrous dysplasia of bone

756.55 Chondroectodermal dysplasia
Ellis-van Creveld syndrome

756.56 Multiple epiphyseal dysplasia

756.59 Other
Albright (-McCune)-Sternberg syndrome

● Code new
  to this edition

▲ Revision of
  existing code

④ ⑤ Fourth or fifth
  digit required

756.6 Anomalies of diaphragm
    Absence of diaphragm   Eventration of diaphragm
    Congenital hernia:
      diaphragmatic
      foramen of Morgagni

> Excludes: *congenital hiatus hernia (750.6)*

⑤ **756.7 Anomalies of abdominal wall**
    Omphalocele
    Exomphalos   Prune belly (syndrome)
    Gastroschisis

    756.70 Anomaly of abdominal wall, unspecified

    756.71 Prune belly syndrome
        Eagle-Barrett syndrome
        Prolapse of bladder mucosa

    756.79 Other congenital anomalies of abdominal wall
        Exomphalos
        Gastroschisis
        Omphalocele

> Excludes: *umbilical hernia (551-553 with .1)*

⑤ **756.8 Other specified anomalies of muscle, tendon, fascia, and connective tissue**

    756.81 Absence of muscle and tendon
        Absence of muscle (pectoral)

    756.82 Accessory muscle

    756.83 Ehlers-Danlos syndrome

    756.89 Other
        Amyotrophia congenita
        Congenital shortening of tendon

756.9 Other and unspecified anomalies of musculoskeletal system
    Congenital:
      anomaly NOS
      deformity NOS   } of musculoskeletal system, not elsewhere classified

757 Congenital anomalies of the integument
    Includes: anomalies of skin, subcutaneous tissue, hair, nails, and breast

> Excludes: *hemangioma (228.00-228.09)*
>
> *pigmented nevus (216.0-216.9)*

757.0 Hereditary edema of legs
    Congenital lymphedema   Milroy's disease
    Hereditary trophedema

757.1 Ichthyosis congenita
    Congenital ichthyosis
    Harlequin fetus
    Ichthyosiform erythroderma

757.2 Dermatoglyphic anomalies
    Abnormal palmar creases

⑤ **757.3 Other specified anomalies of skin**

    757.31 Congenital ectodermal dysplasia

    757.32 Vascular hamartomas
        Birthmarks
        Port-wine stain
        Strawberry nevus

    757.33 Congenital pigmentary anomalies of skin
        Congenital poikiloderma
        Urticaria pigmentosa
        Xeroderma pigmentosum

> Excludes: *albinism (270.2)*

🟥 Add 4th or 5th digit	🟧 Nonspecific code	🟨 Unspecified code	🟦 Manifestation code

757.39 Other
Accessory skin tags, congenital
Congenital scar
Epidermolysis bullosa
Keratoderma (congenital)

Excludes: pilonidal cyst (685.0-685.1)

757.4 Specified anomalies of hair

Congenital:
alopecia
atrichosis
beaded hair

Congenital:
hypertrichosis
monilethrix
Persistent lanugo

757.5 Specified anomalies of nails

Anonychia
Congenital:
clubnail
koilonychia

Congenital:
leukonychia
onychauxis
pachyonychia

757.6 Specified anomalies of breast

Absent
Accessory   } breast or nipple
Supernumerary
Hypoplasia of breast

Excludes: absence of pectoral muscle (756.81)

757.8 Other specified anomalies of the integument

757.9 Unspecified anomaly of the integument

Congenital:
anomaly NOS   } of integument
deformity NOS

758 Chromosomal anomalies
Includes: syndromes associated with anomalies in the number and form of chromosomes

758.0 Down's syndrome

Mongolism
Translocation Down's
    syndrome

Trisomy:
21 or 22
G

758.1 Patau's syndrome
Trisomy:
13
D_1

758.2 Edwards' syndrome
Trisomy:
18
E_3

758.3 Autosomal deletion syndromes
Antimongolism syndrome   Cri-du-chat syndrome

758.4 Balanced autosomal translocation in normal individual

758.5 Other conditions due to autosomal anomalies
Accessory autosomes NEC

758.6 Gonadal dysgenesis
Ovarian dysgenesis   XO syndrome
Turner's syndrome

Excludes: pure gonadal dysgenesis (752.7)

758.7 Klinefelter's syndrome
XXY syndrome

⑤ **758.8 Other conditions due to chromosome anomalies**

758.81 Other conditions due to sex chromosome anomalies

758.89 Other

758.9 Conditions due to anomaly of unspecified chromosome

759 Other and unspecified congenital anomalies

759.0 Anomalies of spleen

Aberrant   }
Absent   } spleen
Accessory   }

Congenital splenomegaly
Ectopic spleen
Lobulation of spleen

● Code new
  to this edition

▲ Revision of
  existing code

④ ⑤ Fourth or fifth
    digit required

759.1 Anomalies of adrenal gland
Aberrant
Absent   } adrenal gland
Accessory

Excludes: *adrenogenital disorders (255.2)*
congenital disorders of steroid metabolism (255.2)

759.2 Anomalies of other endocrine glands
Absent parathyroid gland
Accessory thyroid gland
Persistent thyroglossal or thyrolingual duct
Thyroglossal (duct) cyst

Excludes: *congenital:*
goiter (246.1)
hypothyroidism (243)

759.3 Situs inversus
Situs inversus or transversus: Transposition of viscera:
  abdominalis   abdominal
  thoracis   thoracic

Excludes: *dextrocardia without mention of complete transposition (746.87)*

759.4 Conjoined twins
Craniopagus   Thoracopagus
Dicephalus   Xiphopagus
Pygopagus

759.5 Tuberous sclerosis
Bourneville's disease   Epiloia

759.6 Other hamartoses, not elsewhere classified
Syndrome:
  Peutz-Jeghers
  Sturge-Weber (-Dimitri)
  von Hippel-Lindau

Excludes: *neurofibromatosis (237.7)*

759.7 Multiple congenital anomalies, so described
Congenital:
  anomaly, multiple NOS
  deformity, multiple NOS

⑤ **759.8 Other specified anomalies**

759.81 Prader-Willi syndrome

759.82 Marfan syndrome

759.83 Fragile X syndrome

759.89 Other
Congenital malformation syndromes affecting multiple systems, not elsewhere classified
Laurence-Moon-Biedl syndrome

759.9 Congenital anomaly, unspecified

Add 4th or 5th digit	Nonspecific code	Unspecified code	Manifestation code

● Code new
to this edition

▲ Revision of
existing code

④ ⑤ Fourth or fifth
digit required

15. CERTAIN CONDITIONS ORIGINATING IN THE PERINATAL PERIOD (760-779)

Includes: conditions which have their origin in the perinatal period even though death or morbidity occurs later

Use additional code(s) to further specify condition

MATERNAL CAUSES OF PERINATAL MORBIDITY AND MORTALITY (760-763)

760 Fetus or newborn affected by maternal conditions which may be unrelated to present pregnancy
Includes: the listed maternal conditions only when specified as a cause of mortality or morbidity of the fetus or newborn

Excludes: *maternal endocrine and metabolic disorders affecting fetus or newborn (775.0-775.9)*

760.0 Maternal hypertensive disorders
Fetus or newborn affected by maternal conditions classifiable to 642

760.1 Maternal renal and urinary tract diseases
Fetus or newborn affected by maternal conditions classifiable to 580-599

760.2 Maternal infections
Fetus or newborn affected by maternal infectious disease classifiable to 001-136 and 487, but fetus or newborn not manifesting that disease

Excludes: *congenital infectious diseases (771.0-771.8)*
maternal genital tract and other localized infections (760.8)

760.3 Other chronic maternal circulatory and respiratory diseases
Fetus or newborn affected by chronic maternal conditions classifiable to 390-459, 490-519, 745-748

760.4 Maternal nutritional disorders
Fetus or newborn affected by:
maternal disorders classifiable to 260-269
maternal malnutrition NOS

Excludes: *fetal malnutrition (764.10-764.29)*

760.5 Maternal injury
Fetus or newborn affected by maternal conditions classifiable to 800-995

760.6 Surgical operation on mother

Excludes: *cesarean section for present delivery (763.4)*
damage to placenta from amniocentesis, cesarean section, or surgical induction (762.1)
previous surgery to uterus or pelvic organs (763.89)

⑤ **760.7 Noxious influences affecting fetus via placenta or breast milk**
Fetus or newborn affected by noxious substance transmitted via placenta or breast milk

Excludes: *anesthetic and analgesic drugs administered during labor and delivery (763.5)*
drug withdrawal syndrome in newborn (779.5)

760.70 Unspecified noxious substance
Fetus or newborn affected by:
Drug NEC

760.71 Alcohol
Fetal alcohol syndrome

760.72 Narcotics

760.73 Hallucinogenic agents

760.74 Anti-infectives
Antibiotics

760.75 Cocaine

760.76 Diethylstilbestrol (DES)

760.79 Other
Fetus or newborn affected by:
immune sera transmitted via placenta or breast milk
medicinal agents NEC transmitted via placenta or breast milk
toxic substance NEC transmitted via placenta or breast milk

760.8 Other specified maternal conditions affecting fetus or newborn
Maternal genital tract and other localized infection affecting fetus or newborn, but fetus or newborn not manifesting that disease

Excludes: *maternal urinary tract infection affecting fetus or newborn (760.1)*

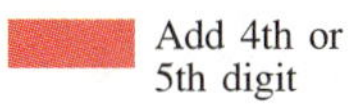
Add 4th or
5th digit

Nonspecific
code

Unspecified
code

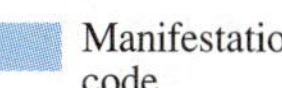
Manifestation
code

760.9 Unspecified maternal condition affecting fetus or newborn

761 Fetus or newborn affected by maternal complications of pregnancy
Includes: the listed maternal conditions only when specified as a cause of mortality or
morbidity of the fetus or newborn

761.0 Incompetent cervix

761.1 Premature rupture of membranes

761.2 Oligohydramnios

Excludes: *that due to premature rupture of membranes (761.1)*

761.3 Polyhydramnios
Hydramnios (acute) (chronic)

761.4 Ectopic pregnancy
Pregnancy:
abdominal
intraperitoneal
tubal

761.5 Multiple pregnancy
Triplet (pregnancy)   Twin (pregnancy)

761.6 Maternal death

761.7 Malpresentation before labor
Breech presentation
External version
Oblique lie   } before labor
Transverse lie
Unstable lie

761.8 Other specified maternal complications of pregnancy affecting fetus or newborn
Spontaneous abortion, fetus

761.9 Unspecified maternal complication of pregnancy affecting fetus or newborn

762 Fetus or newborn affected by complications of placenta, cord, and membranes
Includes: the listed maternal conditions only when specified as a cause of mortality or
morbidity in the fetus or newborn

762.0 Placenta previa

762.1 Other forms of placental separation and hemorrhage
Abruptio placentae
Antepartum hemorrhage
Damage to placenta from amniocentesis, cesarean section, or surgical induction
Maternal blood loss
Premature separation of placenta
Rupture of marginal sinus

762.2 Other and unspecified morphological and functional abnormalities of placenta
Placental:
dysfunction
infarction
insufficiency

762.3 Placental transfusion syndromes
Placental and cord abnormality resulting in twin-to-twin or other transplacental
transfusion

Use additional code, if desired, to indicate resultant condition in fetus or newborn:
fetal blood loss (772.0)
polycythemia neonatorum (776.4)

762.4 Prolapsed cord
Cord presentation

762.5 Other compression of umbilical cord
Cord around neck   Knot in cord
Entanglement of cord   Torsion of cord

762.6 Other and unspecified conditions of umbilical cord
Short cord
Thrombosis
Varices   } of umbilical cord
Velamentous insertion
Vasa previa

Excludes: *infection of umbilical cord (771.4)*
single umbilical artery (747.5)

● Code new   ▲ Revision of   ④ ⑤ Fourth or fifth
  to this edition   existing code   digit required

762.7 Chorioamnionitis
Amnionitis   Placentitis
Membranitis

762.8 Other specified abnormalities of chorion and amnion

762.9 Unspecified abnormality of chorion and amnion

763 Fetus or newborn affected by other complications of labor and delivery
Includes: the listed conditions only when specified as a cause of mortality or morbidity in the
fetus or newborn

763.0 Breech delivery and extraction

763.1 Other malpresentation, malposition, and disproportion during labor and delivery
Fetus or newborn affected by:
abnormality of bony pelvis
contracted pelvis
persistent occipitoposterior position
shoulder presentation
transverse lie
conditions classifiable to 652, 653, and 660

763.2 Forceps delivery
Fetus or newborn affected by forceps extraction

763.3 Delivery by vacuum extractor

763.4 Cesarean delivery

Excludes: placental separation or hemorrhage from cesarean section (762.1)

763.5 Maternal anesthesia and analgesia
Reactions and intoxications from maternal opiates and tranquilizers during labor and
delivery

Excludes: drug withdrawal syndrome in newborn (779.5)

763.6 Precipitate delivery
Rapid second stage

763.7 Abnormal uterine contractions
Fetus or newborn affected by:
contraction ring
hypertonic labor
hypotonic uterine dysfunction
uterine inertia or dysfunction
conditions classifiable to 661, except 661.3

⑤ **763.8 Other specified complications of labor and delivery affecting fetus or newborn**

763.81   Abnormality in fetal heart rate or rhythm before the onset of labor

763.82   Abnormality in fetal heart rate or rhythm during labor

763.83   Abnormality in fetal heart rate or rhythm, unspecified as to time of onset

763.89   Other specified complications of labor and delivery affecting fetus or newborn
Fetus or newborn affected by:
abnormality of maternal soft tissues
destructive operation on live fetus to facilitate delivery
induction of labor (medical)
previous surgery to uterus or pelvic organs
other conditions classifiable to 650-669
other procedures used in labor and delivery

763.9 Unspecified complication of labor and delivery affecting fetus or newborn

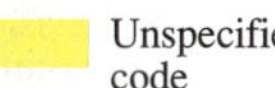

OTHER CONDITIONS ORIGINATING IN THE PERINATAL PERIOD (764-779)

The following fifth-digit subclassification is for use with categories 764-765 to denote birthweight:

0 unspecified [weight]

1 less than 500 grams

2 500-749 grams

3 750-999 grams

4 1,000- 1,249 grams

5 1,250-1,499 grams

6 1,500-1,749 grams

7 1,750-1,999 grams

8 2,000-2,499 grams

9 2,500 grams and over

⑤ **764** **Slow fetal growth and fetal malnutrition**

⑤ **764.0** **"Light-for-dates" without mention of fetal malnutrition**
Infants underweight for gestational age
"Small-for-dates"

⑤ **764.1** **"Light-for-dates" with signs of fetal malnutrition**
Infants "light-for-dates" classifiable to 764.0, who in addition show signs of fetal malnutrition, such as dry peeling skin and loss of subcutaneous tissue

⑤ **764.2** **Fetal malnutrition without mention of "light-for-dates"**
Infants, not underweight for gestational age, showing signs of fetal malnutrition, such as dry peeling skin and loss of subcutaneous tissue
Intrauterine malnutrition

⑤ **764.9** **Fetal growth retardation, unspecified**
Intrauterine growth retardation

⑤ **765** **Disorders relating to short gestation and unspecified low birthweight**
Includes: the listed conditions, without further specification, as causes of mortality, morbidity, or additional care, in fetus or newborn

⑤ **765.0** **Extreme immaturity**
Note: Usually implies a birthweight of less than 1000 grams and/or a gestation of less than 28 completed weeks.

⑤ **765.1** **Other preterm infants**
Note: Usually implies a birthweight of 1000-2499 grams and/or a gestation of 28-37 completed weeks.
Prematurity NOS
Prematurity or small size, not classifiable to 765.0 or as "light-for-dates" in 764

766 **Disorders relating to long gestation and high birthweight**
Includes: the listed conditions, without further specification, as causes of mortality, morbidity, or additional care, in fetus or newborn

766.0 **Exceptionally large baby**
Note: Usually implies a birthweight of 4500 grams or more.

766.1 **Other "heavy-for-dates" infants**
Other fetus or infant "heavy-" or "large-for-dates" regardless of period of gestation

766.2 **Post-term infant, not "heavy-for-dates"**
Fetus or infant with gestation period of 294 days or more [42 or more completed weeks], not "heavy-" or "large-for-dates"
Postmaturity NOS

767 **Birth trauma**

767.0 **Subdural and cerebral hemorrhage**
Subdural and cerebral hemorrhage, whether described as due to birth trauma or to intrapartum anoxia or hypoxia
Subdural hematoma (localized)
Tentorial tear

Use additional code, if desired, to identify cause

Excludes:	*intraventricular hemorrhage (772.1)*
	subarachnoid hemorrhage (772.2)

767.1 Injuries to scalp
Caput succedaneum
Cephalhematoma
Chignon (from vacuum extraction)
Massive epicranial subaponeurotic hemorrhage

767.2 Fracture of clavicle

767.3 Other injuries to skeleton
Fracture of:
long bones
skull

> *Excludes:* congenital dislocation of hip (754.30-754.35)
> fracture of spine, congenital (767.4)

767.4 Injury to spine and spinal cord
Dislocation
Fracture ⎫
Laceration ⎬ of spine or spinal cord due to birth trauma
Rupture ⎭

767.5 Facial nerve injury
Facial palsy

767.6 Injury to brachial plexus
Palsy or paralysis:
brachial
Erb (-Duchenne)
Klumpke (-Déjérine)

767.7 Other cranial and peripheral nerve injuries
Phrenic nerve paralysis

767.8 Other specified birth trauma
Eye damage   Rupture of:
Hematoma of: liver
liver (subcapsular)   spleen
testes   Scalpel wound
vulva   Traumatic glaucoma

> *Excludes:* hemorrhage classifiable to 772.0-772.9

767.9 Birth trauma, unspecified
Birth injury NOS

768 Intrauterine hypoxia and birth asphyxia
Use only when associated with newborn morbidity classifiable elsewhere

768.0 Fetal death from asphyxia or anoxia before onset of labor or at unspecified time

768.1 Fetal death from asphyxia or anoxia during labor

768.2 Fetal distress before onset of labor, in liveborn infant
Fetal metabolic acidemia before onset of labor, in liveborn infant

768.3 Fetal distress first noted during labor, in liveborn infant
Fetal metabolic acidemia first noted during labor, in liveborn infant

768.4 Fetal distress, unspecified as to time of onset, in liveborn infant
Fetal metabolic acidemia unspecified as to time of onset, in liveborn infant

768.5 Severe birth asphyxia
Birth asphyxia with neurologic involvement

768.6 Mild or moderate birth asphyxia
Other specified birth asphyxia (without mention of neurologic involvement)

768.9 Unspecified birth asphyxia in liveborn infant
Anoxia ⎫
Asphyxia ⎬ NOS, in liveborn infant
Hypoxia ⎭

769 Respiratory distress syndrome
Cardiorespiratory distress syndrome of newborn
Hyaline membrane disease (pulmonary)
Idiopathic respiratory distress syndrome [IRDS or RDS] of newborn
Pulmonary hypoperfusion syndrome

> *Excludes:* transient tachypnea of newborn (770.6)

Manifestation
code

770 **Other respiratory conditions of fetus and newborn**

770.0 **Congenital pneumonia**
Infective pneumonia acquired prenatally

Excludes: *pneumonia from infection acquired after birth (480.0-486)*

770.1 **Meconium aspiration syndrome**
Aspiration of contents of birth canal NOS
Meconium aspiration below vocal cords
Pneumonitis:
fetal aspiration
meconium

770.2 **Interstitial emphysema and related conditions**
Pneumomediastinum
Pneumopericardium } originating in the perinatal period
Pneumothorax

770.3 **Pulmonary hemorrhage**
Hemorrhage:
alveolar (lung)
intra-alveolar (lung) } originating in the perinatal period
massive pulmonary

770.4 **Primary atelectasis**
Pulmonary immaturity NOS

770.5 **Other and unspecified atelectasis**
Atelectasis:
NOS
partial
secondary } originating in the perinatal period
Pulmonary collapse

770.6 **Transitory tachypnea of newborn**
Idiopathic tachypnea of newborn
Wet lung syndrome

Excludes: *respiratory distress syndrome (769)*

770.7 **Chronic respiratory disease arising in the perinatal period**
Bronchopulmonary dysplasia
Interstitial pulmonary fibrosis of prematurity
Wilson-Mikity syndrome

770.8 **Other respiratory problems after birth**
Apneic spells NOS originating in the perinatal period
Cyanotic attacks NOS originating in the perinatal period
Fetal acidosis affecting newborn
Fetal anoxia affecting newborn
Fetal asphyxia affecting newborn
Fetal hypercapnia affecting newborn
Fetal hypoxia affecting newborn
Respiratory depression of newborn
Respiratory distress NOS originating in the perinatal period
Respiratory failure NOS originating in the perinatal period

770.9 **Unspecified respiratory condition of fetus and newborn**

771 **Infections specific to the perinatal period**
Includes: infections acquired before or during birth or via the umbilicus

Excludes: *congenital pneumonia (770.0)*
congenital syphilis (090.0-090.9)
maternal infectious disease as a cause of mortality or morbidity in fetus or
newborn, but fetus or newborn not manifesting the disease (760.2)
ophthalmia neonatorum due to gonococcus (098.40)
other infections not specifically classified to this category

771.0 **Congenital rubella**
Congenital rubella pneumonitis

771.1 **Congenital cytomegalovirus infection**
Congenital cytomegalic inclusion disease

● Code new
to this edition

▲ Revision of
existing code

④ ⑤ Fourth or fifth
digit required

771.2 Other congenital infections
Congenital:
  herpes simplex
  listeriosis
  malaria
Congenital:
  toxoplasmosis
  tuberculosis

771.3 Tetanus neonatorum
Tetanus omphalitis

| *Excludes:* | hypocalcemic tetany (775.4) |

771.4 Omphalitis of the newborn
Infection:
  navel cord
  umbilical stump

| *Excludes:* | tetanus omphalitis (771.3) |

771.5 Neonatal infective mastitis

| *Excludes:* | noninfective neonatal mastitis (778.7) |

771.6 Neonatal conjunctivitis and dacryocystitis
Ophthalmia neonatorum NOS

| *Excludes:* | ophthalmia neonatorum due to gonococcus (098.40) |

771.7 Neonatal Candida infection
Neonatal moniliasis
Thrush in newborn

771.8 Other infection specific to the perinatal period
Intra-amniotic infection of fetus:
  NOS
  clostridial
  Escherichia coli [E. coli]
Intrauterine sepsis of fetus
Neonatal urinary tract infection
Septicemia [sepsis] of newborn

772 Fetal and neonatal hemorrhage

| *Excludes:* | hematological disorders of fetus and newborn (776.0-776.9) |

772.0 Fetal blood loss
Fetal blood loss from:
  cut end of co-twin's cord
  placenta
  ruptured cord
  vasa previa
Fetal exsanguination
Fetal hemorrhage into:
  co-twin
  mother's circulation

772.1 Intraventricular hemorrhage
Intraventricular hemorrhage from any perinatal cause

772.2 Subarachnoid hemorrhage
Subarachnoid hemorrhage from any perinatal cause

| *Excludes:* | subdural and cerebral hemorrhage (767.0) |

772.3 Umbilical hemorrhage after birth
Slipped umbilical ligature

772.4 Gastrointestinal hemorrhage

| *Excludes:* | swallowed maternal blood (777.3) |

772.5 Adrenal hemorrhage

772.6 Cutaneous hemorrhage
Bruising
Ecchymoses
Petechiae
Superficial hematoma
} in fetus or newborn

772.8 Other specified hemorrhage of fetus or newborn

| *Excludes:* | hemorrhagic disease of newborn (776.0) |
| | pulmonary hemorrhage (770.3) |

772.9 Unspecified hemorrhage of newborn

773 Hemolytic disease of fetus or newborn, due to isoimmunization

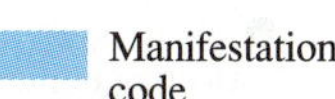

<table>
<tr><td>■ Add 4th or 5th digit</td><td>■ Nonspecific code</td><td>■ Unspecified code</td><td>■ Manifestation code</td></tr>
</table>

773.0 Hemolytic disease due to Rh isoimmunization
Anemia
Erythroblastosis (fetalis)
Hemolytic disease (fetus) (newborn)
Jaundice
Rh hemolytic disease
Rh isoimmunization

} due to RH:
   antibodies
   isoimmunization
   maternal/fetal incompatibility

773.1 Hemolytic disease due to ABO isoimmunization
ABO hemolytic disease
ABO isoimmunization
Anemia
Erythroblastosis (fetalis)
Hemolytic disease (fetus) (newborn)
Jaundice

} due to ABO:
   antibodies
   isoimmunization
   maternal/fetal incompatibility

773.2 Hemolytic disease due to other and unspecified isoimmunization
Erythroblastosis (fetalis) (neonatorum) NOS
Hemolytic disease (fetus) (newborn) NOS
Jaundice or anemia due to other and unspecified blood-group incompatibility

773.3 Hydrops fetalis due to isoimmunization

Use additional code, if desired, to identify type of isoimmunization (773.0-773.2)

773.4 Kernicterus due to isoimmunization

Use additional code, if desired, to identify type of isoimmunization (773.0-773.2)

773.5 Late anemia due to isoimmunization

774 Other perinatal jaundice

774.0 *Perinatal jaundice from hereditary hemolytic anemias*
Code first underlying disease (282.0-282.9)

774.1 Perinatal jaundice from other excessive hemolysis
Fetal or neonatal jaundice from:
   bruising
   drugs or toxins transmitted from mother
   infection
   polycythemia
   swallowed maternal blood

Use additional code, if desired, to identify cause

> Excludes: *jaundice due to isoimmunization (773.0-773.2)*

774.2 Neonatal jaundice associated with preterm delivery
Hyperbilirubinemia of prematurity
Jaundice due to delayed conjugation associated with preterm delivery

⑤ **774.3 Neonatal jaundice due to delayed conjugation from other causes**

774.30 Neonatal jaundice due to delayed conjugation, cause unspecified

774.31 *Neonatal jaundice due to delayed conjugation in diseases classified elsewhere*
Code first underlying diseases, as:
   congenital hypothyroidism (243)
   Crigler-Najjar syndrome (277.4)
   Gilbert's syndrome (277.4)

774.39 Other
Jaundice due to delayed conjugation from causes, such as:
   breast milk inhibitors
   delayed development of conjugating system

774.4 Perinatal jaundice due to hepatocellular damage
Fetal or neonatal hepatitis
Giant cell hepatitis
Inspissated bile syndrome

774.5 *Perinatal jaundice from other causes*
Code first underlying cause, as:
   congenital obstruction of bile duct (751.61)
   galactosemia (271.1)
   mucoviscidosis (277.00-277.01)

774.6 Unspecified fetal and neonatal jaundice
Icterus neonatorum
Neonatal hyperbilirubinemia (transient)
Physiologic jaundice NOS in newborn

> Excludes: *that in preterm infants (774.2)*

● Code new to this edition   ▲ Revision of existing code   ④ ⑤ Fourth or fifth digit required

774.7 Kernicterus not due to isoimmunization
Bilirubin encephalopathy
Kernicterus of newborn NOS

Excludes: *kernicterus due to isoimmunization (773.4)*

775 Endocrine and metabolic disturbances specific to the fetus and newborn
Includes: transitory endocrine and metabolic disturbances caused by the infant's response to maternal endocrine and metabolic factors, its removal from them, or its adjustment to extrauterine existence

775.0 Syndrome of "infant of a diabetic mother"
Maternal diabetes mellitus affecting fetus or newborn (with hypoglycemia)

775.1 Neonatal diabetes mellitus
Diabetes mellitus syndrome in newborn infant

775.2 Neonatal myasthenia gravis

775.3 Neonatal thyrotoxicosis
Neonatal hyperthyroidism (transient)

775.4 Hypocalcemia and hypomagnesemia of newborn
Cow's milk hypocalcemia
Hypocalcemic tetany, neonatal
Neonatal hypoparathyroidism
Phosphate-loading hypocalcemia

775.5 Other transitory neonatal electrolyte disturbances
Dehydration, neonatal

775.6 Neonatal hypoglycemia

Excludes: *infant of mother with diabetes mellitus (775.0)*

775.7 Late metabolic acidosis of newborn

775.8 Other transitory neonatal endocrine and metabolic disturbances
Amino-acid metabolic disorders described as transitory

775.9 Unspecified endocrine and metabolic disturbances specific to the fetus and newborn

776 Hematological disorders of fetus and newborn
Includes: disorders specific to the fetus or newborn

776.0 Hemorrhagic disease of newborn
Hemorrhagic diathesis of newborn
Vitamin K deficiency of newborn

Excludes: *fetal or neonatal hemorrhage (772.0-772.9)*

776.1 Transient neonatal thrombocytopenia
Neonatal thrombocytopenia due to:
exchange transfusion
idiopathic maternal thrombocytopenia
isoimmunization

776.2 Disseminated intravascular coagulation in newborn

776.3 Other transient neonatal disorders of coagulation
Transient coagulation defect, newborn

776.4 Polycythemia neonatorum
Plethora of newborn
Polycythemia due to:
donor twin transfusion
maternal-fetal transfusion

776.5 Congenital anemia
Anemia following fetal blood loss

Excludes: *anemia due to isoimmunization (773.0-773.2, 773.5)*
hereditary hemolytic anemias (282.0-282.9)

776.6 Anemia of prematurity

776.7 Transient neonatal neutropenia
Isoimmune neutropenia
Maternal transfer neutropenia

Excludes: *congenital neutropenia (nontransient) (288.0)*

776.8 Other specified transient hematological disorders

776.9 Unspecified hematological disorder specific to fetus or newborn

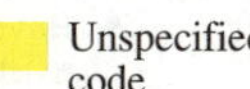
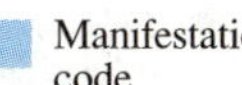

Add 4th or 5th digit   Nonspecific code   Unspecified code   Manifestation code

777 Perinatal disorders of digestive system
Includes: disorders specific to the fetus and newborn

Excludes: *intestinal obstruction classifiable to 560.0-560.9*

777.1 Meconium obstruction
Congenital fecaliths
Delayed passage of meconium
Meconium ileus NOS
Meconium plug syndrome

Excludes: *meconium ileus in cystic fibrosis (277.01)*

777.2 Intestinal obstruction due to inspissated milk

777.3 Hematemesis and melena due to swallowed maternal blood
Swallowed blood syndrome in newborn

Excludes: *that not due to swallowed maternal blood (772.4)*

777.4 Transitory ileus of newborn

Excludes: *Hirschsprung's disease (751.3)*

777.5 Necrotizing enterocolitis in fetus or newborn
Pseudomembranous enterocolitis in newborn

777.6 Perinatal intestinal perforation
Meconium peritonitis

777.8 Other specified perinatal disorders of digestive system

777.9 Unspecified perinatal disorder of digestive system

778 Conditions involving the integument and temperature regulation of fetus and newborn

778.0 Hydrops fetalis not due to isoimmunization
Idiopathic hydrops

Excludes: *hydrops fetalis due to isoimmunization (773.3)*

778.1 Sclerema neonatorum
Subcutaneous fat necrosis

778.2 Cold injury syndrome of newborn

778.3 Other hypothermia of newborn

778.4 Other disturbances of temperature regulation of newborn
Dehydration fever in newborn
Environmentally-induced pyrexia
Hyperthermia in newborn
Transitory fever of newborn

778.5 Other and unspecified edema of newborn
Edema neonatorum

778.6 Congenital hydrocele
Congenital hydrocele of tunica vaginalis

778.7 Breast engorgement in newborn
Noninfective mastitis of newborn

Excludes: *infective mastitis of newborn (771.5)*

778.8 Other specified conditions involving the integument of fetus and newborn
Urticaria neonatorum

Excludes: *impetigo neonatorum (684)*
pemphigus neonatorum (684)

778.9 Unspecified condition involving the integument and temperature regulation of fetus and newborn

779 Other and ill-defined conditions originating in the perinatal period

779.0 Convulsions in newborn
Fits
Seizures } in newborn

779.1 Other and unspecified cerebral irritability in newborn

779.2 Cerebral depression, coma, and other abnormal cerebral signs
CNS dysfunction in newborn NOS

● Code new
to this edition

▲ Revision of
existing code

④ ⑤ Fourth or fifth
digit required

779.3 Feeding problems in newborn
Regurgitation of food
Slow feeding } in newborn
Vomiting

779.4 Drug reactions and intoxications specific to newborn
Gray syndrome from chloramphenicol administration in newborn

Excludes: *fetal alcohol syndrome (760.71)*
reactions and intoxications from maternal opiates and tranquilizers (763.5)

779.5 Drug withdrawal syndrome in newborn
Drug withdrawal syndrome in infant of dependent mother

Excludes: *fetal alcohol syndrome (760.71)*

779.6 Termination of pregnancy (fetus)
Fetus death due to:
    induced abortion
    termination of pregnancy

Excludes: *spontaneous abortion (fetus) (761.8)*

779.8 Other specified conditions originating in the perinatal period

779.9 Unspecified condition originating in the perinatal period
Congenital debility NOS
Stillbirth NEC

● Code new
to this edition

▲ Revision of
existing code

④ ⑤ Fourth or fifth
digit required

16.   SYMPTOMS, SIGNS, AND ILL-DEFINED CONDITIONS (780-799)

This section includes symptoms, signs, abnormal results of laboratory or other investigative procedures, and ill-defined conditions regarding which no diagnosis classifiable elsewhere is recorded.

Signs and symptoms that point rather definitely to a given diagnosis are assigned to some category in the preceding part of the classification. In general, categories 780-796 include the more ill-defined conditions and symptoms that point with perhaps equal suspicion to two or more diseases or to two or more systems of the body, and without the necessary study of the case to make a final diagnosis. Practically all categories in this group could be designated as "not otherwise specified," or as "unknown etiology," or as "transient." The Alphabetic Index should be consulted to determine which symptoms and signs are to be allocated here and which to more specific sections of the classification; the residual subcategories numbered .9 are provided for other relevant symptoms which cannot be allocated elsewhere in the classification.

The conditions and signs or symptoms included in categories 780-796 consist of: (a) cases for which no more specific diagnosis can be made even after all facts bearing on the case have been investigated; (b) signs or symptoms existing at the time of initial encounter that proved to be transient and whose causes could not be determined; (c) provisional diagnoses in a patient who failed to return for further investigation or care; (d) cases referred elsewhere for investigation or treatment before the diagnosis was made; (e) cases in which a more precise diagnosis was not available for any other reason; (f) certain symptoms which represent important problems in medical care and which it might be desired to classify in addition to a known cause.

SYMPTOMS (780-789)

780   General symptoms

⑤ **780.0   Alteration of consciousness**

> *Excludes:* coma:
>> *diabetic (250.2-250.3)*
>> *hepatic (572.2)*
>> *originating in the perinatal period (779.2)*

780.01   Coma

780.02   Transient alteration of awareness

780.03   Persistent vegetative state

780.09   Other
> Drowsiness   Somnolence
> Semicoma   Stupor
> Unconsciousness

780.1   Hallucinations
> Hallucinations: Hallucinations:
>   NOS   olfactory
>   auditory   tactile
>   gustatory

> *Excludes:* those associated with mental disorders, as functional psychoses (295.0-298.9)
>> *organic brain syndromes (290.0-294.9, 310.0-310.9)*
>> *visual hallucinations (368.16)*

780.2   Syncope and collapse
> Blackout   (Near) (Pre) syncope
> Fainting   Vasovagal attack

> *Excludes:* carotid sinus syncope (337.0)
>> *heat syncope (992.1)*
>> *neurocirculatory asthenia (306.2)*
>> *orthostatic hypotension (458.0)*
>> *shock NOS (785.50)*

⑤ **780.3   Convulsions**

> *Excludes:* convulsions:
>> *epileptic (345.10-345.91)*
>> *in newborn (779.0)*

780.31   Febrile convulsions
> Febrile seizure

780.39   Other convulsions
> Convulsive disorder NOS
> Fit NOS
> Seizure NOS

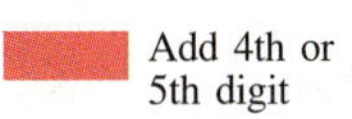

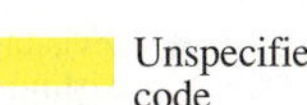

780.4 Dizziness and giddiness
Light-headedness   Vertigo NOS

| Excludes: | *Ménière's disease and other specified vertiginous syndromes (386.0-386.9)* |

⑤ **780.5 Sleep disturbances**

| Excludes: | *that of nonorganic origin (307.40-307.49)* |

    780.50 Sleep disturbance, unspecified

    780.51 Insomnia with sleep apnea

    780.52 Other insomnia
Insomnia NOS

    780.53 Hypersomnia with sleep apnea

    780.54 Other hypersomnia
Hypersomnia NOS

    780.55 Disruptions of 24-hour sleep-wake cycle
Inversion of sleep rhythm
Irregular sleep-wake rhythm NOS
Non-24-hour sleep-wake rhythm

    780.56 Dysfunctions associated with sleep stages or arousal from sleep

    780.57 Other and unspecified sleep apnea

    780.59 Other

780.6 Fever
Chills with fever   Hyperpyrexia NOS
Fever NOS   Pyrexia NOS
Fever of unknown origin   Pyrexia of unknown origin
(FUO)

| Excludes: | *pyrexia of unknown origin (during):* |

    in newborn (778.4)
    labor (659.2)
    the puerperium (672)

⑤ **780.7 Malaise and fatigue**

| Excludes: | *debility, unspecified (799.3)* |

    fatigue (during):
      combat (308.0-308.9)
      heat (992.6)
      pregnancy (646.8)
    neurasthenia (300.5)
    senile asthenia (797.5)

    780.71 Chronic fatigue syndrome

    780.79 Other malaise and fatigue
Asthenia NOS
Lethargy
Postviral (asthenic) syndrome
Tiredness

780.8 Hyperhidrosis
Diaphoresis
Excessive sweating

780.9 Other general symptoms
Amnesia (retrograde)
Chill(s) NOS
Generalized pain
Hypothermia, not associated with low environmental temperature

| Excludes: | *hypothermia:* |

    NOS (accidental) (991.6)
    due to anesthesia (995.89)
    of newborn (778.2-778.3)
    memory disturbance as part of a pattern of mental disorder

● Code new   ▲ Revision of   ④ ⑤ Fourth or fifth
  to this edition   existing code   digit required

781 Symptoms involving nervous and musculoskeletal systems

> *Excludes:* *depression NOS (311)*
>
> > *disorders specifically relating to:*
> > *back (724.0-724.9)*
> > *hearing (388.0-389.9)*
> > *joint (718.0-719.9)*
> > *limb (729.0-729.9)*
> > *neck (723.0-723.9)*
> > *vision (368.0-369.9)*
> > *pain in limb (729.5)*

781.0 Abnormal involuntary movements
Abnormal head movements
Fasciculation
Spasms NOS
Tremor NOS

> *Excludes:* *abnormal reflex (796.1)*
>
> > *chorea NOS (333.5)*
> > *infantile spasms (345.60-345.61)*
> > *spastic paralysis (342.1, 343.0-344.9)*
> > *specified movement disorders classifiable to 333 (333.0-333.9)*
> > *that of nonorganic origin (307.2-307.3)*

781.1 Disturbances of sensation of smell and taste
Anosmia   Parosmia
Parageusia

781.2 Abnormality of gait
Gait: Gait:
  ataxic   spastic
  paralytic   staggering

> *Excludes:* *ataxia:*
>
> > *NOS (781.3)*
> > *locomotor (progressive) (094.0)*
> > *difficulty in walking (719.7)*

781.3 Lack of coordination
Ataxia NOS   Muscular incoordination

> *Excludes:* *ataxic gait (781.2)*
>
> > *cerebellar ataxia (334.0-334.9)*
> > *difficulty in walking (719.7)*
> > *vertigo NOS (780.4)*

781.4 Transient paralysis of limb
Monoplegia, transient NOS

> *Excludes:* *paralysis (342.0-344.9)*

781.5 Clubbing of fingers

781.6 Meningismus
Dupré's syndrome
Meningism

781.7 Tetany
Carpopedal spasm

> *Excludes:* *tetanus neonatorum (771.3)*
>
> > *tetany:*
> > *hysterical (300.11)*
> > *newborn (hypocalcemic) (775.4)*
> > *parathyroid (252.1)*
> > *psychogenic (306.0)*

781.8 Neurologic neglect syndrome
Asomatognosia   Left-sided neglect
Hemi-akinesia   Sensory extinction
Hemi-inattention   Sensory neglect
Hemispatial neglect Visuospatial neglect

⑤ **781.9 Other symptoms involving nervous and musculoskeletal systems**

  ● **781.91 Loss of height**

> *Excludes:* *osteoporosis (733.00-733.09)*

  ● **781.92 Abnormal posture**

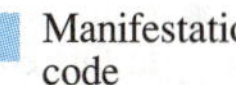

Manifestation
code

● **781.99** **Other symptoms involving nervous and musculoskeletal systems**

782 **Symptoms involving skin and other integumentary tissue**

> *Excludes:* *symptoms relating to breast (611.71-611.79)*

782.0 **Disturbance of skin sensation**
Anesthesia of skin	Hypoesthesia
Burning or prickling	Numbness
sensation	Paresthesia
Hyperesthesia	Tingling

782.1 **Rash and other nonspecific skin eruption**
Exanthem

> *Excludes:* *vesicular eruption (709.8)*

782.2 **Localized superficial swelling, mass, or lump**
Subcutaneous nodules

> *Excludes:* *localized adiposity (278.1)*

782.3 **Edema**
Anasarca	Localized edema NOS
Dropsy	

> *Excludes:* *ascites (789.5)*
>   *edema of:*
>   *newborn NOS (778.5)*
>   *pregnancy (642.0-642.9, 646.1)*
>   *fluid retention (276.6)*
>   *hydrops fetalis (773.3, 778.0)*
>   *hydrothorax (511.8)*
>   *nutritional edema (260, 262)*

782.4 **Jaundice, unspecified, not of newborn**
Cholemia NOS	Icterus NOS

> *Excludes:* *jaundice in newborn (774.0-774.7)*
>   *due to isoimmunization (773.0-773.2, 773.4)*

782.5 **Cyanosis**

> *Excludes:* *newborn (770.8)*

⑤ **782.6** **Pallor and flushing**

    782.61 **Pallor**

    782.62 **Flushing**
      Excessive blushing

782.7 **Spontaneous ecchymoses**
Petechiae

> *Excludes:* *ecchymosis in fetus or newborn (772.6)*
>   *purpura (287.0-287.9)*

782.8 **Changes in skin texture**
Induration of skin
Thickening of skin

782.9 **Other symptoms involving skin and integumentary tissues**

783 **Symptoms concerning nutrition, metabolism, and development**

783.0 **Anorexia**
Loss of appetite

> *Excludes:* *anorexia nervosa (307.1)*
>   *loss of appetite of nonorganic origin (307.59)*

783.1 **Abnormal weight gain**

> *Excludes:* *excessive weight gain in pregnancy (646.1)*
>   *obesity (278.00)*
>   *morbid (278.01)*

▲ **783.2** **Abnormal loss of weight and underweight**

  ● **783.21** **Loss of weight**

  ● **783.22** **Underweight**

● Code new to this edition	▲ Revision of existing code	④ ⑤ Fourth or fifth digit required

783.3 Feeding difficulties and mismanagement
Feeding problem (elderly) (infant)

Excludes: *feeding disturbance or problems:*
in newborn (779.3)
of nonorganic origin (307.50-307.59)

▲ **783.4 Lack of expected normal physiological development in childhood**

Excludes: *delay in sexual development and puberty (259.0)*
gonadal dysgenesis (758.6)
pituitary dwarfism (259.4)
slow fetal growth and fetal malnutrition (764.00-764.99)
specific delays in mental development (315.0-315.9)

● **783.40 Lack of normal physiological development, unspecified**
Inadequate development
Lack of development

● **783.41 Failure to thrive**
Failure to gain weight

● **783.42 Delayed milestones**
Late talker
Late walker

● **783.43 Short stature**
Growth failure
Growth retardation
Lack of growth
Physical retardation

783.5 Polydipsia
Excessive thirst

783.6 Polyphagia
Excessive eating
Hyperalimentation NOS

Excludes: *disorders of eating of nonorganic origin (307.50-307.59)*

● **783.7 Adult failure to thrive**

783.9 Other symptoms concerning nutrition, metabolism, and development
Hypometabolism

Excludes: *abnormal basal metabolic rate (794.7)*
dehydration (276 5)
other disorders of fluid, electrolyte, and acid-base balance (276.0-276.9)

784 Symptoms involving head and neck

Excludes: *encephalopathy NOS (348.3)*
specific symptoms involving neck classifiable to 723 (723.0-723.9)

784.0 Headache
Facial pain   Pain in head NOS

Excludes: *atypical face pain (350.2)*
migraine (346.0-346.9)
tension headache (307.81)

784.1 Throat pain

Excludes: *dysphagia (787.2)*
neck pain (723.1)
sore throat (462)
chronic (472.1)

784.2 Swelling, mass, or lump in head and neck
Space-occupying lesion, intracranial NOS

784.3 Aphasia

Excludes: *developmental aphasia (315.31)*

⑤ **784.4 Voice disturbance**

784.40 Voice disturbance, unspecified

784.41 Aphonia
Loss of voice

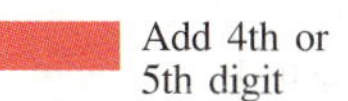

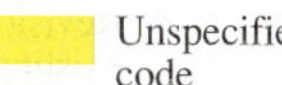

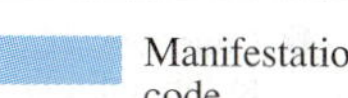

784.49 Other
Change in voice
Dysphonia
Hoarseness
Hypernasality
Hyponasality

784.5 Other speech disturbance
Dysarthria
Dysphasia
Slurred speech

Excludes: *stammering and stuttering (307.0)*
that of nonorganic origin (307.0, 307.9)

⑤ **784.6 Other symbolic dysfunction**

Excludes: *developmental learning delays (315.0-315.9)*

784.60 Symbolic dysfunction, unspecified

784.61 Alexia and dyslexia
Alexia (with agraphia)

784.69 Other
Acalculia
Agnosia
Agraphia NOS
Apraxia

784.7 Epistaxis
Hemorrhage from nose
Nosebleed

784.8 Hemorrhage from throat

Excludes: *hemoptysis (786.3)*

784.9 Other symptoms involving head and neck
Choking sensation
Halitosis
Mouth breathing
Sneezing

785 Symptoms involving cardiovascular system

Excludes: *heart failure NOS (428.9)*

785.0 Tachycardia, unspecified
Rapid heart beat

Excludes: *paroxysmal tachycardia (427.0-427.2)*

785.1 Palpitations
Awareness of heart beat

Excludes: *specified dysrhythmias (427.0-427.9)*

785.2 Undiagnosed cardiac murmurs
Heart murmur NOS

785.3 Other abnormal heart sounds
Cardiac dullness, increased or decreased
Friction fremitus, cardiac
Precordial friction

785.4 *Gangrene*
Gangrenous cellulitis
Gangrene NOS
Gangrene spreading cutaneous
Phagedena

Code first any associated underlying condition, as:
diabetes (250.7)
Raynaud's syndrome (443.0)

Excludes: *gangrene of certain sites—see Alphabetic Index*
gangrene with atherosclerosis of the extremities (440.24)
gas gangrene (040.0)

⑤ **785.5 Shock without mention of trauma**

785.50 Shock, unspecified
Failure of peripheral circulation

785.51 Cardiogenic shock

● Code new
to this edition   ▲ Revision of
existing code   ④ ⑤ Fourth or fifth
digit required

785.59 **Other**
Shock: Shock:
  endotoxic   hypovolemic
  gram-negative   septic

Excludes: *shock (due to):*
  anesthetic (995.4)
  anaphylactic (995.0)
   due to serum (999.4)
  electric (994.8)
  following abortion (639.5)
  lightning (994.0)
  obstetrical (669.1)
  postoperative (998.0)
  traumatic (958.4)

785.6 Enlargement of lymph nodes
Lymphadenopathy   "Swollen glands"

Excludes: *lymphadenitis (chronic) (289.1-289.3)*
  acute (683)

785.9 Other symptoms involving cardiovascular system
Bruit (arterial)   Weak pulse

786 Symptoms involving respiratory system and other chest symptoms

⑤ **786.0 Dyspnea and respiratory abnormalities**

    786.00 Respiratory abnormality, unspecified

    786.01 Hyperventilation

Excludes: *hyperventilation, psychogenic (306.1)*

    786.02 Orthopnea

    786.03 Apnea

Excludes: *sleep apnea (780.51, 780.53, 780.57)*

    786.04 Cheyne-Stokes respiration

    786.05 Shortness of breath

    786.06 Tachypnea

Excludes: *transitory tachypnea of newborn (770.6)*

    786.07 Wheezing

Excludes: *asthma (493.00-493.92)*

    786.09 Other
Respiratory:
  distress
  insufficiency

Excludes: *respiratory distress:*
  following trauma and surgery (518.5)
  newborn (770.8)
  syndrome (newborn) (769)
   adult (518.5)
  respiratory failure (518.81, 518.83-518.84)
  newborn (770.8)

786.1 Stridor

Excludes: *congenital laryngeal stridor (748.3)*

786.2 Cough

Excludes: *cough:*
  psychogenic (306.1)
  smokers' (491.0)
  with hemorrhage (786.3)

786.3 Hemoptysis
Cough with hemorrhage
Pulmonary hemorrhage NOS

Excludes: *pulmonary hemorrhage of newborn (770.3)*

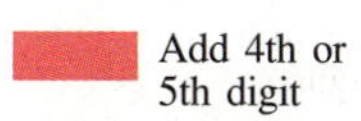

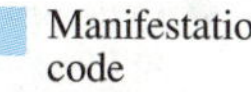

786.4 Abnormal sputum
Abnormal:
amount
color   } (of) sputum
odor
Excessive

⑤ **786.5 Chest pain**

786.50   Chest pain, unspecified

786.51   Precordial pain

786.52   Painful respiration
Pain:
anterior chest wall
pleuritic
Pleurodynia

Excludes: epidemic pleurodynia (074.1)

786.59   Other
Discomfort
Pressure   } in chest
Tightness

Excludes: pain in breast (611.71)

786.6 Swelling, mass, or lump in chest

Excludes: lump in breast (611.72)

786.7 Abnormal chest sounds
Abnormal percussion, chest   Rales
Friction sounds, chest   Tympany, chest

Excludes: wheezing (786.07)

786.8 Hiccough

Excludes: psychogenic hiccough (306.1)

786.9 Other symptoms involving respiratory system and chest
Breath-holding spell

787 Symptoms involving digestive system

Excludes: constipation (564.0)

pylorospasm (537.81)

congenital (750.5)

⑤ **787.0 Nausea and vomiting**
Emesis

Excludes: hematemesis NOS (578.0)

vomiting:
bilious, following gastrointestinal surgery (564.3)
cyclical (536.2)
psychogenic (306.4)
excessive, in pregnancy (643.0-643.9)
habit (536.2)
of newborn (779.3)
psychogenic NOS (307.54)

787.01   Nausea with vomiting

787.02   Nausea alone

787.03   Vomiting alone

787.1 Heartburn
Pyrosis
Waterbrash

Excludes: dyspepsia or indigestion (536.8)

787.2 Dysphagia
Difficulty in swallowing

787.3 Flatulence, eructation, and gas pain
Abdominal distention (gaseous)
Bloating
Tympanites (abdominal) (intestinal)

Excludes: aerophagy (306.4)

     ● Code new   ▲ Revision of   ④ ⑤ Fourth or fifth
      to this edition   existing code   digit required

787.4 Visible peristalsis
Hyperperistalsis

787.5 Abnormal bowel sounds
Absent bowel sounds
Hyperactive bowel sounds

787.6 Incontinence of feces
Encopresis NOS
Incontinence of sphincter ani

Excludes: *that of nonorganic origin (307.7)*

787.7 Abnormal feces
Bulky stools

Excludes: *abnormal stool content (792.1)*
melena:
NOS (578.1)
newborn (772.4, 777.3)

⑤ **787.9 Other symptoms involving digestive system**

Excludes: *gastrointestinal hemorrhage (578.0-578.9)*
intestinal obstruction (560.0-560.9)
specific functional digestive disorders:
esophagus (530.0-530.9)
stomach and duodenum (536.0-536.9)
those not elsewhere classified (564.0-564.9)

    787.91 Diarrhea
Diarrhea NOS

    787.99 Other
Change in bowel habits
Tenesmus (rectal)

788 Symptoms involving urinary system

Excludes: *hematuria (599.7)*
nonspecific findings on examination of the urine (791.0-791.9)
small kidney of unknown cause (589.0-589.9)
uremia NOS (586)

788.0 Renal colic
Colic (recurrent) of:
kidney
ureter

788.1 Dysuria
Painful urination
Strangury

⑤ **788.2 Retention of urine**

    788.20 Retention of urine, unspecified

    788.21 Incomplete bladder emptying

    788.29 Other specified retention of urine

⑤ **788.3 *Incontinence of urine***

Excludes: *that of nonorganic origin (307.6)*
Code first any underlying condition, such as:
congenital ureterocele (753.23)
genital prolapse (618.0-618.9)

    788.30 *Urinary incontinence, unspecified*
Enuresis NOS

    788.31 *Urge incontinence*

    788.32 *Stress incontinence, male*

Excludes: *stress incontinence (female) (625.6)*

    788.33 *Mixed incontinence (male) (female)*
Urge and stress

    788.34 *Incontinence without sensory awareness*

    788.35 *Post-void dribbling*

    788.36 *Nocturnal enuresis*

    788.37 *Continuous leakage*

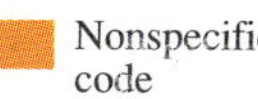

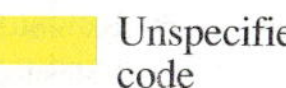

Manifestation
code

788.39 *Other urinary incontinence*

⑤ **788.4 Frequency of urination and polyuria**

    788.41 Urinary frequency
        Frequency of micturition

    788.42 Polyuria

    788.43 Nocturia

788.5 Oliguria and anuria
    Deficient secretion of urine
    Suppression of urinary secretion

    | Excludes: | *that complicating:* |
        abortion (634-638 with .3, 639.3)
        ectopic or molar pregnancy (639.3)
        pregnancy, childbirth, or the puerperium (642.0-642.9, 646.2)

⑤ **788.6 Other abnormality of urination**

    788.61 Splitting of urinary stream
        Intermittent urinary stream

    788.62 Slowing of urinary stream
        Weak stream

    788.69 Other

788.7 Urethral discharge
    Penile discharge   Urethrorrhea

788.8 Extravasation of urine

788.9 Other symptoms involving urinary system
    Extrarenal uremia
    Vesical:
      pain
      tenesmus

789 Other symptoms involving abdomen and pelvis

The following fifth-digit subclassification is to be used for codes 789.0, 789.3, 789.4, 789.6

    0 **unspecified site**

    1 **right upper quadrant**

    2 **left upper quadrant**

    3 **right lower quadrant**

    4 **left lower quadrant**

    5 **periumbilic**

    6 **epigastric**

    7 **generalized**

    9 **other specified site**
        multiple sites

    | Excludes: | *symptoms referable to genital organs:* |
        female (625.0-625.9)
        male (607.0-608.9)
        psychogenic (302.70-302.79)

⑤ **789.0 Abdominal pain**
    Colic:
      NOS
      infantile
    Cramps, abdominal

    | Excludes: | *renal colic (788.0)* |

789.1 Hepatomegaly
    Enlargement of liver

789.2 Splenomegaly
    Enlargement of spleen

⑤ **789.3 Abdominal or pelvic swelling, mass, or lump**
    Diffuse or generalized swelling or mass:
      abdominal NOS
      umbilical

    | Excludes: | *abdominal distention (gaseous) (787.3)* |
        ascites (789.5)

  ● Code new   ▲ Revision of   ④ ⑤ Fourth or fifth
     to this edition   existing code   digit required

⑤ **789.4 Abdominal rigidity**

789.5 Ascites
Fluid in peritoneal cavity

⑤ **789.6 Abdominal tenderness**
Rebound tenderness

789.9 Other symptoms involving abdomen and pelvis
Umbilical:
  bleeding
  discharge

NONSPECIFIC ABNORMAL FINDINGS (790-796)

790 Nonspecific findings on examination of blood

> *Excludes:* *abnormality of:*
>
> > *platelets (287.0-287.9)*
> > *thrombocytes (287.0-287.9)*
> > *white blood cells (288.0-288.9)*

⑤ **790.0 Abnormality of red blood cells**

> *Excludes:* *anemia:*
>
> > *congenital (776.5)*
> > *newborn, due to isoimmunization (773.0-773.2, 773.5)*
> > *of premature infant (776.6)*
> > *other specified types (280.0-285.9)*
> >
> > *hemoglobin disorders (282.5-282.7)*
> > *polycythemia:*
> > > *familial (289.6)*
> > > *neonatorum (776.4)*
> > > *secondary (289.0)*
> > > *vera (238.4)*

● **790.01 Precipitous drop in hematocrit**
Drop in hematocrit

● **790.09 Other abnormality of red blood cells**
Abnormal red cell morphology NOS
Abnormal red cell volume NOS
Anisocytosis
Poikilocytosis

790.1 Elevated sedimentation rate

790.2 Abnormal glucose tolerance test

> *Excludes:* *that complicating pregnancy, childbirth, or the puerperium (648.8)*

790.3 Excessive blood level of alcohol
Elevated blood-alcohol

790.4 Nonspecific elevation of levels of transaminase or lactic acid dehydrogenase [LDH]

790.5 Other nonspecific abnormal serum enzyme levels
Abnormal serum level of: Abnormal serum level of:
  acid phosphatase   amylase
  alkaline phosphatase   lipase

> *Excludes:* *deficiency of circulating enzymes (277.6)*

790.6 Other abnormal blood chemistry
Abnormal blood level of: Abnormal blood level of:
  cobalt   magnesium
  copper   mineral
  iron   zinc
  lithium

> *Excludes:* *abnormality of electrolyte or acid-base balance (276.0-276.9)*
>
> > *hypoglycemia NOS (251.2)*
> > *specific finding indicating abnormality of:*
> > > *amino-acid transport and metabolism (270.0-270.9)*
> > > *carbohydrate transport and metabolism (271.0-271.9)*
> > > *lipid metabolism (272.0-272.9)*
> >
> > *uremia NOS (586)*

790.7 Bacteremia

> *Excludes:* *septicemia (038)*

Use additional code, if desired, to identify organism (041)

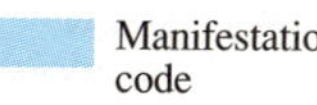

Manifestation
code

790.8 Viremia, unspecified

⑤ **790.9 Other nonspecific findings on examination of blood**

    790.91 Abnormal arterial blood gases

    790.92 Abnormal coagulation profile
        Abnormal or prolonged:
          bleeding time
          coagulation time
          partial thromboplastin time [PTT]
          prothrombin time [PT]

    Excludes: *coagulation (hemorrhagic) disorders (286.0-286.9)*

    790.93 Elevated prostate specific antigen (PSA)

    790.94 Euthyroid sick syndrome

    790.99 Other

791 Nonspecific findings on examination of urine

    Excludes: *hematuria NOS (599.7)*

        specific findings indicating abnormality of:
         amino-acid transport and metabolism (270.0-270.9)
         carbohydrate transport and metabolism (271.0-271.9)

791.0 Proteinuria
    Albuminuria   Bence-Jones proteinuria

    Excludes: *postural proteinuria (593.6)*
        that arising during pregnancy or the puerperium (642.0-642.9, 646.2)

791.1 Chyluria

    Excludes: *filarial (125.0-125.9)*

791.2 Hemoglobinuria

791.3 Myoglobinuria

791.4 Biliuria

791.5 Glycosuria

    Excludes: *renal glycosuria (271.4)*

791.6 Acetonuria
    Ketonuria

791.7 Other cells and casts in urine

791.9 Other nonspecific findings on examination of urine
    Crystalluria
    Elevated urine levels of:
      17-ketosteroids
      catecholamines
      indolacetic acid
      vanillylmandelic acid [VMA]
    Melanuria

792 Nonspecific abnormal findings in other body substances

    Excludes: *that in chromosomal analysis (795.2)*

792.0 Cerebrospinal fluid

792.1 Stool contents
    Abnormal stool color
    Fat in stool   Occult blood
    Mucus in stool   Pus in stool

    Excludes: *blood in stool [melena] (578.1)*
        newborn (772.4, 777.3)

792.2 Semen
    Abnormal spermatozoa

    Excludes: *azoospermia (606.0)*
        oligospermia (606.1)

792.3 Amniotic fluid

792.4 Saliva

    Excludes: *that in chromosomal analysis (795.2)*

● Code new to this edition   ▲ Revision of existing code   ④ ⑤ Fourth or fifth digit required

● **792.5 Cloudy (hemodialysis) (peritoneal) dialysis effluent**

792.9 Other nonspecific abnormal findings in body substances

| Peritoneal fluid | Synovial fluid |
| Pleural fluid | Vaginal fluids |

793 Nonspecific abnormal findings on radiological and other examination of body structure

Includes: nonspecific abnormal findings of:
thermography
ultrasound examination [echogram]
x-ray examination

Excludes: *abnormal results of function studies and radioisotope scans (794.0-794.9)*

793.0 Skull and head

Excludes: *nonspecific abnormal echoencephalogram (794.01)*

793.1 Lung field

Coin lesion
Shadow } (of) lung

793.2 Other intrathoracic organ

Abnormal: Mediastinal shift
echocardiogram
heart shadow
ultrasound cardiogram

793.3 Biliary tract

Nonvisualization of gallbladder

793.4 Gastrointestinal tract

793.5 Genitourinary organs

Filling defect:
bladder
kidney
ureter

793.6 Abdominal area, including retroperitoneum

793.7 Musculoskeletal system

793.8 Breast

Abnormal mammogram

793.9 Other

Abnormal:
placental finding by x-ray or ultrasound method
radiological findings in skin and subcutaneous tissue

Excludes: *abnormal finding by radioisotope localization of placenta (794.9)*

794 Nonspecific abnormal results of function studies

Includes: radioisotope:
scans
uptake studies
scintiphotography

⑤ **794.0 Brain and central nervous system**

794.00 Abnormal function study, unspecified

794.01 Abnormal echoencephalogram

794.02 Abnormal electroencephalogram [EEG]

794.09 Other

Abnormal brain scan

⑤ **794.1 Peripheral nervous system and special senses**

794.10 Abnormal response to nerve stimulation, unspecified

794.11 Abnormal retinal function studies

Abnormal electroretinogram [ERG]

794.12 Abnormal electro-oculogram [EOG]

794.13 Abnormal visually evoked potential

794.14 Abnormal oculomotor studies

794.15 Abnormal auditory function studies

794.16 Abnormal vestibular function studies

794.17 Abnormal electromyogram [EMG]

Excludes: *that of eye (794.14)*

| Add 4th or 5th digit | Nonspecific code | Unspecified code | Manifestation code |

794.19 Other

794.2 Pulmonary
Abnormal lung scan
Reduced:
   ventilatory capacity
   vital capacity

⑤ **794.3 Cardiovascular**

   794.30 Abnormal function study, unspecified

   794.31 Abnormal electrocardiogram [ECG] [EKG]

   794.39 Other
      Abnormal:
         ballistocardiogram
         phonocardiogram
         vectorcardiogram

794.4 Kidney
Abnormal renal function test

794.5 Thyroid
Abnormal thyroid:
   scan
   uptake

794.6 Other endocrine function study

794.7 Basal metabolism
Abnormal basal metabolic rate [BMR]

794.8 Liver
Abnormal liver scan

794.9 Other
Bladder
Pancreas
Placenta
Spleen

795 Nonspecific abnormal histological and immunological findings

> **Excludes:** *nonspecific abnormalities of red blood cells (790.01-790.09)*

795.0 Nonspecific abnormal Papanicolaou smear of cervix
Dyskaryotic cervical smear

795.1 Nonspecific abnormal Papanicolaou smear of other site

795.2 Nonspecific abnormal findings on chromosomal analysis
Abnormal karyotype

795.3 Nonspecific positive culture findings
Positive culture findings in:
   nose
   sputum
   throat
   wound

> **Excludes:** *that of:*
>   *blood (790.7-790.8)*
>   *urine (791.9)*

795.4 Other nonspecific abnormal histological findings

795.5 Nonspecific reaction to tuberculin skin test without active tuberculosis
Abnormal result of Mantoux test
PPD positive
Tuberculin (skin test):
   positive
   reactor

795.6 False positive serological test for syphilis
False positive Wassermann reaction

⑤ **795.7 Other nonspecific immunological findings**

> **Excludes:** *isoimmunization, in pregnancy (656.1-656.2)*
>   *affecting fetus or newborn (773.0-773.2)*

● Code new to this edition   ▲ Revision of existing code   ④ ⑤ Fourth or fifth digit required

795.71 Nonspecific serologic evidence of human immunodeficiency virus [HIV]
Inconclusive human immunodeficiency virus [HIV] test (adult) (infant)

Note: This code is ONLY to be used when a test finding is reported as nonspecific. Asymptomatic positive findings are coded to V08. If any HIV infection symptom or condition is present, see code 042. Negative findings are not coded.

Excludes: *acquired immunodeficiency syndrome [AIDS] (042)*
asymptomatic human immunodeficiency virus, [HIV] infection status (V08)
HIV infection, symptomatic (042)
human immunodeficiency virus [HIV] disease (042)
positive (status) NOS (V08)

795.79 Other and unspecified nonspecific immunological findings
Raised antibody titer
Raised level of immunoglobulins

796 Other nonspecific abnormal findings

796.0 Nonspecific abnormal toxicological findings
Abnormal levels of heavy metals or drugs in blood, urine, or other tissue

Excludes: *excessive blood level of alcohol (790.3)*

796.1 Abnormal reflex

796.2 Elevated blood pressure reading without diagnosis of hypertension

Note: This category is to be used to record an episode of elevated blood pressure in a patient in whom no formal diagnosis of hypertension has been made, or as an incidental finding.

796.3 Nonspecific low blood pressure reading

796.4 Other abnormal clinical findings

796.5 Abnormal finding on antenatal screening

796.9 Other

ILL-DEFINED AND UNKNOWN CAUSES OF MORBIDITY AND MORTALITY (797-799)

797 Senility without mention of psychosis
Old age
Senescence
Senile asthenia
Senile debility
Senile exhaustion

Excludes: *senile psychoses (290.0-290.9)*

798 Sudden death, cause unknown

798.0 Sudden infant death syndrome
Cot death
Crib death
Sudden death of nonspecific cause in infancy

798.1 Instantaneous death

798.2 Death occurring in less than 24 hours from onset of symptoms, not otherwise explained
Death known not to be violent or instantaneous, for which no cause could be discovered
Died without sign of disease

798.9 Unattended death
Death in circumstances where the body of the deceased was found and no cause could be discovered
Found dead

799 Other ill-defined and unknown causes of morbidity and mortality

799.0 Asphyxia

Excludes: *asphyxia (due to):*
carbon monoxide (986)
inhalation of food or foreign body (932-934.9)
newborn (768.0-768.9)
traumatic (994.7)

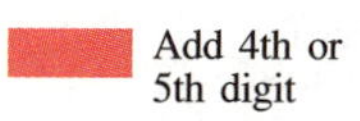

799.1 Respiratory arrest
Cardiorespiratory failure

Excludes: *cardiac arrest (427.5)*
failure of peripheral circulation (785.50)
respiratory distress:
  NOS (786.09)
  acute (518.82)
  following trauma and surgery (518.5)
  newborn (770.8)
  syndrome (newborn) (769)
    adult (following trauma and surgery) (518.5)
      other (518.82)
respiratory failure (518.81, 518.83-518.84)
  newborn (770.8)
respiratory insufficiency (786.09)
  acute (518.82)

799.2 Nervousness
"Nerves"

799.3 Debility, unspecified

Excludes: *asthenia (780.79)*
nervous debility (300.5)
neurasthenia (300.5)
senile asthenia (797)

799.4 Cachexia
Wasting disease

Excludes: *nutritional marasmus (261)*

799.8 Other ill-defined conditions

799.9 Other unknown and unspecified cause
Undiagnosed disease, not specified as to site or system involved
Unknown cause of morbidity or mortality

● Code new
to this edition

▲ Revision of
existing code

④ ⑤ Fourth or fifth
digit required

17. INJURY AND POISONING (800-999)

Use E code(s) to identify the cause and intent of the injury or poisoning (E800-E999)

Note:

1. The principle of multiple coding of injuries should be followed wherever possible. Combination categories for multiple injuries are provided for use when there is insufficient detail as to the nature of the individual conditions, or for primary tabulation purposes when it is more convenient to record a single code; otherwise, the component injuries should be coded separately.

   Where multiple sites of injury are specified in the titles, the word "with" indicates involvement of both sites, and the word "and" indicates involvement of either or both sites. The word "finger" includes thumb.

2. Categories for "late effect" of injuries are to be found at 905-909.

FRACTURES (800-829)

Excludes: *malunion (733.81)*
nonunion (733.82)
pathologic or spontaneous fracture (733.10-733.19)

The terms "condyle," "coronoid process," "ramus," and "symphysis" indicate the portion of the bone fractured, not the name of the bone involved.

The descriptions "closed" and "open" used in the fourth-digit subdivisions include the following terms:

closed (with or without delayed healing):

comminuted	impacted
depressed	linear
elevated	march
fissured	simple
fracture NOS	slipped epiphysis
greenstick	spiral

open (with or without delayed healing):

compound	puncture
infected	with foreign body
missile	

A fracture not indicated as closed or open should be classified as closed.

FRACTURE OF SKULL (800-804)

The following fifth-digit subclassification is for use with the appropriate codes in categories 800, 801, 803, and 804:

0 unspecified state of consciousness

1 with no loss of consciousness

2 with brief [less than one hour] loss of consciousness

3 with moderate [1-24 hours] loss of consciousness and return to pre-existing conscious level

4 with prolonged [more than 24 hours] loss of consciousness and return to pre-existing conscious level

5 with prolonged [more than 24 hours] loss of consciousness, without return to pre-existing conscious level
Use fifth-digit 5 to designate when a patient is unconscious and dies before regaining consciousness, regardless of the duration of the loss of consciousness

6 with loss of consciousness of unspecified duration

9 with concussion, unspecified

⑤ **800 Fracture of vault of skull**
Includes: frontal bone
parietal bone

⑤ **800.0** Closed without mention of intracranial injury

⑤ **800.1** Closed with cerebral laceration and contusion

⑤ **800.2** Closed with subarachnoid, subdural, and extradural hemorrhage

⑤ **800.3** Closed with other and unspecified intracranial hemorrhage

⑤ **800.4** Closed with intracranial injury of other and unspecified nature

⑤ **800.5** Open without mention of intracranial injury

⑤ **800.6** Open with cerebral laceration and contusion

⑤ **800.7** Open with subarachnoid, subdural, and extradural hemorrhage

Add 4th or 5th digit	Nonspecific code	Unspecified code	Medicare secondary payer(MSP) alert

⑤ **800.8** **Open with other and unspecified intracranial hemorrhage**

⑤ **800.9** **Open with intracranial injury of other and unspecified nature**

⑤ **801** **Fracture of base of skull**
Includes:

fossa:	sinus:
anterior	ethmoid
middle	frontal
posterior	sphenoid bone
occiput bone	temporal bone
orbital roof	

⑤ **801.0** **Closed without mention of intracranial injury**

⑤ **801.1** **Closed with cerebral laceration and contusion**

⑤ **801.2** **Closed with subarachnoid, subdural, and extradural hemorrhage**

⑤ **801.3** **Closed with other and unspecified intracranial hemorrhage**

⑤ **801.4** **Closed with intracranial injury of other and unspecified nature**

⑤ **801.5** **Open without mention of intracranial injury**

⑤ **801.6** **Open with cerebral laceration and contusion**

⑤ **801.7** **Open with subarachnoid, subdural, and extradural hemorrhage**

⑤ **801.8** **Open with other and unspecified intracranial hemorrhage**

⑤ **801.9** **Open with intracranial injury of other and unspecified nature**

802 **Fracture of face bones**

802.0 **Nasal bones, closed**

802.1 **Nasal bones, open**

⑤ **802.2** **Mandible, closed**
Inferior maxilla   Lower jaw (bone)

802.20 **Unspecified site**

802.21 **Condylar process**

802.22 **Subcondylar**

802.23 **Coronoid process**

802.24 **Ramus, unspecified**

802.25 **Angle of jaw**

802.26 **Symphysis of body**

802.27 **Alveolar border of body**

802.28 **Body, other and unspecified**

802.29 **Multiple sites**

⑤ **802.3** **Mandible, open**

802.30 **Unspecified site**

802.31 **Condylar process**

802.32 **Subcondylar**

802.33 **Coronoid process**

802.34 **Ramus, unspecified**

802.35 **Angle of jaw**

802.36 **Symphysis of body**

802.37 **Alveolar border of body**

802.38 **Body, other and unspecified**

802.39 **Multiple sites**

802.4 **Malar and maxillary bones, closed**
Superior maxilla   Zygoma
Upper jaw (bone)   Zygomatic arch

802.5 **Malar and maxillary bones, open**

802.6 **Orbital floor (blow-out), closed**

802.7 **Orbital floor (blow-out), open**

● Code new to this edition   ▲ Revision of existing code   ④ ⑤ Fourth or fifth digit required

802.8 **Other facial bones, closed**
    Alveolus
    Orbit:
      NOS
      part other than roof or floor
    Palate

    Excludes: *orbital:*
        floor (802.6)
        roof (801.0-801.9)

802.9 **Other facial bones, open**

⑤ **803** **Other and unqualified skull fractures**
    Includes: skull NOS
              skull multiple NOS

⑤ **803.0** **Closed without mention of intracranial injury**

⑤ **803.1** **Closed with cerebral laceration and contusion**

⑤ **803.2** **Closed with subarachnoid, subdural, and extradural hemorrhage**

⑤ **803.3** **Closed with other and unspecified intracranial hemorrhage**

⑤ **803.4** **Closed with intracranial injury of other and unspecified nature**

⑤ **803.5** **Open without mention of intracranial injury**

⑤ **803.6** **Open with cerebral laceration and contusion**

⑤ **803.7** **Open with subarachnoid, subdural, and extradural hemorrhage**

⑤ **803.8** **Open with other and unspecified intracranial hemorrhage**

⑤ **803.9** **Open with intracranial injury of other and unspecified nature**

⑤ **804** **Multiple fractures involving skull or face with other bones**

⑤ **804.0** **Closed without mention of intracranial injury**

⑤ **804.1** **Closed with cerebral laceration and contusion**

⑤ **804.2** **Closed with subarachnoid, subdural, and extradural hemorrhage**

⑤ **804.3** **Closed with other and unspecified intracranial hemorrhage**

⑤ **804.4** **Closed with intracranial injury of other and unspecified nature**

⑤ **804.5** **Open without mention of intracranial injury**

⑤ **804.6** **Open with cerebral laceration and contusion**

⑤ **804.7** **Open with subarachnoid, subdural, and extradural hemorrhage**

⑤ **804.8** **Open with other and unspecified intracranial hemorrhage**

⑤ **804.9** **Open with intracranial injury of other and unspecified nature**

FRACTURE OF NECK AND TRUNK (805-809)

805 **Fracture of vertebral column without mention of spinal cord injury**
    Includes:

        neural arch   transverse process
        spine   vertebra
        spinous process

The following fifth-digit subclassification is for use with codes 805.0-805.1:

    0 **cervical vertebra, unspecified level**

    1 **first cervical vertebra**

    2 **second cervical vertebra**

    3 **third cervical vertebra**

    4 **fourth cervical vertebra**

    5 **fifth cervical vertebra**

    6 **sixth cervical vertebra**

    7 **seventh cervical vertebra**

    8 **multiple cervical vertebrae**

⑤ **805.0** **Cervical, closed**
    Atlas   Axis

⑤ **805.1** **Cervical, open**

805.2 **Dorsal [thoracic], closed**

805.3 **Dorsal [thoracic], open**

Add 4th or 5th digit	Nonspecific code	Unspecified code	Medicare secondary payer(MSP) alert

805.4 **Lumbar, closed**

805.5 **Lumbar, open**

805.6 **Sacrum and coccyx, closed**

805.7 **Sacrum and coccyx, open**

805.8 **Unspecified, closed**

805.9 **Unspecified, open**

806 **Fracture of vertebral column with spinal cord injury**
Includes: any condition classifiable to 805 with:
complete or incomplete transverse lesion (of cord)
hematomyelia
injury to:
cauda equina
nerve
paralysis
paraplegia
quadriplegia
spinal concussion

⑤ **806.0 Cervical, closed**

806.00 **C_1-C_4 level with unspecified spinal cord injury**
Cervical region NOS with spinal cord injury NOS

806.01 **C_1-C_4 level with complete lesion of cord**

806.02 **C_1-C_4 level with anterior cord syndrome**

806.03 **C_1-C_4 level with central cord syndrome**

806.04 **C_1-C_4 level with other specified spinal cord injury**
C_1-C_4 level with:
incomplete spinal cord lesion NOS
posterior cord syndrome

806.05 **C_5-C_7 level with unspecified spinal cord injury**

806.06 **C_5-C_7 level with complete lesion of cord**

806.07 **C_5-C_7 level with anterior cord syndrome**

806.08 **C_5-C_7 level with central cord syndrome**

806.09 **C_5-C_7 level with other specified spinal cord injury**
C_5-C_7 level with:
incomplete spinal cord lesion NOS
posterior cord syndrome

⑤ **806.1 Cervical, open**

806.10 **C_1-C_4 level with unspecified spinal cord injury**

806.11 **C_1-C_4 level with complete lesion of cord**

806.12 **C_1-C_4 level with anterior cord syndrome**

806.13 **C_1-C_4 level with central cord syndrome**

806.14 **C_1-C_4 level with other specified spinal cord injury**
C_1-C_4 level with:
incomplete spinal cord lesion NOS
posterior cord syndrome

806.15 **C_5-C_7 level with unspecified spinal cord injury**

806.16 **C_5-C_7 level with complete lesion of cord**

806.17 **C_5-C_7 level with anterior cord syndrome**

806.18 **C_5-C_7 level with central cord syndrome**

806.19 **C_5-C_7 level with other specified spinal cord injury**
C_5-C_7 level with:
incomplete spinal cord lesion NOS
posterior cord syndrome

⑤ **806.2 Dorsal [thoracic], closed**

806.20 **T_1-T_6 level with unspecified spinal cord injury**
Thoracic region NOS with spinal cord injury NOS

806.21 **T_1-T_6 level with complete lesion of cord**

806.22 **T_1-T_6 level with anterior cord syndrome**

806.23 **T_1-T_6 level with central cord syndrome**

● Code new
to this edition   ▲ Revision of
existing code   ④ ⑤ Fourth or fifth
digit required

806.24 T_1-T_6 level with other specified spinal cord injury
     T_1-T_6 level with:
       incomplete spinal cord lesion NOS
       posterior cord syndrome

806.25 T_7-T_{12} level with unspecified spinal cord injury

806.26 T_7-T_{12} level with complete lesion of cord

806.27 T_7-T_{12} level with anterior cord syndrome

806.28 T_7-T_{12} level with central cord syndrome

806.29 T_7-T_{12} level with other specified spinal cord injury
     T_7-T_{12} level with:
       incomplete spinal cord lesion NOS
       posterior cord syndrome

⑤ **806.3   Dorsal [thoracic], open**

806.30 T_1-T_6 level with unspecified spinal cord injury

806.31 T_1-T_6 level with complete lesion of cord

806.32 T_1-T_6 level with anterior cord syndrome

806.33 T_1-T_6 level with central cord syndrome

806.34 T_1-T_6 level with other specified spinal cord injury
     T_1-T_6 level with:
       incomplete spinal cord lesion NOS
       posterior cord syndrome

806.35 T_7-T_{12} level with unspecified spinal cord injury

806.36 T_7-T_{12} level with complete lesion of cord

806.37 T_7-$T1_2$ level with anterior cord syndrome

806.38 T_7-T_{12} level with central cord syndrome

806.39 T_7-T_{12} level with other specified spinal cord injury
     T_7-T_{12} level with:
       incomplete spinal cord lesion NOS
       posterior cord syndrome

806.4   Lumbar, closed

806.5   Lumbar, open

⑤ **806.6   Sacrum and coccyx, closed**

806.60   **With unspecified spinal cord injury**

806.61   **With complete cauda equina lesion**

806.62   **With other cauda equina injury**

806.69   **With other spinal cord injury**

⑤ **806.7   Sacrum and coccyx, open**

806.70   **With unspecified spinal cord injury**

806.71   **With complete cauda equina lesion**

806.72   **With other cauda equina injury**

806.79   **With other spinal cord injury**

806.8   Unspecified, closed

806.9   Unspecified, open

807   Fracture of rib(s), sternum, larynx, and trachea

The following fifth-digit subclassification is for use with codes 807.0-807.1:

   0   rib(s), unspecified

   1   one rib

   2   two ribs

   3   three ribs

   4   four ribs

   5   five ribs

   6   six ribs

   7   seven ribs

   8   eight or more ribs

   9   multiple ribs, unspecified

	Add 4th or 5th digit		Nonspecific code		Unspecified code		Medicare secondary payer(MSP) alert

⑤ **807.0 Rib(s), closed**

⑤ **807.1 Rib(s), open**

807.2 Sternum, closed

807.3 Sternum, open

807.4 Flail chest

807.5 Larynx and trachea, closed
   Hyoid bone   Trachea
   Thyroid cartilage

807.6 Larynx and trachea, open

808 Fracture of pelvis

808.0 Acetabulum, closed

808.1 Acetabulum, open

808.2 Pubis, closed

808.3 Pubis, open

⑤ **808.4 Other specified part, closed**

  808.41 Ilium

  808.42 Ischium

  808.43 Multiple pelvic fractures with disruption of pelvic circle

  808.49 Other
     Innominate bone   Pelvic rim

⑤ **808.5 Other specified part, open**

  808.51 Ilium

  808.52 Ischium

  808.53 Multiple pelvic fractures with disruption of pelvic circle

  808.59 Other

808.8 Unspecified, closed

808.9 Unspecified, open

809 Ill-defined fractures of bones of trunk
  Includes: bones of trunk with other bones except those of skull and face
       multiple bones of trunk

   | Excludes: | *multiple fractures of:*
       pelvic bones alone (808.0-808.9)
       ribs alone (807.0-807.1, 807.4)
       ribs or sternum with limb bones (819.0-819.1, 828.0-828.1)
       skull or face with other bones (804.0-804.9)

809.0 Fracture of bones of trunk, closed

809.1 Fracture of bones of trunk, open

FRACTURE OF UPPER LIMB (810-819)

⑤ **810 Fracture of clavicle**
  Includes: collar bone
       interligamentous part of clavicle

The following fifth-digit subclassification is for use with category 810:

  0 unspecified part
     Clavicle NOS

  1 sternal end of clavicle

  2 shaft of clavicle

  3 acromial end of clavicle

⑤ **810.0 Closed**

⑤ **810.1 Open**

⑤ **811 Fracture of scapula**
  Includes: shoulder blade

The following fifth-digit subclassification is for use with category 811:

  0 unspecified part

  1 acromial process
     Acromion (process)

continued

● Code new   ▲ Revision of   ④ ⑤ Fourth or fifth
 to this edition   existing code   digit required

    2 coracoid process

    3 glenoid cavity and neck of scapula

    9 other
       Scapula body

⑤ **811.0** **Closed**

⑤ **811.1** **Open**

812 **Fracture of humerus**

⑤ **812.0** **Upper end, closed**

    812.00 **Upper end, unspecified part**
       Proximal end
       Shoulder

    812.01 **Surgical neck**
       Neck of humerus NOS

    812.02 **Anatomical neck**

    812.03 **Greater tuberosity**

    812.09 **Other**
       Head   Upper epiphysis

⑤ **812.1** **Upper end, open**

    812.10 **Upper end, unspecified part**

    812.11 **Surgical neck**

    812.12 **Anatomical neck**

    812.13 **Greater tuberosity**

    812.19 **Other**

⑤ **812.2** **Shaft or unspecified part, closed**

    812.20 **Unspecified part of humerus**
       Humerus NOS   Upper arm NOS

    812.21 **Shaft of humerus**

⑤ **812.3** **Shaft or unspecified part, open**

    812.30 **Unspecified part of humerus**

    812.31 **Shaft of humerus**

⑤ **812.4** **Lower end, closed**
    Distal end of humerus   Elbow

    812.40 **Lower end, unspecified part**

    812.41 **Supracondylar fracture of humerus**

    812.42 **Lateral condyle**
       External condyle

    812.43 **Medial condyle**
       Internal epicondyle

    812.44 **Condyle(s), unspecified**
       Articular process NOS
       Lower epiphysis NOS

    812.49 **Other**
       Multiple fractures of lower end
       Trochlea

⑤ **812.5** **Lower end, open**

    812.50 **Lower end, unspecified part**

    812.51 **Supracondylar fracture of humerus**

    812.52 **Lateral condyle**

    812.53 **Medial condyle**

    812.54 **Condyle(s), unspecified**

    812.59 **Other**

813 **Fracture of radius and ulna**

⑤ **813.0** **Upper end, closed**
    Proximal end

    813.00 **Upper end of forearm, unspecified**

    813.01 **Olecranon process of ulna**

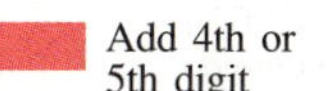

813.02 **Coronoid process of ulna**

813.03 **Monteggia's fracture**

813.04 **Other and unspecified fractures of proximal end of ulna (alone)**
Multiple fractures of ulna, upper end

813.05 **Head of radius**

813.06 **Neck of radius**

813.07 **Other and unspecified fractures of proximal end of radius (alone)**
Multiple fractures of radius, upper end

813.08 **Radius with ulna, upper end [any part]**

⑤ **813.1 Upper end, open**

813.10 **Upper end of forearm, unspecified**

813.11 **Olecranon process of ulna**

813.12 **Coronoid process of ulna**

813.13 **Monteggia's fracture**

813.14 **Other and unspecified fractures of proximal end of ulna (alone)**

813.15 **Head of radius**

813.16 **Neck of radius**

813.17 **Other and unspecified fractures of proximal end of radius (alone)**

813.18 **Radius with ulna, upper end [any part]**

⑤ **813.2 Shaft, closed**

813.20 **Shaft, unspecified**

813.21 **Radius (alone)**

813.22 **Ulna (alone)**

813.23 **Radius with ulna**

⑤ **813.3 Shaft, open**

813.30 **Shaft, unspecified**

813.31 **Radius (alone)**

813.32 **Ulna (alone)**

813.33 **Radius with ulna**

⑤ **813.4 Lower end, closed**
Distal end

813.40 **Lower end of forearm, unspecified**

813.41 **Colles' fracture**
Smith's fracture

813.42 **Other fractures of distal end of radius (alone)**
Dupuytren's fracture, radius
Radius, lower end

813.43 **Distal end of ulna (alone)**
Ulna: Ulna:
  head   lower epiphysis
  lower end   styloid process

813.44 **Radius with ulna, lower end**

⑤ **813.5 Lower end, open**

813.50 **Lower end of forearm, unspecified**

813.51 **Colles' fracture**

813.52 **Other fractures of distal end of radius (alone)**

813.53 **Distal end of ulna (alone)**

813.54 **Radius with ulna, lower end**

⑤ **813.8 Unspecified part, closed**

813.80 **Forearm, unspecified**

813.81 **Radius (alone)**

813.82 **Ulna (alone)**

813.83 **Radius with ulna**

⑤ **813.9 Unspecified part, open**

813.90 **Forearm, unspecified**

● Code new
to this edition   ▲ Revision of
existing code   ④ ⑤ Fourth or fifth
digit required

813.91 Radius (alone)

813.92 Ulna (alone)

813.93 Radius with ulna

⑤ **814 Fracture of carpal bone(s)**

The following fifth-digit subclassification is for use with category 814:

  0 carpal bone, unspecified
Wrist NOS

  1 navicular [scaphoid] of wrist

  2 lunate [semilunar] bone of wrist

  3 triquetral [cuneiform] bone of wrist

  4 pisiform

  5 trapezium bone [larger multangular]

  6 trapezoid bone [smaller multangular]

  7 capitate bone [os magnum]

  8 hamate [unciform] bone

  9 other

⑤ **814.0 Closed**

⑤ **814.1 Open**

⑤ **815 Fracture of metacarpal bone(s)**
Includes:hand [except finger]
metacarpus

The following fifth-digit subclassification is for use with category 815:

  0 metacarpal bone(s), site unspecified

  1 base of thumb [first] metacarpal
Bennett's fracture

  2 base of other metacarpal bone(s)

  3 shaft of metacarpal bone(s)

  4 neck of metacarpal bone(s)

  9 multiple sites of metacarpus

⑤ **815.0 Closed**

⑤ **815.1 Open**

⑤ **816 Fracture of one or more phalanges of hand**
Includes: finger(s)
thumb

The following fifth-digit subclassification is for use with category 816:

  0 phalanx or phalanges, unspecified

  1 middle or proximal phalanx or phalanges

  2 distal phalanx or phalanges

  3 multiple sites

⑤ **816.0 Closed**

⑤ **816.1 Open**

817 Multiple fractures of hand bones
Includes: metacarpal bone(s) with phalanx or phalanges of same hand

817.0 Closed

817.1 Open

818 Ill-defined fractures of upper limb
Includes: arm NOS
multiple bones of same upper limb

Excludes: multiple fractures of:
metacarpal bone(s) with phalanx or phalanges (817.0-817.1)
phalanges of hand alone (816.0-816.1)
radius with ulna (813.0-813.9)

818.0 Closed

818.1 Open

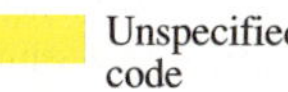

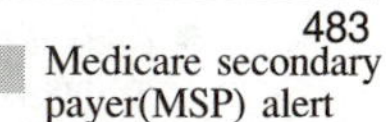

Medicare secondary
payer(MSP) alert

819 **Multiple fractures involving both upper limbs, and upper limb with rib(s) and sternum**
Includes: arm(s) with rib(s) or sternum
both arms [any bones]

819.0 **Closed**

819.1 **Open**

FRACTURE OF LOWER LIMB (820-829)

820 **Fracture of neck of femur**

⑤ **820.0** **Transcervical fracture, closed**

820.00 **Intracapsular section, unspecified**

820.01 **Epiphysis (separation) (upper)**
Transepiphyseal

820.02 **Midcervical section**
Transcervical NOS

820.03 **Base of neck**
Cervicotrochanteric section

820.09 **Other**
Head of femur
Subcapital

⑤ **820.1** **Transcervical fracture, open**

820.10 **Intracapsular section, unspecified**

820.11 **Epiphysis (separation) (upper)**

820.12 **Midcervical section**

820.13 **Base of neck**

820.19 **Other**

⑤ **820.2** **Pertrochanteric fracture, closed**

820.20 **Trochanteric section, unspecified**
Trochanter:
NOS
greater
lesser

820.21 **Intertrochanteric section**

820.22 **Subtrochanteric section**

⑤ **820.3** **Pertrochanteric fracture, open**

820.30 **Trochanteric section, unspecified**

820.31 **Intertrochanteric section**

820.32 **Subtrochanteric section**

820.8 **Unspecified part of neck of femur, closed**
Hip NOS   Neck of femur NOS

820.9 **Unspecified part of neck of femur, open**

821 **Fracture of other and unspecified parts of femur**

⑤ **821.0** **Shaft or unspecified part, closed**

821.00 **Unspecified part of femur**
Thigh   Upper leg

Excludes: hip NOS (820.8)

821.01 **Shaft**

⑤ **821.1** **Shaft or unspecified part, open**

821.10 **Unspecified part of femur**

821.11 **Shaft**

⑤ **821.2** **Lower end, closed**
Distal end

821.20 **Lower end, unspecified part**

821.21 **Condyle, femoral**

821.22 **Epiphysis, lower (separation)**

821.23 **Supracondylar fracture of femur**

● Code new
to this edition

▲ Revision of
existing code

④ ⑤ Fourth or fifth
digit required

821.29　Other
　　　Multiple fractures of lower end

⑤ **821.3**　Lower end, open

821.30　Lower end, unspecified part

821.31　Condyle, femoral

821.32　Epiphysis, lower (separation)

821.33　Supracondylar fracture of femur

821.39　Other

822　Fracture of patella

822.0　Closed

822.1　Open

⑤ **823**　Fracture of tibia and fibula

> $\boxed{Excludes:}$ *Dupuytren's fracture (824.4-824.5)*
> 　　　　*ankle (824.4-824.5)*
> 　　　　*radius (813.42, 813.52)*
> 　　*Pott's fracture (824.4-824.5)*
> 　　*that involving ankle (824.0-824.9)*

The following fifth-digit subclassification is for use with category 823:

0　tibia alone

1　fibula alone

2　fibula with tibia

⑤ **823.0**　Upper end, closed
　　Head　　　　　　　　　　　Tibia:
　　Proximal end　　　　　　　　condyles
　　　　　　　　　　　　　　　　tuberosity

⑤ **823.1**　Upper end, open

⑤ **823.2**　Shaft, closed

⑤ **823.3**　Shaft, open

⑤ **823.8**　Unspecified part, closed
　　Lower leg NOS

⑤ **823.9**　Unspecified part, open

824　Fracture of ankle

824.0　Medial malleolus, closed
　　Tibia involving:
　　　ankle
　　　malleolus

824.1　Medial malleolus, open

824.2　Lateral malleolus, closed
　　Fibula involving:
　　　ankle
　　　malleolus

824.3　Lateral malleolus, open

824.4　Bimalleolar, closed
　　Dupuytren's fracture, fibula
　　Pott's fracture

824.5　Bimalleolar, open

824.6　Trimalleolar, closed
　　Lateral and medial malleolus with anterior or posterior lip of tibia

824.7　Trimalleolar, open

824.8　Unspecified, closed
　　Ankle NOS

824.9　Unspecified, open

825　Fracture of one or more tarsal and metatarsal bones

825.0　Fracture of calcaneus, closed
　　Heel bone　　　　　　　　Os calcis

825.1　Fracture of calcaneus, open

⑤ **825.2**　Fracture of other tarsal and metatarsal bones, closed

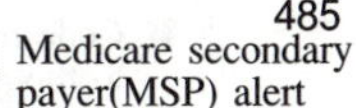

825.20 Unspecified bone(s) of foot [except toes]
Instep

825.21 Astragalus
Talus

825.22 Navicular [scaphoid], foot

825.23 Cuboid

825.24 Cuneiform, foot

825.25 Metatarsal bone(s)

825.29 Other
Tarsal with metatarsal bone(s) only

Excludes: calcaneus (825.0)

⑤ **825.3 Fracture of other tarsal and metatarsal bones, open**

825.30 Unspecified bone(s) of foot [except toes]

825.31 Astragalus

825.32 Navicular [scaphoid], foot

825.33 Cuboid

825.34 Cuneiform, foot

825.35 Metatarsal bone(s)

825.39 Other

826 Fracture of one or more phalanges of foot
Includes: toe(s)

826.0 Closed

826.1 Open

827 Other, multiple, and ill-defined fractures of lower limb
Includes: leg NOS
multiple bones of same lower limb

Excludes: multiple fractures of:
ankle bones alone (824.4-824.9)
phalanges of foot alone (826.0-826.1)
tarsal with metatarsal bones (825.29, 825.39)
tibia with fibula (823.0-823.9 with fifth-digit 2)

827.0 Closed

827.1 Open

828 Multiple fractures involving both lower limbs, lower with upper limb, and lower limb(s) with rib(s) and sternum
Includes: arm(s) with leg(s) [any bones]
both legs [any bones]
leg(s) with rib(s) or sternum

828.0 Closed

828.1 Open

829 Fracture of unspecified bones

829.0 Unspecified bone, closed

829.1 Unspecified bone, open

DISLOCATION (830-839)

Includes: displacement
subluxation

Excludes: congenital dislocation (754.0-755.8)
pathological dislocation (718.2)
recurrent dislocation (718.3)

The descriptions "closed" and "open", used in the fourth-digit subdivisions, include the following terms:

closed:	open:
complete	compound
dislocation NOS	infected
partial	with foreign body
simple	
uncomplicated	

A dislocation not indicated as closed or open should be classified as closed.

● Code new to this edition   ▲ Revision of existing code   ④ ⑤ Fourth or fifth digit required

830 Dislocation of jaw

    Includes: jaw (cartilage) (meniscus)
                mandible
                maxilla (inferior)
                temporomandibular (joint)

830.0 Closed dislocation

830.1 Open dislocation

⑤ **831 Dislocation of shoulder**

    Excludes: *sternoclavicular joint (839.61, 839.71)*
                 sternum (839.61, 839.71)

The following fifth-digit subclassification is for use with category 831:

    0 **shoulder, unspecified**
        Humerus NOS

    1 **anterior dislocation of humerus**

    2 **posterior dislocation of humerus**

    3 **inferior dislocation of humerus**

    4 **acromioclavicular (joint)**
        Clavicle

    9 **other**
        Scapula

⑤ **831.0 Closed dislocation**

⑤ **831.1 Open dislocation**

⑤ **832 Dislocation of elbow**

The following fifth-digit subclassification is for use with category 832:

    0 **elbow unspecified**

    1 **anterior dislocation of elbow**

    2 **posterior dislocation of elbow**

    3 **medial dislocation of elbow**

    4 **lateral dislocation of elbow**

    9 **other**

⑤ **832.0 Closed dislocation**

⑤ **832.1 Open dislocation**

⑤ **833 Dislocation of wrist**

The following fifth-digit subclassification is for use with category 833:

    0 **wrist, unspecified part**
        Carpal (bone)   Radius, distal end

    1 **radioulnar (joint), distal**

    2 **radiocarpal (joint)**

    3 **midcarpal (joint)**

    4 **carpometacarpal (joint)**

    5 **metacarpal (bone), proximal end**

    9 **other**
        Ulna, distal end

⑤ **833.0 Closed dislocation**

⑤ **833.1 Open dislocation**

⑤ **834 Dislocation of finger**

    Includes: finger(s)
               phalanx of hand
              thumb

The following fifth-digit subclassification is for use with category 834:

    0 **finger, unspecified part**

    1 **metacarpophalangeal (joint)**
        Metacarpal (bone), distal end

    2 **interphalangeal (joint), hand**

⑤ **834.0 Closed dislocation**

⑤ **834.1 Open dislocation**

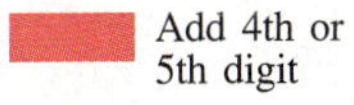 Add 4th or 5th digit

 Nonspecific code

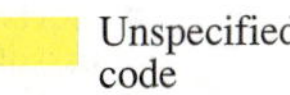 Unspecified code

Medicare secondary payer(MSP) alert

⑤ **835 Dislocation of hip**

The following fifth-digit subclassification is for use with category 835:

0 **dislocation of hip, unspecified**

1 **posterior dislocation**

2 **obturator dislocation**

3 **other anterior dislocation**

⑤ **835.0 Closed dislocation**

⑤ **835.1 Open dislocation**

836 Dislocation of knee

Excludes: *dislocation of knee:*
old or pathological (718.2)
recurrent (718.3)
internal derangement of knee joint (717.0-717.5, 717.8-717.9)
old tear of cartilage or meniscus of knee (717.0-717.5, 717.8-717.9)

836.0 Tear of medial cartilage or meniscus of knee, current
Bucket handle tear:
NOS
medial meniscus
} current injury

836.1 Tear of lateral cartilage or meniscus of knee, current

836.2 Other tear of cartilage or meniscus of knee, current
Tear of:
cartilage (semilunar)
meniscus
} current injury, not specified as medial or lateral

836.3 Dislocation of patella, closed

836.4 Dislocation of patella, open

⑤ **836.5 Other dislocation of knee, closed**

836.50 **Dislocation of knee, unspecified**

836.51 **Anterior dislocation of tibia, proximal end**
Posterior dislocation of femur, distal end

836.52 **Posterior dislocation of tibia, proximal end**
Anterior dislocation of femur, distal end

836.53 **Medial dislocation of tibia, proximal end**

836.54 **Lateral dislocation of tibia, proximal end**

836.59 **Other**

⑤ **836.6 Other dislocation of knee, open**

836.60 **Dislocation of knee, unspecified**

836.61 **Anterior dislocation of tibia, proximal end**

836.62 **Posterior dislocation of tibia, proximal end**

836.63 **Medial dislocation of tibia, proximal end**

836.64 **Lateral dislocation of tibia, proximal end**

836.69 **Other**

837 Dislocation of ankle
Includes:

astragalus
fibula, distal end
navicular, foot
scaphoid, foot
tibia, distal end

837.0 Closed dislocation

837.1 Open dislocation

⑤ **838 Dislocation of foot**

The following fifth-digit subclassification is for use with category 838:

0 **foot, unspecified**

1 **tarsal (bone), joint unspecified**

2 **midtarsal (joint)**

3 **tarsometatarsal (joint)**

4 **metatarsal (bone), joint unspecified**

5 **metatarsophalangeal (joint)**

● Code new
to this edition

▲ Revision of
existing code

④ ⑤ Fourth or fifth
digit required

    6 **interphalangeal (joint), foot**

    9 **other**
        Phalanx of foot   Toe(s)

⑤ **838.0** **Closed dislocation**

⑤ **838.1** **Open dislocation**

839 **Other, multiple, and ill-defined dislocations**

⑤ **839.0** **Cervical vertebra, closed**
      Cervical spine   Neck

    839.00 **Cervical vertebra, unspecified**

    839.01 **First cervical vertebra**

    839.02 **Second cervical vertebra**

    839.03 **Third cervical vertebra**

    839.04 **Fourth cervical vertebra**

    839.05 **Fifth cervical vertebra**

    839.06 **Sixth cervical vertebra**

    839.07 **Seventh cervical vertebra**

    839.08 **Multiple cervical vertebrae**

⑤ **839.1** **Cervical vertebra, open**

    839.10 **Cervical vertebra, unspecified**

    839.11 **First cervical vertebra**

    839.12 **Second cervical vertebra**

    839.13 **Third cervical vertebra**

    839.14 **Fourth cervical vertebra**

    839.15 **Fifth cervical vertebra**

    839.16 **Sixth cervical vertebra**

    839.17 **Seventh cervical vertebra**

    839.18 **Multiple cervical vertebrae**

⑤ **839.2** **Thoracic and lumbar vertebra, closed**

    839.20 **Lumbar vertebra**

    839.21 **Thoracic vertebra**
        Dorsal [thoracic] vertebra

⑤ **839.3** **Thoracic and lumbar vertebra, open**

    839.30 **Lumbar vertebra**

    839.31 **Thoracic vertebra**

⑤ **839.4** **Other vertebra, closed**

    839.40 **Vertebra, unspecified site**
        Spine NOS

    839.41 **Coccyx**

    839.42 **Sacrum**
        Sacroiliac (joint)

    839.49 **Other**

⑤ **839.5** **Other vertebra, open**

    839.50 **Vertebra, unspecified site**

    839.51 **Coccyx**

    839.52 **Sacrum**

    839.59 **Other**

⑤ **839.6** **Other location, closed**

    839.61 **Sternum**
        Sternoclavicular joint

    839.69 **Other**
        Pelvis

⑤ **839.7** **Other location, open**

    839.71 **Sternum**

    839.79 **Other**

Add 4th or 5th digit	Nonspecific code	Unspecified code	Medicare secondary payer(MSP) alert

839.8 **Multiple and ill-defined, closed**
Arm
Back
Hand
Multiple locations, except fingers or toes alone
Other ill-defined locations
Unspecified location

839.9 **Multiple and ill-defined, open**

SPRAINS AND STRAINS OF JOINTS AND ADJACENT MUSCLES (840-848)

Includes:

avulsion		joint capsule
hemarthrosis		ligament
laceration	of:	muscle
rupture		tendon
sprain		
strain		
tear		

Excludes: *laceration of tendon in open wounds (880-884 and 890-894 with .2)*

840 **Sprains and strains of shoulder and upper arm**

840.0 **Acromioclavicular (joint) (ligament)**

840.1 **Coracoclavicular (ligament)**

840.2 **Coracohumeral (ligament)**

840.3 **Infraspinatus (muscle) (tendon)**

840.4 **Rotator cuff (capsule)**

Excludes: *complete rupture of rotator cuff, nontraumatic (727.61)*

840.5 **Subscapularis (muscle)**

840.6 **Supraspinatus (muscle) (tendon)**

840.8 **Other specified sites of shoulder and upper arm**

840.9 **Unspecified site of shoulder and upper arm**
Arm NOS   Shoulder NOS

841 **Sprains and strains of elbow and forearm**

841.0 **Radial collateral ligament**

841.1 **Ulnar collateral ligament**

841.2 **Radiohumeral (joint)**

841.3 **Ulnohumeral (joint)**

841.8 **Other specified sites of elbow and forearm**

841.9 **Unspecified site of elbow and forearm**
Elbow NOS

842 **Sprains and strains of wrist and hand**

⑤ **842.0** **Wrist**

842.00 **Unspecified site**

842.01 **Carpal (joint)**

842.02 **Radiocarpal (joint) (ligament)**

842.09 **Other**
Radioulnar joint, distal

⑤ **842.1** **Hand**

842.10 **Unspecified site**

842.11 **Carpometacarpal (joint)**

842.12 **Metacarpophalangeal (joint)**

842.13 **Interphalangeal (joint)**

842.19 **Other**
Midcarpal (joint)

843 **Sprains and strains of hip and thigh**

843.0 **Iliofemoral (ligament)**

843.1 **Ischiocapsular (ligament)**

843.8 **Other specified sites of hip and thigh**

● Code new to this edition   ▲ Revision of existing code   ④ ⑤ Fourth or fifth digit required

843.9 Unspecified site of hip and thigh
Hip NOS   Thigh NOS

844 Sprains and strains of knee and leg

844.0 Lateral collateral ligament of knee

844.1 Medial collateral ligament of knee

844.2 Cruciate ligament of knee

844.3 Tibiofibular (joint) (ligament), superior

844.8 Other specified sites of knee and leg

844.9 Unspecified site of knee and leg
Knee NOS   Leg NOS

845 Sprains and strains of ankle and foot

⑤ **845.0** Ankle

845.00 Unspecified site

845.01 Deltoid (ligament), ankle
Internal collateral (ligament), ankle

845.02 Calcaneofibular (ligament)

845.03 Tibiofibular (ligament), distal

845.09 Other
Achilles tendon

⑤ **845.1** Foot

845.10 Unspecified site

845.11 Tarsometatarsal (joint) (ligament)

845.12 Metatarsophalangeal (joint)

845.13 Interphalangeal (joint), toe

845.19 Other

846 Sprains and strains of sacroiliac region

846.0 Lumbosacral (joint) (ligament)

846.1 Sacroiliac ligament

846.2 Sacrospinatus (ligament)

846.3 Sacrotuberous (ligament)

846.8 Other specified sites of sacroiliac region

846.9 Unspecified site of sacroiliac region

847 Sprains and strains of other and unspecified parts of back

Excludes: lumbosacral (846.0)

847.0 Neck
Anterior longitudinal (ligament), cervical
Atlanto-axial (joints)
Atlanto-occipital (joints)
Whiplash injury

Excludes: neck injury NOS (959.0)
thyroid region (848.2)

847.1 Thoracic

847.2 Lumbar

847.3 Sacrum
Sacrococcygeal (ligament)

847.4 Coccyx

847.9 Unspecified site of back
Back NOS

848 Other and ill-defined sprains and strains

848.0 Septal cartilage of nose

848.1 Jaw
Temporomandibular (joint) (ligament)

848.2 Thyroid region
Cricoarytenoid (joint) (ligament)
Cricothyroid (joint) (ligament)
Thyroid cartilage

Add 4th or 5th digit	Nonspecific code	Unspecified code	Medicare secondary payer(MSP) alert

848.3 Ribs
Chondrocostal (joint)
Costal cartilage   } without mention of injury to sternum

⑤ **848.4 Sternum**

848.40 Unspecified site

848.41 Sternoclavicular (joint) (ligament)

848.42 Chondrosternal (joint)

848.49 Other
Xiphoid cartilage

848.5 Pelvis
Symphysis pubis

Excludes: *that in childbirth (665.6)*

848.8 Other specified sites of sprains and strains

848.9 Unspecified site of sprain and strain

INTRACRANIAL INJURY, EXCLUDING THOSE WITH SKULL FRACTURE (850-854)

Excludes: *intracranial injury with skull fracture (800-801 and 803-804, except .0 and .5)*
open wound of head without intracranial injury (870.0-873.9)
skull fracture alone (800-801 and 803-804 with .0, .5)

The description "with open intracranial wound," used in the fourth-digit subdivisions, includes those specified as open or with mention of infection or foreign body.

The following fifth-digit subclassification is for use with categories 851-854:

0 unspecified state of consciousness

1 with no loss of consciousness

2 with brief [less than one hour] loss of consciousness

3 with moderate [1-24 hours] loss of consciousness

4 with prolonged [more than 24 hours] loss of consciousness and return to pre-existing conscious level

5 with prolonged [more than 24 hours] loss of consciousness, without return to pre-existing conscious level

Use fifth-digit 5 to designate when a patient is unconscious and dies before regaining consciousness, regardless of the duration of the loss of consciousness

6 with loss of consciousness of unspecified duration

9 with concussion, unspecified

850 Concussion
Includes: commotio cerebri

Excludes: *concussion with:*
cerebral laceration or contusion (851.0-851.9)
cerebral hemorrhage (852-853)
head injury NOS (959.01)

850.0 With no loss of consciousness
Concussion with mental confusion or disorientation, without loss of consciousness

850.1 With brief loss of consciousness
Loss of consciousness for less than one hour

850.2 With moderate loss of consciousness
Loss of consciousness for 1-24 hours

850.3 With prolonged loss of consciousness and return to pre-existing conscious level
Loss of consciousness for more than 24 hours with complete recovery

850.4 With prolonged loss of consciousness, without return to pre-existing conscious level

850.5 With loss of consciousness of unspecified duration

850.9 Concussion, unspecified

⑤ **851 Cerebral laceration and contusion**

⑤ **851.0 Cortex (cerebral) contusion without mention of open intracranial wound**

⑤ **851.1 Cortex (cerebral) contusion with open intracranial wound**

⑤ **851.2 Cortex (cerebral) laceration without mention of open intracranial wound**

⑤ **851.3 Cortex (cerebral) laceration with open intracranial wound**

⑤ **851.4 Cerebellar or brain stem contusion without mention of open intracranial wound**

● Code new
to this edition

▲ Revision of
existing code

④ ⑤ Fourth or fifth
digit required

⑤ **851.5** Cerebellar or brain stem contusion with open intracranial wound

⑤ **851.6** Cerebellar or brain stem laceration without mention of open intracranial wound

⑤ **851.7** Cerebellar or brain stem laceration with open intracranial wound

⑤ **851.8** Other and unspecified cerebral laceration and contusion, without mention of open intracranial wound
    Brain (membrane) NOS

⑤ **851.9** Other and unspecified cerebral laceration and contusion, with open intracranial wound

⑤ **852** Subarachnoid, subdural, and extradural hemorrhage, following injury

> *Excludes:* *Cerebral contusion or laceration (with hemorrhage) (851.0-851.9)*

⑤ **852.0** Subarachnoid hemorrhage following injury without mention of open intracranial wound
    Middle meningeal hemorrhage following injury

⑤ **852.1** Subarachnoid hemorrhage following injury with open intracranial wound

⑤ **852.2** Subdural hemorrhage following injury without mention of open intracranial wound

⑤ **852.3** Subdural hemorrhage following injury with open intracranial wound

⑤ **852.4** Extradural hemorrhage following injury without mention of open intracranial wound
    Epidural hematoma following injury

⑤ **852.5** Extradural hemorrhage following injury with open intracranial wound

⑤ **853** Other and unspecified intracranial hemorrhage following injury

⑤ **853.0** Without mention of open intracranial wound
    Cerebral compression due to injury
    Intracranial hematoma following injury
    Traumatic cerebral hemorrhage

⑤ **853.1** With open intracranial wound

⑤ **854** Intracranial injury of other and unspecified nature
    Includes: brain injury NOS
              cavernous sinus
              intracranial injury

> *Excludes:* *any condition classifiable to 850-853*
> *head injury NOS (959.01)*

⑤ **854.0** Without mention of open intracranial wound

⑤ **854.1** With open intracranial wound

INTERNAL INJURY OF THORAX, ABDOMEN, AND PELVIS (860-869)

    Includes:

      blast injuries
      blunt trauma
      bruise
      concussion injuries (except cerebral)
      crushing
      hematoma   } of internal organs
      laceration
      puncture
      tear
      traumatic rupture

> *Excludes:* *concussion NOS (850.0-850.9)*
> *flail chest (807.4)*
> *foreign body entering through orifice (930.0-939.9)*
> *injury to blood vessels (901.0-902.9)*

The description "with open wound," used in the fourth-digit subdivisions, includes those with mention of infection or foreign body.

860 Traumatic pneumothorax and hemothorax

  860.0 Pneumothorax without mention of open wound into thorax

  860.1 Pneumothorax with open wound into thorax

  860.2 Hemothorax without mention of open wound into thorax

  860.3 Hemothorax with open wound into thorax

  860.4 Pneumohemothorax without mention of open wound into thorax

  860.5 Pneumohemothorax with open wound into thorax

861 **Injury to heart and lung**

  Excludes: injury to blood vessels of thorax (901.0-901.9)

⑤ **861.0** **Heart, without mention of open wound into thorax**

  861.00 **Unspecified injury**

  861.01 **Contusion**
    Cardiac contusion   Myocardial contusion

  861.02 **Laceration without penetration of heart chambers**

  861.03 **Laceration with penetration of heart chambers**

⑤ **861.1** **Heart, with open wound into thorax**

  861.10 **Unspecified injury**

  861.11 **Contusion**

  861.12 **Laceration without penetration of heart chambers**

  861.13 **Laceration with penetration of heart chambers**

⑤ **861.2** **Lung, without mention of open wound into thorax**

  861.20 **Unspecified injury**

  861.21 **Contusion**

  861.22 **Laceration**

⑤ **861.3** **Lung, with open wound into thorax**

  861.30 **Unspecified injury**

  861.31 **Contusion**

  861.32 **Laceration**

862 **Injury to other and unspecified intrathoracic organs**

  Excludes: injury to blood vessels of thorax (901.0-901.9)

862.0 **Diaphragm, without mention of open wound into cavity**

862.1 **Diaphragm, with open wound into cavity**

⑤ **862.2** **Other specified intrathoracic organs, without mention of open wound into cavity**

  862.21 **Bronchus**

  862.22 **Esophagus**

  862.29 **Other**
    Pleura   Thymus gland

⑤ **862.3** **Other specified intrathoracic organs, with open wound into cavity**

  862.31 **Bronchus**

  862.32 **Esophagus**

  862.39 **Other**

862.8 **Multiple and unspecified intrathoracic organs, without mention of open wound into cavity**
  Crushed chest
  Multiple intrathoracic organs

862.9 **Multiple and unspecified intrathoracic organs, with open wound into cavity**

863 **Injury to gastrointestinal tract**

  Excludes: anal sphincter laceration during delivery (664.2)
    bile duct (868.0-868.1 with fifth-digit 2)
    gallbladder (868.0-868.1 with fifth-digit 2)

863.0 **Stomach, without mention of open wound into cavity**

863.1 **Stomach, with open wound into cavity**

⑤ **863.2** **Small intestine, without mention of open wound into cavity**

  863.20 **Small intestine, unspecified site**

  863.21 **Duodenum**

  863.29 **Other**

⑤ **863.3** **Small intestine, with open wound into cavity**

  863.30 **Small intestine, unspecified site**

  863.31 **Duodenum**

  863.39 **Other**

  ● Code new   ▲ Revision of   ④ ⑤ Fourth or fifth
    to this edition   existing code   digit required

⑤ **863.4** **Colon or rectum, without mention of open wound into cavity**

863.40 Colon, unspecified site

863.41 Ascending [right] colon

863.42 Transverse colon

863.43 Descending [left] colon

863.44 Sigmoid colon

863.45 Rectum

863.46 Multiple sites in colon and rectum

863.49 Other

⑤ **863.5** **Colon or rectum, with open wound into cavity**

863.50 Colon, unspecified site

863.51 Ascending [right] colon

863.52 Transverse colon

863.53 Descending [left] colon

863.54 Sigmoid colon

863.55 Rectum

863.56 Multiple sites in colon and rectum

863.59 Other

⑤ **863.8** **Other and unspecified gastrointestinal sites, without mention of open wound into cavity**

863.80 Gastrointestinal tract, unspecified site

863.81 Pancreas, head

863.82 Pancreas, body

863.83 Pancreas, tail

863.84 Pancreas, multiple and unspecified sites

863.85 Appendix

863.89 Other
Intestine NOS

⑤ **863.9** **Other and unspecified gastrointestinal sites, with open wound into cavity**

863.90 Gastrointestinal tract, unspecified site

863.91 Pancreas, head

863.92 Pancreas, body

863.93 Pancreas, tail

863.94 Pancreas, multiple and unspecified sites

863.95 Appendix

863.99 Other

⑤ **864** **Injury to liver**

The following fifth-digit subclassification is for use with category 864:

0 unspecified injury

1 hematoma and contusion

2 laceration, minor
Laceration involving capsule only, or without significant involvement of hepatic parenchyma [i.e., less than 1 cm deep]

3 laceration, moderate
Laceration involving parenchyma but without major disruption of parenchyma [i.e., less than 10 cm long and less than 3 cm deep]

4 laceration, major
Laceration with significant disruption of hepatic parenchyma [i.e., 10 cm long and 3 cm deep]
Multiple moderate lacerations, with or without hematoma
Stellate lacerations of liver

5 laceration, unspecified

9 other

⑤ **864.0** **Without mention of open wound into cavity**

Add 4th or 5th digit	Nonspecific code	Unspecified code	Medicare secondary payer(MSP) alert

⑤ **864.1** **With open wound into cavity**

⑤ **865** **Injury to spleen**

The following fifth-digit subclassification is for use with category 865:

0 **unspecified injury**

1 **hematoma without rupture of capsule**

2 **capsular tears, without major disruption of parenchyma**

3 **laceration extending into parenchyma**

4 **massive parenchymal disruption**

9 **other**

⑤ **865.0** **Without mention of open wound into cavity**

⑤ **865.1** **With open wound into cavity**

⑤ **866** **Injury to kidney**

The following fifth-digit subclassification is for use with category 866:

0 **unspecified injury**

1 **hematoma without rupture of capsule**

2 **laceration**

3 **complete disruption of kidney parenchyma**

⑤ **866.0** **Without mention of open wound into cavity**

⑤ **866.1** **With open wound into cavity**

867 **Injury to pelvic organs**

Excludes: *injury during delivery (664.0-665.9)*

867.0 **Bladder and urethra, without mention of open wound into cavity**

867.1 **Bladder and urethra, with open wound into cavity**

867.2 **Ureter, without mention of open wound into cavity**

867.3 **Ureter, with open wound into cavity**

867.4 **Uterus, without mention of open wound into cavity**

867.5 **Uterus, with open wound into cavity**

867.6 **Other specified pelvic organs, without mention of open wound into cavity**
Fallopian tube   Seminal vesicle
Ovary   Vas deferens
Prostate

867.7 **Other specified pelvic organs, with open wound into cavity**

867.8 **Unspecified pelvic organs, without mention of open wound into cavity**

867.9 **Unspecified pelvic organ, with open wound into cavity**

⑤ **868** **Injury to other intra-abdominal organs**

The following fifth-digit subclassification is for use with category 868:

0 **unspecified intra-abdominal organ**

1 **adrenal gland**

2 **bile duct and gallbladder**

3 **peritoneum**

4 **retroperitoneum**

9 **other and multiple intra-abdominal organs**

⑤ **868.0** **Without mention of open wound into cavity**

⑤ **868.1** **With open wound into cavity**

869 **Internal injury to unspecified or ill-defined organs**
Includes: internal injury NOS
          multiple internal injury NOS

869.0 **Without mention of open wound into cavity**

869.1 **With open wound into cavity**

● Code new to this edition   ▲ Revision of existing code   ④ ⑤ Fourth or fifth digit required

OPEN WOUND (870-897)

Includes:

animal bite	laceration
avulsion	puncture wound
cut	traumatic amputation

Excludes: *burn (940.0-949.5)*
crushing (925-929.9)
puncture of internal organs (860.0-869.1)
superficial injury (910.0-919.9)
that incidental to:
  dislocation (830.0-839.9)
  fracture (800.0-829.1)
  internal injury (860.0-869.1)
  intracranial injury (851.0-854.1)

The description "complicated" used in the fourth-digit subdivisions includes those with mention of delayed healing, delayed treatment, foreign body, or major infection.

OPEN WOUND OF HEAD, NECK, AND TRUNK (870-879)

870 Open wound of ocular adnexa

870.0 Laceration of skin of eyelid and periocular area

870.1 Laceration of eyelid, full-thickness, not involving lacrimal passages

870.2 Laceration of eyelid involving lacrimal passages

870.3 Penetrating wound of orbit, without mention of foreign body

870.4 Penetrating wound of orbit with foreign body

Excludes: *retained (old) foreign body in orbit (376.6)*

870.8 Other specified open wounds of ocular adnexa

870.9 Unspecified open wound of ocular adnexa

871 Open wound of eyeball

Excludes: *2nd cranial nerve [optic] injury (950.0-950.9)*
3rd cranial nerve [oculomotor] injury (951.0)

871.0 Ocular laceration without prolapse of intraocular tissue

871.1 Ocular laceration with prolapse or exposure of intraocular tissue

871.2 Rupture of eye with partial loss of intraocular tissue

871.3 Avulsion of eye
Traumatic enucleation

871.4 Unspecified laceration of eye

871.5 Penetration of eyeball with magnetic foreign body

Excludes: *retained (old) magnetic foreign body in globe (360.50-360.59)*

871.6 Penetration of eyeball with (nonmagnetic) foreign body

Excludes: *retained (old) (nonmagnetic) foreign body in globe (360.60-360.69)*

871.7 Unspecified ocular penetration

871.9 Unspecified open wound of eyeball

872 Open wound of ear

⑤ **872.0 External ear, without mention of complication**

 872.00 External ear, unspecified site

 872.01 Auricle, ear
 Pinna

 872.02 Auditory canal

⑤ **872.1 External ear, complicated**

 872.10 External ear, unspecified site

 872.11 Auricle, ear

 872.12 Auditory canal

⑤ **872.6 Other specified parts of ear, without mention of complication**

 872.61 Ear drum
 Drumhead   Tympanic membrane

 872.62 Ossicles

872.63   Eustachian tube

872.64   Cochlea

`872.69`   Other and multiple sites

⑤ 872.7   Other specified parts of ear, complicated

872.71   Ear drum

872.72   Ossicles

872.73   Eustachian tube

872.74   Cochlea

`872.79`   Other and multiple sites

`872.8`   Ear, part unspecified, without mention of complication
     Ear NOS

`872.9`   Ear, part unspecified, complicated

`873`   **Other open wound of head**

873.0   Scalp, without mention of complication

873.1   Scalp, complicated

⑤ 873.2   Nose, without mention of complication

`873.20`   Nose, unspecified site

873.21   Nasal septum

873.22   Nasal cavity

873.23   Nasal sinus

`873.29`   Multiple sites

⑤ 873.3   Nose, complicated

`873.30`   Nose, unspecified site

873.31   Nasal septum

873.32   Nasal cavity

873.33   Nasal sinus

`873.39`   Multiple sites

⑤ 873.4   Face, without mention of complication

`873.40`   Face, unspecified site

873.41   Cheek

873.42   Forehead
     Eyebrow

873.43   Lip

873.44   Jaw

`873.49`   Other and multiple sites

⑤ 873.5   Face, complicated

`873.50`   Face, unspecified site

873.51   Cheek

873.52   Forehead

873.53   Lip

873.54   Jaw

`873.59`   Other and multiple sites

⑤ 873.6   Internal structures of mouth, without mention of complication

`873.60`   Mouth, unspecified site

873.61   Buccal mucosa

873.62   Gum (alveolar process)

873.63   Tooth (broken)

873.64   Tongue and floor of mouth

873.65   Palate

`873.69`   Other and multiple sites

⑤ 873.7   Internal structures of mouth, complicated

`873.70`   Mouth, unspecified site

873.71   Buccal mucosa

● Code new
to this edition   ▲ Revision of existing code   ④ ⑤ Fourth or fifth digit required

873.72   **Gum (alveolar process)**

873.73   **Tooth (broken)**

873.74   **Tongue and floor of mouth**

873.75   **Palate**

873.79   **Other and multiple sites**

873.8 Other and unspecified open wound of head without mention of complication
    Head NOS

873.9 Other and unspecified open wound of head, complicated

874 Open wound of neck

⑤ **874.0 Larynx and trachea, without mention of complication**

874.00   **Larynx with trachea**

874.01   **Larynx**

874.02   **Trachea**

⑤ **874.1 Larynx and trachea, complicated**

874.10   **Larynx with trachea**

874.11   **Larynx**

874.12   **Trachea**

874.2 Thyroid gland, without mention of complication

874.3 Thyroid gland, complicated

874.4 Pharynx, without mention of complication
    Cervical esophagus

874.5 Pharynx, complicated

874.8 Other and unspecified parts, without mention of complication
    Nape of neck   Throat NOS
    Supraclavicular region

874.9 Other and unspecified parts, complicated

875 Open wound of chest (wall)

> Excludes: *open wound into thoracic cavity (860.0-862.9)*
>   *traumatic pneumothorax and hemothorax (860.1, 860.3, 860.5)*

875.0 Without mention of complication

875.1 Complicated

876 Open wound of back
    Includes: loin   lumbar region

> Excludes: *open wound into thoracic cavity (860.0-862.9)*
>   *traumatic pneumothorax and hemothorax (860.1, 860.3, 860.5)*

876.0 Without mention of complication

876.1 Complicated

877 Open wound of buttock
    Includes: sacroiliac region

877.0 Without mention of complication

877.1 Complicated

878 Open wound of genital organs (external), including traumatic amputation

> Excludes: *injury during delivery (664.0-665.9)*
>   *internal genital organs (867.0-867.9)*

878.0 Penis, without mention of complication

878.1 Penis, complicated

878.2 Scrotum and testes, without mention of complication

878.3 Scrotum and testes, complicated

878.4 Vulva, without mention of complication
    Labium (majus) (minus)

878.5 Vulva, complicated

878.6 Vagina, without mention of complication

878.7 Vagina, complicated

878.8 Other and unspecified parts, without mention of complication

878.9 Other and unspecified parts, complicated

879 Open wound of other and unspecified sites, except limbs

879.0 Breast, without mention of complication

879.1 Breast, complicated

879.2 Abdominal wall, anterior, without mention of complication
Abdominal wall NOS	Pubic region
Epigastric region	Umbilical region
Hypogastric region	

879.3 Abdominal wall, anterior, complicated

879.4 Abdominal wall, lateral, without mention of complication
Flank	Iliac (region)
Groin	Inguinal region
Hypochondrium	

879.5 Abdominal wall, lateral, complicated

879.6 Other and unspecified parts of trunk, without mention of complication
Pelvic region	Trunk NOS
Perineum	

879.7 Other and unspecified parts of trunk, complicated

879.8 Open wound(s) (multiple) of unspecified site(s) without mention of complication
Multiple open wounds NOS
Open wound NOS

879.9 Open wound(s) (multiple) of unspecified site(s), complicated

OPEN WOUND OF UPPER LIMB (880-887)

⑤ **880** Open wound of shoulder and upper arm

The following fifth-digit subclassification is for use with category 880:

    0 shoulder region

    1 scapular region

    2 axillary region

    3 upper arm

    9 multiple sites

⑤ **880.0** Without mention of complication

⑤ **880.1** Complicated

⑤ **880.2** With tendon involvement

⑤ **881** Open wound of elbow, forearm, and wrist

The following fifth-digit subclassification is for use with category 881:

    0 forearm

    1 elbow

    2 wrist

⑤ **881.0** Without mention of complication

⑤ **881.1** Complicated

⑤ **881.2** With tendon involvement

882 Open wound of hand except finger(s) alone

882.0 Without mention of complication

882.1 Complicated

882.2 With tendon involvement

883 Open wound of finger(s)
Includes: fingernail	thumb (nail)

883.0 Without mention of complication

883.1 Complicated

883.2 With tendon involvement

884 Multiple and unspecified open wound of upper limb
Includes: arm NOS
              multiple sites of one upper limb
              upper limb NOS

884.0 Without mention of complication

884.1 Complicated

● Code new
to this edition ▲ Revision of
existing code ④ ⑤ Fourth or fifth
digit required

884.2 With tendon involvement

885 Traumatic amputation of thumb (complete) (partial)
Includes: thumb(s) (with finger(s) of either hand)

885.0 Without mention of complication

885.1 Complicated

886 Traumatic amputation of other finger(s) (complete) (partial)
Includes: finger(s) of one or both hands, without mention of thumb(s)

886.0 Without mention of complication

886.1 Complicated

887 Traumatic amputation of arm and hand (complete) (partial)

887.0 Unilateral, below elbow, without mention of complication

887.1 Unilateral, below elbow, complicated

887.2 Unilateral, at or above elbow, without mention of complication

887.3 Unilateral, at or above elbow, complicated

887.4 Unilateral, level not specified, without mention of complication

887.5 Unilateral, level not specified, complicated

887.6 Bilateral [any level], without mention of complication
One hand and other arm

887.7 Bilateral [any level], complicated

OPEN WOUND OF LOWER LIMB (890-897)

890 Open wound of hip and thigh

890.0 Without mention of complication

890.1 Complicated

890.2 With tendon involvement

891 Open wound of knee, leg [except thigh], and ankle
Includes: leg NOS
multiple sites of leg, except thigh

Excludes: *that of thigh (890.0-890.2)*
with multiple sites of lower limb (894.0-894.2)

891.0 Without mention of complication

891.1 Complicated

891.2 With tendon involvement

892 Open wound of foot except toe(s) alone
Includes: heel

892.0 Without mention of complication

892.1 Complicated

892.2 With tendon involvement

893 Open wound of toe(s)
Includes: toenail

893.0 Without mention of complication

893.1 Complicated

893.2 With tendon involvement

894 Multiple and unspecified open wound of lower limb
Includes: lower limb NOS
multiple sites of one lower limb, with thigh

894.0 Without mention of complication

894.1 Complicated

894.2 With tendon involvement

895 Traumatic amputation of toe(s) (complete) (partial)
Includes: toe(s) of one or both feet

895.0 Without mention of complication

895.1 Complicated

896 Traumatic amputation of foot (complete) (partial)

896.0 Unilateral, without mention of complication

896.1 Unilateral, complicated

896.2 Bilateral, without mention of complication

> *Excludes:* *one foot and other leg (897.6-897.7)*

896.3 Bilateral, complicated

897 Traumatic amputation of leg(s) (complete) (partial)

897.0 Unilateral, below knee, without mention of complication

897.1 Unilateral, below knee, complicated

897.2 Unilateral, at or above knee, without mention of complication

897.3 Unilateral, at or above knee, complicated

897.4 Unilateral, level not specified, without mention of complication

897.5 Unilateral, level not specified, complicated

897.6 Bilateral [any level], without mention of complication
      One foot and other leg

897.7 Bilateral [any level], complicated

INJURY TO BLOOD VESSELS (900-904)

Includes:

    arterial hematoma
    avulsion
    cut   } of blood vessel, secondary to
    laceration   other injuries e.g., fracture or
    rupture   open wound
    traumatic aneurysm or fistula (arteriovenous)

> *Excludes:* *accidental puncture or laceration during medical procedure (998.2)*
> *intracranial hemorrhage following injury (851.0-854.1)*

900 Injury to blood vessels of head and neck

⑤ **900.0** Carotid artery

    900.00 Carotid artery, unspecified

    900.01 Common carotid artery

    900.02 External carotid artery

    900.03 Internal carotid artery

900.1 Internal jugular vein

⑤ **900.8** Other specified blood vessels of head and neck

    900.81 External jugular vein
                Jugular vein NOS

    900.82 Multiple blood vessels of head and neck

    900.89 Other

900.9 Unspecified blood vessel of head and neck

901 Injury to blood vessels of thorax

> *Excludes:* *traumatic hemothorax (860.2-860.5)*

901.0 Thoracic aorta

901.1 Innominate and subclavian arteries

901.2 Superior vena cava

901.3 Innominate and subclavian veins

⑤ **901.4** Pulmonary blood vessels

    901.40 Pulmonary vessel(s), unspecified

    901.41 Pulmonary artery

    901.42 Pulmonary vein

⑤ **901.8** Other specified blood vessels of thorax

    901.81 Intercostal artery or vein

    901.82 Internal mammary artery or vein

    901.83 Multiple blood vessels of thorax

    901.89 Other
                Azygos vein   Hemiazygos vein

● Code new to this edition   ▲ Revision of existing code   ④ ⑤ Fourth or fifth digit required

901.9 Unspecified blood vessel of thorax

902 Injury to blood vessels of abdomen and pelvis

902.0 Abdominal aorta

⑤ 902.1 Inferior vena cava

902.10 Inferior vena cava, unspecified

902.11 Hepatic veins

902.19 Other

⑤ 902.2 Celiac and mesenteric arteries

902.20 Celiac and mesenteric arteries, unspecified

902.21 Gastric artery

902.22 Hepatic artery

902.23 Splenic artery

902.24 Other specified branches of celiac axis

902.25 Superior mesenteric artery (trunk)

902.26 Primary branches of superior mesenteric artery
Ileo-colic artery

902.27 Inferior mesenteric artery

902.29 Other

⑤ 902.3 Portal and splenic veins

902.31 Superior mesenteric vein and primary subdivisions
Ileo-colic vein

902.32 Inferior mesenteric vein

902.33 Portal vein

902.34 Splenic vein

902.39 Other
Cystic vein   Gastric vein

⑤ 902.4 Renal blood vessels

902.40 Renal vessel(s), unspecified

902.41 Renal artery

902.42 Renal vein

902.49 Other
Suprarenal arteries

⑤ 902.5 Iliac blood vessels

902.50 Iliac vessel(s), unspecified

902.51 Hypogastric artery

902.52 Hypogastric vein

902.53 Iliac artery

902.54 Iliac vein

902.55 Uterine artery

902.56 Uterine vein

902.59 Other

⑤ 902.8 Other specified blood vessels of abdomen and pelvis

902.81 Ovarian artery

902.82 Ovarian vein

902.87 Multiple blood vessels of abdomen and pelvis

902.89 Other

902.9 Unspecified blood vessel of abdomen and pelvis

903 Injury to blood vessels of upper extremity

⑤ 903.0 Axillary blood vessels

903.00 Axillary vessel(s), unspecified

903.01 Axillary artery

903.02 Axillary vein

903.1 Brachial blood vessels

Add 4th or 5th digit   Nonspecific code   Unspecified code   Medicare secondary payer(MSP) alert

903.2 Radial blood vessels

903.3 Ulnar blood vessels

903.4 Palmar artery

903.5 Digital blood vessels

903.8 Other specified blood vessels of upper extremity
Multiple blood vessels of upper extremity

903.9 Unspecified blood vessel of upper extremity

904 Injury to blood vessels of lower extremity and unspecified sites

904.0 Common femoral artery
Femoral artery above profunda origin

904.1 Superficial femoral artery

904.2 Femoral veins

904.3 Saphenous veins
Saphenous vein (greater) (lesser)

⑤ **904.4 Popliteal blood vessels**

904.40 Popliteal vessel(s), unspecified

904.41 Popliteal artery

904.42 Popliteal vein

⑤ **904.5 Tibial blood vessels**

904.50 Tibial vessel(s), unspecified

904.51 Anterior tibial artery

904.52 Anterior tibial vein

904.53 Posterior tibial artery

904.54 Posterior tibial vein

904.6 Deep plantar blood vessels

904.7 Other specified blood vessels of lower extremity
Multiple blood vessels of lower extremity

904.8 Unspecified blood vessel of lower extremity

904.9 Unspecified site
Injury to blood vessel NOS

LATE EFFECTS OF INJURIES, POISONINGS, TOXIC EFFECTS, AND OTHER EXTERNAL CAUSES (905-909)

Note: These categories are to be used to indicate conditions classifiable to 800-999 as the cause of late effects, which are themselves classified elsewhere. The "late effects" include those specified as such, or as sequelae, which may occur at any time after the acute injury.

905 Late effects of musculoskeletal and connective tissue injuries

905.0 Late effect of fracture of skull and face bones
Late effect of injury classifiable to 800-804

905.1 Late effect of fracture of spine and trunk without mention of spinal cord lesion
Late effect of injury classifiable to 805, 807-809

905.2 Late effect of fracture of upper extremities
Late effect of injury classifiable to 810-819

905.3 Late effect of fracture of neck of femur
Late effect of injury classifiable to 820

905.4 Late effect of fracture of lower extremities
Late effect of injury classifiable to 821-827

905.5 Late effect of fracture of multiple and unspecified bones
Late effect of injury classifiable to 828-829

905.6 Late effect of dislocation
Late effect of injury classifiable to 830-839

905.7 Late effect of sprain and strain without mention of tendon injury
Late effect of injury classifiable to 840-848, except tendon injury

● Code new to this edition   ▲ Revision of existing code   ④ ⑤ Fourth or fifth digit required

905.8 Late effect of tendon injury
Late effect of tendon injury due to:
open wound [injury classifiable to 880-884 with .2, 890-894 with .2]
sprain and strain [injury classifiable to 840-848]

905.9 Late effect of traumatic amputation
Late effect of injury classifiable to 885-887, 895-897

Excludes: *late amputation stump complication (997.60-997.69)*

906 Late effects of injuries to skin and subcutaneous tissues

906.0 Late effect of open wound of head, neck, and trunk
Late effect of injury classifiable to 870-879

906.1 Late effect of open wound of extremities without mention of tendon injury
Late effect of injury classifiable to 880-884, 890-894 except .2

906.2 Late effect of superficial injury
Late effect of injury classifiable to 910-919

906.3 Late effect of contusion
Late effect of injury classifiable to 920-924

906.4 Late effect of crushing
Late effect of injury classifiable to 925-929

906.5 Late effect of burn of eye, face, head, and neck
Late effect of injury classifiable to 940-941

906.6 Late effect of burn of wrist and hand
Late effect of injury classifiable to 944

906.7 Late effect of burn of other extremities
Late effect of injury classifiable to 943 or 945

906.8 Late effect of burns of other specified sites
Late effect of injury classifiable to 942, 946-947

906.9 Late effect of burn of unspecified site
Late effect of injury classifiable to 948-949

907 Late effects of injuries to the nervous system

907.0 Late effect of intracranial injury without mention of skull fracture
Late effect of injury classifiable to 850-854

907.1 Late effect of injury to cranial nerve
Late effect of injury classifiable to 950-951

907.2 Late effect of spinal cord injury
Late effect of injury classifiable to 806, 952

907.3 Late effect of injury to nerve root(s), spinal plexus(es), and other nerves of trunk
Late effect of injury classifiable to 953-954

907.4 Late effect of injury to peripheral nerve of shoulder girdle and upper limb
Late effect of injury classifiable to 955

907.5 Late effect of injury to peripheral nerve of pelvic girdle and lower limb
Late effect of injury classifiable to 956

907.9 Late effect of injury to other and unspecified nerve
Late effect of injury classifiable to 957

908 Late effects of other and unspecified injuries

908.0 Late effect of internal injury to chest
Late effect of injury classifiable to 860-862

908.1 Late effect of internal injury to intra-abdominal organs
Late effect of injury classifiable to 863-866, 868

908.2 Late effect of internal injury to other internal organs
Late effect of injury classifiable to 867 or 869

908.3 Late effect of injury to blood vessel of head, neck, and extremities
Late effect of injury classifiable to 900, 903-904

908.4 Late effect of injury to blood vessel of thorax, abdomen, and pelvis
Late effect of injury classifiable to 901-902

908.5 Late effect of foreign body in orifice
Late effect of injury classifiable to 930-939

908.6 Late effect of certain complications of trauma
Late effect of complications classifiable to 958

908.9 Late effect of unspecified injury
Late effect of injury classifiable to 959

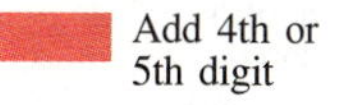 Add 4th or 5th digit

 Nonspecific code

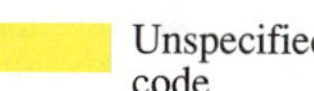 Unspecified code

Medicare secondary payer(MSP) alert

909 **Late effects of other and unspecified external causes**

909.0 **Late effect of poisoning due to drug, medicinal or biological substance**
Late effect of conditions classifiable to 960-979

Excludes: *late effect of adverse effect of drug, medicinal or biological substance (909.5)*

909.1 **Late effect of toxic effects of nonmedical substances**
Late effect of conditions classifiable to 980-989

909.2 **Late effect of radiation**
Late effect of conditions classifiable to 990

909.3 **Late effect of complications of surgical and medical care**
Late effect of conditions classifiable to 996-999

909.4 **Late effect of certain other external causes**
Late effect of conditions classifiable to 991-994

909.5 **Late effect of adverse effect of drug, medicinal or biological substance**

Excludes: *late effect of poisoning due to drug, medicinal or biological substance (909.0)*

909.9 **Late effect of other and unspecified external causes**

SUPERFICIAL INJURY (910-919)

Excludes: *burn (blisters) (940.0-949.5)*
contusion (920-924.9)
foreign body:
  granuloma (728.82)
  inadvertently left in operative wound (998.4)
  residual, in soft tissue (729.6)
insect bite, venomous (989.5)
open wound with incidental foreign body (870.0-897.7)

910 **Superficial injury of face, neck, and scalp except eye**
Includes:

cheek	lip
ear	nose
gum	throat

Excludes: *eye and adnexa (918.0-918.9)*

910.0 **Abrasion or friction burn without mention of infection**

910.1 **Abrasion or friction burn, infected**

910.2 **Blister without mention of infection**

910.3 **Blister, infected**

910.4 **Insect bite, nonvenomous, without mention of infection**

910.5 **Insect bite, nonvenomous, infected**

910.6 **Superficial foreign body (splinter) without major open wound and without mention of infection**

910.7 **Superficial foreign body (splinter) without major open wound, infected**

910.8 **Other and unspecified superficial injury of face, neck, and scalp without mention of infection**

910.9 **Other and unspecified superficial injury of face, neck, and scalp, infected**

911 **Superficial injury of trunk**
Includes:

abdominal wall	interscapular region
anus	labium (majus) (minus)
back	penis
breast	perineum
buttock	scrotum
chest wall	testis
flank	vagina
groin	vulva

Excludes: *hip (916.0-916.9)*
scapular region (912.0-912.9)

911.0 **Abrasion or friction burn without mention of infection**

911.1 **Abrasion or friction burn, infected**

911.2 **Blister without mention of infection**

911.3 **Blister, infected**

● Code new
to this edition   ▲ Revision of
existing code   ④ ⑤ Fourth or fifth
digit required

911.4 Insect bite, nonvenomous, without mention of infection

911.5 Insect bite, nonvenomous, infected

911.6 Superficial foreign body (splinter) without major open wound and without mention of infection

911.7 Superficial foreign body (splinter) without major open wound, infected

911.8 Other and unspecified superficial injury of trunk without mention of infection

911.9 Other and unspecified superficial injury of trunk, infected

912 Superficial injury of shoulder and upper arm
    Includes: axilla   scapular region

912.0 Abrasion or friction burn without mention of infection

912.1 Abrasion or friction burn, infected

912.2 Blister without mention of infection

912.3 Blister, infected

912.4 Insect bite, nonvenomous, without mention of infection

912.5 Insect bite, nonvenomous, infected

912.6 Superficial foreign body (splinter) without major open wound and without mention of infection

912.7 Superficial foreign body (splinter) without major open wound, infected

912.8 Other and unspecified superficial injury of shoulder and upper arm without mention of infection

912.9 Other and unspecified superficial injury of shoulder and upper arm, infected

913 Superficial injury of elbow, forearm, and wrist

913.0 Abrasion or friction burn without mention of infection

913.1 Abrasion or friction burn, infected

913.2 Blister without mention of infection

913.3 Blister, infected

913.4 Insect bite, nonvenomous, without mention of infection

913.5 Insect bite, nonvenomous, infected

913.6 Superficial foreign body (splinter) without major open wound and without mention of infection

913.7 Superficial foreign body (splinter) without major open wound, infected

913.8 Other and unspecified superficial injury of elbow, forearm, and wrist without mention of infection

913.9 Other and unspecified superficial injury of elbow, forearm, and wrist, infected

914 Superficial injury of hand(s) except finger(s) alone

914.0 Abrasion or friction burn without mention of infection

914.1 Abrasion or friction burn, infected

914.2 Blister without mention of infection

914.3 Blister, infected

914.4 Insect bite, nonvenomous, without mention of infection

914.5 Insect bite, nonvenomous, infected

914.6 Superficial foreign body (splinter) without major open wound and without mention of infection

914.7 Superficial foreign body (splinter) without major open wound, infected

914.8 Other and unspecified superficial injury of hand without mention of infection

914.9 Other and unspecified superficial injury of hand, infected

915 Superficial injury of finger(s)
    Includes: fingernail   thumb (nail)

915.0 Abrasion or friction burn without mention of infection

915.1 Abrasion or friction burn, infected

915.2 Blister without mention of infection

915.3 Blister, infected

915.4 Insect bite, nonvenomous, without mention of infection

915.5 Insect bite, nonvenomous, infected

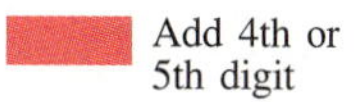

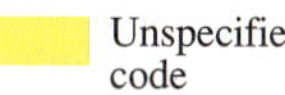

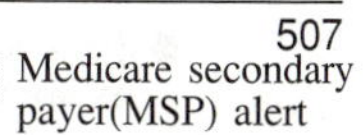

915.6 Superficial foreign body (splinter) without major open wound and without mention of infection

915.7 Superficial foreign body (splinter) without major open wound, infected

915.8 Other and unspecified superficial injury of fingers without mention of infection

915.9 Other and unspecified superficial injury of fingers, infected

916 Superficial injury of hip, thigh, leg, and ankle

916.0 Abrasion or friction burn without mention of infection

916.1 Abrasion or friction burn, infected

916.2 Blister without mention of infection

916.3 Blister, infected

916.4 Insect bite, nonvenomous, without mention of infection

916.5 Insect bite, nonvenomous, infected

916.6 Superficial foreign body (splinter) without major open wound and without mention of infection

916.7 Superficial foreign body (splinter) without major open wound, infected

916.8 Other and unspecified superficial injury of hip, thigh, leg, and ankle without mention of infection

916.9 Other and unspecified superficial injury of hip, thigh, leg, and ankle, infected

917 Superficial injury of foot and toe(s)

Includes: heel   toenail

917.0 Abrasion or friction burn without mention of infection

917.1 Abrasion or friction burn, infected

917.2 Blister without mention of infection

917.3 Blister, infected

917.4 Insect bite, nonvenomous, without mention of infection

917.5 Insect bite, nonvenomous, infected

917.6 Superficial foreign body (splinter) without major open wound and without mention of infection

917.7 Superficial foreign body (splinter) without major open wound, infected

917.8 Other and unspecified superficial injury of foot and toes without mention of infection

917.9 Other and unspecified superficial injury of foot and toes, infected

918 Superficial injury of eye and adnexa

Excludes: burn (940.0-940.9)

foreign body on external eye (930.0-930.9)

918.0 Eyelids and periocular area

Abrasion   Superficial foreign body (splinter)

Insect bite

918.1 Cornea

Corneal abrasion   Superficial laceration

Excludes: corneal injury due to contact lens (371.82)

918.2 Conjunctiva

918.9 Other and unspecified superficial injuries of eye

Eye (ball) NOS

919 Superficial injury of other, multiple, and unspecified sites

Excludes: multiple sites classifiable to the same three-digit category (910.0-918.9)

919.0 Abrasion or friction burn without mention of infection

919.1 Abrasion or friction burn, infected

919.2 Blister without mention of infection

919.3 Blister, infected

919.4 Insect bite, nonvenomous, without mention of infection

919.5 Insect bite, nonvenomous, infected

919.6 Superficial foreign body (splinter) without major open wound and without mention of infection

919.7 Superficial foreign body (splinter) without major open wound, infected

● Code new to this edition   ▲ Revision of existing code   ④ ⑤ Fourth or fifth digit required

919.8 Other and unspecified superficial injury without mention of infection

919.9 Other and unspecified superficial injury, infected

CONTUSION WITH INTACT SKIN SURFACE (920-924)

Includes:

bruise
hematoma } without fracture or open wound

Excludes: *concussion (850.0-850.9)*
hemarthrosis (840.0-848.9)
internal organs (860.0-869.1)
that incidental to:
   crushing injury (925-929.9)
   dislocation (830.0-839.9)
   fracture (800.0-829.1)
   internal injury (860.0-869.1)
   intracranial injury (850.0-854.1)
   nerve injury (950.0-957.9)
   open wound (870.0-897.7)

920 Contusion of face, scalp, and neck except eye(s)

Cheek	Mandibular joint area
Ear (auricle)	Nose
Gum	Throat
Lip	

921 Contusion of eye and adnexa

921.0 Black eye, not otherwise specified

921.1 Contusion of eyelids and periocular area

921.2 Contusion of orbital tissues

921.3 Contusion of eyeball

921.9 Unspecified contusion of eye
Injury of eye NOS

922 Contusion of trunk

922.0 Breast

922.1 Chest wall

922.2 Abdominal wall

Flank	Groin

⑤ **922.3 Back**

Excludes: *scapular region (923.01)*

922.31 Back

Excludes: *interscapular region (922.33)*

922.32 Buttock

922.33 Interscapular region

922.4 Genital organs

Labium (majus) (minus)	Testis
Penis	Vagina
Perineum	Vulva
Scrotum	

922.8 Multiple sites of trunk

922.9 Unspecified part
Trunk NOS

923 Contusion of upper limb

⑤ **923.0 Shoulder and upper arm**

923.00 Shoulder region

923.01 Scapular region

923.02 Axillary region

923.03 Upper arm

923.09 Multiple sites

⑤ **923.1 Elbow and forearm**

923.10 Forearm

Add 4th or 5th digit	Nonspecific code	Unspecified code	Medicare secondary payer(MSP) alert

    923.11   **Elbow**

⑤ **923.2** **Wrist and hand(s), except finger(s) alone**

    923.20   **Hand(s)**

    923.21   **Wrist**

923.3 **Finger**
    Fingernail   Thumb (nail)

923.8 **Multiple sites of upper limb**

923.9 **Unspecified part of upper limb**
    Arm NOS

924 **Contusion of lower limb and of other and unspecified sites**

⑤ **924.0** **Hip and thigh**

    924.00   **Thigh**

    924.01   **Hip**

⑤ **924.1** **Knee and lower leg**

    924.10   **Lower leg**

    924.11   **Knee**

⑤ **924.2** **Ankle and foot, excluding toe(s)**

    924.20   **Foot**
         Heel

    924.21   **Ankle**

924.3 **Toe**
    Toenail

924.4 **Multiple sites of lower limb**

924.5 **Unspecified part of lower limb**
    Leg NOS

924.8 **Multiple sites, not elsewhere classified**

924.9 **Unspecified site**

CRUSHING INJURY (925-929)

    Excludes: *concussion (850.0-850.9)*
            fractures (800-829)
            internal organs (860.0-869.1)
            that incidental to:
                internal injury (860.0-869.1)
                intracranial injury (850.0-854.1)

925 **Crushing injury of face, scalp, and neck**
    Cheek   Pharynx
    Ear   Throat
    Larynx

925.1 **Crushing injury of face and scalp**
    Cheek   Ear

925.2 **Crushing injury of neck**
    Larynx   Throat
    Pharynx

926 **Crushing injury of trunk**

    Excludes: *crush injury of internal organs (860.0-869.1)*

926.0 **External genitalia**
    Labium (majus) (minus)   Testis
    Penis   Vulva
    Scrotum

⑤ **926.1** **Other specified sites**

    926.11   **Back**

    926.12   **Buttock**

    926.19   **Other**
         Breast

    Excludes: *crushing of chest (860.0-862.9)*

926.8 **Multiple sites of trunk**

● Code new   ▲ Revision of   ④ ⑤ Fourth or fifth
  to this edition   existing code   digit required

926.9 Unspecified site
Trunk NOS

927 Crushing injury of upper limb

⑤ **927.0** Shoulder and upper arm

    927.00 Shoulder region

    927.01 Scapular region

    927.02 Axillary region

    927.03 Upper arm

    927.09 Multiple sites

⑤ **927.1** Elbow and forearm

    927.10 Forearm

    927.11 Elbow

⑤ **927.2** Wrist and hand(s), except finger(s) alone

    927.20 Hand(s)

    927.21 Wrist

927.3 Finger(s)

927.8 Multiple sites of upper limb

927.9 Unspecified site
Arm NOS

928 Crushing injury of lower limb

⑤ **928.0** Hip and thigh

    928.00 Thigh

    928.01 Hip

⑤ **928.1** Knee and lower leg

    928.10 Lower leg

    928.11 Knee

⑤ **928.2** Ankle and foot, excluding toe(s) alone

    928.20 Foot
        Heel

    928.21 Ankle

928.3 Toe(s)

928.8 Multiple sites of lower limb

928.9 Unspecified site
Leg NOS

929 Crushing injury of multiple and unspecified sites

    Excludes: multiple internal injury NOS (869.0-869.1)

929.0 Multiple sites, not elsewhere classified

929.9 Unspecified site

EFFECTS OF FOREIGN BODY ENTERING THROUGH ORIFICE (930-939)

    Excludes: foreign body:

        granuloma (728.82)
        inadvertently left in operative wound (998.4, 998.7)
        in open wound (800-839, 851-897)
        residual, in soft tissues (729.6)
        superficial without major open wound (910-919 with .6 or .7)

930 Foreign body on external eye

    Excludes: foreign body in penetrating wound of:

        eyeball (871.5-871.6)
          retained (old) (360.5-360.6)
        ocular adnexa (870.4)
          retained (old) (376.6)

930.0 Corneal foreign body

930.1 Foreign body in conjunctival sac

930.2 Foreign body in lacrimal punctum

930.8 Other and combined sites

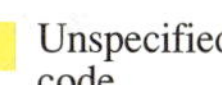

Add 4th or 5th digit	Nonspecific code	Unspecified code	Medicare secondary payer(MSP) alert

930.9 Unspecified site
External eye NOS

931 Foreign body in ear
Auditory canal   Auricle

932 Foreign body in nose
Nasal sinus   Nostril

933 Foreign body in pharynx and larynx

933.0 Pharynx
Nasopharynx   Throat NOS

933.1 Larynx
Asphyxia due to   Choking due to:
  foreign body   food (regurgitated)
                                                        phlegm

934 Foreign body in trachea, bronchus, and lung

934.0 Trachea

934.1 Main bronchus

934.8 Other specified parts
Bronchioles   Lung

934.9 Respiratory tree, unspecified
Inhalation of liquid or vomitus, lower respiratory tract NOS

935 Foreign body in mouth, esophagus, and stomach

935.0 Mouth

935.1 Esophagus

935.2 Stomach

936 Foreign body in intestine and colon

937 Foreign body in anus and rectum
Rectosigmoid (junction)

938 Foreign body in digestive system, unspecified
Alimentary tract NOS   Swallowed foreign body

939 Foreign body in genitourinary tract

939.0 Bladder and urethra

939.1 Uterus, any part

> *Excludes:* *intrauterine contraceptive device:*
> *complications from (996.32, 996.65)*
> *presence of (V45.51)*

939.2 Vulva and vagina

939.3 Penis

939.9 Unspecified site

BURNS (940-949)

Includes: burns from:
        electrical heating appliance
        electricity
        flame
        hot object
        lightning
        radiation
    chemical burns (external) (internal)
    scalds

> *Excludes:* *friction burns (910-919 with .0, .1)*
> *sunburn (692.71)*

940 Burn confined to eye and adnexa

940.0 Chemical burn of eyelids and periocular area

940.1 Other burns of eyelids and periocular area

940.2 Alkaline chemical burn of cornea and conjunctival sac

940.3 Acid chemical burn of cornea and conjunctival sac

940.4 Other burn of cornea and conjunctival sac

940.5 Burn with resulting rupture and destruction of eyeball

● Code new
to this edition   ▲ Revision of
existing code   ④ ⑤ Fourth or fifth
digit required

⑤ **940.9** Unspecified burn of eye and adnexa

⑤ **941** Burn of face, head, and neck

> Excludes: mouth (947.0)

The following fifth-digit subclassification is for use with category 941:

0 face and head, unspecified site

1 ear [any part]

2 eye (with other parts of face, head, and neck)

3 lip(s)

4 chin

5 nose (septum)

6 scalp [any part]
Temple (region)

7 forehead and cheek

8 neck

9 multiple sites [except with eye] of face, head, and neck

⑤ **941.0** Unspecified degree

⑤ 941.1 Erythema [first degree]

⑤ 941.2 Blisters, epidermal loss [second degree]

⑤ 941.3 Full-thickness skin loss [third degree NOS]

⑤ 941.4 Deep necrosis of underlying tissues [deep third degree] without mention of loss of a body part

⑤ 941.5 Deep necrosis of underlying tissues [deep third degree] with loss of a body part

⑤ **942** Burn of trunk

> Excludes: scapular region (943.0-943.5 with fifth-digit 6)

The following fifth-digit subclassification is for use with category 942:

0 trunk, unspecified site

1 breast

2 chest wall, excluding breast and nipple

3 abdominal wall
Flank   Groin

4 back [any part]
Buttock   Interscapular region

5 genitalia
Labium (majus) (minus)   Scrotum
Penis   Testis
Perineum   Vulva

9 other and multiple sites of trunk

⑤ **942.0** Unspecified degree

⑤ 942.1 Erythema [first degree]

⑤ 942.2 Blisters, epidermal loss [second degree]

⑤ 942.3 Full-thickness skin loss [third degree NOS]

⑤ 942.4 Deep necrosis of underlying tissues [deep third degree] without mention of loss of a body part

⑤ 942.5 Deep necrosis of underlying tissues [deep third degree] with loss of a body part

⑤ **943** Burn of upper limb, except wrist and hand

The following fifth-digit subclassification is for use with category 943:

0 upper limb, unspecified site

1 forearm

2 elbow

3 upper arm

4 axilla

5 shoulder

6 scapular region

9 multiple sites of upper limb, except wrist and hand

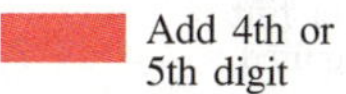

⑤ **943.0** **Unspecified degree**

⑤ 943.1 **Erythema [first degree]**

⑤ 943.2 **Blisters, epidermal loss [second degree]**

⑤ 943.3 **Full-thickness skin loss [third degree NOS]**

⑤ 943.4 **Deep necrosis of underlying tissues [deep third degree] without mention of loss of a body part**

⑤ 943.5 **Deep necrosis of underlying tissues [deep third degree] with loss of a body part**

⑤ **944** **Burn of wrist(s) and hand(s)**

The following fifth-digit subclassification is for use with category 944:

    0 **hand, unspecified site**

    1 **single digit [finger (nail)] other than thumb**

    2 **thumb (nail)**

    3 **two or more digits, not including thumb**

    4 **two or more digits including thumb**

    5 **palm**

    6 **back of hand**

    7 **wrist**

    8 **multiple sites of wrist(s) and hand(s)**

⑤ **944.0** **Unspecified degree**

⑤ 944.1 **Erythema [first degree]**

⑤ 944.2 **Blisters, epidermal loss [second degree]**

⑤ 944.3 **Full-thickness skin loss [third degree NOS]**

⑤ 944.4 **Deep necrosis of underlying tissues [deep third degree] without mention of loss of a body part**

⑤ 944.5 **Deep necrosis of underlying tissues [deep third degree] with loss of a body part**

⑤ **945** **Burn of lower limb(s)**

The following fifth-digit subclassification is for use with category 945:

    0 **lower limb [leg], unspecified site**

    1 **toe(s) (nail)**

    2 **foot**

    3 **ankle**

    4 **lower leg**

    5 **knee**

    6 **thigh [any part]**

    9 **multiple sites of lower limb(s)**

⑤ **945.0** **Unspecified degree**

⑤ 945.1 **Erythema [first degree]**

⑤ 945.2 **Blisters, epidermal loss [second degree]**

⑤ 945.3 **Full-thickness skin loss [third degree NOS]**

⑤ 945.4 **Deep necrosis of underlying tissues [deep third degree] without mention of loss of a body part**

⑤ 945.5 **Deep necrosis of underlying tissues [deep third degree] with loss of a body part**

946 **Burns of multiple specified sites**

Includes: burns of sites classifiable to more than one three-digit category in 940-945

Excludes: *multiple burns NOS (949.0-949.5)*

946.0 **Unspecified degree**

946.1 **Erythema [first degree]**

946.2 **Blisters, epidermal loss [second degree]**

946.3 **Full-thickness skin loss [third degree NOS]**

946.4 **Deep necrosis of underlying tissues [deep third degree] without mention of loss of a body part**

946.5 **Deep necrosis of underlying tissues [deep third degree] with loss of a body part**

● Code new to this edition   ▲ Revision of existing code   ④ ⑤ Fourth or fifth digit required

947 Burn of internal organs
Includes: burns from chemical agents (ingested)

947.0 Mouth and pharynx
Gum   Tongue

947.1 Larynx, trachea, and lung

947.2 Esophagus

947.3 Gastrointestinal tract
Colon   Small intestine
Rectum   Stomach

947.4 Vagina and uterus

947.8 Other specified sites

947.9 Unspecified site

⑤ **948 Burns classified according to extent of body surface involved**

Excludes: sunburn (692.71)

Note: This category is to be used when the site of the burn is unspecified, or with categories 940-947 when the site is specified.

The following fifth-digit subclassification is for use with category 948 to indicate the percent of *body surface* with *third degree* burn; valid digits are in [brackets] under each code:

0 less than 10 percent or unspecified

1 10-19%

2 20-29%

3 30-39%

4 40-49%

5 50-59%

6 60-69%

7 70-79%

8 80-89%

9 90% or more of body surface

⑤ **948.0 Burn [any degree] involving less than 10 percent of body surface**
[0]

⑤ **948.1 10-19 percent of body surface**
[0-1]

⑤ **948.2 20-29 percent of body surface**
[0-2]

⑤ **948.3 30-39 percent of body surface**
[0-3]

⑤ **948.4 40-49 percent of body surface**
[0-4]

⑤ **948.5 50-59 percent of body surface**
[0-5]

⑤ **948.6 60-69 percent of body surface**
[0-6]

⑤ **948.7 70-79 percent of body surface**
[0-7]

⑤ **948.8 80-89 percent of body surface**
[0-8]

⑤ **948.9 90 percent or more of body surface**
[0-9]

949 Burn, unspecified
Includes:
burn NOS   multiple burns NOS

Excludes: burn of unspecified site but with statement of the extent of body surface involved (948.0-948.9)

949.0 Unspecified degree

949.1 Erythema [first degree]

949.2 Blisters, epidermal loss [second degree]

949.3 Full-thickness skin loss [third degree NOS]

Add 4th or 5th digit   Nonspecific code

Unspecified code   Medicare secondary payer(MSP) alert

949.4 Deep necrosis of underlying tissues [deep third degree] without mention of loss of a body part

949.5 Deep necrosis of underlying tissues [deep third degree] with loss of a body part

INJURY TO NERVES AND SPINAL CORD (950-957)

Includes:

division of nerve
lesion in continuity
traumatic neuroma
traumatic transient paralysis
} (with open wound)

Excludes: *accidental puncture or laceration during medical procedure (998.2)*

950 Injury to optic nerve and pathways

950.0 Optic nerve injury
Second cranial nerve

950.1 Injury to optic chiasm

950.2 Injury to optic pathways

950.3 Injury to visual cortex

950.9 Unspecified
Traumatic blindness NOS

951 Injury to other cranial nerve(s)

951.0 Injury to oculomotor nerve
Third cranial nerve

951.1 Injury to trochlear nerve
Fourth cranial nerve

951.2 Injury to trigeminal nerve
Fifth cranial nerve

951.3 Injury to abducens nerve
Sixth cranial nerve

951.4 Injury to facial nerve
Seventh cranial nerve

951.5 Injury to acoustic nerve
Auditory nerve   Traumatic deafness NOS
Eighth cranial nerve

951.6 Injury to accessory nerve
Eleventh cranial nerve

951.7 Injury to hypoglossal nerve
Twelfth cranial nerve

951.8 Injury to other specified cranial nerves
Glossopharyngeal [9th cranial] nerve
Olfactory [1st cranial] nerve
Pneumogastric [10th cranial] nerve
Traumatic anosmia NOS
Vagus [10th cranial] nerve

951.9 Injury to unspecified cranial nerve

952 Spinal cord injury without evidence of spinal bone injury

⑤ **952.0** Cervical

952.00 C_1-C_4 level with unspecified spinal cord injury
Spinal cord injury, cervical region NOS

952.01 C_1-C_4 level with complete lesion of spinal cord

952.02 C_1-C_4 level with anterior cord syndrome

952.03 C_1-C_4 level with central cord syndrome

952.04 C_1-C_4 level with other specified spinal cord injury
Incomplete spinal cord lesion at C_1-C_4 level:
NOS
with posterior cord syndrome

952.05 C_5-C_7 level with unspecified spinal cord injury

952.06 C_5-C_7 level with complete lesion of spinal cord

952.07 C_5-C_7 level with anterior cord syndrome

952.08 C_5-C_7 level with central cord syndrome

● Code new
to this edition

▲ Revision of
existing code

④ ⑤ Fourth or fifth
digit required

952.09 C$_5$-C$_7$ level with other specified spinal cord injury
Incomplete spinal cord lesion at C$_5$-C$_7$ level:
NOS
with posterior cord syndrome

⑤ **952.1 Dorsal [thoracic]**

952.10 T$_1$-T$_6$ level with unspecified spinal cord injury
Spinal cord injury, thoracic region NOS

952.11 T$_1$-T$_6$ level with complete lesion of spinal cord

952.12 T$_1$-T$_6$ level with anterior cord syndrome

952.13 T$_1$-T$_6$ level with central cord syndrome

952.14 T$_1$-T$_6$ level with other specified spinal cord injury
Incomplete spinal cord lesion at T$_1$-T$_6$ level:
NOS
with posterior cord syndrome

952.15 T$_7$-T$_{12}$ level with unspecified spinal cord injury

952.16 T$_7$-T$_{12}$ level with complete lesion of spinal cord

952.17 T$_7$-T$_{12}$ level with anterior cord syndrome

952.18 T$_7$-T$_{12}$ level with central cord syndrome

952.19 T$_7$-T$_{12}$ level with other specified spinal cord injury
Incomplete spinal cord lesion at T$_7$-T$_{12}$ level:
NOS
with posterior cord syndrome

952.2 Lumbar

952.3 Sacral

952.4 Cauda equina

952.8 Multiple sites of spinal cord

952.9 Unspecified site of spinal cord

953 Injury to nerve roots and spinal plexus

953.0 Cervical root

953.1 Dorsal root

953.2 Lumbar root

953.3 Sacral root

953.4 Brachial plexus

953.5 Lumbosacral plexus

953.8 Multiple sites

953.9 Unspecified site

954 Injury to other nerve(s) of trunk, excluding shoulder and pelvic girdles

954.0 Cervical sympathetic

954.1 Other sympathetic
Celiac ganglion or plexus   Splanchnic nerve(s)
Inferior mesenteric plexus   Stellate ganglion

954.8 Other specified nerve(s) of trunk

954.9 Unspecified nerve of trunk

955 Injury to peripheral nerve(s) of shoulder girdle and upper limb

955.0 Axillary nerve

955.1 Median nerve

955.2 Ulnar nerve

955.3 Radial nerve

955.4 Musculocutaneous nerve

955.5 Cutaneous sensory nerve, upper limb

955.6 Digital nerve

955.7 Other specified nerve(s) of shoulder girdle and upper limb

955.8 Multiple nerves of shoulder girdle and upper limb

955.9 Unspecified nerve of shoulder girdle and upper limb

	Add 4th or 5th digit		Nonspecific code		Unspecified code		Medicare secondary payer(MSP) alert

956 **Injury to peripheral nerve(s) of pelvic girdle and lower limb**

956.0 **Sciatic nerve**

956.1 **Femoral nerve**

956.2 **Posterior tibial nerve**

956.3 **Peroneal nerve**

956.4 **Cutaneous sensory nerve, lower limb**

956.5 **Other specified nerve(s) of pelvic girdle and lower limb**

956.8 **Multiple nerves of pelvic girdle and lower limb**

956.9 **Unspecified nerve of pelvic girdle and lower limb**

957 **Injury to other and unspecified nerves**

957.0 **Superficial nerves of head and neck**

957.1 **Other specified nerve(s)**

957.8 **Multiple nerves in several parts**
Multiple nerve injury NOS

957.9 **Unspecified site**
Nerve injury NOS

CERTAIN TRAUMATIC COMPLICATIONS AND UNSPECIFIED INJURIES (958-959)

958 **Certain early complications of trauma**

Excludes: *adult respiratory distress syndrome (518.5)*
flail chest (807.4)
shock lung (518.5)
that occurring during or following medical procedures (996.0-999.9)

958.0 **Air embolism**
Pneumathemia

Excludes: *that complicating:*
abortion (634-638 with .6, 639.6)
ectopic or molar pregnancy (639.6)
pregnancy, childbirth, or the puerperium (673.0)

958.1 **Fat embolism**

Excludes: *that complicating:*
abortion (634-638 with .6, 639.6)
pregnancy, childbirth, or the puerperium (673.8)

958.2 **Secondary and recurrent hemorrhage**

958.3 **Posttraumatic wound infection, not elsewhere classified**

958.4 **Traumatic shock**
Shock (immediate) (delayed) following injury

Excludes: *shock:*
anaphylactic (995.0)
due to serum (999.4)
anesthetic (995.4)
electric (994.8)
following abortion (639.5)
lightning (994.0)
nontraumatic NOS (785.50)
obstetric (669.1)
postoperative (998.0)

958.5 **Traumatic anuria**
Crush syndrome
Renal failure following crushing

Excludes: *that due to a medical procedure (997.5)*

958.6 **Volkmann's ischemic contracture**
Posttraumatic muscle contracture

958.7 **Traumatic subcutaneous emphysema**

Excludes: *subcutaneous emphysema resulting from a procedure (998.81)*

958.8 **Other early complications of trauma**

959 **Injury, other and unspecified**
    Includes: injury NOS

    Excludes: *injury NOS of:*
        blood vessels (900.0-904.9)
        eye (921.0-921.9)
        internal organs (860.0-869.1)
        intracranial sites (854.0-854.1)
        nerves (950.0-951.9, 953.0-957.9)
        spinal cord (952.0-952.9)

⑤ **959.0** **Head, face and neck**

Cheek	Mouth
Ear	Nose
Eyebrow	Throat
Lip	

    959.01 **Head injury, unspecified**

    Excludes: *concussion (850.1-850.9)*
        with head injury NOS (850.1-850.9)
        specified intracranial injuries (850.0-854.1)

    959.09 **Injury of face and neck**

959.1 **Trunk**

Abdominal wall	External genital organs
Back	Flank
Breast	Groin
Buttock	Interscapular region
Chest wall	Perineum

    Excludes: *scapular region (959.2)*

959.2 **Shoulder and upper arm**
    Axilla   Scapular region

959.3 **Elbow, forearm, and wrist**

959.4 **Hand, except finger**

959.5 **Finger**
    Fingernail   Thumb (nail)

959.6 **Hip and thigh**
    Upper leg

959.7 **Knee, leg, ankle, and foot**

959.8 **Other specified sites, including multiple**

    Excludes: *multiple sites classifiable to the same four-digit category (959.0-959.7)*

959.9 **Unspecified site**

POISONING BY DRUGS, MEDICINAL AND BIOLOGICAL SUBSTANCES (960-979)

    Includes: overdose of these substances
              wrong substances given or taken in error

    Excludes: *adverse effects ["hypersensitivity," "reaction," etc.] of correct substance properly*
        administered. Such cases are to be classified according to the nature of the
        adverse effect, such as:
        adverse effect NOS (995.2)
        allergic lymphadenitis (289.3)
        aspirin gastritis (535.4)
        blood disorders (280.0-289.9)
        dermatitis:
          contact (692.0-692.9)
          due to ingestion (693.0-693.9)
        nephropathy (583.9)
        [The drug giving rise to the adverse effect may be identified by use of categories
          E930-E949]
        drug dependence (304.0-304.9)
        drug reaction and poisoning affecting the newborn (760.0-779.9)
        nondependent abuse of drugs (305.0-305.9)
        pathological drug intoxication (292.2)
    Use additional code to specify the effects of the poisoning

---

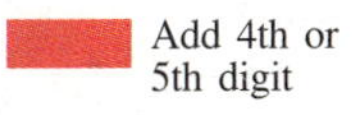 Add 4th or 5th digit	 Nonspecific code	 Unspecified code	Medicare secondary payer(MSP) alert

960 Poisoning by antibiotics

> *Excludes:* antibiotics:
>> ear, nose, and throat (976.6)
>> eye (976.5)
>> local (976.0)

960.0 Penicillins

Ampicillin	Cloxacillin
Carbenicillin	Penicillin G

960.1 Antifungal antibiotics

Amphotericin B	Nystatin
Griseofulvin	Trichomycin

> *Excludes:* preparations intended for topical use (976.0-976.9)

960.2 Chloramphenicol group

Chloramphenicol	Thiamphenicol

960.3 Erythromycin and other macrolides

Oleandomycin	Spiramycin

960.4 Tetracycline group

Doxycycline	Oxytetracycline
Minocycline	

960.5 Cephalosporin group

Cephalexin	Cephaloridine
Cephaloglycin	Cephalothin

960.6 Antimycobacterial antibiotics

Cycloserine	Rifampin
Kanamycin	Streptomycin

960.7 Antineoplastic antibiotics

Actinomycin such as:	Bleomycin
Cactinomycin	Daunorubicin
Dactinomycin	Mitomycin

960.8 Other specified antibiotics

960.9 Unspecified antibiotic

961 Poisoning by other anti-infectives

> *Excludes:* anti-infectives:
>> ear, nose, and throat (976.6)
>> eye (976.5)
>> local (976.0)

961.0 Sulfonamides

Sulfadiazine	Sulfamethoxazole
Sulfafurazole	

961.1 Arsenical anti-infectives

961.2 Heavy metal anti-infectives

Compounds of:	Compounds of:
antimony	lead
bismuth	mercury

> *Excludes:* mercurial diuretics (974.0)

961.3 Quinoline and hydroxyquinoline derivatives

Chiniofon	Diiodohydroxyquin

> *Excludes:* antimalarial drugs (961.4)

961.4 Antimalarials and drugs acting on other blood protozoa

Chloroquine	Proguanil [chloroguanide]
Cycloguanil	Pyrimethamine
Primaquine	Quinine

961.5 Other antiprotozoal drugs

Emetine

961.6 Anthelmintics

Hexylresorcinol	Thiabendazole
Piperazine	

● Code new to this edition   ▲ Revision of existing code   ④ ⑤ Fourth or fifth digit required

961.7 Antiviral drugs
Methisazone

> *Excludes:* *amantadine (966.4)*
> *cytarabine (963.1)*
> *idoxuridine (976.5)*

961.8 Other antimycobacterial drugs
Ethambutol Para-aminosalicylic acid derivatives
Ethionamide Sulfones
Isoniazid

961.9 Other and unspecified anti-infectives
Flucytosine Nitrofuran derivatives

962 Poisoning by hormones and synthetic substitutes

> *Excludes:* *oxytocic hormones (975.0)*

962.0 Adrenal cortical steroids
Cortisone derivatives
Desoxycorticosterone derivatives
Fluorinated corticosteroids

962.1 Androgens and anabolic congeners
Methandriol Oxymetholone
Nandrolone Testosterone

962.2 Ovarian hormones and synthetic substitutes
Contraceptives, oral
Estrogens
Estrogens and progestogens, combined
Progestogens

962.3 Insulins and antidiabetic agents
Acetohexamide Insulin
Biguanide derivatives, oral Phenformin
Chlorpropamide Sulfonylurea derivatives, oral
Glucagon Tolbutamide

962.4 Anterior pituitary hormones
Corticotropin
Gonadotropin
Somatotropin [growth hormone]

962.5 Posterior pituitary hormones
Vasopressin

> *Excludes:* *oxytocic hormones (975.0)*

962.6 Parathyroid and parathyroid derivatives

962.7 Thyroid and thyroid derivatives
Dextrothyroxin Liothyronine
Levothyroxine sodium Thyroglobulin

962.8 Antithyroid agents
Iodides Thiourea
Thiouracil

962.9 Other and unspecified hormones and synthetic substitutes

963 Poisoning by primarily systemic agents

963.0 Antiallergic and antiemetic drugs
Antihistamines Diphenylpyraline
Chlorpheniramine Thonzylamine
Diphenhydramine Tripelennamine

> *Excludes:* *phenothiazine-based tranquilizers (969.1)*

963.1 Antineoplastic and immunosuppressive drugs
Azathioprine Cytarabine
Busulfan Fluorouracil
Chlorambucil Mercaptopurine
Cyclophosphamide thio-TEPA

> *Excludes:* *antineoplastic antibiotics (960.7)*

963.2 Acidifying agents

963.3 Alkalizing agents

963.4 Enzymes, not elsewhere classified
Penicillinase

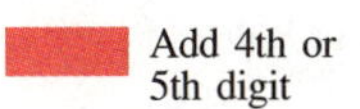

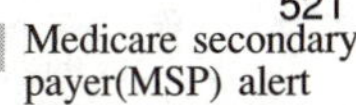

963.5 Vitamins, not elsewhere classified
Vitamin A   Vitamin D

> *Excludes:* *nicotinic acid (972.2)*
> *vitamin K (964.3)*

963.8 Other specified systemic agents
Heavy metal antagonists

963.9 Unspecified systemic agent

964 Poisoning by agents primarily affecting blood constituents

964.0 Iron and its compounds
Ferric salts
Ferrous sulfate and other ferrous salts

964.1 Liver preparations and other antianemic agents
Folic acid

964.2 Anticoagulants
Coumarin   Phenindione
Heparin   Warfarin sodium

964.3 Vitamin K [phytonadione]

964.4 Fibrinolysis-affecting drugs
Aminocaproic acid   Streptokinase
Streptodornase   Urokinase

964.5 Anticoagulant antagonists and other coagulants
Hexadimethrine   Protamine sulfate

964.6 Gamma globulin

964.7 Natural blood and blood products
Blood plasma   Packed red cells
Human fibrinogen   Whole blood

> *Excludes:* *transfusion reactions (999.4-999.8)*

964.8 Other specified agents affecting blood constituents
Macromolecular blood substitutes
Plasma expanders

964.9 Unspecified agent affecting blood constituents

965 Poisoning by analgesics, antipyretics, and antirheumatics

> *Excludes:* *drug dependence (304.0-304.9)*
> *nondependent abuse (305.0-305.9)*

⑤ **965.0 Opiates and related narcotics**

    965.00 Opium (alkaloids), unspecified

    965.01 Heroin
        Diacetylmorphine

    965.02 Methadone

    965.09 Other
        Codeine [methylmorphine]
        Meperidine [pethidine]
        Morphine

965.1 Salicylates
Acetylsalicylic acid [aspirin]
Salicylic acid salts

965.4 Aromatic analgesics, not elsewhere classified
Acetanilid
Paracetamol [acetaminophen]
Phenacetin [acetophenetidin]

965.5 Pyrazole derivatives
Aminophenazone [aminopyrine]
Phenylbutazone

⑤ **965.6 Antirheumatics [antiphlogistics]**

> *Excludes:* *salicylates (965.1)*
> *steroids (962.0-962.9)*

● Code new to this edition   ▲ Revision of existing code   ④ ⑤ Fourth or fifth digit required

965.61 Propionic acid derivatives
Fenoprofen   Ketoprofen
Flurbiprofen   Naproxen
Ibuprofen   Oxaprozin

965.69 Other antirheumatics
Gold salts
Indomethacin

965.7 Other non-narcotic analgesics
Pyrabital

965.8 Other specified analgesics and antipyretics
Pentazocine

965.9 Unspecified analgesic and antipyretic

966 Poisoning by anticonvulsants and anti-Parkinsonism drugs

966.0 Oxazolidine derivatives
Paramethadione   Trimethadione

966.1 Hydantoin derivatives
Phenytoin

966.2 Succinimides
Ethosuximide   Phensuximide

966.3 Other and unspecified anticonvulsants
Primidone

Excludes: *barbiturates (967.0)*
              sulfonamides (961.0)

966.4 Anti-Parkinsonism drugs
Amantadine
Ethopropazine [profenamine]
Levodopa [L-dopa]

967 Poisoning by sedatives and hypnotics

Excludes: *drug dependence (304.0-304.9)*
              nondependent abuse (305.0-305.9)

967.0 Barbiturates
Amobarbital [amylobarbitone]
Barbital [barbitone]
Butabarbital [butabarbitone]
Pentobarbital [pentobarbitone]
Phenobarbital [phenobarbitone]
Secobarbital [quinalbarbitone]

Excludes: *thiobarbiturate anesthetics (968.3)*

967.1 Chloral hydrate group

967.2 Paraldehyde

967.3 Bromine compounds
Bromide   Carbromal (derivatives)

967.4 Methaqualone compounds

967.5 Glutethimide group

967.6 Mixed sedatives, not elsewhere classified

967.8 Other sedatives and hypnotics

967.9 Unspecified sedative or hypnotic
Sleeping:
   drug
   pill   } NOS
   tablet

968 Poisoning by other central nervous system depressants and anesthetics

Excludes: *drug dependence (304.0-304.9)*
              nondependent abuse (305.0-305.9)

968.0 Central nervous system muscle-tone depressants
Chlorphenesin (carbamate)   Methocarbamol
Mephenesin

968.1 Halothane

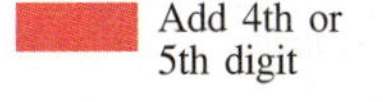

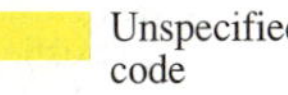

Medicare secondary
payer(MSP) alert

968.2 Other gaseous anesthetics
    Ether
    Halogenated hydrocarbon derivatives, except halothane
    Nitrous oxide

968.3 Intravenous anesthetics

    Excludes: *Methohexital [methohexitone]*
            Thiobarbiturates, such as thiopental sodium

968.4 Other and unspecified general anesthetics

968.5 Surface [topical] and infiltration anesthetics
    Cocaine   Procaine
    Lidocaine [lignocaine]   Tetracaine

968.6 Peripheral nerve and plexus-blocking anesthetics

968.7 Spinal anesthetics

968.9 Other and unspecified local anesthetics

969 Poisoning by psychotropic agents

    Excludes: *drug dependence (304.0-304.9)*
            nondependent abuse (305.0-305.9)

969.0 Antidepressants
    Amitriptyline   Monoamine oxidase [MAO] inhibitors
    Imipramine

969.1 Phenothiazine-based tranquilizers
    Chlorpromazine   Prochlorperazine
    Fluphenazine   Promazine

969.2 Butyrophenone-based tranquilizers
    Haloperidol   Trifluperidol
    Spiperone

969.3 Other antipsychotics, neuroleptics, and major tranquilizers

969.4 Benzodiazepine-based tranquilizers
    Chlordiazepoxide   Lorazepam
    Diazepam   Medazepam
    Flurazepam   Nitrazepam

969.5 Other tranquilizers
    Hydroxyzine   Meprobamate

969.6 Psychodysleptics [hallucinogens]
    Cannabis (derivatives)   Mescaline
    Lysergide [LSD]   Psilocin
    Marihuana (derivatives) Psilocybin

969.7 Psychostimulants
    Amphetamine   Caffeine

    Excludes: *central appetite depressants (977.0)*

969.8 Other specified psychotropic agents

969.9 Unspecified psychotropic agent

970 Poisoning by central nervous system stimulants

970.0 Analeptics
    Lobeline   Nikethamide

970.1 Opiate antagonists
    Levallorphan   Naloxone
    Nalorphine

970.8 Other specified central nervous system stimulants

970.9 Unspecified central nervous system stimulant

971 Poisoning by drugs primarily affecting the autonomic nervous system

971.0 Parasympathomimetics [cholinergics]
    Acetylcholine   Pilocarpine
    Anticholinesterase:
      organophosphorus
      reversible

● Code new to this edition   ▲ Revision of existing code   ④ ⑤ Fourth or fifth digit required

971.1 Parasympatholytics [anticholinergics and antimuscarinics] and spasmolytics
Atropine | Hyoscine [scopolamine]
Homatropine | Quaternary ammonium derivatives

Excludes: papaverine (972.5)

971.2 Sympathomimetics [adrenergics]
Epinephrine [adrenalin]
Levarterenol [noradrenalin]

971.3 Sympatholytics [antiadrenergics]
Phenoxybenzamine | Tolazoline hydrochloride

971.9 Unspecified drug primarily affecting autonomic nervous system

972 Poisoning by agents primarily affecting the cardiovascular system

972.0 Cardiac rhythm regulators
Practolol | Propranolol
Procainamide | Quinidine

Excludes: lidocaine (968.5)

972.1 Cardiotonic glycosides and drugs of similar action
Digitalis glycosides | Strophanthins
Digoxin

972.2 Antilipemic and antiarteriosclerotic drugs
Clofibrate
Nicotinic acid derivatives

972.3 Ganglion-blocking agents
Pentamethonium bromide

972.4 Coronary vasodilators
Dipyridamole | Nitrites
Nitrates [nitroglycerin]

972.5 Other vasodilators
Cyclandelate | Papaverine
Diazoxide

Excludes: nicotinic acid (972.2)

972.6 Other antihypertensive agents
Clonidine | Rauwolfia alkaloids
Guanethidine | Reserpine

972.7 Antivaricose drugs, including sclerosing agents
Sodium morrhuate | Zinc salts

972.8 Capillary-active drugs
Adrenochrome derivatives
Metaraminol

972.9 Other and unspecified agents primarily affecting the cardiovascular system

973 Poisoning by agents primarily affecting the gastrointestinal system

973.0 Antacids and antigastric secretion drugs
Aluminum hydroxide | Magnesium trisilicate

973.1 Irritant cathartics
Bisacodyl | Phenolphthalein
Castor oil

973.2 Emollient cathartics
Dioctyl sulfosuccinates

973.3 Other cathartics, including intestinal atonia drugs
Magnesium sulfate

973.4 Digestants
Pancreatin | Pepsin
Papain

973.5 Antidiarrheal drugs
Kaolin | Pectin

Excludes: anti-infectives (960.0-961.9)

973.6 Emetics

973.8 Other specified agents primarily affecting the gastrointestinal system

973.9 Unspecified agent primarily affecting the gastrointestinal system

974 Poisoning by water, mineral, and uric acid metabolism drugs

▮ Add 4th or 5th digit	▮ Nonspecific code	▮ Unspecified code	▮ Medicare secondary payer(MSP) alert

974.0 Mercurial diuretics
    Chlormerodrin   Mersalyl
    Mercaptomerin

974.1 Purine derivative diuretics
    Theobromine   Theophylline

    Excludes: *aminophylline [theophylline ethylenediamine] (975.7)*
                caffeine (969.7)

974.2 Carbonic acid anhydrase inhibitors
    Acetazolamide

974.3 Saluretics
    Benzothiadiazides   Chlorothiazide group

974.4 Other diuretics
    Ethacrynic acid   Furosemide

974.5 Electrolytic, caloric, and water-balance agents

974.6 Other mineral salts, not elsewhere classified

974.7 Uric acid metabolism drugs
    Allopurinol   Probenecid
    Colchicine

975 Poisoning by agents primarily acting on the smooth and skeletal muscles and respiratory system

975.0 Oxytocic agents
    Ergot alkaloids   Prostaglandins
    Oxytocin

975.1 Smooth muscle relaxants
    Adiphenine
    Metaproterenol [orciprenaline]

    Excludes: *papaverine (972.5)*

975.2 Skeletal muscle relaxants

975.3 Other and unspecified drugs acting on muscles

975.4 Antitussives
    Dextromethorphan   Pipazethate

975.5 Expectorants
    Acetylcysteine   Terpin hydrate
      Guaifenesin

975.6 Anti-common cold drugs

975.7 Antiasthmatics
    Aminophylline [theophylline ethylenediamine]

975.8 Other and unspecified respiratory drugs

976 Poisoning by agents primarily affecting skin and mucous membrane, ophthalmological, otorhinolaryngological, and dental drugs

976.0 Local anti-infectives and anti-inflammatory drugs

976.1 Antipruritics

976.2 Local astringents and local detergents

976.3 Emollients, demulcents, and protectants

976.4 Keratolytics, keratoplastics, other hair treatment drugs and preparations

976.5 Eye anti-infectives and other eye drugs
    Idoxuridine

976.6 Anti-infectives and other drugs and preparations for ear, nose, and throat

976.7 Dental drugs topically applied

    Excludes: *anti-infectives (976.0)*
                local anesthetics (968.5)

976.8 Other agents primarily affecting skin and mucous membrane
    Spermicides [vaginal contraceptives]

976.9 Unspecified agent primarily affecting skin and mucous membrane

977 Poisoning by other and unspecified drugs and medicinal substances

977.0 Dietetics
    Central appetite depressants

977.1 Lipotropic drugs

● Code new to this edition   ▲ Revision of existing code   ④ ⑤ Fourth or fifth digit required

977.2 Antidotes and chelating agents, not elsewhere classified

977.3 Alcohol deterrents

977.4 Pharmaceutical excipients
Pharmaceutical adjuncts

977.8 Other specified drugs and medicinal substances
Contrast media used for diagnostic x-ray procedures
Diagnostic agents and kits

977.9 Unspecified drug or medicinal substance

978 Poisoning by bacterial vaccines

978.0 BCG

978.1 Typhoid and paratyphoid

978.2 Cholera

978.3 Plague

978.4 Tetanus

978.5 Diphtheria

978.6 Pertussis vaccine, including combinations with a pertussis component

978.8 Other and unspecified bacterial vaccines

978.9 Mixed bacterial vaccines, except combinations with a pertussis component

979 Poisoning by other vaccines and biological substances

> Excludes: *gamma globulin (964.6)*

979.0 Smallpox vaccine

979.1 Rabies vaccine

979.2 Typhus vaccine

979.3 Yellow fever vaccine

979.4 Measles vaccine

979.5 Poliomyelitis vaccine

979.6 Other and unspecified viral and rickettsial vaccines
Mumps vaccine

979.7 Mixed viral-rickettsial and bacterial vaccines, except combinations with a pertussis component

> Excludes: *combinations with a pertussis component (978.6)*

979.9 Other and unspecified vaccines and biological substances

TOXIC EFFECTS OF SUBSTANCES CHIEFLY NONMEDICAL AS TO SOURCE (980-989)

> Excludes: *burns from chemical agents (ingested) (947.0-947.9)*
> *localized toxic effects indexed elsewhere (001.0-799.9)*
> *respiratory conditions due to external agents (506.0-508.9)*

Use additional code to specify the nature of the toxic effect

980 Toxic effect of alcohol

980.0 Ethyl alcohol
Denatured alcohol
Ethanol
Grain alcohol
Use additional code to identify any associated:
acute alcohol intoxication (305.0)
in alcoholism (303.0)
drunkenness (simple) (305.0)
pathological (291.4)

980.1 Methyl alcohol
Methanol   Wood alcohol

980.2 Isopropyl alcohol
Dimethyl carbinol   Rubbing alcohol
Isopropanol

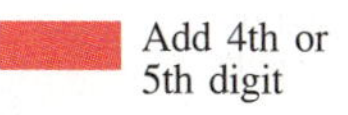 Add 4th or 5th digit    Nonspecific code   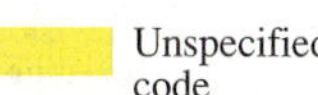 Unspecified code   Medicare secondary payer(MSP) alert

980.3 Fusel oil
Alcohol:
amyl
butyl
propyl

980.8 Other specified alcohols

980.9 Unspecified alcohol

981 Toxic effect of petroleum products

Benzine	Petroleum:
Gasoline	ether
Kerosene	naphtha
Paraffin wax	spirit

982 Toxic effect of solvents other than petroleum-based

982.0 Benzene and homologues

982.1 Carbon tetrachloride

982.2 Carbon disulfide
Carbon bisulfide

982.3 Other chlorinated hydrocarbon solvents
Tetrachloroethylene   Trichloroethylene

Excludes: *chlorinated hydrocarbon preparations other than solvents (989.2)*

982.4 Nitroglycol

982.8 Other nonpetroleum-based solvents
Acetone

983 Toxic effect of corrosive aromatics, acids, and caustic alkalis

983.0 Corrosive aromatics
Carbolic acid or phenol   Cresol

983.1 Acids
Acid:
hydrochloric
nitric
sulfuric

983.2 Caustic alkalis
Lye   Sodium hydroxide
Potassium hydroxide

983.9 Caustic, unspecified

984 Toxic effect of lead and its compounds (including fumes)
Includes: that from all sources except medicinal substances

984.0 Inorganic lead compounds
Lead dioxide   Lead salts

984.1 Organic lead compounds
Lead acetate   Tetraethyl lead

984.8 Other lead compounds

984.9 Unspecified lead compound

985 Toxic effect of other metals
Includes: that from all sources except medicinal substances

985.0 Mercury and its compounds
Minamata disease

985.1 Arsenic and its compounds

985.2 Manganese and its compounds

985.3 Beryllium and its compounds

985.4 Antimony and its compounds

985.5 Cadmium and its compounds

985.6 Chromium

985.8 Other specified metals
Brass fumes   Iron compounds
Copper salts   Nickel compounds

985.9 Unspecified metal

● Code new
to this edition

▲ Revision of
existing code

④ ⑤ Fourth or fifth
digit required

986 Toxic effect of carbon monoxide
    Carbon monoxide from any source

987 Toxic effect of other gases, fumes, or vapors

    987.0 Liquefied petroleum gases
        Butane   Propane

    987.1 Other hydrocarbon gas

    987.2 Nitrogen oxides
        Nitrogen dioxide   Nitrous fumes

    987.3 Sulfur dioxide

    987.4 Freon
        Dichloromonofluoromethane

    987.5 Lacrimogenic gas
        Bromobenzyl cyanide   Ethyliodoacetate
        Chloroacetophenone

    987.6 Chlorine gas

    987.7 Hydrocyanic acid gas

    987.8 Other specified gases, fumes, or vapors
        Phosgene   Polyester fumes

    987.9 Unspecified gas, fume, or vapor

988 Toxic effect of noxious substances eaten as food

> *Excludes:* *allergic reaction to food, such as:*
>   *gastroenteritis (558.3)*
>   *rash (692.5, 693.1)*
>   *food poisoning (bacterial) (005.0-005.9)*
>   *toxic effects of food contaminants, such as:*
>   *aflatoxin and other mycotoxin (989.7)*
>   *mercury (985.0)*

    988.0 Fish and shellfish

    988.1 Mushrooms

    988.2 Berries and other plants

    988.8 Other specified noxious substances eaten as food

    988.9 Unspecified noxious substance eaten as food

989 Toxic effect of other substances, chiefly nonmedicinal as to source

    989.0 Hydrocyanic acid and cyanides
        Potassium cyanide   Sodium cyanide

> *Excludes:* *gas and fumes (987.7)*

    989.1 Strychnine and salts

    989.2 Chlorinated hydrocarbons
        Aldrin   DDT
        Chlordane   Dieldrin

> *Excludes:* *chlorinated hydrocarbon solvents (982.0-982.3)*

    989.3 Organophosphate and carbamate
        Carbaryl   Parathion
        Dichlorvos   Phorate
        Malathion   Phosdrin

    989.4 Other pesticides, not elsewhere classified
        Mixtures of insecticides

    989.5 Venom
        Bites of venomous snakes, lizards, and spiders
        Tick paralysis

    989.6 Soaps and detergents

    989.7 Aflatoxin and other mycotoxin [food contaminants]

  ⑤ **989.8 Other substances, chiefly nonmedicinal as to source**

        989.81 Asbestos

> *Excludes:* *asbestosis (501)*
>   *exposure to asbestos (V15.84)*

        989.82 Latex

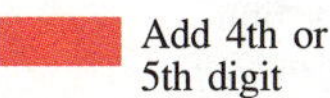

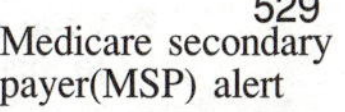

989.83   Silicone

Excludes: *silicone used in medical devices, implants and grafts (996.00-996.79)*

989.84   Tobacco

989.89   Other

989.9   Unspecified substance, chiefly nonmedicinal as to source

OTHER AND UNSPECIFIED EFFECTS OF EXTERNAL CAUSES (990-995)

990   Effects of radiation, unspecified

Complication of phototherapy   Radiation sickness
Complication of radiation therapy

Excludes: *specified adverse effects of radiation*

> *Such conditions are to be classified according to the nature of the adverse effect, as:*
> *burns (940.0-949.5)*
> *dermatitis (692.7-692.8)*
> *leukemia (204.0-208.9)*
> *pneumonia (508.0)*
> *sunburn (692.71)*
> *[The type of radiation giving rise to the adverse effect may be identified by use of the E codes.]*

991   Effects of reduced temperature

991.0   Frostbite of face

991.1   Frostbite of hand

991.2   Frostbite of foot

991.3   Frostbite of other and unspecified sites

991.4   Immersion foot
Trench foot

991.5   Chilblains
Erythema pernio   Perniosis

991.6   Hypothermia
Hypothermia (accidental)

Excludes: *hypothermia following anesthesia (995.89)*
hypothermia not associated with low environmental temperature (780.9)

991.8   Other specified effects of reduced temperature

991.9   Unspecified effect of reduced temperature
Effects of freezing or excessive cold NOS

992   Effects of heat and light

Excludes: *burns (940.0-949.5)*
diseases of sweat glands due to heat (705.0-705.9)
malignant hyperpyrexia following anesthesia (995.86)
sunburn (692.71)

992.0   Heat stroke and sunstroke
Heat apoplexy   Siriasis
Heat pyrexia   Thermoplegia
Ictus solaris

992.1   Heat syncope
Heat collapse

992.2   Heat cramps

992.3   Heat exhaustion, anhydrotic
Heat prostration due to water depletion

Excludes: *that associated with salt depletion (992.4)*

992.4   Heat exhaustion due to salt depletion
Heat prostration due to salt (and water) depletion

992.5   Heat exhaustion, unspecified
Heat prostration NOS

992.6   Heat fatigue, transient

992.7   Heat edema

992.8   Other specified heat effects

992.9   Unspecified

● Code new to this edition   ▲ Revision of existing code   ④ ⑤ Fourth or fifth digit required

993 Effects of air pressure

993.0 Barotrauma, otitic
Aero-otitis media
Effects of high altitude on ears

993.1 Barotrauma, sinus
Aerosinusitis
Effects of high altitude on sinuses

993.2 Other and unspecified effects of high altitude
Alpine sickness
Andes disease
Anoxia due to high altitude
Hypobaropathy
Mountain sickness

993.3 Caisson disease
Bends
Compressed-air disease
Decompression sickness
Divers' palsy or paralysis

993.4 Effects of air pressure caused by explosion

993.8 Other specified effects of air pressure

993.9 Unspecified effect of air pressure

994 Effects of other external causes

Excludes: certain adverse effects not elsewhere classified (995.0-995.8)

994.0 Effects of lightning
Shock from lightning
Struck by lightning NOS

Excludes: burns (940.0-949.5)

994.1 Drowning and nonfatal submersion
Bathing cramp
Immersion

994.2 Effects of hunger
Deprivation of food
Starvation

994.3 Effects of thirst
Deprivation of water

994.4 Exhaustion due to exposure

994.5 Exhaustion due to excessive exertion
Overexertion

994.6 Motion sickness
Air sickness
Seasickness
Travel sickness

994.7 Asphyxiation and strangulation
Suffocation (by):
  bedclothes
  cave-in
  constriction
  mechanical
Suffocation (by):
  plastic bag
  pressure
  strangulation

Excludes: asphyxia from:
      carbon monoxide (986)
      inhalation of food or foreign body (932-934.9)
      other gases, fumes, and vapors (987.0-987.9)

994.8 Electrocution and nonfatal effects of electric current
Shock from electric current

Excludes: electric burns (940.0-949.5)

994.9 Other effects of external causes
Effects of:
  abnormal gravitational [G] forces or states
  weightlessness

995 Certain adverse effects not elsewhere classified

Excludes: complications of surgical and medical care (996.0-999.9)

Add 4th or
5th digit

Nonspecific
code

Unspecified
code

Medicare secondary
payer(MSP) alert

995.0 Other anaphylactic shock
Allergic shock
Anaphylactic reaction
Anaphylaxis
} NOS or due to adverse effect of correct medicinal substance properly administered

Excludes: *anaphylactic reaction to serum (999.4)*
anaphylactic shock due to adverse food reaction (995.60-995.69)

Code first any underlying condition such as:
poisoning by drugs, medicinals and biologic substances (960-979)
toxic effects of substances chiefly nonmedical as to source (980-989)
Use additional E code, if desired, to identify external cause, such as:
adverse effects of correct medicinal substance properly administered (E930-E949)

995.1 Angioneurotic edema
Giant urticaria

Excludes: *Urticaria:*
due to serum (999.5)
other specified (698.2, 708.0-708.9, 757.33)

995.2 Unspecified adverse effect of drug, medicinal and biological substance
Adverse effect
Allergic reaction
Hypersensitivity
Idiosyncrasy
} (due) to correct medicinal substance properly administered

Drug:
hypersensitivity NOS
reaction NOS

Excludes: *pathological drug intoxication (292.2)*

995.3 Allergy, unspecified
Allergic reaction NOS   Idiosyncrasy NOS
Hypersensitivity NOS

Excludes: *allergic reaction NOS to correct medicinal substance properly administered (995.2)*
specific types of allergic reaction, such as:
allergic diarrhea (558.3)
dermatitis (691.0-693.9)
hay fever (477.0-477.9)

995.4 Shock due to anesthesia
Shock due to anesthesia in which the correct substance was properly administered

Excludes: *complications of anesthesia in labor or delivery (668.0-668.9)*
overdose or wrong substance given (968.0-969.9)
postoperative shock NOS (998.0)
specified adverse effects of anesthesia classified elsewhere, such as:
anoxic brain damage (348.1)
hepatitis (070.0-070.9), etc.
unspecified adverse effect of anesthesia (995.2)

⑤ **995.5 Child maltreatment syndrome**
Use additional code(s), if applicable, to identify any associated injuries
Use additional E code to identify:
nature of abuse (E960-E968)
perpetrator (E967.0-E967.9)

995.50 Child abuse, unspecified

995.51 Child emotional/psychological abuse

995.52 Child neglect (nutritional)

995.53 Child sexual abuse

995.54 Child physical abuse
Battered baby or child syndrome

Excludes: *Shaken infant syndrome (995.55)*

995.55 Shaken infant syndrome
Use additional code(s) to identify any associated injuries

995.59 Other child abuse and neglect
Multiple forms of abuse

● Code new
to this edition
▲ Revision of
existing code
④ ⑤ Fourth or fifth
digit required

⑤ **995.6 Anaphylactic shock due to adverse food reaction**
Anaphylactic shock due to nonpoisonous foods

995.60 **Due to unspecified food**

995.61 **Due to peanuts**

995.62 **Due to crustaceans**

995.63 **Due to fruits and vegetables**

995.64 **Due to tree nuts and seeds**

995.65 **Due to fish**

995.66 **Due to food additives**

995.67 **Due to milk products**

995.68 **Due to eggs**

995.69 **Due to other specified food**

● **995.7 Other adverse food reactions, not elsewhere classified**
Use additional code to identify the type of reaction, such as:
hives (708.0)
wheezing (786.07)

Excludes: *anaphylactic shock due to adverse food reaction (995.60-995.69)*
asthma (493.0, 493.9)
dermatitis due to food (693.1)
in contact with the skin (692.5)
gastroenteritis and colitis due to food (558.3)
rhinitis due to food (477.1)

⑤ **995.8 Other specified adverse effects, not elsewhere classified**

995.80 **Adult maltreatment, unspecified**
Abused person NOS
Use additional code to identify:
any associated injury
perpetrator (E967.0-E967.9)

995.81 **Adult physical abuse**
Battered:
person syndrome NEC
man
spouse
woman
Use additional code to identify:
any associated injury
nature of abuse (E960-E968)
perpetrator (E967.0-E967.9)

995.82 **Adult emotional/psychological abuse**
Use additional E code to identify perpetrator (E967.0-E967.9)

995.83 **Adult sexual abuse**
Use additional code to identify:
any associated injury
perpetrator (E967.0-E967.9)

995.84 **Adult neglect (nutritional)**
Use additional code to identify:
intent of neglect (E904.0, E968.4)
perpetrator (E967.0-967.9)

995.85 **Other adult abuse and neglect**
Multiple forms of abuse and neglect
Use additional code to identify:
any associated injury
intent of neglect (E904.0, E968.4)
nature of abuse (E960-E968)
perpetrator (E967.0-E967.9)

995.86 **Malignant hyperthermia**
Malignant hyperpyrexia due to anesthesia

995.89 **Other**
Hypothermia due to anesthesia

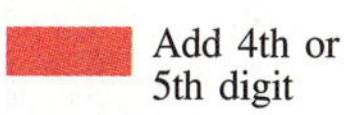

Medicare secondary
payer(MSP) alert

COMPLICATIONS OF SURGICAL AND MEDICAL CARE, NOT ELSEWHERE CLASSIFIED (996-999)

Excludes: *adverse effects of medicinal agents (001.0-799.9, 995.0-995.8)*
burns from local applications and irradiation (940.0-949.5)
complications of:
conditions for which the procedure was performed
surgical procedures during abortion, labor, and delivery (630-676.9)
poisoning and toxic effects of drugs and chemicals (960.0-989.9)
postoperative conditions in which no complications are present, such as:
artificial opening status (V44.0-V44.9)
closure of external stoma (V55.0-V55.9)
fitting of prosthetic device (V52.0-V52.9)
specified complications classified elsewhere
anesthetic shock (995.4)
electrolyte imbalance (276.0-276.9)
postlaminectomy syndrome (772.80-722.83)
postmastectomy lymphedema syndrome (457.0)
postoperative psychosis (293.0-293.9)
any other condition classified elsewhere in the Alphabetic Index when described
as due to a procedure

996 Complications peculiar to certain specified procedures

Includes: complications, not elsewhere classified, in the use of artificial substitutes [e.g., Dacron, metal, Silastic, Teflon] or natural sources [e.g., bone] involving:
anastomosis (internal)
graft (bypass) (patch)
implant
internal device:
catheter
electronic
fixation
prosthetic
reimplant
transplant

Excludes: *accidental puncture or laceration during procedure (998.2)*
complications of internal anastomosis of:
gastrointestinal tract (997.4)
urinary tract (997.5)
other specified complications classified elsewhere, such as:
hemolytic anemia (283.1)
functional cardiac disturbances (429.4)
serum hepatitis (070.2-070.3)

⑤ **996.0 Mechanical complication of cardiac device, implant, and graft**

Breakdown (mechanical)   Obstruction, mechanical
Displacement   Perforation
Leakage   Protrusion

996.00   Unspecified device, implant, and graft

996.01   Due to cardiac pacemaker (electrode)

996.02   Due to heart valve prosthesis

996.03   Due to coronary bypass graft

Excludes: *atherosclerosis of graft (414.02, 414.03)*
embolism [occlusion NOS] [thrombus] of graft (996.72)

996.04   Due to automatic implantable cardiac defibrillator

996.09   Other

● Code new to this edition   ▲ Revision of existing code   ④ ⑤ Fourth or fifth digit required

996.1 Mechanical complication of other vascular device, implant, and graft
Mechanical complications involving:
aortic (bifurcation) graft (replacement)
arteriovenous:
dialysis catheter
fistula surgically created
shunt surgicall created
balloon (counterpulsation) device, intra-aortic
carotid artery bypass graft
femoral-popliteal bypass graft
umbrella device, vena cava

Excludes: *atherosclerosis of biological graft (440.30-440.32)*
embolism [occlusion NOS] [thrombus] of (biological) (synthetic) graft (996.74)
peritoneal dialysis catheter (996.56)

996.2 Mechanical complication of nervous system device, implant, and graft
Mechanical complications involving:
dorsal column stimulator
electrodes implanted in brain [brain "pacemaker"]
peripheral nerve graft
ventricular (communicating) shunt

⑤ **996.3 Mechanical complication of genitourinary device, implant, and graft**

996.30 Unspecified device, implant, and graft

996.31 Due to urethral [indwelling] catheter

996.32 Due to intrauterine contraceptive device

996.39 Other
Cystostomy catheter
Prosthetic reconstruction of vas deferens
Repair (graft) of ureter without mention of resection

Excludes: *complications due to:*
external stoma of urinary tract (997.5)
internal anastomosis of urinary tract (997.5)

996.4 Mechanical complication of internal orthopedic device, implant, and graft
Mechanical complications involving:
external (fixation) device utilizing internal screw(s), pin(s) or other methods of fixation
grafts of bone, cartilage, muscle, or tendon
internal (fixation) device such as nail, plate, rod, etc.

Excludes. *complications of external orthopedic device, such as:*
pressure ulcer due to cast (707.0)

⑤ **996.5 Mechanical complication of other specified prosthetic device, implant, and graft**
Mechanical complications involving:
prosthetic implant in:
bile duct
breast
chin
orbit of eye
nonabsorbable surgical material NOS
other graft, implant, and internal device, not elsewhere classified

996.51 Due to corneal graft

996.52 Due to graft of other tissue, not elsewhere classified
Skin graft failure or rejection

Excludes: *failure of artificial skin graft (996.55)*
failure of decellularized allodermis (996.55)
sloughing of temporary skin allografts or xenografts (pigskin)—omit code

996.53 Due to ocular lens prosthesis

Excludes: *contact lenses—code to condition*

996.54 Due to breast prosthesis
Breast capsule (prosthesis)
Mammary implant

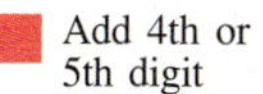 Add 4th or 5th digit    Nonspecific code   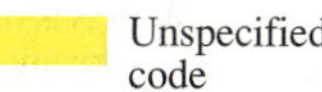 Unspecified code    Medicare secondary payer(MSP) alert

996.55 Due to artificial skin graft and decellularized allodermis
Dislodgement
Displacement
Failure
Non-adherence
Poor incorporation
Shearing

996.56 Due to peritoneal dialysis catheter

Excludes: _mechanical complication of arteriovenous dialysis catheter (996.1)_

996.59 Due to other implant and internal device, not elsewhere classified
Nonabsorbable surgical material NOS
Prosthetic implant in:
bile duct
chin
orbit of eye

⑤ **996.6 Infection and inflammatory reaction due to internal prosthetic device, implant, and graft**
Infection (causing obstruction) due to (presence of) any device, implant and graft classifiable to 996.0-996.5
Inflammation due to (presence of) any device, implant and graft classifiable to 996.0-996.5

Use additional code to identify specified infections

996.60 Due to unspecified device, implant, and graft

996.61 Due to cardiac device, implant, and graft
Cardiac pacemaker or defibrillator:
electrode(s), lead(s)
pulse generator
subcutaneous pocket
Coronary artery bypass graft
Heart valve prosthesis

996.62 Due to other vascular device, implant, and graft
Arterial graft
Arteriovenous fistula or shunt
Infusion pump
Vascular catheter (arterial) (dialysis) (venous)

996.63 Due to nervous system device, implant, and graft
Electrodes implanted in brain
Peripheral nerve graft
Spinal canal catheter
Ventricular (communicating) shunt (catheter)

996.64 Due to indwelling urinary catheter
Use additional code to identify specified infections, such as:
Cystitis (595.0-595.9)
Sepsis (038.0-038.9)

996.65 Due to other genitourinary device, implant, and graft
Intrauterine contraceptive device

996.66 Due to internal joint prosthesis

996.67 Due to other internal orthopedic device, implant, and graft
Bone growth stimulator (electrode)
Internal fixation device (pin) (rod) (screw)

996.68 Due to peritoneal dialysis catheter
Exit-site infection or inflammation

996.69 Due to other internal prosthetic device, implant, and graft
Breast prosthesis
Ocular lens prosthesis
Prosthetic orbital implant

     ● Code new   ▲ Revision of   ④ ⑤ Fourth or fifth
       to this edition   existing code   digit required

⑤ **996.7** **Other complications of internal (biological) (synthetic) prosthetic device, implant, and graft**

Complication NOS
 occlusion NOS
Embolism
Fibrosis   due to (presence of) any device, implant, and graft
Hemorrhage   classifiable to 996.0-996.5
Pain
Stenosis
Thrombus

Excludes: *transplant rejection (996.8)*

996.70 **Due to unspecified device, implant, and graft**

996.71 **Due to heart valve prosthesis**

996.72 **Due to other cardiac device, implant, and graft**
Cardiac pacemaker or defibrillator:
 electrode(s), lead(s)
 subcutaneous pocket
Coronary artery bypass (graft)

Excludes: *occlusion due to atherosclerosis (414.02-414.03)*

996.73 **Due to renal dialysis device, implant, and graft**

996.74 **Due to other vascular device, implant, and graft**

Excludes: *occlusion of biological graft due to atherosclerosis (440.30-440.32)*

996.75 **Due to nervous system device, implant, and graft**

996.76 **Due to genitourinary device, implant, and graft**

996.77 **Due to internal joint prosthesis**

996.78 **Due to other internal orthopedic device, implant, and graft**

996.79 **Due to other internal prosthetic device, implant, and graft**

⑤ **996.8** **Complications of transplanted organ**
Use additional code, if desired, to identify nature of complication, such as:
Cytomegalovirus (CMV) infection (078.5)
Transplant failure or rejection

996.80 **Transplanted organ, unspecified**

996.81 **Kidney**

996.82 **Liver**

996.83 **Heart**

996.84 **Lung**

996.85 **Bone Marrow**
Graft-versus-host disease (acute) (chronic)

996.86 **Pancreas**

● **996.87** **Intestine**

996.89 **Other specified transplanted organ**

⑤ **996.9** **Complications of reattached extremity or body part**

996.90 **Unspecified extremity**

996.91 **Forearm**

996.92 **Hand**

996.93 **Finger(s)**

996.94 **Upper extremity, other and unspecified**

996.95 **Foot and toe(s)**

996.96 **Lower extremity, other and unspecified**

996.99 **Other specified body part**

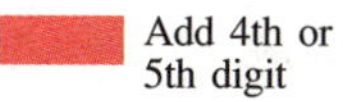
Add 4th or
5th digit

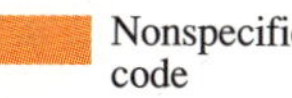
Nonspecific
code

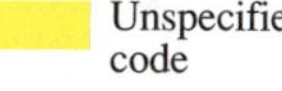
Unspecified
code

Medicare secondary
payer(MSP) alert

997 **Complications affecting specified body systems, not elsewhere classified**
Use additional code to identify complication

Excludes: *the listed conditions when specified as:*
causing shock (998.0)
complications of:
anesthesia:
adverse effect (001.0-799.9, 995.0-995.8)
in labor or delivery (668.0-668.9)
poisoning (968.0-969.9)
implanted device or graft (996.0-996.9)
obstetrical procedures (669.0-669.4)
reattached extremity (996.90-996.96)
transplanted organ (996.80-996.89)

⑤ **997.0** **Nervous system complications**

997.00 **Nervous system complication, unspecified**

997.01 **Central nervous system complication**
Anoxic brain damage
Cerebral hypoxia

Excludes: *cerebrovascular hemorrhage or infarction (997.02)*

997.02 **Iatrogenic cerebrovascular infarction or hemorrhage**
Postoperative stroke

997.09 **Other nervous system complications**

997.1 **Cardiac complications**
Cardiac arrest during or resulting from a procedure
Cardiac insufficiency during or resulting from a procedure
Cardiorespiratory failure during or resulting from a procedure
Heart failure during or resulting from a procedure

Excludes: *the listed conditions as long-term effects of cardiac surgery or due to the*
presence of cardiac prosthetic device (429.4)

997.2 **Peripheral vascular complications**
Phlebitis or thrombophlebitis during or resulting from a procedure

Excludes: *the listed conditions due to:*
implant or catheter device (996.62)
infusion, perfusion, or transfusion (999.2)
complications affecting internal blood vessels, such as:
mesenteric artery (997.4)
renal artery (997.5)

997.3 **Respiratory complications**
Mendelson's syndrome ⎤
Pneumonia (aspiration) ⎦ resulting from a procedure

Excludes: *iatrogenic [postoperative] pneumothorax (512.1)*
iatrogenic pulmonary embolism (415.11)
Mendelson's syndrome in labor and delivery (668.0)
specified complications classified elsewhere, such as:
adult respiratory distress syndrome (518.5)
pulmonary edema, postoperative (518.4)
respiratory insufficiency, acute, postoperative (518.5)
shock lung (518.5)
tracheostomy complications (519.00-519.09)

    ● Code new
to this edition   ▲ Revision of
existing code   ④ ⑤ Fourth or fifth
digit required

997.4 Digestive system complications
Complications of intestinal (internal) anastomosis and bypass, not elsewhere classified, except that involving urinary tract
Hepatic failure
Hepatorenal syndrome ⎫ specified as due to a procedure
Intestinal obstruction NOS ⎭

> *Excludes:* specified gastrointestinal complications classified elsewhere, such as:
> blind loop syndrome (579.2)
> colostomy or enterostomy complications (569.60-569.69)
> gastrostomy complications (536.40-536.49)
> gastrojejunal ulcer (534.0-534.9)
> infection of external stoma (569.61)
> pelvic peritoneal adhesions, female (614.6)
> peritoneal adhesions (568.0)
> peritoneal adhesions with obstruction (560.81)
> postcholecystectomy syndrome (576.0)
> postgastric surgery syndromes (564.2)

997.5 Urinary complications
Complications of:
  external stoma of urinary tract
  internal anastomosis and bypass of urinary tract, including that involving intestinal tract
Oliguria or anuria
Renal: ⎫
  failure (acute) ⎬ specified as due to procedure
  insufficiency (acute) ⎪
Tubular necrosis (acute) ⎭

> *Excludes:* specified complications classified elsewhere, such as:
> postoperative stricture of:
> ureter (593.3)
> urethra (598.2)

⑤ **997.6 Amputation stump complication**

> *Excludes:* admission for treatment for a current traumatic amputation; code to complicated traumatic amputation
> phantom limb (syndrome) (353.6)

997.60 Unspecified complication

997.61 Neuroma of amputation stump

997.62 Infection (chronic)

Use additional code to identify the organism

997.69 Other

⑤ **997.9 Complications affecting other specified body systems, not elsewhere classified**

> *Excludes:* specified complications classified elsewhere, such as:
> broad ligament laceration syndrome (620.6)
> postartificial menopause syndrome (627.4)
> postoperative stricture of vagina (623.2)

997.91 Hypertension

> *Excludes:* essential hypertension (401.0-401.9)

997.99 Other
Vitreous touch syndrome

998 Other complications of procedures, NEC

998.0 Postoperative shock
Collapse NOS ⎫
Shock (endotoxic) (hypo- ⎬ during or resulting from a surgical procedure
  volemic) (septic) ⎭

> *Excludes:* shock:
> anaphylactic due to serum (999.4)
> anesthetic (995.4)
> electric (994.8)
> following abortion (639.5)
> obstetric (669.1)
> traumatic (958.4)

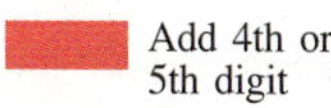 Add 4th or 5th digit
 Nonspecific code
 Unspecified code
 Medicare secondary payer(MSP) alert

⑤ **998.1 Hemorrhage or hematoma or seroma complicating a procedure**

> **Excludes:** *hemorrhage due to implanted device or graft (996.70-996.79)*
> *hemorrhage, hematoma or seroma complicating cesarean section or puerperal perineal wound (674.3)*

    998.11 Hemorrhage complicating a procedure

    998.12 Hematoma complicating a procedure

    998.13 Seroma complicating a procedure

998.2 Accidental puncture or laceration during a procedure

Accidental perforation by catheter or other instrument during a procedure on:
   blood vessel
   nerve
   organ

> **Excludes:** *iatrogenic [postoperative] pneumothorax (512.1)*
> *puncture or laceration caused by implanted device intentionally left in operation wound (996.0-996.5)*
> *specified complications classified elsewhere, such as:*
>   *broad ligament laceration syndrome (620.6)*
> *trauma from instruments during delivery (664.0-665.9)*

998.3 Disruption of operation wound

Dehiscence
Rupture   } of operation wound

> **Excludes:** *disruption of:*
>   *cesarean wound (674.1)*
>   *perineal wound, puerperal (674.2)*

998.4 Foreign body accidentally left during a procedure

Adhesions
Obstruction   } due to foreign body accidentally left in operative
Perforation   wound
                  or body cavity during a procedure

> **Excludes:** *obstruction or perforation caused by implanted device intentionally left in body (996.0-996.5)*

⑤ **998.5 Postoperative infection**

> **Excludes:** *infection due to:*
>   *implanted device (996.60-996.69)*
>   *infusion, perfusion, or transfusion (999.3)*
> *postoperative obstetrical wound infection (674.3)*

    998.51 Infected postoperative seroma

Use additional code to identify organism

    998.59 Other postoperative infection

Abscess: postoperative
  intra-abdominal postoperative
  stitch postoperative
  subphrenic postoperative
  wound postoperative
Septicemia postoperative

Use additional code to identify infection

998.6 Persistent postoperative fistula

998.7 Acute reaction to foreign substance accidentally left during a procedure

Peritonitis:
  aseptic
  chemical

⑤ **998.8 Other specified complications of procedures, not elsewhere classified**

    998.81 Emphysema (subcutaneous) (surgical) resulting from a procedure

    998.82 Cataract fragments in eye following cataract surgery

    998.83 Non-healing surgical wound

    998.89 Other specified complications

998.9 Unspecified complication of procedure, not elsewhere classified

Postoperative complication NOS

> **Excludes:** *complication NOS of obstetrical surgery or procedure (669.4)*

● Code new to this edition   ▲ Revision of existing code   ④ ⑤ Fourth or fifth digit required

999 **Complications of medical care, not elsewhere classified**
Includes: complications, not elsewhere classified, of:
dialysis (hemodialysis) (peritoneal) (renal)
extracorporeal circulation
hyperalimentation therapy
immunization
infusion
inhalation therapy
injection
inoculation
perfusion
transfusion
vaccination
ventilation therapy

Excludes: specified complications classified elsewhere such as:
complications of implanted device (996.0-996.9)
contact dermatitis due to drugs (692.3)
dementia dialysis (294.8)
transient (293.9)
dialysis disequilibrium syndrome (276.0-276.9)
poisoning and toxic effects of drugs and chemicals (960.0-989.9)
postvaccinal encephalitis (323.5)
water and electrolyte imbalance (276.0-276.9)

999.0 Generalized vaccinia

999.1 Air embolism
Air embolism to any site following infusion, perfusion, or transfusion

Excludes: embolism specified as:
complicating:
abortion (634-638 with .6, 639.6)
ectopic or molar pregnancy (639.6)
pregnancy, childbirth, or the puerperium (673.0)
due to implanted device (996.7)
traumatic (958.0)

999.2 Other vascular complications
Phlebitis
Thromboembolism } following infusion, perfusion, or transfusion
Thrombophlebitis

Excludes: the listed conditions when specified as:
due to implanted device (996.61-996.62, 996.72-996.74)
postoperative NOS (997.2)

999.3 Other infection
Infection
Sepsis } following infusion, injection, transfusion, or vaccination
Septicemia

Excludes: the listed conditions when specified as:
due to implanted device (996.60-996.69)
postoperative NOS (998.51-998.59)

999.4 Anaphylactic shock due to serum

Excludes: shock:
allergic NOS (995.0)
anaphylactic:
NOS (995.0)
due to drugs and chemicals (995.0)

999.5 Other serum reaction
Intoxication by serum   Serum sickness
Protein sickness   Urticaria due to serum
Serum rash

Excludes: serum hepatitis (070.2-070.3)

999.6 ABO incompatibility reaction
Incompatible blood transfusion
Reaction to blood group incompatibility in infusion or transfusion

999.7 Rh incompatibility reaction
Reactions due to Rh factor in infusion or transfusion

Add 4th or
5th digit

Nonspecific
code

Unspecified
code

Medicare secondary
payer(MSP) alert

999.8 **Other transfusion reaction**
Septic shock due to transfusion
Transfusion reaction NOS

Excludes: *postoperative shock (998.0)*

999.9 **Other and unspecified complications of medical care, not elsewhere classified**
Complications, not elsewhere classified, of:
electroshock
inhalation
ultrasound } therapy
ventilation
Unspecified misadventure of medical care

Excludes: *unspecified complication of:*
phototherapy (990)
radiation therapy (990)

● Code new
to this edition
▲ Revision of
existing code
④ ⑤ Fourth or fifth
digit required

SUPPLEMENTARY CLASSIFICATION OF FACTORS INFLUENCING HEALTH STATUS AND CONTACT WITH HEALTH SERVICES (V01-V82)

This classification is provided to deal with occasions when circumstances other than a disease or injury classifiable to categories 001-999 (the main part of ICD)are recorded as "diagnoses" or "problems." This can arise mainly in three ways:

a) When a person who is not currently sick encounters the health services for some specific purpose, such as to act as a donor of an organ or tissue, to receive prophylactic vaccination, or to discuss a problem which is in itself not a disease or injury. This will be a fairly rare occurrence among hospital inpatients, but will be relatively more common among hospital outpatients and patients of family practitioners, health clinics, etc.

b) When a person with a known disease or injury, whether it is current or resolving, encounters the health care system for a specific treatment of that disease or injury (e.g., dialysis for renal disease; chemotherapy for malignancy; cast change).

c) When some circumstance or problem is present which influences the person's health status but is not in itself a current illness or injury. Such factors may be elicited during population surveys, when the person may or may not be currently sick, or be recorded as an additional factor to be borne in mind when the person is receiving care for some current illness or injury classifiable to categories 001-999.

In the latter circumstances the V code should be used only as a supplementary code and should not be the one selected for use in primary, single cause tabulations. Examples of these circumstances are a personal history of certain diseases, or a person with an artificial heart valve in situ.

PERSONS WITH POTENTIAL HEALTH HAZARDS RELATED TO COMMUNICABLE DISEASES (V01-V06)

> *Excludes:* family history of infectious and parasitic diseases (V18.8)
> personal history of infectious and parasitic diseases (V12.0)

V01 **Contact with or exposure to communicable diseases**

V01.0 **Cholera**
Conditions classifiable to 001

V01.1 **Tuberculosis**
Conditions classifiable to 010-018

V01.2 **Poliomyelitis**
Conditions classifiable to 045

V01.3 **Smallpox**
Conditions classifiable to 050

V01.4 **Rubella**
Conditions classifiable to 056

V01.5 **Rabies**
Conditions classifiable to 071

V01.6 **Venereal diseases**
Conditions classifiable to 090-099

V01.7 **Other viral diseases**
Conditions classifiable to 042-078 and V08, except as above

V01.8 **Other communicable diseases**
Conditions classifiable to 001-136, except as above

V01.9 **Unspecified communicable disease**

V02 **Carrier or suspected carrier of infectious diseases**

V02.0 **Cholera**

V02.1 **Typhoid**

V02.2 **Amebiasis**

V02.3 **Other gastrointestinal pathogens**

V02.4 **Diphtheria**

⑤ **V02.5** **Other specified bacterial diseases**

V02.51 **Group B streptococcus**

V02.52 **Other streptococcus**

V02.59 **Other specified bacterial diseases**
Meningococcal
Staphylococcal

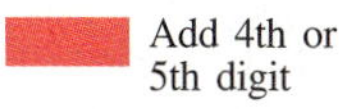

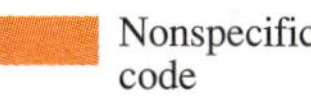

Unspecified
code

Manifestation
code

⑤ **V02.6 Viral hepatitis**
Hepatitis Australian-antigen [HAA] [SH] carrier
Serum hepatitis carrier

V02.60 Viral hepatitis carrier, unspecified

V02.61 Hepatitis B carrier

V02.62 Hepatitis C carrier

V02.69 Other viral hepatitis carrier

V02.7 Gonorrhea

V02.8 Other venereal diseases

V02.9 Other specified infectious organism

V03 Need for prophylactic vaccination and inoculation against bacterial diseases

Excludes: vaccination not carried out because of contraindication (V64.0)
vaccines against combinations of diseases (V06.0-V06.9)

V03.0 Cholera alone

V03.1 Typhoid-paratyphoid alone [TAB]

V03.2 Tuberculosis [BCG]

V03.3 Plague

V03.4 Tularemia

V03.5 Diphtheria alone

V03.6 Pertussis alone

V03.7 Tetanus toxoid alone

⑤ **V03.8 Other specified vaccinations against single bacterial diseases**

V03.81 Hemophilus influenza, type B [Hib]

V03.82 Streptococcus pneumoniae [pneumococcus]

V03.89 Other specified vaccination

V03.9 Unspecified single bacterial disease

V04 Need for prophylactic vaccination and inoculation against certain viral diseases

Excludes: vaccines against combinations of diseases (V06.0-V06.9)

V04.0 Poliomyelitis

V04.1 Smallpox

V04.2 Measles alone

V04.3 Rubella alone

V04.4 Yellow fever

V04.5 Rabies

V04.6 Mumps alone

V04.7 Common cold

V04.8 Influenza

V05 Need for other prophylactic vaccination and inoculation against single diseases

Excludes: vaccines against combinations of diseases (V06.0-V06.9)

V05.0 Arthropod-borne viral encephalitis

V05.1 Other arthropod-borne viral diseases

V05.2 Leishmaniasis

V05.3 Viral hepatitis

V05.4 Varicella
Chickenpox

V05.8 Other specified disease

V05.9 Unspecified single disease

V06 Need for prophylactic vaccination and inoculation against combinations of diseases
Note: Use additional single vaccination codes from categories V03-V05 to identify any
vaccinations not included in a combination code.

V06.0 Cholera with typhoid-paratyphoid [cholera + TAB]

V06.1 Diphtheria-tetanus-pertussis, combined [DTP]

V06.2 Diphtheria-tetanus-pertussis with typhoid-paratyphoid [DTP + TAB]

● Code new
to this edition

▲ Revision of
existing code

④ ⑤ Fourth or fifth
digit required

V06.3 Diphtheria-tetanus-pertussis with poliomyelitis [DTP + polio]

V06.4 Measles-mumps-rubella [MMR]

V06.5 Tetanus-diphtheria [Td]

V06.6 Streptococcus pneumoniae [pneumococcus] and influenza

V06.8 Other combinations

> *Excludes:* *multiple single vaccination codes (V03.0-V05.9)*

V06.9 Unspecified combined vaccine

PERSONS WITH NEED FOR ISOLATION, OTHER POTENTIAL HEALTH HAZARDS AND PROPHYLACTIC MEASURES (V07-V09)

V07 Need for isolation and other prophylactic measures

> *Excludes:* *prophylactic organ removal (V50.41-V50.49)*

V07.0 Isolation
Admission to protect the individual from his surroundings or for isolation of individual after contact with infectious diseases

V07.1 Desensitization to allergens

V07.2 Prophylactic immunotherapy
Administration of:
antivenin
immune sera [gamma globulin]
RhoGAM
tetanus antitoxin

⑤ **V07.3 Other prophylactic chemotherapy**

V07.31 Prophylactic fluoride administration

V07.39 Other prophylactic chemotherapy

> *Excludes:* *maintenance chemotherapy following disease (V58.1)*

V07.4 Postmenopausal hormone replacement therapy

V07.8 Other specified prophylactic measure

V07.9 Unspecified prophylactic measure

V08 Asymptomatic human immunodeficiency virus [HIV] infection status
HIV positive NOS

Note: This code is ONLY to be used when NO HIV infection symptoms or conditions are present. If any HIV infection symptoms or conditions are present, see code 042.

> *Excludes:* *AIDS (042)*
> *human immunodeficiency virus [HIV] disease (042)*
> *exposure to HIV (V01.7)*
> *nonspecific serologic evidence of HIV (795.71)*
> *symptomatic human immunodeficiency virus [HIV] infection (042)*

V09 Infection with drug-resistant microorganisms

Note: This category is intended for use as an additional code for infectious conditions classified elsewhere to indicate the presence of drug-resistance of the infectious organism.

V09.0 Infection with microorganisms resistant to penicillins

V09.1 Infection with microorganisms resistant to cephalosporins and other B-lactam antibiotics

V09.2 Infection with microorganisms resistant to macrolides

V09.3 Infection with microorganisms resistant to tetracyclines

V09.4 Infection with microorganisms resistant to aminoglycosides

V09.5 Infection with microorganisms resistant to quinolones and fluoroquinolones

V09.50 Without mention of resistance to multiple quinolones and fluoroquinolones

V09.51 With resistance to multiple quinolones and fluoroquinolones

V09.6 Infection with microorganisms resistant to sulfonamides

⑤ **V09.7 Infection with microorganisms resistant to other specified antimycobacterial agents**

> *Excludes:* *Amikacin (V09.4)*
> *Kanamycin (V09.4)*
> *Streptomycin [SM] (V09.4)*

V09.70 Without mention of resistance to multiple antimycobacterial agents

V09.71 With resistance to multiple antimycobacterial agents

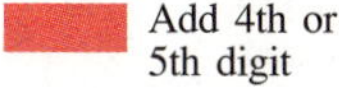

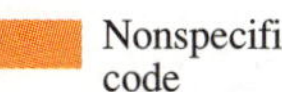

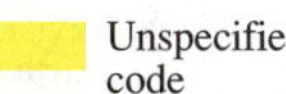

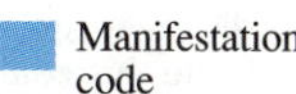

⑤ **V09.8 Infection with microorganisms resistant to other specified drugs**

    V09.80 Without mention of resistance to multiple drugs

    V09.81 With resistance to multiple drugs

⑤ **V09.9 Infection with drug-resistant microorganisms, unspecified**
    Drug resistance NOS

    V09.90 Without mention of multiple drug resistance

    V09.91 With multiple drug resistance
        Multiple drug resistance NOS

PERSONS WITH POTENTIAL HEALTH HAZARDS RELATED TO PERSONAL AND FAMILY HISTORY (V10-V19)

    Excludes: obstetric patients where the possibility that the fetus might be affected is the reason for observation or management during pregnancy (655.0-655.9)

V10 **Personal history of malignant neoplasm**

⑤ **V10.0 Gastrointestinal tract**
    History of conditions classifiable to 140-159

    V10.00 Gastrointestinal tract, unspecified

    V10.01 Tongue

    V10.02 Other and unspecified oral cavity and pharynx

    V10.03 Esophagus

    V10.04 Stomach

    V10.05 Large intestine

    V10.06 Rectum, rectosigmoid junction, and anus

    V10.07 Liver

    V10.09 Other

⑤ **V10.1 Trachea, bronchus, and lung**
    History of conditions classifiable to 162

    V10.11 Bronchus and lung

    V10.12 Trachea

⑤ **V10.2 Other respiratory and intrathoracic organs**
    History of conditions classifiable to 160, 161, 163-165

    V10.20 Respiratory organ, unspecified

    V10.21 Larynx

    V10.22 Nasal cavities, middle ear, and accessory sinuses

    V10.29 Other

V10.3 Breast
    History of conditions classifiable to 174 and 175

⑤ **V10.4 Genital organs**
    History of conditions classifiable to 179-187

    V10.40 Female genital organ, unspecified

    V10.41 Cervix uteri

    V10.42 Other parts of uterus

    V10.43 Ovary

    V10.44 Other female genital organs

    V10.45 Male genital organ, unspecified

    V10.46 Prostate

    V10.47 Testis

    V10.48 Epididymis

    V10.49 Other male genital organs

⑤ **V10.5 Urinary organs**
    History of conditions classifiable to 188 and 189

    V10.50 Urinary organ, unspecified

    V10.51 Bladder

    V10.52 Kidney

    V10.59 Other

● Code new to this edition   ▲ Revision of existing code   ④ ⑤ Fourth or fifth digit required

⑤ **V10.6 Leukemia**
Conditions classifiable to 204-208

Excludes: *leukemia in remission (204-208)*

V10.60 **Leukemia, unspecified**
V10.61 **Lymphoid leukemia**
V10.62 **Myeloid leukemia**
V10.63 **Monocytic leukemia**
V10.69 **Other**

⑤ **V10.7 Other lymphatic and hematopoietic neoplasms**
Conditions classifiable to 200-203

Excludes: *listed conditions in 200-203 in remission*

V10.71 **Lymphosarcoma and reticulosarcoma**
V10.72 **Hodgkin's disease**
V10.79 **Other**

⑤ **V10.8 Personal history of malignant neoplasm of other sites**
History of conditions classifiable to 170-173, 190-195

V10.81 **Bone**
V10.82 **Malignant melanoma of skin**
V10.83 **Other malignant neoplasm of skin**
V10.84 **Eye**
V10.85 **Brain**
V10.86 **Other parts of nervous system**

Excludes: *peripheral, sympathetic, and parasympathetic nerves (V10.89)*

V10.87 **Thyroid**
V10.88 **Other endocrine glands and related structures**
V10.89 **Other**

V10.9 **Unspecified personal history of malignant neoplasm**

V11 **Personal history of mental disorder**

V11.0 Schizophrenia

Excludes: *that in remission (295.0-295.9 with fifth-digit 5)*

V11.1 Affective disorders
Personal history of manic-depressive psychosis

Excludes: *that in remission (296.0-296.6 with fifth-digit
5, 6)*

V11.2 Neurosis

V11.3 Alcoholism

V11.8 Other mental disorders

V11.9 Unspecified mental disorder

V12 **Personal history of certain other diseases**

⑤ **V12.0 Infectious and parasitic diseases**

V12.00 **Unspecified infectious and parasitic disease**
V12.01 **Tuberculosis**
V12.02 **Poliomyelitis**
V12.03 **Malaria**
V12.09 **Other**

V12.1 Nutritional deficiency

V12.2 Endocrine, metabolic, and immunity disorders

Excludes: *history of allergy (V14.0-V14.9, V15.01-V15.09)*

V12.3 Diseases of blood and blood-forming organs

⑤ **V12.4 Disorders of nervous system and sense organs**

V12.40 **Unspecified disorder of nervous system and sense organs**
V12.41 **Benign neoplasm of the brain**

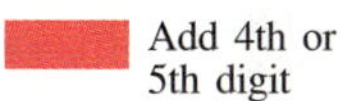

V12.49 **Other disorders of nervous system and sense organs**

⑤ **V12.5** **Diseases of circulatory system**

> Excludes: old myocardial infarction (412)
> postmyocardial infarction syndrome (411.0)

  V12.50 **Unspecified circulatory disease**

  V12.51 **Venous thrombosis and embolism**
Pulmonary embolism

  V12.52 **Thrombophlebitis**

  V12.59 **Other**
Note: Assign code V12.59 (and not a code from category 438) as an additional code for history of cerebrovascular disease when no neurologic deficits are present.

V12.6 **Diseases of respiratory system**

⑤ **V12.7** **Diseases of digestive system**

  V12.70 **Unspecified digestive disease**

  V12.71 **Peptic ulcer disease**

  V12.72 **Colonic polyps**

  V12.79 **Other**

V13 **Personal history of other diseases**

⑤ **V13.0** **Disorders of urinary system**

  V13.00 **Unspecified urinary disorder**

  V13.01 **Urinary calculi**

  V13.09 **Other**

V13.1 **Trophoblastic disease**

> Excludes: supervision during a current pregnancy (V23.1)

V13.2 **Other genital system and obstetric disorders**

> Excludes: supervision during a current pregnancy of a woman with poor obstetric history (V23.0-V23.9)
> habitual aborter (646.3)
> without current history (629.9)

V13.3 **Diseases of skin and subcutaneous tissue**

V13.4 **Arthritis**

V13.5 **Other musculoskeletal disorders**

⑤ **V13.6** **Congenital malformations**

  V13.61 **Hypospadias**

  V13.69 **Other congenital malformations**

V13.7 **Perinatal problems**

> Excludes: low birth weight status (V21.30-V21.35)

V13.8 **Other specified diseases**

V13.9 **Unspecified disease**

V14 **Personal history of allergy to medicinal agents**

V14.0 **Penicillin**

V14.1 **Other antibiotic agent**

V14.2 **Sulfonamides**

V14.3 **Other anti-infective agent**

V14.4 **Anesthetic agent**

V14.5 **Narcotic agent**

V14.6 **Analgesic agent**

V14.7 **Serum or vaccine**

V14.8 **Other specified medicinal agents**

V14.9 **Unspecified medicinal agent**

V15 **Other personal history presenting hazards to health**

⑤ **V15.0** **Allergy, other than to medicinal agents**

> Excludes: allergy to food substance used as base for medicinal agent (V14.0-V14.9)

● Code new to this edition   ▲ Revision of existing code   ④ ⑤ Fourth or fifth digit required

- ● **V15.01 Allergy to peanuts**
- ● **V15.02 Allergy to milk products**

> *Excludes:* *lactose intolerance (271.3)*

- ● **V15.03 Allergy to eggs**
- ● **V15.04 Allergy to seafood**
  Seafood (octopus) (squid) ink
  Shellfish
- ● **V15.05 Allergy to other foods**
  Food additives
  Nuts other than peanuts
- ● **V15.06 Allergy to insects**
  Bugs
  Insect bites and stings
  Spiders
- ● **V15.07 Allergy to latex**
  Latex sensitivity
- ● **V15.08 Allergy to radiographic dye**
  Contrast media used for diagnostic x-ray procedures
- ● **V15.09 Other allergy, other than to medicinal agents**

V15.1 Surgery to heart and great vessels

> *Excludes:* *replacement by transplant or other means (V42.1-V42.2, V43.2-V43.4)*

V15.2 Surgery to other major organs

> *Excludes:* *replacement by transplant or other means (V42.0-V43.8)*

V15.3 Irradiation
Previous exposure to therapeutic or other ionizing radiation

⑤ **V15.4 Psychological trauma**

> *Excludes:* *history of condition classifiable to 290-316 (V11.0-V11.9)*

V15.41 History of physical abuse
Rape

V15.42 History of emotional abuse
Neglect

V15.49 Other

V15.5 Injury

V15.6 Poisoning

V15.7 Contraception

> *Excludes:* *current contraceptive management (V25.0-V25.4)*
> *presence of intrauterine contraceptive device as incidental finding (V45.5)*

⑤ **V15.8 Other specified personal history presenting hazards to health**

V15.81 Noncompliance with medical treatment

V15.82 History of tobacco use

> *Excludes:* *tobacco dependence (305.1)*

V15.84 Exposure to asbestos

V15.85 Exposure to potentially hazardous body fluids

V15.86 Exposure to lead

V15.89 Other

V15.9 Unspecified personal history presenting hazards to health

V16 Family history of malignant neoplasm

V16.0 Gastrointestinal tract
Family history of condition classifiable to 140-159

V16.1 Trachea, bronchus, and lung
Family history of condition classifiable to 162

V16.2 Other respiratory and intrathoracic organs
Family history of condition classifiable to 160-161, 163-165

V16.3 Breast
Family history of condition classifiable to 174

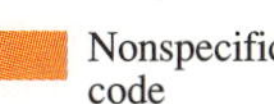

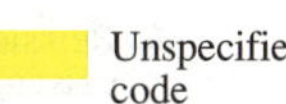

⑤ **V16.4 Genital organs**
Family history of condition classifiable to 179-187

    V16.40 Genital organ, unspecified

    V16.41 Ovary

    V16.42 Prostate

    V16.43 Testis

    V16.49 Other

⑤ **V16.5 Urinary organs**
Family history of condition classifiable to 189

    V16.51 Kidney

    V16.59 Other

V16.6 Leukemia
Family history of condition classifiable to 204-208

V16.7 Other lymphatic and hematopoietic neoplasms
Family history of condition classifiable to 200-203

V16.8 Other specified malignant neoplasm
Family history of other condition classifiable to 140-199

V16.9 Unspecified malignant neoplasm

V17 Family history of certain chronic disabling diseases

V17.0 Psychiatric condition

    Excludes: *family history of mental retardation (V18.4)*

V17.1 Stroke (cerebrovascular)

V17.2 Other neurological diseases
Epilepsy   Huntington's chorea

V17.3 Ischemic heart disease

V17.4 Other cardiovascular diseases

V17.5 Asthma

V17.6 Other chronic respiratory conditions

V17.7 Arthritis

V17.8 Other musculoskeletal diseases

V18 Family history of certain other specific conditions

V18.0 Diabetes mellitus

V18.1 Other endocrine and metabolic diseases

V18.2 Anemia

V18.3 Other blood disorders

V18.4 Mental retardation

V18.5 Digestive disorders

⑤ **V18.6 Kidney diseases**

    V18.61 Polycystic kidney

    V18.69 Other kidney diseases

V18.7 Other genitourinary diseases

V18.8 Infectious and parasitic diseases

V19 Family history of other conditions

V19.0 Blindness or visual loss

V19.1 Other eye disorders

V19.2 Deafness or hearing loss

V19.3 Other ear disorders

V19.4 Skin conditions

V19.5 Congenital anomalies

V19.6 Allergic disorders

V19.7 Consanguinity

V19.8 Other condition

● Code new to this edition   ▲ Revision of existing code   ④ ⑤ Fourth or fifth digit required

PERSONS ENCOUNTERING HEALTH SERVICES IN CIRCUMSTANCES RELATED TO REPRODUCTION AND DEVELOPMENT (V20-V29)

V20 Health supervision of infant or child

V20.0 Foundling

V20.1 Other healthy infant or child receiving care
Medical or nursing care supervision of healthy infant in cases of:
maternal illness, physical or psychiatric
socioeconomic adverse condition at home
too many children at home preventing or interfering with normal care

V20.2 Routine infant or child health check
Developmental testing of infant or child
Immunizations appropriate for age
Routine vision and hearing testing

Excludes: *special screening for developmental handicaps (V79.3)*
Use additional code(s) to identify:
Special screening examination(s) performed (V73.0-V82.9)

V21 Constitutional states in development

V21.0 Period of rapid growth in childhood

V21.1 Puberty

V21.2 Other adolescence

● **V21.3 Low birth weight status**

Excludes: *history of perinatal problems (V13.7)*

● **V21.30 Low birth weight status, unspecified**
● **V21.31 Low birth weight status, less than 500 grams**
● **V21.32 Low birth weight status, 500-999 grams**
● **V21.33 Low birth weight status, 1000-1499 grams**
● **V21.34 Low birth weight status, 1500-1999 grams**
● **V21.35 Low birth weight status, 2000-2500 grams**

V21.8 Other specified constitutional states in development

V21.9 Unspecified constitutional state in development

V22 Normal pregnancy

Excludes: *pregnancy examination or test, pregnancy unconfirmed (V72.4)*

V22.0 Supervision of normal first pregnancy

V22.1 Supervision of other normal pregnancy

V22.2 Pregnant state, incidental
Pregnant state NOS

V23 Supervision of high-risk pregnancy

V23.0 Pregnancy with history of infertility

V23.1 Pregnancy with history of trophoblastic disease
Pregnancy with history of:
hydatidiform mole
vesicular mole

Excludes: *that without current pregnancy (V13.1)*

V23.2 Pregnancy with history of abortion
Pregnancy with history of conditions classifiable to 634-638

Excludes: *habitual aborter:*
care during pregnancy (646.3)
that without current pregnancy (629.9)

V23.3 Grand multiparity

Excludes: *care in relation to labor and delivery (659.4)*
that without current pregnancy (V61.5)

V23.4 Pregnancy with other poor obstetric history
Pregnancy with history of other conditions classifiable to 630-676

V23.5 Pregnancy with other poor reproductive history
Pregnancy with history of stillbirth or neonatal death

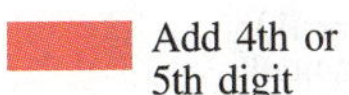

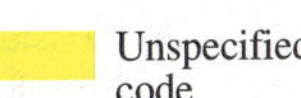

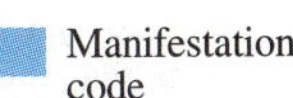

V23.7 Insufficient prenatal care
History of little or no prenatal care

⑤ **V23.8 Other high-risk pregnancy**

V23.81 Elderly primigravida
First pregnancy in a woman who will be 35 years of age or older at expected date of delivery

| Excludes: | *elderly primigravida complicating pregnancy (659.5)* |

V23.82 Elderly multigravida
Second or more pregnancy in a woman who will be 35 years of age or older at expected date of delivery

| Excludes: | *elderly multigravida complicating pregnancy (659.6)* |

V23.83 Young primigravida
First pregnancy in a female less than 16 years old at expected date of delivery

| Excludes: | *young primigravida complicating pregnancy (659.8)* |

V23.84 Young multigravida
Second or more pregnancy in a female less than 16 years old at expected date of delivery

| Excludes: | *young multigravida complicating pregnancy (659.8)* |

V23.89 Other high-risk pregnancy

V23.9 Unspecified high-risk pregnancy

V24 Postpartum care and examination

V24.0 Immediately after delivery
Care and observation in uncomplicated cases

V24.1 Lactating mother
Supervision of lactation

V24.2 Routine postpartum follow-up

V25 Encounter for contraceptive management

⑤ **V25.0 General counseling and advice**

V25.01 Prescription of oral contraceptives

V25.02 Initiation of other contraceptive measures
Fitting of diaphragm
Prescription of foams, creams, or other agents

V25.09 Other
Family planning advice

V25.1 Insertion of intrauterine contraceptive device

V25.2 Sterilization
Admission for interruption of fallopian tubes or vas deferens

V25.3 Menstrual extraction
Menstrual regulation

⑤ **V25.4 Surveillance of previously prescribed contraceptive methods**
Checking, reinsertion, or removal of contraceptive device
Repeat prescription for contraceptive method
Routine examination in connection with contraceptive maintenance

| Excludes: | *presence of intrauterine contraceptive device as incidental finding (V45.5)* |

V25.40 Contraceptive surveillance, unspecified

V25.41 Contraceptive pill

V25.42 Intrauterine contraceptive device
Checking, reinsertion, or removal of intrauterine device

V25.43 Implantable subdermal contraceptive

V25.49 Other contraceptive method

V25.5 Insertion of implantable subdermal contraceptive

V25.8 Other specified contraceptive management
Postvasectomy sperm count

| Excludes: | *sperm count following sterilization reversal (V26.22)* |
| | *sperm count for fertility testing (V26.21)* |

V25.9 Unspecified contraceptive management

● Code new
  to this edition

▲ Revision of
  existing code

④ ⑤ Fourth or fifth
  digit required

V26 **Procreative management**

V26.0 **Tuboplasty or vasoplasty after previous sterilization**

V26.1 **Artificial insemination**

⑤ **V26.2** **Investigation and testing**

> Excludes: *postvasectomy sperm count (V25.8)*

● **V26.21** **Fertility testing**
Fallopian insufflation
Sperm count for fertility testing

> Excludes: *Genetic counseling and testing (V26.3)*

● **V26.22** **Aftercare following sterilization reversal**
Fallopian insufflation following sterilization reversal
Sperm count following sterilization reversal

● **V26.29** **Other investigation and testing**

▲ **V26.3** **Genetic counseling and testing**

> Excludes: *fertility testing (V26.21)*

V26.4 **General counseling and advice**

⑤ **V26.5** **Sterilization status**

V26.51 **Tubal ligation status**

> Excludes: *infertility not due to previous tubal ligation (628.0-628.9)*

V26.52 **Vasectomy status**

V26.8 **Other specified procreative management**

V26.9 **Unspecified procreative management**

V27 **Outcome of delivery**

Note: This category is intended for the coding of the outcome of delivery on the mother's record.

V27.0 **Single liveborn**

V27.1 **Single stillborn**

V27.2 **Twins, both liveborn**

V27.3 **Twins, one liveborn and one stillborn**

V27.4 **Twins, both stillborn**

V27.5 **Other multiple birth, all liveborn**

V27.6 **Other multiple birth, some liveborn**

V27.7 **Other multiple birth, all stillborn**

V27.9 **Unspecified outcome of delivery**
Single birth, outcome to infant unspecified
Multiple birth, outcome to infant unspecified

V28 **Antenatal screening**

> Excludes: *abnormal findings on screening—code to findings*
> *routine prenatal care (V22.0-V23.9)*

V28.0 **Screening for chromosomal anomalies by amniocentesis**

V28.1 **Screening for raised alpha-fetoprotein levels in amniotic fluid**

V28.2 **Other screening based on amniocentesis**

V28.3 **Screening for malformation using ultrasonics**

V28.4 **Screening for fetal growth retardation using ultrasonics**

V28.5 **Screening for isoimmunization**

V28.6 **Screening for Streptococcus B**

V28.8 **Other specified antenatal screening**

V28.9 **Unspecified antenatal screening**

V29 **Observation and evaluation of newborns for suspected condition not found**

Note: This category is to be used for newborns, within the neonatal period, (the first 28 days of life) who are suspected of having an abnormal condition resulting from exposure from the mother or the birth process, but without signs or symptoms, and, which after examination and observation, is found not to exist.

V29.0 **Observation for suspected infectious condition**

V29.1 **Observation for suspected neurological condition**

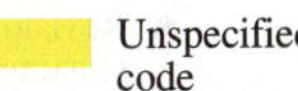

V29.2 Observation for suspected respiratory condition

V29.3 Observation for suspected genetic or metabolic condition

V29.8 Observation for other specified suspected condition

V29.9 Observation for unspecified suspected condition

LIVEBORN INFANTS ACCORDING TO TYPE OF BIRTH (V30-V39)

Note: These categories are intended for the coding of liveborn infants who are consuming health care [e.g., crib or bassinet occupancy].

The following fourth-digit subdivisions are for use with categories V30-V39:

    .0 Born in hospital

    .1 Born before admission to hospital

    .2 Born outside hospital and not hospitalized

The following two fifth-digits are for use with the fourth-digit .0, Born in hospital:

    0 delivered without mention of cesarean delivery

    1 delivered by cesarean delivery

④ **V30 Single liveborn**

④ **V31 Twin, mate liveborn**

④ **V32 Twin, mate stillborn**

④ **V33 Twin, unspecified**

④ **V34 Other multiple, mates all liveborn**

④ **V35 Other multiple, mates all stillborn**

④ **V36 Other multiple, mates live- and stillborn**

④ **V37 Other multiple, unspecified**

④ **V39 Unspecified**

PERSONS WITH A CONDITION INFLUENCING THEIR HEALTH STATUS (V40-V49)

Note: These categories are intended for use when these conditions are recorded as "diagnoses" or "problems."

V40 Mental and behavioral problems

V40.0 Problems with learning

V40.1 Problems with communication [including speech]

V40.2 Other mental problems

V40.3 Other behavioral problems

V40.9 Unspecified mental or behavioral problem

V41 Problems with special senses and other special functions

V41.0 Problems with sight

V41.1 Other eye problems

V41.2 Problems with hearing

V41.3 Other ear problems

V41.4 Problems with voice production

V41.5 Problems with smell and taste

V41.6 Problems with swallowing and mastication

V41.7 Problems with sexual function

    Excludes: *marital problems (V61.10)*

           psychosexual disorders (302.0-302.9)

V41.8 Other problems with special functions

V41.9 Unspecified problem with special functions

V42 Organ or tissue replaced by transplant

    Includes: homologous or heterologous (animal) (human) transplant organ status

V42.0 Kidney

V42.1 Heart

V42.2 Heart valve

V42.3 Skin

V42.4 Bone

● Code new to this edition   ▲ Revision of existing code   ④ ⑤ Fourth or fifth digit required

V42.5 Cornea

V42.6 Lung

V42.7 Liver

⑤ **V42.8 Other specified organ or tissue**

      V42.81 Bone marrow

      V42.82 Peripheral stem cells

      V42.83 Pancreas

    ● **V42.84 Intestines**

      V42.89 Other

V42.9 Unspecified organ or tissue

V43 Organ or tissue replaced by other means

    Includes: replacement of organ by:
          artificial device
          mechanical device
          prosthesis

    Excludes: *cardiac pacemaker in situ (V45.01)*
        fitting and adjustment of prosthetic device (V52.0-V52.9)
        renal dialysis status (V45.1)

V43.0 Eye globe

V43.1 Lens

    Pseudophakos

V43.2 Heart

V43.3 Heart valve

V43.4 Blood vessel

V43.5 Bladder

⑤ **V43.6 Joint**

      V43.60 Unspecified joint

      V43.61 Shoulder

      V43.62 Elbow

      V43.63 Wrist

      V43.64 Hip

      V43.65 Knee

      V43.66 Ankle

      V43.69 Other

V43.7 Limb

⑤ **V43.8 Other organ or tissue**

      V43.81 Larynx

      V43.82 Breast

      V43.83 Artificial skin

      V43.89 Other

V44 Artificial opening status

    Excludes: *artificial openings requiring attention or management (V55.0-V55.9)*

V44.0 Tracheostomy

V44.1 Gastrostomy

V44.2 Ileostomy

V44.3 Colostomy

V44.4 Other artificial opening of gastrointestinal tract

⑤ **V44.5 Cystostomy**

      V44.50 Cystostomy, unspecified

      V44.51 Cutaneous-vesicostomy

      V44.52 Appendico-vesicostomy

      V44.59 Other cystostomy

Manifestation
code

V44.6 Other artificial opening of urinary tract
Nephrostomy
Ureterostomy
Urethrostomy

V44.7 Artificial vagina

V44.8 Other artificial opening status

V44.9 Unspecified artificial opening status

V45 Other postsurgical states

> Excludes: *aftercare management (V51-V58.9)*
> *malfunction or other complication—code to condition*

⑤ **V45.0 Cardiac device in situ**

V45.00 Unspecified cardiac device

V45.01 Cardiac pacemaker

V45.02 Automatic implantable cardiac defibrillator

V45.09 Other specified cardiac device
Carotid sinus pacemaker in situ

V45.1 Renal dialysis status
Patient requiring intermittent renal dialysis
Presence of arterial-venous shunt (for dialysis)

> Excludes: *admission for dialysis treatment, or session (V56.0)*

V45.2 Presence of cerebrospinal fluid drainage device
Cerebral ventricle (communicating) shunt, valve, or device in situ

> Excludes: *malfunction (996.2)*

V45.3 Intestinal bypass or anastomosis status

V45.4 Arthrodesis status

⑤ **V45.5 Presence of contraceptive device**

> Excludes: *checking, reinsertion, or removal of device (V25.42)*
> *complication from device (996.32)*
> *insertion of device (V25.1)*

V45.51 Intrauterine contraceptive device

V45.52 Subdermal contraceptive implant

V45.59 Other

⑤ **V45.6 States following surgery of eye and adnexa**
Cataract extraction
Filtering bleb   } state following eye surgery
Surgical eyelid adhesion

> Excludes: *aphakia (379.31)*
> *artificial eye globe (V43.0)*

V45.61 Cataract extraction status
Use additional code for associated artificial lens status (V43.1)

V45.69 Other states following surgery of eye and adnexa

⑤ **V45.7 Acquired absence of organ**

V45.71 Acquired absence of breast

V45.72 Acquired absence of intestine (large) (small)

V45.73 Acquired absence of kidney

● **V45.74 Other parts of urinary tract**
Bladder

● **V45.75 Stomach**

● **V45.76 Lung**

● **V45.77 Genital organs**

● **V45.78 Eye**

● **V45.79 Other acquired absence of organ**

⑤ **V45.8 Other postsurgical status**

V45.81 Aortocoronary bypass status

V45.82 Percutaneous transluminal coronary angioplasty status

● Code new to this edition   ▲ Revision of existing code   ④ ⑤ Fourth or fifth digit required

V45.83　Breast implant removal status

V45.89　Other
　　　Presence of neuropacemaker or other electronic device

　Excludes: *artificial heart valve in situ (V43.3)*
　　　vascular prosthesis in situ (V43.4)

V46　Other dependence on machines

V46.0　Aspirator

V46.1　Respirator
　　Iron lung

V46.8　Other enabling machines
　　Hyperbaric chamber
　　Possum [Patient-Operated-Selector-Mechanism]

　Excludes: *cardiac pacemaker (V45.0)*
　　　kidney dialysis machine (V45.1)

V46.9　Unspecified machine dependence

V47　Other problems with internal organs

V47.0　Deficiencies of internal organs

V47.1　Mechanical and motor problems with internal organs

V47.2　Other cardiorespiratory problems
　　Cardiovascular exercise intolerance with pain (with):
　　　at rest
　　　less than ordinary activity
　　　ordinary activity

V47.3　Other digestive problems

V47.4　Other urinary problems

V47.5　Other genital problems

V47.9　Unspecified

V48　Problems with head, neck, and trunk

V48.0　Deficiencies of head

　　Excludes: *deficiencies of ears, eyelids, and nose (V48.8)*

V48.1　Deficiencies of neck and trunk

V48.2　Mechanical and motor problems with head

V48.3　Mechanical and motor problems with neck and trunk

V48.4　Sensory problem with head

V48.5　Sensory problem with neck and trunk

V48.6　Disfigurements of head

V48.7　Disfigurements of neck and trunk

V48.8　Other problems with head, neck, and trunk

V48.9　Unspecified problem with head, neck, or trunk

▲ V49　Other conditions influencing health status

V49.0　Deficiencies of limbs

V49.1　Mechanical problems with limbs

V49.2　Motor problems with limbs

V49.3　Sensory problems with limbs

V49.4　Disfigurements of limbs

V49.5　Other problems of limbs

⑤　**V49.6　Upper limb amputation status**

　　V49.60　Unspecified level

　　V49.61　Thumb

　　V49.62　Other finger(s)

　　V49.63　Hand

　　V49.64　Wrist
　　　　Disarticulation of wrist

　　V49.65　Below elbow

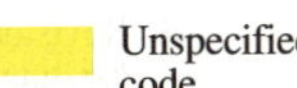

V49.66 Above elbow
Disarticulation of elbow

V49.67 Shoulder
Disarticulation of shoulder

⑤ **V49.7 Lower limb amputation status**

V49.70 Unspecified level

V49.71 Great toe

V49.72 Other toe(s)

V49.73 Foot

V49.74 Ankle
Disarticulation of ankle

V49.75 Below knee

V49.76 Above knee
Disarticulation of knee

V49.77 Hip
Disarticulation of hip

▲ **V49.8 Other specified conditions influencing health status**

● **V49.81 Postmenopausal status (age-related) (natural)**

Excludes: *menopausal and premenopausal disorders (627.0-627.9)*
postsurgical menopause (256.2)
premature menopause (256.3)
symptomatic menopause (627.0-627.9)

● **V49.89 Other specified conditions influencing health status**

V49.9 Unspecified

PERSONS ENCOUNTERING HEALTH SERVICES FOR SPECIFIC PROCEDURES AND AFTERCARE (V50-V59)

Note: Categories V51-V58 are intended for use to indicate a reason for care in patients who may have already been treated for some disease or injury not now present, but who are receiving care to consolidate the treatment, to deal with residual states, or to prevent recurrence.

Excludes: *follow-up examination for medical surveillance following treatment (V67.0-V67.9)*

V50 Elective surgery for purposes other than remedying health states

V50.0 Hair transplant

V50.1 Other plastic surgery for unacceptable cosmetic appearance
Breast augmentation or reduction
Face-lift

Excludes: *plastic surgery following healed injury or operation (V51)*

V50.2 Routine or ritual circumcision
Circumcision in the absence of significant medical indication

V50.3 Ear piercing

⑤ **V50.4 Prophylactic organ removal**

Excludes: *organ donations (V59.0-V59.9)*
therapeutic organ removal—code to condition

V50.41 Breast

V50.42 Ovary

V50.49 Other

V50.8 Other

V50.9 Unspecified

V51 Aftercare involving the use of plastic surgery
Plastic surgery following healed injury or operation

Excludes: *cosmetic plastic surgery (V50.1)*
plastic surgery as treatment for current injury—code to condition
repair of scarred tissue—code to scar

● Code new
to this edition

▲ Revision of
existing code

④ ⑤ Fourth or fifth
digit required

V52 Fitting and adjustment of prosthetic device and implant
Includes: removal of device

> Excludes: *malfunction or complication of prosthetic device (996.0-996.7)*
> *status only, without need for care (V43.0-V43.8)*

V52.0 Artificial arm (complete) (partial)

V52.1 Artificial leg (complete) (partial)

V52.2 Artificial eye

V52.3 Dental prosthetic device

V52.4 Breast prosthesis and implant

> Excludes: *admission for implant insertion (V50.1)*

V52.8 Other specified prosthetic device

V52.9 Unspecified prosthetic device

V53 Fitting and adjustment of other device
Includes: removal of device
replacement of device

> Excludes: *status only, without need for care (V45.0-V45.8)*

⑤ **V53.0 Devices related to nervous system and special senses**

    V53.01 Fitting and adjustment of cerebral ventricular (communicating) shunt

    V53.02 Neuropacemaker (brain) (peripheral nerve) (spinal cord)

    V53.09 Fitting and adjustment of other devices related to nervous system and special senses
Auditory substitution device
Visual substitution device

V53.1 Spectacles and contact lenses

V53.2 Hearing aid

⑤ **V53.3 Cardiac device**
Reprogramming

    V53.31 Cardiac pacemaker

> Excludes: *mechanical complication of cardiac pacemaker (996.01)*

    V53.32 Automatic implantable cardiac defibrillator

    V53.39 Other cardiac device

V53.4 Orthodontic devices

V53.5 Other intestinal appliance

> Excludes: *colostomy (V55.3)*
> *ileostomy (V55.2)*
> *other artificial opening of digestive tract (V55.4)*

V53.6 Urinary devices
Urinary catheter

> Excludes: *cystostomy (V55.5)*
> *nephrostomy (V55.6)*
> *ureterostomy (V55.6)*
> *urethrostomy (V55.6)*

V53.7 Orthopedic devices

Orthopedic:
  brace
  cast

Orthopedic:
  corset
  shoes

> Excludes: *other orthopedic aftercare (V54)*

V53.8 Wheelchair

V53.9 Other and unspecified device

V54 Other orthopedic aftercare

> Excludes: *fitting and adjustment of orthopedic devices (V53.7)*
> *malfunction of internal orthopedic device (996.4)*
> *other complication of nonmechanical nature (996.60-996.79)*

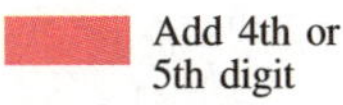

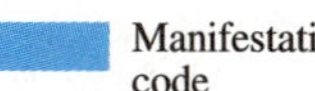

V54.0 Aftercare involving removal of fracture plate or other internal fixation device
Removal of:
  pins
  plates
Removal of:
  rods
  screws

Excludes: *removal of external fixation device (V54.8)*

V54.8 Other orthopedic aftercare
Change, checking, or removal of:
  Kirschner wire
  plaster cast
  splint, external
  other external fixation or traction device

V54.9 Unspecified orthopedic aftercare

V55 Attention to artificial openings
Includes: adjustment or repositioning of catheter
        closure
        passage of sounds or bougies
        reforming
        removal or replacement of catheter
        toilet or cleansing

Excludes: *complications of external stoma (519.00-519.09, 569.60-569.69, 997.4, 997.5)*
status only, without need for care (V44.0-V44.9)

V55.0 Tracheostomy

V55.1 Gastrostomy

V55.2 Ileostomy

V55.3 Colostomy

V55.4 Other artificial opening of digestive tract

V55.5 Cystostomy

V55.6 Other artificial opening of urinary tract
Nephrostomy   Urethrostomy
Ureterostomy

V55.7 Artificial vagina

V55.8 Other specified artificial opening

V55.9 Unspecified artificial opening

V56 Encounter for dialysis and dialysis catheter care
Use additional code to identify the associated condition

Excludes: *dialysis preparation—code to condition*

V56.0 Extracorporeal dialysis
Dialysis (renal) NOS

Excludes: *dialysis status (V45.1)*

V56.1 Fitting and adjustment of extracorporeal dialysis catheter
Removal or replacement of catheter
Toilet or cleansing
Use additional code for any concurrent extracorporeal dialysis (V56.0)

V56.2 Fitting and adjustment of peritoneal dialysis catheter
Use additional code for any concurrent peritoneal dialysis (V56.8)

● **V56.3 Encounter for adequacy testing for dialysis**

   ● **V56.31 Encounter for adequacy testing for hemodialysis**

   ● **V56.32 Encounter for adequacy testing for peritoneal dialysis**
       Peritoneal equilibration test

V56.8 Other dialysis
Peritoneal dialysis

V57 Care involving use of rehabilitation procedures
Use additional code to identify underlying condition

V57.0 Breathing exercises

V57.1 Other physical therapy
Therapeutic and remedial exercises, except breathing

⑤ **V57.2 Occupational therapy and vocational rehabilitation**

   V57.21 Encounter for occupational therapy

● Code new
  to this edition
▲ Revision of
  existing code
④ ⑤ Fourth or fifth
    digit required

V57.22 Encounter for vocational therapy

V57.3 Speech therapy

V57.4 Orthoptic training

⑤ **V57.8 Other specified rehabilitation procedure**

V57.81 Orthotic training
Gait training in the use of artificial limbs

V57.89 Other
Multiple training or therapy

V57.9 Unspecified rehabilitation procedure

V58 Encounter for other and unspecified procedures and aftercare

Excludes: *convalescence and palliative care (V66)*

V58.0 Radiotherapy
Encounter or admission for radiotherapy

Excludes: *encounter for radioactive implant—code to condition*
radioactive iodine therapy—code to condition

V58.1 Chemotherapy
Encounter or admission for chemotherapy

Excludes: *prophylactic chemotherapy against disease which has never been present (V03.0-V07.9)*

V58.2 Blood transfusion, without reported diagnosis

V58.3 Attention to surgical dressings and sutures
Change of dressings   Removal of sutures

⑤ **V58.4 Other aftercare following surgery**

Excludes: *aftercare following sterilization reversal surgery (V26.22)*
attention to artificial openings (V55.0-V55.9)
orthopedic aftercare (V54.0-V54.9)

V58.41 Encounter for planned postoperative wound closure

Excludes: *disruption of operative wound (998.3)*

V58.49 Other specified aftercare following surgery

V58.5 Orthodontics

Excludes: *fitting and adjustment of orthodontic device (V53.4)*

⑤ **V58.6 Long-term (current) drug use**

Excludes: *drug abuse (305.00-305.93)*
drug dependence (304.00-304.93)

V58.61 Long-term (current) use of anticoagulants

V58.62 Long-term (current) use of antibiotics

V58.69 Long-term (current) use of other medications
High-risk medications

⑤ **V58.8 Other specified procedures and aftercare**

V58.81 Fitting and adjustment of vascular catheter
Removal or replacement of catheter
Toilet or cleansing

Excludes: *complication of renal dialysis catheter (996.73)*
complication of vascular catheter (996.74)
dialysis preparation -- code to condition
encounter for dialysis (V56.0-V56.8)
fitting and adjustment of dialysis catheter (V56.1)

V58.82 Fitting and adjustment of non-vascular catheter NEC
Removal or replacement of catheter
Toilet or cleansing

Excludes: *fitting and adjustment of peritoneal dialysis catheter (V56.2)*
fitting and adjustment of urinary catheter (V53.6)

● **V58.83 Encounter for therapeutic drug monitoring**

Excludes: *blood-drug testing for medicolegal reasons (V70.4)*

V58.89 Other specified aftercare

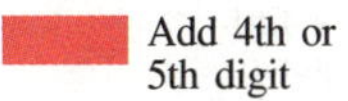

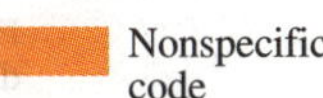

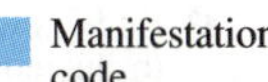

V58.9 Unspecified aftercare

V59 Donors

> Excludes: *examination of potential donor (V70.8)*
> *self-donation of organ or tissue -- code to condition*

⑤ **V59.0 Blood**

    V59.01 Whole blood

    V59.02 Stem cells

    V59.09 Other

V59.1 Skin

V59.2 Bone

V59.3 Bone marrow

V59.4 Kidney

V59.5 Cornea

V59.6 Liver

V59.8 Other specified organ or tissue

V59.9 Unspecified organ or tissue

PERSONS ENCOUNTERING HEALTH SERVICES IN OTHER CIRCUMSTANCES (V60-V68)

V60 Housing, household, and economic circumstances

V60.0 Lack of housing

Hobos	Transients
Social migrants	Vagabonds
Tramps	

V60.1 Inadequate housing
Lack of heating
Restriction of space
Technical defects in home preventing adequate care

V60.2 Inadequate material resources

Economic problem	Poverty NOS

V60.3 Person living alone

V60.4 No other household member able to render care
Person requiring care (has) (is):
    family member too handicapped, ill, or otherwise unsuited to render care
    partner temporarily away from home
    temporarily away from usual place of abode

> Excludes: *holiday relief care (V60.5)*

V60.5 Holiday relief care
Provision of health care facilities to a person normally cared for at home, to enable relatives to take a vacation

V60.6 Person living in residential institution
Boarding school resident

V60.8 Other specified housing or economic circumstances

V60.9 Unspecified housing or economic circumstance

V61 Other family circumstances
Includes: when these circumstances or fear of them, affecting the person directly involved or others, are mentioned as the reason, justified or not, for seeking or receiving medical advice or care

V61.0 Family disruption

Divorce	Estrangement

⑤ **V61.1 Counseling for marital and partner problems**

> Excludes: *problems related to:*
> *psychosexual disorders (302.0-302.9)*
> *sexual function (V41.7)*

    V61.10 Counseling for marital and partner problems, unspecified
    Marital conflict
    Partner conflict

    V61.11 Counseling for victim of spousal and partner abuse

> Excludes: *encounter for treatment of current injuries due to abuse (995.80-995.85)*

● Code new to this edition	▲ Revision of existing code	④ ⑤ Fourth or fifth digit required

V61.12 Counseling for perpetrator of spousal and partner abuse

⑤ **V61.2 Parent-child problems**

V61.20 Counseling for parent-child problem, unspecified
Concern about behavior of child
Parent-child conflict

V61.21 Counseling for victim of child abuse
Child battering
Child neglect

| Excludes: | current injuries due to abuse (995.50-995.59) |

V61.22 Counseling for perpetrator of parental child abuse

| Excludes: | counseling for non-parental abuser (V62.83) |

V61.29 Other
Problem concerning adopted or foster child

V61.3 Problems with aged parents or in-laws

⑤ **V61.4 Health problems within family**

V61.41 Alcoholism in family

V61.49 Other
Care of
Presence of } sick or handicapped person in family or household

V61.5 Multiparity

V61.6 Illegitimacy or illegitimate pregnancy

V61.7 Other unwanted pregnancy

V61.8 Other specified family circumstances
Problems with family members NEC

V61.9 Unspecified family circumstance

V62 Other psychosocial circumstances
Includes: those circumstances or fear of them, affecting the person directly involved or others, mentioned as the reason, justified or not, for seeking or receiving medical advice or care

| Excludes: | previous psychological trauma (V15.41-V15.49) |

V62.0 Unemployment

| Excludes: | circumstances when main problem is economic inadequacy or poverty (V60.2) |

V62.1 Adverse effects of work environment

V62.2 Other occupational circumstances or maladjustment
Career choice problem
Dissatisfaction with employment

V62.3 Educational circumstances
Dissatisfaction with school environment
Educational handicap

V62.4 Social maladjustment

Cultural deprivation	Social:
Political, religious, or sex discrimination	isolation
	persecution

V62.5 Legal circumstances

| Imprisonment | Litigation |
| Legal investigation | Prosecution |

V62.6 Refusal of treatment for reasons of religion or conscience

⑤ **V62.8 Other psychological or physical stress, not elsewhere classified**

V62.81 Interpersonal problems, not elsewhere classified

V62.82 Bereavement, uncomplicated

| Excludes: | bereavement as adjustment reaction (309.0) |

V62.83 Counseling for perpetrator of physical/sexual abuse

| Excludes: | counseling for perpetrator of parental child abuse (V61.22) |
| | counseling for perpetrator of spousal and partner abuse (V61.12) |

V62.89 Other
Life circumstance problems
Phase of life problems

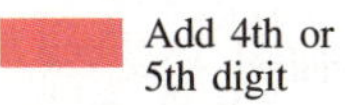

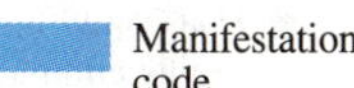

V62.9 Unspecified psychosocial circumstance

V63 Unavailability of other medical facilities for care

V63.0 Residence remote from hospital or other health care facility

V63.1 Medical services in home not available

> Excludes: *no other household member able to render care (V60.4)*

V63.2 Person awaiting admission to adequate facility elsewhere

V63.8 Other specified reasons for unavailability of medical facilities
Person on waiting list undergoing social agency investigation

V63.9 Unspecified reason for unavailability of medical facilities

V64 Persons encountering health services for specific procedures, not carried out

V64.0 Vaccination not carried out because of contraindication

V64.1 Surgical or other procedure not carried out because of contraindication

V64.2 Surgical or other procedure not carried out because of patient's decision

V64.3 Procedure not carried out for other reasons

V64.4 Laparoscopic surgical procedure converted to open procedure

V65 Other persons seeking consultation without complaint or sickness

V65.0 Healthy person accompanying sick person
Boarder

V65.1 Person consulting on behalf of another person
Advice or treatment for nonattending third party

> Excludes: *concern (normal) about sick person in family (V61.41-V61.49)*

V65.2 Person feigning illness
Malingerer   Peregrinating patient

V65.3 Dietary surveillance and counseling
Dietary surveillance and counseling (in):
NOS
colitis
diabetes mellitus
food allergies or intolerance
gastritis
hypercholesterolemia
hypoglycemia
obesity

⑤ **V65.4** Other counseling, not elsewhere classified
Health:
advice
education
instruction

> Excludes: *counseling (for):*
> *contraception (V25.40-V25.49)*
> *genetic (V26.3)*
> *on behalf of third party (V65.1)*
> *procreative management (V26.4)*

V65.40 Counseling NOS

V65.41 Exercise counseling

V65.42 Counseling on substance use and abuse

V65.43 Counseling on injury prevention

V65.44 Human immunodeficiency virus [HIV] counseling

V65.45 Counseling on other sexually transmitted diseases

V65.49 Other specified counseling

V65.5 Person with feared complaint in whom no diagnosis was made
Feared condition not demonstrated
Problem was normal state
"Worried well"

V65.8 Other reasons for seeking consultation

> Excludes: *specified symptoms*

V65.9 Unspecified reason for consultation

V66 Convalescence and palliative care

  ● Code new
to this edition   ▲ Revision of
existing code   ④ ⑤ Fourth or fifth
digit required

V66.0 Following surgery

V66.1 Following radiotherapy

V66.2 Following chemotherapy

V66.3 Following psychotherapy and other treatment for mental disorder

V66.4 Following treatment of fracture

V66.5 Following other treatment

V66.6 Following combined treatment

V66.7 *Encounter for palliative care*
    End-of-life care
    Hospice care
    Terminal care

Code first underlying disease

V66.9 Unspecified convalescence

V67 Follow-up examination
    Includes: surveillance only following completed treatment

    Excludes: *surveillance of contraception (V25.40-V25.49)*

⑤ **V67.0 Following surgery**

● **V67.00 Following surgery, unspecified**

● **V67.01 Follow-up vaginal pap smear**
    Vaginal pap smear, status-post hysterectomy for malignant condition
Use additional code to identify:
    acquired absence of uterus (V45.77)
    personal history of malignant neoplasm (V10.40-V10.44)

    Excludes: *vaginal pap smear status-post hysterectomy for non-malignant condition (V76.47)*

● **V67.09 Following other surgery**

    Excludes: *sperm count following sterilization reversal (V26.22)*
        sperm count for fertility testing (V26.21)

V67.1 Following radiotherapy

V67.2 Following chemotherapy
    Cancer chemotherapy follow-up

V67.3 Following psychotherapy and other treatment for mental disorder

V67.4 Following treatment of healed fracture

    Excludes: *current (healing) fracture aftercare (V54.0-V54.9)*

⑤ **V67.5 Following other treatment**

    V67.51 Following completed treatment with high-risk medication, NEC

    Excludes: *long-term (current) drug use (V58.61-V58.69)*

    V67.59 Other

V67.6 Following combined treatment

V67.9 Unspecified follow-up examination

V68 Encounters for administrative purposes

V68.0 Issue of medical certificates
    Issue of medical certificate of: cause of death
                         fitness
                         incapacity

    Excludes: *encounter for general medical examination (V70.0-V70.9)*

V68.1 Issue of repeat prescriptions
    Issue of repeat prescription for: appliance
                           glasses
                           medications

    Excludes: *repeat prescription for contraceptives (V25.41-V25.49)*

V68.2 Request for expert evidence

⑤ **V68.8 Other specified administrative purpose**

    V68.81 Referral of patient without examination or treatment

    V68.89 Other

V68.9 Unspecified administrative purpose

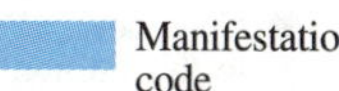

V69 Problems related to lifestyle

V69.0 Lack of physical exercise

V69.1 Inappropriate diet and eating habits

> *Excludes:* *anorexia nervosa (307.1)*
> *bulimia (783.6)*
> *malnutrition and other nutritional deficiencies (260-269.9)*
> *other and unspecified eating disorders (307.50-307.59)*

V69.2 High-risk sexual behavior

V69.3 Gambling and betting

> *Excludes:* *pathological gambling (312.31)*

V69.8 Other problems related to lifestyle
Self-damaging behavior

V69.9 Problem related to lifestyle, unspecified

PERSONS WITHOUT REPORTED DIAGNOSIS ENCOUNTERED DURING EXAMINATION AND INVESTIGATION OF INDIVIDUALS AND POPULATIONS (V70-V82)

Note: Nonspecific abnormal findings disclosed at the time of these examinations are classifiable to categories 790-796.

V70 General medical examination

Use additional code(s) to identify any special screening examination(s) performed (V73.0-V82.9)

V70.0 Routine general medical examination at a health care facility
Health checkup

> *Excludes:* *health checkup of infant or child (V20.2)*

V70.1 General psychiatric examination, requested by the authority

V70.2 General psychiatric examination, other and unspecified

V70.3 Other medical examination for administrative purposes
General medical examination for:

admission to old age home	marriage
adoption	prison
camp	school admission
driving license	sports competition
immigration and naturalization	
insurance certification	

> *Excludes:* *attendance for issue of medical certificates (V68.0)*
> *pre-employment screening (V70.5)*

V70.4 Examination for medicolegal reasons
Blood-alcohol tests
Blood-drug tests
Paternity testing

> *Excludes:* *examination and observation following:*
> *accidents (V71.3, V71.4)*
> *assault (V71.6)*
> *rape (V71.5)*

V70.5 Health examination of defined subpopulations

Armed forces personnel	Preschool children
Inhabitants of institutions	Prisoners
Occupational health	Prostitutes
examinations	Refugees
Pre-employment screening	School children
	Students

V70.6 Health examination in population surveys

> *Excludes:* *special screening (V73.0-V82.9)*

V70.7 Examination for normal comparison or control in clinical research

V70.8 Other specified general medical examinations
Examination of potential donor of organ or tissue

V70.9 Unspecified general medical examination

● Code new
to this edition
▲ Revision of
existing code
④ ⑤ Fourth or fifth
digit required

V71 Observation and evaluation for suspected conditions not found

Note: This category is to be used when persons without a diagnosis are suspected of having an abnormal condition, without signs or symptoms, which requires study, but after examination and observation, is found not to exist. This category is also for use for administrative and legal observation status.

⑤ **V71.0 Observation for suspected mental condition**

V71.01 Adult antisocial behavior

Dyssocial behavior or gang activity in adult without manifest psychiatric disorder

V71.02 Childhood or adolescent antisocial behavior

Dyssocial behavior or gang activity in child or adolescent without manifest psychiatric disorder

V71.09 Other suspected mental condition

V71.1 Observation for suspected malignant neoplasm

V71.2 Observation for suspected tuberculosis

V71.3 Observation following accident at work

V71.4 Observation following other accident

Examination of individual involved in motor vehicle traffic accident

V71.5 Observation following alleged rape or seduction

Examination of victim or culprit

V71.6 Observation following other inflicted injury

Examination of victim or culprit

V71.7 Observation for suspected cardiovascular disease

⑤ **V71.8 Observation for other specified suspected conditions**

● **V71.81 Abuse and neglect**

Excludes: *adult abuse and neglect (995.80-995.85)*

child abuse and neglect (995.50-995.59)

● **V71.89 Other specified suspected conditions**

V71.9 Observation for unspecified suspected condition

V72 Special investigations and examinations

Includes: routine examination of specific system

Excludes: *general medical examination (V70.0-V70.4)*

general screening examination of defined population groups (V70.5, V70.6, V70.7)
routine examination of infant or child (V20.2)

Use additional code(s) to identify any special screening examination(s) performed (V73.0-V82.9)

V72.0 Examination of eyes and vision

V72.1 Examination of ears and hearing

V72.2 Dental examination

V72.3 Gynecological examination

Papanicolaou cervical smear as part of general gynecological examination
Pelvic examination (annual) (periodic)

Use additional code to identify routine vaginal Papanicolaou smear (V76.47)

Excludes: *cervical Papanicolaou smear without general gynecological examination (V76.2)*

routine examination in contraceptive management (V25.40-V25.49)

V72.4 Pregnancy examination or test, pregnancy unconfirmed

Possible pregnancy, not (yet) confirmed

Excludes: *pregnancy examination with immediate confirmation (V22.0-V22.1)*

V72.5 Radiological examination, not elsewhere classified

Routine chest x-ray

Excludes: *examination for suspected tuberculosis (V71.2)*

V72.6 Laboratory examination

Excludes: *that for suspected disorder (V71.0-V71.9)*

V72.7 Diagnostic skin and sensitization tests

Allergy tests
Skin tests for hypersensitivity

Excludes: *diagnostic skin tests for bacterial diseases (V74.0-V74.9)*

⑤ **V72.8 Other specified examinations**

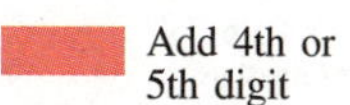

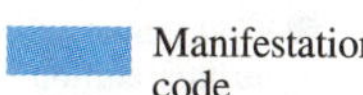

V72.81   Pre-operative cardiovascular examination

V72.82   Pre-operative respiratory examination

`V72.83`   Other specified pre-operative examination

`V72.84`   Pre-operative examination, unspecified

`V72.85`   Other specified examination

`V72.9` Unspecified examination

`V73` Special screening examination for viral and chlamydial diseases

V73.0 Poliomyelitis

V73.1 Smallpox

V73.2 Measles

V73.3 Rubella

V73.4 Yellow fever

`V73.5` Other arthropod-borne viral diseases
> Dengue fever   Viral encephalitis:
> Hemorrhagic fever   mosquito-borne
>   tick-borne

V73.6 Trachoma

⑤ V73.8 Other specified viral and chlamydial diseases

        `V73.88` Other specified chlamydial diseases

        `V73.89` Other specified viral diseases

⑤ V73.9 Unspecified viral and chlamydial disease

        `V73.98` Unspecified chlamydial disease

        `V73.99` Unspecified viral disease

`V74` Special screening examination for bacterial and spirochetal diseases
> Includes: diagnostic skin tests for these diseases

V74.0 Cholera

V74.1 Pulmonary tuberculosis

V74.2 Leprosy [Hansen's disease]

V74.3 Diphtheria

V74.4 Bacterial conjunctivitis

V74.5 Venereal disease

V74.6 Yaws

`V74.8` Other specified bacterial and spirochetal diseases
> Brucellosis   Tetanus
> Leptospirosis   Whooping cough
> Plague

`V74.9` Unspecified bacterial and spirochetal disease

`V75` Special screening examination for other infectious diseases

V75.0 Rickettsial diseases

V75.1 Malaria

V75.2 Leishmaniasis

V75.3 Trypanosomiasis
> Chagas' disease   Sleeping sickness

V75.4 Mycotic infections

V75.5 Schistosomiasis

V75.6 Filariasis

V75.7 Intestinal helminthiasis

`V75.8` Other specified parasitic infections

`V75.9` Unspecified infectious disease

`V76` Special screening for malignant neoplasms

V76.0 Respiratory organs

⑤ V76.1 Breast

        `V76.10` Breast screening, unspecified

        V76.11 Screening mammogram for high-risk patient

    ● Code new   ▲ Revision of   ④ ⑤ Fourth or fifth
               to this edition   existing code   digit required

V76.12 Other screening mammogram

V76.19 Other screening breast examination

V76.2 Cervix
Routine cervical Papanicolaou smear

Excludes: *that as part of a general gynecological examination (V72.3)*

V76.3 Bladder

⑤ **V76.4 Other sites**

V76.41 Rectum

V76.42 Oral cavity

V76.43 Skin

V76.44 Prostate

V76.45 Testis

● **V76.46 Ovary**

● **V76.47 Vagina**
Vaginal pap smear status-post hysterectomy for non-malignant condition
Use additional code to identify acquired absence of uterus (V45.77)

Excludes: *vaginal pap smear status-post hysterectomy for malignant condition (V67.01)*

▲ **V76.49 Other sites**

● **V76.5 Intestine**

● **V76.50 Intestine, unspecified**

● **V76.51 Colon**

Excludes: *rectum (V76.41)*

● **V76.52 Small intestine**

⑤ **V76.8 Other neoplasm**

● **V76.81 Nervous system**

● **V76.89 Other neoplasm**

V76.9 Unspecified

V77 Special screening for endocrine, nutritional, metabolic, and immunity disorders

V77.0 Thyroid disorders

V77.1 Diabetes mellitus

V77.2 Malnutrition

V77.3 Phenylketonuria [PKU]

V77.4 Galactosemia

V77.5 Gout

V77.6 Cystic fibrosis
Screening for mucoviscidosis

V77.7 Other inborn errors of metabolism

V77.8 Obesity

⑤ **V77.9 Other and unspecified endocrine, nutritional, metabolic, and immunity disorders**

● **V77.91 Screening for lipoid disorders**
Screening cholesterol level
Screening for hypercholesterolemia
Screening for hyperlipidemia

● **V77.99 Other and unspecified endocrine, nutritional, metabolic, and immunity disorders**

V78 Special screening for disorders of blood and blood-forming organs

V78.0 Iron deficiency anemia

V78.1 Other and unspecified deficiency anemia

V78.2 Sickle-cell disease or trait

V78.3 Other hemoglobinopathies

V78.8 Other disorders of blood and blood-forming organs

V78.9 Unspecified disorder of blood and blood-forming organs

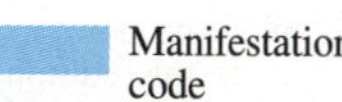

Manifestation
code

V79 Special screening for mental disorders and developmental handicaps

V79.0 Depression

V79.1 Alcoholism

V79.2 Mental retardation

V79.3 Developmental handicaps in early childhood

V79.8 Other specified mental disorders and developmental handicaps

V79.9 Unspecified mental disorder and developmental handicap

V80 Special screening for neurological, eye, and ear diseases

V80.0 Neurological conditions

V80.1 Glaucoma

V80.2 Other eye conditions

    Screening for:
      cataract
      congenital anomaly of eye
      senile macular lesions

    | *Excludes:* | *general vision examination (V72.0)* |

V80.3 Ear diseases

    | *Excludes:* | *general hearing examination (V72.1)* |

V81 Special screening for cardiovascular, respiratory, and genitourinary diseases

V81.0 Ischemic heart disease

V81.1 Hypertension

V81.2 Other and unspecified cardiovascular conditions

V81.3 Chronic bronchitis and emphysema

V81.4 Other and unspecified respiratory conditions

    | *Excludes:* | *screening for:* |

        lung neoplasm (V76.0)
        pulmonary tuberculosis (V74.1)

V81.5 Nephropathy

    Screening for asymptomatic bacteriuria

V81.6 Other and unspecified genitourinary conditions

V82 Special screening for other conditions

V82.0 Skin conditions

V82.1 Rheumatoid arthritis

V82.2 Other rheumatic disorders

V82.3 Congenital dislocation of hip

V82.4 Maternal postnatal screening for chromosomal anomalies

    | *Excludes:* | *antenatal screening by amniocentesis (V28.0)* |

V82.5 Chemical poisoning and other contamination

    Screening for:
      heavy metal poisoning
      ingestion of radioactive substance
      poisoning from contaminated water supply
      radiation exposure

V82.6 Multiphasic screening

⑤ V82.8 Other specified conditions

    ● V82.81 Osteoporosis

Use additional code to identify:
    postmenopausal hormone replacement therapy status (V07.4)
    postmenopausal (natural) status (V49.81)

    ● V82.89 Other specified conditions

V82.9 Unspecified condition

● Code new to this edition   ▲ Revision of existing code   ④ ⑤ Fourth or fifth digit required

SUPPLEMENTARY CLASSIFICATION OF EXTERNAL CAUSES OF INJURY AND POISONING (E800-E999)

This section is provided to permit the classification of environmental events, circumstances, and conditions as the cause of injury, poisoning, and other adverse effects. Where a code from this section is applicable, it is intended that it shall be used in addition to a code from one of the main chapters of *ICD-9-CM*, indicating the nature of the condition. Certain other conditions which may be stated to be due to external causes are classified in Chapters 1 to 16 of *ICD-9-CM*. For these, the "E" code classification should be used for more detailed analysis.

Machinery accidents [other than those connected with transport] are classifiable to category E919, in which the fourth-digit allows a broad classification of the type of machinery involved. If a more detailed classification of type of machinery is required, it is suggested that the "Classification of Industrial Accidents according to Agency," prepared by the International Labor Office, be used in addition. This is reproduced on page 571, for optional use.

Categories for "late effects" of accidents and other external causes are to be found at E929, E959, E969, E977, E989, and E999.

Definitions and examples related to transport accidents

(a) A **transport accident** (E800-E848) is any accident involving a device designed primarily for, or being used at the time primarily for, conveying persons or goods from one place to another.

Includes: accidents involving:
aircraft and spacecraft (E840-E845)
watercraft (E830-E838)
motor vehicle (E810-E825)
railway (E800-E807)
other road vehicles (E826-E829)

In classifying accidents which involve more than one kind of transport, the above order of precedence of transport accidents should be used.

Accidents involving agriculture and construction machines, such as tractors, cranes, and bulldozers, are regarded as transport accidents only when these vehicles are under their own power on a highway [otherwise the vehicles are regarded as machinery]. Vehicles which can travel on land or water, such as hovercraft and other amphibious vehicles, are regarded as watercraft when on the water, as motor vehicles when on the highway, and as off-road motor vehicles when on land, but off the highway.

Excludes: *accidents:*

in sports which involve the use of transport but where the transport vehicle itself was not involved in the accident
involving vehicles which are part of industrial equipment used entirely on industrial premises
occurring during transportation but unrelated to the hazards associated with the means of transportation [e.g., injuries received in a fight on board ship; transport vehicle involved in a cataclysm such as an earthquake]
to persons engaged in the maintenance or repair of transport equipment or vehicle not in motion, unless injured by another vehicle in motion

(b) A **railway accident** is a transport accident involving a railway train or other railway vehicle operated on rails, whether in motion or not.

Excludes: *accidents:*

in repair shops
in roundhouse or on turntable
on railway premises but not involving a train or other railway vehicle

(c) A **railway train** or **railway vehicle** is any device with or without cars coupled to it, designed for traffic on a railway.

Includes: interurban:
electric car   } (operated chiefly on its own right-of-way, not open to
streetcar   }   other traffic)
railway train, any power [diesel] [electric] [steam]
funicular
monorail or two-rail
subterranean or elevated
other vehicle designed to run on a railway track

Excludes: *interurban electric cars [streetcars] specified to be operating on a right-of-way that forms part of the public street or highway [definition (n)]*

(d) A **railway** or **railroad** is a right-of-way designed for traffic on rails, which is used by carriages or wagons transporting passengers or freight, and by other rolling stock, and which is not open to other public vehicular traffic.

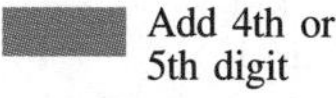 Add 4th or 5th digit   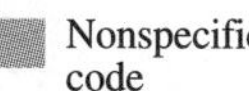 Nonspecific code   Unspecified code   Manifestation code

(e) A **motor vehicle accident** is a transport accident involving a motor vehicle. It is defined as a motor vehicle traffic accident or as a motor vehicle nontraffic accident according to whether the accident occurs on a public highway or elsewhere.

> Excludes: *injury or damage due to cataclysm*
>
> *injury or damage while a motor vehicle, not under its own power, is being loaded on, or unloaded from, another conveyance*

(f) A **motor vehicle traffic accident** is any motor vehicle accident occurring on a public highway [i.e., originating, terminating, or involving a vehicle partially on the highway]. A motor vehicle accident is assumed to have occurred on the highway unless another place is specified, except in the case of accidents involving only off-road motor vehicles which are classified as nontraffic accidents unless the contrary is stated.

(g) A **motor vehicle nontraffic accident** is any motor vehicle accident which occurs entirely in any place other than a public highway.

(h) A **public highway [trafficway]** or **street** is the entire width between property lines [or other boundary lines] of every way or place, of which any part is open to the use of the public for purposes of vehicular traffic as a matter of right or custom. A roadway is that part of the public highway designed, improved, and ordinarily used, for vehicular travel.

Includes: approaches (public) to:
docks
public building
station

> Excludes: *driveway (private)*
>
> *parking lot*
> *ramp*
> *roads in:*
> *airfield*
> *farm*
> *industrial premises*
> *mine*
> *private grounds*
> *quarry*

(i) A **motor vehicle** is any mechanically or electrically powered device, not operated on rails, upon which any person or property may be transported or drawn upon a highway. Any object such as a trailer, coaster, sled, or wagon being towed by a motor vehicle is considered a part of the motor vehicle.

Includes: automobile [any type]
bus
construction machinery, farm and industrial machinery, steam roller, tractor, army tank, highway grader, or similar vehicle on wheels or treads, while in transport under own power
fire engine (motorized)
motorcycle
motorized bicycle [moped] or scooter
trolley bus not operating on rails
truck
van

> Excludes: *devices used solely to move persons or materials within the confines of a building and its premises, such as:*
> *building elevator*
> *coal car in mine*
> *electric baggage or mail truck used solely within a railroad station*
> *electric truck used solely within an industrial plant*
> *moving overhead crane*

(j) A **motorcycle** is a two-wheeled motor vehicle having one or two riding saddles and sometimes having a third wheel for the support of a sidecar. The sidecar is considered part of the motorcycle.

Includes: motorized:
bicycle [moped]
scooter
tricycle

(k) An **off-road motor vehicle** is a motor vehicle of special design, to enable it to negotiate rough or soft terrain or snow. Examples of special design are high construction, special wheels and tires, driven by treads, or support on a cushion of air.

Includes: all terrain vehicle [ATV]
army tank
hovercraft, on land or swamp
snowmobile

● Code new to this edition   ▲ Revision of existing code   ④ ⑤ Fourth or fifth digit required

(l) A **driver** of a motor vehicle is the occupant of the motor vehicle operating it or intending to operate it. A **motorcyclist** is the driver of a motorcycle. Other authorized occupants of a motor vehicle are **passengers**.

(m) An **other road vehicle** is any device, except a motor vehicle, in, on, or by which any person or property may be transported on a highway.

    Includes: animal carrying a person or goods
            animal-drawn vehicle
            animal harnessed to conveyance
            bicycle [pedal cycle]
            streetcar
            tricycle (pedal)

      Excludes: *pedestrian conveyance [definition (q)]*

(n) A **streetcar** is a device designed and used primarily for transporting persons within a municipality, running on rails, usually subject to normal traffic control signals, and operated principally on a right-of-way that forms part of the traffic way. A trailer being towed by a streetcar is considered a part of the streetcar.

    Includes: interurban or intraurban electric or streetcar, when specified to be operating on a
              street or public highway
            tram (car)
            trolley (car)

(o) A **pedal cycle** is any road transport vehicle operated solely by pedals.

    Includes: bicycle
            pedal cycle
            tricycle

      Excludes: *motorized bicycle [definition (i)]*

(p) A **pedal cyclist** is any person riding on a pedal cycle or in a sidecar attached to such a vehicle.

(q) A **pedestrian conveyance** is any human powered device by which a pedestrian may move other than by walking or by which a walking person may move another pedestrian.

    Includes:

baby carriage	roller skates
coaster wagon	scooter
ice skates	skateboard
perambulator	skis
pushcart	sled
pushchair	wheelchair

(r) A **pedestrian** is any person involved in an accident who was not at the time of the accident riding in or on a motor vehicle, railroad train, streetcar, animal-drawn or other vehicle, or on a bicycle or animal.

    Includes: person:
            changing tire of vehicle
            in or operating a pedestrian conveyance
            making adjustment to motor of vehicle
            on foot

(s) A **watercraft** is any device for transporting passengers or goods on the water.

(t) A **small boat** is any watercraft propelled by paddle, oars, or small motor, with a passenger capacity of less than ten.

    Includes:

boat NOS	rowboat
canoe	rowing shell
coble	scull
dinghy	skiff
punt	small motorboat
raft	

      Excludes: *barge*
              lifeboat (used after abandoning ship)
              raft (anchored) being used as diving platform
              yacht

(u) An **aircraft** is any device for transporting passengers or goods in the air.

    Includes: airplane [any type]
            balloon
            bomber
            dirigible
            glider (hang)
            military aircraft
            parachute

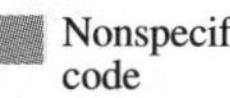 Add 4th or 5th digit   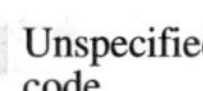 Nonspecific code   Unspecified code   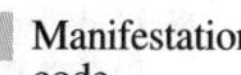 Manifestation code

(v) A **commercial transport aircraft** is any device for collective passenger or freight transportation by air, whether run on commercial lines for profit or by government authorities, with the exception of military craft.

RAILWAY ACCIDENTS (E800-E807)

Note: For definitions of railway accident and related terms see definitions (a) to (d).

> *Excludes:* *accidents involving railway train and:*
> *aircraft (E840.0-E845.9)*
> *motor vehicle (E810.0-E825.9)*
> *watercraft (E830.0-E838.9)*

The following fourth-digit subdivisions are for use with categories E800-E807 to identify the injured person:

.0 Railway employee
Any person who by virtue of his employment in connection with a railway, whether by the railway company or not, is at increased risk of involvement in a railway accident, such as:
catering staff of train
driver
guard
porter
postal staff on train
railway fireman
shunter
sleeping car attendant

.1 Passenger on railway
Any authorized person traveling on a train, except a railway employee.

> *Excludes:* *intending passenger waiting at station (.8)*
> *unauthorized rider on railway vehicle (.8)*

.2 Pedestrian
See definition (r)

.3 Pedal cyclist
See definition (p)

.8 Other specified person
Intending passenger or bystander waiting at station
Unauthorized rider on railway vehicle

.9 Unspecified person

④ **E800 Railway accident involving collision with rolling stock**
Includes: collision between railway trains or railway vehicles, any kind
collision NOS on railway
derailment with antecedent collision with rolling stock or NOS

④ **E801 Railway accident involving collision with other object**
Includes: collision of railway train with:
buffers
fallen tree on railway
gates
platform
rock on railway
streetcar
other nonmotor vehicle
other object

> *Excludes:* *collision with:*
> *aircraft (E840.0-E842.9)*
> *motor vehicle (E810.0-E810.9, E820.0-E822.9)*

④ **E802 Railway accident involving derailment without antecedent collision**

④ **E803 Railway accident involving explosion, fire, or burning**

> *Excludes:* *explosion or fire, with antecedent derailment (E802.0-E802.9)*
> *explosion or fire, with mention of antecedent collision (E800.0-E801.9)*

④ **E804 Fall in, on, or from railway train**
Includes: fall while alighting from or boarding railway train

> *Excludes:* *fall related to collision, derailment, or explosion of railway train (E800.0-E803.9)*

● Code new
to this edition
▲ Revision of
existing code
④ ⑤ Fourth or fifth
digit required

④ **E805 Hit by rolling stock**

    Includes:

        crushed
        injured
        killed } by railway train or part
        knocked down
        run over

    Excludes: *pedestrian hit by object set in motion by railway train (E806.0-E806.9)*

④ **E806 Other specified railway accident**

    Includes: hit by object falling in railway train
        injured by door or window on railway train
        nonmotor road vehicle or pedestrian hit by object set in motion by railway train
        railway train hit by falling:
        earth NOS
        rock
        tree
        other object

    Excludes: *railway accident due to cataclysm (E908-E909)*

④ **E807 Railway accident of unspecified nature**

    Includes:

        found dead } on railway right-of-way NOS
        injured
        railway accident NOS

MOTOR VEHICLE TRAFFIC ACCIDENTS (E810-E819)

    Note: For definitions of motor vehicle traffic accident, and related terms, see definitions (e) to (k).

    Excludes: *accidents involving motor vehicle and aircraft (E840.0-E845.9)*

The following fourth-digit subdivisions are for use with categories E810-E819 to identify the injured person:

    .0 Driver of motor vehicle other than motorcycle
        See definition (l)

    .1 Passenger in motor vehicle other than motorcycle
        See definition (l)

    .2 Motorcyclist
        See definition (l)

    .3 Passenger on motorcycle
        See definition (l)

    .4 Occupant of streetcar

    .5 Rider of animal; occupant of animal-drawn vehicle

    .6 Pedal cyclist
        See definition (p)

    .7 Pedestrian
        See definition (r)

    .8 Other specified person
        Occupant of vehicle other than above
        Person in railway train involved in accident
        Unauthorized rider of motor vehicle

    .9 Unspecified person

④ **E810 Motor vehicle traffic accident involving collision with train**

    Excludes: *motor vehicle collision with object set in motion by railway train (E815.0-E815.9)*
        railway train hit by object set in motion by motor vehicle (E818.0-E818.9)

④ **E811 Motor vehicle traffic accident involving re-entrant collision with another motor vehicle**

    Includes: collision between motor vehicle which accidentally leaves the roadway then re-enters the same roadway, or the opposite roadway on a divided highway, and another motor vehicle

    Excludes: *collision on the same roadway when none of the motor vehicles involved have left and re-entered the roadway (E812.0-E812.9)*

④ **E812 Other motor vehicle traffic accident involving collision with motor vehicle**

    Includes: collision with another motor vehicle parked, stopped, stalled, disabled, or abandoned on the highway
        motor vehicle collision NOS

continued

 Add 4th or 5th digit
 Nonspecific code
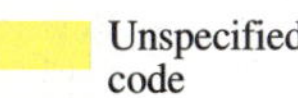 Unspecified code
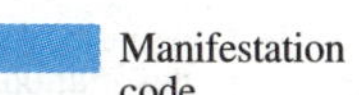 Manifestation code

Excludes:	*collision with object set in motion by another motor vehicle (E815.0-E815.9)*
	re-entrant collision with another motor vehicle (E811.0-E811.9)

④ **E813** **Motor vehicle traffic accident involving collision with other vehicle**

Includes: collision between motor vehicle, any kind, and:
other road (nonmotor transport) vehicle, such as:
animal carrying a person
animal-drawn vehicle
pedal cycle
streetcar

Excludes:	*collision with:*
	object set in motion by nonmotor road vehicle (E815.0-E815.9)
	pedestrian (E814.0-E814.9)
	nonmotor road vehicle hit by object set in motion by motor vehicle (E818.0-E818.9)

④ **E814** **Motor vehicle traffic accident involving collision with pedestrian**

Includes: collision between motor vehicle, any kind, and pedestrian
pedestrian dragged, hit, or run over by motor vehicle, any kind

Excludes:	*pedestrian hit by object set in motion by motor vehicle (E818.0-E818.9)*

④ **E815** **Other motor vehicle traffic accident involving collision on the highway**

Includes: collision (due to loss of control) (on highway) between motor vehicle, any kind, and:
abutment (bridge) (overpass)
animal (herded) (unattended)
fallen stone, traffic sign, tree, utility pole
guard rail or boundary fence
interhighway divider
landslide (not moving)
object set in motion by railway train or road vehicle (motor) (nonmotor)
object thrown in front of motor vehicle
safety island
temporary traffic sign or marker
wall of cut made for road
other object, fixed, movable, or moving

Excludes:	*collision with:*
	any object off the highway (resulting from loss of control) (E816.0-E816.9)
	any object which normally would have been off the highway and is not stated to have been on it (E816.0-E816.9)
	motor vehicle parked, stopped, stalled, disabled, or abandoned on highway (E812.0-E812.9)
	moving landslide (E909)
	motor vehicle hit by object:
	set in motion by railway train or road vehicle (motor) (nonmotor) (E818.0-E818.9)
	thrown into or on vehicle (E818.0-E818.9)

④ **E816** **Motor vehicle traffic accident due to loss of control, without collision on the highway**

Includes: motor vehicle:
failing to make curve
going out of control (due to):
blowout
burst tire   and:
driver falling asleep   colliding with object off the
driver inattention   highway
excessive speed   overturning
failure of mechanical part   stopping abruptly off the highway

Excludes:	*collision on highway following loss of control (E810.0-E815.9)*
	loss of control of motor vehicle following collision on the highway (E810.0-E815.9)

④ **E817** **Noncollision motor vehicle traffic accident while boarding or alighting**

Includes:

fall down stairs of motor bus
fall from car in street   while boarding or alighting
injured by moving part of the vehicle
trapped by door of motor bus

● Code new to this edition   ▲ Revision of existing code   ④ ⑤ Fourth or fifth digit required

④ **E818 Other noncollision motor vehicle traffic accident**

Includes:

accidental poisoning from exhaust gas generated by
breakage of any part of
explosion of any part of
fall, jump, or being accidentally pushed from
fire starting in
hit by object thrown into or on
injured by being thrown against some part of, or object in
injury from moving part of
object falling in or on
object thrown on

} motor vehicle while in motion

collision of railway train or road vehicle except motor vehicle, with object set in motion by motor vehicle

motor vehicle hit by object set in motion by railway train or road vehicle (motor) (nonmotor)

pedestrian, railway train, or road vehicle (motor) (nonmotor) hit by object set in motion by motor vehicle

Excludes: *collision between motor vehicle and:*

> *object set in motion by railway train or road vehicle (motor) (nonmotor) (E815.0-E815.9)*
> *object thrown towards the motor vehicle (E815.0-E815.9)*
> *person overcome by carbon monoxide generated by stationary motor vehicle off the roadway with motor running (E868.2)*

④ **E819 Motor vehicle traffic accident of unspecified nature**

Includes: motor vehicle traffic accident NOS
traffic accident NOS

MOTOR VEHICLE NONTRAFFIC ACCIDENTS (E820-E825)

Note: For definitions of motor vehicle nontraffic accident and related terms see definitions (a) to (k).

Includes: accidents involving motor vehicles being used in recreational or sporting activities off the highway

collision and noncollision motor vehicle accidents occurring entirely off the highway

Excludes: *accidents involving motor vehicle and:*

> *aircraft (E840.0-E845.9)*
> *watercraft (E830.0-E838.9)*
> *accidents, not on the public highway, involving agricultural and construction machinery but not involving another motor vehicle (E919.0, E919.2, E919.7)*

The following fourth-digit subdivisions are for use with categories E820-E825 to identify the injured person:

.0 Driver of motor vehicle other than motorcycle
See definition (l)

.1 Passenger in motor vehicle other than motorcycle
See definition (l)

.2 Motorcyclist
See definition (l)

.3 Passenger on motorcycle
See definition (l)

.4 Occupant of streetcar

.5 Rider of animal; occupant of animal-drawn vehicle

.6 Pedal cyclist
See definition (p)

.7 Pedestrian
See definition (r)

.8 Other specified person
Occupant of vehicle other than above
Person on railway train involved in accident
Unauthorized rider of motor vehicle

.9 Unspecified person

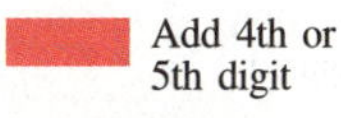

④ **E820** **Nontraffic accident involving motor-driven snow vehicle**

Includes:

breakage of part of
fall from
hit by
overturning of
run over or dragged by   } motor-driven snow vehicle (not on public highway)

collision of motor-driven snow vehicle with:
  animal (being ridden) (-drawn vehicle)
  another off-road motor vehicle
  other motor vehicle, not on public highway
  railway train
  other object, fixed or movable
injury caused by rough landing of motor-driven snow vehicle (after leaving
    ground on rough terrain)

Excludes: *accident on the public highway involving motor driven snow vehicle*
    (E810.0-E819.9)

④ **E821** **Nontraffic accident involving other off-road motor vehicle**

Includes:

breakage of part of
fall from
hit by
overturning of
run over or dragged by
thrown against some part of or object in   } off-road motor vehicle, except snow vehicle (not on public highway)

collision with:
  animal (being ridden) (-drawn vehicle)
  another off-road motor vehicle, except snow vehicle
  other motor vehicle, not on public highway
  other object, fixed or movable

Excludes: *accident on public highway involving off-road motor vehicle (E810.0-E819.9)*

collision between motor driven snow vehicle and other off-road motor vehicle
    (E820.0-E820.9)

hovercraft accident on water (E830.0-E838.9)

④ **E822** **Other motor vehicle nontraffic accident involving collision with moving object**

Includes: collision, not on public highway, between motor vehicle, except off-road motor
     vehicle and:
    animal
    nonmotor vehicle
    other motor vehicle, except off-road motor vehicle
    pedestrian
    railway train
    other moving object

Excludes: *collision with:*
    motor-driven snow vehicle (E820.0-E820.9)
    other off-road motor vehicle (E821.0-E821.9)

④ **E823** **Other motor vehicle nontraffic accident involving collision with stationary object**

Includes: collision, not on public highway, between motor vehicle, except off-road motor
     vehicle, and any object, fixed or movable, but not in motion

④ **E824** **Other motor vehicle nontraffic accident while boarding and alighting**

Includes:

fall
injury from moving part of motor vehicle
trapped by door of motor vehicle   } while boarding or alighting from motor vehicle, except off-road motor vehicle, not on public highway

● Code new
to this edition

▲ Revision of
existing code

④ ⑤ Fourth or fifth
digit required

④ **E825** **Other motor vehicle nontraffic accident of other and unspecified nature**

> Includes:
>
> accidental poisoning from carbon monoxide
>   generated by
> breakage of any part of
> explosion of any part of
> fall, jump, or being accidentally pushed from   } motor vehicle while in motion, not
> fire starting in   on public highway
> hit by object thrown into, towards, or on
> injured by being thrown against some part of,
>   or object in
> injury from moving part of
> object falling in or on
> motor vehicle nontraffic accident NOS

> *Excludes:* *fall from or in stationary motor vehicle (E884.9, E885.9)*
>
> *overcome by carbon monoxide or exhaust gas generated by stationary motor*
>   *vehicle off the roadway with motor running (E868.2)*
> *struck by falling object from or in stationary motor vehicle (E916)*

OTHER ROAD VEHICLE ACCIDENTS (E826-E829)

Note: Other road vehicle accidents are transport accidents involving road vehicles other than motor
vehicles. For definitions of other road vehicle and related terms see definitions (m) to (o).
Includes: accidents involving other road vehicles being used in recreational or sporting activities

> *Excludes:* *collision of other road vehicle [any] with:*
>
> *aircraft (E840.0-E845.9)*
> *motor vehicle (E813.0-E813.9, E820.0-E822.9)*
> *railway train (E801.0-E801.9)*

The following fourth-digit subdivisions are for use with categories E826-E829 to identify the
injured person:

.0 Pedestrian
See definition (r)

.1 Pedal cyclist
See definition (p)

.2 Rider of animal

.3 Occupant of animal-drawn vehicle

.4 Occupant of streetcar

.8 Other specified person

.9 Unspecified person

④ **E826** **Pedal cycle accident**

[0-9]

> Includes: breakage of any part of pedal cycle
> collision between pedal cycle and:
>   animal (being ridden) (herded) (unattended)
>   another pedal cycle
>   nonmotor road vehicle, any
>   pedestrian
>   other object, fixed, movable, or moving, not set in motion by motor vehicle,
>   railway train, or aircraft
> entanglement in wheel of pedal cycle
> fall from pedal cycle
> hit by object falling or thrown on the pedal cycle
> pedal cycle accident NOS
> pedal cycle overturned

 Add 4th or 5th digit

 Nonspecific code

 Unspecified code

Manifestation code

④ **E827** **Animal-drawn vehicle accident**
[0,2-4,8,9]
    Includes   breakage of any part of vehicle
                 collision between animal-drawn vehicle and:
                   animal (being ridden) (herded) (unattended)
                   nonmotor road vehicle, except pedal cycle
                   pedestrian, pedestrian conveyance, or pedestrian vehicle
                   other object, fixed, movable, or moving, not set in motion by motor vehicle,
                      railway train, or aircraft

fall from
knocked down by
overturning of   } animal-drawn vehicle
run over by
thrown from

> *Excludes:* *collision of animal-drawn vehicle with pedal cycle (E826.0-E826.9)*

④ **E828** **Accident involving animal being ridden**
[0,2,4,8,9]
    Includes: collision between animal being ridden and:
                   another animal
                   nonmotor road vehicle, except pedal cycle, and animal-drawn vehicle
                   pedestrian, pedestrian conveyance, or pedestrian vehicle
                   other object, fixed, movable, or moving, not set in motion by motor vehicle,
                      railway train, or aircraft

fall from
knocked down by
thrown from   } animal being ridden
trampled by

                   ridden animal stumbled and fell

> *Excludes:* *collision of animal being ridden with:*
> *animal-drawn vehicle (E827.0-E827.9)*
> *pedal cycle (E826.0-E826.9)*

④ **E829** **Other road vehicle accidents**
[0,4,8,9]
    Includes:

accident while boarding or alighting from
blow from object in
breakage of any part of   } streetcar nonmotor road vehicle
caught in door of   not classifiable to E826-E828
derailment of
fall in, on, or from
fire in

                 collision between streetcar or nonmotor road vehicle, except as in E826-E828, and:
                   animal (not being ridden)
                   another nonmotor road vehicle not classifiable to E826-E828
                   pedestrian
                   other object, fixed, movable, or moving, not set in motion by motor vehicle,
                      railway train, or aircraft
                 nonmotor road vehicle accident NOS
                 streetcar accident NOS

> *Excludes:* *collision with:*
> *animal being ridden (E828.0-E828.9)*
> *animal-drawn vehicle (E827.0-E827.9)*
> *pedal cycle (E826.0-E826.9)*

WATER TRANSPORT ACCIDENTS (E830-E838)

    Note: For definitions of water transport accident and related terms see definitions (a), (s), and (t).

    Includes: watercraft accidents in the course of recreational activities

> *Excludes:* *accidents involving both aircraft, including objects set in motion by aircraft, and*
> *watercraft (E840.0-E845.9)*

    The following fourth-digit subdivisions are for use with categories E830-E838 to identify the injured person:

    .0 Occupant of small boat, unpowered

    .1 Occupant of small boat, powered
       See definition (t)

continued

● Code new   ▲ Revision of   ④ ⑤ Fourth or fifth
  to this edition   existing code   digit required

.2 Occupant of other watercraft—crew
Persons:
  engaged in operation of watercraft
  providing passenger services [cabin attendants, ship's physician, catering personnel]
  working on ship during voyage in other capacity [musician in band, operators of
    shops and beauty parlors]

.3 Occupant of other watercraft—other than crew
Passenger
Occupant of lifeboat, other than crew, after abandoning ship

.4 Water skier

.5 Swimmer

.6 Dockers, stevedores
Longshoreman employed on the dock in loading and unloading ships

.8 Other specified person
Immigration and custom officials on board ship
Person:
  accompanying passenger or member of crew
  visiting boat
Pilot (guiding ship into port)

.9 Unspecified person

④ E830 Accident to watercraft causing submersion
Includes: submersion and drowning due to:
      boat overturning
      boat submerging
      falling or jumping from burning ship
      falling or jumping from crushed watercraft
      ship sinking
      other accident to watercraft

④ E831 Accident to watercraft causing other injury
Includes: any injury, except submersion and drowning, as a result of an accident to watercraft
      burned while ship on fire
      crushed between ships in collision
      crushed by lifeboat after abandoning ship
      fall due to collision or other accident to watercraft
      hit by falling object due to accident to watercraft
      injured in watercraft accident involving collision
      struck by boat or part thereof after fall or jump from damaged boat

Excludes: burns from localized fire or explosion on board ship (E837.0-E837.9)

④ E832 Other accidental submersion or drowning in water transport accident
Includes: submersion or drowning as a result of an accident other than accident to the
        watercraft, such as:
      fall:
        from gangplank
        from ship
        overboard
      thrown overboard by motion of ship
      washed overboard

Excludes: submersion or drowning of swimmer or diver who voluntarily jumps from boat not
        involved in an accident (E910.0-E910.9)

④ E833 Fall on stairs or ladders in water transport

Excludes: fall due to accident to watercraft (E831.0-E831.9)

④ E834 Other fall from one level to another in water transport

Excludes: fall due to accident to watercraft (E831.0-E831.9)

④ E835 Other and unspecified fall in water transport

Excludes: fall due to accident to watercraft (E831.0-E831.9)

Add 4th or 5th digit

Nonspecific code

Unspecified code

Manifestation code

④ **E836 Machinery accident in water transport**
Includes: injuries in water transport caused by:
deck
engine room
galley   } machinery
laundry
loading

④ **E837 Explosion, fire, or burning in watercraft**
Includes: explosion of boiler on steamship
localized fire on ship

Excludes: *burning ship (due to collision or explosion) resulting in:*
submersion or drowning (E830.0-E830.9)
other injury (E831.0-E831.9)

④ **E838 Other and unspecified water transport accident**
Includes: accidental poisoning by gases or fumes on ship
atomic power plant malfunction in watercraft
crushed between ship and stationary object [wharf]
crushed between ships without accident to watercraft
crushed by falling object on ship or while loading or unloading
hit by boat while water skiing
struck by boat or part thereof (after fall from boat)
watercraft accident NOS

AIR AND SPACE TRANSPORT ACCIDENTS (E840-E845)

Note: For definition of aircraft and related terms see definitions (u) and (v).

The following fourth-digit subdivisions are for use with categories E840-E845 to identify the
injured person:

.0 Occupant of spacecraft

.1 Occupant of military aircraft, any
Crew
Passenger (civilian)   } in military aircraft [air force]
(military)   [army] [national guard] [navy]
Troops

Excludes: *occupants of aircraft operated under jurisdiction of police departments (.5)*
parachutist (.7)

.2 Crew of commercial aircraft (powered) in surface to surface transport

.3 Other occupant of commercial aircraft (powered) in surface to surface transport
Flight personnel:
not part of crew
on familiarization flight
Passenger on aircraft (powered) NOS

.4 Occupant of commercial aircraft (powered) in surface to air transport
Occupant [crew] [passenger] of aircraft (powered) engaged in activities, such as:
aerial spraying (crops) (fire retardants)
air drops of emergency supplies
air drops of parachutists, except from military craft
crop dusting
lowering of construction material [bridge or telephone pole]
sky writing

.5 Occupant of other powered aircraft
Occupant [crew] [passenger] of aircraft [powered] engaged in activities, such as:
aerobatic flying
aircraft racing
rescue operation
storm surveillance
traffic surveillance
Occupant of private plane NOS

.6 Occupant of unpowered aircraft, except parachutist
Occupant of aircraft classifiable to E842

.7 Parachutist (military) (other)
Person making voluntary descent

Excludes: *person making descent after accident to aircraft (.1-.6)*

● Code new   ▲ Revision of   ④ ⑤ Fourth or fifth
   to this edition   existing code   digit required

.8 Ground crew, airline employee
Persons employed at airfields (civil) (military) or launching pads, not occupants of aircraft

.9 Other person

④ **E840 Accident to powered aircraft at takeoff or landing**
Includes:

collision of aircraft with any object, fixed, movable, or moving crash explosion on aircraft fire on aircraft forced landing	while taking off or landing

④ **E841 Accident to powered aircraft, other and unspecified**
Includes: aircraft accident NOS
aircraft crash or wreck NOS
any accident to powered aircraft while in transit or when not specified whether in transit, taking off, or landing
collision of aircraft with another aircraft, bird, or any object, while in transit
explosion on aircraft while in transit
fire on aircraft while in transit

④ **E842 Accident to unpowered aircraft**
[6-9]
Includes: any accident, except collision with powered aircraft, to:
balloon
glider
hang glider
kite carrying a person
hit by object falling from unpowered aircraft

④ **E843 Fall in, on, or from aircraft**
[0-9]
Includes: accident in boarding or alighting from aircraft, any kind
fall in, on, or from aircraft [any kind], while in transit, taking off, or landing, except when as a result of an accident to aircraft

④ **E844 Other specified air transport accidents**
[0-9]
Includes:

hit by:
  aircraft
  object falling from aircraft
injury by or from:
  machinery on aircraft
  rotating propeller
  voluntary parachute descent
poisoning by carbon monoxide from aircraft
  while in transit
sucked into jet
	without accident to aircraft

any accident involving other transport vehicle (motor) (nonmotor) due to being hit by object set in motion by aircraft (powered)

> Excludes: *air sickness (E903)*
> *effects of:*
>   *high altitude (E902.0-E902.1)*
>   *pressure change (E902.0-E902.1)*
> *injury in parachute descent due to accident to aircraft (840.0-E842.9)*

④ **E845 Accident involving spacecraft**
[0,8,9]
Includes: launching pad accident

> Excludes: *effects of weightlessness in spacecraft (E928.0)*

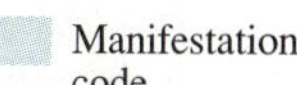

VEHICLE ACCIDENTS NOT ELSEWHERE CLASSIFIABLE (E846-E848)

E846 **Accidents involving powered vehicles used solely within the buildings and premises of industrial or commercial establishment**
Accident to, on, or involving:
battery powered airport passenger vehicle
battery powered trucks (baggage) (mail)
coal car in mine
logging car
self propelled truck, industrial
station baggage truck (powered)
tram, truck, or tub (powered) in mine or quarry
Breakage of any part of vehicle
Collision with:
pedestrian
other vehicle or object within premises
Explosion of
Fall from   } powered vehicle, industrial or commercial
Overturning of
Struck by

Excludes: *accidental poisoning by exhaust gas from vehicle not elsewhere classifiable (E868.2)*
injury by crane, lift (fork), or elevator (E919.2)

E847 **Accidents involving cable cars not running on rails**
Accident to, on, or involving:
cable car, not on rails
ski chair-lift
ski-lift with gondola
téléférique
Breakage of cable
Caught or dragged by
Fall or jump from   } cable car, not on rails
Object thrown from or in

E848 **Accidents involving other vehicles, not elsewhere classifiable**
Accident to, on, or involving:
ice yacht
land yacht
nonmotor, nonroad vehicle NOS

E849 *Place of occurrence*
The following category is for use to denote the place where the injury or poisoning occurred.

E849.0 *Home*

Apartment	*Private:*
Boarding house	*driveway*
Farm house	*garage*
Home premises	*garden*
House (residential)	*home*
Noninstitutional place	*walk*
of residence	*Swimming pool in private house or garden*
	Yard of home

Excludes: *home under construction but not yet occupied (E849.3)*
institutional place of residence (E849.7)

E849.1 *Farm*
Farm:
buildings
land under cultivation

Excludes: *farm house and home premises of farm (E849.0)*

E849.2 *Mine and quarry*
Gravel pit   *Tunnel under construction*
Sand pit

● Code new   ▲ Revision of   ④ ⑤ Fourth or fifth
to this edition   existing code   digit required

E849.3 Industrial place and premises

Building under construction	Industrial yard
Dockyard	Loading platform (factory) (store)
Dry dock	Plant, industrial
Factory	Railway yard
building	Shop (place of work)
premises	Warehouse
Garage (place of work)	Workhouse

E849.4 Place for recreation and sport

Amusement park	Public park
Baseball field	Racecourse
Basketball court	Resort NOS
Beach resort	Riding school
Cricket ground	Rifle range
Fives court	Seashore resort
Football field	Skating rink
Golf course	Sports ground
Gymnasium	Sports palace
Hockey field	Stadium
Holiday camp	Swimming pool, public
Ice palace	Tennis court
Lake resort	Vacation resort
Mountain resort	
Playground, including	
school playground	

Excludes: that in private house or garden (E849.0)

E849.5 Street and highway

E849.6 Public building

Building (including adjacent grounds) used by the general public or by a particular
group of the public, such as:

airport	nightclub
bank	office
café	office building
casino	opera house
church	post office
cinema	public hall
clubhouse	radio broadcasting station
courthouse	restaurant
dance hall	school (state) (public) (private)
garage building (for car	shop, commercial
storage)	station (bus) (railway)
hotel	store
market (grocery or other	theater
commodity)	
movie house	
music hall	

Excludes: home garage (E849.0)
        industrial building or workplace (E849.3)

E849.7 Residential institution

Children's home	Old people's home
Dormitory	Orphanage
Hospital	Prison
Jail	Reform school

E849.8 Other specified places

Beach NOS	Pond or pool (natural)
Canal	Prairie
Caravan site NOS	Public place NOS
Derelict house	Railway line
Desert	Reservoir
Dock	River
Forest	Sea
Harbor	Seashore NOS
Hill	Stream
Lake NOS	Swamp
Mountain	Trailer court
Parking lot	Woods
Parking place	

E849.9 Unspecified place

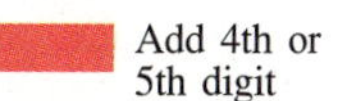
Add 4th or
5th digit

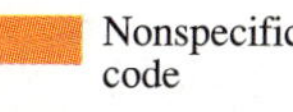
Nonspecific
code

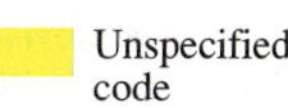
Unspecified
code

Manifestation
code

ACCIDENTAL POISONING BY DRUGS, MEDICINAL SUBSTANCES, AND BIOLOGICALS (E850-E858)

Includes: accidental overdose of drug, wrong drug given or taken in error, and drug taken inadvertently

accidents in the use of drugs and biologicals in medical and surgical procedures

Excludes: *administration with suicidal or homicidal intent or intent to harm, or in circumstances classifiable to E980-E989 (E950.0-E950.5, E962.0, E980.0-E980.5)*

correct drug properly administered in therapeutic or prophylactic dosage, as the cause of adverse effect (E930.0-E949.9)

See Alphabetic Index for more complete list of specific drugs to be classified under the fourth-digit subdivisions. The American Hospital Formulary numbers can be used to classify new drugs listed by the American Hospital Formulary Service (AHFS). See appendix C.

E850 **Accidental poisoning by analgesics, antipyretics, and antirheumatics**

E850.0 **Heroin**
Diacetylmorphine

E850.1 **Methadone**

E850.2 **Other opiates and related narcotics**
Codeine [methylmorphine]   Morphine
Meperidine [pethidine]   Opium (alkaloids)

E850.3 **Salicylates**
Acetylsalicylic acid [aspirin]
Amino derivatives of salicylic acid
Salicylic acid salts

E850.4 **Aromatic analgesics, not elsewhere classified**
Acetanilid
Paracetamol [acetaminophen]
Phenacetin [acetophenetidin]

E850.5 **Pyrazole derivatives**
Aminophenazone [amidopyrine]
Phenylbutazone

E850.6 **Antirheumatics [antiphlogistics]**
Gold salts   Indomethacin

Excludes: *salicylates (E850.3)*
steroids (E858.0)

E850.7 **Other non-narcotic analgesics**
Pyrabital

E850.8 **Other specified analgesics and antipyretics**
Pentazocine

E850.9 **Unspecified analgesic or antipyretic**

E851 **Accidental poisoning by barbiturates**
Amobarbital [amylobarbitone]
Barbital [barbitone]
Butabarbital [butabarbitone]
Pentobarbital [pentobarbitone]
Phenobarbital [phenobarbitone]
Secobarbital [quinalbarbitone]

Excludes: *thiobarbiturates (E855.1)*

E852 **Accidental poisoning by other sedatives and hypnotics**

E852.0 **Chloral hydrate group**

E852.1 **Paraldehyde**

E852.2 **Bromine compounds**
Bromides   Carbromal (derivatives)

E852.3 **Methaqualone compounds**

E852.4 **Glutethimide group**

E852.5 **Mixed sedatives, not elsewhere classified**

E852.8 **Other specified sedatives and hypnotics**

● Code new to this edition   ▲ Revision of existing code   ④ ⑤ Fourth or fifth digit required

E852.9 Unspecified sedative or hypnotic
    Sleeping:
      drug
      pill   } NOS
      tablet

E853 Accidental poisoning by tranquilizers

E853.0 Phenothiazine-based tranquilizers
Chlorpromazine	Prochlorperazine
Fluphenazine	Promazine

E853.1 Butyrophenone-based tranquilizers
Haloperidol	Trifluperidol
Spiperone	

E853.2 Benzodiazepine-based tranquilizers
Chlordiazepoxide	Lorazepam
Diazepam	Medazepam
Flurazepam	Nitrazepam

E853.8 Other specified tranquilizers
Hydroxyzine	Meprobamate

E853.9 Unspecified tranquilizer

E854 Accidental poisoning by other psychotropic agents

E854.0 Antidepressants
Amitriptyline	Monoamine oxidase [MAO] inhibitors
Imipramine	

E854.1 Psychodysleptics [hallucinogens]
Cannabis derivatives	Mescaline
Lysergide [LSD]	Psilocin
Marihuana (derivatives)	Psilocybin

E854.2 Psychostimulants
Amphetamine	Caffeine

    Excludes: *central appetite depressants (E858.8)*

E854.3 Central nervous system stimulants
Analeptics	Opiate antagonists

E854.8 Other psychotropic agents

E855 Accidental poisoning by other drugs acting on central and autonomic nervous system

E855.0 Anticonvulsant and anti-Parkinsonism drugs
    Amantadine
    Hydantoin derivatives
    Levodopa [L-dopa]
    Oxazolidine derivatives [paramethadione] [trimethadione]
    Succinimides

E855.1 Other central nervous system depressants
Ether	Intravenous anesthetics
Gaseous anesthetics	Thiobarbiturates, such as thiopental sodium
Halogenated hydrocarbon derivatives	

E855.2 Local anesthetics
Cocaine	Procaine
Lidocaine [lignocaine]	Tetracaine

E855.3 Parasympathomimetics [cholinergics]
Acetylcholine	Pilocarpine
Anticholinesterase:	
organophosphorus	
reversible	

E855.4 Parasympatholytics [anticholinergics and antimuscarinics] and spasmolytics
Atropine	Hyoscine [scopolamine]
Homatropine	Quaternary ammonium derivatives

E855.5 Sympathomimetics [adrenergics]
    Epinephrine [adrenalin]
    Levarterenol [noradrenalin]

E855.6 Sympatholytics [antiadrenergics]
Phenoxybenzamine	Tolazoline hydrochloride

E855.8 Other specified drugs acting on central and autonomic nervous systems

Add 4th or 5th digit	**Nonspecific code**	**Unspecified code**	**Manifestation code**

E855.9 Unspecified drug acting on central and autonomic nervous systems

E856 Accidental poisoning by antibiotics

E857 Accidental poisoning by other anti-infectives

E858 Accidental poisoning by other drugs

    E858.0 Hormones and synthetic substitutes

    E858.1 Primarily systemic agents

    E858.2 Agents primarily affecting blood constituents

    E858.3 Agents primarily affecting cardiovascular system

    E858.4 Agents primarily affecting gastrointestinal system

    E858.5 Water, mineral, and uric acid metabolism drugs

    E858.6 Agents primarily acting on the smooth and skeletal muscles and respiratory system

    E858.7 Agents primarily affecting skin and mucous membrane, ophthalmological, otorhinolaryngological, and dental drugs

    E858.8 Other specified drugs
        Central appetite depressants

    E858.9 Unspecified drug

ACCIDENTAL POISONING BY OTHER SOLID AND LIQUID SUBSTANCES, GASES, AND VAPORS (E860-E869)

    Note: Categories in this section are intended primarily to indicate the external cause of poisoning states classifiable to 980-989. They may also be used to indicate external causes of localized effects classifiable to 001-799.

E860 Accidental poisoning by alcohol, not elsewhere classified

    E860.0 Alcoholic beverages
        Alcohol in preparations intended for consumption

    E860.1 Other and unspecified ethyl alcohol and its products
        Denatured alcohol   Grain alcohol NOS
        Ethanol NOS   Methylated spirit

    E860.2 Methyl alcohol
        Methanol   Wood alcohol

    E860.3 Isopropyl alcohol
        Dimethyl carbinol   Secondary propyl alcohol
        Isopropanol
        Rubbing alcohol substitute

    E860.4 Fusel oil
        Alcohol:
          amyl
          butyl
          propyl

    E860.8 Other specified alcohols

    E860.9 Unspecified alcohol

E861 Accidental poisoning by cleansing and polishing agents, disinfectants, paints, and varnishes

    E861.0 Synthetic detergents and shampoos

    E861.1 Soap products

    E861.2 Polishes

    E861.3 Other cleansing and polishing agents
        Scouring powders

    E861.4 Disinfectants
        Household and other disinfectants not ordinarily used on the person

        Excludes: carbolic acid or phenol (E864.0)

    E861.5 Lead paints

    E861.6 Other paints and varnishes
        Lacquers   Paints, other than lead
        Oil colors   White washes

    E861.9 Unspecified

E862 Accidental poisoning by petroleum products, other solvents and their vapors, not elsewhere classified

    E862.0 Petroleum solvents

● Code new to this edition   ▲ Revision of existing code   ④ ⑤ Fourth or fifth digit required

Petroleum:
  ether
  benzine
  naphtha

E862.1 Petroleum fuels and cleaners
Antiknock additives to petroleum fuels
Gas oils
Gasoline or petrol
Kerosene

Excludes: *kerosene insecticides (E863.4)*

E862.2 Lubricating oils

E862.3 Petroleum solids
Paraffin wax

E862.4 Other specified solvents
Benzene

E862.9 Unspecified solvent

E863 Accidental poisoning by agricultural and horticultural chemical and pharmaceutical preparations other than plant foods and fertilizers

Excludes: *plant foods and fertilizers (E866.5)*

E863.0 Insecticides of organochlorine compounds

Benzene hexachloride	Dieldrin
Chlordane	Endrine
DDT	Toxaphene

E863.1 Insecticides of organophosphorus compounds

Demeton	Parathion
Diazinon	Phenylsulphthion
Dichlorvos	Phorate
Malathion	Phosdrin
Methyl parathion	

E863.2 Carbamates

Aldicarb	Propoxur
Carbaryl	

E863.3 Mixtures of insecticides

E863.4 Other and unspecified insecticides
Kerosene insecticides

E863.5 Herbicides
2, 4-Dichlorophenoxyacetic acid [2, 4-D]
2, 4, 5-Trichlorophenoxyacetic acid [2, 4, 5-T]
Chlorates
Diquat
Mixtures of plant food and fertilizers with herbicides
Paraquat

E863.6 Fungicides
Organic mercurials (used in seed dressing)
Pentachlorophenols

E863.7 Rodenticides

Fluoroacetates	Warfarin
Squill and derivatives	Zinc phosphide
Thallium	

E863.8 Fumigants

Cyanides	Phosphine
Methyl bromide	

E863.9 Other and unspecified

E864 Accidental poisoning by corrosives and caustics, not elsewhere classified

Excludes: *those as components of disinfectants (E861.4)*

E864.0 Corrosive aromatics
Carbolic acid or phenol

E864.1 Acids
Acid:
  hydrochloric
  nitric
  sulfuric

E864.2 Caustic alkalis
    Lye

E864.3 Other specified corrosives and caustics

E864.4 Unspecified corrosives and caustics

E865 Accidental poisoning from poisonous foodstuffs and poisonous plants
    Includes: any meat, fish, or shellfish
              plants, berries, and fungi eaten as, or in mistake for, food, or by a child

    Excludes: *anaphylactic shock due to adverse food reaction (995.6)*
           food poisoning (bacterial) (005.0-005.9)
           poisoning and toxic reactions to venomous plants (E905.6-E905.7)

E865.0 Meat

E865.1 Shellfish

E865.2 Other fish

E865.3 Berries and seeds

E865.4 Other specified plants

E865.5 Mushrooms and other fungi

E865.8 Other specified foods

E865.9 Unspecified foodstuff or poisonous plant

E866 Accidental poisoning by other and unspecified solid and liquid substances

    Excludes: *these substances as a component of:*
        medicines (E850.0-E858.9)
        paints (E861.5-E861.6)
        pesticides (E863.0-E863.9)
        petroleum fuels (E862.1)

E866.0 Lead and its compounds and fumes

E866.1 Mercury and its compounds and fumes

E866.2 Antimony and its compounds and fumes

E866.3 Arsenic and its compounds and fumes

E866.4 Other metals and their compounds and fumes
    Beryllium (compounds)   Iron (compounds)
    Brass fumes   Manganese (compounds)
    Cadmium (compounds)   Nickel (compounds)
    Copper salts   Thallium (compounds)

E866.5 Plant foods and fertilizers
    Excludes: *mixtures with herbicides (E863.5)*

E866.6 Glues and adhesives

E866.7 Cosmetics

E866.8 Other specified solid or liquid substances

E866.9 Unspecified solid or liquid substance

E867 Accidental poisoning by gas distributed by pipeline
    Carbon monoxide from incomplete combustion of piped gas
    Coal gas NOS
    Liquefied petroleum gas distributed through pipes (pure or mixed with air)
    Piped gas (natural) (manufactured)

E868 Accidental poisoning by other utility gas and other carbon monoxide

E868.0 Liquefied petroleum gas distributed in mobile containers
    Butane   or carbon monoxide from
    Liquefied hydrocarbon gas NOS   incomplete combustion of
    Propane   these gases

E868.1 Other and unspecified utility gas
    Acetylene
    Gas NOS used for
      lighting,   or carbon monoxide from incomplete combustion of these gases
      heating, or
      cooking
    Water gas

● Code new to this edition   ▲ Revision of existing code   ④ ⑤ Fourth or fifth digit required

E868.2 Motor vehicle exhaust gas
Exhaust gas from:
farm tractor, not in transit
gas engine
motor pump
motor vehicle, not in transit
any type of combustion engine not in watercraft

Excludes: *poisoning by carbon monoxide from:*
aircraft while in transit (E844.0-E844.9)
motor vehicle while in transit (E818.0-E818.9)
watercraft whether or not in transit (E838.0-E838.9)

E868.3 Carbon monoxide from incomplete combustion of other domestic fuels
Carbon monoxide from incomplete combustion of:
coal
coke
kerosene } in domestic stove or fireplace
wood

Excludes: *carbon monoxide from smoke and fumes due to conflagration (E890.0-E893.9)*

E868.8 Carbon monoxide from other sources
Carbon monoxide from:
blast furnace gas
incomplete combustion of fuels in industrial use
kiln vapor

E868.9 Unspecified carbon monoxide

E869 Accidental poisoning by other gases and vapors

Excludes: *effects of gases used as anesthetics (E855.1, E938.2)*
fumes from heavy metals (E866.0-E866.4)
smoke and fumes due to conflagration or explosion (E890.0-E899)

E869.0 Nitrogen oxides

E869.1 Sulfur dioxide

E869.2 Freon

E869.3 Lacrimogenic gas [tear gas]
Bromobenzyl cyanide   Ethyliodoacetate
Chloroacetophenone

E869.4 Second-hand tobacco smoke

E869.8 Other specified gases and vapors
Chlorine   Hydrocyanic acid gas

E869.9 Unspecified gases and vapors

MISADVENTURES TO PATIENTS DURING SURGICAL AND MEDICAL CARE (E870-E876)

Excludes: *accidental overdose of drug and wrong drug given in error (E850.0-E858.9)*
surgical and medical procedures as the cause of abnormal reaction by the patient,
without mention of misadventure at the time of procedure (E878.0-E879.9)

E870 Accidental cut, puncture, perforation, or hemorrhage during medical care

E870.0 Surgical operation

E870.1 Infusion or transfusion

E870.2 Kidney dialysis or other perfusion

E870.3 Injection or vaccination

E870.4 Endoscopic examination

E870.5 Aspiration of fluid or tissue, puncture, and catheterization
Abdominal paracentesis   Lumbar puncture
Aspirating needle biopsy   Thoracentesis
Blood sampling

Excludes: *heart catheterization (E870.6)*

E870.6 Heart catheterization

E870.7 Administration of enema

E870.8 Other specified medical care

E870.9 Unspecified medical care

E871 Foreign object left in body during procedure

Add 4th or 5th digit   Nonspecific code   Unspecified code   Manifestation code

E871.0   **Surgical operation**

E871.1   **Infusion or transfusion**

E871.2   **Kidney dialysis or other perfusion**

E871.3   **Injection or vaccination**

E871.4   **Endoscopic examination**

E871.5   **Aspiration of fluid or tissue, puncture, and catheterization**
    Abdominal paracentesis   Lumbar puncture
    Aspiration needle biopsy   Thoracentesis
    Blood sampling

> *Excludes:* *heart catheterization (E871.6)*

E871.6   **Heart catheterization**

E871.7   **Removal of catheter or packing**

E871.8   **Other specified procedures**

E871.9   **Unspecified procedure**

E872   **Failure of sterile precautions during procedure**

E872.0   **Surgical operation**

E872.1   **Infusion or transfusion**

E872.2   **Kidney dialysis and other perfusion**

E872.3   **Injection or vaccination**

E872.4   **Endoscopic examination**

E872.5   **Aspiration of fluid or tissue, puncture, and catheterization**
    Abdominal paracentesis   Lumbar puncture
    Aspirating needle biopsy   Thoracentesis
    Blood sampling

> *Excludes:* *heart catheterization (E872.6)*

E872.6   **Heart catheterization**

E872.8   **Other specified procedures**

E872.9   **Unspecified procedure**

E873   **Failure in dosage**

> *Excludes:* *accidental overdose of drug, medicinal or biological substance (E850.0-E858.9)*

E873.0   **Excessive amount of blood or other fluid during transfusion or infusion**

E873.1   **Incorrect dilution of fluid during infusion**

E873.2   **Overdose of radiation in therapy**

E873.3   **Inadvertent exposure of patient to radiation during medical care**

E873.4   **Failure in dosage in electroshock or insulin-shock therapy**

E873.5   **Inappropriate [too hot or too cold] temperature in local application and packing**

E873.6   **Nonadministration of necessary drug or medicinal substance**

E873.8   **Other specified failure in dosage**

E873.9   **Unspecified failure in dosage**

E874   **Mechanical failure of instrument or apparatus during procedure**

E874.0   **Surgical operation**

E874.1   **Infusion and transfusion**
    Air in system

E874.2   **Kidney dialysis and other perfusion**

E874.3   **Endoscopic examination**

E874.4   **Aspiration of fluid or tissue, puncture, and catheterization**
    Abdominal paracentesis   Lumbar puncture
    Aspirating needle biopsy   Thoracentesis
    Blood sampling

> *Excludes:* *heart catheterization (E874.5)*

E874.5   **Heart catheterization**

E874.8   **Other specified procedures**

E874.9   **Unspecified procedure**

  ● Code new to this edition   ▲ Revision of existing code   ④ ⑤ Fourth or fifth digit required

E875 **Contaminated or infected blood, other fluid, drug, or biological substance**

Includes: presence of:
bacterial pyrogens
endotoxin-producing bacteria
serum hepatitis-producing agent

E875.0 **Contaminated substance transfused or infused**

E875.1 **Contaminated substance injected or used for vaccination**

E875.2 **Contaminated drug or biological substance administered by other means**

E875.8 **Other**

E875.9 **Unspecified**

E876 **Other and unspecified misadventures during medical care**

E876.0 **Mismatched blood in transfusion**

E876.1 **Wrong fluid in infusion**

E876.2 **Failure in suture and ligature during surgical operation**

E876.3 **Endotracheal tube wrongly placed during anesthetic procedure**

E876.4 **Failure to introduce or to remove other tube or instrument**

Excludes: *foreign object left in body during procedure (E871.0-E871.9)*

E876.5 **Performance of inappropriate operation**

E876.8 **Other specified misadventures during medical care**
Performance of inappropriate treatment NEC

E876.9 **Unspecified misadventure during medical care**

SURGICAL AND MEDICAL PROCEDURES AS THE CAUSE OF ABNORMAL REACTION OF PATIENT OR LATER COMPLICATION, WITHOUT MENTION OF MISADVENTURE AT THE TIME OF PROCEDURE (E878-E879)

Includes: procedures as the cause of abnormal reaction, such as:
displacement or malfunction of prosthetic device
hepatorenal failure, postoperative
malfunction of external stoma
postoperative intestinal obstruction
rejection of transplanted organ

Excludes: *anesthetic management properly carried out as the cause of adverse effect (E937.0-E938.9)*
infusion and transfusion, without mention of misadventure in the technique of procedure (E930.0-E949.9)

E878 **Surgical operation and other surgical procedures as the cause of abnormal reaction of patient, or of later complication, without mention of misadventure at the time of operation**

E878.0 **Surgical operation with transplant of whole organ**
Transplantation of:
heart
kidney
liver

E878.1 **Surgical operation with implant of artificial internal device**
Cardiac pacemaker   Heart valve prosthesis
Electrodes implanted in brain   Internal orthopedic device

E878.2 **Surgical operation with anastomosis, bypass, or graft, with natural or artificial tissues used as implant**
Anastomosis: Graft of blood vessel, tendon, or skin
arteriovenous
gastrojejunal

Excludes: *external stoma (E878.3)*

E878.3 **Surgical operation with formation of external stoma**
Colostomy   Gastrostomy
Cystostomy   Ureterostomy
Duodenostomy

E878.4 **Other restorative surgery**

E878.5 **Amputation of limb(s)**

E878.6 **Removal of other organ (partial) (total)**

E878.8 **Other specified surgical operations and procedures**

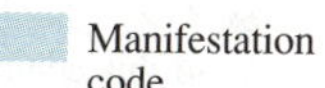

Manifestation
code

E878.9 Unspecified surgical operations and procedures

E879 Other procedures, without mention of misadventure at the time of procedure, as the cause of abnormal reaction of patient, or of later complication

E879.0 Cardiac catheterization

E879.1 Kidney dialysis

E879.2 Radiological procedure and radiotherapy

> Excludes: radio-opaque dyes for diagnostic x-ray procedures (E947.8)

E879.3 Shock therapy
Electroshock therapy   Insulin-shock therapy

E879.4 Aspiration of fluid
Lumbar puncture   Thoracentesis

E879.5 Insertion of gastric or duodenal sound

E879.6 Urinary catheterization

E879.7 Blood sampling

E879.8 Other specified procedures
Blood transfusion

E879.9 Unspecified procedure

ACCIDENTAL FALLS (E880-E888)

> Excludes: falls (in or from):
> burning building (E890.8, E891.8)
> into fire (E890.0-E899)
> into water (with submersion or drowning) (E910.0-E910.9)
> machinery (in operation) (E919.0-E919.9)
> on edged, pointed, or sharp object (E920.0-E920.9)
> transport vehicle (E800.0-E845.9)
> vehicle not elsewhere classifiable (E846-E848)

E880 Fall on or from stairs or steps

E880.0 Escalator

E880.1 Fall on or from sidewalk curb

> Excludes: fall from moving sidewalk (E885.9)

E880.9 Other stairs or steps

E881 Fall on or from ladders or scaffolding

E881.0 Fall from ladder

E881.1 Fall from scaffolding

E882 Fall from or out of building or other structure
Fall from: Fall from:
balcony   turret
bridge   viaduct
building   wall
flagpole   window
tower   Fall through roof

> Excludes: collapse of a building or structure (E916)
> fall or jump from burning building (E890.8, E891.8)

E883 Fall into hole or other opening in surface
Includes:
fall into: fall into:
cavity   shaft
dock   swimming pool
hole   tank
pit   well
quarry

> Excludes: fall into water NOS (E910.9)
> that resulting in drowning or submersion without mention of injury (E910.0-E910.9)

E883.0 Accident from diving or jumping into water [swimming pool]
Strike or hit:
against bottom when jumping or diving into water
wall or board of swimming pool
water surface

● Code new
to this edition

▲ Revision of
existing code

④ ⑤ Fourth or fifth
digit required

     Excludes: *diving with insufficient air supply (E913.2)*
                effects of air pressure from diving (E902.2)

E883.1   **Accidental fall into well**

E883.2   **Accidental fall into storm drain or manhole**

E883.9   **Fall into other hole or other opening in surface**

E884   **Other fall from one level to another**

E884.0   **Fall from playground equipment**

     Excludes: *recreational machinery (E919.8)*

E884.1   **Fall from cliff**

E884.2   **Fall from chair**

E884.3   **Fall from wheelchair**

E884.4   **Fall from bed**

E884.5   **Fall from other furniture**

E884.6   **Fall from commode**
      Toilet

E884.9   **Other fall from one level to another**
      Fall from: Fall from:
        embankment   stationary vehicle
        haystack   tree

E885   **Fall on same level from slipping, tripping, or stumbling**

● **E885.1**   **Fall from roller skates**
      In-line skates

● **E885.2**   **Fall from skateboard**

● **E885.3**   **Fall from skis**

● **E885.4**   **Fall from snowboard**

● **E885.9**   **Fall from other slipping, tripping or stumbling**
      Fall on moving sidewalk

E886   **Fall on same level from collision, pushing, or shoving, by or with other person**

     Excludes: *crushed or pushed by a crowd or human stampede (E917.1)*

E886.0   **In sports**
      Tackles in sports

     Excludes: *kicked, stepped on, struck by object, in sports (E917.0)*

E886.9   **Other and unspecified**
      Fall from collision of pedestrian (conveyance) with another pedestrian (conveyance)

E887   **Fracture, cause unspecified**

E888   **Other and unspecified fall**
     Accidental fall NOS
     Fall from bumping against object
     Fall on same level NOS

ACCIDENTS CAUSED BY FIRE AND FLAMES (E890-E899)

     Includes: asphyxia or poisoning due to conflagration or ignition
                burning by fire
                secondary fires resulting from explosion

     Excludes: *arson (E968.0)*

          fire in or on:
            machinery (in operation) (E919.0-E919.9)
            transport vehicle other than stationary vehicle (E800.0-E845.9)
            vehicle not elsewhere classifiable (E846-E848)

E890 Conflagration in private dwelling
      Includes: conflagration in:
            apartment
            boarding house
            camping place
            caravan
            farmhouse
            house
            lodging house
            mobile home
            private garage
            rooming house
            tenement
        conflagration originating from sources classifiable to E893–E898 in the above
            buildings

E890.0 Explosion caused by conflagration

E890.1 Fumes from combustion of polyvinylchloride [PVC] and similar material in conflagration

E890.2 Other smoke and fumes from conflagration
    Carbon monoxide
    Fumes NOS   } from conflagration in private building
    Smoke NOS

E890.3 Burning caused by conflagration

E890.8 Other accident resulting from conflagration
    Collapse of
    Fall from
    Hit by object falling from   } burning private building
    Jump from

E890.9 Unspecified accident resulting from conflagration in private dwelling

E891 Conflagration in other and unspecified building or structure
Conflagration in:
  barn
  church
  convalescent and other
    residential home
  dormitory of educational
    institution
  factory
Conflagration in:
  farm outbuildings
  hospital
  hotel
  school
  store
  theater
Conflagration originating from sources classifiable to E893–E898, in the above buildings

E891.0 Explosion caused by conflagration

E891.1 Fumes from combustion of polyvinylchloride [PVC] and similar material in conflagration

E891.2 Other smoke and fumes from conflagration
    Carbon monoxide
    Fumes NOS   } from conflagration in building or structure
    Smoke NOS

E891.3 Burning caused by conflagration

E891.8 Other accident resulting from conflagration
    Collapse of
    Fall from
    Hit by object falling from   } burning building or structure
    Jump from

E891.9 Unspecified accident resulting from conflagration of other and unspecified building or structure

E892 Conflagration not in building or structure
Fire (uncontrolled) (in) (of):
  forest
  grass
  hay
  lumber
  mine
  prairie
  transport vehicle [any], except while in transit
  tunnel

● Code new
  to this edition
▲ Revision of
  existing code
④ ⑤ Fourth or fifth
  digit required

E893 Accident caused by ignition of clothing

> *Excludes:* *ignition of clothing:*
> > *from highly inflammable material (E894)*
> > *with conflagration (E890.0-E892)*

E893.0 From controlled fire in private dwelling

Ignition of clothing from:
normal fire (charcoal) (coal) (electric) (gas)
  (wood) in:
brazier
fireplace — in private dwelling (as listed in
furnace   E890)
stove

E893.1 From controlled fire in other building or structure

Ignition of clothing from:
normal fire (charcoal) (coal) (electric)
  (gas) (wood) in:
brazier
fireplace — in other building or structure (as
furnace   listed in E891)
stove

E893.2 From controlled fire not in building or structure

Ignition of clothing from:
bonfire (controlled)
brazier fire (controlled), not in building or structure
trash fire (controlled)

> *Excludes:* *conflagration not in building (E892)*
> > *trash fire out of control (E892)*

E893.8 From other specified sources

Ignition of clothing from:
blowlamp
blowtorch
burning bedspread
candle
cigar

Ignition of clothing from:
cigarette
lighter
matches
pipe
welding torch

E893.9 Unspecified source

Ignition of clothing (from controlled fire NOS) (in building NOS) NOS

E894 Ignition of highly inflammable material

Ignition of:
benzine
gasoline
fat
kerosene — (with ignition of clothing)
paraffin
petrol

> *Excludes:* *ignition of highly inflammable material with:*
> > *conflagration (E890.0-E892)*
> > *explosion (E923.0-E923.9)*

E895 Accident caused by controlled fire in private dwelling

Burning by (flame of) normal fire (charcoal) (coal)
  (electric) (gas) (wood) in:
brazier
fireplace — in private dwelling (as listed in
furnace   E890)
stove

> *Excludes:* *burning by hot objects not producing fire or flames (E924.0-E924.9)*
> > *ignition of clothing from these sources (E893.0)*
> > *poisoning by carbon monoxide from incomplete combustion of fuel (E867-E868.9)*
> > *that with conflagration (E890.0-E890.9)*

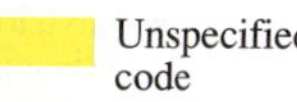

E896 **Accident caused by controlled fire in other and unspecified building or structure**
 Burning by (flame of) normal fire (charcoal) (coal)
  (electric) (gas) (wood) in:
  brazier
  fireplace   in other building or structure (as
  furnace   listed in E891)
  stove

   Excludes: *burning by hot objects not producing fire or flames (E924.0-E924.9)*
       ignition of clothing from these sources (E893.1)
       poisoning by carbon monoxide from incomplete combustion of fuel (E867-E868.9)
       that with conflagration (E891.0-E891.9)

E897 **Accident caused by controlled fire not in building or structure**
 Burns from flame of:
  bonfire (controlled)
  brazier fire (controlled), not in building or structure
  trash fire (controlled)

   Excludes: *ignition of clothing from these sources (E893.2)*
       trash fire out of control (E892)
       that with conflagration (E892)

E898 **Accident caused by other specified fire and flames**

   Excludes: *conflagration (E890.0-E892)*
       that with ignition of:
        clothing (E893.0-E893.9)
        highly inflammable material (E894)

 E898.0 **Burning bedclothes**
   Bed set on fire NOS

 E898.1 **Other**
   Burning by: Burning by:
    blowlamp   lamp
    blowtorch   lighter
    candle   matches
    cigar   pipe
    cigarette   welding torch
    fire in room NOS

E899 **Accident caused by unspecified fire**
  Burning NOS

ACCIDENTS DUE TO NATURAL AND ENVIRONMENTAL FACTORS (E900-E909)

E900 **Excessive heat**

 E900.0 **Due to weather conditions**
   Excessive heat as the external cause of:
    ictus solaris
    siriasis
    sunstroke

 E900.1 **Of man-made origin**
   Heat (in):   Heat (in):
    boiler room   generated in transport vehicle
    drying room   kitchen
    factory
    furnace room

 E900.9 **Of unspecified origin**

E901 **Excessive cold**

 E901.0 **Due to weather conditions**
   Excessive cold as the cause of:
    chilblains NOS
    immersion foot

● Code new   ▲ Revision of   ④ ⑤ Fourth or fifth
 to this edition   existing code   digit required

E901.1 Of man-made origin
Contact with or inhalation of:
  dry ice
  liquid air
  liquid hydrogen
  liquid nitrogen
Prolonged exposure in:
  deep freeze unit
  refrigerator

E901.8 Other specified origin

E901.9 Of unspecified origin

E902 High and low air pressure and changes in air pressure

E902.0 Residence or prolonged visit at high altitude
Residence or prolonged visit at high altitude as the cause of:
  Acosta syndrome
  Alpine sickness
  altitude sickness
  Andes disease
  anoxia, hypoxia
  barotitis, barodontalgia, barosinusitis, otitic barotrauma
  hypobarism, hypobaropathy
  mountain sickness
  range disease

E902.1 In aircraft
Sudden change in air pressure in aircraft during ascent or descent as the cause of:
  aeroneurosis
  aviators' disease

E902.2 Due to diving
High air pressure from rapid descent in water
Reduction in atmospheric pressure while
  surfacing from deep water diving
} as the cause of:
  caisson disease
  divers' disease
  divers' palsy or paralysis

E902.8 Due to other specified causes
Reduction in atmospheric pressure while surfacing from underground

E902.9 Unspecified cause

E903 Travel and motion

E904 Hunger, thirst, exposure, and neglect

Excludes: any condition resulting from homicidal intent (E968.0-E968.9)
    hunger, thirst, and exposure resulting from accidents connected with transport (E800.0-E848)

E904.0 Abandonment or neglect of infants and helpless persons
Exposure to weather
  conditions
Hunger or thirst
} resulting from abandonment or neglect

Desertion of newborn
Inattention at or after birth
Lack of care (helpless person) (infant)

Excludes: criminal [purposeful] neglect (E968.4)

E904.1 Lack of food
Lack of food as the cause of:
  inanition
  insufficient nourishment
  starvation

Excludes: hunger resulting from abandonment or neglect (E904.0)

E904.2 Lack of water
Lack of water as the cause of:
  dehydration
  inanition

Excludes: dehydration due to acute fluid loss (276.5)

E904.3 Exposure (to weather conditions), not elsewhere classifiable
Exposure NOS   Struck by hailstones
Humidity

Excludes: struck by lightning (E907)

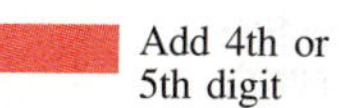

Manifestation
code

E904.9 Privation, unqualified
Destitution

E905 Venomous animals and plants as the cause of poisoning and toxic reactions
Includes: chemical released by animal
insects
release of venom through fangs, hairs, spines, tentacles, and other venom apparatus

Excludes: *eating of poisonous animals or plants (E865.0-E865.9)*

E905.0 Venomous snakes and lizards

Cobra	Mamba
Copperhead snake	Rattlesnake
Coral snake	Sea snake
Fer de lance	Snake (venomous)
Gila monster	Viper
Krait	Water moccasin

Excludes: *bites of snakes and lizards known to be nonvenomous (E906.2)*

E905.1 Venomous spiders
Black widow spider   Tarantula (venomous)
Brown spider

E905.2 Scorpion

E905.3 Hornets, wasps, and bees
Yellow jacket

E905.4 Centipede and venomous millipede (tropical)

E905.5 Other venomous arthropods
Sting of:
ant
caterpillar

E905.6 Venomous marine animals and plants
Puncture by sea urchin spine   Sting of:
Sting of: nematocysts
coral   sea anemone
jelly fish   sea cucumber
other marine animal or plant

Excludes: *bites and other injuries caused by nonvenomous marine animal (E906.2-E906.8)*
bite of sea snake (venomous) (E905.0)

E905.7 Poisoning and toxic reactions caused by other plants
Injection of poisons or toxins into or through skin by plant thorns, spines, or other
mechanisms

Excludes: *puncture wound NOS by plant thorns or spines (E920.8)*

E905.8 Other specified

E905.9 Unspecified
Sting NOS   Venomous bite NOS

E906 Other injury caused by animals

Excludes: *poisoning and toxic reactions caused by venomous animals and insects
(E905.0-E905.9)*
road vehicle accident involving animals (E827.0-E828.9)
tripping or falling over an animal (E885.9)

E906.0 Dog bite

E906.1 Rat bite

E906.2 Bite of nonvenomous snakes and lizards

E906.3 Bite of other animal except arthropod
Cats   Rodents, except rats
Moray eel   Shark

E906.4 Bite of nonvenomous arthropod
Insect bite NOS

E906.5 Bite by unspecified animal
Animal bite NOS

● Code new   ▲ Revision of   ④ ⑤ Fourth or fifth
to this edition   existing code   digit required

E906.8 **Other specified injury caused by animal**
Butted by animal
Fallen on by horse or other animal, not being ridden
Gored by animal
Implantation of quills of porcupine
Pecked by bird
Run over by animal, not being ridden
Stepped on by animal, not being ridden

Excludes: *injury by animal being ridden (E828.0-E828.9)*

E906.9 **Unspecified injury caused by animal**

E907 **Lightning**

Excludes: *injury from:*
fall of tree or other object caused by lightning (E916)
fire caused by lightning (E890.0-E892)

E908 **Cataclysmic storms, and floods resulting from storms**

Excludes: *collapse of dam or man-made structure causing flood (E909.3)*

E908.0 **Hurricane**
Storm surge
"Tidal wave" caused by storm action
Typhoon

E908.1 **Tornado**
Cyclone
Twisters

E908.2 **Floods**
Torrential rainfall
Flash flood

Excludes: *collapse of dam or man-made structure causing flood (909.3)*

E908.3 **Blizzard (snow) (ice)**

E908.4 **Dust storm**

E908.8 **Other cataclysmic storms**

E908.9 **Unspecified cataclysmic storms, and floods resulting from storms**
Storm NOS

E909 **Cataclysmic earth surface movements and eruptions**

Excludes: *"tidal wave" caused by storm action (E908.0)*
transport accident involving collision with avalanche or landslide not in motion (E800.0-E848)

E909.0 **Earthquakes**

E909.1 **Volcanic eruptions**
Burns from lava
Ash inhalation

E909.2 **Avalanche, landslide, or mudslide**

E909.3 **Collapse of dam or man-made structure**

E909.4 **Tidal wave caused by earthquake**
Tidal wave NOS
Tsunami

Excludes: *tidal wave caused by tropical storm (E908.0)*

E909.8 **Other cataclysmic earth surface movements and eruptions**

E909.9 **Unspecified cataclysmic earth surface movements and eruptions**

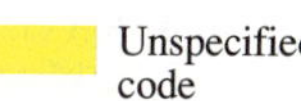

ACCIDENTS CAUSED BY SUBMERSION, SUFFOCATION, AND FOREIGN BODIES (E910-E915)

E910 Accidental drowning and submersion

Includes: immersion
swimmers' cramp

Excludes: *diving accident (NOS) (resulting in injury except drowning) (E883.0)*
diving with insufficient air supply (E913.2)
drowning and submersion due to:
cataclysm (E908-E909)
machinery accident (E919.0-E919.9)
transport accident (E800.0-E845.9)
effect of high and low air pressure (E902.2)
injury from striking against objects while in running water (E917.2)

E910.0 While water-skiing

Fall from water skis with submersion or drowning

Excludes: *accident to water-skier involving a watercraft and resulting in submersion or other injury (E830.4, E831.4)*

E910.1 While engaged in other sport or recreational activity with diving equipment

Scuba diving NOS
Skin diving NOS
Underwater spear fishing NOS

E910.2 While engaged in other sport or recreational activity without diving equipment

Fishing or hunting, except from boat or with diving equipment
Ice skating
Playing in water
Surfboarding
Swimming NOS
Voluntarily jumping from boat, not involved in accident, for swim NOS
Wading in water

Excludes: *jumping into water to rescue another person (E910.3)*

E910.3 While swimming or diving for purposes other than recreation or sport

Marine salvage
Pearl diving
Placement of fishing nets   } (with diving equipment)
Rescue (attempt) of another person
Underwater construction or repairs

E910.4 In bathtub

E910.8 Other accidental drowning or submersion

Drowning in:
quenching tank
swimming pool

E910.9 Unspecified accidental drowning or submersion

Accidental fall into water NOS
Drowning NOS

E911 Inhalation and ingestion of food causing obstruction of respiratory tract or suffocation

Aspiration and inhalation of food [any] (into respiratory tract) NOS
Asphyxia by
Choked on   } food [including bone, seed in food, regurgitated food]
Suffocation by

Compression of trachea
Interruption of respiration   } by food lodged in esophagus
Obstruction of respiration

Obstruction of pharynx by food (bolus)

Excludes: *injury, except asphyxia and obstruction of respiratory passage, caused by food (E915)*
obstruction of esophagus by food without mention of asphyxia or obstruction of respiratory passage (E915)

● Code new
to this edition

▲ Revision of
existing code

④ ⑤ Fourth or fifth
digit required

E912 Inhalation and ingestion of other object causing obstruction of respiratory tract or suffocation

Aspiration and inhalation of foreign body except food (into respiratory tract) NOS
Foreign object [bean] [marble] in nose
Obstruction of pharynx by foreign body
Compression ⎫
Interruption of respiration ⎬ by foreign body in esophagus
Obstruction of respiration ⎭

Excludes: *injury, except asphyxia and obstruction of respiratory passage, caused by foreign body (E915)*
obstruction of esophagus by foreign body without mention of asphyxia or obstruction in respiratory passage (E915)

E913 Accidental mechanical suffocation

Excludes: *mechanical suffocation from or by:*
accidental inhalation or ingestion of:
food (E911)
foreign object (E912)
cataclysm (E908-E909)
explosion (E921.0-E921.9, E923.0-E923.9)
machinery accident (E919.0-E919.9)

E913.0 In bed or cradle

Excludes: *suffocation by plastic bag (E913.1)*

E913.1 By plastic bag

E913.2 Due to lack of air (in closed place)
Accidentally closed up in refrigerator or other airtight enclosed space
Diving with insufficient air supply

Excludes: *suffocation by plastic bag (E913.1)*

E913.3 By falling earth or other substance
Cave-in NOS

Excludes: *cave-in caused by cataclysmic earth surface movements and eruptions (E909)*
struck by cave-in without asphyxiation or suffocation (E916)

E913.8 Other specified means
Accidental hanging, except in bed or cradle

E913.9 Unspecified means
Asphyxia, mechanical NOS
Strangulation NOS
Suffocation NOS

E914 Foreign body accidentally entering eye and adnexa

Excludes: *corrosive liquid (E924.1)*

E915 Foreign body accidentally entering other orifice

Excludes: *aspiration and inhalation of foreign body, any, (into respiratory tract) NOS (E911-E912)*

OTHER ACCIDENTS (E916-E928)

E916 Struck accidentally by falling object
Collapse of building, except on fire
Falling:
rock
snowslide NOS
stone
tree
Object falling from:
machine, not in operation
stationary vehicle
Code first: collapse of building on fire (E890.0-E891.9)
falling object in:
cataclysm (E908-E909)
machinery accidents (E919.0-E919.9)
transport accidents (E800.0-E845.9)
vehicle accidents not elsewhere classifiable (E846-E848)
object set in motion by:
explosion (E921.0-E921.9, E923.0-E923.9)
firearm (E922.0-E922.9)
projected object (E917.0-E917.9)

 Add 4th or 5th digit

 Nonspecific code

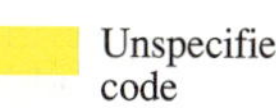 Unspecified code

Manifestation code

E917   Striking against or struck accidentally by objects or persons
Includes:

bumping into or against	object (moving) (projected) (stationary)
colliding with	pedestrian conveyance
kicking against	person
stepping on	
struck by	

Excludes: *fall from:*
bumping into or against object (E888)
collision with another person, except when caused by a crowd (E886.0-E886.9)
stumbling over object (E885.9)
injury caused by:
assault (E960.0-E960.1, E967.0-E967.9)
cutting or piercing instrument (E920.0-E920.9)
explosion (E921.0-E921.9, E923.0-E923.9)
firearm (E922.0-E922.9)
machinery (E919.0-E919.9)
transport vehicle (E800.0-E845.9)
vehicle not elsewhere classifiable (E846-E848)

E917.0   In sports
Kicked or stepped on during game (football) (rugby)
Knocked down while boxing
Struck by hit or thrown ball
Struck by hockey stick or puck

E917.1   Caused by a crowd, by collective fear or panic

Crushed	
Pushed	by crown or human stampede
Stepped on	

E917.2   In running water

Excludes: *drowning or submersion (E910.0-E910.9)*
that in sports (E917.0)

E917.9   Other

E918   Caught accidentally in or between objects
Caught, crushed, jammed, or pinched in or between moving or stationary objects, such as:
escalator
folding object
hand tools, appliances, or implements
sliding door and door frame
under packing crate
washing machine wringer

Excludes: *injury caused by:*
cutting or piercing instrument (E920.0-E920.9)
machinery (E919.0-E919.9)
transport vehicle (E800.0-E845.9)
vehicle not elsewhere classifiable (E846-E848)
struck accidentally by:
falling object (E916)
object (moving) (projected) (E917.0-E917.9)

● Code new to this edition   ▲ Revision of existing code   ④ ⑤ Fourth or fifth digit required

E919 **Accidents caused by machinery**

Includes:

burned by
caught in (moving parts of)
collapse of
crushed by
cut or pierced by
drowning or submersion caused by
explosion of, on, in
fall from or into moving part of
fire starting in or on
mechanical suffocation caused by   } machinery (accident)
object falling from, on, in motion by
overturning of
pinned under
run over by
struck by
thrown from
caught between machinery and other object
machinery accident NOS

Excludes: *accidents involving machinery, not in operation (E884.9, E916-E918)*

injury caused by:
electric current in connection with machinery (E925.0-E925.9)
escalator (E880.0, E918)
explosion of pressure vessel in connection with machinery (E921.0-E921.9)
moving sidewalk (E885.9)
powered hand tools, appliances, and implements (E916-E918, E920.0-E921.9,
E923.0-E926.9)
transport vehicle accidents involving machinery (E800.0-E848.9)
poisoning by carbon monoxide generated by machine (E868.8)

E919.0 **Agriculture machines**

Animal-powered	Farm tractor
agricultural machine	Harvester
Combine	Hay mower or rake
Derrick, hay	Reaper
Farm machinery NOS	Thresher

Excludes: *that in transport under own power on the highway (E810.0-E819.9)*
that being towed by another vehicle on the highway (E810.0-E819.9,
E827.0-E827.9, E829.0-E829.9)
that involved in accident classifiable to E820-E829 (E820.0-E829.9)

E919.1 **Mining and earth-drilling machinery**

Bore or drill (land) (seabed)	Shaft lift
Shaft hoist	Under-cutter

Excludes: *coal car, tram, truck, and tub in mine (E846)*

E919.2 **Lifting machines and appliances**

Chain hoist
Crane
Derrick
Elevator (building) (grain)   } except in agricultural or mining operations
Forklift truck
Lift
Pulley block
Winch

Excludes: *that being towed by another vehicle on the highway (E810.0-E819.9,*
E827.0-E827.9, E829.0-E829.9)
that in transport under own power on the highway (E810.0-E819.9)
that involved in accident classifiable to E820-E829 (E820.0-E829.9)

E919.3 **Metalworking machines**

Abrasive wheel	Metal:
Forging machine	drilling machine
Lathe	milling machine
Mechanical shears	power press
	rolling-mill
	sawing machine

Add 4th or 5th digit	Nonspecific code	Unspecified code	Manifestation code

E919.4 Woodworking and forming machines
- Band saw
- Bench saw
- Circular saw
- Molding machine
- Overhead plane
- Powered saw
- Radial saw
- Sander

Excludes: hand saw (E920.1)

E919.5 Prime movers, except electrical motors
- Gas turbine
- Internal combustion engine
- Steam engine
- Water driven turbine

Excludes: that being towed by other vehicle on the highway (E810.0-E819.9, E827.0-E827.9, E829.0-E829.9)
that in transport under own power on the highway (E810.0-E819.9)

E919.6 Transmission machinery
- Transmission:
  - belt
  - cable
  - chain
  - gear
- Transmission:
  - pinion
  - pulley
  - shaft

E919.7 Earth moving, scraping, and other excavating machines
- Bulldozer
- Road scraper
- Steam shovel

Excludes: that being towed by other vehicle on the highway (E810.0-E819.9, E827.0-E827.9, E829.0-E829.9)
that in transport under own power on the highway (E810.0-E819.9)

E919.8 Other specified machinery
- Machines for manufacture of:
  - clothing
  - foodstuffs and beverages
  - paper
- Printing machine
- Recreational machinery
- Spinning, weaving, and textile machines

E919.9 Unspecified machinery

E920 Accidents caused by cutting and piercing instruments or objects
Includes: accidental injury by fall on object:
- edged
- pointed
- sharp

E920.0 Powered lawn mower

E920.1 Other powered hand tools
Any powered hand tool [compressed air] [electric] [explosive cartridge] [hydraulic power], such as:
- drill
- hand saw
- hedge clipper
- rivet gun
- snow blower
- staple gun

Excludes: band saw (E919.4)
bench saw (E919.4)

E920.2 Powered household appliances and implements
- Blender
- Electric:
  - beater or mixer
  - can opener
  - fan
- Electric:
  - knife
  - sewing machine
- Garbage disposal appliance

E920.3 Knives, swords, and daggers

E920.4 Other hand tools and implements
- Axe
- Can opener NOS
- Chisel
- Fork
- Hand saw
- Hoe
- Ice pick
- Needle (sewing)
- Paper cutter
- Pitchfork
- Rake
- Scissors
- Screwdriver
- Sewing machine, not powered
- Shovel

● Code new to this edition ▲ Revision of existing code ④ ⑤ Fourth or fifth digit required

E920.5 Hypodermic needle
    Contaminated needle
    Needle stick

E920.8 Other specified cutting and piercing instruments or objects
    Arrow   Nail
    Broken glass   Plant thorn
    Dart   Splinter
    Edge of stiff paper   Tin can lid
    Lathe turnings

> *Excludes:* *animal spines or quills (E906.8)*
> *flying glass due to explosion (E921.0-E923.9)*

E920.9 Unspecified cutting and piercing instrument or object

E921 Accident caused by explosion of pressure vessel
    Includes: accidental explosion of pressure vessels, whether or not part of machinery

> *Excludes:* *explosion of pressure vessel on transport vehicle (E800.0-E845.9)*

E921.0 Boilers

E921.1 Gas cylinders
    Air tank   Pressure gas tank

E921.8 Other specified pressure vessels
    Aerosol can   Pressure cooker
    Automobile tire

E921.9 Unspecified pressure vessel

E922 Accident caused by firearm and air gun missile

E922.0 Handgun
    Pistol   Revolver

> *Excludes:* *Verey pistol (E922.8)*

E922.1 Shotgun (automatic)

E922.2 Hunting rifle

E922.3 Military firearms
    Army rifle   Machine gun

E922.4 Air gun
    BB gun   Pellet gun

E922.8 Other specified firearm missile
    Verey pistol [flare]

E922.9 Unspecified firearm missile
    Gunshot wound NOS   Shot NOS

E923 Accident caused by explosive material
    Includes: flash burns and other injuries resulting from explosion of explosive material
    ignition of highly explosive material with explosion

> *Excludes:* *explosion:*
> *in or on machinery (E919.0-E919.9)*
> *on any transport vehicle, except stationary motor vehicle (E800.0-E848)*
> *with conflagration (E890.0, E891.0, E892)*
> *secondary fires resulting from explosion (E890.0-E899)*

E923.0 Fireworks

E923.1 Blasting materials
    Blasting cap   Explosive [any] used in blasting operations
    Detonator
    Dynamite

E923.2 Explosive gases
    Acetylene   Fire damp
    Butane   Gasoline fumes
    Coal gas   Methane
    Explosion in mine NOS   Propane

E923.8 Other explosive materials
    Bomb   Torpedo
    Explosive missile   Explosion in munitions:
    Grenade   dump
    Mine   factory
    Shell

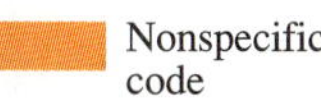

E923.9 **Unspecified explosive material**
Explosion NOS

E924 **Accident caused by hot substance or object, caustic or corrosive material, and steam**

Excludes: *burning NOS (E899)*
chemical burn resulting from swallowing a corrosive substance (E860.0-E864.4)
fire caused by these substances and objects (E890.0-E894)
radiation burns (E926.0-E926.9)
therapeutic misadventures (E870.0-E876.9)

E924.0 **Hot liquids and vapors, including steam**
Burning or scalding by:
boiling water
hot or boiling liquids not primarily caustic or corrosive
liquid metal
steam
other hot vapor

Excludes: *hot (boiling) tap water (E924.2)*

E924.1 **Caustic and corrosive substances**
Burning by:
acid [any kind]
ammonia
caustic oven cleaner or other substance
corrosive substance
lye
vitriol

E924.2 **Hot (boiling) tap water**

E924.8 **Other**
Burning by:
heat from electric heating appliance
hot object NOS
light bulb
steam pipe

E924.9 **Unspecified**

E925 **Accident caused by electric current**
Includes: electric current from exposed wire, faulty appliance, high voltage cable, live rail, or
open electric socket as the cause of:
burn
cardiac fibrillation
convulsion
electric shock
electrocution
puncture wound
respiratory paralysis

Excludes: *burn by heat from electrical appliance (E924.8)*
lightning (E907)

E925.0 **Domestic wiring and appliances**

E925.1 **Electric power generating plants, distribution stations, transmission lines**
Broken power line

E925.2 **Industrial wiring, appliances, and electrical machinery**
Conductors   Electrical equipment and machinery
Control apparatus   Transformers

E925.8 **Other electric current**
Wiring and appliances in   Wiring and appliances in or on:
or on: residential institutions
farm [not farmhouse]   schools
outdoors
public building

E925.9 **Unspecified electric current**
Burns or other injury from electric current NOS
Electric shock NOS
Electrocution NOS

● Code new   ▲ Revision of   ④ ⑤ Fourth or fifth
to this edition   existing code   digit required

E926 Exposure to radiation

> *Excludes:* *abnormal reaction to or complication of treatment without mention of misadventure (E879.2)*
> *atomic power plant malfunction in water transport (E838.0-E838.9)*
> *misadventure to patient in surgical and medical procedures (E873.2-E873.3)*
> *use of radiation in war operations (E996-E997.9)*

E926.0 Radiofrequency radiation

Overexposure to:
microwave radiation
radar radiation
radiofrequency
radiofrequency radiation [any]

from:
high-powered radio and
television transmitters
industrial radiofrequency induction
heaters
radar installations

E926.1 Infra-red heaters and lamps

Exposure to infra-red radiation from heaters and lamps as the cause of:
blistering
burning
charring
inflammatory change

> *Excludes:* *physical contact with heater or lamp (E924.8)*

E926.2 Visible and ultraviolet light sources

Arc lamps
Black light sources
Electrical welding arc

Oxygas welding torch
Sun rays

> *Excludes:* *excessive heat from these sources (E900.1-E900.9)*

E926.3 X-rays and other electromagnetic ionizing radiation

Gamma rays
X-rays (hard) (soft)

E926.4 Lasers

E926.5 Radioactive isotopes

Radiobiologicals
Radiopharmaceuticals

E926.8 Other specified radiation

Artificially accelerated beams of ionized particles generated by:
betatrons
synchrotrons

E926.9 Unspecified radiation

Radiation NOS

E927 Overexertion and strenuous movements

Excessive physical exercise
Overexertion (from):
lifting
pulling
pushing

Strenuous movements in:
recreational activities
other activities

E928 Other and unspecified environmental and accidental causes

E928.0 Prolonged stay in weightless environment

Weightlessness in spacecraft (simulator)

E928.1 Exposure to noise

Noise (pollution)
Sound waves

Supersonic waves

E928.2 Vibration

● **E928.3 Human bite**

E928.8 Other

E928.9 Unspecified accident

Accident NOS
Blow NOS
Casualty (not due to war)
Decapitation
Injury [any part of body, or unspecified]
Killed
Knocked down
Mangled
Wound

stated as accidentally inflicted,
but not otherwise specified

> *Excludes:* *fracture, cause unspecified (E887)*
> *injuries undetermined whether accidentally or purposely inflicted (E980.0-E989)*

Add 4th or
5th digit

Nonspecific
code

Unspecified
code

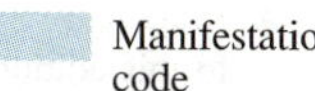
Manifestation
code

LATE EFFECTS OF ACCIDENTAL INJURY (E929)

Note: This category is to be used to indicate accidental injury as the cause of death or disability from late effects, which are themselves classifiable elsewhere. The "late effects" include conditions reported as such or as sequelae which may occur at any time after the acute injury.

E929 Late effects of accidental injury

> | Excludes: | *late effects of:*
>
> *surgical and medical procedures (E870.0-E879.9)*
> *therapeutic use of drugs and medicines (E930.0-E949.9)*

E929.0 Late effects of motor vehicle accident
Late effects of accidents classifiable to E810-E825

E929.1 Late effects of other transport accident
Late effects of accidents classifiable to E800-E807, E826-E838, E840-E848

E929.2 Late effects of accidental poisoning
Late effects of accidents classifiable to E850-E858, E860-E869

E929.3 Late effects of accidental fall
Late effects of accidents classifiable to E880-E888

E929.4 Late effects of accident caused by fire
Late effects of accidents classifiable to E890-E899

E929.5 Late effects of accident due to natural and environmental factors
Late effects of accidents classifiable to E900-E909

E929.8 Late effects of other accidents
Late effects of accidents classifiable to E910-E928.8

E929.9 Late effects of unspecified accident
Late effects of accidents classifiable to E928.9

DRUGS, MEDICINAL AND BIOLOGICAL SUBSTANCES CAUSING ADVERSE EFFECTS IN THERAPEUTIC USE (E930-E949)

Includes: correct drug properly administered in therapeutic or prophylactic dosage, as the cause of any adverse effect including allergic or hypersensitivity reactions

> | Excludes: | *accidental overdose of drug and wrong drug given or taken in error (E850.0-E858.9)*
> *accidents in the technique of administration of drug or biological substance, such as accidental puncture during injection, or contamination of drug (E870.0-E876.9)*
> *administration with suicidal or homicidal intent or intent to harm, or in circumstances classifiable to E980-E989 (E950.0-E950.5, E962.0, E980.0-E980.5)*

See Alphabetic Index for more complete list of specific drugs to be classified under the fourth-digit subdivisions. The American Hospital Formulary numbers can be used to classify new drugs listed by the American Hospital Formulary Service (AHFS). See appendix C.

E930 Antibiotics

> | Excludes: | *that used as eye, ear, nose, and throat [ENT], and local anti-infectives (E946.0-E946.9)*

E930.0 Penicillins

Natural	Semisynthetic, such as:
Synthetic	ampicillin
	cloxacillin
	nafcillin
	oxacillin

E930.1 Antifungal antibiotics

Amphotericin B	Hachimycin [trichomycin]
Griseofulvin	Nystatin

E930.2 Chloramphenicol group

Chloramphenicol	Thiamphenicol

E930.3 Erythromycin and other macrolides

Oleandomycin	Spiramycin

E930.4 Tetracycline group
Doxycycline
Minocycline
Oxytetracycline

● Code new to this edition   ▲ Revision of existing code   ④ ⑤ Fourth or fifth digit required

E930.5 Cephalosporin group
Cephalexin   Cephaloridine
Cephaloglycin   Cephalothin

E930.6 Antimycobacterial antibiotics
Cycloserine   Rifampin
Kanamycin   Streptomycin

E930.7 Antineoplastic antibiotics
Actinomycins, such as: Bleomycin
  Cactinomycin   Daunorubicin
  Dactinomycin   Mitomycin

Excludes: *other antineoplastic drugs (E933.1)*

E930.8 Other specified antibiotics

E930.9 Unspecified antibiotic

E931 Other anti-infectives

Excludes: *ENT, and local anti-infectives (E946.0-E946.9)*

E931.0 Sulfonamides
Sulfadiazine   Sulfamethoxazole
Sulfafurazole

E931.1 Arsenical anti-infectives

E931.2 Heavy metal anti-infectives
Compounds of: Compounds of:
  antimony   lead
  bismuth   mercury

Excludes: *mercurial diuretics (E944.0)*

E931.3 Quinoline and hydroxyquinoline derivatives
Chiniofon   Diiodohydroxyquin

Excludes: *antimalarial drugs (E931.4)*

E931.4 Antimalarials and drugs acting on other blood protozoa
Chloroquine phosphate   Proguanil [chloroguanide]
Cycloguanil   Pyrimethamine
Primaquine   Quinine (sulphate)

E931.5 Other antiprotozoal drugs
Emetine

E931.6 Anthelmintics
Hexylresorcinol   Piperazine
Male fern oleoresin   Thiabendazole

E931.7 Antiviral drugs
Methisazone

Excludes: *amantadine (E936.4)*
cytarabine (E933.1)
idoxuridine (E946.5)

E931.8 Other antimycobacterial drugs
Ethambutol   Para-aminosalicylic acid derivatives
Ethionamide   Sulfones
Isoniazid

E931.9 Other and unspecified anti-infectives
Flucytosine   Nitrofuran derivatives

E932 Hormones and synthetic substitutes

E932.0 Adrenal cortical steroids
Cortisone derivatives
Desoxycorticosterone derivatives
Fluorinated corticosteroids

E932.1 Androgens and anabolic congeners
Nandrolone phenpropionate
Oxymetholone
Testosterone and preparations

E932.2 Ovarian hormones and synthetic substitutes
Contraceptives, oral
Estrogens
Estrogens and progestogens combined
Progestogens

E932.3 Insulins and antidiabetic agents
Acetohexamide
Biguanide derivatives, oral
Chlorpropamide
Glucagon
Insulin
Phenformin
Sulfonylurea derivatives, oral
Tolbutamide

> *Excludes:* *adverse effect of insulin administered for shock therapy (E879.3)*

E932.4 Anterior pituitary hormones
Corticotropin
Gonadotropin
Somatotropin [growth hormone]

E932.5 Posterior pituitary hormones
Vasopressin

> *Excludes:* *oxytocic agents (E945.0)*

E932.6 Parathyroid and parathyroid derivatives

E932.7 Thyroid and thyroid derivatives
Dextrothyroxine
Levothyroxine sodium
Liothyronine
Thyroglobulin

E932.8 Antithyroid agents
Iodides
Thiouracil
Thiourea

E932.9 Other and unspecified hormones and synthetic substitutes

E933 Primarily systemic agents

E933.0 Antiallergic and antiemetic drugs
Antihistamines
Chlorpheniramine
Diphenhydramine
Diphenylpyraline
Thonzylamine
Tripelennamine

> *Excludes:* *phenothiazine-based tranquilizers (E939.1)*

E933.1 Antineoplastic and immunosuppressive drugs
Azathioprine
Busulfan
Chlorambucil
Cyclophosphamide
Cytarabine
Fluorouracil
Mechlorethamine hydrochloride
Mercaptopurine
Triethylenethiophosphoramide [thio-TEPA]

> *Excludes:* *antineoplastic antibiotics (E930.7)*

E933.2 Acidifying agents

E933.3 Alkalizing agents

E933.4 Enzymes, not elsewhere classified
Penicillinase

E933.5 Vitamins, not elsewhere classified
Vitamin A
Vitamin D

> *Excludes:* *nicotinic acid (E942.2)*
> *vitamin K (E934.3)*

E933.8 Other systemic agents, not elsewhere classified
Heavy metal antagonists

E933.9 Unspecified systemic agent

E934 Agents primarily affecting blood constituents

E934.0 Iron and its compounds
Ferric salts
Ferrous sulphate and other ferrous salts

E934.1 Liver preparations and other antianemic agents
Folic acid

E934.2 Anticoagulants
Coumarin
Heparin
Phenindione
Prothrombin synthesis inhibitor
Warfarin sodium

E934.3 Vitamin K [phytonadione]

E934.4 Fibrinolysis-affecting drugs
Aminocaproic acid
Streptodornase
Streptokinase
Urokinase

● Code new
to this edition

▲ Revision of
existing code

④ ⑤ Fourth or fifth
digit required

E934.5 Anticoagulant antagonists and other coagulants
Hexadimethrine bromide   Protamine sulfate

E934.6 Gamma globulin

E934.7 Natural blood and blood products
Blood plasma   Packed red cells
Human fibrinogen   Whole blood

E934.8 Other agents affecting blood constituents
Macromolecular blood substitutes

E934.9 Unspecified agent affecting blood constituents

E935 Analgesics, antipyretics, and antirheumatics

E935.0 Heroin
Diacetylmorphine

E935.1 Methadone

E935.2 Other opiates and related narcotics
Codeine [methylmorphine]   Opium (alkaloids)
Morphine   Meperidine [pethidine]

E935.3 Salicylates
Acetylsalicylic acid [aspirin]
Amino derivatives of salicylic acid
Salicylic acid salts

E935.4 Aromatic analgesics, not elsewhere classified
Acetanilid
Paracetamol [acetaminophen]
Phenacetin [acetophenetidin]

E935.5 Pyrazole derivatives
Aminophenazone [aminopyrine]
Phenylbutazone

E935.6 Antirheumatics [antiphlogistics]
Gold salts   Indomethacin

Excludes: salicylates (E935.3)
steroids (E932.0)

E935.7 Other non-narcotic analgesics
Pyrabital

E935.8 Other specified analgesics and antipyretics
Pentazocine

E935.9 Unspecified analgesic and antipyretic

E936 Anticonvulsants and anti-Parkinsonism drugs

E936.0 Oxazolidine derivatives
Paramethadione   Trimethadione

E936.1 Hydantoin derivatives
Phenytoin

E936.2 Succinimides
Ethosuximide   Phensuximide

E936.3 Other and unspecified anticonvulsants
Beclamide   Primidone

E936.4 Anti-Parkinsonism drugs
Amantadine
Ethopropazine [profenamine]
Levodopa [L-dopa]

E937 Sedatives and hypnotics

E937.0 Barbiturates
Amobarbital [amylobarbitone]
Barbital [barbitone]
Butabarbital [butabarbitone]
Pentobarbital [pentobarbitone]
Phenobarbital [phenobarbitone]
Secobarbital [quinalbarbitone]

Excludes: thiobarbiturates (E938.3)

E937.1 Chloral hydrate group

E937.2 Paraldehyde

 Add 4th or 5th digit

 Nonspecific code

 Unspecified code

Manifestation code

E937.3 Bromine compounds
    Bromide   Carbromal (derivatives)

E937.4 Methaqualone compounds

E937.5 Glutethimide group

E937.6 Mixed sedatives, not elsewhere classified

E937.8 Other sedatives and hypnotics

E937.9 Unspecified
    Sleeping:
        drug
        pill   } NOS
        tablet

E938 Other central nervous system depressants and anesthetics

E938.0 Central nervous system muscle-tone depressants
    Chlorphenesin (carbamate)   Methocarbamol
    Mephenesin

E938.1 Halothane

E938.2 Other gaseous anesthetics
    Ether
    Halogenated hydrocarbon derivatives, except halothane
    Nitrous oxide

E938.3 Intravenous anesthetics
    Ketamine   Thiobarbiturates, such as thiopental sodium
    Methohexital
    [methohexitone]

E938.4 Other and unspecified general anesthetics

E938.5 Surface and infiltration anesthetics
    Cocaine   Procaine
    Lidocaine [lignocaine]   Tetracaine

E938.6 Peripheral nerve- and plexus-blocking anesthetics

E938.7 Spinal anesthetics

E938.9 Other and unspecified local anesthetics

E939 Psychotropic agents

E939.0 Antidepressants
    Amitriptyline   Monoamine oxidase [MAO] inhibitors
    Imipramine

E939.1 Phenothiazine-based tranquilizers
    Chlorpromazine   Prochlorperazine
    Fluphenazine   Promazine
    Phenothiazine

E939.2 Butyrophenone-based tranquilizers
    Haloperidol   Trifluperidol
    Spiperone

E939.3 Other antipsychotics, neuroleptics, and major tranquilizers

E939.4 Benzodiazepine-based tranquilizers
    Chlordiazepoxide   Lorazepam
    Diazepam   Medazepam
    Flurazepam   Nitrazepam

E939.5 Other tranquilizers
    Hydroxyzine   Meprobamate

E939.6 Psychodysleptics [hallucinogens]
    Cannabis (derivatives)   Mescaline
    Lysergide [LSD]   Psilocin
    Marihuana (derivatives)   Psilocybin

E939.7 Psychostimulants
    Amphetamine   Caffeine

        Excludes: *central appetite depressants (E947.0)*

E939.8 Other psychotropic agents

E939.9 Unspecified psychotropic agent

    ● Code new   ▲ Revision of   ④ ⑤ Fourth or fifth
          to this edition   existing code   digit required

E940 Central nervous system stimulants

    E940.0 Analeptics
        Lobeline   Nikethamide

    E940.1 Opiate antagonists
        Levallorphan   Naloxone
        Nalorphine

    E940.8 Other specified central nervous system stimulants

    E940.9 Unspecified central nervous system stimulant

E941 Drugs primarily affecting the autonomic nervous system

    E941.0 Parasympathomimetics [cholinergics]
        Acetylcholine   Pilocarpine
        Anticholinesterase:
          organophosphorus
          reversible

    E941.1 Parasympatholytics [anticholinergics and antimuscarinics] and spasmolytics
        Atropine   Hyoscine [scopolamine]
        Homatropine   Quaternary ammonium derivatives

        Excludes: *papaverine (E942.5)*

    E941.2 Sympathomimetics [adrenergics]
        Epinephrine [adrenalin]
        Levarterenol [noradrenalin]

    E941.3 Sympatholytics [antiadrenergics]
        Phenoxybenzamine   Tolazoline hydrochloride

    E941.9 Unspecified drug primarily affecting the autonomic nervous system

E942 Agents primarily affecting the cardiovascular system

    E942.0 Cardiac rhythm regulators
        Practolol   Propranolol
        Procainamide   Quinidine

    E942.1 Cardiotonic glycosides and drugs of similar action
        Digitalis glycosides   Strophanthins
        Digoxin

    E942.2 Antilipemic and antiarteriosclerotic drugs
        Cholestyramine   Nicotinic acid derivatives
        Clofibrate   Sitosterols

        Excludes: *dextrothyroxine (E932.7)*

    E942.3 Ganglion-blocking agents
        Pentamethonium bromide

    E942.4 Coronary vasodilators
        Dipyridamole   Nitrites
        Nitrates [nitroglycerin] Prenylamine

    E942.5 Other vasodilators
        Cyclandelate   Hydralazine
        Diazoxide   Papaverine

    E942.6 Other antihypertensive agents
        Clonidine   Rauwolfia alkaloids
        Guanethidine   Reserpine

    E942.7 Antivaricose drugs, including sclerosing agents
        Monoethanolamine   Zinc salts

    E942.8 Capillary-active drugs
        Adrenochrome derivatives Metaraminol
        Bioflavonoids

    E942.9 Other and unspecified agents primarily affecting the cardiovascular system

E943 Agents primarily affecting gastrointestinal system

    E943.0 Antacids and antigastric secretion drugs
        Aluminum hydroxide   Magnesium trisilicate

    E943.1 Irritant cathartics
        Bisacodyl   Phenolphthalein
        Castor oil

    E943.2 Emollient cathartics
        Sodium dioctyl sulfosuccinate

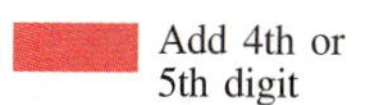

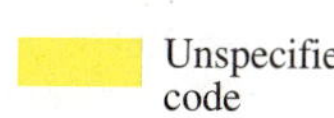

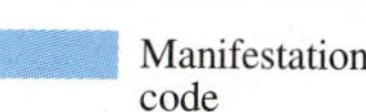

E943.3 **Other cathartics, including intestinal atonia drugs**
Magnesium sulfate

E943.4 **Digestants**
Pancreatin
Papain
Pepsin

E943.5 **Antidiarrheal drugs**
Bismuth subcarbonate
Kaolin
Pectin

Excludes: *anti-infectives (E930.0-E931.9)*

E943.6 **Emetics**

E943.8 **Other specified agents primarily affecting the gastrointestinal system**

E943.9 **Unspecified agent primarily affecting the gastrointestinal system**

E944 **Water, mineral, and uric acid metabolism drugs**

E944.0 **Mercurial diuretics**
Chlormerodrin
Mercaptomerin
Mercurophylline
Mersalyl

E944.1 **Purine derivative diuretics**
Theobromine
Theophylline

Excludes: *aminophylline [theophylline ethylenediamine] (E945.7)*

E944.2 **Carbonic acid anhydrase inhibitors**
Acetazolamide

E944.3 **Saluretics**
Benzothiadiazides
Chlorothiazide group

E944.4 **Other diuretics**
Ethacrynic acid
Furosemide

E944.5 **Electrolytic, caloric, and water-balance agents**

E944.6 **Other mineral salts, not elsewhere classified**

E944.7 **Uric acid metabolism drugs**
Cinchophen and congeners
Colchicine
Phenoquin
Probenecid

E945 **Agents primarily acting on the smooth and skeletal muscles and respiratory system**

E945.0 **Oxytocic agents**
Ergot alkaloids
Prostaglandins

E945.1 **Smooth muscle relaxants**
Adiphenine
Metaproterenol [orciprenaline]

Excludes: *papaverine (E942.5)*

E945.2 **Skeletal muscle relaxants**
Alcuronium chloride
Suxamethonium chloride

E945.3 **Other and unspecified drugs acting on muscles**

E945.4 **Antitussives**
Dextromethorphan
Pipazethate hydrochloride

E945.5 **Expectorants**
Acetylcysteine
Cocillana
Guaifenesin [glyceryl guaiacolate]
Ipecacuanha
Terpin hydrate

E945.6 **Anti-common cold drugs**

E945.7 **Antiasthmatics**
Aminophylline [theophylline ethylenediamine]

E945.8 **Other and unspecified respiratory drugs**

E946 **Agents primarily affecting skin and mucous membrane, ophthalmological, otorhinolaryngological, and dental drugs**

E946.0 **Local anti-infectives and anti-inflammatory drugs**

E946.1 **Antipruritics**

E946.2 **Local astringents and local detergents**

E946.3 **Emollients, demulcents, and protectants**

E946.4 **Keratolytics, keratoplastics, other hair treatment drugs and preparations**

● Code new
to this edition

▲ Revision of
existing code

④ ⑤ Fourth or fifth
digit required

E946.5 Eye anti-infectives and other eye drugs
Idoxuridine

E946.6 Anti-infectives and other drugs and preparations for ear, nose, and throat

E946.7 Dental drugs topically applied

E946.8 Other agents primarily affecting skin and mucous membrane
Spermicides

E946.9 Unspecified agent primarily affecting skin and mucous membrane

E947 Other and unspecified drugs and medicinal substances

E947.0 Dietetics

E947.1 Lipotropic drugs

E947.2 Antidotes and chelating agents, not elsewhere classified

E947.3 Alcohol deterrents

E947.4 Pharmaceutical excipients

E947.8 Other drugs and medicinal substances
Contrast media used for diagnostic x-ray procedures
Diagnostic agents and kits

E947.9 Unspecified drug or medicinal substance

E948 Bacterial vaccines

E948.0 BCG vaccine

E948.1 Typhoid and paratyphoid

E948.2 Cholera

E948.3 Plague

E948.4 Tetanus

E948.5 Diphtheria

E948.6 Pertussis vaccine, including combinations with a pertussis component

E948.8 Other and unspecified bacterial vaccines

E948.9 Mixed bacterial vaccines, except combinations with a pertussis component

E949 Other vaccines and biological substances

Excludes: *gamma globulin (E934.6)*

E949.0 Smallpox vaccine

E949.1 Rabies vaccine

E949.2 Typhus vaccine

E949.3 Yellow fever vaccine

E949.4 Measles vaccine

E949.5 Poliomyelitis vaccine

E949.6 Other and unspecified viral and rickettsial vaccines
Mumps vaccine

E949.7 Mixed viral-rickettsial and bacterial vaccines, except combinations with a pertussis component

Excludes: *combinations with a pertussis component (E948.6)*

E949.9 Other and unspecified vaccines and biological substances

SUICIDE AND SELF-INFLICTED INJURY (E950-E959)

Includes: injuries in suicide and attempted suicide
self-inflicted injuries specified as intentional

E950 Suicide and self-inflicted poisoning by solid or liquid substances

E950.0 Analgesics, antipyretics, and antirheumatics

E950.1 Barbiturates

E950.2 Other sedatives and hypnotics

E950.3 Tranquilizers and other psychotropic agents

E950.4 Other specified drugs and medicinal substances

E950.5 Unspecified drug or medicinal substances

E950.6 Agricultural and horticultural chemical and pharmaceutical preparations other than plant foods and fertilizers

| Add 4th or 5th digit | Nonspecific code | Unspecified code | Manifestation code |

E950.7 Corrosive and caustic substances
Suicide and self-inflicted poisoning by substances classifiable to E864

E950.8 Arsenic and its compounds

E950.9 Other and unspecified solid and liquid substances

E951 Suicide and self-inflicted poisoning by gases in domestic use

E951.0 Gas distributed by pipeline

E951.1 Liquefied petroleum gas distributed in mobile containers

E951.8 Other utility gas

E952 Suicide and self-inflicted poisoning by other gases and vapors

E952.0 Motor vehicle exhaust gas

E952.1 Other carbon monoxide

E952.8 Other specified gases and vapors

E952.9 Unspecified gases and vapors

E953 Suicide and self-inflicted injury by hanging, strangulation, and suffocation

E953.0 Hanging

E953.1 Suffocation by plastic bag

E953.8 Other specified means

E953.9 Unspecified means

E954 Suicide and self-inflicted injury by submersion [drowning]

E955 Suicide and self-inflicted injury by firearms, air guns and explosives

E955.0 Handgun

E955.1 Shotgun

E955.2 Hunting rifle

E955.3 Military firearms

E955.4 Other and unspecified firearm
Gunshot NOS   Shot NOS

E955.5 Explosives

E955.6 Air gun
BB gun   Pellet gun

E955.9 Unspecified

E956 Suicide and self-inflicted injury by cutting and piercing instrument

E957 Suicide and self-inflicted injuries by jumping from high place

E957.0 Residential premises

E957.1 Other man-made structures

E957.2 Natural sites

E957.9 Unspecified

E958 Suicide and self-inflicted injury by other and unspecified means

E958.0 Jumping or lying before moving object

E958.1 Burns, fire

E958.2 Scald

E958.3 Extremes of cold

E958.4 Electrocution

E958.5 Crashing of motor vehicle

E958.6 Crashing of aircraft

E958.7 Caustic substances, except poisoning

> Excludes: *poisoning by caustic substance (E950.7)*

E958.8 Other specified means

E958.9 Unspecified means

E959 Late effects of self-inflicted injury
Note: This category is to be used to indicate circumstances classifiable to E950-E958 as the cause of death or disability from late effects, which are themselves classifiable elsewhere. The "late effects" include conditions reported as such or as sequelae which may occur at any time after the attempted suicide or self-inflicted injury.

     ● Code new
to this edition   ▲ Revision of
existing code   ④ ⑤ Fourth or fifth
digit required

HOMICIDE AND INJURY PURPOSELY INFLICTED BY OTHER PERSONS (E960-E969)

Includes: injuries inflicted by another person with intent to injure or kill, by any means

Excludes: *injuries due to:*
legal intervention (E970-E978)
operations of war (E990-E999)

E960 Fight, brawl, rape

E960.0 Unarmed fight or brawl
Beatings NOS
Brawl or fight with hands, fists, feet
Injured or killed in fight NOS

Excludes: *homicidal:*
injury by weapons (E965.0-E966, E969)
strangulation (E963)
submersion (E964)

E960.1 Rape

E961 Assault by corrosive or caustic substance, except poisoning
Injury or death purposely caused by corrosive or caustic substance, such as:
acid [any]
corrosive substance
vitriol

Excludes: *burns from hot liquid (E968.3)*
chemical burns from swallowing a corrosive substance (E962.0-E962.9)

E962 Assault by poisoning

E962.0 Drugs and medicinal substances
Homicidal poisoning by any drug or medicinal substance

E962.1 Other solid and liquid substances

E962.2 Other gases and vapors

E962.9 Unspecified poisoning

E963 Assault by hanging and strangulation
Homicidal (attempt):
garrotting or ligature
hanging
strangulation
suffocation

E964 Assault by submersion [drowning]

E965 Assault by firearms and explosives

E965.0 Handgun
Pistol   Revolver

E965.1 Shotgun

E965.2 Hunting rifle

E965.3 Military firearms

E965.4 Other and unspecified firearm

E965.5 Antipersonnel bomb

E965.6 Gasoline bomb

E965.7 Letter bomb

E965.8 Other specified explosive
Bomb NOS (placed in) car
Bomb NOS (placed in) house
Dynamite

E965.9 Unspecified explosive

E966 Assault by cutting and piercing instrument
Assassination (attempt), homicide (attempt) by any instrument classifiable under E920
Homicidal cut, any part of the body
Homicidal puncture, any part of the body
Homicidal stab, any part of the body
Stabbed, any part of the body

▲ E967 Perpetrator of child and adult abuse

Note: selection of the correct perpetrator code is based on the relationship between the perpetrator and the victim

Add 4th or 5th digit

Nonspecific code

Unspecified code

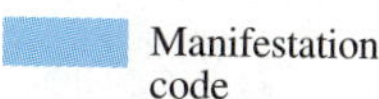
Manifestation code

▲ **E967.0 By father, stepfather or boyfriend**
Male partner of child's parent or guardian

E967.1 By other specified person

▲ **E967.2 By mother, stepmother or girlfriend**
Female partner of child's parent or guardian

E967.3 By spouse or partner
Abuse of spouse or partner by ex-spouse or ex-partner

E967.4 By child

E967.5 By sibling

E967.6 By grandparent

E967.7 By other relative

E967.8 By non-related caregiver

E967.9 By unspecified person

E968 Assault by other and unspecified means

E968.0 Fire
Arson   Homicidal burns NOS

Excludes: *burns from hot liquid (E968.3)*

E968.1 Pushing from a high place

E968.2 Striking by blunt or thrown object

E968.3 Hot liquid
Homicidal burns by scalding

E968.4 Criminal neglect
Abandonment of child, infant, or other helpless person with intent to injure or kill

E968.5 Transport vehicle
Being struck by other vehicle or run down with intent to injure
Pushed in front of, thrown from, or dragged by moving vehicle with intent to injure

E968.6 Air gun
BB gun
Pellet gun

● **E968.7 Human bite**

E968.8 Other specified means

E968.9 Unspecified means
Assassination (attempt) NOS   Manslaughter (nonaccidental)
Homicidal (attempt):   Murder (attempt) NOS
  injury NOS   Violence, non-accidental
  wound NOS

E969 Late effects of injury purposely inflicted by other person
Note: This category is to be used to indicate circumstances classifiable to E960-E968 as the cause of death or disability from late effects, which are themselves classifiable elsewhere. The "late effects" include conditions reported as such, or as sequelae which may occur at any time after the acute injury.

LEGAL INTERVENTION (E970-E978)

Includes: injuries inflicted by the police or other law-enforcing agents, including military on duty, in the course of arresting or attempting to arrest lawbreakers, suppressing disturbances, maintaining order, and other legal action
legal execution

Excludes: *injuries caused by civil insurrections (E990.0-E999)*

E970 Injury due to legal intervention by firearms
Gunshot wound   Injury by:
Injury by: rifle pellet or rubber bullet
  machine gun   shot NOS
  revolver

E971 Injury due to legal intervention by explosives
Injury by:
  dynamite
  explosive shell
  grenade
  mortar bomb

● Code new to this edition   ▲ Revision of existing code   ④ ⑤ Fourth or fifth digit required

E972 Injury due to legal intervention by gas
    Asphyxiation by gas
    Injury by tear gas
    Poisoning by gas

E973 Injury due to legal intervention by blunt object
    Hit, struck by:
        baton (nightstick)
        blunt object
        stave

E974 Injury due to legal intervention by cutting and piercing instrument
    Cut   Incised wound
    Injured by bayonet   Stab wound

E975 Injury due to legal intervention by other specified means
    Blow
    Manhandling

E976 Injury due to legal intervention by unspecified means

E977 Late effects of injuries due to legal intervention
    Note: This category is to be used to indicate circumstances classifiable to E970-E976 as the cause of death or disability from late effects, which are themselves classifiable elsewhere. The "late effects" include conditions reported as such, or as sequelae which may occur at any time after the acute injury due to legal intervention.

E978 Legal execution
    All executions performed at the behest of the judiciary or ruling authority [whether permanent or temporary] as:
    asphyxiation by gas   hanging
    beheading, decapitation   poisoning
       (by guillotine)   shooting
    capital punishment   other specified means
    electrocution

INJURY UNDETERMINED WHETHER ACCIDENTALLY OR PURPOSELY INFLICTED (E980-E989)

    Note: Categories E980-E989 are for use when it is unspecified or it cannot be determined whether the injuries are accidental (unintentional), suicide (attempted), or assault.

E980 Poisoning by solid or liquid substances, undetermined whether accidentally or purposely inflicted

E980.0 Analgesics, antipyretics, and antirheumatics

E980.1 Barbiturates

E980.2 Other sedatives and hypnotics

E980.3 Tranquilizers and other psychotropic agents

E980.4 Other specified drugs and medicinal substances

E980.5 Unspecified drug or medicinal substance

E980.6 Corrosive and caustic substances
    Poisoning, undetermined whether accidental or purposeful, by substances classifiable to E864

E980.7 Agricultural and horticultural chemical and pharmaceutical preparations other than plant foods and fertilizers

E980.8 Arsenic and its compounds

E980.9 Other and unspecified solid and liquid substances

E981 Poisoning by gases in domestic use, undetermined whether accidentally or purposely inflicted

E981.0 Gas distributed by pipeline

E981.1 Liquefied petroleum gas distributed in mobile containers

E981.8 Other utility gas

E982 Poisoning by other gases, undetermined whether accidentally or purposely inflicted

E982.0 Motor vehicle exhaust gas

E982.1 Other carbon monoxide

E982.8 Other specified gases and vapors

E982.9 Unspecified gases and vapors

Add 4th or 5th digit

Nonspecific code

Unspecified code

Manifestation code

E983 **Hanging, strangulation, or suffocation, undetermined whether accidentally or purposely inflicted**

    E983.0 **Hanging**

    E983.1 **Suffocation by plastic bag**

    E983.8 **Other specified means**

    E983.9 **Unspecified means**

E984 **Submersion [drowning], undetermined whether accidentally or purposely inflicted**

E985 **Injury by firearms, air guns and explosives, undetermined whether accidentally or purposely inflicted**

    E985.0 **Handgun**

    E985.1 **Shotgun**

    E985.2 **Hunting rifle**

    E985.3 **Military firearms**

    E985.4 **Other and unspecified firearm**

    E985.5 **Explosives**

    E985.6 **Air gun**
        BB gun
        Pellet gun

E986 **Injury by cutting and piercing instruments, undetermined whether accidentally or purposely inflicted**

E987 **Falling from high place, undetermined whether accidentally or purposely inflicted**

    E987.0 **Residential premises**

    E987.1 **Other man-made structures**

    E987.2 **Natural sites**

    E987.9 **Unspecified site**

E988 **Injury by other and unspecified means, undetermined whether accidentally or purposely inflicted**

    E988.0 **Jumping or lying before moving object**

    E988.1 **Burns, fire**

    E988.2 **Scald**

    E988.3 **Extremes of cold**

    E988.4 **Electrocution**

    E988.5 **Crashing of motor vehicle**

    E988.6 **Crashing of aircraft**

    E988.7 **Caustic substances, except poisoning**

    E988.8 **Other specified means**

    E988.9 **Unspecified means**

E989 **Late effects of injury, undetermined whether accidentally or purposely inflicted**

    Note: This category is to be used to indicate circumstances classifiable to E980-E988 as the cause of death or disability from late effects, which are themselves classifiable elsewhere. The "late effects" include conditions reported as such or as sequelae which may occur at any time after the acute injury, undetermined whether accidentally or purposely inflicted.

INJURY RESULTING FROM OPERATIONS OF WAR (E990-E999)

    Includes: injuries to military personnel and civilians caused by war and civil insurrections and occurring during the time of war and insurrection

    Excludes: *accidents during training of military personnel, manufacture of war material and transport, unless attributable to enemy action*

E990 **Injury due to war operations by fires and conflagrations**
    Includes: asphyxia, burns, or other injury originating from fire caused by a fire-producing device or indirectly by any conventional weapon

    E990.0 **From gasoline bomb**

    E990.9 **From other and unspecified source**

E991 **Injury due to war operations by bullets and fragments**

    E991.0 **Rubber bullets (rifle)**

    E991.1 **Pellets (rifle)**

● Code new to this edition   ▲ Revision of existing code   ④ ⑤ Fourth or fifth digit required

E991.2 Other bullets

Bullet [any, except rubber bullets and pellets]
carbine
machine gun
pistol
rifle
shotgun

E991.3 Antipersonnel bomb (fragments)

E991.9 Other and unspecified fragments

Fragments from:
artillery shell
bombs, except antipersonnel
grenade
guided missile

Fragments from:
land mine
rockets
shell
Shrapnel

E992 Injury due to war operations by explosion of marine weapons

Depth charge
Marine mines
Mine NOS, at sea or in harbor

Sea-based artillery shell
Torpedo
Underwater blast

E993 Injury due to war operations by other explosion

Accidental explosion of munitions
being used in war
Accidental explosion of own weapons
Air blast NOS
Blast NOS
Explosion NOS

Explosion of:
artillery shell
breech block
cannon block
mortar bomb
Injury by weapon burst

E994 Injury due to war operations by destruction of aircraft

Airplane:
burned
exploded
shot down

Crushed by falling airplane

E995 Injury due to war operations by other and unspecified forms of conventional warfare

Battle wounds
Bayonet injury

Drowned in war operations

E996 Injury due to war operations by nuclear weapons

Blast effects
Exposure to ionizing radiation from nuclear weapons
Fireball effects
Heat
Other direct and secondary effects of nuclear weapons

E997 Injury due to war operations by other forms of unconventional warfare

E997.0 Lasers

E997.1 Biological warfare

E997.2 Gases, fumes, and chemicals

E997.8 Other specified forms of unconventional warfare

E997.9 Unspecified form of unconventional warfare

E998 Injury due to war operations but occurring after cessation of hostilities

Injuries due to operations of war but occurring after cessation of hostilities by any means classifiable under E990-E997
Injuries by explosion of bombs or mines placed in the course of operations of war, if the explosion occurred after cessation of hostilities

E999 Late effect of injury due to war operations

Note: This category is to be used to indicate circumstances classifiable to E990-E998 as the cause of death or disability from late effects, which are themselves classifiable elsewhere. The "late effects" include conditions reported as such or as sequelae which may occur at any time after the acute injury, resulting from operations of war.

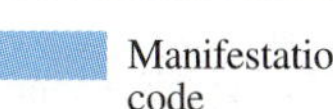

● Code new
to this edition

▲ Revision of
existing code

④ ⑤ Fourth or fifth
digit required

MORPHOLOGY OF NEOPLASMS

The World Health Organization has published an adaptation of the International Classification of Diseases for oncology (ICD-O). It contains a coded nomenclature for the morphology of neoplasms, which is reproduced here for those who wish to use it in conjunction with Chapter 2 of the *International Classification of Diseases, 9th Revision, Clinical Modification.*

The morphology code numbers consist of five digits; the first four identify the histological type of the neoplasm and the fifth indicates its behavior. The one-digit behavior code is as follows:

/0 Benign

/1 Uncertain whether benign or malignant
 Borderline malignancy

/2 Carcinoma in situ
 Intraepithelial
 Noninfiltrating
 Noninvasive

/3 Malignant, primary site

/6 Malignant, metastatic site
 Secondary site

/9 Malignant, uncertain whether primary or metastatic site

In the nomenclature below, the morphology code numbers include the behavior code appropriate to the histological type of neoplasm, but this behavior code should be changed if other reported information makes this necessary. For example, "chordoma (M9370/3)" is assumed to be malignant; the term "benign chordoma" should be coded M9370/0. Similarly, "superficial spreading adenocarcinoma (M8143/3)" described as "noninvasive" should be coded M8143/2 and "melanoma (M8720/3)" described as "secondary" should be coded M8720/6.

The following table shows the correspondence between the morphology code and the different sections of Chapter 2:

Morphology code Histology/Behavior			ICD-9-CM Chapter 2
Any	0	210-229	Benign neoplasms
M8000-M8004	1	239	Neoplasms of unspecified nature
M8010+	1	235-238	Neoplasms of uncertain behavior
Any	2	230-234	Carcinoma in situ
Any	3	140-195 200-208	Malignant neoplasms, stated or presumed to be primary
Any	6	196-198	Malignant neoplasms, stated or presumed to be secondary

The ICD-O behavior digit /9 is inapplicable in an ICD context, since all malignant neoplasms are presumed to be primary (/3) or secondary (/6) according to other information on the medical record.

Only the first-listed term of the full ICD-O morphology nomenclature appears against each code number in the list below. The ICD-9-CM Alphabetical Index (Volume 2), however, includes all the ICD-O synonyms as well as a number of other morphological names still likely to be encountered on medical records but omitted from ICD-O as outdated or otherwise undesirable.

A coding difficulty sometimes arises where a morphological diagnosis contains two qualifying adjectives that have different code numbers. An example is "transitional cell epidermoid carcinoma." "Transitional cell carcinoma NOS" is M8120/3 and "epidermoid carcinoma NOS" is M8070/3. In such circumstances, the higher number (M8120/3 in this example) should be used, as it is usually more specific.

CODED NOMENCLATURE FOR MORPHOLOGY OF NEOPLASMS

M800 **Neoplasms NOS**
M8000/0 *Neoplasm, benign*
M8000/1 *Neoplasm, uncertain whether benign or malignant*
M8000/3 *Neoplasm, malignant*
M8000/6 *Neoplasm, metastatic*
M8000/9 *Neoplasm, malignant, uncertain whether primary or metastatic*
M8001/0 *Tumor cells, benign*
M8001/1 *Tumor cells, uncertain whether benign or malignant*
M8001/3 *Tumor cells, malignant*
M8002/3 *Malignant tumor, small cell type*
M8003/3 *Malignant tumor, giant cell type*
M8004/3 *Malignant tumor, fusiform cell type*

M801-M804 Epithelial neoplasms NOS
M8010/0 *Epithelial tumor, benign*
M8010/2 *Carcinoma in situ NOS*
M8010/3 *Carcinoma NOS*
M8010/6 *Carcinoma, metastatic NOS*
M8010/9 *Carcinomatosis*
M8011/0 *Epithelioma, benign*
M8011/3 *Epithelioma, malignant*
M8012/3 *Large cell carcinoma NOS*
M8020/3 *Carcinoma, undifferentiated type NOS*
M8021/3 *Carcinoma, anaplastic type NOS*
M8022/3 *Pleomorphic carcinoma*
M8030/3 *Giant cell and spindle cell carcinoma*
M8031/3 *Giant cell carcinoma*
M8032/3 *Spindle cell carcinoma*
M8033/3 *Pseudosarcomatous carcinoma*
M8034/3 *Polygonal cell carcinoma*
M8035/3 *Spheroidal cell carcinoma*
M8040/1 *Tumorlet*
M8041/3 *Small cell carcinoma NOS*
M8042/3 *Oat cell carcinoma*
M8043/3 *Small cell carcinoma, fusiform cell type*

M805-M808 Papillary and squamous cell neoplasms
M8050/0 *Papilloma NOS (except Papilloma of urinary bladder M8120/1)*
M8050/2 *Papillary carcinoma in situ*
M8050/3 *Papillary carcinoma NOS*
M8051/0 *Verrucous papilloma*
M8051/3 *Verrucous carcinoma NOS*
M8052/0 *Squamous cell papilloma*
M8052/3 *Papillary squamous cell carcinoma*
M8053/0 *Inverted papilloma*
M8060/0 *Papillomatosis NOS*
M8070/2 *Squamous cell carcinoma in situ NOS*
M8070/3 *Squamous cell carcinoma NOS*
M8070/6 *Squamous cell carcinoma, metastatic NOS*
M8071/3 *Squamous cell carcinoma, keratinizing type NOS*
M8072/3 *Squamous cell carcinoma, large cell, nonkeratinizing type*
M8073/3 *Squamous cell carcinoma, small cell, nonkeratinizing type*
M8074/3 *Squamous cell carcinoma, spindle cell type*
M8075/3 *Adenoid squamous cell carcinoma*
M8076/2 *Squamous cell carcinoma in situ with questionable stromal invasion*
M8076/3 *Squamous cell carcinoma, microinvasive*
M8080/2 *Queyrat's erythroplasia*
M8081/2 *Bowen's disease*
M8082/3 *Lymphoepithelial carcinoma*

M809-M811 Basal cell neoplasms
M8090/1 *Basal cell tumor*
M8090/3 *Basal cell carcinoma NOS*
M8091/3 *Multicentric basal cell carcinoma*
M8092/3 *Basal cell carcinoma, morphea type*
M8093/3 *Basal cell carcinoma, fibroepithelial type*
M8094/3 *Basosquamous carcinoma*
M8095/3 *Metatypical carcinoma*
M8096/0 *Intraepidermal epithelioma of Jadassohn*
M8100/0 *Trichoepithelioma*
M8101/0 *Trichofolliculoma*

M8102/0	*Tricholemmoma*
M8110/0	*Pilomatrixoma*

M812-M813 Transitional cell papillomas and carcinomas

M8120/0	*Transitional cell papilloma NOS*
M8120/1	*Urothelial papilloma*
M8120/2	*Transitional cell carcinoma in situ*
M8120/3	*Transitional cell carcinoma NOS*
M8121/0	*Schneiderian papilloma*
M8121/1	*Transitional cell papilloma, inverted type*
M8121/3	*Schneiderian carcinoma*
M8122/3	*Transitional cell carcinoma, spindle cell type*
M8123/3	*Basaloid carcinoma*
M8124/3	*Cloacogenic carcinoma*
M8130/3	*Papillary transitional cell carcinoma*

M814-M838 Adenomas and adenocarcinomas

M8140/0	*Adenoma NOS*
M8140/1	*Bronchial adenoma NOS*
M8140/2	*Adenocarcinoma in situ*
M8140/3	*Adenocarcinoma NOS*
M8140/6	*Adenocarcinoma, metastatic NOS*
M8141/3	*Scirrhous adenocarcinoma*
M8142/3	*Linitis plastica*
M8143/3	*Superficial spreading adenocarcinoma*
M8144/3	*Adenocarcinoma, intestinal type*
M8145/3	*Carcinoma, diffuse type*
M8146/0	*Monomorphic adenoma*
M8147/0	*Basal cell adenoma*
M8150/0	*Islet cell adenoma*
M8150/3	*Islet cell carcinoma*
M8151/0	*Insulinoma NOS*
M8151/3	*Insulinoma, malignant*
M8152/0	*Glucagonoma NOS*
M8152/3	*Glucagonoma, malignant*
M8153/1	*Gastrinoma NOS*
M8153/3	*Gastrinoma, malignant*
M8154/3	*Mixed islet cell and exocrine adenocarcinoma*
M8160/0	*Bile duct adenoma*
M8160/3	*Cholangiocarcinoma*
M8161/0	*Bile duct cystadenoma*
M8161/3	*Bile duct cystadenocarcinoma*
M8170/0	*Liver cell adenoma*
M8170/3	*Hepatocellular carcinoma NOS*
M8180/0	*Hepatocholangioma, benign*
M8180/3	*Combined hepatocellular carcinoma and cholangiocarcinoma*
M8190/0	*Trabecular adenoma*
M8190/3	*Trabecular adenocarcinoma*
M8191/0	*Embryonal adenoma*
M8200/0	*Eccrine dermal cylindroma*
M8200/3	*Adenoid cystic carcinoma*
M8201/3	*Cribriform carcinoma*
M8210/0	*Adenomatous polyp NOS*
M8210/3	*Adenocarcinoma in adenomatous polyp*
M8211/0	*Tubular adenoma NOS*
M8211/3	*Tubular adenocarcinoma*
M8220/0	*Adenomatous polyposis coli*
M8220/3	*Adenocarcinoma in adenomatous polyposis coli*
M8221/0	*Multiple adenomatous polyps*
M8230/3	*Solid carcinoma NOS*
M8231/3	*Carcinoma simplex*
M8240/1	*Carcinoid tumor NOS*
M8240/3	*Carcinoid tumor, malignant*
M8241/1	*Carcinoid tumor, argentaffin NOS*
M8241/3	*Carcinoid tumor, argentaffin, malignant*
M8242/1	*Carcinoid tumor, nonargentaffin NOS*
M8242/3	*Carcinoid tumor, nonargentaffin, malignant*
M8243/3	*Mucocarcinoid tumor, malignant*
M8244/3	*Composite carcinoid*
M8250/1	*Pulmonary adenomatosis*
M8250/3	*Bronchiolo-alveolar adenocarcinoma*
M8251/0	*Alveolar adenoma*

M8251/3	*Alveolar adenocarcinoma*
M8260/0	*Papillary adenoma NOS*
M8260/3	*Papillary adenocarcinoma NOS*
M8261/1	*Villous adenoma NOS*
M8261/3	*Adenocarcinoma in villous adenoma*
M8262/3	*Villous adenocarcinoma*
M8263/0	*Tubulovillous adenoma*
M8270/0	*Chromophobe adenoma*
M8270/3	*Chromophobe carcinoma*
M8280/0	*Acidophil adenoma*
M8280/3	*Acidophil carcinoma*
M8281/0	*Mixed acidophil-basophil adenoma*
M8281/3	*Mixed acidophil-basophil carcinoma*
M8290/0	*Oxyphilic adenoma*
M8290/3	*Oxyphilic adenocarcinoma*
M8300/0	*Basophil adenoma*
M8300/3	*Basophil carcinoma*
M8310/0	*Clear cell adenoma*
M8310/3	*Clear cell adenocarcinoma NOS*
M8311/1	*Hypernephroid tumor*
M8312/3	*Renal cell carcinoma*
M8313/0	*Clear cell adenofibroma*
M8320/3	*Granular cell carcinoma*
M8321/0	*Chief cell adenoma*
M8322/0	*Water-clear cell adenoma*
M8322/3	*Water-clear cell adenocarcinoma*
M8323/0	*Mixed cell adenoma*
M8323/3	*Mixed cell adenocarcinoma*
M8324/0	*Lipoadenoma*
M8330/0	*Follicular adenoma*
M8330/3	*Follicular adenocarcinoma NOS*
M8331/3	*Follicular adenocarcinoma, well differentiated type*
M8332/3	*Follicular adenocarcinoma, trabecular type*
M8333/0	*Microfollicular adenoma*
M8334/0	*Macrofollicular adenoma*
M8340/3	*Papillary and follicular adenocarcinoma*
M8350/3	*Nonencapsulated sclerosing carcinoma*
M8360/1	*Multiple endocrine adenomas*
M8361/1	*Juxtaglomerular tumor*
M8370/0	*Adrenal cortical adenoma NOS*
M8370/3	*Adrenal cortical carcinoma*
M8371/0	*Adrenal cortical adenoma, compact cell type*
M8372/0	*Adrenal cortical adenoma, heavily pigmented variant*
M8373/0	*Adrenal cortical adenoma, clear cell type*
M8374/0	*Adrenal cortical adenoma, glomerulosa cell type*
M8375/0	*Adrenal cortical adenoma, mixed cell type*
M8380/0	*Endometrioid adenoma NOS*
M8380/1	*Endometrioid adenoma, borderline malignancy*
M8380/3	*Endometrioid carcinoma*
M8381/0	*Endometrioid adenofibroma NOS*
M8381/1	*Endometrioid adenofibroma, borderline malignancy*
M8381/3	*Endometrioid adenofibroma, malignant*

M839-M842 Adnexal and skin appendage neoplasms

M8390/0	*Skin appendage adenoma*
M8390/3	*Skin appendage carcinoma*
M8400/0	*Sweat gland adenoma*
M8400/1	*Sweat gland tumor NOS*
M8400/3	*Sweat gland adenocarcinoma*
M8401/0	*Apocrine adenoma*
M8401/3	*Apocrine adenocarcinoma*
M8402/0	*Eccrine acrospiroma*
M8403/0	*Eccrine spiradenoma*
M8404/0	*Hidrocystoma*
M8405/0	*Papillary hydradenoma*
M8406/0	*Papillary syringadenoma*
M8407/0	*Syringoma NOS*
M8410/0	*Sebaceous adenoma*
M8410/3	*Sebaceous adenocarcinoma*
M8420/0	*Ceruminous adenoma*
M8420/3	*Ceruminous adenocarcinoma*

M843	**Mucoepidermoid neoplasms**
M8430/1	*Mucoepidermoid tumor*
M8430/3	*Mucoepidermoid carcinoma*

M844-M849	**Cystic, mucinous, and serous neoplasms**
M8440/0	*Cystadenoma NOS*
M8440/3	*Cystadenocarcinoma NOS*
M8441/0	*Serous cystadenoma NOS*
M8441/1	*Serous cystadenoma, borderline malignancy*
M8441/3	*Serous cystadenocarcinoma NOS*
M8450/0	*Papillary cystadenoma NOS*
M8450/1	*Papillary cystadenoma, borderline malignancy*
M8450/3	*Papillary cystadenocarcinoma NOS*
M8460/0	*Papillary serous cystadenoma NOS*
M8460/1	*Papillary serous cystadenoma, borderline malignancy*
M8460/3	*Papillary serous cystadenocarcinoma*
M8461/0	*Serous surface papilloma NOS*
M8461/1	*Serous surface papilloma, borderline malignancy*
M8461/3	*Serous surface papillary carcinoma*
M8470/0	*Mucinous cystadenoma NOS*
M8470/1	*Mucinous cystadenoma, borderline malignancy*
M8470/3	*Mucinous cystadenocarcinoma NOS*
M8471/0	*Papillary mucinous cystadenoma NOS*
M8471/1	*Papillary mucinous cystadenoma, borderline malignancy*
M8471/3	*Papillary mucinous cystadenocarcinoma*
M8480/0	*Mucinous adenoma*
M8480/3	*Mucinous adenocarcinoma*
M8480/6	*Pseudomyxoma peritonei*
M8481/3	*Mucin-producing adenocarcinoma*
M8490/3	*Signet ring cell carcinoma*
M8490/6	*Metastatic signet ring cell carcinoma*

M850-M854	**Ductal, lobular, and medullary neoplasms**
M8500/2	*Intraductal carcinoma, noninfiltrating NOS*
M8500/3	*Infiltrating duct carcinoma*
M8501/2	*Comedocarcinoma, noninfiltrating*
M8501/3	*Comedocarcinoma NOS*
M8502/3	*Juvenile carcinoma of the breast*
M8503/0	*Intraductal papilloma*
M8503/2	*Noninfiltrating intraductal papillary adenocarcinoma*
M8504/0	*Intracystic papillary adenoma*
M8504/2	*Noninfiltrating intracystic carcinoma*
M8505/0	*Intraductal papillomatosis NOS*
M8506/0	*Subareolar duct papillomatosis*
M8510/3	*Medullary carcinoma NOS*
M8511/3	*Medullary carcinoma with amyloid stroma*
M8512/3	*Medullary carcinoma with lymphoid stroma*
M8520/2	*Lobular carcinoma in situ*
M8520/3	*Lobular carcinoma NOS*
M8521/3	*Infiltrating ductular carcinoma*
M8530/3	*Inflammatory carcinoma*
M8540/3	*Paget's disease, mammary*
M8541/3	*Paget's disease and infiltrating duct carcinoma of breast*
M8542/3	*Paget's disease, extramammary (except Paget's disease of bone)*

M855	**Acinar cell neoplasms**
M8550/0	*Acinar cell adenoma*
M8550/1	*Acinar cell tumor*
M8550/3	*Acinar cell carcinoma*

M856-M858	**Complex epithelial neoplasms**
M8560/3	*Adenosquamous carcinoma*
M8561/0	*Adenolymphoma*
M8570/3	*Adenocarcinoma with squamous metaplasia*
M8571/3	*Adenocarcinoma with cartilaginous and osseous metaplasia*
M8572/3	*Adenocarcinoma with spindle cell metaplasia*
M8573/3	*Adenocarcinoma with apocrine metaplasia*
M8580/0	*Thymoma, benign*
M8580/3	*Thymoma, malignant*

M859-M867	**Specialized gonadal neoplasms**
M8590/1	*Sex cord-stromal tumor*
M8600/0	*Thecoma NOS*
M8600/3	*Theca cell carcinoma*

M8610/0	*Luteoma NOS*
M8620/1	*Granulosa cell tumor NOS*
M8620/3	*Granulosa cell tumor, malignant*
M8621/1	*Granulosa cell-theca cell tumor*
M8630/0	*Androblastoma, benign*
M8630/1	*Androblastoma NOS*
M8630/3	*Androblastoma, malignant*
M8631/0	*Sertoli-Leydig cell tumor*
M8632/1	*Gynandroblastoma*
M8640/0	*Tubular androblastoma NOS*
M8640/3	*Sertoli cell carcinoma*
M8641/0	*Tubular androblastoma with lipid storage*
M8650/0	*Leydig cell tumor, benign*
M8650/1	*Leydig cell tumor NOS*
M8650/3	*Leydig cell tumor, malignant*
M8660/0	*Hilar cell tumor*
M8670/0	*Lipid cell tumor of ovary*
M8671/0	*Adrenal rest tumor*

M868-M871 Paragangliomas and glomus tumors

M8680/1	*Paraganglioma NOS*
M8680/3	*Paraganglioma, malignant*
M8681/1	*Sympathetic paraganglioma*
M8682/1	*Parasympathetic paraganglioma*
M8690/1	*Glomus jugulare tumor*
M8691/1	*Aortic body tumor*
M8692/1	*Carotid body tumor*
M8693/1	*Extra-adrenal paraganglioma NOS*
M8693/3	*Extra-adrenal paraganglioma, malignant*
M8700/0	*Pheochromocytoma NOS*
M8700/3	*Pheochromocytoma, malignant*
M8710/3	*Glomangiosarcoma*
M8711/0	*Glomus tumor*
M8712/0	*Glomangioma*

M872-M879 Nevi and melanomas

M8720/0	*Pigmented nevus NOS*
M8720/3	*Malignant melanoma NOS*
M8721/3	*Nodular melanoma*
M8722/0	*Balloon cell nevus*
M8722/3	*Balloon cell melanoma*
M8723/0	*Halo nevus*
M8724/0	*Fibrous papule of the nose*
M8725/0	*Neuronevus*
M8726/0	*Magnocellular nevus*
M8730/0	*Nonpigmented nevus*
M8730/3	*Amelanotic melanoma*
M8740/0	*Junctional nevus*
M8740/3	*Malignant melanoma in junctional nevus*
M8741/2	*Precancerous melanosis NOS*
M8741/3	*Malignant melanoma in precancerous melanosis*
M8742/2	*Hutchinson's melanotic freckle*
M8742/3	*Malignant melanoma in Hutchinson's melanotic freckle*
M8743/3	*Superficial spreading melanoma*
M8750/0	*Intradermal nevus*
M8760/0	*Compound nevus*
M8761/1	*Giant pigmented nevus*
M8761/3	*Malignant melanoma in giant pigmented nevus*
M8770/0	*Epithelioid and spindle cell nevus*
M8771/3	*Epithelioid cell melanoma*
M8772/3	*Spindle cell melanoma NOS*
M8773/3	*Spindle cell melanoma, type A*
M8774/3	*Spindle cell melanoma, type B*
M8775/3	*Mixed epithelioid and spindle cell melanoma*
M8780/0	*Blue nevus NOS*
M8780/3	*Blue nevus, malignant*
M8790/0	*Cellular blue nevus*

M880 Soft tissue tumors and sarcomas NOS

M8800/0	*Soft tissue tumor, benign*
M8800/3	*Sarcoma NOS*
M8800/9	*Sarcomatosis NOS*
M8801/3	*Spindle cell sarcoma*

M8802/3   *Giant cell sarcoma (except of bone M9250/3)*
M8803/3   *Small cell sarcoma*
M8804/3   *Epithelioid cell sarcoma*

M881-M883 Fibromatous neoplasms
M8810/0   *Fibroma NOS*
M8810/3   *Fibrosarcoma NOS*
M8811/0   *Fibromyxoma*
M8811/3   *Fibromyxosarcoma*
M8812/0   *Periosteal fibroma*
M8812/3   *Periosteal fibrosarcoma*
M8813/0   *Fascial fibroma*
M8813/3   *Fascial fibrosarcoma*
M8814/3   *Infantile fibrosarcoma*
M8820/0   *Elastofibroma*
M8821/1   *Aggressive fibromatosis*
M8822/1   *Abdominal fibromatosis*
M8823/1   *Desmoplastic fibroma*
M8830/0   *Fibrous histiocytoma NOS*
M8830/1   *Atypical fibrous histiocytoma*
M8830/3   *Fibrous histiocytoma, malignant*
M8831/0   *Fibroxanthoma NOS*
M8831/1   *Atypical fibroxanthoma*
M8831/3   *Fibroxanthoma, malignant*
M8832/0   *Dermatofibroma NOS*
M8832/1   *Dermatofibroma protuberans*
M8832/3   *Dermatofibrosarcoma NOS*

M884   Myxomatous neoplasms
M8840/0   *Myxoma NOS*
M8840/3   *Myxosarcoma*

M885-M888 Lipomatous neoplasms
M8850/0   *Lipoma NOS*
M8850/3   *Liposarcoma NOS*
M8851/0   *Fibrolipoma*
M8851/3   *Liposarcoma, well differentiated type*
M8852/0   *Fibromyxolipoma*
M8852/3   *Myxoid liposarcoma*
M8853/3   *Round cell liposarcoma*
M8854/3   *Pleomorphic liposarcoma*
M8855/3   *Mixed type liposarcoma*
M8856/0   *Intramuscular lipoma*
M8857/0   *Spindle cell lipoma*
M8860/0   *Angiomyolipoma*
M8860/3   *Angiomyoliposarcoma*
M8861/0   *Angiolipoma NOS*
M8861/1   *Angiolipoma, infiltrating*
M8870/0   *Myelolipoma*
M8880/0   *Hibernoma*
M8881/0   *Lipoblastomatosis*

M889-M892 Myomatous neoplasms
M8890/0   *Leiomyoma NOS*
M8890/1   *Intravascular leiomyomatosis*
M8890/3   *Leiomyosarcoma NOS*
M8891/1   *Epithelioid leiomyoma*
M8891/3   *Epithelioid leiomyosarcoma*
M8892/1   *Cellular leiomyoma*
M8893/0   *Bizarre leiomyoma*
M8894/0   *Angiomyoma*
M8894/3   *Angiomyosarcoma*
M8895/0   *Myoma*
M8895/3   *Myosarcoma*
M8900/0   *Rhabdomyoma NOS*
M8900/3   *Rhabdomyosarcoma NOS*
M8901/3   *Pleomorphic rhabdomyosarcoma*
M8902/3   *Mixed type rhabdomyosarcoma*
M8903/0   *Fetal rhabdomyoma*
M8904/0   *Adult rhabdomyoma*
M8910/3   *Embryonal rhabdomyosarcoma*
M8920/3   *Alveolar rhabdomyosarcoma*

M893-M899 Complex mixed and stromal neoplasms
M8930/3 *Endometrial stromal sarcoma*
M8931/1 *Endolymphatic stromal myosis*
M8932/0 *Adenomyoma*
M8940/0 *Pleomorphic adenoma*
M8940/3 *Mixed tumor, malignant NOS*
M8950/3 *Mullerian mixed tumor*
M8951/3 *Mesodermal mixed tumor*
M8960/1 *Mesoblastic nephroma*
M8960/3 *Nephroblastoma NOS*
M8961/3 *Epithelial nephroblastoma*
M8962/3 *Mesenchymal nephroblastoma*
M8970/3 *Hepatoblastoma*
M8980/3 *Carcinosarcoma NOS*
M8981/3 *Carcinosarcoma, embryonal type*
M8982/0 *Myoepithelioma*
M8990/0 *Mesenchymoma, benign*
M8990/1 *Mesenchymoma, NOS*
M8990/3 *Mesenchymoma, malignant*
M8991/3 *Embryonal sarcoma*

M900-M903 Fibroepithelial neoplasms
M9000/0 *Brenner tumor NOS*
M9000/1 *Brenner tumor, borderline malignancy*
M9000/3 *Brenner tumor, malignant*
M9010/0 *Fibroadenoma NOS*
M9011/0 *Intracanalicular fibroadenoma NOS*
M9012/0 *Pericanalicular fibroadenoma*
M9013/0 *Adenofibroma NOS*
M9014/0 *Serous adenofibroma*
M9015/0 *Mucinous adenofibroma*
M9020/0 *Cellular intracanalicular fibroadenoma*
M9020/1 *Cystosarcoma phyllodes NOS*
M9020/3 *Cystosarcoma phyllodes, malignant*
M9030/0 *Juvenile fibroadenoma*

M904 Synovial neoplasms
M9040/0 *Synovioma, benign*
M9040/3 *Synovial sarcoma NOS*
M9041/3 *Synovial sarcoma, spindle cell type*
M9042/3 *Synovial sarcoma, epithelioid cell type*
M9043/3 *Synovial sarcoma, biphasic type*
M9044/3 *Clear cell sarcoma of tendons and aponeuroses*

M905 Mesothelial neoplasms
M9050/0 *Mesothelioma, benign*
M9050/3 *Mesothelioma, malignant*
M9051/0 *Fibrous mesothelioma, benign*
M9051/3 *Fibrous mesothelioma, malignant*
M9052/0 *Epithelioid mesothelioma, benign*
M9052/3 *Epithelioid mesothelioma, malignant*
M9053/0 *Mesothelioma, biphasic type, benign*
M9053/3 *Mesothelioma, biphasic type, malignant*
M9054/0 *Adenomatoid tumor NOS*

M906-M909 Germ cell neoplasms
M9060/3 *Dysgerminoma*
M9061/3 *Seminoma NOS*
M9062/3 *Seminoma, anaplastic type*
M9063/3 *Spermatocytic seminoma*
M9064/3 *Germinoma*
M9070/3 *Embryonal carcinoma NOS*
M9071/3 *Endodermal sinus tumor*
M9072/3 *Polyembryoma*
M9073/1 *Gonadoblastoma*
M9080/0 *Teratoma, benign*
M9080/1 *Teratoma NOS*
M9080/3 *Teratoma, malignant NOS*
M9081/3 *Teratocarcinoma*
M9082/3 *Malignant teratoma, undifferentiated type*
M9083/3 *Malignant teratoma, intermediate type*
M9084/0 *Dermoid cyst*
M9084/3 *Dermoid cyst with malignant transformation*

M9090/0	*Struma ovarii NOS*
M9090/3	*Struma ovarii, malignant*
M9091/1	*Strumal carcinoid*

M910   **Trophoblastic neoplasms**
M9100/0	*Hydatidiform mole NOS*
M9100/1	*Invasive hydatidiform mole*
M9100/3	*Choriocarcinoma*
M9101/3	*Choriocarcinoma combined with teratoma*
M9102/3	*Malignant teratoma, trophoblastic*

M911   **Mesonephromas**
M9110/0	*Mesonephroma, benign*
M9110/1	*Mesonephric tumor*
M9110/3	*Mesonephroma, malignant*
M9111/1	*Endosalpingioma*

M912-M916   **Blood vessel tumors**
M9120/0	*Hemangioma NOS*
M9120/3	*Hemangiosarcoma*
M9121/0	*Cavernous hemangioma*
M9122/0	*Venous hemangioma*
M9123/0	*Racemose hemangioma*
M9124/3	*Kupffer cell sarcoma*
M9130/0	*Hemangioendothelioma, benign*
M9130/1	*Hemangioendothelioma NOS*
M9130/3	*Hemangioendothelioma, malignant*
M9131/0	*Capillary hemangioma*
M9132/0	*Intramuscular hemangioma*
M9140/3	*Kaposi's sarcoma*
M9141/0	*Angiokeratoma*
M9142/0	*Verrucous keratotic hemangioma*
M9150/0	*Hemangiopericytoma, benign*
M9150/1	*Hemangiopericytoma NOS*
M9150/3	*Hemangiopericytoma, malignant*
M9160/0	*Angiofibroma NOS*
M9161/1	*Hemangioblastoma*

M917   **Lymphatic vessel tumors**
M9170/0	*Lymphangioma NOS*
M9170/3	*Lymphangiosarcoma*
M9171/0	*Capillary lymphangioma*
M9172/0	*Cavernous lymphangioma*
M9173/0	*Cystic lymphangioma*
M9174/0	*Lymphangiomyoma*
M9174/1	*Lymphangiomyomatosis*
M9175/0	*Hemolymphangioma*

M918-M920   **Osteomas and osteosarcomas**
M9180/0	*Osteoma NOS*
M9180/3	*Osteosarcoma NOS*
M9181/3	*Chondroblastic osteosarcoma*
M9182/3	*Fibroblastic osteosarcoma*
M9183/3	*Telangiectatic osteosarcoma*
M9184/3	*Osteosarcoma in Paget's disease of bone*
M9190/3	*Juxtacortical osteosarcoma*
M9191/0	*Osteoid osteoma NOS*
M9200/0	*Osteoblastoma*

M921-M924   **Chondromatous neoplasms**
M9210/0	*Osteochondroma*
M9210/1	*Osteochondromatosis NOS*
M9220/0	*Chondroma NOS*
M9220/1	*Chondromatosis NOS*
M9220/3	*Chondrosarcoma NOS*
M9221/0	*Juxtacortical chondroma*
M9221/3	*Juxtacortical chondrosarcoma*
M9230/0	*Chondroblastoma NOS*
M9230/3	*Chondroblastoma, malignant*
M9240/3	*Mesenchymal chondrosarcoma*
M9241/0	*Chondromyxoid fibroma*

M925   **Giant cell tumors**
| M9250/1 | *Giant cell tumor of bone NOS* |
| M9250/3 | *Giant cell tumor of bone, malignant* |

M9251/1	*Giant cell tumor of soft parts NOS*
M9251/3	*Malignant giant cell tumor of soft parts*

M926 **Miscellaneous bone tumors**
M9260/3   *Ewing's sarcoma*
M9261/3   *Adamantinoma of long bones*
M9262/0   *Ossifying fibroma*

M927-M934 Odontogenic tumors
M9270/0   *Odontogenic tumor, benign*
M9270/1   *Odontogenic tumor NOS*
M9270/3   *Odontogenic tumor, malignant*
M9271/0   *Dentinoma*
M9272/0   *Cementoma NOS*
M9273/0   *Cementoblastoma, benign*
M9274/0   *Cementifying fibroma*
M9275/0   *Gigantiform cementoma*
M9280/0   *Odontoma NOS*
M9281/0   *Compound odontoma*
M9282/0   *Complex odontoma*
M9290/0   *Ameloblastic fibro-odontoma*
M9290/3   *Ameloblastic odontosarcoma*
M9300/0   *Adenomatoid odontogenic tumor*
M9301/0   *Calcifying odontogenic cyst*
M9310/0   *Ameloblastoma NOS*
M9310/3   *Ameloblastoma, malignant*
M9311/0   *Odontoameloblastoma*
M9312/0   *Squamous odontogenic tumor*
M9320/0   *Odontogenic myxoma*
M9321/0   *Odontogenic fibroma NOS*
M9330/0   *Ameloblastic fibroma*
M9330/3   *Ameloblastic fibrosarcoma*
M9340/0   *Calcifying epithelial odontogenic tumor*

M935-M937 Miscellaneous tumors
M9350/1   *Craniopharyngioma*
M9360/1   *Pinealoma*
M9361/1   *Pineocytoma*
M9362/3   *Pineoblastoma*
M9363/0   *Melanotic neuroectodermal tumor*
M9370/3   *Chordoma*

M938-M948 Gliomas
M9380/3   *Glioma, malignant*
M9381/3   *Gliomatosis cerebri*
M9382/3   *Mixed glioma*
M9383/1   *Subependymal glioma*
M9384/1   *Subependymal giant cell astrocytoma*
M9390/0   *Choroid plexus papilloma NOS*
M9390/3   *Choroid plexus papilloma, malignant*
M9391/3   *Ependymoma NOS*
M9392/3   *Ependymoma, anaplastic type*
M9393/1   *Papillary ependymoma*
M9394/1   *Myxopapillary ependymoma*
M9400/3   *Astrocytoma NOS*
M9401/3   *Astrocytoma, anaplastic type*
M9410/3   *Protoplasmic astrocytoma*
M9411/3   *Gemistocytic astrocytoma*
M9420/3   *Fibrillary astrocytoma*
M9421/3   *Pilocytic astrocytoma*
M9422/3   *Spongioblastoma NOS*
M9423/3   *Spongioblastoma polare*
M9430/3   *Astroblastoma*
M9440/3   *Glioblastoma NOS*
M9441/3   *Giant cell glioblastoma*
M9442/3   *Glioblastoma with sarcomatous component*
M9443/3   *Primitive polar spongioblastoma*
M9450/3   *Oligodendroglioma NOS*
M9451/3   *Oligodendroglioma, anaplastic type*
M9460/3   *Oligodendroblastoma*
M9470/3   *Medulloblastoma NOS*
M9471/3   *Desmoplastic medulloblastoma*
M9472/3   *Medullomyoblastoma*

M9480/3	*Cerebellar sarcoma NOS*
M9481/3	*Monstrocellular sarcoma*

M949-M952 Neuroepitheliomatous neoplasms

M9490/0	*Ganglioneuroma*
M9490/3	*Ganglioneuroblastoma*
M9491/0	*Ganglioneuromatosis*
M9500/3	*Neuroblastoma NOS*
M9501/3	*Medulloepithelioma NOS*
M9502/3	*Teratoid medulloepithelioma*
M9503/3	*Neuroepithelioma NOS*
M9504/3	*Spongioneuroblastoma*
M9505/1	*Ganglioglioma*
M9506/0	*Neurocytoma*
M9507/0	*Pacinian tumor*
M9510/3	*Retinoblastoma NOS*
M9511/3	*Retinoblastoma, differentiated type*
M9512/3	*Retinoblastoma, undifferentiated type*
M9520/3	*Olfactory neurogenic tumor*
M9521/3	*Esthesioneurocytoma*
M9522/3	*Esthesioneuroblastoma*
M9523/3	*Esthesioneuroepithelioma*

M953 Meningiomas

M9530/0	*Meningioma NOS*
M9530/1	*Meningiomatosis NOS*
M9530/3	*Meningioma, malignant*
M9531/0	*Meningotheliomatous meningioma*
M9532/0	*Fibrous meningioma*
M9533/0	*Psammomatous meningioma*
M9534/0	*Angiomatous meningioma*
M9535/0	*Hemangioblastic meningioma*
M9536/0	*Hemangiopericytic meningioma*
M9537/0	*Transitional meningioma*
M9538/1	*Papillary meningioma*
M9539/3	*Meningeal sarcomatosis*

M954-M957 Nerve sheath tumor

M9540/0	*Neurofibroma NOS*
M9540/1	*Neurofibromatosis NOS*
M9540/3	*Neurofibrosarcoma*
M9541/0	*Melanotic neurofibroma*
M9550/0	*Plexiform neurofibroma*
M9560/0	*Neurilemmoma NOS*
M9560/1	*Neurinomatosis*
M9560/3	*Neurilemmoma, malignant*
M9570/0	*Neuroma NOS*

M958 Granular cell tumors and alveolar soft part sarcoma

M9580/0	*Granular cell tumor NOS*
M9580/3	*Granular cell tumor, malignant*
M9581/3	*Alveolar soft part sarcoma*

M959-M963 Lymphomas, NOS or diffuse

M9590/0	*Lymphomatous tumor, benign*
M9590/3	*Malignant lymphoma NOS*
M9591/3	*Malignant lymphoma, non Hodgkin's type*
M9600/3	*Malignant lymphoma, undifferentiated cell type NOS*
M9601/3	*Malignant lymphoma, stem cell type*
M9602/3	*Malignant lymphoma, convoluted cell type NOS*
M9610/3	*Lymphosarcoma NOS*
M9611/3	*Malignant lymphoma, lymphoplasmacytoid type*
M9612/3	*Malignant lymphoma, immunoblastic type*
M9613/3	*Malignant lymphoma, mixed lymphocytic-histiocytic NOS*
M9614/3	*Malignant lymphoma, centroblastic-centrocytic, diffuse*
M9615/3	*Malignant lymphoma, follicular center cell NOS*
M9620/3	*Malignant lymphoma, lymphocytic, well differentiated NOS*
M9621/3	*Malignant lymphoma, lymphocytic, intermediate differentiation NOS*
M9622/3	*Malignant lymphoma, centrocytic*
M9623/3	*Malignant lymphoma, follicular center cell, cleaved NOS*
M9630/3	*Malignant lymphoma, lymphocytic, poorly differentiated NOS*
M9631/3	*Prolymphocytic lymphosarcoma*
M9632/3	*Malignant lymphoma, centroblastic type NOS*
M9633/3	*Malignant lymphoma, follicular center cell, noncleaved NOS*

M964	**Reticulosarcomas**
M9640/3	*Reticulosarcoma NOS*
M9641/3	*Reticulosarcoma, pleomorphic cell type*
M9642/3	*Reticulosarcoma, nodular*

M965-M966 Hodgkin's disease

M9650/3	*Hodgkin's disease NOS*
M9651/3	*Hodgkin's disease, lymphocytic predominance*
M9652/3	*Hodgkin's disease, mixed cellularity*
M9653/3	*Hodgkin's disease, lymphocytic depletion NOS*
M9654/3	*Hodgkin's disease, lymphocytic depletion, diffuse fibrosis*
M9655/3	*Hodgkin's disease, lymphocytic depletion, reticular type*
M9656/3	*Hodgkin's disease, nodular sclerosis NOS*
M9657/3	*Hodgkin's disease, nodular sclerosis, cellular phase*
M9660/3	*Hodgkin's paragranuloma*
M9661/3	*Hodgkin's granuloma*
M9662/3	*Hodgkin's sarcoma*

M969	**Lymphomas, nodular or follicular**
M9690/3	*Malignant lymphoma, nodular NOS*
M9691/3	*Malignant lymphoma, mixed lymphocytic-histiocytic, nodular*
M9692/3	*Malignant lymphoma, centroblastic-centrocytic, follicular*
M9693/3	*Malignant lymphoma, lymphocytic, well differentiated, nodular*
M9694/3	*Malignant lymphoma, lymphocytic, intermediate differentiation, nodular*
M9695/3	*Malignant lymphoma, follicular center cell, cleaved, follicular*
M9696/3	*Malignant lymphoma, lymphocytic, poorly differentiated, nodular*
M9697/3	*Malignant lymphoma, centroblastic type, follicular*
M9698/3	*Malignant lymphoma, follicular center cell, noncleaved, follicular*

M970	**Mycosis fungoides**
M9700/3	*Mycosis fungoides*
M9701/3	*Sezary's disease*

M971-M972 Miscellaneous reticuloendothelial neoplasms

M9710/3	*Microglioma*
M9720/3	*Malignant histiocytosis*
M9721/3	*Histiocytic medullary reticulosis*
M9722/3	*Letterer-Siwe's disease*

M973	**Plasma cell tumors**
M9730/3	*Plasma cell myeloma*
M9731/0	*Plasma cell tumor, benign*
M9731/1	*Plasmacytoma NOS*
M9731/3	*Plasma cell tumor, malignant*

M974	**Mast cell tumors**
M9740/1	*Mastocytoma NOS*
M9740/3	*Mast cell sarcoma*
M9741/3	*Malignant mastocytosis*

M975	**Burkitt's tumor**
M9750/3	*Burkitt's tumor*

M980-M994 Leukemias

M980	**Leukemias NOS**
M9800/3	*Leukemia NOS*
M9801/3	*Acute leukemia NOS*
M9802/3	*Subacute leukemia NOS*
M9803/3	*Chronic leukemia NOS*
M9804/3	*Aleukemic leukemia NOS*

M981	**Compound leukemias**
M9810/3	*Compound leukemia*

M982	**Lymphoid leukemias**
M9820/3	*Lymphoid leukemia NOS*
M9821/3	*Acute lymphoid leukemia*
M9822/3	*Subacute lymphoid leukemia*
M9823/3	*Chronic lymphoid leukemia*
M9824/3	*Aleukemic lymphoid leukemia*
M9825/3	*Prolymphocytic leukemia*

M983	**Plasma cell leukemias**
M9830/3	*Plasma cell leukemia*

M984	**Erythroleukemias**
M9840/3	*Erythroleukemia*
M9841/3	*Acute erythremia*

M9842/3	*Chronic erythremia*

M985   **Lymphosarcoma cell leukemias**
M9850/3   *Lymphosarcoma cell leukemia*

M986   **Myeloid leukemias**
M9860/3   *Myeloid leukemia NOS*
M9861/3   *Acute myeloid leukemia*
M9862/3   *Subacute myeloid leukemia*
M9863/3   *Chronic myeloid leukemia*
M9864/3   *Aleukemic myeloid leukemia*
M9865/3   *Neutrophilic leukemia*
M9866/3   *Acute promyelocytic leukemia*

M987   **Basophilic leukemias**
M9870/3   *Basophilic leukemia*

M988   **Eosinophilic leukemias**
M9880/3   *Eosinophilic leukemia*

M989   **Monocytic leukemias**
M9890/3   *Monocytic leukemia NOS*
M9891/3   *Acute monocytic leukemia*
M9892/3   *Subacute monocytic leukemia*
M9893/3   *Chronic monocytic leukemia*
M9894/3   *Aleukemic monocytic leukemia*

M990-M994   **Miscellaneous leukemias**
M9900/3   *Mast cell leukemia*
M9910/3   *Megakaryocytic leukemia*
M9920/3   *Megakaryocytic myelosis*
M9930/3   *Myeloid sarcoma*
M9940/3   *Hairy cell leukemia*

M995-M997   **Miscellaneous myeloproliferative and lymphoproliferative disorders**
M9950/1   *Polycythemia vera*
M9951/1   *Acute panmyelosis*
M9960/1   *Chronic myeloproliferative disease*
M9961/1   *Myelosclerosis with myeloid metaplasia*
M9962/1   *Idiopathic thrombocythemia*
M9970/1   *Chronic lymphoproliferative disease*

GLOSSARY OF MENTAL DISORDERS

The psychiatric terms which appear in Chapter 5, "Mental Disorders," are listed here in alphabetic sequence. Many of the glossary descriptions originally appeared in the section on Mental Disorders in the *International Classification of Diseases, 9th Revision,*[1] and others are included to define the psychiatric conditions added to *ICD-9-CM*. The additional definitions are based on material furnished by the American Psychiatric Association's Task Force on Nomenclature and Statistics[2] and from *A Psychiatric Glossary.*[3] In a few instances definitions were obtained from *Dorland's Illustrated Medical Dictionary*[4] *and from Stedman's Medical Dictionary, Illustrated.*[5]

1. Manual of the *International Classification of Diseases, Injuries, and Causes of Death*, 9th Revision. World Health Organization, Geneva, Switzerland, 1975.
2. American Psychiatric Association, Task Force on Nomenclature and Statistics, Robert L. Spitzer, Chairman.
3. A *Psychiatric Glossary*, Fourth Edition, American Psychiatric Association, Washington, D.C., 1975.
4. *Dorland's Illustrated Medical Dictionary*, Twenty-fifth Edition, W.B. Saunders Company, Philadelphia, 1974.
5. *Stedman's Medical Dictionary*, Illustrated, Twenty-third Edition, Williams and Wilkins, Baltimore, 1976.

Academic underachievement disorder: Failure to achieve in most school tasks despite adequate intellectual capacity, a supportive and encouraging social environment, and apparent effort. The failure occurs in the absence of a demonstrable specific learning disability and is caused by emotional conflict not clearly associated with any other mental disorder.[2]

Adaptation reaction—*see* Adjustment reaction

Adjustment reaction or disorder: Mild or transient disorders lasting longer than acute stress reactions which occur in individuals of any age without any apparent pre-existing mental disorder. Such disorders are often relatively circumscribed or situation-specific, are generally reversible, and usually last only a few months. They are usually closely related in time and content to stresses such as bereavement, migration, or other experiences. Reactions to major stress that last longer than a few days are also included. In children such disorders are associated with no significant distortion of development.[1]

> **conduct disturbance:** Mild or transient disorders in which the main disturbance predominantly involves a disturbance of conduct (e.g., an adolescent grief reaction resulting in aggressive or antisocial disorder).[1]

> **depressive reaction:** States of depression, not specifiable as manic-depressive, psychotic, or neurotic.[1]

>> **brief:** Generally transient, in which the depressive symptoms are usually closely related in time and content to some stressful event.[1]

>> **prolonged:** Generally long-lasting, usually developing in association with prolonged exposure to a stressful situation.[1]

> **emotional disturbance:** An adjustment disorder in which the main symptoms are emotional in type (e.g., anxiety, fear, worry) but not specifically depressive.[1]

> **mixed conduct and emotional disturbance:** An adjustment reaction in which both emotional disturbance and disturbance of conduct are prominent features.[1]

Affective psychoses: Mental disorders, usually recurrent, in which there is a severe disturbance of mood (mostly compounded of depression and anxiety but also manifested as elation, and excitement) which is accompanied by one or more of the following: delusions, perplexity, disturbed attitude to self, disorder of perception and behavior; these are all in keeping with the individual's prevailing mood (as are hallucinations when they occur). There is a strong tendency to suicide. For practical reasons, mild disorders of mood may also be included here if the symptoms match closely the descriptions given; this applies particularly to mild hypomania.[1]

> **bipolar:** A manic-depressive psychosis which has appeared in both the depressive and manic form, either alternating or separated by an interval of normality.[1]

>> **atypical:** An episode of affective psychosis with some, but not all, of the features of the one form of the disorder in individuals who have had a previous episode of the other form of the disorder.[2]

>> **depressed:** A manic-depressive psychosis, circular type, in which the depressive form is currently present.[1]

>> **manic:** A manic-depressive psychosis, circular type, in which the manic form is currently present.[1]

>> **mixed:** A manic-depressive psychosis, circular type, in which both manic and depressive symptoms are present at the same time.[1]

> **depressed type:** A manic-depressive psychosis in which there is a widespread depressed mood of gloom and wretchedness with some degree of anxiety. There is often reduced activity but there may be restlessness and agitation. There is marked tendency to recurrence; in a few cases this may be at regular intervals.[1]

atypical: An affective depressive disorder that cannot be classified as a manic-depressive psychosis, depressed type, or chronic depressive personality disorder, or as an adjustment disorder.[2]

manic type: A manic-depressive psychosis characterized by states of elation or excitement out of keeping with the individual's circumstances and varying from enhanced liveliness (hypomania) to violent, almost uncontrollable, excitement. Aggression and anger, flight of ideas, distractibility, impaired judgement, and grandiose ideas are common.[1]

mixed type: Manic-depressive psychosis syndromes corresponding to both the manic and depressed types, but which for other reasons cannot be classified more specifically.[1]

Aggressive personality—*see* Personality disorder, explosive type

Agoraphobia—*see* agoraphobia under Phobia

Alcohol dependence syndrome: A state, psychic and usually also physical, resulting from taking alcohol, characterized by behavioral and other responses that always include a compulsion to take alcohol on a continuous or periodic basis in order to experience its psychic effects, and sometimes to avoid the discomfort of its absence; tolerance may or may not be present. A person may be dependent on alcohol and other drugs; if so, also record the diagnosis of drug dependence to identify the agent. If alcohol dependence is associated with alcoholic psychosis or with physical complications, *both* diagnoses should be recorded.[1]

Alcohol intoxication

acute: A psychic and physical state resulting from alcohol ingestion characterized by slurred speech, unsteady gait, poor coordination, flushed facies, nystagmus, sluggish reflexes, fetor alcoholica, loud speech, emotional instability (e.g., jollity followed by lugubriousness), excessive conviviality, loquacity, and poorly inhibited sexual and aggressive behavior.[2]

idiosyncratic: Acute psychotic episodes induced by relatively small amounts of alcohol. These are regarded as individual idiosyncratic reactions to alcohol, not due to excessive consumption and without conspicuous neurological signs of intoxication.[1]

pathological—*see* Alcohol intoxication, idiosyncratic

Alcoholic psychoses: Organic psychotic states due mainly to excessive consumption of alcohol; defects of nutrition are thought to play an important role.[1]

alcohol abstinence syndrome—*see* alcohol withdrawal syndrome below

alcohol amnestic syndrome: A syndrome of prominent and lasting reduction of memory span, including striking loss of recent memory, disordered time appreciation and confabulation, occurring in alcoholics as the sequel to an acute alcoholic psychosis (especially delirium tremens) or, more rarely, in the course of chronic alcoholism. It is usually accompanied by peripheral neuritis and may be associated with Wernicke's encephalopathy.[1]

alcohol withdrawal delirium [delirium tremens]: Acute or subacute organic psychotic states in alcoholics, characterized by clouded consciousness, disorientation, fear, illusions, delusions, hallucinations of any kind, notably visual and tactile, and restlessness, tremor and sometimes fever.[1]

alcohol withdrawal hallucinosis: A psychosis usually of less than six months' duration, with slight or no clouding of consciousness and much anxious restlessness in which auditory hallucinations, mostly of voices uttering insults and threats, predominate.[1]

alcohol withdrawal syndrome: Tremor of hands, tongue, and eyelids following cessation of prolonged heavy drinking of alcohol. Nausea and vomiting, dry mouth, headache, heavy perspiration, fitful sleep, acute anxiety attacks, mood depression, feelings of guilt and remorse, and irritability are associated features.[2]

alcohol delirium—*see* alcohol withdrawal delirium above

alcoholic dementia: Nonhallucinatory dementias occurring in association with alcoholism, but not characterized by the features of either alcohol withdrawal delirium [delirium tremens] or alcohol amnestic syndrome [Korsakoff's alcoholic psychosis].[1]

alcoholic hallucinosis—*see* alcohol withdrawal hallucinosis above

alcoholic jealousy: Chronic paranoid psychosis characterized by delusional jealousy and associated with alcoholism.[1]

alcoholic paranoia—*see* Alcoholic jealousy

alcoholic polyneuritic psychosis—*see* alcohol amnestic syndrome above

Alcoholism

acute—*see* Alcohol intoxication, acute

chronic—*see* Alcohol dependence syndrome

Alexia: Loss of a previously possessed reading facility that cannot be explained by defective visual acuity.[3]

Amnesia, psychogenic: A form of dissociative hysteria in which there is a temporary disturbance in the ability to recall important personal information which has already been registered and stored in memory. The sudden onset of this disturbance in the absence of an underlying organic mental disorder, and the extent of the disturbance being too great to be explained by ordinary forgetfulness, are the essential features.[2]

Amnestic syndrome: A syndrome of prominent and lasting reduction of memory span, including striking loss of recent memory, disordered time appreciation, and confabulation. The commonest causes are chronic alcoholism [alcohol amnestic syndrome; Korsakoff's alcoholic psychosis], chronic barbiturate dependence, and malnutrition. An amnestic syndrome may be the predominating disturbance in the early states of presenile and senile dementia, arteriosclerotic dementia, and in encephalitis and other inflammatory and degenerative diseases in which there is particular bilateral involvement of the temporal lobes, and certain temporal lobe tumors.[2]

    alcoholic—*see* alcohol amnestic syndrome under Alcoholic psychoses

Amoral personality—*see* Personality disorder, antisocial type

Anancastic [anankastic] neurosis—*see* Neurotic disorder, obsessive-compulsive

Anancastic [anankastic] personality—*see* Personality disorder, compulsive type

Anorexia nervosa: A disorder in which the main features are persistent active refusal to eat and marked loss of weight. The level of activity and alertness is characteristically high in relation to the degree of emaciation. Typically the disorder begins in teenage girls but it may sometimes begin before puberty and rarely it occurs in males. Amenorrhea is usual and there may be a variety of other physiological changes including slow pulse and respiration, low body temperature, and dependent edema. Unusual eating habits and attitudes toward food are typical and sometimes starvation follows or alternates with periods of overeating. The accompanying psychiatric symptoms are diverse.[1]

Anxiety hysteria—*see* phobia under Neurotic disorders

Anxiety state (neurotic): Apprehension, tension, or uneasiness that stems from the anticipation of danger, the source of which is largely unknown or unrecognized.[3]

    atypical: An anxiety disorder that does not fulfill the criteria of generalized or panic attack anxiety. An example might be an individual with a single morbid fear.[2]

    generalized: A disorder of at least six months' duration in which the predominant feature is limited to diffuse and persistent anxiety without the specific symptoms that characterize phobic disorders, panic disorder, or obsessive-compulsive disorder.[2]

    panic attack: An episodic and often chronic, recurrent disorder in which the predominant features are anxiety attacks and nervousness. The anxiety attacks are manifested by discrete periods of sudden onset of intense apprehension, fearfulness, or terror often associated with feelings of impending doom.[2]

Aphasia, developmental: A delay in the production of spoken language. Rarely, there is also a developmental delay in the comprehension of speech sounds.[1]

Arteriosclerotic dementia: Dementia attributable, because of physical signs (on examination of the central nervous system), to degenerative arterial disease of the brain. Symptoms suggesting a focal lesion in the brain are common. There may be a fluctuating or patchy intellectual defect with insight, and an intermittent course is common. Clinical differentiation from senile or presenile dementia, which may coexist with it, may be very difficult or impossible. The diagnosis of cerebral atherosclerosis should also be recorded.[1]

Asocial personality—*see* Personality disorder, antisocial type

Astasia-abasia, hysterical: A form of conversion hysteria in which the individual is unable to stand or walk although the legs are otherwise under control.[4]

Asthenia, psychogenic—*see* neurasthenia under Neurotic disorders

Asthenic personality—*see* Personality disorder, dependent type

Attention deficit disorder—*see* attention deficit disorder under Hyperkinetic syndrome of childhood.

Autism, infantile: A syndrome present from birth or beginning almost invariably in the first 30 months. Responses to auditory and sometimes to visual stimuli are abnormal, and there are usually severe problems in the understanding of spoken language. Speech is delayed and, if it develops, is characterized by echolalia, the reversal of pronouns, immature grammatical structure, and inability to use abstract terms. There is generally an impairment in the social use of both verbal and gestural language. Problems in social relationships are most severe before the age of five years and include an impairment in the development of eye-to-eye gaze, social attachments, and cooperative play. Ritualistic behavior is usual and may include abnormal routines, resistance to change, attachment to odd objects and stereotyped patterns of play. The capacity for abstract or symbolic thought and for imaginative play is diminished. Intelligence ranges from severely subnormal to normal or above. Performance is usually better on tasks involving rote memory or visuospatial skills than on those requiring symbolic or linguistic skills.[1]

Avoidant personality—*see* Personality disorder, avoidant type

"Bad trips": Acute intoxication from hallucinogen abuse, manifested by hallucinatory states lasting only a few days or less.[1]

Barbiturate abuse: Cases where an individual has taken the drug to the detriment of his health or social functioning, in doses above or for periods beyond those normally regarded as therapeutic.[1]

Bestiality—*see* Zoophilia

Bipolar disorder—*see* Affective psychosis, bipolar

    atypical—*see* Affective psychosis, bipolar, atypical

Body-rocking—*see* Stereotyped repetitive movements

Borderline personality—*see* Personality disorder, borderline type

Borderline psychosis of childhood—*see* Psychosis, atypical childhood

Borderline schizophrenia—*see* Schizophrenia, latent

Bouffée délirante—*see* Paranoid reaction, acute

Briquet's disorder—*see* somatization disorder under Neurotic disorders

Bulimia: An episodic pattern of overeating [binge eating] accompanied by an awareness of the disordered eating pattern with a fear of not being able to stop eating voluntarily. Depressive moods and self-deprecating thoughts follow the episodes of binge eating.[2]

Catalepsy schizophrenia—*see* Schizophrenia, catatonic type

Catastrophic stress—*see* Gross stress reaction

Catatonia (schizophrenic)—*see* Schizophrenia, catatonic type

Character neurosis—*see* Personality disorders

Childhood autism—*see* Autism, infantile

Childhood type schizophrenia—*see* Psychosis, child

Chronic alcoholic brain syndrome—*see* alcoholic dementia under Alcoholic psychoses

Clay-eating—*see* Pica

Clumsiness syndrome—*see* coordination disorder under Developmental delay disorders, specific

Combat fatigue—*see* Posttraumatic disorder, acute

Compensation neurosis—*see* compensation neurosis under Neurotic disorders

Compulsive conduct disorder—*see* impulse control disorders under Conduct disorders

Compulsive neurosis—*see* Neurotic disorder, obsessive-compulsive

Compulsive personality—*see* Personality disorder, compulsive type

Concentration camp syndrome—*see* Posttraumatic stress disorder, prolonged

Conduct disorders: Disorders mainly involving aggressive and destructive behavior and disorders involving delinquency. It should be used for abnormal behavior, in individuals of any age, which gives rise to social disapproval but which is not part of any other psychiatric condition. Minor emotional disturbances may also be present. To be included, the behavior, as judged by its frequency, severity, and type of associations with other symptoms, must be abnormal in its context. Disturbances of conduct are distinguished from an adjustment reaction by a longer duration and by a lack of close relationship in time and content to some stress. They differ from a personality disorder by the absence of deeply ingrained maladaptive patterns of behavior present from adolescence or earlier.[1]

    impulse control disorders: A failure to resist an impulse, drive, or temptation to perform some action which is harmful to the individual or to others. The impulse may or may not be consciously resisted, and the act may or may not be premeditated or planned. Prior to committing the act, there is an increasing sense of tension, and at the time of committing the act, there is an experience of either pleasure, gratification, or release. Immediately following the act, there may or may not be genuine regret, self-reproach, or guilt.[2] *See also* Intermittent explosive disorder, Isolated explosive disorder, Kleptomania, Pathological gambling, and Pyromania.

    mixed disturbance of conduct and emotions: A disorder characterized by features of undersocialized and socialized disturbance of conduct, but in which there is also considerable emotional disturbance as shown, for example, by anxiety, misery, or obsessive manifestations.[1]

    socialized conduct disorder: Conduct disorders in individuals who have acquired the values or behavior of a delinquent peer group to whom they are loyal and with whom they characteristically steal, play truant, and stay out late at night. There may also be sexual promiscuity.[1]

    undersocialized conduct disturbance

        aggressive type: A disorder characterized by a persistent pattern of disrespect for the feelings and well-being of others (bullying, physical aggression, cruel behavior, hostility, verbal abusiveness, impudence, defiance, negativism), aggressive antisocial behavior (destructiveness, stealing, persistent lying, frequent truancy, and vandalism), and failure to develop close and stable relationships with others.[2]

unaggressive type: A disorder in which there is a lack of concern for the rights and feelings of others to a degree which indicates a failure to establish a normal degree of affection, empathy, or bond with others. There are two patterns of behavior found. In one, the child is fearful and timid, lacking self-assertiveness, resorts to self-protective and manipulative lying, indulges in whining demandingness and temper tantrums, feels rejected and unfairly treated, and is mistrustful of others. In the other pattern of the disorder, the child approaches others strictly for his own gains and acts exclusively because of exploitative and extractive goals. The child lies brazenly and steals, appearing to feel no guilt, and forms no social bonds to other individuals.[2]

Confusion, psychogenic—*see* Psychosis, reactive confusion

Confusion, reactive—*see* Psychosis, reactive confusion

Confusional state

    acute—*see* Delirium, acute

    epileptic—*see* Delirium, acute

    subacute—*see* Delirium, subacute

Conversion hysteria—*see* hysteria, conversion type under Neurotic disorders

Coordination disorder—*see* coordination disorder under Developmental delay disorders, specific

Culture shock: A form of stress reaction associated with an individual's assimilation into a new culture which is vastly different from that in which he was raised.[5]

Cyclic schizophrenia—*see* Schizophrenia, schizo-affective type

Cyclothymic personality or disorder—*see* Personality disorder, cyclothymic type

Delirium: Transient organic psychotic conditions with a short course in which there is a rapidly developing onset of disorganization of higher mental processes manifested by some degree of impairment of information processing, impaired or abnormal attention, perception, memory, and thinking. Clouded consciousness, confusion, disorientation, delusions, illusions, and often vivid hallucinations predominate in the clinical picture.[1,2]

    acute: short-lived states, lasting hours or days, of the above type.[1]

    subacute: states of the above type in which the symptoms, usually less florid, last for several weeks or longer, during which they may show marked fluctuations in intensity.[1]

Delirium tremens—*see* alcohol withdrawal delirium under Alcoholic psychoses

Delusions, systematized—*see* Paranoia

Dementia: A decrement in intellectual functioning of sufficient severity to interfere with occupational or social performance, or both. There is impairment of memory and abstract thinking, the ability to learn new skills, problem solving, and judgment. There is often also personality change or impairment in impulse control. Dementia in organic psychoses may be of a chronic or progressive nature, which if untreated are usually irreversible and terminal.[1,2]

    alcoholic—*see* alcoholic dementia under Alcoholic psychoses

    arteriosclerotic—*see* Arteriosclerotic dementia

    multi-infarct—*see* Arteriosclerotic dementia

    presenile—*see* Presenile dementia

    repeated infarct—*see* Arteriosclerotic dementia

    senile—*see* Senile dementia

Depersonalization syndrome—*see* depersonalization syndrome under Neurotic disorders

Depression: States of depression, usually of moderate but occasionally of marked intensity, which have no specifically manic-depressive or other psychotic depressive features, and which do not appear to be associated with stressful events or other features specified under neurotic depression.[1]

    anxiety—*see* depression under Neurotic disorders

    endogenous—*see* Affective psychosis, depressed type

    monopolar—*see* Affective psychosis, depressed type

    neurotic—*see* depression under Neurotic disorders

    psychotic—*see* Affective psychosis, depressed type

    psychotic reactive—*see* Psychosis, depressive

    reactive—*see* depression under Neurotic disorders

    reactive psychotic—*see* Psychosis, depressive

Depressive personality or character—*see* Personality disorder, chronic depressive type

Depressive reaction—*see* depressive reaction under Adjustment reaction

Depressive psychosis—*see* Affective psychosis, depressed type

Derealization (neurotic)—*see* depersonalization syndrome under Neurotic disorders

Developmental delay disorders, specific: A group of disorders in which a specific delay in development is the main feature. For many the delay is not explicable in terms of general intellectual retardation or of inadequate schooling. In each case development is related to biological maturation, but it is also influenced by nonbiological factors. A diagnosis of a specific developmental delay carries no etiological implications. A diagnosis of specific delay in development should not be made if it is due to a known neurological disorder.[1]

    arithmetical disorder: Disorders in which the main feature is a serious impairment in the development of arithmetical skills.[1]

    articulation disorder: A delay in the development of normal word-sound production resulting in defects of articulation. Omissions or substitutions of consonants are most frequent.[1]

    coordination disorder: Disorders in which the main feature is a serious impairment in the development of motor coordination which is not explicable in terms of general intellectual retardation. The clumsiness is commonly associated with perceptual difficulties.[1]

    mixed development disorder: A delay in the development of one specific skill (e.g., reading, arithmetic, speech, or coordination) is frequently associated with lesser delays in other skills. When this occurs the diagnosis should be made according to the skill most seriously impaired. The mixed category should be used only where the mixture of delayed skills is such that no one skill is preponderantly affected.[1]

    motor retardation—*see* coordination disorder above

    reading disorder or retardation: Disorders in which the main feature is a serious impairment in the development of reading or spelling skills which is not explicable in terms of general intellectual retardation or of inadequate schooling. Speech or language difficulties, impaired right-left differentiation, perceptuo-motor problems, and coding difficulties are frequently associated. Similar problems are often present in other members of the family. Adverse psychosocial factors may be present.[1]

    speech or language disorder: Disorders in which the main feature is a serious impairment in the development of speech or language (syntax or semantic) which is not explicable in terms of general intellectual retardation. Most commonly there is a delay in the development of normal word-sound production resulting in defects of articulation. Omissions or substitutions of consonants are most frequent. There may also be a delay in the production of spoken language. Rarely, there is also a developmental delay in the comprehension of sounds. Includes cases in which delay is largely due to environmental privation.[1]

Dipsomania—*see* Alcohol dependence syndrome

Disorganized schizophrenia—*see* Schizophrenia, disorganized type

Dissociative hysteria—*see* hysteria, dissociative type under Neurotic disorders

Drug abuse: Includes cases where an individual, for whom no other diagnosis is possible, has come under medical care because of the maladaptive effect of a drug on which he is not dependent (*see* Drug dependence) and that he has taken on his own initiative to the detriment of his health or social functioning. When drug abuse is secondary to a psychiatric disorder, record the disorder as an additional diagnosis.[1]

Drug dependence: A state, psychic and sometimes also physical, resulting from taking a drug, characterized by behavioral and other responses that always include a compulsion to take a drug on a continuous or periodic basis in order to experience its psychic effects, and sometimes to avoid the discomfort of its absence. Tolerance may or may not be present. A person may be dependent on more than one drug.[1]

Drug psychoses: Organic mental syndromes which are due to consumption of drugs (notably amphetamines, barbiturates, and opiate and LSD groups) and solvents. Some of the syndromes in this group are not as severe as most conditions labeled "psychotic," but they are included here for practical reasons. The drug should be identified, and also a diagnosis of drug dependence should be recorded, if present.[1]

    drug-induced hallucinosis: Hallucinatory states of more than a few days, but not more than a few months' duration, associated with large or prolonged intake of drugs, notably of the amphetamine and LSD groups. Auditory hallucinations usually predominate and there may be anxiety or restlessness. States following LSD or other hallucinogens lasting only a few days or less ["bad trips"] are not included.[1]

    drug-induced organic delusional syndrome: Paranoid states of more than a few days, but not more than a few months' duration, associated with large or prolonged intake of drugs, notably of the amphetamine and LSD groups.[1]

    drug withdrawal syndrome: States associated with drug withdrawal ranging from severe, as specified for alcohol withdrawal delirium [delirium tremens], to less severe states characterized by one or more symptoms such as convulsions, tremor, anxiety, restlessness, gastrointestinal and muscular complaints, and mild disorientation and memory disturbance.[1]

Drunkenness:

acute—*see* Alcohol intoxication, acute

pathologic—*see* Alcohol intoxication, idiosyncratic

simple: A state of inebriation due to alcohol consumption without conspicuous neurological signs of intoxication.[2]

sleep: An inability to fully arouse from the sleep state characterized by failure to attain full consciousness after arousal.[2]

Dyscalculia—*see* arithmetical disorder under Developmental delay disorders, specific

Dyslalia—*see* articulation disorder under Developmental delay disorders, specific

Dyslexia, developmental: A disorder in which the main feature is a serious impairment of reading skills which is not explicable in terms of general intellectual retardation or of inadequate schooling. Word-blindness and strephosymbolia (tendency to reverse letters and words in reading) are included.[1,3]

Dysmenorrhea, psychogenic: Painful menstruation due to disturbance of psychic control.[4]

Dyspareunia, functional—*see* functional dyspareunia under Psychosexual dysfunctions

Dyspraxia syndrome—*see* coordination disorder under Developmental delay disorders, specific

Dyssocial personality—*see* Personality disorder, antisocial type

Dysuria, psychogenic: Difficulty in passing urine due to psychic factors.[4]

Eating disorders: A group of disorders characterized by a conspicuous disturbance in eating behavior.[2] *See also* Bulimia, Pica, and Rumination, psychogenic.

Eccentric personality—*see* Personality disorder, eccentric type

Elective mutism: A pervasive and persistent refusal to speak in situations not attributable to a mental disorder. In some cases the behavior may manifest a form of withdrawal reaction to a specific stressful situation, or as a predominant feature in children exhibiting shyness or social withdrawal disorders.[2]

Emancipation disorder: An adjustment reaction in adolescents or young adults in which there is symptomatic expression (e.g., difficulty in making independent decisions, increased dependence on parental advice, adoption of values deliberately oppositional to parents) of a conflict over independence following the recent assumption of a status in which the individual is more independent of parental control or supervision.[2]

Emotional disturbances specific to childhood and adolescence: Less well-differentiated emotional disorders characteristic of the childhood period. When the emotional disorder takes the form of a neurosis, the appropriate diagnosis should be made. These disorders differ from adjustment reactions in terms of longer duration and by the lack of close relationship in time and content to some stress.[1] *See also* Academic underachievement disorder, Elective mutism, Identity disorder, Introverted disorder of childhood, Misery and unhappiness disorder, Oppositional disorder, Overanxious disorder, and Shyness disorder of childhood.

Encopresis: A disorder in which the main manifestation is the persistent voluntary or involuntary passage of formed stools of normal or near-normal consistency into places not intended for that purpose in the individual's own sociocultural setting. Sometimes the child has failed to gain bowel control, and sometimes he has gained control but then later again became encopretic. There may be a variety of associated psychiatric symptoms and there may be smearing of feces. The condition would not usually be diagnosed under the age of four years.[1]

Endogenous depression—*see* Affective psychosis, depressed type

Enuresis: A disorder in which the main manifestation is a persistent involuntary voiding of urine by day or night which is considered abnormal for the age of the individual. Sometimes the child will have failed to gain bladder control and in other cases he will have gained control and then lost it. Episodic or fluctuating enuresis should be included. The disorder would not usually be diagnosed under the age of four years.[1]

Epileptic confusional or twilight state—*see* Delirium, acute

Excitation

catatonic—*see* Schizophrenia, catatonic type

psychogenic—*see* Psychosis, excitative type

reactive—*see* Psychosis, excitative type

Exhaustion delirium—*see* Stress reaction, acute

Exhibitionism: Sexual deviation in which the main sexual pleasure and gratification is derived from exposure of the genitals to a person of the opposite sex.[1]

Explosive personality disorder—*see* Personality disorder, explosive type

Factitious illness: A form of hysterical neurosis in which there are physical or psychological symptoms that are not real, genuine, or natural, which are produced by the individual and are under his voluntary control.[2]

physical symptom type: The presentation of physical symptoms that may be total fabrication, self-inflicted, an exaggeration or exacerbation of a pre-existing physical condition, or any combination or variation of these.[2]

psychological symptom type: The voluntary production of symptoms suggestive of a mental disorder. Behavior may mimic psychosis or, rather, the individual's idea of psychosis.[2]

Fanatic personality—*see* Personality disorder, paranoid type

Fatigue neurosis—*see* neurasthenia under Neurotic disorders

Feeble-minded—*see* Mental retardation, mild

Fetishism: A sexual deviation in which nonliving objects are utilized as a preferred or exclusive method of stimulating erotic arousal.[2]

Finger-flicking—*see* Stereotyped repetitive movements

Folie à deux—*see* Shared paranoid disorder

Frigidity: A psychosexual dysfunction in which there is partial or complete failure to attain or maintain the lubrication-swelling response of sexual excitement until completion of the sexual act.[2]

Frontal lobe syndrome: Changes in behavior following damage to the frontal areas of the brain or following interference with the connections of those areas. There is a general diminution of self-control, foresight, creativity, and spontaneity, which may be manifest as increased irritability, selfishness, restlessness and lack of concern for others. Conscientiousness and powers of concentration are often diminished, but measurable deterioration of intellect or memory is not necessarily present. The overall picture is often one of emotional dullness, lack of drive, and slowness; but, particularly in persons previously with energetic, restless, or aggressive characteristics, there may be a change towards impulsiveness, boastfulness, temper outbursts, silly fatuous humor, and the development of unrealistic ambitions; the direction of change usually depends upon the previous personality. A considerable degree of recovery is possible and may continue over the course of several years.[1]

Fugue, psychogenic: A form of dissociative hysteria characterized by an episode of wandering with inability to recall one's prior identity. Both onset and recovery are rapid. Following recovery there is no recollection of events which took place during the fugue state.[2]

Ganser's syndrome (hysterical): A form of factitious illness in which the patient voluntarily produces symptoms suggestive of a mental disorder.[2]

Gender identity disorder—*see* gender identity disorder under Psychosexual identity disorders

Gilles de la Tourette's disorder or syndrome—*see* Gilles de la Tourette's disorder under Tics

Grief reaction—*see* depressive reaction, brief under Adjustment reaction

Gross stress reaction—*see* Stress reaction, acute

Group delinquency—*see* socialized conduct disorder under Conduct disorders

Habit spasm—*see* chronic motor tic disorder under Tics

Hangover (alcohol)—*see* Drunkenness, simple

Head-banging—*see* Stereotyped repetitive movements

Hebephrenia—*see* Schizophrenia, disorganized type

Heller's syndrome—*see* Psychosis, disintegrative

High grade defect—*see* Mental retardation, mild

Homosexuality: Exclusive or predominant sexual attraction for persons of the same sex with or without physical relationship. Record homosexuality as a diagnosis whether or not it is considered as a mental disorder.[1]

Hospital addiction syndrome—*see* Munchausen syndrome

Hospital hoboes—*see* Munchausen syndrome

Hospitalism: A mild or transient adjustment reaction characterized by withdrawal seen in hospitalized patients. In young children this may be manifested by elective mutism.[1]

Hyperkinetic syndrome of childhood: Disorders in which the essential features are short attention-span and distractibility. In early childhood the most striking symptom is disinhibited, poorly organized and poorly regulated extreme overactivity but in adolescence this may be replaced by underactivity. Impulsiveness, marked mood fluctuations, and aggression are also common symptoms. Delays in the development of specific skills are often present and disturbed, poor relationships are common. If the hyperkinesis is symptomatic of an underlying disorder, the diagnosis of the underlying disorder is recorded instead.[1]

attention deficit disorder: Cases of hyperkinetic syndrome in which short attention span, distractibility, and overactivity are the main manifestations without significant disturbance of conduct or delay in specific skills.[1]

hyperkinesis with developmental delay: Cases in which the hyperkinetic syndrome is associated with speech delay, clumsiness, reading difficulties, or other delays of specific skills.[1]

hyperkinetic conduct disorder: Cases in which the hyperkinetic syndrome is associated with marked conduct disturbance but not developmental delay.[1]

Hypersomnia: A disorder of initiating arousal from sleep or maintaining wakefulness.

persistent: Chronic difficulty in initiating arousal from sleep or maintaining wakefulness associated with major or minor depressive mental disorders.[2]

transient: Episodes of difficulty in arousal from sleep or maintaining wakefulness associated with acute or intermittent emotional reactions or conflicts.[2]

Hypochondriasis—*see* hypochondriasis under Neurotic disorders

Hypomania—*see* Affective psychosis, manic type

Hypomanic personality—*see* Personality disorder, chronic hypomanic type

Hyposomnia—*see* Insomnia

Hysteria—*see* hysteria under Neurotic disorders

anxiety—*see* phobia under Neurotic disorders

psychosis—*see* Psychosis, reactive

acute—*see* Psychosis, excitative type

Hysterical personality—*see* Personality disorder, histrionic type

Identity disorder: An emotional disorder caused by distress over the inability to reconcile aspects of the self into a relatively coherent and acceptable sense of self, not secondary to another mental disorder. The disturbance is manifested by intense subjective distress regarding uncertainty about a variety of issues relating to identity, including long-term goals, career choice, friendship patterns, values, and loyalties.[2]

Idiocy—*see* Mental retardation, profound

Imbecile—*see* Mental retardation, moderate

Impotence: A psychosexual dysfunction in which there is partial or complete failure to attain or maintain erection until completion of the sexual act.[2]

Impulse control disorder—*see* impulse control disorders under Conduct disorders

Inadequate personality—*see* Personality disorder, dependent type

Induced paranoid disorder—*see* Shared paranoid disorder

Inebriety—*see* Drunkenness, simple

Infantile autism—*see* Autism, infantile

Insomnia: A disorder of initiating or maintaining sleep.[2]

persistent: A chronic state of sleeplessness associated with chronic anxiety, major or minor depressive disorders, or psychoses.[2]

transient: Episodes of sleeplessness associated with acute or intermittent emotional reactions or conflicts.[2]

Intermittent explosive disorder: Recurrent episodes of sudden and significant loss of control of aggressive impulses, not accounted for by any other mental disorder, which results in serious assault or destruction of property. The magnitude of the behavior during an episode is grossly out of proportion to any psychosocial stressors which may have played a role in eliciting the episode of lack of control. Following each episode there is genuine regret or self-reproach at the consequences of the action and the inability to control the aggressive impulse.[2]

Introverted disorder of childhood: An emotional disturbance in children chiefly manifested by a lack of interest in social relationships and indifference to social praise or criticism.[2]

Introverted personality—*see* Personality disorder, introverted type

Involutional melancholia—*see* Affective psychosis, depressed type

Involutional paranoid state—*see* Paraphrenia

Isolated explosive disorder: A disorder of impulse control in which there is a single discrete episode characterized by failure to resist an impulse which leads to a single, violent externally- directed act, which has a catastrophic impact on others, and for which the available information does not justify the diagnosis of another mental disorder.[2]

Isolated phobia—*see* simple phobia under Phobia

Jet lag syndrome: A phase-shift disruption of the 24-hour sleep-wake cycle due to rapid time-zone changes experienced in long-distance travel.[2]

Kanner's syndrome—*see* Autism, infantile

Kleptomania: A disorder of impulse control characterized by a recurrent failure to resist impulses to steal objects not for immediate use or their monetary value. An increasing sense of tension is experienced prior to committing the act, with an intense experience of gratification at the time of committing the theft.[2]

Korsakoff's psychosis:

> **alcoholic**—*see* alcohol amnestic syndrome under Alcoholic psychoses

> **nonalcoholic**—*see* Amnestic syndrome

Latent schizophrenia—*see* Schizophrenia, latent

Lesbianism—*see* Homosexuality

Lobotomy syndrome—*see* Frontal lobe syndrome

LSD reaction: Acute intoxication from hallucinogen abuse, manifested by hallucinatory states lasting only a few days or less.[1]

Major depressive disorder—*see* Affective psychosis, depressed type

Malingering: A clinical picture in which the predominant feature is the presentation of fake or grossly exaggerated physical or psychiatric illness apparently under voluntary control. In contrast to factitious illness, the symptoms produced in malingering are in pursuit of a goal which, when known, is recognizable and obviously understandable in light of knowledge of the individual's circumstances. Examples of understandable goals include, but are not limited to, becoming a "patient" in order to avoid conscription or military duty, avoid work, obtain financial compensation, evade criminal prosecution, and obtain drugs.[2]

Mania (monopolar)—*see* Affective psychosis, manic type

Manic-depressive psychosis

> **circular type**—*see* Affective psychosis, bipolar

> **depressed type**—*see* Affective psychosis, depressed type

> **manic type**—*see* Affective psychosis, manic type

> **mixed type**—*see* Affective psychosis, mixed type

Manic disorder—*see* Affective psychosis, manic type

> **atypical**—*see* Affective psychosis, manic type, atypical

Masochistic personality—*see* Personality disorder, masochistic type

Melancholia—*see* Affective psychoses

> **involutional**—*see* Affective psychosis, depressed type

Mental retardation: A condition of arrested or incomplete development of mind which is especially characterized by subnormality of intelligence. The coding should be made on the individual's *current* level of functioning *without regard to its nature* or causation, such as psychosis, cultural deprivation, Down's syndrome, etc. Where there is a specific cognitive handicap—such as in speech—the diagnosis of mental retardation should be based on assessments of cognition *outside the area of specific handicap*. The assessment of intellectual level should be based on whatever information is available, including clinical evidence, adaptive behavior, and psychometric findings. The IQ levels given are based on a test with a mean of 100 and a standard deviation of 15, such as the Wechsler scales. They are provided only as a guide and should not be applied rigidly. Mental retardation often involves psychiatric disturbances and may often develop as a result of some physical disease or injury. In these cases, an additional diagnosis should be recorded to identify any associated condition, psychiatric or physical.[1]

> **mild mental retardation:** IQ criteria 50-70. Individuals with this level of retardation are usually educable. During the pre-school period they can develop social and communication skills, have minimal retardation in sensorimotor areas, and often are not distinguished from normal children until a later age. During the school age period they can learn academic skills up to approximately the sixth-grade level. During the adult years, they can usually achieve social and vocational skills adequate for minimum self-support, but may need guidance and assistance when under social or economic stress.[2]

> **moderate mental retardation:** IQ criteria 35-49. Individuals with this level of retardation are usually trainable. During the pre-school period they can talk or learn to communicate. They have poor social awareness and fair motor development. During the school age period they can profit from training in social and occupational skills, but they are unlikely to progress beyond the second-grade level in academic subjects. During their adult years they may achieve self-maintenance in unskilled or semi-skilled work under sheltered conditions. They need supervision and guidance when under mild social or economic stress.[2]

> **severe mental retardation:** IQ criteria 20-34. Individuals with this level of retardation evidence poor motor development, minimal speech, and are generally unable to profit from training and self-help during the pre-school period. During the school age period they can talk or learn to communicate, can be trained in elementary health habits, and may profit from systematic habit training. During the adult years they may contribute partially to self-maintenance under complete supervision.[2]

profound mental retardation: IQ criteria under 20. Individuals with this level of retardation evidence minimal capacity for sensorimotor functioning and need nursing care during the pre-school period. During the school age period some further motor development may occur, and they may respond to minimal or limited training in self-help. During the adult years some motor and speech development may occur, and they may achieve very limited self-care and need nursing care.[2]

Merycism—*see* Rumination, psychogenic

Minimal brain dysfunction [MBD]—*see* Hyperkinetic syndrome of childhood

Misery and unhappiness disorder: An emotional disorder characteristic of childhood in which the main symptoms involve misery and unhappiness. There may also be eating and sleep disturbances.[1]

Mood swings (brief compensatory) (rebound): Mild disorders of mood (depression and anxiety or elation and excitement, occurring alternatingly or episodically) seen in affective psychosis.[1]

Motor tic disorders—*see* Tics

Motor-verbal tic disorder—*see* Gilles de la Tourette's disorder under Tics

Multi-infarct dementia or psychosis—*see* Arteriosclerotic dementia

Multiple operations syndrome—*see* Munchausen syndrome

Multiple personality: A form of dissociative hysteria in which there is the domination of the individual at any one time by one of two or more distinct personalities. Each personality is a full-integrated and complex unit with memories, behavior patterns, and social friendships which determine the nature of the individual's acts when uppermost in consciousness.[2]

Munchausen syndrome: A chronic form of factitious illness in which the individual demonstrates a plausible presentation of voluntarily produced physical symptomatology of such a degree that he is able to obtain and sustain multiple hospitalizations.[2]

Narcissistic personality—*see* Personality disorder, narcissistic type

Nervous debility—*see* neurasthenia under Neurotic disorders

Neurasthenia—*see* neurasthenia under Neurotic disorders

Neurotic delinquency—*see* mixed disturbance of conduct and emotions under Conduct disorders

Neurotic disorders: Neurotic disorders are mental disorders without any demonstrable organic basis in which the individual may have considerable insight and has unimpaired reality testing, in that he usually does not confuse his morbid subjective experiences and fantasies with external reality. Behavior may be greatly affected although usually remaining within socially acceptable limits, but personality is not disorganized. The principal manifestations include excessive anxiety, hysterical symptoms, phobias, obsessional and compulsive symptoms, and depression.[1]

> **anxiety states:** Various combinations of physical and mental manifestations of anxiety, not attributable to real danger and occurring either in attacks [*see* Anxiety state, panic attacks] or as a persisting state [*see* Anxiety state, generalized]. The anxiety is usually diffuse and may extend to panic. Other neurotic features such as obsessional or hysterical symptoms may be present but do not dominate the clinical picture.[1]

> **compensation neurosis:** Certain unconscious neurotic reactions in which features of secondary gain, such as a situational or financial advantage, are prominent.[3]

> **depersonalization:** A neurotic disorder with an unpleasant state of disturbed perception in which external objects or parts of one's own body are experienced as changed in their quality, unreal, remote, or automatized. The patient is aware of the subjective nature of the change he experiences. If depersonalization occurs as a feature of anxiety, schizophrenia, or other mental disorder, the condition is classified according to the major psychiatric disorder.[1]

> **depression:** A neurotic disorder characterized by disproportionate depression which has usually recognizably ensued on a distressing experience; it does not include among its features delusions or hallucinations, and there is often preoccupation with the psychic trauma which preceded the illness, e.g., loss of a cherished person or possession. Anxiety is also frequently present and mixed states of anxiety and depression should be included here. The distinction between depressive neurosis and psychosis should be made not only upon the degree of depression but also on the presence or absence of other neurotic and psychotic characteristics, and upon the degree of disturbance of the individual's behavior.[1]

> **hypochondriasis:** A neurotic disorder in which the conspicuous features are excessive concern with one's health in general or the integrity and functioning of some part of one's body, or less frequently, one's mind. It is usually associated with anxiety and depression. It may occur as a feature of some other severe mental disorder (e.g., manic-depressive psychosis, depressed type, schizophrenia, hysteria) and in that case should be classified according to the corresponding major disorder.[1]

> **hysteria:** A neurotic mental disorder in which motives, of which the patient seems unaware, produce either a restriction of the field of consciousness or disturbances of motor or sensory function which may seem to have psychological advantage or symbolic value.[1] There are three subtypes:

> **conversion type:** The chief or only symptoms of the hysterical neurosis consist of psychogenic disturbance of function in some part of the body, e.g., paralysis, tremor, blindness, deafness, seizures.[1]
>
> **dissociative type:** The most prominent feature of the hysterical neurosis is a narrowing of the field of consciousness which seems to serve an unconscious purpose and is commonly accompanied or followed by a selective amnesia. There may be dramatic but essentially superficial changes of personality [multiple personality], or sometimes the patient enters into a wandering state [fugue].[1]
>
> **factitious illness:** Physical or psychological symptoms that are not real, genuine, or natural, which are produced by the individual and are under his voluntary control.[2]

neurasthenia: A neurotic disorder characterized by fatigue, irritability, headache, depression, insomnia, difficulty in concentration, and lack of capacity for enjoyment [anhedonia]. It may follow or accompany an infection or exhaustion, or arise from continued emotional stress. If neurasthenia is associated with a physical disorder, the latter should also be recorded as a diagnosis.[1]

obsessive-compulsive: States in which the outstanding symptom is a feeling of subjective compulsion, which must be resisted, to carry out some action, to dwell on an idea, to recall an experience, or to ruminate on an abstract topic. Unwanted thoughts which intrude, the insistency of words or ideas, ruminations or trains of thought are perceived by the individual to be inappropriate or nonsensical. The obsessional urge or idea is recognized as alien to the personality but as coming from within the self. Obsessional actions may be quasi-ritual performances designed to relieve anxiety, e.g., washing the hands to cope with contamination. Attempts to dispel the unwelcome thought or urges may lead to a severe inner struggle, with intense anxiety.[1]

occupational: A neurosis characterized by a functional disorder of a group of muscles used chiefly in one's occupation, marked by the occurrence of spasm, paresis, or incoordination on attempt to repeat the habitual movements (e.g., writers' cramp).[5]

phobic disorders: Neurotic states with abnormally intense dread of certain objects or specific situations which would not normally have that effect. If the anxiety tends to spread from a specified situation or object to a wider range of circumstances, it becomes akin to or identical with anxiety state and should be classified as such.[1] *See also* Phobia.

somatization disorder: A chronic, but fluctuating, neurotic disorder which begins early in life and is characterized by recurrent and multiple somatic complaints for which medical attention is sought but which are not apparently due to any physical illness. Complaints are presented in a dramatic, vague, or exaggerated way, or are part of a complicated medical history in which often many specific diagnoses have allegedly been made by other physicians. Complaints invariably refer to many organ systems (headache, fatigue, palpitations, fainting, nausea and vomiting, abdominal pains, bowel trouble, allergies, menstrual and sexual difficulties), and the individual frequently receives medical care from a number of physicians, sometimes simultaneously.[2]

Neurosis—*see* Neurotic disorders

Nightmares: Anxiety attacks occurring in dreams during REM sleep.[2]

Night terrors: A pathology of arousal from stage 4 sleep in which the individual experiences excessive terror and extreme panic (screaming, verbalizations), symptoms of autonomic activity, confusion, and poor recall for event.[2]

Nymphomania: Abnormal and excessive need or desire in the woman for sexual intercourse.[3]

Obsessional personality—*see* Personality disorder, compulsive type

Occupational neurosis—*see* Neurotic disorder, occupational

Oneirophrenia—*see* Schizophrenia, acute episode

Oppositional disorder of childhood or adolescence: A disorder characterized by pervasive opposition to all in authority regardless of self-interest, a continuous argumentativeness, and an unwillingness to respond to reasonable persuasion, not accounted for by a conduct disorder, adjustment disorder, or a psychosis of childhood. The oppositional behavior in this disorder is evoked by any demand, rule, suggestion, request, or admonishment placed on the individual.[2]

Organic affective syndrome: A clinical picture in which the predominating symptoms closely resemble those seen in either the depressive or manic affective disorders, occurring in the presence of evidence or history of a specific organic factor which is etiologically related to the disturbance, such as head trauma, endocranial tumors, and exocranial tumors secreting neurotoxic diatheses (e.g., pancreatic carcinoma). Excessive use of steroids, Cushing's syndrome, and other endocrine disorders may lead to an organic affective syndrome.[2]

Organic personality syndrome: Chronic, mild states of memory disturbance and intellectual deterioration, of nonpsychotic nature, often accompanied by increased irritability, querulousness, lassitude, and complaints of physical weakness. These states are often associated with old age, and may precede more severe states due to brain damage classifiable under senile or presenile dementia, dementia associated with other chronic organic psychotic brain syndromes, or delirium, delusions, hallucinosis, and depression in transient organic psychotic conditions.[1]

Organic psychosyndrome, focal (partial): A nonpsychotic organic mental disorder resembling the postconcussion syndrome associated with localized diseases of the brain or surrounding tissues.[1]

Organic psychotic conditions: Syndromes in which there is impairment of orientation, memory, comprehension, calculation, learning capacity, and judgment. These are the essential features but there may also be shallowness or lability of affect, or a more persistent disturbance of mood, lowering of ethical standards and exaggeration or emergence of personality traits, and diminished capacity for independent decision.[1] See also Alcohol psychoses, Arteriosclerotic dementia, Drug psychoses, Presenile dementia, and Senile dementia.

    mixed paranoid and affective: Organic psychosis in which depressive and paranoid symptoms are the main features.[1]

    transient: States characterized by clouded consciousness, confusion, disorientation, illusions, and often vivid hallucinations. They are usually due to some intra- or extracerebral toxic, infectious, metabolic or other systemic disturbance and are generally reversible. Depressive and paranoid symptoms may also be present but are not the main feature. The diagnosis of the associated physical or neurological condition should also be recorded.[1]

    acute delirium: Short-lived states, lasting hours or days, of the above type.[1]

    subacute delirium: States of the above type in which the symptoms, usually less florid, last for several weeks or longer during which they may show marked fluctuations in intensity.[1]

Organic reaction—*see* Organic psychotic conditions, transient

Overanxious disorder: An ill-defined emotional disorder characteristic of childhood in which the main symptoms involve anxiety and fearfulness.[1]

Panic disorder—*see* panic attack under Anxiety state

Paranoia: A rare chronic psychosis in which logically constructed systematized delusions have developed gradually without concomitant hallucinations or the schizophrenic type of disordered thinking. The delusions are mostly of grandeur (the paranoiac prophet or inventor), persecution, or somatic abnormality.[1]

    alcoholic—*see* alcoholic jealousy under Alcoholic psychoses

    querulans: A paranoid state which, though in many ways akin to schizophrenic or affective states, differs from other paranoid states and psychogenic paranoid psychosis.[1]

    senile—*see* Paraphrenia

Paranoid personality—*see* Personality disorder, paranoid type

Paranoid reaction, acute: Paranoid states apparently provoked by some emotional stress. The stress is often misconstrued as an attack or threat. Such states are particularly prone to occur in prisoners or as acute reactions to a strange and threatening environment, e.g., in immigrants.[1]

Paranoid schizophrenia—*see* Schizophrenia, paranoid type

Paranoid state

    involutional—*see* Paraphrenia

    senile—*see* Paraphrenia

    simple: A psychosis, acute or chronic, not classifiable as schizophrenia or affective psychosis, in which delusions, especially of being influenced, persecuted, or treated in some special way, are the main symptoms. The delusions are of a fairly fixed, elaborate, and systematized kind.[1]

Paranoid traits—*see* Personality disorder, paranoid type

Paraphilia—*see* Sexual deviations

Paraphrenia: Paranoid psychosis in which there are conspicuous hallucinations, often in several modalities. Affective symptoms and disordered thinking, if present, do not dominate the clinical picture, and the personality is well preserved.[1]

Paraphrenic schizophrenia—*see* Schizophrenia, paranoid type

Passive-aggressive personality — *see* Personality disorder, passive-aggressive type

Passive personality—*see* Personality disorder, dependent type

Pathological

    alcohol intoxication—*see* Alcohol intoxication, idiosyncratic

    drug intoxication: Individual idiosyncratic reactions to comparatively small quantities of a drug, which take the form of acute, brief psychotic states of any type.[1]

    drunkenness—*see* Alcohol intoxication, idiosyncratic

    gambling: A disorder of impulse control characterized by a chronic and progressive preoccupation with gambling and urge to gamble, with subsequent gambling behavior that compromises, disrupts, or damages personal, family, and vocational pursuits.[2]

    personality—*see* Personality disorder

Pedophilia: Sexual deviations in which an adult engages in sexual activity with a child of the same or opposite sex.[1]

Peregrinating patient—*see* Malingering

Personality disorders: Deeply ingrained maladaptive patterns of behavior generally recognizable by the time of adolescence or earlier and continuing throughout most of adult life, although often becoming less obvious in middle or old age. The personality is abnormal either in the balance of its components, their quality and expression, or in its total aspect. Because of this deviation or psychopathy the patient suffers or others have to suffer, and there is an adverse effect upon the individual or on society. It includes what is sometimes called psychopathic personality, but if this is determined primarily by malfunctioning of the brain, it should be classified as one of the nonpsychotic organic brain syndromes. When the patient exhibits an anomaly of personality directly related to his neurosis or psychosis, e.g., schizoid personality and schizophrenia or anancastic personality and obsessive compulsive neurosis, the relevant neurosis or psychosis which is in evidence should be diagnosed in addition.[1]

    affective type: A chronic personality disorder characterized by lifelong predominance of a pronounced mood. The illness does not have a clear onset, and there may be intermittent periods of disturbed mood separated by periods of normal mood.[1]

    anancastic [anankastic] type—*see* Personality disorder, compulsive type

    antisocial type: A personality disorder characterized by disregard for social obligations, lack of feeling for others, and impetuous violence or callous unconcern. There is a gross disparity between behavior and the prevailing social norms. Behavior is not readily modifiable by experience, including punishment. People with this personality are often affectively cold, and may be abnormally aggressive or irresponsible. Their tolerance to frustration is low; they blame others or offer plausible rationalizations for the behavior which brings them into conflict with society.[1]

    asthenic type—*see* Personality disorder, dependent type

    avoidant type: Individuals with this disorder exhibit excessive social inhibitions and shyness, a tendency to withdraw from opportunities for developing close relationships, and a fearful expectation that they will be belittled and humiliated. Desires for affection and acceptance are strong, but they are unwilling to enter relationships unless given unusually strong guarantees that they will be uncritically accepted. Therefore, they have few close relationships and suffer from feelings of loneliness and isolation.[2]

    borderline type: Individuals with this disorder are characterized by instability in a variety of areas, including interpersonal relationships, behavior, mood, and self image. Interpersonal relationships are often intense and unstable with marked shifts of attitude over time. Frequently there is impulsive and unpredictable behavior which is potentially physically self-damaging. There may be problems tolerating being alone, and chronic feelings of emptiness or boredom.[2]

    chronic depressive type: An affective personality disorder characterized by lifelong predominance of a chronic nonpsychotic disturbance involving either intermittent or sustained periods of depressed mood (marked by worry, pessimism, low output of energy, and a sense of futility).[2]

    chronic hypomanic type: An affective personality disorder characterized by lifelong predominance of a chronic nonpsychotic disturbance involving either intermittent or sustained periods of abnormally elevated mood (unshakable optimism and an enhanced zest for life and activity).[2]

    compulsive type: A personality disorder characterized by feelings of personal insecurity, doubt, and incompleteness leading to excessive conscientiousness, checking, stubbornness, and caution. There may be insistent and unwelcome thoughts or impulses which do not attain the severity of an obsessional neurosis. There is perfectionism and meticulous accuracy and a need to check repeatedly in an attempt to ensure this. Rigidity and excessive doubt may be conspicuous.[1]

    cyclothymic type: A chronic nonpsychotic disturbance involving depressed and elevated mood, lasting at least two years, separated by periods of normal mood.[2]

    dependent type: A personality disorder characterized by passive compliance with the wishes of elders and others and a weak inadequate response to the demands of daily life. Lack of vigor may show itself in the intellectual or emotional spheres; there is little capacity for enjoyment.[1]

    eccentric type: A personality disorder characterized by oddities of behavior which do not conform to the clinical syndromes of personality disorders described elsewhere.[2]

    explosive type: A personality disorder characterized by instability of mood with liability to intemperate outbursts of anger, hate, violence, or affection. Aggression may be expressed in words or in physical violence. The outbursts cannot readily be controlled by the affected persons, who are not otherwise prone to antisocial behavior.[1]

    histrionic type: A personality disorder characterized by shallow, labile affectivity, dependence on others, craving for appreciation and attention, suggestibility, and theatricality. There is often sexual immaturity, e.g., frigidity and over-responsiveness to stimuli. Under stress hysterical symptoms [neurosis] may develop.[1]

    hysterical type—*see* Personality disorder, histrionic type

    inadequate type—*see* Personality disorder, dependent type

introverted type: A form of schizoid personality in which the essential features are a profound defect in the ability to form social relationships and to respond to the usual forms of social reinforcements. Such patients are characteristically "loners" who do not appear distressed by their social distance and are not interested in greater social involvements.[2]

masochistic type: A personality disorder in which the individual appears to arrange life situations so as to be defeated and humiliated.[2]

narcissistic type: A personality disorder in which interpersonal difficulties are caused by an inflated sense of self-worth, and indifference to the welfare of others. Achievement deficits and social irresponsibilities are justified and sustained by a boastful arrogance, expansive fantasies, facile rationalization, and frank prevarication.[2]

paranoid type: A personality disorder in which there is excessive sensitiveness to setbacks or to what are taken to be humiliations and rebuffs, a tendency to distort experience by misconstruing the neutral or friendly actions of others as hostile or contemptuous, and a combative and tenacious sense of personal rights. There may be a proneness to jealousy or excessive self-importance. Such persons may feel helplessly humiliated and put upon; others, likewise excessively sensitive, are aggressive and insistent. In all cases there is excessive self-reference.[1]

passive-aggressive type: A personality disorder characterized by aggressive behavior manifested in passive ways, such as obstructionism, pouting, procrastination, intentional inefficiency, or stubbornness. The *aggression* often arises from resentment at failing to find gratification in a relationship with an individual or institution upon which the individual is overdependent.[3]

passive type—*see* Personality disorder, dependent type

schizoid type: A personality disorder in which there is withdrawal from affectional, social, and other contacts with autistic preference for fantasy and introspective reserve. Behavior may be slightly eccentric or indicate avoidance of competitive situations. Apparent coolness and detachment may mask an incapacity to express feeling.

schizotypal type: A form of schizoid personality in which individuals with this disorder manifest various oddities of thinking, perception, communication, and behavior. The disturbance in thinking may be expressed as magical thinking, ideas of reference, or paranoid ideation. Perceptual disturbances may include recurrent illusions and derealization [depersonalization]. Frequently, but not invariably, the behavioral manifestations include social isolation and constricted or inappropriate affect which interferes with rapport in face-to-face interaction without any of the frank psychotic features which characterize schizophrenia.[2]

Phobia: Neurotic states with abnormally intense dread of certain objects or specific situations which would not normally have that effect. If the anxiety tends to spread from a specified situation or object to a wider range of circumstances, it becomes akin to or identical with anxiety state, and should be classified as such.[1]

acrophobia: Fear of heights[3]

agoraphobia: fear of leaving the familiar setting of the home, and is almost always preceded by a phase during which there are recurrent panic attacks. Because of the anticipatory fear of helplessness when having a panic attack, the patient is reluctant or refuses to be alone, travel or walk alone, or to be in situations where there is no ready access to help, such as in crowds, closed or open spaces, or crowded stores.[2]

ailurophobia: Fear of cats[3]

algophobia: Fear of pain[3]

claustrophobia: Fear of closed spaces[3]

isolated phobia—*see* simple phobia below

mysophobia: Fear of dirt or germs[3]

obsessional—*see* Neurotic disorder, obsessive-compulsive

panphobia: Fear of everything[3]

simple phobia: Fear of a discrete object or situation which is neither fear of leaving the familiar setting of the home [agoraphobia], or of being observed by others in certain situations [social phobia]. Examples of simple phobia are fear of animals, acrophobia, and claustrophobia.

social phobia: Fear of situations in which the subject is exposed to possible scrutiny by others, and the possibility exists that he may act in a fashion that will be considered shameful. The most common social phobias are fears of public speaking, blushing, eating in public, writing in front of others, or using public lavatories.[2]

xenophobia: Fear of strangers[3]

Pica: Perverted appetite of nonorganic origin in which there is persistent eating of non-nutritional substances. Typically, infants ingest paint, plaster, string, hair, or cloth. Older children may have access to animal droppings, sand, bugs, leaves, or pebbles. In the adult, eating of starch or clay-earth has been observed.[2]

Postconcussion syndrome: States occurring after generalized contusion of the brain, in which the symptom picture may resemble that of the frontal lobe syndrome or that of any of the neurotic disorders, but in which in addition, headache, giddiness, fatigue, insomnia, and a subjective feeling of impaired intellectual ability are usually prominent. Mood may fluctuate, and quite ordinary stress may produce exaggerated fear and apprehension. There may be marked intolerance of mental and physical exertion, undue sensitivity to noise, and hypochondriacal preoccupation. The symptoms are more common in persons who have previously suffered from neurotic or personality disorders, or when there is a possibility of compensation. This syndrome is particularly associated with the closed type of head injury when signs of localized brain damage are slight or absent, but it may also occur in other conditions.[1]

Postcontusion syndrome or encephalopathy—*see* Postconcussion syndrome

Postencephalitic syndrome: A nonpsychotic organic mental disorder resembling the postconcussion syndrome associated with central nervous system infections.[1]

Postleucotomy syndrome—*see* Frontal lobe syndrome

Posttraumatic brain syndrome, nonpsychotic—*see* Postconcussion syndrome

Posttraumatic organic psychosis—*see* Organic psychotic conditions, transient

Posttraumatic stress disorder: The development of characteristic symptoms (re-experiencing the traumatic event, numbing of responsiveness to or involvement with the external world, and a variety of other autonomic, dysphoric, or cognitive symptoms) after experiencing a psychologically traumatic event or events outside the normal range of human experience (e.g., rape or assault, military combat, natural catastrophes such as flood or earthquake, or other disaster, such as airplane crash, fires, bombings).[2]

    acute: Brief, episodic, or recurrent disorders lasting less than six months' duration after the onset of trauma.[2]

    prolonged: Chronic disorders of the above type lasting six months or more following the trauma.[2]

Premature ejaculation—*see* premature ejaculation under Psychosexual dysfunction.

Prepsychotic schizophrenia—*see* Schizophrenia, latent

Presbyophrenia—*see* Organic personality syndrome

Presenile dementia: Dementia occuring usually before the age of 65 in patients with the relatively rare forms of diffuse or lobar cerebral atrophy. The associated neurological condition (e.g., Alzheimer's disease, Pick's disease, Jakob-Creutzfeldt disease) should also be recorded as a diagnosis.[1]

Prodromal schizophrenia—*see* Schizophrenia, latent

Pseudoneurotic schizophrenia—*see* Schizophrenia, latent

Psychalgia: Pains of mental origin, e.g., headache or backache, for which a more precise medical or psychiatric diagnosis cannot be made.[1]

Psychasthenia: A functional neurosis marked by stages of pathological fear or anxiety, obsessions, fixed ideas, tics, feelings of inadequacy, self-accusation, and peculiar feelings of strangeness, unreality, and depersonalization.[4]

Psychic shock: A sudden disturbance of mental equilibrium produced by strong emotion in response to physical or mental stress.[4]

Psychic factors associated with physical diseases: Mental disturbances or psychic factors of any type thought to have played a major part in the etiology of physical conditions, usually involving tissue damage, classified elsewhere. The mental disturbance is usually mild and nonspecific, and the psychic factors (worry, fear, conflict, etc.) may be present without any overt psychiatric disorder. Examples of these conditions are asthma, dermatitis, eczema, duodenal ulcer, ulcerative colitis, and urticaria, specified as due to psychogenic factors.
Use an additional diagnosis to identify the physical condition. In the rare instance that an overt psychiatric disorder is thought to have caused the physical condition, the psychiatric diagnosis should be recorded in addition.[1]

Psychoneurosis—*see* Neurotic disorders

Psycho-organic syndrome—*see* Organic psychotic conditions, transient

Psychopathic constitutional state—*see* Personality disorders

Psychopathic personality—*see* Personality disorders

Psychophysiological disorders: A variety of physical symptoms or types of physiological malfunctions of mental origin, not involving tissue damage, and usually mediated through the autonomic nervous system. The disorders are classified according to the body system involved. If the physical symptom is secondary to a psychiatric disorder classifiable elsewhere, the physical symptom is not classified as a psychophysiological disorder. If tissue damage is involved, then the diagnosis is classified as a *Psychic factor associated with diseases classified elsewhere.*[1]

Psychosexual dysfunctions: A group of disorders in which there is recurrent and persistent dysfunction encountered during sexual activity. The dysfunction may be lifelong or acquired, generalized or situational, and total or partial.[2]

functional dyspareunia: Recurrent and persistent genital pain associated with coitus.[2]

functional vaginismus: A history of recurrent and persistent involuntary spasm of the musculature of the outer one-third of the vagina that interferes with sexual activity.[2]

inhibited female orgasm: Recurrent and persistent inhibition of the female orgasm as manifested by a delay or absence of orgasm following a normal sexual excitement phase during sexual activity.[2]

inhibited male orgasm: Recurrent and persistent inhibition of the male orgasm as manifested by a delay or absence of either the emission or ejaculation phases, or more usually, both following an adequate phase of sexual excitement.[2]

inhibited sexual desire: Persistent inhibition of desire for engaging in a particular form of sexual activity.[2]

inhibited sexual excitement: Recurrent and persistent inhibition of sexual excitement during sexual activity, manifested either by partial or complete failure to attain or maintain erection until completion of the sexual act [impotence], or partial or complete failure to attain or maintain the lubrication-swelling response of sexual excitement until completion of the sexual act [frigidity].[2]

premature ejaculation: Ejaculation occurs before the individual wishes it, because of recurrent and persistent absence of reasonable voluntary control of ejaculation and orgasm during sexual activity.[2]

Psychosexual gender identity disorders: Behavior occurring in preadolescents of immature psychosexuality, or in adults, in which there is an incongruence between the individual's anatomic sex and gender identity.[2]

gender identity disorder: In children or in adults a condition in which the individual would prefer to be of the other sex, and strongly prefers the clothes, toys, activities, and companionship of the other sex. Cross-dressing is intermittent, although it may be frequent. In children the commonest form is feminism in boys.[2]

trans-sexualism: A psychosexual identity disorder centered around fixed beliefs that the overt bodily sex is wrong. The resulting behavior is directed towards either changing the sexual organs by operation, or completely concealing the bodily sex by adopting both the dress and behavior of the opposite sex.[1]

Psychosomatic disorders—*see* Psychophysiological disorders

Psychosis: Mental disorders in which impairment of mental function has developed to a degree that interferes grossly with insight, ability to meet some ordinary demands of life or to maintain adequate contact with reality. It is not an exact or well defined term. Mental retardation is excluded.[1]

affective—*see* Affective psychoses

alcoholic—*see* Alcoholic psychoses

atypical childhood: A variety of atypical infantile psychoses which may show some, but not all, of the features of infantile autism. Symptoms may include stereotyped repetitive movements, hyperkinesis, self-injury, retarded speech development, echolalia, and impaired social relationships. Such disorders may occur in children of any level of intelligence but are particularly common in those with mental retardation.[1]

borderline, of childhood—*see* Psychosis, atypical childhood

child: A group of disorders in children, characterized by distortions in the timing, rate, and sequence of many psychological functions involving language development and social relations in which the severe qualitative abnormalities are not normal for any stage of development.[2] See also Autism, infantile, Psychosis, disintegrative, Psychosis, atypical childhood.

depressive—*see* Affective psychosis, depressed type

depressive type: A depressive psychosis which can be similar in its symptoms to manic-depressive psychosis, depressed type but is apparently provoked by saddening stress such as a bereavement, or a severe disappointment or frustration. There may be less diurnal variation of symptoms than in manic-depressive psychosis, depressed type, and the delusions are more often understandable in the context of the life experiences. There is usually a serious disturbance of behavior, e.g., major suicidal attempt.[1]

disintegrative: A disorder in which normal or near-normal development for the first few years is followed by a loss of social skills and of speech, together with a severe disorder of emotions, behavior, and relationships. Usually this loss of speech and of social competence takes place over a period of a few months and is accompanied by the emergence of overactivity and of stereotypies. In most cases there is intellectual impairment, but this is not a necessary part of the disorder. The condition may follow overt brain disease, such as measles encephalitis, but it may also occur in the absence of any known organic brain disease or damage. Any associated neurological disorder should also be recorded.[1]

epileptic: An organic psychotic condition associated with epilepsy.[1]

excitative type: An affective psychosis similar in its symptoms to manic-depressive psychosis, manic type, but apparently provoked by emotional stress.[1]

hypomanic—*see* Affective psychosis, manic type

hysterical—*see* Psychosis, reactive

    acute—*see* Psychosis, excitative type

induced—*see* Shared paranoid disorder

infantile—*see* Autism, infantile

infective—*see* Organic psychotic conditions, transient

Korsakoff's:

    alcoholic—*see* alcohol amnestic syndrome under Alcoholic psychoses

    nonalcoholic—*see* Amnestic syndrome

manic-depressive—*see* Affective psychoses

multi-infarct—*see* Arteriosclerotic dementia

paranoid

    chronic—*see* Paranoia

    protracted reactive—*see* Psychosis, paranoid, psychogenic

    psychogenic: Psychogenic or reactive paranoid psychosis of any type which is more protracted than the reactions described under paranoid reaction, acute.[1]
    acute—*see* Paranoid reaction, acute

postpartum—*see* Psychosis, puerperal

psychogenic—*see* Psychosis, reactive

    depressive—*see* Psychosis, depressive type

puerperal: Any psychosis occurring within a fixed period (approximately 90 days) after childbirth.[3] The diagnosis should be classified according to the predominant symptoms or characteristics, such as schizophrenia, affective psychosis, paranoid states, or other specified psychosis.

reactive: A psychotic condition which is largely or entirely attributable to a recent life experience. This diagnosis is not used for the wider range of psychoses in which environmental factors play some, but not the *major,* part in etiology.[1]

    brief: A florid psychosis of at least a few hours' duration but lasting no more than two weeks, with sudden onset immediately following a severe environmental stress and eventually terminating in complete recovery to the pre-psychotic state.[2]

    confusion: Mental disorders with clouded consciousness, disorientation (though less marked than in organic confusion), and diminished accessibility often accompanied by excessive activity and apparently provoked by emotional stress.[1]

    depressive—*see* Psychosis, depressive type

schizo-affective—*see* Schizophrenia, schizo-affective type

schizophrenic—*see* Schizophrenia

schizophreniform—*see* Schizophrenia

    affective type—*See* Schizophrenia, schizo-affective type

    confusional type—*see* Schizophrenia, acute episode

senile—*see* Senile dementia, delusional type

Pyromania: A disorder of impulse control characterized by a recurrent failure to resist impulses to set fires without regard for the consequences, or with deliberate destructive intent. Invariably there is intense fascination with the setting of fires, seeing fires burn, and a satisfaction with the resultant destruction.[2]

Relationship problems of childhood: Emotional disorders characteristic of childhood in which the main symptoms involve relationship problems.[1]

Repeated infarct dementia—*see* Arteriosclerotic dementia

Residual schizophrenia—.*see* Schizophrenia, residual type

Restzustand (schizophrenia)—*see* Schizophrenia, residual type

Rumination:

    obsessional: The constant preoccupation with certain thoughts, with inability to dismiss them from the mind.[4] *see* Neurotic disorder, obsessive-compulsive.

    psychogenic: In children the regurgitation of food, with failure to thrive or weight loss developing after a period of normal functioning. Food is brought up without nausea, retching, or disgust. The food is then ejected from the mouth, or chewed and reswallowed.[2]

Sander's disease—*see* Paranoia

Satyriasis: Pathologic or exaggerated sexual desire or excitement in the man.[3]

Schizoid personality disorder—*see* Personality disorder, schizoid type

Schizophrenia: A group of psychoses in which there is a fundamental disturbance of personality, a characteristic distortion of thinking, often a sense of being controlled by alien forces, delusions which may be bizarre, disturbed perception, abnormal affect out of keeping with the real situation, and autism. Nevertheless, clear consciousness and intellectual capacity are usually maintained. The disturbance of personality involves its most basic functions which give the normal person his feeling of individuality, uniqueness, and self-direction. The most intimate thoughts, feelings, and acts are often felt to be known to or shared by others and explanatory delusions may develop, to the effect that natural or supernatural forces are at work to influence the schizophrenic person's thoughts and actions in ways that are often bizarre. He may see himself as the pivot of all that happens. Hallucinations, especially of hearing, are common and may comment on the patient or address him. Perception is frequently disturbed in other ways; there may be perplexity, irrelevant features may become all-important and accompanied by passivity feeling, may lead the patient to believe that everyday objects and situations possess a special, usually sinister, meaning intended for him. In the characteristic schizophrenic disturbance of thinking, peripheral and irrelevant features of a total concept, which are inhibited in normal directed mental activity, are brought to the forefront and utilized in place of the elements relevant and appropriate to the situation. Thus, thinking becomes vague, elliptical and obscure, and its expression in speech sometimes incomprehensible. Breaks and interpolations in the flow of consecutive thought are frequent, and the patient may be convinced that his thoughts are being withdrawn by some outside agency. Mood may be shallow, capricious, or incongruous. Ambivalence and disturbance of volition may appear as inertia, negativism, or stupor. Catatonia may be present. The diagnosis "schizophrenia" should not be made unless there is, or has been evident during the same illness, characteristic disturbance of thought, perception, mood, conduct, or personality—preferably in at least two of these areas. The diagnosis should not be restricted to conditions running a protracted, deteriorating, or chronic course. In addition to making the diagnosis on the criteria just given, effort should be made to specify one of the following subtypes of schizophrenia, according to the predominant symptoms.[1]

acute (undifferentiated): Schizophrenia of florid nature which cannot be classified as simple, catatonic, hebephrenic, paranoid, or any other types.[1]

acute episode: Schizophrenic disorders, other than simple, hebephrenic, catatonic, and paranoid, in which there is a dream-like state with slight clouding of consciousness and perplexity. External things, people, and events may become charged with personal significance for the patient. There may be ideas of reference and emotional turmoil. In many such cases remission occurs within a few weeks or months, even without treatment.[1]

atypical—*see* Schizophrenia, acute (undifferentiated)

borderline—*see* Schizophrenia, latent

catatonic type: Includes as an essential feature prominent psychomotor disturbances often alternating between extremes such as hyperkinesis and stupor, or automatic obedience and negativism. Constrained attitudes may be maintained for long periods: if the patient's limbs are put in some unnatural position they may be held there for some time after the external force has been removed. Severe excitement may be a striking feature of the condition. Depressive or hypomanic concomitants may be present.[1]

cenesthopathic—*see* Schizophrenia, acute (undifferentiated)

childhood type—*see* Psychosis, child

chronic undifferentiated—*see* Schizophrenia, residual

cyclic—*see* Schizophrenia, schizo-affective type

disorganized type: A form of schizophrenia in which affective changes are prominent, delusions and hallucinations fleeting and fragmentary, behavior irresponsible and unpredictable, and mannerisms common. The mood is shallow and inappropriate, accompanied by giggling or self-satisfied, self—absorbed smiling, or by a lofty manner, grimaces, mannerisms, pranks, hypochondriacal complaints, and reiterated phrases. Thought is disorganized. There is a tendency to remain solitary, and behavior seems empty of purpose and feeling. This form of schizophrenia usually starts between the ages of 15 and 25 years.[1]

hebephrenic type:—*see* Schizophrenia, disorganized type

latent: It has not been possible to produce a generally acceptable description for this condition. It is not recommended for general use, but a description is provided for those who believe it to be useful: a condition of eccentric or inconsequent behavior and anomalies of affect which give the impression of schizophrenia though no definite and characteristic schizophrenic anomalies, present or past, have been manifest.[1]

paranoid type: The form of schizophrenia in which relatively stable delusions, which may be accompanied by hallucinations, dominate the clinical picture. The delusions are frequently of persecution, but may take other forms (for example, of jealousy, exalted birth, Messianic mission, or bodily change). Hallucinations and erratic behavior may occur; in some cases conduct is seriously disturbed from the outset, thought disorder may be gross, and affective flattening with fragmentary delusions and hallucinations may develop.[1]

prepsychotic—*see* Schizophrenia, latent

prodromal—*see* Schizophrenia, latent

pseudoneurotic—*see* Schizophrenia, latent

residual: A chronic form of schizophrenia in which the symptoms that persist from the acute phase have mostly lost their sharpness. Emotional response is blunted and thought disorder, even when gross, does not prevent the accomplishment of routine work.[1]

schizo-affective type: A psychosis in which pronounced manic or depressive features are intermingled with schizophrenic features and which tends towards remission without permanent defect, but which is prone to recur. The diagnosis should be made only when both the affective and schizophrenic symptoms are pronounced.[1]

simple type: A psychosis in which there is insidious development of oddities of conduct, inability to meet the demands of society, and decline in total performance. Delusions and hallucinations are not in evidence and the condition is less obviously psychotic than are the hebephrenic, catatonic, and paranoid types of schizophrenia. With increasing social impoverishment vagrancy may ensue and the patient becomes self-absorbed, idle, and aimless. Because the schizophrenic symptoms are not clear-cut, diagnosis of this form should be made sparingly, if at all.[1]

simplex—*see* Schizophrenia, simple type

Schizophrenic syndrome of childhood—*see* Psychosis, child

Schizophreniform

attack—*see* Schizophrenia, acute episode

disorder—*see* Schizophrenia, acute episode

psychosis—*see* Schizophrenia

    affective type—*see* Schizophrenia, schizo-affective type

    confusional type—*see* Schizophrenia, acute episode

Schizotypal personality—Dementia occurring usually after the age of 65 in which any cerebral pathology other than that of senile atrophic change can be reasonably excluded.[1]

delirium: Senile dementia with a superimposed reversible episode of acute confusional state.[1]

delusional type: A type of senile dementia characterized by development in advanced old age, progressive in nature, in which delusions, varying from simple poorly formed paranoid delusions to highly formed paranoid delusional states, and hallucinations are also present.[1,2]

depressed type: A type of senile dementia characterized by development in advanced old age, progressive in nature, in which depressive features, ranging from mild to severe forms of manic-depressive affective psychosis, are also present. Disturbance of the sleep-waking cycle and preoccupation with dead people are often particularly prominent.[1,2]

paranoid type—*see* Senile dementia, delusional type

simple type—*see* Senile dementia

Sensitiver Beziehungswahn: A paranoid state which, though in many ways akin to schizophrenic or affective states, differs from paranoia, simple paranoid state, shared paranoid disorder, or psychogenic psychosis.[1]

Sensitivity reaction of childhood or adolescence—*see* Shyness disorder of childhood

Separation anxiety disorder: A clinical disorder in children in which the predominant disturbance is exaggerated distress at separation from parents, home, or other familial surroundings. When separation is instituted, the child may experience anxiety to the point of panic. In adults a similar disorder is seen in agoraphobic reactions.[2]

Sexual deviations: Abnormal sexual inclinations or behavior which are part of a referral problem. The limits and features of normal sexual behavior have not been stated absolutely in different societies and cultures, but are broadly such as serve approved social and biological purposes. The sexual activity of affected persons is directed primarily either towards people not of the opposite sex, or towards sexual acts not associated with coitus normally, or towards coitus performed under abnormal circumstances. If the anomalous behavior becomes manifest only during psychosis or other mental illness the condition should be classified under the major illness. It is common for more than one anomaly to occur together in the same individual; in that case the predominant deviation is classified. It is preferable not to diagnose sexual deviation in individuals who perform deviant sexual acts when normal sexual outlets are not available to them.[1] *see also* exhibitionism, Fetishism, Homosexuality, Nymphomania, Pedophilia, Satyriasis, Sexual masochism, Sexual sadism, Transvestism, Voyeurism, and Zoophilia.

Gender identity disorder and trans-sexualism are considered to be psychosexual gender identity disorders and are not included here.

Sexual masochism: A sexual deviation in which sexual arousal and pleasure is produced in an individual by his own physical or psychological suffering, and in which there are insistent and persistent fantasies wherein sexual excitement is produced as a result of suffering.[2]

Sexual sadism: A sexual deviation in which physical or psychological suffering inflicted on another person is utilized as a method of stimulating erotic excitement and orgasm, and in which there are insistent and persistent fantasies wherein sexual excitement is produced as a result of suffering inflicted on the partner.[2]

Shared paranoid disorder: Mainly delusional psychosis, usually chronic and often without florid features, which appears to have developed as a result of a close, if not dependent, relationship with another person who already has an established similar psychosis. The delusions are at least partly shared. The rare cases in which several persons are affected should also be included here.[1]

Shifting sleep-work schedule: A sleep disorder in which the phase- shift disruption of the 24-hour sleep-wake cycle occurs due to rapid changes in the individual's work schedule.[2]

Short sleeper: Individuals who typically need only 4-6 hours of sleep within the 24-hour cycle.[2]

Shyness disorder of childhood: A persistent and excessive shrinking from familiarity or contact with all strangers of sufficient severity as to interfere with peer functioning, yet there are warm and satisfying relationships with family members. A critical feature of this disorder is that the avoidant behavior with strangers persists even after prolonged exposure or contact.[2]

Sibling jealousy or rivalry: An emotional disorder related to competition between siblings for the love of a parent or for other recognition or gain.[3]

Simple phobia—*see* simple phobia under Phobia

Situational disturbance, acute—*see* Stress reaction, acute

Social phobia—*see* social phobia under Phobia

Social withdrawal of childhood—*see* Introverted disorder of childhood

Socialized conduct disorder—*see* socialized conduct disorder under Conduct disorders

Somatization disorder—*see* somatization disorder under Neurotic disorders

Somatoform disorder, atypical—*see* hypochondriasis under Neurotic disorders

Spasmus nutans—*see* Stereotyped repetitive movements

Specific academic or work inhibition: An adjustment reaction in which a specific academic or work inhibition occurs in an individual whose intellectual capacity, skills, and previous academic or work performance have been at least adequate, and in which the inhibition occurs despite apparent effort and is not due to any other mental disorder.[2]

Stammering—*see* Stuttering

Starch-eating—*see* Pica

Status postcommotio cerebri—*see* Postconcussion syndrome

Stereotyped repetitive movements: Disorders in which voluntary repetitive stereotyped movements, which are not due to any psychiatric or neurological condition, constitute the main feature. Includes head-banging, spasmus nutans, rocking, twirling, finger-flicking mannerisms, and eye poking. Such movements are particularly common in cases of mental retardation with sensory impairment or with environmental monotony.[1]

Stereotypies—*see* Stereotyped repetitive movements

Stress reaction

    acute: Acute transient disorders of any severity and nature of emotions, consciousness, and psychomotor states (singly or in combination) which occur in individuals, without any apparent pre-existing mental disorder, in response to exceptional physical or mental stress, such as natural catastrophe or battle, and which usually subside within hours or days.[1]

    chronic—*see* Adjustment reaction

Stupor

    catatonic—*see* Schizophrenia, catatonic type

    psychogenic—*see* Psychosis, reactive

Stuttering: Disorders in the rhythm of speech, in which the individual knows precisely what he wishes to say, but at the time is unable to say it because of an involuntary, repetitive prolongation or cessation of a sound.[1]

Subjective insomnia complaint: a complaint of insomnia made by the individual, which has not been investigated or proven.[2]

Systematized delusions—*see* Paranoia

Tension headache: Headache of mental origin for which a more precise medical or psychiatric diagnosis cannot be made.[1]

Tics: Disorders of no known organic origin in which the outstanding feature consists of quick, involuntary, apparently purposeless, and frequently repeated movements which are not due to any neurological condition. Any part of the body may be involved but the face is most frequently affected. Only one form of tic may be present, or there may be a combination of tics which are carried out simultaneously, alternatively, or consecutively.[1]

    chronic motor tic disorder: A tic disorder starting in childhood and persisting into adult life. The tic is limited to no more than three motor areas, and rarely has a verbal component.[2]

Gilles de la Tourette's disorder [motor-verbal tic disorder]: a rare disorder occurring in individuals of any level of intelligence in which facial tics and tic-like throat noises become more marked and more generalized, and in which later whole words or short sentences (often with obscene content) are ejaculated spasmodically and involuntarily. There is some overlap with other varieties of tic.[1]

transient tic disorder of childhood: Facial or other tics beginning in childhood, but limited to one year in duration.[2]

Tobacco use disorder: Cases in which tobacco is used to the detriment of a person's health or social functioning or in which there is tobacco dependence. Dependence is included here rather than under drug dependence because tobacco differs from other drugs of dependence in its psychotoxic effects.[1]

Tranquilizer abuse: Cases where an individual has taken the drug to the detriment of his health or social functioning, in doses above or for periods beyond those normally regarded as therapeutic.[1]

Transient organic psychotic condition—*see* Organic psychotic conditions, transient

Trans-sexualism—*see* trans-sexualism under Psychosexual identity disorders

Transvestism: Sexual deviation in which there is recurrent and persistent dressing in clothes of the opposite sex, and initially in the early stage of the illness, for the purpose of sexual arousal.[2]

Twilight state

confusional—*see* Delirium, acute

psychogenic—*see* Psychosis, reactive confusion

Undersocialized conduct disorder—*see* undersocialized conduct disorder under Conduct disorders

Unsocialized aggressive disorder—*see* undersocialized conduct disorder, aggressive type under Conduct disorders

Vaginismus, functional—*see* functional vaginismus under Psychosexual dysfunctions

Vorbeireden: The symptom of the approximate answer or talking past the point, seen in the Ganser syndrome, a form of factitious illness.[2]

Voyeurism: A sexual deviation in which the individual repetitively seeks out situations in which he engages in looking at unsuspecting women who are either naked, in the act of disrobing, or engaging in sexual activity. The act of looking is accompanied by sexual excitement, frequently with orgasm. In its severe form, the act of peeping constitutes the preferred or exclusive sexual activity of the individual.[2]

Wernicke-Korsakoff syndrome—*see* alcohol amnestic syndrome under Alcoholic psychoses

Withdrawal reaction of childhood or adolescence—*see* Introverted disorder of childhood

Word-deafness: A developmental delay in the comprehension of speech sounds.[1]

Zoophilia: Sexual or anal intercourse with animals.[1]

1. Manual of the *International Classification of Diseases, Injuries, and Causes of Death*. 9th Revision. World Health Organization, Geneva, Switzerland, 1975.
2. American Psychiatric Association, Task Force on Nomenclature and Statistics, Robert L. Spitzer, Chairman.
3. *A Psychiatric Glossary*, Fourth Edition, American Psychiatric Association, Washington, D.C., 1975.
4. *Dorland's Illustrated Medical Dictionary*. Twenty-fifth Edition, W. B. Saunders Company, Philadelphia, 1974.
5. *Stedman's Medical Dictionary. Illustrated,* Twenty-third Edition, Williams and Wilkins, Baltimore, 1976.

CLASSIFICATION OF DRUGS BY AMERICAN HOSPITAL FORMULARY SERVICE LIST NUMBER AND THEIR ICD-9-CM EQUIVALENTS

The coding of adverse effects of drugs is keyed to the continually revised Hospital Formulary of the American Hospital Formulary Service (AHFS) published under the direction of the American Society of Hospital Pharmacists.

The following section gives the ICD-9-CM diagnosis code for each AHFS list.

	AHFS* LIST	ICD-9-CM Diagnosis Code
4:00	**ANTIHISTAMINE DRUGS**	963.0
8:00	**ANTI-INFECTIVE AGENTS**	
8:04	Amebacides	961.5
	hydroxyquinoline derivatives	961.3
	arsenical anti-infectives	961.1
8:08	Anthelmintics	961.6
	quinoline derivatives	961.3
8:12.04	Antifungal Antibiotics	960.1
	nonantibiotics	961.9
8:12.06	Cephalosporins	960.5
8:12.08	Chloramphenicol	960.2
8:12.12	The Erythromycins	960.3
8:12.16	The Penicillins	960.0
8:12.20	The Streptomycins	960.6
8:12.24	The Tetracyclines	960.4
8:12.28	Other Antibiotics	960.8
	antimycobacterial antibiotics	960.6
	macrolides	960.3
8:16	Antituberculars	961.8
	antibiotics	960.6
8:18	Antivirals	961.7
8:20	Plasmodicides (antimalarials)	961.4
8:24	Sulfonamides	961.0
8:26	The Sulfones	961.8
8:28	Treponemicides	961.2
8:32	Trichomonacides	961.5
	hydroxyquinoline derivatives	961.3
	nitrofuran derivatives	961.9
8:36	Urinary Germicides	961.9
	quinoline derivatives	961.3
8:40	Other Anti-Infectives	961.9
10:00	**ANTINEOPLASTIC AGENTS**	963.1
	antibiotics	960.7
	progestogens	962.2
12:00	**AUTONOMIC DRUGS**	
12:04	Parasympathomimetic (Cholinergic) Agents	971.0
12:08	Parasympatholytic (Cholinergic Blocking) Agents	971.1
12:12	Sympathomimetic (Adrenergic) Agents	971.2
12:16	Sympatholytic (Adrenergic Blocking) Agents	971.3
12:20	Skeletal Muscle Relaxants	975.2
	central nervous system muscle-tone depressants	968.0

	AHFS* LIST	ICD-9-CM Diagnosis Code
16:00	**BLOOD DERIVATIVES**	964.7
20:00	**BLOOD FORMATION AND COAGULATION**	
20:04	Antianemia Drugs	964.1
20:04.04	Iron Preparations	964.0
20:04.08	Liver and Stomach Preparations	964.1
20:12.04	Anticoagulants	964.2
20:12.08	Antiheparin agents	964.5
20:12.12	Coagulants	964.5
20:12.16	Hemostatics	964.5
	capillary-active drugs	972.8
	fibrinolysis-affecting agents	964.4
	natural products	964.7
24:00	**CARDIOVASCULAR DRUGS**	
24:04	Cardiac Drugs	972.9
	cardiotonic agents	972.1
	rhythm regulators	972.0
24:06	Antilipemic Agents	972.2
	thyroid derivatives	962.7
24:08	Hypotensive Agents	972.6
	adrenergic blocking agents	971.3
	ganglion-blocking agents	972.3
	vasodilators	972.5
24:12	Vasodilating Agents	972.5
	coronary	972.4
	nicotinic acid derivatives	972.2
24:16	Sclerosing Agents	972.7
28:00	**CENTRAL NERVOUS SYSTEM DRUGS**	
28:04	General Anesthetics	968.4
	gaseous anesthetics	968.2
	halothane	968.1
	intravenous anesthetics	968.3
28:08	Analgesics and Antipyretics	965.9
	antirheumatics	965.6
	aromatic analgesics	965.4
	non-narcotics NEC	965.7
	opium alkaloids	965.00
	heroin	965.01
	methadone	965.02
	specified type NEC	965.09
	pyrazole derivatives	965.5
	salicylates	965.1
	specified type NEC	965.8
28:10	Narcotic Antagonists	970.1
28:12	Anticonvulsants	966.3
	barbiturates	967.0
	benzodiazepine-based tranquilizers	969.4
	bromides	967.3
	hydantoin derivatives	966.1
	oxazolidine derivative	966.0
	succinimides	966.2
28:16.04	Antidepressants	969.0
28:16.08	Tranquilizers	969.5
	benzodiazepine-based	969.4
	butyrophenone-based	969.2
	major NEC	969.3
	phenothiazine-based	969.1

AHFS* LIST		ICD-9-CM Diagnosis Code
28:16.12	Other Psychotherapeutic Agents	969.8
28:20	Respiratory and Cerebral Stimulants	970.9
	analeptics	970.0
	anorexigenic agents	977.0
	psychostimulants	969.7
	specified type NEC	970.8
28:24	Sedatives and Hypnotics	967.9
	barbiturates	967.0
	benzodiazepine-based tranquilizers	969.4
	chloral hydrate group	967.1
	glutethamide group	967.5
	intravenous anesthetics	968.3
	methaqualone	967.4
	paraldehyde	967.2
	phenothiazine-based tranquilizers	969.1
	specified type NEC	967.8
	thiobarbiturates	968.3
	tranquilizer NEC	969.5
36:00	**DIAGNOSTIC AGENTS**	977.8
40:00	**ELECTROLYTE, CALORIC, AND WATER BALANCE AGENTS NEC**	974.5
40:04	Acidifying Agents	963.2
40:08	Alkalinizing Agents	963.3
40:10	Ammonia Detoxicants	974.5
40:12	Replacement Solutions NEC	974.5
	plasma volume expanders	964.8
40:16	Sodium-Removing Resins	974.5
40:18	Potassium-Removing Resins	974.5
40:20	Caloric Agents	974.5
40:24	Salt and Sugar Substitutes	974.5
40:28	Diuretics NEC	974.4
	carbonic acid anhydrase inhibitors	974.2
	mercurials	974.0
	purine derivatives	974.1
	saluretics	974.3
40:36	Irrigating Solutions	974.5
40:40	Uricosuric Agents	974.7
44:00	**ENZYMES NEC**	963.4
	fibrinolysis-affecting agents	964.4
	gastric agents	973.4
48:00	**EXPECTORANTS AND COUGH PREPARATIONS**	
	antihistamine agents	963.0
	antitussives	975.4
	codeine derivatives	965.09
	expectorants	975.5
	narcotic agents NEC	965.09
52:00	**EYE, EAR, NOSE, AND THROAT PREPARATIONS**	
52:04	Anti-Infectives	
	ENT	976.6
	ophthalmic	976.5
52:04.04	Antibiotics	
	ENT	976.6
	ophthalmic	976.5

	AHFS* LIST	ICD-9-CM Diagnosis Code
52:04.06	Antivirals	
	ENT	976.6
	ophthalmic	976.5
52:04.08	Sulfonamides	
	ENT	976.6
	ophthalmic	976.5
52:04.12	Miscellaneous Anti-Infectives	
	ENT	976.6
	ophthalmic	976.5
52:08	Anti-Inflammatory Agents	
	ENT	976.6
	ophthalmic	976.5
52:10	Carbonic Anhydrase Inhibitors	974.2
52:12	Contact Lens Solutions	976.5
52:16	Local Anesthetics	968.5
52:20	Miotics	971.0
52:24	Mydriatics	
	adrenergics	971.2
	anticholinergics	971.1
	antimuscarinics	971.1
	parasympatholytics	971.1
	spasmolytics	971.1
	sympathomimetics	971.2
52:28	Mouth Washes and Gargles	976.6
52:32	Vasoconstrictors	971.2
52:36	Unclassified Agents	
	ENT	976.6
	ophthalmic	976.5
56:00	**GASTROINTESTINAL DRUGS**	
56:04	Antacids and Absorbants	973.0
56:08	Anti-Diarrhea Agents	973.5
56:10	Antiflatulents	973.8
56:12	Cathartics NEC	973.3
	emollients	973.2
	irritants	973.1
56:16	Digestants	973.4
56:20	Emetics and Antiemetics	
	antiemetics	963.0
	emetics	973.6
56:24	Lipotropic Agents	977.1
60:00	**GOLD COMPOUNDS**	965.6
64:00	**HEAVY METAL ANTAGONISTS**	963.8
68:00	**HORMONES AND SYNTHETIC SUBSTITUTES**	
68:04	Adrenals	962.0
68:08	Androgens	962.1
68:12	Contraceptives	962.2
68:16	Estrogens	962.2
68:18	Gonadotropins	962.4
68:20	Insulins and Antidiabetic Agents	962.3
68:20.08	Insulins	962.3
68:24	Parathyroid	962.6

* American Hospital Formulary Service

	AHFS* LIST	ICD-9-CM Diagnosis Code
68:28	Pituitary	
	anterior	962.4
	posterior	962.5
68:32	Progestogens	962.2
68:34	Other Corpus Luteum Hormones	962.2
68:36	Thyroid and Antithyroid	
	antithyroid	962.8
	thyroid	962.7
72:00	**LOCAL ANESTHETICS NEC**	968.9
	topical (surface) agents	968.5
	infiltrating agents (intradermal) (subcutaneous)	
	(submucosal)	968.5
	nerve blocking agents (peripheral)	968.6
	(plexus)(regional)	
	spinal	968.7
76:00	**OXYTOCICS**	975.0
78:00	**RADIOACTIVE AGENTS**	990
80:00	**SERUMS, TOXOIDS, AND VACCINES**	
80:04	Serums	979.9
	immune globulin (gamma) (human)	964.6
80:08	Toxoids NEC	978.8
	diphtheria	978.5
	and tetanus	978.9
	with pertussis component	978.6
	tetanus	978.4
	and diphtheria	978.9
	with pertussis component	978.6
80:12	Vaccines NEC	979.9
	bacterial NEC	978.8
	with	
	other bacterial component	978.9
	pertussis component	978.6
	viral and rickettsial component	979.7
	rickettsial NEC	979.6
	with	
	bacterial component	979.7
	pertussis component	978.6
	viral component	979.7
	viral NEC	979.6
	with	
	bacterial component	979.7
	pertussis component	978.6
	rickettsial component	979.7
84:00	**SKIN AND MUCOUS MEMBRANE PREPARATIONS**	
84:04	Anti-Infectives	976.0
84:04.04	Antibiotics	976.0
84:04.08	Fungicides	976.0
84:04.12	Scabicides and Pediculicides	976.0
84:04.16	Miscellaneous Local Anti-Infectives	976.0
84:06	Anti-Inflammatory Agents	976.0
84:08	Antipruritics and Local Anesthetics	
	antipruritics	976.1
	local anesthetics	968.5
84:12	Astringents	976.2
84:16	Cell Stimulants and Proliferants	976.8
84:20	Detergents	976.2

	AHFS* LIST	ICD-9-CM Diagnosis Code
84:24	Emollients, Demulcents, and Protectants	976.3
84:28	Keratolytic Agents	976.4
84:32	Keratoplastic Agents	976.4
84:36	Miscellaneous Agents	976.8
86:00	**SPASMOLYTIC AGENTS**	975.1
	antiasthmatics	975.7
	papaverine	972.5
	theophyllin	974.1
88:00	**VITAMINS**	
88:04	Vitamin A	963.5
88:08	Vitamin B Complex	963.5
	hematopoietic vitamin	964.1
	nicotinic acid derivatives	972.2
88:12	Vitamin C	963.5
88:16	Vitamin D	963.5
88:20	Vitamin E	963.5
88:24	Vitamin K Activity	964.3
88:28	Multivitamin Preparations	963.5
92:00	**UNCLASSIFIED THERAPEUTIC AGENTS**	977.8

* American Hospital Formulary Service

CLASSIFICATION OF INDUSTRIAL ACCIDENTS ACCORDING TO AGENCY

Annex B to the Resolution concerning Statistics of Employment Injuries adopted by the Tenth International Conference of Labor Statisticians on 12 October 1962

1 MACHINES

11 Prime-Movers, except Electrical Motors
111 Steam engines
112 Internal combustion engines
119 Others

12 Transmission Machinery
121 Transmission shafts
122 Transmission belts, cables, pulleys, pinions, chains, gears
129 Others

13 Metalworking Machines
131 Power presses
132 Lathes
133 Milling machines
134 Abrasive wheels
135 Mechanical shears
136 Forging machines
137 Rolling-mills
139 Others

14 Wood and Assimilated Machines
141 Circular saws
142 Other saws
143 Molding machines
144 Overhand planes
149 Others

15 Agricultural Machines
151 Reapers (including combine reapers)
152 Threshers
159 Others

16 Mining Machinery
161 Under-cutters
169 Others

19 Other Machines Not Elsewhere Classified
191 Earth-moving machines, excavating and scraping machines, except means of transport
192 Spinning, weaving and other textile machines
193 Machines for the manufacture of foodstuffs and beverages
194 Machines for the manufacture of paper
195 Printing machines
199 Others

2 MEANS OF TRANSPORT AND LIFTING EQUIPMENT

21 Lifting Machines and Appliances
211 Cranes
212 Lifts and elevators
213 Winches
214 Pulley blocks
219 Others

22 Means of Rail Transport
221 Inter-urban railways
222 Rail transport in mines, tunnels, quarries, industrial establishments, docks, etc.
229 Others

23 Other Wheeled Means of Transport, Excluding Rail Transport
231 Tractors
232 Lorries
233 Trucks
234 Motor vehicles, not elsewhere classified
235 Animal-drawn vehicles

2 MEANS OF TRANSPORT AND LIFTING EQUIPMENT *continued*

236 Hand-drawn vehicles
239 Others

24 Means of Air Transport

25 Means of Water Transport
251 Motorized means of water transport
252 Non-motorized means of water transport

26 Other Means of Transport
261 Cable-cars
262 Mechanical conveyors, except cable-cars
269 Others

3 OTHER EQUIPMENT

31 Pressure Vessels
311 Boilers
312 Pressurized containers
313 Pressurized piping and accessories
314 Gas cylinders
315 Caissons, diving equipment
319 Others

32 Furnaces, Ovens, Kilns
321 Blast furnaces
322 Refining furnaces
323 Other furnaces
324 Kilns
325 Ovens

33 Refrigerating Plants

34 Electrical Installations, Including Electric Motors, but Excluding Electric Hand Tools
341 Rotating machines
342 Conductors
343 Transformers
344 Control apparatus
349 Others

35 Electric Hand Tools

36 Tools, Implements, and Appliances, Except Electric Hand Tools
361 Power-driven hand tools, except electric hand tools
362 Hand tools, not power-driven
369 Others

37 Ladders, Mobile Ramps

38 Scaffolding

39 Other Equipment, Not Elsewhere Classified

4 MATERIALS, SUBSTANCES AND RADIATIONS

41 Explosives

42 Dusts, Gases, Liquids and Chemicals, Excluding Explosives
421 Dusts
422 Gases, vapors, fumes
423 Liquids, not elsewhere classified
424 Chemicals, not elsewhere classified

43 Flying Fragments

44 Radiations
441 Ionizing radiations
449 Others

49 Other Materials and Substances Not Elsewhere Classified

5 WORKING ENVIRONMENT

51 Outdoor
511 Weather

5 WORKING ENVIRONMENT *continued*

512 Traffic and working surfaces
513 Water
519 Others

52 Indoor

521 Floors
522 Confined quarters
523 Stairs
524 Other traffic and working surfaces
525 Floor openings and wall openings
526 Environmental factors (lighting, ventilation, temperature, noise, etc.)
529 Others

53 Underground

531 Roofs and faces of mine roads and tunnels, etc.
532 Floors of mine roads and tunnels, etc.
533 Working-faces of mines, tunnels, etc.
534 Mine shafts
535 Fire
536 Water
539 Others

6 OTHER AGENCIES, NOT ELSEWHERE CLASSIFIED

61 Animals

611 Live animals
612 Animals products

69 Other Agencies, Not Elsewhere Classified

7 AGENCIES NOT CLASSIFIED FOR LACK OF SUFFICIENT DATA

LIST OF THREE-DIGIT CATEGORIES

1. INFECTIOUS AND PARASITIC DISEASES

Intestinal infectious diseases (001-009)

001   Cholera
002   Typhoid and paratyphoid fevers
003   Other salmonella infections
004   Shigellosis
005   Other food poisoning (bacterial)
006   Amebiasis
007   Other protozoal intestinal diseases
008   Intestinal infections due to other organisms
009   Ill-defined intestinal infections

Tuberculosis (010-018)

010   Primary tuberculous infection
011   Pulmonary tuberculosis
012   Other respiratory tuberculosis
013   Tuberculosis of meninges and central nervous system
014   Tuberculosis of intestines, peritoneum, and mesenteric glands
015   Tuberculosis of bones and joints
016   Tuberculosis of genitourinary system
017   Tuberculosis of other organs
018   Miliary tuberculosis

Zoonotic bacterial diseases (020-027)

020   Plague
021   Tularemia
022   Anthrax
023   Brucellosis
024   Glanders
025   Melioidosis
026   Rat-bite fever
027   Other zoonotic bacterial diseases

Other bacterial diseases (030-041)

030   Leprosy
031   Diseases due to other mycobacteria
032   Diphtheria
033   Whooping cough
034   Streptococcal sore throat and scarlet fever
035   Erysipelas
036   Meningococcal infection
037   Tetanus
038   Septicemia
039   Actinomycotic infections
040   Other bacterial diseases
041   Bacterial infection in conditions classified elsewhere and of unspecified site

Human immunodeficiency virus (042)

042   Human immunodeficiency virus [HIV] disease

Poliomyelitis and other non-arthropod-borne viral diseases of central nervous system (045-049)

045   Acute poliomyelitis
046   Slow virus infection of central nervous system
047   Meningitis due to enterovirus
048   Other enterovirus diseases of central nervous system
049   Other non-arthropod-borne viral diseases of central nervous system

Viral diseases accompanied by exanthem (050-057)

050   Smallpox
051   Cowpox and paravaccinia
052   Chickenpox
053   Herpes zoster
054   Herpes simplex
055   Measles
056   Rubella
057   Other viral exanthemata

1. INFECTIOUS AND PARASITIC DISEASES *continued*

Arthropod-borne viral diseases (060-066)

- 060 Yellow fever
- 061 Dengue
- 062 Mosquito-borne viral encephalitis
- 063 Tick-borne viral encephalitis
- 064 Viral encephalitis transmitted by other and unspecified arthropods
- 065 Arthropod-borne hemorrhagic fever
- 066 Other arthropod-borne viral diseases

Other diseases due to viruses and Chlamydiae (070-079)

- 070 Viral hepatitis
- 071 Rabies
- 072 Mumps
- 073 Ornithosis
- 074 Specific diseases due to Coxsackie virus
- 075 Infectious mononucleosis
- 076 Trachoma
- 077 Other diseases of conjunctiva due to viruses and Chlamydiae
- 078 Other diseases due to viruses and Chlamydiae
- 079 Viral and Chlamydial infection in conditions classified elsewhere and of unspecified site

Rickettsioses and other arthropod-borne diseases (080-088)

- 080 Louse-borne [epidemic] typhus
- 081 Other typhus
- 082 Tick-borne rickettsioses
- 083 Other rickettsioses
- 084 Malaria
- 085 Leishmaniasis
- 086 Trypanosomiasis
- 087 Relapsing fever
- 088 Other arthropod-borne diseases

Syphilis and other venereal diseases (090-099)

- 090 Congenital syphilis
- 091 Early syphilis, symptomatic
- 092 Early syphilis, latent
- 093 Cardiovascular syphilis
- 094 Neurosyphilis
- 095 Other forms of late syphilis, with symptoms
- 096 Late syphilis, latent
- 097 Other and unspecified syphilis
- 098 Gonococcal infections
- 099 Other venereal diseases

Other spirochetal diseases (100-104)

- 100 Leptospirosis
- 101 Vincent's angina
- 102 Yaws
- 103 Pinta
- 104 Other spirochetal infection

Mycoses (110-118)

- 110 Dermatophytosis
- 111 Dermatomycosis, other and unspecified
- 112 Candidiasis
- 114 Coccidioidomycosis
- 115 Histoplasmosis
- 116 Blastomycotic infection
- 117 Other mycoses
- 118 Opportunistic mycoses

Helminthiases (120-129)

- 120 Schistosomiasis [bilharziasis]
- 121 Other trematode infections
- 122 Echinococcosis
- 123 Other cestode infection
- 124 Trichinosis
- 125 Filarial infection and dracontiasis

1. INFECTIOUS AND PARASITIC DISEASES *continued*

126 Ancylostomiasis and necatoriasis
127 Other intestinal helminthiases
128 Other and unspecified helminthiases
129 Intestinal parasitism, unspecified

Other infectious and parasitic diseases (130-136)

130 Toxoplasmosis
131 Trichomoniasis
132 Pediculosis and phthirus infestation
133 Acariasis
134 Other infestation
135 Sarcoidosis
136 Other and unspecified infectious and parasitic diseases

Late effects of infectious and parasitic diseases (137-139)

137 Late effects of tuberculosis
138 Late effects of acute poliomyelitis
139 Late effects of other infectious and parasitic diseases

2. NEOPLASMS

Malignant neoplasm of lip, oral cavity, and pharynx (140-149)

140 Malignant neoplasm of lip
141 Malignant neoplasm of tongue
142 Malignant neoplasm of major salivary glands
143 Malignant neoplasm of gum
144 Malignant neoplasm of floor of mouth
145 Malignant neoplasm of other and unspecified parts of mouth
146 Malignant neoplasm of oropharynx
147 Malignant neoplasm of nasopharynx
148 Malignant neoplasm of hypopharynx
149 Malignant neoplasm of other and ill-defined sites within the lip, oral cavity, and pharynx

Malignant neoplasm of digestive organs and peritoneum (150-159)

150 Malignant neoplasm of esophagus
151 Malignant neoplasm of stomach
152 Malignant neoplasm of small intestine, including duodenum
153 Malignant neoplasm of colon
154 Malignant neoplasm of rectum, rectosigmoid junction, and anus
155 Malignant neoplasm of liver and intrahepatic bile ducts
156 Malignant neoplasm of gallbladder and extrahepatic bile ducts
157 Malignant neoplasm of pancreas
158 Malignant neoplasm of retroperitoneum and peritoneum
159 Malignant neoplasm of other and ill-defined sites within the digestive organs and peritoneum

Malignant neoplasm of respiratory and intrathoracic organs (160-165)

160 Malignant neoplasm of nasal cavities, middle ear, and accessory sinuses
161 Malignant neoplasm of larynx
162 Malignant neoplasm of trachea, bronchus, and lung
163 Malignant neoplasm of pleura
164 Malignant neoplasm of thymus, heart, and mediastinum
165 Malignant neoplasm of other and ill-defined sites within the respiratory system and intrathoracic organs

Malignant neoplasm of bone, connective tissue, skin, and breast (170-176)

170 Malignant neoplasm of bone and articular cartilage
171 Malignant neoplasm of connective and other soft tissue
172 Malignant melanoma of skin
173 Other malignant neoplasm of skin
174 Malignant neoplasm of female breast
175 Malignant neoplasm of male breast
176 Kaposi's sarcoma

Malignant neoplasm of genitourinary organs (179-189)

179 Malignant neoplasm of uterus, part unspecified
180 Malignant neoplasm of cervix uteri
181 Malignant neoplasm of placenta
182 Malignant neoplasm of body of uterus

2. NEOPLASMS *continued*

183   Malignant neoplasm of ovary and other uterine adnexa
184   Malignant neoplasm of other and unspecified female genital organs
185   Malignant neoplasm of prostate
186   Malignant neoplasm of testis
187   Malignant neoplasm of penis and other male genital organs
188   Malignant neoplasm of bladder
189   Malignant neoplasm of kidney and other and unspecified urinary organs

Malignant neoplasm of other and unspecified sites (190-199)

190   Malignant neoplasm of eye
191   Malignant neoplasm of brain
192   Malignant neoplasm of other and unspecified parts of nervous system
193   Malignant neoplasm of thyroid gland
194   Malignant neoplasm of other endocrine glands and related structures
195   Malignant neoplasm of other and ill-defined sites
196   Secondary and unspecified malignant neoplasm of lymph nodes
197   Secondary malignant neoplasm of respiratory and digestive systems
198   Secondary malignant neoplasm of other specified sites
199   Malignant neoplasm without specification of site

Malignant neoplasm of lymphatic and hematopoietic tissue (200-208)

200   Lymphosarcoma and reticulosarcoma
201   Hodgkin's disease
202   Other malignant neoplasm of lymphoid and histiocytic tissue
203   Multiple myeloma and immunoproliferative neoplasms
204   Lymphoid leukemia
205   Myeloid leukemia
206   Monocytic leukemia
207   Other specified leukemia
208   Leukemia of unspecified cell type

Benign neoplasms (210-229)

210   Benign neoplasm of lip, oral cavity, and pharynx
211   Benign neoplasm of other parts of digestive system
212   Benign neoplasm of respiratory and intrathoracic organs
213   Benign neoplasm of bone and articular cartilage
214   Lipoma
215   Other benign neoplasm of connective and other soft tissue
216   Benign neoplasm of skin
217   Benign neoplasm of breast
218   Uterine leiomyoma
219   Other benign neoplasm of uterus
220   Benign neoplasm of ovary
221   Benign neoplasm of other female genital organs
222   Benign neoplasm of male genital organs
223   Benign neoplasm of kidney and other urinary organs
224   Benign neoplasm of eye
225   Benign neoplasm of brain and other parts of nervous system
226   Benign neoplasm of thyroid gland
227   Benign neoplasm of other endocrine glands and related structures
228   Hemangioma and lymphangioma, any site
229   Benign neoplasm of other and unspecified sites

Carcinoma in situ (230-234)

230   Carcinoma in situ of digestive organs
231   Carcinoma in situ of respiratory system
232   Carcinoma in situ of skin
233   Carcinoma in situ of breast and genitourinary system
234   Carcinoma in situ of other and unspecified sites

Neoplasms of uncertain behavior (235-238)

235   Neoplasm of uncertain behavior of digestive and respiratory systems
236   Neoplasm of uncertain behavior of genitourinary organs
237   Neoplasm of uncertain behavior of endocrine glands and nervous system
238   Neoplasm of uncertain behavior of other and unspecified sites and tissues

Neoplasm of unspecified nature (239)

239   Neoplasm of unspecified nature

3. ENDOCRINE, NUTRITIONAL AND METABOLIC DISEASES, AND IMMUNITY DISORDERS

Disorders of thyroid gland (240-246)

240 Simple and unspecified goiter
241 Nontoxic nodular goiter
242 Thyrotoxicosis with or without goiter
243 Congenital hypothyroidism
244 Acquired hypothyroidism
245 Thyroiditis
246 Other disorders of thyroid

Diseases of other endocrine glands (250-259)

250 Diabetes mellitus
251 Other disorders of pancreatic internal secretion
252 Disorders of parathyroid gland
253 Disorders of the pituitary gland and its hypothalamic control
254 Diseases of thymus gland
255 Disorders of adrenal glands
256 Ovarian dysfunction
257 Testicular dysfunction
258 Polyglandular dysfunction and related disorders
259 Other endocrine disorders

Nutritional deficiencies (260-269)

260 Kwashiorkor
261 Nutritional marasmus
262 Other severe protein-calorie malnutrition
263 Other and unspecified protein-calorie malnutrition
264 Vitamin A deficiency
265 Thiamine and niacin deficiency states
266 Deficiency of B-complex components
267 Ascorbic acid deficiency
268 Vitamin D deficiency
269 Other nutritional deficiencies

Other metabolic disorders and immunity disorders (270-279)

270 Disorders of amino-acid transport and metabolism
271 Disorders of carbohydrate transport and metabolism
272 Disorders of lipoid metabolism
273 Disorders of plasma protein metabolism
274 Gout
275 Disorders of mineral metabolism
276 Disorders of fluid, electrolyte, and acid-base balance
277 Other and unspecified disorders of metabolism
278 Obesity and other hyperalimentation
279 Disorders involving the immune mechanism

4. DISEASES OF THE BLOOD AND BLOOD-FORMING ORGANS

Diseases of blood and blood-forming organs (280-289)

280 Iron deficiency anemias
281 Other deficiency anemias
282 Hereditary hemolytic anemias
283 Acquired hemolytic anemias
284 Aplastic anemia
285 Other and unspecified anemias
286 Coagulation defects
287 Purpura and other hemorrhagic conditions
288 Diseases of white blood cells
289 Other diseases of blood and blood-forming organs

5. MENTAL DISORDERS

Organic psychotic conditions (290-294)

290 Senile and presenile organic psychotic conditions
291 Alcoholic psychoses
292 Drug psychoses
293 Transient organic psychotic conditions
294 Other organic psychotic conditions (chronic)

5. MENTAL DISORDERS *continued*

Other psychoses (295-299)

- 295 Schizophrenic psychoses
- 296 Affective psychoses
- 297 Paranoid states (Delusional disorders)
- 298 Other nonorganic psychoses
- 299 Psychoses with origin specific to childhood

Neurotic disorders, personality disorders, and other nonpsychotic mental disorders (300-316)

- 300 Neurotic disorders
- 301 Personality disorders
- 302 Sexual deviations and disorders
- 303 Alcohol dependence syndrome
- 304 Drug dependence
- 305 Nondependent abuse of drugs
- 306 Physiological malfunction arising from mental factors
- 307 Special symptoms or syndromes, not elsewhere classified
- 308 Acute reaction to stress
- 309 Adjustment reaction
- 310 Specific nonpsychotic mental disorders due to organic brain damage
- 311 Depressive disorder, not elsewhere classified
- 312 Disturbance of conduct, not elsewhere classified
- 313 Disturbance of emotions specific to childhood and adolescence
- 314 Hyperkinetic syndrome of childhood
- 315 Specific delays in development
- 316 Psychic factors associated with diseases classified elsewhere

Mental retardation (317-319)

- 317 Mild mental retardation
- 318 Other specified mental retardation
- 319 Unspecified mental retardation

6. DISEASES OF THE NERVOUS SYSTEM AND SENSE ORGANS

Inflammatory diseases of the central nervous system (320-326)

- 320 Bacterial meningitis
- 321 Meningitis due to other organisms
- 322 Meningitis of unspecified cause
- 323 Encephalitis, myelitis, and encephalomyelitis
- 324 Intracranial and intraspinal abscess
- 325 Phlebitis and thrombophlebitis of intracranial venous sinuses
- 326 Late effects of intracranial abscess or pyogenic infection

Hereditary and degenerative diseases of the central nervous system (330-337)

- 330 Cerebral degenerations usually manifest in childhood
- 331 Other cerebral degenerations
- 332 Parkinson's disease
- 333 Other extrapyramidal disease and abnormal movement disorders
- 334 Spinocerebellar disease
- 335 Anterior horn cell disease
- 336 Other diseases of spinal cord
- 337 Disorders of the autonomic nervous system

Other disorders of the central nervous system (340-349)

- 340 Multiple sclerosis
- 341 Other demyelinating diseases of central nervous system
- 342 Hemiplegia and hemiparesis
- 343 Infantile cerebral palsy
- 344 Other paralytic syndromes
- 345 Epilepsy
- 346 Migraine
- 347 Cataplexy and narcolepsy
- 348 Other conditions of brain
- 349 Other and unspecified disorders of the nervous system

Disorders of the peripheral nervous system (350-359)

- 350 Trigeminal nerve disorders
- 351 Facial nerve disorders
- 352 Disorders of other cranial nerves
- 353 Nerve root and plexus disorders

6. DISEASES OF THE NERVOUS SYSTEM AND SENSE ORGANS *continued*

354 Mononeuritis of upper limb and mononeuritis multiplex
355 Mononeuritis of lower limb and unspecified site
356 Hereditary and idiopathic peripheral neuropathy
357 Inflammatory and toxic neuropathy
358 Myoneural disorders
359 Muscular dystrophies and other myopathies

Disorders of the eye and adnexa (360-379)
360 Disorders of the globe
361 Retinal detachments and defects
362 Other retinal disorders
363 Chorioretinal inflammations and scars and other disorders of choroid
364 Disorders of iris and ciliary body
365 Glaucoma
366 Cataract
367 Disorders of refraction and accommodation
368 Visual disturbances
369 Blindness and low vision
370 Keratitis
371 Corneal opacity and other disorders of cornea
372 Disorders of conjunctiva
373 Inflammation of eyelids
374 Other disorders of eyelids
375 Disorders of lacrimal system
376 Disorders of the orbit
377 Disorders of optic nerve and visual pathways
378 Strabismus and other disorders of binocular eye movements
379 Other disorders of eye

Diseases of the ear and mastoid process (380-389)
380 Disorders of external ear
381 Nonsuppurative otitis media and Eustachian tube disorders
382 Suppurative and unspecified otitis media
383 Mastoiditis and related conditions
384 Other disorders of tympanic membrane
385 Other disorders of middle ear and mastoid
386 Vertiginous syndromes and other disorders of vestibular system
387 Otosclerosis
388 Other disorders of ear
389 Hearing loss

7. DISEASES OF THE CIRCULATORY SYSTEM

Acute rheumatic fever (390-392)
390 Rheumatic fever without mention of heart involvement
391 Rheumatic fever with heart involvement
392 Rheumatic chorea

Chronic rheumatic heart disease (393-398)
393 Chronic rheumatic pericarditis
394 Diseases of mitral valve
395 Diseases of aortic valve
396 Diseases of mitral and aortic valves
397 Diseases of other endocardial structures
398 Other rheumatic heart disease

Hypertensive disease (401-405)
401 Essential hypertension
402 Hypertensive heart disease
403 Hypertensive renal disease
404 Hypertensive heart and renal disease
405 Secondary hypertension

Ischemic heart disease (410-414)
410 Acute myocardial infarction
411 Other acute and subacute form of ischemic heart disease
412 Old myocardial infarction
413 Angina pectoris
414 Other forms of chronic ischemic heart disease

7. DISEASES OF THE CIRCULATORY SYSTEM *continued*

Diseases of pulmonary circulation (415-417)
- 415 Acute pulmonary heart disease
- 416 Chronic pulmonary heart disease
- 417 Other diseases of pulmonary circulation

Other forms of heart disease (420-429)
- 420 Acute pericarditis
- 421 Acute and subacute endocarditis
- 422 Acute myocarditis
- 423 Other diseases of pericardium
- 424 Other diseases of endocardium
- 425 Cardiomyopathy
- 426 Conduction disorders
- 427 Cardiac dysrhythmias
- 428 Heart failure
- 429 Ill-defined descriptions and complications of heart disease

Cerebrovascular disease (430-438)
- 430 Subarachnoid hemorrhage
- 431 Intracerebral hemorrhage
- 432 Other and unspecified intracranial hemorrhage
- 433 Occlusion and stenosis of precerebral arteries
- 434 Occlusion of cerebral arteries
- 435 Transient cerebral ischemia
- 436 Acute but ill-defined cerebrovascular disease
- 437 Other and ill-defined cerebrovascular disease
- 438 Late effects of cerebrovascular disease

Diseases of arteries, arterioles, and capillaries (440-448)
- 440 Atherosclerosis
- 441 Aortic aneurysm and dissection
- 442 Other aneurysm
- 443 Other peripheral vascular disease
- 444 Arterial embolism and thrombosis
- 446 Polyarteritis nodosa and allied conditions
- 447 Other disorders of arteries and arterioles
- 448 Diseases of capillaries

Diseases of veins and lymphatics, and other diseases of circulatory system (451-459)
- 451 Phlebitis and thrombophlebitis
- 452 Portal vein thrombosis
- 453 Other venous embolism and thrombosis
- 454 Varicose veins of lower extremities
- 455 Hemorrhoids
- 456 Varicose veins of other sites
- 457 Noninfective disorders of lymphatic channels
- 458 Hypotension
- 459 Other disorders of circulatory system

8. DISEASES OF THE RESPIRATORY SYSTEM

Acute respiratory infections (460-466)
- 460 Acute nasopharyngitis [common cold]
- 461 Acute sinusitis
- 462 Acute pharyngitis
- 463 Acute tonsillitis
- 464 Acute laryngitis and tracheitis
- 465 Acute upper respiratory infections of multiple or unspecified sites
- 466 Acute bronchitis and bronchiolitis

Other diseases of upper respiratory tract (470-478)
- 470 Deviated nasal septum
- 471 Nasal polyps
- 472 Chronic pharyngitis and nasopharyngitis
- 473 Chronic sinusitis
- 474 Chronic disease of tonsils and adenoids
- 475 Peritonsillar abscess
- 476 Chronic laryngitis and laryngotracheitis
- 477 Allergic rhinitis

8. DISEASES OF THE RESPIRATORY SYSTEM *continued*

478 Other diseases of upper respiratory tract

Pneumonia and influenza (480-487)

480 Viral pneumonia
481 Pneumococcal pneumonia [Streptococcus pneumoniae pneumonia]
482 Other bacterial pneumonia
483 Pneumonia due to other specified organism
484 Pneumonia in infectious diseases classified elsewhere
485 Bronchopneumonia, organism unspecified
486 Pneumonia, organism unspecified
487 Influenza

Chronic obstructive pulmonary disease and allied conditions (490-496)

490 Bronchitis, not specified as acute or chronic
491 Chronic bronchitis
492 Emphysema
493 Asthma
494 Bronchiectasis
495 Extrinsic allergic alveolitis
496 Chronic airway obstruction, not elsewhere classified

Pneumoconioses and other lung diseases due to external agents (500-508)

500 Coalworkers' pneumoconiosis
501 Asbestosis
502 Pneumoconiosis due to other silica or silicates
503 Pneumoconiosis due to other inorganic dust
504 Pneumopathy due to inhalation of other dust
505 Pneumoconiosis, unspecified
506 Respiratory conditions due to chemical fumes and vapors
507 Pneumonitis due to solids and liquids
508 Respiratory conditions due to other and unspecified external agents

Other diseases of respiratory system (510-519)

510 Empyema
511 Pleurisy
512 Pneumothorax
513 Abscess of lung and mediastinum
514 Pulmonary congestion and hypostasis
515 Postinflammatory pulmonary fibrosis
516 Other alveolar and parietoalveolar pneumopathy
517 Lung involvement in conditions classified elsewhere
518 Other diseases of lung
519 Other diseases of respiratory system

9. DISEASES OF THE DIGESTIVE SYSTEM

Diseases of oral cavity, salivary glands, and jaws (520-529)

520 Disorders of tooth development and eruption
521 Diseases of hard tissues of teeth
522 Diseases of pulp and periapical tissues
523 Gingival and periodontal diseases
524 Dentofacial anomalies, including malocclusion
525 Other diseases and conditions of the teeth and supporting structures
526 Diseases of the jaws
527 Diseases of the salivary glands
528 Diseases of the oral soft tissues, excluding lesions specific for gingiva and tongue
529 Diseases and other conditions of the tongue

Diseases of esophagus, stomach, and duodenum (530-537)

530 Diseases of esophagus
531 Gastric ulcer
532 Duodenal ulcer
533 Peptic ulcer, site unspecified
534 Gastrojejunal ulcer
535 Gastritis and duodenitis
536 Disorders of function of stomach
537 Other disorders of stomach and duodenum

9. DISEASES OF THE DIGESTIVE SYSTEM *continued*

Appendicitis (540-543)
- 540 Acute appendicitis
- 541 Appendicitis, unqualified
- 542 Other appendicitis
- 543 Other diseases of appendix

Hernia of abdominal cavity (550-553)
- 550 Inguinal hernia
- 551 Other hernia of abdominal cavity, with gangrene
- 552 Other hernia of abdominal cavity, with obstruction, but without mention of gangrene
- 553 Other hernia of abdominal cavity without mention of obstruction or gangrene

Noninfectious enteritis and colitis (555-558)
- 555 Regional enteritis
- 556 Ulcerative colitis
- 557 Vascular insufficiency of intestine
- 558 Other noninfectious gastroenteritis and colitis

Other diseases of intestines and peritoneum (560-569)
- 560 Intestinal obstruction without mention of hernia
- 562 Diverticula of intestine
- 564 Functional digestive disorders, not elsewhere classified
- 565 Anal fissure and fistula
- 566 Abscess of anal and rectal regions
- 567 Peritonitis
- 568 Other disorders of peritoneum
- 569 Other disorders of intestine

Other diseases of digestive system (570-579)
- 570 Acute and subacute necrosis of liver
- 571 Chronic liver disease and cirrhosis
- 572 Liver abscess and sequelae of chronic liver disease
- 573 Other disorders of liver
- 574 Cholelithiasis
- 575 Other disorders of gallbladder
- 576 Other disorders of biliary tract
- 577 Diseases of pancreas
- 578 Gastrointestinal hemorrhage
- 579 Intestinal malabsorption

10. DISEASES OF THE GENITOURINARY SYSTEM

Nephritis, nephrotic syndrome, and nephrosis (580-589)
- 580 Acute glomerulonephritis
- 581 Nephrotic syndrome
- 582 Chronic glomerulonephritis
- 583 Nephritis and nephropathy, not specified as acute or chronic
- 584 Acute renal failure
- 585 Chronic renal failure
- 586 Renal failure, unspecified
- 587 Renal sclerosis, unspecified
- 588 Disorders resulting from impaired renal function
- 589 Small kidney of unknown cause

Other diseases of urinary system (590-599)
- 590 Infections of kidney
- 591 Hydronephrosis
- 592 Calculus of kidney and ureter
- 593 Other disorders of kidney and ureter
- 594 Calculus of lower urinary tract
- 595 Cystitis
- 596 Other disorders of bladder
- 597 Urethritis, not sexually transmitted, and urethral syndrome
- 598 Urethral stricture
- 599 Other disorders of urethra and urinary tract

Diseases of male genital organs (600-608)
- 600 Hyperplasia of prostate
- 601 Inflammatory diseases of prostate

10. DISEASES OF THE GENITOURINARY SYSTEM *continued*

602   Other disorders of prostate
603   Hydrocele
604   Orchitis and epididymitis
605   Redundant prepuce and phimosis
606   Infertility, male
607   Disorders of penis
608   Other disorders of male genital organs

Disorders of breast (610-611)

610   Benign mammary dysplasias
611   Other disorders of breast

Inflammatory disease of female pelvic organs (614-616)

614   Inflammatory disease of ovary, fallopian tube, pelvic cellular tissue, and peritoneum
615   Inflammatory diseases of uterus, except cervix
616   Inflammatory disease of cervix, vagina, and vulva

Other disorders of female genital tract (617-629)

617   Endometriosis
618   Genital prolapse
619   Fistula involving female genital tract
620   Noninflammatory disorders of ovary, fallopian tube, and broad ligament
621   Disorders of uterus, not elsewhere classified
622   Noninflammatory disorders of cervix
623   Noninflammatory disorders of vagina
624   Noninflammatory disorders of vulva and perineum
625   Pain and other symptoms associated with female genital organs
626   Disorders of menstruation and other abnormal bleeding from female genital tract
627   Menopausal and postmenopausal disorders
628   Infertility, female
629   Other disorders of female genital organs

11. COMPLICATIONS OF PREGNANCY, CHILDBIRTH AND THE PUERPERIUM

Ectopic and molar pregnancy (630-633)

630   Hydatidiform mole
631   Other abnormal product of conception
632   Missed abortion
633   Ectopic pregnancy

Other pregnancy with abortive outcome (634-639)

634   Abortion
635   Legally induced abortion
636   Illegally induced abortion
637   Unspecified abortion
638   Failed attempted abortion
639   Complications following abortion and ectopic and molar pregnancies

Complications mainly related to pregnancy (640-648)

640   Hemorrhage in early pregnancy
641   Antepartum hemorrhage, abruptio placentae, and placenta previa
642   Hypertension complicating pregnancy, childbirth, and the puerperium
643   Excessive vomiting in pregnancy
644   Early or threatened labor
645   Late pregnancy
646   Other complications of pregnancy, not elsewhere classified
647   Infective and parasitic conditions in the mother classifiable elsewhere but complicating pregnancy, childbirth, and the puerperium
648   Other current conditions in the mother classifiable elsewhere but complicating pregnancy, childbirth, and the puerperium

Normal delivery, and other indications for care in pregnancy, labor, and delivery (650-659)

650   Normal delivery
651   Multiple gestation
652   Malposition and malpresentation of fetus
653   Disproportion
654   Abnormality of organs and soft tissues of pelvis
655   Known or suspected fetal abnormality affecting management of mother
656   Other fetal and placental problems affecting management of mother
657   Polyhydramnios

11. COMPLICATIONS OF PREGNANCY, CHILDBIRTH AND THE PUERPERIUM *continued*

    658   Other problems associated with amniotic cavity and membranes
    659   Other indications for care or intervention related to labor and delivery and not elsewhere classified

Complications occurring mainly in the course of labor and delivery (660-669)

    660   Obstructed labor
    661   Abnormality of forces of labor
    662   Long labor
    663   Umbilical cord complications
    664   Trauma to perineum and vulva during delivery
    665   Other obstetrical trauma
    666   Postpartum hemorrhage
    667   Retained placenta or membranes, without hemorrhage
    668   Complications of the administration of anesthetic or other sedation in labor and delivery
    669   Other complications of labor and delivery, not elsewhere classified

Complications of the puerperium (670-677)

    670   Major puerperal infection
    671   Venous complications in pregnancy and the puerperium
    672   Pyrexia of unknown origin during the puerperium
    673   Obstetrical pulmonary embolism
    674   Other and unspecified complications of the puerperium, not elsewhere classified
    675   Infections of the breast and nipple associated with childbirth
    676   Other disorders of the breast associated with childbirth, and disorders of lactation
    677   Late effect of complication of pregnancy, childbirth, and the puerperium

12. DISEASES OF THE SKIN AND SUBCUTANEOUS TISSUE

Infections of skin and subcutaneous tissue (680-686)

    680   Carbuncle and furuncle
    681   Cellulitis and abscess of finger and toe
    682   Other cellulitis and abscess
    683   Acute lymphadenitis
    684   Impetigo
    685   Pilonidal cyst
    686   Other local infections of skin and subcutaneous tissue

Other inflammatory conditions of skin and subcutaneous tissue (690-698)

    690   Erythematosquamous dermatosis
    691   Atopic dermatitis and related conditions
    692   Contact dermatitis and other eczema
    693   Dermatitis due to substances taken internally
    694   Bullous dermatoses
    695   Erythematous conditions
    696   Psoriasis and similar disorders
    697   Lichen
    698   Pruritus and related conditions

Other diseases of skin and subcutaneous tissue (700-709)

    700   Corns and callosities
    701   Other hypertrophic and atrophic conditions of skin
    702   Other dermatoses
    703   Diseases of nail
    704   Diseases of hair and hair follicles
    705   Disorders of sweat glands
    706   Diseases of sebaceous glands
    707   Chronic ulcer of skin
    708   Urticaria
    709   Other disorders of skin and subcutaneous tissue

13. DISEASES OF THE MUSCULOSKELETAL SYSTEM AND CONNECTIVE TISSUE

Arthropathies and related disorders (710-719)

    710   Diffuse diseases of connective tissue
    711   Arthropathy associated with infections
    712   Crystal arthropathies
    713   Arthropathy associated with other disorders classified elsewhere
    714   Rheumatoid arthritis and other inflammatory polyarthropathies
    715   Osteoarthrosis and allied disorders

13. DISEASES OF THE MUSCULOSKELETAL SYSTEM AND CONNECTIVE TISSUE
continued

716   Other and unspecified arthropathies
717   Internal derangement of knee
718   Other derangement of joint
719   Other and unspecified disorder of joint

Dorsopathies (720-724)
720   Ankylosing spondylitis and other inflammatory spondylopathies
721   Spondylosis and allied disorders
722   Intervertebral disc disorders
723   Other disorders of cervical region
724   Other and unspecified disorders of back

Rheumatism, excluding the back (725-729)
725   Polymyalgia rheumatica
726   Peripheral enthesopathies and allied syndromes
727   Other disorders of synovium, tendon, and bursa
728   Disorders of muscle, ligament, and fascia
729   Other disorders of soft tissues

Osteopathies, chondropathies, and acquired musculoskeletal deformities (730-739)
730   Osteomyelitis, periostitis, and other infections involving bone
731   Osteitis deformans and osteopathies associated with other disorders classified elsewhere
732   Osteochondropathies
733   Other disorders of bone and cartilage
734   Flat foot
735   Acquired deformities of toe
736   Other acquired deformities of limbs
737   Curvature of spine
738   Other acquired deformity
739   Nonallopathic lesions, not elsewhere classified

14. CONGENITAL ANOMALIES

740   Anencephalus and similar anomalies
741   Spina bifida
742   Other congenital anomalies of nervous system
743   Congenital anomalies of eye
744   Congenital anomalies of ear, face, and neck
745   Bulbus cordis anomalies and anomalies of cardiac septal closure
746   Other congenital anomalies of heart
747   Other congenital anomalies of circulatory system
748   Congenital anomalies of respiratory system
749   Cleft palate and cleft lip
750   Other congenital anomalies of upper alimentary tract
751   Other congenital anomalies of digestive system
752   Congenital anomalies of genital organs
753   Congenital anomalies of urinary system
754   Certain congenital musculoskeletal deformities
755   Other congenital anomalies of limbs
756   Other congenital musculoskeletal anomalies
757   Congenital anomalies of the integument
758   Chromosomal anomalies
759   Other and unspecified congenital anomalies

15. CERTAIN CONDITIONS ORIGINATING IN THE PERINATAL PERIOD

Maternal causes of perinatal morbidity and mortality (760-763)
760   Fetus or newborn affected by maternal conditions which may be unrelated to present pregnancy
761   Fetus or newborn affected by maternal complications of pregnancy
762   Fetus or newborn affected by complications of placenta, cord, and membranes
763   Fetus or newborn affected by other complications of labor and delivery

Other conditions originating in the perinatal period (764-779)
764   Slow fetal growth and fetal malnutrition
765   Disorders relating to short gestation and unspecified low birthweight
766   Disorders relating to long gestation and high birthweight
767   Birth trauma

15. CERTAIN CONDITIONS ORIGINATING IN THE PERINATAL PERIOD *continued*

- 768 Intrauterine hypoxia and birth asphyxia
- 769 Respiratory distress syndrome
- 770 Other respiratory conditions of fetus and newborn
- 771 Infections specific to the perinatal period
- 772 Fetal and neonatal hemorrhage
- 773 Hemolytic disease of fetus or newborn, due to isoimmunization
- 774 Other perinatal jaundice
- 775 Endocrine and metabolic disturbances specific to the fetus and newborn
- 776 Hematological disorders of fetus and newborn
- 777 Perinatal disorders of digestive system
- 778 Conditions involving the integument and temperature regulation of fetus and newborn
- 779 Other and ill-defined conditions originating in the perinatal period

16. SYMPTOMS, SIGNS, AND ILL-DEFINED CONDITIONS

Symptoms (780-789)

- 780 General symptoms
- 781 Symptoms involving nervous and musculoskeletal systems
- 782 Symptoms involving skin and other integumentary tissue
- 783 Symptoms concerning nutrition, metabolism, and development
- 784 Symptoms involving head and neck
- 785 Symptoms involving cardiovascular system
- 786 Symptoms involving respiratory system and other chest symptoms
- 787 Symptoms involving digestive system
- 788 Symptoms involving urinary system
- 789 Other symptoms involving abdomen and pelvis

Nonspecific abnormal findings (790-796)

- 790 Nonspecific findings on examination of blood
- 791 Nonspecific findings on examination of urine
- 792 Nonspecific abnormal findings in other body substances
- 793 Nonspecific abnormal findings on radiological and other examination of body structure
- 794 Nonspecific abnormal results of function studies
- 795 Nonspecific abnormal histological and immunological findings
- 796 Other nonspecific abnormal findings

Ill-defined and unknown causes of morbidity and mortality (797-799)

- 797 Senility without mention of psychosis
- 798 Sudden death, cause unknown
- 799 Other ill-defined and unknown causes of morbidity and mortality

17. INJURY AND POISONING

Fracture of skull (800-804)

- 800 Fracture of vault of skull
- 801 Fracture of base of skull
- 802 Fracture of face bones
- 803 Other and unqualified skull fractures
- 804 Multiple fractures involving skull or face with other bones

Fracture of neck and trunk (805-809)

- 805 Fracture of vertebral column without mention of spinal cord injury
- 806 Fracture of vertebral column with spinal cord injury
- 807 Fracture of rib(s), sternum, larynx, and trachea
- 808 Fracture of pelvis
- 809 Ill-defined fractures of bones of trunk

Fracture of upper limb (810-819)

- 810 Fracture of clavicle
- 811 Fracture of scapula
- 812 Fracture of humerus
- 813 Fracture of radius and ulna
- 814 Fracture of carpal bone(s)
- 815 Fracture of metacarpal bone(s)
- 816 Fracture of one or more phalanges of hand
- 817 Multiple fractures of hand bones
- 818 Ill-defined fractures of upper limb
- 819 Multiple fractures involving both upper limbs, and upper limb with rib(s) and sternum

17. INJURY AND POISONING *continued*

Fracture of lower limb (820-829)

820 Fracture of neck of femur
821 Fracture of other and unspecified parts of femur
822 Fracture of patella
823 Fracture of tibia and fibula
824 Fracture of ankle
825 Fracture of one or more tarsal and metatarsal bones
826 Fracture of one or more phalanges of foot
827 Other, multiple, and ill-defined fractures of lower limb
828 Multiple fractures involving both lower limbs, lower with upper limb, and lower limb(s) with rib(s) and sternum
829 Fracture of unspecified bones

Dislocation (830-839)

830 Dislocation of jaw
831 Dislocation of shoulder
832 Dislocation of elbow
833 Dislocation of wrist
834 Dislocation of finger
835 Dislocation of hip
836 Dislocation of knee
837 Dislocation of ankle
838 Dislocation of foot
839 Other, multiple, and ill-defined dislocations

Sprains and strains of joints and adjacent muscles (840-848)

840 Sprains and strains of shoulder and upper arm
841 Sprains and strains of elbow and forearm
842 Sprains and strains of wrist and hand
843 Sprains and strains of hip and thigh
844 Sprains and strains of knee and leg
845 Sprains and strains of ankle and foot
846 Sprains and strains of sacroiliac region
847 Sprains and strains of other and unspecified parts of back
848 Other and ill-defined sprains and strains

Intracranial injury, excluding those with skull fracture (850-854)

850 Concussion
851 Cerebral laceration and contusion
852 Subarachnoid, subdural, and extradural hemorrhage, following injury
853 Other and unspecified intracranial hemorrhage following injury
854 Intracranial injury of other and unspecified nature

Internal injury of thorax, abdomen, and pelvis (860-869)

860 Traumatic pneumothorax and hemothorax
861 Injury to heart and lung
862 Injury to other and unspecified intrathoracic organs
863 Injury to gastrointestinal tract
864 Injury to liver
865 Injury to spleen
866 Injury to kidney
867 Injury to pelvic organs
868 Injury to other intra-abdominal organs
869 Internal injury to unspecified or ill-defined organs

Open wound of head, neck, and trunk (870-879)

870 Open wound of ocular adnexa
871 Open wound of eyeball
872 Open wound of ear
873 Other open wound of head
874 Open wound of neck
875 Open wound of chest (wall)
876 Open wound of back
877 Open wound of buttock
878 Open wound of genital organs (external), including traumatic amputation
879 Open wound of other and unspecified sites, except limbs

Open wound of upper limb (880-887)

880 Open wound of shoulder and upper arm

17. INJURY AND POISONING *continued*

881 Open wound of elbow, forearm, and wrist
882 Open wound of hand except finger(s) alone
883 Open wound of finger(s)
884 Multiple and unspecified open wound of upper limb
885 Traumatic amputation of thumb (complete) (partial)
886 Traumatic amputation of other finger(s) (complete) (partial)
887 Traumatic amputation of arm and hand (complete) (partial)

Open wound of lower limb (890-897)

890 Open wound of hip and thigh
891 Open wound of knee, leg [except thigh], and ankle
892 Open wound of foot except toe(s) alone
893 Open wound of toe(s)
894 Multiple and unspecified open wound of lower limb
895 Traumatic amputation of toe(s) (complete) (partial)
896 Traumatic amputation of foot (complete) (partial)
897 Traumatic amputation of leg(s) (complete) (partial)

Injury to blood vessels (900-904)

900 Injury to blood vessels of head and neck
901 Injury to blood vessels of thorax
902 Injury to blood vessels of abdomen and pelvis
903 Injury to blood vessels of upper extremity
904 Injury to blood vessels of lower extremity and unspecified sites

Late effects of injuries, poisonings, toxic effects, and other external causes (905-909)

905 Late effects of musculoskeletal and connective tissue injuries
906 Late effects of injuries to skin and subcutaneous tissues
907 Late effects of injuries to the nervous system
908 Late effects of other and unspecified injuries
909 Late effects of other and unspecified external causes

Superficial injury (910-919)

910 Superficial injury of face, neck, and scalp except eye
911 Superficial injury of trunk
912 Superficial injury of shoulder and upper arm
913 Superficial injury of elbow, forearm, and wrist
914 Superficial injury of hand(s) except finger(s) alone
915 Superficial injury of finger(s)
916 Superficial injury of hip, thigh, leg, and ankle
917 Superficial injury of foot and toe(s)
918 Superficial injury of eye and adnexa
919 Superficial injury of other, multiple, and unspecified sites

Contusion with intact skin surface (920-924)

920 Contusion of face, scalp, and neck except eye(s)
921 Contusion of eye and adnexa
922 Contusion of trunk
923 Contusion of upper limb
924 Contusion of lower limb and of other and unspecified sites

Crushing injury (925-929)

925 Crushing injury of face, scalp, and neck
926 Crushing injury of trunk
927 Crushing injury of upper limb
928 Crushing injury of lower limb
929 Crushing injury of multiple and unspecified sites

Effects of foreign body entering through orifice (930-939)

930 Foreign body on external eye
931 Foreign body in ear
932 Foreign body in nose
933 Foreign body in pharynx and larynx
934 Foreign body in trachea, bronchus, and lung
935 Foreign body in mouth, esophagus, and stomach
936 Foreign body in intestine and colon
937 Foreign body in anus and rectum
938 Foreign body in digestive system, unspecified
939 Foreign body in genitourinary tract

17. INJURY AND POISONING *continued*

Burns (940-949)

    940   Burn confined to eye and adnexa
    941   Burn of face, head, and neck
    942   Burn of trunk
    943   Burn of upper limb, except wrist and hand
    944   Burn of wrist(s) and hand(s)
    945   Burn of lower limb(s)
    946   Burns of multiple specified sites
    947   Burn of internal organs
    948   Burns classified according to extent of body surface involved
    949   Burn, unspecified

Injury to nerves and spinal cord (950-957)

    950   Injury to optic nerve and pathways
    951   Injury to other cranial nerve(s)
    952   Spinal cord injury without evidence of spinal bone injury
    953   Injury to nerve roots and spinal plexus
    954   Injury to other nerve(s) of trunk excluding shoulder and pelvic girdles
    955   Injury to peripheral nerve(s) of shoulder girdle and upper limb
    956   Injury to peripheral nerve(s) of pelvic girdle and lower limb
    957   Injury to other and unspecified nerves

Certain traumatic complications and unspecified injuries (958-959)

    958   Certain early complications of trauma
    959   Injury, other and unspecified

Poisoning by drugs, medicinal and biological substances (960-979)

    960   Poisoning by antibiotics
    961   Poisoning by other anti-infectives
    962   Poisoning by hormones and synthetic substitutes
    963   Poisoning by primarily systemic agents
    964   Poisoning by agents primarily affecting blood constituents
    965   Poisoning by analgesics, antipyretics, and antirheumatics
    966   Poisoning by anticonvulsants and anti-Parkinsonism drugs
    967   Poisoning by sedatives and hypnotics
    968   Poisoning by other central nervous system depressants and anesthetics
    969   Poisoning by psychotropic agents
    970   Poisoning by central nervous system stimulants
    971   Poisoning by drugs primarily affecting the autonomic nervous system
    972   Poisoning by agents primarily affecting the cardiovascular system
    973   Poisoning by agents primarily affecting the gastrointestinal system
    974   Poisoning by water, mineral, and uric acid metabolism drugs
    975   Poisoning by agents primarily acting on the smooth and skeletal muscles and respiratory system
    976   Poisoning by agents primarily affecting skin and mucous membrane, ophthalmological, otorhinolaryngological, and dental drugs
    977   Poisoning by other and unspecified drugs and medicinals
    978   Poisoning by bacterial vaccines
    979   Poisoning by other vaccines and biological substances

Toxic effects of substances chiefly nonmedicinal as to source (980-989)

    980   Toxic effect of alcohol
    981   Toxic effect of petroleum products
    982   Toxic effect of solvents other than petroleum-based
    983   Toxic effect of corrosive aromatics, acids, and caustic alkalis
    984   Toxic effect of lead and its compounds (including fumes)
    985   Toxic effect of other metals
    986   Toxic effect of carbon monoxide
    987   Toxic effect of other gases, fumes, or vapors
    988   Toxic effect of noxious substances eaten as food
    989   Toxic effect of other substances, chiefly nonmedicinal as to source

Other and unspecified effects of external causes (990-995)

    990   Effects of radiation, unspecified
    991   Effects of reduced temperature
    992   Effects of heat and light
    993   Effects of air pressure
    994   Effects of other external causes

17. INJURY AND POISONING *continued*

    995   Certain adverse effects, not elsewhere classified

Complications of surgical and medical care, not elsewhere classified (996-999)

    996   Complications peculiar to certain specified procedures
    997   Complications affecting specified body systems, not elsewhere classified
    998   Other complications of procedures, not elsewhere classified
    999   Complications of medical care, not elsewhere classified

SUPPLEMENTARY CLASSIFICATION OF FACTORS INFLUENCING HEALTH STATUS AND CONTACT WITH HEALTH SERVICES

Persons with potential health hazards related to communicable diseases (V01-V09)

    V01   Contact with or exposure to communicable diseases
    V02   Carrier or suspected carrier of infectious diseases
    V03   Need for prophylactic vaccination and inoculation against bacterial diseases
    V04   Need for prophylactic vaccination and inoculation against certain viral diseases
    V05   Need for other prophylactic vaccination and inoculation against single diseases
    V06   Need for prophylactic vaccination and inoculation against combinations of diseases
    V07   Need for isolation and other prophylactic measures
    V08   Asymptomatic human immunodeficiency virus (HIV) infection status
    V09   Infection with drug-resistant microorganisms

Persons with potential health hazards related to personal and family history (V10-V19)

    V10   Personal history of malignant neoplasm
    V11   Personal history of mental disorder
    V12   Personal history of certain other diseases
    V13   Personal history of other diseases
    V14   Personal history of allergy to medicinal agents
    V15   Other personal history presenting hazards to health
    V16   Family history of malignant neoplasm
    V17   Family history of certain chronic disabling diseases
    V18   Family history of certain other specific conditions
    V19   Family history of other conditions

Persons encountering health services in circumstances related to reproduction and development (V20-V29)

    V20   Health supervision of infant or child
    V21   Constitutional states in development
    V22   Normal pregnancy
    V23   Supervision of high-risk pregnancy
    V24   Postpartum care and examination
    V25   Encounter for contraceptive management
    V26   Procreative management
    V27   Outcome of delivery
    V28   Antenatal screening
    V29   Observation and evaluation of newborns and infants for suspected condition not found

Liveborn infants according to type of birth (V30-V39)

    V30   Single liveborn
    V31   Twin, mate liveborn
    V32   Twin, mate stillborn
    V33   Twin, unspecified
    V34   Other multiple, mates all liveborn
    V35   Other multiple, mates all stillborn
    V36   Other multiple, mates live- and stillborn
    V37   Other multiple, unspecified
    V39   Unspecified

Persons with a condition influencing their health status (V40-V49)

    V40   Mental and behavioral problems
    V41   Problems with special senses and other special functions
    V42   Organ or tissue replaced by transplant
    V43   Organ or tissue replaced by other means
    V44   Artificial opening status
    V45   Other postsurgical states
    V46   Other dependence on machines
    V47   Other problems with internal organs
    V48   Problems with head, neck, and trunk
    V49   Other conditions influencing health status

SUPPLEMENTARY CLASSIFICATION...HEALTH STATUS/HEALTH SERVICES *continued*

Persons encountering health services for specific procedures and aftercare (V50-V59)

V50 Elective surgery for purposes other than remedying health states
V51 Aftercare involving the use of plastic surgery
V52 Fitting and adjustment of prosthetic device and implant
V53 Fitting and adjustment of other device
V54 Other orthopedic aftercare
V55 Attention to artificial openings
V56 Encounter for dialysis and dialysis catheter care
V57 Care involving use of rehabilitation procedures
V58 Encounter for other and unspecified procedures and aftercare
V59 Donors

Persons encountering health services in other circumstances (V60-V69)

V60 Housing, household, and economic circumstances
V61 Other family circumstances
V62 Other psychosocial circumstances
V63 Unavailability of other medical facilities for care
V64 Persons encountering health services for specific procedures, not carried out
V65 Other persons seeking consultation without complaint or sickness
V66 Convalescence and palliative care
V67 Follow-up examination
V68 Encounters for administrative purposes
V69 Problems related to lifestyle

Persons without reported diagnosis encountered during examination and investigation of individuals and populations (V70-V82)

V70 General medical examination
V71 Observation and evaluation for suspected conditions not found
V72 Special investigations and examinations
V73 Special screening examination for viral and chlamydial diseases
V74 Special screening examination for bacterial and spirochetal diseases
V75 Special screening examination for other infectious diseases
V76 Special screening for malignant neoplasms
V77 Special screening for endocrine, nutritional, metabolic, and immunity disorders
V78 Special screening for disorders of blood and blood-forming organs
V79 Special screening for mental disorders and developmental handicaps
V80 Special screening for neurological, eye, and ear diseases
V81 Special screening for cardiovascular, respiratory, and genitourinary diseases
V82 Special screening for other conditions

SUPPLEMENTARY CLASSIFICATION OF EXTERNAL CAUSES OF INJURY AND POISONING

Railway accidents (E800-E807)

E800 Railway accident involving collision with rolling stock
E801 Railway accident involving collision with other object
E802 Railway accident involving derailment without antecedent collision
E803 Railway accident involving explosion, fire, or burning
E804 Fall in, on, or from railway train
E805 Hit by rolling stock
E806 Other specified railway accident
E807 Railway accident of unspecified nature

Motor vehicle traffic accidents (E810-E819)

E810 Motor vehicle traffic accident involving collision with train
E811 Motor vehicle traffic accident involving re-entrant collision with another motor vehicle
E812 Other motor vehicle traffic accident involving collision with another motor vehicle
E813 Motor vehicle traffic accident involving collision with other vehicle
E814 Motor vehicle traffic accident involving collision with pedestrian
E815 Other motor vehicle traffic accident involving collision on the highway
E816 Motor vehicle traffic accident due to loss of control, without collision on the highway
E817 Noncollision motor vehicle traffic accident while boarding or alighting
E818 Other noncollision motor vehicle traffic accident
E819 Motor vehicle traffic accident of unspecified nature

Motor vehicle nontraffic accidents (E820-E825)

E820 Nontraffic accident involving motor-driven snow vehicle
E821 Nontraffic accident involving other off-road motor vehicle

SUPPLEMENTARY CLASSIFICATION...INJURY AND POISONING *continued*

E822 Other motor vehicle nontraffic accident involving collision with moving object
E823 Other motor vehicle nontraffic accident involving collision with stationary object
E824 Other motor vehicle nontraffic accident while boarding and alighting
E825 Other motor vehicle nontraffic accident of other and unspecified nature

Other road vehicle accidents (E826-E829)

E826 Pedal cycle accident
E827 Animal-drawn vehicle accident
E828 Accident involving animal being ridden
E829 Other road vehicle accidents

Water transport accidents (E830-E838)

E830 Accident to watercraft causing submersion
E831 Accident to watercraft causing other injury
E832 Other accidental submersion or drowning in water transport accident
E833 Fall on stairs or ladders in water transport
E834 Other fall from one level to another in water transport
E835 Other and unspecified fall in water transport
E836 Machinery accident in water transport
E837 Explosion, fire, or burning in watercraft
E838 Other and unspecified water transport accident

Air and space transport accidents (E840-E845)

E840 Accident to powered aircraft at takeoff or landing
E841 Accident to powered aircraft, other and unspecified
E842 Accident to unpowered aircraft
E843 Fall in, on, or from aircraft
E844 Other specified air transport accidents
E845 Accident involving spacecraft

Vehicle accidents, not elsewhere classifiable (E846-E849)

E846 Accidents involving powered vehicles used solely within the buildings and premises
of an industrial or commercial establishment
E847 Accidents involving cable cars not running on rails
E848 Accidents involving other vehicles, not elsewhere classifiable
E849 Place of occurrence

Accidental poisoning by drugs, medicinal substances, and biologicals (E850-E858)

E850 Accidental poisoning by analgesics, antipyretics, and antirheumatics
E851 Accidental poisoning by barbiturates
E852 Accidental poisoning by other sedatives and hypnotics
E853 Accidental poisoning by tranquilizers
E854 Accidental poisoning by other psychotropic agents
E855 Accidental poisoning by other drugs acting on central and autonomic nervous systems
E856 Accidental poisoning by antibiotics
E857 Accidental poisoning by other anti-infectives
E858 Accidental poisoning by other drugs

Accidental poisoning by other solid and liquid substances, gases, and vapors (E860-E869)

E860 Accidental poisoning by alcohol, not elsewhere classified
E861 Accidental poisoning by cleansing and polishing agents, disinfectants, paints, and
varnishes
E862 Accidental poisoning by petroleum products, other solvents and their vapors, not
elsewhere classified
E863 Accidental poisoning by agricultural and horticultural chemical and pharmaceutical
preparations other than plant foods and fertilizers
E864 Accidental poisoning by corrosives and caustics, not elsewhere classified
E865 Accidental poisoning from poisonous foodstuffs and poisonous plants
E866 Accidental poisoning by other and unspecified solid and liquid substances
E867 Accidental poisoning by gas distributed by pipeline
E868 Accidental poisoning by other utility gas and other carbon monoxide
E869 Accidental poisoning by other gases and vapors

Misadventures to patients during surgical and medical care (E870-E876)

E870 Accidental cut, puncture, perforation, or hemorrhage during medical care
E871 Foreign object left in body during procedure
E872 Failure of sterile precautions during procedure
E873 Failure in dosage
E874 Mechanical failure of instrument or apparatus during procedure

SUPPLEMENTARY CLASSIFICATION...INJURY AND POISONING *continued*

E875 Contaminated or infected blood, other fluid, drug, or biological substance
E876 Other and unspecified misadventures during medical care

Surgical and medical procedures as the cause of abnormal reaction of patient or later complication, without mention of misadventure at the time of procedure (E878-E879)

E878 Surgical operation and other surgical procedures as the cause of abnormal reaction of patient, or of later complication, without mention of misadventure at the time of operation
E879 Other procedures, without mention of misadventure at the time of procedure, as the cause of abnormal reaction of patient, or of later complication

Accidental falls (E880-E888)

E880 Fall on or from stairs or steps
E881 Fall on or from ladders or scaffolding
E882 Fall from or out of building or other structure
E883 Fall into hole or other opening in surface
E884 Other fall from one level to another
E885 Fall on same level from slipping, tripping, or stumbling
E886 Fall on same level from collision, pushing or shoving, by or with other person
E887 Fracture, cause unspecified
E888 Other and unspecified fall

Accidents caused by fire and flames (E890-E899)

E890 Conflagration in private dwelling
E891 Conflagration in other and unspecified building or structure
E892 Conflagration not in building or structure
E893 Accident caused by ignition of clothing
E894 Ignition of highly inflammable material
E895 Accident caused by controlled fire in private dwelling
E896 Accident caused by controlled fire in other and unspecified building or structure
E897 Accident caused by controlled fire not in building or structure
E898 Accident caused by other specified fire and flames
E899 Accident caused by unspecified fire

Accidents due to natural and environmental factors (E900-E909)

E900 Excessive heat
E901 Excessive cold
E902 High and low air pressure and changes in air pressure
E903 Travel and motion
E904 Hunger, thirst, exposure, and neglect
E905 Venomous animals and plants as the cause of poisoning and toxic reactions
E906 Other injury caused by animals
E907 Lightning
E908 Cataclysmic storms, and floods resulting from storms
E909 Cataclysmic earth surface movements and eruptions

Accidents caused by submersion, suffocation, and foreign bodies (E910-E915)

E910 Accidental drowning and submersion
E911 Inhalation and ingestion of food causing obstruction of respiratory tract or suffocation
E912 Inhalation and ingestion of other object causing obstruction of respiratory tract or suffocation
E913 Accidental mechanical suffocation
E914 Foreign body accidentally entering eye and adnexa
E915 Foreign body accidentally entering other orifice

Other accidents (E916-E928)

E916 Struck accidentally by falling object
E917 Striking against or struck accidentally by objects or persons
E918 Caught accidentally in or between objects
E919 Accidents caused by machinery
E920 Accidents caused by cutting and piercing instruments or objects
E921 Accident caused by explosion of pressure vessel
E922 Accident caused by firearm and air gun missile
E923 Accident caused by explosive material
E924 Accident caused by hot substance or object, caustic or corrosive material, and steam
E925 Accident caused by electric current
E926 Exposure to radiation
E927 Overexertion and strenuous movements
E928 Other and unspecified environmental and accidental causes

SUPPLEMENTARY CLASSIFICATION...INJURY AND POISONING *continued*

Late effects of accidental injury (E929)
E929 Late effects of accidental injury

Drugs, medicinal and biological substances causing adverse effects in therapeutic use (E930-E949)
E930 Antibiotics
E931 Other anti-infectives
E932 Hormones and synthetic substitutes
E933 Primarily systemic agents
E934 Agents primarily affecting blood constituents
E935 Analgesics, antipyretics, and antirheumatics
E936 Anticonvulsants and anti-Parkinsonism drugs
E937 Sedatives and hypnotics
E938 Other central nervous system depressants and anesthetics
E939 Psychotropic agents
E940 Central nervous system stimulants
E941 Drugs primarily affecting the autonomic nervous system
E942 Agents primarily affecting the cardiovascular system
E943 Agents primarily affecting gastrointestinal system
E944 Water, mineral, and uric acid metabolism drugs
E945 Agents primarily acting on the smooth and skeletal muscles and respiratory system
E946 Agents primarily affecting skin and mucous membrane, ophthalmological, otorhinolaryngological, and dental drugs
E947 Other and unspecified drugs and medicinal substances
E948 Bacterial vaccines
E949 Other vaccines and biological substances

Suicide and self-inflicted injury (E950-E959)
E950 Suicide and self-inflicted poisoning by solid or liquid substances
E951 Suicide and self-inflicted poisoning by gases in domestic use
E952 Suicide and self-inflicted poisoning by other gases and vapors
E953 Suicide and self inflicted injury by hanging, strangulation, and suffocation
E954 Suicide and self-inflicted injury by submersion [drowning]
E955 Suicide and self-inflicted injury by firearms, air guns and explosives
E956 Suicide and self-inflicted injury by cutting and piercing instruments
E957 Suicide and self-inflicted injuries by jumping from high place
E958 Suicide and self-inflicted injury by other and unspecified means
E959 Late effects of self-inflicted injury

Homicide and injury purposely inflicted by other persons (E960-E969)
E960 Fight, brawl, and rape
E961 Assault by corrosive or caustic substance, except poisoning
E962 Assault by poisoning
E963 Assault by hanging and strangulation
E964 Assault by submersion [drowning]
E965 Assault by firearms and explosives
E966 Assault by cutting and piercing instrument
E967 Perpetrator of child and adult abuse
E968 Assault by other and unspecified means
E969 Late effects of injury purposely inflicted by other person

Legal intervention (E970-E978)
E970 Injury due to legal intervention by firearms
E971 Injury due to legal intervention by explosives
E972 Injury due to legal intervention by gas
E973 Injury due to legal intervention by blunt object
E974 Injury due to legal intervention by cutting and piercing instruments
E975 Injury due to legal intervention by other specified means
E976 Injury due to legal intervention by unspecified means
E977 Late effects of injuries due to legal intervention
E978 Legal execution

Injury undetermined whether accidentally or purposely inflicted (E980-E989)
E980 Poisoning by solid or liquid substances, undetermined whether accidentally or purposely inflicted
E981 Poisoning by gases in domestic use, undetermined whether accidentally or purposely inflicted

SUPPLEMENTARY CLASSIFICATION...INJURY AND POISONING *continued*

E982 Poisoning by other gases, undetermined whether accidentally or purposely inflicted
E983 Hanging, strangulation, or suffocation, undetermined whether accidentally or purposely inflicted
E984 Submersion [drowning], undetermined whether accidentally or purposely inflicted
E985 Injury by firearms, air guns and explosives, undetermined whether accidentally or purposely inflicted
E986 Injury by cutting and piercing instruments, undetermined whether accidentally or purposely inflicted
E987 Falling from high place, undetermined whether accidentally or purposely inflicted
E988 Injury by other and unspecified means, undetermined whether accidentally or purposely inflicted
E989 Late effects of injury, undetermined whether accidentally or purposely inflicted

Injury resulting from operations of war (E990-E999)

E990 Injury due to war operations by fires and conflagrations
E991 Injury due to war operations by bullets and fragments
E992 Injury due to war operations by explosion of marine weapons
E993 Injury due to war operations by other explosion
E994 Injury due to war operations by destruction of aircraft
E995 Injury due to war operations by other and unspecified forms of conventional warfare
E996 Injury due to war operations by nuclear weapons
E997 Injury due to war operations by other forms of unconventional warfare
E998 Injury due to war operations but occurring after cessation of hostilities
E999 Late effects of injury due to war operations

DISEASES: ALPHABETIC INDEX
VOLUME 2

A

AAV (disease) (illness) (infection)—*see* Human immunodeficiency virus (disease) (illness) (infection)
Abactio —*see* Abortion, induced
Abactus venter —*see* Abortion, induced
Abarognosis 781.99
Abasia (-astasia) 307.9
  atactica 781.3
  choreic 781.3
  hysterical 300.11
  paroxysmal trepidant 781.3
  spastic 781.3
  trembling 781.3
  trepidans 781.3
Abderhalden-Kaufmann-Lignac syndrome (cystinosis) 270.0
Abdomen, abdominal —*see also* condition
  accordion 306.4
  acute 789.0
  angina 557.1
  burst 868.00
  convulsive equivalent (*see also* Epilepsy) 345.5
  heart 746.87
  muscle deficiency syndrome 756.79
  obstipum 756.79
Abdominalgia 789.0
  periodic 277.3
Abduction contracture, hip or other joint —*see* Contraction, joint
Abercrombie's syndrome (amyloid degeneration) 277.3
Aberrant (congenital)—*see also* Malposition, congenital
  adrenal gland 759.1
  blood vessel NEC 747.60
    arteriovenous NEC 747.60
    cerebrovascular 747.81
    gastrointestinal 747.61
    lower limb 747.64
    renal 747.62
    spinal 747.82
    upper limb 747.63
  breast 757.6
  endocrine gland NEC 759.2
  gastrointestinal vessel (peripheral) 747.61
  hepatic duct 751.69
  lower limb vessel (peripheral) 747.64
  pancreas 751.7
  parathyroid gland 759.2
  peripheral vascular vessel NEC 747.60
  pituitary gland (pharyngeal) 759.2
  renal blood vessel 747.62
  sebaceous glands, mucous membrane, mouth 750.26
  spinal vessel 747.82
  spleen 759.0
  testis (descent) 752.51
  thymus gland 759.2
  thyroid gland 759.2
  upper limb vessel (peripheral) 747.63
Aberratio
  lactis 757.6
  testis 752.51
Aberration —*see also* Anomaly
  chromosome—*see* Anomaly, chromosome(s)
  distantial 368.9
  mental (*see also* Disorder, mental, nonpsychotic) 300.9

Abetalipoproteinemia 272.5
Abionarce 780.79
Abiotrophy 799.8
Ablatio
  placentae—*see* Placenta, ablatio
  retinae (*see also* Detachment, retina) 361.9
Ablation
  pituitary (gland) (with hypofunction) 253.7
  placenta—*see* Placenta, ablatio
  uterus 621.8
Ablepharia, ablepharon, ablephary 743.62
Ablepsia —*see* Blindness
Ablepsy —*see* Blindness
Ablutomania 300.3
Abnormal, abnormality, abnormalities —*see also* Anomaly
  acid-base balance 276.4
    fetus or newborn—*see* Distress, fetal
  adaptation curve, dark 368.63
  alveolar ridge 525.9
  amnion 658.9
    affecting fetus or newborn 762.9
  anatomical relationship NEC 759.9
  apertures, congenital, diaphragm 756.6
  auditory perception NEC 388.40
  autosomes NEC 758.5
    13 758.1
    18 758.2
    21 or 22 758.0
    D$_1$ 758.1
    E$_3$ 758.2
    G 758.0
  ballistocardiogram 794.39
  basal metabolic rate (BMR) 794.7
  biosynthesis, testicular androgen 257.2
  blood level (of)
    cobalt 790.6
    copper 790.6
    iron 790.6
    lithium 790.6
    magnesium 790.6
    mineral 790.6
    zinc 790.6
  blood pressure
    elevated (without diagnosis of hypertension) 796.2
    low (*see also* Hypotension) 458.9
      reading (incidental) (isolated) (nonspecific) 796.3
  bowel sounds 787.5
  breathing behavior—*see* Respiration
  caloric test 794.19
  cervix (acquired) NEC 622.9
    congenital 752.40
    in pregnancy or childbirth 654.6
      causing obstructed labor 660.2
        affecting fetus or newborn 763.1
  chemistry, blood NEC 790.6
  chest sounds 786.7
  chorion 658.9
    affecting fetus or newborn 762.9
  chromosomal NEC 758.89
    analysis, nonspecific result 795.2
    autosomes (*see also* Abnormal, autosomes NEC) 758.5
    fetal, (suspected) affecting management of pregnancy 655.1
    sex 758.81

Abnormal, abnormality . . .—*continued*
  clinical findings NEC 796.4
  communication—*see* Fistula
  configuration of pupils 379.49
  coronary
    artery 746.85
    vein 746.9
  cortisol-binding globulin 255.8
  course, Eustachian tube 744.24
  dentofacial NEC 524.9
    functional 524.5
    specified type NEC 524.8
  development, developmental NEC 759.9
    bone 756.9
    central nervous system 742.9
  direction, teeth 524.3
  Dynia (see also Defect, coagulation) 286.9
  Ebstein 746.2
  echocardiogram 793.2
  echoencephalogram 794.01
  echogram NEC—*see* Findings, abnormal,
    structure
  electrocardiogram (ECG) (EKG) 794.31
  electroencephalogram (EEG) 794.02
  electromyogram (EMG) 794.17
    ocular 794.14
  electro-oculogram (EOG) 794.12
  electroretinogram (ERG) 794.11
  erythrocytes 289.9
    congenital, with perinatal jaundice 282.9
      [774.0]
  Eustachian valve 746.9
  excitability under minor stress 301.9
  fat distribution 782.9
  feces 787.7
  fetal heart rate—*see* Distress, fetal
  fetus NEC
    affecting management of pregnancy—*see*
      Pregnancy, management affected by, fetal
    causing disproportion 653.7
      affecting fetus or newborn 763.1
      causing obstructed labor 660.1
        affecting fetus or newborn 763.1
  findings without manifest disease—*see*
    Findings, abnormal
  fluid
    amniotic 792.3
    cerebrospinal 792.0
    peritoneal 792.9
    pleural 792.9
    synovial 792.9
    vaginal 792.9
  forces of labor NEC 661.9
    affecting fetus or newborn 763.7
  form, teeth 520.2
  function studies
    auditory 794.15
    bladder 794.9
    brain 794.00
    cardiovascular 794.30
    endocrine NEC 794.6
    kidney 794.4
    liver 794.8
    nervous system
      central 794.00
      peripheral 794.19
    oculomotor 794.14
    pancreas 794.9
    placenta 794.9
    pulmonary 794.2

Abnormal, abnormality . . .—*continued*
  retina 794.11
  special senses 794.19
  spleen 794.9
  thyroid 794.5
  vestibular 794.16
  gait 781.2
    hysterical 300.11
  gastrin secretion 251.5
  globulin
    cortisol-binding 255.8
    thyroid-binding 246.8
  glucagon secretion 251.4
  glucose tolerance test 790.2
    in pregnancy, childbirth, or puerperium 648.8
      fetus or newborn 775.0
  gravitational (G) forces or states 994.9
  hair NEC 704.2
  hard tissue formation in pulp 522.3
  head movement 781.0
  heart
    rate
      fetus, affecting liveborn infant
        before the onset of labor 763.81
        during labor 763.82
        unspecified as to time of onset 763.83
      intrauterine
        before the onset of labor 763.81
        during labor 763.82
        unspecified as to time of onset 763.83
      newborn
        before the onset of labor 763.81
        during labor 763.82
        unspecified as to time of onset 763.83
    shadow 793.2
    sounds NEC 785.3
  hemoglobin (*see also* Disease, hemoglobin)
    282.7
    trait—*see* Trait, hemoglobin, abnormal
  hemorrhage, uterus—*see* Hemorrhage, uterus
  histology NEC 795.4
  increase in
    appetite 783.6
    development 783.9
  involuntary movement 781.0
  jaw closure 524.5
  karyotype 795.2
  knee jerk 796.1
  labor NEC 661.9
    affecting fetus or newborn 763.7
  laboratory findings—*see* Findings, abnormal
  length, organ or site, congenital—*see* Distortion
  loss of height 781.91
  loss of weight 783.21
  lung shadow 793.1
  mammogram 793.8
  Mantoux test 795.5
  membranes (fetal)
    affecting fetus or newborn 762.9
    complicating pregnancy 658.8
  menstruation—*see* Menstruation
  metabolism (*see also* condition) 783.9
  movement 781.0
    disorder, NEC 333.90
      specified, NEC 333.99
    head 781.0
    involuntary 781.0
    specified type NEC 333.99
  muscle contraction, localized 728.85
  myoglobin (Aberdeen) (Annapolis) 289.9
  narrowness, eyelid 743.62

Abnormal, abnormality . . .—*continued*
uterine hemorrhage (*see also* Hemorrhage,
        uterus) 626.9
    climacteric 627.0
    postmenopausal 627.1
vagina (acquired) (congenital)
    in pregnancy or childbirth 654.7
        affecting fetus or newborn 763.89
        causing obstructed labor 660.2
            affecting fetus or newborn 763.1
vascular sounds 785.9
vectorcardiogram 794.39
visually evoked potential (VEP) 794.13
vulva (acquired) (congenital)
    in pregnancy or childbirth 654.8
        affecting fetus or newborn 763.89
        causing obstructed labor 660.2
            affecting fetus or newborn 763.1
weight
    gain 783.1
        of pregnancy 646.1
            with hypertension—see Toxemia, of
                pregnancy
    loss 783.21
x-ray examination—*see* Abnormal, radiological
    examination
Abnormally formed uterus —*see* Anomaly,
    uterus
Abnormity (any organ or part)—*see* Anomaly
ABO
hemolytic disease 773.1
incompatibility reaction 999.6
Abocclusion 524.2
Abolition, language 784.69
Aborter, habitual or recurrent NEC
without current pregnancy 629.9
current abortion (*see also* Abortion,
    spontaneous) 634.9
    affecting fetus or newborn 761.8
observation in current pregnancy 646.3
Abortion (complete) (incomplete) (inevitable)
    (with retained products of conception) 637.9

Note—Use the following fifth-digit
subclassification with categories 634-637:

0 unspecified
1 incomplete
2 complete

---

with
    complication(s) (any) following previous
        abortion—*see* category 639
    damage to pelvic organ (laceration) (rupture)
        (tear) 637.2
    embolism (air) (amniotic fluid) (blood clot)
        (pulmonary) (pyemic) (septic) (soap) 637.6
    genital tract and pelvic infection 637.0
    hemorrhage, delayed or excessive 637.1
    metabolic disorder 637.4
    renal failure (acute) 637.3
    sepsis (genital tract) (pelvic organ) 637.0
        urinary tract 637.7
    shock (postoperative) (septic) 637.5
    specified complication NEC 637.7
    toxemia 637.3
    unspecified complication(s) 637.8
    urinary tract infection 637.7
accidental—*see* Abortion, spontaneous
artificial—*see* Abortion, induced
attempted (failed)—*see* Abortion, failed
criminal—*see* Abortion, illegal

Abortion—*continued*
early—*see* Abortion, spontaneous
elective—*see* Abortion, legal
failed (legal) 638.9
    with
        damage to pelvic organ (laceration)
            (rupture) (tear) 638.2
        embolism (air) (amniotic fluid) (blood clot)
            (pulmonary) (pyemic) (septic) (soap)
            638.6
        genital tract and pelvic infection 638.0
        hemorrhage, delayed or excessive 638.1
        metabolic disorder 638.4
        renal failure (acute) 638.3
        sepsis (genital tract) (pelvic organ) 638.0
            urinary tract 638.7
        shock (postoperative) (septic) 638.5
        specified complication NEC 638.7
        toxemia 638.3
        unspecified complication(s) 638.8
        urinary tract infection 638.7
fetal indication—*see* Abortion, legal
fetus 779.6
following threatened abortion—*see* Abortion,
    by type
habitual or recurrent (care during pregnancy)
    646.3
    with current abortion (*see also* Abortion,
        spontaneous) 634.9
        affecting fetus or newborn 761.8
    without current pregnancy 629.9
homicidal—*see* Abortion, illegal
illegal 636.9
    with
        damage to pelvic organ (laceration)
            (rupture) (tear) 636.2
        embolism (air) (amniotic fluid) (blood clot)
            (pulmonary) (pyemic) (septic) (soap)
            636.6
        genital tract and pelvic infection 636.0
        hemorrhage, delayed or excessive 636.1
        metabolic disorder 636.4
        renal failure 636.3
        sepsis (genital tract) (pelvic organ) 636.0
            urinary tract 636.7
        shock (postoperative) (septic) 636.5
        specified complication NEC 636.7
        toxemia 636.3
        unspecified complication(s) 636.8
        urinary tract infection 636.7
    fetus 779.6
induced 637.9
    illegal—*see* Abortion, illegal
    legal indications—*see* Abortion, legal
    medical indications—*see* Abortion, legal
    therapeutic—*see* Abortion, legal
late—*see* Abortion, spontaneous
legal (legal indication) (medical indication)
    (under medical supervision) 635.9
    with
        damage to pelvic organ (laceration)
            (rupture) (tear) 635.2
        embolism (air) (amniotic fluid) (blood clot)
            (pulmonary) (pyemic) (septic) (soap)
            635.6
        genital tract and pelvic infection 635.0
        hemorrhage, delayed or excessive 635.1
        metabolic disorder 635.4
        renal failure (acute) 635.3
        sepsis (genital tract) (pelvic organ) 635.0
            urinary tract 635.7

Abortion—*continued*
    shock (postoperative) (septic) 635.5
    specified complication NEC 635.7
    toxemia 635.3
    unspecified complication(s) 635.8
    urinary tract infection 635.7
  fetus 779.6
medical indication—*see* Abortion, legal
mental hygiene problem—*see* Abortion, legal
missed 632
operative—*see* Abortion, legal
psychiatric indication—*see* Abortion, legal
recurrent—*see* Abortion, spontaneous
self-induced—*see* Abortion, illegal
septic—*see* Abortion, by type, with sepsis
spontaneous 634.9
  with
    damage to pelvic organ (laceration)
      (rupture) (tear) 634.2
    embolism (air) (amniotic fluid) (blood clot)
      (pulmonary) (pyemic) (septic) (soap)
      634.6
    genital tract and pelvic infection 634.0
    hemorrhage, delayed or excessive 634.1
    metabolic disorder 634.4
    renal failure 634.3
    sepsis (genital tract) (pelvic organ) 634.0
      urinary tract 634.7
    shock (postoperative) (septic) 634.5
    specified complication NEC 634.7
    toxemia 634.3
    unspecified complication(s) 634.8
    urinary tract infection 634.7
  fetus 761.8
  threatened 640.0
    affecting fetus or newborn 762.1
surgical—*see* Abortion, legal
therapeutic—*see* Abortion, legal
threatened 640.0
  affecting fetus or newborn 762.1
tubal—*see* Pregnancy, tubal
voluntary—*see* Abortion, legal
Abortus fever 023.9
Aboulomania 301.6
Abrachia 755.20
Abrachiatism 755.20
Abrachiocephalia 759.89
Abrachiocephalus 759.89
Abrami's disease (acquired hemolytic jaundice)
  283.9
Abramov-Fiedler myocarditis (acute isolated
  myocarditis) 422.91
Abrasion —*see also* Injury, superficial, by site
cornea 918.1
dental 521.2
teeth, tooth (dentifrice) (habitual) (hard tissues)
  (occupational) (ritual) (traditional) (wedge
  defect) 521.2
Abrikossov's tumor (M9580/0)—*see also*
  Neoplasm, connective tissue, benign
malignant (M9580/3)—*see* Neoplasm,
  connective tissue, malignant
Abrism 988.8
Abruption, placenta —*see* Placenta, abruptio
Abruptio placentae —*see* Placenta, abruptio
Abscess (acute) (chronic) (infectional)
  (lymphangitic) (metastatic) (multiple)
  (pyogenic) (septic) (with lymphangitis) (*see
  also* Cellulitis) 682.9
abdomen, abdominal
  cavity—*see* Abscess, peritoneum

Abscess—*continued*
wall 682.2
abdominopelvic—*see* Abscess, peritoneum
accessory sinus (chronic) (*see also* Sinusitis)
  473.9
adrenal (capsule) (gland) 255.8
alveolar 522.5
  with sinus 522.7
amebic 006.3
  bladder 006.8
  brain (with liver or lung abscess) 006.5
  liver (without mention of brain or lung
    abscess) 006.3
    with
      brain abscess (and lung abscess) 006.5
      lung abscess 006.4
  lung (with liver abscess) 006.4
    with brain abscess 006.5
  seminal vesicle 006.8
  specified site NEC 006.8
  spleen 006.8
anaerobic 040.0
ankle 682.6
anorectal 566
antecubital space 682.3
antrum (chronic) (Highmore) (*see also*
  Sinusitis, maxillary) 473.0
anus 566
apical (tooth) 522.5
  with sinus (alveolar) 522.7
appendix 540.1
areola (acute) (chronic) (nonpuerperal) 611.0
  puerperal, postpartum 675.1
arm (any part, above wrist) 682.3
artery (wall) 447.2
atheromatous 447.2
auditory canal (external) 380.10
auricle (ear) (staphylococcal) (streptococcal)
  380.10
axilla, axillary (region) 682.3
  lymph gland or node 683
back (any part) 682.2
Bartholin's gland 616.3
  with
    abortion—*see* Abortion, by type, with sepsis
    ectopic pregnancy (*see also* categories
      633.0-633.9) 639.0
    molar pregnancy (*see also* categories
      630-632) 639.0
  complicating pregnancy or puerperium 646.6
  following
    abortion 639.0
    ectopic or molar pregnancy 639.0
bartholinian 616.3
Bezold's 383.01
bile, biliary, duct or tract (*see also*
  Cholecystitis) 576.8
bilharziasis 120.1
bladder (wall) 595.89
  amebic 006.8
bone (subperiosteal) (*see also* Osteomyelitis)
  730.0
  accessory sinus (chronic) (*see also* Sinusitis)
    473.9
  acute 730.0
  chronic or old 730.1
  jaw (lower) (upper) 526.4
  mastoid—*see* Mastoiditis, acute
  petrous (*see also* Petrositis) 383.20
  spinal (tuberculous) (*see also* Tuberculosis)
    015.0 *[730.88]*

Abscess—*continued*
  gland, glandular (lymph) (acute) NEC 683
  glottis 478.79
  gluteal (region) 682.5
  gonorrheal NEC (*see also* Gonococcus) 098.0
  groin 682.2
  gum 523.3
  hand (except finger or thumb) 682.4
  head (except face) 682.8
  heart 429.89
  heel 682.7
  helminthic (*see also* Infestation, by specific
    parasite) 128.9
  hepatic 572.0
    amebic (*see also* Abscess, liver, amebic) 006.3
    duct 576.8
  hip 682.6
    tuberculous (active) (*see also* Tuberculosis)
      015.1
  ileocecal 540.1
  ileostomy (bud) 569.6
  iliac (region) 682.2
    fossa 540.1
  iliopsoas (tuberculous) (*see also* Tuberculosis)
    015.0 *[730.88]*
    nontuberculous 728.89
  infraclavicular (fossa) 682.3
  inguinal (region) 682.2
    lymph gland or node 683
  intersphincteric (anus) 566
  intestine, intestinal 569.5
    rectal 566
  intra-abdominal (*see also* Abscess, peritoneum)
    567.2
    postoperative 998.59
  intracranial 324.0
    late effect—*see* category 326
  intramammary—*see* Abscess, breast
  intramastoid (*see also* Mastoiditis, acute) 383.00
  intraorbital 376.01
  intraperitoneal—*see* Abscess, peritoneum
  intraspinal 324.1
    late effect—*see* category 326
  intratonsillar 475
  iris 364.3
  ischiorectal 566
  jaw (bone) (lower) (upper) 526.4
    skin 682.0
  joint (*see also* Arthritis, pyogenic) 711.0
    vertebral (tuberculous) (*see also* Tuberculosis)
      015.0 *[730.88]*
    nontuberculous 724.8
  kidney 590.2
    with
      abortion—*see* Abortion, by type, with
        urinary tract infection
      calculus 592.0
      ectopic pregnancy (*see also* categories
        633.0-633.9) 639.8
      molar pregnancy (*see also* categories
        630-632) 639.8
     complicating pregnancy or puerperium 646.6
      affecting fetus or newborn 760.1
     following
      abortion 639.8
      ectopic or molar pregnancy 639.8
  knee 682.6
    joint 711.06
    tuberculous (active) (*see also* Tuberculosis)
      015.2
  labium (majus) (minus) 616.4

Abscess—*continued*
  complicating pregnancy, childbirth, or
    puerperium 646.6
  lacrimal (passages) (sac) (*see also*
    Dacryocystitis) 375.30
    caruncle 375.30
    gland (*see also* Dacryoadenitis) 375.00
  lacunar 597.0
  larynx 478.79
  lateral (alveolar) 522.5
    with sinus 522.7
  leg, except foot 682.6
  lens 360.00
  lid 373.13
  lingual 529.0
    tonsil 475
  lip 528.5
  Littre's gland 597.0
  liver 572.0
    amebic 006.3
      with
        brain abscess (and lung abscess) 006.5
        lung abscess 006.4
    due to Entamoeba histolytica 006.3
    dysenteric (*see also* Abscess, liver, amebic)
      006.3
    pyogenic 572.0
    tropical (*see also* Abscess, liver, amebic) 006.3
  loin (region) 682.2
  lumbar (tuberculous) (*see also* Tuberculosis)
    015.0 *[730.88]*
    nontuberculous 682.2
  lung (miliary) (putrid) 513.0
    amebic (with liver abscess) 006.4
      with brain abscess 006.5
  lymph, lymphatic, gland or node (acute) 683
    any site, except mesenteric 683
    mesentery 289.2
  lymphangitic, acute—*see* Cellulitis
  malar 526.4
  mammary gland—*see* Abscess, breast
  marginal (anus) 566
  mastoid (process) (*see also* Mastoiditis, acute)
    383.00
    subperiosteal 383.01
  maxilla, maxillary 526.4
    molar (tooth) 522.5
      with sinus 522.7
    premolar 522.5
    sinus (chronic) (*see also* Sinusitis, maxillary)
      473.0
  mediastinum 513.1
  meibomian gland 373.12
  meninges (*see also* Meningitis) 320.9
  mesentery, mesenteric—*see* Abscess,
    peritoneum
  mesosalpinx (*see also* Salpingo-oophoritis)
    614.2
  milk 675.1
  Monro's (psoriasis) 696.1
  mons pubis 682.2
  mouth (floor) 528.3
  multiple sites NEC 682.9
  mural 682.2
  muscle 728.89
  myocardium 422.92
  nabothian (follicle) (*see also* Cervicitis) 616.0
  nail (chronic) (with lymphangitis) 681.9
    finger 681.02
    toe 681.11
  nasal (fossa) (septum) 478.1

Abscess—*continued*
  pouch of Douglas (chronic) (*see also* Disease, pelvis, inflammatory) 614.4
  premammary—*see* Abscess, breast
  prepatellar 682.6
  prostate (*see also* Prostatitis) 601.2
    gonococcal (acute) 098.12
      chronic or duration of 2 months or over 098.32
  psoas (tuberculous) (*see also* Tuberculosis) 015.0 *[730.88]*
    nontuberculous 728.89
  pterygopalatine fossa 682.8
  pubis 682.2
  puerperal—Puerperal, abscess, by site
  pulmonary—*see* Abscess, lung
  pulp, pulpal (dental) 522.0
    finger 681.01
    toe 681.10
  pyemic—*see* Septicemia
  pyloric valve 535.0
  rectovaginal septum 569.5
  rectovesical 595.89
  rectum 566
  regional NEC 682.9
  renal (*see also* Abscess, kidney) 590.2
  retina 363.00
  retrobulbar 376.01
  retrocecal—*see* Abscess, peritoneum
  retrolaryngeal 478.79
  retromammary—*see* Abscess, breast
  retroperineal 682.2
  retroperitoneal—*see* Abscess, peritoneum
  retropharyngeal 478.24
    tuberculous (*see also* Tuberculosis) 012.8
  retrorectal 566
  retrouterine (*see also* Disease, pelvis, inflammatory) 614.4
    acute 614.3
  retrovesical 595.89
  root, tooth 522.5
    with sinus (alveolar) 522.7
  round ligament (*see also* Disease, pelvis, inflammatory) 614.4
    acute 614.3
  rupture (spontaneous) NEC 682.9
  sacrum (tuberculous) (*see also* Tuberculosis) 015.0 *[730.88]*
    nontuberculous 730.08
  salivary duct or gland 527.3
  scalp (any part) 682.8
  scapular 730.01
  sclera 379.09
  scrofulous (*see also* Tuberculosis) 017.2
  scrotum 608.4
  seminal vesicle 608.0
    amebic 006.8
  septal, dental 522.5
    with sinus (alveolar) 522.7
  septum (nasal) 478.1
  serous (*see also* Periostitis) 730.3
  shoulder 682.3
  side 682.2
  sigmoid 569.5
  sinus (accessory) (chronic) (nasal) (*see also* Sinusitis) 473.9
    intracranial venous (any) 324.0
      late effect—*see* category 326
  Skene's duct or gland 597.0
  skin NEC 682.9

Abscess—*continued*
  tuberculous (primary) (*see also* Tuberculosis) 017.0
  sloughing NEC 682.9
  specified site NEC 682.8
    amebic 006.8
  spermatic cord 608.4
  sphenoidal (sinus) (*see also* Sinusitis, sphenoidal) 473.3
  spinal
    cord (any part) (staphylococcal) 324.1
      tuberculous (*see also* Tuberculosis) 013.5
    epidural 324.1
  spine (column) (tuberculous) (*see also* Tuberculosis) 015.0 *[730.88]*
    nontuberculous 730.08
  spleen 289.59
    amebic 006.8
  staphylococcal NEC 682.9
  stitch 998.59
  stomach (wall) 535.0
  strumous (tuberculous) (*see also* Tuberculosis) 017.2
  subarachnoid 324.9
    brain 324.0
    cerebral 324.0
    late effect—*see* category 326
    spinal cord 324.1
  subareolar—*see also* Abscess, breast
    puerperal, postpartum 675.1
  subcecal 540.1
  subcutaneous NEC 682.9
  subdiaphragmatic—*see* Abscess, peritoneum
  subdorsal 682.2
  subdural 324.9
    brain 324.0
    late effect—*see* category 326
    spinal cord 324.1
  subgaleal 682.8
  subhepatic—*see* Abscess, peritoneum
  sublingual 528.3
    gland 527.3
  submammary—*see* Abscess, breast
  submandibular (region) (space) (triangle) 682.0
    gland 527.3
  submaxillary (region) 682.0
    gland 527.3
  submental (pyogenic) 682.0
    gland 527.3
  subpectoral 682.2
  subperiosteal—*see* Abscess, bone
  subperitoneal—*see* Abscess, peritoneum
  subphrenic—*see also* Abscess, peritoneum
    postoperative 998.59
  subscapular 682.2
  subungual 681.9
  suburethral 597.0
  sudoriparous 705.89
  suppurative NEC 682.9
  supraclavicular (fossa) 682.3
  suprahepatic—*see* Abscess, peritoneum
  suprapelvic (*see also* Disease, pelvis, inflammatory) 614.4
    acute 614.3
  suprapubic 682.2
  suprarenal (capsule) (gland) 255.8
  sweat gland 705.89
  syphilitic 095.8
  teeth, tooth (root) 522.5
    with sinus (alveolar) 522.7
      supporting structures NEC 523.3

Absence—*continued*
  with
    complete absence of distal elements 755.21
    ulna 755.25
      with
        complete absence of distal elements 755.21
        humerus (incomplete) 755.23
  ray, congenital 755.4
    lower limb (complete) (partial) (*see also* Deformity, reduction, lower limb) 755.38
      meaning all rays 755.31
      transverse 755.31
    upper limb (complete) (partial) (*see also* Deformity, reduction, upper limb) 755.28
      meaning all rays 755.21
      transverse 755.21
  rectum (congenital) 751.2
    acquired V45.79
  red cell 284.9
    acquired (secondary) 284.8
    congenital 284.0
    hereditary 284.0
    idiopathic 284.9
  respiratory organ (congenital) NEC 748.9
  rib (acquired) 738.3
    congenital 756.3
  roof of orbit (congenital) 742.0
  round ligament (congenital) 752.8
  sacrum, congenital 756.13
  salivary gland(s) (congenital) 750.21
  scapula 755.59
  scrotum, congenital 752.8
  seminal tract or duct (congenital) 752.8
    acquired V45.77
  septum (congenital)—*see also* Imperfect, closure, septum
    atrial 745.69
      and ventricular 745.7
    between aorta and pulmonary artery 745.0
    ventricular 745.3
      and atrial 745.7
  sex chromosomes 758.81
  shoulder girdle, congenital (complete) (partial) 755.59
  skin (congenital) 757.39
  skull bone 756.0
    with
      anencephalus 740.0
      encephalocele 742.0
      hydrocephalus 742.3
        with spina bifida (*see also* Spina bifida) 741.0
      microcephalus 742.1
  spermatic cord (congenital) 752.8
  spinal cord 742.59
  spine, congenital 756.13
  spleen (congenital) 759.0
    acquired V45.79
  sternum, congenital 756.3
  stomach (acquired) (partial) (postoperative) V45.75
    congenital 750.7
    with postgastric surgery syndrome 564.2
  submaxillary gland(s) (congenital) 750.21
  superior vena cava (congenital) 747.49
  tarsal(s), congenital (complete) (partial) (with absence of distal elements, incomplete) (*see also* Deformity, reduction, lower limb) 755.38

Absence—*continued*
  teeth, tooth (congenital) 520.0
    with abnormal spacing 524.3
    acquired 525.1
      with malocclusion 524.3
  tendon (congenital) 756.81
  testis (congenital) 752.8
    acquired V45.77
  thigh (acquired) 736.89
  thumb (acquired) V49.61
    congenital 755.29
  thymus gland (congenital) 759.2
  thyroid (gland) (surgical) 246.8
    with hypothyroidism 244.0
    cartilage, congenital 748.3
    congenital 243
  tibia, congenital (complete) (partial) (with absence of distal elements, incomplete) (*see also* Deformity, reduction, lower limb) 755.36
    with
      complete absence of distal elements 755.31
      fibula 755.35
        with
          complete absence of distal elements 755.31
          femur (incomplete) 755.33
            with complete absence of distal elements 755.31
  toe (acquired) V49.72
    congenital (complete) (partial) 755.39
      meaning all toes 755.31
      transverse 755.31
    great V49.71
  tongue (congenital) 750.11
  tooth, teeth, (congenital) 520.0
    with abnormal spacing 524.3
    acquired 525.1
      with malocclusion 524.3
  trachea (cartilage) (congenital) (rings) 748.3
  transverse aortic arch (congenital) 747.21
  tricuspid valve 746.1
  ulna, congenital (complete) (partial) (with absence of distal elements, incomplete) (*see also* Deformity, reduction, upper limb) 755.27
    with
      complete absence of distal elements 755.21
      radius 755.25
        with
          complete absence of distal elements 755.21
          humerus (incomplete) 755.23
  umbilical artery (congenital) 747.5
  ureter (congenital) 753.4
    acquired V45.74
  urethra, congenital 753.8
    acquired V45.74
  urinary system, part NEC, congenital 753.8
    acquired V45.74
  uterus (acquired) V45.77
    congenital 752.3
  uvula (congenital) 750.26
  vagina, congenital 752.49
    acquired V45.77
  vas deferens (congenital) 752.8
    acquired V45.77
  vein (congenital) (peripheral) NEC (*see also* Anomaly, peripheral vascular system) 747.60
    brain 747.81

Absence—*continued*
   great 747.49
   portal 747.49
   pulmonary 747.49
  vena cava (congenital) (inferior) (superior)
    747.49
  ventral horn cell 742.59
  ventricular septum 745.3
  vermis of cerebellum 742.2
  vertebra, congenital 756.13
  vulva, congenital 752.49
Absentia epileptica (*see also* Epilepsy) 345.0
Absinthemia (*see also* Dependence) 304.6
Absinthism (*see also* Dependence) 304.6
Absorbent system disease 459.89
Absorption
  alcohol, through placenta or breast milk 760.71
  antibiotics, through placenta or breast milk
    760.74
  anti-infective, through placenta or breast milk
    760.74
  chemical NEC 989.9
   specified chemical or substance—*see* Table of
     drugs and chemicals
   through placenta or breast milk (fetus or
     newborn) 760.70
    alcohol 760.71
    anti-infective agents 760.74
    cocaine 760.75
    "crack" 760.75
    diethylstilbestrol [DES] 760.76
    hallucinogenic agents 760.73
    medicinal agents NEC 760.79
    narcotics 760.72
    obstetric anesthetic or analgesic drug 763.5
    specified agent NEC 760.79
    suspected, affecting management of
     pregnancy 655.5
  cocaine, through placenta or breast milk 760.75
  drug NEC (*see also* Reaction, drug)
   through placenta or breast milk (fetus or
     newborn) 760.70
    alcohol 760.71
    anti-infective agents 760.74
    cocaine 760.75
    "crack" 760.75
    diethylstilbestrol (DES) 760.76
    hallucinogenic agents 760.73
    medicinal agents NEC 760.79
    narcotics 760.72
    obstetric anesthetic or analgesic drug 763.5
    specified agent NEC 760.79
    suspected, affecting management of
     pregnancy 655.5
  fat, disturbance 579.8
  hallucinogenic agents, through placenta or
    breast milk 760.73
  immune sera, through placenta or breast milk
    760.79
  lactose defect 271.3
  medicinal agents NEC, through placenta or
    breast milk 760.79
  narcotics, through placenta or breast milk 760.72
  noxious substance,—*see* Absorption, chemical
  protein, disturbance 579.8
  pus or septic, general—*see* Septicemia
  quinine, through placenta or breast milk 760.74
  toxic substance—*see* Absorption, chemical
  uremic—*see* Uremia
Abstinence symptoms or syndrome
  alcohol 291.81
  drug 292.0

Abt-Letterer-Siwe syndrome (acute
  histiocytosis X) (M9722/3) 202.5
Abulia 799.8
Abulomania 301.6
Abuse
  adult 995.80
   emotional 995.82
   multiple forms 995.85
   neglect (nutritional) 995.84
   physical 995.81
   psychological 995.82
   sexual 995.83
  alcohol (*see also* Alcoholism) 305.0
   dependent 303.9
   non-dependent 305.0
  child 995.50
   counseling
    perpetrator
     non-parent V62.83
     parent V61.22
    victim V61.21
   emotional 995.51
   multiple forms 995.59
   neglect (nutritional) 995.52
   physical 995.54
    shaken infant syndrome 995.55
   psychological 995.51
   sexual 995.53
  drugs, nondependent 305.9

> *Note—Use the following fifth-digit
> subclassification with the following codes:
> 305.0, 305.2-305.9:*
>
> *0 unspecified*
> *1 continuous*
> *2 episodic*
> *3 in remission*

   amphetamine type 305.7
   antidepressants 305.8
   barbiturates 305.4
   caffeine 305.9
   cannabis 305.2
   cocaine type 305.6
   hallucinogens 305.3
   hashish 305.2
   LSD 305.3
   marijuana 305.2
   mixed 305.9
   morphine type 305.5
   opioid type 305.5
   phencyclidine (PCP) 305.9
   specified NEC 305.9
   tranquilizers 305.4
  spouse 995.80
  tobacco 305.1
Acalcerosis 275.40
Acalcicosis 275.40
Acalculia 784.69
  developmental 315.1
Acanthocheilonemiasis 125.4
Acanthocytosis 272.5
Acanthokeratodermia 701.1
Acantholysis 701.8
  bullosa 757.39
Acanthoma (benign) (M8070/0)—*see also*
  Neoplasm, by site, benign
  malignant (M8070/3)—*see* Neoplasm, by site,
   malignant

Acanthosis (acquired) (nigricans) 701.2
  adult 701.2
  benign (congenital) 757.39
  congenital 757.39
  glycogenic
    esophagus 530.8
  juvenile 701.2
  tongue 529.8
Acanthrocytosis 272.5
Acapnia 276.3
Acarbia 276.2
Acardia 759.89
Acardiacus amorphus 759.89
Acardiotrophia 429.1
Acardius 759.89
Acariasis 133.9
  sarcoptic 133.0
Acaridiasis 133.9
Acarinosis 133.9
Acariosis 133.9
Acarodermatitis 133.9
  urticarioides 133.9
Acarophobia 300.29
Acatalasemia 277.8
Acatalasia 277.8
Acatamathesia 784.69
Acataphasia 784.5
Acathisia 781.0
  due to drugs 333.99
Acceleration, accelerated
  atrioventricular conduction 426.7
  idioventricular rhythm 427.89
Accessory (congenital)
  adrenal gland 759.1
  anus 751.5
  appendix 751.5
  atrioventricular conduction 426.7
  auditory ossicles 744.04
  auricle (ear) 744.1
  autosome(s) NEC 758.5
    21 or 22 758.0
  biliary duct or passage 751.69
  bladder 753.8
  blood vessels (peripheral) (congenital) NEC
    (*see also* Anomaly, peripheral vascular
    system) 747.60
    cerebral 747.81
    coronary 746.85
  bone NEC 756.9
    foot 755.67
  breast tissue, axilla 757.6
  carpal bones 755.56
  cecum 751.5
  cervix 752.49
  chromosome(s) NEC 758.5
    13-15 758.1
    16-18 758.2
    21 or 22 758.0
    autosome(s) NEC 758.5
    D_1 758.1
    E_3 758.2
    G 758.0
    sex 758.81
  coronary artery 746.85
  cusp(s), heart valve NEC 746.89
    pulmonary 746.09
  cystic duct 751.69
  digits 755.00
  ear (auricle) (lobe) 744.1
  endocrine gland NEC 759.2
  external os 752.49

Accessory—*continued*
  eyelid 743.62
  eye muscle 743.69
  face bone(s) 756.0
  fallopian tube (fimbria) (ostium) 752.19
  fingers 755.01
  foreskin 605
  frontonasal process 756.0
  gallbladder 751.69
  genital organ(s)
    female 752.8
      external 752.49
      internal NEC 752.8
    male NEC 752.8
      penis 752.69
  genitourinary organs NEC 752.8
  heart 746.89
    valve NEC 746.89
      pulmonary 746.09
  hepatic ducts 751.69
  hymen 752.49
  intestine (large) (small) 751.5
  kidney 753.3
  lacrimal canal 743.65
  leaflet, heart valve NEC 746.89
    pulmonary 746.09
  ligament, broad 752.19
  liver (duct) 751.69
  lobule (ear) 744.1
  lung (lobe) 748.69
  muscle 756.82
  navicular of carpus 755.56
  nervous system, part NEC 742.8
  nipple 757.6
  nose 748.1
  organ or site NEC—*see* Anomaly, specified
    type NEC
  ovary 752.0
  oviduct 752.19
  pancreas 751.7
  parathyroid gland 759.2
  parotid gland (and duct) 750.22
  pituitary gland 759.2
  placental lobe—*see* Placenta, abnormal
  preauricular appendage 744.1
  prepuce 605
  renal arteries (multiple) 747.62
  rib 756.3
    cervical 756.2
  roots (teeth) 520.2
  salivary gland 750.22
  sesamoids 755.8
  sinus—*see* condition
  skin tags 757.39
  spleen 759.0
  sternum 756.3
  submaxillary gland 750.22
  tarsal bones 755.67
  teeth, tooth 520.1
    causing crowding 524.3
  tendon 756.89
  thumb 755.01
  thymus gland 759.2
  thyroid gland 759.2
  toes 755.02
  tongue 750.13
  tragus 744.1
  ureter 753.4
  urethra 753.8
  urinary organ or tract NEC 753.8
  uterus 752.2

Accessory—*continued*
  vagina 752.49
  valve, heart NEC 746.89
    pulmonary 746.09
  vertebra 756.19
  vocal cords 748.3
  vulva 752.49
Accident, accidental —*see also* condition
  birth NEC 767.9
  cardiovascular (*see also* Disease,
      cardiovascular) 429.2
  cerebral (*see also* Disease, cerebrovascular,
      acute) 436
  cerebrovascular (current) (CVA) (*see also*
      Disease, cerebrovascular, acute) 436
    healed or old V12.59
    impending 435.9
    late effect—*see* Late effect(s) (of)
        cerebrovascular disease
  coronary (*see also* Infarct, myocardium) 410.9
  craniovascular (*see also* Disease,
      cerebrovascular, acute) 436
  during pregnancy, to mother
    affecting fetus or newborn 760.5
  heart, cardiac (*see also* Infarct, myocardium)
      410.9
  intrauterine 779.8
  vascular—*see* Disease, cerebrovascular, acute
Accommodation
  disorder of 367.51
    drug-induced 367.89
    toxic 367.89
  insufficiency of 367.4
  paralysis of 367.51
    hysterical 300.11
  spasm of 367.53
Accouchement —*see* Delivery
Accreta placenta (without hemorrhage) 667.0
  with hemorrhage 666.0
Accretio cordis (nonrheumatic) 423.1
Accretions on teeth 523.6
Accumulation secretion, prostate 602.8
Acephalia, acephalism, acephaly 740.0
Acephalic monster 740.0
Acephalobrachia monster 759.89
Acephalocardia 759.89
Acephalocardius 759.89
Acephalochiria 759.89
Acephalochirus monster 759.89
Acephalogaster 759.89
Acephalostomus monster 759.89
Acephalothorax 759.89
Acephalus 740.0
Acetonemia 790.6
  diabetic 250.1
Acetonglycosuria 982.8
Acetonuria 791.6
Achalasia 530.0
  cardia 530.0
  digestive organs congenital NEC 751.8
  esophagus 530.0
  pelvirectal 751.3
  psychogenic 306.4
  pylorus 750.5
  sphincteral NEC 564.89
Achard-Thiers syndrome (adrenogenital) 255.2
Ache (s)—*see* Pain
Acheilia 750.26
Acheiria 755.21
Achilloburitis 726.71
Achillodynia 726.71

Achlorhydria, achlorhydric 536.0
  anemia 280.9
  diarrhea 536.0
  neurogenic 536.0
  postvagotomy 564.2
  psychogenic 306.4
  secondary to vagotomy 564.2
Achloroblepsia 368.52
Achloropsia 368.52
Acholia 575.8
Acholuric jaundice (familial) (splenomegalic)
    (*see also* Spherocytosis) 282.0
  acquired 283.9
Achondroplasia 756.4
Achrestic anemia 281.8
Achroacytosis, lacrimal gland 375.00
  tuberculous (*see also* Tuberculosis) 017.3
Achroma, cutis 709.00
Achromate (congenital) 368.54
Achromatopia 368.54
Achromatopsia (congenital) 368.54
Achromia
  congenital 270.2
  parasitica 111.0
  unguium 703.8
Achylia
  gastrica 536.8
    neurogenic 536.3
    psychogenic 306.4
  pancreatica 577.1
Achylosis 536.8
Acid
  burn—*see also* Burn, by site
    from swallowing acid—*see* Burn, internal
        organs
  deficiency
    amide nicotinic 265.2
    amino 270.9
    ascorbic 267
    folic 266.2
    nicotinic (amide) 265.2
    pantothenic 266.2
  intoxication 276.2
  peptic disease 536.8
  stomach 536.8
    psychogenic 306.4
Acidemia 276.2
  arginosuccinic 270.6
  fetal
    affecting management of pregnancy 656.3
    before onset of labor, in liveborn infant 768.2
    during labor, in liveborn infant 768.3
    intrauterine—*see* Distress, fetal 656.3
    unspecified as to time of onset, in liveborn
        infant 768.4
  pipecolic 270.7
Acidity, gastric (high) (low) 536.8
  psychogenic 306.4
Acidocytopenia 288.0
Acidocytosis 288.3
Acidopenia 288.0
Acidosis 276.2
  diabetic 250.1
  fetal, affecting newborn 770.8
  fetal, affecting management of pregnancy 656.8
  kidney tubular 588.8
  lactic 276.2
  metabolic NEC 276.2
    with respiratory acidosis 276.4
    late, of newborn 775.7

Actinomyces
  israelii (infection)—*see* Actinomycosis
  muris-ratti (infection) 026.1
Actinomycosis actinomycotic 039.9
  with
    pneumonia 039.1
  abdominal 039.2
  cervicofacial 039.3
  cutaneous 039.0
  pulmonary 039.1
  specified site NEC 039.8
  thoracic 039.1
Actinoneuritis 357.8
Action, heart
  disorder 427.9
    postoperative 997.1
  irregular 427.9
    postoperative 997.1
    psychogenic 306.2
Active —*see* condition
Activity decrease, functional 780.9
Acute —*see also* condition
  abdomen NEC 789.0
  gallbladder (*see also* Cholecystitis, acute) 575.0
Acyanoblepsia 368.53
Acyanopsia 368.53
Acystia 753.8
Acystinervia —*see* Neurogenic, bladder
Acystineuria —*see* Neurogenic, bladder
Adactylia, adactyly (congenital) 755.4
  lower limb (complete) (intercalary) (partial)
    (terminal) (*see also* Deformity, reduction,
    lower limb) 755.39
Adactylia, adactyly—*continued*
    meaning all digits (complete) (partial) 755.31
    transverse (complete) (partial) 755.31
  upper limb (complete) (intercalary) (partial)
    (terminal) (*see also* Deformity, reduction,
    upper limb) 755.29
    meaning all digits (complete) (partial) 755.21
    transverse (complete) (partial) 755.21
Adair-Dighton syndrome (brittle bones and blue
  sclera, deafness) 756.51
Adamantinoblastoma (M9310/0)—*see*
  Ameloblastoma
Adamantinoma (M9310/0)—*see* Ameloblastoma
Adamantoblastoma (M9310/0)—*see*
  Ameloblastoma
Adams-Stokes (-Morgagni) disease or syndrome
  (syncope with heart block) 426.9
Adaptation reaction (*see also* Reaction,
  adjustment) 309.9
Addiction —*see also* Dependence
  absinthe 304.6
  alcoholic (ethyl) (methyl) (wood) 303.9
    complicating pregnancy, childbirth, or
      puerperium 648.4
      affecting fetus or newborn 760.71
      suspected damage to fetus affecting
        management of pregnancy 655.4
  drug (*see also* Dependence) 304.9
  ethyl alcohol 303.9
  heroin 304.0
  hospital 301.51
  methyl alcohol 303.9
  methylated spirit 303.9
  morphine (-like substances) 304.0
  nicotine 305.1
  opium 304.0
  tobacco 305.1
  wine 303.9

Addison's
  anemia (pernicious) 281.0
  disease (bronze) (primary adrenal insufficiency)
    255.4
    tuberculous (*see also* Tuberculosis) 017.6
  keloid (morphea) 701.0
  melanoderma (adrenal cortical hypofunction)
    255.4
Addison-Biermer anemia (pernicious) 281.0
Addison-Gull disease —*see* Xanthoma
Addisonian crisis or melanosis (acute
  adrenocortical insufficiency) 255.4
Additional —*see also* Accessory
  chromosome(s) 758.5
    13-15 758.1
    16-18 758.2
    21 758.0
    autosome(s) NEC 758.5
    sex 758.81
Adduction contracture, hip or other joint
  —*see* Contraction, joint
Adenasthenia gastrica 536.0
Aden fever 061
Adenitis (*see also* Lymphadenitis) 289.3
  acute, unspecified site 683
    epidemic infectious 075
  axillary 289.3
    acute 683
    chronic or subacute 289.1
  Bartholin's gland 616.8
  bulbourethral gland (*see also* Urethritis) 597.89
  cervical 289.3
    acute 683
    chronic or subacute 289.1
  chancroid (Ducrey's bacillus) 099.0
  chronic (any lymph node, except mesenteric)
    289.1
    mesenteric 289.2
  Cowper's gland (*see also* Urethritis) 597.89
  epidemic, acute 075
  gangrenous 683
  gonorrheal NEC 098.89
  groin 289.3
    acute 683
    chronic or subacute 289.1
  infectious 075
  inguinal (region) 289.3
    acute 683
    chronic or subacute 289.1
  lymph gland or node, except mesenteric 289.3
    acute 683
    chronic or subacute 289.1
    mesenteric (acute) (chronic) (nonspecific)
      (subacute) 289.2
  mesenteric (acute) (chronic) (nonspecific)
    (subacute) 289.2
    due to Pasteurella multocida (P. septica) 027.2
  parotid gland (suppurative) 527.2
  phlegmonous 683
  salivary duct or gland (any) (recurring)
    (suppurative) 527.2
  scrofulous (*see also* Tuberculosis) 017.2
  septic 289.3
  Skene's duct or gland (*see also* Urethritis)
    597.89
  strumous, tuberculous (*see also* Tuberculosis)
    017.2
  subacute, unspecified site 289.1
  sublingual gland (suppurative) 527.2
  submandibular gland (suppurative) 527.2
  submaxillary gland (suppurative) 527.2

Adenitis—*continued*
  suppurative 683
  tuberculous—*see* Tuberculosis, lymph gland
  urethral gland (*see also* Urethritis) 597.89
  venereal NEC 099.8
  Wharton's duct (suppurative) 527.2
Adenoacanthoma (M8570/3)—*see* Neoplasm,
  by site, malignant
Adenoameloblastoma (M9300/0) 213.1
  upper jaw (bone) 213.0
Adenocarcinoma (M8140/3)—*see also*
  Neoplasm, by site, malignant

> *Note*—*The list of adjectival modifiers below is
> not exhaustive. A description of
> adenocarcinoma that does not appear in this list
> should be coded in the same manner as
> carcinoma with that description. Thus, "mixed
> acidophil-basophil adenocarcinoma," should
> be coded in the same manner as "mixed
> acidophil-basophil carcinoma," which appears
> in the list under "Carcinoma."*
>
> *Except where otherwise indicated, the
> morphological varieties of adenocarcinoma in
> the list below should be coded by site as for
> "Neoplasm, malignant."*

  with
    apocrine metaplasia (M8573/3)
    cartilaginous (and osseous) metaplasia
      (M8571/3)
    osseous (and cartilaginous) metaplasia
      (M8571/3)
    spindle cell metaplasia (M8572/3)
    squamous metaplasia (M8570/3)
  acidophil (M8280/3)
    specified site—*see* Neoplasm, by site,
      malignant
    unspecified site 194.3
  acinar (M8550/3)
  acinic cell (M8550/3)
  adrenal cortical (M8370/3) 194.0
  alveolar (M8251/3)
  and
    epidermoid carcinoma, mixed (M8560/3)
    squamous cell carcinoma, mixed (M8560/3)
  apocrine (M8401/3)
    breast—*see* Neoplasm, breast, malignant
    specified site NEC—*see* Neoplasm, skin,
      malignant
    unspecified site 173.9
  basophil (M8300/3)
    specified site—*see* Neoplasm, by site,
      malignant
    unspecified site 194.3
  bile duct type (M8160/3)
    liver 155.1
    specified site NEC—*see* Neoplasm, by site,
      malignant
    unspecified site 155.1
  bronchiolar (M8250/3)—*see* Neoplasm, lung,
    malignant
  ceruminous (M8420/3) 173.2
  chromophobe (M8270/3)
    specified site—*see* Neoplasm, by site,
      malignant
    unspecified site 194.3
  clear cell (mesonephroid type) (M8310/3)
  colloid (M8480/3)
  cylindroid type (M8200/3)
  diffuse type (M8145/3)

Adenocarcinoma—*continued*
  specified site—*see* Neoplasm, by site,
    malignant
  unspecified site 151.9
  duct (infiltrating) (M8500/3)
    with Paget's disease (M8541/3)—*see*
      Neoplasm, breast, malignant
    specified site—*see* Neoplasm, by site,
      malignant
    unspecified site 174.9
  embryonal (M9070/3)
  endometrioid (M8380/3)—*see* Neoplasm, by
    site, malignant
  eosinophil (M8280/3)
    specified site—*see* Neoplasm, by site,
      malignant
    unspecified site 194.3
  follicular (M8330/3)
    and papillary (M8340/3) 193
    moderately differentiated type (M8332/3) 193
    pure follicle type (M8331/3) 193
    specified site—*see* Neoplasm, by site,
      malignant
    trabecular type (M8332/3) 193
    unspecified type 193
    well differentiated type (M8331/3) 193
  gelatinous (M8480/3)
  granular cell (M8320/3)
  Hürthle cell (M8290/3) 193
  in
    adenomatous
      polyp (M8210/3)
      polyposis coli (M8220/3) 153.9
    polypoid adenoma (M8210/3)
    tubular adenoma (M8210/3)
    villous adenoma (M8261/3)
  infiltrating duct (M8500/3)
    with Paget's disease (M8541/3)—*see*
      Neoplasm, breast, malignant
    specified site—*see* Neoplasm, by site,
      malignant
    unspecified site 174.9
  inflammatory (M8530/3)
    specified site—*see* Neoplasm, by site,
      malignant
    unspecified site 174.9
  in situ (M8140/2)—*see* Neoplasm, by site, in
    situ
  intestinal type (M8144/3)
    specified site—*see* Neoplasm, by site,
      malignant
    unspecified site 151.9
  intraductal (noninfiltrating) (M8500/2)
    papillary (M8503/2)
      specified site—*see* Neoplasm, by site, in situ
      unspecified site 233.0
    specified site—*see* Neoplasm, by site, in situ
    unspecified site 233.0
  islet cell (M8150/3)
    and exocrine, mixed (M8154/3)
      specified site—*see* Neoplasm, by site,
        malignant
      unspecified site 157.9
    pancreas 157.4
    specified site NEC—*see* Neoplasm, by site,
      malignant
    unspecified site 157.4
  lobular (M8520/3)
    specified site—*see* Neoplasm, by site,
      malignant
    unspecified site 174.9

Adenocarcinoma—*continued*
medullary (M8510/3)
mesonephric (M9110/3)
mixed cell (M8323/3)
mucinous (M8480/3)
mucin-producing (M8481/3)
mucoid (M8480/3)—*see also* Neoplasm, by
   site, malignant
  cell (M8300/3)
    specified site—*see* Neoplasm, by site,
     malignant
    unspecified site 194.3
nonencapsulated sclerosing (M8350/3) 193
oncocytic (M8290/3)
oxyphilic (M8290/3)
papillary (M8260/3)
  and follicular (M8340/3) 193
  intraductal (noninfiltrating) (M8503/2)
    specified site—*see* Neoplasm, by site, in situ
    unspecified site 233.0
  serous (M8460/3)
    specified site—*see* Neoplasm, by site,
     malignant
    unspecified site 183.0
papillocystic (M8450/3)
  specified site—*see* Neoplasm, by site,
    malignant
  unspecified site 183.0
pseudomucinous (M8470/3)
  specified site—*see* Neoplasm, by site,
    malignant
  unspecified site 183.0
renal cell (M8312/3) 189.0
sebaceous (M8410/3)
serous (M8441/3)—*see also* Neoplasm, by site,
  malignant
  papillary
    specified site—*see* Neoplasm, by site,
     malignant
    unspecified site 183.0
signet ring cell (M8490/3)
superficial spreading (M8143/3)
sweat gland (M8400/3)—*see* Neoplasm, skin,
  malignant
trabecular (M8190/3)
tubular (M8211/3)
villous (M8262/3)
water-clear cell (M8322/3) 194.1
Adenofibroma (M9013/0)
clear cell (M8313/0)—*see* Neoplasm, by site,
  benign
endometrioid (M8381/0) 220
  borderline malignancy (M8381/1) 236.2
  malignant (M8381/3) 183.0
mucinous (M9015/0)
  specified site—*see* Neoplasm, by site, benign
  unspecified site 220
prostate 600.2
serous (M9014/0)
  specified site—*see* Neoplasm, by site, benign
  unspecified site 220
specified site—*see* Neoplasm, by site, benign
unspecified site 220
Adenofibrosis
breast 610.2
endometrioid 617.0
Adenoiditis 474.01
acute 463
chronic 474.01
  with chronic tonsillitis 474.02

Adenoids (congenital) (of nasal fossa) 474.9
hypertrophy 474.12
vegetations 474.2
Adenolipomatosis (symmetrical) 272.8
Adenolymphoma (M8561/0)
specified site—*see* Neoplasm, by site, benign
unspecified 210.2
Adenoma (sessile) (M8140/0)—*see also*
  Neoplasm, by site, benign

> *Note—Except where otherwise indicated, the morphological varieties of adenoma in the list below should be coded by site as for "Neoplasm, benign."*

acidophil (M8280/0)
  specified site—*see* Neoplasm, by site, benign
  unspecified site 227.3
acinar (cell) (M8550/0)
acinic cell (M8550/0)
adrenal (cortex) (cortical) (functioning)
  (M8370/0) 227.0
  clear cell type (M8373/0) 227.0
  compact cell type (M8371/0) 227.0
  glomerulosa cell type (M8374/0) 227.0
  heavily pigmented variant (M8372/0) 227.0
  mixed cell type (M8375/0) 227.0
alpha cell (M8152/0)
  pancreas 211.7
  specified site NEC—*see* Neoplasm, by site,
    benign
  unspecified site 211.7
alveolar (M8251/0)
apocrine (M8401/0)
  breast 217
  specified site NEC—*see* Neoplasm, skin,
    benign
  unspecified site 216.9
basal cell (M8147/0)
basophil (M8300/0)
  specified site—*see* Neoplasm, by site, benign
  unspecified site 227.3
beta cell (M8151/0)
  pancreas 211.7
  specified site NEC—*see* Neoplasm, by site,
    benign
  unspecified site 211.7
bile duct (M8160/0) 211.5
black (M8372/0) 227.0
bronchial (M8140/1) 235.7
  carcinoid type (M8240/3)—*see* Neoplasm,
    lung, malignant
  cylindroid type (M8200/3)—*see* Neoplasm,
    lung, malignant
ceruminous (M8420/0) 216.2
chief cell (M8321/0) 227.1
chromophobe (M8270/0)
  (specified site—*see* Neoplasm, by site, benign
  unspecified site 227.3
clear cell (M8310/0)
colloid (M8334/0)
  specified site—*see* Neoplasm, by site, benign
  unspecified site 226
cylindroid type, bronchus (M8200/3)—*see*
  Neoplasm, lung, malignant
duct (M8503/0)
embryonal (M8191/0)
endocrine, multiple (M8360/1)
  single specified site—*see* Neoplasm, by site,
    uncertain behavior
  two or more specified sites 237.4
  unspecified site 237.4

Adherent
  labium (minus) 624.4
  pericardium (nonrheumatic) 423.1
    rheumatic 393
  placenta 667.0
    with hemorrhage 666.0
  prepuce 605
  scar (skin) NEC 709.2
  tendon in scar 709.2
Adhesion(s), adhesive (postinfectional)(postoperative)
  abdominal (wall) (*see also* Adhesions, peritoneum) 568.0
  amnion to fetus 658.8
    affecting fetus or newborn 762.8
  appendix 543.9
  arachnoiditis—*see* Meningitis
  auditory tube (Eustachian) 381.89
  bands—*see also* Adhesions, peritoneum
    cervix 622.3
    uterus 621.5
  bile duct (any) 576.8
  bladder (sphincter) 596.8
  bowel (*see also* Adhesions, peritoneum) 568.0
  cardiac 423.1
    rheumatic 398.99
  cecum (*see also* Adhesions, peritoneum) 568.0
  cervicovaginal 622.3
    congenital 752.49
    postpartal 674.8
      old 622.3
  cervix 622.3
  clitoris 624.4
  colon (*see also* Adhesions, peritoneum) 568.0
  common duct 576.8
  congenital—*see also* Anomaly, specified type NEC
    fingers (*see also* Syndactylism, fingers) 755.11
    labium (majus) (minus) 752.49
    omental, anomalous 751.4
    ovary 752.0
    peritoneal 751.4
    toes (*see also* Syndactylism, toes) 755.13
    tongue (to gum or roof of mouth) 750.12
  conjunctiva (acquired) (localized) 372.62
    congenital 743.63
    extensive 372.63
  cornea—*see* Opacity, cornea
  cystic duct 575.8
  diaphragm (*see also* Adhesions, peritoneum) 568.0
  due to foreign body—*see* Foreign body
  duodenum (*see also* Adhesions, peritoneum) 568.0
    with obstruction 537.3
  ear, middle—*see* Adhesions, middle ear
  epididymis 608.89
  epidural—*see* Adhesions, meninges
  epiglottis 478.79
  Eustachian tube 381.89
  eyelid 374.46
    postoperative 997.99
      surgically created V45.69
  gallbladder (*see also* Disease, gallbladder) 575.8
  globe 360.89
  heart 423.1
    rheumatic 398.99
  ileocecal (coil) (*see also* Adhesions, peritoneum) 568.0
  ileum (*see also* Adhesions, peritoneum) 568.0

Adhesion—*continued*
  intestine (postoperative) (*see also* Adhesions, peritoneum) 568.0
    with obstruction 560.81
      with hernia—*see also* Hernia, by site, with obstruction
        gangrenous—*see* Hernia, by site, with gangrene
  intra-abdominal (*see also* Adhesions, peritoneum) 568.0
  iris 364.70
    to corneal graft 996.79
  joint (*see also* Ankylosis) 718.5
  kidney 593.89
  labium (majus) (minus), congenital 752.49
  liver 572.8
  lung 511.0
  mediastinum 519.3
  meninges 349.2
    cerebral (any) 349.2
      congenital 742.4
    congenital 742.8
    spinal (any) 349.2
      congenital 742.59
    tuberculous (cerebral) (spinal) (*see also* Tuberculosis, meninges) 013.0
  mesenteric (*see also* Adhesions, peritoneum) 568.0
  middle ear (fibrous) 385.10
    drum head 385.19
      to
        incus 385.11
        promontorium 385.13
        stapes 385.12
    specified NEC 385.19
  nasal (septum) (to turbinates) 478.1
  nerve NEC 355.9
    spinal 355.9
      root 724.9
        cervical NEC 723.4
        lumbar NEC 724.4
        lumbosacral 724.4
        thoracic 724.4
  ocular muscle 378.60
  omentum (*see also* Adhesions, peritoneum) 568.0
  organ or site, congenital NEC—*see* Anomaly, specified type NEC
  ovary 614.6
    congenital (to cecum, kidney, or omentum) 752.0
  parauterine 614.6
  parovarian 614.6
  pelvic (peritoneal)
    female 614.6
    male (*see also* Adhesions, peritoneum) 568.0
    postpartal (old) 614.6
    tuberculous (*see also* Tuberculosis) 016.9
  penis to scrotum (congenital) 752.69
  periappendiceal (*see also* Adhesions, peritoneum) 568.0
  pericardium (nonrheumatic) 423.1
    rheumatic 393
    tuberculous (*see also* Tuberculosis) 017.9
      [420.0]
  pericholecystic 575.8
  perigastric (*see also* Adhesions, peritoneum) 568.0
  periovarian 614.6
  periprostatic 602.8

Adhesion—*continued*
  perirectal (*see also* Adhesions, peritoneum)
    568.0
  perirenal 593.89
  peritoneum, peritoneal (fibrous) (postoperative)
    568.0
    with obstruction (intestinal) 560.81
      with hernia—*see also* Hernia, by site, with
        obstruction
        gangrenous—*see* Hernia, by site, with
          gangrene
        duodenum 537.3
    congenital 751.4
    female, (postoperative) (postinfective) 614.6
    pelvic, female 614.6
    pelvic, male 568.0
    postpartal, pelvic 614.6
    to uterus 614.6
  peritubal 614.6
  periureteral 593.89
  periuterine 621.5
  perivesical 596.8
  perivesicular (seminal vesicle) 608.89
  pleura, pleuritic 511.0
    tuberculous (*see also* Tuberculosis, pleura)
      012.0
  pleuropericardial 511.0
  postoperative (gastrointestinal tract) (*See also*
    Adhesions, peritoneum) 568.0
    eyelid 997.99
      surgically created V45.69
    urethra 598.2
  postpartal, old 624.4
  preputial, prepuce 605
  pulmonary 511.0
  pylorus (*see also* Adhesions, peritoneum) 568.0
  Rosenmüller's fossa 478.29
  sciatic nerve 355.0
  seminal vesicle 608.89
  shoulder (joint) 726.0
  sigmoid flexure (*see also* Adhesions,
    peritoneum) 568.0
  spermatic cord (acquired) 608.89
    congenital 752.8
  spinal canal 349.2
    nerve 355.9
      root 724.9
        cervical NEC 723.4
        lumbar NEC 724.4
        lumbosacral 724.4
        thoracic 724.4
  stomach (*see also* Adhesions, peritoneum) 568.0
  subscapular 726.2
  tendonitis 726.90
    shoulder 726.0
  testicle 608.89
  tongue (congenital) (to gum or roof of mouth)
    750.12
    acquired 529.8
  trachea 519.1
  tubo-ovarian 614.6
  tunica vaginalis 608.89
  ureter 593.89
  uterus 621.5
    to abdominal wall 614.6
      in pregnancy or childbirth 654.4
        affecting fetus or newborn 763.89
  vagina (chronic) (postoperative) (postradiation)
    623.2
  vaginitis (congenital) 752.49
  vesical 596.8
  vitreous 379.29

Adie (-Holmes) syndrome (tonic pupillary
  reaction) 379.46
Adiponecrosis neonatorum 778.1
Adiposa dolorosa 272.8
Adiposalgia 272.8
Adiposis 278.0
  cerebralis 253.8
  dolorosa 272.8
  tuberosa simplex 272.8
Adiposity 278.0
  heart (*see also* Degeneration, myocardial) 429.1
  localized 278.1
Adiposogenital dystrophy 253.8
Adjustment
  prosthesis or other device—*see* Fitting of
  reaction—*see* Reaction, adjustment
Administration, prophylactic
  antibiotics V07.39
  antitoxin, any V07.2
  antivenin V07.2
  chemotherapeutic agent NEC V07.39
  chemotherapy NEC V07.39
  diphtheria antitoxin V07.2
  fluoride V07.31
  gamma globulin V07.2
  immune sera (gamma globulin) V07.2
  passive immunization agent V07.2
  RhoGAM V07.2
Admission (encounter)
  as organ donor—*see* Donor
  by mistake V68.9
  for
    adequacy testing (for)
      hemodialysis V56.31
      peritoneal dialysis V56.32
    adjustment (of)
      artificial
        arm (complete) (partial) V52.0
        eye V52.2
        leg (complete) (partial) V52.1
      brain neuropacemaker V53.02
      breast
        implant V50.1
        prosthesis V52.4
      cardiac device V53.39
        defibrillator, automatic implantable V53.32
        pacemaker V53.31
          carotid sinus V53.39
      catheter
        non-vascular V58.82
        vascular V58.81
      cerebral ventricle (communicating) shunt
        V53.01
      colostomy belt V53.5
      contact lenses V53.1
      cystostomy device V53.6
      dental prosthesis V52.3
      device NEC V53.9
        abdominal V53.5
        cardiac V53.39
          defibrillator, automatic implantable
            V53.32
          pacemaker V53.31
            carotid sinus V53.39
        cerebral ventricle (communicating) shunt
          V53.01
        intrauterine contraceptive V25.1
        nervous system V53.09
        orthodontic V53.4

Admission—*continued*
  cosmetic surgery NEC V50.1
    following healed injury or operation V51
  counseling (*see also* Counseling) V65.40
    without complaint or sickness V65.49
    contraceptive management V25.09
    dietary V65.3
    exercise V65.41
    for
      nonattending third party V65.1
      victim of abuse
        child V61.21
        partner or spouse V61.11
    genetic V26.3
    gonorrhea V65.45
    HIV V65.44
    human immunodeficiency virus V65.44
    injury prevention V65.43
    procreative management V26.4
    sexually transmitted disease NEC V65.45
      HIV V65.44
    specified reason NEC V65.49
    substance use and abuse V65.42
    syphilis V65.45
    victim of abuse
      child V61.21
      partner or spouse V61.11
  desensitization to allergens V07.1
  dialysis V56.0
    catheter
      fitting and adjustment
        extracorporeal V56.1
        peritoneal V56.2
      removal or replacement
        extracorporeal V56.1
        peritoneal V56.2
    extracorporeal (renal) V56.0
    peritoneal V56.8
    renal V56.0
  dietary surveillance and counseling V65.3
  drug monitoring, therapeutic V58.83
  ear piercing V50.3
  elective surgery V50.9
    breast
      augmentation or reduction V50.1
      removal, prophylactic V50.41
    circumcision, ritual or routine (in absence of
      medical indication) V50.2
    cosmetic NEC V50.1
      following healed injury or operation V51
    ear piercing V50.3
    face-lift V50.1
    hair transplant V50.0
    plastic
      cosmetic NEC V50.1
      following healed injury or operation V51
    prophylactic organ removal V50.49
      breast V50.41
      ovary V50.42
    repair of scarred tissue (following healed
      injury or operation) V51
    specified type NEC V50.8
  end-of-life care V66.7
  examination (*see also* Examination) V70.9
    administrative purpose NEC V70.3
    adoption V70.3
    allergy V72.7
    at health care facility V70.0
    athletic team V70.3
    camp V70.3
    cardiovascular, preoperative V72.81

Admission—*continued*
    clinical research investigation V70.7
    dental V72.2
    developmental testing (child) (infant) V20.2
    donor (potential) V70.8
    driver's license V70.3
    ear V72.1
    employment V70.5
    eye V72.0
    follow-up (routine)—*see* Examination,
      follow-up
    for admission to
      old age home V70.3
      school V70.3
    general V70.9
      specified reason NEC V70.8
    gynecological V72.3
    health supervision (child) (infant) V20.2
    hearing V72.1
    immigration V70.3
    insurance certification V70.3
    laboratory V72.6
    marriage license V70.3
    medical (general) (*see also* Examination,
      medical) V70.9
    medicolegal reasons V70.4
    naturalization V70.3
    pelvic (annual) (periodic) V72.3
    postpartum checkup V24.2
    pregnancy (possible) (unconfirmed) V72.4
    preoperative V72.84
      cardiovascular V72.81
      respiratory V72.82
      specified NEC V72.83
    prison V70.3
    psychiatric (general) V70.2
      requested by authority V70.1
    radiological NEC V72.5
    respiratory, preoperative V72.82
    school V70.3
    screening—*see* Screening
    skin hypersensitivity V72.7
    specified type NEC V72.85
    sport competition V70.3
    vision V72.0
    well baby and child care V20.2
  exercise therapy V57.1
  face-lift, cosmetic reason V50.1
  fitting (of)
    artificial
      arm (complete) (partial) V52.0
      eye V52.2
      leg (complete) (partial) V52.1
    biliary drainage tube V58.82
    brain neuropacemaker V53.02
    breast V52.4
      implant V50.1
      prosthesis V52.4
    cardiac pacemaker V53.31
    catheter
      non-vascular V58.82
      vascular V58.81
    cerebral ventricle (communicating) shunt
      V53.01
    chest tube V58.82
    colostomy belt V53.5
    contact lenses V53.1
    cystostomy device V53.6
    dental prosthesis V52.3

Admission—*continued*
- plastic surgery
  - cosmetic NEC V50.1
  - following healed injury or operation V51
- postmenopausal hormone replacement therapy V07.4
- postpartum observation
  - immediately after delivery V24.0
  - routine follow-up V24.2
- poststerilization (for restoration) V26.0
- procreative management V26.9
  - specified type NEC V26.8
- prophylactic
  - administration of
    - antibiotics V07.39
    - antitoxin, any V07.2
    - antivenin V07.2
    - chemotherapeutic agent NEC V07.39
    - chemotherapy NEC V07.39
    - diphtheria antitoxin V07.2
    - fluoride V07.31
    - gamma globulin V07.2
    - immune sera (gamma globulin) V07.2
    - RhoGAM V07.2
    - tetanus antitoxin V07.2
  - breathing exercises V57.0
  - chemotherapy NEC V07.39
    - fluoride V07.31
  - measure V07.9
    - specified type NEC V07.8
  - organ removal V50.49
    - breast V50.41
    - ovary V50.42
- psychiatric examination (general) V70.2
  - requested by authority V70.1
- radiation management V58.0
- radiotherapy V58.0
- reforming of artificial opening—*see* Attention to, artificial, opening
- rehabilitation V57.9
  - multiple types V57.89
  - occupational V57.21
  - orthoptic V57.4
  - orthotic V57.81
  - physical NEC V57.1
  - specified type NEC V57.89
  - speech V57.3
  - vocational V57.22
- removal of
  - cardiac pacemaker V53.31
  - cast (plaster) V54.8
  - catheter from artificial opening—*see* Attention to, artificial, opening
  - cerebral ventricle (communicating) shunt V53.01
  - cystostomy catheter V55.5
  - device
    - cerebral ventricle (communicating) shunt V53.01
    - fixation
      - external V54.8
      - internal V54.0
    - intrauterine contraceptive V25.42
    - traction, external V54.8
  - dressing V58.3
  - fixation device
    - external V54.8
    - internal V54.0
  - intrauterine contraceptive device V25.42
  - Kirschner wire V54.8

Admission—*continued*
- neuropacemaker (brain) (peripheral nerve) (spinal cord) V53.02
- orthopedic fixation device
  - external V54.8
  - internal V54.0
- pacemaker device
  - brain V53.02
  - cardiac V53.31
  - carotid sinus V53.39
  - nervous system V53.02
- plaster cast V54.8
- plate (fracture) V54.0
- rod V54.0
- screw (fracture) V54.0
- splint, traction V54.8
- Steinmann pin V54.8
- subdermal implantable contraceptive V25.43
- surgical dressing V58.3
- sutures V58.3
- traction device, external V54.8
- ureteral stent V53.6
- repair of scarred tissue (following healed injury or operation) V51
- reprogramming of cardiac pacemaker V53.31
- restoration of organ continuity (poststerilization) (tuboplasty) (vasoplasty) V26.0
- sensitivity test—*see also* Test, skin
  - allergy NEC V72.7
  - bacterial disease NEC V74.9
  - Dick V74.8
  - Kveim V82.89
  - Mantoux V74.1
  - mycotic infection NEC V75.4
  - parasitic disease NEC V75.8
  - Schick V74.3
  - Schultz-Charlton V74.8
- social service (agency) referral or evaluation V63.8
- speech therapy V57.3
- sterilization V25.2
- suspected disorder (ruled out) (without need for further care)—*see* Observation
- terminal care V66.7
- tests only—*see* Test
- therapeutic drug monitoring V58.83
- therapy
  - blood transfusion, without reported diagnosis V58.2
  - breathing exercises V57.0
  - chemotherapy V58.1
    - prophylactic NEC V07.39
    - fluoride V07.31
  - dialysis (intermittent) (treatment)
    - extracorporeal V56.0
    - peritoneal V56.8
    - renal V56.0
    - specified type NEC V56.8
  - exercise (remedial) NEC V57.1
    - breathing V57.0
  - long-term (current) drug use NEC V58.69
    - antibiotics V58.62
    - anticoagulant V58.61
  - occupational V57.21
  - orthoptic V57.4
  - physical NEC V57.1
  - radiation V58.0
  - speech V57.3
  - vocational V57.22

Admission—*continued*
  toilet or cleaning
    of artificial opening — *see* Attention to,
      artificial, opening
    of non-vascular catheter V58.82
    of vascular catheter V58.81
  tubal ligation V25.2
  tuboplasty for previous sterilization V26.0
  vaccination, prophylactic (against)
    arthropod-borne virus, viral NEC V05.1
      disease NEC V05.1
      encephalitis V05.0
    Bacille Calmette Guérin (BCG) V03.2
    BCG V03.2
    chickenpox V05.4
    cholera alone V03.0
      with typhoid-paratyphoid (cholera + TAB)
        V06.0
    common cold V04.7
    dengue V05.1
    diphtheria alone V03.5
    diphtheria-tetanus [Td] without pertussis
      V06.5
    diphtheria-tetanus-pertussis (DTP) V06.1
      with
        poliomyelitis (DTP + polio) V06.3
        typhoid-paratyphoid (DTP + TAB)
          V06.2
    disease (single) NEC V05.9
      bacterial NEC V03.9
        specified type NEC V03.89
      combinations NEC V06.9
        specified type NEC V06.8
      specified type NEC V05.8
    encephalitis, viral, arthropod-borne V05.0
    Hemophilus influenzae, type B [Hib] V03.81
    hepatitis, viral V05.3
    immune sera (gamma globulin) V07.2
    influenza V04.8
      with
        Streptococcus pneumoniae
          [pneumococcus] V06.6
    Leishmaniasis V05.2
    measles alone V04.2
    measles-mumps-rubella (MMR) V06.4
    mumps alone V04.6
      with measles and rubella (MMR) V06.4
    not done because of contraindication V64.0
    pertussis alone V03.6
    plague V03.3
    pneumonia V03.82
    poliomyelitis V04.0
      with diphtheria-tetanus-pertussis (DTP +
        polio) V06.3
    rabies V04.5
    rubella alone V04.3
      with measles and mumps (MMR) V06.4
    smallpox V04.1
    specified type NEC V05.8
    Streptococcus pneumoniae [pneumococcus]
      V03.82
      with
        influenza V06.6
    tetanus toxoid alone V03.7
      with diphtheria [Td] V06.5
        and pertussis (DTP) V06.1
    tuberculosis (BCG) V03.2
    tularemia V03.4
    typhoid alone V03.1
      with diphtheria-tetanus-pertussis (TAB +
        DTP) V06.2

Admission—*continued*
    typhoid-paratyphoid alone (TAB) V03.1
    typhus V05.8
    varicella V05.4
    viral encephalitis, arthropod-borne V05.0
    viral hepatitis V05.3
    yellow fever V04.4
  vasectomy V25.2
  vasoplasty for previous sterilization V26.0
  vision examination V72.0
  vocational therapy V57.22
  waiting period for admission to other facility
    V63.2
    undergoing social agency investigation
      V63.8
  well baby and child care V20.2
  x-ray of chest
    for suspected tuberculosis V71.2
    routine V72.5
Adnexitis (suppurative) (*see also*
  Salpingo-oophoritis) 614.2
Adolescence NEC V21.2
Adoption
  agency referral V68.89
  examination V70.3
  held for V68.89
Adrenal gland —*see* condition
Adrenalism 255.9
  tuberculous (*see also* Tuberculosis) 017.6
Adrenalitis, adrenitis 255.8
  meningococcal hemorrhagic 036.3
Adrenarche, precocious 259.1
Adrenocortical syndrome 255.2
Adrenogenital syndrome (acquired) (congenital)
  255.2
  iatrogenic, fetus or newborn 760.79
Adventitious bursa —*see* Bursitis
Adynamia (episodica) (hereditary) (periodic)
  359.3
Adynamic
  ileus or intestine (see also ileus) 560.1
  ureter 753.22
Aeration lung imperfect, newborn 770.5
Aerobullosis 993.3
Aerocele —*see* Embolism, air
Aerodermectasia
  subcutaneous (traumatic) 958.7
    surgical 998.81
  surgical 998.81
Aerodontalgia 993.2
Aeroembolism 993.3
Aerogenes capsulatus infection (*see also*
  Gangrene, gas) 040.0
Aero-otitis media 993.0
Aerophagy, aerophagia 306.4
  psychogenic 306.4
Aerosinusitis 993.1
Aerotitis 993.0
Affection, affections —*see also* Disease
  sacroiliac (joint), old 724.6
  shoulder region NEC 726.2
Afibrinogenemia 286.3
  acquired 286.6
  congenital 286.3
  postpartum 666.3
African
  sleeping sickness 086.5
  tick fever 087.1
  trypanosomiasis 086.5
    Gambian 086.3
    Rhodesian 086.4

Aftercare V58.9
artificial openings—*see* Attention to, artificial, opening
blood transfusion without reported diagnosis V58.2
breathing exercise V57.0
cardiac device V53.39
 defibrillator, automatic implantable V53.32
 pacemaker V53.31
  carotid sinus V53.39
carotid sinus pacemaker V53.39
cerebral ventricle (communicating) shunt V53.01
chemotherapy session (adjunctive) (maintenance) V58.1
defibrillator, automatic implantable cardiac V53.32
exercise (remedial) (therapeutic) V57.1
 breathing V57.0
extracorporeal dialysis (intermittent) (treatment) V56.0
following surgery NEC V58.49
 wound closure, planned V58.41
fracture V54.9
 removal of
  external fixation device V54.8
  internal fixation device V54.0
 specified care NEC V54.8
gait training V57.1
 for use of artificial limb(s) V57.81
involving
 dialysis (intermittent) (treatment)
  extracorporeal V56.0
  peritoneal V56.8
  renal V56.0
 gait training V57.1
  for use of artificial limb(s) V57.81
 orthoptic training V57.4
 orthotic training V57.81
 radiotherapy session V58.0
 removal of
  dressings V58.3
  fixation device
   external V54.8
   internal V54.0
  fracture plate V54.0
  pins V54.0
  plaster cast V54.8
  rods V54.0
  screws V54.0
  surgical dressings V58.3
  sutures V58.3
  traction device, external V54.8
neuropacemaker (brain) (peripheral nerve) (spinal cord) V53.02
occupational therapy V57.21
orthodontic V58.5
orthopedic V54.9
 change of external fixation or traction device V54.8
 removal of fixation device
  external V54.8
  internal V54.0
 specified care NEC V54.8
orthoptic training V57.4
orthotic training V57.81
pacemaker
 brain V53.02
 cardiac V53.31
 carotid sinus V53.39
 peripheral nerve V53.02

Aftercare—*continued*
spinal cord V53.02
peritoneal dialysis (intermittent) (treatment) V56.8
physical therapy NEC V57.1
 breathing exercises V57.0
radiotherapy session V58.0
rehabilitation procedure V57.9
 breathing exercises V57.0
 multiple types V57.89
 occupational V57.21
 orthoptic V57.4
 orthotic V57.81
 physical therapy NEC V57.1
 remedial exercises V57.1
 specified type NEC V57.89
 speech V57.3
 therapeutic exercises V57.1
 vocational V57.22
renal dialysis (intermittent) (treatment) V56.0
specified type NEC V58.89
 removal of non-vascular catheter V58.82
 removal of vascular catheter V58.81
speech therapy V57.3
vocational rehabilitation V57.22
After-cataract 366.50
obscuring vision 366.53
specified type, not obscuring vision 366.52
Agalactia 676.4
Agammaglobulinemia 279.00
with lymphopenia 279.2
acquired (primary) (secondary) 279.06
Bruton's X-linked 279.04
infantile sex-linked (Bruton's) (congenital) 279.04
Swiss-type 279.2
Aganglionosis (bowel) (colon) 751.3
Age (old) (*see also* Senile) 797
Agenesis —*see also* Absence, by site, congenital
acoustic nerve 742.8
adrenal (gland) 759.1
alimentary tract (complete) (partial) NEC 751.8
 lower 751.2
 upper 750.8
anus, anal (canal) 751.2
aorta 747.22
appendix 751.2
arm (complete) (partial) (*see also* Deformity, reduction, upper limb) 755.20
artery (peripheral) NEC (*see also* Anomaly, peripheral vascular system) 747.60
 brain 747.81
 coronary 746.85
 pulmonary 747.3
 umbilical 747.5
auditory (canal) (external) 744.01
auricle (ear) 744.01
bile, biliary duct or passage 751.61
bone NEC 756.9
brain 740.0
 specified part 742.2
breast 757.6
bronchus 748.3
canaliculus lacrimalis 743.65
carpus NEC (*see also* Deformity, reduction, upper limb) 755.28
cartilage 756.9
cecum 751.2
cerebellum 742.2
cervix 752.49
chin 744.89

Agenesis—*continued*
  skull (bone) 756.0
    with
      anencephalus 740.0
      encephalocele 742.0
      hydrocephalus 742.3
        with spina bifida (*see also* Spina bifida) 741.0
      microcephalus 742.1
  spermatic cord 752.8
  spinal cord 742.59
  spine 756.13
    lumbar 756.13
      isthmus 756.11
        pars articularis 756.11
  spleen 759.0
  sternum 756.3
  stomach 750.7
  tarsus NEC 755.38
  tendon 756.81
  testicular 752.8
  testis 752.8
  thymus (gland) 759.2
  thyroid (gland) 243
    cartilage 748.3
  tibia NEC (*see also* Absence, tibia, congenital) 755.36
  tibiofibular NEC 755.35
  toe (complete) (partial) (*see also* Absence, toe, congenital) 755.39
  tongue 750.11
  trachea (cartilage) 748.3
  ulna NEC (*see also* Absence, ulna, congenital) 755.27
  ureter 753.4
  urethra 753.8
  urinary tract NEC 753.8
  uterus 752.3
  uvula 750.26
  vagina 752.49
  vas deferens 752.8
  vein(s) (peripheral) NEC (*see also* Anomaly, peripheral vascular system) 747.60
    brain 747.81
    great 747.49
    portal 747.49
    pulmonary 747.49
  vena cava (inferior) (superior) 747.49
  vermis of cerebellum 742.2
  vertebra 756.13
    lumbar 756.13
      isthmus 756.11
        pars articularis 756.11
  vulva 752.49
Ageusia (*see also* Disturbance, sensation) 781.1
Aggressiveness 301.3
Aggressive outburst (*see also* Disturbance, conduct) 312.0
  in children and adolescents 313.9
Aging skin 701.8
Agitated —*see* condition
Agitation 307.9
  catatonic (*see also* Schizophrenia) 295.2
Aglossia (congenital) 750.11
Aglycogenosis 271.0
Agnail (finger) (with lymphangitis) 681.02
Agnosia (body image) (tactile) 784.69
  verbal 784.69
    auditory 784.69
      secondary to organic lesion 784.69
    developmental 315.8

Agnosia—*continued*
    secondary to organic lesion 784.69
  visual 784.69
    developmental 315.8
    secondary to organic lesion 784.69
  visual 368.16
    developmental 315.31
Agoraphobia 300.22
  with panic attacks 300.21
Agrammatism 784.69
Agranulocytopenia 288.0
Agranulocytosis (angina) (chronic) (cyclical) (genetic) (infantile) (periodic) (pernicious) 288.0
Agraphia (absolute) 784.69
  with alexia 784.61
  developmental 315.39
Agrypnia (*see also* Insomnia) 780.52
Ague (*see also* Malaria) 084.6
  brass-founders' 985.8
  dumb 084.6
  tertian 084.1
Agyria 742.2
Ahumada-del Castillo syndrome (nonpuerperal galactorrhea and amenorrhea) 253.1
AIDS 042
AIDS-associated retrovirus (disease) (illness) 042
  infection—*see* Human immunodeficiency virus, infection
AIDS-associated virus (disease) (illness) 042
  infection—*see* Human immunodeficiency virus, infection
AIDS-like disease (illness) (syndrome) 042
AIDS-related complex 042
AIDS-related conditions 042
AIDS-related virus (disease) (illness) 042
  infection—*see* Human immunodeficiency virus, infection
AIDS virus (disease) (illness) 042
  infection—*see* Human immunodeficiency virus, infection
Ailment, heart —*see* Disease, heart
Ailurophobia 300.29
Ainhum (disease) 136.0
Air
  anterior mediastinum 518.1
  compressed, disease 993.3
  embolism (any site) (artery) (cerebral) 958.0
    with
      abortion—*see* Abortion, by type, with embolism
      ectopic pregnancy (*see also* categories 633.0-633.9) 639.6
      molar pregnancy (*see also* categories 630-632) 639.6
    due to implanted device—*see* Complications, due to (presence of) any device, implant, or graft classified to 996.0-996.5 NEC
    following
      abortion 639.6
      ectopic or molar pregnancy 639.6
    infusion, perfusion, or transfusion 999.1
    in pregnancy, childbirth, or puerperium 673.0
    traumatic 958.0
  hunger 786.09
    psychogenic 306.1
  leak (lung) (pulmonary) (thorax) 512.8
    iatrogenic 512.1
    postoperative 512.1

Air —*continued*
rarefied, effects of—*see* Effect, adverse, high
altitude
sickness 994.6
Airplane sickness 994.6
Akathisia, acathisia 781.0
due to drugs 333.99
Akinesia algeria 352.6
Akiyami 100.89
Akureyri disease (epidemic neuromyasthenia)
049.8
Alacrima (congenital) 743.65
Alactasia (hereditary) 271.3
Alalia 784.3
developmental 315.31
receptive-expressive 315.32
secondary to organic lesion 784.3
Alaninemia 270.8
Alastrim 050.1
Albarrán's disease (colibacilluria) 791.9
Albers-Schönberg's disease (marble bones)
756.52
Albert's disease 726.71
Albinism, albino (choroid) (cutaneous) (eye)
(generalized) (isolated) (ocular)
(oculocutaneous) (partial) 270.2
Albinismus 270.2
Albright (-Martin) (-Bantam) disease
(pseudohypoparathyroidism) 275.49
Albright (-McCune) (-Sternberg) syndrome
(osteitis fibrosa disseminata) 756.59
Albuminous —*see* condition
Albuminuria, albuminuric (acute) (chronic)
(subacute) 791.0
Bence-Jones 791.0
cardiac 785.9
complicating pregnancy, childbirth, or
puerperium 646.2
with hypertension—*see* Toxemia, of
pregnancy
affecting fetus or newborn 760.1
cyclic 593.6
gestational 646.2
gravidarum 646.2
with hypertension—*see* Toxemia, of
pregnancy
affecting fetus or newborn 760.1
heart 785.9
idiopathic 593.6
orthostatic 593.6
postural 593.6
pre-eclamptic (mild) 642.4
affecting fetus or newborn 760.0
severe 642.5
affecting fetus or newborn 760.0
recurrent physiologic 593.6
scarlatinal 034.1
Albumosuria 791.0
Bence-Jones 791.0
myelopathic (M9730/3) 203.0
Alcaptonuria 270.2
Alcohol, alcoholic
abstinance 291.81
acute intoxication 305.0
with dependence 303.0
addiction (*see also* Alcoholism) 303.9
maternal
with suspected fetal damage affecting
management of pregnancy 655.4
affecting fetus or newborn 760.71
amnestic disorder, persisting 291.1

Alcohol, alcoholic—*continued*
anxiety 291.89
brain syndrome, chronic 291.2
cardiopathy 425.5
chronic (*see also* Alcoholism) 303.9
cirrhosis (liver) 571.2
delirium 291.0
acute 291.0
chronic 291.1
tremens 291.0
withdrawal 291.0
dementia NEC 291.2
deterioration 291.2
drunkenness (simple) 305.0
hallucinosis (acute) 291.3
insanity 291.9
intoxication (acute) 305.0
with dependence 303.0
pathological 291.4
jealousy 291.5
Korsakoff's, Korsakov's, Korsakow's 291.1
liver NEC 571.3
acute 571.1
chronic 571.2
mania (acute) (chronic) 291.9
mood 291.89
paranoia 291.5
paranoid (type) psychosis 291.5
pellagra 265.2
poisoning, accidental (acute) NEC 980.9
specified type of alcohol—*see* Table of drugs
and chemicals
psychosis (*see also* Psychosis, alcoholic) 291.9
Korsakoff's, Korsakov's, Korsakow's 291.1
polyneuritic 291.1
with
delusions 291.5
hallucinations 291.3
withdrawal symptoms, syndrome NEC 291.81
delirium 291.0
hallucinosis 291.3
Alcoholism 303.9

*Note—Use the following fifth-digit
subclassification with category 303:*

0   *unspecified*
1   *continuous*
2   *episodic*
3   *in remission*

with psychosis (*see also* Psychosis, alcoholic)
291.9
acute 303.0
chronic 303.9
with psychosis 291.9
complicating pregnancy, childbirth, or
puerperium 648.4
affecting fetus or newborn 760.71
history V11.3
Korsakoff's, Korsakov's, Korsakow's 291.1
suspected damage to fetus affecting
management of pregnancy 655.4
Alder's anomaly or syndrome (leukocyte
granulation anomaly) 288.2
Alder-Reilly anomaly (leukocyte granulation)
288.2
Aldosteronism (primary) (secondary) 255.1
congenital 255.1
Aldosteronoma (M8370/1) 237.2
Aldrich (-Wiskott) syndrome
(eczema-thrombocytopenia) 279.12
Aleppo boil 085.1

Aleukemic —*see* condition
Aleukia
  congenital 288.0
  hemorrhagica 284.9
    acquired (secondary) 284.8
    congenital 284.0
    idiopathic 284.9
  splenica 289.4
Alexia (congenital) (developmental) 315.01
  secondary to organic lesion 784.61
Algoneurodystrophy 733.7
Algophobia 300.29
Alibert's disease (mycosis fungoides) (M9700/3)
  202.1
Alibert-Bazin disease (M9700/3) 202.1
Alice in Wonderland syndrome 293.89
Alienation, mental (*see also* Psychosis) 298.9
Alkalemia 276.3
Alkalosis 276.3
  metabolic 276.3
    with respiratory acidosis 276.4
  respiratory 276.3
Alkaptonuria 270.2
Allen-Masters syndrome 620.6
Allergic bronchopulmonary aspergillosis 518.6
Allergy, allergic (reaction) 995.3
  air-borne substance (*see also* Fever, hay) 477.9
    specified allergen NEC 477.8
  alveolitis (extrinsic) 495.9
    due to
      Aspergillus clavatus 495.4
      cryptostroma corticale 495.6
      organisms (fungal, thermophilic
        actinomycete, other) growing in
        ventilation (air conditioning systems)
        495.7
    specified type NEC 495.8
  anaphylactic shock 999.4
    due to
      food—*see* Anaphylactic shock, due to, food
  angioneurotic edema 995.1
  animal (dander) (epidermal) (hair) 477.8
  arthritis (*see also* Arthritis, allergic) 716.2
  asthma—*see* Asthma
  bee sting (anaphylactic shock) 989.5
  biological—*see* Allergy, drug
  bronchial asthma—*see* Asthma
  conjunctivitis (eczematous) 372.14
  dander (animal) 477.8
  dandruff 477.8
  dermatitis (venenata)—*see* Dermatitis
  diathesis V15.09
  drug, medicinal substance, and biological (any)
    (correct medicinal substance properly
    administered) (external) (internal) 995.2
    wrong substance given or taken NEC 977.9
      specified drug or substance—*see* Table of
        drugs and chemicals
  dust (house) (stock) 477.8
  eczema—*see* Eczema
  endophthalmitis 360.19
  epidermal (animal) 477.8
  feathers 477.8
  food (any) (ingested) 693.1
    atopic 691.8
    in contact with skin 692.5
  gastritis 535.4
  gastroenteritis 558.3
  gastrointestinal 558.3
  grain 477.0

Allergy, allergic—*continued*
  grass (pollen) 477.0
    asthma (*see also* Asthma) 493.0
    hay fever 477.0
  hair (animal) 477.8
  hay fever (grass) (pollen) (ragweed) (tree) (*see*
    also Fever, hay) 477.9
  history (of) V15.09
    to
      eggs V15.03
      food additives V15.05
      insect bite V15.06
      latex V15.07
      milk products V15.02
      nuts V15.05
        peanuts V15.01
      radiographic dye V15.08
      seafood V15.04
      specified food NEC V15.05
      spider bite V15.06
  horse serum—*see* Allergy, serum
  inhalant 477.9
    dust 477.8
    pollen 477.0
    specified allergen other than pollen 477.8
  kapok 477.8
  medicine—*see* Allergy, drug
  migraine 346.2
  pannus 370.62
  pneumonia 518.3
  pollen (any) (hay fever) 477.0
    asthma (*see also* Asthma) 493.0
  primrose 477.0
  primula 477.0
  purpura 287.0
  ragweed (pollen) (Senecio jacobae) 477.0
    asthma (*see also* Asthma) 493.0
    hay fever 477.0
  respiratory (*see also* Allergy, inhalant) 477.9
    due to
      drug—*see* Allergy, drug
      food—*see* Allergy, food
  rhinitis (*see also* Fever, hay) 477.9
    due to food 477.1
  rose 477.0
  Senecio jacobae 477.0
  serum (prophylactic) (therapeutic) 999.5
    anaphylactic shock 999.4
  shock (anaphylactic)
    due to
      adverse effect of correct medicinal
        substance properly administered 995.0
      food—*see* Anaphylactic shock, due to, food
    from serum or immunization 999.5
      anaphylactic 999.4
  sinusitis (*see also* Fever, hay) 477.9
  skin reaction 692.9
    specified substance—*see* Dermatitis, due to
  tree (any) (hay fever) (pollen) 477.0
    asthma (*see also* Asthma) 493.0
  upper respiratory (*see also* Fever, hay) 477.9
  urethritis 597.89
  urticaria 708.0
  vaccine—*see* Allergy, serum
Allescheriosis 117.6
Alligator skin disease (ichthyosis congenita)
  757.1
  acquired 701.1
Allocheiria, allochiria (*see also* Disturbance,
  sensation) 782.0
Almeida's disease (Brazilian blastomycosis)
  116.1

Alopecia (atrophicans) (pregnancy) (premature)
(senile) 704.00
adnata 757.4
areata 704.01
(celsi 704.01
cicatrisata 704.09
circumscripta 704.01
congenital, congenitalis 757.4
disseminata 704.01
effluvium (telogen) 704.02
febrile 704.09
generalisata 704.09
hereditaria 704.09
marginalis 704.01
mucinosa 704.09
postinfectional 704.09
seborrheica 704.09
specific 091.82
syphilitic (secondary) 091.82
telogen effluvium 704.02
totalis 704.09
toxica 704.09
universalis 704.09
x-ray 704.09
Alper's disease 330.8
Alpha-lipoproteinemia 272.4
Alpha thalassemia 282.4
Alphos 696.1
Alpine sickness 993.2
Alport's syndrome (hereditary
hematuria-nephropathy-deafness) 759.89
Alteration (of) altered
awareness 780.09
transient 780.02
consciousness 780.09
persistent vegetative state 780.03
transient 780.02
mental status 780.9
Alternaria (infection) 118
Alternating —*see* condition
Altitude, high (effects)—*see* Effect, adverse,
high altitude
Aluminosis (of lung) 503
Alvarez syndrome (transient cerebral ischemia)
435.9
Alveolar capillary block syndrome 516.3
Alveolitis
allergic (extrinsic) 495.9
due to organisms (fungal, thermophilic
actinomycete, other) growing in
ventilation (air conditioning systems)
495.7
specified type NEC 495.8
due to
Aspergillus clavatus 495.4
Cryptostroma corticale 495.6
fibrosing (chronic) (cryptogenic) (lung) 516.3
idiopathic 516.3
rheumatoid 714.81
jaw 526.5
sicca dolorosa 526.5
Alveolus, alveolar —*see* condition
Alymphocytosis (pure) 279.2
Alymphoplasia, thymic 279.2
Alzheimer's
dementia (senile)
with behavioral disturbance 331.0 *[294.11]*
without behavioral disturbance 331.0 *[294.10]*
disease or sclerosis 331.0
with dementia—*see* Alzheimer's, dementia
Amastia (*see also* Absence, breast) 611.8

Amaurosis (acquired) (congenital) (*see also*
Blindness) 369.00
fugax 362.34
hysterical 300.11
Leber's (congenital) 362.76
tobacco 377.34
uremic—*see* Uremia
Amaurotic familial idiocy (infantile) (juvenile)
(late) 330.1
Ambisexual 752.7
Amblyopia (acquired) (congenital) (partial)
368.00
color 368.59
acquired 368.55
deprivation 368.02
ex anopsia 368.00
hysterical 300.11
nocturnal 368.60
vitamin A deficiency 264.5
refractive 368.03
strabismic 368.01
suppression 368.01
tobacco 377.34
toxic NEC 377.34
uremic—*see* Uremia
Ameba, amebic (histolytica)–*see also* Amebiasis
abscess 006.3
bladder 006.8
brain (with liver and lung abscess) 006.5
liver 006.3
with
brain abscess (and lung abscess) 006.5
lung abscess 006.4
lung (with liver abscess) 006.4
with brain abscess 006.5
seminal vesicle 006.8
spleen 006.8
carrier (suspected of) V02.2
meningoencephalitis
due to Naegleria (gruberi) 136.2
primary 136.2
Amebiasis NEC 006.9
with
brain abscess (with liver or lung abscess)
006.5
liver abscess (without mention of brain or
lung abscess) 006.3
lung abscess (with liver abscess) 006.4
with brain abscess 006.5
acute 006.0
bladder 006.8
chronic 006.1
cutaneous 006.6
cutis 006.6
due to organism other than Entamoeba
histolytica 007.8
hepatic (*see also* Abscess, liver, amebic) 006.3
nondysenteric 006.2
seminal vesicle 006.8
specified
organism NEC 007.8
site NEC 006.8
Ameboma 006.8
Amelia 755.4
lower limb 755.31
upper limb 755.21
Ameloblastoma (M9310/0) 213.1
jaw (bone) (lower) 213.1
upper 213.0
long bones (M9261/3)—*see* Neoplasm, bone,
malignant

Note—*"Complicated" includes traumatic amputation with delayed healing, delayed treatment, foreign body, or major infection.*

Anomaly, anomalous—*continued*
  leukocyte 288.2
  gum 750.9
  gyri 742.9
  hair 757.9
    specified type NEC 757.4
  hand 755.50
  hard tissue formation in pulp 522.3
  head (*see also* Anomaly, skull) 756.0
  heart 746.9
    auricle 746.9
    bands 746.9
    fibroelastosis cordis 425.3
    folds 746.9
    malposition 746.87
    maternal, affecting fetus or newborn 760.3
    obstructive NEC 746.84
    patent ductus arteriosus (Botalli) 747.0
    septum 745.9
      acquired 429.71
      aortic 745.0
      aorticopulmonary 745.0
      atrial 745.5
      auricular 745.5
      between aorta and pulmonary artery 745.0
      endocardial cushion type 745.60
        specified type NEC 745.69
      interatrial 745.5
      interventricular 745.4
        with pulmonary stenosis or atresia,
          dextraposition of aorta, and
          hypertrophy of right ventricle 745.2
        acquired 429.71
      specified type NEC 745.8
      ventricular 745.4
        with pulmonary stenosis or atresia,
          dextraposition of aorta, and
          hypertrophy of right ventricle 745.2
        acquired 429.71
    specified type NEC 746.89
    tetralogy of Fallot 745.2
    valve NEC 746.9
      aortic 746.9
        atresia 746.89
        bicuspid valve 746.4
        insufficiency 746.4
        specified type NEC 746.89
        stenosis 746.3
          subaortic 746.81
          supravalvular 747.22
      mitral 746.9
        atresia 746.89
        insufficiency 746.6
        specified type NEC 746.89
        stenosis 746.5
      pulmonary 746.00
        atresia 746.01
        insufficiency 746.09
        stenosis 746.02
          infundibular 746.83
          subvalvular 746.83
      tricuspid 746.9
        atresia 746.1
        stenosis 746.1
    ventricle 746.9
  heel 755.67
  Hegglin's 288.2
  hemianencephaly 740.0
  hemicephaly 740.0
  hemicrania 740.0
  hepatic duct 751.60

Anomaly, anomalous—*continued*
  hip (joint) 755.63
  hourglass
    bladder 753.8
    gallbladder 751.69
    stomach 750.7
  humerus 755.50
  hymen 752.40
  hypersegmentation of neutrophils, hereditary
    288.2
  hypophyseal 759.2
  ileocecal (coil) (valve) 751.5
  ileum (intestine) 751.5
  ilium 755.60
  integument 757.9
    specified type NEC 757.8
  intervertebral cartilage or disc 756.10
  intestine (large) (small) 751.5
    fixational type 751.4
  iris 743.9
    specified type NEC 743.46
  ischium 755.60
  jaw NEC 524.9
    closure 524.5
    size NEC 524.00
    specified type NEC 524.8
  jaw-cranial base relationship 524.10
    specified NEC 524.19
  jejunum 751.5
  joint 755.9
    hip
      dislocation (*see also* Dislocation, hip,
        congenital) 754.30
      predislocation (*see also* Subluxation,
        congenital, hip) 754.32
      preluxation (*see also* Subluxation,
        congenital, hip) 754.32
      subluxation (*see also* Subluxation,
        congenital, hip) 754.32
    lumbosacral 756.10
      spondylolisthesis 756.12
      spondylosis 756.11
    multiple arthrogryposis 754.89
    sacroiliac 755.69
  Jordan's 288.2
  kidney(s) (calyx) (pelvis) 753.9
    vessel 747.62
  Klippel-Feil (brevicollis) 756.16
  knee (joint) 755.64
  labium (majus) (minus) 752.40
  labyrinth, membranous (causing impairment of
    hearing) 744.05
  lacrimal
    apparatus, duct or passage 743.9
      specified type NEC 743.65
    gland 743.9
      specified type NEC 743.64
  Langdon Down (mongolism) 758.0
  larynx, laryngeal (muscle) 748.3
    web, webbed 748.2
  leg (lower) (upper) 755.60
    reduction NEC (*see also* Deformity,
      reduction, lower limb) 755.30
  lens 743.9
    shape 743.36
    specified type NEC 743.39
  leukocytes, genetic 288.2
    granulation (constitutional) 288.2
  lid (fold) 743.9
  ligament 756.9
    broad 752.10

Anomaly, anomalous—*continued*
  round 752.9
  limb, except reduction deformity 755.9
    lower 755.60
      reduction deformity (*see also* Deformity,
        reduction, lower limb) 755.30
      specified type NEC 755.69
    upper 755.50
      reduction deformity (*see also* Deformity,
        reduction, upper limb) 755.20
      specified type NEC 755.59
  lip 750.9
    harelip (*see also* Cleft, lip) 749.10
    specified type NEC 750.26
  liver (duct) 751.60
    atresia 751.69
  lower extremity 755.60
    vessel 747.64
  lumbosacral (joint) (region) 756.10
  lung (fissure) (lobe) NEC 748.60
    agenesis 748.5
    specified type NEC 748.69
  lymphatic system 759.9
  Madelung's (radius) 755.54
  mandible 524.9
    size NEC 524.00
  maxilla 524.9
    size NEC 524.00
  May (-Hegglin) 288.2
  meatus urinarius 753.9
    specified type NEC 753.8
  meningeal bands or folds, constriction of 742.8
  meninges 742.9
    brain 742.4
    spinal 742.59
  meningocele (*see also* Spina bifida) 741.9
  mesentery 751.9
  metacarpus 755.50
  metatarsus 755.67
  middle ear, except ossicles (causing impairment
    of hearing) 744.03
    ossicles 744.04
  mitral (leaflets) (valve) 746.9
    atresia 746.89
    insufficiency 746.6
    specified type NEC 746.89
    stenosis 746.5
  mouth 750.9
    specified type NEC 750.26
  multiple NEC 759.7
    specified type NEC 759.89
  muscle 756.9
    eye 743.9
      specified type NEC 743.69
    specified type NEC 756.89
  musculoskeletal system, except limbs 756.9
    specified type NEC 756.9
  nail 757.9
    specified type NEC 757.5
  narrowness, eyelid 743.62
  nasal sinus or septum 748.1
  neck (any part) 744.9
    specified type NEC 744.89
  nerve 742.9
    acoustic 742.9
      specified type NEC 742.8
    optic 742.9
      specified type NEC 742.8
    specified type NEC 742.8
  nervous system NEC 742.9
    brain 742.9

Anomaly, anomalous—*continued*
    specified type NEC 742.4
    specified type NEC 742.8
  neurological 742.9
  nipple 757.9
  nonteratogenic NEC 754.89
  nose, nasal (bone) (cartilage) (septum) (sinus)
    748.1
  ocular muscle 743.9
  omphalomesenteric duct 751.0
  opening, pulmonary veins 747.49
  optic
    disc 743.9
      specified type NEC 743.57
    nerve 742.9
  opticociliary vessels 743.9
  orbit (eye) 743.9
    specified type NEC 743.66
  organ
    of Corti (causing impairment of hearing)
      744.05
    or site 759.9
      specified type NEC 759.89
  origin
    both great arteries from same ventricle 745.11
    coronary artery 746.85
    innominate artery 747.69
    left coronary artery from pulmonary artery
      746.85
    pulmonary artery 747.3
    renal vessels 747.62
    subclavian artery (left) (right) 747.21
  osseous meatus (ear) 744.03
  ovary 752.0
  oviduct 752.10
  palate (hard) (soft) 750.9
    cleft (*see also* Cleft, palate) 749.00
  pancreas (duct) 751.7
  papillary muscles 746.9
  parathyroid gland 759.2
  paraurethral ducts 753.9
  parotid (gland) 750.9
  patella 755.64
  Pelger-Huët (hereditary hyposegmentation)
    288.2
  pelvic girdle 755.60
    specified type NEC 755.69
  pelvis (bony) 755.60
    complicating delivery 653.0
    rachitic 268.1
      fetal 756.4
  penis (glans) 752.69
  pericardium 746.89
  peripheral vascular system NEC 747.60
    gastrointestinal 747.61
    lower limb 747.64
    renal 747.62
    specified site NEC 747.69
    spinal 747.82
    upper limb 747.63
  Peter's 743.44
  pharynx 750.9
    branchial cleft 744.41
    specified type NEC 750.29
  Pierre Robin 756.0
  pigmentation NEC 709.00
    congenital 757.33
  pituitary (gland) 759.2
  pleural folds 748.8
  portal vein 747.40
  position tooth, teeth 524.3

Anomaly, anomalous—*continued*
　preauricular sinus 744.46
　prepuce 752.9
　prostate 752.9
　pulmonary 748.60
　　artery 747.3
　　circulation 747.3
　　specified type NEC 748.69
　　valve 746.00
　　　atresia 746.01
　　　insufficiency 746.09
　　　specified type NEC 746.09
　　　stenosis 746.02
　　　　infundibular 746.83
　　　　subvalvular 746.83
　　vein 747.40
　　venous
　　　connection 747.49
　　　　partial 747.42
　　　　total 747.41
　　　return 747.49
　　　　partial 747.42
　　　　total (TAPVR) (complete)
　　　　　(subdiaphragmatic)
　　　　　(supradiaphragmatic) 747.41
　pupil 743.9
　pylorus 750.9
　　hypertrophy 750.5
　　stenosis 750.5
　rachitic, fetal 756.4
　radius 755.50
　rectovaginal (septum) 752.40
　rectum 751.5
　refraction 367.9
　renal 753.9
　　vessel 747.62
　respiratory system 748.9
　　specified type NEC 748.8
　rib 756.3
　　cervical 756.2
　Rieger's 743.44
　rings, trachea 748.3
　rotation—*see also* Malrotation
　　hip or thigh (*see also* Subluxation, congenital,
　　　hip) 754.32
　round ligament 752.9
　sacroiliac (joint) 755.69
　sacrum 756.10
　saddle
　　back 754.2
　　nose 754.0
　　　syphilitic 090.5
　salivary gland or duct 750.9
　　specified type NEC 750.26
　scapula 755.50
　sclera 743.9
　　specified type NEC 743.47
　scrotum 752.9
　sebaceous gland 757.9
　seminal duct or tract 752.9
　sense organs 742.9
　　specified type NEC 742.8
　septum
　　heart—*see* Anomaly, heart, septum
　　nasal 748.1
　sex chromosomes NEC (*see also* Anomaly,
　　chromosomes) 758.81
　shoulder (girdle) (joint) 755.50
　　specified type NEC 755.59
　sigmoid (flexure) 751.5
　sinus of Valsalva 747.29

Anomaly, anomalous—*continued*
　site NEC 759.9
　skeleton generalized NEC 756.50
　skin (appendage) 757.9
　　specified type NEC 757.39
　skull (bone) 756.0
　　with
　　　anencephalus 740.0
　　　encephalocele 742.0
　　　hydrocephalus 742.3
　　　　with spina bifida (*see also* Spina bifida)
　　　　　741.0
　　　microcephalus 742.1
　specified type NEC
　　adrenal (gland) 759.1
　　alimentary tract (complete) (partial) 751.8
　　　lower 751.5
　　　upper 750.8
　　ankle 755.69
　　anus, anal (canal) 751.5
　　aorta, aortic 747.29
　　　arch 747.21
　　appendix 751.5
　　arm 755.59
　　artery (peripheral) NEC (*see also* Anomaly,
　　　peripheral vascular system) 747.60
　　　brain 747.81
　　　coronary 746.85
　　　eye 743.58
　　　pulmonary 747.3
　　　retinal 743.58
　　　umbilical 747.5
　　auditory canal 744.29
　　　causing impairment of hearing 744.02
　　bile duct or passage 751.69
　　bladder 753.8
　　　neck 753.8
　　bone(s) 756.9
　　　arm 755.59
　　　face 756.0
　　　leg 755.69
　　　pelvic girdle 755.69
　　　shoulder girdle 755.59
　　　skull 756.0
　　　　with
　　　　　anencephalus 740.0
　　　　　encephalocele 742.0
　　　　　hydrocephalus 742.3
　　　　　　with spina bifida (*see also* Spina
　　　　　　　bifida) 741.0
　　　　　microcephalus 742.1
　　brain 742.4
　　breast 757.6
　　broad ligament 752.19
　　bronchus 748.3
　　canal of Nuck 752.8
　　cardiac septal closure 745.8
　　carpus 755.59
　　cartilaginous 756.9
　　cecum 751.5
　　cervix 752.49
　　chest (wall) 756.3
　　chin 744.89
　　ciliary body 743.46
　　circulatory system 747.89
　　clavicle 755.51
　　clitoris 752.49
　　coccyx 756.19
　　colon 751.5
　　common duct 751.69
　　connective tissue 756.89

Anomaly, anomalous—*continued*
  venous return (pulmonary) 747.49
    partial 747.42
    total 747.41
  ventricle, ventricular (heart) 746.9
    bands 746.9
    folds 746.9
    septa 745.4
  vertebra 756.10
  vesicourethral orifice 753.9
  vessels NEC (*see also* Anomaly, peripheral
    vascular system) 747.60
    optic papilla 743.9
  vitelline duct 751.0
  vitreous humor 743.9
    specified type NEC 743.51
  vulva 752.40
  wrist (joint) 755.50
Anomia 784.69
Anonychia 757.5
  acquired 703.8
Anophthalmos, anophthalmus (clinical)
  (congenital) (globe) 743.00
  acquired V45.78
Anopsia (altitudinal) (quadrant) 368.46
Anorchia 752.8
Anorchism, anorchidism 752.8
Anorexia 783.0
  hysterical 300.11
  nervosa 307.1
Anosmia (*see also* Disturbance, sensation) 781.1
  hysterical 300.11
  postinfectional 478.9
  psychogenic 306.7
  traumatic 951.8
Anosognosia 780.9
Anosphrasia 781.1
Anosteoplasia 756.50
Anotia 744.09
Anovulatory cycle 628.0
Anoxemia 799.0
  newborn 770.8
Anoxia 799.0
  altitude 993.2
  cerebral 348.1
    with
      abortion—*see* Abortion, by type,
        with specified complication NEC
      ectopic pregnancy (*see also* categories
        633.0-633.9) 639.8
      molar pregnancy (*see also* categories
        630-632) 639.8
    complicating
      delivery (cesarean) (instrumental) 669.4
      ectopic or molar pregnancy 639.8
      obstetric anesthesia or sedation 668.2
    during or resulting from a procedure 997.01
    following
      abortion 639.8
      ectopic or molar pregnancy 639.8
    newborn (*see also* Distress, fetal, liveborn
      infant) 768.9
  due to drowning 994.1
  fetal, affecting newborn 770.8
  heart—*see* Insufficiency, coronary
  high altitude 993.2
  intrauterine
    fetal death (before onset of labor) 768.0
      during labor 768.1
    liveborn infant—*see* Distress, fetal, liveborn
      infant

Anoxia—*continued*
  myocardial—*see* Insufficiency, coronary
  newborn 768.9
    mild or moderate 768.6
    severe 768.5
  pathological 799.0
Anteflexion —*see* Anteversion
Antenatal
  care, normal pregnancy V22.1
    first V22.0
  screening (for) V28.9
    based on amniocentesis NEC V28.2
      chromosomal anomalies V28.0
      raised alphafetoprotein levels V28.1
    chromosomal anomalies V28.0
    fetal growth retardation using ultrasonics
      V28.4
    isoimmunization V28.5
    malformations using ultrasonics V28.3
    raised alphafetoprotein levels in amniotic fluid
      V28.1
    specified condition NEC V28.8
    Streptococcus B V28.6
Antepartum —*see* condition
Anterior —*see also* condition
  spinal artery compression syndrome 721.1
Antero-occlusion 524.2
Anteversion
  cervix (*see also* Anteversion, uterus) 621.6
  femur (neck), congenital 755.63
  uterus, uterine (cervix) (postinfectional)
    (postpartal, old) 621.6
    congenital 752.3
    in pregnancy or childbirth 654.4
      affecting fetus or newborn 763.89
      causing obstructed labor 660.2
        affecting fetus or newborn 763.1
Anthracosilicosis (occupational) 500
Anthracosis (lung) (occupational) 500
  lingua 529.3
Anthrax 022.9
  with pneumonia 022.1 *[484.5]*
  colitis 022.2
  cutaneous 022.0
  gastrointestinal 022.2
  intestinal 022.2
  pulmonary 022.1
  respiratory 022.1
  septicemia 022.3—
  specified manifestation NEC 022.8
Anthropoid pelvis 755.69
  with disproportion (fetopelvic) 653.2
    affecting fetus or newborn 763.1
    causing obstructed labor 660.1
      affecting fetus or newborn 763.1
Anthropophobia 300.29
Antibioma, breast 611.0
Antibodies
  maternal (blood group) (*see also*
    Incompatibility) 656.2
    anti-D, cord blood 656.1
      fetus or newborn 773.0
Antibody deficiency syndrome
  agammaglobulinemic 279.00
  congenital 279.04
  hypogammaglobulinemic 279.00
Anticoagulant, circulating (*see also* Circulating
  anticoagulants) 286.5
Antimongolism syndrome 758.3
Antimonial cholera 985.4
Antisocial personality 301.7

Antithrombinemia (*see also* Circulating anticoagulants) 286.5
Antithromboplastinemia (*see also* Circulating anticoagulants) 286.5
Antithromboplastinogenemia (*see also* Circulating anticoagulants) 286.5
Antitoxin complication or reaction —*see* Complications, vaccination
Anton (-Babinski) syndrome (hemiasomatognosia) 307.9
Antritis (chronic) 473.0
  acute 461.0
Antrum, antral —*see* condition
Anuria 788.5
  with
    abortion—*see* Abortion, by type, with renal failure
    ectopic pregnancy (*see also* categories 633.0-633.9) 639.3
    molar pregnancy (*see also* categories 630-632) 639.3
  calculus (impacted) (recurrent) 592.9
    kidney 592.0
    ureter 592.1
  congenital 753.3
  due to a procedure 997.5
  following
    abortion 639.3
    ectopic or molar pregnancy 639.3
  newborn 753.3
  postrenal 593.4
  puerperal, postpartum, childbirth 669.3
  specified as due to a procedure 997.5
  sulfonamide
    correct substance properly administered 788.5
    overdose or wrong substance given or taken 961.0
  traumatic (following crushing) 958.5
Anus, anal —*see* condition
Anusitis 569.49
Anxiety (neurosis) (reaction) (state) 300.00
  alcohol-induced 291.89
  depression 300.4
  drug-induced 292.89
  due to or associated with physical condition 293.84
  generalized 300.02
  hysteria 300.20
  in
    acute stress reaction 308.0
    transient adjustment reaction 309.24
  panic type 300.01
  separation, abnormal 309.21
  syndrome (organic) (transient) 293.84
Aorta, aortic —*see* condition
Aortectasia 441.9
Aortitis (nonsyphilitic) 447.6
  arteriosclerotic 440.0
  calcific 447.6
  Döhle-Heller 093.1
  luetic 093.1
  rheumatic (*see also* Endocarditis, acute, rheumatic) 391.1
  rheumatoid—*see* Arthritis, rheumatoid
  specific 093.1
  syphilitic 093.1
    congenital 090.5
Apathetic thyroid storm (*see also* Thyrotoxicosis) 242.9
Apepsia 536.8
  achlorhydric 536.0
  psychogenic 306.4

Aperistalsis, esophagus 530.0
Apert's syndrome (acrocephalosyndactyly) 755.55
Apert-Gallais syndrome (adrenogenital) 255.2
Apertognathia 524.2
Aphagia 787.2
  psychogenic 307.1
Aphakia (acquired) (bilateral) (postoperative) (unilateral) 379.31
  congenital 743.35
Aphalangia (congenital) 755.4
  lower limb (complete) (intercalary) (partial) (terminal) 755.39
    meaning all digits (complete) (partial) 755.31
    transverse 755.31
  upper limb (complete) (intercalary) (partial) (terminal) 755.29
    meaning all digits (complete) (partial) 755.21
    transverse 755.21
Aphasia (amnestic) (ataxic) (auditory) (Broca's) (choreatic) (classic) (expressive) (global) (ideational) (ideokinetic) (ideomotor) (jargon) (motor) (nominal) (receptive) (semantic) (sensory) (syntactic) (verbal) (visual) (Wernicke's) 784.3
  developmental 315.31
  syphilis, tertiary 094.89
  uremic—*see* Uremia
Aphemia 784.3
  uremic—*see* Uremia
Aphonia 784.41
  clericorum 784.49
  hysterical 300.11
  organic 784.41
  psychogenic 306.1
Aphthae, aphthous —*see also* condition
  Bednar's 528.2
  cachectic 529.0
  epizootic 078.4
  fever 078.4
  oral 528.2
  stomatitis 528.2
  thrush 112.0
  ulcer (oral) (recurrent) 528.2
    genital organ(s) NEC
      female 629.8
      male 608.89
    larynx 478.79
Apical —*see* condition
Aplasia —*see also* Agenesis
  alveolar process (acquired) 525.8
    congenital 750.26
  aorta (congenital) 747.22
  aortic valve (congenital) 746.89
  axialis extracorticalis (congenital) 330.0
  bone marrow (myeloid) 284.9
    acquired (secondary) 284.8
    congenital 284.0
    idiopathic 284.9
  brain 740.0
    specified part 742.2
  breast 757.6
  bronchus 748.3
  cementum 520.4
  cerebellar 742.2
  congenital pure red cell 284.0
  corpus callosum 742.2
  erythrocyte 284.8
    congenital 284.0
  extracortical axial 330.0
  eye (congenital) 743.00

Aplasia—*continued*
  fovea centralis (congenital) 743.55
  germinal (cell) 606.0
  iris 743.45
  labyrinth, membranous 744.05
  limb (congenital) 755.4
    lower NEC 755.30
    upper NEC 755.20
  lung (bilateral) (congenital) (unilateral) 748.5
  nervous system NEC 742.8
  nuclear 742.8
  ovary 752.0
  Pelizaeus-Merzbacher 330.0
  prostate (congenital) 752.8
  red cell (pure) (with thymoma) 284.8
    acquired (secondary) 284.8
    congenital 284.0
    hereditary 284.0
    of infants 284.0
    primary 284.0
  round ligament (congenital) 752.8
  salivary gland 750.21
  skin (congenital) 757.39
  spinal cord 742.59
  spleen 759.0
  testis (congenital) 752.8
  thymic, with immunodeficiency 279.2
  thyroid 243
  uterus 752.3
  ventral horn cell 742.59
Apleuria 756.3
Apnea, apneic (spells) 786.03
  newborn, neonatorum 770.8
  psychogenic 306.1
  sleep NEC 780.57
    with
      hypersomnia 780.53
      hyposomnia 780.51
      insomnia 780.51
      sleep disturbance NEC 780.57
Apneumatosis newborn 770.4
Apodia 755.31
Apophysitis (bone) (*see also* Osteochondrosis)
    732.9
  calcaneus 732.5
  juvenile 732.6
Apoplectiform convulsions (*see also* Disease,
    cerebrovascular, acute) 436
Apoplexia, apoplexy, apoplectic (*see also*
    Disease, cerebrovascular, acute) 436
  abdominal 569.89
  adrenal 036.3
  attack 436
  basilar (*see also* Disease, cerebrovascular,
    acute) 436
  brain (*see also* Disease, cerebrovascular, acute)
    436
  bulbar (*see also* Disease, cerebrovascular,
    acute) 436
  capillary (*see also* Disease, cerebrovascular,
    acute) 436
  cardiac (*see also* Infarct, myocardium) 410.9
  cerebral (*see also* Disease, cerebrovascular,
    acute) 436
  chorea (*see also* Disease, cerebrovascular,
    acute) 436
  congestive (*see also* Disease, cerebrovascular,
    acute) 436
    newborn 767.4
  embolic (*see also* Embolism, brain) 434.1
  fetus 767.0

Apoplexia, apoplexy, apoplectic—*continued*
  fit (*see also* Disease, cerebrovascular, acute) 436
  healed or old V12.59
  heart (auricle) (ventricle) (*see also* Infarct,
    myocardium) 410.9
  heat 992.0
  hemiplegia (*see also* Disease, cerebrovascular,
    acute) 436
  hemorrhagic (stroke) (*see also* Hemorrhage,
    brain) 432.9
  ingravescent (*see also* Disease, cerebrovascular,
    acute) 436
  late effect—*see* Late effect(s) (of)
    cerebrovascular disease
  lung—*see* Embolism, pulmonary
  meninges, hemorrhagic (*see also* Hemorrhage,
    subarachnoid) 430
  neonatorum 767.0
  newborn 767.0
  pancreatitis 577.0
  placenta 641.2
  progressive (*see also* Disease, cerebrovascular,
    acute) 436
  pulmonary (artery) (vein)—*see* Embolism,
    pulmonary
  sanguineous (*see also* Disease, cerebrovascular,
    acute) 436
  seizure (*see also* Disease, cerebrovascular,
    acute) 436
  serous (*see also* Disease, cerebrovascular,
    acute) 436
  spleen 289.59
  stroke (*see also* Disease, cerebrovascular, acute)
    436
  thrombotic (*see also* Thrombosis, brain) 434.0
  uremic—*see* Uremia
  uteroplacental 641.2
Appendage
  fallopian tube (cyst of Morgagni) 752.11
  intestine (epiploic) 751.5
  preauricular 744.1
  testicular (organ of Morgagni) 752.8
Appendicitis 541
  with
    perforation, peritonitis (generalized), or
      rupture 540.0
      with peritoneal abscess 540.1
    peritoneal abscess 540.1
  acute (catarrhal) (fulminating) (gangrenous)
      (inflammatory) (obstructive) (retrocecal)
      (suppurative) 540.9
    with
      perforation, peritonitis, or rupture 540.0
        with peritoneal abscess 540.1
      peritoneal abscess 540.1
  amebic 006.8
  chronic (recurrent) 542
  exacerbation—*see* Appendicitis, acute
  fulminating—*see* Appendicitis, acute
  gangrenous—*see* Appendicitis, acute
  healed (obliterative) 542
  interval 542
  neurogenic 542
  obstructive 542
  pneumococcal 541
  recurrent 542
  relapsing 542
  retrocecal 541
  subacute (adhesive) 542
  subsiding 542
  suppurative—*see* Appendicitis, acute
  tuberculous (*see also* Tuberculosis) 014.8

Appendiclausis 543.9
Appendicolithiasis 543.9
Appendicopathia oxyurica 127.4
Appendix, appendicular —*see also* condition
  Morgagni (male) 752.8
    fallopian tube 752.11
Appetite
  depraved 307.52
  excessive 783.6
    psychogenic 307.51
  lack or loss (*see also* Anorexia) 783.0
    nonorganic origin 307.59
  perverted 307.52
    hysterical 300.11
Apprehension, apprehensiveness (abnormal)
    (state) 300.00
  specified type NEC 300.09
Approximal wear 521.1
Apraxia (classic) (ideational) (ideokinetic)
    (ideomotor) (motor) 784.69
  oculomotor, congenital 379.51
  verbal 784.69
Aptyalism 527.7
Arabicum elephantiasis (*see also* Infestation,
    filarial) 125.9
Arachnidism 989.5
Arachnitis —*see* Meningitis
Arachnodactyly 759.82
Arachnoidism 989.5
Arachnoiditis (acute) (adhesive) (basic) (brain)
    (cerebrospinal) (chiasmal) (chronic) (spinal)
    (*see also* Meningitis) 322.9
  meningococcal (chronic) 036.0
  syphilitic 094.2
  tuberculous (*see also* Tuberculosis, meninges)
    013.0
Araneism 989.5
Arboencephalitis, Australian 062.4
Arborization block (heart) 426.6
Arbor virus, arbovirus (infection) NEC 066.9
ARC 042
Arches —*see* condition
Arcuatus uterus 752.3
Arcus (cornea)
  juvenilis 743.43
    interfering with vision 743.42
  senilis 371.41
Arc-welders' lung 503
Arc-welders' syndrome (photokeratitis) 370.24
Areflexia 796.1
Areola —*see* condition
Argentaffinoma (M8241/1)—*see also*
    Neoplasm, by site, uncertain behavior
  benign (M8241/0)—*see* Neoplasm, by site,
    benign
  malignant (M8241/3)—*see* Neoplasm, by site,
    malignant
  syndrome 259.2
Argentinian hemorrhagic fever 078.7
Arginosuccinicaciduria 270.6
Argonz-Del Castillo syndrome (nonpuerperal
    galactorrhea and amenorrhea) 253.1
Argyll-Robertson phenomenon pupil, or
  syndrome (syphilitic) 094.89
  atypical 379.45
  nonluetic 379.45
  nonsyphilitic 379.45
  reversed 379.45
Argyria, argyriasis NEC 985.8
  conjunctiva 372.55
  cornea 371.16

Argyria, argyriasis—*continued*
  from drug or medicinal agent
    correct substance properly administered
      709.09
    overdose or wrong substance given or taken
      961.2
Arhinencephaly 742.2
Arias-Stella phenomenon 621.3
Ariboflavinosis 266.0
Arizona enteritis 008.1
Arm —*see* condition
Armenian disease 277.3
Arnold-Chiari obstruction or syndrome (*see
    also* Spina bifida) 741.0
  type I 348.4
  type II (*see also* Spina bifida) 741.0
  type III 742.0
  type IV 742.2
Arrest, arrested
  active phase of labor 661.1
    affecting fetus or newborn 763.7
  any plane in pelvis
    complicating delivery 660.1
      affecting fetus or newborn 763.1
  bone marrow (*see also* Anemia, aplastic) 284.9
  cardiac 427.5
    with
      abortion—*see* Abortion, by type, with
        specified complication NEC
      ectopic pregnancy (*see also* categories
        633.0-633.9) 639.8
      molar pregnancy (*see also* categories
        630-632) 639.8
    complicating
      anesthesia
        correct substance properly administered
          427.5
        obstetric 668.1
        overdose or wrong substance given 968.4
          specified anesthetic—*see* Table of drugs
          and chemicals
      delivery (cesarean) (instrumental) 669.4
      ectopic or molar pregnancy 639.8
      surgery (nontherapeutic) (therapeutic) 997.1
    fetus or newborn 779.8
    following
      abortion 639.8
      ectopic or molar pregnancy 639.8
    postoperative (immediate) 997.1
      long-term effect of cardiac surgery 429.4
  cardiorespiratory (*see also* Arrest, cardiac) 427.5
  deep transverse 660.3
    affecting fetus or newborn 763.1
  development or growth
    bone 733.91
    child 783.40
    fetus 764.9
      affecting management of pregnancy 656.5
    tracheal rings 748.3
  epiphyseal 733.91
  granulopoiesis 288.0
  heart—*see* Arrest, cardiac
  respiratory 799.1
    newborn 770.8
  sinus 426.6
  transverse (deep) 660.3
    affecting fetus or newborn 763.1

Arrhenoblastoma (M8630.1)
　benign (M8630/0)
　　specified site—*see* Neoplasm, by site, benign
　　unspecified site
　　　female 220
　　　male 222.0
　malignant (M8630/3)
　　specified site— *see* Neoplasm, by site,
　　　malignant
　　unspecified site
　　　female 183.0
　　　male 186.9
　specified site—*see* Neoplasm, by site, uncertain
　　behavior
　unspecified site
　　female 236.2
　　male 236.4
Arrhinencephaly 742.2
　due to
　　trisomy 13 (13-15) 758.1
　　trisomy 18 (16-l8) 758.2
Arrhythmia (auricle) (cardiac) (cordis) (gallop
　rhythm) (juvenile) (nodal) (reflex) (sinus)
　(supraventricular) (transitory) (ventricle) 427.9
　bigeminal rhythm 427.89
　block 426.9
　bradycardia 427.89
　contractions, premature 427.60
　coronary sinus 427.89
　ectopic 427.89
　extrasystolic 427.60
　postoperative 997.1
　psychogenic 306.2
　vagal 780.2
Arrillaga-Ayerza syndrome (pulmonary artery
　sclerosis with pulmonary hypertension) 416.0
Arsenical
　dermatitis 692.4
　keratosis 692.4
　pigmentation 985.1
　　from drug or medicinal agent
　　　correct substance properly administered
　　　　709.09
　　　overdose or wrong substance given or taken
　　　　961.1
Arsenism 985.1
　from drug or medicinal agent
　　correct substance properly administered 692.4
　　overdose or wrong substance given or taken
　　　961.1
Arterial —*see* condition
Arteriectasis 447.8
Arteriofibrosis —*see* Arteriosclerosis
Arteriolar sclerosis —*see* Arteriosclerosis
Arteriolith —*see* Arteriosclerosis
Arteriolitis 447.6
　necrotizing, kidney 447.5
　renal—*see* Hypertension, kidney
Arteriolosclerosis —*see* Arteriosclerosis
Arterionephrosclerosis (*see also* Hypertension,
　kidney) 403.90
Arteriopathy 447.9
Arteriosclerosis, arteriosclerotic (artery)
　(deformans) (diffuse) (disease) (endarteritis)
　(general) (obliterans) (obliterative) (occlusive)
　(senile) (with calcification) 440.9
　with
　　gangrene 440.24
　　psychosis (*see also* Psychosis,
　　　arteriosclerotic) 290.40
　　ulceration 440.23

Arteriosclerosis, arteriosclerotic—*continued*
　aorta 440.0
　arteries of extremities NEC — *see*
　　Arteriosclerosis, extremities
　basilar (artery) (*see also* Occlusion, artery,
　　basilar) 433.0
　brain 437.0
　bypass graft
　　coronary artery 414.05
　　　autologous artery (gastroepiploic) (internal
　　　　mammary) 414.04
　　　autologous vein 414.02
　　　nonautologous biological 414.03
　　extremity 440.30
　　　autologous vein 440.31
　　　nonautologous biological 440.32
　cardiac — *see* Arteriosclerosis, coronary
　cardiopathy — *see* Arteriosclerosis, coronary
　cardiorenal (*see also* Hypertension, cardiorenal)
　　404.90
　cardiovascular (*see also* Disease,
　　cardiovascular) 429.2
　carotid (artery) (common) (internal) (*see also*
　　Occlusion, artery, carotid) 433.1
　central nervous system 437.0
　cerebral 437.0
　　late effect—*see* Late effect(s) (of)
　　　cerebrovascular disease
　cerebrospinal 437.0
　cerebrovascular 437.0
　coronary (artery) 414.00
　　graft—*see* Arteriosclerosis, bypass graft
　　native artery 414.01
　extremities (native artery) 440.20
　　bypass graft 440.30
　　　autologous vein 440.31
　　　nonautologous biological 440.32
　　claudication (intermittent) 440.21
　　　and
　　　　gangrene 440.24
　　　　rest pain 440.22
　　　　　and
　　　　　　gangrene 440.24
　　　　　　ulceration 440.23
　　　　　　　and gangrene 440.24
　　　　　ulceration 440.23
　　　　　　and gangrene 440.24
　　gangrene 440.24
　　rest pain 440.22
　　　and
　　　　gangrene 440.24
　　　　ulceration 440.23
　　　　　and gangrene 440.24
　　specified site NEC 440.29
　　ulceration 440.23
　　　and gangrene 440.24
　heart (disease) — *see also* Arteriosclerosis,
　　coronary
　valve 424.99
　　aortic 424.1
　　mitral 424.0
　　pulmonary 424.3
　　tricuspid 424.2
　kidney (*see also* Hypertension, kidney) 403.90
　labyrinth, labyrinthine 388.00
　medial NEC 440.20
　mesentery (artery) 557.1
　Mönckeberg's 440.20
　myocarditis 429.0
　nephrosclerosis (*see also* Hypertension, kidney)
　　403.90

Arteriosclerosis, arteriosclerotic—*continued*
  peripheral (of extremities) *see* Arteriosclerosis,
      extremities
  precerebral 433.9
    specified artery NEC 433.8
  pulmonary (idiopathic) 416.0
  renal (*see also* Hypertension, kidney) 403.90
    arterioles (*see also* Hypertension, kidney)
        403.90
    artery 440.1
  retinal (vascular) 440.8 *[362.13]*
  specified artery NEC 440.8
    with gangrene 440.8 *[785.4]*
  spinal (cord) 437.0
  vertebral (artery) (*see also* Occlusion, artery,
      vertebral) 433.2
Arteriospasm 443.9
Arteriovenous —*see* condition
Arteritis 447.6
  allergic (*see also* Angiitis, hypersensitivity)
      446.20
  aorta (nonsyphilitic) 447.6
    syphilitic 093.1
  aortic arch 446.7
  brachiocephalica 446.7
  brain 437.4
    syphilitic 094.89
  branchial 446.7
  cerebral 437.4
    late effect—*see* Late effect(s) (of)
        cerebrovascular disease
    syphilitic 094.89
  coronary (artery) —*see also* Arteriosclerosis,
        coronary
      rheumatic 391.9
        chronic 398.99
      syphilitic 093.89
  cranial (left) (right) 446.5
  deformans—*see* Arteriosclerosis
  giant cell 446.5
  necrosing or necrotizing 446.0
  nodosa 446.0
  obliterans—*see also* Arteriosclerosis
    subclaviocarotica 446.7
  pulmonary 417.8
  retina 362.18
  rheumatic—*see* Fever, rheumatic
  senile—*see* Arteriosclerosis
  suppurative 447.2
  syphilitic (general) 093.89
    brain 094.89
    coronary 093.89
    spinal 094.89
  temporal 446.5
  young female, syndrome 446.7
Artery, arterial —*see* condition
Arthralgia (*see also* Pain, joint) 719.4
  allergic (*see also* Pain, joint) 719.4
  in caisson disease 993.3—
  psychogenic 307.89
  rubella 056.71
  Salmonella 003.23
  temporomandibular joint 524.62

Arthritis, arthritic (acute) (chronic) (subacute)
    716.9

Note—Use the following fifth-digit
subclassification with categories 711-712,
715-716:

0 site unspecified
1 shoulder region
2 upper arm
3 forearm
4 hand
5 pelvic region and thigh
6 lower leg
7 ankle and foot
8 other specified sites
9 multiple sites

---

  allergic 716.2
  ankylosing (crippling) (spine) 720.0
    sites other than spine 716.9
  atrophic 714.0
    spine 720.9
  back (*see also* Arthritis, spine) 721.90
  Bechterew's (ankylosing spondylitis) 720.0
  blennorrhagic 098.50
  cervical, cervicodorsal (*see also* Spondylosis,
      cervical) 721.0
  Charcot's 094.0 *[713.5]*
    diabetic 250.6 *[713.5]*
    syringomyelic 336.0 *[713.5]*
    tabetic 094.0 *[713.5]*
  chylous (*see also* Filariasis) 125.9 *[711.7]*
  climacteric NEC 716.3
  coccyx 721.8
  cricoarytenoid 478.79
  crystal (-induced)—*see* Arthritis, due to crystals
  deformans (*see also* Osteoarthrosis) 715.9
    spine 721.90
      with myelopathy 721.91
  degenerative (*see also* Osteoarthrosis) 715.9
    idiopathic 715.09
    polyarticular 715.09
    spine 721.90
      with myelopathy 721.91
  dermatoarthritis, lipoid 272.8 *[713.0]*
  due to or associated with
    acromegaly 253.0 *[713.0]*
    actinomycosis 039.8 *[711.4]*
    amyloidosis 277.3 *[713.7]*
    bacterial disease NEC 040.89 *[711.4]*
    Behçet's syndrome 136.1 *[711.2]*
    blastomycosis 116.0 *[711.6]*
    brucellosis (*see also* Brucellosis) 023.9
        [711.4]
    caisson disease 993.3
    coccidioidomycosis 114.3 *[711.6]*
    coliform (Escherichia coli) 711.0
    colitis, ulcerative (*see also* Colitis, ulcerative)
        556.9 *[713.1]*
    cowpox 051.0 *[711.5]*
    crystals (*see also* Gout)
      dicalcium phosphate 275.49 *[712.1]*
        pyrophosphate 275.49 *[712.2]*
        specified NEC 275.49 *[712.8]*
    dermatoarthritis, lipoid 272.8 *[713.0]*
    dermatological disorder NEC 709.9 *[713.3]*
    diabetes 250.6 *[713.5]*
    diphtheria 032.89 *[711.4]*
    dracontiasis 125.7 *[711.7]*
    dysentery 009.0 *[711.3]*

Arthritis, arthritic—*continued*
  endocrine disorder NEC 259.9 *[713.0]*
  enteritis NEC 009.1 *[711.3]*
    infectious (*see also* Enteritis, infectious)
      009.0 *[711.3]*
      specified organism NEC 008.8 *[711.3]*
      regional (*see also* Enteritis, regional) 555.9
        [713.1]
      specified organism NEC 008.8 *[711.3]*
  epiphyseal slip, nontraumatic (old) 716.8
  erysipelas 035 *[711.4]*
  erythema
    epidemic 026.1
    multiforme 695.1 *[713.3]*
    nodosum 695.2 *[713.3]*
  Escherichia coli 711.0
  filariasis NEC 125.9 *[711.7]*
  gastrointestinal condition NEC 569.9 *[713.1]*
  glanders 024 *[711.4]*
  Gonococcus 098.50
  gout 274.0
  H. influenzae 711.0
  helminthiasis NEC 128.9 *[711.7]*
  hematological disorder NEC 289.9 *[713.2]*
  hemochromatosis 275.0 *[713.0]*
  hemoglobinopathy NEC (*see also* Disease,
    hemoglobin) 282.7 *[713.2]*
  hemophilia (*see also* Hemophilia) 286.0
    [713.2]
  Hemophilus influenzae (H. influenzae) 711.0
  Henoch (-Schönlein) purpura 287.0 *[713.6]*
  histoplasmosis NEC (*see also* Histoplasmosis)
    115.99 *[711.6]*
  hyperparathyroidism 252.0 *[713.0]*
  hypersensitivity reaction NEC 995.3 *[713.6]*
  hypogammaglobulinemia (*see also*
    Hypogammaglobulinemia) 279.00 *[713.0]*
  hypothyroidism NEC 244.9 *[713.0]*
  infection (*see also* Arthritis, infectious) 711.9
  infectious disease NEC 136.9 *[711.8]*
  leprosy (*see also* Leprosy) 030.9 *[711.4]*
  leukemia NEC (M9800/3) 208.9 *[713.2]*
  lipoid dermatoarthritis 272.8 *[713.0]*
  Lyme disease 088.81 *[711.8]*
  meaning Osteoarthritis—*see* Osteoarthrosis
  Mediterranean fever, familial 277.3 *[713.7]*
  meningococcal infection 036.82
  metabolic disorder NEC 277.9 *[713.0]*
  multiple myelomatosis (M9730/3) 203.0
    [713.2]
  mumps 072.79 *[711.5]*
  mycobacteria 031.8 *[711.4]*
  mycosis NEC 117.9 *[711.6]*
  neurological disorder NEC 349.9 *[713.5]*
  ochronosis 270.2 *[713.0]*
  O'Nyong Nyong 066.3 *[711.5]*
  parasitic disease NEC 136.9 *[711.8]*
  paratyphoid fever (*see also* Fever,
    paratyphoid) 002.9 *[711.3]*
  Pneumococcus 711.0
  poliomyelitis (*see also* Poliomyelitis) 045.9
    [711.5]
  Pseudomonas 711.0
  psoriasis 696.0
  pyogenic organism (E. coli) (H. influenzae)
    (Pseudomonas) (Streptococcus) 711.0
  rat-bite fever 026.1 *[711.4]*
  regional enteritis (*see also* Enteritis, regional)
    555.9 *[713.1]*
  Reiter's disease 099.3 *[711.1]*
  respiratory disorder NEC 519.9 *[713.4]*

Arthritis, arthritic—*continued*
  reticulosis, malignant (M9720/3) 202.3
    [713.2]
  rubella 056.71
  salmonellosis 003.23
  sarcoidosis 135 *[713.7]*
  serum sickness 999.5 *[713.6]*
  Staphylococcus 711.0
  Streptococcus 711.0
  syphilis (*see also* Syphilis) 094.0 *[711.4]*
  syringomyelia 336.0 *[713.5]*
  thalassemia 282.4 *[713.2]*
  tuberculosis (*see also* Tuberculosis, arthritis)
    015.9 *[711.4]*
  typhoid fever 002.0 *[711.3]*
  ulcerative colitis (*see also* Colitis, ulcerative)
    556.9 *[713.1]*
  urethritis
    nongonococcal (*see also* Urethritis,
      nongonococcal) 099.40 *[711.1]*
    nonspecific (*see also* Urethritis,
      nongonococcal) 099.40 *[711.1]*
    Reiter's 099.3 *[711.1]*
  viral disease NEC 079.99 *[711.5]*
 erythema epidemic 026.1
 gonococcal 098.50
 gouty (acute) 274.0
 hypertrophic (*see also* Osteoarthrosis) 715.9
  spine 721.90
    with myelopathy 721.91
 idiopathic, blennorrheal 099.3
 in caisson disease 993.3 *[713.8]*
 infectious or infective (acute) (chronic)
  (subacute) NEC 711.9
  nonpyogenic 711.9
  spine 720.9
 inflammatory NEC 714.9
 juvenile rheumatoid (chronic) (polyarticular)
  714.30
  acute 714.31
  monoarticular 714.33
  pauciarticular 714.32
 lumbar (*see also* Spondylosis, lumbar) 721.3
 meningococcal 036.82
 menopausal NEC 716.3
 migratory—*see* Fever, rheumatic
 neuropathic (Charcot's) 094.0 *[713.5]*
  diabetic 250.6 *[713.5]*
  nonsyphilitic NEC 349.9 *[713.5]*
  syringomyelic 336.0 *[713.5]*
  tabetic 094.0 *[713.5]*
 nodosa (*see also* Osteoarthrosis) 715.9
  spine 721.90
    with myelopathy 721.91
 nonpyogenic NEC 716.9
  spine 721.90
    with myelopathy 721.91
 ochronotic 270.2 *[713.0]*
 palindromic (*see also* Rheumatism,
  palindromic) 719.3
 pneumococcal 711.0
 postdysenteric 009.0 *[711.3]*
 postrheumatic, chronic (Jaccoud's) 714.4
 primary progressive 714.0
  spine 720.9
 proliferative 714.0
  spine 720.0
 psoriatic 696.0
 purulent 711.0
 pyogenic or pyemic 711.0

Arthritis, arthritic—*continued*
  rheumatic 714.0
    acute or subacute—*see* Fever, rheumatic
    chronic 714.0
    spine 720.9
  rheumatoid (nodular) 714.0
    with
      splenoadenomegaly and leukopenia 714.1
      visceral or systemic involvement 714.2
    aortitis 714.89
    carditis 714.2
    heart disease 714.2
    juvenile (chronic) (polyarticular) 714.30
      acute 714.31
        monoarticular 714.33
        pauciarticular 714.32
    spine 720.0
  rubella 056.71
  sacral, sacroiliac, sacrococcygeal (*see also*
    Spondylosis, sacral) 721.3
  scorbutic 267
  senile or senescent (*see also* Osteoarthrosis)
    715.9
    spine 721.90
      with myelopathy 721.91
  septic 711.0
  serum (nontherapeutic) (therapeutic) 999.5
    [713.6]
  specified form NEC 716.8
  spine 721.90
    with myelopathy 721.91
    atrophic 720.9
    degenerative 721.90
      with myelopathy 721.91
    hypertrophic (with deformity) 721.90
      with myelopathy 721.91
    infectious or infective NEC 720.9
    Marie-Strümpell 720.0
    nonpyogenic 721.90
      with myelopathy 721.91
    pyogenic 720.9
    rheumatoid 720.0
    traumatic (old) 721.7
    tuberculous (*see also* Tuberculosis) 015.0
      [720.81]
  staphylococcal 711.0
  streptococcal 711.0
  suppurative 711.0
  syphilitic 094.0 *[713.5]*
    congenital 090.49 *[713.5]*
  syphilitica deformans (Charcot) 094.0 *[713.5]*
  temporomandibular joint 524.69
  thoracic (*see also* Spondylosis, thoracic) 721.2
  toxic of menopause 716.3
  transient 716.4
  traumatic (chronic) (old) (post) 716.1
    current injury—*see* nature of injury
  tuberculous (*see also* Tuberculosis, arthritis)
    015.9 *[711.4]*
  urethritica 099.3 *[711.1]*
  urica, uratic 274.0
  venereal 099.3 *[711.1]*
  vertebral (*see also* Arthritis, spine) 721.90
  villous 716.8
  von Bechterew's 720.0
Arthrocele (*see also* Effusion, joint) 719.0
Arthrochondritis —*see* Arthritis
Arthrodesis status V45.4
Arthrodynia (*see also* Pain, joint) 719.4
  psychogenic 307.89
Arthrodysplasia 755.9
Arthrofibrosis, joint (*see also* Ankylosis) 718.5

Arthrogryposis 728.3
  multiplex, congenita 754.89
Arthrokatadysis 715.35
Arthrolithiasis 274.0
Arthro-onychodysplasia 756.89
Arthro-osteo-onychodysplasia 756.89
Arthropathy (*see also* Arthritis) 716.9

> *Note—Use the following fifth-digit*
> *subclassification with categories 711-712, 716:*
>
> *0 site unspecified*
> *1 shoulder region*
> *2 upper arm*
> *3 forearm*
> *4 hand*
> *5 pelvic region and thigh*
> *6 lower leg*
> *7 ankle and foot*
> *8 other specified sites*
> *9 multiple sites*

  Behçet's 136.1 *[711.2]*
  Charcot's 094.0 *[713.5]*
    diabetic 250.6 *[713.5]*
    syringomyelic 336.0 *[713.5]*
    tabetic 094.0 *[713.5]*
  crystal (-induced)—*see* Arthritis, due to crystals
  gouty 274.0
  neurogenic, neuropathic (Charcot's) (tabetic)
    094.0 *[713.5]*
    diabetic 250.6 *[713.5]*
    nonsyphilitic NEC 349.9 *[713.5]*
    syringomyelic 336.0 *[713.5]*
  postdysenteric NEC 009.0 *[711.3]*
  postrheumatic, chronic (Jaccoud's) 714.4
  psoriatic 696.0
  pulmonary 731.2
  specified NEC 716.8
  syringomyelia 336.0 *[713.5]*
  tabes dorsalis 094.0 *[713.5]*
  tabetic 094.0 *[713.5]*
  transient 716.4
  traumatic 716.1
  uric acid 274.0
Arthrophyte (*see also* Loose, body, joint) 718.1
Arthrophytis 719.80
  ankle 719.87
  elbow 719.82
  foot 719.87
  hand 719.84
  hip 719.85
  knee 719.86
  multiple sites 719.89
  pelvic region 719.85
  shoulder (region) 719.81
  specified site NEC 719.88
  wrist 719.83
Arthropyosis (*see also* Arthritis, pyogenic) 711.0
Arthrosis (deformans) (degenerative) (*see also*
  Osteoarthrosis) 715.9
  Charcot's 094.0 *[713.5]*
  polyarticular 715.09
  spine (*see also* Spondylosis) 721.90
Arthus' phenomenon 995.2
  due to
    correct substance properly administered 995.2
    overdose or wrong substance given or taken
      977.9
      specified drug—*see* Table of drugs and
        chemicals
    serum 999.5

Articular —*see also* condition
  disc disorder (reducing or non-reducing) 524.63
  spondylolisthesis 756.12
Artificial
  device (prosthetic)—*see* Fitting, device
  insemination V26.1
  menopause (states) (symptoms) (syndrome)
      627.4
  opening status (functioning) (without
      complication) V44.9
    anus (colostomy) V44.3
    colostomy V44.3
    cystostomy V44.50
      appendico-vesicostomy V44.52
      cutaneous-vesicostomy V44.51
      specified type NEC V44.59
    enterostomy V44.4
    gastrostomy V44.1
    ileostomy V44.2
    intestinal tract NEC V44.4
    jejunostomy V44.4
    nephrostomy V44.6
    specified site NEC V44.8
    tracheostomy V44.0
    ureterostomy V44.6
    urethrostomy V44.6
    urinary tract NEC V44.6
    vagina V44.7
  vagina status V44.7
ARV (disease) (illness) (infection)—*see* Human
    immunodeficiency virus (disease) (illness)
    (infection)
Arytenoid —*see* condition
Asbestosis (occupational) 501
Asboe-Hansen's disease (incontinentia
    pigmenti) 757.33
Ascariasis (intestinal) (lung) 127.0
Ascaridiasis 127.0
Ascaridosis 127.0
Ascaris 127.0
  lumbricoides (infestation) 127.0
  pneumonia 127.0
Ascending —*see* condition
Aschoff's bodies (*see also* Myocarditis,
    rheumatic) 398.0
Ascites 789.5
  abdominal NEC 789.5
  cancerous (M8000/6) 197.6
  cardiac 428.0
  chylous (nonfilarial) 457.8
    filarial (*see also* Infestation, filarial) 125.9
  congenital 778.0
  due to S. japonicum 120.2
  fetal, causing fetopelvic disproportion 653.7
  heart 428.0
  joint (*see also* Effusion, joint) 719.0
  malignant (M8000/6) 197.6
  pseudochylous 789.5
  syphilitic 095.2
  tuberculous (*see also* Tuberculosis) 014.0
Ascorbic acid (vitamin C) deficiency (scurvy)
    267
ASCVD (arteriosclerotic cardiovascular disease)
    429.2
Aseptic —*see* condition
Asherman's syndrome 621.5
Asialia 527.7
Asiatic cholera (*see also* Cholera) 001.9
Asocial personality or trends 301.7
Asomatognosia 781.8

Aspergillosis 117.3
  with pneumonia 117.3 *[484.6]*
  allergic bronchopulmonary 518.6
  nonsyphilitic NEC 117.3
Aspergillus (flavus) (fumigatus) (infection)
    (terreus) 117.3
Aspermatogenesis 606.0
Aspermia (testis) 606.0
Asphyxia, asphyxiation (by) 799.0
  antenatal—*see* Distress, fetal
  bedclothes 994.7
  birth (*see also* Asphyxia, newborn) 768.9
  bunny bag 994.7
  carbon monoxide 986
  caul (*see also* Asphyxia, newborn) 768.9
  cave-in 994.7
    crushing—*see* Injury, internal, intrathoracic
      organs
  constriction 994.7
  crushing—*see* Injury, internal, intrathoracic
      organs
  drowning 994.1
  fetal, affecting newborn 770.8
  food or foreign body (in larynx) 933.1
    bronchioles 934.8
    bronchus (main) 934.1
    lung 934.8
    nasopharynx 933.0
    nose, nasal passages 932
    pharynx 933.0
    respiratory tract 934.9
      specified part NEC 934.8
    throat 933.0
    trachea 934.0
  gas, fumes, or vapor NEC 987.9
    specified—*see* Table of drugs and chemicals
  gravitational changes 994.7
  hanging 994.7
  inhalation—*see* Inhalation
  intrauterine
    fetal death (before onset of labor) 768.0
      during labor 768.1
    liveborn infant—*see* Distress, fetal, liveborn
      infant
  local 443.0
  mechanical 994.7
    during birth (*see also* Distress, fetal) 770.8
  mucus 933.1
    bronchus (main) 934.1
    larynx 933.1
    lung 934.8
    nasal passages 932
    newborn 770.1
    pharynx 933.0
    respiratory tract 934.9
      specified part NEC 934.8
    throat 933.0
    trachea 934.0
    vaginal (fetus or newborn) 770.1
  newborn 768.9
    blue 768.6
    livida 768.6
    mild or moderate 768.6
    pallida 768.5
    severe 768.5
    white 768.5
    with neurologic involvement 768.5
  pathological 799.0
  plastic bag 994.7
  postnatal (*see also* Asphyxia, newborn) 768.9
    mechanical 994.7

Asphyxia, Asphyxiation—*continued*
 pressure 994.7
 reticularis 782.61
 strangulation 994.7
 submersion 994.1
 traumatic NEC—*see* Injury, internal,
  intrathoracic organs
 vomiting, vomitus—*see* Asphyxia, food or
  foreign body
Aspiration
 acid pulmonary (syndrome) 997.3
  obstetric 668.0
 amniotic fluid 770.1
 bronchitis 507.0
 contents of birth canal 770.1
 fetal pneumonitis 770.1
 food, foreign body, or gasoline (with
  asphyxiation)—*see* Asphyxia, food or
  foreign body
 meconium 770.1
 mucus 933.1
  into
   bronchus (main) 934.1
   lung 934.8
   respiratory tract 934.9
    specified part NEC 934.8
   trachea 934.0
  newborn 770.1
  vaginal (fetus or newborn) 770.1
 newborn 770.1
 pneumonia 507.0
 pneumonitis 507.0
  fetus or newborn 770.1
  obstetric 668.0
 syndrome of newborn (massive) (meconium)
  770.1
 vernix caseosa 770.1
Asplenia 759.0
 with mesocardia 746.87
Assam fever 085.0
Assimilation, pelvis
 with disproportion 653.2
  affecting fetus or newborn 763.1
  causing obstructed labor 660.1
   affecting fetus or newborn 763.1
Assmann's focus (*see also* Tuberculosis) 011.0
Astasia (-abasia) 307.9
 hysterical 300.11
Asteatosis 706.8
 cutis 706.8
Astereognosis 780.9
Asterixis 781.3
 in liver disease 572.8
Asteroid hyalitis 379.22
Asthenia, asthenic 780.79
 cardiac (*see also* Failure, heart) 428.9
  psychogenic 306.2
 cardiovascular (*see also* Failure, heart) 428.9
  psychogenic 306.2
 heart (*see also* Failure, heart) 428.9
  psychogenic 306.2
 hysterical 300.11
 myocardial (*see also* Failure, heart) 428.9
  psychogenic 306.2
 nervous 300.5
 neurocirculatory 306.2
 neurotic 300.5
 psychogenic 300.5
 psychoneurotic 300.5
 psychophysiologic 300.5
 reaction, psychoneurotic 300.5

Asthenia, asthenic—*continued*
 senile 797
 Stiller's 780.79
 tropical anhidrotic 705.1
Asthenopia 368.13
 accommodative 367.4
 hysterical (muscular) 300.11
 psychogenic 306.7
Asthenospermia 792.2
Asthma, asthmatic (bronchial) (catarrh)
 (spasmodic) 493.9

> *Note—Use the following fifth-digit
> subclassification with category 493:*
>
> 0 *without mention of status asthmaticus*
> 1 *with status asthmaticus*
> 2 with acute exacerbation

 with
  chronic obstructive pulmonary disease
   (COPD) 493.2
  hay fever 493.0
  rhinitis, allergic 493.0
 allergic 493.9
  stated cause (external allergen) 493.0
 atopic 493.0
 cardiac (*see also* Failure, ventricular, left) 428.1
 cardiobronchial (*see also* Failure, ventricular,
  left) 428.1
 cardiorenal (*see also* Hypertension, cardiorenal)
  404.90
 childhood 493.0
 colliers' 500
 croup 493.9
 detergent 507.8
 due to
  detergent 507.8
  inhalation of fumes 506.3
  internal immunological process 493.0
 endogenous (intrinsic) 493.1
 eosinophilic 518.3
 exogenous (cosmetics) (dander or dust) (drugs)
  (dust) (feathers) (food) (hay) (platinum)
  (pollen) 493.0
 extrinsic 493.0
 grinders' 502
 hay 493.0
 heart (*see also* Failure, ventricular, left) 428.1
 IgE 493.0
 infective 493.1
 intrinsic 493.1
 Kopp's 254.8
 late-onset 493.1
 meat-wrappers' 506.9
 Millar's (laryngismus stridulus) 478.75
 millstone makers' 502
 miners' 500
 Monday morning 504
 New Orleans (epidemic) 493.0
 platinum 493.0
 pneumoconiotic (occupational) NEC 505
 potters' 502
 psychogenic 316 *[493.9]*
 pulmonary eosinophilic 518.3
 red cedar 495.8
 Rostan's (*see also* Failure, ventricular, left)
  428.1
 sandblasters' 502
 sequoiosis 495.8
 stonemasons' 502
 thymic 254.8

Asthma, asthmatic—*continued*
  tuberculous (*see also* Tuberculosis, pulmonary)
      011.9
  Wichmann's (laryngismus stridulus) 478.75
  wood 495.8
Astigmatism (compound) (congenital) 367.20
  irregular 367.22
  regular 367.21
Astroblastoma (M9430/3)
  nose 748.1
  specified site—*see* Neoplasm, by site,
      malignant
  unspecified site 191.9
Astrocytoma (cystic) (M9400/3)
  anaplastic type (M9401/3)
      specified site—*see* Neoplasm, by site,
          malignant
      unspecified site 191.9
  fibrillary (M9420/3)
      specified site—*see* Neoplasm, by site,
          malignant
      unspecified site 191.9
  fibrous (M9420/3)
      specified site—*see* Neoplasm, by site,
          malignant
      unspecified site 191.9
  gemistocytic (M9411/3)
      specified site—*see* Neoplasm, by site,
          malignant
      unspecified site 191.9
  juvenile (M9421/3)
      specified site—*see* Neoplasm, by site,
          malignant
      unspecified site 191.9
  nose 748.1
  pilocytic (M9421/3)
      specified site—*see* Neoplasm, by site,
          malignant
      unspecified site 191.9
  piloid (M9421/3)
      specified site—*see* Neoplasm, by site,
          malignant
      unspecified site 191.9
  protoplasmic (M9410/3)
      specified site—*see* Neoplasm, by site,
          malignant
      unspecified site 191.9
  specified site—*see* Neoplasm, by site, malignant
  subependymal (M9383/1) 237.5
      giant cell (M9384/1) 237.5
  unspecified site 191.9
Astroglioma (M9400/3)
  nose 748.1
  specified site—*see* Neoplasm, by site, malignant
  unspecified site 191.9
Asymbolia 784.60
Asymmetrical breathing 786.09
Asymmetry —*see also* Distortion
  chest 786.9
  face 754.0
  jaw NEC 524.12
      maxillary 524.11
  pelvis with disproportion 653.0
      affecting fetus or newborn 763.1
      causing obstructed labor 660.1
          affecting fetus or newborn 763.1
Asynergia 781.3
Asynergy 781.3
  ventricular 429.89
Asystole (heart) (*see also* Arrest, cardiac) 427.5

Ataxia, ataxy, ataxic 781.3
  acute 781.3
  brain 331.89
  cerebellar 334.3
      hereditary (Marie's) 334.2
      in
          alcoholism 303.9 *[334.4]*
          myxedema (*see also* Myxedema) 244.9
              [334.4]
          neoplastic disease NEC 239.9 *[334.4]*
  cerebral 331.89
  family, familial 334.2
      cerebral (Marie's) 334.2
      spinal (Friedreich's) 334.0
  Friedreich's (heredofamilial) (spinal) 334.0
  frontal lobe 781.3
  gait 781.2
      hysterical 300.11
  general 781.3
  hereditary NEC 334.2
      cerebellar 334.2
      spastic 334.1
      spinal 334.0
  heredofamilial (Marie's) 334.2
  hysterical 300.11
  locomotor (progressive) 094.0
      diabetic 250.6 *[337.1]*
  Marie's (cerebellar) (heredofamilial) 334.2
  nonorganic origin 307.9
  partial 094.0
  postchickenpox 052.7
  progressive locomotor 094.0
  psychogenic 307.9
  Sanger-Brown's 334.2
  spastic 094.0
      hereditary 334.1
      syphilitic 094.0
  spinal
      hereditary 334.0
      progressive locomotor 094.0
  telangiectasia 334.8
Ataxia-telangiectasia 334.8
Atelectasis (absorption collapse) (complete)
      (compression) (massive) (partial)
      (postinfective) (pressure collapse)
      (pulmonary) (relaxation) 518.0
  newborn (congenital) (partial) 770.5
      primary 770.4
  primary 770.4
  tuberculous (*see also* Tuberculosis, pulmonary)
      011.9
Ateleiosis, ateliosis 253.3
Atelia —*see* Distortion
Ateliosis 253.3
Atelocardia 746.9
Atelomyelia 742.59
Athelia 757.6
Atheroembolism *see* Atherosclerosis
Atheroma, atheromatous (*see also*
      Arteriosclerosis) 440.9
  aorta, aortic 440.0
      valve (*see also* Endocarditis, aortic) 424.1
  artery—*see* Arteriosclerosis
  basilar, (artery) (*see also* Occlusion, artery,
      basilar) 433.0
  carotid (artery) (common) (internal) (*see also*
      Occlusion, artery, carotid) 433.1
  cerebral (arteries) 437.0
  coronary (artery)—*see* Arteriosclerosis,
      coronary
  degeneration—*see* Arteriosclerosis

Atrophy, atrophic—*continued*
  senile 331.2
  breast 611.4
    puerperal, postpartum 676.3
  buccal cavity 528.9
  cardiac (brown) (senile) (*see also* Degeneration,
    myocardial) 429.1
  cartilage (infectional) (joint) 733.99
  cast, plaster of Paris 728.2
  cerebellar—*see* Atrophy, brain
  cerebral—*see* Atrophy, brain
  cervix (endometrium) (mucosa) (myometrium)
    (senile) (uteri) 622.8
    menopausal 627.8
  Charcot-Marie-Tooth 356.1
  choroid 363.40
    diffuse secondary 363.42
    hereditary (*see also* Dystrophy, choroid)
      363.50
      gyrate
        central 363.54
        diffuse 363.57
        generalized 363.57
    senile 363.41
  ciliary body 364.57
  colloid, degenerative 701.3
  conjunctiva (senile) 372.89
  corpus cavernosum 607.89
  cortical (*see also* Atrophy, brain) 331.9
  Cruveilhier's 335.21
  cystic duct 576.8
  dacryosialadenopathy 710.2
  degenerative
    colloid 701.3
    senile 701.3
  Déjérine-Thomas 333.0
  diffuse idiopathic, dermatological 701.8
  disuse
    bone 733.7
    muscle 728.2
  Duchenne-Aran 335.21
  ear 388.9
  edentulous alveolar ridge 525.2
  emphysema, lung 492.8
  endometrium (senile) 621.8
    cervix 622.8
  enteric 569.89
  epididymis 608.3
  eyeball, cause unknown 360.41
  eyelid (senile) 374.50
  facial (skin) 701.9
  facioscapulohumeral (Landouzy-Déjérine) 359.1
  fallopian tube (senile), acquired 620.3
  fatty, thymus (gland) 254.8
  gallbladder 575.8
  gastric 537.89
  gastritis (chronic) 535.1
  gastrointestinal 569.89
  genital organ, male 608.89
  glandular 289.3
  globe (phthisis bulbi) 360.41
  gum 523.2
  hair 704.2
  heart (brown) (senile) (*see also* Degeneration,
    myocardial) 429.1
  hemifacial 754.0
    Romberg 349.89
  hydronephrosis 591
  infantile 261
    paralysis, acute (*see also* Poliomyelitis, with
      paralysis) 045.1

Atrophy, atrophic—*continued*
  intestine 569.89
  iris (generalized) (postinfectional) (sector
    shaped) 364.59
    essential 364.51
    progressive 364.51
    sphincter 364.54
  kidney (senile) (*see also* Sclerosis, renal) 587
    with hypertension (*see also* Hypertension,
      kidney) 403.90
    congenital 753.0
    hydronephrotic 591
    infantile 753.0
  lacrimal apparatus (primary) 375.13
    secondary 375.14
  Landouzy-Déjérine 359.1
  laryngitis, infection 476.0
  larynx 478.79
  Leber's optic 377.16
  lip 528.5
  liver (acute) (subacute) (*see also* Necrosis,
    liver) 570
    chronic (yellow) 571.8
    yellow (congenital) 570
      with
        abortion—*see* Abortion, by type, with
          specified complication NEC
        ectopic pregnancy (*see also* categories
          633.0-633.9) 639.8
        molar pregnancy (*see also* categories
          630-632) 639.8
      chronic 571.8
      complicating pregnancy 646.7
      following
        abortion 639.8
        ectopic or molar pregnancy 639.8
      from injection, inoculation or transfusion
        (onset within 8 months after
        administration)—*see* Hepatitis, viral
      healed 571.5
      obstetric 646.7
      postabortal 639.8
      postimmunization—*see* Hepatitis, viral
      posttransfusion—*see* Hepatitis, viral
      puerperal, postpartum 674.8
  lung (senile) 518.89
    congenital 748.69
  macular (dermatological) 701.3
    syphilitic, skin 091.3
      striated 095.8
  muscle, muscular 728.2
    disuse 728.2
    Duchenne-Aran 335.21
    extremity (lower) (upper) 728.2
    familial spinal 335.11
    general 728.2
    idiopathic 728.2
    infantile spinal 335.0
    myelopathic (progressive) 335.10
    myotonic 359.2
    neuritic 356.1
    neuropathic (peroneal) (progressive) 356.1
    peroneal 356.1
    primary (idiopathic) 728.2
    progressive (familial) (hereditary) (pure)
      335.21
      adult (spinal) 335.19
      infantile (spinal) 335.0
      juvenile (spinal) 335.11
      spinal 335.10
        adult 335.19

Atrophy, atrophic—*continued*
　　　hereditary or familial 335.11
　　　　infantile 335.0
　　pseudohypertrophic 359.1
　　spinal (progressive) 335.10
　　　adult 335.19
　　　Aran-Duchenne 335.21
　　　familial 335.11
　　　hereditary 335.11
　　　infantile 335.0
　　　juvenile 335.11
　　　syphilitic 095.6
　myocardium (*see also* Degeneration,
　　　myocardial) 429.1
　myometrium (senile) 621.8
　　cervix 622.8
　myotatic 728.2
　myotonia 359.2
　nail 703.8
　　congenital 757.5
　nasopharynx 472.2
　nerve—*see also* Disorder, nerve
　　abducens 378.54
　　accessory 352.4
　　acoustic or auditory 388.5
　　cranial 352.9
　　　first (olfactory) 352.0
　　　second (optic) (*see also* Atrophy, optic
　　　　nerve) 377.10
　　　third (oculomotor) (partial) 378.51
　　　　total 378.52
　　　fourth (trochlear) 378.53
　　　fifth (trigeminal) 350.8
　　　sixth (abducens) 378.54
　　　seventh (facial) 351.8
　　　eighth (auditory) 388.5
　　　ninth (glossopharyngeal) 352.2
　　　tenth (pneumogastric) (vagus) 352.3
　　　eleventh (accessory) 352.4
　　　twelfth (hypoglossal) 352.5
　　facial 351.8
　　glossopharyngeal 352.2
　　hypoglossal 352.5
　　oculomotor (partial) 378.51
　　　total 378.52
　　olfactory 352.0
　　peripheral 355.9
　　pneumogastric 352.3
　　trigeminal 350.8
　　trochlear 378.53
　　vagus (pneumogastric) 352.3
　nervous system, congenital 742.8
　neuritic (*see also* Disorder, nerve) 355.9
　neurogenic NEC 355.9
　　bone
　　　tabetic 094.0
　nutritional 261
　old age 797
　olivopontocerebellar 333.0
　optic nerve (ascending) (descending)
　　　(infectional) (nonfamilial) (papillomacular
　　　bundle) (postretinal) (secondary NEC)
　　　(simple) 377.10
　　associated with retinal dystrophy 377.13
　　dominant hereditary 377.16
　　glaucomatous 377.14
　　hereditary (dominant) (Leber's) 377.16
　　Leber's (hereditary) 377.16
　　partial 377.15
　　postinflammatory 377.12
　　primary 377.11

Atrophy, atrophic—*continued*
　syphilitic 094.84
　　congenital 090.49
　　tabes dorsalis 094.0
　orbit 376.45
　ovary (senile), acquired 620.3
　oviduct (senile), acquired 620.3
　palsy, diffuse 335.20
　pancreas (duct) (senile) 577.8
　papillary muscle 429.81
　paralysis 355.9
　parotid gland 527.0
　patches skin 701.3
　　senile 701.8
　penis 607.89
　pharyngitis 472.1
　pharynx 478.29
　pluriglandular 258.8
　polyarthritis 714.0
　prostate 602.2
　pseudohypertrophic 359.1
　renal (*see also* Sclerosis, renal) 587
　reticulata 701.8
　retina (*see also* Degeneration, retina) 362.60
　　hereditary (*see also* Dystrophy, retina) 362.70
　rhinitis 472.0
　salivary duct or gland 527.0
　scar NEC 709.2
　sclerosis, lobar (of brain) 331.0
　　with dementia
　　　with behavioral disturbance 331.1 *[294.11]*
　　　without behavioral disturbance 331.1
　　　　[294.10]
　scrotum 608.89
　seminal vesicle 608.89
　senile 797
　　degenerative, of skin 701.3
　skin (patches) (senile) 701.8
　spermatic cord 608.89
　spinal (cord) 336.8
　　acute 336.8
　　muscular (chronic) 335.10
　　　adult 335.19
　　　familial 335.11
　　　juvenile 335.10
　　paralysis 335.10
　　　acute (*see also* Poliomyelitis, with paralysis)
　　　　045.1
　spine (column) 733.99
　spleen (senile) 289.59
　spots (skin) 701.3
　　senile 701.8
　stomach 537.89
　striate and macular 701.3
　　syphilitic 095.8
　subcutaneous 701.9
　　due to injection 999.9
　sublingual gland 527.0
　submaxillary gland 527.0
　Sudeck's 733.7
　suprarenal (autoimmune) (capsule) (gland) 255.4
　　with hypofunction 255.4
　tarso-orbital fascia, congenital 743.66
　testis 608.3
　thenar, partial 354.0
　throat 478.29
　thymus (fat) 254.8
　thyroid (gland) 246.8
　　with
　　　cretinism 243
　　　myxedema 244.9

Avitaminosis (multiple NEC) (*see also*
    Deficiency, vitamin) 269.2
  A 264.9
  B 266.9
    with
      beriberi 265.0
      pellagra 265.2
  B_1 265.1
  B_2 266.0
  B_6 266.1
  B_{12} 266.2
  C (with scurvy) 267
  D 268.9
    with
      osteomalacia 268.2
      rickets 268.0
  E 269.1
  G 266.0
  H 269.1
  K 269.0
  multiple 269.2
  nicotinic acid 265.2
  P 269.1
Avulsion (traumatic) 879.8
  blood vessel—*see* Injury, blood vessel, by site
  cartilage—*see also* Dislocation, by site
    knee, current (*see also* Tear, meniscus) 836.2
    symphyseal (inner), complicating delivery
      665.6
  complicated 879.9
  diaphragm—*see* Injury, internal, diaphragm
  ear—*see* Wound, open, ear
  epiphysis of bone—*see* Fracture, by site
  external site other than limb—*see* Wound, open,
    by site
  eye 871.3
  fingernail—*see* Wound, open, finger
  fracture—*see* Fracture, by site
  genital organs, external—*see* Wound, open,
    genital organs
  head (intracranial) NEC—*see also* Injury,
    intracranial, with open intracranial wound
    complete 874.9
    external site NEC 873.8
      complicated 873.9
  internal organ or site—*see* Injury, internal, by
    site
  joint—*see also* Dislocation, by site
    capsule—*see* Sprain, by site
  ligament—*see* Sprain, by site
  limb—*see also* Amputation, traumatic, by site
    skin and subcutaneous tissue—*see* Wound,
      open, by site
  muscle—*see* Sprain, by site
  nerve (root)—*see* Injury, nerve, by site
  scalp—*see* Wound, open, scalp
  skin and subcutaneous tissue—*see* Wound,
    open, by site
  symphyseal cartilage (inner), complicating
    delivery 665.6
  tendon—*see also* Sprain, by site
    with open wound—*see* Wound, open, by site
  toenail—*see* Wound, open, toe(s)
  tooth 873.63
    complicated 873.73
Awareness of heart beat 785.1
Axe grinders' disease 502
Axenfeld's anomaly or syndrome 743.44
Axilla, axillary —*see also* condition
  breast 757.6
Axonotmesis —*see* Injury, nerve, by site
Ayala's disease 756.89

Ayerza's disease or syndrome (pulmonary
  artery sclerosis with pulmonary hypertension)
  416.0
Azoospermia 606.0
Azorean disease (of the nervous system) 334.8
Azotemia 790.6
  meaning uremia (*see also* Uremia) 586
Aztec ear 744.29
Azygos lobe, lung (fissure) 748.69

B

Baader's syndrome (erythema multiforme exudativum) 695.1
Baastrup's syndrome 721.5
Babesiasis 088.82
Babesiosis 088.82
Babington's disease (familial hemorrhagic telangiectasia) 448.0
Babinski's syndrome (cardiovascular syphilis) 093.89
Babinski-Fröhlich syndrome (adiposogenital dystrophy) 253.8
Babinski-Nageotte syndrome 344.89
Bacillary —*see* condition
Bacilluria 791.9
  asymptomatic, in pregnancy or puerperium 646.5
  tuberculous (*see also* Tuberculosis) 016.9
Bacillus—*see also* **Infection, bacillus**
  abortus infection 023.1
  anthracis infection 022.9
  coli
    infection 041.4
      generalized 038.42
      intestinal 008.00
    pyemia 038.42
    septicemia 038.42
  Flexner's 004.1
  fusiformis infestation 101
  mallei infection 024
  Shiga's 004.0
  suipestifer infection (*see also* Infection, Salmonella) 003.9
Back —*see* condition
Backache (postural) 724.5
  psychogenic 307.89
  sacroiliac 724.6
Backflow (pyelovenous) (*see also* Disease, renal) 593.9
Backknee (*see also* Genu, recurvatum) 736.5
Bacteremia (*see also* Infection, bacillus) 790.7
  with
    sepsis—*see* Septicemia
  during
    labor 659.3
    pregnancy 647.8
  newborn 771.8
Bacteria
  in blood (*see also* Bacteremia) 790.7
  in urine (*see also* Bacteriuria) 599.0
Bacterial —*see* condition
Bactericholia (*see also* Cholecystitis, acute) 575.0
Bacterid, bacteride (Andrews' pustular) 686.8
Bacteriuria, bacteruria 791.9
  with
    urinary tract infection 599.0
  asymptomatic 791.9
    in pregnancy or puerperium 646.5
      affecting fetus or newborn 760.1
Bad
  breath 784.9
  heart—*see* Disease, heart
  trip (*see also* Abuse, drugs, nondependent) 305.3
Baehr-Schiffrin disease (thrombotic thrombocytopenic purpura) 446.6
Baelz's disease (cheilitis glandularis apostematosa) 528.5
Baerensprung's disease (eczema marginatum) 110.3

Bagassosis (occupational) 495.1
Baghdad boil 085.1
Bagratuni's syndrome (temporal arteritis) 446.5
Baker's
  cyst (knee) 727.51
    tuberculous (*see also* Tuberculosis) 015.2
  itch 692.89
Bakwin-Krida syndrome (craniometaphyseal dysplasia) 756.89
Balanitis (circinata) (gangraenosa) (infectious) (vulgaris) 607.1
  amebic 006.8
  candidal 112.2
  chlamydial 099.53
  due to Ducrey's bacillus 099.0
  erosiva circinata et gangraenosa 607.1
  gangrenous 607.1
  gonococcal (acute) 098.0
    chronic or duration of 2 months or over 098.2
  nongonococcal 607.1
  phagedenic 607.1
  venereal NEC 099.8
  xerotica obliterans 607.81
Balanoposthitis 607.1
  chlamydial 099.53
  gonococcal (acute) 098.0
    chronic or duration of 2 months or over 098.2
  ulcerative NEC 099.8
Balanorrhagia —*see* Balanitis
Balantidiasis 007.0
Balantidiosis 007.0
Balbuties, balbutio 307.0
Bald
  patches on scalp 704.00
  tongue 529.4
Baldness (*see also* Alopecia) 704.00
Balfour's disease (chloroma) 205.3
Balint's syndrome (psychic paralysis of visual fixation) 368.16
Balkan grippe 083.0
Ball
  food 938
  hair 938
Ballantyne (-Runge) syndrome (postmaturity) 766.2
Balloon disease (*see also* Effect, adverse, high altitude) 993.2
Ballooning posterior leaflet syndrome 424.0
Baló's disease or concentric sclerosis 341.1
Bamberger's disease (hypertrophic pulmonary osteoarthropathy) 731.2
Bamberger-Marie disease (hypertrophic pulmonary osteoarthropathy) 731.2
Bamboo spine 720.0
Bancroft's filariasis 125.0
Band(s)
  adhesive (*see also* Adhesions, peritoneum) 568.0
  amniotic 658.8
    affecting fetus or newborn 762.8
  anomalous or congenital—*see also* Anomaly, specified type NEC
    atrial 746.9
    heart 746.9
    intestine 751.4
    omentum 751.4
    ventricular 746.9
  cervix 622.3
  gallbladder (congenital) 751.69

Band(s)—*continued*
  intestinal (adhesive) (*see also* Adhesions,
      peritoneum) 568.0
    congenital 751.4
  obstructive (*see also* Obstruction, intestine)
      560.81
  periappendiceal (congenital) 751.4
  peritoneal (adhesive) (*see also* Adhesions,
      peritoneum) 568.0
    with intestinal obstruction 560.81
    congenital 751.4
  uterus 621.5
  vagina 623.2
Bandl's ring (contraction)
  complicating delivery 661.4
    affecting fetus or newborn 763.7
Bang's disease (Brucella abortus) 023.1
Bangkok hemorrhagic fever 065.4
Bannister's disease 995.1
Bantam-Albright-Martin disease
    (pseudohypoparathyroidism) 275.49
Banti's disease or syndrome (with cirrhosis)
    (with portal hypertension)—*see* Cirrhosis,
    liver
Bar
  calcaneocuboid 755.67
  calcaneonavicular 755.67
  cubonavicular 755.67
  prostate 600.9
  talocalcaneal 755.67
Baragnosis 780.9
Barasheh, barashek 266.2
Barcoo disease or rot (*see also* Ulcer, skin) 707.9
Bard-Pic syndrome (carcinoma, head of
    pancreas) 157.0
Bärensprung's disease (eczema marginatum)
    110.3
Baritosis 503
Barium lung disease 503
Barlow's syndrome (meaning mitral valve
    prolapse) 424.0
Barlow (-Möller) disease or syndrome (meaning
    infantile scurvy) 267
Barodontalgia 993.2
Baron Münchausen syndrome 301.51
Barosinusitis 993.1
Barotitis 993.0
Barotrauma 993.2
  odontalgia 993.2
  otitic 993.0
  sinus 993.1
Barraquer's disease or syndrome (progressive
    lipodystrophy) 272.6
Barré-Guillain syndrome 357.0
Barré-Liéou syndrome (posterior cervical
    sympathetic) 723.2
Barrel chest 738.3
Barrett's syndrome or ulcer (chronic peptic
    ulcer of esophagus) 530.2
Bársony-Polgár syndrome (corkscrew
    esophagus) 530.5
Bársony-Teschendorf syndrome (corkscrew
    esophagus) 530.5
Bartholin's
  adenitis (*see also* Bartholinitis) 616.8
  gland—*see* condition
Bartholinitis (suppurating) 616.8
  gonococcal (acute) 098.0
    chronic or duration of 2 months or over 098.2
Bartonellosis 088.0

Bartter's syndrome (secondary
    hyperaldosteronism with juxtaglomerular
    hyperplasia) 255.1
Basal—*see* **condition**
Basan's (hidrotic) ectodermal dysplasia 757.31
Baseball finger 842.13
Basedow's disease or syndrome (exophthalmic
    goiter) 242.0
Basic —*see* condition
Basilar —*see* condition
Bason's (hidrotic) ectodermal dysplasia 757.31
Basopenia 288.0
Basophilia 288.8
Basophilism (corticoadrenal) (Cushing's)
    (pituitary) (thymic) 255.0
Bassen-Kornzweig syndrome
    (abetalipoproteinemia) 272.5
Bat ear 744.29
Bateman's
  disease 078.0
  purpura (senile) 287.2
Bathing cramp 994.1
Bathophobia 300.23
Batten's disease, retina 330.1 *[362.71]*
Batten-Mayou disease 330.1 *[362.71]*
Batten-Steinert syndrome 359.2
Battered
  adult (syndrome) 995.81
  baby or child (syndrome) 995.54
  spouse (syndrome) 995.81
Battey mycobacterium infection 031.0
Battledore placenta —*see* Placenta, abnormal
Battle exhaustion (*see also* Reaction, stress,
    acute) 308.9
Baumgarten-Cruveilhier (cirrhosis) disease, or
    syndrome 571.5
Bauxite
  fibrosis (of lung) 503
  workers' disease 503
Bayle's disease (dementia paralytica) 094.1
Bazin's disease (primary) (*see also* Tuberculosis)
    017.1
Beach ear 380.12
Beaded hair (congenital) 757.4
Beard's disease (neurasthenia) 300.5
Bearn-Kunkel (-Slater) syndrome (lupoid
    hepatitis) 571.49
Beat
  elbow 727.2
  hand 727.2
  knee 727.2
Beats
  ectopic 427.60
  escaped, heart 427.60
    postoperative 997.1
  premature (nodal) 427.60
    atrial 427.61
    auricular 427.61
    postoperative 997.1
    specified type NEC 427.69
    supraventricular 427.61
    ventricular 427.69
Beau's
  disease or syndrome (*see also* Degeneration,
      myocardial) 429.1
  lines (transverse furrows on fingernails) 703.8
Bechterew's disease (ankylosing spondylitis)
    720.0
Bechterew-Strümpell-Marie syndrome
    (ankylosing spondylitis) 720.0

Beck's syndrome (anterior spinal artery occlusion) 433.8

Becker's
disease (idiopathic mural endomyocardial disease) 425.2
dystrophy 359.1

Beckwith (-Wiedemann) syndrome 759.89

Bedclothes, asphyxiation or suffocation by 994.7

Bednar's aphthae 528.2

Bedsore 707.0
with gangrene 707.0 *[785.4]*

Bedwetting (*see also* Enuresis) 788.36

Beer-drinkers' heart (disease) 425.5

Bee sting (with allergic or anaphylactic shock) 989.5

Begbie's disease (exophthalmic goiter) 242.0

Behavior disorder, disturbance —*see also* Disturbance, conduct
antisocial, without manifest psychiatric disorder
adolescent V71.02
adult V71.01
child V71.02
dyssocial, without manifest psychiatric disorder
adolescent V71.02
adult V71.01
child V71.02
high-risk—*see* Problem

Behçet's syndrome 136.1

Behr's disease 362.50

Beigel's disease or morbus (white piedra) 111.2

Bejel 104.0

Bekhterev's disease (ankylosing spondylitis) 720.0

Bekhterev-Strümpell-Marie syndrome (ankylosing spondylitis) 720.0

Belching (*see also* Eructation) 787.3

Bell's
disease (*see also* Psychosis, affective) 296.0
mania (*see also* Psychosis, affective) 296.0
palsy, paralysis 351.0
infant 767.5
newborn 767.5
syphilitic 094.89
spasm 351.0

Bence-Jones albuminuria, albuminosuria, or proteinuria 791.0

Bends 993.3

Benedikt's syndrome (paralysis) 344.89

Benign —*see also* condition
prostate
hyperplasia 600.0
neoplasm 222.2

Bennett's
disease (leukemia) 208.9
fracture (closed) 815.01
open 815.11

Benson's disease 379.22

Bent
back (hysterical) 300.11
nose 738.0
congenital 754.0

Bereavement V62.82
as adjustment reaction 309.0

Berger's paresthesia (lower limb) 782.0

Bergeron's disease (hysteroepilepsy) 300.11

Beriberi (acute) (atrophic) (chronic) (dry) (subacute) (wet) 265.0
with polyneuropathy 265.0 *[357.4]*
heart (disease) 265.0 *[425.7]*
leprosy 030.1
neuritis 265.0 *[357.4]*

Berlin's disease or edema (traumatic) 921.3

Berloque dermatitis 692.72

Bernard-Horner syndrome (*see also* Neuropathy, peripheral, autonomic) 337.9

Bernard-Sergent syndrome (acute adrenocortical insufficiency) 255.4

Bernard-Soulier disease or thrombopathy 287.1

Bernhardt's disease or paresthesia 355.1

Bernhardt-Roth disease or syndrome (paresthesia) 355.1

Bernheim's syndrome (*see also* Failure, heart, congestive) 428.0

Bertielliasis 123.8

Bertolotti's syndrome (sacralization of fifth lumbar vertebra) 756.15

Berylliosis (acute) (chronic) (lung) (occupational) 503

Besnier's
lupus pernio 135
prurigo (atopic dermatitis) (infantile eczema) 691.8

Besnier-Boeck disease or sarcoid 135

Besnier-Boeck-Schaumann disease (sarcoidosis) 135

Best's disease 362.76

Bestiality 302.1

Beta-adrenergic hyperdynamic circulatory state 429.82

Beta-aminoisobutyric aciduria 277.2

Beta-mercaptolactate-cysteine disulfiduria 270.0

Beta thalassemia (major) (minor) (mixed) 282.4

Beurmann's disease (sporotrichosis) 117.1

Bezoar 938
intestine 936
stomach 935.2

Bezold's abscess (*see also* Mastoiditis) 383.01

Bianchi's syndrome (aphasia-apraxia-alexia) 784.69

Bicornuate or bicornis uterus 752.3
in pregnancy or childbirth 654.0
with obstructed labor 660.2
affecting fetus or newborn 763.1
affecting fetus or newborn 763.89

Bicuspid aortic valve 746.4

Biedl-Bardet syndrome 759.89

Bielschowsky's disease 330.1

Bielschowsky-Jansky
amaurotic familial idiocy 330.1
disease 330.1

Biemond's syndrome (obesity, polydactyly, and mental retardation) 759.89

Biermer's anemia or disease (pernicious anemia) 281.0

Biett's disease 695.4

Bifid (congenital)—*see also* Imperfect, closure
apex, heart 746.89
clitoris 752.49
epiglottis 748.3
kidney 753.3
nose 748.1
patella 755.64
scrotum 752.8
toe 755.66
tongue 750.13
ureter 753.4
uterus 752.3
uvula 749.02
with cleft lip (*see also* Cleft, palate, with cleft lip) 749.20

Biforis uterus (suprasimplex) 752.3
Bifurcation (congenital)—*see also* Imperfect,
   closure
  gallbladder 751.69
  kidney pelvis 753.3
  renal pelvis 753.3
  rib 756.3
  tongue 750.13
  trachea 748.3
  ureter 753.4
  urethra 753.8
  uvula 749.02
    with cleft lip (*see also* Cleft, palate, with cleft
     lip) 749.20
  vertebra 756.19
Bigeminal pulse 427.89
Bigeminy 427.89
Big spleen syndrome 289.4
Bilateral —*see* condition
Bile duct —*see* condition
Bile pigments in urine 791.4
Bilharziasis (*see also* Schistosomiasis) 120.9
  chyluria 120.0
  cutaneous 120.3
  galacturia 120.0
  hematochyluria 120.0
  intestinal 120.1
  lipemia 120.9
  lipuria 120.0
  Oriental 120.2
  piarhemia 120.9
  pulmonary 120.2
  tropical hematuria 120.0
  vesical 120.0
Biliary —*see* condition
Bilious (attack)—*see also* Vomiting
  fever, hemoglobinuric 084.8
Bilirubinuria 791.4
Biliuria 791.4
Billroth's disease
  meningocele (*see also* Spina bifida) 741.9
Bilobate placenta —*see* Placenta, abnormal
Bilocular
  heart 745.7
  stomach 536.8
Bing-Horton syndrome (histamine cephalgia)
  346.2
Binswanger's disease or dementia 290.12
Biörck (-Thorson) syndrome (malignant
  carcinoid) 259.2
Biparta, bipartite —*see also* Imperfect, closure
  carpal scaphoid 755.59
  patella 755.64
  placenta—*see* Placenta, abnormal
  vagina 752.49
Bird
  face 756.0
  fanciers' lung or disease 495.2
Bird's disease (oxaluria) 271.8
Birth
  abnormal fetus or newborn 763.9
  accident, fetus or newborn—*see* Birth, injury
  complications in mother—*see* Delivery,
    complicated
  compression during NEC 767.9
  defect—*see* Anomaly
  delayed, fetus 763.9
  difficult NEC, affecting fetus or newborn 763.9
  dry, affecting fetus or newborn 761.1
  forced, NEC, affecting fetus or newborn 763.89
  forceps, affecting fetus or newborn 763.2

Birth—*continued*
  hematoma of sternomastoid 767.8
  immature 765.1
    extremely 765.0
  inattention, after or at 995.52
  induced, affecting fetus or newborn 763.89
  infant—*see* Newborn
  injury NEC 767.9
    adrenal gland 767.8
    basal ganglia 767.0
    brachial plexus (paralysis) 767.6
    brain (compression) (pressure) 767.0
    cerebellum 767.0
    cerebral hemorrhage 767.0
    conjunctiva 767.8
    eye 767.8
    fracture
      bone, any except clavicle or spine 767.3
      clavicle 767.2
      femur 767.3
      humerus 767.3
      long bone 767.3
      radius and ulna 767.3
      skeleton NEC 767.3
      skull 767.3
      spine 767.4
      tibia and fibula 767.3
    hematoma 767.8
      liver (subcapsular) 767.8
      mastoid 767.8
      skull 767.1
      sternomastoid 767.8
      testes 767.8
      vulva 767.8
    intracranial (edema) 767.0
    laceration
      brain 767.0
      by scalpel 767.8
      peripheral nerve 767.7
    liver 767.8
    meninges
      brain 767.0
      spinal cord 767.4
    nerves (cranial, peripheral) 767.7
      brachial plexus 767.6
      facial 767.5
    paralysis 767.7
      brachial plexus 767.6
      Erb (-Duchenne) 767.6
      facial nerve 767.5
      Klumpke (-Déjérine) 767.6
      radial nerve 767.6
      spinal (cord) (hemorrhage) (laceration)
       (rupture) 767.4
    rupture
      intracranial 767.0
      liver 767.8
      spinal cord 767.4
      spleen 767.8
      viscera 767.8
    scalp 767.1
    scalpel wound 767.8
    skeleton NEC 767.3
    specified NEC 767.8
    spinal cord 767.4
    spleen 767.8
    subdural hemorrhage 767.0
    tentorial, tear 767.0
    testes 767.8
    vulva 767.8

Birth—*continued*
  instrumental, NEC, affecting fetus or newborn 763.2
  lack of care, after or at 995.52
  multiple
    affected by maternal complications of pregnancy 761.5
    healthy liveborn—*see* Newborn, multiple
  neglect, after or at 995.52
  newborn—*see* Newborn
  palsy or paralysis NEC 767.7
  precipitate, fetus or newborn 763.6
  premature (infant) 765.1
  prolonged, affecting fetus or newborn 763.9
  retarded, fetus or newborn 763.9
  shock, newborn 779.8
  strangulation or suffocation
    due to aspiration of amniotic fluid 770.1
    mechanical 767.8
  trauma NEC 767.9
  triplet
    affected by maternal complications of pregnancy 761.5
    healthy liveborn—*see* Newborn, multiple
  twin
    affected by maternal complications of pregnancy 761.5
    healthy liveborn—*see* Newborn, twin
  ventouse, affecting fetus or newborn 763.3
Birthmark 757.32
Bisalbuminemia 273.8
Biskra button 085.1
Bite (s)
  with intact skin surface—*see* Contusion
  animal—*see* Wound, open, by site
    intact skin surface—*see* Contusion
  centipede 989.5
  chigger 133.8
  fire ant 989.5
  flea—*see* Injury, superficial, by site
  human (open wound)—*see also* Wound, open, by site
    intact skin surface—*see* Contusion
  insect
    nonvenomous—*see* Injury, superficial, by site
    venomous 989.5
  mad dog (death from) 071
  poisonous 989.5
  red bug 133.8
  reptile 989.5
    nonvenomous—*see* Wound, open, by site
  snake 989.5
    nonvenomous—*see* Wound, open, by site
  spider (venomous) 989.5
    nonvenomous—*see* Injury, superficial, by site
  venomous 989.5
Biting
  cheek or lip 528.9
  nail 307.9
Black
  death 020.9
  eye NEC 921.0
  hairy tongue 529.3
  lung disease 500
Blackfan-Diamond anemia or syndrome (congenital hypoplastic anemia) 284.0
Blackhead 706.1
Blackout 780.2
Blackwater fever 084.8
Bladder —*see* Condition

Blast
  blindness 921.3
  concussion—*see* Blast, injury
  injury 869.0
    with open wound into cavity 869.1
    abdomen or thorax—*see* Injury, internal, by site
    brain (*see also* Concussion, brain) 850.9
      with skull fracture—*see* Fracture, skull
    ear (acoustic nerve trauma) 951.5
      with perforation, tympanic membrane—*see* Wound, open, ear, drum
    lung (*see also* Injury, internal, lung) 861.20
    otitic (explosive) 388.11
Blastomycosis, blastomycotic (chronic) (cutaneous) (disseminated) (lung) (pulmonary) (systemic) 116.0
  Brazilian 116.1
  European 117.5
  keloidal 116.2
  North American 116.0
  primary pulmonary 116.0
  South American 116.1
Bleb(s) 709.8
  emphysematous (bullous) (diffuse) (lung) (ruptured) (solitary) 492.0
  filtering, eye (postglaucoma) (status) V45.69
    with complication 997.99
    postcataract extraction (complication) 997.99
  lung (ruptured) 492.0
    congenital 770.5
  subpleural (emphysematous) 492.0
Bleeder (familial) (hereditary) (*see also* Defect, coagulation) 286.9
  nonfamilial 286.9
Bleeding (*see also* Hemorrhage) 459.0
  anal 569.3
  anovulatory 628.0
  atonic, following delivery 666.1
  capillary 448.9
  due to subinvolution 621.1
    puerperal 666.2
  ear 388.69
  excessive, associated with menopausal onset 627.0
  familial (*see also* Defect, coagulation) 286.9
  following intercourse 626.7
  gastrointestinal 578.9
  gums 523.8
  hemorrhoids—*see* Hemorrhoids, bleeding
  intermenstrual
    irregular 626.6
    regular 626.5
  intraoperative 998.11
  irregular NEC 626.4
  menopausal 627.0
  mouth 528.9
  nipple 611.79
  nose 784.7
  ovulation 626.5
  postclimacteric 627.1
  postcoital 626.7
  postmenopausal 627.1
    following induced menopause 627.4
  postoperative 998.11
  preclimacteric 627.0
  puberty 626.3
    excessive, with onset of menstrual periods 626.3
  rectum, rectal 569.3
  tendencies (*see also* Defect, coagulation) 286.9

Bleeding—*continued*
  throat 784.8
  umbilical stump 772.3
  umbilicus 789.9
  unrelated to menstrual cycle 626.6
  uterus, uterine 626.9
    climacteric 627.0
    dysfunctional 626.8
    functional 626.8
    unrelated to menstrual cycle 626.6
  vagina, vaginal 623.8
    functional 626.8
  vicarious 625.8
Blennorrhagia, blennorrhagic —*see*
  Blennorrhea
Blennorrhea (acute) 098.0
  adultorum 098.40
  alveolaris 523.4
  chronic or duration of 2 months or over 098.2
  gonococcal (neonatorum) 098.40
  inclusion (neonatal) (newborn) 771.6
  neonatorum 098.40
Blepharelosis (*see also* Entropion) 374.00
Blepharitis (eyelid) 373.00
  angularis 373.01
  ciliaris 373.00
    with ulcer 373.01
  marginal 373.00
    with ulcer 373.01
  scrofulous (*see also* Tuberculosis) 017.3
    [373.00]
  squamous 373.02
  ulcerative 373.01
Blepharochalasis 374.34
  congenital 743.62
Blepharoclonus 333.81
Blepharoconjunctivitis (*see also* Conjunctivitis)
  372.20
  angular 372.21
  contact 372.22
Blepharophimosis (eyelid) 374.46
  congenital 743.62
Blepharoplegia 374.89
Blepharoptosis 374.30
  congenital 743.61
Blepharopyorrhea 098.49
Blepharospasm 333.81
Blessig's cyst 362.62
Blighted ovum 631
Blind
  bronchus (congenital) 748.3
  eye—*see also* Blindness
    hypertensive 360.42
    hypotensive 360.41
  loop syndrome (postoperative) 579.2
  sac, fallopian tube (congenital) 752.19
  spot, enlarged 368.42
  tract or tube (congenital) NEC—*see* Atresia
Blindness (acquired) (congenital) (both eyes)
  369.00
  blast 921.3
    with nerve injury—*see* Injury, nerve, optic
  Bright's—*see* Uremia
  color (congenital) 368.59
    acquired 368.55
    blue 368.53
    green 368.52
    red 368.51
    total 368.54
  concussion 950.9
  cortical 377.75

Blindness—*continued*
  day 368.60
    acquired 368.62
    congenital 368.61
    hereditary 368.61
    specified type NEC 368.69
  due to
    injury NEC 950.9
    refractive error—*see* Error, refractive
  eclipse (total) 363.31
  emotional 300.11
  hysterical 300.11
  legal (both eyes) (USA definition) 369.4
    with impairment of better (less impaired) eye
      near-total 369.02
        with
          lesser eye impairment 369.02
            near-total 369.04
            total 369.03
      profound 369.05
        with
          lesser eye impairment 369.05
            near-total 369.07
            profound 369.08
            total 369.06
      severe 369.21
        with
          lesser eye impairment 369.21
            blind 369.11
            near-total 369.13
            profound 369.14
            severe 369.22
            total 369.12
    total
      with lesser eye impairment total 369.01
  mind 784.69
  moderate
    both eyes 369.25
      with impairment of lesser eye (specified as)
        blind, not further specified 369.15
        low vision, not further specified 369.23
        near-total 369.17
        profound 369.18
        severe 369.24
        total 369.16
    one eye 369.74
      with vision of other eye (specified as)
        near-normal 369.75
        normal 369.76
  near-total
    both eyes 369.04
      with impairment of lesser eye (specified as)
        blind, not further specified 369.02
        total 369.03
    one eye 369.64
      with vision of other eye (specified as)
        near-normal 369.65
        normal 369.66
  night 368.60
    acquired 368.62
    congenital (Japanese) 368.61
    hereditary 368.61
    specified type NEC 368.69
    vitamin A deficiency 264.5
  nocturnal—*see* Blindness, night
  one eye 369.60
    with low vision of other eye 369.10
  profound
    both eyes 369.08
      with impairment of lesser eye (specified as)
        blind, not further specified 369.05

Block—*continued*
  portal (vein) 452
  sinoatrial 426.6
  sinoauricular 426.6
  spinal cord 336.9
  trifascicular 426.54
  tubal 628.2
  vein NEC 453.9
Blocq's disease or syndrome (astasia-abasia)
  307.9
Blood
  constituents, abnormal NEC 790.6
  disease 289.9
    specified NEC 289.8
  donor V59.01
    other blood components V59.09
    stem cells V59.02
    whole blood V59.01
  dyscrasia 289.9
    with
      abortion—*see* Abortion, by type, with
        hemorrhage, delayed or excessive
      ectopic pregnancy (*see also* categories
        633.0-633.9) 639.1
      molar pregnancy (*see also* categories
        630-632) 639.1
    fetus or newborn NEC 776.9
    following
      abortion 639.1
      ectopic or molar pregnancy 639.1
    puerperal, postpartum 666.3
  flukes NEC (*see also* Infestation, Schistosoma)
    120.9
  in
    feces (*see also* Melena) 578.1
      occult 792.1
    urine (*see also* Hematuria) 599.7
  mole 631
  occult 792.1
  poisoning (*see also* Septicemia) 038.9
  pressure
    decreased, due to shock following injury 958.4
    fluctuating 796.4
    high (*see also* Hypertension) 401.9
      incidental reading (isolated) (nonspecific),
        without diagnosis of hypertension 796.2
    low (*see also* Hypotension) 458.9
      incidental reading (isolated) (nonspecific),
        without diagnosis of hypotension 796.3
  spitting (*see also* Hemoptysis) 786.3
  staining cornea 371.12
  transfusion
    without reported diagnosis V58.2
    donor V59.01
      stem cells V59.02
    reaction or complication—*see* Complications,
      transfusion
  tumor—*see* Hematoma
  vessel rupture—*see* Hemorrhage
  vomiting (*see also* Hematemesis) 578.0
Blood-forming organ disease 289.9
Bloodgood's disease 610.1
Bloodshot eye 379.93
Bloom (-Machacek) (-Torre) syndrome 757.39
Blotch, palpebral 372.55
Blount's disease (tibia vara) 732.4
Blount-Barber syndrome (tibia vara) 732.4
Blue
  baby 746.9
  bloater 491.20
    with acute bronchitis or exacerbation 491.21

Blue —*continued*
  diaper syndrome 270.0
  disease 746.9
  dome cyst 610.0
  drum syndrome 381.02
  sclera 743.47
    with fragility of bone and deafness 756.51
  toe syndrome—*see* Atherosclerosi*s*
Blueness (*see also* Cyanosis) 782.5
Blurring, visual 368.8
Blushing (abnormal) (excessive) 782.62
Boarder, hospital V65.0
  infant V65.0
Bockhart's impetigo (superficial folliculitis)
  704.8
Bodechtel-Guttmann disease (subacute
  sclerosing panencephalitis) 046.2
Boder-Sedgwick syndrome (ataxia-
  telangiectasia) 334.8
Body, bodies
  Aschoff (*see also* Myocarditis, rheumatic) 398.0
  asteroid, vitreous 379.22
  choroid, colloid (degenerative) 362.57
    hereditary 362.77
  cytoid (retina) 362.82
  drusen (retina) (*see also* Drusen) 362.57
    optic disc 377.21
  fibrin, pleura 511.0
  foreign—*see* Foreign body
  Hassall-Henle 371.41
  loose
    joint (*see also* Loose, body, joint) 718.1
      knee 717.6
    knee 717.6
    sheath, tendon 727.82
  Mallory's 034.1
  Mooser 081.0
  Negri 071
  rice (joint) (*see also* Loose, body, joint) 718.1
    knee 717.6
  rocking 307.3
Boeck's
  disease (sarcoidosis) 135
  lupoid (miliary) 135
  sarcoid 135
Boerhaave's syndrome (spontaneous esophageal
  rupture) 530.4
Boggy
  cervix 622.8
  uterus 621.8
Boil (*see also* Carbuncle) 680.9
  abdominal wall 680.2
  Aleppo 085.1
  ankle 680.6
  anus 680.5
  arm (any part, above wrist) 680.3
  auditory canal, external 680.0
  axilla 680.3
  back (any part) 680.2
  Baghdad 085.1
  breast 680.2
  buttock 680.5
  chest wall 680.2
  corpus cavernosum 607.2
  Delhi 085.1
  ear (any part) 680.0
  eyelid 373.13
  face (any part, except eye) 680.0
  finger (any) 680.4
  flank 680.2
  foot (any part) 680.7

Boil —*continued*
  forearm 680.3
  Gafsa 085.1
  genital organ, male 608.4
  gluteal (region) 680.5
  groin 680.2
  hand (any part) 680.4
  head (any part, except face) 680.8
  heel 680.7
  hip 680.6
  knee 680.6
  labia 616.4
  lacrimal (*see also* Dacryocystitis) 375.30
    gland (*see also* Dacryoadenitis) 375.00
    passages (duct) (sac) (*see also* Dacryocystitis) 375.30
  leg, any part except foot 680.6
  multiple sites 680.9
  Natal 085.1
  neck 680.1
  nose (external) (septum) 680.0
  orbit, orbital 376.01
  partes posteriores 680.5
  pectoral region 680.2
  penis 607.2
  perineum 680.2
  pinna 680.0
  scalp (any part) 680.8
  scrotum 608.4
  seminal vesicle 608.0
  shoulder 680.3
  skin NEC 680.9
  specified site NEC 680.8
  spermatic cord 608.4
  temple (region) 680.0
  testis 608.4
  thigh 680.6
  thumb 680.4
  toe (any) 680.7
  tropical 085.1
  trunk 680.2
  tunica vaginalis 608.4
  umbilicus 680.2
  upper arm 680.3
  vas deferens 608.4
  vulva 616.4
  wrist 680.4
Bold hives (*see also* Urticaria) 708.9
Bolivian hemorrhagic fever 078.7
Bombé, iris 364.74
Bomford-Rhoads anemia (refractory) 284.9
Bone —*see* condition
Bonnevie-Ullrich syndrome 758.6
Bonnier's syndrome 386.19
Bonvale Dam fever 780.79
Bony block of joint 718.80
  ankle 718.87
  elbow 718.82
  foot 718.87
  hand 718.84
  hip 718.85
  knee 718.86
  multiple sites 718.89
  pelvic region 718.85
  shoulder (region) 718.81
  specified site NEC 718.88
  wrist 718.83
Borderline
  intellectual functioning V62.89
  pelvis 653.1
    with obstruction during labor 660.1

Borderline—*continued*
  affecting fetus or newborn 763.1
  psychosis (*see also* Schizophrenia) 295.5
    of childhood (*see also* Psychosis, childhood) 299.8
  schizophrenia (*see also* Schizophrenia) 295.5
Borna disease 062.9
Bornholm disease (epidemic pleurodynia) 074.1
Borrelia vincentii (mouth) (pharynx) (tonsils) 101
Bostock's catarrh (*see also* Fever, hay) 477.9
Boston exanthem 048
Botalli, ductus (patent) (persistent) 747.0
Bothriocephalus latus infestation 123.4
Botulism 005.1
Bouba (*see also* Yaws) 102.9
Bouffée délirante 298.3
Bouillaud's disease or syndrome (rheumatic heart disease) 391.9
Bourneville's disease (tuberous sclerosis) 759.5
Boutonneuse fever 082.1
Boutonniere
  deformity (finger) 736.21
  hand (intrinsic) 736.21
Bouveret (-Hoffmann) disease or syndrome (paroxysmal tachycardia) 427.2
Bovine heart —*see* Hypertrophy, cardiac
Bowel —*see* condition
Bowen's
  dermatosis (precancerous) (M8081/2)—*see* Neoplasm, skin, in situ
  disease (M8081/2)—*see* Neoplasm, skin, in situ
  epithelioma (M8081/2)—*see* Neoplasm, skin, in situ
  type
    epidermoid carcinoma in situ (M8081/2)—*see* Neoplasm, skin, in situ
    intraepidermal squamous cell carcinoma (M8081/2)–*see* Neoplasm, skin, in situ
Bowing
  femur 736.89
    congenital 754.42
  fibula 736.89
    congenital 754.43
  forearm 736.09
    away from midline (cubitus valgus) 736.01
    toward midline (cubitus varus) 736.02
  leg(s), long bones, congenital 754.44
  radius 736.09
    away from midline (cubitus valgus) 736.01
    toward midline (cubitus varus) 736.02
  tibia 736.89
    congenital 754.43
Bowleg (s) 736.42
  congenital 754.44
  rachitic 268.1
Boyd's dysentery 004.2
Brachial —*see* condition
Brachman-de Lange syndrome (Amsterdam dwarf, mental retardation, and brachycephaly) 759.89
Brachycardia 427.89
Brachycephaly 756.0
Brachymorphism and ectopia lentis 759.89
Bradley's disease (epidemic vomiting) 078.82
Bradycardia 427.89
  chronic (sinus) 427.81
  newborn 763.83
  nodal 427.89
  postoperative 997.1
  reflex 337.0

Broken—*continued*
  implant or internal device—*see* listing under
    Complications, mechanical
  neck—*see* Fracture, vertebra, cervical
  nose 802.0
    open 802.1
  tooth, teeth 873.63
    complicated 873.73
Bromhidrosis 705.89
Bromidism, bromism
  acute 967.3
    correct substance properly administered
      349.82
    overdose or wrong substance given or taken
      967.3
  chronic (*see also* Dependence) 304.1
Bromidrosiphobia 300.23
Bromidrosis 705.89
Bronchi, bronchial —*see* condition
Bronchiectasis (cylindrical) (diffuse) (fusiform)
  (localized) (moniliform) (postinfectious)
  (recurrent) (saccular) 494.0
  with acute exacerbation 494.1
  congenital 748.61
  tuberculosis (*see also* Tuberculosis) 011.5
Bronchiolectasis —*see* Bronchiectasis
Bronchiolitis (acute) (infectious) (subacute)
  466.19
  with
    bronchospasm or obstruction 466.19
    influenza, flu, or grippe 487.1
  catarrhal (acute) (subacute) 466.19
  chemical 506.0
    chronic 506.4
  chronic (obliterative) 491.8
  due to external agent—*see* Bronchitis, acute,
    due to
  fibrosa obliterans 491.8
  influenzal 487.1
  obliterans 491.8
    status post lung transplant 996.84
    with organizing pneumonia (B.O.O.P.) 516.8
  obliterative (chronic) (diffuse) (subacute) 491.8
    due to fumes or vapors 506.4
  respiratory syncytial virus 466.11
  vesicular—*see* Pneumonia, broncho-
Bronchitis (diffuse) (hypostatic) (infectious)
  (inflammatory) (simple) 490
  with
    emphysema—*see* Emphysema
    influenza, flu, or grippe 487.1
    obstruction airway, chronic 491.20
      with acute exacerbation 491.21
    tracheitis 490
      acute or subacute 466.0
        with bronchospasm or obstruction 466.0
      chronic 491.8
  acute or subacute 466.0
    with
      bronchospasm 466.0
      chronic
        bronchitis (obstructive) 491.21
        obstructive pulmonary disease (COPD)
          491.21
      obstruction 466.0
      tracheitis 466.0
    chemical (due to fumes or vapors) 506.0
    due to
      fumes or vapors 506.0
      radiation 508.8
  allergic (acute) (*see also* Asthma) 493.9

Bronchitis—*continued*
  arachidic 934.1
  aspiration 507.0
    due to fumes or vapors 506.0
  asthmatic (acute) (*see also* Asthma) 493.9
    chronic 491.20
      with acute bronchitis or acute exacerbation
        491.21
  capillary 466.19
    with bronchospasm or obstruction 466.19
    chronic 491.8
  caseous (*see also* Tuberculosis) 011.3
  Castellani's 104.8
  catarrhal 490
    acute—*see* Bronchitis, acute
    chronic 491.0
  chemical (acute) (subacute) 506.0
    chronic 506.4
    due to fumes or vapors (acute) (subacute)
      506.0
      chronic 506.4
  chronic 491.9
    with
      tracheitis (chronic) 491.8
    asthmatic 491.20
      with acute bronchitis or acute exacerbation
        491.21
    catarrhal 491.0
    chemical (due to fumes and vapors) 506.4
    due to
      fumes or vapors (chemical) (inhalation)
        506.4
      radiation 508.8
      tobacco smoking 491.0
    mucopurulent 491.1
    obstructive 491.20
      with acute bronchitis or acute exacerbation
        491.21
    purulent 491.1
    simple 491.0
    specified type NEC 491.8
  croupous 466.0
    with bronchospasm or obstruction 466.0
    due to fumes or vapors 506.0
  emphysematous 491.20
    with acute bronchitis or acute exacerbation
      491.21
  exudative 466.0
  fetid (chronic) (recurrent) 491.1
  fibrinous, acute or subacute 466.0
    with bronchospasm or obstruction 466.0
  grippal 487.1
  influenzal 487.1
  membranous, acute or subacute 466.0
    with bronchospasm or obstruction 466.0
  moulders' 502
  mucopurulent (chronic) (recurrent) 491.1
    acute or subacute 466.0
  non-obstructive 491.0
  obliterans 491.8
  obstructive (chronic) 491.20
    with acute bronchitis or acute exacerbation
      491.21
  pituitous 491.1
  plastic (inflammatory) 466.0
  pneumococcal, acute or subacute 466.0
    with bronchospasm or obstruction 466.0
  pseudomembranous 466.0
  purulent (chronic) (recurrent) 491.1
    acute or subacute 466.0
      with bronchospasm or obstruction 466.0

Bulky uterus 621.2
Bulla(e) 709.8
   lung (emphysematous) (solitary) 492.0
Bullet wound —*see also* Wound, open, by site
   fracture—*see* Fracture, by site, open
   internal organ (abdomen, chest, or pelvis)—*see*
      Injury, internal, by site, with open wound
   intracranial—*see* Laceration, brain, with open
      wound
Bullis fever 082.8
Bullying (*see also* Disturbance, conduct) 312.0
Bundle
   branch block (complete) (false) (incomplete)
      426.50
     bilateral 426.53
     left (*see also* Block, bundle branch, left) 426.3
       hemiblock 426.2
     right (*see also* Block, bundle branch, right)
       426.4
   of His—*see* condition
   of Kent syndrome (anomalous atrioventricular
      excitation) 426.7
Bungpagga 040.81
Bunion 727.1
Bunionette 727.1
Bunyamwera fever 066.3
Buphthalmia, buphthalmos (congenital) 743.20
   associated with
     keratoglobus, congenital 743.22
     megalocornea 743.22
     ocular anomalies NEC 743.22
   isolated 743.21
   simple 743.21
Bürger-Grütz disease or syndrome (essential
   familial hyperlipemia) 272.3
Buried roots 525.3
Burke's syndrome 577.8
Burkitt's
   tumor (M9750/3) 200.2
   type malignant, lymphoma, lymphoblastic, or
     undifferentiated (M9750/3) 200.2
Burn (acid) (cathode ray) (caustic) (chemical)
   (electric heating appliance) (electricity) (fire)
   (flame) (hot liquid or object) (irradiation)
   (lime) (radiation) (steam) (thermal) (x-ray)
   949.0

---

*Note—Use the following fifth-digit
subclassification with category 948 to indicate
the percent of body surface with third degree
burn:*

0 less than 10% or unspecified
1 10-19%
2 20-29%
3 30-39%
4 40-49%
5 50-59%
6 60-69%
7 70-79%
8 80-89%
9 90% or more of body surface

---

   with
     blisters—*see* Burn, by site, second degree
     erythema—*see* Burn, by site, first degree
     skin loss (epidermal)—*see also* Burn, by site,
       second degree
      full thickness—*see also* Burn, by site, third
       degree
       with necrosis of underlying tissues—*see*
        Burn, by site, third degree, deep

Burn—*continued*
   first degree—*see* Burn, by site, first degree
   second degree—*see* Burn, by site, second degree
   third degree—*see also* Burn, by site, third
     degree
     deep—*see* Burn, by site, third degree, deep
   abdomen, abdominal (muscle) (wall) 942.03
     with
       trunk—*see* Burn, trunk, multiple sites
     first degree 942.13
     second degree 942.23
     third degree 942.33
      deep 942.43
       with loss of body part 942.53
   ankle 945.03
     with
       lower limb(s)–*see* Burn, leg, multiple sites
     first degree 945.13
     second degree 945.23
     third degree 945.33
      deep 945.43
       with loss of body part 945.53
   anus—*see* Burn, trunk, specified site NEC
   arm(s) 943.00
     first degree 943.10
     second degree 943.20
     third degree 943.30
      deep 943.40
       with loss of body part 943.50
     lower—*see* Burn, forearm(s)
     multiple sites, except hand(s) or wrist(s)
      943.09
      first degree 943.19
      second degree 943.29
      third degree 943.39
       deep 943.49
        with loss of body part 943.59
     upper 943.03
      first degree 943.13
      second degree 943.23
      third degree 943.33
       deep 943.43
        with loss of body part 943.53
   auditory canal (external)—*see* Burn, ear
   auricle (ear)—*see* Burn, ear
   axilla 943.04
     with
       upper limb(s) except hand(s) or
        wrist(s)—*see* Burn, arm(s), multiple sites
     first degree 943.14
     second degree 943.24
     third degree 943.34
      deep 943.44
       with loss of body part 943.54
   back 942.04
     with
       trunk—*see* Burn, trunk, multiple sites
     first degree 942.14
     second degree 942.24
     third degree 942.34
      deep 942.44—
       with loss of body part 942.54
   biceps
     brachii—*see* Burn, arm(s), upper
     femoris—*see* Burn, thigh
   breast(s) 942.01
     with
       trunk—*see* Burn, trunk, multiple sites
     first degree 942.11
     second degree 942.21

Burn—*continued*
  tonsil 947.0
  trachea 947.1
  trunk 942.00
    first degree 942.10
    second degree 942.20
    third degree 942.30
      deep 942.40
        with loss of body part 942.50
    multiple sites 942.09
      first degree 942.19
      second degree 942.29
      third degree 942.39
        deep 942.49
          with loss of body part 942.59
    specified site NEC 942.09
      first degree 942.19
      second degree 942.29
      third degree 942.39
        deep 942.49
          with loss of body part 942.59
  tunica vaginalis—*see* Burn, genitourinary
    organs, external
  tympanic membrane—*see* Burn, ear
  tympanum—*see* Burn, ear
  unspecified site (multiple) 949.0
    with extent of body surface involved specified
      less than 10 percent 948.0
      10-19 percent 948.1
      20-29 percent 948.2
      30-39 percent 948.3
      40-49 percent 948.4
      50-59 percent 948.5
      60-69 percent 948.6
      70-79 percent 948.7
      80-89 percent 948.8
      90 percent or more 948.9
    first degree 949.1
    second degree 949.2
    third degree 949.3
      deep 949.4
        with loss of body part 949.5
  uterus 947.4
  uvula 947.0
  vagina 947.4
  vulva—*see* Burn, genitourinary organs, external
  wrist(s) 944.07
    with
      hand(s)—*see* Burn, hand(s), multiple sites
    first degree 944.17
    second degree 944.27
    third degree 944.37
      deep 944.47
        with loss of body part 944.57
Burnett's syndrome (milk-alkali) 999.9
Burnier's syndrome (hypophyseal dwarfism)
  253.3
Burning
  feet syndrome 266.2
  sensation (*see also* Disturbance, sensation) 782.0
  tongue 529.6
Burns' disease (osteochondrosis, lower ulna)
  732.3
Bursa —*see also* condition
  pharynx 478.29
Bursitis NEC 727.3
  Achilles tendon 726.71
  adhesive 726.90
    shoulder 726.0
  ankle 726.79
  buttock 726.5
  calcaneal 726.79

Bursitis—*continued*
  collateral ligament
    fibular 726.63
    tibial 726.62
  Duplay's 726.2
  elbow 726.33
  finger 726.8
  foot 726.79
  gonococcal 098.52
  hand 726.4
  hip 726.5
  infrapatellar 726.69
  ischiogluteal 726.5
  knee 726.60
  occupational NEC 727.2
  olecranon 726.33
  pes anserinus 726.61
  pharyngeal 478.29
  popliteal 727.51
  prepatellar 726.65
  radiohumeral 727.3
  scapulohumeral 726.19
    adhesive 726.0
  shoulder 726.10
    adhesive 726.0
  subacromial 726.19
    adhesive 726.0
  subcoracoid 726.19
  subdeltoid 726.19
    adhesive 726.0
  subpatellar 726.69
  syphilitic 095.7
  Thornwaldt's, Tornwaldt's (pharyngeal) 478.29
  toe 726.79
  trochanteric area 726.5
  wrist 726.4
Burst stitches or sutures (complication of
  surgery) 998.3
Buruli ulcer 031.1
Bury's disease (erythema elevatum diutinum)
  695.89
Buschke's disease or scleredema (adultorum)
  710.1
Busquet's disease (osteoperiostitis) (*see also*
  Osteomyelitis) 730.1
Busse-Buschke disease (cryptococcosis) 117.5
Buttock —*see* condition
Button
  Biskra 085.1
  Delhi 085.1
  oriental 085.1
Buttonhole hand (intrinsic) 736.21
Bwamba fever (encephalitis) 066.3
Byssinosis (occupational) 504
Bywaters' syndrome 958.5

C

Cacergasia 300.9
Cachexia 799.4
cancerous (M8000/3) 199.1
cardiac—*see* Disease, heart
dehydration 276.5
with
hypernatremia 276.0
hyponatremia 276.1
due to malnutrition 261
exophthalmic 242.0
heart—*see* Disease, heart
hypophyseal 253.2
hypopituitary 253.2
lead 984.9
specified type of lead—*see* Table of drugs and chemicals
malaria 084.9
malignant (M8000/3) 199.1
marsh 084.9
nervous 300.5
old age 797
pachydermic—*see* Hypothyroidism
paludal 084.9
pituitary (postpartum) 253.2
renal (*see also* Disease, renal) 593.9
saturnine 984.9
specified type of lead—*see* Table of drugs and chemicals
senile 797
Simmonds' (pituitary cachexia) 253.2
splenica 289.59
strumipriva (*see also* Hypothyroidism) 244.9
tuberculous NEC (*see also* Tuberculosis) 011.9
café au lait spots 709.09
Caffey's disease or syndrome (infantile cortical hyperostosis) 756.59
Caisson disease 993.3
Caked breast (puerperal, postpartum) 676.2
Cake kidney 753.3
Calabar swelling 125.2
Calcaneal spur 726.73
Calcaneoapophysitis 732.5
Calcaneonavicular bar 755.67
Calcareous —*see* condition
Calcicosis (occupational) 502
Calciferol (vitamin D) deficiency 268.9
with
osteomalacia 268.2
rickets (*see also* Rickets) 268.0
Calcification
adrenal (capsule) (gland) 255.4
tuberculous (*see also* Tuberculosis) 017.6
aorta 440.0
artery (annular)—*see* Arteriosclerosis
auricle (ear) 380.89
bladder 596.8
due to S. hematobium 120.0
brain (cortex)—*see* Calcification, cerebral
bronchus 519.1
bursa 727.82
cardiac (*see also* Degeneration, myocardial) 429.1
cartilage (postinfectional) 733.99
cerebral (cortex) 348.8
artery 437.0
cervix (uteri) 622.8
choroid plexus 349.2
conjunctiva 372.54

Calcification—*continued*
corpora cavernosa (penis) 607.89
cortex (brain)—*see* Calcification, cerebral
dental pulp (nodular) 522.2
dentinal papilla 520.4
disc, intervertebral 722.90
cervical, cervicothoracic 722.91
lumbar, lumbosacral 722.93
thoracic, thoracolumbar 722.92
fallopian tube 620.8
falx cerebri—*see* Calcification, cerebral
fascia 728.89
gallbladder 575.8
general 275.40
heart (*see also* Degeneration, myocardial) 429.1
valve—*see* Endocarditis
intervertebral cartilage or disc (postinfectional) 722.90
cervical, cervicothoracic 722.91
lumbar, lumbosacral 722.93
thoracic, thoracolumbar 722.92
intracranial—*see* Calcification, cerebral
intraspinal ligament 728.89
joint 719.80
ankle 719.87
elbow 719.82
foot 719.87
hand 719.84
hip 719.85
knee 719.86
multiple sites 719.89
pelvic region 719.85
shoulder (region) 719.81
specified site NEC 719.88
wrist 719.83
kidney 593.89
tuberculous (*see also* Tuberculosis) 016.0
larynx (senile) 478.79
lens 366.8
ligament 728.89
intraspinal 728.89
knee (medial collateral) 717.89
lung 518.89
active 518.89
postinfectional 518.89
tuberculous (*see also* Tuberculosis, pulmonary) 011.9
lymph gland or node (postinfectional) 289.3
tuberculous (*see also* Tuberculosis, lymph gland) 017.2
massive (paraplegic) 728.10
medial NEC (*see also* Arteriosclerosis, extremities) 440.20
meninges (cerebral) 349.2
metastatic 275.40
Mönckeberg's—*see* Arteriosclerosis
muscle 728.10
heterotopic, postoperative 728.13
myocardium, myocardial (*see also* Degeneration, myocardial) 429.1
ovary 620.8
pancreas 577.8
penis 607.99
periarticular 728.89
pericardium (*see also* Pericarditis) 423.8
pineal gland 259.8
pleura 511.0
postinfectional 518.89

Calcification—*continued*
 tuberculous (*see also* Tuberculosis, pleura)
  012.0
 pulp (dental) (nodular) 522.2
 renal 593.89
 rider's bone 733.99
 sclera 379.16
 semilunar cartilage 717.89
 spleen 289.59
 subcutaneous 709.3
 suprarenal (capsule) (gland) 255.4
 tendon (sheath) 727.82
  with bursitis, synovitis or tenosynovitis 727.82
 trachea 519.1
 ureter 593.89
 uterus 621.8
 vitreous 379.29
Calcified —*see also* Calcification
 hematoma NEC 959.9
Calcinosis (generalized) (interstitial) (tumoral)
  (universalis) 275.49
 circumscripta 709.3
 cutis 709.3
 intervertebralis 275.49 *[722.90]*
 Raynaud's
  phenomenonsclerodactylytelangiectasis
  (CRST) 710.1
Calcium
 blood
  high (*see also* Hypercalcemia) 275.42
  low (*see also* Hypocalcemia) 275.41
 deposits—*see also* Calcification, by site
  in bursa 727.82
  in tendon (sheath) 727.82
   with bursitis, synovitis or tenosynovitis
    727.82
 salts or soaps in vitreous 379.22
Calciuria 791.9
Calculi —*see* Calculus
Calculosis, intrahepatic —*see*
 Choledocholithiasis
Calculus, calculi, calculous 592.9
 ampulla of Vater—*see* Choledocholithiasis
 anuria (impacted) (recurrent) 592.0
 appendix 543.9
 bile duct (any)—*see* Choledocholithiasis
 biliary—*see* Cholelithiasis
 bilirubin, multiple—*see* Cholelithiasis
 bladder (encysted) (impacted) (urinary) 594.1
  diverticulum 594.0
 bronchus 518.89
 calyx (kidney) (renal) 592.0
  congenital 753.3
 cholesterol (pure) (solitary)—*see* Cholelithiasis
 common duct (bile)—*see* Choledocholithiasis
 conjunctiva 372.54
 cystic 594.1
  duct—*see* Cholelithiasis
 dental 523.6
  subgingival 523.6
  supragingival 523.6
 epididymis 608.89
 gallbladder—*see also* Cholelithiasis
  congenital 751.69
 hepatic (duct)—*see* Choledocholithiasis
 intestine (impaction) (obstruction) 560.39
 kidney (impacted) (multiple) (pelvis) (recurrent)
  (staghorn) 592.0
  congenital 753.3
 lacrimal (passages) 375.57
 liver (impacted)—*see* Choledocholithiasis

Calculus, calculi, calculous—*continued*
 lung 518.89
 nephritic (impacted) (recurrent) 592.0
 nose 478.1
 pancreas (duct) 577.8
 parotid gland 527.5
 pelvis, encysted 592.0
 prostate 602.0
 pulmonary 518.89
 renal (impacted) (recurrent) 592.0
  congenital 753.3
 salivary (duct) (gland) 527.5
 seminal vesicle 608.89
 staghorn 592.0
 Stensen's duct 527.5
 sublingual duct or gland 527.5
  congenital 750.26
 submaxillary duct, gland, or region 527.5
 suburethral 594.8
 tonsil 474.8
 tooth, teeth 523.6
 tunica vaginalis 608.89
 ureter (impacted) (recurrent) 592.1
 urethra (impacted) 594.2
 urinary (duct) (impacted) (passage) (tract) 592.9
  lower tract NEC 594.9
   specified site 594.8
 vagina 623.8
 vesical (impacted) 594.1
 Wharton's duct 527.5
Caliectasis 593.89
California
 disease 114.0
 encephalitis 062.5
Caligo cornea 371.03
Callositas, callosity (infected) 700
Callus (infected) 700
 bone 726.91
 excessive, following fracture—*see also* Late,
  effect (of), fracture
Calvé (-Perthes) disease (osteochondrosis,
 femoral capital) 732.1
Calvities (*see also* Alopecia) 704.00
Cameroon fever (*see also* Malaria) 084.6
Camptocormia 300.11
Camptodactyly (congenital) 755.59
Camurati-Engelmann disease (diaphyseal
 sclerosis) 756.59
Canal— *see* condition
Canaliculitis (lacrimal) (acute) 375.31
 Actinomyces 039.8
 chronic 375.41
Canavan's disease 330.0
Cancer (M8000/3)—*see also* Neoplasm, by site,
 malignant

Note—The term "cancer" when modified by an adjective or adjectival phrase indicating a morphological type should be coded in the same manner as "carcinoma" with that adjective or phrase. Thus, "squamous-cell cancer" should be coded in the same manner as "squamous-cell carcinoma," which appears in the list under "Carcinoma."

 bile duct type (M8160/3), liver 155.1
 hepatocellular (M8170/3) 155.0
Cancerous (M8000/3)—*see* Neoplasm, by site,
 malignant
Cancerphobia 300.29
Cancrum oris 528.1

Candidiasis, candidal 112.9
  with pneumonia 112.4
  balanitis 112.2
  congenital 771.7
  disseminated 112.5
  endocarditis 112.81
  esophagus 112.84
  intertrigo 112.3
  intestine 112.85
  lung 112.4
  meningitis 112.83
  mouth 112.0
  nails 112.3
  neonatal 771.7
  onychia 112.3
  otitis externa 112.82
  otomycosis 112.82
  paronychia 112.3
  perionyxis 112.3
  pneumonia 112.4
  pneumonitis 112.4
  skin 112.3
  specified site NEC 112.89
  systemic 112.5
  urogenital site NEC 112.2
  vagina 112.1
  vulva 112.1
  vulvovaginitis 112.1
Candidiosis —*see* Candidiasis
Candiru infection or infestation 136.8
Canities (premature) 704.3
  congenital 757.4
Canker (mouth) (sore) 528.2
  rash 034.1
Cannabinosis 504
Canton fever 081.9
Cap
  cradle 690.11
Capillariasis 127.5
Capillary —*see* condition
Caplan's syndrome 714.81
Caplan-Colinet syndrome 714.81
Capsule —*see* condition
Capsulitis (joint) 726.90
  adhesive (shoulder) 726.0
  hip 726.5
  knee 726.60
  labyrinthine 387.8
  thyroid 245.9
  wrist 726.4
Caput
  crepitus 756.0
  medusae 456.8
  succedaneum 767.1
Carapata disease 087.1
Carate —*see* Pinta
Carboxyhemoglobinemia 986
Carbuncle 680.9
  abdominal wall 680.2
  ankle 680.6
  anus 680.5
  arm (any part, above wrist) 680.3
  auditory canal, external 680.0
  axilla 680.3
  back (any part) 680.2
  breast 680.2
  buttock 680.5
  chest wall 680.2
  corpus cavernosum 607.2
  ear (any part) (external) 680.0
  eyelid 373.13

Carbuncle—*continued*
  face (any part, except eye) 680.0
  finger (any) 680.4
  flank 680.2
  foot (any part) 680.7
  forearm 680.3
  genital organ (male) 608.4
  gluteal (region) 680.5
  groin 680.2
  hand (any part) 680.4
  head (any part, except face) 680.8
  heel 680.7
  hip 680.6
  kidney (*see also* Abscess, kidney) 590.2
  knee 680.6
  labia 616.4
  lacrimal
    gland (*see also* Dacryoadenitis) 375.00
    passages (duct) (sac) (*see also* Dacryocystitis)
      375.30
  leg, any part except foot 680.6
  lower extremity, any part except foot 680.6
  malignant 022.0
  multiple sites 680.9
  neck 680.1
  nose (external) (septum) 680.0
  orbit, orbital 376.01
  partes posteriores 680.5
  pectoral region 680.2
  penis 607.2
  perineum 680.2
  pinna 680.0
  scalp (any part) 680.8
  scrotum 608.4
  seminal vesicle 608.0
  shoulder 680.3
  skin NEC 680.9
  specified site NEC 680.8
  spermatic cord 608.4
  temple (region) 680.0
  testis 608.4
  thigh 680.6
  thumb 680.4
  toe (any) 680.7
  trunk 680.2
  tunica vaginalis 608.4
  umbilicus 680.2
  upper arm 680.3
  urethra 597.0
  vas deferens 608.4
  vulva 616.4
  wrist 680.4
Carbunculus (*see also* Carbuncle) 680.9
Carcinoid (tumor) (M8240/1)—*see also*
  Neoplasm, by site, uncertain behavior
  and struma ovarii (M9091/1) 236.2
  argentaffin (M8241/1)—*see* Neoplasm, by site
    uncertain behavior
    malignant (M8241/3)—*see* Neoplasm, by site,
      malignant
  benign (M9091/0) 220
  composite (M8244/3)—*see* Neoplasm, by site,
    malignant
  goblet cell (M8243/3)—*see* Neoplasm, by site,
    malignant
  malignant (M8240/3)—*see* Neoplasm, by site,
    malignant
  nonargentaffin (M8242/1)—*see also* Neoplasm,
    by site, uncertain behavior
    malignant (M8242/3)—*see* Neoplasm, by site,
      malignant

Carcinoid—*continued*
  strumal (M9091/1) 236.2
  syndrome (intestinal) (metastatic) 259.2
  type bronchial adenoma (M8240/3)—*see*
    Neoplasm, lung, malignant
Carcinoidosis 259.2
Carcinoma (M8010/3)—*see also* Neoplasm, by
  site, malignant

> *Note—Except where otherwise indicated, the*
> *morphological varieties of carcinoma in the list*
> *below should be coded by site as for*
> *"Neoplasm, malignant."*

  with
    apocrine metaplasia (M8573/3)
    cartilaginous (and osseous) metaplasia
      (M8571/3)
    osseous (and cartilaginous) metaplasia
      (M8571/3)
    productive fibrosis (M8141/3)
    spindle cell metaplasia (M8572/3)
    squamous metaplasia (M8570/3)
  acidophil (M8280/3)
    specified site—*see* Neoplasm, by site,
      malignant
    unspecified site 194.3
  acidophil-basophil, mixed (M8281/3)
    specified site—*see* Neoplasm, by site,
      malignant
    unspecified site 194.3
  acinar (cell) (M8550/3)
  acinic cell (M8550/3)
  adenocystic (M8200/3)
  adenoid
    cystic (M8200/3)
    squamous cell (M8075/3)
  adenosquamous (M8560/3)
  adnexal (skin) (M8390/3)—*see* Neoplasm, skin,
    malignant
  adrenal cortical (M8370/3) 194.0
  alveolar (M8251/3)
    cell (M8250/3)—*see* Neoplasm, lung,
      malignant
  anaplastic type (M8021/3)
  apocrine (M8401/3)
    breast—*see* Neoplasm, breast, malignant
    specified site NEC—*see* Neoplasm, skin,
      malignant
    unspecified site 173.9
  basal cell (pigmented) (M8090/3)—*see also*
    Neoplasm, skin, malignant
    fibro-epithelial type (M8093/3)—*see*
      Neoplasm, skin, malignant
    morphea type (M8092/3)—*see* Neoplasm,
      skin, malignant
    multicentric (M8091/3)—*see* Neoplasm, skin,
      malignant
  basaloid (M8123/3)
  basal-squamous cell, mixed (M8094/3)—*see*
    Neoplasm, skin, malignant
  basophil (M8300/3)
    specified site—*see* Neoplasm, by site,
      malignant
    unspecified site 194.3
  basophil-acidophil, mixed (M8281/3)
    specified site—*see* Neoplasm, by site,
      malignant
    unspecified site 194.3
  basosquamous (M8094/3)—*see* Neoplasm,
    skin, malignant

Carcinoma—*continued*
  bile duct type (M8160/3)
    and hepatocellular, mixed (M8180/3) 155.0
    liver 155.1
    specified site NEC—*see* Neoplasm, by site,
      malignant
    unspecified site 155.1
  branchial or branchiogenic 146.8
  bronchial or bronchogenic—*see* Neoplasm,
    lung, malignant
  bronchiolar (terminal) (M8250/3)—*see*
    Neoplasm, lung, malignant
  bronchiolo-alveolar (M8250/3)—*see* Neoplasm,
    lung, malignant
  bronchogenic (epidermoid) 162.9
  C cell (M8510/3)
    specified site—*see* Neoplasm, by site,
      malignant
    unspecified site 193
  ceruminous (M8420/3) 173.2
  chorionic (M9100/3)
    specified site—*see* Neoplasm, by site,
      malignant
    unspecified site
      female 181
      male 186.9
  chromophobe (M8270/3)
    specified site—*see* Neoplasm, by site,
      malignant
    unspecified site 194.3
  clear cell (mesonephroid type) (M8310/3)
  cloacogenic (M8124/3)
    specified site—*see* Neoplasm, by site,
      malignant
    unspecified site 154.8
  colloid (M8480/3)
  cribriform (M8201/3)
  cylindroid type (M8200/3)
  diffuse type (M8145/3)
    specified site—*see* Neoplasm, by site,
      malignant
    unspecified site 151.9
  duct (cell) (M8500/3)
    with Paget's disease (M8541/3)—*see*
      Neoplasm, breast, malignant
    infiltrating (M8500/3)
      specified site—*see* Neoplasm, by site,
        malignant
      unspecified site 174.9
  ductal (M8500/3)
  ductular, infiltrating (M8521/3)
  embryonal (M9070/3)
    and teratoma, mixed (M9081/3)
    combined with choriocarcinoma
      (M9101/3)—*see* Neoplasm, by site,
      malignant
    infantile type (M9071/3)
    liver 155.0
    polyembryonal type (M9072/3)
  endometrioid (M8380/3)
  eosinophil (M8280/3)
    specified site—*see* Neoplasm, by site,
      malignant
    unspecified site 194.3
  epidermoid (M8070/3)—*see also* Carcinoma,
    squamous cell
    and adenocarcinoma, mixed (M8560/3)
    in situ, Bowen's type (M8081/2)—*see*
      Neoplasm, skin, in situ
    intradermal—*see* Neoplasm, skin, in situ

Carcinoma—*continued*
  fibroepithelial type basal cell (M8093/3)—*see*
    Neoplasm, skin, malignant
  follicular (M8330/3)
    and papillary (mixed) (M8340/3) 193
    moderately differentiated type (M8332/3) 193
    pure follicle type (M8331/3) 193
    specified site—*see* Neoplasm, by site,
      malignant
    trabecular type (M8332/3) 193
    unspecified site 193
    well differentiated type (M8331/3) 193
  gelatinous (M8480/3)
  giant cell (M8031/3)
    and spindle cell (M8030/3)
  granular cell (M8320/3)
  granulosa cell (M8620/3) 183.0
  hepatic cell (M8170/3) 155.0
  hepatocellular (M8170/3) 155.0
    and bile duct, mixed (M8180/3)
      155.0
  hepatocholangiolitic (M8180/3) 155.0
  Hurthle cell (thyroid) 193
  hypernephroid (M8311/3)
  in
    adenomatous
      polyp (M8210/3)
      polyposis coli (M8220/3) 153.9
    pleomorphic adenoma (M8940/3)
    polypoid adenoma (M8210/3)
    situ (M8010/3)—*see* Carcinoma,
      in situ
    tubular adenoma (M8210/3)
    villous adenoma (M8261/3)
  infiltrating duct (M8500/3)
    with Paget's disease (M8541/3)—*see*
      Neoplasm, breast, malignant
    specified site—*see* Neoplasm, by site,
      malignant
    unspecified site 174.9
  inflammatory (M8530/3)
    specified site—*see* Neoplasm, by site,
      malignant
    unspecified site 174.9
  in situ (M8010/2)—*see also* Neoplasm, by site,
    in situ
    epidermoid (M8070/2)—*see also* Neoplasm,
      by site, in situ
      with questionable stromal invasion
        (M8076/2)
        specified site—*see* Neoplasm, by site, in
          situ
        unspecified site 233.1
      Bowen's type (M8081/2)—*see* Neoplasm,
        skin, in situ
    intraductal (M8500/2)
      specified site—*see* Neoplasm, by site, in situ
      unspecified site 233.0
    lobular (M8520/2)
      specified site—*see* Neoplasm, by site, in situ
      unspecified site 233.0
    papillary (M8050/2)—*see* Neoplasm, by site,
      in situ
    squamous cell (M8070/2)—*see also*
      Neoplasm, by site, in situ
  with questionable stromal invasion (M8076/2)
      specified site—*see* Neoplasm, by site, in
        situ
      unspecified site 233.1
    transitional cell (M8120/2)—*see* Neoplasm,
      by site, in situ

Carcinoma—*continued*
  intestinal type (M8144/3)
    specified site—*see* Neoplasm, by site,
      malignant
    unspecified site 151.9
  intraductal (noninfiltrating) (M8500/2)
    papillary (M8503/2)
      specified site—*see* Neoplasm, by site, in situ
      unspecified site 233.0
    specified site—*see* Neoplasm, by site, in situ
    unspecified site 233.0
  intraepidermal (M8070/2)—*see also* Neoplasm,
    skin, in situ
    squamous cell, Bowen's type (M8081/2)—*see*
      Neoplasm, skin, in situ
  intraepithelial (M8010/2)—*see also* Neoplasm,
    by site, in situ
    squamous cell (M8072/2)—*see* Neoplasm, by
      site, in situ
  intraosseous (M9270/3) 170.1
    upper jaw (bone) 170.0
  islet cell (M8150/3)
    and exocrine, mixed (M8154/3)
      specified site—*see* Neoplasm, by site,
        malignant
      unspecified site 157.9
    pancreas 157.4
    specified site NEC—*see* Neoplasm, by site,
      malignant
    unspecified site 157.4
  juvenile, breast (M8502/3)—*see* Neoplasm,
    breast, malignant
  Kulchitsky's cell (carcinoid tumor of intestine)
    259.2
  large cell (M8012/3)
    squamous cell, nonkeratinizing type
      (M8072/3)
  Leydig cell (testis) (M8650/3)
    specified site—*see* Neoplasm, by site,
      malignant
    unspecified site 186.9
      female 183.0
      male 186.9
  liver cell (M8170/3) 155.0
  lobular (infiltrating) (M8520/3)
    non-infiltrating (M8520/3)
      specified site—*see* Neoplasm, by site, in situ
      unspecified site 233.0
    specified site—*see* Neoplasm, by site,
      malignant
    unspecified site 174.9
  lymphoepithelial (M8082/3)
  medullary (M8510/3)
    with
      amyloid stroma (M8511/3)
        specified site—*see* Neoplasm, by site,
          malignant
        unspecified site 193
      lymphoid stroma (M8512/3)
        specified site—*see* Neoplasm, by site,
          malignant
        unspecified site 174.9
  mesometanephric (M9110/3)
  mesonephric (M9110/3)
  metastatic (M8010/6)—*see* Metastasis, cancer
  metatypical (M8095/3)—*see* Neoplasm, skin,
    malignant
  morphea type basal cell (M8092/3)—*see*
    Neoplasm, skin, malignant
  mucinous (M8480/3)
  mucin-producing (M8481/3)

Catalepsy 300.11
  catatonic (acute) (*see also* Schizophrenia) 295.2
  hysterical 300.11
  schizophrenic (*see also* Schizophrenia) 295.2
Cataphasia 307.0
Cataplexy (idiopathic) 347
Cataract (anterior cortical) (anterior polar)
    (black) (capsular) (central) (cortical)
    (hypermature) (immature) (incipient) (mature)
    366.9
  anterior
    and posterior axial embryonal 743.33
    pyramidal 743.31
    subcapsular polar
      infantile, juvenile, or presenile 366.01
      senile 366.13
  associated with
    calcinosis 275.40 *[366.42]*
    craniofacial dysostosis 756.0 *[366.44]*
    galactosemia 271.1 *[366.44]*
    hypoparathyroidism 252.1 *[366.42]*
    myotonic disorders 359.2 *[366.43]*
    neovascularization 366.33
  blue dot 743.39
  cerulean 743.39
  complicated NEC 366.30
  congenital 743.30
    capsular or subcapsular 743.31
    cortical 743.32
    nuclear 743.33
    specified type NEC 743.39
    total or subtotal 743.34
    zonular 743.32
  coronary (congenital) 743.39
    acquired 366.12
  cupuliform 366.14
  diabetic 250.5 *[366.41]*
  drug-induced 366.45
  due to
    chalcosis 360.24 *[366.34]*
    chronic choroiditis (*see also* Choroiditis)
      363.20 *[366.32]*
    degenerative myopia 360.21 *[366.34]*
    glaucoma (*see also* Glaucoma) 365.9 *[366.31]*
    infection, intraocular NEC 366.32
    inflammatory ocular disorder NEC 366.32
    iridocyclitis, chronic 364.10 *[366.33]*
    pigmentary retinal dystrophy 362.74 *[366.34]*
    radiation 366.46
  electric 366.46
  glassblowers' 366.46
  heat ray 366.46
  heterochromic 366.33
  in eye disease NEC 366.30
  infantile (*see also* Cataract, juvenile) 366.00
  intumescent 366.12
  irradiational 366.46
  juvenile 366.00
    anterior subcapsular polar 366.01
    combined forms 366.09
    cortical 366.03
    lamellar 366.03
    nuclear 366.04
    posterior subcapsular polar 366.02
    specified NEC 366.09
    zonular 366.03
  lamellar 743.32
    infantile, juvenile, or presenile 366.03
  morgagnian 366.18
  myotonic 359.2 *[366.43]*
  myxedema 244.9 *[366.44]*

Cataract—*continued*
  nuclear 366.16
  posterior, polar (capsular) 743.31
    infantile, juvenile, or presenile 366.02
    senile 366.14
  presenile (*see also* Cataract, juvenile) 366.00
  punctate
    acquired 366.12
    congenital 743.39
  secondary (membrane) 366.50
    obscuring vision 366.53
    specified type, not obscuring vision 366.52
  senile 366.10
    anterior subcapsular polar 366.13
    combined forms 366.19
    cortical 366.15
    hypermature 366.18
    immature 366.12
    incipient 366.12
    mature 366.17
    nuclear 366.16
    posterior subcapsular polar 366.14
    specified NEC 366.19
    total or subtotal 366.17
  snowflake 250.5 *[366.41]*
  specified NEC 366.8
  subtotal (senile) 366.17
    congenital 743.34
  sunflower 360.24 *[366.34]*
  tetanic NEC 252.1 *[366.42]*
  total (mature) (senile) 366.17
    congenital 743.34
    localized 366.21
    traumatic 366.22
  toxic 366.45
  traumatic 366.20
    partially resolved 366.23
    total 366.22
  zonular (perinuclear) 743.32
    infantile, juvenile, or presenile 366.03
Cataracta 366.10
  brunescens 366.16
  cerulea 743.39
  complicata 366.30
  congenita 743.30
  coralliformis 743.39
  coronaria (congenital) 743.39
    acquired 366.12
  diabetic 250.5 *[366.41]*
  floriformis 360.24 *[366.34]*
  membranacea
    accreta 366.50
    congenita 743.39
  nigra 366.16
Catarrh, catarrhal (inflammation) (*see also*
    condition) 460
  acute 460
  asthma, asthmatic (*see also* Asthma) 493.9
  Bostock's (*see also* Fever, hay) 477.9
  bowel—*see* Enteritis
  bronchial 490
    acute 466.0
    chronic 491.0
    subacute 466.0
  cervix, cervical (canal) (uteri)—*see* Cervicitis
  chest (*see also* Bronchitis) 490
  chronic 472.0
  congestion 472.0
  conjunctivitis 372.03
  due to syphilis 095.9
    congenital 090.0

Cellulitis—*continued*
  face (any part, except eye) 682.0
  finger (intrathecal) (periosteal) (subcutaneous)
      (subcuticular) 681.00
  flank 682.2
  foot (except toe) 682.7
  forearm 682.3
  gangrenous (*see also* Gangrene) 785.4
  genital organ NEC
      female—*see* Abscess, genital organ, female
      male 608.4
  glottis 478.71
  gluteal (region) 682.5
  gonococcal NEC 098.0
  groin 682.2
  hand (except finger or thumb) 682.4
  head (except face) NEC 682.8
  heel 682.7
  hip 682.6
  jaw (region) 682.0
  knee 682.6
  labium (majus) (minus) (*see also* Vulvitis)
      616.10
  larynx 478.71
  leg, except foot 682.6
  lip 528.5
  mammary gland 611.0
  mouth (floor) 528.3
  multiple sites NEC 682.9
  nasopharynx 478.21
  navel 682.2
      newborn NEC 771.4
  neck (region) 682.1
  nipple 611.0
  nose 478.1
      external 682.0
  orbit, orbital 376.01
  palate (soft) 528.3
  pectoral (region) 682.2
  pelvis, pelvic
      with
          abortion—*see* Abortion, by type, with sepsis
          ectopic pregnancy (*see also* categories
              633.0-633.9) 639.0
          molar pregnancy (*see also* categories
              630-632) 639.0
      female (*see also* Disease, pelvis,
          inflammatory) 614.4
          acute 614.3
      following
          abortion 639.0
          ectopic or molar pregnancy 639.0
      male (*see also* Abscess, peritoneum) 567.2
      puerperal, postpartum, childbirth 670
  penis 607.2
  perineal, perineum 682.2
  perirectal 566
  peritonsillar 475
  periurethral 597.0
  periuterine (*see also* Disease, pelvis,
      inflammatory) 614.4
      acute 614.3
  pharynx 478.21
  phlegmonous NEC 682.9
  rectum 566
  retromammary 611.0
  retroperitoneal (*see also* Peritonitis) 567.2
  round ligament (*see also* Disease, pelvis,
      inflammatory) 614.4
      acute 614.3

Cellulitis—*continued*
  scalp (any part) 682.8
      dissecting 704.8
  scrotum 608.4
  seminal vesicle 608.0
  septic NEC 682.9
  shoulder 682.3
  specified sites NEC 682.8
  spermatic cord 608.4
  submandibular (region) (space) (triangle) 682.0
      gland 527.3
  submaxillary 528.3
      gland 527.3
  submental (pyogenic) 682.0
      gland 527.3
  suppurative NEC 682.9
  testis 608.4
  thigh 682.6
  thumb (intrathecal) (periosteal) (subcutaneous)
      (subcuticular) 681.00
  toe (intrathecal) (periosteal) (subcutaneous)
      (subcuticular) 681.10
  tonsil 475
  trunk 682.2
  tuberculous (primary) (*see also* Tuberculosis)
      017.0
  tunica vaginalis 608.4
  umbilical 682.2
      newborn NEC 771.4
  vaccinal 999.3
  vagina—*see* Vaginitis
  vas deferens 608.4
  vocal cords 478.5
  vulva (*see also* Vulvitis) 616.10
  wrist 682.4
Cementoblastoma, benign (M9273/0) 213.1
  upper jaw (bone) 213.0
Cementoma (M9273/0) 213.1
  gigantiform (M9276/0) 213.1
      upper jaw (bone) 213.0
  upper jaw (bone) 213.0
Cementoperiostitis 523.4
Cephalgia, cephalalgia (*see also* Headache)
      784.0
  histamine 346.2
  nonorganic origin 307.81
  psychogenic 307.81
  tension 307.81
Cephalhematocele, cephalematocele
  due to birth injury 767.1
  fetus or newborn 767.1
  traumatic (*see also* Contusion, head) 920
Cephalhematoma, cephalematoma (calcified)
  due to birth injury 767.1
  fetus or newborn 767.1
  traumatic (*see also* Contusion, head) 920
Cephalic —*see* condition
Cephalitis —*see* Encephalitis
Cephalocele 742.0
Cephaloma —*see* Neoplasm, by site,
  malignant
Cephalomenia 625.8
Cephalopelvic —*see* condition
Cercomoniasis 007.3
Cerebellitis —*see* Encephalitis
Cerebellum (cerebellar)—*see* condition
Cerebral —*see* condition
Cerebritis —*see* Encephalitis
Cerebrohepatorenal syndrome 759.89
Cerebromacular degeneration 330.1
Cerebromalacia (*see also* Softening, brain) 434.9
Cerebrosidosis 272.7

Change(s) (of)—*continued*
  inflammatory—*see* Inflammation
  joint (*see also* Derangement, joint) 718.90
    sacroiliac 724.6
  Kirschner wire V54.8
  knee 717.9
  macular, congenital 743.55
  malignant (M——/3)—*see also* Neoplasm, by
    site, malignant

> *Note—for malignant change occurring in a neoplasm, use the appropriate M code with behavior digit /3 e.g., malignant change in uterine fibroid—M8890/3. For malignant change occurring in a nonneoplastic condition (e.g., gastric ulcer) use the M code M8000/3.*

  mental (status) NEC 780.9
    due to or associated with physical
      condition—*see* Syndrome, brain
  myocardium, myocardial—*see* Degeneration,
    myocardial
  of life (*see also* Menopause) 627.2
  pacemaker battery (cardiac) V53.31
  peripheral nerve 355.9
  personality (nonpsychotic) NEC 310.1
  plaster cast V54.8
  refractive, transient 367.81
  regressive, dental pulp 522.2
  retina 362.9
    myopic (degenerative) (malignant) 360.21
    vascular appearance 362.13
  sacroiliac joint 724.6
  scleral 379.19
    degenerative 379.16
  senile (*see also* Senility) 797
  sensory (*see also* Disturbance, sensation) 782.0
  skin texture 782.8
  spinal cord 336.9
  splint, external V54.8
  subdermal implantable contraceptive V25.5
  suture V58.3
  traction device V54.8
  trophic 355.9
    arm NEC 354.9
    leg NEC 355.8
    lower extremity NEC 355.8
    upper extremity NEC 354.9
  vascular 459.9
  vasomotor 443.9
  voice 784.49
    psychogenic 306.1
Changing sleep-work schedule, affecting sleep
  307.45
Changuinola fever 066.0
Chapping skin 709.8
Character
  depressive 301.12
Charcot's
  arthropathy 094.0 *[713.5]*
  cirrhosis—*see* Cirrhosis, biliary
  disease 094.0
    spinal cord 094.0
  fever (biliary) (hepatic) (intermittent)—*see*
    Choledocholithiasis
  joint (disease) 094.0 *[713.5]*
    diabetic 250.6 *[713.5]*
    syringomyelic 336.0 *[713.5]*
  syndrome (intermittent claudication) 443.9
    due to atherosclerosis 440.21
Charcot-Marie-Tooth disease, paralysis, or syndrome 356.1

Charleyhorse (quadriceps) 843.8
  muscle, except quadriceps—*see* Sprain, by site
Charlouis' disease (*see also* Yaws) 102.9
Chauffeur's fracture —*see* Fracture, ulna,
  lower end
Cheadle (-Möller) (-Barlow) disease or
  syndrome (infantile scurvy) 267
Checking (of)
  contraceptive device (intrauterine) V25.42
  device
    fixation V54.8
      external V54.8
      internal V54.0
    traction V54.8
  Kirschner wire V54.8
  plaster cast V54.8
  splint, external V54.8
Checkup
  following treatment—*see* Examination
  health V70.0
  infant (not sick) V20.2
  pregnancy (normal) V22.1
    first V22.0
    high risk pregnancy V23.9
      specified problem NEC V23.8
Chédiak-Higashi (-Steinbrinck) anomaly,
  disease, or syndrome (congenital gigantism of
  peroxidase granules) 288.2
Cheek —*see also* condition
  biting 528.9
Cheese itch 133.8
Cheese washers' lung 495.8
Cheilitis 528.5
  actinic (due to sun) 692.72
    chronic NEC 692.74
      due to radiation, except from sun 692.82
    due to radiation, except from sun 692.82
  acute 528.5
  angular 528.5
  catarrhal 528.5
  chronic 528.5
  exfoliative 528.5
  gangrenous 528.5
  glandularis apostematosa 528.5
  granulomatosa 351.8
  infectional 528.5
  membranous 528.5
  Miescher's 351.8
  suppurative 528.5
  ulcerative 528.5
  vesicular 528.5
Cheilodynia 528.5
Cheilopalatoschisis (*see also* Cleft, palate, with
  cleft lip) 749.20
Cheilophagia 528.9
Cheiloschisis (*see also* Cleft, lip) 749.10
Cheilosis 528.5
  with pellagra 265.2
  angular 528.5
  due to
    dietary deficiency 266.0
    vitamin deficiency 266.0
Cheiromegaly 729.89
Cheiropompholyx 705.81
Cheloid (*see also* Keloid) 701.4
Chemical burn —*see also* Burn, by site
  from swallowing chemical—*see* Burn, internal
    organs
Chemodectoma (M8693/1)—*see*
  Paraganglioma, nonchromaffin
Chemoprophylaxis NEC V07.39
Chemosis, conjunctiva 372.73

Chemotherapy
  convalescence V66.2
  encounter (for) V58.1
  maintenance V58.l
  prophylactic NEC V07.39
    fluoride V07.31
Cherubism 526.89
Chest —*see* condition
Cheyne-Stokes respiration (periodic) 786.04
Chiari's
  disease or syndrome (hepatic vein thrombosis)
    453.0
  malformation
    type I 348.4
    type II (*see also* Spina bifida) 741.0
    type III 742.0
    type IV 742.2
  network 746.89
Chiari-Frommel syndrome 676.6
Chicago disease (North American
    blastomycosis) 116.0
Chickenpox (*see also* Varicella) 052.9
  vaccination and inoculation (prophylactic) V05.4
Chiclero ulcer 085.4
Chiggers 133.8
Chignon 111.2
  fetus or newborn (from vacuum extraction)
    767.1
Chigoe disease 134.1
Chikungunya fever 066.3
Chilaiditi's syndrome (subphrenic displacement,
    colon) 751.4
Chilblains 991.5
  lupus 991.5
Child
  behavior causing concern V61.20
Childbed fever 670
Childbirth —*see also* Delivery
  puerperal complications—*see* Puerperal
Childhood, period of rapid growth V21.0
Chill (s) 780.9
  with fever 780.6
  congestive 780.9
    in malarial regions 084.6
  septic—*see* Septicemia
  urethral 599.84
Chilomastigiasis 007.8
Chin —*see* condition
Chinese dysentery 004.9
Chiropractic dislocation (*see also* Lesion,
    nonallopathic, by site) 739.9
Chitral fever 066.0
Chlamydia, chlamydial -*see* **condition**
Chloasma 709.09
  cachecticorum 709.09
  eyelid 374.52
    congenital 757.33
    hyperthyroid 242.0
  gravidarum 646.8
  idiopathic 709.09
  skin 709.09
  symptomatic 709.09
Chloroma (M9930/3) 205.3
Chlorosis 280.9
  Egyptian (*see also* Ancylostomiasis) 126.9
  miners' (*see also* Ancylostomiasis) 126.9
Chlorotic anemia 280.9
Chocolate cyst (ovary) 617.1

Choked
  disk or disc—*see* Papilledema
  on food, phlegm, or vomitus NEC (*see also*
    Asphyxia, food) 933.1
  phlegm 933.1
  while vomiting NEC (*see also* Asphyxia, food)
    933.1
Chokes (resulting from bends) 993.3
Choking sensation 784.9
Cholangiectasis (*see also* Disease, gallbladder)
    575.8
Cholangiocarcinoma (M8160/3)
  and hepatocellular carcinoma, combined
    (M8180/3) 155.0
  liver 155.1
  specified site NEC—*see* Neoplasm, by site,
    malignant
  unspecified site 155.1
Cholangiohepatitis 575.8
  due to fluke infestation 121.1
Cholangiohepatoma (M8180/3) 155.0
Cholangiolitis (acute) (chronic) (extrahepatic)
    (gangrenous) 576.1
  intrahepatic 575.8
  paratyphoidal (*see also* Fever, paratyphoid)
    002.9
  typhoidal 002.0
Cholangioma (M8160/0) 211.5
  malignant—*see* Cholangiocarcinoma
Cholangitis (acute) (ascending) (catarrhal)
    (chronic) (infective) (malignant) (primary)
    (recurrent) (sclerosing) (secondary)
    (stenosing) (suppurative) 576.1
  chronic nonsuppurative destructive 571.6
  nonsuppurative destructive (chronic) 571.6
Cholecystdocholithiasis —*see*
    Choledocholithiasis
Cholecystitis 575.10
  with
    calculus, stones in
      bile duct (common) (hepatic)—*see*
        Choledocholithiasis
      gallbladder—*see* Cholelithiasis
  acute and chronic 575.12
  chronic 575.11
  emphysematous (acute) (*see also* Cholecystitis,
    acute) 575.0
  gangrenous (*see also* Cholecystitis, acute) 575.0
  paratyphoidal, current (*see also* Fever,
    paratyphoid) 002.9
  suppurative (*see also* Cholecystitis, acute) 575.0
  typhoidal 002.0
Choledochitis (suppurative) 576.1
Choledocholith —*see* Choledocholithiasis
Choledocholithiasis 574.5

> *Note—Use the following fifth-digit*
> *subclassification with category 574:*
>
> *0 without mention of obstruction*
> *1 with obstruction*

  with
    cholecystitis 574.4
      acute 574.3
      chronic 574.4
    cholelithiasis 574.9
      with
        cholecystitis 574.7
          acute 574.6
            and chronic 574.8
          chronic 574.7

Cholelithiasis (impacted) (multiple) 574.2

*Note—Use the following fifth-digit
subclassification with category 574:*

0 *without mention of obstruction*
1 *with obstruction*

with
   cholecystitis 574.1
      acute 574.0
      chronic 574.1
   choledocholithiasis 574.9
      with
         cholecystitis 574.7
            acute 574.6
               and chronic 574.8
         chronic cholecystitis 574.7
Cholemia (*see also* Jaundice) 782.4
   familial 277.4
   Gilbert's (familial nonhemolytic) 277.4
Cholemic gallstone —*see* Cholelithiasis
Choleperitoneum, choleperitonitis (*see also*
      Disease, gallbladder) 567.8
Cholera (algid) (Asiatic) (asphyctic) (epidemic)
      (gravis) (Indian) (malignant) (morbus)
      (pestilential) (spasmodic) 001.9
   antimonial 985.4
   carrier (suspected) of V02.0
   classical 001.0
   contact V01.0
   due to
      Vibrio
         cholerae (Inaba, Ogawa, Hikojima
            serotypes) 001.0
            El Tor 001.1
      El Tor 001.1
   exposure to V01.0
   vaccination, prophylactic (against) V03.0
Cholerine (*see also* Cholera) 001.9
Cholestasis 576.8
Cholesteatoma (ear) 385.30
   attic (primary) 385.31
   diffuse 385.35
   external ear (canal) 380.21
   marginal (middle ear) 385.32
      with involvement of mastoid cavity 385.33
      secondary (with middle ear involvement)
         385.33
   mastoid cavity 385.30
   middle ear (secondary) 385.32
      with involvement of mastoid cavity 385.33
   postmastoidectomy cavity (recurrent) 383.32
   primary 385.31
   recurrent, postmastoidectomy cavity 383.32
   secondary (middle ear) 385.32
      with involvement of mastoid cavity 385.33
Cholesteatosis (middle ear) (*see also*
      Cholesteatoma) 385.30
   diffuse 385.35
Cholesteremia 272.0
Cholesterin
   granuloma, middle ear 385.82
   in vitreous 379.22
Cholesterol
   deposit
      retina 362.82
      vitreous 379.22
   imbibition of gallbladder (*see also* Disease,
      gallbladder) 575.6

Cholesterolemia 272.0
   essential 272.0
   familial 272.0
   hereditary 272.0
Cholesterosis, cholesterolosis (gallbladder) 575.6
   middle ear (*see also* Cholesteatoma) 385.30
   with
      cholecystitis—*see* Cholecystitis
      cholelithiasis—*see* Cholelithiasis
Cholocolic fistula (*see also* Fistula, gallbladder)
      575.5
Choluria 791.4
Chondritis (purulent) 733.99
   costal 733.6
      Tietze's 733.6
   patella, posttraumatic 717.7
   posttraumatica patellae 717.7
   tuberculous (active) (*see also* Tuberculosis)
      015.9
      intervertebral 015.0 *[730.88]*
Chondroangiopathia calcarea seu punctate
      756.59
Chondroblastoma (M9230/0)—*see also*
      Neoplasm, bone, benign
   malignant (M9230/3)—*see* Neoplasm, bone,
      malignant
Chondrocalcinosis (articular) (crystal
      deposition) (dihydrate) (*see also* Arthritis, due
      to, crystals) 275.49 *[712.3]*
   due to
      calcium pyrophosphate 275.49 *[712.2]*
      dicalcium phosphate crystals 275.49 *[712.1]*
      pyrophosphate crystals 275.4 *[712.2]*
Chondrodermatitis nodularis helicis 380.00
Chondrodysplasia 756.4
   angiomatose 756.4
   calcificans congenita 756.59
   epiphysialis punctata 756.59
   hereditary deforming 756.4
Chondrodystrophia (fetalis) 756.4
   calcarea 756.4
   calcificans congenita 756.59
   fetalis hypoplastica 756.59
   hypoplastica calcinosa 756.59
   punctata 756.59
   tarda 277.5
Chondrodystrophy (familial) (hypoplastic) 756.4
Chondroectodermal dysplasia 756.55
Chondrolysis 733.99
Chondroma (M9220/0)—*see also* Neoplasm
      cartilage, benign
   juxtacortical (M9221/0)—*see* Neoplasm, bone,
      benign
   periosteal (M9221/0)—*see* Neoplasm, bone,
      benign
Chondromalacia 733.92
   epiglottis (congenital) 748.3
   generalized 733.92
   knee 717.7
   larynx (congenital) 748.3
   localized, except patella 733.92
   patella, patellae 717.7
   systemic 733.92
   tibial plateau 733.92
   trachea (congenital) 748.3
Chondromatosis (M9220/1)—*see* Neoplasm,
      cartilage, uncertain behavior
Chondromyxosarcoma (M9220/3)—*see*
      Neoplasm, cartilage, malignant
Chondro-osteodysplasia (Morquio-Brailsford
      type) 277.5

Chondro-osteodystrophy 277.5
Chondro-osteodystrophy 277.5
Chondro-osteoma (M9210/0)—*see* Neoplasm,
   bone, benign
Chondropathia tuberosa 733.6
Chondrosarcoma (M9220/3)—*see also*
   Neoplasm, cartilage, malignant
   juxtacortical (M9221/3)—*see* Neoplasm, bone,
      malignant
   mesenchymal (M9240/3)—*see* Neoplasm,
      connective tissue, malignant
Chordae tendineae rupture (chronic) 429.5
Chordee (nonvenereal) 607.89
   congenital 752.63
   gonococcal 098.2
Chorditis (fibrinous) (nodosa) (tuberosa) 478.5
Chordoma (M9370/3)—*see* Neoplasm, by site,
   malignant
Chorea (gravis) (minor) (spasmodic) 333.5
   with
      heart involvement—*see* Chorea with
         rheumatic heart disease
      rheumatic heart disease (chronic, inactive, or
         quiescent) (conditions classifiable to
         393-398)—*see also* Rheumatic heart
         condition involved
      active or acute (conditions classifiable to
         391) 392.0
   acute—*see* Chorea, Sydenham's
   apoplectic (*see also* Disease, cerebrovascular,
      acute) 436
   chronic 333.4
   electric 049.8
   gravidarum—*see* Eclampsia, pregnancy
   habit 307.22
   hereditary 333.4
   Huntington's 333.4
   posthemiplegic 344.89
   pregnancy—*see* Eclampsia, pregnancy
   progressive 333.4
      chronic 333.4
      hereditary 333.4
   rheumatic (chronic) 392.9
      with heart disease or involvement—*see*
         Chorea, with rheumatic heart disease
   senile 333.5
   Sydenham's 392.9
      with heart involvement—*see* Chorea, with
         rheumatic heart disease
      nonrheumatic 333.5
   variabilis 307.23
Choreoathetosis (paroxysmal) 333.5
Chorioadenoma (destruens) (M9100/1) 236.1
Chorioamnionitis 658.4
   affecting fetus or newborn 762.7
Chorioangioma (M9120/0) 219.8
Choriocarcinoma (M9100/3)
   combined with
      embryonal carcinoma (M9101/3)—*see*
         Neoplasm, by site, malignant
      teratoma (M9101/3)—*see* Neoplasm, by site,
         malignant
   specified site—*see* Neoplasm, by site, malignant
   unspecified site
      female 181
      male 186.9
Chorioencephalitis, lymphocytic (acute)
   (serous) 049.0
Chorioepithelioma (M9100/3)—*see*
   Choriocarcinoma
Choriomeningitis (acute) (benign) (lymphocytic)
   (serous) 049.0

Chorionepithelioma (M9100/3)—*see*
   Choriocarcinoma
Chorionitis (*see also* Scleroderma) 710.1
Chorioretinitis 363.20
   disseminated 363.10
      generalized 363.13
      in
         neurosyphilis 094.83
         secondary syphilis 091.51
      peripheral 363.12
      posterior pole 363.11
      tuberculous (*see also* Tuberculosis) 017.3
         [363.13]
   due to
      histoplasmosis (*see also* Histoplasmosis)
         115.92
      toxoplasmosis (acquired) 130.2
         congenital (active) 771.2
   focal 363.00
      juxtapapillary 363.01
      peripheral 363.04
      posterior pole NEC 363.03
   juxtapapillaris, juxtapapillary 363.01
   progressive myopia (degeneration) 360.21
   syphilitic (secondary) 091.51
      congenital (early) 090.0 *[363.13]*
         late 090.5 *[363.13]*
      late 095.8 *[363.13]*
   tuberculous (*see also* Tuberculosis) 017.3
      [363.13]
Choristoma —*see* Neoplasm, by site, benign
Choroid —*see* condition
Choroideremia, choroidermia (initial stage)
   (late stage) (partial or total atrophy) 363.55
Choroiditis (*see also* Chorioretinitis) 363.20
   leprous 030.9 *[363.13]*
   senile guttate 363.41
   sympathetic 360.11
   syphilitic (secondary) 091.51
      congenital (early) 090.0 *[363.13]*
         late 090.5 *[363.13]*
      late 095.8 *[363.13]*
   Tay's 363.41
   tuberculous (*see also* Tuberculosis) 017.3
      [363.13]
Choroidopathy NEC 363.9
   degenerative (*see also* Degeneration, choroid)
      363.40
   hereditary (*see also* Dystrophy, choroid) 363.50
   specified type NEC 363.8
Choroidoretinitis —*see* Chorioretinitis
Choroidosis, central serous 362.41
Choroidretinopathy, serous 362.41
Christian's syndrome (chronic histiocytosis X)
   277.8
Christian-Weber disease (nodular
   nonsuppurative panniculitis) 729.30
Christmas disease 286.1
Chromaffinoma (M8700/0)—*see also*
   Neoplasm, by site, benign
   malignant (M8700/3)—*see* Neoplasm, by site,
      malignant
Chromatopsia 368.59
Chromhidrosis, chromidrosis 705.89
Chromoblastomycosis 117.2
Chromomycosis 117.2
Chromophytosis 111.0
Chromotrichomycosis 111.8
Chronic —*see* condition
Churg-Strauss syndrome 446.4
Chyle cyst, mesentery 457.8

Chylocele (nonfilarial) 457.8
  filarial (*see also* Infestation, filarial) 125.9
  tunica vaginalis (nonfilarial) 608.84
    filarial (*see also* Infestation, filarial) 125.9
Chylomicronemia (fasting) (with
    hyperprebetalipoproteinemia) 272.3
Chylopericardium (acute) 420.90
Chylothorax (nonfilarial) 457.8
  filarial (*see also* Infestation, filarial) 125.9
Chylous
  ascites 457.8
  cyst of peritoneum 457.8
  hydrocele 603.9
  hydrothorax (nonfilarial) 457.8
    filarial (*see also* Infestation, filarial) 125.9
Chyluria 791.1
  bilharziasis 120.0
  due to
    Brugia (malayi) 125.1
    Wuchereria (bancrofti) 125.0
      malayi 125.1
  filarial (*see also* Infestation, filarial) 125.9
  filariasis (*see also* Infestation, filarial) 125.9
  nonfilarial 791.1
Cicatricial (deformity)—*see* Cicatrix
Cicatrix (adherent) (contracted) (painful)
    (vicious) 709.2
  adenoid 474.8
  alveolar process 525.8
  anus 569.49
  auricle 380.89
  bile duct (*see also* Disease, biliary) 576.8
  bladder 596.8
  bone 733.99
  brain 348.8
  cervix (postoperative) (postpartal) 622.3
    in pregnancy or childbirth 654.6
      causing obstructed labor 660.2
  chorioretinal 363.30
    disseminated 363.35
    macular 363.32
    peripheral 363.34
    posterior pole NEC 363.33
  choroid—*see* Cicatrix, chorioretinal
  common duct (*see also* Disease, biliary) 576.8
  congenital 757.39
  conjunctiva 372.64
  cornea 371.00
    tuberculous (*see also* Tuberculosis) 017.3
      [371.05]
  duodenum (bulb) 537.3
  esophagus 530.3
  eyelid 374.46
    with
      ectropion—*see* Ectropion
      entropion—*see* Entropion
  hypopharynx 478.29
  knee, semilunar cartilage 717.5
  lacrimal
    canaliculi 375.53
    duct
      acquired 375.56
      neonatal 375.55
    punctum 375.52
    sac 375.54
  larynx 478.79
  limbus (cystoid) 372.64
  lung 518.89
  macular 363.32
    disseminated 363.35
    peripheral 363.34

Cicatrix—*continued*
  middle ear 385.89
  mouth 528.9
  muscle 728.89
  nasolacrimal duct
    acquired 375.56
    neonatal 375.55
  nasopharynx 478.29
  palate (soft) 528.9
  penis 607.89
  prostate 602.8
  rectum 569.49
  retina 363.30
    disseminated 363.35
    macular 363.32
    peripheral 363.34
    posterior pole NEC 363.33
  semilunar cartilage—*see* Derangement,
    meniscus
  seminal vesicle 608.89
  skin 709.2
    infected 686.8
    postinfectional 709.2
    tuberculous (*see also* Tuberculosis) 017.0
  specified site NEC 709.2
  throat 478.29
  tongue 529.8
  tonsil (and adenoid) 474.8
  trachea 478.9
  tuberculous NEC (*see also* Tuberculosis) 011.9
  ureter 593.89
  urethra 599.84
  uterus 621.8
  vagina 623.4
    in pregnancy or childbirth 654.7
      causing obstructed labor 660.2
  vocal cord 478.5
  wrist, constricting (annular) 709.2
CIN I [cervical intraepithelial neoplasia I] 622.1
CIN II [cervical intraepithelial neoplasia II] 622.1
CIN III [cervical intraepithelial neoplasia III]
  233.1
Cinchonism
  correct substance properly administered 386.9
  overdose or wrong substance given or taken
    961.4
Circine herpes 110.5
Circle of Willis —*see* condition
Circular —*see also* condition
  hymen 752.49
Circulating anticoagulants 286.5
  following childbirth 666.3
  postpartum 666.3
Circulation
  collateral (venous), any site 459.89
  defective 459.9
    congenital 747.9
    lower extremity 459.89
  embryonic 747.9
  failure 799.8
    fetus or newborn 779.8
    peripheral 785.59
  fetal, persistent 747.89
  heart, incomplete 747.9
Circulatory system —*see* condition
Circulus senilis 371.41
Circumcision
  in absence of medical indication V50.2
  ritual V50.2
  routine V50.2
Circumscribed —*see* condition

Circumvallata placenta —*see* Placenta,
   abnormal
Cirrhosis, cirrhotic 571.5
  with alcoholism 571.2
  alcoholic (liver) 571.2
  atrophic (of liver)—*see* Cirrhosis, portal
  Baumgarten-Cruveilhier 571.5
  biliary (cholangiolitic) (cholangitic)
     (cholestatic) (extrahepatic) (hypertrophic)
     (intrahepatic) (nonobstructive) (obstructive)
     (pericholangiolitic) (posthepatic) (primary)
     (secondary) (xanthomatous) 571.6
    due to
      clonorchiasis 121.1
      flukes 121.3
  brain 331.9
  capsular—*see* Cirrhosis, portal
  cardiac 571.5
    alcoholic 571.2
  central (liver)—*see* Cirrhosis, liver
  Charcot's 571.6
  cholangiolitic—*see* Cirrhosis, biliary
  cholangitic—*see* Cirrhosis, biliary
  cholestatic—*see* Cirrhosis, biliary
  clitoris (hypertrophic) 624.2
  coarsely nodular 571.5
  congestive (liver)—*see* Cirrhosis, cardiac
  Cruveilhier-Baumgarten 571.5
  cryptogenic (of liver) 571.5
    alcoholic 571.2
  dietary (*see also* Cirrhosis, portal) 571.5
  due to
    bronzed diabetes 275.0
    congestive hepatomegaly—*see* Cirrhosis,
      cardiac
    cystic fibrosis 277.00
    hemochromatosis 275.0
    hepatolenticular degeneration 275.1
    passive congestion (chronic)—*see* Cirrhosis,
      cardiac
    Wilson's disease 275.1
    xanthomatosis 272.2
  extrahepatic (obstructive)—*see* Cirrhosis, biliary
  fatty 571.8
    alcoholic 571.0
  florid 571.2
  Glisson's—*see* Cirrhosis, portal
  Hanot's (hypertrophic)—*see* Cirrhosis, biliary
  hepatic—*see* Cirrhosis, liver
  hepatolienal—*see* Cirrhosis, liver
  hobnail—*see* Cirrhosis, portal
  hypertrophic—*see also* Cirrhosis, liver
    biliary—*see* Cirrhosis, biliary
    Hanot's—*see* Cirrhosis, biliary
  infectious NEC—*see* Cirrhosis, portal
  insular—*see* Cirrhosis, portal
  intrahepatic (obstructive) (primary)
    (secondary)—*see* Cirrhosis, biliary
  juvenile (*see also* Cirrhosis, portal) 571.5
  kidney (*see also* Sclerosis, renal) 587
  Laennec's (of liver) 571.2
    nonalcoholic 571.5
  liver (chronic) (hepatolienal) (hypertrophic)
    (nodular) (splenomegalic) (unilobar) 571.5
    with alcoholism 571.2
    alcoholic 571.2
    congenital (due to failure of obliteration of
      umbilical vein) 777.8
    cryptogenic 571.5
      alcoholic 571.2

Cirrhosis, cirrhotic—*continued*
  fatty 571.8
    alcoholic 571.0
  macronodular 571.5
    alcoholic 571.2
  micronodular 571.5
    alcoholic 571.2
  nodular, diffuse 571.5
    alcoholic 571.2
  pigmentary 275.0
  portal 571.5
    alcoholic 571.2
  postnecrotic 571.5
    alcoholic 571.2
  syphilitic 095.3
  lung (chronic) (*see also* Fibrosis, lung) 515
  macronodular (of liver) 571.5
    alcoholic 571.2
  malarial 084.9
  metabolic NEC 571.5
  micronodular (of liver) 571.5
    alcoholic 571.2
  monolobular—*see* Cirrhosis, portal
  multilobular—*see* Cirrhosis, portal
  nephritis (*see also* Sclerosis, renal) 587
  nodular—*see* Cirrhosis, liver
  nutritional (fatty) 571.5
  obstructive (biliary) (extrahepatic)
    (intrahepatic)—*see* Cirrhosis, biliary
  ovarian 620.8
  paludal 084.9
  pancreas (duct) 577.8
  pericholangiolitic—*see* Cirrhosis, biliary
  periportal—*see* Cirrhosis, portal
  pigment, pigmentary (of liver) 275.0
  portal (of liver) 571.5
    alcoholic 571.2
  posthepatitic (*see also* Cirrhosis, postnecrotic)
    571.5
  postnecrotic (of liver) 571.5
    alcoholic 571.2
  primary (intrahepatic)—*see* Cirrhosis, biliary
  pulmonary (*see also* Fibrosis, lung) 515
  renal (*see also* Sclerosis, renal) 587
  septal (*see also* Cirrhosis, postnecrotic) 571.5
  spleen 289.51
  splenomegalic (of liver)—*see* Cirrhosis, liver
  stasis (liver)—*see* Cirrhosis, liver
  stomach 535.4
  Todd's (*see also* Cirrhosis, biliary) 571.6
  toxic (nodular)—*see* Cirrhosis, postnecrotic
  trabecular—*see* Cirrhosis, postnecrotic
  unilobar—*see* Cirrhosis, liver
  vascular (of liver)—*see* Cirrhosis, liver
  xanthomatous (biliary) (*see also* Cirrhosis,
    biliary) 571.6
    due to xanthomatosis (familial) (metabolic)
      (primary) 272.2
Cistern, subarachnoid 793.0
Citrullinemia 270.6
Citrullinuria 270.6
Ciuffini-Pancoast tumor (M8010/3) (carcinoma,
  pulmonary apex) 162.3
Civatte's disease or poikiloderma 709.09
Clam diggers' itch 120.3
Clap —*see* Gonorrhea
Clark's paralysis 343.9
Clarke-Hadfield syndrome (pancreatic
  infantilism) 577.8
Clastothrix 704.2
Claude's syndrome 352.6

Claude Bernard-Horner syndrome (*see also* Neuropathy, peripheral, autonomic) 337.9
Claudication, intermittent 443.9
  cerebral (artery) (*see also* Ischemia, cerebral, transient) 435.9
  due to atherosclerosis 440.21
  spinal cord (arteriosclerotic) 435.1
    syphilitic 094.89
  spinalis 435.1
  venous (axillary) 453.8
Claudicatio venosa intermittens 453.8
Claustrophobia 300.29
Clavus (infected) 700
Claw foot (congenital) 754.71
  acquired 736.74
Claw hand (acquired) 736.06
  congenital 755.59
Clawtoe (congenital) 754.71
  acquired 735.5
Clay eating 307.52
Clay shovelers' fracture —*see* Fracture, vertebra, cervical
Cleansing of artificial opening (*see also* Attention to artificial opening) V55.9
Cleft (congenital)—*see also* Imperfect, closure
  alveolar process 525.8
  branchial (persistent) 744.41
    cyst 744.42
  clitoris 752.49
  cricoid cartilage, posterior 748.3
  facial (*see also* Cleft, lip) 749.10
  lip 749.10
    with cleft palate 749.20
      bilateral (lip and palate) 749.24
        with unilateral lip or palate 749.25
        complete 749.23
        incomplete 749.24
      unilateral (lip and palate) 749.22
        with bilateral lip or palate 749.25
        complete 749.21
        incomplete 749.22
    bilateral 749.14
      with cleft palate, unilateral 749.25
      complete 749.13
      incomplete 749.14
    unilateral 749.12
      with cleft palate, bilateral 749.25
      complete 749.11
      incomplete 749.12
  nose 748.1
  palate 749.00
    with cleft lip 749.20
      bilateral (lip and palate) 749.24
        with unilateral lip or palate 749.25
        complete 749.23
        incomplete 749.24
      unilateral (lip and palate) 749.22
        with bilateral lip or palate 749.25
        complete 749.21
        incomplete 749.22
    bilateral 749.04
      with cleft lip, unilateral 749.25
      complete 749.03
      incomplete 749.04
    unilateral 749.02
      with cleft lip, bilateral 749.25
      complete 749.01
      incomplete 749.02
  penis 752.69
  posterior, cricoid cartilage 748.3
  scrotum 752.8

Cleft—*continued*
  sternum (congenital) 756.3
  thyroid cartilage (congenital) 748.3
  tongue 750.13
  uvula 749.02
    with cleft lip (*see also* Cleft, lip, with cleft palate) 749.20
  water 366.12
Cleft hand (congenital) 755.58
Cleidocranial dysostosis 755.59
Cleidotomy, fetal 763.89
Cleptomania 312.32
Clérambault's syndrome 297.8
  erotomania 302.89
Clergyman's sore throat 784.49
Click, clicking
  systolic syndrome 785.2
Clifford's syndrome (postmaturity) 766.2
Climacteric (*see also* Menopause) 627.2
  arthritis NEC (*see also* Arthritis, climacteric) 716.3
  depression (*see also* Psychosis, affective) 296.2
  disease 627.2
    recurrent episode 296.3
    single episode 296.2
  female (symptoms) 627.2
  male (symptoms) (syndrome) 608.89
  melancholia (*see also* Psychosis, affective) 296.2
    recurrent episode 296.3
    single episode 296.2
  paranoid state 297.2
  paraphrenia 297.2
  polyarthritis NEC 716.39
    male 608.89
  symptoms (female) 627.2
Clinical research investigation V70.7
Clinodactyly 755.59
Clitoris —*see* condition
Cloaca, persistent 751.5
Clonorchiasis 121.1
Clonorchiosis 121.1
Clonorchis infection, liver 121.1
Clonus 781.0
Closed bite 524.2
Closure
  artificial opening (*see also* Attention to artificial opening) V55.9
  congenital, nose 748.0
  cranial sutures, premature 756.0
  defective or imperfect NEC—*see* Imperfect, closure
  fistula, delayed—*see* Fistula
  fontanelle, delayed 756.0
  foramen ovale, imperfect 745.5
  hymen 623.3
  interauricular septum, defective 745.5
  interventricular septum, defective 745.4
  lacrimal duct 375.56
    congenital 743.65
    neonatal 375.55
  nose (congenital) 748.0
    acquired 738.0
  vagina 623.2
  valve—*see* Endocarditis
  vulva 624.8
Clot (blood)
  artery (obstruction) (occlusion) (*see also* Embolism) 444.9
  bladder 596.7

Clot —*continued*
  brain (extradural or intradural) (*see also*
      Thrombosis, brain) 434.0
    late effect—*see* Late effect(s) (of)
        cerebrovascular disease
  circulation 444.9
  heart (*see also* Infarct, myocardium) 410.9
  vein (*see also* Thrombosis) 453.9
Clotting defect NEC (*see also* Defect,
    coagulation) 286.9
Clouded state 780.09
  epileptic (*see also* Epilepsy) 345.9
  paroxysmal (idiopathic) (*see also* Epilepsy)
      345.9
Clouding
  corneal graft 996.51
Cloudy
  antrum, antra 473.0
  dialysis effluent 792.5
Clouston's (hidrotic) ectodermal dysplasia 757.31
Clubbing of fingers 781.5
Clubfinger 736.29
  acquired 736.29
  congenital 754.89
Clubfoot (congenital) 754.70
  acquired 736.71
  equinovarus 754.51
  paralytic 736.71
Club hand (congenital) 754.89
  acquired 736.07
Clubnail (acquired) 703.8
  congenital 757.5
Clump kidney 753.3
Clumsiness 781.3
  syndrome 315.4
Cluttering 307.0
Clutton's joints 090.5
Coagulation, intravascular (diffuse)
      (disseminated) (*see also* Fibrinolysis) 286.6
  newborn 776.2
Coagulopathy (*see also* Defect, coagulation)
      286.9
  consumption 286.6
  intravascular (disseminated) NEC 286.6
    newborn 776.2
Coalition
  calcaneoscaphoid 755.67
  calcaneus 755.67
  tarsal 755.67
Coal miners'
  elbow 727.2
  lung 500
Coal workers' lung or pneumoconiosis 500
Coarctation
  aorta (postductal) (preductal) 747.10
  pulmonary artery 747.3
Coated tongue 529.3
Coats' disease 362.12
Cocainism (*see also* Dependence) 304.2
Coccidioidal granuloma 114.3
Coccidioidomycosis 114.9
  with pneumonia 114.0
  cutaneous (primary) 114.1
  disseminated 114.3
  extrapulmonary (primary) 114.1
  lung 114.5
    acute 114.0
    chronic 114.4
    primary 114.0
  meninges 114.2
  primary (pulmonary) 114.0

Coccidioidomycosis—*continued*
  acute 114.0
  prostate 114.3
  pulmonary 114.5
    acute 114.0
    chronic 114.4
    primary 114.0
  specified site NEC 114.3
Coccidioidosis 114.9
  lung 114.5
    acute 114.0
    chronic 114.4
    primary 114.0
  meninges 114.2
Coccidiosis (colitis) (diarrhea) (dysentery) 007.2
Cocciuria 791.9
Coccus in urine 791.9
Coccydynia 724.79
Coccygodynia 724.79
Coccyx —*see* condition
Cochin-China
  diarrhea 579.1
    anguilluliasis 127.2
  ulcer 085.1
Cock's peculiar tumor 706.2
Cockayne's disease or syndrome (microcephaly
    and dwarfism) 759.89
Cockayne-Weber syndrome (epidermolysis
    bullosa) 757.39
Cocked-up toe 735.2
Codman's tumor (benign chondroblastoma)
    (M9230/0)—*see* Neoplasm, bone, benign
Coenurosis 123.8
Coffee workers' lung 495.8
Cogan's syndrome 370.52
  congenital oculomotor apraxia 379.51
  nonsyphilitic interstitial keratitis 370.52
Coiling, umbilical cord —*see* Complications,
    umbilical cord
Coitus, painful (female) 625.0
  male 608.89
  psychogenic 302.76
Cold 460
  with influenza, flu, or grippe 487.1
  abscess—*see also* Tuberculosis, abscess
    articular—*see* Tuberculosis, joint
  agglutinin
    disease (chronic) or syndrome 283.0
    hemoglobinuria 283.0
      paroxysmal (cold) (nocturnal) 283.2
  allergic (*see also* Fever, hay) 477.9
  bronchus or chest—*see* Bronchitis
    with grippe or influenza 487.1
  common (head) 460
    vaccination, prophylactic (against) V04.7
  deep 464.10
  effects of 991.9
    specified effect NEC 991.8
  excessive 991.9
    specified effect NEC 991.8
  exhaustion from 991.8
  exposure to 991.9
    specified effect NEC 991.8
  grippy 487.1
  head 460
  injury syndrome (newborn) 778.2
  intolerance 780.9
  on lung—*see* Bronchitis
  rose 477.0
  sensitivity, autoimmune 283.0
  virus 460
Coldsore (*see also* Herpes, simplex) 054.9

Colibacillosis 041.4
 generalized 038.42
Colibacilluria 791.9
Colic (recurrent) 789.0
 abdomen 789.0
  (recurrent)psychogenic 307.89
 appendicular 543.9
 appendix 543.9
 bile duct—*see* Choledocholithiasis
 biliary—*see* Cholelithiasis
 bilious—*see* Cholelithiasis
 common duct—*see* Choledocholithiasis
 Devonshire NEC 984.9
  specified type of lead—*see* Table of drugs and
   chemicals
 flatulent 787.3
 gallbladder or gallstone—*see* Cholelithiasis
 gastric 536.8
 hepatic (duct)—*see* Choledocholithiasis
 hysterical 300.11
 infantile 789.0
 intestinal 789.0
 kidney 788.0
 lead NEC 984.9
  specified type of lead—*see* Table of drugs and
   chemicals
 liver (duct)—*see* Choledocholithiasis
 mucous 564.9
  psychogenic 316 *[564.9]*
 nephritic 788.0
 painter's NEC 984.9
 pancreas 577.8
 psychogenic 306.4
 renal 788.0
 saturnine NEC 984.9
  specified type of lead—*see* Table of drugs and
   chemicals
 spasmodic 789.0
 ureter 788.0
 urethral 599.84
  due to calculus 594.2
 uterus 625.8
  menstrual 625.3
 vermicular 543.9
 virus 460
 worm NEC 128.9
Colicystitis (*see also* Cystitis) 595.9
Colitis (acute) (catarrhal) (croupous) (cystica
  superficialis) (exudative) (hemorrhagic)
  (noninfectious) (phlegmonous) (presumed
  noninfectious) 558.9
 adaptive 564.9
 allergic 558.3
 amebic (*see also* Amebiasis) 006.9
  nondysenteric 006.2
 anthrax 022.2
 bacillary (*see also* Infection, Shigella) 004.9
 balantidial 007.0
 chronic 558.9
  ulcerative (*see also* Colitis, ulcerative) 556.9
 coccidial 007.2
 dietetic 558.9
 due to radiation 558.1
 functional 558.9
 gangrenous 009.0
 giardial 007.1
 granulomatous 555.1
 gravis (*see also* Colitis, ulcerative) 556.9
 infectious (*see also* Enteritis, due to, specific
   organism) 009.0
  presumed 009.1

Colitis—*continued*
 ischemic 557.9
  acute 557.0
  chronic 557.1
  due to mesenteric artery insufficiency 557.1
 membranous 564.9
  psychogenic 316 *[564.9]*
 mucous 564.9
  psychogenic 316 *[564.9]*
 necrotic 009.0
 polyposa (*see also* Colitis, ulcerative) 556.9
 protozoal NEC 007.9
 pseudomembranous 008.45
 pseudomucinous 564.9
 regional 555.1
 segmental 555.1
 septic (*see also* Enteritis, due to, specific
   organism) 009.0
 spastic 564.9
  psychogenic 316 *[564.9]*
 staphylococcus 008.41
  food 005.0
 thromboulcerative 557.0
 toxic 558.2
 transmural 555.1
 trichomonal 007.3
 tuberculous (ulcerative) 014.8
 ulcerative (chronic) (idiopathic) (nonspecific)
   556.9
  entero- 556.0
  fulminant 557.0
  ileo- 556.1
  left-sided 556.5
  procto- 556.2
  proctosigmoid 556.3
  psychogenic 316 *[556]*
  specified NEC 556.8
  universal 556.6
Collagen disease NEC 710.9
 nonvascular 710.9
 vascular (allergic) (*see also* Angiitis,
   hypersensitivity) 446.20
Collagenosis (*see also* Collagen disease) 710.9
 cardiovascular 425.4
 mediastinal 519.3
Collapse 780.2
 adrenal 255.8
 cardiorenal (*see also* Hypertension, cardiorenal)
   404.90
 cardiorespiratory 785.51
  fetus or newborn 779.8
 cardiovascular (*see also* Disease, heart) 785.51
  fetus or newborn 779.8
 circulatory (peripheral) 785.59
  with
   abortion—*see* Abortion, by type, with shock
   ectopic pregnancy (*see also* categories
    633.0-633.9) 639.5
   molar pregnancy (*see also* categories
    630-632) 639.5
  during or after labor and delivery 669.1
  fetus or newborn 779.8
  following
   abortion 639.5
   ectopic or molar pregnancy 639.5
 during or after labor and delivery 669.1
  fetus or newborn 779.8

Collapse—*continued*
  external ear canal 380.50
    secondary to
      inflammation 380.53
      surgery 380.52
      trauma 380.51
  general 780.2
  heart—*see* Disease, heart
  heat 992.1
  hysterical 300.11
  labyrinth, membranous (congenital) 744.05
  lung (massive) (*see also* Atelectasis) 518.0
    pressure, during labor 668.0
  myocardial—*see* Disease, heart
  nervous (*see also* Disorder, mental,
    nonpsychotic) 300.9
  neurocirculatory 306.2
  nose 738.0
  postoperative (cardiovascular) 998.0
  pulmonary (*see also* Atelectasis) 518.0
    fetus or newborn 770.5
      partial 770.5
      primary 770.4
  thorax 512.8
    iatrogenic 512.1
    postoperative 512.1
  trachea 519.1
  valvular—*see* Endocarditis
  vascular (peripheral) 785.59
    with
      abortion—*see* Abortion, by type, with shock
      ectopic pregnancy (*see also* categories
        633.0-633.9) 639.5
      molar pregnancy (*see also* categories
        630-632) 639.5
    cerebral (*see also* Disease, cerebrovascular,
      acute) 436
    during or after labor and delivery 669.1
    fetus or newborn 779.8
    following
      abortion 639.5
      ectopic or molar pregnancy 639.5
  vasomotor 785.59
  vertebra 733.13
Collateral —*see also* condition
  circulation (venous) 459.89
  dilation, veins 459.89
Colles' fracture (closed) (reversed) (separation)
  813.41
  open 813.51
Collet's syndrome 352.6
Collet-Sicard syndrome 352.6
Colliculitis urethralis (*see also* Urethritis) 597.89
Colliers'
  asthma 500
  lung 500
  phthisis (*see also* Tuberculosis) 011.4
Collodion baby (ichthyosis congenita) 757.1
Colloid milium 709.3
Coloboma NEC 743.49
  choroid 743.59
  fundus 743.52
  iris 743.46
  lens 743.36
  lids 743.62
  optic disc (congenital) 743.57
    acquired 377.23
  retina 743.56
  sclera 743.47
Coloenteritis —*see* Enteritis
Colon —*see* condition
Coloptosis 569.89

Color
  amblyopia NEC 368.59
    acquired 368.55
  blindness NEC (congenital) 368.59
    acquired 368.55
Colostomy
  attention to V55.3
  fitting or adjustment V53.5
  malfunctioning 569.62
  status V44.3
Colpitis (*see also* Vaginitis) 616.10
Colpocele 618.6
Colpocystitis (*see also* Vaginitis) 616.10
Colporrhexis 665.4
Colpospasm 625.1
Column, spinal, vertebral —*see* condition
Coma 780.01
  apoplectic (*see also* Disease, cerebrovascular,
    acute) 436
  diabetic (with ketoacidosis) 250.3
    hyperosmolar 250.2
  eclamptic (*see also* Eclampsia) 780.39
  epileptic 345.3
  hepatic 572.2
  hyperglycemic 250.2
  hyperosmolar (diabetic) (nonketotic) 250.2
  hypoglycemic 251.0
    diabetic 250.3
  insulin 250.3
    hyperosmolar 250.2
    non-diabetic 251.0
    organic hyperinsulinism 251.0
  Kussmaul's (diabetic) 250.3
  liver 572.2
  newborn 779.2
  prediabetic 250.2
  uremic—*see* Uremia
Combat fatigue (*see also* Reaction, stress, acute)
  308.9
Combined —*see* condition
Comedo 706.1
Comedocarcinoma (M8501/3)—*see also*
  Neoplasm, breast, malignant
  noninfiltrating (M8501/2)
    specified site—*see* Neoplasm, by site, in situ
    unspecified site 233.0
Comedomastitis 610.4
Comedones 706.1
  lanugo 757.4
Comma bacillus, carrier (suspected) of V02.3
Comminuted fracture —*see* Fracture, by site
Common
  aortopulmonary trunk 745.0
  atrioventricular canal (defect) 745.69
  atrium 745.69
  cold (head) 460
    vaccination, prophylactic (against) V04.7
  truncus (arteriosus) 745.0
  ventricle 745.3
Commotio (current)
  cerebri (*see also* Concussion, brain) 850.9
    with skull fracture—*see* Fracture, skull, by site
  retinae 921.3
  spinalis—*see* Injury, spinal, by site
Commotion (current)
  brain (without skull fracture) (*see also*
    Concussion, brain) 850.9
    with skull fracture—*see* Fracture, skull, by site
  spinal cord—*see* Injury, spinal, by site

Communication
  abnormal—*see also* Fistula
    between
      base of aorta and pulmonary artery 745.0
      left ventricle and right atrium 745.4
      pericardial sac and pleural sac 748.8
      pulmonary artery and pulmonary vein 747.3
    congenital, between uterus and anterior
      abdominal wall 752.3
      bladder 752.3
      intestine 752.3
      rectum 752.3
  left ventricular-right atrial 745.4
  pulmonary artery-pulmonary vein 747.3
Compensation
  broken—*see* Failure, heart, congestive
  failure—*see* Failure, heart, congestive
  neurosis, psychoneurosis 300.11
Complaint —*see also* Disease
  bowel, functional 564.9
    psychogenic 306.4
  intestine, functional 564.9
    psychogenic 306.4
  kidney (*see also* Disease, renal) 593.9
  liver 573.9
  miners' 500
Complete —*see* condition
Complex
  cardiorenal (*see also* Hypertension, cardiorenal)
    404.90
  castration 300.9
  Costen's 524.60
  ego-dystonic homosexuality 302.0
  Eisenmenger's (ventricular septal defect) 745.4
  homosexual, ego-dystonic 302.0
  hypersexual 302.89
  inferiority 301.9
  jumped process
    spine—*see* Dislocation, vertebra
  primary, tuberculosis (*see also* Tuberculosis)
    010.0
  Taussig-Bing (transposition, aorta and
    overriding pulmonary artery) 745.11
Complications
  abortion NEC—*see* categories 634-639
  accidental puncture or laceration during a
    procedure 998.2
  amputation stump (late) (surgical) 997.60
    traumatic—*see* Amputation, traumatic
  anastomosis (and bypass)—*see also*
    Complications, due to (presence of) any
    device, implant, or graft classified to
    996.0-996.5 NEC
    hemorrhage NEC 998.11
    intestinal (internal) NEC 997.4
      involving urinary tract 997.5
    mechanical—*see* Complications, mechanical,
      graft
    urinary tract (involving intestinal tract) 997.5
  anesthesia, anesthetic NEC (*see also*
    Anesthesia, complication) 995.2
    in labor and delivery 668.9
      affecting fetus or newborn 763.5
      cardiac 668.1
      central nervous system 668.2
      pulmonary 668.0
      specified type NEC 668.8
  aortocoronary (bypass) graft 996.03
    atherosclerosis —*see* Arteriosclerosis,
      coronary
    embolism 996.72

Complications—*continued*
    occlusion NEC 996.72
    thrombus 996.72
  arthroplasty 996.4
  artificial opening
    cecostomy 569.60
    colostomy 569.6
    cystostomy 997.5
    enterostomy 569.60
    gastrostomy 536.40
    ileostomy 569.60
    jejunostomy 569.60
    nephrostomy 997.5
    tracheostomy 519.00
    ureterostomy 997.5
    urethrostomy 997.5
  bile duct implant (prosthetic) NEC 996.79
    infection or inflammation 996.69
    mechanical 996.59
  bleeding (intraoperative) (postoperative) 998.11
  blood vessel graft 996.1
    aortocoronary 996.03
      atherosclerosis —*see* Arteriosclerosis,
        coronary
      embolism 996.72
      occlusion NEC 996.72
      thrombus 996.72
    atherosclerosis —*see* Arteriosclerosis,
      extremities
    embolism 996.74
    occlusion NEC 996.74
    thrombus 996.74
  bone growth stimulator NEC 996.78
    infection or inflammation 996.67
  bone marrow transplant 996.85
  breast implant (prosthetic) NEC 996.79
    infection or inflammation 996.69
    mechanical 996.54
  bypass—*see also* Complications, anastomosis
    aortocoronary 996.03
      atherosclerosis —*see* Arteriosclerosis,
        coronary
      embolism 996.72
      occlusion NEC 996.72
      thrombus 996.72
    carotid artery 996.1
      atherosclerosis —*see* Arteriosclerosis,
        extremities
      embolism 996.74
      occlusion NEC 996.74
      thrombus 996.74
  cardiac (*see also* Disease, heart) 429.9
    device, implant, or graft NEC 996.72
      infection or inflammation 996.61
      long-term effect 429.4
      mechanical (*see also* Complications,
        mechanical, by type) 996.00
      valve prosthesis 996.71
        infection or inflammation 996.61
    postoperative NEC 997.1
      long-term effect 429.4
  cardiorenal (*see also* Hypertension, cardiorenal)
    404.90
  carotid artery bypass graft 996.1
    atherosclerosis —*see* Arteriosclerosis,
      extremities
    embolism 996.74
    occlusion NEC 996.74
    thrombus 996.74
  cataract fragments in eye 998.82

Complications—*continued*
  organ (immune or nonimmune cause) (partial)
    (total) 996.80
    bone marrow 996.85
    heart 996.83
    intestines 996.87
    kidney 996.81
    liver 996.82
    lung 996.84
    pancreas 996.86
    specified NEC 996.89
   skin NEC 996.79
    infection or inflammation 996.69
    rejection 996.52
     artificial 996.55
     decellularized allodermis 996.55
  heart—*see also* Disease, heart
   transplant (immune or nonimmune cause)
    996.83
  hematoma (intraoperative) (postoperative)
   998.12
  hemorrhage (intraoperative) (postoperative)
   998.11
  hyperalimentation therapy NEC 999.9
  immunization (procedure)—*see* Complications,
   vaccination
  implant—*see also* Complications, due to
   (presence of) any device, implant, or graft
   classified to 996.0-996.5 NEC
   mechanical—*see* Complications, mechanical,
    implant
  infection and inflammation
   due to (presence of) any device, implant, or
    graft classified to 996.0-996.5 NEC 996.50
    arterial NEC 996.62
     coronary 996.61
     renal dialysis 996.62
    arteriovenous fistula or shunt 996.62
    bone growth stimulator 996.67
    breast 996.69
    cardiac 996.61
    catheter NEC 996.69
     peritoneal 996.68
     spinal 996.63
     urinary, indwelling 996.64
     vascular NEC 996.62
     ventricular shunt 996.63
    coronary artery bypass 996.61
    electrodes
     brain 996.63
     heart 996.61
    gastrointestinal NEC 996.69
    genitourinary NEC 996.65
     indwelling urinary catheter 996.64
    heart valve 996.61
    infusion pump 996.62
    intrauterine contraceptive device 996.65
    joint prosthesis, internal 996.66
    ocular lens 996.69
    orbital (implant) 996.69
    orthopedic NEC 996.67
     joint, internal 996.66
    specified type NEC 996.69
    urinary catheter, indwelling 996.64
    ventricular shunt 996.63
  infusion (procedure) 999.9
   blood—*see* Complications, transfusion
   infection NEC 999.3
   sepsis NEC 999.3
  inhalation therapy NEC 999.9

Complications—*continued*
  injection (procedure) 999.9
   drug reaction (*see also* Reaction, drug) 995.2
   infection NEC 999.3
   sepsis NEC 999.3
   serum (prophylactic) (therapeutic)—*see*
    Complications, vaccination
   vaccine (any)—*see* Complications, vaccination
  inoculation (any)—*see* Complications,
   vaccination
  internal device (catheter) (electronic) (fixation)
   (prosthetic) NEC—*see also* Complications,
   due to (presence of) any device, implant, or
   graft classified to 996.0-996.5 NEC
   mechanical—*see* Complications, mechanical
  intestinal transplant (immune or nonimmune
   cause) 996.87
  intraoperative bleeding or hemorrhage 998.11
  intrauterine contraceptive device (*see also*
   Complications, contraceptive device) 996.76
   infection or inflammation 996.65
   with fetal damage affecting management of
    pregnancy 655.8
  jejunostomy 569.60
  kidney transplant (immune or nonimmune
   cause) 996.81
  labor 669.9
   specified condition NEC 669.8
  liver transplant (immune or nonimmune cause)
   996.82
  lumbar puncture 349.0
  mechanical
   anastomosis—*see* Complications, mechanical,
    graft
   bypass—*see* Complications, mechanical, graft
   catheter NEC 996.59
    cardiac 996.09
    cystostomy 996.39
    dialysis (hemodialysis) 996.1
     peritoneal 996.56
    during a procedure 998.2
    urethral, indwelling 996.31
   colostomy 569.62
   device NEC 996.59
    balloon (counterpulsation), intra-aortic 996.1
    cardiac 996.00
     long-term effect 429.4
     specified NEC 996.09
    contraceptive, intrauterine 996.32
    counterpulsation, intra-aortic 996.1
    fixation, external, with internal components
     996.4
    fixation, internal (nail, rod, plate) 996.4
    genitourinary 996.30
     specified NEC 996.39
    nervous system 996.2
    orthopedic, internal 996.4
    prosthetic NEC 996.59
    umbrella, vena cava 996.1
    vascular 996.1
   dorsal column stimulator 996.2
   electrode NEC 996.59
    brain 996.2
    cardiac 996.01
    spinal column 996.2
   enterostomy 569.62
   fistula, arteriovenous, surgically created 996.1
   gastrostomy 536.42

Complications—*continued*
  graft NEC 996.52
    aortic (bifurcation) 996.1
    aortocoronary bypass 996.03
    blood vessel NEC 996.1
    bone 996.4
    cardiac 996.00
    carotid artery bypass 996.1
    cartilage 996.4
    corneal 996.51
    coronary bypass 996.03
    decellularized allodermis 996.55
    genitourinary 996.30
      specified NEC 996.39
    muscle 996.4
    nervous system 996.2
    organ (immune or nonimmune cause) 996.80
      heart 996.83
      intestines 996.87
      kidney 996.81
      liver 996.82
      lung 996.84
      pancreas 996.86
      specified NEC 996.89
    orthopedic, internal 996.4
    peripheral nerve 996.2
    prosthetic NEC 996.59
    skin 996.52
      artificial 996.55
    specified NEC 996.59
    tendon 996.4
    tissue NEC 996.52
    tooth 996.59
    ureter, without mention of resection 996.39
    vascular 996.1
  heart valve prosthesis 996.02
    long-term effect 429.4
  implant NEC 996.59
    cardiac 996.00
      long-term effect 429.4
      specified NEC 996.09
    electrode NEC 996.59
      brain 996.2
      cardiac 996.01
      spinal column 996.2
    genitourinary 996.30
    nervous system 996.2
    orthopedic, internal 996.4
    prosthetic NEC 996.59
      in
        bile duct 996.59
        breast 996.54
        chin 996.59
        eye
          ocular lens 996.53
          orbital globe 996.59
    vascular 996.1
  nonabsorbable surgical material 996.59
  pacemaker NEC 996.59
    brain 996.2
    cardiac 996.01
    nerve (phrenic) 996.2
  patch—*see* Complications, mechanical, graft
  prosthesis NEC 996.59
    bile duct 996.59
    breast 996.54
    chin 996.59
    ocular lens 996.53
    reconstruction, vas deferens 996.39
  reimplant NEC 996.59

Complications—*continued*
    extremity (*see also* Complications,
      reattached, extremity) 996.90
    organ (*see also* Complications, transplant,
      organ, by site) 996.80
    repair—*see* Complications, mechanical, graft
    shunt NEC 996.59
      arteriovenous, surgically created 996.1
      ventricular (communicating) 996.2
    stent NEC 996.59
    tracheostomy 519.02
    vas deferens reconstruction 996.39
  medical care NEC 999.9
    cardiac NEC 997.1
    gastrointestinal NEC 997.4
    nervous system NEC 997.00
    peripheral vascular NEC 997.2
    respiratory NEC 997.3
    urinary NEC 997.5
  nephrostomy 997.5
  nervous system
    device, implant, or graft NEC 349.1
      mechanical 996.2
    postoperative NEC 997.00
  obstetric 669.9
    procedure (instrumental) (manual) (surgical)
      669.4
    specified NEC 669.8
    surgical wound 674.3
  ocular lens implant NEC 996.79
    infection or inflammation 996.69
    mechanical 996.53
  organ transplant—*see* Complications,
    transplant, organ, by site
  orthopedic device, implant, or graft
    internal (fixation) (nail) (plate) (rod) NEC
      996.78
      infection or inflammation 996.67
      joint prosthesis 996.77
        infection or inflammation 996.66
      mechanical 996.4
  pacemaker (cardiac) 996.72
    infection or inflammation 996.61
    mechanical 996.01
  pancreas transplant (immune or nonimmune
    cause) 996.86
  perfusion NEC 999.9
  perineal repair (obstetrical) 674.3
    disruption 674.2
  pessary (uterus) (vagina)—*see* Complications,
    contraceptive device
  phototherapy 990
  postcystoscopic 997.5
  postmastoidectomy NEC 383.30
  postoperative—*see* Complications, surgical
    procedures
  pregnancy NEC 646.9
    affecting fetus or newborn 761.9
  prosthetic device, internal—*see also*
    Complications, due to (presence of) any
    device, implant, or graft classified to
    996.0-996.5 NEC
    mechanical NEC (*see also* Complications,
      mechanical) 996.59
  puerperium NEC (*see also* Puerperal) 674.9
  puncture, spinal 349.0
  pyelogram 997.5
  radiation 990
  radiotherapy 990
  reattached
    body part, except extremity 996.99

Complications—*continued*
    extremity (infection) (rejection) 996.90
      arm(s) 996.94
      digit(s) (hand) 996.93
        foot 996.95
      finger(s) 996.93
      foot 996.95
      forearm 996.91
      hand 996.92
      leg 996.96
      lower NEC 996.96
      toe(s) 996.95
      upper NEC 996.94
    reimplant—*see also* Complications, due to
      (presence of) any device, implant, or graft
      classified to 996.0-996.5 NEC
      bone marrow 996.85
      extremity (*see also* Complications, reattached,
        extremity) 996.90
      due to infection 996.90
      mechanical—*see* Complications, mechanical,
        reimplant
      organ (immune or nonimmune cause) (partial)
        (total) (*see also* Complications, transplant,
        organ, by site) 996.80
    renal allograft 996.81
    renal dialysis—*see* Complications, dialysis
    respiratory 519.9
      device, implant or graft NEC 996.79
        infection or inflammation 996.69
        mechanical 996.59
      distress syndrome, adult, following trauma or
        surgery 518.5
      insufficiency, acute, postoperative 518.5
      postoperative NEC 997.3
      therapy NEC 999.9
    sedation during labor and delivery 668.9
      affecting fetus or newborn 763.5
      cardiac 668.1
      central nervous system 668.2
      pulmonary 668.0
      specified type NEC 668.8
    seroma (intraoperative) (postoperative)
      (noninfected) 998.13
      infected 998.51
    shunt—*see also* Complications, due to
      (presence of) any device, implant, or graft
      classified to 996.0-996.5 NEC
      mechanical—*see* Complications, mechanical,
        shunt
    specified body system NEC
      device, implant, or graft—*see* Complications,
        due to (presence of) any device, implant,
        or graft classified to 996.0-996.5 NEC
      postoperative NEC 997.99
    spinal puncture or tap 349.0
    stoma, external
      gastrointestinal tract
        colostomy 569.60
        enterostomy 569.60
        gastrostomy 536.40
      urinary tract 997.5
    surgical procedures 998.9
      accidental puncture or laceration 998.2
      amputation stump (late) 997.60
      anastomosis—*see* Complications, anastomosis
      burst stitches or sutures 998.3
      cardiac 997.1
        long-term effect following cardiac surgery
          429.4
      cataract fragments in eye 998.82

Complications—*continued*
    catheter device—*see* Complications, catheter
      device
    cecostomy malfunction 569.62
    colostomy malfunction 569.62
    cystostomy malfunction 997.5
    dehiscence (of incision) 998.3
    dialysis NEC (*see also* Complications,
      dialysis) 999.9
    disruption
      anastomosis (internal)—*see* Complications,
        mechanical, graft
      internal suture (line) 998.3
      wound 998.3
    dumping syndrome (postgastrectomy) 564.2
    elephantiasis or lymphedema 997.99
      postmastectomy 457.0
    emphysema (surgical) 998.81
    enterostomy malfunction 569.62
    evisceration 998.3
    fistula (persistent postoperative) 998.6
    foreign body inadvertently left in wound
      (sponge) (suture) (swab) 998.4
    from nonabsorbable surgical material
      (Dacron) (mesh) (permanent suture)
      (reinforcing) (Teflon)—*see*
      Complications, due to (presence of) any
      device, implant, or graft classified to
      996.0-996.5 NEC
    gastrointestinal NEC 997.4
    gastrostomy malfunction 536.42
    hematoma 998.12
    hemorrhage 998.11
    ileostomy malfunction 569.62
    internal prosthetic device NEC (*see also*
      Complications, internal device) 996.70
      hemolytic anemia 283.19
      infection or inflammation 996.60
      malfunction—*see* Complications,
        mechanical
      mechanical complication—*see*
        Complications, mechanical
      thrombus 996.70
    jejunostomy malfunction 569.62
    nervous system NEC 997.00
    obstruction, internal anastomosis—*see*
      Complications, mechanical, graft
    other body system NEC 997.99
    peripheral vascular NEC 997.2
    postcardiotomy syndrome 429.4
    postcholecystectomy syndrome 576.0
    postcommissurotomy syndrome 429.4
    postgastrectomy dumping syndrome 564.2
    postmastectomy lymphedema syndrome 457.0
    postmastoidectomy 383.30
      cholesteatoma, recurrent 383.32
      cyst, mucosal 383.31
      granulation 383.33
      inflammation, chronic 383.33
    postvagotomy syndrome 564.2
    postvalvulotomy syndrome 429.4
    reattached extremity (infection) (rejection)
      (*see also* Complications, reattached,
      extremity) 996.90
    respiratory NEC 997.3
    seroma 998.13
    shock (endotoxic) (hypovolemic) (septic)
      998.0

Compression—*continued*
  esophagus 530.3
    congenital, external 750.3
  Eustachian tube 381.63
  facies (congenital) 754.0
  fracture—*see* Fracture, by site
  heart—*see* Disease, heart
  intestine (*see also* Obstruction, intestine) 560.9
    with hernia—*see* Hernia, by site, with
      obstruction
  laryngeal nerve, recurrent 478.79
  leg NEC 355.8
  lower extremity NEC 355.8
  lumbosacral plexus 353.1
  lung 518.89
  lymphatic vessel 457.1
  medulla—*see* Compression, brain
  nerve NEC—*see also* Disorder, nerve
    arm NEC 354.9
    autonomic nervous system (*see also*
      Neuropathy, peripheral, autonomic) 337.9
    axillary 353.0
    cranial NEC 352.9
    due to displacement of intervertebral disc
      722.2
      with myelopathy 722.70
      cervical 722.0
        with myelopathy 722.71
      lumbar, lumbosacral 722.10
        with myelopathy 722.73
      thoracic, thoracolumbar 722.11
        with myelopathy 722.72
    iliohypogastric 355.79
    ilioinguinal 355.79
    leg NEC 355.8
    lower extremity NEC 355.8
    median (in carpal tunnel) 354.0
    obturator 355.79
    optic 377.49
    plantar 355.6
    posterior tibial (in tarsal tunnel) 355.5
    root (by scar tissue) NEC 724.9
      cervical NEC 723.4
      lumbar NEC 724.4
      lumbosacral 724.4
      thoracic 724.4
    saphenous 355.79
    sciatic (acute) 355.0
    sympathetic 337.9
    traumatic—*see* Injury, nerve
    ulnar 354.2
    upper extremity NEC 354.9
  peripheral—*see* Compression, nerve
  spinal (cord) (old or nontraumatic) 336.9
    by displacement of intervertebral disc—*see*
      Displacement, intervertebral disc
    nerve
      root NEC 724.9
        postoperative 722.80
          cervical region 722.81
          lumbar region 722.83
          thoracic region 722.82
        traumatic—*see* Injury, nerve, spinal
      traumatic—*see* Injury, nerve, spinal
    spondylogenic 721.91
      cervical 721.1
      lumbar, lumbosacral 721.42
      thoracic 721.41
    traumatic—*see also* Injury, spinal, by site
      with fracture, vertebra—*see* Fracture,
        vertebra, by site, with spinal cord injury

Compression—*continued*
  spondylogenic—*see* Compression, spinal cord,
    spondylogenic
  subcostal nerve (syndrome) 354.8
  sympathetic nerve NEC 337.9
  syndrome 958.5
  thorax 512.8
    iatrogenic 512.1
    postoperative 512.1
  trachea 519.1
    congenital 748.3
  ulnar nerve (by scar tissue) 354.2
  umbilical cord
    affecting fetus or newborn 762.5
      cord prolapsed 762.4
    complicating delivery 663.2
      cord around neck 663.1
      cord prolapsed 663.0
  upper extremity NEC 354.9
  ureter 593.3
  urethra—*see* Stricture, urethra
  vein 459.2
  vena cava (inferior) (superior) 459.2
  vertebral NEC—*see* Compression, spinal (cord)
Compulsion, compulsive
  eating 307.51
  neurosis (obsessive) 300.3
  personality 301.4
  states (mixed) 300.3
  swearing 300.3
    in Gilles de la Tourette's syndrome 307.23
  tics and spasms 307.22
  water drinking NEC (syndrome) 307.9
Concato's disease (pericardial polyserositis)
  423.2
  peritoneal 568.82
  pleural—*see* Pleurisy
Concavity, chest wall 738.3
Concealed
  hemorrhage NEC 459.0
  penis 752.65
Concentric fading 368.12
Concern (normal) about sick person in family
  V61.49
Concrescence (teeth) 520.2
Concretio cordis 423.1
  rheumatic 393
Concretion —*see also* Calculus
  appendicular 543.9
  canaliculus 375.57
  clitoris 624.8
  conjunctiva 372.54
  eyelid 374.56
  intestine (impaction) (obstruction) 560.39
  lacrimal (passages) 375.57
  prepuce (male) 605
    female (clitoris) 624.8
  salivary gland (any) 527.5
  seminal vesicle 608.89
  stomach 537.89
  tonsil 474.8
Concussion (current) 850.9
  with
    loss of consciousness 850.5
      brief (less than one hour) 850.1
      moderate (1-24 hours) 850.2
      prolonged (more than 24 hours) (with
        complete recovery) (with return to
        pre-existing conscious level) 850.3
        without return to pre-existing conscious
          level 850.4

Concussion—*continued*
　mental confusion or disorientation (without
　　loss of consciousness) 850.0
　　with loss of consciousness—*see*
　　　Concussion, with, loss of consciousness
　without loss of consciousness 850.0
　blast (air) (hydraulic) (immersion) (underwater)
　　869.0
　with open wound into cavity 869.1
　abdomen or thorax—*see* Injury, internal, by
　　site
　brain—*see* Concussion, brain
　ear (acoustic nerve trauma) 951.5
　　with perforation, tympanic membrane—*see*
　　　Wound, open, ear drum
　thorax—*see* Injury, internal, intrathoracic
　　organs NEC
　brain or cerebral (without skull fracture) 850.9
　　with
　　　loss of consciousness 850.5
　　　　brief (less than one hour) 850.1
　　　　moderate (1-24 hours) 850.2
　　　　prolonged (more than 24 hours) (with
　　　　　complete recovery) (with return to
　　　　　pre-existing conscious level) 850.3
　　　　without return to pre-existing conscious
　　　　　level 850.4
　　　mental confusion or disorientation (without
　　　　loss of consciousness) 850.0
　　　　with loss of consciousness—*see*
　　　　　Concussion, brain, with, loss of
　　　　　consciousness
　　　skull fracture—*see* Fracture, skull, by site
　　without loss of consciousness 850.0
　cauda equina 952.4
　cerebral—*see* Concussion, brain
　conus medullaris (spine) 952.4
　hydraulic—*see* Concussion, blast
　internal organs—*see* Injury, internal, by site
　labyrinth—*see* Injury, intracranial
　ocular 921.3
　osseous labyrinth—*see* Injury, intracranial
　spinal (cord)—*see also* Injury, spinal, by site
　　due to
　　　broken
　　　　back—*see* Fracture, vertebra, by site, with
　　　　　spinal cord injury
　　　　neck—*see* Fracture, vertebra, cervical,
　　　　　with spinal cord injury
　　　fracture, fracture dislocation, or
　　　　compression fracture of spine or
　　　　vertebra—*see* Fracture, vertebra, by site,
　　　　with spinal cord injury
　syndrome 310.2
　underwater blast—*see* Concussion, blast
Condition —*see also* Disease
　psychiatric 298.9
　respiratory NEC 519.9
　　acute or subacute NEC 519.9
　　　due to
　　　　external agent 508.9
　　　　　specified type NEC 508.8
　　　　fumes or vapors (chemical) (inhalation)
　　　　　506.3
　　　　radiation 508.0
　　chronic NEC 519.9
　　　due to
　　　　external agent 508.9
　　　　　specified type NEC 508.8
　　　　fumes or vapors (chemical) (inhalation)
　　　　　506.4

Condition—*continued*
　　radiation 508.1
　　due to
　　　external agent 508.9
　　　　specified type NEC 508.8
　　　fumes or vapors (chemical) (inhalation)
　　　　506.9
Conduct disturbance (*see also* Disturbance,
　conduct) 312.9
　adjustment reaction 309.3
　hyperkinetic 314.2
Condyloma NEC 078.10
　acuminatum 078.11
　gonorrheal 098.0
　latum 091.3
　syphilitic 091.3
　　congenital 090.0
　venereal, syphilitic 091.3
Confinement —*see* Delivery
Conflagration —*see also* Burn, by site
　asphyxia (by inhalation of smoke, gases, fumes,
　　or vapors) 987.9
　　specified agent—*see* Table of drugs and
　　　chemicals
Conflict
　family V61.9
　　specified circumstance NEC V61.8
　interpersonal NEC V62.81
　marital V61.10
　　involving divorce or estrangement V61.0
　parent-child V61.20
　partner V61.10
Confluent —*see* condition
Confusion, confused (mental) (state) (*see also*
　State, confusional) 298.9
　acute 293.0
　epileptic 293.0
　postoperative 293.9
　psychogenic 298.2
　reactive (from emotional stress, psychological
　　trauma) 298.2
　subacute 293.1
Congelation 991.9
Congenital —*see also* condition
　aortic septum 747.29
　intrinsic factor deficiency 281.0
　malformation—*see* Anomaly
Congestion, congestive (chronic) (passive)
　asphyxia, newborn 768.9
　bladder 596.8
　bowel 569.89
　brain (*see also* Disease, cerebrovascular NEC)
　　437.8
　　malarial 084.9
　breast 611.79
　bronchi 519.1
　bronchial tube 519.1
　catarrhal 472.0
　cerebral—*see* Congestion, brain
　cerebrospinal—*see* Congestion, brain
　chest 514
　chill 780.9
　　malarial (*see also* Malaria) 084.6
　circulatory NEC 459.9
　conjunctiva 372.71
　due to disturbance of circulation 459.9
　duodenum 537.3
　enteritis—*see* Enteritis
　eye 372.71
　fibrosis syndrome (pelvic) 625.5
　gastroenteritis—*see* Enteritis

Conjunctivitis—*continued*
sunlamp 372.04
swimming pool 077.0
trachomatous (follicular) 076.1
acute 076.0
late effect 139.1
traumatic NEC 372.39
tuberculous (*see also* Tuberculosis) 017.3
[370.31]
tularemic 021.3
tularensis 021.3
vernal 372.13
limbar 372.13 *[370.32]*
viral 077.99
acute hemorrhagic 077.4
specified NEC 077.8
Conjunctivochalasis 372.81
Conjunctoblepharitis —*see* Conjunctivitis
Conn (-Louis) syndrome (primary aldosteronism)
255.1
Connective tissue —*see* condition
Conradi (-Hünermann) syndrome or disease
(chondrodysplasia calcificans congenita)
756.59
Consanguinity V19.7
Consecutive —*see* condition
Consolidated lung (base)—*see* Pneumonia, lobar
Constipation (atonic) (neurogenic) (simple)
(spastic) 564.0
drug induced
correct substance properly administered 564.0
overdose or wrong substance given or taken
977.9
specified drug—*see* Table of drugs and
chemicals
neurogenic 564.0
psychogenic 306.4
Constitutional —*see also* condition
arterial hypotension (*see also* Hypotension)
458.9
obesity 278.00
morbid 278.01
psychopathic state 301.9
short stature in childhood 783.43
state, developmental V21.9
specified development NEC V21.8
substandard 301.6
Constitutionally substandard 301.6
Constriction
anomalous, meningeal bands or folds 742.8
aortic arch (congenital) 747.10
asphyxiation or suffocation by 994.7
bronchus 519.1
canal, ear (*see also* Stricture, ear canal,
acquired) 380.50
duodenum 537.3
gallbladder (*see also* Obstruction, gallbladder)
575.2
congenital 751.69
intestine (*see also* Obstruction, intestine) 560.9
larynx 478.74
congenital 748.3
meningeal bands or folds, anomalous 742.8
organ or site, congenital NEC—*see* Atresia
prepuce (congenital) 605
pylorus 537.0
adult hypertrophic 537.0
congenital or infantile 750.5
newborn 750.5
ring (uterus) 661.4
affecting fetus or newborn 763.7

Constriction—*continued*
spastic—*see also* Spasm
ureter 593.3
urethra—*see* Stricture, urethra
stomach 537.89
ureter 593.3
urethra—*see* Stricture, urethra
visual field (functional) (peripheral) 368.45
Constrictive —*see* condition
Consultation V65.9
medical—*see also* Counseling, medical
specified reason NEC V65.8
without complaint or sickness V65.9
feared complaint unfounded V65.5
specified reason NEC V65.8
Consumption —*see* Tuberculosis
Contact
with
AIDS virus V01.7
cholera V01.0
communicable disease V01.9
specified type NEC V01.8
viral NEC V01.7
German measles V01.4
gonorrhea V01.6
HIV V01.7
human immunodeficiency virus V01.7
parasitic disease NEC V01.8
poliomyelitis V01.2
rabies V01.5
rubella V01.4
smallpox V01.3
syphilis V01.6
tuberculosis V01.1
venereal disease V01.6
viral disease NEC V01.7
dermatitis—*see* Dermatitis
Contamination, food (*see also* Poisoning, food)
005.9
Contraception, contraceptive
advice NEC V25.09
family planning V25.09
fitting of diaphragm V25.02
prescribing or use of
oral contraceptive agent V25.01
specified agent NEC V25.02
counseling NEC V25.09
family planning V25.09
fitting of diaphragm V25.02
prescribing or use of
oral contraceptive agent V25.01
specified agent NEC V25.02
device (in situ) V45.59
causing menorrhagia 996.76
checking V25.42
complications 996.32
insertion V25.1
intrauterine V45.51
reinsertion V25.42
removal V25.42
subdermal V45.52
fitting of diaphragm V25.02
insertion
intrauterine contraceptive device V25.1
subdermal implantable V25.5
maintenance V25.40
examination V25.40
intrauterine device V25.42
oral contraceptive V25.41
specified method NEC V25.49
subdermal implantable V25.43

Contraception, contraceptive—*continued*
   intrauterine device V25.42
   oral contraceptive V25.41
   specified method NEC V25.49
   subdermal implantable V25.43
  management NEC V25.49
  prescription
   oral contraceptive agent V25.01
    repeat V25.41
   specified agent NEC V25.02
    repeat V25.49
  sterilization V25.2
  surveillance V25.40
   intrauterine device V25.42
   oral contraceptive agent V25.41
   specified method NEC V25.49
   subdermal implantable V25.43

Contraction, contracture, contracted
  Achilles tendon (*see also* Short, tendon,
    Achilles) 727.81
  anus 564.89
  axilla 729.9
  bile duct (*see also* Disease, biliary) 576.8
  bladder 596.8
   neck or sphincter 596.0
  bowel (*see also* Obstruction, intestine) 560.9
  Braxton Hicks 644.1
  bronchus 519.1
  burn (old)—*see* Cicatrix
  cecum (*see also* Obstruction, intestine) 560.9
  cervix (*see also* Stricture, cervix) 622.4
   congenital 752.49
  cicatricial—*see* Cicatrix
  colon (*see also* Obstruction, intestine) 560.9
  conjunctiva trachomatous, active 076.1
   late effect 139.1
  Dupuytren's 728.6
  eyelid 374.41
  eye socket (after enucleation) 372.64
  face 729.9
  fascia (lata) (postural) 728.89
   Dupuytren's 728.6
   palmar 728.6
   plantar 728.71
  finger NEC 736.29
   congenital 755.59
   joint (*see also* Contraction, joint) 718.44
  flaccid, paralytic
   joint (*see also* Contraction, joint) 718.4
   muscle 728.85
    ocular 378.50
  gallbladder (*see also* Obstruction, gallbladder)
    575.2
  hamstring 728.89
   tendon 727.81
  heart valve—*see* Endocarditis
  Hicks' 644.1
  hip (*see also* Contraction, joint) 718.4
  hourglass
   bladder 596.8
    congenital 753.8
   gallbladder (*see also* Obstruction, gallbladder)
    575.2
    congenital 751.69
   stomach 536.8
    congenital 750.7
    psychogenic 306.4
   uterus 661.4
    affecting fetus or newborn 763.7
  hysterical 300.11
  infantile (*see also* Epilepsy) 345.6

Contraction—*continued*
  internal os (*see also* Stricture, cervix) 622.4
  intestine (*see also* Obstruction, intestine) 560.9
  joint (abduction) (acquired) (adduction)
    (flexion) (rotation) 718.40
   ankle 718.47
   congenital NEC 755.8
    generalized or multiple 754.89
     lower limb joints 754.89
    hip (*see also* Subluxation, congenital, hip)
     754.32
    lower limb (including pelvic girdle) not
     involving hip 754.89
    upper limb (including shoulder girdle) 755.59
   elbow 718.42
   foot 718.47
   hand 718.44
   hip 718.45
   hysterical 300.11
   knee 718.46
   multiple sites 718.49
   pelvic region 718.45
   shoulder (region) 718.41
   specified site NEC 718.48
   wrist 718.43
  kidney (granular) (secondary) (*see also*
    Sclerosis, renal) 587
   congenital 753.3
   hydronephritic 591
   pyelonephritic (*see also* Pyelitis, chronic)
    590.00
   tuberculous (*see also* Tuberculosis) 016.0
  ligament 728.89
   congenital 756.89
  liver—*see* Cirrhosis, liver
  muscle (postinfectional) (postural) NEC 728.85
   congenital 756.89
    sternocleidomastoid 754.1
   extraocular 378.60
   eye (extrinsic) (*see also* Strabismus) 378.9
    paralytic (*see also* Strabismus, paralytic)
     378.50
   flaccid 728.85
   hysterical 300.11
   ischemic (Volkmann's) 958.6
   paralytic 728.85
   posttraumatic 958.6
   psychogenic 306.0
    specified as conversion reaction 300.11
  myotonic 728.85
  neck (*see also* Torticollis) 723.5
   congenital 754.1
   psychogenic 306.0
  ocular muscle (*see also* Strabismus) 378.9
   paralytic (*see also* Strabismus, paralytic)
    378.50
  organ or site, congenital NEC—*see* Atresia
  outlet (pelvis)—*see* Contraction, pelvis
  palmar fascia 728.6
  paralytic
   joint (*see also* Contraction, joint) 718.4
   muscle 728.85
    ocular (*see also* Strabismus, paralytic)
     378.50
  pelvis (acquired) (general) 738.6
   affecting fetus or newborn 763.1
   complicating delivery 653.1
    causing obstructed labor 660.1
    generally contracted 653.1
     causing obstructed labor 660.1
   inlet 653.2

Contraction—*continued*
    causing obstructed labor 660.1
    midpelvic 653.8
      causing obstructed labor 660.1
    midplane 653.8
      causing obstructed labor 660.1
    outlet 653.3
      causing obstructed labor 660.1
plantar fascia 728.71
premature
  atrial 427.61
  auricular 427.61
  auriculoventricular 427.61
  heart (junctional) (nodal) 427.60
  supraventricular 427.61
  ventricular 427.69
prostate 602.8
pylorus (*see also* Pylorospasm) 537.81
rectosigmoid (*see also* Obstruction, intestine) 560.9
rectum, rectal (sphincter) 564.89
  psychogenic 306.4
ring (Bandl's) 661.4
  affecting fetus or newborn 763.7
scar—*see* Cicatrix
sigmoid (*see also* Obstruction, intestine) 560.9
socket, eye 372.64
spine (*see also* Curvature, spine) 737.9
stomach 536.8
  hourglass 536.8
    congenital 750.7
    psychogenic 306.4
  psychogenic 306.4
tendon (sheath) (*see also* Short, tendon) 727.81
toe 735.8
ureterovesical orifice (postinfectional) 593.3
urethra 599.84
uterus 621.8
  abnormal 661.9
    affecting fetus or newborn 763.7
  clonic, hourglass or tetanic 661.4
    affecting fetus or newborn 763.7
  dyscoordinate 661.4
    affecting fetus or newborn 763.7
  hourglass 661.4
    affecting fetus or newborn 763.7
  hypotonic NEC 661.2
    affecting fetus or newborn 763.7
  incoordinate 661.4
    affecting fetus or newborn 763.7
  inefficient or poor 661.2
    affecting fetus or newborn 763.7
  irregular 661.2
    affecting fetus or newborn 763.7
  tetanic 661.4
    affecting fetus or newborn 763.7
vagina (outlet) 623.2
vesical 596.8
  neck or urethral orifice 596.0
visual field, generalized 368.45
Volkmann's (ischemic) 958.6

Contusion (skin surface intact) 924.9
with
  crush injury—*see* Crush
  dislocation—*see* Dislocation, by site
  fracture—*see* Fracture, by site
  internal injury—*see also* Injury, internal, by site
    heart—*see* Contusion, cardiac
    kidney—*see* Contusion, kidney
    liver—*see* Contusion, liver

Contusion—*continued*
  lung—*see* Contusion, lung
  spleen—*see* Contusion, spleen
  intracranial injury—*see* Injury, intracranial
  nerve injury—*see* Injury, nerve
  open wound—*see* Wound, open, by site
abdomen, abdominal (muscle) (wall) 922.2
  organ(s) NEC 868.00
adnexa, eye NEC 921.9
ankle 924.21
  with other parts of foot 924.20
arm 923.9
  lower (with elbow) 923.10
  upper 923.03
    with shoulder or axillary region 923.09
auditory canal (external) (meatus) (and other part(s) of neck, scalp, or face, except eye) 920
auricle, ear (and other part(s) of neck, scalp, or face except eye) 920
axilla 923.02
  with shoulder or upper arm 923.09
back 922.31
bone NEC 924.9
brain (cerebral) (membrane) (with hemorrhage) 851.8

Note—Use the following fifth-digit subclassification with categories 851-854:

0 unspecified state of consciousness
1 with no loss of consciousness
2 with brief [less than one hour] loss of consciousness
3 with moderate [1-24 hours] loss of consciousness
4 with prolonged [more than 24 hours] loss of consciousness and return to pre-existing conscious level
5 with prolonged [more than 24 hours] loss of consciousness, without return to pre-existing conscious level
Use fifth-digit 5 to designate when a patient is unconscious and dies before regaining conciousness, regardless of the duration of the loss of conciousness
6 with loss of consciousness of unspecified duration
9 with concussion, unspecified

---

with
  open intracranial wound 851.9
  skull fracture—*see* Fracture, skull, by site
cerebellum 851.4
  with open intracranial wound 851.5
cortex 851.0
  with open intracranial wound 851.1
occipital lobe 851.4
  with open intracranial wound 851.5
stem 851.4
  with open intracranial wound 851.5
breast 922.0
brow (and other part(s) of neck, scalp, or face, except eye) 920
buttock 922.32
canthus 921.1
cardiac 861.01
  with open wound into thorax 861.11
cauda equina (spine) 952.4
cerebellum—*see* Contusion, brain, cerebellum
cerebral—*see* Contusion, brain

Contusion—*continued*
cheek(s) (and other part(s) of neck, scalp, or
    face, except eye) 920
chest (wall) 922.1
chin (and other part(s) of neck, scalp, or face,
    except eye) 920
clitoris 922.4
conjunctiva 921.1
conus medullaris (spine) 952.4
cornea 921.3
corpus cavernosum 922.4
cortex (brain) (cerebral)—*see* Contusion, brain,
    cortex
costal region 922.1
ear (and other part(s) of neck, scalp, or face
    except eye) 920
elbow 923.11
    with forearm 923.10
epididymis 922.4
epigastric region 922.2
eye NEC 921.9
eyeball 921.3
eyelid(s) (and periocular area) 921.1
face (and neck, or scalp any part, except eye)
    920
femoral triangle 922.2
fetus or newborn 772.6
finger(s) (nail) (subungual) 923.3
flank 922.2
foot (with ankle) (excluding toe(s)) 924.20
forearm (and elbow) 923.10
forehead (and other part(s) of neck, scalp, or
    face, except eye) 920
genital organs, external 922.4
globe (eye) 921.3
groin 922.2
gum(s) (and other part(s) of neck, scalp, or face.
    except eye) 920
hand(s) (except fingers alone) 923.20
head (any part, except eye) (and face) (and
    neck) 920
heart—*see* Contusion, cardiac
heel 924.20
hip 924.01
    with thigh 924.00
iliac region 922.2
inguinal region 922.2
internal organs (abdomen, chest, or pelvis)
    NEC—*see* Injury, internal, by site
interscapular region 922.33
iris (eye) 921.3
kidney 866.01
    with open wound into cavity 866.11
knee 924.11
    with lower leg 924.10
labium (majus) (minus) 922.4
lacrimal apparatus, gland, or sac 921.1
larynx (and other part(s) of neck, scalp, or face.
    except eye) 920
late effect—*see* Late, effects (of), contusion
leg 924.5
    lower (with knee) 924.10
lens 921.3
lingual (and other part(s) of neck, scalp, or face,
    except eye) 920
lip(s) (and other part(s) of neck, scalp, or face,
    except eye) 920
liver 864.01
    with
        laceration—*see* Laceration, liver
        open wound into cavity 864.11

Contusion—*continued*
lower extremity 924.5
    multiple sites 924.4
lumbar region 922.31
lung 861.21
    with open wound into thorax 861.31
malar region (and other part(s) of neck, scalp, or
    face, except eye) 920
mandibular joint (and other part(s) of neck,
    scalp, or face, except eye) 920
mastoid region (and other part(s) of neck, scalp,
    or face, except eye) 920
membrane, brain—*see* Contusion, brain
midthoracic region 922.1
mouth (and other part(s) of neck, scalp, or face,
    except eye) 920
multiple sites (not classifiable to same
    three-digit category) 924.8
    lower limb 924.4
    trunk 922.8
    upper limb 923.8
muscle NEC 924.9
myocardium—*see* Contusion, cardiac
nasal (septum) (and other part(s) of neck, scalp,
    or face, except eye) 920
neck (and scalp, or face any part, except eye)
    920
nerve—*see* Injury, nerve, by site
continuednose (and other part(s) of neck, scalp,
    or face, except eye) 920
occipital region (scalp) (and neck or face,
    except eye) 920
    lobe—*see* Contusion, brain, occipital lobe
orbit (region) (tissues) 921.2
palate (soft) (and other part(s) of neck, scalp, or
    face, except eye) 920
parietal region (scalp) (and neck, or face, except
    eye) 920
    lobe—*see* Contusion, brain
penis 922.4
pericardium—*see* Contusion, cardiac
perineum 922.4
periocular area 921.1
pharynx (and other part(s) of neck, scalp, or
    face, except eye) 920
popliteal space (*see also* Contusion, knee)
    924.11
prepuce 922.4
pubic region 922.4
pudenda 922.4
pulmonary—*see* Contusion, lung
quadriceps femoralis 924.00
rib cage 922.1
sacral region 922.32
salivary ducts or glands (and other part(s) of
    neck, scalp, or face, except eye) 920
scalp (and neck, or face any part, except eye)
    920
scapular region 923.01
    with shoulder or upper arm 923.09
sclera (eye) 921.3
scrotum 922.4
shoulder 923.00
    with upper arm or axillar regions 923.09
skin NEC 924.9
skull 920
spermatic cord 922.4
spinal cord—*see also* Injury, spinal, by site
    cauda equina 952.4
    conus medullaris 952.4

Cor —*continued*
  triloculare 745.8
    biatriatum 745.3
    biventriculare 745.69
Corbus' disease 607.1
Cord —*see also* condition
  around neck (tightly) (with compression)
    affecting fetus or newborn 762.5
    complicating delivery 663.1
      without compression 663.3
        affecting fetus or newborn 762.6
  bladder NEC 344.61
    tabetic 094.0
  prolapse
    affecting fetus or newborn 762.4
    complicating delivery 663.0
Cord's angiopathy (*see also* Tuberculosis) 017.3
  [362.18]
Cordis ectopia 746.87
Corditis (spermatic) 608.4
Corectopia 743.46
Cori type glycogen storage disease —*see*
  Disease, glycogen storage
Cork-handlers' disease or lung 495.3
Corkscrew esophagus 530.5
Corlett's pyosis (impetigo) 684
Corn (infected) 700
Cornea—*see also* condition
  donor V59.5
  guttata (dystrophy) 371.57
  plana 743.41
Cornelia de Lange's syndrome (Amsterdam
  dwarf, mental retardation, and brachycephaly)
  759.89
Cornual gestation or pregnancy —*see*
  Pregnancy, cornual
Cornu cutaneum 702.8
Coronary (artery)—*see also* condition
  arising from aorta or pulmonary trunk 746.85
Corpora —*see also* condition
  amylacea (prostate) 602.8
  cavernosa—*see* condition
Corpulence (*see also* Obesity) 278.0
Corpus —*see* condition
Corrigan's disease —*see* Insufficiency, aortic
Corrosive burn —*see* Burn, by site
Corsican fever (*see also* Malaria) 084.6
Cortical —*see also* condition
  blindness 377.75
  necrosis, kidney (bilateral) 583.6
Corticoadrenal —*see* condition
Corticosexual syndrome 255.2
Coryza (acute) 460
  with grippe or influenza 487.1
  syphilitic 095.8
    congenital (chronic) 090.0
Costen's syndrome or complex 524.60
Costiveness (*see also* Constipation) 564.0
Costochondritis 733.6
Cotard's syndrome (paranoia) 297.1
Cot death 798.0
Cotungo's disease 724.3
Cough 786.2
  with hemorrhage (*see also* Hemoptysis) 786.3
  affected 786.2
  bronchial 786.2
    with grippe or influenza 487.1
  chronic 786.2
  epidemic 786.2
  functional 306.1
  hemorrhagic 786.3

Cough—*continued*
  hysterical 300.11
  laryngeal, spasmodic 786.2
  nervous 786.2
  psychogenic 306.1
  smokers' 491.0
  tea tasters' 112.89
Counseling NEC V65.40
  without complaint or sickness V65.49
  abuse victim NEC V62.89
    child V61.21
    partner V61.11
    spouse V61.11
  child abuse, maltreatment, or neglect V61.21
  contraceptive NEC V25.09
    device (intrauterine) V25.02
    maintenance V25.40
      intrauterine contraceptive device V25.42
      oral contraceptive (pill) V25.41
      specified type NEC V25.49
      subdermal implantable V25.43
    management NEC V25.9
    oral contraceptive (pill) V25.01
    prescription NEC V25.02
      oral contraceptive (pill) V25.01
        repeat prescription V25.41
      repeat prescription V25.40
    subdermal implantable V25.43
    surveillance V25.40
  dietary V65.3
  exercise V65.41
  explanation of
    investigation finding NEC V65.49
    medication NEC V65.49
  family planning V25.09
  for nonattending third party V65.1
  genetic V26.3
  gonorrhea V65.45
  health (advice) (education) (instruction) NEC
    V65.49
  HIV V65.44
  human immunodeficiency virus V65.44
  injury prevention V65.43
  marital V61.10
  medical (for) V65.9
    boarding school resident V60.6
    condition not demonstrated V65.5
    feared complaint and no disease found V65.5
    institutional resident V60.1
    on behalf of another V65.1
    person living alone V60.3
  parent-child conflict V61.20
    specified problem NEC V61.29
  partner abuse
    perpetrator V61.12
    victim V61.11
  perpetrator of
    child abuse V62.83
      parental V61.22
    partner abuse V61.12
    spouse abuse V61.12
  procreative V65.49
  sex NEC V65.49
    transmitted disease NEC V65.45
      HIV V65.44
  specified reason NEC V65.49
  spousal abuse
    perpetrator V61.12
    victim V61.11
  substance use and abuse V65.42
  syphilis V65.45

Counseling—*continued*
 victim (of)
  abuse NEC V62.89
  child abuse V61.21
  partner abuse V61.11
  spousal abuse V61.11
Coupled rhythm 427.89
Couvelaire uterus (complicating delivery)—*see*
  Placenta, separation
Cowper's gland —*see* condition
Cowperitis (*see also* Urethritis) 597.89
 gonorrheal (acute) 098.0
  chronic or duration of 2 months or over 098.2
Cowpox (abortive) 051.0
 due to vaccination 999.0
 eyelid 051.0 *[373.5]*
  postvaccination 999.0 *[373.5]*
Coxa
 plana 732.1
 valga (acquired) 736.31
  congenital 755.61
  late effect of rickets 268.1
 vara (acquired) 736.32
  congenital 755.62
  late effect of rickets 268.1
Coxae malum senilis 715.25
Coxalgia (nontuberculous) 719.45
 tuberculous (*see also* Tuberculosis) 015.1
  [730.85]
Coxalgic pelvis 736.30
Coxitis 716.65
Coxsackie (infection) (virus) 079.2
 central nervous system NEC 048
 endocarditis 074.22
 enteritis 008.67
 meningitis (aseptic) 047.0
 myocarditis 074.23
 pericarditis 074.21
 pharyngitis 074.0
 pleurodynia 074.1
 specific disease NEC 074.8
Crabs, meaning pubic lice 132.2
Crack baby 760.75
Cracked nipple 611.2
 puerperal, postpartum 676.1
Cradle cap 690.11
Craft neurosis 300.89
Craigiasis 007.8
Cramp (s) 729.82
 abdominal 789.0
 bathing 994.1
 colic 789.0
  psychogenic 306.4
 due to immersion 994.1
 extremity (lower) (upper) NEC 729.82
 fireman 992.2
 heat 992.2
 hysterical 300.11
 immersion 994.1
 intestinal 789.0
  psychogenic 306.4
 linotypist's 300.89
  organic 333.84
 muscle (extremity) (general) 729.82
  due to immersion 994.1
  hysterical 300.11
 occupational (hand) 300.89
  organic 333.84

Cramp(s)—*continued*
 psychogenic 307.89
 salt depletion 276.1
 stoker 992.2
 stomach 789.0
 telegraphers' 300.89
  organic 333.84
 typists' 300.89
  organic 333.84
 uterus 625.8
  menstrual 625.3
 writers' 333.84
  organic 333.84
  psychogenic 300.89
Cranial —*see* condition
Cranioclasis, fetal 763.89
Craniocleidodysostosis 755.59
Craniofenestria (skull) 756.0
Craniolacunia (skull) 756.0
Craniopagus 759.4
Craniopathy, metabolic 733.3
Craniopharyngeal —*see* condition
Craniopharyngioma (M9350/1) 237.0
Craniorachischisis (totalis) 740.1
Cranioschisis 756.0
Craniostenosis 756.0
Craniosynostosis 756.0
Craniotabes (cause unknown) 733.3
 rachitic 268.1
 syphilitic 090.5
Craniotomy, fetal 763.89
Cranium —*see* condition
Craw-craw 125.3
Creaking joint 719.60
 ankle 719.67
 elbow 719.62
 foot 719.67
 hand 719.64
 hip 719.65
 knee 719.66
 multiple sites 719.69
 pelvic region 719.65
 shoulder (region) 719.61
 specified site NEC 719.68
 wrist 719.63
Creeping
 eruption 126.9
 palsy 335.21
 paralysis 335.21
Crenated tongue 529.8
Creotoxism 005.9
Crepitus
 caput 756.0
 joint 719.60
  ankle 719.67
  elbow 719.62
  foot 719.67
  hand 719.64
  hip 719.65
  knee 719.66
  multiple sites 719.69
  pelvic region 719.65
  shoulder (region) 719.61
  specified site NEC 719.68
  wrist 719.63
Crescent or conus choroid, congenital 743.57

Cretin, cretinism (athyrotic) (congenital) (endemic) (metabolic) (nongoitrous) (sporadic) 243
  goitrous (sporadic) 246.1
  pelvis (dwarf type) (male type) 243
    with disproportion (fetopelvic) 653.1
      affecting fetus or newborn 763.1
      causing obstructed labor 660.1
        affecting fetus or newborn 763.1
  pituitary 253.3
Cretinoid degeneration 243
Creutzfeldt-Jakob disease (syndrome) 046.1
  with dementia
    with behavioral disturbance 046.1 *[294.11]*
    without behavioral disturbance 046.1 *[294.10]*
Crib death 798.0
Cribriform hymen 752.49
Cri-du-chat syndrome 758.3
Crigler-Najjar disease or syndrome (congenital hyperbilirubinemia) 277.4
Crimean hemorrhagic fever 065.0
Criminalism 301.7
Crisis
  abdomen 789.0
  addisonian (acute adrenocortical insufficiency) 255.4
  adrenal (cortical) 255.4
  asthmatic—*see* Asthma
  brain, cerebral (*see also* Disease, cerebrovascular, acute) 436
  celiac 579.0
  Dietl's 593.4
  emotional NEC 309.29
    acute reaction to stress 308.0
    adjustment reaction 309.9
    specific to childhood and adolescence 313.9
  gastric (tabetic) 094.0
  glaucomatocyclitic 364.22
  heart (*see also* Failure, heart) 428.9
  hypertensive—*see* Hypertension
  nitritoid
    correct substance properly administered 458.2
    overdose or wrong substance given or taken 961.1
  oculogyric 378.87
    psychogenic 306.7
  Pel's 094.0
  psychosexual identity 302.6
  rectum 094.0
  renal 593.81
  sickle cell 282.62
  stomach (tabetic) 094.0
  tabetic 094.0
  thyroid (*see also* Thyrotoxicosis) 242.9
  thyrotoxic (*see also* Thyrotoxicosis) 242.9
  vascular—*see* Disease, cerebrovascular, acute
Crocq's disease (acrocyanosis) 443.89
Crohn's disease (*see also* Enteritis, regional) 555.9
Cronkhite-Canada syndrome 211.3
Crooked septum, nasal 470
Cross
  birth (of fetus) complicating delivery 652.3
    with successful version 652.1
    causing obstructed labor 660.0
  bite, anterior or posterior 524.2
  eye (*see also* Esotropia) 378.00
Crossed ectopia of kidney 753.3
Crossfoot 754.50

Croup, croupus (acute) (angina) (catarrhal) (infective) (inflammatory) (laryngeal) (membranous) (nondiphtheritic) (pseudomembranous) 464.4
  asthmatic (*see also* Asthma) 493.9
  bronchial 466.0
  diphtheritic (membranous) 032.3
  false 478.75
  spasmodic 478.75
    diphtheritic 032.3
  stridulous 478.75
    diphtheritic 032.3
Crouzon's disease (craniofacial dysostosis) 756.0
Crowding, teeth 524.3
CRST syndrome (cutaneous systemic sclerosis) 710.1
Cruchet's disease (encephalitis lethargica) 049.8
Cruelty in children (*see also* Disturbance, conduct) 312.9
Crural ulcer (*see also* Ulcer, lower extremity) 707.10
Crush, crushed, crushing (injury) 929.9
  with
    fracture—*see* Fracture, by site
  abdomen 926.19
    internal—*see* Injury, internal, abdomen
  ankle 928.21
    with other parts of foot 928.20
  arm 927.9
    lower (and elbow) 927.10
    upper 927.03
      with shoulder or axillary region 927.09
  axilla 927.02
    with shoulder or upper arm 927.09
  back 926.11
  breast 926.19
  buttock 926.12
  cheek 925.1
  chest—*see* Injury, internal, chest
  ear 925.1
  elbow 927.11
    with forearm 927.10
  face 925.1
  finger(s) 927.3
    with hand(s) 927.20
      and wrist(s) 927.21
  flank 926.19
  foot, excluding toe(s) alone (with ankle) 928.20
  forearm (and elbow) 927.10
  genitalia, external (female) (male) 926.0
    internal—*see* Injury, internal, genital organ NEC
  hand, except finger(s) alone (and wrist) 927.20
  head—*see* Fracture, skull, by site
  heel 928.20
  hip 928.01
    with thigh 928.00
  internal organ (abdomen, chest, or pelvis)—*see* Injury, internal, by site
  knee 928.11
    with leg, lower 928.10
  labium (majus) (minus) 926.0
  larynx 925.2
  late effect—*see* Late, effects (of), crushing
  leg 928.9
    lower 928.10
      and knee 928.11
    upper 928.00

Crush, crushed, crushing—*continued*
  limb
    lower 928.9
      multiple sites 928.8
    upper 927.9
      multiple sites 927.8
  multiple sites NEC 929.0
  neck 925.2
  nerve—*see* Injury, nerve, by site
  nose 802.0
    open 802.1
  penis 926.0
  pharynx 925.2
  scalp 925.2
  scapular region 927.01
    with shoulder or upper arm 927.09
  scrotum 926.0
  shoulder 927.00
    with upper arm or axillary region 927.09
  skull or cranium—*see* Fracture, skull, by site
  spinal cord—*see* Injury, spinal, by site
  syndrome (complication of trauma) 958.5
  testis 926.0
  thigh (with hip) 928.00
  throat 925.2
  thumb(s) (and fingers) 927.3
  toe(s) 928.3
    with foot 928.20
      and ankle 928.21
  tonsil 925.2
  trunk 926.9
    chest—*see* Injury, internal, intrathoracic
      organs NEC
    internal organ—*see* Injury, internal, by site
    multiple sites 926.8
    specified site NEC 926.19
  vulva 926.0
  wrist 927.21
    with hand(s), except fingers alone 927.20
Crusta lactea 690.11
Crusts 782.8
Crutch paralysis 953.4
Cruveilhier's disease 335.21
**Cruveilhier-Baumgarten cirrhosis, disease, or
  syndrome** 571.5
Cruz-Chagas disease (*see also*
  Trypanosomiasis) 086.2
Cryoglobulinemia (mixed) 273.2
Crypt (anal) (rectal) 569.49
Cryptitis (anal) (rectal) 569.49
Cryptococcosis (European) (pulmonary)
  (systemic) 117.5
Cryptococcus 117.5
  epidermicus 117.5
  neoformans, infection by 117.5
Cryptopapillitis (anus) 569.49
Cryptophthalmos (eyelid) 743.06
Cryptorchid, cryptorchism, cryptorchidism
  752.51
Cryptosporidiosis 007.4
Cryptotia 744.29
Crystallopathy
  calcium pyrophosphate (*see also* Arthritis)
    275.49 *[712.2]*
  dicalcium phosphate (*see also* Arthritis) 275.49
    [712.1]
  gouty 274.0
  pyrophosphate NEC (*see also* Arthritis) 275.49
    [712.2]
  uric acid 274.0
Crystalluria 791.9

Csillag's disease (lichen sclerosus et atrophicus)
  701.0
Cuban itch 050.1
Cubitus
  valgus (acquired) 736.01
    congenital 755.59
    late effect of rickets 268.1
  varus (acquired) 736.02
    congenital 755.59
    late effect of rickets 268.1
Cultural deprivation V62.4
Cupping of optic disc 377.14
Curling's ulcer —*see* Ulcer, duodenum
Curling esophagus 530.5
Curschmann (-Batten) (-Steinert) disease or
  syndrome 359.2
Curvature
  organ or site, congenital NEC—*see* Distortion
  penis (lateral) 752.69
  Pott's (spinal) (*see also* Tuberculosis) 015.0
    [737.43]
  radius, idiopathic, progressive (congenital)
    755.54
  spine (acquired) (angular) (idiopathic)
    (incorrect) (postural) 737.9
    congenital 754.2
    due to or associated with
      Charcot-Marie-Tooth disease 356.1 *[737.40]*
      mucopolysaccharidosis 277.5 *[737.40]*
      neurofibromatosis 237.71 *[737.40]*
      osteitis
        deformans 731.0 *[737.40]*
        fibrosa cystica 252.0 *[737.40]*
      osteoporosis (*see also* Osteoporosis) 733.00
        [737.40]
      poliomyelitis (*see also* Poliomyelitis) 138
        [737.40]
      tuberculosis (Pott's curvature) (*see also*
        Tuberculosis) 015.0 *[737.43]*
    kyphoscoliotic (*see also* Kyphoscoliosis)
      737.30
    kyphotic (*see also* Kyphosis) 737.10
    late effect of rickets 268.1 *[737.40]*
    Pott's 015.0 *[737.40]*
    scoliotic (*see also* Scoliosis) 737.30
    specified NEC 737.8
    tuberculous 015.0 *[737.40]*
Cushing's
  basophilism, disease, or syndrome (iatrogenic)
    (idiopathic) (pituitary basophilism)
    (pituitary dependent) 255.0
  ulcer—*see* Ulcer, peptic
Cushingoid due to steroid therapy
  correct substance properly administered 255.0
  overdose or wrong substance given or taken
    962.0
Cut (external)—*see* Wound, open, by site
Cutaneous —*see also* condition
  hemorrhage 782.7
  horn (cheek) (eyelid) (mouth) 702.8
  larva migrans 126.9
Cutis —*see also* condition
  hyperelastic 756.83
    acquired 701.8
  laxa 756.83
    senilis 701.8
  marmorata 782.61
  osteosis 709.3
  pendula 756.83
    acquired 701.8
  rhomboidalis nuchae 701.8

Cutis—*continued*
  verticis gyrata 757.39
    acquired 701.8
Cyanopathy, newborn 770.8
Cyanosis 782.5
  autotoxic 289.7
  common atrioventricular canal 745.69
  congenital 770.8
  conjunctiva 372.71
  due to
    endocardial cushion defect 745.60
    nonclosure, foramen botalli 745.5
    patent foramen botalli 745.5
    persistent foramen ovale 745.5
  enterogenous 289.7
  fetus or newborn 770.8
  ostium primum defect 745.61
  paroxysmal digital 443.0
  retina, retinal 362.10
Cycle
  anovulatory 628.0
  menstrual, irregular 626.4
Cyclencephaly 759.89
Cyclical vomiting 536.2
  psychogenic 306.4
Cyclitic membrane 364.74
Cyclitis (*see also* Iridocyclitis) 364.3
  acute 364.00
    primary 364.01
    recurrent 364.02
  chronic 364.10
    in
        sarcoidosis 135 *[364.11]*
        tuberculosis (*see also* Tuberculosis) 017.3
          [364.11]
  Fuchs' heterochromic 364.21
  granulomatous 364.10
  lens induced 364.23
  nongranulomatous 364.00
  posterior 363.21
  primary 364.01
  recurrent 364.02
  secondary (noninfectious) 364.04
    infectious 364.03
  subacute 364.00
    primary 364.01
    recurrent 364.02
Cyclokeratitis —*see* Keratitis
Cyclophoria 378.44
Cyclopia, cyclops 759.89
Cycloplegia 367.51
Cyclospasm 367.53
Cyclosporiasis 007.5
Cyclothymia 301.13
Cyclothymic personality 301.13
Cyclotropia 378.33
Cyesis —*see* Pregnancy
Cylindroma (M8200/3)—*see also* Neoplasm, by
    site, malignant
  eccrine dermal (M8200/0)—*see* Neoplasm,
    skin, benign
  skin (M8200/0)—*see* Neoplasm, skin, benign
Cylindruria 791.7
Cyllosoma 759.89
Cynanche
  diphtheritic 032.3
  tonsillaris 475
Cynorexia 783.6
Cyphosis —*see* Kyphosis
Cyprus fever (*see also* Brucellosis) 023.9
Cyriax's syndrome (slipping rib) 733.99

Cyst (mucus) (retention) (serous) (simple)

> *Note—In general, cysts are not neoplastic and
> are classified to the appropriate category for
> disease of the specified anatomical site. This
> generalization does not apply to certain types of
> cysts which are neoplastic in nature, for
> example, dermoid, nor does it apply to cysts of
> certain structures, for example, branchial cleft,
> which are classified as developmental
> anomalies. The following listing includes some
> of the most frequently reported sites of cysts as
> well as qualifiers which indicate the type of
> cyst. The latter qualifiers usually are not
> repeated under the anatomical sites. Since the
> code assignment for a given site may vary
> depending upon the type of cyst, the coder
> should refer to the listings under the specified
> type of cyst before consideration is given to the
> site.*

  accessory, fallopian tube 752.11
  adenoid (infected) 474.8
  adrenal gland 255.8
    congenital 759.1
  air, lung 518.89
  allantoic 753.7
  alveolar process (jaw bone) 526.2
  amnion, amniotic 658.8
  anterior chamber (eye) 364.60
    exudative 364.62
    implantation (surgical) (traumatic) 364.61
    parasitic 360.13
  anterior nasopalatine 526.1
  antrum 478.1
  anus 569.49
  apical (periodontal) (tooth) 522.8
  appendix 543.9
  arachnoid, brain 348.0
  arytenoid 478.79
  auricle 706.2
  Baker's (knee) 727.51
    tuberculous (*see also* Tuberculosis) 015.2
  Bartholin's gland or duct 616.2
  bile duct (*see also* Disease, biliary) 576.8
  bladder (multiple) (trigone) 596.8
  Blessig's 362.62
  blood, endocardial (*see also* Endocarditis)
      424.90
  blue dome 610.0
  bone (local) 733.20
    aneurysmal 733.22
    jaw 526.2
      developmental (odontogenic) 526.0
      fissural 526.1
      latent 526.89
    solitary 733.21
    unicameral 733.21
  brain 348.0
    congenital 742.4
    hydatid (*see also* Echinococcus) 122.9
    third ventricle (colloid) 742.4
  branchial (cleft) 744.42
  branchiogenic 744.42
  breast (benign) (blue dome) (pedunculated)
      (solitary) (traumatic) 610.0
    involution 610.4
    sebaceous 610.8
  broad ligament (benign) 620.8
    embryonic 752.11

Cyst —*continued*
  ethmoid sinus 478.1
  eye (retention) 379.8
    congenital 743.03
    posterior segment, congenital 743.54
  eyebrow 706.2
  eyelid (sebaceous) 374.84
    infected 373.13
    sweat glands or ducts 374.84
  falciform ligament (inflammatory) 573.8
  fallopian tube 620.8
  female genital organs NEC 629.8
  fimbrial (congenital) 752.11
  fissural (oral region) 526.1
  follicle (atretic) (graafian) (ovarian) 620.0
    nabothian (gland) 616.0
  follicular (atretic) (ovarian) 620.0
    dentigerous 526.0
  frontal sinus 478.1
  gallbladder or duct 575.8
  ganglion 727.43
  Gartner's duct 752.11
  gas, of mesentery 568.89
  gingiva 523.8
  gland of moll 374.84
  globulomaxillary 526.1
  graafian follicle 620.0
  granulosal lutein 620.2
  hemangiomatous (M9121/0) (*see also*
    Hemangioma) 228.00
  hydatid (*see also* Echinococcus) 122.9
    fallopian tube (Morgagni) 752.11
    liver NEC 122.8
    lung NEC 122.9
    Morgagni 752.8
      fallopian tube 752.11
    specified site NEC 122.9
  hymen 623.8
    embryonal 752.41
  hypopharynx 478.26
  hypophysis, hypophyseal (duct) (recurrent)
    253.8
    cerebri 253.8
  implantation (dermoid)
    anterior chamber (eye) 364.61
    external area or site (skin) NEC 709.8
    iris 364.61
    vagina 623.8
    vulva 624.8
  incisor, incisive canal 526.1
  inclusion (epidermal) (epithelial) (epidermoid)
    (mucous) (squamous) (*see also* Cyst, skin)
    706.2
  not of skin—*see* Neoplasm, by site, benign
  intestine (large) (small) 569.89
  intracranial—*see* Cyst, brain
  intraligamentous 728.89
    knee 717.89
  intrasellar 253.8
  iris (idiopathic) 364.60
    exudative 364.62
    implantation (surgical) (traumatic) 364.61
    miotic pupillary 364.55
    parasitic 360.13
  Iwanoff's 362.62
  jaw (bone) (aneurysmal) (extravasation)
    (hemorrhagic) (traumatic) 526.2
    developmental (odontogenic) 526.0
    fissural 526.1
  keratin 706.2

Cyst —*continued*
  kidney (congenital) 753.10
    acquired 593.2
    calyceal (*see also* Hydronephrosis) 591
    multiple 753.19
    pyelogenic (*see also* Hydronephrosis) 591
    simple 593.2
    single 753.11
    solitary (not congenital) 593.2
  labium (majus) (minus) 624.8
    sebaceous 624.8
  lacrimal
    apparatus 375.43
    gland or sac 375.12
  larynx 478.79
  lens 379.39
    congenital 743.39
  lip (gland) 528.5
  liver 573.8
    congenital 751.62
    hydatid (*see also* Echinococcus) 122.8
      granulosis 122.0
      multilocularis 122.5
  lung 518.89
    congenital 748.4
    giant bullous 492.0
  lutein 620.1
  lymphangiomatous (M9173/0) 228.1
  lymphoepithelial
    mouth 528.4
    oral soft tissue 528.4
  macula 362.54
  malignant (M8000/3)—*see* Neoplasm, by site,
    malignant
  mammary gland (sweat gland) (*see also* Cyst,
    breast) 610.0
  mandible 526.2
    dentigerous 526.0
    radicular 522.8
  maxilla 526.2
    dentigerous 526.0
    radicular 522.8
  median
    anterior maxillary 526.1
    palatal 526.1
  mediastinum (congenital) 748.8
  meibomian (gland) (retention) 373.2
    infected 373.12
  membrane, brain 348.0
  meninges (cerebral) 348.0
    spinal 349.2
  meniscus knee 717.5
  mesentery, mesenteric (gas) 568.89
    chyle 457.8
    gas 568.89
  mesonephric duct 752.8
  mesothelial
    peritoneum 568.89
    pleura (peritoneal) 568.89
  milk 611.5
  miotic pupillary (iris) 364.55
  Morgagni (hydatid) 752.8
    fallopian tube 752.11
  mouth 528.4
  mullerian duct 752.8
  multilocular (ovary) (M8000/1) 239.5
  myometrium 621.8
  nabothian (follicle) (ruptured) 616.0
  nasal sinus 478.1
  nasoalveolar 528.4
  nasolabial 528.4

Cyst —*continued*
  seminal vesicle 608.89
  serous (ovary) 620.2
  sinus (antral) (ethmoidal) (frontal) (maxillary)
      (nasal) (sphenoidal) 478.1
  Skene's gland 599.89
  skin (epidermal) (epidermoid, inclusion)
      (epithelial) (inclusion) (retention)
      (sebaceous) 706.2
    breast 610.8
    eyelid 374.84
    genital organ NEC
      female 629.8
      male 608.89
    neoplastic 216.3
    scrotum 706.2
    sweat gland or duct 705.89
  solitary
    bone 733.21
    kidney 593.2
  spermatic cord 608.89
  sphenoid sinus 478.1
  spinal meninges 349.2
  spine (*see also* Cyst, bone) 733.20
  spleen NEC 289.59
    congenital 759.0
    hydatid (*see also* Echinococcus) 122.9
  spring water (pericardium) 746.89
  subarachnoid 348.0
    intrasellar 793.0
  subdural (cerebral) 348.0
    spinal cord 349.2
  sublingual gland 527.6
    mucous extravasation or retention 527.6
  submaxillary gland 527.6
    mucous extravasation or retention 527.6
  suburethral 599.89
  suprarenal gland 255.8
  suprasellar—*see* Cyst, brain
  sweat gland or duct 705.89
  sympathetic nervous system 337.9
  synovial 727.40
    popliteal space 727.51
  Tarlov's 355.9
  tarsal 373.2
  tendon (sheath) 727.42
  testis 608.89
  theca-lutein (ovary) 620.2
  Thornwaldt's, Tornwaldt's 478.26
  thymus (gland) 254.8
  thyroglossal (duct) (infected) (persistent) 759.2
  thyroid (gland) 246.2
    adenomatous—*see* Goiter, nodular
    colloid (*see also* Goiter) 240.9
  thyrolingual duct (infected) (persistent) 759.2
  tongue (mucous) 529.8
  tonsil 474.8
  tooth (dental root) 522.8
  tubo-ovarian 620.8
    inflammatory 614.1
  tunica vaginalis 608.89
  turbinate (nose) (*see also* Cyst, bone) 733.20
  Tyson's gland (benign) (infected) 607.89
  umbilicus 759.89
  urachus 753.7
  ureter 593.89
  ureterovesical orifice 593.89
    congenital 753.4
  urethra 599.84
  urethral gland (Cowper's) 599.89

Cyst —*continued*
  uterine
    ligament 620.8
      embryonic 752.11
    tube 620.8
  uterus (body) (corpus) (recurrent) 621.8
    embryonal 752.3
  utricle (ear) 386.8
    prostatic 599.89
  utriculus masculinus 599.89
  vagina, vaginal (squamous cell) (wall) 623.8
    embryonal 752.41
    implantation 623.8
    inclusion 623.8
  vallecula, vallecular 478.79
  ventricle, neuroepithelial 348.0
  verumontanum 599.89
  vesical (orifice) 596.8
  vitreous humor 379.29
  vulva (sweat glands) 624.8
    congenital 752.41
    implantation 624.8
    inclusion 624.8
    sebaceous gland 624.8
  vulvovaginal gland 624.8
  wolffian 752.8
Cystadenocarcinoma (M8440/3)—*see also*
    Neoplasm, by site, malignant
  bile duct type (M8161/3) 155.1
  endometrioid (M8380/3)—*see* Neoplasm, by
    site, malignant
  mucinous (M8470/3)
    papillary (M8471/3)
      specified site—*see* Neoplasm, by site,
        malignant
      unspecified site 183.0
    specified site—*see* Neoplasm, by site,
      malignant
    unspecified site 183.0
  papillary (M8450/3)
    mucinous (M8471/3)
      specified site—*see* Neoplasm, by site,
        malignant
      unspecified site 183.0
    pseudomucinous (M8471/3)
      specified site—*see* Neoplasm, by site,
        malignant
      unspecified site 183.0
    serous (M8460/3)
      specified site—*see* Neoplasm, by site,
        malignant
      unspecified site 183.0
    specified site—*see* Neoplasm, by site,
      malignant
    unspecified 183.0
  pseudomucinous (M8470/3)
    papillary (M8471/3)
      specified site—*see* Neoplasm, by site,
        malignant
      unspecified site 183.0
    specified site—*see* Neoplasm, by site,
      malignant
    unspecified site 183.0
  serous (M8441/3)
    papillary (M8460/3)
      specified site—*see* Neoplasm, by site,
        malignant
      unspecified site 183.0
    specified site—*see* Neoplasm, by site,
      malignant
    unspecified site 183.0

Cystadenofibroma (M9013/0)
  clear cell (M8313/0)—*see* Neoplasm, by site,
    benign
  endometrioid (M8381/0) 220
    borderline malignancy (M8381/1) 236.2
    malignant (M8381/3) 183.0
  mucinous (M9015/0)
    specified site—*see* Neoplasm, by site, benign
    unspecified site 220
  serous (M9014/0)
    specified site—*see* Neoplasm, by site, benign
    unspecified site 220
  specified site—*see* Neoplasm, by site, benign
  unspecified site 220
Cystadenoma (M8440/0)—*see also* Neoplasm,
  by site, benign
  bile duct (M8161/0) 211.5
  endometrioid (M8380/0)—*see also* Neoplasm,
    by site, benign
    borderline malignancy (M8380/1)—*see*
      Neoplasm, by site, uncertain behavior
  malignant (M8440/3)—*see* Neoplasm, by site,
    malignant
  mucinous (M8470/0)
    borderline malignancy (M8470/1)
      specified site—*see* Neoplasm, uncertain
        behavior
      unspecified site 236.2
    papillary (M8471/0)
      borderline malignancy (M8471/1)
        specified site—*see* Neoplasm, by site,
          uncertain behavior
        unspecified site 236.2
      specified site—*see* Neoplasm, by site,
        benign
      unspecified site 220
    specified site—*see* Neoplasm, by site, benign
    unspecified site 220
  papillary (M8450/0)
    borderline malignancy (M8450/1)
      specified site—*see* Neoplasm, by site,
        uncertain behavior
      unspecified site 236.2
    lymphomatosum (M8561/0) 210.2
    mucinous (M8471/0)
      borderline malignancy (M8471/1)
        specified site—*see* Neoplasm, by site,
          uncertain behavior
        unspecified site 236.2
      specified site—*see* Neoplasm, by site,
        benign
      unspecified site 220
    pseudomucinous (M8471/0)
      borderline malignancy (M8471/1)
        specified site—*see* Neoplasm, by site,
          uncertain behavior
        unspecified site 236.2
      specified site—*see* Neoplasm, by site,
        benign
      unspecified site 220
    serous (M8460/0)
      borderline malignancy (M8460/1)
        specified site—*see* Neoplasm, by site,
          uncertain behavior
        unspecified site 236.2
      specified site—*see* Neoplasm, by site,
        benign
      unspecified site 220
    specified site—*see* Neoplasm, by site, benign
    unspecified site 220

Cystadenoma—*continued*
  pseudomucinous (M8470/0)
    borderline malignancy (M8470/1)
      specified site—*see* Neoplasm, by site,
        uncertain behavior
      unspecified site 236.2
    papillary (M8471/0)
      borderline malignancy (M8471/1)
        specified site—*see* Neoplasm, by site,
          uncertain behavior
        unspecified site 236.2
      specified site—*see* Neoplasm, by site,
        benign
      unspecified site 220
    specified site—*see* Neoplasm, by site, benign
    unspecified site 220
  serous (M8441/0)
    borderline malignancy (M8441/1)
      specified site—*see* Neoplasm, by site,
        uncertain behavior
      unspecified site 236.2
    papillary (M8460/0)
      borderline malignancy (M8460/1)
        specified site—*see* Neoplasm, by site,
          uncertain behavior
        unspecified site 236.2
      specified site—*see* Neoplasm, by site,
        benign
      unspecified site 220
    specified site—*see* Neoplasm, by site, benign
    unspecified site 220
  thyroid 226
Cystathioninemia 270.4
Cystathioninuria 270.4
Cystic —*see also* condition
  breast, chronic 610.1
  corpora lutea 620.1
  degeneration, congenital
    brain 742.4
    kidney (*see also* Cystic, disease, kidney)
      753.10
  disease
    breast, chronic 610.1
    kidney, congenital 753.10
      medullary 753.16
      multiple 753.19
      polycystic—*see* Polycystic, kidney
      single 753.11
      specified NEC 753.19
    liver, congenital 751.62
    lung 518.89
      congenital 748.4
    pancreas, congenital 751.7
    semilunar cartilage 717.5
  duct—*see* condition
  eyeball, congenital 743.03
  fibrosis (pancreas) 277.00
  hygroma (M9173/0) 228.1
  kidney, congenital 753.10
    medullary 753.16
    multiple 753.19
    polycystic—*see* Polycystic, kidney
    single 753.11
    specified NEC 753.19
  liver, congenital 751.62
  lung 518.89
    congenital 748.4
  mass—*see* Cyst
  mastitis, chronic 610.1
  ovary 620.2
  pancreas, congenital 751.7
Cysticerciasis 123.1

Cysticercosis (mammary) (subretinal) 123.1
Cysticercus 123.1
  cellulosae infestation 123.1
Cystinosis (malignant) 270.0
Cystinuria 270.0
Cystitis (bacillary) (colli) (diffuse) (exudative)
    (hemorrhagic) (purulent) (recurrent) (septic)
    (suppurative) (ulcerative) 595.9
  with
    abortion—*see* Abortion, by type, with urinary
      tract infection
    ectopic pregnancy (*see also* categories
      633.0-633.9) 639.8
    fibrosis 595.1
    leukoplakia 595.1
    malakoplakia 595.1
    metaplasia 595.1
    molar pregnancy (*see also* categories
      630-632) 639.8
  actinomycotic 039.8 *[595.4]*
  acute 595.0
    of trigone 595.3
  allergic 595.89
  amebic 006.8 *[595.4]*
  bilharzial 120.9 *[595.4]*
  blennorrhagic (acute) 098.11
    chronic or duration of 2 months or more
      098.31
  bullous 595.89
  calculous 594.1
  chlamydial 099.53
  chronic 595.2
    interstitial 595.1
    of trigone 595.3
  complicating pregnancy, childbirth, or
    puerperium 646.6
    affecting fetus or newborn 760.1
  cystic(a) 595.81
  diphtheritic 032.84
  echinococcal
    granulosus 122.3 *[595.4]*
    multilocularis 122.6 *[595.4]*
  emphysematous 595.89
  encysted 595.81
  follicular 595.3
  following
    abortion 639.8
    ectopic or molar pregnancy 639.8
  gangrenous 595.89
  glandularis 595.89
  gonococcal (acute) 098.11
    chronic or duration of 2 months or more
      098.31
  incrusted 595.89
  interstitial 595.1
  irradiation 595.82
  irritation 595.89
  malignant 595.89
  monilial 112.2
  of trigone 595.3
  panmural 595.1
  polyposa 595.89
  prostatic 601.3
  radiation 595.82
  Reiter's (abacterial) 099.3
  specified NEC 595.89
  subacute 595.2
  submucous 595.1
  syphilitic 095.8
  trichomoniasis 131.09
  tuberculous (*see also* Tuberculosis) 016.1
  ulcerative 595.1

Cystocele (-rectocele)
  female (without uterine prolapse) 618.0
    with uterine prolapse 618.4
      complete 618.3
      incomplete 618.2
  in pregnancy or childbirth 654.4
    affecting fetus or newborn 763.89
    causing obstructed labor 660.2
      affecting fetus or newborn 763.1
  male 596.8
Cystoid
  cicatrix limbus 372.64
  degeneration macula 362.53
Cystolithiasis 594.1
Cystoma (M8440/0)—*see also* Neoplasm, by
  site, benign
  endometrial, ovary 617.1
  mucinous (M8470/0)
    specified site—*see* Neoplasm, by site, benign
    unspecified site 220
  serous (M8441/0)
    specified site—*see* Neoplasm, by site, benign
    unspecified site 220
  simple (ovary) 620.2
Cystoplegia 596.53
Cystoptosis 596.8
Cystopyelitis (*see also* Pyelitis) 590.80
Cystorrhagia 596.8
Cystosarcoma phyllodes (M9020/1) 238.3
  benign (M9020/0) 217
  malignant (M9020/3)—*see* Neoplasm, breast,
    malignant
Cystostomy status V44.50
  appendico-vesicostomy V44.52
  cutaneous-vesicostomy V44.51
  specified type NEC V44.59
  with complication 997.5
Cystourethritis (*see also* Urethritis) 597.89
Cystourethrocele (*see also* Cystocele)
  female (without uterine prolapse) 618.0
    with uterine prolapse 618.4
      complete 618.3
      incomplete 618.2
  male 596.8
Cytomegalic inclusion disease 078.5
  congenital 771.1
Cytomycosis, reticuloendothelial (*see also*
  Histoplasmosis, American) 115.00

D

Daae (-Finsen) disease (epidemic pleurodynia) 074.1
Dabney's grip 074.1
Da Costa's syndrome (neurocirculatory asthenia) 306.2
Dacryoadenitis, dacryadenitis 375.00
  acute 375.01
  chronic 375.02
Dacryocystitis 375.30
  acute 375.32
  chronic 375.42
  neonatal 771.6
  phlegmonous 375.33
  syphilitic 095.8
    congenital 090.0
  trachomatous, active 076.1
    late effect 139.1
  tuberculous (see also Tuberculosis) 017.3
Dacryocystoblennorrhea 375.42
Dacryocystocele 375.43
Dacryolith, dacryolithiasis 375.57
Dacryoma 375.43
Dacryopericystitis (acute) (subacute) 375.32
  chronic 375.42
Dacryops 375.11
Dacryosialadenopathy, atrophic 710.2
Dacryostenosis 375.56
  congenital 743.65
Dactylitis 686.9
  bone (see also Osteomyelitis) 730.2
  sickle-cell 282.61
  syphilitic 095.5
  tuberculous (see also Tuberculosis) 015.5
Dactylolysis spontanea 136.0
Dactylosymphysis (see also Syndactylism) 755.10
Damage
  arteriosclerotic—see Arteriosclerosis
  brain 348.9
    anoxic, hypoxic 348.1
      during or resulting from a procedure 997.01
    child NEC 343.9
    due to birth injury 767.0
    minimal (child) (see also Hyperkinesia) 314.9
    newborn 767.0
  cardiac—see also Disease, heart
  cardiorenal (vascular) (see also Hypertension, cardiorenal) 404.90
  central nervous system—see Damage, brain
  cerebral NEC—see Damage, brain
  coccyx, complicating delivery 665.6
  coronary (see also Ischemia, heart) 414.9
  eye, birth injury 767.8
  heart—see also Disease, heart
    valve—see Endocarditis
  hypothalamus NEC 348.9
  liver 571.9
    alcoholic 571.3
  myocardium (see also Degeneration, myocardial) 429.1
  pelvic
    joint or ligament, during delivery 665.6
    organ NEC
      with
        abortion—see Abortion, by type, with damage to pelvic organs
        ectopic pregnancy (see also categories 633.0-633.9) 639.2

Damage—continued
        molar pregnancy (see also categories 630-632) 639.2
    during delivery 665.5
    following
      abortion 639.2
      ectopic or molar pregnancy 639.2
  renal (see also Disease, renal) 593.9
  skin, solar 692.79
    acute 692.72
    chronic 692.74
  subendocardium, subendocardial (see also Degeneration, myocardial) 429.1
  vascular 459.9
Dameshek's syndrome (erythroblastic anemia) 282.4
Dana-Putnam syndrome (subacute combined sclerosis with pernicious anemia) 281.0 [336.2]
Danbolt (-Closs) syndrome (acrodermatitis enteropathica) 686.8
Dandruff 690.18
Dandy fever 061
Dandy-Walker deformity or syndrome (atresia, foramen of Magendie) 742.3
  with spina bifida (see also Spina bifida) 741.0
Dangle foot 736.79
Danielssen's disease (anesthetic leprosy) 030.1
Danlos' syndrome 756.83
Darier's disease (congenital) (keratosis follicularis) 757.39
  due to vitamin A deficiency 264.8
  meaning erythema annulare centrifugum 695.0
Darier-Roussy sarcoid 135
Darling's
  disease (see also Histoplasmosis, American) 115.00
  histoplasmosis (see also Histoplasmosis, American) 115.00
Dartre 054.9
Darwin's tubercle 744.29
Davidson's anemia (refractory) 284.9
Davies' disease 425.0
Davies-Colley syndrome (slipping rib) 733.99
Dawson's encephalitis 046.2
Day blindness (see also Blindness, day) 368.60
Dead
  fetus
    retained (in utero) 656.4
      early pregnancy (death before 22 completed weeks gestation) 632
      late (death after 22 completed weeks gestation) 656.4
    syndrome 641.3
  labyrinth 386.50
  ovum, retained 631
Deaf and dumb NEC 389.7
Deaf mutism (acquired) (congenital) NEC 389.7
  endemic 243
  hysterical 300.11
  syphilitic, congenital 090.0

Deafness (acquired) (bilateral) (both ears) (complete) (congenital) (hereditary) (middle ear) (partial) (unilateral) 389.9
  with blue sclera and fragility of bone 756.51
  auditory fatigue 389.9
  aviation 993.0
    nerve injury 951.5
  boilermakers' 951.5
  central 389.14
    with conductive hearing loss 389.2
  conductive (air) 389.00
    with sensorineural hearing loss 389.2
    combined types 389.08
    external ear 389.01
    inner ear 389.04
    middle ear 389.03
    multiple types 389.08
    tympanic membrane 389.02
  emotional (complete) 300.11
  functional (complete) 300.11
  high frequency 389.8
  hysterical (complete) 300.11
  injury 951.5
  low frequency 389.8
  mental 784.69
  mixed conductive and sensorineural 389.2
  nerve 389.12
    with conductive hearing loss 389.2
  neural 389.12
    with conductive hearing loss 389.2
  noise-induced 388.12
    nerve injury 951.5
  nonspeaking 389.7
  perceptive 389.10
    with conductive hearing loss 389.2
    central 389.14
    combined types 389.18
    multiple types 389.18
    neural 389.12
    sensory 389.11
  psychogenic (complete) 306.7
  sensorineural (*see also* Deafness, perceptive) 389.10
  sensory 389.11
    with conductive hearing loss 389.2
  specified type NEC 389.8
  sudden NEC 388.2
  syphilitic 094.89
  transient ischemic 388.02
  transmission—*see* Deafness, conductive
  traumatic 951.5
  word (secondary to organic lesion) 784.69
    developmental 315.31
Death
  after delivery (cause not stated) (sudden) 674.9
  anesthetic
    due to
      correct substance properly administered 995.4
      overdose or wrong substance given 968.4
        specified anesthetic—*see* Table of drugs and chemicals
    during delivery 668.9
  brain 348.8
  cardiac—*see* Disease, heart
  cause unknown 798.2
  cot (infant) 798.0
  crib (infant) 798.0

Death—*continued*
  fetus, fetal (cause not stated) (intrauterine) 779.9
    early, with retention (before 22 completed weeks gestation) 632
    from asphyxia or anoxia (before labor) 768.0
      during labor 768.1
    late, affecting management of pregnancy (after 22 completed weeks gestation) 656.4
  from pregnancy NEC 646.9
  instantaneous 798.1
  intrauterine (*see also* Death, fetus) 779.9
    complicating pregnancy 656.4
  maternal, affecting fetus or newborn 761.6
  neonatal NEC 779.9
  sudden (cause unknown) 798.1
    during delivery 669.9
      under anesthesia NEC 668.9
    infant, syndrome (SIDS) 798.0
    puerperal, during puerperium 674.9
  unattended (cause unknown) 798.9
  under anesthesia NEC
    due to
      correct substance properly administered 995.4
      overdose or wrong substance given 968.4
        specified anesthetic—*see* Table of drugs and chemicals
    during delivery 668.9
  violent 798.1
de Beurmann-Gougerot disease (sporotrichosis) 117.1
Debility (general) (infantile) (postinfectional) 799.3
  with nutritional difficulty 269.9
  congenital or neonatal NEC 779.9
  nervous 300.5
  old age 797
  senile 797
Débove's disease (splenomegaly) 789.2
Decalcification
  bone (*see also* Osteoporosis) 733.00
  teeth 521.8
Decapitation 874.9
  fetal (to facilitate delivery) 763.89
Decapsulation, kidney 593.89
Decay
  dental 521.0
  senile 797
  tooth, teeth 521.0
Decensus, uterus —*see* Prolapse, uterus
Deciduitis (acute)
  with
    abortion—*see* Abortion, by type, with sepsis
    ectopic pregnancy (*see also* categories 633.0-633.9) 639.0
    molar pregnancy (*see also* categories 630-632) 639.0
  affecting fetus or newborn 760.8
  following
    abortion 639.0
    ectopic or molar pregnancy 639.0
  in pregnancy 646.6
  puerperal, postpartum 670
Deciduoma malignum (M9100/3) 181
Deciduous tooth (retained) 520.6
Decline (general) (*see also* Debility) 799.3

Decompensation
cardiac (acute) (chronic) (*see also* Disease, heart) 429.9
  failure—*see* Failure, heart, congestive
cardiorenal (*see also* Hypertension, cardiorenal) 404.90
cardiovascular (*see also* Disease, cardiovascular) 429.2
heart (*see also* Disease, heart) 429.9
  failure—*see* Failure, heart, congestive
hepatic 572.2
myocardial (acute) (chronic) (*see also* Disease, heart) 429.9
  failure—*see* Failure, heart, congestive
respiratory 519.9
Decompression sickness 993.3
Decrease, decreased
blood
  platelets (*see also* Thrombocytopenia) 287.5
  pressure 796.3
    due to shock following
      injury 958.4
      operation 998.0
cardiac reserve—*see* Disease, heart
estrogen 256.3
  postablative 256.2
fetal movements 655.7
fragility of erythrocytes 289.8
function
  adrenal (cortex) 255.4
    medulla 255.5
  ovary in hypopituitarism 253.4
  parenchyma of pancreas 577.8
  pituitary (gland) (lobe) (anterior) 253.2
    posterior (lobe) 253.8
functional activity 780.9
glucose 790.2
haptoglobin (serum) NEC 273.8
platelets (*see also* Thrombocytopenia) 287.5
pulse pressure 785.9
respiration due to shock following injury 958.4
tear secretion NEC 375.15
tolerance
  fat 579.8
  glucose 790.2
  salt and water 276.9
vision NEC 369.9
Decubital gangrene 707.0 *[785.4]*
Decubiti (*see also* Decubitus) 707.0
Decubitus (ulcer) 707.0
with gangrene 707.0 *[785.4]*
Deepening acetabulum 718.85
Defect, defective 759.9
3-beta-hydroxysteroid dehydrogenase 255.2
11-hydroxylase 255.2
21-hydroxylase 255.2
abdominal wall, congenital 756.70
aorticopulmonary septum 745.0
aortic septal 745.0
atrial septal (ostium secundum type) 745.5
  acquired 429.71
  ostium primum type 745.61
  sinus venosus 745.8
atrioventricular
  canal 745.69
  septum 745.4
    acquired 429.71
atrium secundum 745.5
  acquired 429.71
auricular septal 745.5
  acquired 429.71

Defect, defective—*continued*
bilirubin excretion 277.4
biosynthesis, testicular androgen 257.2
bulbar septum 745.0
butanol-insoluble iodide 246.1
chromosome—*see* Anomaly, chromosome
circulation (acquired) 459.9
  congenital 747.9
  newborn 747.9
clotting NEC (*see also* Defect, coagulation) 286.9
coagulation (factor) (*see also* Deficiency, coagulation factor) 286.9
with
  abortion—*see* Abortion, by type, with hemorrhage
  ectopic pregnancy (*see also* categories 634-638) 639.1
  molar pregnancy (*see also* categories 630-632) 639.1
acquired (any) 286.7
antepartum or intrapartum 641.3
  affecting fetus or newborn 762.1
causing hemorrhage of pregnancy or delivery 641.3
due to
  liver disease 286.7
  vitamin K deficiency 286.7
newborn, transient 776.3
postpartum 666.3
specified type NEC 286.3
conduction (heart) 426.9
bone (*see also* Deafness, conductive) 389.00
congenital, organ or site NEC—*see also* Anomaly
circulation 747.9
Descemet's membrane 743.9
  specified type NEC 743.49
diaphragm 756.6
ectodermal 757.9
esophagus 750.9
pulmonic cusps—*see* Anomaly, heart valve
respiratory system 748.9
  specified type NEC 748.8
cushion endocardial 745.60
dentin (hereditary) 520.5
Descemet's membrane (congenital) 743.9
acquired 371.30
specific type NEC 743.49
deutan 368.52
developmental—*see also* Anomaly, by site
cauda equina 742.59
left ventricle 746.9
  with atresia or hypoplasia of aortic orifice or valve, with hypoplasia of ascending aorta 746.7
  in hypoplastic left heart syndrome 746.7
testis 752.9
vessel 747.9
diaphragm
with elevation, eventration, or hernia—*see* Hernia, diaphragm
congenital 756.6
  with elevation, eventration, or hernia 756.6
  gross (with elevation, eventration, or hernia) 756.6
ectodermal, congenital 757.9
Eisenmenger's (ventricular septal defect) 745.4
endocardial cushion 745.60
specified type NEC 745.69

Defect, defective—*continued*
  esophagus, congenital 750.9
  extensor retinaculum 728.9
  fibrin polymerization (*see also* Defect,
    coagulation) 286.3
  filling
    biliary tract 793.3
    bladder 793.5
    gallbladder 793.3
    kidney 793.5
    stomach 793.4
    ureter 793.5
  fossa ovalis 745.5
  gene, carrier (suspected) of V19.8
  Gerbode 745.4
  glaucomatous, without elevated tension 365.89
  Hageman (factor) (*see also* Defect, coagulation)
    286.3
  hearing (*see also* Deafness) 389.9
  high grade 317
  homogentisic acid 270.2
  interatrial septal 745.5
    acquired 429.71
  interauricular septal 745.5
    acquired 429.71
  interventricular septal 745.4
    with pulmonary stenosis or atresia,
      dextroposition of aorta, and hypertrophy
      of right ventricle 745.2
    acquired 429.71
    in tetralogy of Fallot 745.2
  iodide trapping 246.1
  iodotyrosine dehalogenase 246.1
  kynureninase 270.2
  learning, specific 315.2
  mental (*see also* Retardation, mental) 319
  osteochondral NEC 738.8
  ostium
    primum 745.61
    secundum 745.5
  pericardium 746.89
  peroxidase-binding 246.1
  placental blood supply—*see* Placenta,
    insufficiency
  platelet (qualitative) 287.1
    constitutional 286.4
  postural, spine 737.9
  protan 368.51
  pulmonic cusps, congenital 746.00
  renal pelvis 753.9
    obstructive 753.29
    specified type NEC 753.3
  respiratory system, congenital 748.9
    specified type NEC 748.8
  retina, retinal 361.30
    with detachment (*see also* Detachment, retina,
      with retinal defect) 361.00
    multiple 361.33
      with detachment 361.02
    nerve fiber bundle 362.85
    single 361.30
      with detachment 361.01
  septal (closure) (heart) NEC 745.9
    acquired 429.71
    atrial 745.5
    specified type NEC 745.8
  speech NEC 784.5
    developmental 315.39
    secondary to organic lesion 784.5
  Taussig-Bing (transposition, aorta and
    overriding pulmonary artery) 745.11

Defect, defective—*continued*
  teeth, wedge 521.2
  thyroid hormone synthesis 246.1
  tritan 368.53
  ureter 753.9
    obstructive 753.29
  vascular (acquired) (local) 459.9
    congenital (peripheral) NEC 747.60
      gastrointestinal 747.61
      lower limb 747.64
      renal 747.62
      specified NEC 747.69
      spinal 747.82
      upper limb 747.63
  ventricular septal 745.4
    with pulmonary stenosis or atresia,
      dextraposition of aorta, and hypertrophy
      of right ventricle 745.2
    acquired 429.71
    atrioventricular canal type 745.69
    between infundibulum and anterior portion
      745.4
    in tetralogy of Fallot 745.2
    isolated anterior 745.4
  vision NEC 369.9
  visual field 368.40
    arcuate 368.43
    heteronymous, bilateral 368.47
    homonymous, bilateral 368.46
    localized NEC 368.44
    nasal step 368.44
    peripheral 368.44
    sector 368.43
  voice 784.40
  wedge, teeth (abrasion) 521.2
Defeminization syndrome 255.2
Deferentitis 608.4
  gonorrheal (acute) 098.14
    chronic or duration of 2 months or over 098.34
Defibrination syndrome (*see also* Fibrinolysis)
  286.6
Deficiency, deficient
  3-beta-hydroxysteroid dehydrogenase 255.2
  6-phosphogluconic dehydrogenase (anemia)
    282.2
  11-beta-hydroxylase 255.2
  17-alpha-hydroxylase 255.2
  18-hydroxysteroid dehydrogenase 255.2
  20-alpha-hydroxylase 255.2
  21-hydroxylase 255.2
  abdominal muscle syndrome 756.79
  accelerator globulin (Ac G) (blood) (*see also*
    Defect, coagulation) 286.3
  AC globulin (congenital) (*see also* Defect,
    coagulation) 286.3
    acquired 286.7
  activating factor (blood) (*see also* Defect,
    coagulation) 286.3
  adenohypophyseal 253.2
  adenosine deaminase 277.2
  aldolase (hereditary) 271.2
  alpha-1-antitrypsin 277.6
  alpha-1-trypsin inhibitor 277.6
  alpha-fucosidase 271.8
  alpha-lipoprotein 272.5
  alpha-mannosidase 271.8
  amino acid 270.9
  anemia—*see* Anemia, deficiency
  aneurin 265.1
    with beriberi 265.0

Deficiency, deficient—*continued*
  antibody NEC 279.00
  antidiuretic hormone 253.5
  antihemophilic
    factor (A) 286.0
      B 286.1
      C 286.2
    globulin (AHG) NEC 286.0
  antitrypsin 277.6
  argininosuccinate synthetase or lyase 270.6
  ascorbic acid (with scurvy) 267
  autoprothrombin
    I (*see also* Defect, coagulation) 286.3
    II 286.1
    C (*see also* Defect, coagulation) 286.3
  bile salt 579.8
  biotin 266.2
  biotinidase 277.6
  bradykinase-1 277.6
  brancher enzyme (amylopectinosis) 271.0
  calciferol 268.9
    with
      osteomalacia 268.2
      rickets (*see also* Rickets) 268.0
  calcium 275.40
    dietary 269.3
  calorie, severe 261
  carbamyl phosphate synthetase 270.6
  cardiac (*see also* Insufficiency, myocardial)
    428.0
  carnitine palmityl transferase 791.3
  carotene 264.9
  Carr factor (*see also* Defect, coagulation) 286.9
  central nervous system 349.9
  ceruloplasmin 275.1
  cevitamic acid (with scurvy) 267
  choline 266.2
  Christmas factor 286.1
  chromium 269.3
  citrin 269.1
  clotting (blood) (*see also* Defect, coagulation)
    286.9
  coagulation factor NEC 286.9
    with
      abortion—*see* Abortion, by type, with
        hemorrhage
      ectopic pregnancy (*see also* categories
        634-638) 639.1
      molar pregnancy (*see also* categories
        630-632) 639.1
    acquired (any) 286.7
    antepartum or intrapartum 641.3
      affecting fetus or newborn 762.1
    due to
      liver disease 286.7
      vitamin K deficiency 286.7
    newborn, transient 776.3
    postpartum 666.3
    specified type NEC 286.3
  color vision (congenital) 368.59
    acquired 368.55
  combined, two or more coagulation factors (*see
    also* Defect, coagulation) 286.9
  complement factor NEC 279.8
  contact factor (*see also* Defect, coagulation)
    286.3
  copper NEC 275.1
  corticoadrenal 255.4
  craniofacial axis 756.0
  cyanocobalamin (vitamin B12) 266.2

Deficiency, deficient—*continued*
  debrancher enzyme (limit dextrinosis) 271.0
  desmolase 255.2
  diet 269.9
  dihydrofolate reductase 281.2
  dihydropteridine reductase 270.1
  disaccharidase (intestinal) 271.3
  disease NEC 269.9
  ear(s) V48.8
  edema 262
  endocrine 259.9
  enzymes, circulating NEC (*see also* Deficiency,
    by specific enzyme) 277.6
  ergosterol 268.9
    with
      osteomalacia 268.2
      rickets (*see also* Rickets) 268.0
  erythrocytic glutathione (anemia) 282.2
  eyelid(s) V48.8
  factor (*see also* Defect, coagulation) 286.9
    I (congenital) (fibrinogen) 286.3
      antepartum or intrapartum 641.3
        affecting fetus or newborn 762.1
      newborn, transient 776.3
      postpartum 666.3
    II (congenital) (prothrombin) 286.3
    V (congenital) (labile) 286.3
    VII (congenital) (stable) 286.3
    VIII (congenital) (functional) 286.0
      with
        functional defect 286.0
        vascular defect 286.4
    IX (Christmas) (congenital) (functional) 286.1
    X (congenital) (Stuart-Prower) 286.3
    XI (congenital) (plasma thromboplastin
      antecedent) 286.2
    XII (congenital) (Hageman) 286.3
    XIII (congenital) (fibrin stabilizing) 286.3
    Hageman 286.3
    multiple (congenital) 286.9
      acquired 286.7
  fibrinase (*see also* Defect, coagulation) 286.3
  fibrinogen (congenital) (*see also* Defect,
    coagulation) 286.3
    acquired 286.6
  fibrin stabilizing factor (congenital) (*see also*
    Defect, coagulation) 286.3
    acquired 286.7
  finger—*see* Absence, finger
  Fletcher factor (*see also* Defect, coagulation)
    286.9
  fluorine 269.3
  folate, anemia 281.2
  folic acid (vitamin Bc) 266.2
    anemia 281.2
  follicle-stimulating hormone (FSH) 253.4
  fructokinase 271.2
  fructose-1, 6-diphosphate 271.2
  fructose-1-phosphate aldolase 271.2
  FSH (follicle-stimulating hormone) 253.4
  fucosidase 271.8
  galactokinase 271.1
  galactose-1-phosphate uridyl transferase 271.1
  gamma globulin in blood 279.00
  glass factor (*see also* Defect, coagulation) 286.3
  glucocorticoid 255.4
  glucose-6-phosphatase 271.0
  glucose-6-phosphate dehydrogenase anemia
    282.2
  glucuronyl transferase 277.4
  glutathione-reductase (anemia) 282.2

Deficiency, deficient—*continued*
glycogen synthetase 271.0
growth hormone 253.3
Hageman factor (congenital) (*see also* Defect,
coagulation) 286.3
head V48.0
hemoglobin (*see also* Anemia) 285.9
hepatophosphorylase 271.0
hexose monophosphate (HMP) shunt 282.2
HGH (human growth hormone) 253.3
HG-PRT 277.2
homogentisic acid oxidase 270.2
hormone—*see also* Deficiency, by specific
hormone
anterior pituitary (isolated) (partial) NEC
253.4
growth (human) 253.3
follicle-stimulating 253.4
growth (human) (isolated) 253.3
human growth 253.3
interstitial cell-stimulating 253.4
luteinizing 253.4
melanocyte-stimulating 253.4
testicular 257.2
human growth hormone 253.3
humoral 279.00
with
hyper-IgM 279.05
autosomal recessive 279.05
X-linked 279.05
increased IgM 279.05
congenital hypogammaglobulinemia 279.04
non-sex-linked 279.06
selective immunoglobulin NEC 279.03
IgA 279.01
IgG 279.03
IgM 279.02
increased 279.05
specified NEC 279.09
hydroxylase 255.2
hypoxanthine-guanine
phosphoribosyltransferase (HG-PRT) 277.2
ICSH (interstitial cell-stimulating hormone)
253.4
immunity NEC 279.3
cell-mediated 279.10
with
hyperimmunoglobulinemia 279.2
thrombocytopenia and eczema 279.12
specified NEC 279.19
combined (severe) 279.2
syndrome 279.2
common variable 279.06
humoral NEC 279.00
IgA (secretory) 279.01
IgG 279.03
IgM 279.02
immunoglobulin, selective NEC 279.03
IgA 279.01
IgG 279.03
IgM 279.02
inositol (B complex) 266.2
interferon 279.4
internal organ V47.0
interstitial cell-stimulating hormone (ICSH)
253.4
intrinsic (urethral) sphincter (ISD) 599.82
intrinsic factor (Castle's) (congenital) 281.0
invertase 271.3
iodine 269.3
iron, anemia 280.9

Deficiency, deficient—*continued*
labile factor (congenital) (*see also* Defect,
coagulation) 286.3
acquired 286.7
lacrimal fluid (acquired) 375.15
congenital 743.64
lactase 271.3
Laki-Lorand factor (*see also* Defect,
coagulation) 286.3
lecithin-cholesterol acyltranferase 272.5
LH (luteinizing hormone) 253.4
limb V49.0
lower V49.0
congenital (*see also* Deficiency, lower limb,
congenital) 755.30
upper V49.0
congenital (*see also* Deficiency, upper limb,
congenital) 755.20
lipocaic 577.8
lipoid (high-density) 272.5
lipoprotein (familial) (high density) 272.5
liver phosphorylase 271.0
lower limb V49.0
congenital 755.30
with complete absence of distal elements
755.31
longitudinal (complete) (partial) (with distal
deficiencies, incomplete) 755.32
with complete absence of distal elements
755.31
combined femoral, tibial, fibular
(incomplete) 755.33
femoral 755.34
fibular 755.37
metatarsal(s) 755.38
phalange(s) 755.39
meaning all digits 755.31
tarsal(s) 755.38
tibia 755.36
tibiofibular 755.35
transverse 755.31
luteinizing hormone (LH) 253.4
lysosomal alpha-1, 4 glucosidase 271.0
magnesium 275.2
mannosidase 271.8
melanocyte-stimulating hormone (MSH) 253.4
menadione (vitamin K) 269.0
newborn 776.0
mental (familial) (hereditary) (*see also*
Retardation, mental) 319
mineral NEC 269.3
molybdenum 269.3
moral 301.7
multiple, syndrome 260
myocardial (*see also* Insufficiency myocardial)
428.0
myophosphorylase 271.0
NADH (DPNH) -methemoglobin-reductase
(congenital) 289.7
NADH diaphorase or reductase (congenital)
289.7
neck V48.1
niacin (amide) (-tryptophan) 265.2
nicotinamide 265.2
nicotinic acid (amide) 265.2
nose V48.8
number of teeth (*see also* Anodontia) 520.0
nutrition, nutritional 269.9
specified NEC 269.8

Deficiency, deficient—*continued*
> ornithine transcarbamylase 270.6
> ovarian 256.3
> oxygen (*see also* Anoxia) 799.0
> pantothenic acid 266.2
> parathyroid (gland) 252.1
> phenylalanine hydroxylase 270.1
> phosphofructokinase 271.2
> phosphoglucomutase 271.0
> phosphohexosisomerase 271.0
> phosphorylase kinase, liver 271.0
> pituitary (anterior) 253.2
>> posterior 253.5
> placenta—*see* Placenta, insufficiency
> plasma
>> cell 279.00
>> protein (paraproteinemia) (pyroglobulinemia) 273.8
>>> gamma globulin 279.00
>> thromboplastin
>>> antecedent (PTA) 286.2
>>> component (PTC) 286.1
> platelet NEC 287.1
>> constitutional 286.4
> polyglandular 258.9
> potassium (K) 276.8
> proaccelerin (congenital) (*see also* Defect, congenital) 286.3
>> acquired 286.7
> proconvertin factor (congenital) (*see also* Defect, coagulation) 286.3
>> acquired 286.7
> prolactin 253.4
> protein 260
>> anemia 281.4
>> plasma—*see* Deficiency, plasma, protein
> prothrombin (congenital) (*see also* Defect, coagulation) 286.3
>> acquired 286.7
> Prower factor (*see also* Defect, coagulation) 286.3
> PRT 277.2
> pseudocholinesterase 289.8
> psychobiological 301.6
> PTA 286.2
> PTC 286.1
> purine nucleoside phosphorylase 277.2
> pyracin (alpha) (beta) 266.1
> pyridoxal 266.1
> pyridoxamine 266.1
> pyridoxine (derivatives) 266.1
> pyruvate kinase (PK) 282.3
> riboflavin (vitamin B_2) 266.0
> saccadic eye movements 379.57
> salivation 527.7
> salt 276.1
> secretion
>> ovary 256.3
>> salivary gland (any) 527.7
>> urine 788.5
> selenium 269.3
> serum
>> antitrypsin, familial 277.6
>> protein (congenital) 273.8
> smooth pursuit movements (eye) 379.58
> sodium (Na) 276.1
> SPCA (*see also* Defect, coagulation) 286.3
> specified NEC 269.8
> stable factor (congenital) (*see also* Defect, coagulation) 286.3
> acquired 286.7

Deficiency, deficient—*continued*
> Stuart (-Prower) factor (*see also* Defect, coagulation) 286.3
> sucrase 271.3
> sucrase-isomaltase 271.3
> sulfite oxidase 270.0
> syndrome, multiple 260
> thiamine, thiaminic (chloride) 265.1
> thrombokinase (*see also* Defect, coagulation) 286.3
>> newborn 776.0
> thrombopoieten 287.3
> thymolymphatic 279.2
> thyroid (gland) 244.9
> tocopherol 269.1
> toe—*see* Absence, toe
> tooth bud (*see also* Anodontia) 520.0
> trunk V48.1
> UDPG-glycogen transferase 271.0
> upper limb V49.0
>> congenital 755.20
>>> with complete absence of distal elements 755.21
>>> longitudinal (complete) (partial) (with distal deficiencies, incomplete) 755.22
>>>> carpal(s) 755.28
>>>> combined humeral, radial, ulnar (incomplete) 755.23
>>>> humeral 755.24
>>>> metacarpal(s) 755.28
>>>> phalange(s) 755.29
>>>>> meaning all digits 755.21
>>>> radial 755.26
>>>> radioulnar 755.25
>>>> ulnar 755.27
>>> transverse (complete) (partial) 755.21
> vascular 459.9
> vasopressin 253.5
> viosterol (*see also* Deficiency, calciferol) 268.9
> vitamin (multiple) NEC 269.2
>> A 264.9
>>> with
>>>> Bitôt's spot 264.1
>>>>> corneal 264.2
>>>>>> with corneal ulceration 264.3
>>>> keratomalacia 264.4
>>>> keratosis, follicular 264.8
>>>> night blindness 264.5
>>>> scar of cornea, xerophthalmic 264.6
>>>> specified manifestation NEC 264.8
>>>>> ocular 264.7
>>>> xeroderma 264.8
>>>> xerophthalmia 264.7
>>>> xerosis
>>>>> conjunctival 264.0
>>>>>> with Bitôt's spot 264.1
>>>>> corneal 264.2
>>>>>> with corneal ulceration 264.3
>> B (complex) NEC 266.9
>>> with
>>>> beriberi 265.0
>>>> pellagra 265.2
>>> specified type NEC 266.2
>> B_1 NEC 265.1
>>> beriberi 265.0
>> B_2 266.0
>> B_6 266.1
>> B_{12} 266.2
>> B_c (folic acid) 266.2

Deformity—*continued*
  foot (acquired) 736.70
    cavovarus 736.75
      congenital 754.59
    congenital NEC 754.70
      specified type NEC 754.79
    valgus (acquired) 736.79
      congenital 754.60
        specified type NEC 754.69
    varus (acquired) 736.79
      congenital 754.50
        specified type NEC 754.59
  forearm (acquired) 736.00
    congenital 755.50
  forehead (acquired) 738.19
    congenital (*see also* Deformity, skull,
      congenital) 756.0
  frontal bone (acquired) 738.19
    congenital (*see also* Deformity, skull,
      congenital) 756.0
  gallbladder (congenital) 751.60
    acquired 575.8
  gastrointestinal tract (congenital) NEC 751.9
    acquired 569.89
    specified type NEC 751.8
  genitalia, genital organ(s) or system NEC
    congenital 752.9
      female (congenital) 752.9
        acquired 629.8
        external 752.40
        internal 752.9
      male (congenital) 752.9
        acquired 608.89
  globe (eye) (congenital) 743.9
    acquired 360.89
  gum (congenital) 750.9
    acquired 523.9
  gunstock 736.02
  hand (acquired) 736.00
    claw 736.06
    congenital 755.50
    minus (and plus) (intrinsic) 736.09
    pill roller (intrinsic) 736.09
    plus (and minus) (intrinsic) 736.09
    swan neck (intrinsic) 736.09
  head (acquired) 738.10
    congenital (*see also* Deformity, skull,
      congenital) 756.0
    specified NEC 738.19
  heart (congenital) 746.9
    auricle (congenital) 746.9
    septum 745.9
      auricular 745.5
      specified type NEC 745.8
      ventricular 745.4
    valve (congenital) NEC 746.9
      acquired—*see* Endocarditis
      pulmonary (congenital) 746.00
      specified type NEC 746.89
    ventricle (congenital) 746.9
  heel (acquired) 736.76
    congenital 755.67
  hepatic duct (congenital) 751.60
    acquired 576.8
      with calculus, choledocholithiasis, or
        stones—*see* Choledocholithiasis
  hip (joint) (acquired) 736.30
    congenital NEC 755.63
    flexion 718.45
      congenital (*see also* Subluxation,
        congenital, hip) 754.32

Deformity—*continued*
  hourglass—*see* Contraction, hourglass
  humerus (acquired) 736.89
    congenital 755.50
  hymen (congenital) 752.40
  hypophyseal (congenital) 759.2
  ileocecal (coil) (valve) (congenital) 751.5
    acquired 569.89
  ileum (intestine) (congenital) 751.5
    acquired 569.89
  ilium (acquired) 738.6
    congenital 755.60
  integument (congenital) 757.9
  intervertebral cartilage or disc (acquired)—*see*
    also Displacement, intervertebral disc
    congenital 756.10
  intestine (large) (small) (congenital) 751.5
    acquired 569.89
  iris (acquired) 364.75
    congenital 743.9
    prolapse 364.8
  ischium (acquired) 738.6
    congenital 755.60
  jaw (acquired) (congenital) NEC 524.9
    due to intrauterine malposition and pressure
      754.0
  joint (acquired) NEC 738.8
    congenital 755.9
    contraction (abduction) (adduction)
      (extension) (flexion)—*see* Contraction,
      joint
  kidney(s) (calyx) (pelvis) (congenital) 753.9
    acquired 593.89
    vessel 747.62
      acquired 459.9
  Klippel-Feil (brevicollis) 756.16
  knee (acquired) NEC 736.6
    congenital 755.64
  labium (majus) (minus) (congenital) 752.40
    acquired 624.8
  lacrimal apparatus or duct (congenital) 743.9
    acquired 375.69
  larynx (muscle) (congenital) 748.3
    acquired 478.79
    web (glottic) (subglottic) 748.2
  leg (lower) (upper) (acquired) NEC 736.89
    congenital 755.60
    reduction—*see* Deformity, reduction, lower
      limb
  lens (congenital) 743.9
    acquired 379.39
  lid (fold) (congenital) 743.9
    acquired 374.89
  ligament (acquired) 728.9
    congenital 756.9
  limb (acquired) 736.9
    congenital, except reduction deformity 755.9
      lower 755.60
        reduction (*see also* Deformity, reduction,
          lower limb) 755.30
      upper 755.50
        reduction (*see also* Deformity, reduction,
          lower limb) 755.20
    specified NEC 736.89
  lip (congenital) NEC 750.9
    acquired 528.5
    specified type NEC 750.26

Deformity—*continued*
  liver (congenital) 751.60
    acquired 573.8
    duct (congenital) 751.60
      acquired 576.8
        with calculus, choledocholithiasis, or
          stones—*see* Choledocholithiasis
  lower extremity—*see* Deformity, leg
  lumbosacral (joint) (region) (congenital) 756.10
    acquired 738.5
  lung (congenital) 748.60
    acquired 518.89
    specified type NEC 748.69
  lymphatic system, congenital 759.9
  Madelung's (radius) 755.54
  maxilla (acquired) (congenital) 524.9
  meninges or membrane (congenital) 742.9
    brain 742.4
      acquired 349.2
    spinal (cord) 742.59
      acquired 349.2
  mesentery (congenital) 751.9
    acquired 568.89
  metacarpus (acquired) 736.00
    congenital 755.50
  metatarsus (acquired) 736.70
    congenital 754.70
  middle ear, except ossicles (congenital) 744.03
    ossicles 744.04
  mitral (leaflets) (valve) (congenital) 746.9
    acquired—*see* Endocarditis, mitral
    Ebstein's 746.89
    parachute 746.5
    specified type NEC 746.89
    stenosis, congenital 746.5
  mouth (acquired) 528.9
    congenital NEC 750.9
      specified type NEC 750.26
  multiple, congenital NEC 759.7
    specified type NEC 759.89
  muscle (acquired) 728.9
    congenital 756.9
      specified type NEC 756.89
      sternocleidomastoid (due to intrauterine
        malposition and pressure) 754.1
  musculoskeletal system, congenital NEC 756.9
    specified type NEC 756.9
  nail (acquired) 703.9
    congenital 757.9
  nasal—*see* Deformity, nose
  neck (acquired) NEC 738.2
    congenital (any part) 744.9
      sternocleidomastoid 754.1
  nervous system (congenital) 742.9
  nipple (congenital) 757.9
    acquired 611.8
  nose, nasal (cartilage) (acquired) 738.0
    bone (turbinate) 738.0
    congenital 748.1
      bent 754.0
      squashed 754.0
    saddle 738.0
      syphilitic 090.5
    septum 470
      congenital 748.1
    sinus (wall) (congenital) 748.1
      acquired 738.0
    syphilitic (congenital) 090.5
      late 095.8
  ocular muscle (congenital) 743.9
    acquired 378.60

Deformity—*continued*
  opticociliary vessels (congenital) 743.9
  orbit (congenital) (eye) 743.9
    acquired NEC 376.40
      associated with craniofacial deformities
        376.44
      due to
        bone disease 376.43
        surgery 376.47
        trauma 376.47
  organ of Corti (congenital) 744.05
  ovary (congenital) 752.0
    acquired 620.8
  oviduct (congenital) 752.10
    acquired 620.8
  palate (congenital) 750.9
    acquired 526.89
    cleft (congenital) (*see also* Cleft, palate)
      749.00
    hard, acquired 526.89
    soft, acquired 528.9
  pancreas (congenital) 751.7
    acquired 577.8
  parachute, mitral valve 746.5
  parathyroid (gland) 759.2
  parotid (gland) (congenital) 750.9
    acquired 527.8
  patella (acquired) 736.6
    congenital 755.64
  pelvis, pelvic (acquired) (bony) 738.6
    with disproportion (fetopelvic) 653.0
      affecting fetus or newborn 763.1
      causing obstructed labor 660.1
        affecting fetus or newborn 763.1
    congenital 755.60
    rachitic (late effect) 268.1
  penis (glans) (congenital) 752.9
    acquired 607.89
  pericardium (congenital) 746.9
    acquired—*see* Pericarditis
  pharynx (congenital) 750.9
    acquired 478.29
  Pierre Robin (congenital) 756.0
  pinna (acquired) 380.32
    congenital 744.3
  pituitary (congenital) 759.2
  pleural folds (congenital) 748.8
  portal vein (congenital) 747.40
  posture—*see* Curvature, spine
  prepuce (congenital) 752.9
    acquired 607.89
  prostate (congenital) 752.9
    acquired 602.8
  pulmonary valve—*see* Endocarditis, pulmonary
  pupil (congenital) 743.9
    acquired 364.75
  pylorus (congenital) 750.9
    acquired 537.89
  rachitic (acquired), healed or old 268.1
  radius (acquired) 736.00
    congenital 755.50
    reduction—*see* Deformity, reduction, upper
      limb
  rectovaginal septum (congenital) 752.40
    acquired 623.8
  rectum (congenital) 751.5
    acquired 569.49

Deformity—*continued*
  thumb (acquired) 736.20
    congenital 755.50
  thymus (tissue) (congenital) 759.2
  thyroid (gland) (congenital) 759.2
    cartilage 748.3
      acquired 478.79
  tibia (acquired) 736.89
    congenital 755.60
    saber 090.5
  toe (acquired) 735.9
    congenital 755.66
    specified NEC 735.8
  tongue (congenital) 750.10
    acquired 529.8
  tooth, teeth NEC 520.9
  trachea (rings) (congenital) 748.3
    acquired 519.1
  transverse aortic arch (congenital) 747.21
  tricuspid (leaflets) (valve) (congenital) 746.9
    acquired—*see* Endocarditis, tricuspid
    atresia or stenosis 746.1
    specified type NEC 746.89
  trunk (acquired) 738.3
    congenital 759.9
  ulna (acquired) 736.00
    congenital 755.50
  upper extremity—*see* Deformity, arm
  urachus (congenital) 753.7
  ureter (opening) (congenital) 753.9
    acquired 593.89
  urethra (valve) (congenital) 753.9
    acquired 599.84
  urinary tract or system (congenital) 753.9
    urachus 753.7
  uterus (congenital) 752.3
    acquired 621.8
  uvula (congenital) 750.9
    acquired 528.9
  vagina (congenital) 752.40
    acquired 623.8
  valve, valvular (heart) (congenital) 746.9
    acquired—*see* Endocarditis
    pulmonary 746.00
    specified type NEC 746.89
  vascular (congenital) (peripheral) NEC 747.60
    acquired 459.9
    gastrointestinal 747.61
    lower limb 747.64
    renal 747.62
    specified site NEC 747.69
    spinal 747.82
    upper limb 747.63
  vas deferens (congenital) 752.9
    acquired 608.89
  vein (congenital) NEC (*see also* Deformity,
      vascular) 747.60
    brain 747.81
    coronary 746.9
    great 747.40
  vena cava (inferior) (superior) (congenital)
      747.40
  vertebra—*see* Deformity, spine
  vesicourethral orifice (acquired) 596.8
    congenital NEC 753.9
      specified type NEC 753.8
  vessels of optic papilla (congenital) 743.9
  visual field (contraction) 368.45
  vitreous humor (congenital) 743.9
    acquired 379.29

Deformity—*continued*
  vulva (congenital) 752.40
    acquired 624.8
  wrist (joint) (acquired) 736.00
    congenital 755.50
    contraction 718.43
    valgus 736.03
      congenital 755.59
    varus 736.04
      congenital 755.59
Degeneration, degenerative
  adrenal (capsule) (gland) 255.8
    with hypofunction 255.4
    fatty 255.8
    hyaline 255.8
    infectional 255.8
    lardaceous 277.3
  amyloid (any site) (general) 277.3
  anterior cornua, spinal cord 336.8
  aorta, aortic 440.0
    fatty 447.8
    valve (heart) (*see also* Endocarditis, aortic)
      424.1
  arteriovascular—*see* Arteriosclerosis
  artery, arterial (atheromatous) (calcareous)—*see
      also* Arteriosclerosis
    amyloid 277.3
    lardaceous 277.3
    medial NEC (*see also* Arteriosclerosis,
      extremities) 440.20
  articular cartilage NEC (*see also* Disorder,
      cartilage, articular) 718.0
    elbow 718.02
    knee 717.5
    patella 717.7
    shoulder 718.01
    spine (*see also* Spondylosis) 721.90
  atheromatous—*see* Arteriosclerosis
  bacony (any site) 277.3
  basal nuclei or ganglia NEC 333.0
  bone 733.90
  brachial plexus 353.0
  brain (cortical) (progressive) 331.9
    arteriosclerotic 437.0
    childhood 330.9
      specified type NEC 330.8
    congenital 742.4
    cystic 348.0
      congenital 742.4
    familial NEC 331.89
    grey matter 330.8
    heredofamilial NEC 331.89
    in
      alcoholism 303.9 *[331.7]*
      beriberi 265.0 *[331.7]*
      cerebrovascular disease 437.9 *[331.7]*
      congenital hydrocephalus 742.3 *[331.7]*
        with spina bifida (*see also* Spina bifida)
          741.0 *[331.7]*
      Fabry's disease 272.7 *[330.2]*
      Gaucher's disease 272.7 *[330.2]*
      Hunter's disease or syndrome 277.5 *[330.3]*
      lipidosis
        cerebral 330.1
        generalized 272.7 *[330.2]*
      mucopolysaccharidosis 277.5 *[330.3]*
      myxedema (*see also* Myxedema) 244.9
        [331.7]
      neoplastic disease NEC (M8000/1) 239.9
        [331.7]
      Niemann-Pick disease 272.7 *[330.2]*

Degeneration, degenerative—*continued*
  spine (*see also* Spondylosis) 721.90
  kidney (*see also* Sclerosis, renal) 587
    amyloid 277.3 *[583.81]*
    cyst, cystic (multiple) (solitary) 593.2
      congenital (*see also* Cystic, disease, kidney)
        753.10
    fatty 593.89
    fibrocystic (congenital) 753.19
    lardaceous 277.3 *[583.81]*
    polycystic (congenital) 753.12
      adult type (APKD) 753.13
      autosomal dominant 753.13
      autosomal recessive 753.14
      childhood type (CPKD) 753.14
      infantile type 753.14
    waxy 277.3 *[583.81]*
  Kuhnt-Junius (retina) 362.52
  labyrinth, osseous 386.8
  lacrimal passages, cystic 375.12
  lardaceous (any site) 277.3
  lateral column (posterior), spinal cord (*see also*
    Degeneration, combined) 266.2 *[336.2]*
  lattice 362.63
  lens 366.9
    infantile, juvenile, or presenile 366.00
    senile 366.10
  lenticular (familial) (progressive) (Wilson's)
    (with cirrhosis of liver) 275.1
    striate artery 437.0
  lethal ball, prosthetic heart valve 996.02
  ligament
    collateral (knee) (medial) 717.82
      lateral 717.81
    cruciate (knee) (posterior) 717.84
      anterior 717.83
  liver (diffuse) 572.8
    amyloid 277.3
    congenital (cystic) 751.62
    cystic 572.8
      congenital 751.62
    fatty 571.8
      alcoholic 571.0
    hypertrophic 572.8
    lardaceous 277.3
    parenchymatous, acute or subacute (*see also*
      Necrosis, liver) 570
    pigmentary 572.8
    toxic (acute) 573.8
    waxy 277.3
  lung 518.8
  lymph gland 289.3
    hyaline 289.3
    lardaceous 277.3
  macula (acquired) (senile) 362.50
    atrophic 362.51
    Best's 362.76
    congenital 362.75
    cystic 362.54
    cystoid 362.53
    disciform 362.52
    dry 362.51
    exudative 362.52
    familial pseudoinflammatory 362.77
    hereditary 362.76
    hole 362.54
    juvenile (Stargardt's) 362.75
    nonexudative 362.51
    pseudohole 362.54
    wet 362.52

Degeneration, degenerative—*continued*
  medullary—*see* Degeneration, brain
  membranous labyrinth, congenital (causing
    impairment of hearing) 744.05
  meniscus—*see* Derangement, joint
  microcystoid 362.62
  mitral—*see* Insufficiency, mitral
  Mönckeberg's (*see also* Arteriosclerosis,
    extremities) 440.20
  moral 301.7
  motor centers, senile 331.2
  mural (*see also* Degeneration, myocardial) 429.1
    heart, cardiac (*see also* Degeneration,
      myocardial) 429.1
    myocardium, myocardial (*see also*
      Degeneration, myocardial) 429.1
  muscle 728.9
    fatty 728.9
    fibrous 728.9
    heart (*see also* Degeneration, myocardial)
      429.1
    hyaline 728.9
  muscular progressive 728.2
  myelin, central nervous system NEC 341.9
  myocardium, myocardial (brown) (calcareous)
    (fatty) (fibrous) (hyaline) (mural)
    (muscular) (pigmentary) (senile) (with
    arteriosclerosis) 429.1
    with rheumatic fever (conditions classifiable
      to 390) 398.0
      active, acute, or subacute 391.2
        with chorea 392.0
      inactive or quiescent (with chorea) 398.0
    amyloid 277.3 *[425.7]*
    congenital 746.89
    fetus or newborn 779.8
    gouty 274.82
    hypertensive (*see also* Hypertension, heart)
      402.90
    ischemic 414.8
    rheumatic (*see also* Degeneration,
      myocardium, with rheumatic fever) 398.0
    syphilitic 093.82
  nasal sinus (mucosa) (*see also* Sinusitis) 473.9
    frontal 473.1
    maxillary 473.0
  nerve—*see* Disorder, nerve
  nervous system 349.89
    amyloid 277.3 *[357.4]*
    autonomic (*see also* Neuropathy, peripheral,
      autonomic) 337.9
    fatty 349.89
    peripheral autonomic NEC (*see also*
      Neuropathy, peripheral, autonomic) 337.9
  nipple 611.9
  nose 478.1
  oculoacousticocerebral, congenital (progressive)
    743.8
  olivopontocerebellar (familial) (hereditary)
    333.0
  osseous labyrinth 386.8
  ovary 620.8
    cystic 620.2
    microcystic 620.2
  pallidal, pigmentary (progressive) 333.0
  pancreas 577.8
    tuberculous (*see also* Tuberculosis) 017.9
  papillary muscle 429.81
  paving stone 362.61
  penis 607.89
  peritoneum 568.89

Degeneration, degenerative—*continued*
  pigmentary (diffuse) (general)
    localized—*see* Degeneration, by site
    pallidal (progressive) 333.0
    secondary 362.65
  pineal gland 259.8
  pituitary (gland) 253.8
  placenta (fatty) (fibrinoid) (fibroid)—*see*
    Placenta, abnormal
  popliteal fat pad 729.31
  posterolateral (spinal cord) (*see also*
    Degeneration, combined) 266.2 *[336.2]*
  pulmonary valve (heart) (*see also* Endocarditis,
    pulmonary) 424.3
  pulp (tooth) 522.2
  pupillary margin 364.54
  renal (*see also* Sclerosis, renal) 587
    fibrocystic 753.19
    polycystic 753.12
      adult type (APKD) 753.13
      autosomal dominant 753.13
      autosomal recessive 753.14
      childhood type (CPKD) 753.14
      infantile type 753.14
  reticuloendothelial system 289.8
  retina (peripheral) 362.60
    with retinal defect (*see also* Detachment,
      retina, with retinal defect) 361.00
    cystic (senile) 362.50
    cystoid 362.53
    hereditary (*see also* Dystrophy, retina) 362.70
      cerebroretinal 362.71
      congenital 362.75
      juvenile (Stargardt's) 362.75
      macula 362.76
    Kuhnt-Junius 362.52
    lattice 362.63
    macular (*see also* Degeneration, macula)
      362.50
    microcystoid 362.62
    palisade 362.63
    paving stone 362.61
    pigmentary (primary) 362.74
      secondary 362.65
    posterior pole (*see also* Degeneration, macula)
      362.50
    secondary 362.66
    senile 362.60
      cystic 362.53
      reticular 362.64
  saccule, congenital (causing impairment of
    hearing) 744.05
  sacculocochlear 386.8
  senile 797
    brain 331.2
    cardiac, heart, or myocardium (*see also*
      Degeneration, myocardial) 429.1
    motor centers 331.2
    reticule 362.64
    retina, cystic 362.50
    vascular—*see* Arteriosclerosis
  silicone rubber poppet (prosthetic valve) 996.02
  sinus (cystic) (*see also* Sinusitis) 473.9
    polypoid 471.1
  skin 709.3
    amyloid 277.3
    colloid 709.3

Degeneration, degenerative—*continued*
  spinal (cord) 336.8
    amyloid 277.3
    column 733.90
    combined (subacute) (*see also* Degeneration,
      combined) 266.2 *[336.2]*
      with anemia (pernicious) 281.0 *[336.2]*
    dorsolateral (*see also* Degeneration,
      combined) 266.2 *[336.2]*
    familial NEC 336.8
    fatty 336.8
    funicular (*see also* Degeneration, combined)
      266.2 *[336.2]*
    heredofamilial NEC 336.8
    posterolateral (*see also* Degeneration,
      combined) 266.2 *[336.2]*
    subacute combined—*see* Degeneration,
      combined
    tuberculous (*see also* Tuberculosis) 013.8
  spine 733.90
  spleen 289.59
    amyloid 277.3
    lardaceous 277.3
  stomach 537.89
    lardaceous 277.3
  strionigral 333.0
  sudoriparous (cystic) 705.89
  suprarenal (capsule) (gland) 255.8
    with hypofunction 255.4
  sweat gland 705.89
  synovial membrane (pulpy) 727.9
  tapetoretinal 362.74
    adult or presenile form 362.50
  testis (postinfectional) 608.89
  thymus (gland) 254.8
    fatty 254.8
    lardaceous 277.3
  thyroid (gland) 246.8
  tricuspid (heart) (valve)—*see* Endocarditis,
    tricuspid
  tuberculous NEC (*see also* Tuberculosis) 011.9
  turbinate 733.90
  uterus 621.8
    cystic 621.8
  vascular (senile)—*see also* Arteriosclerosis
    hypertensive—*see* Hypertension
  vitreoretinal (primary) 362.73
    secondary 362.66
  vitreous humor (with infiltration) 379.21
  wallerian NEC—*see* Disorder, nerve
  waxy (any site) 277.3
  Wilson's hepatolenticular 275.1
Deglutition
  paralysis 784.9
    hysterical 300.11
  pneumonia 507.0
Degos' disease or syndrome 447.8
**Degradation disorder, branched-chain
  amino-acid** 270.3
Dehiscence
  anastomosis—*see* Complications, anastomosis
  cesarean wound 674.1
  episiotomy 674.2
  operation wound 998.3
  perineal wound (postpartum) 674.2
  postoperative 998.3
    abdomen 998.3
  uterine wound 674.1

Dehydration (cachexia) 276.5
  newborn 775.5
Deiters' nucleus syndrome 386.19
Déjérine's disease 356.0
Déjérine-Klumpke paralysis 767.6
Déjérine-Roussy syndrome 348.8
Déjérine-Sottas disease or neuropathy
  (hypertrophic) 356.0
Déjérine-Thomas atrophy or syndrome 333.0
de Lange's syndrome (Amsterdam dwarf,
  mental retardation, and brachycephaly) 759.89
Delay, delayed
  adaptation, cones or rods 368.63
  any plane in pelvis
    affecting fetus or newborn 763.1
    complicating delivery 660.1
  birth or delivery NEC 662.1
    affecting fetus or newborn 763.9
    second twin, triplet, or multiple mate 662.3
  closure—*see also* Fistula
    cranial suture 756.0
    fontanel 756.0
  coagulation NEC 790.92
  conduction (cardiac) (ventricular) 426.9
  delivery NEC 662.1
    second twin, triplet, etc. 662.3
      affecting fetus or newborn 763.89
  development
    in childhood 783.40
      physiological 783.40
    intellectual NEC 315.9
    learning NEC 315.2
    reading 315.00
    sexual 259.0
    speech 315.39
      associated with hyperkinesis 314.1
    spelling 315.09
  gastric emptying 536.8
  menarche 256.3
    due to pituitary hypofunction 253.4
  menstruation (cause unknown) 626.8
  milestone in childhood 783.42
  motility—*see* Hypomotility
  passage of meconium (newborn) 777.1
  primary respiration 768.9
  puberty 259.0
  sexual maturation, female 259.0
Del Castillo's syndrome (germinal aplasia) 606.0
Deleage's disease 359.8
Delhi (boil) (button) (sore) 085.1
Delinquency (juvenile) 312.9
  group (*see also* Disturbance, conduct) 312.2
  neurotic 312.4
Delirium, delirious 780.09
  acute (psychotic) 293.0
  alcoholic 291.0
    acute 291.0
    chronic 291.1
  alcoholicum 291.0
  chronic (*see also* Psychosis) 293.89
    due to or associated with physical
      condition—*see* Psychosis, organic
  drug-induced 292.81
  eclamptic (*see also* Eclampsia) 780.39
  exhaustion (*see also* Reaction, stress, acute)
    308.9
  hysterical 300.11

Delirium, delirious—*continued*
  in
    presenile dementia 290.11
    senile dementia 290.3
  induced by drug 292.81
  manic, maniacal (acute) (*see also* Psychosis,
    affective) 296.0
    recurrent episode 296.1
    single episode 296.0
  puerperal 293.9
  senile 290.3
  subacute (psychotic) 293.1
  thyroid (*see also* Thyrotoxicosis) 242.9
  traumatic—*see also* Injury, intracranial
    with
      lesion, spinal cord—*see* Injury, spinal, by
        site
      shock, spinal—*see* Injury, spinal, by site
  tremens (impending) 291.0
  uremic—*see* Uremia
  withdrawal
    alcoholic (acute) 291.0
      chronic 291.1
    drug 292.0
Delivery

> Note—Use the following fifth-digit
> subclassification with categories 640-648,
> 651-676:
>
> 0 *unspecified as to episode of care*
> 1 *delivered, with or without mention of*
>   *antepartum condition*
> 2 *delivered, with mention of*
>   *postpartum complication*
> 3 *antepartum condition or complication*
> 4 *postpartum condition or*
>   *complication*

  breech (assisted) (spontaneous) 652.2
    affecting fetus or newborn 763.0
    extraction NEC 669.6
  cesarean (for) 669.7
    abnormal
      cervix 654.6
      pelvic organs or tissues 654.9
      pelvis (bony) (major) NEC 653.0
      presentation or position 652.9
        in multiple gestation 652.6
      size, fetus 653.5
      soft parts (of pelvis) 654.9
      uterus, congenital 654.0
      vagina 654.7
      vulva 654.8
    abruptio placentae 641.2
    acromion presentation 652.8
    affecting fetus or newborn 763.4
    anteversion, cervix or uterus 654.4
    atony, uterus 666.1
    bicornis or bicornuate uterus 654.0
    breech presentation 652.2
    brow presentation 652.4
    cephalopelvic disproportion (normally formed
      fetus) 653.4
    chin presentation 652.4
    cicatrix of cervix 654.6
    contracted pelvis (general) 653.1
      inlet 653.2
      outlet 653.3
    cord presentation or prolapse 663.0
    cystocele 654.4

Delivery—*continued*
    vulva 654.8
  primary uterine inertia 661.0
  primipara, elderly or old 659.5
  prolapse
    arm or hand 652.7
      causing obstructed labor 660.0
    cord (umbilical) 663.0
    fetal extremity 652.8
    foot or leg 652.8
      causing obstructed labor 660.0
    umbilical cord (complete) (occult) (partial)
      663.0
    uterus 654.4
      causing obstructed labor 660.2
  prolonged labor 662.1
    first stage 662.0
    second stage 662.2
    active phase 661.2
    due to
      cervical dystocia 661.0
      contraction ring 661.4
      tetanic uterus 661.4
      uterine inertia 661.2
        primary 661.0
        secondary 661.1
    latent phase 661.0
  pyrexia during labor 659.2
  rachitic pelvis 653.2
    causing obstructed labor 660.1
  rectocele 654.4
    causing obstructed labor 660.2
  retained membranes or portions of placenta
    666.2
    without hemorrhage 667.1
  retarded (prolonged) birth 662.1
  retention secundines (with hemorrhage) 666.2
    without hemorrhage 667.1
  retroversion, uterus or cervix 654.3
    causing obstructed labor 660.2
  rigid
    cervix 654.6
      causing obstructed labor 660.2
    pelvic floor 654.4
      causing obstructed labor 660.2
    perineum or vulva 654.8
      causing obstructed labor 660.2
    vagina 654.7
      causing obstructed labor 660.2
  Robert's pelvis 653.0
    causing obstructed labor 660.1
  rupture—*see also* Delivery, complicated,
    laceration
    bladder (urinary) 665.5
    cervix 665.3
    marginal sinus 641.2
    membranes, premature 658.1
    pelvic organ NEC 665.5
    perineum (without mention of other
      laceration)—*see* Delivery, complicated,
      laceration, perineum
    peritoneum 665.5
    urethra 665.5
    uterus (during labor) 665.1
      before labor 665.0
  sacculation, pregnant uterus 654.4
  sacral teratomas, fetal 653.7
    causing obstructed labor 660.1
  scar(s)
    cervix 654.6
      causing obstructed labor 660.2

Delivery—*continued*
  cesarean delivery 654.2
    causing obstructed labor 660.2
  perineum 654.8
    causing obstructed labor 660.2
  uterus NEC 654.9
    causing obstructed labor 660.2
    due to previous cesarean delivery 654.2
  vagina 654.7
    causing obstructed labor 660.2
  vulva 654.8
    causing obstructed labor 660.2
  scoliotic pelvis 653.0
    causing obstructed labor 660.1
  secondary uterine inertia 661.1
  secundines, retained—*see* Delivery,
    complicated, placenta, retained
  separation
    placenta (premature) 641.2
    pubic bone 665.6
    symphysis pubis 665.6
  septate vagina 654.7
    causing obstructed labor 660.2
  shock (birth) (obstetric) (puerperal) 669.1
  short cord syndrome 663.4
  shoulder
    girdle dystocia 660.4
    presentation 652.8
      causing obstructed labor 660.0
  Siamese twins 653.7
    causing obstructed labor 660.1
  slow slope active phase 661.2
  spasm
    cervix 661.4
    uterus 661.4
  spondylolisthesis, pelvis 653.3
    causing obstructed labor 660.1
  spondylolysis (lumbosacral) 653.3
    causing obstructed labor 660.1
  spondylosis 653.0
    causing obstructed labor 660.1
  stenosis or stricture
    cervix 654.6
      causing obstructed labor 660.2
    vagina 654.7
      causing obstructed labor 660.2
  sudden death, unknown cause 669.9
  tear (pelvic organ) (*see also* Delivery,
    complicated, laceration) 664.9
  teratomas, sacral, fetal 653.7
    causing obstructed labor 660.1
  tetanic uterus 661.4
  tipping pelvis 653.0
    causing obstructed labor 660.1
  transverse
    arrest (deep) 660.3
    presentation or lie 652.3
      with successful version 652.1
      causing obstructed labor 660.0
  trauma (obstetrical) NEC 665.9
  tumor
    abdominal, fetal 653.7
      causing obstructed labor 660.1
    pelvic organs or tissues NEC 654.9
      causing obstructed labor 660.2
  umbilical cord (*see also* Delivery,
    complicated, cord) 663.9
    around neck tightly, or with compression
      663.1
    entanglement NEC 663.3
      with compression 663.2

Delivery—*continued*
   prolapse (complete) (occult) (partial) 663.0
   unstable lie 652.0
     causing obstructed labor 660.0
   uterine
     inertia (*see also* Delivery, complicated,
       inertia, uterus) 661.2
       spasm 661.4
     vasa previa 663.5
     velamentous insertion of cord 663.8
     young maternal age 659.8
   delayed NEC 662.1
     following rupture of membranes
       (spontaneous) 658.2
       artificial 658.3
     second twin, triplet, etc. 662.3
   difficult NEC 669.9
     previous, affecting management of pregnancy
       or childbirth V23.4
     specified type NEC 669.8
   early onset (spontaneous) 644.2
   forceps NEC 669.5
     affecting fetus or newborn 763.2
   footling 652.8
     with successful version 652.1
   missed (at or near term) 656.4
   multiple gestation NEC 651.9
     with fetal loss and retention of one or more
       fetus(es) 651.6
     specified type NEC 651.8
       with fetal loss and retention of one or more
        fetus(es) 651.6
   nonviable infant 656.4
   normal—*see* category 650
   precipitate 661.3
     affecting fetus or newborn 763.6
   premature NEC (before 37 completed weeks
     gestation) 644.2
     previous, affecting management of pregnancy
       V23.4
   quadruplet NEC 651.2
     with fetal loss and retention of one or more
       fetus(es) 651.5
   quintuplet NEC 651.8
     with fetal loss and retention of one or more
       fetus(es) 651.6
   sextuplet NEC 651.8
     with fetal loss and retention of one or more
       fetus(es) 651.6
   specified complication NEC 669.8
   stillbirth (near term) NEC 656.4
     early (before 22 completed weeks' gestation)
       632
   term pregnancy (live birth) NEC—*see* category
     650
     stillbirth NEC 656.4
   threatened premature 644.2
   triplets NEC 651.1
     with fetal loss and retention of one or more
       fetus(es) 651.4
     delayed delivery (one or more mates) 662.3
     locked mates 660.5
   twins NEC 651.0
     with fetal loss and retention of one or more
       fetus(es) 651.3
     delayed delivery (one or more mates) 662.3
     locked mates 660.5
   uncomplicated—*see* category 650
   vacuum extractor NEC 669.5
     affecting fetus or newborn 763.3
   ventouse NEC 669.5
     affecting fetus or newborn 763.3

Dellen, cornea 371.41
Delusions (paranoid) 297.9
  grandiose 297.1
  parasitosis 300.29
  systematized 297.1
Dementia 294.8
  alcoholic (*see also* Psychosis, alcoholic) 291.2
  Alzheimer's—*see* Alzheimer's dementia
  arteriosclerotic (simple type) (uncomplicated)
    290.40
    with
      acute confusional state 290.41
      delirium 290.41
      delusional features 290.42
      depressive features 290.43
     depressed type 290.43
     paranoid type 290.42
  Binswanger's 290.12
  catatonic (acute) (*see also* Schizophrenia) 295.2
  congenital (*see also* Retardation, mental) 319
  degenerative 290.9
    presenile-onset—*see* Dementia, presenile
    senile-onset—*see* Dementia, senile
  developmental (*see also* Schizophrenia) 295.9
  dialysis 294.8
    transient 293.9
  due to or associated with condition(s) classified
    elsewhere
    Alzheimer's
      with behavioral disturbance 331.0 *[294.11]*
      without behavioral disturbance 331.0
        [294.10]
    cerebral lipidoses
      with behavioral disturbance 330.1 *[294.11]*
      without behavioral disturbance 330.1
        [294.10]
    epilepsy
      with behavioral disturbance 345.9 *[294.11]*
      without behavioral disturbance 345.9
        [294.10]
    hepatolenticular degeneration
      with behavioral disturbance 275.1 *[294.11]*
      without behavioral disturbance 275.1
        [294.10]
    HIV
      with behavioral disturbance 042 *[294.11]*
      without behavioral disturbance 042 *[294.10]*
    Huntington's chorea
      with behavioral disturbance 333.4 *[294.11]*
      without behavioral disturbance 333.4
        [294.10]
    Jakob-Creutzfeldt disease
      with behavioral disturbance 046.1 *[294.11]*
      without behavioral disturbance 046.1
        [294.10]
    multiple sclerosis
      with behavioral disturbance 340 *[294.11]*
      without behavioral disturbance 340 *[294.10]*
    neurosyphilis
      with behavioral disturbance 094.9 *[294.11]*
      without behavioral disturbance 094.9
        [294.10]
    Pelizaeus-Merzbacher disease
      with behavioral disturbance 333.0 *[294.11]*
      without behavioral disturbance 333.0
        [294.10]
    Pick's disease
      with behavioral disturbance 331.1 *[294.11]*
      without behavioral disturbance 331.1
        [294.10]

Dementia—*continued*
  polyarteritis nodosa
    with behavioral disturbance 446.0 *[294.11]*
    without behavioral disturbance 446.0
      [294.10]
  syphilis
    with behavioral disturbance 094.1 *[294.11]*
    without behavioral disturbance 094.1
      [294.10]
  Wilson's disease
    with behavioral disturbance 275.1 *[294.11]*
    without behavioral disturbance 275.1
      [294.10]
  hebephrenic (acute) 295.1
  Heller's (infantile psychosis) (*see also*
    Psychosis, childhood) 299.1
  idiopathic 290.9
    presenile-onset—*see* Dementia, presenile
    senile-onset—*see* Dementia, senile
  in
    arteriosclerotic brain disease 290.40
    senility 290.0
  induced by drug 292.82
  infantile, infantilia (*see also* Psychosis,
    childhood) 299.0
  multi-infarct (cerebrovascular) (*see also*
    Dementia, arteriosclerotic) 290.40
  old age 290.0
  paralytica, paralytic 094.1
    juvenilis 090.40
    syphilitic 094.1
      congenital 090.40
    tabetic form 094.1
  paranoid (*see also* Schizophrenia) 295.3
  paraphrenic (*see also* Schizophrenia) 295.3
  paretic 094.1
  praecox (*see also* Schizophrenia) 295.9
  presenile 290.10
    with
      acute confusional state 290.11
      delirium 290.11
      delusional features 290.12
      depressive features 290.13
    depressed type 290.13
    paranoid type 290.12
    simple type 290.10
    uncomplicated 290.10
  primary (acute) (*see also* Schizophrenia) 295.0
  progressive, syphilitic 094.1
  puerperal—*see* Psychosis, puerperal
  schizophrenic (*see also* Schizophrenia) 295.9
  senile 290.0
    with
      acute confusional state 290.3
      delirium 290.3
      delusional features 290.20
      depressive features 290.21
    depressed type 290.21
    exhaustion 290.0
    paranoid type 290.20
  simple type (acute) (*see also* Schizophrenia)
    295.0
  simplex (acute) (*see also* Schizophrenia) 295.0
  syphilitic 094.1
  uremic—*see* Uremia
  vascular 290.40
Demerol dependence (*see also* Dependence)
  304.0
Demineralization, ankle (*see also* Osteoporosis)
  733.00
Demodex folliculorum (infestation) 133.8
de Morgan's spots (senile angiomas) 448.1

Demyelinating
  polyneuritis, chronic inflammatory 357.8
Demyelination, demyelinization
  central nervous system 341.9
    specified NEC 341.8
  corpus callosum (central) 341.8
  global 340
Dengue (fever) 061
  sandfly 061
  vaccination, prophylactic (against) V05.1
  virus hemorrhagic fever 065.4
Dens
  evaginatus 520.2
  in dente 520.2
  invaginatus 520.2
Density
  increased, bone (disseminated) (generalized)
    (spotted) 733.99
  lung (nodular) 518.89
Dental —*see also* condition
  examination only V72.2
Dentia praecox 520.6
Denticles (in pulp) 522.2
Dentigerous cyst 526.0
Dentin
  irregular (in pulp) 522.3
  opalescent 520.5
  secondary (in pulp) 522.3
  sensitive 521.8
Dentinogenesis imperfecta 520.5
Dentinoma (M9271/0) 213.1
  upper jaw (bone) 213.0
Dentition 520.7
  abnormal 520.6
  anomaly 520.6
  delayed 520.6
  difficult 520.7
  disorder of 520.6
  precocious 520.6
  retarded 520.6
Denture sore (mouth) 528.9
Dependence

> *Note—Use the following fifth-digit*
> *subclassification with category 304:*
>
> *0 unspecified*
> *1 continuous*
> *2 episodic*
> *3 in remission*

  with
    withdrawal symptoms
      alcohol 291.81
      drug 292.0
  14-hydroxy-dihydromorphinone 304.0
  absinthe 304.6
  acemorphan 304.0
  acetanilid(e) 304.6
  acetophenetidin 304.6
  acetorphine 304.0
  acetyldihydrocodeine 304.0
  acetyldihydrocodeinone 304.0
  Adalin 304.1
  Afghanistan black 304.3
  agrypnal 304.1
  alcohol, alcoholic (ethyl) (methyl) (wood) 303.9
    maternal, with suspected fetal damage
      affecting management of pregnancy 655.4
  allobarbitone 304.1
  allonal 304.1
  allylisopropylacetylurea 304.1

Dependence—*continued*
  alphaprodine (hydrochloride) 304.0
  Alurate 304.1
  Alvodine 304.0
  amethocaine 304.6
  amidone 304.0
  amidopyrine 304.6
  aminopyrine 304.6
  amobarbital 304.1
  amphetamine(s) (type) (drugs classifiable to 969.7) 304.4
  amylene hydrate 304.6
  amylobarbitone 304.1
  amylocaine 304.6
  Amytal (sodium) 304.1
  analgesic (drug) NEC 304.6
    synthetic with morphine-like effect 304.0
  anesthetic (agent) (drug) (gas) (general) (local) NEC 304.6
  Angel dust 304.6
  anileridine 304.0
  antipyrine 304.6
  aprobarbital 304.1
  aprobarbitone 304.1
  atropine 304.6
  Avertin (bromide) 304.6
  barbenyl 304.1
  barbital(s) 304.1
  barbitone 304.1
  barbiturate(s) (compounds) (drugs classifiable to 967.0) 304.1
  barbituric acid (and compounds) 304.1
  benzedrine 304.4
  benzylmorphine 304.0
  Beta-chlor 304.1
  bhang 304.3
  blue velvet 304.0
  Brevital 304.1
  bromal (hydrate) 304.1
  bromide(s) NEC 304.1
  bromine compounds NEC 304.1
  bromisovalum 304.1
  bromoform 304.1
  Bromo-seltzer 304.1
  bromural 304.1
  butabarbital (sodium) 304.1
  butabarpal 304.1
  butallylonal 304.1
  butethal 304.1
  buthalitone (sodium) 304.1
  Butisol 304.1
  butobarbitone 304.1
  butyl chloral (hydrate) 304.1
  caffeine 304.4
  cannabis (indica) (sativa) (resin) (derivatives) (type) 304.3
  carbamazepine 304.6
  Carbrital 304.1
  carbromal 304.1
  carisoprodol 304.6
  Catha (edulis) 304.4
  chloral (betaine) (hydrate) 304.1
  chloralamide 304.1
  chloralformamide 304.1
  chloralose 304.1
  chlordiazepoxide 304.1
  Chloretone 304.1
  chlorobutanol 304.1
  chlorodyne 304.1
  chloroform 304.6
  Cliradon 304.0

Dependence—*continued*
  coca (leaf) and derivatives 304.2
  cocaine 304.2
    hydrochloride 304.2
    salt (any) 304.2
  codeine 304.0
  combination of drugs (excluding morphine or opioid type drug) NEC 304.8
    morphine or opioid type drug with any other drug 304.7
  croton-chloral 304.1
  cyclobarbital 304.1
  cyclobarbitone 304.1
  dagga 304.3
  Delvinal 304.1
  Demerol 304.0
  desocodeine 304.0
  desomorphine 304.0
  desoxyephedrine 304.4
  DET 304.5
  dexamphetamine 304.4
  dexedrine 304.4
  dextromethorphan 304.0
  dextromoramide 304.0
  dextronorpseudophedrine 304.4
  dextrorphan 304.0
  diacetylmorphine 304.0
  Dial 304.1
  diallylbarbituric acid 304.1
  diamorphine 304.0
  diazepam 304.1
  dibucaine 304.6
  dichloroethane 304.6
  diethyl barbituric acid 304.1
  diethylsulfone-diethylmethane 304.1
  difencloxazine 304.0
  dihydrocodeine 304.0
  dihydrocodeinone 304.0
  dihydrohydroxycodeinone 304.0
  dihydroisocodeine 304.0
  dihydromorphine 304.0
  dihydromorphinone 304.0
  dihydroxcodeinone 304.0
  Dilaudid 304.0
  dimenhydrinate 304.6
  dimethylmeperidine 304.0
  dimethyltriptamine 304.5
  Dionin 304.0
  diphenoxylate 304.6
  dipipanone 304.0
  d-lysergic acid diethylamide 304.5
  DMT 304.5
  Dolophine 304.0
  DOM 304.2
  Doriden 304.1
  dormiral 304.1
  Dormison 304.1
  Dromoran 304.0
  drug NEC 304.9
    analgesic NEC 304.6
    combination (excluding morphine or opioid type drug) NEC 304.8
      morphine or opioid type drug with any other drug 304.7
    complicating pregnancy, childbirth, or puerperium 648.3
      affecting fetus or newborn 779.5
    hallucinogenic 304.5
    hypnotic NEC 304.1
    narcotic NEC 304.9
    psychostimulant NEC 304.4

Dependence—*continued*
  sedative 304.1
  soporific NEC 304.1
  specified type NEC 304.6
  suspected damage to fetus affecting
    management of pregnancy 655.5
  synthetic, with morphine-like effect 304.0
  tranquilizing 304.1
duboisine 304.6
ectylurea 304.1
Endocaine 304.6
Equanil 304.1
Eskabarb 304.1
ethchlorvynol 304.1
ether (ethyl) (liquid) (vapor) (vinyl) 304.6
ethidene 304.6
ethinamate 304.1
ethoheptazine 304.6
ethyl
  alcohol 303.9
  bromide 304.6
  carbamate 304.6
  chloride 304.6
  morphine 304.0
ethylene (gas) 304.6
  dichloride 304.6
ethylidene chloride 304.6
etilfen 304.1
etorphine 304.0
etoval 304.1
eucodal 304.0
euneryl 304.1
Evipal 304.1
Evipan 304.1
fentanyl 304.0
ganja 304.3
gardenal 304.1
gardenpanyl 304.1
gelsemine 304.6
Gelsemium 304.6
Gemonil 304.1
glucochloral 304.1
glue (airplane) (sniffing) 304.6
glutethimide 304.1
hallucinogenics 304.5
hashish 304.3
headache powder NEC 304.6
Heavenly Blue 304.5
hedonal 304.1
hemp 304.3
heptabarbital 304.1
Heptalgin 304.0
heptobarbitone 304.1
heroin 304.0
  salt (any) 304.0
hexethal (sodium) 304.1
hexobarbital 304.1
Hycodan 304.0
hydrocodone 304.0
hydromorphinol 304.0
hydromorphinone 304.0
hydromorphone 304.0
hydroxycodeine 304.0
hypnotic NEC 304.1
Indian hemp 304.3
intranarcon 304.1
Kemithal 304.1
ketobemidone 304.0
khat 304.4
kif 304.3
Lactuca (virosa) extract 304.1

Dependence—*continued*
lactucarium 304.1
laudanum 304.0
Lebanese red 304.3
Leritine 304.0
lettuce opium 304.1
Levanil 304.1
Levo-Dromoran 304.0
levo-iso-methadone 304.0
levorphanol 304.0
Librium 304.1
Lomotil 304.6
Lotusate 304.1
LSD (-25) (and derivatives) 304.5
Luminal 304.1
lysergic acid 304.5
  amide 304.5
maconha 304.3
magic mushroom 304.5
marihuana 304.3
MDA (methylene dioxyamphetamine) 304.4
Mebaral 304.1
Medinal 304.1
Medomin 304.1
megahallucinogenics 304.5
meperidine 304.0
mephobarbital 304.1
meprobamate 304.1
mescaline 304.5
methadone 304.0
methamphetamine(s) 304.4
methaqualone 304.1
metharbital 304.1
methitural 304.1
methobarbitone 304.1
methohexital 304.1
methopholine 304.6
methyl
  alcohol 303.9
  bromide 304.6
  morphine 304.0
  sulfonal 304.1
methylated spirit 303.9
methylbutinol 304.6
methyldihydromorphinone 304.0
methylene
  chloride 304.6
  dichloride 304.6
  dioxyamphetamine (MDA) 304.4
methylparafynol 304.1
methylphenidate 304.4
methyprylone 304.1
metopon 304.0
Miltown 304.1
morning glory seeds 304.5
morphinan(s) 304.0
morphine (sulfate) (sulfite) (type) (drugs
  classifiable to 965.00-965.09) 304.0
morphine or opioid type drug (drugs classifiable
  to 965.00-965.09) with any other drug 304.7
morphinol(s) 304.0
morphinon 304.0
morpholinylethylmorphine 304.0
mylomide 304.1
myristicin 304.5
narcotic (drug) NEC 304.9
nealbarbital 304.1
nealbarbitone 304.1
Nembutal 304.1
Neonal 304.1
Neraval 304.1

Dependence—*continued*
  Neravan 304.1
  neurobarb 304.1
  nicotine 305.1
  Nisentil 304.0
  nitrous oxide 304.6
  Noctec 304.1
  Noludar 304.1
  nonbarbiturate sedatives and tranquilizers with
     similar effect 304.1
  noptil 304.1
  normorphine 304.0
  noscapine 304.0
  Novocaine 304.6
  Numorphan 304.0
  nunol 304.1
  Nupercaine 304.6
  Oblivon 304.1
  on
    aspirator V46.0
    hyperbaric chamber V46.8
    iron lung V46.1
    machine (enabling) V46.9
      specified type NEC V46.8
    Possum (Patient-Operated-Selector-
      Mechanism) V46.8
    renal dialysis machine V45.1
    respirator V46.1
  opiate 304.0
  opioids 304.0
  opioid type drug 304.0
    with any other drug 304.7
  opium (alkaloids) (derivatives) (tincture) 304.0
  ortal 304.1
  Oxazepam 304.1
  oxycodone 304.0
  oxymorphone 304.0
  Palfium 304.0
  Panadol 304.6
  pantopium 304.0
  pantopon 304.0
  papaverine 304.0
  paracetamol 304.6
  paracodin 304.0
  paraldehyde 304.1
  paregoric 304.0
  Parzone 304.0
  PCP (phencyclidine) 304.6
  Pearly Gates 304.5
  pentazocine 304.0
  pentobarbital 304.1
  pentobarbitone (sodium) 304.1
  Pentothal 304.1
  Percaine 304.6
  Percodan 304.0
  Perichlor 304.1
  Pernocton 304.1
  Pernoston 304.1
  peronine 304.0
  pethidine (hydrochloride) 304.0
  petrichloral 304.1
  peyote 304.5
  Phanodorn 304.1
  phenacetin 304.6
  phenadoxone 304.0
  phenaglycodol 304.1
  phenazocine 304.0
  phencyclidine 304.6
  phenmetrazine 304.4
  phenobal 304.1
  phenobarbital 304.1

Dependence—*continued*
  phenobarbitone 304.1
  phenomorphan 304.0
  phenonyl 304.1
  phenoperidine 304.0
  pholcodine 304.0
  piminodine 304.0
  Pipadone 304.0
  Pitkin's solution 304.6
  Placidyl 304.1
  polysubstance 304.8
  Pontocaine 304.6
  pot 304.3
  potassium bromide 304.1
  Preludin 304.4
  Prinadol 304.0
  probarbital 304.1
  procaine 304.6
  propanal 304.1
  propoxyphene 304.6
  psilocibin 304.5
  psilocin 304.5
  psilocybin 304.5
  psilocyline 304.5
  psilocyn 304.5
  psychedelic agents 304.5
  psychostimulant NEC 304.4
  psychotomimetic agents 304.5
  pyrahexyl 304.3
  Pyramidon 304.6
  quinalbarbitone 304.1
  racemoramide 304.0
  racemorphan 304.0
  Rela 304.6
  scopolamine 304.6
  secobarbital 304.1
  Seconal 304.1
  sedative NEC 304.1
    nonbarbiturate with barbiturate effect 304.1
  Sedormid 304.1
  sernyl 304.1
  sodium bromide 304.1
  Soma 304.6
  Somnal 304.1
  Somnos 304.1
  Soneryl 304.1
  soporific (drug) NEC 304.1
  specified drug NEC 304.6
  speed 304.4
  spinocaine 304.6
  Stovaine 304.6
  STP 304.5
  stramonium 304.6
  Sulfonal 304.1
  sulfonethylmethane 304.1
  sulfonmethane 304.1
  Surital 304.1
  synthetic drug with morphine-like effect 304.0
  talbutal 304.1
  tetracaine 304.6
  tetrahydrocannabinol 304.3
  tetronal 304.1
  THC 304.3
  thebacon 304.0
  thebaine 304.0
  thiamil 304.1
  thiamylal 304.1
  thiopental 304.1
  tobacco 305.1
  toluene, toluol 304.6

Dependence—*continued*
tranquilizer NEC 304.1
nonbarbiturate with barbiturate effect 304.1
tribromacetaldehyde 304.6
tribromethanol 304.6
tribromomethane 304.6
trichloroethanol 304.6
trichoroethyl phosphate 304.1
triclofos 304.1
Trional 304.1
Tuinal 304.1
Turkish Green 304.3
urethan(e) 304.6
Valium 304.1
Valmid 304.1
veganin 304.0
veramon 304.1
Veronal 304.1
versidyne 304.6
vinbarbital 304.1
vinbarbitone 304.1
vinyl bitone 304.1
vitamin B_6 266.1
wine 303.9
Zactane 304.6
Dependency
passive 301.6
reactions 301.6
Depersonalization (episode, in neurotic state) (neurotic) (syndrome) 300.6
Depletion
carbohydrates 271.9
complement factor 279.8
extracellular fluid 276.5
plasma 276.5
potassium 276.8
nephropathy 588.8
salt or sodium 276.1
causing heat exhaustion or prostration 992.4
nephropathy 593.9
volume 276.5
extracellular fluid 276.5
plasma 276.5
Deposit
argentous, cornea 371.16
bone, in Boeck's sarcoid 135
calcareous, calcium—*see* Calcification
cholesterol
retina 362.82
skin 709.3
vitreous (humor) 379.22
conjunctival 372.56
cornea, corneal NEC 371.10
argentous 371.16
in
cystinosis 270.0 *[371.15]*
mucopolysaccharidosis 277.5 *[371.15]*
crystalline, vitreous (humor) 379.22
hemosiderin, in old scars of cornea 371.11
metallic, in lens 366.45
skin 709.3
teeth, tooth (betel) (black) (green) (materia alba) (orange) (soft) (tobacco) 523.6
urate, in kidney (*see also* Disease, renal) 593.9
Depraved appetite 307.52

Depression 311
acute (*see also* Psychosis, affective) 296.2
recurrent episode 296.3
single episode 296.2
agitated (*see also* Psychosis, affective) 296.2
recurrent episode 296.3
single episode 296.2
anaclitic 309.21
anxiety 300.4
arches 734
congenital 754.61
autogenous (*see also* Psychosis, affective) 296.2
recurrent episode 296.3
single episode 296.2
basal metabolic rate (BMR) 794.7
bone marrow 289.9
central nervous system 799.1
newborn 779.2
cerebral 331.9
newborn 779.2
cerebrovascular 437.8
newborn 779.2
chest wall 738.3
endogenous (*see also* Psychosis, affective) 296.2
recurrent episode 296.3
single episode 296.2
functional activity 780.9
hysterical 300.11
involutional, climacteric, or menopausal (*see also* Psychosis, affective) 296.2
recurrent episode 296.3
single episode 296.2
manic (*see also* Psychosis, affective) 296.80
medullary 348.8
newborn 779.2
mental 300.4
metatarsal heads—*see* Depression, arches
metatarsus—*see* Depression, arches
monopolar (*see also* Psychosis, affective) 296.2
recurrent episode 296.3
single episode 296.2
nervous 300.4
neurotic 300.4
nose 738.0
postpartum 648.4
psychogenic 300.4
reactive 298.0
psychoneurotic 300.4
psychotic (*see also* Psychosis, affective) 296.2
reactive 298.0
recurrent episode 296.3
single episode 296.2
reactive 300.4
neurotic 300.4
psychogenic 298.0
psychoneurotic 300.4
psychotic 298.0
recurrent 296.3
respiratory center 348.8
newborn 770.8
scapula 736.89
senile 290.21
situational (acute) (brief) 309.0
prolonged 309.1
skull 754.0
sternum 738.3
visual field 368.40

Depressive reaction —*see also* Reaction,
  depressive
  acute (transient) 309.0
    with anxiety 309.28
  prolonged 309.1
  situational (acute) 309.0
    prolonged 309.1
Deprivation
  cultural V62.4
  emotional V62.89
    affecting
      adult 995.82
      infant or child 995.51
  food 994.2
    specific substance NEC 269.8
  protein (familial) (kwashiorkor) 260
  social V62.4
    affecting
      adult 995.82
      infant or child 995.51
  symptoms, syndrome
    alcohol 291.81
    drug 292.0
  vitamins (*see also* Deficiency, vitamin) 269.2
  water 994.3
de Quervain's
  disease (tendon sheath) 727.04
  thyroiditis (subacute granulomatous thyroiditis)
    245.1
Derangement
  ankle (internal) 718.97
    current injury (*see also* Dislocation, ankle)
      837.0
    recurrent 718.37
  cartilage (articular) NEC (*see also* Disorder,
    cartilage, articular) 718.0
    knee 717.9
      recurrent 718.36
    recurrent 718.3
  collateral ligament (knee) (medial) (tibial)
    717.82
    current injury 844.1
      lateral (fibular) 844.0
    lateral (fibular) 717.81
      current injury 844.0
  cruciate ligament (knee) (posterior) 717.84
    anterior 717.83
      current injury 844.2
    current injury 844.2
  elbow (internal) 718.92
    current injury (*see also* Dislocation, elbow)
      832.00
    recurrent 718.32
  gastrointestinal 536.9
  heart—*see* Disease, heart
  hip (joint) (internal) (old) 718.95
    current injury (*see also* Dislocation, hip)
      835.00
    recurrent 718.35
  intervertebral disc—*see* Displacement,
    intervertebral disc
  joint (internal) 718.90
    ankle 718.97
    current injury—*see also* Dislocation, by site
      knee, meniscus or cartilage (*see also* Tear,
        meniscus) 836.2
    elbow 718.92
    foot 718.97
    hand 718.94
    hip 718.95
    knee 717.9

Derangement—*continued*
    multiple sites 718.99
    pelvic region 718.95
    recurrent 718.30
      ankle 718.37
      elbow 718.32
      foot 718.37
      hand 718.34
      hip 718.35
      knee 718.36
      multiple sites 718.39
      pelvic region 718.35
      shoulder (region) 718.31
      specified site NEC 718.38
      temporomandibular (old) 524.69
      wrist 718.33
    shoulder (region) 718.91
    specified site NEC 718.98
    spine NEC 724.9
    temporomandibular 524.69
    wrist 718.93
  knee (cartilage) (internal) 717.9
    current injury (*see also* Tear, meniscus) 836.2
    ligament 717.89
      capsular 717.85
      collateral—*see* Derangement, collateral
        ligament
      cruciate—*see* Derangement, cruciate
        ligament
      specified NEC 717.85
    recurrent 718.36
  low back NEC 724.9
  meniscus NEC (knee) 717.5
    current injury (*see also* Tear, meniscus) 836.2
    lateral 717.40
      anterior horn 717.42
      posterior horn 717.43
      specified NEC 717.49
    medial 717.3
      anterior horn 717.1
      posterior horn 717.2
    recurrent 718.3
    site other than knee—*see* Disorder, cartilage,
      articular
  mental (*see also* Psychosis) 298.9
  rotator cuff (recurrent) (tear) 726.10
    current 840.4
  sacroiliac (old) 724.6
    current—*see* Dislocation, sacroiliac
  semilunar cartilage (knee) 717.5
    current injury 836.2
      lateral 836.1
      medial 836.0
    recurrent 718.3
  shoulder (internal) 718.91
    current injury (*see also* Dislocation, shoulder)
      831.00
    recurrent 718.31
  spine (recurrent) NEC 724.9
    current—*see* Dislocation, spine
  temporomandibular (internal) (joint) (old)
    524.69
    current—*see* Dislocation, jaw
Dercum's disease or syndrome (adiposis
  dolorosa) 272.8
Derealization (neurotic) 300.6
Dermal —*see* condition
Dermaphytid —*see* Dermatophytosis
Dermatergosis —*see* Dermatitis

Dermatitis (allergic) (contact) (occupational)
    (venenata) 692.9
  ab igne 692.82
  acneiform 692.9
  actinic (due to sun) 692.70
    acute 692.72
    chronic NEC 692.74
    other than from sun NEC 692.82
  ambustionis
    due to
      burn or scald—*see* Burn, by site
      sunburn 692.71
  amebic 006.6
  ammonia 691.0
  anaphylactoid NEC 692.9
  arsenical 692.4
  artefacta 698.4
    psychogenic 316 *[698.4]*
  asthmatic 691.8
  atopic (allergic) (intrinsic) 691.8
    psychogenic 316 *[691.8]*
  atrophicans 701.8
    diffusa 701.8
    maculosa 701.3
  berlock, berloque 692.72
  blastomycetic 116.0
  blister beetle 692.89
  Brucella NEC 023.9
  bullosa 694.9
    striata pratensis 692.6
  bullous 694.9
    mucosynechial, atrophic 694.60
      with ocular involvement 694.61
    seasonal 694.8
  calorica
    due to
      burn or scald—*see* Burn, by site
      cold 692.89
      sunburn 692.71
  caterpillar 692.89
  cercarial 120.3
  combustionis
    due to
      burn or scald—*see* Burn, by site
      sunburn 692.71
  congelationis 991.5
  contusiformis 695.2
  diabetic 250.8
  diaper 691.0
  diphtheritica 032.85
  due to
    acetone 692.2
    acids 692.4
    adhesive plaster 692.4
    alcohol (skin contact) (substances classifiable
      to 980.0-980.9) 692.4
      taken internally 693.8
    alkalis 692.4
    allergy NEC 692.9
    ammonia (household) (liquid) 692.4
    arnica 692.3
    arsenic 692.4
      taken internally 693.8
    blister beetle 692.89
    cantharides 692.3
    carbon disulphide 692.2
    caterpillar 692.89
    caustics 692.4
    cereal (ingested) 693.1
      contact with skin 692.5

Dermatitis—*continued*
  chemical(s) NEC 692.4
    internal 693.8
    irritant NEC 692.4
    taken internally 693.8
  chlorocompounds 692.2
  coffee (ingested) 693.1
    contact with skin 692.5
  cold weather 692.89
  cosmetics 692.81
  cyclohexanes 692.2
  deodorant 692.81
  detergents 692.0
  dichromate 692.4
  drugs and medicinals (correct substance
    properly administered) (internal use) 693.0
    external (in contact with skin) 692.3
      wrong substance given or taken 976.9
        specified substance—*see* Table of drugs
          and chemicals
      wrong substance given or taken 977.9
        specified substance—*see* Table of drugs
          and chemicals
  dyes 692.89
    hair 692.89
  epidermophytosis—*see* Dermatophytosis
  esters 692.2
  external irritant NEC 692.9
    specified agent NEC 692.89
  eye shadow 692.81
  fish (ingested) 693.1
    contact with skin 692.5
  flour (ingested) 693.1
    contact with skin 692.5
  food (ingested) 693.1
    in contact with skin 692.5
  fruit (ingested) 693.1
    contact with skin 692.5
  fungicides 692.3
  furs 692.89
  glycols 692.2
  greases NEC 692.1
  hair dyes 692.89
  hot
    objects and materials—*see* Burn, by site
    weather or places 692.89
  hydrocarbons 692.2
  infrared rays, except from sun 692.82
    solar NEC (*see* also Dermatitis, due to, sun)
      692.70
  ingested substance 693.9
    drugs and medicinals (*see also* Dermatitis,
      due to, drugs and medicinals) 693.0
    food 693.1
    specified substance NEC 693.8
  ingestion or injection of
    chemical 693.8
    drug (correct substance properly
      administered) 693.0
      wrong substance given or taken 977.9
        specified substance—*see* Table of drugs
          and chemicals
  insecticides 692.4
  internal agent 693.9
    drugs and medicinals (*see also* Dermatitis,
      due to, drugs and medicinals) 693.0
    food (ingested) 693.1
      in contact with skin 692.5
    specified agent NEC 693.8
  iodine 692.3
  iodoform 692.3

Dermatitis—*continued*
irradiation 692.82
jewelry 692.83
keratolytics 692.3
ketones 692.2
lacquer tree (Rhus verniciflua) 692.6
light (sun) NEC (*see also* Dermatitis, due to, sun) 692.70
other 692.82
low temperature 692.89
mascara 692.81
meat (ingested) 693.1
contact with skin 692.5
mercury, mercurials 692.3
metals 692.83
milk (ingested) 693.1
contact with skin 692.5
Neomycin 692.3
nylon 692.4
oils NEC 692.1
paint solvent 692.2
pediculocides 692.3
petroleum products (substances classifiable to 981) 692.4
phenol 692.3
photosensitiveness, photosensitivity (sun) 692.72
other light 692.82
plants NEC 692.6
plasters, medicated (any) 692.3
plastic 692.4
poison
ivy (Rhus toxicodendron) 692.6
oak (Rhus diversiloba) 692.6
plant or vine 692.6
sumac (Rhus venenata) 692.6
vine (Rhus radicans) 692.6
preservatives 692.89
primrose (primula) 692.6
primula 692.6
radiation 692.82
sun NEC (*see also* Dermatitis, due to, sun) 692.70
radioactive substance 692.82
radium 692.82
ragweed (Senecio jacobae) 692.6
Rhus (diversiloba) (radicans) (toxicodendron) (venenata) (verniciflua) 692.6
rubber 692.4
scabicides 692.3
Senecio jacobae 692.6
solar radiation—*see* Dermatitis, due to, sun
solvents (any) (substances classifiable to 982.0-982.8) 692.2
chlorocompound group 692.2
cyclohexane group 692.2
ester group 692.2
glycol group 692.2
hydrocarbon group 692.2
ketone group 692.2
paint 692.2
specified agent NEC 692.89
sun 692.70
acute 692.72
chronic NEC 692.74
specified NEC 692.79
sunburn 692.71
sunshine NEC (*see also* Dermatitis, due to, sun) 692.70
tetrachlorethylene 692.2
toluene 692.2

Dermatitis—*continued*
topical medications 692.3
turpentine 692.2
ultraviolet rays, except from sun 692.82
sun NEC (*see also* Dermatitis, due to, sun) 692.70
vaccine or vaccination (correct substance properly administered) 693.0
wrong substance given or taken
bacterial vaccine 978.8
specified—*see* Table of drugs and chemicals
other vaccines NEC 979.9
specified—*see* Table of drugs and chemicals
varicose veins (*see also* Varicose, vein, inflamed or infected) 454.1
x-rays 692.82
dyshydrotic 705.81
dysmenorrheica 625.8
eczematoid NEC 692.9
infectious 690.8
eczematous NEC 692.9
epidemica 695.89
erysipelatosa 695.81
escharotica—*see* Burn, by site
exfoliativa, exfoliative 695.89
generalized 695.89
infantum 695.81
neonatorum 695.81
eyelid 373.31
allergic 373.32
contact 373.32
eczematous 373.31
herpes (zoster) 053.20
simplex 054.41
infective 373.5
due to
actinomycosis 039.3 [373.5]
herpes
simplex 054.41
zoster 053.20
impetigo 684 [373.5]
leprosy (*see also* Leprosy) 030.0 [373.4]
lupus vulgaris (tuberculous) (*see also* Tuberculosis) 017.0 [373.4]
mycotic dermatitis (*see also* Dermatomycosis) 111.9 [373.5]
vaccinia 051.0 [373.5]
postvaccination 999.0 [373.5]
yaws (*see also* Yaws) 102.9 [373.4]
facta, factitia 698.4
psychogenic 316 [698.4]
ficta 698.4
psychogenic 316 [698.4]
flexural 691.8
follicularis 704.8
friction 709.8
fungus 111.9
specified type NEC 111.8
gangrenosa, gangrenous (infantum) (*see also* Gangrene) 785.4
gestationis 646.8
gonococcal 098.89
gouty 274.89
harvest mite 133.8
heat 692.89
herpetiformis (bullous) (erythematous) (pustular) (vesicular) 694.0
juvenile 694.2
senile 694.5

Dermatosis—*continued*
occupational (*see also* Dermatitis) 692.9
papulosa nigra 709.8
pigmentary NEC 709.00
progressive 709.09
Schamberg's 709.09
Siemens-Bloch 757.33
progressive pigmentary 709.09
psychogenic 316
pustular subcorneal 694.1
Schamberg's (progressive pigmentary) 709.09
senile NEC 709.3
Unna's (seborrheic dermatitis) 690.10
Dermographia 708.3
Dermographism 708.3
Dermoid (cyst) (M9084/0)—*see also* Neoplasm,
by site, benign
with malignant transformation (M9084/3) 183.0
Dermopathy
infiltrative, with thyrotoxicosis 242.0
senile NEC 709.3
Dermophytosis —*see* Dermatophytosis
Descemet's membrane —*see* condition
Descemetocele 371.72
Descending —*see* condition
Descensus uteri (complete) (incomplete)
(partial) (without vaginal wall prolapse) 618.1
with mention of vaginal wall prolapse—*see*
Prolapse, uterovaginal
Desensitization to allergens V07.1
Desert
rheumatism 114.0
sore (*see also* Ulcer, skin) 707.9
Desertion (child) (newborn) 995.52
adult 995.84
Desmoid (extra-abdominal) (tumor)
(M8821/1)—*see also* Neoplasm, connective
tissue, uncertain behavior
abdominal (M8822/1)—*see* Neoplasm,
connective tissue, uncertain behavior
Despondency 300.4
Desquamative dermatitis NEC 695.89
Destruction
articular facet (*see also* Derangement, joint)
718.9
vertebra 724.9
bone 733.90
syphilitic 095.5
joint (*see also* Derangement, joint) 718.9
sacroiliac 724.6
kidney 593.89
live fetus to facilitate birth NEC 763.89
ossicles (ear) 385.24
rectal sphincter 569.49
septum (nasal) 478.1
tuberculous NEC (*see also* Tuberculosis) 011.9
tympanic membrane 384.82
tympanum 385.89
vertebral disc—*see* Degeneration, intervertebral
disc
Destructiveness (*see also* Disturbance, conduct)
312.9
adjustment reaction 309.3
Detachment
cartilage—*see also* Sprain, by site
knee—*see* Tear, meniscus
cervix, annular 622.8
complicating delivery 665.3

Detachment—*continued*
choroid (old) (postinfectional) (simple)
(spontaneous) 363.70
hemorrhagic 363.72
serous 363.71
knee, medial meniscus (old) 717.3
current injury 836.0
ligament—*see* Sprain, by site
placenta (premature)—*see* Placenta, separation
retina (recent) 361.9
with retinal defect (rhegmatogenous) 361.00
giant tear 361.03
multiple 361.02
partial
with
giant tear 361.03
multiple defects 361.02
retinal dialysis (juvenile) 361.04
single defect 361.01
retinal dialysis (juvenile) 361.04
single 361.01
subtotal 361.05
total 361.05
delimited (old) (partial) 361.06
old
delimited 361.06
partial 361.06
total or subtotal 361.07
pigment epithelium (RPE) (serous) 362.42
exudative 362.42
hemorrhagic 362.43
rhegmatogenous (*see also* Detachment, retina,
with retinal defect) 361.00
serous (without retinal defect) 361.2
specified type NEC 361.89
traction (with vitreoretinal organization)
361.81
vitreous humor 379.21
Detergent asthma 507.8
Deterioration
epileptic
with behavioral disturbance 345.9 *[294.11]*
without behavioral disturbance 345.9 *[294.10]*
heart, cardiac (*see also* Degeneration,
myocardial) 429.1
mental (*see also* Psychosis) 298.9
myocardium, myocardial (*see also*
Degeneration, myocardial) 429.1
senile (simple) 797
transplanted organ—*see* Complications,
transplant, organ, by site
de Toni-Fanconi syndrome (cystinosis) 270.0
Deuteranomaly 368.52
Deuteranopia (anomalous trichromat)
(complete) (incomplete) 368.52
Deutschländer's disease —*see* Fracture, foot
Development
abnormal, bone 756.9
arrested 783.40
bone 733.91
child 783.40
due to malnutrition (protein-calorie) 263.2
fetus or newborn 764.9
tracheal rings (congenital) 748.3
defective, congenital—*see also* Anomaly
cauda equina 742.59
left ventricle 746.9
with atresia or hypoplasia of aortic orifice or
valve with hypoplasia of ascending aorta
746.7
in hypoplastic left heart syndrome 746.7

Development—*continued*
  delayed (*see also* Delay, development) 783.40
    arithmetical skills 315.1
    language (skills) 315.31
      expressive 315.31
      mixed receptive-expressive 315.32
    learning skill, specified NEC 315.2
    mixed skills 315.5
    motor coordination 315.4
    reading 315.00
    specified
      learning skill NEC 315.2
      type NEC, except learning 315.8
    speech 315.39
      associated with hyperkinesia 314.1
      phonological 315.39
    spelling 315.09
    written expression 315.2
  imperfect, congenital—*see also* Anomaly
    heart 746.9
    lungs 748.60
  improper (fetus or newborn) 764.9
  incomplete (fetus or newborn) 764.9
    affecting management of pregnancy 656.5
    bronchial tree 748.3
    organ or site not listed—*see* Hypoplasia
    respiratory system 748.9
  sexual, precocious NEC 259.1
  tardy, mental (*see also* Retardation, mental) 319
Developmental —*see* condition
Devergie's disease (pityriasis rubra pilaris) 696.4
Deviation
  conjugate (eye) 378.87
    palsy 378.81
    spasm, spastic 378.82
  esophagus 530.89
  eye, skew 378.87
  midline (jaw) (teeth) 524.2
    specified site NEC—*see* Malposition
  organ or site, congenital NEC—*see*
    Malposition, congenital
  septum (acquired) (nasal) 470
    congenital 754.0
  sexual 302.9
    bestiality 302.1
    coprophilia 302.89
    ego-dystonic
      homosexuality 302.0
      lesbianism 302.0
    erotomania 302.89
      Clérambault's 297.8
    exhibitionism (sexual) 302.4
    fetishism 302.81
      transvestic 302.3
    frotteurism 302.89
    homosexuality, ego-dystonic 302.0
      pedophilic 302.2
    lesbianism, ego-dystonic 302.0
    masochism 302.83
    narcissism 302.89
    necrophilia 302.89
    nymphomania 302.89
    pederosis 302.2
    pedophilia 302.2
    sadism 302.84
    sadomasochism 302.84
    satyriasis 302.89
    specified type NEC 302.89
    transvestic fetishism 302.3
    transvestism 302.3
    voyeurism 302.82

Deviation—*continued*
    zoophilia (erotica) 302.1
  teeth, midline 524.2
  trachea 519.1
  ureter (congenital) 753.4
Devic's disease 341.0
Device
  cerebral ventricle (communicating) in situ V45.2
  contraceptive—*see* Contraceptive, device
  drainage, cerebrospinal fluid V45.2
Devil's
  grip 074.1
  pinches (purpura simplex) 287.2
Devitalized tooth 522.9
Devonshire colic 984.9
  specified type of lead—*see* Table of drugs and
    chemicals
Dextraposition, aorta 747.21
  with ventricular septal defect, pulmonary
    stenosis or atresia, and hypertrophy of right
    ventricle 745.2
  in tetralogy of Fallot 745.2
Dextratransposition, aorta 745.11
Dextrinosis, limit (debrancher enzyme
  deficiency) 271.0
Dextrocardia (corrected) (false) (isolated)
  (secondary) (true) 746.87
  with
  complete transposition of viscera 759.3
  situs inversus 759.3
Dextroversion, kidney (left) 753.3
Dhobie itch 110.3
Diabetes, diabetic (brittle) (congenital) (familial)
  (mellitus) (severe) (slight) (without
  complication) 250.0

> *Note—Use the following fifth-digit*
> *subclassification with category 250:*
>
> 0 *type II [non-insulin dependent type]*
>   *[NIDDM type] [adult-onset type] or*
>   *unspecified type, not stated as uncontrolled*
> 1 *type I [insulin dependent type]*
>   *[IDDM] [juvenile type], not stated as uncon-*
>   *trolled*
> 2 *type II [non-insulin dependent type] [NIDDM*
>   *type] [adult-onset type] or unspecified type,*
>   *uncontrolled*
> 3 *type I [insulin dependent type] [IDDM]*
>   *[juvenile type], uncontrolled*

  with
    coma (with ketoacidosis) 250.3
      hyperosmolar (nonketotic) 250.2
    complication NEC 250.9
      specified NEC 250.8
    gangrene 250.7 *[785.4]*
    hyperosmolarity 250.2
    ketosis, ketoacidosis 250.1
    osteomyelitis 250.8 *[731.8]*
    specified manifestations NEC 250.8
  acetonemia 250.1
  acidosis 250.1
  amyotrophy 250.6 *[358.1]*
  angiopathy, peripheral 250.7 *[443.81]*
  asymptomatic 790.2
  autonomic neuropathy (peripheral) 250.6
    [337.1]
  bone change 250.8 *[731.8]*
  bronze, bronzed 275.0
  cataract 250.5 *[366.41]*
  chemical 790.2

Diarrhea, diarrheal—*continued*
  due to
    achylia gastrica 536.8
    Aerobacter aerogenes 008.2
    Bacillus coli—*see* Enteritis, E. coli
    bacteria NEC 008.5
    bile salts 579.8
    Capillaria
      hepatica 128.8
      philippinensis 127.5
    Clostridium perfringens (C) (F) 008.46
    Enterobacter aerogenes 008.2
    enterococci 008.49
    Escherichia coli—*see* Enteritis, E. coli
    Giardia lamblia 007.1
    Heterophyes heterophyes 121.6
    irritating foods 558.9
    Metagonimus yokogawai 121.5
    Necator americanus 126.1
    Paracolobactrum arizonae 008.1
    Paracolon bacillus NEC 008.47
      Arizona 008.1
    Proteus (bacillus) (mirabilis) (Morganii) 008.3
    Pseudomonas aeruginosa 008.42
    S. japonicum 120.2
    specified organism NEC 008.8
      bacterial 008.49
      viral NEC 008.69
    Staphylococcus 008.41
    Streptococcus 008.49
      anaerobic 008.46
    Strongyloides stercoralis 127.2
    Trichuris trichiuria 127.3
    virus NEC (*see also* Enteritis, viral) 008.69
  dysenteric 009.2
    due to specified organism NEC 008.8
  dyspeptic 558.9
  endemic 009.3
  epidemic 009.3
  fermentative 558.9
  flagellate 007.9
  Flexner's (ulcerative) 004.1
  functional 564.5
    following gastrointestinal surgery 564.4
    psychogenic 306.4
  giardial 007.1
  Giardia lamblia 007.1
  hill 579.1
  hyperperistalsis (nervous) 306.4
  infectious 009.2
    presumed 009.3
  inflammatory 558.9
    due to specified organism NEC 008.8
  malarial (*see also* Malaria) 084.6
  mite 133.8
  mycotic 117.9
  nervous 306.4
  neurogenic 564.5
  parenteral NEC 009.2
  postgastrectomy 564.4
  postvagotomy 564.4
  prostaglandin induced 579.8
  protozoal NEC 007.9
  psychogenic 306.4
  septic 009.2
    due to specified organism NEC 008.8
  specified organism NEC 008.8
    bacterial 008.49
    viral NEC 008.69
  Staphylococcus 008.41

Diarrhea, diarrheal—*continued*
  Streptococcus 008.49
    anaerobic 088.46
  toxic 558.2
  travelers' 009.2
    due to specified organism NEC 008.8
  trichomonal 007.3
  tropical 579.1
  tuberculous 014.8
  ulcerative (chronic) (*see also* Colitis, ulcerative)
    556.9
  viral (*see also* Enteritis, viral) 008.8
  zymotic NEC 009.2
Diastasis
  cranial bones 733.99
    congenital 756.0
  joint (traumatic)—*see* Dislocation, by site
  muscle 728.84
    congenital 756.89
  recti (abdomen) 728.84
    complicating delivery 665.8
    congenital 756.79
Diastema, teeth, tooth 524.3
Diastematomyelia 742.51
Diataxia, cerebral, infantile 343.0
Diathesis
  allergic V15.09
  bleeding (familial) 287.9
  cystine (familial) 270.0
  gouty 274.9
  hemorrhagic (familial) 287.9
    newborn NEC 776.0
  oxalic 271.8
  scrofulous (*see also* Tuberculosis) 017.2
  spasmophilic (*see also* Tetany) 781.7
  ulcer 536.9
  uric acid 274.9
Diaz's disease or osteochondrosis 732.5
Dibothriocephaliasis 123.4
  larval 123.5
Dibothriocephalus (infection) (infestation)
    (latus) 123.4
  larval 123.5
Dicephalus 759.4
Dichotomy, teeth 520.2
Dichromat, dichromata (congenital) 368.59
Dichromatopsia (congenital) 368.59
Dichuchwa 104.0
Dicroceliasis 121.8
Didelphys, didelphic (*see also* Double uterus)
    752.2
Didymitis (*see also* Epididymitis) 604.90
Died —*see also* Death
  without
    medical attention (cause unknown) 798.9
    sign of disease 798.2
Dientamoeba diarrhea 007.8
Dietary
  inadequacy or deficiency 269.9
  surveillance and counseling V65.3
Dietl's crisis 593.4
Dieulafoy's ulcer —*see* Ulcer, stomach
Difficult
  birth, affecting fetus or newborn 763.9
  delivery NEC 669.9
Difficulty
  feeding 783.3
    breast 676.8
    newborn 779.3
  nonorganic (infant) NEC 307.59
  mechanical, gastroduodenal stoma 537.89

Difficulty—*continued*
  reading 315.00
  specific, spelling 315.09
  swallowing (*see also* Dysphagia) 787.2
  walking 719.7
Diffuse —*see* condition
Diffused ganglion 727.42
DiGeorge's syndrome (thymic hypoplasia)
  279.11
Digestive —*see* condition
Di Guglielmo's disease or syndrome (M9841/3)
  207.0
Diktyoma (M9051/3)—*see* Neoplasm, by site,
  malignant
Dilaceration, tooth 520.4
Dilatation
  anus 564.89
    venule—*see* Hemorrhoids
  aorta (focal) (general) (*see also* Aneurysm,
    aorta) 441.9
    congenital 747.29
    infectional 093.0
    ruptured 441.5
    syphilitic 093.0
  appendix (cystic) 543.9
  artery 447.8
  bile duct (common) (cystic) (congenital) 751.69
    acquired 576.8
  bladder (sphincter) 596.8
    congenital 753.8
    in pregnancy or childbirth 654.4
      causing obstructed labor 660.2
        affecting fetus or newborn 763.1
  blood vessel 459.89
  bronchus, bronchi 494.0
    with acute exacerbation 494.1
  calyx (due to obstruction) 593.89
  capillaries 448.9
  cardiac (acute) (chronic) (*see also* Hypertrophy,
    cardiac) 429.3
    congenital 746.89
      valve NEC 746.89
        pulmonary 746.09
    hypertensive (*see also* Hypertension, heart)
      402.90
  cavum septi pellucidi 742.4
  cecum 564.89
    psychogenic 306.4
  cervix (uteri)—*see also* Incompetency, cervix
    incomplete, poor, slow
      affecting fetus or newborn 763.7
      complicating delivery 661.0
        affecting fetus or newborn 763.7
  colon 564.7
    congenital 751.3
    due to mechanical obstruction 560.89
    psychogenic 306.4
  common bile duct (congenital) 751.69
    acquired 576.8
      with calculus, choledocholithiasis, or
        stones—*see* Choledocholithiasis
  cystic duct 751.69
    acquired (any bile duct) 575.8
  duct, mammary 610.4
  duodenum 564.89
  esophagus 530.89
    congenital 750.4
    due to
      achalasia 530.0
      cardiospasm 530.0
  Eustachian tube, congenital 744.24

Dilatation—*continued*
  fontanel 756.0
  gallbladder 575.8
    congenital 751.69
  gastric 536.8
    acute 536.1
    psychogenic 306.4
  heart (acute) (chronic) (*see also* Hypertrophy,
    cardiac) 429.3
    congenital 746.89
    hypertensive (*see also* Hypertension, heart)
      402.90
    valve—*see also* Endocarditis
      congenital 746.89
  ileum 564.89
    psychogenic 306.4
  inguinal rings—*see* Hernia, inguinal
  jejunum 564.89
    psychogenic 306.4
  kidney (calyx) (collecting structures) (cystic)
    (parenchyma) (pelvis) 593.89
  lacrimal passages 375.69
  lymphatic vessel 457.1
  mammary duct 610.4
  Meckel's diverticulum (congenital) 751.0
  meningeal vessels, congenital 742.8
  myocardium (acute) (chronic) (*see also*
    Hypertrophy, cardiac) 429.3
  organ or site, congenital NEC—*see* Distortion
  pancreatic duct 577.8
  pelvis, kidney 593.89
  pericardium—*see* Pericarditis
  pharynx 478.29
  prostate 602.8
  pulmonary
    artery (idiopathic) 417.8
      congenital 747.3
    valve, congenital 746.09
  pupil 379.43
  rectum 564.89
  renal 593.89
  saccule vestibularis, congenital 744.05
  salivary gland (duct) 527.8
  sphincter ani 564.89
  stomach 536.8
    acute 536.1
    psychogenic 306.4
  submaxillary duct 527.8
  trachea, congenital 748.3
  ureter (idiopathic) 593.89
    congenital 753.20
    due to obstruction 593.5
  urethra (acquired) 599.84
  vasomotor 443.9
  vein 459.89
  ventricular, ventricle (acute) (chronic) (*see also*
    Hypertrophy, cardiac) 429.3
    cerebral, congenital 742.4
    hypertensive (*see also* Hypertension, heart)
      402.90
  venule 459.89
    anus—*see* Hemorrhoids
  vesical orifice 596.8
Dilated, dilation —*see* Dilatation
Diminished
  hearing (acuity) (*see also* Deafness) 389.9
  pulse pressure 785.9
  vision NEC 369.9
  vital capacity 794.2
Diminuta taenia 123.6

Diminution, sense or sensation (cold) (heat)
(tactile) (vibratory) (*see also* Disturbance,
sensation) 782.0
Dimitri-Sturge-Weber disease
(encephalocutaneous angiomatosis) 759.6
Dimple
parasacral 685.1
with abscess 685.0
pilonidal 685.1
with abscess 685.0
postanal 685.1
with abscess 685.0
Dioctophyma renale (infection) (infestation)
128.8
Dipetalonemiasis 125.4
Diphallus 752.69
Diphtheria, diphtheritic (gangrenous)
(hemorrhagic) 032.9
carrier (suspected) of V02.4
cutaneous 032.85
cystitis 032.84
faucial 032.0
infection of wound 032.85
inoculation (anti) (not sick) V03.5
laryngeal 032.3
myocarditis 032.82
nasal anterior 032.2
nasopharyngeal 032.1
neurological complication 032.89
peritonitis 032.83
specified site NEC 032.89
Diphyllobothriasis (intestine) 123.4
larval 123.5
Diplacusis 388.41
Diplegia (upper limbs) 344.2
brain or cerebral 437.8
congenital 343.0
facial 351.0
congenital 352.6
infantile or congenital (cerebral) (spastic)
(spinal) 343.0
lower limbs 344.1
syphilitic, congenital 090.49
Diplococcus, diplococcal —*see* condition
Diplomyelia 742.59
Diplopia 368.2
refractive 368.15
Dipsomania (*see also* Alcoholism) 303.9
with psychosis (*see also* Psychosis, alcoholic)
291.9
Dipylidiasis 123.8
intestine 123.8
Direction, teeth, abnormal 524.3
Dirt-eating child 307.52
Disability
heart—*see* Disease, heart
learning NEC 315.2
special spelling 315.09
Disarticulation (*see also* Derangement, joint)
718.9
meaning
amputation
status—*see* Absence, by site
traumatic —*see* Amputation, traumatic
dislocation, traumatic or congenital—*see*
Dislocation
Disaster, cerebrovascular (*see also* Disease,
cerebrovascular, acute) 436

Discharge
anal NEC 787.99
breast (female) (male) 611.79
conjunctiva 372.89
continued locomotor idiopathic (*see also*
Epilepsy) 345.5
diencephalic autonomic idiopathic (*see also*
Epilepsy) 345.5
ear 388.60
blood 388.69
cerebrospinal fluid 388.61
excessive urine 788.42
eye 379.93
nasal 478.1
nipple 611.79
patterned motor idiopathic (*see also* Epilepsy)
345.5
penile 788.7
postnasal—*see* Sinusitis
sinus, from mediastinum 510.0
umbilicus 789.9
urethral 788.7
bloody 599.84
vaginal 623.5
Discitis 722.90
cervical, cervicothoracic 722.91
lumbar, lumbosacral 722.93
thoracic, thoracolumbar 722.92
Discogenic syndrome —*see* Displacement,
intervertebral disc
Discoid
kidney 753.3
meniscus, congenital 717.5
semilunar cartilage 717.5
Discoloration
mouth 528.9
nails 703.8
teeth 521.7
due to
drugs 521.7
metals (copper) (silver) 521.7
pulpal bleeding 521.7
during formation 520.8
posteruptive 521.7
Discomfort
chest 786.59
visual 368.13
Discomycosis —*see* Actinomycosis
Discontinuity, ossicles, ossicular chain 385.23
Discrepancy
leg length (acquired) 736.81
congenital 755.30
uterine size-date 646.8
Discrimination
political V62.4
racial V62.4
religious V62.4
sex V62.4
Disease, diseased —*see also* Syndrome
Abrami's (acquired hemolytic jaundice) 283.9
absorbent system 459.89
accumulation—*see* Thesaurismosis
acid-peptic 536.8
Acosta's 993.2
Adams-Stokes (-Morgagni) (syncope with heart
block) 426.9
Addison's (bronze) (primary adrenal
insufficiency) 255.4
anemia (pernicious) 281.0
tuberculous (*see also* Tuberculosis) 017.6
Addison-Gull—*see* Xanthoma

Disease, diseased—*continued*
  adenoids (and tonsils) (chronic) 474.9
  adrenal (gland) (capsule) (cortex) 255.9
    hyperfunction 255.3
    hypofunction 255.4
    specified type NEC 255.8
  ainhum (dactylolysis spontanea) 136.0
  akamushi (scrub typhus) 081.2
  Akureyri (epidemic neuromyasthenia) 049.8
  Albarrán's (colibacilluria) 791.9
  Albers-Schönberg's (marble bones) 756.52
  Albert's 726.71
  Albright (-Martin) (-Bantam) 275.49
  Alibert's (mycosis fungoides) (M9700/3) 202.1
  Alibert-Bazin (M9700/3) 202.1
  alimentary canal 569.9
  alligator skin (ichthyosis congenital) 757.1
    acquired 701.1
  Almeida's (Brazilian blastomycosis) 116.1
  Alpers' 330.8
  alpine 993.2
  altitude 993.2
  alveoli, teeth 525.9
  Alzheimer's—*see* Alzheimer's
  amyloid (any site) 277.3
  anarthritic rheumatoid 446.5
  Anders' (adiposis tuberosa simplex) 272.8
  Andersen's (glycogenosis IV) 271.0
  Anderson's (angiokeratoma corporis diffusum) 272.7
  Andes 993.2
  Andrews' (bacterid) 686.8
  angiospastic, angiospasmodic 443.9
    cerebral 435.9
      with transient neurologic deficit 435.9
    vein 459.89
  anterior
    chamber 364.9
    horn cell 335.9
      specified type NEC 335.8
  antral (chronic) 473.0
    acute 461.0
  anus NEC 569.49
  aorta (nonsyphilitic) 447.9
    syphilitic NEC 093.89
  aortic (heart) (valve) (*see also* Endocarditis, aortic) 424.1
  apollo 077.4
  aponeurosis 726.90
  appendix 543.9
  aqueous (chamber) 364.9
  arc-welders' lung 503
  Armenian 277.3
  Arnold-Chiari (*see also* Spina bifida) 741.0
  arterial 447.9
    occlusive (*see also* Occlusion, by site) 444.22
      with embolus or thrombus—*see* Occlusion, by site
      due to stricture or stenosis 447.1
    specified type NEC 447.8
  arteriocardiorenal (*see also* Hypertension, cardiorenal) 404.90
  arteriolar (generalized) (obliterative) 447.9
    specified type NEC 447.8
  arteriorenal—*see* Hypertension, kidney
  arteriosclerotic—*see also* Arteriosclerosis
    cardiovascular 429.2
    coronary —*see* Arteriosclerosis, coronary
    heart —*see* Arteriosclerosis, coronary
    vascular—*see* Arteriosclerosis

Disease, diseased—*continued*
  artery 447.9
    cerebral 437.9
    coronary —*see* Arteriosclerosis, coronary
    specified type NEC 447.8
  arthropod-borne NEC 088.9
    specified type NEC 088.89
  Asboe-Hansen's (incontinentia pigmenti) 757.33
  atticoantral, chronic (with posterior or superior marginal perforation of ear drum) 382.2
  auditory canal, ear 380.9
  Aujeszky's 078.89
  auricle, ear NEC 380.30
  Australian X 062.4
  autoimmune NEC 279.4
    hemolytic (cold type) (warm type) 283.0
    parathyroid 252.1
    thyroid 245.2
  aviators' (*see also* Effect, adverse, high altitude) 993.2
  ax(e)-grinders' 502
  Ayala's 756.89
  Ayerza's (pulmonary artery sclerosis with pulmonary hypertension) 416.0
  Azorean (of the nervous system) 334.8
  Babington's (familial hemorrhagic telangiectasia) 448.0
  back bone NEC 733.90
  bacterial NEC 040.89
    zoonotic NEC 027.9
      specified type NEC 027.8
  Baehr-Schiffrin (thrombotic thrombocytopenic purpura) 446.6
  Baelz's (cheilitis glandularis apostematosa) 528.5
  Baerensprung's (eczema marginatum) 110.3
  Balfour's (chloroma) 205.3
  balloon (*see also* Effect, adverse, high altitude) 993.2
  Baló's 341.1
  Bamberger (-Marie) (hypertrophic pulmonary osteoarthropathy) 731.2
  Bang's (Brucella abortus) 023.1
  Bannister's 995.1
  Banti's (with cirrhosis) (with portal hypertension)—*see* Cirrhosis, liver
  Barcoo (*see also* Ulcer, skin) 707.9
  barium lung 503
  Barlow (-Möller) (infantile scurvy) 267
  barometer makers' 985.0
  Barraquer (-Simons) (progressive lipodystrophy) 272.6
  basal ganglia 333.90
    degenerative NEC 333.0
    specified NEC 333.89
  Basedow's (exophthalmic goiter) 242.0
  basement membrane NEC 583.89
    with
      pulmonary hemorrhage (Goodpasture's syndrome) 446.21 *[583.81]*
  Bateman's 078.0
    purpura (senile) 287.2
  Batten's 330.1 *[362.71]*
  Batten-Mayou (retina) 330.1 *[362.71]*
  Batten-Steinert 359.2
  Battey 031.0
  Baumgarten-Cruveilhier (cirrhosis of liver) 571.5
  bauxite-workers' 503
  Bayle's (dementia paralytica) 094.1
  Bazin's (primary) (*see also* Tuberculosis) 017.1

Disease, diseased—*continued*
  Beard's (neurasthenia) 300.5
  Beau's (*see also* Degeneration, myocardial)
    429.1
  Bechterew's (ankylosing spondylitis) 720.0
  Becker's (idiopathic mural endomyocardial
    disease) 425.2
  Begbie's (exophthalmic goiter) 242.0
  Behr's 362.50
  Beigel's (white piedra) 111.2
  Bekhterev's (ankylosing spondylitis) 720.0
  Bell's (*see also* Psychosis, affective) 296.0
  Bennett's (leukemia) 208.9
  Benson's 379.22
  Bergeron's (hysteroepilepsy) 300.11
  Berlin's 921.3
  Bernard-Soulier (thrombopathy) 287.1
  Bernhardt (-Roth) 355.1
  beryllium 503
  Besnier-Boeck (-Schaumann) (sarcoidosis) 135
  Best's 362.76
  Beurmann's (sporotrichosis) 117.1
  Bielschowsky (-Jansky) 330.1
  Biermer's (pernicious anemia) 281.0
  Biett's (discoid lupus erythematosus) 695.4
  bile duct (*see also* Disease, biliary) 576.9
  biliary (duct) (tract) 576.9
    with calculus, choledocholithiasis, or
      stones—*see* Choledocholithiasis
  Billroth's (meningocele) (*see also* Spina bifida)
    741.9
  Binswanger's 290.12
  Bird's (oxaluria) 271.8
  bird fanciers' 495.2
  black lung 500
  bladder 596.9
    specified NEC 596.8
  bleeder's 286.0
  Bloch-Sulzberger (incontinentia pigmenti)
    757.33
  Blocq's (astasia-abasia) 307.9
  blood (-forming organs) 289.9
    specified NEC 289.8
    vessel 459.9
  Bloodgood's 610.1
  Blount's (tibia vara) 732.4
  blue 746.9
  Bodechtel-Guttmann (subacute sclerosing
    panencephalitis) 046.2
  Boeck's (sarcoidosis) 135
  bone 733.90
    fibrocystic NEC 733.29
      jaw 526.2
    marrow 289.9
    Paget's (osteitis deformans) 731.0
    specified type NEC 733.99
    von Recklinghausen's (osteitis fibrosa cystica)
      252.0
  Bonfils'—*see* Disease, Hodgkin's
  Borna 062.9
  Bornholm (epidemic pleurodynia) 074.1
  Bostock's (*see also* Fever, hay) 477.9
  Bouchard's (myopathic dilatation of the
    stomach) 536.1
  Bouillaud's (rheumatic heart disease) 391.9
  Bourneville (-Brissaud) (tuberous sclerosis)
    759.5
  Bouveret (-Hoffmann) (paroxysmal
    tachycardia) 427.2

Disease, diseased—*continued*
  bowel 569.9
    functional 564.9
      psychogenic 306.4
  Bowen's (M8081/2)—*see* Neoplasm, skin, in
    situ
  Bozzolo's (multiple myeloma) (M9730/3) 203.0
  Bradley's (epidemic vomiting) 078.82
  Brailsford's 732.3
    radius, head 732.3
    tarsal, scaphoid 732.5
  Brailsford-Morquio (mucopolysaccharidosis
    IV) 277.5
  brain 348.9
    Alzheimer's 331.0
      with dementia—*see* Alzheimer's, dementia
    arterial, artery 437.9
    arteriosclerotic 437.0
    congenital 742.9
    degenerative—*see* Degeneration, brain
    inflammatory—*see also* Encephalitis
      late effect—*see* category 326
    organic 348.9
      arteriosclerotic 437.0
    parasitic NEC 123.9
    Pick's 331.1
      with dementia
        with behavioral disturbance 331.1 *[294.11]*
        without behavioral disturbance 331.1
          [294.10]
    senile 331.2
  braziers' 985.8
  breast 611.9
    cystic (chronic) 610.1
    fibrocystic 610.1
    inflammatory 611.0
    Paget's (M8540/3) 174.0
    puerperal, postpartum NEC 676.3
    specified NEC 611.8
  Breda's (*see also* Yaws) 102.9
  Breisky's (kraurosis vulvae) 624.0
  Bretonneau's (diphtheritic malignant angina)
    032.0
  Bright's (*see also* Nephritis) 583.9
    arteriosclerotic (*see also* Hypertension,
      kidney) 403.90
  Brill's (recrudescent typhus) 081.1
    flea-borne 081.0
    louse-borne 081.1
  Brill-Symmers (follicular lymphoma)
    (M9690/3) 202.0
  Brill-Zinsser (recrudescent typhus) 081.1
  Brinton's (leather bottle stomach) (M8142/3)
    151.9
  Brion-Kayser (*see also* Fever, paratyphoid)
    002.9
  broad
    beta 272.2
    ligament, noninflammatory 620.9
      specified NEC 620.8
  Brocq's 691.8
    meaning
      atopic (diffuse) neurodermatitis 691.8
      dermatitis herpetiformis 694.0
      lichen simplex chronicus 698.3
      parapsoriasis 696.2
      prurigo 698.2
  Brocq-Duhring (dermatitis herpetiformis) 694.0
  Brodie's (joint) (*see also* Osteomyelitis) 730.1
  bronchi 519.1
  bronchopulmonary 519.1

Disease, diseased—*continued*
  bronze (Addison's) 255.4
    tuberculous (*see also* Tuberculosis) 017.6
  Brown-Séquard 344.89
  Bruck's 733.99
  Bruck-de Lange (Amsterdam dwarf, mental
    retardation, and brachycephaly) 759.89
  Bruhl's (splenic anemia with fever) 285.8
  Bruton's (X-linked agammaglobulinemia)
    279.04
  buccal cavity 528.9
  Buchanan's (juvenile osteochondrosis, iliac
    crest) 732.1
  Buchman's (osteochondrosis juvenile) 732.1
  Budgerigar-fanciers' 495.2
  Büdinger-Ludloff-Läwen 717.89
  Buerger's (thromboangiitis obliterans) 443.1
  Bürger-Grütz (essential familial hyperlipemia)
    272.3
  Burns' (lower ulna) 732.3
  bursa 727.9
  Bury's (erythema elevatum diutinum) 695.89
  Buschke's 710.1
  Busquet's (*see also* Osteomyelitis) 730.1
  Busse-Buschke (cryptococcosis) 117.5
  C$_2$ (*see also* Alcoholism) 303.9
  Caffey's (infantile cortical hyperostosis) 756.59
  caisson 993.3
  calculous 592.9
  California 114.0
  Calvé (-Perthes) (osteochondrosis, femoral
    capital) 732.1
  Camurati-Engelmann (diaphyseal sclerosis)
    756.59
  Canavan's 330.0
  capillaries 448.9
  Carapata 087.1
  cardiac-*see* Disease, heart
  cardiopulmonary, chronic 416.9
  cardiorenal (arteriosclerotic) (hepatic)
    (hypertensive) (vascular) (*see also*
    Hypertension, cardiorenal) 404.90
  cardiovascular (arteriosclerotic) 429.2
    congenital 746.9
    hypertensive (*see also* Hypertension, heart)
      402.90
      benign 402.10
      malignant 402.00
    renal (*see also* Hypertension, cardiorenal)
      404.90
    syphilitic (asymptomatic) 093.9
  carotid gland 259.8
  Carrión's (Bartonellosis) 088.0
  cartilage NEC 733.90
    specified NEC 733.99
  Castellani's 104.8
  cat-scratch 078.3
  Cavare's (familial periodic paralysis) 359.3
  Cazenave's (pemphigus) 694.4
  cecum 569.9
  celiac (adult) 579.0
    infantile 579.0
  cellular tissue NEC 709.9
  central core 359.0
  cerebellar, cerebellum—*see* Disease, brain
  cerebral (*see also* Disease, brain) 348.9
    arterial, artery 437.9
    degenerative—*see* Degeneration, brain
  cerebrospinal 349.9
  cerebrovascular NEC 437.9
    acute 436

Disease, diseased—*continued*
    embolic—*see* Embolism, brain
    late effect—*see* Late effect(s) (of)
      cerebrovascular disease
    puerperal, postpartum, childbirth 674.0
    thrombotic—*see* Thrombosis, brain
    arteriosclerotic 437.0
    embolic—*see* Embolism, brain
    ischemic, generalized NEC 437.1
    late effect—*see* Late effect(s) (of)
      cerebrovascular disease
    occlusive 437.1
    puerperal, postpartum, childbirth 674.0
    specified type NEC 437.8
    thrombotic—*see* Thrombosis, brain
  ceroid storage 272.7
  cervix (uteri)
    inflammatory 616.9
      specified NEC 616.8
    noninflammatory 622.9
      specified NEC 622.8
  Chabert's 022.9
  Chagas' (*see also* Trypanosomiasis, American)
    086.2
  Chandler's (osteochondritis dissecans, hip)
    732.7
  Charcot's (joint) 094.0 *[713.5]*
    spinal cord 094.0
  Charcot-Marie-Tooth 356.1
  Charlouis' (*see also* Yaws) 102.9
  Cheadle (-Möller) (-Barlow) (infantile scurvy)
    267
  Chédiak-Steinbrinck (-Higashi) (congenital
    gigantism of peroxidase granules) 288.2
  cheek, inner 528.9
  chest 519.9
  Chiari's (hepatic vein thrombosis) 453.0
  Chicago (North American blastomycosis) 116.0
  chignon (white piedra) 111.2
  chigoe, chigo (jigger) 134.1
  childhood granulomatous 288.1
  Chinese liver fluke 121.1
  chlamydial NEC 078.88
  cholecystic (*see also* Disease, gallbladder) 575.9
  choroid 363.9
    degenerative (*see also* Degeneration, choroid)
      363.40
    hereditary (*see also* Dystrophy, choroid)
      363.50
    specified type NEC 363.8
  Christian's (chronic histiocytosis X) 277.8
  Christian-Weber (nodular nonsuppurative
    panniculitis) 729.30
  Christmas 286.1
  ciliary body 364.9
  circulatory (system) NEC 459.9
    chronic, maternal, affecting fetus or newborn
      760.3
    specified NEC 459.89
    syphilitic 093.9
      congenital 090.5
  Civatte's (poikiloderma) 709.09
  climacteric 627.2
    male 608.89
  coagulation factor deficiency (congenital) (*see
    also* Defect, coagulation) 286.9
  Coats' 362.12
  coccidioidal pulmonary 114.5
    acute 114.0
    chronic 114.4
    primary 114.0

Disease, diseased—*continued*
  residual 114.4
  Cockayne's (microcephaly and dwarfism)
    759.89
  Cogan's 370.52
  cold
    agglutinin 283.0
      or hemoglobinuria 283.0
        paroxysmal (cold) (nocturnal) 283.2
    hemagglutinin (chronic) 283.0
  collagen NEC 710.9
    nonvascular 710.9
    specified NEC 710.8
    vascular (allergic) (*see also* Angiitis,
      hypersensitivity) 446.20
  colon 569.9
    functional 564.9
      congenital 751.3
    ischemic 557.0
  combined system (of spinal cord) 266.2 *[336.2]*
    with anemia (pernicious) 281.0 *[336.2]*
  compressed air 993.3
  Concato's (pericardial polyserositis) 423.2
    peritoneal 568.82
    pleural—*see* Pleurisy
  congenital NEC 799.8
  conjunctiva 372.9
    chlamydial 077.98
      specified NEC 077.8
    specified type NEC 372.89
    viral 077.99
      specified NEC 077.8
  connective tissue, diffuse (*see also* Disease,
    collagen) 710.9
  Conor and Bruch's (boutonneuse fever) 082.1
  Conradi (-Hünermann) 756.59
  Cooley's (erythroblastic anemia) 282.4
  Cooper's 610.1
  Corbus' 607.1
  cork-handlers' 495.3
  cornea (*see also* Keratopathy) 371.9
  coronary (*see also* Ischemia, heart) 414.9
    congenital 746.85
    ostial, syphilitic 093.20
      aortic 093.22
      mitral 093.21
      pulmonary 093.24
      tricuspid 093.23
  Corrigan's—*see* Insufficiency, aortic
  Cotugno's 724.3
  Coxsackie (virus) NEC 074.8
  cranial nerve NEC 352.9
  Creutzfeldt-Jakob 046.1
    with dementia
      with behavioral disturbance 046.1 *[294.11]*
      without behavioral disturbance 046.1
        [294.10]
  Crigler-Najjar (congenital hyperbilirubinemia)
    277.4
  Crocq's (acrocyanosis) 443.89
  Crohn's (intestine) (*see also* Enteritis, regional)
    555.9
  Crouzon's (craniofacial dysostosis) 756.0
  Cruchet's (encephalitis lethargica) 049.8
  Cruveilhier's 335.21
  Cruz-Chagas (*see also* Trypanosomiasis,
    American) 086.2
  crystal deposition (*see also* Arthritis, due to,
    crystals) 712.9
  Csillag's (lichen sclerosus et atrophicus) 701.0
  Curschmann's 359.2

Disease, diseased—*continued*
  Cushing's (pituitary basophilism) 255.0
  cystic
    breast (chronic) 610.1
    kidney, congenital (*see also* Cystic, disease,
      kidney) 753.10
    liver, congenital 751.62
    lung 518.89
      congenital 748.4
    pancreas 577.2
      congenital 751.7
    renal, congenital (*see also* Cystic, disease,
      kidney) 753.10
    semilunar cartilage 717.5
  cysticercus 123.1
  cystine storage (with renal sclerosis) 270.0
  cytomegalic inclusion (generalized) 078.5
    with
      pneumonia 078.5 *[484.1]*
    congenital 771.1
  Daae (-Finsen) (epidemic pleurodynia) 074.1
  dancing 297.8
  Danielssen's (anesthetic leprosy) 030.1
  Darier's (congenital) (keratosis follicularis)
    757.39
    erythema annulare centrifugum 695.0
    vitamin A deficiency 264.8
  Darling's (histoplasmosis) (*see also*
    Histoplasmosis, American) 115.00
  Davies' 425.0
  de Beurmann-Gougerot (sporotrichosis) 117.1
  Débove's (splenomegaly) 789.2
  deer fly (*see also* Tularemia) 021.9
  deficiency 269.9
  degenerative—*see also* Degeneration
    disc—*see* Degeneration, intervertebral disc
  Degos' 447.8
  Déjérine (-Sottas) 356.0
  Deleage's 359.8
  demyelinating, demyelinizing (brain stem)
    (central nervous system) 341.9
    multiple sclerosis 340
    specified NEC 341.8
  de Quervain's (tendon sheath) 727.04
    thyroid (subacute granulomatous thyroiditis)
      245.1
  Dercum's (adiposis dolorosa) 272.8
  Deutschländer's—*see* Fracture, foot
  Devergie's (pityriasis rubra pilaris) 696.4
  Devic's 341.0
  diaphorase deficiency 289.7
  diaphragm 519.4
  diarrheal, infectious 009.2
  diatomaceous earth 502
  Diaz's (osteochondrosis astragalus) 732.5
  digestive system 569.9
  Di Guglielmo's (erythemic myelosis)
    (M9841/3) 207.0
  Dimitri-Sturge-Weber (encephalocutaneous
    angiomatosis) 759.6
  disc, degenerative—*see* Degeneration,
    intervertebral disc
  discogenic (*see also* Disease, intervertebral
    disc) 722.90
  diverticular—*see* Diverticula
  Down's (mongolism) 758.0
  Dubini's (electric chorea) 049.8
  Dubois' (thymus gland) 090.5
  Duchenne's 094.0
    locomotor ataxia 094.0
    muscular dystrophy 359.1

Disease, diseased—*continued*
  paralysis 335.22
  pseudohypertrophy, muscles 359.1
  Duchenne-Griesinger 359.1
  ductless glands 259.9
  Duhring's (dermatitis herpetiformis) 694.0
  Dukes (-Filatov) 057.8
  duodenum NEC 537.9
    specified NEC 537.89
  Duplay's 726.2
  Dupré's (meningism) 781.6
  Dupuytren's (muscle contracture) 728.6
  Durand-Nicolas-Favre (climatic bubo) 099.1
  Duroziez's (congenital mitral stenosis) 746.5
  Dutton's (trypanosomiasis) 086.9
  Eales' 362.18
  ear (chronic) (inner) NEC 388.9
    middle 385.9
      adhesive (*see also* Adhesions, middle ear)
        385.10
      specified NEC 385.89
  Eberth's (typhoid fever) 002.0
  Ebstein's
    heart 746.2
    meaning diabetes 250.4 *[581.81]*
  Echinococcus (*see also* Echinococcus) 122.9
  ECHO virus NEC 078.89
  Economo's (encephalitis lethargica) 049.8
  Eddowes' (brittle bones and blue sclera) 756.51
  Edsall's 992.2
  Eichstedt's (pityriasis versicolor) 111.0
  Ellis-van Creveld (chondroectodermal
    dysplasia) 756.55
  endocardium—*see* Endocarditis
  endocrine glands or system NEC 259.9
    specified NEC 259.8
  endomyocardial, idiopathic mural 425.2
  Engel-von Recklinghausen (osteitis fibrosa
    cystica) 252.0
  Engelmann's (diaphyseal sclerosis) 756.59
  English (rickets) 268.0
  Engman's (infectious eczematoid dermatitis)
    690.8
  enteroviral, enterovirus NEC 078.89
    central nervous system NEC 048
  epidemic NEC 136.9
  epididymis 608.9
  epigastric, functional 536.9
    psychogenic 306.4
  Erb (-Landouzy) 359.1
  Erb-Goldflam 358.0
  Erichsen's (railway spine) 300.16
  esophagus 530.9
    functional 530.5
    psychogenic 306.4
  Eulenburg's (congenital paramyotonia) 359.2
  Eustachian tube 381.9
  Evans' (thrombocytopenic purpura) 287.3
  external auditory canal 380.9
  extrapyramidal NEC 333.90
  eye 379.90
    anterior chamber 364.9
    inflammatory NEC 364.3
    muscle 378.9
  eyeball 360.9
  eyelid 374.9
  eyeworm of Africa 125.2
  Fabry's (angiokeratoma corporis diffusum)
    272.7
  facial nerve (seventh) 351.9
    newborn 767.5

Disease, diseased—*continued*
  Fahr-Volhard (malignant nephrosclerosis)
    403.00
  fallopian tube, noninflammatory 620.9
    specified NEC 620.8
  familial periodic 277.3
    paralysis 359.3
  Fanconi's (congenital pancytopenia) 284.0
  Farber's (disseminated lipogranulomatosis)
    272.8
  fascia 728.9
    inflammatory 728.9
  Fauchard's (periodontitis) 523.4
  Favre-Durand-Nicolas (climatic bubo) 099.1
  Favre-Racouchot (elastoidosis cutanea
    nodularis) 701.8
  Fede's 529.0
  Feer's 985.0
  Felix's (juvenile osteochondrosis, hip) 732.1
  Fenwick's (gastric atrophy) 537.89
  Fernels' (aortic aneurysm) 441.9
  fibrocaseous, of lung (*see also* Tuberculosis,
    pulmonary) 011.9
  fibrocystic—*see also* Fibrocystic, disease
    newborn 277.01
  Fiedler's (leptospiral jaundice) 100.0
  fifth 057.0
  Filatoff's (infectious mononucleosis) 075
  Filatov's (infectious mononucleosis) 075
  file-cutters' 984.9
    specified type of lead—*see* Table of drugs and
      chemicals
  filterable virus NEC 078.89
  fish skin 757.1
    acquired 701.1
  Flajani (-Basedow) (exophthalmic goiter) 242.0
  Flatau-Schilder 341.1
  flax-dressers' 504
  Fleischner's 732.3
  flint 502
  fluke—*see* Infestation, fluke
  Følling's (phenylketonuria) 270.1
  foot and mouth 078.4
  foot process 581.3
  Forbes' (glycogenosis III) 271.0
  Fordyce's (ectopic sebaceous glands) (mouth)
    750.26
  Fordyce-Fox (apocrine miliaria) 705.82
  Fothergill's
    meaning scarlatina anginosa 034.1
    neuralgia (*see also* Neuralgia, trigeminal)
      350.1
  Fournier's 608.83
  fourth 057.8
  Fox (-Fordyce) (apocrine miliaria) 705.82
  Francis' (*see also* Tularemia) 021.9
  Franklin's (heavy chain) 273.2
  Frei's (climatic bubo) 099.1
  Freiberg's (flattening metatarsal) 732.5
  Friedländer's (endarteritis obliterans)—*see*
    Arteriosclerosis
  Friedreich's
    combined systemic or ataxia 334.0
    facial hemihypertrophy 756.0
    myoclonia 333.2
  Fröhlich's (adiposogenital dystrophy) 253.8
  Frommel's 676.6
  frontal sinus (chronic) 473.1
    acute 461.1
  Fuller's earth 502
  fungus, fungous NEC 117.9

Disease, diseased—*continued*
  Gaisböck's (polycythemia hypertonica) 289.0
  gallbladder 575.9
    congenital 751.60
  Gamna's (siderotic splenomegaly) 289.51
  Gamstorp's (adynamia episodica hereditaria)
    359.3
  Gandy-Nanta (siderotic splenomegaly) 289.51
  gannister (occupational) 502
  Garré's (*see also* Osteomyelitis) 730.1
  gastric (*see also* Disease, stomach) 537.9
  gastrointestinal (tract) 569.9
    amyloid 277.3
    functional 536.9
      psychogenic 306.4
  Gaucher's (adult) (cerebroside lipidosis)
    (infantile) 272.7
  Gayet's (superior hemorrhagic
    polioencephalitis) 265.1
  Gee (-Herter) (-Heubner) (-Thaysen)
    (nontropical sprue) 579.0
  generalized neoplastic (M8000/6) 199.0
  genital organs NEC
    female 629.9
      specified NEC 629.8
    male 608.9
  Gerhardt's (erythromelalgia) 443.89
  Gerlier's (epidemic vertigo) 078.81
  Gibert's (pityriasis rosea) 696.3
  Gibney's (perispondylitis) 720.9
  Gierke's (glycogenosis I) 271.0
  Gilbert's (familial nonhemolytic jaundice) 277.4
  Gilchrist's (North American blastomycosis)
    116.0
  Gilford (-Hutchinson) (progeria) 259.8
  Gilles de la Tourette's (motor-verbal tic) 307.23
  Giovannini's 117.9
  gland (lymph) 289.9
  Glanzmann's (hereditary hemorrhagic
    thrombasthenia) 287.1
  glassblowers' 527.1
  Glénard's (enteroptosis) 569.89
  Glisson's (*see also* Rickets) 268.0
  glomerular
    membranous, idiopathic 581.1
    minimal change 581.3
  glycogen storage (Andersen's) (Cori types 1-7)
    (Forbes') (McArdle-Schmid-Pearson)
    (Pompe's) (types I-VII) 271.0
    cardiac 271.0 *[425.7]*
    generalized 271.0
    glucose-6-phosphatase deficiency 271.0
    heart 271.0 *[425.7]*
    hepatorenal 271.0
    liver and kidneys 271.0
    myocardium 271.0 *[425.7]*
    von Gierke's (glycogenosis I) 271.0
  Goldflam-Erb 358.0
  Goldscheider's (epidermolysis bullosa) 757.39
  Goldstein's (familial hemorrhagic
    telangiectasia) 448.0
  gonococcal NEC 098.0
  Goodall's (epidemic vomiting) 078.82
  Gordon's (exudative enteropathy) 579.8
  Gougerot's (trisymptomatic) 709.1
  Gougerot-Carteaud (confluent reticulate
    papillomatosis) 701.8
  Gougerot-Hailey-Hailey (benign familial
    chronic pemphigus) 757.39

Disease, diseased—*continued*
  graft-versus-host (bone marrow) 996.85
    due to organ transplant NEC—*see*
      Complications, transplant, organ
  grain-handlers' 495.8
  Grancher's (splenopneumonia)—*see* Pneumonia
  granulomatous (childhood) (chronic) 288.1
  graphite lung 503
  Graves' (exophthalmic goiter) 242.0
  Greenfield's 330.0
  green monkey 078.89
  Griesinger's (*see also* Ancylostomiasis) 126.9
  grinders' 502
  Grisel's 723.5
  Gruby's (tinea tonsurans) 110.0
  Guertin's (electric chorea) 049.8
  Guillain-Barré 357.0
  Guinon's (motor-verbal tic) 307.23
  Gull's (thyroid atrophy with myxedema) 244.8
  Gull and Sutton's—*see* Hypertension, kidney
  gum NEC 523.9
  Günther's (congenital erythropoietic porphyria)
    277.1
  gynecological 629.9
    specified NEC 629.8
  H 270.0
  Haas' 732.3
  Habermann's (acute parapsoriasis varioliformis)
    696.2
  Haff 985.1
  Hageman (congenital factor XII deficiency) (*see
    also* Defect, congenital) 286.3
  Haglund's (osteochondrosis os tibiale
    externum) 732.5
  Hagner's (hypertrophic pulmonary
    osteoarthropathy) 731.2
  Hailey-Hailey (benign familial chronic
    pemphigus) 757.39
  hair (follicles) NEC 704.9
    specified type NEC 704.8
  Hallervorden-Spatz 333.0
  Hallopeau's (lichen sclerosus et atrophicus)
    701.0
  Hamman's (spontaneous mediastinal
    emphysema) 518.1
  hand, foot, and mouth 074.3
  Hand-Schüller-Christian (chronic histiocytosis
    X) 277.8
  Hanot's—*see* Cirrhosis, biliary
  Hansen's (leprosy) 030.9
    benign form 030.1
    malignant form 030.0
  Harada's 363.22
  Harley's (intermittent hemoglobinuria) 283.2
  Hart's (pellagra-cerebellar ataxia renal
    aminoaciduria) 270.0
  Hartnup (pellagra-cerebellar ataxia-renal
    aminoaciduria) 270.0
  Hashimoto's (struma lymphomatosa) 245.2
  Hb—*see* Disease, hemoglobin
  heart (organic) 429.9
    with
      acute pulmonary edema (*see also* Failure,
        ventricular, left) 428.1
      hypertensive 402.91
        with renal failure 404.92
        benign 402.11
          with renal failure 404.12
        malignant 402.01
          with renal failure 404.02

Disease, diseased—*continued*
  kidney disease—*see* Hypertension,
    cardiorenal
  rheumatic fever (conditions classifiable to
    390)
    active 391.9
      with chorea 392.0
    inactive or quiescent (with chorea) 398.90
  amyloid 277.3 *[425.7]*
  aortic (valve) (*see also* Endocarditis, aortic)
    424.1
  arteriosclerotic or sclerotic (minimal)
    (senile)—*see* Arteriosclerosis, coronary
  artery, arterial —*see* Arteriosclerosis, coronary
  atherosclerotic —*see* Arteriosclerosis,
    coronary
  beer drinkers' 425.5
  beriberi 265.0 *[425.7]*
  black 416.0
  congenital NEC 746.9
    cyanotic 746.9
    maternal, affecting fetus or newborn 760.3
    specified type NEC 746.89
  congestive (*see also* Failure, heart,
    congestive) 428.0
  coronary 414.9
  cryptogenic 429.9
  due to
    amyloidosis 277.3 *[425.7]*
    beriberi 265.0 *[425.7]*
    cardiac glycogenosis 271.0 *[425.7]*
    Friedreich's ataxia 334.0 *[425.8]*
    gout 274.82
    mucopolysaccharidosis 277.5 *[425.7]*
    myotonia atrophica 359.2 *[425.8]*
    progressive muscular dystrophy 359.1
      [425.8]
    sarcoidosis 135 *[425.8]*
  fetal 746.9
    inflammatory 746.89
  fibroid (*see also* Myocarditis) 429.0
  functional 427.9
    postoperative 997.1
    psychogenic 306.2
  glycogen storage 271.0 *[425.7]*
  gonococcal NEC 098.85
  gouty 274.82
  hypertensive (*see also* Hypertension, heart)
    402.90
    benign 402.10
    malignant 402.00
  hyperthyroid (*see also* Hyperthyroidism)
    242.9 *[425.7]*
  incompletely diagnosed—*see* Disease, heart
  ischemic (chronic) (*see also* Ischemia, heart)
    414.9
    acute (*see also* Infarct, myocardium) 410.9
      without myocardial infarction 411.89
        with coronary (artery) occlusion 411.81
    asymptomatic 412
    diagnosed on ECG or other special
      investigation but currently presenting no
      symptoms 412
  kyphoscoliotic 416.1
  mitral (*see also* Endocarditis, mitral) 394.9
  muscular (*see also* Degeneration, myocardial)
    429.1
  postpartum 674.8
  psychogenic (functional) 306.2
  pulmonary (chronic) 416.9
    acute 415.0

Disease, diseased—*continued*
  specified NEC 416.8
  rheumatic (chronic) (inactive) (old)
    (quiescent) (with chorea) 398.90
    active or acute 391.9
      with chorea (active) (rheumatic)
        (Sydenham's) 392.0
      specified type NEC 391.8
    maternal, affecting fetus or newborn 760.3
  rheumatoid—*see* Arthritis, rheumatoid
  sclerotic —*see* Arteriosclerosis, coronary
  senile (*see also* Myocarditis) 429.0
  specified type NEC 429.89
  syphilitic 093.89
    aortic 093.1
      aneurysm 093.0
    asymptomatic 093.89
    congenital 090.5
  thyroid (gland) (*see also* Hyperthyroidism)
    242.9 *[425.7]*
  thyrotoxic (*see also* Thyrotoxicosis) 242.9
    [425.7]
  tuberculous (*see also* Tuberculosis) 017.9
    [425.8]
  valve, valvular (obstructive)
    (regurgitant)—*see also* Endocarditis
    congenital NEC (*see also* Anomaly, heart,
      valve) 746.9
      pulmonary 746.00
      specified type NEC 746.89
  vascular—*see* Disease, cardiovascular
heavy-chain (gamma G) 273.2
Heberden's 715.04
Hebra's
  dermatitis exfoliativa 695.89
  erythema multiforme exudativum 695.1
  pityriasis
    maculata et circinata 696.3
    rubra 695.89
    pilaris 696.4
  prurigo 698.2
Heerfordt's (uveoparotitis) 135
Heidenhain's 290.10
  with dementia 290.10
Heilmeyer-Schöner (M9842/3) 207.1
Heine-Medin (*see also* Poliomyelitis) 045.9
Heller's (*see also* Psychosis, childhood) 299.1
Heller-Döhle (syphilitic aortitis) 093.1
hematopoietic organs 289.9
hemoglobin (Hb) 282.7
  with thalassemia 282.4
  abnormal (mixed) NEC 282.7
    with thalassemia 282.4
  AS genotype 282.5
  Bart's 282.7
  C (Hb-C) 282.7
    with other abnormal hemoglobin NEC 282.7
    elliptocytosis 282.7
    Hb-S 282.63
    sickle-cell 282.63
    thalassemia 282.4
  constant spring 282.7
  D (Hb-D) 282.7
    with other abnormal hemoglobin NEC 282.7
    Hb-S 282.69
    sickle-cell 282.69
    thalassemia 282.4
  E (Hb-E) 282.7
    with other abnormal hemoglobin NEC 282.7
    Hb-S 282.69
    sickle-cell 282.69

> *Note—Use the following fifth-digit*
> *subclassification with categories 201:*
>
> *0 unspecified site*
> *1 lymph nodes of head, face, and neck*
> *2 intrathoracic lymph nodes*
> *3 intra-abdominal lymph nodes*
> *4 lymph nodes of axilla and upper limb*
> *5 lymph nodes of inguinal region and*
> *   lower limb*
> *6 intrapelvic lymph nodes*
> *7 spleen*
> *8 lymph nodes of multiple sites*

Disease, diseased—*continued*
  lumbar, lumbosacral 722.93
    with myelopathy 722.73
  thoracic, thoracolumbar 722.92
    with myelopathy 722.72
  intestine 569.9
    functional 564.9
      congenital 751.3
      psychogenic 306.4
    lardaceous 277.3
    organic 569.9
    protozoal NEC 007.9
  iris 364.9
  iron
    metabolism 275.0
    storage 275.0
  Isambert's (*see also* Tuberculosis, larynx) 012.3
  Iselin's (osteochondrosis, fifth metatarsal) 732.5
  Island (scrub typhus) 081.2
  itai-itai 985.5
  Jadassohn's (maculopapular erythroderma)
    696.2
  Jadassohn-Pellizari's (anetoderma) 701.3
  Jakob-Creutzfeldt 046.1
    with dementia
      with behavioral disturbance 046.1 *[294.11]*
      without behavioral disturbance 046.1
        [294.10]
  Jaksch (-Luzet) (pseudoleukemia infantum)
    285.8
  Janet's 300.89
  Jansky-Bielschowsky 330.1
  jaw NEC 526.9
    fibrocystic 526.2
  Jensen's 363.05
  Jeune's (asphyxiating thoracic dystrophy) 756.4
  jigger 134.1
  Johnson-Stevens (erythema multiforme
    exudativum) 695.1
  joint NEC 719.9
    ankle 719.97
    Charcot 094.0 *[713.5]*
    degenerative (*see also* Osteoarthrosis) 715.9
      multiple 715.09
      spine (*see also* Spondylosis) 721.90
    elbow 719.92
    foot 719.97
    hand 719.94
    hip 719.95
    hypertrophic (chronic) (degenerative) (*see
      also* Osteoarthrosis) 715.9
      spine (*see also* Spondylosis) 721.90
    knee 719.96
    Luschka 721.90
    multiple sites 719.99
    pelvic region 719.95
    sacroiliac 724.6
    shoulder (region) 719.91
    specified site NEC 719.98
    spine NEC 724.9
      pseudarthrosis following fusion 733.82
      sacroiliac 724.6
    wrist 719.93
  Jourdain's (acute gingivitis) 523.0
  Jüngling's (sarcoidosis) 135
  Kahler (-Bozzolo) (multiple myeloma)
    (M9730/3) 203.0
  Kalischer's 759.6
  Kaposi's 757.33
    lichen ruber 697.8
      acuminatus 696.4

Disease, diseased—*continued*
  moniliformis 697.8
  xeroderma pigmentosum 757.33
  Kaschin-Beck (endemic polyarthritis) 716.00
    ankle 716.07
    arm 716.02
      lower (and wrist) 716.03
      upper (and elbow) 716.02
    foot (and ankle) 716.07
    forearm (and wrist) 716.03
    hand 716.04
    leg 716.06
      lower 716.06
      upper 716.05
    multiple sites 716.09
    pelvic region (hip) (thigh) 716.05
    shoulder region 716.01
    specified site NEC 716.08
  Katayama 120.2
  Kawasaki 446.1
  Kedani (scrub typhus) 081.2
  kidney (functional) (pelvis) (*see also* Disease,
    renal) 593.9
    cystic (congenital) 753.10
      multiple 753.19
      single 753.11
      specified NEC 753.19
    fibrocystic (congenital) 753.19
    in gout 274.10
    polycystic (congenital) 753.12
      adult type (APKD) 753.13
      autosomal dominant 753.13
      autosomal recessive 753.14
      childhood type (CPKD) 753.14
      infantile type 753.14
  Kienböck's (carpal lunate) (wrist) 732.3
  Kimmelstiel (-Wilson) (intercapillary
    glomerulosclerosis) 250.4 *[581.81]*
  Kinnier Wilson's (hepatolenticular
    degeneration) 275.1
  kissing 075
  Kleb's (*see also* Nephritis) 583.9
  Klinger's 446.4
  Klippel's 723.8
  Klippel-Feil (brevicollis) 756.16
  knight's 911.1
  Köbner's (epidermolysis bullosa) 757.39
  Koenig-Wichmann (pemphigus) 694.4
  Köhler's
    first (osteoarthrosis juvenilis) 732.5
    second (Freiberg's infraction, metatarsal
      head) 732.5
    patellar 732.4
    tarsal navicular (bone) (osteoarthrosis
      juvenilis) 732.5
  Köhler-Freiberg (infraction, metatarsal head)
    732.5
  Köhler-Mouchet (osteoarthrosis juvenilis) 732.5
  Köhler-Pellegrini-Stieda (calcification, knee
    joint) 726.62
  König's (osteochondritis dissecans) 732.7
  Korsakoff's (nonalcoholic) 294.0
    alcoholic 291.1
  Kostmann's (infantile genetic agranulocytosis)
    288.0
  Krabbe's 330.0
  Kraepelin-Morel (*see also* Schizophrenia) 295.9
  Kraft-Weber-Dimitri 759.6
  Kufs' 330.1
  Kugelberg-Welander 335.11
  Kuhnt-Junius 362.52

Disease, diseased—*continued*
 Kümmell's (-Verneuil) (spondylitis) 721.7
 Kundrat's (lymphosarcoma) 200.1
 kuru 046.0
 Kussmaul (-Meier) (polyarteritis nodosa) 446.0
 Kyasanur Forest 065.2
 Kyrle's (hyperkeratosis follicularis in cutem
  penetrans) 701.1
 labia
  inflammatory 616.9
   specified NEC 616.8
  noninflammatory 624.9
   specified NEC 624.8
 labyrinth, ear 386.8
 lacrimal system (apparatus) (passages) 375.9
  gland 375.00
  specified NEC 375.89
 Lafora's 333.2
 Lagleyze-von Hippel (retinocerebral
  angiomatosis) 759.6
 Lancereaux-Mathieu (leptospiral jaundice) 100.0
 Landry's 357.0
 Lane's 569.89
 lardaceous (any site) 277.3
 Larrey-Weil (leptospiral jaundice) 100.0
 Larsen (-Johansson) (juvenile osteopathia
  patellae) 732.4
 larynx 478.70
 Lasègue's (persecution mania) 297.9
 Leber's 377.16
 Lederer's (acquired infectious hemolytic
  anemia) 283.19
 Legg's (capital femoral osteochondrosis) 732.1
 Legg-Calvé-Perthes (capital femoral
  osteochondrosis) 732.1
 Legg-Calvé-Waldenström (femoral capital
  osteochondrosis) 732.1
 Legg-Perthes (femoral capital osteochondrosis)
  732.1
 Legionnaires' 482.84
 Leigh's 330.8
 Leiner's (exfoliative dermatitis) 695.89
 Leloir's (lupus erythematosus) 695.4
 Lenegre's 426.0
 lens (eye) 379.39
 Leriche's (osteoporosis, posttraumatic) 733.7
 Letterer-Siwe (acute histiocytosis X) (M9722/3)
  202.5
 Lev's (acquired complete heart block) 426.0
 Lewandowski's (*see also* Tuberculosis) 017.0
 Lewandowski-Lutz (epidermodysplasia
  verruciformis) 078.19
 Leyden's (periodic vomiting) 536.2
 Libman-Sacks (verrucous endocarditis) 710.0
  [424.91]
 Lichtheim's (subacute combined sclerosis with
  pernicious anemia) 281.0 *[336.2]*
 ligament 728.9
 light chain 203.0
 Lightwood's (renal tubular acidosis) 588.8
 Lignac's (cystinosis) 270.0
 Lindau's (retinocerebral angiomatosis) 759.6
 Lindau-von Hippel (angiomatosis
  retinocerebellosa) 759.6
 lip NEC 528.5
 lipidosis 272.7
 lipoid storage NEC 272.7
 Lipschültz's 616.50
 Little's—*see* Palsy, cerebral

Disease, diseased—*continued*
 liver 573.9
  alcoholic 571.3
   acute 571.1
   chronic 571.3
  chronic 571.9
   alcoholic 571.3
  cystic, congenital 751.62
  drug-induced 573.3
  due to
   chemicals 573.3
   fluorinated agents 573.3
   hypersensitivity drugs 573.3
   isoniazids 573.3
  fibrocystic (congenital) 751.62
  glycogen storage 271.0
  organic 573.9
  polycystic (congenital) 751.62
 Lobo's (keloid blastomycosis) 116.2
 Lobstein's (brittle bones and blue sclera) 756.61
 locomotor system 334.9
 Lorain's (pituitary dwarfism) 253.3
 Lou Gehrig's 335.20
 Lucas-Championnière (fibrinous bronchitis)
  466.0
 Ludwig's (submaxillary cellulitis) 528.3
 luetic—*see* Syphilis
 lumbosacral region 724.6
 lung NEC 518.89
  black 500
  congenital 748.60
  cystic 518.89
   congenital 748.4
  fibroid (chronic) (*see also* Fibrosis, lung) 515
  fluke 121.2
   Oriental 121.2
  in
   amyloidosis 277.3 *[517.8]*
   polymyositis 710.4 *[517.8]*
   sarcoidosis 135 *[517.8]*
   Sjögren's syndrome 710.2 *[517.8]*
   syphilis 095.1
   systemic lupus erythematosus 710.0 *[517.8]*
   systemic sclerosis 710.1 *[517.2]*
  interstitial (chronic) 515
   acute 136.3
  nonspecific, chronic 496
  obstructive (chronic) (COPD) 496
   with
    acute exacerbation NEC 491.21
    alveolitis, allergic (*see also* Alveolitis,
     allergic) 495.9
    asthma (chronic) (obstructive) 493.2
    bronchiectasis 494.0
     with acute exacerbation 494.1
    bronchitis (chronic) 491.20
     with acute exacerbation 491.21
    emphysema NEC 492.8
   diffuse (with fibrosis) 496
  polycystic 518.89
   asthma (chronic) (obstructive) 493.2
   congenital 748.4
  purulent (cavitary) 513.0
  restrictive 518.89
  rheumatoid 714.81
   diffuse interstitial 714.81
  specified NEC 518.89
 Lutembacher's (atrial septal defect with mitral
  stenosis) 745.5
 Lutz-Miescher (elastosis perforans serpiginosa)
  701.1

Disease, diseased—*continued*
  Lutz-Splendore-de Almeida (Brazilian
      blastomycosis) 116.1
  Lyell's (toxic epidermal necrolysis) 695.1
    due to drug
      correct substance properly administered
          695.1
        overdose or wrong substance given or taken
          977.9
          specific drug—*see* Table of drugs and
              chemicals
  Lyme 088.81
  lymphatic (gland) (system) 289.9
    channel (noninfective) 457.9
    vessel (noninfective) 457.9
      specified NEC 457.8
  lymphoproliferative (chronic) (M9970/1) 238.7
  Machado-Joseph 334.8
  Madelung's (lipomatosis) 272.8
  Madura (actinomycotic) 039.9
    mycotic 117.4
  Magitot's 526.4
  Majocchi's (purpura annularis telangiectodes)
      709.1
  malarial (*see also* Malaria) 084.6
  Malassez's (cystic) 608.89
  Malibu 919.8
    infected 919.9
  malignant (M8000/3)—*see also* Neoplasm, by
      site, malignant
    previous, affecting management of pregnancy
        V23.8
  Manson's 120.1
  maple bark 495.6
  maple syrup (urine) 270.3
  Marburg (virus) 078.89
  Marchiafava (-Bignami) 341.8
  Marfan's 090.49
    congenital syphilis 090.49
    meaning Marfan's syndrome 759.82
  Marie-Bamberger (hypertrophic pulmonary
      osteoarthropathy) (secondary) 731.2
    primary or idiopathic (acropachyderma)
        757.39
    pulmonary (hypertrophic osteoarthropathy)
        731.2
  Marie-Strümpell (ankylosing spondylitis) 720.0
  Marion's (bladder neck obstruction) 596.0
  Marsh's (exophthalmic goiter) 242.0
  Martin's 715.27
  mast cell 757.33
    systemic (M9741/3) 202.6
  mastoid (*see also* Mastoiditis) 383.9
    process 385.9
  maternal, unrelated to pregnancy NEC,
      affecting fetus or newborn 760.9
  Mathieu's (leptospiral jaundice) 100.0
  Mauclaire's 732.3
  Mauriac's (erythema nodosum syphiliticum)
      091.3
  Maxcy's 081.0
  McArdle (-Schmid-Pearson) (glycogenosis V)
      271.0
  mediastinum NEC 519.3
  Medin's (*see also* Poliomyelitis) 045.9
  Mediterranean (with hemoglobinopathy) 282.4
  medullary center (idiopathic) (respiratory) 348.8
  Meige's (chronic hereditary edema) 757.0
  Meleda 757.39
  Ménétrier's (hypertrophic gastritis) 535.2

Disease, diseased—*continued*
  Ménière's (active) 386.00
    cochlear 386.02
    cochleovestibular 386.01
    inactive 386.04
    in remission 386.04
    vestibular 386.03
  meningeal—*see* Meningitis
  mental (*see also* Psychosis) 298.9
  Merzbacher-Pelizaeus 330.0
  mesenchymal 710.9
  mesenteric embolic 557.0
  metabolic NEC 277.9
  metal polishers' 502
  metastatic—*see* Metastasis
  Mibelli's 757.39
  microdrepanocytic 282.4
  Miescher's 709.3
  Mikulicz's (dryness of mouth, absent or
      decreased lacrimation) 527.1
  Milkman (-Looser) (osteomalacia with
      pseudofractures) 268.2
  Miller's (osteomalacia) 268.2
  Mills' 335.29
  Milroy's (chronic hereditary edema) 757.0
  Minamata 985.0
  Minor's 336.1
  Minot's (hemorrhagic disease, newborn) 776.0
  Minot-von Willebrand-Jürgens
      (angiohemophilia) 286.4
  Mitchell's (erythromelalgia) 443.89
  mitral—*see* Endocarditis, mitral
  Mljet (mal de Meleda) 757.39
  Möbius', Moebius' 346.8
  Moeller's 267
  Möller (-Barlow) (infantile scurvy) 267
  Mönckeberg's (*see also* arteriosclerosis,
      extremities) 440.20
  Mondor's (thrombophlebitis of breast) 451.89
  Monge's 993.2
  Morel-Kraepelin (*see also* Schizophrenia) 295.9
  Morgagni's (syndrome) (hyperostosis frontalis
      interna) 733.3
  Morgagni-Adams-Stokes (syncope with heart
      block) 426.9
  Morquio (-Brailsford) (-Ullrich)
      (mucopolysaccharidosis IV) 277.5
  Morton's (with metatarsalgia) 355.6
  Morvan's 336.0
  motor neuron (bulbar) (mixed type) 335.20
  Mouchet's (juvenile osteochondrosis, foot)
      732.5
  mouth 528.9
  Moyamoya 437.5
  Mucha's (acute parapsoriasis varioliformis)
      696.2
  mu-chain 273.2
  mucolipidosis (I) (II) (III) 272.7
  Münchmeyer's (exostosis luxurians) 728.11
  Murri's (intermittent hemoglobinuria) 283.2
  muscle 359.9
    inflammatory 728.9
    ocular 378.9
  musculoskeletal system 729.9
  mushroom workers' 495.5
  Myà's (congenital dilation, colon) 751.3
  mycotic 117.9
  myeloproliferative (chronic) (M9960/1) 238.7
  myocardium, myocardial (*see also*
      Degeneration, myocardial) 429.1

Disease, diseased—*continued*
  hypertensive (*see also* Hypertension, heart)
    402.90
    primary (idiopathic) 425.4
  myoneural 358.9
  Naegeli's 287.1
  nail 703.9
    specified type NEC 703.8
  Nairobi sheep 066.1
  nasal 478.1
    cavity NEC 478.1
    sinus (chronic)—*see* Sinusitis
  navel (newborn) NEC 779.8
  nemaline body 359.0
  neoplastic, generalized (M8000/6) 199.0
  nerve—*see* Disorder, nerve
  nervous system (central) 349.9
    autonomic, peripheral (*see also* Neuropathy,
      peripheral, autonomic) 337.9
    congenital 742.9
    inflammatory—*see* Encephalitis
    parasympathetic (*see also* Neuropathy,
      peripheral, autonomic) 337.9
    peripheral NEC 355.9
    specified NEC 349.89
    sympathetic (*see also* Neuropathy, peripheral,
      autonomic) 337.9
    vegetative (*see also* Neuropathy, peripheral,
      autonomic) 337.9
  Nettleship's (urticaria pigmentosa) 757.33
  Neumann's (pemphigus vegetans) 694.4
  neurologic (central) NEC (*see also* Disease,
    nervous system) 349.9
    peripheral NEC 355.9
  neuromuscular system NEC 358.9
  Newcastle 077.8
  Nicolas (-Durand) -Favre (climatic bubo) 099.1
  Niemann-Pick (lipid histiocytosis) 272.7
  nipple 611.9
    Paget's (M8540/3) 174.0
  Nishimoto (-Takeuchi) 437.5
  nonarthropod-borne NEC 078.89
    central nervous system NEC 049.9
    enterovirus NEC 078.89
  non-autoimmune hemolytic NEC 283.10
  Nonne-Milroy-Meige (chronic hereditary
    edema) 757.0
  Norrie's (congenital progressive
    oculoacousticocerebral degeneration) 743.8
  nose 478.1
  nucleus pulposus—*see* Disease, intervertebral
    disc
  nutritional 269.9
    maternal, affecting fetus or newborn 760.4
  oasthouse, urine 270.2
  obliterative vascular 447.1
  Odelberg's (juvenile osteochondrosis) 732.1
  Oguchi's (retina) 368.61
  Ohara's (*see also* Tularemia) 021.9
  Ollier's (chondrodysplasia) 756.4
  Opitz's (congestive splenomegaly) 289.51
  Oppenheim's 358.8
  Oppenheim-Urbach (necrobiosis lipoidica
    diabeticorum) 250.8 *[709.3]*
  optic nerve NEC 377.49
  orbit 376.9
    specified NEC 376.89
  Oriental liver fluke 121.1
  Oriental lung fluke 121.2
  Ormond's 593.4
  Osgood's tibia (tubercle) 732.4

Disease, diseased—*continued*
  Osgood-Schlatter 732.4
  Osler (-Vaquez) (polycythemia vera) (M9950/1)
    238.4
  Osler-Rendu (familial hemorrhagic
    telangiectasia) 448.0
  osteofibrocystic 252.0
  Otto's 715.35
  outer ear 380.9
  ovary (noninflammatory) NEC 620.9
    cystic 620.2
    polycystic 256.4
    specified NEC 620.8
  Owren's (congenital) (*see also* Defect,
    coagulation) 286.3
  Paas' 756.59
  Paget's (osteitis deformans) 731.0
    with infiltrating duct carcinoma of the breast
      (M8541/3)—*see* Neoplasm, breast,
      malignant
    bone 731.0
      osteosarcoma in (M9184/3)—*see*
        Neoplasm, bone, malignant
    breast (M8540/3) 174.0
    extramammary (M8542/3)—*see also*
      Neoplasm, skin, malignant
      anus 154.3
      skin 173.5
    malignant (M8540/3)
      breast 174.0
      specified site NEC (M8542/3)—*see*
        Neoplasm, skin, malignant
      unspecified site 174.0
    mammary (M8540/3) 174.0
    nipple (M8540/3) 174.0
  palate (soft) 528.9
  Paltauf-Sternberg 201.9
  pancreas 577.9
    cystic 577.2
      congenital 751.7
    fibrocystic 277.00
  Panner's 732.3
    capitellum humeri 732.3
    head of humerus 732.3
    tarsal navicular (bone) (osteochondrosis) 732.5
  panvalvular—*see* Endocarditis, mitral
  parametrium 629.9
  parasitic NEC 136.9
    cerebral NEC 123.9
    intestinal NEC 129
    mouth 112.0
    skin NEC 134.9
    specified type—*see* Infestation
    tongue 112.0
  parathyroid (gland) 252.9
    specified NEC 252.8
  Parkinson's 332.0
  parodontal 523.9
  Parrot's (syphilitic osteochondritis) 090.0
  Parry's (exophthalmic goiter) 242.0
  Parson's (exophthalmic goiter) 242.0
  Pavy's 593.6
  Paxton's (white piedra) 111.2
  Payr's (splenic flexure syndrome) 569.89
  pearl-workers' (chronic osteomyelitis) (*see also*
    Osteomyelitis) 730.1
  Pel-Ebstein—*see* Disease, Hodgkin's

Disease, diseased—*continued*
  Pelizaeus-Merzbacher 330.0
    with dementia
      with behavioral disturbance 330.0 *[294.11]*
      without behavioral disturbance 330.0
        [294.10]
  Pellegrini-Stieda (calcification, knee joint)
    726.62
  pelvis, pelvic
    female NEC 629.9
      specified NEC 629.8
    gonococcal (acute) 098.19
      chronic or duration of 2 months or over
        098.39
    infection (*see also* Disease, pelvis,
      inflammatory) 614.9
    inflammatory (female) (PID) 614.9
      with
        abortion—*see* Abortion, by type, with
          sepsis
        ectopic pregnancy (*see also* categories
          633.0-633.9) 639.0
        molar pregnancy (*see also* categories
          630-632) 639.0
      acute 614.3
      chronic 614.4
      complicating pregnancy 646.6
        affecting fetus or newborn 760.8
      following
        abortion 639.0
        ectopic or molar pregnancy 639.0
      peritonitis (acute) 614.5
        chronic NEC 614.7
      puerperal, postpartum, childbirth 670
      specified NEC 614.8
    organ, female NEC 629.9
      specified NEC 629.8
    peritoneum, female NEC 629.9
      specified NEC 629.8
  penis 607.9
    inflammatory 607.2
  peptic NEC 536.9
    acid 536.8
  periapical tissues NEC 522.9
  pericardium 423.9
    specified type NEC 423.8
  perineum
    female
      inflammatory 616.9
        specified NEC 616.8
      noninflammatory 624.9
        specified NEC 624.8
    male (inflammatory) 682.2
  periodic (familial) (Reimann's) NEC 277.3
    paralysis 359.3
  periodontal NEC 523.9
    specified NEC 523.8
  periosteum 733.90
  peripheral
    arterial 443.9
    autonomic nervous system (*see also*
      Neuropathy, autonomic) 337.9
    nerve NEC (*see also* Neuropathy) 356.9
      multiple—*see* Polyneuropathy
    vascular 443.9
      specified type NEC 443.89
  peritoneum 568.9
    pelvic, female 629.9
      specified NEC 629.8
  Perrin-Ferraton (snapping hip) 719.65

Disease, diseased—*continued*
  persistent mucosal (middle ear) (with posterior
    or superior marginal perforation of ear
    drum) 382.2
  Perthes' (capital femoral osteochondrosis) 732.1
  Petit's (*see also* Hernia, lumbar) 553.8
  Peutz-Jeghers 759.6
  Peyronie's 607.89
  Pfeiffer's (infectious mononucleosis) 075
  pharynx 478.20
  Phocas' 610.1
  photochromogenic (acid-fast bacilli)
    (pulmonary) 031.0
    nonpulmonary 031.9
  Pick's
    brain 331.1
      with dementia
        with behavioral disturbance 331.1 *[294.11]*
        without behavioral disturbance 331.1
          [294.10]
    cerebral atrophy 331.1
      with dementia
        with behavioral disturbance 331.1 *[294.11]*
        without behavioral disturbance 331.1
          [294.10]
    lipid histiocytosis 272.7
    liver (pericardial pseudocirrhosis of liver)
      423.2
    pericardium (pericardial pseudocirrhosis of
      liver) 423.2
    polyserositis (pericardial pseudocirrhosis of
      liver) 423.2
  Pierson's (osteochondrosis) 732.1
  pigeon fancier's or breeders' 495.2
  pineal gland 259.8
  pink 985.0
  Pinkus' (lichen nitidus) 697.1
  pinworm 127.4
  pituitary (gland) 253.9
    hyperfunction 253.1
    hypofunction 253.2
  pituitary snuff-takers' 495.8
  placenta
    affecting fetus or newborn 762.2
    complicating pregnancy or childbirth 656.7
  pleura (cavity) (*see also* Pleurisy) 511.0
  Plummer's (toxic nodular goiter) 242.3
  pneumatic
    drill 994.9
    hammer 994.9
  policeman's 729.2
  Pollitzer's (hidradenitis suppurativa) 705.83
  polycystic (congenital) 759.89
    kidney or renal 753.12
      adult type (APKD) 753.13
      autosomal dominant 753.13
      autosomal recessive 753.14
      childhood type (CPKD) 753.14
      infantile type 753.14
    liver or hepatic 751.62
    lung or pulmonary 518.89
      congenital 748.4
    ovary, ovaries 256.4
    spleen 759.0
  Pompe's (glycogenosis II) 271.0
  Poncet's (tuberculous rheumatism) (*see also*
    Tuberculosis) 015.9
  Posada-Wernicke 114.9
  Potain's (pulmonary edema) 514

Disease, diseased—*continued*
  Pott's (*see also* Tuberculosis) 015.0 *[730.88]*
    osteomyelitis 015.0 *[730.88]*
    paraplegia 015.0 *[730.88]*
    spinal curvature 015.0 *[737.43]*
    spondylitis 015.0 *[720.81]*
  Potter's 753.0
  Poulet's 714.2
  pregnancy NEC (*see also* Pregnancy) 646.9
  Preiser's (osteoporosis) 733.09
  Pringle's (tuberous sclerosis) 759.5
  Profichet's 729.9
  prostate 602.9
    specified type NEC 602.8
  protozoal NEC 136.8
    intestine, intestinal NEC 007.9
  pseudo-Hurler's (mucolipidosis III) 272.7
  psychiatric (*see also* Psychosis) 298.9
  psychotic (*see also* Psychosis) 298.9
  Puente's (simple glandular cheilitis) 528.5
  puerperal NEC (*see also* Puerperal) 674.9
  pulmonary—*see also* Disease, lung
    amyloid 277.3 *[517.8]*
    artery 417.9
    circulation, circulatory 417.9
      specified NEC 417.8
    diffuse obstructive (chronic) 496
      with
        acute exacerbation NEC 491.21
        asthma (chronic) (obstructive) 493.2
        bronchitis (chronic) 491.20
          with acute exacerbation 491.21
    heart (chronic) 416.9
      specified NEC 416.8
    hypertensive (vascular) 416.0
      cardiovascular 416.0
    obstructive diffuse (chronic) 496
      with
        acute exacerbation NEC 491.21
        asthma (chronic) (obstructive) 493.2
    valve (*see also* Endocarditis, pulmonary) 424.3
  pulp (dental) NEC 522.9
  pulseless 446.7
  Putnam's (subacute combined sclerosis with
    pernicious anemia) 281.0 *[336.2]*
  Pyle (-Cohn) (craniometaphyseal dysplasia)
    756.89
  pyramidal tract 333.90
  Quervain's
    tendon sheath 727.04
    thyroid (subacute granulomatous thyroiditis)
      245.1
  Quincke's—*see* Edema, angioneurotic
  Quinquaud (acne decalvans) 704.09
  rag sorters' 022.1
  Raynaud's (Paroxysmal digital cyanosis) 443.0
  reactive airway—*see* Asthma
  Recklinghausen's (M9540/1) 237.71
    bone (osteitis fibrosa cystica) 252.0
  Recklinghausen-Applebaum (hemochromatosis)
    275.0
  Reclus' (cystic) 610.1
  rectum NEC 569.49
  Refsum's (heredopathia atactica
    polyneuritiformis) 356.3
  Reichmann's (gastrosuccorrhea) 536.8
  Reimann's (periodic) 277.3
  Reiter's 099.3
  renal (functional) (pelvis) 593.9
    with
      edema (*see also* Nephrosis) 581.9

Disease, diseased—*continued*
    exudative nephritis 583.89
    lesion of interstitial nephritis 583.89
    stated generalized cause—*see* Nephritis
  acute—*see* Nephritis, acute
  basement membrane NEC 583.89
    with
      pulmonary hemorrhage (Goodpasture's
        syndrome) 446.21 *[583.81]*
  chronic—*see* Nephritis, chronic
  complicating pregnancy or puerperium NEC
    646.2
    with hypertension—*see* Toxemia, of
      pregnancy
    affecting fetus or newborn 760.1
  cystic, congenital (*see also* Cystic, disease,
    kidney) 753.10
  diabetic 250.4 *[583.81]*
  due to
    amyloidosis 277.3 *[583.81]*
    diabetes mellitus 250.4 *[583.81]*
    systemic lupus erythematosis 710.0 *[583.81]*
  end-stage 585
  exudative 583.89
  fibrocystic (congenital) 753.19
  gonococcal 098.19 *[583.81]*
  gouty 274.10
  hypertensive (*see also* Hypertension, kidney)
    403.90
  immune complex NEC 583.89
  interstitial (diffuse) (focal) 583.89
  lupus 710.0 *[583.81]*
  maternal, affecting fetus or newborn 760.1
    hypertensive 760.0
  phosphate-losing (tubular) 588.0
  polycystic (congenital) 753.12
    adult type (APKD) 753.13
    autosomal dominant 753.13
    autosomal recessive 753.14
    childhood type (CPKD) 753.14
    infantile type 753.14
  specified lesion or cause NEC (*see also*
    Glomerulonephritis) 583.89
  subacute 581.9
  syphilitic 095.4
  tuberculous (*see also* Tuberculosis) 016.0
    [583.81]
  tubular (*see also* Nephrosis, tubular) 584.5
  Rendu-Olser-Weber (familial hemorrhagic
    telangiectasia) 448.0
  renovascular (arteriosclerotic) (*see also*
    Hypertension, kidney) 403.90
  respiratory (tract) 519.9
    acute or subacute (upper) NEC 465.9
      due to fumes or vapors 506.3
      multiple sites NEC 465.8
      noninfectious 478.9
      streptococcal 034.0
    chronic 519.9
      arising in the perinatal period 770.7
      due to fumes or vapors 506.4
    due to
      aspiration of liquids or solids 508.9
      external agents NEC 508.9
        specified NEC 508.8
      fumes or vapors 506.9
        acute or subacute NEC 506.3
        chronic 506.4
    fetus or newborn NEC 770.9
    obstructive 496
    specified type NEC 519.8

Disease, diseased—*continued*
  upper (acute) (infectious) NEC 465.9
    multiple sites NEC 465.8
    noninfectious NEC 478.9
    streptococcal 034.0
  retina, retinal NEC 362.9
    Batten's or Batten-Mayou 330.1 *[362.71]*
    degeneration 362.89
    vascular lesion 362.17
  rheumatic (*see also* Arthritis) 716.8
    heart—*see* Disease, heart, rheumatic
  rheumatoid (heart)—*see* Arthritis, rheumatoid
  rickettsial NEC 083.9
    specified type NEC 083.8
  Riedel's (ligneous thyroiditis) 245.3
  Riga (-Fede) (cachectic aphthae) 529.0
  Riggs' (compound periodontitis) 523.4
  Ritter's 695.81
  Rivalta's (cervicofacial actinomycosis) 039.3
  Robles' (onchocerciasis) 125.3 *[360.13]*
  Roger's (congenital interventricular septal
    defect) 745.4
  Rokitansky's (*see also* Necrosis, liver) 570
  Romberg's 349.89
  Rosenthal's (factor XI deficiency) 286.2
  Rossbach's (hyperchlorhydria) 536.8
    psychogenic 306.4
  Roth (-Bernhardt) 355.1
  Runeberg's (progressive pernicious anemia)
    281.0
  Rust's (tuberculous spondylitis) (*see also*
    Tuberculosis) 015.0 *[720.81]*
  Rustitskii's (multiple myeloma) (M9730/3)
    203.0
  Ruysch's (Hirschsprung's disease) 751.3
  Sachs (-Tay) 330.1
  sacroiliac NEC 724.6
  salivary gland or duct NEC 527.9
    inclusion 078.5
      streptococcal 034.0
    virus 078.5
  Sander's (paranoia) 297.1
  Sandhoff's 330.1
  sandworm 126.9
  Savill's (epidemic exfoliative dermatitis) 695.89
  Schamberg's (progressive pigmentary
    dermatosis) 709.09
  Schaumann's (sarcoidosis) 135
  Schenck's (sporotrichosis) 117.1
  Scheuermann's (osteochondrosis) 732.0
  Schilder (-Flatau) 341.1
  Schimmelbusch's 610.1
  Schlatter's tibia (tubercle) 732.4
  Schlatter-Osgood 732.4
  Schmorl's 722.30
    cervical 722.39
    lumbar, lumbosacral 722.32
    specified region NEC 722.39
    thoracic, thoracolumbar 722.31
  Scholz's 330.0
  Schönlein (-Henoch) (purpura rheumatica) 287.0
  Schottmüller's (*see also* Fever, paratyphoid)
    002.9
  Schüller-Christian (chronic histiocytosis X)
    277.8
  Schultz's (agranulocytosis) 288.0
  Schwalbe-Ziehen-Oppenheimer 333.6
  Schweninger-Buzzi (macular atrophy) 701.3
  sclera 379.19
  scrofulous (*see also* Tuberculosis) 017.2
  scrotum 608.9

Disease, diseased—*continued*
  sebaceous glands NEC 706.9
  Secretan's (posttraumatic edema) 782.3
  semilunar cartilage, cystic 717.5
  seminal vesicle 608.9
  Senear-Usher (pemphigus erythematosus) 694.4
  serum NEC 999.5
  Sever's (osteochondrosis calcaneum) 732.5
  Sézary's (reticulosis) (M9701/3) 202.2
  Shaver's (bauxite pneumoconiosis) 503
  Sheehan's (postpartum pituitary necrosis) 253.2
  shimamushi (scrub typhus) 081.2
  shipyard 077.1
  sickle-cell 282.60
    with
      crisis 282.62
      Hb-S disease 282.61
      other abnormal hemoglobin (Hb-D) (Hb-E)
        (Hb-G) (Hb-J) (Hb-K) (Hb-O) (Hb-P)
        (high fetal gene) 282.69
    elliptocytosis 282.60
    Hb-C 282.63
    Hb-S 282.61
      with
        crisis 282.62
        Hb-C 282.63
        other abnormal hemoglobin (Hb-D)
          (Hb-E) (Hb-G) (Hb-J) (Hb-K) (Hb-O)
          (Hb-P) (high fetal gene) 282.69
    spherocytosis 282.60
    thalassemia 282.4
  Siegal-Cattan-Mamou (periodic) 277.3
  silo fillers' 506.9
  Simian B 054.3
  Simmonds' (pituitary cachexia) 253.2
  Simons' (progressive lipodystrophy) 272.6
  Sinding-Larsen (juvenile osteopathia patellae)
    732.4
  sinus—*see also* Sinusitis
    brain 437.9
    specified NEC 478.1
  Sirkari's 085.0
  sixth 057.8
  Sjögren (-Gougerot) 710.2
    with lung involvement 710.2 *[517.8]*
  Skevas-Zerfus 989.5
  skin NEC 709.9
    due to metabolic disorder 277.9
    specified type NEC 709.8
  sleeping 347
    meaning sleeping sickness (*see also*
      Trypanosomiasis) 086.5
  small vessel 443.9
  Smith-Strang (oasthouse urine) 270.2
  Sneddon-Wilkinson (subcorneal pustular
    dermatosis) 694.1
  South African creeping 133.8
  Spencer's (epidemic vomiting) 078.82
  Spielmeyer-Stock 330.1
  Spielmeyer-Vogt 330.1
  spine, spinal 733.90
    combined system (*see also* Degeneration,
      combined) 266.2 *[336.2]*
      with pernicious anemia 281.0 *[336.2]*
    cord NEC 336.9
      congenital 742.9
    demyelinating NEC 341.8
    joint (*see also* Disease, joint, spine) 724.9
    tuberculous 015.0 *[730.8]*
  spinocerebellar 334.9
    specified NEC 334.8

Disease, diseased—*continued*
　spleen (organic) (postinfectional) 289.50
　　amyloid 277.3
　　lardaceous 277.3
　　polycystic 759.0
　　specified NEC 289.59
　sponge divers' 989.5
　Stanton's (melioidosis) 025
　Stargardt's 362.75
　Steinert's 359.2
　Sternberg's—*see* Disease, Hodgkin's
　Stevens-Johnson (erythema multiforme
　　　exudativum) 695.1
　Sticker's (erythema infectiosum) 057.0
　Stieda's (calcification, knee joint) 726.62
　Still's (juvenile rheumatoid arthritis) 714.30
　Stiller's (asthenia) 780.79
　Stokes' (exophthalmic goiter) 242.0
　Stokes-Adams (syncope with heart block) 426.9
　Stokvis (-Talma) (enterogenous cyanosis) 289.7
　stomach NEC (organic) 537.9
　　functional 536.9
　　　psychogenic 306.4
　　lardaceous 277.3
　stonemasons' 502
　storage
　　glycogen (*see also* Disease, glycogen storage)
　　　271.0
　　lipid 272.7
　　mucopolysaccharide 277.5
　striatopallidal system 333.90
　　specified NEC 333.89
　Strümpell-Marie (ankylosing spondylitis) 720.0
　Stuart's (congenital factor X deficiency) (*see*
　　　also Defect, coagulation) 286.3
　Stuart-Prower (congenital factor X deficiency)
　　　(*see also* Defect, coagulation) 286.3
　Sturge (-Weber) (-Dimitri) (encephalocutaneous
　　　angiomatosis) 759.6
　Stuttgart 100.89
　Sudeck's 733.7
　supporting structures of teeth NEC 525.9
　suprarenal (gland) (capsule) 255.9
　　hyperfunction 255.3
　　hypofunction 255.4
　Sutton's 709.09
　Sutton and Gull's—*see* Hypertension, kidney
　sweat glands NEC 705.9
　　specified type NEC 705.89
　sweating 078.2
　Sweeley-Klionsky 272.4
　Swift (-Feer) 985.0
　swimming pool (bacillus) 031.1
　swineherd's 100.89
　Sylvest's (epidemic pleurodynia) 074.1
　Symmers (follicular lymphoma) (M9690/3)
　　　202.0
　sympathetic nervous system (*see also*
　　　Neuropathy, peripheral, autonomic) 337.9
　synovium 727.9
　syphilitic—*see* Syphilis
　systemic tissue mast cell (M9741/3) 202.6
　Taenzer's 757.4
　Takayasu's (pulseless) 446.7
　Talma's 728.85
　Tangier (familial high-density lipoprotein
　　　deficiency) 272.5
　Tarral-Besnier (pityriasis rubra pilaris) 696.4
　Tay-Sachs 330.1
　Taylor's 701.8
　tear duct 375.69

Disease, diseased—*continued*
　teeth, tooth 525.9
　　hard tissues NEC 521.9
　　pulp NEC 522.9
　tendon 727.9
　　inflammatory NEC 727.9
　terminal vessel 443.9
　testis 608.9
　Thaysen-Gee (nontropical sprue) 579.0
　Thomsen's 359.2
　Thomson's (congenital poikiloderma) 757.33
　Thornwaldt's, Tornwaldt's (pharyngeal bursitis)
　　　478.29
　throat 478.20
　　septic 034.0
　thromboembolic (*see also* Embolism) 444.9
　thymus (gland) 254.9
　　specified NEC 254.8
　thyroid (gland) NEC 246.9
　　heart (*see also* Hyperthyroidism) 242.9 [*425.7*]
　　lardaceous 277.3
　　specified NEC 246.8
　Tietze's 733.6
　Tommaselli's
　　correct substance properly administered 599.7
　　overdose or wrong substance given or taken
　　　961.4
　tongue 529.9
　tonsils, tonsillar (and adenoids) (chronic) 474.9
　　specified NEC 474.8
　tooth, teeth 525.9
　　hard tissues NEC 521.9
　　pulp NEC 522.9
　Tornwaldt's (pharyngeal bursitis) 478.29
　Tourette's 307.23
　trachea 519.1
　tricuspid—*see* Endocarditis, tricuspid
　triglyceride-storage, type I, II, III 272.7
　triple vessel (coronary arteries) —*see*
　　　Arteriosclerosis, coronary
　trisymptomatic, Gougerot's 709.1
　trophoblastic (*see also* Hydatidiform mole) 630
　　previous, affecting management of pregnancy
　　　V23.1
　tsutsugamushi (scrub typhus) 081.2
　tube (fallopian), noninflammatory 620.9
　　specified NEC 620.8
　tuberculous NEC (*see also* Tuberculosis) 011.9
　tubo-ovarian
　　inflammatory (*see also* Salpingo-oophoritis)
　　　614.2
　　noninflammatory 620.9
　　　specified NEC 620.8
　tubotympanic, chronic (with anterior perforation
　　　of ear drum) 382.1
　tympanum 385.9
　Uhl's 746.84
　umbilicus (newborn) NEC 779.8
　Underwood's (sclerema neonatorum) 778.1
　undiagnosed 799.9
　Unna's (seborrheic dermatitis) 690.18
　unstable hemoglobin hemolytic 282.7
　Unverricht (-Lundborg) 333.2
　Urbach-Oppenheim (necrobiosis lipoidica
　　　diabeticorum) 250.8 [*709.3*]
　Urbach-Wiethe (lipoid proteinosis) 272.8
　ureter 593.9
　urethra 599.9
　　specified type NEC 599.84
　urinary (tract) 599.9
　　bladder 596.9

Disease, diseased—*continued*
    specified NEC 596.8
    maternal, affecting fetus or newborn 760.1
  Usher-Senear (pemphigus erythematosus) 694 4
  uterus (organic) 621.9
    infective (*see also* Endometritis) 615.9
    inflammatory (*see also* Endometritis) 615.9
    noninflammatory 621.9
      specified type NEC 621.8
  uveal tract
    anterior 364.9
    posterior 363.9
  vagabonds' 132.1
  vagina, vaginal
    inflammatory 616.9
      specified NEC 616.8
    noninflammatory 623.9
      specified NEC 623.8
  Valsuani's (progressive pernicious anemia,
    puerperal) 648.2
    complicating pregnancy or puerperium 648.2
  valve, valvular—*see* Endocarditis
  van Bogaert-Nijssen (-Peiffer) 330.0
  van Creveld-von Gierke (glycogenosis I) 271 0
  van den Bergh's (enterogenous cyanosis) 289.7
  van Neck's (juvenile osteochondrosis) 732.1
  Vaquez (-Osler) (polycythemia vera) (M995C/1)
    238.4
  vascular 459.9
    arteriosclerotic—*see* Arteriosclerosis
    hypertensive—*see* Hypertension
    obliterative 447.1
      peripheral 443.9
    occlusive 459.9
    peripheral (occlusive) 443.9
      in diabetes mellitus 250.7 *[443.81]*
      specified type NEC 443.89
  vas deferens 608.9
  vasomotor 443.9
  vasospastic 443.9
  vein 459.9
  venereal 099.9
    fifth 099.1
    sixth 099.1
    chlamydial NEC 099.50
      anus 099.52
      bladder 099.53
      cervix 099.53
      epididymis 099.54
      genitourinary NEC 099.55
        lower 099.53
        specified NEC 099.54
      pelvic inflammatory disease 099.54
      perihepatic 099.56
      peritoneum 099.56
      pharynx 099.51
      rectum 099.52
      specified site NEC 099.59
      testis 099.54
      vagina 099.53
      vulva 099.53
    complicating pregnancy, childbirth, or
      puerperium 647.2
    specified nature or type NEC 099.8
      chlamydial—*see* Disease, venereal,
        chlamydial
  Verneuil's (syphilitic bursitis) 095.7
  Verse's (calcinosis intervertebralis) 275.49
    [722.90]
  vertebra, vertebral NEC 733.90
    disc—*see* Disease, Intervertebral disc

Disease, diseased—*continued*
  vibration NEC 994.9
  Vidal's (lichen simplex chronicus) 698.3
  Vincent's (trench mouth) 101
  Virchow's 733.99
  virus (filterable) NEC 078.89
    arbovirus NEC 066.9
    arthropod-borne NEC 066.9
    central nervous system NEC 049.9
      specified type NEC 049.8
    complicating pregnancy, childbirth, or
      puerperium 647.6
    contact (with) V01.7
    exposure to V01.7
    Marburg 078.89
    maternal
      with fetal damage affecting management of
        pregnancy 655.3
    nonarthropod-borne NEC 078.89
      central nervous system NEC 049.9
        specified NEC 049.8
  vitreous 379.29
  vocal cords NEC 478.5
  Vogt's (Cecile) 333.7
  Vogt-Spielmeyer 330.1
  Volhard-Fahr (malignant nephrosclerosis)
    403.00
  Volkmann's
    acquired 958.6
  von Bechterew's (ankylosing spondylitis) 720.0
  von Economo's (encephalitis lethargica) 049.8
  von Eulenburg's (congenital paramyotonia)
    359.2
  von Gierke's (glycogenosis I) 271.0
  von Graefe's 378.72
  von Hippel's (retinocerebral angiomatosis) 759.6
  von Hippel-Lindau (angiomatosis
    retinocerebellosa) 759.6
  von Jaksch's (pseudoleukemia infantum) 285.8
  von Recklinghausen's (M9540/1) 237.71
    bone (osteitis fibrosa cystica) 252.0
  von Recklinghausen-Applebaum
    (hemochromatosis) 275.0
  von Willebrand (-Jürgens) (angiohemophilia)
    286.4
  von Zambusch's (lichen sclerosus et atrophicus)
    701.0
  Voorhoeve's (dyschondroplasia) 756.4
  Vrolik's (osteogenesis imperfecta) 756.51
  vulva
    noninflammatory 624.9
      specified NEC 624.8
  Wagner's (colloid milium) 709.3
  Waldenström's (osteochondrosis capital
    femoral) 732.1
  Wallgren's (obstruction of splenic vein with
    collateral circulation) 459.89
  Wardrop's (with lymphangitis) 681.9
    finger 681.02
    toe 681.11
  Wassilieff's (leptospiral jaundice) 100.0
  wasting NEC 799.4
    due to malnutrition 261
    paralysis 335.21
  Waterhouse-Friderichsen 036.3
  waxy (any site) 277.3
  Weber-Christian (nodular nonsuppurative
    panniculitis) 729.30
  Wegner's (syphilitic osteochondritis) 090.0
  Weil's (leptospiral jaundice) 100.0
    of lung 100.0

Disease, diseased—*continued*
  Weir Mitchell's (erythromelalgia) 443.89
  Werdnig-Hoffmann 335.0
  Werlhof's (*see also* Purpura, thrombocytopenic)
    287.3
  Wermer's 258.0
  Werner's (progeria adultorum) 259.8
  Werner-His (trench fever) 083.1
  Werner-Schultz (agranulocytosis) 288.0
  Wernicke's (superior hemorrhagic
    polioencephalitis) 265.1
  Wernicke-Posadas 114.9
  Whipple's (intestinal lipodystrophy) 040.2
  whipworm 127.3
  white
    blood cell 288.9
      specified NEC 288.8
    spot 701.0
  White's (congenital) (keratosis follicularis)
    757.39
  Whitmore's (melioidosis) 025
  Widal-Abrami (acquired hemolytic jaundice)
    283.9
  Wilkie's 557.1
  Wilkinson-Sneddon (subcorneal pustular
    dermatosis) 694.1
  Willis' (diabetes mellitus) (*see also* Diabetes)
    250.0
  Wilson's (hepatolenticular degeneration) 275.1
  Wilson-Brocq (dermatitis exfoliativa) 695.89
  winter vomiting 078.82
  Wise's 696.2
  Wohlfart-Kugelberg-Welander 335.11
  Woillez's (acute idiopathic pulmonary
    congestion) 518.5
  Wolman's (primary familial xanthomatosis)
    272.7
  wool-sorters' 022.1
  Zagari's (xerostomia) 527.7
  Zahorsky's (exanthem subitum) 057.8
  Ziehen-Oppenheim 333.6
  zoonotic, bacterial NEC 027.9
    specified type NEC 027.8
Disfigurement (due to scar) 709.2
  head V48.6
  limb V49.4
  neck V48.7
  trunk V48.7
Disgerminoma —*see* Dysgerminoma
Disinsertion, retina 361.04
Disintegration, complete, of the body 799.8
  traumatic 869.1
Disk kidney 753.3
Dislocatable hip, congenita l (*see also*
  Dislocation, hip, congenital) 754.30
Dislocation (articulation) (closed) (displacement)
  (simple) (subluxation) 839.8

---

*Note—"Closed" includes simple, complete,
partial, uncomplicated, and unspecified
dislocation. "Open" includes dislocation
specified as infected or compound and
dislocation with foreign body. "Chronic,"
"habitual," "old," or "recurrent" dislocations
should be coded as indicated under the entry
"Dislocation, recurrent"; and "pathological"
as indicated under the entry "Dislocation,
pathological." For late effect of dislocation see
Late, effect, dislocation.*

---

  with fracture—*see* Fracture, by site

Dislocation—*continued*
  acromioclavicular (joint) (closed) 831.04
    open 831.14
  anatomical site (closed)
    specified NEC 839.69
      open 839.79
    unspecified or ill-defined 839.8
      open 839.9
  ankle (scaphoid bone) (closed) 837.0
    open 837.1
  arm (closed) 839.8
    open 839.9
  astragalus (closed) 837.0
    open 837.1
  atlanto-axial (closed) 839.01
    open 839.11
  atlas (closed) 839.01
    open 839.11
  axis (closed) 839.02
    open 839.12
  back (closed) 839.8
    open 839.9
  Bell-Daly 723.8
  breast bone (closed) 839.61
    open 839.71
  capsule, joint—*see* Dislocation, by site
  carpal (bone)—*see* Dislocation, wrist
  carpometacarpal (joint) (closed) 833.04
    open 833.14
  cartilage (joint)—*see also* Dislocation, by site
    knee—*see* Tear, meniscus
  cervical, cervicodorsal, or cervicothoracic
    (spine) (vertebra)—*see* Dislocation,
    vertebra, cervical
  chiropractic (*see also* Lesion, nonallopathic)
    739.9
  chondrocostal—*see* Dislocation, costochondral
  chronic—*see* Dislocation, recurrent
  clavicle (closed) 831.04
    open 831.14
  coccyx (closed) 839.41
    open 839.51
  collar bone (closed) 831.04
    open 831.14
  compound (open) NEC 839.9
  congenital NEC 755.8
    hip (*see also* Dislocation, hip, congenital)
      754.30
    lens 743.37
    rib 756.3
    sacroiliac 755.69
    spine NEC 756.19
    vertebra 756.19
  coracoid (closed) 831.09
    open 831.19
  costal cartilage (closed) 839.69
    open 839.79
  costochondral (closed) 839.69
    open 839.79
  cricoarytenoid articulation (closed) 839.69
    open 839.79
  cricothyroid (cartilage) articulation (closed)
    839.69
    open 839.79
  dorsal vertebrae (closed) 839.21
    open 839.31
  ear ossicle 385.23
  elbow (closed) 832.00
    anterior (closed) 832.01
      open 832.11
    congenital 754.89

Dislocation—*continued*
  coccyx 839.41
    open 839.51
    congenital 756.19
    due to birth trauma 767.4
    open 839.50
    recurrent 724.9
    sacroiliac 839.42
      recurrent 724.6
    sacrum (sacrococcygeal) (sacroiliac) 839.42
      open 839.52
  spontaneous—*see* Dislocation, pathological
  sternoclavicular (joint) (closed) 839.61
    open 839.71
  sternum (closed) 839.61
    open 839.71
  subastragalar—*see* Dislocation, foot
  subglenoid (closed) 831.01
    open 831.11
  symphysis
    jaw (closed) 830.0
      open 830.1
    mandibular (closed) 830.0
      open 830.1
    pubis (closed) 839.69
      open 839.79
  tarsal (bone) (joint) 838.01
    open 838.11
  tarsometatarsal (joint) 838.03
    open 838.13
  temporomandibular (joint) (closed) 830.0
    open 830.1
    recurrent 524.69
  thigh
    distal end (*see also* Dislocation, femur, distal
      end) 836.50
    proximal end (*see also* Dislocation, hip)
      835.00
  thoracic (vertebrae) (closed) 839.21
    open 839.31
  thumb(s) (*see also* Dislocation, finger) 834.00
  thyroid cartilage (closed) 839.69
    open 839.79
  tibia
    distal end (closed) 837.0
      open 837.1
    proximal end (closed) 836.50
      anterior 836.51
        open 836.61
      lateral 836.54
        open 836.64
      medial 836.53
        open 836.63
      open 836.60
      posterior 836.52
        open 836.62
      rotatory 836.59
        open 836.69
  tibiofibular
    distal (closed) 837.0
      open 837.1
    superior (closed) 836.59
      open 836.69
  toe(s) (closed) 838.09
    open 838.19
  trachea (closed) 839.69
    open 839.79
  ulna
    distal end (closed) 833.09
      open 833.19
    proximal end—*see* Dislocation, elbow

Dislocation—*continued*
  vertebra (articular process) (body) (closed)
    839.40
    cervical, cervicodorsal or cervicothoracic
      (closed) 839.00
      first (atlas) 839.01
        open 839.11
      second (axis) 839.02
        open 839.12
      third 839.03
        open 839.13
      fourth 839.04
        open 839.14
      fifth 839.05
        open 839.15
      sixth 839.06
        open 839.16
      seventh 839.07
        open 839.17
      congenital 756.19
      multiple sites 839.08
        open 839.18
      open 839.10
    congenital 756.19
    dorsal 839.21
      open 839.31
      recurrent 724.9
    lumbar, lumbosacral 839.20
      open 839.30
    open NEC 839.50
    recurrent 724.9
    specified region NEC 839.49
      open 839.59
    thoracic 839.21
      open 839.31
  wrist (carpal bone) (scaphoid) (semilunar)
    (closed) 833.00
    carpometacarpal (joint) 833.04
      open 833.14
    metacarpal bone, proximal end 833.05
      open 833.15
    midcarpal (joint) 833.03
      open 833.13
    open 833.10
    radiocarpal (joint) 833.02
      open 833.12
    radioulnar (joint) 833.01
      open 833.11
    recurrent 718.33
    specified site NEC 833.09
      open 833.19
  xiphoid cartilage (closed) 839.61
    open 839.71
Dislodgement
  artificial skin graft 996.55
  decellularized allodermis graft 996.55
Disobedience, hostile (covert) (overt) (*see also*
  Disturbance, conduct) 312.0
Disorder —*see also* Disease
  academic underachievement, childhood and
    adolescence 313.83
  accommodation 367.51
    drug-induced 367.89
    toxic 367.89
  adjustment (*see also* Reaction, adjustment) 309.9
  adrenal (capsule) (cortex) (gland) 255.9
    specified type NEC 255.8
  adrenogenital 255.2
  affective (*see also* Psychosis, affective) 296.90
    atypical 296.81

Disorder—*continued*
  aggressive, unsocialized (*see also* Disturbance, conduct) 312.0
  alcohol, alcoholic (*see also* Alcohol) 291.9
  allergic—*see* Allergy
  amino acid (metabolic) (*see also* Disturbance, metabolism, amino acid) 270.9
    albinism 270.2
    alkaptonuria 270.2
    argininosuccinicaciduria 270.6
    beta-amino-isobutyricaciduria 277.2
    cystathioninuria 270.4
    cystinosis 270.0
    cystinuria 270.0
    glycinuria 270.0
    homocystinuria 270.4
    imidazole 270.5
    maple syrup (urine) disease 270.3
    neonatal, transitory 775.8
    oasthouse urine disease 270.2
    ochronosis 270.2
    phenylketonuria 270.1
    phenylpyruvic oligophrenia 270.1
    purine NEC 277.2
    pyrimidine NEC 277.2
    renal transport NEC 270.0
    specified type NEC 270.8
    transport NEC 270.0
      renal 270.0
    xanthinuria 277.2
  amnestic (*see also* Amnestic syndrome) 294.0
  anaerobic glycolysis with anemia 282.3
  anxiety (*see also* Anxiety) 300.00
    due to or associated with physical condition 293.84
  arteriole 447.9
    specified type NEC 447.8
  artery 447.9
    specified type NEC 447.8
  articulation—*see* Disorder, joint
  Asperger's 299.8
  attachment of infancy 313.89
  attention deficit 314.00
    with hyperactivity 314.01
    predominantly
      combined hyperactive/inattentive 314.01
      hyperactive/impulsive 314.01
      inattentive 314.00
    residual type 314.8
  autistic 299.0
  autoimmune NEC 279.4
    hemolytic (cold type) (warm type) 283.0
    parathyroid 252.1
    thyroid 245.2
  avoidant, childhood or adolescence 313.21
  balance
    acid-base 276.9
      mixed (with hypercapnia) 276.4
    electrolyte 276.9
    fluid 276.9
  behavior NEC (*see also* Disturbance, conduct) 312.9
  bilirubin excretion 277.4
  bipolar (affective) (alternating) (Type I) (*see also* Psychosis, affective) 296.7
    atypical 296.7
    currently
      depressed 296.5
      hypomanic 296.4
      manic 296.4
      mixed 296.6

Disorder—*continued*
    Type II (recurrent major depressive episodes with hypomania) 296.89
  bladder 596.9
    functional NEC 596.59
    specified NEC 596.8
  bone NEC 733.90
    specified NEC 733.99
  brachial plexus 353.0
  branched-chain amino-acid degradation 270.3
  breast 611.9
    puerperal, postpartum 676.3
    specified NEC 611.8
  Briquet's 300.81
  bursa 727.9
    shoulder region 726.10
  carbohydrate metabolism, congenital 271.9
  cardiac, functional 427.9
    postoperative 997.1
    psychogenic 306.2
  cardiovascular, psychogenic 306.2
  cartilage NEC 733.90
    articular 718.00
      ankle 718.07
      elbow 718.02
      foot 718.07
      hand 718.04
      hip 718.05
      knee 717.9
      multiple sites 718.09
      pelvic region 718.05
      shoulder region 718.01
      specified
        site NEC 718.08
        type NEC 733.99
      wrist 718.03
  catatonic—see Catatonia
  cervical region NEC 723.9
  cervical root (nerve) NEC 353.2
  character NEC (*see also* Disorder, personality) 301.9
  coagulation (factor) (*see also* Defect, coagulation) 286.9
    factor VIII (congenital) (functional) 286.0
    factor IX (congenital) (functional) 286.1
    neonatal, transitory 776.3
  coccyx 724.70
    specified NEC 724.79
  cognitive 294.9
  colon 569.9
    functional 564.9
      congenital 751.3
  conduct (*see also* Disturbance, conduct) 312.9
    adjustment reaction 309.3
    adolescent onset type 312.82
    childhood onset type 312.81
    compulsive 312.30
      specified type NEC 312.39
    hyperkinetic 314.2
    socialized (type) 312.20
      aggressive 312.23
      unaggressive 312.21
    specified NEC 312.89
  conduction, heart 426.9
    specified NEC 426.89
  convulsive (secondary) (*see also* Convulsions) 780.39
    due to injury at birth 767.0
    idiopathic 780.39
  coordination 781.3

Disorder—*continued*
  cornea NEC 371.89
    due to contact lens 371.82
  corticosteroid metabolism NEC 255.2
  cranial nerve—*see* Disorder, nerve, cranial
  cyclothymic 301.13
  degradation, branched-chain amino acid 270.3
  delusional 297.9
  dentition 520.6
  depressive NEC 311
    atypical 296.82
    major (*see also* Psychosis, affective) 296.2
      recurrent episode 296.3
      single episode 296.2
  development, specific 315.9
    associated with hyperkinesia 314.1
    language 315.31
    learning 315.2
      arithmetical 315.1
      reading 315.00
    mixed 315.5
    motor coordination 315.4
    specified type NEC 315.8
    speech 315.39
  diaphragm 519.4
  digestive 536.9
    fetus or newborn 777.9
      specified NEC 777.8
    psychogenic 306.4
  disintegrative (childhood) 299.1
  dissociative 300.14
    identity 300.14
  dysmorphic body 300.7
  dysthymic 300.4
  ear 388.9
    degenerative NEC 388.00
    external 380.9
      specified 380.89
    pinna 380.30
    specified type NEC 388.8
    vascular NEC 388.00
  eating NEC 307.50
  electrolyte NEC 276.9
    with
      abortion—*see* Abortion, by type, with
        metabolic disorder
      ectopic pregnancy (*see also* categories
        633.0-633.9) 639.4
      molar pregnancy (*see also* categories
        630-632) 639.4
    acidosis 276.2
      metabolic 276.2
      respiratory 276.2
    alkalosis 276.3
      metabolic 276.3
      respiratory 276.3
    following
      abortion 639.4
      ectopic or molar pregnancy 639.4
    neonatal, transitory NEC 775.5
  emancipation as adjustment reaction 309.22
  emotional (*see also* Disorder, mental,
    nonpsychotic) V40.9
  endocrine 259.9
    specified type NEC 259.8
  esophagus 530.9
    functional 530.5
    psychogenic 306.4
  explosive
    intermittent 312.34
    isolated 312.35

Disorder—*continued*
  expressive language 315.31
  eye 379.90
    globe—*see* Disorder, globe
    ill-defined NEC 379.99
    limited duction NEC 378.63
    specified NEC 379.8
  eyelid 374.9
    degenerative 374.50
    sensory 374.44
    specified type NEC 374.89
    vascular 374.85
  factitious —*see* Illness, factitious
  factor, coagulation (*see also* Defect,
    coagulation) 286.9
    VIII (congenital) (functional) 286.0
    IX (congenital) (functional) 286.1
  fascia 728.9
  feeding —*see* Feeding
  female sexual arousal 302.72
  fluid NEC 276.9
  gastric (functional) 536.9
    motility 536.8
    psychogenic 306.4
    secretion 536.8
  gastrointestinal (functional) NEC 536.9
    newborn (neonatal) 777.9
      specified NEC 777.8
    psychogenic 306.4
  gender (child) 302.6
    adult 302.85
  gender identity (childhood) 302.6
    adult-life 302.85
  genitourinary system, psychogenic 306.50
  globe 360.9
    degenerative 360.20
      specified NEC 360.29
    specified type NEC 360.89
  hearing—*see also* Deafness
    conductive type (air) (*see also* Deafness,
      conductive) 389.00
    mixed conductive and sensorineural 389.2
    nerve 389.12
    perceptive (*see also* Deafness, perceptive)
      389.10
    sensorineural type NEC (*see also* Deafness,
      perceptive) 389.10
  heart action 427.9
    postoperative 997.1
  hematological, transient neonatal 776.9
    specified type NEC 776.8
  hematopoietic organs 289.9
  hemorrhagic NEC 287.9
    due to circulating anticoagulants 286.5
    specified type NEC 287.8
  hemostasis (*see also* Defect, coagulation) 286.9
  homosexual conflict 302.0
  hypomanic (chronic) 301.11
  identity
    childhood and adolescence 313.82
      gender 302.6
    gender 302.6
  immune mechanism (immunity) 279.9
    single complement (C_1-C_9) 279.8
    specified type NEC 279.8
  impulse control (*see also* Disturbance, conduct,
    compulsive) 312.30
  infant sialic acid storage 271.8
  integument, fetus or newborn 778.9
    specified type NEC 778.8

Disorder—*continued*
  iron 275.0
  lactose 271.3
  lipid 272.9
    specified type NEC 272.8
    storage 272.7
  lipoprotein—*see also* Hyperlipemia
    deficiency (familial) 272.5
  lysine 270.7
  magnesium 275.2
  mannosidosis 271.8
  mineral 275.9
    specified type NEC 275.8
  mucopolysaccharide 277.5
  nitrogen 270.9
  ornithine 270.6
  oxalosis 271.8
  pentosuria 271.8
  phenylketonuria 270.1
  phosphate 275.3
  phosphorus 275.3
  plasma protein 273.9
    specified type NEC 273.8
  porphyrin 277.1
  purine 277.2
  pyrimidine 277.2
  serine 270.7
  sodium 276.9
  specified type NEC 277.8
  steroid 255.2
  threonine 270.7
  urea cycle 270.6
  xylose 271.8
 micturition NEC 788.69
  psychogenic 306.53
 misery and unhappiness, of childhood and
  adolescence 313.1
 mitral valve 424.0
 mood—*see* Psychosis, affective
 motor tic 307.20
  chronic 307.22
  transient, childhood 307.21
 movement NEC 333.90
  hysterical 300.11
  specified type NEC 333.99
  stereotypic 307.3
 mucopolysaccharide 277.5
 muscle 728.9
  psychogenic 306.0
  specified type NEC 728.3
 muscular attachments, peripheral—*see also*
  Enthesopathy
  spine 720.1
 musculoskeletal system NEC 729.9
  psychogenic 306.0
 myeloproliferative (chronic) NEC (M9960/1)
  238.7
 myoneural 358.9
  due to lead 358.2
  specified type NEC 358.8
  toxic 358.2
 myotonic 359.2
 neck region NEC 723.9
 nerve 349.9
  abducens NEC 378.54
  accessory 352.4
  acoustic 388.5
  auditory 388.5
  auriculotemporal 350.8
  axillary 353.0
  cerebral—*see* Disorder, nerve, cranial

Disorder—*continued*
  cranial 352.9
    first 352.0
    second 377.49
    third
      partial 378.51
      total 378.52
    fourth 378.53
    fifth 350.9
    sixth 378.54
    seventh NEC 351.9
    eighth 388.5
    ninth 352.2
    tenth 352.3
    eleventh 352.4
    twelfth 352.5
    multiple 352.6
  entrapment—*see* Neuropathy, entrapment
  facial 351.9
    specified NEC 351.8
  femoral 355.2
  glossopharyngeal NEC 352.2
  hypoglossal 352.5
  iliohypogastric 355.79
  ilioinguinal 355.79
  intercostal 353.8
  lateral
    cutaneous of thigh 355.1
    popliteal 355.3
  lower limb NEC 355.8
  medial, popliteal 355.4
  median NEC 354.1
  obturator 355.79
  oculomotor
    partial 378.51
    total 378.52
  olfactory 352.0
  optic 377.49
    ischemic 377.41
    nutritional 377.33
    toxic 377.34
  peroneal 355.3
  phrenic 354.8
  plantar 355.6
  pneumogastric 352.3
  posterior tibial 355.5
  radial 354.3
  recurrent laryngeal 352.3
  root 353.9
    specified NEC 353.8
  saphenous 355.79
  sciatic NEC 355.0
  specified NEC 355.9
    lower limb 355.79
    upper limb 354.8
  spinal 355.9
  sympathetic NEC 337.9
  trigeminal 350.9
    specified NEC 350.8
  trochlear 378.53
  ulnar 354.2
  upper limb NEC 354.9
  vagus 352.3
 nervous system NEC 349.9
  autonomic (peripheral) (*see also* Neuropathy,
    peripheral, autonomic) 337.9
  cranial 352.9
  parasympathetic (*see also* Neuropathy,
    peripheral, autonomic) 337.9
  specified type NEC 349.89

Disorder—*continued*
    sympathetic (*see also* Neuropathy, peripheral, autonomic) 337.9
    vegetative (*see also* Neuropathy, peripheral, autonomic) 337.9
  neurohypophysis NEC 253.6
  neurological NEC 781.99
    peripheral NEC 355.9
  neuromuscular NEC 358.9
    hereditary NEC 359.1
    specified NEC 358.8
    toxic 358.2
  neurotic 300.9
    specified type NEC 300.89
  neutrophil, polymorphonuclear (functional) 288.1
  obsessive-compulsive 300.3
  oppositional, childhood and adolescence 313.81
  optic
    chiasm 377.54
      associated with
        inflammatory disorders 377.54
        neoplasm NEC 377.52
          pituitary 377.51
        pituitary disorders 377.51
        vascular disorders 377.53
    nerve 377.49
    radiations 377.63
    tracts 377.63
  orbit 376.9
    specified NEC 376.89
  overanxious, of childhood and adolescence 313.0
  pancreas, internal secretion (other than diabetes mellitus) 251.9
    specified type NEC 251.8
  panic 300.01
    with agoraphobia 300.21
  papillary muscle NEC 429.81
  paranoid 297.9
    induced 297.3
    shared 297.3
  parathyroid 252.9
    specified type NEC 252.8
  paroxysmal, mixed 780.39
  pentose phosphate pathway with anemia 282.2
  personality 301.9
    affective 301.10
    aggressive 301.3
    amoral 301.7
    anancastic, anankastic 301.4
    antisocial 301.7
    asocial 301.7
    asthenic 301.6
    borderline 301.83
    compulsive 301.4
    cyclothymic 301.13
    dependent-passive 301.6
    dyssocial 301.7
    emotional instability 301.59
    epileptoid 301.3
    explosive 301.3
    following organic brain damage 310.1
    histrionic 301.50
    hyperthymic 301.11
    hypomanic (chronic) 301.11
    hypothymic 301.12
    hysterical 301.50
    immature 301.89
    inadequate 301.6
    introverted 301.21

Disorder—*continued*
    labile 301.59
    moral deficiency 301.7
    obsessional 301.4
    obsessive (-compulsive) 301.4
    overconscientious 301.4
    paranoid 301.0
    passive (-dependent) 301.6
    passive-aggressive 301.84
    pathological NEC 301.9
    pseudosocial 301.7
    psychopathic 301.9
    schizoid 301.20
      introverted 301.21
      schizotypal 301.22
    schizotypal 301.22
    seductive 301.59
    type A 301.4
    unstable 301.59
  pervasive developmental, childhood-onset 299.8
  pigmentation, choroid (congenital) 743.53
  pinna 380.30
    specified type NEC 380.39
  pituitary, thalamic 253.9
    anterior NEC 253.4
    iatrogenic 253.7
    postablative 253.7
    specified NEC 253.8
  pityriasis-like NEC 696.8
  platelets (blood) 287.1
  polymorphonuclear neutrophils (functional) 288.1
  porphyrin metabolism 277.1
  postmenopausal 627.9
    specified type NEC 627.8
  posttraumatic stress 309.81
    acute 308.3
    brief 308.3
    chronic 309.81
  psoriatic-like NEC 696.8
  psychic, with diseases classified elsewhere 316
  psychogenic NEC (*see also* condition) 300.9
    allergic NEC
      respiratory 306.1
    anxiety 300.00
      atypical 300.00
      generalized 300.02
    appetite 307.50
    articulation, joint 306.0
    asthenic 300.5
    blood 306.8
    cardiovascular (system) 306.2
    compulsive 300.3
    cutaneous 306.3
    depressive 300.4
    digestive (system) 306.4
    dysmenorrheic 306.52
    dyspneic 306.1
    eczematous 306.3
    endocrine (system) 306.6
    eye 306.7
    feeding 307.59
    functional NEC 306.9
    gastric 306.4
    gastrointestinal (system) 306.4
    genitourinary (system) 306.50
    heart (function) (rhythm) 306.2
    hemic 306.8
    hyperventilatory 306.1
    hypochondriacal 300.7
    hysterical 300.10

Disorder—*continued*
  steroid metabolism NEC 255.2
  stomach (functional) (*see also* Disorder, gastric)
    536.9
    psychogenic 306.4
  storage, iron 275.0
  stress (*see also* Reaction, stress, acute) 308.9
    posttraumatic
      acute 308.3
      brief 308.3
      chronic 309.81
  substitution 300.11
  suspected—*see* Observation
  synovium 727.9
  temperature regulation, fetus or newborn 778.4
  temporomandibular joint NEC 524.60
    specified NEC 524.69
  tendon 727.9
    shoulder region 726.10
  thoracic root (nerve) NEC 353.3
  thyrocalcitonin secretion 246.0
  thyroid (gland) NEC 246.9
    specified type NEC 246.8
  tic 307.20
    chronic (motor or vocal) 307.22
    motor-verbal 307.23
    organic origin 333.1
    transient of childhood 307.21
  tooth NEC 525.9
    development NEC 520.9
      specified type NEC 520.8
    eruption 520.6
      with abnormal position 524.3
    specified type NEC 525.8
  transport, carbohydrate 271.9
    specified type NEC 271.8
  tubular, phosphate-losing 588.0
  tympanic membrane 384.9
  unaggressive, unsocialized (*see also*
    Disturbance, conduct) 312.1
  undersocialized, unsocialized—*see also*
    Disturbance, conduct
    aggressive (type) 312.0
    unaggressive (type) 312.1
  vision, visual NEC 368.9
    binocular NEC 368.30
    cortex 377.73
      associated with
        inflammatory disorders 377.73
        neoplasms 377.71
        vascular disorders 377.72
    pathway NEC 377.63
      associated with
        inflammatory disorders 377.63
        neoplasms 377.61
        vascular disorders 377.62
  wakefulness (*see also* Hypersomnia) 780.54
    nonorganic origin (transient) 307.43
    persistent 307.44
Disorganized globe 360.29
Displacement, displaced

> *Note—For acquired displacement of*
> *bones,cartilage, joints, tendons, due to injury,*
> *see also Dislocation. Displacements at ages*
> *under one year should be considered*
> *congenital, provided there is no indication the*
> *condition was acquired after birth.*

  acquired traumatic of bond, cartilage, joint,
    tendon NEC (without fracture) (*see also*
    Dislocation) 839.8

Displacement, displaced—*continued*
  with fracture—*see* Fracture, by site
  adrenal gland (congenital) 759.1
  appendix, retrocecal (congenital) 751.5
  auricle (congenital) 744.29
  bladder (acquired) 596.8
    congenital 753.8
  brachial plexus (congenital) 742.8
  brain stem, caudal 742.4
  canaliculus lacrimalis 743.65
  cardia, through esophageal hiatus 750.6
  cerebellum, caudal 742.4
  cervix (*see also* Malposition, uterus) 621.6
  colon (congenital) 751.4
  device, implant, or graft—*see* Complications,
    mechanical
  epithelium
    columnar of cervix 622.1
    cuboidal, beyond limits of external os (uterus)
      752.49
  esophageal mucosa into cardia of stomach,
    congenital 750.4
  esophagus (acquired) 530.89
    congenital 750.4
  eyeball (acquired) (old) 376.36
    congenital 743.8
    current injury 871.3
    lateral 376.36
  fallopian tube (acquired) 620.4
    congenital 752.19
    opening (congenital) 752.19
  gallbladder (congenital) 751.69
  gastric mucosa 750.7
    into
      duodenum 750.7
      esophagus 750.7
      Meckel's diverticulum, congenital 750.7
  globe (acquired) (lateral) (old) 376.36
    current injury 871.3
  graft
    artificial skin graft 996.55
    decellularized allodermis graft 996.55
  heart (congenital) 746.87
    acquired 429.89
  hymen (congenital) (upward) 752.49
  internal prosthesis NEC—*see* Complications,
    mechanical
  intervertebral disc (with neuritis, radiculitis,
    sciatica, or other pain) 722.2
    with myelopathy 722.70
    cervical, cervicodorsal, cervicothoracic 722.0
      with myelopathy 722.71
      due to major trauma—*see* Dislocation,
        vertebra, cervical
    due to major trauma—*see* Dislocation,
      vertebra
    lumbar, lumbosacral 722.10
      with myelopathy 722.73
      due to major trauma—*see* Dislocation,
        vertebra, lumbar
    thoracic, thoracolumbar 722.11
      with myelopathy 722.72
      due to major trauma—*see* Dislocation,
        vertebra, thoracic
  intrauterine device 996.32
  kidney (acquired) 593.0
    congenital 753.3
  lacrimal apparatus or duct (congenital) 743.65
  macula (congenital) 743.55
  Meckel's diverticulum (congenital) 751.0

Displacement, displaced—*continued*
  nail (congenital) 757.5
    acquired 703.8
  opening of Wharton's duct in mouth 750.26
  organ or site, congenital NEC—*see*
    Malposition, congenital
  ovary (acquired) 620.4
    congenital 752.0
    free in peritoneal cavity (congenital) 752.0
    into hernial sac 620.4
  oviduct (acquired) 620.4
    congenital 752.19
  parathyroid (gland) 252.8
  parotid gland (congenital) 750.26
  punctum lacrimale (congenital) 743.65
  sacroiliac (congenital) (joint) 755.69
    current injury—*see* Dislocation, sacroiliac
    old 724.6
  spine (congenital) 756.19
  spleen, congenital 759.0
  stomach (congenital) 750.7
    acquired 537.89
  subglenoid (closed) 831.01
  sublingual duct (congenital) 750.26
  teeth, tooth 524.3
  tongue (congenital) (downward) 750.19
  trachea (congenital) 748.3
  ureter or ureteric opening or orifice (congenital)
    753.4
  uterine opening of oviducts or fallopian tubes
    752.19
  uterus, uterine (*see also* Malposition, uterus)
    621.6
    congenital 752.3
  ventricular septum 746.89
    with rudimentary ventricle 746.89
  xyphoid bone (process) 738.3
Disproportion 653.9
  affecting fetus or newborn 763.1
  caused by
    conjoined twins 653.7
    contraction, pelvis (general) 653.1
      inlet 653.2
      midpelvic 653.8
      midplane 653.8
      outlet 653.3
    fetal
      ascites 653.7
      hydrocephalus 653.6
      hydrops 653.7
      meningomyelocele 653.7
      sacral teratoma 653.7
      tumor 653.7
    hydrocephalic fetus 653.6
    pelvis, pelvic, abnormality (bony) NEC 653.0
    unusually large fetus 653.5
  causing obstructed labor 660.1
  cephalopelvic, normally formed fetus 653.4
    causing obstructed labor 660.1
  fetal NEC 653.5
    causing obstructed labor 660.1
  fetopelvic, normally formed fetus 653.4
    causing obstructed labor 660.1
  mixed maternal and fetal origin, normally
    formed fetus 653.4
  pelvis, pelvic (bony) NEC 653.1
    causing obstructed labor 660.1
  specified type NEC 653.8

Disruption
  cesarean wound 674.1
  family V61.0
  gastrointestinal anastomosis 997.4
  ligament(s)—*see also* Sprain
    knee
      current injury—*see* Dislocation, knee
      old 717.89
        capsular 717.85
        collateral (medial) 717.82
          lateral 717.81
        cruciate (posterior) 717.84
          anterior 717.83
        specified site NEC 717.85
  marital V61.10
    involving divorce or estrangement V61.0
  operation wound 998.3
  organ transplant, anastomosis site—*see*
    Complications, transplant, organ, by site
  ossicles, ossicular chain 385.23
    traumatic—*see* Fracture, skull, base
  parenchyma
    liver (hepatic)—*see* Laceration, liver, major
    spleen—*see* Laceration, spleen, parenchyma,
      massive
  phase-shift, of 24-hour sleep-wake cycle 780.55
    nonorganic origin 307.45
  sleep-wake cycle (24-hour) 780.55
    circadian rhythm 307.45
    nonorganic origin 307.45
  suture line (external) 998.3
    internal 998.3
  wound
    cesarean operation 674.1
    episiotomy 674.2
    operation 998.3
      cesarean 674.1
    perineal (obstetric) 674.2
    uterine 674.1
Disruptio uteri —*see also* Rupture, uterus
  complicating delivery—*see* Delivery,
    complicated, rupture, uterus
Dissatisfaction with
  employment V62.2
  school environment V62.3
Dissecting —*see* condition
Dissection
  aorta 441.00
    abdominal 441.02
    thoracic 441.01
    thoracoabdominal 441.03
  vascular 459.9
  wound—*see* Wound, open, by site
Disseminated —*see* condition
Dissociated personality NEC 300.15
Dissociation
  auriculoventricular or atrioventricular (any
    degree) (AV) 426.89
    with heart block 426.0
  interference 426.89
  isorhythmic 426.89
  rhythm
    atrioventricular (AV) 426.89
    interference 426.89
Dissociative
  identity disorder 300.14
  reaction NEC 300.15
Dissolution, vertebra (*see also* Osteoporosis)
  733.00

Distention
abdomen (gaseous) 787.3
bladder 596.8
cecum 569.89
colon 569.89
gallbladder 575.8
gaseous (abdomen) 787.3
intestine 569.89
kidney 593.89
liver 573.9
seminal vesicle 608.89
stomach 536.8
acute 536.1
psychogenic 306.4
ureter 593.5
uterus 621.8
Distichia, distichiasis (eyelid) 743.63
Distoma hepaticum infestation 121.3
Distomiasis 121.9
bile passages 121.3
due to Clonorchis sinensis 121.1
hemic 120.9
hepatic (liver) 121.3
due to Clonorchis sinensis (clonorchiasis)
121.1
intestinal 121.4
liver 121.3
due to Clonorchis sinensis 121.1
lung 121.2
pulmonary 121.2
Distomolar (fourth molar) 520.1
causing crowding 524.3
Disto-occlusion 524.2
Distortion (congenital)
adrenal (gland) 759.1
ankle (joint) 755.69
anus 751.5
aorta 747.29
appendix 751.5
arm 755.59
artery (peripheral) NEC (*see also* Distortion,
peripheral vascular system) 747.60
cerebral 747.81
coronary 746.85
pulmonary 747.3
retinal 743.58
umbilical 747.5
auditory canal 744.29
causing impairment of hearing 744.02
bile duct or passage 751.69
bladder 753.8
brain 742.4
bronchus 748.3
cecum 751.5
cervix (uteri) 752.49
chest (wall) 756.3
clavicle 755.51
clitoris 752.49
coccyx 756.19
colon 751.5
common duct 751.69
cornea 743.41
cricoid cartilage 748.3
cystic duct 751.69
duodenum 751.5
ear 744.29
auricle 744.29
causing impairment of hearing 744.02
causing impairment of hearing 744.09
external 744.29
causing impairment of hearing 744.02

Distortion—*continued*
inner 744.05
middle, except ossicles 744.03
ossicles 744.04
ossicles 744.04
endocrine (gland) NEC 759.2
epiglottis 748.3
Eustachian tube 744.24
eye 743.8
adnexa 743.69
face bone(s) 756.0
fallopian tube 752.19
femur 755.69
fibula 755.69
finger(s) 755.59
foot 755.67
gallbladder 751.69
genitalia, genital organ(s)
female 752.8
external 752.49
internal NEC 752.8
male 752.8
penis 752.69
glottis 748.3
gyri 742.4
hand bone(s) 755.59
heart (auricle) (ventricle) 746.89
valve (cusp) 746.89
hepatic duct 751.69
humerus 755.59
hymen 752.49
ileum 751.5
intestine (large) (small) 751.5
with anomalous adhesions, fixation or
malrotation 751.4
jaw NEC 524.8
jejunum 751.5
kidney 753.3
knee (joint) 755.64
labium (majus) (minus) 752.49
larynx 748.3
leg 755.69
lens 743.36
liver 751.69
lumbar spine 756.19
with disproportion (fetopelvic) 653.0
affecting fetus or newborn 763.1
causing obstructed labor 660.1
lumbosacral (joint) (region) 756.19
lung (fissures) (lobe) 748.69
nerve 742.8
nose 748.1
organ
of Corti 744.05
or site not listed—*see* Anomaly, specified
type NEC
ossicles, ear 744.04
ovary 752.0
oviduct 752.19
pancreas 751.7
parathyroid (gland) 759.2
patella 755.64
peripheral vascular system NEC 747.60
gastrointestinal 747.61
lower limb 747.64
renal 747.62
spinal 747.82
upper limb 747.63
pituitary (gland) 759.2
radius 755.59
rectum 751.5

Distortion—*continued*
rib 756.3
sacroiliac joint 755.69
sacrum 756.19
scapula 755.59
shoulder girdle 755.59
site not listed—*see* Anomaly, specified type
NEC
skull bone(s) 756.0
with
anencephalus 740.0
encephalocele 742.0
hydrocephalus 742.3
with spina bifida (*see also* Spina bifida)
741.0
microcephalus 742.1
spinal cord 742.59
spine 756.19
spleen 759.0
sternum 756.3
thorax (wall) 756.3
thymus (gland) 759.2
thyroid (gland) 759.2
cartilage 748.3
tibia 755.69
toe(s) 755.66
tongue 750.19
trachea (cartilage) 748.3
ulna 755.59
ureter 753.4
causing obstruction 753.20
urethra 753.8
causing obstruction 753.6
uterus 752.3
vagina 752.49
vein (peripheral) NEC (*see also* Distortion,
peripheral vascular system) 747.60
great 747.49
portal 747.49
pulmonary 747.49
vena cava (inferior) (superior) 747.49
vertebra 756.19
visual NEC 368.15
shape or size 368.14
vulva 752.49
wrist (bones) (joint) 755.59
Distress
abdomen 789.0
colon 789.0
emotional V40.9
epigastric 789.0
fetal (syndrome) 768.4
affecting management of pregnancy or
childbirth 656.3
liveborn infant 768.4
first noted
before onset of labor 768.2
during labor or delivery 768.3
stillborn infant (death before onset of labor)
768.0
death during labor 768.1
gastrointestinal (functional) 536.9
psychogenic 306.4
intestinal (functional) NEC 564.9
psychogenic 306.4
intrauterine (*see* Distress, fetal)
leg 729.5
maternal 669.0
mental V40.9
respiratory 786.09
acute (adult) 518.82

Distress—*continued*
adult syndrome (following shock, surgery, or
trauma) 518.5
specified NEC 518.82
fetus or newborn 770.8
syndrome (idiopathic) (newborn) 769
stomach 536.9
psychogenic 306.4
Distribution vessel, atypical NEC 747.60
coronary artery 746.85
spinal 747.82
Districhiasis 704.2
Disturbance —*see also* Disease
absorption NEC 579.9
calcium 269.3
carbohydrate 579.8
fat 579.8
protein 579.8
specified type NEC 579.8
vitamin (*see also* Deficiency, vitamin) 269.2
acid-base equilibrium 276.9
activity and attention, simple, with hyperkinesis
314.01
amino acid (metabolic) (*see also* Disorder,
amino acid) 270.9
imidazole 270.5
maple syrup (urine) disease 270.3
transport 270.0
assimilation, food 579.9
attention, simple 314.00
with hyperactivity 314.01
auditory, nerve, except deafness 388.5
behavior (*see also* Disturbance, conduct) 312.9
blood clotting (hypoproteinemia) (mechanism)
(*see also* Defect, coagulation) 286.9
central nervous system NEC 349.9
cerebral nerve NEC 352.9
circulatory 459.9
conduct 312.9

> *Note—Use the following fifth-digit*
> *subclassification with categories 312.0-312.2:*
>
> 0 *unspecified*
> 1 *mild*
> 2 *moderate*
> 3 *severe*

adjustment reaction 309.3
adolescent onset type 312.82
childhood onset type 312.81
compulsive 312.30
intermittent explosive disorder 312.34
isolated explosive disorder 312.35
kleptomania 312.32
pathological gambling 312.31
pyromania 312.33
hyperkinetic 314.2
intermittent explosive 312.34
isolated explosive 312.35
mixed with emotions 312.4
socialized (type) 312.20
aggressive 312.23
unaggressive 312.21
specified type NEC 312.89
undersocialized, unsocialized
aggressive (type) 312.0
unaggressive (type) 312.1
coordination 781.3
cranial nerve NEC 352.9
deep sensibility—*see* Disturbance, sensation

Disturbance—*continued*
  digestive 536.9
    psychogenic 306.4
  electrolyte—*see* Imbalance, electrolyte
  emotions specific to childhood and adolescence
      313.9
    with
      academic underachievement 313.83
      anxiety and fearfulness 313.0
      elective mutism 313.23
      identity disorder 313.82
      jealousy 313.3
      misery and unhappiness 313.1
      oppositional disorder 313.81
      overanxiousness 313.0
      sensitivity 313.21
      shyness 313.21
      social withdrawal 313.22
      withdrawal reaction 313.22
    involving relationship problems 313.3
    mixed 313.89
    specified type NEC 313.89
  endocrine (gland) 259.9
    neonatal, transitory 775.9
      specified NEC 775.8
  equilibrium 780.4
  feeding (elderly) (infant) 783.3
    newborn 779.3
    nonorganic origin NEC 307.59
    psychogenic NEC 307.59
  fructose metabolism 271.2
  gait 781.2
    hysterical 300.11
  gastric (functional) 536.9
    motility 536.8
    psychogenic 306.4
    secretion 536.8
  gastrointestinal (functional) 536.9
    psychogenic 306.4
  habit, child 307.9
  hearing, except deafness 388.40
  heart, functional (conditions classifiable to 426,
      427, 428)
    due to presence of (cardiac) prosthesis 429.4
    postoperative (immediate) 997.1
      long-term effect of cardiac surgery 429.4
    psychogenic 306.2
  hormone 259.9
  innervation uterus, sympathetic,
      parasympathetic 621.8
  keratinization NEC
    gingiva 523.1
    lip 528.5
    oral (mucosa) (soft tissue) 528.7
    tongue 528.7
  labyrinth, labyrinthine (vestibule) 386.9
  learning, specific NEC 315.2
  memory (*see also* Amnesia) 780.9
    mild, following organic brain damage 310.1
  mental (*see also* Disorder, mental) 300.9
    associated with diseases classified elsewhere
      316
  metabolism (acquired) (congenital) (*see also*
      Disorder, metabolism) 277.9
    with
      abortion—*see* Abortion, by type, with
        metabolic disorder
      ectopic pregnancy (*see also* categories
        633.0-633.9) 639.4
      molar pregnancy (*see also* categories
        630-632) 639.4

Disturbance—*continued*
  amino acid (*see also* Disorder, amino acid)
      270.9
    aromatic NEC 270.2
    branched-chain 270.3
    specified type NEC 270.8
    straight-chain NEC 270.7
    sulfur-bearing 270.4
    transport 270.0
  ammonia 270.6
  arginine 270.6
  argininosuccinic acid 270.6
  carbohydrate NEC 271.9
  cholesterol 272.9
  citrulline 270.6
  cystathionine 270.4
  fat 272.9
  following
    abortion 639.4
    ectopic or molar pregnancy 639.4
  general 277.9
    carbohydrate 271.9
    iron 275.0
    phosphate 275.3
    sodium 276.9
  glutamine 270.7
  glycine 270.7
  histidine 270.5
  homocystine 270.4
  in labor or delivery 669.0
  iron 275.0
  isoleucine 270.3
  leucine 270.3
  lipoid 272.9
    specified type NEC 272.8
  lysine 270.7
  methionine 270.4
  neonatal, transitory 775.9
    specified type NEC 775.8
  nitrogen 788.9
  ornithine 270.6
  phosphate 275.3
  phosphatides 272.7
  serine 270.7
  sodium NEC 276.9
  threonine 270.7
  tryptophan 270.2
  tyrosine 270.2
  urea cycle 270.6
  valine 270.3
  motor 796.1
  nervous functional 799.2
  neuromuscular mechanism (eye) due to syphilis
      094.84
  nutritional 269.9
    nail 703.8
  ocular motion 378.87
    psychogenic 306.7
  oculogyric 378.87
    psychogenic 306.7
  oculomotor NEC 378.87
    psychogenic 306.7
  olfactory nerve 781.1
  optic nerve NEC 377.49
  oral epithelium, including tongue 528.7
  personality (pattern) (trait) (*see also* Disorder,
      personality) 301.9
    following organic brain damage 310.1
  polyglandular 258.9
  psychomotor 307.9

Disturbance—*continued*
pupillary 379.49
reflex 796.1
rhythm, heart 427.9
postoperative (immediate) 997.1
long-term effect of cardiac surgery 429.4
psychogenic 306.2
salivary secretion 527.7
sensation (cold) (heat) (localization) (tactile
discrimination localization) (texture)
(vibratory) NEC 782.0
hysterical 300.11
skin 782.0
smell 781.1
taste 781.1
sensory (*see also* Disturbance, sensation) 782.0
innervation 782.0
situational (transient) (*see also* Reaction,
adjustment) 309.9
acute 308.3
sleep 780.50
initiation or maintenance (*see also* Insomnia)
780.52
nonorganic origin 307.41
nonorganic origin 307.40
specified type NEC 307.49
specified NEC 780.59
nonorganic origin 307.49
wakefulness (*see also* Hypersomnia) 780.54
nonorganic origin 307.43
with apnea—*see* Apnea, sleep
sociopathic 301.7
speech NEC 784.5
developmental 315.39
associated with hyperkinesis 314.1
secondary to organic lesion 784.5
stomach (functional) (*see also* Disturbance,
gastric) 536.9
sympathetic (nerve) (*see also* Neuropathy,
peripheral, autonomic) 337.9
temperature sense 782.0
hysterical 300.11
tooth
eruption 520.6
formation 520.4
structure, hereditary NEC 520.5
touch (*see also* Disturbance, sensation) 782.0
vascular 459.9
arteriosclerotic—*see* Arteriosclerosis
vasomotor 443.9
vasospastic 443.9
vestibular labyrinth 386.9
vision, visual NEC 368.9
psychophysical 368.16
specified NEC 368.8
subjective 368.10
voice 784.40
wakefulness (initiation or maintenance) (*see
also* Hypersomnia) 780.54
nonorganic origin 307.43
Disulfiduria, beta-mercaptolactate-cysteine 270.0
Disuse atrophy, bone 733.7
Ditthomska syndrome 307.81
Diuresis 788.42
Divers'
palsy or paralysis 993.3
squeeze 993.3

Diverticula, diverticulosis, diverticulum (acute)
(multiple) (perforated) (ruptured) 562.10
with diverticulitis 562.11
aorta (Kommerell's) 747.21
appendix (noninflammatory) 543.9
bladder (acquired) (sphincter) 596.3
congenital 753.8
broad ligament 620.8
bronchus (congenital) 748.3
acquired 494.0
with acute exacerbation 494.1
calyx, calyceal (kidney) 593.89
cardia (stomach) 537.1
cecum 562.10
with
diverticulitis 562.11
with hemorrhage 562.13
hemorrhage 562.12
congenital 751.5
colon (acquired) 562.10
with
diverticulitis 562.11
with hemorrhage 562.13
hemorrhage 562.12
congenital 751.5
duodenum 562.00
with
diverticulitis 562.01
with hemorrhage 562.03
hemorrhage 562.02
congenital 751.5
epiphrenic (esophagus) 530.6
esophagus (congenital) 750.4
acquired 530.6
epiphrenic 530.6
pulsion 530.6
traction 530.6
Zenker's 530.6
Eustachian tube 381.89
fallopian tube 620.8
gallbladder (congenital) 751.69
gastric 537.1
heart (congenital) 746.89
ileum 562.00
with
diverticulitis 562.01
with hemorrhage 562.03
hemorrhage 562.02
intestine (large) 562.10
with
diverticulitis 562.11
with hemorrhage 562.13
hemorrhage 562.12
congenital 751.5
small 562.00
with
diverticulitis 562.01
with hemorrhage 562.03
hemorrhage 562.02
congenital 751.5
jejunum 562.00
with
diverticulitis 562.01
with hemorrhage 562.03
hemorrhage 562.02
kidney (calyx) (pelvis) 593.89
with calculus 592.0
Kommerell's 747.21
laryngeal ventricle (congenital) 748.3
Meckel's (displaced) (hypertrophic) 751.0
midthoracic 530.6

Diverticula, diverticulosis—*continued*
  organ or site, congenital NEC—*see* Distortion
  pericardium (congenital) (cyst) 746.89
    acquired (true) 423.8
  pharyngoesophageal (pulsion) 530.6
  pharynx (congenital) 750.27
  pulsion (esophagus) 530.6
  rectosigmoid 562.10
    with
      diverticulitis 562.11
        with hemorrhage 562.13
      hemorrhage 562.12
    congenital 751.5
  rectum 562.10
    with
      diverticulitis 562.11
        with hemorrhage 562.13
      hemorrhage 562.12
  renal (calyces) (pelvis) 593.89
    with calculus 592.0
  Rokitansky's 530.6
  seminal vesicle 608.0
  sigmoid 562.10
    with
      diverticulitis 562.11
        with hemorrhage 562.13
      hemorrhage 562.12
    congenital 751.5
  small intestine 562.00
    with
      diverticulitis 562.01
        with hemorrhage 562.03
      hemorrhage 562.02
  stomach (cardia) (juxtacardia) (juxtapyloric)
      (acquired) 537.1
    congenital 750.7
  subdiaphragmatic 530.6
  trachea (congenital) 748.3
    acquired 519.1
  traction (esophagus) 530.6
  ureter (acquired) 593.89
    congenital 753.4
  ureterovesical orifice 593.89
  urethra (acquired) 599.2
    congenital 753.8
  ventricle, left (congenital) 746.89
  vesical (urinary) 596.3
    congenital 753.8
  Zenker's (esophagus) 530.6
Diverticulitis (acute) (*see also* Diverticula)
      562.11
  with hemorrhage 562.13
  bladder (urinary) 596.3
  cecum (perforated) 562.11
    with hemorrhage 562.13
  colon (perforated) 562.11
    with hemorrhage 562.13
  duodenum 562.01
    with hemorrhage 562.03
  esophagus 530.6
  ileum (perforated) 562.01
    with hemorrhage 562.03
  intestine (large) (perforated) 562.11
    with hemorrhage 562.13
    small 562.01
      with hemorrhage 562.03
  jejunum (perforated) 562.01
    with hemorrhage 562.03
  Meckel's (perforated) 751.0
  pharyngoesophageal 530.6

Diverticulitis—*continued*
  rectosigmoid (perforated) 562.11
    with hemorrhage 562.13
  rectum 562.11
    with hemorrhage 562.13
  sigmoid (old) (perforated) 562.11
    with hemorrhage 562.13
  small intestine (perforated) 562.01
    with hemorrhage 562.03
  vesical (urinary) 596.3
Diverticulosis —*see* Diverticula
Division
  cervix uteri 622.8
    external os into two openings by frenum
        752.49
  external (cervical) into two openings by frenum
      752.49
  glans penis 752.69
  hymen 752.49
  labia minora (congenital) 752.49
  ligament (partial or complete) (current)—*see
      also* Sprain, by site
    with open wound—*see* Wound, open, by site
  muscle (partial or complete) (current)—*see also*
      Sprain, by site
    with open wound—*see* Wound, open, by site
  nerve—*see* Injury, nerve, by site
  penis glans 752.69
  spinal cord—*see* Injury, spinal, by site
  vein 459.9
    traumatic—*see* Injury, vascular, by site
Divorce V61.0
Dix-Hallpike neurolabyrinthitis 386.12
Dizziness 780.4
  hysterical 300.11
  psychogenic 306.9
Doan-Wiseman syndrome (primary splenic
      neutropenia) 288.0
Dog bite —*see* Wound, open, by site
Döhle-Heller aortitis 093.1
Döhle body-panmyelopathic syndrome 288.2
Dolichocephaly, dolichocephalus 754.0
Dolichocolon 751.5
Dolichostenomelia 759.82
Donohue's syndrome (leprechaunism) 259.8
Donor
  blood V59.01
    other blood components V59.09
    stem cells V59.02
    whole blood V59.01
  bone V59.2
    marrow V59.3
  cornea V59.5
  heart V59.8
  kidney V59.4
  liver V59.6
  lung V59.8
  lymphocyte V59.8
  organ V59.9
    specified NEC V59.8
  potential, examination of V70.8
  skin V59.1
  specified organ or tissue NEC V59.8
  stem cells V59.02
  tissue V59.9
    specified type NEC V59.8
Donovanosis (granuloma venereum) 099.2
DOPS (diffuse obstructive pulmonary syndrome)
      496

Double
albumin 273.8
aortic arch 747.21
auditory canal 744.29
auricle (heart) 746.82
bladder 753.8
external (cervical) os 752.49
kidney with double pelvis (renal) 753.3
larynx 748.3
meatus urinarius 753.8
organ or site NEC—*see* Accessory
orifice
heart valve NEC 746.89
pulmonary 746.09
outlet, right ventricle 745.11
pelvis (renal) with double ureter 753.4
penis 752.69
tongue 750.13
ureter (one or both sides) 753.4
with double pelvis (renal) 753.4
urethra 753.8
urinary meatus 753.8
uterus (any degree) 752.2
with doubling of cervix and vagina 752.2
in pregnancy or childbirth 654.0
affecting fetus or newborn 763.89
vagina 752.49
with doubling of cervix and uterus 752.2
vision 368.2
vocal cords 748.3
vulva 752.49
whammy (syndrome) 360.81
Douglas' pouch, cul-de-sac —*see* condition
Down's disease or syndrome (mongolism) 758.0
Down-growth, epithelial (anterior chamber)
364.61
Dracontiasis 125.7
Dracunculiasis 125.7
Dracunculosis 125.7
Drainage
abscess (spontaneous)—*see* Abscess
anomalous pulmonary veins to hepatic veins or
right atrium 747.41
stump (amputation) (surgical) 997.62
suprapubic, bladder 596.8
Dream state, hysterical 300.13
Drepanocytic anemia (*see also* Disease, sickle
cell) 282.60
Dresbach's syndrome (elliptocytosis) 282.1
Dreschlera (infection) 118
hawaiiensis 117.8
Dressler's syndrome (postmyocardial infarction)
411.0
Dribbling (post-void) 788.35
Drift, ulnar 736.09
Drinking (alcohol)—*see also* Alcoholism
excessive, to excess NEC (*see also* Abuse,
drugs, nondependent) 305.0
bouts, periodic 305.0
continual 303.9
episodic 305.0
habitual 303.9
periodic 305.0
Drip, postnasal (chronic)—*see* Sinusitis
Drivers' license examination V70.3
Droop, Cooper's 611.8
Drop
finger 736.29
foot 736.79
hematocrit (precipitous) 790.01
toe 735.8
wrist 736.05

Dropped
dead 798.1
heart beats 426.6
Dropsy, dropsical (*see also* Edema) 782.3
abdomen 789.5
amnion (*see also* Hydramnios) 657
brain—*see* Hydrocephalus
cardiac (*see also* Failure, heart, congestive)
428.0
cardiorenal (*see also* Hypertension, cardiorenal)
404.90
chest 511.9
fetus or newborn 778.0
due to isoimmunization 773.3
gangrenous (*see also* Gangrene) 785.4
heart (*see also* Failure, heart, congestive) 428.0
hepatic—*see* Cirrhosis, liver
infantile—*see* Hydrops, fetalis
kidney (*see also* Nephrosis) 581.9
liver—*see* Cirrhosis, liver
lung 514
malarial (*see also* Malaria) 084.9
neonatorum—*see* Hydrops, fetalis
nephritic 581.9
newborn—*see* Hydrops, fetalis
nutritional 269.9
ovary 620.8
pericardium (*see also* Pericarditis) 423.9
renal (*see also* Nephrosis) 581.9
uremic—*see* Uremia
Drowned, drowning 994.1
lung 518.5
Drowsiness 780.09
Drug —*see also* condition
addiction (*see also* listing under Dependence)
304.9
adverse effect NEC, correct substance properly
administered 995.2
dependence (*see also* listing under Dependence)
304.9
habit (*see also* listing under Dependence) 304.9
overdose—*see* Table of drugs and chemicals
poisoning—*see* Table of drugs and chemicals
therapy (maintenance) status NEC V58.1
long-term (current) use V58.69
antibiotics V58.62
anticoagulant V58.61
wrong substance given or taken in error—*see*
Table of drugs and chemicals
Drunkenness (*see also* Abuse, drugs,
nondependent) 305.0
acute in alcoholism (*see also* Alcoholism) 303.0
chronic (*see also* Alcoholism) 303.9
pathologic 291.4
simple (acute) 305.0
in alcoholism 303.0
sleep 307.47
Drusen
optic disc or papilla 377.21
retina (colloid) (hyaloid degeneration) 362.57
hereditary 362.77
Drusenfieber 075
Dry, dryness —*see also* condition
eye 375.15
syndrome 375.15
larynx 478.79
mouth 527.7
nose 478.1
skin syndrome 701.1
socket (teeth) 526.5
throat 478.29

DSAP (disseminated superficial actinic
  porokeratosis) 692.75
Duane's retraction syndrome 378.71
Duane-Stilling-Turk syndrome (ocular
  retraction syndrome) 378.71
Dubin-Johnson disease or syndrome 277.4
Dubini's disease (electric chorea) 049.8
Dubois' abscess or disease 090.5
Duchenne's
  disease 094.0
    locomotor ataxia 094.0
    muscular dystrophy 359.1
    pseudohypertrophy, muscles 359.1
  paralysis 335.22
  syndrome 335.22
Duchenne-Aran myelopathic muscular atrophy
  (nonprogressive) (progressive) 335.21
Duchenne-Griesinger disease 359.1
Ducrey's
  bacillus 099.0
  chancre 099.0
  disease (chancroid) 099.0
Duct, ductus —*see* condition
Duengero 061
Duhring's disease (dermatitis herpetiformis)
  694.0
Dukes (-Filatov) disease 057.8
Dullness
  cardiac (decreased) (increased) 785.3
Dumb ague (*see also* Malaria) 084.6
Dumbness (*see also* Aphasia) 784.3
Dumdum fever 085.0
Dumping syndrome (postgastrectomy) 564.2
  nonsurgical 536.8
Duodenitis (nonspecific) (peptic) 535.60
  due to
    Strongyloides stercoralis 127.2
  with hemorrhage 535.61
Duodenocholangitis 575.8
Duodenum, duodenal —*see* condition
Duplay's disease, periarthritis, or syndrome 726.2
Duplex —*see also* Accessory
  kidney 753.3
  placenta—*see* Placenta, abnormal
  uterus 752.2
Duplication —*see also* Accessory
  anus 751.5
  aortic arch 747.21
  appendix 751.5
  biliary duct (any) 751.69
  bladder 753.8
  cecum 751.5
    and appendix 751.5
  clitoris 752.49
  cystic duct 751.69
  digestive organs 751.8
  duodenum 751.5
  esophagus 750.4
  fallopian tube 752.19
  frontonasal process 756.0
  gallbladder 751.69
  ileum 751.5
  intestine (large) (small) 751.5
  jejunum 751.5
  kidney 753.3
  liver 751.69
  nose 748.1
  pancreas 751.7
  penis 752.69
  respiratory organs NEC 748.9
  salivary duct 750.22

Duplication—*continued*
  spinal cord (incomplete) 742.51
  stomach 750.7
  ureter 753.4
  vagina 752.49
  vas deferens 752.8
  vocal cords 748.3
Dupré's disease or syndrome (meningism) 781.6
Dupuytren's
  contraction 728.6
  disease (muscle contracture) 728.6
  fracture (closed) 824.4
    ankle (closed) 824.4
      open 824.5
    fibula (closed) 824.4
      open 824.5
    open 824.5
    radius (closed) 813.42
      open 813.52
  muscle contracture 728.6
Durand-Nicolas-Favre disease (climatic bubo)
  099.1
Duroziez's disease (congenital mitral stenosis)
  746.5
Dust
  conjunctivitis 372.05
  reticulation (occupational) 504
Dutton's
  disease (trypanosomiasis) 086.9
  relapsing fever (West African) 087.1
Dwarf, dwarfism 259.4
  with infantilism (hypophyseal) 253.3
  achondroplastic 756.4
  Amsterdam 759.89
  bird-headed 759.89
  congenital 259.4
  constitutional 259.4
  hypophyseal 253.3
  infantile 259.4
  Levi type 253.3
  Lorain-Levi (pituitary) 253.3
  Lorain type (pituitary) 253.3
  metatropic 756.4
  nephrotic-glycosuric, with hypophosphatemic
    rickets 270.0
  nutritional 263.2
  ovarian 758.6
  pancreatic 577.8
  pituitary 253.3
  polydystrophic 277.5
  primordial 253.3
  psychosocial 259.4
  renal 588.0
    with hypertension—*see* Hypertension, kidney
  Russell's (uterine dwarfism and craniofacial
    dysostosis) 759.89
Dyke-Young anemia or syndrome (acquired
  macrocytic hemolytic anemia) (secondary)
  (symptomatic) 283.9
Dynia abnormality (*see also* Defect,
  coagulation) 286.9
Dysacousis 388.40
Dysadrenocortism 255.9
  hyperfunction 255.3
  hypofunction 255.4
Dysarthria 784.5
Dysautonomia (*see also* Neuropathy, peripheral,
  autonomic) 337.9
  familial 742.8
Dysbarism 993.3

Dysbasia 719.7
  angiosclerotica intermittens 443.9
    due to atherosclerosis 440.21
  hysterical 300.11
  lordotica (progressiva) 333.6
  nonorganic origin 307.9
  psychogenic 307.9
Dysbetalipoproteinemia (familial) 272.2
Dyscalculia 315.1
Dyschezia (*see also* Constipation) 564.0
Dyschondroplasia (with hemangiomata) 756.4
  Voorhoeve's 756.4
Dyschondrosteosis 756.59
Dyschromia 709.00
Dyscollagenosis 710.9
Dyscoria 743.41
Dyscraniopyophalangy 759.89
Dyscrasia
  blood 289.9
    with antepartum hemorrhage 641.3
    fetus or newborn NEC 776.9
    hemorrhage, subungual 287.8
    puerperal, postpartum 666.3
  ovary 256.8
  plasma cell 273.9
  pluriglandular 258.9
  polyglandular 258.9
Dysdiadochokinesia 781.3
Dysectasia, vesical neck 596.8
Dysendocrinism 259.9
Dysentery, dysenteric (bilious) (catarrhal)
    (diarrhea) (epidemic) (gangrenous)
    (hemorrhagic) (infectious) (sporadic)
    (tropical) (ulcerative) 009.0
  abscess, liver (*see also* Abscess, amebic) 006.3
  amebic (*see also* Amebiasis) 006.9
    with abscess—*see* Abscess, amebic
    acute 006.0
    carrier (suspected) of V02.2
    chronic 006.1
  arthritis (*see also* Arthritis, due to, dysentery)
    009.0 *[711.3]*
    bacillary 004.9 *[711.3]*
  asylum 004.9
  bacillary 004.9
    arthritis 004.9 *[711.3]*
    Boyd 004.2
    Flexner 004.1
    Schmitz (-Stutzer) 004.0
    Shiga 004.0
    Shigella 004.9
      group A 004.0
      group B 004.1
      group C 004.2
      group D 004.3
      specified type NEC 004.8
    Sonne 004.3
    specified type NEC 004.8
  bacterium 004.9
  balantidial 007.0
  Balantidium coli 007.0
  Boyd's 004.2
  Chilomastix 007.8
  Chinese 004.9
  choleriform 001.1
  coccidial 007.2
  Dientamoeba fragilis 007.8
  due to specified organism NEC—*see* Enteritis,
    due to, by organism
  Embadomonas 007.8
  Endolimax nana—*see* Dysentery, amebic

Dysentery, dysenteric—*continued*
  Entamoba, entamebic—*see* Dysentery, amebic
  Flexner's 004.1
  Flexner-Boyd 004.2
  giardial 007.1
  Giardia lamblia 007.1
  Hiss-Russell 004.1
  lamblia 007.1
  leishmanial 085.0
  malarial (*see also* Malaria) 084.6
  metazoal 127.9
  Monilia 112.89
  protozoal NEC 007.9
  Russell's 004.8
  salmonella 003.0
  schistosomal 120.1
  Schmitz (-Stutzer) 004.0
  Shiga 004.0
  Shigella NEC (*see also* Dysentery, bacillary)
    004.9
    boydii 004.2
    dysenteriae 004.0
      Schmitz 004.0
      Shiga 004.0
    flexneri 004.1
    Group A 004.0
    Group B 004.1
    Group C 004.2
    Group D 004.3
    Schmitz 004.0
    Shiga 004.0
    Sonnei 004.3
  Sonne 004.3
  strongyloidiasis 127.2
  trichomonal 007.3
  tuberculous (*see also* Tuberculosis) 014.8
  viral (*see also* Enteritis, viral) 008.8
Dysequilibrium 780.4
Dysesthesia 782.0
  hysterical 300.11
Dysfibrinogenemia (congenital) (*see also*
  Defect, coagulation) 286.3
Dysfunction
  adrenal (cortical) 255.9
    hyperfunction 255.3
    hypofunction 255.4
  associated with sleep stages or arousal from
    sleep 780.56
    nonorganic origin 307.47
  bladder NEC 596.59
  bleeding, uterus 626.8
  brain, minimal (*see also* Hyperkinesia) 314.9
  cerebral 348.3
  colon 564.9
    psychogenic 306.4
  colostomy or enterostomy 569.62
  cystic duct 575.8
  diastolic 429.9
    with heart failure—*see* Failure, heart
    due to
      cardiomyopathy—*see* Cardiomyopathy
      hypertension—*see* Hypertension, heart
  endocrine NEC 259.9
  endometrium 621.8
  enteric stoma 569.62
  enterostomy 569.62
  Eustachian tube 381.81
  gallbladder 575.8
  gastrointestinal 536.9
  gland, glandular NEC 259.9

Dysfunction—*continued*
  heart 427.9
    postoperative (immediate) 997.1
      long-term effect of cardiac surgery 429.4
  hemoglobin 288.8
  hepatic 573.9
  hepatocellular NEC 573.9
  hypophysis 253.9
    hyperfunction 253.1
    hypofunction 253.2
    posterior lobe 253.6
      hypofunction 253.5
  kidney (*see also* Disease, renal) 593.9
  labyrinthine 386.50
    specified NEC 386.58
  liver 573.9
    constitutional 277.4
  minimal brain (child) (*see also* Hyperkinesia)
    314.9
  ovary, ovarian 256.9
    hyperfunction 256.1
      estrogen 256.0
    hypofunction 256.3
      postablative 256.2
    postablative 256.2
    specified NEC 256.8
  papillary muscle 429.81
    with myocardial infarction 410.8
  parathyroid 252.8
    hyperfunction 252.0
    hypofunction 252.1
  pineal gland 259.8
  pituitary (gland) 253.9
    hyperfunction 253.1
    hypofunction 253.2
    posterior 253.6
      hypofunction 253.5
  placental—*see* Placenta, insufficiency
  platelets (blood) 287.1
  polyglandular 258.9
    specified NEC 258.8
  psychosexual 302.70
    with
      dyspareunia (functional) (psychogenic)
        302.76
      frigidity 302.72
      impotence 302.72
      inhibition
        orgasm
          female 302.73
          male 302.74
        sexual
          desire 302.71
          excitement 302.72
      premature ejaculation 302.75
      sexual aversion 302.79
      specified disorder NEC 302.79
      vaginismus 306.51
  pylorus 537.9
  rectum 564.9
    psychogenic 306.4
  segmental (*see also* Dysfunction, somatic) 739.9
  senile 797
  sinoatrial node 427.81
  somatic 739.9
    abdomen 739.9
    acromioclavicular 739.7
    cervical 739.1
    cervicothoracic 739.1
    costochondral 739.8
    costovertebral 739.8

Dysfunction—*continued*
  extremities
    lower 739.6
    upper 739.7
  head 739.0
  hip 739.5
  umbar, lumbosacral 739.3
  occipitocervical 739.0
  pelvic 739.5
  pubic 739.5
  rib cage 739.8
  sacral 739.4
  sacrococcygeal 739.4
  sacroiliac 739.4
  specified site NEC 739.9
  sternochondral 739.8
  sternoclavicular 739.7
  temporomandibular 739.0
  thoracic, thoracolumbar 739.2
  stomach 536.9
    psychogenic 306.4
  suprarenal 255.9
    hyperfunction 255.3
    hypofunction 255.4
  symbolic NEC 784.60
    specified type NEC 784.69
  temporomandibular (joint)
    (joint-pain-syndrome) NEC 524.60
    specified NEC 524.69
  testicular 257.9
    hyperfunction 257.0
    hypofunction 257.2
    specified type NEC 257.8
  thymus 254.9
  thyroid 246.9
    complicating pregnancy, childbirth, or
      puerperium 648.1
    hyperfunction—*see* Hyperthyroidism
    hypofunction—*see* Hypothyroidism
  uterus, complicating delivery 661.9
    affecting fetus or newborn 763.7
    hypertonic 661.4
    hypotonic 661.2
      primary 661.0
      secondary 661.1
  velopharyngeal (acquired) 528.9
    congenital 750.29
  ventricular 429.9
    with congestive heart failure (*see also* Failure,
      heart, congestive) 428.0
    due to
      cardiomyopathy—*see* Cardiomyopathy
      hypertension—*see* Hypertension, heart
  vesicourethral NEC 596.59
  vestibular 386.50
    specified type NEC 386.58
Dysgammaglobulinemia 279.06
Dysgenesis
  gonadal (due to chromosomal anomaly) 758.6
    pure 752.7
  kidney(s) 753.0
  ovarian 758.6
  renal 753.0
  reticular 279.2
  seminiferous tubules 758.6
  tidal platelet 287.3
Dysgerminoma (M9060/3)
  specified site—*see* Neoplasm, by site, malignant
  unspecified site
    female 183.0
    male 186.9
Dysgeusia 781.1

Dysgraphia 781.3
Dyshidrosis 705.81
Dysidrosis 705.81
Dysinsulinism 251.8
Dyskaryotic cervical smear 795.0
Dyskeratosis (*see also* Keratosis) 701.1
  bullosa hereditaria 757.39
  cervix 622.1
  congenital 757.39
  follicularis 757.39
    vitamin A deficiency 264.8
  gingiva 523.8
  oral soft tissue NEC 528.7
  tongue 528.7
  uterus NEC 621.8
Dyskinesia 781.3
  biliary 575.8
  esophagus 530.5
  hysterical 300.11
  intestinal 564.89
  nonorganic origin 307.9
  orofacial 333.82
  psychogenic 307.9
  tardive (oral) 333.82
Dyslalia 784.5
  developmental 315.39
Dyslexia 784.61
  developmental 315.02
  secondary to organic lesion 784.61
Dysmaturity (*see also* Immaturity) 765.1
  lung 770.4
  pulmonary 770.4
Dysmenorrhea (essential) (exfoliative)
  (functional) (intrinsic) (membranous)
  (primary) (secondary) 625.3
  psychogenic 306.52
Dysmetria 781.3
Dysmorodystrophia mesodermalis congenita
  759.82
Dysnomia 784.3
Dysorexia 783.0
  hysterical 300.11
Dysostosis
  cleidocranial, cleidocranialis 755.59
  craniofacial 756.0
  Fairbank's (idiopathic familial generalized
    osteophytosis) 756.50
  mandibularis 756.0
  mandibulofacial, incomplete 756.0
  multiplex 277.5
  orodigitofacial 759.89
Dyspareunia (female) 625.0
  male 608.89
  psychogenic 302.76
Dyspepsia (allergic) (congenital) (fermentative)
  (flatulent) (functional) (gastric)
  (gastrointestinal) (neurogenic) (occupational)
  (reflex) 536.8
  acid 536.8
  atonic 536.3
    psychogenic 306.4
  diarrhea 558.9
    psychogenic 306.4
  intestinal 564.89
    psychogenic 306.4
  nervous 306.4
  neurotic 306.4
  psychogenic 306.4

Dysphagia 787.2
  functional 300.11
  hysterical 300.11
  nervous 300.11
  psychogenic 306.4
  sideropenic 280.8
  spastica 530.5
Dysphagocytosis, congenital 288.1
Dysphasia 784.5
Dysphonia 784.49
  clericorum 784.49
  functional 300.11
  hysterical 300.11
  psychogenic 306.1
  spastica 478.79
Dyspigmentation —*see also* Pigmentation
  eyelid (acquired) 374.52
Dyspituitarism 253.9
  hyperfunction 253.1
  hypofunction 253.2
  posterior lobe 253.6
Dysplasia —*see also* Anomaly
  artery
    fibromuscular NEC 447.8
      carotid 447.8
      renal 447.3
  bladder 596.8
  bone (fibrous) NEC 733.29
    diaphyseal, progressive 756.59
    jaw 526.89
    monostotic 733.29
    polyostotic 756.54
    solitary 733.29
  brain 742.9
  bronchopulmonary, fetus or newborn 770.7
  cervix (uteri) 622.1
    cervical intraepithelial neoplasia I [CIN 1]
      622.1
    cervical intraepithelial neoplasia II [CIN II]
      622.1
    cervical intraepithelial neoplasia III [CIN III]
      233.1
    CIN I 622.1
    CIN II 622.1
    CIN III 233.1
  chondroectodermal 756.55
  chondromatose 756.4
  craniocarpotarsal 759.89
  craniometaphyseal 756.89
  dentinal 520.5
  diaphyseal, progressive 756.59
  ectodermal (anhidrotic) (Bason) (Clouston's)
    (congenital) (Feinmesser) (hereditary)
    (hidrotic) (Marshall) (Robinson's) 757.31
  epiphysealis 756.9
    multiplex 756.56
    punctata 756.59
  epiphysis 756.9
    multiple 756.56
  epithelial
    epiglottis 478.79
    uterine cervix 622.1
  erythroid NEC 289.8
  eye (*see also* Microphthalmos) 743.10
  familial metaphyseal 756.89
  fibromuscular, artery NEC 447.8
    carotid 447.8
    renal 447.3
  fibrous
    bone NEC 733.29
    diaphyseal, progressive 756.59

E

Eagle-Barrett syndrome 756.71
Eales' disease (syndrome) 362.18
Ear —*see also* condition
  ache 388.70
    otogenic 388.71
    referred 388.72
  lop 744.29
  piercing V50.3
  swimmers' acute 380.12
  tank 380.12
  tropical 111.8 *[380.15]*
  wax 380.4
Earache 388.70
  otogenic 388.71
  referred 388.72
Eaton-Lambert syndrome (*see also* Neoplasm,
  by site, malignant) 199.1 *[358.1]*
Eberth's disease (typhoid fever) 002.0
Ebstein's
  anomaly or syndrome (downward displacement,
    tricuspid valve into right ventricle) 746.2
  disease (diabetes) 250.4 *[581.81]*
Eccentro-osteochondrodysplasia 277.5
Ecchondroma (M9210/0)—*see* Neoplasm, bone,
  benign
Ecchondrosis (M9210/1) 238.0
Ecchordosis physaliphora 756.0
Ecchymosis (multiple) 459.89
  conjunctiva 372.72
  eye (traumatic) 921.0
  eyelids (traumatic) 921.1
  newborn 772.6
  spontaneous 782.7
  traumatic—*see* Contusion
Echinococciasis —*see* Echinococcus
Echinococcosis —*see* Echinococcus
Echinococcus (infection) 122.9
  granulosus 122.4
    liver 122.0
    lung 122.1
    orbit 122.3 *[376.13]*
    specified site NEC 122.3
    thyroid 122.2
  liver NEC 122.8
    granulosus 122.0
    multilocularis 122.5
  lung NEC 122.9
    granulosus 122.1
    multilocularis 122.6
  multilocularis 122.7
    liver 122.5
    specified site NEC 122.6
  orbit 122.9 *[376.13]*
    granulosus 122.3 *[376.13]*
    multilocularis 122.6 *[376.13]*
  specified site NEC 122.9
    granulosus 122.3
    multilocularis 122.6 *[376.13]*
  thyroid NEC 122.9
    granulosus 122.2
    multilocularis 122.6
Echinorhynchiasis 127.7
Echinostomiasis 121.8
Echolalia 784.69
ECHO virus infection NEC 079.1

Eclampsia, eclamptic (coma) (convulsions)
  (delirium) 780.39
  female, child-bearing age NEC—*see* Eclampsia,
    pregnancy
  gravidarum—*see* Eclampsia, pregnancy
  male 780.39
  not associated with pregnancy or childbirth
    780.39
  pregnancy, childbirth or puerperium 642.6
    with pre-existing hypertension 642.7
    affecting fetus or newborn 760.0
  uremic 586
Eclipse blindness (total) 363.31
Economic circumstance affecting care V60.9
  specified type NEC V60.8
Economo's disease (encephalitis lethargica)
  049.8
Ectasia, ectasis
  aorta (*see also* Aneurysm, aorta) 441.9
    ruptured 441.5
  breast 610.4
  capillary 448.9
  cornea (marginal) (postinfectional) 371.71
  duct (mammary) 610.4
  kidney 593.89
  mammary duct (gland) 610.4
  papillary 448.9
  renal 593.89
  salivary gland (duct) 527.8
  scar, cornea 371.71
  sclera 379.11
Ecthyma 686.8
  contagiosum 051.2
  gangrenosum 686.09
  infectiosum 051.2
Ectocardia 746.87
Ectodermal dysplasia, congenital 757.31
Ectodermosis erosiva pluriorificialis 695.1
Ectopic, ectopia (congenital) 759.89
  abdominal viscera 751.8
    due to defect in anterior abdominal wall
      756.79
  ACTH syndrome 255.0
  adrenal gland 759.1
  anus 751.5
  auricular beats 427.61
  beats 427.60
  bladder 753.5
  bone and cartilage in lung 748.69
  brain 742.4
  breast tissue 757.6
  cardiac 746.87
  cerebral 742.4
  cordis 746.87
  endometrium 617.9
  gallbladder 751.69
  gastric mucosa 750.7
  gestation—*see* Pregnancy, ectopic
  heart 746.87
  hormone secretion NEC 259.3
  hyperparathyroidism 259.3
  kidney (crossed) (intrathoracic) (pelvis) 753.3
    in pregnancy or childbirth 654.4
      causing obstructed labor 660.2
  lens 743.37
  lentis 743.37
  mole—*see* Pregnancy, ectopic

Ectopic, ectopia—*continued*
  organ or site NEC—*see* Malposition, congenital
  ovary 752.0
  pancreas, pancreatic tissue 751.7
  pregnancy—*see* Pregnancy, ectopic
  pupil 364.75
  renal 753.3
  sebaceous glands of mouth 750.26
  secretion
    ACTH 255.0
    adrenal hormone 259.3
    adrenalin 259.3
    adrenocorticotropin 255.0
    antidiuretic hormone (ADH) 259.3
    epinephrine 259.3
    hormone NEC 259.3
    norepinephrine 259.3
    pituitary (posterior) 259.3
  spleen 759.0
  testis 752.51
  thyroid 759.2
  ureter 753.4
  ventricular beats 427.69
  vesicae 753.5
Ectrodactyly 755.4
  finger (*see also* Absence, finger, congenital)
    755.29
  toe (*see also* Absence, toe, congenital) 755.39
Ectromelia 755.4
  lower limb 755.30
  upper limb 755.20
Ectropion 374.10
  anus 569.49
  cervix 622.0
    with mention of cervicitis 616.0
  cicatricial 374.14
  congenital 743.62
  eyelid 374.10
    cicatricial 374.14
    congenital 743.62
    mechanical 374.12
    paralytic 374.12
    senile 374.11
    spastic 374.13
  iris (pigment epithelium) 364.54
  lip (congenital) 750.26
    acquired 528.5
  mechanical 374.12
  paralytic 374.12
  rectum 569.49
  senile 374.11
  spastic 374.13
  urethra 599.84
  uvea 364.54
Eczema (acute) (allergic) (chronic)
    (erythematous) (fissum) (occupational)
    (rubrum) (squamous) 692.9
  asteatotic 706.8
  atopic 691.8
  contact NEC 692.9
  dermatitis NEC 692.9
  due to specified cause—*see* Dermatitis, due to
  dyshidrotic 705.81
  external ear 380.22
  flexural 691.8
  gouty 274.89
  herpeticum 054.0
  hypertrophicum 701.8
  hypostatic—*see* Varicose, vein

Eczema—*continued*
  impetiginous 684
  infantile (acute) (chronic) (due to any
    substance) (intertriginous) (seborrheic)
    690.12
  intertriginous NEC 692.9
    infantile 690.12
  intrinsic 691.8
  lichenified NEC 692.9
  marginatum 110.3
  nummular 692.9
  pustular 686.8
  seborrheic 690.18
    infantile 690.12
  solare 692.72
  stasis (lower extremity) 454.1
    ulcerated 454.2
  vaccination, vaccinatum 999.0
  varicose (lower extremity)—*see* Varicose, vein
  verrucosum callosum 698.3
Eczematoid, exudative 691.8
Eddowes' syndrome (brittle bones and blue
  sclera) 756.51
Edema, edematous 782.3
  with nephritis (*see also* Nephrosis) 581.9
  allergic 995.1
  angioneurotic (allergic) (any site) (with
    urticaria) 995.1
    hereditary 277.6
  angiospastic 443.9
  Berlin's (traumatic) 921.3
  brain 348.5
    due to birth injury 767.8
    fetus or newborn 767.8
  cardiac (*see also* Failure, heart, congestive)
    428.0
  cardiovascular (*see also* Failure, heart,
    congestive) 428.0
  cerebral—*see* Edema, brain
  cerebrospinal vessel—*see* Edema, brain
  cervix (acute) (uteri) 622.8
    puerperal, postpartum 674.8
  chronic hereditary 757.0
  circumscribed, acute 995.1
    hereditary 277.6
  complicating pregnancy (gestational) 646.1
    with hypertension—*see* Toxemia, of
      pregnancy
  conjunctiva 372.73
  connective tissue 782.3
  cornea 371.20
    due to contact lenses 371.24
    idiopathic 371.21
    secondary 371.22
  due to
    lymphatic obstruction—*see* Edema, lymphatic
    salt retention 276.0
  epiglottis—*see* Edema, glottis
  essential, acute 995.1
    hereditary 277.6
  extremities, lower—*see* Edema, legs
  eyelid NEC 374.82
  familial, hereditary (legs) 757.0
  famine 262
  fetus or newborn 778.5
  genital organs
    female 629.8
    male 608.86

Edema, edematous—*continued*
  gestational 646.1
    with hypertension—*see* Toxemia, of
      pregnancy
  glottis, glottic, glottides (obstructive) (passive)
    478.6
    allergic 995.1
      hereditary 277.6
    due to external agent—*see* Condition,
      respiratory, acute, due to specified agent
  heart (*see also* Failure, heart, congestive) 428.0
    newborn 779.8
  heat 992.7
  hereditary (legs) 757.0
  inanition 262
  infectious 782.3
  intracranial 348.5
    due to injury at birth 767.8
  iris 364.8
  joint (*see also* Effusion, joint) 719.0
  larynx (*see also* Edema, glottis) 478.6
  legs 782.3
    due to venous obstruction 459.2
    hereditary 757.0
  localized 782.3
    due to venous obstruction 459.2
      lower extremity 459.2
  lower extremities—*see* Edema, legs
  lungs 514
    acute 518.4
      with heart disease or failure (*see also*
        Failure, ventricular, left) 428.1
        congestive 428.0
      chemical (due to fumes or vapors) 506.1
      due to
        external agent(s) NEC 508.9
          specified NEC 508.8
        fumes and vapors (chemical) (inhalation)
          506.1
        radiation 508.0
    chemical (acute) 506.1
      chronic 506.4
    chronic 514
      chemical (due to fumes or vapors) 506.4
      due to
        external agent(s) NEC 508.9
          specified NEC 508.8
        fumes or vapors (chemical) (inhalation)
          506.4
        radiation 508.1
    due to
      external agent 508.9
        specified NEC 508.8
      high altitude 993.2
      near drowning 994.1
    postoperative 518.4
    terminal 514
  lymphatic 457.1
    due to mastectomy operation 457.0
  macula 362.83
    cystoid 362.53
    diabetic 250.5 *[362.01]*
  malignant (*see also* Gangrene, gas) 040.0
  Milroy's 757.0
  nasopharynx 478.25
  neonatorum 778.5
  nutritional (newborn) 262
    with dyspigmentation, skin and hair 260
  optic disc or nerve—*see* Papilledema

Edema, edematous—*continued*
  orbit 376.33
    circulatory 459.89
  palate (soft) (hard) 528.9
  pancreas 577.8
  penis 607.83
  periodic 995.1
    hereditary 277.6
  pharynx 478.25
  pitting 782.3
  pulmonary—*see* Edema, lung
  Quincke's 995.1
    hereditary 277.6
  renal (*see also* Nephrosis) 581.9
  retina (localized) (macular) (peripheral) 362.83
    cystoid 362.53
    diabetic 250.5 *[362.01]*
  salt 276.0
  scrotum 608.86
  seminal vesicle 608.86
  spermatic cord 608.86
  spinal cord 336.1
  starvation 262
  subconjunctival 372.73
  subglottic (*see also* Edema, glottis) 478.6
  supraglottic (*see also* Edema, glottis) 478.6
  testis 608.86
  toxic NEC 782.3
  traumatic NEC 782.3
  tunica vaginalis 608.86
  vas deferens 608.86
  vocal cord—*see* Edema, glottis
  vulva (acute) 624.8
Edentia (complete) (partial) (*see also* Absence,
  tooth) 520.0
  causing malocclusion 524.3
  congenital (deficiency of tooth buds) 520.0
  due to accident, extraction, or local periodontal
    disease 525.1
Edsall's disease 992.2
Educational handicap V62.3
Edwards' syndrome 758.2
Effect, adverse NEC
  abnormal gravitational (G) forces or states 994.9
  air pressure—*see* Effect, adverse, atmospheric
    pressure
  altitude (high)—*see* Effect, adverse, high
    altitude
  anesthetic
    in labor and delivery NEC 668.9
      affecting fetus or newborn 763.5
  antitoxin—*see* Complications, vaccination
  atmospheric pressure 993.9
    due to explosion 993.4
    high 993.3
    low—*see* Effect, adverse, high altitude
    specified effect NEC 993.8
  biological, correct substance properly
    administered (*see also* Effect, adverse, drug)
    995.2
  blood (derivatives) (serum) (transfusion)—*see*
    Complications, transfusion
  chemical substance NEC 989.9
    specified—*see* Table of drugs and chemicals
  cobalt, radioactive (*see also* Effect, adverse,
    radioactive substance) 990
  cold (temperature) (weather) 991.9
    chilblains 991.5
    frostbite—*see* Frostbite
    specified effect NEC 991.8

Effect, adverse—*continued*
  drugs and medicinals NEC 995.2
    correct substance properly administered 995.2
    overdose or wrong substance given or taken
      977.9
      specified drug—*see* Table of drugs and
        chemicals
  electric current (shock) 994.8
    burn—*see* Burn, by site
  electricity (electrocution) (shock) 994.8
    burn—*see* Burn, by site
  exertion (excessive) 994.5
  exposure 994.9
    exhaustion 994.4
  external cause NEC 994.9
  fallout (radioactive) NEC 990
  fluoroscopy NEC 990
  foodstuffs
    allergic reaction (*see also* Allergy, food) 693.1
      anaphylactic shock due to food NEC 995.60
    noxious 988.9
      specified type NEC (*see also* Poisoning, by
        name of noxious foodstuff) 988.8
  gases, fumes, or vapors—*see* Table of drugs
    and chemicals
  glue (airplane) sniffing 304.6
  heat—*see* Heat
  high altitude NEC 993.2
    anoxia 993.2
    on
      fears 993.0
      sinuses 993.1
    polycythemia 289.0
  hot weather—*see* Heat
  hunger 994.2
  immersion, foot 991.4
  immunization—*see* Complications, vaccination
  immunological agents—*see* Complications,
    vaccination
  implantation (removable) of isotope or radium
    NEC 990
  infrared (radiation) (rays) NEC 990
    burn—*see* Burn, by site
    dermatitis or eczema 692.82
  infusion—*see* Complications, infusion
  ingestion or injection of isotope (therapeutic)
    NEC 990
  irradiation NEC (*see also* Effect, adverse,
    radiation) 990
  isotope (radioactive) NEC 990
  lack of care (child) (infant) (newborn) 995.52
    adult 995.84
  lightning 994.0
    burn—*see* Burn, by site
  Lirugin—*see* Complications, vaccination
  medicinal substance, correct, properly
    administered (*see also* Effect, adverse,
    drugs) 995.2
  mesothorium NEC 990
  motion 994.6
  noise, inner ear 388.10
  overheated places—*see* Heat
  polonium NEC 990
  psychosocial, of work environment V62.1

Effect, adverse—*continued*
  radiation (diagnostic) (fallout) (infrared)
    (natural source) (therapeutic) (tracer)
    (ultraviolet) (x-ray) NEC 990
    with pulmonary manifestations
      acute 508.0
      chronic 508.1
    dermatitis or eczema 692.82
      due to sun NEC (*see also* Dermatitis, due to,
        sun) 692.70
    fibrosis of lungs 508.1
    maternal with suspected damage to fetus
      affecting management of pregnancy 655.6
    pneumonitis 508.0
  radioactive substance NEC 990
    dermatitis or eczema 692.82
  radioactivity NEC 990
  radiotherapy NEC 990
    dermatitis or eczema 692.82
  radium NEC 990
  reduced temperature 991.9
    frostbite—*see* Frostbite
    immersion, foot (hand) 991.4
    specified effect NEC 991.8
  roentgenography NEC 990
  roentgenoscopy NEC 990
  roentgen rays NEC 990
  serum (prophylactic) (therapeutic) NEC 999.5
  specified NEC 995.89
    external cause NEC 994.9
  strangulation 994.7
  submersion 994.1
  teletherapy NEC 990
  thirst 994.3
  transfusion—*see* Complications, transfusion
  ultraviolet (radiation) (rays) NEC 990
    burn—*see also* Burn, by site
      from sun 692.71
    dermatitis or eczema 692.82
      due to sun NEC (*see also* Dermatitis, due to,
        sun) 692.70
  uranium NEC 990
  vaccine (any)—*see* Complications, vaccination
  weightlessness 994.9
  whole blood—*see also* Complications,
    transfusion
    overdose or wrong substance given (*see also*
      Table of drugs and chemicals) 964.7
  working environment V62.1
  x-rays NEC 990
    dermatitis or eczema 692.82

Effect, remote
  of cancer, —*see* condition

Effects, late —*see* Late, effect (of)

Effluvium, telogen 704.02

Effort
  intolerance 306.2
  syndrome (aviators) (psychogenic) 306.2

Effusion
  Amniotic fluid (*see also* Rupture, membranes,
    premature) 658.1
  brain (serous) 348.5
  bronchial (*see also* Bronchitis) 490
  cerebral 348.5
  cerebrospinal (*see also* Meningitis) 322.9
    vessel 348.5
  chest—*see* Effusion, pleura
  intracranial 348.5

Effusion—*continued*
  joint 719.00
    ankle 719.07
    elbow 719.02
    foot 719.07
    hand 719.04
    hip 719.05
    knee 719.06
    multiple sites 719.09
    pelvic region 719.05
    shoulder (region) 719.01
    specified site NEC 719.08
    wrist 719.03
  meninges (*see also* Meningitis) 322.9
  pericardium, pericardial (*see also* Pericarditis)
    423.9
    acute 420.90
  peritoneal (chronic) 568.82
  pleura, pleurisy, pleuritic, pleuropericardial
    511.9
    bacterial, nontuberculous 511.1
    fetus or newborn 511.9
    malignant 197.2
    nontuberculous 511.9
      bacterial 511.1
    pneumococcal 511.1
    staphylococcal 511.1
    streptococcal 511.1
    tuberculous (*see also* Tuberculosis, pleura)
      012.0
      primary progressive 010.1
    traumatic 862.29
      with open wound 862.39
  pulmonary—*see* Effusion, pleura
  spinal (*see also* Meningitis) 322.9
  thorax, thoracic—*see* Effusion, pleura
Eggshell nails 703.8
  congenital 757.5
Ego-dystonic
  homosexuality 302.0
  lesbianism 302.0
Egyptian splenomegaly 120.1
Ehlers-Danlos syndrome 756.83
Ehrlichiosis 082.40
  chafeensis 082.41
  specified type NEC 082.49
Eichstedt's disease (pityriasis versicolor) 111.0
Eisenmenger's complex or syndrome
  (ventricular septal defect) 745.4
Ejaculation, semen
  painful 608.89
    psychogenic 306.59
  premature 302.75
Ekbom syndrome (restless legs) 333.99
Ekman's syndrome (brittle bones and blue
  sclera) 756.51
Elastic skin 756.83
  acquired 701.8
Elastofibroma (M8820/0)—*see* Neoplasm,
  connective tissue, benign
Elastoidosis
  cutanea nodularis 701.8
  cutis cystica et comedonica 701.8
Elastoma 757.39
  juvenile 757.39
  Miescher's (elastosis perforans serpiginosa)
    701.1
Elastomyofibrosis 425.3
Elastosis 701.8
  atrophicans 701.8
  perforans serpiginosa 701.1

Elastosis—*continued*
  reactive perforating 701.1
  senilis 701.8
  solar (actinic) 692.74
Elbow —*see* condition
Electric
  current, electricity, effects (concussion) (fatal)
    (nonfatal) (shock) 994.8
    burn—*see* Burn, by site
  feet (foot) syndrome 266.2
Electrocution 994.8
Electrolyte imbalance 276.9
  with
    abortion—*see* Abortion, by type, with
      metabolic disorder
    ectopic pregnancy (*see also* categories
      633.0-633.9) 639.4
    hyperemesis gravidarum (before 22 completed
      weeks gestation) 643.1
    molar pregnancy (*see also* categories
      630-632) 639.4
  following
    abortion 639.4
    ectopic or molar pregnancy 639.4
Elephant man syndrome 237.71
Elephantiasis (nonfilarial) 457.1
  arabicum (*see also* Infestation, filarial) 125.9
  congenita hereditaria 757.0
  congenital (any site) 757.0
  due to
    Brugia (malayi) 125.1
    mastectomy operation 457.0
    Wuchereria (bancrofti) 125.0
      malayi 125.1
  eyelid 374.83
  filarial (*see also* Infestation, filarial) 125.9
  filariensis (*see also* Infestation, filarial) 125.9
  gingival 523.8
  glandular 457.1
  graecorum 030.9
  lymphangiectatic 457.1
  lymphatic vessel 457.1
    due to mastectomy operation 457.0
  neuromatosa 237.71
  postmastectomy 457.0
  scrotum 457.1
  streptococcal 457.1
  surgical 997.99
    postmastectomy 457.0
  telangiectodes 457.1
  vulva (nonfilarial) 624.8
Elevated —*see* Elevation
Elevation
  17-ketosteroids 791.9
  acid phosphatase 790.5
  alkaline phosphatase 790.5
  amylase 790.5
  antibody titers 795.79
  basal metabolic rate (BMR) 794.7
  blood pressure (*see also* Hypertension) 401.9
    reading (incidental) (isolated) (nonspecific),
      no diagnosis of hypertension 796.2
  body temperature (of unknown origin) (*see also*
    Pyrexia) 780.6
  conjugate, eye 378.81
  diaphragm, congenital 756.6
  immunoglobulin level 795.79
  indolacetic acid 791.9
  lactic acid dehydrogenase (LDH) level 790.4
  lipase 790.5
  prostate specific antigen (PSA) 790.93

Elevation—*continued*
  renin 790.99
    in hypertension (*see also* Hypertension,
      renovascular) 405.91
  Rh titer 999.7
  scapula, congenital 755.52
  sedimentation rate 790.1
  SGOT 790.4
  SGPT 790.4
  transaminase 790.4
  vanillylmandelic acid 791.9
  venous pressure 459.89
  VMA 791.9
Elliptocytosis (congenital) (hereditary) 282.1
  Hb-C (disease) 282.7
  hemoglobin disease 282.7
  sickle-cell (disease) 282.60
    trait 282.5
Ellis-van Creveld disease or syndrome
  (chondroectodermal dysplasia) 756.55
Ellison-Zollinger syndrome (gastric
  hypersecretion with pancreatic islet cell
  tumor) 251.5
Elongation, elongated (congenital)—*see also*
  Distortion
  bone 756.9
  cervix (uteri) 752.49
    acquired 622.6
    hypertrophic 622.6
  colon 751.5
  common bile duct 751.69
  cystic duct 751.69
  frenulum, penis 752.69
  labia minora, acquired 624.8
  ligamentum patellae 756.89
  petiolus (epiglottidis) 748.3
  styloid bone (process) 733.99
  tooth, teeth 520.2
  uvula 750.26
    acquired 528.9
Elschnig bodies or pearls 366.51
El Tor cholera 001.1
Emaciation (due to malnutrition) 261
Emancipation disorder 309.22
Embadomoniasis 007.8
Embarrassment heart, cardiac —*see* Disease,
  heart
Embedded tooth, teeth 520.6
  with abnormal position (same or adjacent tooth)
    524.3
  root only 525.3
Embolic —*see* condition
Embolism
  with
    abortion—*see* Abortion, by type, with
      embolism
    ectopic pregnancy (*see also* categories
      633.0-633.9) 639.6
    molar pregnancy (*see also* categories
      630-632) 639.6
  air (any site) 958.0
    with
      abortion—*see* Abortion, by type, with
        embolism
      ectopic pregnancy (*see also* categories
        633.0-633.9) 639.6
      molar pregnancy (*see also* categories
        630-632) 639.6
    due to implanted device—*see* Complications,
      due to (presence of) any device, implant,
      or graft classified to 996.0-996.5 NEC

Embolism—*continued*
  following
    abortion 639.6
    ectopic or molar pregnancy 639.6
    infusion, perfusion, or transfusion 999.1
  in pregnancy, childbirth, or puerperium 673.0
  traumatic 958.0
  amniotic fluid (pulmonary) 673.1
    with
      abortion—*see* Abortion, by type, with
        embolism
      ectopic pregnancy (*see also* categories
        633.0-633.9) 639.6
      molar pregnancy (*see also* categories
        630-632) 639.6
    following
      abortion 639.6
      ectopic or molar pregnancy 639.6
  aorta, aortic 444.1
    abdominal 444.0
    bifurcation 444.0
    saddle 444.0
    thoracic 444.1
  artery 444.9
    auditory, internal 433.8
    basilar (*see also* Occlusion, artery, basilar)
      433.0
    bladder 444.89
    carotid (common) (internal) (*see also*
      Occlusion, artery, carotid) 433.1
    cerebellar (anterior inferior) (posterior
      inferior) (superior) 433.8
    cerebral (*see also* Embolism, brain) 434.1
    choroidal (anterior) 433.8
    communicating posterior 433.8
    coronary (*see also* Infarct, myocardium) 410.9
      without myocardial infarction 411.81
    extremity 444.22
      lower 444.22
      upper 444.21
    hypophyseal 433.8
    mesenteric (with gangrene) 557.0
    ophthalmic (*see also* Occlusion, retina) 362.30
    peripheral 444.22
    pontine 433.8
    precerebral NEC—*see* Occlusion, artery,
      precerebral
    pulmonary—*see* Embolism, pulmonary
    renal 593.81
    retinal (*see also* Occlusion, retina) 362.30
    specified site NEC 444.89
    vertebral (*see also* Occlusion, artery,
      vertebral) 433.2
  auditory, internal 433.8
  basilar (artery) (*see also* Occlusion, artery,
    basilar) 433.0
  birth, mother—*see* Embolism, obstetrical
  blood-clot
    with
      abortion—*see* Abortion, by type, with
        embolism
      ectopic pregnancy (*see also* categories
        633.0-633.9) 639.6
      molar pregnancy (*see also* categories
        630-632) 639.6
    following
      abortion 639.6
      ectopic or molar pregnancy 639.6
    in pregnancy, childbirth, or puerperium 673.2

Embolism—*continued*
  brain 434.1
    with
      abortion—*see* Abortion, by type, with
        embolism
      ectopic pregnancy (*see also* categories
        633.0-633.9) 639.6
      molar pregnancy (*see also* categories
        630-632) 639.6
    following
      abortion 639.6
      ectopic or molar pregnancy 639.6
    late effect—*see* Late effect(s) (of)
      cerebrovascular disease
    puerperal, postpartum, childbirth 674.0
  capillary 448.9
  cardiac (*see also* Infarct, myocardium) 410.9
  carotid (artery) (common) (internal) (*see also*
    Occlusion, artery, carotid) 433.1
  cavernous sinus (venous)—*see* Embolism,
    intracranial venous sinus
  cerebral (*see also* Embolism, brain) 434.1
  choroidal (anterior) (artery) 433.8
  coronary (artery or vein) (systemic) (*see also*
    Infarct, myocardium) 410.9
    without myocardial infarction 411.81
  due to (presence of) any device, implant, or
    graft classifiable to 996.0-996.5 —*see*
    Complications, due to (presence of) any
    device, implant, or graft classified to
    996.0-996.5 NEC
  encephalomalacia (*see also* Embolism, brain)
    434.1
  extremities 444.22
    lower 444.22
    upper 444.21
  eye 362.30
  fat (cerebral) (pulmonary) (systemic) 958.1
    with
      abortion—*see* Abortion, by type, with
        embolism
      ectopic pregnancy (*see also* categories
        633.0-633.9) 639.6
      molar pregnancy (*see also* categories
        630-632) 639.6
    complicating delivery or puerperium 673.8
    following
      abortion 639.6
      ectopic or molar pregnancy 639.6
    in pregnancy, childbirth, or the puerperium
      673.8
  femoral (artery) 444.22
    vein 453.8
  following
    abortion 639.6
    ectopic or molar pregnancy 639.6
    infusion, perfusion, or transfusion
      air 999.1
      thrombus 999.2
  heart (fatty) (*see also* Infarct, myocardium)
    410.9
  hepatic (vein) 453.0
  iliac (artery) 444.81
  iliofemoral 444.81
  in pregnancy, childbirth, or puerperium
    (pulmonary)—*see* Embolism, obstetrical
  intestine (artery) (vein) (with gangrene) 557.0
  intracranial (*see also* Embolism, brain) 434.1
    venous sinus (any) 325
      late effect—*see* category 326

Embolism—*continued*
  nonpyogenic 437.6
    in pregnancy or puerperium 671.5
  kidney (artery) 593.81
  lateral sinus (venous)—*see* Embolism,
    intracranial venous sinus
  longitudinal sinus (venous)—*see* Embolism,
    intracranial venous sinus
  lower extremity 444.22
  lung (massive)—*see* Embolism, pulmonary
  meninges (*see also* Embolism, brain) 434.1
  mesenteric (artery) (with gangrene) 557.0
  multiple NEC 444.9
  obstetrical (pulmonary) 673.2
    air 673.0
    amniotic fluid (pulmonary) 673.1
    blood-clot 673.2
    cardiac 674.8
    fat 673.8
    heart 674.8
    pyemic 673.3
    septic 673.3
    specified NEC 674.8
  ophthalmic (*see also* Occlusion, retina) 362.30
  paradoxical NEC 444.9
  penis 607.82
  peripheral arteries NEC 444.22
    lower 444.22
    upper 444.21
  pituitary 253.8
  popliteal (artery) 444.22
  portal (vein) 452
  postoperative NEC 997.2
    cerebral 997.02
    peripheral vascular 997.2
    pulmonary 415.11
  precerebral artery (*see also* Occlusion, artery,
    precerebral) 433.9
  puerperal—*see* Embolism, obstetrical
  pulmonary (artery) (vein) 415.1
    with
      abortion—*see* Abortion, by type, with
        embolism
      ectopic pregnancy (*see also* categories
        633.0-633.9) 639.6
      molar pregnancy (*see also* categories
        630-632) 639.6
    following
      abortion 639.6
      ectopic or molar pregnancy 639.6
    iatrogenic 415.11
    in pregnancy, childbirth, or puerperium—*see*
      Embolism, obstetrical
    postoperative 415.11
  pyemic (multiple) 038.9
    with
      abortion—*see* Abortion, by type, with
        embolism
      ectopic pregnancy (*see also* categories
        633.0-633.9) 639.6
      molar pregnancy (*see also* categories
        630-632) 639.6
    Aerobacter aerogenes 038.49
    enteric gram-negative bacilli 038.40
    Enterobacter aerogenes 038.49
    Escherichia coli 038.42
    following
      abortion 639.6
      ectopic or molar pregnancy 639.6
    Hemophilus influenzae 038.41
    pneumococcal 038.2

Empyema (chest) (diaphragmatic) (double)
(encapsulated) (general) (interlobar) (lung)
(medial) (necessitatis) (perforating chest wall)
(pleura) (pneumococcal) (residual)
(sacculated) (streptococcal)
(supradiaphragmatic) 510.9
  with fistula 510.0
  accessory sinus (chronic) (*see also* Sinusitis)
    473.9
  acute 510.9
    with fistula 510.0
  antrum (chronic) (*see also* Sinusitis, maxillary)
    473.0
  brain (any part) (*see also* Abscess, brain) 324.0
  ethmoidal (sinus) (chronic) (*see also* Sinusitis,
    ethmoidal) 473.2
  extradural (*see also* Abscess, extradural) 324.9
  frontal (sinus) (chronic) (*see also* Sinusitis,
    frontal) 473.1
  gallbladder (*see also* Cholecystitis, acute) 575.0
  mastoid (process) (acute) (*see also* Mastoiditis,
    acute) 383.00
  maxilla, maxillary 526.4
    sinus (chronic) (*see also* Sinusitis, maxillary)
      473.0
  nasal sinus (chronic) (*see also* Sinusitis) 473.9
  sinus (accessory) (nasal) (*see also* Sinusitis)
    473.9
  sphenoidal (chronic) (sinus) (*see also* Sinusitis,
    sphenoidal) 473.3
  subarachnoid (*see also* Abscess, extradural)
    324.9
  subdural (*see also* Abscess, extradural) 324.9
  tuberculous (*see also* Tuberculosis, pleura)
    012.0
  ureter (*see also* Ureteritis) 593.89
  ventricular (*see also* Abscess, brain) 324.0
Enameloma 520.2
Encephalitis (bacterial) (chronic) (hemorrhagic)
(idiopathic) (nonepidemic) (spurious)
(subacute) 323.9
  acute—*see also* Encephalitis, viral
    disseminated (postinfectious) NEC 136.9
      [323.6]
      postimmunization or postvaccination 323.5
    inclusional 049.8
    inclusion body 049.8
    necrotizing 049.8
  arboviral, arbovirus NEC 064
  arthropod-borne (*see also* Encephalitis, viral,
    arthropod-borne) 064
  Australian X 062.4
  Bwamba fever 066.3
  California (virus) 062.5
  Central European 063.2
  Czechoslovakian 063.2
  Dawson's (inclusion body) 046.2
  diffuse sclerosing 046.2
  due to
    actinomycosis 039.8 *[323.4]*
    cat-scratch disease 078.3 *[323.0]*
    infectious mononucleosis 075 *[323.0]*
    malaria (*see also* Malaria) 084.6 *[323.2]*
    Negishi virus 064
    ornithosis 073.7 *[323.0]*
    prophylactic inoculation against smallpox
      323.5
    rickettsiosis (*see also* Rickettsiosis) 083.9
      [323.1]

Encephalitis—*continued*
  rubella 056.01
    toxoplasmosis (acquired) 130.0
      congenital (active) 771.2 *[323.4]*
    typhus (fever) (*see also* Typhus) 081.9 *[323.1]*
    vaccination (smallpox) 323.5
  Eastern equine 062.2
  endemic 049.8
  epidemic 049.8
  equine (acute) (infectious) (viral) 062.9
    Eastern 062.2
    Venezuelan 066.2
    Western 062.1
  Far Eastern 063.0
  following vaccination or other immunization
    procedure 323.5
  herpes 054.3
  Ilheus (virus) 062.8
  inclusion body 046.2
  infectious (acute) (virus) NEC 049.8
  influenzal 487.8 *[323.4]*
    lethargic 049.8
  Japanese (B type) 062.0
  La Crosse 062.5
  Langat 063.8
  late effect—*see* Late, effect, encephalitis
  lead 984.9 *[323.7]*
  lethargic (acute) (infectious) (influenzal) 049.8
  lethargica 049.8
  louping ill 063.1
  lupus 710.0 *[323.8]*
  lymphatica 049.0
  Mengo 049.8
  meningococcal 036.1
  mumps 072.2
  Murray Valley 062.4
  myoclonic 049.8
  Negishi virus 064
  otitic NEC 382.4 *[323.4]*
  parasitic NEC 123.9 *[323.4]*
  periaxialis (concentrica) (diffusa) 341.1
  postchickenpox 052.0
  postexanthematous NEC 057.9 *[323.6]*
  postimmunization 323.5
  postinfectious NEC 136.9 *[323.6]*
  postmeasles 055.0
  posttraumatic 323.8
  postvaccinal (smallpox) 323.5
  postvaricella 052.0
  postviral NEC 079.99 *[323.6]*
    postexanthematous 057.9 *[323.6]*
      specified NEC 057.8 *[323.6]*
  Powassan 063.8
  progressive subcortical (Binswanger's) 290.12
  Rio Bravo 049.8
  rubella 056.01
  Russian
    autumnal 062.0
    spring-summer type (taiga) 063.0
  saturnine 984.9 *[323.7]*
  Semliki Forest 062.8
  serous 048
  slow-acting virus NEC 046.8
  specified cause NEC 323.8
  St. Louis type 062.3
  subacute sclerosing 046.2
  subcorticalis chronica 290.12
  summer 062.0
  suppurative 324.0

Encephalitis—*continued*
 syphilitic 094.81
  congenital 090.41
 tick-borne 063.9
 torula, torular 117.5 *[323.4]*
 toxic NEC 989.9 *[323.7]*
 toxoplasmic (acquired) 130.0
  congenital (active) 771.2 *[323.4]*
 trichinosis 124 *[323.4]*
 Trypanosomiasis (*see also* Trypanosomiasis)
  086.9 *[323.2]*
 tuberculous (*see also* Tuberculosis) 013.6
 type B (Japanese) 062.0
 type C 062.3
 van Bogaert's 046.2
 Venezuelan 066.2
 Vienna type 049.8
 viral, virus 049.9
  arthropod-borne NEC 064
   mosquito-borne 062.9
    Australian X disease 062.4
    California virus 062.5
    Eastern equine 062.2
    Ilheus virus 062.8
    Japanese (B type) 062.0
    Murray Valley 062.4
    specified type NEC 062.8
    St. Louis 062.3
    type B 062.0
    type C 062.3
    Western equine 062.1
   tick-borne 063.9
    biundulant 063.2
    Central European 063.2
    Czechoslovakian 063.2
    diphasic meningoencephalitis 063.2
    Far Eastern 063.0
    Langat 063.8
    louping ill 063.1
    Powassan 063.8
    Russian spring-summer (taiga) 063.0
    specified type NEC 063.8
   vector unknown 064
  slow acting NEC 046.8
  specified type NEC 049.8
  vaccination, prophylactic (against) V05.0
 von Economo's 049.8
 Western equine 062.1
 West Nile type 066.3
Encephalocele 742.0
 orbit 376.81
Encephalocystocele 742.0
Encephalomalacia (brain) (cerebellar) (cerebral)
  (cerebrospinal) (*see also* Softening, brain)
  434.9
 due to
  hemorrhage (*see also* Hemorrhage, brain) 431
  recurrent spasm of artery 435.9
 embolic (cerebral) (*see also* Embolism, brain)
  434.1
 subcorticalis chronicus arteriosclerotica 290.12
 thrombotic (*see also* Thrombosis, brain) 434.0
Encephalomeningitis —*see* Meningoencephalitis
Encephalomeningocele 742.0
Encephalomeningomyelitis —*see*
  Meningoencephalitis
Encephalomeningopathy (*see also*
  Meningoencephalitis) 349.9

Encephalomyelitis (chronic) (granulomatous)
  (hemorrhagic necrotizing, acute) (myalgic,
  benign) (*see also* Encephalitis) 323.9
 abortive disseminated 049.8
 acute disseminated (postinfectious) 136.9
  [323.6]
  postimmunization 323.5
 due to or resulting from vaccination (any) 323.5
 equine (acute) (infectious) 062.9
  Eastern 062.2
  Venezuelan 066.2
  Western 062.1
 funicularis infectiosa 049.8
 late effect—*see* Late, effect, encephalitis
 Munch-Peterson's 049.8
 postchickenpox 052.0
 postimmunization 323.5
 postmeasles 055.0
 postvaccinal (smallpox) 323.5
 rubella 056.01
 specified cause NEC 323.8
 syphilitic 094.81
Encephalomyelocele 742.0
Encephalomyelomeningitis —*see*
  Meningoencephalitis
Encephalomyeloneuropathy 349.9
Encephalomyelopathy 349.9
 subacute necrotizing (infantile) 330.8
Encephalomyeloradiculitis (acute) 357.0
Encephalomyeloradiculoneuritis (acute) 357.0
Encephalomyeloradiculopathy 349.9
Encephalomyocarditis 074.23
Encephalopathia hyperbilirubinemica
  newborn 774.7
 due to isoimmunization (conditions classifiable
  to 773.0-773.2) 773.4
Encephalopathy (acute) 348.3
 alcoholic 291.2
 anoxic—*see* Damage, brain, anoxic
 arteriosclerotic 437.0
  late effect—*see* Late effect(s) (of)
   cerebrovascular disease
 bilirubin, newborn 774.7
  due to isoimmunization 773.4
 congenital 742.9
 demyelinating (callosal) 341.8
 due to
  birth injury (intracranial) 767.8
  dialysis 294.8
   transient 293.9
  hyperinsulinism—*see* Hyperinsulinism
  influenza (virus) 487.8
  lack of vitamin (*see also* Deficiency, vitamin)
   269.2
  nicotinic acid deficiency 291.2
  serum (nontherapeutic) (therapeutic) 999.5
  syphilis 094.81
  trauma (postconcussional) 310.2
   current (*see also* Concussion, brain) 850.9
    with skull fracture—*see* Fracture, skull, by
     site, with intracranial injury
  vaccination 323.5
 hepatic 572.2
 hyperbilirubinemic, newborn 774.7
  due to isoimmunization (conditions
   classifiable to 773.0-773.2) 773.4
 hypertensive 437.2
 hypoglycemic 251.2
 hypoxic—*see* Damage, brain, anoxic
 infantile cystic necrotizing (congenital) 341.8

Encephalopathy—*continued*
  lead 984.9 *[323.7]*
  leukopolio 330.0
  metabolic (toxic)—*see* Delirium
  necrotizing, subacute 330.8
  pellagrous 265.2
  portal-systemic 572.2
  postcontusional 310.2
  posttraumatic 310.2
  saturnine 984.9 *[323.7]*
  spongioform, subacute (viral) 046.1
  subacute
    necrotizing 330.8
    spongioform 046.1
    viral, spongioform 046.1
  subcortical progressive (Schilder) 341.1
    chronic (Binswanger's) 290.12
  toxic 349.82
    metabolic—*see* Delirium
  traumatic (postconcussional) 310.2
    current (*see also* Concussion, brain) 850.9
      with skull fracture—*see* Fracture, skull, by
        site, with intracranial injury
  vitamin B deficiency NEC 266.9
  Wernicke's (superior hemorrhagic
    polioencephalitis) 265.1
Enchephalorrhagia (*see also* Hemorrhage,
    brain) 432.9
  healed or old V12.59
  late effect—*see* Late effect(s) (of)
    cerebrovascular disease
Encephalosis, posttraumatic 310.2
Enchondroma (M9220/0)—*see also* Neoplasm,
    bone, benign
  multiple, congenital 756.4
Enchondromatosis (cartilaginous) (congenital)
    (multiple) 756.4
Enchondroses, multiple (cartilaginous)
    (congenital) 756.4
Encopresis (*see also* Incontinence, feces) 787.6
  nonorganic origin 307.7
Encounter for —*see also* Admission for
  administrative purpose only V68.9
    referral of patient without examination or
      treatment V68.81
    specified purpose NEC V68.89
  chemotherapy V58.1
  end-of-life care V66.7
  hospice care V66.7
  palliative care V66.7
  radiotherapy V58.0
  screening mammogram NEC V76.12
    for high-risk patient V76.11
  paternity testing V70.4
  terminal care V66.7
Encystment —*see* Cyst
End-of-life care V66.7
Endamebiasis —*see* Amebiasis
Endamoeba —*see* Amebiasis
Endarteritis (bacterial, subacute) (infective)
    (septic) 447.6
  brain, cerebral or cerebrospinal 437.4
    late effect—*see* Late effect(s) (of)
      cerebrovascular disease
  coronary (artery) —*see* Arteriosclerosis,
    coronary
  deformans—*see* Arteriosclerosis
  embolic (*see also* Embolism) 444.9
  obliterans—*see also* Arteriosclerosis
    pulmonary 417.8
  pulmonary 417.8

Endarteritis—*continued*
  retina 362.18
  senile—*see* Arteriosclerosis
  syphilitic 093.89
    brain or cerebral 094.89
    congenital 090.5
    spinal 094.89
  tuberculous (*see also* Tuberculosis) 017.9
Endemic —*see* condition
Endocarditis (chronic) (indeterminate)
    (interstitial) (marantis) (nonbacterial
    thrombotic) (residual) (sclerotic) (sclerous)
    (senile) (valvular) 424.90
  with
    rheumatic fever (conditions classifiable to 390)
      active—*see* Endocarditis, acute, rheumatic
      inactive or quiescent (with chorea) 397.9
  acute or subacute 421.9
    rheumatic (aortic) (mitral) (pulmonary)
      (tricuspid) 391.1
      with chorea (acute) (rheumatic)
        (Sydenham's) 392.0
  aortic (heart) (nonrheumatic) (valve) 424.1
    with
      mitral (valve) disease 396.9
        active or acute 391.1
          with chorea (acute) (rheumatic)
            (Sydenham's) 392.0
        rheumatic fever (conditions classifiable to
          390)
        active—*see* Endocarditis, acute, rheumatic
        inactive or quiescent (with chorea) 395.9
          with mitral disease 396.9
    acute or subacute 421.9
    arteriosclerotic 424.1
    congenital 746.89
    hypertensive 424.1
    rheumatic (chronic) (inactive) 395.9
      with mitral (valve) disease 396.9
        active or acute 391.1
          with chorea (acute) (rheumatic)
            (Sydenham's) 392.0
        active or acute 391.1
          with chorea (acute) (rheumatic)
            (Sydenham's) 392.0
    specified cause, except rheumatic 424.1
    syphilitic 093.22
  arteriosclerotic or due to arteriosclerosis 424.99
  atypical verrucous (Libman-Sacks) 710.0
    [424.91]
  bacterial (acute) (any valve) (chronic)
    (subacute) 421.0
  blastomycotic 116.0 *[421.1]*
  candidal 112.81
  congenital 425.3
  constrictive 421.0
  Coxsackie 074.22
  due to
    blastomycosis 116.0 *[421.1]*
    candidiasis 112.81
    Coxsackie (virus) 074.22
    disseminated lupus erythematosus 710.0
      [424.91]
    histoplasmosis (*see also* Histoplasmosis)
      115.94
    hypertension (benign) 424.99
    moniliasis 112.81
    prosthetic cardiac valve 996.61
    Q fever 083.0 *[421.1]*
    serratia marcescens 421.0
    typhoid (fever) 002.0 *[421.1]*

Endocarditis—*continued*
  fetal 425.3
  gonococcal 098.84
  hypertensive 424.99
  infectious or infective (acute) (any valve)
      (chronic) (subacute) 421.0
  lenta (acute) (any valve) (chronic) (subacute)
      421.0
  Libman-Sacks 710.0 *[424.91]*
  Loeffler's (parietal fibroplastic) 421.0
  malignant (acute) (any valve) (chronic)
      (subacute) 421.0
  meningococcal 036.42
  mitral (chronic) (double) (fibroid) (heart)
      (inactive) (valve) (with chorea) 394.9
    with
      aortic (valve) disease 396.9
        active or acute 391.1
          with chorea (acute) (rheumatic)
              (Sydenham's) 392.0
        rheumatic fever (conditions classifiable to
            390)
          active—*see* Endocarditis, acute, rheumatic
          inactive or quiescent (with chorea) 394.9
            with aortic valve disease 396.9
      active or acute 391.1
        bacterial 421.0
        with chorea (acute) (rheumatic)
            (Sydenham's) 392.0
      arteriosclerotic 424.0
      congenital 746.89
      hypertensive 424.0
      nonrheumatic 424.0
        acute or subacute 421.9
      syphilitic 093.21
  monilial 112.81
  mycotic (acute) (any valve) (chronic) (subacute)
      421.0
  pneumococcic (acute) (any valve) (chronic)
      (subacute) 421.0
  pulmonary (chronic) (heart) (valve) 424.3
    with
      rheumatic fever (conditions classifiable to
          390)
        active—*see* Endocarditis, acute, rheumatic
        inactive or quiescent (with chorea) 397.1
    acute or subacute 421.9
      rheumatic 391.1
        with chorea (acute) (rheumatic)
            (Sydenham's) 392.0
    arteriosclerotic or due to arteriosclerosis 424.3
    congenital 746.09
    hypertensive or due to hypertension (benign)
        424.3
    rheumatic (chronic) (inactive) (with chorea)
        397.1
      active or acute 391.1
        with chorea (acute) (rheumatic)
            (Sydenham's) 392.0
    syphilitic 093.24
  purulent (acute) (any valve) (chronic)
      (subacute) 421.0
  rheumatic (chronic) (inactive) (with chorea)
      397.9
    active or acute (aortic) (mitral) (pulmonary)
        (tricuspid) 391.1
      with chorea (acute) (rheumatic)
          (Sydenham's) 392.0
  septic (acute) (any valve) (chronic) (subacute)
      421.0
  specified cause, except rheumatic 424.99

Endocarditis—*continued*
  streptococcal (acute) (any valve) (chronic)
      (subacute) 421.0
  subacute—*see* Endocarditis, acute
  suppurative (any valve) (acute) (chronic)
      (subacute) 421.0
  syphilitic NEC 093.20
  toxic (*see also* Endocarditis, acute) 421.9
  tricuspid (chronic) (heart) (inactive) (rheumatic)
      (valve) (with chorea) 397.0
    with
      rheumatic fever (conditions classifiable to
          390)
        active—*see* Endocarditis, acute, rheumatic
        inactive or quiescent (with chorea) 397.0
    active or acute 391.1
      with chorea (acute) (rheumatic)
          (Sydenham's) 392.0
    arteriosclerotic 424.2
    congenital 746.89
    hypertensive 424.2
    nonrheumatic 424.2
      acute or subacute 421.9
    specified cause, except rheumatic 424.2
    syphilitic 093.23
  tuberculous (*see also* Tuberculosis) 017.9
      [424.91]
  typhoid 002.0 *[421.1]*
  ulcerative (acute) (any valve) (chronic)
      (subacute) 421.0
  vegetative (acute) (any valve) (chronic)
      (subacute) 421.0
  verrucous (acute) (any valve) (chronic)
      (subacute) NEC 710.0 *[424.91]*
    nonbacterial 710.0 *[424.91]*
    nonrheumatic 710.0 *[424.91]*
Endocardium, endocardial —*see also* condition
  cushion defect 745.60
    specified type NEC 745.69
Endocervicitis (*see also* Cervicitis) 616.0
  due to
    intrauterine (contraceptive) device 996.65
  gonorrheal (acute) 098.15
    chronic or duration of 2 months or over 098.35
  hyperplastic 616.0
  syphilitic 095.8
  trichomonal 131.09
  tuberculous (*see also* Tuberculosis) 016.7
Endocrine —*see* condition
Endocrinopathy, pluriglandular 258.9
Endodontitis 522.0
Endomastoiditis (*see also* Mastoiditis) 383.9
Endometrioma 617.9
Endometriosis 617.9
  appendix 617.5
  bladder 617.8
  bowel 617.5
  broad ligament 617.3
  cervix 617.0
  colon 617.5
  cul-de-sac (Douglas') 617.3
  exocervix 617.0
  fallopian tube 617.2
  female genital organ NEC 617.8
  gallbladder 617.8
  in scar of skin 617.6
  internal 617.0
  intestine 617.5
  lung 617.8
  myometrium 617.0
  ovary 617.1

Endometriosis—*continued*
   parametrium 617.3
   pelvic peritoneum 617.3
   peritoneal (pelvic) 617.3
   rectovaginal septum 617.4
   rectum 617.5
   round ligament 617.3
   skin 617.6
   specified site NEC 617.8
   stromal (M8931/1) 236.0
   umbilicus 617.8
   uterus 617.0
      internal 617.0
   vagina 617.4
   vulva 617.8
Endometritis (nonspecific) (purulent) (septic) (suppurative) 615.9
   with
      abortion—*see* Abortion, by type, with sepsis
      ectopic pregnancy (*see also* categories 633.0-633.9) 639.0
      molar pregnancy (*see also* categories 630-632) 639.0
   acute 615.0
   blennorrhagic 098.16
      acute 098.16
      chronic or duration of 2 months or over 098.36
   cervix, cervical (*see also* Cervicitis) 616.0
      hyperplastic 616.0
   chronic 615.1
   complicating pregnancy 646.6
      affecting fetus or newborn 760.8
   decidual 615.9
   following
      abortion 639.0
      ectopic or molar pregnancy 639.0
   gonorrheal (acute) 098.16
      chronic or duration of 2 months or over 098.36
   hyperplastic 621.3
      cervix 616.0
   polypoid—*see* Endometritis, hyperplastic
   puerperal, postpartum, childbirth 670
   senile (atrophic) 615.9
   subacute 615.0
   tuberculous (*see also* Tuberculosis) 016.7
Endometrium —*see* condition
Endomyocardiopathy, South African 425.2
Endomyocarditis —*see* Endocarditis
Endomyofibrosis 425.0
Endomyometritis (*see also* Endometritis) 615.9
Endopericarditis —*see* Endocarditis
Endoperineuritis —*see* Disorder, nerve
Endophlebitis (*see also* Phlebitis) 451.9
   leg 451.2
      deep (vessels) 451.19
      superficial (vessels) 451.0
   portal (vein) 572.1
   retina 362.18
   specified site NEC 451.89
   syphilitic 093.89
Endophthalmia (*see also* Endophthalmitis) 360.00
   gonorrheal 098.42
Endophthalmitis (globe) (infective) (metastatic) (purulent) (subacute) 360.00
   acute 360.01
   chronic 360.03
   parasitic 360.13
   phacoanaphylactic 360.19
   specified type NEC 360.19
   sympathetic 360.11

Endosalpingioma (M9111/1) 236.2
Endosteitis —*see* Osteomyelitis
Endothelioma, bone (M9260/3)—*see* Neoplasm, bone, malignant
Endotheliosis 287.8
   hemorrhagic infectional 287.8
Endotoxic shock 785.59
Endotrachelitis (*see also* Cervicitis) 616.0
Enema rash 692.89
Engel-von Recklinghausen disease or syndrome (osteitis fibrosa cystica) 252.0
Engelmann's disease (diaphyseal sclerosis) 756.59
English disease (*see also* Rickets) 268.0
Engman's disease (infectious eczematoid dermatitis) 690.8
Engorgement
   breast 611.79
      newborn 778.7
      puerperal, postpartum 676.2
   liver 573.9
   lung 514
   pulmonary 514
   retina, venous 362.37
   stomach 536.8
   venous, retina 362.37
Enlargement, enlarged —*see also* Hypertrophy
   abdomen 789.3
   adenoids 474.12
      and tonsils 474.10
   alveolar process or ridge 525.8
   apertures of diaphragm (congenital) 756.6
   blind spot, visual field 368.42
   gingival 523.8
   heart, cardiac (*see also* Hypertrophy, cardiac) 429.3
   lacrimal gland, chronic 375.03
   liver (*see also* Hypertrophy, liver) 789.1
   lymph gland or node 785.6
   orbit 376.46
   organ or site, congenital NEC—*see* Anomaly, specified type NEC
   parathyroid (gland) 252.0
   pituitary fossa 793.0
   prostate, simple 600.0
      soft 600.0
   sella turcica 793.0
   spleen (*see also* Splenomegaly) 789.2
      congenital 759.0
   thymus (congenital) (gland) 254.0
   thyroid (gland) (*see also* Goiter) 240.9
   tongue 529.8
   tonsils 474.11
      and adenoids 474.10
   uterus 621.2
Enophthalmos 376.50
   due to
      atrophy of orbital tissue 376.51
      surgery 376.52
      trauma 376.52
Enostosis 526.89
Entamebiasis —*see* Amebiasis
Entamebic —*see* Amebiasis
Entanglement, umbilical cord (s) 663.3
   with compression 663.2
   affecting fetus or newborn 762.5
   around neck with compression 663.1
   twins in monoamniotic sac 663.2
Enteralgia 789.0
Enteric —*see* condition

Enteritis (acute) (catarrhal) (choleraic) (chronic)
(congestive) (diarrheal) (exudative)
(follicular) (hemorrhagic) (infantile)
(lienteric) (noninfectious) (perforative)
(phlegmonous) (presumed noninfectious)
(pseudomembranous) 558.9
  adaptive 564.9
  aertrycke infection 003.0
  allergic 558.3
  amebic (*see also* Amebiasis) 006.9
    with abscess—*see* Abscess, amebic
    acute 006.0
      with abscess—*see* Abscess, amebic
      nondysenteric 006.2
    chronic 006.1
      with abscess—*see* Abscess, amebic
      nondysenteric 006.2
    nondysenteric 006.2
  anaerobic (cocci) (gram-negative)
(gram-positive) (mixed) NEC 008.46
  bacillary NEC 004.9
  bacterial NEC 008.5
    specified NEC 008.49
  Bacteroides (fragilis) (melaninogeniscus)
(oralis) 008.46
  Butyrivibrio (fibriosolvens) 008.46
  Campylobacter 008.43
  Candida 112.85
  Chilomastix 007.8
  choleriformis 001.1
  chronic 558.9
    ulcerative (*see also* Colitis, ulcerative) 556.9
  cicatrizing (chronic) 555.0
  Clostridium
    botulinum 005.1
    difficile 008.45
    haemolyticum 008.46
    novyi 008.46
    perfringens (C) (F) 008.46
    specified type NEC 008.46
  coccidial 007.2
  dietetic 558.9
  due to
    achylia gastrica 536.8
    adenovirus 008.62
    Aerobacter aerogenes 008.2
    anaerobes—*see* Enteritis, anaerobic 008.46
    Arizona (bacillus) 008.1
    astrovirus 008.66
    Bacillus coli—*see* Enteritis, E. coli 008.0
    bacteria NEC 008.5
      specified NEC 008.49
    Bacteroides 008.46
    Butyrivibrio (fibriosolvens) 008.46
    Calcivirus 008.65
    Campylobacter 008.43
    Clostridium—*see* Enteritis, Clostridium
    Cockle agent 008.64
    Coxsackie (virus) 008.67
    Ditchling agent 008.64
    ECHO virus 008.67
    Enterobacter aerogenes 008.2
    enterococci 008.49
    enterovirus NEC 008.67
    Escherichia coli—*see* Enteritis, E. coli
    Eubacterium 008.46
    Fusobacterium (nucleatum) 008.46
    gram-negative bacteria NEC 008.47
      anaerobic NEC 008.46

Enteritis—*continued*
    Hawaii agent 008.63
    irritating foods 558.9
    Klebsiella aerogenes 008.47
    Marin County agent 008.66
    Montgomery County agent 008.63
    Norwalk-like agent 008.63
    Norwalk virus 008.63
    Otofuke agent 008.63
    Paracolobactrum arizonae 008.1
    paracolon bacillus NEC 008.47
      Arizona 008.1
    Paramatta agent 008.64
    Peptococcus 008.46
    Peptostreptococcus 008.46
    Propionibacterium 008.46
    Proteus (bacillus) (mirabilis) (morganii) 008.3
    Pseudomonas aeruginosa 008.42
    Rotavirus 008.61
    Sapporo agent 008.63
    small round virus (SRV) NEC 008.64
      featureless NEC 008.63
      structured NEC 008.63
    Snow Mountain (SM) agent 008.63
    specified
      bacteria NEC 008.49
      organism, nonbacterial NEC 008.8
      virus NEC 008.69
    Staphylococcus 008.41
    Streptococcus 008.49
      anaerobic 008.46
    Taunton agent 008.63
    Torovirus 008.69
    Treponema 008.46
    Veillonella 008.46
    virus 008.8
      specified type NEC 008.69
    Wollan (W) agent 008.64
    Yersinia enterocolitica 008.44
  dysentery—*see* Dysentery
  E. coli 008.00
    enterohemorrhagic 008.04
    enteroinvasive 008.03
    enteropathogenic 008.01
    enterotoxigenic 008.02
    specified type NEC 008.09
  el tor 001.1
  embadomonial 007.8
  epidemic 009.0
  Eubacterium 008.46
  fermentative 558.9
  fulminant 557.0
  Fusobacterium (nucleatum) 008.46
  gangrenous (*see also* Enteritis, due to, by
organism) 009.0
  giardial 007.1
  gram-negative bacteria NEC 008.47
    anaerobic NEC 008.46
  infectious NEC (*see also* Enteritis, due to, by
organism) 009.0
    presumed 009.1
  influenzal 487.8
  ischemic 557.9
    acute 557.0
    chronic 557.1
    due to mesenteric artery insufficiency 557.1
  membranous 564.9
  mucous 564.9
  myxomembranous 564.9

Ependymoma (epithelial) (malignant) (M9391/3)
anaplastic type (M9392/3)
   specified site—*see* Neoplasm, by site,
      malignant
   unspecified site 191.9
benign (M9391/0)
   specified site—*see* Neoplasm, by site, benign
   unspecified site 225.0
myxopapillary (M9394/1) 237.5
papillary (M9393/1) 237.5
specified site—*see* Neoplasm, by site, malignant
unspecified site 191.9
Ependymopathy 349.2
spinal cord 349.2
Ephelides, ephelis 709.09
Ephemeral fever (*see also* Pyrexia) 780.6
Epiblepharon (congenital) 743.62
Epicanthus, epicanthic fold (congenital)
   (eyelid) 743.63
Epicondylitis (elbow) (lateral) 726.32
medial 726.31
Epicystitis (*see also* Cystitis) 595.9
Epidemic —*see* condition
Epidermidalization, cervix —*see* condition
Epidermidization, cervix *see* condition
Epidermis, epidermal —*see* condition
Epidermization, cervix —*see* condition
Epidermodysplasia verruciformis 078.19
Epidermoid
cholesteatoma—*see* Cholesteatoma
inclusion (*see also* Cyst, skin) 706.2
Epidermolysis
acuta (combustiformis) (toxica) 695.1
bullosa 757.39
necroticans combustiformis 695.1
   due to drug
      correct substance properly administered
         695.1
      overdose or wrong substance given or taken
         977.9
         specified drug—*see* Table of drugs and
            chemicals
Epidermophytid —*see* Dermatophytosis
Epidermophytosis (infected)—*see*
   Dermatophytosis
Epidermosis, ear (middle) (*see also*
   Cholesteatoma) 385.30
Epididymis —*see* condition
Epididymitis (nonvenereal) 604.90
with abscess 604.0
acute 604.99
blennorrhagic (acute) 098.0
   chronic or duration of 2 months or over 098.2
caseous (*see also* Tuberculosis) 016.4
chlamydial 099.54
diphtheritic 032.89 *[604.91]*
filarial 125.9 *[604.91]*
gonococcal (acute) 098.0
   chronic or duration of 2 months or over 098.2
recurrent 604.99
residual 604.99
syphilitic 095.8 *[604.91]*
tuberculous (*see also* Tuberculosis) 016.4
Epididymo-orchitis (*see also* Epididymitis)
   604.90
with abscess 604.0
chlamydial 099.54
gonococcal (acute) 098.13
   chronic or duration of 2 months or over 098.33
Epidural —*see* condition
Epigastritis (*see also* Gastritis) 535.5

Epigastrium, epigastric —*see* condition
Epigastrocele (*see also* Hernia, epigastric) 553.29
Epiglottiditis (acute) 464.30
with obstruction 464.31
chronic 476.1
viral 464.30
   with obstruction 464.31
Epiglottis —*see* condition
Epiglottitis (acute) 464.30
with obstruction 464.31
chronic 476.1
viral 464.30
   with obstruction 464.31
Epignathus 759.4
Epilepsia
partialis continua (*see also* Epilepsy) 345.7
procursiva (*see also* Epilepsy) 345.8
Epilepsy, epileptic (idiopathic) 345.9

> *Note—use the following fifth-digit*
> *subclassification with categories 345.0, 345.1,*
> *345.4-345.9*
>
> *0   without mention of intractable epilepsy*
> *1   with intractable epilepsy*

abdominal 345.5
absence (attack) 345.0
akinetic 345.0
   psychomotor 345.4
automatism 345.4
autonomic diencephalic 345.5
brain 345.9
Bravais-Jacksonian 345.5
cerebral 345.9
climacteric 345.9
clonic 345.1
clouded state 345.9
coma 345.3
communicating 345.4
congenital 345.9
convulsions 345.9
cortical (focal) (motor) 345.5
cursive (running) 345.8
cysticercosis 123.1
deterioration
   with behavioral disturbance 345.9 *[294.11]*
   without behavioral disturbance 345.9 *[294.10]*
due to syphilis 094.89
equivalent 345.5
fit 345.9
focal (motor) 345.5
gelastic 345.8
generalized 345.9
   convulsive 345.1
      flexion 345.1
   nonconvulsive 345.0
grand mal (idiopathic) 345.1
Jacksonian (motor) (sensory) 345.5
Kojevnikoff's, Kojevnikov's, Kojewnikoff's
   345.7
laryngeal 786.2
limbic system 345.4
major (motor) 345.1
minor 345.0
mixed (type) 345.9
motor partial 345.5
musicogenic 345.1
myoclonus, myoclonic 345.1
   progressive (familial) 333.2
nonconvulsive, generalized 345.0

Epilepsy, epileptic—*continued*
  parasitic NEC 123.9
  partial (focalized) 345.5
    with
        impairment of consciousness 345.4
        memory and ideational disturbances 345.4
      abdominal type 345.5
      motor type 345.5
      psychomotor type 345.4
      psychosensory type 345.4
      secondarily generalized 345.4
      sensory type 345.5
      somatomotor type 345.5
      somatosensory type 345.5
      temporal lobe type 345.4
      visceral type 345.5
      visual type 345.5
  peripheral 345.9
  petit mal 345.0
  photokinetic 345.8
  progressive myoclonic (familial) 333.2
  psychic equivalent 345.5
  psychomotor 345.4
  psychosensory 345.4
  reflex 345.1
  seizure 345.9
  senile 345.9
  sensory-induced 345.5
  sleep 347
  somatomotor type 345.5
  somatosensory 345.5
  specified type NEC 345.8
  status (grand mal) 345.3
    focal motor 345.7
    petit mal 345.2
    psychomotor 345.7
    temporal lobe 345.7
  symptomatic 345.9
  temporal lobe 345.4
  tonic (-clonic) 345.1
  traumatic (injury unspecified) 907.0
    injury specified—*see* Late, effect (of)
        specified injury
  twilight 293.0
  uncinate (gyrus) 345.4
  Unverricht (-Lundborg) (familial myoclonic)
      333.2
  visceral 345.5
  visual 345.5
Epileptiform
  convulsions 780.39
  seizure 780.39
Epiloia 759.5
Epimenorrhea 626.2
Epipharyngitis (*see also* Nasopharyngitis) 460
Epiphora 375.20
  due to
    excess lacrimation 375.21
    insufficient drainage 375.22
Epiphyseal arrest 733.91
  femoral head 732.2
Epiphyseolysis, epiphysiolysis (*see also*
    Osteochondrosis) 732.9
Epiphysitis (*see also* Osteochondrosis) 732.9
  juvenile 732.6
  marginal (Scheuermann's) 732.0
  os calcis 732.5
  syphilitic (congenital) 090.0
  vertebral (Scheuermann's) 732.0
Epiplocele (*see also* Hernia) 553.9
Epiploitis (*see also* Peritonitis) 567.9

Epiplosarcomphalocele (*see also* Hernia,
    umbilicus) 553.1
Episcleritis 379.00
  gouty 274.89 *[379.09]*
  nodular 379.02
  periodica fugax 379.01
    angioneurotic—*see* Edema, angioneurotic
  specified NEC 379.09
  staphylococcal 379.00
  suppurative 379.00
  syphilitic 095.0
  tuberculous (*see also* Tuberculosis) 017.3
    [379.09]
Episode
  brain (*see also* Disease, cerebrovascular, acute)
      436
  cerebral (*see also* Disease, cerebrovascular,
      acute) 436
  depersonalization (in neurotic state) 300.6
  psychotic (*see also* Psychosis) 298.9
    organic, transient 293.9
  schizophrenic (acute) NEC (*see also*
      Schizophrenia) 295.4
Epispadias
  female 753.8
  male 752.62
Episplenitis 289.59
Epistaxis (multiple) 784.7
  hereditary 448.0
  vicarious menstruation 625.8
Epithelioma (malignant) (M8011/3)—*see also*
    Neoplasm, by site, malignant
  adenoides cysticum (M8100/0)—*see* Neoplasm,
      skin, benign
  basal cell (M8090/3)—*see* Neoplasm, skin,
      malignant
  benign (M8011/0)—*see* Neoplasm, by site,
      benign
  Bowen's (M8081/2)—*see* Neoplasm, skin, in
      situ
  calcifying (benign) (Malherbe's)
      (M8110/0)—*see* Neoplasm, skin, benign
  external site—*see* Neoplasm, skin, malignant
  intraepidermal, Jadassohn (M8096/0)—*see*
      Neoplasm, skin, benign
  squamous cell (M8070/3)—*see* Neoplasm, by
      site, malignant
Epitheliopathy
  pigment, retina 363.15
  posterior multifocal placoid (acute) 363.15
Epithelium, epithelial —*see* condition
Epituberculosis (allergic) (with atelectasis) (*see
    also* Tuberculosis) 010.8
Eponychia 757.5
Epstein's
  nephrosis or syndrome (*see also* Nephrosis)
      581.9
  pearl (mouth) 528.4
Epstein-Barr infection (viral) 075
  chronic 780.79 *[139.8]*
Epulis (giant cell) (gingiva) 523.8
Equinia 024
Equinovarus (congenital) 754.51
  acquired 736.71
Equivalent
  convulsive (abdominal) (*see also* Epilepsy)
      345.5
  epileptic (psychic) (*see also* Epilepsy) 345.5

Erb's
  disease 359.1
  palsy, paralysis (birth) (brachial) (newborn)
      767.6
    spinal (spastic) syphilitic 094.89
  pseudohypertrophic muscular dystrophy 359.1
Erb (-Duchenne) paralysis (birth injury)
    (newborn) 767.6
Erb-Goldflam disease or syndrome 358.0
Erdheim's syndrome (acromegalic
    macrospondylitis) 253.0
Erection, painful (persistent) 607.3
Ergosterol deficiency (vitamin D) 268.9
  with
    osteomalacia 268.2
    rickets (*see also* Rickets) 268.0
Ergotism (ergotized grain) 988.2
  from ergot used as drug (migraine therapy)
    correct substance properly administered
        349.82
    overdose or wrong substance given or taken
        975.0
Erichsen's disease (railway spine) 300.16
Erlacher-Blount syndrome (tibia vara) 732.4
Erosio interdigitalis blastomycetica 112.3
Erosion
  arteriosclerotic plaque—*see* Arteriosclerosis, by
    site
  artery NEC 447.2
    without rupture 447.8
  bone 733.99
  bronchus 519.1
  cartilage (joint) 733.99
  cervix (uteri) (acquired) (chronic) (congenital)
      622.0
    with mention of cervicitis 616.0
  cornea (recurrent) (*see also* Keratitis) 371.42
    traumatic 918.1
  dental (idiopathic) (occupational) 521.3
  duodenum, postpyloric—*see* Ulcer, duodenum
  esophagus 530.89
  gastric 535.4
  intestine 569.89
  lymphatic vessel 457.8
  pylorus, pyloric (ulcer) 535,4
  sclera 379.16
  spine, aneurysmal 094.89
  spleen 289.59
  stomach 535.4
  teeth (idiopathic) (occupational) 521.3
    due to
      medicine 521.3
      persistent vomiting 521.3
  urethra 599.84
  uterus 621.8
  vertebra 733.99
Erotomania 302.89
  Clérambault's 297.8
Error
  in diet 269.9
  refractive 367.9
    astigmatism (*see also* Astigmatism) 367.20
    drug-induced 367.89
    hypermetropia 367.0
    hyperopia 367.0
    myopia 367.1
    presbyopia 367.4
    toxic 367.89
Eructation 787.3
  nervous 306.4
  psychogenic 306.4

Eruption
  creeping 126.9
  drug—*see* Dermatitis, due to, drug
  Hutchinson, summer 692.72
  Kaposi's varicelliform 054.0
  napkin (psoriasiform) 691.0
  polymorphous
    light (sun) 692.72
      other source 692.82
  psoriasiform, napkin 691.0
  recalcitrant pustular 694.8
  ringed 695.89
  skin (*see also* Dermatitis) 782.1
    creeping (meaning hookworm) 126.9
    due to
      chemical(s) NEC 692.4
        internal use 693.8
      drug—*see* Dermatitis, due to, drug
      prophylactic inoculation or vaccination
          against disease—*see* Dermatitis, due to,
          vaccine
      smallpox vaccination NEC—*see* Dermatitis,
          due to, vaccine
    erysipeloid 027.1
    feigned 698.4
    Hutchinson, summer 692.72
    Kaposi's, varicelliform 054.0
      vaccinia 999.0
    lichenoid, axilla 698.3
    polymorphous, due to light 692.72
    toxic NEC 695.0
    vesicular 709.8
  teeth, tooth
    accelerated 520.6
    delayed 520.6
    difficult 520.6
    disturbance of 520.6
    in abnormal sequence 520.6
    incomplete 520.6
    late 520.6
    natal 520.6
    neonatal 520.6
    obstructed 520.6
    partial 520.6
    persistent primary 520.6
    premature 520.6
  vesicular 709.8
Erysipelas (gangrenous) (infantile) (newborn)
    (phlegmonous) (suppurative) 035
  external ear 035 [380.13]
  puerperal, postpartum, childbirth 670
Erysipelatoid (Rosenbach's) 027.1
Erysipeloid (Rosenbach's) 027.1
Erythema, erythematous (generalized) 695.9
  ab igne—*see* Burn, by site, first degree
  annulare (centrifugum) (rheumaticum) 695.0
  arthriticum epidemicum 026.1
  brucellum (*see also* Brucellosis) 023.9
  bullosum 695.1
  caloricum—*see* Burn, by site, first degree
  chronicum migrans 088.81
    chronicum 088.81
  circinatum 695.1
  diaper 691.0
  due to
    chemical (contact) NEC 692.4
      internal 693.8
    drug (internal use) 693.0
      contact 692.3

Erythema, erythematous—*continued*
  elevatum diutinum 695.89
  endemic 265.2
  epidemic, arthritic 026.1
  figuratum perstans 695.0
  gluteal 691.0
  gyratum (perstans) (repens) 695.1
  heat—*see* Burn, by site, first degree
  ichthyosiforme congenitum 757.1
  induratum (primary) (scrofulosorum) (*see also*
    Tuberculosis) 017.1
    nontuberculous 695.2
  infantum febrile 057.8
  infectional NEC 695.9
  infectiosum 057.0
  inflammation NEC 695.9
  intertrigo 695.89
  iris 695.1
  lupus (discoid) (localized) (*see also* Lupus,
    erythematosus) 695.4
  marginatum 695.0
    rheumaticum—*see* Fever, rheumatic
  medicamentosum—*see* Dermatitis, due to, drug
  migrans 529.1
  multiforme 695.1
    bullosum 695.1
    conjunctiva 695.1
    exudativum (Hebra) 695.1
    pemphigoides 694.5
  napkin 691.0
  neonatorum 778.8
  nodosum 695.2
    tuberculous (*see also* Tuberculosis) 017.1
  nummular, nummulare 695.1
  palmar 695.0
  palmaris hereditarium 695.0
  pernio 991.5
  perstans solare 692.72
  rash, newborn 778.8
  scarlatiniform (exfoliative) (recurrent) 695.0
  simplex marginatum 057.8
  solare 692.71
  streptogenes 696.5
  toxic, toxicum NEC 695.0
    newborn 778.8
  tuberculous (primary) (*see also* Tuberculosis)
    017.0
  venenatum 695.0
Erythematosus —*see* condition
Erythematous —*see* condition
Erythermalgia (primary) 443.89
Erythralgia 443.89
Erythrasma 039.0
Erythredema 985.0
  polyneuritica 985.0
  polyneuropathy 985.0
Erythremia (acute) (M9841/3) 207.0
  chronic (M9842/3) 207.1
  secondary 289.0
Erythroblastopenia (acquired) 284.8
  congenital 284.0
Erythroblastophthisis 284.0
Erythroblastosis (fetalis) (newborn) 773.2
  due to
    ABO
      antibodies 773.1
      incompatibility, maternal/fetal 773.1
      isoimmunization 773.1
    Rh
      antibodies 773.0
      incompatibility, maternal/fetal 773.0
      isoimmunization 773.0

Erythrocyanosis (crurum) 443.89
Erythrocythemia —*see* Erythremia
Erythrocytopenia 285.9
Erythrocytosis (megalosplenic)
  familial 289.6
  oval, hereditary (*see also* Elliptocytosis) 282.1
  secondary 289.0
  stress 289.0
Erythroderma (*see also* Erythema) 695.9
  desquamativa (in infants) 695.89
  exfoliative 695.89
  ichthyosiform, congenital 757.1
  infantum 695.89
  maculopapular 696.2
  neonatorum 778.8
  psoriaticum 696.1
  secondary 695.9
Erythrogenesis imperfecta 284.0
Erythroleukemia (M9840/3) 207.0
Erythromelalgia 443.89
Erythromelia 701.8
Erythropenia 285.9
Erythrophagocytosis 289.9
Erythrophobia 300.23
Erythroplakia
  oral mucosa 528.7
  tongue 528.7
Erythroplasia (Queyrat) (M8080/2)
  specified site—*see* Neoplasm, skin, in situ
  unspecified site 233.5
Erythropoiesis, idiopathic ineffective 285.0
Escaped beats, heart 427.60
  postoperative 997.1
Esoenteritis —*see* Enteritis
Esophagalgia 530.89
Esophagectasis 530.89
  due to cardiospasm 530.0
Esophagismus 530.5
Esophagitis (acute) (alkaline) (chemical)
    (chronic) (infectional) (necrotic) (peptic)
    (postoperative) (regurgitant) 530.10
  candidal 112.84
  reflux 530.11
  specified NEC 530.19
  tuberculous (*see also* Tuberculosis) 017.8
Esophagocele 530.6
Esophagodynia 530.89
Esophagomalacia 530.89
Esophagoptosis 530.89
Esophagospasm 530.5
Esophagostenosis 530.3
Esophagostomiasis 127.7
Esophagotracheal —*see* condition
Esophagus —*see* condition
Esophoria 378.41
  convergence, excess 378.84
  divergence, insufficiency 378.85
Esotropia (nonaccommodative) 378.00
  accommodative 378.35
  alternating 378.05
    with
      A pattern 378.06
      specified noncomitancy NEC 378.08
      V pattern 378.07
      X pattern 378.08
      Y pattern 378.08
    intermittent 378.22
  intermittent 378.20
    alternating 378.22
    monocular 378.21

Examination—*continued*
  health (of)
    armed forces personnel V70.5
    checkup V70.0
    child, routine V20.2
    defined subpopulation NEC V70.5
    inhabitants of institutions V70.5
    occupational V70.5
    pre-employment screening V70.5
    preschool children V70.5
      for admission to school V70.3
    prisoners V70.5
      for entrance into prison V70.3
    prostitutes V70.5
    refugees V70.5
    school children V70.5
    students V70.5
  hearing V72.1
  infant V20.2
  laboratory V72.6
  lactating mother V24.1
  medical (for) (of) V70.9
    administrative purpose NEC V70.3
    admission to
      old age home V70.3
      prison V70.3
      school V70.3
    adoption V70.3
    armed forces personnel V70.5
    at health care facility V70.0
    camp V70.3
    child, routine V20.2
    clinical research, normal comparison in V70.7
    control subject in clinical research V70.7
    defined subpopulation NEC V70.5
    donor (potential) V70.8
    driving license V70.3
    general V70.9
      routine V70.0
      specified reason NEC V70.8
    immigration V70.3
    inhabitants of institutions V70.5
    insurance certification V70.3
    marriage V70.3
    medicolegal reasons V70.4
    naturalization V70.3
    occupational V70.5
    population survey V70.6
    pre-employment V70.5
    preschool children V70.5
      for admission to school V70.3
    prison V70.3
    prisoners V70.5
      for entrance into prison V70.3
    prostitutes V70.5
    refugees V70.5
    school children V70.5
    specified reason NEC V70.8
    sport competition V70.3
    students V70.5
  medicolegal reason V70.4
  pelvic (annual) (periodic) V72.3
  periodic (annual) (routine) V70.0
  postpartum
    immediately after delivery V24.0
    routine follow-up V24.2
  pregnancy (unconfirmed) (possible) V72.4
  prenatal V22.1
    first pregnancy V22.0
    high-risk pregnancy V23.9
      specified problem NEC V23.8

Examination—*continued*
  preoperative V72.84
    cardiovascular V72.81
    respiratory V72.82
    specified NEC V72.83
  psychiatric V70.2
    follow-up not needing further care V67.3
    requested by authority V70.1
  radiological NEC V72.5
  respiratory preoperative V72.82
  screening—*see* Screening
  sensitization V72.7
  skin V72.7
    hypersensitivity V72.7
  special V72.9
  specified type or reason NEC V72.85
    preoperative V72.83
      specified NEC V72.83
  teeth V72.2
  vaginal Papanicolaou smear V76.47
    following hysterectomy for malignant
      condition V67.01
  victim or culprit following
    alleged rape or seduction V71.5
    inflicted injury NEC V71.6
  vision V72.0
  well baby V20.2
Exanthem, exanthema (*see also* Rash) 782.1
  Boston 048
  epidemic, with meningitis 048
  lichenoid psoriasiform 696.2
  subitum 057.8
  viral, virus NEC 057.9
    specified type NEC 057.8
Excess, excessive, excessively
  alcohol level in blood 790.3
  carbohydrate tissue, localized 278.1
  carotene (dietary) 278.3
  cold 991.9
    specified effect NEC 991.8
  convergence 378.84
  development, breast 611.1
  diaphoresis 780.8
  divergence 378.85
  drinking (alcohol) NEC (*see also* Abuse, drugs,
    nondependent) 305.0
    continual (*see also* Alcoholism) 303.9
    habitual (*see also* Alcoholism) 303.9
  eating 783.6
  eyelid fold (congenital) 743.62
  fat 278.00
    in heart (*see also* Degeneration, myocardial)
      429.1
    tissue, localized 278.1
  foreskin 605
  gas 787.3
  gastrin 251.5
  glucagon 251.4
  heat (*see also* Heat) 992.9
  large
    colon 564.7
      congenital 751.3
    fetus or infant 766.0
      with obstructed labor 660.1
      affecting management of pregnancy 656.6
      causing disproportion 653.5
    newborn (weight of 4500 grams or more)
      766.0
    organ or site, congenital NEC—*see* Anomaly,
      specified type NEC
  lid fold (congenital) 743.62

Excess, excessive, excessively—*continued*
long
  colon 751.5
  organ or site, congenital NEC—*see* Anomaly,
    specified type NEC
  umbilical cord (entangled)
    affecting fetus or newborn 762.5
    in pregnancy or childbirth 663.3
      with compression 663.2
menstruation 626.2
number of teeth 520.1
  causing crowding 524.3
nutrients (dietary) NEC 783.6
potassium (K) 276.7
salivation (*see also* Ptyalism) 527.7
secretion—*see also* Hypersecretion
  milk 676.6
  sputum 786.4
  sweat 780.8
short
  organ or site, congenital NEC—*see* Anomaly,
    specified type NEC
  umbilical cord
    affecting fetus or newborn 762.6
    in pregnancy or childbirth 663.4
skin NEC 701.9
  eyelid 743.62
    acquired 374.30
sodium (Na) 276.0
sputum 786.4
sweating 780.8
tearing (ducts) (eye) (*see also* Epiphora) 375.20
thirst 783.5
  due to deprivation of water 994.3
vitamin
  A (dietary) 278.2
    administered as drug (chronic) (prolonged
      excessive intake) 278.2
    reaction to sudden overdose 963.5
  D (dietary) 278.4
    administered as drug (chronic) (prolonged
      excessive intake) 278.4
    reaction to sudden overdose 963.5
weight 278.00
  gain 783.1
    of pregnancy 646.1
  loss 783.21
Excitability, abnormal , under minor stress
  309.29
Excitation
catatonic (*see also* Schizophrenia) 295.2
psychogenic 298.1
reactive (from emotional stress, psychological
  trauma) 298.1
Excitement
manic (*see also* Psychosis, affective) 296.0
  recurrent episode 296.1
  single episode 296.0
mental, reactive (from emotional stress,
  psychological trauma) 298.1
state, reactive (from emotional stress,
  psychological trauma) 298.1
Excluded pupils 364.76
Excoriation (traumatic) (*see also* Injury,
  superficial, by site) 919.8
neurotic 698.4
Excyclophoria 378.44
Excyclotropia 378.33
Exencephalus, exencephaly 742.0

Exercise
breathing V57.0
remedial NEC V57.1
therapeutic NEC V57.1
Exfoliation, teeth due to systemic causes 525.0
Exfoliative —*see also* condition
dermatitis 695.89
Exhaustion, exhaustive (physical NEC) 780.79
battle (*see also* Reaction, stress, acute) 308.9
cardiac (*see also* Failure, heart) 428.9
delirium (*see also* Reaction, stress, acute) 308.9
due to
  cold 991.8
  excessive exertion 994.5
  exposure 994.4
fetus or newborn 779.8
heart (*see also* Failure, heart) 428.9
heat 992.5
  due to
    salt depletion 992.4
    water depletion 992.3
manic (*see also* Psychosis, affective) 296.0
  recurrent episode 296.1
  single episode 296.0
maternal, complicating delivery 669.8
  affecting fetus or newborn 763.89
mental 300.5
myocardium, myocardial (*see also* Failure,
  heart) 428.9
nervous 300.5
old age 797
postinfectional NEC 780.79
psychogenic 300.5
psychosis (*see also* Reaction, stress, acute) 308.9
senile 797
  dementia 290.0
Exhibitionism (sexual) 302.4
Exomphalos 756.79
Exophoria 378.42
convergence, insufficiency 378.83
divergence, excess 378.85
Exophthalmic
cachexia 242.0
goiter 242.0
ophthalmoplegia 242.0 *[376.22]*
Exophthalmos 376.30
congenital 743.66
constant 376.31
endocrine NEC 259.9 *[376.22]*
hyperthyroidism 242.0 *[376.21]*
intermittent NEC 376.34
malignant 242.0 *[376.21]*
pulsating 376.35
  endocrine NEC 259.9 *[376.22]*
thyrotoxic 242.0 *[376.21]*
Exostosis 726.91
cartilaginous (M9210/0)—*see* Neoplasm, bone,
  benign
congenital 756.4
ear canal, external 380.81
gonococcal 098.89
hip 726.5
intracranial 733.3
jaw (bone) 526.81
luxurians 728.11
multiple (cancellous) (congenital) (hereditary)
  756.4
nasal bones 726.91
orbit, orbital 376.42
osteocartilaginous (M9210/0)—*see* Neoplasm,
  bone, benign

Exostosis—*continued*
  spine 721.8
    with spondylosis—*see* Spondylosis
  syphilitic 095.5
  wrist 726.4
Exotropia 378.10
  alternating 378.15
    with
      A pattern 378.16
      specified noncomitancy 378.18
      V pattern 378.17
      X pattern 378.18
      Y pattern 378.18
      intermittent 378.24
  intermittent 378.20
    alternating 378.24
    monocular 378.23
  monocular 378.11
    with
      A pattern 378.12
      specified noncomitancy NEC 378.14
      V pattern 378.13
      X pattern 378.14
      Y pattern 378.14
      intermittent 378.23
Explanation of
  investigation finding V65.4
  medication V65.4
Exposure 994.9
  cold 991.9
    specified effect NEC 991.8
  effects of 994.9
  exhaustion due to 994.4
  to
    AIDS virus V01.7
    asbestos V15.84
    body fluids (hazardous) V15.85
    cholera V01.0
    communicable disease V01.9
      specified type NEC V01.8
    German measles V01.4
    gonorrhea V01.6
    hazardous body fluids V15.85
    HIV V01.7
    human immunodeficiency virus V01.7
    lead V15.86
    parasitic disease V01.8
    poliomyelitis V01.2
    potentially hazardous body fluids V15.85
    rabies V01.5
    rubella V01.4
    smallpox V01.3
    syphilis V01.6
    tuberculosis V01.1
    venereal disease V01.6
    viral disease NEC V01.7
Exsanguination, fetal 772.0
Exstrophy
  abdominal content 751.8
  bladder (urinary) 753.5
Extensive —*see* condition
Extra —*see also* Accessory
  rib 756.3
    cervical 756.2
Extraction
  with hook 763.89
  breech NEC 669.6
    affecting fetus or newborn 763.0
  cataract postsurgical V45.61
  manual NEC 669.8
    affecting fetus or newborn 763.89

Extrasystole 427.60
  atrial 427.61
  postoperative 997.1
  ventricular 427.69
Extrauterine gestation or pregnancy —*see*
  Pregnancy, ectopic
Extravasation
  blood 459.0
    lower extremity 459.0
  chyle into mesentery 457.8
  pelvicalyceal 593.4
  pyelosinus 593.4
  urine 788.8
    from ureter 788.8
Extremity —*see* condition
Extrophy —*see* Exstrophy
Extroversion
  bladder 753.5
  uterus 618.1
    complicating delivery 665.2
      affecting fetus or newborn 763.89
    postpartal (old) 618.1
Extrusion
  breast implant (prosthetic) 996.54
  device, implant, or graft—*see* Complications,
    mechanical
  eye implant (ball) (globe) 996.59
  intervertebral disc—*see* Displacement,
    intervertebral disc
  lacrimal gland 375.43
  mesh (reinforcing) 996.59
  ocular lens implant 996.53
  prosthetic device NEC—*see* Complications,
    mechanical
  vitreous 379.26
Exudate, pleura —*see* Effusion, pleura
Exudates, retina 362.82
Exudative —*see* condition
Eye, eyeball, eyelid —*see* condition
Eyestrain 368.13
Eyeworm disease of Africa 125.2

F

Faber's anemia or syndrome (achlorhydric anemia) 280.9
Fabry's disease (angiokeratoma corporis diffusum) 272.7
Face, facial —*see* condition
Facet of cornea 371.44
Faciocephalalgia, autonomic (*see also* Neuropathy, peripheral, autonomic) 337.9
Facioscapulohumeral myopathy 359.1
Factitious disorder, illness —*see* Illness, factitious
Factor
  deficiency—*see* Deficiency, factor
  psychic, associated with diseases classified elsewhere 316
  risk—*see* Problem
Fahr-Volhard disease (malignant nephrosclerosis) 403.00
Failure, failed
  adenohypophyseal 253.2
  attempted abortion (legal) (*see also* Abortion, failed) 638.9
  bone marrow (anemia) 284.9
    acquired (secondary) 284.8
    congenital 284.0
    idiopathic 284.9
  cardiac (*see also* Failure, heart) 428.9
    newborn 779.8
  cardiorenal (chronic) 428.9
    hypertensive (*see also* Hypertension, cardiorenal) 404.93
  cardiorespiratory 799.1
    specified during or due to a procedure 997.1
      long-term effect of cardiac surgery 429.4
  cardiovascular (chronic) 428.9
  cerebrovascular 437.8
  cervical dilatation in labor 661.0
    affecting fetus or newborn 763.7
  circulation, circulatory 799.8
    fetus or newborn 779.8
    peripheral 785.50
  compensation—*see* Disease, heart
  congestive (*see also* Failure, heart, congestive) 428.0
  coronary (*see also* Insufficiency, coronary) 411.89
  descent of head (at term) 652.5
    affecting fetus or newborn 763.1
    in labor 660.0
      affecting fetus or newborn 763.1
  device, implant, or graft—*see* Complications, mechanical
  engagement of head NEC 652.5
    in labor 660.0
  extrarenal 788.9
  fetal head to enter pelvic brim 652.5
    affecting fetus or newborn 763.1
    in labor 660.0
      affecting fetus or newborn 763.1
  forceps NEC 660.7
    affecting fetus or newborn 763.1
  fusion (joint) (spinal) 996.4
  growth in childhood 783.43
  heart (acute) (sudden) 428.9
    with
      abortion—*see* Abortion, by type, with specified complication NEC

Failure, failed—*continued*
    acute pulmonary edema (*see also* Failure, ventricular, left) 428.1
      with congestion 428.0
    decompensation (*see also* Failure, heart, congestive) 428.0
    dilation—*see* Disease, heart
    ectopic pregnancy (*see also* categories 633.0-633.9) 639.8
    molar pregnancy (*see also* categories 630-632) 639.8
   arteriosclerotic 440.9
   combined left-right sided 428.0
   compensated (*see also* Failure, heart, congestive) 428.0
   complicating
    abortion—*see* Abortion, by type, with specified complication NEC
    delivery (cesarean) (instrumental) 669.4
    ectopic pregnancy (*see also* categories 633.0-633.9) 639.8
    molar pregnancy (*see also* categories 630-632) 639.8
    obstetric anesthesia or sedation 668.1
    surgery 997.1
   congestive (compensated) (decompensated) 428.0
    with rheumatic fever (conditions classifiable to 390)
      active 391.8
      inactive or quiescent (with chorea) 398.91
    fetus or newborn 779.8
    hypertensive (*see also* Hypertension, heart) 402.91
      with renal disease (*see also* Hypertension, cardiorenal) 404.91
        with renal failure 404.93
      benign 402.11
      malignant 402.01
    rheumatic (chronic) (inactive) (with chorea) 398.91
      active or acute 391.8
        with chorea (Sydenham's) 392.0
   decompensated (*see also* Failure, heart, congestive) 428.0
   degenerative (*see also* Degeneration, myocardial) 429.1
   due to presence of (cardiac) prosthesis 429.4
   fetus or newborn 779.8
   following
    abortion 639.8
    cardiac surgery 429.4
    ectopic or molar pregnancy 639.8
   high output NEC 428.9
   hypertensive (*see also* Hypertension, heart) 402.91
    with renal disease (*see also* Hypertension, cardiorenal) 404.91
      with renal failure 404.93
    benign 402.11
    malignant 402.01
   left (ventricular) (*see also* Failure, ventricular, left) 428.1
    with right-sided failure 428.0
   low output (syndrome) NEC 428.9

Failure, failed—*continued*
  organic—*see* Disease, heart
  postoperative (immediate) 997.1
    long term effect of cardiac surgery 429.4
  rheumatic (chronic) (congestive) (inactive)
    398.91
  right (secondary to left heart failure,
    conditions classifiable to 428.1)
    (ventricular) (*see also* Failure, heart,
    congestive) 428.0
  senile 797
  specified during or due to a procedure 997.1
    long-term effect of cardiac surgery 429.4
  thyrotoxic (*see also* Thyrotoxicosis) 242.9
    [425.7]
  valvular—*see* Endocarditis
hepatic 572.8
  acute 570
  due to a procedure 997.4
hepatorenal 572.4
hypertensive heart (*see also* Hypertension,
  heart) 402.91
  benign 402.11
  malignant 402.01
induction (of labor) 659.1
  abortion (legal) (*see also* Abortion, failed)
    638.9
  affecting fetus or newborn 763.89
  by oxytocic drugs 659.1
  instrumental 659.0
  mechanical 659.0
  medical 659.1
  surgical 659.0
initial alveolar expansion, newborn 770.4
involution, thymus (gland) 254.8
kidney—*see* Failure, renal
lactation 676.4
Leydig's cell, adult 257.2
liver 572.8
  acute 570
medullary 799.8
mitral—*see* Endocarditis, mitral
myocardium, myocardial (*see also* Failure,
  heart) 428.9
  chronic (*see also* Failure, heart, congestive)
    428.0
  congestive (*see also* Failure, heart,
    congestive) 428.0
ovarian (primary) 256.3
  iatrogenic 256.2
  postablative 256.2
  postirradiation 256.2
  postsurgical 256.2
ovulation 628.0
prerenal 788.9
renal 586
  with
    abortion—*see* Abortion, by type, with renal
      failure
    ectopic pregnancy (*see also* categories
      633.0-633.9) 639.3
    edema (*see also* Nephrosis) 581.9
    hypertension (*see also* Hypertension,
      kidney) 403.91
    hypertensive heart disease (conditions
      classifiable to 402) 404.92
      with heart failure 404.93
      benign 404.12
        with heart failure 404.13
      malignant 404.02
        with heart failure 404.03

Failure, failed—*continued*
  molar pregnancy (*see also* categories
    630-632) 639.3
  tubular necrosis (acute) 584.5
  acute 584.9
    with lesion of
      necrosis
        cortical (renal) 584.6
        medullary (renal) (papillary) 584.7
        tubular 584.5
      specified pathology NEC 584.8
  chronic 585
    hypertensive or with hypertension (*see also*
      Hypertension, kidney) 403.91
  due to a procedure 997.5
  following
    abortion 639.3
    crushing 958.5
    ectopic or molar pregnancy 639.3
    labor and delivery (acute) 669.3
  hypertensive (*see also* Hypertension, kidney)
    403.91
  puerperal, postpartum 669.3
respiration, respiratory 518.81
  acute 518.81
  acute and chronic 518.84
  center 348.8
    newborn 770.8
  chronic 518.83
  due to trauma, surgery or shock 518.5
  newborn 770.8
rotation
  cecum 751.4
  colon 751.4
  intestine 751.4
  kidney 753.3
segmentation—*see also* Fusion
  fingers (*see also* Syndactylism, fingers) 755.11
  toes (*see also* Syndactylism, toes) 755.13
seminiferous tubule, adult 257.2
senile (general) 797
  with psychosis 290.20
testis, primary (seminal) 257.2
to progress 661.2
to thrive
  adult 783.7
  child 783.41
transplant 996.80
  bone marrow 996.85
  organ (immune or nonimmune cause) 996.80
    bone marrow 996.85
    heart 996.83
    intestines 996.87
    kidney 996.81
    liver 996.82
    lung 996.84
    pancreas 996.86
    specified NEC 996.89
  skin 996.52
    artificial 996.55
    decellularized allodermis 996.55
    temporary allograft or pigskin graft—*omit*
      code
trial of labor NEC 660.6
  affecting fetus or newborn 763.1
urinary 586
vacuum extraction
  abortion—*see* Abortion, failed
  delivery NEC 660.7
    affecting fetus or newborn 763.1

Failure, failed—*continued*
  ventouse NEC 660.7
    affecting fetus or newborn 763.1
  ventricular (*see also* Failure, heart) 428.9
    left 428.1
      with rheumatic fever (conditions classifiable
        to 390)
        active 391.8
          with chorea 392.0
        inactive or quiescent (with chorea) 398.91
      hypertensive (*see also* Hypertension, heart)
        402.91
        benign 402.11
        malignant 402.01
      rheumatic (chronic) (inactive) (with chorea)
        398.91
        active or acute 391.8
          with chorea 392.0
    right (*see also* Failure, heart, congestive) 428.0
  vital centers, fetus or newborn 779.8
  weight gain in childhood 783.41
Fainting (fit) (spell) 780.2
Falciform hymen 752.49
Fall, maternal, affecting fetus or newborn
  760.5
Fallen arches 734
Falling, any organ or part —*see* Prolapse
Fallopian
  insufflation
    fertility testing V26.21
    following sterilization reversal V26.22
  tube—*see* condition
Fallot's
  pentalogy 745.2
  tetrad or tetralogy 745.2
  triad or trilogy 746.09
Fallout, radioactive (adverse effect) NEC 990
False —*see also* condition
  bundle branch block 426.50
  bursa 727.89
  croup 478.75
  joint 733.82
  labor (pains) 644.1
  opening, urinary, male 752.69
  passage, urethra (prostatic) 599.4
  positive
    serological test for syphilis 795.6
    Wassermann reaction 795.6
  pregnancy 300.11
Family, familial —*see also* condition
  disruption V61.0
  planning advice V25.09
  problem V61.9
    specified circumstance NEC V61.8
Famine 994.2
  edema 262
Fanconi's anemia (congenital pancytopenia)
  284.0
Fanconi (-de Toni) (-Debré) syndrome
  (cystinosis) 270.0
Farber (-Uzman) syndrome or disease
  (disseminated lipogranulomatosis) 272.8
Farcin 024
Farcy 024
Farmers '
  lung 495.0
  skin 692.74
Farsightedness 367.0
Fascia —*see* condition
Fasciculation 781.0
Fasciculitis optica 377.32

Fasciitis 729.4
  eosinophilic 728.89
  necrotizing 728.86
  nodular 728.79
  perirenal 593.4
  plantar 728.71
  pseudosarcomatous 728.79
  traumatic (old) NEC 728.79
    current—*see* Sprain, by site
Fasciola hepatica infestation 121.3
Fascioliasis 121.3
Fasciolopsiasis (small intestine) 121.4
Fasciolopsis (small intestine) 121.4
Fast pulse 785.0
Fat
  embolism (cerebral) (pulmonary) (systemic)
    958.1
    with
      abortion—*see* Abortion, by type, with
        embolism
      ectopic pregnancy (*see also* categories
        633.0-633.9) 639.6
      molar pregnancy (*see also* categories
        630-632) 639.6
    complicating delivery or puerperium 673.8
    following
      abortion 639.6
      ectopic or molar pregnancy 639.6
    in pregnancy, childbirth, or the puerperium
      673.8
  excessive 278.00
    in heart (*see also* Degeneration, myocardial)
      429.1
  general 278.00
  hernia, herniation 729.30
    eyelid 374.34
    knee 729.31
    orbit 374.34
    retro-orbital 374.34
    retropatellar 729.31
    specified site NEC 729.39
  indigestion 579.8
  in stool 792.1
  localized (pad) 278.1
    heart (*see also* Degeneration, myocardial)
      429.1
    knee 729.31
    retropatellar 729.31
  necrosis—*see also* Fatty, degeneration
    breast (aseptic) (segmental) 611.3
    mesentery 567.8
    omentum 567.8
  pad 278.1
Fatal syncope 798.1
Fatigue 780.79
  auditory deafness (*see also* Deafness) 389.9
  chronic, syndrome 780.71
  combat (*see also* Reaction, stress, acute) 308.9
  during pregnancy 646.8
  general 780.79
    psychogenic 300.5
  heat (transient) 992.6
  muscle 729.89
  myocardium (*see also* Failure, heart) 428.9
  nervous 300.5
  neurosis 300.5
  operational 300.89
  postural 729.89
  posture 729.89
  psychogenic (general) 300.5

Fever—*continued*
    pericarditis 393
  Rift Valley (viral) 066.3
  Rocky Mountain spotted 082.0
  rose 477.0
  Ross river (viral) 066.3
  Russian hemorrhagic 078.6
  sandfly 066.0
  San Joaquin (valley) 114.0
  São Paulo 082.0
  scarlet 034.1
  septic—*see* Septicemia
  seven-day 061
    Japan 100.89
    Queensland 100.89
  shin bone 083.1
  Singapore hemorrhagic 065.4
  solar 061
  sore 054.9
  South African tick-bite 087.1
  Southeast Asia hemorrhagic 065.4
  spinal—*see* Meningitis
  spirillary 026.0
  splenic (*see also* Anthrax) 022.9
  spotted (Rocky Mountain) 082.0
    American 082.0
    Brazilian 082.0
    Colombian 082.0
    meaning
      cerebrospinal meningitis 036.0
      typhus 082.9
  spring 309.23
  steroid
    correct substance properly administered 780.6
    overdose or wrong substance given or taken
      962.0
  streptobacillary 026.1
  subtertian 084.0
  Sumatran mite 081.2
  sun 061
  swamp 100.89
  sweating 078.2
  swine 003.8
  sylvatic yellow 060.0
  Tahyna 062.5
  tertian—*see* Malaria, tertian
  Thailand hemorrhagic 065.4
  thermic 992.0
  three day 066.0
    with Coxsackie exanthem 074.8
  tick
    American mountain 066.1
    Colorado 066.1
    Kemerovo 066.1
    Mediterranean 082.1
    mountain 066.1
    nonexanthematous 066.1
    Quaranfil 066.1
  tick-bite NEC 066.1
  tick-borne NEC 066.1
    hemorrhagic NEC 065.3
  transitory of newborn 778.4
  trench 083.1
  tsutsugamushi 081.2
  typhogastric 002.0
  typhoid (abortive) (ambulant) (any site)
    (hemorrhagic) (infection) (intermittent)
    (malignant) (rheumatic) 002.0
  typhomalarial (*see also* Malaria) 084.6
  typhus—*see* Typhus
  undulant (*see also* Brucellosis) 023.9

Fever—*continued*
  unknown origin (*see also* Pyrexia) 780.6
  uremic—*see* Uremia
  uveoparotid 135
  valley (Coccidioidomycosis) 114.0
  Venezuelan equine 066.2
  Volhynian 083.1
  Wesselsbron (viral) 066.3
  West
    African 084.8
    Nile (viral) 066.3
  Whitmore's 025
  Wolhynian 083.1
  worm 128.9
  Yaroslav hemorrhagic 078.6
  yellow 060.9
    jungle 060.0
    sylvatic 060.0
    urban 060.1
    vaccination, prophylactic (against) V04.4
  Zika (viral) 066.3
Fibrillation
  atrial (established) (paroxysmal) 427.31
  auricular (atrial) (established) 427.31
  cardiac (ventricular) 427.41
  coronary (*see also* Infarct, myocardium) 410.9
  heart (ventricular) 427.41
  muscular 728.9
  postoperative 997.1
  ventricular 427.41
Fibrin
  ball or bodies, pleural (sac) 511.0
  chamber, anterior (eye) (gelatinous exudate)
    364.04
Fibrinogenolysis (hemorrhagic)—*see*
  Fibrinolysis
Fibrinogenopenia (congenital) (hereditary) (*see*
  also Defect, coagulation) 286.3
  acquired 286.6
Fibrinolysis (acquired) (hemorrhagic)
  (pathologic) 286.6
  with
    abortion—*see* Abortion, by type, with
      hemorrhage, delayed or excessive
    ectopic pregnancy (*see also* categories
      633.0-633.9) 639.1
    molar pregnancy (*see also* categories
      630-632) 639.1
  antepartum or intrapartum 641.3
    affecting fetus or newborn 762.1
  following
    abortion 639.1
    ectopic or molar pregnancy 639.1
  newborn, transient 776.2
  postpartum 666.3
Fibrinopenia (hereditary) (*see also* Defect,
  coagulation) 286.3
  acquired 286.6
Fibrinopurulent —*see* condition
Fibrinous —*see* condition
Fibroadenoma (M9010/0)
  cellular intracanalicular (M9020/0) 217
  giant (intracanalicular) (M9020/0) 217
  intracanalicular (M9011/0)
    cellular (M9020/0) 217
    giant (M9020/0) 217
    specified site—*see* Neoplasm, by site, benign
    unspecified site 217
  juvenile (M9030/0) 217

Fibroadenoma—*continued*
  pericanalicular (M9012/0)
    specified site—*see* Neoplasm, by site, benign
    unspecified site 217
  phyllodes (M9020/0) 217
  prostate 600.2
  specified site—*see* Neoplasm, by site, benign
  unspecified site 217
Fibroadenosis, breast (chronic) (cystic) (diffuse)
  (periodic) (segmental) 610.2
Fibroangioma (M9160/0)—*see also* Neoplasm,
  by site, benign
  juvenile (M9160/0)
    specified site—*see* Neoplasm, by site, benign
    unspecified site 210.7
Fibrocellulitis progressiva ossificans 728.11
Fibrochondrosarcoma (M9220/3)—*see*
  Neoplasm, cartilage, malignant
Fibrocystic
  disease 277.00
    bone NEC 733.29
    breast 610.1
    jaw 526.2
    kidney (congenital) 753.19
    liver 751.62
    lung 518.89
      congenital 748.4
    pancreas 277.00
  kidney (congenital) 753.19
Fibrodysplasia ossificans multiplex
  (progressiva) 728.11
Fibroelastosis (cordis) (endocardial)
  (endomyocardial) 425.3
Fibroid (tumor) (M8890/0)—*see also* Neoplasm,
  connective tissue, benign
  disease, lung (chronic) (*see also* Fibrosis, lung)
    515
  heart (disease) (*see also* Myocarditis) 429.0
  induration, lung (chronic) (*see also* Fibrosis,
    lung) 515
  in pregnancy or childbirth 654.1
    affecting fetus or newborn 763.89
    causing obstructed labor 660.2
      affecting fetus or newborn 763.1
  liver—*see* Cirrhosis, liver
  lung (*see also* Fibrosis, lung) 515
  pneumonia (chronic) (*see also* Fibrosis, lung)
    515
  uterus (M8890/0) (*see also* Leiomyoma, uterus)
    218.9
Fibrolipoma (M8851/0) (*see also* Lipoma, by
  site) 214.9
Fibroliposarcoma (M8850/3)—*see* Neoplasm,
  connective tissue, malignant
Fibroma (M8810/0)—*see also* Neoplasm,
  connective tissue, benign
  ameloblastic (M9330/0) 213.1
    upper jaw (bone) 213.0
  bone (nonossifying) 733.99
    ossifying (M9262/0)—*see* Neoplasm, bone,
      benign
  cementifying (M9274/0)—*see* Neoplasm, bone,
    benign
  chondromyxoid (M9241/0)—*see* Neoplasm,
    bone, benign
  desmoplastic (M8823/1)—*see* Neoplasm,
    connective tissue, uncertain behavior
  facial (M8813/0)—*see* Neoplasm, connective
    tissue, benign
  invasive (M8821/1)—*see* Neoplasm, connective
    tissue, uncertain behavior

Fibroma—*continued*
  molle (M8851/0) (*see also* Lipoma, by site)
    214.9
  myxoid (M8811/0)—*see* Neoplasm, connective
    tissue, benign
  nasopharynx, nasopharyngeal (juvenile)
    (M9160/0) 210.7
  nonosteogenic (nonossifying)—*see* Dysplasia,
    fibrous
  odontogenic (M9321/0) 213.1
    upper jaw (bone) 213.0
  ossifying (M9262/0)—*see* Neoplasm, bone,
    benign
  periosteal (M8812/0)—*see* Neoplasm, bone,
    benign
  prostate 600.2
  soft (M8851/0) (*see also* Lipoma, by site) 214.9
Fibromatosis
  abdominal (M8822/1)—*see* Neoplasm,
    connective tissue, uncertain behavior
  aggressive (M8821/1)—*see* Neoplasm,
    connective tissue, uncertain behavior
  Dupuytren's 728.6
  gingival 523.8
  plantar fascia 728.71
  proliferative 728.79
  pseudosarcomatous (proliferative)
    (subcutaneous) 728.79
  subcutaneous pseudosarcomatous (proliferative)
    728.79
Fibromyalgia 729.1
Fibromyoma (M8890/0)—*see also* Neoplasm,
  connective tissue, benign
  uterus (corpus) (*see also* Leiomyoma, uterus)
    218.9
    in pregnancy or childbirth 654.1
      affecting fetus or newborn 763.89
      causing obstructed labor 660.2
        affecting fetus or newborn 763.1
Fibromyositis (*see also* Myositis) 729.1
  scapulohumeral 726.2
Fibromyxolipoma (M8852/0) (*see also* Lipoma,
  by site) 214.9
Fibromyxoma (M8811/0)—*see* Neoplasm,
  connective tissue, benign
Fibromyxosarcoma (M8811/3)—*see* Neoplasm,
  connective tissue, malignant
Fibro-odontoma, ameloblastic (M9290/0) 213.1
  upper jaw (bone) 213.0
Fibro-osteoma (M9262/0)—*see* Neoplasm,
  bone, benign
Fibroplasia, retrolental 362.21
Fibropurulent —*see* condition
Fibrosarcoma (M8810/3)—*see also* Neoplasm,
  connective tissue, malignant
  ameloblastic (M9330/3) 170.1
    upper jaw (bone) 170.0
  congenital (M8814/3)—*see* Neoplasm,
    connective tissue, malignant
  fascial (M8813/3)—*see* Neoplasm, connective
    tissue, malignant
  infantile (M8814/3)—*see* Neoplasm, connective
    tissue, malignant
  odontogenic (M9330/3) 170.1
    upper jaw (bone) 170.0
  periosteal (M8812/3)—*see* Neoplasm, bone,
    malignant

Fibrosis, fibrotic—*continued*
  vagina 623.8
  valve, heart (*see also* Endocarditis) 424.90
  vas deferens 608.89
  vein 459.89
    lower extremities 459.89
  vesical 595.1
Fibrositis (periarticular) (rheumatoid) 729.0
  humeroscapular region 726.2
  nodular, chronic
    Jaccoud's 714.4
    rheumatoid 714.4
  ossificans 728.11
  scapulohumeral 726.2
Fibrothorax 511.0
Fibrotic —*see* Fibrosis
Fibrous —*see* condition
Fibroxanthoma (M8831/0)—*see also* Neoplasm,
    connective tissue, benign
  atypical (M8831/1)—*see* Neoplasm, connective
    tissue, uncertain behavior
  malignant (M8831/3)—*see* Neoplasm,
    connective tissue, malignant
Fibroxanthosarcoma (M8831/3)—*see*
    Neoplasm, connective tissue, malignant
Fiedler's
  disease (leptospiral jaundice) 100.0
  myocarditis or syndrome (acute isolated
    myocarditis) 422.91
Fiessinger-Leroy (-Reiter) syndrome 099.3
Fiessinger-Rendu syndrome (erythema
    muliforme exudativum) 695.1
Fifth disease (eruptive) 057.0
  venereal 099.1
Filaria, filarial —*see* Infestation, filarial
Filariasis (*see also* Infestation, filarial) 125.9
  bancroftian 125.0
  Brug's 125.1
  due to
    bancrofti 125.0
    Brugia (Wuchereria) (malayi) 125.1
    Loa loa 125.2
    malayi 125.1
    organism NEC 125.6
    Wuchereria (bancrofti) 125.0
      malayi 125.1
  Malayan 125.1
  ozzardi 125.5
  specified type NEC 125.6
Filatoff's, Filatov's, Filatow's disease
    (infectious mononucleosis) 075
File-cutters' disease 984.9
  specified type of lead—*see* Table of drugs and
    chemicals
Filling defect
  biliary tract 793.3
  bladder 793.5
  duodenum 793.4
  gallbladder 793.3
  gastrointestinal tract 793.4
  intestine 793.4
  kidney 793.5
  stomach 793.4
  ureter 793.5
Filtering bleb, eye (postglaucoma) (status)
    V45.69
  with complication or rupture 997.99
  postcataract extraction (complication) 997.99
Fimbrial cyst (congenital) 752.11
Fimbriated hymen 752.49
Financial problem affecting care V60.2

Findings, abnormal, without diagnosis
    (examination) (laboratory test) 796.4
  17-ketosteroids, elevated 791.9
  acetonuria 791.6
  acid phosphatase 790.5
  albumin-globulin ratio 790.99
  albuminuria 791.0
  alcohol in blood 790.3
  alkaline phosphatase 790.5
  amniotic fluid 792.3
  amylase 790.5
  anisocytosis 790.09
  antenatal screening 796.5
  antibody titers, elevated 795.79
  anticardiolipin antibody 795.79
  antigen-antibody reaction 795.79
  antiphospholipid antibody 795.79
  bacteriuria 791.9
  ballistocardiogram 794.39
  bicarbonate 276.9
  bile in urine 791.4
  bilirubin 277.4
  bleeding time (prolonged) 790.92
  blood culture, positive 790.7
  blood gas level 790.91
  blood sugar level 790.2
    high 790.2
    low 251.2
  calcium 275.40
  carbonate 276.9
  casts, urine 791.7
  catecholamines 791.9
  cells, urine 791.7
  cerebrospinal fluid (color) (content) (pressure)
    792.0
  chloride 276.9
  cholesterol 272.9
  chromosome analysis 795.2
  chyluria 791.1
  circulation time 794.39
  cloudy dialysis effluent 792.5
  cloudy urine 791.9
  coagulation study 790.92
  cobalt, blood 790.6
  color of urine (unusual) NEC 791.9
  copper, blood 790.6
  crystals, urine 791.9
  culture, positive NEC 795.3
    blood 790.7
    HIV V08
    human immunodeficiency virus V08
    nose 795.3
    skin lesion NEC 795.3
    spinal fluid 792.0
    sputum 795.3
    stool 792.1
    throat 795.3
    urine 791.9
    viral
      human immunodeficiency V08
    wound 795.3
  echocardiogram 793.2
  echoencephalogram 794.01
  echogram NEC—*see* Findings, abnormal,
    structure
  electrocardiogram (ECG) (EKG) 794.31
  electroencephalogram (EEG) 794.02
  electrolyte level, urinary 791.9
  electromyogram (EMG) 794.17
    ocular 794.14
  electro-oculogram (EOG) 794.12

Fistula—*continued*
 appendix, appendicular 543.9
 arteriovenous (acquired) 447.0
  brain 437.3
   congenital 747.81
    ruptured (*see also* Hemorrhage,
      subarachnoid) 430
    ruptured (*see also* Hemorrhage,
      subarachnoid) 430
   cerebral 437.3
    congenital 747.81
   congenital (peripheral) 747.60
    brain—*see* Fistula, arteriovenous, brain,
      congenital
    coronary 746.85
    gastrointestinal 747.61
    lower limb 747.64
    pulmonary 747.3
    renal 747.62
    specified NEC 747.69
    upper limb 747.63
   coronary 414.19
    congenital 746.85
   heart 414.19
   pulmonary (vessels) 417.0
    congenital 747.3
   surgically created (for dialysis) V45.1
    complication NEC 996.73
     atherosclerosis —*see* Arteriosclerosis,
       extremities
     embolism 996.74
     infection or inflammation 996.62
     mechanical 996.1
     occlusion NEC 996.74
     thrombus 996.74
   traumatic—*see* Injury, blood vessel, by site
 artery 447.2
 aural 383.81
  congenital 744.49
 auricle 383.81
  congenital 744.49
 Bartholin's gland 619.8
 bile duct (*see also* Fistula, biliary) 576.4
 biliary (duct) (tract) 576.4
  congenital 751.69
 bladder (neck) (sphincter) 596.2
  into seminal vesicle 596.2
 bone 733.99
 brain 348.8
  arteriovenous—*see* Fistula, arteriovenous,
    brain
 branchial (cleft) 744.41
 branchiogenous 744.41
 breast 611.0
  puerperal, postpartum 675.1
 bronchial 510.0
 bronchocutaneous, bronchomediastinal,
   bronchopleural, bronchopleuromediastinal
   (infective) 510.0
  tuberculous (*see also* Tuberculosis) 011.3
 bronchoesophageal 530.89
  congenital 750.3
 buccal cavity (infective) 528.3
 canal, ear 380.89
 carotid-cavernous
  congenital 747.81
   with hemorrhage 430
  traumatic 900.82
   with hemorrhage (see also Hemorrhage,
     brain, traumatic) 853.0
   late effect 908.3

Fistula—*continued*
 cecosigmoidal 569.81
 cecum 569.81
 cerebrospinal (fluid) 349.81
 cervical, lateral (congenital) 744.41
 cervicoaural (congenital) 744.49
 cervicosigmoidal 619.1
 cervicovesical 619.0
 cervix 619.8
 chest (wall) 510.0
 cholecystocolic (*see also* Fistula, gallbladder)
   575.5
 cholecystocolonic (*see also* Fistula, gallbladder)
   575.5
 cholecystoduodenal (*see also* Fistula,
   gallbladder) 575.5
 cholecystoenteric (*see also* Fistula, gallbladder)
   575.5
 cholecystogastric (*see also* Fistula, gallbladder)
   575.5
 cholecystointestinal (*see also* Fistula,
   gallbladder) 575.5
 choledochoduodenal 576.4
 cholocolic (*see also* Fistula, gallbladder) 575.5
 coccyx 685.1
  with abscess 685.0
 colon 569.81
 colostomy 569.69
 colovaginal (acquired) 619.1
 common duct (bile duct) 576.4
 congenital, NEC—*see* Anomaly, specified type
   NEC
 cornea, causing hypotony 360.32
 coronary, arteriovenous 414.19
  congenital 746.85
 costal region 510.0
 cul-de-sac, Douglas' 619.8
 cutaneous 686.9
 cystic duct (*see also* Fistula, gallbladder) 575.5
  congenital 751.69
 dental 522.7
 diaphragm 510.0
  bronchovisceral 510.0
  pleuroperitoneal 510.0
  pulmonoperitoneal 510.0
 duodenum 537.4
 ear (canal) (external) 380.89
 enterocolic 569.81
 enterocutaneous 569.81
 enteroenteric 569.81
 entero-uterine 619.1
  congenital 752.3
 enterovaginal 619.1
  congenital 752.49
 enterovesical 596.1
 epididymis 608.89
  tuberculous (*see also* Tuberculosis) 016.4
 esophagobronchial 530.89
  congenital 750.3
 esophagocutaneous 530.89
 esophagopleurocutaneous 530.89
 esophagotracheal 530.84
  congenital 750.3
 esophagus 530.89
  congenital 750.4
 ethmoid (*see also* Sinusitis, ethmoidal) 473.2
 eyeball (cornea) (sclera) 360.32
 eyelid 373.11
 fallopian tube (external) 619.2
 fecal 569.81
  congenital 751.5

Fistula—*continued*
from periapical lesion 522.7
frontal sinus (*see also* Sinusitis, frontal) 473.1
gallbladder 575.5
  with calculus, cholelithiasis, stones (*see also*
    Cholelithiasis) 574.2
  congenital 751.69
gastric 537.4
gastrocolic 537.4
  congenital 750.7
  tuberculous (*see also* Tuberculosis) 014.8
gastroenterocolic 537.4
gastroesophageal 537.4
gastrojejunal 537.4
gastrojejunocolic 537.4
genital
  organs
    female 619.9
      specified site NEC 619.8
    male 608.89
  tract-skin (female) 619.2
hepatopleural 510.0
hepatopulmonary 510.0
horseshoe 565.1
ileorectal 569.81
ileosigmoidal 569.81
ileostomy 569.69
ileovesical 596.1
ileum 569.81
in ano 565.1
  tuberculous (*see also* Tuberculosis) 014.8
inner ear (*see also* Fistula, labyrinth) 386.40
intestine 569.81
intestinocolonic (abdominal) 569.81
intestinoureteral 593.82
intestinouterine 619.1
intestinovaginal 619.1
  congenital 752.49
intestinovesical 596.1
involving female genital tract 619.9
  digestive-genital 619.1
  genital tract-skin 619.2
  specified site NEC 619.8
  urinary-genital 619.0
ischiorectal (fossa) 566
jejunostomy 569.69
jejunum 569.81
joint 719.80
  ankle 719.87
  elbow 719.82
  foot 719.87
  hand 719.84
  hip 719.85
  knee 719.86
  multiple sites 719.89
  pelvic region 719.85
  shoulder (region) 719.81
  specified site NEC 719.88
  tuberculous—*see* Tuberculosis, joint
  wrist 719.83
kidney 593.89
labium (majus) (minus) 619.8
labyrinth, labyrinthine NEC 386.40
  combined sites 386.48
  multiple sites 386.48
  oval window 386.42
  round window 386.41
  semicircular canal 386.43
lacrimal, lachrymal (duct) (gland) (sac) 375.61
lacrimonasal duct 375.61
laryngotracheal 748.3

Fistula—*continued*
larynx 478.79
lip 528.5
  congenital 750.25
lumbar, tuberculous (*see also* Tuberculosis)
  015.0 *[730.8]*
lung 510.0
lymphatic (node) (vessel) 457.8
mamillary 611.0
mammary (gland) 611.0
  puerperal, postpartum 675.1
mastoid (process) (region) 383.1
maxillary (*see also* Sinusitis, maxillary) 473.0
mediastinal 510.0
mediastinobronchial 510.0
mediastinocutaneous 510.0
middle ear 385.89
mouth 528.3
nasal 478.1
  sinus (*see also* Sinusitis) 473.9
nasopharynx 478.29
nipple—*see* Fistula, breast
nose 478.1
oral (cutaneous) 528.3
  maxillary (*see also* Sinusitis, maxillary) 473.0
  nasal (with cleft palate) (*see also* Cleft, palate)
    749.00
orbit, orbital 376.10
oro-antral (*see also* Sinusitis, maxillary) 473.0
oval window (internal ear) 386.42
oviduct (external) 619.2
palate (hard) 526.89
  soft 528.9
pancreatic 577.8
pancreaticoduodenal 577.8
parotid (gland) 527.4
  region 528.3
pelvoabdominointestinal 569.81
penis 607.89
perianal 565.1
pericardium (pleura) (sac) (*see also* Pericarditis)
  423.8
pericecal 569.81
perineal—*see* Fistula, perineum
perineorectal 569.81
perineosigmoidal 569.81
perineo-urethroscrotal 608.89
perineum, perineal (with urethral involvement)
  NEC 599.1
  tuberculous (*see also* Tuberculosis) 017.9
  ureter 593.82
perirectal 565.1
  tuberculous (*see also* Tuberculosis) 014.8
peritoneum (*see also* Peritonitis) 567.2
periurethral 599.1
pharyngo-esophageal 478.29
pharynx 478.29
  branchial cleft (congenital) 744.41
pilonidal (infected) (rectum) 685.1
  with abscess 685.0
pleura, pleural, pleurocutaneous,
  pleuroperitoneal 510.0
  stomach 510.0
  tuberculous (*see also* Tuberculosis) 012.0
pleuropericardial 423.8
postauricular 383.81
postoperative, persistent 998.6
preauricular (congenital) 744.46
prostate 602.8

Fistula—*continued*
  pulmonary 510.0
    arteriovenous 417.0
      congenital 747.3
      tuberculous (*see also* Tuberculosis,
        pulmonary) 011.9
  pulmonoperitoneal 510.0
  rectolabial 619.1
  rectosigmoid (intercommunicating) 569.81
  rectoureteral 593.82
  rectourethral 599.1
    congenital 753.8
  rectouterine 619.1
    congenital 752.3
  rectovaginal 619.1
    congenital 752.49
    old, postpartal 619.1
    tuberculous (*see also* Tuberculosis) 014.8
  rectovesical 596.1
    congenital 753.8
  rectovesicovaginal 619.1
  rectovulvar 619.1
    congenital 752.49
  rectum (to skin) 565.1
    tuberculous (*see also* Tuberculosis) 014.8
  renal 593.89
  retroauricular 383.81
  round window (internal ear) 386.41
  salivary duct or gland 527.4
    congenital 750.24
  sclera 360.32
  scrotum (urinary) 608.89
    tuberculous (*see also* Tuberculosis) 016.5
  semicircular canals (internal ear) 386.43
  sigmoid 569.81
    vesicoabdominal 596.1
  sigmoidovaginal 619.1
    congenital 752.49
  skin 686.9
    ureter 593.82
    vagina 619.2
  sphenoidal sinus (*see also* Sinusitis, sphenoidal)
    473.3
  splenocolic 289.59
  stercoral 569.81
  stomach 537.4
  sublingual gland 527.4
    congenital 750.24
  submaxillary
    gland 527.4
      congenital 750.24
    region 528.3
  thoracic 510.0
    duct 457.8
  thoracicoabdominal 510.0
  thoracicogastric 510.0
  thoracicointestinal 510.0
  thoracoabdominal 510.0
  thoracogastric 510.0
  thorax 510.0
  thyroglossal duct 759.2
  thyroid 246.8
  trachea (congenital) (external) (internal) 748.3
  tracheoesophageal 530.84
    congenital 750.3
    following tracheostomy 519.09
  traumatic
    arteriovenous (*see also* Injury, blood vessel,
      by site) 904.9
    brain—*see* Injury, intracranial

Fistula—*continued*
  tuberculous—*see* Tuberculosis, by site
  typhoid 002.0
  umbilical 759.89
  umbilico-urinary 753.8
  urachal, urachus 753.7
  ureter (persistent) 593.82
  ureteroabdominal 593.82
  ureterocervical 593.82
  ureterorectal 593.82
  ureterosigmoido-abdominal 593.82
  ureterovaginal 619.0
  ureterovesical 596.2
  urethra 599.1
    congenital 753.8
    tuberculous (*see also* Tuberculosis) 016.3
  urethroperineal 599.1
  urethroperineovesical 596.2
  urethrorectal 599.1
    congenital 753.8
  urethroscrotal 608.89
  urethrovaginal 619.0
  urethrovesical 596.2
  urethrovesicovaginal 619.0
  urinary (persistent) (recurrent) 599.1
  uteroabdominal (anterior wall) 619.2
    congenital 752.3
  uteroenteric 619.1
  uterofecal 619.1
  uterointestinal 619.1
    congenital 752.3
  uterorectal 619.1
    congenital 752.3
  uteroureteric 619.0
  uterovaginal 619.8
  uterovesical 619.0
    congenital 752.3
  uterus 619.8
  vagina (wall) 619.8
    postpartal, old 619.8
  vaginocutaneous (postpartal) 619.2
  vaginoileal (acquired) 619.1
  vaginoperineal 619.2
  vesical NEC 596.2
  vesicoabdominal 596.2
  vesicocervicovaginal 619.0
  vesicocolic 596.1
  vesicocutaneous 596.2
  vesicoenteric 596.1
  vesicointestinal 596.1
  vesicometrorectal 619.1
  vesicoperineal 596.2
  vesicorectal 596.1
    congenital 753.8
  vesicosigmoidal 596.1
  vesicosigmoidovaginal 619.1
  vesicoureteral 596.2
  vesicoureterovaginal 619.0
  vesicourethral 596.2
  vesicourethrorectal 596.1
  vesicouterine 619.0
    congenital 752.3
  vesicovaginal 619.0
  vulvorectal 619.1
    congenital 752.49
Fit 780.39
  apoplectic (*see also* Disease, cerebrovascular,
    acute) 436
    late effect—*see* Late effect(s) (of)
      cerebrovascular disease
  epileptic (*see also* Epilepsy) 345.9

Fit —*continued*
  fainting 780.2
  hysterical 300.11
  newborn 779.0
Fitting (of)
  artificial
    arm (complete) (partial) V52.0
    breast V52.4
    eye(s) V52.2
    leg(s) (complete) (partial) V52.1
  brain neuropacemaker V53.02
  cardiac pacemaker V53.31
  carotid sinus pacemaker V53.39
  cerebral ventricle (communicating) shunt
    V53.01
  colostomy belt V53.5
  contact lenses V53.1
  cystostomy device V53.6
  defibrillator, automatic implantable V53.32
  dentures V52.3
  device NEC V53.9
    abdominal V53.5
    cardiac
      defibrillator, automatic implantable V53.32
      pacemaker V53.31
      specified NEC V53.39
    cerebral ventricle (communicating) shunt
      V53.01
    intrauterine contraceptive V25.1
    nervous system V53.09
    orthodontic V53.4
    orthoptic V53.1
    prosthetic V52.9
      breast V52.4
      dental V52.3
      eye V52.2
      specified type NEC V52.8
    special senses V53.09
    substitution
      auditory V53.09
      nervous system V53.09
      visual V53.09
    urinary V53.6
  diaphragm (contraceptive) V25.02
  glasses (reading) V53.1
  hearing aid V53.2
  ileostomy device V53.5
  intestinal appliance or device NEC V53.5
  intrauterine contraceptive device V25.1
  neuropacemaker (brain) (peripheral nerve)
    (spinal cord) V53.02
  orthodontic device V53.4
  orthopedic (device) V53.7
    brace V53.7
    cast V53.7
    corset V53.7
    shoes V53.7
  pacemaker (cardiac) V53.31
    brain V53.02
    carotid sinus V53.39
    peripheral nerve V53.02
    spinal cord V53.02
  prosthesis V52.9
    arm (complete) (partial) V52.0
    breast V52.4
    dental V52.3
    eye V52.2
    leg (complete) (partial) V52.1
    specified type NEC V52.8
  spectacles V53.1
  wheelchair V53.8

Fitz's syndrome (acute hemorrhagic
  pancreatitis) 577.0
Fitz-Hugh and Curtis syndrome (gonococcal
  peritonitis) 098.86
Fixation
  joint—*see* Ankylosis
  larynx 478.79
  pupil 364.76
  stapes 385.22
    deafness (*see also* Deafness, conductive)
      389.04
  uterus (acquired)—*see* Malposition, uterus
  vocal cord 478.5
Flaccid —*see* condition
  foot 736.79
  forearm 736.09
  palate, congenital 750.26
Flail
  chest 807.4
    newborn 767.3
  joint (paralytic) 718.80
    ankle 718.87
    elbow 718.82
    foot 718.87
    hand 718.84
    hip 718.85
    knee 718.86
    multiple sites 718.89
    pelvic region 718.85
    shoulder (region) 718.81
    specified site NEC 718.88
    wrist 718.83
Flajani (-Basedow) syndrome or disease
  (exophthalmic goiter) 242.0
Flap, liver 572.8
Flare, anterior chamber (aqueous) (eye) 364.04
Flashback phenomena (drug) (hallucinogenic)
  292.89
Flat
  chamber (anterior) (eye) 360.34
  chest, congenital 754.89
  electroencephalogram (EEG) 348.8
  foot (acquired) (fixed type) (painful) (postural)
    (spastic) 734
    congenital 754.61
      rocker bottom 754.61
      vertical talus 754.61
    rachitic 268.1
    rocker bottom (congenital) 754.61
    vertical talus, congenital 754.61
  organ or site, congenital NEC—*see* Anomaly,
    specified type NEC
  pelvis 738.6
    with disproportion (fetopelvic) 653.2
      affecting fetus or newborn 763.1
      causing obstructed labor 660.1
        affecting fetus or newborn 763.1
    congenital 755.69
Flatau-Schilder disease 341.1
Flattening
  head, femur 736.39
  hip 736.39
  lip (congenital) 744.89
  nose (congenital) 754.0
    acquired 738.0
Flatulence 787.3
Flatus 787.3
  vaginalis 629.8
Flax dressers' disease 504
Flea bite —*see* Injury, superficial, by site
Fleischer (-Kayser) ring (corneal pigmentation)
  275.1 *[371.14]*

Fleischner's disease 732.3
Fleshy mole 631
Flexibilitas cerea (*see also* Catalepsy) 300.11
Flexion
    cervix (*see also* Malposition, uterus) 621.6
    contracture, joint (*see also* Contraction, joint) 718.4
    deformity, joint (*see also* Contraction, joint) 718.4
        hip, congenital (*see also* Subluxation, congenital, hip) 754.32
    uterus (*see also* Malposition, uterus) 621.6
Flexner's
    bacillus 004.1
    diarrhea (ulcerative) 004.1
    dysentery 004.1
Flexner-Boyd dysentery 004.2
Flexure —*see* condition
Floater, vitreous 379.24
Floating
    cartilage (joint) (*see also* Disorder, cartilage, articular) 718.0
        knee 717.6
    gallbladder (congenital) 751.69
    kidney 593.0
        congenital 753.3
    liver (congenital) 751.69
    rib 756.3
    spleen 289.59
Flooding 626.2
Floor —*see* condition
Floppy
    infant NEC 781.99
    valve syndrome (mitral) 424.0
Flu —*see also* Influenza
    gastric NEC 008.8
Fluctuating blood pressure 796.4
Fluid
    abdomen 789.5
    chest (*see also* Pleurisy, with effusion) 511.9
    heart (*see also* Failure, heart, congestive) 428.0
    joint (*see also* Effusion, joint) 719.0
    loss (acute) 276.5
        with
            hypernatremia 276.0
            hyponatremia 276.1
    lung—*see also* Edema, lung
        encysted 511.8
    peritoneal cavity 789.5
    pleural cavity (*see also* Pleurisy, with effusion) 511.9
    retention 276.6
Flukes NEC (*see also* Infestation, fluke) 121.9
    blood NEC (*see also* Infestation, Schistosoma) 120.9
    liver 121.3
Fluor (albus) (vaginalis) 623.5
    trichomonal (Trichomonas vaginalis) 131.00
Fluorosis (dental) (chronic) 520.3
Flushing 782.62
    menopausal 627.2
Flush syndrome 259.2
Flutter
    atrial or auricular 427.32
    heart (ventricular) 427.42
        atrial 427.32
    impure 427.32
    postoperative 997.1
    ventricular 427.42
Flux (bloody) (serosanguineous) 009.0
Focal —*see* condition
Fochier's abscess —*see* Abscess, by site

Focus, Assmann's (*see also* Tuberculosis) 011.0
Fogo selvagem 694.4
Foix-Alajouanine syndrome 336.1
Folds, anomalous —*see also* Anomaly, specified type NEC
    Bowman's membrane 371.31
    Descemet's membrane 371.32
    epicanthic 743.63
    heart 746.89
    posterior segment of eye, congenital 743.54
Folie à deux 297.3
Follicle
    cervix (nabothian) (ruptured) 616.0
    graafian, ruptured, with hemorrhage 620.0
    nabothian 616.0
Folliclis (primary) (*see also* Tuberculosis) 017.0
Follicular —*see also* condition
    cyst (atretic) 620.0
Folliculitis 704.8
    abscedens et suffodiens 704.8
    decalvans 704.09
    gonorrheal (acute) 098.0
        chronic or duration of 2 months or more 098.2
    keloid, keloidalis 706.1
    pustular 704.8
    ulerythematosa reticulata 701.8
Folliculosis, conjunctival 372.02
Folling's disease (phenylketonuria) 270.1
Follow-up (examination) (routine) (following) V67.9
    cancer chemotherapy V67.2
    chemotherapy V67.2
    fracture V67.4
    high-risk medication V67.51
    injury NEC V67.59
    postpartum
        immediately after delivery V24.0
        routine V24.2
    psychiatric V67.3
    psychotherapy V67.3
    radiotherapy V67.1
    specified condition NEC V67.59
    specified surgery NEC V67.09
    surgery V67.00
        vaginal pap smear V67.01
    treatment V67.9
        combined NEC V67.6
        fracture V67.4
        involving high-risk medication NEC V67.51
        mental disorder V67.3
        specified NEC V67.59
Fong's syndrome (hereditary osteoonychodysplasia) 756.89
Food
    allergy 693.1
    anaphylactic shock—*see* Anaphylactic shock, due to, food
    asphyxia (from aspiration or inhalation) (*see also* Asphyxia, food) 933.1
    choked on (*see also* Asphyxia, food) 933.1
    deprivation 994.2
        specified kind of food NEC 269.8
    intoxication (*see also* Poisoning, food) 005.9
    lack of 994.2
    poisoning (*see also* Poisoning, food) 005.9
    refusal or rejection NEC 307.59
    strangulation or suffocation (*see also* Asphyxia, food) 933.1
    toxemia (*see also* Poisoning, food) 005.9
Foot —*see also* condition
    and mouth disease 078.4
    process disease 581.3

Foramen ovale (nonclosure) (patent) (persistent) 745.5
Forbes' (glycogen storage) disease 271.0
Forbes-Albright syndrome (nonpuerperal amenorrhea and lactation associated with pituitary tumor) 253.1
Forced birth or delivery NEC 669.8
  affecting fetus or newborn NEC 763.89
Forceps
  delivery NEC 669.5
    affecting fetus or newborn 763.2
Fordyce's disease (ectopic sebaceous glands) (mouth) 750.26
Fordyce-Fox disease (apocrine miliaria) 705.82
Forearm —*see* condition
Foreign body

> *Note—For foreign body with open wound or other injury, see Wound, open, or the type of injury specified.*

  accidentally left during a procedure 998.4
  anterior chamber (eye) 871.6
    magnetic 871.5
      retained or old 360.51
    retained or old 360.61
  ciliary body (eye) 871.6
    magnetic 871.5
      retained or old 360.52
    retained or old 360.62
  entering through orifice (current) (old)
    accessory sinus 932
    air passage (upper) 933.0
      lower 934.8
    alimentary canal 938
    alveolar process 935.0
    antrum (Highmore) 932
    anus 937
    appendix 936
    asphyxia due to (*see also* Asphyxia, food) 933.1
    auditory canal 931
    auricle 931
    bladder 939.0
    bronchioles 934.8
    bronchus (main) 934.1
    buccal cavity 935.0
    canthus (inner) 930.1
    cecum 936
    cervix (canal) uterine 939.1
    coil, ileocecal 936
    colon 936
    conjunctiva 930.1
    conjunctival sac 930.1
    cornea 930.0
    digestive organ or tract NEC 938
    duodenum 936
    ear (external) 931
    esophagus 935.1
    eye (external) 930.9
      combined sites 930.8
      intraocular—*see* Foreign body, by site
      specified site NEC 930.8
    eyeball 930.8
      intraocular—*see* Foreign body, intraocular
    eyelid 930.1
      retained or old 374.86
    frontal sinus 932
    gastrointestinal tract 938
    genitourinary tract 939.9

Foreign body—*continued*
  globe 930.8
    penetrating 871.6
      magnetic 871.5
        retained or old 360.50
      retained or old 360.60
  gum 935.0
  Highmore's antrum 932
  hypopharynx 933.0
  ileocecal coil 936
  ileum 936
  inspiration (of) 933.1
  intestine (large) (small) 936
  lacrimal apparatus, duct, gland, or sac 930.2
  larynx 933.1
  lung 934.8
  maxillary sinus 932
  mouth 935.0
  nasal sinus 932
  nasopharynx 933.0
  nose (passage) 932
  nostril 932
  oral cavity 935.0
  palate 935.0
  penis 939.3
  pharynx 933.0
  pyriform sinus 933.0
  rectosigmoid 937
    junction 937
  rectum 937
  respiratory tract 934.9
    specified part NEC 934.8
  sclera 930.1
  sinus 932
    accessory 932
    frontal 932
    maxillary 932
    nasal 932
    pyriform 933.0
  small intestine 936
  stomach (hairball) 935.2
  suffocation by (*see also* Asphyxia, food) 933.1
  swallowed 938
    tongue 933.0
  tear ducts or glands 930.2
  throat 933.0
  tongue 935.0
    swallowed 933.0
  tonsil, tonsillar 933.0
    fossa 933.0
  trachea 934.0
  ureter 939.0
  urethra 939.0
  uterus (any part) 939.1
  vagina 939.2
  vulva 939.2
  wind pipe 934.0
  granuloma (old) 728.82
    bone 733.99
    in operative wound (inadvertently left) 998.4
      due to surgical material intentionally left—*see* Complications, due to (presence of) any device, implant, or graft classified to 996.0-996.5 NEC
    muscle 728.82
    skin 709.4
    soft tissue 709.1
    subcutaneous tissue 709.4
  in
    bone (residual) 733.99

Foreign body—*continued*
   open wound—*see* Wound, open, by site
      complicated
   soft tissue (residual) 729.6
   inadvertently left in operation wound (causing
      adhesions, obstruction, or perforation) 998.4
   ingestion, ingested NEC 938
   inhalation or inspiration (*see also* Asphyxia,
      food) 933.1
   internal organ, not entering through an
      orifice—*see* Injury, internal, by site, with
      open wound
   intraocular (nonmagnetic) 871.6
     combined sites 871.6
       magnetic 871.5
         retained or old 360.59
       retained or old 360.69
     magnetic 871.5
       retained or old 360.50
     retained or old 360.60
     specified site NEC 871.6
       magnetic 871.5
         retained or old 360.59
       retained or old 360.69
   iris (nonmagnetic) 871.6
     magnetic 871.5
       retained or old 360.52
     retained or old 360.62
   lens (nonmagnetic) 871.6
     magnetic 871.5
       retained or old 360.53
     retained or old 360.63
   lid, eye 930.1
   ocular muscle 870.4
     retained or old 376.6
   old or residual
     bone 733.99
     eyelid 374.86
     middle ear 385.83
     muscle 729.6
       ocular 376.6
     retrobulbar 376.6
     skin 729.6
       with granuloma 709.4
     soft tissue 729.6
       with granuloma 709.4
     subcutaneous tissue 729.6
       with granuloma 709.4
   operation wound, left accidentally 998.4
   orbit 870.4
     retained or old 376.6
   posterior wall, eye 871.6
     magnetic 871.5
       retained or old 360.55
     retained or old 360.65
   respiratory tree 934.9
     specified site NEC 934.8
   retained (old) (nonmagnetic) (in)
     anterior chamber (eye) 360.61
       magnetic 360.51
     ciliary body 360.62
       magnetic 360.52
     eyelid 374.86
     globe 360.60
       magnetic 360.50
     intraocular 360.60
       magnetic 360.50
       specified site NEC 360.69
         magnetic 360.59

Foreign body—*continued*
   iris 360.62
     magnetic 360.52
   lens 360.63
     magnetic 360.53
   muscle 729.6
   orbit 376.6
   posterior wall of globe 360.65
     magnetic 360.55
   retina 360.65
     magnetic 360.55
   retrobulbar 376.6
   skin 729.6
     with granuloma 709.4
   soft tissue 729.6
     with granuloma 709.4
   subcutaneous tissue 729.6
     with granuloma 709.4
   vitreous 360.64
     magnetic 360.54
  retina 871.6
   magnetic 871.5
     retained or old 360.55
   retained or old 360.65
  superficial, without major open wound (*see also*
     Injury, superficial, by site) 919.6
  swallowed NEC 938
  vitreous (humor) 871.6
   magnetic 871.5
     retained or old 360.54
   retained or old 360.64
Forking, aqueduct of Sylvius 742.3
  with spina bifida (*see also* Spina bifida) 741.0
Formation
  bone in scar tissue (skin) 709.3
  connective tissue in vitreous 379.25
  Elschnig pearls (postcataract extraction) 366.51
  hyaline in cornea 371.49
  sequestrum in bone (due to infection) (*see also*
     Osteomyelitis) 730.1
  valve
   colon, congenital 751.5
   ureter (congenital) 753.29
Formication 782.0
Fort Bragg fever 100.89
Fossa —*see also* condition
  pyriform—*see* condition
Foster-Kennedy syndrome 377.04
Fothergill's
  disease, meaning scarlatina anginosa 034.1
  neuralgia (*see also* Neuralgia, trigeminal) 350.1
Foul breath 784.9
Found dead (cause unknown) 798.9
Foundling V20.0
Fournier's disease (idiopathic gangrene) 608.83
Fourth
  cranial nerve—*see* condition
  disease 057.8
  molar 520.1
Foville's syndrome 344.89
Fox's
  disease (apocrine miliaria) 705.82
  impetigo (contagiosa) 684
Fox-Fordyce disease (apocrine miliaria) 705.82

Fracture (abduction) (adduction) (avulsion) (compression) (crush) (dislocation) (oblique) (separation) (closed) 829.0

> *Note—For fracture of any of the following sites with fracture of other bones—see Fracture, multiple.*
>
> *"Closed" includes the following descriptions of fractures, with or without delayed healing, unless they are specified as open or compound:*
>
> > *comminuted*
> > *depressed*
> > *elevated*
> > *fissured*
> > *greenstick*
> > *impacted*
> > *linear*
> > *march*
> > *simple*
> > *slipped epiphysis*
> > *spiral*
> > *unspecified*
>
> *"Open" includes the following descriptions of fractures, with or without delayed healing:*
>
> > *compound*
> > *infected*
> > *missile*
> > *puncture*
> > *with foreign body*
>
> *For late effect of fracture, see Late, effect, fracture, by site.*

with
    internal injuries in same region (conditions
        classifiable to 860-869)—*see also* Injury,
        internal, by site
    pelvic region—*see* Fracture, pelvis
acetabulum (with visceral injury) (closed) 808.0
    open 808.1
acromion (process) (closed) 811.01
    open 811.11
alveolus (closed) 802.8
    open 802.9
ankle (malleolus) (closed) 824.8
    bimalleolar (Dupuytren's) (Pott's) 824.4
        open 824.5
    bone 825.21
        open 825.31
    lateral malleolus only (fibular) 824.2
        open 824.3
    medial malleolus only (tibial) 824.0
        open 824.1
    open 824.9
    pathologic 733.16
    talus 825.21
        open 825.31
    trimalleolar 824.6
        open 824.7
antrum—*see* Fracture, skull, base
arm (closed) 818.0
    and leg(s) (any bones) 828.0
        open 828.1
    both (any bones) (with rib(s)) (with sternum)
        819.0
        open 819.1
    lower 813.80
        open 813.90

Fracture—*continued*
    open 818.1
    upper—*see* Fracture, humerus
astragalus (closed) 825.21
    open 825.31
atlas—*see* Fracture, vertebra, cervical, first
axis—*see* Fracture, vertebra, cervical, second
back—*see* Fracture, vertebra, by site
Barton's—*see* Fracture, radius, lower end
basal (skull)—*see* Fracture, skull, base
Bennett's (closed) 815.01
    open 815.11
bimalleolar (closed) 824.4
    open 824.5
bone (closed) NEC 829.0
    birth injury NEC 767.3
    open 829.1
    pathologic NEC (*see also* Fracture,
        pathologic) 733.10
boot top—*see* Fracture, fibula
boxers'—*see* Fracture, metacarpal bone(s)
breast bone—*see* Fracture, sternum
bucket handle (semilunar cartilage)—*see* Tear,
    meniscus
bursting—*see* Fracture, phalanx, hand, distal
calcaneus (closed) 825.0
    open 825.1
capitate (bone) (closed) 814.07
    open 814.17
capitellum (humerus) (closed) 812.49
    open 812.59
carpal bone(s) (wrist NEC) (closed) 814.00
    open 814.10
    specified site NEC 814.09
        open 814.19
cartilage, knee (semilunar)—*see* Tear, meniscus
cervical—*see* Fracture, vertebra, cervical
chauffeur's—*see* Fracture, ulna, lower end
chisel—*see* Fracture, radius, upper end
clavicle (interligamentous part) (closed) 810.00
    acromial end 810.03
        open 810.13
    due to birth trauma 767.2
    open 810.10
    shaft (middle third) 810.02
        open 810.12
    sternal end 810.01
        open 810.11
clayshovelers'—*see* Fracture, vertebra, cervical
coccyx—*see also* Fracture, vertebra, coccyx
    complicating delivery 665.6
collar bone—*see* Fracture, clavicle
Colles' (reversed) (closed) 813.41
    open 813.51
comminuted—*see* Fracture, by site
compression—*see also* Fracture, by site
    nontraumatic—*see* Fracture, pathologic
congenital 756.9
coracoid process (closed) 811.02
    open 811.12
coronoid process (ulna) (closed) 813.02
    mandible (closed) 802.23
        open 802.33
    open 813.12
costochondral junction—*see* Fracture, rib
costosternal junction—*see* Fracture, rib
cranium—*see* Fracture, skull, by site
cricoid cartilage (closed) 807.5
    open 807.6
cuboid (ankle) (closed) 825.23
    open 825.33

Fracture—*continued*
  cuneiform
    foot (closed) 825.24
      open 825.34
    wrist (closed) 814.03
      open 814.13
  due to
    birth injury—*see* Birth injury, fracture
    gunshot—*see* Fracture, by site, open
    neoplasm—*see* Fracture, pathologic
    osteoporosis—*see* Fracture, pathologic
  Dupuytren's (ankle) (fibula) (closed) 824.4
    open 824.5
    radius 813.42
      open 813.52
  Duverney's—*see* Fracture, ilium
  elbow—*see also* Fracture, humerus, lower end
    olecranon (process) (closed) 813.01
      open 813.11
    supracondylar (closed) 812.41
      open 812.51
  ethmoid (bone) (sinus)—*see* Fracture, skull,
    base
  face bone(s) (closed) NEC 802.8
    with
      other bone(s)—*see also* Fracture, multiple,
        skull
      skull—*see also* Fracture, skull
        involving other bones—*see* Fracture,
          multiple, skull
    open 802.9
  fatigue—*see* Fracture, march
  femur, femoral (closed) 821.00
    cervicotrochanteric 820.03
      open 820.13
    condyles, epicondyles 821.21
      open 821.31
    distal end—*see* Fracture, femur, lower end
    epiphysis (separation)
      capital 820.01
        open 820.11
      head 820.01
        open 820.11
      lower 821.22
        open 821.32
      trochanteric 820.01
        open 820.11
      upper 820.01
        open 820.11
    head 820.09
      open 820.19
    lower end or extremity (distal end) (closed)
      821.20
      condyles, epicondyles 821.21
        open 821.31
      epiphysis (separation) 821.22
        open 821.32
      multiple sites 821.29
        open 821.39
      open 821.30
      specified site NEC 821.29
        open 821.39
      supracondylar 821.23
        open 821.33
      T-shaped 821.21
        open 821.31
    neck (closed) 820.8
      base (cervicotrochanteric) 820.03
        open 820.13
      extracapsular 820.20
        open 820.30

Fracture—*continued*
      intertrochanteric (section) 820.21
        open 820.31
      intracapsular 820.00
        open 820.10
      intratrochanteric 820.21
        open 821.31
      midcervical 820.02
        open 820.12
      open 820.9
      pathologic 733.14
        specified part NEC 733.15
      specified site NEC 820.09
        open 820.19
      transcervical 820.02
        open 820.12
      transtrochanteric 820.20
        open 820.30
    open 821.10
    pathologic 733.14
      specified part NEC 733.15
    peritrochanteric (section) 820.20
      open 820.30
    shaft (lower third) (middle third) (upper third)
      821.01
      open 821.11
    subcapital 820.09
      open 820.19
    subtrochanteric (region) (section) 820.22
      open 820.32
    supracondylar 821.23
      open 821.33
    transepiphyseal 820.01
      open 820.11
    trochanter (greater) (lesser) (*see also* Fracture,
      femur, neck, by site) 820.20
      open 820.30
    T-shaped, into knee joint 821.21
      open 821.31
    upper end 820.8
      open 820.9
  fibula (closed) 823.81
    with tibia 823.82
      open 823.92
    distal end 824.8
      open 824.9
    epiphysis
      lower 824.8
        open 824.9
      upper—*see* Fracture, fibula, upper end
    head—*see* Fracture, fibula, upper end
    involving ankle 824.2
      open 824.3
    lower end or extremity 824.8
      open 824.9
    malleolus (external) (lateral) 824.2
      open 824.3
    open NEC 823.91
    pathologic 733.16
    proximal end—*see* Fracture, fibula, upper end
    shaft 823.21
      with tibia 823.22
        open 823.32
      open 823.31
    upper end or extremity (epiphysis) (head)
      (proximal end) (styloid) 823.01
      with tibia 823.02
        open 823.12
      open 823.11

Fracture—*continued*
  finger(s), of one hand (closed) (*see also*
      Fracture, phalanx, hand) 816.00
    with
      metacarpal bone(s), of same hand 817.0
        open 817.1
      thumb of same hand 816.03
        open 816.13
    open 816.10
  foot, except toe(s) alone (closed) 825.20
    open 825.30
  forearm (closed) NEC 813.80
    lower end (distal end) (lower epiphysis)
      813.40
      open 813.50
    open 813.90
    shaft 813.20
      open 813.30
    upper end (proximal end) (upper epiphysis)
      813.00
      open 813.10
  fossa, anterior, middle, or posterior—*see*
    Fracture, skull, base
  frontal (bone)—*see also* Fracture, skull, vault
    sinus—*see* Fracture, skull base
  Galeazzi's—*see* Fracture, radius, lower end
  glenoid (cavity) (fossa) (scapula) (closed)
    811.03
    open 811.13
  Gosselin's—*see* Fracture, ankle
  greenstick—*see* Fracture, by site
  grenade-throwers'—*see* Fracture, humerus, shaft
  gutter—*see* Fracture, skull, vault
  hamate (closed) 814.08
    open 814.18
  hand, one (closed) 815.00
    carpals 814.00
      open 814.10
      specified site NEC 814.09
        open 814.19
    metacarpals 815.00
      open 815.10
    multiple, bones of one hand 817.0
      open 817.1
    open 815.10
    phalanges (*see also* Fracture, phalanx, hand)
      816.00
    open 816.10
  healing or old
    aftercare or convalescence V54.9
    change of cast V54.8
    complications—*see* condition
    removal of
      cast V54.8
      fixation device
        external V54.8
        internal V54.0
  heel bone (closed) 825.0
    open 825.1
  hip (closed) (*see also* Fracture, femur, neck)
    820.8
    open 820.9
    pathologic 733.14
  humerus (closed) 812.20
    anatomical neck 812.02
      open 812.12
    articular process (*see also* Fracture, humerus,
      condyle(s) 812.44
      open 812.54

Fracture—*continued*
  capitellum 812.49
    open 812.59
  condyle(s) 812.44
    lateral (external) 812.42
      open 812.52
    medial (internal epicondyle) 812.43
      open 812.53
    open 812.54
  distal end—*see* Fracture, humerus, lower end
  epiphysis
    lower (*see also* Fracture, humerus,
      condyle(s)) 812.44
      open 812.54
    upper 812.09
      open 812.19
  external condyle 812.42
    open 812.52
  great tuberosity 812.03
    open 812.13
  head 812.09
    open 812.19
  internal epicondyle 812.43
    open 812.53
  lesser tuberosity 812.09
    open 812.19
  lower end or extremity (distal end) (*see also*
    Fracture, humerus, by site) 812.40
    multiple sites NEC 812.49
      open 812.59
    open 812.50
    specified site NEC 812.49
      open 812.59
  neck 812.01
    open 812.11
  open 812.30
  pathologic 733.11
  proximal end—*see* Fracture, humerus, upper
    end
  shaft 812.21
    open 812.31
  supracondylar 812.41
    open 812.51
  surgical neck 812.01
    open 812.11
  trochlea 812.49
    open 812.59
  T-shaped 812.44
    open 812.54
  tuberosity—*see* Fracture, humerus, upper end
  upper end or extremity (proximal end) (*see*
    also Fracture, humerus, by site) 812.00
    open 812.10
    specified site NEC 812.09
      open 812.19
  hyoid bone (closed) 807.5
    open 807.6
  hyperextension—*see* Fracture, radius, lower end
  ilium (with visceral injury) (closed) 808.41
    open 808.51
  impaction, impacted—*see* Fracture, by site
  incus—*see* Fracture, skull, base
  innominate bone (with visceral injury) (closed)
    808.49
    open 808.59
  instep, of one foot (closed) 825.20
    with toe(s) of same foot 827.0
      open 827.1
    open 825.30

Fracture—*continued*
  internal
    ear—*see* Fracture, skull, base
    semilunar cartilage, knee—*see* Tear,
      meniscus, medial
  intertrochanteric—*see* Fracture, femur, neck,
    intertrochanteric
  ischium (with visceral injury) (closed) 808.42
    open 808.52
  jaw (bone) (lower) (closed) (*see also* Fracture,
    mandible) 802.20
    angle 802.25
      open 802.35
    open 802.30
    upper—*see* Fracture, maxilla
  knee
    cap (closed) 822.0
      open 822.1
    cartilage (semilunar)—*see* Tear, meniscus
  labyrinth (osseous)—*see* Fracture, skull, base
  larynx (closed) 807.5
    open 807.6
  late effect—*see* Late, effects (of), fracture
  Le Fort's—*see* Fracture, maxilla
  leg (closed) 827.0
    with rib(s) or sternum 828.0
      open 828.1
    both (any bones) 828.0
      open 828.1
    lower—*see* Fracture, tibia
    open 827.1
    upper—*see* Fracture, femur
  limb
    lower (multiple) (closed) NEC 827.0
      open 827.1
    upper (multiple) (closed) NEC 818.0
      open 818.1
  long bones, due to birth trauma—*see* Birth
    injury, fracture
  lumbar—*see* Fracture, vertebra, lumbar
  lunate bone (closed) 814.02
    open 814.12
  malar bone (closed) 802.4
    open 802.5
  Malgaigne's (closed) 808.43
    open 808.53
  malleolus (closed)0 824.8
    bimalleolar 824.4
      open 824.5
    lateral 824.2
      and medial—*see also* Fracture, malleolus,
        bimalleolar
        with lip of tibia—*see* Fracture, malleolus,
          trimalleolar
      open 824.3
    medial (closed) 824.0
      and lateral—*see also* Fracture, malleolus,
        bimalleolar
        with lip of tibia—*see* Fracture, malleolus,
          trimalleolar
      open 824.1
    open 824.9
    trimalleolar (closed) 824.6
      open 824.7
  malleus—*see* Fracture, skull, base
  malunion 733.81

Fracture—*continued*
  mandible (closed) 802.20
    angle 802.25
      open 802.35
    body 802.28
      alveolar border 802.27
        open 802.37
      open 802.38
      symphysis 802.26
        open 802.36
    condylar process 802.21
      open 802.31
    coronoid process 802.23
      open 802.33
    multiple sites 802.29
      open 802.39
    open 802.30
    ramus NEC 802.24
      open 802.34
    subcondylar 802.22
      open 802.32
  manubrium—*see* Fracture, sternum
  march (closed) 825.20
    open 825.30
  maxilla, maxillary (superior) (upper jaw)
    (closed) 802.4
    inferior—*see* Fracture, mandible
    open 802.5
  meniscus, knee—*see* Tear, meniscus
  metacarpus, metacarpal (bone(s)), of one hand
    (closed) 815.00
    with phalanx, phalanges, hand (finger(s))
      (thumb) of same hand 817.0
      open 817.1
    base 815.02
      first metacarpal 815.01
        open 815.11
      open 815.12
      thumb 815.01
        open 815.11
    multiple sites 815.09
      open 815.19
    neck 815.04
      open 815.14
    open 815.10
    shaft 815.03
      open 815.13
  metatarsus, metatarsal (bone(s)), of one foot
    (closed) 825.25
    with tarsal bone(s) 825.29
      open 825.39
    open 825.35
  Monteggia's (closed) 813.03
    open 813.13
  Moore's—*see* Fracture, radius, lower end
  multangular bone (closed)
    larger 814.05
      open 814.15
    smaller 814.06
      open 814.16
  multiple (closed) 829.0

Fracture—*continued*

> *Note*—*Multiple fractures of sites classifiable to the same three- or four-digit category are coded to that category, except for sites classifiable to 810-818 or 820-827 in different limbs.*
>
> *Multiple fractures of sites classifiable to different fourth-digit subdivisions within the same three- digit category should be dealt with according to coding rules.*
>
> *Multiple fractures of sites classifiable to different three-digit categories (identifiable from the listing under "Fracture"), and of sites classifiable to 810-818 or 820-827 in different limbs should be coded according to the following list, which should be referred to in the following priority order: skull or face bones, pelvis or vertebral column, legs, arms.*

arm (multiple bones in same arm except in hand alone) (sites classifiable to 810-817 with sites classifiable to a different three-digit category in 810-817 in same arm) (closed) 818.0
  open 818.1
arms, both or arm(s) with rib(s) or sternum (sites classifiable to 810-818 with sites classifiable to same range of categories in other limb or to 807) (closed) 819.0
  open 819.1
bones of trunk NEC (closed) 809.0
  open 809.1
hand, metacarpal bone(s) with phalanx or phalanges of same hand (sites classifiable to 815 with sites classifiable to 816 in same hand) (closed) 817.0
  open 817.1
leg (multiple bones in same leg) (sites classifiable to 820-826 with sites classifiable to a different three-digit category in that range in same leg) (closed) 827.0
  open 827.1
legs, both or leg(s) with arm(s), rib(s), or sternum (sites classifiable to 820-827 with sites classifiable to same range of categories in other leg or to 807 or 810-819) (closed) 828.0
  open 828.1
open 829.1
pelvis with other bones except skull or face bones (sites classifiable to 808 with sites classifiable to 805-807 or 810-829) (closed) 809.0
  open 809.1
skull, specified or unspecified bones, or face bone(s) with any other bone(s) (sites classifiable to 800-803 with sites classifiable to 805-829) (closed) 804.0

Fracture—*continued*

> *Note*—*Use the following fifth-digit subclassification with categories 800, 801, 803, and 804:*
>
> 0 *unspecified state of consciousness*
> 1 *with no loss of consciousness*
> 2 *with brief [less than one hour] loss of consciousness*
> 3 *with moderate [1-24 hours] loss of consciousness*
> 4 *with prolonged [more than 24 hours] loss of consciousness and return to pre-existing conscious level*
> 5 *with prolonged [more than 24 hours] loss of consciousness, without return to pre-existing conscious level*
> *Use fifth-digit 5 to designate when a patient is unconcious and dies before regaining conciousness, regardless of the duration of the loss of conciousness*
> 6 *with loss of consciousness of unspecified duration*
> 9 *with concussion, unspecified*

with
  contusion, cerebral 804.1
  epidural hemorrhage 804.2
  extradural hemorrhage 804.2
  hemorrhage (intracranial) NEC 804.3
  intracranial injury NEC 804.4
  laceration, cerebral 804.1
  subarachnoid hemorrhage 804.2
  subdural hemorrhage 804.2
open 804.5
  with
    contusion, cerebral 804.6
    epidural hemorrhage 804.7
    extradural hemorrhage 804.7
    hemorrhage (intracranial) NEC 804.8
    intracranial injury NEC 804.9
    laceration, cerebral 804.6
    subarachnoid hemorrhage 804.7
    subdural hemorrhage 804.7
vertebral column with other bones, except skull or face bones (sites classifiable to 805 or 806 with sites classifiable to 807-808 or 810-829) (closed) 809.0
  open 809.1
nasal (bone(s)) (closed) 802.0
  open 802.1
  sinus—Fracture, skull, base
navicular
  carpal (wrist) (closed) 814.01
    open 814.11
  tarsal (ankle) (closed) 825.22
    open 825.32
neck—*see* Fracture, vertebra, cervical
neural arch—*see* Fracture, vertebra, by site
nonunion 733.82
nose, nasal, (bone) (septum) (closed) 802.0
  open 802.1
occiput—*see* Fracture, skull, base
odontoid process—*see* Fracture, vertebra, cervical
olecranon (process) (ulna) (closed) 813.01
  open 813.11
open 829.1
orbit, orbital (bone) (region) (closed) 802.8
  floor (blow-out) 802.6
    open 802.7

Fracture—*continued*
  open 802.9
  roof—*see* Fracture, skull, base
  specified part NEC 802.8
    open 802.9
  os
    calcis (closed) 825.0
      open 825.1
    magnum (closed) 814.07
      open 814.17
    pubis (with visceral injury) (closed) 808.2
      open 808.3
    triquetrum (closed) 814.03
      open 814.13
  osseous
    auditory meatus—*see* Fracture, skull, base
    labyrinth—*see* Fracture, skull, base
  ossicles, auditory (incus) (malleus)
    (stapes)—*see* Fracture, skull, base
  osteoporotic—*see* Fracture, pathologic
  palate (closed) 802.8
    open 802.9
  paratrooper—*see* Fracture, tibia, lower end
  parietal bone—*see* Fracture, skull, vault
  parry—*see* Fracture, Monteggia's
  patella (closed) 822.0
    open 822.1
  pathologic (cause unknown) 733.10
    ankle 733.16
    femur (neck) 733.14
      specified NEC 733.15
    fibula 733.16
    hip 733.14
    humerus 733.11
    radius 733.12
    specified site NEC 733.19
    tibia 733.16
    ulna 733.12
    vertebrae (collapse) 733.13
    wrist 733.12
  pedicle (of vertebral arch)—*see* Fracture,
    vertebra, by site
  pelvis, pelvic (bone(s)) (with visceral injury)
    (closed) 808.8
    multiple (with disruption of pelvic circle)
      808.43
      open 808.53
    open 808.9
    rim (closed) 808.49
      open 808.59
  peritrochanteric (closed) 820.20
    open 820.30
  phalanx, phalanges, of one
    foot (closed) 826.0
      with bone(s) of same lower limb 827.0
        open 827.1
      open 826.1
    hand (closed) 816.00
      with metacarpal bone(s) of same hand 817.0
        open 817.1
      distal 816.02
        open 816.12
      middle 816.01
        open 816.11
      multiple sites NEC 816.03
        open 816.13
      open 816.10
      proximal 816.01
        open 816.11
  pisiform (closed) 814.04
    open 814.14

Fracture—*continued*
  pond—Fracture, skull, vault
  Pott's (closed) 824.4
    open 824.5
  prosthetic device, internal—*see* Complications,
    mechanical
  pubis (with visceral injury) (closed) 808.2
    open 808.3
  Quervain's (closed) 814.01
    open 814.11
  radius (alone) (closed) 813.81
    with ulna NEC 813.83
      open 813.93
    distal end—*see* Fracture, radius, lower end
    epiphysis
      lower—*see* Fracture, radius, lower end
      upper—*see* Fracture, radius, upper end
    head—*see* Fracture, radius, upper end
    lower end or extremity (distal end) (lower
      epiphysis) 813.42
      with ulna (lower end) 813.44
        open 813.54
      open 813.52
    neck—*see* Fracture, radius, upper end
    open NEC 813.91
    pathologic 733.12
    proximal end—*see* Fracture, radius, upper end
    shaft (closed) 813.21
      with ulna (shaft) 813.23
        open 813.33
      open 813.31
    upper end 813.07
      with ulna (upper end) 813.08
        open 813.18
      epiphysis 813.05
        open 813.15
      head 813.05
        open 813.15
      multiple sites 813.07
        open 813.17
      neck 813.06
        open 813.16
      open 813.17
      specified site NEC 813.07
        open 813.17
  ramus
    inferior or superior (with visceral injury)
      (closed) 808.2
      open 808.3
    ischium—*see* Fracture, ischium
    mandible 802.24
      open 802.34
  rib(s) (closed) 807.0

> *Note—Use the following fifth-digit*
> *subclassification with categories 807.0-807.1:*
>
> *0　rib(s), unspecified*
> *1　one rib*
> *2　two ribs*
> *3　three ribs*
> *4　four ribs*
> *5　five ribs*
> *6　six ribs*
> *7　seven ribs*
> *8　eight or more ribs*
> *9　multiple ribs, unspecified*

    with flail chest (open) 807.4
      open 807.1
  root, tooth 873.63
    complicated 873.73

Fracture—*continued*
  sacrum—*see* Fracture, vertebra, sacrum
  scaphoid
    ankle (closed) 825.22
      open 825.32
    wrist (closed) 814.01
      open 814.11
  scapula (closed) 811.00
    acromial, acromion (process) 811.01
      open 811.11
    body 811.09
      open 811.19
    coracoid process 811.02
      open 811.12
    glenoid (cavity) (fossa) 811.03
      open 811.13
    neck 811.03
      open 811.13
    open 811.10
  semilunar
    bone, wrist (closed) 814.02
      open 814.12
    cartilage (interior) (knee)—*see* Tear, meniscus
  sesamoid bone—*see* Fracture, by site
  Shepherd's (closed) 825.21
    open 825.31
  shoulder—*see also* Fracture, humerus, upper end
    blade—*see* Fracture, scapula
  silverfork—*see* Fracture, radius, lower end
  sinus (ethmoid) (frontal) (maxillary) (nasal)
    (sphenoidal)—*see* Fracture, skull, base
    maxillary—*see* Fracture, maxilla
  Skillern's—*see* Fracture, radius, shaft
  skull (multiple NEC) (with face bones) (closed)
    803.0

Note—Use the following fifth-digit subclassification with categories 800, 801, 803, and 804:

0 unspecified state of consciousness
1 with no loss of consciousness
2 with brief [less than one hour] loss of consciousness
3 with moderate [1-24 hours] loss of consciousness
4 with prolonged [more than 24 hours] loss of consciousness and return to pre-existing conscious level
5 with prolonged [more than 24 hours] loss of consciousness, without return to pre-existing conscious level
Use fifth-digit 5 to designate when a patient is unconscious and dies before regaining consciousness, regardless of the duration of the loss of consciousness
6 with loss of consciousness of unspecified duration
9 with concussion, unspecified

---

    with
      contusion, cerebral 803.1
      epidural hemorrhage 803.2
      extradural hemorrhage 803.2
      hemorrhage (intracranial) NEC 803.3
      intracranial injury NEC 803.4
      laceration, cerebral 803.1
      other bones—*see* Fracture, multiple, skull
      subarachnoid hemorrhage 803.2
      subdural hemorrhage 803.2

Fracture—*continued*
  base (antrum) (ethmoid bone) (fossa) (internal
    ear) (nasal sinus) (occiput) (sphenoid)
    (temporal bone) (closed) 801.0
    with
      contusion, cerebral 801.1
      epidural hemorrhage 801.2
      extradural hemorrhage 801.2
      hemorrhage (intracranial) NEC 801.3
      intracranial injury NEC 801.4
      laceration, cerebral 801.1
      subarachnoid hemorrhage 801.2
      subdural hemorrhage 801.2
    open 801.5
      with
        contusion, cerebral 801.6
        epidural hemorrhage 801.7
        extradural hemorrhage 801.7
        hemorrhage (intracranial) NEC 801.8
        intracranial injury NEC 801.9
        laceration, cerebral 801.6
        subarachnoid hemorrhage 801.7
        subdural hemorrhage 801.7
  birth injury 767.3
  face bones—*see* Fracture, face bones
  open 803.5
    with
      contusion, cerebral 803.6
      epidural hemorrhage 803.7
      extradural hemorrhage 803.7
      hemorrhage (intracranial) NEC 803.8
      intracranial injury NEC 803.9
      laceration, cerebral 803.6
      subarachnoid hemorrhage 803.7
      subdural hemorrhage 803.7
  vault (frontal bone) (parietal bone) (vertex)
    (closed) 800.0
    with
      contusion, cerebral 800.1
      epidural hemorrhage 800.2
      extradural hemorrhage 800.2
      hemorrhage (intracranial) NEC 800.3
      intracranial injury NEC 800.4
      laceration, cerebral 800.1
      subarachnoid hemorrhage 800.2
      subdural hemorrhage 800.2
    open 800.5
      with
        contusion, cerebral 800.6
        epidural hemorrhage 800.7
        extradural hemorrhage 800.7
        hemorrhage (intracranial) NEC 800.8
        intracranial injury NEC 800.9
        laceration, cerebral 800.6
        subarachnoid hemorrhage 800.7
        subdural hemorrhage 800.7
  Smith's 813.41
    open 813.51
  sphenoid (bone) (sinus)—*see* Fracture, skull,
    base
  spine—*see also* Fracture, vertebra, by site
    due to birth trauma 767.4
  spinous process—*see* Fracture, vertebra, by site
  spontaneous—*see* Fracture, pathologic
  sprinters'—*see* Fracture, ilium
  stapes—*see* Fracture, skull, base
  stave—*see also* Fracture, metacarpus,
    metacarpal bone(s)
    spine—*see* Fracture, tibia, upper end
  sternum (closed) 807.2
    with flail chest (open) 807.4

Fracture—*continued*
    paraplegia—*see* Fracture, vertebra, by site,
        with spinal cord injury
    quadriplegia—*see* Fracture, vertebra, by
        site, with spinal cord injury
    spinal concussion—*see* Fracture, vertebra,
        by site, with spinal cord injury
    spinal cord injury (closed) NEC 806.8

Note—Use the following fifth-digit
subclassification with categories 806.0-806.3:

C_1-C_4 *or unspecified level and D_1-D_6 (T_1-T_6) or*
unspecified level with:

0 unspecified spinal cord injury
1 complete lesion of cord
2 anterior cord syndrome
3 central cord syndrome
4 specified injury NEC

C_5-C_7 *level and D_7-D_{12} level with:*

5 unspecified spinal cord injury
6 complete lesion of cord
7 anterior cord syndrome
8 central cord syndrome
9 specified injury NEC

      cervical 806.0
        open 806.1
      dorsal, dorsolumbar 806.2
        open 806.3
        open 806.9
      thoracic, thoracolumbar 806.2
        open 806.3
    atlanto-axial—*see* Fracture, vertebra, cervical
    cervical (hangman) (teardrop) (closed) 805.00
      with spinal cord injury—*see* Fracture,
        vertebra, with spinal cord injury, cervical
      first (atlas) 805.01
        open 805.11
      second (axis) 805.02
        open 805.12
      third 805.03
        open 805.13
      fourth 805.04
        open 805.14
      fifth 805.05
        open 805.15
      sixth 805.06
        open 805.16
      seventh 805.07
        open 805.17
      multiple sites 805.08
        open 805.18
      open 805.10
    coccyx (closed) 805.6
      with spinal cord injury (closed) 806.60
        cauda equina injury 806.62
          complete lesion 806.61
            open 806.71
          open 806.72
        open 806.70
        specified type NEC 806.69
          open 806.79
      open 805.7
    collapsed 733.13
    compression, not due to trauma 733.13
    dorsal (closed) 805.2
      with spinal cord injury—*see* Fracture,
        vertebra, with spinal cord injury, dorsal

Fracture—*continued*
    open 805.3
    dorsolumbar (closed) 805.2
      with spinal cord injury—*see* Fracture,
        vertebra, with spinal cord injury, dorsal
    open 805.3
    due to osteoporosis 733.13
    fetus or newborn 767.4
    lumbar (closed) 805.4
      with spinal cord injury (closed) 806.4
        open 806.5
      open 805.5
    nontraumatic 733.13
    open NEC 805.9
    pathologic 733.13
    sacrum (closed) 805.6
      with spinal cord injury 806.60
        cauda equina injury 806.62
          complete lesion 806.61
            open 806.71
          open 806.72
        open 806.70
        specified type NEC 806.69
          open 806.79
      open 805.7
    site unspecified (closed) 805.8
      with spinal cord injury (closed) 806.8
        open 806.9
      open 805.9
    thoracic (closed) 805.2
      with spinal cord injury—*see* Fracture,
        vertebra, with spinal cord injury, thoracic
      open 805.3
    vertex—*see* Fracture, skull, vault
    vomer (bone) 802.0
      open 802.1
    Wagstaffe's—*see* Fracture, ankle
    wrist (closed) 814.00
      open 814.10
      pathologic 733.12
    xiphoid (process)—*see* Fracture, sternum
    zygoma (zygomatic arch) (closed) 802.4
      open 802.5
Fragile X syndrome 759.83
Fragilitas
    crinium 704.2
    hair 704.2
    ossium 756.51
      with blue sclera 756.51
    unguium 703.8
      congenital 757.5
Fragility
    bone 756.51
      with deafness and blue sclera 756.51
    capillary (hereditary) 287.8
    hair 704.2
    nails 703.8
Fragmentation —*see* Fracture, by site
Frambesia, frambesial (tropica) (*see also* Yaws)
    102.9
    initial lesion or ulcer 102.0
    primary 102.0
Frambeside
    gummatous 102.4
    of early yaws 102.2
Frambesioma 102.1
Franceschetti's syndrome (mandibulofacial
    dysostosis) 756.0
Francis' disease (*see also* Tularemia) 021.9
Frank's essential thrombocytopenia (*see also*
    Purpura, thrombocytopenic) 287.3

Franklin's disease (heavy chain) 273.2
Fraser's syndrome 759.89
Freckle 709.09
  malignant melanoma in (M8742/3)—*see*
    Melanoma
  melanotic (of Hutchinson) (M8742/2)—*see*
    Neoplasm, skin, in situ
Freeman-Sheldon syndrome 759.89
Freezing 991.9
  specified effect NEC 991.8
Frei's disease (climatic bubo) 099.1
Freiberg's
  disease (osteochondrosis, second metatarsal)
    732.5
  infraction of metatarsal head 732.5
  osteochondrosis 732.5
Fremitus, friction, cardiac 785.3
Frenulum lingua 750.0
Frenum
  external os 752.49
  tongue 750.0
Frequency (urinary) NEC 788.41
  micturition 788.41
  nocturnal 788.43
  psychogenic 306.53
Frey's syndrome (auriculotemporal syndrome)
    350.8
Friction
  burn (*see also* Injury, superficial, by site) 919.0
  fremitus, cardiac 785.3
  precordial 785.3
  sounds, chest 786.7
Friderichsen-Waterhouse syndrome or disease
    036.3
Friedländer's
  B (bacillus) NEC (*see also* condition) 041.3
    sepsis or septicemia 038.49
  disease (endarteritis obliterans)—*see*
    Arteriosclerosis
Friedreich's
  ataxia 334.0
  combined systemic disease 334.0
  disease 333.2
    combined systemic 334.0
  myoclonia 333.2
  sclerosis (spinal cord) 334.0
Friedrich-Erb-Arnold syndrome
    (acropachyderma) 757.39
Frigidity 302.72
  psychic or psychogenic 302.72
Fröhlich's disease or syndrome (adiposogenital
    dystrophy) 253.8
Froin's syndrome 336.8
Frommel's disease 676.6
Frommel-Chiari syndrome 676.6
Frontal —*see also* condition
  lobe syndrome 310.0
Frostbite 991.3
  face 991.0
  foot 991.2
  hand 991.1
  specified site NEC 991.3
Frotteurism 302.89
Frozen 991.9
  pelvis 620.8
  shoulder 726.0
Fructosemia 271.2
Fructosuria (benign) (essential) 271.2

Fuchs'
  black spot (myopic) 360.21
  corneal dystrophy (endothelial) 371.57
  heterochromic cyclitis 364.21
Fucosidosis 271.8
Fugue 780.9
  hysterical (dissociative) 300.13
  reaction to exceptional stress (transient) 308.1
Fuller Albright's syndrome (osteitis fibrosa
    disseminata) 756.59
Fuller's earth disease 502
Fulminant, fulminating —*see* condition
Functional —*see* condition
Fundus —*see also* condition
  flavimaculatus 362.76
Fungemia 117.9
Fungus, fungous
  cerebral 348.8
  disease NEC 117.9
  infection—*see* Infection, fungus
  testis (*see also* Tuberculosis) 016.5 *[608.81]*
Funiculitis (acute) 608.4
  chronic 608.4
  endemic 608.4
  gonococcal (acute) 098.14
    chronic or duration of 2 months or over 098.34
  tuberculous (*see also* Tuberculosis) 016.5
F.U.O. (*see also* Pyrexia) 780.6
Funnel
  breast (acquired) 738.3
    congenital 754.81
    late effect of rickets 268.1
  chest (acquired) 738.3
    congenital 754.81
    late effect of rickets 268.1
  pelvis (acquired) 738.6
    with disproportion (fetopelvic) 653.3
      affecting fetus or newborn 763.1
      causing obstructed labor 660.1
        affecting fetus or newborn 763.1
    congenital 755.69
  tuberculous (*see also* Tuberculosis) 016.9
Furfur 690.18
  microsporon 111.0
Furor, paroxysmal (idiopathic) (*see also*
    Epilepsy) 345.8
Furriers' lung 495.8
Furrowed tongue 529.5
  congenital 750.13
Furrowing nail (s) (transverse) 703.8
  congenital 757.5
Furuncle 680.9
  abdominal wall 680.2
  ankle 680.6
  anus 680.5
  arm (any part, above wrist) 680.3
  auditory canal, external 680.0
  axilla 680.3
  back (any part) 680.2
  breast 680.2
  buttock 680.5
  chest wall 680.2
  corpus cavernosum 607.2
  ear (any part) 680.0
  eyelid 373.13
  face (any part, except eye) 680.0
  finger (any) 680.4
  flank 680.2
  foot (any part) 680.7
  forearm 680.3
  gluteal (region) 680.5

Furuncle—*continued*
  groin 680.2
  hand (any part) 680.4
  head (any part, except face) 680.8
  heel 680.7
  hip 680.6
  kidney (*see also* Abscess, kidney) 590.2
  knee 680.6
  labium (majus) (minus) 616.4
  lacrimal
    gland (*see also* Dacryoadenitis) 375.00
    passages (duct) (sac) (see *also* Dacryocystitis) 375.30
  leg, any part except foot 680.6
  malignant 022.0
  multiple sites 680.9
  neck 680.1
  nose (external) (septum) 680.0
  orbit 376.01
  partes posteriores 680.5
  pectoral region 680.2
  penis 607.2
  perineum 680.2
  pinna 680.0
  scalp (any part) 680.8
  scrotum 608.4
  seminal vesicle 608.0
  shoulder 680.3
  skin NEC 680.9
  specified site NEC 680.8
  spermatic cord 608.4
  temple (region) 680.0
  testis 604.90
  thigh 680.6
  thumb 680.4
  toe (any) 680.7
  trunk 680.2
  tunica vaginalis 608.4
  umbilicus 680.2
  upper arm 680.3
  vas deferens 608.4
  vulva 616.4
  wrist 680.4
Furunculosis (*see also* Furuncle) 680.9
  external auditory meatus 680.0 *[380.13]*
Fusarium (infection) 118
Fusion, fused (congenital)
  anal (with urogenital canal) 751.5
  aorta and pulmonary artery 745.0
  astragaloscaphoid 755.67
  atria 745.5
  atrium and ventricle 745.69
  auditory canal 744.02
  auricles, heart 745.5
  binocular, with defective stereopsis 368.33
  bone 756.9
  cervical spine—*see* Fusion, spine
  choanal 748.0
  commissure, mitral valve 746.5
  cranial sutures, premature 756.0
  cusps, heart valve NEC 746.89
    mitral 746.5
    tricuspid 746.89
  ear ossicles 744.04
  fingers (*see also* Syndactylism, fingers) 755.11
  hymen 752.42
  hymeno-urethral 599.89
    causing obstructed labor 660.1
      affecting fetus or newborn 763.1
  joint (acquired)—*see also* Ankylosis
    congenital 755.8

Fusion, fused—*continued*
  kidneys (incomplete) 753.3
  labium (majus) (minus) 752.49
  larynx and trachea 748.3
  limb 755.8
    lower 755.69
    upper 755.59
  lobe, lung 748.5
  lumbosacral (acquired) 724.6
    congenital 756.15
    surgical V45.4
  nares (anterior) (posterior) 748.0
  nose, nasal 748.0
  nostril(s) 748.0
  organ or site NEC—*see* Anomaly, specified type NEC
  ossicles 756.9
    auditory 744.04
  pulmonary valve segment 746.02
  pulmonic cusps 746.02
  ribs 756.3
  sacroiliac (acquired) (joint) 724.6
    congenital 755.69
    surgical V45.4
  skull, imperfect 756.0
  spine (acquired) 724.9
    arthrodesis status V45.4
    congenital (vertebra) 756.15
    postoperative status V45.4
  sublingual duct with submaxillary duct at opening in mouth 750.26
  talonavicular (bar) 755.67
  teeth, tooth 520.2
  testes 752.8
  toes (*see also* Syndactylism, toes) 755.13
  trachea and esophagus 750.3
  twins 759.4
  urethral-hymenal 599.89
  vagina 752.49
  valve cusps—*see* Fusion, cusps, heart valve
  ventricles, heart 745.4
  vertebra (arch)—*see* Fusion, spine
  vulva 752.49
Fusospirillosis (mouth) (tongue) (tonsil) 101

G

Gafsa boil 085.1
Gain, weight (abnormal) (excessive) (*see also* Weight, gain) 783.1
Gaisböck's disease or syndrome (polycythemia hypertonica) 289.0
Gait
  abnormality 781.2
    hysterical 300.11
  ataxic 781.2
    hysterical 300.11
  disturbance 781.2
    hysterical 300.11
  paralytic 781.2
  scissor 781.2
  spastic 781.2
  staggering 781.2
    hysterical 300.11
Galactocele (breast) (infected) 611.5
  puerperal, postpartum 676.8
Galactophoritis 611.0
  puerperal, postpartum 675.2
Galactorrhea 676.6
  not associated with childbirth 611.6
Galactosemia (classic) (congenital) 271.1
Galactosuria 271.1
Galacturia 791.1
  bilharziasis 120.0
Galen's vein —*see* condition
Gallbladder —*see also* condition
  acute (*see also* Disease, gallbladder) 575.0
Gall duct —*see* condition
Gallop rhythm 427.89
Gallstone (cholemic) (colic) (impacted)—*see also* Cholelithiasis
  causing intestinal obstruction 560.31
Gambling, pathological 312.31
Gammaloidosis 277.3
Gammopathy 273.9
  macroglobulinemia 273.3
  monoclonal (benign) (essential) (idiopathic) (with lymphoplasmacytic dyscrasia) 273.1
Gamna's disease (siderotic splenomegaly) 289.51
Gampsodactylia (congenital) 754.71
Gamstorp's disease (adynamia episodica hereditaria) 359.3
Gandy-Nanta disease (siderotic splenomegaly) 289.51
Gang activity without manifest psychiatric disorder V71.09
  adolescent V71.02
  adult V71.01
  child V71.02
Gangliocytoma (M9490/0)—*see* Neoplasm, connective tissue, benign
Ganglioglioma (M9505/1)—*see* Neoplasm, by site, uncertain behavior
Ganglion 727.43
  joint 727.41
  of yaws (early) (late) 102.6
  periosteal (*see also* Periostitis) 730.3
  tendon sheath (compound) (diffuse) 727.42
  tuberculous (*see also* Tuberculosis) 015.9
Ganglioneuroblastoma (M9490/3)—*see* Neoplasm, connective tissue, malignant

Ganglioneuroma (M9490/0)—*see also* Neoplasm, connective tissue, benign
  malignant (M9490/3)—*see* Neoplasm, connective tissue, malignant
Ganglioneuromatosis (M9491/0)—*see* Neoplasm, connective tissue, benign
Ganglionitis
  fifth nerve (*see also* Neuralgia, trigeminal) 350.1
  gasserian 350.1
  geniculate 351.1
    herpetic 053.11
    newborn 767.5
  herpes zoster 053.11
  herpetic geniculate (Hunt's syndrome) 053.11
Gangliosidosis 330.1
Gangosa 102.5
Gangrene, gangrenous (anemia) (artery) (cellulitis) (dermatitis) (dry) (infective) (moist) (pemphigus) (septic) (skin) (stasis) (ulcer) 785.4
  with
    arteriosclerosis (native artery) 440.24
      bypass graft 440.30
        autologous vein 440.31
        nonautologous biological 440.32
    diabetes (mellitus) 250.7 *[785.4]*
  abdomen (wall) 785.4
    arteriosclerotic 440.29 *[785.4]*
  adenitis 683
  alveolar 526.5
  angina 462
    diphtheritic 032.0
  anus 569.49
  appendices epiploicae—*see* Gangrene, mesentery
  appendix—*see* Appendicitis, acute
  arteriosclerotic —*see* Arteriosclerosis, with, gangrene
  auricle 785.4
  Bacillus welchii (*see also* Gangrene, gas) 040.0
  bile duct (*see also* Cholangitis) 576.8
  bladder 595.89
  bowel—*see* Gangrene, intestine
  cecum—*see* Gangrene, intestine
  Clostridium perfringens or welchii (*see also* Gangrene, gas) 040.0
  colon—*see* Gangrene, intestine
  connective tissue 785.4
  cornea 371.40
  corpora cavernosa (infective) 607.2
    noninfective 607.89
  cutaneous, spreading 785.4
  decubital 707.0 *[785.4]*
  diabetic (any site) 250.7 *[785.4]*
  dropsical 785.4
  emphysematous (*see also* Gangrene, gas) 040.0
  epidemic (ergotized grain) 988.2
  epididymis (infectional) (*see also* Epididymitis) 604.99
  erysipelas (*see also* Erysipelas) 035
  extremity (lower) (upper) 785.4
  gallbladder or duct (*see also* Cholecystitis, acute) 575.0

Gastritis 535.5

> *Note—Use the following fifth-digit subclassification for category 535:*
>
> *0 without mention of hemorrhage*
> *1 with hemorrhage*

acute 535.0
alcoholic 535.3
allergic 535.4
antral 535.4
atrophic 535.1
atrophic-hyperplastic 535.1
bile-induced 535.4
catarrhal 535.0
chronic (atrophic) 535.1
cirrhotic 535.4
corrosive (acute) 535.4
dietetic 535.4
due to diet deficiency 269.9 *[535.4]*
eosinophilic 535.4
erosive 535.4
follicular 535.4
  chronic 535.1
giant hypertrophic 535.2
glandular 535.4
  chronic 535.1
hypertrophic (mucosa) 535.2
  chronic giant 211.1
irritant 535.4
nervous 306.4
phlegmonous 535.0
psychogenic 306.4
sclerotic 535.4
spastic 536.8
subacute 535.0
superficial 535.4
suppurative 535.0
toxic 535.4
tuberculous (*see also* Tuberculosis) 017.9
Gastrocarcinoma (M8010/3) 151.9
Gastrocolic —*see* condition
Gastrocolitis —*see* Enteritis
Gastrodisciasis 121.8
Gastroduodenitis (*see also* Gastritis) 535.5
catarrhal 535.0
infectional 535.0
virus, viral 008.8
  specified type NEC 008.69
Gastrodynia 536.8
Gastroenteritis (acute) (catarrhal) (congestive) (hemorrhagic) (noninfectious) (*see also* Enteritis) 558.9
aertrycke infection 003.0
allergic 558.3
chronic 558.9
  ulcerative (*see also* Colitis, ulcerative) 556.9
dietetic 558.9
due to
  food poisoning (*see also* Poisoning, food) 005.9
  radiation 558.1
epidemic 009.0
functional 558.9
infectious (*see also* Enteritis, due to, by organism) 009.0
  presumed 009.1
salmonella 003.0
septic (*see also* Enteritis, due to, by organism) 009.0
toxic 558.2

Gastroenteritis—*continued*
tuberculous (*see also* Tuberculosis) 014.8
ulcerative (*see also* Colitis, ulcerative) 556.9
viral NEC 008.8
  specified type NEC 008.69
zymotic 009.0
Gastroenterocolitis —*see* Enteritis
Gastroenteropathy, protein-losing 579.8
Gastroenteroptosis 569.89
Gastroesophageal laceration-hemorrhage syndrome 530.7
Gastroesophagitis 530.19
Gastrohepatitis (*see also* Gastritis) 535.5
Gastrointestinal —*see* condition
Gastrojejunal —*see* condition
Gastrojejunitis (*see also* Gastritis) 535.5
Gastrojejunocolic —*see* condition
Gastroliths 537.89
Gastromalacia 537.89
Gastroparalysis 536.8
diabetic 250.6 *[337.1]*
Gastroparesis 536.3
diabetic 250.6 *[536.3]*
Gastropathy, exudative 579.8
Gastroptosis 537.5
Gastrorrhagia 578.0
Gastrorrhea 536.8
psychogenic 306.4
Gastroschisis (congenital) 756.79
acquired 569.89
Gastrospasm (neurogenic) (reflex) 536.8
neurotic 306.4
psychogenic 306.4
Gastrostaxis 578.0
Gastrostenosis 537.89
Gastrostomy
attention to V55.1
complication 536.40
  specified type 536.49
infection 536.41
malfunctioning 536.42
status V44.1
Gastrosuccorrhea (continuous) (intermittent) 536.8
neurotic 306.4
psychogenic 306.4
Gaucher's
disease (adult) (cerebroside lipidosis) (infantile) 272.7
hepatomegaly 272.7
splenomegaly (cerebroside lipidosis) 272.7
Gayet's disease (superior hemorrhagic polioencephalitis) 265.1
Gayet-Wernicke's syndrome (superior hemorrhagic polioencephalitis) 265.1
Gee (-Herter) (-Heubner) (-Thaysen) disease or syndrome (nontropical sprue) 579.0
Gélineau's syndrome 347
Gemination, teeth 520.2
Gemistocytoma (M9411/3)
specified site—*see* Neoplasm, by site, malignant
unspecified site 191.9
General, generalized —*see* condition
Genital —*see* condition
Genito-anorectal syndrome 099.1
Genitourinary system —*see* condition
Genu
congenital 755.64
extrorsum (acquired) 736.42
  congenital 755.64
  late effects of rickets 268.1

Genu—*continued*
  introrsum (acquired) 736.41
    congenital 755.64
    late effects of rickets 268.1
  rachitic (old) 268.1
  recurvatum (acquired) 736.5
    congenital 754.40
      with dislocation of knee 754.41
    late effects of rickets 268.1
  valgum (acquired) (knock-knee) 736.41
    congenital 755.64
    late effects of rickets 268.1
  varum (acquired) (bowleg) 736.42
    congenital 755.64
    late effects of rickets 268.1
Geographic tongue 529.1
Geophagia 307.52
Geotrichosis 117.9
  intestine 117.9
  lung 117.9
  mouth 117.9
Gephyrophobia 300.29
Gerbode defect 745.4
Gerhardt's
  disease (erythromelalgia) 443.89
  syndrome (vocal cord paralysis) 478.30
Gerlier's disease (epidemic vertigo) 078.81
German measles 056.9
  exposure to V01.4
Germinoblastoma (diffuse) (M9614/3) 202.8
  follicular (M9692/3) 202.0
Germinoma (M9064/3)—*see* Neoplasm, by site,
  malignant
Gerontoxon 371.41
Gerstmann's syndrome (finger agnosia) 784.69
Gestation (period)—*see also* Pregnancy
  ectopic NEC (*see also* Pregnancy, ectopic) 633.9
Gestational proteinuria 646.2
  with hypertension—*see* Toxemia, of pregnancy
Ghon tubercle primary infection (*see also*
  Tuberculosis) 010.0
Ghost
  teeth 520.4
  vessels, cornea 370.64
Ghoul hand 102.3
Giant
  cell
    epulis 523.8
    peripheral (gingiva) 523.8
    tumor, tendon sheath 727.02
  colon (congenital) 751.3
  esophagus (congenital) 750.4
  kidney 753.3
  urticaria 995.1
    hereditary 277.6
Giardia lamblia infestation 007.1
Giardiasis 007.1
Gibert's disease (pityriasis rosea) 696.3
Gibraltar fever —*see* Brucellosis
Giddiness 780.4
  hysterical 300.11
  psychogenic 306.9
Gierke's disease (glycogenosis I) 271.0
Gigantism (cerebral) (hypophyseal) (pituitary)
  253.0
Gilbert's disease or cholemia (familial
  nonhemolytic jaundice) 277.4
Gilchrist's disease (North American
  blastomycosis) 116.0
Gilford (-Hutchinson) disease or syndrome
  (progeria) 259.8

Gilles de la Tourette's disease (motor-verbal tic)
  307.23
Gillespie's syndrome (dysplasia
  oculodentodigitalis) 759.89
Gingivitis 523.1
  acute 523.0
    necrotizing 101
  catarrhal 523.0
  chronic 523.1
  desquamative 523.1
  expulsiva 523.4
  hyperplastic 523.1
  marginal, simple 523.1
  necrotizing, acute 101
  pellagrous 265.2
  ulcerative 523.1
    acute necrotizing 101
  Vincent's 101
Gingivoglossitis 529.0
Gingivopericementitis 523.4
Gingivosis 523.1
Gingivostomatitis 523.1
  herpetic 054.2
Giovannini's disease 117.9
Gland, glandular —*see* condition
Glanders 024
Glanzmann (-Naegeli) disease or thrombasthenia
  287.1
Glassblowers' disease 527.1
Glaucoma (capsular) (inflammatory)
  (noninflammatory) (primary) 365.9
  with increased episcleral venous pressure 365.82
  absolute 360.42
  acute 365.22
    narrow angle 365.22
    secondary 365.60
  angle closure 365.20
    acute 365.22
    chronic 365.23
    intermittent 365.21
    interval 365.21
    residual stage 365.24
    subacute 365.21
  border line 365.00
  chronic 365.11
    noncongestive 365.11
    open angle 365.11
    simple 365.11
  closed angle—*see* Glaucoma, angle closure
  congenital 743.20
    associated with other eye anomalies 743.22
    simple 743.21
  congestive—*see* Glaucoma, narrow angle
  corticosteroid-induced (glaucomatous stage)
    365.31
    residual stage 365.32
  hemorrhagic 365.60
  hypersecretion 365.81
  in or with
    aniridia 743.45 *[365.42]*
    Axenfeld's anomaly 743.44 *[365.41]*
    concussion of globe 921.3 *[365.65]*
    congenital syndromes NEC 759.89 *[365.44]*
    dislocation of lens
      anterior 379.33 *[365.59]*
      posterior 379.34 *[365.59]*
    disorder of lens NEC 365.59
    epithelial down-growth 364.61 *[365.64]*
    glaucomatocyclitic crisis 364.22 *[365.62]*
    hypermature cataract 366.18 *[365.51]*
    hyphema 364.41 *[365.63]*

Glomerulonephritis—*continued*
   renal necrosis 583.9
      cortical 583.6
      medullary 583.7
     specified pathology NEC 583.89
      acute 580.89
      chronic 582.89
   necrosis, renal 583.9
     cortical 583.6
     medullary (papillary) 583.7
   specified pathology or lesion NEC 583.89
  acute 580.9
   with
     exudative nephritis 580.89
     interstitial nephritis (diffuse) (focal) 580.89
     necrotizing glomerulitis 580.4
   extracapillary with epithelial crescents 580.4
   poststreptococcal 580.0
   proliferative (diffuse) 580.0
   rapidly progressive 580.4
   specified pathology NEC 580.89
  arteriolar (*see also* Hypertension, kidney) 403.90
  arteriosclerotic (*see also* Hypertension, kidney) 403.90
  ascending (*see also* Pyelitis) 590.80
  basement membrane NEC 583.89
   with
     pulmonary hemorrhage (Goodpasture's syndrome) 446.21 *[583.81]*
  chronic 582.9
   with
     exudative nephritis 582.89
     interstitial nephritis (diffuse) (focal) 582.89
     necrotizing glomerulitis 582.4
     specified pathology or lesion NEC 582.89
   endothelial 582.2
   extracapillary with epithelial crescents 582.4
   hypocomplementemic persistent 582.2
   lobular 582.2
   membranoproliferative 582.2
   membranous 582.1
    and proliferative (mixed) 582.2
    sclerosing 582.1
   mesangiocapillary 582.2
   mixed membranous and proliferative 582.2
   proliferative (diffuse) 582.0
   rapidly progressive 582.4
   sclerosing 582.1
  cirrhotic—*see* Sclerosis, renal
  desquamative—*see* Nephrosis
  due to or associated with
   amyloidosis 277.3 *[583.81]*
    with nephrotic syndrome 277.3 *[581.81]*
    chronic 277.3 *[582.81]*
   diabetes mellitus 250.4 *[583.81]*
    with nephrotic syndrome 250.4 *[581.81]*
   diphtheria 032.89 *[580.81]*
   gonococcal infection (acute) 098.19 *[583.81]*
    chronic or duration or 2 months or over 098.39 *[583.81]*
   infectious hepatitis 070.9 *[580.81]*
   malaria (with nephrotic syndrome) 084.9 *[581.81]*
   mumps 072.79 *[580.81]*
   polyarteritis (nodosa) (with nephrotic syndrome) 446.0 *[581.81]*
   specified pathology NEC 583.89
    acute 580.89
    chronic 582.89
   streptotrichosis 039.8 *[583.81]*

Glomerulonephritis—*continued*
  subacute bacterial endocarditis 421.0 *[580.81]*
  syphilis (late) 095.4
   congenital 090.5 *[583.81]*
   early 091.69 *[583.81]*
  systemic lupus erythematosus 710.0 *[583.81]*
   with nephrotic syndrome 710.0 *[581.81]*
   chronic 710.0 *[582.81]*
  tuberculosis (*see also* Tuberculosis) 016.0 *[583.81]*
  typhoid fever 002.0 *[580.81]*
  extracapillary with epithelial crescents 583.4
   acute 580.4
   chronic 582.4
  exudative 583.89
   acute 580.89
   chronic 582.89
  focal (*see also* Nephritis) 583.9
   embolic 580.4
  granular 582.89
  granulomatous 582.89
  hydremic (*see also* Nephrosis) 581.9
  hypocomplementemic persistent 583.2
   with nephrotic syndrome 581.2
   chronic 582.2
  immune complex NEC 583.89
  infective (*see also* Pyelitis) 590.80
  interstitial (diffuse) (focal) 583.89
   with nephrotic syndrome 581.89
   acute 580.89
   chronic 582.89
  latent or quiescent 582.9
  lobular 583.2
   with nephrotic syndrome 581.2
   chronic 582.2
  membranoproliferative 583.2
   with nephrotic syndrome 581.2
   chronic 582.2
  membranous 583.1
   with nephrotic syndrome 581.1
   and proliferative (mixed) 583.2
    with nephrotic syndrome 581.2
    chronic 582.2
   chronic 582.1
   sclerosing 582.1
    with nephrotic syndrome 581.1
  mesangiocapillary 583.2
   with nephrotic syndrome 581.2
   chronic 582.2
  minimal change 581.3
  mixed membranous and proliferative 583.2
   with nephrotic syndrome 581.2
   chronic 582.2
  necrotizing 583.4
   acute 580.4
   chronic 582.4
  nephrotic (*see also* Nephrosis) 581.9
  old—*see* Glomerulonephritis, chronic
  parenchymatous 581.89
  poststreptococcal 580.0
  proliferative (diffuse) 583.0
   with nephrotic syndrome 581.0
   acute 580.0
   chronic 582.0
  purulent (*see also* Pyelitis) 590.80
  quiescent—*see* Nephritis, chronic
  rapidly progressive 583.4
   acute 580.4
   chronic 582.4
  sclerosing membranous (chronic) 582.1
   with nephrotic syndrome 581.1

Glomerulonephritis—*continued*
  septic (*see also* Pyelitis) 590.80
  specified pathology or lesion NEC 583.89
    with nephrotic syndrome 581.89
      acute 580.89
      chronic 582.89
  suppurative (acute) (disseminated) (*see also*
    Pyelitis) 590.80
  toxic—*see* Nephritis, acute
  tubal, tubular—*see* Nephrosis, tubular
  type II (Ellis)—*see* Nephrosis
  vascular—*see* Hypertension, kidney
Glomerulosclerosis (*see also* Sclerosis, renal)
  587
  focal 582.1
    with nephrotic syndrome 581.1
  intercapillary (nodular) (with diabetes) 250.4
    [581.81]
Glossagra 529.6
Glossalgia 529.6
Glossitis 529.0
  areata exfoliativa 529.1
  atrophic 529.4
  benign migratory 529.1
  gangrenous 529.0
  Hunter's 529.4
  median rhomboid 529.2
  Moeller's 529.4
  pellagrous 265.2
Glossocele 529.8
Glossodynia 529.6
  exfoliativa 529.4
Glossoncus 529.8
Glossophytia 529.3
Glossoplegia 529.8
Glossoptosis 529.8
Glossopyrosis 529.6
Glossotrichia 529.3
Glossy skin 701.9
Glottis —*see* condition
Glottitis —*see* Glossitis
Glucagonoma (M8152/0)
  malignant (M8152/3)
    pancreas 157.4
    specified site NEC—*see* Neoplasm, by site,
      malignant
    unspecified site 157.4
  pancreas 211.7
  specified site NEC—*see* Neoplasm, by site,
    benign
  unspecified site 211.7
Glucoglycinuria 270.7
Glue ear syndrome 381.20
Glue sniffing (airplane glue) (*see also*
  Dependence) 304.6
Glycinemia (with methylmalonic acidemia) 270.7
Glycinuria (renal) (with ketosis) 270.0
Glycogen
  infiltration (*see also* Disease, glycogen storage)
    271.0
  storage disease (*see also* Disease, glycogen
    storage) 271.0
Glycogenosis (*see also* Disease, glycogen
  storage) 271.0
  cardiac 271.0 *[425.7]*
  Cori, types I-VII 271.0
  diabetic, secondary 250.8 *[259.8]*
  diffuse (with hepatic cirrhosis) 271.0
  generalized 271.0
  glucose-6-phosphatase deficiency 271.0
  hepatophosphorylase deficiency 271.0

Glycogenosis—*continued*
  hepatorenal 271.0
  myophosphorylase deficiency 271.0
Glycopenia 251.2
Glycoprolinuria 270.8
Glycosuria 791.5
  renal 271.4
Gnathostoma (spinigerum) (infection)
  (infestation) 128.1
  wandering swellings from 128.1
Gnathostomiasis 128.1
Goiter (adolescent) (colloid) (diffuse) (dipping)
  (due to iodine deficiency) (endemic)
  (euthyroid) (heart) (hyperplastic) (internal)
  (intrathoracic) (juvenile) (mixed type)
  (nonendemic) (parenchymatous) (plunging)
  (sporadic) (subclavicular) (substernal) 240.9
  with
    hyperthyroidism (recurrent) (*see also* Goiter,
      toxic) 242.0
    thyrotoxicosis (*see also* Goiter, toxic) 242.0
  adenomatous (*see also* Goiter, nodular) 241.9
  cancerous (M8000/3) 193
  complicating pregnancy, childbirth, or
    puerperium 648.1
  congenital 246.1
  cystic (*see also* Goiter, nodular) 241.9
  due to enzyme defect in synthesis of thyroid
    hormone (butane-insoluble iodine)
    (coupling) (deiodinase) (iodide trapping or
    organification) (iodotyrosine dehalogenase)
    (peroxidase) 246.1
  dyshormonogenic 246.1
  exophthalmic (*see also* Goiter, toxic) 242.0
  familial (with deaf-mutism) 243
  fibrous 245.3
  lingual 759.2
  lymphadenoid 245.2
  malignant (M8000/3) 193
  multinodular (nontoxic) 241.1
    toxic or with hyperthyroidism (*see also*
      Goiter, toxic) 242.2
  nodular (nontoxic) 241.9
    with
      hyperthyroidism (*see also* Goiter, toxic)
        242.3
      thyrotoxicosis (*see also* Goiter, toxic) 242.3
    endemic 241.9
    exophthalmic (diffuse) (*see also* Goiter, toxic)
      242.0
    multinodular (nontoxic) 241.1
    sporadic 241.9
    toxic (*see also* Goiter, toxic) 242.3
    uninodular (nontoxic) 241.0
  nontoxic (nodular) 241.9
    multinodular 241.1
    uninodular 241.0
  pulsating (*see also* Goiter, toxic) 242.0
  simple 240.0
  toxic 242.0

Note—Use the following fifth-digit subclassification with category 242:

0 without mention of thyrotoxic crisis or storm
1 with mention of thyrotoxic crisis or storm

---

    adenomatous 242.3
      multinodular 242.2
      uninodular 242.1
    multinodular 242.2

Goiter—*continued*
  nodular 242.3
    multinodular 242.2
    uninodular 242.1
   uninodular 242.1
  uninodular (nontoxic) 241.0
   toxic or with hyperthyroidism (*see also*
    Goiter, toxic) 242.1
Goldberg (-Maxwell) (-Morris) syndrome
  (testicular feminization) 257.8
Goldblatt's
  hypertension 440.1
  kidney 440.1
Goldenhar's syndrome (oculoauriculovertebral
  dysplasia) 756.0
Goldflam-Erb disease or syndrome 358.0
Goldscheider's disease (epidermolysis bullosa)
  757.39
Goldstein's disease (familial hemorrhagic
  telangiectasia) 448.0
Golfer's elbow 726.32
Goltz-Gorlin syndrome (dermal hypoplasia)
  757.39
Gonadoblastoma (M9073/1)
  specified site—*see* Neoplasm, by site uncertain
   behavior
  unspecified site
   female 236.2
   male 236.4
Gonecystitis (*see also* Vesiculitis) 608.0
Gongylonemiasis 125.6
  mouth 125.6
Goniosynechiae 364.73
Gonococcemia 098.89
Gonococcus, gonococcal (disease) (infection)
  (*see also* condition) 098.0
  anus 098.7
  bursa 098.52
  chronic NEC 098.2
  complicating pregnancy, childbirth, or
   puerperium 647.1
   affecting fetus or newborn 760.2
  conjunctiva, conjunctivitis (neonatorum) 098.40
  dermatosis 098.89
  endocardium 098.84
  epididymo-orchitis 098.13
   chronic or duration of 2 months or over 098.33
  eye (newborn) 098.40
  fallopian tube (chronic) 098.37
   acute 098.17
  genitourinary (acute) (organ) (system) (tract)
   (*see also* Gonorrhea) 098.0
   lower 098.0
    chronic 098.2
   upper 098.10
    chronic 098.30
  heart NEC 098.85
  joint 098.50
  keratoderma 098.81
  keratosis (blennorrhagica) 098.81
  lymphatic (gland) (node) 098.89
  meninges 098.82
  orchitis (acute) 098.13
   chronic or duration of 2 months or over 098.33
  pelvis (acute) 098.19
   chronic or duration of 2 months or over 098.39
  pericarditis 098.83
  peritonitis 098.86
  pharyngitis 098.6
  pharynx 098.6

Gonococcus, gonococcal—*continued*
  proctitis 098.7
  pyosalpinx (chronic) 098.37
   acute 098.17
  rectum 098.7
  septicemia 098.89
  skin 098.89
  specified site NEC 098.89
  synovitis 098.51
  tendon sheath 098.51
  throat 098.6
  urethra (acute) 098.0
   chronic of duration of 2 months or over 098.2
  vulva (acute) 098.0
   chronic or duration of 2 months or over 098.2
Gonocytoma (M9073/1)
  specified site—*see* Neoplasm, by site, uncertain
   behavior
  unspecified site
   female 236.2
   male 236.4
Gonorrhea 098.0
  acute 098.0
  Bartholin's gland (acute) 098.0
   chronic or duration of 2 months or over 098.2
  bladder (acute) 098.11
   chronic or duration of 2 months or over 098.31
  carrier (suspected of) V02.7
  cervix (acute) 098.15
   chronic or duration of 2 months or over 098.35
  chronic 098.2
  complicating pregnancy, childbirth, or
   puerperium 647.1
   affecting fetus or newborn 760.2
  conjunctiva, conjunctivitis (neonatorum) 098.40
  contact V01.6
  Cowper's gland (acute) 098.0
   chronic or duration of 2 months or over 098.2
  duration of two months or over 098.2
  exposure to V01.6
  fallopian tube (chronic) 098.37
   acute 098.17
  genitourinary (acute) (organ) (system) (tract)
   098.0
   chronic 098.2
   duration of two months or over 098.2
  kidney (acute) 098.19
   chronic or duration of 2 months or over 098.39
  ovary (acute) 098.19
   chronic or duration of 2 months or over 098.39
  pelvis (acute) 098.19
   chronic or duration of 2 months or over 098.39
  penis (acute) 098.0
   chronic or duration of 2 months or over 098.2
  prostate (acute) 098.12
   chronic or duration of 2 months or over 098.32
  seminal vesicle (acute) 098.14
   chronic or duration of 2 months or over 098.34
  specified site NEC—*see* Gonococcus
  spermatic cord (acute) 098.14
   chronic or duration of 2 months or over 098.34
  urethra (acute) 098.0
   chronic or duration of 2 months or over 098.2
  vagina (acute) 098.0
   chronic or duration of 2 months or over 098.2
  vas deferens (acute) 098.14
   chronic or duration of 2 months or over 098.34
  vulva (acute) 098.0
   chronic or duration of 2 months or over 098.2
Goodpasture's syndrome (pneumorenal) 446.21

Gopalan's syndrome (burning feet) 266.2
Gordon's disease (exudative enteropathy) 579.8
Gorlin-Chaudhry-Moss syndrome 759.89
Gougerot's syndrome (trisymptomatic) 709.1
Gougerot-Blum syndrome (pigmented purpuric lichenoid dermatitis) 709.1
Gougerot-Carteaud disease or syndrome (confluent reticulate papillomatosis) 701.8
Gougerot-Hailey-Hailey disease (benign familial chronic pemphigus) 757.39
Gougerot (-Houwer) -Sjögren syndrome (keratoconjunctivitis sicca) 710.2
Gouley's syndrome (constrictive pericarditis) 423.2
Goundou 102.6
Gout, gouty 274.9
    with specified manifestations NEC 274.89
    arthritis (acute) 274.0
    arthropathy 274.0
    degeneration, heart 274.82
    diathesis 274.9
    eczema 274.89
    episcleritis 274.89 *[379.09]*
    external ear (tophus) 274.81
    glomerulonephritis 274.10
    iritis 274.89 *[364.11]*
    joint 274.0
    kidney 274.10
    lead 984.9
        specified type of lead—*see* Table of drugs and chemicals
    nephritis 274.10
    neuritis 274.89 *[357.4]*
    phlebitis 274.89 *[451.9]*
    rheumatic 714.0
    saturnine 984.9
        specified type of lead—*see* Table of drugs and chemicals
    spondylitis 274.0
    synovitis 274.0
    syphilitic 095.8
    tophi 274.0
        ear 274.81
        heart 274.82
        specified site NEC 274.82
Gowers'
    muscular dystrophy 359.1
    syndrome (vasovagal attack) 780.2
Gowers-Paton-Kennedy syndrome 377.04
Gradenigo's syndrome 383.02
Graft-versus-host disease (bone marrow) 996.85
    due to organ transplant NEC—*see* Complications, transplant, organ
Graham Steell's murmur (pulmonic regurgitation) (*see also* Endocarditis, pulmonary) 424.3
Grain-handlers' disease or lung 495.8
Grain mite (itch) 133.8
Grand
    mal (idiopathic) (*see also* Epilepsy) 345.1
        hysteria of Charcot 300.11
        nonrecurrent or isolated 780.39
    multipara
        affecting management of labor and delivery 659.4
        status only (not pregnant) V61.5
Granite workers' lung 502

Granular —*see also* condition
    inflammation, pharynx 472.1
    kidney (contracting) (*see also* Sclerosis, renal) 587
    liver—*see* Cirrhosis, liver
    nephritis—*see* Nephritis
Granulation tissue, abnormal —*see also* Granuloma
    abnormal or excessive 701.5
    postmastoidectomy cavity 383.33
    postoperative 701.5
    skin 701.5
Granulocytopenia, granulocytopenic (primary) 288.0
    malignant 288.0
Granuloma NEC 686.1
    abdomen (wall) 568.89
        skin (pyogenicum) 686.1
            from residual foreign body 709.4
    annulare 695.89
    anus 569.49
    apical 522.6
    appendix 543.9
    aural 380.23
    beryllium (skin) 709.4
        lung 503
    bone (*see also* Osteomyelitis) 730.1
        eosinophilic 277.8
        from residual foreign body 733.99
    canaliculus lacrimalis 375.81
    cerebral 348.8
    cholesterin, middle ear 385.82
    coccidioidal (progressive) 114.3
        lung 114.4
        meninges 114.2
        primary (lung) 114.0
    colon 569.89
    conjunctiva 372.61
    dental 522.6
    ear, middle (cholesterin) 385.82
        with otitis media—*see* Otitis media
    eosinophilic 277.8
        bone 277.8
        lung 277.8
        oral mucosa 528.9
    exuberant 701.5
    eyelid 374.89
    facial
        lethal midline 446.3
        malignant 446.3
    faciale 701.8
    fissuratum (gum) 523.8
    foot NEC 686.1
    foreign body (in soft tissue) NEC 728.82
        bone 733.99
        in operative wound 998.4
        muscle 728.82
        skin 709.4
        subcutaneous tissue 709.4
    fungoides 202.1
    gangraenescens 446.3
    giant cell (central) (jaw) (reparative) 526.3
        gingiva 523.8
        peripheral (gingiva) 523.8
    gland (lymph) 289.3
    Hodgkin's (M9661/3) 201.1
    ileum 569.89
    infectious NEC 136.9
    inguinale (Donovan) 099.2
        venereal 099.2
    intestine 569.89

H

Haas' disease (osteochondrosis head of humerus) 732.3
Habermann's disease (acute parapsoriasis varioliformis) 696.2
Habit, habituation
  chorea 307.22
  disturbance, child 307.9
  drug (*see also* Dependence) 304.9
  laxative (*see also* Abuse, drugs, nondependent) 305.9
  spasm 307.20
    chronic 307.22
    transient of childhood 307.21
  tic 307.20
    chronic 307.22
    transient of childhood 307.21
  use of
    nonprescribed drugs (*see also* Abuse, drugs, nondependent) 305.9
    patent medicines (*see also* Abuse, drugs, nondependent) 305.9
  vomiting 536.2
Hadfield-Clarke syndrome (pancreatic infantilism) 577.8
Haff disease 985.1
Hageman factor defect, deficiency, or disease (*see also* Defect, coagulation) 286.3
Haglund's disease (osteochondrosis os tibiale externum) 732.5
Haglund-Läwen-Fründ syndrome 717.89
Hagner's disease (hypertrophic pulmonary osteoarthropathy) 731.2
Hag teeth, tooth 524.3
Hailey-Hailey disease (benign familial chronic pemphigus) 757.39
Hair —*see also* condition
  plucking 307.9
Hairball in stomach 935.2
Hairy black tongue 529.3
Half vertebra 756.14
Halitosis 784.9
Hallermann-Streiff syndrome 756.0
Hallervorden-Spatz disease or syndrome 333.0
Hallopeau's
  acrodermatitis (continua) 696.1
  disease (lichen sclerosis et atrophicus) 701.0
Hallucination (auditory) (gustatory) (olfactory) (tactile) 780.1
  alcoholic 291.3
  drug-induced 292.12
  visual 368.16
Hallucinosis 298.9
  alcoholic (acute) 291.3
  drug-induced 292.12
Hallus —*see* Hallux
Hallux 735.9
  malleus (acquired) 735.3
  rigidus (acquired) 735.2
    congenital 755.66
    late effects of rickets 268.1
  valgus (acquired) 735.0
    congenital 755.66
  varus (acquired) 735.1
    congenital 755.66
Halo, visual 368.15
Hamartoblastoma 759.6

Hamartoma 759.6
  epithelial (gingival), odontogenic, central, or peripheral (M9321/0) 213.1
  upper jaw (bone) 213.0
  vascular 757.32
Hamartosis, hamartoses NEC 759.6
Hamman's disease or syndrome (spontaneous mediastinal emphysema) 518.1
Hamman-Rich syndrome (diffuse interstitial pulmonary fibrosis) 516.3
Hammer toe (acquired) 735.4
  congenital 755.66
  late effects of rickets 268.1
Hand —*see* condition
Hand-Schüller-Christian disease or syndrome (chronic histiocytosis x) 277.8
Hand-foot syndrome 282.61
Hanging (asphyxia) (strangulation) (suffocation) 994.7
Hangnail (finger) (with lymphangitis) 681.02
Hangover (alcohol) (*see also* Abuse, drugs, nondependent) 305.0
Hanot's cirrhosis or disease —*see* Cirrhosis, biliary
Hanot-Chauffard (-Troisier) syndrome (bronze diabetes) 275.0
Hansen's disease (leprosy) 030.9
  benign form 030.1
  malignant form 030.0
Harada's disease or syndrome 363.22
Hard chancre 091.0
Hard firm prostate 600.1
Hardening
  artery—*see* Arteriosclerosis
  brain 348.8
  liver 571.8
Hare's syndrome (M8010/3) (carcinoma, pulmonary apex) 162.3
Harelip (*see also* Cleft, lip) 749.10
Harkavy's syndrome 446.0
Harlequin (fetus) 757.1
  color change syndrome 779.8
Harley's disease (intermittent hemoglobinuria) 283.2
Harris'
  lines 733.91
  syndrome (organic hyperinsulinism) 251.1
Hart's disease or syndrome (pellagra-cerebellar ataxia-renal aminoaciduria) 270.0
Hartmann's pouch (abnormal sacculation of gallbladder neck) 575.8
Hartnup disease (pellagra-cerebellar ataxia-renal aminoaciduria) 270.0
Harvester lung 495.0
Hashimoto's disease or struma (struma lymphomatosa) 245.2
Hassall-Henle bodies (corneal warts) 371.41
Haut mal (*see also* Epilepsy) 345.1
Haverhill fever 026.1
Hawaiian wood rose dependence 304.5
Hawkins' keloid 701.4
Hay
  asthma (*see also* Asthma) 493.0
  fever (allergic) (with rhinitis) 477.9
    with asthma (bronchial) (*see also* Asthma) 493.0

Hay —*continued*
  allergic, due to grass, pollen, ragweed, or tree
      477.0
  conjunctivitis 372.05
  due to
      dander 477.8
      dust 477.8
      fowl 477.8
      pollen 477.0
      specified allergen other than pollen 477.8
Hayem-Faber syndrome (achlorhydric anemia)
    280.9
Hayem-Widal syndrome (acquired hemolytic
    jaundice) 283.9
Haygarth's nodosities 715.04
Hazard-Crile tumor (M8350/3) 193
Hb (abnormal)
  disease—*see* Disease, hemoglobin
  trait—*see* Trait
H disease 270.0
Head —*see also* condition
  banging 307.3
Headache 784.0
  allergic 346.2
  cluster 346.2
  due to
      loss, spinal fluid 349.0
      lumbar puncture 349.0
      saddle block 349.0
  emotional 307.81
  histamine 346.2
  lumbar puncture 349.0
  menopausal 627.2
  migraine 346.9
  nonorganic origin 307.81
  postspinal 349.0
  psychogenic 307.81
  psychophysiologic 307.81
  sick 346.1
  spinal 349.0
  spinal fluid loss 349.0
  tension 307.81
  vascular 784.0
      migraine type 346.9
  vasomotor 346.9
Health
  advice V65.4
  audit V70.0
  checkup V70.0
  education V65.4
  hazard (*see also* History of) V15.9
      specified cause NEC V15.89
  instruction V65.4
  services provided because (of)
      boarding school residence V60.6
      holiday relief for person providing home care
          V60.5
      inadequate
          housing V60.1
          resources V60.2
      lack of housing V60.0
      no care available in home V60.4
      person living alone V60.3
      poverty V60.3
      residence in institution V60.6
      specified cause NEC V60.8
      vacation relief for person providing home care
          V60.5

Healthy
  donor (*see also* Donor) V59.9
  infant or child
      accompanying sick mother V65.0
      receiving care V20.1
  person
      accompanying sick relative V65.0
      admitted for sterilization V25.2
      receiving prophylactic inoculation or
          vaccination (*see also* Vaccination,
          prophylactic) V05.9
Hearing examination V72.1
Heart —*see* condition
Heartburn 787.1
  psychogenic 306.4
Heat (effects) 992.9
  apoplexy 992.0
  burn—*see also* Burn, by site
      from sun 692.71
  collapse 992.1
  cramps 992.2
  dermatitis or eczema 692.89
  edema 992.7
  erythema—*see* Burn, by site
  excessive 992.9
      specified effect NEC 992.8
  exhaustion 992.5
      anhydrotic 992.3
      due to
          salt (and water) depletion 992.4
          water depletion 992.3
  fatigue (transient) 992.6
  fever 992.0
  hyperpyrexia 992.0
  prickly 705.1
  prostration—*see* Heat, exhaustion
  pyrexia 992.0
  rash 705.1
  specified effect NEC 992.8
  stroke 992.0
  sunburn 692.71
  syncope 992.1
Heavy-chain disease 273.2
Heavy-for-dates (fetus or infant) 766.1
  4500 grams or more 766.0
  exceptionally 766.0
Hebephrenia, hebephrenic (acute) (*see also*
    Schizophrenia) 295.1
  dementia (praecox) (*see also* Schizophrenia)
      295.1
  schizophrenia (*see also* Schizophrenia) 295.1
Heberden's
  disease or nodes 715.04
  syndrome (angina pectoris) 413.9
Hebra's disease
  dermatitis exfoliativa 695.89
  erythema multiforme exudativum 695.1
  pityriasis 695.89
      maculata et circinata 696.3
      rubra 695.89
          pilaris 696.4
  prurigo 698.2
Hebra, nose 040.1
Hedinger's syndrome (malignant carcinoid)
    259.2
Heel —*see* condition
Heerfordt's disease or syndrome
    (uveoparotitis) 135
Hegglin's anomaly or syndrome 288.2
Heidenhain's disease 290.10
  with dementia 290.10

Heilmeyer-Schöner disease (M9842/3) 207.1
Heine-Medin disease (*see also* Poliomyelitis)
   045.9
Heinz-body anemia, congenital 282.7
Heller's disease or syndrome (infantile
   psychosis) (*see also* Psychosis, childhood)
   299.1
H.E.L.L.P. 642.5
Helminthiasis (*see also* Infestation, by specific
   parasite) 128.9
  Ancylostoma (*see also* Ancylostoma) 126.9
  intestinal 127.9
    mixed types (types classifiable to more than
      one of the titles 120.0-127.7) 127.8
    specified type 127.7
    mixed types (intestinal) (types classifiable to
      more than one of the titles 120.0-127.7)
      127.8
  Necator americanus 126.1
  specified type NEC 128.8
  Trichinella 124
Heloma 700
Hemangioblastoma (M9161/1)—*see also*
   Neoplasm, connective tissue, uncertain
   behavior
  malignant (M9161//3)—*see* Neoplasm,
    connective tissue, malignant
Hemangioblastomatosis, cerebelloretinal 759.6
Hemangioendothelioma (M9130/1)—*see also*
   Neoplasm, by site, uncertain behavior
  benign (M9130/0) 228.00
  bone (diffuse) (M9130/3)—*see* Neoplasm,
    bone, malignant
  malignant (M9130/3)—*see* Neoplasm,
    connective tissue, malignant
  nervous system (M9130/0) 228.09
Hemangioendotheliosarcoma (M9130/3)—*see*
   Neoplasm, connective tissue, malignant
Hemangiofibroma (M9160/0)—*see* Neoplasm,
   by site, benign
Hemangiolipoma (M8861/0)—*see* Lipoma
Hemangioma (M9120/0) 228.00
  arteriovenous (M9123/0)—*see* Hemangioma,
    by site
  brain 228.02
  capillary (M9131/0)—*see* Hemangioma, by site
  cavernous (M9121/0)—*see* Hemangioma, by
    site
  central nervous system NEC 228.09
  choroid 228.09
  heart 228.09
  infantile (M9131/0)—*see* Hemangioma, by site
  intra-abdominal structures 228.04
  intracranial structures 228.02
  intramuscular (M9132/0)—*see* Hemangioma,
    by site
  iris 228.09
  juvenile (M9131/0)—*see* Hemangioma, by site
  malignant (M9120/3)—*see* Neoplasm,
    connective tissue, malignant
  meninges 228.09
    brain 228.02
    spinal cord 228.09
  peritoneum 228.04
  placenta—*see* Placenta, abnormal
  plexiform (M9131/0)—*see* Hemangioma, by site
  racemose (M9123/0)—*see* Hemangioma, by site
  retina 228.03
  retroperitoneal tissue 228.04
  sclerosing (M8832/0)—*see* Neoplasm, skin,
    benign

Hemangioma—*continued*
  simplex (M9131/0)—*see* Hemangioma, by site
  skin and subcutaneous tissue 228.01
  specified site NEC 228.09
  spinal cord 228.09
  venous (M9122/0)—*see* Hemangioma, by site
  verrucous keratotic (M9142/0)—*see*
    Hemangioma, by site
Hemangiomatosis (systemic) 757.32
  involving single site—*see* Hemangioma
Hemangiopericytoma (M9150/1)—*see also*
   Neoplasm, connective tissue, uncertain
   behavior
  benign (M9150/0)—*see* Neoplasm, connective
    tissue, benign
  malignant (M9150/3)—*see* Neoplasm,
    connective tissue, malignant
Hemangiosarcoma (M9120/3)—*see* Neoplasm,
   connective tissue, malignant
Hemarthrosis (nontraumatic) 719.0
  ankle 719.17
  elbow 719.12
  foot 719.17
  hand 719.14
  hip 719.15
  knee 719.16
  multiple sites 719.19
  pelvic region 719.15
  shoulder (region) 719.11
  specified site NEC 719.18
  traumatic—*see* Sprain, by site
  wrist 719.13
Hematemesis 578.0
  with ulcer—*see* Ulcer, by site, with hemorrhage
  due to S. japonicum 120.2
  Goldstein's (familial hemorrhagic
    telangiectasia) 448.0
  newborn 772.4
    due to swallowed maternal blood 777.3
Hematidrosis 705.89
Hematinuria (*see also* Hemoglobinuria) 791.2
  malarial 084.8
  paroxysmal 283.2
Hematite miners' lung 503
Hematobilia 576.8
Hematocele (congenital) (diffuse) (idiopathic)
   608.83
  broad ligament 620.7
  canal of Nuck 629.0
  cord, male 608.83
  fallopian tube 620.8
  female NEC 629.0
  ischiorectal 569.89
  male NEC 608.83
  ovary 629.0
  pelvis, pelvic
    female 629.0
      with ectopic pregnancy (*see also* Pregnancy,
        ectopic) 633.9
    male 608.83
  periuterine 629.0
  retrouterine 629.0
  scrotum 608.83
  spermatic cord (diffuse) 608.83
  testis 608.84
  traumatic—*see* Injury, internal, pelvis
  tunica vaginalis 608.83
  uterine ligament 629.0
  uterus 621.4
  vagina 623.6
  vulva 624.5

Hematocephalus 742.4
Hematochezia (*see also* Melena) 578.1
Hematochyluria (*see also* Infestation, filarial) 125.9
Hematocolpos 626.8
Hematocornea 371.12
Hematogenous —*see* condition
Hematoma (skin surface intact) (traumatic)—*see also* Contusion

> *Note—Hematomas are coded according to origin and the nature and site of the hematoma or the accompanying injury. Hematomas of unspecified origin are coded as injuries of the sites involved, except:*
> *(a) hematomas of genital organs which are coded as diseases of the organ involved unless they complicate pregnancy or delivery*
> *(b) hematomas of the eye which are coded as diseases of the eye.*
>
> *For late effect of hematoma classifiable to 920-924 see Late, effect, contusion*

with
　crush injury—*see* Crush
　fracture—*see* Fracture, by site
　injury of internal organs—*see also* Injury, internal, by site
　　kidney—*see* Hematoma, kidney, traumatic
　　liver—*see* Hematoma, liver, traumatic
　　spleen—*see* Hematoma, spleen
　nerve injury—*see* Injury, nerve
　open wound—*see* Wound, open, by site
　skin surface intact—*see* Contusion
abdomen (wall)—*see* Contusion, abdomen
amnion 658.8
aorta, dissecting 441.00
　abdominal 441.02
　thoracic 441.01
　thoracoabdominal 441.03
arterial (complicating trauma) 904.9
　specified site—*see* Injury, blood vessel, by site
auricle (ear) 380.31
birth injury 767.8
　skull 767.1
brain (traumatic) 853.0

> *Note—Use the following fifth-digit subclassification with categories 851-854:*
>
> *0 unspecified state of consciousness*
> *1 with no loss of consciousness*
> *2 with brief [less than one hour] loss of consciousness*
> *3 with moderate [1-24 hours] loss of consciousness*
> *4 with prolonged [more than 24 hours] loss of consciousness and return to pre-existing conscious level*
> *5 with prolonged [more than 24 hours] loss of consciousness, without return to pre-existing conscious level*
> *Use fifth-digit 5 to designate when a patient is unconscious and dies before regaining consciousness, regardless of the duration of the loss of consciousness*
> *6 with loss of consciousness of unspecified duration*
> *9 with concussion, unspecified*

Hematoma—*continued*
with
　cerebral
　　contusion—*see* Contusion, brain
　　laceration—*see* Laceration, brain
　　open intracranial wound 853.1
　　skull fracture—*see* Fracture, skull, by site
　extradural or epidural 852.4
　　with open intracranial wound 852.5
　　fetus or newborn 767.0
　　nontraumatic 432.0
　fetus or newborn NEC 767.0
　nontraumatic (*see also* Hemorrhage, brain) 431
　　epidural or extradural 432.0
　　newborn NEC 772.8
　　subarachnoid, arachnoid, or meningeal (*see also* Hemorrhage, subarachnoid) 430
　　subdural (*see also* Hemorrhage, subdural) 432.1
　subarachnoid, arachnoid, or meningeal 852.0
　　with open intracranial wound 852.1
　　fetus or newborn 772.2
　　nontraumatic (*see also* Hemorrhage, subarachnoid) 430
　subdural 852.2
　　with open intracranial wound 852.3
　　fetus or newborn (localized) 767.0
　　nontraumatic (*see also* Hemorrhage, subdural) 432.1
breast (nontraumatic) 611.8
broad ligament (nontraumatic) 620.7
　complicating delivery 665.7
　traumatic—*see* Injury, internal, broad ligament
calcified NEC 959.9
capitis 920
　due to birth injury 767.1
　newborn 767.1
cerebral—*see* Hematoma, brain
cesarean section wound 674.3
chorion—*see* Placenta, abnormal
complicating delivery (perineum) (vulva) 664.5
　pelvic 665.7
　vagina 665.7
corpus
　cavernosum (nontraumatic) 607.82
　luteum (nontraumatic) (ruptured) 620.1
dura (mater)—*see* Hematoma, brain, subdural
epididymis (nontraumatic) 608.83
epidural (traumatic)—*see also* Hematoma, brain, extradural
　spinal—*see* Injury, spinal, by site
episiotomy 674.3
external ear 380.31
extradural—*see also* Hematoma, brain, extradural
　fetus or newborn 767.0
　nontraumatic 432.0
　　fetus or newborn 767.0
fallopian tube 620.8
genital organ (nontraumatic)
　female NEC 629.8
　male NEC 608.83
　traumatic (external site) 922.4
　　internal—*see* Injury, internal, genital organ
graafian follicle (ruptured) 620.0
internal organs (abdomen, chest, or pelvis)—*see also* Injury, internal, by site
　kidney—*see* Hematoma, kidney, traumatic
　liver—*see* Hematoma, liver, traumatic
　spleen—*see* Hematoma, spleen

Hematoma—*continued*
  intracranial—*see* Hematoma, brain
  kidney, cystic 593.81
    traumatic 866.01
      with open wound into cavity 866.11
  labia (nontraumatic) 624.5
  lingual (and other parts of neck, scalp, or face, except eye) 920
  liver (subcapsular) 573.8
    birth injury 767.8
    fetus or newborn 767.8
    traumatic NEC 864.01
      with
        laceration—*see* Laceration, liver
        open wound into cavity 864.11
  mediastinum—*see* Injury, internal, mediastinum
  meninges, meningeal (brain)—*see also* Hematoma, brain, subarachnoid
    spinal—*see* Injury, spinal, by site
  mesosalpinx (nontraumatic) 620.8
    traumatic—*see* Injury, internal, pelvis
  muscle (traumatic)—*see* Contusion, by site
  nasal (septum) (and other part(s) of neck, scalp, or face, except eye) 920
  obstetrical surgical wound 674.3
  orbit, orbital (nontraumatic) 376.32
    traumatic 921.2
  ovary (corpus luteum) (nontraumatic) 620.1
    traumatic—*see* Injury, internal, ovary
  pelvis (female) (nontraumatic) 629.8
    complicating delivery 665.7
    male 608.83
    traumatic—*see also* Injury, internal, pelvis
      specified organ NEC (*see also* Injury, internal, pelvis) 867.6
  penis (nontraumatic) 607.82
  pericranial (and neck, or face any part, except eye) 920
    due to injury at birth 767.1
  perineal wound (obstetrical) 674.3
    complicating delivery 664.5
  perirenal, cystic 593.81
  pinna 380.31
  placenta—*see* Placenta, abnormal
  postoperative 998.12
  retroperitoneal (nontraumatic) 568.81
    traumatic—*see* Injury, internal, retroperitoneum
  retropubic, male 568.81
  scalp (and neck, or face any part, except eye) 920
    fetus or newborn 767.1
  scrotum (nontraumatic) 608.83
    traumatic 922.4
  seminal vesicle (nontraumatic) 608.83
    traumatic—*see* Injury, internal, seminal vesicle
  spermatic cord—*see also* Injury, internal, spermatic cord
    nontraumatic 608.83
  spinal (cord) (meninges)—*see also* Injury, spinal, by site
    fetus or newborn 767.4
    nontraumatic 336.1
  spleen 865.01
    with
      laceration—*see* Laceration, spleen
      open wound into cavity 865.11
  sternocleidomastoid, birth injury 767.8

Hematoma—*continued*
  sternomastoid, birth injury 767.8
  subarachnoid—*see also* Hematoma, brain, subarachnoid
    fetus or newborn 772.2
    nontraumatic (*see also* Hemorrhage, subarachnoid) 430
    newborn 772.2
  subdural—*see also* Hematoma, brain, subdural
    fetus or newborn (localized) 767.0
    nontraumatic (*see also* Hemorrhage, subdural) 432.1
  subperiosteal (syndrome) 267
    traumatic—*see* Hematoma, by site
  superficial, fetus or newborn 772.6
  syncytium—*see* Placenta, abnormal
  testis (nontraumatic) 608.83
    birth injury 767.8
    traumatic 922.4
  tunica vaginalis (nontraumatic) 608.83
  umbilical cord 663.6
    affecting fetus or newborn 762.6
  uterine ligament (nontraumatic) 620.7
    traumatic—*see* Injury, internal, pelvis
  uterus 621.4
    traumatic—*see* Injury, internal, pelvis
  vagina (nontraumatic) (ruptured) 623.6
    complicating delivery 665.7
    traumatic 922.4
  vas deferens (nontraumatic) 608.83
    traumatic—*see* Injury, internal, vas deferens
  vitreous 379.23
  vocal cord 920
  vulva (nontraumatic) 624.5
    complicating delivery 664.5
    fetus or newborn 767.8
    traumatic 922.4
Hematometra 621.4
Hematomyelia 336.1
  with fracture of vertebra (*see also* Fracture, vertebra, by site, with spinal cord injury) 806.8
  fetus or newborn 767.4
Hematomyelitis 323.9
  late effect—*see* category 326
Hematoperitoneum (*see also* Hemoperitoneum) 568.81
Hematopneumothorax (*see also* Hemothorax) 511.8
Hematoporphyria (acquired) (congenital) 277.1
Hematoporphyrinuria (acquired) (congenital) 277.1
Hematorachis, hematorrhachis 336.1
  fetus or newborn 767.4
Hematosalpinx 620.8
  with
    ectopic pregnancy (*see also* categories 633.0-633.9) 639.2
    molar pregnancy (*see also* categories 630-632) 639.2
  infectional (*see also* Salpingo-oophoritis) 614.2
Hematospermia 608.83
Hematothorax (*see also* Hemothorax) 511.8
Hematotympanum 381.03
Hematuria (benign) (essential) (idiopathic) 599.7
  due to S. hematobium 120.0
  endemic 120.0
  intermittent 599.7
  malarial 084.8
  paroxysmal 599.7

Hematuria—*continued*
  sulfonamide
    correct substance properly administered 599.7
    overdose or wrong substance given or taken
      961.0
  tropical (bilharziasis) 120.0
  tuberculous (*see also* Tuberculosis) 016.9
Hematuric bilious fever 084.8
Hemeralopia 368.60
  meaning day blindness 368.10
  vitamin A deficiency 264.5
Hemiabiotrophy 799.8
Hemi-akinesia 781.8
Hemianalgesia (*see also* Disturbance, sensation)
    782.0
Hemianencephaly 740.0
Hemianesthesia (*see also* Disturbance,
    sensation) 782.0
Hemianopia, hemianopsia (altitudinal)
    (homonymous) 368.46
  binasal 368.47
  bitemporal 368.47
  heteronymous 368.47
  syphilitic 095.8
Hemiasomatognosia 307.9
Hemiathetosis 781.0
Hemiatrophy 799.8
  cerebellar 334.8
  face 349.89
    progressive 349.89
  fascia 728.9
  leg 728.2
  tongue 529.8
Hemiballism (us) 333.5
Hemiblock (cardiac) (heart) (left) 426.2
Hemicardia 746.89
Hemicephalus, hemicephaly 740.0
Hemichorea 333.5
Hemicrania 346.9
  congenital malformation 740.0
Hemidystrophy —*see* Hemiatrophy
Hemiectromelia 755.4
Hemihypalgesia (*see also* Disturbance,
    sensation) 782.0
Hemihypertrophy (congenital) 759.89
  cranial 756.0
Hemihypesthesia (*see also* Disturbance,
    sensation) 782.0
Hemi-inattention 781.8
Hemimelia 755.4
  lower limb 755.30
    paraxial (complete) (incomplete) (intercalary)
      (terminal) 755.32
      fibula 755.37
      tibia 755.36
    transverse (complete) (partial) 755.31
  upper limb 755.20
    paraxial (complete) (incomplete) (intercalary)
      (terminal) 755.22
      radial 755.26
      ulnar 755.27
    transverse (complete) (partial) 755.21
Hemiparalysis (*see also* Hemiplegia) 342.9
Hemiparesis (*see also* Hemiplegia) 342.9
Hemiparesthesia (*see also* Disturbance,
    sensation) 782.0

Hemiplegia 342.9
  acute (*see also* Disease, cerebrovascular, acute)
    436
  alternans facialis 344.89
  apoplectic (*see also* Disease, cerebrovascular,
    acute) 436
    late effect or residual
      affecting
        dominant side 438.21
        nondominant side 438.22
        unspecfied side 438.20
  arteriosclerotic 437.0
    late effect or residual
      affecting
        dominant side 438.21
        nondominant side 438.22
        unspecified side 438.20
  ascending (spinal) NEC 344.89
  attack (*see also* Disease, cerebrovascular, acute)
    436
  brain, cerebral (current episode) 437.8
    congenital 343.1
  cerebral—*see* Hemiplegia, brain
  congenital (cerebral) (spastic) (spinal) 343.1
  conversion neurosis (hysterical) 300.11
  cortical—*see* Hemiplegia, brain
  due to
    arteriosclerosis 437.0
      late effect or residual
        affecting
          dominant side 438.21
          nondominant side 438.22
          unspecified side 438.20
    cerebrovascular lesion (*see also* Disease,
      cerebrovascular, acute) 436
      late effect
        affecting
          dominant side 438.21
          nondominant side 438.22
          unspecified side 438.20
  embolic (current) (*see also* Embolism, brain)
    434.1
    late effect
      affecting
        dominant side 438.21
        nondominant side 438.22
        unspecified side 438.20
  flaccid 342.0
  hypertensive (current episode) 437.8
  infantile (postnatal) 343.4
  late effect
    birth injury, intracranial or spinal 343.4
    cerebrovascular lesion—*see* Late effect(s) (of)
      cerebrovascular disease
    viral encephalitis 139.0
  middle alternating NEC 344.89
  newborn NEC 767.0
  seizure (current episode) (*see also* Disease,
    cerebrovascular, acute) 436
  spastic 342.1
    congenital or infantile 343.1
  specified NEC 342.8
  thrombotic (current) (*see also* Thrombosis,
    brain) 434.0
    late effect—*see* late effect(s) (of)
      cerebrovascular disease
Hemisection, spinal cord —*see* Fracture,
    vertebra, by site, with spinal cord injury
Hemispasm 781.0
  facial 781.0
Hemispatial neglect 781.8

Hemisporosis 117.9
Hemitremor 781.0
Hemivertebra 756.14
Hemobilia 576.8
Hemocholecyst 575.8
Hemochromatosis (acquired) (diabetic)
    (hereditary) (liver) (myocardium) (primary
    idiopathic) (secondary) 275.0
  with refractory anemia 285.0
Hemodialysis V56.0
Hemoglobin —*see also* condition
  abnormal (disease)—*see* Disease, hemoglobin
  AS genotype 282.5
  fetal, hereditary persistence 282.7
  high-oxygen-affinity 289.0
  low NEC 285.9
  S (Hb-S), heterozygous 282.5
Hemoglobinemia 283.2
  due to blood transfusion NEC 999.8
    bone marrow 996.85
  paroxysmal 283.2
Hemoglobinopathy (mixed) (*see also* Disease,
    hemoglobin) 282.7
  with thalassemia 282.4
  sickle-cell 282.60
    with thalassemia 282.4
Hemoglobinuria, hemoglobinuric 791.2
  with anemia, hemolytic, acquired (chronic)
    NEC 283.2
  cold (agglutinin) (paroxysmal) (with Raynaud's
    syndrome) 283.2
  due to
    exertion 283.2
    hemolysis (from external causes) NEC 283.2
  exercise 283.2
  fever (malaria) 084.8
  infantile 791.2
  intermittent 283.2
  malarial 084.8
  march 283.2
  nocturnal (paroxysmal) 283.2
  paroxysmal (cold) (nocturnal) 283.2
Hemolymphangioma (M9175/0) 228.1
Hemolysis
  fetal—*see* Jaundice, fetus or newborn
  intravascular (disseminated) NEC 286.6
    with
      abortion—*see* Abortion, by type, with
        hemorrhage, delayed or excessive
      ectopic pregnancy (*see also* categories
        633.0-633.9) 639.1
      hemorrhage of pregnancy 641.3
        affecting fetus or newborn 762.1
      molar pregnancy (*see also* categories
        630-632) 639.1
    acute 283.2
    following
      abortion 639.1
      ectopic or molar pregnancy 639.1
  neonatal—*see* Jaundice, fetus or newborn
  transfusion NEC 999.8
    bone marrow 996.85
Hemolytic —*see also* condition
  anemia—*see* Anemia, hemolytic
  uremic syndrome 283.11
Hemometra 621.4
Hemopericardium (with effusion) 423.0
  newborn 772.8
  traumatic (*see also* Hemothorax, traumatic)
    860.2
    with open wound into thorax 860.3

Hemoperitoneum 568.81
  infectional (*see also* Peritonitis) 567.2
  traumatic—*see* Injury, internal, peritoneum
Hemophilia (familial) (hereditary) 286.0
  A 286.0
  B (Leyden) 286.1
  C 286.2
  calcipriva (*see also* Fibrinolysis) 286.7
  classical 286.0
  nonfamilial 286.7
  vascular 286.4
Hemophilus influenzae NEC 041.5
  arachnoiditis (basic) (brain) (spinal) 320.0
    late effect—*see* category 326
  bronchopneumonia 482.2
  cerebral ventriculitis 320.0
    late effect—*see* category 326
  cerebrospinal inflammation 320.0
    late effect—*see* category 326
  infection NEC 041.5
  leptomeningitis 320.0
    late effect—*see* category 326
  meningitis (cerebral) (cerebrospinal) (spinal)
    320.0
    late effect—*see* category 326
  meningomyelitis 320.0
    late effect—*see* category 326
  pachymeningitis (adhesive) (fibrous)
    (hemorrhagic) (hypertrophic) (spinal) 320.0
    late effect—*see* category 326
  pneumonia (broncho-) 482.2
Hemophthalmos 360.43
Hemopneumothorax (*see also* Hemothorax)
    511.8
  traumatic 860.4
    with open wound into thorax 860.5
Hemoptysis 786.3
  due to Paragonimus (westermani) 121.2
  newborn 770.3
  tuberculous (*see also* Tuberculosis, pulmonary)
    011.9
Hemorrhage, hemorrhagic (nontraumatic) 459.0
  abdomen 459.0
  accidental (antepartum) 641.2
    affecting fetus or newborn 762.1
  adenoid 474.8
  adrenal (capsule) (gland) (medulla) 255.4
    newborn 772.5
  after labor—*see* Hemorrhage, postpartum
  alveolar
    lung, newborn 770.3
    process 525.8
  alveolus 525.8
  amputation stump (surgical) 998.11
    secondary, delayed 997.69
  anemia (chronic) 280.0
    acute 285.1
  antepartum—*see* Hemorrhage, pregnancy
  anus (sphincter) 569.3
  apoplexy (stroke) 432.9
  arachnoid—*see* Hemorrhage, subarachnoid
  artery NEC 459.0
    brain (*see also* Hemorrhage, brain) 431
    middle meningeal—*see* Hemorrhage,
      subarachnoid
  basilar (ganglion) (*see also* Hemorrhage, brain)
    431
  bladder 596.8
  blood dyscrasia 289.9

Hemorrhage, hemorrhagic—*continued*
  bowel 578.9
    newborn 772.4
  brain (miliary) (nontraumatic) 431
    with
      birth injury 767.0
    arachnoid—*see* Hemorrhage, subarachnoid
    due to
      birth injury 767.0
      rupture of aneurysm (congenital) (*see also*
        Hemorrhage, subarachnoid) 430
        mycotic 431
        syphilis 094.89
    epidural or extradural—*see* Hemorrhage,
      extradural
    fetus or newborn (anoxic) (hypoxic) (due to
      birth trauma) (nontraumatic) 767.0
    iatrogenic 997.02
    postoperative 997.02
    puerperal, postpartum, childbirth 674.0
    stem 431
    subarachnoid, arachnoid or meningeal—*see*
      Hemorrhage, subarachnoid
    subdural—*see* Hemorrhage, subdural
    traumatic NEC 853.0

> *Note—Use the following fifth-digit*
> *subclassification with categories 851-854:*
>
> *0 unspecified state of consciousness*
> *1 with no loss of consciousness*
> *2 with brief [less than one hour] loss of*
> *consciousness*
> *3 with moderate [1-24 hours] loss of*
> *consciousness*
> *4 with prolonged [more than 24 hours] loss of*
> *consciousness and return to pre-existing*
> *conscious level*
> *5 with prolonged [more than 24 hours] loss of*
> *consciousness, without return to pre-existing*
> *conscious level*
> *Use fifth-digit 5 to designate when a patient is*
> *unconscious and dies before regaining*
> *consciousness, regardless of the duration of the*
> *loss of consciousness*
> *6 with loss of consciousness of unspecified*
> *duration*
> *9 with concussion, unspecified*

      with
        cerebral
          contusion—*see* Contusion, brain
          laceration—*see* Laceration, brain
        open intracranial wound 853.1
        skull fracture—*see* Fracture, skull, by site
      extradural or epidural 852.4
        with open intracranial wound 852.5
      subarachnoid 852.0
        with open intracranial wound 852.1
      subdural 852.2
        with open intracranial wound 852.3
  breast 611.79
  bronchial tube—*see* Hemorrhage, lung
  bronchopulmonary—*see* Hemorrhage, lung
  bronchus (cause unknown) (*see also*
    Hemorrhage, lung) 786.3
  bulbar (*see also* Hemorrhage, brain) 431
  bursa 727.89
  capillary 448.9
    primary 287.8
  capsular—*see* Hemorrhage, brain
  cardiovascular 429.89

Hemorrhage, hemorrhagic—*continued*
  cecum 578.9
  cephalic (*see also* Hemorrhage, brain) 431
  cerebellar (*see also* Hemorrhage, brain) 431
  cerebellum (*see also* Hemorrhage, brain) 431
  cerebral (*see also* Hemorrhage, brain) 431
    fetus or newborn (anoxic) (traumatic) 767.0
  cerebromeningeal (*see also* Hemorrhage, brain)
    431
  cerebrospinal (*see also* Hemorrhage, brain) 431
  cerebrum (*see also* Hemorrhage, brain) 431
  cervix (stump) (uteri) 622.8
  cesarean section wound 674.3
  chamber, anterior (eye) 364.41
  childbirth—*see* Hemorrhage, complicating,
    delivery
  choroid 363.61
    expulsive 363.62
  ciliary body 364.41
  cochlea 386.8
  colon—*see* Hemorrhage, intestine
  complicating
    delivery 641.9
      affecting fetus or newborn 762.1
      associated with
        afibrinogenemia 641.3
          affecting fetus or newborn 763.89
        coagulation defect 641.3
          affecting fetus or newborn 763.89
        hyperfibrinolysis 641.3
          affecting fetus or newborn 763.89
        hypofibrinogenemia 641.3
          affecting fetus or newborn 763.89
      due to
        low-lying placenta 641.1
          affecting fetus or newborn 762.0
        placenta previa 641.1
          affecting fetus or newborn 762.0
        premature separation of placenta 641.2
          affecting fetus or newborn 762.1
        retained
          placenta 666.0
          secundines 666.2
        trauma 641.8
          affecting fetus or newborn 763.89
        uterine leiomyoma 641.8
          affecting fetus or newborn 763.89
    surgical procedure 998.11
  concealed NEC 459.0
  congenital 772.9
  conjunctiva 372.72
    newborn 772.8
  cord, newborn 772.0
    slipped ligature 772.3
    stump 772.3
  corpus luteum (ruptured) 620.1
  cortical (*see also* Hemorrhage, brain) 431
  cranial 432.9
  cutaneous 782.7
    newborn 772.6
  cyst, pancreas 577.2
  cystitis—*see* Cystitis
  delayed
    with
      abortion—*see* Abortion, by type, with
        hemorrhage, delayed or excessive
      ectopic pregnancy (*see also* categories
        633.0-633.9) 639.1
      molar pregnancy (*see also* categories
        630-632) 639.1

Hemorrhage, hemorrhagic—*continued*
　following
　　abortion 639.1
　　ectopic or molar pregnancy 639.1
　　postpartum 666.2
　diathesis (familial) 287.9
　　newborn 776.0
　disease 287.9
　　newborn 776.0
　　specified type NEC 287.8
　disorder 287.9
　　due to circulating anticoagulants 286.5
　　specified type NEC 287.8
　due to
　　any device, implant, or graft (presence of)
　　　classifiable to 996.0-996.5—*see*
　　　Complications, due to (presence of) any
　　　device, implant, or graft classified to
　　　996.0—996.5 NEC
　　circulating anticoagulant 286.5
　duodenum, duodenal 537.89
　　ulcer—*see* Ulcer, duodenum, with hemorrhage
　dura mater—*see* Hemorrhage, subdural
　endotracheal—*see* Hemorrhage, lung
　epidural—*see* Hemorrhage, extradural
　episiotomy 674.3
　esophagus 530.82
　　varix (*see also* Varix, esophagus, bleeding)
　　　456.0
　excessive
　　with
　　　abortion—*see* Abortion, by type, with
　　　　hemorrhage, delayed or excessive
　　　ectopic pregnancy (*see also* categories
　　　　633.0-633.9) 639.1
　　　molar pregnancy (*see also* categories
　　　　630-632) 639.1
　　following
　　　abortion 639.1
　　　ectopic or molar pregnancy 639.1
　external 459.0
　extradural (traumatic)—*see also* Hemorrhage,
　　brain, traumatic, extradural
　　birth injury 767.0
　　fetus or newborn (anoxic) (traumatic) 767.0
　　nontraumatic 432.0
　eye 360.43
　　chamber (anterior) (aqueous) 364.41
　　fundus 362.81
　eyelid 374.81
　fallopian tube 620.8
　fetomaternal 772.0
　　affecting management of pregnancy or
　　　puerperium 656.0
　fetus, fetal 772.0
　　from
　　　cut end of co-twin's cord 772.0
　　　placenta 772.0
　　　ruptured cord 772.0
　　　vasa previa 772.0
　　into
　　　co-twin 772.0
　　　mother's circulation 772.0
　　　　affecting management of pregnancy or
　　　　　puerperium 656.0
　fever (*see also* Fever, hemorrhagic) 065.9
　　with renal syndrome 078.6
　　arthropod-borne NEC 065.9
　　Bangkok 065.4
　　Crimean 065.0
　　dengue virus 065.4

Hemorrhage, hemorrhagic—*continued*
　　epidemic 078.6
　　Junin virus 078.7
　　Korean 078.6
　　Machupo virus 078.7
　　mite-borne 065.8
　　mosquito-borne 065.4
　　Philippine 065.4
　　Russian (Yaroslav) 078.6
　　Singapore 065.4
　　southeast Asia 065.4
　　Thailand 065.4
　　tick-borne NEC 065.3
　fibrinogenolysis (*see also* Fibrinolysis) 286.6
　fibrinolytic (acquired) (*see also* Fibrinolysis)
　　286.6
　fontanel 767.1
　from tracheostomy stoma 519.09
　fundus, eye 362.81
　funis
　　affecting fetus or newborn 772.0
　　complicating delivery 663.8
　gastric (*see also* Hemorrhage, stomach) 578.9
　gastroenteric 578.9
　　newborn 772.4
　gastrointestinal (tract) 578.9
　　newborn 772.4
　genitourinary (tract) NEC 599.89
　gingiva 523.8
　globe 360.43
　gravidarum—*see* Hemorrhage, pregnancy
　gum 523.8
　heart 429.89
　hypopharyngeal (throat) 784.8
　intermenstrual 626.6
　　irregular 626.6
　　regular 626.5
　internal (organs) 459.0
　　capsule (*see also* Hemorrhage brain) 431
　　ear 386.8
　　newborn 772.8
　intestine 578.9
　　congenital 772.4
　　newborn 772.4
　into
　　bladder wall 596.7
　　bursa 727.89
　　corpus luysii (*see also* Hemorrhage, brain) 431
　intra-abdominal 459.0
　　during or following surgery 998.11
　intra-alveolar, newborn (lung) 770.3
　intracerebral (*see also* Hemorrhage, brain) 431
　intracranial NEC 432.9
　　puerperal, postpartum, childbirth 674.0
　　traumatic—*see* Hemorrhage, brain, traumatic
　intramedullary NEC 336.1
　intraocular 360.43
　intraoperative 998.11
　intrapartum—*see* Hemorrhage, complicating,
　　delivery
　intrapelvic
　　female 629.8
　　male 459.0
　intraperitoneal 459.0
　intrapontine (*see also* Hemorrhage, brain) 431
　intrauterine 621.4
　　complicating delivery—*see* Hemorrhage,
　　　complicating, delivery
　　in pregnancy or childbirth—*see* Hemorrhage,
　　　pregnancy

Hemorrhage, hemorrhagic—*continued*
  postpartum (*see also* Hemorrhage,
      postpartum) 666.1
  intraventricular (*see also* Hemorrhage, brain)
      431
    fetus or newborn (anoxic) (traumatic) 772.1
  intravesical 596.7
  iris (postinfectional) (postinflammatory) (toxic)
      364.41
  joint (nontraumatic) 719.10
    ankle 719.17
    elbow 719.12
    foot 719.17
    forearm 719.13
    hand 719.14
    hip 719.15
    knee 719.16
    lower leg 719.16
    multiple sites 719.19
    pelvic region 719.15
    shoulder (region) 719.11
    specified site NEC 719.18
    thigh 719.15
    upper arm 719.12
    wrist 719.13
  kidney 593.81
  knee (joint) 719.16
  labyrinth 386.8
  leg NEC 459.0
  lenticular striate artery (*see also* Hemorrhage,
      brain) 431
  ligature, vessel 998.11
  liver 573.8
  lower extremity NEC 459.0
  lung 786.3
    newborn 770.3
    tuberculous (*see also* Tuberculosis,
        pulmonary) 011.9
  malaria 084.8
  marginal sinus 641.2
  massive subaponeurotic, birth injury 767.1
  maternal, affecting fetus or newborn 762.1
  mediastinum 786.3
  medulla (*see also* Hemorrhage, brain) 431
  membrane (brain) (*see also* Hemorrhage,
      subarachnoid) 430
    spinal cord—*see* Hemorrhage, spinal cord
  meninges, meningeal (brain) (middle) (*see also*
      Hemorrhage, subarachnoid) 430
    spinal cord—*see* Hemorrhage, spinal cord
  mesentery 568.81
  metritis 626.8
  midbrain (*see also* Hemorrhage, brain) 431
  mole 631
  mouth 528.9
  mucous membrane NEC 459.0
    newborn 772.8
  muscle 728.89
  nail (subungual) 703.8
  nasal turbinate 784.7
    newborn 772.8
  nasopharynx 478.29
  navel, newborn 772.3
  newborn 772.9
    adrenal 772.5
    alveolar (lung) 770.3
    brain (anoxic) (hypoxic) (due to birth trauma)
        767.0
    cerebral (anoxic) (hypoxic) (due to birth
        trauma) 767.0
    conjunctiva 772.8

Hemorrhage, hemorrhagic—*continued*
  cutaneous 772.6
  diathesis 776.0
  due to vitamin K deficiency 776.0
  gastrointestinal 772.4
  internal (organs) 772.8
  intestines 772.4
  intra-alveolar (lung) 770.3
  intracranial (from any perinatal cause) 767.0
  intraventricular (from any perinatal cause)
      772.1
  lung 770.3
  pulmonary (massive) 770.3
  spinal cord, traumatic 767.4
  stomach 772.4
  subaponeurotic (massive) 767.1
  subarachnoid (from any perinatal cause) 772.2
  subconjunctival 772.8
  umbilicus 772.0
    slipped ligature 772.3
    vasa previa 772.0
  nipple 611.79
  nose 784.7
    newborn 772.8
  obstetrical surgical wound 674.3
  omentum 568.89
    newborn 772.4
  optic nerve (sheath) 377.42
  orbit 376.32
  ovary 620.1
  oviduct 620.8
  pancreas 577.8
  parathyroid (gland) (spontaneous) 252.8
  parturition—*see* Hemorrhage, complicating,
      delivery
  penis 607.82
  pericardium, pericarditis 423.0
  perineal wound (obstetrical) 674.3
  peritoneum, peritoneal 459.0
  peritonsillar tissue 474.8
    after operation on tonsils 998.11
    due to infection 475
  petechial 782.7
  pituitary (gland) 253.8
  placenta NEC 641.9
    affecting fetus or newborn 762.1
    from surgical or instrumental damage 641.8
      affecting fetus or newborn 762.1
    previa 641.1
      affecting fetus or newborn 762.0
  pleura—*see* Hemorrhage, lung
  polioencephalitis, superior 265.1
  polymyositis—*see* Polymyositis
  pons (*see also* Hemorrhage, brain) 431
  pontine (*see also* Hemorrhage, brain) 431
  popliteal 459.0
  postcoital 626.7
  postextraction (dental) 998.11
  postmenopausal 627.1
  postnasal 784.7
  postoperative 998.11
  postpartum (atonic) (following delivery of
      placenta) 666.1
    delayed or secondary (after 24 hours) 666.2
    retained placenta 666.0
    third stage 666.0
  pregnancy (concealed) 641.9
    accidental 641.2
      affecting fetus or newborn 762.1
    affecting fetus or newborn 762.1

Hemorrhage, hemorrhagic—*continued*
   before 22 completed weeks gestation 640.9
      affecting fetus or newborn 762.1
     due to
      abruptio placenta 641.2
        affecting fetus or newborn 762.1
      afibrinogenemia or other coagulation defect
        (conditions classifiable to 286.0-286.9)
        641.3
        affecting fetus or newborn 762.1
      coagulation defect 641.3
        affecting fetus or newborn 762.1
      hyperfibrinolysis 641.3
        affecting fetus or newborn 762.1
      hypofibrinogenemia 641.3
        affecting fetus or newborn 762.1
      leiomyoma, uterus 641.8
        affecting fetus or newborn 762.1
      low-lying placenta 641.1
        affecting fetus or newborn 762.1
      marginal sinus (rupture) 641.2
        affecting fetus or newborn 762.1
      placenta previa 641.1
        affecting fetus or newborn 762.0
      premature separation of placenta (normally
        implanted) 641.2
        affecting fetus or newborn 762.1
      threatened abortion 640.0
        affecting fetus or newborn 762.1
      trauma 641.8
        affecting fetus or newborn 762.1
   early (before 22 completed weeks gestation)
      640.9
     affecting fetus or newborn 762.1
   previous, affecting management of pregnancy
     or childbirth V23.4
   unavoidable—*see* Hemorrhage, pregnancy,
     due to placenta previa
   prepartum (mother)—*see* Hemorrhage,
     pregnancy
   preretinal, cause unspecified 362.81
   prostate 602.1
   puerperal (*see also* Hemorrhage, postpartum)
     666.1
   pulmonary—*see also* Hemorrhage, lung
    newborn (massive) 770.3
    renal syndrome 446.21
   purpura (primary) (*see also* Purpura,
     thrombocytopenic) 287.3
   rectum (sphincter) 569.3
   recurring, following initial hemorrhage at time
     of injury 958.2
   renal 593.81
    pulmonary syndrome 446.21
   respiratory tract (*see also* Hemorrhage, lung)
     786.3
   retina, retinal (deep) (superficial) (vessels)
     362.81
    diabetic 250.5 *[362.01]*
    due to birth injury 772.8
   retrobulbar 376.89
   retroperitoneal 459.0
   retroplacental (*see also* Placenta, separation)
     641.2
   scalp 459.0
    due to injury at birth 767.1
   scrotum 608.83
   secondary (nontraumatic) 459.0
    following initial hemorrhage at time of injury
     958.2
   seminal vesicle 608.83

Hemorrhage, hemorrhagic—*continued*
   skin 782.7
    newborn 772.6
   spermatic cord 608.83
   spinal (cord) 336.1
    aneurysm (ruptured) 336.1
     syphilitic 094.89
    due to birth injury 767.4
    fetus or newborn 767.4
   spleen 289.59
   spontaneous NEC 459.0
    petechial 782.7
   stomach 578.9
    newborn 772.4
    ulcer—*see* Ulcer, stomach, with hemorrhage
   subaponeurotic, newborn 767.1
    massive (birth injury) 767.1
   subarachnoid (nontraumatic) 430
    fetus or newborn (anoxic) (traumatic) 772.2
    puerperal, postpartum, childbirth 674.0
    traumatic—*see* Hemorrhage, brain, traumatic,
     subarachnoid
   subconjunctival 372.72
    due to birth injury 772.8
    newborn 772.8
   subcortical (*see also* Hemorrhage, brain) 431
   subcutaneous 782.7
   subdiaphragmatic 459.0
   subdural (nontraumatic) 432.1
    due to birth injury 767.0
    fetus or newborn (anoxic) (hypoxic) (due to
     birth trauma) 767.0
    puerperal, postpartum, childbirth 674.0
    spinal 336.1
    traumatic—*see* Hemorrhage, brain, traumatic,
     subdural
   subhyaloid 362.81
   subperiosteal 733.99
   subretinal 362.81
   subtentorial (*see also* Hemorrhage, subdural)
     432.1
   subungual 703.8
    due to blood dyscrasia 287.8
   suprarenal (capsule) (gland) 255.4
    fetus or newborn 772.5
   tentorium (traumatic)—*see also* Hemorrhage,
     brain, traumatic
    fetus or newborn 767.0
    nontraumatic—*see* Hemorrhage, subdural
   testis 608.83
   thigh 459.0
   third stage 666.0
   thorax—*see* Hemorrhage, lung
   throat 784.8
   thrombocythemia 238.7
   thymus (gland) 254.8
   thyroid (gland) 246.3
    cyst 246.3
   tongue 529.8
   tonsil 474.8
    postoperative 998.11
   tooth socket (postextraction) 998.11
   trachea—*see* Hemorrhage, lung
   traumatic—*see also* nature of injury
    brain—*see* Hemorrhage, brain, traumatic
    recurring or secondary (following initial
     hemorrhage at time of injury) 958.2
   tuberculous NEC (*see also* Tuberculosis,
     pulmonary) 011.9
   tunica vaginalis 608.83
   ulcer—*see* Ulcer, by site, with hemorrhage

Hemorrhage, hemorrhagic—*continued*
  umbilicus, umbilical cord 772.0
    after birth, newborn 772.3
    complicating delivery 663.8
      affecting fetus or newborn 772.0
    slipped ligature 772.3
    stump 772.3
  unavoidable (due to placenta previa) 641.1
    affecting fetus or newborn 762.0
  upper extremity 459.0
  urethra (idiopathic) 599.84
  uterus, uterine (abnormal) 626.9
    climacteric 627.0
    complicating delivery—*see* Hemorrhage,
      complicating, delivery
    due to
      intrauterine contraceptive device 996.76
        perforating uterus 996.32
    functional or dysfunctional 626.8
    in pregnancy—*see* Hemorrhage, pregnancy
    intermenstrual 626.6
      irregular 626.6
      regular 626.5
    postmenopausal 627.1
    postpartum (*see also* Hemorrhage,
      postpartum) 666.1
    prepubertal 626.8
    pubertal 626.3
    puerperal (immediate) 666.1
  vagina 623.8
  vasa previa 663.5
    affecting fetus or newborn 772.0
  vas deferens 608.83
  ventricular (*see also* Hemorrhage, brain) 431
  vesical 596.8
  viscera 459.0
    newborn 772.8
  vitreous (humor) (intraocular) 379.23
  vocal cord 478.5
  vulva 624.8
Hemorrhoids (anus) (rectum) (without
    complication) 455.6
  bleeding, prolapsed, strangulated, or ulcerated
    NEC 455.8
    external 455.5
    internal 455.2
  complicated NEC 455.8
  complicating pregnancy and puerperium 671.8
  external 455.3
    with complication NEC 455.5
    bleeding, prolapsed, strangulated, or ulcerated
      455.5
    thrombosed 455.4
  internal 455.0
    with complication NEC 455.2
    bleeding, prolapsed, strangulated, or ulcerated
      455.2
    thrombosed 455.1
  residual skin tag 455.9
  sentinel pile 455.9
  thrombosed NEC 455.7
    external 455.4
    internal 455.1
Hemosalpinx 620.8
Hemosiderosis 275.0
  dietary 275.0
  pulmonary (idiopathic) 275.0 *[516.1]*
  transfusion NEC 999.8
    bone marrow 996.85
Hemospermia 608.83

Hemothorax 511.8
  bacterial, nontuberculous 511.1
  newborn 772.8
  nontuberculous 511.8
    bacterial 511.1
  pneumococcal 511.1
  postoperative 998.11
  staphylococcal 511.1
  streptococcal 511.1
  traumatic 860.2
    with
      open wound into thorax 860.3
      pneumothorax 860.4
        with open wound into thorax 860.5
  tuberculous (*see also* Tuberculosis, pleura)
    012.0
Hemotympanum 385.89
Hench-Rosenberg syndrome (palindromic
    arthritis) (*see also* Rheumatism, palindromic)
    719.3
Henle's warts 371.41
Henoch (-Schönlein)
  disease or syndrome (allergic purpura) 287.0
  purpura (allergic) 287.0
Henpue, henpuye 102.6
Heparitinuria 277.5
Hepar lobatum 095.3
Hepatalgia 573.8
Hepatic —*see also* condition
  flexure syndrome 569.89
Hepatitis 573.3
  acute (*see also* Necrosis, liver) 570
    alcoholic 571.1
    infective 070.1
      with hepatic coma 070.0
  alcoholic 571.1
  amebic—*see* Abscess, liver, amebic
  anicteric (acute)—*see* Hepatitis, viral
  antigen-associated (HAA) *see* Hepatitis, viral,
    type B
  Australian antigen (positive) *see* Hepatitis, viral,
    type B
  catarrhal (acute) 070.1
    with hepatic coma 070.0
    chronic 571.40
    newborn 070.1
      with hepatic coma 070.0
  chemical 573.3
  cholangiolitic 573.8
  cholestatic 573.8
  chronic 571.40
    active 571.49
      viral—*see* Hepatitis, viral
    aggressive 571.49
    persistent 571.41
    viral—*see* Hepatitis, viral
  cytomegalic inclusion virus 078.5 *[573.1]*
  diffuse 573.3
  "dirty needle"—*see* Hepatitis, viral
    with hepatic coma 070.2
  drug-induced 573.3
  due to
    Coxsackie 074.8 *[573.1]*
    cytomegalic inclusion virus 078.5 *[573.1]*
    infectious mononucleosis 075 *[573.1]*
    malaria 084.9 *[573.2]*
    mumps 072.71
    secondary syphilis 091.62
    toxoplasmosis (acquired) 130.5
      congenital (active) 771.2
  epidemic—*see* Hepatitis, viral, type A

Hepatitis—*continued*
  fetus or newborn 774.4
  fibrous (chronic) 571.49
    acute 570
  from injection, inoculation, or transfusion
    (blood) (other substance) (plasma) (serum)
    (onset within 8 months after administration)
    see Hepatitis, viral
  fulminant (viral) (*see also* Hepatitis, viral) 070.9
    with hepatic coma 070.6
    type A 070.1
      with hepatic coma 070.0
    type B—*see* Hepatitis, viral, Type B
  giant cell (neonatal) 774.4
  hemorrhagic 573.8
  homologous serum—*see* Hepatitis, viral
  hypertrophic (chronic) 571.49
    acute 570
  infectious, infective (acute) (chronic) (subacute)
    070.1
    with hepatic coma 070.0
  inoculation—*see* Hepatitis, viral
  interstitial (chronic) 571.49
    acute 570
  lupoid 571.49
  malarial 084.9 *[573.2]*
  malignant (*see also* Necrosis, liver) 570
  neonatal (toxic) 774.4
  newborn 774.4
  parenchymatous (acute) (*see also* Necrosis,
    liver) 570
  peliosis 573.3
  persistent, chronic 571.41
  plasma cell 571.49
  postimmunization—*see* Hepatitis, viral
  postnecrotic 571.49
  posttransfusion—*see* Hepatitis, viral
  recurrent 571.49
  septic 573.3
  serum—*see* Hepatitis, viral
    carrier (suspected) of V02.61
  subacute (*see also* Necrosis, liver) 570
  suppurative (diffuse) 572.0
  syphilitic (late) 095.3
    congenital (early) 090.0 *[573.2]*
      late 090.5 *[573.2]*
    secondary 091.62
  toxic (noninfectious) 573.3
    fetus or newborn 774.4
  tuberculous (*see also* Tuberculosis) 017.9
  viral (acute) (anicteric) (cholangiolitic)
    (cholestatic) (chronic) (subacute) 070.9
    with hepatic coma 070.6
    AU-SH type virus—*see* Hepatitis, viral, type B
    Australian antigen—*see* Hepatitis, viral, type
      B
    B-antigen—*see* Hepatitis, viral, type B
    Coxsackie 074.8 *[573.1]*
    cytomegalic inclusion 078.5 *[573.1]*
    IH (virus)—*see* Hepatitis, viral, type A
    infectious hepatitis virus—*see* Hepatitis, viral,
      type A
    serum hepatitis virus—*see* Hepatitis, viral,
      type B
    SH—*see* Hepatitis, viral, type B
    specified type NEC 070.59
      with hepatic coma 070.49
    type A 070.1
      with hepatic coma 070.0

Hepatitis—*continued*
  type B (acute) 070.30
    with
      hepatic coma 070.20
        with hepatitis delta 070.21
      hepatitis delta 070.31
        with hepatic coma 070.21
    carrier status V02.61
    chronic 070.32
      with
        hepatic coma 070.22
          with hepatitis delta 070.23
        hepatitis delta 070.33
          with hepatic coma 070.23
  type C (acute) 070.51
    with hepatic coma 070.41
    carrier status V02.62
    chronic 070.54
      with hepatic coma 070.44
  type delta (with hepatitis B carrier state)
    070.52
    with
      active hepatitis B disease—*see* Hepatitis,
        viral, type B
      hepatic coma 070.42
  type E 070.53
    with hepatic coma 070.43
  vaccination and inoculation (prophylactic)
    V05.3
Hepatization, lung (acute)—*see also*
  Pneumonia, lobar
  chronic (*see also* Fibrosis, lung) 515
Hepatoblastoma (M8970/3) 155.0
Hepatocarcinoma (M8170/3) 155.0
Hepatocholangiocarcinoma (M8180/3) 155.0
Hepatocholangioma, benign (M8180/0) 211.5
Hepatocholangitis 573.8
Hepatocystitis (*see also* Cholecystitis) 575.10
Hepatodystrophy 570
Hepatolenticular degeneration 275.1
Hepatolithiasis —*see* Choledocholithiasis
Hepatoma (malignant) (M8170/3) 155.0
  benign (M8170/0) 211.5
  congenital (M8970/3) 155.0
  embryonal (M8970/3) 155.0
Hepatomegalia glycogenica diffusa 271.0
Hepatomegaly (*see also* Hypertrophy, liver)
  789.1
  congenital 751.69
    syphilitic 090.0
  due to Clonorchis sinensis 121.1
  Gaucher's 272.7
  syphilitic (congenital) 090.0
Hepatoptosis 573.8
Hepatorrhexis 573.8
Hepatosis, toxic 573.8
Hepatosplenomegaly 571.8
  due to S. japonicum 120.2
  hyperlipemic (Burger-Grutz type) 272.3
Herald patch 696.3
Hereditary —*see* condition
Heredodegeneration 330.9
  macular 362.70
Heredopathia atactica polyneuritiformis 356.3
Heredosyphilis (*see also* Syphilis, congenital)
  090.9
Hermaphroditism (true) 752.7
  with specified chromosomal anomaly—*see*
    Anomaly, chromosomes, sex

Hernia, hernial (acquired) (recurrent) 553.9
 with
  gangrene (obstructed) NEC 551.9
  obstruction NEC 552.9
   and gangrene 551.9
 abdomen (wall)—*see* Hernia, ventral
 abdominal, specified site NEC 553.8
  with
   gangrene (obstructed) 551.8
   obstruction 552.8
    and gangrene 551.8
 appendix 553.8
  with
   gangrene (obstructed) 551.8
   obstruction 552.8
    and gangrene 551.8
 bilateral (inguinal)—*see* Hernia, inguinal
 bladder (sphincter)
  congenital (female) (male) 756.71
  female 618.0
  male 596.8
 brain 348.4
  congenital 742.0
 broad ligament 553.8
 cartilage, vertebral—*see* Displacement,
   intervertebral disc
 cerebral 348.4
  congenital 742.0
  endaural 742.0
 ciliary body 364.8
  traumatic 871.1
 colic 553.9
  with
   gangrene (obstructed) 551.9
   obstruction 552.9
    and gangrene 551.9
 colon 553.9
  with
   gangrene (obstructed) 551.9
   obstruction 552.9
   and gangrene 551.9
 colostomy (stoma) 569.69
 Cooper's (retroperitoneal) 553.8
  with
   gangrene (obstructed) 551.8
   obstruction 552.8
   and gangrene 551.8
 crural—*see* Hernia, femoral
 diaphragm, diaphragmatic 553.3
  with
   gangrene (obstructed) 551.3
   obstruction 552.3
    and gangrene 551.3
  congenital 756.6
  due to gross defect of diaphragm 756.6
  traumatic 862.0
  with open wound into cavity 862.1
 direct (inguinal)—*see* Hernia, inguinal
 disc, intervertebral—*see* Displacement,
   intervertebral disc
 diverticulum, intestine 553.9
  with
   gangrene (obstructed) 551.9
   obstruction 552.9
    and gangrene 551.9
 double (inguinal)—*see* Hernia, inguinal
 duodenojejunal 553.8
  with
   gangrene (obstructed) 551.8
   obstruction 552.8
    and gangrene 551.8

Hernia, hernial—*continued*
 en glissade—*see* Hernia, inguinal
 enterostomy (stoma) 569.69
 epigastric 553.29
  with
   gangrene (obstruction) 551.29
   obstruction 552.29
    and gangrene 551.29
  recurrent 553.21
   with
    gangrene (obstructed) 551.21
    obstruction 552.21
     and gangrene 551.21
 esophageal hiatus (sliding) 553.3
  with
   gangrene (obstructed) 551.3
   obstruction 552.3
    and gangrene 551.3
  congenital 750.6
 external (inguinal)—*see* Hernia, inguinal
 fallopian tube 620.4
 fascia 728.89
 fat 729.30
  eyelid 374.34
  orbital 374.34
  pad 729.30
   eye, eyelid 374.34
   knee 729.31
   orbit 374.34
   popliteal (space) 729.31
   specified site NEC 729.39
 femoral (unilateral) 553.00
  with
   gangrene (obstructed) 551.00
   obstruction 552.00
    with gangrene 551.00
  bilateral 553.02
   gangrenous (obstructed) 551.02
   obstructed 552.02
    with gangrene 551.02
   recurrent 553.03
    gangrenous (obstructed) 551.03
    obstructed 552.03
     with gangrene 551.03
  recurrent (unilateral) 553.01
   bilateral 553.03
    gangrenous (obstructed) 551.03
    obstructed 552.03
     with gangrene 551.03
   gangrenous (obstructed) 551.01
   obstructed 552.01
    with gangrene 551.01
 foramen
  Bochdalek 553.3
   with
    gangrene (obstructed) 551.3
    obstruction 552.3
     and gangrene 551.3
   congenital 756.6
  magnum 348.4
  Morgagni, morgagnian 553.3
   with
    gangrene 551.3
    obstruction 552.3
     and gangrene 551.3
   congenital 756.6
 funicular (umbilical) 553.1
  with
   gangrene (obstructed) 551.1
   obstruction 552.1
    and gangrene 551.1

Hernia, hernial—*continued*
   spermatic cord—*see* Hernia, inguinal
   gangrenous—*see* Hernia, by site, with gangrene
   gastrointestinal tract 553.9
     with
       gangrene (obstructed) 551.9
       obstruction 552.9
         and gangrene 551.9
   gluteal—*see* Hernia, femoral
   Gruber's (internal mesogastric) 553.8
     with
       gangrene (obstructed) 551.8
       obstruction 552.8
         and gangrene 551.8
   Hesselbach's 553.8
     with
       gangrene (obstructed) 551.8
       obstruction 552.8
         and gangrene 551.8
   hiatal (esophageal) (sliding) 553.3
     with
       gangrene (obstructed) 551.3
       obstruction 552.3
         and gangrene 551.3
     congenital 750.6
   incarcerated (*see also* Hernia, by site, with
     obstruction) 552.9
   gangrenous (*see also* Hernia, by site, with
     gangrene) 551.9
   incisional 553.21
     with
       gangrene (obstructed) 551.21
       obstruction 552.21
         and gangrene 551.21
     lumbar—*see* Hernia, lumbar
     recurrent 553.21
       with
         gangrene (obstructed) 551.21
         obstruction 552.21
           and gangrene 551.21
   indirect (inguinal)—*see* Hernia, inguinal
   infantile—*see* Hernia, inguinal
   infrapatellar fat pad 729.31
   inguinal (direct) (double) (encysted) (external)
     (funicular) (indirect) (infantile) (internal)
     (interstitial) (oblique) (scrotal) (sliding)
     550.9

Note—Use the following fifth-digit
subclassification with category 550:

0　unilateral or unspecified (not specified as
*　　recurrent)*
1　unilateral or unspecified, recurrent
2　bilateral (not specified as recurrent)
3　bilateral, recurrent

---

     with
       gangrene (obstructed) 550.0
       obstruction 550.1
         and gangrene 550.0
   internal 553.8
     with
       gangrene (obstructed) 551.8
       obstruction 552.8
         and gangrene 551.8
     inguinal—*see* Hernia, inguinal
   interstitial 553.9
     with
       gangrene (obstructed) 551.9
       obstruction 552.9
         and gangrene 551.9

Hernia, hernial—*continued*
   inguinal—*see* Hernia, inguinal
   intervertebral cartilage or disc—*see*
     Displacement, intervertebral disc
   intestine, intestinal 553.9
     with
       gangrene (obstructed) 551.9
       obstruction 552.9
         and gangrene 551.9
   intra-abdominal 553.9
     with
       gangrene (obstructed) 551.9
       obstruction 552.9
         and gangrene 551.9
   intraparietal 553.9
     with
       gangrene (obstructed) 551.9
       obstruction 552.9
         and gangrene 551.9
   iris 364.8
     traumatic 871.1
   irreducible (*see also* Hernia, by site, with
     obstruction) 552.9
   gangrenous (with obstruction) (*see also*
     Hernia, by site, with gangrene) 551.9
   ischiatic 553.8
     with
       gangrene (obstructed) 551.8
       obstruction 552.8
         and gangrene 551.8
   ischiorectal 553.8
     with
       gangrene (obstructed) 551.8
       obstruction 552.8
         and gangrene 551.8
   lens 379.32
     traumatic 871.1
   linea
     alba—*see* Hernia, epigastric
     semilunaris—*see* Hernia, spigelian
   Littre's (diverticular) 553.9
     with
       gangrene (obstructed) 551.9
       obstruction 552.9
         and gangrene 551.9
   lumbar 553.8
     with
       gangrene (obstructed) 551.8
       obstruction 552.8
         and gangrene 551.8
     intervertebral disc 722.10
   lung (subcutaneous) 518.89
     congenital 748.69
   mediastinum 519.3
   mesenteric (internal) 553.8
     with
       gangrene (obstructed) 551.8
       obstruction 552.8
         and gangrene 551.8
   mesocolon 553.8
     with
       gangrene (obstructed) 551.8
       obstruction 552.8
         and gangrene 551.8
   muscle (sheath) 728.89
   nucleus pulposus—*see* Displacement,
     intervertebral disc
   oblique (inguinal)—*see* Hernia, inguinal

Heterotropia 378.30
  intermittent 378.20
    vertical 378.31
  vertical (constant) (intermittent) 378.31
Heubner's disease 094.89
Heubner-Herter disease or syndrome
  (nontropical sprue) 579.0
Hexadactylism 755.00
Heyd's syndrome (hepatorenal) 572.4
Hibernoma (M8880/0)—*see* Lipoma
Hiccough 786.8
  epidemic 078.89
  psychogenic 306.1
Hiccup (*see also* Hiccough) 786.8
Hicks (-Braxton) contractures 644.1
Hidden penis 752.65
Hidradenitis (axillaris) (suppurative) 705.83
Hidradenoma (nodular) (M8400/0)—*see also*
  Neoplasm, skin, benign
  clear cell (M8402/0)—*see* Neoplasm, skin,
    benign
  papillary (M8405/0)—*see* Neoplasm, skin,
    benign
Hidrocystoma (M8404/0)—*see* Neoplasm, skin,
  benign
High
  A₂ anemia 282.4
  altitude effects 993.2
    anoxia 993.2
    on
      ears 993.0
      sinuses 993.1
    polycythemia 289.0
  arch
    foot 755.67
    palate 750.26
  artery (arterial) tension (*see also* Hypertension)
    401.9
    without diagnosis of hypertension 796.2
  basal metabolic rate (BMR) 794.7
  blood pressure (*see also* Hypertension) 401.9
    incidental reading (isolated) (nonspecific), no
      diagnosis of hypertension 796.2
  compliance bladder 596.4
  diaphragm (congenital) 756.6
  frequency deafness (congenital) (regional) 389.8
  head at term 652.5
  output failure (cardiac) (*see also* Failure, heart)
    428.9
  oxygen-affinity hemoglobin 289.0
  palate 750.26
  risk
    behavior —*see* Problem
    family situation V61.9
      specified circumstance NEC V61.8
    individual NEC V62.89
    infant NEC V20.1
    patient taking drugs (prescribed) V67.51
      nonprescribed (*see also* Abuse, drugs,
        nondependent) 305.9
    pregnancy V23.9
      inadequate prenatal care V23.7
      specified problem NEC V23.8
  temperature (of unknown origin) (*see also*
    Pyrexia) 780.6
  thoracic rib 756.3
Hildenbrand's disease (typhus) 081.9
Hilger's syndrome 337.0
Hill diarrhea 579.1
Hilliard's lupus (*see also* Tuberculosis) 017.0
Hilum —*see* condition

Hip —*see* condition
Hippel's disease (retinocerebral angiomatosis)
  759.6
Hippus 379.49
Hirschfeld's disease (acute diabetes mellitus)
  (*see also* Diabetes) 250.0
Hirschsprung's disease or megacolon
  (congenital) 751.3
Hirsuties (*see also* Hypertrichosis) 704.1
Hirsutism (*see also* Hypertrichosis) 704.1
Hirudiniasis (external) (internal) 134.2
His-Werner disease (trench fever) 083.1
Hiss-Russell dysentery 004.1
Histamine cephalgia 346.2
Histidinemia 270.5
Histidinuria 270.5
Histiocytoma (M8832/0)—*see also* Neoplasm,
  skin, benign
  fibrous (M8830/0)—*see also* Neoplasm, skin,
    benign
    atypical (M8830/1)—*see* Neoplasm,
      connective tissue, uncertain behavior
    malignant (M8830/0)—*see* Neoplasm,
      connective tissue, malignant
Histiocytosis (acute) (chronic) (subacute) 277.8
  acute differentiated progressive (M9722/3) 202.5
  cholesterol 277.8
  essential 277.8
  lipid, lipoid (essential) 272.7
  lipochrome (familial) 288.1
  malignant (M9720/3) 202.3
  X (chronic) 277.8
    acute (progressive) (M9722/3) 202.5
Histoplasmosis 115.90
  with
    endocarditis 115.94
    meningitis 115.91
    pericarditis 115.93
    pneumonia 115.95
    retinitis 115.92
    specified manifestation NEC 115.99
  African (due to Histoplasma duboisii) 115.10
    with
      endocarditis 115.14
      meningitis 115.11
      pericarditis 115.13
      pneumonia 115.15
      retinitis 115.12
      specified manifestation NEC 115.19
  American (due to Histoplasma capsulatum)
    115.00
    with
      endocarditis 115.04
      meningitis 115.01
      pericarditis 115.03
      pneumonia 115.05
      retinitis 115.02
      specified manifestation NEC 115.09
  Darling's—*see* Histoplasmosis, American
  large form (*see also* Histoplasmosis, African)
    115.10
  lung 115.05
  small form (*see also* Histoplasmosis, American)
    115.00
History (personal) of
  abuse
    emotional V15.42
    neglect V15.42
    physical V15.41
    sexual V15.41

History—*continued*
  affective psychosis V11.1
  alcoholism V11.3
    specified as drinking problem (*see also*
      Abuse, drugs, nondependent) 305.0
  allergy to
    analgesic agent NEC V14.6
    anesthetic NEC V14.4
    antibiotic agent NEC V14.1
      penicillin V14.0
    anti-infective agent NEC V14.3
    diathesis V15.09
    drug V14.9
      specified type NEC V14.8
    eggs V15.03
    food additives V15.05
    insect bite V15.06
    latex V15.07
    medicinal agents V14.9
      specified type NEC V14.8
    milk products V15.02
    narcotic agent NEC V14.5
    nuts V15.05
      peanuts V15.01
    penicillin V14.0
    radiographic dye V15.08
    seafood V15.04
    serum V14.7
    specified food NEC V15.05
    specified nonmedicinal agents NEC V15.09
    spider bite V15.06
    sulfa V14.2
    sulfonamides V14.2
    therapeutic agent NEC V15.09
    vaccine V14.7
  anemia V12.3
  arthritis V13.4
  benign neoplasm of brain V12.41
  blood disease V12.3
  calculi, urinary V13.01
  cardiovascular disease V12.50
    myocardial infarction 412
  child abuse V15.41
  cigarette smoking V15.82
  circulatory system disease V12.50
    myocardial infarction 412
  congenital malformation V13.69
  contraception V15.7
  diathesis, allergic V15.09
  digestive system disease V12.70
    peptic ulcer V12.71
    polyps, colonic V12.72
    specified NEC V12.79
  disease (of) V13.9
    blood V12.3
    blood-forming organs V12.3
    cardiovascular system V12.50
    circulatory system V12.50
    digestive system V12.70
      peptic ulcer V12.71
      polyps, colonic V12.72
      specified NEC V12.79
    infectious V12.00
      malaria V12.03
      poliomyelitis V12.02
      specified NEC V12.09
      tuberculosis V12.01
    parasitic V12.00
      specified NEC V12.09
    respiratory system V12.6
    skin V13.3

History—*continued*
    specified site NEC V13.8
    subcutaneous tissue V13.3
    trophoblastic V13.1
      affecting management of pregnancy V23.1
  disorder (of) V13.9
    endocrine V12.2
    genital system V13.2
    hematological V12.3
    immunity V12.2
    mental V11.9
      affective type V11.1
      manic-depressive V11.1
      neurosis V11.2
      schizophrenia V11.0
      specified type NEC V11.8
    metabolic V12.2
    musculoskeletal NEC V13.5
    nervous system V12.40
      specified type NEC V12.49
    obstetric V13.2
      affecting management of current pregnancy
        V23.4
    sense organs V12.40
      specified type NEC V12.49
    specified site NEC V13.8
    urinary system V13.00
      calculi V13.01
      specified NEC V13.09
  drug use
    nonprescribed (*see also* Abuse, drugs,
      nondependent) 305.9
    patent (*see also* Abuse, drugs, nondependent)
      305.9
  effect NEC of external cause V15.89
  embolism (pulmonary) V12.51
  emotional abuse V15.42
  endocrine disorder V12.2
  family
    allergy V19.6
    anemia V18.2
    arteriosclerosis V17.4
    arthritis V17.7
    asthma V17.5
    blindness V19.0
    blood disorder NEC V18.3
    cardiovascular disease V17.4
    cerebrovascular disease V17.1
    chronic respiratory condition NEC V17.6
    congenital anomalies V19.5
    consanguinity V19.7
    coronary artery disease V17.3
    cystic fibrosis V18.1
    deafness V19.2
    diabetes mellitus V18.0
    digestive disorders V18.5
    disease or disorder (of)
      allergic V19.6
      blood NEC V18.3
      cardiovascular NEC V17.4
      cerebrovascular V17.1
      coronary artery V17.3
      digestive V18.5
      ear NEC V19.3
      endocrine V18.1
      eye NEC V19.1
      genitourinary NEC V18.7
      hypertensive V17.4
      infectious V18.8
      ischemic heart V17.3
      kidney V18.69

History—*continued*
    polycystic V18.61
    mental V17.0
    metabolic V18.1
    musculoskeletal NEC V17.8
    neurological NEC V17.2
    parasitic V18.8
    psychiatric condition V17.0
    skin condition V19.4
  ear disorder NEC V19.3
  endocrine disease V18.1
  epilepsy V17.2
  eye disorder NEC V19.1
  genitourinary disease NEC V18.7
  glomerulonephritis V18.69
  gout V18.1
  hay fever V17.6
  hearing loss V19.2
  hematopoietic neoplasia V16.7
  Hodgkin's disease V16.7
  Huntington's chorea V17.2
  hydrocephalus V19.5
  hypertension V17.4
  hypospadias V13.61
  infectious disease V18.8
  ischemic heart disease V17.3
  kidney disease V18.69
    polycystic V18.61
  leukemia V16.6
  lymphatic malignant neoplasia NEC V16.7
  malignant neoplasm (of) NEC V16.9
    anorectal V16.0
    anus V16.0
    appendix V16.0
    bladder V16.59
    bone V16.8
    brain V16.8
    breast V16.3
      male V16.8
    bronchus V16.1
    cecum V16.0
    cervix V16.49
    colon V16.0
    duodenum V16.0
    esophagus V16.0
    eye V16.8
    gallbladder V16.0
    gastrointestinal tract V16.0
    genital organs V16.40
    hemopoietic NEC V16.7
    ileum V16.0
    ilium V16.8
    intestine V16.0
    intrathoracic organs NEC V16.2
    kidney V16.51
    larynx V16.2
    liver V16.0
    lung V16.1
    lymphatic NEC V16.7
    ovary V16.41
    oviduct V16.41
    pancreas V16.0
    penis V16.49
    prostate V16.42
    rectum V16.0
    respiratory organs NEC V16.2
    skin V16.8
    specified site NEC V16.8
    stomach V16.0
    testis V16.43
    trachea V16.1

History—*continued*
    ureter V16.59
    urethra V16.59
    urinary organs V16.59
    uterus V16.49
    vagina V16.49
    vulva V16.49
  mental retardation V18.4
  metabolic disease NEC V18.1
  mongolism V19.5
  multiple myeloma V16.7
  musculoskeletal disease NEC V17.8
  nephritis V18.69
  nephrosis V18.69
  parasitic disease V18.8
  polycystic kidney disease V18.61
  psychiatric disorder V17.0
  psychosis V17.0
  retardation, mental V18.4
  retinitis pigmentosa V19.1
  schizophrenia V17.0
  skin conditions V19.4
  specified condition NEC V19.8
  stroke (cerebrovascular) V17.1
  visual loss V19.0
 genital system disorder V13.2
 health hazard V15.9
  specified cause NEC V15.89
 Hodgkin's disease V10.72
 immunity disorder V12.2
 infectious disease V12.00
  malaria V12.03
  poliomyelitis V12.02
  specified NEC V12.09
  tuberculosis V12.01
 injury NEC V15.5
 insufficient prenatal care V23.7
 irradiation V15.3
 leukemia V10.60
  lymphoid V10.61
  monocytic V10.63
  myeloid V10.62
  specified type NEC V10.69
 little or no prenatal care V23.7
 low birth weight (*see also* Status, low birth
    weight) V21.30
 lymphosarcoma V10.71
 malaria V12.03
 malignant neoplasm (of) V10.9
  accessory sinus V10.22
  adrenal V10.88
  anus V10.06
  bile duct V10.09
  bladder V10.51
  bone V10.81
  brain V10.85
  breast V10.3
  bronchus V10.11
  cervix uteri V10.41
  colon V10.05
  connective tissue NEC V10.89
  corpus uteri V10.42
  digestive system V10.00
    specified part NEC V10.09
  duodenum V10.09
  endocrine gland NEC V10.88
  epididymis V10.48
  esophagus V10.03
  eye V10.84
  fallopian tube V10.44
  female genital organ V10.40

Hunt's
neuralgia 053.11
syndrome (herpetic geniculate ganglionitis)
053.11
dyssynergia cerebellaris myoclonica 334.2
Hunter's glossitis 529.4
Hunter (-Hurler) syndrome
(mucopolysaccharidosis II) 277.5
Hunterian chancre 091.0
Huntington's
chorea 333.4
disease 333.4
Huppert's disease (multiple myeloma)
(M9730/3) 203.0
Hurler (-Hunter) disease or syndrome
(mucopolysaccharidosis II) 277.5
Hürthle cell
adenocarcinoma (M8290/3) 193
adenoma (M8290/0) 226
carcinoma (M8290/3) 193
tumor (M8290/0) 226
Hutchinson's
disease meaning
angioma serpiginosum 709.1
cheiropompholyx 705.81
prurigo estivalis 692.72
summer eruption, or summer prurigo 692.72
incisors 090.5
melanotic freckle (M8742/2)—*see also*
Neoplasm, skin, in situ
malignant melanoma in (M8742/3)—*see*
Melanoma
teeth or incisors (congenital syphilis) 090.5
Hutchinson-Boeck disease or syndrome
(sarcoidosis) 135
Hutchinson-Gilford disease or syndrome
(progeria) 259.8
Hyaline
degeneration (diffuse) (generalized) 728.9
localized—*see* Degeneration, by site
membrane (disease) (lung) (newborn) 769
Hyalinosis cutis et mucosae 272.8
Hyalin plaque, sclera, senile 379.16
Hyalitis (asteroid) 379.22
syphilitic 095.8
Hydatid
cyst or tumor—*see also* Echinococcus
fallopian tube 752.11
Hydatid—*continued*
mole—*see* Hydatidiform mole
Morgagni (congenital) 752.8
fallopian tube 752.11
Hydatidiform mole (benign) (complicating
pregnancy) (delivered) (undelivered) 630
invasive (M9100/1) 236.1
malignant (M9100/1) 236.1
previous, affecting management of pregnancy
V23.1
Hydatidosis —*see* Echinococcus
Hyde's disease (prurigo nodularis) 698.3
Hydradenitis 705.83
Hydradenoma (M8400/0)—*see* Hidradenoma
Hydralazine lupus or syndrome
correct substance properly administered 695.4
overdose or wrong substance given or taken
972.6
Hydramnios 657
affecting fetus or newborn 761.3
Hydrancephaly 742.3
with spina bifida (*see also* Spina bifida) 741.0
Hydranencephaly 742.3
with spina bifida (*see also* Spina bifida) 741.0

Hydrargyrism NEC 985.0
Hydrarthrosis (*see also* Effusion, joint) 719.0
gonococcal 098.50
intermittent (*see also* Rheumatism, palindromic)
719.3
of yaws (early) (late) 102.6
syphilitic 095.8
congenital 090.5
Hydremia 285.9
Hydrencephalocele (congenital) 742.0
Hydrencephalomeningocele (congenital) 742.0
Hydroa 694.0
aestivale 692.72
gestationis 646.8
herpetiformis 694.0
pruriginosa 694.0
vacciniforme 692.72
Hydroadenitis 705.83
Hydrocalycosis (*see also* Hydronephrosis) 591
congenital 753.29
Hydrocalyx (*see also* Hydronephrosis) 591
Hydrocele (calcified) (chylous) (idiopathic)
(infantile) (inguinal canal) (recurrent) (senile)
(spermatic cord) (testis) (tunica vaginalis)
603.9
canal of Nuck (female) 629.1
male 603.9
congenital 778.6
encysted 603.0
congenital 778.6
female NEC 629.8
infected 603.1
round ligament 629.8
specified type NEC 603.8
congenital 778.6
spinalis (*see also* Spina bifida) 741.9
vulva 624.8
Hydrocephalic fetus
affecting management of pregnancy 655.0
causing disproportion 653.6
with obstructed labor 660.1
affecting fetus or newborn 763.1
Hydrocephalus (acquired) (external) (internal)
(malignant) (noncommunicating) (obstructive)
(recurrent) 331.4
aqueduct of Sylvius stricture 742.3
with spina bifida (*see also* Spina bifida) 741.0
chronic 742.3
with spina bifida (*see also* Spina bifida) 741.0
communicating 331.3
congenital (external) (internal) 742.3
with spina bifida (*see also* Spina bifida) 741.0
due to
stricture of aqueduct of Sylvius 742.3
with spina bifida (*see also* Spina bifida)
741.0
toxoplasmosis (congenital) 771.2
fetal affecting management of pregnancy 655.0
foramen Magendie block (acquired) 331.3
congenital 742.3
with spina bifida (*see also* Spina bifida)
741.0
newborn 742.3
with spina bifida (*see also* Spina bifida) 741.0
otitic 331.4
syphilitic, congenital 090.49
tuberculous (*see also* Tuberculosis) 013.8
Hydrocolpos (congenital) 623.8
Hydrocystoma (M8404/0)—*see* Neoplasm, skin,
benign
Hydroencephalocele (congenital) 742.0
Hydroencephalomeningocele (congenital) 742.0

Hypergammaglobulinemia 289.8
  monoclonal, benign (BMH) 273.1
  polyclonal 273.0
  Waldenström's 273.0
Hyperglobulinemia 273.8
Hyperglycemia 790.6
  maternal
    affecting fetus or newborn 775.0
    manifest diabetes in infant 775.1
  postpancreatectomy (complete) (partial) 251.3
Hyperglyceridemia 272.1
  endogenous 272.1
  essential 272.1
  familial 272.1
  hereditary 272.1
  mixed 272.3
  pure 272.1
Hyperglycinemia 270.7
Hypergonadism
  ovarian 256.1
  testicular (infantile) (primary) 257.0
Hyperheparinemia (*see also* Circulating
  anticoagulants) 286.5
Hyperhidrosis, hyperidrosis 780.8
  psychogenic 306.3
Hyperhistidinemia 270.5
Hyperinsulinism (ectopic) (functional) (organic)
  NEC 251.1
  iatrogenic 251.0
  reactive 251.2
  spontaneous 251.2
  therapeutic misadventure (from administration
    of insulin) 962.3
Hyperiodemia 276.9
Hyperirritability (cerebral), in newborn 779.1
Hyperkalemia 276.7
Hyperkeratosis (*see also* Keratosis) 701.1
  cervix 622.1
  congenital 757.39
  cornea 371.89
  due to yaws (early) (late) (palmar or plantar)
    102.3
  eccentrica 757.39
  figurata centrifuga atrophica 757.39
  follicularis 757.39
    in cutem penetrans 701.1
  limbic (cornea) 371.89
  palmoplantaris climacterica 701.1
  pinta (carate) 103.1
  senile (with pruritus) 702.0
  tongue 528.7
  universalis congenita 757.1
  vagina 623.1
  vocal cord 478.5
  vulva 624.0
Hyperkinesia, hyperkinetic (disease) (reaction)
  (syndrome) 314.9
  with
    attention deficit —*see* Disorder, attention
      deficit
    conduct disorder 314.2
    developmental delay 314.1
    simple disturbance of activity and attention
      314.01
    specified manifestation NEC 314.8
  heart (disease) 429.82
  of childhood or adolescence NEC 314.9
Hyperlacrimation (*see also* Epiphora) 375.20
Hyperlipemia (*see also* Hyperlipidemia) 272.4

Hyperlipidemia 272.4
  carbohydrate-induced 272.1
  combined 272.4
  endogenous 272.1
  exogenous 272.3
  fat-induced 272.3
  group
    A 272.0
    B 272.1
    C 272.2
    D 272.3
  mixed 272.2
  specified type NEC 272.4
Hyperlipidosis 272.7
  hereditary 272.7
Hyperlipoproteinemia (acquired) (essential)
  (familial) (hereditary) (primary) (secondary)
  272.4
  Fredrickson type
    I 272.3
    IIa 272.0
    IIb 272.2
    III 272.2
    IV 272.1
    V 272.3
  low-density-lipoid-type (LDL) 272.0
  very-low-density-lipoid-type [VLDL] 272.1
Hyperlucent lung, unilateral 492.8
Hyperluteinization 256.1
Hyperlysinemia 270.7
Hypermagnesemia 275.2
  neonatal 775.5
Hypermaturity (fetus or newborn) 766.2
Hypermenorrhea 626.2
Hypermetabolism 794.7
Hypermethioninemia 270.4
Hypermetropia (congenital) 367.0
Hypermobility
  cecum 564.9
  coccyx 724.71
  colon 564.9
    psychogenic 306.4
  ileum 564.89
  joint (acquired) 718.80
    ankle 718.87
    elbow 718.82
    foot 718.87
    hand 718.84
    hip 718.85
    knee 718.86
    multiple sites 718.89
    pelvic region 718.85
    shoulder (region) 718.81
    specified site NEC 718.88
    wrist 718.83
  kidney, congenital 753.3
  meniscus (knee) 717.5
  scapula 718.81
  stomach 536.8
    psychogenic 306.4
  syndrome 728.5
  testis, congenital 752.52
  urethral 599.81
Hypermotility
  gastrointestinal 536.8
  intestine 564.9
    psychogenic 306.4
  stomach 536.8
Hypernasality 784.49
Hypernatremia 276.0
  with water depletion 276.0
Hypernephroma (M8312/3) 189.0

Hyperopia 367.0
Hyperorexia 783.6
Hyperornithinemia 270.6
Hyperosmia (*see also* Disturbance, sensation)
      781.1
Hyperosmolality 276.0
Hyperosteogenesis 733.99
Hyperostosis 733.99
   calvarial 733.3
   cortical 733.3
      infantile 756.59
   frontal, internal of skull 733.3
   interna frontalis 733.3
   monomelic 733.99
   skull 733.3
      congenital 756.0
   vertebral 721.8
      with spondylosis—*see* Spondylosis
      ankylosing 721.6
Hyperovarianism 256.1
Hyperovarism, hyperovaria 256.1
Hyperoxaluria (primary) 271.8
Hyperoxia 987.8
Hyperparathyroidism 252.0
   ectopic 259.3
   secondary, of renal origin 588.8
Hyperpathia (*see also* Disturbance, sensation)
      782.0
   psychogenic 307.80
Hyperperistalsis 787.4
   psychogenic 306.4
Hyperpermeability, capillary 448.9
Hyperphagia 783.6
Hyperphenylalaninemia 270.1
Hyperphoria 378.40
   alternating 378.45
Hyperphosphatemia 275.3
Hyperpiesia (*see also* Hypertension) 401.9
Hyperpiesis (*see also* Hypertension) 401.9
Hyperpigmentation —*see* Pigmentation
Hyperpinealism 259.8
Hyperpipecolatemia 270.7
Hyperpituitarism 253.1
Hyperplasia, hyperplastic
   adenoids (lymphoid tissue) 474.12
      and tonsils 474.10
   adrenal (capsule) (cortex) (gland) 255.8
      with
         sexual precocity (male) 255.2
         virilism, adrenal 255.2
         virilization (female) 255.2
      congenital 255.2
      due to excess ACTH (ectopic) (pituitary) 255.0
      medulla 255.8
   alpha cells (pancreatic)
      with
         gastrin excess 251.5
         glucagon excess 251.4
   appendix (lymphoid) 543.0
   artery, fibromuscular NEC 447.8
      carotid 447.8
      renal 447.3
   bone 733.99
      marrow 289.9
   breast (*see also* Hypertrophy, breast) 611.1
   carotid artery 447.8
   cementation, cementum (teeth) (tooth) 521.5
   cervical gland 785.6
   cervix (uteri) 622.1
      basal cell 622.1
      congenital 752.49

Hyperplasia, hyperplastic—*continued*
   endometrium 622.1
      polypoid 622.1
   chin 524.05
   clitoris, congenital 752.49
   dentin 521.5
   endocervicitis 616.0
   endometrium, endometrial (adenomatous)
         (atypical) (cystic) (glandular) (polypoid)
         (uterus) 621.3
      cervix 622.1
   epithelial 709.8
      focal, oral, including tongue 528.7
      mouth (focal) 528.7
      nipple 611.8
      skin 709.8
      tongue (focal) 528.7
      vaginal wall 623.0
   erythroid 289.9
   fascialis ossificans (progressiva) 728.11
   fibromuscular, artery NEC 447.8
      carotid 447.8
      renal 447.3
   genital
      female 629.8
      male 608.89
   gingiva 523.8
   glandularis
      cystica uteri 621.3
      endometrium (uterus) 621.3
      interstitialis uteri 621.3
   granulocytic 288.8
   gum 523.8
   hymen, congenital 752.49
   islands of Langerhans 251.1
   islet cell (pancreatic) 251.9
      alpha cells
         with excess
            gastrin 251.5
            glucagon 251.4
      beta cells 251.1
   juxtaglomerular (complex) (kidney) 593.89
   kidney (congenital) 753.3
   liver (congenital) 751.69
   lymph node (gland) 785.6
   lymphoid (diffuse) (nodular) 785.6
      appendix 543.0
      intestine 569.89
   mandibular 524.02
      alveolar 524.72
      unilateral condylar 526.89
   Marchand multiple nodular (liver)—*see*
         Cirrhosis, postnecrotic
   maxillary 524.01
      alveolar 524.71
   medulla, adrenal 255.8
   myometrium, myometrial 621.2
   nose (lymphoid) (polypoid) 478.1
   oral soft tissue (inflammatory) (irritative)
         (mucosa) NEC 528.9
      gingiva 523.8
      tongue 529.8
   organ or site, congenital NEC—*see* Anomaly,
         specified type NEC
   ovary 620.8
   palate, papillary 528.9
   pancreatic islet cells 251.9
      alpha
         with excess
            gastrin 251.5
            glucagon 251.4

*—"H" listing resumes after
Hypertension table...*

Hypertension, hypertensive

	Malignant	Benign	Unspecified
(arterial) (arteriolar) (crisis) (degeneration) (disease) (essential) (fluctuating) (idiopathic) (intermittent) (labile) (low renin) (orthostatic) (paroxysmal) (primary) (systemic) (uncontrolled) (vascular)	401.0	401.1	401.9
with			
heart involvement (conditions classifiable to 425.8, 428, 429.0-429.3, 429.8, 429.9 due to hypertension) (*see also* Hypertension, heart)	402.00	402.10	402.90
with kidney involvement—*see* Hypertension, cardiorenal			
renal involvement (only conditions classifiable to 585, 586, 587) (excludes conditions classifiable to 584) (*see also* Hypertension, kidney)	403.00	403.10	403.90
with heart involvement—*see* Hypertension, cardiorenal			
failure (and sclerosis) (*see also* Hypertension, kidney)	403.01	403.11	403.91
sclerosis without failure (*see also* Hypertension, kidney)	403.00	403.10	403.90
accelerated (*see also* Hypertension, by type, malignant)	401.0	—	—
antepartum—*see* Hypertension complicating pregnancy, childbirth, or the puerperium			
cardiorenal (disease)	404.00	404.10	404.90
with			
heart failure (congestive)	404.01	404.11	404.91
and renal failure	404.03	404.13	404.93
renal failure	404.02	404.12	404.92
and heart failure (congestive)	404.03	404.13	404.93
cardiovascular disease (arteriosclerotic) (sclerotic)	402.00	402.10	402.90
with			
heart failure (congestive)	402.01	402.11	402.91
renal involvement (conditions classifiable to 403) (*see also* Hypertension, cardiorenal)	404.00	404.10	404.90
cardiovascular renal (disease) (sclerosis) (*see also* Hypertension cardiorenal)	404.00	404.10	404.90
cerebrovascular disease NEC	437.2	437.2	437.2
complicating pregnancy, childbirth, or the puerperium	642.2	642.0	642.9
with			
albuminuria (and edema) (mild)	—	—	642.4
severe	—	—	642.5
edema (mild)	—	—	642.4
severe	—	—	642.5
heart disease	642.2	642.2	642.2
and renal disease	642.2	642.2	642.2
renal disease	642.2	642.2	642.2
and heart disease	642.2	642.2	642.2
chronic	642.2	642.0	642.0
with pre-eclampsia or eclampsia	642.7	642.7	642.7
fetus or newborn	760.0	760.0	760.0
essential	—	642.0	642.0
with pre-eclampsia or eclampsia	—	642.7	642.7
fetus or newborn	760.0	760.0	760.0
fetus or newborn	760.0	760.0	760.0
gestational	—	—	642.3
pre-existing	642.2	642.0	642.0
with pre-eclampsia or eclampsia	642.7	642.7	642.7
fetus or newborn	760.0	760.0	760.0
secondary to renal disease	642.1	642.1	642.1
with pre-eclampsia or eclampsia	642.7	642.7	642.7
fetus or newborn	760.0	760.0	760.0
transient	—	—	642.3
due to			
aldosteronism, primary	405.09	405.19	405.99
brain tumor	405.09	405.19	405.99
bulbar poliomyelitis	405.09	405.19	405.99
calculus			
kidney	405.09	405.19	405.99
ureter	405.09	405.19	405.99
coarctation, aorta	405.09	405.19	405.99
Cushing's disease	405.09	405.19	405.99
glomerulosclerosis (*see also* Hypertension, kidney)	403.00	403.10	403.90
periarteritis nodosa	405.09	405.19	405.99
pheochromocytoma	405.09	405.19	405.99
polycystic kidney(s)	405.09	405.19	405.99
polycythemia	405.09	405.19	405.99
porphyria	405.09	405.19	405.99
pyelonephritis	405.09	405.19	405.99

	Malignant	Benign	Unspecified
renal (artery)			
aneurysm	405.01	405.11	405.91
anomaly	405.01	405.11	405.91
embolism	405.01	405.11	405.91
fibromuscular hyperplasia	405.01	405.11	405.91
occlusion	405.01	405.11	405.91
stenosis	405.01	405.11	405.91
thrombosis	405.01	405.11	405.91
encephalopathy	437.2	437.2	437.2
gestational (transient) NEC	—	—	642.3
Goldblatt's	440.1	440.1	440.1
heart (disease) (conditions classifiable to 425.8, 428,			
429.0-429.3, 429.8, 429.9 due to hypertension)	402.00	402.10	402.90
with			
heart failure	402.01	402.11	402.91
congestive	402.01	402.11	402.91
hypertensive kidney disease (conditions classifiable to 403)			
(*see also* Hypertension, cardiorenal)	404.00	404.10	404.90
renal sclerosis (*see also* Hypertension, cardiorenal)	404.00	404.10	404.90
intracranial, benign	—	348.2	—
intraocular	—	—	365.04
kidney	403.00	403.10	403.90
with			
heart involvement (conditions classifiable to 425.8, 428,			
429.0-429.3, 429.8, 429.9 due to hypertension) (*see*			
also Hypertension cardiorenal)	404.00	404.10	404.90
hypertensive heart (disease) (conditions classifiable to 402)			
(*see also* Hypertension, cardiorenal)	404.00	404.10	404.90
lesser circulation	—	—	416.0
necrotizing	401.0	—	—
ocular	—	—	365.04
portal (due to chronic liver disease)	—	—	572.3
postoperative 997.91			
psychogenic	—	—	306.2
puerperal, postpartum—*see* Hypertension, complicating			
pregnancy, childbirth, or the puerperium			
pulmonary (artery)	—	—	416.8
idiopathic	—	—	416.0
primary	—	—	416.0
with cor pulmonale (chronic)	—	—	416.8
acute	—	—	415.0
secondary	—	—	416.8
renal (disease) (*see also* Hypertension, kidney)	403.00	403.10	403.90
renovascular NEC	405.01	405.11	405.91
secondary NEC	405.09	405.19	405.99
due to			
aldosteronism, primary	405.09	405.19	405.99
brain tumor	405.09	405.19	405.99
bulbar poliomyelitis	405.09	405.19	405.99
calculus			
kidney	405.09	405.19	405.99
ureter	405.09	405.19	405.99
coarctation, aorta	405.09	405.19	405.99
Cushing's disease	405.09	405.19	405.99
glomerulosclerosis (*see also* Hypertension, kidney)	403.00	403.10	403.90
periarteritis nodosa	405.09	405.19	405.99
pheochromocytoma	405.09	405.19	405.99
polycystic kidney(s)	405.09	405.19	405.99
polycythemia	405.09	405.19	405.99
porphyria	405.09	405.19	405.99
pyelonephritis	405.09	405.19	405.99
renal (artery)			
aneurysm	405.01	405.11	405.91
anomaly	405.01	405.11	405.91
embolism	405.01	405.11	405.91
fibromuscular hyperplasia	405.01	405.11	405.91
occlusion	405.01	405.11	405.91
stenosis	405.01	405.11	405.91
thrombosis	405.01	405.11	405.91
transient	—	—	796.2
of pregnancy	—	—	642.3

Hyperthecosis, ovary 256.8
Hyperthermia (of unknown origin) (*see also*
Pyrexia) 780.6
malignant (due to anesthesia) 995.86
newborn 778.4
Hyperthymergasia (*see also* Psychosis,
affective) 296.0
reactive (from emotional stress, psychological
trauma) 298.1
recurrent episode 296.1
single episode 296.0
Hyperthymism 254.8
Hyperthyroid (recurrent)—*see* Hyperthyroidism
Hyperthyroidism (latent) (preadult) (recurrent)
(without goiter) 242.9

Note—Use the following fifth-digit
subclassification with category 242:

0 *without mention of thyrotoxic crisis or storm*
1 *with mention of thyrotoxic crisis or storm*

---

with
goiter (diffuse) 242.0
adenomatous 242.3
multinodular 242.2
uninodular 242.1
nodular 242.3
multinodular 242.2
uninodular 242.1
thyroid nodule 242.1
complicating pregnancy, childbirth, or
puerperium 648.1
neonatal (transient) 775.3
Hypertonia —Hypertonicity
Hypertonicity
bladder 596.51
fetus or newborn 779.8
gastrointestinal (tract) 536.8
infancy 779.8
due to electrolyte imbalance 779.8
muscle 728.85
stomach 536.8
psychogenic 306.4
uterus, uterine (contractions) 661.4
affecting fetus or newborn 763.7
Hypertony —*see* Hypertonicity
Hypertransaminemia 790.4
Hypertrichosis 704.1
congenital 757.4
eyelid 374.54
lanuginosa 757.4
acquired 704.1
Hypertriglyceridemia, essential 272.1
Hypertrophy, hypertrophic
adenoids (infectional) 474.12
and tonsils (faucial) (infective) (lingual)
(lymphoid) 474.10
adrenal 255.8
alveolar process or ridge 525.8
anal papillae 569.49
apocrine gland 705.82
artery NEC 447.8
carotid 447.8
congenital (peripheral) NEC 747.60
gastrointestinal 747.61
lower limb 747.64
renal 747.62
specified NEC 747.69
spinal 747.82
upper limb 747.63

Hypertrophy, hypertrophic—*continued*
arthritis (chronic) (*see also* Osteoarthrosis) 715.9
spine (*see also* Spondylosis) 721.90
arytenoid 478.79
asymmetrical (heart) 429.9
auricular—*see* Hypertrophy, cardiac
Bartholin's gland 624.8
bile duct 576.8
bladder (sphincter) (trigone) 596.8
blind spot, visual field 368.42
bone 733.99
brain 348.8
breast 611.1
cystic 610.1
fetus or newborn 778.7
fibrocystic 610.1
massive pubertal 611.1
puerperal, postpartum 676.3
senile (parenchymatous) 611.1
cardiac (chronic) (idiopathic) 429.3
with
rheumatic fever (conditions classifiable to
390)
active 391.8
with chorea 392.0
inactive or quiescent (with chorea) 398.99
congenital NEC 746.89
fatty (*see also* Degeneration, myocardial)
429.1
hypertensive (*see also* Hypertension, heart)
402.90
rheumatic (with chorea) 398.99
active or acute 391.8
with chorea 392.0
valve (*see also* Endocarditis) 424.90
congenital NEC 746.89
cartilage 733.99
cecum 569.89
cervix (uteri) 622.6
congenital 752.49
elongation 622.6
clitoris (cirrhotic) 624.2
congenital 752.49
colon 569.89
congenital 751.3
conjunctiva, lymphoid 372.73
cornea 371.89
corpora cavernosa 607.89
duodenum 537.89
endometrium (uterus) 621.3
cervix 622.6
epididymis 608.89
esophageal hiatus (congenital) 756.6
with hernia—*see* Hernia, diaphragm
eyelid 374.30
falx, skull 733.99
fat pad 729.30
infrapatellar 729.31
knee 729.31
orbital 374.34
popliteal 729.31
prepatellar 729.31
retropatellar 729.31
specified site NEC 729.39
foot (congenital) 755.67
frenum, frenulum (tongue) 529.8
linguae 529.8
lip 528.5
gallbladder or cystic duct 575.8
gastric mucosa 535.2
gingiva 523.8

Hypofunction—*continued*
  postablative 257.1
  postirradiation 257.1
  postsurgical 257.1
Hypogammaglobulinemia 279.00
 acquired primary 279.06
 non-sex-linked, congenital 279.06
 sporadic 279.06
 transient of infancy 279.09
Hypogenitalism (congenital) (female) (male)
  752.8
 penis 752.69
Hypoglycemia (spontaneous) 251.2
 coma 251.0
  diabetic 250.3
 diabetic 250.8
 due to insulin 251.0
  therapeutic misadventure 962.3
 familial (idiopathic) 251.2
 following gastrointestinal surgery 579.3
 infantile (idiopathic) 251.2
 in infant of diabetic mother 775.0
 leucine-induced 270.3
 neonatal 775.6
 reactive 251.2
 specified NEC 251.1
Hypoglycemic shock 251.0
 diabetic 250.8
 due to insulin 251.0
 functional (syndrome) 251.1
Hypogonadism
 female 256.3
 gonadotrophic (isolated) 253.4
 hypogonadotropic (isolated) (with anosmia)
  253.4
 isolated 253.4
 male 257.2
 ovarian (primary) 256.3
 pituitary (secondary) 253.4
 testicular (primary) (secondary) 257.2
Hypohidrosis 705.0
Hypohidrotic ectodermal dysplasia 757.31
Hypoidrosis 705.0
Hypoinsulinemia, postsurgical 251.3
 postpancreatectomy (complete) (partial) 251.3
Hypokalemia 276.8
Hypokinesia 780.9
Hypoleukia splenica 289.4
Hypoleukocytosis 288.8
Hypolipidemia 272.5
Hypolipoproteinemia 272.5
Hypomagnesemia 275.2
 neonatal 775.4
Hypomania, hypomanic reaction (*see also*
  Psychosis, affective) 296.0
 recurrent episode 296.1
 single episode 296.0
Hypomastia (congenital) 757.6
Hypomenorrhea 626.1
Hypometabolism 783.9
Hypomotility
 gastrointestinal tract 536.8
  psychogenic 306.4
 intestine 564.89
  psychogenic 306.4
 stomach 536.8
  psychogenic 306.4
Hyponasality 784.49
Hyponatremia 276.1
Hypo-ovarianism 256.3
Hypo-ovarism 256.3

Hypoparathyroidism (idiopathic) (surgically
  induced) 252.1
 neonatal 775.4
Hypopharyngitis 462
Hypophoria 378.40
Hypophosphatasia 275.3
Hypophosphatemia (acquired) (congenital)
  (familial) 275.3
 renal 275.3
Hypophyseal, hypophysis —*see also* condition
 dwarfism 253.3
 gigantism 253.0
 syndrome 253.8
Hypophyseothalamic syndrome 253.8
Hypopiesis —*see* Hypotension
Hypopigmentation 709.00
 eyelid 374.53
Hypopinealism 259.8
Hypopituitarism (juvenile) (syndrome) 253.2
 due to
  hormone therapy 253.7
  hypophysectomy 253.7
  radiotherapy 253.7
 postablative 253.7
 postpartum hemorrhage 253.2
Hypoplasia, hypoplasis 759.89
 adrenal (gland) 759.1
 alimentary tract 751.8
  lower 751.2
  upper 750.8
 anus, anal (canal) 751.2
 aorta 747.22
 aortic
  arch (tubular) 747.10
  orifice or valve with hypoplasia of ascending
   aorta and defective development of left
   ventricle (with mitral valve atresia) 746.7
 appendix 751.2
 areola 757.6
 arm (*see also* Absence, arm, congenital) 755.20
 artery (congenital) (peripheral) NEC 747.60
  brain 747.81
  cerebral 747.81
  coronary 746.85
  gastrointestinal 747.61
  lower limb 747.64
  pulmonary 747.3
  renal 747.62
  retinal 743.58
  specified NEC 747.69
  spinal 747.82
  umbilical 747.5
  upper limb 747.63
 auditory canal 744.29
  causing impairment of hearing 744.02
 biliary duct (common) or passage 751.61
 bladder 753.8
 bone NEC 756.9
  face 756.0
  malar 756.0
  mandible 524.04
   alveolar 524.74
  marrow 284.9
   acquired (secondary) 284.8
   congenital 284.0
   idiopathic 284.9
  maxilla 524.03
   alveolar 524.73
  skull (*see also* Hypoplasia, skull) 756.0
 brain 742.1
  gyri 742.2

Hypoplasia, hypoplasis—*continued*
  radioulnar (*see also* Absence, radius,
      congenital, with ulna) 755.25
  radius (*see also* Absence, radius, congenital)
      755.26
  rectum 751.2
  respiratory system NEC 748.9
  rib 756.3
  sacrum 756.19
  scapula 755.59
  shoulder girdle 755.59
  skin 757.39
  skull (bone) 756.0
    with
        anencephalus 740.0
        encephalocele 742.0
        hydrocephalus 742.3
            with spina bifida (*see also* Spina bifida)
                741.0
        microcephalus 742.1
  spinal (cord) (ventral horn cell) 742.59
    vessel 747.82
  spine 756.19
  spleen 759.0
  sternum 756.3
  tarsus (*see also* Absence, tarsal, congenital)
      755.38
  testis, testicle 752.8
  thymus (gland) 279.11
  thyroid (gland) 243
    cartilage 748.3
  tibiofibular (*see also* Absence, tibia, congenital,
      with fibula) 755.35
  toe (*see also* Absence, toe, congenital) 755.39
  tongue 750.16
  trachea (cartilage) (rings) 748.3
  Turner's (tooth) 520.4
  ulna (*see also* Absence, ulna, congenital) 755.27
  umbilical artery 747.5
  ureter 753.29
  uterus 752.3
  vagina 752.49
  vascular (peripheral) NEC (*see also* Hypoplasia,
      peripheral vascular system) 747.60
    brain 747.81
  vein(s) (peripheral) NEC (*see also* Hypoplasia,
      peripheral vascular system 747.60
    brain 747.81
    cardiac 746.89
    great 747.49
    portal 747.49
    pulmonary 747.49
  vena cava (inferior) (superior) 747.49
  vertebra 756.19
  vulva 752.49
  zonule (ciliary) 743.39
  zygoma 738.12
Hypopotassemia 276.8
Hypoproaccelerinemia (*see also* Defect,
    coagulation) 286.3
Hypoproconvertinemia (congenital) (*see also*
    Defect, coagulation) 286.3
Hypoproteinemia (essential) (hypermetabolic)
    (idiopathic) 273.8
Hypoproteinosis 260
Hypoprothrombinemia (congenital) (hereditary)
    (idiopathic) (*see also* Defect, coagulation)
    286.3
  acquired 286.7
  newborn 776.3
Hypopselaphesia 782.0

Hypopyon (anterior chamber) (eye) 364.05
  iritis 364.05
  ulcer (cornea) 370.04
Hypopyrexia 780.9
Hyporeflex 796.1
Hyporeninemia, extreme 790.99
  in primary aldosteronism 255.1
Hyposecretion
  ACTH 253.4
    ovary 256.3
    postablative 256.2
  salivary gland (any) 527.7
Hyposegmentation of neutrophils, hereditary
    288.2
Hyposiderinemia 280.9
Hyposmolality 276.1
  syndrome 276.1
Hyposomatotropism 253.3
Hyposomnia (*see also* Insomnia) 780.52
Hypospadias (male) 752.61
  female 753.8
Hypospermatogenesis 606.1
Hyposphagma 372.72
Hyposplenism 289.59
Hypostasis, pulmonary 514
Hypostatic —*see* condition
Hyposthenuria 593.89
Hyposuprarenalism 255.4
Hypo-TBG-nemia 246.8
Hypotension (arterial) (constitutional) 458.9
  chronic 458.1
  iatrogenic 458.2
  maternal, syndrome (following labor and
      delivery) 669.2
  orthostatic (chronic) 458.0
    dysautonomic-dyskinetic syndrome 333.0
  permanent idiopathic 458.1
  postoperative 458.2
  postural 458.0
  specified type NEC 458.8
  transient 796.3
Hypothermia (accidental) 991.6
  anesthetic 995.89
  newborn NEC 778.3
  not associated with low environmental
      temperature 780.9
Hypothymergasia (*see also* Psychosis, affective)
    296.2
  recurrent episode 296.3
  single episode 296.2
Hypothyroidism (acquired) 244.9
  complicating pregnancy, childbirth, or
      puerperium 648.1
  congenital 243
  due to
    ablation 244.1
      radioactive iodine 244.1
      surgical 244.0
    iodine (administration) (ingestion) 244.2
      radioactive 244.1
    irradiation therapy 244.1
    p-aminosalicylic acid (PAS) 244.3
    phenylbutazone 244.3
    resorcinol 244.3
    specified cause NEC 244.8
    surgery 244.0
  goitrous (sporadic) 246.1
  iatrogenic NEC 244.3
  iodine 244.2
  pituitary 244.8
  postablative NEC 244.1

Hypothyroidism—*continued*
  postsurgical 244.0
  primary 244.9
  secondary NEC 244.8
  specified cause NEC 244.8
  sporadic goitrous 246.1
Hypotonia, hypotonicity, hypotony 781.3
  benign congenital 358.8
  bladder 596.4
  congenital 779.8
    benign 358.8
  eye 360.30
    due to
      fistula 360.32
      ocular disorder NEC 360.33
    following loss of aqueous or vitreous 360.33
    primary 360.31
  infantile muscular (benign) 359.0
  muscle 728.9
  uterus, uterine (contractions)—*see* Inertia, uterus
Hypotrichosis 704.09
  congenital 757.4
  lid (congenital) 757.4
    acquired 374.55
  postinfectional NEC 704.09
Hypotropia 378.32
Hypoventilation 786.09
Hypovitaminosis (*see also* Deficiency, vitamin)
    269.2
Hypovolemia 276.5
  surgical shock 998.0
  traumatic (shock) 958.4
Hypoxemia (*see also* Anoxia) 799.0
Hypoxia (*see also* Anoxia) 799.0
  cerebral 348.1
    during or resulting from a procedure 997.01
    newborn 768.9
      mild or moderate 768.6
      severe 768.5
  fetal, affecting newborn 770.8
  intrauterine—*see* Distress, fetal
  myocardial (*see also* Insufficiency, coronary)
    411.89
    arteriosclerotic —*see* Arteriosclerosis,
      coronary
  newborn 770.8
Hypsarrhythmia (*see also* Epilepsy) 345.6
Hysteralgia, pregnant uterus 646.8
Hysteria, hysterical 300.10
  anxiety 300.20
  Charcot's gland 300.11
  conversion (any manifestation) 300.11
  dissociative type NEC 300.15
  psychosis, acute 298.1
Hysteroepilepsy 300.11
Hysterotomy , affecting fetus or newborn
    763.89

I

Iatrogenic syndrome of excess cortisol 255.0
Iceland disease (epidemic neuromyasthenia)
   049.8
Ichthyosis (congenita) 757.1
   acquired 701.1
   fetalis gravior 757.1
   follicularis 757.1
   hystrix 757.39
   lamellar 757.1
   lingual 528.6
   palmaris and plantaris 757.39
   simplex 757.1
   vera 757.1
   vulgaris 757.1
Ichthyotoxism 988.0
   bacterial (*see also* Poisoning, food) 005.9
Icteroanemia, hemolytic (acquired) 283.9
   congenital (*see also* Spherocytosis) 282.0
Icterus (*see also* Jaundice) 782.4
   catarrhal—*see* Icterus, infectious
   conjunctiva 782.4
      newborn 774.6
   epidemic—*see* Icterus, infectious
   febrilis—*see* Icterus, infectious
   fetus or newborn—*see* Jaundice, fetus or
      newborn
   gravis (*see also* Necrosis, liver) 570
      complicating pregnancy 646.7
         affecting fetus or newborn 760.8
      fetus or newborn NEC 773.0
      obstetrical 646.7
         affecting fetus or newborn 760.8
   hematogenous (acquired) 283.9
   hemolytic (acquired) 283.9
      congenital (*see also* Spherocytosis) 282.0
   hemorrhagic (acute) 100.0
      leptospiral 100.0
      newborn 776.0
      spirochetal 100.0
   infectious 070.1
      with hepatic coma 070.0
      leptospiral 100.0
      spirochetal 100.0
   intermittens juvenilis 277.4
   malignant (*see also* Necrosis, liver) 570
   neonatorum (*see also* Jaundice, fetus or
      newborn) 774.6
   pernicious (*see also* Necrosis, liver) 570
   spirochetal 100.0
Ictus solaris, solis 992.0
Identity disorder 313.82
   dissociative 300.14
   gender role (child) 302.6
      adult 302.85
   psychosexual (child) 302.6
      adult 302.85
Idioglossia 307.9
Idiopathic —*see* condition
Idiosyncrasy (*see also* Allergy) 995.3
   drug, medicinal substance, and biological—*see*
      Allergy, drug
Idiot, idiocy (congenital) 318.2
   amaurotic (Bielschowsky) (-Jansky) (family)
      (infantile (late)) (juvenile (late))
      (Vogt-Spielmeyer) 330.1
   microcephalic 742.1
   Mongolian 758.0
   oxycephalic 756.0
Id reaction (due to bacteria) 692.89

IgE asthma 493.0
Ileitis (chronic) (*see also* Enteritis) 558.9
   infectious 009.0
   noninfectious 558.9
   regional (ulcerative) 555.0
      with large intestine 555.2
   segmental 555.0
      with large intestine 555.2
   terminal (ulcerative) 555.0
      with large intestine 555.2
Ileocolitis (*see also* Enteritis) 558.9
   infectious 009.0
   regional 555.2
   ulcerative 556.1
Ileostomy status V44.2
   with complication 569.60
Ileotyphus 002.0
Ileum —*see* condition
Ileus (adynamic) (bowel) (colon) (inhibitory)
      (intestine) (neurogenic) (paralytic) 560.1
   arteriomesenteric duodenal 537.2
   due to gallstone (in intestine) 560.31
   duodenal, chronic 537.2
   following gastrointestinal surgery 997.4
   gallstone 560.31
   mechanical (*see also* Obstruction, intestine)
      560.9
   meconium 777.1
      due to cystic fibrosis 277.01
   myxedema 564.89
   postoperative 997.4
   transitory, newborn 777.4
Iliac —*see* condition
Iliotibial band friction syndrome 728.89
Ill, louping 063.1
Illegitimacy V61.6
Illness —*see also* Disease
   factitious 300.19
      with
         combined physical and psychological
            symptoms 300.19
         physical symptoms 300.19
         psychological symptoms 300.16
      chronic (with physical symptoms) 301.51
   heart—*see* Disease, heart
   manic-depressive (*see also* Psychosis, affective)
      296.80
   mental (*see also* Disorder, mental) 300.9
Imbalance 781.2
   autonomic (*see also* Neuropathy, peripheral,
      autonomic) 337.9
   electrolyte 276.9
      with
         abortion—*see* Abortion, by type, with
            metabolic disorder
         ectopic pregnancy (*see also* categories
            633.0-633.9) 639.4
         hyperemesis gravidarum (before 22
            completed weeks gestation) 643.1
         molar pregnancy (*see also* categories
            630-632) 639.4
      following
         abortion 639.4
         ectopic or molar pregnancy 639.4
      neonatal, transitory NEC 775.5
   endocrine 259.9
   eye muscle NEC 378.9
      heterophoria—*see* Heterophoria

Imbalance—*continued*
  glomerulotubular NEC 593.89
  hormone 259.9
  hysterical (*see also* Hysteria) 300.10
  labyrinth NEC 386.50
  posture 729.9
  sympathetic (*see also* Neuropathy, peripheral,
      autonomic) 337.9
Imbecile, imbecility 318.0
  moral 301.7
  old age 290.9
  senile 290.9
  specified IQ—*see* IQ
  unspecified IQ 318.0
Imbedding, intrauterine device 996.32
Imbibition, cholesterol (gallbladder) 575.6
Imerslund (-Gräsbeck) syndrome (anemia due to
    familial selective vitamin B_{12} malabsorption)
    281.1
Iminoacidopathy 270.8
Iminoglycinuria, familial 270.8
Immature —*see also* Immaturity
  personality 301.89
Immaturity 765.1
  extreme 765.0
  fetus or infant light-for-dates—*see*
      Light-for-dates
  lung, fetus or newborn 770.4
  organ or site NEC—*see* Hypoplasia
  pulmonary, fetus or newborn 770.4
  reaction 301.89
  sexual (female) (male) 259.0
Immersion 994.1
  foot 991.4
  hand 991.4
Immobile, immobility
  intestine 564.89
  joint—*see* Ankylosis
  syndrome (paraplegic) 728.3
Immunization
  ABO
    affecting management of pregnancy 656.2
      fetus or newborn 773.1
  complication—*see* Complications, vaccination
  Rh factor
    affecting management of pregnancy 656.1
      fetus or newborn 773.0
    from transfusion 999.7
Immunodeficiency 279.3
  with
    adenosine-deaminase deficiency 279.2
    defect, predominant
      B-cell 279.00
      T-cell 279.10
    hyperimmunoglobulinemia 279.2
    lymphopenia, hereditary 279.2
    thrombocytopenia and eczema 279.12
    thymic
      aplasia 279.2
      dysplasia 279.2
  autosomal recessive, Swiss-type 279.2
  common variable 279.06
  severe combined (SCID) 279.2
  to Rh factor
    affecting management of pregnancy 656.1
      fetus or newborn 773.0
  X-linked, with increased IgM 279.05
Immunotherapy, prophylactic V07.2

Impaction, impacted
  bowel, colon, rectum 560.30
    with hernia—*see also* Hernia, by site, with
        obstruction
      gangrenous—*see* Hernia, by site, with
          gangrene
    by
      calculus 560.39
      gallstone 560.31
    fecal 560.39
    specified type NEC 560.39
  calculus—*see* Calculus
  cerumen (ear) (external) 380.4
  cuspid 520.6
    with abnormal position (same or adjacent
        tooth) 524.3
  dental 520.6
    with abnormal position (same or adjacent
        tooth) 524.3
  fecal, feces 560.39
    with hernia—*see also* Hernia, by site, with
        obstruction
      gangrenous—*see* Hernia, by site, with
          gangrene
  fracture—*see* Fracture, by site
  gallbladder—*see* Cholelithiasis
  gallstone(s)—*see* Cholelithiasis
    in intestine (any part) 560.31
  intestine(s) 560.30
    with hernia—*see also* Hernia, by site, with
        obstruction
      gangrenous—*see* Hernia, by site, with
          gangrene
    by
      calculus 560.39
      gallstone 560.31
    fecal 560.39
    specified type NEC 560.39
  intrauterine device (IUD) 996.32
  molar 520.6
    with abnormal position (same or adjacent
        tooth) 524.3
  shoulder 660.4
    affecting fetus or newborn 763.1
  tooth, teeth 520.6
    with abnormal position (same or adjacent
        tooth) 524.3
  turbinate 733.99
Impaired, impairment (function)
  arm V49.1
    movement, involving
      musculoskeletal system V49.1
      nervous system V49.2
  auditory discrimination 388.43
  back V48.3
  body (entire) V49.89
  hearing (*see also* Deafness) 389.9
  heart—*see* Disease, heart
  kidney (*see also* Disease, renal) 593.9
    disorder resulting from 588.9
      specified NEC 588.8
  leg V49.1
    movement, involving
      musculoskeletal system V49.1
      nervous system V49.2
  limb V49.1
    movement, involving
      musculoskeletal system V49.1
      nervous system V49.2
  liver 573.8
  mastication 524.9

Impaired, impairment—*continued*
  mobility
    ear ossicles NEC 385.22
    incostapedial joint 385.22
    malleus 385.21
  myocardium, myocardial (*see also*
    Insufficiency, myocardial) 428.0
  neuromusculoskeletal NEC V49.89
    back V48.3
    head V48.2
    limb V49.2
    neck V48.3
    spine V48.3
    trunk V48.3
  rectal sphincter 787.99
  renal (*see also* Disease, renal) 593.9
    disorder resulting from 588.9
      specified NEC 588.8
  spine V48.3
  vision NEC 369.9
    both eyes NEC 369.3
    moderate 369.74
      both eyes 369.25
        with impairment of lesser eye (specified
          as)
          blind, not further specified 369.15
          low vision, not further specified 369.23
          near-total 369.17
          profound 369.18
          severe 369.24
          total 369.16
      one eye 369.74
        with vision of other eye (specified as)
          near-normal 369.75
          normal 369.76
    near-total 369.64
      both eyes 369.04
        with impairment of lesser eye (specified
          as)
          blind, not further specified 369.02
          total 369.03
      one eye 369.64
        with vision of other eye (specified as)
          near-normal 369.65
          normal 369.66
    one eye 369.60
      with low vision of other eye 369.10
    profound 369.67
      both eyes 369.08
        with impairment of lesser eye (specified
          as)
          blind, not further specified 369.05
          near-total 369.07
          total 369.06
      one eye 369.67
        with vision of other eye (specified as)
          near-normal 369.68
          normal 369.69
    severe 369.71
      both eyes 369.22
        with impairment of lesser eye (specified
          as)
          blind, not further specified 369.11
          low vision, not further specified 369.21
          near-total 369.13
          profound 369.14
          total 369.12
      one eye 369.71
        with vision of other eye (specified as)
          near-normal 369.72
          normal 369.73

Impaired, impairment—*continued*
  total
    both eyes 369.01
    one eye 369.61
      with vision of other eye (specified as)
        near-normal 369.62
        normal 369.63
Impaludism —*see* Malaria
Impediment, speech NEC 784.5
  psychogenic 307.9
  secondary to organic lesion 784.5
Impending
  cerebrovascular accident or attack 435.9
  coronary syndrome 411.1
  delirium tremens 291.0
  myocardial infarction 411.1
Imperception, auditory (acquired) (congenital)
  389.9
Imperfect
  aeration, lung (newborn) 770.5
  closure (congenital)
    alimentary tract NEC 751.8
      lower 751.5
      upper 750.8
    atrioventricular ostium 745.69
    atrium (secundum) 745.5
      primum 745.61
    branchial cleft or sinus 744.41
    choroid 743.59
    cricoid cartilage 748.3
    cusps, heart valve NEC 746.89
      pulmonary 746.09
    ductus
      arteriosus 747.0
      Botalli 747.0
    ear drum 744.29
      causing impairment of hearing 744.03
    endocardial cushion 745.60
    epiglottis 748.3
    esophagus with communication to bronchus
      or trachea 750.3
    Eustachian valve 746.89
    eyelid 743.62
    face, facial (*see also* Cleft, lip) 749.10
    foramen
      Botalli 745.5
      ovale 745.5
    genitalia, genital organ(s) or system
      female 752.8
        external 752.49
        internal NEC 752.8
        uterus 752.3
      male 752.8
        penis 752.69
    glottis 748.3
    heart valve (cusps) NEC 746.89
    interatrial ostium or septum 745.5
    interauricular ostium or septum 745.5
    interventricular ostium or septum 745.4
    iris 743.46
    kidney 753.3
    larynx 748.3
    lens 743.36
    lip (*see also* Cleft, lip) 749.10
    nasal septum or sinus 748.1
    nose 748.1
    omphalomesenteric duct 751.0
    optic nerve entry 743.57
    organ or site NEC—*see* Anomaly, specified
      type, by site

Imperfect—*continued*
  ostium
    interatrial 745.5
    interauricular 745.5
    interventricular 745.4
  palate (*see also* Cleft, palate) 749.00
  preauricular sinus 744.46
  retina 743.56
  roof of orbit 742.0
  sclera 743.47
  septum
    aortic 745.0
    aorticopulmonary 745.0
    atrial (secundum) 745.5
      primum 745.61
    between aorta and pulmonary artery 745.0
    heart 745.9
    interatrial (secundum) 745.5
      primum 745.61
    interauricular (secundum) 745.5
      primum 745.61
    interventricular 745.4
      with pulmonary stenosis or atresia,
        dextraposition of aorta, and
        hypertrophy of right ventricle 745.2
      in tetralogy of Fallot 745.2
    nasal 748.1
    ventricular 745.4
      with pulmonary stenosis or atresia,
        dextraposition of aorta, and
        hypertrophy of right ventricle 745.2
      in tetralogy of Fallot 745.2
  skull 756.0
    with
      anencephalus 740.0
      encephalocele 742.0
      hydrocephalus 742.3
        with spina bifida (*see also* Spina bifida)
          741.0
      microcephalus 742.1
  spine (with meningocele) (*see also* Spina
    bifida) 741.90
  thyroid cartilage 748.3
  trachea 748.3
  tympanic membrane 744.29
    causing impairment of hearing 744.03
  uterus (with communication to bladder,
    intestine, or rectum) 752.3
  uvula 749.02
    with cleft lip (*see also* Cleft, palate, with
      cleft lip) 749.20
  vitelline duct 751.0
  development—*see* Anomaly, by site
  erection 607.84
  fusion—*see* Imperfect, closure
  inflation lung (newborn) 770.5
  intestinal canal 751.5
  poise 729.9
  rotation—*see* Malrotation
  septum, ventricular 745.4
Imperfectly descended testis 752.51
Imperforate (congenital)—*see also* Atresia
  anus 751.2
  bile duct 751.61
  cervix (uteri) 752.49
  esophagus 750.3
  hymen 752.42
  intestine (small) 751.1
    large 751.2
  jejunum 751.1
  pharynx 750.29

Imperforate—*continued*
  rectum 751.2
  salivary duct 750.23
  urethra 753.6
  urinary meatus 753.6
  vagina 752.49
Impervious (congenital)—*see also* Atresia
  anus 751.2
  bile duct 751.61
  esophagus 750.3
  intestine (small) 751.1
    large 751.5
  rectum 751.2
  urethra 753.6
Impetiginization of other dermatoses 684
Impetigo (any organism) (any site) (bullous)
    (circinate) (contagiosa) (neonatorum)
    (simplex) 684
  Bockhart's (superficial folliculitis) 704.8
  external ear 684 *[380.13]*
  eyelid 684 *[373.5]*
  Fox's (contagiosa) 684
  furfuracea 696.5
  herpetiformis 694.3
    nonobstetrical 694.3
  staphylococcal infection 684
  ulcerative 686.8
  vulgaris 684
Impingement, soft tissue between teeth 524.2
Implant, endometrial 617.9
Implantation
  anomalous—*see also* Anomaly, specified type,
    by site
    ureter 753.4
  cyst
    external area or site (skin) NEC 709.8
    iris 364.61
    vagina 623.8
    vulva 624.8
  dermoid (cyst)
    external area or site (skin) NEC 709.8
    iris 364.61
    vagina 623.8
    vulva 624.8
  placenta, low or marginal—*see* Placenta previa
Impotence (sexual) (psychogenic) 302.72
  organic origin NEC 607.84
Impoverished blood 285.9
Impression, basilar 756.0
Imprisonment V62.5
Improper
  development, infant 764.9
Improperly tied umbilical cord (causing
    hemorrhage) 772.3
Impulses, obsessional 300.3
Impulsive neurosis 300.3
Inaction, kidney (*see also* Disease, renal) 593.9
Inactive —*see* condition
Inadequate, inadequacy
  biologic 301.6
  cardiac and renal—*see* Hypertension,
    cardiorenal
  constitutional 301.6
  development
    child 783.40
    fetus 764.9
      affecting management of pregnancy 656.5
    genitalia
      after puberty NEC 259.0
      congenital—*see* Hypoplasia, genitalia
    lungs 748.5

Inadequate, inadequacy—*continued*
  organ or site NEC—*see* Hypoplasia, by site
  dietary 269.9
  education V62.3
  environment
    economic problem V60.2
    household condition NEC V60.1
    poverty V60.2
    unemployment V62.0
  functional 301.6
  household care, due to
    family member
      handicapped or ill V60.4
      temporarily away from home V60.4
        on vacation V60.5
    technical defects in home V60.1
    temporary absence from home of person
      rendering care V60.4
  housing (heating) (space) V60.1
  material resources V60.2
  mental (*see also* Retardation, mental) 319
  nervous system 799.2
  personality 301.6
  prenatal care in current pregnancy V23.7
  pulmonary
    function 786.09
      newborn 770.8
    ventilation, newborn 770.8
  respiration 786.09
    newborn 770.8
  social 301.6
Inanition 263.9
  with edema 262
  due to
    deprivation of food 994.2
    malnutrition 263.9
  fever 780.6
Inappropriate secretion
  ACTH 255.0
  antidiuretic hormone (ADH) (excessive) 253.6
    deficiency 253.5
  ectopic hormone NEC 259.3
  pituitary (posterior) 253.6
Inattention after or at birth 995.52
Inborn errors of metabolism —*see* Disorder,
  metabolism
Incarceration, incarcerated
  bubonocele—*see also* Hernia, inguinal, with
    obstruction
    gangrenous—*see* Hernia, inguinal, with
      gangrene
  colon (by hernia)—*see also* Hernia, by site,
    with obstruction
    gangrenous—*see* Hernia, by site, with
      gangrene
  enterocele 552.9
    gangrenous 551.9
  epigastrocele 552.29
    gangrenous 551.29
  epiplocele 552.9
    gangrenous 551.9
  exomphalos 552.1
    gangrenous 551.1
  fallopian tube 620.8
  hernia—*see also* Hernia, by site, with
    obstruction

Incarceration, incarcerated—*continued*
  gangrenous—*see* Hernia, by site, with
    gangrene
  iris, in wound 871.1
  lens, in wound 871.1
  merocele (*see also* Hernia, femoral, with
    obstruction) 552.00
  Omentum (by hernia)—*see also* Hernia, by site,
    with obstruction
    gangrenous—*see* Hernia, by site, with
      gangrene
  omphalocele 756.79
  rupture (meaning hernia) (*see also* Hernia, by
    site, with obstruction) 552.9
    gangrenous (*see also* Hernia, by site, with
      gangrene) 551.9
  sarcoepiplocele 552.9
    gangrenous 551.9
  sarcoepiplomphalocele 552.1
    with gangrene 551.1
  uterus 621.8
    gravid 654.3
      causing obstructed labor 660.2
        affecting fetus or newborn 763.1
Incident, cerebrovascular (*see also* Disease,
  cerebrovascular, acute) 436
Incineration (entire body) (from fire,
  conflagration, electricity, or lightning)—*see*
  Burn, multiple, specified sites
Incised wound
  external—*see* Wound, open, by site
  internal organs (abdomen, chest, or pelvis)—*see*
    Injury, internal, by site, with open wound
Incision, incisional
  hernia—*see* Hernia, incisional
  surgical, complication—*see* Complications,
    surgical procedures
  traumatic
    external—*see* Wound, open, by site
    internal organs (abdomen, chest or
      pelvis)—*see* Injury, internal, by site, with
      open wound
Inclusion
  azurophilic leukocytic 288.2
  blennorrhea (neonatal) (newborn) 771.6
  cyst—*see* Cyst, skin
  gallbladder in liver (congenital) 751.69
Incompatibility
  ABO
    affecting management of pregnancy 656.2
    fetus or newborn 773.1
    infusion or transfusion reaction 999.6
  blood (group) (Duffy) (E) (K(ell)) (Kidd)
    (Lewis) (M) (N) (P) (S) NEC
    affecting management of pregnancy 656.2
    fetus or newborn 773.2
    infusion or transfusion reaction 999.6
  marital V61.10
    involving divorce or estrangement V61.0
  Rh (blood group) (factor)
    affecting management of pregnancy 656.1
    fetus or newborn 773.0
    infusion or transfusion reaction 999.7
  Rhesus—*see* Incompatibility, Rh
Incompetency, incompetence, incompetent
  annular
    aortic (valve) (*see also* Insufficiency, aortic)
      424.1
    mitral (valve)—(*see also* Insufficiency,
      mitral) 424.0

Incompetency, Incompetence—*continued*
   pulmonary valve (heart) (*see also*
      Endocarditis, pulmonary) 424.3
   aortic (valve) (*see also* Insufficiency, aortic)
      424.1
   syphilitic 093.22
   cardiac (orifice) 530.0
     valve—*see* Endocarditis
   cervix, cervical (os) 622.5
     in pregnancy 654.5
       affecting fetus or newborn 761.0
   esophagogastric (junction) (sphincter) 530.0
   heart valve, congenital 746.89
   mitral (valve)—*see* Insufficiency, mitral
   papillary muscle (heart) 429.81
   pelvic fundus 618.8
   pulmonary valve (heart) (*see also* Endocarditis,
      pulmonary) 424.3
     congenital 746.09
   tricuspid (annular) (rheumatic) (valve) (*see also*
      Endocarditis, tricuspid) 397.0
   valvular—*see* Endocarditis
   vein, venous (saphenous) (varicose) (*see also*
      Varicose, vein) 454.9
   velopharyngeal (closure)
     acquired 528.9
     congenital 750.29
Incomplete —*see also* condition
   bladder emptying 788.21
   expansion lungs (newborn) 770.5
   gestation (liveborn)—*see* Immaturity
   rotation—*see* Malrotation
Incontinence 788.30
   without sensory awareness 788.34
   anal sphincter 787.6
   continuous leakage 788.37
   feces 787.6
     due to hysteria 300.11
     nonorganic origin 307.7
   hysterical 300.11
   mixed (male) (female) (urge and stress) 788.33
   overflow 788.39
   paradoxical 788.39
   rectal 787.6
   specified NEC 788.39
   stress (female) 625.6
     male NEC 788.32
   urethral sphincter 599.84
   urge 788.31
     and stress (male) (female) 788.33
   urine 788.30
     active 788.30
     male 788.30
       stress 788.32
         and urge 788.33
       neurogenic 788.39
       nonorganic origin 307.6
       stress (female) 625.6
         male NEC 788.32
       urge 788.31
         and stress 788.33
Incontinentia pigmenti 757.33
Incoordinate
   uterus (action) (contractions) 661.4
     affecting fetus or newborn 763.7
Incoordination
   esophageal-pharyngeal (newborn) 787.2
   muscular 781.3
   papillary muscle 429.81

Increase, increased
   abnormal, in development 783.9
   androgens (ovarian) 256.1
   anticoagulants (antithrombin) (anti-VIIIa)
      (anti-IXa) (anti-Xa) (anti-XIa) 286.5
     postpartum 666.3
   cold sense (*see also* Disturbance, sensation)
      782.0
   estrogen 256.0
   function
     adrenal (cortex) 255.3
       medulla 255.6
     pituitary (anterior) (gland) (lobe) 253.1
       posterior 253.6
   heat sense (*see also* Disturbance, sensation)
      782.0
   intracranial pressure 781.99
     injury at birth 767.8
   light reflex of retina 362.13
   permeability, capillary 448.9
   pressure
     intracranial 781.99
       injury at birth 767.8
     intraocular 365.00
   pulsations 785.9
   pulse pressure 785.9
   sphericity, lens 743.36
   splenic activity 289.4
   venous pressure 459.89
     portal 572.3
Incrustation, cornea, lead or zinc 930.0
Incyclophoria 378.44
Incyclotropia 378.33
Indeterminate sex 752.7
India rubber skin 756.83
Indicanuria 270.2
Indigestion (bilious) (functional) 536.8
   acid 536.8
   catarrhal 536.8
   due to decomposed food NEC 005.9
   fat 579.8
   nervous 306.4
   psychogenic 306.4
Indirect —*see* condition
Indolent bubo NEC 099.8
Induced
   abortion—*see* Abortion, induced
   birth, affecting fetus or newborn 763.89
   delivery—*see* Delivery
   labor—*see* Delivery
Induration, indurated
   brain 348.8
   breast (fibrous) 611.79
     puerperal, postpartum 676.3
   broad ligament 620.8
   chancre 091.0
     anus 091.1
     congenital 090.0
     extragenital NEC 091.2
   corpora cavernosa (penis) (plastic) 607.89
   liver (chronic) 573.8
     acute 573.8
   lung (black) (brown) (chronic) (fibroid) (*see*
      also Fibrosis, lung) 515
     essential brown 275.0 *[516.1]*
   penile 607.89
   phlebitic—*see* Phlebitis
   skin 782.8
   stomach 537.89
Induratio penis plastica 607.89
Industrial —*see* condition

Inebriety (*see also* Abuse, drugs, nondependent) 305.0
Inefficiency
  kidney (*see also* Disease, renal) 593.9
  thyroid (acquired) (gland) 244.9
Inelasticity, skin 782.8
Inequality, leg (acquired) (length) 736.81
  congenital 755.30
Inertia
  bladder 596.4
    neurogenic 596.54
      with cauda equina syndrome 344.61
  stomach 536.8
    psychogenic 306.4
  uterus, uterine 661.2
    affecting fetus or newborn 763.7
    primary 661.0
    secondary 661.1
  vesical 596.4
    neurogenic 596.54
      with cauda equina 344.61
Infant —*see also* condition
  held for adoption V68.89
  newborn—*see* Newborn
  syndrome of diabetic mother 775.0
"Infant Hercules" syndrome 255.2
Infantile —*see also* condition
  genitalia, genitals 259.0
    in pregnancy or childbirth NEC 654.4
      affecting fetus or newborn 763.89
      causing obstructed labor 660.2
        affecting fetus or newborn 763.1
  heart 746.9
  kidney 753.3
  lack of care 995.52
  macula degeneration 362.75
  melanodontia 521.0
  os, uterus (*see also* Infantile, genitalia) 259.0
  pelvis 738.6
    with disproportion (fetopelvic) 653.1
      affecting fetus or newborn 763.1
      causing obstructed labor 660.1
        affecting fetus or newborn 763.1
  penis 259.0
  testis 257.2
  uterus (*see also* Infantile, genitalia) 259.0
  vulva 752.49
Infantilism 259.9
  with dwarfism (hypophyseal) 253.3
  Brissaud's (infantile myxedema) 244.9
  celiac 579.0
  Herter's (nontropical sprue) 579.0
  hypophyseal 253.3
  hypothalamic (with obesity) 253.8
  idiopathic 259.9
  intestinal 579.0
  pancreatic 577.8
  pituitary 253.3
  renal 588.0
  sexual (with obesity) 259.0
Infants, healthy liveborn —*see* Newborn
Infarct, infarction
  adrenal (capsule) (gland) 255.4
  amnion 658.8
  anterior (with contiguous portion of
    intraventricular septum) NEC (*see also*
    Infarct, myocardium) 410.1
  appendices epiploicae 557.0
  bowel 557.0

Infarct, infarction—*continued*
  brain (stem) 434.91
    embolic (*see also* Embolism, brain) 434.11
    healed or old, without residuals V12.59
      iatrogenic 997.02
      postoperative 997.02
    puerperal, postpartum, childbirth 674.0
    thrombotic (*see also* Thrombosis, brain)
      434.01
  breast 611.8
  Brewer's (kidney) 593.81
  cardiac (*see also* Infarct, myocardium) 410.9
  cerebellar (*see also* Infarct, brain) 434.91
    embolic (*see also* Embolism, brain) 434.11
  cerebral (*see also* Infarct, brain) 434.91
    embolic (*see also* Embolism, brain) 434.11
  chorion 658.8
  colon (acute) (agnogenic) (embolic)
    (hemorrhagic) (nonocclusive)
    (nonthrombotic) (occlusive) (segmental)
    (thrombotic) (with gangrene) 557.0
  coronary artery (*see also* Infarct, myocardium)
    410.9
  embolic (*see also* Embolism) 444.9
  fallopian tube 620.8
  gallbladder 575.8
  heart (*see also* Infarct, myocardium) 410.9
  hepatic 573.4
  hypophysis (anterior lobe) 253.8
  impending (myocardium) 411.1
  intestine (acute) (agnogenic) (embolic)
    (hemorrhagic) (nonocclusive)
    (nonthrombotic) (occlusive) (thrombotic)
    (with gangrene) 557.0
  kidney 593.81
  liver 573.4
  lung (embolic) (thrombotic) 415.19
    with
      abortion—*see* Abortion, by type, with,
        embolism
      ectopic pregnancy (*see also* categories
        633.0-633.9) 639.6
      molar pregnancy (*see also* categories
        630-632) 639.6
    following
      abortion 639.6
      ectopic or molar pregnancy 639.6
    iatrogenic 415.11
    in pregnancy, childbirth, or puerperium—*see*
      Embolism, obstetrical
    postoperative 415.11
  lymph node or vessel 457.8
  medullary (brain)—*see* Infarct, brain
  meibomian gland (eyelid) 374.85
  mesentery, mesenteric (embolic) (thrombotic)
    (with gangrene) 557.0
  midbrain—*see* Infarct, brain
  myocardium, myocardial (acute or with a stated
    duration of 8 weeks or less) (with
    hypertension) 410.9

<table>
<tr><td>

*Note—use the following fifth-digit
subclassification with category 410*

0 episode unspecified
1 initial episode
2 subsequent episode without recurrence

</td></tr>
</table>

Infarct, infarction—*continued*
  with symptoms after 8 weeks from date of infarction 414.8
  anterior (wall) (with contiguous portion of intraventricular septum) NEC 410.1
  anteroapical (with contiguous portion of intraventricular septum) 410.1
  anterolateral (wall) 410.0
  anteroseptal (with contiguous portion of intraventricular septum) 410.1
  apical-lateral 410.5
  atrial 410.8
  basal-lateral 410.5
  chronic (with symptoms after 8 weeks from date of infarction) 414.8
  diagnosed on ECG, but presenting no symptoms 412
  diaphragmatic wall (with contiguous portion of intraventricular septum) 410.4
  healed or old, currently presenting no symptoms 412
  high lateral 410.5
  impending 411.1
  inferior (wall) (with contiguous portion of intraventricular septum) 410.4
  inferolateral (wall) 410.2
  inferoposterior wall 410.3
  lateral wall 410.5
  nontransmural 410.7
  papillary muscle 410.8
  past (diagnosed on ECG or other special investigation, but correctly presenting no symptoms) 412
    with symptoms NEC 414.8
  posterior (strictly) (true) (wall) 410.6
  posterobasal 410.6
  posteroinferior 410.3
  posterolateral 410.5
  previous, currently presenting no symptoms 412
  septal 410.8
  specified site NEC 410.8
  subendocardial 410.7
  syphilitic 093.82
 nontransmural 410.7
 omentum 557.0
 ovary 620.8
 pancreas 577.8
 papillary muscle (*see also* Infarct, myocardium) 410.8
 parathyroid gland 252.8
 pituitary (gland) 253.8
 placenta (complicating pregnancy) 656.7
  affecting fetus or newborn 762.2
 pontine—*see* Infarct, brain
 posterior NEC (*see also* Infarct, myocardium) 410.6
 prostate 602.8
 pulmonary (artery) (hemorrhagic) (vein) 415.19
  with
    abortion—*see* Abortion, by type, with embolism
    ectopic pregnancy (*see also* categories 633.0-633.9) 639.6
    molar pregnancy (*see also* categories 630-632) 639.6
    following
      abortion 639.6
      ectopic or molar pregnancy 639.6
    iatrogenic 415.11

Infarct, infarction—*continued*
 in pregnancy, childbirth, or puerperium—*see* Embolism, obstetrical
 postoperative 415.11
 renal 593.81
  embolic or thrombotic 593.81
 retina, retinal 362.84
  with occlusion—*see* Occlusion, retina
 spinal (acute) (cord) (embolic) (nonembolic) 336.1
 spleen 289.59
  embolic or thrombotic 444.89
 subchorionic—*see* Infarct, placenta
 subendocardial (*see also* Infarct, myocardium) 410.7
 suprarenal (capsule) (gland) 255.4
 syncytium—*see* Infarct, placenta
 testis 608.83
 thrombotic (*see also* Thrombosis) 453.9
  artery, arterial—*see* Embolism
 thyroid (gland) 246.3
 ventricle (heart) (*see also* Infarct, myocardium) 410.9
Infecting —*see* condition
Infection, infected, infective (opportunistic) 136.9
 with lymphangitis—*see* Lymphangitis
 abortion—*see* Abortion, by type, with sepsis
 abscess (skin)—*see* Abscess, by site
 Absidia 117.7
 Acanthocheilonema (perstans) 125.4
  streptocerca 125.6
 accessory sinus (chronic) (*see also* Sinusitis) 473.9
 Achorion—*see* Dermatophytosis
 Acremonium falciforme 117.4
 acromioclavicular (joint) 711.91
 actinobacillus
  lignieresii 027.8
  mallei 024
  muris 026.1
 actinomadura—*see* Actinomycosis
 Actinomyces (israelii)—*see also* Actinomycosis
  muris-ratti 026.1
 Actinomycetales (actinomadura) (Actinomyces) (Nocardia) (Streptomyces)—*see* Actinomycosis
 actinomycotic NEC (*see also* Actinomycosis) 039.9
 adenoid (chronic) 474.01
  acute 463
  and tonsil (chronic) 474.02
  acute or subacute 463
 adenovirus NEC 079.0
  in diseases classified elsewhere—*see* category 079
  unspecified nature or site 079.0
 Aerobacter aerogenes NEC 041.85
  enteritis 008.2
 aerogenes capsulatus (*see also* Gangrene, gas) 040.0
 aertrycke (*see also* Infection, Salmonella) 003.9
 ajellomyces dermatitidis 116.0
 alimentary canal NEC (*see also* Enteritis, due to, by organism) 009.0
 Allescheria boydii 117.6
 Alternaria 118
 alveolus, alveolar (process) (pulpal origin) 522.4
 ameba, amebic (histolytica) (*see also* Amebiasis) 006.9
  acute 006.0

Infection, infected, infective—*continued*
  chronic 006.1
  free-living 136.2
  hartmanni 007.8
  specified
    site NEC 006.8
    type NEC 007.8
  amniotic fluid or cavity 658.4
    affecting fetus or newborn 762.7
  anaerobes (cocci) (gram-negative) (gram
    positive) (mixed) NEC 041.84
  anal canal 569.49
  Ancylostoma braziliense 126.2
  Angiostrongylus cantonensis 128.8
  anisakiasis 127.1
  Anisakis larva 127.1
  anthrax (*see also* Anthrax) 022.9
  antrum (chronic) (*see also* Sinusitis, maxillary)
    473.0
  anus (papillae) (sphincter) 569.49
  arbor virus NEC 066.9
  arbovirus NEC 066.9
  argentophil-rod 027.0
  Ascaris lumbricoides 127.0
  ascomycetes 117.4
  Aspergillus (flavus) (fumigatus) (terreus) 117.3
  atypical
    acid-fast (bacilli) (*see also* Mycobacterium,
      atypical) 031.9
    mycobacteria (*see also* Mycobacterium,
      atypical) 031.9
  auditory meatus (circumscribed) (diffuse)
    (external) (*see also* Otitis, externa) 380.10
  auricle (ear) (*see also* Otitis, externa) 380.10
  axillary gland 683
  Babesiasis 088.82
  Babesiosis 088.82
  Bacillus NEC 041.89
    abortus 023.1
    anthracis (*see also* Anthrax) 022.9
    cereus (food poisoning) 005.89
    coli—*see* Infection, Escherichia coli
    coliform NEC 041.85
    Ducrey's (any location) 099.0
    Flexner's 004.1
    fragilis NEC 041.82
    Friedländer's NEC 041.3
    fusiformis 101
    gas (gangrene) (*see also* Gangrene, gas) 040.0
    mallei 024
    melitensis 023.0
    paratyphoid, paratyphosus 002.9
      A 002.1
      B 002.2
      C 002.3
    Schmorl's 040.3
    Shiga 004.0
    suipestifer (*see also* Infection, Salmonella)
      003.9
    swimming pool 031.1
    typhosa 002.0
    welchii (*see also* Gangrene, gas) 040.0
    Whitmore's 025
  bacterial NEC 041.9
    specified NEC 041.89
      anaerobic NEC 041.84
      gram-negative NEC 041.85
      anaerobic NEC 041.84
  Bacterium
    paratyphosum 002.9
      A 002.1

Infection, infected, infective—*continued*
      B 002.2
      C 002.3
    typhosum 002.0
  Bacteroides (fragilis) (melaninogenicus) (oralis)
    NEC 041.84
  balantidium coli 007.0
  Bartholin's gland 616.8
  Basidiobolus 117.7
  Bedsonia 079.98
    specified NEC 079.88
  bile duct 576.1
  bladder (*see also* Cystitis) 595.9
  Blastomyces, blastomycotic 116.0
    brasiliensis 116.1
    dermatitidis 116.0
    European 117.5
    Loboi 116.2
    North American 116.0
    South American 116.1
  blood stream—*see* Septicemia
  bone 730.9
    specified—*see* Osteomyelitis
  Bordetella 033.9
    bronchiseptica 033.8
    parapertussis 033.1
    pertussis 033.0
  Borrelia
    bergdorfi 088.81
    vincentii (mouth) (pharynx) (tonsil) 101
  brain (*see also* Encephalitis) 323.9
    late effect—*see* category 326
    membranes—(*see also* Meningitis) 322.9
    septic 324.0
      late effect—*see* category 326
      meninges (*see also* Meningitis) 320.9
  branchial cyst 744.42
  breast 611.0
    puerperal, postpartum 675.2
      with nipple 675.9
        specified type NEC 675.8
      nonpurulent 675.2
      purulent 675.1
  bronchus (*see also* Bronchitis) 490
    fungus NEC 117.9
  Brucella 023.9
    abortus 023.1
    canis 023.3
    melitensis 023.0
    mixed 023.8
    suis 023.2
  Brugia (Wuchereria) malayi 125.1
  bursa—*see* Bursitis
  buttocks (skin) 686.9
  Candida (albicans) (tropicalis) (*see also*
    Candidiasis) 112.9
    congenital 771.7
  Candiru 136.8
  Capillaria
    hepatica 128.8
    philippinensis 127.5
  cartilage 733.99
  cat liver fluke 121.0
  cellulitis—*see* Cellulitis, by site
  Cephalosporum falciforme 117.4
  Cercomonas hominis (intestinal) 007.3
  cerebrospinal (*see also* Meningitis) 322.9
    late effect—*see* category 326
  cervical gland 683
  cervix (*see also* Cervicitis) 616.0
  cesarean section wound 674.3

Infection, infected, infective—*continued*
　Epstein-Barr virus 075
　　chronic 780.79 *[139.8]*
　erysipeloid 027.1
　Erysipelothrix (insidiosa) (rhusiopathiae) 027.1
　erythema infectiosum 057.0
　Escherichia coli NEC 041.4
　　congenital 771.8
　　enteritis—*see* Enteritis, E. coli
　　generalized 038.42
　　intestinal—*see* Enteritis, E. coli
　ethmoidal (chronic) (sinus) (*see also* Sinusitis,
　　　ethmoidal) 473.2
　Eubacterium 041.84
　Eustachian tube (ear) 381.50
　　acute 381.51
　　chronic 381.52
　exanthema subitum 057.8
　external auditory canal (meatus) (*see also* Otitis,
　　　externa) 380.10
　eye NEC 360.00
　eyelid 373.9
　　specified NEC 373.8
　fallopian tube (*see also* Salpingo-oophoritis)
　　　614.2
　fascia 728.89
　Fasciola
　　gigantica 121.3
　　hepatica 121.3
　Fasciolopsis (buski) 121.4
　fetus (intra-amniotic)—*see* Infection, congenital
　filarial—*see* Infestation, filarial
　finger (skin) 686.9
　　abscess (with lymphangitis) 681.00
　　　pulp 681.01
　　cellulitis (with lymphangitis) 681.00
　　distal closed space (with lymphangitis) 681.00
　　nail 681.02
　　　fungus 110.1
　fish tapeworm 123.4
　　larval 123.5
　flagellate, intestinal 007.9
　fluke—*see* Infestation, fluke
　focal
　　teeth (pulpal origin) 522.4
　　tonsils 474.00
　　　and adenoids 474.02
　Fonsecaea
　　compactum 117.2
　　pedrosoi 117.2
　food (*see also* Poisoning, food) 005.9
　foot (skin) 686.9
　　fungus 110.4
　Francisella tularensis (*see also* Tularemia) 021.9
　frontal sinus (chronic) (*see also* Sinusitis,
　　　frontal) 473.1
　fungus NEC 117.9
　　beard 110.0
　　body 110.5
　　dermatiacious NEC 117.8
　　foot 110.4
　　groin 110.3
　　hand 110.2
　　nail 110.1
　　pathogenic to compromised host only 118
　　perianal (area) 110.3
　　scalp 110.0
　　scrotum 110.8
　　skin 111.9
　　　foot 110.4
　　　hand 110.2

Infection, infected, infective—*continued*
　toenails 110.1
　trachea 117.9
　Fusarium 118
　Fusobacterium 041.84
　gallbladder (*see also* Cholecystitis, acute) 575.0
　gas bacillus (*see also* Gas, gangrene) 040.0
　gastric (*see also* Gastritis) 535.5
　Gastrodiscoides hominis 121.8
　gastroenteric (*see also* Enteritis, due to, by
　　　organism) 009.0
　gastrointestinal (*see also* Enteritis, due to, by
　　　organism) 009.0
　gastrostomy 536.41
　generalized NEC (*see also* Septicemia) 038.9
　genital organ or tract NEC
　　female 614.9
　　　with
　　　　abortion—*see* Abortion, by type, with
　　　　　sepsis
　　　　ectopic pregnancy (*see also* categories
　　　　　633.0-633.9) 639.0
　　　　molar pregnancy (*see also* categories
　　　　　630-632) 639.0
　　　complicating pregnancy 646.6
　　　　affecting fetus or newborn 760.8
　　　following
　　　　abortion 639.0
　　　　ectopic or molar pregnancy 639.0
　　　puerperal, postpartum, childbirth 670
　　　　minor or localized 646.6
　　　　　affecting fetus or newborn 760.8
　　male 608.4
　genitourinary tract NEC 599.0
　Ghon tubercle, primary (*see also* Tuberculosis)
　　　010.0
　Giardia lamblia 007.1
　gingival (chronic) 523.1
　　acute 523.0
　　Vincent's 101
　glanders 024
　Glenosporopsis amazonica 116.2
　Gnathostoma spinigerum 128.1
　Gongylonema 125.6
　gonococcal NEC (*see also* Gonococcus) 098.0
　gram-negative bacilli NEC 041.85
　　anaerobic 041.84
　guinea worm 125.7
　gum (*see also* Infection, gingival) 523.1
　Hantavirus 079.81
　heart 429.89
　Helicobacter pylori (H. pylori) 041.86
　helminths NEC 128.9
　　intestinal 127.9
　　　mixed (types classifiable to more than one
　　　　category in 120.0-127.7) 127.8
　　　specified type NEC 127.7
　　specified type NEC 128.8
　Hemophilus influenzae NEC 041.5
　　generalized 038.41
　Herpes (simplex) (*see also* Herpes, simplex)
　　　054.9
　　congenital 771.2
　　zoster (*see also* Herpes, zoster) 053.9
　　　eye NEC 053.29
　Heterophyes heterophyes 121.6
　Histoplasma (*see also* Histoplasmosis) 115.90
　　capsulatum (*see also* Histoplasmosis,
　　　American) 115.00
　　duboisii (*see also* Histoplasmosis, African)
　　　115.10

Infection, infected, infective—*continued*
  HIV V08
    with symptoms, symptomatic 042
  hookworm (*see also* Ancylostomiasis) 126.9
  human immunodeficiency virus V08
    with symptoms, symptomatic 042
  human papillomavirus 079.4
  hydrocele 603.1
  hydronephrosis 591
  Hymenolepis 123.6
  hypopharynx 478.29
  inguinal glands 683
    due to soft chancre 099.0
  intestine, intestinal (*see also* Enteritis, due to, by
    organism) 009.0
  intrauterine (*see also* Endometritis) 615.9
    complicating delivery 646.6
  isospora belli or hominis 007.2
  Japanese B encephalitis 062.0
  jaw (bone) (acute) (chronic) (lower) (subacute)
    (upper) 526.4
  joint—*see* Arthritis, infectious or infective
  kidney (cortex) (hematogenous) 590.9
    with
      abortion—*see* Abortion, by type, with
        urinary tract infection
      calculus 592.0
      ectopic pregnancy (*see also* categories
        633.0-633.9) 639.8
      molar pregnancy (*see also* categories
        630-632) 639.8
    complicating pregnancy or puerperium 646.6
      affecting fetus or newborn 760.1
    following
      abortion 639.8
      ectopic or molar pregnancy 639.8
    pelvis and ureter 590.3
  Klebsiella pneumoniae NEC 041.3
  knee (skin) NEC 686.9
    joint—*see* Arthritis, infectious
  Koch's (*see also* Tuberculosis, pulmonary)
    011.9
  labia (majora) (minora) (*see also* Vulvitis)
    616.10
  lacrimal
    gland (*see also* Dacryoadenitis) 375.00
    passages (duct) (sac) (*see also* Dacryocystitis)
      375.30
  larynx NEC 478.79
  leg (skin) NEC 686.9
  Leishmania (*see also* Leishmaniasis) 085.9
    braziliensis 085.5
    donovani 085.0
    Ethiopica 085.3
    furunculosa 085.1
    infantum 085.0
    mexicana 085.4
    tropica (minor) 085.1
      major 085.2
  Leptosphaeria senegalensis 117.4
  leptospira (*see also* Leptospirosis) 100.9
    Australis 100.89
    Bataviae 100.89
    pyrogenes 100.89
    specified type NEC 100.89
  leptospirochetal NEC (*see also* Leptospirosis)
    100.9
  Leptothrix—*see* Actinomycosis
  Listeria monocytogenes (listeriosis) 027.0
    congenital 771.2
  liver fluke—*see* Infestation, fluke, liver

Infection, infected, infective—*continued*
  Loa loa 125.2
    eyelid 125.2 *[373.6]*
  Loboa loboi 116.2
  local, skin (staphylococcal) (streptococcal) NEC
    686.9
    abscess—*see* Abscess, by site
    cellulitis—*see* Cellulitis, by site
    ulcer (*see also* Ulcer, skin) 707.9
  Loefflerella
    mallei 024
    whitmori 025
  lung 518.89
    atypical Mycobacterium 031.0
      tuberculous (*see also* Tuberculosis,
        pulmonary) 011.9
    basilar 518.89
    chronic 518.89
    fungus NEC 117.9
    spirochetal 104.8
    virus—*see* Pneumonia, virus
  lymph gland (axillary) (cervical) (inguinal) 683
    mesenteric 289.2
  lymphoid tissue, base of tongue or posterior
    pharynx, NEC 474.00
  madurella
    grisea 117.4
    mycetomii 117.4
  major
    with
      abortion—*see* Abortion, by type, with sepsis
      ectopic pregnancy (*see also* categories
        633.0-633.9) 639.0
      molar pregnancy (*see also* categories
        630-632) 639.0
    following
      abortion 639.0
      ectopic or molar pregnancy 639.0
    puerperal, postpartum, childbirth 670
  malarial—*see* Malaria
  Malassezia furfur 111.0
  Malleomyces
    mallei 024
    pseudomallei 025
  mammary gland 611.0
    puerperal, postpartum 675.2
  Mansonella (ozzardi) 125.5
  mastoid (suppurative)—*see* Mastoiditis
  maxilla, maxillary 526.4
    sinus (chronic) (*see also* Sinusitis, maxillary)
      473.0
  mediastinum 519.2
  medina 125.7
  meibomian
    cyst 373.12
    gland 373.12
  melioidosis 025
  meninges (*see also* Meningitis) 320.9
  meningococcal (*see also* condition) 036.9
    brain 036.1
    cerebrospinal 036.0
    endocardium 036.42
    generalized 036.2
    meninges 036.0
    meningococcemia 036.2
    specified site NEC 036.89
  mesenteric lymph nodes or glands NEC 289.2
  Metagonimus 121.5
  metatarsophalangeal 711.97
  microorganism resistant to drugs—*see*
    Resistance (to), drugs by microorganisms

Infection, infected, infective—*continued*
  Microsporidia 136.8
  microsporum, microsporic—*see*
    Dermatophytosis
  Mima polymorpha NEC 041.85
  mixed flora NEC 041.89
  Monilia (*see also* Candidiasis) 112.9
    neonatal 771.7
  Monosporium apiospermum 117.6
  mouth (focus) NEC 528.9
    parasitic 112.0
  Mucor 117.7
  muscle NEC 728.89
  mycelium NEC 117.9
  mycetoma
    actinomycotic NEC (*see also* Actinomycosis)
      039.9
    mycotic NEC 117.4
  Mycobacterium, mycobacterial (*see also*
    Mycobacterium) 031.9
  mycoplasma NEC 041.81
  mycotic NEC 117.9
    pathogenic to compromised host only 118
    skin NEC 111.9
    systemic 117.9
  myocardium NEC 422.90
  nail (chronic) (with lymphangitis) 681.9
    finger 681.02
      fungus 110.1
    ingrowing 703.0
    toe 681.11
      fungus 110.1
  nasal sinus (chronic) (*see also* Sinusitis) 473.9
  nasopharynx (chronic) 478.29
    acute 460
  navel 686.9
    newborn 771.4
  Neisserian—*see* Gonococcus
  Neotestudina rosatii 117.4
  newborn, generalized 771.8
  nipple 611.0
    puerperal, postpartum 675.0
      with breast 675.9
        specified type NEC 675.8
  Nocardia—*see* Actinomycosis
  nose 478.1
  nostril 478.1
  obstetrical surgical wound 674.3
  Oesophagostomum (apiostomum) 127.7
  Oestrus ovis 134.0
  Oidium albicans (*see also* Candidiasis) 112.9
  Onchocerca (volvulus) 125.3
    eye 125.3 *[360.13]*
    eyelid 125.3 *[373.6]*
  operation wound 998.59
  Opisthorchis (felineus) (tenuicollis) (viverrini)
    121.0
  orbit 376.00
    chronic 376.10
  ovary (*see also* Salpingo-oophoritis) 614.2
  Oxyuris vermicularis 127.4
  pancreas 577.0
  Paracoccidioides brasiliensis 116.1
  Paragonimus (westermani) 121.2
  parainfluenza virus 079.89
  parameningococcus NEC 036.9
    with meningitis 036.0
  parasitic NEC 136.9
  paratyphoid 002.9
    Type A 002.1
    Type B 002.2

Infection, infected, infective—*continued*
    Type C 002.3
  paraurethral ducts 597.89
  parotid gland 527.2
  Pasteurella NEC 027.2
    multocida (cat-bite) (dog-bite) 027.2
    pestis (*see also* Plague) 020.9
    pseudotuberculosis 027.2
    septica (cat-bite) (dog-bite) 027.2
    tularensis (*see also* Tularemia) 021.9
  pelvic, female (*see also* Disease, pelvis,
    inflammatory) 614.9
  penis (glans) (retention) NEC 607.2
    herpetic 054.13
  Peptococcus 041.84
  Peptostreptococcus 041.84
  periapical (pulpal origin) 522.4
  peridental 523.3
  perineal wound (obstetrical) 674.3
  periodontal 523.3
  periorbital 376.00
    chronic 376.10
  perirectal 569.49
  perirenal (*see also* Infection, kidney) 590.9
  peritoneal (*see also* Peritonitis) 567.9
  periureteral 593.89
  periurethral 597.89
  Petriellidium boydii 117.6
  pharynx 478.29
    Coxsackie virus 074.0
    phlegmonous 462
    posterior, lymphoid 474.00
  Phialophora
    gougerotii 117.8
    jeanselmei 117.8
    verrucosa 117.2
  Piedraia hortai 111.3
  pinna, acute 380.11
  pinta 103.9
    intermediate 103.1
    late 103.2
    mixed 103.3
    primary 103.0
  pinworm 127.4
  pityrosporum furfur 111.0
  pleuropneumonia-like organisms NEC (PPLO)
    041.81
  pneumococcal NEC 041.2
    generalized (purulent) 038.2
  Pneumococcus NEC 041.2
  postoperative wound 998.59
  posttraumatic NEC 958.3
  postvaccinal 999.3
  prepuce NEC 607.1
  Propionibacterium 041.84
  prostate (capsule) (*see also* Prostatitis) 601.9
  Proteus (mirabilis) (morganii) (vulgaris) NEC
    041.6
    enteritis 008.3
  protozoal NEC 136.8
    intestinal NEC 007.9
  Pseudomonas NEC 041.7
    mallei 024
    pneumonia 482.1
    pseudomallei 025
  psittacosis 073.9
  puerperal, postpartum (major) 670
    minor 646.6
  pulmonary—*see* Infection, lung
  purulent—*see* Abscess
  putrid, generalized—*see* Septicemia

Infection, infected, infective—*continued*
  morsus muris 026.0
  obermeieri 087.0
  spirochetal NEC 104.9
    lung 104.8
    specified nature or site NEC 104.8
  spleen 289.59
  Sporothrix schenckii 117.1
  Sporotrichum (schenckii) 117.1
  Sporozoa 136.8
  staphylococcal NEC 041.10
    aureus 041.11
    food poisoning 005.0
    generalized (purulent) 038.10
      aureus 038.11
      specified organism NEC 038.19
    pneumonia 482.40
      aureus 482.41
      specified type NEC 482.49
    septicemia 038.10
      aureus 038.11
      specified organism NEC 038.19
    specified NEC 041.19
  steatoma 706.2
  Stellantchasmus falcatus 121.6
  Streptobacillus moniliformis 026.1
  streptococcal NEC 041.00
    congenital 771.8
    generalized (purulent) 038.0
    group
      A 041.01
      B 041.02
      C 041.03
      D [enterococcus] 041.04
      G 041.05
    pneumonia—*see* Pneumonia, streptococcal
      482.3
    septicemia 038.0
    sore throat 034.0
    specified NEC 041.09
  Streptomyces—*see* Actinomycosis
  streptotrichosis—*see* Actinomycosis
  Strongyloides (stercoralis) 127.2
  stump (amputation) (posttraumatic) (surgical)
    997.62
    traumatic—*see* Amputation, traumatic, by
      site, complicated
  subcutaneous tissue, local NEC 686.9
  submaxillary region 528.9
  suipestifer (*see also* Infection, Salmonella) 003.9
  swimming pool bacillus 031.1
  syphilitic—*see* Syphilis
  systemic—*see* Septicemia
  Taenia—*see* Infestation, Taenia
  Taeniarhynchus saginatus 123.2
  tapeworm—*see* Infestation, tapeworm
  tendon (sheath) 727.89
  Ternidens diminutus 127.7
  testis (*see also* Orchitis) 604.90
  thigh (skin) 686.9
  threadworm 127.4
  throat 478.29
    pneumococcal 462
    staphylococcal 462
    streptococcal 034.0
    viral NEC (*see also* Pharyngitis) 462
  thumb (skin) 686.9
    abscess (with lymphangitis) 681.00
      pulp 681.01
    cellulitis (with lymphangitis) 681.00
    nail 681.02

Infection, infected, infective—*continued*
  thyroglossal duct 529.8
  toe (skin) 686.9
    abscess (with lymphangitis) 681.10
    cellulitis (with lymphangitis) 681.10
    nail 681.11
      fungus 110.1
  tongue NEC 529.0
    parasitic 112.0
  tonsil (faucial) (lingual) (pharyngeal) 474.00
    acute or subacute 463
    and adenoid 474.02
    tag 474.00
  tooth, teeth 522.4
    periapical (pulpal origin) 522.4
    peridental 523.3
    periodontal 523.3
    pulp 522.0
    socket 526.5
  Torula histolytica 117.5
  Toxocara (cani) (cati) (felis) 128.0
  Toxoplasma gondii (*see also* Toxoplasmosis)
    130.9
  trachea, chronic 491.8
    fungus 117.9
  traumatic NEC 958.3
  trematode NEC 121.9
  trench fever 083.1
  Treponema
    denticola 041.84
    macrodenticum 041.84
    pallidum (*see also* Syphilis) 097.9
  Trichinella (spiralis) 124
  Trichomonas 131.9
    bladder 131.09
    cervix 131.09
    hominis 007.3
    intestine 007.3
    prostate 131.03
    specified site NEC 131.8
    urethra 131.02
    urogenitalis 131.00
    vagina 131.01
    vulva 131.01
  Trichophyton, trichophytid—*see*
    Dermatophytosis
  Trichosporon (beigelii) cutaneum 111.2
  Trichostrongylus 127.6
  Trichuris (trichiuria) 127.3
  Trombicula (irritans) 133.8
  Trypanosoma (*see also* Trypanosomiasis) 086.9
    cruzi 086.2
  tubal (*see also* Salpingo-oophoritis) 614.2
  tuberculous NEC (*see also* Tuberculosis) 011.9
  tubo-ovarian (*see also* Salpingo-oophoritis)
    614.2
  tunica vaginalis 608.4
  tympanic membrane—*see* Myringitis
  typhoid (abortive) (ambulant) (bacillus) 002.0
  typhus 081.9
    flea-borne (endemic) 081.0
    louse-borne (epidemic) 080
    mite-borne 081.2
    recrudescent 081.1
    tick-borne 082.9
      African 082.1
      North Asian 082.2
  umbilicus (septic) 686.9
    newborn NEC 771.4
  ureter 593.89
  urethra (*see also* Urethritis) 597.80

Infestation—*continued*
  Toxocara (cani) (cati) (felis) 128.0
  trematode(s) NEC 121.9
  Trichina spiralis 124
  Trichinella spiralis 124
  Trichocephalus 127.3
  Trichomonas 131.9
    bladder 131.09
    cervix 131.09
    intestine 007.3
    prostate 131.03
    specified site NEC 131.8
    urethra (female) (male) 131.02
    urogenital 131.00
    vagina 131.01
    vulva 131.01
  Trichophyton—*see* Dermatophytosis
  Trichostrongylus instabilis 127.6
  Trichuris (trichiuria) 127.3
  Trombicula (irritans) 133.8
  Trypanosoma—*see* Trypanosomiasis
  Tunga penetrans 134.1
  Uncinaria americana 126.1
  whipworm 127.3
  worms NEC 128.9
    intestinal 127.9
  Wuchereria 125.0
    bancrofti 125.0
    malayi 125.1
Infiltrate, infiltration
  with an iron compound 275.0
  amyloid (any site) (generalized) 277.3
  calcareous (muscle) NEC 275.49
    localized—*see* Degeneration, by site
  calcium salt (muscle) 275.49
  corneal (*see also* Edema, cornea) 371.20
  eyelid 373.9
  fatty (diffuse) (generalized) 272.8
    localized—*see* Degeneration, by site, fatty
  glycogen, glycogenic (*see also* Disease,
      glycogen storage) 271.10
  heart, cardiac
    fatty (*see also* Degeneration, myocardial)
      429.1
    glycogenic 271.0 *[425.7]*
  inflammatory in vitreous 379.29
  kidney (*see also* Disease, renal) 593.9
  leukemic (M9800/3)—*see* Leukemia
  liver 573.8
    fatty—*see* Fatty, liver
    glycogen (*see also* Disease, glycogen storage)
      271.0
  lung (*see also* Infiltrate, pulmonary) 518.3
    eosinophilic 518.3
    x-ray finding only 793.1
  lymphatic (*see also* Leukemia, lymphatic) 204.9
    gland, pigmentary 289.3
  muscle, fatty 728.9
  myelogenous (*see also* Leukemia, myeloid)
      205.9
  myocardium, myocardial
    fatty (*see also* Degeneration, myocardial)
      429.1
    glycogenic 271.0 *[425.7]*
  pulmonary 518.3
    with
      eosinophilia 518.3
      pneumonia—*see* Pneumonia, by type
    x-ray finding only 793.1
  Ranke's primary (*see also* Tuberculosis) 010.0
  skin, lymphocyctic (benign) 709.8

Infiltrate, infiltration—*continued*
  thymus (gland) (fatty) 254.8
  urine 788.8
  vitreous humor 379.29
Infirmity 799.8
  senile 797
Inflammation, inflamed, inflammatory (with
    exudation)
  abducens (nerve) 378.54
  accessory sinus (chronic) (*see also* Sinusitis)
    473.9
  adrenal (gland) 255.8
  alimentary canal—*see* Enteritis
  alveoli (teeth) 526.5
    scorbutic 267
  amnion—*see* Amnionitis
  anal canal 569.49
  antrum (chronic) (*see also* Sinusitis, maxillary)
    473.0
  anus 569.49
  appendix (*see also* Appendicitis) 541
  arachnoid—*see* Meningitis
  areola 611.0
    puerperal, postpartum 675.0
  areolar tissue NEC 686.9
  artery—*see* Arteritis
  auditory meatus (external) (*see also* Otitis,
    externa) 380.10
  Bartholin's gland 616.8
  bile duct or passage 576.1
  bladder (*see also* Cystitis) 595.9
  bone—*see* Osteomyelitis
  bowel (*see also* Enteritis) 558.9
  brain (*see also* Encephalitis) 323.9
    late effect—*see* category 326
    membrane—*see* Meningitis
  breast 611.0
    puerperal, postpartum 675.2
  broad ligament (*see also* Disease, pelvis,
      inflammatory) 614.4
    acute 614.3
  bronchus—*see* Bronchitis
  bursa—*see* Bursitis
  capsule
    liver 573.3
    spleen 289.59
  catarrhal (*see also* Catarrh) 460
    vagina 616.10
  cecum (*see also* Appendicitis) 541
  cerebral (*see also* Encephalitis) 323.9
    late effect—*see* category 326
    membrane—*see* Meningitis
  cerebrospinal (*see also* Meningitis) 322.9
    late effect—*see* category 326
    meningococcal 036.0
    tuberculous (*see also* Tuberculosis) 013.6
  cervix (uteri) (*see also* Cervicitis) 616.0
  chest 519.9
  choroid NEC (*see also* Choroiditis) 363.20
  cicatrix (tissue)—*see* Cicatrix
  colon (*see also* Enteritis) 558.9
    granulomatous 555.1
    newborn 558.9
  connective tissue (diffuse) NEC 728.9
  cornea (*see also* Keratitis) 370.9
    with ulcer (*see also* Ulcer, cornea) 370.00
  corpora cavernosa (penis) 607.2
  cranial nerve—*see* Disorder, nerve, cranial
  diarrhea—*see* Diarrhea

Inflammation, inflamed, inflammatory—*cont.*
  disc (intervertebral) (space) 722.90
    cervical, cervicothoracic 722.91
    lumbar, lumbosacral 722.93
    thoracic, thoracolumbar 722.93
  Douglas' cul-de-sac or pouch (chronic) (*see also* Disease, pelvis, inflammatory) 614.4
    acute 614.3
  due to (presence of) any device, implant, or graft classifiable to 996.0-996.5—*see* Complications, infection and inflammation, due to (presence of) any device, implant, or graft classified to 996.0-996.5 NEC
  duodenum 535.6
  dura mater—*see* Meningitis
  ear—*see also* Otitis
    external (*see also* Otitis, externa) 380.10
    inner (*see also* Labyrinthitis) 386.30
    middle—*see* Otitis media
  esophagus 530.10
  ethmoidal (chronic) (sinus) (*see also* Sinusitis, ethmoidal) 473.2
  Eustachian tube (catarrhal) 381.50
    acute 381.51
    chronic 381.52
  extrarectal 569.49
  eye 379.99
  eyelid 373.9
    specified NEC 373.8
  fallopian tube (*see also* Salpingo-oophoritis) 614.2
  fascia 728.9
  fetal membranes (acute) 658.4
    affecting fetus or newborn 762.7
  follicular, pharynx 472.1
  frontal (chronic) (sinus) (*see also* Sinusitis, frontal) 473.1
  gallbladder (*see also* Cholecystitis, acute) 575.0
  gall duct (*see also* Cholecystitis) 575.10
  gastrointestinal (*see also* Enteritis) 558.9
  genital organ (diffuse) (internal)
    female 614.9
      with
        abortion—*see* Abortion, by type, with sepsis
        ectopic pregnancy (*see also* categories 633.0-633.9) 639.0
        molar pregnancy (*see also* categories 630-632) 639.0
      complicating pregnancy, childbirth, or puerperium 646.6
        affecting fetus or newborn 760.8
      following
        abortion 639.0
        ectopic or molar pregnancy 639.0
    male 608.4
  gland (lymph) (*see also* Lymphadenitis) 289.3
  glottis (*see also* Laryngitis) 464.0
  granular, pharynx 472.1
  gum 523.1
  heart (*see also* Carditis) 429.89
  hepatic duct 576.8
  hernial sac—*see* Hernia, by site
  ileum (*see also* Enteritis) 558.9
    terminal or regional 555.0
      with large intestine 555.2
  intervertebral disc 722.90
    cervical, cervicothoracic 722.91
    lumbar, lumbosacral 722.93
    thoracic, thoracolumbar 722.92
  intestine (*see also* Enteritis) 558.9

Inflammation, inflamed, inflammatory—*cont.*
  jaw (acute) (bone) (chronic) (lower) (suppurative) (upper) 526.4
  jejunum—*see* Enteritis
  joint NEC (*see also* Arthritis) 716.9
    sacroiliac 720.2
  kidney (*see also* Nephritis) 583.9
  knee (joint) 716.66
    tuberculous (active) (*see also* Tuberculosis) 015.2
  labium (majus) (minus) (*see also* Vulvitis) 616.10
  lacrimal
    gland (*see also* Dacryoadenitis) 375.00
    passages (duct) (sac) (*see also* Dacryocystitis) 375.30
  larynx (*see also* Laryngitis) 464.0
    diphtheritic 032.3
  leg NEC 686.9
  lip 528.5
  liver (capsule) (*see also* Hepatitis) 573.3
    acute 570
    chronic 571.40
    suppurative 572.0
  lung (acute) (*see also* Pneumonia) 486
    chronic (interstitial) 518.89
  lymphatic vessel (*see also* Lymphangitis) 457.2
  lymph node or gland (*see also* Lymphadenitis) 289.3
  mammary gland 611.0
    puerperal, postpartum 675.2
  maxilla, maxillary 526.4
    sinus (chronic) (*see also* Sinusitis, maxillary) 473.0
  membranes of brain or spinal cord—*see* Meningitis
  meninges—*see* Meningitis
  mouth 528.0
  muscle 728.9
  myocardium (*see also* Myocarditis) 429.0
  nasal sinus (chronic) (*see also* Sinusitis) 473.9
  nasopharynx—*see* Nasopharyngitis
  navel 686.9
    newborn NEC 771.4
  nerve NEC 729.2
  nipple 611.0
    puerperal, postpartum 675.0
  nose 478.1
    suppurative 472.0
  oculomotor nerve 378.51
  optic nerve 377.30
  orbit (chronic) 376.10
    acute 376.00
    chronic 376.10
  ovary (*see also* Salpingo-oophoritis) 614.2
  oviduct (*see also* Salpingo-oophoritis) 614.2
  pancreas—*see* Pancreatitis
  parametrium (chronic) (*see also* Disease, pelvis, inflammatory) 614.4
    acute 614.3
  parotid region 686.9
    gland 527.2
  pelvis, female (*see also* Disease, pelvis, inflammatory) 614.9
  penis (corpora cavernosa) 607.2
  perianal 569.49
  pericardium (*see also* Pericarditis) 423.9
  perineum (female) (male) 686.9
  perirectal 569.49
  peritoneum (*see also* Peritonitis) 567.9

Inflammation, inflamed, inflammatory—*cont.*
  periuterine (*see also* Disease, pelvis, inflammatory) 614.9
  perivesical (*see also* Cystitis) 595.9
  petrous bone (*see also* Petrositis) 383.20
  pharynx (*see also* Pharyngitis) 462
    follicular 472.1
    granular 472.1
  pia mater—*see* Meningitis
  pleura—*see* Pleurisy
  postmastoidectomy cavity 383.30
    chronic 383.33
  prostate (*see also* Prostatitis) 601.9
  rectosigmoid—*see* Rectosigmoiditis
  rectum (*see also* Proctitis) 569.49
  respiratory, upper (*see also* Infection, respiratory, upper) 465.9
    chronic, due to external agent—*see* Condition, respiratory, chronic, due to, external agent
    due to
      fumes or vapors (chemical) (inhalation) 506.2
      radiation 508.1
  retina (*see also* Retinitis) 363.20
  retrocecal (*see also* Appendicitis) 541
  retroperitoneal (*see also* Peritonitis) 567.9
  salivary duct or gland (any) (suppurative) 527.2
  scorbutic, alveoli, teeth 267
  scrotum 608.4
  sigmoid—*see* Enteritis
  sinus (*see also* Sinusitis) 473.9
  Skene's duct or gland (*see also* Urethritis) 597.89
  skin 686.9
  spermatic cord 608.4
  sphenoidal (sinus) (*see also* Sinusitis, sphenoidal) 473.3
  spinal
    cord (*see also* Encephalitis) 323.9
      late effect—*see* category 326
    membrane—*see* Meningitis
    nerve—*see* Disorder, nerve
  spine (*see also* Spondylitis) 720.9
  spleen (capsule) 289.59
  stomach—*see* Gastritis
  stricture, rectum 569.49
  subcutaneous tissue NEC 686.9
  suprarenal (gland) 255.8
  synovial (fringe) (membrane)—*see* Bursitis
  tendon (sheath) NEC 726.90
  testis (*see also* Orchitis) 604.90
  thigh 686.9
  throat (*see also* Sore throat) 462
  thymus (gland) 254.8
  thyroid (gland) (*see also* Thyroiditis) 245.9
  tongue 529.0
  tonsil—*see* Tonsillitis
  trachea—*see* Tracheitis
  trochlear nerve 378.53
  tubal (*see also* Salpingo-oophoritis) 614.2
  tuberculous NEC (*see also* Tuberculosis) 011.9
  tubo-ovarian (*see also* Salpingo-oophoritis) 614.2
  tunica vaginalis 608.4
  tympanic membrane—*see* Myringitis
  umbilicus, umbilical 686.9
    newborn NEC 771.4
  uterine ligament (*see also* Disease, pelvis, inflammatory) 614.4
    acute 614.3

Inflammation, inflamed, inflammatory—*cont.*
  uterus (catarrhal) (*see also* Endometritis) 615.9
  uveal tract (anterior) (*see also* Iridocyclitis) 364.3
    posterior—*see* Chorioretinitis
    sympathetic 360.11
  vagina (*see also* Vaginitis) 616.10
  vas deferens 608.4
  vein (*see also* Phlebitis) 451.9
    thrombotic 451.9
      cerebral (*see also* Thrombosis, brain) 434.0
      leg 451.2
        deep (vessels) NEC 451.19
        superficial (vessels) 451.0
      lower extremity 451.2
        deep (vessels) NEC 451.19
        superficial (vessels) 451.0
  vocal cord 478.5
  vulva (*see also* Vulvitis) 616.10
Inflation, lung imperfect (newborn) 770.5
Influenza, influenzal 487.1
  with
    bronchitis 487.1
    bronchopneumonia 487.0
    cold (any type) 487.1
    digestive manifestations 487.8
    hemoptysis 487.1
    involvement of
      gastrointestinal tract 487.8
      nervous system 487.8
    laryngitis 487.1
    manifestations NEC 487.8
      respiratory 487.1
        pneumonia 487.0
    pharyngitis 487.1
    pneumonia (any form classifiable to 480-483, 485-486) 487.0
    respiratory manifestations NEC 487.1
    sinusitis 487.1
    sore throat 487.1
    tonsillitis 487.1
    tracheitis 487.1
    upper respiratory infection (acute) 487.1
  abdominal 487.8
  Asian 487.1
  bronchial 487.1
  bronchopneumonia 487.0
  catarrhal 487.1
  epidemic 487.1
  gastric 487.8
  intestinal 487.8
  laryngitis 487.1
  maternal affecting fetus or newborn 760.2
    manifest influenza in infant 771.2
  pharyngitis 487.1
  pneumonia (any form) 487.0
  respiratory (upper) 487.1
  stomach 487.8
  vaccination, prophylactic (against) V04.8
Influenza-like disease 487.1
Infraction, Freiberg's (metatarsal head) 732.5
Infusion complication, misadventure or reaction —*see* Complication, infusion
Ingestion
  chemical—*see* Table of drugs and chemicals
  drug or medicinal substance
    overdose or wrong substance given or taken 977.9
      specified drug—*see* Table of drugs and chemicals
  foreign body NEC (*see also* Foreign body) 938

Ingrowing
hair 704.8
nail (finger) (toe) (infected) 703.0
Inguinal —*see also* condition
testis 752.51
Inhalation
carbon monoxide 986
flame
mouth 947.0
lung 947.1
food or foreign body (*see also* Asphyxia, food
or foreign body) 933.1
gas, fumes, or vapor (noxious) 987.9
specified agent—*see* Table of drugs and
chemicals
liquid or vomitus (*see also* Asphyxia, food or
foreign body) 933.1
lower respiratory tract NEC 934.9
meconium (fetus or newborn) 770.1
mucus (*see also* Asphyxia, mucus) 933.1
oil (causing suffocation) (*see also* Asphyxia,
food or foreign body) 933.1
pneumonia—*see* Pneumonia, aspiration
smoke 987.9
steam 987.9
stomach contents or secretions (*see also*
Asphyxia, food or foreign body) 933.1
in labor and deliver 668.0
Inhibition, inhibited
academic as adjustment reaction 309.23
orgasm
female 302.73
male 302.74
sexual
desire 302.71
excitement 302.72
work as adjustment reaction 309.23
Inhibitor, systemic lupus erythematosus
(presence of) 286.5
Iniencephalus, iniencephaly 740.2
Injected eye 372.74
Injury 959.9

---

*Note—For abrasion, insect bite (nonvenomous),
blister, or scratch, see Injury, superficial. For
laceration, traumatic rupture, tear, or
penetrating wound of internal organs, such as
heart, lung, liver, kidney, pelvic organs,
whether or not accompanied by open wound in
the same region, see Injury, internal. For nerve
injury, see Injury, nerve. For late effect of
injuries classifiable to 850-854, 860-869,
900-919, 950-959, see Late, effect, injury, by
type.*

---

abdomen, abdominal (viscera)—*see also* Injury,
internal, abdomen
muscle or wall 959.1
acoustic, resulting in deafness 951.5
adenoid 959.09
adrenal (gland)—*see* Injury, internal, adrenal
alveolar (process) 959.09
ankle (and foot) (and knee) (and leg, except
thigh) 959.7
anterior chamber, eye 921.3
anus 959.1
aorta (thoracic) 901.0
abdominal 902.0
appendix—*see* Injury, internal, appendix
arm, upper (and shoulder) 959.2
artery (complicating trauma) (*see also* Injury,
blood vessel, by site) 904.9

Injury—*continued*
cerebral or meningeal (*see also* Hemorrhage,
brain, traumatic, subarachnoid) 852.0
auditory canal (external) (meatus) 959.09
auricle, auris, ear 959.09
axilla 959.2
back 959.1
bile duct—*see* Injury, internal, bile duct
birth—*see also* Birth, injury
canal NEC, complicating delivery 665.9
bladder (sphincter)—*see* Injury, internal, bladder
blast (air) (hydraulic) (immersion) (underwater)
NEC 869.0
with open wound into cavity NEC 869.1
abdomen or thorax—*see* Injury, internal, by
site
brain—*see* Concussion, brain
ear (acoustic nerve trauma) 951.5
with perforation of tympanic
membrane—*see* Wound, open, ear, drum
blood vessel NEC 904.9
abdomen 902.9
multiple 902.87
specified NEC 902.89
aorta (thoracic) 901.0
abdominal 902.0
arm NEC 903.9
axillary 903.00
artery 903.01
vein 903.02
azygos vein 901.89
basilic vein 903.1
brachial (artery) (vein) 903.1
bronchial 901.89
carotid artery 900.00
common 900.01
external 900.02
internal 900.03
celiac artery 902.20
specified branch NEC 902.24
cephalic vein (arm) 903.1
colica dextra 902.26
cystic
artery 902.24
vein 902.39
deep plantar 904.6
digital (artery) (vein) 903.5
due to accidental puncture or laceration during
procedure 998.2
extremity
lower 904.8
multiple 904.7
specified NEC 904.7
upper 903.9
multiple 903.8
specified NEC 903.8
femoral
artery (superficial) 904.1
above profunda origin 904.0
common 904.0
vein 904.2
gastric
artery 902.21
vein 902.39
head 900.9
intracranial—*see* Injury, intracranial
multiple 900.82
specified NEC 900.89
hemiazygos vein 901.89
hepatic
artery 902.22

Injury—*continued*
  diaphragm—*see* Injury, internal, diaphragm
  duodenum—*see* Injury, internal, duodenum
  ear (auricle) (canal) (drum) (external) 959.09
  elbow (and forearm) (and wrist) 959.3
  epididymis 959.1
  epigastric region 959.1
  epiglottis 959.09
  epiphyseal, current—*see* Fracture, by site
  esophagus—*see* Injury, internal, esophagus
  Eustachian tube 959.09
  extremity (lower) (upper) NEC 959.8
  eye 921.9
    penetrating eyeball—*see* Injury, eyeball,
        penetrating
    superficial 918.9
  eyeball 921.3
    penetrating 871.7
      with
        partial loss (of intraocular tissue) 871.12
        prolapse or exposure (of intraocular
            tissue) 871.1
      without prolapse 871.0
      foreign body (nonmagnetic) 871.6
        magnetic 871.5
    superficial 918.9
  eyebrow 959.09
  eyelid(s) 921.1
    laceration—*see* Laceration, eyelid
    superficial 918.0
  face (and neck) 959.09
  fallopian tube—*see* Injury, internal, fallopian
      tube
  finger(s) (nail) 959.5
  flank 959.1
  foot (and ankle) (and knee) (and leg except
      thigh) 959.7
  forceps NEC 767.9
    scalp 767.1
  forearm (and elbow) (and wrist) 959.3
  forehead 959.09
  gallbladder—*see* Injury, internal, gallbladder
  gasserian ganglion 951.2
  gastrointestinal tract—*see* Injury, internal,
      gastrointestinal tract
  genital organ(s)
    with
      abortion—*see* Abortion, by type, with,
          damage to pelvic organs
      ectopic pregnancy (*see also* categories
          633.0-633.9) 639.2
      molar pregnancy (*see also* categories
          630-632) 639.2
    external 959.1
    following
      abortion 639.2
      ectopic or molar pregnancy 639.2
    internal—*see* Injury, internal, genital organs
    obstetrical trauma NEC 665.9
      affecting fetus or newborn 763.89
  gland
    lacrimal 921.1
      laceration 870.8
    parathyroid 959.09
    salivary 959.09
    thyroid 959.09
  globe (eye) (*see also* Injury, eyeball) 921.3
  grease gun—*see* Wound, open, by site,
      complicated
  groin 959.1

Injury—*continued*
  gum 959.09
  hand(s) (except fingers) 959.4
  head NEC 959.01
    with
      skull fracture—*see* Fracture, skull, by site
  heart—*see* Injury, internal, heart
  heel 959.7
  hip (and thigh) 959.6
  hymen 959.1
  hyperextension (cervical) (vertebra) 847.0
  ileum—*see* Injury, internal, ileum
  iliac region 959.1
  infrared rays NEC 990
  instrumental (during surgery) 998.2
    birth injury—*see* Birth, injury
    nonsurgical (*see also* Injury, by site) 959.9
    obstetrical 665.9
      affecting fetus or newborn 763.89
      bladder 665.5
      cervix 665.3
      high vaginal 665.4
      perineal NEC 664.9
      urethra 665.5
      uterus 665.5
  internal 869.0

---

*Note—For injury of internal organ(s) by foreign
body entering through a natural orifice (e.g.,
inhaled, ingested, or swallowed)—see Foreign
body, entering through orifice.*

*For internal injury of any of the following sites
with internal injury of any other of the sites—
see Injury, internal, multiple.*

---

    with
      fracture
        pelvis—*see* Fracture, pelvis
        specified site, except pelvis—*see* Injury,
            internal, by site
      open wound into cavity 869.1
    abdomen, abdominal (viscera) NEC 868.00
      with
        fracture, pelvis—*see* Fracture, pelvis
        open wound into cavity 868.10
      specified site NEC 868.09
        with open wound into cavity 868.19
    adrenal (gland) 868.01
      with open wound into cavity 868.11
    aorta (thoracic) 901.0
      abdominal 902.0
    appendix 863.85
      with open wound into cavity 863.95
    bile duct 868.02
      with open wound into cavity 868.12
    bladder (sphincter) 867.0
      with
        abortion—*see* Abortion, by type, with,
            damage to pelvic organs
        ectopic pregnancy (*see also* categories
            633.0-633.9) 639.2
        molar pregnancy (*see also* categories
            630-632) 639.2
        open wound into cavity 867.1
      following
        abortion 639.2
        ectopic or molar pregnancy 639.2
      obstetrical trauma 665.5
        affecting fetus or newborn 763.89
    blood vessel—*see* Injury, blood vessel, by site

Injury—*continued*
  broad ligament 867.6
    with open wound into cavity 867.7
  bronchus, bronchi 862.21
    with open wound into cavity 862.31
  cecum 863.89
    with open wound into cavity 863.99
  cervix (uteri) 867.4
    with
      abortion—*see* Abortion, by type, with
        damage to pelvic organs
      ectopic pregnancy (*see also* categories
        633.0-633.9) 639.2
      molar pregnancy (*see also* categories
        630-632) 639.2
      open wound into cavity 867.5
    following
      abortion 639.2
      ectopic or molar pregnancy 639.2
    obstetrical trauma 665.3
      affecting fetus or newborn 763.89
  chest (*see also* Injury, internal, intrathoracic
    organs) 862.8
    with open wound into cavity 862.9
  colon 863.40
    with
      open wound into cavity 863.50
        rectum 863.46
          with open wound into cavity 863.56
      ascending (right) 863.41
        with open wound into cavity 863.51
      descending (left) 863.43
        with open wound into cavity 863.53
      multiple sites 863.46
        with open wound into cavity 863.56
      sigmoid 863.44
        with open wound into cavity 863.54
      specified site NEC 863.49
        with open wound into cavity 863.59
      transverse 863.42
        with open wound into cavity 863.52
  common duct 868.02
    with open wound into cavity 868.12
  complicating delivery 665.9
    affecting fetus or newborn 763.89
  diaphragm 862.0
    with open wound into cavity 862.1
  duodenum 863.21
    with open wound into cavity 863.31
  esophagus (intrathoracic) 862.22
    with open wound into cavity 862.32
    cervical region 874.4
      complicated 874.5
  fallopian tube 867.6
    with open wound into cavity 867.7
  gallbladder 868.02
    with open wound into cavity 868.12
  gastrointestinal tract NEC 863.80
    with open wound into cavity 863.90
  genital organ NEC 867.6
    with open wound into cavity 867.7
  heart 861.00
    with open wound into thorax 861.10
  ileum 863.29
    with open wound into cavity 863.39
  intestine NEC 863.89
    with open wound into cavity 863.99
    large NEC 863.40
      with open wound into cavity 863.50
    small NEC 863.20
      with open wound into cavity 863.30

Injury—*continued*
  intra-abdominal (organ) 868.00
    with open wound into cavity 868.10
    multiple sites 868.09
      with open wound into cavity 868.19
    specified site NEC 868.09
      with open wound into cavity 868.19
  intrathoracic organs (multiple) 862.8
    with open wound into cavity 862.9
    diaphragm (only)—*see* Injury, internal,
      diaphragm
    heart (only)—*see* Injury, internal, heart
    lung (only)—*see* Injury, internal, lung
    specified site NEC 862.29
      with open wound into cavity 862.39
  intrauterine (*see also* Injury, internal, uterus)
    867.4
    with open wound into cavity 867.5
  jejunum 863.29
    with open wound into cavity 863.39
  kidney (subcapsular) 866.00
    with
      disruption of parenchyma (complete)
        866.03
        with open wound into cavity 866.13
      hematoma (without rupture of capsule)
        866.01
        with open wound into cavity 866.11
      laceration 866.02
        with open wound into cavity 866.12
      open wound into cavity 866.10
  liver 864.00
    with
      contusion 864.01
        with open wound into cavity 864.11
      hematoma 864.01
        with open wound into cavity 864.11
      laceration 864.05
        with open wound into cavity 864.15
        major (disruption of hepatic
          parenchyma) 864.04
          with open wound into cavity 864.14
        minor (capsule only) 864.02
          with open wound into cavity 864.12
        moderate (involving parenchyma) 864.03
          with open wound into cavity 864.13
        multiple 864.04
        stellate 864.04
          with open wound in cavity 864.14
      open wound into cavity 864.10
  lung 861.20
    with open wound into thorax 861.30
    hemopneumothorax—*see*
      Hemopneumothorax, traumatic
    hemothorax—*see* Hemothorax, traumatic
    pneumohemothorax—*see*
      Pneumohemothorax, traumatic
    pneumothorax—*see* Pneumothorax,
      traumatic
  mediastinum 862.29
    with open wound into cavity 862.39
  mesentery 863.89
    with open wound into cavity 863.99
  mesosalpinx 867.6
    with open wound into cavity 867.7

Injury—*continued*
   multiple 869.0

> *Note—Multiple internal injuries of sites*
> *classifiable to the same three- or four- digit*
> *category should be classified to that category.*
> *Multiple injuries classifiable to different*
> *fourth-digit subdivisions of 861 (heart and lung*
> *injuries) should be dealt with according to*
> *coding rules.*

     with open wound into cavity 869.1
    intra-abdominal organ (sites classifiable to
      863-868)
     with
       intrathoracic organ(s) (sites classifiable
         to 861-862) 869.0
        with open wound into cavity 869.1
       other intra-abdominal organ(s) (sites
         classifiable to 863-868, except
         where classifiable to the same
         three-digit category) 868.09
        with open wound into cavity 868.19
    intrathoracic organ (sites classifiable to
      861-862)
     with
       intra-abdominal organ(s) (sites
         classifiable to 863-868) 869.0
        with open wound into cavity 869.1
       other intrathoracic organ(s) (sites
         classifiable to 861-862, except
         where classifiable to the same
         three-digit category) 862.8
        with open wound into cavity 862.9
   myocardium—*see* Injury, internal, heart
   ovary 867.6
    with open wound into cavity 867.7
   pancreas (multiple sites) 863.84
    with open wound into cavity 863.94
    body 863.82
     with open wound into cavity 863.92
    head 863.81
     with open wound into cavity 863.91
    tail 863.83
     with open wound into cavity 863.93
   pelvis, pelvic (organs) (viscera) 867.8
    with
     fracture, pelvis—*see* Fracture, pelvis
     open wound into cavity 867.9
    specified site NEC 867.6
     with open wound into cavity 867.7
   peritoneum 868.03
    with open wound into cavity 868.13
   pleura 862.29
    with open wound into cavity 862.39
   prostate 867.6
   with open wound into cavity 867.7
   rectum 863.45
    with
     colon 863.46
      with open wound into cavity 863.56
     open wound into cavity 863.55
   retroperitoneum 868.04
    with open wound into cavity 868.14
   round ligament 867.6
    with open wound into cavity 867.7
   seminal vesicle 867.6
    with open wound into cavity 867.7
   spermatic cord 867.6
    with open wound into cavity 867.7
    scrotal—*see* Wound, open, spermatic cord

Injury—*continued*
   spleen 865.00
    with
     disruption of parenchyma (massive)
      865.04
      with open wound into cavity 865.14
     hematoma (without rupture of capsule)
      865.01
      with open wound into cavity 865.11
     open wound into cavity 865.10
     tear, capsular 865.02
      with open wound into cavity 865.12
      extending into parenchyma 865.03
       with open wound into cavity 865.13
   stomach 863.0
    with open wound into cavity 863.1
   suprarenal gland (multiple) 868.01
    with open wound into cavity 868.11
   thorax, thoracic (cavity) (organs) (multiple)
    (*see also* Injury, internal, intrathoracic
    organs) 862.8
    with open wound into cavity 862.9
   thymus (gland) 862.29
    with open wound into cavity 862.39
   trachea (intrathoracic) 862.29
    with open wound into cavity 862.39
    cervical region (*see also* Wound, open,
     trachea) 874.02
   ureter 867.2
    with open wound into cavity 867.3
   urethra (sphincter) 867.0
    with
     abortion—*see* Abortion, by type, with,
      damage to pelvic organs
     ectopic pregnancy (*see also* categories
      633.0-633.9) 639.2
     molar pregnancy (*see also* categories
      630-632) 639.2
     open wound into cavity 867.1
    following
     abortion 639.2
     ectopic or molar pregnancy 639.2
    obstetrical trauma 665.5
     affecting fetus or newborn 763.89
   uterus 867.4
    with
     abortion—*see* Abortion, by type, with,
      damage to pelvic organs
     ectopic pregnancy (*see also* categories
      633.0-633.9) 639.2
     molar pregnancy (*see also* categories
      630-632) 639.2
     open wound into cavity 867.5
    following
     abortion 639.2
     ectopic or molar pregnancy 639.2
    obstetrical trauma NEC 665.5
     affecting fetus or newborn 763.89
   vas deferens 867.6
    with open wound into cavity 867.7
   vesical (sphincter) 867.0
    with open wound into cavity 867.1
   viscera (abdominal) (*see also* Injury, internal,
    multiple) 868.00
    with
     fracture, pelvis—*see* Fracture, pelvis
     open wound into cavity 868.10
    thoracic NEC (*see also* Injury, internal,
     intrathoracic organs) 862.8
     with open wound into cavity 862.9

Injury—*continued*
interscapular region 959.1
intervertebral disc 959.1
intestine—*see* Injury, internal, intestine
intra-abdominal (organs) NEC—*see* Injury,
    internal, intra-abdominal
intracranial 854.0

---

*Note—Use the following fifth-digit
subclassification with categories 851-854:*

0 unspecified state of consciousness
1 with no loss of consciousness
*2 with brief [less than one hour] loss of
    consciousness*
*3 with moderate [1-24 hours] loss of
    consciousness*
*4 with prolonged [more than 24 hours] loss of
    consciousness and return to pre-existing
    conscious level*
*5 with prolonged [more than 24 hours] loss of
    consciousness, without return to pre-existing
    conscious level*
*Use fifth-digit 5 to designate when a patient is
unconscious and dies before regaining
consciousness, regardless of the duration of the
loss of consciousness*
*6 with loss of consciousness of unspecified
    duration*
9 with concussion, unspecified

---

    with
        open intracranial wound 854.1
        skull fracture—*see* Fracture, skull, by site
    contusion 851.8
        with open intracranial wound 851.9
        brain stem 851.4
            with open intracranial wound 851.5
        cerebellum 851.4
            with open intracranial wound 851.5
        cortex (cerebral) 851.0
            with open intracranial wound 851.2
    hematoma—*see* Injury, intracranial,
        hemorrhage
    hemorrhage 853.0
        with
            laceration—*see* Injury, intracranial,
                laceration
            open intracranial wound 853.1
        extradural 852.4
            with open intracranial wound 852.5
        subarachnoid 852.0
            with open intracranial wound 852.1
        subdural 852.2
            with open intracranial wound 852.3
    laceration 851.8
        with open intracranial wound 851.9
        brain stem 851.6
            with open intracranial wound 851.7
        cerebellum 851.6
            with open intracranial wound 851.7
        cortex (cerebral) 851.2
            with open intracranial wound 851.3
    intraocular—*see* Injury, eyeball, penetrating
    intrathoracic organs (multiple)—*see* Injury,
        internal, intrathoracic organs
    intrauterine—*see* Injury, internal, intrauterine
    iris 921.3
        penetrating—*see* Injury, eyeball, penetrating
    jaw 959.09
    jejunum—*see* Injury, internal, jejunum

Injury—*continued*
joint NEC 959.9
    old or residual 718.80
        ankle 718.87
        elbow 718.82
        foot 718.87
        hand 718.84
        hip 718.85
        knee 718.86
        multiple sites 718.89
        pelvic region 718.85
        shoulder (region) 718.81
        specified site NEC 718.88
        wrist 718.83
kidney—*see* Injury, internal, kidney
knee (and ankle) (and foot) (and leg, except
    thigh) 959.7
labium (majus) (minus) 959.1
labyrinth, ear 959.09
lacrimal apparatus, gland, or sac 921.1
    laceration 870.8
larynx 959.09
late effect—*see* Late, effects (of), injury
leg except thigh (and ankle) (and foot) (and
    knee) 959.7
    upper or thigh 959.6
lens, eye 921.3
    penetrating—*see* Injury, eyeball, penetrating
lid, eye—*see* Injury, eyelid
lip 959.09
liver—*see* Injury, internal, liver
lobe, parietal—*see* Injury, intracranial
lumbar (region) 959.1
    plexus 953.5
lumbosacral (region) 959.1
    plexus 953.5
lung—*see* Injury, internal, lung
malar region 959.09
mastoid region 959.09
maternal, during pregnancy, affecting fetus or
    newborn 760.5
maxilla 959.09
mediastinum—*see* Injury, internal, mediastinum
membrane
    brain (*see also* Injury, intracranial) 854.0
    tympanic 959.09
meningeal artery—*see* Hemorrhage, brain,
    traumatic, subarachnoid
meninges (cerebral)—*see* Injury, intracranial
mesenteric
    artery—*see* Injury, blood vessel, mesenteric,
        artery
    plexus, inferior 954.1
    vein—*see* Injury, blood vessel, mesenteric,
        vein
mesentery—*see* Injury, internal, mesentery
mesosalpinx—*see* Injury, internal, mesosalpinx
middle ear 959.09
midthoracic region 959.1
mouth 959.09
multiple (sites not classifiable to the same
    four-digit category in 959.0-959.7) 959.8
    internal 869.0
        with open wound into cavity 869.1
musculocutaneous nerve 955.4
nail
    finger 959.5
    toe 959.7
nasal (septum) (sinus) 959.09
nasopharynx 959.09

Injury—*continued*
  paint-gun—*see* Wound, open, by site,
     complicated
  palate (soft) 959.09
  pancreas—*see* Injury, internal, pancreas
  parathyroid (gland) 959.09
  parietal (region) (scalp) 959.09
    lobe—*see* Injury, intracranial
  pelvic
    floor 959.1
      complicating delivery 664.1
        affecting fetus or newborn 763.89
      joint or ligament, complicating delivery 665.6
        affecting fetus or newborn 763.89
      organs—*see also* Injury, internal, pelvis
        with
          abortion—*see* Abortion, by type, with
            damage to pelvic organs
          ectopic pregnancy (*see also* categories
            633.0-633.9) 639.2
          molar pregnancy (*see also* categories
            633.0-633.9) 639.2
        following
          abortion 639.2
          ectopic or molar pregnancy 639.2
        obstetrical trauma 665.5
        affecting fetus or newborn 763.89
  pelvis 959.1
  penis 959.1
  perineum 959.1
  peritoneum—*see* Injury, internal, peritoneum
  periurethral tissue
    with
      abortion—*see* Abortion, by type, with
        damage to pelvic organs
      ectopic pregnancy (*see also* categories
        633.0-633.9) 639.2
      molar pregnancy (*see also* categories
        630-632) 639.2
      complicating delivery 665.5
        affecting fetus or newborn 763.89
      following
        abortion 639.2
        ectopic or molar pregnancy 639.2
  phalanges
    foot 959.7
    hand 959.5
  pharynx 959.09
  pleura—*see* Injury, internal, pleura
  popliteal space 959.7
  prepuce 959.1
  prostate—*see* Injury, internal, prostate
  pubic region 959.1
  pudenda 959.1
  radiation NEC 990
  radioactive substance or radium NEC 990
  rectovaginal septum 959.1
  rectum—*see* Injury, internal, rectum
  retina 921.3
    penetrating—*see* Injury, eyeball, penetrating
  retroperitoneal—*see* Injury, internal,
    retroperitoneum
  roentgen rays NEC 990
  round ligament—*see* Injury, internal, round
    ligament
  sacral (region) 959.1
    plexus 953.5
  sacroiliac ligament NEC 959.1
  sacrum 959.1

Injury—*continued*
  salivary ducts or glands 959.09
  scalp 959.09
    due to birth trauma 767.1
    fetus or newborn 767.1
  scapular region 959.2
  sclera 921.3
    penetrating—*see* Injury, eyeball, penetrating
    superficial 918.2
  scrotum 959.1
  seminal vesicle—*see* Injury, internal, seminal
    vesicle
  shoulder (and upper arm) 959.2
  sinus
    cavernous (*see also* Injury, intracranial) 854.0
    nasal 959.09
  skeleton NEC, birth injury 767.3
  skin NEC 959.9
  skull—*see* Fracture, skull, by site
  soft tissue (of external sites) (severe)—*see*
    Wound, open, by site
  specified site NEC 959.8
  spermatic cord—*see* Injury, internal, spermatic
    cord
  spinal (cord) 952.9
    with fracture, vertebra—*see* Fracture,
      vertebra, by site, with spinal cord injury
    cervical (C_1-C_4) 952.00
      with
        anterior cord syndrome 952.02
        central cord syndrome 952.03
        complete lesion of cord 952.01
        incomplete lesion NEC 952.04
        posterior cord syndrome 952.04
      C_5-C_7 level 952.05
        with
          anterior cord syndrome 952.07
          central cord syndrome 952.08
          complete lesion of cord 952.06
          incomplete lesion NEC 952.09
          posterior cord syndrome 952.09
        specified type NEC 952.09
      specified type NEC 952.04
    dorsal (D_1-D_6) (T_1-T_6) (thoracic) 952.10
      with
        anterior cord syndrome 952.12
        central cord syndrome 952.13
        complete lesion of cord 952.11
        incomplete lesion NEC 952.14
        posterior cord syndrome 952.14
      D_7-D_{12} level (T_7-T_{12}) 952.15
        with
          anterior cord syndrome 952.17
          central cord syndrome 952.18
          complete lesion of cord 952.16
          incomplete lesion NEC 952.19
          posterior cord syndrome 952.19
        specified type NEC 952.19
      specified type NEC 952.14
    lumbar 952.2
    multiple sites 952.8
    nerve (root) NEC—*see* Injury, nerve, spinal,
      root
    plexus 953.9
      brachial 953.4
      lumbosacral 953.5
      multiple sites 953.8
    sacral 952.3
    thoracic (*see also* Injury, spinal, dorsal) 952.10

Injury—*continued*
  spleen—*see* Injury, internal, spleen
  stellate ganglion 954.1
  sternal region 959.1
  stomach—*see* Injury, internal, stomach
  subconjunctival 921.1
  subcutaneous 959.9
  subdural—*see* Injury, intracranial
  submaxillary region 959.09
  submental region 959.09
  subungual
    fingers 959.5
    toes 959.7
  superficial 919

Note—Use the following fourth-digit subdivisions with categories 910-919:

.0 Abrasion or friction burn without mention of infection
.1 Abrasion or friction burn, infected
.2 Blister without mention of infection
.3 Blister, infected
.4 Insect bite, nonvenomous, without mention of infection
.5 Insect bite, nonvenomous, infected
.6 Superficial foreign body (splinter) without major open wound and without mention of infection
.7 Superficial foreign body (splinter) without major open wound, infected
.8 Other and unspecified superficial injury without mention of infection
.9 Other and unspecified superficial injury, infected

For late effects of superficial injury, *see* category 906.2.

---

    abdomen, abdominal (muscle) (wall) (and other part(s) of trunk) 911
    ankle (and hip, knee, leg, or thigh) 916
    anus (and other part(s) of trunk) 911
    arm 913
      upper (and shoulder) 912
    auditory canal (external) (meatus) (and other part(s) of face, neck, or scalp, except eye) 910
    axilla (and upper arm) 912
    back (and other part(s) of trunk) 911
    breast (and other part(s) of trunk) 911
    brow (and other part(s) of face, neck or scalp, except eye) 910
    buttock (and other part(s) of trunk) 911
    canthus, eye 918.0
    cheek(s) (and other part(s) of face, neck, or scalp, except eye) 910
    chest wall (and other part(s) of trunk) 911
    chin (and other part(s) of face, neck, or scalp, except eye) 910
    clitoris (and other part(s) of trunk) 911
    conjunctiva 918.2
    cornea 918.1
      due to contact lens 371.82
    costal region (and other part(s) of trunk) 911
    ear(s) (auricle) (canal) (drum) (external) (and other part(s) of face, neck, or scalp, except eye) 910
    elbow (and forearm) (and wrist) 913
    epididymis (and other part(s) of trunk) 911

Injury—*continued*
  epigastric region (and other part(s) of trunk) 911
  epiglottis (and other part(s) of face, neck, or scalp, except eye) 910
  eye(s) (and adnexa) NEC 918.9
  eyelid(s) (and periocular area) 918.0
  face (any part(s), except eye) (and neck or scalp) 910
  finger(s) (nail) (any) 915
  flank (and other part(s) of trunk) 911
  foot (phalanges) (and toe(s)) 917
  forearm (and elbow) (and wrist) 913
  forehead (and other part(s) of face, neck, or scalp, except eye) 910
  globe (eye) 918.9
  groin (and other part(s) of trunk) 911
  gum(s) (and other part(s) of face, neck, or scalp, except eye) 910
  hand(s) (except fingers alone) 914
  head (and other part(s) of face, neck, or scalp, except eye) 910
  heel (and foot or toe) 917
  hip (and ankle, knee, leg, or thigh) 916
  iliac region (and other part(s) of trunk) 911
  interscapular region (and other part(s) of trunk) 911
  iris 918.9
  knee (and ankle, hip, leg, or thigh) 916
  labium (majus) (minus) (and other part(s) of trunk) 911
  lacrimal (apparatus) (gland) (sac) 918.0
  leg (lower) (upper) (and ankle, hip, knee, or thigh) 916
  lip(s) (and other part(s) of face, neck, or scalp, except eye) 910
  lower extremity (except foot) 916
  lumbar region (and other part(s) of trunk) 911
  malar region (and other part(s) of face, neck, or scalp, except eye) 910
  mastoid region (and other part(s) of face, neck, or scalp, except eye) 910
  midthoracic region (and other part(s) of trunk) 911
  mouth (and other part(s) of face, neck, or scalp, except eye) 910
  multiple sites (not classifiable to the same three-digit category) 919
  nasal (septum) (and other part(s) of face, neck, or scalp, except eye) 910
  neck (and face or scalp, any part(s), except eye) 910
  nose (septum) (and other part(s) of face, neck, or scalp, except eye) 910
  occipital region (and other part(s) of face, neck, or scalp, except eye) 910
  orbital region 918.0
  palate (soft) (and other part(s) of face, neck, or scalp, except eye) 910
  parietal region (and other part(s) of face, neck, or scalp, except eye) 910
  penis (and other part(s) of trunk) 911
  perineum (and other part(s) of trunk) 911
  periocular area 918.0
  pharynx (and other part(s) of face, neck, or scalp, except eye) 910
  popliteal space (and ankle, hip, leg, or thigh) 916
  prepuce (and other part(s) of trunk) 911
  pubic region (and other part(s) of trunk) 911

Injury—*continued*
    pudenda (and other part(s) of trunk) 911
    sacral region (and other part(s) of trunk) 911
    salivary (ducts) (glands) (and other part(s) of face, neck, or scalp, except eye) 910
    scalp (and other part(s) of face or neck, except eye) 910
    scapular region (and upper arm) 912
    sclera 918.2
    scrotum (and other part(s) of trunk) 911
    shoulder (and upper arm) 912
    skin NEC 919
    specified site(s) NEC 919
    sternal region (and other part(s) of trunk) 911
    subconjunctival 918.2
    subcutaneous NEC 919
    submaxillary region (and other part(s) of face, neck, or scalp, except eye) 910
    submental region (and other part(s) of face, neck, or scalp, except eye) 910
    supraclavicular fossa (and other part(s) of face, neck or scalp, except eye) 910
    supraorbital 918.0
    temple (and other part(s) of face, neck, or scalp, except eye) 910
    temporal region (and other part(s) of face, neck, or scalp, except eye) 910
    testis (and other part(s) of trunk) 911
    thigh (and ankle, hip, knee, or leg) 916
    thorax, thoracic (external) (and other part(s) of trunk) 911
    throat (and other part(s) of face, neck, or scalp, except eye) 910
    thumb(s) (nail) 915
    toe(s) (nail) (subungual) (and foot) 917
    tongue (and other part(s) of face, neck, or scalp, except eye) 910
    tooth, teeth 521.2
    trunk (any part(s)) 911
    tunica vaginalis (and other part(s) of trunk) 911
    tympanum, tympanic membrane (and other part(s) of face, neck, or scalp, except eye) 910
    upper extremity NEC 913
    uvula (and other part(s) of face, neck, or scalp, except eye) 910
    vagina (and other part(s) of trunk) 911
    vulva (and other part(s) of trunk) 911
    wrist (and elbow) (and forearm) 913
  supraclavicular fossa 959.1
  supraorbital 959.09
  surgical complication (external or internal site) 998.2
  symphysis pubis 959.1
    complicating delivery 665.6
    affecting fetus or newborn 763.89
  temple 959.09
  temporal region 959.09
  testis 959.1
  thigh (and hip) 959.6
  thorax, thoracic (external) 959.1
    cavity—*see* Injury, internal, thorax
    internal—*see* Injury, internal, intrathoracic organs
  throat 959.09
  thumb(s) (nail) 959.5
  thymus—*see* Injury, internal, thymus
  thyroid (gland) 959.09
  toe (nail) (any) 959.7

Injury—*continued*
  tongue 959.09
  tonsil 959.09
  tooth NEC 873.63
    complicated 873.73
  trachea—*see* Injury, internal, trachea
  trunk 959.1
  tunica vaginalis 959.1
  tympanum, tympanic membrane 959.09
  ultraviolet rays NEC 990
  ureter—*see* Injury, internal, ureter
  urethra (sphincter)—*see* Injury, internal, urethra
  uterus—*see* Injury, internal, uterus
  uvula 959.09
  vagina 959.1
  vascular—*see* Injury, blood vessel
  vas deferens—*see* Injury, internal, vas deferens
  vein (*see also* Injury, blood vessel, by site) 904.9
  vena cava
    inferior 902.10
    superior 901.2
  vesical (sphincter)—*see* Injury, internal, vesical
  viscera (abdominal)—*see* Injury, internal, viscera
    with fracture, pelvis—*see* Fracture, pelvis
  visual 950.9
    cortex 950.3
  vitreous (humor) 871.2
  vulva 959.1
  whiplash (cervical spine) 847.0
  wringer—*see* Crush, by site
  wrist (and elbow) (and forearm) 959.3
  x-ray NEC 990
Inoculation —*see also* Vaccination
  complication or reaction—*see* Complication, vaccination
Insanity, insane (*see also* Psychosis) 298.9
  adolescent (*see also* Schizophrenia) 295.9
  alternating (*see also* Psychosis, affective, circular) 296.7
  confusional 298.9
    acute 293.0
    subacute 293.1
  delusional 298.9
  paralysis, general 094.1
    progressive 094.1
  paresis, general 094.1
  senile 290.20
Insect
  bite—*see* Injury, superficial, by site
  venomous, poisoning by 989.5
Insemination, artificial V26.1
Insertion
  cord (umbilical) lateral or velamentous 663.8
    affecting fetus or newborn 762.6
  intrauterine contraceptive device V25.1
  placenta, vicious—*see* Placenta, previa
  subdermal implantable contraceptive V25.5
  velamentous, umbilical cord 663.8
    affecting fetus or newborn 762.6
Insolation 992.0
  meaning sunstroke 992.0
Insomnia 780.52
  with sleep apnea 780.51
  nonorganic origin 307.41
    persistent (primary) 307.42
    transient 307.41
  subjective complaint 307.49

Inspiration
  food or foreign body (*see also* Asphyxia, food
    or foreign body) 933.1
  mucus (*see also* Asphyxia, mucus) 933.1
Inspissated bile syndrome, newborn 774.4
Instability
  detrusor 596.59
  emotional (excessive) 301.3
  joint (posttraumatic) 718.80
    ankle 718.87
    elbow 718.82
    foot 718.87
    hand 718.84
    hip 718.85
    knee 718.86
    lumbosacral 724.6
    multiple sites 718.89
    pelvic region 718.85
    sacroiliac 724.6
    shoulder (region) 718.81
    specified site NEC 718.88
    wrist 718.83
  lumbosacral 724.6
  nervous 301.89
  personality (emotional) 301.59
  thyroid, paroxysmal 242.9
  urethral 599.83
  vasomotor 780.2
Insufficiency, insufficient
  accommodation 367.4
  adrenal (gland) (acute) (chronic) 255.4
    medulla 255.5
    primary 255.4
    specified NEC 255.5
  adrenocortical 255.4
  anus 569.49
  aortic (valve) 424.1
    with
      mitral (valve) disease 396.1
        insufficiency, incompetence, or
          regurgitation 396.3
        stenosis or obstruction 396.1
      stenosis or obstruction 424.1
        with mitral (valve) disease 396.8
    congenital 746.4
    rheumatic 395.1
      with
        mitral (valve) disease 396.1
          insufficiency, incompetence, or
            regurgitation 396.3
          stenosis or obstruction 396.1
        stenosis or obstruction 395.2
          with mitral (valve) disease 396.8
    specified cause NEC 424.1
    syphilitic 093.22
  arterial 447.1
    basilar artery 435.0
    carotid artery 435.8
    cerebral 437.1
    coronary (acute or subacute) 411.89
    mesenteric 557.1
    peripheral 443.9
    precerebral 435.9
    vertebral artery 435.1
    vertibrobasilar 435.3
  arteriovenous 459.9
  basilar artery 435.0
  biliary 575.8

Insufficiency, insufficient—*continued*
  cardiac (*see also* Insufficiency, myocardial)
    428.0
    complicating surgery 997.1
    due to presence of (cardiac) prosthesis 429.4
    postoperative 997.1
      long-term effect of cardiac surgery 429.4
      specified during or due to a procedure 997.1
      long-term effect of cardiac surgery 429.4
  cardiorenal (*see also* Hypertension, cardiorenal)
    404.90
  cardiovascular (*see also* Disease,
    cardiovascular) 429.2
    renal (*see also* Hypertension, cardiorenal)
      404.90
  carotid artery 435.8
  cerebral (vascular) 437.9
  cerebrovascular 437.9
    with transient focal neurological signs and
      symptoms 435.9
    acute 437.1
      with transient focal neurological signs and
        symptoms 435.9
  circulatory NEC 459.9
    fetus or newborn 779.8
  convergence 378.83
  coronary (acute or subacute) 411.89
    chronic or with a stated duration of over 8
      weeks 414.8
  corticoadrenal 255.4
  dietary 269.9
  divergence 378.85
  food 994.2
  gastroesophageal 530.89
  gonadal
    ovary 256.3
    testis 257.2
  gonadotropic hormone secretion 253.4
  heart—*see also* Insufficiency, myocardial
    fetus or newborn 779.8
    valve (*see also* Endocarditis) 424.90
      congenital NEC 746.89
  hepatic 573.8
  idiopathic autonomic 333.0
  kidney (*see also* Disease, renal) 593.9
  labyrinth, labyrinthine (function) 386.53
    bilateral 386.54
    unilateral 386.53
  lacrimal 375.15
  liver 573.8
  lung (acute) (*see also* Insufficiency, pulmonary)
    518.82
    following trauma, surgery, or shock 518.5
    newborn 770.8
  mental (congenital) (*see also* Retardation,
    mental) 319
  mesenteric 557.1
  mitral (valve) 424.0
    with
      aortic (valve) disease 396.3
        insufficiency, incompetence, or
          regurgitation 396.3
        stenosis or obstruction 396.2
      obstruction or stenosis 394.2
        with aortic valve disease 396.8
    congenital 746.6

Insufficiency, insufficient—*continued*
  rheumatic 394.1
    with
      aortic (valve) disease 396.3
        insufficiency, incompetence, or
          regurgitation 396.3
        stenosis or obstruction 396.2
      obstruction or stenosis 394.2
        with aortic valve disease 396.8
      active or acute 391.1
        with chorea, rheumatic (Sydenham's)
          392.0
    specified cause, except rheumatic 424.0
  muscle
    heart—*see* Insufficiency, myocardial
    ocular (*see also* Strabismus) 378.9
  myocardial, myocardium (with arteriosclerosis)
    428.0
    with rheumatic fever (conditions classifiable
      to 390)
      active, acute, or subacute 391.2
        with chorea 392.0
      inactive or quiescent (with chorea) 398.0
    congenital 746.89
    due to presence of (cardiac) prosthesis 429.4
    fetus or newborn 779.8
    following cardiac surgery 429.4
    hypertensive (*see also* Hypertension, heart)
      402.91
      benign 402.11
      malignant 402.01
    postoperative 997.1
      long-term effect of cardiac surgery 429.4
    rheumatic 398.0
      active, acute, or subacute 391.2
        with chorea (Sydenham's) 392.0
    syphilitic 093.82
  nourishment 994.2
  organic 799.8
  ovary 256.3
    postablative 256.2
  pancreatic 577.8
  parathyroid (gland) 252.1
  peripheral vascular (arterial) 443.9
  pituitary (anterior) 253.2
    posterior 253.5
  placental—*see* Placenta, insufficiency
  platelets 287.5
  prenatal care in current pregnancy V23.7
  progressive pluriglandular 258.9
  pseudocholinesterase 289.8
  pulmonary (acute) 518.82
    following
      shock 518.5
      surgery 518.5
      trauma 518.5
    newborn 770.8
    valve (*see also* Endocarditis, pulmonary) 424.3
      congenital 746.09
  pyloric 537.0
  renal 593.9
    due to a procedure 997.5
  respiratory 786.09
    acute 518.82
      following shock, surgery, or trauma 518.5
    newborn 770.8
  rotation—*see* Malrotation
  suprarenal 255.4
    medulla 255.5
  tarso-orbital fascia, congenital 743.66

Insufficiency, insufficient—*continued*
  tear film 375.15
  testis 257.2
  thyroid (gland) (acquired)—*see also*
    Hypothyroidism
    congenital 243
  tricuspid (*see also* Endocarditis, tricuspid) 397.0
    congenital 746.89
    syphilitic 093.23
  urethral sphincter 599.84
  valve, valvular (heart) (*see also* Endocarditis)
    424.90
  vascular 459.9
    intestine NEC 557.9
    mesenteric 557.1
    peripheral 443.9
    renal (*see also* Hypertension, kidney) 403.90
  velopharyngeal
    acquired 528.9
    congenital 750.29
  venous (peripheral) 459.81
  ventricular—*see* Insufficiency, myocardial
  vertebral artery 435.1
  vertibrobasilar artery 435.3
  weight gain during pregnancy 646.8
  zinc 269.3
Insufflation
  fallopian
    fertility testing V26.21
    following sterilization reversal V26.22
  meconium 770.1
Insular —*see* condition
Insulinoma (M8151/0)
  malignant (M8151/3)
    pancreas 157.4
    specified site—*see* Neoplasm, by site,
      malignant
    unspecified site 157.4
  pancreas 211.7
  specified site—*see* Neoplasm, by site, benign
  unspecified site 211.7
Insuloma —*see* Insulinoma
Insult
  brain 437.9
    acute 436
  cerebral 437.9
    acute 436
  cerebrovascular 437.9
    acute 436
  vascular NEC 437.9
    acute 436
Insurance examination (certification) V70.3
Intemperance (*see also* Alcoholism) 303.9
Interception of pregnancy (menstrual
  extraction) V25.3
Intermenstrual
  bleeding 626.6
    irregular 626.6
    regular 626.5
  hemorrhage 626.6
    irregular 626.6
    regular 626.5
  pain(s) 625.2
Intermittent— *see* condition
Internal —*see* condition
Interproximal wear 521.1
Interruption
  aortic arch 747.11
  bundle of His 426.50
  fallopian tube (for sterilization) V25.2

Interruption—*continued*
  phase-shift, sleep cycle 307.45
  repeated REM-sleep 307.48
  sleep
    due to perceived environmental disturbances
      307.48
    phase-shift, of 24-hour sleep-wake cycle
      307.45
    repeated REM-sleep type 307.48
  vas deferens (for sterilization) V25.2
Intersexuality 752.7
Interstitial —*see* condition
Intertrigo 695.89
  labialis 528.5
Intervertebral disc —*see* condition
Intestine, intestinal —*see also* condition
  flu 487.8
Intolerance
  carbohydrate NEC 579.8
  cardiovascular exercise, with pain (at rest) (with
    less than ordinary activity) (with ordinary
    activity) V47.2
  cold 780.9
  disaccharide (hereditary) 271.3
  drug
    correct substance properly administered 995.2
    wrong substance given or taken in error 977.9
      specified drug—*see* Table of drugs and
        chemicals
  effort 306.2
  fat NEC 579.8
  foods NEC 579.8
  fructose (hereditary) 271.2
  glucose (-galactose) (congenital) 271.3
  gluten 579.0
  lactose (hereditary) (infantile) 271.3
  lysine (congenital) 270.7
  milk NEC 579.8
  protein (familial) 270.7
  starch NEC 579.8
  sucrose (-isomaltose) (congenital) 271.3
Intoxicated NEC (*see also* Alcoholism) 305.0
Intoxication
  acid 276.2
  acute
    alcoholic 305.0
      with alcoholism 303.0
      hangover effects 305.0
    caffeine 305.9
    hallucinogenic (*see also* Abuse, drugs,
      nondependent) 305.3
  alcohol (acute) 305.0
    with alcoholism 303.0
    hangover effects 305.0
    idiosyncratic 291.4
    pathological 291.4
  alimentary canal 558.2
  ammonia (hepatic) 572.2
  chemical—*see also* Table of drugs and
    chemicals
    via placenta or breast milk 760.70
      alcohol 760.71
      anti-infective agents 760.74
      cocaine 760.75
      "crack" 760.75
      hallucinogenic agents NEC 760.73
      medicinal agents NEC 760.79
      narcotics 760.72
      obstetric anesthetic or analgesic drug 763.5
      specified agent NEC 760.79

Intoxication—*continued*
    suspected, affecting management of
      pregnancy 655.5
  cocaine, through placenta or breast milk 760.75
  delirium
    alcohol 291.0
    drug 292.81
  drug
    with delirium 292.81
    correct substance properly administered (*see
      also* Allergy, drug) 995.2
    newborn 779.4
    obstetric anesthetic or sedation 668.9
      affecting fetus or newborn 763.5
    overdose or wrong substance given or
      taken—*see* Table of drugs and chemicals
    pathologic 292.2
    specific to newborn 779.4
    via placenta or breast milk 760.70
      alcohol 760.71
      anti-infective agents 760.74
      cocaine 760.75
      "crack" 760.75
      hallucinogenic agents 760.73
      medicinal agents NEC 760.79
      narcotics 760.72
      obstetric anesthetic or analgesic drug 763.5
      specified agent NEC 760.79
      suspected, affecting management of
        pregnancy 655.5
  enteric—*see* Intoxication, intestinal
  fetus or newborn, via placenta or breast milk
    760.70
    alcohol 760.71
    anti-infective agents 760.74
    cocaine 760.75
    "crack" 760.75
    hallucinogenic agents 760.73
    medicinal agents NEC 760.79
    narcotics 760.72
    obstetric anesthetic or analgesic drug 763.5
    specified agent NEC 760.79
    suspected, affecting management of
      pregnancy 655.5
  food—*see* Poisoning, food
  gastrointestinal 558.2
  hallucinogenic (acute) 305.3
  hepatocerebral 572.2
  idiosyncratic alcohol 291.4
  intestinal 569.89
    due to putrefaction of food 005.9
  methyl alcohol (*see also* Alcoholism) 305.0
    with alcoholism 303.0
  pathologic 291.4
    drug 292.2
  potassium (K) 276.7
  septic
    with
      abortion—*see* Abortion, by type, with sepsis
      ectopic pregnancy (*see also* categories
        633.0-633.9) 639.0
      molar pregnancy (*see also* categories
        630-632) 639.0
    during labor 659.3
    following
      abortion 639.0
      ectopic or molar pregnancy 639.0
    generalized—*see* Septicemia
    puerperal, postpartum, childbirth 670
  serum (prophylactic) (therapeutic) 999.5
  uremic—*see* Uremia
  water 276.6

Intracranial —*see* condition
Intrahepatic gallbladder 751.69
Intraligamentous —*see also* condition
  pregnancy—*see* Pregnancy, cornual
Intraocular —*see also* condition
  sepsis 360.00
Intrathoracic —*see also* condition
  kidney 753.3
  stomach—*see* Hernia, diaphragm
Intrauterine contraceptive device
  checking V25.42
  insertion V25.1
  in situ V45.51
  management V25.42
  prescription V25.02
    repeat V25.42
  reinsertion V25.42
  removal V25.42
Intraventricular —*see* condition
Intrinsic deformity —*see* Deformity
Intrusion, repetitive, of sleep (due to
    environmental disturbances) (with atypical
    polysomnographic features) 307.48
Intumescent, lens (eye) NEC 366.9
  senile 366.12
Intussusception (colon) (enteric) (intestine)
    (rectum) 560.0
  appendix 543.9
  congenital 751.5
  fallopian tube 620.8
  ileocecal 560.0
  ileocolic 560.0
  ureter (with obstruction) 593.4
Invagination
  basilar 756.0
  colon or intestine 560.0
Invalid (since birth) 799.8
Invalidism (chronic) 799.8
Inversion
  albumin-globulin (A-G) ratio 273.8
  bladder 596.8
  cecum (*see also* Intussusception) 560.0
  cervix 622.8
  nipple 611.79
    congenital 757.6
    puerperal, postpartum 676.3
  optic papilla 743.57
  organ or site, congenital NEC—*see* Anomaly,
    specified type NEC
  sleep rhythm 780.55
    nonorganic origin 307.45
  testis (congenital) 752.51
  uterus (postinfectional) (postpartal, old) 621.7
    chronic 621.7
    complicating delivery 665.2
      affecting fetus or newborn 763.89
  vagina—*see* Prolapse, vagina
Investigation
  allergens V72.7
  clinical research V70.7
Inviability —*see* Immaturity
Involuntary movement, abnormal 781.0
Involution, involutional —*see also* condition
  breast, cystic or fibrocystic 610.1
  depression (*see also* Psychosis, affective) 296.2
    recurrent episode 296.3
    single episode 296.2
  melancholia (*see also* Psychosis, affective)
    296.2
    recurrent episode 296.3
    single episode 296.2

Involution, involutional—*continued*
  ovary, senile 620.3
  paranoid state (reaction) 297.2
  paraphrenia (climacteric) (menopause) 297.2
  psychosis 298.8
  thymus failure 254.8
IQ
  under 20 318.2
  20-34 318.1
  35-49 318.0
  50-70 317
IRDS 769
Irideremia 743.45
Iridis rubeosis 364.42
  diabetic 250.5 *[364.42]*
Iridochoroiditis (panuveitis) 360.12
Iridocyclitis NEC 364.3
  acute 364.00
    primary 364.01
    recurrent 364.02
  chronic 364.10
    in
      lepromatous leprosy 030.0 *[364.11]*
      sarcoidosis 135 *[364.11]*
      tuberculosis (*see also* Tuberculosis) 017.3
        [364.11]
  due to allergy 364.04
  endogenous 364.01
  gonococcal 098.41
  granulomatous 364.10
  herpetic (simplex) 054.44
    zoster 053.22
  hypopyon 364.05
  lens induced 364.23
  nongranulomatous 364.00
  primary 364.01
  recurrent 364.02
  rheumatic 364.10
  secondary 364.04
    infectious 364.03
    noninfectious 364.04
  subacute 364.00
    primary 364.01
    recurrent 364.02
  sympathetic 360.11
  syphilitic (secondary) 091.52
  tuberculous (chronic) (*see also* Tuberculosis)
    017.3 *[364.11]*
Iridocyclochoroiditis (panuveitis) 360.12
Iridodialysis 364.76
Iridodonesis 364.8
Iridoplegia (complete) (partial) (reflex) 379.49
Iridoschisis 364.52
Iris —*see* condition
Iritis 364.3
  acute 364.00
    primary 364.01
    recurrent 364.02
  chronic 364.10
    in
      sarcoidosis 135 *[364.11]*
      tuberculosis (*see also* Tuberculosis) 017.3
        [364.11]
  diabetic 250.5 *[364.42]*
  due to
    allergy 364.04
    herpes simplex 054.44
    leprosy 030.0 *[364.11]*
  endogenous 364.01
  gonococcal 098.41
  gouty 274.89 *[364.11]*

Iritis—*continued*
  granulomatous 364.10
  hypopyon 364.05
  lens induced 364.23
  nongranulomatous 364.00
  papulosa 095.8 *[364.11]*
  primary 364.01
  recurrent 364.02
  rheumatic 364.10
  secondary 364.04
    infectious 364.03
    noninfectious 364.04
  subacute 364.00
    primary 364.01
    recurrent 364.02
  sympathetic 360.11
  syphilitic (secondary) 091.52
    congenital 090.0 *[364.11]*
    late 095.8 *[364.11]*
  tuberculous (*see also* Tuberculosis) 017.3
    [364.11]
  uratic 274.89 *[364.11]*
Iron
  deficiency anemia 280.9
  metabolism disease 275.0
  storage disease 275.0
Iron-miners' lung 503
Irradiated enamel (tooth, teeth) 521.8
Irradiation
  burn—*see* Burn, by site
  effects, adverse 990
Irreducible, irreducibility —*see* condition
Irregular, irregularity
  action, heart 427.9
  alveolar process 525.8
  bleeding NEC 626.4
  breathing 786.09
  colon 569.89
  contour of cornea 743.41
    acquired 371.70
  dentin in pulp 522.3
  eye movements NEC 379.59
  menstruation (cause unknown) 626.4
  periods 626.4
  prostate 602.9
  pupil 364.75
  respiratory 786.09
  septum (nasal) 470
  shape, organ or site, congenital NEC—*see*
    Distortion
  sleep-wake rhythm (non-24-hour) 780.55
    nonorganic origin 307.45
  vertebra 733.99
Irritability (nervous) 799.2
  bladder 596.8
    neurogenic 596.54
      with cauda equina syndrome 344.61
  bowel (syndrome) 564.1
  bronchial (*see also* Bronchitis) 490
  cerebral, newborn 779.1
  colon 564.1
    psychogenic 306.4
  duodenum 564.89
  heart (psychogenic) 306.2
  ileum 564.89
  jejunum 564.89
  myocardium 306.2
  rectum 564.89
  stomach 536.9
    psychogenic 306.4

Irritability—*continued*
  sympathetic (nervous system) (*see also*
    Neuropathy, peripheral, autonomic) 337.9
  urethra 599.84
  ventricular (heart) (psychogenic) 306.2
Irritable —*see* Irritability
Irritation
  anus 569.49
  axillary nerve 353.0
  bladder 596.8
  brachial plexus 353.0
  brain (traumatic) (*see also* Injury, intracranial)
    854.0
    nontraumatic—*see* Encephalitis
  bronchial (*see also* Bronchitis) 490
  cerebral (traumatic) (*see also* Injury,
    intracranial) 854.0
    nontraumatic—*see* Encephalitis
  cervical plexus 353.2
  cervix (*see also* Cervicitis) 616.0
  choroid, sympathetic 360.11
  cranial nerve—*see* Disorder, nerve, cranial
  digestive tract 536.9
    psychogenic 306.4
  gastric 536.9
    psychogenic 306.4
  gastrointestinal (tract) 536.9
    functional 536.9
    psychogenic 306.4
  globe, sympathetic 360.11
  intestinal (bowel) 564.9
  labyrinth 386.50
  lumbosacral plexus 353.1
  meninges (traumatic) (*see also* Injury,
    intracranial) 854.0
    nontraumatic—*see* Meningitis
  myocardium 306.2
  nerve—*see* Disorder, nerve
  nervous 799.2
  nose 478.1
  penis 607.89
  perineum 709.9
  peripheral
    autonomic nervous system (*see also*
      Neuropathy, peripheral, autonomic) 337.9
    nerve—*see* Disorder, nerve
  peritoneum (*see also* Peritonitis) 567.9
  pharynx 478.29
  plantar nerve 355.6
  spinal (cord) (traumatic)—*see also* Injury,
    spinal, by site
    nerve—*see also* Disorder, nerve
      root NEC 724.9
      traumatic—*see* Injury, nerve, spinal
    nontraumatic—*see* Myelitis
  stomach 536.9
    psychogenic 306.4
  sympathetic nerve NEC (*see also* Neuropathy,
    peripheral, autonomic) 337.9
  ulnar nerve 354.2
  vagina 623.9
Isambert's disease 012.3
Ischemia, ischemic 459.9
  basilar artery (with transient neurologic deficit)
    435.0
  bone NEC 733.40
  bowel (transient) 557.9
    acute 557.0
    chronic 557.1
    due to mesenteric artery insufficiency 557.1

J

Jaccoud's nodular fibrositis, chronic
(Jaccoud's syndrome) 714.4
Jackson's
membrane 751.4
paralysis or syndrome 344.89
veil 751.4
Jacksonian
epilepsy (*see also* Epilepsy) 345.5
seizures (focal) (*see also* Epilepsy) 345.5
Jacob's ulcer (M8090/3)—*see* Neoplasm, skin,
malignant, by site
Jacquet's dermatitis (diaper dermatitis) 691.0
Jadassohn's
blue nevus (M8780/0)—*see* Neoplasm, skin,
benign
disease (maculopapular erythroderma) 696.2
intraepidermal epithelioma (M8096/0)—*see*
Neoplasm, skin, benign
Jadassohn-Lewandowski syndrome
(pachyonychia congenita) 757.5
Jadassohn-Pellizari's disease (anetoderma)
701.3
Jadassohn-Tièche nevus (M8780/0)—*see*
Neoplasm, skin, benign
Jaffe-Lichtenstein (-Uehlinger) syndrome 252.0
Jahnke's syndrome (encephalocutaneous
angiomatosis) 759.6
Jakob-Creutzfeldt disease or syndrome 046.1
with dementia
with behavioral disturbance 046.1 *[294.11]*
without behavioral disturbance 046.1 *[294.10]*
Jaksch (-Luzet) disease or syndrome
(pseudoleukemia infantum) 285.8
Jamaican
neuropathy 349.82
paraplegic tropical ataxic-spastic syndrome
349.82
Janet's disease (psychasthenia) 300.89
Janiceps 759.4
Jansky-Bielschowsky amaurotic familial idiocy
330.1
Japanese
B type encephalitis 062.0
river fever 081.2
seven-day fever 100.89
Jaundice (yellow) 782.4
acholuric (familial) (splenomegalic) (*see also*
Spherocytosis) 282.0
acquired 283.9
breast milk 774.39
catarrhal (acute) 070.1
with hepatic coma 070.0
chronic 571.9
epidemic—*see* Jaundice, epidemic
cholestatic (benign) 782.4
chronic idiopathic 277.4
epidemic (catarrhal) 070.1
with hepatic coma 070.0
leptospiral 100.0
spirochetal 100.0
febrile (acute) 070.1
with hepatic coma 070.0
leptospiral 100.0
spirochetal 100.0

Jaundice—*continued*
fetus or newborn 774.6
due to or associated with
ABO
antibodies 773.1
incompatibility, maternal/fetal 773.1
isoimmunization 773.1
absence or deficiency of enzyme system for
bilirubin conjugation (congenital) 774.39
blood group incompatibility NEC 773.2
breast milk inhibitors to conjugation 774.39
associated with preterm delivery 774.2
bruising 774.1
Crigler-Najjar syndrome 277.4 *[774.31]*
delayed conjugation 774.30
associated with preterm delivery 774.2
development 774.39
drugs or toxins transmitted from mother
774.1
G-6-PD deficiency 282.2 *[774.0]*
galactosemia 271.1 *[774.5]*
Gilbert's syndrome 277.4 *[774.31]*
hepatocellular damage 774.4
hereditary hemolytic anemia (*see also*
Anemia, hemolytic) 282.9 *[774.0]*
hypothyroidism, congenital 243 *[774.31]*
incompatibility, maternal/fetal NEC 773.2
infection 774.1
inspissated bile syndrome 774.4
isoimmunization NEC 773.2
mucoviscidosis 277.01 *[774.5]*
obliteration of bile duct, congenital 751.61
[774.5]
polycythemia 774.1
preterm delivery 774.2
red cell defect 282.9 *[774.0]*
Rh
antibodies 773.0
incompatibility, maternal/fetal 773.0
isoimmunization 773.0
spherocytosis (congenital) 282.0 *[774.0]*
swallowed maternal blood 774.1
physiological NEC 774.6
from injection, inoculation, infusion, or
transfusion (blood) (plasma) (serum) (other
substance) (onset within 8 months after
administration)—*see* Hepatitis, viral
Gilbert's (familial nonhemolytic) 277.4
hematogenous 283.9
hemolytic (acquired) 283.9
congenital (*see also* Spherocytosis) 282.0
hemorrhagic (acute) 100.0
leptospiral 100.0
newborn 776.0
spirochetal 100.0
hepatocellular 573.8
homologous (serum)—*see* Hepatitis, viral
idiopathic, chronic 277.4
infectious (acute) (subacute) 070.1
with hepatic coma 070.0
leptospiral 100.0
spirochetal 100.0
leptospiral 100.0
malignant (*see also* Necrosis, liver) 570
newborn (physiological) (*see also* Jaundice,
fetus or newborn) 774.6

K

Kahler (-Bozzolo) disease (multiple myeloma)
  (M9730/3) 203.0
Kakergasia 300.9
Kakke 265.0
Kala-azar (Indian) (infantile) (Mediterranean)
  (Sudanese) 085.0
Kalischer's syndrome (encephalocutaneous
  angiomatosis) 759.6
Kallmann's syndrome (hypogonadotropic
  hypogonadism with anosmia) 253.4
Kanner's syndrome (autism) (*see also*
  Psychosis, childhood) 299.0
Kaolinosis 502
Kaposi's
  disease 757.33
    lichen ruber 696.4
      acuminatus 696.4
      moniliformis 697.8
    xeroderma pigmentosum 757.33
  sarcoma (M9140/3) 176.9
    adipose tissue 176.1
    aponeurosis 176.1
    artery 176.1
    blood vessel 176.1
    bursa 176.1
    connective tissue 176.1
    external genitalia 176.8
    fascia 176.1
    fatty tissue 176.1
    fibrous tissue 176.1
    gastrointestinal tract NEC 176.3
    ligament 176.1
    lung 176.4
    lymph
      gland(s) 176.5
      node(s) 176.5
    lymphatic(s) NEC 176.1
    muscle (skeletal) 176.1
    oral cavity NEC 176.8
    palate 176.2
    scrotum 176.8
    skin 176.0
    soft tissue 176.1
    specified site NEC 176.8
    subcutaneous tissue 176.1
    synovia 176.1
    tendon (sheath) 176.1
    vein 176.1
    vessel 176.1
    viscera NEC 176.9
    vulva 176.8
  varicelliform eruption 054.0
  vaccinia 999.0
Kartagener's syndrome or triad (sinusitis,
  bronchiectasis, situs inversus) 759.3
Kasabach-Merritt syndrome (capillary
  hemangioma associated with
  thrombocytopenic purpura) 287.3
Kaschin-Beck disease (endemic
  polyarthritis)—*see* Disease, Kaschin-Beck
Kast's syndrome (dyschondroplasia with
  hemangiomas) 756.4
Katatonia (*see also* Schizophrenia) 295.2
Katayama disease or fever 120.2
Kathisophobia 781.0
Kawasaki disease 446.1
Kayser-Fleischer ring (cornea)
  (pseudosclerosis) 275.1 *[371.14]*

Kaznelson's syndrome (congenital hypoplastic
  anemia) 284.0
Kedani fever 081.2
Kelis 701.4
Kelly (-Patterson) syndrome (sideropenic
  dysphagia) 280.8
Keloid, cheloid 701.4
  Addison's (morphea) 701.0
  cornea 371.00
  Hawkins' 701.4
  scar 701.4
Keloma 701.4
Kenya fever 082.1
Keratectasia 371.71
  congenital 743.41
Keratitis (nodular) (nonulcerative) (simple)
  (zonular) NEC 370.9
  with ulceration (*see also* Ulcer, cornea) 370.00
  actinic 370.24
  arborescens 054.42
  areolar 370.22
  bullosa 370.8
  deep—*see* Keratitis, interstitial
  dendritic(a) 054.42
  desiccation 370.34
  diffuse interstitial 370.52
  disciform(is) 054.43
    varicella 052.7 *[370.44]*
  epithelialis vernalis 372.13 *[370.32]*
  exposure 370.34
  filamentary 370.23
  gonococcal (congenital) (prenatal) 098.43
  herpes, herpetic (simplex) NEC 054.43
    zoster 053.21
  hypopyon 370.04
  in
    chickenpox 052.7 *[370.44]*
    exanthema (*see also* Exanthem) 057.9
      [370.44]
    paravaccinia (*see also* Paravaccinia) 051.9
      [370.44]
    smallpox (*see also* Smallpox) 050.9 *[370.44]*
    vernal conjunctivitis 372.13 *[370.32]*
  interstitial (nonsyphilitic) 370.50
    with ulcer (*see also* Ulcer, cornea) 370.00
    diffuse 370.52
    herpes, herpetic (simplex) 054.43
      zoster 053.21
    syphilitic (congenital) (hereditary) 090.3
    tuberculous (*see also* Tuberculosis) 017.3
      [370.59]
  lagophthalmic 370.34
  macular 370.22
  neuroparalytic 370.35
  neurotrophic 370.35
  nummular 370.22
  oyster-shuckers' 370.8
  parenchymatous—*see* Keratitis, interstitial
  petrificans 370.8
  phlyctenular 370.31
  postmeasles 055.71
  punctata, punctate 370.21
    leprosa 030.0 *[370.21]*
    profunda 090.3
    superficial (Thygeson's) 370.21
  purulent 370.8
  pustuliformis profunda 090.3

Kyphoscoliosis, kyphoscoliotic—*continued*
　idiopathic 737.30
　　infantile
　　　progressive 737.32
　　　resolving 737.31
　late effect of rickets 268.1 *[737.43]*
　specified NEC 737.39
　thoracogenic 737.34
　tuberculous (*see also* Tuberculosis) 015.0
　　[737.43]
Kyphosis, kyphotic (acquired) (postural) 737.10
　adolescent postural 737.0
　congenital 756.19
　dorsalis juvenilis 732.0
　due to or associated with
　　Charcot-Marie-Tooth disease 356.1 *[737.41]*
　　mucopolysaccharidosis 277.5 *[737.41]*
　　neurofibromatosis 237.71 *[737.41]*
　　osteitis
　　　deformans 731.0 *[737.41]*
　　　fibrosa cystica 252.0 *[737.41]*
　　osteoporosis (*see also* Osteoporosis) 733.0
　　　[737.41]
　　poliomyelitis (*see also* Poliomyelitis) 138
　　　[737.41]
　　radiation 737.11
　　tuberculosis (*see also* Tuberculosis) 015.0
　　　[737.41]
　Kümmell's 721.7
　late effect of rickets 268.1 *[737.41]*
　Morquio-Brailsford type (spinal) 277.5 *[737.41]*
　pelvis 738.6
　postlaminectomy 737.12
　specified cause NEC 737.19
　syphilitic, congenital 090.5 *[737.41]*
　tuberculous (*see also* Tuberculosis) 015.0
　　[737.41]
Kyrle's disease (hyperkeratosis follicularis in
　cutem penetrans) 701.1

L

Labia, labium —*see* condition
Labiated hymen 752.49
Labile
  blood pressure 796.2
  emotions, emotionality 301.3
  vasomotor system 443.9
Labioglossal paralysis 335.22
Labium leporinum (*see also* Cleft, lip) 749.10
Labor (*see also* Delivery)
  with complications—*see* Delivery, complicated
  abnormal NEC 661.9
    affecting fetus or newborn 763.7
  arrested active phase 661.1
    affecting fetus or newborn 763.7
  desultory 661.2
    affecting fetus or newborn 763.7
  dyscoordinate 661.4
    affecting fetus or newborn 763.7
  early onset (22-36 weeks gestation) 644.2
  failed
    induction 659.1
      mechanical 659.0
      medical 659.1
      surgical 659.0
    trial (vaginal delivery) 660.6
  false 644.1
  forced or induced, affecting fetus or newborn 763.89
  hypertonic 661.4
    affecting fetus or newborn 763.7
  hypotonic 661.2
    affecting fetus or newborn 763.7
    primary 661.0
      affecting fetus or newborn 763.7
    secondary 661.1
      affecting fetus or newborn 763.7
  incoordinate 661.4
    affecting fetus or newborn 763.7
  irregular 661.2
    affecting fetus or newborn 763.7
  long—*see* Labor, prolonged
  missed (at or near term) 656.4
  obstructed NEC 660.9
    affecting fetus or newborn 763.1
    specified cause NEC 660.8
      affecting fetus or newborn 763.1
  pains, spurious 644.1
  precipitate 661.3
    affecting fetus or newborn 763.6
  premature 644.2
    threatened 644.0
  prolonged or protracted 662.1
    affecting fetus or newborn 763.89
    first stage 662.0
      affecting fetus or newborn 763.89
    second stage 662.2
      affecting fetus or newborn 763.89
  threatened NEC 644.1
  undelivered 644.1

Labored breathing (*see also* Hyperventilation) 786.09
Labyrinthitis (inner ear) (destructive) (latent) 386.30
  circumscribed 386.32
  diffuse 386.31
  focal 386.32
  purulent 386.33
  serous 386.31
  suppurative 386.33
  syphilitic 095.8
  toxic 386.34
  viral 386.35
Laceration —*see also* Wound, open, by site
  accidental, complicating surgery 998.2
  Achilles tendon 845.09
    with open wound 892.2
  anus (sphincter) 863.89
    with
      abortion—*see* Abortion, by type, with damage to pelvic organs
      ectopic pregnancy (*see also* categories 633.0-633.9) 639.2
      molar pregnancy (*see also* categories 630-632) 639.2
    complicating delivery 664.2
      with laceration of anal or rectal mucosa 664.3
    following
      abortion 639.2
      ectopic or molar pregnancy 639.2
    nontraumatic, nonpuerperal 565.0
  bladder (urinary)
    with
      abortion—*see* Abortion, by type, with damage to pelvic organs
      ectopic pregnancy (*see also* categories 633.0-633.9) 639.2
      molar pregnancy (*see also* categories 630-632) 639.2
    following
      abortion 639.2
      ectopic or molar pregnancy 639.2
    obstetrical trauma 665.5
  blood vessel—*see* Injury, blood vessel, by site
  bowel
    with
      abortion—*see* Abortion, by type, with damage to pelvic organs
      ectopic pregnancy (*see also* categories 633.0-633.9) 639.2
      molar pregnancy (*see also* categories 630-632) 639.2
    following
      abortion 639.2
      ectopic or molar pregnancy 639.2
    obstetrical trauma 665.5

Laceration—*continued*
  tendon 848.9
    with open wound–*see* Wound, open, by site
    Achilles 845.09
      with open wound 892.2
    lower limb NEC 844.9
      with open wound NEC 894.2
    upper limb NEC 840.9
      with open wound NEC 884.2
  tentorium cerebelli—*see* Laceration, brain,
    cerebellum
  tongue 873.64
    complicated 873.74
  urethra
    with
      abortion—*see* Abortion, by type, with
        damage to pelvic organs
      ectopic pregnancy (*see also* categories
        633.0- 633.9) 639.2
      molar pregnancy (*see also* categories
        630-632) 639.2
    following
      abortion 639.2
      ectopic or molar pregnancy 639.2
    nonpuerperal, nontraumatic 599.84
    obstetrical trauma 665.5
  uterus
    with
      abortion—*see* Abortion, by type, with
        damage to pelvic organs
      ectopic pregnancy (*see also* categories
        633.0-633.9) 639.2
      molar pregnancy (*see also* categories
        630-632) 639.2
    following
      abortion 639.2
      ectopic or molar pregnancy 639.2
    nonpuerperal, nontraumatic 621.8
    obstetrical trauma NEC 665.1
    old (postpartal) 621.8
  vagina
    with
      abortion—*see* Abortion, by type, with
        damage to pelvic organs
      ectopic pregnancy (*see also* categories
        633.0-633.9) 639.2
      molar pregnancy (*see also* categories
        630-632) 639.2
      perineal involvement, complicating delivery
        664.0
    complicating delivery 665.4
      first degree 664.0
      second degree 664.1
      third degree 664.2
      fourth degree 664.3
      high 665.4
      muscles 664.1
      sulcus 665.4
      wall 665.4
    following
      abortion 639.2
      ectopic or molar pregnancy 639.2
    nonpuerperal, nontraumatic 623.4
    old (postpartal) 623.4
  valve, heart—*see* Endocarditis
  vulva
    with
      abortion—*see* Abortion, by type, with
        damage to pelvic organs
      ectopic pregnancy (*see also* categories
        633.0-633.9) 639.2

Laceration—*continued*
    molar pregnancy (*see also* categories
      630-632) 639.2
    complicating delivery 664.0
    following
      abortion 639.2
      ectopic or molar pregnancy 639.2
    nonpuerperal, nontraumatic 624.4
    old (postpartal) 624.4
Lachrymal —*see* condition
Lachrymonasal duct —*see* condition
Lack of
  appetite (*see also* Anorexia) 783.0
  care
    in home V60.4
    of adult 995.84
    of infant (at or after birth) 995.52
  coordination 781.3
  development—*see also* Hypoplasia
    physiological in childhood 783.40
  education V62.3
  energy 780.79
  financial resources V60.2
  food 994.2
    in environment V60.8
  growth in childhood 783.43
  heating V60.1
  housing (permanent) (temporary) V60.0
    adequate V60.1
  material resources V60.2
  medical attention 799.8
  memory (*see also* Amnesia) 780.9
    mild, following organic brain damage 310.1
  ovulation 628.0
  person able to render necessary care V60.4
  physical exercise V69.0
  physiologic development in childhood 783.40
  prenatal care in current pregnancy V23.7
  shelter V60.0
  water 994.3
Lacrimal —*see* condition
Lacrimation, abnormal (*see also* Epiphora)
  375.20
Lacrimonasal duct —*see* condition
Lactation, lactating (breast) (puerperal)
  (postpartum)
  defective 676.4
  disorder 676.9
    specified type NEC 676.8
  excessive 676.6
  failed 676.4
  mastitis NEC 675.2
  mother (care and/or examination) V24.1
  nonpuerperal 611.6
  suppressed 676.5
Lacticemia 271.3
  excessive 276.2
Lactosuria 271.3
Lacunar skull 756.0
Laennec's cirrhosis (alcoholic) 571.2
  nonalcoholic 571.5
Lafora's disease 333.2
Lag, lid (nervous) 374.41
Lagleyze-von Hippel disease (retinocerebral
  angiomatosis) 759.6
Lagophthalmos (eyelid) (nervous) 374.20
  cicatricial 374.23
  keratitis (*see also* Keratitis) 370.34
  mechanical 374.22
  paralytic 374.21

Laryngotracheitis—*continued*
  streptococcal 034.0
  stridulous 478.75
  syphilitic 095.8
    congenital 090.5
  tuberculous (*see also* Tuberculosis, larynx)
    012.3
  Vincent's 101
Laryngotracheobronchitis (*see also* Bronchitis)
  490
  acute 466.0
  chronic 491.8
  viral 466.0
Laryngotracheobronchopneumonitis —*see*
  Pneumonia, broncho-
Larynx, laryngeal —*see* condition
Lasègue's disease (persecution mania) 297.9
Lassa fever 078.89
Lassitude (*see also* Weakness) 780.79
Late —*see also* condition
  effect(s) (of)—*see also* condition
    abscess
      intracranial or intraspinal (conditions
        classifiable to 324)–*see* category 326
    adverse effect of drug, medicinal or biological
      substance 909.5
    allergic reaction 909.9
    amputation
      postoperative (late) 997.60
      traumatic (injury classifiable to 885-887 and
        895-897) 905.9
    burn (injury classifiable to 948-949) 906.9
      extremities NEC (injury classifiable to 943
        or 945) 906.7
        hand or wrist (injury classifiable to 944)
          906.6
      eye (injury classifiable to 940) 906.5
      face, head, and neck (injury classifiable to
        941) 906.5
      specified site NEC (injury classifiable to
        942 and 946-947) 906.8
    cerebrovascular disease (conditions
      classifiable to 430-437) 438.9
      with
        aphasia 438.11
        apraxia 438.81
        cognitive deficits 438.0
        dysphagia 438.82
        dysphasia 438.12
        hemiplegia/hemiparesis
          affecting
            dominant side 438.21
            nondominant side 438.22
            unspecified side 438.20
        monoplegia of lower limb
          affecting
            dominant side 438.41
            nondominant side 438.42
            unspecified side 438.40
        monoplegia of upper limb
          affecting
            dominant side 438.31
            nondominant side 438.32
            unspecified side 438.30
        paralytic syndrome NEC
          affecting
            bilateral 438.53
            dominant side 438.51
            nondominant side 438.52
            unspecified side 438.50
        speech and language deficit 438.10

Late —*continued*
    specified type NEC 438.19
    specified type NEC 438.89
  childbirth complication(s) 677
  complication(s) of
    childbirth 677
    delivery 677
    pregnancy 677
    puerperium 677
    surgical and medical care (conditions
      classifiable to 996-999) 909.3
    trauma (conditions classifiable to 958) 908.6
  contusion (injury classifiable to 920-924)
    906.3
  crushing (injury classifiable to 925-929) 906.4
  delivery complication(s) 677
  dislocation (injury classifiable to 830-839)
    905.6
  encephalitis or encephalomyelitis (conditions
    classifiable to 323)—*see* category 326
    in infectious diseases 139.8
      viral (conditions classifiable to 049.8,
        049.9, 062-064) 139.0
  external cause NEC (conditions classifiable to
    995) 909.9
    certain conditions classifiable to categories
      991-994 909.4
  foreign body in orifice (injury classifiable to
    930-939) 908.5
  fracture (multiple) (injury classifiable to
    828-829) 905.5
    extremity
      lower (injury classifiable to 821-827)
        905.4
        neck of femur (injury classifiable to
          820) 905.3
      upper (injury classifiable to 810-819)
        905.2
    face and skull (injury classifiable to
      800-804) 905.0
    skull and face (injury classifiable to
      800-804) 905.0
    spine and trunk (injury classifiable to 805
      and 807-809) 905.1
      with spinal cord lesion (injury classifiable
        to 806) 907.2
  infection
    pyogenic, intracranial—*see* category 326
  infectious diseases (conditions classifiable to
    001-136) NEC 139.8
  injury (injury classifiable to 959) 908.9
    blood vessel 908.3
      abdomen and pelvis (injury classifiable to
        902) 908.4
      extremity (injury classifiable to 903-904)
        908.3
      head and neck (injury classifiable to 900)
        908.3
      intracranial (injury classifiable to
        850-854) 907.0
        with skull fracture 905.0
      thorax (injury classifiable to 901) 908.4
    internal organ NEC (injury classifiable to
      867 and 869) 908.2
      abdomen (injury classifiable to 863-866
        and 868) 908.1
      thorax (injury classifiable to 860-862)
        908.0
    intracranial (injury classifiable to 850-854)
      907.0

Late —*continued*
  with skull fracture (injury classifiable to
      800-801 and 803-804) 905.0
  nerve NEC (injury classifiable to 957) 907.9
    cranial (injury classifiable to 950-951)
        907.1
    peripheral NEC (injury classifiable to 957)
        907.9
      lower limb and pelvic girdle (injury
          classifiable to 956) 907.5
      upper limb and shoulder girdle (injury
          classifiable to 955) 907.4
    roots and plexus(es), spinal (injury
        classifiable to 953) 907.3
    trunk (injury classifiable to 954) 907.3
  pregnancy complication(s) 677
  puerperal complication(s) 677
  spinal
    cord (injury classifiable to 806 and 952)
        907.2
    nerve root(s) and plexus(es) (injury
        classifiable to 953) 907.3
  superficial (injury classifiable to 910-919)
      906.2
  tendon (tendon injury classifiable to
      840-848, 880-884 with .2, and 890-894
      with .2) 905.8
  meningitis
    bacterial (conditions classifiable to
        320)—*see* category 326
    unspecified cause (conditions classifiable to
        322)—*see* category 326
  myelitis (*see also* Late, effect(s) (of),
      encephalitis)—*see* category 326
  parasitic diseases (conditions classifiable to
      001-136 NEC) 139.8
  phlebitis or thrombophlebitis of intracranial
      venous sinuses (conditions classifiable to
      325)—*see* category 326
  poisoning due to drug, medicinal or biological
      substance (conditions classifiable to
      960-979) 909.0
  poliomyelitis, acute (conditions classifiable to
      045) 138
  radiation (conditions classifiable to 990) 909.2
  rickets 268.1
  sprain and strain without mention of tendon
      injury (injury classifiable to 840-848,
      except tendon injury) 905.7
    tendon involvement 905.8
  toxic effect of
    drug, medicinal or biological substance
        (conditions classifiable to 960-979)
        909.0
    nonmedical substance (conditions
        classifiable to 980-989) 909.1
  trachoma (conditions classifiable to 076) 139.1
  tuberculosis 137.0
    bones and joints (conditions classifiable to
        015) 137.3
    central nervous system (conditions
        classifiable to 013) 137.1
    genitourinary (conditions classifiable to
        016) 137.2
    pulmonary (conditions classifiable to
        010-012) 137.0
    specified organs NEC (conditions
        classifiable to 014, 017-018) 137.4
  viral encephalitis (conditions classifiable to
      049.8, 049.9, 062-064) 139.0

Late —*continued*
  wound, open
    extremity (injury classifiable to 880-884 and
        890-894, except .2) 906.1
      tendon (injury classifiable to 880-884 with
          .2 and 890-894 with .2) 905.8
    head, neck, and trunk (injury classifiable to
        870-879) 906.0
Latent —*see* condition
Lateral —*see* condition
Laterocession —*see* Lateroversion
Lateroflexion —*see* Lateroversion
Lateroversion
  cervix—*see* Lateroversion, uterus
  uterus, uterine (cervix) (postinfectional)
      (postpartal, old) 621.6
    congenital 752.3
    in pregnancy or childbirth 654.4
      affecting fetus or newborn 763.89
Lathyrism 988.2
Launois' syndrome (pituitary gigantism) 253.0
Launois-Bensaude's lipomatosis 272.8
Launois-Cléret syndrome (adiposogenital
    dystrophy) 253.8
Laurence-Moon-Biedl syndrome (obesity,
    polydactyly, and mental retardation) 759.89
LAV (disease) (illness) (infection)—*see* Human
    immunodeficiency virus (disease) (illness)
    (infection)
LAV/HTLV-III (disease) (illness)
    (infection)—*see* Human immunodeficiency
    virus (disease) (illness) (infection)
Lawford's syndrome (encephalocutaneous
    angiomatosis) 759.6
Lax, laxity —*see also* Relaxation
  ligament 728.4
  skin (acquired) 701.8
    congenital 756.83
Laxative habit (*see also* Abuse, drugs,
    nondependent) 305.9
Lazy leukocyte syndrome 288.0
Lead —*see also* condition
  exposure to V15.86
  incrustation of cornea 371.15
  poisoning 984.9
    specified type of lead—*see* Table of drugs and
        chemicals
Lead miner's lung 503
Leakage
  amniotic fluid 658.1
    with delayed delivery 658.2
    affecting fetus or newborn 761.1
  bile from drainage tube (T tube) 997.4
  blood (microscopic), fetal, into maternal
      circulation 656.0
    affecting management of pregnancy or
        puerperium 656.0
  device, implant, or graft—*see* Complications,
      mechanical
  spinal fluid at lumbar puncture site 997.09
  urine, continuous 788.37
Leaky heart —*see* Endocarditis
Learning defect, specific NEC
    (strephosymbolia) 315.2
Leather bottle stomach (M8142/3) 151.9
Leber's
  congenital amaurosis 362.76
  optic atrophy (hereditary) 377.16
Lederer's anemia or disease (acquired
    infectious hemolytic anemia) 283.19
Lederer-Brill syndrome (acquired infectious
    hemolytic anemia) 283.19

Leeches (aquatic) (land) 134.2
Left-sided neglect 781.8
Leg —*see* condition
Legal investigation V62.5
Legg (-Calvé) -Perthes disease or syndrome
   (osteochondrosis, femoral capital) 732.1
Legionnaires' disease 482.84
Leigh's disease 330.8
Leiner's disease (exfoliative dermatitis) 695.89
Leiofibromyoma (M8890/0)—*see also*
   Leiomyoma
  uterus (cervix) (corpus) (*see also* Leiomyoma,
   uterus) 218.9
Leiomyoblastoma (M8891/1)—*see* Neoplasm,
  connective tissue, uncertain behavior
Leiomyofibroma (M8890/0)—*see also*
  Neoplasm, connective tissue, benign
  uterus (cervix) (corpus) (*see also* Leiomyoma,
   uterus) 218.9
Leiomyoma (M8890/0)—*see also* Neoplasm,
  connective tissue, benign
  bizarre (M8893/0)—*see* Neoplasm, connective
   tissue, benign
  cellular (M8892/1)—*see* Neoplasm, connective
   tissue, uncertain behavior
  epithelioid (M8891/1)—*see* Neoplasm,
   connective tissue, uncertain behavior
  prostate (polypoid) 600.2
  uterus (cervix) (corpus) 218.9
   interstitial 218.1
   intramural 218.1
   submucous 218.0
   subperitoneal 218.2
   subserous 218.2
   vascular (M8894/0)—*see* Neoplasm,
    connective tissue, benign
Leiomyomatosis (intravascular) (M8890/1)—*see*
  Neoplasm, connective tissue, uncertain
  behavior
Leiomyosarcoma (M8890/3)—*see also*
  Neoplasm, connective tissue, malignant
  epithelioid (M8891/3)—*see* Neoplasm,
   connective tissue, malignant
Leishmaniasis 085.9
  American 085.5
   cutaneous 085.4
   mucocutaneous 085.5
  Asian desert 085.2
  Brazilian 085.5
  cutaneous 085.9
   acute necrotizing 085.2
   American 085.4
   Asian desert 085.2
   diffuse 085.3
   dry form 085.1
   Ethiopian 085.3
   eyelid 085.5 *[373.6]*
   late 085.1
   lepromatous 085.3
   recurrent 085.1
   rural 085.2
   ulcerating 085.1
   urban 085.1
   wet form 085.2
   zoonotic form 085.2
  dermal—*see also* Leishmaniasis, cutaneous
   post kala-azar 085.0
  eyelid 085.5 *[373.6]*
  infantile 085.0
  Mediterranean 085.0
  mucocutaneous (American) 085.5

Leishmaniasis—*continued*
  naso-oral 085.5
  nasopharyngeal 085.5
  Old World 085.1
  tegumentaria diffusa 085.4
  vaccination, prophylactic (against) V05.2
  visceral (Indian) 085.0
Leishmanoid, dermal —*see also* Leishmaniasis,
  cutaneous
  post kala-azar 085.0
Leloir's disease 695.4
Lenegre's disease 426.0
Lengthening, leg 736.81
Lennox's syndrome (*see also* Epilepsy) 345.0
Lens —*see* condition
Lenticonus (anterior) (posterior) (congenital)
  743.36
Lenticular degeneration, progressive 275.1
Lentiglobus (posterior) (congenital) 743.36
Lentigo (congenital) 709.09
  juvenile 709.09
  Maligna (M8742/2)—*see also* Neoplasm, skin,
   in situ
   melanoma (M8742/3)—*see* Melanoma
  senile 709.09
Leonine leprosy 030.0
Leontiasis
  ossium 733.3
  syphilitic 095.8
   congenital 090.5
Léopold-Lévi's syndrome (paroxysmal thyroid
  instability) 242.9
Lepore hemoglobin syndrome 282.4
Lepothrix 039.0
Lepra 030.9
  Willan's 696.1
Leprechaunism 259.8
Lepromatous leprosy 030.0
Leprosy 030.9
  anesthetic 030.1
  beriberi 030.1
  borderline (group B) (infiltrated) (neuritic) 030.3
  cornea (*see also* Leprosy, by type) 030.9
   [371.89]
  dimorphous (group B) (infiltrated)
   (lepromatous) (neuritic) (tuberculoid) 030.3
  eyelid 030.0 *[373.4]*
  indeterminate (group I) (macular) (neuritic)
   (uncharacteristic) 030.2
  leonine 030.0
  lepromatous (diffuse) (infiltrated) (macular)
   (neuritic) (nodular) (type L) 030.0
  macular (early) (neuritic) (simple) 030.2
  maculoanesthetic 030.1
  mixed 030.0
  neuro 030.1
  nodular 030.0
  primary neuritic 030.3
  specified type or group NEC 030.8
  tubercular 030.1
  tuberculoid (macular) (maculoanesthetic)
   (major) (minor) (neuritic) (type T) 030.1
Leptocytosis, hereditary 282.4
Leptomeningitis (chronic) (circumscribed)
  (hemorrhagic) (nonsuppurative) (*see also*
  Meningitis) 322.9
  aseptic 047.9
   adenovirus 049.1
   Coxsackie virus 047.0
   ECHO virus 047.1
   enterovirus 047.9

Leptomeningitis—*continued*
lymphocytic choriomeningitis 049.0
epidemic 036.0
late effect—*see* category 326
meningococcal 036.0
pneumococcal 320.1
syphilitic 094.2
tuberculous (*see also* Tuberculosis, meninges)
013.0
Leptomeningopathy (*see also* Meningitis) 322.9
Leptospiral —*see* condition
Leptospirochetal —*see* condition
Leptospirosis 100.9
autumnalis 100.89
canicula 100.89
grippotyphosa 100.89
hebdomidis 100.89
icterohemorrhagica 100.0
nanukayami 100.89
pomona 100.89
Weil's disease 100.0
Leptothricosis —*see* Actinomycosis
Leptothrix infestation —*see* Actinomycosis
Leptotricosis —*see* Actinomycosis
Leptus dermatitis 133.8
Léri's pleonosteosis 756.89
Léri-Weill syndrome 756.59
Leriche syndrome (aortic bifurcation occlusion)
444.0
Lermoyez's syndrome (*see also* Disease,
Ménière's) 386.00
Lesbianism —*omit code*
egodystonic 302.0
problems with 302.0
Lesch-Nyhan syndrome (hypoxanthine-guanine-
phosphoribosyltransferase deficiency) 277.2
Lesion
abducens nerve 378.54
alveolar process 525.8
anorectal 569.49
aortic (valve)—*see* Endocarditis, aortic
auditory nerve 388.5
basal ganglion 333.90
bile duct (*see also* Disease, biliary) 576.8
bladder 596.9
bone 733.90
brachial plexus 353.0
brain 348.8
congenital 742.9
vascular (*see also* Lesion, cerebrovascular)
437.9
degenerative 437.1
healed or old without residuals V12.59
hypertensive 437.2
late effect—*see* Late effect(s) (of)
cerebrovascular disease
buccal 528.9
calcified—*see* Calcification
canthus 373.9
carate—*see* Pinta, lesions
cardia 537.89
cardiac—*see also* Disease, heart congenital
746.9
valvular—*see* Endocarditis
cauda equina 344.60
with neurogenic bladder 344.61
cecum 569.89
cerebral—*see* Lesion, brain
cerebrovascular (*see also* Disease,
cerebrovascular NEC) 437.9

Lesion—*continued*
degenerative 437.1
healed or old without residuals V12.59
hypertensive 437.2
specified type NEC 437.8
cervical root (nerve) NEC 353.2
chiasmal 377.54
associated with
inflammatory disorders 377.54
neoplasm NEC 377.52
pituitary 377.51
pituitary disorders 377.51
vascular disorders 377.53
chorda tympani 351.8
coin, lung 793.1
colon 569.89
congenital—*see* Anomaly
conjunctiva 372.9
coronary artery (*see also* Ischemia, heart) 414.9
cranial nerve 352.9
first 352.0
second 377.49
third
partial 378.51
total 378.52
fourth 378.53
fifth 350.9
sixth 378.54
seventh 351.9
eighth 388.5
ninth 352.2
tenth 352.3
eleventh 352.4
twelfth 352.5
cystic—*see* Cyst
degenerative—*see* Degeneration
dermal (skin) 709.9
duodenum 537.89
with obstruction 537.3
eyelid 373.9
gasserian ganglion 350.8
gastric 537.89
gastroduodenal 537.89
gastrointestinal 569.89
glossopharyngeal nerve 352.2
heart (organic)—*see also* Disease, heart
vascular—*see* Disease, cardiovascular
helix (ear) 709.9
hyperchromic, due to pinta (carate) 103.1
hyperkeratotic (*see also* Hyperkeratosis) 701.1
hypoglossal nerve 352.5
hypopharynx 478.29
hypothalamic 253.9
ileocecal coil 569.89
ileum 569.89
iliohypogastric nerve 355.79
ilioinguinal nerve 355.79
in continuity—*see* Injury, nerve, by site
inflammatory—*see* Inflammation
intestine 569.89
intracerebral—*see* Lesion, brain
intrachiasmal (optic) (*see also* Lesion,
chiasmal) 377.54
intracranial, space-occupying NEC 784.2
joint 719.90
ankle 719.97
elbow 719.92
foot 719.97

Letterer-Siwe disease (acute histiocytosis X)
  (M9722/3) 202.5
Leucinosis 270.3
Leucocoria 360.44
Leucosarcoma (M9850/3) 207.8
Leukasmus 270.2
Leukemia, leukemic (congenital) (M9800/3)
  208.9

> *Note—Use the following fifth-digit*
> *subclassification for categories 203-208:*
>
> *0 without mention of remission*
> *1 with remission*

  acute NEC (M9801/3) 208.0
  aleukemic NEC (M9804/3) 208.8
    granulocytic (M9864/3) 205.8
  basophilic (M9870/3) 205.1
  blast (cell) (M9801/3) 208.0
  blastic (M9801/3) 208.0
    granulocytic (M9861/3) 205.0
  chronic NEC (M9803/3) 208.1
  compound (M9810/3) 207.8
  eosinophilic (M9880/3) 205.1
  giant cell (M9910/3) 207.2
  granulocytic (M9860/3) 205.9
    acute (M9861/3) 205.0
    aleukemic (M9864/3) 205.8
    blastic (M9861/3) 205.0
    chronic (M9863/3) 205.1
    subacute (M9862/3) 205.2
    subleukemic (M9864/3) 205.8
  hairy cell (M9940/3) 202.4
  hemoblastic (M9801/3) 208.0
  histiocytic (M9890/3) 206.9
  lymphatic (M9820/3) 204.9
    acute (M9821/3) 204.0
    aleukemic (M9824/3) 204.8
    chronic (M9823/3) 204.1
    subacute (M9822/3) 204.2
    subleukemic (M9824/3) 204.8
  lymphoblastic (M9821/3) 204.0
  lymphocytic (M9820/3) 204.9
    acute (M9821/3) 204.0
    aleukemic (M9824/3) 204.8
    chronic (M9823/3) 204.1
    subacute (M9822/3) 204.2
    subleukemic (M9824/3) 204.8
  lymphogenous (M9820/3)—*see* Leukemia,
    lymphoid
  lymphoid (M9820/3) 204.9
    acute (M9821/3) 204.0
    aleukemic (M9824/3) 204.8
    blastic (M9821/3) 204.0
    chronic (M9823/3) 204.1
    subacute (M9822/3) 204.2
    subleukemic (M9824/3) 204.8
  lymphosarcoma cell (M9850/3) 207.8
  mast cell (M9900/3) 207.8
  megakaryocytic (M9910/3) 207.2
  megakaryocytoid (M9910/3) 207.2
  mixed (cell) (M9810/3) 207.8
  monoblastic (M9891/3) 206.0
  monocytic (Schilling-type) (M9890/3) 206.9
    acute (M9891/3) 206.0
    aleukemic (M9894/3) 206.8
    chronic (M9893/3) 206.1
    Naegeli-type (M9863/3) 205.1
    subacute (M9892/3) 206.2
    subleukemic (M9894/3) 206.8

Leukemia, leukemic—*continued*
  monocytoid (M9890/3) 206.9
    acute (M9891/3) 206.0
    aleukemic (M9894/3) 206.8
    chronic (M9893/3) 206.1
    myelogenous (M9863/3) 205.1
    subacute (M9892/3) 206.2
    subleukemic (M9894/3) 206.8
  monomyelocytic (M9860/3)—*see* Leukemia,
    myelomonocytic
  myeloblastic (M9861/3) 205.0
  myelocytic (M9863/3) 205.1
    acute (M9861/3) 205.0
  myelogenous (M9860/3) 205.9
    acute (M9861/3) 205.0
    aleukemic (M9864/3) 205.8
    chronic (M9863/3) 205.1
    monocytoid (M9863/3) 205.1
    subacute (M9862/3) 205.2
    subleukemic (M9864) 205.8
  myeloid (M9860/3) 205.9
    acute (M9861/3) 205.0
    aleukemic (M9864/3) 205.8
    chronic (M9863/3) 205.1
    subacute (M9862/3) 205.2
    subleukemic (M9864/3) 205.8
  myelomonocytic (M9860/3) 205.9
    acute (M9861/3) 205.0
    chronic (M9863/3) 205.1
  Naegeli-type monocytic (M9863/3) 205.1
  neutrophilic (M9865/3) 205.1
  plasma cell (M9830/3) 203.1
  plasmacytic (M9830/3) 203.1
  prolymphocytic (M9825/3)—*see* Leukemia,
    lymphoid
  promyelocytic, acute (M9866/3) 205.0
  Schilling-type monocytic (M9890/3)—*see*
    Leukemia, monocytic
  stem cell (M9801/3) 208.0
  subacute NEC (M9802/3) 208.2
  subleukemic NEC (M9804/3) 208.8
  thrombocytic (M9910/3) 207.2
  undifferentiated (M9801/3) 208.0
Leukemoid reaction (lymphocytic) (monocytic)
  (myelocytic) 288.8
Leukoclastic vasculitis 446.29
Leukocoria 360.44
Leukocythemia —*see* Leukemia
Leukocytosis 288.8
  basophilic 288.8
  eosinophilic 288.3
  lymphocytic 288.8
  monocytic 288.8
  neutrophilic 288.8
Leukoderma 709.09
  syphilitic 091.3
  late 095.8
Leukodermia (*see also* Leukoderma) 709.09
Leukodystrophy (cerebral) (globoid cell)
  (metachromatic) (progressive) (sudanophilic)
  330.0
Leukoedema, mouth or tongue 528.7
Leukoencephalitis
  acute hemorrhagic (postinfectious) NEC 136.9
    [323.6]
    postimmunization or postvaccinal 323.5
  subacute sclerosing 046.2
    van Bogaert's 046.2
  van Bogaert's (sclerosing) 046.2

Leukoencephalopathy (*see also* Encephalitis)
323.9
  acute necrotizing hemorrhagic (postinfectious)
    136.9 *[323.6]*
    postimmunization or postvaccinal 323.5
  metachromatic 330.0
  multifocal (progressive) 046.3
  progressive multifocal 046.3
Leukoerythroblastosis 289.0
Leukoerythrosis 289.0
Leukokeratosis (*see also* Leukoplakia) 702.8
  mouth 528.6
  nicotina palati 528.7
  tongue 528.6
Leukokoria 360.44
Leukokoraurosis vulva, vulvae 624.0
Leukolymphosarcoma (M9850/3) 207.8
Leukoma (cornea) (interfering with central
    vision) 371.03
  adherent 371.04
Leukomelanopathy, hereditary 288.2
Leukonychia (punctata) (striata) 703.8
  congenital 757.5
Leukopathia
  unguium 703.8
    congenital 757.5
Leukopenia 288.0
  cyclic 288.0
  familial 288.0
  malignant 288.0
  periodic 288.0
  transitory neonatal 776.7
Leukopenic —*see* condition
Leukoplakia 702.8
  anus 569.49
  bladder (postinfectional) 596.8
  buccal 528.6
  cervix (uteri) 622.2
  esophagus 530.83
  gingiva 528.6
  kidney (pelvis) 593.89
  larynx 478.79
  lip 528.6
  mouth 528.6
  oral soft tissue (including tongue) (mucosa)
    528.6
  palate 528.6
  pelvis (kidney) 593.89
  penis (infectional) 607.0
  rectum 569.49
  syphilitic 095.8
  tongue 528.6
  tonsil 478.29
  ureter (postinfectional) 593.89
  urethra (postinfectional) 599.84
  uterus 621.8
  vagina 623.1
  vesical 596.8
  vocal cords 478.5
  vulva 624.0
Leukopolioencephalopathy 330.0
Leukorrhea (vagina) 623.5
  due to trichomonas (vaginalis) 131.00
  trichomonal (Trichomonas vaginalis) 131.00
Leukosarcoma (M9850/3) 207.8
Leukosis (M9800/3)—*see* Leukemia
Lev's disease or syndrome (acquired complete
    heart block) 426.0
Levi's syndrome (pituitary dwarfism) 253.3
Levocardia (isolated) 746.87
  with situs inversus 759.3
Levulosuria 271.2

Lewandowski's disease (primary) (*see also*
    Tuberculosis) 017.0
Lewandowski-Lutz disease (epidermodysplasia
    verruciformis) 078.19
Leyden's disease (periodic vomiting) 536.2
Leyden's-Möbius dystrophy 359.1
Leydig cell
  carcinoma (M8650/3)
    specified site—*see* Neoplasm, by site,
      malignant
    unspecified site
      female 183.0
      male 186.9
  tumor (M8650/1)
    benign (M8650/0)
      specified site—*see* Neoplasm, by site,
        benign
      unspecified site
        female 220
        male 222.0
    malignant (M8650/3)
      specified site—*see* Neoplasm, by site,
        malignant
      unspecified site
        female 183.0
        male 186.9
    specified site—*see* Neoplasm, by site,
      uncertain behavior
    unspecified site
      female 236.2
      male 236.4
Leydig-Sertoli cell tumor (M8631/0)
  specified site—*see* Neoplasm, by site, benign
  unspecified site
    female 220
    male 222.0
Liar, pathologic 301.7
Libman-Sacks disease or syndrome 710.0
  [424.91]
Lice (infestation) 132.9
  body (pediculus corporis) 132.1
  crab 132.2
  head (pediculus capitis) 132.0
  mixed (classifiable to more than one of the
    categories 132.0-132.2) 132.3
  pubic (pediculus pubis) 132.2
Lichen 697.9
  albus 701.0
  annularis 695.89
  atrophicus 701.0
  corneus obtusus 698.3
  myxedematous 701.8
  nitidus 697.1
  pilaris 757.39
    acquired 701.1
  planopilaris 697.0
  planus (acute) (chronicus) (hypertrophic)
    (verrucous) 697.0
    morphoeicus 701.0
    sclerosus (et atrophicus) 701.0
  ruber 696.4
    acuminatus 696.4
    moniliformis 697.8
    obtusus corneus 698.3
    of Wilson 697.0
    planus 697.0
  sclerosus (et atrophicus) 701.0
  scrofulosus (primary) (*see also* Tuberculosis)
    017.0
  simplex (Vidal's) 698.3
    chronicus 698.3

Lipomyxoma (M8852/0)—*see* Lipoma, by site
Lipomyxosarcoma (M8852/3)—*see* Neoplasm,
 connective tissue, malignant
Lipophagocytosis 289.8
Lipoproteinemia (alpha) 272.4
 broad-beta 272.2
 floating-beta 272.2
 hyper-pre-beta 272.1
Lipoproteinosis (Rössle-Urbach-Wiethe) 272.8
Liposarcoma (M8850/3)—*see also* Neoplasm,
 connective tissue, malignant
 differentiated type (M8851/3)—*see* Neoplasm,
  connective tissue, malignant
 embryonal (M8852/3)—*see* Neoplasm,
  connective tissue, malignant
 mixed type (M8855/3)—*see* Neoplasm,
  connective tissue, malignant
 myxoid (M8852/3)—*see* Neoplasm, connective
  tissue, malignant
 pleomorphic (M8854/3)—*see* Neoplasm,
  connective tissue, malignant
 round cell (M8853/3)—*see* Neoplasm,
  connective tissue, malignant
 well differentiated type (M8851/3)—*see*
  Neoplasm, connective tissue, malignant
Liposynovitis prepatellaris 272.8
Lipping
 cervix 622.0
 spine (*see also* Spondylosis) 721.90
 vertebra (*see also* Spondylosis) 721.90
Lip pits (mucus), congenital 750.25
Lipschütz disease or ulcer 616.50
Lipuria 791.1
 bilharziasis 120.0
Liquefaction, vitreous humor 379.21
Lisping 307.9
Lissauer's paralysis 094.1
Lissencephalia, lissencephaly 742.2
Listerellose 027.0
Listeriose 027.0
Listeriosis 027.0
 congenital 771.2
 fetal 771.2
 suspected fetal damage affecting management
  of pregnancy 655.4
Listlessness 780.79
Lithemia 790.6
Lithiasis —*see also* Calculus
 hepatic (duct)—*see* Choledocholithiasis
 urinary 592.9
Lithopedion 779.9
 affecting management of pregnancy 656.8
Lithosis (occupational) 502
 with tuberculosis—*see* Tuberculosis, pulmonary
Lithuria 791.9
Litigation V62.5
Little
 league elbow 718.82
 stroke syndrome 435.9
Little's disease —*see* Palsy, cerebral
Littre's
 gland—*see* condition
 hernia—*see* Hernia, Littre's
Littritis (*see also* Urethritis) 597.89
Livedo 782.61
 annularis 782.61
 racemose 782.61
 reticularis 782.61
Live flesh 781.0
Liver —*see also* condition
 donor V59.8

Livida, asphyxia
 newborn 768.6
Living
 alone V60.3
 with handicapped person V60.4
Lloyd's syndrome 258.1
Loa loa 125.2
Loasis 125.2
Lobe, lobar —*see* condition
Lobo's disease or blastomycosis 116.2
Lobomycosis 116.2
Lobotomy syndrome 310.0
Lobstein's disease (brittle bones and blue sclera)
 756.51
Lobster-claw hand 755.58
Lobulation (congenital)—*see also* Anomaly,
 specified type NEC, by site
 kidney, fetal 753.3
 liver, abnormal 751.69
 spleen 759.0
Lobule, lobular —*see* condition
Local, localized —*see* condition
Locked bowel or intestine (*see also* Obstruction,
 intestine) 560.9
Locked twins 660.5
 affecting fetus or newborn 763.1
Locked-in state 344.81
Locking
 joint (*see also* Derangement, joint) 718.90
 knee 717.9
Lockjaw (*see also* Tetanus) 037
Locomotor ataxia (progressive) 094.0
Löffler's
 endocarditis 421.0
 eosinophilia or syndrome 518.3
 pneumonia 518.3
 syndrome (eosinophilic pneumonitis) 518.3
Löfgren's syndrome (sarcoidosis) 135
Loiasis 125.2
 eyelid 125.2 *[373.6]*
Loneliness V62.89
Lone star fever 082.8
Long labor 662.1
 affecting fetus or newborn 763.89
 first stage 662.0
 second stage 662.2
Long-term (current) drug use V58.69
 antibiotics V58.62
 anticoagulants V58.61
Longitudinal stripes or grooves, nails 703.8
 congenital 757.5
Loop
 intestine (*see also* Volvulus) 560.2
 intrascleral nerve 379.29
 vascular on papilla (optic) 743.57
Loose —*see also* condition
 body
  in tendon sheath 727.82
  joint 718.10
   ankle 718.17
   elbow 718.12
   foot 718.17
   hand 718.14
   hip 718.15
   knee 717.6
   multiple sites 718.19
   pelvic region 718.15
   prosthetic implant—*see* Complications,
    mechanical
   shoulder (region) 718.11
   specified site NEC 718.18

Loose—*continued*
    wrist 718.13
  cartilage (joint) (*see also* Loose, body, joint) 718.1
    knee 717.6
  facet (vertebral) 724.9
  prosthetic implant—*see* Complications, mechanical
  sesamoid, joint (*see also* Loose, body, joint) 718.1
  tooth, teeth 525.8
Loosening epiphysis 732.9
Looser (-Debray) -Milkman syndrome (osteomalacia with pseudofractures) 268.2
Lop ear (deformity) 744.29
Lorain's disease or syndrome (pituitary dwarfism) 253.3
Lorain-Levi syndrome (pituitary dwarfism) 253.3
Lordosis (acquired) (postural) 737.20
  congenital 754.2
  due to or associated with
    Charcot-Marie-Tooth disease 356.1 *[737.42]*
    mucopolysaccharidosis 277.5 *[737.42]*
    neurofibromatosis 237.71 *[737.42]*
    osteitis
      deformans 731.0 *[737.42]*
      fibrosa cystica 252.0 *[737.42]*
    osteoporosis (*see also* Osteoporosis) 733.00 *[737.42]*
    poliomyelitis (*see also* Poliomyelitis) 138 *[737.42]*
    tuberculosis (*see also* Tuberculosis) 015.0 *[737.42]*
  late effect of rickets 268.1 *[737.42]*
  postlaminectomy 737.21
  postsurgical NEC 737.22
  rachitic 268.1 *[737.42]*
  specified NEC 737.29
  tuberculous (*see also* Tuberculosis) 015.0 *[737.42]*
Loss
  appetite 783.0
    hysterical 300.11
    nonorganic origin 307.59
    psychogenic 307.59
  blood—*see* Hemorrhage
  central vision 368.41
  consciousness 780.09
    transient 780.2
  control, sphincter, rectum 787.6
    nonorganic origin 307.7
  ear ossicle, partial 385.24
  elasticity, skin 782.8
  extremity or member, traumatic, current—*see* Amputation, traumatic
  fluid (acute) 276.5
    with
      hypernatremia 276.0
      hyponatremia 276.1
    fetus or newborn 775.5
  hair 704.00
  hearing—*see also* Deafness
    central 389.14
    conductive (air) 389.00
      with sensorineural hearing loss 389.2
      combined types 389.08
      external ear 389.01
      inner ear 389.04
      middle ear 389.03
      multiple types 389.08

Loss —*continued*
    tympanic membrane 389.02
    mixed type 389.2
    nerve 389.12
    neural 389.12
    noise-induced 388.12
    perceptive NEC (*see also* Loss, hearing, sensorineural) 389.10
    sensorineural 389.10
      with conductive hearing loss 389.2
      central 389.14
      combined types 389.18
      multiple types 389.18
      neural 389.12
      sensory 389.11
    sensory 389.11
    specified type NEC 389.8
    sudden NEC 388.2
  height 781.91
  labyrinthine reactivity (unilateral) 386.55
    bilateral 386.56
  memory (*see also* Amnesia) 780.9
    mild, following organic brain damage 310.1
  mind (*see also* Psychosis) 298.9
  organ or part—*see* Absence, by site, acquired
  sensation 782.0
  sense of
    smell (*see also* Disturbance, sensation) 781.1
    taste (*see also* Disturbance, sensation) 781.1
    touch (*see also* Disturbance, sensation) 781.1
  sight (acquired) (complete) (congenital)—*see* Blindness
  spinal fluid
    headache 349.0
  substance of
    bone (*see also* Osteoporosis) 733.00
    cartilage 733.99
      ear 380.32
    vitreous (humor) 379.26
  tooth, teeth, due to accident, extraction, or local periodontal disease 525.1
  vision, visual (*see also* Blindness) 369.9
    both eyes (*see also* Blindness, both eyes) 369.3
    complete (*see also* Blindness, both eyes) 369.00
    one eye 369.8
    sudden 368.11
    transient 368.12
  vitreous 379.26
  voice (*see also* Aphonia) 784.41
  weight (cause unknown) 783.21
Lou Gehrig's disease 335.20
Louis-Bar syndrome (ataxia-telangiectasia) 334.8
Louping ill 063.1
Lousiness —*see* Lice
Low
  back syndrome 724.2
  basal metabolic rate (BMR) 794.7
  birthweight 765.1
    extreme (less than 1000 grams) 765.0
    for gestational age 764.0
    status (*see also* Status, low birth weight) V21.30
  bladder compliance 596.52
  blood pressure (*see also* Hypotension) 458.9
    reading (incidental) (isolated) (nonspecific) 796.3
  cardiac reserve—*see* Disease, heart
  compliance bladder 596.52
  frequency deafness—*see* Disorder, hearing

M

Macacus ear 744.29
Maceration
  fetus (cause not stated) 779.9
  wet feet, tropical (syndrome) 991.4
Machado-Joseph disease 334.8
Machupo virus hemorrhagic fever 078.7
Macleod's syndrome (abnormal transradiancy, one lung) 492.8
Macrocephalia, macrocephaly 756.0
Macrocheilia (congenital) 744.81
Macrochilia (congenital) 744.81
Macrocolon (congenital) 751.3
Macrocornea 743.41
  associated with buphthalmos 743.22
Macrocytic —*see* condition
Macrocytosis 289.8
Macrodactylia, macrodactylism (fingers) (thumbs) 755.57
  toes 755.65
Macrodontia 520.2
Macroencephaly 742.4
Macrogenia 524.05
Macrogenitosomia (female) (male) (praecox) 255.2
Macrogingivae 523.8
Macroglobulinemia (essential) (idiopathic) (monoclonal) (primary) (syndrome) (Waldenström's) 273.3
Macroglossia (congenital) 750.15
  acquired 529.8
Macrognathia, macrognathism (congenital) 524.00
  mandibular 524.02
    alveolar 524.72
  maxillary 524.01
    alveolar 524.71
Macrogyria (congenital) 742.4
Macrohydrocephalus (*see also* Hydrocephalus) 331.4
Macromastia (*see also* Hypertrophy, breast) 611.1
Macropsia 368.14
Macrosigmoid 564.7
  congenital 751.3
Macrospondylitis, acromegalic 253.0
Macrostomia (congenital) 744.83
Macrotia (external ear) (congenital) 744.22
Macula
  cornea, corneal
    congenital 743.43
      interfering with vision 743.42
    interfering with central vision 371.03
    not interfering with central vision 371.02
  degeneration (*see also* Degeneration, macula) 362.50
    hereditary (*see also* Dystrophy, retina) 362.70
  edema, cystoid 362.53
Maculae ceruleae 132.1
Macules and papules 709.8
Maculopathy, toxic 362.55
Madarosis 374.55
Madelung's
  deformity (radius) 755.54
  disease (lipomatosis) 272.8
  lipomatosis 272.8
Madness (*see also* Psychosis) 298.9
  myxedema (acute) 293.0
    subacute 293.1

Madura
  disease (actinomycotic) 039.9
    mycotic 117.4
  foot (actinomycotic) 039.4
    mycotic 117.4
Maduromycosis (actinomycotic) 039.9
  mycotic 117.4
Maffucci's syndrome (dyschondroplasia with hemangiomas) 756.4
Magenblase syndrome 306.4
Main en griffe (acquired) 736.06
  congenital 755.59
Maintenance
  chemotherapy regimen or treatment V58.1
  dialysis regimen or treatment
    extracorporeal (renal) V56.0
    peritoneal V56.8
    renal V56.0
  drug therapy or regimen V58.1
  external fixation NEC V54.8
  radiotherapy V58.0
  traction NEC V54.8
Majocchi's
  disease (purpura annularis telangiectodes) 709.1
  granuloma 110.6
Major —*see* condition
Mal
  cerebral (idiopathic) (*see also* Epilepsy) 345.9
  comital (*see also* Epilepsy) 345.9
  de los pintos (*see also* Pinta) 103.9
  de Meleda 757.39
  de mer 994.6
  lie—*see* Presentation, fetal
  perforant (*see also* Ulcer, lower extremity) 707.15
Malabar itch 110.9
  beard 110.0
  foot 110.4
  scalp 110.0
Malabsorption 579.9
  calcium 579.8
  carbohydrate 579.8
  disaccharide 271.3
  drug-induced 579.8
  due to bacterial overgrowth 579.8
  fat 579.8
  folate, congenital 281.2
  galactose 271.1
  glucose-galactose (congenital) 271.3
  intestinal 579.9
  isomaltose 271.3
  lactose (hereditary) 271.3
  methionine 270.4
  monosaccharide 271.8
  postgastrectomy 579.3
  postsurgical 579.3
  protein 579.8
  sucrose (-isomaltose) (congenital) 271.3
  syndrome 579.9
    postgastrectomy 579.3
    postsurgical 579.3
Malacia, bone 268.2
  juvenile (*see also* Rickets) 268.0
  Kienböck's (juvenile) (lunate) (wrist) 732.3
    adult 732.8

Malposition—*continued*
  foot 755.67
  gallbladder 751.69
  gastrointestinal tract 751.8
  genitalia, genital organ(s) or tract
    female 752.8
      external 752.49
      internal NEC 752.8
    male 752.8
      penis 752.69
  glottis 748.3
  hand 755.59
  heart 746.87
    dextrocardia 746.87
      with complete transposition of viscera
        759.3
  hepatic duct 751.69
  hip (joint) (*see also* Dislocation, hip,
    congenital) 754.30
  intestine (large) (small) 751.5
    with anomalous adhesions, fixation, or
      malrotation 751.4
  joint NEC 755.8
  kidney 753.3
  larynx 748.3
  limb 755.8
    lower 755.69
    upper 755.59
  liver 751.69
  lung (lobe) 748.69
  nail(s) 757.5
  nerve 742.8
  nervous system NEC 742.8
  nose, nasal (septum) 748.1
  organ or site NEC—*see* Anomaly, specified
    type NEC, by site
  ovary 752.0
  pancreas 751.7
  parathyroid (gland) 759.2
  patella 755.64
  peripheral vascular system 747.60
    gastrointestinal 747.61
    lower limb 747.64
    renal 747.62
    specified NEC 747.69
    spinal 747.82
    upper limb 747.63
  pituitary (gland) 759.2
  respiratory organ or system NEC 748.9
  rib (cage) 756.3
    supernumerary in cervical region 756.2
  scapula 755.59
  shoulder 755.59
  spinal cord 742.59
  spine 756.19
  spleen 759.0
  sternum 756.3
  stomach 750.7
  symphysis pubis 755.69
  testis (undescended) 752.51
  thymus (gland) 759.2
  thyroid (gland) (tissue) 759.2
    cartilage 748.3
  toe(s) 755.66
    supernumerary 755.02
  tongue 750.19
  trachea 748.3
  uterus 752.3

Malposition—*continued*
  vein(s) (peripheral) NEC (*see also*
    Malposition, congenital, peripheral
    vascular system) 747.60
    great 747.49
    portal 747.49
    pulmonary 747.49
  vena cava (inferior) (superior) 747.49
  device, implant, or graft—*see* Complications,
    mechanical
  fetus NEC (*see also* Presentation, fetal) 652.9
    with successful version 652.1
    affecting fetus or newborn 763.1
    before labor, affecting fetus or newborn 761.7
    causing obstructed labor 660.0
    in multiple gestation (one fetus or more) 652.6
      with locking 660.5
    causing obstructed labor 660.0
  gallbladder (*see also* Disease, gallbladder) 575.8
  gastrointestinal tract 569.89
    congenital 751.8
  heart (*see also* Malposition, congenital, heart)
    746.87
  intestine 569.89
    congenital 751.5
  pelvic organs or tissues
    in pregnancy or childbirth 654.4
      affecting fetus or newborn 763.89
      causing obstructed labor 660.2
        affecting fetus or newborn 763.1
  placenta—*see* Placenta, previa
  stomach 537.89
    congenital 750.7
  tooth, teeth (with impaction) 524.3
  uterus or cervix (acquired) (acute) (adherent)
    (any degree) (asymptomatic)
    (postinfectional) (postpartal, old) 621.6
    anteflexion or anteversion (*see also*
      Anteversion, uterus) 621.6
    congenital 752.3
    flexion 621.6
      lateral (*see also* Lateroversion, uterus) 621.6
    in pregnancy or childbirth 654.4
      affecting fetus or newborn 763.89
      causing obstructed labor 660.2
        affecting fetus or newborn 763.1
    inversion 621.6
    lateral (flexion) (version) (*see also*
      Lateroversion, uterus) 621.6
    lateroflexion (*see also* Lateroversion, uterus)
      621.6
    lateroversion (*see also* Lateroversion, uterus)
      621.6
    retroflexion or retroversion (*see also*
      Retroversion, uterus) 621.6
Malposture 729.9
Malpresentation, fetus (*see also* Presentation,
  fetal) 652.9
Malrotation
  cecum 751.4
  colon 751.4
  intestine 751.4
  kidney 753.3
Malta fever (*see also* Brucellosis) 023.9
Maltosuria 271.3
Maltreatment (of)
  adult 995.80
    emotional 995.82
    multiple forms 995.85
    neglect (nutritional) 995.84
    physical 995.81

Mastoiditis—*continued*
> with
>> Gradenigo's syndrome 383.02
>> petrositis 383.02
>> specified complication NEC 383.02
>> subperiosteal abscess 383.01
> chronic (necrotic) (recurrent) 383.1
> tuberculous (*see also* Tuberculosis) 015.6

Mastopathy, mastopathia 611.9
> chronica cystica 610.1
> diffuse cystic 610.1
> estrogenic 611.8
> ovarian origin 611.8

Mastoplasia 611.1

Masturbation 307.9

Maternal condition, affecting fetus or newborn
> acute yellow atrophy of liver 760.8
> albuminuria 760.1
> anesthesia or analgesia 763.5
> blood loss 762.1
> chorioamnionitis 762.7
> circulatory disease, chronic (conditions classifiable to 390-459, 745-747) 760.3
> congenital heart disease (conditions classifiable to 745-746) 760.3
> cortical necrosis of kidney 760.1
> death 761.6
> diabetes mellitus 775.0
>> manifest diabetes in the infant 775.1
> disease NEC 760.9
>> circulatory system, chronic (conditions classifiable to 390-459, 745-747) 760.3
>> genitourinary system (conditions classifiable to 580-599) 760.1
>> respiratory (conditions classifiable to 490-519, 748) 760.3
> eclampsia 760.0
> hemorrhage NEC 762.1
> hepatitis acute, malignant, or subacute 760.8
> hyperemesis (gravidarum) 761.8
> hypertension (arising during pregnancy) (conditions classifiable to 642) 760.0
> infection
>> disease classifiable to 001-136 760.2
>> genital tract NEC 760.8
>> urinary tract 760.1
> influenza 760.2
>> manifest influenza in the infant 771.2
> injury (conditions classifiable to 800-996) 760.5
> malaria 760.2
>> manifest malaria in infant or fetus 771.2
> malnutrition 760.4
> necrosis of liver 760.8
> nephritis (conditions classifiable to 580-583) 760.1
> nephrosis (conditions classifiable to 581) 760.1
> noxious substance transmitted via breast milk or placenta 760.70
>> alcohol 760.71
>> anti-infective agents 760.74
>> cocaine 760.75
>> "crack" 760.75
>> diethylstilbestrol [DES] 760.76
>> hallucinogenic agents 760.73
>> medicinal agents NEC 760.79
>> narcotics 760.72
>> obstetric anesthetic or analgesic drug 760.72
>> specified agent NEC 760.79
> nutritional disorder (conditions classifiable to 260-269) 760.4
> operation unrelated to current delivery 760.6

Maternal condition, affecting fetus. . .—*cont.*
> pre-eclampsia 760.0
> pyelitis or pyelonephritis, arising during pregnancy (conditions classifiable to 590) 760.1
> renal disease or failure 760.1
> respiratory disease, chronic (conditions classifiable to 490-519, 748) 760.3
> rheumatic heart disease (chronic) (conditions classifiable to 393-398) 760.3
> rubella (conditions classifiable to 056) 760.2
>> manifest rubella in the infant or fetus 771.0
> surgery unrelated to current delivery 760.6
>> to uterus or pelvic organs 763.89
> syphilis (conditions classifiable to 090-097) 760.2
>> manifest syphilis in the infant or fetus 090.0
> thrombophlebitis 760.3
> toxemia (of pregnancy) 760.0
>> pre-eclamptic 760.0
> toxoplasmosis (conditions classifiable to 130) 760.2
>> manifest toxoplasmosis in the infant or fetus 771.2
> transmission of chemical substance through the placenta 760.70
>> alcohol 760.71
>> anti-infective 760.74
>> cocaine 760.75
>> "crack" 760.75
>> diethylstilbestrol [DES] 760.76
>> hallucinogenic agents 760.73
>> narcotics 760.72
>> specified substance NEC 760.79
> uremia 760.1
> urinary tract conditions (conditions classifiable to 580-599) 760.1
> vomiting (pernicious) (persistent) (vicious) 761.8

Maternity —*see* Delivery

Matheiu's disease (leptospiral jaundice) 100.0

Mauclaire's disease or osteochondrosis 732.3

Maxcy's disease 081.0

Maxilla, maxillary —*see* condition

May (-Hegglin) anomaly or syndrome 288.2

Mayaro fever 066.3

Mazoplasia 610.8

MBD (minimal brain dysfunction), child (*see also* Hyperkinesia) 314.9

McArdle (-Schmid-Pearson) disease or syndrome (glycogenosis V) 271.0

McCune-Albright syndrome (osteitis fibrosa disseminata) 756.59

MCLS (mucocutaneous lymph node syndrome) 446.1

McQuarrie's syndrome (idiopathic familial hypoglycemia) 251.2

Measles (black) (hemorrhagic) (suppressed) 055.9
> with
>> encephalitis 055.0
>> keratitis 055.71
>> keratoconjunctivitis 055.71
>> otitis media 055.2
>> pneumonia 055.1
> complication 055.8
>> specified type NEC 055.79
> encephalitis 055.0
> French 056.9
> German 056.9
> keratitis 055.71
> keratoconjunctivitis 055.71

Measles—*continued*
  liberty 056.9
  otitis media 055.2
  pneumonia 055.1
  specified complications NEC 055.79
  vaccination, prophylactic (against) V04.2
Meatitis, urethral (*see also* Urethritis) 597.89
Meat poisoning —*see* Poisoning, food
Meatus, meatal —*see* condition
Meat-wrappers' asthma 506.9
Meckel's
  diverticulitis 751.0
  diverticulum (displaced) (hypertrophic) 751.0
Meconium
  aspiration 770.1
  delayed passage in newborn 777.1
  ileus 777.1
    due to cystic fibrosis 277.01
  in liquor 792.3
    noted during delivery 656.8
  insufflation 770.1
  obstruction
    fetus or newborn 777.1
      in mucoviscidosis 277.01
  passage of 792.3
    noted during delivery—*omit code*
  peritonitis 777.6
  plug syndrome (newborn) NEC 777.1
Median —*see also* condition
  arcuate ligament syndrome 447.4
  bar (prostate) 600.9
    vesical orifice 600.9
  rhomboid glossitis 529.2
Mediastinal shift 793.2
Mediastinitis (acute) (chronic) 519.2
  actinomycotic 039.8
  syphilitic 095.8
  tuberculous (*see also* Tuberculosis) 012.8
Mediastinopericarditis (*see also* Pericarditis)
    423.9
  acute 420.90
  chronic 423.8
    rheumatic 393
  rheumatic, chronic 393
Mediastinum, mediastinal —*see* condition
Medical services provided for —*see* Health,
    services provided because (of)
Medicine poisoning (by overdose) (wrong
    substance given or taken in error) 977.9
  specified drug or substance—*see* Table of drugs
    and chemicals
Medin's disease (poliomyelitis) 045.9
Mediterranean
  anemia (with other hemoglobinopathy) 282.4
  disease or syndrome (hemipathic) 282.4
  fever (*see also* Brucellosis) 023.9
    familial 277.3
  kala-azar 085.0
  leishmaniasis 085.0
  tick fever 082.1
Medulla —*see* condition
Medullary
  cystic kidney 753.16
  sponge kidney 753.17
Medullated fibers
  optic (nerve) 743.57
  retina 362.85
Medulloblastoma (M9470/3)
  desmoplastic (M9471/3) 191.6
  specified site—*see* Neoplasm, by site, malignant
  unspecified site 191.6

Medulloepithelioma (M9501/3)—*see also*
    Neoplasm, by site, malignant
  teratoid (M9502/3)—*see* Neoplasm, by site,
    malignant
Medullomyoblastoma (M9472/3)
  specified site—*see* Neoplasm, by site, malignant
  unspecified site 191.6
Meekeren-Ehlers-Danlos syndrome 756.83
Megacaryocytic —*see* condition
Megacolon (acquired) (functional) (not
    Hirschsprung's disease) 564.7
  aganglionic 751.3
  congenital, congenitum 751.3
  Hirschsprung's (disease) 751.3
  psychogenic 306.4
  toxic (*see also* Colitis, ulcerative) 556.9
Megaduodenum 537.3
Megaesophagus (functional) 530.0
  congenital 750.4
Megakaryocytic —*see* condition
Megalencephaly 742.4
Megalerythema (epidermicum) (infectiosum)
    057.0
Megalia, cutis et ossium 757.39
Megaloappendix 751.5
Megalocephalus, megalocephaly NEC 756.0
Megalocornea 743.41
  associated with buphthalmos 743.22
Megalocytic anemia 281.9
Megalodactylia (fingers) (thumbs) 755.57
  toes 755.65
Megaloduodenum 751.5
Megaloesophagus (functional) 530.0
  congenital 750.4
Megalogastria (congenital) 750.7
Megalomania 307.9
Megalophthalmos 743.8
Megalopsia 368.14
Megalosplenia (*see also* Splenomegaly) 789.2
Megaloureter 593.89
  congenital 753.22
Megarectum 569.49
Megasigmoid 564.7
  congenital 751.3
Megaureter 593.89
  congenital 753.22
Megrim 346.9
Meibomian
  cyst 373.2
    infected 373.12
  gland—*see* condition
  infarct (eyelid) 374.85
  stye 373.11
Meibomitis 373.12
Meige
  -Milroy disease (chronic hereditary edema)
    757.0
  syndrome (blepharospasm-oromandibular
    dystonia) 333.82
Melalgia, nutritional 266.2
Melancholia (*see also* Psychosis, affective)
    296.90
  climacteric 296.2
    recurrent episode 296.3
    single episode 296.2
  hypochondriac 300.7
  intermittent 296.2
    recurrent episode 296.3
    single episode 296.2
  involutional 296.2
    recurrent episode 296.3

Melanoma—*continued*
  superficial spreading (M8743/3)—*see*
    Melanoma, by site
  temple 172.3
  thigh 172.7
  toe 172.7
  trunk NEC 172.5
  umbilicus 172.5
  upper limb NEC 172.6
  vagina vault 184.0
  vulva 184.4
Melanoplakia 528.9
Melanosarcoma (M8720/3)—*see also* Melanoma
  epithelioid cell (M8771/3)—*see* Melanoma
Melanosis 709.09
  addisonian (primary adrenal insufficiency) 255.4
    tuberculous (*see also* Tuberculosis) 017.6
  adrenal 255.4
  colon 569.89
  conjunctiva 372.55
    congenital 743.49
  corii degenerativa 757.33
  cornea (presenile) (senile) 371.12
    congenital 743.43
      interfering with vision 743.42
    prenatal 743.43
      interfering with vision 743.42
  eye 372.55
    congenital 743.49
  jute spinners' 709.09
  lenticularis progressiva 757.33
  liver 573.8
  precancerous (M8741/2)—*see also* Neoplasm,
    skin, in situ
    malignant melanoma in (M8741/3)—*see*
      Melanoma
  Riehl's 709.09
  sclera 379.19
    congenital 743.47
  suprarenal 255.4
  tar 709.09
  toxic 709.09
Melanuria 791.9
MELAS 758.89
Melasma 709.09
  adrenal (gland) 255.4
  suprarenal (gland) 255.4
Melena 578.1
  due to
    swallowed maternal blood 777.3
    ulcer—*see* Ulcer, by site, with hemorrhage
  newborn 772.4
    due to swallowed maternal blood 777.3
Meleney's
  gangrene (cutaneous) 686.09
  ulcer (chronic undermining) 686.09
Melioidosis 025
Melitensis, febris 023.0
Melitococcosis 023.0
Melkersson (-Rosenthal) syndrome 351.8
Mellitus, diabetes —*see* Diabetes
Melorheostosis (bone) (leri) 733.99
Meloschisis 744.83
Melotia 744.29
Membrana
  capsularis lentis posterior 743.39
  epipapillaris 743.57
Membranacea placenta —*see* Placenta,
  abnormal
Membranaceous uterus 621.8

Membrane, membranous —*see also* condition
  folds, congenital—*see* Web
  Jackson's 751.4
  over face (causing asphyxia), fetus or newborn
    768.9
  premature rupture—*see* Rupture, membranes,
    premature
  pupillary 364.74
    persistent 743.46
  retained (complicating delivery) (with
    hemorrhage) 666.2
    without hemorrhage 667.1
  secondary (eye) 366.50
  unruptured (causing asphyxia) 768.9
  vitreous humor 379.25
Membranitis, fetal 658.4
  affecting fetus or newborn 762.7
Memory disturbance, loss or lack (*see also*
  Amnesia) 780.9
  mild, following organic brain damage 310.1
Menadione (vitamin K) deficiency 269.0
Menarche, precocious 259.1
Mendacity, pathologic 301.7
Mende's syndrome (ptosis-epicanthus) 270.2
Mendelson's syndrome (resulting from a
  procedure) 997.3
  obstetric 668.0
Ménétrier's disease or syndrome (hypertrophic
  gastritis) 535.2
Ménière's disease, syndrome, or vertigo 386.00
  cochlear 386.02
  cochleovestibular 386.01
  inactive 386.04
  in remission 386.04
  vestibular 386.03
Meninges, meningeal —*see* condition
Meningioma (M9530/0)—*see also* Neoplasm,
  meninges, benign
  angioblastic (M9535/0)—*see* Neoplasm,
    meninges, benign
  angiomatous (M9534/0)—*see* Neoplasm,
    meninges, benign
  endotheliomatous (M9531/0)—*see* Neoplasm,
    meninges, benign
  fibroblastic (M9532/0)—*see* Neoplasm,
    meninges, benign
  fibrous (M9532/0)—*see* Neoplasm, meninges,
    benign
  hemangioblastic (M9535/0)—*see* Neoplasm,
    meninges, benign
  hemangiopericytic (M9536/0)—*see* Neoplasm,
    meninges, benign
  malignant (M9530/3)—*see* Neoplasm,
    meninges, malignant
  meningiothelial (M9531/0)—*see* Neoplasm,
    meninges, benign
  meningotheliomatous (M9531/0)—*see*
    Neoplasm, meninges, benign
  mixed (M9537/0)—*see* Neoplasm, meninges,
    benign
  multiple (M9530/1) 237.6
  papillary (M9538/1) 237.6
  psammomatous (M9533/0)—*see* Neoplasm,
    meninges, benign
  syncytial (M9531/0)—*see* Neoplasm, meninges,
    benign
  transitional (M9537/0)—*see* Neoplasm,
    meninges, benign
Meningiomatosis (diffuse) (M9530/1) 237.6
Meningism (*see also* Meningismus) 781.6

Meningismus (infectional) (pneumococcal) 781.6
  due to serum or vaccine 997.09 *[321.8]*
  influenzal NEC 487.8
Meningitis (basal) (basic) (basilar) (brain)
    (cerebral) (cervical) (congestive) (diffuse)
    (hemorrhagic) (infantile) (membranous)
    (metastatic) (nonspecific) (pontine)
    (progressive) (simple) (spinal) (subacute)
    (sympathetica) (toxic) 322.9
  abacterial NEC (*see also* Meningitis, aseptic)
    047.9
  actinomycotic 039.8 *[320.7]*
  adenoviral 049.1
  Aerobacter aerogenes 320.82
  anaerobes (cocci) (gram-negative)
    (gram-positive) (mixed) (NEC) 320.81
  arbovirus NEC 066.9 *[321.2]*
    specified type NEC 066.8 *[321.2]*
  aseptic (acute) NEC 047.9
    adenovirus 049.1
    Coxsackie virus 047.0
    due to
      adenovirus 049.1
      Coxsackie virus 047.0
      ECHO virus 047.1
      enterovirus 047.9
      mumps 072.1
      poliovirus (*see also* Poliomyelitis) 045.2
        [321.2]
    ECHO virus 047.1
    herpes (simplex) virus 054.72
      zoster 053.0
    leptospiral 100.81
    lymphocytic choriomeningitis 049.0
    noninfective 322.0
  Bacillus pyocyaneus 320.89
  bacterial NEC 320.9
    anaerobic 320.81
    gram-negative 320.82
      anaerobic 320.81
  Bacteroides (fragilis) (oralis) (melaninogenicus)
    320.81
  cancerous (M8000/6) 198.4
  candidal 112.83
  carcinomatous (M8010/6) 198.4
  caseous (*see also* Tuberculosis, meninges) 013.0
  cerebrospinal (acute) (chronic) (diplococcal)
    (endemic) (epidemic) (fulminant)
    (infectious) (malignant) (meningococcal)
    (sporadic) 036.0
    carrier (suspected) of V02.59
  chronic NEC 322.2
  clear cerebrospinal fluid NEC 322.0
  Clostridium (haemolyticum) (novyi) NEC
    320.81
  coccidioidomycosis 114.2
  Coxsackie virus 047.0
  cryptococcal 117.5 *[321.0]*
  diplococcal 036.0
    gram-negative 036.0
    gram-positive 320.1
  Diplococcus pneumoniae 320.1
  due to
    actinomycosis 039.8 *[320.7]*
    adenovirus 049.1
    coccidiomycosis 114.2
    enterovirus 047.9
      specified NEC 047.8
    histoplasmosis (*see also* Histoplasmosis)
      115.91
    Listerosis 027.0 *[320.7]*

Meningitis—*continued*
  Lyme disease 088.81 *[320.7]*
  moniliasis 112.83
  mumps 072.1
  neurosyphilis 094.2
  nonbacterial organisms NEC 321.8
  oidiomycosis 112.83
  poliovirus (*see also* Poliomyelitis) 045.2
    [321.2]
  preventive immunization, inoculation, or
    vaccination 997.09 *[321.8]*
  sarcoidosis 135 *[321.4]*
  sporotrichosis 117.1 *[321.1]*
  syphilis 094.2
    acute 091.81
    congenital 090.42
    secondary 091.81
  trypanosomiasis (*see also* Trypanosomiasis)
    086.9 *[321.3]*
  whooping cough 033.9 *[320.7]*
  E. coli 320.82
  ECHO virus 047.1
  endothelial-leukocytic, benign, recurrent 047.9
  Enterobacter aerogenes 320.82
  enteroviral 047.9
    specified type NEC 047.8
  enterovirus 047.9
    specified NEC 047.8
  eosinophilic 322.1
  epidemic NEC 036.0
  Escherichia coli (E. coli) 320.82
  Eubacterium 320.81
  fibrinopurulent NEC 320.9
    specified type NEC 320.89
  Friedländer (bacillus) 320.82
  fungal NEC 117.9 *[321.1]*
  Fusobacterium 320.81
  gonococcal 098.82
  gram-negative bacteria NEC 320.82
    anaerobic 320.81
    cocci 036.0
      specified NEC 320.82
  gram-negative cocci NEC 036.0
    specified NEC 320.82
  gram-positive cocci NEC 320.9
  H. influenzae 320.0
  herpes (simplex) virus 054.72
    zoster 053.0
  infectious NEC 320.9
  influenzal 320.0
  Klebsiella pneumoniae 320.82
  late effect—*see* Late, effect, meningitis
  leptospiral (aseptic) 100.81
  Listerella (monocytogenes) 027.0 *[320.7]*
  Listeria monocytogenes 027.0 *[320.7]*
  lymphocytic (acute) (benign) (serous) 049.0
    choriomeningitis virus 049.0
  meningococcal (chronic) 036.0
  Mima polymorpha 320.82
  Mollaret's 047.9
  monilial 112.83
  mumps (virus) 072.1
  mycotic NEC 117.9 *[321.1]*
  Neisseria 036.0
  neurosyphilis 094.2
  nonbacterial NEC (*see also* Meningitis, aseptic)
    047.9
  nonpyogenic NEC 322.0
  oidiomycosis 112.83
  ossificans 349.2
  Peptococcus 320.81

Meningitis—*continued*
  Peptostreptococcus 320.81
  pneumococcal 320.1
  poliovirus (*see also* Poliomyelitis) 045.2 *[321.2]*
  Proprionibacterium 320.81
  Proteus morganii 320.82
  Pseudomonas (aeruginosa) (pyocyaneus) 320.82
  purulent NEC 320.9
    specified organism NEC 320.89
  pyogenic NEC 320.9
    specified organism NEC 320.89
  Salmonella 003.21
  septic NEC 320.9
    specified organism NEC 320.89
  serosa circumscripta NEC 322.0
  serous NEC (*see also* Meningitis, aseptic) 047.9
    lymphocytic 049.0—
    syndrome 348.2
  Serratia (marcescens) 320.82
  specified organism NEC 320.89
  sporadic cerebrospinal 036.0
  sporotrichosis 117.1 *[321.1]*
  staphylococcal 320.3
  sterile 997.09
  streptococcal (acute) 320.2
  suppurative 320.9
    specified organism NEC 320.89
  syphilitic 094.2
    acute 091.81
    congenital 090.42
    secondary 091.81
  torula 117.5 *[321.0]*
  traumatic (complication of injury) 958.8
  Treponema (denticola) (macrodenticum) 320.81
  trypanosomiasis 086.1 *[321.3]*
  tuberculous (*see also* Tuberculosis, meninges)
    013.0
  typhoid 002.0 *[320.7]*
  Veillonella 320.81
  Vibrio vulnificus 320.82
  viral, virus NEC (*see also* Meningitis, aseptic)
    047.9
  Wallgren's (*see also* Meningitis, aseptic) 047.9
Meningocele (congenital) (spinal) (*see also*
    Spina bifida) 741.9
  acquired (traumatic) 349.2
  cerebral 742.0
  cranial 742.0
Meningocerebritis —*see* Meningoencephalitis
Meningococcemia (acute) (chronic) 036.2
Meningococcus, meningococcal (*see also*
    condition) 036.9
  adrenalitis, hemorrhagic 036.3
  carditis 036.40
  carrier (suspected) of V02.59
  cerebrospinal fever 036.0
  encephalitis 036.1
  endocarditis 036.42
  infection NEC 036.9
  meningitis (cerebrospinal) 036.0
  myocarditis 036.43
  optic neuritis 036.81
  pericarditis 036.41
  septicemia (chronic) 036.2
Meningoencephalitis (*see also* Encephalitis)
    323.9
  acute NEC 048
  bacterial, purulent, pyogenic, or septic—*see*
    Meningitis
  chronic NEC 094.1
  diffuse NEC 094.1

Meningoencephalitis—*continued*
  diphasic 063.2
  due to
    actinomycosis 039.8 *[320.7]*
    blastomycosis NEC (*see also* Blastomycosis)
      116.0 *[323.4]*
    free-living amebae 136.2
    Listeria monocytogenes 027.0 *[320.7]*
    Lyme disease 088.81 *[320.7]*
    mumps 072.2
    Naegleria (amebae) (gruberi) (organisms)
      136.2
    rubella 056.01
    sporotrichosis 117.1 *[321.1]*
    toxoplasmosis (acquired) 130.0
      congenital (active) 771.2 *[323.4]*
    Trypanosoma 086.1 *[323.2]*
  epidemic 036.0
  herpes 054.3
  herpetic 054.3
  H. influenzae 320.0
  infectious (acute) 048
  influenzal 320.0
  late effect—*see* category 326
  Listeria monocytogenes 027.0 *[320.7]*
  lymphocytic (serous) 049.0
  mumps 072.2
  parasitic NEC 123.9 *[323.4]*
  pneumococcal 320.1
  primary amebic 136.2
  rubella 056.01
  serous 048
    lymphocytic 049.0
  specific 094.2
  staphylococcal 320.3
  streptococcal 320.2
  syphilitic 094.2
  toxic NEC 989.9 *[323.7]*
    due to
      carbon tetrachloride 987.8 *[323.7]*
      hydroxyquinoline derivatives poisoning
        961.3 *[323.7]*
      lead 984.9 *[323.7]*
      mercury 985.0 *[323.7]*
      thallium 985.8 *[323.7]*
  toxoplasmosis (acquired) 130.0
  trypanosomic 086.1 *[323.2]*
  tuberculous (*see also* Tuberculosis, meninges)
    013.0
  virus NEC 048
Meningoencephalocele 742.0
  syphilitic 094.89
    congenital 090.49
Meningoencephalomyelitis (*see also*
    Meningoencephalitis) 323.9
  acute NEC 048
    disseminated (postinfectious) 136.9 *[323.6]*
      postimmunization or postvaccination 323.5
  due to
    actinomycosis 039.8 *[320.7]*
    torula 117.5 *[323.4]*
    toxoplasma or toxoplasmosis (acquired) 130.0
      congenital (active) 771.2 *[323.4]*
  late effect—*see* category 326
Meningoencephalomyelopathy (*see also*
    Meningoencephalomyelitis) 349.9
Meningoencephalopathy (*see also*
    Meningoencephalitis) 348.3
Meningoencephalopoliomyelitis (*see also*
    Poliomyelitis, bulbar) 045.0
  late effect 138

Meningomyelitis (*see also* Meningoencephalitis) 323.9
  blastomycotic NEC (*see also* Blastomycosis) 116.0 *[323.4]*
  due to
    actinomycosis 039.8 *[320.7]*
    blastomycosis (*see also* Blastomycosis) 116.0 *[323.4]*
    Meningococcus 036.0
    sporotrichosis 117.1 *[323.4]*
    torula 117.5 *[323.4]*
  late effect—*see* category 326
  lethargic 049.8
  meningococcal 036.0
  syphilitic 094.2
  tuberculous (*see also* Tuberculosis, meninges) 013.0
Meningomyelocele (*see also* Spina bifida) 741.9
  syphilitic 094.89
Meningomyeloneuritis —*see* Meningoencephalitis
Meningoradiculitis —*see* Meningitis
Meningovascular —*see* condition
Meniscocytosis 282.60
Menkes' syndrome —*see* Syndrome, Menkes'
Menolipsis 626.0
Menometrorrhagia 626.2
Menopause, menopausal (symptoms) (syndrome) 627.2
  arthritis (any site) NEC 716.3
  artificial 627.4
  bleeding 627.0
  crisis 627.2
  depression (*see also* Psychosis, affective) 296.2
    agitated 296.2
      recurrent episode 296.3
      single episode 296.2
    psychotic 296.2
      recurrent episode 296.3
      single episode 296.2
    recurrent episode 296.3
    single episode 296.2
  melancholia (*see also* Psychosis, affective) 296.2
    recurrent episode 296.3
    single episode 296.2
  paranoid state 297.2
  paraphrenia 297.2
  postsurgical 627.4
  premature 256.3
    postirradiation 256.2
    postsurgical 256.2
  psychoneurosis 627.2
  psychosis NEC 298.8
  surgical 627.4
  toxic polyarthritis NEC 716.39
Menorrhagia (primary) 626.2
  climacteric 627.0
  menopausal 627.0
  postclimacteric 627.1
  postmenopausal 627.1
  preclimacteric 627.0
  premenopausal 627.0
  puberty (menses retained) 626.3
Menorrhalgia 625.3
Menoschesis 626.8
Menostaxis 626.2
Menses, retention 626.8
Menstrual —*see* Menstruation
  cycle, irregular 626.4
  disorders NEC 626.9

Menstrual—*continued*
  extraction V25.3
  fluid, retained 626.8
  molimen 625.4
  period, normal V65.5
  regulation V25.3
Menstruation
  absent 626.0
  anovulatory 628.0
  delayed 626.8
  difficult 625.3
  disorder 626.9
    psychogenic 306.52
    specified NEC 626.8
  during pregnancy 640.8
  excessive 626.2
  frequent 626.2
  infrequent 626.1
  irregular 626.4
  latent 626.8
  membranous 626.8
  painful (primary) (secondary) 625.3
    psychogenic 306.52
  passage of clots 626.2
  precocious 626.8
  protracted 626.8
  retained 626.8
  retrograde 626.8
  scanty 626.1
  suppression 626.8
  vicarious (nasal) 625.8
Mentagra (*see also* Sycosis) 704.8
Mental —*see also* condition
  deficiency (*see also* Retardation, mental) 319
  deterioration (*see also* Psychosis) 298.9
  disorder (*see also* Disorder, mental) 300.9
  exhaustion 300.5
  insufficiency (congenital) (*see also* Retardation, mental) 319
  observation without need for further medical care NEC V71.09
  retardation (*see also* Retardation, mental) 319
  subnormality (*see also* Retardation, mental) 319
    mild 317
    moderate 318.0
    profound 318.2
    severe 318.1
  upset (*see also* Disorder, mental) 300.9
Meralgia paresthetica 355.1
Mercurial —*see* condition
Mercurialism NEC 985.0
Merergasia 300.9
MERFF 758.89
Merkel cell tumor —*see* Neoplasm, by site, malignant
Merocele (*see also* Hernia, femoral) 553.00
Meromelia 755.4
  lower limb 755.30
    intercalary 755.32
      femur 755.34
        tibiofibular (complete) (incomplete) 755.33
      fibula 755.37
      metatarsal(s) 755.38
      tarsal(s) 755.38
      tibia 755.36
      tibiofibular 755.35
    terminal (complete) (partial) (transverse) 755.31
      longitudinal 755.32
        metatarsal(s) 755.38
        phalange(s) 755.39

Mole—*continued*
malignant
meaning
malignant hydatidiform mole (M9100/1) 236.1
melanoma (M8720/3)—*see* Melanoma
nonpigmented (M8730/0)—*see* Neoplasm, skin, benign
pregnancy NEC 631
skin (M8720/0)—*see* Neoplasm, skin, benign
tubal—*see* Pregnancy, tubal
vesicular (*see also* Hydatidiform mole) 630
Molimen, molimina (menstrual) 625.4
Mollaret's meningitis 047.9
Mollities (cerebellar) (cerebral) 437.8
ossium 268.2
Molluscum
contagiosum 078.0
epitheliale 078.0
fibrosum (M8851/0)—*see* Lipoma, by site
pendulum (M8851/0)—*see* Lipoma, by site
Mönckeberg's arteriosclerosis, degeneration disease, or sclerosis (*see also* Arteriosclerosis, extremities) 440.20
Monday fever 504
Monday morning dyspnea or asthma 504
Mondini's malformation (cochlea) 744.05
Mondor's disease (thrombophlebitis of breast) 451.89
Mongolian, mongolianism, mongolism mongoloid 758.0
spot 757.33
Monilethrix (congenital) 757.4
Monilia infestation —*see* Candidiasis
Moniliasis —*see also* Candidiasis
neonatal 771.7
vulvovaginitis 112.1
Monoarthritis 716.60
ankle 716.67
arm 716.62
lower (and wrist) 716.63
upper (and elbow) 716.62
foot (and ankle) 716.67
forearm (and wrist) 716.63
hand 716.64
leg 716.66
lower 716.66
upper 716.65
pelvic region (hip) (thigh) 716.65
shoulder (region) 716.61
specified site NEC 716.68
Monoblastic —*see* condition
Monochromatism (cone) (rod) 368.54
Monocytic —*see* condition
Monocytosis (symptomatic) 288.8
Monofixation syndrome 378.34
Monomania (*see also* Psychosis) 298.9
Mononeuritis 355.9
cranial nerve—*see* Disorder, nerve, cranial
femoral nerve 355.2
lateral
cutaneous nerve of thigh 355.1
popliteal nerve 355.3
lower limb 355.8
specified nerve NEC 355.79
medial popliteal nerve 355.4
median nerve 354.1
multiplex 354.5
plantar nerve 355.6
posterior tibial nerve 355.5
radial nerve 354.3

Mononeuritis—*continued*
sciatic nerve 355.0
ulnar nerve 354.2
upper limb 354.9
specified nerve NEC 354.8
vestibular 388.5
Mononeuropathy (*see also* Mononeuritis) 355.9
diabetic NEC 250.6 *[355.9]*
lower limb 250.6 *[355.8]*
upper limb 250.6 *[354.9]*
iliohypogastric nerve 355.79
ilioinguinal nerve 355.79
obturator nerve 355.79
saphenous nerve 355.79
Mononucleosis, infectious 075
with hepatitis 075 *[573.1]*
Monoplegia 344.5
brain (current episode) (*see also* Paralysis, brain) 437.8
fetus or newborn 767.8
cerebral (current episode) (*see also* Paralysis, brain) 437.8
congenital or infantile (cerebral) (spastic) (spinal) 343.3
embolic (current) (*see also* Embolism, brain) 434.1
late effect—*see* Late effect(s) (of) cerebrovascular disease
infantile (cerebral) (spastic) (spinal) 343.3
lower limb 344.30
affecting
dominant side 344.31
nondominant side 344.32
due to late effect of cerebrovascular accident —*see* Late effect(s) (of) cerebrovascular accident
newborn 767.8
psychogenic 306.0
specified as conversion reaction 300.11
thrombotic (current) (*see also* Thrombosis, brain) 434.0
late effect—*see* Late effect(s) (of) cerebrovascular disease
transient 781.4
upper limb 344.40
affecting
dominant side 344.41
nondominant side 344.42
due to late effect of cerebrovascular accident —*see* Late effect(s) (of) cerebrovascular accident
Monorchism, monorchidism 752.8
Monteggia's fracture (closed) 813.03
open 813.13
Mood swings
brief compensatory 296.99
rebound 296.99
Moore's syndrome (*see also* Epilepsy) 345.5
Mooren's ulcer (cornea) 370.07
Mooser-Neill reaction 081.0
Mooser bodies 081.0
Moral
deficiency 301.7
imbecility 301.7
Morax-Axenfeld conjunctivitis 372.03
Morbilli (*see also* Measles) 055.9
Morbus
anglicus, anglorum 268.0
Beigel 111.2
caducus (*see also* Epilepsy) 345.9
caeruleus 746.89

Morbus—*continued*
  celiacus 579.0
  comitialis (*see also* Epilepsy) 345.9
  cordis—*see also* Disease, heart
    valvulorum—*see* Endocarditis
  coxae 719.95
    tuberculous (*see also* Tuberculosis) 015.1
  hemorrhagicus neonatorum 776.0
  maculosus neonatorum 772.6
  renum 593.0
  senilis (*see also* Osteoarthrosis) 715.9
Morel-Kraepelin disease (*see also*
    Schizophrenia) 295.9
Morel-Moore syndrome (hyperostosis frontalis
    interna) 733.3
Morel-Morgagni syndrome (hyperostosis
    frontalis interna) 733.3
Morgagni
  cyst, organ, hydatid, or appendage 752.8
    fallopian tube 752.11
  disease or syndrome (hyperostosis frontalis
    interna) 733.3
Morgagni-Adams-Stokes syndrome (syncope
    with heart block) 426.9
Morgagni-Stewart-Morel syndrome
    (hyperostosis frontalis interna) 733.3
Moria (*see also* Psychosis) 298.9
Morning sickness 643.0
Moron 317
Morphea (guttate) (linear) 701.0
Morphine dependence (*see also* Dependence)
    304.0
Morphinism (*see also* Dependence) 304.0
Morphinomania (*see also* Dependence) 304.0
Morphoea 701.0
Morquio (-Brailsford) (-Ullrich) disease or
    syndrome (mucopolysaccharidosis IV) 277.5
  kyphosis 277.5
Morris syndrome (testicular feminization) 257.8
Morsus humanus (open wound)—*see also*
    Wound, open, by site
  skin surface intact—*see* Contusion
Mortification (dry) (moist) (*see also* Gangrene)
    785.4
Morton's
  disease 355.6
  foot 355.6
  metatarsalgia (syndrome) 355.6
  neuralgia 355.6
  neuroma 355.6
  syndrome (metatarsalgia) (neuralgia) 355.6
  toe 355.6
Morvan's disease 336.0
Mosaicism, mosaic (chromosomal) 758.9
  autosomal 758.5
  sex 758.81
Moschcowitz's syndrome (thrombotic
    thrombocytopenic purpura) 446.6
Mother yaw 102.0
Motion sickness (from travel, any vehicle) (from
    roundabouts or swings) 994.6
Mottled teeth (enamel) (endemic) (nonendemic)
    520.3
Mottling enamel (endemic) (nonendemic) (teeth)
    520.3
Mouchet's disease 732.5
Mould (s) (in vitreous) 117.9
Moulders'
  bronchitis 502
  tuberculosis (*see also* Tuberculosis) 011.4
Mounier-Kuhn syndrome 494.0
  with acute exacerbation 494.1

Mountain
  fever—*see* Fever, mountain
  sickness 993.2
    with polycythemia, acquired 289.0
    acute 289.0
  tick fever 066.1
Mouse, joint (*see also* Loose, body, joint) 718.1
  knee 717.6
Mouth —*see* condition
Movable
  coccyx 724.71
  kidney (*see also* Disease, renal) 593.0
    congenital 753.3
  organ or site, congenital NEC—*see*
    Malposition, congenital
  spleen 289.59
Movement
  abnormal (dystonic) (involuntary) 781.0
  decreased fetal 655.7
  paradoxical facial 374.43
Moya Moya disease 437.5
Mozart's ear 744.29
Mucha's disease (acute parapsoriasis
    varioliformis) 696.2
Mucha-Haberman syndrome (acute
    parapsoriasis varioliformis) 696.2
Mu-chain disease 273.2
Mucinosis (cutaneous) (papular) 701.8
Mucocele
  appendix 543.9
  buccal cavity 528.9
  gallbladder (*see also* Disease, gallbladder) 575.3
  lacrimal sac 375.43
  orbit (eye) 376.81
  salivary gland (any) 527.6
  sinus (accessory) (nasal) 478.1
  turbinate (bone) (middle) (nasal) 478.1
  uterus 621.8
Mucocutaneous lymph node syndrome (acute)
    (febrile) (infantile) 446.1
Mucoenteritis 564.9
Mucolipidosis I, II, III 272.7
Mucopolysaccharidosis (types 1-6) 277.5
  cardiopathy 277.5 *[425.7]*
Mucormycosis (lung) 117.7
Mucositis —*see also* Inflammation by site
  necroticans agranulocytica 288.0
Mucous —*see also* condition
  patches (syphilitic) 091.3
    congenital 090.0
Mucoviscidosis 277.00
  with meconium obstruction 277.01
Mucus
  asphyxia or suffocation (*see also* Asphyxia,
    mucus) 933.1
    newborn 770.1
  in stool 792.1
  plug (*see also* Asphyxia, mucus) 933.1
    aspiration, of newborn 770.1
    tracheobronchial 519.1
      newborn 770.1
Muguet 112.0
Mulberry molars 090.5
Mullerian mixed tumor (M8950/3)—*see*
    Neoplasm, by site, malignant
Multicystic kidney 753.19
Multilobed placenta —*see* Placenta, abnormal
Multinodular prostate 600.1

Multiparity V61.5
  affecting
    fetus or newborn 763.89
    management of
      labor and delivery 659.4
      pregnancy V23.3
  requiring contraceptive management (*see also* Contraception) V25.9
Multipartita placenta —*see* Placenta, abnormal
Multiple, multiplex —*see also* condition
  birth
    affecting fetus or newborn 761.5
    healthy liveborn—*see* Newborn, multiple
  digits (congenital) 755.00
    fingers 755.01
    toes 755.02
  organ or site NEC—*see* Accessory
  personality 300.14
  renal arteries 747.62
Mumps 072.9
  with complication 072.8
    specified type NEC 072.79
  encephalitis 072.2
  hepatitis 072.71
  meningitis (aseptic) 072.1
  meningoencephalitis 072.2
  oophoritis 072.79
  orchitis 072.0
  pancreatitis 072.3
  polyneuropathy 072.72
  vaccination, prophylactic (against) V04.6
Mumu (*see also* Infestation, filarial) 125.9
Münchausen syndrome 301.51
Münchmeyer's disease or syndrome (exostosis luxurians) 728.11
Mural —*see* condition
Murmur (cardiac) (heart) (nonorganic) (organic) 785.2
  abdominal 787.5
  aortic (valve) (*see also* Endocarditis, aortic) 424.1
  benign—*omit code*
  cardiorespiratory 785.2
  diastolic—*see* condition
  Flint (*see also* Endocarditis, aortic) 424.1
  functional—*omit code*
  Graham Steell (pulmonic regurgitation) (*see also* Endocarditis, pulmonary) 424.3
  innocent—*omit code*
  insignificant—*omit code*
  midsystolic 785.2
  mitral (valve)—*see* stenosis, mitral
  physiologic—*see* condition
  presystolic, mitral—*see* Insufficiency, mitral
  pulmonic (valve) (*see also* Endocarditis, pulmonary) 424.3
  Still's (vibratory)—*omit code*
  systolic (valvular)—*see* condition
  tricuspid (valve)—*see* Endocarditis, tricuspid
  valvular—*see* condition
  vibratory—*omit code*
  undiagnosed 785.2
Murri's disease (intermittent hemoglobinuria) 283.2
Muscae volitantes 379.24
Muscle, muscular —*see* condition
Musculoneuralgia 729.1
Mushrooming hip 718.95
Mushroom workers' (pickers') lung 495.5

Mutism (*see also* Aphasia) 784.3
  akinetic 784.3
  deaf (acquired) (congenital) 389.7
  elective (selective) 313.23
    adjustment reaction 309.83
  hysterical 300.11
Myà's disease (congenital dilation, colon) 751.3
Myalgia (intercostal) 729.1
  eosinophilia syndrome 710.5
  epidemic 074.1
    cervical 078.89
  psychogenic 307.89
  traumatic NEC 959.9
Myasthenia, myasthenic 358.0
  cordis—*see* Failure, heart
  gravis 358.0
    neonatal 775.2
    pseudoparalytica 358.0
  stomach 536.8
    psychogenic 306.4
  syndrome in
    botulism 005.1 *[358.1]*
    diabetes mellitus 250.6 *[358.1]*
    hypothyroidism (*see also* Hypothyroidism) 244.9 *[358.1]*
    malignant neoplasm NEC 199.1 *[358.1]*
    pernicious anemia 281.0 *[358.1]*
    thyrotoxicosis (*see also* Thyrotoxicosis) 242.9 *[358.1]*
Mycelium infection NEC 117.9
Mycetismus 988.1
Mycetoma (actinomycotic) 039.9
  bone 039.8
    mycotic 117.4
  foot 039.4
    mycotic 117.4
  madurae 039.9
    mycotic 117.4
  maduromycotic 039.9
    mycotic 117.4
  mycotic 117.4
  nocardial 039.9
Mycobacteriosis —*see* Mycobacterium
Mycobacterium, mycobacterial (infection) 031.9
  acid-fast (bacilli) 031.9
  anonymous (*see also* Mycobacterium, atypical) 031.9
  atypical (acid-fast bacilli) 031.9
    cutaneous 031.1
    pulmonary 031.0
      tuberculous (*see also* Tuberculosis, pulmonary) 011.9
    specified site NEC 031.8
  avium 031.0
    intracellulare complex bacteremia (MAC) 031.2
  balnei 031.1
  Battey 031.0
  cutaneous 031.1
  disseminated 031.2
    avium-intracellulare complex (DMAC) 031.2
  fortuitum 031.0
  intracellulare (battey bacillus) 031.0
  kakerifu 031.8
  kansasii 031.0
  kasongo 031.8
  leprae—*see* Leprosy
  luciflavum 031.0
  marinum 031.1
  pulmonary 031.0

Mycobacterium, mycobacterial—*continued*
  tuberculous (*see also* Tuberculosis,
    pulmonary) 011.9
  scrofulaceum 031.1
  tuberculosis (human, bovine)—*see also*
    Tuberculosis
    avian type 031.0
  ulcerans 031.1
  xenopi 031.0
Mycosis, mycotic 117.9
  cutaneous NEC 111.9
  ear 111.8 *[380.15]*
  fungoides (M9700/3) 202.1
  mouth 112.0
  pharynx 117.9
  skin NEC 111.9
  stomatitis 112.0
  systemic NEC 117.9
  tonsil 117.9
  vagina, vaginitis 112.1
Mydriasis (persistent) (pupil) 379.43
Myelatelia 742.59
Myelinoclasis, perivascular, acute
  (postinfectious) NEC 136.9 *[323.6]*
  postimmunization or postvaccinal 323.5
Myelinosis, central pontine 341.8
Myelitis (acute) (ascending) (cerebellar)
  (childhood) (chronic) (descending) (diffuse)
  (disseminated) (pressure) (progressive) (spinal
  cord) (subacute) (transverse) (*see also*
  Encephalitis) 323.9
  late effect—*see* category 326
  optic neuritis in 341.0
  postchickenpox 052.7
  postvaccinal 323.5
  syphilitic (transverse) 094.89
  tuberculous (*see also* Tuberculosis) 013.6
  virus 049.9
Myeloblastic —*see* condition
Myelocele (*see also* Spina bifida) 741.9
  with hydrocephalus 741.0
Myelocystocele (*see also* Spina bifida) 741.9
Myelocytic —*see* condition
Myelocytoma 205.1
Myelodysplasia (spinal cord) 742.59
  meaning myelodysplastic syndrome—*see*
    Syndrome, myelodysplastic
Myeloencephalitis —*see* Encephalitis
Myelofibrosis (osteosclerosis) 289.8
Myelogenous —*see* condition
Myeloid —*see* condition
Myelokathexis 288.0
Myeloleukodystrophy 330.0
Myelolipoma (M8870/0)—*see* Neoplasm, by
  site, benign
Myeloma (multiple) (plasma cell) (plasmacytic)
  (M9730/3) 203.0
  monostotic (M9731/1) 238.6
  solitary (M9731/1) 238.6
Myelomalacia 336.8
Myelomata, multiple (M9730/3) 203.0
Myelomatosis (M9730/3) 203.0
Myelomeningitis —*see* Meningoencephalitis
Myelomeningocele (spinal cord) (*see also* Spina
  bifida) 741.9
  fetal, causing fetopelvic disproportion 653.7
Myelo-osteo-musculodysplasia hereditaria
  756.89
Myelopathic —*see* condition

Myelopathy (spinal cord) 336.9
  cervical 721.1
  diabetic 250.6 *[336.3]*
  drug-induced 336.8
  due to or with
    carbon tetrachloride 987.8 *[323.7]*
    degeneration or displacement, intervertebral
      disc 722.70
      cervical, cervicothoracic 722.71
      lumbar, lumbosacral 722.73
      thoracic, thoracolumbar 722.72
    hydroxyquinoline derivatives 961.3 *[323.7]*
    infection—*see* Encephalitis
    intervertebral disc disorder 722.70
      cervical, cervicothoracic 722.71
      lumbar, lumbosacral 722.73
      thoracic, thoracolumbar 722.72
    lead 984.9 *[323.7]*
    mercury 985.0 *[323.7]*
    neoplastic disease (*see also* Neoplasm, by
      site) 239.9 *[336.3]*
    pernicious anemia 281.0 *[336.3]*
    spondylosis 721.91
      cervical 721.1
      lumbar, lumbosacral 721.42
      thoracic 721.41
    thallium 985.8 *[323.7]*
  lumbar, lumbosacral 721.42
  necrotic (subacute) 336.1
  radiation-induced 336.8
  spondylogenic NEC 721.91
    cervical 721.1
    lumbar, lumbosacral 721.42
    thoracic 721.41
  thoracic 721.41
  toxic NEC 989.9 *[323.7]*
  transverse (*see also* Encephalitis) 323.9
  vascular 336.1
Myeloproliferative disease (M9960/1) 238.7
Myeloradiculitis (*see also* Polyneuropathy) 357.0
Myeloradiculodysplasia (spinal) 742.59
Myelosarcoma (M9930/3) 205.3
Myelosclerosis 289.8
  with myeloid metaplasia (M9961/1) 238.7
  disseminated, of nervous system 340
  megakaryocytic (M9961/1) 238.7
Myelosis (M9860/3) (*see also* Leukemia,
  myeloid) 205.9
  acute (M9861/3) 205.0
  aleukemic (M9864/3) 205.8
  chronic (M9863/3) 205.1
  erythremic (M9840/3) 207.0
    acute (M9841/3) 207.0
  megakaryocytic (M9920/3) 207.2
  nonleukemic (chronic) 288.8
  subacute (M9862/3) 205.2
Myesthenia —*see* Myasthenia
Myiasis (cavernous) 134.0
  orbit 134.0 *[376.13]*
Myoadenoma, prostate 600.2
Myoblastoma
  granular cell (M9580/0)—*see also* Neoplasm,
    connective tissue, benign
    malignant (M9580/3)—*see* Neoplasm,
      connective tissue, malignant
  tongue (M9580/0) 210.1
Myocardial —*see* condition

Myokymia —*see also* Myoclonus
  facial 351.8
Myolipoma (M8860/0)
  specified site—*see* Neoplasm, connective
    tissue, benign
  unspecified site 223.0
Myoma (M8895/0)—*see also* Neoplasm,
    connective tissue, benign
  cervix (stump) (uterus) (*see also* Leiomyoma)
    218.9
  malignant (M8895/3)—*see* Neoplasm,
    connective tissue, malignant
  prostate 600.2
  uterus (cervix) (corpus) (*see also* Leiomyoma)
    218.9
    in pregnancy or childbirth 654.1
      affecting fetus or newborn 763.89
      causing obstructed labor 660.2
        affecting fetus or newborn 763.1
Myomalacia 728.9
  cordis, heart (*see also* Degeneration,
    myocardial) 429.1
Myometritis (*see also* Endometritis) 615.9
Myometrium —*see* condition
Myonecrosis, clostridial 040.0
Myopathy 359.9
  alcoholic 359.4
  amyloid 277.3 *[359.6]*
  benign congenital 359.0
  central core 359.0
  centronuclear 359.0
  congenital (benign) 359.0
  distal 359.1
  due to drugs 359.4
  endocrine 259.9 *[359.5]*
    specified type NEC 259.8 *[359.5]*
  extraocular muscles 376.82
  facioscapulohumeral 359.1
  in
    Addison's disease 255.4 *[359.5]*
    amyloidosis 277.3 *[359.6]*
    cretinism 243 *[359.5]*
    Cushing's syndrome 255.0 *[359.5]*
    disseminated lupus erythematosus 710.0
      [359.6]
    giant cell arteritis 446.5 *[359.6]*
    hyperadrenocorticism NEC 255.3 *[359.5]*
    hyperparathyroidism 252.0 *[359.5]*
    hypopituitarism 253.2 *[359.5]*
    hypothyroidism (*see also* Hypothyroidism)
      244.9 *[359.5]*
    malignant neoplasm NEC (M8000/3) 199.1
      [359.6]
    myxedema (*see also* Myxedema) 244.9
      [359.5]
    polyarteritis nodosa 446.0 *[359.6]*
    rheumatoid arthritis 714.0 *[359.6]*
    sarcoidosis 135 *[359.6]*
    scleroderma 710.1 *[359.6]*
    Sjögren's disease 710.2 *[359.6]*
    thyrotoxicosis (*see also* Thyrotoxicosis) 242.9
      [359.5]
  inflammatory 359.8
  limb-girdle 359.1
  myotubular 359.0
  nemaline 359.0
  ocular 359.1
  oculopharyngeal 359.1
  primary 359.8
  progressive NEC 359.8
  rod body 359.0

Myopathy—*continued*
  scapulohumeral 359.1
  specified type NEC 359.8
  toxic 359.4
Myopericarditis (*see also* Pericarditis) 423.9
Myopia (axial) (congenital) (increased curvature
    or refraction, nucleus of lens) 367.1
  degenerative, malignant 360.21
  malignant 360.21
  progressive high (degenerative) 360.21
Myosarcoma (M8895/3)—*see* Neoplasm,
    connective tissue, malignant
Myosis (persistent) 379.42
  stromal (endolymphatic) (M8931/1) 236.0
Myositis 729.1
  clostridial 040.0
  due to posture 729.1
  epidemic 074.1
  fibrosa or fibrous (chronic) 728.2
    Volkmann's (complicating trauma) 958.6
  infective 728.0
  interstitial 728.81
  multiple—*see* Polymyositis
  occupational 729.1
  orbital, chronic 376.12
  ossificans 728.12
    circumscribed 728.12
    progressive 728.11
    traumatic 728.12
  progressive fibrosing 728.11
  purulent 728.0
  rheumatic 729.1
  rheumatoid 729.1
  suppurative 728.0
  syphilitic 095.6
  traumatic (old) 729.1
Myospasia impulsiva 307.23
Myotonia (acquisita) (intermittens) 728.85
  atrophica 359.2
  congenita 359.2
  dystrophica 359.2
Myotonic pupil 379.46
Myriapodiasis 134.1
Myringitis
  with otitis media—*see* Otitis media
  acute 384.00
    specified type NEC 384.09
  bullosa hemorrhagica 384.01
  bullous 384.01
  chronic 384.1
Mysophobia 300.29
Mytilotoxism 988.0
Myxadenitis labialis 528.5
Myxedema (adult) (idiocy) (infantile) (juvenile)
    (thyroid gland) (*see also* Hypothyroidism)
    244.9
  circumscribed 242.9
  congenital 243
  cutis 701.8
  localized (pretibial) 242.9
  madness (acute) 293.0
    subacute 293.1
  papular 701.8
  pituitary 244.8
  postpartum 674.8
  pretibial 242.9
  primary 244.9
Myxochondrosarcoma (M9220/3)—*see*
    Neoplasm, cartilage, malignant

Myxofibroma (M8811/0)—*see also* Neoplasm,
connective tissue, benign
odontogenic (M9320/0) 213.1
upper jaw (bone) 213.0
Myxofibrosarcoma (M8811/3)—*see* Neoplasm,
connective tissue, malignant
Myxolipoma (M8852/0) (*see also* Lipoma, by
site) 214.9
Myxoliposarcoma (M8852/3)—*see* Neoplasm,
connective tissue, malignant
Myxoma (M8840/0)—*see also* Neoplasm,
connective tissue, benign
odontogenic (M9320/0) 213.1
upper jaw (bone) 213.0
Myxosarcoma (M8840/3)—*see* Neoplasm,
connective tissue, malignant

N

Naegeli's
  disease (hereditary hemorrhagic
    thrombasthenia) 287.1
  leukemia, monocytic (M9863/3) 205.1
  syndrome (incontinentia pigmenti) 757.33
Naffziger's syndrome 353.0
Naga sore (*see also* Ulcer, skin) 707.9
Nägele's pelvis 738.6
  with disproportion (fetopelvic) 653.0
    affecting fetus or newborn 763.1
    causing obstructed labor 660.1
      affecting fetus or newborn 763.1
Nager-de Reynier syndrome (dysostosis
  mandibularis) 756.0
Nail —*see also* condition
  biting 307.9
  patella syndrome (hereditary
    osteo-onychodysplasia) 756.89
Nanism, nanosomia (*see also* Dwarfism) 259.4
  hypophyseal 253.3
  pituitary 253.3
  renis, renalis 588.0
Nanukayami 100.89
Napkin rash 691.0
Narcissism 301.81
Narcolepsy 347
Narcosis
  carbon dioxide (respiratory) 786.09
  due to drug
    correct substance properly administered
      780.09
    overdose or wrong substance given or taken
      977.9
      specified drug—*see* Table of drugs and
        chemicals
Narcotism (chronic) (*see also* listing under
  Dependence) 304.9
  acute
    correct substance properly administered
      349.82
    overdose or wrong substance given or taken
      967.8
      specified drug—*see* Table of drugs and
        chemicals
Narrow
  anterior chamber angle 365.02
  pelvis (inlet) (outlet)—*see* Contraction, pelvis
Narrowing
  artery NEC 447.1
    auditory, internal 433.8
    basilar 433.0
      with other precerebral artery 433.3
      bilateral 433.3
    carotid 433.1
      with other precerebral artery 433.3
      bilateral 433.3
    cerebellar 433.8
    choroidal 433.8
    communicating posterior 433.8
    coronary —*see also* Arteriosclerosis, coronary
      congenital 746.85
      due to syphilis 090.5
    hypophyseal 433.8
    pontine 433.8
    precerebral NEC 433.9
      multiple or bilateral 433.3
      specified NEC 433.8

Narrowing—*continued*
    vertebral 433.2
      with other precerebral artery 433.3
      bilateral 433.3
  auditory canal (external) (*see also* Stricture, ear
    canal, acquired) 380.50
  cerebral arteries 437.0
  cicatricial—*see* Cicatrix
  congenital—*see* Anomaly, congenital
  coronary artery—*see* Narrowing, artery,
    coronary
  ear, middle 385.22
  Eustachian tube (*see also* Obstruction,
    Eustachian tube) 381.60
  eyelid 374.46
    congenital 743.62
  intervertebral disc or space NEC—*see*
    Degeneration, intervertebral disc
  joint space, hip 719.85
  larynx 478.74
  lids 374.46
    congenital 743.62
  mesenteric artery (with gangrene) 557.0
  palate 524.8
  palpebral fissure 374.46
  retinal artery 362.13
  ureter 593.3
  urethra (*see also* Stricture, urethra) 598.9
Narrowness, abnormal, eyelid 743.62
Nasal —*see* condition
Nasolacrimal —*see* condition
Nasopharyngeal —*see also* condition
  bursa 478.29
  pituitary gland 759.2
  torticollis 723.5
Nasopharyngitis (acute) (infective) (subacute)
  460
  chronic 472.2
    due to external agent—*see* Condition,
      respiratory, chronic, due to
  due to external agent—*see* Condition,
    respiratory, due to
  septic 034.0
  streptococcal 034.0
  suppurative (chronic) 472.2
  ulcerative (chronic) 472.2
Nasopharynx, nasopharyngeal —*see* condition
Natal tooth, teeth 520.6
Nausea (*see also* Vomiting) 787.02
  epidemic 078.82
  gravidarum—*see* Hyperemesis, gravidarum
  marina 994.6
  with vomiting 787.01
Naval —*see* condition
Neapolitan fever (*see also* Brucellosis) 023.9
Nearsightedness 367.1
Near-syncope 780.2
Nebécourt's syndrome 253.3
Nebula, cornea (eye) 371.01
  congenital 743.43
    interfering with vision 743.42
Necator americanus infestation 126.1
Necatoriasis 126.1
Neck —*see* condition
Necrencephalus (*see also* Softening, brain) 437.8
Necrobacillosis 040.3

Necrobiosis 799.8
  brain or cerebral (*see also* Softening, brain)
      437.8
  lipoidica 709.3
      diabeticorum 250.8 *[709.3]*
Necrodermolysis 695.1
Necrolysis, toxic epidermal 695.1
  due to drug
      correct substance properly administered 695.1
      overdose or wrong substance given or taken
          977.9
          specified drug—*see* Table of drugs and
              chemicals
Necrophilia 302.89
Necrosis, necrotic
  adrenal (capsule) (gland) 255.8
  antrum, nasal sinus 478.1
  aorta (hyaline) (*see also* Aneurysm, aorta) 441.9
      cystic medial 441.00
          abdominal 441.02
          thoracic 441.01
          thoracoabdominal 441.03
      ruptured 441.5
  arteritis 446.0
  artery 447.5
  aseptic, bone 733.40
      femur (head) (neck) 733.42
          medial condyle 733.43
      humoral head 733.41
      medial femoral condyle 733.43
      specified site NEC 733.49
      talus 733.44
  avascular, bone NEC (*see also* Necrosis,
      aseptic, bone) 733.40
  bladder (aseptic) (sphincter) 596.8
  bone (*see also* Osteomyelitis) 730.1
      acute 730.0
      aseptic or avascular 733.40
          femur (head) (neck) 733.42
              medial condyle 733.43
          humoral head 733.41
          medial femoral condyle 733.43
          specified site NEC 733.49
          talus 733.44
      ethmoid 478.1
      ischemic 733.40
      jaw 526.4
      marrow 289.8
      Paget's (osteitis deformans) 731.0
      tuberculous—*see* Tuberculosis, bone
  brain (softening) (*see also* Softening, brain)
      437.8
  breast (aseptic) (fat) (segmental) 611.3
  bronchus, bronchi 519.1
  central nervous system NEC (*see also*
      Softening, brain) 437.8
  cerebellar (*see also* Softening, brain) 437.8
  cerebral (softening) (*see also* Softening, brain)
      437.8
  cerebrospinal (softening) (*see also* Softening,
      brain) 437.8
  cornea (*see also* Keratitis) 371.40
  cortical, kidney 583.6
  cystic medial (aorta) 441.00
      abdominal 441.02
      thoracic 441.01
      thoracoabdominal 441.03
  dental 521.0
      pulp 522.1

Necrosis, necrotic—*continued*
  due to swallowing corrosive substance—*see*
      Burn, by site
  ear (ossicle) 385.24
  esophagus 530.89
  ethmoid (bone) 478.1
  eyelid 374.50
  fat, fatty (generalized) (*see also* Degeneration,
      fatty) 272.8
      breast (aseptic) (segmental) 611.3
      intestine 569.89
      localized—*see* Degeneration, by site, fatty
      mesentery 567.8
      omentum 567.8
      pancreas 577.8
      peritoneum 567.8
      skin (subcutaneous) 709.3
          newborn 778.1
  femur (aseptic) (avascular) 733.42
      head 733.42
      medial condyle 733.43
      neck 733.42
  gallbladder (*see also* Cholecystitis, acute) 575.0
  gangrenous 785.4
  gastric 537.89
  glottis 478.79
  heart (myocardium)—*see* Infarct, myocardium
  hepatic (*see also* Necrosis, liver) 570
  hip (aseptic) (avascular) 733.42
  intestine (acute) (hemorrhagic) (massive) 557.0
  ischemic 785.4
  jaw 526.4
  kidney (bilateral) 583.9
      acute 584.9
      cortical 583.6
          acute 584.6
          with
              abortion—*see* Abortion, by type, with
                  renal failure
              ectopic pregnancy (*see also* categories
                  633.0-633.9) 639.3
              molar pregnancy (*see also* categories
                  630-632) 639.3
          complicating pregnancy 646.2
              affecting fetus or newborn 760.1
          following labor and delivery 669.3
      medullary (papillary) (*see also* Pyelitis) 590.80
          in
              acute renal failure 584.7
              nephritis, nephropathy 583.7
      papillary (*see also* Pyelitis) 590.80
          in
              acute renal failure 584.7
              nephritis, nephropathy 583.7
      tubular 584.5
          with
              abortion—*see* Abortion, by type, with
                  renal failure
              ectopic pregnancy (*see also* categories
                  633.0-633.9) 639.3
              molar pregnancy (*see also* categories
                  630-632) 639.3
          complicating
              abortion 639.3
              ectopic or molar pregnancy 639.3
              pregnancy 646.2
                  affecting fetus or newborn 760.1
          following labor and delivery 669.3
          traumatic 958.5
  larynx 478.79

Necrosis, necrotic—*continued*
  liver (acute) (congenital) (diffuse) (massive)
    (subacute) 570
    with
      abortion—*see* Abortion, by type, with
        specified complication NEC
      ectopic pregnancy (*see also* categories
        633.0-633.9) 639.8
        molar pregnancy (*see also* categories
          630-632) 639.8
      complicating pregnancy 646.7
        affecting fetus or newborn 760.8
      following
        abortion 639.8
        ectopic or molar pregnancy 639.8
      obstetrical 646.7
      postabortal 639.8
      puerperal, postpartum 674.8
      toxic 573.3
  lung 513.0
  lymphatic gland 683
  mammary gland 611.3
  mastoid (chronic) 383.1
  mesentery 557.0
    fat 567.8
  mitral valve—*see* Insufficiency, mitral
  myocardium, myocardial—*see* Infarct,
    myocardium
  nose (septum) 478.1
  omentum 557.0
    with mesenteric infarction 557.0
    fat 567.8
  orbit, orbital 376.10
  ossicles, ear (aseptic) 385.24
  ovary (*see also* Salpingo-oophoritis) 614.2
  pancreas (aseptic) (duct) (fat) 577.8
    acute 577.0
    infective 577.0
  papillary, kidney (*see also* Pyelitis) 590.80
  peritoneum 557.0
    with mesenteric infarction 557.0
    fat 567.8
  pharynx 462
    in granulocytopenia 288.0
  phosphorus 983.9
  pituitary (gland) (postpartum) (Sheehan) 253.2
  placenta (*see also* Placenta, abnormal) 656.7
  pneumonia 513.0
  pulmonary 513.0
  pulp (dental) 522.1
  pylorus 537.89
  radiation—*see* Necrosis, by site
  radium—*see* Necrosis, by site
  renal—*see* Necrosis, kidney
  sclera 379.19
  scrotum 608.89
  skin or subcutaneous tissue 709.8
    due to burn—*see* Burn, by site
    gangrenous 785.4
  spine, spinal (column) 730.18
    acute 730.18
    cord 336.1
  spleen 289.59
  stomach 537.89
  stomatitis 528.1
  subcutaneous fat 709.3
    fetus or newborn 778.1
  subendocardial—*see* Infarct, myocardium
  suprarenal (capsule) (gland) 255.8

Necrosis, necrotic—*continued*
  teeth, tooth 521.0
  testis 608.89
  thymus (gland) 254.8
  tonsil 474.8
  trachea 519.1
  tuberculous NEC—*see* Tuberculosis
  tubular (acute) (anoxic) (toxic) 584.5
    due to a procedure 997.5
  umbilical cord, affecting fetus or newborn 762.6
  vagina 623.8
  vertebra (lumbar) 730.18
    acute 730.18
    tuberculous (*see also* Tuberculosis) 015.0
      [730.8]
  vesical (aseptic) (bladder) 596.8
  x-ray—*see* Necrosis, by site
Necrospermia 606.0
Necrotizing angiitis 446.0
Negativism 301.7
Neglect (child) (newborn) NEC 995.52
  adult 995.84
  after or at birth 995.52
  hemispatial 781.8
  left-sided 781.8
  sensory 781.8
  visuospatial 781.8
Negri bodies 071
Neill-Dingwall syndrome (microcephaly and
  dwarfism) 759.89
Neisserian infection NEC—*see* Gonococcus
Nematodiasis NEC (*see also* Infestation,
  Nematode) 127.9
  ancylostoma (*see also* Ancylostomiasis) 126.9
Neoformans cryptococcus infection 117.5
Neonatal —*see also* condition
  teeth, tooth 520.6
Neonatorum —*see* condition

"N" listing resumes after
"Neoplasm, neoplastic" table…

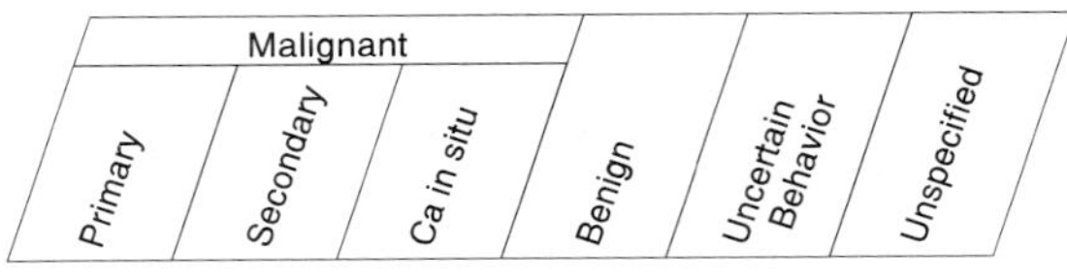

	Malignant			Benign	Uncertain Behavior	Unspecified
	Primary	Secondary	Ca in situ			
Neoplasm, neoplastic	**199.1**	**199.1**	**234.9**	**229.9**	**238.9**	**239.9**

Note—1. The list below gives the code numbers for neoplasms by anatomical site. For each site there are six possible code numbers according to whether the neoplasm in question is malignant, benign, in situ, of uncertain behavior, or of unspecified nature. The description of the neoplasm will often indicate which of the six columns is appropriate; e.g., malignant melanoma of skin, benign fibroadenoma of breast, carcinoma in situ of cervix uteri.

Where such descriptors are not present, the remainder of the Index should be consulted where guidance is given to the appropriate column for each morphological (histological) variety listed; e.g., Mesonephroma—see Neoplasm, malignant; Embryoma—see also Neoplasm, uncertain behavior; Disease, Bowen's—see Neoplasm, skin, in situ. However, the guidance in the Index can be overridden if one of the descriptors mentioned above is present; e.g., malignant adenoma of colon is coded to 153.9 and not to 211.3 as the adjective "malignant" overrides the Index entry "Adenoma—see also Neoplasm, benign."

*Note—2. Sites marked with the sign * (e.g., face NEC*) should be classified to malignant neoplasm of skin of these sites if the variety of neoplasm is a squamous cell carcinoma or an epidermoid carcinoma and to benign neoplasm of skin of these sites if the variety of neoplasm is a papilloma (any type).*

	Primary	Secondary	Ca in situ	Benign	Uncertain Behavior	Unspecified
abdomen, abdominal	195.2	198.89	234.8	229.8	238.8	239.8
cavity	195.2	198.89	234.8	229.8	238.8	239.8
organ	195.2	198.89	234.8	229.8	238.8	239.8
viscera	195.2	198.89	234.8	229.8	238.8	239.8
wall	173.5	198.2	232.5	216.5	238.2	239.2
connective tissue	171.5	198.89	—	215.5	238.1	239.2
abdominopelvic	195.8	198.89	234.8	229.8	238.8	239.8
accessory sinus—*see* Neoplasm, sinus						
acoustic nerve	192.0	198.4	—	225.1	237.9	239.7
acromion (process)	170.4	198.5	—	213.4	238.0	239.2
adenoid (pharynx) (tissue)	147.1	198.89	230.0	210.7	235.1	239.0
adipose tissue (*see also* Neoplasm,						
connective tissue)	171.9	198.89	—	215.9	238.1	239.2
adnexa (uterine)	183.9	198.82	233.3	221.8	236.3	239.5
adrenal (cortex) (gland) (medulla)	194.0	198.7	234.8	227.0	237.2	239.7
ala nasi (external)	173.3	198.2	232.3	216.3	238.2	239.2
alimentary canal or tract NEC	159.9	197.8	230.9	211.9	235.5	239.0
alveolar	143.9	198.89	230.0	210.4	235.1	239.0
mucosa	143.9	198.89	230.0	210.4	235.1	239.0
lower	143.1	198.89	230.0	210.4	235.1	239.0
upper	143.0	198.89	230.0	210.4	235.1	239.0
ridge or process	170.1	198.5	—	213.1	238.0	239.2
carcinoma	143.9	—	—	—	—	—
lower	143.1	—	—	—	—	—
upper	143.0	—	—	—	—	—
lower	170.1	198.5	—	213.1	238.0	239.2
mucosa	143.9	198.89	230.0	210.4	235.1	239.0
lower	143.1	198.89	230.0	210.4	235.1	239.0
upper	143.0	198.89	230.0	210.4	235.1	239.0
upper	170.0	198.5	—	213.0	238.0	239.2
sulcus	145.1	198.89	230.0	210.4	235.1	239.0
alveolus	143.9	198.89	230.0	210.4	235.1	239.0
lower	143.1	198.89	230.0	210.4	235.1	239.0
upper	143.0	198.89	230.0	210.4	235.1	239.0
ampulla of Vater	156.2	197.8	230.8	211.5	235.3	239.0
ankle NEC*	195.5	198.89	232.7	229.8	238.8	239.8
anorectum, anorectal (junction)	154.8	197.5	230.7	211.4	235.2	239.0
antecubital fossa or space*	195.4	198.89	232.6	229.8	238.8	239.8
antrum (Highmore) (maxillary)	160.2	197.3	231.8	212.0	235.9	239.1
pyloric	151.2	197.8	230.2	211.1	235.2	239.0
tympanicum	160.1	197.3	231.8	212.0	235.9	239.1
anus, anal	154.3	197.5	230.6	211.4	235.5	239.0
canal	154.2	197.5	230.5	211.4	235.5	239.0

| | Malignant | | | | | |
---	Primary	Secondary	Ca in situ	Benign	Uncertain Behavior	Unspecified
anus, anal—*continued*						
contiguous sites with rectosigmoid junction or rectum	154.8	—	—	—	—	—
margin	173.5	198.2	232.5	216.5	238.2	239.2
skin	173.5	198.2	232.5	216.5	238.2	239.2
sphincter	154.2	197.5	230.5	211.4	235.5	239.0
aorta (thoracic)	171.4	198.89	—	215.4	238.1	239.2
abdominal	171.5	198.89	—	215.5	238.1	239.2
aortic body	194.6	198.89	—	227.6	237.3	239.7
aponeurosis	171.9	198.89	—	215.9	238.1	239.2
palmar	171.2	198.89	—	215.2	238.1	239.2
plantar	171.3	198.89	—	215.3	238.1	239.2
appendix	153.5	197.5	230.3	211.3	235.2	239.0
arachnoid (cerebral)	192.1	198.4	—	225.2	237.6	239.7
spinal	192.3	198.4	—	225.4	237.6	239.7
areola (female)	174.0	198.81	233.0	217	238.3	239.3
male	175.0	198.81	233.0	217	238.3	239.3
arm NEC*	195.4	198.89	232.6	229.8	238.8	239.8
artery—*see* Neoplasm, connective tissue						
aryepiglottic fold	148.2	198.89	230.0	210.8	235.1	239.0
hypopharyngeal aspect	148.2	198.89	230.0	210.8	235.1	239.0
laryngeal aspect	161.1	197.3	231.0	212.1	235.6	239.1
marginal zone	148.2	198.89	230.0	210.8	235.1	239.0
arytenoid (cartilage)	161.3	197.3	231.0	212.1	235.6	239.1
fold—*see* Neoplasm, aryepiglottic						
atlas	170.2	198.5	—	213.2	238.0	239.2
atrium, cardiac	164.1	198.89	—	212.7	238.8	239.8
auditory						
canal (external) (skin)	173.2	198.2	232.2	216.2	238.2	239.2
internal	160.1	197.3	231.8	212.0	235.9	239.1
nerve	192.0	198.4	—	225.1	237.9	239.7
tube	160.1	197.3	231.8	212.0	235.9	239.1
opening	147.2	198.89	230.0	210.7	235.1	239.0
auricle, ear	173.2	198.2	232.2	216.2	238.2	239.2
cartilage	171.0	198.89	—	215.0	238.1	239.2
auricular canal (external)	173.2	198.2	232.2	216.2	238.2	239.2
internal	160.1	197.3	231.8	212.0	235.9	239.1
autonomic nerve or nervous system NEC	171.9	198.89	—	215.9	238.1	239.2
axilla, axillary	195.1	198.89	234.8	229.8	238.8	239.8
fold	173.5	198.2	232.5	216.5	238.2	239.2
back NEC*	195.8	198.89	232.5	229.8	238.8	239.8
Bartholin's gland	184.1	198.82	233.3	221.2	236.3	239.5
basal ganglia	191.0	198.3	—	225.0	237.5	239.6
basis pedunculi	191.7	198.3	—	225.0	237.5	239.6
bile or biliary (tract)	156.9	197.8	230.8	211.5	235.3	239.0
canaliculi (biliferi) (intrahepatic)	155.1	197.8	230.8	211.5	235.3	239.0
canals, interlobular	155.1	197.8	230.8	211.5	235.3	239.0
contiguous sites	156.8	—	—	—	—	—
duct or passage (common) (cyst) (extrahepatic)	156.1	197.8	230.8	211.5	235.3	239.0
contiguous sites with gallbladder	156.8	—	—	—	—	—
interlobular	155.1	197.8	230.8	211.5	235.3	239.0
intrahepatic	155.1	197.8	230.8	211.5	235.3	239.0
and extrahepatic	156.9	197.8	230.8	211.5	235.3	239.0
bladder (urinary)	188.9	198.1	233.7	223.3	236.7	239.4
contiguous sites	188.8	—	—	—	—	—
dome	188.1	198.1	233.7	223.3	236.7	239.4
neck	188.5	198.1	233.7	223.3	236.7	239.4
orifice	188.9	198.1	233.7	223.3	236.7	239.4
ureteric	188.6	198.1	233.7	223.3	236.7	239.4
urethral	188.5	198.1	233.7	223.3	236.7	239.4
sphincter	188.8	198.1	233.7	223.3	236.7	239.4
trigone	188.0	198.1	233.7	223.3	236.7	239.4

	Malignant					
	Primary	Secondary	Ca in situ	Benign	Uncertain Behavior	Unspecified
urachus	188.7	—	233.7	223.3	236.7	239.4
wall	188.9	198.1	233.7	223.3	236.7	239.4
anterior	188.3	198.1	233.7	223.3	236.7	239.4
lateral	188.2	198.1	233.7	223.3	236.7	239.4
posterior	188.4	198.1	233.7	223.3	236.7	239.4
blood vessel—*see* Neoplasm, connective tissue						

> *Note—Carcinomas and adenocarcinomas, of any type other than intraosseous or odontogenic, of the sites listed under "Neoplasm, bone" should be considered as constituting metastatic spread from an unspecified primary site and coded to 198.5 for morbidity coding and to 199.1 for underlying cause of death coding.*

	Primary	Secondary	Ca in situ	Benign	Uncertain Behavior	Unspecified
bone (periosteum)	170.9	198.5	—	213.9	238.0	239.2
acetabulum	170.6	198.5	—	213.6	238.0	239.2
acromion (process)	170.4	198.5	—	213.4	238.0	239.2
ankle	170.8	198.5	—	213.8	238.0	239.2
arm NEC	170.4	198.5	—	213.4	238.0	239.2
astragalus	170.8	198.5	—	213.8	238.0	239.2
atlas	170.2	198.5	—	213.2	238.0	239.2
axis	170.2	198.5	—	213.2	238.0	239.2
back NEC	170.2	198.5	—	213.2	238.0	239.2
calcaneus	170.8	198.5	—	213.8	238.0	239.2
calvarium	170.0	198.5	—	213.0	238.0	239.2
carpus (any)	170.5	198.5	—	213.5	238.0	239.2
cartilage NEC	170.9	198.5	—	213.9	238.0	239.2
clavicle	170.3	198.5	—	213.3	238.0	239.2
clivus	170.0	198.5	—	213.0	238.0	239.2
coccygeal vertebra	170.6	198.5	—	213.6	238.0	239.2
coccyx	170.6	198.5	—	213.6	238.0	239.2
costal cartilage	170.3	198.5	—	213.3	238.0	239.2
costovertebral joint	170.3	198.5	—	213.3	238.0	239.2
cranial	170.0	198.5	—	213.0	238.0	239.2
cuboid	170.8	198.5	—	213.8	238.0	239.2
cuneiform	170.9	198.5	—	213.9	238.0	239.2
ankle	170.8	198.5	—	213.8	238.0	239.2
wrist	170.5	198.5	—	213.5	238.0	239.2
digital	170.9	198.5	—	213.9	238.0	239.2
finger	170.5	198.5	—	213.5	238.0	239.2
toe	170.8	198.5	—	213.8	238.0	239.2
elbow	170.4	198.5	—	213.4	238.0	239.2
ethmoid (labyrinth)	170.0	198.5	—	213.0	238.0	239.2
face	170.0	198.5	—	213.0	238.0	239.2
lower jaw	170.1	198.5	—	213.1	238.0	239.2
femur (any part)	170.7	198.5	—	213.7	238.0	239.2
fibula (any part)	170.7	198.5	—	213.7	238.0	239.2
finger (any)	170.5	198.5	—	213.5	238.0	239.2
foot	170.8	198.5	—	213.8	238.0	239.2
forearm	170.4	198.5	—	213.4	238.0	239.2
frontal	170.0	198.5	—	213.0	238.0	239.2
hand	170.5	198.5	—	213.5	238.0	239.2
heel	170.8	198.5	—	213.8	238.0	239.2
hip	170.6	198.5	—	213.6	238.0	239.2
humerus (any part)	170.4	198.5	—	213.4	238.0	239.2
hyoid	170.0	198.5	—	213.0	238.0	239.2
ilium	170.6	198.5	—	213.6	238.0	239.2
innominate	170.6	198.5	—	213.6	238.0	239.2
intervertebral cartilage or disc	170.2	198.5	—	213.2	238.0	239.2
ischium	170.6	198.5	—	213.6	238.0	239.2
jaw (lower)	170.1	198.5	—	213.1	238.0	239.2
upper	170.0	198.5	—	213.0	238.0	239.2
knee	170.7	198.5	—	213.7	238.0	239.2
leg NEC	170.7	198.5	—	213.7	238.0	239.2
limb NEC	170.9	198.5	—	213.9	238.0	239.2
lower (long bones)	170.7	198.5	—	213.7	238.0	239.2

bone—*continued*

	Malignant					
	Primary	Secondary	Ca in situ	Benign	Uncertain Behavior	Unspecified
short bones	170.8	198.5	—	213.8	238.0	239.2
upper (long bones)	170.4	198.5	—	213.4	238.0	239.2
short bones	170.5	198.5	—	213.5	238.0	239.2
long	170.9	198.5	—	213.9	238.0	239.2
lower limbs NEC	170.7	198.5	—	213.7	238.0	239.2
upper limbs NEC	170.4	198.5	—	213.4	238.0	239.2
malar	170.0	198.5	—	213.0	238.0	239.2
mandible	170.1	198.5	—	213.1	238.0	239.2
marrow NEC	202.9	198.5	—	—	—	238.7
mastoid	170.0	198.5	—	213.0	238.0	239.2
maxilla, maxillary (superior)	170.0	198.5	—	213.0	238.0	239.2
inferior	170.1	198.5	—	213.1	238.0	239.2
metacarpus (any)	170.5	198.5	—	213.5	238.0	239.2
metatarsus (any)	170.8	198.5	—	213.8	238.0	239.2
navicular (ankle)	170.8	198.5	—	213.8	238.0	239.2
hand	170.5	198.5	—	213.5	238.0	239.2
nose, nasal	170.0	198.5	—	213.0	238.0	239.2
occipital	170.0	198.5	—	213.0	238.0	239.2
orbit	170.0	198.5	—	213.0	238.0	239.2
parietal	170.0	198.5	—	213.0	238.0	239.2
patella	170.8	198.5	—	213.8	238.0	239.2
pelvic	170.6	198.5	—	213.6	238.0	239.2
phalanges	170.9	198.5	—	213.9	238.0	239.2
foot	170.8	198.5	—	213.8	238.0	239.2
hand	170.5	198.5	—	213.5	238.0	239.2
pubic	170.6	198.5	—	213.6	238.0	239.2
radius (any part)	170.4	198.5	—	213.4	238.0	239.2
rib	170.3	198.5	—	213.3	238.0	239.2
sacral vertebra	170.6	198.5	—	213.6	238.0	239.2
sacrum	170.6	198.5	—	213.6	238.0	239.2
scaphoid (of hand)	170.5	198.5	—	213.5	238.0	239.2
of ankle	170.8	198.5	—	213.8	238.0	239.2
scapula (any part)	170.4	198.5	—	213.4	238.0	239.2
sella turcica	170.0	198.5	—	213.0	238.0	239.2
short	170.9	198.5	—	213.9	238.0	239.2
lower limb	170.8	198.5	—	213.8	238.0	239.2
upper limb	170.5	198.5	—	213.5	238.0	239.2
shoulder	170.4	198.5	—	213.4	238.0	239.2
skeleton, skeletal NEC	170.9	198.5	—	213.9	238.0	239.2
skull	170.0	198.5	—	213.0	238.0	239.2
sphenoid	170.0	198.5	—	213.0	238.0	239.2
spine, spinal (column)	170.2	198.5	—	213.2	238.0	239.2
coccyx	170.6	198.5	—	213.6	238.0	239.2
sacrum	170.6	198.5	—	213.6	238.0	239.2
sternum	170.3	198.5	—	213.3	238.0	239.2
tarsus (any)	170.8	198.5	—	213.8	238.0	239.2
temporal	170.0	198.5	—	213.0	238.0	239.2
thumb	170.5	198.5	—	213.5	238.0	239.2
tibia (any part)	170.7	198.5	—	213.7	238.0	239.2
toe (any)	170.8	198.5	—	213.8	238.0	239.2
trapezium	170.5	198.5	—	213.5	238.0	239.2
trapezoid	170.5	198.5	—	213.5	238.0	239.2
turbinate	170.0	198.5	—	213.0	238.0	239.2
ulna (any part)	170.4	198.5	—	213.4	238.0	239.2
unciform	170.5	198.5	—	213.5	238.0	239.2
vertebra (column)	170.2	198.5	—	213.2	238.0	239.2
coccyx	170.6	198.5	—	213.6	238.0	239.2
sacrum	170.6	198.5	—	213.6	238.0	239.2
vomer	170.0	198.5	—	213.0	238.0	239.2
wrist	170.5	198.5	—	213.5	238.0	239.2
xiphoid process	170.3	198.5	—	213.3	238.0	239.2
zygomatic	170.0	198.5	—	213.0	238.0	239.2

| | Malignant | | | | | |
	Primary	Secondary	Ca in situ	Benign	Uncertain Behavior	Unspecified
book-leaf (mouth)	145.8	198.89	230.0	210.4	235.1	239.0
bowel—*see* Neoplasm, intestine						
brachial plexus	171.2	198.89	—	215.2	238.1	239.2
brain NEC	191.9	198.3	—	225.0	237.5	239.6
basal ganglia	191.0	198.3	—	225.0	237.5	239.6
cerebellopontine angle	191.6	198.3	—	225.0	237.5	239.6
cerebellum NOS	191.6	198.3	—	225.0	237.5	239.6
cerebrum	191.0	198.3	—	225.0	237.5	239.6
choroid plexus	191.5	198.3	—	225.0	237.5	239.6
contiguous sites	191.8	—	—	—	—	—
corpus callosum	191.8	198.3	—	225.0	237.5	239.6
corpus striatum	191.0	198.3	—	225.0	237.5	239.6
cortex (cerebral)	191.0	198.3	—	225.0	237.5	239.6
frontal lobe	191.1	198.3	—	225.0	237.5	239.6
globus pallidus	191.0	198.3	—	225.0	237.5	239.6
hippocampus	191.2	198.3	—	225.0	237.5	239.6
hypothalamus	191.0	198.3	—	225.0	237.5	239.6
internal capsule	191.0	198.3	—	225.0	237.5	239.6
medulla oblongata	191.7	198.3	—	225.0	237.5	239.6
meninges	192.1	198.4	—	225.2	237.6	239.7
midbrain	191.7	198.3	—	225.0	237.5	239.6
occipital lobe	191.4	198.3	—	225.0	237.5	239.6
parietal lobe	191.3	198.3	—	225.0	237.5	239.6
peduncle	191.7	198.3	—	225.0	237.5	239.6
pons	191.7	198.3	—	225.0	237.5	239.6
stem	191.7	198.3	—	225.0	237.5	239.6
tapetum	191.8	198.3	—	225.0	237.5	239.6
temporal lobe	191.2	198.3	—	225.0	237.5	239.6
thalamus	191.0	198.3	—	225.0	237.5	239.6
uncus	191.2	198.3	—	225.0	237.5	239.6
ventricle (floor)	191.5	198.3	—	225.0	237.5	239.6
branchial (cleft) (vestiges)	146.8	198.89	230.0	210.6	235.1	239.0
breast (connective tissue) (female)						
(glandular tissue) (soft parts)	174.9	198.81	233.0	217	238.3	239.3
areola	174.0	198.81	233.0	217	238.3	239.3
male	175.0	198.81	233.0	217	238.3	239.3
axillary tail	174.6	198.81	233.0	217	238.3	239.3
central portion	174.1	198.81	233.0	217	238.3	239.3
contiguous sites	174.8	—	—	—	—	—
ectopic sites	174.8	198.81	233.0	217	238.3	239.3
inner	174.8	198.81	233.0	217	238.3	239.3
lower	174.8	198.81	233.0	217	238.3	239.3
lower-inner quadrant	174.3	198.81	233.0	217	238.3	239.3
lower-outer quadrant	174.5	198.81	233.0	217	238.3	239.3
male	175.9	198.81	233.0	217	238.3	239.3
areola	175.0	198.81	233.0	217	238.3	239.3
ectopic tissue	175.9	198.81	233.0	217	238.3	239.3
nipple	175.0	198.81	233.0	217	238.3	239.3
mastectomy site (skin)	173.5	198.2	—	—	—	—
specified as breast tissue	174.8	198.81	—	—	—	—
midline	174.8	198.81	233.0	217	238.3	239.3
nipple	174.0	198.81	233.0	217	238.3	239.3
male	175.0	198.81	233.0	217	238.3	239.3
outer	174.8	198.81	233.0	217	238.3	239.3
skin	173.5	198.2	232.5	216.5	238.2	239.2
tail (axillary)	174.6	198.81	233.0	217	238.3	239.3
upper	174.8	198.81	233.0	217	238.3	239.3
upper-inner quadrant	174.2	198.81	233.0	217	238.3	239.3
upper-outer quadrant	174.4	198.81	233.0	217	238.3	239.3
broad ligament	183.3	198.82	233.3	221.0	236.3	239.5
bronchiogenic, bronchogenic (lung)	162.9	197.0	231.2	212.3	235.7	239.1
bronchiole	162.9	197.0	231.2	212.3	235.7	239.1

| | Malignant | | | | | |
	Primary	Secondary	Ca in situ	Benign	Uncertain Behavior	Unspecified
bronchus	162.9	197.0	231.2	212.3	235.7	239.1
carina	162.2	197.0	231.2	212.3	235.7	239.1
contiguous sites with lung or trachea	162.8	—	—	—	—	—
lower lobe of lung	162.5	197.0	231.2	212.3	235.7	239.1
main	162.2	197.0	231.2	212.3	235.7	239.1
middle lobe of lung	162.4	197.0	231.2	212.3	235.7	239.1
upper lobe of lung	162.3	197.0	231.2	212.3	235.7	239.1
brow	173.3	198.2	232.3	216.3	238.2	239.2
buccal (cavity)	145.9	198.89	230.0	210.4	235.1	239.0
commissure	145.0	198.89	230.0	210.4	235.1	239.0
groove (lower) (upper)	145.1	198.89	230.0	210.4	235.1	239.0
mucosa	145.0	198.89	230.0	210.4	235.1	239.0
sulcus (lower) (upper)	145.1	198.89	230.0	210.4	235.1	239.0
bulbourethral gland	189.3	198.1	233.9	223.81	236.99	239.5
bursa—*see* Neoplasm, connective tissue						
buttock NEC*	195.3	198.89	232.5	229.8	238.8	239.8
calf*	195.5	198.89	232.7	229.8	238.8	239.8
calvarium	170.0	198.5	—	213.0	238.0	239.2
calyx, renal	189.1	198.0	233.9	223.1	236.91	239.5
canal						
anal	154.2	197.5	230.5	211.4	235.5	239.0
auditory (external)	173.2	198.2	232.2	216.2	238.2	239.2
auricular (external)	173.2	198.2	232.2	216.2	238.2	239.2
canaliculi, biliary (biliferi) (intrahepatic)	155.1	197.8	230.8	211.5	235.3	239.0
canthus (eye) (inner) (outer)	173.1	198.2	232.1	216.1	238.2	239.2
capillary—*see* Neoplasm, connective tissue						
caput coli	153.4	197.5	230.3	211.3	235.2	239.0
cardia (gastric)	151.0	197.8	230.2	211.1	235.2	239.0
cardiac orifice (stomach)	151.0	197.8	230.2	211.1	235.2	239.0
cardio-esophageal junction	151.0	197.8	230.2	211.1	235.2	239.0
cardio-esophagus	151.0	197.8	230.2	211.1	235.2	239.0
carina (bronchus)	162.2	197.0	231.2	212.3	235.7	239.1
carotid (artery)	171.0	198.89	—	215.0	238.1	239.2
body	194.5	198.89	—	227.5	237.3	239.7
carpus (any bone)	170.5	198.5	—	213.5	238.0	239.2
cartilage (articular) (joint) NEC—*see also*						
Neoplasm, bone	170.9	198.5	—	213.9	238.0	239.2
arytenoid	161.3	197.3	231.0	212.1	235.6	239.1
auricular	171.0	198.89	—	215.0	238.1	239.2
bronchi	162.2	197.3	—	212.3	235.7	239.1
connective tissue—*see* Neoplasm, connective tissue						
costal	170.3	198.5	—	213.3	238.0	239.2
cricoid	161.3	197.3	231.0	212.1	235.6	239.1
cuneiform	161.3	197.3	231.0	212.1	235.6	239.1
ear (external)	171.0	198.89	—	215.0	238.1	239.2
ensiform	170.3	198.5	—	213.3	238.0	239.2
epiglottis	161.1	197.3	231.0	212.1	235.6	239.1
anterior surface	146.4	198.89	230.0	210.6	235.1	239.0
eyelid	171.0	198.89	—	215.0	238.1	239.2
intervertebral	170.2	198.5	—	213.2	238.0	239.2
larynx, laryngeal	161.3	197.3	231.0	212.1	235.6	239.1
nose, nasal	160.0	197.3	231.8	212.0	235.9	239.1
pinna	171.0	198.89	—	215.0	238.1	239.2
rib	170.3	198.5	—	213.3	238.0	239.2
semilunar (knee)	170.7	198.5	—	213.7	238.0	239.2
thyroid	161.3	197.3	231.0	212.1	235.6	239.1
trachea	162.0	197.3	231.1	212.2	235.7	239.1
cauda equina	192.2	198.3	—	225.3	237.5	239.7
cavity						
buccal	145.9	198.89	230.0	210.4	235.1	239.0
nasal	160.0	197.3	231.8	212.0	235.9	239.1
oral	145.9	198.89	230.0	210.4	235.1	239.0

	Malignant			Benign	Uncertain Behavior	Unspecified
	Primary	Secondary	Ca in situ			
cavity—*continued*						
peritoneal	158.9	197.6	—	211.8	235.4	239.0
tympanic	160.1	197.3	231.8	212.0	235.9	239.1
cecum	153.4	197.5	230.3	211.3	235.2	239.0
central						
nervous system—*see* Neoplasm,						
nervous system						
white matter	191.0	198.3	—	225.0	237.5	239.6
cerebellopontine (angle)	191.6	198.3	—	225.0	237.5	239.6
cerebellum, cerebellar	191.6	198.3	—	225.0	237.5	239.6
cerebrum, cerebral (cortex) (hemisphere)						
(white matter)	191.0	198.3	—	225.0	237.5	239.6
meninges	192.1	198.4	—	225.2	237.6	239.7
peduncle	191.7	198.3	—	225.0	237.5	239.6
ventricle (any)	191.5	198.3	—	225.0	237.5	239.6
cervical region	195.0	198.89	234.8	229.8	238.8	239.8
cervix (cervical) (uteri) (uterus)	180.9	198.82	233.1	219.0	236.0	239.5
canal	180.0	198.82	233.1	219.0	236.0	239.5
contiguous sites	180.8	—	—	—	—	—
endocervix (canal) (gland)	180.0	198.82	233.1	219.0	236.0	239.5
exocervix	180.1	198.82	233.1	219.0	236.0	239.5
external os	180.1	198.82	233.1	219.0	236.0	239.5
internal os	180.0	198.82	233.1	219.0	236.0	239.5
nabothian gland	180.0	198.82	233.1	219.0	236.0	239.5
squamocolumnar junction	180.8	198.82	233.1	219.0	236.0	239.5
stump	180.8	198.82	233.1	219.0	236.0	239.5
cheek	195.0	198.89	234.8	229.8	238.8	239.8
external	173.3	198.2	232.3	216.3	238.2	239.2
inner aspect	145.0	198.89	230.0	210.4	235.1	239.0
internal	145.0	198.89	230.0	210.4	235.1	239.0
mucosa	145.0	198.89	230.0	210.4	235.1	239.0
chest (wall) NEC	195.1	198.89	234.8	229.8	238.8	239.8
chiasma opticum	192.0	198.4	—	225.1	237.9	239.7
chin	173.3	198.2	232.3	216.3	238.2	239.2
choana	147.3	198.89	230.0	210.7	235.1	239.0
cholangiole	155.1	197.8	230.8	211.5	235.3	239.0
choledochal duct	156.1	197.8	230.8	211.5	235.3	239.0
choroid	190.6	198.4	234.0	224.6	238.8	239.8
plexus	191.5	198.3	—	225.0	237.5	239.6
ciliary body	190.0	198.4	234.0	224.0	238.8	239.8
clavicle	170.3	198.5	—	213.3	238.0	239.2
clitoris	184.3	198.82	233.3	221.2	236.3	239.5
clivus	170.0	198.5	—	213.0	238.0	239.2
cloacogenic zone	154.8	197.5	230.7	211.4	235.5	239.0
coccygeal						
body or glomus	194.6	198.89	—	227.6	237.3	239.7
vertebra	170.6	198.5	—	213.6	238.0	239.2
coccyx	170.6	198.5	—	213.6	238.0	239.2
colon—*see also* Neoplasm, intestine, large						
and rectum	154.0	197.5	230.4	211.4	235.2	239.0
column, spinal—*see* Neoplasm, spine						
columnella	173.3	198.2	232.3	216.3	238.2	239.2
commissure						
labial, lip	140.6	198.89	230.0	210.4	235.1	239.0
laryngeal	161.0	197.3	231.0	212.1	235.6	239.1
common (bile) duct	156.1	197.8	230.8	211.5	235.3	239.0
concha	173.2	198.2	232.2	216.2	238.2	239.2
nose	160.0	197.3	231.8	212.0	235.9	239.1
conjunctiva	190.3	198.4	234.0	224.3	238.8	239.8

| | Malignant | | | | | |
---	Primary	Secondary	Ca in situ	Benign	Uncertain Behavior	Unspecified
connective tissue NEC	171.9	198.89	—	215.9	238.1	239.2

Note—For neoplasms of connective tissue (blood vessel, bursa, fasica, ligament, muscle, peripheral nerves, sympathetic and parasympathetic nerves, and ganglia, synovia, tendon, etc.) or of morphological types that indicate connective tissue, code according to the list under "Neoplasm, connective tissue;" for sites that do not appear in this list, code to neoplasm of that site; e.g.: liposarcoma, shoulder 171.2; leiomyosarcoma,stomach 151.9; neurofibroma,chest wall 215.4.

Morphological types that indicate connective tissue appear in their proper place in the alphabetic index with the instruction "see Neoplasm, connective tissue..."

	Primary	Secondary	Ca in situ	Benign	Uncertain Behavior	Unspecified
abdomen	171.5	198.89	—	215.5	238.1	239.2
abdominal wall	171.5	198.89	—	215.5	238.1	239.2
ankle	171.3	198.89	—	215.3	238.1	239.2
antecubital fossa or space	171.2	198.89	—	215.2	238.1	239.2
arm	171.2	198.89	—	215.2	238.1	239.2
auricle (ear)	171.0	198.89	—	215.0	238.1	239.2
axilla	171.4	198.89	—	215.4	238.1	239.2
back	171.7	198.89	—	215.7	238.1	239.2
breast (female) *(see also* Neoplasm, breast)	174.9	198.81	233.0	217	238.3	239.3
male	175.9	198.81	233.0	217	238.3	239.3
buttock	171.6	198.89	—	215.6	238.1	239.2
calf	171.3	198.89	—	215.3	238.1	239.2
cervical region	171.0	198.89	—	215.0	238.1	239.2
cheek	171.0	198.89	—	215.0	238.1	239.2
chest (wall)	171.4	198.89	—	215.4	238.1	239.2
chin	171.0	198.89	—	215.0	238.1	239.2
contiguous sites	171.8	—	—	—	—	—
diaphragm	171.4	198.89	—	215.4	238.1	239.2
ear (external)	171.0	198.89	—	215.0	238.1	239.2
elbow	171.2	198.89	—	215.2	238.1	239.2
extrarectal	171.6	198.89	—	215.6	238.1	239.2
extremity	171.8	198.89	—	215.8	238.1	239.2
lower	171.3	198.89	—	215.3	238.1	239.2
upper	171.2	198.89	—	215.2	238.1	239.2
eyelid	171.0	198.89	—	215.0	238.1	239.2
face	171.0	198.89	—	215.0	238.1	239.2
finger	171.2	198.89	—	215.2	238.1	239.2
flank	171.7	198.89	—	215.7	238.1	239.2
foot	171.3	198.89	—	215.3	238.1	239.2
forearm	171.2	198.89	—	215.2	238.1	239.2
forehead	171.0	198.89	—	215.0	238.1	239.2
gluteal region	171.6	198.89	—	215.6	238.1	239.2
great vessels NEC	171.4	198.89	—	215.4	238.1	239.2
groin	171.6	198.89	—	215.6	238.1	239.2
hand	171.2	198.89	—	215.2	238.1	239.2
head	171.0	198.89	—	215.0	238.1	239.2
heel	171.3	198.89	—	215.3	238.1	239.2
hip	171.3	198.89	—	215.3	238.1	239.2
hypochondrium	171.5	198.89	—	215.5	238.1	239.2
iliopsoas muscle	171.6	198.89	—	215.5	238.1	239.2
infraclavicular region	171.4	198.89	—	215.4	238.1	239.2
inguinal (canal) (region)	171.6	198.89	—	215.6	238.1	239.2
intrathoracic	171.4	198.89	—	215.4	238.1	239.2
ischorectal fossa	171.6	198.89	—	215.6	238.1	239.2
jaw	143.9	198.89	230.0	210.4	235.1	239.0
knee	171.3	198.89	—	215.3	238.1	239.2
leg	171.3	198.89	—	215.3	238.1	239.2

| | Malignant | | | | | |
	Primary	Secondary	Ca in situ	Benign	Uncertain Behavior	Unspecified
connective tissue—*continued*						
limb NEC	171.9	198.89	—	215.8	238.1	239.2
lower	171.3	198.89	—	215.3	238.1	239.2
upper	171.2	198.89	—	215.2	238.1	239.2
nates	171.6	198.89	—	215.6	238.1	239.2
neck	171.0	198.89	—	215.0	238.1	239.2
orbit	190.1	198.4	234.0	224.1	238.8	239.8
pararectal	171.6	198.89	—	215.6	238.1	239.2
para-urethral	171.6	198.89	—	215.6	238.1	239.2
paravaginal	171.6	198.89	—	215.6	238.1	239.2
pelvis (floor)	171.6	198.89	—	215.6	238.1	239.2
pelvo-abdominal	171.8	198.89	—	215.8	238.1	239.2
perineum	171.6	198.89	—	215.6	238.1	239.2
perirectal (tissue)	171.6	198.89	—	215.6	238.1	239.2
periurethral (tissue)	171.6	198.89	—	215.6	238.1	239.2
popliteal fossa or space	171.3	198.89	—	215.3	238.1	239.2
presacral	171.6	198.89	—	215.6	238.1	239.2
psoas muscle	171.5	198.89	—	215.5	238.1	239.2
pterygoid fossa	171.0	198.89	—	215.0	238.1	239.2
rectovaginal septum or wall	171.6	198.89	—	215.6	238.1	239.2
rectovesical	171.6	198.89	—	215.6	238.1	239.2
retroperitoneum	158.0	197.6	—	211.8	235.4	239.0
sacrococcygeal region	171.6	198.89	—	215.6	238.1	239.2
scalp	171.0	198.89	—	215.0	238.1	239.2
scapular region	171.4	198.89	—	215.4	238.1	239.2
shoulder	171.2	198.89	—	215.2	238.1	239.2
skin (dermis) NEC	173.9	198.2	232.9	216.9	238.2	239.2
submental	171.0	198.89	—	215.0	238.1	239.2
supraclavicular region	171.0	198.89	—	215.0	238.1	239.2
temple	171.0	198.89	—	215.0	238.1	239.2
temporal region	171.0	198.89	—	215.0	238.1	239.2
thigh	171.3	198.89	—	215.3	238.1	239.2
thoracic (duct) (wall)	171.4	198.89	—	215.4	238.1	239.2
thorax	171.4	198.89	—	215.4	238.1	239.2
thumb	171.2	198.89	—	215.2	238.1	239.2
toe	171.3	198.89	—	215.3	238.1	239.2
trunk	171.7	198.89	—	215.7	238.1	239.2
umbilicus	171.5	198.89	—	215.5	238.1	239.2
vesicorectal	171.6	198.89	—	215.6	238.1	239.2
wrist	171.2	198.89	—	215.2	238.1	239.2
conus medullaris	192.2	198.3	—	225.3	237.5	239.7
cord (true) (vocal)	161.0	197.3	231.0	212.1	235.6	239.1
false	161.1	197.3	231.0	212.1	235.6	239.1
spermatic	187.6	198.82	233.6	222.8	236.6	239.5
spinal (cervical) (lumbar) (thoracic)	192.2	198.3	—	225.3	237.5	239.7
cornea (limbus)	190.4	198.4	234.0	224.4	238.8	239.8
corpus						
albicans	183.0	198.6	233.3	220	236.2	239.5
callosum, brain	191.8	198.3	—	225.0	237.5	239.6
cavernosum	187.3	198.82	233.5	222.1	236.6	239.5
gastric	151.4	197.8	230.2	211.1	235.2	239.0
penis	187.3	198.82	233.5	222.1	236.6	239.5
striatum, cerebrum	191.0	198.3	—	225.0	237.5	239.6
uteri	182.0	198.82	233.2	219.1	236.0	239.5
isthmus	182.1	198.82	233.2	219.1	236.0	239.5
cortex						
adrenal	194.0	198.7	234.8	227.0	237.2	239.7
cerebral	191.0	198.3	—	225.0	237.5	239.6
costal cartilage	170.3	198.5	—	213.3	238.0	239.2
costovertebral joint	170.3	198.5	—	213.3	238.0	239.2

	Malignant					
	Primary	Secondary	Ca in situ	Benign	Uncertain Behavior	Unspecified
Cowper's gland	189.3	198.1	233.9	223.81	236.99	239.5
cranial (fossa, any)	191.9	198.3	—	225.0	237.5	239.6
meninges	192.1	198.4	—	225.2	237.6	239.7
nerve (any)	192.0	198.4	—	225.1	237.9	239.7
craniobuccal pouch	194.3	198.89	234.8	227.3	237.0	239.7
craniopharyngeal (duct) (pouch)	194.3	198.89	234.8	227.3	237.0	239.7
cricoid	148.0	198.89	230.0	210.8	235.1	239.0
cartilage	161.3	197.3	231.0	212.1	235.6	239.1
cricopharynx	148.0	198.89	230.0	210.8	235.1	239.0
crypt of Morgagni	154.8	197.5	230.7	211.4	235.2	239.0
crystalline lens	190.0	198.4	234.0	224.0	238.8	239.8
cul-de-sac (Douglas')	158.8	197.6	—	211.8	235.4	239.0
cuneiform cartilage	161.3	197.3	231.0	212.1	235.6	239.1
cutaneous—*see* Neoplasm, skin						
cutis—*see* Neoplasm, skin						
cystic (bile) duct (common)	156.1	197.8	230.8	211.5	235.3	239.0
dermis—*see* Neoplasm, skin						
diaphragm	171.4	198.89	—	215.4	238.1	239.2
digestive organs, system, tube, tract NEC	159.9	197.8	230.9	211.9	235.5	239.0
contiguous sites with peritoneum	159.8	—	—	—	—	—
disc, intervertebral	170.2	198.5	—	213.2	238.0	239.2
disease, generalized	199.0	199.0	234.9	229.9	238.9	199.0
disseminated	199.0	199.0	234.9	229.9	238.9	199.0
Douglas' cul-de-sac or pouch	158.8	197.6	—	211.8	235.4	239.0
duodenojejunal junction	152.8	197.4	230.7	211.2	235.2	239.0
duodenum	152.0	197.4	230.7	211.2	235.2	239.0
dura (cranial) (mater)	192.1	198.4	—	225.2	237.6	239.7
cerebral	192.1	198.4	—	225.2	237.6	239.7
spinal	192.3	198.4	—	225.4	237.6	239.7
ear (external)	173.2	198.2	232.2	216.2	238.2	239.2
auricle or auris	173.2	198.2	232.2	216.2	238.2	239.2
canal, external	173.2	198.2	232.2	216.2	238.2	239.2
cartilage	171.0	198.89	—	215.0	238.1	239.2
external meatus	173.2	198.2	232.2	216.2	238.2	239.2
inner	160.1	197.3	231.8	212.0	235.9	239.1
lobule	173.2	198.2	232.2	216.2	238.2	239.2
middle	160.1	197.3	231.8	212.0	235.9	239.1
contiguous sites with accessory sinuses or nasal cavities	160.8	—	—	—	—	—
skin	173.2	198.2	232.2	216.2	238.2	239.2
earlobe	173.2	198.2	232.2	216.2	238.2	239.2
ejaculatory duct	187.8	198.82	233.6	222.8	236.6	239.5
elbow NEC*	195.4	198.89	232.6	229.8	238.8	239.8
endocardium	164.1	198.89	—	212.7	238.8	239.8
endocervix (canal) (gland)	180.0	198.82	233.1	219.0	236.0	239.5
endocrine gland NEC	194.9	198.89	—	227.9	237.4	239.7
pluriglandular NEC	194.8	198.89	234.8	227.8	237.4	239.7
endometrium (gland) (stroma)	182.0	198.82	233.2	219.1	236.0	239.5
ensiform cartilage	170.3	198.5	—	213.3	238.0	239.2
enteric—*see* Neoplasm, intestine						
ependyma (brain)	191.5	198.3	—	225.0	237.5	239.6
epicardium	164.1	198.89	—	212.7	238.8	239.8
epididymis	187.5	198.82	233.6	222.3	236.6	239.5
epidural	192.9	198.4	—	225.9	237.9	239.7
epiglottis	161.1	197.3	231.0	212.1	235.6	239.1
anterior aspect or surface	146.4	198.89	230.0	210.6	235.1	239.0
cartilage	161.3	197.3	231.0	212.1	235.6	239.1
free border (margin)	146.4	198.89	230.0	210.6	235.1	239.0
junctional region	146.5	198.89	230.0	210.6	235.1	239.0
posterior (laryngeal) surface	161.1	197.3	231.0	212.1	235.6	239.1
suprahyoid portion	161.1	197.3	231.0	212.1	235.6	239.1

	Malignant					
	Primary	Secondary	Ca in situ	Benign	Uncertain Behavior	Unspecified
esophagogastric junction	151.0	197.8	230.2	211.1	235.2	239.0
esophagus	150.9	197.8	230.1	211.0	235.5	239.0
abdominal	150.2	197.8	230.1	211.0	235.5	239.0
cervical	150.0	197.8	230.1	211.0	235.5	239.0
contiguous sites	150.8	—	—	—	—	—
distal (third)	150.5	197.8	230.1	211.0	235.5	239.0
lower (third)	150.5	197.8	230.1	211.0	235.5	239.0
middle (third)	150.4	197.8	230.1	211.0	235.5	239.0
proximal (third)	150.3	197.8	230.1	211.0	235.5	239.0
specified part NEC	150.8	197.8	230.1	211.0	235.5	239.0
thoracic	150.1	197.8	230.1	211.0	235.5	239.0
upper (third)	150.3	197.8	230.1	211.0	235.5	239.0
ethmoid (sinus)	160.3	197.3	231.8	212.0	235.9	239.1
bone or labyrinth	170.0	198.5	—	213.0	238.0	239.2
Eustachian tube	160.1	197.3	231.8	212.0	235.9	239.1
exocervix	180.1	198.82	233.1	219.0	236.0	239.5
external						
meatus (ear)	173.2	198.2	232.2	216.2	238.2	239.2
os, cervix uteri	180.1	198.82	233.1	219.0	236.0	239.5
extradural	192.9	198.4	—	225.9	237.9	239.7
extrahepatic (bile) duct	156.1	197.8	230.8	211.5	235.3	239.0
contiguous sites with gallbladder	156.8	—	—	—	—	—
extraocular muscle	190.1	198.4	234.0	224.1	238.8	239.8
extrarectal	195.3	198.89	234.8	229.8	238.8	239.8
extremity*	195.8	198.89	232.8	229.8	238.8	239.8
lower*	195.5	198.89	232.7	229.8	238.8	239.8
upper*	195.4	198.89	232.6	229.8	238.8	239.8
eye NEC	190.9	198.4	234.0	224.9	238.8	239.8
contiguous sites	190.8	—	—	—	—	—
specified sites NEC	190.8	198.4	234.0	224.8	238.8	239.8
eyeball	190.0	198.4	234.0	224.0	238.8	239.8
eyebrow	173.3	198.2	232.3	216.3	238.2	239.2
eyelid (lower) (skin) (upper)	173.1	198.2	232.1	216.1	238.2	239.2
cartilage	171.0	198.89	—	215.0	238.1	239.2
face NEC*	195.0	198.89	232.3	229.8	238.8	239.8
fallopian tube (accessory)	183.2	198.82	233.3	221.0	236.3	239.5
falx (cerebelli) (cerebri)	192.1	198.4	—	225.2	237.6	239.7
fascia—*see also* Neoplasm, connective tissue						
palmar	171.2	198.89	—	215.2	238.1	239.2
plantar	171.3	198.89	—	215.3	238.1	239.2
fatty tissue—*see* Neoplasm, connective tissue						
fauces, faucial NEC	146.9	198.89	230.0	210.6	235.1	239.0
pillars	146.2	198.89	230.0	210.6	235.1	239.0
tonsil	146.0	198.89	230.0	210.5	235.1	239.0
femur (any part)	170.7	198.5	—	213.7	238.0	239.2
fetal membrane	181	198.82	233.2	219.8	236.1	239.5
fibrous tissue—*see* Neoplasm, connective tissue						
fibula (any part)	170.7	198.5	—	213.7	238.0	239.2
filum terminale	192.2	198.3	—	225.3	237.5	239.7
finger NEC*	195.4	198.89	232.6	229.8	238.8	239.8
flank NEC*	195.8	198.89	232.5	229.8	238.8	239.8
follicle, nabothian	180.0	198.82	233.1	219.0	236.0	239.5
foot NEC*	195.5	198.89	232.7	229.8	238.8	239.8
forearm NEC*	195.4	198.89	232.6	229.8	238.8	239.8
forehead (skin)	173.3	198.2	232.3	216.3	238.2	239.2
foreskin	187.1	198.82	233.5	222.1	236.6	239.5

| | Malignant | | | | | |
	Primary	Secondary	Ca in situ	Benign	Uncertain Behavior	Unspecified
fornix						
pharyngeal	147.3	198.89	230.0	210.7	235.1	239.0
vagina	184.0	198.82	233.3	221.1	236.3	239.5
fossa (of)						
anterior (cranial)	191.9	198.3	—	225.0	237.5	239.6
cranial	191.9	198.3	—	225.0	237.5	239.6
ischiorectal	195.3	198.89	234.8	229.8	238.8	239.8
middle (cranial)	191.9	198.3	—	225.0	237.5	239.6
pituitary	194.3	198.89	234.8	227.3	237.0	239.7
posterior (cranial)	191.9	198.3	—	225.0	237.5	239.6
pterygoid	171.0	198.89	—	215.0	238.1	239.2
pyriform	148.1	198.89	230.0	210.8	235.1	239.0
Rosenmüller	147.2	198.89	230.0	210.7	235.1	239.0
tonsillar	146.1	198.89	230.0	210.6	235.1	239.0
fourchette	184.4	198.82	233.3	221.2	236.3	239.5
frenulum						
labii—*see* Neoplasm, lip, internal						
linguae	141.3	198.89	230.0	210.1	235.1	239.0
frontal						
bone	170.0	198.5	—	213.0	238.0	239.2
lobe, brain	191.1	198.3	—	225.0	237.5	239.6
meninges	192.1	198.4	—	225.2	237.6	239.7
pole	191.1	198.3	—	225.0	237.5	239.6
sinus	160.4	197.3	231.8	212.0	235.9	239.1
fundus						
stomach	151.3	197.8	230.2	211.1	235.2	239.0
uterus	182.0	198.82	233.2	219.1	236.0	239.5
gall duct (extrahepatic)	156.1	197.8	230.8	211.5	235.3	239.0
intrahepatic	155.1	197.8	230.8	211.5	235.3	239.0
gallbladder	156.0	197.8	230.8	211.5	235.3	239.0
contiguous sites with extrahepatic						
bile ducts	156.8	—	—	—	—	—
ganglia *(see also* Neoplasm, connective						
tissue)	171.9	198.89	—	215.9	238.1	239.2
basal	191.0	198.3	—	225.0	237.5	239.6
ganglion *(see also* Neoplasm, connective						
tissue)	171.9	198.89	—	215.9	238.1	239.2
cranial nerve	192.0	198.4	—	225.1	237.9	239.7
Gartner's duct	184.0	198.82	233.3	221.1	236.3	239.5
gastric—*see* Neoplasm, stomach						
gastrocolic	159.8	197.8	230.9	211.9	235.5	239.0
gastroesophageal junction	151.0	197.8	230.2	211.1	235.2	239.0
gastrointestinal (tract) NEC	159.9	197.8	230.9	211.9	235.5	239.0
generalized	199.0	199.0	234.9	229.9	238.9	199.0
genital organ or tract						
female NEC	184.9	198.82	233.3	221.9	236.3	239.5
contiguous sites	184.8	—	—	—	—	—
specified site NEC	184.8	198.82	233.3	221.8	236.3	239.5
male NEC	187.9	198.82	233.6	222.9	236.6	239.5
contiguous sites	187.8	—	—	—	—	—
specified site NEC	187.8	198.82	233.6	222.8	236.6	239.5
genitourinary tract						
female	184.9	198.82	233.3	221.9	236.3	239.5
male	187.9	198.82	233.6	222.9	236.6	239.5
gingiva (alveolar) (marginal)	143.9	198.89	230.0	210.4	235.1	239.0
lower	143.1	198.89	230.0	210.4	235.1	239.0
mandibular	143.1	198.89	230.0	210.4	235.1	239.0
maxillary	143.0	198.89	230.0	210.4	235.1	239.0
upper	143.0	198.89	230.0	210.4	235.1	239.0

| | Malignant | | | | | |
	Primary	Secondary	Ca in situ	Benign	Uncertain Behavior	Unspecified
gland, glandular (lymphatic) (system)— *see also* Neoplasm, lymph gland						
endocrine NEC	194.9	198.89	—	227.9	237.4	239.7
salivary—*see* Neoplasm, salivary, gland						
glans penis	187.2	198.82	233.5	222.1	236.6	239.5
globus pallidus	191.0	198.3	—	225.0	237.5	239.6
glomus						
coccygeal	194.6	198.89	—	227.6	237.3	239.7
jugularis	194.6	198.89	—	227.6	237.3	239.7
glosso-epiglottic fold(s)	146.4	198.89	230.0	210.6	235.1	239.0
glossopalatine fold	146.2	198.89	230.0	210.6	235.1	239.0
glossopharyngeal sulcus	146.1	198.89	230.0	210.6	235.1	239.0
glottis	161.0	197.3	231.0	212.1	235.6	239.1
gluteal region*	195.3	198.89	232.5	229.8	238.8	239.8
great vessels NEC	171.4	198.89	—	215.4	238.1	239.2
groin NEC*	195.3	198.89	232.5	229.8	238.8	239.8
gum	143.9	198.89	230.0	210.4	235.1	239.0
contiguous sites	143.8	—	—	—	—	—
lower	143.1	198.89	230.0	210.4	235.1	239.0
upper	143.0	198.89	230.0	210.4	235.1	239.0
hand NEC*	195.4	198.89	232.6	229.8	238.8	239.8
head NEC*	195.0	198.89	232.4	229.8	238.8	239.8
heart	164.1	198.89	—	212.7	238.8	239.8
contiguous sites with mediastinum or thymus	164.8	—	—	—	—	—
heel NEC*	195.5	198.89	232.7	229.8	238.8	239.8
helix	173.2	198.2	232.2	216.2	238.2	239.2
hematopoietic, hemopoietic tissue NEC	202.8	198.89	—	—	—	238.7
hemisphere, cerebral	191.0	198.3	—	225.0	237.5	239.6
hemorrhoidal zone	154.2	197.5	230.5	211.4	235.5	239.0
hepatic	155.2	197.7	230.8	211.5	235.3	239.0
duct (bile)	156.1	197.8	230.8	211.5	235.3	239.0
flexure (colon)	153.0	197.5	230.3	211.3	235.2	239.0
primary	155.0	—	—	—	—	—
hilus of lung	162.2	197.0	231.2	212.3	235.7	239.1
hip NEC*	195.5	198.89	232.7	229.8	238.8	239.8
hippocampus, brain	191.2	198.3	—	225.0	237.5	239.6
humerus (any part)	170.4	198.5	—	213.4	238.0	239.2
hymen	184.0	198.82	233.3	221.1	236.3	239.5
hypopharynx, hypopharyngeal NEC	148.9	198.89	230.0	210.8	235.1	239.0
contiguous sites	148.8	—	—	—	—	—
postcricoid region	148.0	198.89	230.0	210.8	235.1	239.0
posterior wall	148.3	198.89	230.0	210.8	235.1	239.0
pyriform fossa (sinus)	148.1	198.89	230.0	210.8	235.1	239.0
specified site NEC	148.8	198.89	230.0	210.8	235.1	239.0
wall	148.9	198.89	230.0	210.8	235.1	239.0
posterior	148.3	198.89	230.0	210.8	235.1	239.0
hypophysis	194.3	198.89	234.8	227.3	237.0	239.7
hypothalamus	191.0	198.3	—	225.0	237.5	239.6
ileocecum, ileocecal (coil, junction, valve)	153.4	197.5	230.3	211.3	235.2	239.0
ileum	152.2	197.4	230.7	211.2	235.2	239.0
ilium	170.6	198.5	—	213.6	238.0	239.2
immunoproliferative NEC	203.8	—	—	—	—	—
infraclavicular (region)*	195.1	198.89	232.5	229.8	238.8	239.8
inguinal (region)*	195.3	198.89	232.5	229.8	238.8	239.8
insula	191.0	198.3	—	225.0	237.5	239.6
insular tissue (pancreas)	157.4	197.8	230.9	211.7	235.5	239.0
brain	191.0	198.3	—	225.0	237.5	239.6

	Malignant			Benign	Uncertain Behavior	Unspecified
	Primary	Secondary	Ca in situ			
interarytenoid fold	148.2	198.89	230.0	210.8	235.1	239.0
hypopharyngeal aspect	148.2	198.89	230.0	210.8	235.1	239.0
laryngeal aspect	161.1	197.3	231.0	212.1	235.6	239.1
marginal zone	148.2	198.89	230.0	210.8	235.1	239.0
interdental papillae	143.9	198.89	230.0	210.4	235.1	239.0
lower	143.1	198.89	230.0	210.4	235.1	239.0
upper	143.0	198.89	230.0	210.4	235.1	239.0
internal						
capsule	191.0	198.3	—	225.0	237.5	239.6
os (cervix)	180.0	198.82	233.1	219.0	236.0	239.5
intervertebral cartilage or disc	170.2	198.5	—	213.2	238.0	239.2
intestine, intestinal	159.0	197.8	230.7	211.9	235.2	239.0
large	153.9	197.5	230.3	211.3	235.2	239.0
appendix	153.5	197.5	230.3	211.3	235.2	239.0
caput coli	153.4	197.5	230.3	211.3	235.2	239.0
cecum	153.4	197.5	230.3	211.3	235.2	239.0
colon	153.9	197.5	230.3	211.3	235.2	239.0
and rectum	154.0	197.5	230.4	211.4	235.2	239.0
ascending	153.6	197.5	230.3	211.3	235.2	239.0
caput	153.4	197.5	230.3	211.3	235.2	239.0
contiguous sites	153.8	—	—	—	—	—
descending	153.2	197.5	230.3	211.3	235.2	239.0
distal	153.2	197.5	230.3	211.3	235.2	239.0
left	153.2	197.5	230.3	211.3	235.2	239.0
pelvic	153.3	197.5	230.3	211.3	235.2	239.0
right	153.6	197.5	230.3	211.3	235.2	239.0
sigmoid (flexure)	153.3	197.5	230.3	211.3	235.2	239.0
transverse	153.1	197.5	230.3	211.3	235.2	239.0
contiguous sites	153.8	—	—	—	—	—
hepatic flexure	153.0	197.5	230.3	211.3	235.2	239.0
ileocecum,ileocecal (coil, valve)	153.4	197.5	230.3	211.3	235.2	239.0
sigmoid flexure (lower) (upper)	153.3	197.5	230.3	211.3	235.2	239.0
splenic flexure	153.7	197.5	230.3	211.3	235.2	239.0
small	152.9	197.4	230.7	211.2	235.2	239.0
contiguous sites	152.8	—	—	—	—	—
duodenum	152.0	197.4	230.7	211.2	235.2	239.0
ileum	152.2	197.4	230.7	211.2	235.2	239.0
jejunum	152.1	197.4	230.7	211.2	235.2	239.0
tract NEC	159.0	197.8	230.7	211.9	235.2	239.0
intra-abdominal	195.2	198.89	234.8	229.8	238.8	239.8
intracranial NEC	191.9	198.3	—	225.0	237.5	239.6
intrahepatic (bile) duct	155.1	197.8	230.8	211.5	235.3	239.0
intraocular	190.0	198.4	234.0	224.0	238.8	239.8
intraorbital	190.1	198.4	234.0	224.1	238.8	239.8
intrasellar	194.3	198.89	234.8	227.3	237.0	239.7
intrathoracic (cavity) (organs NEC)	195.1	198.89	234.8	229.8	238.8	239.8
contiguous sites with respiratory						
organs	165.8	—	—	—	—	—
iris	190.0	198.4	234.0	224.0	238.8	239.8
ischiorectal (fossa)	195.3	198.89	234.8	229.8	238.8	239.8
ischium	170.6	198.5	—	213.6	238.0	239.2
island of Reil	191.0	198.3	—	225.0	237.5	239.6
islands or islets of Langerhans	157.4	197.8	230.9	211.7	235.5	239.0
isthmus uteri	182.1	198.82	233.2	219.1	236.0	239.5
jaw	195.0	198.89	234.8	229.8	238.8	239.8
bone	170.1	198.5	—	213.1	238.0	239.2
carcinoma	143.9	—	—	—	—	—
lower	143.1	—	—	—	—	—
upper	143.0	—	—	—	—	—
lower	170.1	198.5	—	213.1	238.0	239.2
upper	170.0	198.5	—	213.0	238.0	239.2

	Malignant					
	Primary	Secondary	Ca in situ	Benign	Uncertain Behavior	Unspecified
jaw—*continued*						
carcinoma (any type) (lower) (upper) .	195.0	—	—	—	—	—
skin	173.3	198.2	232.3	216.3	238.2	239.2
soft tissues	143.9	198.89	230.0	210.4	235.1	239.0
lower	143.1	198.89	230.0	210.4	235.1	239.0
upper	143.0	198.89	230.0	210.4	235.1	239.0
jejunum	152.1	197.4	230.7	211.2	235.2	239.0
joint NEC *(see also* Neoplasm, bone) .	170.9	198.5	—	213.9	238.0	239.2
acromioclavicular	170.4	198.5	—	213.4	238.0	239.2
bursa or synovial membrane—*see* Neoplasm, connective tissue						
costovertebral	170.3	198.5	—	213.3	238.0	239.2
sternocostal	170.3	198.5	—	213.3	238.0	239.2
temporomandibular	170.1	198.5	—	213.1	238.0	239.2
junction						
anorectal	154.8	197.5	230.7	211.4	235.5	239.0
cardioesophageal	151.0	197.8	230.2	211.1	235.2	239.0
esophagogastric	151.0	197.8	230.2	211.1	235.2	239.0
gastroesophageal	151.0	197.8	230.2	211.1	235.2	239.0
hard and soft palate	145.5	198.89	230.0	210.4	235.1	239.0
ileocecal	153.4	197.5	230.3	211.3	235.2	239.0
pelvirectal	154.0	197.5	230.4	211.4	235.2	239.0
pelviureteric	189.1	198.0	233.9	223.1	236.91	239.5
rectosigmoid	154.0	197.5	230.4	211.4	235.2	239.0
squamocolumnar, of cervix	180.8	198.82	233.1	219.0	236.0	239.5
kidney (parenchyma)	189.0	198.0	233.9	223.0	236.91	239.5
calyx	189.1	198.0	233.9	223.1	236.91	239.5
hilus	189.1	198.0	233.9	223.1	236.91	239.5
pelvis	189.1	198.0	233.9	223.1	236.91	239.5
knee NEC*	195.5	198.89	232.7	229.8	238.8	239.8
labia (skin)	184.4	198.82	233.3	221.2	236.3	239.5
majora	184.1	198.82	233.3	221.2	236.3	239.5
minora	184.2	198.82	233.3	221.2	236.3	239.5
labial—*see also* Neoplasm, lip						
sulcus (lower) (upper)	145.1	198.89	230.0	210.4	235.1	239.0
labium (skin)	184.4	198.82	233.3	221.2	236.3	239.5
majus	184.1	198.82	233.3	221.2	236.3	239.5
minus	184.2	198.82	233.3	221.2	236.3	239.5
lacrimal						
canaliculi	190.7	198.4	234.0	224.7	238.8	239.8
duct (nasal)	190.7	198.4	234.0	224.7	238.8	239.8
gland	190.2	198.4	234.0	224.2	238.8	239.8
punctum	190.7	198.4	234.0	224.7	238.8	239.8
sac	190.7	198.4	234.0	224.7	238.8	239.8
Langerhans, islands or islets	157.4	197.8	230.9	211.7	235.5	239.0
laryngopharynx	148.9	198.89	230.0	210.8	235.1	239.0
larynx, laryngeal NEC	161.9	197.3	231.0	212.1	235.6	239.1
aryepiglottic fold	161.1	197.3	231.0	212.1	235.6	239.1
cartilage (arytenoid) (cricoid) (cuneiform) (thyroid)	161.3	197.3	231.0	212.1	235.6	239.1
commissure (anterior) (posterior) . . .	161.0	197.3	231.0	212.1	235.6	239.1
contiguous sites	161.8	—	—	—	—	—
extrinsic NEC	161.1	197.3	231.0	212.1	235.6	239.1
meaning hypopharynx	148.9	198.89	230.0	210.8	235.1	239.0
interarytenoid fold	161.1	197.3	231.0	212.1	235.6	239.1
intrinsic	161.0	197.3	231.0	212.1	235.6	239.1
ventricular band	161.1	197.3	231.0	212.1	235.6	239.1
leg NEC*	195.5	198.89	232.7	229.8	238.8	239.8
lens, crystalline	190.0	198.4	234.0	224.0	238.8	239.8

| | Malignant | | | | | |
---	Primary	Secondary	Ca in situ	Benign	Uncertain Behavior	Unspecified
lid (lower) (upper)	173.1	198.2	232.1	216.1	238.2	239.2
ligament—*see also* Neoplasm, connective tissue						
broad	183.3	198.82	233.3	221.0	236.3	239.5
Mackenrodt's	183.8	198.82	233.3	221.8	236.3	239.5
non-uterine—*see* Neoplasm, connective tissue						
round	183.5	198.82	—	221.0	236.3	239.5
sacro-uterine	183.4	198.82	—	221.0	236.3	239.5
uterine	183.4	198.82	—	221.0	236.3	239.5
utero-ovarian	183.8	198.82	233.3	221.8	236.3	239.5
uterosacral	183.4	198.82	—	221.0	236.3	239.5
limb*	195.8	198.89	232.8	229.8	238.8	239.8
lower*	195.5	198.89	232.7	229.8	238.8	239.8
upper*	195.4	198.89	232.6	229.8	238.8	239.8
limbus of cornea	190.4	198.4	234.0	224.4	238.8	239.8
lingual NEC (*see also* Neoplasm, tongue)	141.9	198.89	230.0	210.1	235.1	239.0
lingula, lung	162.3	197.0	231.2	212.3	235.7	239.1
lip (external) (lipstick area) (vermillion border)	140.9	198.89	230.0	210.0	235.1	239.0
buccal aspect—*see* Neoplasm, lip, internal						
commissure	140.6	198.89	230.0	210.4	235.1	239.0
contiguous sites	140.8	—	—	—	—	—
with oral cavity or pharynx	149.8	—	—	—	—	—
frenulum—*see* Neoplasm, lip, internal						
inner aspect—*see* Neoplasm, lip, internal						
internal (buccal) (frenulum) (mucosa) (oral)	140.5	198.89	230.0	210.0	235.1	239.0
lower	140.4	198.89	230.0	210.0	235.1	239.0
upper	140.3	198.89	230.0	210.0	235.1	239.0
lower	140.1	198.89	230.0	210.0	235.1	239.0
internal (buccal) (frenulum) (mucosa) (oral)	140.4	198.89	230.0	210.0	235.1	239.0
mucosa—*see* Neoplasm, lip, internal						
oral aspect—*see* Neoplasm, lip, internal						
skin (commissure) (lower) (upper)	173.0	198.2	232.0	216.0	238.2	239.2
upper	140.0	198.89	230.0	210.0	235.1	239.0
internal (buccal) (frenulum) (mucosa) (oral)	140.3	198.89	230.0	210.0	235.1	239.0
liver	155.2	197.7	230.8	211.5	235.3	239.0
primary	155.0	—	—	—	—	—
lobe						
azygos	162.3	197.0	231.2	212.3	235.7	239.1
frontal	191.1	198.3	—	225.0	237.5	239.6
lower	162.5	197.0	231.2	212.3	235.7	239.1
middle	162.4	197.0	231.2	212.3	235.7	239.1
occipital	191.4	198.3	—	225.0	237.5	239.6
parietal	191.3	198.3	—	225.0	237.5	239.6
temporal	191.2	198.3	—	225.0	237.5	239.6
upper	162.3	197.0	231.2	212.3	235.7	239.1
lumbosacral plexus	171.6	198.4	—	215.6	238.1	239.2
lung	162.9	197.0	231.2	212.3	235.7	239.1
azygos lobe	162.3	197.0	231.2	212.3	235.7	239.1
carina	162.2	197.0	231.2	212.3	235.7	239.1
contiguous sites with bronchus or trachea	162.8	—	—	—	—	—
hilus	162.2	197.0	231.2	212.3	235.7	239.1

| | Malignant | | | | | |
	Primary	Secondary	Ca in situ	Benign	Uncertain Behavior	Unspecified
lung—*continued*						
lingula	162.3	197.0	231.2	212.3	235.7	239.1
lobe NEC	162.9	197.0	231.2	212.3	235.7	239.1
lower lobe	162.5	197.0	231.2	212.3	235.7	239.1
main bronchus	162.2	197.0	231.2	212.3	235.7	239.1
middle lobe	162.4	197.0	231.2	212.3	235.7	239.1
upper lobe	162.3	197.0	231.2	212.3	235.7	239.1
lymph, lymphatic						
channel NEC *(see also* Neoplasm, connective tissue)	171.9	198.89	—	215.9	238.1	239.2
gland (secondary)	—	196.9	—	229.0	238.8	239.8
abdominal	—	196.2	—	229.0	238.8	239.8
aortic	—	196.2	—	229.0	238.8	239.8
arm	—	196.3	—	229.0	238.8	239.8
auricular (anterior) (posterior)	—	196.0	—	229.0	238.8	239.8
axilla, axillary	—	196.3	—	229.0	238.8	239.8
brachial	—	196.3	—	229.0	238.8	239.8
bronchial	—	196.1	—	229.0	238.8	239.8
bronchopulmonary	—	196.1	—	229.0	238.8	239.8
celiac	—	196.2	—	229.0	238.8	239.8
cervical	—	196.0	—	229.0	238.8	239.8
cervicofacial	—	196.0	—	229.0	238.8	239.8
Cloquet	—	196.5	—	229.0	238.8	239.8
colic	—	196.2	—	229.0	238.8	239.8
common duct	—	196.2	—	229.0	238.8	239.8
cubital	—	196.3	—	229.0	238.8	239.8
diaphragmatic	—	196.1	—	229.0	238.8	239.8
epigastric, inferior	—	196.6	—	229.0	238.8	239.8
epitrochlear	—	196.3	—	229.0	238.8	239.8
esophageal	—	196.1	—	229.0	238.8	239.8
face	—	196.0	—	229.0	238.8	239.8
femoral	—	196.5	—	229.0	238.8	239.8
gastric	—	196.2	—	229.0	238.8	239.8
groin	—	196.5	—	229.0	238.8	239.8
head	—	196.0	—	229.0	238.8	239.8
hepatic	—	196.2	—	229.0	238.8	239.8
hilar (pulmonary)	—	196.1	—	229.0	238.8	239.8
splenic	—	196.2	—	229.0	238.8	239.8
hypogastric	—	196.6	—	229.0	238.8	239.8
ileocolic	—	196.2	—	229.0	238.8	239.8
iliac	—	196.6	—	229.0	238.8	239.8
infraclavicular	—	196.3	—	229.0	238.8	239.8
inguina, inguinal	—	196.5	—	229.0	238.8	239.8
innominate	—	196.1	—	229.0	238.8	239.8
intercostal	—	196.1	—	229.0	238.8	239.8
intestinal	—	196.2	—	229.0	238.8	239.8
intrabdominal	—	196.2	—	229.0	238.8	239.8
intrapelvic	—	196.6	—	229.0	238.8	239.8
intrathoracic	—	196.1	—	229.0	238.8	239.9
jugular	—	196.0	—	229.0	238.8	239.8
leg	—	196.5	—	229.0	238.8	239.8
limb						
lower	—	196.5	—	229.0	238.8	239.8
upper	—	196.3	—	229.0	238.8	239.8
lower limb	—	196.5	—	229.0	238.8	238.9
lumbar	—	196.2	—	229.0	238.8	239.8
mandibular	—	196.0	—	229.0	238.8	239.8
mediastinal	—	196.1	—	229.0	238.8	239.8
mesenteric (inferior) (superior)	—	196.2	—	229.0	238.8	239.8
midcolic	—	196.2	—	229.0	238.8	239.8

| | Malignant | | | | | |
	Primary	Secondary	Ca in situ	Benign	Uncertain Behavior	Unspecified
lymph, lymphatic—*continued*						
multiple sites in categories						
196.0-196.6	—	196.8	—	229.0	238.8	239.8
neck	—	196.0	—	229.0	238.8	239.8
obturator	—	196.6	—	229.0	238.8	239.8
occipital	—	196.0	—	229.0	238.8	239.8
pancreatic	—	196.2	—	229.0	238.8	239.8
para-aortic	—	196.2	—	229.0	238.8	239.8
paracervical	—	196.6	—	229.0	238.8	239.8
parametrial	—	196.6	—	229.0	238.8	239.8
parasternal	—	196.1	—	229.0	238.8	239.8
parotid	—	196.0	—	229.0	238.8	239.8
pectoral	—	196.3	—	229.0	238.8	239.8
pelvic	—	196.6	—	229.0	238.8	239.8
peri-aortic	—	196.2	—	229.0	238.8	239.8
peripancreatic	—	196.2	—	229.0	238.8	239.8
popliteal	—	196.5	—	229.0	238.8	239.8
porta hepatis	—	196.2	—	229.0	238.8	239.8
portal	—	196.2	—	229.0	238.8	239.8
preauricular	—	196.0	—	229.0	238.8	239.8
prelaryngeal	—	196.0	—	229.0	238.8	239.8
presymphysial	—	196.6	—	229.0	238.8	239.8
pretracheal	—	196.0	—	229.0	238.8	239.8
primary (any site) NEC	202.9	—	—	—	—	—
pulmonary (hiler)	—	196.1	—	229.0	238.8	239.8
pyloric	—	196.2	—	229.0	238.8	239.8
retroperitoneal	—	196.2	—	229.0	238.8	239.8
retropharyngeal	—	196.0	—	229.0	238.8	239.8
Rosenmüller's	—	196.5	—	229.0	238.8	239.8
sacral	—	196.6	—	229.0	238.8	239.8
scalene	—	196.0	—	229.0	238.8	239.8
site NEC	—	196.9	—	229.0	238.8	239.8
splenic (hilar)	—	196.2	—	229.0	238.8	239.8
subclavicular	—	196.3	—	229.0	238.8	239.8
subinguinal	—	196.5	—	229.0	238.8	239.8
sublingual	—	196.0	—	229.0	238.8	239.8
submandibular	—	196.0	—	229.0	238.8	239.8
submaxillary	—	196.0	—	229.0	238.8	239.8
submental	—	196.0	—	229.0	238.8	239.8
subscapular	—	196.3	—	229.0	238.8	239.8
supraclavicular	—	196.0	—	229.0	238.8	239.8
thoracic	—	196.1	—	229.0	238.8	239.8
tibial	—	196.5	—	229.0	238.8	239.8
tracheal	—	196.1	—	229.0	238.8	239.8
tracheobronchial	—	196.1	—	229.0	238.8	239.8
upper limb	—	196.3	—	229.0	238.8	239.8
Virchow's	—	196.0	—	229.0	238.8	239.8
node—*see also* Neoplasm, lymph gland						
primary NEC	202.9	—	—	—	—	—
vessel (*see also* Neoplasm, connective						
tissue)	171.9	198.89	—	215.9	238.1	239.2
Mackenrodt's ligament	183.8	198.82	233.3	221.8	236.3	239.5
malar	170.0	198.5	—	213.0	238.0	239.2
region—*see* Neoplasm, cheek						
mammary gland—*see* Neoplasm, breast						
mandible	170.1	198.5	—	213.1	238.0	239.2
alveolar						
mucose	143.1	198.89	230.0	210.4	235.1	239.0
ridge or process	170.1	198.5	—	213.1	238.0	239.2
carcinoma	143.1	—	—	—	—	—
carcinoma	143.1	—	—	—	—	—

	Malignant					
	Primary	Secondary	Ca in situ	Benign	Uncertain Behavior	Unspecified
marrow (bone) NEC	202.9	198.5	—	—	—	238.7
mastectomy site (skin)	173.5	198.2	—	—	—	—
specified as breast tissue	174.8	198.81	—	—	—	—
mastoid (air cells) (antrum) (cavity)	160.1	197.3	231.8	212.0	235.9	239.1
bone or process	170.0	198.5	—	213.0	238.0	239.2
maxilla, maxillary (superior)	170.0	198.5	—	213.0	238.0	239.2
alveolar						
mucosa	143.0	198.89	230.0	210.4	235.1	239.0
ridge or process	170.0	198.5	—	213.0	238.0	239.2
carcinoma	143.0	—	—	—	—	—
antrum	160.2	197.3	231.8	212.0	235.9	239.1
carcinoma	143.0	—	—	—	—	—
inferior—*see* Neoplasm, mandible						
sinus	160.2	197.3	231.8	212.0	235.9	239.1
meatus						
external (ear)	173.2	198.2	232.2	216.2	238.2	239.2
Meckel's diverticulum	152.3	197.4	230.7	211.2	235.2	239.0
mediastinum, mediastinal	164.9	197.1	—	212.5	235.8	239.8
anterior	164.2	197.1	—	212.5	235.8	239.8
contiguous sites with heart and						
thymus	164.8	—	—	—	—	—
posterior	164.3	197.1	—	212.5	235.8	239.8
medulla						
adrenal	194.0	198.7	234.8	227.0	237.2	239.7
oblongata	191.7	198.3	—	225.0	237.5	239.6
meibomian gland	173.1	198.2	232.1	216.1	238.2	239.2
melanoma —*see* Melanoma						
meninges (brain) (cerebral) (cranial)						
(intracranial)	192.1	198.4	—	225.2	237.6	239.7
spinal (cord)	192.3	198.4	—	225.4	237.6	239.7
meniscus, knee joint (lateral) (medial)	170.7	198.5	—	213.7	238.0	239.2
mesentery, mesenteric	158.8	197.6	—	211.8	235.4	239.0
mesoappendix	158.8	197.6	—	211.8	235.4	239.0
mesocolon	158.8	197.6	—	211.8	235.4	239.0
mesopharynx—*see* Neoplasm, oropharynx						
mesosalpinx	183.3	198.82	233.3	221.0	236.3	239.5
mesovarium	183.3	198.82	233.3	221.0	236.3	239.5
metacarpus (any bone)	170.5	198.5	—	213.5	238.0	239.2
metastatic NEC—*see also* Neoplasm,						
by site, secondary	—	199.1	—	—	—	—
metatarsus (any bone)	170.8	198.5	—	213.8	238.0	239.2
midbrain	191.7	198.3	—	225.0	237.5	239.6
milk duct—*see* Neoplasm, breast						
mons						
pubis	184.4	198.82	233.3	221.2	236.3	239.5
veneris	184.4	198.82	233.3	221.2	236.3	239.5
motor tract	192.9	198.4	—	225.9	237.9	239.7
brain	191.9	198.3	—	225.0	237.5	239.6
spinal	192.2	198.3	—	225.3	237.5	239.7
mouth	145.9	198.89	230.0	210.4	235.1	239.0
contiguous sites	145.8	—	—	—	—	—
floor	144.9	198.89	230.0	210.3	235.1	239.0
anterior portion	144.0	198.89	230.0	210.3	235.1	239.0
contiguous sites	144.8	—	—	—	—	—
lateral portion	144.1	198.89	230.0	210.3	235.1	239.0
roof	145.5	198.89	230.0	210.4	235.1	239.0
specified part NEC	145.8	198.89	230.0	210.4	235.1	239.0
vestibule	145.1	198.89	230.0	210.4	235.1	239.0
mucosa						
alveolar (ridge or process)	143.9	198.89	230.0	210.4	235.1	239.0
lower	143.1	198.89	230.0	210.4	235.1	239.0
upper	143.0	198.89	230.0	210.4	235.1	239.0

	Malignant					
	Primary	Secondary	Ca in situ	Benign	Uncertain Behavior	Unspecified
mucosa—*continued*						
buccal	145.0	198.89	230.0	210.4	235.1	239.0
cheek	145.0	198.89	230.0	210.4	235.1	239.0
lip—*see* Neoplasm, lip, internal						
nasal	160.0	197.3	231.8	212.0	235.9	239.1
oral	145.0	198.89	230.0	210.4	235.1	239.0
Müllerian duct						
female	184.8	198.82	233.3	221.8	236.3	239.5
male	187.8	198.82	233.6	222.8	236.6	239.5
multiple sites NEC	199.0	199.0	234.9	229.9	238.9	199.0
muscle—*see also* Neoplasm, connective tissue						
extraocular	190.1	198.4	234.0	224.1	238.8	239.8
myocardium	164.1	198.89	—	212.7	238.8	239.8
myometrium	182.0	198.82	233.2	219.1	236.0	239.5
myopericardium	164.1	198.89	—	212.7	238.8	239.8
nabothian gland (follicle)	180.0	198.82	233.1	219.0	236.0	239.5
nail	173.9	198.2	232.9	216.9	238.2	239.2
finger	173.6	198.2	232.6	216.6	238.2	239.2
toe	173.7	198.2	232.7	216.7	238.2	239.2
nares, naris (anterior) (posterior)	160.0	197.3	231.8	212.0	235.9	239.1
nasal—*see* Neoplasm, nose						
nasolabial groove	173.3	198.2	232.3	216.3	238.2	239.2
nasolacrimal duct	190.7	198.4	234.0	224.7	238.8	239.8
nasopharynx, nasopharyngeal	147.9	198.89	230.0	210.7	235.1	239.0
contiguous sites	147.8	—	—	—	—	—
floor	147.3	198.89	230.0	210.7	235.1	239.0
roof	147.0	198.89	230.0	210.7	235.1	239.0
specified site NEC	147.8	198.89	230.0	210.7	235.1	239.0
wall	147.9	198.89	230.0	210.7	235.1	239.0
anterior	147.3	198.89	230.0	210.7	235.1	239.0
lateral	147.2	198.89	230.0	210.7	235.1	239.0
posterior	147.1	198.89	230.0	210.7	235.1	239.0
superior	147.0	198.89	230.0	210.7	235.1	239.0
nates	173.5	198.2	232.5	216.5	238.2	239.2
neck NEC*	195.0	198.89	234.8	229.8	238.8	239.8
nerve (autonomic) (ganglion) (parasympathetic) (peripheral) (sympathetic)—*see also* Neoplasm, connective tissue						
abducens	192.0	198.4	—	225.1	237.9	239.7
accessory (spinal)	192.0	198.4	—	225.1	237.9	239.7
acoustic	192.0	198.4	—	225.1	237.9	239.7
auditory	192.0	198.4	—	225.1	237.9	239.7
brachial	171.2	198.89	—	215.2	238.1	239.2
cranial (any)	192.0	198.4	—	225.1	237.9	239.7
facial	192.0	198.4	—	225.1	237.9	239.7
femoral	171.3	198.89	—	215.3	238.1	239.2
glossopharyngeal	192.0	198.4	—	225.1	237.9	239.7
hypoglossal	192.0	198.4	—	225.1	237.9	239.7
intercostal	171.4	198.89	—	215.4	238.1	239.2
lumbar	171.7	198.89	—	215.7	238.1	239.2
median	171.2	198.89	—	215.2	238.1	239.2
obturator	171.3	198.89	—	215.3	238.1	239.2
oculomotor	192.0	198.4	—	225.1	237.9	239.7
olfactory	192.0	198.4	—	225.1	237.9	239.7
optic	192.0	198.4	—	225.1	237.9	239.7
peripheral NEC	171.9	198.89	—	215.9	238.1	239.2
radial	171.2	198.89	—	215.2	238.1	239.2
sacral	171.6	198.89	—	215.6	238.1	239.2
sciatic	171.3	198.89	—	215.3	238.1	239.2
spinal NEC	171.9	198.89	—	215.9	238.1	239.2

| | Malignant | | | | | |
	Primary	Secondary	Ca in situ	Benign	Uncertain Behavior	Unspecified
nerve—*continued*						
trigeminal	192.0	198.4	—	225.1	237.9	239.7
trochlear	192.0	198.4	—	225.1	237.9	239.7
ulnar	171.2	198.89	—	215.2	238.1	239.2
vagus	192.0	198.4	—	225.1	237.9	239.7
nervous system (central) NEC	192.9	198.4	—	225.9	237.9	239.7
autonomic NEC	171.9	198.89	—	215.9	238.1	239.2
brain—*see also* Neoplasm, brain						
membrane or meninges	192.1	198.4	—	225.2	237.6	239.7
contiguous sites	192.8	—	—	—	—	—
parasympathetic NEC	171.9	198.89	—	215.9	238.1	239.2
sympathetic NEC	171.9	198.89	—	215.9	238.1	239.2
nipple (female)	174.0	198.81	233.0	217	238.3	239.3
male	175.0	198.81	233.0	217	238.3	239.3
nose, nasal	195.0	198.89	234.8	229.8	238.8	239.8
ala (external)	173.3	198.2	232.3	216.3	238.2	239.2
bone	170.0	198.5	—	213.0	238.0	239.2
cartilage	160.0	197.3	231.8	212.0	235.9	239.1
cavity	160.0	197.3	231.8	212.0	235.9	239.1
contiguous sites with accessory sinuses or middle ear	160.8	—	—	—	—	—
choana	147.3	198.89	230.0	210.7	235.1	239.0
external (skin)	173.3	198.2	232.3	216.3	238.2	239.2
fossa	160.0	197.3	231.8	212.0	235.9	239.1
internal	160.0	197.3	231.8	212.0	235.9	239.1
mucosa	160.0	197.3	231.8	212.0	235.9	239.1
septum	160.0	197.3	231.8	212.0	235.9	239.1
posterior margin	147.3	198.89	230.0	210.7	235.1	239.0
sinus—*see* Neoplasm, sinus						
skin	173.3	198.2	232.3	216.3	238.2	239.2
turbinate (mucosa)	160.0	197.3	231.8	212.0	235.9	239.1
bone	170.0	198.5	—	213.0	238.0	239.2
vestibule	160.0	197.3	231.8	212.0	235.9	239.1
nostril	160.0	197.3	231.8	212.0	235.9	239.1
nucleus pulposus	170.2	198.5	—	213.2	238.0	239.2
occipital						
bone	170.0	198.5	—	213.0	238.0	239.2
lobe or pole, brain	191.4	198.3	—	225.0	237.5	239.6
odontogenic—*see* Neoplasm, jaw bone						
oesophagus—*see* Neoplasm, esophagus						
olfactory nerve or bulb	192.0	198.4	—	225.1	237.9	239.7
olive (brain)	191.7	198.3	—	225.0	237.5	239.6
omentum	158.8	197.6	—	211.8	235.4	239.0
operculum (brain)	191.0	198.3	—	225.0	237.5	239.6
optic nerve, chiasm, or tract	192.0	198.4	—	225.1	237.9	239.7
oral (cavity)	145.9	198.89	230.0	210.4	235.1	239.0
contiguous sites with lip or pharynx	149.8	—	—	—	—	—
ill-defined	149.9	198.89	230.0	210.4	235.1	239.0
mucosa	145.9	198.89	230.0	210.4	235.1	239.0
orbit	190.1	198.4	234.0	224.1	238.8	239.8
bone	170.0	198.5	—	213.0	238.0	239.2
eye	190.1	198.4	234.0	224.1	238.8	239.8
soft parts	190.1	198.4	234.0	224.1	238.8	239.8
organ of Zuckerkandl	194.6	198.89	—	227.6	237.3	239.7
oropharynx	146.9	198.89	230.0	210.6	235.1	239.0
branchial cleft (vestige)	146.8	198.89	230.0	210.6	235.1	239.0
contiguous sites	146.8	—	—	—	—	—
junctional region	146.5	198.89	230.0	210.6	235.1	239.0
lateral wall	146.6	198.89	230.0	210.6	235.1	239.0
pillars of fauces	146.2	198.89	230.0	210.6	235.1	239.0

| | Malignant | | | | | |
	Primary	Secondary	Ca in situ	Benign	Uncertain Behavior	Unspecified
oropharynx—*continued*						
posterior wall	146.7	198.89	230.0	210.6	235.1	239.0
specified part NEC	146.8	198.89	230.0	210.6	235.1	239.0
vallecula	146.3	198.89	230.0	210.6	235.1	239.0
os						
external	180.1	198.82	233.1	219.0	236.0	239.5
internal	180.0	198.82	233.1	219.0	236.0	239.5
ovary	183.0	198.6	233.3	220	236.2	239.5
oviduct	183.2	198.82	233.3	221.0	236.3	239.5
palate	145.5	198.89	230.0	210.4	235.1	239.0
hard	145.2	198.89	230.0	210.4	235.1	239.0
junction of hard and soft palate	145.5	198.89	230.0	210.4	235.1	239.0
soft	145.3	198.89	230.0	210.4	235.1	239.0
nasopharyngeal surface	147.3	198.89	230.0	210.7	235.1	239.0
posterior surface	147.3	198.89	230.0	210.7	235.1	239.0
superior surface	147.3	198.89	230.0	210.7	235.1	239.0
palatoglossal arch	146.2	198.89	230.0	210.6	235.1	239.0
palatopharyngeal arch	146.2	198.89	230.0	210.6	235.1	239.0
pallium	191.0	198.3	—	225.0	237.5	239.6
palpebra	173.1	198.2	232.1	216.1	238.2	239.2
pancreas	157.9	197.8	230.9	211.6	235.5	239.0
body	157.1	197.8	230.9	211.6	235.5	239.0
contiguous sites	157.8	—	—	—	—	—
duct (of Santorini) (of Wirsung)	157.3	197.8	230.9	211.6	235.5	239.0
ectopic tissue	157.8	197.8	230.9	211.6	235.5	239.0
head	157.0	197.8	230.9	211.6	235.5	239.0
islet cells	157.4	197.8	230.9	211.7	235.5	239.0
neck	157.8	197.8	230.9	211.6	235.5	239.0
tail	157.2	197.8	230.9	211.6	235.5	239.0
para-aortic body	194.6	198.89	—	227.6	237.3	239.7
paraganglion NEC	194.6	198.89	—	227.6	237.3	239.7
parametrium	183.4	198.82	—	221.0	236.3	239.5
paranephric	158.0	197.6	—	211.8	235.4	239.0
pararectal	195.3	198.89	—	229.8	238.8	239.8
parasagittal (region)	195.0	198.89	234.8	229.8	238.8	239.8
parasellar	192.9	198.4	—	225.9	237.9	239.7
parathyroid (gland)	194.1	198.89	234.8	227.1	237.4	239.7
paraurethral	195.3	198.89	—	229.8	238.8	239.8
gland	189.4	198.1	233.9	223.89	236.99	239.5
paravaginal	195.3	198.89	—	229.8	238.8	239.8
parenchyma, kidney	189.0	198.0	233.9	223.0	236.91	239.5
parietal						
bone	170.0	198.5	—	213.0	238.0	239.2
lobe, brain	191.3	198.3	—	225.0	237.5	239.6
paroophoron	183.3	198.82	233.3	221.0	236.3	239.5
parotid (duct) (gland)	142.0	198.89	230.0	210.2	235.0	239.0
parovarium	183.3	198.82	233.3	221.0	236.3	239.5
patella	170.8	198.5	—	213.8	238.0	239.2
peduncle, cerebral	191.7	198.3	—	225.0	237.5	239.6
pelvirectal junction	154.0	197.5	230.4	211.4	235.2	239.0
pelvis, pelvic	195.3	198.89	234.8	229.8	238.8	239.8
bone	170.6	198.5	—	213.6	238.0	239.2
floor	195.3	198.89	234.8	229.8	238.8	239.8
renal	189.1	198.0	233.9	223.1	236.91	239.5
viscera	195.3	198.89	234.8	229.8	238.8	239.8
wall	195.3	198.89	234.8	229.8	238.8	239.8
pelvo-abdominal	195.8	198.89	234.8	229.8	238.8	239.8
penis	187.4	198.82	233.5	222.1	236.6	239.5
body	187.3	198.82	233.5	222.1	236.6	239.5
corpus (cavernosum)	187.3	198.82	233.5	222.1	236.6	239.5
glans	187.2	198.82	233.5	222.1	236.6	239.5
skin NEC	187.4	198.82	233.5	222.1	236.6	239.5

	Malignant					
	Primary	Secondary	Ca in situ	Benign	Uncertain Behavior	Unspecified
periadrenal (tissue)	158.0	197.6	—	211.8	235.4	239.0
perianal (skin)	173.5	198.2	232.5	216.5	238.2	239.2
pericardium	164.1	198.89	—	212.7	238.8	239.8
perinephric	158.0	197.6	—	211.8	235.4	239.0
perineum	195.3	198.89	234.8	229.8	238.8	239.8
periodontal tissue NEC	143.9	198.89	230.0	210.4	235.1	239.0
periosteum—*see* Neoplasm, bone						
peripancreatic	158.0	197.6	—	211.8	235.4	239.0
peripheral nerve NEC	171.9	198.89	—	215.9	238.1	239.2
perirectal (tissue)	195.3	198.89	—	229.8	238.8	239.8
perirenal (tissue)	158.0	197.6	—	211.8	235.4	239.0
peritoneum, peritoneal (cavity)	158.9	197.6	—	211.8	235.4	239.0
contiguous sites	158.8	—	—	—	—	—
with digestive organs	159.8	—	—	—	—	—
parietal	158.8	197.6	—	211.8	235.4	239.0
pelvic	158.8	197.6	—	211.8	235.4	239.0
specified part NEC	158.8	197.6	—	211.8	235.4	239.0
peritonsillar (tissue)	195.0	198.89	234.8	229.8	238.8	239.8
periurethral tissue	195.3	198.89	—	229.8	238.8	239.8
phalanges	170.9	198.5	—	213.9	238.0	239.2
foot	170.8	198.5	—	213.8	238.0	239.2
hand	170.5	198.5	—	213.5	238.0	239.2
pharynx, pharyngeal	149.0	198.89	230.0	210.9	235.1	239.0
bursa	147.1	198.89	230.0	210.7	235.1	239.0
fornix	147.3	198.89	230.0	210.7	235.1	239.0
recess	147.2	198.89	230.0	210.7	235.1	239.0
region	149.0	198.89	230.0	210.9	235.1	239.0
tonsil	147.1	198.89	230.0	210.7	235.1	239.0
wall (lateral) (posterior)	149.0	198.89	230.0	210.9	235.1	239.0
pia mater (cerebral) (cranial)	192.1	198.4	—	225.2	237.6	239.7
spinal	192.3	198.4	—	225.4	237.6	239.7
pillars of fauces	146.2	198.89	230.0	210.6	235.1	239.0
pineal (body) (gland)	194.4	198.89	234.8	227.4	237.1	239.7
pinna (ear) NEC	173.2	198.2	232.2	216.2	238.2	239.2
cartilage	171.0	198.89	—	215.0	238.1	239.2
piriform fossa or sinus	148.1	198.89	230.0	210.8	235.1	239.0
pituitary (body) (fossa) (gland) (lobe)	194.3	198.89	234.8	227.3	237.0	239.7
placenta	181	198.82	233.2	219.8	236.1	239.5
pleura, pleural (cavity)	163.9	197.2	—	212.4	235.8	239.1
contiguous sites	163.8	—	—	—	—	—
parietal	163.0	197.2	—	212.4	235.8	239.1
visceral	163.1	197.2	—	212.4	235.8	239.1
plexus						
brachial	171.2	198.89	—	215.2	238.1	239.2
cervical	171.0	198.89	—	215.0	238.1	239.2
choroid	191.5	198.3	—	225.0	237.5	239.6
lumbosacral	171.6	198.89	—	215.6	238.1	239.2
sacral	171.6	198.89	—	215.6	238.1	239.2
pluri-endocrine	194.8	198.89	234.8	227.8	237.4	239.7
pole						
frontal	191.1	198.3	—	225.0	237.5	239.6
occipital	191.4	198.3	—	225.0	237.5	239.6
pons (varolii)	191.7	198.3	—	225.0	237.5	239.6
popliteal fossa or space*	195.5	198.89	234.8	229.8	238.8	239.8
postcricoid (region)	148.0	198.89	230.0	210.8	235.1	239.0
posterior fossa (cranial)	191.6	198.3	—	225.0	237.5	239.6
postnasal space	147.9	198.89	230.0	210.7	235.1	239.0
prepuce	187.1	198.82	233.5	222.1	236.6	239.5
prepylorus	151.1	197.8	230.2	211.1	235.2	239.0
presacral (region)	195.3	198.89	—	229.8	238.8	239.8

	Malignant					
	Primary	Secondary	Ca in situ	Benign	Uncertain Behavior	Unspecified
prostate (gland)	185	198.82	233.4	222.2	236.5	239.5
utricle	189.3	198.1	233.9	223.81	236.99	239.5
pterygoid fossa	171.0	198.89	—	215.0	238.1	239.2
pubic bone	170.6	198.5	—	213.6	238.0	239.2
pudenda, pudendum (female)	184.4	198.82	233.3	221.2	236.3	239.5
pulmonary	162.9	197.0	231.2	212.3	235.7	239.1
putamen	191.0	198.3	—	225.0	237.5	239.6
pyloric						
antrum	151.2	197.8	230.2	211.1	235.2	239.0
canal	151.1	197.8	230.2	211.1	235.2	239.0
pylorus	151.1	197.8	230.2	211.1	235.2	239.0
pyramid (brain)	191.7	198.3	—	225.0	237.5	239.6
pyriform fossa or sinus	148.1	198.89	230.0	210.8	235.1	239.0
radius (any part)	170.4	198.5	—	213.4	238.0	239.2
Rathke's pouch	194.3	198.89	234.8	227.3	237.0	239.7
rectosigmoid (colon) (junction)	154.0	197.5	230.4	211.4	235.2	239.0
contiguous sites with anus or rectum	154.8	—	—	—	—	—
rectouterine pouch	158.8	197.6	—	211.8	235.4	239.0
rectovaginal septum or wall	195.3	198.89	234.8	229.8	238.8	239.8
rectovesical septum	195.3	198.89	234.8	229.8	238.8	239.8
rectum (ampulla)	154.1	197.5	230.4	211.4	235.2	239.0
and colon	154.0	197.5	230.4	211.4	235.2	239.0
contiguous sites with anus or rectosigmoid junction	154.8	—	—	—	—	—
renal	189.0	198.0	233.9	223.0	236.91	239.5
calyx	189.1	198.0	233.9	223.1	236.91	239.5
hilus	189.1	198.0	233.9	223.1	236.91	239.5
parenchyma	189.0	198.0	233.9	223.0	236.91	239.5
pelvis	189.1	198.0	233.9	223.1	236.91	239.5
respiratory						
organs or system NEC	165.9	197.3	231.9	212.9	235.9	239.1
contiguous sites with intrathoracic organs	165.8	—	—	—	—	—
specified sites NEC	165.8	197.3	231.8	212.8	235.9	239.1
tract NEC	165.9	197.3	231.9	212.9	235.9	239.1
upper	165.0	197.3	231.9	212.9	235.9	239.1
retina	190.5	198.4	234.0	224.5	238.8	239.8
retrobulbar	190.1	198.4	—	224.1	238.8	239.8
retrocecal	158.0	197.6	—	211.8	235.4	239.0
retromolar (area) (triangle) (trigone)	145.6	198.89	230.0	210.4	235.1	239.0
retro-orbital	195.0	198.89	234.8	229.8	238.8	239.8
retroperitoneal (space) (tissue)	158.0	197.6	—	211.8	235.4	239.0
contiguous sites	158.8	—	—	—	—	—
retroperitoneum	158.0	197.6	—	211.8	235.4	239.0
contiguous sites	158.8	—	—	—	—	—
retropharyngeal	149.0	198.89	230.0	210.9	235.1	239.0
retrovesical (septum)	195.3	198.89	234.8	229.8	238.8	239.8
rhinencephalon	191.0	198.3	—	225.0	237.5	239.6
rib	170.3	198.5	—	213.3	238.0	239.2
Rosenmüller's fossa	147.2	198.89	230.0	210.7	235.1	239.0
round ligament	183.5	198.82	—	221.0	236.3	239.5
sacrococcyx, sacrococcygeal	170.6	198.5	—	213.6	238.0	239.2
region	195.3	198.89	234.8	229.8	238.8	239.8
sacrouterine ligament	183.4	198.82	—	221.0	236.3	239.5
sacrum, sacral (vertebra)	170.6	198.5	—	213.6	238.0	239.2
salivary gland or duct (major)	142.9	198.89	230.0	210.2	235.0	239.0
contiguous sites	142.8	—	—	—	—	—
minor NEC	145.9	198.89	230.0	210.4	235.1	239.0
parotid	142.0	198.89	230.0	210.2	235.0	239.0
pluriglandular	142.8	198.89	230.0	210.2	235.0	239.0

| | Malignant | | | | | |
	Primary	Secondary	Ca in situ	Benign	Uncertain Behavior	Unspecified
salivary gland or duct (major)—*continued*						
sublingual	142.2	198.89	230.0	210.2	235.0	239.0
submandibular	142.1	198.89	230.0	210.2	235.0	239.0
submaxillary	142.1	198.89	230.0	210.2	235.0	239.0
salpinx (uterine)	183.2	198.82	233.3	221.0	236.3	239.5
Santorini's duct	157.3	197.8	230.9	211.6	235.5	239.0
scalp	173.4	198.2	232.4	216.4	238.2	239.2
scapula (any part)	170.4	198.5	—	213.4	238.0	239.2
scapular region	195.1	198.89	234.8	229.8	238.8	239.8
scar NEC *(see also* Neoplasm, skin)	173.9	198.2	232.9	216.9	238.2	239.2
sciatic nerve	171.3	198.89	—	215.3	238.1	239.2
sclera	190.0	198.4	234.0	224.0	238.8	239.8
scrotum (skin)	187.7	198.82	233.6	222.4	236.6	239.5
sebaceous gland—*see* Neoplasm, skin						
sella turcica	194.3	198.89	234.8	227.3	237.0	239.7
bone	170.0	198.5	—	213.0	238.0	239.2
semilunar cartilage (knee)	170.7	198.5	—	213.7	238.0	239.2
seminal vesicle	187.8	198.82	233.6	222.8	236.6	239.5
septum						
nasal	160.0	197.3	231.8	212.0	235.9	239.1
posterior margin	147.3	198.89	230.0	210.7	235.1	239.0
rectovaginal	195.3	198.89	234.8	229.8	238.8	239.8
rectovesical	195.3	198.89	234.8	229.8	238.8	239.8
urethrovaginal	184.9	198.82	233.3	221.9	236.3	239.5
vesicovaginal	184.9	198.82	233.3	221.9	236.3	239.5
shoulder NEC*	195.4	198.89	232.6	229.8	238.8	239.8
sigmoid flexure (lower) (upper)	153.3	197.5	230.3	211.3	235.2	239.0
sinus (accessory)	160.9	197.3	231.8	212.0	235.9	239.1
bone (any)	170.0	198.5	—	213.0	238.0	239.2
contiguous sites with middle ear or						
nasal cavities	160.8	—	—	—	—	—
ethmoidal	160.3	197.3	231.8	212.0	235.9	239.1
frontal	160.4	197.3	231.8	212.0	235.9	239.1
maxillary	160.2	197.3	231.8	212.0	235.9	239.1
nasal, paranasal NEC	160.9	197.3	231.8	212.0	235.9	239.1
pyriform	148.1	198.89	230.0	210.8	235.1	239.0
sphenoidal	160.5	197.3	231.8	212.0	235.9	239.1
skeleton, skeletal NEC	170.9	198.5	—	213.9	238.0	239.2
Skene's gland	189.4	198.1	233.9	223.89	236.99	239.5
skin NEC	173.9	198.2	232.9	216.9	238.2	239.2
abdominal wall	173.5	198.2	232.5	216.5	238.2	239.2
ala nasi	173.3	198.2	232.3	216.3	238.2	239.2
ankle	173.7	198.2	232.7	216.7	238.2	239.2
antecubital space	173.6	198.2	232.6	216.6	238.2	239.2
anus	173.5	198.2	232.5	216.5	238.2	239.2
arm	173.6	198.2	232.6	216.6	238.2	239.2
auditory canal (external)	173.2	198.2	232.2	216.2	238.2	239.2
auricle (ear)	173.2	198.2	232.2	216.2	238.2	239.2
auricular canal (external)	173.2	198.2	232.2	216.2	238.2	239.2
axilla, axillary fold	173.5	198.2	232.5	216.5	238.2	239.2
back	173.5	198.2	232.5	216.5	238.2	239.2
breast	173.5	198.2	232.5	216.5	238.2	239.2
brow	173.3	198.2	232.3	216.3	238.2	239.2
buttock	173.5	198.2	232.5	216.5	238.2	239.2
calf	173.7	198.2	232.7	216.7	238.2	239.2
canthus (eye) (inner) (outer)	173.1	198.2	232.1	216.1	238.2	239.2
cervical region	173.4	198.2	232.4	216.4	238.2	239.2
cheek (external)	173.3	198.2	232.3	216.3	238.2	239.2
chest (wall)	173.5	198.2	232.5	216.5	238.2	239.2
chin	173.3	198.2	232.3	216.3	238.2	239.2

	Malignant					
	Primary	Secondary	Ca in situ	Benign	Uncertain Behavior	Unspecified
skin NEC—*continued*						
clavicular area	173.5	198.2	232.5	216.5	238.2	239.2
clitoris	184.3	198.82	233.3	221.2	236.3	239.5
columnella	173.3	198.2	232.3	216.3	238.2	239.2
concha	173.2	198.2	232.2	216.2	238.2	239.2
contiguous sites	173.8	—	—	—	—	—
ear (external)	173.2	198.2	232.2	216.2	238.2	239.2
elbow	173.6	198.2	232.6	216.6	238.2	239.2
eyebrow	173.3	198.2	232.3	216.3	238.2	239.2
eyelid	173.1	198.2	232.1	216.1	238.2	239.2
face NEC	173.3	198.2	232.3	216.3	238.2	239.2
female genital organs (external)	184.4	198.82	233.3	221.2	236.3	239.5
clitoris	184.3	198.82	233.3	221.2	236.3	239.5
labium NEC	184.4	198.82	233.3	221.2	236.3	239.5
majus	184.1	198.82	233.3	221.2	236.3	239.5
minus	184.2	198.82	233.3	221.2	236.3	239.5
pudendum	184.4	198.82	233.3	221.2	236.3	239.5
vulva	184.4	198.82	233.3	221.2	236.3	239.5
finger	173.6	198.2	232.6	216.6	238.2	239.2
flank	173.5	198.2	232.5	216.5	238.2	239.2
foot	173.7	198.2	232.7	216.7	238.2	239.2
forearm	173.6	198.2	232.6	216.6	238.2	239.2
forehead	173.3	198.2	232.3	216.3	238.2	239.2
glabella	173.3	198.2	232.3	216.3	238.2	239.2
gluteal region	173.5	198.2	232.5	216.5	238.2	239.2
groin	173.5	198.2	232.5	216.5	238.2	239.2
hand	173.6	198.2	232.6	216.6	238.2	239.2
head NEC	173.4	198.2	232.4	216.4	238.2	239.2
heel	173.7	198.2	232.7	216.7	238.2	239.2
helix	173.2	198.2	232.2	216.2	238.2	239.2
hip	173.7	198.2	232.7	216.7	238.2	239.2
infraclavicular region	173.5	198.2	232.5	216.5	238.2	239.2
inguinal region	173.5	198.2	232.5	216.5	238.2	239.2
jaw	173.3	198.2	232.3	216.3	238.2	239.2
knee	173.7	198.2	232.7	216.7	238.2	239.2
labia						
majora	184.1	198.82	233.3	221.2	236.3	239.5
minora	184.2	198.82	233.3	221.2	236.3	239.5
leg	173.7	198.2	232.7	216.7	238.2	239.2
lid (lower) (upper)	173.1	198.2	232.1	216.1	238.2	239.2
limb NEC	173.9	198.2	232.9	216.9	238.2	239.5
lower	173.7	198.2	232.7	216.7	238.2	239.2
upper	173.6	198.2	232.6	216.6	238.2	239.2
lip (lower) (upper)	173.0	198.2	232.0	216.0	238.2	239.2
male genital organs	187.9	198.82	233.6	222.9	236.6	239.5
penis	187.4	198.82	233.5	222.1	236.6	239.5
prepuce	187.1	198.82	233.5	222.1	236.6	239.5
scrotum	187.7	198.82	233.6	222.4	236.6	239.5
mastectomy site	173.5	198.2	—	—	—	—
specified as breast tissue	174.8	198.81	—	—	—	—
meatus, acoustic (external)	173.2	198.2	232.2	216.2	238.2	239.2
melanoma —*see* Melanoma						
nates	173.5	198.2	232.5	216.5	238.2	239.2
neck	173.4	198.2	232.4	216.4	238.2	239.2
nose (external)	173.3	198.2	232.3	216.3	238.2	239.2
palm	173.6	198.2	232.6	216.6	238.2	239.2
palpebra	173.1	198.2	232.1	216.1	238.2	239.2
penis NEC	187.4	198.82	233.5	222.1	236.6	239.5
perianal	173.5	198.2	232.5	216.5	238.2	239.2
perineum	173.5	198.2	232.5	216.5	238.2	239.2

	Malignant					
	Primary	Secondary	Ca in situ	Benign	Uncertain Behavior	Unspecified
skin NEC—*continued*						
pinna	173.2	198.2	232.2	216.2	238.2	239.2
plantar	173.7	198.2	232.7	216.7	238.2	239.2
popliteal fossa or space	173.7	198.2	232.7	216.7	238.2	239.2
prepuce	187.1	198.82	233.5	222.1	236.6	239.5
pubes	173.5	198.2	232.5	216.5	238.2	239.2
sacrococcygeal region	173.5	198.2	232.5	216.5	238.2	239.2
scalp	173.4	198.2	232.4	216.4	238.2	239.2
scapular region	173.5	198.2	232.5	216.5	238.2	239.2
scrotum	187.7	198.82	233.6	222.4	236.6	239.5
shoulder	173.6	198.2	232.6	216.6	238.2	239.2
sole (foot)	173.7	198.2	232.7	216.7	238.2	239.2
specified sites NEC	173.8	198.2	232.8	216.8	232.8	239.2
submammary fold	173.5	198.2	232.5	216.5	238.2	239.2
supraclavicular region	173.4	198.2	232.4	216.4	238.2	239.2
temple	173.3	198.2	232.3	216.3	238.2	239.2
thigh	173.7	198.2	232.7	216.7	238.2	239.2
thoracic wall	173.5	198.2	232.5	216.5	238.2	239.2
thumb	173.6	198.2	232.6	216.6	238.2	239.2
toe	173.7	198.2	232.7	216.7	238.2	239.2
tragus	173.2	198.2	232.2	216.2	238.2	239.2
trunk	173.5	198.2	232.5	216.5	238.2	239.2
umbilicus	173.5	198.2	232.5	216.5	238.2	239.2
vulva	184.4	198.82	233.3	221.2	236.3	239.5
wrist	173.6	198.2	232.6	216.6	238.2	239.2
skull	170.0	198.5	—	213.0	238.0	239.2
soft parts or tissues—*see* Neoplasm, connective tissue						
specified site NEC	195.8	198.89	234.8	229.8	238.8	239.8
spermatic cord	187.6	198.82	233.6	222.8	236.6	239.5
sphenoid	160.5	197.3	231.8	212.0	235.9	239.1
bone	170.0	198.5	—	213.0	238.0	239.2
sinus	160.5	197.3	231.8	212.0	235.9	239.1
sphincter						
anal	154.2	197.5	230.5	211.4	235.5	239.0
of Oddi	156.1	197.8	230.8	211.5	235.3	239.0
spine, spinal (column)	170.2	198.5	—	213.2	238.0	239.2
bulb	191.7	198.3	—	225.0	237.5	239.6
coccyx	170.6	198.5	—	213.6	238.0	239.2
cord (cervical) (lumbar) (sacral) (thoracic)	192.2	198.3	—	225.3	237.5	239.7
dura mater	192.3	198.4	—	225.4	237.6	239.7
lumbosacral	170.2	198.5	—	213.2	238.0	239.2
membrane	192.3	198.4	—	225.4	237.6	239.7
meninges	192.3	198.4	—	225.4	237.6	239.7
nerve (root)	171.9	198.89	—	215.9	238.1	239.2
pia mater	192.3	198.4	—	225.4	237.6	239.7
root	171.9	198.89	—	215.9	238.1	239.2
sacrum	170.6	198.5	—	213.6	238.0	239.2
spleen, splenic NEC	159.1	197.8	230.9	211.9	235.5	239.0
flexure (colon)	153.7	197.5	230.3	211.3	235.2	239.0
stem, brain	191.7	198.3	—	225.0	237.5	239.6
Stensen's duct	142.0	198.89	230.0	210.2	235.0	239.0
sternum	170.3	198.5	—	213.3	238.0	239.2
stomach	151.9	197.8	230.2	211.1	235.2	239.0
antrum (pyloric)	151.2	197.8	230.2	211.1	235.2	239.0
body	151.4	197.8	230.2	211.1	235.2	239.0
cardia	151.0	197.8	230.2	211.1	235.2	239.0
cardiac orifice	151.0	197.8	230.2	211.1	235.2	239.0
contiguous sites	151.8	—	—	—	—	—
corpus	151.4	197.8	230.2	211.1	235.2	239.0

	Malignant			Benign	Uncertain Behavior	Unspecified
	Primary	Secondary	Ca in situ			
stomach—*continued*						
fundus	151.3	197.8	230.2	211.1	235.2	239.0
greater curvature NEC	151.6	197.8	230.2	211.1	235.2	239.0
lesser curvature NEC	151.5	197.8	230.2	211.1	235.2	239.0
prepylorus	151.1	197.8	230.2	211.1	235.2	239.0
pylorus	151.1	197.8	230.2	211.1	235.2	239.0
wall NEC	151.9	197.8	230.2	211.1	235.2	239.0
anterior NEC	151.8	197.8	230.2	211.1	235.2	239.0
posterior NEC	151.8	197.8	230.2	211.1	235.2	239.0
stroma, endometrial	182.0	198.82	233.2	219.1	236.0	239.5
stump, cervical	180.8	198.82	233.1	219.0	236.0	239.5
subcutaneous (nodule) (tissue) NEC—*see* Neoplasm, connective tissue						
subdural	192.1	198.4	—	225.2	237.6	239.7
subglottis, subglottic	161.2	197.3	231.0	212.1	235.6	239.1
sublingual	144.9	198.89	230.0	210.3	235.1	239.0
gland or duct	142.2	198.89	230.0	210.2	235.0	239.0
submandibular gland	142.1	198.89	230.0	210.2	235.0	239.0
submaxillary gland or duct	142.1	198.89	230.0	210.2	235.0	239.0
submental	195.0	198.89	234.8	229.8	238.8	239.8
subpleural	162.9	197.0	—	212.3	235.7	239.1
substernal	164.2	197.1	—	212.5	235.8	239.8
sudoriferous, sudoriparous gland, site unspecified	173.9	198.2	232.9	216.9	238.2	239.2
specified site—*see* Neoplasm, skin						
supraclavicular region	195.0	198.89	234.8	229.8	238.8	239.8
supraglottis	161.1	197.3	231.0	212.1	235.6	239.1
suprarenal (capsule) (cortex) (gland) (medulla)	194.0	198.7	234.8	227.0	237.2	239.7
suprasellar (region)	191.9	198.3	—	225.0	237.5	239.6
sweat gland (apocrine) (eccrine), site unspecified	173.9	198.2	232.9	216.9	238.2	239.2
specified site—*see* Neoplasm, skin						
sympathetic nerve or nervous system NEC	171.9	198.89	—	215.9	238.1	239.2
symphysis pubis	170.6	198.5	—	213.6	238.0	239.2
synovial membrane—*see* Neoplasm, connective tissue						
tapetum, brain	191.8	198.3	—	225.0	237.5	239.6
tarsus (any bone)	170.8	198.5	—	213.8	238.0	239.2
temple (skin)	173.3	198.2	232.3	216.3	238.2	239.2
temporal						
bone	170.0	198.5	—	213.0	238.0	239.2
lobe or pole	191.2	198.3	—	225.0	237.5	239.6
region	195.0	198.89	234.8	229.8	238.8	239.8
skin	173.3	198.2	232.3	216.3	238.2	239.2
tendon (sheath)—*see* Neoplasm, connective tissue						
tentorium (cerebelli)	192.1	198.4	—	225.2	237.6	239.7
testis, testes (descended) (scrotal)	186.9	198.82	233.6	222.0	236.4	239.5
ectopic	186.0	198.82	233.6	222.0	236.4	239.5
retained	186.0	198.82	233.6	222.0	236.4	239.5
undescended	186.0	198.82	233.6	222.0	236.4	239.5
thalamus	191.0	198.3	—	225.0	237.5	239.6
thigh NEC*	195.5	198.89	234.8	229.8	238.8	239.8
thorax, thoracic (cavity) (organs NEC)	195.1	198.89	234.8	229.8	238.8	239.8
duct	171.4	198.89	—	215.4	238.1	239.2
wall NEC	195.1	198.89	234.8	229.8	238.8	239.8
throat	149.0	198.89	230.0	210.9	235.1	239.0
thumb NEC*	195.4	198.89	232.6	229.8	238.8	239.8

| | Malignant | | | | | |
---	Primary	Secondary	Ca in situ	Benign	Uncertain Behavior	Unspecified
thymus (gland)	164.0	198.89	—	212.6	235.8	239.8
contiguous sites with heart and mediastinum	164.8	—	—	—	—	—
thyroglossal duct	193	198.89	234.8	226	237.4	239.7
thyroid (gland)	193	198.89	234.8	226	237.4	239.7
cartilage	161.3	197.3	231.0	212.1	235.6	239.1
tibia (any part)	170.7	198.5	—	213.7	238.0	239.2
toe NEC*	195.5	198.89	232.7	229.8	238.8	239.8
tongue	141.9	198.89	230.0	210.1	235.1	239.0
anterior (two-thirds) NEC	141.4	198.89	230.0	210.1	235.1	239.0
dorsal surface	141.1	198.89	230.0	210.1	235.1	239.0
ventral surface	141.3	198.89	230.0	210.1	235.1	239.0
base (dorsal surface)	141.0	198.89	230.0	210.1	235.1	239.0
border (lateral)	141.2	198.89	230.0	210.1	235.1	239.0
contiguous sites	141.8	—	—	—	—	—
dorsal surface NEC	141.1	198.89	230.0	210.1	235.1	239.0
fixed part NEC	141.0	198.89	230.0	210.1	235.1	239.0
foramen cecum	141.1	198.89	230.0	210.1	235.1	239.0
frenulum linguae	141.3	198.89	230.0	210.1	235.1	239.0
junctional zone	141.5	198.89	230.0	210.1	235.1	239.0
margin (lateral)	141.2	198.89	230.0	210.1	235.1	239.0
midline NEC	141.1	198.89	230.0	210.1	235.1	239.0
mobile part NEC	141.4	198.89	230.0	210.1	235.1	239.0
posterior (third)	141.0	198.89	230.0	210.1	235.1	239.0
root	141.0	198.89	230.0	210.1	235.1	239.0
surface (dorsal)	141.1	198.89	230.0	210.1	235.1	239.0
base	141.0	198.89	230.0	210.1	235.1	239.0
ventral	141.3	198.89	230.0	210.1	235.1	239.0
tip	141.2	198.89	230.0	210.1	235.1	239.0
tonsil	141.6	198.89	230.0	210.1	235.1	239.0
tonsil	146.0	198.89	230.0	210.5	235.1	239.0
fauces, faucial	146.0	198.89	230.0	210.5	235.1	239.0
lingual	141.6	198.89	230.0	210.1	235.1	239.0
palatine	146.0	198.89	230.0	210.5	235.1	239.0
pharyngeal	147.1	198.89	230.0	210.7	235.1	239.0
pillar (anterior) (posterior)	146.2	198.89	230.0	210.6	235.1	239.0
tonsillar fossa	146.1	198.89	230.0	210.6	235.1	239.0
tooth socket NEC	143.9	198.89	230.0	210.4	235.1	239.0
trachea (cartilage) (mucosa)	162.0	197.3	231.1	212.2	235.7	239.1
contiguous sites with bronchus or lung	162.8	—	—	—	—	—
tracheobronchial	162.8	197.3	231.1	212.2	235.7	239.1
contiguous sites with lung	162.8	—	—	—	—	—
tragus	173.2	198.2	232.2	216.2	238.2	239.2
trunk NEC*	195.8	198.89	232.5	229.8	238.8	239.8
tubo-ovarian	183.8	198.82	233.3	221.8	236.3	239.5
tunica vaginalis	187.8	198.82	233.6	222.8	236.6	239.5
turbinate (bone)	170.0	198.5	—	213.0	238.0	239.2
nasal	160.0	197.3	231.8	212.0	235.9	239.1
tympanic cavity	160.1	197.3	231.8	212.0	235.9	239.1
ulna (any part)	170.4	198.5	—	213.4	238.0	239.2
umbilicus, umbilical	173.5	198.2	232.5	216.5	238.2	239.2
uncus, brain	191.2	198.3	—	225.0	237.5	239.6
unknown site or unspecified	199.1	199.1	234.9	229.9	238.9	239.9
urachus	188.7	198.1	233.7	223.3	236.7	239.4
ureter, ureteral	189.2	198.1	233.9	223.2	236.91	239.5
orifice (bladder)	188.6	198.1	233.7	223.3	236.7	239.4
ureter-bladder (junction)	188.6	198.1	233.7	223.3	236.7	239.4
urethra, urethral (gland)	189.3	198.1	233.9	223.81	236.99	239.5
orifice, internal	188.5	198.1	233.7	223.3	236.7	239.4
urethrovaginal (septum)	184.9	198.82	233.3	221.9	236.3	239.5

| | Malignant | | | | |
	Primary	Secondary	Ca in situ	Benign	Uncertain Behavior	Unspecified
urinary organ or system NEC	189.9	198.1	233.9	223.9	236.99	239.5
bladder—*see* Neoplasm, bladder						
contiguous sites	189.8	—	—	—	—	—
specified sites NEC	189.8	198.1	233.9	223.89	236.99	239.5
utero-ovarian	183.8	198.82	233.3	221.8	236.3	239.5
ligament	183.3	198.82	—	221.0	236.3	239.5
uterosacral ligament	183.4	198.82	—	221.0	236.3	239.5
uterus, uteri, uterine	179	198.82	233.2	219.9	236.0	239.5
adnexa NEC	183.9	198.82	233.3	221.8	236.3	239.5
contiguous sites	183.8	—	—	—	—	—
body	182.0	198.82	233.2	219.1	236.0	239.5
contiguous sites	182.8	—	—	—	—	—
cervix	180.9	198.82	233.1	219.0	236.0	239.5
cornu	182.0	198.82	233.2	219.1	236.0	239.5
corpus	182.0	198.82	233.2	219.1	236.0	239.5
endocervix (canal) (gland)	180.0	198.82	233.1	219.0	236.0	239.5
endometrium	182.0	198.82	233.2	219.1	236.0	239.5
exocervix	180.1	198.82	233.1	219.0	236.0	239.5
external os	180.1	198.82	233.1	219.0	236.0	239.5
fundus	182.0	198.82	233.2	219.1	236.0	239.5
internal os	180.0	198.82	233.1	219.0	236.0	239.5
isthmus	182.1	198.82	233.2	219.1	236.0	239.5
ligament	183.4	198.82	—	221.0	236.3	239.5
broad	183.3	198.82	233.3	221.0	236.3	239.5
round	183.5	198.82	—	221.0	236.3	239.5
lower segment	182.1	198.82	233.2	219.1	236.0	239.5
myometrium	182.0	198.82	233.2	219.1	236.0	239.5
squamocolumnar junction	180.8	198.82	233.1	219.0	236.0	239.5
tube	183.2	198.82	233.3	221.0	236.3	239.5
utricle, prostatic	189.3	198.1	233.9	223.81	236.99	239.5
uveal tract	190.0	198.4	234.0	224.0	238.8	239.8
uvula	145.4	198.89	230.0	210.4	235.1	239.0
vagina, vaginal (fornix) (vault) (wall)	184.0	198.82	233.3	221.1	236.3	239.5
vaginovesical	184.9	198.82	233.3	221.9	236.3	239.5
septum	194.9	198.82	233.3	221.9	236.3	239.5
vallecula (epiglottis)	146.3	198.89	230.0	210.6	235.1	239.0
vascular—*see* Neoplasm, connective tissue						
vas deferens	187.6	198.82	233.6	222.8	236.6	239.5
Vater's ampulla	156.2	197.8	230.8	211.5	235.3	239.0
vein, venous—*see* Neoplasm, connective tissue						
vena cava (abdominal) (inferior)	171.5	198.89	—	215.5	238.1	239.2
superior	171.4	198.89	—	215.4	238.1	239.2
ventricle (cerebral) (floor) (fourth) (lateral) (third)	191.5	198.3	—	225.0	237.5	239.6
cardiac (left) (right)	164.1	198.89	—	212.7	238.8	239.8
ventricular band of larynx	161.1	197.3	231.0	212.1	235.6	239.1
ventriculus—*see* Neoplasm, stomach						
vermillion border—*see* Neoplasm, lip						
vermis, cerebellum	191.6	198.3	—	225.0	237.5	239.6
vertebra (column)	170.2	198.5	—	213.2	238.0	239.2
coccyx	170.6	198.5	—	213.6	238.0	239.2
sacrum	170.6	198.5	—	213.6	238.0	239.2
vesical—*see* Neoplasm, bladder						
vesicle, seminal	187.8	198.82	233.6	222.8	236.6	239.5
vesicocervical tissue	184.9	198.82	233.3	221.9	236.3	239.5
vesicorectal	195.3	198.89	234.8	229.8	238.8	239.8
vesicovaginal	184.9	198.82	233.3	221.9	236.3	239.5
septum	184.9	198.82	233.3	221.9	236.3	239.5
vessel (blood)—*see* Neoplasm, connective tissue						

	Malignant					
	Primary	Secondary	Ca in situ	Benign	Uncertain Behavior	Unspecified
vestibular gland, greater	184.1	198.82	233.3	221.2	236.3	239.5
vestibule						
mouth	145.1	198.89	230.0	210.4	235.1	239.0
nose	160.0	197.3	231.8	212.0	235.9	239.1
Virchow's gland	—	196.0	—	229.0	238.8	239.8
viscera NEC	195.8	198.89	234.8	229.8	238.8	239.8
vocal cords (true)	161.0	197.3	231.0	212.1	235.6	239.1
false	161.1	197.3	231.0	212.1	235.6	239.1
vomer	170.0	198.5	—	213.0	238.0	239.2
vulva	184.4	198.82	233.3	221.2	236.3	239.5
vulvovaginal gland	184.4	198.82	233.3	221.2	236.3	239.5
Waldeyer's ring	149.1	198.89	230.0	210.9	235.1	239.0
Wharton's duct	142.1	198.89	230.0	210.2	235.0	239.0
white matter (central) (cerebral)	191.0	198.3	—	225.0	237.5	239.6
windpipe	162.0	197.3	231.1	212.2	235.7	239.1
Wirsung's duct	157.3	197.8	230.9	211.6	235.5	239.0
wolffian (body) (duct)						
female	184.8	198.82	233.3	221.8	236.3	239.5
male	187.8	198.82	233.6	222.8	236.6	239.5
womb—*see* Neoplasm, uterus						
wrist NEC*	195.4	198.89	232.6	229.8	238.8	239.8
xiphoid process	170.3	198.5	—	213.3	238.0	239.2
Zuckerkandl's organ	194.6	198.89	—	227.6	237.3	239.7

Neovascularization
choroid 362.16
ciliary body 364.42
cornea 370.60
deep 370.63
localized 370.61
iris 364.42
retina 362.16
subretinal 362.16
Nephralgia 788.0
Nephritis, nephritic (albuminuric) (azotemic)
(congenital) (degenerative) (diffuse)
(disseminated) (epithelial) (familial) (focal)
(granulomatous) (hemorrhagic) (infantile)
(nonsuppurative, excretory) (uremic) 583.9
with
edema—*see* Nephrosis
lesion of
glomerulonephritis
hypocomplementemic persistent 583.2
with nephrotic syndrome 581.2
chronic 582.2
lobular 583.2
with nephrotic syndrome 581.2
chronic 582.2
membranoproliferative 583.2
with nephrotic syndrome 581.2
chronic 582.2
membranous 583.1
with nephrotic syndrome 581.1
chronic 582.1
mesangiocapillary 583.2
with nephrotic syndrome 581.2
chronic 582.2
mixed membranous and proliferative 583.2
with nephrotic syndrome 581.2
chronic 582.2
proliferative (diffuse) 583.0
with nephrotic syndrome 581.0
acute 580.0
chronic 582.0
rapidly progressive 583.4
acute 580.4
chronic 582.4
interstitial nephritis (diffuse) (focal) 583.89
with nephrotic syndrome 581.89
acute 580.89
chronic 582.89
necrotizing glomerulitis 583.4
acute 580.4
chronic 582.4
renal necrosis 583.9
cortical 583.6
medullary 583.7
specified pathology NEC 583.89
with nephrotic syndrome 581.89
acute 580.89
chronic 582.89
necrosis, renal 583.9
cortical 583.6
medullary (papillary) 583.7
nephrotic syndrome (*see also* Nephrosis) 581.9
papillary necrosis 583.7
specified pathology NEC 583.89
acute 580.9
extracapillary with epithelial crescents 580.4
hypertensive (*see also* Hypertension, kidney)
403.90
necrotizing 580.4
poststreptococcal 580.0
proliferative (diffuse) 580.0

Nephritis, nephritic—*continued*
rapidly progressive 580.4
specified pathology NEC 580.89
amyloid 277.3 *[583.81]*
chronic 277.3 *[582.81]*
arteriolar (*see also* Hypertension, kidney) 403.90
arteriosclerotic (*see also* Hypertension, kidney)
403.90
ascending (*see also* Pyelitis) 590.80
atrophic 582.9
basement membrane NEC 583.89
with
pulmonary hemorrhage (Goodpasture's
syndrome) 446.21 *[583.81]*
calculous, calculus 592.0
cardiac (*see also* Hypertension, kidney) 403.90
cardiovascular (*see also* Hypertension, kidney)
403.90
chronic 582.9
arteriosclerotic (*see also* Hypertension,
kidney) 403.90
hypertensive (*see also* Hypertension, kidney)
403.90
cirrhotic (*see also* Sclerosis, renal) 587
complicating pregnancy, childbirth, or
puerperium 646.2
with hypertension 642.1
affecting fetus or newborn 760.0
affecting fetus or newborn 760.1
croupous 580.9
desquamative—*see* Nephrosis
due to
amyloidosis 277.3 *[583.81]*
chronic 277.3 *[582.81]*
arteriosclerosis (*see also* Hypertension,
kidney) 403.90
diabetes mellitus 250.4 *[583.81]*
with nephrotic syndrome 250.4 *[581.81]*
diphtheria 032.89 *[580.81]*
gonococcal infection (acute) 098.19 *[583.81]*
chronic or duration of 2 months or over
098.39 *[583.81]*
gout 274.10
infectious hepatitis 070.9 *[580.81]*
mumps 072.79 *[580.81]*
specified kidney pathology NEC 583.89
acute 580.89
chronic 582.89
streptotrichosis 039.8 *[583.81]*
subacute bacterial endocarditis 421.0 *[580.81]*
systemic lupus erythematosus 710.0 *[583.81]*
chronic 710.0 *[582.81]*
typhoid fever 002.0 *[580.81]*
endothelial 582.2
end stage (chronic) (terminal) NEC 585
epimembranous 581.1
exudative 583.89
with nephrotic syndrome 581.89
acute 580.89
chronic 582.89
gonococcal (acute) 098.19 *[583.81]*
chronic or duration of 2 months or over
098.39 *[583.81]*
gouty 274.10
hereditary (Alport's syndrome) 759.89
hydremic—*see* Nephrosis
hypertensive (*see also* Hypertension, kidney)
403.90
hypocomplementemic persistent 583.2
with nephrotic syndrome 581.2
chronic 582.2

Nephritis, nephritic—*continued*
  immune complex NEC 583.89
  infective (*see also* Pyelitis) 590.80
  interstitial (diffuse) (focal) 583.89
    with nephrotic syndrome 581.89
    acute 580.89
    chronic 582.89
  latent or quiescent—*see* Nephritis, chronic
  lead 984.9
    specified type of lead—*see* Table of drugs and
      chemicals
  lobular 583.2
    with nephrotic syndrome 581.2
    chronic 582.2
  lupus 710.0 *[583.81]*
    acute 710.0 *[580.81]*
    chronic 710.0 *[582.81]*
  membranoproliferative 583.2
    with nephrotic syndrome 581.2
    chronic 582.2
  membranous 583.1
    with nephrotic syndrome 581.1
    chronic 582.1
  mesangiocapillary 583.2
    with nephrotic syndrome 581.2
    chronic 582.2
  minimal change 581.3
  mixed membranous and proliferative 583.2
    with nephrotic syndrome 581.2
    chronic 582.2
  necrotic, necrotizing 583.4
    acute 580.4
    chronic 582.4
  nephrotic—*see* Nephrosis
  old—*see* Nephritis, chronic
  parenchymatous 581.89
  polycystic 753.12
    adult type (APKD) 753.13
    autosomal dominant 753.13
    autosomal recessive 753.14
    childhood type (CPKD) 753.14
    infantile type 753.14
  poststreptococcal 580.0
  pregnancy—*see* Nephritis, complicating
    pregnancy
  proliferative 583.0
    with nephrotic syndrome 581.0
    acute 580.0
    chronic 582.0
  purulent (*see also* Pyelitis) 590.80
  rapidly progressive 583.4
    acute 580.4
    chronic 582.4
  salt-losing or salt-wasting (*see also* Disease,
    renal) 593.9
  saturnine 984.9
    specified type of lead—*see* Table of drugs and
      chemicals
  septic (*see also* Pyelitis) 590.80
  specified pathology NEC 583.89
    acute 580.89
    chronic 582.89
  staphylococcal (*see also* Pyelitis) 590.80
  streptotrichosis 039.8 *[583.81]*
  subacute (*see also* Nephrosis) 581.9
  suppurative (*see also* Pyelitis) 590.80
  syphilitic (late) 095.4
    congenital 090.5 *[583.81]*
    early 091.69 *[583.81]*
  terminal (chronic) (end-stage) NEC 585
  toxic—*see* Nephritis, acute

Nephritis, nephritic—*continued*
  tubal, tubular—*see* Nephrosis, tubular
  tuberculous (*see also* Tuberculosis) 016.0
    [583.81]
  type II (Ellis)—*see* Nephrosis
  vascular—*see* Hypertension, kidney
  war 580.9
Nephroblastoma (M8960/3) 189.0
  epithelial (M8961/3) 189.0
  mesenchymal (M8962/3) 189.0
Nephrocalcinosis 275.49
Nephrocystitis, pustular (*see also* Pyelitis)
  590.80
Nephrolithiasis (congenital) (pelvis) (recurrent)
  592.0
  uric acid 274.11
Nephroma (M8960/3) 189.0
  mesoblastic (M8960/1) 236.9
Nephronephritis (*see also* Nephrosis) 581.9
Nephronopthisis 753.16
Nephropathy (*see also* Nephritis) 583.9
  with
    exudative nephritis 583.89
    interstitial nephritis (diffuse) (focal) 583.89
    medullary necrosis 583.7
    necrosis 583.9
      cortical 583.6
      medullary or papillary 583.7
    papillary necrosis 583.7
    specified lesion or cause NEC 583.89
  analgesic 583.89
    with medullary necrosis, acute 584.7
  arteriolar (*see also* Hypertension, kidney) 403.90
  arteriosclerotic (*see also* Hypertension, kidney)
    403.90
  complicating pregnancy 646.2
  diabetic 250.4 *[583.81]*
  gouty 274.10
    specified type NEC 274.19
  hypercalcemic 588.8
  hypertensive (*see also* Hypertension, kidney)
    403.90
  hypokalemic (vacuolar) 588.8
  obstructive 593.89
    congenital 753.20
  phenacetin 584.7
  phosphate-losing 588.0
  potassium depletion 588.8
  proliferative (*see also* Nephritis, proliferative)
    583.0
  protein-losing 588.8
  salt-losing or salt-wasting (*see also* Disease,
    renal) 593.9
  sickle-cell (*see also* Disease, sickle-cell) 282.60
    [583.81]
  toxic 584.5
  vasomotor 584.5
  water-losing 588.8
Nephroptosis (*see also* Disease, renal) 593.0
  congenital (displaced) 753.3
Nephropyosis (*see also* Abscess, kidney) 590.2
Nephrorrhagia 593.81
Nephrosclerosis (arteriolar) (arteriosclerotic)
    (chronic) (hyaline) (*see also* Hypertension,
    kidney) 403.90
  gouty 274.10
  hyperplastic (arteriolar) (*see also* Hypertension,
    kidney) 403.90
  senile (*see also* Sclerosis, renal) 587

Nephrosis, nephrotic (Epstein's) (syndrome) 581.9
  with
    lesion of
      focal glomerulosclerosis 581.1
      glomerulonephritis
        endothelial 581.2
        hypocomplementemic persistent 581.2
        lobular 581.2
        membranoproliferative 581.2
        membranous 581.1
        mesangiocapillary 581.2
        minimal change 581.3
        mixed membranous and proliferative 581.2
        proliferative 581.0
      segmental hyalinosis 581.1
      specified pathology NEC 581.89
  acute—*see* Nephrosis, tubular
  anoxic—*see* Nephrosis, tubular
  arteriosclerotic (*see also* Hypertension, kidney) 403.90
  chemical—*see* Nephrosis, tubular
  cholemic 572.4
  complicating pregnancy, childbirth, or puerperium—*see* Nephritis, complicating pregnancy
  diabetic 250.4 *[581.81]*
  hemoglobinuric—*see* Nephrosis, tubular
  in
    amyloidosis 277.3 *[581.81]*
    diabetes mellitus 250.4 *[581.81]*
    epidemic hemorrhagic fever 078.6
    malaria 084.9 *[581.81]*
    polyarteritis 446.0 *[581.81]*
    systemic lupus erythematosus 710.0 *[581.81]*
  ischemic—*see* Nephrosis, tubular
  lipoid 581.3
  lower nephron—*see* Nephrosis, tubular
  lupoid 710.0 *[581.81]*
  lupus 710.0 *[581.81]*
  malarial 084.9 *[581.81]*
  minimal change 581.3
  necrotizing—*see* Nephrosis, tubular
  osmotic (sucrose) 588.8
  polyarteritic 446.0 *[581.81]*
  radiation 581.9
  specified lesion or cause NEC 581.89
  syphilitic 095.4
  toxic—*see* Nephrosis, tubular
  tubular (acute) 584.5
    due to a procedure 997.5
    radiation 581.9
Nephrosonephritis hemorrhagic (endemic) 078.6
Nephrostomy status V44.6
  with complication 997.5
Nerve —*see* condition
Nerves 799.2
Nervous (*see also* condition) 799.2
  breakdown 300.9
  heart 306.2
  stomach 306.4
  tension 799.2
Nervousness 799.2
Nesidioblastoma (M8150/0)
  pancreas 211.7
  specified site NEC—*see* Neoplasm, by site, benign
  unspecified site 211.7
Netherton's syndrome (ichthyosiform erythroderma) 757.1
Nettle rash 708.8

Nettleship's disease (urticaria pigmentosa) 757.33
Neumann's disease (pemphigus vegetans) 694.4
Neuralgia, neuralgic (acute) (*see also* Neuritis) 729.2
  accessory (nerve) 352.4
  acoustic (nerve) 388.5
  ankle 355.8
  anterior crural 355.8
  anus 787.99
  arm 723.4
  auditory (nerve) 388.5
  axilla 353.0
  bladder 788.1
  brachial 723.4
  brain—*see* Disorder, nerve, cranial
  broad ligament 625.9
  cerebral—*see* Disorder, nerve, cranial
  ciliary 346.2
  cranial nerve—*see also* Disorder, nerve, cranial
    fifth or trigeminal (*see also* Neuralgia, trigeminal) 350.1
  ear 388.71
    middle 352.1
  facial 351.8
  finger 354.9
  flank 355.8
  foot 355.8
  forearm 354.9
  Fothergill's (*see also* Neuralgia, trigeminal) 350.1
    postherpetic 053.12
  glossopharyngeal (nerve) 352.1
  groin 355.8
  hand 354.9
  heel 355.8
  Horton's 346.2
  Hunt's 053.11
  hypoglossal (nerve) 352.5
  iliac region 355.8
  infraorbital (*see also* Neuralgia, trigeminal) 350.1
  inguinal 355.8
  intercostal (nerve) 353.8
    postherpetic 053.19
  jaw 352.1
  kidney 788.0
  knee 355.8
  loin 355.8
  malarial (*see also* Malaria) 084.6
  mastoid 385.89
  maxilla 352.1
  median thenar 354.1
  metatarsal 355.6
  middle ear 352.1
  migrainous 346.2
  Morton's 355.6
  nerve, cranial—*see* Disorder, nerve, cranial
  nose 352.0
  occipital 723.8
  olfactory (nerve) 352.0
  ophthalmic 377.30
    postherpetic 053.19
  optic (nerve) 377.30
  penis 607.9
  perineum 355.8
  pleura 511.0
  postherpetic NEC 053.19
    geniculate ganglion 053.11
    ophthalmic 053.19
    trifacial 053.12

Neuralgia, neuralgic—*continued*
  trigeminal 053.12
  pubic region 355.8
  radial (nerve) 723.4
  rectum 787.99
  sacroiliac joint 724.3
  sciatic (nerve) 724.3
  scrotum 608.9
  seminal vesicle 608.9
  shoulder 354.9
  Sluder's 337.0
  specified nerve NEC—*see* Disorder, nerve
  spermatic cord 608.9
  sphenopalatine (ganglion) 337.0
  subscapular (nerve) 723.4
  suprascapular (nerve) 723.4
  testis 608.89
  thenar (median) 354.1
  thigh 355.8
  tongue 352.5
  trifacial (nerve) (*see also* Neuralgia, trigeminal)
    350.1
  trigeminal (nerve) 350.1
    postherpetic 053.12
  tympanic plexus 388.71
  ulnar (nerve) 723.4
  vagus (nerve) 352.3
  wrist 354.9
  writers' 300.89
    organic 333.84
Neurapraxia —*see* Injury, nerve
Neurasthenia 300.5
  cardiac 306.2
  gastric 306.4
  heart 306.2
  postfebrile 780.79
  postviral 780.79
Neurilemmoma (M9560/0)—*see also* Neoplasm,
  connective tissue, benign
  acoustic (nerve) 225.1
  malignant (M9560/3)—*see also* Neoplasm,
    connective tissue, malignant
    acoustic (nerve) 192.0
Neurilemmosarcoma (M9560/3)—*see*
  Neoplasm, connective tissue, malignant
Neurilemoma —*see* Neurilemmoma
Neurinoma (M9560/0)—*see* Neurilemmoma
Neurinomatosis (M9560/1)—*see also*
  Neoplasm, connective tissue, uncertain
  behavior
  centralis 759.5
Neuritis (*see also* Neuralgia) 729.2
  abducens (nerve) 378.54
  accessory (nerve) 352.4
  acoustic (nerve) 388.5
    syphilitic 094.86
  alcoholic 357.5
    with psychosis 291.1
  amyloid, any site 277.3 *[357.4]*
  anterior crural 355.8
  arising during pregnancy 646.4
  arm 723.4
  ascending 355.2
  auditory (nerve) 388.5
  brachial (nerve) NEC 723.4
    due to displacement, intervertebral disc 722.0
  cervical 723.4
  chest (wall) 353.8
  costal region 353.8

Neuritis—*continued*
  cranial nerve—*see also* Disorder, nerve, cranial
    first or olfactory 352.0
    second or optic 377.30
    third or oculomotor 378.52
    fourth or trochlear 378.53
    fifth or trigeminal (*see also* Neuralgia,
      trigeminal) 350.1
    sixth or abducens 378.54
    seventh or facial 351.8
      newborn 767.5
    eighth or acoustic 388.5
    ninth or glossopharyngeal 352.1
    tenth or vagus 352.3
    eleventh or accessory 352.4
    twelfth or hypoglossal 352.5
  Déjérine-Sottas 356.0
  diabetic 250.6 *[357.2]*
  diphtheritic 032.89 *[357.4]*
  due to
    beriberi 265.0 *[357.4]*
    displacement, prolapse, protrusion, or rupture
      of intervertebral disc 722.2
      cervical 722.0
      lumbar, lumbosacral 722.10
      thoracic, thoracolumbar 722.11
    herniation, nucleus pulposus 722.2
      cervical 722.0
      lumbar, lumbosacral 722.10
      thoracic, thoracolumbar 722.11
  endemic 265.0 *[357.4]*
  facial (nerve) 351.8
    newborn 767.5
  general—*see* Polyneuropathy
  geniculate ganglion 351.1
    due to herpes 053.11
  glossopharyngeal (nerve) 352.1
  gouty 274.89 *[357.4]*
  hypoglossal (nerve) 352.5
  ilioinguinal (nerve) 355.8
  in diseases classified elsewhere—*see*
    Polyneuropathy, in
  infectious (multiple) 357.0
  intercostal (nerve) 353.8
  interstitial hypertrophic progressive NEC 356.9
  leg 355.8
  lumbosacral NEC 724.4
  median (nerve) 354.1
    thenar 354.1
  multiple (acute) (infective) 356.9
    endemic 265.0 *[357.4]*
  multiplex endemica 265.0 *[357.4]*
  nerve root (*see also* Radiculitis) 729.2
  oculomotor (nerve) 378.52
  olfactory (nerve) 352.0
  optic (nerve) 377.30
    in myelitis 341.0
    meningococcal 036.81
  pelvic 355.8
  peripheral (nerve)—*see also* Neuropathy,
    peripheral
    complicating pregnancy or puerperium 646.4
    specified nerve NEC—*see* Mononeuritis
  pneumogastric (nerve) 352.3
  postchickenpox 052.7
  postherpetic 053.19
  progressive hypertrophic interstitial NEC 356.9
  puerperal, postpartum 646.4
  radial (nerve) 723.4
  retrobulbar 377.32
    syphilitic 094.85

Neuritis—*continued*
  rheumatic (chronic) 729.2
  sacral region 355.8
  sciatic (nerve) 724.3
    due to displacement of intervertebral disc
        722.10
  serum 999.5
  specified nerve NEC—*see* Disorder, nerve
  spinal (nerve) 355.9
    root (*see also* Radiculitis) 729.2
  subscapular (nerve) 723.4
  suprascapular (nerve) 723.4
  syphilitic 095.8
  thenar (median) 354.1
  thoracic NEC 724.4
  toxic NEC 357.7
  trochlear (nerve) 378.53
  ulnar (nerve) 723.4
  vagus (nerve) 352.3
Neuroangiomatosis, encephalofacial 759.6
Neuroastrocytoma (M9505/1)—*see* Neoplasm,
    by site, uncertain behavior
Neuro-avitaminosis 269.2
Neuroblastoma (M9500/3)
  olfactory (M9522/3) 160.0
  specified site—*see* Neoplasm, by site, malignant
  unspecified site 194.0
Neurochorioretinitis (*see also* Chorioretinitis)
    363.20
Neurocirculatory asthenia 306.2
Neurocytoma (M9506/0)—*see* Neoplasm, by
    site, benign
Neurodermatitis (circumscribed) (circumscripta)
    (local) 698.3
  atopic 691.8
  diffuse (Brocq) 691.8
  disseminated 691.8
  nodulosa 698.3
Neuroencephalomyelopathy, optic 341.0
Neuroepithelioma (M9503/3)—*see also*
    Neoplasm, by site, malignant
  olfactory (M9521/3) 160.0
Neurofibroma (M9540/0)—*see also* Neoplasm,
    connective tissue, benign
  melanotic (M9541/0)—*see* Neoplasm,
    connective tissue, benign
  multiple (M9540/1) 237.70
    Type 1 237.71
    Type 2 237.72
  plexiform (M9550/0)—*see* Neoplasm,
    connective tissue, benign
Neurofibromatosis (multiple) (M9540/1) 237.70
  acoustic 237.72
  malignant (M9540/3)—*see* Neoplasm,
    connective tissue, malignant
  Type 1 237.71
  Type 2 237.72
  von Recklinghausen's 237.71
Neurofibrosarcoma (M9540/3)—*see* Neoplasm,
    connective tissue, malignant
Neurogenic —*see also* condition
  bladder (atonic) (automatic) (autonomic)
      (flaccid) (hypertonic) (hypotonic) (inertia)
      (infranuclear) (irritable) (motor) (nonreflex)
      (nuclear) (paralysis) (reflex) (sensory)
      (spastic) (supranuclear) (uninhibited) 596.54
    with cauda equina syndrome 344.61
  bowel 564.81
  heart 306.2
Neuroglioma (M9505/1)—*see* Neoplasm, by
    site, uncertain behavior
Neurolabyrinthitis (of Dix and Hallpike) 386.12

Neurolathyrism 988.2
Neuroleprosy 030.1
Neuroleptic malignant syndrome 333.92
Neurolipomatosis 272.8
Neuroma (M9570/0)—*see also* Neoplasm,
    connective tissue, benign
  acoustic (nerve) (M9560/0) 225.1
  amputation (traumatic)—*see also* Injury, nerve,
      by site
    surgical complication (late) 997.61
  appendix 211.3
  auditory nerve 225.1
  digital 355.6
    toe 355.6
  interdigital (toe) 355.6
  intermetatarsal 355.6
  Morton's 355.6
  multiple 237.70
    Type 1 237.71
    Type 2 237.72
  nonneoplastic 355.9
    arm NEC 354.9
    leg NEC 355.8
    lower extremity NEC 355.8
    specified site NEC—*see* Mononeuritis, by site
    upper extremity NEC 354.9
  optic (nerve) 225.1
  plantar 355.6
  plexiform (M9550/0)—*see* Neoplasm,
    connective tissue, benign
  surgical (nonneoplastic) 355.9
    arm NEC 354.9
    leg NEC 355.8
    lower extremity NEC 355.8
    upper extremity NEC 354.9
  traumatic—*see also* Injury, nerve, by site
    old—*see* Neuroma, nonneoplastic
Neuromyalgia 729.1
Neuromyasthenia (epidemic) 049.8
Neuromyelitis 341.8
  ascending 357.0
  optica 341.0
Neuromyopathy NEC 358.9
Neuromyositis 729.1
Neuronevus (M8725/0)—*see* Neoplasm, skin,
    benign
Neuronitis 357.0
  ascending (acute) 355.2
  vestibular 386.12
Neuroparalytic —*see* condition
Neuropathy, neuropathic (*see also* Disorder,
    nerve) 355.9
  alcoholic 357.5
    with psychosis 291.1
  arm NEC 354.9
  autonomic (peripheral)—*see* Neuropathy,
    peripheral, autonomic
  axillary nerve 353.0
  brachial plexus 353.0
  cervical plexus 353.2
  chronic
    progressive segmentally demyelinating 357.8
    relapsing demyelinating 357.8
  congenital sensory 356.2
  Déjérine-Sottas 356.0
  diabetic 250.6 *[357.2]*
  entrapment 355.9
    iliohypogastric nerve 355.79
    ilioinguinal nerve 355.79
    lateral cutaneous nerve of thigh 355.1
    median nerve 354.0

Neurosis, neurotic—*continued*
  railroad 300.16
  rectum 306.4
  respiratory 306.1
  rumination 306.4
  senile 300.89
  sexual 302.70
  situational 300.89
  specified type NEC 300.89
  state 300.9
    with depersonalization episode 300.6
  stomach 306.4
  vasomotor 306.2
  visceral 306.4
  war 300.16
Neurospongioblastosis diffusa 759.5
Neurosyphilis (arrested) (early) (inactive) (late)
    (latent) (recurrent) 094.9
  with ataxia (cerebellar) (locomotor) (spastic)
    (spinal) 094.0
  acute meningitis 094.2
  aneurysm 094.89
  arachnoid (adhesive) 094.2
  arteritis (any artery) 094.89
  asymptomatic 094.3
  congenital 090.40
  dura (mater) 094.89
  general paresis 094.1
  gumma 094.9
  hemorrhagic 094.9
  juvenile (asymptomatic) (meningeal) 090.40
  leptomeninges (aseptic) 094.2
  meningeal 094.2
  meninges (adhesive) 094.2
  meningovascular (diffuse) 094.2
  optic atrophy 094.84
  parenchymatous (degenerative) 094.1
  paresis (*see also* Paresis, general) 094.1
  paretic (*see also* Paresis, general) 094.1
  relapse 094.9
  remission in (sustained) 094.9
  serological 094.3
  specified nature or site NEC 094.89
  tabes (dorsalis) 094.0
    juvenile 090.40
  tabetic 094.0
    juvenile 090.40
  taboparesis 094.1
    juvenile 090.40
  thrombosis 094.89
  vascular 094.89
Neurotic (*see also* Neurosis) 300.9
  excoriation 698.4
    psychogenic 306.3
Neurotmesis —*see* Injury, nerve, by site
Neurotoxemia —*see* Toxemia
Neutroclusion 524.2
Neutropenia, neutropenic (chronic) (cyclic)
    (drug-induced) (genetic) (idiopathic)
    (immune) (infantile) (malignant) (periodic)
    (pernicious) (primary) (splenic)
    (splenomegaly) (toxic) 288.0
  chronic hypoplastic 288.0
  congenital (nontransient) 288.0
  fever 288.0
  neonatal, transitory (isoimmune) (maternal
    transfer) 776.7
Neutrophilia, hereditary giant 288.2
Nevocarcinoma (M8720/3)—*see* Melanoma

Nevus (M8720/0)—*see also* Neoplasm, skin,
    benign

> *Note—Except where otherwise indicated, the*
> *varieties of nevus in the list below that are*
> *followed by a morphology code number (M——*
> *-/0) should be coded by site as for "Neoplasm,*
> *skin, benign."*

  acanthotic 702.8
  achromic (M8730/0)
  amelanotic (M8730/0)
  anemic, anemicus 709.09
  angiomatous (M9120/0) (*see also*
    Hemangioma) 228.00
  araneus 448.1
  avasculosus 709.09
  balloon cell (M8722/0)
  bathing trunk (M8761/1) 238.2
  blue (M8780/0)
    cellular (M8790/0)
    giant (M8790/0)
    Jadassohn's (M8780/0)
    malignant (M8780/3)—*see* Melanoma
  capillary (M9131/0) (*see also* Hemangioma)
    228.00
  cavernous (M9121/0) (*see also* Hemangioma)
    228.00
  cellular (M8720/0)
    blue (M8790/0)
  comedonicus 757.33
  compound (M8760/0)
  conjunctiva (M8720/0) 224.3
  dermal (M8750/0)
    and epidermal (M8760/0)
  epithelioid cell (and spindle cell) (M8770/0)
  flammeus 757.32
    osteohypertrophic 759.89
  hairy (M8720/0)
  halo (M8723/0)
  hemangiomatous (M9120/0) (*see also*
    Hemangioma) 228.00
  intradermal (M8750/0)
  intraepidermal (M8740/0)
  involuting (M8724/0)
  Jadassohn's (blue) (M8780/0)
  junction, junctional (M8740/0)
    malignant melanoma in (M8740/3)—*see*
      Melanoma
  juvenile (M8770/0)
  lymphatic (M9170/0) 228.1
  magnocellular (M8726/0)
    specified site—*see* Neoplasm, by site, benign
    unspecified site 224.0
  malignant (M8720/3)—*see* Melanoma
  meaning hemangioma (M9120/0) (*see also*
    Hemangioma) 228.00
  melanotic (pigmented) (M8720/0)
  multiplex 759.5
  nonneoplastic 448.1
  nonpigmented (M8730/0)
  nonvascular (M8720/0)
  oral mucosa, white sponge 750.26
  osteohypertrophic, flammeus 759.89
  papillaris (M8720/0)
  papillomatosus (M8720/0)
  pigmented (M8720/0)
    giant (M8761/1)—*see also* Neoplasm, skin,
      uncertain behavior
    malignant melanoma in (M8761/3)—*see*
      Melanoma
  systematicus 757.33

Nevus—*continued*
  pilosus (M8720/0)
  port wine 757.32
  sanguineous 757.32
  sebaceous (senile) 702.8
  senile 448.1
  spider 448.1
  spindle cell (and epithelioid cell) (M8770/0)
  stellar 448.1
  strawberry 757.32
  syringocystadenomatous papilliferous
    (M8406/0)
  unius lateris 757.33
  Unna's 757.32
  vascular 757.32
  verrucous 757.33
  white sponge (oral mucosa) 750.26
Newborn (infant) (liveborn)
  multiple NEC
    born in hospital (without mention of cesarean
      delivery or section) V37.00
      with cesarean delivery or section V37.01
    born outside hospital
      hospitalized V37.1
      not hospitalized V37.2
    mates all liveborn
      born in hospital (without mention of
        cesarean delivery or section) V34.00
        with cesarean delivery or section V34.01
      born outside hospital
        hospitalized V34.1
        not hospitalized V34.2
    mates all stillborn
      born in hospital (without mention of
        cesarean delivery or section) V35.00
        with cesarean delivery or section V35.01
      born outside hospital
        hospitalized V35.1
        not hospitalized V35.2
    mates liveborn and stillborn
      born in hospital (without mention of
        cesarean delivery or section) V36.00
        with cesarean delivery or section V36.01
      born outside hospital
        hospitalized V36.1
        not hospitalized V36.2
  single
    born in hospital (without mention of cesarean
      delivery or section) V30.00
      with cesarean delivery or section V30.01
    born outside hospital
      hospitalized V30.1
      not hospitalized V30.2
  twin NEC
    born in hospital (without mention of cesarean
      delivery or section) V33.00
      with cesarean delivery or section V33.01
    born outside hospital
      hospitalized V33.1
      not hospitalized V33.2
    mate liveborn
      born in hospital V31.0
      born outside hospital
        hospitalized V31.1
        not hospitalized V31.2
    mate stillborn
      born in hospital V32.0
      born outside hospital
        hospitalized V32.1
        not hospitalized V32.2

Newborn—*continued*
  unspecified as to single or multiple birth
    born in hospital (without mention of cesarean
      delivery or section) V39.00
      with cesarean delivery or section V39.01
    born outside hospital
      hospitalized V39.1
      not hospitalized V39.2
Newcastle's conjunctivitis or disease 077.8
Nezelof's syndrome (pure alymphocytosis)
    279.13
Niacin (amide) deficiency 265.2
Nicolas-Durand-Favre disease (climatic bubo)
    099.1
Nicolas-Favre disease (climatic bubo) 099.1
Nicotinic acid (amide) deficiency 265.2
Niemann-Pick disease (lipid histiocytosis)
    (splenomegaly) 272.7
Night
  blindness (*see also* Blindness, night) 368.60
    congenital 368.61
    vitamin A deficiency 264.5
  cramps 729.82
  sweats 780.8
  terrors, child 307.46
Nightmare 307.47
  REM-sleep type 307.47
Nipple —*see* condition
Nisbet's chancre 099.0
Nishimoto (-Takeuchi) disease 437.5
Nitritoid crisis or reaction —*see* Crisis, nitritoid
Nitrogen retention, extrarenal 788.9
Nitrosohemoglobinemia 289.8
Njovera 104.0
No
  diagnosis 799.9
  disease (found) V71.9
  room at the inn V65.0
Nocardiasis —*see* Nocardiosis
Nocardiosis 039.9
  with pneumonia 039.1
  lung 039.1
  specified type NEC 039.8
Nocturia 788.43
  psychogenic 306.53
Nocturnal —*see also* condition
  dyspnea (paroxysmal) 786.09
  emissions 608.89
  enuresis 788.36
    psychogenic 307.6
  frequency (micturition) 788.43
    psychogenic 306.53
Nodal rhythm disorder 427.89
Nodding of head 781.0
Node (s)—*see also* Nodule
  Heberden's 715.04
  larynx 478.79
  lymph—*see* condition
  milkers' 051.1
  Osler's 421.0
  rheumatic 729.89
  Schmorl's 722.30
    lumbar, lumbosacral 722.32
    specified region NEC 722.39
    thoracic, thoracolumbar 722.31
  singers' 478.5
  skin NEC 782.2
  tuberculous—*see* Tuberculosis, lymph gland
  vocal cords 478.5
Nodosities, Haygarth's 715.04

Nodule(s), nodular
  actinomycotic (*see also* Actinomycosis) 039.9
  arthritic—*see* Arthritis, nodosa
  cutaneous 782.2
  Haygarth's 715.04
  inflammatory—*see* Inflammation
  juxta-articular 102.7
    syphilitic 095.7
    yaws 102.7
  larynx 478.79
  lung, solitary 518.89
    emphysematous 492.8
  milkers' 051.1
  prostate 600.1
  rheumatic 729.89
  rheumatoid—*see* Arthritis rheumatoid
  scrotum (inflammatory) 608.4
  singers' 478.5
  skin NEC 782.2
  solitary, lung 518.89
    emphysematous 492.8
  subcutaneous 782.2
  thyroid (gland) (nontoxic) (uninodular) 241.0
    with
      hyperthyroidism 242.1
      thyrotoxicosis 242.1
    toxic or with hyperthyroidism 242.1
  vocal cords 478.5
Noma (gangrenous) (hospital) (infective) 528.1
  auricle (*see also* Gangrene) 785.4
  mouth 528.1
  pudendi (*see also* Vulvitis) 616.10
  vulvae (*see also* Vulvitis) 616.10
Nomadism V60.0
Non-adherence
  artificial skin graft 996.55
  decellularized allodermis graft 996.55
Non-autoimmune hemolytic anemia NEC
  283.10
Nonclosure —*see also* Imperfect, closure
  ductus
    arteriosus 747.0
    Botalli 747.0
  Eustachian valve 746.89
  foramen
    Botalli 745.5
    ovale 745.5
Noncompliance with medical treatment V15.81
Nondescent (congenital)—*see also* Malposition,
  congenital
  cecum 751.4
  colon 751.4
  testis 752.51
Nondevelopment
  brain 742.1
    specified part 742.2
  heart 746.89
  organ or site, congenital NEC—*see* Hypoplasia
Nonengagement
  head NEC 652.5
    in labor 660.1
      affecting fetus or newborn 763.1
Nonexanthematous tick fever 066.1
Nonexpansion, lung (newborn) NEC 770.4
Nonfunctioning
  cystic duct (*see also* Disease, gallbladder) 575.8
  gallbladder (*see also* Disease, gallbladder) 575.8
  kidney (*see also* Disease, renal) 593.9
  labyrinth 386.58
Nonhealing
  stump (surgical) 997.60
  wound, surgical 998.83

Nonimplantation of ovum, causing infertility
  628.3
Noninsufflation, fallopian tube 628.2
Nonne-Milroy-Meige syndrome (chronic
  hereditary edema) 757.0
Nonovulation 628.0
Nonpatent fallopian tube 628.2
Nonpneumatization, lung NEC 770.4
Nonreflex bladder 596.54
  with cauda equina 344.61
Nonretention of food —*see also* Vomiting
Nonrotation —*see* Malrotation
Nonsecretion, urine (*see also* Anuria) 788.5
  newborn 753.3
Nonunion
  fracture 733.82
  organ or site, congenital NEC—*see* Imperfect,
    closure
  symphysis pubis, congenital 755.69
  top sacrum, congenital 756.19
Nonviability 765.0
Nonvisualization, gallbladder 793.3
Nonvitalized tooth 522.9
Normal
  delivery—*see* category 650
  menses V65.5
  state (feared complaint unfounded) V65.5
Normoblastosis 289.8
Normocytic anemia (infectional) 285.9
  due to blood loss (chronic) 280.0
    acute 285.1
Norrie's disease (congenital) (progressive
  oculoacousticocerebral degeneration) 743.8
North American blastomycosis 116.0
Norwegian itch 133.0
Nose, nasal —*see* condition
Nosebleed 784.7
Nosomania 298.9
Nosophobia 300.29
Nostalgia 309.89
Notch of iris 743.46
Notched lip, congenital (*see also* Cleft, lip)
  749.10
Notching nose, congenital (tip) 748.1
Nothnagel's
  syndrome 378.52
  vasomotor acroparesthesia 443.89
Novy's relapsing fever (American) 087.1
Noxious
  foodstuffs, poisoning by
    fish 988.0
    fungi 988.1
    mushrooms 988.1
    plants (food) 988.2
    shellfish 988.0
    specified type NEC 988.8
    toadstool 988.1
  substances transmitted through placenta or
      breast milk 760.70
    alcohol 760.71
    anti-infective agents 760.74
    cocaine 760.75
    "crack" 760.75
    diethylstilbestrol (DES) 760.76
    hallucinogenic agents NEC 760.73
    medicinal agents NEC 760.79
    narcotics 760.72
    obstetric anesthetic or analgesic 763.5
    specified agent NEC 760.79
    suspected, affecting management of
        pregnancy 655.5
Nuchal hitch (arm) 652.8

Nucleus pulposus —*see* condition
Numbness 782.0
Nuns' knee 727.2
Nursemaid's
  elbow 832.0
  shoulder 831.0
Nutmeg liver 573.8
Nutrition, deficient or insufficient (particular
    kind of food) 269.9
  due to
    insufficient food 994.2
    lack of
      care (child) (infant) 995.52
        adult 995.84
      food 994.2
Nyctalopia (*see also* Blindness, night) 368.60
  vitamin A deficiency 264.5
Nycturia 788.43
  psychogenic 306.53
Nymphomania 302.89
Nystagmus 379.50
  associated with vestibular system disorders
    379.54
  benign paroxysmal positional 386.11
  central positional 386.2
  congenital 379.51
  deprivation 379.53
  dissociated 379.55
  latent 379.52
  miners' 300.89
  positional
    benign paroxysmal 386.11
    central 386.2
  specified NEC 379.56
  vestibular 379.54
  visual deprivation 379.53

O

Oasthouse urine disease 270.2
Obermeyer's relapsing fever (European) 087.0
Obesity (constitutional) (exogenous) (familial)
(nutritional) (simple) 278.00
adrenal 255.8
due to hyperalimentation 278.00
endocrine NEC 259.9
endogenous 259.9
Fröhlich's (adiposogenital dystrophy) 253.8
glandular NEC 259.9
hypothyroid (*see also* Hypothyroidism) 244.9
morbid 278.01
of pregnancy 646.1
pituitary 253.8
thyroid (*see also* Hypothyroidism) 244.9
Oblique —*see also* condition
lie before labor, affecting fetus or newborn 761.7
Obliquity, pelvis 738.6
Obliteration
abdominal aorta 446.7
appendix (lumen) 543.9
artery 447.1
ascending aorta 446.7
bile ducts 576.8
with calculus, choledocholithiasis, or
stones—*see* Choledocholithiasis
congenital 751.61
jaundice from 751.61 *[774.5]*
common duct 576.8
with calculus, choledocholithiasis, or
stones—*see* Choledocholithiasis
congenital 751.61
cystic duct 575.8
with calculus, choledocholithiasis, or
stones—*see* Choledocholithiasis
disease, arteriolar 447.1
endometrium 621.8
eye, anterior chamber 360.34
fallopian tube 628.2
lymphatic vessel 457.1
postmastectomy 457.0
organ or site, congenital NEC—*see* Atresia
placental blood vessels—*see* Placenta, abnormal
supra-aortic branches 446.7
ureter 593.89
urethra 599.84
vein 459.9
vestibule (oral) 525.8
Observation (for) V71.9
without need for further medical care V71.9
accident NEC V71.4
at work V71.3
criminal assault V71.6
deleterious agent ingestion V71.89
disease V71.9
cardiovascular V71.7
heart V71.7
mental V71.09
specified condition NEC V71.89
foreign body ingestion V71.89
growth and development variations V21.8
injuries (accidental) V71.4
inflicted NEC V71.6
during alleged rape or seduction V71.5
malignant neoplasm, suspected V71.1
postpartum
immediately after delivery V24.0
routine follow-up V24.2

Observation—*continued*
pregnancy
high-risk V23.9
specified problem NEC V23.8
normal (without complication) V22.1
with nonobstetric complication V22.2
first V22.0
rape or seduction, alleged V71.5
injury during V71.5
suicide attempt, alleged V71.89
suspected (undiagnosed) (unproven)
abuse V71.81
cardiovascular disease V71.7
child or wife battering victim V71.6
concussion (cerebral) V71.6
condition NEC V71.89
infant—*see* Observation, suspected,
condition, newborn
newborn V29.9
cardiovascular disease V29.8
congenital anomaly V29.8
genetic V29.3
infectious V29.0
ingestion foreign object V29.8
injury V29.8
metabolic V29.3
neoplasm V29.8
neurological V29.1
poison, poisoning V29.8
respiratory V29.2
specified NEC V29.8
infectious disease not requiring isolation
V71.89
malignant neoplasm V71.1
mental disorder V71.09
neglect V71.81
neoplasm
benign V71.89
malignant V71.1
specified condition NEC V71.89
tuberculosis V71.2
tuberculosis, suspected V71.2
Obsession, obsessional 300.3
ideas and mental images 300.3
impulses 300.3
neurosis 300.3
phobia 300.3
psychasthenia 300.3
ruminations 300.3
state 300.3
syndrome 300.3
Obsessive-compulsive 300.3
neurosis 300.3
reaction 300.3
Obstetrical trauma NEC (complicating
delivery) 665.9
with
abortion—*see* Abortion, by type, with damage
to pelvic organs
ectopic pregnancy (*see also* categories
633.0-633.9) 639.2
molar pregnancy (*see also* categories
630-632) 639.2
affecting fetus or newborn 763.89
following
abortion 639.2
ectopic or molar pregnancy 639.2
Obstipation (*see also* Constipation) 564.0
psychogenic 306.4

Obstruction, obstructed, obstructive
  airway NEC 519.8
    with
      allergic alveolitis NEC 495.9
      asthma NEC (*see also* Asthma) 493.9
      bronchiectasis 494.0
        with acute exacerbation 494.1
      bronchitis (*see also* Bronchitis, with,
          obstruction) 491.20
      emphysema NEC 492.8
    chronic 496
      with
        allergic alveolitis NEC 495.5
        asthma NEC (*see also* Asthma) 493.2
        bronchiectasis 494.0
          with acute exacerbation 494.1
        bronchitis (*see also* Bronchitis, chronic,
            obstructive) 491.20
        emphysema NEC 492.8
    due to
      bronchospasm 519.1
      foreign body 934.9
      inhalation of fumes or vapors 506.9
      laryngospasm 478.75
  alimentary canal (*see also* Obstruction,
      intestine) 560.9
  ampulla of Vater 576.2
    with calculus, cholelithiasis, or stones—*see*
        Choledocholithiasis
  aortic (heart) (valve) (*see also* Stenosis, aortic)
      424.1
    rheumatic (*see also* Stenosis, aortic,
        rheumatic) 395.0
  aortoiliac 444.0
  aqueduct of Sylvius 331.4
    congenital 742.3
      with spina bifida (*see also* Spina bifida)
          741.0
  Arnold-Chiari (*see also* Spina bifida) 741.0
  artery (*see also* Embolism, artery) 444.9
    basilar (complete) (partial) (*see also*
        Occlusion, artery, basilar) 433.0
    carotid (complete) (partial) (*see also*
        Occlusion, artery, carotid) 433.1
    precerebral—*see* Occlusion, artery,
        precerebral NEC
    retinal (central) (*see also* Occlusion, retina)
        362.30
    vertebral (complete) (partial) (*see also*
        Occlusion, artery, vertebral) 433.2
  asthma (chronic) (with obstructive pulmonary
      disease) 493.2
  band (intestinal) 560.81
  bile duct or passage (*see also* Obstruction,
      biliary) 576.2
    congenital 751.61
      jaundice from 751.61 *[774.5]*
  biliary (duct) (tract) 576.2
    with calculus 574.51
      with cholecystitis (chronic) 574.41
        acute 574.31
    congenital 751.61
      jaundice from 751.61 *[774.5]*
    gallbladder 575.2
      with calculus 574.21
        with cholecystitis (chronic) 574.11
          acute 574.01
  bladder neck (acquired) 596.0
    congenital 753.6
  bowel (*see also* Obstruction, intestine) 560.9
  bronchus 519.1

Obstruction, obstructed, . . .—*continued*
  canal, ear (*see also* Stricture, ear canal,
      acquired) 380.50
  cardia 537.89
  caval veins (inferior) (superior) 459.2
  cecum (*see also* Obstruction, intestine) 560.9
  circulatory 459.9
  colon (*see also* Obstruction, intestine) 560.9
    sympathicotonic 560.89
  common duct (*see also* Obstruction, biliary)
      576.2
    congenital 751.61
  coronary —*see* Arteriosclerosis, coronary
  cystic duct (*see also* Obstruction, gallbladder)
      575.2
    congenital 751.61
  device, implant, or graft—*see* Complications,
      due to (presence of) any device, implant, or
      graft classified to 996.0-996.5 NEC
  due to foreign body accidentally left in
      operation wound 998.4
  duodenum 537.3
    congenital 751.1
    due to
      compression NEC 537.3
      cyst 537.3
      intrinsic lesion or disease NEC 537.3
      scarring 537.3
      torsion 537.3
      ulcer 532.91
      volvulus 537.3
  ejaculatory duct 608.89
  endocardium 424.90
    arteriosclerotic 424.99
    specified cause, except rheumatic 424.99
  esophagus 530.3
  Eustachian tube (complete) (partial) 381.60
    cartilaginous
      extrinsic 381.63
      intrinsic 381.62
    due to
      cholesteatoma 381.61
      osseous lesion NEC 381.61
      polyp 381.61
    osseous 381.61
  fallopian tube (bilateral) 628.2
  fecal 560.39
    with hernia—*see also* Hernia, by site, with
        obstruction
      gangrenous—*see* Hernia, by site, with
          gangrene
  foramen of Monro (congenital) 742.3
    with spina bifida (*see also* Spina bifida) 741.0
  foreign body—*see* Foreign body
  gallbladder 575.2
    with calculus, cholelithiasis, or stones 574.21
      with cholecystitis (chronic) 574.11
        acute 574.01
    congenital 751.69
      jaundice from 751.69 *[774.5]*
  gastric outlet 537.0
  gastrointestinal (*see also* Obstruction, intestine)
      560.9
  glottis 478.79
  hepatic 573.8
    duct (*see also* Obstruction, biliary) 576.2
      congenital 751.61
  icterus (*see also* Obstruction, biliary) 576.8
    congenital 751.61
  ileocecal coil (*see also* Obstruction, intestine)
      560.9

Occlusion—*continued*
  without thrombus or embolus (*see also*
      Arteriosclerosis, extremities) 440.20
    due to stricture or stenosis 447.1
    upper extremity 444.21
      without thrombus or embolus (*see also*
          Arteriosclerosis, extremities) 440.20
      due to stricture or stenosis 447.1
  pontine (artery) 433.8
  posterior lingual, of mandibular teeth 524.2
  precerebral artery—*see* Occlusion, artery,
      precerebral NEC
  puncta lacrimalia 375.52
  pupil 364.74
  pylorus (*see also* Stricture, pylorus) 537.0
  renal artery 593.81
  retina, retinal (vascular) 362.30
    artery, arterial 362.30
      branch 362.32
      central (total) 362.31
      partial 362.33
      transient 362.34
      tributary 362.32
    vein 362.30
      branch 362.36
      central (total) 362.35
      incipient 362.37
      partial 362.37
      tributary 362.36
  spinal artery 433.8
  stent
    coronary 996.72
  teeth (mandibular) (posterior lingual) 524.2
  thoracic duct 457.1
  tubal 628.2
  ureter (complete) (partial) 593.4
    congenital 753.29
  urethra (*see also* Stricture, urethra) 598.9
    congenital 753.6
  uterus 621.8
  vagina 623.2
  vascular NEC 459.9
  vein—*see* Thrombosis
  vena cava (inferior) (superior) 453.2
  ventricle (brain) NEC 331.4
  vertebral (artery)—*see* Occlusion, artery,
      vertebral
  vessel (blood) NEC 459.9
  vulva 624.8
Occlusio pupillae 364.74
Occupational
  problems NEC V62.2
  therapy V57.21
Ochlophobia 300.29
Ochronosis (alkaptonuric) (congenital)
      (endogenous) 270.2
  with chloasma of eyelid 270.2
Ocular muscle —*see also* condition
  myopathy 359.1
Oculoauriculovertebral dysplasia 756.0
Oculogyric
  crisis or disturbance 378.87
    psychogenic 306.7
Oculomotor syndrome 378.81
Oddi's sphincter spasm 576.5
Odelberg's disease (juvenile osteochondrosis)
      732.1
Odontalgia 525.9
Odontoameloblastoma (M9311/0) 213.1
  upper jaw (bone) 213.0
Odontoclasia 521.0

Odontoclasis 873.63
  complicated 873.73
Odontodysplasia, regional 520.4
Odontogenesis imperfecta 520.5
Odontoma (M9280/0) 213.1
  ameloblastic (M9311/0) 213.1
    upper jaw (bone) 213.0
  calcified (M9280/0) 213.1
    upper jaw (bone) 213.0
  complex (M9282/0) 213.1
    upper jaw (bone) 213.0
  compound (M9281/0) 213.1
    upper jaw (bone) 213.0
  fibroameloblastic (M9290/0) 213.1
    upper jaw (bone) 213.0
  follicular 526.0
  upper jaw (bone) 213.0
Odontomyelitis (closed) (open) 522.0
Odontonecrosis 521.0
Odontorrhagia 525.8
Odontosarcoma, ameloblastic (M9290/3) 170.1
  upper jaw (bone) 170.0
Odynophagia 787.2
Oesophagostomiasis 127.7
Oesophagostomum infestation 127.7
Oestriasis 134.0
Ogilvie's syndrome (sympathicotonic colon
      obstruction) 560.89
Oguchi's disease (retina) 368.61
Ohara's disease (*see also* Tularemia) 021.9
Oidiomycosis (*see also* Candidiasis) 112.9
Oidiomycotic meningitis 112.83
Oidium albicans infection (*see also* Candidiasis)
      112.9
Old age 797
  dementia (of) 290.0
Olfactory —*see* condition
Oligemia 285.9
Oligergasia (*see also* Retardation, mental) 319
Oligoamnios 658.0
  affecting fetus or newborn 761.2
Oligoastrocytoma, mixed (M9382/3)
  specified site—*see* Neoplasm, by site, malignant
  unspecified site 191.9
Oligocythemia 285.9
Oligodendroblastoma (M9460/3)
  specified site—*see* Neoplasm, by site, malignant
  unspecified site 191.9
Oligodendroglioma (M9450/3)
  anaplastic type (M9451/3)
    specified site—*see* Neoplasm, by site,
        malignant
    unspecified site 191.9
  specified site—*see* Neoplasm, by site, malignant
  unspecified site 191.9
Oligodendroma —*see* Oligodendroglioma
Oligodontia (*see also* Anodontia) 520.0
Oligoencephalon 742.1
Oligohydramnios 658.0
  affecting fetus or newborn 761.2
  due to premature rupture of membranes 658.1
    affecting fetus or newborn 761.2
Oligohydrosis 705.0
Oligomenorrhea 626.1
Oligophrenia (*see also* Retardation, mental) 319
  phenylpyruvic 270.1
Oligospermia 606.1
Oligotrichia 704.09
  congenita 757.4

Oliguria 788.5
  with
    abortion—*see* Abortion, by type, with renal
      failure
    ectopic pregnancy (*see also* categories
      633.0-633.9) 639.3
    molar pregnancy (*see also* categories
      630-632) 639.3
    complicating
      abortion 639.3
      ectopic or molar pregnancy 639.3
      pregnancy 646.2
        with hypertension—*see* Toxemia, of
          pregnancy
    due to a procedure 997.5
    following labor and delivery 669.3
    heart or cardiac—*see* Failure, heart, congestive
    puerperal, postpartum 669.3
    specified due to a procedure 997.5
Ollier's disease (chondrodysplasia) 756.4
Omentitis (*see also* Peritonitis) 567.9
Omentocele (*see also* Hernia, omental) 553.8
Omentum, omental —*see* condition
Omphalitis (congenital) (newborn) 771.4
  not of newborn 686.9
  tetanus 771.3
Omphalocele 756.79
Omphalomesenteric duct, persistent 751.0
Omphalorrhagia, newborn 772.3
Omsk hemorrhagic fever 065.1
Onanism 307.9
Onchocerciasis 125.3
  eye 125.3 *[360.13]*
Onchocercosis 125.3
Oncocytoma (M8290/0)—*see* Neoplasm, by site,
  benign
Ondine's curse 348.8
Oneirophrenia (*see also* Schizophrenia) 295.4
Onychauxis 703.8
  congenital 757.5
Onychia (with lymphangitis) 681.9
  dermatophytic 110.1
  finger 681.02
  toe 681.11
Onychitis (with lymphangitis) 681.9
  finger 681.02
  toe 681.11
Onychocryptosis 703.0
Onychodystrophy 703.8
  congenital 757.5
Onychogryphosis 703.8
Onychogryposis 703.8
Onycholysis 703.8
Onychomadesis 703.8
Onychomalacia 703.8
Onychomycosis 110.1
  finger 110.1
  toe 110.1
Onycho-osteodysplasia 756.89
Onychophagy 307.9
Onychoptosis 703.8
Onychorrhexis 703.8
  congenital 757.5
Onychoschizia 703.8
Onychotrophia (*see also* Atrophy, nail) 703.8
O'nyong-nyong fever 066.3
Onyxis (finger) (toe) 703.0
Onyxitis (with lymphangitis) 681.9
  finger 681.02
  toe 681.11

Oophoritis (cystic) (infectional) (interstitial) (*see*
  also Salpingo-oophoritis) 614.2
  complicating pregnancy 646.6
  fetal (acute) 752.0
  gonococcal (acute) 098.19
    chronic or duration of 2 months or over 098.39
  tuberculous (*see also* Tuberculosis) 016.6
Opacity, opacities
  cornea 371.00
    central 371.03
    congenital 743.43
      interfering with vision 743.42
    degenerative (*see also* Degeneration, cornea)
      371.40
    hereditary (*see also* Dystrophy, cornea) 371.50
    inflammatory (*see also* Keratitis) 370.9
    late effect of trachoma (healed) 139.1
    minor 371.01
    peripheral 371.02
  enamel (fluoride) (nonfluoride) (teeth) 520.3
  lens (*see also* Cataract) 366.9
  snowball 379.22
  vitreous (humor) 379.24
    congenital 743.51
Opalescent dentin (hereditary) 520.5
Open, opening
  abnormal, organ or site, congenital—*see*
    Imperfect, closure
  angle with
    borderline intraocular pressure 365.01
    cupping of discs 365.01
  bite (anterior) (posterior) 524.2
  false—*see* Imperfect, closure
  wound—*see* Wound, open, by site
Operation
  causing mutilation of fetus 763.89
  destructive, on live fetus, to facilitate birth
    763.89
  for delivery, fetus or newborn 763.89
  maternal, unrelated to current delivery, affecting
    fetus or newborn 760.6
Operational fatigue 300.89
Operative —*see* condition
Operculitis (chronic) 523.4
  acute 523.3
Operculum, retina 361.32
  with detachment 361.01
Ophiasis 704.01
Ophthalmia (*see also* Conjunctivitis) 372.30
  actinic rays 370.24
  allergic (acute) 372.05
    chronic 372.14
  blennorrhagic (neonatorum) 098.40
  catarrhal 372.03
  diphtheritic 032.81
  Egyptian 076.1
  electric, electrica 370.24
  gonococcal (neonatorum) 098.40
  metastatic 360.11
  migraine 346.8
  neonatorum, newborn 771.6
    gonococcal 098.40
  nodosa 360.14
  phlyctenular 370.31
    with ulcer (*see also* Ulcer, cornea) 370.00
  sympathetic 360.11
Ophthalmitis —*see* Ophthalmia
Ophthalmocele (congenital) 743.66
Ophthalmoneuromyelitis 341.0
Ophthalmopathy, infiltrative with
  thyrotoxicosis 242.0

Ophthalmoplegia (*see also* Strabismus) 378.9
  anterior internuclear 378.86
  ataxia-areflexia syndrome 357.0
  bilateral 378.9
  diabetic 250.5 *[378.86]*
  exophthalmic 242.0 *[376.22]*
  external 378.55
    progressive 378.72
    total 378.56
  interna(l) (complete) (total) 367.52
  internuclear 378.86
  migraine 346.8
  painful 378.55
  Parinaud's 378.81
  progressive external 378.72
  supranuclear, progressive 333.0
  total (external) 378.56
    internal 367.52
  unilateral 378.9
Opisthognathism 524.00
Opisthorchiasis (felineus) (tenuicollis)
  (viverrini) 121.0
Opisthotonos, opisthotonus 781.0
Opitz's disease (congestive splenomegaly)
  289.51
Opiumism (*see also* Dependence) 304.0
Oppenheim's disease 358.8
Oppenheim-Urbach disease or syndrome
  (necrobiosis lipoidica diabeticorum) 250.8
  [709.3]
Opsoclonia 379.59
Optic nerve —*see* condition
Orbit —*see* condition
Orchioblastoma (M9071/3) 186.9
Orchitis (nonspecific) (septic) 604.90
  with abscess 604.0
  blennorrhagic (acute) 098.13
    chronic or duration of 2 months or over 098.33
  diphtheritic 032.89 *[604.91]*
  filarial 125.9 *[604.91]*
  gangrenous 604.99
  gonococcal (acute) 098.13
    chronic or duration of 2 months or over 098.33
  mumps 072.0
  parotidea 072.0
  suppurative 604.99
  syphilitic 095.8 *[604.91]*
  tuberculous (*see also* Tuberculosis) 016.5
    [608.81]
Orf 051.2
Organic —*see also* condition
  heart—*see* Disease, heart
  insufficiency 799.8
Oriental
  bilharziasis 120.2
  schistosomiasis 120.2
  sore 085.1
Orifice —*see* condition
Origin, both great vessels from right ventricle
  745.11
Ormond's disease or syndrome 593.4
Ornithosis 073.9
  with
    complication 073.8
      specified NEC 073.7
    pneumonia 073.0
    pneumonitis (lobular) 073.0
Orodigitofacial dysostosis 759.89
Oropouche fever 066.3
Orotaciduria, oroticaciduria (congenital)
  (hereditary) (pyrimidine deficiency) 281.4
Oroya fever 088.0

Orthodontics V58.5
  adjustment V53.4
  aftercare V58.5
  fitting V53.4
Orthopnea 786.02
Orthoptic training V57.4
Os, uterus —*see* condition
Osgood-Schlatter
  disease 732.4
  osteochondrosis 732.4
Osler's
  disease (M9950/1) (polycythemia vera) 238.4
  nodes 421.0
Osler-Rendu disease (familial hemorrhagic
  telangiectasia) 448.0
Osler-Vaquez disease (M9950/1) (polycythemia
  vera) 238.4
Osler-Weber-Rendu syndrome (familial
  hemorrhagic telangiectasia) 448.0
Osmidrosis 705.89
Osseous —*see* condition
Ossification
  artery—*see* Arteriosclerosis
  auricle (ear) 380.39
  bronchus 519.1
  cardiac (*see also* Degeneration, myocardial)
    429.1
  cartilage (senile) 733.99
  coronary —*see* Arteriosclerosis, coronary
  diaphragm 728.10
  ear 380.39
    middle (*see also* Otosclerosis) 387.9
  falx cerebri 349.2
  fascia 728.10
  fontanel
    defective or delayed 756.0
    premature 756.0
  heart (*see also* Degeneration, myocardial) 429.1
    valve—*see* Endocarditis
  larynx 478.79
  ligament
    posterior longitudinal 724.8
      cervical 723.7
  meninges (cerebral) 349.2
    spinal 336.8
  multiple, eccentric centers 733.99
  muscle 728.10
    heterotopic, postoperative 728.13
  myocardium, myocardial (*see also*
    Degeneration, myocardial) 429.1
  penis 607.81
  periarticular 728.89
  sclera 379.16
  tendon 727.82
  trachea 519.1
  tympanic membrane (*see also*
    Tympanosclerosis) 385.00
  vitreous (humor) 360.44
Osteitis (*see also* Osteomyelitis) 730.2
  acute 730.0
  alveolar 526.5
  chronic 730.1
  condensans (ilii) 733.5
  deformans (Paget's) 731.0
    due to or associated with malignant neoplasm
      (*see also* Neoplasm, bone, malignant)
      170.9 *[731.1]*
  due to yaws 102.6
  fibrosa NEC 733.29
    cystica (generalisata) 252.0
    disseminata 756.59

> *Note—Use the following fifth-digit subclassification with category 715:*
>
> *0 site unspecified*
> *1 shoulder region*
> *2 upper arm*
> *3 forearm*
> *4 hand*
> *5 pelvic region and thigh*
> *6 lower leg*
> *7 ankle and foot*
> *8 other specified sites except spine*
> *9 multiple sites*

Osteochondrosis— *continued*
  patella 732.4
  primary patellar center (of Köhler) 732.4
  specified site NEC 732.6
  spine 732.0
  tarsal scaphoid 732.5
  tibia (epiphysis) (tuberosity) 732.4
  upper extremity 732.3
  vertebra (body) (Calvé) 732.0
    epiphyseal plates (of Scheuermann) 732.0
  Kienböck's (disease) 732.3
  Köhler's (disease) (navicular, ankle) 732.5
    patellar 732.4
    tarsal navicular 732.5
  Legg-Calvé-Perthes (disease) 732.1
  lower extremity (juvenile) 732.4
  lunate bone 732.3
  Mauclaire's 732.3
  metacarpal heads (of Mauclaire) 732.3
  metatarsal (fifth) (head) (second) 732.5
  navicular, ankle 732.5
  os calcis 732.5
  Osgood-Schlatter 732.4
  os tibiale externum 732.5
  Panner's 732.3
  patella (juvenile) 732.4
  patellar center
    primary (of Köhler) 732.4
    secondary (of Sinding-Larsen) 732.4
  pelvis (juvenile) 732.1
  Pierson's 732.1
  radial head (juvenile) 732.3
  Scheuermann's 732.0
  Sever's (calcaneum) 732.5
  Sinding-Larsen (secondary patellar center) 732.4
  spine (juvenile) 732.0
    adult 732.8
  symphysis pubis (of Pierson) (juvenile) 732.1
  syphilitic (congenital) 090.0
  tarsal (navicular) (scaphoid) 732.5
  tibia (proximal) (tubercle) 732.4
  tuberculous—*see* Tuberculosis, bone
  ulna 732.3
  upper extremity (juvenile) 732.3
  van Neck's (juvenile osteochondrosis) 732.1
  vertebral (juvenile) 732.0
    adult 732.8
Osteoclastoma (M9250/1) 238.0
  malignant (M9250/3)—*see* Neoplasm, bone,
    malignant
Osteocopic pain 733.90
Osteodynia 733.90
Osteodystrophy
  azotemic 588.0
  chronica deformans hypertrophica 731.0
  congenital 756.50
    specified type NEC 756.59
  deformans 731.0
  fibrosa localisata 731.0
  parathyroid 252.0
  renal 588.0
Osteofibroma (M9262/0)—*see* Neoplasm, bone,
  benign
Osteofibrosarcoma (M9182/3)—*see* Neoplasm,
  bone, malignant
Osteogenesis imperfecta 756.51
Osteogenic —*see* condition
Osteoma (M9180/0)—*see also* Neoplasm, bone,
  benign
  osteoid (M9191/0)—*see also* Neoplasm, bone,
    benign
    giant (M9200/0)—*see* Neoplasm, bone, benign

Osteomalacia 268.2
  chronica deformans hypertrophica 731.0
  due to vitamin D deficiency 268.2
  infantile (*see also* Rickets) 268.0
  juvenile (*see also* Rickets) 268.0
  pelvis 268.2
  vitamin D-resistant 275.3
Osteomalacic bone 268.2
Osteomalacosis 268.2
Osteomyelitis (general) (infective) (localized)
  (neonatal) (purulent) (pyogenic) (septic)
  (staphylococcal) (streptococcal) (suppurative)
  (with periostitis) 730.2

> *Note—Use the following fifth-digit*
> *subclassification with category 730:*
>
> 0 *site unspecified*
> 1 *shoulder region*
> 2 *upper arm*
> 3 *forearm*
> 4 *hand*
> 5 *pelvic region and thigh*
> 6 *lower leg*
> 7 *ankle and foot*
> 8 *other specified sites*
> 9 *multiple sites*

  acute or subacute 730.0
  chronic or old 730.1
  due to or associated with
    diabetes mellitus 250.8 *[731.8]*
    tuberculosis (*see also* Tuberculosis, bone)
      015.9 *[730.8]*
      limb bones 015.5 *[730.8]*
      specified bones NEC 015.7 *[730.8]*
      spine 015.0 *[730.8]*
    typhoid 002.0 *[730.8]*
  Garré's 730.1
  jaw (acute) (chronic) (lower) (neonatal)
    (suppurative) (upper) 526.4
  nonsuppurating 730.1
  orbital 376.03
  petrous bone (*see also* Petrositis) 383.20
  Salmonella 003.24
  sclerosing, nonsuppurative 730.1
  sicca 730.1
  syphilitic 095.5
    congenital 090.0 *[730.8]*
  tuberculous—*see* Tuberculosis, bone
  typhoid 002.0 *[730.8]*
Osteomyelofibrosis 289.8
Osteomyelosclerosis 289.8
Osteonecrosis (*see also* Osteomyelitis) 730.1
Osteo-onycho-arthro dysplasia 756.89
Osteo-onychodysplasia, hereditary 756.89
Osteopathia
  condensans disseminata 756.53
  hyperostotica multiplex infantilis 756.59
  hypertrophica toxica 731.2
  striata 756.4
Osteopathy resulting from poliomyelitis (*see*
  also Poliomyelitis) 045.9 *[730.7]*
  familial dysplastic 731.2
Osteopecilia 756.53
Osteopenia 733.90
Osteoperiostitis (*see also* Osteomyelitis) 730.2
  ossificans toxica 731.2
  toxica ossificans 731.2
Osteopetrosis (familial) 756.52
Osteophyte —*see* Exostosis
Osteophytosis —*see* Exostosis

Otitis—*continued*
  catarrhal 381.4
    acute 381.00
    chronic (simple) 381.10
  chronic 382.9
    with effusion 381.3
    adhesive (*see also* Adhesions, middle ear)
      385.10
    allergic 381.3
    atticoantral, suppurative (with posterior or
      superior marginal perforation of ear
      drum) 382.2
    benign suppurative (with anterior
      perforation of ear drum) 382.1
    catarrhal 381.10
    exudative 381.3
    mucinous 381.20
    mucoid, mucous (simple) 381.20
    mucosanguineous 381.29
    nonsuppurative 381.3
    purulent 382.3
    secretory 381.3
    seromucinous 381.3
    serosanguineous 381.19
    serous (simple) 381.10
    suppurative 382.3
      atticoantral (with posterior or superior
        marginal perforation of ear drum)
        382.2
      benign (with anterior perforation of ear
        drum) 382.1
      tuberculous (*see also* Tuberculosis) 017.4
      tubotympanic 382.1
    transudative 381.3
  exudative 381.4
    acute 381.00
    chronic 381.3
  fibrotic (*see also* Adhesions, middle ear)
    385.10
  mucoid, mucous 381.4
    acute 381.02
    chronic (simple) 381.20
  mucosanguineous, chronic 381.29
  nonsuppurative 381.4
    acute 381.00
    chronic 381.3
  postmeasles 055.2
  purulent 382.4
    acute 382.00
      with spontaneous rupture of ear drum
        382.01
    chronic 382.3
  sanguineous, acute 381.03
    allergic 381.06
  secretory 381.4
    acute or subacute 381.01
    chronic 381.3
  seromucinous 381.4
    acute or subacute 381.02
    chronic 381.3
  serosanguineous, chronic 381.19
  serous 381.4
    acute or subacute 381.01
    chronic (simple) 381.10
  subacute—*see* Otitis, media, acute
  suppurative 382.4
    acute 382.00
      with spontaneous rupture of ear drum
        382.01

Otitis—*continued*
  chronic 382.3
    atticoantral 382.2
    benign 382.1
    tuberculous (*see also* Tuberculosis) 017.4
    tubotympanic 382.1
  transudative 381.4
    acute 381.00
    chronic 381.3
  tuberculous (*see also* Tuberculosis) 017.4
  postmeasles 055.2
Otoconia 386.8
Otolith syndrome 386.19
Otomycosis 111.8 *[380.15]*
  in
    aspergillosis 117.3 *[380.15]*
    moniliasis 112.82
Otopathy 388.9
Otoporosis (*see also* Otosclerosis) 387.9
Otorrhagia 388.69
  traumatic—*see* nature of injury
Otorrhea 388.60
  blood 388.69
  cerebrospinal (fluid) 388.61
Otosclerosis (general) 387.9
  cochlear (endosteal) 387.2
  involving
    otic capsule 387.2
    oval window
      nonobliterative 387.0
      obliterative 387.1
    round window 387.2
  nonobliterative 387.0
  obliterative 387.1
  specified type NEC 387.8
Otospongiosis (*see also* Otosclerosis) 387.9
Otto's disease or pelvis 715.35
Outburst, aggressive (*see also* Disturbance,
  conduct) 312.0
  in children and adolescents 313.9
Outcome of delivery
  multiple birth NEC V27.9
    all liveborn V27.5
    all stillborn V27.7
    some liveborn V27.6
    unspecified V27.9
  single V27.9
    liveborn V27.0
    stillborn V27.1
  twins V27.9
    both liveborn V27.2
    both stillborn V27.4
    one liveborn, one stillborn V27.3
Outlet —*see also* condition
  syndrome (thoracic) 353.0
Outstanding ears (bilateral) 744.29
Ovalocytosis (congenital) (hereditary) (*see also*
  Elliptocytosis) 282.1
Ovarian —*see also* condition
  pregnancy—*see* Pregnancy, ovarian
  remnant syndrome 620.8
  vein syndrome 593.4
Ovaritis (cystic) (*see also* Salpingo-oophoritis)
  614.2
Ovary, ovarian —*see* condition
Overactive —*see also* Hyperfunction
  bladder 596.51
  eye muscle (*see also* Strabismus) 378.9
  hypothalamus 253.8
  thyroid (*see also* Thyrotoxicosis) 242.9
Overactivity, child 314.01

P

Pacemaker syndrome 429.4
Pachyderma, pachydermia 701.8
  laryngis 478.5
  laryngitis 478.79
  larynx (verrucosa) 478.79
Pachydermatitis 701.8
Pachydermatocele (congenital) 757.39
  acquired 701.8
Pachydermatosis 701.8
Pachydermoperiostitis
  secondary 731.2
Pachydermoperiostosis
  primary idiopathic 757.39
  secondary 731.2
Pachymeningitis (adhesive) (basal) (brain)
  (cerebral) (cervical) (chronic) (circumscribed)
  (external) (fibrous) (hemorrhagic)
  (hypertrophic) (internal) (purulent) (spinal)
  (suppurative) (*see also* Meningitis) 322.9
  gonococcal 098.82
Pachyonychia (congenital) 757.5
  acquired 703.8
Pachyperiosteodermia
  primary or idiopathic 757.39
  secondary 731.2
Pachyperiostosis
  primary or idiopathic 757.39
  secondary 731.2
Pacinian tumor (M9507/0)—*see* Neoplasm,
  skin, benign
Pads, knuckle or Garrod's 728.79
Paget's disease (osteitis deformans) 731.0
  with infiltrating duct carcinoma of the breast
    (M8541/3)—*see* Neoplasm, breast,
    malignant
  bone 731.0
    osteosarcoma in (M9184/3)—*see* Neoplasm,
      bone, malignant
  breast (M8540/3) 174.0
  extramammary (M8542/3)—*see also* Neoplasm,
    skin, malignant
  anus 154.3
    skin 173.5
  malignant (M8540/3)
    breast 174.0
    specified site NEC (M8542/3)—*see*
      Neoplasm, skin, malignant
    unspecified site 174.0
  mammary (M8540/3) 174.0
  necrosis of bone 731.0
  nipple (M8540/3) 174.0
  osteitis deformans 731.0
Paget-Schroetter syndrome (intermittent venous
  claudication) 453.8
Pain(s)
  abdominal 789.0
  adnexa (uteri) 625.9
  alimentary, due to vascular insufficiency 557.9
  anginoid (*see also* Pain, precordial) 786.51
  anus 569.42
  arch 729.5
  arm 729.5
  back (postural) 724.5
    low 724.2
    psychogenic 307.89
  bile duct 576.9
  bladder 788.9

Pain(s)—*continued*
  bone 733.90
  breast 611.71
    psychogenic 307.89
  broad ligament 625.9
  cartilage NEC 733.90
  cecum 789.0
  cervicobrachial 723.3
  chest (central) 786.50
    atypical 786.59
    midsternal 786.51
    musculoskeletal 786.59
    noncardiac 786.59
    substernal 786.51
    wall (anterior) 786.52
  coccyx 724.79
  colon 789.0
  common duct 576.9
  coronary—*see* Angina
  costochondral 786.52
  diaphragm 786.52
  due to (presence of) any device, implant, or
    graft classifiable to 996.0-996.5—*see*
    Complications, due to (presence of) any
    device, implant, or graft classified to
    996.0-996.5 NEC
  ear (*see also* Otalgia) 388.70
  epigastric, epigastrium 789.0
  extremity (lower) (upper) 729.5
  eye 379.91
  face, facial 784.0
    atypical 350.2
    nerve 351.8
  false (labor) 644.1
  female genital organ NEC 625.9
    psychogenic 307.89
  finger 729.5
  flank 789.0
  foot 729.5
  gallbladder 575.9
  gas (intestinal) 787.3
  gastric 536.8
  generalized 780.9
  genital organ
    female 625.9
    male 608.9
    psychogenic 307.89
  groin 789.0
  growing 781.99
  hand 729.5
  head (*see also* Headache) 784.0
  heart (*see also* Pain, precordial) 786.51
  infraorbital (*see also* Neuralgia, trigeminal)
    350.1
  intermenstrual 625.2
  jaw 526.9
  joint 719.40
    ankle 719.47
    elbow 719.42
    foot 719.47
    hand 719.44
    hip 719.45
    knee 719.46
    multiple sites 719.49
    pelvic region 719.45
    psychogenic 307.89
    shoulder (region) 719.41
    specified site NEC 719.48

Pain(s)—*continued*
  wrist 719.43
  kidney 788.0
  labor, false or spurious 644.1
  laryngeal 784.1
  leg 729.5
  limb 729.5
  low back 724.2
  lumbar region 724.2
  mastoid (*see also* Otalgia) 388.70
  maxilla 526.9
  metacarpophalangeal (joint) 719.44
  metatarsophalangeal (joint) 719.47
  mouth 528.9
  muscle 729.1
    intercostal 786.59
  nasal 478.1
  nasopharynx 478.29
  neck NEC 723.1
    psychogenic 307.89
  nerve NEC 729.2
  neuromuscular 729.1
  nose 478.1
  ocular 379.91
  ophthalmic 379.91
  orbital region 379.91
  osteocopic 733.90
  ovary 625.9
    psychogenic 307.89
  over heart (*see also* Pain, precordial) 786.51
  ovulation 625.2
  pelvic (female) 625.9
    male NEC 789.0
      psychogenic 307.89
    psychogenic 307.89
  penis 607.9
    psychogenic 307.89
  pericardial (*see also* Pain, precordial) 786.51
  perineum
    female 625.9
    male 608.9
  pharynx 478.29
  pleura, pleural, pleuritic 786.52
  post-operative —*see* Pain, by site
  preauricular 388.70
  precordial (region) 786.51
    psychogenic 307.89
  psychogenic 307.80
    cardiovascular system 307.89
    gastrointestinal system 307.89
    genitourinary system 307.89
    heart 307.89
    musculoskeletal system 307.89
    respiratory system 307.89
    skin 306.3
  radicular (spinal) (*see also* Radiculitis) 729.2
  rectum 569.42
  respiration 786.52
  retrosternal 786.51
  rheumatic NEC 729.0
    muscular 729.1
  rib 786.50
  root (spinal) (*see also* Radiculitis) 729.2
  round ligament (stretch) 625.9
  sacroiliac 724.6
  sciatic 724.3
  scrotum 608.9
    psychogenic 307.89
  seminal vesicle 608.9
  sinus 478.1
  skin 782.0

Pain(s)—*continued*
  spermatic cord 608.9
  spinal root (*see also* Radiculitis) 729.2
  stomach 536.8
    psychogenic 307.89
  substernal 786.51
  temporomandibular (joint) 524.62
  temporomaxillary joint 524.62
  testis 608.9
    psychogenic 307.89
  thoracic spine 724.1
    with radicular and visceral pain 724.4
  throat 784.1
  tibia 733.90
  toe 729.5
  tongue 529.6
  tooth 525.9
  trigeminal (*see also* Neuralgia, trigeminal) 350.1
  umbilicus 789.0
  ureter 788.0
  urinary (organ) (system) 788.0
  uterus 625.9
    psychogenic 307.89
  vagina 625.9
  vertebrogenic (syndrome) 724.5
  vesical 788.9
  vulva 625.9
  xiphoid 733.90
Painful —*see also* Pain
  arc syndrome 726.19
  coitus
    female 625.0
    male 608.89
    psychogenic 302.76
  ejaculation (semen) 608.89
    psychogenic 302.79
  erection 607.3
  feet syndrome 266.2
  menstruation 625.3
    psychogenic 306.52
  micturition 788.1
  ophthalmoplegia 378.55
  respiration 786.52
  scar NEC 709.2
  urination 788.1
  wire sutures 998.89
Painters' colic 984.9
  specified type of lead—*see* Table of drugs and chemicals
Palate —*see* condition
Palatoplegia 528.9
Palatoschisis (*see also* Cleft, palate) 749.00
Palilalia 784.69
Palindromic arthritis (*see also* Rheumatism, palindromic) 719.3
Palliative care V66.7
Pallor 782.61
  temporal, optic disc 377.15
Palmar —*see also* condition
  fascia—*see* condition
Palpable
  cecum 569.89
  kidney 593.89
  liver 573.9
  lymph nodes 785.6
  ovary 620.8
  prostate 602.9
  spleen (*see also* Splenomegaly) 789.2
  uterus 625.8
Palpitation (heart) 785.1
  psychogenic 306.2

Palsy (*see also* Paralysis) 344.9
atrophic diffuse 335.20
Bell's 351.0
  newborn 767.5
birth 767.7
brachial plexus 353.0
  fetus or newborn 767.6
brain—*see also* Palsy, cerebral
  noncongenital or noninfantile 344.89
    due to vascular lesion—*see* category 438
    late effect—*see* Late effect(s) (of) cerebrovascular disease
  syphilitic 094.89
    congenital 090.49
bulbar (chronic) (progressive) 335.22
  pseudo NEC 335.23
  supranuclear NEC 344.89
cerebral (congenital) (infantile) (spastic) 343.9
  athetoid 333.7
  diplegic 343.0
    due to previous vascular lesion—*see* category 438
    late effect—*see* Late effect(s) (of) cerebrovascular disease
  hemiplegic 343.1
  monoplegic 343.3
  noncongenital or noninfantile 437.8
    due to previous vascular lesion—*see* category 438
    late effect—*see* Late effect(s) (of) cerebrovascular disease
  paraplegic 343.0
  quadriplegic 343.2
  spastic, not congenital or infantile 344.89
  syphilitic 094.89
    congenital 090.49
  tetraplegic 343.2
cranial nerve—*see also* Disorder, nerve, cranial
  multiple 352.6
creeping 335.21
divers' 993.3
Erb's (birth injury) 767.6
facial 351.0
  newborn 767.5
glossopharyngeal 352.2
Klumpke (-Déjérine) 767.6
lead 984.9
  specified type of lead—*see* Table of drugs and chemicals
median nerve (tardy) 354.0
peroneal nerve (acute) (tardy) 355.3
progressive supranuclear 333.0
pseudobulbar NEC 335.23
radial nerve (acute) 354.3
seventh nerve 351.0
  newborn 767.5
shaking (*see also* Parkinsonism) 332.0
spastic (cerebral) (spinal) 343.9
  hemiplegic 343.1
specified nerve NEC—*see* Disorder, nerve
supranuclear NEC 356.8
  progressive 333.0
ulnar nerve (tardy) 354.2
wasting 335.21
Paltauf-Sternberg disease 201.9
Paludism —*see* Malaria
Panama fever 084.0
Panaris (with lymphangitis) 681.9
finger 681.02
toe 681.11

Panaritium (with lymphangitis) 681.9
finger 681.02
toe 681.11
Panarteritis (nodosa) 446.0
brain or cerebral 437.4
Pancake heart 793.2
with cor pulmonale (chronic) 416.9
Pancarditis (acute) (chronic) 429.89
with
  rheumatic
    fever (active) (acute) (chronic) (subacute) 391.8
      inactive or quiescent 398.99
  rheumatic, acute 391.8
    chronic or inactive 398.99
Pancoast's syndrome or tumor (carcinoma, pulmonary apex) (M8010/3) 162.3
Pancoast-Tobias syndrome (M8010/3) (carcinoma, pulmonary apex) 162.3
Pancolitis 556.6
Pancreas, pancreatic —*see* condition
Pancreatitis 577.0
acute (edematous) (hemorrhagic) (recurrent) 577.0
annular 577.0
apoplectic 577.0
calcereous 577.0
chronic (infectious) 577.1
  recurrent 577.1
cystic 577.2
fibrous 577.8
gangrenous 577.0
hemorrhagic (acute) 577.0
interstitial (chronic) 577.1
  acute 577.0
malignant 577.0
mumps 072.3
painless 577.1
recurrent 577.1
relapsing 577.1
subacute 577.0
suppurative 577.0
syphilitic 095.8
Pancreatolithiasis 577.8
Pancytolysis 289.9
Pancytopenia (acquired) 284.8
with malformations 284.0
congenital 284.0
Panencephalitis —*see also* Encephalitis
subacute, sclerosing 046.2
Panhematopenia 284.8
congenital 284.0
constitutional 284.0
splenic, primary 289.4
Panhemocytopenia 284.8
congenital 284.0
constitutional 284.0
Panhypogonadism 257.2
Panhypopituitarism 253.2
prepubertal 253.3
Panic (attack) (state) 300.01
reaction to exceptional stress (transient) 308.0
Panmyelopathy, familial constitutional 284.0
Panmyelophthisis 284.9
acquired (secondary) 284.8
congenital 284.0
idiopathic 284.9
Panmyelosis (acute) (M9951/1) 238.7
Panner's disease 732.3
capitellum humeri 732.3
head of humerus 732.3
tarsal navicular (bone) (osteochondrosis) 732.5

Panneuritis endemica 265.0 *[357.4]*
Panniculitis 729.30
  back 724.8
  knee 729.31
  neck 723.6
  nodular, nonsuppurative 729.30
  sacral 724.8
  specified site NEC 729.39
Panniculus adiposus (abdominal) 278.1
Pannus 370.62
  allergic eczematous 370.62
  degenerativus 370.62
  keratic 370.62
  rheumatoid—*see* Arthritis, rheumatoid
  trachomatosus, trachomatous (active) 076.1
      [370.62]
    late effect 139.1
Panophthalmitis 360.02
Panotitis —*see* Otitis media
Pansinusitis (chronic) (hyperplastic)
      (nonpurulent) (purulent) 473.8
  acute 461.8
  due to fungus NEC 117.9
  tuberculous (*see also* Tuberculosis) 012.8
Panuveitis 360.12
  sympathetic 360.11
Panvalvular disease —*see* Endocarditis, mitral
Papageienkrankheit 073.9
Papanicolaou smear
  cervix (screening test) V76.2
    as part of gynecological examination V72.3
    for suspected malignant neoplasm V76.2
      no disease found V71.1
    nonspecific abnormal finding 795.0
  other specified site—*see also* Screening,
      malignant neoplasm
    for suspected malignant neoplasm—*see also*
      Screening, malignant neoplasm
    no disease found V71.1
    nonspecific abnormal finding 795.1
  vagina V76.47
    following hysterectomy for malignant
      condition V67.01
Papilledema 377.00
  associated with
    decreased ocular pressure 377.02
    increased intracranial pressure 377.01
    retinal disorder 377.03
  choked disc 377.00
  infectional 377.00
Papillitis 377.31
  anus 569.49
  chronic lingual 529.4
  necrotizing, kidney 584.7
  optic 377.31
  rectum 569.49
  renal, necrotizing 584.7
  tongue 529.0
Papilloma (M8050/0)—*see also* Neoplasm, by
      site, benign

---

*Note—Except where otherwise indicated, the
morphological varieties of papilloma in the list
below should be coded by site as for
"Neoplasm, benign."*

---

  acuminatum (female) (male) 078.11
  bladder (urinary) (transitional cell) (M8120/1)
      236.7
    benign (M8120/0) 223.3
  choroid plexus (M9390/0) 225.0
    anaplastic type (M9390/3) 191.5

Papilloma—*continued*
  malignant (M9390/3) 191.5
  ductal (M8503/0)
  dyskeratotic (M8052/0)
  epidermoid (M8052/0)
  hyperkeratotic (M8052/0)
  intracystic (M8504/0)
  intraductal (M8503/0)
  inverted (M8053/0)
  keratotic (M8052/0)
  parakeratotic (M8052/0)
  pinta (primary) 103.0
  renal pelvis (transitional cell) (M8120/1) 236.99
    benign (M8120/0) 223.1
  Schneiderian (M8121/0)
    specified site—*see* Neoplasm, by site, benign
    unspecified site 212.0
  serous surface (M8461/0)
    borderline malignancy (M8461/1)
      specified site—*see* Neoplasm, by site,
        uncertain behavior
      unspecified site 236.2
    specified site—*see* Neoplasm, by site, benign
    unspecified site 220
  squamous (cell) (M8052/0)
  transitional (cell) (M8120/0)
    bladder (urinary) (M8120/1) 236.7
    inverted type (M8121/1)—*see* Neoplasm, by
      site, uncertain behavior
    renal pelvis (M8120/1) 236.91
    ureter (M8120/1) 236.91
  ureter (transitional cell) (M8120/1) 236.91
    benign (M8120/0) 223.2
  urothelial (M8120/1)—*see* Neoplasm, by site,
    uncertain behavior
  verrucous (M8051/0)
  villous (M8261/1)—*see* Neoplasm, by site,
    uncertain behavior
  yaws, plantar or palmar 102.1
Papillomata, multiple, of yaws 102.1
Papillomatosis (M8060/0)—*see also* Neoplasm,
      by site, benign
  confluent and reticulate 701.8
  cutaneous 701.8
  ductal, breast 610.1
  Gougerot-Carteaud (confluent reticulate) 701.8
  intraductal (diffuse) (M8505/0)—*see* Neoplasm,
      by site, benign
  subareolar duct (M8506/0) 217
Papillon-Léage and Psaume syndrome
      (orodigitofacial dysostosis) 759.89
Papule 709.8
  carate (primary) 103.0
  fibrous, of nose (M8724/0) 216.3
  pinta (primary) 103.0
Papulosis, malignant 447.8
Papyraceous fetus 779.8
  complicating pregnancy 646.0
Paracephalus 759.7
Parachute mitral valve 746.5
Paracoccidioidomycosis 116.1
  mucocutaneous-lymphangitic 116.1
  pulmonary 116.1
  visceral 116.1
Paracoccidiomycosis —*see*
      Paracoccidioidomycosis
Paracusis 388.40
Paradentosis 523.5
Paradoxical facial movements 374.43
Paraffinoma 999.9

Paraganglioma (M8680/1)
  adrenal (M8700/0) 227.0
    malignant (M8700/3) 194.0
  aortic body (M8691/1) 237.3
    malignant (M8691/3) 194.6
  carotid body (M8692/1) 237.3
    malignant (M8692/3) 194.5
  chromaffin (M8700/0)—*see also* Neoplasm, by
    site, benign
    malignant (M8700/3)—*see* Neoplasm, by site,
      malignant
  extra-adrenal (M8693/1)
    malignant (M8693/3)
      specified site—*see* Neoplasm, by site,
        malignant
      unspecified site 194.6
    specified site—*see* Neoplasm, by site,
      uncertain behavior
    unspecified site 237.3
  glomus jugulare (M8690/1) 237.3
    malignant (M8690/3) 194.6
  jugular (M8690/1) 237.3
    malignant (M8680/3)
      specified site—*see* Neoplasm, by site,
        malignant
      unspecified site 194.6
  nonchromaffin (M8693/1)
    malignant (M8693/3)
      specified site—*see* Neoplasm, by site,
        malignant
      unspecified site 194.6
    specified site—*see* Neoplasm, by site,
      uncertain behavior
    unspecified site 237.3
  parasympathetic (M8682/1)
    specified site—*see* Neoplasm, by site,
      uncertain behavior
    unspecified site 237.3
  specified site—*see* Neoplasm, by site, uncertain
    behavior
  sympathetic (M8681/1)
    specified site—*see* Neoplasm, by site,
      uncertain behavior
    unspecified site 237.3
  unspecified site 237.3
Parageusia 781.1
  psychogenic 306.7
Paragonimiasis 121.2
Paragranuloma, Hodgkin's (M9660/3) 201.0
Parahemophilia (*see also* Defect, coagulation)
  286.3
Parakeratosis 690.8
  psoriasiformis 696.2
  variegata 696.2
Paralysis, paralytic (complete) (incomplete)
  344.9
  with
    broken
      back—*see* Fracture, vertebra, by site, with
        spinal cord injury
      neck—*see* Fracture, vertebra, cervical, with
        spinal cord injury
    fracture, vertebra—*see* Fracture, vertebra, by
      site, with spinal cord injury
    syphilis 094.89
  abdomen and back muscles 355.9
  abdominal muscles 355.9
  abducens (nerve) 378.54
  abductor 355.9
    lower extremity 355.8
    upper extremity 354.9

Paralysis, paralytic—*continued*
  accessory nerve 352.4
  accommodation 367.51
    hysterical 300.11
  acoustic nerve 388.5
  agitans 332.0
    arteriosclerotic 332.0
  alternating 344.89
    oculomotor 344.89
  amyotrophic 335.20
  ankle 355.8
  anterior serratus 355.9
  anus (sphincter) 569.49
  apoplectic (current episode) (*see also* Disease,
    cerebrovascular, acute) 436
    late effect—*see* Late effect(s) (of)
      cerebrovascular disease
    category 438
  arm 344.40
    affecting
      dominant side 344.41
      nondominant side 344.42
    both 344.2
    due to old CVA—*see* category 438
    hysterical 300.11
    late effect—*see* Late effect(s) (of)
      cerebrovascular disease
    psychogenic 306.0
    transient 781.4
      traumatic NEC (*see also* Injury, nerve,
        upper limb) 955.9
  arteriosclerotic (current episode) 437.0
    late effect—*see* Late effect(s) (of)
      cerebrovascular disease
  ascending (spinal), acute 357.0
  associated, nuclear 344.89
  asthenic bulbar 358.0
  ataxic NEC 334.9
    general 094.1
  athetoid 333.7
  atrophic 356.9
    infantile, acute (*see also* Poliomyelitis, with
      paralysis) 045.1
    muscle NEC 355.9
    progressive 335.21
    spinal (acute) (*see also* Poliomyelitis, with
      paralysis) 045.1
  attack (*see also* Disease, cerebrovascular, acute)
    436
  axillary 353.0
  Babinski-Nageotte's 344.89
  Bell's 351.0
    newborn 767.5
  Benedikt's 344.89
  birth (injury) 767.7
    brain 767.0
    intracranial 767.0
    spinal cord 767.4
  bladder (sphincter) 596.53
    neurogenic 596.54
      with cauda equina syndrome 344.61
    puerperal, postpartum, childbirth 665.5
    sensory 596.54
      with cauda equina 344.61
    spastic 596.54
      with cauda equina 344.61
  bowel, colon, or intestine (*see also* Ileus) 560.1
  brachial plexus 353.0
    due to birth injury 767.6
    newborn 767.6

Paralysis, paralytic—*continued*
- brain
  - congenital—*see* Palsy, cerebral
  - current episode 437.8
  - diplegia 344.2
  - due to previous vascular lesion—*see* category 438
  - hemiplegia 342.9
    - due to previous vascular lesion—*see* category 438
    - late effect—*see* Late effect(s) (of) cerebrovascular disease
  - infantile—*see* Palsy, cerebral
  - late effect—*see* Late effect(s) (of) cerebrovascular disease
  - monoplegia—*see also* Monoplegia
    - due to previous vascular lesion—*see* category 438
    - late effect—*see* Late effect(s) (of) cerebrovascular disease
  - paraplegia 344.1
  - quadriplegia —*see* Quadriplegia
  - syphilitic, congenital 090.49
  - triplegia 344.89
- bronchi 519.1
- Brown-Séquard's 344.89
- bulbar (chronic) (progressive) 335.22
  - infantile (*see also* Poliomyelitis, bulbar) 045.0
  - poliomyelitic (*see also* Poliomyelitis, bulbar) 045.0
  - pseudo 335.23
  - supranuclear 344.89
- bulbospinal 358.0
- cardiac (*see also* Failure, heart) 428.9
- cerebral
  - current episode 437.8
  - spastic, infantile—*see* Palsy, cerebral
- cerebrocerebellar 437.8
  - diplegic infantile 343.0
- cervical
  - plexus 353.2
  - sympathetic NEC 337.0
- Céstan-Chenais 344.89
- Charcot-Marie-Tooth type 356.1
- childhood—*see* Palsy, cerebral
- Clark's 343.9
- colon (*see also* Ileus) 560.1
- compressed air 993.3
- compression
  - arm NEC 354.9
  - cerebral—*see* Paralysis, brain
  - leg NEC 355.8
  - lower extremity NEC 355.8
  - upper extremity NEC 354.9
- congenital (cerebral) (spastic) (spinal)—*see* Palsy, cerebral
- conjugate movement (of eye) 378.81
  - cortical (nuclear) (supranuclear) 378.81
- convergence 378.83
- cordis (*see also* Failure, heart) 428.9
- cortical (*see also* Paralysis, brain) 437.8
- cranial or cerebral nerve (*see also* Disorder, nerve, cranial) 352.9
- creeping 335.21
- crossed leg 344.89
- crutch 953.4
- deglutition 784.9
  - hysterical 300.11
- dementia 094.1
- descending (spinal) NEC 335.9
- diaphragm (flaccid) 519.4

Paralysis, paralytic—*continued*
- due to accidental section of phrenic nerve during procedure 998.2
- digestive organs NEC 564.89
- diplegic—*see* Diplegia
- divergence (nuclear) 378.85
- divers' 993.3
- Duchenne's 335.22
- due to intracranial or spinal birth injury—*see* Palsy, cerebral
- embolic (current episode) (*see also* Embolism, brain) 434.1
  - late effect —*see* Late effect(s) (of) cerebrovascular disease
- enteric (*see also* Ileus) 560.1
  - with hernia—*see* Hernia, by site, with obstruction
- Erb's syphilitic spastic spinal 094.89
- Erb (-Duchenne) (birth) (newborn) 767.6
- esophagus 530.89
- essential, infancy (*see also* Poliomyelitis) 045.9
- extremity
  - lower —*see* Paralysis, leg
  - spastic (hereditary) 343.3
    - noncongenital or noninfantile 344.1
  - transient (cause unknown) 781.4
  - upper —*see* Paralysis, arm
- eye muscle (extrinsic) 378.55
  - intrinsic 367.51
- facial (nerve) 351.0
  - birth injury 767.5
  - congenital 767.5
  - following operation NEC 998.2
  - newborn 767.5
- familial 359.3
  - periodic 359.3
  - spastic 334.1
- fauces 478.29
- finger NEC 354.9
- foot NEC 355.8
- gait 781.2
- gastric nerve 352.3
- gaze 378.81
- general 094.1
  - ataxic 094.1
  - insane 094.1
  - juvenile 090.40
  - progressive 094.1
  - tabetic 094.1
- glossopharyngeal (nerve) 352.2
- glottis (*see also* Paralysis, vocal cord) 478.30
- gluteal 353.4
- Gubler (-Millard) 344.89
- hand 354.9
  - hysterical 300.11
  - psychogenic 306.0
- heart (*see also* Failure, heart) 428.9
- hemifacial, progressive 349.89
- hemiplegic—*see* Hemiplegia
- hyperkalemic periodic (familial) 359.3
- hypertensive (current episode) 437.8
- hypoglossal (nerve) 352.5
- hypokalemic periodic 359.3
- Hyrtl's sphincter (rectum) 569.49
- hysterical 300.11
- ileus (*see also* Ileus) 560.1
- infantile (*see also* Poliomyelitis) 045.9
  - atrophic acute 045.1
  - bulbar 045.0
  - cerebral—*see* Palsy, cerebral
  - paralytic 045.1

Paralysis, paralytic—*continued*
    progressive acute 045.9
      spastic—*see* Palsy, cerebral
      spinal 045.9
    infective (*see also* Poliomyelitis) 045.9
    inferior nuclear 344.9
    insane, general or progressive 094.1
    internuclear 378.86
    interosseous 355.9
    intestine (*see also* Ileus) 560.1
    intracranial (current episode) (*see also*
      Paralysis, brain) 437.8
      due to birth injury 767.0
    iris 379.49
      due to diphtheria (toxin) 032.81 *[379.49]*
    ischemic, Volkmann's (complicating trauma)
      958.6
    Jackson's 344.89
    jake 357.7
    Jamaica ginger (jake) 357.7
    juvenile general 090.40
    Klumpke (-Déjérine) (birth) (newborn) 767.6
    labioglossal (laryngeal) (pharyngeal) 335.22
    Landry's 357.0
    laryngeal nerve (recurrent) (superior) (*see also*
      Paralysis, vocal cord) 478.30
    larynx (*see also* Paralysis, vocal cord) 478.30
      due to diphtheria (toxin) 032.3
    late effect
      due to
        birth injury, brain or spinal (cord)—*see*
          Palsy, cerebral
        edema, brain or cerebral—*see* Paralysis,
          brain
        lesion
          cerebrovascular—*see* category 438
          late effect—*see* Late effect(s) (of)
            cerebrovascular disease
          spinal (cord)—*see* Paralysis, spinal
    lateral 335.24
    lead 984.9
      specified type of lead—*see* Table of drugs and
        chemicals
    left side—*see* Hemiplegia
    leg 344.30
      affecting
        dominant side 344.31
        nondominant side 344.32
      both (*see also* Paraplegia) 344.1
      crossed 344.89
      hysterical 300.11
      psychogenic 306.0
      transient or transitory 781.4
        traumatic NEC (*see also* Injury, nerve,
          lower limb) 956.9
    levator palpebrae superioris 374.31
    limb NEC 344.5
      all four—*see* Quadriplegia
      quadriplegia—*see* Quadriplegia
    lip 528.5
    Lissauer's 094.1
    local 355.9
    lower limb—*see also* Paralysis, leg
      both (*see also* Paraplegia) 344.1
    lung 518.89
      newborn 770.8
    median nerve 354.1
    medullary (tegmental) 344.89
    mesencephalic NEC 344.89
      tegmental 344.89
    middle alternating 344.89

Paralysis, paralytic—*continued*
  Millard-Gubler-Foville 344.89
  monoplegic—*see* Monoplegia
  motor NEC 344.9
    cerebral—*see* Paralysis, brain
    spinal—*see* Paralysis, spinal
  multiple
    cerebral—*see* Paralysis, brain
    spinal—*see* Paralysis, spinal
  muscle (flaccid) 359.9
    due to nerve lesion NEC 355.9
    eye (extrinsic) 378.55
      intrinsic 367.51
      oblique 378.51
    iris sphincter 364.8
    ischemic (complicating trauma) (Volkmann's)
      958.6
    pseudohypertrophic 359.1
  muscular (atrophic) 359.9
    progressive 335.21
  musculocutaneous nerve 354.9
  musculospiral 354.9
  nerve—*see also* Disorder, nerve
    third or oculomotor (partial) 378.51
      total 378.52
    fourth or trochlear 378.53
    sixth or abducens 378.54
    seventh or facial 351.0
      birth injury 767.5
      due to
        injection NEC 999.9
        operation NEC 997.09
      newborn 767.5
    accessory 352.4
    auditory 388.5
    birth injury 767.7
    cranial or cerebral (*see also* Disorder, nerve,
      cranial) 352.9
    facial 351.0
      birth injury 767.5
      newborn 767.5
    laryngeal (*see also* Paralysis, vocal cord)
      478.30
    newborn 767.7
    phrenic 354.8
      newborn 767.7
    radial 354.3
      birth injury 767.6
      newborn 767.6
    syphilitic 094.89
    traumatic NEC (*see also* Injury, nerve, by
      site) 957.9
    trigeminal 350.9
    ulnar 354.2
  newborn NEC 767.0
  normokalemic periodic 359.3
  obstetrical, newborn 767.7
  ocular 378.9
  oculofacial, congenital 352.6
  oculomotor (nerve) (partial) 378.51
    alternating 344.89
    external bilateral 378.55
    total 378.52
  olfactory nerve 352.0
  palate 528.9
  palatopharyngolaryngeal 352.6
  paratrigeminal 350.9
  periodic (familial) (hyperkalemic)
    (hypokalemic) (normokalemic) (secondary)
    359.3

Paralysis, paralytic—*continued*
peripheral
  autonomic nervous system—*see* Neuropathy,
    peripheral, autonomic
  nerve NEC 355.9
peroneal (nerve) 355.3
pharynx 478.29
phrenic nerve 354.8
plantar nerves 355.6
pneumogastric nerve 352.3
poliomyelitis (current) (*see also* Poliomyelitis,
  with paralysis) 045.1
  bulbar 045.0
popliteal nerve 355.3
pressure (*see also* Neuropathy, entrapment)
  355.9
progressive 335.21
  atrophic 335.21
  bulbar 335.22
  general 094.1
  hemifacial 349.89
  infantile, acute (*see also* Poliomyelitis) 045.9
  multiple 335.20
pseudobulbar 335.23
pseudohypertrophic 359.1
  muscle 359.1
psychogenic 306.0
pupil, pupillary 379.49
quadriceps 355.8
quadriplegic (*see also* Quadriplegia) 344.0
radial nerve 354.3
  birth injury 767.6
rectum (sphincter) 569.49
rectus muscle (eye) 378.55
recurrent laryngeal nerve (*see also* Paralysis,
  vocal cord) 478.30
respiratory (muscle) (system) (tract) 786.09
  center NEC 344.89
    fetus or newborn 770.8
  congenital 768.9
  newborn 768.9
right side—*see* Hemiplegia
Saturday night 354.3
saturnine 984.9
  specified type of lead—*see* Table of drugs and
    chemicals
sciatic nerve 355.0
secondary—*see* Paralysis, late effect
seizure (cerebral) (current episode) (*see also*
  Disease, cerebrovascular, acute) 436
  late effect—*see* Late effect(s) (of)
    cerebrovascular disease
senile NEC 344.9
serratus magnus 355.9
shaking (*see also* Parkinsonism) 332.0
shock (*see also* Disease, cerebrovascular, acute)
  436
  late effect—*see* Late effect(s) (of)
    cerebrovascular disease
shoulder 354.9
soft palate 528.9
spasmodic—*see* Paralysis, spastic
spastic 344.9
  cerebral infantile—*see* Palsy, cerebral
  congenital (cerebral)—*see* Palsy, cerebral
  familial 334.1
  hereditary 334.1
  infantile 343.9
  noncongenital or noninfantile, cerebral 344.9
  syphilitic 094.0
    spinal 094.89

Paralysis, paralytic—*continued*
sphincter, bladder (*see also* Paralysis, bladder)
  596.53
spinal (cord) NEC 344.1
  accessory nerve 352.4
  acute (*see also* Poliomyelitis) 045.9
  ascending acute 357.0
  atrophic (acute) (*see also* Poliomyelitis, with
    paralysis) 045.1
    spastic, syphilitic 094.89
  congenital NEC 343.9
  hemiplegic —*see* Hemiplegia
  hereditary 336.8
  infantile (*see also* Poliomyelitis) 045.9
  late effect NEC 344.89
  monoplegic—*see* Monoplegia
  nerve 355.9
  progressive 335.10
  quadriplegic —*see* Quadriplegia
  spastic NEC 343.9
  traumatic—*see* Injury, spinal, by site
sternomastoid 352.4
stomach 536.3
  nerve 352.3
stroke (current episode) (*see also* Disease,
  cerebrovascular, acute) 436
  late effect—*see* Late effect(s) (of)
    cerebrovascular disease
subscapularis 354.8
superior nuclear NEC 334.9
supranuclear 356.8
sympathetic
  cervical NEC 337.0
  nerve NEC (*see also* Neuropathy, peripheral,
    autonomic) 337.9
  nervous system—*see* Neuropathy, peripheral,
    autonomic
syndrome 344.9
  specified NEC 344.89
syphilitic spastic spinal (Erb's) 094.89
tabetic general 094.1
thigh 355.8
throat 478.29
  diphtheritic 032.0
  muscle 478.29
thrombotic (current episode) (*see also*
  Thrombosis, brain) 434.0
  late effect—*see* Late effect(s) (of)
    cerebrovascular disease
thumb NEC 354.9
tick (-bite) 989.5
Todd's (postepileptic transitory paralysis)
  344.89
toe 355.6
tongue 529.8
transient
  arm or leg NEC 781.4
  traumatic NEC (*see also* Injury, nerve, by
    site) 957.9
trapezius 352.4
traumatic, transient NEC (*see also* Injury, nerve,
  by site) 957.9
trembling (*see also* Parkinsonism) 332.0
triceps brachii 354.9
trigeminal nerve 350.9
trochlear nerve 378.53
ulnar nerve 354.2
upper limb —*see also* Paralysis, arm
  both (*see also* Diplegia) 344.2
uremic—*see* Uremia
uveoparotitic 135

Paralysis, paralytic—*continued*
  uvula 528.9
    hysterical 300.11
      postdiphtheritic 032.0
  vagus nerve 352.3
  vasomotor NEC 337.9
  velum palati 528.9
  vesical (*see also* Paralysis, bladder) 596.53
  vestibular nerve 388.5
  visual field, psychic 368.16
  vocal cord 478.30
    bilateral (partial) 478.33
      complete 478.34
    complete (bilateral) 478.34
    unilateral (partial) 478.31
      complete 478.32
  Volkmann's (complicating trauma) 958.6
  wasting 335.21
  Weber's 344.89
  wrist NEC 354.9
Paramedial orifice, urethrovesical 753.8
Paramenia 626.9
Parametritis (chronic) (*see also* Disease, pelvis,
  inflammatory) 614.4
  acute 614.3
  puerperal, postpartum, childbirth 670
Parametrium, parametric —*see* condition
Paramnesia (*see also* Amnesia) 780.9
Paramolar 520.1
  causing crowding 524.3
Paramyloidosis 277.3
Paramyoclonus multiplex 333.2
Paramyotonia 359.2
  congenita 359.2
Paraneoplastic syndrome —*see* condition
Parangi (*see also* Yaws) 102.9
Paranoia 297.1
  alcoholic 291.5
  querulans 297.8
  senile 290.20
Paranoid
  dementia (*see also* Schizophrenia) 295.3
    praecox (acute) 295.3
    senile 290.20
  personality 301.0
  psychosis 297.9
    alcoholic 291.5
    climacteric 297.2
    drug-induced 292.11
    involutional 297.2
    menopausal 297.2
    protracted reactive 298.4
    psychogenic 298.4
      acute 298.3
    senile 290.20
  reaction (chronic) 297.9
    acute 298.3
  schizophrenia (acute) (*see also* Schizophrenia)
    295.3
  state 297.9
    alcohol-induced 291.5
    climacteric 297.2
    drug-induced 292.11
    due to or associated with
      arteriosclerosis (cerebrovascular) 290.42
      presenile brain disease 290.12
      senile brain disease 290.20
    involutional 297.2
    menopausal 297.2
    senile 290.20
    simple 297.0

Paranoid— *continued*
  specified type NEC 297.8
  tendencies 301.0
  traits 301.0
  trends 301.0
  type, psychopathic personality 301.0
Paraparesis (*see also* Paralysis) 344.9
Paraphasia 784.3
Paraphilia (*see also* Deviation, sexual) 302.9
Paraphimosis (congenital) 605
  chancroidal 099.0
Paraphrenia, paraphrenic (late) 297.2
  climacteric 297.2
  dementia (*see also* Schizophrenia) 295.3
  involutional 297.2
  menopausal 297.2
  schizophrenia (acute) (*see also* Schizophrenia)
    295.3
Paraplegia 344.1
  with
    broken back—*see* Fracture, vertebra, by site,
      with spinal cord injury
    fracture, vertebra—*see* Fracture, vertebra, by
      site, with spinal cord injury
  ataxic—*see* Degeneration, combined, spinal cord
  brain (current episode) (*see also* Paralysis,
    brain) 437.8
  cerebral (current episode) (*see also* Paralysis,
    brain) 437.8
  congenital or infantile (cerebral) (spastic)
    (spinal) 343.0
  cortical—*see* Paralysis, brain
  familial spastic 334.1
  functional (hysterical) 300.11
  hysterical 300.11
  infantile 343.0
  late effect 344.1
  Pott's (*see also* Tuberculosis) 015.0 *[730.88]*
  psychogenic 306.0
  spastic
    Erb's spinal 094.89
    hereditary 334.1
    not infantile or congenital 344.1
  spinal (cord)
    traumatic NEC—*see* Injury, spinal, by site
  syphilitic (spastic) 094.89
  traumatic NEC—*see* Injury, spinal, by site
Paraproteinemia 273.2
  benign (familial) 273.1
  monoclonal 273.1
  secondary to malignant or inflammatory disease
    273.1
Parapsoriasis 696.2
  en plaques 696.2
  guttata 696.2
  lichenoides chronica 696.2
  retiformis 696.2
  varioliformis (acuta) 696.2
Parascarlatina 057.8
Parasitic —*see also* condition
  disease NEC (*see also* Infestation, parasitic)
    136.9
    contact V01.8
    exposure to V01.8
    intestinal NEC 129
    skin NEC 134.9
  stomatitis 112.0
  sycosis 110.0
    beard 110.0
    scalp 110.0
  twin 759.4

Parasitism NEC 136.9
  intestinal NEC 129
  skin NEC 134.9
  specified—*see* Infestation
Parasitophobia 300.29
Parasomnia 780.59
  nonorganic origin 307.47
Paraspadias 752.69
Paraspasm facialis 351.8
Parathyroid gland —*see* condition
Parathyroiditis (autoimmune) 252.1
Parathyroprival tetany 252.1
Paratrachoma 077.0
Paratyphilitis (*see also* Appendicitis) 541
Paratyphoid (fever)—*see* Fever, paratyphoid
Paratyphus —*see* Fever, paratyphoid
Paraurethral duct 753.8
Para-urethritis 597.89
  gonococcal (acute) 098.0
    chronic or duration of 2 months or over 098.2
Paravaccinia NEC 051.9
  milkers' node 051.1
Paravaginitis (*see also* Vaginitis) 616.10
Parencephalitis (*see also* Encephalitis) 323.9
  late effect—*see* category 326
Parergasia 298.9
Paresis (*see also* Paralysis) 344.9
  accommodation 367.51
  bladder (spastic) (sphincter) (*see also* Paralysis,
    bladder) 596.53
    tabetic 094.0
  bowel, colon, or intestine (*see also* Ileus) 560.1
  brain or cerebral—*see* Paralysis, brain
  extrinsic muscle, eye 378.55
  general 094.1
    arrested 094.1
    brain 094.1
    cerebral 094.1
    insane 094.1
    juvenile 090.40
      remission 090.49
    progressive 094.1
    remission (sustained) 094.1
    tabetic 094.1
  heart (*see also* Failure, heart) 428.9
  infantile (*see also* Poliomyelitis) 045.9
  insane 094.1
  juvenile 090.40
  late effect—*see* Paralysis, late effect
  luetic (general) 094.1
  peripheral progressive 356.9
  pseudohypertrophic 359.1
  senile NEC 344.9
  stomach 536.3
  syphilitic (general) 094.1
    congenital 090.40
  transient, limb 781.4
  vesical (sphincter) NEC 596.53
Paresthesia (*see also* Disturbance, sensation)
    782.0
  Berger's (paresthesia of lower limb) 782.0
  Bernhardt 355.1
  Magnan's 782.0
Paretic —*see* condition
Parinaud's
  conjunctivitis 372.02
  oculoglandular syndrome 372.02
  ophthalmoplegia 378.81
  syndrome (paralysis of conjugate upward gaze)
    378.81
Parkes Weber and Dimitri syndrome
    (encephalocutaneous angiomatosis) 759.6

Parkinson's disease, syndrome, or tremor
  —*see* Parkinsonism
Parkinsonism (arteriosclerotic) (idiopathic)
    (primary) 332.0
  associated with orthostatic hypotension
    (idiopathic) (symptomatic) 333.0
  due to drugs 332.1
  secondary 332.1
  syphilitic 094.82
Parodontitis 523.4
Parodontosis 523.5
Paronychia (with lymphangitis) 681.9
  candidal (chronic) 112.3
  chronic 681.9
    candidal 112.3
    finger 681.02
    toe 681.11
  finger 681.02
  toe 681.11
  tuberculous (primary) (*see also* Tuberculosis)
    017.0
Parorexia NEC 307.52
  hysterical 300.11
Parosmia 781.1
  psychogenic 306.7
Parotid gland —*see* condition
Parotiditis (*see also* Parotitis) 527.2
  epidemic 072.9
  infectious 072.9
Parotitis 527.2
  allergic 527.2
  chronic 527.2
  epidemic (*see also* Mumps) 072.9
  infectious (*see also* Mumps) 072.9
  noninfectious 527.2
  nonspecific toxic 527.2
  not mumps 527.2
  postoperative 527.2
  purulent 527.2
  septic 527.2
  suppurative (acute) 527.2
  surgical 527.2
  toxic 527.2
Paroxysmal —*see also* condition
  dyspnea (nocturnal) 786.09
Parrot's disease (syphilitic osteochondritis) 090.0
Parrot fever 073.9
Parry's disease or syndrome (exophthalmic
    goiter) 242.0
Parry-Romberg syndrome 349.89
Parson's disease (exophthalmic goiter) 242.0
Parsonage-Aldren-Turner syndrome 353.5
Parsonage-Turner syndrome 353.5
Pars planitis 363.21
Particolored infant 757.39
Parturition —*see* Delivery
Passage
  false, urethra 599.4
  of sounds or bougies (*see also* Attention to
    artificial opening) V55.9
Passive —*see* condition
Pasteurella septica 027.2
Pasteurellosis (*see also* Infection, Pasteurella)
    027.2
PAT (paroxysmal atrial tachycardia) 427.0
Patau's syndrome (trisomy D_1) 758.1
Patch
  herald 696.3
Patches
  mucous (syphilitic) 091.3
    congenital 090.0
  smokers' (mouth) 528.6

Pendred's syndrome (familial goiter with
deaf-mutism) 243
Pendulous
abdomen 701.9
in pregnancy or childbirth 654.4
affecting fetus or newborn 763.89
breast 611.8
Penetrating wound —*see also* Wound, open, by
site
with internal injury—*see* Injury, internal, by
site, with open wound
eyeball 871.7
with foreign body (nonmagnetic) 871.6
magnetic 871.5
ocular (*see also* Penetrating wound, eyeball)
871.7
adnexa 870.3
with foreign body 870.4
orbit 870.3
with foreign body 870.4
Penetration, pregnant uterus by instrument
with
abortion—*see* Abortion, by type, with damage
to pelvic organs
ectopic pregnancy (*see also* categories
633.0-633.9) 639.2
molar pregnancy (*see also* categories
630-632) 639.2
complication of delivery 665.1
affecting fetus or newborn 763.89
following
abortion 639.2
ectopic or molar pregnancy 639.2
Penfield's syndrome (*see also* Epilepsy) 345.5
Penicilliosis of lung 117.3
Penis —*see* condition
Penitis 607.2
Penta X syndrome 758.81
Pentalogy (of Fallot) 745.2
Pentosuria (benign) (essential) 271.8
Peptic acid disease 536.8
Peregrinating patient V65.2
Perforated —*see* Perforation
Perforation, perforative (nontraumatic)
antrum (*see also* Sinusitis, maxillary) 473.0
appendix 540.0
with peritoneal abscess 540.1
atrial septum, multiple 745.5
attic, ear 384.22
healed 384.81
bile duct, except cystic (*see also* Disease,
biliary) 576.3
cystic 575.4
bladder (urinary) 596.6
with
abortion—*see* Abortion, by type, with
damage to pelvic organs
ectopic pregnancy (*see also* categories
633.0-633.9) 639.2
molar pregnancy (*see also* categories
630-632) 639.2
following
abortion 639.2
ectopic or molar pregnancy 639.2
obstetrical trauma 665.5
bowel 569.83
with
abortion—*see* Abortion, by type, with
damage to pelvic organs
ectopic pregnancy (*see also* categories
633.0-633.9) 639.2

Perforation, perforative—*continued*
molar pregnancy (*see also* categories
630-632) 639.2
fetus or newborn 777.6
following
abortion 639.2
ectopic or molar pregnancy 639.2
obstetrical trauma 665.5
broad ligament
with
abortion—*see* Abortion, by type, with
damage to pelvic organs
ectopic pregnancy (*see also* categories
633.0-633.9) 639.2
molar pregnancy (*see also* categories
630-632) 639.2
following
abortion 639.2
ectopic or molar pregnancy 639.2
obstetrical trauma 665.6
by
device, implant, or graft—*see* Complications,
mechanical
foreign body left accidentally in operation
wound 998.4
instrument (any) during a procedure,
accidental 998.2
cecum 540.0
with peritoneal abscess 540.1
cervix (uteri)—*see also* Injury, internal, cervix
with
abortion—*see* Abortion, by type, with
damage to pelvic organs
ectopic pregnancy (*see also* categories
633.0-633.9) 639.2
molar pregnancy (*see also* categories
630-632) 639.2
following
abortion 639.2
ectopic or molar pregnancy 639.2
obstetrical trauma 665.3
colon 569.83
common duct (bile) 576.3
cornea (*see also* Ulcer, cornea) 370.00
due to ulceration 370.06
cystic duct 575.4
diverticulum (*see also* Diverticula) 562.10
small intestine 562.00
duodenum, duodenal (ulcer)—*see* Ulcer,
duodenum, with perforation
ear drum—*see* Perforation, tympanum
enteritis—*see* Enteritis
esophagus 530.4
ethmoidal sinus (*see also* Sinusitis, ethmoidal)
473.2
foreign body (external site)—*see also* Wound,
open, by site, complicated
internal site, by ingested object—*see* Foreign
body
frontal sinus (*see also* Sinusitis, frontal) 473.1
gallbladder or duct (*see also* Disease,
gallbladder) 575.4
gastric (ulcer)—*see* Ulcer, stomach, with
perforation
heart valve—*see* Endocarditis
ileum (*see also* Perforation, intestine) 569.83
instrumental
external—*see* Wound, open, by site
pregnant uterus, complicating delivery 665.9
surgical (accidental) (blood vessel) (nerve)
(organ) 998.2

Perforation, perforative—*continued*
  intestine 569.83
    with
      abortion—*see* Abortion, by type, with
        damage to pelvic organs
      ectopic pregnancy (*see also* categories
        633.0-633.9) 639.2
      molar pregnancy (*see also* categories
        630-632) 639.2
      fetus or newborn 777.6
      obstetrical trauma 665.5
      ulcerative NEC 569.83
  jejunum, jejunal 569.83
    ulcer—*see* Ulcer, gastrojejunal, with
      perforation
  mastoid (antrum) (cell) 383.89
  maxillary sinus (*see also* Sinusitis, maxillary)
    473.0
  membrana tympani—*see* Perforation, tympanum
  nasal
    septum 478.1
      congenital 748.1
      syphilitic 095.8
    sinus (*see also* Sinusitis) 473.9
      congenital 748.1
  palate (hard) 526.89
    soft 528.9
      syphilitic 095.8
    syphilitic 095.8
  palatine vault 526.89
    syphilitic 095.8
      congenital 090.5
  pelvic
    floor
      with
        abortion—*see* Abortion, by type, with
          damage to pelvic organs
        ectopic pregnancy (*see also* categories
          633.0-633.9) 639.2
        molar pregnancy (*see also* categories
          630-632) 639.2
      obstetrical trauma 664.1
    organ
      with
        abortion—*see* Abortion, by type, with
          damage to pelvic organs
        ectopic pregnancy (*see also* categories
          633.0-633.9) 639.2
        molar pregnancy (*see also* categories
          630-632) 639.2
      following
        abortion 639.2
        ectopic or molar pregnancy 639.2
      obstetrical trauma 665.5
  perineum—*see* Laceration, perineum
  periurethral tissue
    with
      abortion—*see* Abortion, by type, with
        damage to pelvic organs
      ectopic pregnancy (*see also* categories
        630-632) 639.2
      molar pregnancy (*see also* categories
        630-632) 639.2
  pharynx 478.29
  pylorus, pyloric (ulcer)—*see* Ulcer, stomach,
    with perforation
  rectum 569.49
  sigmoid 569.83
  sinus (accessory) (chronic) (nasal) (*see also*
    Sinusitis) 473.9

Perforation, perforative—*continued*
  sphenoidal sinus (*see also* Sinusitis, sphenoidal)
    473.3
  stomach (due to ulcer)—*see* Ulcer, stomach,
    with perforation
  surgical (accidental) (by instrument) (blood
    vessel) (nerve) (organ) 998.2
  traumatic
    external—*see* Wound, open, by site
    eye (*see also* Penetrating wound, ocular) 871.7
    internal organ—*see* Injury, internal, by site
  tympanum (membrane) (persistent
    posttraumatic) (postinflammatory) 384.20
    with
      otitis media—*see* Otitis media
    attic 384.22
    central 384.21
    healed 384.81
    marginal NEC 384.23
    multiple 384.24
    pars flaccida 384.22
    total 384.25
    traumatic—*see* Wound, open, ear, drum
  typhoid, gastrointestinal 002.0
  ulcer—*see* Ulcer, by site, with perforation
  ureter 593.89
  urethra
    with
      abortion—*see* Abortion, by type, with
        damage to pelvic organs
      ectopic pregnancy (*see also* categories
        633.0-633.9) 639.2
      molar pregnancy (*see also* categories
        630-632) 639.2
    following
      abortion 639.2
      ectopic or molar pregnancy 639.2
    obstetrical trauma 665.5
  uterus—*see also* Injury, internal, uterus
    with
      abortion—*see* Abortion, by type, with
        damage to pelvic organs
      ectopic pregnancy (*see also* categories
        633.0-633.9) 639.2
      molar pregnancy (*see also* categories
        630-632) 639.2
    by intrauterine contraceptive device 996.32
    following
      abortion 639.2
      ectopic or molar pregnancy 639.2
    obstetrical trauma—*see* Injury, internal,
      uterus, obstetrical trauma
  uvula 528.9
    syphilitic 095.8
  vagina—*see* Laceration, vagina
  viscus NEC 799.8
    traumatic 868.00
    with open wound into cavity 868.10
Periadenitis mucosa necrotica recurrens 528.2
Periangiitis 446.0
Periantritis 535.4
Periappendicitis (acute) (*see also* Appendicitis)
  541
Periarteritis (disseminated) (infectious)
  (necrotizing) (nodosa) 446.0
Periarthritis (joint) 726.90
  Duplay's 726.2
  gonococcal 098.50
  humeroscapularis 726.2
  scapulohumeral 726.2
  shoulder 726.2
  wrist 726.4

Periarthrosis (angioneural)—*see* Periarthritis
Peribronchitis 491.9
  tuberculous (*see also* Tuberculosis) 011.3
Pericapsulitis, adhesive (shoulder) 726.0
Pericarditis (granular) (with decompensation)
    (with effusion) 423.9
  with
    rheumatic fever (conditions classifiable to 390)
      active (*see also* Pericarditis, rheumatic)
        391.0
      inactive or quiescent 393
  actinomycotic 039.8 *[420.0]*
  acute (nonrheumatic) 420.90
    with chorea (acute) (rheumatic) (Sydenham's)
      392.0
    bacterial 420.99
    benign 420.91
    hemorrhagic 420.90
    idiopathic 420.91
    infective 420.90
    nonspecific 420.91
    rheumatic 391.0
      with chorea (acute) (rheumatic)
        (Sydenham's) 392.0
    sicca 420.90
    viral 420.91
  adhesive or adherent (external) (internal) 423.1
    acute—*see* Pericarditis, acute
    rheumatic (external) (internal) 393
  amebic 006.8 *[420.0]*
  bacterial (acute) (subacute) (with serous or
    seropurulent effusion) 420.99
  calcareous 423.2
  cholesterol (chronic) 423.8
    acute 420.90
  chronic (nonrheumatic) 423.8
    rheumatic 393
  constrictive 423.2
  Coxsackie 074.21
  due to
    actinomycosis 039.8 *[420.0]*
    amebiasis 006.8 *[420.0]*
    Coxsackie (virus) 074.21
    histoplasmosis (*see also* Histoplasmosis)
      115.93
    nocardiosis 039.8 *[420.0]*
    tuberculosis (*see also* Tuberculosis) 017.9
      [420.0]
  fibrinocaseous (*see also* Tuberculosis) 017.9
    [420.0]
  fibrinopurulent 420.99
  fibrinous—*see* Pericarditis, rheumatic
  fibropurulent 420.99
  fibrous 423.1
  gonococcal 098.83
  hemorrhagic 423.0
  idiopathic (acute) 420.91
  infective (acute) 420.90
  meningococcal 036.41
  neoplastic (chronic) 423.8
    acute 420.90
  nonspecific 420.91
  obliterans, obliterating 423.1
  plastic 423.1
  pneumococcal (acute) 420.99
  postinfarction 411.0
  purulent (acute) 420.99
  rheumatic (active) (acute) (with effusion) (with
    pneumonia) 391.0
    with chorea (acute) (rheumatic) (Sydenham's)
      392.0

Pericarditis—*continued*
  chronic or inactive (with chorea) 393
  septic (acute) 420.99
  serofibrinous—*see* Pericarditis, rheumatic
  staphylococcal (acute) 420.99
  streptococcal (acute) 420.99
  suppurative (acute) 420.99
  syphilitic 093.81
  tuberculous (acute) (chronic) (*see also*
    Tuberculosis) 017.9 *[420.0]*
  uremic 585 *[420.0]*
  viral (acute) 420.91
Pericardium, pericardial —*see* condition
Pericellulitis (*see also* Cellulitis) 682.9
Pericementitis 523.4
  acute 523.3
  chronic (suppurative) 523.4
Pericholecystitis (*see also* Cholecystitis) 575.10
Perichondritis
  auricle 380.00
    acute 380.01
    chronic 380.02
  bronchus 491.9
  ear (external) 380.00
    acute 380.01
    chronic 380.02
  larynx 478.71
    syphilitic 095.8
    typhoid 002.0 *[478.71]*
  nose 478.1
  pinna 380.00
    acute 380.01
    chronic 380.02
  trachea 478.9
Periclasia 523.5
Pericolitis 569.89
Pericoronitis (chronic) 523.4
  acute 523.3
Pericystitis (*see also* Cystitis) 595.9
Pericytoma (M9150/1)—*see also* Neoplasm,
    connective tissue, uncertain behavior
  benign (M9150/0)—*see* Neoplasm, connective
    tissue, benign
  malignant (M9150/3)—*see* Neoplasm,
    connective tissue, malignant
Peridacryocystitis, acute 375.32
Peridiverticulitis (*see also* Diverticulitis) 562.11
Periduodenitis 535.6
Periendocarditis (*see also* Endocarditis) 424.90
  acute or subacute 421.9
Periepididymitis (*see also* Epididymitis) 604.90
Perifolliculitis (abscedens) 704.8
  capitis, abscedens et suffodiens 704.8
  dissecting, scalp 704.8
  scalp 704.8
  superficial pustular 704.8
Perigastritis (acute) 535.0
Perigastrojejunitis (acute) 535.0
Perihepatitis (acute) 573.3
  chlamydial 099.56
  gonococcal 098.86
Peri-ileitis (subacute) 569.89
Perilabyrinthitis (acute)—*see* Labyrinthitis
Perimeningitis —*see* Meningitis
Perimetritis (*see also* Endometritis) 615.9
Perimetrosalpingitis (*see also*
    Salpingo-oophoritis) 614.2
Perinephric —*see* condition
Perinephritic —*see* condition
Perinephritis (*see also* Infection, kidney) 590.9
  purulent (*see also* Abscess, kidney) 590.2
Perineum, perineal —*see* condition

Person—*continued*
  concern (normal) about sick person in family V61.49
  consulting on behalf of another V65.1
  feared
    complaint in whom no diagnosis was made V65.5
    condition not demonstrated V65.5
  feigning illness V65.2
  healthy, accompanying sick person V65.0
  living (in)
    alone V60.3
    boarding school V60.6
    residence remote from hospital or medical care facility V63.0
    residential institution V60.6
    without
      adequate
        financial resources V60.2
          housing (heating) (space) V60.1
        housing (permanent) (temporary) V60.0
        material resources V60.2
        person able to render necessary care V60.4
        shelter V60.0
  medical services in home not available V63.1
  on waiting list V63.2
    undergoing social agency investigation V63.8
  sick or handicapped in family V61.49
  "worried well" V65.5
Personality
  affective 301.10
  aggressive 301.3
  amoral 301.7
  anancastic, anankastic 301.4
  antisocial 301.7
  asocial 301.7
  asthenic 301.6
  avoidant 301.82
  borderline 301.83
  change 310.1
  compulsive 301.4
  cycloid 301.13
  cyclothymic 301.13
  dependent 301.6
  depressive (chronic) 301.12
  disorder, disturbance NEC 301.9
    with
      antisocial disturbance 301.7
      pattern disturbance NEC 301.9
      sociopathic disturbance 301.7
      trait disturbance 301.9
  dual 300.14
  dyssocial 301.7
  eccentric 301.89
    "haltlose" type 301.89
  emotionally unstable 301.59
  epileptoid 301.3
  explosive 301.3
  fanatic 301.0
  histrionic 301.50
  hyperthymic 301.11
  hypomanic 301.11
  hypothymic 301.12
  hysterical 301.50
  immature 301.89
  inadequate 301.6
  labile 301.59
  masochistic 301.89
  morally defective 301.7
  multiple 300.14
  narcissistic 301.81

Personality—*continued*
  obsessional 301.4
  obsessive (-compulsive) 301.4
  overconscientious 301.4
  paranoid 301.0
  passive (-dependent) 301.6
  passive-aggressive 301.84
  pathologic NEC 301.9
  pattern defect or disturbance 301.9
  pseudosocial 301.7
  psychoinfantile 301.59
  psychoneurotic NEC 301.89
  psychopathic 301.9
    with
      amoral trend 301.7
      antisocial trend 301.7
      asocial trend 301.7
      pathologic sexuality (*see also* Deviation, sexual) 302.9
    mixed types 301.9
  schizoid 301.20
    introverted 301.21
    schizotypal 301.22
    with sexual deviation (*see also* Deviation, sexual) 302.9
    antisocial 301.7
    dyssocial 301.7
  type A 301.4
  unstable (emotional) 301.59
Perthes' disease (capital femoral osteochondrosis) 732.1
Pertussis (*see also* Whooping cough) 033.9
  vaccination, prophylactic (against) V03.6
Peruvian wart 088.0
Perversion, perverted
  appetite 307.52
    hysterical 300.11
  function
    pineal gland 259.8
    pituitary gland 253.9
      anterior lobe
        deficient 253.2
        excessive 253.1
      posterior lobe 253.6
    placenta—*see* Placenta, abnormal
  sense of smell or taste 781.1
    psychogenic 306.7
  sexual (*see also* Deviation, sexual) 302.9
Pervious, congenital —*see also* Imperfect, closure
  ductus arteriosus 747.0
Pes (congenital) (*see also* Talipes) 754.70
  abductus (congenital) 754.60
    acquired 736.79
  acquired NEC 736.79
    planus 734
  adductus (congenital) 754.79
    acquired 736.79
  cavus 754.71
    acquired 736.73
  planovalgus (congenital) 754.69
    acquired 736.79
  planus (acquired) (any degree) 734
    congenital 754.61
    rachitic 268.1
  valgus (congenital) 754.61
    acquired 736.79
  varus (congenital) 754.50
    acquired 736.79
Pest (*see also* Plague) 020.9

Phosphatemia 275.3
Phosphaturia 275.3
Photoallergic response 692.72
Photocoproporphyria 277.1
Photodermatitis (sun) 692.72
  light other than sun 692.82
Photokeratitis 370.24
Photo-ophthalmia 370.24
Photophobia 368.13
Photopsia 368.15
Photoretinitis 363.31
Photoretinopathy 363.31
Photosensitiveness (sun) 692.72
  light other than sun 692.82
Photosensitization (sun) skin 692.72
  light other than sun 692.82
Phototoxic response 692.72
Phrenitis 323.9
Phrynoderma 264.8
Phthiriasis (pubis) (any site) 132.2
  with any infestation classifiable to 132.0
    and 132.1 132.3
Phthirus infestation —*see* Phthiriasis
Phthisis (*see also* Tuberculosis) 011.9
  bulbi (infectional) 360.41
  colliers' 011.4
  cornea 371.05
  eyeball (due to infection) 360.41
  millstone makers' 011.4
  miners' 011.4
  potters' 011.4
  sandblasters' 011.4
  stonemasons' 011.4
Phycomycosis 117.7
Physalopteriasis 127.7
Physical therapy NEC V57.1
  breathing exercises V57.0
Physiological cup, optic papilla
  borderline, glaucoma suspect 365.00
  enlarged 377.14
  glaucomatous 377.14
Phytobezoar 938
  intestine 936
  stomach 935.2
Pian (*see also* Yaws) 102.9
Pianoma 102.1
Piarhemia, piarrhemia (*see also* Hyperlipemia)
  272.4
  bilharziasis 120.9
Pica 307.52
  hysterical 300.11
Pick's
  cerebral atrophy 331.1
    with dementia
      with behavioral disturbance 331.1 *[294.11]*
      without behavioral disturbance 331.1
        [294.10]
  disease
    brain 331.1
      dementia in
        with behavioral disturbance 331.1 *[294.11]*
        without behavioral disturbance 331.1
          [294.10]
    lipid histiocytosis 272.7
    liver (pericardial pseudocirrhosis of liver)
      423.2
    pericardium (pericardial pseudocirrhosis of
      liver) 423.2
    polyserositis (pericardial pseudocirrhosis of
      liver) 423.2

Pick's—*continued*
  syndrome
    heart (pericardial pseudocirrhosis of liver)
      423.2
    liver (pericardial pseudocirrhosis of liver)
      423.2
  tubular adenoma (M8640/0)
    specified site—*see* Neoplasm, by site, benign
    unspecified site
      female 220
      male 222.0
Pick-Herxheimer syndrome (diffuse idiopathic
  cutaneous atrophy) 701.8
Pick-Niemann disease (lipid histiocytosis) 272.7
Pickwickian syndrome (cardiopulmonary
  obesity) 278.8
Piebaldism, classic 709.09
Piedra 111.2
  beard 111.2
    black 111.3
    white 111.2
  black 111.3
  scalp 111.3
    black 111.3
    white 111.2
  white 111.2
Pierre Marie's syndrome (pulmonary
  hypertrophic osteoarthropathy) 731.2
Pierre Marie-Bamberger syndrome
  (hypertrophic pulmonary osteoarthropathy)
  731.2
Pierre Mauriac's syndrome
  (diabetes-dwarfism-obesity) 258.1
Pierre Robin deformity or syndrome
  (congenital) 756.0
Pierson's disease or osteochondrosis 732.1
Pigeon
  breast or chest (acquired) 738.3
    congenital 754.82
    rachitic (*see also* Rickets) 268.0
  breeders' disease or lung 495.2
  fanciers' disease or lung 495.2
  toe 735.8
Pigmentation (abnormal) 709.00
  anomaly 709.00
    congenital 757.33
    specified NEC 709.09
  conjunctiva 372.55
  cornea 371.10
    anterior 371.11
    posterior 371.13
    stromal 371.12
  lids (congenital) 757.33
    acquired 374.52
  limbus corneae 371.10
  metals 709.00
  optic papilla, congenital 743.57
  retina (congenital) (grouped) (nevoid) 743.53
    acquired 362.74
  scrotum, congenital 757.33
Piles —*see* Hemorrhoids
Pili
  annulati or torti (congenital) 757.4
  incarnati 704.8
Pill roller hand (intrinsic) 736.09
Pilomatrixoma (M8110/0)—*see* Neoplasm, skin,
  benign
Pilonidal —*see* condition
Pimple 709.8
Pinched nerve —*see* Neuropathy, entrapment
Pineal body or gland —*see* condition
Pinealoblastoma (M9362/3) 194.4

Pinealoma (M9360/1) 237.1
  malignant (M9360/3) 194.4
Pineoblastoma (M9362/3) 194.4
Pineocytoma (M9361/1) 237.1
Pinguecula 372.51
Pinhole meatus (*see also* Stricture, urethra) 598.9
Pink
  disease 985.0
  eye 372.03
  puffer 492.8
Pinkus' disease (lichen nitidus) 697.1
Pinpoint
  meatus (*see also* Stricture, urethra) 598.9
  os (uteri) (*see also* Stricture, cervix) 622.4
Pinselhaare (congenital) 757.4
Pinta 103.9
  cardiovascular lesions 103.2
  chancre (primary) 103.0
  erythematous plaques 103.1
  hyperchromic lesions 103.1
  hyperkeratosis 103.1
  lesions 103.9
    cardiovascular 103.2
    hyperchromic 103.1
    intermediate 103.1
    late 103.2
    mixed 103.3
    primary 103.0
    skin (achromic) (cicatricial) (dyschromic) 103.2
      hyperchromic 103.1
      mixed (achromic and hyperchromic) 103.3
  papule (primary) 103.0
  skin lesions (achromic) (cicatricial) (dyschromic) 103.2
    hyperchromic 103.1
    mixed (achromic and hyperchromic) 103.3
  vitiligo 103.2
Pintid 103.0
Pinworms (disease) (infection) (infestation) 127.4
Piry fever 066.8
Pistol wound —*see* Gunshot wound
Pit, lip (mucus), congenital 750.25
Pitchers' elbow 718.82
Pithecoid pelvis 755.69
  with disproportion (fetopelvic) 653.2
    affecting fetus or newborn 763.1
    causing obstructed labor 660.1
Pithiatism 300.11
Pitted —*see also* Pitting
  teeth 520.4
Pitting (edema) (*see also* Edema) 782.3
  lip 782.3
  nail 703.8
    congenital 757.5
Pituitary gland —*see* condition
Pituitary snuff-takers' disease 495.8
Pityriasis 696.5
  alba 696.5
  capitis 690.11
  circinata (et maculata) 696.3
  Hebra's (exfoliative dermatitis) 695.89
  lichenoides et varioliformis 696.2
  maculata (et circinata) 696.3
  nigra 111.1
  pilaris 757.39
    acquired 701.1
    Hebra's 696.4
  rosea 696.3
  rotunda 696.3

Pityriasis—*continued*
  rubra (Hebra) 695.89
    pilaris 696.4
  sicca 690.18
  simplex 690.18
  specified type NEC 696.5
  streptogenes 696.5
  versicolor 111.0
    scrotal 111.0
Placenta, placental
  ablatio 641.2
    affecting fetus or newborn 762.1
  abnormal, abnormality 656.7
    with hemorrhage 641.8
      affecting fetus or newborn 762.1
    affecting fetus or newborn 762.2
  abruptio 641.2
    affecting fetus or newborn 762.1
  accessory lobe—*see* Placenta, abnormal
  accreta (without hemorrhage) 667.0
    with hemorrhage 666.0
  adherent (without hemorrhage) 667.0
    with hemorrhage 666.0
  apoplexy—*see* Placenta, separation
  battledore—*see* Placenta, abnormal
  bilobate—*see* Placenta, abnormal
  bipartita—*see* Placenta, abnormal
  carneous mole 631
  centralis—*see* Placenta, previa
  circumvallata—*see* Placenta, abnormal
  cyst (amniotic)—*see* Placenta, abnormal
  deficiency—*see* Placenta insufficiency
  degeneration—*see* Placenta, insufficiency
  detachment (partial) (premature) (with hemorrhage) 641.2
    affecting fetus or newborn 762.1
  dimidiata—*see* Placenta, abnormal
  disease 656.7
    affecting fetus or newborn 762.2
  duplex—*see* Placenta, abnormal
  dysfunction—*see* Placenta, insufficiency
  fenestrata—*see* Placenta, abnormal
  fibrosis—*see* Placenta, abnormal
  fleshy mole 631
  hematoma—*see* Placenta, abnormal
  hemorrhage NEC—*see* Placenta, separation
  hormone disturbance or malfunction—*see* Placenta, abnormal
  hyperplasia—*see* Placenta, abnormal
  increta (without hemorrhage) 667.0
    with hemorrhage 666.0
  infarction 656.7
    affecting fetus or newborn 762.2
  insertion, vicious—*see* Placenta, previa
  insufficiency
    affecting
      fetus or newborn 762.2
      management of pregnancy 656.5
  lateral—*see* Placenta, previa
  low implantation or insertion—*see* Placenta, previa
  low-lying—*see* Placenta, previa
  malformation—*see* Placenta, abnormal
  malposition—*see* Placenta, previa
  marginalis, marginata—*see* Placenta, previa
  marginal sinus (hemorrhage) (rupture) 641.2
    affecting fetus or newborn 762.1
  membranacea—*see* Placenta, abnormal
  multilobed—*see* Placenta, abnormal
  multipartita—*see* Placenta, abnormal
  necrosis—*see* Placenta, abnormal

Placenta, placental—*continued*
  percreta (without hemorrhage) 667.0
    with hemorrhage 666.0
  polyp 674.4
  previa (central) (centralis) (complete) (lateral)
    (marginal) (marginalis) (partial) (partialis)
    (total) (with hemorrhage) 641.1
    affecting fetus or newborn 762.0
    noted
      before labor, without hemorrhage (with
        cesarean delivery) 641.0
      during pregnancy (without hemorrhage)
        641.0
      without hemorrhage (before labor and
        delivery) (during pregnancy) 641.0
  retention (with hemorrhage) 666.0
    fragments, complicating puerperium (delayed
      hemorrhage) 666.2
      without hemorrhage 667.1
    postpartum, puerperal 666.2
    without hemorrhage 667.0
  separation (normally implanted) (partial)
    (premature) (with hemorrhage) 641.2
    affecting fetus or newborn 762.1
  septuplex—*see* Placenta, abnormal
  small—*see* Placenta, insufficiency
  softening (premature)—*see* Placenta, abnormal
  spuria—*see* Placenta, abnormal
  succenturiata—*see* Placenta, abnormal
  syphilitic 095.8
  transfusion syndromes 762.3
  transmission of chemical substance—*see*
    Absorption, chemical, through placenta
  trapped (with hemorrhage) 666.0
    without hemorrhage 667.0
  trilobate—*see* Placenta, abnormal
  tripartita—*see* Placenta, abnormal
  triplex—*see* Placenta, abnormal
  varicose vessel—*see* Placenta, abnormal
  vicious insertion—*see* Placenta, previa
Placentitis
  affecting fetus or newborn 762.7
  complicating pregnancy 658.4
Plagiocephaly (skull) 754.0
Plague 020.9
  abortive 020.8
  ambulatory 020.8
  bubonic 020.0
  cellulocutaneous 020.1
  lymphatic gland 020.0
  pneumonic 020.5
    primary 020.3
    secondary 020.4
  pulmonary—*see* Plague, pneumonic
  pulmonic—*see* Plague, pneumonic
  septicemic 020.2
  tonsillar 020.9
    septicemic 020.2
  vaccination, prophylactic (against) V03.3
Planning, family V25.09
  contraception V25.9
  procreation V26.4
Plaque
  artery, arterial—*see* Arteriosclerosis
  calcareous—*see* Calcification
  Hollenhorst's (retinal) 362.33
  tongue 528.6
Plasma cell myeloma 203.0

Plasmacytoma, plasmocytoma (solitary)
  (M9731/1) 238.6
  benign (M9731/0)—*see* Neoplasm, by site,
    benign
  malignant (M9731/3) 203.8
Plasmacytosis 288.8
Plaster ulcer (*see also* Decubitus) 707.0
Platybasia 756.0
Platyonychia (congenital) 757.5
  acquired 703.8
Platypelloid pelvis 738.6
  with disproportion (fetopelvic) 653.2
    affecting fetus or newborn 763.1
    causing obstructed labor 660.1
      affecting fetus or newborn 763.1
  congenital 755.69
Platyspondylia 756.19
Plethora 782.62
  newborn 776.4
Pleura, pleural —*see* condition
Pleuralgia 786.52
Pleurisy (acute) (adhesive) (chronic) (costal)
  (diaphragmatic) (double) (dry) (fetid)
  (fibrinous) (fibrous) (interlobar) (latent) (lung)
  (old) (plastic) (primary) (residual) (sicca)
  (sterile) (subacute) (unresolved) (with
  adherent pleura) 511.0
  with
    effusion (without mention of cause) 511.9
      bacterial, nontuberculous 511.1
      nontuberculous NEC 511.9
        bacterial 511.1
      pneumococcal 511.1
      specified type NEC 511.8
      staphylococcal 511.1
      streptococcal 511.1
      tuberculous (*see also* Tuberculosis, pleura)
        012.0
        primary, progressive 010.1
    influenza, flu, or grippe 487.1
    tuberculosis—*see* Pleurisy, tuberculous
  encysted 511.8
  exudative (*see also* Pleurisy, with effusion)
    511.9
    bacterial, nontuberculous 511.1
  fibrinopurulent 510.9
    with fistula 510.0
  fibropurulent 510.9
    with fistula 510.0
  hemorrhagic 511.8
  influenzal 487.1
  pneumococcal 511.0
    with effusion 511.1
  purulent 510.9
    with fistula 510.0
  septic 510.9
    with fistula 510.0
  serofibrinous (*see also* Pleurisy, with effusion)
    511.9
    bacterial, nontuberculous 511.1
  seropurulent 510.9
    with fistula 510.0
  serous (*see also* Pleurisy, with effusion) 511.9
    bacterial, nontuberculous 511.1
  staphylococcal 511.0
    with effusion 511.1
  streptococcal 511.0
    with effusion 511.1
  suppurative 510.9
    with fistula 510.0

Pneumonia—*continued*
in
  actinomycosis 039.1
  anthrax 022.1 *[484.5]*
  aspergillosis 117.3 *[484.6]*
  candidiasis 112.4
  coccidioidomycosis 114.0
  cytomegalic inclusion disease 078.5 *[484.1]*
  histoplasmosis (*see also* Histoplasmosis)
    115.95
  infectious disease NEC 136.9 *[484.8]*
  measles 055.1
  mycosis, systemic NEC 117.9 *[484.7]*
  nocardiasis, nocardiosis 039.1
  ornithosis 073.0
  pneumocystosis 136.3
  psittacosis 073.0
  Q fever 083.0 *[484.8]*
  salmonellosis 003.22
  toxoplasmosis 130.4
  tularemia 021.2
  typhoid (fever) 002.0 *[484.8]*
  varicella 052.1
  whooping cough (*see also* Whooping cough)
    033.9 *[484.3]*
infective, acquired prenatally 770.0
influenzal (broncho) (lobar) (virus) 487.0
inhalation (*see also* Pneumonia, aspiration)
  507.0
  fumes or vapors (chemical) 506.0
interstitial 516.8
  with influenzal 487.0
  acute 136.3
  chronic (*see also* Fibrosis, lung) 515
  desquamative 516.8
  hypostatic 514
  lipoid 507.1
  lymphoid 516.8
  plasma cell 136.3
  pseudomonas 482.1
intrauterine (infective) 770.0
  aspiration 770.1
Klebsiella pneumoniae 482.0
Legionnaires' 482.84
lipid, lipoid (exogenous) (interstitial) 507.1
  endogenous 516.8
lobar (diplococcal) (disseminated) (double)
  (interstitial) (pneumococcal, any type) 481
  with influenza 487.0
  bacterial 482.9
    specified type NEC 482.89
  chronic (*see also* Fibrosis, lung) 515
  Escherichia coli (E. coli) 482.82
  Friedländer's bacillus 482.0
  Hemophilus influenzae (H. influenzae) 482.2
  hypostatic 514
  influenzal 487.0
  Klebsiella 482.0
  ornithosis 073.0
  Proteus 482.83
  pseudomonas 482.1
  psittacosis 073.0
  specified organism NEC 483.8
    bacterial NEC 482.89
  staphylococcal 482.40
    aureus 482.41
    specified type NEC 482.49
  streptococcal—*see* Pneumonia, streptococcal
  viral, virus (*see also* Pneumonia, viral) 480.9
lobular (confluent)—*see* Pneumonia, broncho-
Löffler's 518.3

Pneumonia—*continued*
  massive—*see* Pneumonia, lobar
  meconium 770.1
  metastatic NEC 038.8 *[484.8]*
  Mycoplasma (pneumoniae) 483.0
  necrotic 513.0
  nitrogen dioxide 506.9
  orthostatic 514
  parainfluenza virus 480.2
  parenchymatous (*see also* Fibrosis, lung) 515
  passive 514
  patchy—*see* Pneumonia, broncho
  Peptococcus 482.81
  Peptostreptococcus 482.81
  plasma cell 136.3
  pleurolobar—*see* Pneumonia, lobar
  pleuropneumonia-like organism (PPLO) 483.0
  pneumococcal (broncho) (lobar) 481
  Pneumocystis (carinii) 136.3
  postinfectional NEC 136.9 *[484.8]*
  postmeasles 055.1
  postoperative 997.3
  primary atypical 486
  Proprionibacterium 482.81
  Proteus 482.83
  pseudomonas 482.1
  psittacosis 073.0
  radiation 508.0
  respiratory syncytial virus 480.1
  resulting from a procedure 997.3
  rheumatic 390 *[517.1]*
  Salmonella 003.22
  segmented, segmental—*see* Pneumonia,
    broncho-
  Serratia (marcescens) 482.83
  specified
    bacteria NEC 482.89
    organism NEC 483.8
    virus NEC 480.8
  spirochetal 104.8 *[484.8]*
  staphylococcal (broncho) (lobar) 482.40
    aureus 482.41
    specified type NEC 482.49
  static, stasis 514
  streptococcal (broncho) (lobar) NEC 482.30
    Group
      A 482.31
      B 482.32
      specified NEC 482.39
    pneumoniae 481
    specified type NEC 482.39
  Streptococcus pneumoniae 481
  traumatic (complication) (early) (secondary)
    958.8
  tuberculous (any) (*see also* Tuberculosis) 011.6
  tularemic 021.2
  TWAR agent 483.1
  varicella 052.1
  Veillonella 482.81
  viral, virus (broncho) (interstitial) (lobar) 480.9
    with influenza, flu, or grippe 487.0
    adenoviral 480.0
    parainfluenza 480.2
    respiratory syncytial 480.1
    specified type NEC 480.8
  white (congenital) 090.0
Pneumonic —*see* condition
Pneumonitis (acute) (primary) (*see also*
  Pneumonia) 486
allergic 495.9
  specified type NEC 495.8

Pneumonitis—*continued*
  aspiration 507.0
    due to fumes or gases 506.0
    newborn 770.1
    obstetric 668.0
  chemical 506.0
    due to fumes or gases 506.0
  cholesterol 516.8
  chronic (*see also* Fibrosis, lung) 515
  congenital rubella 771.0
  due to
    fumes or vapors 506.0
    inhalation
      food (regurgitated), milk, vomitus 507.0
      oils, essences 507.1
      saliva 507.0
      solids, liquids NEC 507.8
    toxoplasmosis (acquired) 130.4
      congenital (active) 771.2 *[484.8]*
  eosinophilic 518.3
  fetal aspiration 770.1
  hypersensitivity 495.9
  interstitial (chronic) (*see also* Fibrosis, lung) 515
    lymphoid 516.8
  lymphoid, interstitial 516.8
  meconium 770.1
  postanesthetic
    correct substance properly administered 507.0
    obstetric 668.0
    overdose or wrong substance given 968.4
      specified anesthetic—*see* Table of drugs
        and chemicals
  postoperative 997.3
    obstetric 668.0
  radiation 508.0
  rubella, congenital 771.0
  "ventilation" 495.7
  wood-dust 495.8
Pneumonoconiosis —*see* Pneumoconiosis
Pneumoparotid 527.8
Pneumopathy NEC 518.89
  alveolar 516.9
    specified NEC 516.8
  due to dust NEC 504
  parietoalveolar 516.9
    specified condition NEC 516.8
Pneumopericarditis (*see also* Pericarditis) 423.9
  acute 420.90
Pneumopericardium —*see also* Pericarditis
  congenital 770.2
  fetus or newborn 770.2
  traumatic (post) (*see also* Pneumothorax,
    traumatic) 860.0
    with open wound into thorax 860.1
Pneumoperitoneum 568.89
  fetus or newborn 770.2
Pneumophagia (psychogenic) 306.4
Pneumopleurisy, pneumopleuritis (*see also*
  Pneumonia) 486
Pneumopyopericardium 420.99
Pneumopyothorax (*see also* Pyopneumothorax)
  510.9
  with fistula 510.0
Pneumorrhagia 786.3
  newborn 770.3
  tuberculous (*see also* Tuberculosis, pulmonary)
    011.9
Pneumosiderosis (occupational) 503
Pneumothorax (acute) (chronic) 512.8
  congenital 770.2

Pneumothorax—*continued*
  due to operative injury of chest wall or lung
    512.1
    accidental puncture or laceration 512.1
  fetus or newborn 770.2
  iatrogenic 512.1
  postoperative 512.1
  spontaneous 512.8
    fetus or newborn 770.2
    tension 512.0
  sucking 512.8
    iatrogenic 512.1
    postoperative 512.1
  tense valvular, infectional 512.0
  tension 512.0
    iatrogenic 512.1
    postoperative 512.1
    spontaneous 512.0
  traumatic 860.0
    with
      hemothorax 860.4
        with open wound into thorax 860.5
      open wound into thorax 860.1
  tuberculous (*see also* Tuberculosis) 011.7
Pocket (s)
  endocardial (*see also* Endocarditis) 424.90
  periodontal 523.8
Podagra 274.9
Podencephalus 759.89
Poikilocytosis 790.09
Poikiloderma 709.09
  Civatte's 709.09
  congenital 757.33
  vasculare atrophicans 696.2
Poikilodermatomyositis 710.3
Pointed ear 744.29
Poise imperfect 729.9
Poisoned —*see* Poisoning
Poisoning (acute)—*see also* Table of drugs and
  chemicals
  Bacillus, B.
    aertrycke (*see also* Infection, Salmonella)
      003.9
    botulinus 005.1
    cholerae (suis) (*see also* Infection,
      Salmonella) 003.9
    paratyphosus (*see also* Infection, Salmonella)
      003.9
    suipestifer (*see also* Infection, Salmonella)
      003.9
  bacterial toxins NEC 005.9
  berries, noxious 988.2
  blood (general)—*see* Septicemia
  botulism 005.1
  bread, moldy, mouldy—*see* Poisoning, food
  damaged meat—*see* Poisoning, food
  death-cap (Amanita phalloides) (Amanita
    verna) 988.1
  decomposed food—*see* Poisoning, food
  diseased food—*see* Poisoning, food
  drug—*see* Table of drugs and chemicals
  epidemic, fish, meat, or other food—*see*
    Poisoning, food
  fava bean 282.2
  fish (bacterial)—*see also* Poisoning, food
    noxious 988.0

Poisoning—*continued*
　food (acute) (bacterial) (diseased) (infected)
　　NEC 005.9
　　due to
　　　Bacillus
　　　　aertrycke (*see also* Poisoning, food, due to
　　　　　Salmonella) 003.9
　　　　botulinus 005.1
　　　　cereus 005.89
　　　　choleraesuis (*see also* Poisoning, food,
　　　　　due to Salmonella) 003.9
　　　　paratyphosus (*see also* Poisoning, food,
　　　　　due to Salmonella) 003.9
　　　　suipestifer (*see also* Poisoning, food, due
　　　　　to Salmonella) 003.9
　　　Clostridium 005.3
　　　　botulinum 005.1
　　　　perfringens 005.2
　　　　welchii 005.2
　　　Salmonella (aertrycke) (callinarum)
　　　　(choleraesuis) (enteritidis) (paratyphi)
　　　　(suipestifer) 003.9
　　　　with
　　　　　gastroenteritis 003.0
　　　　　localized infection(s) (*see also* Infection,
　　　　　　Salmonella) 003.20
　　　　　septicemia 003.1
　　　　　specified manifestation NEC 003.8
　　　specified bacterium NEC 005.89
　　　Staphylococcus 005.0
　　　Streptococcus 005.8
　　　Vibrio parahaemolyticus 005.4
　　　Vibrio vulnificus 005.81
　　noxious or naturally toxic 988.0
　　　berries 988.2
　　　fish 988.0
　　　mushroom 988.1
　　　plants NEC 988.2
　　ice cream—*see* Poisoning, food
　　ichthyotoxism (bacterial) 005.9
　　kreotoxism, food 005.9
　　malarial—*see* Malaria
　　meat—*see* Poisoning, food
　　mushroom (noxious) 988.1
　　mussel—*see also* Poisoning, food
　　　noxious 988.0
　　noxious foodstuffs (*see also* Poisoning, food,
　　　noxious) 988.9
　　　specified type NEC 988.8
　　plants, noxious 988.2
　　pork—*see also* Poisoning, food
　　　specified NEC 988.8
　　　Trichinosis 124
　　ptomaine—*see* Poisoning, food
　　putrefaction, food—*see* Poisoning, food
　　radiation 508.0
　　Salmonella (*see also* Infection, Salmonella)
　　　003.9
　　sausage—*see also* Poisoning, food
　　　Trichinosis 124
　　saxitoxin 988.0
　　shellfish—*see also* Poisoning, food
　　　noxious 988.0
　　Staphylococcus, food 005.0
　　toxic, from disease NEC 799.8
　　truffles—*see* Poisoning, food
　　uremic—*see* Uremia
　　uric acid 274.9
Poison ivy, oak, sumac or other plant
　dermatitis 692.6
Poker spine 720.0
Policeman's disease 729.2

Polioencephalitis (acute) (bulbar) (*see also*
　Poliomyelitis, bulbar) 045.0
　inferior 335.22
　influenzal 487.8
　superior hemorrhagic (acute) (Wernicke's) 265.1
　Wernicke's (superior hemorrhagic) 265.1
Polioencephalomyelitis (acute) (anterior)
　(bulbar) (*see also* Polioencephalitis) 045.0
Polioencephalopathy, superior hemorrhagic
　265.1
　with
　　beriberi 265.0
　　pellagra 265.2
Poliomeningoencephalitis —*see*
　Meningoencephalitis
Poliomyelitis (acute) (anterior) (epidemic) 045.9

*Note—Use the following fifth-digit
subclassification with category 045:*

0　poliovirus, unspecified type
1　poliovirus, type I
2　poliovirus, type II
3　poliovirus, type III

　with
　　paralysis 045.1
　　　bulbar 045.0
　　abortive 045.2
　　ascending 045.9
　　　progressive 045.9
　　bulbar 045.0
　　cerebral 045.0
　　chronic 335.21
　　congenital 771.2
　　contact V01.2
　　deformities 138
　　exposure to V01.2
　　late effect 138
　　nonepidemic 045.9
　　nonparalytic 045.2
　　old with deformity 138
　　posterior, acute 053.19
　　residual 138
　　sequelae 138
　　spinal, acute 045.9
　　syphilitic (chronic) 094.89
　　vaccination, prophylactic (against) V04.0
Poliosis (eyebrow) (eyelashes) 704.3
　circumscripta (congenital) 757.4
　　acquired 704.3
　congenital 757.4
Pollakiuria 788.41
　psychogenic 306.53
Pollinosis 477.0
Pollitzer's disease (hidradenitis suppurativa)
　705.83
Polyadenitis (*see also* Adenitis) 289.3
　malignant 020.0
Polyalgia 729.9
Polyangiitis (essential) 446.0
Polyarteritis (nodosa) (renal) 446.0
Polyarthralgia 719.49
　psychogenic 306.0
Polyarthritis, polyarthropathy NEC 716.59
　due to or associated with other specified
　　conditions—*see* Arthritis, due to or
　　associated with
　endemic (*see also* Disease, Kaschin-Beck) 716.0
　inflammatory 714.9
　　specified type NEC 714.89

Polyarthritis, polyarthropathy—*continued*
  juvenile (chronic) 714.30
    acute 714.31
  migratory—*see* Fever, rheumatic
  rheumatic 714.0
    fever (acute)—*see* Fever, rheumatic
Polycarential syndrome of infancy 260
Polychondritis (atrophic) (chronic) (relapsing) 733.99
Polycoria 743.46
Polycystic (congenital) (disease) 759.89
  degeneration, kidney—*see* Polycystic, kidney
  kidney (congenital) 753.12
    adult type (APKD) 753.13
    autosomal dominant 753.13
    autosomal recessive 753.14
    childhood type (CPKD) 753.14
    infantile type 753.14
  liver 751.62
  lung 518.89
    congenital 748.4
  ovary, ovaries 256.4
  spleen 759.0
Polycythemia (primary) (rubra) (vera) (M9950/1) 238.4
  acquired 289.0
  benign 289.0
    familial 289.6
  due to
    donor twin 776.4
    fall in plasma volume 289.0
    high altitude 289.0
    maternal-fetal transfusion 776.4
    stress 289.0
  emotional 289.0
  erythropoietin 289.0
  familial (benign) 289.6
  Gaisböck's (hypertonica) 289.0
  high altitude 289.0
  hypertonica 289.0
  hypoxemic 289.0
  neonatorum 776.4
  nephrogenous 289.0
  relative 289.0
  secondary 289.0
  spurious 289.0
  stress 289.0
Polycytosis cryptogenica 289.0
Polydactylism, polydactyly 755.00
  fingers 755.01
  toes 755.02
Polydipsia 783.5
Polydystrophic oligophrenia 277.5
Polyembryoma (M9072/3)—*see* Neoplasm, by site, malignant
Polygalactia 676.6
Polyglandular
  deficiency 258.9
  dyscrasia 258.9
  dysfunction 258.9
  syndrome 258.8
Polyhydramnios (*see also* Hydramnios) 657
Polymastia 757.6
Polymenorrhea 626.2
Polymicrogyria 742.2
Polymyalgia 725
  arteritica 446.5
  rheumatica 725

Polymyositis (acute) (chronic) (hemorrhagic) 710.4
  with involvement of
    lung 710.4 *[517.8]*
    skin 710.3
  ossificans (generalisata) (progressiva) 728.19
  Wagner's (dermatomyositis) 710.3
Polyneuritis, polyneuritic (*see also* Polyneuropathy) 356.9
  alcoholic 357.5
    with psychosis 291.1
  cranialis 352.6
  demyelinating, chronic inflammatory 357.8
  diabetic 250.6 *[357.2]*
  due to lack of vitamin NEC 269.2 *[357.4]*
  endemic 265.0 *[357.4]*
  erythredema 985.0
  febrile 357.0
  hereditary ataxic 356.3
  idiopathic, acute 357.0
  infective (acute) 357.0
  nutritional 269.9 *[357.4]*
  postinfectious 357.0
Polyneuropathy (peripheral) 356.9
  alcoholic 357.5
  amyloid 277.3 *[357.4]*
  arsenical 357.7
  diabetic 250.6 *[357.2]*
  due to
    antitetanus serum 357.6
    arsenic 357.7
    drug or medicinal substance 357.6
      correct substance properly administered 357.6
      overdose or wrong substance given or taken 977.9
      specified drug—*see* Table of drugs and chemicals
    lack of vitamin NEC 269.2 *[357.4]*
    lead 357.7
    organophosphate compounds 357.7
    pellagra 265.2 *[357.4]*
    porphyria 277.1 *[357.4]*
    serum 357.6
    toxic agent NEC 357.7
  hereditary 356.0
  idiopathic 356.9
    progressive 356.4
  in
    amyloidosis 277.3 *[357.4]*
    avitaminosis 269.2 *[357.4]*
      specified NEC 269.1 *[357.4]*
    beriberi 265.0 *[357.4]*
    collagen vascular disease NEC 710.9 *[357.1]*
    deficiency
      B-complex NEC 266.2 *[357.4]*
      vitamin B 266.9 *[357.4]*
      vitamin B_6 266.1 *[357.4]*
    diabetes 250.6 *[357.2]*
    diphtheria (*see also* Diphtheria) 032.89 *[357.4]*
    disseminated lupus erythematosus 710.0 *[357.1]*
    herpes zoster 053.13
    hypoglycemia 251.2 *[357.4]*
    malignant neoplasm (M8000/3) NEC 199.1 *[357.3]*
    mumps 072.72
    pellagra 265.2 *[357.4]*
    polyarteritis nodosa 446.0 *[357.1]*
    porphyria 277.1 *[357.4]*

Polyneuropathy—*continued*
  rheumatoid arthritis 714.0 *[357.1]*
  sarcoidosis 135 *[357.4]*
  uremia 585 *[357.4]*
  lead 357.7
  nutritional 269.9 *[357.4]*
    specified NEC 269.8 *[357.4]*
  postherpetic 053.13
  progressive 356.4
  sensory (hereditary) 356.2
Polyonychia 757.5
Polyopia 368.2
  refractive 368.15
Polyorchism, polyorchidism (three testes) 752.8
Polyorrhymenitis (peritoneal) (*see also*
    Polyserositis) 568.82
  pericardial 423.2
Polyostotic fibrous dysplasia 756.54
Polyotia 744.1
Polyp, polypus

> *Note—Polyps of organs or sites that do not appear in the list below should be coded to the residual category for diseases of the organ or site concerned.*

  accessory sinus 471.8
  adenoid tissue 471.0
  adenomatous (M8210/0)—*see also* Neoplasm,
    by site, benign
    adenocarcinoma in (M8210/3)—*see*
      Neoplasm, by site, malignant
    carcinoma in (M8210/3)—*see* Neoplasm, by
      site, malignant
    multiple (M8221/0)—*see* Neoplasm, by site,
      benign
  antrum 471.8
  anus, anal (canal) (nonadenomatous) 569.0
    adenomatous 211.4
  Bartholin's gland 624.6
  bladder (M8120/1) 236.7
  broad ligament 620.8—
  cervix (uteri) 622.7
    adenomatous 219.0
    in pregnancy or childbirth 654.6
      affecting fetus or newborn 763.89
      causing obstructed labor 660.2
    mucous 622.7
    nonneoplastic 622.7
  choanal 471.0
  cholesterol 575.6
  clitoris 624.6
  colon (M8210/0) (*see also* Polyp, adenomatous)
    211.3
  corpus uteri 621.0
  dental 522.0
  ear (middle) 385.30
  endometrium 621.0
  ethmoidal (sinus) 471.8
  fallopian tube 620.8
  female genital organs NEC 624.8
  frontal (sinus) 471.8
  gallbladder 575.6
  gingiva 523.8
  gum 523.8
  labia 624.6
  larynx (mucous) 478.4
  malignant (M8000/3)—*see* Neoplasm, by site,
    malignant
  maxillary (sinus) 471.8
  middle ear 385.30
  myometrium 621.0

Polyp, polypus—*continued*
  nares
    anterior 471.9
    posterior 471.0
  nasal (mucous) 471.9
    cavity 471.0
    septum 471.9
  nasopharyngeal 471.0
  neoplastic (M8210/0)—*see* Neoplasm, by site,
    benign
  nose (mucous) 471.9
  oviduct 620.8
  paratubal 620.8
  pharynx 478.29
    congenital 750.29
  placenta, placental 674.4
  prostate 600.2
  pudenda 624.6
  pulp (dental) 522.0
  rectosigmoid 211.4
  rectum (nonadenomatous) 569.0
    adenomatous 211.4
  septum (nasal) 471.9
  sinus (accessory) (ethmoidal) (frontal)
    (maxillary) (sphenoidal) 471.8
  sphenoidal (sinus) 471.8
  stomach (M8210/0) 211.1
  tube, fallopian 620.8
  turbinate, mucous membrane 471.8
  ureter 593.89
  urethra 599.3
  uterine
    ligament 620.8
    tube 620.8
  uterus (body) (corpus) (mucous) 621.0
    in pregnancy or childbirth 654.1
      affecting fetus or newborn 763.89
      causing obstructed labor 660.2
  vagina 623.7—
  vocal cord (mucous) 478.4
  vulva 624.6
Polyphagia 783.6
Polypoid —*see* condition
Polyposis —*see also* Polyp
  coli (adenomatous) (M8220/0) 211.3
    adenocarcinoma in (M8220/3) 153.9
    carcinoma in (M8220/3) 153.9
  familial (M8220/0) 211.3
  intestinal (adenomatous) (M8220/0) 211.3
  multiple (M8221/0)—*see* Neoplasm, by site,
    benign
Polyradiculitis (acute) 357.0
Polyradiculoneuropathy (acute) (segmentally
    demyelinating) 357.0
Polysarcia 278.00
Polyserositis (peritoneal) 568.82
  due to pericarditis 423.2
  paroxysmal (familial) 277.3
  pericardial 423.2
  periodic 277.3
  pleural—*see* Pleurisy
  recurrent 277.3
  tuberculous (*see also* Tuberculosis,
    polyserositis) 018.9
Polysialia 527.7
Polysplenia syndrome 759.0
Polythelia 757.6
Polytrichia (*see also* Hypertrichosis) 704.1
Polyunguia (congenital) 757.5
  acquired 703.8
Polyuria 788.42
Pompe's disease (glycogenosis II) 271.0

Postmenopausal
　endometrium (atrophic) 627.8
　　suppurative (*see also* Endometritis) 615.9
　hormone replacement therapy V07.4
　status (age related) (natural) V49.81
Postnasal drip —*see* Sinusitis
Postnatal —*see* condition
Postoperative —*see also* condition
　confusion state 293.9
　psychosis 293.9
　status NEC (*see also* Status (post)) V45.89
Postpancreatectomy hyperglycemia 251.3
Postpartum —*see also* condition
　observation
　　immediately after delivery V24.0
　　routine follow-up V24.2
Postperfusion syndrome NEC 999.8
　bone marrow 996.85
Postpoliomyelitic —*see* condition
Postsurgery status NEC (*see also* Status (post))
　V45.89
Post-term (pregnancy) 645.1
　infant (294 days or more gestation) 766.2
Posttraumatic —*see* condition
Posttraumatic brain syndrome, nonpsychotic
　310.2
Post-typhoid abscess 002.0
Postures, hysterical 300.11
Postvaccinal reaction or complication —*see*
　Complications, vaccination
Postvagotomy syndrome 564.2
Postvalvulotomy syndrome 429.4
Postvasectomy sperm count V25.8
Potain's disease (pulmonary edema) 514
Potain's syndrome (gastrectasis with dyspepsia)
　536.1
Pott's
　curvature (spinal) (*see also* Tuberculosis) 015.0
　　[737.43]
　disease or paraplegia (*see also* Tuberculosis)
　　015.0 *[730.88]*
　fracture (closed) 824.4
　　open 824.5
　gangrene 440.24
　osteomyelitis (*see also* Tuberculosis) 015.0
　　[730.88]
　spinal curvature (*see also* Tuberculosis) 015.0
　　[737.43]
　tumor, puffy (*see also* Osteomyelitis) 730.2
Potter's
　asthma 502
　disease 753.0
　facies 754.0
　lung 502
　syndrome (with renal agenesis) 753.0
Pouch
　bronchus 748.3
　Douglas'—*see* condition
　esophagus, esophageal (congenital) 750.4
　　acquired 530.6
　gastric 537.1
　Hartmann's (abnormal sacculation of
　　gallbladder neck) 575.8
　pharynx, pharyngeal (congenital) 750.27
Poulet's disease 714.2
Poultrymen's itch 133.8
Poverty V60.2
Prader-Labhart-Willi-Fanconi syndrome
　(hypogenital dystrophy with diabetic
　tendency) 759.81
Prader-Willi syndrome (hypogenital dystrophy
　with diabetic tendency) 759.81

Preachers' voice 784.49
Pre-AIDS —*see* Human immunodeficiency virus
　(disease) (illness) (infection)
Preauricular appendage 744.1
Prebetalipoproteinemia (acquired) (essential)
　(familial) (hereditary) (primary) (secondary)
　272.1
　with chylomicronemia 272.3
Precipitate labor 661.3
　affecting fetus or newborn 763.6
Preclimacteric bleeding 627.0
　menorrhagia 627.0
Precocious
　adrenarche 259.1
　menarche 259.1
　menstruation 626.8
　pubarche 259.1
　puberty NEC 259.1
　sexual development NEC 259.1
　thelarche 259.1
Precocity, sexual (constitutional) (cryptogenic)
　(female) (idiopathic) (male) NEC 259.1
　with adrenal hyperplasia 255.2
Precordial pain 786.51
　psychogenic 307.89
Predeciduous teeth 520.2
Prediabetes, prediabetic 790.2
　complicating pregnancy, childbirth, or
　　puerperium 648.8
　fetus or newborn 775.8
Predislocation status of hip, at birth (*see also*
　Subluxation, congenital, hip) 754.32
Pre-eclampsia (mild) 642.4
　with pre-existing hypertension 642.7
　affecting fetus or newborn 760.0
　severe 642.5
　superimposed on pre-existing hypertensive
　　disease 642.7
Preeruptive color change, teeth, tooth 520.8
Preexcitation 426.7
　atrioventricular conduction 426.7
　ventricular 426.7
Preglaucoma 365.00
Pregnancy (single) (uterine) (without sickness)
　V22.2

> *Note—Use the following fifth-digit*
> *subclassification with categories 640-648,*
> *651-676:*
>
> *0　unspecified as to episode of care*
> *1　delivered, with or without mention of*
> *　antepartum condition*
> *2　delivered, with mention of postpartum*
> *　complication*
> *3　antepartum condition or complication*
> *4　postpartum condition or complication*

　abdominal (ectopic) 633.0
　　affecting fetus or newborn 761.4
　abnormal NEC 646.9
　ampullar—*see* Pregnancy, tubal
　broad ligament—*see* Pregnancy, cornual
　cervical—*see* Pregnancy, cornual
　combined (extrauterine and intrauterine)—*see*
　　Pregnancy, cornual
　complicated (by) 646.9
　　abnormal, abnormality NEC 646.9
　　　cervix 654.6
　　　cord (umbilical) 663.9
　　　glucose tolerance (conditions classifiable to
　　　　790.2) 648.8

Pressure
- area, skin ulcer (*see also* Decubitus) 707.0
- atrophy, spine 733.99
- birth, fetus or newborn NEC 767.9
- brachial plexus 353.0
- brain 348.4
  - injury at birth 767.0
- cerebral—*see* Pressure, brain
- chest 786.59
- cone, tentorial 348.4
  - injury at birth 767.0
- funis—*see* Compression, umbilical cord
- hyposystolic (*see also* Hypotension) 458.9
- increased
  - intracranial 781.99
    - due to
      - benign intracranial hypertension 348.2
      - hydrocephalus—*see* hydrocephalus
      - injury at birth 767.8
    - intraocular 365.00
- lumbosacral plexus 353.1
- mediastinum 519.3
- necrosis (chronic) (skin) (*see also* Decubitus) 707.0
- nerve—*see* Compression, nerve
- paralysis (*see also* Neuropathy, entrapment) 355.9
- sore (chronic) (*see also* Decubitus) 707.0
- spinal cord 336.9
- ulcer (chronic) (*see also* Decubitus) 707.0
- umbilical cord—*see* Compression, umbilical cord
- venous, increased 459.89

Pre-syncope 780.2

Preterm infant NEC 765.1
- extreme 765.0

Priapism (penis) 607.3

Prickling sensation (*see also* Disturbance, sensation) 782.0

Prickly heat 705.1

Primary —*see* condition

Primigravida, elderly
- affecting
  - fetus or newborn 763.89
  - management of pregnancy, labor, and delivery 659.5

Primipara, old
- affecting
  - fetus or newborn 763.89
  - management of pregnancy, labor, and delivery 659.5

Primula dermatitis 692.6

Primus varus (bilateral) (metatarsus) 754.52

P.R.I.N.D. 436

Pringle's disease (tuberous sclerosis) 759.5

Prinzmetal's angina 413.1

Prinzmetal-Massumi syndrome (anterior chest wall) 786.52

Prizefighter ear 738.7

Problem (with) V49.9
- academic V62.3
- acculturation V62.4
- adopted child V61.29
- aged
  - in-law V61.3
  - parent V61.3
  - person NEC V61.8
- alcoholism in family V61.41
- anger reaction (*see also* Disturbance, conduct) 312.0
- behavior, child 312.9

Problem—*continued*
- behavioral V40.9
  - specified NEC V40.3
- betting V69.3
- cardiorespiratory NEC V47.2
- care of sick or handicapped person in family or household V61.49
- career choice V62.2
- communication V40.1
- conscience regarding medical care V62.6
- delinquency (juvenile) 312.9
- diet, inappropriate V69.1
- digestive NEC V47.3
- ear NEC V41.3
- eating habits, inappropriate V69.1
- economic V60.2
  - affecting care V60.9
    - specified type NEC V60.8
- educational V62.3
- enuresis, child 307.6
- exercise, lack of V69.0
- eye NEC V41.1
- family V61.9
  - specified circumstance NEC V61.8
- fear reaction, child 313.0
- feeding (elderly) (infant) 783.3
  - newborn 779.3
  - nonorganic 307.50
- fetal, affecting management of pregnancy 656.9
  - specified type NEC 656.8
- financial V60.2
- foster child V61.29
  - specified NEC V41.8
- functional V41.9
  - specified type NEC V41.8
- gambling V69.3
- genital NEC V47.5
- head V48.9
  - deficiency V48.0
  - disfigurement V48.6
  - mechanical V48.2
  - motor V48.2
  - movement of V48.2
  - sensory V48.4
  - specified condition NEC V48.8
- hearing V41.2
- high-risk sexual behavior V69.2
- influencing health status NEC V49.89
- internal organ NEC V47.9
  - deficiency V47.0
  - mechanical or motor V47.1
- interpersonal NEC V62.81
- jealousy, child 313.3
- learning V40.0
- legal V62.5
- life circumstance NEC V62.89
- lifestyle V69.9
  - specified NEC V69.8
- limb V49.9
  - deficiency V49.0
  - disfigurement V49.4
  - mechanical V49.1
  - motor V49.2
  - movement, involving
    - musculoskeletal system V49.1
    - nervous system V49.2
  - sensory V49.3
  - specified condition NEC V49.5
- litigation V62.5
- living alone V60.3
- loneliness NEC V62.89

Problem—*continued*
  marital V61.10
    involving
      divorce V61.0
      estrangement V61.0
      psychosexual disorder 302.9
      sexual function V41.7
  mastication V41.6
  medical care, within family V61.49
  mental V40.9
    specified NEC V40.2
  mental hygiene, adult V40.9
  multiparity V61.5
  nail biting, child 307.9
  neck V48.9
    deficiency V48.1
    disfigurement V48.7
    mechanical V48.3
    motor V48.3
    movement V48.3
    sensory V48.5
    specified condition NEC V48.8
  neurological NEC 781.99
  none (feared complaint unfounded) V65.5
  occupational V62.2
  parent-child V61.20
  partner V61.10
  personal NEC V62.89
    interpersonal conflict NEC V62.81
  personality (*see also* Disorder, personality)
    301.9
  phase of life V62.89
  placenta, affecting management of pregnancy
    656.9
    specified type NEC 656.8
  poverty V60.2
  presence of sick or handicapped person in
    family or household V61.49
  psychiatric 300.9
  psychosocial V62.9
    specified type NEC V62.89
  relational NEC V62.81
  relationship, childhood 313.3
  religious or spiritual belief
    other than medical care V62.89
    regarding medical care V62.6
  self-damaging behavior V69.8
  sexual
    behavior, high-risk V69.2
    function NEC V41.7
  sibling, relational V61.8
  sight V41.0
  sleep disorder, child 307.40
  smell V41.5
  speech V40.1
  spite reaction, child (*see also* Disturbance,
    conduct) 312.0
  spoiled child reaction (*see also* Disturbance,
    conduct) 312.1
  swallowing V41.6
  tantrum, child (*see also* Disturbance, conduct)
    312.1
  taste V41.5
  thumb sucking, child 307.9
  tic, child 307.21
  trunk V48.9
    deficiency V48.1
    disfigurement V48.7
    mechanical V48.3
    motor V48.3
    movement V48.3

Problem—*continued*
  sensory V48.5
  specified condition NEC V48.8
  unemployment V62.0
  urinary NEC V47.4
  voice production V41.4
Procedure (surgical) not done NEC V64.3
  because of
    contraindication V64.1
    patient's decision V64.2
      for reasons of conscience or religion V62.6
    specified reason NEC V64.3
Procidentia
  anus (sphincter) 569.1
  rectum (sphincter) 569.1
  stomach 537.89
  uteri 618.1
Proctalgia 569.42
  fugax 564.6
  spasmodic 564.6
    psychogenic 307.89
Proctitis 569.49
  amebic 006.8
  chlamydial 099.52
  gonococcal 098.7
  granulomatous 555.1
  idiopathic 556.2
    with ulcerative sigmoiditis 556.3
  tuberculous (*see also* Tuberculosis) 014.8
  ulcerative (chronic) (nonspecific) 556.2
    with ulcerative sigmoiditis 556.3
Proctocele
  female (without uterine prolapse) 618.0
    with uterine prolapse 618.4
      complete 618.3
      incomplete 618.2
  male 569.49
Proctocolitis, idiopathic 556.2
  with ulcerative sigmoiditis 556.3
Proctoptosis 569.1
Proctosigmoiditis 569.89
  ulcerative (chronic) 556.3
Proctospasm 564.6
  psychogenic 306.4
Prodromal-AIDS —*see* Human
  immunodeficiency virus (disease) (illness)
  (infection)
Profichet's disease or syndrome 729.9
Progeria (adultorum) (syndrome) 259.8
Prognathism (mandibular) (maxillary) 524.00
Progonoma (melanotic) (M9363/0)—*see*
  Neoplasm, by site, benign
Progressive —*see* condition
Prolapse, prolapsed
  anus, anal (canal) (sphincter) 569.1
  arm or hand, complicating delivery 652.7
    causing obstructed labor 660.0
      affecting fetus or newborn 763.1
    fetus or newborn 763.1
  bladder (acquired) (mucosa) (sphincter)
    congenital (female) (male) 756.71
    female 618.0
    male 596.8
  breast implant (prosthetic) 996.54
  cecostomy 569.69
  cecum 569.89
  cervix, cervical (stump) (hypertrophied) 618.1
    anterior lip, obstructing labor 660.2
      affecting fetus or newborn 763.1
    congenital 752.49
    postpartal (old) 618.1

Propulsion
eyeball 360.81
Prosecution, anxiety concerning V62.5
Prostate, prostatic —*see* condition
Prostatism 600.9
Prostatitis (congestive) (suppurative) 601.9
acute 601.0
cavitary 601.8
chlamydial 099.54
chronic 601.1
diverticular 601.8
due to Trichomonas (vaginalis) 131.03
fibrous 600.9
gonococcal (acute) 098.12
chronic or duration of 2 months or over 098.32
granulomatous 601.8
hypertrophic 600.0
specified type NEC 601.8
subacute 601.1
trichomonal 131.03
tuberculous (*see also* Tuberculosis) 016.5
[601.4]
Prostatocystitis 601.3
Prostatorrhea 602.8
Prostatoseminovesiculitis, trichomonal 131.03
Prostration 780.79
heat 992.5
anhydrotic 992.3
due to
salt (and water) depletion 992.4
water depletion 992.3
nervous 300.5
newborn 779.8
senile 797
Protanomaly 368.51
Protanopia (anomalous trichromat) (complete)
(incomplete) 368.51
Protein
deficiency 260
malnutrition 260
sickness (prophylactic) (therapeutic) 999.5
Proteinemia 790.99
Proteinosis
alveolar, lung or pulmonary 516.0
lipid 272.8
Proteinosis
lipoid (of Urbach) 272.8
Proteinuria (*see also* Albuminuria) 791.0
Bence-Jones NEC 791.0
gestational 646.2
with hypertension—*see* Toxemia, of
pregnancy
orthostatic 593.6
postural 593.6
Proteolysis, pathologic 286.6
Protocoproporphyria 277.1
Protoporphyria (erythrohepatic) (erythropoietic)
277.1
Protrusio acetabuli 718.65
Protrusion
acetabulum (into pelvis) 718.65
device, implant, or graft—*see* Complications,
mechanical
ear, congenital 744.29
intervertebral disc—*see* Displacement,
intervertebral disc
nucleus pulposus—*see* Displacement,
intervertebral disc
Proud flesh 701.5
Prune belly (syndrome) 756.71

Prurigo (ferox) (gravis) (Hebra's) (hebrae)
(mitis) (simplex) 698.2
agria 698.3
asthma syndrome 691.8
Besnier's (atopic dermatitis) (infantile eczema)
691.8
eczematodes allergicum 691.8
estivalis (Hutchinson's) 692.72
Hutchinson's 692.72
nodularis 698.3
psychogenic 306.3
Pruritus, pruritic 698.9
ani 698.0
psychogenic 306.3
conditions NEC 698.9
psychogenic 306.3
due to Onchocerca volvulus 125.3
ear 698.9
essential 698.9
genital organ(s) 698.1
psychogenic 306.3
gravidarum 646.8
hiemalis 698.8
neurogenic (any site) 306.3
perianal 698.0
psychogenic (any site) 306.3
scrotum 698.1
psychogenic 306.3
senile, senilis 698.8
Trichomonas 131.9
vulva, vulvae 698.1
psychogenic 306.3
Psammocarcinoma (M8140/3)—*see* Neoplasm,
by site, malignant
Pseudarthrosis, pseudoarthrosis (bone) 733.82
joint following fusion V45.4
Pseudoacanthosis
nigricans 701.8
Pseudoaneurysm —*see* Aneurysm
Pseudoangina (pectoris)—*see* Angina
Pseudoangioma 452
Pseudo-Argyll-Robertson pupil 379.45
Pseudoarteriosus 747.89
Pseudoarthrosis —*see* Pseudarthrosis
Pseudoataxia 799.8
Pseudobursa 727.89
Pseudocholera 025
Pseudochromidrosis 705.89
Pseudocirrhosis, liver, pericardial 423.2
Pseudocoarctation 747.21
Pseudocowpox 051.1
Pseudocoxalgia 732.1
Pseudocroup 478.75
Pseudocyesis 300.11
Pseudocyst
lung 518.89
pancreas 577.2
retina 361.19
Pseudodementia 300.16
Pseudoelephantiasis neuroarthritica 757.0
Pseudoemphysema 518.89
Pseudoencephalitis
superior (acute) hemorrhagic 265.1
Pseudoerosion cervix, congenital 752.49
Pseudoexfoliation, lens capsule 366.11
Pseudofracture (idiopathic) (multiple)
(spontaneous) (symmetrical) 268.2
Pseudoglanders 025
Pseudoglioma 360.44
Pseudogout —*see* Chondrocalcinosis
Pseudohallucination 780.1
Pseudohemianesthesia 782.0

Pseudohemophilia (Bernuth's) (hereditary) (type
B) 286.4
   type A 287.8
   vascular 287.8
Pseudohermaphroditism 752.7
   with chromosomal anomaly—*see* Anomaly,
      chromosomal
   adrenal 255.2
   female (without adrenocortical disorder) 752.7
      with adrenocortical disorder 255.2
      adrenal 255.2
   male (without gonadal disorder) 752.7
      with
         adrenocortical disorder 255.2
         cleft scrotum 752.7
         feminizing testis 257.8
         gonadal disorder 257.9
      adrenal 255.2
Pseudohole, macula 362.54
Pseudo-Hurler's disease (mucolipidosis III)
   272.7
Pseudohydrocephalus 348.2
Pseudohypertrophic muscular dystrophy
   (Erb's) 359.1
Pseudohypertrophy, muscle 359.1
Pseudohypoparathyroidism 275.49
Psuedopseudohypoparathyroidism 275.49
Pseudoinfluenza 487.1
Pseudoinsomnia 307.49
Pseudoleukemia 288.8
   infantile 285.8
Pseudomembranous —*see* condition
Pseudomeningocele (cerebral) (infective)
   (surgical) 349.2
   spinal 349.2
Pseudomenstruation 626.8
Pseudomucinous
   cyst (ovary) (M8470/0) 220
   peritoneum 568.89
Pseudomyeloma 273.1
Pseudomyxoma peritonei (M8480/6) 197.6
Pseudoneuritis optic (nerve) 377.24
   papilla 377.24
      congenital 743.57
Pseudoneuroma —*see* Injury, nerve, by site
Pseudo-obstruction
   intestine 564.89
Pseudopapilledema 377.24
Pseudoparalysis
   arm or leg 781.4
   atonic, congenital 358.8
Pseudopelade 704.09
Pseudophakia V43.1
Pseudopolycythemia 289.0
Pseudopolyposis, colon 556.4
Pseudoporencephaly 348.0
Pseudopseudohypoparathyroidism 275.49
Pseudopsychosis 300.16
Pseudopterygium 372.52
Pseudoptosis (eyelid) 374.34
Pseudorabies 078.89
Pseudoretinitis, pigmentosa 362.65
Pseudorickets 588.0
   senile (Pozzi's) 731.0
Pseudorubella 057.8
Pseudoscarlatina 057.8
Pseudosclerema 778.1

Pseudosclerosis (brain)
   Jakob's 046.1
   of Westphal (-Strümpell) (hepatolenticular
      degeneration) 275.1
   spastic 046.1
      with dementia
         with behavioral disturbance 046.1 *[294.11]*
         without behavioral disturbance 046.1
            [294.10]
Pseudoseizure 780.39
   non-psychiatric 780.39
   psychiatric 300.11
Pseudotabes 799.8
   diabetic 250.6 *[337.1]*
Pseudotetanus (*see also* Convulsions) 780.39
Pseudotetany 781.7
   hysterical 300.11
Pseudothalassemia 285.0
Pseudotrichinosis 710.3
Pseudotruncus arteriosus 747.29
Pseudotuberculosis, pasteurella (infection)
   027.2
Pseudotumor
   cerebri 348.2
   orbit (inflammatory) 376.11
Pseudo-Turner's syndrome 759.89
Pseudoxanthoma elasticum 757.39
Psilosis (sprue) (tropical) 579.1
   Monilia 112.89
   nontropical 579.0
   not sprue 704.00
Psittacosis 073.9
Psoitis 728.89
Psora NEC 696.1
Psoriasis 696.1
   any type, except arthropathic 696.1
   arthritic, arthropathic 696.0
   buccal 528.6
   flexural 696.1
   follicularis 696.1
   guttate 696.1
   inverse 696.1
   mouth 528.6
   nummularis 696.1
   psychogenic 316 *[696.1]*
   punctata 696.1
   pustular 696.1
   rupioides 696.1
   vulgaris 696.1
Psorospermiasis 136.4
Psorospermosis 136.4
   follicularis (vegetans) 757.39
Psychalgia 307.80
Psychasthenia 300.89
   compulsive 300.3
   mixed compulsive states 300.3
   obsession 300.3
Psychiatric disorder or problem NEC 300.9
Psychogenic —*see also* condition
   factors associated with physical conditions 316
Psychoneurosis, psychoneurotic (*see also*
   Neurosis) 300.9
   anxiety (state) 300.00
   climacteric 627.2
   compensation 300.16
   compulsion 300.3
   conversion hysteria 300.11
   depersonalization 300.6
   depressive type 300.4
   dissociative hysteria 300.15
   hypochondriacal 300.7

Note—Use the following fifth-digit
subclassification with categories 296.0-296.6:

0 unspecified
1 mild
2 moderate
3 severe, without mention of psychotic
*   behavior*
4 severe, specified as with psychotic behavior
5 in partial or unspecified remission
6 in full remission

Note—Use the following fifth-digit
subclassification with category 299:

0 current or active state
1 residual state

Psychosis—*continued*
  drug 292.9
    with
      affective syndrome 292.84
      amnestic syndrome 292.83
      anxiety 292.89
      delirium 292.81
        withdrawal 292.0
      delusional syndrome 292.11
      dementia 292.82
      depressive state 292.84
      hallucinosis 292.12
      mood disturbance 292.84
      organic personality syndrome NEC 292.89
      sexual dysfunction 292.89
      sleep disturbance 292.89
      withdrawal syndrome (and delirium) 292.0
    affective syndrome 292.84
    delusional state 292.11
    hallucinatory state 292.12
    hallucinosis 292.12
    paranoid state 292.11
    specified type NEC 292.89
    withdrawal syndrome (and delirium) 292.0
  due to or associated with physical condition (*see also* Psychosis, organic) 293.9
  epileptic NEC 294.8
  excitation (psychogenic) (reactive) 298.1
  exhaustive (*see also* Reaction, stress, acute) 308.9
  hypomanic (*see also* Psychosis, affective) 296.0
    recurrent episode 296.1
    single episode 296.0
  hysterical 298.8
    acute 298.1
  incipient 298.8
    schizophrenic (*see also* Schizophrenia) 295.5
  induced 297.3
  infantile (*see also* Psychosis, childhood) 299.0
  infective 293.9
    acute 293.0
    subacute 293.1
  in pregnancy, childbirth, or puerperium 648.4
  interactional (childhood) (*see also* Psychosis, childhood) 299.1
  involutional 298.8
    depressive (*see also* Psychosis, affective) 296.2
      recurrent episode 296.3
      single episode 296.2
    melancholic 296.2
      recurrent episode 296.3
      single episode 296.2
    paranoid state 297.2
    paraphrenia 297.2
  Korsakoff's, Korakov's, Korsakow's (nonalcoholic) 294.0
    alcoholic 291.1
  mania (phase) (*see also* Psychosis, affective) 296.0
    recurrent episode 296.1
    single episode 296.0
  manic (*see also* Psychosis, affective) 296.0
    atypical 296.81
    recurrent episode 296.1
    single episode 296.0
  manic-depressive 296.80
    circular 296.7
      currently
        depressed 296.5
        manic 296.4

Psychosis—*continued*
    mixed 296.6
    depressive 296.2
      recurrent episode 296.3
        with hypomania (bipolar II) 296.89
      single episode 296.2
    hypomanic 296.0
      recurrent episode 296.1
      single episode 296.0
    manic 296.0
      atypical 296.81
      recurrent episode 296.1
      single episode 296.0
    mixed NEC 296.89
    perplexed 296.89
    stuporous 296.89
  menopausal (*see also* Psychosis, involutional) 298.8
  mixed schizophrenic and affective (*see also* Schizophrenia) 295.7
  multi-infarct (cerebrovascular) (*see also* Psychosis, arteriosclerotic) 290.40
  organic NEC 294.9
    due to or associated with
      addiction
        alcohol (*see also* Psychosis, alcoholic) 291.9
        drug (*see also* Psychosis, drug) 292.9
      alcohol intoxication, acute (*see also* Psychosis, alcoholic) 291.9
      alcoholism (*see also* Psychosis, alcoholic) 291.9
      arteriosclerosis (cerebral) (*see also* Psychosis, arteriosclerotic) 290.40
      cerebrovascular disease
        acute (psychosis) 293.0
        arteriosclerotic (*see also* Psychosis, arteriosclerotic) 290.40
      childbirth—*see* Psychosis, puerperal
      dependence
        alcohol (*see also* Psychosis, alcoholic) 291.9
        drug 292.9
      disease
        alcoholic liver (*see also* Psychosis, alcoholic) 291.9
        brain
          arteriosclerotic (*see also* Psychosis, arteriosclerotic) 290.40
          cerebrovascular
            acute (psychosis) 293.0
            arteriosclerotic (*see also* Psychosis, arteriosclerotic) 290.40
        endocrine or metabolic 293.9
          acute (psychosis) 293.0
          subacute (psychosis) 293.1
        Jakob-Creutzfeldt
          with behavioral disturbance 046.1 *[294.11]*
          without behavioral disturbance 046.1 *[294.10]*
        liver, alcoholic (*see also* Psychosis, alcoholic) 291.9
      disorder
        cerebrovascular
          acute (psychosis) 293.0
        endocrine or metabolic 293.9
          acute (psychosis) 293.0
          subacute (psychosis) 293.1

Psychosis—*continued*
  epilepsy
    with behavioral disturbance 345.9 *[294.11]*
    without behavioral disturbance 345.9
      [294.10]
    transient (acute) 293.0
  Huntington's chorea
    with behavioral disturbance 333.4 *[294.11]*
    without behavioral disturbance 333.4
      [294.10]
  infection
    brain 293.9
      acute (psychosis) 293.0
      chronic 294.8
      subacute (psychosis) 293.1
    intracranial NEC 293.9
      acute (psychosis) 293.0
      chronic 294.8
      subacute (psychosis) 293.1
  intoxication
    alcoholic (acute) (*see also* Psychosis,
      alcoholic) 291.9
      pathological 291.4
    drug (*see also* Psychosis, drug) 292.9
  ischemia
    cerebrovascular (generalized) (*see also*
      Psychosis, arteriosclerotic) 290.40
  Jakob-Creutzfeldt disease or syndrome
    with behavioral disturbance 046.1 *[294.11]*
    without behavioral disturbance 046.1
      [294.10]
  multiple sclerosis
    with behavioral disturbance 340 *[294.11]*
    without behavioral disturbance 340
      [294.10]
  physical condition NEC 293.9
    with
      delusions 293.81
      hallucinations 293.82
  presenility 290.10
  puerperium—*see* Psychosis, puerperal
  sclerosis, multiple
    with behavioral disturbance 340 *[294.11]*
    without behavioral disturbance 340
      [294.10]
  senility 290.20
  status epilepticus
    with behavioral disturbance 345.3 *[294.11]*
    without behavioral disturbance 345.3
      [294.10]
  trauma
    brain (birth) (from electrical current)
      (surgical) 293.9
      acute (psychosis) 293.0
      chronic 294.8
      subacute (psychosis) 293.1
    unspecified physical condition 293.9
      with
        delusions 293.81
        hallucinations 293.82
  infective 293.9
    acute (psychosis) 293.0
    subacute 293.1
  posttraumatic 293.9
    acute 293.0
    subacute 293.1
  specified type NEC 294.8

Psychosis—*continued*
  transient 293.9
    with
      anxiety 293.84
      delusions 293.81
      depression 293.83
      hallucinations 293.82
    depressive type 293.83
    hallucinatory type 293.82
    paranoid type 293.81
    specified type NEC 293.89
  paranoic 297.1
  paranoid (chronic) 297.9
    alcoholic 291.5
    chronic 297.1
    climacteric 297.2
    involutional 297.2
    menopausal 297.2
    protracted reactive 298.4
    psychogenic 298.4
      acute 298.3
    schizophrenic (*see also* Schizophrenia) 295.3
    senile 290.20
  paroxysmal 298.9
    senile 290.20
  polyneuritic, alcoholic 291.1
  postoperative 293.9
  postpartum—*see* Psychosis, puerperal
  prepsychotic (*see also* Schizophrenia) 295.5
  presbyophrenic (type) 290.8
  presenile (*see also* Dementia, presenile) 290.10
  prison 300.16
  psychogenic 298.8
    depressive 298.0
    paranoid 298.4
      acute 298.3
  puerperal
    specified type—*see* categories 295-298
    unspecified type 293.89
      acute 293.0
      chronic 293.89
      subacute 293.1
  reactive (emotional stress) (psychological
    trauma) 298.8
    brief 298.8
    confusion 298.2
    depressive 298.0
    excitation 298.1
  schizo-affective (depressed) (excited) (*see also*
    Schizophrenia) 295.7
  schizophrenia, schizophrenic (*see also*
    Schizophrenia) 295.9
    borderline type 295.5
      of childhood (*see also* Psychosis, childhood)
        299.8
    catatonic (excited) (withdrawn) 295.2
    childhood type (*see also* Psychosis,
      childhood) 299.9
    hebephrenic 295.1
    incipient 295.5
    latent 295.5
    paranoid 295.3
    prepsychotic 295.5
    prodromal 295.5
    pseudoneurotic 295.5
    pseudopsychopathic 295.5
    schizophreniform 295.4
    simple 295.0
  schizophreniform 295.4

Psychosis—*continued*
  senile NEC 290.20
    with
      delusional features 290.20
      depressive features 290.21
    depressed type 290.21
    paranoid type 290.20
    simple deterioration 290.20
    specified type—*see* categories 295-298
  shared 297.3
  situational (reactive) 298.8
  symbiotic (childhood) (*see also* Psychosis,
    childhood) 299.1
  toxic (acute) 293.9
Psychotic (*see also* condition) 298.9
  episode 298.9
    due to or associated with physical conditions
      (*see also* Psychosis, organic) 293.9
Pterygium (eye) 372.40
  central 372.43
  colli 744.5
  double 372.44
  peripheral (stationary) 372.41
    progressive 372.42
  recurrent 372.45
Ptilosis 374.55
Ptomaine (poisoning) (*see also* Poisoning, food)
  005.9
Ptosis (adiposa) 374.30
  breast 611.8
  cecum 569.89
  colon 569.89
  congenital (eyelid) 743.61
    specified site NEC—*see* Anomaly, specified
      type NEC
  epicanthus syndrome 270.2
  eyelid 374.30
    congenital 743.61
    mechanical 374.33
    myogenic 374.32
    paralytic 374.31
  gastric 537.5
  intestine 569.89
  kidney (*see also* Disease, renal) 593.0
    congenital 753.3
  liver 573.8
  renal (*see also* Disease, renal) 593.0
    congenital 753.3
  splanchnic 569.89
  spleen 289.59
  stomach 537.5
  viscera 569.89
Ptyalism 527.7
  hysterical 300.11
  periodic 527.2
  pregnancy 646.8
  psychogenic 306.4
Ptyalolithiasis 527.5
Pubalgia 848.8
Pubarche, precocious 259.1
Pubertas praecox 259.1

Puberty V21.1
  abnormal 259.9
  bleeding 626.3
  delayed 259.0
  precocious (constitutional) (cryptogenic)
    (idiopathic) NEC 259.1
    due to
      adrenal
        cortical hyperfunction 255.2
          hyperplasia 255.2
      cortical hyperfunction 255.2
      ovarian hyperfunction 256.1
        estrogen 256.0
      pineal tumor 259.8
      testicular hyperfunction 257.0
  premature 259.1
    due to
      adrenal cortical hyperfunction 255.2
      pineal tumor 259.8
      pituitary (anterior) hyperfunction 253.1
Puckering, macula 362.56
Pudenda, pudendum —*see* condition
Puente's disease (simple glandular cheilitis)
  528.5
Puerperal
  abscess
    areola 675.1
    Bartholin's gland 646.6
    breast 675.1
    cervix (uteri) 670
    fallopian tube 670
    genital organ 670
    kidney 646.6
    mammary 675.1
    mesosalpinx 670
    nabothian 646.6
    nipple 675.0
    ovary, ovarian 670
    oviduct 670
    parametric 670
    para-uterine 670
    pelvic 670
    perimetric 670
    periuterine 670
    retro-uterine 670
    subareolar 675.1
    suprapelvic 670
    tubal (ruptured) 670
    tubo-ovarian 670
    urinary tract NEC 646.6
    uterine, uterus 670
    vagina (wall) 646.6
    vaginorectal 646.6
    vulvovaginal gland 646.6
  accident 674.9
  adnexitis 670
  afibrinogenemia, or other coagulation defect
    666.3
  albuminuria (acute) (subacute) 646.2
    pre-eclamptic 642.4
  anemia (conditions classifiable to 280-285)
    648.2
  anuria 669.3
  apoplexy 674.0
  asymptomatic bacteriuria 646.5
  atrophy, breast 676.3
  blood dyscrasia 666.3
  caked breast 676.2
  cardiomyopathy 674.8
  cellulitis—*see* Puerperal, abscess

Puerperal—*continued*
  cerebrovascular disorder (conditions classifiable
    to 430-434, 436-437) 674.0
  cervicitis (conditions classifiable to 616.0) 646.6
  coagulopathy (any) 666.3
  complications 674.9
    specified type NEC 674.8
  convulsions (eclamptic) (uremic) 642.6
    with pre-existing hypertension 642.7
  cracked nipple 676.1
  cystitis 646.6
  cystopyelitis 646.6
  deciduitis (acute) 670
  delirium NEC 293.9
  diabetes (mellitus) (conditions classifiable to
    250) 648.0
  disease 674.9
    breast NEC 676.3
    cerebrovascular (acute) 674.0
    nonobstetric NEC (*see also* Pregnancy,
      complicated, current disease or condition)
      648.9
    pelvis inflammatory 670
    renal NEC 646.2
    tubo-ovarian 670
    Valsuani's (progressive pernicious anemia)
      648.2
  disorder
    lactation 676.9
      specified type NEC 676.8
    nonobstetric NEC (*see also* Pregnancy,
      complicated, current disease or condition)
      648.9
  disruption
    cesarean wound 674.1
    episiotomy wound 674.2
    perineal laceration wound 674.2
  drug dependence (conditions classifiable to 304)
    648.3
  eclampsia 642.6
    with pre-existing hypertension 642.7
  embolism (pulmonary) 673.2
    air 673.0
    amniotic fluid 673.1
    blood-clot 673.2
    brain or cerebral 674.0
    cardiac 674.8
    fat 673.8
    intracranial sinus (venous) 671.5
    pyemic 673.3
    septic 673.3
    spinal cord 671.5
  endometritis (conditions classifiable to
    615.0-615.9) 670
  endophlebitis—*see* Puerperal, phlebitis
  endotrachelitis 646.6
  engorgement, breasts 676.2
  erysipelas 670
  failure
    lactation 676.4
    renal, acute 669.3
  fever 670
    meaning pyrexia (of unknown origin) 672
    meaning sepsis 670
  fissure, nipple 676.1
  fistula
    breast 675.1
    mammary gland 675.1
    nipple 675.0
  galactophoritis 675.2
  galactorrhea 676.6

Puerperal—*continued*
  gangrene
    gas 670
    uterus 670
  gonorrhea (conditions classifiable to 098) 647.1
  hematoma, subdural 674.0
  hematosalpinx, infectional 670
  hemiplegia, cerebral 674.0
  hemorrhage 666.1
    brain 674.0
    bulbar 674.0
    cerebellar 674.0
    cerebral 674.0
    cortical 674.0
    delayed (after 24 hours) (uterine) 666.2
    extradural 674.0
    internal capsule 674.0
    intracranial 674.0
    intrapontine 674.0
    meningeal 674.0
    pontine 674.0
    subarachnoid 674.0
    subcortical 674.0
    subdural 674.0
    uterine, delayed 666.2
    ventricular 674.0
  hemorrhoids 671.8
  hepatorenal syndrome 674.8
  hypertrophy
    breast 676.3
    mammary gland 676.3
  induration breast (fibrous) 676.3
  infarction
    lung—*see* Puerperal, embolism
    pulmonary—*see* Puerperal, embolism
  infection
    Bartholin's gland 646.6
    breast 675.2
      with nipple 675.9
        specified type NEC 675.8
    cervix 646.6
    endocervix 646.6
    fallopian tube 670
    generalized 670
    genital tract (major) 670
      minor or localized 646.6
    kidney (bacillus coli) 646.6
    mammary gland 675.2
      with nipple 675.9
        specified type NEC 675.8
    nipple 675.0
      with breast 675.9
        specified type NEC 675.8
    ovary 670
    pelvic 670
    peritoneum 670
    renal 646.6
    tubo-ovarian 670
    urinary (tract) NEC 646.6
      asymptomatic 646.5
    uterus, uterine 670
    vagina 646.6
  inflammation—*see also* Puerperal, infection
    areola 675.1
    Bartholin's gland 646.6
    breast 675.2
    broad ligament 670
    cervix (uteri) 646.6
    fallopian tube 670
    genital organs 670
      localized 646.6

Puerperal—*continued*
  mammary gland 675.2
  nipple 675.0
  ovary 670
  oviduct 670
  pelvis 670
  periuterine 670
  tubal 670
  vagina 646.6
  vein—*see* Puerperal, phlebitis
  inversion, nipple 676.3
  ischemia, cerebral 674.0
  lymphangitis 670
    breast 675.2
  malaria (conditions classifiable to 084) 647.4
  malnutrition 648.9
  mammillitis 675.0
  mammitis 675.2
  mania 296.0
    recurrent episode 296.1
    single episode 296.0
  mastitis 675.2
    purulent 675.1
    retromammary 675.1
    submammary 675.1
  melancholia 296.2
    recurrent episode 296.3
    single episode 296.2
  mental disorder (conditions classifiable to
    290-303, 305-316, 317-319) 648.4
  metritis (septic) (suppurative) 670
  metroperitonitis 670
  metrorrhagia 666.2
  metrosalpingitis 670
  metrovaginitis 670
  milk leg 671.4
  monoplegia, cerebral 674.0
  necrosis
    kidney, tubular 669.3
    liver (acute) (subacute) (conditions
      classifiable to 570) 674.8
    ovary 670
    renal cortex 669.3
  nephritis or nephrosis (conditions classifiable to
    580-589) 646.2
    with hypertension 642.1
  nutritional deficiency (conditions classifiable to
    260-269) 648.9
  occlusion, precerebral artery 674.0
  oliguria 669.3
  oophoritis 670
  ovaritis 670
  paralysis
    bladder (sphincter) 665.5
    cerebral 674.0
  paralytic stroke 674.0
  parametritis 670
  paravaginitis 646.6
  pelviperitonitis 670
  perimetritis 670
  perimetrosalpingitis 670
  perinephritis 646.6
  perioophoritis 670
  periphlebitis—*see* Puerperal, phlebitis
  perisalpingitis 670
  peritoneal infection 670
  peritonitis (pelvic) 670
  perivaginitis 646.6
  phlebitis 671.9
    deep 671.4
    intracranial sinus (venous) 671.5

Puerperal—*continued*
  pelvic 671.4
  specified site NEC 671.5
  superficial 671.2
  phlegmasia alba dolens 671.4
  placental polyp 674.4
  pneumonia, embolic—*see* Puerperal, embolism
  prediabetes 648.8
  pre-eclampsia (mild) 642.4
    with pre-existing hypertension 642.7
    severe 642.5
  psychosis, unspecified (*see also* Psychosis,
    puerperal) 293.89
  pyelitis 646.6
  pyelocystitis 646.6
  pyelohydronephrosis 646.6
  pyelonephritis 646.6
  pyelonephrosis 646.6
  pyemia 670
  pyocystitis 646.6
  pyohemia 670
  pyometra 670
  pyonephritis 646.6
  pyonephrosis 646.6
  pyo-oophoritis 670
  pyosalpingitis 670
  pyosalpinx 670
  pyrexia (of unknown origin) 672
  renal
    disease NEC 646.2
    failure, acute 669.3
  retention
    decidua (fragments) (with delayed
      hemorrhage) 666.2
      without hemorrhage 667.1
    placenta (fragments) (with delayed
      hemorrhage) 666.2
      without hemorrhage 667.1
    secundines (fragments) (with delayed
      hemorrhage) 666.2
      without hemorrhage 667.1
  retracted nipple 676.0
  rubella (conditions classifiable to 056) 647.5
  salpingitis 670
  salpingo-oophoritis 670
  salpingo-ovaritis 670
  salpingoperitonitis 670
  sapremia 670
  secondary perineal tear 674.2
  sepsis (pelvic) 670
  septicemia 670
  subinvolution (uterus) 674.8
  sudden death (cause unknown) 674.9
  suppuration—*see* Puerperal, abscess
  syphilis (conditions classifiable to 090-097)
    647.0
  tetanus 670
  thelitis 675.0
  thrombocytopenia 666.3
  thrombophlebitis (superficial) 671.2
    deep 671.4
    pelvic 671.4
    specified site NEC 671.5
  thrombosis (venous)—*see* Thrombosis,
    puerperal
  thyroid dysfunction (conditions classifiable to
    240-246) 648.1
  toxemia (*see also* Toxemia, of pregnancy) 642.4
    eclamptic 642.6
      with pre-existing hypertension 642.7
    pre-eclamptic (mild) 642.4

Puerperal—*continued*
   with
      convulsions 642.6
      pre-existing hypertension 642.7
      severe 642.5
   tuberculosis (conditions classifiable to 010-018) 647.3
   uremia 669.3
   vaginitis (conditions classifiable to 616.1) 646.6
   varicose veins (legs) 671.0
     vulva or perineum 671.1
   vulvitis (conditions classifiable to 616.1) 646.6
   vulvovaginitis (conditions classifiable to 616.1) 646.6
   white leg 671.4
Pulled muscle —*see* Sprain, by site
Pulmolithiasis 518.89
Pulmonary —*see* condition
Pulmonitis (unknown etiology) 486
Pulpitis (acute) (anachoretic) (chronic) (hyperplastic) (putrescent) (suppurative) (ulcerative) 522.0
Pulpless tooth 522.9
Pulse
   alternating 427.89
     psychogenic 306.2
   bigeminal 427.89
   fast 785.0
   feeble, rapid, due to shock following injury 958.4
   rapid 785.0
   slow 427.89
   strong 785.9
   trigeminal 427.89
   water-hammer (*see also* Insufficiency, aortic) 424.1
   weak 785.9
Pulseless disease 446.7
Pulsus
   alternans or trigeminy 427.89
     psychogenic 306.2
Punch drunk 310.2
Puncta lacrimalia occlusion 375.52
Punctiform hymen 752.49
Puncture (traumatic)—*see also* Wound, open, by site
   accidental, complicating surgery 998.2
   bladder, nontraumatic 596.6
   by
     device, implant, or graft—*see* Complications, mechanical
     foreign body
       internal organs—*see also* Injury, internal, by site
       by ingested object—*see* Foreign body
     left accidentally in operation wound 998.4
     instrument (any) during a procedure, accidental 998.2
   internal organs, abdomen, chest, or pelvis—*see* Injury, internal, by site
   kidney, nontraumatic 593.89
Pupil —*see* condition
Pupillary membrane 364.74
   persistent 743.46
Pupillotonia 379.46
   pseudotabetic 379.46
Purpura 287.2
   abdominal 287.0
   allergic 287.0
   anaphylactoid 287.0
   annularis telangiectodes 709.1

Purpura—*continued*
   arthritic 287.0
   autoerythrocyte sensitization 287.2
   autoimmune 287.0
   bacterial 287.0
   Bateman's (senile) 287.2
   capillary fragility (hereditary) (idiopathic) 287.8
   cryoglobulinemic 273.2
   devil's pinches 287.2
   fibrinolytic (*see also* Fibrinolysis) 286.6
   fulminans, fulminous 286.6
   gangrenous 287.0
   hemorrhagic (*see also* Purpura, thrombocytopenic) 287.3
     nodular 272.7
     nonthrombocytopenic 287.0
     thrombocytopenic 287.3
   Henoch's (purpura nervosa) 287.0
   Henoch-Schönlein (allergic) 287.0
   hypergammaglobulinemic (benign primary) (Waldenström's) 273.0
   idiopathic 287.3
     nonthrombocytopenic 287.0
     thrombocytopenic 287.3
   infectious 287.0
   malignant 287.0
   neonatorum 772.6
   nervosa 287.0
   newborn NEC 772.6
   nonthrombocytopenic 287.2
     hemorrhagic 287.0
     idiopathic 287.0
   nonthrombopenic 287.2
   peliosis rheumatica 287.0
   pigmentaria, progressiva 709.09
   posttransfusion 287.4
   primary 287.0
   primitive 287.0
   red cell membrane sensitivity 287.2
   rheumatica 287.0
   Schönlein (-Henoch) (allergic) 287.0
   scorbutic 267
   senile 287.2
   simplex 287.2
   symptomatica 287.0
   telangiectasia annularis 709.1
   thrombocytopenic (congenital) (essential) (hereditary) (idiopathic) (primary) (*see also* Thrombocytopenia) 287.3
     neonatal, transitory (*see also* Thrombocytopenia, neonatal transitory) 776.1
     puerperal, postpartum 666.3
     thrombotic 446.6
   thrombohemolytic (*see also* Fibrinolysis) 286.6
   thrombopenic (congenital) (essential) (*see also* Thrombocytopenia) 287.3
   thrombotic 446.6
     thrombocytic 446.6
     thrombocytopenic 446.6
   toxic 287.0
   variolosa 050.0
   vascular 287.0
   visceral symptoms 287.0
   Werlhof's (*see also* Purpura, thrombocytopenic) 287.3
Purpuric spots 782.7
Purulent —*see* condition

Pus
  absorption, general—*see* Septicemia
  in
    stool 792.1
    urine 791.9
  tube (rupture) (*see also* Salpingo-oophoritis)
    614.2
Pustular rash 782.1
Pustule 686.9
  malignant 022.0
  nonmalignant 686.9
Putnam's disease (subacute combined sclerosis
  with pernicious anemia) 281.0 *[336.2]*
Putnam-Dana syndrome (subacute combined
  sclerosis with pernicious anemia) 281.0
  [336.2]
Putrefaction, intestinal 569.89
Putrescent pulp (dental) 522.1
Pyarthritis —*see* Pyarthrosis
Pyarthrosis (*see also* Arthritis, pyogenic) 711.0
  tuberculous—*see* Tuberculosis, joint
Pycnoepilepsy, pycnolepsy (idiopathic) (*see also*
  Epilepsy) 345.0
Pyelectasia 593.89
Pyelectasis 593.89
Pyelitis (congenital) (uremic) 590.80
  with
    abortion—*see* Abortion, by type, with
      specified complication NEC
    contracted kidney 590.00
    ectopic pregnancy (*see also* categories
      633.0-633.9) 639.8
    molar pregnancy (*see also* categories
      630-632) 639.8
  acute 590.10
    with renal medullary necrosis 590.11
  chronic 590.00
    with
      renal medullary necrosis 590.01
  complicating pregnancy, childbirth, or
    puerperium 646.6
    affecting fetus or newborn 760.1
  cystica 590.3
  following
    abortion 639.8
    ectopic or molar pregnancy 639.8
  gonococcal 098.19
    chronic or duration of 2 months or over 098.39
  tuberculous (*see also* Tuberculosis) 016.0
    [590.81]
Pyelocaliectasis 593.89
Pyelocystitis (*see also* Pyelitis) 590.80
Pyelohydronephrosis 591
Pyelonephritis (*see also* Pyelitis) 590.80
  acute 590.10
    with renal medullary necrosis 590.11
  chronic 590.00
  syphilitic (late) 095.4
  tuberculous (*see also* Tuberculosis) 016.0
    [590.81]
Pyelonephrosis (*see also* Pyelitis) 590.80
  chronic 590.00
Pyelophlebitis 451.89
Pyelo-ureteritis cystica 590.3

Pyemia, pyemic (purulent) (*see also* Septicemia)
  038.9
  abscess—*see* Abscess
  arthritis (*see also* Arthritis, pyogenic) 711.0
  Bacillus coli 038.42
  embolism—*see* Embolism, pyemic
  fever 038.9
  infection 038.9
  joint (*see also* Arthritis, pyogenic) 711.0
  liver 572.1
  meningococcal 036.2
  newborn 771.8
  phlebitis—*see* Phlebitis
  pneumococcal 038.2
  portal 572.1
  postvaccinal 999.3
  specified organism NEC 038.8
  staphylococcal 038.10
    aureus 038.11
    specified organism NEC 038.19
  streptococcal 038.0
  tuberculous—*see* Tuberculosis, miliary
Pygopagus 759.4
Pykno-epilepsy, pyknolepsy (idiopathic) (*see
  also* Epilepsy) 345.0
Pyle (-Cohn) disease (craniometaphyseal
  dysplasia) 756.89
Pylephlebitis (suppurative) 572.1
Pylethrombophlebitis 572.1
Pylethrombosis 572.1
Pyloritis (*see also* Gastritis) 535.5
Pylorospasm (reflex) 537.81
  congenital or infantile 750.5
  neurotic 306.4
  newborn 750.5
  psychogenic 306.4
Pylorus, pyloric —*see* condition
Pyoarthrosis —*see* Pyarthrosis
Pyocele
  mastoid 383.00
  sinus (accessory) (nasal) (*see also* Sinusitis)
    473.9
  turbinate (bone) 473.9
  urethra (*see also* Urethritis) 597.0
Pyococcal dermatitis 686.00
Pyococcide, skin 686.00
Pyocolpos (*see also* Vaginitis) 616.10
Pyocyaneus dermatitis 686.09
Pyocystitis (*see also* Cystitis) 595.9
Pyoderma, pyodermia NEC 686.00
  gangrenosum 686.01
  specified type NEC 686.09
  vegetans 686.8
Pyodermatitis 686.00
  vegetans 686.8
Pyogenic —*see* condition
Pyohemia —*see* Septicemia
Pyohydronephrosis (*see also* Pyelitis) 590.80
Pyometra 615.9
Pyometritis (*see also* Endometritis) 615.9
Pyometrium (*see also* Endometritis) 615.9
Pyomyositis 728.0
  ossificans 728.19
  tropical (bungpagga) 040.81
Pyonephritis (*see also* Pyelitis) 590.80
  chronic 590.00
Pyonephrosis (congenital) (*see also* Pyelitis)
  590.80
  acute 590.10
Pyo-oophoritis (*see also* Salpingo-oophoritis)
  614.2

Pyo-ovarium (*see also* Salpingo-oophoritis)
   614.2
Pyopericarditis 420.99
Pyopericardium 420.99
Pyophlebitis —*see* Phlebitis
Pyopneumopericardium 420.99
Pyopneumothorax (infectional) 510.9
   with fistula 510.0
   subdiaphragmatic (*see also* Peritonitis) 567.2
   subphrenic (*see also* Peritonitis) 567.2
   tuberculous (*see also* Tuberculosis, pleura)
      012.0
Pyorrhea (alveolar) (alveolaris) 523.4
   degenerative 523.5
Pyosalpingitis (*see also* Salpingo-oophoritis)
   614.2
Pyosalpinx (*see also* Salpingo-oophoritis) 614.2
Pyosepticemia —*see* Septicemia
Pyosis
   Corlett's (impetigo) 684
   Manson's (pemphigus contagiosus) 684
Pyothorax 510.9
   with fistula 510.0
   tuberculous (*see also* Tuberculosis, pleura)
      012.0
Pyoureter 593.89
   tuberculous (*see also* Tuberculosis) 016.2
Pyramidopallidonigral syndrome 332.0
Pyrexia (of unknown origin) (P.U.O.) 780.6
   atmospheric 992.0
   during labor 659.2
   environmentally-induced
      newborn 778.4
   heat 992.0
   newborn, environmentally-induced 778.4
   puerperal 672
Pyroglobulinemia 273.8
Pyromania 312.33
Pyrosis 787.1
Pyrroloporphyria 277.1
Pyuria (bacterial) 791.9

Q

Q fever 083.0
  with pneumonia 083.0 *[484.8]*
Quadricuspid aortic valve 746.89
Quadrilateral fever 083.0
Quadriparesis *—see* Quadriplegia
Quadriplegia 344.00
  with fracture, vertebra (process)—*see* Fracture,
      vertebra, cervical, with spinal cord injury
  brain (current episode) 437.8
  cerebral (current episode) 437.8
  C1-C4
    complete 344.01
    incomplete 344.02
  C5-C7
    complete 344.03
    incomplete 344.04
  congenital or infantile (cerebral) (spastic)
      (spinal) 343.2
  cortical 437.8
  embolic (current episode) (*see also* Embolism,
      brain) 434.1
  infantile (cerebral) (spastic) (spinal) 343.2
  newborn NEC 767.0
  specified NEC 344.09
  thrombotic (current episode) (*see also*
      Thrombosis, brain) 434.0
  traumatic—*see* Injury, spinal, cervical
Quadruplet
  affected by maternal complications of
      pregnancy 761.5
  healthy liveborn—*see* Newborn, multiple
  pregnancy (complicating delivery) NEC 651.8
    with fetal loss and retention of one or more
        fetus(es) 651.5
Quarrelsomeness 301.3
Quartan
  fever 084.2
  malaria (fever) 084.2
Queensland fever 083.0
  coastal 083.0
  seven-day 100.89
Quervain's disease 727.04
  thyroid (subacute granulomatous thyroiditis)
      245.1
Queyrat's erythroplasia (M8080/2)
  specified site—*see* Neoplasm, skin, in situ
  unspecified site 233.5
Quincke's disease or edema *—see* Edema,
    angioneurotic
Quinquaud's disease (acne decalvans) 704.09
Quinsy (gangrenous) 475
Quintan fever 083.1
Quintuplet
  affected by maternal complications of
      pregnancy 761.5
  healthy liveborn—*see* Newborn, multiple
  pregnancy (complicating delivery) NEC 651.2
    with fetal loss and retention of one or more
        fetus(es) 651.6
Quotidian
  fever 084.0
  malaria (fever) 084.0

R

Rabbia 071
Rabbit fever (*see also* Tularemia) 021.9
Rabies 071
  contact V01.5
  exposure to V01.5
  inoculation V04.5
    reaction—*see* Complications, vaccination
  vaccination, prophylactic (against) V04.5
Rachischisis (*see also* Spina bifida) 741.9
Rachitic *—see also* condition
  deformities of spine 268.1
  pelvis 268.1
    with disproportion (fetopelvic) 653.2
      affecting fetus or newborn 763.1
      causing obstructed labor 660.1
        affecting fetus or newborn 763.1
Rachitis, rachitism *—see also* Rickets
  acute 268.0
  fetalis 756.4
  renalis 588.0
  tarda 268.0
Racket nail 757.5
Radial nerve *—see* condition
Radiation effects or sickness *—see also* Effect,
    adverse, radiation
  cataract 366.46
  dermatitis 692.82
    sunburn 692.71
Radiculitis (pressure) (vertebrogenic) 729.2
  accessory nerve 723.4
  anterior crural 724.4
  arm 723.4
  brachial 723.4
  cervical NEC 723.4
  due to displacement of intervertebral disc—*see*
      Neuritis, due to, displacement intervertebral
      disc
  leg 724.4
  lumbar NEC 724.4
  lumbosacral 724.4
  rheumatic 729.2
  syphilitic 094.89
  thoracic (with visceral pain) 724.4
Radiculomyelitis 357.0
  toxic, due to
    Clostridium tetani 037
    Corynebacterium diphtheriae 032.89
Radiculopathy (*see also* Radiculitis) 729.2
Radioactive substances, adverse effect *—see*
    Effect, adverse, radioactive substance
Radiodermal burns (acute) (chronic)
    (occupational)—*see* Burn, by site
Radiodermatitis 692.82
Radionecrosis *—see* Effect, adverse, radiation
Radiotherapy session V58.0
Radium, adverse effect *—see* Effect, adverse,
    radioactive substance
Raeder-Harbitz syndrome (pulseless disease)
    446.7
Rage (*see also* Disturbance, conduct) 312.0
  meaning rabies 071
Rag sorters' disease 022.1
Raillietiniasis 123.8
Railroad neurosis 300.16
Railway spine 300.16
Raised *—see* Elevation
Raiva 071
Rake teeth, tooth 524.3

Rales 786.7
Ramifying renal pelvis 753.3
Ramsay Hunt syndrome (herpetic geniculate
    ganglionitis) 053.11
  meaning dyssynergia cerebellaris myoclonica
    334.2
Ranke's primary infiltration (*see also*
    Tuberculosis) 010.0
Ranula 527.6
  congenital 750.26
Rape (*see* Injury, by site)
  alleged, observation or examination V71.5
Rapid
  feeble pulse, due to shock, following injury
    958.4
  heart (beat) 785.0
    psychogenic 306.2
  respiration 786.06
    psychogenic 306.1
  second stage (delivery) 661.3
    affecting fetus or newborn 763.6
  time-zone change syndrome 307.45
Rarefaction, bone 733.99
Rash 782.1
  canker 034.1
  diaper 691.0
  drug (internal use) 693.0
    contact 692.3
  ECHO 9 virus 078.89
  enema 692.89
  food (*see also* Allergy, food) 693.1
  heat 705.1
  napkin 691.0
  nettle 708.8
  pustular 782.1
  rose 782.1
    epidemic 056.9
    of infants 057.8
  scarlet 034.1
  serum (prophylactic) (therapeutic) 999.5
  toxic 782.1
  wandering tongue 529.1
Rasmussen's aneurysm (*see also* Tuberculosis)
    011.2
Rat-bite fever 026.9
  due to Streptobacillus moniliformis 026.1
  spirochetal (morsus muris) 026.0
Rathke's pouch tumor (M9350/1) 237.0
Raymond (-Céstan) syndrome 433.8
Raynaud's
  disease or syndrome (paroxysmal digital
    cyanosis) 443.0
  gangrene (symmetric) 443.0 *[785.4]*
  phenomenon (paroxysmal digital cyanosis)
    (secondary) 443.0
RDS 769
Reaction
  acute situational maladjustment (*see also*
    Reaction, adjustment) 309.9
  adaptation (*see also* Reaction, adjustment) 309.9
  adjustment 309.9
    with
      anxious mood 309.24
        with depressed mood 309.28
      conduct disturbance 309.3
        combined with disturbance of emotions
          309.4
      depressed mood 309.0
        brief 309.0
          with anxious mood 309.28
        prolonged 309.1

Reaction—*continued*
    elective mutism 309.83
    mixed emotions and conduct 309.4
    mutism, elective 309.83
    physical symptoms 309.82
    predominant disturbance (of)
      conduct 309.3
      emotions NEC 309.29
        mixed 309.28
      mixed, emotions and conduct 309.4
      specified type NEC 309.89
    specific academic or work inhibition 309.23
    withdrawal 309.83
    depressive 309.0
      with conduct disturbance 309.4
      brief 309.0
      prolonged 309.1
    specified type NEC 309.89
  adverse food NEC 995.7
  affective (*see also* Psychosis, affective) 296.90
    specified type NEC 296.99
  aggressive 301.3
    unsocialized (*see also* Disturbance, conduct)
      312.0
  allergic (*see also* Allergy) 995.3
    drug, medicinal substance, and
      biological—*see* Allergy, drug
    food—*see* Allergy, food
    serum 999.5
  anaphylactic—*see* Shock, anaphylactic
  anesthesia—*see* Anesthesia, complication
  anger 312.0
  antisocial 301.7
  antitoxin (prophylactic) (therapeutic)—*see*
    Complications, vaccination
  anxiety 300.00
  asthenic 300.5
  compulsive 300.3
  conversion (anesthetic) (autonomic)
    (hyperkinetic) (mixed paralytic)
    (paresthetic) 300.11
  deoxyribonuclease (DNA) (DNase)
    hypersensitivity NEC 287.2
  depressive 300.4
    acute 309.0
    affective (*see also* Psychosis, affective) 296.2
      recurrent episode 296.3
      single episode 296.2
    brief 309.0
    manic (*see also* Psychosis, affective) 296.80
    neurotic 300.4
    psychoneurotic 300.4
    psychotic 298.0
  dissociative 300.15
  drug NEC (*see also* Table of drugs and
    chemicals) 995.2
    allergic—*see* Allergy, drug
    correct substance properly administered 995.2
    obstetric anesthetic or analgesic NEC 668.9
      affecting fetus or newborn 763.5
      specified drug—*see* Table of drugs and
        chemicals
    overdose or poisoning 977.9
      specified drug—*see* Table of drugs and
        chemicals
    specific to newborn 779.4
    transmitted via placenta or breast milk—*see*
      Absorption, drug, through placenta
    withdrawal NEC 292.0
      infant of dependent mother 779.5
    wrong substance given or taken in error 977.9

Reaction—*continued*
  runaway—*see also* Disturbance, conduct
    socialized 312.2
    undersocialized, unsocialized 312.1
  scarlet fever toxin—*see* Complications,
    vaccination
  schizophrenic (*see also* Schizophrenia) 295.9
    latent 295.5
  serological for syphilis—*see* Serology for
    syphilis
  serum (prophylactic) (therapeutic) 999.5
    immediate 999.4
  situational (*see also* Reaction, adjustment) 309.9
    acute, to stress 308.3
    adjustment (*see also* Reaction, adjustment)
      309.9
  somatization (*see also* Disorder, psychosomatic)
    306.9
  spinal puncture 349.0
  spite, child (*see also* Disturbance, conduct)
    312.0
  stress, acute 308.9
    with predominant disturbance (of)
      consciousness 308.1
      emotions 308.0
      mixed 308.4
      psychomotor 308.2
      specified type NEC 308.3
  surgical procedure—*see* Complications,
    surgical procedure
  tetanus antitoxin—*see* Complications,
    vaccination
  toxin-antitoxin—*see* Complications, vaccination
  transfusion (blood) (bone marrow)
    (lymphocytes) (allergic)—*see*
    Complications, transfusion
  tuberculin skin test, nonspecific (without active
    tuberculosis) 795.5
    positive (without active tuberculosis) 795.5
  ultraviolet—*see* Effect, adverse, ultraviolet
  undersocialized, unsocialized—*see also*
    Disturbance, conduct
    aggressive (type) 312.0
    unaggressive (type) 312.1
  vaccination (any)—*see* Complications,
    vaccination
  white graft (skin) 996.52
  withdrawing, child or adolescent 313.22
  x-ray—*see* Effect, adverse, x-rays
Reactive depression (*see also* Reaction,
  depressive) 300.4
  neurotic 300.4
  psychoneurotic 300.4
  psychotic 298.0
Rebound tenderness 789.6
Recalcitrant patient V15.81
Recanalization, thrombus —*see* Thrombosis
Recession, receding
  chamber angle (eye) 364.77
  chin 524.06
  gingival (generalized) (localized) (postinfective)
    (postoperative) 523.2
Recklinghausen's disease (M9540/1) 237.71
  bones (osteitis fibrosa cystica) 252.0
Recklinghausen-Applebaum disease
  (hemochromatosis) 275.0
Reclus' disease (cystic) 610.1
Recrudescent typhus (fever) 081.1
Recruitment, auditory 388.44
Rectalgia 569.42
Rectitis 569.49

Rectocele
  female (without uterine prolapse) 618.0
    with uterine prolapse 618.4
      complete 618.3
      incomplete 618.2
  in pregnancy or childbirth 654.4
    causing obstructed labor 660.2
      affecting fetus or newborn 763.1
  male 569.49
  vagina, vaginal (outlet) 618.0
Rectosigmoiditis 569.89
  ulcerative (chronic) 556.3
Rectosigmoid junction —*see* condition
Rectourethral —*see* condition
Rectovaginal —*see* condition
Rectovesical —*see* condition
Rectum, rectal —*see* condition
Recurrent —*see* condition
Red bugs 133.8
Red cedar asthma 495.8
Redness
  conjunctiva 379.93
  eye 379.93
  nose 478.1
Reduced ventilatory or vital capacity 794.2
Reduction
  function
    kidney (*see also* Disease, renal) 593.9
    liver 573.8
  ventilatory capacity 794.2
  vital capacity 794.2
Redundant, redundancy
  abdomen 701.9
  anus 751.5
  cardia 537.89
  clitoris 624.2
  colon (congenital) 751.5
  foreskin (congenital) 605
  intestine 751.5
  labia 624.3
  organ or site, congenital NEC—*see* Accessory
  panniculus (abdominal) 278.1
  prepuce (congenital) 605
  pylorus 537.89
  rectum 751.5
  scrotum 608.89
  sigmoid 751.5
  skin (of face) 701.9
    eyelids 374.30
  stomach 537.89
  uvula 528.9
  vagina 623.8
Reduplication —*see* Duplication
Referral
  adoption (agency) V68.89
  nursing care V63.8
  patient without examination or treatment V68.81
  social services V63.8
Reflex —*see also* condition
  blink, deficient 374.45
  hyperactive gag 478.29
  neurogenic bladder NEC 596.54
    atonic 596.54
      with cauda equina syndrome 344.61
  vasoconstriction 443.9
  vasovagal 780.2
Reflux
  esophageal 530.81
  esophagitis 530.11
  gastroesophageal 530.81
  mitral—*see* Insufficiency, mitral

Reflux—*continued*
  ureteral —*see* Reflux, vesicoureteral
  vesicoureteral 593.70
    with
      reflux nephropathy 593.73
        bilateral 593.72
        unilateral 593.71
Reformed gallbladder 576.0
Reforming, artificial openings (*see also*
    Attention to, artificial, opening) V55.9
Refractive error (*see also* Error, refractive) 367.9
Refsum's disease or syndrome (heredopathia
    atactica polyneuritiformis) 356.3
Refusal of
  food 307.59
    hysterical 300.11
  treatment because of, due to
    patient's decision NEC V64.2
    reason of conscience or religion V62.6
Regaud
  tumor (M8082/3)—*see* Neoplasm,
    nasopharynx, malignant
  type carcinoma (M8082/3)—*see* Neoplasm,
    nasopharynx, malignant
Regional —*see* condition
Regulation feeding (elderly) (infant) 783.3
  newborn 779.3
Regurgitated
  food, choked on 933.1
  stomach contents, choked on 933.1
Regurgitation
  aortic (valve) (*see also* Insufficiency, aortic)
    424.1
    congenital 746.4
    syphilitic 093.22
  food—*see also* Vomiting
    with reswallowing—*see* Rumination
    newborn 779.3
  gastric contents—*see* Vomiting
  heart—*see* Endocarditis
  mitral (valve)—*see also* Insufficiency, mitral
    congenital 746.6
  myocardial—*see* Endocarditis
  pulmonary (heart) (valve) (*see also*
    Endocarditis, pulmonary) 424.3
  stomach—*see* Vomiting
  tricuspid—*see* Endocarditis, tricuspid
  valve, valvular—*see* Endocarditis
  vesicoureteral —*see* Reflux, vesicoureteral
Rehabilitation V57.9
  multiple types V57.89
  occupational V57.21
  specified type NEC V57.89
  speech V57.3
  vocational V57.22
Reichmann's disease or syndrome
    (gastrosuccorrhea) 536.8
Reifenstein's syndrome (hereditary familial
    hypogonadism, male) 257.2
Reilly's syndrome or phenomenon (*see also*
    Neuropathy, peripheral, autonomic) 337.9
Reimann's periodic disease 277.3
Reinsertion, contraceptive device V25.42
Reiter's disease, syndrome, or urethritis 099.3
    [711.1]
Rejection
  food, hysterical 300.11
  transplant 996.80
    bone marrow 996.85
    corneal 996.51

Rejection—*continued*
  organ (immune or nonimmune cause) 996.80
    bone marrow 996.85
    heart 996.83
    intestines 996.87
    kidney 996.81
    liver 996.82
    lung 996.84
    pancreas 996.86
    specified NEC 996.89
  skin 996.52
    artificial 996.55
    decellularized allodermis 996.55
Relapsing fever 087.9
  Carter's (Asiatic) 087.0
  Dutton's (West African) 087.1
  Koch's 087.9
  louse-borne (epidemic) 087.0
  Novy's (American) 087.1
  Obermeyer's (European) 087.0
  Spirillum 087.9
  tick-borne (endemic) 087.1
Relaxation
  anus (sphincter) 569.49
    due to hysteria 300.11
  arch (foot) 734
    congenital 754.61
  back ligaments 728.4
  bladder (sphincter) 596.59
  cardio-esophageal 530.89
  cervix (*see also* Incompetency, cervix) 622.5
  diaphragm 519.4
  inguinal rings—*see* Hernia, inguinal
  joint (capsule) (ligament) (paralytic) (*see also*
    Derangement, joint) 718.90
    congenital 755.8
  lumbosacral joint 724.6
  pelvic floor 618.8
  pelvis 618.8
  perineum 618.8
  posture 729.9
  rectum (sphincter) 569.49
  sacroiliac (joint) 724.6
  scrotum 608.89
  urethra (sphincter) 599.84
  uterus (outlet) 618.8
  vagina (outlet) 618.8
  vesical 596.59
Remains
  canal of Cloquet 743.51
  capsule (opaque) 743.51
Remittent fever (malarial) 084.6
Remnant
  canal of Cloquet 743.51
  capsule (opaque) 743.51
  cervix, cervical stump (acquired)
    (postoperative) 622.8
  cystic duct, postcholecystectomy 576.0
  fingernail 703.8
    congenital 757.5
  meniscus, knee 717.5
  thyroglossal duct 759.2
  tonsil 474.8
    infected 474.00
  urachus 753.7
Remote effect of cancer —*see* Condition
Removal (of)
  catheter (urinary) (indwelling) V53.6
    from artificial opening—*see* Attention to,
      artificial, opening
    non-vascular V58.82

Removal (of)—*continued*
   vascular V58.81
  cerebral ventricle (communicating) shunt
    V53.01
  device—*see also* Fitting (of)
   contraceptive V25.42
   fixation
    external V54.8
    internal V54.0
    traction V54.8
  dressing V58.3
  ileostomy V55.2
  Kirschner wire V54.8
  non-vascular catheter V58.82
  pin V54.0
  plaster cast V54.8
  plate (fracture) V54.0
  rod V54.0
  screw V54.0
  splint, external V54.8
  subdermal implantable contraceptive V25.43
  suture V58.3
  traction device, external V54.8
  vascular catheter V58.81
Ren
  arcuatus 753.3
  mobile, mobilis (*see also* Disease, renal) 593.0
   congenital 753.3
  unguliformis 753.3
Renal —*see also* condition
  glomerulohyalinosis-diabetic syndrome 250.4
   [581.81]
Rendu-Osler-Weber disease or syndrome
  (familial hemorrhagic telangiectasia) 448.0
Reninoma (M8361/1) 236.91
Rénon-Delille syndrome 253.8
Repair
  pelvic floor, previous, in pregnancy or
   childbirth 654.4
   affecting fetus or newborn 763.89
  scarred tissue V51
Replacement by artificial or mechanical device
  or prosthesis of (*see also* Fitting (of))
  artificial skin V43.83
  bladder V43.5
  blood vessel V43.4
  breast V43.82
  eye globe V43.0
  heart V43.2
   valve V43.3
  intestine V43.89
  joint V43.60
   ankle 43.66
   elbow V43.62
   finger V43.69
   hip (partial) (total) V43.64
   knee V43.65
   shoulder V43.61
   specified NEC V43.69
   wrist V43.63
  kidney V43.89
  larynx V43.81
  lens V43.1
  limb(s) V43.7
  liver V43.89
  lung V43.89
  organ NEC V43.89
  pancreas V43.89
  skin (artificial) V43.83
  tissue NEC V43.89
Reprogramming
  cardiac pacemaker V53.31

Request for expert evidence V68.2
Reserve, decreased or low
  cardiac—*see* Disease, heart
  kidney (*see also* Disease, renal) 593.9
Residual —*see also* condition
  bladder 596.8
  foreign body—*see* Retention, foreign body
  state, schizophrenic (*see also* Schizophrenia)
   295.6
  urine 788.69
Resistance, resistant (to)

> *Note—Use the following subclassification for
> categories V09.5, V09.7, V09.8, V09.9.:*
>
> *0 without mention of resistance to multiple
>   drugs*
> *1 with resistance to multiple drugs*
>
> *V09.5 quinolones and fluoroquinolones*
> *V09.7 antimycobacterial agents*
> *V09.8 specified drugs NEC*
> *V09.9 unspecified drugs*
>
> *9 multiple sites*

  drugs by microorganisms V09.9
   Amikacin V09.4
   aminoglycosides V09.4
   Amodiaquine V09.5
   Amoxicillin V09.0
   Ampicillin V09.0
   antimycobacterial agents V09.7
   Azithromycin V09.2
   Azlocillin V09.0
   Aztreonam V09.1
   B-lactam antibiotics V09.1
   Bacampicillin V09.0
   Bacitracin V09.8
   Benznidazole V09.8
   Capreomycin V09.7
   Carbenicillin V09.0
   Cefaclor V09.1
   Cefadroxil V09.1
   Cefamandole V09.1
   Cefatetan V09.1
   Cefazolin V09.1
   Cefixime V09.1
   Cefonicid V09.1
   Cefoperazone V09.1
   Ceforanide V09.1
   Cefotaxime V09.1
   Cefoxitin V09.1
   Ceftazidine V09.1
   Ceftizoxime V09.1
   Ceftriaxone V09.1
   Cefuroxime V09.1
   Cephalexin V09.1
   Cephaloglycin V09.1
   Cephaloridine V09.1
   cephalosporins V09.1
   Cephalothin V09.1
   Cephapirin V09.1
   Cephradine V09.1
   Chloramphenicol V09.8
   Chloraquine V09.5
   Chlorguanide V09.8
   Chlorproguanil V09.8
   Chlortetracycline V09.3
   Cinoxacin V09.5
   Ciprofloxacin V09.5
   Clarithromycin V09.2

Resistance, resistant (to)—*continued*
    Clindamycin V09.8
    Clioquinol V09.5
    Clofazimine V09.7
    Cloxacillin V09.0
    Cyclacillin V09.0
    Cycloserine V09.7
    Dapsone [DZ] V09.7
    Demeclocycline V09.3
    Dicloxacillin V09.0
    Doxycycline V09.3
    Enoxacin V09.5
    Erythromycin V09.2
    Ethambutol [EMB] V09.7
    Ethionamide [ETA] V09.7
    fluoroquinolones NEC V09.5
    Gentamicin V09.4
    Halofantrine V09.8
    ImipenemV09.1
    Iodoquinol V09.5
    Isoniazid [INH] V09.7
    Kanamycin V09.4
    macrolides V09.2
    Mafenide V09.6
    Mefloquine V09.8
    Melassoprol V09.8
    Methacillin V09.0
    Methacycline V09.3
    Methenamine V09.8
    Metronidazole V09.8
    Mezlocillin V09.0
    Minocycline V09.3
    Nafcillin V09.0
    Nalidixic Acid V09.5
    Natamycin V09.2
    Neomycin V09.4
    Netilmicin V09.4
    Nimorazole V09.8
    Nitrofurantoin V09.8
    Nitrofurtimox V09.8
    Norfloxacin V09.5
    Nystatin V09.2
    Ofloxacin V09.5
    Oleandomycin V09.2
    Oxacillin V09.0
    Oxytetracycline V09.3
    Para-amino salicylic acid [PAS] V09.7
    Paromomycin V09.4
    Penicillin (G)(V)(VK) V09.0
    penicillins V09.0
    Pentamidine V09.8
    Piperacillin V09.0
    Primaquine V09.5
    Proguanil V09.8
    Pyrazinamide [PZA] V09.7
    Pyrimethamine/Sulfalene V09.8
    Pyrimethamine/Sulfodoxine V09.8
    Quinacrine V09.5
    Quinidine V09.8
    Quinine V09.8
    quinolones V09.5
    Rifabutin V09.7
    Rifampin [RIF] V09.7
    Rifamycin V09.7
    Rolitetracycline V09.3
    specified drugs NEC V09.8
    Spectinomycin V09.8
    Spiramycin V09.2
    Streptomycin [SM] V09.4
    Sulfacetamide V09.6
    Sulfacytine V90.6

Resistance, resistant (to)—*continued*
    Sulfadiazine V09.6
    Sulfadoxine V09.6
    Sulfamethoxazole V09.6
    Sulfapyridine V09.6
    Sulfasalizine V09.6
    Sulfasoxazole V09.6
    sulfonamides V09.6
    Sulfoxone V09.7
    Tetracycline V09.3
    tetracyclines V09.3
    Thiamphenicol V09.8
    Ticarcillin V09.0
    Tinidazole V09.8
    Tobramycin V09.4
    Triamphenicol V09.8
    Trimethoprim V09.8
    Vancomycin V09.8
Resorption
  biliary 576.8
    purulent or putrid (*see also* Cholecystitis) 576.8
  dental (roots) 521.4
    alveoli 525.8
  septic—*see* Septicemia
  teeth (external) (internal) (pathological) (roots) 521.4
Respiration
  asymmetrical 786.09
  bronchial 786.09
  Cheyne-Stokes (periodic respiration) 786.04
  decreased, due to shock following injury 958.4
  disorder of 786.00
    psychogenic 306.1
    specified NEC 786.09
  failure 518.81
    acute 518.81
    acute and chronic 518.84
    chronic 518.83
    newborn 770.8
  insufficiency 786.09
    acute 518.82
    newborn NEC 770.8
  Kussmaul (air hunger) 786.09
  painful 786.52
  periodic 786.09
  poor 786.09
    newborn NEC 770.8
  sighing 786.7
    psychogenic 306.1
  wheezing 786.07
Respiratory —*see also* condition
  distress 786.09
    acute 518.82
    fetus or newborn NEC 770.8
    syndrome (newborn) 769
      adult (following shock, surgery, or trauma) 518.5
      specified NEC 518.82
  failure 518.81
    acute 518.81
    acute and chronic 518.84
    chronic 518.83
Respiratory syncytial virus (RSV) 079.6
  bronchiolitis 466.11
  pneumonia 480.1
Response
  photoallergic 692.72
  phototoxic 692.72

Rest, rests
　mesonephric duct 752.8
　　fallopian tube 752.11
　ovarian, in fallopian tubes 752.19
　wolffian duct 752.8
Restless leg (syndrome) 333.99
Restlessness 799.2
Restoration of organ continuity from previous
　sterilization (tuboplasty) (vasoplasty) V26.0
Restriction of housing space V60.1
Restzustand, schizophrenic (*see also*
　Schizophrenia) 295.6
Retained —*see* Retention
Retardation
　development, developmental, specific (*see also*
　　Disorder, development, specific) 315.9
　　learning, specific 315.2
　　　arithmetical 315.1
　　　language (skills) 315.31
　　　　expressive 315.31
　　　　mixed receptive-expressive 315.32
　　　mathematics 315.1
　　　reading 315.00
　　　　phonological 315.39
　　　written expression 315.2
　　motor 315.4
　endochondral bone growth 733.91
　growth (physical) in childhood 783.43
　　due to malnutrition 263.2
　　fetal (intrauterine) 764.9
　　　affecting management of pregnancy 656.5
　intrauterine growth 764.9
　　affecting management of pregnancy 656.5
　mental 319
　　borderline V62.89
　　mild, IQ 50-70 317
　　moderate, IQ 35-49 318.0
　　profound, IQ under 20 318.2
　　severe, IQ 20-34 318.1
　motor, specific 315.4
　physical 783.43
　　child 783.43
　　due to malnutrition 263.2
　　fetus (intrauterine) 764.9
　　　affecting management of pregnancy 656.5
　psychomotor NEC 307.9
　reading 315.00
Retching —*see* Vomiting
Retention, retained
　bladder NEC (*see also* Retention, urine) 788.20
　　psychogenic 306.53
　carbon dioxide 276.2
　cyst—*see* Cyst
　dead
　　fetus (after 22 completed weeks gestation)
　　　656.4
　　　early fetal death (before 22 completed
　　　　weeks gestation) 632
　　ovum 631
　decidua (following delivery) (fragments) (with
　　hemorrhage) 666.2
　　without hemorrhage 667.1
　deciduous tooth 520.6
　dental root 525.3
　fecal (*see also* Constipation) 564.0
　fluid 276.6
　foreign body—*see also* Foreign body, retained
　　bone 733.99
　　current trauma—*see* Foreign body, by site or
　　　type
　　middle ear 385.83

Retention, retained—*continued*
　muscle 729.6
　　soft tissue NEC 729.6
　gastric 536.8
　membranes (following delivery) (with
　　hemorrhage) 666.2
　　with abortion—*see* Abortion, by type
　　without hemorrhage 667.1
　menses 626.8
　milk (puerperal) 676.2
　nitrogen, extrarenal 788.9
　placenta (total) (with hemorrhage) 666.0
　　with abortion—*see* Abortion, by type
　　portions or fragments 666.2
　　　without hemorrhage 667.1
　　without hemorrhage 667.0
　products of conception
　　early pregnancy (fetal death before 22
　　　completed weeks gestation) 632
　　following
　　　abortion—*see* Abortion, by type
　　　delivery 666.2
　　　　with hemorrhage 666.2
　　　　without hemorrhage 667.1
　secundines (following delivery) (with
　　hemorrhage) 666.2
　　with abortion—*see* Abortion, by type
　　complicating puerperium (delayed
　　　hemorrhage) 666.2
　　without hemorrhage 667.1
　smegma, clitoris 624.8
　urine NEC 788.20
　　bladder, incomplete emptying 788.21
　　psychogenic 306.53
　　specified NEC 788.29
　water (in tissue) (*see also* Edema) 782.3
Reticulation, dust (occupational) 504
Reticulocytosis NEC 790.99
Reticuloendotheliosis
　acute infantile (M9722/3) 202.5
　leukemic (M9940/3) 202.4
　malignant (M9720/3) 202.3
　nonlipid (M9722/3) 202.5
Reticulohistiocytoma (giant cell) 277.8
Reticulohistiocytosis, multicentric 272.8
Reticulolymphosarcoma (diffuse) (M9613/3)
　200.8
　follicular (M9691/3) 202.0
　nodular (M9691/3) 202.0
Reticulosarcoma (M9640/3) 200.0
　odular (M9642/3) 200.0
　pleomorphic cell type (M9641/3) 200.0
Reticulosis (skin)
　acute of infancy (M9722/3) 202.5
　histiocytic medullary (M9721/3) 202.3
　lipomelanotic 695.89
　malignant (M9720/3) 202.3
　Sézary's (M9701/3) 202.2
Retina, retinal —*see* condition
Retinitis (*see also* Chorioretinitis) 363.20
　albuminurica 585 *[363.10]*
　arteriosclerotic 440.8 *[362.13]*
　central angiospastic 362.41
　Coat's 362.12
　diabetic 250.5 *[362.01]*
　disciformis 362.52
　disseminated 363.10
　　metastatic 363.14
　　neurosyphilitic 094.83
　　pigment epitheliopathy 363.15
　exudative 362.12

Rh (factor)—*continued*
  titer elevated 999.7
  transfusion reaction 999.7
Rhabdomyolysis (idiopathic) 728.89
Rhabdomyoma (M8900/0)—*see also* Neoplasm,
  connective tissue, benign
  adult (M8904/0)—*see* Neoplasm, connective
    tissue, benign
  fetal (M8903/0)—*see* Neoplasm, connective
    tissue, benign
  glycogenic (M8904/0)—*see* Neoplasm,
    connective tissue, benign
Rhabdomyosarcoma (M8900/3)—*see also*
  Neoplasm connective tissue, malignant
  alveolar (M8920/3)—*see* Neoplasm, connective
    tissue, malignant
  embryonal (M8910/3)—*see* Neoplasm,
    connective tissue malignant
  mixed type (M8902/3)—*see* Neoplasm,
    connective tissue, malignant
  pleomorphic (M8901/3)—*see* Neoplasm,
    connective tissue, malignant
Rhabdosarcoma (M8900/3)—*see*
  Rhabdomyosarcoma
Rhesus (factor) (Rh) incompatibility—*see* Rh,
  incompatibility
Rheumaticosis —*see* Rheumatism
Rheumatism, rheumatic (acute NEC) 729.0
  adherent pericardium 393
  arthritis
    acute or subacute—*see* Fever, rheumatic
    chronic 714.0
      spine 720.0
  articular (chronic) NEC (*see also* Arthritis)
    716.9
    acute or subacute—*see* Fever, rheumatic
  back 724.9
  blennorrhagic 098.59
  carditis—*see* Disease, heart, rheumatic
  cerebral—*see* Fever, rheumatic
  chorea (acute)—*see* Chorea, rheumatic
  chronic NEC 729.0
  coronary arteritis 391.9
    chronic 398.99
  degeneration, myocardium (*see also*
    Degeneration, myocardium, with rheumatic
    fever) 398.0
  desert 114.0
  febrile—*see* Fever, rheumatic
  fever—*see* Fever, rheumatic
  gonococcal 098.59
  gout 274.0
  heart
    disease (*see also* Disease, heart, rheumatic)
      398.90
    failure (chronic) (congestive) (inactive) 398.91
  hemopericardium—*see* Rheumatic, pericarditis
  hydropericardium—*see* Rheumatic, pericarditis
  inflammatory (acute) (chronic) (subacute)—*see*
    Fever, rheumatic
  intercostal 729.0
    meaning Tietze's disease 733.6
  joint (chronic) NEC (*see also* Arthritis) 716.9
    acute—*see* Fever, rheumatic
  mediastinopericarditis—*see* Rheumatic,
    pericarditis
  muscular 729.0
  myocardial degeneration (*see also*
    Degeneration, myocardium, with rheumatic
    fever) 398.0

Rheumatism, rheumatic—*continued*
  myocarditis (chronic) (inactive) (with chorea)
    398.0
    active or acute 391.2
      with chorea (acute) (rheumatic)
        (Sydenham's) 392.0
  myositis 729.1
  neck 724.9
  neuralgic 729.0
  neuritis (acute) (chronic) 729.2
  neuromuscular 729.0
  nodose—*see* Arthritis, nodosa
  nonarticular 729.0
  palindromic 719.30
    ankle 719.37
    elbow 719.32
    foot 719.37
    hand 719.34
    hip 719.35
    knee 719.36
    multiple sites 719.39
    pelvic region 719.35
    shoulder (region) 719.31
    specified site NEC 719.38
    wrist 719.33
  pancarditis, acute 391.8
    with chorea (acute) (rheumatic) (Sydenham's)
      392.0
    chronic or inactive 398.99
  pericarditis (active) (acute) (with effusion) (with
    pneumonia) 391.0
    with chorea (acute) (rheumatic) (Sydenham's)
      392.0
    chronic or inactive 393
  pericardium—*see* Rheumatic, pericarditis
  pleuropericarditis—*see* Rheumatic, pericarditis
  pneumonia 390 *[517.1]*
  pneumonitis 390 *[517.1]*
  pneumopericarditis—*see* Rheumatic, pericarditis
  polyarthritis
    acute or subacute—*see* Fever, rheumatic
    chronic 714.0
  polyarticular NEC (*see also* Arthritis) 716.9
  psychogenic 306.0
  radiculitis 729.2
  sciatic 724.3
  septic—*see* Fever, rheumatic
  spine 724.9
  subacute NEC 729.0
  torticollis 723.5
  tuberculous NEC (*see also* Tuberculosis) 015.9
  typhoid fever 002.0
Rheumatoid —*see also* condition
  lungs 714.81
Rhinitis (atrophic) (catarrhal) (chronic)
  (croupous) (fibrinous) (hyperplastic)
  (hypertrophic) (membranous) (purulent)
  (suppurative) (ulcerative) 472.0
  with
    hay fever (*see also* Fever, hay) 477.9
      with asthma (bronchial) 493.0
    sore throat—*see* Nasopharyngitis
  acute 460
  allergic (nonseasonal) (seasonal) (*see also*
    Fever, hay) 477.9
    due to food 477.1
    with asthma (*see also* Asthma) 493.0
  granulomatous 472.0
  infective 460
  obstructive 472.0
  pneumococcal 460

Ring(s)—*continued*
hymenal, tight (acquired) (congenital) 623.3
Kayser-Fleischer (cornea) 275.1 *[371.14]*
retraction, uterus, pathological 661.4
  affecting fetus or newborn 763.7
Schatzki's (esophagus) (congenital) (lower)
  750.3
  acquired 530.3
Soemmering's 366.51
trachea, abnormal 748.3
vascular (congenital) 747.21
Vossius' 921.3
  late effect 366.21
Ringed hair (congenital) 757.4
Ringing in the ear (*see also* Tinnitus) 388.30
Ringworm 110.9
beard 110.0
body 110.5
Burmese 110.9
corporeal 110.5
foot 110.4
groin 110.3
hand 110.2
honeycomb 110.0
nails 110.1
perianal (area) 110.3
scalp 110.0
specified site NEC 110.8
Tokelau 110.5
Rise, venous pressure 459.89
Risk
factor —*see* Problem
suicidal 300.9
Ritter's disease (dermatitis exfoliativa
  neonatorum) 695.81
Rivalry, sibling 313.3
Rivalta's disease (cervicofacial actinomycosis)
  039.3
River blindness 125.3 *[360.13]*
Robert's pelvis 755.69
with disproportion (fetopelvic) 653.0
  affecting fetus or newborn 763.1
  causing obstructed labor 660.1
    affecting fetus or newborn 763.1
Robin's syndrome 756.0
Robinson's (hidrotic) ectodermal dysplasia
  757.31
Robles' disease (onchocerciasis) 125.3 *[360.13]*
Rochalimea —*see* Rickettsial disease
Rocky Mountain fever (spotted) 082.0
Rodent ulcer (M8090/3)—*see also* Neoplasm,
  skin, malignant
cornea 370.07
Roentgen ray, adverse effect —*see* Effect,
  adverse, x-ray
Roetheln 056.9
Roger's disease (congenital interventricular
  septal defect) 745.4
Rokitansky's
disease (*see also* Necrosis, liver) 570
tumor 620.2
Rokitansky-Aschoff sinuses (mucosal
  outpouching of gallbladder) (*see also* Disease,
  gallbladder) 575.8
Rokitansky-Kuster-Hauser syndrome
  (congenital absence vagina) 752.49
Rollet's chancre (syphilitic) 091.0
Rolling of head 781.0
Romano-Ward syndrome (prolonged Q-T
  interval) 794.31
Romanus lesion 720.1
Romberg's disease or syndrome 349.89

Roof, mouth —*see* condition
Rosacea 695.3
acne 695.3
keratitis 695.3 *[370.49]*
Rosary, rachitic 268.0
Rose
cold 477.0
fever 477.0
rash 782.1
  epidemic 056.9
  of infants 057.8
Rosen-Castleman-Liebow syndrome
  (pulmonary proteinosis) 516.0
Rosenbach's erysipelatoid or erysipeloid 027.1
Rosenthal's disease (factor XI deficiency) 286.2
Roseola 057.8
infantum, infantilis 057.8
Rossbach's disease (hyperchlorhydria) 536.8
psychogenic 306.4
Rössle-Urbach-Wiethe lipoproteinosis 272.8
Ross river fever 066.3
Rostan's asthma (cardiac) (*see also* Failure,
  ventricular, left) 428.1
Rot
Barcoo (*see also* Ulcer, skin) 707.9
knife-grinders' (*see also* Tuberculosis) 011.4
Rot-Bernhardt disease 355.1
Rotation
anomalous, incomplete or insufficient—*see*
  Malrotation
cecum (congenital) 751.4
colon (congenital) 751.4
manual, affecting fetus or newborn 763.89
spine, incomplete or insufficient 737.8
tooth, teeth 524.3
vertebra, incomplete or insufficient 737.8
Röteln 056.9
Roth's disease or meralgia 355.1
Roth-Bernhardt disease or syndrome 355.1
Rothmund (-Thomson) syndrome 757.33
Rotor's disease or syndrome (idiopathic
  hyperbilirubinemia) 277.4
Rotundum ulcus —*see* Ulcer, stomach
Round
back (with wedging of vertebrae) 737.10
  late effect of rickets 268.1
hole, retina 361.31
  with detachment 361.01
ulcer (stomach)—*see* Ulcer, stomach
worms (infestation) (large) NEC 127.0
Roussy-Lévy syndrome 334.3
Routine postpartum follow-up V24.2
Roy (-Jutras) syndrome (acropachyderma) 757.39
Rubella (German measles) 056.9
complicating pregnancy, childbirth, or
  puerperium 647.5
complication 056.8
  neurological 056.00
    encephalomyelitis 056.01
    specified type NEC 056.09
    specified type NEC 056.79
congenital 771.0
contact V01.4
exposure to V01.4
maternal
  with suspected fetal damage affecting
    management of pregnancy 655.3
  affecting fetus or newborn 760.2
    manifest rubella in infant 771.0
specified complications NEC 056.79
vaccination, prophylactic (against) V04.3

Rubeola (measles) (*see also* Measles) 055.9
  complicated 055.8
  meaning rubella (*see also* Rubella) 056.9
  scarlatinosis 057.8
Rubeosis iridis 364.42
  diabetica 250.5 *[364.42]*
Rubinstein-Taybi's syndrome (brachydactylia,
  short stature and mental retardation) 759.89
Rud's syndrome (mental deficiency, epilepsy,
  and infantilism) 759.89
Rudimentary (congenital)—*see also* Agenesis
  arm 755.22
  bone 756.9
  cervix uteri 752.49
  eye (*see also* Microphthalmos) 743.10
  fallopian tube 752.19
  leg 755.32
  lobule of ear 744.21
  patella 755.64
  respiratory organs in thoracopagus 759.4
  tracheal bronchus 748.3
  uterine horn 752.3
  uterus 752.3
    in male 752.7
    solid or with cavity 752.3
  vagina 752.49
Ruiter-Pompen (-Wyers) syndrome
  (angiokeratoma corporis diffusum) 272.7
Ruled out condition (*see also* Observation,
  suspected) V71.9
Rumination —*see also* Vomiting
  neurotic 300.3
  obsessional 300.3
  psychogenic 307.53
Runaway reaction —*see also* Disturbance,
  conduct
  socialized 312.2
  undersocialized, unsocialized 312.1
Runeberg's disease (progressive pernicious
  anemia) 281.0
Runge's syndrome (postmaturity) 766.2
Rupia 091.3
  congenital 090.0
  tertiary 095.9
Rupture, ruptured 553.9
  abdominal viscera NEC 799.8
    obstetrical trauma 665.5
  abscess (spontaneous)—*see* Abscess, by site
  amnion—*see* Rupture, membranes
  aneurysm—*see* Aneurysm
  anus (sphincter)—*see* Laceration, anus
  aorta, aortic 441.5
    abdominal 441.3
    arch 441.1
    ascending 441.1
    descending 441.5
      abdominal 441.3
      thoracic 441.1
    syphilitic 093.0
    thoracoabdominal 441.6
    thorax, thoracic 441.1
    transverse 441.1
    traumatic (thoracic) 901.0
      abdominal 902.0
    valve or cusp (*see also* Endocarditis, aortic)
      424.1
  appendix (with peritonitis) 540.0
    traumatic—*see* Injury, internal,
      gastrointestinal tract
    with peritoneal abscess 540.1
  arteriovenous fistula, brain (congenital) 430

Rupture, ruptured—*continued*
  artery 447.2
    brain (*see also* Hemorrhage, brain) 431
    coronary (*see also* Infarct, myocardium) 410.9
    heart (*see also* Infarct, myocardium) 410.9
    pulmonary 417.8
    traumatic (complication) (*see also* Injury,
      blood vessel, by site) 904.9
  bile duct, except cystic (*see also* Disease,
    biliary) 576.3
    cystic 575.4
    traumatic—*see* Injury, internal,
      intra-abdominal
  bladder (sphincter) 596.6
    with
      abortion—*see* Abortion, by type, with
        damage to pelvic organs
      ectopic pregnancy (*see also* categories
        633.0-633.9) 639.2
      molar pregnancy (*see also* categories
        630-632) 639.2
    following
      abortion 639.2
      ectopic or molar pregnancy 639.2
    nontraumatic 596.6
    obstetrical trauma 665.5
    spontaneous 596.6
    traumatic—*see* Injury, internal, bladder
  blood vessel (*see also* Hemorrhage) 459.0
    brain (*see also* Hemorrhage, brain) 431
    heart (*see also* Infarct, myocardium) 410.9
    traumatic (complication) (*see also* Injury,
      blood vessel, by site) 904.9
  bone—*see* Fracture, by site
  bowel 569.89
    traumatic—*see* Injury, internal, intestine
  Bowman's membrane 371.31
  brain
    aneurysm (congenital) (*see also* Hemorrhage,
      subarachnoid) 430
      late effect—*see* Late effect(s) (of)
        cerebrovascular disease
      syphilitic 094.87
    hemorrhagic (*see also* Hemorrhage, brain) 431
    injury at birth 767.0
    syphilitic 094.89
  capillaries 448.9
  cardiac (*see also* Infarct, myocardium) 410.9
  cartilage (articular) (current)—*see also* Sprain,
    by site
    knee—*see* Tear, meniscus
    semilunar—*see* Tear, meniscus
  cecum (with peritonitis) 540.0
    traumatic 863.89
      with open wound into cavity 863.99
    with peritoneal abscess 540.1
  cerebral aneurysm (congenital) (*see also*
    Hemorrhage, subarachnoid) 430
    late effect—*see* Late effect(s) (of)
      cerebrovascular disease
  cervix (uteri)
    with
      abortion—*see* Abortion, by type, with
        damage to pelvic organs
      ectopic pregnancy (*see also* categories
        633.0-633.9) 639.2
      molar pregnancy (*see also* categories
        630-632) 639.2
    following
      abortion 639.2
      ectopic or molar pregnancy 639.2

Rupture, ruptured—*continued*
   with otitis media—*see* Otitis media
   traumatic—*see* Wound, open, ear, drum
  umbilical cord 663.8
   fetus or newborn 772.0
  ureter (traumatic) (*see also* Injury, internal,
     ureter) 867.2
   nontraumatic 593.89
  urethra 599.84
   with
    abortion—*see* Abortion, by type, with
      damage to pelvic organs
    ectopic pregnancy (*see also* categories
      633.0-633.9) 639.2
    molar pregnancy (*see also* categories
      630-632) 639.2
   following
    abortion 639.2
    ectopic or molar pregnancy 639.2
   obstetrical trauma 665.5
   traumatic—*see* Injury, internal urethra
  uterosacral ligament 620.8
  uterus (traumatic)—*see also* Injury, internal
     uterus
   affecting fetus or newborn 763.89
   during labor 665.1
   nonpuerperal, nontraumatic 621.8
   nontraumatic 621.8
   pregnant (during labor) 665.1
    before labor 665.0
  vaginal 878.6
   complicated 878.7
   complicating delivery—*see* Laceration,
     vagina, complicating delivery
  valve, valvular (heart)—*see* Endocarditis
  varicose vein—*see* Varicose, vein
  varix—*see* Varix
  vena cava 459.0
  ventricle (free wall) (left) (*see also* Infarct,
     myocardium) 410.9
  vesical (urinary) 596.6
   traumatic—*see* Injury, internal, bladder
  vessel (blood) 459.0
   pulmonary 417.8
  viscus 799.8
  vulva 878.4
   complicated 878.5
   complicating delivery 664.0
Russell's dwarf (uterine dwarfism and
  craniofacial dysostosis) 759.89
Russell's dysentery 004.8
Russell (-Silver) syndrome (congenital
  hemihypertrophy and short stature) 759.89
Russian spring-summer type encephalitis 063.0
Rust's disease (tuberculous spondylitis) 015.0
  [720.81]
Rustitskii's disease (multiple myeloma)
  (M9730/3) 203.0
Ruysch's disease (Hirschsprung's disease) 751.3
Rytand-Lipsitch syndrome (complete
  atrioventricular block) 426.0

S

Saber
  shin 090.5
  tibia 090.5
Sac, lacrimal —*see* condition
Saccharomyces infection (*see also* Candidiasis)
  112.9
Saccharopinuria 270.7
Saccular —*see* condition
Sacculation
  aorta (nonsyphilitic) (*see also* Aneurysm, aorta)
    441.9
    ruptured 441.5
    syphilitic 093.0
  bladder 596.3
  colon 569.89
  intralaryngeal (congenital) (ventricular) 748.3
  larynx (congenital) (ventricular) 748.3
  organ or site, congenital—*see* Distortion
  pregnant uterus, complicating delivery 654.4
    affecting fetus or newborn 763.1
      causing obstructed labor 660.2
        affecting fetus or newborn 763.1
  rectosigmoid 569.89
  sigmoid 569.89
  ureter 593.89
  urethra 599.2
  vesical 596.3
Sachs (-Tay) disease (amaurotic familial idiocy)
  330.1
Sacks-Libman disease 710.0 *[424.91]*
Sacralgia 724.6
Sacralization
  fifth lumbar vertebra 756.15
  incomplete (vertebra) 756.15
Sacrodynia 724.6
Sacroiliac joint —*see* condition
Sacroiliitis NEC 720.2
Sacrum —*see* condition
Saddle
  back 737.8
  embolus, aorta 444.0
  nose 738.0
    congenital 754.0
    due to syphilis 090.5
Sadism (sexual) 302.84
Saemisch's ulcer 370.04
Saenger's syndrome 379.46
Sago spleen 277.3
Sailors' skin 692.74
Saint
  Anthony's fire (*see also* Erysipelas) 035
  Guy's dance—*see* Chorea
  Louis-type encephalitis 062.3
  triad (*see also* Hernia, diaphragm) 553.3
  Vitus' dance—*see* Chorea
Salicylism
  correct substance properly administered 535.4
  overdose or wrong substance given or taken
    965.1
Salivary duct or gland —*see also* condition
  virus disease 078.5
Salivation (excessive) (*see also* Ptyalism) 527.7
Salmonella (aertrycke) (choleraesuis)
  (enteritidis) (gallinarum) (suipestifer)
  (typhimurium) (*see also* Infection,
  Salmonella) 003.9
  arthritis 003.23
  carrier (suspected) of V02.3

Salmonella—*continued*
  meningitis 003.21
  osteomyelitis 003.24
  pneumonia 003.22
  septicemia 003.1
  typhosa 002.0
  carrier (suspected) of V02.1
Salmonellosis 003.0
  with pneumonia 003.22
Salpingitis (catarrhal) (fallopian tube) (nodular)
  (pseudofollicular) (purulent) (septic) (*see also*
  Salpingo-oophoritis) 614.2
  ear 381.50
    acute 381.51
    chronic 381.52
  Eustachian (tube) 381.50
    acute 381.51
    chronic 381.52
  follicularis 614.1
  gonococcal (chronic) 098.37
    acute 098.17
  interstitial, chronic 614.1
  isthmica nodosa 614.1
  old—*see* Salpingo-oophoritis, chronic
  puerperal, postpartum, childbirth 670
  specific (chronic) 098.37
    acute 098.17
  tuberculous (acute) (chronic) (*see also*
    Tuberculosis) 016.6
  venereal (chronic) 098.37
    acute 098.17
Salpingocele 620.4
Salpingo-oophoritis (catarrhal) (purulent)
  (ruptured) (septic) (suppurative) 614.2
  acute 614.0
    with
      abortion—*see* Abortion, by type, with sepsis
      ectopic pregnancy (*see also* categories
        633.0-633.9) 639.0
      molar pregnancy (*see also* categories
        630-632) 639.0
    following
      abortion 639.0
      ectopic or molar pregnancy 639.0
    gonococcal 098.17
    puerperal, postpartum, childbirth 670
    tuberculous (*see also* Tuberculosis) 016.6
  chronic 614.1
    gonococcal 098.37
    tuberculous (*see also* Tuberculosis) 016.6
  complicating pregnancy 646.6
    affecting fetus or newborn 760.8
  gonococcal (chronic) 098.37
    acute 098.17
  old—*see* Salpingo-oophoritis, chronic
  puerperal 670
  specific—*see* Salpingo-oophoritis, gonococcal
  subacute (*see also* Salpingo-oophoritis, acute)
    614.0
  tuberculous (acute) (chronic) (*see also*
    Tuberculosis) 016.6
  venereal—*see* Salpingo-oophoritis, gonococcal
Salpingo-ovaritis (*see also* Salpingo-oophoritis)
  614.2
Salpingoperitonitis (*see also*
  Salpingo-oophoritis) 614.2

Salt-losing
   nephritis (*see also* Disease, renal) 593.9
   syndrome (*see also* Disease, renal) 593.9
Salt-rheum (*see also* Eczema) 692.9
Salzmann's nodular dystrophy 371.46
Sampson's cyst or tumor 617.1
Sandblasters'
   asthma 502
   lung 502
Sander's disease (paranoia) 297.1
Sandfly fever 066.0
Sandhoff's disease 330.1
Sanfilippo's syndrome (mucopolysaccharidosis
      III) 277.5
Sanger-Brown's ataxia 334.2
San Joaquin Valley fever 114.0
São Paulo fever or typhus 082.0
Saponification, mesenteric 567.8
Sapremia —*see* Septicemia
Sarcocele (benign)
   syphilitic 095.8
      congenital 090.5
Sarcoepiplocele (*see also* Hernia) 553.9
Sarcoepiplomphalocele (*see also* Hernia,
      umbilicus) 553.1
Sarcoid (any site) 135
   with lung involvement 135 *[517.8]*
      Boeck's 135
      Darier-Roussy 135
      Spiegler-Fendt 686.8
Sarcoidosis 135
   cardiac 135 *[425.8]*
   lung 135 *[517.8]*
Sarcoma (M8800/3)—*see also* Neoplasm,
      connective tissue, malignant
   alveolar soft part (M9581/3)—*see* Neoplasm,
      connective tissue, malignant
   ameloblastic (M9330/3) 170.1
      upper jaw (bone) 170.0
   botryoid (M8910/3)—*see* Neoplasm, connective
      tissue, malignant
   botryoides (M8910/3)—*see* Neoplasm,
      connective tissue, malignant
   cerebellar (M9480/3) 191.6
      circumscribed (arachnoidal) (M9471/3) 191.6
   circumscribed (arachnoidal) cerebellar
      (M9471/3) 191.6
   clear cell, of tendons and aponeuroses
      (M9044/3)—*see* Neoplasm, connective
      tissue, malignant
   embryonal (M8991/3)—*see* Neoplasm,
      connective tissue, malignant
   endometrial (stromal) (M8930/3) 182.0
      isthmus 182.1
   endothelial (M9130/3)—*see also* Neoplasm,
      connective tissue, malignant
      bone (M9260/3)—*see* Neoplasm, bone,
         malignant
   epithelioid cell (M8804/3)—*see* Neoplasm,
      connective tissue, malignant
   Ewing's (M9260/3)—*see* Neoplasm, bone,
      malignant
   germinoblastic (diffuse) (M9632/3) 202.8
      follicular (M9697/3) 202.0
   giant cell (M8802/3)—*see also* Neoplasm,
      connective tissue, malignant
      bone (M9250/3)—*see* Neoplasm, bone,
         malignant
      glomoid (M8710/3)—*see* Neoplasm, connective
         tissue, malignant

Sarcoma—*continued*
   granulocytic (M9930/3) 205.3
   hemangioendothelial (M9130/3)—*see*
      Neoplasm, connective tissue, malignant
   hemorrhagic, multiple (M9140/3)—*see*
      Kaposi's, sarcoma
   Hodgkin's (M9662/3) 201.2
   immunoblastic (M9612/3) 200.8
   Kaposi's (M9140/3)—*see* Kaposi's, sarcoma
   Kupffer cell (M9124/3) 155.0
   leptomeningeal (M9530/3)—*see* Neoplasm,
      meninges, malignant
   lymphangioendothelial (M9170/3)—*see*
      Neoplasm, connective tissue, malignant
   lymphoblastic (M9630/3) 200.1
   lymphocytic (M9620/3) 200.1
   mast cell (M9740/3) 202.6
   melanotic (M8720/3)—*see* Melanoma
   meningeal (M9530/3)—*see* Neoplasm,
      meninges, malignant
   meningothelial (M9530/3)—*see* Neoplasm,
      meninges, malignant
   mesenchymal (M8800/3)—*see also* Neoplasm,
      connective tissue, malignant
      mixed (M8990/3)—*see* Neoplasm, connective
         tissue, malignant
   mesothelial (M9050/3)—*see* Neoplasm, by site,
      malignant
   monstrocellular (M9481/3)
      specified site—*see* Neoplasm, by site,
         malignant
      unspecified site 191.9
   myeloid (M9930/3) 205.3
   neurogenic (M9540/3)—*see* Neoplasm,
      connective tissue, malignant
   odontogenic (M9270/3) 170.1
      upper jaw (bone) 170.0
   osteoblastic (M9180/3)—*see* Neoplasm, bone,
      malignant
   osteogenic (M9180/3)—*see also* Neoplasm,
      bone, malignant
      juxtacortical (M9190/3)—*see* Neoplasm,
         bone, malignant
      periosteal (M9190/3)—*see* Neoplasm, bone,
         malignant
   periosteal (M8812/3)—*see also* Neoplasm,
      bone, malignant
      osteogenic (M9190/3)—*see* Neoplasm, bone,
         malignant
   plasma cell (M9731/3) 203.8
   pleomorphic cell (M8802/3)—*see* Neoplasm,
      connective tissue, malignant
   reticuloendothelial (M9720/3) 202.3
   reticulum cell (M9640/3) 200.0
      nodular (M9642/3) 200.0
      pleomorphic cell type (M9641/3) 200.0
   round cell (M8803/3)—*see* Neoplasm,
      connective tissue, malignant
   small cell (M8803/3)—*see* Neoplasm,
      connective tissue, malignant
   spindle cell (M8801/3)—*see* Neoplasm,
      connective tissue, malignant
   stromal (endometrial) (M8930/3) 182.0
      isthmus 182.1
   synovial (M9040/3)—*see also* Neoplasm,
      connective tissue, malignant
      biphasic type (M9043/3)—*see* Neoplasm,
         connective tissue, malignant
      epithelioid cell type (M9042/3)—*see*
         Neoplasm, connective tissue, malignant
      spindle cell type (M9041/3)—*see* Neoplasm,
         connective tissue, malignant

Sarcomatosis
  meningeal (M9539/3)—*see* Neoplasm,
    meninges, malignant
  specified site NEC (M8800/3)—*see* Neoplasm,
    connective tissue, malignant
  unspecified site (M8800/6) 171.9
Sarcosinemia 270.8
Sarcosporidiosis 136.5
Saturnine —*see* condition
Saturnism 984.9
  specified type of lead—*see* Table of drugs and
    chemicals
Satyriasis 302.89
Sauriasis —*see* Ichthyosis
Sauriderma 757.39
Sauriosis —*see* Ichthyosis
Savill's disease (epidemic exfoliative dermatitis)
  695.89
SBE (subacute bacterial endocarditis) 421.0
Scabies (any site) 133.0
Scabs 782.8
Scaglietti-Dagnini syndrome (acromegalic
  macrospondylitis) 253.0
Scald, scalded —*see also* Burn, by site
  skin syndrome 695.1
Scalenus anticus (anterior) syndrome 353.0
Scales 782.8
Scalp —*see* condition
Scaphocephaly 756.0
Scaphoiditis, tarsal 732.5
Scapulalgia 733.90
Scapulohumeral myopathy 359.1
Scar, scarring (*see also* Cicatrix) 709.2
  adherent 709.2
  atrophic 709.2
  cervix
    in pregnancy or childbirth 654.6
      affecting fetus or newborn 763.89
      causing obstructed labor 660.2
        affecting fetus or newborn 763.1
  cheloid 701.4
  chorioretinal 363.30
    disseminated 363.35
    macular 363.32
    peripheral 363.34
    posterior pole NEC 363.33
  choroid (*see also* Scar, chorioretinal) 363.30
  compression, pericardial 423.9
  congenital 757.39
  conjunctiva 372.64
  cornea 371.00
    xerophthalmic 264.6
  due to previous cesarean delivery, complicating
    pregnancy or childbirth 654.2
    affecting fetus or newborn 763.89
  duodenal (bulb) (cap) 537.3
  hypertrophic 701.4
  keloid 701.4
  labia 624.4
  lung (base) 518.89
  macula 363.32
    disseminated 363.35
    peripheral 363.34
  muscle 728.89
  myocardium, myocardial 412
  painful 709.2
  papillary muscle 429.81
  posterior pole NEC 363.33
    macular—*see* Scar, macula
  postnecrotic (hepatic) (liver) 571.9

Scar, scarring—*continued*
  psychic V15.49
  retina (*see also* Scar, chorioretinal) 363.30
  trachea 478.9
  uterus 621.8
    in pregnancy or childbirth NEC 654.9
      affecting fetus or newborn 763.89
      due to previous cesarean delivery 654.2
  vulva 624.4
Scarabiasis 134.1
Scarlatina 034.1
  anginosa 034.1
  maligna 034.1
  myocarditis, acute 034.1 *[422.0]*
    old (*see also* Myocarditis) 429.0
  otitis media 034.1 *[382.02]*
  ulcerosa 034.1
Scarlatinella 057.8
Scarlet fever (albuminuria) (angina)
  (convulsions) (lesions of lid) (rash) 034.1
Schamberg's disease, dermatitis, or dermatosis
  (progressive pigmentary dermatosis) 709.09
Schatzki's ring (esophagus) (lower) (congenital)
  750.3
  acquired 530.3
Schaufenster krankheit 413.9
Schaumann's
  benign lymphogranulomatosis 135
  disease (sarcoidosis) 135
  syndrome (sarcoidosis) 135
Scheie's syndrome (mucopolysaccharidosis IS)
  277.5
Schenck's disease (sporotrichosis) 117.1
Scheuermann's disease or osteochondrosis
  732.0
Scheuthauer-Marie-Sainton syndrome
  (cleidocranialis dysostosis) 755.59
Schilder (-Flatau) disease 341.1
Schilling-type monocytic leukemia (M9890/3)
  206.9
Schimmelbusch's disease, cystic mastitis, or hy-
  perplasia 610.1
Schirmer's syndrome (encephalocutaneous
  angiomatosis) 759.6
Schistocelia 756.79
Schistoglossia 750.13
Schistosoma infestation —*see* Infestation,
  Schistosoma
Schistosomiasis 120.9
  Asiatic 120.2
  bladder 120.0
  chestermani 120.8
  colon 120.1
  cutaneous 120.3
  due to
    S. hematobium 120.0
    S. japonicum 120.2
    S. mansoni 120.1
    S. mattheii 120.8
  eastern 120.2
  genitourinary tract 120.0
  intestinal 120.1
  lung 120.2
  Manson's (intestinal) 120.1
  Oriental 120.2
  pulmonary 120.2
  specified type NEC 120.8
  vesical 120.0
Schizencephaly 742.4
Schizo-affective psychosis (*see also*
  Schizophrenia) 295.7
Schizodontia 520.2

Schizoid personality 301.20
introverted 301.21
schizotypal 301.22
Schizophrenia, schizophrenic (reaction) 295.9

> *Note—Use the following fifth-digit*
> *subclassification with category 295:*
>
> *0 unspecified*
> *1 subchronic*
> *2 chronic*
> *3 subchronic with acute exacerbation*
> *4 chronic with acute exacerbation*
> *5 in remission*

acute (attack) NEC 295.8
episode 295.4
atypical form 295.8
borderline 295.5
catalepsy 295.2
catatonic (type) (acute) (excited) (withdrawn)
295.2
childhood (type) (*see also* Psychosis,
childhood) 299.9
chronic NEC 295.6
coenesthesiopathic 295.8
cyclic (type) 295.7
disorganized (type) 295.1
flexibilitas cerea 295.2
hebephrenic (type) (acute) 295.1
incipient 295.5
latent 295.5
paranoid (type) (acute) 295.3
paraphrenic (acute) 295.3
prepsychotic 295.5
primary (acute) 295.0
prodromal 295.5
pseudoneurotic 295.5
pseudopsychopathic 295.5
reaction 295.9
residual (state) (type) 295.6
restzustand 295.6
schizo-affective (type) (depressed) (excited)
295.7
schizophreniform type 295.4
simple (type) (acute) 295.0
simplex (acute) 295.0
specified type NEC 295.8
syndrome of childhood NEC (*see also*
Psychosis, childhood) 299.9
undifferentiated 295.9
acute 295.8
chronic 295.6
Schizothymia 301.20
introverted 301.21
schizotypal 301.22
Schlafkrankheit 086.5
Schlatter's tibia (osteochondrosis) 732.4
Schlatter-Osgood disease (osteochondrosis,
tibial tubercle) 732.4
Schloffer's tumor (*see also* Peritonitis) 567.2
Schmidt's syndrome
sphallo-pharyngo-laryngeal hemiplegia 352.6
thyroid-adrenocortical insufficiency 258.1
vagoaccessory 352.6
Schmincke
carcinoma (M8082/3)—*see* Neoplasm,
nasopharynx, malignant
tumor (M8082/3)—*see* Neoplasm,
nasopharynx, malignant
Schmitz (-Stutzer) dysentery 004.0

Schmorl's disease or nodes 722.30
lumbar, lumbosacral 722.32
specified region NEC 722.39
thoracic, thoracolumbar 722.31
Schneider's syndrome 047.9
Schneiderian
carcinoma (M8121/3)
specified site—*see* Neoplasm, by site,
malignant
unspecified site 160.0
papilloma (M8121/0)
specified site—*see* Neoplasm, by site, benign
unspecified site 212.0
Schoffer's tumor (*see also* Peritonitis) 567.2
Scholte's syndrome (malignant carcinoid) 259.2
Scholz's disease 330.0
Scholz (-Bielschowsky-Henneberg) syndrome
330.0
Schönlein (-Henoch) disease (primary) (purpura)
(rheumatic) 287.0
School examination V70.3
Schottmüller's disease (*see also* Fever,
paratyphoid) 002.9
Schroeder's syndrome (endocrine-hypertensive)
255.3
Schüller-Christian disease or syndrome
(chronic histiocytosis X) 277.8
Schultz's disease or syndrome (agranulocytosis)
288.0
Schultze's acroparesthesia, simple 443.89
Schwalbe-Ziehen-Oppenheimer disease 333.6
Schwannoma (M9560/0)—*see also* Neoplasm,
connective tissue, benign
malignant (M9560/3)—*see* Neoplasm,
connective tissue, malignant
Schwartz (-Jampel) syndrome 756.89
Schwartz-Bartter syndrome (inappropriate
secretion of antidiuretic hormone) 253.6
Schweninger-Buzzi disease (macular atrophy)
701.3
Sciatic —*see* condition
Sciatica (infectional) 724.3
due to
displacement of intervertebral disc 722.10
herniation, nucleus pulposus 722.10
Scimitar syndrome (anomalous venous
drainage, right lung to inferior vena cava)
747.49
Sclera —*see* condition
Sclerectasia 379.11
Scleredema
adultorum 710.1
Buschke's 710.1
newborn 778.1
Sclerema
adiposum (newborn) 778.1
adultorum 710.1
edematosum (newborn) 778.1
neonatorum 778.1
newborn 778.1
Scleriasis —*see* Scleroderma
Scleritis 379.00
with corneal involvement 379.05
anterior (annular) (localized) 379.03
brawny 379.06
granulomatous 379.09
posterior 379.07
specified NEC 379.09
suppurative 379.09
syphilitic 095.0
tuberculous (nodular) (*see also* Tuberculosis)
017.3 *[379.09]*

Sclerochoroiditis (*see also* Scleritis) 379.00
Scleroconjunctivitis (*see also* Scleritis) 379.00
Sclerocystic ovary (syndrome) 256.4
Sclerodactylia 701.0
Scleroderma, sclerodermia (acrosclerotic)
   (diffuse) (generalized) (progressive)
   (pulmonary) 710.1
   circumscribed 701.0
   linear 701.0
   localized (linear) 701.0
   newborn 778.1
Sclerokeratitis 379.05
   meaning sclerosing keratitis 370.54
   tuberculous (*see also* Tuberculosis) 017.3
      [379.09]
Scleroma, trachea 040.1
Scleromalacia
   multiple 731.0
   perforans 379.04
Scleromyxedema 701.8
Scleroperikeratitis 379.05
Sclerose en plaques 340
Sclerosis, sclerotic
   adrenal (gland) 255.8
   Alzheimer's 331.0
      with dementia—*see* Alzheimer's, demential
   amyotrophic (lateral) 335.20
   annularis fibrosi
      aortic 424.1
      mitral 424.0
   aorta, aortic 440.0
      valve (*see also* Endocarditis, aortic) 424.1
   artery, arterial, arteriolar, arteriovascular—*see*
      Arteriosclerosis
   ascending multiple 340
   Baló's (concentric) 341.1
   basilar—*see* Sclerosis, brain
   bone (localized) NEC 733.99
   brain (general) (lobular) 341.9
      Alzheimer's—*see* Alzheimer's dementia
      artery, arterial 437.0
      atrophic lobar 331.0
         with dementia
            with behavioral disturbance 331.0 *[294.11]*
            without behavioral disturbance 331.0
               [294.10]
      diffuse 341.1
         familial (chronic) (infantile) 330.0
         infantile (chronic) (familial) 330.0
         Pelizaeus-Merzbacher type 330.0
      disseminated 340
      hereditary 334.2
      infantile, (degenerative) (diffuse) 330.0
      insular 340
      Krabbe's 330.0
      miliary 340
      multiple 340
      Pelizaeus-Merzbacher 330.0
      progressive familial 330.0
      senile 437.0
      tuberous 759.5
   bulbar, progressive 340
   bundle of His 426.50
      left 426.3
      right 426.4
   cardiac —*see* Arteriosclerosis, coronary
   cardiorenal (*see also* Hypertension, cardiorenal)
      404.90
   cardiovascular (*see also* Disease,
      cardiovascular) 429.2

Sclerosis, sclerotic—*continued*
   renal (*see also* Hypertension, cardiorenal)
      404.90
   centrolobar, familial 330.0
   cerebellar—*see* Sclerosis, brain
   cerebral—*see* Sclerosis, brain
   cerebrospinal 340
      disseminated 340
      multiple 340
   cerebrovascular 437.0
   choroid 363.40
      diffuse 363.56
   combined (spinal cord)—*see also* Degeneration,
      combined
      multiple 340
   concentric, Baló's 341.1
   cornea 370.54
   coronary (artery) —*see* Arteriosclerosis,
      coronary
   corpus cavernosum
      female 624.8
      male 607.89
   Dewitzky's
      aortic 424.1
      mitral 424.0
   diffuse NEC 341.1
   disease, heart —*see* Arteriosclerosis, coronary
   disseminated 340
   dorsal 340
   dorsolateral (spinal cord)—*see* Degeneration,
      combined
   endometrium 621.8
   extrapyramidal 333.90
   eye, nuclear (senile) 366.16
   Friedreich's (spinal cord) 334.0
   funicular (spermatic cord) 608.89
   gastritis 535.4
   general (vascular)—*see* Arteriosclerosis
   gland (lymphatic) 457.8
   hepatic 571.9
   hereditary
      cerebellar 334.2
      spinal 334.0
   idiopathic cortical (Garré's) (*see also*
      Osteomyelitis) 730.1
   ilium, piriform 733.5
   insular 340
      pancreas 251.8
   Islands of Langerhans 251.8
   kidney—*see* Sclerosis, renal
   larynx 478.79
   lateral 335.24
      amyotrophic 335.20
      descending 335.24
      primary 335.24
      spinal 335.24
   liver 571.9
   lobar, atrophic (of brain) 331.0
      with dementia
         with behavioral disturbance 331.0 *[294.11]*
         without behavioral disturbance 331.0
            [294.10]
   lung (*see also* Fibrosis, lung) 515
   mastoid 383.1
   mitral—*see* Endocarditis, mitral
   Mönckeberg's (medial) (*see also*
      Arteriosclerosis, extremities) 440.20
   multiple (brain stem) (cerebral) (generalized)
      (spinal cord) 340
   myocardium, myocardial —*see*
      Arteriosclerosis, coronary

Screening (for)—*continued*
cardiovascular disease NEC V81.2
cataract V80.2
Chagas' disease V75.3
chemical poisoning V82.5
cholera V74.0
cholesterol V77.91
chromosomal
  anomalies
    by amniocentesis, antenatal V28.0
    maternal postnatal V82.4
  athletes V70.3
condition
  cardiovascular NEC V81.2
  eye NEC V80.2
  genitourinary NEC V81.6
  neurological V80.0
  respiratory NEC V81.4
  skin V82.0
  specified NEC V82.89
congenital
  anomaly V82.89
    eye V80.2
  dislocation of hip V82.3
  eye condition or disease V80.2
conjunctivitis, bacterial V74.4
contamination NEC (*see also* Poisoning) V82.5
coronary artery disease V81.0
cystic fibrosis V77.6
deficiency anemia NEC V78.1
  iron V78.0
dengue fever V73.5
depression V79.0
developmental handicap V79.9
  in early childhood V79.3
  specified type NEC V79.8
diabetes mellitus V77.1
diphtheria V74.3
disease or disorder V82.9
  bacterial V74.9
    specified NEC V74.8
  blood V78.9
    specified type NEC V78.8
  blood-forming organ V78.9
    specified type NEC V78.8
  cardiovascular NEC V81.2
    hypertensive V81.1
    ischemic V81.0
  Chagas' V75.3
  chlamydial V73.98
    specified NEC V73.88
  ear NEC V80.3
  endocrine NEC V77.99
  eye NEC V80.2
  genitourinary NEC V81.6
  heart NEC V81.2
    hypertensive V81.1
    ischemic V81.0
  immunity NEC V77.99
  infectious NEC V75.9
  lipoid NEC V77.91
  mental V79.9
    specified type NEC V79.8
  metabolic NEC V77.99
    inborn NEC V77.7
  neurological V80.0
  nutritional NEC V77.99
  rheumatic NEC V82.2
  rickettsial V75.0
  sickle-cell V78.2
    trait V78.2

Screening (for)—*continued*
specified type NEC V82.89
thyroid V77.0
vascular NEC V81.2
  ischemic V81.0
venereal V74.5
viral V73.99
  arthropod-borne NEC V73.5
  specified type NEC V73.89
dislocation of hip, congenital V82.3
drugs in athletes V70.3
emphysema (chronic) V81.3
encephalitis, viral (mosquito or tick borne)
  V73.5
endocrine disorder NEC V77.99
eye disorder NEC V80.2
  congenital V80.2
fever
  dengue V73.5
  hemorrhagic V73.5
  yellow V73.4
filariasis V75.6
galactosemia V77.4
genitourinary condition NEC V81.6
glaucoma V80.1
gonorrhea V74.5
gout V77.5
Hansen's disease V74.2
heart disease NEC V81.2
  hypertensive V81.1
  ischemic V81.0
heavy metal poisoning V82.5
helminthiasis, intestinal V75.7
hematopoietic malignancy V76.89
hemoglobinopathies NEC V78.3
hemorrhagic fever V73.5
Hodgkin's disease V76.89
hormones in athletes V70.3
hypercholesterolemia V77.91
hyperlipidemia V77.91
hypertension V81.1
immunity disorder NEC V77.99
inborn errors of metabolism NEC V77.7
infection
  bacterial V74.9
    specified type NEC V74.8
  mycotic V75.4
  parasitic NEC V75.8
infectious disease V75.9
  specified type NEC V75.8
ingestion of radioactive substance V82.5
intestinal helminthiasis V75.7
iron deficiency anemia V78.0
ischemic heart disease V81.0
lead poisoning V82.5
leishmaniasis V75.2
leprosy V74.2
leptospirosis V74.8
leukemia V76.89
lipoid disorder NEC V77.91
lymphoma V76.89
malaria V75.1
malignant neoplasm (of) V76.9
  bladder V76.3
  blood V76.89
  breast V76.10
    mammogram NEC V76.12
      for high-risk patient V76.11
    specified type NEC V76.19
  cervix V76.2
  colon V76.51

Screening (for)—*continued*
  hematopoietic system V76.89
  intestine V76.50
    colon V76.51
    small V76.52
  lung V76.0
  lymph (glands) V76.89
  nervous system V76.81
  oral cavity V76.42
  other specified neoplasm NEC V76.89
  ovary V76.46
  prostate V76.44
  rectum V76.41
  respiratory organs V76.0
  skin V76.43
  specified sites NEC V76.49
  testis V76.45
  vagina V76.47
    following hysterectomy for malignant
      condition V67.01
  malnutrition V77.2
  mammogram NEC V76.12
    for high-risk patient V76.11
  maternal postnatal chromosomal anomalies
    V82.4
  measles V73.2
  mental
    disorder V79.9
      specified type NEC V79.8
    retardation V79.2
  metabolic errors, inborn V77.7
  metabolic disorder NEC V77.99
  mucoviscidosis V77.6
  multiphasic V82.6
  mycosis V75.4
  mycotic infection V75.4
  nephropathy V81.5
  neurological condition V80.0
  nutritional disorder V77.99
    obesity V77.8
  obesity V77.8
  osteoporosis V82.81
  parasitic infection NEC V75.8
  phenylketonuria V77.3
  plague V74.8
  poisoning
    chemical NEC V82.5
    contaminated water supply V82.5
    heavy metal V82.5
  poliomyelitis V73.0
  postnatal chromosomal anomalies, maternal
    V82.4
  prenatal—*see* Screening, antenatal
  pulmonary tuberculosis V74.1
  radiation exposure V82.5
  renal disease V81.5
  respiratory condition NEC V81.4
  rheumatic disorder NEC V82.2
  rheumatoid arthritis V82.1
  rickettsial disease V75.0
  rubella V73.3
  schistosomiasis V75.5
  senile macular lesions of eye V80.2
  sickle-cell anemia, disease, or trait V78.2
  skin condition V82.0
  sleeping sickness V75.3
  smallpox V73.1
  special V82.9
    specified condition NEC V82.89
  specified type NEC V82.89
  spirochetal disease V74.9

Screening (for)—*continued*
  specified type NEC V74.8
  stimulants in athletes V70.3
  syphilis V74.5
  tetanus V74.8
  thyroid disorder V77.0
  trachoma V73.6
  trypanosomiasis V75.3
  tuberculosis, pulmonary V74.1
  venereal disease V74.5
  viral encephalitis
    mosquito-borne V73.5
    tick-borne V73.5
  whooping cough V74.8
  worms, intestinal V75.7
  yaws V74.6
  yellow fever V73.4
Scrofula (*see also* Tuberculosis) 017.2
Scrofulide (primary) (*see also* Tuberculosis)
  017.0
Scrofuloderma, scrofulodermia (any site)
  (primary) (*see also* Tuberculosis) 017.0
Scrofulosis (universal) (*see also* Tuberculosis)
  017.2
Scrofulosis lichen (primary) (*see also*
  Tuberculosis) 017.0
Scrofulous —*see* condition
Scrotal tongue 529.5
  congenital 750.13
Scrotum —*see* condition
Scurvy (gum) (infantile) (rickets) (scorbutic) 267
Sea-blue histiocyte syndrome 272.7
Seabright-Bantam syndrome
  (pseudohypoparathyroidism) 275.49
Seasickness 994.6
Seatworm 127.4
Sebaceous
  cyst (*see also* Cyst, sebaceous) 706.2
  gland disease NEC 706.9
Sebocystomatosis 706.2
Seborrhea, seborrheic 706.3
  adiposa 706.3
  capitis 690.11
  congestiva 695.4
  corporis 706.3
  dermatitis 690.10
    infantile 690.12
  diathesis in infants 695.89
  eczema 690.18
    infantile 690.12
  keratosis 702.19
    inflamed 702.11
  nigricans 705.89
  sicca 690.18
  wart 702.19
    inflamed 702.11
Seckel's syndrome 759.89
Seclusion pupil 364.74
Seclusiveness, child 313.22
Secondary —*see also* condition
  neoplasm—*see* Neoplasm, by site, malignant,
    secondary
Secretan's disease or syndrome (posttraumatic
  edema) 782.3
Secretion
  antidiuretic hormone, inappropriate (syndrome)
    253.6
  catecholamine, by pheochromocytoma 255.6
  hormone
    antidiuretic, inappropriate (syndrome) 253.6

Secretion—*continued*
　by
　　carcinoid tumor 259.2
　　pheochromocytoma 255.6
　　ectopic NEC 259.3
　urinary
　　excessive 788.42
　　suppression 788.5
Section
　cesarean
　　affecting fetus or newborn 763.4
　　post mortem, affecting fetus or newborn 761.6
　　previous, in pregnancy or childbirth 654.2
　　　affecting fetus or newborn 763.89
　nerve, traumatic—*see* Injury, nerve, by site
Seeligmann's syndrome (ichthyosis congenita)
　757.1
Segmentation, incomplete (congenital)—*see*
　also Fusion
　bone NEC 756.9
　lumbosacral (joint) 756.15
　vertebra 756.15
　　lumbosacral 756.15
Seizure 780.39
　akinetic (idiopathic) (*see also* Epilepsy) 345.0
　　psychomotor 345.4
　apoplexy, apoplectic (*see also* Disease,
　　cerebrovascular, acute) 436
　atonic (*see also* Epilepsy) 345.0
　autonomic 300.11
　brain or cerebral (*see also* Disease,
　　cerebrovascular, acute) 436
　convulsive (*see also* Convulsions) 780.39
　cortical (focal) (motor) (*see also* Epilepsy) 345.5
　epilepsy, epileptic (cryptogenic) (*see also*
　　Epilepsy) 345.9
　epileptiform, epileptoid 780.39
　　focal (*see also* Epilepsy) 345.5
　febrile 780.31
　heart—*see* Disease, heart
　hysterical 300.11
　Jacksonian (focal) (*see also* Epilepsy) 345.5
　　motor type 345.5
　　sensory type 345.5
　newborn 779.0
　paralysis (*see also* Disease, cerebrovascular,
　　acute) 436
　recurrent 780.39
　　epileptic—*see* Epilepsy
　repetitive 780.39
　　epileptic—*see* Epilepsy
　salaam (*see also* Epilepsy) 345.6
　uncinate (*see also* Epilepsy) 345.4
Self-mutilation 300.9
Semicoma 780.09
Semiconsciousness 780.09
Seminal
　vesicle—*see* condition
　vesiculitis (*see also* Vesiculitis) 608.0
Seminoma (M9061/3)
　anaplastic type (M9062/3)
　　specified site—*see* Neoplasm, by site,
　　　malignant
　　unspecified site 186.9
　specified site—*see* Neoplasm, by site, malignant
　spermatocytic (M9063/3)
　　specified site—*see* Neoplasm, by site,
　　　malignant
　　unspecified site 186.9
　unspecified site 186.9
Semliki Forest encephalitis 062.8

Senear-Usher disease or syndrome (pemphigus
　erythematosus) 694.4
Senecio jacobae dermatitis 692.6
Senectus 797
Senescence 797
Senile (*see also* condition) 797
　cervix (atrophic) 622.8
　degenerative atrophy, skin 701.3
　endometrium (atrophic) 621.8
　fallopian tube (atrophic) 620.3
　heart (failure) 797
　lung 492.8
　ovary (atrophic) 620.3
　syndrome 259.8
　vagina, vaginitis (atrophic) 627.3
　wart 702.0
Senility 797
　with
　　acute confusional state 290.3
　　delirium 290.3
　　mental changes 290.9
　　psychosis NEC (*see also* Psychosis, senile)
　　　290.20
　premature (syndrome) 259.8
Sensation
　burning (*see also* Disturbance, sensation) 782.0
　　tongue 529.6
　choking 784.9
　loss of (*see also* Disturbance, sensation) 782.0
　prickling (*see also* Disturbance, sensation) 782.0
　tingling (*see also* Disturbance, sensation) 782.0
Sense loss (touch) (*see also* Disturbance,
　sensation) 782.0
　smell 781.1
　taste 781.1
Sensibility disturbance NEC (cortical) (deep)
　(vibratory) (*see also* Disturbance, sensation)
　782.0
Sensitive dentine 521.8
Sensitiver Beziehungswahn 297.8
Sensitivity, sensitization —*see also* Allergy
　autoerythrocyte 287.2
　carotid sinus 337.0
　child (excessive) 313.21
　cold, autoimmune 283.0
　methemoglobin 289.7
　suxamethonium 289.8
　tuberculin, without clinical or radiological
　　symptoms 795.5
Sensory
　extinction 781.8
　neglect 781.8
Separation
　acromioclavicular—*see* Dislocation, shoulder
　anxiety, abnormal 309.21
　apophysis, traumatic—*see* Fracture, by site
　choroid 363.70
　　hemorrhagic 363.72
　　serous 363.71
　costochondral (simple) (traumatic)—*see*
　　Dislocation, costochondral
　epiphysis, epiphyseal
　　nontraumatic 732.9
　　　upper femoral 732.2
　　traumatic—*see* Fracture, by site
　fracture—*see* Fracture, by site
　infundibulum cardiac from right ventricle by a
　　partition 746.83
　joint (current) (traumatic)—*see* Dislocation, by
　　site

Separation—*continued*
  placenta (normally implanted)—*see* Placenta,
      separation
  pubic bone, obstetrical trauma 665.6
  retina, retinal (*see also* Detachment, retina)
      361.9
    layers 362.40
      sensory (*see also* Retinoschisis) 361.10
      pigment epithelium (exudative) 362.42
      hemorrhagic 362.43
  sternoclavicular (traumatic)—*see* Dislocation,
      sternoclavicular
  symphysis pubis, obstetrical trauma 665.6
  tracheal ring, incomplete (congenital) 748.3
Sepsis (generalized) (*see also* Septicemia) 038.9
  with
    abortion—*see* Abortion, by type, with sepsis
    ectopic pregnancy (*see also* categories
        633.0-633.9) 639.0
    molar pregnancy (*see also* categories
        630-632) 639.0
  buccal 528.3
  complicating labor 659.3
  dental (pulpal origin) 522.4
  female genital organ NEC 614.9
  fetus (intrauterine) 771.8
  following
    abortion 639.0
    ectopic or molar pregnancy 639.0
    infusion, perfusion, or transfusion 999.3
  Friedländer's 038.49
  intraocular 360.00
  localized
    in operation wound 998.59
    skin (*see also* Abscess) 682.9
  malleus 024
  nadir 038.9
  newborn (umbilical) (organism unspecified)
      NEC 771.8
  oral 528.3
  puerperal, postpartum, childbirth (pelvic) 670
  resulting from infusion, injection, transfusion,
      or vaccination 999.3
  skin, localized (*see also* Abscess) 682.9
  umbilical (newborn) (organism unspecified)
      771.8
    tetanus 771.3
  urinary 599.0
Septate —*see also* Septum
Septic —*see also* condition
  adenoids 474.01
    and tonsils 474.02
  arm (with lymphangitis) 682.3
  embolus—*see* Embolism
  finger (with lymphangitis) 681.00
  foot (with lymphangitis) 682.7
  gallbladder (*see also* Cholecystitis) 575.8
  hand (with lymphangitis) 682.4
  joint (*see also* Arthritis, septic) 711.0
  kidney (*see also* Infection, kidney) 590.9
  leg (with lymphangitis) 682.6
  mouth 528.3
  nail 681.9
    finger 681.02
    toe 681.11
  shock (endotoxic) 785.59
  sore (*see also* Abscess) 682.9
    throat 034.0
      milk-borne 034.0
      streptococcal 034.0
  spleen (acute) 289.59

Septic—*continued*
  teeth (pulpal origin) 522.4
  throat 034.0
  thrombus—*see* Thrombosis
  toe (with lymphangitis) 681.10
  tonsils 474.00
    and adenoids 474.02
  umbilical cord (newborn) (organism
      unspecified) 771.8
  uterus (*see also* Endometritis) 615.9
Septicemia, septicemic (generalized)
    (suppurative) 038.9
  with
    abortion—*see* Abortion, by type, with sepsis
    ectopic pregnancy (*see also* categories
        633.0-633.9) 639.0
    molar pregnancy (*see also* categories
        630-632) 639.0
  Aerobacter aerogenes 038.49
  anaerobic 038.3
  anthrax 022.3
  Bacillus coli 038.42
  Bacteroides 038.3
  Clostridium 038.3
  complicating labor 659.3
  cryptogenic 038.9
  enteric gram-negative bacilli 038.40
  Enterobacter aerogenes 038.49
  Erysipelothrix (insidiosa) (rhusiopathiae) 027.1
  Escherichia coli 038.42
  following
    abortion 639.0
    ectopic or molar pregnancy 639.0
    infusion, injection, transfusion, or vaccination
        999.3
  Friedländer's (bacillus) 038.49
  gangrenous 038.9
  gonococcal 098.89
  gram-negative (organism) 038.40
    anaerobic 038.3
  Hemophilus influenzae 038.41
  herpes (simplex) 054.5
  herpetic 054.5
  Listeria monocytogenes 027.0
  meningeal—*see* Meningitis
  meningococcal (chronic) (fulminating) 036.2
  navel, newborn (organism unspecified) 771.8
  newborn (umbilical) (organism unspecified)
      771.8
  plague 020.2
  pneumococcal 038.2
  postabortal 639.0
  postoperative 998.59
  Proteus vulgaris 038.49
  Pseudomonas (aeruginosa) 038.43
  puerperal, postpartum 670
  Salmonella (aertrycke) (callinarum)
      (choleraesuis) (enteritidis) (suipestifer) 003.1
  Serratia 038.44
  Shigella (*see also* Dysentery, bacillary) 004.9
  specified organism NEC 038.8
  staphylococcal 038.10
    aureus 038.11
    specified organism NEC 038.19
  streptococcal (anaerobic) 038.0
  suipestifer 003.1
  umbilicus, newborn (organism unspecified)
      771.8
  viral 079.99
  Yersinia enterocolitica 038.49

Septum, septate (congenital)—*see also*
Anomaly, specified type NEC
anal 751.2
aqueduct of Sylvius 742.3
with spina bifida (*see also* Spina bifida) 741.0
hymen 752.49
uterus (*see also* Double, uterus) 752.2
vagina 752.49
in pregnancy or childbirth 654.7
affecting fetus or newborn 763.89
causing obstructed labor 660.2
affecting fetus or newborn 763.1
Sequestration
lung (congenital) (extralobar) (intralobar) 748.5
orbit 376.10
pulmonary artery (congenital) 747.3
Sequestrum
bone (*see also* Osteomyelitis) 730.1
jaw 526.4
dental 525.8
jaw bone 526.4
sinus (accessory) (nasal) (*see also* Sinusitis)
473.9
maxillary 473.0
Sequoiosis asthma 495.8
Serology for syphilis
doubtful
with signs or symptoms—*see* Syphilis, by site
and stage
follow-up of latent syphilis—*see* Syphilis,
latent
false positive 795.6
negative, with signs or symptoms—*see*
Syphilis, by site and stage
positive 097.1
with signs or symptoms—*see* Syphilis, by site
and stage
false 795.6
follow-up of latent syphilis—*see* Syphilis,
latent
only finding—*see* Syphilis, latent
reactivated 097.1
Seroma (postoperative) (non-infected) 998.13
infected 998.51
Seropurulent —*see* condition
Serositis, multiple 569.89
pericardial 423.2
peritoneal 568.82
pleural—*see* Pleurisy
Serotonin syndrome 333.99
Serous —*see* condition
Sertoli cell
adenoma (M8640/0)
specified site—*see* Neoplasm, by site, benign
unspecified site
female 220
male 222.0
carcinoma (M8640/3)
specified site—*see* Neoplasm, by site,
malignant
unspecified site 186.9
syndrome (germinal aplasia) 606.0
tumor (M8640/0)
with lipid storage (M8641/0)
specified site—*see* Neoplasm, by site,
benign
unspecified site
female 220
male 222.0
specified site—*see* Neoplasm, by site, benign

Sertoli cell—*continued*
unspecified site
female 220
male 222.0
Sertoli-Leydig cell tumor (M8631/0)
specified site—*see* Neoplasm, by site, benign
unspecified site
female 220
male 222.0
Serum
allergy, allergic reaction 999.5
shock 999.4
arthritis 999.5 *[713.6]*
complication or reaction NEC 999.5
disease NEC 999.5
hepatitis 070.3
intoxication 999.5
jaundice (homologous) *see* Hepatitis, viral
neuritis 999.5
poisoning NEC 999.5
rash NEC 999.5
reaction NEC 999.5
sickness NEC 999.5
Sesamoiditis 733.99
Seven-day fever 061
of
Japan 100.89
Queensland 100.89
Sever's disease or osteochondrosis (calcaneum)
732.5
Sex chromosome mosaics 758.81
Sextuplet
affected by maternal complications of
pregnancy 761.5
healthy liveborn—*see* Newborn, multiple
pregnancy (complicating delivery) NEC 651.8
with fetal loss and retention of one or more
fetus(es) 651.6
Sexual
anesthesia 302.72
deviation (*see also* Deviation, sexual) 302.9
disorder (*see also* Deviation, sexual) 302.9
frigidity (female) 302.72
function, disorder of (psychogenic) 302.70
specified type NEC 302.79
immaturity (female) (male) 259.0
impotence (psychogenic) 302.72
organic origin NEC 607.84
precocity (constitutional) (cryptogenic) (female)
(idiopathic) (male) NEC 259.1
with adrenal hyperplasia 255.2
sadism 302.84
Sexuality, pathological (*see also* Deviation,
sexual) 302.9
Sézary's disease, reticulosis, or syndrome
(M9701/3) 202.2
Shadow, lung 793.1
Shaken infant syndrome 995.55
Shaking
head (tremor) 781.0
palsy or paralysis (*see also* Parkinsonism) 332.0
Shallowness, acetabulum 736.39
Shaver's disease or syndrome (bauxite
pneumoconiosis) 503
Shearing
artificial skin graft 996.55
decellularized allodermis graft 996.55
Sheath (tendon)—*see* condition
Shedding
nail 703.8
teeth, premature, primary (deciduous) 520.6

Sheehan's disease or syndrome (postpartum
    pituitary necrosis) 253.2
Shelf, rectal 569.49
Shell
  shock (current) (*see also* Reaction, stress, acute)
      308.9
    lasting state 300.16
  teeth 520.5
Shield kidney 753.3
Shift, mediastinal 793.2
Shifting
  pacemaker 427.89
  sleep-work schedule (affecting sleep) 307.45
Shiga's
  bacillus 004.0
  dysentery 004.0
Shigella (dysentery) (*see also* Dysentery,
    bacillary) 004.9
  carrier (suspected) of V02.3
Shigellosis (*see also* Dysentery, bacillary) 004.9
Shingles (*see also* Herpes, zoster) 053.9
  eye NEC 053.29
Shin splints 844.9
Shipyard eye or disease 077.1
Shirodkar suture, in pregnancy 654.5
Shock 785.50
  with
    abortion—*see* Abortion, by type, with shock
    ectopic pregnancy (*see also* categories
        633.0-633.9) 639.5
    molar pregnancy (*see also* categories
        630-632) 639.5
  allergic—*see* Shock, anaphylactic
  anaclitic 309.21
  anaphylactic 995.0
    chemical—*see* Table of drugs and chemicals
    correct medicinal substance properly
        administered 995.0
    drug or medicinal substance
      correct substance properly administered
          995.0
      overdose or wrong substance given or taken
          977.9
        specified drug—*see* Table of drugs and
            chemicals
    food—*see* Anaphylactic shock, due to, food
    following sting(s) 989.5
    immunization 999.4
    serum 999.4
  anaphylactoid—*see* Shock, anaphylactic
  anesthetic
    correct substance properly administered 995.4
    overdose or wrong substance given 968.4
      specified anesthetic—*see* Table of drugs
          and chemicals
  birth, fetus or newborn NEC 779.8
  cardiogenic 785.51
  chemical substance—*see* Table of drugs and
      chemicals
  circulatory 785.59
  complicating
    abortion—*see* Abortion, by type, with shock
    ectopic pregnancy (*see also* categories
        633.0-633.9) 639.5
    labor and delivery 669.1
    molar pregnancy (*see also* categories
        630-632) 639.5
  culture 309.29

Shock—*continued*
  due to
    drug 995.0
      correct substance properly administered
          995.0
      overdose or wrong substance given or taken
          977.9
        specified drug—*see* Table of drugs and
            chemicals
    food—*see* Anaphylactic shock, due to, food
  during labor and delivery 669.1
  electric 994.8
  endotoxic 785.59
    due to surgical procedure 998.0
  following
    abortion 639.5
    ectopic or molar pregnancy 639.5
    injury (immediate) (delayed) 958.4
    labor and delivery 669.1
  gram-negative 785.59
  hematogenic 785.59
  hemorrhagic
    due to
      disease 785.59
      surgery (intraoperative) (postoperative)
          998.0
      trauma 958.4
  hypovolemic NEC 785.59
    surgical 998.0
    traumatic 958.4
  insulin 251.0
    therapeutic misadventure 962.3
  kidney 584.5
    traumatic (following crushing) 958.5
  lightning 994.0
  lung 518.5
  nervous (*see also* Reaction, stress, acute) 308.9
  obstetric 669.1
    with
      abortion—*see* Abortion, by type, with shock
      ectopic pregnancy (*see also* categories
          633.0-633.9) 639.5
      molar pregnancy (*see also* categories
          630-632) 639.5
    following
      abortion 639.5
      ectopic or molar pregnancy 639.5
  paralysis, paralytic (*see also* Disease,
      cerebrovascular, acute) 436
    late effect—*see* Late effect(s) (of)
        cerebrovascular disease
  pleural (surgical) 998.0
    due to trauma 958.4
  postoperative 998.0
    with
      abortion—*see* Abortion, by type, with shock
      ectopic pregnancy (*see also* categories
          633.0-633.9) 639.5
      molar pregnancy (*see also* categories
          630-632) 639.5
    following
      abortion 639.5
      ectopic or molar pregnancy 639.5
  psychic (*see also* Reaction, stress, acute) 308.9
    past history (of) V15.49
  psychogenic (*see also* Reaction, stress, acute)
      308.9
  septic 785.59
    with
      abortion—*see* Abortion, by type, with shock

Sirenomelia 759.89
Siriasis 992.0
Sirkari's disease 085.0
Siti 104.0
Sitophobia 300.29
Situation, psychiatric 300.9
Situational
  disturbance (transient) (*see also* Reaction,
    adjustment) 309.9
    acute 308.3
  maladjustment, acute (*see also* Reaction,
    adjustment) 309.9
  reaction (*see also* Reaction, adjustment) 309.9
    acute 308.3
Situs inversus or transversus 759.3
  abdominalis 759.3
  thoracis 759.3
Sixth disease 057.8
Sjögren (-Gougerot) syndrome or disease
    (keratoconjunctivitis sicca) 710.2
  with lung involvement 710.2 *[517.8]*
Sjögren-Larsson syndrome (ichthyosis
    congenita) 757.1
Skeletal —*see* condition
Skene's gland —*see* condition
Skenitis (*see also* Urethritis) 597.89
  gonorrheal (acute) 098.0
    chronic or duration of 2 months or over 098.2
Skerljevo 104.0
Skevas-Zerfus disease 989.5
Skin —*see also* condition
  donor V59.1
  hidebound 710.9
Slate-dressers' lung 502
Slate-miners' lung 502
Sleep
  disorder 780.50
    with apnea—*see* Apnea, sleep
    child 307.40
      nonorganic origin 307.40
        specified type NEC 307.49
    disturbance 780.50
      with apnea—*see* Apnea, sleep
      nonorganic origin 307.40
        specified type NEC 307.49
  drunkenness 307.47
  paroxysmal 347
  rhythm inversion 780.55
    nonorganic origin 307.45
  walking 307.46
    hysterical 300.13
Sleeping sickness 086.5
  late effect 139.8
Sleeplessness (*see also* Insomnia) 780.52
  menopausal 627.2
  nonorganic origin 307.41
Slipped, slipping
  epiphysis (postinfectional) 732.9
    traumatic (old) 732.9
      current—*see* Fracture, by site
    upper femoral (nontraumatic) 732.2
  intervertebral disc—*see* Displacement,
    intervertebral disc
  ligature, umbilical 772.3
  patella 717.89
  rib 733.99
  sacroiliac joint 724.6
  tendon 727.9
  ulnar nerve, nontraumatic 354.2
  vertebra NEC (*see also* Spondylolisthesis)
    756.12
Slocumb's syndrome 255.3

Sloughing (multiple) (skin) 686.9
  abscess—*see* Abscess, by site
  appendix 543.9
  bladder 596.8
  fascia 728.9
  graft—*see* Complications, graft
  phagedena (*see also* Gangrene) 785.4
  reattached extremity (*see also* Complications,
    reattached extremity) 996.90
  rectum 569.49
  scrotum 608.89
  tendon 727.9
  transplanted organ (*see also* Rejection,
    transplant, organ, by site) 996.80
  ulcer (*see also* Ulcer, skin) 707.9
Slow
  feeding newborn 779.3
  fetal, growth NEC 764.9
    affecting management of pregnancy 656.5
Slowing
  heart 427.89
  urinary stream 788.62
Sluder's neuralgia or syndrome 337.0
Slurred, slurring, speech 784.5
Small, smallness
  cardiac reserve—*see* Disease, heart
  for dates
    fetus or newborn 764.0
      with malnutrition 764.1
      affecting management of pregnancy 656.5
    infant, term 764.0
      with malnutrition 764.1
      affecting management of pregnancy 656.5
  introitus, vagina 623.3
  kidney, unknown cause 589.9
    bilateral 589.1
    unilateral 589.0
  ovary 620.8
  pelvis
    with disproportion (fetopelvic) 653.1
      affecting fetus or newborn 763.1
    causing obstructed labor 660.1
      affecting fetus or newborn 763.1
  placenta—*see* Placenta, insufficiency
  uterus 621.8
  white kidney 582.9
Small-for-dates (*see also* Light-for-dates) 764.0
  affecting management of pregnancy 656.5
Smallpox 050.9
  contact V01.3
  exposure to V01.3
  hemorrhagic (pustular) 050.0
  malignant 050.0
  modified 050.2
  vaccination
    complications—*see* Complications,
      vaccination
    prophylactic (against) V04.1
Smith's fracture (separation) (closed) 813.41
  open 813.51
Smith-Lemli-Opitz syndrome
    (cerebrohepatorenal syndrome) 759.89
Smith-Strang disease (oasthouse urine) 270.2
Smokers'
  bronchitis 491.0
  cough 491.0
  syndrome (*see also* Abuse, drugs,
    nondependent) 305.1
  throat 472.1
  tongue 528.6
Smothering spells 786.09
Snaggle teeth, tooth 524.3

Snapping
  finger 727.05
  hip 719.65
  jaw 524.69
  knee 717.9
  thumb 727.05
Sneddon-Wilkinson disease or syndrome
  (subcorneal pustular dermatosis) 694.1
Sneezing 784.9
  intractable 478.1
Sniffing
  cocaine (*see also* Dependence) 304.2
  ether (*see also* Dependence) 304.6
  glue (airplane) (*see also* Dependence) 304.6
Snoring 786.09
Snow blindness 370.24
Snuffles (nonsyphilitic) 460
  syphilitic (infant) 090.0
Social migrant V60.0
Sodoku 026.0
Soemmering's ring 366.51
Soft —*see also* condition
  enlarged prostate 600.0
  nails 703.8
Softening
  bone 268.2
  brain (necrotic) (progressive) 434.9
    arteriosclerotic 437.0
Softening—*continued*
    congenital 742.4
    embolic (*see also* Embolism, brain) 434.1
    hemorrhagic (*see also* Hemorrhage, brain) 431
    occlusive 434.9
    thrombotic (*see also* Thrombosis, brain) 434.0
  cartilage 733.92
  cerebellar—*see* Softening, brain
  cerebral—*see* Softening, brain
  cerebrospinal—*see* Softening, brain
  myocardial, heart (*see also* Degeneration,
    myocardial) 429.1
  nails 703.8
  spinal cord 336.8
  stomach 537.89
Solar fever 061
Soldier's
  heart 306.2
  patches 423.1
Solitary
  cyst
    bone 733.21
    kidney 593.2
  kidney (congenital) 753.0
  tubercle, brain (*see also* Tuberculosis, brain)
    013.2
  ulcer, bladder 596.8
Somatization reaction, somatic reaction (*see*
  also Disorder, psychosomatic) 306.9
  disorder 300.81
Somatoform disorder 300.82
  atypical 300.82
  severe 300.81
  undifferentiated 300.82
Somnambulism 307.46
  hysterical 300.13
Somnolence 780.09
  nonorganic origin 307.43
  periodic 349.89
Sonne dysentery 004.3
Soor 112.0

Sore
  Delhi 085.1
  desert (*see also* Ulcer, skin) 707.9
  eye 379.99
  Lahore 085.1
  mouth 528.9
    canker 528.2
    due to dentures 528.9
  muscle 729.1
  Naga (*see also* Ulcer, skin) 707.9
  oriental 085.1
  pressure 707.0
    with gangrene 707.0 *[785.4]*
  skin NEC 709.9
  soft 099.0
  throat 462
    with influenza, flu, or grippe 487.1
    acute 462
    chronic 472.1
    clergyman's 784.49
    coxsackie (virus) 074.0
    diphtheritic 032.0
    epidemic 034.0
    gangrenous 462
    herpetic 054.79
    influenzal 487.1
    malignant 462
    purulent 462
    putrid 462
    septic 034.0
    streptococcal (ulcerative) 034.0
    ulcerated 462
    viral NEC 462
      Coxsackie 074.0
  tropical (*see also* Ulcer, skin) 707.9
  veldt (*see also* Ulcer, skin) 707.9
Sotos' syndrome (cerebral gigantism) 253.0
Sounds
  friction, pleural 786.7
  succussion, chest 786.7
South African cardiomyopathy syndrome 425.2
South American
  blastomycosis 116.1
  trypanosomiasis—*see* Trypanosomiasis
Southeast Asian hemorrhagic fever 065.4
Spacing, teeth, abnormal 524.3
Spade-like hand (congenital) 754.89
Spading nail 703.8
  congenital 757.5
Spanemia 285.9
Spanish collar 605
Sparganosis 123.5
Spasm, spastic, spasticity (*see also* condition)
  781.0
  accommodation 367.53
  ampulla of Vater (*see also* Disease, gallbladder)
    576.8
  anus, ani (sphincter) (reflex) 564.6
    psychogenic 306.4
  artery NEC 443.9
    basilar 435.0
    carotid 435.8
    cerebral 435.9
      specified artery NEC 435.8
    retinal (*see also* Occlusion, retinal, artery)
      362.30
    vertebral 435.1
    vertebrobasilar 435.3
  Bell's 351.0
  bladder (sphincter, external or internal) 596.8

Spasm, spastic, spasticity—*continued*
 bowel 564.9
  psychogenic 306.4
 bronchus, bronchiole 519.1
 cardia 530.0
 cardiac—*see* Angina
 carpopedal (*see also* Tetany) 781.7
 cecum 564.9
  psychogenic 306.4
 cerebral (arteries) (vascular) 435.9
  specified artery NEC 435.8
 cerebrovascular 435.9
 cervix, complicating delivery 661.4
  affecting fetus or newborn 763.7
 ciliary body (of accommodation) 367.53
 colon 564.1
  psychogenic 306.4
 common duct (*see also* Disease, biliary) 576.8
 compulsive 307.22
 conjugate 378.82
 convergence 378.84
 coronary (artery)—*see* Angina
 diaphragm (reflex) 786.8
  psychogenic 306.1
 duodenum, duodenal (bulb) 564.89
 esophagus (diffuse) 530.5
  psychogenic 306.4
 facial 351.8
 fallopian tube 620.8
 gait 781.2
 gastrointestinal (tract) 536.8
  psychogenic 306.4
 glottis 478.75
  hysterical 300.11
  psychogenic 306.1
   specified as conversion reaction 300.11
  reflex through recurrent laryngeal nerve
    478.75
 habit 307.20
  chronic 307.22
  transient of childhood 307.21
 heart—*see* Angina
 hourglass—*see* Contraction, hourglass
 hysterical 300.11
 infantile (*see also* Epilepsy) 345.6
 internal oblique, eye 378.51
 intestinal 564.9
  psychogenic 306.4
 larynx, laryngeal 478.75
  hysterical 300.11
  psychogenic 306.1
   specified as conversion reaction 300.11
 levator palpebrae superioris 333.81
 lightning (*see also* Epilepsy) 345.6
 mobile 781.0
 muscle 728.85
  back 724.8
  psychogenic 306.0
 nerve, trigeminal 350.1
 nervous 306.0
 nodding 307.3
  infantile (*see also* Epilepsy) 345.6
 occupational 300.89
 oculogyric 378.87
 ophthalmic artery 362.30
 orbicularis 781.0
 perineal 625.8
 peroneo-extensor (*see also* Flat, foot) 734
 pharynx (reflex) 478.29
  hysterical 300.11
  psychogenic 306.1

Spasm, spastic, spasticity—*continued*
  specified as conversion reaction 300.11
 pregnant uterus, complicating delivery 661.4
 psychogenic 306.0
 pylorus 537.81
  adult hypertrophic 537.0
  congenital or infantile 750.5
  psychogenic 306.4
 rectum (sphincter) 564.6
  psychogenic 306.4
 retinal artery NEC (*see also* Occlusion, retina,
   artery) 362.30
 sacroiliac 724.6
 salaam (infantile) (*see also* Epilepsy) 345.6
 saltatory 781.0
 sigmoid 564.9
  psychogenic 306.4
 sphincter of Oddi (*see also* Disease,
   gallbladder) 576.5
 stomach 536.8
  neurotic 306.4
 throat 478.29
  hysterical 300.11
  psychogenic 306.1
   specified as conversion reaction 300.11
 tic 307.20
  chronic 307.22
  transient of childhood 307.21
 tongue 529.8
 torsion 333.6
 trigeminal nerve 350.1
  postherpetic 053.12
 ureter 593.89
 urethra (sphincter) 599.84
 uterus 625.8
  complicating labor 661.4
   affecting fetus or newborn 763.7
 vagina 625.1
  psychogenic 306.51
 vascular NEC 443.9
 vasomotor NEC 443.9
 vein NEC 459.89
 vesical (sphincter, external or internal) 596.8
 viscera 789.0
Spasmodic —*see* condition
Spasmophilia (*see also* Tetany) 781.7
Spasmus nutans 307.3
Spastic —*see also* Spasm
 child 343.9
Spasticity —*see also* Spasm
 cerebral, child 343.9
Speakers' throat 784.49
Specific, specified —*see* condition
Speech
 defect, disorder, disturbance, impediment NEC
   784.5
  psychogenic 307.9
 therapy V57.3
Spells 780.39
 breath-holding 786.9
Spencer's disease (epidemic vomiting) 078.82
Spens' syndrome (syncope with heart block)
   426.9
Spermatic cord —*see* condition
Spermatocele 608.1
 congenital 752.8
Spermatocystitis 608.4
Spermatocytoma (M9063/3)
 specified site—*see* Neoplasm, by site, malignant
 unspecified site 186.9
Spermatorrhea 608.89

Sperm counts
  fertility testing V26.21
  following sterilization reversal V26.22
  postvasectomy V25.8
Sphacelus (*see also* Gangrene) 785.4
Sphenoidal —*see* condition
Sphenoiditis (chronic) (*see also* Sinusitis,
    sphenoidal) 473.3
Sphenopalatine ganglion neuralgia 337.0
Sphericity, increased, lens 743.36
Spherocytosis (congenital) (familial) (hereditary)
    282.0
  hemoglobin disease 287.7
  sickle-cell (disease) 282.60
Spherophakia 743.36
Sphincter —*see* condition
Sphincteritis, sphincter of Oddi (*see also*
    Cholecystitis) 576.8
Sphingolipidosis 272.7
Sphingolipodystrophy 272.7
Sphingomyelinosis 272.7
Spicule tooth 520.2
Spider
  finger 755.59
  nevus 448.1
  vascular 448.1
Spiegler-Fendt sarcoid 686.8
Spielmeyer-Stock disease 330.1
Spielmeyer-Vogt disease 330.1
Spina bifida (aperta) 741.9

> *Note—Use the following fifth-digit*
> *subclassification with category 741:*
>
> *0 unspecified region*
> *1 cervical region*
> *2 dorsal [thoracic] region*
> *3 lumbar region*

  with hydrocephalus 741.0
  fetal (suspected), affecting management of
      pregnancy 655.0
  occulta 756.17
Spindle, Krukenberg's 371.13
Spine, spinal —*see* condition
Spiradenoma (eccrine) (M8403/0)—*see*
    Neoplasm, skin, benign
Spirillosis NEC (*see also* Fever, relapsing) 087.9
Spirillum minus 026.0
Spirillum obermeieri infection 087.0
Spirochetal —*see* condition
Spirochetosis 104.9
  arthritic, arthritica 104.9 *[711.8]*
  bronchopulmonary 104.8
  icterohemorrhagica 100.0
  lung 104.8
Spitting blood (*see also* Hemoptysis) 786.3
Splanchnomegaly 569.89
Splanchnoptosis 569.89
Spleen, splenic —*see also* condition
  agenesis 759.0
  flexure syndrome 569.89
  neutropenia syndrome 288.0
  sequestration syndrome 282.60
Splenectasis (*see also* Splenomegaly) 789.2
Splenitis (interstitial) (malignant) (nonspecific)
    289.59
  malarial (*see also* Malaria) 084.6
  tuberculous (*see also* Tuberculosis) 017.7
Splenocele 289.59
Splenomegalia —*see* Splenomegaly
Splenomegalic —*see* condition

Splenomegaly 789.2
  Bengal 789.2
  cirrhotic 289.51
  congenital 759.0
  congestive, chronic 289.51
  cryptogenic 789.2
  Egyptian 120.1
  Gaucher's (cerebroside lipidosis) 272.7
  idiopathic 789.2
  malarial (*see also* Malaria) 084.6
  neutropenic 288.0
  Niemann-Pick (lipid histiocytosis) 272.7
  siderotic 289.51
  syphilitic 095.8
    congenital 090.0
  tropical (Bengal) (idiopathic) 789.2
Splenopathy 289.50
Splenopneumonia —*see* Pneumonia
Splenoptosis 289.59
Splinter —*see* Injury, superficial, by site
Split, splitting
  heart sounds 427.89
  lip, congenital (*see also* Cleft, lip) 749.10
  nails 703.8
  urinary stream 788.61
Spoiled child reaction (*see also* Disturbance,
    conduct) 312.1
Spondylarthritis (*see also* Spondylosis) 721.90
Spondylarthrosis (*see also* Spondylosis) 721.90
Spondylitis 720.9
  ankylopoietica 720.0
  ankylosing (chronic) 720.0
  atrophic 720.9
    ligamentous 720.9
  chronic (traumatic) (*see also* Spondylosis)
      721.90
  deformans (chronic) (*see also* Spondylosis)
      721.90
  gonococcal 098.53
  gouty 274.0
  hypertrophic (*see also* Spondylosis) 721.90
  infectious NEC 720.9
  juvenile (adolescent) 720.0
  Kümmell's 721.7
  Marie-Strümpell (ankylosing) 720.0
  muscularis 720.9
  ossificans ligamentosa 721.6
  osteoarthritica (*see also* Spondylosis) 721.90
  posttraumatic 721.7
  proliferative 720.0
  rheumatoid 720.0
  rhizomelica 720.0
  sacroiliac NEC 720.2
  senescent (*see also* Spondylosis) 721.90
  senile (*see also* Spondylosis) 721.90
  static (*see also* Spondylosis) 721.90
  traumatic (chronic) (*see also* Spondylosis)
      721.90
  tuberculous (*see also* Tuberculosis) 015.0
      [720.81]
  typhosa 002.0 *[720.81]*
Spondyloarthrosis (*see also* Spondylosis) 721.90
Spondylolisthesis (congenital) (lumbosacral)
    756.12
  with disproportion (fetopelvic) 653.3
    affecting fetus or newborn 763.1
    causing obstructed labor 660.1
      affecting fetus or newborn 763.1
  acquired 738.4
  degenerative 738.4
  traumatic 738.4

Spondylolisthesis—*continued*
   acute (lumbar)—*see* Fracture, vertebra, lumbar
   site other than lumbosacral—*see* Fracture,
      vertebra, by site
Spondylolysis (congenital) 756.11
   acquired 738.4
   cervical 756.19
   lumbosacral region 756.11
     with disproportion (fetopelvic) 653.3
       affecting fetus or newborn 763.1
       causing obstructed labor 660.1
        affecting fetus or newborn 763.1
Spondylopathy
   inflammatory 720.9
     specified type NEC 720.89
   traumatic 721.7
Spondylose rhizomelique 720.0
Spondylosis 721.90
   with
     disproportion 653.3
       affecting fetus or newborn 763.1
       causing obstructed labor 660.1
        affecting fetus or newborn 763.1
     myelopathy NEC 721.91
   cervical, cervicodorsal 721.0
     with myelopathy 721.1
   inflammatory 720.9
   lumbar, lumbosacral 721.3
     with myelopathy 721.42
   sacral 721.3
     with myelopathy 721.42
   thoracic 721.2
     with myelopathy 721.41
   traumatic 721.7
Sponge
   divers' disease 989.5
   inadvertently left in operation wound 998.4
   kidney (medullary) 753.17
Spongioblastoma (M9422/3)
   multiforme (M9440/3)
     specified site—*see* Neoplasm, by site,
       malignant
     unspecified site 191.9
   polare (M9423/3)
     specified site—*see* Neoplasm, by site,
       malignant
     unspecified site 191.9
   primitive polar (M9443/3)
     specified site—*see* Neoplasm, by site,
       malignant
     unspecified site 191.9
   specified site—*see* Neoplasm, by site, malignant
   unspecified site 191.9
Spongiocytoma (M9400/3)
   specified site—*see* Neoplasm, by site, malignant
   unspecified site 191.9
Spongioneuroblastoma (M9504/3)—*see*
   Neoplasm, by site, malignant
Spontaneous —*see also* condition
   fracture—*see* Fracture, pathologic
Spoon nail 703.8
   congenital 757.5
Sporadic —*see* condition
Sporotrichosis (bones) (cutaneous)
   (disseminated) (epidermal) (lymphatic)
   (lymphocutaneous) (mucous membranes)
   (pulmonary) (skeletal) (visceral) 117.1
Sporotrichum schenckii infection 117.1

Spots, spotting
   atrophic (skin) 701.3
   Bitôt's (in the young child) 264.1
   café au lait 709.09
   cayenne pepper 448.1
   cotton wool (retina) 362.83
   de Morgan's (senile angiomas) 448.1
   Fúchs' black (myopic) 360.21
   intermenstrual
     irregular 626.6
     regular 626.5
   interpalpebral 372.53
   Koplik's 055.9
   liver 709.09
   Mongolian (pigmented) 757.33
   of pregnancy 641.9
   purpuric 782.7
   ruby 448.1
Spotted fever —*see* Fever, spotted
Sprain, strain (joint) (ligament) (muscle)
   (tendon) 848.9
   abdominal wall (muscle) 848.8
   Achilles tendon 845.09
   acromioclavicular 840.0
   ankle 845.00
     and foot 845.00
   anterior longitudinal, cervical 847.0
   arm 840.9
     upper 840.9
       and shoulder 840.9
   astragalus 845.00
   atlanto-axial 847.0
   atlanto-occipital 847.0
   atlas 847.0
   axis 847.0
   back (*see also* Sprain, spine) 847.9
   breast bone 848.40
   broad ligament—*see* Injury, internal, broad
     ligament
   calcaneofibular 845.02
   carpal 842.01
   carpometacarpal 842.11
   cartilage
     costal, without mention of injury to sternum
       848.3
       involving sternum 848.42
     ear 848.8
     knee 844.9
       with current tear (*see also* Tear, meniscus)
        836.2
     semilunar (knee) 844.8
       with current tear (*see also* Tear, meniscus)
        836.2
     septal, nose 848.0
     thyroid region 848.2
     xiphoid 848.49
   cervical, cervicodorsal, cervicothoracic 847.0
   chondrocostal, without mention of injury to
     sternum 848.3
     involving sternum 848.42
   chondrosternal 848.42
   chronic (joint)—*see* Derangement, joint
   clavicle 840.9
   coccyx 847.4
   collar bone 840.9
   collateral, knee (medial) (tibial) 844.1
     lateral (fibular) 844.0
     recurrent or old 717.89
       lateral 717.81
       medial 717.82
   coracoacromial 840.8

Stenosis—*continued*
  cervix, cervical (canal) 622.4
    congenital 752.49
    in pregnancy or childbirth 654.6
      affecting fetus or newborn 763.89
      causing obstructed labor 660.2
        affecting fetus or newborn 763.1
  colon (*see also* Obstruction, intestine) 560.9
    congenital 751.2
  colostomy 569.62
  common bile duct (*see also* Obstruction, biliary)
      576.2
    congenital 751.61
  coronary (artery) —*see* Arteriosclerosis,
      coronary
  cystic duct (*see also* Obstruction, gallbladder)
      575.2
    congenital 751.61
  due to (presence of) any device, implant, or
      graft classifiable to 996.0-996.5—*see*
      Complications, due to (presence of) any
      device, implant, or graft classified to
      996.0-996.5 NEC
  duodenum 537.3
    congenital 751.1
  ejaculatory duct NEC 608.89
  endocervical os—*see* Stenosis, cervix
  enterostomy 569.62
  esophagus 530.3
    congenital 750.3
    syphilitic 095.8
      congenital 090.5
  external ear canal 380.50
    secondary to
      inflammation 380.53
      surgery 380.52
      trauma 380.51
  gallbladder (*see also* Obstruction, gallbladder)
      575.2
  glottis 478.74
  heart valve (acquired)—*see also* Endocarditis
    congenital NEC 746.89
      aortic 746.3
      mitral 746.5
      pulmonary 746.02
      tricuspid 746.1
  hepatic duct (*see also* Obstruction, biliary) 576.2
  hymen 623.3
  hypertrophic subaortic (idiopathic) 425.1
  infundibulum cardiac 746.83
  intestine (*see also* Obstruction, intestine) 560.9
    congenital (small) 751.1
      large 751.2
  lacrimal
    canaliculi 375.53
    duct 375.56
      congenital 743.65
    punctum 375.52
      congenital 743.65
    sac 375.54
      congenital 743.65
  lacrimonasal duct 375.56
    congenital 743.65
    neonatal 375.55
  larynx 478.74
    congenital 748.3
    syphilitic 095.8
      congenital 090.5
  mitral (valve) (chronic) (inactive) 394.0
    with
      aortic (valve)

Stenosis—*continued*
    disease (insufficiency) 396.1
      insufficiency or incompetence 396.1
      stenosis or obstruction 396.0
    incompetency, insufficiency or regurgitation
        394.2
      with aortic valve disease 396.8
    active or acute 391.1
      with chorea (acute) (rheumatic)
          (Sydenham's) 392.0
    congenital 746.5
    specified cause, except rheumatic 424.0
    syphilitic 093.21
  myocardium, myocardial (*see also*
      Degeneration, myocardial) 429.1
    hypertrophic subaortic (idiopathic) 425.1
  nares (anterior) (posterior) 478.1
    congenital 748.0
  nasal duct 375.56
    congenital 743.65
  nasolacrimal duct 375.56
    congenital 743.65
    neonatal 375.55
  organ or site, congenital NEC—*see* Atresia
  papilla of Vater 576.2
    with calculus, cholelithiasis, or stones—*see*
        Choledocholithiasis
  pulmonary (artery) (congenital) 747.3
    with ventricular septal defect, dextraposition
        of aorta and hypertrophy of right ventricle
        745.2
    acquired 417.8
    infundibular 746.83
    in tetralogy of Fallot 745.2
    subvalvular 746.83
    valve (*see also* Endocarditis, pulmonary) 424.3
      congenital 746.02
    vein 747.49
      acquired 417.8
    vessel NEC 417.8
  pulmonic (congenital) 746.02
    infundibular 746.83
    subvalvular 746.83
  pylorus (hypertrophic) 537.0
    adult 537.0
    congenital 750.5
    infantile 750.5
  rectum (sphincter) (*see also* Stricture, rectum)
      569.2
  renal artery 440.1
  salivary duct (any) 527.8
  sphincter of Oddi (*see also* Obstruction, biliary)
      576.2
  spinal 724.00
    cervical 723.0
    lumbar, lumbosacral 724.02
    nerve (root) NEC 724.9
    specified region NEC 724.09
    thoracic, thoracolumbar 724.01
  stomach, hourglass 537.6
  subaortic 746.81
    hypertrophic (idiopathic) 425.1
  supra (valvular)-aortic 747.22
  trachea 519.1
    congenital 748.3
    syphilitic 095.8
    tuberculous (*see also* Tuberculosis) 012.8
  tracheostomy 519.02
  tricuspid (valve) (*see also* Endocarditis,
      tricuspid) 397.0
    congenital 746.1

Stomatitis 528.0
  angular 528.5
    due to dietary or vitamin deficiency 266.0
  aphthous 528.2
  candidal 112.0
  catarrhal 528.0
  denture 528.9
  diphtheritic (membranous) 032.0
  due to
    dietary deficiency 266.0
    thrush 112.0
    vitamin deficiency 266.0
  epidemic 078.4
  epizootic 078.4
  follicular 528.0
  gangrenous 528.1
  herpetic 054.2
  herpetiformis 528.2
  malignant 528.0
  membranous acute 528.0
  monilial 112.0
  mycotic 112.0
  necrotic 528.1
    ulcerative 101
  necrotizing ulcerative 101
  parasitic 112.0
  septic 528.0
  spirochetal 101
  suppurative (acute) 528.0
  ulcerative 528.0
    necrotizing 101
  ulceromembranous 101
  vesicular 528.0
    with exanthem 074.3
  Vincent's 101
Stomatocytosis 282.8
Stomatomycosis 112.0
Stomatorrhagia 528.9
Stone(s) —*see also* Calculus
  bladder 594.1
    diverticulum 594.0
  cystine 270.0
  heart syndrome (*see also* Failure, ventricular,
    left) 428.1
  kidney 592.0
  prostate 602.0
  pulp (dental) 522.2
  renal 592.0
  salivary duct or gland (any) 527.5
  ureter 592.1
  urethra (impacted) 594.2
  urinary (duct) (impacted) (passage) 592.9
    bladder 594.1
      diverticulum 594.0
    lower tract NEC 594.9
    specified site 594.8
  xanthine 277.2
Stonecutters' lung 502
  tuberculous (*see also* Tuberculosis) 011.4
Stonemasons'
  asthma, disease, or lung 502
    tuberculous (*see also* Tuberculosis) 011.4
  phthisis (*see also* Tuberculosis) 011.4
Stoppage
  bowel (*see also* Obstruction, intestine) 560.9
  heart (*see also* Arrest, cardiac) 427.5
  intestine (*see also* Obstruction, intestine) 560.9
  urine NEC (*see also* Retention, urine) 788.20
Storm, thyroid (apathetic) (*see also*
  Thyrotoxicosis) 242.9

Strabismus (alternating) (congenital)
  (nonparalytic) 378.9
  concomitant (*see also* Heterotropia) 378.30
    convergent (*see also* Esotropia) 378.00
    divergent (*see also* Exotropia) 378.10
  convergent (*see also* Esotropia) 378.00
  divergent (*see also* Exotropia) 378.10
  due to adhesions, scars—*see* Strabismus,
    mechanical
  in neuromuscular disorder NEC 378.73
    intermittent 378.20
      vertical 378.31
  latent 378.40
    convergent (esophoria) 378.41
    divergent (exophoria) 378.42
    vertical 378.43
  mechanical 378.60
    due to
      Brown's tendon sheath syndrome 378.61
      specified musculofascial disorder NEC
        378.62
  paralytic 378.50
    third or oculomotor nerve (partial) 378.51
      total 378.52
    fourth or trochlear nerve 378.53
    sixth or abducens nerve 378.54
  specified type NEC 378.73
  vertical (hypertropia) 378.31
Strain —*see also* Sprain, by site
  eye NEC 368.13
  heart—*see* Disease, heart
  meaning gonorrhea—*see* Gonorrhea
  physical NEC V62.89
  postural 729.9
  psychological NEC V62.89
Strands
  conjunctiva 372.62
  vitreous humor 379.25
Strangulation, strangulated 994.7
  appendix 543.9
  asphyxiation or suffocation by 994.7
  bladder neck 596.0
  bowel—*see* Strangulation, intestine
  colon—*see* Strangulation, intestine
  cord (umbilical)—*see* Compression, umbilical
    cord
  due to birth injury 767.8
  food or foreign body (*see also* Asphyxia, food)
    933.1
  hemorrhoids 455.8
    external 455.5
    internal 455.2
  hernia—*see also* Hernia, by site, with
    obstruction
    gangrenous—*see* Hernia, by site, with
      gangrene
  intestine (large) (small) 560.2
    with hernia—*see also* Hernia, by site, with
      obstruction
      gangrenous—*see* Hernia, by site, with
        gangrene
    congenital (small) 751.1
      large 751.2
  mesentery 560.2
  mucus (*see also* Asphyxia, mucus) 933.1
    newborn 770.1
  omentum 560.2
  organ or site, congenital NEC—*see* Atresia
  ovary 620.8
    due to hernia 620.4

Stricture—*continued*
  tricuspid (valve) (*see also* Endocarditis,
      tricuspid) 397.0
    congenital 746.1
    nonrheumatic 424.2
  tunica vaginalis 608.85
  ureter (postoperative) 593.3
    congenital 753.29
    tuberculous (*see also* Tuberculosis) 016.2
  ureteropelvic junction 593.3
    congenital 753.21
  ureterovesical orifice 593.3
    congenital 753.22
  urethra (anterior) (meatal) (organic) (posterior)
      (spasmodic) 598.9
    associated with schistosomiasis (*see also*
      Schistosomiasis) 120.9 *[598.01]*
    congenital (valvular) 753.6
    due to
      infection 598.00
        syphilis 095.8 *[598.01]*
      trauma 598.1
    gonococcal 098.2 *[598.01]*
    gonorrheal 098.2 *[598.01]*
    infective 598.00
    late effect of injury 598.1
    postcatheterization 598.2
    postobstetric 598.1
    postoperative 598.2
    specified cause NEC 598.8
    syphilitic 095.8 *[598.01]*
    traumatic 598.1
    valvular, congenital 753.6
  urinary meatus (*see also* Stricture, urethra) 598.9
    congenital 753.6
  uterus, uterine 621.5
    os (external) (internal)—*see* Stricture, cervix
  vagina (outlet) 623.2
    congenital 752.49
  valve (cardiac) (heart) (*see also* Endocarditis)
      424.90
    congenital (cardiac) (heart) NEC 746.89
      aortic 746.3
      mitral 746.5
      pulmonary 746.02
      tricuspid 746.1
      urethra 753.6
  valvular (*see also* Endocarditis) 424.90
  vascular graft or shunt 996.1
    atherosclerosis —*see* Arteriosclerosis,
      extremities
    embolism 996.74
    occlusion NEC 996.74
    thrombus 996.74
  vas deferens 608.85
    congenital 752.8
  vein 459.2
  vena cava (inferior) (superior) NEC 459.2
    congenital 747.49
  ventricular shunt 996.2
  vesicourethral orifice 596.0
    congenital 753.6
  vulva (acquired) 624.8
Stridor 786.1
  congenital (larynx) 748.3
Stridulous —*see* condition
Strippling of nails 703.8

Stroke (*see also* Disease, cerebrovascular, acute)
  436
  apoplectic (*see also* Disease, cerebrovascular,
    acute) 436
  brain (*see also* Disease, cerebrovascular, acute)
    436
  epileptic—*see* Epilepsy
  healed or old V12.59
  heart—*see* Disease, heart
  heat 992.0
  iatrogenic 997.02
  in evolution 435.9
  late effect—*see* Late effect(s) (of)
    cerebrovascular disease
  lightning 994.0
  paralytic (*see also* Disease, cerebrovascular,
    acute) 436
  postoperative 997.02
  progressive 435.9
Stromatosis, endometrial (M8931/1) 236.0
Strong pulse 785.9
Strongyloides stercoralis infestation 127.2
Strongyloidiasis 127.2
Strongyloidosis 127.2
Strongylus (gibsoni) infestation 127.7
Strophulus (newborn) 779.8
  pruriginosus 698.2
Struck by lightning 994.0
Struma (*see also* Goiter) 240.9
  fibrosa 245.3
  Hashimoto (struma lymphomatosa) 245.2
  lymphomatosa 245.2
  nodosa (simplex) 241.9
    endemic 241.9
    multinodular 241.1
    sporadic 241.9
    toxic or with hyperthyroidism 242.3
      multinodular 242.2
      uninodular 242.1
    toxicosa 242.3
      multinodular 242.2
      uninodular 242.1
    uninodular 241.0
  ovarii (M9090/0) 220
    and carcinoid (M9091/1) 236.2
    malignant (M9090/3) 183.0
  Riedel's (ligneous thyroiditis) 245.3
  scrofulous (*see also* Tuberculosis) 017.2
  tuberculous (*see also* Tuberculosis) 017.2
    abscess 017.2
    adenitis 017.2
    lymphangitis 017.2
    ulcer 017.2
Strumipriva cachexia (*see also*
  Hypothyroidism) 244.9
Strümpell-Marie disease or spine (ankylosing
  spondylitis) 720.0
Strümpell-Westphal pseudosclerosis
  (hepatolenticular degeneration) 275.1
Stuart's disease (congenital factor X deficiency)
  (*see also* Defect, coagulation) 286.3
Stuart-Prower factor deficiency (congenital
  factor X deficiency) (*see also* Defect,
  coagulation) 286.3
Students' elbow 727.2
Stuffy nose 478.1
Stump —*see also* Amputation
  cervix, cervical (healed) 622.8

Stupor 780.09
  catatonic (*see also* Schizophrenia) 295.2
  circular (*see also* Psychosis, manic-depressive,
      circular) 296.7
  manic 296.89
  manic-depressive (*see also* Psychosis, affective)
      296.89
  mental (anergic) (delusional) 298.9
  psychogenic 298.8
  reaction to exceptional stress (transient) 308.2
  traumatic NEC—*see also* Injury, intracranial
      with spinal (cord)
          lesion—*see* Injury, spinal, by site
          shock—*see* Injury, spinal, by site
Sturge (-Weber) (-Dimitri) disease or syndrome
      (encephalocutaneous angiomatosis) 759.6
Sturge-Kalischer-Weber syndrome
      (encephalocutaneous angiomatosis) 759.6
Stuttering 307.0
Sty, stye 373.11
  external 373.11
  internal 373.12
  meibomian 373.12
Subacidity, gastric 536.8
  psychogenic 306.4
Subacute —*see* condition
Subarachnoid —*see* condition
Subclavian steal syndrome 435.2
Subcortical —*see* condition
Subcostal syndrome 098.86
  nerve compression 354.8
Subcutaneous, subcuticular —*see* condition
Subdelirium 293.1
Subdural —*see* condition
Subendocardium —*see* condition
Subependymoma (M9383/1) 237.5
Suberosis 495.3
Subglossitis —*see* Glossitis
Subhemophilia 286.0
Subinvolution (uterus) 621.1
  breast (postlactational) (postpartum) 611.8
  chronic 621.1
  puerperal, postpartum 674.8
Sublingual —*see* condition
Sublinguitis 527.2
Subluxation —*see also* Dislocation, by site
  congenital NEC—*see also* Malposition,
      congenital
      hip (unilateral) 754.32
        with dislocation of other hip 754.35
        bilateral 754.33
      joint
        lower limb 755.69
        shoulder 755.59
        upper limb 755.59
      lower limb (joint) 755.69
      shoulder (joint) 755.59
      upper limb (joint) 755.59
  lens 379.32
      anterior 379.33
      posterior 379.34
  rotary, cervical region of spine—*see* Fracture,
      vertebra, cervical
Submaxillary —*see* condition
Submersion (fatal) (nonfatal) 994.1
Submissiveness (undue), in child 313.0
Submucous —*see* condition

Subnormal, subnormality
  accommodation (*see also* Disorder,
      accommodation) 367.9
  mental (*see also* Retardation, mental) 319
      mild 317
      moderate 318.0
      profound 318.2
      severe 318.1
  temperature (accidental) 991.6
      not associated with low environmental
          temperature 780.9
Subphrenic —*see* condition
Subscapular nerve —*see* condition
Subseptus uterus 752.3
Subsiding appendicitis 542
Substernal thyroid (*see also* Goiter) 240.9
  congenital 759.2
Substitution disorder 300.11
Subtentorial —*see* condition
Subtertian
  fever 084.0
  malaria (fever) 084.0
Subthyroidism (acquired) (*see also*
      Hypothyroidism) 244.9
  congenital 243
Succenturiata placenta —*see* Placenta, abnormal
Succussion sounds, chest 786.7
Sucking thumb, child 307.9
Sudamen 705.1
Sudamina 705.1
Sudanese kala-azar 085.0
Sudden
  death, cause unknown (less than 24 hours) 798.1
      during childbirth 669.9
      infant 798.0
      puerperal, postpartum 674.9
  hearing loss NEC 388.2
  heart failure (*see also* Failure, heart) 428.9
  infant death syndrome 798.0
Sudeck's atrophy, disease, or syndrome 733.7
SUDS (Sudden unexplained death) 798.2
Suffocation (*see also* Asphyxia) 799.0
  by
      bed clothes 994.7
      bunny bag 994.7
      cave-in 994.7
      constriction 994.7
      drowning 994.1
      inhalation
          food or foreign body (*see also* Asphyxia,
              food or foreign body) 933.1
          oil or gasoline (*see also* Asphyxia, food or
              foreign body) 933.1
      overlying 994.7
      plastic bag 994.7
      pressure 994.7
      strangulation 994.7
  during birth 768.1
  mechanical 994.7
Sugar
  blood
      high 790.6
      low 251.2
  in urine 791.5
Suicide, suicidal (attempted)
  by poisoning—*see* Table of drugs and chemicals
  risk 300.9
  tendencies 300.9
  trauma NEC (*see also* nature and site of injury)
      959.9
Suipestifer infection (*see also* Infection,
      Salmonella) 003.9

Sulfatidosis 330.0
Sulfhemoglobinemia, sulphemoglobinemia
(acquired) (congenital) 289.7
Sumatran mite fever 081.2
Summer —*see* condition
Sunburn 692.71
dermatitis 692.71
Sunken
acetabulum 718.85
fontanels 756.0
Sunstroke 992.0
Superfecundation 651.9
with fetal loss and retention of one or more
fetus(es) 651.6
Superfetation 651.9
with fetal loss and retention of one or more
fetus(es) 651.6
Supernumerary (congenital)
aortic cusps 746.89
auditory ossicles 744.04
bone 756.9
breast 757.6
carpal bones 755.56
cusps, heart valve NEC 746.89
mitral 746.5
pulmonary 746.09
digit(s) 755.00
finger 755.01
toe 755.02
ear (lobule) 744.1
fallopian tube 752.19
finger 755.01
hymen 752.49
kidney 753.3
lacrimal glands 743.64
lacrimonasal duct 743.65
lobule (ear) 744.1
mitral cusps 746.5
muscle 756.82
nipples 757.6
organ or site NEC—*see* Accessory
ossicles, auditory 744.04
ovary 752.0
oviduct 752.19
pulmonic cusps 746.09
rib 756.3
cervical or first 756.2
syndrome 756.2
roots (of teeth) 520.2
spinal vertebra 756.19
spleen 759.0
tarsal bones 755.67
teeth 520.1
causing crowding 524.3
testis 752.8
thumb 755.01
toe 755.02
uterus 752.2
vagina 752.49
vertebra 756.19
Supervision (of)
contraceptive method previously prescribed
V25.40
intrauterine device V25.42
oral contraceptive (pill) V25.41
specified type NEC V25.49
subdermal implantable contraceptive V25.43
dietary (for) V65.3
allergy (food) V65.3
colitis V65.3
diabetes mellitus V65.3

Supervision (of)—*continued*
food allergy intolerance V65.3
gastritis V65.3
hypercholesterolemia V65.3
hypoglycemia V65.3
intolerance (food) V65.3
obesity V65.3
specified NEC V65.3
lactation V24.1
pregnancy—*see* Pregnancy, supervision of
Supplemental teeth 520.1
causing crowding 524.3
Suppression
binocular vision 368.31
lactation 676.5
menstruation 626.8
ovarian secretion 256.3
renal 586
urinary secretion 788.5
urine 788.5
Suppuration, suppurative —*see also* condition
accessory sinus (chronic) (*see also* Sinusitis)
473.9
adrenal gland 255.8
antrum (chronic) (*see also* Sinusitis, maxillary)
473.0
bladder (*see also* Cystitis) 595.89
bowel 569.89
brain 324.0
late effect 326
breast 611.0
puerperal, postpartum 675.1
dental periosteum 526.5
diffuse (skin) 686.00
ear (middle) (*see also* Otitis media) 382.4
external (*see also* Otitis, externa) 380.10
internal 386.33
ethmoidal (sinus) (chronic) (*see also* Sinusitis,
ethmoidal) 473.2
fallopian tube (*see also* Salpingo-oophoritis)
614.2
frontal (sinus) (chronic) (*see also* Sinusitis,
frontal) 473.1
gallbladder (*see also* Cholecystitis, acute) 575.0
gum 523.3
hernial sac—*see* Hernia, by site
intestine 569.89
joint (*see also* Arthritis, suppurative) 711.0
labyrinthine 386.33
lung 513.0
mammary gland 611.0
puerperal, postpartum 675.1
maxilla, maxillary 526.4
sinus (chronic) (*see also* Sinusitis, maxillary)
473.0
muscle 728.0
nasal sinus (chronic) (*see also* Sinusitis) 473.9
pancreas 577.0
parotid gland 527.2
pelvis, pelvic
female (*see also* Disease, pelvis,
inflammatory) 614.4
acute 614.3
male (*see also* Peritonitis) 567.2
pericranial (*see also* Osteomyelitis) 730.2
salivary duct or gland (any) 527.2
sinus (nasal) (*see also* Sinusitis) 473.9
sphenoidal (sinus) (chronic) (*see also* Sinusitis,
sphenoidal) 473.3
thymus (gland) 254.1
thyroid (gland) 245.0

Suppuration, suppurative—*continued*
tonsil 474.8
uterus (*see also* Endometritis) 615.9
vagina 616.10
wound—*see also* Wound, open, by site,
complicated
dislocation—*see* Dislocation, by site,
compound
fracture—*see* Fracture, by site, open
scratch or other superficial injury—*see* Injury,
superficial, by site
Suprapubic drainage 596.8
Suprarenal (gland)—*see* condition
Suprascapular nerve —*see* condition
Suprasellar —*see* condition
Supraspinatus syndrome 726.10
Surfer knots 919.8
infected 919.9
Surgery
cosmetic NEC V50.1
following healed injury or operation V51
hair transplant V50.0
elective V50.9
breast augmentation reduction V50.1
circumcision, ritual or routine (in absence of
medical indication) V50.2
cosmetic NEC V50.1
ear piercing V50.3
face-lift V50.1
following healed injury or operation V51
hair transplant V50.0
not done because of
contraindication V64.1
patient's decision V64.2
specified reason NEC V64.3
plastic
breast augmentation or reduction V50.1
cosmetic V50.1
face-lift V50.1
following healed injury or operation V51
repair of scarred tissue (following healed
injury or operation) V51
specified type NEC V50.8
previous, in pregnancy or childbirth
cervix 654.6
affecting fetus or newborn 763.89
causing obstructed labor 660.2
affecting fetus or newborn 763.1
pelvic soft tissues NEC 654.9
affecting fetus or newborn 763.89
causing obstructed labor 660.2
affecting fetus or newborn 763.1
perineum or vulva 654.8
uterus NEC 654.9
affecting fetus or newborn 763.89
causing obstructed labor 660.2
affecting fetus or newborn 763.1
due to previous cesarean delivery 654.2
vagina 654.7
Surgical
abortion—*see* Abortion, legal
emphysema 998.81
kidney (*see also* Pyelitis) 590.80
operation NEC 799.9
procedures, complication or misadventure—*see*
Complications, surgical procedure
shock 998.0
Suspected condition, ruled out (*see also*
Observation, suspected) V71.9
specified condition NEC V71.89

Suspended uterus, in pregnancy or childbirth
654.4
affecting fetus or newborn 763.89
causing obstructed labor 660.2
affecting fetus or newborn 763.1
Sutton's disease 709.09
Sutton and Gull's disease (arteriolar
nephrosclerosis) (*see also* Hypertension,
kidney) 403.90
Suture
burst (in operation wound) 998.3
inadvertently left in operation wound 998.4
removal V58.3
Shirodkar, in pregnancy (with or without
cervical incompetence) 654.5
Swab inadvertently left in operation wound
998.4
Swallowed, swallowing
difficulty (*see also* Dysphagia) 787.2
foreign body NEC (*see also* Foreign body) 938
Swamp fever 100.89
Swan neck hand (intrinsic) 736.09
Sweat (s), sweating
disease or sickness 078.2
excessive 780.8
fetid 705.89
fever 078.2
gland disease 705.9
specified type NEC 705.89
miliary 078.2
night 780.8
Sweeley-Klionsky disease (angiokeratoma
corporis diffusum) 272.7
Sweet's syndrome (acute febrile neutrophilic
dermatosis) 695.89
Swelling
abdominal (not referable to specific organ) 789.3
adrenal gland, cloudy 255.8
ankle 719.07
anus 787.99
arm 729.81
breast 611.72
Calabar 125.2
cervical gland 785.6
cheek 784.2
chest 786.6
ear 388.8
epigastric 789.3
extremity (lower) (upper) 729.81
eye 379.92
female genital organ 625.8
finger 729.81
foot 729.81
glands 785.6
gum 784.2
hand 729.81
head 784.2
inflammatory—*see* Inflammation
joint (*see also* Effusion, joint) 719.0
tuberculous—*see* Tuberculosis, joint
kidney, cloudy 593.89
leg 729.81
limb 729.81
liver 573.8
lung 786.6
lymph nodes 785.6
mediastinal 786.6
mouth 784.2
muscle (limb) 729.81
neck 784.2
nose or sinus 784.2

Swelling—*continued*
　palate 784.2
　pelvis 789.3
　penis 607.83
　perineum 625.8
　rectum 787.99
　scrotum 608.86
　skin 782.2
　splenic (*see also* Splenomegaly) 789.2
　substernal 786.6
　superficial, localized (skin) 782.2
　testicle 608.86
　throat 784.2
　toe 729.81
　tongue 784.2
　tubular (*see also* Disease, renal) 593.9
　umbilicus 789.3
　uterus 625.8
　vagina 625.8
　vulva 625.8
　wandering, due to Gnathostoma (spinigerum)
　　128.1
　white—*see* Tuberculosis, arthritis
Swift's disease 985.0
Swimmers'
　ear (acute) 380.12
　itch 120.3
Swimming in the head 780.4
Swollen —*see also* Swelling
　glands 785.6
Swyer-James syndrome (unilateral hyperlucent
　lung) 492.8
Swyer's syndrome (XY pure gonadal
　dysgenesis) 752.7
Sycosis 704.8
　barbae (not parasitic) 704.8
　contagiosa 110.0
　lupoid 704.8
　mycotic 110.0
　parasitic 110.0
　vulgaris 704.8
Sydenham's chorea —*see* Chorea, Sydenham's
Sylvatic yellow fever 060.0
Sylvest's disease (epidemic pleurodynia) 074.1
Symblepharon 372.63
　congenital 743.62
Symonds' syndrome 348.2
Sympathetic —*see* condition
Sympatheticotonia (*see also* Neuropathy,
　peripheral, autonomic) 337.9
Sympathicoblastoma (M9500/3)
　specified site—*see* Neoplasm, by site, malignant
　unspecified site 194.0
Sympathicogonioma (M9500/3)—*see*
　Sympathicoblastoma
Sympathoblastoma (M9500/3)—*see*
　Sympathicoblastoma
Sympathogonioma (M9500/3)—*see*
　Sympathicoblastoma
Symphalangy (*see also* Syndactylism) 755.10
Symptoms, specified (general) NEC 780.9
　abdomen NEC 789.9
　bone NEC 733.90
　breast NEC 611.79
　cardiac NEC 785.9
　cardiovascular NEC 785.9
　chest NEC 786.9
　development NEC 783.9
　digestive system NEC 787.99
　eye NEC 379.99
　gastrointestinal tract NEC 787.99

Symptoms, specified—*continued*
　genital organs NEC
　　female 625.9
　　male 608.9
　head and neck NEC 784.9
　heart NEC 785.9
　joint NEC 719.60
　　ankle 719.67
　　elbow 719.62
　　foot 719.67
　　hand 719.64
　　hip 719.65
　　knee 719.66
　　multiple sites 719.69
　　pelvic region 719.65
　　shoulder (region) 719.61
　　specified site NEC 719.68
　　wrist 719.63
　larynx NEC 784.9
　limbs NEC 729.89
　lymphatic system NEC 785.9
　menopausal 627.2
　metabolism NEC 783.9
　mouth NEC 528.9
　muscle NEC 728.9
　musculoskeletal NEC 781.99
　　limbs NEC 729.89
　nervous system NEC 781.99
　neurotic NEC 300.9
　nutrition, metabolism, and development NEC
　　783.9
　pelvis NEC 789.9
　　female 625.9
　peritoneum NEC 789.9
　respiratory system NEC 786.9
　skin and integument NEC 782.9
　subcutaneous tissue NEC 782.9
　throat NEC 784.9
　tonsil NEC 784.9
　urinary system NEC 788.9
　vascular NEC 785.9
Sympus 759.89
Synarthrosis 719.80
　ankle 719.87
　elbow 719.82
　foot 719.87
　hand 719.84
　hip 719.85
　knee 719.86
　multiple sites 719.89
　pelvic region 719.85
　shoulder (region) 719.81
　specified site NEC 719.88
　wrist 719.83
Syncephalus 759.4
Synchondrosis 756.9
　abnormal (congenital) 756.9
　ischiopubic (van Neck's) 732.1
Synchysis (senile) (vitreous humor) 379.21
　scintillans 379.22
Syncope (near) (pre-) 780.2
　anginosa 413.9
　bradycardia 427.89
　cardiac 780.2
　carotid sinus 337.0
　complicating delivery 669.2
　due to lumbar puncture 349.0
　fatal 798.1
　heart 780.2
　heat 992.1
　laryngeal 786.2

Syndrome—*continued*
　Gougerot (-Houwer) -Sjögren
　　(keratoconjunctivitis sicca) 710.2
　Gougerot-Blum (pigmented purpuric lichenoid
　　dermatitis) 709.1
　Gougerot-Carteaud (confluent reticulate
　　papillomatosis) 701.8
　Gouley's (constrictive pericarditis) 423.2
　Gowers' (vasovagal attack) 780.2
　Gowers-Paton-Kennedy 377.04
　Gradenigo's 383.02
　Gray or grey (chloramphenicol) (newborn) 779.4
　Greig's (hypertelorism) 756.0
　Gubler-Millard 344.89
　Guérin-Stern (arthrogryposis multiplex
　　congenita) 754.89
　Guillain-Barré (-Strohl) 357.0
　Gunn's (jaw-winking syndrome) 742.8
　Günther's (congenital erythropoietic porphyria)
　　277.1
　gustatory sweating 350.8
　H3O 759.81
　Hadfield-Clarke (pancreatic infantilism) 577.8
　Haglund-Läwen-Fründ 717.89
　hairless women 257.8
　Hallermann-Streiff 756.0
　Hallervorden-Spatz 333.0
　Hamman's (spontaneous mediastinal
　　emphysema) 518.1
　Hamman-Rich (diffuse interstitial pulmonary
　　fibrosis) 516.3
　Hand-Schüller-Christian (chronic histiocytosis
　　X) 277.8
　hand-foot 282.61
　Hanot-Chauffard (-Troisier) (bronze diabetes)
　　275.0
　Harada's 363.22
　Hare's (M8010/3) (carcinoma, pulmonary apex)
　　162.3
　Harkavy's 446.0
　harlequin color change 779.8
　Harris' (organic hyperinsulinism) 251.1
　Hart's (pellagra-cerebellar ataxia-renal
　　aminoaciduria) 270.0
　Hayem-Faber (achlorhydric anemia) 280.9
　Hayem-Widal (acquired hemolytic jaundice)
　　283.9
　Heberden's (angina pectoris) 413.9
　Hedinger's (malignant carcinoid) 259.2
　Hegglin's 288.2
　Heller's (infantile psychosis) (*see also*
　　Psychosis, childhood) 299.1
　H.E.L.L.P. 642.5
　hemolytic-uremic (adult) (child) 283.11
　Hench-Rosenberg (palindromic arthritis) (*see
　　also* Rheumatism, palindromic) 719.3
　Henoch-Schönlein (allergic purpura) 287.0
　hepatic flexure 569.89
　hepatorenal 572.4
　　due to a procedure 997.4
　　following delivery 674.8
　hepatourologic 572.4
　Herrick's (hemoglobin S disease) 282.61
　Herter (-Gee) (nontropical sprue) 579.0
　Heubner-Herter (nontropical sprue) 579.0
　Heyd's (hepatorenal) 572.4
　HHHO 759.81
　Hilger's 337.0
　Hoffa (-Kastert) (liposynovitis prepatellaris)
　　272.8
　Hoffmann's 244.9 *[359.5]*

Syndrome—*continued*
　Hoffmann-Bouveret (paroxysmal tachycardia)
　　427.2
　Hoffmann-Werdnig 335.0
　Holländer-Simons (progressive lipodystrophy)
　　272.6
　Holmes' (visual disorientation) 368.16
　Holmes-Adie 379.46
　Hoppe-Goldflam 358.0
　Horner's (*see also* Neuropathy, peripheral,
　　autonomic) 337.9
　　traumatic—*see* Injury, nerve, cervical
　　　sympathetic
　hospital addiction 301.51
　Hunt's (herpetic geniculate ganglionitis) 053.11
　　dyssynergia cerebellaris myoclonica 334.2
　Hunter (-Hurler) (mucopolysaccharidosis II)
　　277.5
　hunterian glossitis 529.4
　Hurler (-Hunter) (mucopolysaccharidosis II)
　　277.5
　Hutchinson's incisors or teeth 090.5
　Hutchinson-Boeck (sarcoidosis) 135
　Hutchinson-Gilford (progeria) 259.8
　hydralazine
　　correct substance properly administered 695.4
　　overdose or wrong substance given or taken
　　　972.6
　hydraulic concussion (abdomen) (*see also*
　　Injury, internal, abdomen) 868.00
　hyperabduction 447.8
　hyperactive bowel 564.9
　hyperaldosteronism with hypokalemic alkalosis
　　(Bartter's) 255.1
　hypercalcemic 275.42
　hypercoagulation NEC 289.8
　hypereosinophilic (idiopathic) 288.3
　hyperkalemic 276.7
　hyperkinetic—*see also* Hyperkinesia
　　heart 429.82
　hyperlipemia-hemolytic anemia-icterus 571.1
　hypermobility 728.5
　hypernatremia 276.0
　hyperosmolarity 276.0
　hypersomnia-bulimia 349.89
　hypersplenic 289.4
　hypersympathetic (*see also* Neuropathy,
　　peripheral, autonomic) 337.9
　hypertransfusion, newborn 776.4
　hyperventilation, psychogenic 306.1
　hyperviscosity (of serum) NEC 273.3
　　polycythemic 289.0
　　sclerothymic 282.8
　hypoglycemic (familial) (neonatal) 251.2
　　functional 251.1
　hypokalemic 276.8
　hypophyseal 253.8
　hypophyseothalamic 253.8
　hypopituitarism 253.2
　hypoplastic left heart 746.7
　hypopotassemia 276.8
　hyposmolality 276.1
　hypotension, maternal 669.2
　hypotonia-hypomentia-hypogonadism-obesity
　　759.81
　ICF (intravascular coagulation-fibrinolysis) (*see
　　also* Fibrinolysis) 286.6
　idiopathic cardiorespiratory distress, newborn
　　769
　idiopathic nephrotic (infantile) 581.9

Syndrome—*continued*
  Imerslund (-Gräsbeck) (anemia due to familial
    selective vitamin B_{12} malabsorption) 281.1
  immobility (paraplegic) 728.3
  immunity deficiency, combined 279.2
  impending coronary 411.1
  impingement
    shoulder 726.2
    vertebral bodies 724.4
  inappropriate secretion of antidiuretic hormone
    (ADH) 253.6
  incomplete
    mandibulofacial 756.0
  infant
    death, sudden (SIDS) 798.0
    Hercules 255.2
    of diabetic mother 775.0
    shaken 995.55
  infantilism 253.3
  inferior vena cava 459.2
  influenza-like 487.1
  inspissated bile, newborn 774.4
  intermediate coronary (artery) 411.1
  internal carotid artery (*see also* Occlusion,
    artery, carotid) 433.1
  interspinous ligament 724.8
  intestinal
    carcinoid 259.2
    gas 787.3
    knot 560.2
  intravascular
    coagulation-fibrinolysis (ICF) (*see also*
      Fibrinolysis) 286.6
    coagulopathy (*see also* Fibrinolysis) 286.6
  inverted Marfan's 759.89
  IRDS (idiopathic respiratory distress, newborn)
    769
  irritable
    bowel 564.1
    heart 306.2
    weakness 300.5
  ischemic bowel (transient) 557.9
    chronic 557.1
    due to mesenteric artery insufficiency 557.1
  Itsenko-Cushing (pituitary basophilism) 255.0
  IVC (intravascular coagulopathy) (*see also*
    Fibrinolysis) 286.6
  Ivemark's (asplenia with congenital heart
    disease) 759.0
  Jaccoud's 714.4
  Jackson's 344.89
  Jadassohn-Lewandowski (pachyonychia
    congenita) 757.5
  Jaffe-Lichtenstein (-Uehlinger) 252.0
  Jahnke's (encephalocutaneous angiomatosis)
    759.6
  Jakob-Creutzfeldt 046.1
    with dementia
      with behavioral disturbance 046.1 *[294.11]*
      without behavioral disturbance 046.1
        [294.10]
  Jaksch's (pseudoleukemia infantum) 285.8
  Jaksch-Hayem (-Luzet) (pseudoleukemia
    infantum) 285.8
  jaw-winking 742.8
  jejunal 564.2
  jet lag 307.45
  Jeune's (asphyxiating thoracic dystrophy of
    newborn) 756.4
  Job's (chronic granulomatous disease) 288.1
  Jordan's 288.2

Syndrome—*continued*
  Joseph-Diamond-Blackfan (congenital
    hypoplastic anemia) 284.0
  jugular foramen 352.6
  Kahler's (multiple myeloma) (M9730/3) 203.0
  Kalischer's (encephalocutaneous angiomatosis)
    759.6
  Kallmann's (hypogonadotropic hypogonadism
    with anosmia) 253.4
  Kanner's (autism) (*see also* Psychosis,
    childhood) 299.0
  Kartagener's (sinusitis, bronchiectasis, situs
    inversus) 759.3
  Kasabach-Merritt (capillary hemangioma
    associated with thrombocytopenic purpura)
    287.3
  Kast's (dyschondroplasia with hemangiomas)
    756.4
  Kaznelson's (congenital hypoplastic anemia)
    284.0
  Kelly's (sideropenic dysphagia) 280.8
  Kimmelstiel-Wilson (intercapillary
    glomerulosclerosis) 250.4 *[581.81]*
  Klauder's (erythema multiforme exudativum)
    695.1
  Klein-Waardenburg (ptosis-epicanthus) 270.2
  Kleine-Levin 349.89
  Klinefelter's 758.7
  Klippel-Feil (brevicollis) 756.16
  Klippel-Trenaunay 759.89
  Klumpke (-Déjérine) (injury to brachial plexus
    at birth) 767.6
  Klüver-Bucy (-Terzian) 310.0
  Köhler-Pellegrini-Stieda (calcification, knee
    joint) 726.62
  König's 564.89
  Korsakoff's (nonalcoholic) 294.0
    alcoholic 291.1
  Korsakoff (-Wernicke) (nonalcoholic) 294.0
    alcoholic 291.1
  Kostmann's (infantile genetic agranulocytosis)
    288.0
  Krabbe's
    congenital muscle hypoplasia 756.89
    cutaneocerebral angioma 759.6
  Kunkel (lupoid hepatitis) 571.49
  labyrinthine 386.50
  laceration, broad ligament 620.6
  Langdon Down (mongolism) 758.0
  Larsen's (flattened facies and multiple
    congenital dislocations) 755.8
  lateral
    cutaneous nerve of thigh 355.1
    medullary (*see also* Disease, cerebrovascular
      acute) 436
  Launois' (pituitary gigantism) 253.0
  Launois-Cléret (adiposogenital dystrophy) 253.8
  Laurence-Moon (-Bardet) -Biedl (obesity,
    polydactyly, and mental retardation) 759.8
  Lawford's (encephalocutaneous angiomatosis)
    759.6
  lazy
    leukocyte 288.0
    posture 728.3
  Lederer-Brill (acquired infectious hemolytic
    anemia) 283.19
  Legg-Calvé-Perthes (osteochondrosis capital
    femoral) 732.1
  Lennox's (*see also* Epilepsy) 345.0
  lenticular 275.1

Syndrome—*continued*
  Michotte's 721.5
  micrognathia-glossoptosis 756.0
  microphthalmos (congenital) 759.89
  midbrain 348.8
  middle
    lobe (lung) (right) 518.0
    radicular 353.0
  Miescher's
    familial acanthosis nigricans 701.2
    granulomatosis disciformis 709.3
  Mieten's 759.89
  migraine 346.0
  Mikity-Wilson (pulmonary dysmaturity) 770.7
  Mikulicz's (dryness of mouth, absent or
    decreased lacrimation) 527.1
  milk alkali (milk drinkers') 999.9
  Milkman (-Looser) (osteomalacia with
    pseudofractures) 268.2
  Millard-Gubler 344.89
  Miller Fisher's 357.0
  Milles' (encephalocutaneous angiomatosis)
    759.6
  Minkowski-Chauffard (*see also* Spherocytosis)
    282.0
  Mirizzi's (hepatic duct stenosis) 576.2
    with calculus, cholelithiasis, or stones—*see*
      Choledocholithiasis
  mitral
    click (-murmur) 785.2
    valve prolapse 424.0
  Möbius'
    congenital oculofacial paralysis 352.6
    ophthalmoplegic migraine 346.8
  Mohr's (Types I and II) 759.89
  monofixation 378.34
  Moore's (*see also* Epilepsy) 345.5
  Morel-Moore (hyperostosis frontalis interna)
    733.3
  Morel-Morgagni (hyperostosis frontalis interna)
    733.3
  Morgagni (-Stewart-Morel) (hyperostosis
    frontalis interna) 733.3
  Morgagni-Adams-Stokes (syncope with heart
    block) 426.9
  Morquio (-Brailsford) (-Ullrich)
    (mucopolysaccharidosis IV) 277.5
  Morris (testicular feminization) 257.8
  Morton's (foot) (metatarsalgia) (metatarsal
    neuralgia) (neuralgia) (neuroma) (toe) 355.6
  Moschcowitz (-Singer-Symmers) (thrombotic
    thrombocytopenic purpura) 446.6
  Mounier-Kuhn 494.0
    with acute exacerbation 494.1
  Mucha-Haberman (acute parapsoriasis
    varioliformis) 696.2
  mucocutaneous lymph node (acute) (febrile)
    (infantile) (MCLS) 446.1
  multiple
    deficiency 260
    operations 301.51
  Munchausen's 301.51
  Münchmeyer's (exostosis luxurians) 728.11
  Murchison-Sanderson—*see* Disease, Hodgkin's
  myasthenic—*see* Myasthenia, syndrome
  myelodysplastic 238.7
  myeloproliferative (chronic) (M9960/1) 238.7
  myofascial pain NEC 729.1
  Naffziger's 353.0
  Nager-de Reynier (dysostosis mandibularis)
    756.0

Syndrome—*continued*
  nail-patella (hereditary osteo-onychodysplasia)
    756.89
  Nebécourt's 253.3
  Neill-Dingwall (microencephaly and dwarfism)
    759.89
  nephrotic (*see also* Nephrosis) 581.9
    diabetic 250.4 *[581.81]*
  Netherton's (ichthyosiform erythroderma) 757.1
  neurocutaneous 759.6
  neuroleptic malignant 333.92
  Nezelof's (pure alymphocytosis) 279.13
  Niemann-Pick (lipid histiocytosis) 272.7
  Nonne-Milroy-Meige (chronic hereditary
    edema) 757.0
  nonsense 300.16
  Noonan's 759.89
  Nothnagel's
    ophthalmoplegia-cerebellar ataxia 378.52
    vasomotor acroparesthesia 443.89
  nucleus ambiguous-hypoglossal 352.6
  OAV (oculoauriculovertebral dysplasia) 756.0
  obsessional 300.3
  oculocutaneous 364.24
  oculomotor 378.81
  oculourethroarticular 099.3
  Ogilvie's (sympathicotonic colon obstruction)
    560.89
  ophthalmoplegia-cerebellar ataxia 378.52
  Oppenheim-Urbach (necrobiosis lipoidica
    diabeticorum) 250.8 *[709.3]*
  oral-facial-digital 759.89
  organic
    affective NEC 293.83
      drug-induced 292.84
    anxiety 293.84
    delusional 293.81
      alcohol-induced 291.5
      drug-induced 292.11
      due to or associated with
        arteriosclerosis 290.42
        presenile brain disease 290.12
        senility 290.20
    depressive 293.83
      drug-induced 292.84
      due to or associated with
        arteriosclerosis 290.43
        presenile brain disease 290.13
        senile brain disease 290.21
    hallucinosis 293.82
      drug-induced 292.84
  organic affective 293.83
    induced by drug 292.84
  organic personality 310.1
    induced by drug 292.89
  Ormond's 593.4
  orodigitofacial 759.89
  orthostatic hypotensive-dysautonomic-
    dyskinetic 333.0
  Osler-Weber-Rendu (familial hemorrhagic
    telangiectasia) 448.0
  osteodermopathic hyperostosis 757.39
  osteoporosis-osteomalacia 268.2
  Österreicher-Turner (hereditary
    osteo-onychodysplasia) 756.89
  Ostrum-Furst 756.59
  otolith 386.19
  otopalatodigital 759.89
  outlet (thoracic) 353.0
  ovarian remnant 620.8
  ovarian vein 593.4

Syndrome—*continued*
  postvagotomy 564.2
  postvalvulotomy 429.4
  postviral (asthenia) NEC 780.79
  Potain's (gastrectasis with dyspepsia) 536.1
  potassium intoxication 276.7
  Potter's 753.0
  Prader (-Labhart) -Willi (-Fanconi) 759.81
  preinfarction 411.1
  preleukemic 238.7
  premature senility 259.8
  premenstrual 625.4
  premenstrual tension 625.4
  pre ulcer 536.9
  Prinzmetal-Massumi (anterior chest wall
      syndrome) 786.52
  Profichet's 729.9
  progeria 259.8
  progressive pallidal degeneration 333.0
  prolonged gestation 766.2
  Proteus (dermal hypoplasia) 757.39
  prune belly 756.71
  prurigo-asthma 691.8
  pseudocarpal tunnel (sublimis) 354.0
  pseudohermaphroditism-virilism-hirsutism 255.2
  pseudoparalytica 358.0
  pseudo-Turner's 759.89
  psycho-organic 293.9
    acute 293.0
    anxiety type 293.84
    depressive type 293.83
    hallucinatory type 293.82
    nonpsychotic severity 310.1
      specified focal (partial) NEC 310.8
    paranoid type 293.81
    specified type NEC 293.89
    subacute 293.1
  pterygolymphangiectasia 758.6
  ptosis-epicanthus 270.2
  pulmonary
    arteriosclerosis 416.0
    hypoperfusion (idiopathic) 769
    renal (hemorrhagic) 446.21
  pulseless 446.7
  Putnam-Dana (subacute combined sclerosis
      with pernicious anemia) 281.0 *[336.2]*
  pyloroduodenal 537.89
  pyramidopallidonigral 332.0
  pyriformis 355.0
  Q-T interval prolongation 794.31
  radicular NEC 729.2
    lower limbs 724.4
    upper limbs 723.4
      newborn 767.4
  Raeder-Harbitz (pulseless disease) 446.7
  Ramsay Hunt's
    dyssynergia cerebellaris myoclonica 334.2
    herpetic geniculate ganglionitis 053.11
  rapid time-zone change 307.45
  Raymond (-Céstan) 433.8
  Raynaud's (paroxysmal digital cyanosis) 443.0
  RDS (respiratory distress syndrome, newborn)
      769
  Refsum's (heredopathia atactica
      polyneuritiformis) 356.3
  Reichmann's (gastrosuccorrhea) 536.8
  Reifenstein's (hereditary familial
      hypogonadism, male) 257.2
  Reilly's (*see also* Neuropathy, peripheral,
      autonomic) 337.9
  Reiter's 099.3

Syndrome—*continued*
  renal glomerulohyalinosis-diabetic 250.4
      [581.81]
  Rendu-Osler-Weber (familial hemorrhagic
      telangiectasia) 448.0
  renofacial (congenital biliary fibroangiomatosis)
      753.0
  Rénon-Delille 253.8
  respiratory distress (idiopathic) (newborn) 769
    adult (following shock, surgery, or trauma)
        518.5
      specified NEC 518.82
  restless leg 333.99
  retraction (Duane's) 378.71
  retroperitoneal fibrosis 593.4
  Rett's 330.8
  Reye's 331.81
  Reye-Sheehan (postpartum pituitary necrosis)
      253.2
  Riddoch's (visual disorientation) 368.16
  Ridley's (*see also* Failure, ventricular, left)
      428.1
  Rieger's (mesodermal dysgenesis, anterior
      ocular segment) 743.44
  Rietti-Greppi-Micheli (thalassemia minor) 282.4
  right ventricular obstruction—*see* Failure heart,
      congestive
  Riley-Day (familial dysautonomia) 742.8
  Robin's 756.0
  Rokitansky-Kuster-Hauser (congenital absence,
      vagina) 752.49
  Romano-Ward (prolonged Q-T interval) 794.31
  Romberg's 349.89
  Rosen-Castleman-Liebow (pulmonary
      proteinosis) 516.0
  rotator cuff, shoulder 726.10
  Roth's 355.1
  Rothmund's (congenital poikiloderma) 757.33
  Rotor's (idiopathic hyperbilirubinemia) 277.4
  Roussy-Lévy 334.3
  Roy (-Jutras) (acropachyderma) 757.39
  rubella (congenital) 771.0
  Rubinstein-Taybi's (brachydactylia, short
      stature, and mental retardation) 759.89
  Rud's (mental deficiency, epilepsy, and
      infantilism) 759.89
  Ruiter-Pompen (-Wyers) (angiokeratoma
      corporis diffusum) 272.7
  Runge's (postmaturity) 766.2
  Russell (-Silver) (congenital hemihypertrophy
      and short stature) 759.89
  Rytand-Lipsitch (complete atrioventricular
      block) 426.0
  sacralization-scoliosis-sciatica 756.15
  sacroiliac 724.6
  Saenger's 379.46
  salt
    depletion (*see also* Disease, renal) 593.9
      due to heat NEC 992.8
        causing heat exhaustion or prostration
            992.4
    low (*see also* Disease, renal) 593.9
  salt-losing (*see also* Disease, renal) 593.9
  Sanfilippo's (mucopolysaccharidosis III) 277.5
  Scaglietti-Dagnini (acromegalic
      macrospondylitis) 253.0
  scalded skin 695.1
  scalenus anticus (anterior) 353.0
  scapulocostal 354.8
  scapuloperoneal 359.1
  scapulovertebral 723.4

Syndrome—*continued*
  Sturge-Weber (-Dimitri) (encephalocutaneous
      angiomatosis) 759.6
  subclavian-carotid obstruction (chronic) 446.7
  subclavian steal 435.2
  subcoracoid-pectoralis minor 447.8
  subcostal 098.86
    nerve compression 354.8
  subperiosteal hematoma 267
  subphrenic interposition 751.4
  sudden infant death (SIDS) 798.0
  Sudeck's 733.7
  Sudeck-Leriche 733.7
  superior
    cerebellar artery (*see also* Disease,
        cerebrovascular, acute) 436
      mesenteric artery 557.1
      pulmonary sulcus (tumor) (M8010/3) 162.3
      vena cava 459.2
  suprarenal cortical 255.3
  supraspinatus 726.10
  swallowed blood 777.3
  sweat retention 705.1
  Sweet's (acute febrile neutrophilic dermatosis)
      695.89
  Swyer-James (unilateral hyperlucent lung) 492.8
  Swyer's (XY pure gonadal dysgenesis) 752.7
  Symonds' 348.2
  sympathetic
    cervical paralysis 337.0
    pelvic 625.5
  syndactylic oxycephaly 755.55
  syphilitic-cardiovascular 093.89
  systemic fibrosclerosing 710.8
  systolic click (-murmur) 785.2
  Tabagism 305.1
  tachycardia-bradycardia 427.81
  Takayasu (-Onishi) (pulseless disease) 446.7
  Tapia's 352.6
  tarsal tunnel 355.5
  Taussig-Bing (transposition, aorta and
      overriding pulmonary artery) 745.11
  Taybi's (otopalatodigital) 759.89
  Taylor's 625.5
  teething 520.7
  tegmental 344.89
  telangiectasis-pigmentation-cataract 757.33
  temporal 383.02
    lobectomy behavior 310.0
  temporomandibular joint-pain-dysfunction
      [TMJ] NEC 524.60
    specified NEC 524.69
  Terry's 362.21
  testicular feminization 257.8
  testis, nonvirilizing 257.8
  tethered (spinal) cord 742.59
  thalamic 348.8
  Thibierge-Weissenbach (cutaneous systemic
      sclerosis) 710.1
  Thiele 724.6
  thoracic outlet (compression) 353.0
  thoracogenous rheumatic (hypertrophic
      pulmonary osteoarthropathy) 731.2
  Thorn's (*see also* Disease, renal) 593.9
  Thorson-Biörck (malignant carcinoid) 259.2
  thrombopenia-hemangioma 287.3
  thyroid-adrenocortical insufficiency 258.1
  Tietze's 733.6
  time-zone (rapid) 307.45
  Tobias' (carcinoma, pulmonary apex)
      (M8010/3) 162.3

Syndrome—*continued*
  toilet seat 926.0
  Tolosa-Hunt 378.55
  Toni-Fanconi (cystinosis) 270.0
  Touraine's (hereditary osteo-onychodysplasia)
      756.89
  Touraine-Solente-Golé (acropachyderma)
      757.39
  toxic
    oil 710.5
    shock 040.89
  transfusion
    fetal-maternal 772.0
    twin
      donor (infant) 772.0
      recipient (infant) 776.4
  Treacher Collins' (incomplete mandibulofacial
      dysostosis) 756.0
  trigeminal plate 259.8
  triple X female 758.81
  trisomy NEC 758.5
    13 or D₁ 758.1
    16-18 or E 758.2
    18 or E₃ 758.2
    20 758.5
    21 or G (mongolism) 758.0
    22 or G (mongolism) 758.0
    G 758.0
  Troisier-Hanot-Chauffard (bronze diabetes)
      275.0
  tropical wet feet 991.4
  Trousseau's (thrombophlebitis migrans visceral
      cancer) 453.1
  Türk's (ocular retraction syndrome) 378.71
  Turner's 758.6
  Turner-Varny 758.6
  twin-to-twin transfusion 762.3
    recipient twin 776.4
  Uehlinger's (acropachyderma) 757.39
  Ullrich (-Bonnevie) (-Turner) 758.6
  Ullrich-Feichtiger 759.89
  underwater blast injury (abdominal) (*see also*
      Injury, internal, abdomen) 868.00
  universal joint, cervix 620.6
  Unverricht (-Lundborg) 333.2
  Unverricht-Wagner (dermatomyositis) 710.3
  upward gaze 378.81
  Urbach-Oppenheim (necrobiosis lipoidica
      diabeticorum) 250.8 *[709.3]*
  Urbach-Wiethe (lipoid proteinosis) 272.8
  uremia, chronic 585
  urethral 597.81
  urethro-oculoarticular 099.3
  urethro-oculosynovial 099.3
  urohepatic 572.4
  uveocutaneous 364.24
  uveomeningeal, uveomeningitis 363.22
  vagohypoglossal 352.6
  vagovagal 780.2
  van Buchem's (hyperostosis corticalis) 733.3
  van der Hoeve's (brittle bones and blue sclera,
      deafness) 756.51
  van der Hoeve-Halbertsma-Waardenburg
      (ptosis-epicanthus) 270.2
  van der Hoeve-Waardenburg-Gualdi
      (ptosis-epicanthus) 270.2
  van Neck-Odelberg (juvenile osteochondrosis)
      732.1
  vanishing twin 651.33
  vascular splanchnic 557.0
  vasomotor 443.9

Syndrome—*continued*
- vasovagal 780.2
- VATER 759.89
- vena cava (inferior) (superior) (obstruction) 459.2
- Verbiest's (claudicatio intermittens spinalis) 435.1
- Vernet's 352.6
- vertebral
  - artery 435.1
    - compression 721.1
    - lumbar 724.4
    - steal 435.1
- vertebrogenic (pain) 724.5
- vertiginous NEC 386.9
- video display tube 723.8
- Villaret's 352.6
- Vinson-Plummer (sideropenic dysphagia) 280.8
- virilizing adrenocortical hyperplasia, congenital 255.2
- virus, viral 079.99
- visceral larval migrans 128.0
- visual disorientation 368.16
- vitamin B$_6$ deficiency 266.1
- vitreous touch 997.99
- Vogt's (corpus striatum) 333.7
- Vogt-Koyanagi 364.24
- Volkmann's 958.6
- von Bechterew-Strümpell (ankylosing spondylitis) 720.0
- von Graefe's 378.72
- von Hippel-Lindau (angiomatosis retinocerebellosa) 759.6
- von Schroetter's (intermittent venous claudication) 453.8
- von Willebrand (-Jürgens) (angiohemophilia) 286.4
- Waardenburg-Klein (ptosis epicanthus) 270.2
- Wagner (-Unverricht) (dermatomyositis) 710.3
- Waldenström's (macroglobulinemia) 273.3
- Waldenström-Kjellberg (sideropenic dysphagia) 280.8
- Wallenberg's (posterior inferior cerebellar artery) (*see also* Disease, cerebrovascular, acute) 436
- Waterhouse (-Friderichsen) 036.3
- water retention 276.6
- Weber's 344.89
- Weber-Christian (nodular nonsuppurative panniculitis) 729.30
- Weber-Cockayne (epidermolysis bullosa) 757.39
- Weber-Dimitri (encephalocutaneous angiomatosis) 759.6
- Weber-Gubler 344.89
- Weber-Leyden 344.89
- Weber-Osler (familial hemorrhagic telangiectasia) 448.0
- Wegener's (necrotizing respiratory granulomatosis) 446.4
- Weill-Marchesani (brachymorphism and ectopia lentis) 759.89
- Weingarten's (tropical eosinophilia) 518.3
- Weiss-Baker (carotid sinus syncope) 337.0
- Weissenbach-Thibierge (cutaneous systemic sclerosis) 710.1
- Werdnig-Hoffmann 335.0
- Werlhof-Wichmann (*see also* Purpura, thrombocytopenic) 287.3
- Werner's (polyendocrine adenomatosis) 258.0
- Werner's (progeria adultorum) 259.8

Syndrome—*continued*
- Wernicke's (nonalcoholic) (superior hemorrhagic polioencephalitis) 265.1
- Wernicke-Korsakoff (nonalcoholic) 294.0
  - alcoholic 291.1
- Westphal-Strümpell (hepatolenticular degeneration) 275.1
- wet
  - brain (alcoholic) 303.9
  - feet (maceration) (tropical) 991.4
  - lung
    - adult 518.5
    - newborn 770.6
- whiplash 847.0
- Whipple's (intestinal lipodystrophy) 040.2
- "whistling face" (craniocarpotarsal dystrophy) 759.89
- Widal (-Abrami) (acquired hemolytic jaundice) 283.9
- Wilkie's 557.1
- Wilkinson-Sneddon (subcorneal pustular dermatosis) 694.1
- Willan-Plumbe (psoriasis) 696.1
- Willebrand (-Jürgens) (angiohemophilia) 286.4
- Willi-Prader (hypogenital dystrophy with diabetic tendency) 759.81
- Wilson's (hepatolenticular degeneration) 275.1
- Wilson-Mikity 770.7
- Wiskott-Aldrich (eczema-thrombocytopenia) 279.12
- withdrawal
  - alcohol 291.81
  - drug 292.0
    - infant of dependent mother 779.5
- Woakes' (ethmoiditis) 471.1
- Wolff-Parkinson-White (anomalous atrioventricular excitation) 426.7
- Wright's (hyperabduction) 447.8
- X 413.9
- xiphoidalgia 733.99
- XO 758.6
- XXX 758.81
- XXXXY 758.81
- XXY 758.7
- yellow vernix (placental dysfunction) 762.2
- Zahorsky's 074.0
- Zieve's (jaundice, hyperlipemia and hemolytic anemia) 571.1
- Zollinger-Ellison (gastric hypersecretion with pancreatic islet cell tumor) 251.5
- Zuelzer-Ogden (nutritional megaloblastic anemia) 281.2

Synechia (iris) (pupil) 364.70
- anterior 364.72
  - peripheral 364.73
- intrauterine (traumatic) 621.5
- posterior 364.71
- vulvae, congenital 752.49

Synesthesia (*see also* Disturbance, sensation) 782.0

Synodontia 520.2

Synophthalmus 759.89

Synorchidism 752.8

Synorchism 752.8

Synostosis (congenital) 756.59
- astragaloscaphoid 755.67
- radioulnar 755.53
- talonavicular (bar) 755.67
- tarsal 755.67

Synovial —*see* condition

Synovioma (M9040/3)—*see also* Neoplasm, connective tissue, malignant
  benign (M9040/3)—*see* Neoplasm, connective tissue, benign
Synoviosarcoma (M9040/3)—*see* Neoplasm, connective tissue, malignant
Synovitis 727.00
  chronic crepitant, wrist 727.2
  due to crystals—*see* Arthritis, due to crystals
  gonococcal 098.51
  gouty 274.0
  syphilitic 095.7
    congenital 090.0
  traumatic, current—*see* Sprain, by site
  tuberculous—*see* Tuberculosis, synovitis
  villonodular 719.20
    ankle 719.27
    elbow 719.22
    foot 719.27
    hand 719.24
    hip 719.25
    knee 719.26
    multiple sites 719.29
    pelvic region 719.25
    shoulder (region) 719.21
    specified site NEC 719.28
    wrist 719.23
Syphilide 091.3
  congenital 090.0
  newborn 090.0
  tubercular 095.8
    congenital 090.0
Syphilis, syphilitic (acquired) 097.9
  with lung involvement 095.1
  abdomen (late) 095.2
  acoustic nerve 094.86
  adenopathy (secondary) 091.4
  adrenal (gland) 095.8
    with cortical hypofunction 095.8
  age under 2 years NEC (*see also* Syphilis, congenital) 090.9
    acquired 097.9
  alopecia (secondary) 091.82
  anemia 095.8
  aneurysm (artery) (ruptured) 093.89
    aorta 093.0
    central nervous system 094.89
    congenital 090.5
  anus 095.8
    primary 091.1
    secondary 091.3
  aorta, aortic (arch) (abdominal) (insufficiency) (pulmonary) (regurgitation) (stenosis) (thoracic) 093.89
    aneurysm 093.0
  arachnoid (adhesive) 094.2
  artery 093.89
    cerebral 094.89
    spinal 094.89
  arthropathy (neurogenic) (tabetic) 094.0 *[713.5]*
  asymptomatic—*see* Syphilis, latent
  ataxia, locomotor (progressive) 094.0
  atrophoderma maculatum 091.3
  auricular fibrillation 093.89
  Bell's palsy 094.89
  bladder 095.8
  bone 095.5
    secondary 091.61
  brain 094.89
  breast 095.8
  bronchus 095.8

Syphilis, syphilitic—*continued*
  bubo 091.0
  bulbar palsy 094.89
  bursa (late) 095.7
  cardiac decompensation 093.89
  cardiovascular (early) (late) (primary) (secondary) (tertiary) 093.9
    specified type and site NEC 093.89
  causing death under 2 years of age (*see also* Syphilis, congenital) 090.9
    stated to be acquired NEC 097.9
  central nervous system (any site) (early) (late) (latent) (primary) (recurrent) (relapse) (secondary) (tertiary) 094.9
    with
      ataxia 094.0
      paralysis, general 094.1
        juvenile 090.40
      paresis (general) 094.1
        juvenile 090.40
      tabes (dorsalis) 094.0
        juvenile 090.40
      taboparesis 094.1
        juvenile 090.40
      aneurysm (ruptured) 094.87
    congenital 090.40
    juvenile 090.40
    remission in (sustained) 094.9
    serology doubtful, negative, or positive 094.9
    specified nature or site NEC 094.89
    vascular 094.89
  cerebral 094.89
    meningovascular 094.2
    nerves 094.89
    sclerosis 094.89
    thrombosis 094.89
  cerebrospinal 094.89
    tabetic 094.0
  cerebrovascular 094.89
  cervix 095.8
  chancre (multiple) 091.0
    extragenital 091.2
    Rollet's 091.0
  Charcot's joint 094.0 *[713.5]*
  choked disc 094.89 *[377.00]*
  chorioretinitis 091.51
    congenital 090.0 *[363.13]*
    late 094.83
  choroiditis 091.51
    congenital 090.0 *[363.13]*
    late 094.83
    prenatal 090.0 *[363.13]*
  choroidoretinitis (secondary) 091.51
    congenital 090.0 *[363.13]*
    late 094.83
  ciliary body (secondary) 091.52
    late 095.8 *[364.11]*
  colon (late) 095.8
  combined sclerosis 094.89
  complicating pregnancy, childbirth or puerperium 647.0
    affecting fetus or newborn 760.2
  condyloma (latum) 091.3
  congenital 090.9
    with
      encephalitis 090.41
      paresis (general) 090.40
      tabes (dorsalis) 090.40
      taboparesis 090.40
    chorioretinitis, choroiditis 090.0 *[363.13]*
    early or less than 2 years after birth NEC 090.2

Syphilis, syphilitic—*continued*
  fingers 091.2
  genital 091.0
  lip 091.2
  specified site NEC 091.2
  tonsils 091.2
 prostate 095.8
 psychosis (intracranial gumma) 094.89
 ptosis (eyelid) 094.89
 pulmonary (late) 095.1
  artery 093.89
 pulmonum 095.1
 pyelonephritis 095.4
 recently acquired, symptomatic NEC 091.89
 rectum 095.8
 respiratory tract 095.8
 retina
  late 094.83
  neurorecidive 094.83
 retrobulbar neuritis 094.85
 salpingitis 095.8
 sclera (late) 095.0
 sclerosis
  cerebral 094.89
  coronary 093.89
  multiple 094.89
  subacute 094.89
 scotoma (central) 095.8
 scrotum 095.8
 secondary (and primary) 091.9
  adenopathy 091.4
  anus 091.3
  bone 091.61
  cardiovascular 093.9
  central nervous system 094.9
  chorioretinitis, choroiditis 091.51
  hepatitis 091.62
  liver 091.62
  lymphadenitis 091.4
  meningitis, acute 091.81
  mouth 091.3
  mucous membranes 091.3
  periosteum 091.61
  periostitis 091.61
  pharynx 091.3
  relapse (treated) (untreated) 091.7
  skin 091.3
  specified form NEC 091.89
  tonsil 091.3
  ulcer 091.3
  viscera 091.69
  vulva 091.3
 seminal vesicle (late) 095.8
 seronegative
  with signs or symptoms—*see* Syphilis, by site
    and stage
 seropositive
  with signs or symptoms—*see* Syphilis, by site
    and stage
  follow-up of latent syphilis—*see* Syphilis,
    latent
  only finding—*see* Syphilis, latent
 seventh nerve (paralysis) 094.89
 sinus 095.8
 sinusitis 095.8
 skeletal system 095.5
 skin (early) (secondary) (with ulceration) 091.3
  late or tertiary 095.8
 small intestine 095.8
 spastic spinal paralysis 094.0
 spermatic cord (late) 095.8

Syphilis, syphilitic—*continued*
 spinal (cord) 094.89
  with
    paresis 094.1
    tabes 094.0
 spleen 095.8
 splenomegaly 095.8
 spondylitis 095.5
 staphyloma 095.8
 stigmata (congenital) 090.5
 stomach 095.8
 synovium (late) 095.7
 tabes dorsalis (early) (late) 094.0
  juvenile 090.40
 tabetic type 094.0
  juvenile 090.40
 taboparesis 094.1
  juvenile 090.40
 tachycardia 093.89
 tendon (late) 095.7
 tertiary 097.0
  with symptoms 095.8
  cardiovascular 093.9
  central nervous system 094.9
  multiple NEC 095.8
  specified site NEC 095.8
 testis 095.8
 thorax 095.8
 throat 095.8
 thymus (gland) 095.8
 thyroid (late) 095.8
 tongue 095.8
 tonsil (lingual) 095.8
  primary 091.2
  secondary 091.3
 trachea 095.8
 tricuspid valve 093.23
 tumor, brain 094.89
 tunica vaginalis (late) 095.8
 ulcer (any site) (early) (secondary) 091.3
  late 095.9
  perforating 095.9
    foot 094.0
 urethra (stricture) 095.8
 urogenital 095.8
 uterus 095.8
 uveal tract (secondary) 091.50
  late 095.8 *[363.13]*
 uveitis (secondary) 091.50
  late 095.8 *[363.13]*
 uvula (late) 095.8
  perforated 095.8
 vagina 091.0
  late 095.8
 valvulitis NEC 093.20
 vascular 093.89
  brain or cerebral 094.89
 vein 093.89
  cerebral 094.89
 ventriculi 095.8
 vesicae urinariae 095.8
 viscera (abdominal) 095.2
  secondary 091.69
 vitreous (hemorrhage) (opacities) 095.8
 vulva 091.0
  late 095.8
  secondary 091.3
Syphiloma 095.9
 cardiovascular system 093.9
 central nervous system 094.9
 circulatory system 093.9
 congenital 090.5

Syphilophobia 300.29
Syringadenoma (M8400/0)—*see also*
   Neoplasm, skin, benign
   papillary (M8406/0)—*see* Neoplasm, skin,
      benign
Syringobulbia 336.0
Syringocarcinoma (M8400/3)—*see* Neoplasm,
   skin, malignant
Syringocystadenoma (M8400/0)—*see also*
   Neoplasm, skin, benign
   papillary (M8406/0)—*see* Neoplasm. skin,
      benign
Syringocystoma (M8407/0)—*see* Necplasm,
   skin, benign
Syringoma (M8407/0)—*see also* Neoplasm,
   skin, benign
   chondroid (M8940/0)—*see* Neoplasm, by site,
      benign
Syringomyelia 336.0
Syringomyelitis 323.9
   late effect—*see* category 326
Syringomyelocele (*see also* Spina bifida) 741.9
Syringopontia 336.0
System, systemic —*see also* condition
   disease, combined—*see* Degeneration,
      combined
   fibrosclerosing syndrome 710.8
   lupus erythematosus 710.0
      inhibitor 286.5

T

Tab —*see* Tag
Tabacism 989.8
Tabacosis 989.8
Tabardillo 080
  flea-borne 081.0
  louse-borne 080
Tabes, tabetic
  with
      central nervous system syphilis 094.0
      Charcot's joint 094.0 *[713.5]*
      cord bladder 094.0
      crisis, viscera (any) 094.0
      paralysis, general 094.1
      paresis (general) 094.1
      perforating ulcer 094.0
  arthropathy 094.0 *[713.5]*
  bladder 094.0
  bone 094.0
  cerebrospinal 094.0
  congenital 090.40
  conjugal 094.0
  dorsalis 094.0
      neurosyphilis 094.0
  early 094.0
  juvenile 090.40
  latent 094.0
  mesenterica (*see also* Tuberculosis) 014.8
  paralysis insane, general 094.1
  peripheral (nonsyphilitic) 799.8
  spasmodic 094.0
      not dorsal or dorsalis 343.9
  syphilis (cerebrospinal) 094.0
Taboparalysis 094.1
Taboparesis (remission) 094.1
  with
      Charcot's joint 094.1 *[713.5]*
      cord bladder 094.1
      perforating ulcer 094.1
  juvenile 090.40
Tachyalimentation 579.3
Tachyarrhythmia, tachyrhythmia —*see also*
  Tachycardia
  paroxysmal with sinus bradycardia 427.81
Tachycardia 785.0
  atrial 427.89
  auricular 427.89
  nodal 427.89
      nonparoxysmal atrioventricular 426.89
  nonparoxysmal atrioventricular (nodal) 426.89
  paroxysmal 427.2
      with sinus bradycardia 427.81
      atrial (PAT) 427.0
          psychogenic 316 *[427.0]*
      atrioventricular (AV) 427.0
          psychogenic 316 *[427.0]*
      essential 427.2
      junctional 427.0
      nodal 427.0
      psychogenic 316 *[427.2]*
          atrial 316 *[427.0]*
          supraventricular 316 *[427.0]*
          ventricular 316 *[427.1]*
      supraventricular 427.0
          psychogenic 316 *[427.0]*
      ventricular 427.1
          psychogenic 316 *[427.1]*
  postoperative 997.1

Tachycardia—*continued*
  psychogenic 306.2
  sick sinus 427.81
  sinoauricular 427.89
  sinus 427.89
  supraventricular 427.89
  ventricular (paroxysmal) 427.1
      psychogenic 316 *[427.1]*
Tachypnea 786.06
  hysterical 300.11
  newborn (idiopathic) (transitory) 770.6
  psychogenic 306.1
  transitory, of newborn 770.6
Taenia (infection) (infestation) (*see also*
      Infestation, taenia) 123.3
  diminuta 123.6
  echinococcal infestation (*see also*
      Echinococcus) 122.9
  nana 123.6
  saginata infestation 123.2
  solium (intestinal form) 123.0
      larval form 123.1
Taeniasis (intestine) (*see also* Infestation,
      Taenia) 123.3
  saginata 123.2
  solium 123.0
Taenzer's disease 757.4
Tag (hypertrophied skin) (infected) 701.9
  adenoid 474.8
  anus 455.9
  endocardial (*see also* Endocarditis) 424.90
  hemorrhoidal 455.9
  hymen 623.8
  perineal 624.8
  preauricular 744.1
  rectum 455.9
  sentinel 455.9
  skin 701.9
      accessory 757.39
      anus 455.9
      congenital 757.39
      preauricular 744.1
      rectum 455.9
  tonsil 474.8
  urethra, urethral 599.84
  vulva 624.8
Tahyna fever 062.5
Takayasu (-Onishi) disease or syndrome
      (pulseless disease) 446.7
Talc granuloma 728.82
Talcosis 502
Talipes (congenital) 754.70
  acquired NEC 736.79
      planus 734
  asymmetric 754.79
      acquired 736.79
  calcaneovalgus 754.62
      acquired 736.76
  calcaneovarus 754.59
      acquired 736.76
  calcaneus 754.79
      acquired 736.76
  cavovarus 754.59
      acquired 736.75
  cavus 754.71
      acquired 736.73
  equinovalgus 754.69
      acquired 736.72

Talipes—*continued*
equinovarus 754.51
  acquired 736.71
equinus 754.79
  acquired, NEC 736.72
percavus 754.71
  acquired 736.73
planovalgus 754.69
  acquired 736.79
planus (acquired) (any degree) 734
  congenital 754.61
  due to rickets 268.1
valgus 754.60
  acquired 736.79
varus 754.50
  acquired 736.79
Talma's disease 728.85
Tamponade heart (Rose's) (*see also*
  Pericarditis) 423.9
Tanapox 078.89
Tangier disease (familial high-density
  lipoprotein deficiency) 272.5
Tank ear 380.12
Tantrum (childhood) (*see also* Disturbance,
  conduct) 312.1
Tapeworm (infection) (infestation) (*see also*
  Infestation, tapeworm) 123.9
Tapia's syndrome 352.6
Tarantism 297.8
Target-oval cell anemia 282.4
Tarlov's cyst 355.9
Tarral-Besnier disease (pityriasis rubra pilaris)
  696.4
Tarsalgia 729.2
Tarsal tunnel syndrome 355.5
Tarsitis (eyelid) 373.00
  syphilitic 095.8 *[373.00]*
  tuberculous (*see also* Tuberculosis) 017.0
  [373.4]
Tartar (teeth) 523.6
Tattoo (mark) 709.09
Taurodontism 520.2
Taussig-Bing defect, heart, or syndrome
  (transposition, aorta and overriding pulmonary
  artery) 745.11
Tay's choroiditis 363.41
Tay-Sachs
  amaurotic familial idiocy 330.1
  disease 330.1
Taybi's syndrome (otopalatodigital) 759.89
Taylor's
disease (diffuse idiopathic cutaneous atrophy)
  701.8
syndrome 625.5
Tear, torn (traumatic)—*see also* Wound, open,
  by site
anus, anal (sphincter) 863.89
  with open wound in cavity 863.99
  complicating delivery 664.2
    with mucosa 664.3
  nontraumatic, nonpuerperal 565.0
articular cartilage, old (*see also* Disorder,
  cartilage, articular) 718.0
bladder
  with
    abortion—*see* Abortion, by type, with
      damage to pelvic organs
    ectopic pregnancy (*see also* categories
      633.0-633.9) 639.2
    molar pregnancy (*see also* categories
      630-632) 639.2

Tear, torn—*continued*
following
  abortion 639.2
  ectopic or molar pregnancy 639.2
obstetrical trauma 665.5
bowel
  with
    abortion—*see* Abortion, by type, with
      damage to pelvic organs
    ectopic pregnancy (*see also* categories
      633.0-633.9) 639.2
    molar pregnancy (*see also* categories
      630-632) 639.2
  following
    abortion 639.2
    ectopic or molar pregnancy 639.2
  obstetrical trauma 665.5
broad ligament
  with
    abortion—*see* Abortion, by type, with
      damage to pelvic organs
    ectopic pregnancy (*see also* categories
      633.0-633.9) 639.2
    molar pregnancy (*see also* categories
      630-632) 639.2
  following
    abortion 639.2
    ectopic or molar pregnancy 639.2
  obstetrical trauma 665.6
bucket handle (knee) (meniscus)—*see* Tear,
  meniscus
capsule
  joint—*see* Sprain, by site
  spleen—*see* Laceration, spleen, capsule
cartilage—*see also* Sprain, by site
  articular, old (*see also* Disorder, cartilage,
    articular) 718.0
  knee—*see* Tear, meniscus
  semilunar (knee) (current injury)—*see* Tear,
    meniscus
cervix
  with
    abortion—*see* Abortion, by type, with
      damage to pelvic organs
    ectopic pregnancy (*see also* categories
      633.0-633.9) 639.2
    molar pregnancy (*see also* categories
      630-632) 639.2
  following
    abortion 639.2
    ectopic or molar pregnancy 639.2
  obstetrical trauma (current) 665.3
  old 622.3
internal organ (abdomen, chest, or pelvis)—*see*
  Injury, internal, by site
ligament—*see also* Sprain, by site
  with open wound—*see* Wound, open by site
meniscus (knee) (current injury) 836.2
  bucket handle 836.0
    old 717.0
  lateral 836.1
    anterior horn 836.1
      old 717.42
    bucket handle 836.1
      old 717.41
    old 717.40
    posterior horn 836.1
      old 717.43
    specified site NEC 836.1
      old 717.49

Tear, torn—*continued*
medial 836.0
anterior horn 836.0
old 717.1
bucket handle 836.0
old 717.0
old 717.3
posterior horn 836.0
old 717.2
old NEC 717.5
site other than knee—*see* Sprain, by site
muscle—*see also* Sprain, by site
with open wound—*see* Wound, open by site
pelvic
floor, complicating delivery 664.1
organ NEC
with
abortion—*see* Abortion, by type, with
damage to pelvic organs
ectopic pregnancy (*see also* categories
633.0-633.9) 639.2
molar pregnancy (*see also* categories
630-632) 639.2
following
abortion 639.2
ectopic or molar pregnancy 639.2
obstetrical trauma 665.5
perineum—*see also* Laceration, perineum
obstetrical trauma 665.5
periurethral tissue
with
abortion—*see* Abortion, by type, with
damage to pelvic organs
ectopic pregnancy (*see also* categories
633.0-633.9) 639.2
molar pregnancy (*see also* categories
630-632) 639.2
following
abortion 639.2
ectopic or molar pregnancy 639.2
obstetrical trauma 665.5
rectovaginal septum—*see* Laceration,
rectovaginal septum
retina, retinal (recent) (with detachment) 361.00
without detachment 361.30
dialysis (juvenile) (with detachment) 361.04
giant (with detachment) 361.03
horseshoe (without detachment) 361.32
multiple (with detachment) 361.02
without detachment 361.33
old
delimited (partial) 361.06
partial 361.06
total or subtotal 361.07
partial (without detachment)
giant 361.03
multiple defects 361.02
old (delimited) 361.06
single defect 361.01
round hole (without detachment) 361.31
single defect (with detachment) 361.01
total or subtotal (recent) 361.05
old 361.07
rotator cuff (traumatic) 840.4
current injury 840.4
degenerative 726.10
nontraumatic 727.61
semilunar cartilage, knee (*see also* Tear,
meniscus) 836.2
old 717.5

Tear, torn—*continued*
tendon—*see also* Sprain, by site
with open wound—*see* Wound, open by site
tentorial, at birth 767.0
umbilical cord
affecting fetus or newborn 772.0
complicating delivery 663.8
urethra
with
abortion—*see* Abortion, by type, with
damage to pelvic organs
ectopic pregnancy (*see also* categories
633.0-633.9) 639.2
molar pregnancy (*see also* categories
630-632) 639.2
following
abortion 639.2
ectopic or molar pregnancy 639.2
obstetrical trauma 665.5
uterus—*see* Injury, internal, uterus
vagina—*see* Laceration, vagina
vessel, from catheter 998.2
vulva, complicating delivery 664.0
Tear stone 375.57
Teeth, tooth —*see also* condition
grinding 306.8
Teething 520.7
syndrome 520.7
Tegmental syndrome 344.89
Telangiectasia, telangiectasis (verrucous) 448.9
ataxic (cerebellar) 334.8
familial 448.0
hemorrhagic, hereditary (congenital) (senile)
448.0
hereditary hemorrhagic 448.0
retina 362.15
spider 448.1
Telecanthus (congenital) 743.63
Telescoped bowel or intestine (*see also*
Intussusception) 560.0
Teletherapy, adverse effect NEC 990
Telogen effluvium 704.02
Temperature
body, high (of unknown origin) (*see also*
Pyrexia) 780.6
cold, trauma from 991.9
newborn 778.2
specified effect NEC 991.8
high
body (of unknown origin) (*see also* Pyrexia)
780.6
trauma from—*see* Heat
Temper tantrum (childhood) (*see also*
Disturbance, conduct) 312.1
Temple —*see* condition
Temporal —*see also* condition
lobe syndrome 310.0
**Temporomandibular joint-pain-dysfunction
syndrome** 524.60
Temporosphenoidal —*see* condition
Tendency
bleeding (*see also* Defect, coagulation) 286.9
homosexual, ego-dystonic 302.0
paranoid 301.0
suicide 300.9
Tenderness
abdominal (generalized) (localized) 789.6
rebound 789.6
skin 782.0

Tendinitis, tendonitis (*see also* Tenosynovitis)
726.90
  Achilles 726.71
  adhesive 726.90
    shoulder 726.0
  calcific 727.82
    shoulder 726.11
  gluteal 726.5
  patellar 726.64
  peroneal 726.79
  pes anserinus 726.61
  psoas 726.5
  tibialis (anterior) (posterior) 726.72
  trochanteric 726.5
Tendon —*see* condition
Tendosynovitis —*see* Tenosynovitis
Tendovaginitis —*see* Tenosynovitis
Tenesmus 787.99
  rectal 787.99
  vesical 788.9
Tenia —*see* Taenia
Teniasis —*see* Taeniasis
Tennis elbow 726.32
Tenonitis —*see also* Tenosynovitis
  eye (capsule) 376.04
Tenontosynovitis —*see* Tenosynovitis
Tenontothecitis —*see* Tenosynovitis
Tenophyte 727.9
Tenosynovitis 727.00
  adhesive 726.90
    shoulder 726.0
  ankle 727.06
  bicipital (calcifying) 726.12
  buttock 727.09
  due to crystals—*see* Arthritis, due to crystals
  elbow 727.09
  finger 727.05
  foot 727.06
  gonococcal 098.51
  hand 727.05
  hip 727.09
  knee 727.09
  radial styloid 727.04
  shoulder 726.10
    adhesive 726.0
  spine 720.1
  supraspinatus 726.10
  toe 727.06
  tuberculous—*see* Tuberculosis, tenosynovitis
  wrist 727.05
Tenovaginitis —*see* Tenosynovitis
Tension
  arterial, high (*see also* Hypertension) 401.9
    without diagnosis of hypertension 796.2
  headache 307.81
  intraocular (elevated) 365.00
  nervous 799.2
  ocular (elevated) 365.00
  pneumothorax 512.0
    iatrogenic 512.1
      postoperative 512.1
      spontaneous 512.0
  premenstrual 625.4
  state 300.9
Tentorium —*see* condition
Teratencephalus 759.89
Teratism 759.7
Teratoblastoma (malignant) (M9080/3)—*see*
Neoplasm, by site, malignant
Teratocarcinoma (M9081/3)—*see also*
Neoplasm, by site, malignant
  liver 155.0

Teratoma (solid) (M9080/1)—*see also*
Neoplasm, by site, uncertain behavior
  adult (cystic) (M9080/0)—*see* Neoplasm, by
site, benign
  and embryonal carcinoma, mixed
(M9081/3)—*see* Neoplasm, by site,
malignant
  benign (M9080/0)—*see* Neoplasm, by site,
benign
  combined with choriocarcinoma
(M9101/3)—*see* Neoplasm, by site,
malignant
  cystic (adult) (M9080/0)—*see* Neoplasm, by
site, benign
  differentiated type (M9080/0)—*see* Neoplasm,
by site, benign
  embryonal (M9080/3)—*see also* Neoplasm, by
site, malignant
    liver 155.0
  fetal
    sacral, causing fetopelvic disproportion 653.7
  immature (M9080/3)—*see* Neoplasm, by site,
malignant
  liver (M9080/3) 155.0
    adult, benign, cystic, differentiated type or
mature (M9080/0) 211.5
  malignant (M9080/3)—*see also* Neoplasm, by
site, malignant
    anaplastic type (M9082/3)—*see* Neoplasm, by
site, malignant
    intermediate type (M9083/3)—*see* Neoplasm,
by site, malignant
    liver (M9080/3) 155.0
    trophoblastic (M9102/3)
      specified site—*see* Neoplasm, by site,
malignant
      unspecified site 186.9
    undifferentiated type (M9082/3)—*see*
Neoplasm, by site, malignant
  mature (M9080/0)—*see* Neoplasm, by site,
benign
  ovary (M9080/0) 220
    embryonal, immature, or malignant
(M9080/3) 183.0
  suprasellar (M9080/3)—*see* Neoplasm, by site,
malignant
  testis (M9080/3) 186.9
    adult, benign, cystic, differentiated type or
mature (M9080/0) 222.0
    undescended 186.0
Terminal care V66.7
Termination
  anomalous—*see also* Malposition, congenital
    portal vein 747.49
    right pulmonary vein 747.42
  pregnancy (legal) (therapeutic) (*see* Abortion,
legal) 635.9
    fetus NEC 779.6
    illegal (*see also* Abortion, illegal) 636.9
Ternidens diminutus infestation 127.7
Terrors, night (child) 307.46
Terry's syndrome 362.21
Tertiary —*see* condition
Tessellated fundus, retina (tigroid) 362.89
Test(s)
  adequacy
    hemodialysis V56.31
    peritoneal dialysis V56.32
  AIDS virus V72.6
  allergen V72.7

Test(s)—*continued*
bacterial disease NEC (*see also* Screening, by name of disease) V74.9
basal metabolic rate V72.6
blood-alcohol V70.4
blood-drug V70.4
for therapeutic drug monitoring V58.83
developmental, infant or child V20.2
Dick V74.8
fertility V26.21
genetic V26.3
hearing V72.1
HIV V72.6
human immunodeficiency virus V72.6
Kveim V82.89
laboratory V72.6
for medicolegal reason V70.4
Mantoux (for tuberculosis) V74.1
mycotic organism V75.4
parasitic agent NEC V75.8
paternity V70.4
peritoneal equilibration V56.32
pregnancy
positive V22.1
first pregnancy V22.0
unconfirmed V72.4
preoperative V72.84
cardiovascular V72.81
respiratory V72.82
specified NEC V72.83
procreative management NEC V26.29
sarcoidosis V82.89
Schick V74.3
Schultz-Charlton V74.8
skin, diagnostic
allergy V72.7
bacterial agent NEC (*see also* Screening, by name of disease) V74.9
Dick V74.8
hypersensitivity V72.7
Kveim V82.89
Mantoux V74.1
mycotic organism V75.4
parasitic agent NEC V75.8
sarcoidosis V82.89
Schick V74.3
Schultz-Charlton V74.8
tuberculin V74.1
specified type NEC V72.85
tuberculin V74.1
vision V72.0
Wassermann
positive (*see also* Serology for syphilis, positive) 097.1
false 795.6
Testicle, testicular, testis —*see also* condition
feminization (syndrome) 257.8
Tetanus, tetanic (cephalic) (convulsions) 037
with
abortion—*see* Abortion, by type, with sepsis
ectopic pregnancy (*see also* categories 633.0-633.9) 639.0
molar pregnancy (*see* categories 630-632) 639.0
following
abortion 639.0
ectopic or molar pregnancy 639.0
inoculation V03.7
reaction (due to serum)—*see* Complications, vaccination
neonatorum 771.3
puerperal, postpartum, childbirth 670

Tetany, tetanic 781.7
alkalosis 276.3
associated with rickets 268.0
convulsions 781.7
hysterical 300.11
functional (hysterical) 300.11
hyperkinetic 781.7
hysterical 300.11
hyperpnea 786.01
hysterical 300.11
psychogenic 306.1
hyperventilation 786.01
hysterical 300.11
psychogenic 306.1
hypocalcemic, neonatal 775.4
hysterical 300.11
neonatal 775.4
parathyroid (gland) 252.1
parathyroprival 252.1
postoperative 252.1
postthyroidectomy 252.1
pseudotetany 781.7
hysterical 300.11
psychogenic 306.1
specified as conversion reaction 300.11
Tetralogy of Fallot 745.2
Tetraplegia —*see* Quadriplegia
Thailand hemorrhagic fever 065.4
Thalassanemia 282.4
Thalassemia (alpha) (beta) (disease) (Hb-C) (Hb-D) (Hb-E) (Hb-H) (Hb-I) (Hb-S) (high fetal gene) (high fetal hemoglobin) (intermedia) (major) (minima) (minor) (mixed) (sickle-cell) (trait) (with other hemoglobinopathy) 282.4
Thalassemic variants 282.4
Thaysen-Gee disease (nontropical sprue) 579.0
Thecoma (M8600/0) 220
malignant (M8600/3) 183.0
Thelarche, precocious 259.1
Thelitis 611.0
puerperal, postpartum 675.0
Therapeutic —*see* condition
Therapy V57.9
blood transfusion, without reported diagnosis V58.2
breathing V57.0
chemotherapy V58.1
fluoride V07.31
prophylactic NEC V07.39
dialysis (intermittent) (treatment)
extracorporeal V56.0
peritoneal V56.8
renal V56.0
specified type NEC V56.8
exercise NEC V57.1
breathing V57.0
extracorporeal dialysis (renal) V56.0
fluoride prophylaxis V07.31
hemodialysis V56.0
occupational V57.21
orthoptic V57.4
orthotic V57.81
peritoneal dialysis V56.8
physical NEC V57.1
postmenopausal hormone replacement V07.4
radiation V58.0
speech V57.3
vocational V57.22
Thermalgesia 782.0
Thermalgia 782.0
Thermanalgesia 782.0

Thrombophlebitis—*continued*
  cavernous (venous) sinus—*see*
    Thrombophlebitis, intracranial venous sinus
  cephalic vein 451.82
  cerebral (sinus) (vein) 325
    late effect—*see* category 326
    nonpyogenic 437.6
      in pregnancy or puerperium 671.5
      late effect—*see* Late effect(s) (of)
        cerebrovascular disease
  due to implanted device—*see* Complications,
    due to (presence of) any device, implant, or
    graft classified to 996.0-996.5 NEC
  during or resulting from a procedure NEC 997.2
  femoral 451.11
  femoropopliteal 451.19
  following infusion, perfusion, or transfusion
    999.2
  hepatic (vein) 451.89
  idiopathic, recurrent 453.1
  iliac vein 451.81
  iliofemoral 451.11
  intracranial venous sinus (any) 325
    late effect—*see* category 326
    nonpyogenic 437.6
      in pregnancy or puerperium 671.5
      late effect—*see* Late effect(s) (of)
        cerebrovascular disease
  jugular vein 451.89
  lateral (venous) sinus—*see* Thrombophlebitis,
    intracranial venous sinus
  leg 451.2
    deep (vessels) 451.19
      femoral vein 451.11
      specified vessel NEC 451.19
    superficial (vessels) 451.0
      femoral vein 451.11
  longitudinal (venous) sinus—*see*
    Thrombophlebitis, intracranial venous sinus
  lower extremity 451.2
    deep (vessels) 451.19
      femoral vein 451.11
      specified vessel NEC 451.19
    superficial (vessels) 451.0
  migrans, migrating 453.1
  pelvic
    with
      abortion—*see* Abortion, by type, with sepsis
      ectopic pregnancy (*see also* categories
        633.0-633.9) 639.0
      molar pregnancy (*see also* categories
        630-632) 639.0
    following
      abortion 639.0
      ectopic or molar pregnancy 639.0
    puerperal 671.4
  popliteal vein 451.19
  portal (vein) 572.1
  postoperative 997.2
  pregnancy (superficial) 671.2
    affecting fetus or newborn 760.3
    deep 671.3
  puerperal, postpartum, childbirth (extremities)
    (superficial) 671.2
    deep 671.4
    pelvic 671.4
    specified site NEC 671.5
  radial vein 451.83
  saphenous (greater) (lesser) 451.0
  sinus (intracranial)—*see* Thrombophlebitis,
    intracranial venous sinus

Thrombophlebitis—*continued*
  specified site NEC 451.89
  tibial vein 451.19
Thrombosis, thrombotic (marantic) (multiple)
  (progressive) (septic) (vein) (vessel) 453.9
  with childbirth or during the puerperium—*see*
    Thrombosis, puerperal, postpartum
  antepartum—*see* Thrombosis, pregnancy
  aorta, aortic 444.1
    abdominal 444.0
    bifurcation 444.0
    saddle 444.0
    terminal 444.0
    thoracic 444.1
    valve—*see* Endocarditis, aortic
  apoplexy (*see also* Thrombosis, brain) 434.0
    late effect—*see* Late effect(s) (of)
      cerebrovascular disease
  appendix, septic—*see* Appendicitis, acute
  arteriolar-capillary platelet, disseminated 446.6
  artery, arteries (postinfectional) 444.9
    auditory, internal 433.8
    basilar (*see also* Occlusion, artery, basilar)
      433.0
    carotid (common) (internal) (*see also*
      Occlusion, artery, carotid) 433.1
      with other precerebral artery 433.3
    cerebellar (anterior inferior) (posterior
      inferior) (superior) 433.8
    cerebral (*see also* Thrombosis, brain) 434.0
    choroidal (anterior) 433.8
    communicating posterior 433.8
    coronary (*see also* Infarct, myocardium) 410.9
      due to syphilis 093.89
      healed or specified as old 412
      without myocardial infarction 411.81
    extremities 444.22
      lower 444.22
      upper 444.21
    femoral 444.22
    hepatic 444.89
    hypophyseal 433.8
    meningeal, anterior or posterior 433.8
    mesenteric (with gangrene) 557.0
    ophthalmic (*see also* Occlusion, retina) 362.30
    pontine 433.8
    popliteal 444.22
    precerebral—*see* Occlusion, artery,
      precerebral NEC
    pulmonary 415.19
      iatrogenic 415.11
      postoperative 415.11
    renal 593.81
    retinal (*see also* Occlusion, retina) 362.30
    specified site NEC 444.89
    spinal, anterior or posterior 433.8
    traumatic (complication) (early) (*see also*
      Injury, blood vessel, by site) 904.9
    vertebral (*see also* Occlusion, artery,
      vertebral) 433.2
      with other precerebral artery 433.3
  atrial (endocardial) 424.90
    due to syphilis 093.89
  auricular (*see also* Infarct, myocardium) 410.9
  axillary (vein) 453.8
  basilar (artery) (*see also* Occlusion, artery,
    basilar) 433.0
  bland NEC 453.9
  brain (artery) (stem) 434.0
    due to syphilis 094.89
    iatrogenic 997.02

Thrombosis, thrombotic—*continued*
  late effect—*see* Late effect(s) (of)
    cerebrovascular disease
  postoperative 997.02
  puerperal, postpartum, childbirth 674.0
  sinus (*see also* Thrombosis, intracranial
    venous sinus) 325
  capillary 448.9
  arteriolar, generalized 446.6
  cardiac (*see also* Infarct, myocardium) 410.9
    due to syphilis 093.89
    healed or specified as old 412
    valve—*see* Endocarditis
  carotid (artery) (common) (internal) (*see also*
    Occlusion, artery, carotid) 433.1
    with other precerebral artery 433.3
  cavernous sinus (venous)—*see* Thrombosis,
    intracranial venous sinus
  cerebellar artery (anterior inferior) (posterior
    inferior) (superior) 433.8
    late effect—*see* Late effect(s) (of)
      cerebrovascular disease
  cerebral (arteries) (*see also* Thrombosis, brain)
    434.0
    late effect—*see* Late effect(s) (of)
      cerebrovascular disease
  coronary (artery) (*see also* Infarct, myocardium)
    410.9
    due to syphilis 093.89
    healed or specified as old 412
    without myocardial infarction 411.81
  corpus cavernosum 607.82
  cortical (*see also* Thrombosis, brain) 434.0
  due to (presence of) any device, implant, or
    graft classifiable to 996.0-996.5—*see*
    Complications, due to (presence of) any
    device, implant, or graft classified to
    996.0-996.5 NEC
  effort 453.8
  endocardial—*see* Infarct, myocardium
  eye (*see also* Occlusion, retina) 362.30
  femoral (vein) (deep) 453.8
    with inflammation or phlebitis 451.11
    artery 444.22
  genital organ, male 608.83
  heart (chamber) (*see also* Infarct, myocardium)
    410.9
  hepatic (vein) 453.0
    artery 444.89
    infectional or septic 572.1
  iliac (vein) 453.8
    with inflammation or phlebitis 451.81
    artery (common) (external) (internal) 444.81
  inflammation, vein—*see* Thrombophlebitis
  internal carotid artery (*see also* Occlusion,
    artery, carotid) 433.1
    with other precerebral artery 433.3
  intestine (with gangrene) 557.0
  intracranial (*see also* Thrombosis, brain) 434.0
    venous sinus (any) 325
      nonpyogenic origin 437.6
        in pregnancy or puerperium 671.5
  intramural (*see also* Infarct, myocardium) 410.9
    without
      cardiac condition 429.89
      coronary artery disease 429.89
      myocardial infarction 429.89
    healed or specified as old 412
  jugular (bulb) 453.8
  kidney 593.81
    artery 593.81

Thrombosis, thrombotic—*continued*
  lateral sinus (venous)—*see* Thrombosis,
    intracranial venous sinus
  leg 453.8
    with inflammation or phlebitis—*see*
      Thrombophlebitis
    deep (vessels) 453.8
    superficial (vessels) 453.8
  liver (venous) 453.0
    artery 444.89
    infectional or septic 572.1
    portal vein 452
  longitudinal sinus (venous)—*see* Thrombosis,
    intracranial venous sinus
  lower extremity—*see* Thrombosis, leg
  lung 415.19
    iatrogenic 415.11
    postoperative 415.11
  marantic, dural sinus 437.6
  meninges (brain) (*see also* Thrombosis, brain)
    434.0
  mesenteric (artery) (with gangrene) 557.0
    vein (inferior) (superior) 557.0
  mitral—*see* Insufficiency, mitral
  mural (heart chamber) (*see also* Infarct,
    myocardium) 410.9
    without
      cardiac condition 429.89
      coronary artery disease 429.89
      myocardial infarction 429.89
    due to syphilis 093.89
    following myocardial infarction 429.79
    healed or specified as old 412
  omentum (with gangrene) 557.0
  ophthalmic (artery) (*see also* Occlusion, retina)
    362.30
  pampiniform plexus (male) 608.83
    female 620.8
  parietal (*see also* Infarct, myocardium) 410.9
  penis, penile 607.82
  peripheral arteries 444.22
    lower 444.22
    upper 444.21
  platelet 446.6
  portal 452
    due to syphilis 093.89
    infectional or septic 572.1
  precerebral artery—*see also* Occlusion, artery,
    precerebral NEC
  pregnancy 671.9
    deep (vein) 671.3
    superficial (vein) 671.2
  puerperal, postpartum, childbirth 671.9
    brain (artery) 674.0
      venous 671.5
    cardiac 674.8
    cerebral (artery) 674.0
      venous 671.5
    deep (vein) 671.4
    intracranial sinus (nonpyogenic) (venous)
      671.5
    pelvic 671.4
    pulmonary (artery) 673.2
    specified site NEC 671.5
    superficial 671.2
  pulmonary (artery) (vein) 415.19
    iatrogenic 415.11
    postoperative 415.11
  radial vein 451.83
  renal (artery) 593.81
    vein 453.3

Thrombosis, thrombotic—*continued*
  resulting from presence of shunt or other internal prosthetic device—*see* Complications, due to (presence of) any device, implant, or graft classified to 996.0-996.5 NEC
  retina, retinal (artery) 362.30
    arterial branch 362.32
    central 362.31
    partial 362.33
    vein
      central 362.35
      tributary (branch) 362.36
  scrotum 608.83
  seminal vesicle 608.83
  sigmoid (venous) sinus (*see* Thrombosis, intracranial venous sinus) 325
  silent NEC 453.9
  sinus, intracranial (venous) (any) (*see also* Thrombosis, intracranial venous sinus) 325
  softening, brain (*see also* Thrombosis, brain) 434.0
  specified site NEC 453.8
  spermatic cord 608.83
  spinal cord 336.1
    due to syphilis 094.89
    in pregnancy or puerperium 671.5
    pyogenic origin 324.1
      late effect—*see* category 326
  spleen, splenic 289.59
    artery 444.89
  testis 608.83
  traumatic (complication) (early) (*see also* Injury, blood vessel, by site) 904.9
  tricuspid—*see* Endocarditis, tricuspid
  tunica vaginalis 608.83
  umbilical cord (vessels) 663.6
    affecting fetus or newborn 762.6
  vas deferens 608.83
  vena cava (inferior) (superior) 453.2
Thrombus —*see* Thrombosis
Thrush 112.0
  newborn 771.7
Thumb —*see also* condition
  gamekeeper's 842.12
  sucking (child problem) 307.9
Thygeson's superficial punctate keratitis 370.21
Thymergasia (*see also* Psychosis, affective) 296.80
Thymitis 254.8
Thymoma (benign) (M8580/0) 212.6
  malignant (M8580/3) 164.0
Thymus, thymic (gland)—*see* condition
Thyrocele (*see also* Goiter) 240.9
Thyroglossal —*see also* condition
  cyst 759.2
  duct, persistent 759.2
Thyroid (body) (gland)—*see also* condition
  lingual 759.2
Thyroiditis 245.9
  acute (pyogenic) (suppurative) 245.0
    nonsuppurative 245.0
  autoimmune 245.2
  chronic (nonspecific) (sclerosing) 245.8
    fibrous 245.3
    lymphadenoid 245.2
    lymphocytic 245.2
    lymphoid 245.2
  complicating pregnancy, childbirth, or puerperium 648.1

Thyroiditis—*continued*
  de Quervain's (subacute granulomatous) 245.1
  fibrous (chronic) 245.3
  giant (cell) (follicular) 245.1
  granulomatous (de Quervain's) (subacute) 245.1
  Hashimoto's (struma lymphomatosa) 245.2
  iatrogenic 245.4
  invasive (fibrous) 245.3
  ligneous 245.3
  lymphocytic (chronic) 245.2
  lymphoid 245.2
  lymphomatous 245.2
  pseudotuberculous 245.1
  pyogenic 245.0
  radiation 245.4
  Riedel's (ligneous) 245.3
  subacute 245.1
  suppurative 245.0
  tuberculous (*see also* Tuberculosis) 017.5
  viral 245.1
  woody 245.3
Thyrolingual duct, persistent 759.2
Thyromegaly 240.9
Thyrotoxic
  crisis or storm (*see also* Thyrotoxicosis) 242.9
  heart failure (*see also* Thyrotoxicosis) 242.9 *[425.7]*
Thyrotoxicosis 242.9

Note—Use the following fifth-digit subclassification with category 242:

0 without mention of thyrotoxic crisis or storm
1 with mention of thyrotoxic crisis or storm

---

  with
    goiter (diffuse) 242.0
      adenomatous 242.3
        multinodular 242.2
        uninodular 242.1
      nodular 242.3
        multinodular 242.2
        uninodular 242.1
    infiltrative
      dermopathy 242.0
      ophthalmopathy 242.0
      thyroid acropachy 242.0
  complicating pregnancy, childbirth, or puerperium 648.1
  due to
    ectopic thyroid nodule 242.4
    ingestion of (excessive) thyroid material 242.8
    specified cause NEC 242.8
  factitia 242.8
  heart 242.9 *[425.7]*
  neonatal (transient) 775.3
TIA (transient ischemic attack) 435.9
  with transient neurologic deficit 435.9
  late effect—*see* Late effect(s) (of) cerebrovascular disease
Tibia vara 732.4
Tic 307.20
  breathing 307.20
  child problem 307.21
  compulsive 307.22
  convulsive 307.20
  degenerative (generalized) (localized) 333.3
    facial 351.8
  douloureux (*see also* Neuralgia, trigeminal) 350.1
    atypical 350.2

Toxicity—*continued*
  symptomatic—*see* Table of Drugs and
      Chemicals
  fava bean 282.2
  from drug or poison
      asymptomatic 796.0
      symptomatic—*see* Table of Drugs and
          Chemicals
Toxicosis (*see also* Toxemia) 799.8
  capillary, hemorrhagic 287.0
Toxinfection 799.8
  gastrointestinal 558.2
Toxocariasis 128.0
Toxoplasma infection, generalized 130.9
Toxoplasmosis (acquired) 130.9
  with pneumonia 130.4
  congenital, active 771.2
  disseminated (multisystemic) 130.8
  maternal
      with suspected damage to fetus affecting
          management of pregnancy 655.4
      affecting fetus or newborn 760.2
          manifest toxoplasmosis in fetus or newborn
              771.2
  multiple sites 130.8
  multisystemic disseminated 130.8
  specified site NEC 130.7
Trabeculation, bladder 596.8
Trachea —*see* condition
Tracheitis (acute) (catarrhal) (infantile)
    (membranous) (plastic) (pneumococcal)
    (septic) (suppurative) (viral) 464.10
  with
      bronchitis 490
          acute or subacute 466.0
          chronic 491.8
          tuberculosis—*see* Tuberculosis, pulmonary
      laryngitis (acute) 464.20
          with obstruction 464.21
          chronic 476.1
          tuberculous (*see also* Tuberculosis, larynx)
              012.3
      obstruction 464.11
  chronic 491.8
      with
          bronchitis (chronic) 491.8
          laryngitis (chronic) 476.1
      due to external agent—*see* Condition,
          respiratory, chronic, due to
  diphtheritic (membranous) 032.3
      due to external agent—*see* Inflammation,
          respiratory, upper, due to
  edematous 464.11
  influenzal 487.1
  streptococcal 034.0
  syphilitic 095.8
  tuberculous (*see also* Tuberculosis) 012.8
Trachelitis (nonvenereal) (*see also* Cervicitis)
    616.0
  trichomonal 131.09
Tracheobronchial —*see* condition
Tracheobronchitis (*see also* Bronchitis) 490
  acute or subacute 466.0
      with bronchospasm or obstruction 466.0
  chronic 491.8
  influenzal 487.1
  senile 491.8
Tracheobronchomegaly (congenital) 748.3
Tracheobronchopneumonitis —*see* Pneumonia,
    broncho
Tracheocele (external) (internal) 519.1
  congenital 748.3

Tracheomalacia 519.1
  congenital 748.3
Tracheopharyngitis (acute) 465.8
  chronic 478.9
      due to external agent—*see* Condition,
          respiratory, chronic, due to
  due to external agent—*see* Inflammation,
      respiratory, upper, due to
Tracheostenosis 519.1
  congenital 748.3
Tracheostomy
  attention to V55.0
  complication 519.00
  hemorrhage 519.09
  infection 519.01
  malfunctioning 519.02
  obstruction 519.09
  sepsis 519.01
  status V44.0
  stenosis 519.02
Trachoma, trachomatous 076.9
  active (stage) 076.1
  contraction of conjunctiva 076.1
  dubium 076.0
  healed or late effect 139.1
  initial (stage) 076.0
  Türck's (chronic catarrhal laryngitis) 476.0
Trachyphonia 784.49
Training
  orthoptic V57.4
  orthotic V57.81
Train sickness 994.6
Trait
  hemoglobin
      abnormal NEC 282.7
          with thalassemia 282.4
      C (*see also* Disease, hemoglobin, C) 282.7
          with elliptocytosis 282.7
      S (Hb-S) 282.5
      Lepore 282.4
          with other abnormal hemoglobin NEC 282.4
  paranoid 301.0
  sickle-cell 282.5
      with
          elliptocytosis 282.5
          spherocytosis 282.5
Traits, paranoid 301.0
Tramp V60.0
Trance 780.09
  hysterical 300.13
Transaminasemia 790.4
Transfusion, blood
  donor V59.01
      stem cells V59.02
  incompatible 999.6
  reaction or complication—*see* Complications,
      transfusion
  syndrome
      fetomaternal 772.0
      twin-to-twin
          blood loss (donor twin) 772.0
          recipient twin 776.4
  without reported diagnosis V58.2
Transient —*see also* condition
  alteration of awareness 780.02
  blindness 368.12
  deafness (ischemic) 388.02
  global amnesia 437.7
  person (homeless) NEC V60.0
Transitional, lumbosacral joint of vertebra
    756.19

Translocation
  autosomes NEC 758.5
    13-15 758.1
    16-18 758.2
    21 or 22 758.0
    balanced in normal individual 758.4
    D₁ 758.1
    E₃ 758.2
    G 758.0
  balanced autosomal in normal individual 758.4
  chromosomes NEC 758.89
  Down's syndrome 758.0
Translucency, iris 364.53
Transmission of chemical substances through the placenta
  (affecting fetus or newborn) 760.70
  alcohol 760.71
  anti-infective agents 760.74
  cocaine 760.75
  "crack" 760.75
  diethylstilbestrol [DES] 760.76
  hallucinogenic agents 760.73
  medicinal agents NEC 760.79
  narcotics 760.72
  obstetric anesthetic or analgesic drug 763.5
  specified agent NEC 760.79
  suspected, affecting management of pregnancy 655.5
Transplant(ed)
  bone V42.4
    marrow V42.81
  complication—*see also* Complications, due to (presence of) any device, implant, or graft classified to 996.0-996.5 NEC
    bone marrow 996.85
    corneal graft NEC 996.79
      infection or inflammation 996.69
      reaction 996.51
      rejection 996.51
    organ (failure) (immune or nonimmune cause) (infection) (rejection) 996.80
      bone marrow 996.85
      heart 996.83
      intestines 996.87
      kidney 996.81
      liver 996.82
      lung 996.84
      pancreas 996.86
      specified NEC 996.89
    skin NEC 996.79
      infection or inflammation 996.69
      rejection 996.52
        artificial 996.55
        decellularized allodermis 996.55
  cornea V42.5
  hair V50.0
  heart V42.1
    valve V42.2
  intestine V42.84
  kidney V42.0
  liver V42.7
  lung V42.6
  organ V42.9
    specified NEC V42.89
  pancreas V42.83
  peripheral stem cells V42.82
  skin V42.3
  stem cells, peripheral V42.82
  tissue V42.9
    specified NEC V42.89
Transplants, ovarian, endometrial 617.1
Transposed —*see* Transposition

Transposition (congenital)—*see also* Malposition, congenital
  abdominal viscera 759.3
  aorta (dextra) 745.11
  appendix 751.5
  arterial trunk 745.10
  colon 751.5
  great vessels (complete) 745.10
    both originating from right ventricle 745.11
    corrected 745.12
    double outlet right ventricle 745.11
    incomplete 745.11
    partial 745.11
    specified type NEC 745.19
  heart 746.87
    with complete transposition of viscera 759.3
  intestine (large) (small) 751.5
  pulmonary veins 747.49
  reversed jejunal (for bypass) (status) V45.3
  stomach 750.7
    with general transposition of viscera 759.3
  teeth, tooth 524.3
  vessels (complete) 745.10
    partial 745.11
  viscera (abdominal) (thoracic) 759.3
Trans-sexualism 302.50
  with
    asexual history 302.51
    heterosexual history 302.53
    homosexual history 302.52
Transverse —*see also* condition
  arrest (deep), in labor 660.3
    affecting fetus or newborn 763.1
  lie 652.3
    before labor, affecting fetus or newborn 761.7
    causing obstructed labor 660.0
      affecting fetus or newborn 763.1
    during labor, affecting fetus or newborn 763.1
Transvestism, transvestitism (transvestic fetishism) 302.3
Trapped placenta (with hemorrhage) 666.0
  without hemorrhage 667.0
Trauma, traumatism (*see also* Injury, by site) 959.9
  birth—*see* Birth, injury NEC
  causing hemorrhage of pregnancy or delivery 641.8
  complicating
    abortion—*see* Abortion, by type, with damage to pelvic organs
    ectopic pregnancy (*see also* categories 633.0-633.9) 639.2
    molar pregnancy (*see also* categories 630-632) 639.2
  during delivery NEC 665.9
  following
    abortion 639.2
    ectopic or molar pregnancy 639.2
  maternal, during pregnancy, affecting fetus or newborn 760.5
  neuroma—*see* Injury, nerve, by site
  previous major, affecting management of pregnancy, childbirth, or puerperium V23.8
  psychic (current)—*see also* Reaction, adjustment
    previous (history) V15.49
  psychologic, previous (affecting health) V15.49
  transient paralysis—*see* Injury, nerve, by site
Traumatic —*see* condition
Treacher Collins' syndrome (incomplete facial dysostosis) 756.0
Treitz's hernia —*see* Hernia, Treitz's

Trematode infestation NEC 121.9
Trematodiasis NEC 121.9
Trembles 988.8
Trembling paralysis (*see also* Parkinsonism)
    332.0
Tremor 781.0
  essential (benign) 333.1
  familial 333.1
  flapping (liver) 572.8
  hereditary 333.1
  hysterical 300.11
  intention 333.1
  mercurial 985.0
  muscle 728.85
  Parkinson's (*see also* Parkinsonism) 332.0
  psychogenic 306.0
    specified as conversion reaction 300.11
  senilis 797
  specified type NEC 333.1
Trench
  fever 083.1
  foot 991.4
  mouth 101
  nephritis—*see* Nephritis, acute
Treponema pallidum infection (*see also*
    Syphilis) 097.9
Treponematosis 102.9
  due to
    T. pallidum—*see* Syphilis
    T. pertenue (yaws) (*see also* Yaws) 102.9
Triad
  Kartagener's 759.3
  Reiter's (complete) (incomplete) 099.3
  Saint's (*see also* Hernia, diaphragm) 553.3
Trichiasis 704.2
  cicatricial 704.2
  eyelid 374.05
    with entropion (*see also* Entropion) 374.00
Trichinella spiralis (infection) (infestation) 124
Trichinelliasis 124
Trichinellosis 124
Trichiniasis 124
Trichinosis 124
Trichobezoar 938
  intestine 936
  stomach 935.2
Trichocephaliasis 127.3
Trichocephalosis 127.3
Trichocephalus infestation 127.3
Trichoclasis 704.2
Trichoepithelioma (M8100/0)—*see also*
    Neoplasm, skin, benign
  breast 217
  genital organ NEC—*see* Neoplasm, by site,
    benign
  malignant (M8100/3)—*see* Neoplasm, skin,
    malignant
Trichofolliculoma (M8101/0)—*see* Neoplasm,
    skin, benign
Tricholemmoma (M8102/0)—*see* Neoplasm,
    skin, benign
Trichomatosis 704.2
Trichomoniasis 131.9
  bladder 131.09
  cervix 131.09
  intestinal 007.3
  prostate 131.03
  seminal vesicle 131.09
  specified site NEC 131.8
  urethra 131.02
  urogenitalis 131.00

Trichomoniasis—*continued*
  vagina 131.01
  vulva 131.01
  vulvovaginal 131.01
Trichomycosis 039.0
  axillaris 039.0
  nodosa 111.2
  nodularis 111.2
  rubra 039.0
Trichonocardiosis (axillaris) (palmellina) 039.0
Trichonodosis 704.2
Trichophytid, trichophyton infection (*see also*
    Dermatophytosis) 110.9
Trichophytide —*see* Dermatophytosis
Trichophytobezoar 938
  intestine 936
  stomach 935.2
Trichophytosis —*see* Dermatophytosis
Trichoptilosis 704.2
Trichorrhexis (nodosa) 704.2
Trichosporosis nodosa 111.2
Trichostasis spinulosa (congenital) 757.4
Trichostrongyliasis (small intestine) 127.6
Trichostrongylosis 127.6
Trichostrongylus (instabilis) infection 127.6
Trichotillomania 312.39
Trichromat, anomalous (congenital) 368.59
Trichromatopsia, anomalous (congenital)
    368.59
Trichuriasis 127.3
Trichuris trichiuria (any site) (infection)
    (infestation) 127.3
Tricuspid (valve)—*see* condition
Trifid —*see also* Accessory
  kidney (pelvis) 753.3
  tongue 750.13
Trigeminal neuralgia (*see also* Neuralgia,
    trigeminal) 350.1
Trigeminoencephaloangiomatosis 759.6
Trigeminy 427.89
  postoperative 997.1
Trigger finger (acquired) 727.03
  congenital 756.89
Trigonitis (bladder) (chronic)
    (pseudomembranous) 595.3
  tuberculous (*see also* Tuberculosis) 016.1
Trigonocephaly 756.0
Trihexosidosis 272.7
Trilobate placenta —*see* Placenta, abnormal
Trilocular heart 745.8
Tripartita placenta —*see* Placenta, abnormal
Triple —*see also* Accessory
  kidneys 753.3
  uteri 752.2
  X female 758.81
Triplegia 344.89
  congenital or infantile 343.8
Triplet
  affected by maternal complications of
    pregnancy 761.5
  healthy liveborn—*see* Newborn, multiple
  pregnancy (complicating delivery) NEC 651.1
    with fetal loss and retention of one or more
      fetus(es) 651.4
Triplex placenta —*see* Placenta, abnormal
Triplication —*see* Accessory
Trismus 781.0
  neonatorum 771.3
  newborn 771.3
Trisomy (syndrome) NEC 758.5
  13 (partial) 758.1

Trisomy—*continued*
16-18 758.2
18 (partial) 758.2
21 (partial) 758.0
22 758.0
autosomes NEC 758.5
D₁ 758.1
E₃ 758.2
G (group) 758.0
group D₁ 758.1
group E 758.2
group G 758.0
Tritanomaly 368.53
Tritanopia 368.53
Troisier-Hanot-Chauffard syndrome (bronze
diabetes) 275.0
Trombidiosis 133.8
Trophedema (hereditary) 757.0
congenital 757.0
Trophoblastic disease (*see also* Hydatidiform
mole) 630
previous, affecting management of pregnancy
V23.1
Tropholymphedema 757.0
Trophoneurosis NEC 356.9
arm NEC 354.9
disseminated 710.1
facial 349.89
leg NEC 355.8
lower extremity NEC 355.8
upper extremity NEC 354.9
Tropical —*see also* condition
maceration feet (syndrome) 991.4
wet foot (syndrome) 991.4
Trouble —*see also* Disease
bowel 569.9
heart—*see* Disease, heart
intestine 569.9
kidney (*see also* Disease, renal) 593.9
nervous 799.2
sinus (*see also* Sinusitis) 473.9
Trousseau's syndrome (thrombophlebitis
migrans) 453.1
Truancy, childhood —*see also* Disturbance,
conduct
socialized 312.2
undersocialized, unsocialized 312.1
Truncus
arteriosus (persistent) 745.0
common 745.0
communis 745.0
Trunk —*see* condition
Trychophytide —*see* Dermatophytosis
Trypanosoma infestation —*see*
Trypanosomiasis
Trypanosomiasis 086.9
with meningoencephalitis 086.9 *[323.2]*
African 086.5
due to Trypanosoma 086.5
gambiense 086.3
rhodesiense 086.4
American 086.2
with
heart involvement 086.0
other organ involvement 086.1
without mention of organ involvement 086.2
Brazilian—*see* Trypanosomiasis, American
Chagas'—*see* Trypanosomiasis, American
due to Trypanosoma
cruzi—*see* Trypanosomiasis, American
gambiense 086.3

Trypanosomiasis—*continued*
rhodesiense 086.4
gambiensis, Gambian 086.3
North American—*see* Trypanosomiasis,
American
rhodesiensis, Rhodesian 086.4
South American—*see* Trypanosomiasis,
American
T-shaped incisors 520.2
Tsutsugamushi fever 081.2
Tube, tubal, tubular —*see also* condition
ligation, admission for V25.2
Tubercle —*see also* Tuberculosis
brain, solitary 013.2
Darwin's 744.29
epithelioid noncaseating 135
Ghon, primary infection 010.0
Tuberculid, tuberculide (indurating) (lichenoid)
(miliary) (papulonecrotic) (primary) (skin)
(subcutaneous) (*see also* Tuberculosis) 017.0
Tuberculoma —*see also* Tuberculosis
brain (any part) 013.2
meninges (cerebral) (spinal) 013.1
spinal cord 013.4
Tuberculosis, tubercular, tuberculous
(calcification) (calcified) (caseous)
(chromogenic acid-fast bacilli) (congenital)
(degeneration) (disease) (fibrocaseous)
(fistula) (gangrene) (interstitial) (isolated
circumscribed lesions) (necrosis)
(parenchymatous) (ulcerative) 011.9

> *Note—Use the following fifth-digit*
> *subclassification with categories 010-018:*
>
> *0   unspecified*
> *1   bacteriological or histological examination*
> *   not done*
> *2   bacteriological or histological examination*
> *   unknown (at present)*
> *3   tubercle bacilli found (in sputum) by*
> *   microscopy*
> *4   tubercle bacilli not found (in sputum) by*
> *   microscopy, but found by bacterial culture*
> *5   tubercle bacilli not found by bacteriological*
> *   examination, but tuberculosis confirmed*
> *   histologically*
> *6   tubercle bacilli not found by bacteriological or*
> *   histological examination, but tuberculosis*
> *   confirmed by other methods [inoculation of*
> *   animals]*
>
> *For tuberculous conditions specified as late*
> *effects or sequelae, see category 137.*

abdomen 014.8
lymph gland 014.8
abscess 011.9
arm 017.9
bone (*see also* Osteomyelitis, due to,
tuberculosis) 015.9 *[730.8]*
hip 015.1 *[730.85]*
knee 015.2 *[730.86]*
sacrum 015.0 *[730.88]*
specified site NEC 015.7 *[730.88]*
spinal 015.0 *[730.88]*
vertebra 015.0 *[730.88]*
brain 013.3
breast 017.9
Cowper's gland 016.5
dura (mater) 013.8
brain 013.3

Tuberculosis, tubercular, tuberculous—*cont.*
　female 016.7
　　male 016.5
　pelvis (bony) 015.7 *[730.85]*
　penis 016.5
　peribronchitis 011.3
　pericarditis 017.9 *[420.0]*
　pericardium 017.9 *[420.0]*
　perichondritis, larynx 012.3
　perineum 017.9
　periostitis (*see also* Tuberculosis, bone) 015.9
　　[730.8]
　periphlebitis 017.9
　　eye vessel 017.3 *[362.18]*
　　retina 017.3 *[362.18]*
　perirectal fistula 014.8
　peritoneal gland 014.8
　peritoneum 014.0
　peritonitis 014.0
　pernicious NEC (*see also* Tuberculosis,
　　pulmonary) 011.9
　pharyngitis 012.8
　pharynx 012.8
　phlyctenulosis (conjunctiva) 017.3 *[370.31]*
　phthisis NEC (*see also* Tuberculosis,
　　pulmonary) 011.9
　pituitary gland 017.9
　placenta 016.7
　pleura, pleural, pleurisy, pleuritis (fibrinous)
　　(obliterative) (purulent) (simple plastic)
　　(with effusion) 012.0
　　primary, progressive 010.1
　pneumonia, pneumonic 011.6
　pneumothorax 011.7
　polyserositis 018.9
　　acute 018.0
　　chronic 018.8
　potters' 011.4
　prepuce 016.5
　primary 010.9
　　complex 010.0
　　complicated 010.8
　　　with pleurisy or effusion 010.1
　　progressive 010.8
　　　with pleurisy or effusion 010.1
　　skin 017.0
　proctitis 014.8
　prostate 016.5 *[601.4]*
　prostatitis 016.5 *[601.4]*
　pulmonaris (*see also* Tuberculosis, pulmonary)
　　011.9
　pulmonary (artery) (incipient) (malignant)
　　(multiple round foci) (pernicious)
　　(reinfection stage) 011.9
　　cavitated or with cavitation 011.2
　　　primary, progressive 010.8
　　childhood type or first infection 010.0
　　chromogenic acid-fast bacilli 795.3
　　fibrosis or fibrotic 011.4
　　infiltrative 011.0
　　　primary, progressive 010.9
　　nodular 011.1
　　specified NEC 011.8
　　sputum positive only 795.3
　　status following surgical collapse of lung
　　　NEC 011.9
　pyelitis 016.0 *[590.81]*
　pyelonephritis 016.0 *[590.81]*
　pyemia—*see* Tuberculosis, miliary
　pyonephrosis 016.0
　pyopneumothorax 012.0

Tuberculosis, tubercular, tuberculous—*cont.*
　pyothorax 012.0
　rectum (with abscess) 014.8
　　fistula 014.8
　reinfection stage (*see also* Tuberculosis,
　　pulmonary) 011.9
　renal 016.0
　renis 016.0
　reproductive organ 016.7
　respiratory NEC (*see also* Tuberculosis,
　　pulmonary) 011.9
　　specified site NEC 012.8
　retina 017.3 *[363.13]*
　retroperitoneal (lymph gland or node) 014.8
　　gland 014.8
　retropharyngeal abscess 012.8
　rheumatism 015.9
　rhinitis 012.8
　sacroiliac (joint) 015.8
　sacrum 015.0 *[730.88]*
　salivary gland 017.9
　salpingitis (acute) (chronic) 016.6
　sandblasters' 011.4
　sclera 017.3 *[379.09]*
　scoliosis 015.0 *[737.43]*
　scrofulous 017.2
　scrotum 016.5
　seminal tract or vesicle 016.5 *[608.81]*
　senile NEC (*see also* Tuberculosis, pulmonary)
　　011.9
　septic NEC (*see also* Tuberculosis, miliary)
　　018.9
　shoulder 015.8
　　blade 015.7 *[730.8]*
　sigmoid 014.8
　sinus (accessory) (nasal) 012.8
　　bone 015.7 *[730.88]*
　　epididymis 016.4
　skeletal NEC (*see also* Osteomyelitis, due to
　　tuberculosis) 015.9 *[730.8]*
　skin (any site) (primary) 017.0
　small intestine 014.8
　soft palate 017.9
　spermatic cord 016.5
　spinal
　　column 015.0 *[730.88]*
　　cord 013.4
　　disease 015.0 *[730.88]*
　　medulla 013.4
　　membrane 013.0
　　meninges 013.0
　spine 015.0 *[730.88]*
　spleen 017.7
　splenitis 017.7
　spondylitis 015.0 *[720.81]*
　spontaneous pneumothorax—*see* Tuberculosis,
　　pulmonary
　sternoclavicular joint 015.8
　stomach 017.9
　stonemasons' 011.4
　struma 017.2
　subcutaneous tissue (cellular) (primary) 017.0
　subcutis (primary) 017.0
　subdeltoid bursa 017.9
　submaxillary 017.9
　　region 017.9
　supraclavicular gland 017.2
　suprarenal (capsule) (gland) 017.6
　swelling, joint (*see also* Tuberculosis, joint)
　　015.9
　symphysis pubis 015.7 *[730.88]*

Tuberculosis, tubercular, tuberculous—*cont.*
  synovitis 015.9 *[727.01]*
    hip 015.1 *[727.01]*
    knee 015.2 *[727.01]*
    specified site NEC 015.8 *[727.01]*
    spine or vertebra 015.0 *[727.01]*
  systemic—*see* Tuberculosis, miliary
  tarsitis (eyelid) 017.0 *[373.4]*
    ankle (bone) 015.5 *[730.87]*
  tendon (sheath)—*see* Tuberculosis,
      tenosynovitis
  tenosynovitis 015.9 *[727.01]*
    hip 015.1 *[727.01]*
    knee 015.2 *[727.01]*
    specified site NEC 015.8 *[727.01]*
    spine or vertebra 015.0 *[727.01]*
  testis 016.5 *[608.81]*
  throat 012.8
  thymus gland 017.9
  thyroid gland 017.5
  toe 017.9
  tongue 017.9
  tonsil (lingual) 012.8
  tonsillitis 012.8
  trachea, tracheal 012.8
    gland 012.1
      primary, progressive 010.8
    isolated 012.2
  tracheobronchial 011.3
    glandular 012.1
      primary, progressive 010.8
    isolated 012.2
    lymph gland or node 012.1
      primary, progressive 010.8
  tubal 016.6
  tunica vaginalis 016.5
  typhlitis 014.8
  ulcer (primary) (skin) 017.0
    bowel or intestine 014.8
    specified site NEC—*see* Tuberculosis, by site
  unspecified site—*see* Tuberculosis, pulmonary
  ureter 016.2
  urethra, urethral 016.3
  urinary organ or tract 016.3
    kidney 016.0
  uterus 016.7
  uveal tract 017.3 *[363.13]*
  uvula 017.9
  vaccination, prophylactic (against) V03.2
  vagina 016.7
  vas deferens 016.5
  vein 017.9
  verruca (primary) 017.0
  verrucosa (cutis) (primary) 017.0
  vertebra (column) 015.0 *[730.88]*
  vesiculitis 016.5 *[608.81]*
  viscera NEC 014.8
  vulva 016.7 *[616.51]*
  wrist (joint) 015.8
    bone 015.5 *[730.83]*
Tuberculum
  auriculae 744.29
  occlusal 520.2
  paramolare 520.2
Tuberous sclerosis (brain) 759.5
Tubo-ovarian —*see* condition
Tuboplasty, after previous sterilization V26.0
Tubotympanitis 381.10

Tularemia 021.9
  with
    conjunctivitis 021.3
    pneumonia 021.2
  bronchopneumonic 021.2
  conjunctivitis 021.3
  cryptogenic 021.1
  disseminated 021.8
  enteric 021.1
  generalized 021.8
  glandular 021.8
  intestinal 021.1
  oculoglandular 021.3
  ophthalmic 021.3
  pneumonia 021.2
  pulmonary 021.2
  specified NEC 021.8
  typhoidal 021.1
  ulceroglandular 021.0
  vaccination, prophylactic (against) V03.4
Tularensis conjunctivitis 021.3
Tumefaction —*see also* Swelling
  liver (*see also* Hypertrophy, liver) 789.1
Tumor (M8000/1)—*see also* Neoplasm, by site,
    unspecified nature
  Abrikossov's (M9580/0)—*see also* Neoplasm,
      connective tissue, benign
    malignant (M9580/3)—*see* Neoplasm,
        connective tissue, malignant
  acinar cell (M8550/1)—*see* Neoplasm, by site,
      uncertain behavior
  acinic cell (M8550/1)—*see* Neoplasm, by site,
      uncertain behavior
  adenomatoid (M9054/0)—*see also* Neoplasm,
      by site, benign
    odontogenic (M9300/0) 213.1
      upper jaw (bone) 213.0
  adnexal (skin) (M8390/0)—*see* Neoplasm, skin,
      benign
  adrenal
    cortical (benign) (M8370/0) 227.0
      malignant (M8370/3) 194.0
    rest (M8671/0)—*see* Neoplasm, by site,
        benign
  alpha cell (M8152/0)
    malignant (M8152/3)
      pancreas 157.4
      specified site NEC—*see* Neoplasm, by site,
          malignant
      unspecified site 157.4
    pancreas 211.7
    specified site NEC—*see* Neoplasm, by site,
        benign
    unspecified site 211.7
  aneurysmal (*see also* Aneurysm) 442.9
  aortic body (M8691/1) 237.3
    malignant (M8691/3) 194.6
  argentaffin (M8241/1)—*see* Neoplasm, by site,
      uncertain behavior
  basal cell (M8090/1)—*see also* Neoplasm, skin,
      uncertain behavior
  benign (M8000/0)—*see* Neoplasm, by site,
      benign
  beta cell (M8151/0)
    malignant (M8151/3)
      pancreas 157.4
      specified site—*see* Neoplasm, by site,
          malignant
      unspecified site 157.4
    pancreas 211.7

Tumor—*continued*
  specified site NEC—*see* Neoplasm, by site,
    benign
  unspecified site 211.7
  blood—*see* Hematoma
  brenner (M9000/0) 220
    borderline malignancy (M9000/1) 236.2
    malignant (M9000/3) 183.0
    proliferating (M9000/1) 236.2
  Brooke's (M8100/0)—*see* Neoplasm, skin,
    benign
  brown fat (M8880/0)—*see* Lipoma, by site
  Burkitt's (M9750/3) 200.2
  calcifying epithelial odontogenic (M9340/0)
    213.1
    upper jaw (bone) 213.0
  carcinoid (M8240/1)—*see* Carcinoid
  carotid body (M8692/1) 237.3
    malignant (M8692/3) 194.5
  Castleman's (mediastinal lymph node
    hyperplasia) 785.6
  cells (M8001/1)—*see also* Neoplasm, by site,
    unspecified nature
    benign (M8001/0)—*see* Neoplasm, by site,
      benign
    malignant (M8001/3)—*see* Neoplasm, by site,
      malignant
    uncertain whether benign or malignant
      (M8001/1)—*see* Neoplasm, by site,
      uncertain nature
  cervix
    in pregnancy or childbirth 654.6
      affecting fetus or newborn 763.89
      causing obstructed labor 660.2
      affecting fetus or newborn 763.1
  chondromatous giant cell (M9230/0)—*see*
    Neoplasm, bone, benign
  chromaffin (M8700/0)—*see also* Neoplasm, by
    site, benign
    malignant (M8700/3)—*see* Neoplasm, by site,
      malignant
  Cock's peculiar 706.2
  Codman's (benign chondroblastoma)
    (M9230/0)—*see* Neoplasm, bone, benign
  dentigerous, mixed (M9282/0) 213.1
    upper jaw (bone) 213.0
  dermoid (M9084/0)—*see* Neoplasm, by site,
    benign
    with malignant transformation (M9084/3)
      183.0
  desmoid (extra-abdominal) (M8821/1)—*see*
    also Neoplasm, connective tissue, uncertain
    behavior
    abdominal (M8822/1)—*see* Neoplasm,
      connective tissue, uncertain behavior
  embryonal (mixed) (M9080/1)—*see also*
    Neoplasm, by site, uncertain behavior
    liver (M9080/3) 155.0
  endodermal sinus (M9071/3)
    specified site—*see* Neoplasm, by site,
      malignant
    unspecified site
      female 183.0
      male 186.9
  epithelial
    benign (M8010/0)—*see* Neoplasm, by site,
      benign
    malignant (M8010/3)—*see* Neoplasm, by site,
      malignant
  Ewing's (M9260/3)—*see* Neoplasm, bone,
    malignant

Tumor—*continued*
  fatty—*see* Lipoma
  fetal, causing disproportion 653.7
    causing obstructed labor 660.1
  fibroid (M8890/0)—*see* Leiomyoma
  G cell (M8153/1)
    malignant (M8153/3)
      pancreas 157.4
      specified site NEC—*see* Neoplasm, by site,
        malignant
      unspecified site 157.4
    specified site—*see* Neoplasm, by site,
      uncertain behavior
    unspecified site 235.5
  giant cell (type) (M8003/1)—*see also*
    Neoplasm, by site, unspecified nature
    bone (M9250/1) 238.0
      malignant (M9250/3)—*see* Neoplasm, bone,
        malignant
    chondromatous (M9230/0)—*see* Neoplasm,
      bone, benign
    malignant (M8003/3)—*see* Neoplasm, by site,
      malignant
    peripheral (gingiva) 523.8
    soft parts (M9251/1)—*see also* Neoplasm,
      connective tissue, uncertain behavior
      malignant (M9251/3)—*see* Neoplasm,
        connective tissue, malignant
    tendon sheath 727.02
  glomus (M8711/0)—*see also* Hemangioma, by
    site
    jugulare (M8690/1) 237.3
      malignant (M8690/3) 194.6
  gonadal stromal (M8590/1)—*see* Neoplasm, by
    site, uncertain behavior
  granular cell (M9580/0)—*see also* Neoplasm,
    connective tissue, benign
    malignant (M9580/3)—*see* Neoplasm,
      connective tissue, malignant
  granulosa cell (M8620/1) 236.2
    malignant (M8620/3) 183.0
  granulosa cell-theca cell (M8621/1) 236.2
    malignant (M8621/3) 183.0
  Grawitz's (hypernephroma) (M8312/3) 189.0
  hazard-crile (M8350/3) 193
  hemorrhoidal—*see* Hemorrhoids
  hilar cell (M8660/0) 220
  hurthle cell (benign) (M8290/0) 226
    malignant (M8290/3) 193
  hydatid (*see also* Echinococcus) 122.9
  hypernephroid (M8311/1)—*see also* Neoplasm,
    by site, uncertain behavior
  interstitial cell (M8650/1)—*see also* Neoplasm,
    by site, uncertain behavior
    benign (M8650/0)—*see* Neoplasm, by site,
      benign
    malignant (M8650/3)—*see* Neoplasm, by site,
      malignant
  islet cell (M8150/0)
    malignant (M8150/3)
      pancreas 157.4
      specified site—*see* Neoplasm, by site,
        malignant
      unspecified site 157.4
    pancreas 211.7
    specified site NEC—*see* Neoplasm, by site,
      benign
    unspecified site 211.7
  juxtaglomerular (M8361/1) 236.91
  Krukenberg's (M8490/6) 198.6
  Leydig cell (M8650/1)

Tumor—*continued*
    female 220
    male 222.0
    sex cord (-stromal) (M8590/1)—*see* Neoplasm, by site, uncertain behavior
    skin appendage (M8390/0)—*see* Neoplasm, skin, benign
    soft tissue
        benign (M8800/0)—*see* Neoplasm, connective tissue, benign
        malignant (M8800/3)—*see* Neoplasm, connective tissue, malignant
    sternomastoid 754.1
    superior sulcus (lung) (pulmonary) (syndrome) (M8010/3) 162.3
    suprasulcus (M8010/3) 162.3
    sweat gland (M8400/1)—*see also* Neoplasm, skin, uncertain behavior
        benign (M8400/0)—*see* Neoplasm, skin, benign
        malignant (M8400/3)—*see* Neoplasm, skin, malignant
    syphilitic brain 094.89
        congenital 090.49
    testicular stromal (M8590/1) 236.4
    theca cell (M8600/0) 220
    theca cell-granulosa cell (M8621/1) 236.2
    theca-lutein (M8610/0) 220
    turban (M8200/0) 216.4
    uterus
        in pregnancy or childbirth 654.1
            affecting fetus or newborn 763.89
            causing obstructed labor 660.2
                affecting fetus or newborn 763.1
    vagina
        in pregnancy or childbirth 654.7
            affecting fetus or newborn 763.89
            causing obstructed labor 660.2
                affecting fetus or newborn 763.1
    varicose (*see also* Varicose, vein) 454.9
    von Recklinghausen's (M9540/1) 237.71
    vulva
        in pregnancy or childbirth 654.8
            affecting fetus or newborn 763.89
            causing obstructed labor 660.2
                affecting fetus or newborn 763.1
    Warthin's (salivary gland) (M8561/0) 210.2
    white—*see also* Tuberculosis, arthritis
    White-Darier 757.39
    Wilms' (nephroblastoma) (M8960/3) 189.0
    yolk sac (M9071/3)
        specified site—*see* Neoplasm, by site, malignant
        unspecified site
            female 183.0
            male 186.9
Tumorlet (M8040/1)—*see* Neoplasm, by site, uncertain behavior
Tungiasis 134.1
Tunica vasculosa lentis 743.39
Tunnel vision 368.45
Turban tumor (M8200/0) 216.4
Türck's trachoma (chronic catarrhal laryngitis) 476.0
Türk's syndrome (ocular retraction syndrome) 378.71
Turner's
  hypoplasia (tooth) 520.4
  syndrome 758.6
  tooth 520.4
Turner-Kieser syndrome (hereditary osteo-onychodysplasia) 756.89

Turner-Varny syndrome 758.6
Turricephaly 756.0
Tussis convulsiva (*see also* Whooping cough) 033.9
Twin
  affected by maternal complications of pregnancy 761.5
  conjoined 759.4
  healthy liveborn—*see* Newborn, twin
  pregnancy (complicating delivery) NEC 651.0
    with fetal loss and retention of one fetus 651.3
Twinning, teeth 520.2
Twist, twisted
  bowel, colon, or intestine 560.2
  hair (congenital) 757.4
  mesentery 560.2
  omentum 560.2
  organ or site, congenital NEC—*see* Anomaly, specified type NEC
  ovarian pedicle 620.5
    congenital 752.0
  umbilical cord—*see* Compression, umbilical cord
Twitch 781.0
Tylosis 700
  buccalis 528.6
  gingiva 523.8
  linguae 528.6
  palmaris et plantaris 757.39
Tympanism 787.3
Tympanites (abdominal) (intestine) 787.3
Tympanitis —*see* Myringitis
Tympanosclerosis 385.00
  involving
    combined sites NEC 385.09
      with tympanic membrane 385.03
    tympanic membrane 385.01
      with ossicles 385.02
        and middle ear 385.03
Tympanum —*see* condition
Tympany
  abdomen 787.3
  chest 786.7
Typhlitis (*see also* Appendicitis) 541
Typhoenteritis 002.0
Typhogastric fever 002.0
Typhoid (abortive) (ambulant) (any site) (fever) (hemorrhagic) (infection) (intermittent) (malignant) (rheumatic) 002.0
  with pneumonia 002.0 *[484.8]*
  abdominal 002.0
  carrier (suspected) of V02.1
  cholecystitis (current) 002.0
  clinical (Widal and blood test negative) 002.0
  endocarditis 002.0 *[421.1]*
  inoculation reaction—*see* Complications, vaccination
  meningitis 002.0 *[320.7]*
  mesenteric lymph nodes 002.0
  myocarditis 002.0 *[422.0]*
  osteomyelitis (*see also* Osteomyelitis, due to, typhoid) 002.0 *[730.8]*
  perichondritis, larynx 002.0 *[478.71]*
  pneumonia 002.0 *[484.8]*
  spine 002.0 *[720.81]*
  ulcer (perforating) 002.0
  vaccination, prophylactic (against) V03.1
  Widal negative 002.0
Typhomalaria (fever) (*see also* Malaria) 084.6
Typhomania 002.0
Typhoperitonitis 002.0

Typhus (fever) 081.9
　abdominal, abdominalis 002.0
　African tick 082.1
　amarillic (*see also* Fever, Yellow) 060.9
　brain 081.9
　cerebral 081.9
　classical 080
　endemic (flea-borne) 081.0
　epidemic (louse-borne) 080
　exanthematic NEC 080
　exanthematicus SAI 080
　　brillii SAI 081.1
　　Mexicanus SAI 081.0
　　pediculo vestimenti causa 080
　　typhus murinus 081.0
　flea-borne 081.0
　Indian tick 082.1
　Kenya tick 082.1
　louse-borne 080
　Mexican 081.0
　　flea-borne 081.0
　　louse-borne 080
　　tabardillo 080
　mite-borne 081.2
　murine 081.0
　North Asian tick-borne 082.2
　petechial 081.9
　Queensland tick 082.3
　rat 081.0
　recrudescent 081.1
　recurrent (*see also* Fever, relapsing) 087.9
　São Paulo 082.0
　scrub (China) (India) (Malaya) (New Guinea)
　　081.2
　shop (of Malaya) 081.0
　Siberian tick 082.2
　tick-borne NEC 082.9
　tropical 081.2
　vaccination, prophylactic (against) V05.8
Tyrosinemia 270.2
　neonatal 775.8
Tyrosinosis (Medes) (Sakai) 270.2
Tyrosinuria 270.2
Tyrosyluria 270.2

U

Uehlinger's syndrome (acropachyderma) 757.39
Uhl's anomaly or disease (hypoplasia of
  myocardium, right ventricle) 746.84
Ulcer, ulcerated, ulcerating, ulceration, ulcera-
  tive 707.9
  with gangrene 707.9 *[785.4]*
  abdomen (wall) (*see also* Ulcer, skin) 707.8
  ala, nose 478.1
  alveolar process 526.5
  amebic (intestine) 006.9
    skin 006.6
  anastomotic—*see* Ulcer, gastrojejunal
  anorectal 569.41
  antral—*see* Ulcer, stomach
  anus (sphincter) (solitary) 569.41
    varicose—*see* Varicose, ulcer, anus
  aphthous (oral) (recurrent) 528.2
    genital organ(s)
      female 616.8
      male 608.89
    mouth 528.2
  arm (*see also* Ulcer, skin) 707.8
  arteriosclerotic plaque—*see* Arteriosclerosis, by
    site
  artery NEC 447.2
    without rupture 447.8
  atrophic NEC—*see* Ulcer, skin
  Barrett's (chronic peptic ulcer of esophagus)
    530.2
  bile duct 576.8
  bladder (solitary) (sphincter) 596.8
    bilharzial (*see also* Schistosomiasis) 120.9
      [595.4]
    submucosal (*see also* Cystitis) 595.1
    tuberculous (*see also* Tuberculosis) 016.1
  bleeding NEC—*see* Ulcer, peptic, with
    hemorrhage
  bone 730.9
  bowel (*see also* Ulcer, intestine) 569.82
  breast 611.0
  bronchitis 491.8
  bronchus 519.1
  buccal (cavity) (traumatic) 528.9
  burn (acute)—*see* Ulcer, duodenum
  Buruli 031.1
  buttock (*see also* Ulcer, skin) 707.8
    decubitus (*see also* Ulcer, decubitus) 707.0
  cancerous (M8000/3)—*see* Neoplasm, by site,
    malignant
  cardia—*see* Ulcer, stomach
  cardio-esophageal (peptic) 530.2
  cecum (*see also* Ulcer, intestine) 569.82
  cervix (uteri) (trophic) 622.0
    with mention of cervicitis 616.0
  chancroidal 099.0
  chest (wall) (*see also* Ulcer, skin) 707.8
  Chiclero 085.4
  chin (pyogenic) (*see also* Ulcer, skin) 707.8
  chronic (cause unknown)—*see also* Ulcer, skin
    penis 607.89
  Cochin-China 085.1
  colitis —*see* Colitis, ulcerative
  colon (*see also* Ulcer, intestine) 569.82
  conjunctiva (acute) (postinfectional) 372.00

Ulcer, ulcerated, ulcerating—*continued*
  cornea (infectional) 370.00
    with perforation 370.06
    annular 370.02
    catarrhal 370.01
    central 370.03
    dendritic 054.42
    marginal 370.01
    mycotic 370.05
    phlyctenular, tuberculous (*see also*
      Tuberculosis) 017.3 *[370.31]*
    ring 370.02
    rodent 370.07
    serpent, serpiginous 370.04
    superficial marginal 370.01
    tuberculous (*see also* Tuberculosis) 017.3
      [370.31]
  corpus cavernosum (chronic) 607.89
  crural—*see* Ulcer, lower extremity
  Curling's—*see* Ulcer, duodenum
  Cushing's—*see* Ulcer, peptic
  cystitis (interstitial) 595.1
  decubitus (any site) 707.0
    with gangrene 707.0 *[785.4]*
  dendritic 054.42
  diabetes, diabetic (mellitus) 250.8 *[707.9]*
    lower limb 250.8 *[707.10]*
      ankle 250.8 *[707.13]*
      calf 250.8 *[707.12]*
      foot 250.8 *[707.15]*
      heel 250.8 *[707.14]*
      knee 250.8 *[707.19]*
      specified site NEC 250.8 *[707.19]*
      thigh 250.8 *[707.11]*
      toes 250.8 *[707.15]*
    specified site NEC 250.8 *[707.8]*
  Dieulafoy's—*see* Ulcer, stomach
  due to
    infection NEC—*see* Ulcer, skin
    radiation, radium—*see* Ulcer, by site
    trophic disturbance (any region)—*see* Ulcer,
      skin
    x-ray—*see* Ulcer, by site
  duodenum, duodenal (eroded) (peptic) 532.9

> *Note—Use the following fifth-digit*
> *subclassification with categories 531-534:*
>
> *0 without mention of obstruction*
> *1 with obstruction*

  with
    hemorrhage (chronic) 532.4
      and perforation 532.6
    perforation (chronic) 532.5
      and hemorrhage 532.6
  acute 532.3
    with
      hemorrhage 532.0
        and perforation 532.2
      perforation 532.1
        and hemorrhage 532.2
    bleeding (recurrent)—*see* Ulcer, duodenum,
      with hemorrhage
  chronic 532.7
    with
      hemorrhage 532.4
        and perforation 532.6

Ulcer, ulcerated, ulcerating—*continued*
      perforation 532.5
        and hemorrhage 532.6
    penetrating—*see* Ulcer, duodenum, with
      perforation
    perforating—*see* Ulcer, duodenum, with
      perforation
  dysenteric NEC 009.0
  elusive 595.1
  endocarditis (any valve) (acute) (chronic)
    (subacute) 421.0
  enteritis —*see* Colitis, ulcerative
  enterocolitis 556.0
  epiglottis 478.79
  esophagus (peptic) 530.2
    due to ingestion
      aspirin 530.2
      chemicals 530.2
      medicinal agents 530.2
    fungal 530.2
    infectional 530.2
    varicose (*see also* Varix, esophagus) 456.1
      bleeding (*see also* Varix, esophagus,
        bleeding) 456.0
  eye NEC 360.00
    dendritic 054.42
  eyelid (region) 373.01
  face (*see also* Ulcer, skin) 707.8
  fauces 478.29
  Fenwick (-Hunner) (solitary) (*see also* Cystitis)
    595.1
  fistulous NEC—*see* Ulcer, skin
  foot (indolent) (*see also* Ulcer, lower extremity)
    707.15
    perforating 707.15
      leprous 030.1
      syphilitic 094.0
    trophic 707.15
    varicose 454.0
      inflamed or infected 454.2
  frambesial, initial or primary 102.0
  gallbladder or duct 575.8
  gall duct 576.8
  gangrenous (*see also* Gangrene) 785.4
  gastric—*see* Ulcer, stomach
  gastrocolic—*see* Ulcer, gastrojejunal
  gastroduodenal—*see* Ulcer, peptic
  gastroesophageal—*see* Ulcer, stomach
  gastrohepatic—*see* Ulcer, stomach
  gastrointestinal—*see* Ulcer, gastrojejunal
  gastrojejunal (eroded) (peptic) 534.9

> *Note—Use the following fifth-digit
> subclassification with categories 531-534:*
>
> 0 *without mention of obstruction*
> 1 *with obstruction*

    with
      hemorrhage (chronic) 534.4
        and perforation 534.6
      perforation 534.5
        and hemorrhage 534.6
    acute 534.3
      with
        hemorrhage 534.0
          and perforation 534.2
        perforation 534.1
          and hemorrhage 534.2
    bleeding (recurrent)—*see* Ulcer, gastrojejunal,
      with hemorrhage

Ulcer, ulcerated, ulcerating—*continued*
  chronic 534.7
    with
      hemorrhage 534.4
        and perforation 534.6
      perforation 534.5
        and hemorrhage 534.6
  penetrating—*see* Ulcer, gastrojejunal, with
    perforation
  perforating—*see* Ulcer, gastrojejunal, with
    perforation
  gastrojejunocolic—*see* Ulcer, gastrojejunal
  genital organ
    female 629.8
    male 608.89
  gingiva 523.8
  gingivitis 523.1
  glottis 478.79
  granuloma of pudenda 099.2
  groin (*see also* Ulcer, skin) 707.8
  gum 523.8
  gumma, due to yaws 102.4
  hand (*see also* Ulcer, skin) 707.8
  hard palate 528.9
  heel (*see also* Ulcer, lower extremity) 707.14
    decubitus (*see also* Ulcer, decubitus) 707.0
  hemorrhoids 455.8
    external 455.5
    internal 455.2
  hip (*see also* Ulcer, skin) 707.8
    decubitus (*see also* Ulcer, decubitus) 707.0
  Hunner's 595.1
  hypopharynx 478.29
  hypopyon (chronic) (subacute) 370.04
  hypostaticum—*see* Ulcer, varicose
  ileocolitis 556.1
  ileum (*see also* Ulcer, intestine) 569.82
  intestine, intestinal 569.82
    with perforation 569.83
    amebic 006.9
    duodenal—*see* Ulcer, duodenum
    granulocytopenic (with hemorrhage) 288.0
    marginal 569.82
    perforating 569.83
    small, primary 569.82
    stercoraceous 569.82
    stercoral 569.82
    tuberculous (*see also* Tuberculosis) 014.8
    typhoid (fever) 002.0
    varicose 456.8
  ischemic 707.9
    lower extremity (*see also* Ulcer, lower
      extremity) 707.10
      ankle 707.13
      calf 707.12
      foot 707.15
      heel 707.14
      knee 707.19
      specified site NEC 707.19
      thigh 707.11
      toes 707.15
  jejunum, jejunal—*see* Ulcer, gastrojejunal
  keratitis (*see also* Ulcer, cornea) 370.00
  knee—*see* Ulcer, lower extremity
  labium (majus) (minus) 616.50
  laryngitis (*see also* Laryngitis) 464.0
  larynx (aphthous) (contact) 478.79
    diphtheritic 032.3
  leg—*see* Ulcer, lower extremity
  lip 528.5
  Lipschütz's 616.50

Ulcer, ulcerated, ulcerating—*continued*
  lower extremity (atrophic) (chronic)
    (neurogenic) (perforating) (pyogenic)
    (trophic) (tropical) 707.10
    with gangrene (*see also* Ulcer, lower
      extremity) 707.10 *[785.4]*
      arteriosclerotic 440.24
    ankle 707.13
    arteriosclerotic 440.23
      with gangrene 440.24
    calf 707.12
    decubitus 707.0
      with gangrene 707.0 *[785.4]*
    foot 707.15
    heel 707.14
    knee 707.19
    specified site NEC 707.19
    thigh 707.11
    toes 707.15
    varicose 454.0
      inflamed or infected 454.2
  luetic—*see* Ulcer, syphilitic
  lung 518.89
    tuberculous (*see also* Tuberculosis) 011.2
  malignant (M8000/3)—*see* Neoplasm, by site,
    malignant
  marginal NEC—*see* Ulcer, gastrojejunal
  meatus (urinarius) 597.89
  Meckel's diverticulum 751.0
  Meleney's (chronic undermining) 686.09
  Mooren's (cornea) 370.07
  mouth (traumatic) 528.9
  mycobacterial (skin) 031.1
  nasopharynx 478.29
  navel cord (newborn) 771.4
  neck (*see also* Ulcer, skin) 707.8
    uterus 622.0
  neurogenic NEC—*see* Ulcer, skin
  nose, nasal (infectional) (passage) 478.1
    septum 478.1
      varicose 456.8
    skin—*see* Ulcer, skin
    spirochetal NEC 104.8
  oral mucosa (traumatic) 528.9
  palate (soft) 528.9
  penetrating NEC—*see* Ulcer, peptic, with
    perforation
  penis (chronic) 607.89
  peptic (site unspecified) 533.9

> *Note—Use the following fifth-digit*
> *subclassification with categories 531-534:*
>
> *0 without mention of obstruction*
> *1 with obstruction*

    with
      hemorrhage 533.4
        and perforation 533.6
      perforation (chronic) 533.5
        and hemorrhage 533.6
    acute 533.3
      with
        hemorrhage 533.0
          and perforation 533.2
        perforation 533.1
          and hemorrhage 533.2
    bleeding (recurrent)—*see* Ulcer, peptic, with
      hemorrhage

Ulcer, ulcerated, ulcerating—*continued*
  chronic 533.7
    with
      hemorrhage 533.4
        and perforation 533.6
      perforation 533.5
        and hemorrhage 533.6
  penetrating—*see* Ulcer, peptic, with
    perforation
  perforating NEC (*see also* Ulcer, peptic, with
    perforation) 533.5
    skin 707.9
  perineum (*see also* Ulcer, skin) 707.8
  peritonsillar 474.8
  phagedenic (tropical) NEC—*see* Ulcer, skin
  pharynx 478.29
  phlebitis—*see* Phlebitis
  plaster (*see also* Ulcer, decubitus) 707.0
  popliteal space—*see* Ulcer, lower extremity
  postpyloric—*see* Ulcer, duodenum
  prepuce 607.89
  prepyloric—*see* Ulcer, stomach
  pressure (*see also* Ulcer, decubitus) 707.0
  primary of intestine 569.82
    with perforation 569.83
  proctitis 556.2
    with ulcerative sigmoiditis 556.3
  prostate 601.8
  pseudopeptic—*see* Ulcer, peptic
  pyloric—*see* Ulcer, stomach
  rectosigmoid 569.82
    with perforation 569.83
  rectum (sphincter) (solitary) 569.41
    stercoraceous, stercoral 569.41
    varicose—*see* Varicose, ulcer, anus
  retina (*see also* Chorioretinitis) 363.20
  rodent (M8090/3)—*see also* Neoplasm, skin,
    malignant
    cornea 370.07
  round—*see* Ulcer, stomach
  sacrum (region) (*see also* Ulcer, skin) 707.8
  Saemisch's 370.04
  scalp (*see also* Ulcer, skin) 707.8
  sclera 379.09
  scrofulous (*see also* Tuberculosis) 017.2
  scrotum 608.89
    tuberculous (*see also* Tuberculosis) 016.5
    varicose 456.4
  seminal vesicle 608.89
  sigmoid 569.82
    with perforation 569.83
  skin (atrophic) (chronic) (neurogenic)
    (non-healing) (perforating) (pyogenic)
    (trophic) 707.9
    with gangrene 707.9 *[785.4]*
    amebic 006.6
    decubitus 707.0
      with gangrene 707.0 *[785.4]*
    in granulocytopenia 288.0
    lower extremity (*see also* Ulcer, lower
      extremity) 707.10
      with gangrene 707.10 *[785.4]*
      arteriosclerotic 440.24
      ankle 707.13
      arteriosclerotic 440.23
        with gangrene 440.24
      calf 707.12
      foot 707.15
      heel 707.14
      knee 707.19
      specified site NEC 707.19

> *Note—Use the following fifth-digit subclassification with categories 531-534:*
>
> 0 *without mention of obstruction*
> 1 *with obstruction*

Ureterolith 592.1
Ureterolithiasis 592.1
Ureterostomy status V44.6
with complication 997.5
Urethra, urethral —*see* condition
Urethralgia 788.9
Urethritis (abacterial) (acute) (allergic) (anterior)
(chronic) (nonvenereal) (posterior) (recurrent)
(simple) (subacute) (ulcerative)
(undifferentiated) 597.80
diplococcal (acute) 098.0
chronic or duration of 2 months or over 098.2
due to Trichomonas (vaginalis) 131.02
gonococcal (acute) 098.0
chronic or duration of 2 months or over 098.2
nongonococcal (sexually transmitted) 099.40
Chlamydia trachomatis 099.41
Reiter's 099.3
specified organism NEC 099.49
nonspecific (sexually transmitted) (*see also*
Urethritis, nongonococcal) 099.40
not sexually transmitted 597.80
Reiter's 099.3
trichomonal or due to Trichomonas (vaginalis)
131.02
tuberculous (*see also* Tuberculosis) 016.3
venereal NEC (*see also* Urethritis,
nongonococcal) 099.40
Urethrocele
female 618.0
with uterine prolapse 618.4
complete 618.3
incomplete 618.2
male 599.5
Urethrolithiasis 594.2
Urethro-oculoarticular syndrome 099.3
Urethro-oculosynovial syndrome 099.3
Urethrorectal —*see* condition
Urethrorrhagia 599.84
Urethrorrhea 788.7
Urethrostomy status V44.6
with complication 997.5
Urethrotrigonitis 595.3
Urethrovaginal —*see* condition
Urhidrosis, uridrosis 705.89
Uric acid
diathesis 274.9
in blood 790.6
Uricacidemia 790.6
Uricemia 790.6
Uricosuria 791.9
Urination
frequent 788.41
painful 788.1
Urine, urinary —*see also* condition
abnormality NEC 788.69
blood in (*see also* Hematuria) 599.7
discharge, excessive 788.42
enuresis 788.30
nonorganic origin 307.6
extravasation 788.8
frequency 788.41
incontinence 788.30
active 788.30
female 788.30
stress 625.6
and urge 788.33
male 788.30
stress 788.32
and urge 788.33
mixed (stress and urge) 788.33

Urine, urinary—*continued*
neurogenic 788.39
nonorganic origin 307.6
stress (female) 625.6
male NEC 788.32
intermittent stream 788.61
pus in 791.9
retention or stasis NEC 788.20
bladder, incomplete emptying 788.21
psychogenic 306.53
specified NEC 788.29
secretion
deficient 788.5
excessive 788.42
frequency 788.41
stream
intermittent 788.61
slowing 788.62
splitting 788.61
weak 788.62
Urinemia —*see* Uremia
Urinoma NEC 599.9
bladder 596.8
kidney 593.89
renal 593.89
ureter 593.89
urethra 599.84
Uroarthritis, infectious 099.3
Urodialysis 788.5
Urolithiasis 592.9
Uronephrosis 593.89
Uropathy 599.9
obstructive 599.6
Urosepsis 599.0
meaning sepsis 038.9
meaning urinary tract infection 599.0
Urticaria 708.9
with angioneurotic edema 995.1
hereditary 277.6
allergic 708.0
cholinergic 708.5
chronic 708.8
cold, familial 708.2
dermatographic 708.3
due to
cold or heat 708.2
drugs 708.0
food 708.0
inhalants 708.0
plants 708.8
serum 999.5
factitial 708.3
giant 995.1
hereditary 277.6
gigantea 995.1
hereditary 277.6
idiopathic 708.1
larynx 995.1
hereditary 277.6
neonatorum 778.8
nonallergic 708.1
papulosa (Hebra) 698.2
perstans hemorrhagica 757.39
pigmentosa 757.33
recurrent periodic 708.8
serum 999.5
solare 692.72
specified type NEC 708.8
thermal (cold) (heat) 708.2
vibratory 708.4
Urticarioides acarodermatitis 133.9

Use of
  nonprescribed drugs (*see also* Abuse, drugs,
      nondependent) 305.9
  patent medicines (*see also* Abuse, drugs,
      nondependent) 305.9
Usher-Senear disease (pemphigus
    erythematosus) 694.4
Uta 085.5
Uterine size-date discrepancy 646.8
Uteromegaly 621.2
Uterovaginal —*see* condition
Uterovesical —*see* condition
Uterus —*see* condition
Utriculitis (utriculus prostaticus) 597.89
Uveal —*see* condition
Uveitis (anterior) (*see also* Iridocyclitis) 364.3
  acute or subacute 364.00
    due to or associated with
      gonococcal infection 098.41
      herpes (simplex) 054.44
        zoster 053.22
    primary 364.01
    recurrent 364.02
    secondary (noninfectious) 364.04
      infectious 364.03
  allergic 360.11
  chronic 364.10
    due to or associated with
      sarcoidosis 135 *[364.11]*
      tuberculosis (*see also* Tuberculosis) 017.3
        [364.11]
Uveitis—*continued*
  due to
    operation 360.11
    toxoplasmosis (acquired) 130.2
      congenital (active) 771.2
  granulomatous 364.10
  heterochromic 364.21
  lens-induced 364.23
  nongranulomatous 364.00
  posterior 363.20
    disseminated—*see* Chorioretinitis,
        disseminated
    focal—*see* Chorioretinitis, focal
  recurrent 364.02
  sympathetic 360.11
  syphilitic (secondary) 091.50
    congenital 090.0 *[363.13]*
    late 095.8 *[363.13]*
  tuberculous (*see also* Tuberculosis) 017.3
      [364.11]
Uveoencephalitis 363.22
Uveokeratitis (*see also* Iridocyclitis) 364.3
Uveoparotid fever 135
Uveoparotitis 135
Uvula —*see* condition
Uvulitis (acute) (catarrhal) (chronic)
    (gangrenous) (membranous) (suppurative)
    (ulcerative) 528.3

V

Vaccination
  complication or reaction—*see* Complications,
    vaccination
  not done (contraindicated) V64.0
    because of patient's decision V64.2
  prophylactic (against) V05.9
    arthropod-borne viral
      disease NEC V05.1
      encephalitis V05.0
    chickenpox V05.4
    cholera (alone) V03.0
      with typhoid-paratyphoid (cholera + TAB)
        V06.0
    common cold V04.7
    diphtheria (alone) V03.5
      with
        poliomyelitis (DTP + polio) V06.3
        tetanus V06.5
          -pertussis combined [DTP] V06.1
        typhoid-paratyphoid (DTP + TAB) V06.2
    disease (single) NEC V05.9
      bacterial NEC V03.9
        specified type NEC V03.89
      combinations NEC V06.9
        specified type NEC V06.8
      specified type NEC V05.8
    encephalitis, viral, arthropod-borne V05.0
    Hemophilus influenzae, type B [Hib] V03.81
    hepatitis, viral V05.3
    influenza V04.8
      with
        Streptococcus pneumoniae
          [pneumococcus] V06.6
    lileishmaniasis V05.2
    measles (alone) V04.2
      with mumps-rubella (MMR) V06.4
    mumps (alone) V04.6
      with measles and rubella (MMR) V06.4
    pertussis alone V03.6
    plague V03.3
    poliomyelitis V04.0
      with diphtheria-tetanus-pertussis (DTP +
        polio) V06.3
    rabies V04.5
    rubella (alone) V04.3
      with measles and mumps (MMR) V06.4
    smallpox V04.1
    Streptococcus pneumoniae [pneumococcus]
      V03.82
      with
        influenza V06.6
    tetanus toxoid (alone) V03.7
      with diphtheria [Td] V06.5
        with
          pertussis (DTP) V06.1
            with poliomyelitis (DTP + polio)
              V06.3
    tuberculosis (BCG) V03.2
    tularemia V03.4
    typhoid-paratyphoid (TAB) (alone) V03.1
      with diphtheria-tetanus-pertussis (TAB +
        DTP) V06.2
    varicella V05.4
    viral
      encephalitis, arthropod-borne V05.0
      hepatitis V05.3
    yellow fever V04.4

Vaccinia (generalized) 999.0
  congenital 771.2
  conjunctiva 999.3
  eyelids 999.0 *[373.5]*
  localized 999.3
  nose 999.3
  not from vaccination 051.0
    eyelid 051.0 *[373.5]*
  sine vaccinatione 051.0
  without vaccination 051.0
Vacuum
  extraction of fetus or newborn 763.3
  in sinus (accessory) (nasal) (*see also* Sinusitis)
    473.9
Vagabond V60.0
Vagabondage V60.0
Vagabonds' disease 132.1
Vagina, vaginal —*see* condition
Vaginalitis (tunica) 608.4
Vaginismus (reflex) 625.1
  functional 306.51
  hysterical 300.11
  psychogenic 306.51
Vaginitis (acute) (chronic) (circumscribed)
    (diffuse) (emphysematous) (Hemophilus
    vaginalis) (nonspecific) (nonvenereal)
    (ulcerative) 616.10
  with
    abortion—*see* Abortion, by type, with sepsis
    ectopic pregnancy (*see also* categories
      633.0-633.9) 639.0
    molar pregnancy (*see also* categories
      630-632) 639.0
  adhesive, congenital 752.49
  atrophic, postmenopausal 627.3
  bacterial 616.10
  blennorrhagic (acute) 098.0
    chronic or duration of 2 months or over 098.2
  candidal 112.1
  chlamydial 099.53
  complicating pregnancy or puerperium 646.6
    affecting fetus or newborn 760.8
  congenital (adhesive) 752.49
  due to
    C. albicans 112.1
    Trichomonas (vaginalis) 131.01
  following
    abortion 639.0
    ectopic or molar pregnancy 639.0
  gonococcal (acute) 098.0
    chronic or duration of 2 months or over 098.2
  granuloma 099.2
  Monilia 112.1
  mycotic 112.1
  pinworm 127.4 *[616.11]*
  postirradiation 616.10
  postmenopausal atrophic 627.3
  senile (atrophic) 627.3
  syphilitic (early) 091.0
    late 095.8
  trichomonal 131.01
  tuberculous (*see also* Tuberculosis) 016.7
  venereal NEC 099.8
Vaginosis —*see* Vaginitis
Vagotonia 352.3
Vagrancy V60.0
Vallecula —*see* condition
Valley fever 114.0

Valsuani's disease (progressive pernicious anemia, puerperal) 648.2

Valve, valvular (formation)—*see also* condition
  cerebral ventricle (communicating) in situ V45.2
  cervix, internal os 752.49
  colon 751.5
  congenital NEC—*see* Atresia
  formation, congenital NEC—*see* Atresia
  heart defect—*see* Anomaly, heart, valve
  ureter 753.29
    pelvic junction 753.21
    vesical orifice 753.22
  urethra 753.6

Valvulitis (chronic) (*see also* Endocarditis) 424.90
  rheumatic (chronic) (inactive) (with chorea) 397.9
    active or acute (aortic) (mitral) (pulmonary) (tricuspid) 391.1
  syphilitic NEC 093.20
    aortic 093.22
    mitral 093.21
    pulmonary 093.24
    tricuspid 093.23

Valvulopathy —*see* Endocarditis

van Bogaert's leukoencephalitis (sclerosing) (subacute) 046.2

van Bogaert-Nijssen (-Peiffer) disease 330.0

van Buchem's syndrome (hyperostosis corticalis) 733.3

van Creveld-von Gierke disease (glycogenosis I) 271.0

van den Bergh's disease (enterogenous cyanosis) 289.7

van der Hoeve's syndrome (brittle bones and blue sclera, deafness) 756.51

van der Hoeve-Halbertsma-Waardenburg syndrome (ptosis-epicanthus) 270.2

van der Hoeve-Waardenburg-Gualdi syndrome (ptosis epicanthus) 270.2

Vanillism 692.89

Vanishing lung 492.0

Vanishing twin 651.33

van Neck (-Odelberg) disease or syndrome (juvenile osteochondrosis) 732.1

Vapor asphyxia or suffocation NEC 987.9
  specified agent—*see* Table of drugs and chemicals

Vaquez's disease (M9950/1) 238.4

Vaquez-Osler disease (polycythemia vera) (M9950/1) 238.4

Variance, lethal ball, prosthetic heart valve 996.02

Variants, thalassemic 282.4

Variations in hair color 704.3

Varicella 052.9
  with
    complication 052.8
      specified NEC 052.7
    pneumonia 052.1
  vaccination and inoculation (prophylactic) V05.4

Varices —*see* Varix

Varicocele (scrotum) (thrombosed) 456.4
  ovary 456.5
  perineum 456.6
  spermatic cord (ulcerated) 456.4

Varicose
  aneurysm (ruptured) (*see also* Aneurysm) 442.9
  dermatitis (lower extremity)—*see* Varicose, vein, inflamed or infected
  eczema—*see* Varicose, vein
  phlebitis—*see* Varicose, vein, inflamed or infected
  placental vessel—*see* Placenta, abnormal
  tumor—*see* Varicose, vein
  ulcer (lower extremity, any part) 454.0
    anus 455.8
      external 455.5
      internal 455.2
    esophagus (*see also* Varix, esophagus) 456.1
      bleeding (*see also* Varix, esophagus, bleeding) 456.0
    inflamed or infected 454.2
    nasal septum 456.8
    perineum 456.6
    rectum—*see* Varicose, ulcer, anus
    scrotum 456.4
    specified site NEC 456.8
  vein (lower extremity) (ruptured) (*see also* Varix) 454.9
    with
      inflammation or infection 454.1
        ulcerated 454.2
      stasis dermatitis 454.1
        with ulcer 454.2
      ulcer 454.0
        inflamed or infected 454.2
    anus—*see* Hemorrhoids
    broad ligament 456.5
    congenital (peripheral) NEC 747.60
      gastrointestinal 747.61
      lower limb 747.64
      renal 747.62
      specified NEC 747.69
      upper limb 747.63
    esophagus (ulcerated) (*see also* Varix, esophagus) 456.1
      bleeding (*see also* Varix, esophagus, bleeding) 456.0
    inflamed or infected 454.1
      with ulcer 454.2
    in pregnancy or puerperium 671.0
      vulva or perineum 671.1
    nasal septum (with ulcer) 456.8
    pelvis 456.5
    perineum 456.6
      in pregnancy, childbirth, or puerperium 671.1
    rectum—*see* Hemorrhoids
    scrotum (ulcerated) 456.4
    specified site NEC 456.8
    sublingual 456.3
    ulcerated 454.0
      inflamed or infected 454.2
    umbilical cord, affecting fetus or newborn 762.6
    urethra 456.8
    vulva 456.6
      in pregnancy, childbirth, or puerperium 671.1
    vessel—*see also* Varix
      placenta—*see* Placenta, abnormal

Varicosis, varicosities, varicosity (*see also* Varix) 454.9

Variola 050.9
  hemorrhagic (pustular) 050.0
  major 050.0
  minor 050.1
  modified 050.2
Varioloid 050.2
Variolosa, purpura 050.0
Varix (lower extremity) (ruptured) 454.9
  with
      inflammation or infection 454.1
          with ulcer 454.2
      stasis dermatitis 454.1
          with ulcer 454.2
      ulcer 454.0
          with inflammation or infection 454.2
  aneurysmal (*see also* Aneurysm) 442.9
  anus—*see* Hemorrhoids
  arteriovenous (congenital) (peripheral) NEC
      747.60
      gastrointestinal 747.61
      lower limb 747.64
      renal 747.62
      specified NEC 747.69
      spinal 747.82
      upper limb 747.63
  bladder 456.5
  broad ligament 456.5
  congenital (peripheral) NEC 747.60
  esophagus (ulcerated) 456.1
      bleeding 456.0
          in
              cirrhosis of liver 571.5 *[456.20]*
              portal hypertension 572.3 *[456.20]*
      congenital 747.69
          in
              cirrhosis of liver 571.5 *[456.21]*
                  with bleeding 571.5 *[456.20]*
              portal hypertension 572.3 *[456.21]*
                  with bleeding 572.3 *[456.20]*
  gastric 456.8
  inflamed or infected 454.1
      ulcerated 454.2
  in pregnancy or puerperium 671.0
      perineum 671.1
      vulva 671.1
  labia (majora) 456.6
  orbit 456.8
      congenital 747.69
  ovary 456.5
  papillary 448.1
  pelvis 456.5
  perineum 456.6
      in pregnancy or puerperium 671.1
  pharynx 456.8
  placenta—*see* Placenta, abnormal
  prostate 456.8
  rectum—*see* Hemorrhoids
  renal papilla 456.8
  retina 362.17
  scrotum (ulcerated) 456.4
  sigmoid colon 456.8
  specified site NEC 456.8
  spinal (cord) (vessels) 456.8
  spleen, splenic (vein) (with phlebolith) 456.8
  sublingual 456.3
  ulcerated 454.0
      inflamed or infected 454.2
  umbilical cord, affecting fetus or newborn 762.6
  uterine ligament 456.5
  vocal cord 456.8

Varix—*continued*
  vulva 456.6
      in pregnancy, childbirth, or puerperium 671.1
Vasa previa 663.5
  affecting fetus or newborn 762.6
  hemorrhage from, affecting fetus or newborn
      772.0
Vascular —*see also* condition
  loop on papilla (optic) 743.57
  sheathing, retina 362.13
  spasm 443.9
  spider 448.1
Vascularity, pulmonary, congenital 747.3
Vascularization
  choroid 362.16
  cornea 370.60
      deep 370.63
      localized 370.61
  retina 362.16
  subretinal 362.16
Vasculitis 447.6
  allergic 287.0
  cryoglobulinemic 273.2
  disseminated 447.6
  kidney 447.8
  leukocytoclastic 446.29
  nodular 695.2
  retinal 362.18
  rheumatic—*see* Fever, rheumatic
Vas deferens —*see* condition
Vas deferentitis 608.4
Vasectomy, admission for V25.2
Vasitis 608.4
  nodosa 608.4
  scrotum 608.4
  spermatic cord 608.4
  testis 608.4
  tuberculous (*see also* Tuberculosis) 016.5
  tunica vaginalis 608.4
  vas deferens 608.4
Vasodilation 443.9
Vasomotor —*see* condition
Vasoplasty, after previous sterilization V26.0
Vasoplegia, splanchnic (*see also* Neuropathy,
      peripheral, autonomic) 337.9
Vasospasm 443.9
  cerebral (artery) 435.9
      with transient neurologic deficit 435.9
  nerve
      arm NEC 354.9
      autonomic 337.9
      brachial plexus 353.0
      cervical plexus 353.2
      leg NEC 355.8
      lower extremity NEC 355.8
      peripheral NEC 355.9
      spinal NEC 355.9
      sympathetic 337.9
      upper extremity NEC 354.9
  peripheral NEC 443.9
  retina (artery) (*see also* Occlusion, retinal,
      artery) 362.30
Vasospastic —*see* condition
Vasovagal attack (paroxysmal) 780.2
  psychogenic 306.2
Vater's ampulla —*see* condition
VATER syndrome 759.89
Vegetation, vegetative
  adenoid (nasal fossa) 474.2
  consciousness (persistent) 780.03

Vegetation, vegetative—*continued*
  endocarditis (acute) (any valve) (chronic)
    (subacute) 421.0
  heart (mycotic) (valve) 421.0
  state (persistent) 780.03
Veil
  Jackson's 751.4
  over face (causing asphyxia) 768.9
Vein, venous —*see* condition
Veldt sore (*see also* Ulcer, skin) 707.9
Velpeau's hernia —*see* Hernia, femoral
Venereal
  balanitis NEC 099.8
  bubo 099.1
  disease 099.9
    specified nature or type NEC 099.8
  granuloma inguinale 099.2
  lymphogranuloma (Durand-Nicolas-Favre), any
    site 099.1
  salpingitis 098.37
  urethritis (*see also* Urethritis, nongonococcal)
    099.40
  vaginitis NEC 099.8
  warts 078.19
Vengefulness, in child (*see also* Disturbance,
  conduct) 312.0
Venofibrosis 459.89
Venom, venomous
  bite or sting (animal or insect) 989.5
  poisoning 989.5
Venous —*see* condition
Ventouse delivery NEC 669.5
  affecting fetus or newborn 763.3
Ventral —*see* condition
Ventricle, ventricular —*see also* condition
  escape 427.69
  standstill (*see also* Arrest, cardiac) 427.5
Ventriculitis, cerebral (*see also* Meningitis)
  322.9
Ventriculostomy status V45.2
Verbiest's syndrome (claudicatio intermittens
  spinalis) 435.1
Vernet's syndrome 352.6
Verneuil's disease (syphilitic bursitis) 095.7
Verruca (filiformis) 078.10
  acuminata (any site) 078.11
  necrogenica (primary) (*see also* Tuberculosis)
    017.0
  peruana 088.0
  peruviana 088.0
  plana (juvenilis) 078.19
  plantaris 078.19
  seborrheica 702.19
    inflamed 702.11
  senilis 702.0
  tuberculosa (primary) (*see also* Tuberculosis)
    017.0
  venereal 078.19
  viral NEC 078.10
Verrucosities (*see also* Verruca) 078.10
Verrucous endocarditis (acute) (any valve)
  (chronic) (subacute) 710.0 *[424.91]*
  nonbacterial 710.0 *[424.91]*
Verruga
  peruana 088.0
  peruviana 088.0
Verse's disease (calcinosis intervertebralis)
  275.49 *[722.90]*

Version
  before labor, affecting fetus or newborn 761.7
  cephalic (correcting previous malposition) 652.1
    affecting fetus or newborn 763.1
  cervix (*see also* Malposition, uterus) 621.6
  uterus (postinfectional) (postpartal, old) (*see*
    also Malposition, uterus) 621.6
    forward—*see* Anteversion, uterus
    lateral—*see* Lateroversion, uterus
Vertebra, vertebral —*see* condition
Vertigo 780.4
  auditory 386.19
  aural 386.19
  benign paroxysmal positional 386.11
  central origin 386.2
  cerebral 386.2
  Dix and Hallpike (epidemic) 386.12
  endemic paralytic 078.81
  epidemic 078.81
    Dix and Hallpike 386.12
    Gerlier's 078.81
    Pedersen's 386.12
    vestibular neuronitis 386.12
  epileptic—*see* Epilepsy
  Gerlier's (epidemic) 078.81
  hysterical 300.11
  labyrinthine 386.10
  laryngeal 786.2
  malignant positional 386.2
  Ménière's (*see also* Disease, Ménière's) 386.00
  menopausal 627.2
  otogenic 386.19
  paralytic 078.81
  paroxysmal positional, benign 386.11
  Pedersen's (epidemic) 386.12
  peripheral 386.10
    specified type NEC 386.19
  positional
    benign paroxysmal 386.11
    malignant 386.2
Verumontanitis (chronic) (*see also* Urethritis)
  597.89
Vesania (*see also* Psychosis) 298.9
Vesical —*see* condition
Vesicle
  cutaneous 709.8
  seminal—*see* condition
  skin 709.8
Vesicocolic —*see* condition
Vesicoperineal —*see* condition
Vesicorectal —*see* condition
Vesicourethrorectal —*see* condition
Vesicovaginal —*see* condition
Vesicular —*see* condition
Vesiculitis (seminal) 608.0
  amebic 006.8
  gonorrheal (acute) 098.14
    chronic or duration of 2 months or over 098.34
  trichomonal 131.09
  tuberculous (*see also* Tuberculosis) 016.5
    [608.81]
Vestibulitis (ear) (*see also* Labyrinthitis) 386.30
  nose (external) 478.1
  vulvar 616.10
Vestibulopathy, acute peripheral (recurrent)
  386.12
Vestige, vestigial —*see also* Persistence
  branchial 744.41
  structures in vitreous 743.51
Vibriosis NEC 027.9
Vidal's disease (lichen simplex chronicus) 698.3
Video display tube syndrome 723.8

Vienna type encephalitis 049.8
Villaret's syndrome 352.6
Villous —*see* condition
VIN I (vulvar intraepithelial neoplasia I) 624.8
VIN II (vulvar intraepithelial neoplasia II) 624.8
VIN III (vulvar intraepithelial neoplasia III) 233.3
Vincent's
  angina 101
  bronchitis 101
  disease 101
  gingivitis 101
  infection (any site) 101
  laryngitis 101
  stomatitis 101
  tonsillitis 101
Vinson-Plummer syndrome (sideropenic dysphagia) 280.8
Viosterol deficiency (*see also* Deficiency, calciferol) 268.9
Virchow's disease 733.99
Viremia 790.8
Virilism (adrenal) (female) NEC 255.2
  with
    3-beta-hydroxysteroid dehydrogenase defect 255.2
    11-hydroxylase defect 255.2
    21-hydroxylase defect 255.2
    adrenal
      hyperplasia 255.2
      insufficiency (congenital) 255.2
    cortical hyperfunction 255.2
Virilization (female) (suprarenal) (*see also* Virilism) 255.2
  isosexual 256.4
Virulent bubo 099.0
Virus, viral —*see also* condition
  infection NEC (*see also* Infection, viral) 079.99
  septicemia 079.99
Viscera, visceral —*see* condition
Visceroptosis 569.89
Visible peristalsis 787.4
Vision, visual
  binocular, suppression 368.31
  blurred, blurring 368.8
    hysterical 300.11
  defect, defective (*see also* Impaired, vision) 369.9
  disorientation (syndrome) 368.16
  disturbance NEC (*see also* Disturbance, vision) 368.9
    hysterical 300.11
  examination V72.0
  field, limitation 368.40
  fusion, with defective steropsis 368.33
  hallucinations 368.16
  halos 368.16
  loss 369.9
    both eyes (*see also* Blindness, both eyes) 369.3
    complete (*see also* Blindness, both eyes) 369.00
    one eye 369.8
    sudden 368.16
  low (both eyes) 369.20
    one eye (other eye normal) (*see also* Impaired, vision) 369.70
      blindness, other eye 369.10
  perception, simultaneous without fusion 368.32
  tunnel 368.45
Vitality, lack or want of 780.79
  newborn 779.8
Vitamin deficiency NEC (*see also* Deficiency, vitamin) 269.2

Vitelline duct, persistent 751.0
Vitiligo 709.01
  due to pinta (carate) 103.2
  eyelid 374.53
  vulva 624.8
Vitium cordis —*see* Disease, heart
Vitreous —*see also* condition
  touch syndrome 997.99
Vocal cord —*see* condition
Vocational rehabilitation V57.22
Vogt's (Cecile) disease or syndrome 333.7
Vogt-Koyanagi syndrome 364.24
Vogt-Spielmeyer disease (amaurotic familial idiocy) 330.1
Voice
  change (*see also* Dysphonia) 784.49
  loss (*see also* Aphonia) 784.41
Volhard-Fahr disease (malignant nephrosclerosis) 403.00
Volhynian fever 083.1
Volkmann's ischemic contracture or paralysis (complicating trauma) 958.6
Voluntary starvation 307.1
Volvulus (bowel) (colon) (intestine) 560.2
  with
    hernia—*see also* Hernia, by site, with obstruction
    gangrenous—*see* Hernia, by site, with gangrene
    perforation 560.2
  congenital 751.5
  duodenum 537.3
  fallopian tube 620.5
  oviduct 620.5
  stomach (due to absence of gastrocolic ligament) 537.89
Vomiting 787.03
  with nausea 787.01
  allergic 535.4
  asphyxia 933.1
  bilious (cause unknown) 787.0
    following gastrointestinal surgery 564.3
  blood (*see also* Hematemesis) 578.0
  causing asphyxia, choking, or suffocation (*see also* Asphyxia, food) 933.1
  cyclical 536.2
    psychogenic 306.4
  epidemic 078.82
  fecal matter 569.89
  following gastrointestinal surgery 564.3
  functional 536.8
    psychogenic 306.4
  habit 536.2
  hysterical 300.11
  nervous 306.4
  neurotic 306.4
  newborn 779.3
  of or complicating pregnancy 643.9
    due to
      organic disease 643.8
      specific cause NEC 643.8
    early—*see* Hyperemesis, gravidarum
    late (after 22 completed weeks of gestation) 643.2
  pernicious or persistent 536.2
    complicating pregnancy—*see* Hyperemesis, gravidarum
    psychogenic 306.4
  physiological 787.0
  psychic 306.4
  psychogenic 307.54

W

Waardenburg's syndrome 756.89
  meaning ptosis-epicanthus 270.2
Waardenburg-Klein syndrome
  (ptosis-epicanthus) 270.2
Wagner's disease (colloid milium) 709.3
Wagner (-Unverricht) syndrome
  (dermatomyositis) 710.3
Waiting list, person on V63.2
  undergoing social agency investigation V63.8
Wakefulness disorder (*see also* Hypersomnia)
  780.54
  nonorganic origin 307.43
Waldenström's
  disease (osteochondrosis, capital femoral) 732.1
  hepatitis (lupoid hepatitis) 571.49
  hypergammaglobulinemia 273.0
  macroglobulinemia 273.3
  purpura, hypergammaglobulinemic 273.0
  syndrome (macroglobulinemia) 273.3
Waldenström-Kjellberg syndrome (sideropenic
  dysphagia) 280.8
Walking
  difficulty 719.7
    psychogenic 307.9
  sleep 307.46
    hysterical 300.13
Wall, abdominal —*see* condition
Wallenberg's syndrome (posterior inferior
  cerebellar artery) (*see also* Disease,
  cerebrovascular, acute) 436
Wallgren's
  disease (obstruction of splenic vein with
    collateral circulation) 459.89
  meningitis (*see also* Meningitis, aseptic) 047.9
Wandering
  acetabulum 736.39
  gallbladder 751.69
  kidney, congenital 753.3
  organ or site, congenital NEC—*see*
    Malposition, congenital
  pacemaker (atrial) (heart) 427.89
  spleen 289.59
Wardrop's disease (with lymphangitis) 681.9
  finger 681.02
  toe 681.11
War neurosis 300.16
Wart (common) (digitate) (filiform) (infectious)
  (juvenile) (plantar) (viral) 078.10
  external genital organs (venereal) 078.19
  fig 078.19
  Hassall-Henle's (of cornea) 371.41
  Henle's (of cornea) 371.41
  juvenile 078.19
  moist 078.10
  Peruvian 088.0
  plantar 078.19
  prosector (*see also* Tuberculosis) 017.0
  seborrheic 702.19
    inflamed 702.11
  senile 702.0
  specified NEC 078.19
  syphilitic 091.3
  tuberculous (*see also* Tuberculosis) 017.0
  venereal (female) (male) 078.19
Warthin's tumor (salivary gland) (M8561/0)
  210.2
Washerwoman's itch 692.4

Wassilieff's disease (leptospiral jaundice) 100.0
Wasting
  disease 799.4
    due to malnutrition 261
  extreme (due to malnutrition) 261
  muscular NEC 728.2
  palsy, paralysis 335.21
Water
  clefts 366.12
  deprivation of 994.3
  in joint (*see also* Effusion, joint) 719.0
  intoxication 276.6
  itch 120.3
  lack of 994.3
  loading 276.6
  on
    brain—*see* Hydrocephalus
    chest 511.8
  poisoning 276.6
Waterbrash 787.1
Water-hammer pulse (*see also* Insufficiency,
  aortic) 424.1
Waterhouse (-Friderichsen) disease or syndrome
  036.3
Water-losing nephritis 588.8
Wax in ear 380.4
Waxy
  degeneration, any site 277.3
  disease 277.3
  kidney 277.3 *[583.81]*
  liver (large) 277.3
  spleen 277.3
Weak, weakness (generalized) 780.79
  arches (acquired) 734
    congenital 754.61
  bladder sphincter 596.59
  congenital 779.8
  eye muscle—*see* Strabismus
  foot (double)—*see* Weak, arches
  heart, cardiac (*see also* Failure, heart) 428.9
    congenital 746.9
  mind 317
  muscle 728.9
  myocardium (*see also* Failure, heart) 428.9
  newborn 779.8
  pelvic fundus 618.8
  pulse 785.9
  senile 797
  valvular—*see* Endocarditis
Wear, worn, tooth, teeth (approximal) (hard
  tissues) (interproximal) (occlusal) 521.1
Weather, weathered
  effects of
    cold NEC 991.9
      specified effect NEC 991.8
    hot (*see also* Heat) 992.9
  skin 692.74
Web, webbed (congenital)—*see also* Anomaly,
  specified type NEC
  canthus 743.63
  digits (*see also* Syndactylism) 755.10
  esophagus 750.3
  fingers (*see also* Syndactylism, fingers) 755.11
  larynx (glottic) (subglottic) 748.2
  neck (pterygium colli) 744.5
  Paterson-Kelly (sideropenic dysphagia) 280.8
  popliteal syndrome 756.89
  toes (*see also* Syndactylism, toes) 755.13

Withdrawal symptoms, syndrome
  alcohol 291.81
    delirium (acute) 291.0
      chronic 291.1
      newborn 760.71
  drug or narcotic 292.0
  newborn, infant of dependent mother 779.5
  steroid NEC
    correct substance properly administered 255.4
    overdose or wrong substance given or taken 962.0
Withdrawing reaction, child or adolescent 313.22
Witts' anemia (achlorhydric anemia) 280.9
Witzelsucht 301.9
Woakes' syndrome (ethmoiditis) 471.1
Wohlfart-Kugelberg-Welander disease 335.11
Woillez's disease (acute idiopathic pulmonary congestion) 518.5
Wolff-Parkinson-White syndrome (anomalous atrioventricular excitation) 426.7
Wolhynian fever 083.1
Wolman's disease (primary familial xanthomatosis) 272.7
Wood asthma 495.8
Woolly, wooly hair (congenital) (nevus) 757.4
Wool-sorters' disease 022.1
Word
  blindness (congenital) (developmental) 315.01
    secondary to organic lesion 784.61
  deafness (secondary to organic lesion) 784.69
    developmental 315.31
Worm (s) (colic) (fever) (infection) (infestation) (*see also* Infestation) 128.9
  guinea 125.7
  in intestine NEC 127.9
Worm-eaten soles 102.3
Worn out (*see also* Exhaustion) 780.79
"Worried well" V65.5
Wound, open (by cutting or piercing instrument) (by firearms) (cut) (dissection) (incised) (laceration) (penetration) (perforating) (puncture) (with initial hemorrhage, not internal) 879.8

Note—For fracture with open wound, see Fracture. For laceration, traumatic rupture, tear or penetrating wound of internal organs, such as heart, lung, liver, kidney, pelvic organs, etc., whether or not accompanied by open wound or fracture in the same region, see Injury, internal. For contused wound, see Contusion. For crush injury, see Crush. For abrasion, insect bite (nonvenomous), blister, or scratch, see Injury, superficial.

Complicated includes wounds with:
  delayed healing
  delayed treatment
  foreign body
  primary infection

For late effect of open wound, see Late, effect, wound, open, by site.

---

  abdomen, abdominal (external) (muscle) 879.2
    complicated 879.3
    wall (anterior) 879.2
      complicated 879.3
      lateral 879.4
        complicated 879.5

Wound, open—*continued*
  alveolar (process) 873.62
    complicated 873.72
  ankle 891.0
    with tendon involvement 891.2
    complicated 891.1
  anterior chamber, eye (*see also* Wound, open, intraocular) 871.9
  anus 879.6
    complicated 879.7
  arm 884.0
    with tendon involvement 884.2
    complicated 884.1
    forearm 881.00
      with tendon involvement 881.20
      complicated 881.10
    multiple sites—*see* Wound, open, multiple, upper limb
    upper 880.03
      with tendon involvement 880.23
      complicated 880.13
      multiple sites (with axillary or shoulder regions) 880.09
        with tendon involvement 880.29
        complicated 880.19
  artery—*see* Injury, blood vessel, by site
  auditory
    canal (external) (meatus) 872.02
      complicated 872.12
    ossicles (incus) (malleus) (stapes) 872.62
      complicated 872.72
  auricle, ear 872.01
    complicated 872.11
  axilla 880.02
    with tendon involvement 880.22
    complicated 880.12
      with tendon involvement 880.29
    involving other sites of upper arm 880.09
      complicated 880.19
  back 876.0
    complicated 876.1
  bladder—*see* Injury, internal, bladder
  blood vessel—*see* Injury, blood vessel, by site
  brain—*see* Injury, intracranial, with open intracranial wound
  breast 879.0
    complicated 879.1
  brow 873.42
    complicated 873.52
  buccal mucosa 873.61
    complicated 873.71
  buttock 877.0
    complicated 877.1
  calf 891.0
    with tendon involvement 891.2
    complicated 891.1
  canaliculus lacrimalis 870.8
    with laceration of eyelid 870.2
  canthus, eye 870.8
    laceration—*see* Laceration, eyelid
  cavernous sinus—*see* Injury, intracranial
  cerebellum—*see* Injury, intracranial
  cervical esophagus 874.4
    complicated 874.5
  cervix—*see* Injury, internal, cervix
  cheek(s) (external) 873.41
    complicated 873.51
    internal 873.61
      complicated 873.71
  chest (wall) (external) 875.0
    complicated 875.1

Wound, open—*continued*
  intracranial—*see* Injury, intracranial, with open
      intracranial wound
  intraocular 871.9
    with
      partial loss (of intraocular tissue) 871.2
      prolapse or exposure (of intraocular tissue)
        871.1
      laceration (*see also* Laceration, eyeball) 871.4
      penetrating 871.7
        with foreign body (nonmagnetic) 871.6
          magnetic 871.5
      without prolapse (of intraocular tissue) 871.0
  iris (*see also* Wound, open, eyeball) 871.9
  jaw (fracture not involved) 873.44
    with fracture—*see* Fracture, jaw
    complicated 873.54
  knee 891.0
    with tendon involvement 891.2
    complicated 891.1
  labium (majus) (minus) 878.4
    complicated 878.5
  lacrimal apparatus, gland, or sac 870.8
    with laceration of eyelid 870.2
  larynx 874.01
    with trachea 874.00
      complicated 874.10
    complicated 874.11
  leg (multiple) 891.0
    with tendon involvement 891.2
    complicated 891.1
    lower 891.0
      with tendon involvement 891.2
      complicated 891.1
    thigh 890.0
      with tendon involvement 890.2
      complicated 890.1
    upper 890.0
      with tendon involvement 890.2
      complicated 890.1
  lens (eye) (alone) (*see also* Cataract, traumatic)
    366.20
    with involvement of other eye structures—*see*
      Wound, open, eyeball
  limb
    lower (multiple) NEC 894.0
      with tendon involvement 894.2
      complicated 894.1
    upper (multiple) NEC 884.0
      with tendon involvement 884.2
      complicated 884.1
  lip 873.43
    complicated 873.53
  loin 876.0
    complicated 876.1
  lumbar region 876.0
    complicated 876.1
  malar region 873.41
    complicated 873.51
  mastoid region 873.49
    complicated 873.59
  mediastinum—*see* Injury, internal, mediastinum
  midthoracic region 875.0
    complicated 875.1
  mouth 873.60
    complicated 873.70
    floor 873.64
      complicated 873.74
    multiple sites 873.69
      complicated 873.79

Wound, open—*continued*
  specified site NEC 873.69
    complicated 873.79
  multiple, unspecified site(s) 879.8

> *Note*—*Multiple open wounds of sites
> classifiable to the same four-digit category
> should be classified to that category unless they
> are in different limbs.*
>
> *Multiple open wounds of sites classifiable to
> different four-digit categories, or to different
> limbs, should be coded separately.*

    complicated 879.9
    lower limb(s) (one or both) (sites classifiable
      to more than one three-digit category in
      890 to 893) 894.0
      with tendon involvement 894.2
      complicated 894.1
    upper limb(s) (one or both) (sites classifiable
      to more than one three-digit category in
      880 to 883) 884.0
      with tendon involvement 884.2
      complicated 884.1
  muscle—*see* Sprain, by site
  nail
    finger(s) 883.0
      complicated 883.1
    thumb 883.0
      complicated 883.1
    toe(s) 893.0
      complicated 893.1
  nape (neck) 874.8
    complicated 874.9
    specified part NEC 874.8
      complicated 874.9
  nasal—*see also* Wound, open, nose
    cavity 873.22
      complicated 873.32
    septum 873.21
      complicated 873.31
    sinuses 873.23
      complicated 873.33
  nasopharynx 873.22
    complicated 873.32
  neck 874.8
    complicated 874.9
    nape 874.8
      complicated 874.9
    specified part NEC 874.8
      complicated 874.9
  nerve—*see* Injury, nerve, by site
  non-healing surgical 998.83
  nose 873.20
    complicated 873.30
    multiple sites 873.29
      complicated 873.39
    septum 873.21
      complicated 873.31
    sinuses 873.23
      complicated 873.33
  occipital region—*see* Wound, open, scalp
  ocular NEC 871.9
    adnexa 870.9
      specified region NEC 870.8
    laceration (*see also* Laceration, ocular) 871.4
    muscle (extraocular) 870.3
      with foreign body 870.4
      eyelid 870.1
      intraocular—*see* Wound, open, eyeball

Wound, open—*continued*
   penetrating (*see also* Penetrating wound,
      ocular) 871.7
   orbit 870.8
     penetrating 870.3
      with foreign body 870.4
   orbital region 870.9
   ovary—*see* Injury, internal, pelvic organs
   palate 873.65
     complicated 873.75
   palm 882.0
     with tendon involvement 882.2
     complicated 882.1
   parathyroid (gland) 874.2
     complicated 874.3
   parietal region—*see* Wound, open, scalp
   pelvic floor or region 879.6
     complicated 879.7
   penis 878.0
     complicated 878.1
   perineum 879.6
     complicated 879.7
   periocular area 870.8
     laceration of skin 870.0
   pharynx 874.4
     complicated 874.5
   pinna 872.01
     complicated 872.11
   popliteal space 891.0
     with tendon involvement 891.2
     complicated 891.1
   prepuce 878.0
     complicated 878.1
   pubic region 879.2
     complicated 879.3
   pudenda 878.8
     complicated 878.9
   rectovaginal septum 878.8
     complicated 878.9
   sacral region 877.0
     complicated 877.1
   sacroiliac region 877.0
     complicated 877.1
   salivary (ducts) (glands) 873.69
     complicated 873.79
   scalp 873.0
     complicated 873.1
   scalpel, fetus or newborn 767.8
   scapular region 880.01
     with tendon involvement 880.21
     complicated 880.11
     involving other sites of upper arm 880.09
      with tendon involvement 880.29
      complicated 880.19
   sclera (*see also* Wound, open, intraocular) 871.9
   scrotum 878.2
     complicated 878.3
   seminal vesicle—*see* Injury, internal, pelvic
     organs
   shin 891.0
     with tendon involvement 891.2
     complicated 891.1
   shoulder 880.00
     with tendon involvement 880.20
     complicated 880.10
     involving other sites of upper arm 880.09
      with tendon involvement 880.29
      complicated 880.19
   skin NEC 879.8
     complicated 879.9

Wound, open—*continued*
   skull—*see also* Injury, intracranial, with open
     intracranial wound
     with skull fracture—*see* Fracture, skull
   spermatic cord (scrotal) 878.2
     complicated 878.3
     pelvic region—*see* Injury, internal, spermatic
      cord
   spinal cord—*see* Injury, spinal
   sternal region 875.0
     complicated 875.1
   subconjunctival—*see* Wound, open, intraocular
   subcutaneous NEC 879.8
     complicated 879.9
   submaxillary region 873.44
     complicated 873.54
   submental region 873.44
     complicated 873.54
   subungual
     finger(s) (thumb)—*see* Wound, open, finger
     toe(s)—*see* Wound, open, toe
   supraclavicular region 874.8
     complicated 874.9
   supraorbital 873.42
     complicated 873.52
   surgical, non-healing 998.83
   temple 873.49
     complicated 873.59
   temporal region 873.49
     complicated 873.59
   testis 878.2
     complicated 878.3
   thigh 890.0
     with tendon involvement 890.2
     complicated 890.1
   thorax, thoracic (external) 875.0
     complicated 875.1
   throat 874.8
     complicated 874.9
   thumb (nail) (subungual) 883.0
     with tendon involvement 883.2
     complicated 883.1
   thyroid (gland) 874.2
     complicated 874.3
   toe(s) (nail) (subungual) 893.0
     with tendon involvement 893.2
     complicated 893.1
   tongue 873.64
     complicated 873.74
   tonsil—*see* Wound, open, neck
   trachea (cervical region) 874.02
     with larynx 874.00
      complicated 874.10
     complicated 874.12
     intrathoracic—*see* Injury, internal, trachea
   trunk (multiple) NEC 879.6
     complicated 879.7
     specified site NEC 879.6
      complicated 879.7
   tunica vaginalis 878.2
     complicated 878.3
   tympanic membrane 872.61
     complicated 872.71
   tympanum 872.61
     complicated 872.71
   umbilical region 879.2
     complicated 879.3
   ureter—*see* Injury, internal, ureter
   urethra—*see* Injury, internal, urethra
   uterus—*see* Injury, internal, uterus

Wound, open—*continued*
  uvula 873.69
    complicated 873.79
  vagina 878.6
    complicated 878.7
  vas deferens—*see* Injury, internal, vas deferens
  vitreous (humor) 871.2
  vulva 878.4
    complicated 878.5
  wrist 881.02
    with tendon involvement 881.22
    complicated 881.12
Wright's syndrome (hyperabduction) 447.8
  pneumonia 390 *[517.1]*
Wringer injury —*see* Crush injury, by site
Wrinkling of skin 701.8
Wrist —*see also* condition
  drop (acquired) 736.05
Wrong drug (given in error) NEC 977.9
  specified drug or substance—*see* Table of drugs
    and chemicals
Wry neck —*see also* Torticollis
  congenital 754.1
Wuchereria infestation 125.0
  bancrofti 125.0
  Brugia malayi 125.1
  malayi 125.1
Wuchereriasis 125.0
Wuchereriosis 125.0
Wuchernde struma langhans (M8332/3) 193

X

Xanthelasma 272.2
  eyelid 272.2 *[374.51]*
  palpebrarum 272.2 *[374.51]*
Xanthelasmatosis (essential) 272.2
Xanthelasmoidea 757.33
Xanthine stones 277.2
Xanthinuria 277.2
Xanthofibroma (M8831/0)—*see* Neoplasm,
  connective tissue, benign
Xanthoma (s), xanthomatosis 272.2
  with
    hyperlipoproteinemia
      type I 272.3
      type III 272.2
      type IV 272.1
      type V 272.3
  bone 272.7
  craniohypophyseal 277.8
  cutaneotendinous 272.7
  diabeticorum 250.8 *[272.2]*
  disseminatum 272.7
  eruptive 272.2
  eyelid 272.2 *[374.51]*
  familial 272.7
  hereditary 272.7
  hypercholesterinemic 272.0
  hypercholesterolemic 272.0
  hyperlipemic 272.4
  hyperlipidemic 272.4
  infantile 272.7
  joint 272.7
  juvenile 272.7
  multiple 272.7
  multiplex 272.7
  primary familial 272.7
  tendon (sheath) 272.7
  tuberosum 272.2
  tuberous 272.2
  tubo-eruptive 272.2
Xanthosis 709.09
  surgical 998.81
Xenophobia 300.29
Xeroderma (congenital) 757.39
  acquired 701.1
    eyelid 373.33
  eyelid 373.33
  pigmentosum 757.33
  vitamin A deficiency 264.8
Xerophthalmia 372.53
  vitamin A deficiency 264.7
Xerosis
  conjunctiva 372.53
    with Bitôt's spot 372.53
      vitamin A deficiency 264.1
    vitamin A deficiency 264.0
  cornea 371.40
    with corneal ulceration 370.00
      vitamin A deficiency 264.3
    vitamin A deficiency 264.2
  cutis 706.8
  skin 706.8
Xerostomia 527.7
Xiphodynia 733.90
Xiphoidalgia 733.90
Xiphoiditis 733.99
Xiphopagus 759.4
XO syndrome 758.6

X-ray
  effects, adverse, NEC 990
  of chest
    for suspected tuberculosis V71.2
    routine V72.5
XXX syndrome 758.81
XXXXY syndrome 758.81
XXY syndrome 758.7
Xyloketosuria 271.8
Xylosuria 271.8
Xylulosuria 271.8
XYY syndrome 758.81

Y

Yawning 786.09
  psychogenic 306.1
Yaws 102.9
  bone or joint lesions 102.6
  butter 102.1
  chancre 102.0
  cutaneous, less than five years after infection
     102.2
  early (cutaneous) (macular) (maculopapular)
     (micropapular) (papular) 102.2
    frambeside 102.2
    skin lesions NEC 102.2
  eyelid 102.9 *[373.4]*
  ganglion 102.6
  gangosis, gangosa 102.5
  gumma, gummata 102.4
    bone 102.6
  gummatous
    frambeside 102.4
    osteitis 102.6
    periostitis 102.6
  hydrarthrosis 102.6
  hyperkeratosis (early) (late) (palmar) (plantar)
     102.3
  initial lesions 102.0
  joint lesions 102.6
  juxta-articular nodules 102.7
  late nodular (ulcerated) 102.4
  latent (without clinical manifestations) (with
     positive serology) 102.8
  mother 102.0
  mucosal 102.7
  multiple papillomata 102.1
  nodular, late (ulcerated) 102.4
  osteitis 102.6
  papilloma, papillomata (palmar) (plantar) 102.1
  periostitis (hypertrophic) 102.6
  ulcers 102.4
  wet crab 102.1
Yeast infection (*see also* Candidiasis) 112.9
Yellow
  atrophy (liver) 570
    chronic 571.8
    resulting from administration of blood,
      plasma, serum, or other biological
      substance (within 8 months of
      administration)—*see* Hepatitis, viral
  fever—*see* Fever, yellow
  jack (*see also* Fever, yellow) 060.9
  jaundice (*see also* Jaundice) 782.4
Yersinia septica 027.8

Z

Zagari's disease (xerostomia) 527.7
Zahorsky's disease (exanthema subitum) 057.8
  syndrome (herpangina) 074.0
Zenker's diverticulum (esophagus) 530.6
Ziehen-Oppenheim disease 333.6
Zieve's syndrome (jaundice, hyperlipemia, and
  hemolytic anemia) 571.1
Zika fever 066.3
Zollinger-Ellison syndrome (gastric
  hypersecretion with pancreatic islet cell
  tumor) 251.5
Zona (*see also* Herpes, zoster) 053.9
Zoophilia (erotica) 302.1
Zoophobia 300.29
Zoster (herpes) (*see also* Herpes, zoster) 053.9
Zuelzer (-Ogden) anemia or syndrome
  (nutritional megaloblastic anemia) 281.2
Zygodactyly (*see also* Syndactylism) 755.10
Zygomycosis 117.7
Zymotic —*see* condition

SECTION 2

ALPHABETIC INDEX TO POISONING AND EXTERNAL CAUSES OF ADVERSE EFFECTS OF DRUGS AND OTHER CHEMICAL SUBSTANCES

TABLE OF DRUGS AND CHEMICALS

This table contains a classification of drugs and other chemical substances to identify poisoning states and external causes of adverse effects.

Each of the listed substances in the table is assigned a code according to the poisoning classification (960–989). These codes are used when there is a statement of poisoning, overdose, wrong substance given or taken, or intoxication.

The table also contains a listing of external causes of adverse effects. An adverse effect is a pathologic manifestation due to ingestion or exposure to drugs or other chemical substances (e.g., dermatitis, hypersensitivity reaction, aspirin gastritis). The adverse effect is to be identified by the appropriate code found in Section 1, Index to Diseases and Injuries. An external cause code can then be used to identify the circumstances involved. The table headings pertaining to external causes are defined below:

Accidental poisoning (E850–E869)—accidental overdose of drug, wrong substance given or taken, drug taken inadvertently, accidents in the usage of drugs and biologicals in medical and surgical procedures, and to show external causes of poisonings classifiable to 980–989.

Therapeutic use (E930–E949)—a correct substance properly administered in therapeutic or prophylactic dosage as the external cause of adverse effects.

Suicide attempt (E950–E952)—instances in which self–inflicted injuries or poisonings are involved.

Assault (E961–E962)—injury or poisoning inflicted by another person with the intent to injure or kill.

Undetermined (E980–E982)—to be used when the intent of the poisoning or injury cannot be determined whether it was intentional or accidental.

The American Hospital Formulary Service list numbers are included in the table to help classify new drugs not identified in the table by name. The AHFS list numbers are keyed to the continually revised American Hospital Formulary Service (AHFS).* These listings are found in the table under the main term **Drug**.

Excluded from the table are radium and other radioactive substances. The classification of adverse effects and complications pertaining to these substances will be found in Section 1, Index to Diseases and Injuries, and Section 3, Index to External Causes of Injuries.

Although certain substances are indexed with one or more subentries, the majority are listed according to one use or state. It is recognized that many substances may be used in various ways, in medicine and in industry, and may cause adverse effects whatever the state of the agent (solid, liquid, or fumes arising from a liquid). In cases in which the reported data indicates a use or state not in the table, or which is clearly different from the one listed, an attempt should be made to classify the substance in the form which most nearly expresses the reported facts.

*American Hospital Formulary Service, 2 vol. (Washington, DC: American Society of Hospital Pharmacists, 1959-)

Substance	Poisoning	Accident	Therapeutic Use	Suicide Attempt	Assault	Undetermined
1–propanol	980.3	E860.4	—	E950.9	E962.1	E980.9
2–propanol	980.2	E860.3	—	E950.9	E962.1	E980.9
2, 4–D (dichlorophenoxyacetic acid)	989.4	E863.5	—	E950.6	E962.1	E980.7
2, 4–toluene diisocyanate	983.0	E864.0	—	E950.7	E962.1	E980.6
2, 4, 5–T (trichlorophenoxyacetic acid)	989.2	E863.5	—	E950.6	E962.1	E980.7
14–hydroxydihydromorphinone	965.09	E850.2	E935.2	E950.0	E962.0	E980.0
ABOB	961.7	E857	E931.7	E950.4	E962.0	E980.4
Abrus (seed)	988.2	E865.3	—	E950.9	E962.1	E980.9
Absinthe	980.0	E860.1	—	E950.9	E962.1	E980.9
beverage	980.0	E860.0	—	E950.9	E962.1	E980.9
Acenocoumarin, acenocoumarol	964.2	E858.2	E934.2	E950.4	E962.0	E980.4
Acepromazine	969.1	E853.0	E939.1	E950.3	E962.0	E980.3
Acetal	982.8	E862.4	—	E950.9	E962.1	E980.9
Acetaldehyde (vapor)	987.8	E869.8	—	E952.8	E962.2	E982.8
liquid	989.89	E866.8	—	E950.9	E962.1	E980.9
Acetaminophen	965.4	E850.4	E935.4	E950.0	E962.0	E980.0
Acetaminosalol	965.1	E850.3	E935.3	E950.0	E962.0	E980.0
Acetanilid(e)	965.4	E850.4	E935.4	E950.0	E962.0	E980.0
Acetarsol, acetarsone	961.1	E857	E931.1	E950.4	E962.0	E980.4
Acetazolamide	974.2	E858.5	E944.2	E950.4	E962.0	E980.4
Acetic						
acid	983.1	E864.1	—	E950.7	E962.1	E980.6
with sodium acetate (ointment)	976.3	E858.7	E946.3	E950.4	E962.0	E980.4
irrigating solution	974.5	E858.5	E944.5	E950.4	E962.0	E980.4
lotion	976.2	E858.7	E946.2	E950.4	E962.0	E980.4
anhydride	983.1	E864.1	—	E950.7	E962.1	E980.6
ether (vapor)	982.8	E862.4	—	E950.9	E962.1	E980.9
Acetohexamide	962.3	E858.0	E932.3	E950.4	E962.0	E980.4
Acetomenaphthone	964.3	E858.2	E934.3	E950.4	E962.0	E980.4
Acetomorphine	965.01	E850.0	E935.0	E950.0	E962.0	E980.0
Acetone (oils) (vapor)	982.8	E862.4	—	E950.9	E962.1	E980.9
Acetophenazine (maleate)	969.1	E853.0	E939.1	E950.3	E962.0	E980.3
Acetophenetidin	965.4	E850.4	E935.4	E950.0	E962.0	E980.0
Acetophenone	982.0	E862.4	—	E950.9	E962.1	E980.9
Acetorphine	965.09	E850.2	E935.2	E950.0	E962.0	E980.0
Acetosulfone (sodium)	961.8	E857	E931.8	E950.4	E962.0	E980.4
Acetrizoate (sodium)	977.8	E858.8	E947.8	E950.4	E962.0	E980.4
Acetylcarbromal	967.3	E852.2	E937.3	E950.2	E962.0	E980.2
Acetylcholine (chloride)	971.0	E855.3	E941.0	E950.4	E962.0	E980.4
Acetylcysteine	975.5	E858.6	E945.5	E950.4	E962.0	E980.4
Acetyldigitoxin	972.1	E858.3	E942.1	E950.4	E962.0	E980.4
Acetyldihydrocodeine	965.09	E850.2	E935.2	E950.0	E962.0	E980.0
Acetyldihydrocodeinone	965.09	E850.2	E935.2	E950.0	E962.0	E980.0
Acetylene (gas) (industrial)	987.1	E868.1	—	E951.8	E962.2	E981.8
incomplete combustion of — *see* Carbon monoxide, fuel, utility						
tetrachloride (vapor)	982.3	E862.4	—	E950.9	E962.1	E980.9
Acetyliodosalicylic acid	965.1	E850.3	E935.3	E950.0	E962.0	E980.0
Acetylphenylhydrazine	965.8	E850.8	E935.8	E950.0	E962.0	E980.0
Acetylsalicylic acid	965.1	E850.3	E935.3	E950.0	E962.0	E980.0
Achromycin	960.4	E856	E930.4	E950.4	E962.0	E980.4
ophthalmic preparation	976.5	E858.7	E946.5	E950.4	E962.0	E980.4
topical NEC	976.0	E858.7	E946.0	E950.4	E962.0	E980.4
Acidifying agents	963.2	E858.1	E933.2	E950.4	E962.0	E980.4
Acids (corrosive) NEC	983.1	E864.1	—	E950.7	E962.1	E980.6
Aconite (wild)	988.2	E865.4	—	E950.9	E962.1	E980.9
Aconitine (liniment)	976.8	E858.7	E946.8	E950.4	E962.0	E980.4

Substance	Poisoning	External Cause (E-Code)				
		Accident	Therapeutic Use	Suicide Attempt	Assault	Undetermined
Aconitum ferox	988.2	E865.4	—	E950.9	E962.1	E980.9
Acridine	983.0	E864.0	—	E950.7	E962.1	E980.6
vapor	987.8	E869.8	—	E952.8	E962.2	E982.8
Acriflavine	961.9	E857	E931.9	E950.4	E962.0	E980.4
Acrisorcin	976.0	E858.7	E946.0	E950.4	E962.0	E980.4
Acrolein (gas)	987.8	E869.8	—	E952.8	E962.2	E982.8
liquid	989.89	E866.8	—	E950.9	E962.1	E980.9
Actaea spicata	988.2	E865.4	—	E950.9	E962.1	E980.9
Acterol	961.5	E857	E931.5	E950.4	E962.0	E980.4
ACTH	962.4	E858.0	E932.4	E950.4	E962.0	E980.4
Acthar	962.4	E858.0	E932.4	E950.4	E962.0	E980.4
Actinomycin (C) (D)	960.7	E856	E930.7	E950.4	E962.0	E980.4
Adalin (acetyl)	967.3	E852.2	E937.3	E950.2	E962.0	E980.2
Adenosine (phosphate)	977.8	E858.8	E947.8	E950.4	E962.0	E980.4
Adhesives	989.89	E866.6	—	E950.9	E962.1	E980.9
ADH	962.5	E858.0	E932.5	E950.4	E962.0	E980.4
Adicillin	960.0	E856	E930.0	E950.4	E962.0	E980.4
Adiphenine	975.1	E855.6	E945.1	E950.4	E962.0	E980.4
Adjunct, pharmaceutical	977.4	E858.8	E947.4	E950.4	E962.0	E980.4
Adrenal (extract, cortex or medulla) (glucocorticoids) (hormones) (mineralocorticoids)	962.0	E858.0	E932.0	E950.4	E962.0	E980.4
ENT agent	976.6	E858.7	E946.6	E950.4	E962.0	E980.4
ophthalmic preparation	976.5	E858.7	E946.5	E950.4	E962.0	E980.4
topical NEC	976.0	E858.7	E946.0	E950.4	E962.0	E980.4
Adrenalin	971.2	E855.5	E941.2	E950.4	E962.0	E980.4
Adrenergic blocking agents	971.3	E855.6	E941.3	E950.4	E962.0	E980.4
Adrenergics	971.2	E855.5	E941.2	E950.4	E962.0	E980.4
Adrenochrome (derivatives)	972.8	E858.3	E942.8	E950.4	E962.0	E980.4
Adrenocorticotropic hormone	962.4	E858.0	E932.4	E950.4	E962.0	E980.4
Adrenocorticotropin	962.4	E858.0	E932.4	E950.4	E962.0	E980.4
Adriamycin	960.7	E856	E930.7	E950.4	E962.0	E980.4
Aerosol spray — *see* Sprays						
Aerosporin	960.8	E856	E930.8	E950.4	E962.0	E980.4
ENT agent	976.6	E858.7	E946.6	E950.4	E962.0	E980.4
ophthalmic preparation	976.5	E858.7	E946.5	E950.4	E962.0	E980.4
topical NEC	976.0	E858.7	E946.0	E950.4	E962.0	E980.4
Aethusa cynapium	988.2	E865.4	—	E950.9	E962.1	E980.9
Afghanistan black	969.6	E854.1	E939.6	E950.3	E962.0	E980.3
Aflatoxin	989.7	E865.9	—	E950.9	E962.1	E980.9
African boxwood	988.2	E865.4	—	E950.9	E962.1	E980.9
Agar (–agar)	973.3	E858.4	E943.3	E950.4	E962.0	E980.4
Agricultural agent NEC	989.89	E863.9	—	E950.6	E962.1	E980.7
Agrypnal	967.0	E851	E937.0	E950.1	E962.0	E980.1
Air contaminant(s), source or type not specified	987.9	E869.9	—	E952.9	E962.2	E982.9
specified type — *see* specific substance						
Akee	988.2	E865.4	—	E950.9	E962.1	E980.9
Akrinol	976.0	E858.7	E946.0	E950.4	E962.0	E980.4
Alantolactone	961.6	E857	E931.6	E950.4	E962.0	E980.4
Albamycin	960.8	E856	E930.8	E950.4	E962.0	E980.4
Albumin (normal human serum)	964.7	E858.2	E934.7	E950.4	E962.0	E980.4
Alcohol	980.9	E860.9	—	E950.9	E962.1	E980.9
absolute	980.0	E860.1	—	E950.9	E962.1	E980.9
beverage	980.0	E860.0	E947.8	E950.9	E962.1	E980.9
amyl	980.3	E860.4	—	E950.9	E962.1	E980.9
antifreeze	980.1	E860.2	—	E950.9	E962.1	E980.9

Substance	Poisoning	External Cause (E-Code)				
		Accident	Therapeutic Use	Suicide Attempt	Assault	Undetermined
butyl	980.3	E860.4	—	E950.9	E962.1	E980.9
dehydrated	980.0	E860.1	—	E950.9	E862.1	E980.9
beverage	980.0	E860.0	E947.8	E950.9	E962.1	E980.9
denatured	980.0	E860.1	—	E950.9	E962.1	E980.9
deterrents	977.3	E858.8	E947.3	E950.4	E962.0	E980.4
diagnostic (gastric function)	977.8	E858.8	E947.8	E950.4	E962.0	E980.4
ethyl	980.0	E860.1	—	E950.9	E962.1	E980.9
beverage	980.0	E860.0	E947.8	E950.9	E962.1	E980.9
grain	980.0	E860.1	—	E950.9	E962.1	E980.9
beverage	980.0	E860.0	E947.8	E950.9	E962.1	E980.9
industrial	980.9	E860.9	—	E950.9	E962.1	E980.9
isopropyl	980.2	E860.3	—	E950.9	E962.1	E980.9
methyl	980.1	E860.2	—	E950.9	E962.1	E980.9
preparation for consumption	980.0	E860.0	E947.8	E950.9	E962.1	E980.9
propyl	980.3	E860.4	—	E950.9	E962.1	E980.9
secondary	980.2	E860.3	—	E950.9	E962.1	E980.9
radiator	980.1	E860.2	—	E950.9	E962.1	E980.9
rubbing	980.2	E860.3	—	E950.9	E962.1	E980.9
specified type NEC	980.8	E860.8	—	E950.9	E962.1	E980.9
surgical	980.9	E860.9	—	E950.9	E962.1	E980.9
vapor (from any type of alcohol)	987.8	E869.8	—	E952.8	E962.2	E982.8
wood	980.1	E860.2	—	E950.9	E962.1	E980.9
Alcuronium chloride	975.2	E858.6	E945.2	E950.4	E962.0	E980.4
Aldactone	974.4	E858.5	E944.4	E950.4	E962.0	E980.4
Aldicarb	989.3	E863.2	—	E950.6	E962.1	E980.7
Aldomet	972.6	E858.3	E942.6	E950.4	E962.0	E980.4
Aldosterone	962.0	E858.0	E932.0	E950.4	E962.0	E980.4
Aldrin (dust)	989.2	E863.0	—	E950.6	E962.1	E980.7
Algeldrate	973.0	E858.4	E943.0	E950.4	E962.0	E980.4
Alidase	963.4	E858.1	E933.4	E950.4	E962.0	E980.4
Aliphatic thiocyanates	989.0	E866.8	—	E950.9	E962.1	E980.9
Alkaline antiseptic solution (aromatic)	976.6	E858.7	E946.6	E950.4	E962.0	E980.4
Alkalinizing agents (medicinal)	963.3	E858.1	E933.3	E950.4	E962.0	E980.4
Alkalis, caustic	983.2	E864.2	—	E950.7	E962.1	E980.6
Alkalizing agents (medicinal)	963.3	E858.1	E933.3	E950.4	E962.0	E980.4
Alka–seltzer	965.1	E850.3	E935.3	E950.0	E962.0	E980.0
Alkavervir	972.6	E858.3	E942.6	E950.4	E962.0	E980.4
Allegron	969.0	E854.0	E939.0	E950.3	E962.0	E980.3
Alleve *see* Naproxen						
Allobarbital, allobarbitone	967.0	E851	E937.0	E950.1	E962.0	E980.1
Allopurinol	974.7	E858.5	E944.7	E950.4	E962.0	E980.4
Allylestrenol	962.2	E858.0	E932.2	E950.4	E962.0	E980.4
Allylisopropylacetylurea	967.8	E852.8	E937.8	E950.2	E962.0	E980.2
Allylisopropylmalonylurea	967.0	E851	E937.0	E950.1	E962.0	E980.1
Allyltribromide	967.3	E852.2	E937.3	E950.2	E962.0	E980.2
Aloe, aloes, aloin	973.1	E858.4	E943.1	E950.4	E962.0	E980.4
Aloxidone	966.0	E855.0	E936.0	E950.4	E962.0	E980.4
Aloxiprin	965.1	E850.3	E935.3	E950.0	E962.0	E980.0
Alpha amylase	963.4	E858.1	E933.4	E950.4	E962.0	E980.4
Alphaprodine (hydrochloride)	965.09	E850.2	E935.2	E950.0	E962.0	E980.0
Alpha tocopherol	963.5	E858.1	E933.5	E950.4	E962.0	E980.4
Alseroxylon	972.6	E858.3	E942.6	E950.4	E962.0	E980.4
Alum (ammonium) (potassium)	983.2	E864.2	—	E950.7	E962.1	E980.6
medicinal (astringent) NEC	976.2	E858.7	E946.2	E950.4	E962.0	E980.4
Aluminium, aluminum (gel) (hydroxide)	973.0	E858.4	E943.0	E950.4	E962.0	E980.4
acetate solution	976.2	E858.7	E946.2	E950.4	E962.0	E980.4
aspirin	965.1	E850.3	E935.3	E950.0	E962.0	E980.0

Substance	Poisoning	External Cause (E-Code)				
		Accident	Therapeutic Use	Suicide Attempt	Assault	Undetermined
carbonate	973.0	E858.4	E943.0	E950.4	E962.0	E980.4
glycinate	973.0	E858.4	E943.0	E950.4	E962.0	E980.4
nicotinate	972.2	E858.3	E942.2	E950.4	E962.0	E980.4
ointment (surgical) (topical)	976.3	E858.7	E946.3	E950.4	E962.0	E980.4
phosphate	973.0	E858.4	E943.0	E950.4	E962.0	E980.4
subacetate	976.2	E858.7	E946.2	E950.4	E962.0	E980.4
topical NEC	976.3	E858.7	E946.3	E950.4	E962.0	E980.4
Alurate	967.0	E851	E937.0	E950.1	E962.0	E980.1
Alverine (citrate)	975.1	E858.6	E945.1	E950.4	E962.0	E980.4
Alvodine	965.09	E850.2	E935.2	E950.0	E962.0	E980.0
Amanita phalloides	988.1	E865.5	—	E950.9	E962.1	E980.9
Amantadine (hydrochloride)	966.4	E855.0	E936.4	E950.4	E962.0	E980.4
Ambazone	961.9	E857	E931.9	E950.4	E962.0	E980.4
Ambenonium	971.0	E855.3	E941.0	E950.4	E962.0	E980.4
Ambutonium bromide	971.1	E855.4	E941.1	E950.4	E962.0	E980.4
Ametazole	977.8	E858.8	E947.8	E950.4	E962.0	E980.4
Amethocaine (infiltration) (topical)	968.5	E855.2	E938.5	E950.4	E962.0	E980.4
nerve block (peripheral) (plexus)	968.6	E855.2	E938.6	E950.4	E962.0	E980.4
spinal	968.7	E855.2	E938.7	E950.4	E962.0	E980.4
Amethopterin	963.1	E858.1	E933.1	E950.4	E962.0	E980.4
Amfepramone	977.0	E858.8	E947.0	E950.4	E962.0	E980.4
Amidon	965.02	E850.1	E935.1	E950.0	E962.0	E980.0
Amidopyrine	965.5	E850.5	E935.5	E950.0	E962.0	E980.0
Aminacrine	976.0	E858.7	E946.0	E950.4	E962.0	E980.4
Aminitrozole	961.5	E857	E931.5	E950.4	E962.0	E980.4
Aminoacetic acid	974.5	E858.5	E944.5	E950.4	E962.0	E980.4
Amino acids	974.5	E858.5	E944.5	E950.4	E962.0	E980.4
Aminocaproic acid	964.4	E858.2	E934.4	E950.4	E962.0	E980.4
Aminoethylisothiourium	963.8	E858.1	E933.8	E950.4	E962.0	E980.4
Aminoglutethimide	966.3	E855.0	E936.3	E950.4	E962.0	E980.4
Aminometradine	974.3	E858.5	E944.3	E950.4	E962.0	E980.4
Aminopentamide	971.1	E855.4	E941.1	E950.4	E962.0	E980.4
Aminophenazone	965.5	E850.5	E935.5	E950.0	E962.0	E980.0
Aminophenol	983.0	E864.0	—	E950.7	E962.1	E980.6
Aminophenylpyridone	969.5	E853.8	E939.5	E950.3	E962.0	E980.3
Aminophyllin	975.7	E858.6	E945.7	E950.4	E962.0	E980.4
Aminopterin	963.1	E858.1	E933.1	E950.4	E962.0	E980.4
Aminopyrine	965.5	E850.5	E935.5	E950.0	E962.0	E980.0
Aminosalicylic acid	961.8	E857	E931.8	E950.4	E962.0	E980.4
Amiphenazole	970.1	E854.3	E940.1	E950.4	E962.0	E980.4
Amiquinsin	972.6	E858.3	E942.6	E950.4	E962.0	E980.4
Amisometradine	974.3	E858.5	E944.3	E950.4	E962.0	E980.4
Amitriptyline	969.0	E854.0	E939.0	E950.3	E962.0	E980.3
Ammonia (fumes) (gas) (vapor)	987.8	E869.8	—	E952.8	E962.2	E982.8
liquid (household) NEC	983.2	E861.4	—	E950.7	E962.1	E980.6
spirit, aromatic	970.8	E854.3	E940.8	E950.4	E962.0	E980.4
Ammoniated mercury	976.0	E858.7	E946.0	E950.4	E962.0	E980.4
Ammonium						
carbonate	983.2	E864.2	—	E950.7	E962.1	E980.6
chloride (acidifying agent)	963.2	E858.1	E933.2	E950.4	E962.0	E980.4
expectorant	975.5	E858.6	E945.5	E950.4	E962.0	E980.4
compounds (household) NEC	983.2	E861.4	—	E950.7	E962.1	E980.6
fumes (any usage)	987.8	E869.8	—	E952.8	E962.2	E982.8
industrial	983.2	E864.2	—	E950.7	E962.1	E980.6
ichthyosulfonate	976.4	E858.7	E946.4	E950.4	E962.0	E980.4
mandelate	961.9	E857	E931.9	E950.4	E962.0	E980.4
Amobarbital	967.0	E851	E937.0	E950.1	E962.0	E980.1

Substance	Poisoning	Accident	Therapeutic Use	Suicide Attempt	Assault	Undetermined
			External Cause (E-Code)			
Amodiaquin(e)	961.4	E857	E931.4	E950.4	E962.0	E980.4
Amopyroquin(e)	961.4	E857	E931.4	E950.4	E962.0	E980.4
Amphenidone	969.5	E853.8	E939.5	E950.3	E962.0	E980.3
Amphetamine	969.7	E854.2	E939.7	E950.3	E962.0	E980.3
Amphomycin	960.8	E856	E930.8	E950.4	E962.0	E980.4
Amphotericin B	960.1	E856	E930.1	E950.4	E962.0	E980.4
topical	976.0	E858.7	E946.0	E950.4	E962.0	E980.4
Ampicillin	960.0	E856	E930.0	E950.4	E962.0	E980.4
Amprotropine	971.1	E855.4	E941.1	E950.4	E962.0	E980.4
Amygdalin	977.8	E858.8	E947.8	E950.4	E962.0	E980.4
Amyl						
acetate (vapor)	982.8	E862.4	—	E950.9	E962.1	E980.9
alcohol	980.3	E860.4	—	E950.9	E962.1	E980.9
nitrite (medicinal)	972.4	E858.3	E942.4	E950.4	E962.0	E980.4
Amylase (alpha)	963.4	E858.1	E933.4	E950.4	E962.0	E980.4
Amylene hydrate	980.8	E860.8	—	E950.9	E962.1	E980.9
Amylobarbitone	967.0	E851	E937.0	E950.1	E962.0	E980.1
Amylocaine	968.9	E855.2	E938.9	E950.4	E962.0	E980.4
infiltration (subcutaneous)	968.5	E855.2	E938.5	E950.4	E962.0	E980.4
nerve block (peripheral) (plexus)	968.6	E855.2	E938.6	E950.4	E962.0	E980.4
spinal	968.7	E855.2	E938.7	E950.4	E962.0	E980.4
topical (surface)	968.5	E855.2	E938.5	E950.4	E962.0	E980.4
Amytal (sodium)	967.0	E851	E937.0	E950.1	E962.0	E980.1
Analeptics	970.0	E854.3	E940.0	E950.4	E962.0	E980.4
Analgesics	965.9	E850.9	E935.9	E950.0	E962.0	E980.0
aromatic NEC	965.4	E850.4	E935.4	E950.0	E962.0	E980.0
non–narcotic NEC	965.7	E850.7	E935.7	E950.0	E962.0	E980.0
specified NEC	965.8	E850.8	E935.8	E950.0	E962.0	E980.0
Anamirta cocculus	988.2	E865.3	—	E950.9	E962.1	E980.9
Ancillin	960.0	E856	E930.0	E950.4	E962.0	E980.4
Androgens (anabolic congeners)	962.1	E858.0	E932.1	E950.4	E962.0	E980.4
Androstalone	962.1	E858.0	E932.1	E950.4	E962.0	E980.4
Androsterone	962.1	E858.0	E932.1	E950.4	E962.0	E980.4
Anemone pulsatilla	988.2	E865.4	—	E950.9	E962.1	E980.9
Anesthesia, anesthetic (general) NEC	968.4	E855.1	E938.4	E950.4	E962.0	E980.4
block (nerve) (plexus)	968.6	E855.2	E938.6	E950.4	E962.0	E980.4
gaseous NEC	968.2	E855.1	E938.2	E950.4	E962.0	E980.4
halogenated hydrocarbon derivatives NEC	968.2	E855.1	E938.2	E950.4	E962.0	E980.4
infiltration (intradermal) (subcutaneous) (submucosal)	968.5	E855.2	E938.5	E950.4	E962.0	E980.4
intravenous	968.3	E855.1	E938.3	E950.4	E962.0	E980.4
local NEC	968.9	E855.2	E938.9	E950.4	E962.0	E980.4
nerve blocking (peripheral) (plexus)	968.6	E855.2	E938.6	E950.4	E962.0	E980.4
rectal NEC	968.3	E855.1	E938.3	E950.4	E962.0	E980.4
spinal	968.7	E855.2	E938.7	E950.4	E962.0	E980.4
surface	968.5	E855.2	E938.5	E950.4	E962.0	E980.4
topical	968.5	E855.2	E938.5	E950.4	E962.0	E980.4
Aneurine	963.5	E858.1	E933.5	E950.4	E962.0	E980.4
Angio–Conray	977.8	E858.8	E947.8	E950.4	E962.0	E980.4
Angininesee Glyceryl trinitrate						
Angiotensin	971.2	E855.5	E941.2	E950.4	E962.0	E980.4
Anhydrohydroxyprogesterone	962.2	E858.0	E932.2	E950.4	E962.0	E980.4
Anhydron	974.3	E858.5	E944.3	E950.4	E962.0	E980.4
Anileridine	965.09	E850.2	E935.2	E950.0	E962.0	E980.0
Aniline (dye) (liquid)	983.0	E864.0	—	E950.7	E962.1	E980.6
analgesic	965.4	E850.4	E935.4	E950.0	E962.0	E980.0

Substance	Poisoning	External Cause (E-Code)				
		Accident	Therapeutic Use	Suicide Attempt	Assault	Undetermined
derivatives, therapeutic NEC	965.4	E850.4	E935.4	E950.0	E962.0	E980.0
vapor	987.8	E869.8	—	E952.8	E962.2	E982.8
Anisindione	964.2	E858.2	E934.2	E950.4	E962.0	E980.4
Anisotropine	971.1	E855.4	E941.1	E950.4	E962.0	E980.4
Anorexic agents	977.0	E858.8	E947.0	E950.4	E962.0	E980.4
Ant (bite) (sting)	989.5	E905.5	—	E950.9	E962.1	E980.9
Antabuse	977.3	E858.8	E947.3	E950.4	E962.0	E980.4
Antacids	973.0	E858.4	E943.0	E950.4	E962.0	E980.4
Antazoline	963.0	E858.1	E933.0	E950.4	E962.0	E980.4
Anthelmintics	961.6	E857	E931.6	E950.4	E962.0	E980.4
Anthralin	976.4	E858.7	E946.4	E950.4	E962.0	E980.4
Anthramycin	960.7	E856	E930.7	E950.4	E962.0	E980.4
Antiadrenergics	971.3	E855.6	E941.3	E950.4	E962.0	E980.4
Antiallergic agents	963.0	E858.1	E933.0	E950.4	E962.0	E980.4
Antianemic agents NEC	964.1	E858.2	E934.1	E950.4	E962.0	E980.4
Antiaris toxicaria	988.2	E865.4	—	E950.9	E962.1	E980.9
Antiarteriosclerotic agents	972.2	E858.3	E942.2	E950.4	E962.0	E980.4
Antiasthmatics	975.7	E858.6	E945.7	E950.4	E962.0	E980.4
Antibiotics	960.9	E856	E930.9	E950.4	E962.0	E980.4
antifungal	960.1	E856	E930.1	E950.4	E962.0	E980.4
antimycobacterial	960.6	E856	E930.6	E950.4	E962.0	E980.4
antineoplastic	960.7	E856	E930.7	E950.4	E962.0	E980.4
cephalosporin (group)	960.5	E856	E930.5	E950.4	E962.0	E980.4
chloramphenicol (group)	960.2	E856	E930.2	E950.4	E962.0	E980.4
macrolides	960.3	E856	E930.3	E950.4	E962.0	E980.4
specified NEC	960.8	E856	E930.8	E950.4	E962.0	E980.4
tetracycline (group)	960.4	E856	E930.4	E950.4	E962.0	E980.4
Anticancer agents NEC	963.1	E858.1	E933.1	E950.4	E962.0	E980.4
antibiotics	960.7	E856	E930.7	E950.4	E962.0	E980.4
Anticholinergics	971.1	E855.4	E941.1	E950.4	E962.0	E980.4
Anticholinesterase (organophosphorus) (reversible)	971.0	E855.3	E941.0	E950.4	E962.0	E980.4
Anticoagulants	964.2	E858.2	E934.2	E950.4	E962.0	E980.4
antagonists	964.5	E858.2	E934.5	E950.4	E962.0	E980.4
Anti–common cold agents NEC	975.6	E858.6	E945.6	E950.4	E962.0	E980.4
Anticonvulsants NEC	966.3	E855.0	E936.3	E950.4	E962.0	E980.4
Antidepressants	969.0	E854.0	E939.0	E950.3	E962.0	E980.3
Antidiabetic agents	962.3	E858.0	E932.3	E950.4	E962.0	E980.4
Antidiarrheal agents	973.5	E858.4	E943.5	E950.4	E962.0	E980.4
Antidiuretic hormone	962.5	E858.0	E932.5	E950.4	E962.0	E980.4
Antidotes NEC	977.2	E858.8	E947.2	E950.4	E962.0	E980.4
Antiemetic agents	963.0	E858.1	E933.0	E950.4	E962.0	E980.4
Antiepilepsy agent NEC	966.3	E855.0	E936.3	E950.4	E962.0	E980.4
Antifertility pills	962.2	E858.0	E932.2	E950.4	E962.0	E980.4
Antiflatulents	973.8	E858.4	E943.8	E950.4	E962.0	E980.4
Antifreeze	989.89	E866.8	—	E950.9	E962.1	E980.9
alcohol	980.1	E860.2	—	E950.9	E962.1	E980.9
ethylene glycol	982.8	E862.4	—	E950.9	E962.1	E980.9
Antifungals (nonmedicinal) (sprays)	989.4	E863.6	—	E950.6	E962.1	E980.7
medicinal NEC	961.9	E857	E931.9	E950.4	E962.0	E980.4
antibiotic	960.1	E856	E930.1	E950.4	E962.0	E980.4
topical	976.0	E858.7	E946.0	E950.4	E962.0	E980.4
Antigastric secretion agents	973.0	E858.4	E943.0	E950.4	E962.0	E980.4
Antihelmintics	961.6	E857	E931.6	E950.4	E962.0	E980.4
Antihemophilic factor (human)	964.7	E858.2	E934.7	E950.4	E962.0	E980.4
Antihistamine	963.0	E858.1	E933.0	E950.4	E962.0	E980.4
Antihypertensive agents NEC	972.6	E858.3	E942.6	E950.4	E962.0	E980.4

Substance	Poisoning	Accident	Therapeutic Use	Suicide Attempt	Assault	Undetermined
Anti–infectives NEC	961.9	E857	E931.9	E950.4	E962.0	E980.4
antibiotics	960.9	E856	E930.9	E950.4	E962.0	E980.4
specified NEC	960.8	E856	E930.8	E950.4	E962.0	E980.4
antihelmintic	961.6	E857	E931.6	E950.4	E962.0	E980.4
antimalarial	961.4	E857	E931.4	E950.4	E962.0	E980.4
antimycobacterial NEC	961.8	E857	E931.8	E950.4	E962.0	E980.4
antibiotics	960.6	E856	E930.6	E950.4	E962.0	E980.4
antiprotozoal NEC	961.5	E857	E931.5	E950.4	E962.0	E980.4
blood	961.4	E857	E931.4	E950.4	E962.0	E980.4
antiviral	961.7	E857	E931.7	E950.4	E962.0	E980.4
arsenical	961.1	E857	E931.1	E950.4	E962.0	E980.4
ENT agents	976.6	E858.7	E946.6	E950.4	E962.0	E980.4
heavy metals NEC	961.2	E857	E931.2	E950.4	E962.0	E980.4
local	976.0	E858.7	E946.0	E950.4	E962.0	E980.4
ophthalmic preparation	976.5	E858.7	E946.5	E950.4	E962.0	E980.4
topical NEC	976.0	E858.7	E946.0	E950.4	E962.0	E980.4
Anti–inflammatory agents (topical)	976.0	E858.7	E946.0	E950.4	E962.0	E980.4
Antiknock (tetraethyl lead)	984.1	E862.1	—	E950.9	E962.1	E980.9
Antilipemics	972.2	E858.3	E942.2	E950.4	E962.0	E980.4
Antimalarials	961.4	E857	E931.4	E950.4	E962.0	E980.4
Antimony (compounds) (vapor) NEC	985.4	E866.2	—	E950.9	E962.1	E980.9
anti–infectives	961.2	E857	E931.2	E950.4	E962.0	E980.4
pesticides (vapor)	985.4	E863.4	—	E950.6	E962.2	E980.7
potassium tartrate	961.2	E857	E931.2	E950.4	E962.0	E980.4
tartrated	961.2	E857	E931.2	E950.4	E962.0	E980.4
Antimuscarinic agents	971.1	E855.4	E941.1	E950.4	E962.0	E980.4
Antimycobacterials NEC	961.8	E857	E931.8	E950.4	E962.0	E980.4
antibiotics	960.6	E856	E930.6	E950.4	E962.0	E980.4
Antineoplastic agents	963.1	E858.1	E933.1	E950.4	E962.0	E980.4
antibiotics	960.7	E856	E930.7	E950.4	E962.0	E980.4
Anti–Parkinsonism agents	966.4	E855.0	E936.4	E950.4	E962.0	E980.4
Antiphlogistics	965.69	E850.6	E935.6	E950.0	E962.0	E980.0
Antiprotozoals NEC	961.5	E857	E931.5	E950.4	E962.0	E980.4
blood	961.4	E857	E931.4	E950.4	E962.0	E980.4
Antipruritics (local)	976.1	E858.7	E946.1	E950.4	E962.0	E980.4
Antipsychotic agents NEC	969.3	E853.8	E939.3	E950.3	E962.0	E980.3
Antipyretics	965.9	E850.9	E935.9	E950.0	E962.0	E980.0
specified NEC	965.8	E850.8	E935.8	E950.0	E962.0	E980.0
Antipyrine	965.5	E850.5	E935.5	E950.0	E962.0	E980.0
Antirabies serum (equine)	979.9	E858.8	E949.9	E950.4	E962.0	E980.4
Antirheumatics	965.69	E850.6	E935.6	E950.0	E962.0	E980.0
Antiseborrheics	976.4	E858.7	E946.4	E950.4	E962.0	E980.4
Antiseptics (external) (medicinal)	976.0	E858.7	E946.0	E950.4	E962.0	E980.4
Antistine	963.0	E858.1	E933.0	E950.4	E962.0	E980.4
Antithyroid agents	962.8	E858.0	E932.8	E950.4	E962.0	E980.4
Antitoxin, any	979.9	E858.8	E949.9	E950.4	E962.0	E980.4
Antituberculars	961.8	E857	E931.8	E950.4	E962.0	E980.4
antibiotics	960.6	E856	E930.6	E950.4	E962.0	E980.4
Antitussives	975.4	E858.6	E945.5	E950.4	E962.0	E980.4
Antivaricose agents (sclerosing)	972.7	E858.3	E942.7	E950.4	E962.0	E980.4
Antivenin (crotaline) (spider–bite)	979.9	E858.8	E949.9	E950.4	E962.0	E980.4
Antivert	963.0	E858.1	E933.0	E950.4	E962.0	E980.4
Antivirals NEC	961.7	E857	E931.7	E950.4	E962.0	E980.4
Ant poisons — *see* Pesticides						
Antrol	989.4	E863.4	—	E950.6	E962.1	E980.7
fungicide	989.4	E863.6	—	E950.6	E962.1	E980.7
Apomorphine hydrochloride (emetic)	973.6	E858.4	E943.6	E950.4	E962.0	E980.4

Substance	Poisoning	Accident	Therapeutic Use	Suicide Attempt	Assault	Undetermined
Appetite depressants, central	977.0	E858.8	E947.0	E950.4	E962.0	E980.4
Apresoline	972.6	E858.3	E942.6	E950.4	E962.0	E980.4
Aprobarbital, aprobarbitone	967.0	E851	E937.0	E950.1	E962.0	E980.1
Apronalide	967.8	E852.8	E937.8	E950.2	E962.0	E980.2
Aqua fortis	983.1	E864.1	—	E950.7	E962.1	E980.6
Arachis oil (topical)	976.3	E858.7	E946.3	E950.4	E962.0	E980.4
cathartic	973.2	E858.4	E943.2	E950.4	E962.0	E980.4
Aralen	961.4	E857	E931.4	E950.4	E962.0	E980.4
Arginine salts	974.5	E858.5	E944.5	E950.4	E962.0	E980.4
Argyrol	976.0	E858.7	E946.0	E950.4	E962.0	E980.4
ENT agent	976.6	E858.7	E946.6	E950.4	E962.0	E980.4
ophthalmic preparation	976.5	E858.7	E946.5	E950.4	E962.0	E980.4
Aristocort	962.0	E858.0	E932.0	E950.4	E962.0	E980.4
ENT agent	976.6	E858.7	E946.6	E950.4	E962.0	E980.4
ophthalmic preparation	976.5	E858.7	E946.5	E950.4	E962.0	E980.4
topical NEC	976.0	E858.7	E946.0	E950.4	E962.0	E980.4
Aromatics, corrosive	983.0	E864.0	—	E950.7	E962.1	E980.6
disinfectants	983.0	E861.4	—	E950.7	E962.1	E980.6
Arsenate of lead (insecticide)	985.1	E863.4	—	E950.8	E962.1	E980.8
herbicide	985.1	E863.5	—	E950.8	E962.1	E980.8
Arsenic, arsenicals (compounds) (dust) (fumes) (vapor) NEC	985.1	E866.3	—	E950.8	E962.1	E980.8
anti–infectives	961.1	E857	E931.1	E950.4	E962.0	E980.4
pesticide (dust) (fumes)	985.1	E863.4	—	E950.8	E962.1	E980.8
Arsine (gas)	985.1	E866.3	—	E950.8	E962.1	E980.8
Arsphenamine (silver)	961.1	E857	E931.1	E950.4	E962.0	E980.4
Arsthinol	961.1	E857	E931.1	E950.4	E962.0	E980.4
Artane	971.1	E855.4	E941.1	E950.4	E962.0	E980.4
Arthropod (venomous) NEC	989.5	E905.5	—	E950.9	E962.1	E980.9
Asbestos	989.81	E866.8	—	E950.9	E962.1	E980.9
Ascaridole	961.6	E857	E931.6	E950.4	E962.0	E980.4
Ascorbic acid	963.5	E858.1	E933.5	E950.4	E962.0	E980.4
Asiaticoside	976.0	E858.7	E946.0	E950.4	E962.0	E980.4
Aspidium (oleoresin)	961.6	E857	E931.6	E950.4	E962.0	E980.4
Aspirin	965.1	E850.3	E935.3	E950.0	E962.0	E980.0
Astringents (local)	976.2	E858.7	E946.2	E950.4	E962.0	E980.4
Atabrine	961.3	E857	E931.3	E950.4	E962.0	E980.4
Ataractics	969.5	E853.8	E939.5	E950.3	E962.0	E980.3
Atonia drug, intestinal	973.3	E858.4	E943.3	E950.4	E962.0	E980.4
Atophan	974.7	E858.5	E944.7	E950.4	E962.0	E980.4
Atropine	971.1	E855.4	E941.1	E950.4	E962.0	E980.4
Attapulgite	973.5	E858.4	E943.5	E950.4	E962.0	E980.4
Attenuvax	979.4	E858.8	E949.4	E950.4	E962.0	E980.4
Aureomycin	960.4	E856	E930.4	E950.4	E962.0	E980.4
ophthalmic preparation	976.5	E858.7	E946.5	E950.4	E962.0	E980.4
topical NEC	976.0	E858.7	E946.0	E950.4	E962.0	E980.4
Aurothioglucose	965.69	E850.6	E935.6	E950.0	E962.0	E980.0
Aurothioglycanide	965.69	E850.6	E935.6	E950.0	E962.0	E980.0
Aurothiomalate	965.69	E850.6	E935.6	E950.0	E962.0	E980.0
Automobile fuel	981	E862.1	—	E950.9	E962.1	E980.9
Autonomic nervous system agents NEC	971.9	E855.9	E941.9	E950.4	E962.0	E980.4
Avlosulfon	961.8	E857	E931.8	E950.4	E962.0	E980.4
Avomine	967.8	E852.8	E937.8	E950.2	E962.0	E980.2
Azacyclonol	969.5	E853.8	E939.5	E950.3	E962.0	E980.3
Azapetine	971.3	E855.6	E941.3	E950.4	E962.0	E980.4
Azaribine	963.1	E858.1	E933.1	E950.4	E962.0	E980.4
Azaserine	960.7	E856	E930.7	E950.4	E962.0	E980.4

Substance	Poisoning	External Cause (E-Code)				
		Accident	Therapeutic Use	Suicide Attempt	Assault	Undetermined
Azathioprine	963.1	E858.1	E933.1	E950.4	E962.0	E980.4
Azosulfamide	961.0	E857	E931.0	E950.4	E962.0	E980.4
Azulfidine	961.0	E857	E931.0	E950.4	E962.0	E980.4
Azuresin	977.8	E858.8	E947.8	E950.4	E962.0	E980.4
Bacimycin	976.0	E858.7	E946.0	E950.4	E962.0	E980.4
ophthalmic preparation	976.5	E858.7	E946.5	E950.4	E962.0	E980.4
Bacitracin	960.8	E856	E930.8	E950.4	E962.0	E980.4
ENT agent	976.6	E858.7	E946.6	E950.4	E962.0	E980.4
ophthalmic preparation	976.5	E858.7	E946.5	E950.4	E962.0	E980.4
topical NEC	976.0	E858.7	E946.0	E950.4	E962.0	E980.4
Baking soda	963.3	E858.1	E933.3	E950.4	E962.0	E980.4
BAL	963.8	E858.1	E933.8	E950.4	E962.0	E980.4
Bamethan (sulfate)	972.5	E858.3	E942.5	E950.4	E962.0	E980.4
Bamipine	963.0	E858.1	E933.0	E950.4	E962.0	E980.4
Baneberry	988.2	E865.4	—	E950.9	E962.1	E980.9
Banewort	988.2	E865.4	—	E950.9	E962.1	E980.9
Barbenyl	967.0	E851	E937.0	E950.1	E962.0	E980.1
Barbital, barbitone	967.0	E851	E937.0	E950.1	E962.0	E980.1
Barbiturates, barbituric acid	967.0	E851	E937.0	E950.1	E962.0	E980.1
anesthetic (intravenous)	968.3	E855.1	E938.3	E950.4	E962.0	E980.4
Barium (carbonate) (chloride) (sulfate)	985.8	E866.4	—	E950.9	E962.1	E980.9
diagnostic agent	977.8	E858.8	E947.8	E950.4	E962.0	E980.4
pesticide	985.8	E863.4	—	E950.6	E962.1	E980.7
rodenticide	985.8	E863.7	—	E950.6	E962.1	E980.7
Barrier cream	976.3	E858.7	E946.3	E950.4	E962.0	E980.4
Battery acid or fluid	983.1	E864.1	—	E950.7	E962.1	E980.6
Bay rum	980.8	E860.8	—	E950.9	E962.1	E980.9
BCG vaccine	978.0	E858.8	E948.0	E950.4	E962.0	E980.4
Bearsfoot	988.2	E865.4	—	E950.9	E962.1	E980.9
Beclamide	966.3	E855.0	E936.3	E950.4	E962.0	E980.4
Bee (sting) (venom)	989.5	E905.3	—	E950.9	E962.1	E980.9
Belladonna (alkaloids)	971.1	E855.4	E941.1	E950.4	E962.0	E980.4
Bemegride	970.0	E854.3	E940.0	E950.4	E962.0	E980.4
Benactyzine	969.8	E855.8	E939.8	E950.3	E962.0	E980.3
Benadryl	963.0	E858.1	E933.0	E950.4	E962.0	E980.4
Bendrofluazide	974.3	E858.5	E944.3	E950.4	E962.0	E980.4
Bendroflumethiazide	974.3	E858.5	E944.3	E950.4	E962.0	E980.4
Benemid	974.7	E858.5	E944.7	E950.4	E962.0	E980.4
Benethamine penicillin G	960.0	E856	E930.0	E950.4	E962.0	E980.4
Benisone	976.0	E858.7	E946.0	E950.4	E962.0	E980.4
Benoquin	976.8	E858.7	E946.8	E950.4	E962.0	E980.4
Benoxinate	968.5	E855.2	E938.5	E950.4	E962.0	E980.4
Bentonite	976.3	E858.7	E946.3	E950.4	E962.0	E980.4
Benzalkonium (chloride)	976.0	E858.7	E946.0	E950.4	E962.0	E980.4
ophthalmic preparation	976.5	E858.7	E946.5	E950.4	E962.0	E980.4
Benzamidosalicylate (calcium)	961.8	E857	E931.8	E950.4	E962.0	E980.4
Benzathine penicillin	960.0	E856	E930.0	E950.4	E962.0	E980.4
Benzcarbimine	963.1	E858.1	E933.1	E950.4	E962.0	E980.4
Benzedrex	971.2	E855.5	E941.2	E950.4	E962.0	E980.4
Benzedrine (amphetamine)	969.7	E854.2	E939.7	E950.3	E962.0	E980.3
Benzene (acetyl) (dimethyl) (methyl) (solvent) (vapor)	982.0	E862.4	—	E950.9	E962.1	E980.9
hexachloride (gamma) (insecticide) (vapor)	989.2	E863.0	—	E950.6	E962.1	E980.7
Benzethonium	976.0	E858.7	E946.0	E950.4	E962.0	E980.4
Benzhexol (chloride)	966.4	E855.0	E936.4	E950.4	E962.0	E980.4
Benzilonium	971.1	E855.4	E941.1	E950.4	E962.0	E980.4

Substance	Poisoning	External Cause (E-Code)				
		Accident	Therapeutic Use	Suicide Attempt	Assault	Undetermined
Benzin(e) — *see* Ligroin						
Benziodarone	972.4	E858.3	E942.4	E950.4	E962.0	E980.4
Benzocaine	968.5	E855.2	E938.5	E950.4	E962.0	E980.4
Benzodiapin	969.4	E853.2	E939.4	E950.3	E962.0	E980.3
Benzodiazepines (tranquilizers) NEC	969.4	E853.2	E939.4	E950.3	E962.0	E980.3
Benzoic acid (with salicylic acid) (anti–infective)	976.0	E858.7	E946.0	E950.4	E962.0	E980.4
Benzoin	976.3	E858.7	E946.3	E950.4	E962.0	E980.4
Benzol (vapor)	982.0	E862.4	—	E950.9	E962.1	E980.9
Benzomorphan	965.09	E850.2	E935.2	E950.0	E962.0	E980.0
Benzonatate	975.4	E858.6	E945.4	E950.4	E962.0	E980.4
Benzothiadiazides	974.3	E858.5	E944.3	E950.4	E962.0	E980.4
Benzoylpas	961.8	E857	E931.8	E950.4	E962.0	E980.4
Benzperidol	969.5	E853.8	E939.5	E950.3	E962.0	E980.3
Benzphetamine	977.0	E858.8	E947.0	E950.4	E962.0	E980.4
Benzpyrinium	971.0	E855.3	E941.0	E950.4	E962.0	E980.4
Benzquinamide	963.0	E858.1	E933.0	E950.4	E962.0	E980.4
Benzthiazide	974.3	E858.5	E944.3	E950.4	E962.0	E980.4
Benztropine	971.1	E855.4	E941.1	E950.4	E962.0	E980.4
Benzyl						
acetate	982.8	E862.4	—	E950.9	E962.1	E980.9
benzoate (anti–infective)	976.0	E858.7	E946.0	E950.4	E962.0	E980.4
morphine	965.09	E850.2	E935.2	E950.0	E962.0	E980.0
penicillin	960.0	E856	E930.0	E950.4	E962.0	E980.4
Bephenium hydroxynapthoate	961.6	E857	E931.6	E950.4	E962.0	E980.4
Bergamot oil	989.89	E866.8	—	E950.9	E962.1	E980.9
Berries, poisonous	988.2	E865.3	—	E950.9	E962.1	E980.9
Beryllium (compounds) (fumes)	985.3	E866.4	—	E950.9	E962.1	E980.9
Beta–carotene	976.3	E858.7	E946.3	E950.4	E962.0	E980.4
Beta–Chlor	967.1	E852.0	E937.1	E950.2	E962.0	E980.2
Betamethasone	962.0	E858.0	E932.0	E950.4	E962.0	E980.4
topical	976.0	E858.7	E946.0	E950.4	E962.0	E980.4
Betazole	977.8	E858.8	E947.8	E950.4	E962.0	E980.4
Bethanechol	971.0	E855.3	E941.0	E950.4	E962.0	E980.4
Bethanidine	972.6	E858.3	E942.6	E950.4	E962.0	E980.4
Betula oil	976.3	E858.7	E946.3	E950.4	E962.0	E980.4
Bhang	969.6	E854.1	E939.6	E950.3	E962.0	E980.3
Bialamicol	961.5	E857	E931.5	E950.4	E962.0	E980.4
Bichloride of mercury — *see* Mercury, chloride						
Bichromates (calcium) (crystals) (potassium) (sodium)	983.9	E864.3	—	E950.7	E962.1	E980.6
fumes	987.8	E869.8	—	E952.8	E962.2	E982.8
Biguanide derivatives, oral	962.3	E858.0	E932.3	E950.4	E962.0	E980.4
Biligrafin	977.8	E858.8	E947.8	E950.4	E962.0	E980.4
Bilopaque	977.8	E858.8	E947.8	E950.4	E962.0	E980.4
Bioflavonoids	972.8	E858.3	E942.8	E950.4	E962.0	E980.4
Biological substance NEC	979.9	E858.8	E949.9	E950.4	E962.0	E980.4
Biperiden	966.4	E855.0	E936.4	E950.4	E962.0	E980.4
Bisacodyl	973.1	E858.4	E943.1	E950.4	E962.0	E980.4
Bishydroxycoumarin	964.2	E858.2	E934.2	E950.4	E962.0	E980.4
Bismarsen	961.1	E857	E931.1	E950.4	E962.0	E980.4
Bismuth (compounds) NEC	985.8	E866.4	—	E950.9	E962.1	E980.9
anti–infectives	961.2	E857	E931.2	E950.4	E962.0	E980.4
subcarbonate	973.5	E858.4	E943.5	E950.4	E962.0	E980.4
sulfarsphenamine	961.1	E857	E931.1	E950.4	E962.0	E980.4
Bithionol	961.6	E857	E931.6	E950.4	E962.0	E980.4

Substance	Poisoning	External Cause (E-Code)				
		Accident	Therapeutic Use	Suicide Attempt	Assault	Undetermined
Bitter almond oil	989.0	E866.8	—	E950.9	E962.1	E980.9
Bittersweet	988.2	E865.4	—	E950.9	E962.1	E980.9
Black						
flag	989.4	E863.4	—	E950.6	E962.1	E980.7
henbane	988.2	E865.4	—	E950.9	E962.1	E980.9
leaf (40)	989.4	E863.4	—	E950.6	E962.1	E980.7
widow spider (bite)	989.5	E905.1	—	E950.9	E962.1	E980.9
antivenin	979.9	E858.8	E949.9	E950.4	E962.0	E980.4
Blast furnace gas (carbon monoxide from)	986	E868.8	—	E952.1	E962.2	E982.1
Bleach NEC	983.9	E864.3	—	E950.7	E962.1	E980.6
Bleaching solutions	983.9	E864.3	—	E950.7	E962.1	E980.6
Bleomycin (sulfate)	960.7	E856	E930.7	E950.4	E962.0	E980.4
Blockain	968.9	E855.2	E938.9	E950.4	E962.0	E980.4
infiltration (subcutaneous)	968.5	E855.2	E938.5	E950.4	E962.0	E980.4
nerve block (peripheral) (plexus)	968.6	E855.2	E938.6	E950.4	E962.0	E980.4
topical (surface)	968.5	E855.2	E938.5	E950.4	E962.0	E980.4
Blood (derivatives) (natural) (plasma)						
(whole)	964.7	E858.2	E934.7	E950.4	E962.0	E980.4
affecting agent	964.9	E858.2	E934.9	E950.4	E962.0	E980.4
specified NEC	964.8	E858.2	E934.8	E950.4	E962.0	E980.4
substitute (macromolecular)	964.8	E858.2	E934.8	E950.4	E962.0	E980.4
Blue velvet	965.09	E850.2	E935.2	E950.0	E962.0	E980.0
Bone meal	989.89	E866.5	—	E950.9	E962.1	E980.9
Bonine	963.0	E858.1	E933.0	E950.4	E962.0	E980.4
Boracic acid	976.0	E858.7	E946.0	E950.4	E962.0	E980.4
ENT agent	976.6	E858.7	E946.6	E950.4	E962.0	E980.4
ophthalmic preparation	976.5	E858.7	E946.5	E950.4	E962.0	E980.4
Borate (cleanser) (sodium)	989.6	E861.3	—	E950.9	E962.1	E980.9
Borax (cleanser)	989.6	E861.3	—	E950.9	E962.1	E980.9
Boric acid	976.0	E858.7	E946.0	E950.4	E962.0	E980.4
ENT agent	976.6	E858.7	E946.6	E950.4	E962.0	E980.4
ophthalmic preparation	976.5	E858.7	E946.5	E950.4	E962.0	E980.4
Boron hydride NEC	989.89	E866.8	—	E950.9	E962.1	E980.9
fumes or gas	987.8	E869.8	—	E952.8	E962.2	E982.8
Brake fluid vapor	987.8	E869.8	—	E952.8	E962.2	E982.8
Brass (compounds) (fumes)	985.8	E866.4	—	E950.9	E962.1	E980.9
Brasso	981	E861.3	—	E950.9	E962.1	E980.9
Bretylium (tosylate)	972.6	E858.3	E942.6	E950.4	E962.0	E980.4
Brevital (sodium)	968.3	E855.1	E938.3	E950.4	E962.0	E980.4
British antilewisite	963.8	E858.1	E933.8	E950.4	E962.0	E980.4
Bromal (hydrate)	967.3	E852.2	E937.3	E950.2	E962.0	E980.2
Bromelains	963.4	E858.1	E933.4	E950.4	E962.0	E980.4
Bromides NEC	967.3	E852.2	E937.3	E950.2	E962.0	E980.2
Bromine (vapor)	987.8	E869.8	—	E952.8	E962.2	E982.8
compounds (medicinal)	967.3	E852.2	E937.3	E950.2	E962.0	E980.2
Bromisovalum	967.3	E852.2	E937.3	E950.2	E962.0	E980.2
Bromobenzyl cyanide	987.5	E869.3	—	E952.8	E962.2	E982.8
Bromodiphenhydramine	963.0	E858.1	E933.0	E950.4	E962.0	E980.4
Bromoform	967.3	E852.2	E937.3	E950.2	E962.0	E980.2
Bromophenol blue reagent	977.8	E858.8	E947.8	E950.4	E962.0	E980.4
Bromosalicylhydroxamic acid	961.8	E857	E931.8	E950.4	E962.0	E980.4
Bromo–seltzer	965.4	E850.4	E935.4	E950.0	E962.0	E980.0
Brompheniramine	963.0	E858.1	E933.0	E950.4	E962.0	E980.4
Bromural	967.3	E852.2	E937.3	E950.2	E962.0	E980.2
Brown spider (bite) (venom)	989.5	E905.1	—	E950.9	E962.1	E980.9
Brucia	988.2	E865.3	—	E950.9	E962.1	E980.9
Brucine	989.1	E863.7	—	E950.6	E962.1	E980.7

Substance	Poisoning	Accident	Therapeutic Use	Suicide Attempt	Assault	Undetermined
Brunswick green — *see* Copper						
Bruten — *see* Ibuperofen						
Bryonia (alba) (dioica)	988.2	E865.4	—	E950.9	E962.1	E980.9
Buclizine	969.5	E853.8	E939.5	E950.3	E962.0	E980.3
Bufferin	965.1	E850.3	E935.3	E950.0	E962.0	E980.0
Bufotenine	969.6	E854.1	E939.6	E950.3	E962.0	E980.3
Buphenine	971.2	E855.5	E941.2	E950.4	E962.0	E980.4
Bupivacaine	968.9	E855.2	E938.9	E950.4	E962.0	E980.4
infiltration (subcutaneous)	968.5	E855.2	E938.5	E950.4	E962.0	E980.4
nerve block (peripheral) (plexus)	968.6	E855.2	E938.6	E950.4	E962.0	E980.4
Busulfan	963.1	E858.1	E933.1	E950.4	E962.0	E980.4
Butabarbital (sodium)	967.0	E851	E937.0	E950.1	E962.0	E980.1
Butabarbitone	967.0	E851	E937.0	E950.1	E962.0	E980.1
Butabarpal	967.0	E851	E937.0	E950.1	E962.0	E980.1
Butacaine	968.5	E855.2	E938.5	E950.4	E962.0	E980.4
Butallylonal	967.0	E851	E937.0	E950.1	E962.0	E980.1
Butane (distributed in mobile container)	987.0	E868.0	—	E951.1	E962.2	E981.1
distributed through pipes	987.0	E867	—	E951.0	E962.2	E981.0
incomplete combustion of — *see*						
Carbon monoxide, butane						
Butanol	980.3	E860.4	—	E950.9	E962.1	E980.9
Butanone	982.8	E862.4	—	E950.9	E962.1	E980.9
Butaperazine	969.1	E853.0	E939.1	E950.3	E962.0	E980.3
Butazolidin	965.5	E850.5	E935.5	E950.0	E962.0	E980.0
Butethal	967.0	E851	E937.0	E950.1	E962.0	E980.1
Butethamate	971.1	E855.4	E941.1	E950.4	E962.0	E980.4
Buthalitone (sodium)	968.3	E855.1	E938.3	E950.4	E962.0	E980.4
Butisol (sodium)	967.0	E851	E937.0	E950.1	E962.0	E980.1
Butobarbital, butobarbitone	967.0	E851	E937.0	E950.1	E962.0	E980.1
Butriptyline	969.0	E854.0	E939.0	E950.3	E962.0	E980.3
Buttercups	988.2	E865.4	—	E950.9	E962.1	E980.9
Butter of antimony — *see* Antimony						
Butyl						
acetate (secondary)	982.8	E862.4	—	E950.9	E962.1	E980.9
alcohol	980.3	E860.4	—	E950.9	E962.1	E980.9
carbinol	980.8	E860.8	—	E950.9	E962.1	E980.9
carbitol	982.8	E862.4	—	E950.9	E962.1	E980.9
cellosolve	982.8	E862.4	—	E950.9	E962.1	E980.9
chloral (hydrate)	967.1	E852.0	E937.1	E950.2	E962.0	E980.2
formate	982.8	E862.4	—	E950.9	E962.1	E980.9
scopolammonium bromide	971.1	E855.4	E941.1	E950.4	E962.0	E980.4
Butyn	968.5	E855.2	E938.5	E950.4	E962.0	E980.4
Butyrophenone (–based tranquilizers)	969.2	E853.1	E939.2	E950.3	E962.0	E980.3
Cacodyl, cacodylic acid — *see* Arsenic						
Cactinomycin	960.7	E856	E930.7	E950.4	E962.0	E980.4
Cade oil	976.4	E858.7	E946.4	E950.4	E962.0	E980.4
Cadmium (chloride) (compounds) (dust)						
(fumes) (oxide)	985.5	E866.4	—	E950.9	E962.1	E980.9
sulfide (medicinal) NEC	976.4	E858.7	E946.4	E950.4	E962.0	E980.4
Caffeine	969.7	E854.2	E939.7	E950.3	E962.0	E980.3
Calabar bean	988.2	E865.4	—	E950.9	E962.1	E980.9
Caladium seguinium	988.2	E865.4	—	E950.9	E962.1	E980.9
Calamine (liniment) (lotion)	976.3	E858.7	E946.3	E950.4	E962.0	E980.4
Calciferol	963.5	E858.1	E933.5	E950.4	E962.0	E980.4
Calcium (salts) NEC	974.5	E858.5	E944.5	E950.4	E962.0	E980.4
acetylsalicylate	965.1	E850.3	E935.3	E950.0	E962.0	E980.0
benzamidosalicylate	961.8	E857	E931.8	E950.4	E962.0	E980.4

Substance	Poisoning	External Cause (E-Code)				
		Accident	Therapeutic Use	Suicide Attempt	Assault	Undetermined
carbaspirin	965.1	E850.3	E935.3	E950.0	E962.0	E980.0
carbamide (citrated)	977.3	E858.8	E947.3	E950.4	E962.0	E980.4
carbonate (antacid)	973.0	E858.4	E943.0	E950.4	E962.0	E980.4
cyanide (citrated)	977.3	E858.8	E947.3	E950.4	E962.0	E980.4
dioctyl sulfosuccinate	973.2	E858.4	E943.2	E950.4	E962.0	E980.4
disodium edathamil	963.8	E858.1	E933.8	E950.4	E962.0	E980.4
disodium edetate	963.8	E858.1	E933.8	E950.4	E962.0	E980.4
EDTA	963.8	E858.1	E933.8	E950.4	E962.0	E980.4
hydrate, hydroxide	983.2	E864.2	—	E950.7	E962.1	E980.6
mandelate	961.9	E857	E931.9	E950.4	E962.0	E980.4
oxide	983.2	E864.2	—	E950.7	E962.1	E980.6
Calomel — *see* Mercury, chloride						
Caloric agents NEC	974.5	E858.5	E944.5	E950.4	E962.0	E980.4
Calusterone	963.1	E858.1	E933.1	E950.4	E962.0	E980.4
Camoquin	961.4	E857	E931.4	E950.4	E962.0	E980.4
Camphor (oil)	976.1	E858.7	E946.1	E950.4	E962.0	E980.4
Candeptin	976.0	E858.7	E946.0	E950.4	E962.0	E980.4
Candicidin	976.0	E858.7	E946.0	E950.4	E962.0	E980.4
Cannabinols	969.6	E854.1	E939.6	E950.3	E962.0	E980.3
Cannabis (derivatives) (indica) (sativa)	969.6	E854.1	E939.6	E950.3	E962.0	E980.3
Canned heat	980.1	E860.2	—	E950.9	E962.1	E980.9
Cantharides, cantharidin, cantharis	976.8	E858.7	E946.8	E950.4	E962.0	E980.4
Capillary agents	972.8	E858.3	E942.8	E950.4	E962.0	E980.4
Capreomycin	960.6	E856	E930.6	E950.4	E962.0	E980.4
Captodiame, captodiamine	969.5	E853.8	E939.5	E950.3	E962.0	E980.3
Caramiphen (hydrochloride)	971.1	E855.4	E941.1	E950.4	E962.0	E980.4
Carbachol	971.0	E855.3	E941.0	E950.4	E962.0	E980.4
Carbacrylamine resins	974.5	E858.5	E944.5	E950.4	E962.0	E980.4
Carbamate (sedative)	967.8	E852.8	E937.8	E950.2	E962.0	E980.2
herbicide	989.3	E863.5	—	E950.6	E962.1	E980.7
insecticide	989.3	E863.2	—	E950.6	E962.1	E980.7
Carbamazepine	966.3	E855.0	E936.3	E950.4	E962.0	E980.4
Carbamic esters	967.8	E852.8	E937.8	E950.2	E962.0	E980.2
Carbamide	974.4	E858.5	E944.4	E950.4	E962.0	E980.4
topical	976.8	E858.7	E946.8	E950.4	E962.0	E980.4
Carbamylcholine chloride	971.0	E855.3	E941.0	E950.4	E962.0	E980.4
Carbarsone	961.1	E857	E931.1	E950.4	E962.0	E980.4
Carbaryl	989.3	E863.2	—	E950.6	E962.1	E980.7
Carbaspirin	965.1	E850.3	E935.3	E950.0	E962.0	E980.0
Carbazochrome	972.8	E858.3	E942.8	E950.4	E962.0	E980.4
Carbenicillin	960.0	E856	E930.0	E950.4	E962.0	E980.4
Carbenoxolone	973.8	E858.4	E943.8	E950.4	E962.0	E980.4
Carbetapentane	975.4	E858.6	E945.4	E950.4	E962.0	E980.4
Carbimazole	962.8	E858.0	E932.8	E950.4	E962.0	E980.4
Carbinol	980.1	E860.2	—	E950.9	E962.1	E980.9
Carbinoxamine	963.0	E858.1	E933.0	E950.4	E962.0	E980.4
Carbitol	982.8	E862.4	—	E950.9	E962.1	E980.9
Carbocaine	968.9	E855.2	E938.9	E950.4	E962.0	E980.4
infiltration (subcutaneous)	968.5	E855.2	E938.5	E950.4	E962.0	E980.4
nerve block (peripheral) (plexus)	968.6	E855.2	E938.6	E950.4	E962.0	E980.4
topical (surface)	968.5	E855.2	E938.5	E950.4	E962.0	E980.4
Carbol–fuchsin solution	976.0	E858.7	E946.0	E950.4	E962.0	E980.4
Carbolic acid (*see also* Phenol)	983.0	E864.0	—	E950.7	E962.1	E980.6
Carbomycin	960.8	E856	E930.8	E950.4	E962.0	E980.4
Carbon						
bisulfide (liquid) (vapor)	982.2	E862.4	—	E950.9	E962.1	E980.9
dioxide (gas)	987.8	E869.8	—	E952.8	E962.2	E982.8

Substance	Poisoning	Accident	Therapeutic Use	Suicide Attempt	Assault	Undetermined
disulfide (liquid) (vapor)	982.2	E862.4	—	E950.9	E962.1	E980.9
monoxide (from incomplete combustion						
of) (in) NEC	986	E868.9	—	E952.1	E962.2	E982.1
blast furnace gas	986	E868.8	—	E952.1	E962.2	E982.1
butane (distributed in mobile						
container)	986	E868.0	—	E951.1	E962.2	E981.1
distributed through pipes	986	E867	—	E951.0	E962.2	E981.0
charcoal fumes	986	E868.3	—	E952.1	E962.2	E982.1
coal						
gas (piped)	986	E867	—	E951.0	E962.2	E981.0
solid (in domestic stoves,						
fireplaces)	986	E868.3	—	E952.1	E962.2	E982.1
coke (in domestic stoves, fireplaces)	986	E868.3	—	E952.1	E962.2	E982.1
exhaust gas (motor) not in transit	986	E868.2	—	E952.0	E962.2	E982.0
combustion engine, any not in						
watercraft	986	E868.2	—	E952.0	E962.2	E982.0
farm tractor, not in transit	986	E868.2	—	E952.0	E962.2	E982.0
gas engine	986	E868.2	—	E952.0	E962.2	E982.0
motor pump	986	E868.2	—	E952.0	E962.2	E982.0
motor vehicle, not in transit	986	E868.2	—	E952.0	E962.2	E982.0
fuel (in domestic use)	986	E868.3	—	E952.1	E962.2	E982.1
gas (piped)	986	E867	—	E951.0	E962.2	E981.0
in mobile container	986	E868.0	—	E951.1	E962.2	E981.1
utility	986	E868.1	—	E951.8	E962.2	E981.1
in mobile container	986	E868.0	—	E951.1	E962.2	E981.1
piped (natural)	986	E867	—	E951.0	E962.2	E981.0
illuminating gas	986	E868.1	—	E951.8	E962.2	E981.8
industrial fuels or gases, any	986	E868.8	—	E952.1	E962.2	E982.1
kerosene (in domestic stoves,						
fireplaces)	986	E868.3	—	E952.1	E962.2	E982.1
kiln gas or vapor	986	E868.8	—	E952.1	E962.2	E982.1
motor exhaust gas, not in transit	986	E868.2	—	E952.0	E962.2	E982.0
piped gas (manufactured) (natural)	986	E867	—	E951.0	E962.2	E981.0
producer gas	986	E868.8	—	E952.1	E962.2	E982.1
propane (distributed in mobile						
container)	986	E868.0	—	E951.1	E962.2	E981.1
distributed through pipes	986	E867	—	E951.0	E962.2	E981.0
specified source NEC	986	E868.8	—	E952.1	E962.2	E982.1
stove gas	986	E868.1	—	E951.8	E962.2	E981.8
piped	986	E867	—	E951.0	E962.2	E981.0
utility gas	986	E868.1	—	E951.8	E962.2	E981.8
piped	986	E867	—	E951.0	E962.2	E981.0
water gas	986	E868.1	—	E951.8	E962.2	E981.8
wood (in domestic stoves, fireplaces)	986	E868.3	—	E952.1	E962.2	E982.1
tetrachloride (vapor) NEC	987.8	E869.8	—	E952.8	E962.2	E982.8
liquid (cleansing agent) NEC	982.1	E861.3	—	E950.9	E961.9	E980.9
solvent	982.1	E862.4	—	E950.9	E961.9	E980.9
Carbonic acid (gas)	987.8	E869.8	—	E952.8	E962.2	E982.8
anhydrase inhibitors	974.2	E858.5	E944.2	E950.4	E962.0	E980.4
Carbowax	976.3	E858.7	E946.3	E950.4	E962.0	E980.4
Carbrital	967.0	E851	E937.0	E950.1	E962.0	E980.1
Carbromal (derivatives)	967.3	E852.2	E937.3	E950.2	E962.0	E980.2
Cardiac						
depressants	972.0	E858.3	E942.0	E950.4	E962.0	E980.4
rhythm regulators	972.0	E858.3	E942.0	E950.4	E962.0	E980.4
Cardiografin	977.8	E858.8	E947.8	E950.4	E962.0	E980.4
Cardio–green	977.8	E858.8	E947.8	E950.4	E962.0	E980.4

Substance	Poisoning	External Cause (E-Code)				
		Accident	Therapeutic Use	Suicide Attempt	Assault	Undetermined
Cardiotonic glycosides	972.1	E858.3	E942.1	E950.4	E962.0	E980.4
Cardiovascular agents NEC	972.9	E858.3	E942.9	E950.4	E962.0	E980.4
Cardrase	974.2	E858.5	E944.2	E950.4	E962.0	E980.4
Carfusin	976.0	E858.7	E946.0	E950.4	E962.0	E980.4
Carisoprodol	968.0	E855.1	E938.0	E950.4	E962.0	E980.4
Carmustine	963.1	E858.1	E933.1	E950.4	E962.0	E980.4
Carotene	963.5	E858.1	E933.5	E950.4	E962.0	E980.4
Carphenazine (maleate)	969.1	E853.0	E939.1	E950.3	E962.0	E980.3
Carter's Little Pills	973.1	E858.4	E943.1	E950.4	E962.0	E980.4
Cascara (sagrada)	973.1	E858.4	E943.1	E950.4	E962.0	E980.4
Cassava	988.2	E865.4	—	E950.9	E962.1	E980.9
Castellani's paint	976.0	E858.7	E946.0	E950.4	E962.0	E980.4
Castor						
bean	988.2	E865.3	—	E950.9	E962.1	E980.9
oil	973.1	E858.4	E943.1	E950.4	E962.0	E980.4
Caterpillar (sting)	989.5	E905.5	—	E950.9	E962.1	E980.9
Catha (edulis)	970.8	E854.3	E940.8	E950.4	E962.0	E980.4
Cathartics NEC	973.3	E858.4	E943.3	E950.4	E962.0	E980.4
contact	973.1	E858.4	E943.1	E950.4	E962.0	E980.4
emollient	973.2	E858.4	E943.2	E950.4	E962.0	E980.4
intestinal irritants	973.1	E858.4	E943.1	E950.4	E962.0	E980.4
saline	973.3	E858.4	E943.3	E950.4	E962.0	E980.4
Cathomycin	960.8	E856	E930.8	E950.4	E962.0	E980.4
Caustic(s)	983.9	E864.4	—	E950.7	E962.1	E980.6
alkali	983.2	E864.2	—	E950.7	E962.1	E980.6
hydroxide	983.2	E864.2	—	E950.7	E962.1	E980.6
potash	983.2	E864.2	—	E950.7	E962.1	E980.6
soda	983.2	E864.2	—	E950.7	E962.1	E980.6
specified NEC	983.9	E864.3	—	E950.7	E962.1	E980.6
Ceepryn	976.0	E858.7	E946.0	E950.4	E962.0	E980.4
ENT agent	976.6	E858.7	E946.6	E950.4	E962.0	E980.4
lozenges	976.6	E858.7	E946.6	E950.4	E962.0	E980.4
Celestone	962.0	E858.0	E932.0	E950.4	E962.0	E980.4
topical	976.0	E858.7	E946.0	E950.4	E962.0	E980.4
Cellosolve	982.8	E862.4	—	E950.9	E962.1	E980.9
Cell stimulants and proliferants	976.8	E858.7	E946.8	E950.4	E962.0	E980.4
Cellulose derivatives, cathartic	973.3	E858.4	E943.3	E950.4	E962.0	E980.4
nitrates (topical)	976.3	E858.7	E946.3	E950.4	E962.0	E980.4
Centipede (bite)	989.5	E905.4	—	E950.9	E962.1	E980.9
Central nervous system						
depressants	968.4	E855.1	E938.4	E950.4	E962.0	E980.4
anesthetic (general) NEC	968.4	E855.1	E938.4	E950.4	E962.0	E980.4
gases NEC	968.2	E855.1	E938.2	E950.4	E962.0	E980.4
intravenous	968.3	E855.1	E938.3	E950.4	E962.0	E980.4
barbiturates	967.0	E851	E937.0	E950.1	E962.0	E980.1
bromides	967.3	E852.2	E937.3	E950.2	E962.0	E980.2
cannabis sativa	969.6	E854.1	E939.6	E950.3	E962.0	E980.3
chloral hydrate	967.1	E852.0	E937.1	E950.2	E962.0	E980.2
hallucinogenics	969.6	E854.1	E939.6	E950.3	E962.0	E980.3
hypnotics	967.9	E852.9	E937.9	E950.2	E962.0	E980.2
specified NEC	967.8	E852.8	E937.8	E950.2	E962.0	E980.2
muscle relaxants	968.0	E855.1	E938.0	E950.4	E962.0	E980.4
paraldehyde	967.2	E852.1	E937.2	E950.2	E962.0	E980.2
sedatives	967.9	E852.9	E937.9	E950.2	E962.0	E980.2
mixed NEC	967.6	E852.5	E937.6	E950.2	E962.0	E980.2
specified NEC	967.8	E852.8	E937.8	E950.2	E962.0	E980.2
muscle–tone depressants	968.0	E855.1	E938.0	E950.4	E962.0	E980.4

Substance	Poisoning	External Cause (E-Code)				
		Accident	Therapeutic Use	Suicide Attempt	Assault	Undetermined
stimulants	970.9	E854.3	E940.9	E950.4	E962.0	E980.4
amphetamines	969.7	E854.2	E939.7	E950.3	E962.0	E980.3
analeptics	970.0	E854.3	E940.0	E950.4	E962.0	E980.4
antidepressants	969.0	E854.0	E939.0	E950.3	E962.0	E980.3
opiate antagonists	970.1	E854.3	E940.0	E950.4	E962.0	E980.4
specified NEC	970.8	E854.3	E940.8	E950.4	E962.0	E980.4
Cephalexin	960.5	E856	E930.5	E950.4	E962.0	E980.4
Cephaloglycin	960.5	E856	E930.5	E950.4	E962.0	E980.4
Cephaloridine	960.5	E856	E930.5	E950.4	E962.0	E980.4
Cephalosporins NEC	960.5	E856	E930.5	E950.4	E962.0	E980.4
N (adicillin)	960.0	E856	E930.0	E950.4	E962.0	E980.4
Cephalothin (sodium)	960.5	E856	E930.5	E950.4	E962.0	E980.4
Cerbera (odallam)	988.2	E865.4	—	E950.9	E962.1	E980.9
Cerberin	972.1	E858.3	E942.1	E950.4	E962.0	E980.4
Cerebral stimulants	970.9	E854.3	E940.9	E950.4	E962.0	E980.4
psychotherapeutic	969.7	E854.2	E939.7	E950.3	E962.0	E980.3
specified NEC	970.8	E854.3	E940.8	E950.4	E962.0	E980.4
Cetalkonium (chloride)	976.0	E858.7	E946.0	E950.4	E962.0	E980.4
Cetoxime	963.0	E858.1	E933.0	E950.4	E962.0	E980.4
Cetrimide	976.2	E858.7	E946.2	E950.4	E962.0	E980.4
Cetylpyridinium	976.0	E858.7	E946.0	E950.4	E962.0	E980.4
ENT agent	976.6	E858.7	E946.6	E950.4	E962.0	E980.4
lozenges	976.6	E858.7	E946.6	E950.4	E962.0	E980.4
Cevadilla — *see* Sabadilla						
Cevitamic acid	963.5	E858.1	E933.5	E950.4	E962.0	E980.4
Chalk, precipitated	973.0	E858.4	E943.0	E950.4	E962.0	E980.4
Charcoal						
fumes (carbon monoxide)	986	E868.3	—	E952.1	E962.2	E982.1
industrial	986	E868.8	—	E952.1	E962.2	E982.1
medicinal (activated)	973.0	E858.4	E943.0	E950.4	E962.0	E980.4
Chelating agents NEC	977.2	E858.8	E947.2	E950.4	E962.0	E980.4
Chelidonium majus	988.2	E865.4	—	E950.9	E962.1	E980.9
Chemical substance	989.9	E866.9	—	E950.9	E962.1	E980.9
specified NEC	989.89	E866.8	—	E950.9	E962.1	E980.9
Chemotherapy, antineoplastic	963.1	E858.1	E933.1	E950.4	E962.0	E980.4
Chenopodium (oil)	961.6	E857	E931.6	E950.4	E962.0	E980.4
Cherry laurel	988.2	E865.4	—	E950.9	E962.1	E980.9
Chiniofon	961.3	E857	E931.3	E950.4	E962.0	E980.4
Chlophedianol	975.4	E858.6	E945.4	E950.4	E962.0	E980.4
Chloral (betaine) (formamide) (hydrate)	967.1	E852.0	E937.1	E950.2	E962.0	E980.2
Chloralamide	967.1	E852.0	E937.1	E950.2	E962.0	E980.2
Chlorambucil	963.1	E858.1	E933.1	E950.4	E962.0	E980.4
Chloramphenicol	960.2	E856	E930.2	E950.4	E962.0	E980.4
ENT agent	976.6	E858.7	E946.6	E950.4	E962.0	E980.4
ophthalmic preparation	976.5	E858.7	E946.5	E950.4	E962.0	E980.4
topical NEC	976.0	E858.7	E946.0	E950.4	E962.0	E980.4
Chlorate(s) (potassium) (sodium) NEC	983.9	E864.3	—	E950.7	E962.1	E980.6
herbicides	989.4	E863.5	—	E950.6	E962.1	E980.7
Chlorcyclizine	963.0	E858.1	E933.0	E950.4	E962.0	E980.4
Chlordan(e) (dust)	989.2	E863.0	—	E950.6	E962.1	E980.7
Chlordantoin	976.0	E858.7	E946.0	E950.4	E962.0	E980.4
Chlordiazepoxide	969.4	E853.2	E939.4	E950.3	E962.0	E980.3
Chloresium	976.8	E858.7	E946.8	E950.4	E962.0	E980.4
Chlorethiazol	967.1	E852.0	E937.1	E950.2	E962.0	E980.2
Chlorethyl — *see* Ethyl, chloride						
Chloretone	967.1	E852.0	E937.1	E950.2	E962.0	E980.2
Chlorex	982.3	E862.4	—	E950.9	E962.1	E980.9

Substance	Poisoning	External Cause (E-Code)				
		Accident	Therapeutic Use	Suicide Attempt	Assault	Undetermined
Chlorhexadol	967.1	E852.0	E937.1	E950.2	E962.0	E980.2
Chlorhexidine (hydrochloride)	976.0	E858.7	E946.0	E950.4	E962.0	E980.4
Chlorhydroxyquinolin	976.0	E858.7	E946.0	E950.4	E962.0	E980.4
Chloride of lime (bleach)	983.9	E864.3	—	E950.7	E962.1	E980.6
Chlorinated						
camphene	989.2	E863.0	—	E950.6	E962.1	E980.7
diphenyl	989.89	E866.8	—	E950.9	E962.1	E980.9
hydrocarbons NEC	989.2	E863.0	—	E950.6	E962.1	E980.7
solvent	982.3	E862.4	—	E950.9	E962.1	E980.9
lime (bleach)	983.9	E864.3	—	E950.7	E962.1	E980.6
naphthalene — *see* Naphthalene						
pesticides NEC	989.2	E863.0	—	E950.6	E962.1	E980.7
soda — *see* Sodium, hypochlorite						
Chlorine (fumes) (gas)	987.6	E869.8	—	E952.8	E962.2	E982.8
bleach	983.9	E864.3	—	E950.7	E962.1	E980.6
compounds NEC	983.9	E864.3	—	E950.7	E962.1	E980.6
disinfectant	983.9	E861.4	—	E950.7	E962.1	E980.6
releasing agents NEC	983.9	E864.3	—	E950.7	E962.1	E980.6
Chlorisondamine	972.3	E858.3	E942.3	E950.4	E962.0	E980.4
Chlormadinone	962.2	E858.0	E932.2	E950.4	E962.0	E980.4
Chlormerodrin	974.0	E858.5	E944.0	E950.4	E962.0	E980.4
Chlormethiazole	967.1	E852.0	E937.1	E950.2	E962.0	E980.2
Chlormethylenecycline	960.4	E856	E930.4	E950.4	E962.0	E980.4
Chlormezanone	969.5	E853.8	E939.5	E950.3	E962.0	E980.3
Chloroacetophenone	987.5	E869.3	—	E952.8	E962.2	E982.8
Chloroaniline	983.0	E864.0	—	E950.7	E962.1	E980.6
Chlorobenzene, chlorobenzol	982.0	E862.4	—	E950.9	E962.1	E980.9
Chlorobutanol	967.1	E852.0	E937.1	E950.2	E962.0	E980.2
Chlorodinitrobenzene	983.0	E864.0	—	E950.7	E962.1	E980.6
dust or vapor	987.8	E869.8	—	E952.8	E962.2	E982.8
Chloroethane — *see* Ethyl, chloride						
Chloroform (fumes) (vapor)	987.8	E869.8	—	E952.8	E962.2	E982.8
anesthetic (gas)	968.2	E855.1	E938.2	E950.4	E962.0	E980.4
liquid NEC	968.4	E855.1	E938.4	E950.4	E962.0	E980.4
solvent	982.3	E862.4	—	E950.9	E962.1	E980.9
Chloroguanide	961.4	E857	E931.4	E950.4	E962.0	E980.4
Chloromycetin	960.2	E856	E930.2	E950.4	E962.0	E980.4
ENT agent	976.6	E858.7	E946.6	E950.4	E962.0	E980.4
ophthalmic preparation	976.5	E858.7	E946.5	E950.4	E962.0	E980.4
otic solution	976.6	E858.7	E946.6	E950.4	E962.0	E980.4
topical NEC	976.0	E858.7	E946.0	E950.4	E962.0	E980.4
Chloronitrobenzene	983.0	E864.0	—	E950.7	E962.1	E980.6
dust or vapor	987.8	E869.8	—	E952.8	E962.2	E982.8
Chlorophenol	983.0	E864.0	—	E950.7	E962.1	E980.6
Chlorophenothane	989.2	E863.0	—	E950.6	E962.1	E980.7
Chlorophyll (derivatives)	976.8	E858.7	E946.8	E950.4	E962.0	E980.4
Chloropicrin (fumes)	987.8	E869.8	—	E952.8	E962.2	E982.8
fumigant	989.4	E863.8	—	E950.6	E962.1	E980.7
fungicide	989.4	E863.6	—	E950.6	E962.1	E980.7
pesticide (fumes)	989.4	E863.4	—	E950.6	E962.1	E980.7
Chloroprocaine	968.9	E855.2	E938.9	E950.4	E962.0	E980.4
infiltration (subcutaneous)	968.5	E855.2	E938.5	E950.4	E962.0	E980.4
nerve block (peripheral) (plexus)	968.6	E855.2	E938.6	E950.4	E962.0	E980.4
Chloroptic	976.5	E858.7	E946.5	E950.4	E962.0	E980.4
Chloropurine	963.1	E858.1	E933.1	E950.4	E962.0	E980.4
Chloroquine (hydrochloride) (phosphate)	961.4	E857	E931.4	E950.4	E962.0	E980.4
Chlorothen	963.0	E858.1	E933.0	E950.4	E962.0	E980.4

Substance	Poisoning	Accident (Therapeutic Use)	Suicide Attempt	Assault	Undetermined
		External Cause (E-Code)			
Chlorothiazide	974.3	E858.5	E944.3	E950.4	E962.0	E980.4
Chlorotrianisene	962.2	E858.0	E932.2	E950.4	E962.0	E980.4
Chlorovinyldichloroarsine	985.1	E866.3	—	E950.8	E962.1	E980.8
Chloroxylenol	976.0	E858.7	E946.0	E950.4	E962.0	E980.4
Chlorphenesin (carbamate)	968.0	E855.1	E938.0	E950.4	E962.0	E980.4
topical (antifungal)	976.0	E858.7	E946.0	E950.4	E962.0	E980.4
Chlorpheniramine	963.0	E858.1	E933.0	E950.4	E962.0	E980.4
Chlorphenoxamine	966.4	E855.0	E936.4	E950.4	E962.0	E980.4
Chlorphentermine	977.0	E858.8	E947.0	E950.4	E962.0	E980.4
Chlorproguanil	961.4	E857	E931.4	E950.4	E962.0	E980.4
Chlorpromazine	969.1	E853.0	E939.1	E950.3	E962.0	E980.3
Chlorpropamide	962.3	E858.0	E932.3	E950.4	E962.0	E980.4
Chlorprothixene	969.3	E853.8	E939.3	E950.3	E962.0	E980.3
Chlorquinaldol	976.0	E858.7	E946.0	E950.4	E962.0	E980.4
Chlortetracycline	960.4	E856	E930.4	E950.4	E962.0	E980.4
Chlorthalidone	974.4	E858.5	E944.4	E950.4	E962.0	E980.4
Chlortrianisene	962.2	E858.0	E932.2	E950.4	E962.0	E980.4
Chlor–Trimeton	963.0	E858.1	E933.0	E950.4	E962.0	E980.4
Chlorzoxazone	968.0	E855.1	E938.0	E950.4	E962.0	E980.4
Choke damp	987.8	E869.8	—	E952.8	E962.2	E982.8
Cholebrine	977.8	E858.8	E947.8	E950.4	E962.0	E980.4
Cholera vaccine	978.2	E858.8	E948.2	E950.4	E962.0	E980.4
Cholesterol–lowering agents	972.2	E858.3	E942.2	E950.4	E962.0	E980.4
Cholestyramine (resin)	972.2	E858.3	E942.2	E950.4	E962.0	E980.4
Cholic acid	973.4	E858.4	E943.4	E950.4	E962.0	E980.4
Choline						
dihydrogen citrate	977.1	E858.8	E947.1	E950.4	E962.0	E980.4
salicylate	965.1	E850.3	E935.3	E950.0	E962.0	E980.0
theophyllinate	974.1	E858.5	E944.1	E950.4	E962.0	E980.4
Cholinergics	971.0	E855.3	E941.0	E950.4	E962.0	E980.4
Cholografin	977.8	E858.8	E947.8	E950.4	E962.0	E980.4
Chorionic gonadotropin	962.4	E858.0	E932.4	E950.4	E962.0	E980.4
Chromates	983.9	E864.3	—	E950.7	E962.1	E980.6
dust or mist	987.8	E869.8	—	E952.8	E962.2	E982.8
lead	984.0	E866.0	—	E950.9	E961.1	E980.9
paint	984.0	E861.5	—	E950.9	E961.1	E980.9
Chromic acid	983.9	E864.3	—	E950.7	E962.1	E980.6
dust or mist	987.8	E869.8	—	E952.8	E962.2	E982.8
Chromium	985.6	E866.4	—	E950.9	E962.1	E980.9
compounds — *see* Chromates						
Chromonar	972.4	E858.3	E942.4	E950.4	E962.0	E980.4
Chromyl chloride	983.9	E864.3	—	E950.7	E962.1	E980.6
Chrysarobin (ointment)	976.4	E858.7	E946.4	E950.4	E962.0	E980.4
Chrysazin	973.1	E858.4	E943.1	E950.4	E962.0	E980.4
Chymar	963.4	E858.1	E933.4	E950.4	E962.0	E980.4
ophthalmic preparation	976.5	E858.7	E946.5	E950.4	E962.0	E980.4
Chymotrypsin	963.4	E858.1	E933.4	E950.4	E962.0	E980.4
ophthalmic preparation	976.5	E858.7	E946.5	E950.4	E962.0	E980.4
Cicuta maculata or virosa	988.2	E865.4	—	E950.9	E962.1	E980.9
Cigarette lighter fluid	981	E862.1	—	E950.9	E962.1	E980.9
Cinchocaine (spinal)	968.7	E855.2	E938.7	E950.4	E962.0	E980.4
topical (surface)	968.5	E855.2	E938.5	E950.4	E962.0	E980.4
Cinchona	961.4	E857	E931.4	E950.4	E962.0	E980.4
Cinchonine alkaloids	961.4	E857	E931.4	E950.4	E962.0	E980.4
Cinchophen	974.7	E858.5	E944.7	E950.4	E962.0	E980.4
Cinnarizine	963.0	E858.1	E933.0	E950.4	E962.0	E980.4
Citanest	968.9	E855.2	E938.9	E950.4	E962.0	E980.4

Substance	Poisoning	External Cause (E-Code)				
		Accident	Therapeutic Use	Suicide Attempt	Assault	Undetermined
infiltration (subcutaneous)	968.5	E855.2	E938.5	E950.4	E962.0	E980.4
nerve block (peripheral) (plexus)	968.6	E855.2	E938.6	E950.4	E962.0	E980.4
Citric acid	989.89	E866.8	—	E950.9	E962.1	E980.9
Citrovorum factor	964.1	E858.2	E934.1	E950.4	E962.0	E980.4
Claviceps purpurea	988.2	E865.4	—	E950.9	E962.1	E980.9
Cleaner, cleansing agent NEC	989.89	E861.3	—	E950.9	E962.1	E980.9
of paint or varnish	982.8	E862.9	—	E950.9	E962.1	E980.9
Clematis vitalba	988.2	E865.4	—	E950.9	E962.1	E980.9
Clemizole	963.0	E858.1	E933.0	E950.4	E962.0	E980.4
penicillin	960.0	E856	E930.0	E950.4	E962.0	E980.4
Clidinium	971.1	E855.4	E941.1	E950.4	E962.0	E980.4
Clindamycin	960.8	E856	E930.8	E950.4	E962.0	E980.4
Cliradon	965.09	E850.2	E935.2	E950.0	E962.0	E980.0
Clocortolone	962.0	E858.0	E932.0	E950.4	E962.0	E980.4
Clofedanol	975.4	E858.6	E945.4	E950.4	E962.0	E980.4
Clofibrate	972.2	E858.3	E942.2	E950.4	E962.0	E980.4
Clomethiazole	967.1	E852.0	E937.1	E950.2	E962.0	E980.2
Clomiphene	977.8	E858.8	E947.8	E950.4	E962.0	E980.4
Clonazepam	969.4	E853.2	E939.4	E950.3	E962.0	E980.3
Clonidine	972.6	E858.3	E942.6	E950.4	E962.0	E980.4
Clopamide	974.3	E858.5	E944.3	E950.4	E962.0	E980.4
Clorazepate	969.4	E853.2	E939.4	E950.3	E962.0	E980.3
Clorexolone	974.4	E858.5	E944.4	E950.4	E962.0	E980.4
Clorox (bleach)	983.9	E864.3	—	E950.7	E962.1	E980.6
Clortermine	977.0	E858.8	E947.0	E950.4	E962.0	E980.4
Clotrimazole	976.0	E858.7	E946.0	E950.4	E962.0	E980.4
Cloxacillin	960.0	E856	E930.0	E950.4	E962.0	E980.4
Coagulants NEC	964.5	E858.2	E934.5	E950.4	E962.0	E980.4
Coal (carbon monoxide from) — *see also* Carbon, monoxide, coal						
oil — *see* Kerosene						
tar NEC	983.0	E864.0	—	E950.7	E962.1	E980.6
fumes	987.8	E869.8	—	E952.8	E962.2	E982.8
medicinal (ointment)	976.4	E858.7	E946.4	E950.4	E962.0	E980.4
analgesics NEC	965.5	E850.5	E935.5	E950.0	E962.0	E980.0
naphtha (solvent)	981	E862.0	—	E950.9	E962.1	E980.9
Cobalt (fumes) (industrial)	985.8	E866.4	—	E950.9	E962.1	E980.9
Cobra (venom)	989.5	E905.0	—	E950.9	E962.1	E980.9
Coca (leaf)	970.8	E854.3	E940.8	E950.4	E962.0	E980.4
Cocaine (hydrochloride) (salt)	968.5	E855.2	E938.5	E950.4	E962.0	E980.4
Coccidioidin	977.8	E858.8	E947.8	E950.4	E962.0	E980.4
Cocculus indicus	988.2	E865.3	—	E950.9	E962.1	E980.9
Cochineal	989.89	E866.8	—	E950.9	E962.1	E980.9
medicinal products	977.4	E858.8	E947.4	E950.4	E962.0	E980.4
Codeine	965.09	E850.2	E935.2	E950.0	E962.0	E980.0
Coffee	989.89	E866.8	—	E950.9	E962.1	E980.9
Cogentin	971.1	E855.4	E941.1	E950.4	E962.0	E980.4
Coke fumes or gas (carbon monoxide)	986	E868.3	—	E952.1	E962.2	E982.1
industrial use	986	E868.8	—	E952.1	E962.2	E982.1
Colace	973.2	E858.4	E943.2	E950.4	E962.0	E980.4
Colchicine	974.7	E858.5	E944.7	E950.4	E962.0	E980.4
Colchicum	988.2	E865.3	—	E950.9	E962.1	E980.9
Cold cream	976.3	E858.7	E946.3	E950.4	E962.0	E980.4
Colestipol	972.2	E858.3	E942.2	E950.4	E962.0	E980.4
Colistimethate	960.8	E856	E930.8	E950.4	E962.0	E980.4
Colistin	960.8	E856	E930.8	E950.4	E962.0	E980.4
Collagen	977.8	E866.8	E947.8	E950.9	E962.1	E980.9

Substance	Poisoning	External Cause (E-Code)				
		Accident	Therapeutic Use	Suicide Attempt	Assault	Undetermined
Collagenase	976.8	E858.7	E946.8	E950.4	E962.0	E980.4
Collodion (flexible)	976.3	E858.7	E946.3	E950.4	E962.0	E980.4
Colocynth	973.1	E858.4	E943.1	E950.4	E962.0	E980.4
Coloring matter — *see* Dye(s)						
Combustion gas — *see* Carbon, monoxide						
Compazine	969.1	E853.0	E939.1	E950.3	E962.0	E980.3
Compound						
42 (warfarin)	989.4	E863.7	—	E950.6	E962.1	E980.7
269 (endrin)	989.2	E863.0	—	E950.6	E962.1	E980.7
497 (dieldrin)	989.2	E863.0	—	E950.6	E962.1	E980.7
1080 (sodium fluoroacetate)	989.4	E863.7	—	E950.6	E962.1	E980.7
3422 (parathion)	989.3	E863.1	—	E950.6	E962.1	E980.7
3911 (phorate)	989.3	E863.1	—	E950.6	E962.1	E980.7
3956 (toxaphene)	989.2	E863.0	—	E950.6	E962.1	E980.7
4049 (malathion)	989.3	E863.1	—	E950.6	E962.1	E980.7
4124 (dicapthon)	989.4	E863.4	—	E950.6	E962.1	E980.7
E (cortisone)	962.0	E858.0	E932.0	E950.4	E962.0	E980.4
F (hydrocortisone)	962.0	E858.0	E932.0	E950.4	E962.0	E980.4
Congo red	977.8	E858.8	E947.8	E950.4	E962.0	E980.4
Coniine, conine	965.7	E850.7	E935.7	E950.0	E962.0	E980.0
Conium (maculatum)	988.2	E865.4	—	E950.9	E962.1	E980.9
Conjugated estrogens (equine)	962.2	E858.0	E932.2	E950.4	E962.0	E980.4
Contac	975.6	E858.6	E945.6	E950.4	E962.0	E980.4
Contact lens solution	976.5	E858.7	E946.5	E950.4	E962.0	E980.4
Contraceptives (oral)	962.2	E858.0	E932.2	E950.4	E962.0	E980.4
vaginal	976.8	E858.7	E946.8	E950.4	E962.0	E980.4
Contrast media (roentgenographic)	977.8	E858.8	E947.8	E950.4	E962.0	E980.4
Convallaria majalis	988.2	E865.4	—	E950.9	E962.1	E980.9
Copper (dust) (fumes) (salts) NEC	985.8	E866.4	—	E950.9	E962.1	E980.9
arsenate, arsenite	985.1	E866.3	—	E950.8	E962.1	E980.8
insecticide	985.1	E863.4	—	E950.8	E962.1	E980.8
emetic	973.6	E858.4	E943.6	E950.4	E962.0	E980.4
fungicide	985.8	E863.6	—	E950.6	E962.1	E980.7
insecticide	985.8	E863.4	—	E950.6	E962.1	E980.7
oleate	976.0	E858.7	E946.0	E950.4	E962.0	E980.4
sulfate	983.9	E864.3	—	E950.7	E962.1	E980.6
fungicide	983.9	E863.6	—	E950.7	E962.1	E980.6
cupric	973.6	E858.4	E943.6	E950.4	E962.0	E980.4
cuprous	983.9	E864.3	—	E950.7	E962.1	E980.6
Copperhead snake (bite) (venom)	989.5	E905.0	—	E950.9	E962.1	E980.9
Coral (sting)	989.5	E905.6	—	E950.9	E962.1	E980.9
snake (bite) (venom)	989.5	E905.0	—	E950.9	E962.1	E980.9
Cordran	976.0	E858.7	E946.0	E950.4	E962.0	E980.4
Corn cures	976.4	E858.7	E946.4	E950.4	E962.0	E980.4
Cornhusker's lotion	976.3	E858.7	E946.3	E950.4	E962.0	E980.4
Corn starch	976.3	E858.7	E946.3	E950.4	E962.0	E980.4
Corrosive	983.9	E864.4	—	E950.7	E962.1	E980.6
acids NEC	983.1	E864.1	—	E950.7	E962.1	E980.6
aromatics	983.0	E864.0	—	E950.7	E962.1	E980.6
disinfectant	983.0	E861.4	—	E950.7	E962.1	E980.6
fumes NEC	987.9	E869.9	—	E952.9	E962.2	E982.9
specified NEC	983.9	E864.3	—	E950.7	E962.1	E980.6
sublimate — *see* Mercury, chloride						
Cortate	962.0	E858.0	E932.0	E950.4	E962.0	E980.4
Cort–Dome	962.0	E858.0	E932.0	E950.4	E962.0	E980.4
ENT agent	976.6	E858.7	E946.6	E950.4	E962.0	E980.4
ophthalmic preparation	976.5	E858.7	E946.5	E950.4	E962.0	E980.4

Substance	Poisoning	External Cause (E-Code)				
		Accident	Therapeutic Use	Suicide Attempt	Assault	Undetermined
topical NEC	976.0	E858.7	E946.0	E950.4	E962.0	E980.4
Cortef	962.0	E858.0	E932.0	E950.4	E962.0	E980.4
ENT agent	976.6	E858.7	E946.6	E950.4	E962.0	E980.4
ophthalmic preparation	976.5	E858.7	E946.5	E950.4	E962.0	E980.4
topical NEC	976.0	E858.7	E946.0	E950.4	E962.0	E980.4
Corticosteroids (fluorinated)	962.0	E858.0	E932.0	E950.4	E962.0	E980.4
ENT agent	976.6	E858.7	E946.6	E950.4	E962.0	E980.4
ophthalmic preparation	976.5	E858.7	E946.5	E950.4	E962.0	E980.4
topical NEC	976.0	E858.7	E946.0	E950.4	E962.0	E980.4
Corticotropin	962.4	E858.0	E932.4	E950.4	E962.0	E980.4
Cortisol	962.0	E858.0	E932.0	E950.4	E962.0	E980.4
ENT agent	976.6	E858.7	E946.6	E950.4	E962.0	E980.4
ophthalmic preparation	976.5	E858.7	E946.5	E950.4	E962.0	E980.4
topical NEC	976.0	E858.7	E946.0	E950.4	E962.0	E980.4
Cortisone derivatives (acetate)	962.0	E858.0	E932.0	E950.4	E962.0	E980.4
ENT agent	976.6	E858.7	E946.6	E950.4	E962.0	E980.4
ophthalmic preparation	976.5	E858.7	E946.5	E950.4	E962.0	E980.4
topical NEC	976.0	E858.7	E946.0	E950.4	E962.0	E980.4
Cortogen	962.0	E858.0	E932.0	E950.4	E962.0	E980.4
ENT agent	976.6	E858.7	E946.6	E950.4	E962.0	E980.4
ophthalmic preparation	976.5	E858.7	E946.5	E950.4	E962.0	E980.4
Cortone	962.0	E858.0	E932.0	E950.4	E962.0	E980.4
ENT agent	976.6	E858.7	E946.6	E950.4	E962.0	E980.4
ophthalmic preparation	976.5	E858.7	E946.5	E950.4	E962.0	E980.4
Cortril	962.0	E858.0	E932.0	E950.4	E962.0	E980.4
ENT agent	976.6	E858.7	E946.6	E950.4	E962.0	E980.4
ophthalmic preparation	976.5	E858.7	E946.5	E950.4	E962.0	E980.4
topical NEC	976.0	E858.7	E946.0	E950.4	E962.0	E980.4
Cosmetics	989.89	E866.7	—	E950.9	E962.1	E980.9
Cosyntropin	977.8	E858.8	E947.8	E950.4	E962.0	E980.4
Cotarnine	964.5	E858.2	E934.5	E950.4	E962.0	E980.4
Cottonseed oil	976.3	E858.7	E946.3	E950.4	E962.0	E980.4
Cough mixtures (antitussives)	975.4	E858.6	E945.4	E950.4	E962.0	E980.4
containing opiates	965.09	E850.2	E935.2	E950.0	E962.0	E980.0
expectorants	975.5	E858.6	E945.5	E950.4	E962.0	E980.4
Coumadin	964.2	E858.2	E934.2	E950.4	E962.0	E980.4
rodenticide	989.4	E863.7	—	E950.6	E962.1	E980.7
Coumarin	964.2	E858.2	E934.2	E950.4	E962.0	E980.4
Coumetarol	964.2	E858.2	E934.2	E950.4	E962.0	E980.4
Cowbane	988.2	E865.4	—	E950.9	E962.1	E980.9
Cozyme	963.5	E858.1	E933.5	E950.4	E962.0	E980.4
Creolin	983.0	E864.0	—	E950.7	E962.1	E980.6
disinfectant	983.0	E861.4	—	E950.7	E962.1	E980.6
Creosol (compound)	983.0	E864.0	—	E950.7	E962.1	E980.6
Creosote (beechwood) (coal tar)	983.0	E864.0	—	E950.7	E962.1	E980.6
medicinal (expectorant)	975.5	E858.6	E945.5	E950.4	E962.0	E980.4
syrup	975.5	E858.6	E945.5	E950.4	E962.0	E980.4
Cresol	983.0	E864.0	—	E950.7	E962.1	E980.6
disinfectant	983.0	E861.4	—	E950.7	E962.1	E980.6
Cresylic acid	983.0	E864.0	—	E950.7	E962.1	E980.6
Cropropamide	965.7	E850.7	E935.7	E950.0	E962.0	E980.0
with crotethamide	970.0	E854.3	E940.0	E950.4	E962.0	E980.4
Crotamiton	976.0	E858.7	E946.0	E950.4	E962.0	E980.4
Crotethamide	965.7	E850.7	E935.7	E950.0	E962.0	E980.0
with cropropamide	970.0	E854.3	E940.0	E950.4	E962.0	E980.4
Croton (oil)	973.1	E858.4	E943.1	E950.4	E962.0	E980.4
chloral	967.1	E852.0	E937.1	E950.2	E962.0	E980.2

Substance	Poisoning	External Cause (E-Code) Accident	Therapeutic Use	Suicide Attempt	Assault	Undetermined
Crude oil	981	E862.1	—	E950.9	E962.1	E980.9
Cryogenine	965.8	E850.8	E935.8	E950.0	E962.0	E980.0
Cryolite (pesticide)	989.4	E863.4	—	E950.6	E962.1	E980.7
Cryptenamine	972.6	E858.3	E942.6	E950.4	E962.0	E980.4
Crystal violet	976.0	E858.7	E946.0	E950.4	E962.0	E980.4
Cuckoopint	988.2	E865.4	—	E950.9	E962.1	E980.9
Cumetharol	964.2	E858.2	E934.2	E950.4	E962.0	E980.4
Cupric sulfate	973.6	E858.4	E943.6	E950.4	E962.0	E980.4
Cuprous sulfate	983.9	E864.3	—	E950.7	E962.1	E980.6
Curare, curarine	975.2	E858.6	E945.2	E950.4	E962.0	E980.4
Cyanic acid — *see* Cyanide(s)						
Cyanide(s) (compounds) (hydrogen) (potassium) (sodium) NEC	989.0	E866.8	—	E950.9	E962.1	E980.9
dust or gas (inhalation) NEC	987.7	E869.8	—	E952.8	E962.2	E982.8
fumigant	989.0	E863.8	—	E950.6	E962.1	E980.7
mercuric — *see* Mercury						
pesticide (dust) (fumes)	989.0	E863.4	—	E950.6	E962.1	E980.7
Cyanocobalamin	964.1	E858.2	E934.1	E950.4	E962.0	E980.4
Cyanogen (chloride) (gas) NEC	987.8	E869.8	—	E952.8	E962.2	E982.8
Cyclaine	968.5	E855.2	E938.5	E950.4	E962.0	E980.4
Cyclamen europaeum	988.2	E865.4	—	E950.9	E962.1	E980.9
Cyclandelate	972.5	E858.3	E942.5	E950.4	E962.0	E980.4
Cyclazocine	965.09	E850.2	E935.2	E950.0	E962.0	E980.0
Cyclizine	963.0	E858.1	E933.0	E950.4	E962.0	E980.4
Cyclobarbital, cyclobarbitone	967.0	E851	E937.0	E950.1	E962.0	E980.1
Cycloguanil	961.4	E857	E931.4	E950.4	E962.0	E980.4
Cyclohexane	982.0	E862.4	—	E950.9	E962.1	E980.9
Cyclohexanol	980.8	E860.8	—	E950.9	E962.1	E980.9
Cyclohexanone	982.8	E862.4	—	E950.9	E962.1	E980.9
Cyclomethycaine	968.5	E855.2	E938.5	E950.4	E962.0	E980.4
Cyclopentamine	971.2	E855.5	E941.2	E950.4	E962.0	E980.4
Cyclopenthiazide	974.3	E858.5	E944.3	E950.4	E962.0	E980.4
Cyclopentolate	971.1	E855.4	E941.1	E950.4	E962.0	E980.4
Cyclophosphamide	963.1	E858.1	E933.1	E950.4	E962.0	E980.4
Cyclopropane	968.2	E855.1	E938.2	E950.4	E962.0	E980.4
Cycloserine	960.6	E856	E930.6	E950.4	E962.0	E980.4
Cyclothiazide	974.3	E858.5	E944.3	E950.4	E962.0	E980.4
Cycrimine	966.4	E855.0	E936.4	E950.4	E962.0	E980.4
Cymarin	972.1	E858.3	E942.1	E950.4	E962.0	E980.4
Cyproheptadine	963.0	E858.1	E933.0	E950.4	E962.0	E980.4
Cyprolidol	969.0	E854.0	E939.0	E950.3	E962.0	E980.3
Cytarabine	963.1	E858.1	E933.1	E950.4	E962.0	E980.4
Cytisus						
laburnum	988.2	E865.4	—	E950.9	E962.1	E980.9
scoparius	988.2	E865.4	—	E950.9	E962.1	E980.9
Cytomel	962.7	E858.0	E932.7	E950.4	E962.0	E980.4
Cytosine (antineoplastic)	963.1	E858.1	E933.1	E950.4	E962.0	E980.4
Cytoxan	963.1	E858.1	E933.1	E950.4	E962.0	E980.4
Dacarbazine	963.1	E858.1	E933.1	E950.4	E962.0	E980.4
Dactinomycin	960.7	E856	E930.7	E950.4	E962.0	E980.4
DADPS	961.8	E857	E931.8	E950.4	E962.0	E980.4
Dakin's solution (external)	976.0	E858.7	E946.0	E950.4	E962.0	E980.4
Dalmane	969.4	E853.2	E939.4	E950.3	E962.0	E980.3
DAM	977.2	E858.8	E947.2	E950.4	E962.0	E980.4
Danilone	964.2	E858.2	E934.2	E950.4	E962.0	E980.4
Danthron	973.1	E858.4	E943.1	E950.4	E962.0	E980.4
Dantrolene	975.2	E858.6	E945.2	E950.4	E962.0	E980.4

Substance	Poisoning	External Cause (E-Code)				
		Accident	Therapeutic Use	Suicide Attempt	Assault	Undetermined
Daphne (gnidium) (mezereum)	988.2	E865.4	—	E950.9	E962.1	E980.9
berry	988.2	E865.3	—	E950.9	E962.1	E980.9
Dapsone	961.8	E857	E931.8	E950.4	E962.0	E980.4
Daraprim	961.4	E857	E931.4	E950.4	E962.0	E980.4
Darnel	988.2	E865.3	—	E950.9	E962.1	E980.9
Darvon	965.8	E850.8	E935.8	E950.0	E962.0	E980.0
Daunorubicin	960.7	E856	E930.7	E950.4	E962.0	E980.4
DBI	962.3	E858.0	E932.3	E950.4	E962.0	E980.4
D–Con (rodenticide)	989.4	E863.7	—	E950.6	E962.1	E980.7
DDS	961.8	E857	E931.8	E950.4	E962.0	E980.4
DDT	989.2	E863.0	—	E950.6	E962.1	E980.7
Deadly nightshade	988.2	E865.4	—	E950.9	E962.1	E980.9
berry	988.2	E865.3	—	E950.9	E962.1	E980.9
Deanol	969.7	E854.2	E939.7	E950.3	E962.0	E980.3
Debrisoquine	972.6	E858.3	E942.6	E950.4	E962.0	E980.4
Decaborane	989.89	E866.8	—	E950.9	E962.1	E980.9
fumes	987.8	E869.8	—	E952.8	E962.2	E982.8
Decadron	962.0	E858.0	E932.0	E950.4	E962.0	E980.4
ENT agent	976.6	E858.7	E946.6	E950.4	E962.0	E980.4
ophthalmic preparation	976.5	E858.7	E946.5	E950.4	E962.0	E980.4
topical NEC	976.0	E858.7	E946.0	E950.4	E962.0	E980.4
Decahydronaphthalene	982.0	E862.4	—	E950.9	E962.1	E980.9
Decalin	982.0	E862.4	—	E950.9	E962.1	E980.9
Decamethonium	975.2	E858.6	E945.2	E950.4	E962.0	E980.4
Decholin	973.4	E858.4	E943.4	E950.4	E962.0	E980.4
sodium (diagnostic)	977.8	E858.8	E947.8	E950.4	E962.0	E980.4
Declomycin	960.4	E856	E930.4	E950.4	E962.0	E980.4
Deferoxamine	963.8	E858.1	E933.8	E950.4	E962.0	E980.4
Dehydrocholic acid	973.4	E858.4	E943.4	E950.4	E962.0	E980.4
DeKalin	982.0	E862.4	—	E950.9	E962.1	E980.9
Delalutin	962.2	E858.0	E932.2	E950.4	E962.0	E980.4
Delphinium	988.2	E865.3	—	E950.9	E962.1	E980.9
Deltasone	962.0	E858.0	E932.0	E950.4	E962.0	E980.4
Deltra	962.0	E858.0	E932.0	E950.4	E962.0	E980.4
Delvinal	967.0	E851	E937.0	E950.1	E962.0	E980.1
Demecarium (bromide)	971.0	E855.3	E941.0	E950.4	E962.0	E980.4
Demeclocycline	960.4	E856	E930.4	E950.4	E962.0	E980.4
Demecolcine	963.1	E858.1	E933.1	E950.4	E962.0	E980.4
Demelanizing agents	976.8	E858.7	E946.8	E950.4	E962.0	E980.4
Demerol	965.09	E850.2	E935.2	E950.0	E962.0	E980.0
Demethylchlortetracycline	960.4	E856	E930.4	E950.4	E962.0	E980.4
Demethyltetracycline	960.4	E856	E930.4	E950.4	E962.0	E980.4
Demeton	989.3	E863.1	—	E950.6	E962.1	E980.7
Demulcents	976.3	E858.7	E946.3	E950.4	E962.0	E980.4
Demulen	962.2	E858.0	E932.2	E950.4	E962.0	E980.4
Denatured alcohol	980.0	E860.1	—	E950.9	E962.1	E980.9
Dendrid	976.5	E858.7	E946.5	E950.4	E962.0	E980.4
Dental agents, topical	976.7	E858.7	E946.7	E950.4	E962.0	E980.4
Deodorant spray (feminine hygiene)	976.8	E858.7	E946.8	E950.4	E962.0	E980.4
Deoxyribonuclease	963.4	E858.1	E933.4	E950.4	E962.0	E980.4
Depressants						
appetite, central	977.0	E858.8	E947.0	E950.4	E962.0	E980.4
cardiac	972.0	E858.3	E942.0	E950.4	E962.0	E980.4
central nervous system (anesthetic)	968.4	E855.1	E938.4	E950.4	E962.0	E980.4
psychotherapeutic	969.5	E853.9	E939.5	E950.3	E962.0	E980.3
Dequalinium	976.0	E858.7	E946.0	E950.4	E962.0	E980.4
Dermolate	976.2	E858.7	E946.2	E950.4	E962.0	E980.4

Substance	Poisoning	External Cause (E-Code)				
		Accident	Therapeutic Use	Suicide Attempt	Assault	Undetermined
DES	962.2	E858.0	E932.2	E950.4	E962.0	E980.4
Desenex	976.0	E858.7	E946.0	E950.4	E962.0	E980.4
Deserpidine	972.6	E858.3	E942.6	E950.4	E962.0	E980.4
Desipramine	969.0	E854.0	E939.0	E950.3	E962.0	E980.3
Deslanoside	972.1	E858.3	E942.1	E950.4	E962.0	E980.4
Desocodeine	965.09	E850.2	E935.2	E950.0	E962.0	E980.0
Desomorphine	965.09	E850.2	E935.2	E950.0	E962.0	E980.0
Desonide	976.0	E858.7	E946.0	E950.4	E962.0	E980.4
Desoxycorticosterone derivatives	962.0	E858.0	E932.0	E950.4	E962.0	E980.4
Desoxyephedrine	969.7	E854.2	E939.7	E950.3	E962.0	E980.3
DET	969.6	E854.1	E939.6	E950.3	E962.0	E980.3
Detergents (ingested) (synthetic)	989.6	E861.0	—	E950.9	E962.1	E980.9
external medication	976.2	E858.7	E946.2	E950.4	E962.0	E980.4
Deterrent, alcohol	977.3	E858.8	E947.3	E950.4	E962.0	E980.4
Detrothyronine	962.7	E858.0	E932.7	E950.4	E962.0	E980.4
Dettol (external medication)	976.0	E858.7	E946.0	E950.4	E962.0	E980.4
Dexamethasone	962.0	E858.0	E932.0	E950.4	E962.0	E980.4
ENT agent	976.6	E858.7	E946.6	E950.4	E962.0	E980.4
ophthalmic preparation	976.5	E858.7	E946.5	E950.4	E962.0	E980.4
topical NEC	976.0	E858.7	E946.0	E950.4	E962.0	E980.4
Dexamphetamine	969.7	E854.2	E939.7	E950.3	E962.0	E980.3
Dexedrine	969.7	E854.2	E939.7	E950.3	E962.0	E980.3
Dexpanthenol	963.5	E858.1	E933.5	E950.4	E962.0	E980.4
Dextran	964.8	E858.2	E934.8	E950.4	E962.0	E980.4
Dextriferron	964.0	E858.2	E934.0	E950.4	E962.0	E980.4
Dextroamphetamine	969.7	E854.2	E939.7	E950.3	E962.0	E980.3
Dextro calcium pantothenate	963.5	E858.1	E933.5	E950.4	E962.0	E980.4
Dextromethorphan	975.4	E858.6	E945.4	E950.4	E962.0	E980.4
Dextromoramide	965.09	E850.2	E935.2	E950.0	E962.0	E980.0
Dextro pantothenyl alcohol	963.5	E858.1	E933.5	E950.4	E962.0	E980.4
topical	976.8	E858.7	E946.8	E950.4	E962.0	E980.4
Dextropropoxyphene (hydrochloride)	965.8	E850.8	E935.8	E950.0	E962.0	E980.0
Dextrorphan	965.09	E850.2	E935.2	E950.0	E962.0	E980.0
Dextrose NEC	974.5	E858.5	E944.5	E950.4	E962.0	E980.4
Dextrothyroxin	962.7	E858.0	E932.7	E950.4	E962.0	E980.4
DFP	971.0	E855.3	E941.0	E950.4	E962.0	E980.4
DHE–45	972.9	E858.3	E942.9	E950.4	E962.0	E980.4
Diabinese	962.3	E858.0	E932.3	E950.4	E962.0	E980.4
Diacetyl monoxime	977.2	E858.8	E947.2	E950.4	E962.0	E980.4
Diacetylmorphine	965.01	E850.0	E935.0	E950.0	E962.0	E980.0
Diagnostic agents	977.8	E858.8	E947.8	E950.4	E962.0	E980.4
Dial (soap)	976.2	E858.7	E946.2	E950.4	E962.0	E980.4
sedative	967.0	E851	E937.0	E950.1	E962.0	E980.1
Diallylbarbituric acid	967.0	E851	E937.0	E950.1	E962.0	E980.1
Diaminodiphenylsulfone	961.8	E857	E931.8	E950.4	E962.0	E980.4
Diamorphine	965.01	E850.0	E935.0	E950.0	E962.0	E980.0
Diamox	974.2	E858.5	E944.2	E950.4	E962.0	E980.4
Diamthazole	976.0	E858.7	E946.0	E950.4	E962.0	E980.4
Diaphenylsulfone	961.8	E857	E931.8	E950.4	E962.0	E980.4
Diasone (sodium)	961.8	E857	E931.8	E950.4	E962.0	E980.4
Diazepam	969.4	E853.2	E939.4	E950.3	E962.0	E980.3
Diazinon	989.3	E863.1	—	E950.6	E962.1	E980.7
Diazomethane (gas)	987.8	E869.8	—	E952.8	E962.2	E982.8
Diazoxide	972.5	E858.3	E942.5	E950.4	E962.0	E980.4
Dibenamine	971.3	E855.6	E941.3	E950.4	E962.0	E980.4
Dibenzheptropine	963.0	E858.1	E933.0	E950.4	E962.0	E980.4
Dibenzyline	971.3	E855.6	E941.3	E950.4	E962.0	E980.4

Substance	Poisoning	External Cause (E-Code)				
		Accident	Therapeutic Use	Suicide Attempt	Assault	Undetermined
Diborane (gas)	987.8	E869.8	—	E952.8	E962.2	E982.8
Dibromomannitol	963.1	E858.1	E933.1	E950.4	E962.0	E980.4
Dibucaine (spinal)	968.7	E855.2	E938.7	E950.4	E962.0	E980.4
topical (surface)	968.5	E855.2	E938.5	E950.4	E962.0	E980.4
Dibunate sodium	975.4	E858.6	E945.4	E950.4	E962.0	E980.4
Dibutoline	971.1	E855.4	E941.1	E950.4	E962.0	E980.4
Dicapthon	989.4	E863.4	—	E950.6	E962.1	E980.7
Dichloralphenazone	967.1	E852.0	E937.1	E950.2	E962.0	E980.2
Dichlorodifluoromethane	987.4	E869.2	—	E952.8	E962.2	E982.8
Dichloroethane	982.3	E862.4	—	E950.9	E962.1	E980.9
Dichloroethylene	982.3	E862.4	—	E950.9	E962.1	E980.9
Dichloroethyl sulfide	987.8	E869.8	—	E952.8	E962.2	E982.8
Dichlorohydrin	982.3	E862.4	—	E950.9	E962.1	E980.9
Dichloromethane (solvent) (vapor)	982.3	E862.4	—	E950.9	E962.1	E980.9
Dichlorophen(e)	961.6	E857	E931.6	E950.4	E962.0	E980.4
Dichlorphenamide	974.2	E858.5	E944.2	E950.4	E962.0	E980.4
Dichlorvos	989.3	E863.1	—	E950.6	E962.1	E980.7
Diclofenac sodium	965.69	E850.6	E935.6	E950.0	E962.0	E980.0
Dicoumarin, dicumarol	964.2	E858.2	E934.2	E950.4	E962.0	E980.4
Dicyanogen (gas)	987.8	E869.8	—	E952.8	E962.2	E982.8
Dicyclomine	971.1	E855.4	E941.1	E950.4	E962.0	E980.4
Dieldrin (vapor)	989.2	E863.0	—	E950.6	E962.1	E980.7
Dienestrol	962.2	E858.0	E932.2	E950.4	E962.0	E980.4
Dietetics	977.0	E858.8	E947.0	E950.4	E962.0	E980.4
Diethazine	966.4	E855.0	E936.4	E950.4	E962.0	E980.4
Diethyl						
barbituric acid	967.0	E851	E937.0	E950.1	E962.0	E980.1
carbamazine	961.6	E857	E931.6	E950.4	E962.0	E980.4
carbinol	980.8	E860.8	—	E950.9	E962.1	E980.9
carbonate	982.8	E862.4	—	E950.9	E962.1	E980.9
ether (vapor) — see Ether(s)						
propion	977.0	E858.8	E947.0	E950.4	E962.0	E980.4
stilbestrol	962.2	E858.0	E932.2	E950.4	E962.0	E980.4
Diethylene						
dioxide	982.8	E862.4	—	E950.9	E962.1	E980.9
glycol (monoacetate) (monoethyl ether)	982.8	E862.4	—	E950.9	E962.1	E980.9
Diethylsulfone–diethylmethane	967.8	E852.8	E937.8	E950.2	E962.0	E980.2
Difencloxazine	965.09	E850.2	E935.2	E950.0	E962.0	E980.0
Diffusin	963.4	E858.1	E933.4	E950.4	E962.0	E980.4
Diflos	971.0	E855.3	E941.0	E950.4	E962.0	E980.4
Digestants	973.4	E858.4	E943.4	E950.4	E962.0	E980.4
Digitalin(e)	972.1	E858.3	E942.1	E950.4	E962.0	E980.4
Digitalis glycosides	972.1	E858.3	E942.1	E950.4	E962.0	E980.4
Digitoxin	972.1	E858.3	E942.1	E950.4	E962.0	E980.4
Digoxin	972.1	E858.3	E942.1	E950.4	E962.0	E980.4
Dihydrocodeine	965.09	E850.2	E935.2	E950.0	E962.0	E980.0
Dihydrocodeinone	965.09	E850.2	E935.2	E950.0	E962.0	E980.0
Dihydroergocristine	972.9	E858.3	E942.9	E950.4	E962.0	E980.4
Dihydroergotamine	972.9	E858.3	E942.9	E950.4	E962.0	E980.4
Dihydroergotoxine	972.9	E858.3	E942.9	E950.4	E962.0	E980.4
Dihydrohydroxycodeinone	965.09	E850.2	E935.2	E950.0	E962.0	E980.0
Dihydrohydroxymorphinone	965.09	E850.2	E935.2	E950.0	E962.0	E980.0
Dihydroisocodeine	965.09	E850.2	E935.2	E950.0	E962.0	E980.0
Dihydromorphine	965.09	E850.2	E935.2	E950.0	E962.0	E980.0
Dihydromorphinone	965.09	E850.2	E935.2	E950.0	E962.0	E980.0
Dihydrostreptomycin	960.6	E856	E930.6	E950.4	E962.0	E980.4
Dihydrotachysterol	962.6	E858.0	E932.6	E950.4	E962.0	E980.4

Substance	Poisoning	External Cause (E-Code)				
		Accident	Therapeutic Use	Suicide Attempt	Assault	Undetermined
Dihydroxyanthraquinone	973.1	E858.4	E943.1	E950.4	E962.0	E980.4
Dihydroxycodeinone	965.09	E850.2	E935.2	E950.0	E962.0	E980.0
Diiodohydroxyquin	961.3	E857	E931.3	E950.4	E962.0	E980.4
topical	976.0	E858.7	E946.0	E950.4	E962.0	E980.4
Diiodohydroxyquinoline	961.3	E857	E931.3	E950.4	E962.0	E980.4
Dilantin	966.1	E855.0	E936.1	E950.4	E962.0	E980.4
Dilaudid	965.09	E850.2	E935.2	E950.0	E962.0	E980.0
Diloxanide	961.5	E857	E931.5	E950.4	E962.0	E980.4
Dimefline	970.0	E854.3	E940.0	E950.4	E962.0	E980.4
Dimenhydrinate	963.0	E858.1	E933.0	E950.4	E962.0	E980.4
Dimercaprol	963.8	E858.1	E933.8	E950.4	E962.0	E980.4
Dimercaptopropanol	963.8	E858.1	E933.8	E950.4	E962.0	E980.4
Dimetane	963.0	E858.1	E933.0	E950.4	E962.0	E980.4
Dimethicone	976.3	E858.7	E946.3	E950.4	E962.0	E980.4
Dimethindene	963.0	E858.1	E933.0	E950.4	E962.0	E980.4
Dimethisoquin	968.5	E855.2	E938.5	E950.4	E962.0	E980.4
Dimethisterone	962.2	E858.0	E932.2	E950.4	E962.0	E980.4
Dimethoxanate	975.4	E858.6	E945.4	E950.4	E962.0	E980.4
Dimethyl						
arsine, arsinic acid — *see* Arsenic						
carbinol	980.2	E860.3	—	E950.9	E962.1	E980.9
diguanide	962.3	E858.0	E932.3	E950.4	E962.0	E980.4
ketone	982.8	E862.4	—	E950.9	E962.1	E980.9
vapor	987.8	E869.8	—	E952.8	E962.2	E982.8
meperidine	965.09	E850.2	E935.2	E950.0	E962.0	E980.0
parathion	989.3	E863.1	—	E950.6	E962.1	E980.7
polysiloxane	973.8	E858.4	E943.8	E950.4	E962.0	E980.4
sulfate (fumes)	987.8	E869.8	—	E952.8	E962.2	E982.8
liquid	983.9	E864.3	—	E950.7	E962.1	E980.6
sulfoxide NEC	982.8	E862.4	—	E950.9	E962.1	E980.9
medicinal	976.4	E858.7	E946.4	E950.4	E962.0	E980.4
triptamine	969.6	E854.1	E939.6	E950.3	E962.0	E980.3
tubocurarine	975.2	E858.6	E945.2	E950.4	E962.0	E980.4
Dindevan	964.2	E858.2	E934.2	E950.4	E962.0	E980.4
Dinitro (–ortho–) cresol (herbicide) (spray)	989.4	E863.5	—	E950.6	E962.1	E980.7
insecticide	989.4	E863.4	—	E950.6	E962.1	E980.7
Dinitrobenzene	983.0	E864.0	—	E950.7	E962.1	E980.6
vapor	987.8	E869.8	—	E952.8	E962.2	E982.8
Dinitro–orthocresol (herbicide)	989.4	E863.5	—	E950.6	E962.1	E980.7
insecticide	989.4	E863.4	—	E950.6	E962.1	E980.7
Dinitrophenol (herbicide) (spray)	989.4	E863.5	—	E950.6	E962.1	E980.7
insecticide	989.4	E863.4	—	E950.6	E962.1	E980.7
Dinoprost	975.0	E858.6	E945.0	E950.4	E962.0	E980.4
Dioctyl sulfosuccinate (calcium) (sodium)	973.2	E858.4	E943.2	E950.4	E962.0	E980.4
Diodoquin	961.3	E857	E931.3	E950.4	E962.0	E980.4
Dione derivatives NEC	966.3	E855.0	E936.3	E950.4	E962.0	E980.4
Dionin	965.09	E850.2	E935.2	E950.0	E962.0	E980.0
Dioxane	982.8	E862.4	—	E950.9	E962.1	E980.9
Dioxin — *see* herbicide						
Dioxyline	972.5	E858.3	E942.5	E950.4	E962.0	E980.4
Dipentene	982.8	E862.4	—	E950.9	E962.1	E980.9
Diphemanil	971.1	E855.4	E941.1	E950.4	E962.0	E980.4
Diphenadione	964.2	E858.2	E934.2	E950.4	E962.0	E980.4
Diphenhydramine	963.0	E858.1	E933.0	E950.4	E962.0	E980.4
Diphenidol	963.0	E858.1	E933.0	E950.4	E962.0	E980.4
Diphenoxylate	973.5	E858.4	E943.5	E950.4	E962.0	E980.4
Diphenylchloroarsine	985.1	E866.3	—	E950.8	E962.1	E980.8

Substance	Poisoning	External Cause (E-Code)				
		Accident	Therapeutic Use	Suicide Attempt	Assault	Undetermined
Diphenylhydantoin (sodium)	966.1	E855.0	E936.1	E950.4	E962.0	E980.4
Diphenylpyraline	963.0	E858.1	E933.0	E950.4	E962.0	E980.4
Diphtheria						
antitoxin	979.9	E858.8	E949.9	E950.4	E962.0	E980.4
toxoid	978.5	E858.8	E948.5	E950.4	E962.0	E980.4
with tetanus toxoid	978.9	E858.8	E948.9	E950.4	E962.0	E980.4
with pertussis component	978.6	E858.8	E948.6	E950.4	E962.0	E980.4
vaccine	978.5	E858.8	E948.5	E950.4	E962.0	E980.4
Dipipanone	965.09	E850.2	E935.2	E950.0	E962.0	E980.0
Diplovax	979.5	E858.8	E949.5	E950.4	E962.0	E980.4
Diprophylline	975.1	E858.6	E945.1	E950.4	E962.0	E980.4
Dipyridamole	972.4	E858.3	E942.4	E950.4	E962.0	E980.4
Dipyrone	965.5	E850.5	E935.5	E950.0	E962.0	E980.0
Diquat	989.4	E863.5	—	E950.6	E962.1	E980.7
Disinfectant NEC	983.9	E861.4	—	E950.7	E962.1	E980.6
alkaline	983.2	E861.4	—	E950.7	E962.1	E980.6
aromatic	983.0	E861.4	—	E950.7	E962.1	E980.6
Disipal	966.4	E855.0	E936.4	E950.4	E962.0	E980.4
Disodium edetate	963.8	E858.1	E933.8	E950.4	E962.0	E980.4
Disulfamide	974.4	E858.5	E944.4	E950.4	E962.0	E980.4
Disulfanilamide	961.0	E857	E931.0	E950.4	E962.0	E980.4
Disulfiram	977.3	E858.8	E947.3	E950.4	E962.0	E980.4
Dithiazanine	961.6	E857	E931.6	E950.4	E962.0	E980.4
Dithioglycerol	963.8	E858.1	E933.8	E950.4	E962.0	E980.4
Dithranol	976.4	E858.7	E946.4	E950.4	E962.0	E980.4
Diucardin	974.3	E858.5	E944.3	E950.4	E962.0	E980.4
Diupres	974.3	E858.5	E944.3	E950.4	E962.0	E980.4
Diuretics NEC	974.4	E858.5	E944.4	E950.4	E962.0	E980.4
carbonic acid anhydrase inhibitors	974.2	E858.5	E944.2	E950.4	E962.0	E980.4
mercurial	974.0	E858.5	E944.0	E950.4	E962.0	E980.4
osmotic	974.4	E858.5	E944.4	E950.4	E962.0	E980.4
purine derivatives	974.1	E858.5	E944.1	E950.4	E962.0	E980.4
saluretic	974.3	E858.5	E944.3	E950.4	E962.0	E980.4
Diuril	974.3	E858.5	E944.3	E950.4	E962.0	E980.4
Divinyl ether	968.2	E855.1	E938.2	E950.4	E962.0	E980.4
D–lysergic acid diethylamide	969.6	E854.1	E939.6	E950.3	E962.0	E980.3
DMCT	960.4	E856	E930.4	E950.4	E962.0	E980.4
DMSO	982.8	E862.4	—	E950.9	E962.1	E980.9
DMT	969.6	E854.1	E939.6	E950.3	E962.0	E980.3
DNOC	989.4	E863.5	—	E950.6	E962.1	E980.7
DOCA	962.0	E858.0	E932.0	E950.4	E962.0	E980.4
Dolophine	965.02	E850.1	E935.1	E950.0	E962.0	E980.0
Doloxene	965.8	E850.8	E935.8	E950.0	E962.0	E980.0
DOM	969.6	E854.1	E939.6	E950.3	E962.0	E980.3
Domestic gas — *see* Gas, utility						
Domiphen (bromide) (lozenges)	976.6	E858.7	E946.6	E950.4	E962.0	E980.4
Dopa (levo)	966.4	E855.0	E936.4	E950.4	E962.0	E980.4
Dopamine	971.2	E855.5	E941.2	E950.4	E962.0	E980.4
Doriden	967.5	E852.4	E937.5	E950.2	E962.0	E980.2
Dormiral	967.0	E851	E937.0	E950.1	E962.0	E980.1
Dormison	967.8	E852.8	E937.8	E950.2	E962.0	E980.2
Dornase	963.4	E858.1	E933.4	E950.4	E962.0	E980.4
Dorsacaine	968.5	E855.2	E938.5	E950.4	E962.0	E980.4
Dothiepin hydrochloride	969.0	E854.0	E939.0	E950.3	E962.0	E980.3
Doxapram	970.0	E854.3	E940.0	E950.4	E962.0	E980.4
Doxepin	969.0	E854.0	E939.0	E950.3	E962.0	E980.3
Doxorubicin	960.7	E856	E930.7	E950.4	E962.0	E980.4

Substance	Poisoning	External Cause (E-Code)				
		Accident	Therapeutic Use	Suicide Attempt	Assault	Undetermined
Doxycycline	960.4	E856	E930.4	E950.4	E962.0	E980.4
Doxylamine	963.0	E858.1	E933.0	E950.4	E962.0	E980.4
Dramamine	963.0	E858.1	E933.0	E950.4	E962.0	E980.4
Drano (drain cleaner)	983.2	E864.2	—	E950.7	E962.1	E980.6
Dromoran	965.09	E850.2	E935.2	E950.0	E962.0	E980.0
Dromostanolone	962.1	E858.0	E932.1	E950.4	E962.0	E980.4
Droperidol	969.2	E853.1	E939.2	E950.3	E962.0	E980.3
Drug	977.9	E858.9	E947.9	E950.5	E962.0	E980.5
specified NEC	977.8	E858.8	E947.8	E950.4	E962.0	E980.4
AHFS List						
4:00 antihistamine drugs	963.0	E858.1	E933.0	E950.4	E962.0	E980.4
8:04 amebacides	961.5	E857	E931.5	E950.4	E962.0	E980.4
arsenical anti–infectives	961.1	E857	E931.1	E950.4	E962.0	E980.4
quinoline derivatives	961.3	E857	E931.3	E950.4	E962.0	E980.4
8:08 anthelmintics	961.6	E857	E931.6	E950.4	E962.0	E980.4
quinoline derivatives	961.3	E857	E931.3	E950.4	E962.0	E980.4
8:12.04 antifungal antibiotics	960.1	E856	E930.1	E950.4	E962.0	E980.4
8:12.06 cephalosporins	960.5	E856	E930.5	E950.4	E962.0	E980.4
8:12.08 chloramphenicol	960.2	E856	E930.2	E950.4	E962.0	E980.4
8:12.12 erythromycins	960.3	E856	E930.3	E950.4	E962.0	E980.4
8:12.16 penicillins	960.0	E856	E930.0	E950.4	E962.0	E980.4
8:12.20 streptomycins	960.6	E856	E930.6	E950.4	E962.0	E980.4
8:12.24 tetracyclines	960.4	E856	E930.4	E950.4	E962.0	E980.4
8:12.28 other antibiotics	960.8	E856	E930.8	E950.4	E962.0	E980.4
antimycobacterial	960.6	E856	E930.6	E950.4	E962.0	E980.4
macrolides	960.3	E856	E930.3	E950.4	E962.0	E980.4
8:16 antituberculars	961.8	E857	E931.8	E950.4	E962.0	E980.4
antibiotics	960.6	E856	E930.6	E950.4	E962.0	E980.4
8:18 antivirals	961.7	E857	E931.7	E950.4	E962.0	E980.4
8:20 plasmodicides (antimalarials)	961.4	E857	E931.4	E950.4	E962.0	E980.4
8:24 sulfonamides	961.0	E857	E931.0	E950.4	E962.0	E980.4
8:26 sulfones	961.8	E857	E931.8	E950.4	E962.0	E980.4
8:28 treponemicides	961.2	E857	E931.2	E950.4	E962.0	E980.4
8:32 trichomonacides	961.5	E857	E931.5	E950.4	E962.0	E980.4
quinoline derivatives	961.3	E857	E931.3	E950.4	E962.0	E980.4
nitrofuran derivatives	961.9	E857	E931.9	E950.4	E962.0	E980.4
8:36 urinary germicides	961.9	E857	E931.9	E950.4	E962.0	E980.4
quinoline derivatives	961.3	E857	E931.3	E950.4	E962.0	E980.4
8:40 other anti–infectives	961.9	E857	E931.9	E950.4	E962.0	E980.4
10:00 antineoplastic agents	963.1	E858.1	E933.1	E950.4	E962.0	E980.4
antibiotics	960.7	E856	E930.7	E950.4	E962.0	E980.4
progestogens	962.2	E858.0	E932.2	E950.4	E962.0	E980.4
12:04 parasympathomimetic (cholinergic) agents	971.0	E855.3	E941.0	E950.4	E962.0	E980.4
12:08 parasympatholytic (cholinergic –blocking) agents	971.1	E855.4	E941.1	E950.4	E962.0	E980.4
12:12 Sympathomimetic (adrenergic) agents	971.2	E855.5	E941.2	E950.4	E962.0	E980.4
12:16 sympatholytic (adrenergic– blocking) agents	971.3	E855.6	E941.3	E950.4	E962.0	E980.4
12:20 skeletal muscle relaxants central nervous system muscle-tone depressants	968.0	E855.1	E938.0	E950.4	E962.0	E980.4
myoneural blocking agents	975.2	E858.6	E945.2	E950.4	E962.0	E980.4
16:00 blood derivatives	964.7	E858.2	E934.7	E950.4	E962.0	E980.4
20:04 antianemia drugs	964.1	E858.2	E934.1	E950.4	E962.0	E980.4
20:04.04 iron preparations	964.0	E858.2	E934.0	E950.4	E962.0	E980.4

Substance	Poisoning	External Cause (E-Code)				
		Accident	Therapeutic Use	Suicide Attempt	Assault	Undetermined
20:04.08 liver and stomach preparations	964.1	E858.2	E934.1	E950.4	E962.0	E980.4
20:12.04 anticoagulants	964.2	E858.2	E934.2	E950.4	E962.0	E980.4
20:12.08 antiheparin agents	964.5	E858.2	E934.5	E950.4	E962.0	E980.4
20:12.12 coagulants	964.5	E858.2	E934.5	E950.4	E962.0	E980.4
20:12.16 hemostatics NEC	964.5	E858.2	E934.5	E950.4	E962.0	E980.4
capillary active drugs	972.8	E858.3	E942.8	E950.4	E962.0	E980.4
24:04 cardiac drugs	972.9	E858.3	E942.9	E950.4	E962.0	E980.4
cardiotonic agents	972.1	E858.3	E942.1	E950.4	E962.0	E980.4
rhythm regulators	972.0	E858.3	E942.0	E950.4	E962.0	E980.4
24:06 antilipemic agents	972.2	E858.3	E942.2	E950.4	E962.0	E980.4
thyroid derivatives	962.7	E858.0	E932.7	E950.4	E962.0	E980.4
24:08 hypotensive agents	972.6	E858.3	E942.6	E950.4	E962.0	E980.4
adrenergic blocking agents	971.3	E855.6	E941.3	E950.4	E962.0	E980.4
ganglion blocking agents	972.3	E858.3	E942.3	E950.4	E962.0	E980.4
vasodilators	972.5	E858.3	E942.5	E950.4	E962.0	E980.4
24:12 vasodilating agents NEC	972.5	E858.3	E942.5	E950.4	E962.0	E980.4
coronary	972.4	E858.3	E942.4	E950.4	E962.0	E980.4
nicotinic acid derivatives	972.2	E858.3	E942.2	E950.4	E962.0	E980.4
24:16 sclerosing agents	972.7	E858.3	E942.7	E950.4	E962.0	E980.4
28:04 general anesthetics	968.4	E855.1	E938.4	E950.4	E962.0	E980.4
gaseous anesthetics	968.2	E855.1	E938.2	E950.4	E962.0	E980.4
halothane	968.1	E855.1	E938.1	E950.4	E962.0	E980.4
intravenous anesthetics	968.3	E855.1	E938.3	E950.4	E962.0	E980.4
28:08 analgesics and antipyretics	965.9	E850.9	E935.9	E950.0	E962.0	E980.0
antirheumatics	965.69	E850.6	E935.6	E950.0	E962.0	E980.0
aromatic analgesics	965.4	E850.4	E935.4	E950.0	E962.0	E980.0
non–narcotic NEC	965.7	E850.7	E935.7	E950.0	E962.0	E980.0
opium alkaloids	965.00	E850.2	E935.2	E950.0	E962.0	E980.0
heroin	965.01	E850.0	E935.0	E950.0	E962.0	E980.0
methadone	965.02	E850.1	E935.1	E950.0	E962.0	E980.0
specified type NEC	965.09	E850.2	E935.2	E950.0	E962.0	E980.0
pyrazole derivatives	965.5	E850.5	E935.5	E950.0	E962.0	E980.0
salicylates	965.1	E850.3	E935.3	E950.0	E962.0	E980.0
specified NEC	965.8	E850.8	E935.8	E950.0	E962.0	E980.0
28:10 narcotic antagonists	970.1	E854.3	E940.1	E950.4	E962.0	E980.4
28:12 anticonvulsants	966.3	E855.0	E936.3	E950.4	E962.0	E980.4
barbiturates	967.0	E851	E937.0	E950.1	E962.0	E980.1
benzodiazepine–based tranquilizers	969.4	E853.2	E939.4	E950.3	E962.0	E980.3
bromides	967.3	E852.2	E937.3	E950.2	E962.0	E980.2
hydantoin derivatives	966.1	E855.0	E936.1	E950.4	E962.0	E980.4
oxazolidine (derivatives)	966.0	E855.0	E936.0	E950.4	E962.0	E980.4
succinimides	966.2	E855.0	E936.2	E950.4	E962.0	E980.4
28:16.04 antidepressants	969.0	E854.0	E939.0	E950.3	E962.0	E980.3
28:16.08 tranquilizers	969.5	E853.9	E939.5	E950.3	E962.0	E980.3
benzodiazepine–based	969.4	E853.2	E939.4	E950.3	E962.0	E980.3
butyrophenone–based	969.2	E853.1	E939.2	E950.3	E962.0	E980.3
major NEC	969.3	E853.8	E939.3	E950.3	E962.0	E980.3
phenothiazine–based	969.1	E853.0	E939.1	E950.3	E962.0	E980.3
28:16.12 other psychotherapeutic agents	969.8	E855.8	E939.8	E950.3	E962.0	E980.3
28:20 respiratory and cerebral stimulants	970.9	E854.3	E940.9	E950.4	E962.0	E980.4
analeptics	970.0	E854.3	E940.0	E950.4	E962.0	E980.4
anorexigenic agents	977.0	E858.8	E947.0	E950.4	E962.0	E980.4
psychostimulants	969.7	E854.2	E939.7	E950.3	E962.0	E980.3
specified NEC	970.8	E854.3	E940.8	E950.4	E962.0	E980.4
28:24 sedatives and hypnotics	967.9	E852.9	E937.9	E950.2	E962.0	E980.2
barbiturates	967.0	E851	E937.0	E950.1	E962.0	E980.1

Substance	Poisoning	External Cause (E-Code)				
		Accident	Therapeutic Use	Suicide Attempt	Assault	Undetermined
benzodiazepine–based tranquilizers	969.4	E853.2	E939.4	E950.3	E962.0	E980.3
chloral hydrate (group)	967.1	E852.0	E937.1	E950.2	E962.0	E980.2
glutethamide group	967.5	E852.4	E937.5	E950.2	E962.0	E980.2
intravenous anesthetics	968.3	E855.1	E938.3	E950.4	E962.0	E980.4
methaqualone (compounds)	967.4	E852.3	E937.4	E950.2	E962.0	E980.2
paraldehyde	967.2	E852.1	E937.2	E950.2	E962.0	E980.2
phenothiazine–based tranquilizers	969.1	E853.0	E939.1	E950.3	E962.0	E980.3
specified NEC	967.8	E852.8	E937.8	E950.2	E962.0	E980.2
thiobarbiturates	968.3	E855.1	E938.3	E950.4	E962.0	E980.4
tranquilizer NEC	969.5	E853.9	E939.5	E950.3	E962.0	E980.3
36:04 to 36:88 diagnostic agents	977.8	E858.8	E947.8	E950.4	E962.0	E980.4
40:00 electrolyte, caloric, and water balance agents NEC	974.5	E858.5	E944.5	E950.4	E962.0	E980.4
40:04 acidifying agents	963.2	E858.1	E933.2	E950.4	E962.0	E980.4
40:08 alkalinizing agents	963.3	E858.1	E933.3	E950.4	E962.0	E980.4
40:10 ammonia detoxicants	974.5	E858.5	E944.5	E950.4	E962.0	E980.4
40:12 replacement solutions	974.5	E858.5	E944.5	E950.4	E962.0	E980.4
plasma expanders	964.8	E858.2	E934.8	E950.4	E962.0	E980.4
40:16 sodium–removing resins	974.5	E858.5	E944.5	E950.4	E962.0	E980.4
40:18 potassium–removing resins	974.5	E858.5	E944.5	E950.4	E962.0	E980.4
40:20 caloric agents	974.5	E858.5	E944.5	E950.4	E962.0	E980.4
40:24 salt and sugar substitutes	974.5	E858.5	E944.5	E950.4	E962.0	E980.4
40:28 diuretics NEC	974.4	E858.5	E944.4	E950.4	E962.0	E980.4
carbonic acid anhydrase inhibitors	974.2	E858.5	E944.2	E950.4	E962.0	E980.4
mercurials	974.0	E858.5	E944.0	E950.4	E962.0	E980.4
purine derivatives	974.1	E858.5	E944.1	E950.4	E962.0	E980.4
saluretics	974.3	E858.5	E944.3	E950.4	E962.0	E980.4
thiazides	974.3	E858.5	E944.3	E950.4	E962.1	E980.4
40:36 irrigating solutions	974.5	E858.5	E944.5	E950.4	E962.0	E980.4
40:40 uricosuric agents	974.7	E858.5	E944.7	E950.4	E962.0	E980.4
44:00 enzymes	963.4	E858.1	E933.4	E950.4	E962.0	E980.4
fibrinolysis–affecting agents	964.4	E858.2	E934.4	E950.4	E962.0	E980.4
gastric agents	973.4	E858.4	E943.4	E950.4	E962.0	E980.4
48:00 expectorants and cough preparations						
antihistamine agents	963.0	E858.1	E933.0	E950.4	E962.0	E980.4
antitussives	975.4	E858.6	E945.4	E950.4	E962.0	E980.4
codeine derivatives	965.09	E850.2	E935.2	E950.0	E962.0	E980.0
expectorants	975.5	E858.6	E945.5	E950.4	E962.0	E980.4
narcotic agents NEC	965.09	E850.2	E935.2	E950.0	E962.0	E980.0
52:04 anti–infectives (EENT)						
ENT agent	976.6	E858.7	E946.6	E950.4	E962.0	E980.4
ophthalmic preparation	976.5	E858.7	E946.5	E950.4	E962.0	E980.4
52:04.04 antibiotics (EENT)						
ENT agent	976.6	E858.7	E946.6	E950.4	E962.0	E980.4
ophthalmic preparation	976.5	E858.7	E946.5	E950.4	E962.0	E980.4
52:04.06 antivirals (EENT)						
ENT agent	976.6	E858.7	E946.6	E950.4	E962.0	E980.4
ophthalmic preparation	976.5	E858.7	E946.5	E950.4	E962.0	E980.4
52:04.08 sulfonamides (EENT)						
ENT agent	976.6	E858.7	E946.6	E950.4	E962.0	E980.4
ophthalmic preparation	976.5	E858.7	E946.5	E950.4	E962.0	E980.4
52:04.12 miscellaneous anti–infectives (EENT)						
ENT agent	976.6	E858.7	E946.6	E950.4	E962.0	E980.4
ophthalmic preparation	976.5	E858.7	E946.5	E950.4	E962.0	E980.4
52:08 anti–inflammatory agents (EENT)						
ENT agent	976.6	E858.7	E946.6	E950.4	E962.0	E980.4
ophthalmic preparation	976.5	E858.7	E946.5	E950.4	E962.0	E980.4

Substance	Poisoning	External Cause (E-Code)				
		Accident (Therapeutic Use)	Therapeutic Use	Suicide Attempt	Assault	Undetermined
52:10 carbonic anhydrase inhibitors	974.2	E858.5	E944.2	E950.4	E962.0	E980.4
52:12 contact lens solutions	976.5	E858.7	E946.5	E950.4	E962.0	E980.4
52:16 local anesthetics (EENT)	968.5	E855.2	E938.5	E950.4	E962.0	E980.4
52:20 miotics	971.0	E855.3	E941.0	E950.4	E962.0	E980.4
52:24 mydriatics						
adrenergics	971.2	E855.5	E941.2	E950.4	E962.0	E980.4
anticholinergics	971.1	E855.4	E941.1	E950.4	E962.0	E980.4
antimuscarinics	971.1	E855.4	E941.1	E950.4	E962.0	E980.4
parasympatholytics	971.1	E855.4	E941.1	E950.4	E962.0	E980.4
spasmolytics	971.1	E855.4	E941.1	E950.4	E962.0	E980.4
sympathomimetics	971.2	E855.5	E941.2	E950.4	E962.0	E980.4
52:28 mouth washes and gargles	976.6	E858.7	E946.6	E950.4	E962.0	E980.4
52:32 vasoconstrictors (EENT)	971.2	E855.5	E941.2	E950.4	E962.0	E980.4
52:36 unclassified agents (EENT)						
ENT agent	976.6	E858.7	E946.6	E950.4	E962.0	E980.4
ophthalmic preparation	976.5	E858.7	E946.5	E950.4	E962.0	E980.4
56:04 antacids and adsorbents	973.0	E858.4	E943.0	E950.4	E962.0	E980.4
56:08 Antidiarrhea agents	973.5	E858.4	E943.5	E950.4	E962.0	E980.4
56:10 antiflatulents	973.8	E858.4	E943.8	E950.4	E962.0	E980.4
56:12 cathartics NEC	973.3	E858.4	E943.3	E950.4	E962.0	E980.4
emollients	973.2	E858.4	E943.2	E950.4	E962.0	E980.4
irritants	973.1	E858.4	E943.1	E950.4	E962.0	E980.4
56:16 digestants	973.4	E858.4	E943.4	E950.4	E962.0	E980.4
56:20 emetics and antiemetics						
antiemetics	963.0	E858.1	E933.0	E950.4	E962.0	E980.4
emetics	973.6	E858.4	E943.6	E950.4	E962.0	E980.4
56:24 lipotropic agents	977.1	E858.8	E947.1	E950.4	E962.0	E980.4
56:40 miscellaneous G.I. drugs	973.8	E858.4	E943.8	E950.4	E962.0	E980.4
60:00 gold compounds	965.69	E850.6	E935.6	E950.0	E962.0	E980.0
64:00 heavy metal antagonists	963.8	E858.1	E933.8	E950.4	E962.0	E980.4
68:04 adrenals	962.0	E858.0	E932.0	E950.4	E962.0	E980.4
68:08 androgens	962.1	E858.0	E932.1	E950.4	E962.0	E980.4
68:12 contraceptives, oral	962.2	E858.0	E932.2	E950.4	E962.0	E980.4
68:16 estrogens	962.2	E858.0	E932.2	E950.4	E962.0	E980.4
68:18 gonadotropins	962.4	E858.0	E932.4	E950.4	E962.0	E980.4
68:20 insulins and antidiabetic agents	962.3	E858.0	E932.3	E950.4	E962.0	E980.4
68:20.08 insulins	962.3	E858.0	E932.3	E950.4	E962.0	E980.4
68:24 parathyroid	962.6	E858.0	E932.6	E950.4	E962.0	E980.4
68:28 pituitary (posterior)	962.5	E858.0	E932.5	E950.4	E962.0	E980.4
anterior	962.4	E858.0	E932.4	E950.4	E962.0	E980.4
68:32 progestogens	962.2	E858.0	E932.2	E950.4	E962.0	E980.4
68:34 other corpus luteum hormones NEC	962.2	E858.0	E932.2	E950.4	E962.0	E980.4
68:36 thyroid and antithyroid						
antithyroid	962.8	E858.0	E932.8	E950.4	E962.0	E980.4
thyroid (derivatives)	962.7	E858.0	E932.7	E950.4	E962.0	E980.4
72:00 local anesthetics NEC	968.9	E855.2	E938.9	E950.4	E962.0	E980.4
topical (surface)	968.5	E855.2	E938.5	E950.4	E962.0	E980.4
infiltration (intradermal) (subcutaneous) (submucosal)	968.5	E855.2	E938.5	E950.4	E962.0	E980.4
nerve blocking (peripheral) (plexus) (regional)	968.6	E855.2	E938.6	E950.4	E962.0	E980.4
spinal	968.7	E855.2	E938.7	E950.4	E962.0	E980.4
76:00 oxytocics	975.0	E858.6	E945.0	E950.4	E962.0	E980.4
78:00 radioactive agents	990	—	—	—	—	—
80:04 serums NEC	979.9	E858.8	E949.9	E950.4	E962.0	E980.4
immune gamma globulin (human)	964.6	E858.2	E934.6	E950.4	E962.0	E980.4

Substance		External Cause (E-Code)				
	Poisoning	Accident	Therapeutic Use	Suicide Attempt	Assault	Undetermined
80:08 toxoids NEC	978.8	E858.8	E948.8	E950.4	E962.0	E980.4
diphtheria	978.5	E858.8	E948.5	E950.4	E962.0	E980.4
and tetanus	978.9	E858.8	E948.9	E950.4	E962.0	E980.4
with pertussis component	978.6	E858.8	E948.6	E950.4	E962.0	E980.4
tetanus	978.4	E858.8	E948.4	E950.4	E962.0	E980.4
and diphtheria	978.9	E858.8	E948.9	E950.4	E962.0	E980.4
with pertussis component	978.6	E858.8	E948.6	E950.4	E962.0	E980.4
80:12 vaccines	979.9	E858.8	E949.9	E950.4	E962.0	E980.4
bacterial NEC	978.8	E858.8	E948.8	E950.4	E962.0	E980.4
with						
other bacterial components	978.9	E858.8	E948.9	E950.4	E962.0	E980.4
pertussis component	978.6	E858.8	E948.6	E950.4	E962.0	E980.4
viral and rickettsial						
components	979.7	E858.8	E949.7	E950.4	E962.0	E980.4
rickettsial NEC	979.6	E858.8	E949.6	E950.4	E962.0	E980.4
with						
bacterial component	979.7	E858.8	E949.7	E950.4	E962.0	E980.4
pertussis component	978.6	E858.8	E948.6	E950.4	E962.0	E980.4
viral component	979.7	E858.8	E949.7	E950.4	E962.0	E980.4
viral NEC	979.6	E858.8	E949.6	E950.4	E962.0	E980.4
with						
bacterial component	979.7	E858.8	E949.7	E950.4	E962.0	E980.4
pertussis component	978.6	E858.8	E948.6	E950.4	E962.0	E980.4
rickettsial component	979.7	E858.8	E949.7	E950.4	E962.0	E980.4
84:04.04 antibiotics (skin and mucous membrane)	976.0	E858.7	E946.0	E950.4	E962.0	E980.4
84:04.08 fungicides (skin and mucous membrane)	976.0	E858.7	E946.0	E950.4	E962.0	E980.4
84:04.12 scabicides and pediculicides (skin and mucous membrane)	976.0	E858.7	E946.0	E950.4	E962.0	E980.4
84:04.16 miscellaneous local anti–infectives (skin and mucous membrane)	976.0	E858.7	E946.0	E950.4	E962.0	E980.4
84:06 anti–inflammatory agents (skin and mucous membrane)	976.0	E858.7	E946.0	E950.4	E962.0	E980.4
84:08 antipruritics and local anesthetics						
antipruritics	976.1	E858.7	E946.1	E950.4	E962.0	E980.4
local anesthetics	968.5	E855.2	E938.5	E950.4	E962.0	E980.4
84:12 astringents	976.2	E858.7	E946.2	E950.4	E962.0	E980.4
84:16 cell stimulants and proliferants	976.8	E858.7	E946.8	E950.4	E962.0	E980.4
84:20 detergents	976.2	E858.7	E946.2	E950.4	E962.0	E980.4
84:24 emollients, demulcents, and protectants	976.3	E858.7	E946.3	E950.4	E962.0	E980.4
84:28 keratolytic agents	976.4	E858.7	E946.4	E950.4	E962.0	E980.4
84:32 keratoplastic agents	976.4	E858.7	E946.4	E950.4	E962.0	E980.4
84:36 miscellaneous agents (skin and mucous membrane)	976.8	E858.7	E946.8	E950.4	E962.0	E980.4
86:00 spasmolytic agents	975.1	E858.6	E945.1	E950.4	E962.0	E980.4
antiasthmatics	975.7	E858.6	E945.7	E950.4	E962.0	E980.4
papaverine	972.5	E858.3	E942.5	E950.4	E962.0	E980.4
theophylline	974.1	E858.5	E944.1	E950.4	E962.0	E980.4
88:04 vitamin A	963.5	E858.1	E933.5	E950.4	E962.0	E980.4
88:08 vitamin B complex	963.5	E858.1	E933.5	E950.4	E962.0	E980.4
hematopoietic vitamin	964.1	E858.2	E934.1	E950.4	E962.0	E980.4
nicotinic acid derivatives	972.2	E858.3	E942.2	E950.4	E962.0	E980.4
88:12 vitamin C	963.5	E858.1	E933.5	E950.4	E962.0	E980.4
88:16 vitamin D	963.5	E858.1	E933.5	E950.4	E962.0	E980.4

Substance	Poisoning	External Cause (E-Code)				
		Accident	Therapeutic Use	Suicide Attempt	Assault	Undetermined
88:20 vitamin E	963.5	E858.1	E933.5	E950.4	E962.0	E980.4
88:24 vitamin K activity	964.3	E858.2	E934.3	E950.4	E962.0	E980.4
88:28 multivitamin preparations	963.5	E858.1	E933.5	E950.4	E962.0	E980.4
92:00 unclassified therapeutic agents	977.8	E858.8	E947.8	E950.4	E962.0	E980.4
Duboisine	971.1	E855.4	E941.1	E950.4	E962.0	E980.4
Dulcolax	973.1	E858.4	E943.1	E950.4	E962.0	E980.4
Duponol (C) (EP)	976.2	E858.7	E946.2	E950.4	E962.0	E980.4
Durabolin	962.1	E858.0	E932.1	E950.4	E962.0	E980.4
Dyclone	968.5	E855.2	E938.5	E950.4	E962.0	E980.4
Dyclonine	968.5	E855.2	E938.5	E950.4	E962.0	E980.4
Dydrogesterone	962.2	E858.0	E932.2	E950.4	E962.0	E980.4
Dyes NEC	989.89	E866.8	—	E950.9	E962.1	E980.9
diagnostic agents	977.8	E858.8	E947.8	E950.4	E962.0	E980.4
pharmaceutical NEC	977.4	E858.8	E947.4	E950.4	E962.0	E980.4
Dyfols	971.0	E855.3	E941.0	E950.4	E962.0	E980.4
Dymelor	962.3	E858.0	E932.3	E950.4	E962.0	E980.4
Dynamite	989.89	E866.8	—	E950.9	E962.1	E980.9
fumes	987.8	E869.8	—	E952.8	E962.2	E982.8
Dyphylline	975.1	E858.6	E945.1	E950.4	E962.0	E980.4
Ear preparations	976.6	E858.7	E946.6	E950.4	E962.0	E980.4
Echothiopate, ecothiopate	971.0	E855.3	E941.0	E950.4	E962.0	E980.4
Ectylurea	967.8	E852.8	E937.8	E950.2	E962.0	E980.2
Edathamil disodium	963.8	E858.1	E933.8	E950.4	E962.0	E980.4
Edecrin	974.4	E858.5	E944.4	E950.4	E962.0	E980.4
Edetate, disodium (calcium)	963.8	E858.1	E933.8	E950.4	E962.0	E980.4
Edrophonium	971.0	E855.3	E941.0	E950.4	E962.0	E980.4
Elase	976.8	E858.7	E946.8	E950.4	E962.0	E980.4
Elaterium	973.1	E858.4	E943.1	E950.4	E962.0	E980.4
Elder	988.2	E865.4	—	E950.9	E962.1	E980.9
berry (unripe)	988.2	E865.3	—	E950.9	E962.1	E980.9
Electrolytes NEC	974.5	E858.5	E944.5	E950.4	E962.0	E980.4
Electrolytic agent NEC	974.5	E858.5	E944.5	E950.4	E962.0	E980.4
Embramine	963.0	E858.1	E933.0	E950.4	E962.0	E980.4
Emetics	973.6	E858.4	E943.6	E950.4	E962.0	E980.4
Emetine (hydrochloride)	961.5	E857	E931.5	E950.4	E962.0	E980.4
Emollients	976.3	E858.7	E946.3	E950.4	E962.0	E980.4
Emylcamate	969.5	E853.8	E939.5	E950.3	E962.0	E980.3
Encyprate	969.0	E854.0	E939.0	E950.3	E962.0	E980.3
Endocaine	968.5	E855.2	E938.5	E950.4	E962.0	E980.4
Endrin	989.2	E863.0	—	E950.6	E962.1	E980.7
Enflurane	968.2	E855.1	E938.2	E950.4	E962.0	E980.4
Enovid	962.2	E858.0	E932.2	E950.4	E962.0	E980.4
ENT preparations (anti–infectives)	976.6	E858.7	E946.6	E950.4	E962.0	E980.4
Enzodase	963.4	E858.1	E933.4	E950.4	E962.0	E980.4
Enzymes NEC	963.4	E858.1	E933.4	E950.4	E962.0	E980.4
Epanutin	966.1	E855.0	E936.1	E950.4	E962.0	E980.4
Ephedra (tincture)	971.2	E855.5	E941.2	E950.4	E962.0	E980.4
Ephedrine	971.2	E855.5	E941.2	E950.4	E962.0	E980.4
Epiestriol	962.2	E858.0	E932.2	E950.4	E962.0	E980.4
Epilim — *see* Sodium valproate						
Epinephrine	971.2	E855.5	E941.2	E950.4	E962.0	E980.4
Epsom salt	973.3	E858.4	E943.3	E950.4	E962.0	E980.4
Equanil	969.5	E853.8	E939.5	E950.3	E962.0	E980.3
Equisetum (diuretic)	974.4	E858.5	E944.4	E950.4	E962.0	E980.4
Ergometrine	975.0	E858.6	E945.0	E950.4	E962.0	E980.4
Ergonovine	975.0	E858.6	E945.0	E950.4	E962.0	E980.4
Ergot NEC	988.2	E865.4	—	E950.9	E962.1	E980.9

Substance	Poisoning	External Cause (E-Code)				
		Accident	Therapeutic Use	Suicide Attempt	Assault	Undetermined
medicinal (alkaloids)	975.0	E858.6	E945.0	E950.4	E962.0	E980.4
Ergotamine (tartrate) (for migraine) NEC	972.9	E858.3	E942.9	E950.4	E962.0	E980.4
Ergotrate	975.0	E858.6	E945.0	E950.4	E962.0	E980.4
Erythrityl tetranitrate	972.4	E858.3	E942.4	E950.4	E962.0	E980.4
Erythrol tetranitrate	972.4	E858.3	E942.4	E950.4	E962.0	E980.4
Erythromycin	960.3	E856	E930.3	E950.4	E962.0	E980.4
ophthalmic preparation	976.5	E858.7	E946.5	E950.4	E962.0	E980.4
topical NEC	976.0	E858.7	E946.0	E950.4	E962.0	E980.4
Eserine	971.0	E855.3	E941.0	E950.4	E962.0	E980.4
Eskabarb	967.0	E851	E937.0	E950.1	E962.0	E980.1
Eskalith	969.8	E855.8	E939.8	E950.3	E962.0	E980.3
Estradiol (cypionate) (dipropionate) (valerate)	962.2	E858.0	E932.2	E950.4	E962.0	E980.4
Estriol	962.2	E858.0	E932.2	E950.4	E962.0	E980.4
Estrogens (with progestogens)	962.2	E858.0	E932.2	E950.4	E962.0	E980.4
Estrone	962.2	E858.0	E932.2	E950.4	E962.0	E980.4
Etafedrine	971.2	E855.5	E941.2	E950.4	E962.0	E980.4
Ethacrynate sodium	974.4	E858.5	E944.4	E950.4	E962.0	E980.4
Ethacrynic acid	974.4	E858.5	E944.4	E950.4	E962.0	E980.4
Ethambutol	961.8	E857	E931.8	E950.4	E962.0	E980.4
Ethamide	974.2	E858.5	E944.2	E950.4	E962.0	E980.4
Ethamivan	970.0	E854.3	E940.0	E950.4	E962.0	E980.4
Ethamsylate	964.5	E858.2	E934.5	E950.4	E962.0	E980.4
Ethanol	980.0	E860.1	—	E950.9	E962.1	E980.9
beverage	980.0	E860.0	—	E950.9	E962.1	E980.9
Ethchlorvynol	967.8	E852.8	E937.8	E950.2	E962.0	E980.2
Ethebenecid	974.7	E858.5	E944.7	E950.4	E962.0	E980.4
Ether(s) (diethyl) (ethyl) (vapor)	987.8	E869.8	—	E952.8	E962.2	E982.8
anesthetic	968.2	E855.1	E938.2	E950.4	E962.0	E980.4
petroleum — see Ligroin						
solvent	982.8	E862.4	—	E950.9	E962.1	E980.9
Ethidine chloride (vapor)	987.8	E869.8	—	E952.8	E962.2	E982.8
liquid (solvent)	982.3	E862.4	—	E950.9	E962.1	E980.9
Ethinamate	967.8	E852.8	E937.8	E950.2	E962.0	E980.2
Ethinylestradiol	962.2	E858.0	E932.2	E950.4	E962.0	E980.4
Ethionamide	961.8	E857	E931.8	E950.4	E962.0	E980.4
Ethisterone	962.2	E858.0	E932.2	E950.4	E962.0	E980.4
Ethobral	967.0	E851	E937.0	E950.1	E962.0	E980.1
Ethocaine (infiltration) (topical)	968.5	E855.2	E938.5	E950.4	E962.0	E980.4
nerve block (peripheral) (plexus)	968.6	E855.2	E938.6	E950.4	E962.0	E980.4
spinal	968.7	E855.2	E938.7	E950.4	E962.0	E980.4
Ethoheptazine (citrate)	965.7	E850.7	E935.7	E950.0	E962.0	E980.0
Ethopropazine	966.4	E855.0	E936.4	E950.4	E962.0	E980.4
Ethosuximide	966.2	E855.0	E936.2	E950.4	E962.0	E980.4
Ethotoin	966.1	E855.0	E936.1	E950.4	E962.0	E980.4
Ethoxazene	961.9	E857	E931.9	E950.4	E962.0	E980.4
Ethoxzolamide	974.2	E858.5	E944.2	E950.4	E962.0	E980.4
Ethyl						
acetate (vapor)	982.8	E862.4	—	E950.9	E962.1	E980.9
alcohol	980.0	E860.1	—	E950.9	E962.1	E980.9
beverage	980.0	E860.0	—	E950.9	E962.1	E980.9
aldehyde (vapor)	987.8	E869.8	—	E952.8	E962.2	E982.8
liquid	989.89	E866.8	—	E950.9	E962.1	E980.9
aminobenzoate	968.5	E855.2	E938.5	E950.4	E962.0	E980.4
biscoumacetate	964.2	E858.2	E934.2	E950.4	E962.0	E980.4
bromide (anesthetic)	968.2	E855.1	E938.2	E950.4	E962.0	E980.4
carbamate (antineoplastic)	963.1	E858.1	E933.1	E950.4	E962.0	E980.4

Substance	Poisoning	External Cause (E-Code)				
		Accident	Therapeutic Use	Suicide Attempt	Assault	Undetermined
carbinol	980.3	E860.4	—	E950.9	E962.1	E980.9
chaulmoograte	961.8	E857	E931.8	E950.4	E962.0	E980.4
chloride (vapor)	987.8	E869.8	—	E952.8	E962.2	E982.8
anesthetic (local)	968.5	E855.2	E938.5	E950.4	E962.0	E980.4
inhaled	968.2	E855.1	E938.2	E950.4	E962.0	E980.4
solvent	982.3	E862.4	—	E950.9	E962.1	E980.9
estranol	962.1	E858.0	E932.1	E950.4	E962.0	E980.4
ether — *see* Ether(s)						
formate (solvent) NEC	982.8	E862.4	—	E950.9	E962.1	E980.9
iodoacetate	987.5	E869.3	—	E952.8	E962.2	E982.8
lactate (solvent) NEC	982.8	E862.4	—	E950.9	E962.1	E980.9
methylcarbinol	980.8	E860.8	—	E950.9	E962.1	E980.9
morphine	965.09	E850.2	E935.2	E950.0	E962.0	E980.0
Ethylene (gas)	987.1	E869.8	—	E952.8	E962.2	E982.8
anesthetic (general)	968.2	E855.1	E938.2	E950.4	E962.0	E980.4
chlorohydrin (vapor)	982.3	E862.4	—	E950.9	E962.1	E980.9
dichloride (vapor)	982.3	E862.4	—	E950.9	E962.1	E980.9
glycol(s) (any) (vapor)	982.8	E862.4	—	E950.9	E962.1	E980.9
Ethylidene						
chloride NEC	982.3	E862.4	—	E950.9	E962.1	E980.9
diethyl ether	982.8	E862.4	—	E950.9	E962.1	E980.9
Ethynodiol	962.2	E858.0	E932.2	E950.4	E962.0	E980.4
Etidocaine	968.9	E855.2	E938.9	E950.4	E962.0	E980.4
infiltration (subcutaneous)	968.5	E855.2	E938.5	E950.4	E962.0	E980.4
nerve (peripheral) (plexus)	968.6	E855.2	E938.6	E950.4	E962.0	E980.4
Etilfen	967.0	E851	E937.0	E950.1	E962.0	E980.1
Etomide	965.7	E850.7	E935.7	E950.0	E962.0	E980.0
Etorphine	965.09	E850.2	E935.2	E950.0	E962.0	E980.0
Etoval	967.0	E851	E937.0	E950.1	E962.0	E980.1
Etryptamine	969.0	E854.0	E939.0	E950.3	E962.0	E980.3
Eucaine	968.5	E855.2	E938.5	E950.4	E962.0	E980.4
Eucalyptus (oil) NEC	975.5	E858.6	E945.5	E950.4	E962.0	E980.4
Eucatropine	971.1	E855.4	E941.1	E950.4	E962.0	E980.4
Eucodal	965.09	E850.2	E935.2	E950.0	E962.0	E980.0
Euneryl	967.0	E851	E937.0	E950.1	E962.0	E980.1
Euphthalmine	971.1	E855.4	E941.1	E950.4	E962.0	E980.4
Eurax	976.0	E858.7	E946.0	E950.4	E962.0	E980.4
Euresol	976.4	E858.7	E946.4	E950.4	E962.0	E980.4
Euthroid	962.7	E858.0	E932.7	E950.4	E962.0	E980.4
Evans blue	977.8	E858.8	E947.8	E950.4	E962.0	E980.4
Evipal	967.0	E851	E937.0	E950.1	E962.0	E980.1
sodium	968.3	E855.1	E938.3	E950.4	E962.0	E980.4
Evipan	967.0	E851	E937.0	E950.1	E962.0	E980.1
sodium	968.3	E855.1	E938.3	E950.4	E962.0	E980.4
Exalgin	965.4	E850.4	E935.4	E950.0	E962.0	E980.0
Excipients, pharmaceutical	977.4	E858.8	E947.4	E950.4	E962.0	E980.4
Exhaust gas — *see* Carbon, monoxide						
Ex–Lax (phenolphthalein)	973.1	E858.4	E943.1	E950.4	E962.0	E980.4
Expectorants	975.5	E858.6	E945.5	E950.4	E962.0	E980.4
External medications (skin) (mucous membrane)	976.9	E858.7	E946.9	E950.4	E962.0	E980.4
dental agent	976.7	E858.7	E946.7	E950.4	E962.0	E980.4
ENT agent	976.6	E858.7	E946.6	E950.4	E962.0	E980.4
ophthalmic preparation	976.5	E858.7	E946.5	E950.4	E962.0	E980.4
specified NEC	976.8	E858.7	E946.8	E950.4	E962.0	E980.4
Eye agents (anti–infective)	976.5	E858.7	E946.5	E950.4	E962.0	E980.4
Factor IX complex (human)	964.5	E858.2	E934.5	E950.4	E962.0	E980.4

Substance	Poisoning	External Cause (E-Code)				
		Accident	Therapeutic Use	Suicide Attempt	Assault	Undetermined
Fecal softeners	973.2	E858.4	E943.2	E950.4	E962.0	E980.4
Fenbutrazate	977.0	E858.8	E947.0	E950.4	E962.0	E980.4
Fencamfamin	970.8	E854.3	E940.8	E950.4	E962.0	E980.4
Fenfluramine	977.0	E858.8	E947.0	E950.4	E962.0	E980.4
Fenoprofen	965.61	E850.6	E935.6	E950.0	E962.0	E980.0
Fentanyl	965.09	E850.2	E935.2	E950.0	E962.0	E980.0
Fentazin	969.1	E853.0	E939.1	E950.3	E962.0	E980.3
Fenticlor, fentichlor	976.0	E858.7	E946.0	E950.4	E962.0	E980.4
Fer de lance (bite) (venom)	989.5	E905.0	—	E950.9	E962.1	E980.9
Ferric — *see* Iron						
Ferrocholinate	964.0	E858.2	E934.0	E950.4	E962.0	E980.4
Ferrous fumerate, gluconate, lactate. salt						
NEC, sulfate (medicinal)	964.0	E858.2	E934.0	E950.4	E962.0	E980.4
Ferrum — *see* Iron						
Fertilizers NEC	989.89	E866.5	—	E950.9	E962.1	E980.4
with herbicide mixture	989.4	E863.5	—	E950.6	E962.1	E980.7
Fibrinogen (human)	964.7	E858.2	E934.7	E950.4	E962.0	E980.4
Fibrinolysin	964.4	E858.2	E934.4	E950.4	E962.0	E980.4
Fibrinolysis–affecting agents	964.4	E858.2	E934.4	E950.4	E962.0	E980.4
Filix mas	961.6	E857	E931.6	E950.4	E962.0	E980.4
Fiorinal	965.1	E850.3	E935.3	E950.0	E962.0	E980.0
Fire damp	987.1	E869.8	—	E952.8	E962.2	E982.8
Fish, nonbacterial or noxious	988.0	E865.2	—	E950.9	E962.1	E980.9
shell	988.0	E865.1	—	E950.9	E962.1	E980.9
Flagyl	961.5	E857	E931.5	E950.4	E962.0	E980.4
Flavoxate	975.1	E858.6	E945.1	E950.4	E962.0	E980.4
Flaxedil	975.2	E858.6	E945.2	E950.4	E962.0	E980.4
Flaxseed (medicinal)	976.3	E858.7	E946.3	E950.4	E962.0	E980.4
Florantyrone	973.4	E858.4	E943.4	E950.4	E962.0	E980.4
Floraquin	961.3	E857	E931.3	E950.4	E962.0	E980.4
Florinef	962.0	E858.0	E932.0	E950.4	E962.0	E980.4
ENT agent	976.6	E858.7	E946.6	E950.4	E962.0	E980.4
ophthalmic preparation	976.5	E858.7	E946.5	E950.4	E962.0	E980.4
topical NEC	976.0	E858.7	E946.0	E950.4	E962.0	E980.4
Flowers of sulfur	976.4	E858.7	E946.4	E950.4	E962.0	E980.4
Floxuridine	963.1	E858.1	E933.1	E950.4	E962.0	E980.4
Flucytosine	961.9	E857	E931.9	E950.4	E962.0	E980.4
Fludrocortisone	962.0	E858.0	E932.0	E950.4	E962.0	E980.4
ENT agent	976.6	E858.7	E946.6	E950.4	E962.0	E980.4
ophthalmic preparation	976.5	E858.7	E946.5	E950.4	E962.0	E980.4
topical NEC	976.0	E858.7	E946.0	E950.4	E962.0	E980.4
Flumethasone	976.0	E858.7	E946.0	E950.4	E962.0	E980.4
Flumethiazide	974.3	E858.5	E944.3	E950.4	E962.0	E980.4
Flumidin	961.7	E857	E931.7	E950.4	E962.0	E980.4
Fluocinolone	976.0	E858.7	E946.0	E950.4	E962.0	E980.4
Fluocortolone	962.0	E858.0	E932.0	E950.4	E962.0	E980.4
Fluohydrocortisone	962.0	E858.0	E932.0	E950.4	E962.0	E980.4
ENT agent	976.6	E858.7	E946.6	E950.4	E962.0	E980.4
ophthalmic preparation	976.5	E858.7	E946.5	E950.4	E962.0	E980.4
topical NEC	976.0	E858.7	E946.0	E950.4	E962.0	E980.4
Fluonid	976.0	E858.7	E946.0	E950.4	E962.0	E980.4
Fluopromazine	969.1	E853.0	E939.1	E950.3	E962.0	E980.3
Fluoracetate	989.4	E863.7	—	E950.6	E962.1	E980.7
Fluorescein (sodium)	977.8	E858.8	E947.8	E950.4	E962.0	E980.4
Fluoride(s) (pesticides) (sodium) NEC	989.4	E863.4	—	E950.6	E962.1	E980.7
hydrogen — *see* Hydrofluoric acid						
medicinal	976.7	E858.7	E946.7	E950.4	E962.0	E980.4

Substance	Poisoning	External Cause (E-Code)				
		Accident	Therapeutic Use	Suicide Attempt	Assault	Undetermined
not pesticide NEC	983.9	E864.4	—	E950.7	E962.1	E980.6
stannous	976.7	E858.7	E946.7	E950.4	E962.0	E980.4
Fluorinated corticosteroids	962.0	E858.0	E932.0	E950.4	E962.0	E980.4
Fluorine (compounds) (gas)	987.8	E869.8	—	E952.8	E962.2	E982.8
salt — *see* Fluoride(s)						
Fluoristan	976.7	E858.7	E946.7	E950.4	E962.0	E980.4
Fluoroacetate	989.4	E863.7	—	E950.6	E962.1	E980.7
Fluorodeoxyuridine	963.1	E858.1	E933.1	E950.4	E962.0	E980.4
Fluorometholone (topical) NEC	976.0	E858.7	E946.0	E950.4	E962.0	E980.4
ophthalmic preparation	976.5	E858.7	E946.5	E950.4	E962.0	E980.4
Fluorouracil	963.1	E858.1	E933.1	E950.4	E962.0	E980.4
Fluothane	968.1	E855.1	E938.1	E950.4	E962.0	E980.4
Fluoxetine hydrochloride	969.0	E854.0	E939.0	E950.3	E962.0	E980.3
Fluoxymesterone	962.1	E858.0	E932.1	E950.4	E962.0	E980.4
Fluphenazine	969.1	E853.0	E939.1	E950.3	E962.0	E980.3
Fluprednisolone	962.0	E858.0	E932.0	E950.4	E962.0	E980.4
Flurandrenolide	976.0	E858.7	E946.0	E950.4	E962.0	E980.4
Flurazepam (hydrochloride)	969.4	E853.2	E939.4	E950.3	E962.0	E980.3
Flurbiprofen	965.61	E850.6	E935.6	E950.0	E962.0	E980.0
Flurobate	976.0	E858.7	E946.0	E950.4	E962.0	E980.4
Flurothyl	969.8	E855.8	E939.8	E950.3	E962.0	E980.3
Fluroxene	968.2	E855.1	E938.2	E950.4	E962.0	E980.4
Folacin	964.1	E858.2	E934.1	E950.4	E962.0	E980.4
Folic acid	964.1	E858.2	E934.1	E950.4	E962.0	E980.4
Follicle stimulating hormone	962.4	E858.0	E932.4	E950.4	E962.0	E980.4
Food, foodstuffs, nonbacterial or noxious	988.9	E865.9	—	E950.9	E962.1	E980.9
berries, seeds	988.2	E865.3	—	E950.9	E962.1	E980.9
fish	988.0	E865.2	—	E950.9	E962.1	E980.9
mushrooms	988.1	E865.5	—	E950.9	E962.1	E980.9
plants	988.2	E865.9	—	E950.9	E962.1	E980.9
specified type NEC	988.2	E865.4	—	E950.9	E962.1	E980.9
shellfish	988.0	E865.1	—	E950.9	E962.1	E980.9
specified NEC	988.8	E865.8	—	E950.9	E962.1	E980.9
Fool's parsley	988.2	E865.4	—	E950.9	E962.1	E980.9
Formaldehyde (solution)	989.89	E861.4	—	E950.9	E962.1	E980.9
fungicide	989.4	E863.6	—	E950.6	E962.1	E980.7
gas or vapor	987.8	E869.8	—	E952.8	E962.2	E982.8
Formalin	989.89	E861.4	—	E950.9	E962.1	E980.9
fungicide	989.4	E863.6	—	E950.6	E962.1	E980.7
vapor	987.8	E869.8	—	E952.8	E962.2	E982.8
Formic acid	983.1	E864.1	—	E950.7	E962.1	E980.6
vapor	987.8	E869.8	—	E952.8	E962.2	E982.8
Fowler's solution	985.1	E866.3	—	E950.8	E962.1	E980.8
Foxglove	988.2	E865.4	—	E950.9	E962.1	E980.9
Fox green	977.8	E858.8	E947.8	E950.4	E962.0	E980.4
Framycetin	960.8	E856	E930.8	E950.4	E962.0	E980.4
Frangula (extract)	973.1	E858.4	E943.1	E950.4	E962.0	E980.4
Frei antigen	977.8	E858.8	E947.8	E950.4	E962.0	E980.4
Freons	987.4	E869.2	—	E952.8	E962.2	E982.8
Fructose	974.5	E858.5	E944.5	E950.4	E962.0	E980.4
Frusemide	974.4	E858.5	E944.4	E950.4	E962.0	E980.4
FSH	962.4	E858.0	E932.4	E950.4	E962.0	E980.4
Fuel						
automobile	981	E862.1	—	E950.9	E962.1	E980.9
exhaust gas, not in transit	986	E868.2	—	E952.0	E962.2	E982.0
vapor NEC	987.1	E869.8	—	E952.8	E962.2	E982.8

Substance	Poisoning	Accident	Therapeutic Use	Suicide Attempt	Assault	Undetermined
gas (domestic use) — *see also* Carbon, monoxide, fuel						
utility	987.1	E868.1	—	E951.8	E962.2	E981.8
incomplete combustion of — *see* Carbon, monoxide, fuel, utility						
in mobile container	987.0	E868.0	—	E951.1	E962.2	E981.1
piped (natural)	987.1	E867	—	E951.0	E962.2	E981.0
industrial, incomplete combustion	986	E868.3	—	E952.1	E962.2	E982.1
Fugillin	960.8	E856	E930.8	E950.4	E962.0	E980.4
Fulminate of mercury	985.0	E866.1	—	E950.9	E962.1	E980.9
Fulvicin	960.1	E856	E930.1	E950.4	E962.0	E980.4
Fumadil	960.8	E856	E930.8	E950.4	E962.0	E980.4
Fumagillin	960.8	E856	E930.8	E950.4	E962.0	E980.4
Fumes (from)	987.9	E869.9	—	E952.9	E962.2	E982.9
carbon monoxide — *see* Carbon, monoxide						
charcoal (domestic use)	986	E868.3	—	E952.1	E962.2	E982.1
chloroform — *see* Chloroform						
coke (in domestic stoves, fireplaces)	986	E868.3	—	E952.1	E962.2	E982.1
corrosive NEC	987.8	E869.8	—	E952.8	E962.2	E982.8
ether — *see* Ether(s)						
freons	987.4	E869.2	—	E952.8	E962.2	E982.8
hydrocarbons	987.1	E869.8	—	E952.8	E962.2	E982.8
petroleum (liquefied)	987.0	E868.0	—	E951.1	E962.2	E981.1
distributed through pipes (pure or mixed with air)	987.0	E867	—	E951.0	E962.2	E981.0
lead — *see* Lead						
metals — *see* specified metal						
nitrogen dioxide	987.2	E869.0	—	E952.8	E962.2	E982.8
pesticides — *see* Pesticides						
petroleum (liquefied)	987.0	E868.0	—	E951.1	E962.2	E981.1
distributed through pipes (pure or mixed with air)	987.0	E867	—	E951.0	E962.2	E981.0
polyester	987.8	E869.8	—	E952.8	E962.2	E982.8
specified source, other (see also substance specified)	987.8	E869.8	—	E952.8	E962.2	E982.8
sulfur dioxide	987.3	E869.1	—	E952.8	E962.2	E982.8
Fumigants	989.4	E863.8	—	E950.6	E962.1	E980.7
Fungi, noxious, used as food	988.1	E865.5	—	E950.9	E962.1	E980.9
Fungicides (*see also* Antifungals)	989.4	E863.6	—	E950.6	E962.1	E980.7
Fungizone	960.1	E856	E930.1	E950.4	E962.0	E980.4
topical	976.0	E858.7	E946.0	E950.4	E962.0	E980.4
Furacin	976.0	E858.7	E946.0	E950.4	E962.0	E980.4
Furadantin	961.9	E857	E931.9	E950.4	E962.0	E980.4
Furazolidone	961.9	E857	E931.9	E950.4	E962.0	E980.4
Furnace (coal burning) (domestic),						
gas from	986	E868.3	—	E952.1	E962.2	E982.1
industrial	986	E868.8	—	E952.1	E962.2	E982.1
Furniture polish	989.89	E861.2	—	E950.9	E962.1	E980.9
Furosemide	974.4	E858.5	E944.4	E950.4	E962.0	E980.4
Furoxone	961.9	E857	E931.9	E950.4	E962.0	E980.4
Fusel oil (amyl) (butyl) (propyl)	980.3	E860.4	—	E950.9	E962.1	E980.9
Fusidic acid	960.8	E856	E930.8	E950.4	E962.0	E980.4
Gallamine	975.2	E858.6	E945.2	E950.4	E962.0	E980.4
Gallotannic acid	976.2	E858.7	E946.2	E950.4	E962.0	E980.4
Gamboge	973.1	E858.4	E943.1	E950.4	E962.0	E980.4
Gamimune	964.6	E858.2	E934.6	E950.4	E962.0	E980.4
Gamma–benzene hexachloride (vapor)	989.2	E863.0	—	E950.6	E962.1	E980.7

Substance	Poisoning	External Cause (E-Code)				
		Accident	Therapeutic Use	Suicide Attempt	Assault	Undetermined
Gamma globulin	964.6	E858.2	E934.6	E950.4	E962.0	E980.4
Gamulin	964.6	E858.2	E934.6	E950.4	E962.0	E980.4
Ganglionic blocking agents	972.3	E858.3	E942.3	E950.4	E962.0	E980.4
Ganja	969.6	E854.1	E939.6	E950.3	E962.0	E980.3
Garamycin	960.8	E856	E930.8	E950.4	E962.0	E980.4
ophthalmic preparation	976.5	E858.7	E946.5	E950.4	E962.0	E980.4
topical NEC	976.0	E858.7	E946.0	E950.4	E962.0	E980.4
Gardenal	967.0	E851	E937.0	E950.1	E962.0	E980.1
Gardepanyl	967.0	E851	E937.0	E950.1	E962.0	E980.1
Gas	987.9	E869.9	—	E952.9	E962.2	E982.9
acetylene	987.1	E868.1	—	E951.8	E962.2	E981.8
incomplete combustion of — *see* Carbon, monoxide, fuel, utility						
air contaminants, source or type not specified	987.9	E869.9	—	E952.9	E962.2	E982.9
anesthetic (general) NEC	968.2	E855.1	E938.2	E950.4	E962.0	E980.4
blast furnace	986	E868.8	—	E952.1	E962.2	E982.1
butane — *see* Butane						
carbon monoxide — *see* Carbon, monoxide						
chlorine	987.6	E869.8	—	E952.8	E962.2	E982.8
coal — *see* Carbon, monoxide, coal						
cyanide	987.7	E869.8	—	E952.8	E962.2	E982.8
dicyanogen	987.8	E869.8	—	E952.8	E962.2	E982.8
domestic — *see* Gas, utility						
exhaust — *see* Carbon, monoxide, exhaust gas						
from wood– or coal–burning stove or fireplace	986	E868.3	—	E952.1	E962.2	E982.1
fuel (domestic use) — *see also* Carbon, monoxide, fuel						
industrial use	986	E868.8	—	E952.1	E962.2	E982.1
utility	987.1	E868.1	—	E951.8	E962.2	E981.8
incomplete combustion of — *see* Carbon, monoxide, fuel, utility						
in mobile container	987.0	E868.0	—	E951.1	E962.2	E981.1
piped (natural)	987.1	E867	—	E951.0	E962.2	E981.0
garage	986	E868.2	—	E952.0	E962.2	E982.0
hydrocarbon NEC	987.1	E869.8	—	E952.8	E962.2	E982.8
incomplete combustion of — *see* Carbon, monoxide, fuel, utility						
liquefied (mobile container)	987.0	E868.0	—	E951.1	E962.2	E981.1
piped	987.0	E867	—	E951.0	E962.2	E981.0
hydrocyanic acid	987.7	E869.8	—	E952.8	E962.2	E982.8
illuminating — *see* Gas, utility						
incomplete combustion, any — *see* Carbon, monoxide						
kiln	986	E868.8	—	E952.1	E962.2	E982.1
lacrimogenic	987.5	E869.3	—	E952.8	E962.2	E982.8
marsh	987.1	E869.8	—	E952.8	E962.2	E982.8
motor exhaust, not in transit	986	E868.8	—	E952.1	E962.2	E982.1
mustard — *see* Mustard, gas						
natural	987.1	E867	—	E951.0	E962.2	E981.0
nerve (war)	987.9	E869.9	—	E952.9	E962.2	E982.9
oils	981	E862.1	—	E950.9	E962.1	E980.9
petroleum (liquefied) (distributed in mobile containers)	987.0	E868.0	—	E951.1	E962.2	E981.1
piped (pure or mixed with air)	987.0	E867	—	E951.1	E962.2	E981.1
piped (manufactured) (natural) NEC	987.1	E867	—	E951.0	E962.2	E981.0

Substance	Poisoning	External Cause (E-Code)				
		Accident	Therapeutic Use	Suicide Attempt	Assault	Undetermined
producer	986	E868.8	—	E952.1	E962.2	E982.1
propane — *see* Propane						
refrigerant (freon)	987.4	E869.2	—	E952.8	E962.2	E982.8
not freon	987.9	E869.9	—	E952.9	E962.2	E982.9
sewer	987.8	E869.8	—	E952.8	E962.2	E982.8
specified source NEC (*see also* substance specified)	987.8	E869.8	—	E952.8	E962.2	E982.8
stove — *see* Gas, utility						
tear	987.5	E869.3	—	E952.8	E962.2	E982.8
utility (for cooking, heating, or lighting) (piped) NEC	987.1	E868.1	—	E951.8	E962.2	E981.8
incomplete combustion of — *see* Carbon, monoxide, fuel, utility						
in mobile container	987.0	E868.0	—	E951.1	E962.2	E981.1
piped (natural)	987.1	E867	—	E951.0	E962.2	E981.0
water	987.1	E868.1	—	E951.8	E962.2	E981.8
incomplete combustion of — *see* Carbon, monoxide, fuel, utility						
Gaseous substance — *see* Gas						
Gasoline, gasolene	981	E862.1	—	E950.9	E962.1	E980.9
vapor	987.1	E869.8	—	E952.8	E962.2	E982.8
Gastric enzymes	973.4	E858.4	E943.4	E950.4	E962.0	E980.4
Gastrografin	977.8	E858.8	E947.8	E950.4	E962.0	E980.4
Gastrointestinal agents	973.9	E858.4	E943.9	E950.4	E962.0	E980.4
specified NEC	973.8	E858.4	E943.8	E950.4	E962.0	E980.4
Gaultheria procumbens	988.2	E865.4	—	E950.9	E962.1	E980.9
Gelatin (intravenous)	964.8	E858.2	E934.8	E950.4	E962.0	E980.4
absorbable (sponge)	964.5	E858.2	E934.5	E950.4	E962.0	E980.4
Gelfilm	976.8	E858.7	E946.8	E950.4	E962.0	E980.4
Gelfoam	964.5	E858.2	E934.5	E950.4	E962.0	E980.4
Gelsemine	970.8	E854.3	E940.8	E950.4	E962.0	E980.4
Gelsemium (sempervirens)	988.2	E865.4	—	E950.9	E962.1	E980.9
Gemonil	967.0	E851	E937.0	E950.1	E962.0	E980.1
Gentamicin	960.8	E856	E930.8	E950.4	E962.0	E980.4
ophthalmic preparation	976.5	E858.7	E946.5	E950.4	E962.0	E980.4
topical NEC	976.0	E858.7	E946.0	E950.4	E962.0	E980.4
Gentian violet	976.0	E858.7	E946.0	E950.4	E962.0	E980.4
Gexane	976.0	E858.7	E946.0	E950.4	E962.0	E980.4
Gila monster (venom)	989.5	E905.0	—	E950.9	E962.1	E980.9
Ginger, Jamaica	989.89	E866.8	—	E950.9	E962.1	E980.9
Gitalin	972.1	E858.3	E942.1	E950.4	E962.0	E980.4
Gitoxin	972.1	E858.3	E942.1	E950.4	E962.0	E980.4
Glandular extract (medicinal) NEC	977.9	E858.9	E947.9	E950.5	E962.0	E980.5
Glaucarubin	961.5	E857	E931.5	E950.4	E962.0	E980.4
Globin zinc insulin	962.3	E858.0	E932.3	E950.4	E962.0	E980.4
Glucagon	962.3	E858.0	E932.3	E950.4	E962.0	E980.4
Glucochloral	967.1	E852.0	E937.1	E950.2	E962.0	E980.2
Glucocorticoids	962.0	E858.0	E932.0	E950.4	E962.0	E980.4
Glucose	974.5	E858.5	E944.5	E950.4	E962.0	E980.4
oxidase reagent	977.8	E858.8	E947.8	E950.4	E962.0	E980.4
Glucosulfone sodium	961.8	E857	E931.8	E950.4	E962.0	E980.4
Glue(s)	989.89	E866.6	—	E950.9	E962.1	E980.9
Glutamic acid (hydrochloride)	973.4	E858.4	E943.4	E950.4	E962.0	E980.4
Glutathione	963.8	E858.1	E933.8	E950.4	E962.0	E980.4
Glutethimide (group)	967.5	E852.4	E937.5	E950.2	E962.0	E980.2
Glycerin (lotion)	976.3	E858.7	E946.3	E950.4	E962.0	E980.4
Glycerol (topical)	976.3	E858.7	E946.3	E950.4	E962.0	E980.4

Substance	Poisoning	Accident	Therapeutic Use	Suicide Attempt	Assault	Undetermined
Glyceryl						
guaiacolate	975.5	E858.6	E945.5	E950.4	E962.0	E980.4
triacetate (topical)	976.0	E858.7	E946.0	E950.4	E962.0	E980.4
trinitrate	972.4	E858.3	E942.4	E950.4	E962.0	E980.4
Glycine	974.5	E858.5	E944.5	E950.4	E962.0	E980.4
Glycobiarsol	961.1	E857	E931.1	E950.4	E962.0	E980.4
Glycols (ether)	982.8	E862.4	—	E950.9	E962.1	E980.9
Glycopyrrolate	971.1	E855.4	E941.1	E950.4	E962.0	E980.4
Glymidine	962.3	E858.0	E932.3	E950.4	E962.0	E980.4
Gold (compounds) (salts)	965.69	E850.6	E935.6	E950.0	E962.0	E980.0
Golden sulfide of antimony	985.4	E866.2	—	E950.9	E962.1	E980.9
Goldylocks	988.2	E865.4	—	E950.9	E962.1	E980.9
Gonadal tissue extract	962.9	E858.0	E932.9	E950.4	E962.0	E980.4
female	962.2	E858.0	E932.2	E950.4	E962.0	E980.4
male	962.1	E858.0	E932.1	E950.4	E962.0	E980.4
Gonadotropin	962.4	E858.0	E932.4	E950.4	E962.0	E980.4
Grain alcohol	980.0	E860.1	—	E950.9	E962.1	E980.9
beverage	980.0	E860.0	—	E950.9	E962.1	E980.9
Gramicidin	960.8	E856	E930.8	E950.4	E962.0	E980.4
Gratiola officinalis	988.2	E865.4	—	E950.9	E962.1	E980.9
Grease	989.89	E866.8	—	E950.9	E962.1	E980.9
Green hellebore	988.2	E865.4	—	E950.9	E962.1	E980.9
Green soap	976.2	E858.7	E946.2	E950.4	E962.0	E980.4
Grifulvin	960.1	E856	E930.1	E950.4	E962.0	E980.4
Griseofulvin	960.1	E856	E930.1	E950.4	E962.0	E980.4
Growth hormone	962.4	E858.0	E932.4	E950.4	E962.0	E980.4
Guaiacol	975.5	E858.6	E945.5	E950.4	E962.0	E980.4
Guaiac reagent	977.8	E858.8	E947.8	E950.4	E962.0	E980.4
Guaifenesin	975.5	E858.6	E945.5	E950.4	E962.0	E980.4
Guaiphenesin	975.5	E858.6	E945.5	E950.4	E962.0	E980.4
Guanatol	961.4	E857	E931.4	E950.4	E962.0	E980.4
Guanethidine	972.6	E858.3	E942.6	E950.4	E962.0	E980.4
Guano	989.89	E866.5	—	E950.9	E962.1	E980.9
Guanochlor	972.6	E858.3	E942.6	E950.4	E962.0	E980.4
Guanoctine	972.6	E858.3	E942.6	E950.4	E962.0	E980.4
Guanoxan	972.6	E858.3	E942.6	E950.4	E962.0	E980.4
Hair treatment agent NEC	976.4	E858.7	E946.4	E950.4	E962.0	E980.4
Halcinonide	976.0	E858.7	E946.0	E950.4	E962.0	E980.4
Halethazole	976.0	E858.7	E946.0	E950.4	E962.0	E980.4
Hallucinogens	969.6	E854.1	E939.6	E950.3	E962.0	E980.3
Haloperidol	969.2	E853.1	E939.2	E950.3	E962.0	E980.3
Haloprogin	976.0	E858.7	E946.0	E950.4	E962.0	E980.4
Halotex	976.0	E858.7	E946.0	E950.4	E962.0	E980.4
Halothane	968.1	E855.1	E938.1	E950.4	E962.0	E980.4
Halquinols	976.0	E858.7	E946.0	E950.4	E962.0	E980.4
Harmonyl	972.6	E858.3	E942.6	E950.4	E962.0	E980.4
Hartmann's solution	974.5	E858.5	E944.5	E950.4	E962.0	E980.4
Hashish	969.6	E854.1	E939.6	E950.3	E962.0	E980.3
Hawaiian wood rose seeds	969.6	E854.1	E939.6	E950.3	E962.0	E980.3
Headache cures, drugs, powders NEC	977.9	E858.9	E947.9	E950.5	E962.0	E980.9
Heavenly Blue (morning glory)	969.6	E854.1	E939.6	E950.3	E962.0	E980.3
Heavy metal						
antagonists	963.8	E858.1	E933.8	E950.4	E962.0	E980.4
anti–infectives	961.2	E857	E931.2	E950.4	E962.0	E980.4
Hedaquinium	976.0	E858.7	E946.0	E950.4	E962.0	E980.4
Hedge hyssop	988.2	E865.4	—	E950.9	E962.1	E980.9
Heet	976.8	E858.7	E946.8	E950.4	E962.0	E980.4

Substance	Poisoning	Accident	Therapeutic Use	Suicide Attempt	Assault	Undetermined
Helenin	961.6	E857	E931.6	E950.4	E962.0	E980.4
Hellebore (black) (green) (white)	988.2	E865.4	—	E950.9	E962.1	E980.9
Hemlock	988.2	E865.4	—	E950.9	E962.1	E980.9
Hemostatics	964.5	E858.2	E934.5	E950.4	E962.0	E980.4
capillary active drugs	972.8	E858.3	E942.8	E950.4	E962.0	E980.4
Henbane	988.2	E865.4	—	E950.9	E962.1	E980.9
Heparin (sodium)	964.2	E858.2	E934.2	E950.4	E962.0	E980.4
Heptabarbital, heptabarbitone	967.0	E851	E937.0	E950.1	E962.0	E980.1
Heptachlor	989.2	E863.0	—	E950.6	E962.1	E980.7
Heptalgin	965.09	E850.2	E935.2	E950.0	E962.0	E980.0
Herbicides	989.4	E863.5	—	E950.6	E962.1	E980.7
Heroin	965.01	E850.0	E935.0	E950.0	E962.0	E980.0
Herplex	976.5	E858.7	E946.5	E950.4	E962.0	E980.4
HES	964.8	E858.2	E934.8	E950.4	E962.0	E980.4
Hetastarch	964.8	E858.2	E934.8	E950.4	E962.0	E980.4
Hexachlorocyclohexane	989.2	E863.0	—	E950.6	E962.1	E980.7
Hexachlorophene	976.2	E858.7	E946.2	E950.4	E962.0	E980.4
Hexadimethrine (bromide)	964.5	E858.2	E934.5	E950.4	E962.0	E980.4
Hexafluorenium	975.2	E858.6	E945.2	E950.4	E962.0	E980.4
Hexa–germ	976.2	E858.7	E946.2	E950.4	E962.0	E980.4
Hexahydrophenol	980.8	E860.8	—	E950.9	E962.1	E980.9
Hexalin	980.8	E860.8	—	E950.9	E962.1	E980.9
Hexamethonium	972.3	E858.3	E942.3	E950.4	E962.0	E980.4
Hexamethyleneamine	961.9	E857	E931.9	E950.4	E962.0	E980.4
Hexamine	961.9	E857	E931.9	E950.4	E962.0	E980.4
Hexanone	982.8	E862.4	—	E950.9	E962.1	E980.9
Hexapropymate	967.8	E852.8	E937.8	E950.2	E962.0	E980.2
Hexestrol	962.2	E858.0	E932.2	E950.4	E962.0	E980.4
Hexethal (sodium)	967.0	E851	E937.0	E950.1	E962.0	E980.1
Hexetidine	976.0	E858.7	E946.0	E950.4	E962.0	E980.4
Hexobarbital, hexobarbitone	967.0	E851	E937.0	E950.1	E962.0	E980.1
sodium (anesthetic)	968.3	E855.1	E938.3	E950.4	E962.0	E980.4
soluble	968.3	E855.1	E938.3	E950.4	E962.0	E980.4
Hexocyclium	971.1	E855.4	E941.1	E950.4	E962.0	E980.4
Hexoestrol	962.2	E858.0	E932.2	E950.4	E962.0	E980.4
Hexone	982.8	E862.4	—	E950.9	E962.1	E980.9
Hexylcaine	968.5	E855.2	E938.5	E950.4	E962.0	E980.4
Hexylresorcinol	961.6	E857	E931.6	E950.4	E962.0	E980.4
Hinkle's pills	973.1	E858.4	E943.1	E950.4	E962.0	E980.4
Histalog	977.8	E858.8	E947.8	E950.4	E962.0	E980.4
Histamine (phosphate)	972.5	E858.3	E942.5	E950.4	E962.0	E980.4
Histoplasmin	977.8	E858.8	E947.8	E950.4	E962.0	E980.4
Holly berries	988.2	E865.3	—	E950.9	E962.1	E980.9
Homatropine	971.1	E855.4	E941.1	E950.4	E962.0	E980.4
Homo–tet	964.6	E858.2	E934.6	E950.4	E962.0	E980.4
Hormones (synthetic substitute) NEC	962.9	E858.0	E932.9	E950.4	E962.0	E980.4
adrenal cortical steroids	962.0	E858.0	E932.0	E950.4	E962.0	E980.4
antidiabetic agents	962.3	E858.0	E932.3	E950.4	E962.0	E980.4
follicle stimulating	962.4	E858.0	E932.4	E950.4	E962.0	E980.4
gonadotropic	962.4	E858.0	E932.4	E950.4	E962.0	E980.4
growth	962.4	E858.0	E932.4	E950.4	E962.0	E980.4
ovarian (substitutes)	962.2	E858.0	E932.2	E950.4	E962.0	E980.4
parathyroid (derivatives)	962.6	E858.0	E932.6	E950.4	E962.0	E980.4
pituitary (posterior)	962.5	E858.0	E932.5	E950.4	E962.0	E980.4
anterior	962.4	E858.0	E932.4	E950.4	E962.0	E980.4
thyroid (derivative)	962.7	E858.0	E932.7	E950.4	E962.0	E980.4
Hornet (sting)	989.5	E905.3	—	E950.9	E962.1	E980.9

Substance	Poisoning	Accident	Therapeutic Use	Suicide Attempt	Assault	Undetermined
			External Cause (E-Code)			
Horticulture agent NEC	989.4	E863.9	—	E950.6	E962.1	E980.7
Hyaluronidase	963.4	E858.1	E933.4	E950.4	E962.0	E980.4
Hyazyme	963.4	E858.1	E933.4	E950.4	E962.0	E980.4
Hycodan	965.09	E850.2	E935.2	E950.0	E962.0	E980.0
Hydantoin derivatives	966.1	E855.0	E936.1	E950.4	E962.0	E980.4
Hydeltra	962.0	E858.0	E932.0	E950.4	E962.0	E980.4
Hydergine	971.3	E855.6	E941.3	E950.4	E962.0	E980.4
Hydrabamine penicillin	960.0	E856	E930.0	E950.4	E962.0	E980.4
Hydralazine, hydrallazine	972.6	E858.3	E942.6	E950.4	E962.0	E980.4
Hydrargaphen	976.0	E858.7	E946.0	E950.4	E962.0	E980.4
Hydrazine	983.9	E864.3	—	E950.7	E962.1	E980.6
Hydriodic acid	975.5	E858.6	E945.5	E950.4	E962.0	E980.4
Hydrocarbon gas	987.1	E869.8	—	E952.8	E962.2	E982.8
incomplete combustion of — *see* Carbon, monoxide, fuel, utility						
liquefied (mobile container)	987.0	E868.0	—	E951.1	E962.2	E981.1
piped (natural)	987.0	E867	—	E951.0	E962.2	E981.0
Hydrochloric acid (liquid)	983.1	E864.1	—	E950.7	E962.1	E980.6
medicinal	973.4	E858.4	E943.4	E950.4	E962.0	E980.4
vapor	987.8	E869.8	—	E952.8	E962.2	E982.8
Hydrochlorothiazide	974.3	E858.5	E944.3	E950.4	E962.0	E980.4
Hydrocodone	965.09	E850.2	E935.2	E950.0	E962.0	E980.0
Hydrocortisone	962.0	E858.0	E932.0	E950.4	E962.0	E980.4
ENT agent	976.6	E858.7	E946.6	E950.4	E962.0	E980.4
ophthalmic preparation	976.5	E858.7	E946.5	E950.4	E962.0	E980.4
topical NEC	976.0	E858.7	E946.0	E950.4	E962.0	E980.4
Hydrocortone	962.0	E858.0	E932.0	E950.4	E962.0	E980.4
ENT agent	976.6	E858.7	E946.6	E950.4	E962.0	E980.4
ophthalmic preparation	976.5	E858.7	E946.5	E950.4	E962.0	E980.4
topical NEC	976.0	E858.7	E946.0	E950.4	E962.0	E980.4
Hydrocyanic acid — *see* Cyanide(s)						
Hydroflumethiazide	974.3	E858.5	E944.3	E950.4	E962.0	E980.4
Hydrofluoric acid (liquid)	983.1	E864.1	—	E950.7	E962.1	E980.6
vapor	987.8	E869.8	—	E952.8	E962.2	E982.8
Hydrogen	987.8	E869.8	—	E952.8	E962.2	E982.8
arsenide	985.1	E866.3	—	E950.8	E962.1	E980.8
arseniureted	985.1	E866.3	—	E950.8	E962.1	E980.8
cyanide (salts)	989.0	E866.8	—	E950.9	E962.1	E980.9
gas	987.7	E869.8	—	E952.8	E962.2	E982.8
fluoride (liquid)	983.1	E864.1	—	E950.7	E962.1	E980.6
vapor	987.8	E869.8	—	E952.8	E962.2	E982.8
peroxide (solution)	976.6	E858.7	E946.6	E950.4	E962.0	E980.4
phosphureted	987.8	E869.8	—	E952.8	E962.2	E982.8
sulfide (gas)	987.8	E869.8	—	E952.8	E962.2	E982.8
arseniureted	985.1	E866.3	—	E950.8	E962.1	E980.8
sulfureted	987.8	E869.8	—	E952.8	E962.2	E982.8
Hydromorphinol	965.09	E850.2	E935.2	E950.0	E962.0	E980.0
Hydromorphinone	965.09	E850.2	E935.2	E950.0	E962.0	E980.0
Hydromorphone	965.09	E850.2	E935.2	E950.0	E962.0	E980.0
Hydromox	974.3	E858.5	E944.3	E950.4	E962.0	E980.4
Hydrophilic lotion	976.3	E858.7	E946.3	E950.4	E962.0	E980.4
Hydroquinone	983.0	E864.0	—	E950.7	E962.1	E980.6
vapor	987.8	E869.8	—	E952.8	E962.2	E982.8
Hydrosulfuric acid (gas)	987.8	E869.8	—	E952.8	E962.2	E982.8
Hydrous wool fat (lotion)	976.3	E858.7	E946.3	E950.4	E962.0	E980.4
Hydroxide, caustic	983.2	E864.2	—	E950.7	E962.1	E980.6
Hydroxocobalamin	964.1	E858.2	E934.1	E950.4	E962.0	E980.4

Substance	Poisoning	External Cause (E-Code)				
		Accident	Therapeutic Use	Suicide Attempt	Assault	Undetermined
Hydroxyamphetamine	971.2	E855.5	E941.2	E950.4	E962.0	E980.4
Hydroxychloroquine	961.4	E857	E931.4	E950.4	E962.0	E980.4
Hydroxydihydrocodeinone	965.09	E850.2	E935.2	E950.0	E962.0	E980.0
Hydroxyethyl starch	964.8	E858.2	E934.8	E950.4	E962.0	E980.4
Hydroxyphenamate	969.5	E853.8	E939.5	E950.3	E962.0	E980.3
Hydroxyphenylbutazone	965.5	E850.5	E935.5	E950.0	E962.0	E980.0
Hydroxyprogesterone	962.2	E858.0	E932.2	E950.4	E962.0	E980.4
Hydroxyquinoline derivatives	961.3	E857	E931.3	E950.4	E962.0	E980.4
Hydroxystilbamidine	961.5	E857	E931.5	E950.4	E962.0	E980.4
Hydroxyurea	963.1	E858.1	E933.1	E950.4	E962.0	E980.4
Hydroxyzine	969.5	E853.8	E939.5	E950.3	E962.0	E980.3
Hyoscine (hydrobromide)	971.1	E855.4	E941.1	E950.4	E962.0	E980.4
Hyoscyamine	971.1	E855.4	E941.1	E950.4	E962.0	E980.4
Hyoscyamus (albus) (niger)	988.2	E865.4	—	E950.9	E962.1	E980.9
Hypaque	977.8	E858.8	E947.8	E950.4	E962.0	E980.4
Hypertussis	964.6	E858.2	E934.6	E950.4	E962.0	E980.4
Hypnotics NEC	967.9	E852.9	E937.9	E950.2	E962.0	E980.2
Hypochlorites — *see* Sodium, hypochlorite						
Hypotensive agents NEC	972.6	E858.3	E942.6	E950.4	E962.0	E980.4
Ibufenac	965.69	E850.6	E935.6	E950.0	E962.0	E980.0
Ibuprofen	965.61	E850.6	E935.6	E950.0	E962.0	E980.0
ICG	977.8	E858.8	E947.8	E950.4	E962.0	E980.4
Ichthammol	976.4	E858.7	E946.4	E950.4	E962.0	E980.4
Ichthyol	976.4	E858.7	E946.4	E950.4	E962.0	E980.4
Idoxuridine	976.5	E858.7	E946.5	E950.4	E962.0	E980.4
IDU	976.5	E858.7	E946.5	E950.4	E962.0	E980.4
Iletin	962.3	E858.0	E932.3	E950.4	E962.0	E980.4
Ilex	988.2	E865.4	—	E950.9	E962.1	E980.9
Illuminating gas — *see* Gas, utility						
Ilopan	963.5	E858.1	E933.5	E950.4	E962.0	E980.4
Ilotycin	960.3	E856	E930.3	E950.4	E962.0	E980.4
ophthalmic preparation	976.5	E858.7	E946.5	E950.4	E962.0	E980.4
topical NEC	976.0	E858.7	E946.0	E950.4	E962.0	E980.4
Imipramine	969.0	E854.0	E939.0	E950.3	E962.0	E980.3
Immu–G	964.6	E858.2	E934.6	E950.4	E962.0	E980.4
Immuglobin	964.6	E858.2	E934.6	E950.4	E962.0	E980.4
Immune serum globulin	964.6	E858.2	E934.6	E950.4	E962.0	E980.4
Immunosuppressive agents	963.1	E858.1	E933.1	E950.4	E962.0	E980.4
Immu–tetanus	964.6	E858.2	E934.6	E950.4	E962.0	E980.4
Indandione (derivatives)	964.2	E858.2	E934.2	E950.4	E962.0	E980.4
Inderal	972.0	E858.3	E942.0	E950.4	E962.0	E980.4
Indian						
hemp	969.6	E854.1	E939.6	E950.3	E962.0	E980.3
tobacco	988.2	E865.4	—	E950.9	E962.1	E980.9
Indigo carmine	977.8	E858.8	E947.8	E950.4	E962.0	E980.4
Indocin	965.69	E850.6	E935.6	E950.0	E962.0	E980.0
Indocyanine green	977.8	E858.8	E947.8	E950.4	E962.0	E980.4
Indomethacin	965.69	E850.6	E935.6	E950.0	E962.0	E980.0
Industrial						
alcohol	980.9	E860.9	—	E950.9	E962.1	E980.9
fumes	987.8	E869.8	—	E952.8	E962.2	E982.8
solvents (fumes) (vapors)	982.8	E862.9	—	E950.9	E962.1	E980.9
Influenza vaccine	979.6	E858.8	E949.6	E950.4	E962.0	E982.8
Ingested substances NEC	989.9	E866.9	—	E950.9	E962.1	E980.9
INH (isoniazid)	961.8	E857	E931.8	E950.4	E962.0	E980.4
Inhalation, gas (noxious) — *see* Gas						
Ink	989.89	E866.8	—	E950.9	E962.1	E980.9

Substance	Poisoning	External Cause (E-Code)				
		Accident	Therapeutic Use	Suicide Attempt	Assault	Undetermined
Innovar	967.6	E852.5	E937.6	E950.2	E962.0	E980.2
Inositol niacinate	972.2	E858.3	E942.2	E950.4	E962.0	E980.4
Inproquone	963.1	E858.1	E933.1	E950.4	E962.0	E980.4
Insect (sting), venomous	989.5	E905.5	—	E950.9	E962.1	E980.9
Insecticides (*see also* Pesticides)	989.4	E863.4	—	E950.6	E962.1	E980.7
chlorinated	989.2	E863.0	—	E950.6	E962.1	E980.7
mixtures	989.4	E863.3	—	E950.6	E962.1	E980.7
organochlorine (compounds)	989.2	E863.0	—	E950.6	E962.1	E980.7
organophosphorus (compounds)	989.3	E863.1	—	E950.6	E962.1	E980.7
Insular tissue extract	962.3	E858.0	E932.3	E950.4	E962.0	E980.4
Insulin (amorphous) (globin) (isophane) (Lente) (NPH) (protamine) (Semilente) (Ultralente) (zinc)	962.3	E858.0	E932.3	E950.4	E962.0	E980.4
Intranarcon	968.3	E855.1	E938.3	E950.4	E962.0	E980.4
Inulin	977.8	E858.8	E947.8	E950.4	E962.0	E980.4
Invert sugar	974.5	E858.5	E944.5	E950.4	E962.0	E980.4
Inza—*see* Naproxen						
Iodide NEC (*see also* Iodine)	976.0	E858.7	E946.0	E950.4	E962.0	E980.4
mercury (ointment)	976.0	E858.7	E946.0	E950.4	E962.0	E980.4
methylate	976.0	E858.7	E946.0	E950.4	E962.0	E980.4
potassium (expectorant) NEC	975.5	E858.6	E945.5	E950.4	E962.0	E980.4
Iodinated glycerol	975.5	E858.6	E945.5	E950.4	E962.0	E980.4
Iodine (antiseptic, external) (tincture) NEC	976.0	E858.7	E946.0	E950.4	E962.0	E980.4
diagnostic	977.8	E858.8	E947.8	E950.4	E962.0	E980.4
for thyroid conditions (antithyroid)	962.8	E858.0	E932.8	E950.4	E962.0	E980.4
vapor	987.8	E869.8	—	E952.8	E962.2	E982.8
Iodized oil	977.8	E858.8	E947.8	E950.4	E962.0	E980.4
Iodobismitol	961.2	E857	E931.2	E950.4	E962.0	E980.4
Iodochlorhydroxyquin	961.3	E857	E931.3	E950.4	E962.0	E980.4
topical	976.0	E858.7	E946.0	E950.4	E962.0	E980.4
Iodoform	976.0	E858.7	E946.0	E950.4	E962.0	E980.4
Iodopanoic acid	977.8	E858.8	E947.8	E950.4	E962.0	E980.4
Iodophthalein	977.8	E858.8	E947.8	E950.4	E962.0	E980.4
Ion exchange resins	974.5	E858.5	E944.5	E950.4	E962.0	E980.4
Iopanoic acid	977.8	E858.8	E947.8	E950.4	E962.0	E980.4
Iophendylate	977.8	E858.8	E947.8	E950.4	E962.0	E980.4
Iothiouracil	962.8	E858.0	E932.8	E950.4	E962.0	E980.4
Ipecac	973.6	E858.4	E943.6	E950.4	E962.0	E980.4
Ipecacuanha	973.6	E858.4	E943.6	E950.4	E962.0	E980.4
Ipodate	977.8	E858.8	E947.8	E950.4	E962.0	E980.4
Ipral	967.0	E851	E937.0	E950.1	E962.0	E980.1
Iproniazid	969.0	E854.0	E939.0	E950.3	E962.0	E980.3
Iron (compounds) (medicinal) (preparations)	964.0	E858.2	E934.0	E950.4	E962.0	E980.4
dextran	964.0	E858.2	E934.0	E950.4	E962.0	E980.4
nonmedicinal (dust) (fumes) NEC	985.8	E866.4	—	E950.9	E962.1	E980.9
Irritant drug	977.9	E858.9	E947.9	E950.5	E962.0	E980.5
Ismelin	972.6	E858.3	E942.6	E950.4	E962.0	E980.4
Isoamyl nitrite	972.4	E858.3	E942.4	E950.4	E962.0	E980.4
Isobutyl acetate	982.8	E862.4	—	E950.9	E962.1	E980.9
Isocarboxazid	969.0	E854.0	E939.0	E950.3	E962.0	E980.3
Isoephedrine	971.2	E855.5	E941.2	E950.4	E962.0	E980.4
Isoetharine	971.2	E855.5	E941.2	E950.4	E962.0	E980.4
Isofluorophate	971.0	E855.3	E941.0	E950.4	E962.0	E980.4
Isoniazid (INH)	961.8	E857	E931.8	E950.4	E962.0	E980.4
Isopentaquine	961.4	E857	E931.4	E950.4	E962.0	E980.4

Substance	Poisoning	External Cause (E-Code)				
		Accident	Therapeutic Use	Suicide Attempt	Assault	Undetermined
Isophane insulin	962.3	E858.0	E932.3	E950.4	E962.0	E980.4
Isopregnenone	962.2	E858.0	E932.2	E950.4	E962.0	E980.4
Isoprenaline	971.2	E855.5	E941.2	E950.4	E962.0	E980.4
Isopropamide	971.1	E855.4	E941.1	E950.4	E962.0	E980.4
Isopropanol	980.2	E860.3	—	E950.9	E962.1	E980.9
topical (germicide)	976.0	E858.7	E946.0	E950.4	E962.0	E980.4
Isopropyl						
acetate	982.8	E862.4	—	E950.9	E962.1	E980.9
alcohol	980.2	E860.3	—	E950.9	E962.1	E980.9
topical (germicide)	976.0	E858.7	E946.0	E950.4	E962.0	E980.4
ether	982.8	E862.4	—	E950.9	E962.1	E980.9
Isoproterenol	971.2	E855.5	E941.2	E950.4	E962.0	E980.4
Isosorbide dinitrate	972.4	E858.3	E942.4	E950.4	E962.0	E980.4
Isothipendyl	963.0	E858.1	E933.0	E950.4	E962.0	E980.4
Isoxazolyl penicillin	960.0	E856	E930.0	E950.4	E962.0	E980.4
Isoxsuprine hydrochloride	972.5	E858.3	E942.5	E950.4	E962.0	E980.4
I–thyroxine sodium	962.7	E858.0	E932.7	E950.4	E962.0	E980.4
Jaborandi (pilocarpus) (extract)	971.0	E855.3	E941.0	E950.4	E962.0	E980.4
Jalap	973.1	E858.4	E943.1	E950.4	E962.0	E980.4
Jamaica						
dogwood (bark)	965.7	E850.7	E935.7	E950.0	E962.0	E980.0
ginger	989.89	E866.8	—	E950.9	E962.1	E980.9
Jatropha	988.2	E865.4	—	E950.9	E962.1	E980.9
curcas	988.2	E865.3	—	E950.9	E962.1	E980.9
Jectofer	964.0	E858.2	E934.0	E950.4	E962.0	E980.4
Jellyfish (sting)	989.5	E905.6	—	E950.9	E962.1	E980.9
Jequirity (bean)	988.2	E865.3	—	E950.9	E962.1	E980.9
Jimson weed	988.2	E865.4	—	E950.9	E962.1	E980.9
seeds	988.2	E865.3	—	E950.9	E962.1	E980.9
Juniper tar (oil) (ointment)	976.4	E858.7	E946.4	E950.4	E962.0	E980.4
Kallikrein	972.5	E858.3	E942.5	E950.4	E962.0	E980.4
Kanamycin	960.6	E856	E930.6	E950.4	E962.0	E980.4
Kantrex	960.6	E856	E930.6	E950.4	E962.0	E980.4
Kaolin	973.5	E858.4	E943.5	E950.4	E962.0	E980.4
Karaya (gum)	973.3	E858.4	E943.3	E950.4	E962.0	E980.4
Kemithal	968.3	E855.1	E938.3	E950.4	E962.0	E980.4
Kenacort	962.0	E858.0	E932.0	E950.4	E962.0	E980.4
Keratolytics	976.4	E858.7	E946.4	E950.4	E962.0	E980.4
Keratoplastics	976.4	E858.7	E946.4	E950.4	E962.0	E980.4
Kerosene, kerosine (fuel) (solvent) NEC	981	E862.1	—	E950.9	E962.1	E980.9
insecticide	981	E863.4	—	E950.6	E962.1	E980.7
vapor	987.1	E869.8	—	E952.8	E962.2	E982.8
Ketamine	968.3	E855.1	E938.3	E950.4	E962.0	E980.4
Ketobemidone	965.09	E850.2	E935.2	E950.0	E962.0	E980.0
Ketols	982.8	E862.4	—	E950.9	E962.1	E980.9
Ketone oils	982.8	E862.4	—	E950.9	E962.1	E980.9
Ketoprofen	965.61	E850.6	E935.6	E950.0	E962.0	E980.0
Kiln gas or vapor (carbon monoxide)	986	E868.8	—	E952.1	E962.2	E982.1
Konsyl	973.3	E858.4	E943.3	E950.4	E962.0	E980.4
Kosam seed	988.2	E865.3	—	E950.9	E962.1	E980.9
Krait (venom)	989.5	E905.0	—	E950.9	E962.1	E980.9
Kwell (insecticide)	989.2	E863.0	—	E950.6	E962.1	E980.7
anti–infective (topical)	976.0	E858.7	E946.0	E950.4	E962.0	E980.4
Laburnum (flowers) (seeds)	988.2	E865.3	—	E950.9	E962.1	E980.9
leaves	988.2	E865.4	—	E950.9	E962.1	E980.9
Lacquers	989.89	E861.6	—	E950.9	E962.1	E980.9
Lacrimogenic gas	987.5	E869.3	—	E952.8	E962.2	E982.8

Substance	Poisoning	External Cause (E-Code)				
		Accident	Therapeutic Use	Suicide Attempt	Assault	Undetermined
Lactic acid	983.1	E864.1	—	E950.7	E962.1	E980.6
Lactobacillus acidophilus	973.5	E858.4	E943.5	E950.4	E962.0	E980.4
Lactoflavin	963.5	E858.1	E933.5	E950.4	E962.0	E980.4
Lactuca (virosa) (extract)	967.8	E852.8	E937.8	E950.2	E962.0	E980.2
Lactucarium	967.8	E852.8	E937.8	E950.2	E962.0	E980.2
Laevulose	974.5	E858.5	E944.5	E950.4	E962.0	E980.4
Lanatoside(C)	972.1	E858.3	E942.1	E950.4	E962.0	E980.4
Lanolin (lotion)	976.3	E858.7	E946.3	E950.4	E962.0	E980.4
Largactil	969.1	E853.0	E939.1	E950.3	E962.0	E980.3
Larkspur	988.2	E865.3	—	E950.9	E962.1	E980.9
Laroxyl	969.0	E854.0	E939.0	E950.3	E962.0	E980.3
Lasix	974.4	E858.5	E944.4	E950.4	E962.0	E980.4
Latex	989.82	E866.8	—	E950.9	E962.1	E980.9
Lathyrus (seed)	988.2	E865.3	—	E950.9	E962.1	E980.9
Laudanum	965.09	E850.2	E935.2	E950.0	E962.0	E980.0
Laudexium	975.2	E858.6	E945.2	E950.4	E962.0	E980.4
Laurel, black or cherry	988.2	E865.4	—	E950.9	E962.1	E980.9
Laurolinium	976.0	E858.7	E946.0	E950.4	E962.0	E980.4
Lauryl sulfoacetate	976.2	E858.7	E946.2	E950.4	E962.0	E980.4
Laxatives NEC	973.3	E858.4	E943.3	E950.4	E962.0	E980.4
emollient	973.2	E858.4	E943.2	E950.4	E962.0	E980.4
L–dopa	966.4	E855.0	E936.4	E950.4	E962.0	E980.4
L Tryptophan—*see* amino acid						
Lead (dust) (fumes) (vapor) NEC	984.9	E866.0	—	E950.9	E962.1	E980.9
acetate (dust)	984.1	E866.0	—	E950.9	E962.1	E980.9
anti–infectives	961.2	E857	E931.2	E950.4	E962.0	E980.4
antiknock compound (tetraethyl)	984.1	E862.1	—	E950.9	E962.1	E980.9
arsenate, arsenite (dust) (insecticide)						
(vapor)	985.1	E863.4	—	E950.8	E962.1	E980.8
herbicide	985.1	E863.5	—	E950.8	E962.1	E980.8
carbonate	984.0	E866.0	—	E950.9	E962.1	E980.9
paint	984.0	E861.5	—	E950.9	E962.1	E980.9
chromate	984.0	E866.0	—	E950.9	E962.1	E980.9
paint	984.0	E861.5	—	E950.9	E962.1	E980.9
dioxide	984.0	E866.0	—	E950.9	E962.1	E980.9
inorganic (compound)	984.0	E866.0	—	E950.9	E962.1	E980.9
paint	984.0	E861.5	—	E950.9	E962.1	E980.9
iodine	984.0	E866.0	—	E950.9	E962.1	E980.9
pigment (paint)	984.0	E861.5	—	E950.9	E962.1	E980.9
monoxide (dust)	984.0	E866.0	—	E950.9	E962.1	E980.9
paint	984.0	E861.5	—	E950.9	E962.1	E980.9
organic	984.1	E866.0	—	E950.9	E962.1	E980.9
oxide	984.0	E866.0	—	E950.9	E962.1	E980.9
paint	984.0	E861.5	—	E950.9	E962.1	E980.9
paint	984.0	E861.5	—	E950.9	E962.1	E980.9
salts	984.0	E866.0	—	E950.9	E962.1	E980.9
specified compound NEC	984.8	E866.0	—	E950.9	E962.1	E980.9
tetra–ethyl	984.1	E862.1	—	E950.9	E962.1	E980.9
Lebanese red	969.6	E854.1	E939.6	E950.3	E962.0	E980.3
Lente Iletin (insulin)	962.3	E858.0	E932.3	E950.4	E962.0	E980.4
Leptazol	970.0	E854.3	E940.0	E950.4	E962.0	E980.4
Leritine	965.09	E850.2	E935.2	E950.0	E962.0	E980.0
Letter	962.7	E858.0	E932.7	E950.4	E962.0	E980.4
Lettuce opium	967.8	E852.8	E937.8	E950.2	E962.0	E980.2
Leucovorin (factor)	964.1	E858.2	E934.1	E950.4	E962.0	E980.4
Leukeran	963.1	E858.1	E933.1	E950.4	E962.0	E980.4
Levallorphan	970.1	E854.3	E940.1	E950.4	E962.0	E980.4

Substance	Poisoning	External Cause (E-Code)				
		Accident	Therapeutic Use	Suicide Attempt	Assault	Undetermined
Levanil	967.8	E852.8	E937.8	E950.2	E962.0	E980.2
Levarterenol	971.2	E855.5	E941.2	E950.4	E962.0	E980.4
Levodopa	966.4	E855.0	E936.4	E950.4	E962.0	E980.4
Levo–dromoran	965.09	E850.2	E935.2	E950.0	E962.0	E980.0
Levoid	962.7	E858.0	E932.7	E950.4	E962.0	E980.4
Levo–iso–methadone	965.02	E850.1	E935.1	E950.0	E962.0	E980.0
Levomepromazine	967.8	E852.8	E937.8	E950.2	E962.0	E980.2
Levoprome	967.8	E852.8	E937.8	E950.2	E962.0	E980.2
Levopropoxyphene	975.4	E858.6	E945.4	E950.4	E962.0	E980.4
Levorphan, levophanol	965.09	E850.2	E935.2	E950.0	E962.0	E980.0
Levothyroxine (sodium)	962.7	E858.0	E932.7	E950.4	E962.0	E980.4
Levsin	971.1	E855.4	E941.1	E950.4	E962.0	E980.4
Levulose	974.5	E858.5	E944.5	E950.4	E962.0	E980.4
Lewisite (gas)	985.1	E866.3	—	E950.8	E962.1	E980.8
Librium	969.4	E853.2	E939.4	E950.3	E962.0	E980.3
Lidex	976.0	E858.7	E946.0	E950.4	E962.0	E980.4
Lidocaine (infiltration) (topical)	968.5	E855.2	E938.5	E950.4	E962.0	E980.4
nerve block (peripheral) (plexus)	968.6	E855.2	E938.6	E950.4	E962.0	E980.4
spinal	968.7	E855.2	E938.7	E950.4	E962.0	E980.4
Lighter fluid	981	E862.1	—	E950.9	E962.1	E980.9
Lignocaine (infiltration) (topical)	968.5	E855.2	E938.5	E950.4	E962.0	E980.4
nerve block (peripheral) (plexus)	968.6	E855.2	E938.6	E950.4	E962.0	E980.4
spinal	968.7	E855.2	E938.7	E950.4	E962.0	E980.4
Ligroin(e) (solvent)	981	E862.0	—	E950.9	E962.1	E980.9
vapor	987.1	E869.8	—	E952.8	E962.2	E982.8
Ligustrum vulgare	988.2	E865.3	—	E950.9	E962.1	E980.9
Lily of the valley	988.2	E865.4	—	E950.9	E962.1	E980.9
Lime (chloride)	983.2	E864.2	—	E950.7	E962.1	E980.6
solution, sulferated	976.4	E858.7	E946.4	E950.4	E962.0	E980.4
Limonene	982.8	E862.4	—	E950.9	E962.1	E980.9
Lincomycin	960.8	E856	E930.8	E950.4	E962.0	E980.4
Lindane (insecticide) (vapor)	989.2	E863.0	—	E950.6	E962.1	E980.7
anti–infective (topical)	976.0	E858.7	E946.0	E950.4	E962.0	E980.4
Liniments NEC	976.9	E858.7	E946.9	E950.4	E962.0	E980.4
Linoleic acid	972.2	E858.3	E942.2	E950.4	E962.0	E980.4
Liothyronine	962.7	E858.0	E932.7	E950.4	E962.0	E980.4
Liotrix	962.7	E858.0	E932.7	E950.4	E962.0	E980.4
Lipancreatin	973.4	E858.4	E943.4	E950.4	E962.0	E980.4
Lipo–Lutin	962.2	E858.0	E932.2	E950.4	E962.0	E980.4
Lipotropic agents	977.1	E858.8	E947.1	E950.4	E962.0	E980.4
Liquefied petroleum gases	987.0	E868.0	—	E951.1	E962.2	E981.1
piped (pure or mixed with air)	987.0	E867	—	E951.0	E962.2	E981.0
Liquid petrolatum	973.2	E858.4	E943.2	E950.4	E962.0	E980.4
substance	989.9	E866.9	—	E950.9	E962.1	E980.9
specified NEC	989.89	E866.8	—	E950.9	E962.1	E980.9
Lirugen	979.4	E858.8	E949.4	E950.4	E962.0	E980.4
Lithane	969.8	E855.8	E939.8	E950.3	E962.0	E980.3
Lithium	985.8	E866.4	—	E950.9	E962.1	E980.9
carbonate	969.8	E855.8	E939.8	E950.3	E962.0	E980.3
Lithonate	969.8	E855.8	E939.8	E950.3	E962.0	E980.3
Liver (extract) (injection) (preparations)	964.1	E858.2	E934.1	E950.4	E962.0	E980.4
Lizard (bite) (venom)	989.5	E905.0	—	E950.9	E962.1	E980.9
LMD	964.8	E858.2	E934.8	E950.4	E962.0	E980.4
Lobelia	988.2	E865.4	—	E950.9	E962.1	E980.9
Lobeline	970.0	E854.3	E940.0	E950.4	E962.0	E980.4
Locorten	976.0	E858.7	E946.0	E950.4	E962.0	E980.4
Lolium temulentum	988.2	E865.3	—	E950.9	E962.1	E980.9

Substance	Poisoning	External Cause (E-Code)				
		Accident	Therapeutic Use	Suicide Attempt	Assault	Undetermined
Lomotil	973.5	E858.4	E943.5	E950.4	E962.0	E980.4
Lomustine	963.1	E858.1	E933.1	E950.4	E962.0	E980.4
Lophophora williamsii	969.6	E854.1	E939.6	E950.3	E962.0	E980.3
Lorazepam	969.4	E853.2	E939.4	E950.3	E962.0	E980.3
Lotions NEC	976.9	E858.7	E946.9	E950.4	E962.0	E980.4
Lotusate	967.0	E851	E937.0	E950.1	E962.0	E980.1
Lowila	976.2	E858.7	E946.2	E950.4	E962.0	E980.4
Loxapine	969.3	E853.8	E939.3	E950.3	E962.0	E980.3
Lozenges (throat)	976.6	E858.7	E946.6	E950.4	E962.0	E980.4
LSD (25)	969.6	E854.1	E939.6	E950.3	E962.0	E980.3
Lubricating oil NEC	981	E862.2	—	E950.9	E962.1	E980.9
Lucanthone	961.6	E857	E931.6	E950.4	E962.0	E980.4
Luminal	967.0	E851	E937.0	E950.1	E962.0	E980.1
Lung irritant (gas) NEC	987.9	E869.9	—	E952.9	E962.2	E982.9
Lutocylol	962.2	E858.0	E932.2	E950.4	E962.0	E980.4
Lutromone	962.2	E858.0	E932.2	E950.4	E962.0	E980.4
Lututrin	975.0	E858.6	E945.0	E950.4	E962.0	E980.4
Lye (concentrated)	983.2	E864.2	—	E950.7	E962.1	E980.6
Lygranum (skin test)	977.8	E858.8	E947.8	E950.4	E962.0	E980.4
Lymecycline	960.4	E856	E930.4	E950.4	E962.0	E980.4
Lymphogranuloma venereum antigen	977.8	E858.8	E947.8	E950.4	E962.0	E980.4
Lynestrenol	962.2	E858.0	E932.2	E950.4	E962.0	E980.4
Lyovac Sodium Edecrin	974.4	E858.5	E944.4	E950.4	E962.0	E980.4
Lypressin	962.5	E858.0	E932.5	E950.4	E962.0	E980.4
Lysergic acid (amide) (diethylamide)	969.6	E854.1	E939.6	E950.3	E962.0	E980.3
Lysergide	969.6	E854.1	E939.6	E950.3	E962.0	E980.3
Lysine vasopressin	962.5	E858.0	E932.5	E950.4	E962.0	E980.4
Lysol	983.0	E864.0	—	E950.7	E962.1	E980.6
Lytta (vitatta)	976.8	E858.7	E946.8	E950.4	E962.0	E980.4
Mace	987.5	E869.3	—	E952.8	E962.2	E982.8
Macrolides (antibiotics)	960.3	E856	E930.3	E950.4	E962.0	E980.4
Mafenide	976.0	E858.7	E946.0	E950.4	E962.0	E980.4
Magaldrate	973.0	E858.4	E943.0	E950.4	E962.0	E980.4
Magic mushroom	969.6	E854.1	E939.6	E950.3	E962.0	E980.3
Magnamycin	960.8	E856	E930.8	E950.4	E962.0	E980.4
Magnesia magma	973.0	E858.4	E943.0	E950.4	E962.0	E980.4
Magnesium (compounds) (fumes) NEC	985.8	E866.4	—	E950.9	E962.1	E980.9
antacid	973.0	E858.4	E943.0	E950.4	E962.0	E980.4
carbonate	973.0	E858.4	E943.0	E950.4	E962.0	E980.4
cathartic	973.3	E858.4	E943.3	E950.4	E962.0	E980.4
citrate	973.3	E858.4	E943.3	E950.4	E962.0	E980.4
hydroxide	973.0	E858.4	E943.0	E950.4	E962.0	E980.4
oxide	973.0	E858.4	E943.0	E950.4	E962.0	E980.4
sulfate (oral)	973.3	E858.4	E943.3	E950.4	E962.0	E980.4
intravenous	966.3	E855.0	E936.3	E950.4	E962.0	E980.4
trisilicate	973.0	E858.4	E943.0	E950.4	E962.0	E980.4
Malathion (insecticide)	989.3	E863.1	—	E950.6	E962.1	E980.7
Male fern (oleoresin)	961.6	E857	E931.6	E950.4	E962.0	E980.4
Mandelic acid	961.9	E857	E931.9	E950.4	E962.0	E980.4
Manganese compounds (fumes) NEC	985.2	E866.4	—	E950.9	E962.1	E980.9
Mannitol (diuretic) (medicinal) NEC	974.4	E858.5	E944.4	E950.4	E962.0	E980.4
hexanitrate	972.4	E858.3	E942.4	E950.4	E962.0	E980.4
mustard	963.1	E858.1	E933.1	E950.4	E962.0	E980.4
Mannomustine	963.1	E858.1	E933.1	E950.4	E962.0	E980.4
MAO inhibitors	969.0	E854.0	E939.0	E950.3	E962.0	E980.3
Mapharsen	961.1	E857	E931.1	E950.4	E962.0	E980.4
Marcaine	968.9	E855.2	E938.9	E950.4	E962.0	E980.4

Substance	Poisoning	Accident	Therapeutic Use	Suicide Attempt	Assault	Undetermined
infiltration (subcutaneous)	968.5	E855.2	E938.5	E950.4	E962.0	E980.4
nerve block (peripheral) (plexus)	968.6	E855.2	E938.6	E950.4	E962.0	E980.4
Marezine	963.0	E858.1	E933.0	E950.4	E962.0	E980.4
Marihuana, marijuana (derivatives)	969.6	E854.1	E939.6	E950.3	E962.0	E980.3
Marine animals or plants (sting)	989.5	E905.6	—	E950.9	E962.1	E980.9
Marplan	969.0	E854.0	E939.0	E950.3	E962.0	E980.3
Marsh gas	987.1	E869.8	—	E952.8	E962.2	E982.8
Marsilid	969.0	E854.0	E939.0	E950.3	E962.0	E980.3
Matulane	963.1	E858.1	E933.1	E950.4	E962.0	E980.4
Mazindol	977.0	E858.8	E947.0	E950.4	E962.0	E980.4
Meadow saffron	988.2	E865.3	—	E950.9	E962.1	E980.9
Measles vaccine	979.4	E858.8	E949.4	E950.4	E962.0	E980.4
Meat, noxious or nonbacterial	988.8	E865.0	—	E950.9	E962.1	E980.9
Mebanazine	969.0	E854.0	E939.0	E950.3	E962.0	E980.3
Mebaral	967.0	E851	E937.0	E950.1	E962.0	E980.1
Mebendazole	961.6	E857	E931.6	E950.4	E962.0	E980.4
Mebeverine	975.1	E858.6	E945.1	E950.4	E962.0	E980.4
Mebhydroline	963.0	E858.1	E933.0	E950.4	E962.0	E980.4
Mebrophenhydramine	963.0	E858.1	E933.0	E950.4	E962.0	E980.4
Mebutamate	969.5	E853.8	E939.5	E950.3	E962.0	E980.3
Mecamylamine (chloride)	972.3	E858.3	E942.3	E950.4	E962.0	E980.4
Mechlorethamine hydrochloride	963.1	E858.1	E933.1	E950.4	E962.0	E980.4
Meclizene (hydrochloride)	963.0	E858.1	E933.0	E950.4	E962.0	E980.4
Meclofenoxate	970.0	E854.3	E940.0	E950.4	E962.0	E980.4
Meclozine (hydrochloride)	963.0	E858.1	E933.0	E950.4	E962.0	E980.4
Medazepam	969.4	E853.2	E939.4	E950.3	E962.0	E980.3
Medicine, medicinal substance	977.9	E858.9	E947.9	E950.5	E962.0	E980.5
specified NEC	977.8	E858.8	E947.8	E950.4	E962.0	E980.4
Medinal	967.0	E851	E937.0	E950.1	E962.0	E980.1
Medomin	967.0	E851	E937.0	E950.1	E962.0	E980.1
Medroxyprogesterone	962.2	E858.0	E932.2	E950.4	E962.0	E980.4
Medrysone	976.5	E858.7	E946.5	E950.4	E962.0	E980.4
Mefenamic acid	965.7	E850.7	E935.7	E950.0	E962.0	E980.0
Megahallucinogen	969.6	E854.1	E939.6	E950.3	E962.0	E980.3
Megestrol	962.2	E858.0	E932.2	E950.4	E962.0	E980.4
Meglumine	977.8	E858.8	E947.8	E950.4	E962.0	E980.4
Meladinin	976.3	E858.7	E946.3	E950.4	E962.0	E980.4
Melanizing agents	976.3	E858.7	E946.3	E950.4	E962.0	E980.4
Melarsoprol	961.1	E857	E931.1	E950.4	E962.0	E980.4
Melia azedarach	988.2	E865.3	—	E950.9	E962.1	E980.9
Mellaril	969.1	E853.0	E939.1	E950.3	E962.0	E980.3
Meloxine	976.3	E858.7	E946.3	E950.4	E962.0	E980.4
Melphalan	963.1	E858.1	E933.1	E950.4	E962.0	E980.4
Menadiol sodium diphosphate	964.3	E858.2	E934.3	E950.4	E962.0	E980.4
Menadione (sodium bisulfate)	964.3	E858.2	E934.3	E950.4	E962.0	E980.4
Menaphthone	964.3	E858.2	E934.3	E950.4	E962.0	E980.4
Meningococcal vaccine	978.8	E858.8	E948.8	E950.4	E962.0	E980.4
Menningovax–C	978.8	E858.8	E948.8	E950.4	E962.0	E980.4
Menotropins	962.4	E858.0	E932.4	E950.4	E962.0	E980.4
Menthol NEC	976.1	E858.7	E946.1	E950.4	E962.0	E980.4
Mepacrine	961.3	E857	E931.3	E950.4	E962.0	E980.4
Meparfynol	967.8	E852.8	E937.8	E950.2	E962.0	E980.2
Mepazine	969.1	E853.0	E939.1	E950.3	E962.0	E980.3
Mepenzolate	971.1	E855.4	E941.1	E950.4	E962.0	E980.4
Meperidine	965.09	E850.2	E935.2	E950.0	E962.0	E980.0
Mephenamin(e)	966.4	E855.0	E936.4	E950.4	E962.0	E980.4
Mephenesin (carbamate)	968.0	E855.1	E938.0	E950.4	E962.0	E980.4

Substance	Poisoning	External Cause (E-Code)				
		Accident	Therapeutic Use	Suicide Attempt	Assault	Undetermined
Mephenoxalone	969.5	E853.8	E939.5	E950.3	E962.0	E980.3
Mephentermine	971.2	E855.5	E941.2	E950.4	E962.0	E980.4
Mephenytoin	966.1	E855.0	E936.1	E950.4	E962.0	E980.4
Mephobarbital	967.0	E851	E937.0	E950.1	E962.0	E980.1
Mepiperphenidol	971.1	E855.4	E941.1	E950.4	E962.0	E980.4
Mepivacaine	968.9	E855.2	E938.9	E950.4	E962.0	E980.4
infiltration (subcutaneous)	968.5	E855.2	E938.5	E950.4	E962.0	E980.4
nerve block (peripheral) (plexus)	968.6	E855.2	E938.6	E950.4	E962.0	E980.4
topical (surface)	968.5	E855.2	E938.5	E950.4	E962.0	E980.4
Meprednisone	962.0	E858.0	E932.0	E950.4	E962.0	E980.4
Meprobam	969.5	E853.8	E939.5	E950.3	E962.0	E980.3
Meprobamate	969.5	E853.8	E939.5	E950.3	E962.0	E980.3
Mepyramine (maleate)	963.0	E858.1	E933.0	E950.4	E962.0	E980.4
Meralluride	974.0	E858.5	E944.0	E950.4	E962.0	E980.4
Merbaphen	974.0	E858.5	E944.0	E950.4	E962.0	E980.4
Merbromin	976.0	E858.7	E946.0	E950.4	E962.0	E980.4
Mercaptomerin	974.0	E858.5	E944.0	E950.4	E962.0	E980.4
Mercaptopurine	963.1	E858.1	E933.1	E950.4	E962.0	E980.4
Mercumatilin	974.0	E858.5	E944.0	E950.4	E962.0	E980.4
Mercuramide	974.0	E858.5	E944.0	E950.4	E962.0	E980.4
Mercuranin	976.0	E858.7	E946.0	E950.4	E962.0	E980.4
Mercurochrome	976.0	E858.7	E946.0	E950.4	E962.0	E980.4
Mercury, mercuric, mercurous (compounds) (cyanide) (fumes) (nonmedicinal) (vapor) NEC	985.0	E866.1	—	E950.9	E962.1	E980.9
ammoniated	976.0	E858.7	E946.0	E950.4	E962.0	E980.4
anti–infective	961.2	E857	E931.2	E950.4	E962.0	E980.4
topical	976.0	E858.7	E946.0	E950.4	E962.0	E980.4
chloride (antiseptic) NEC	976.0	E858.7	E946.0	E950.4	E962.0	E980.4
fungicide	985.0	E863.6	—	E950.6	E962.1	E980.7
diuretic compounds	974.0	E858.5	E944.0	E950.4	E962.0	E980.4
fungicide	985.0	E863.6	—	E950.6	E962.1	E980.7
organic (fungicide)	985.0	E863.6	—	E950.6	E962.1	E980.7
Merethoxylline	974.0	E858.5	E944.0	E950.4	E962.0	E980.4
Mersalyl	974.0	E858.5	E944.0	E950.4	E962.0	E980.4
Merthiolate (topical)	976.0	E858.7	E946.0	E950.4	E962.0	E980.4
ophthalmic preparation	976.5	E858.7	E946.5	E950.4	E962.0	E980.4
Meruvax	979.4	E858.8	E949.4	E950.4	E962.0	E980.4
Mescal buttons	969.6	E854.1	E939.6	E950.3	E962.0	E980.3
Mescaline (salts)	969.6	E854.1	E939.6	E950.3	E962.0	E980.3
Mesoridazine besylate	969.1	E853.0	E939.1	E950.3	E962.0	E980.3
Mestanolone	962.1	E858.0	E932.1	E950.4	E962.0	E980.4
Mestranol	962.2	E858.0	E932.2	E950.4	E962.0	E980.4
Metacresylacetate	976.0	E858.7	E946.0	E950.4	E962.0	E980.4
Metaldehyde (snail killer) NEC	989.4	E863.4	—	E950.6	E962.1	E980.7
Metals (heavy) (nonmedicinal) NEC	985.9	E866.4	—	E950.9	E962.1	E980.9
dust, fumes, or vapor NEC	985.9	E866.4	—	E950.9	E962.1	E980.9
light NEC	985.9	E866.4	—	E950.9	E962.1	E980.9
dust, fumes, or vapor NEC	985.9	E866.4	—	E950.9	E962.1	E980.9
pesticides (dust) (vapor)	985.9	E863.4	—	E950.6	E962.1	E980.7
Metamucil	973.3	E858.4	E943.3	E950.4	E962.0	E980.4
Metaphen	976.0	E858.7	E946.0	E950.4	E962.0	E980.4
Metaproterenol	975.1	E858.6	E945.1	E950.4	E962.0	E980.4
Metaraminol	972.8	E858.3	E942.8	E950.4	E962.0	E980.4
Metaxalone	968.0	E855.1	E938.0	E950.4	E962.0	E980.4
Metformin	962.3	E858.0	E932.3	E950.4	E962.0	E980.4
Methacycline	960.4	E856	E930.4	E950.4	E962.0	E980.4

Substance	Poisoning	External Cause (E-Code)				
		Accident	Therapeutic Use	Suicide Attempt	Assault	Undetermined
Methadone	965.02	E850.1	E935.1	E950.0	E962.0	E980.0
Methallenestril	962.2	E858.0	E932.2	E950.4	E962.0	E980.4
Methamphetamine	969.7	E854.2	E939.7	E950.3	E962.0	E980.3
Methandienone	962.1	E858.0	E932.1	E950.4	E962.0	E980.4
Methandriol	962.1	E858.0	E932.1	E950.4	E962.0	E980.4
Methandrostenolone	962.1	E858.0	E932.1	E950.4	E962.0	E980.4
Methane gas	987.1	E869.8	—	E952.8	E962.2	E982.8
Methanol	980.1	E860.2	—	E950.9	E962.1	E980.9
vapor	987.8	E869.8	—	E952.8	E962.2	E982.8
Methantheline	971.1	E855.4	E941.1	E950.4	E962.0	E980.4
Methaphenilene	963.0	E858.1	E933.0	E950.4	E962.0	E980.4
Methapyrilene	963.0	E858.1	E933.0	E950.4	E962.0	E980.4
Methaqualone (compounds)	967.4	E852.3	E937.4	E950.2	E962.0	E980.2
Metharbital, metharbitone	967.0	E851	E937.0	E950.1	E962.0	E980.1
Methazolamide	974.2	E858.5	E944.2	E950.4	E962.0	E980.4
Methdilazine	963.0	E858.1	E933.0	E950.4	E962.0	E980.4
Methedrine	969.7	E854.2	E939.7	E950.3	E962.0	E980.3
Methenamine (mandelate)	961.9	E857	E931.9	E950.4	E962.0	E980.4
Methenolone	962.1	E858.0	E932.1	E950.4	E962.0	E980.4
Methergine	975.0	E858.6	E945.0	E950.4	E962.0	E980.4
Methiacil	962.8	E858.0	E932.8	E950.4	E962.0	E980.4
Methicillin (sodium)	960.0	E856	E930.0	E950.4	E962.0	E980.4
Methimazole	962.8	E858.0	E932.8	E950.4	E962.0	E980.4
Methionine	977.1	E858.8	E947.1	E950.4	E962.0	E980.4
Methisazone	961.7	E857	E931.7	E950.4	E962.0	E980.4
Methitural	967.0	E851	E937.0	E950.1	E962.0	E980.1
Methixene	971.1	E855.4	E941.1	E950.4	E962.0	E980.4
Methobarbital, methobarbitone	967.0	E851	E937.0	E950.1	E962.0	E980.1
Methocarbamol	968.0	E855.1	E938.0	E950.4	E962.0	E980.4
Methohexital, methohexitone (sodium)	968.3	E855.1	E938.3	E950.4	E962.0	E980.4
Methoin	966.1	E855.0	E936.1	E950.4	E962.0	E980.4
Methopholine	965.7	E850.7	E935.7	E950.0	E962.0	E980.0
Methorate	975.4	E858.6	E945.4	E950.4	E962.0	E980.4
Methoserpidine	972.6	E858.3	E942.6	E950.4	E962.0	E980.4
Methotrexate	963.1	E858.1	E933.1	E950.4	E962.0	E980.4
Methotrimeprazine	967.8	E852.8	E937.8	E950.2	E962.0	E980.2
Methoxa–Dome	976.3	E858.7	E946.3	E950.4	E962.0	E980.4
Methoxamine	971.2	E855.5	E941.2	E950.4	E962.0	E980.4
Methoxsalen	976.3	E858.7	E946.3	E950.4	E962.0	E980.4
Methoxybenzyl penicillin	960.0	E856	E930.0	E950.4	E962.0	E980.4
Methoxychlor	989.2	E863.0	—	E950.6	E962.1	E980.7
Methoxyflurane	968.2	E855.1	E938.2	E950.4	E962.0	E980.4
Methoxyphenamine	971.2	E855.5	E941.2	E950.4	E962.0	E980.4
Methoxypromazine	969.1	E853.0	E939.1	E950.3	E962.0	E980.3
Methoxypsoralen	976.3	E858.7	E946.3	E950.4	E962.0	E980.4
Methscopolamine (bromide)	971.1	E855.4	E941.1	E950.4	E962.0	E980.4
Methsuximide	966.2	E855.0	E936.2	E950.4	E962.0	E980.4
Methyclothiazide	974.3	E858.5	E944.3	E950.4	E962.0	E980.4
Methyl						
acetate	982.8	E862.4	—	E950.9	E962.1	E980.9
acetone	982.8	E862.4	—	E950.9	E962.1	E980.9
alcohol	980.1	E860.2	—	E950.9	E962.1	E980.9
amphetamine	969.7	E854.2	E939.7	E950.3	E962.0	E980.3
androstanolone	962.1	E858.0	E932.1	E950.4	E962.0	E980.4
atropine	971.1	E855.4	E941.1	E950.4	E962.0	E980.4
benzene	982.0	E862.4	—	E950.9	E962.1	E980.9
bromide (gas)	987.8	E869.8	—	E952.8	E962.2	E982.8

Substance	Poisoning	External Cause (E-Code)				
		Accident	Therapeutic Use	Suicide Attempt	Assault	Undetermined
fumigant	987.8	E863.8	—	E950.6	E962.2	E980.7
butanol	980.8	E860.8	—	E950.9	E962.1	E980.9
carbinol	980.1	E860.2	—	E950.9	E962.1	E980.9
cellosolve	982.8	E862.4	—	E950.9	E962.1	E980.9
cellulose	973.3	E858.4	E943.3	E950.4	E962.0	E980.4
chloride (gas)	987.8	E869.8	—	E952.8	E962.2	E982.8
cyclohexane	982.8	E862.4	—	E950.9	E962.1	E980.9
cyclohexanone	982.8	E862.4	—	E950.9	E962.1	E980.9
dihydromorphinone	965.09	E850.2	E935.2	E950.0	E962.0	E980.0
ergometrine	975.0	E858.6	E945.0	E950.4	E962.0	E980.4
ergonovine	975.0	E858.6	E945.0	E950.4	E962.0	E980.4
ethyl ketone	982.8	E862.4	—	E950.9	E962.1	E980.9
hydrazine	983.9	E864.3	—	E950.7	E962.1	E980.6
isobutyl ketone	982.8	E862.4	—	E950.9	E962.1	E980.9
morphine NEC	965.09	E850.2	E935.2	E950.0	E962.0	E980.0
parafynol	967.8	E852.8	E937.8	E950.2	E962.0	E980.2
parathion	989.3	E863.1	—	E950.6	E962.1	E980.7
pentynol NEC	967.8	E852.8	E937.8	E950.2	E962.0	E980.2
peridol	969.2	E853.1	E939.2	E950.3	E962.0	E980.3
phenidate	969.7	E854.2	E939.7	E950.3	E962.0	E980.3
prednisolone	962.0	E858.0	E932.0	E950.4	E962.0	E980.4
ENT agent	976.6	E858.7	E946.6	E950.4	E962.0	E980.4
ophthalmic preparation	976.5	E858.7	E946.5	E950.4	E962.0	E980.4
topical NEC	976.0	E858.7	E946.0	E950.4	E962.0	E980.4
propylcarbinol	980.8	E860.8	—	E950.9	E962.1	E980.9
rosaniline NEC	976.0	E858.7	E946.0	E950.4	E962.0	E980.4
salicylate NEC	976.3	E858.7	E946.3	E950.4	E962.0	E980.4
sulfate (fumes)	987.8	E869.8	—	E952.8	E962.2	E982.8
liquid	983.9	E864.3	—	E950.7	E962.1	E980.6
sulfonal	967.8	E852.8	E937.8	E950.2	E962.0	E980.2
testosterone	962.1	E858.0	E932.1	E950.4	E962.0	E980.4
thiouracil	962.8	E858.0	E932.8	E950.4	E962.0	E980.4
Methylated spirit	980.0	E860.1	—	E950.9	E962.1	E980.9
Methyldopa	972.6	E858.3	E942.6	E950.4	E962.0	E980.4
Methylene						
blue	961.9	E857	E931.9	E950.4	E962.0	E980.4
chloride or dichloride (solvent) NEC	982.3	E862.4	—	E950.9	E962.1	E980.9
Methylhexabital	967.0	E851	E937.0	E950.1	E962.0	E980.1
Methylparaben (ophthalmic)	976.5	E858.7	E946.5	E950.4	E962.0	E980.4
Methyprylon	967.5	E852.4	E937.5	E950.2	E962.0	E980.2
Methysergide	971.3	E855.6	E941.3	E950.4	E962.0	E980.4
Metoclopramide	963.0	E858.1	E933.0	E950.4	E962.0	E980.4
Metofoline	965.7	E850.7	E935.7	E950.0	E962.0	E980.0
Metopon	965.09	E850.2	E935.2	E950.0	E962.0	E980.0
Metronidazole	961.5	E857	E931.5	E950.4	E962.0	E980.4
Metycaine	968.9	E855.2	E938.9	E950.4	E962.0	E980.4
infiltration (subcutaneous)	968.5	E855.2	E938.5	E950.4	E962.0	E980.4
nerve block (peripheral) (plexus)	968.6	E855.2	E938.6	E950.4	E962.0	E980.4
topical (surface)	968.5	E855.2	E938.5	E950.4	E962.0	E980.4
Metyrapone	977.8	E858.8	E947.8	E950.4	E962.0	E980.4
Mevinphos	989.3	E863.1	—	E950.6	E962.1	E980.7
Mezereon (berries)	988.2	E865.3	—	E950.9	E962.1	E980.9
Micatin	976.0	E858.7	E946.0	E950.4	E962.0	E980.4
Miconazole	976.0	E858.7	E946.0	E950.4	E962.0	E980.4
Midol	965.1	E850.3	E935.3	E950.0	E962.0	E980.0
Milk of magnesia	973.0	E858.4	E943.0	E950.4	E962.0	E980.4
Millipede (tropical) (venomous)	989.5	E905.4	—	E950.9	E962.1	E980.9

Substance	Poisoning	External Cause (E-Code)				
		Accident	Therapeutic Use	Suicide Attempt	Assault	Undetermined
Miltown	969.5	E853.8	E939.5	E950.3	E962.0	E980.3
Mineral						
oil (medicinal)	973.2	E858.4	E943.2	E950.4	E962.0	E980.4
nonmedicinal	981	E862.1	—	E950.9	E962.1	E980.9
topical	976.3	E858.7	E946.3	E950.4	E962.0	E980.4
salts NEC	974.6	E858.5	E944.6	E950.4	E962.0	E980.4
spirits	981	E862.0	—	E950.9	E962.1	E980.9
Minocycline	960.4	E856	E930.4	E950.4	E962.0	E980.4
Mithramycin (antineoplastic)	960.7	E856	E930.7	E950.4	E962.0	E980.4
Mitobronitol	963.1	E858.1	E933.1	E950.4	E962.0	E980.4
Mitomycin (antineoplastic)	960.7	E856	E930.7	E950.4	E962.0	E980.4
Mitotane	963.1	E858.1	E933.1	E950.4	E962.0	E980.4
Moderil	972.6	E858.3	E942.6	E950.4	E962.0	E980.4
Mogadon—*see* Nitrazepam						
Molindone	969.3	E853.8	E939.3	E950.3	E962.0	E980.3
Monistat	976.0	E858.7	E946.0	E950.4	E962.0	E980.4
Monkshood	988.2	E865.4	—	E950.9	E962.1	E980.9
Monoamine oxidase inhibitors	969.0	E854.0	E939.0	E950.3	E962.0	E980.3
Monochlorobenzene	982.0	E862.4	—	E950.9	E962.1	E980.9
Monosodium glutamate	989.89	E866.8	—	E950.9	E962.1	E980.9
Monoxide, carbon — *see* Carbon, monoxide						
Moperone	969.2	E853.1	E939.2	E950.3	E962.0	E980.3
Morning glory seeds	969.6	E854.1	E939.6	E950.3	E962.0	E980.3
Moroxydine (hydrochloride)	961.7	E857	E931.7	E950.4	E962.0	E980.4
Morphazinamide	961.8	E857	E931.8	E950.4	E962.0	E980.4
Morphinans	965.09	E850.2	E935.2	E950.0	E962.0	E980.0
Morphine NEC	965.09	E850.2	E935.2	E950.0	E962.0	E980.0
antagonists	970.1	E854.3	E940.1	E950.4	E962.0	E980.4
Morpholinylethylmorphine	965.09	E850.2	E935.2	E950.0	E962.0	E980.0
Morrhuate sodium	972.7	E858.3	E942.7	E950.4	E962.0	E980.4
Moth balls (*see also* Pesticides)	989.4	E863.4	—	E950.6	E962.1	E980.7
naphthalene	983.0	E863.4	—	E950.7	E962.1	E980.6
Motor exhaust gas — *see* Carbon, monoxide, exhaust gas						
Mouth wash	976.6	E858.7	E946.6	E950.4	E962.0	E980.4
Mucolytic agent	975.5	E858.6	E945.5	E950.4	E962.0	E980.4
Mucomyst	975.5	E858.6	E945.5	E950.4	E962.0	E980.4
Mucous membrane agents (external)	976.9	E858.7	E946.9	E950.4	E962.0	E980.4
specified NEC	976.8	E858.7	E946.8	E950.4	E962.0	E980.4
Mumps						
immune globulin (human)	964.6	E858.2	E934.6	E950.4	E962.0	E980.4
skin test antigen	977.8	E858.8	E947.8	E950.4	E962.0	E980.4
vaccine	979.6	E858.8	E949.6	E950.4	E962.0	E980.4
Mumpsvax	979.6	E858.8	E949.6	E950.4	E962.0	E980.4
Muriatic acid — *see* Hydrochloric acid						
Muscarine	971.0	E855.3	E941.0	E950.4	E962.0	E980.4
Muscle affecting agents NEC	975.3	E858.6	E945.3	E950.4	E962.0	E980.4
oxytocic	975.0	E858.6	E945.0	E950.4	E962.0	E980.4
relaxants	975.3	E858.6	E945.3	E950.4	E962.0	E980.4
central nervous system	968.0	E855.1	E938.0	E950.4	E962.0	E980.4
skeletal	975.2	E858.6	E945.2	E950.4	E962.0	E980.4
smooth	975.1	E858.6	E945.1	E950.4	E962.0	E980.4
Mushrooms, noxious	988.1	E865.5	—	E950.9	E962.1	E980.9
Mussel, noxious	988.0	E865.1	—	E950.9	E962.1	E980.9
Mustard (emetic)	973.6	E858.4	E943.6	E950.4	E962.0	E980.4
gas	987.8	E869.8	—	E952.8	E962.2	E982.8
nitrogen	963.1	E858.1	E933.1	E950.4	E962.0	E980.4

Substance	Poisoning	Accident	Therapeutic Use	Suicide Attempt	Assault	Undetermined
Mustine	963.1	E858.1	E933.1	E950.4	E962.0	E980.4
M–vac	979.4	E858.8	E949.4	E950.4	E962.0	E980.4
Mycifradin	960.8	E856	E930.8	E950.4	E962.0	E980.4
topical	976.0	E858.7	E946.0	E950.4	E962.0	E980.4
Mycitracin	960.8	E856	E930.8	E950.4	E962.0	E980.4
ophthalmic preparation	976.5	E858.7	E946.5	E950.4	E962.0	E980.4
Mycostatin	960.1	E856	E930.1	E950.4	E962.0	E980.4
topical	976.0	E858.7	E946.0	E950.4	E962.0	E980.4
Mydriacyl	971.1	E855.4	E941.1	E950.4	E962.0	E980.4
Myelobromal	963.1	E858.1	E933.1	E950.4	E962.0	E980.4
Myleran	963.1	E858.1	E933.1	E950.4	E962.0	E980.4
Myochrysin(e)	965.69	E850.6	E935.6	E950.0	E962.0	E980.0
Myoneural blocking agents	975.2	E858.6	E945.2	E950.4	E962.0	E980.4
Myristica fragrans	988.2	E865.3	—	E950.9	E962.1	E980.9
Myristicin	988.2	E865.3	—	E950.9	E962.1	E980.9
Mysoline	966.3	E855.0	E936.3	E950.4	E962.0	E980.4
Nafcillin (sodium)	960.0	E856	E930.0	E950.4	E962.0	E980.4
Nail polish remover	982.8	E862.4	—	E950.9	E962.1	E980.9
Nalidixic acid	961.9	E857	E931.9	E950.4	E962.0	E980.4
Nalorphine	970.1	E854.3	E940.1	E950.4	E962.0	E980.4
Naloxone	970.1	E854.3	E940.1	E950.4	E962.0	E980.4
Nandrolone (decanoate) (phenproprioate)	962.1	E858.0	E932.1	E950.4	E962.0	E980.4
Naphazoline	971.2	E855.5	E941.2	E950.4	E962.0	E980.4
Naphtha (painter's) (petroleum)	981	E862.0	—	E950.9	E962.1	E980.9
solvent	981	E862.0	—	E950.9	E962.1	E980.9
vapor	987.1	E869.8	—	E952.8	E962.2	E982.8
Naphthalene (chlorinated)	983.0	E864.0	—	E950.7	E962.1	E980.6
insecticide or moth repellent	983.0	E863.4	—	E950.7	E962.1	E980.6
vapor	987.8	E869.8	—	E952.8	E962.2	E982.8
Naphthol	983.0	E864.0	—	E950.7	E962.1	E980.6
Naphthylamine	983.0	E864.0	—	E950.7	E962.1	E980.6
Naprosyn—*see* Naproxen						
Naproxen	965.61	E850.6	E935.6	E950.0	E962.0	E980.0
Narcotic (drug)	967.9	E852.9	E937.9	E950.2	E962.0	E980.2
analgesic NEC	965.8	E850.8	E935.8	E950.0	E962.0	E980.0
antagonist	970.1	E854.3	E940.1	E950.4	E962.0	E980.4
specified NEC	967.8	E852.8	E937.8	E950.2	E962.0	E980.2
Narcotine	975.4	E858.6	E945.4	E950.4	E962.0	E980.4
Nardil	969.0	E854.0	E939.0	E950.3	E962.0	E980.3
Natrium cyanide — *see* Cyanide(s)						
Natural						
blood (product)	964.7	E858.2	E934.7	E950.4	E962.0	E980.4
gas (piped)	987.1	E867	—	E951.0	E962.2	E981.0
incomplete combustion	986	E867	—	E951.0	E962.2	E981.0
Nealbarbital, nealbarbitone	967.0	E851	E937.0	E950.1	E962.0	E980.1
Nectadon	975.4	E858.6	E945.4	E950.4	E962.0	E980.4
Nematocyst (sting)	989.5	E905.6	—	E950.9	E962.1	E980.9
Nembutal	967.0	E851	E937.0	E950.1	E962.0	E980.1
Neoarsphenamine	961.1	E857	E931.1	E950.4	E962.0	E980.4
Neocinchophen	974.7	E858.5	E944.7	E950.4	E962.0	E980.4
Neomycin	960.8	E856	E930.8	E950.4	E962.0	E980.4
ENT agent	976.6	E858.7	E946.6	E950.4	E962.0	E980.4
ophthalmic preparation	976.5	E858.7	E946.5	E950.4	E962.0	E980.4
topical NEC	976.0	E858.7	E946.0	E950.4	E962.0	E980.4
Neonal	967.0	E851	E937.0	E950.1	E962.0	E980.1
Neoprontosil	961.0	E857	E931.0	E950.4	E962.0	E980.4
Neosalvarsan	961.1	E857	E931.1	E950.4	E962.0	E980.4

Substance	Poisoning	External Cause (E-Code)				
		Accident	Therapeutic Use	Suicide Attempt	Assault	Undetermined
Neosilversalvarsan	961.1	E857	E931.1	E950.4	E962.0	E980.4
Neosporin	960.8	E856	E930.8	E950.4	E962.0	E980.4
ENT agent	976.6	E858.7	E946.6	E950.4	E962.0	E980.4
ophthalmic preparation	976.5	E858.7	E946.5	E950.4	E962.0	E980.4
topical NEC	976.0	E858.7	E946.0	E950.4	E962.0	E980.4
Neostigmine	971.0	E855.3	E941.0	E950.4	E962.0	E980.4
Neraval	967.0	E851	E937.0	E950.1	E962.0	E980.1
Neravan	967.0	E851	E937.0	E950.1	E962.0	E980.1
Nerium oleander	988.2	E865.4	—	E950.9	E962.1	E980.9
Nerve gases (war)	987.9	E869.9	—	E952.9	E962.2	E982.9
Nesacaine	968.9	E855.2	E938.9	E950.4	E962.0	E980.4
infiltration (subcutaneous)	968.5	E855.2	E938.5	E950.4	E962.0	E980.4
nerve block (peripheral) (plexus)	968.6	E855.2	E938.6	E950.4	E962.0	E980.4
Neurobarb	967.0	E851	E937.0	E950.1	E962.0	E980.1
Neuroleptics NEC	969.3	E853.8	E939.3	E950.3	E962.0	E980.3
Neuroprotective agent	977.8	E858.8	E947.8	E950.4	E962.0	E980.4
Neutral spirits	980.0	E860.1	—	E950.9	E962.1	E980.9
beverage	980.0	E860.0	—	E950.9	E962.1	E980.9
Niacin, niacinamide	972.2	E858.3	E942.2	E950.4	E962.0	E980.4
Nialamide	969.0	E854.0	E939.0	E950.3	E962.0	E980.3
Nickle (carbonyl) (compounds) (fumes) (tetracarbonyl) (vapor)	985.8	E866.4	—	E950.9	E962.1	E980.9
Niclosamide	961.6	E857	E931.6	E950.4	E962.0	E980.4
Nicomorphine	965.09	E850.2	E935.2	E950.0	E962.0	E980.0
Nicotinamide	972.2	E858.3	E942.2	E950.4	E962.0	E980.4
Nicotine (insecticide) (spray) (sulfate) NEC	989.4	E863.4	—	E950.6	E962.1	E980.7
not insecticide	989.89	E866.8	—	E950.9	E962.1	E980.9
Nicotinic acid (derivatives)	972.2	E858.3	E942.2	E950.4	E962.0	E980.4
Nicotinyl alcohol	972.2	E858.3	E942.2	E950.4	E962.0	E980.4
Nicoumalone	964.2	E858.2	E934.2	E950.4	E962.0	E980.4
Nifenazone	965.5	E850.5	E935.5	E950.0	E962.0	E980.0
Nifuraldezone	961.9	E857	E931.9	E950.4	E962.0	E980.4
Nightshade (deadly)	988.2	E865.4	—	E950.9	E962.1	E980.9
Nikethamide	970.0	E854.3	E940.0	E950.4	E962.0	E980.4
Nilstat	960.1	E856	E930.1	E950.4	E962.0	E980.4
topical	976.0	E858.7	E946.0	E950.4	E962.0	E980.4
Nimodipine	977.8	E858.8	E947.8	E950.4	E962.0	E980.4
Niridazole	961.6	E857	E931.6	E950.4	E962.0	E980.4
Nisentil	965.09	E850.2	E935.2	E950.0	E962.0	E980.0
Nitrates	972.4	E858.3	E942.4	E950.4	E962.0	E980.4
Nitrazepam	969.4	E853.2	E939.4	E950.3	E962.0	E980.3
Nitric						
acid (liquid)	983.1	E864.1	—	E950.7	E962.1	E980.6
vapor	987.8	E869.8	—	E952.8	E962.2	E982.8
oxide (gas)	987.2	E869.0	—	E952.8	E962.2	E982.8
Nitrite, amyl (medicinal) (vapor)	972.4	E858.3	E942.4	E950.4	E962.0	E980.4
Nitroaniline	983.0	E864.0	—	E950.7	E962.1	E980.6
vapor	987.8	E869.8	—	E952.8	E962.2	E982.8
Nitrobenzene, nitrobenzol	983.0	E864.0	—	E950.7	E962.1	E980.6
vapor	987.8	E869.8	—	E952.8	E962.2	E982.8
Nitrocellulose	976.3	E858.7	E946.3	E950.4	E962.0	E980.4
Nitrofuran derivatives	961.9	E857	E931.9	E950.4	E962.0	E980.4
Nitrofurantoin	961.9	E857	E931.9	E950.4	E962.0	E980.4
Nitrofurazone	976.0	E858.7	E946.0	E950.4	E962.0	E980.4
Nitrogen (dioxide) (gas) (oxide)	987.2	E869.0	—	E952.8	E962.2	E982.8
mustard (antineoplastic)	963.1	E858.1	E933.1	E950.4	E962.0	E980.4
Nitroglycerin, nitroglycerol (medicinal)	972.4	E858.3	E942.4	E950.4	E962.0	E980.4

Substance	Poisoning	Accident	Therapeutic Use	Suicide Attempt	Assault	Undetermined
nonmedicinal	989.89	E866.8	—	E950.9	E962.1	E980.9
fumes	987.8	E869.8	—	E952.8	E962.2	E982.8
Nitrohydrochloric acid	983.1	E864.1	—	E950.7	E962.1	E980.6
Nitromersol	976.0	E858.7	E946.0	E950.4	E962.0	E980.4
Nitronaphthalene	983.0	E864.0	—	E950.7	E962.2	E980.6
Nitrophenol	983.0	E864.0	—	E950.7	E962.2	E980.6
Nitrothiazol	961.6	E857	E931.6	E950.4	E962.0	E980.4
Nitrotoluene, nitrotoluol	983.0	E864.0	—	E950.7	E962.1	E980.6
vapor	987.8	E869.8	—	E952.8	E962.2	E982.8
Nitrous	968.2	E855.1	E938.2	E950.4	E962.0	E980.4
acid (liquid)	983.1	E864.1	—	E950.7	E962.1	E980.6
fumes	987.2	E869.0	—	E952.8	E962.2	E982.8
oxide (anesthetic) NEC	968.2	E855.1	E938.2	E950.4	E962.0	E980.4
Nitrozone	976.0	E858.7	E946.0	E950.4	E962.0	E980.4
Noctec	967.1	E852.0	E937.1	E950.2	E962.0	E980.2
Noludar	967.5	E852.4	E937.5	E950.2	E962.0	E980.2
Noptil	967.0	E851	E937.0	E950.1	E962.0	E980.1
Noradrenalin	971.2	E855.5	E941.2	E950.4	E962.0	E980.4
Noramidopyrine	965.5	E850.5	E935.5	E950.0	E962.0	E980.0
Norepinephrine	971.2	E855.5	E941.2	E950.4	E962.0	E980.4
Norethandrolone	962.1	E858.0	E932.1	E950.4	E962.0	E980.4
Norethindrone	962.2	E858.0	E932.2	E950.4	E962.0	E980.4
Norethisterone	962.2	E858.0	E932.2	E950.4	E962.0	E980.4
Norethynodrel	962.2	E858.0	E932.2	E950.4	E962.0	E980.4
Norlestrin	962.2	E858.0	E932.2	E950.4	E962.0	E980.4
Norlutin	962.2	E858.0	E932.2	E950.4	E962.0	E980.4
Normison—*see* Benzodiazepines						
Normorphine	965.09	E850.2	E935.2	E950.0	E962.0	E980.0
Nortriptyline	969.0	E854.0	E939.0	E950.3	E962.0	E980.3
Noscapine	975.4	E858.6	E945.4	E950.4	E962.0	E980.4
Nose preparations	976.6	E858.7	E946.6	E950.4	E962.0	E980.4
Novobiocin	960.8	E856	E930.8	E950.4	E962.0	E980.4
Novocain (infiltration) (topical)	968.5	E855.2	E938.5	E950.4	E962.0	E980.4
nerve block (peripheral) (plexus)	968.6	E855.2	E938.6	E950.4	E962.0	E980.4
spinal	968.7	E855.2	E938.7	E950.4	E962.0	E980.4
Noxythiolin	961.9	E857	E931.9	E950.4	E962.0	E980.4
NPH Iletin (insulin)	962.3	E858.0	E932.3	E950.4	E962.0	E980.4
Numorphan	965.09	E850.2	E935.2	E950.0	E962.0	E980.0
Nunol	967.0	E851	E937.0	E950.1	E962.0	E980.1
Nupercaine (spinal anesthetic)	968.7	E855.2	E938.7	E950.4	E962.0	E980.4
topical (surface)	968.5	E855.2	E938.5	E950.4	E962.0	E980.4
Nutmeg oil (liniment)	976.3	E858.7	E946.3	E950.4	E962.0	E980.4
Nux vomica	989.1	E863.7	—	E950.6	E962.1	E980.7
Nydrazid	961.8	E857	E931.8	E950.4	E962.0	E980.4
Nylidrin	971.2	E855.5	E941.2	E950.4	E962.0	E980.4
Nystatin	960.1	E856	E930.1	E950.4	E962.0	E980.4
topical	976.0	E858.7	E946.0	E950.4	E962.0	E980.4
Nytol	963.0	E858.1	E933.0	E950.4	E962.0	E980.4
Oblivion	967.8	E852.8	E937.8	E950.2	E962.0	E980.2
Octyl nitrite	972.4	E858.3	E942.4	E950.4	E962.0	E980.4
Oestradiol (cypionate) (dipropionate) (valerate)	962.2	E858.0	E932.2	E950.4	E962.0	E980.4
Oestriol	962.2	E858.0	E932.2	E950.4	E962.0	E980.4
Oestrone	962.2	E858.0	E932.2	E950.4	E962.0	E980.4
Oil (of) NEC	989.89	E866.8	—	E950.9	E962.1	E980.9
bitter almond	989.0	E866.8	—	E950.9	E962.1	E980.9
camphor	976.1	E858.7	E946.1	E950.4	E962.0	E980.4

Substance	Poisoning	Accident	Therapeutic Use	Suicide Attempt	Assault	Undetermined
colors	989.89	E861.6	—	E950.9	E962.1	E980.9
fumes	987.8	E869.8	—	E952.8	E962.2	E982.8
lubricating	981	E862.2	—	E950.9	E962.1	E980.9
specified source, other — *see* substance specified						
vitriol (liquid)	983.1	E864.1	—	E950.7	E962.1	E980.6
fumes	987.8	E869.8	—	E952.8	E962.2	E982.8
wintergreen (bitter) NEC	976.3	E858.7	E946.3	E950.4	E962.0	E980.4
Ointments NEC	976.9	E858.7	E946.9	E950.4	E962.0	E980.4
Oleander	988.2	E865.4	—	E950.9	E962.1	E980.9
Oleandomycin	960.3	E856	E930.3	E950.4	E962.0	E980.4
Oleovitamin A	963.5	E858.1	E933.5	E950.4	E962.0	E980.4
Oleum ricini	973.1	E858.4	E943.1	E950.4	E962.0	E980.4
Olive oil (medicinal) NEC	973.2	E858.4	E943.2	E950.4	E962.0	E980.4
OMPA	989.3	E863.1	—	E950.6	E962.1	E980.7
Oncovin	963.1	E858.1	E933.1	E950.4	E962.0	E980.4
Ophthaine	968.5	E855.2	E938.5	E950.4	E962.0	E980.4
Ophthetic	968.5	E855.2	E938.5	E950.4	E962.0	E980.4
Opiates, opioids, opium NEC	965.00	E850.2	E935.2	E950.0	E962.0	E980.0
antagonists	970.1	E854.3	E940.1	E950.4	E962.0	E980.4
Oracon	962.2	E858.0	E932.2	E950.4	E962.0	E980.4
Oragrafin	977.8	E858.8	E947.8	E950.4	E962.0	E980.4
Oral contraceptives	962.2	E858.0	E932.2	E950.4	E962.0	E980.4
Orciprenaline	975.1	E858.6	E945.1	E950.4	E962.0	E980.4
Organidin	975.5	E858.6	E945.5	E950.4	E962.0	E980.4
Organophosphates	989.3	E863.1	—	E950.6	E962.1	E980.7
Orimune	979.5	E858.8	E949.5	E950.4	E962.0	E980.4
Orinase	962.3	E858.0	E932.3	E950.4	E962.0	E980.4
Orphenadrine	966.4	E855.0	E936.4	E950.4	E962.0	E980.4
Ortal (sodium)	967.0	E851	E937.0	E950.1	E962.0	E980.1
Orthoboric acid	976.0	E858.7	E946.0	E950.4	E962.0	E980.4
ENT agent	976.6	E858.7	E946.6	E950.4	E962.0	E980.4
ophthalmic preparation	976.5	E858.7	E946.5	E950.4	E962.0	E980.4
Orthocaine	968.5	E855.2	E938.5	E950.4	E962.0	E980.4
Ortho–Novum	962.2	E858.0	E932.2	E950.4	E962.0	E980.4
Orthotolidine (reagent)	977.8	E858.8	E947.8	E950.4	E962.0	E980.4
Osmic acid (liquid)	983.1	E864.1	—	E950.7	E962.1	E980.6
fumes	987.8	E869.8	—	E952.8	E962.2	E982.8
Osmotic diuretics	974.4	E858.5	E944.4	E950.4	E962.0	E980.4
Ouabain	972.1	E858.3	E942.1	E950.4	E962.0	E980.4
Ovarian hormones (synthetic substitutes)	962.2	E858.0	E932.2	E950.4	E962.0	E980.4
Ovral	962.2	E858.0	E932.2	E950.4	E962.0	E980.4
Ovulation suppressants	962.2	E858.0	E932.2	E950.4	E962.0	E980.4
Ovulen	962.2	E858.0	E932.2	E950.4	E962.0	E980.4
Oxacillin (sodium)	960.0	E856	E930.0	E950.4	E962.0	E980.4
Oxalic acid	983.1	E864.1	—	E950.7	E962.1	E980.6
Oxanamide	969.5	E853.8	E939.5	E950.3	E962.0	E980.3
Oxandrolone	962.1	E858.0	E932.1	E950.4	E962.0	E980.4
Oxaprozin	965.61	E850.6	E935.6	E950.0	E962.0	E980.0
Oxazepam	969.4	E853.2	E939.4	E950.3	E962.0	E980.3
Oxazolidine derivatives	966.0	E855.0	E936.0	E950.4	E962.0	E980.4
Ox bile extract	973.4	E858.4	E943.4	E950.4	E962.0	E980.4
Oxedrine	971.2	E855.5	E941.2	E950.4	E962.0	E980.4
Oxeladin	975.4	E858.6	E945.4	E950.4	E962.0	E980.4
Oxethazaine NEC	968.5	E855.2	E938.5	E950.4	E962.0	E980.4
Oxidizing agents NEC	983.9	E864.3	—	E950.7	E962.1	E980.6
Oxolinic acid	961.3	E857	E931.3	E950.4	E962.0	E980.4

Substance	Poisoning	External Cause (E-Code)				
		Accident	Therapeutic Use	Suicide Attempt	Assault	Undetermined
Oxophenarsine	961.1	E857	E931.1	E950.4	E962.0	E980.4
Oxsoralen	976.3	E858.7	E946.3	E950.4	E962.0	E980.4
Oxtriphylline	975.7	E858.6	E945.7	E950.4	E962.0	E980.4
Oxybuprocaine	968.5	E855.2	E938.5	E950.4	E962.0	E980.4
Oxybutynin	975.1	E858.6	E945.1	E950.4	E962.0	E980.4
Oxycodone	965.09	E850.2	E935.2	E950.0	E962.0	E980.0
Oxygen	987.8	E869.8	—	E952.8	E962.2	E982.8
Oxylone	976.0	E858.7	E946.0	E950.4	E962.0	E980.4
ophthalmic preparation	976.5	E858.7	E946.5	E950.4	E962.0	E980.4
Oxymesterone	962.1	E858.0	E932.1	E950.4	E962.0	E980.4
Oxymetazoline	971.2	E855.5	E941.2	E950.4	E962.0	E980.4
Oxymetholone	962.1	E858.0	E932.1	E950.4	E962.0	E980.4
Oxymorphone	965.09	E850.2	E935.2	E950.0	E962.0	E980.0
Oxypertine	969.0	E854.0	E939.0	E950.3	E962.0	E980.3
Oxyphenbutazone	965.5	E850.5	E935.5	E950.0	E962.0	E980.0
Oxyphencyclimine	971.1	E855.4	E941.1	E950.4	E962.0	E980.4
Oxyphenisatin	973.1	E858.4	E943.1	E950.4	E962.0	E980.4
Oxyphenonium	971.1	E855.4	E941.1	E950.4	E962.0	E980.4
Oxyquinoline	961.3	E857	E931.3	E950.4	E962.0	E980.4
Oxytetracycline	960.4	E856	E930.4	E950.4	E962.0	E980.4
Oxytocics	975.0	E858.6	E945.0	E950.4	E962.0	E980.4
Oxytocin	975.0	E858.6	E945.0	E950.4	E962.0	E980.4
Ozone	987.8	E869.8	—	E952.8	E962.2	E982.8
PABA	976.3	E858.7	E946.3	E950.4	E962.0	E980.4
Packed red cells	964.7	E858.2	E934.7	E950.4	E962.0	E980.4
Paint NEC	989.89	E861.6	—	E950.9	E962.1	E980.9
cleaner	982.8	E862.9	—	E950.9	E962.1	E980.9
fumes NEC	987.8	E869.8	—	E952.8	E962.1	E982.8
lead (fumes)	984.0	E861.5	—	E950.9	E962.1	E980.9
solvent NEC	982.8	E862.9	—	E950.9	E962.1	E980.9
stripper	982.8	E862.9	—	E950.9	E962.1	E980.9
Palfium	965.09	E850.2	E935.2	E950.0	E962.0	E980.0
Paludrine	961.4	E857	E931.4	E950.4	E962.0	E980.4
PAM	977.2	E855.8	E947.2	E950.4	E962.0	E980.4
Pamaquine (naphthoate)	961.4	E857	E931.4	E950.4	E962.0	E980.4
Pamprin	965.1	E850.3	E935.3	E950.0	E962.0	E980.0
Panadol	965.4	E850.4	E935.4	E950.0	E962.0	E980.0
Pancreatic dornase (mucolytic)	963.4	E858.1	E933.4	E950.4	E962.0	E980.4
Pancreatin	973.4	E858.4	E943.4	E950.4	E962.0	E980.4
Pancrelipase	973.4	E858.4	E943.4	E950.4	E962.0	E980.4
Pangamic acid	963.5	E858.1	E933.5	E950.4	E962.0	E980.4
Panthenol	963.5	E858.1	E933.5	E950.4	E962.0	E980.4
topical	976.8	E858.7	E946.8	E950.4	E962.0	E980.4
Pantopaque	977.8	E858.8	E947.8	E950.4	E962.0	E980.4
Pantopon	965.00	E850.2	E935.2	E950.0	E962.0	E980.0
Pantothenic acid	963.5	E858.1	E933.5	E950.4	E962.0	E980.4
Panwarfin	964.2	E858.2	E934.2	E950.4	E962.0	E980.4
Papain	973.4	E858.4	E943.4	E950.4	E962.0	E980.4
Papaverine	972.5	E858.3	E942.5	E950.4	E962.0	E980.4
Para–aminobenzoic acid	976.3	E858.7	E946.3	E950.4	E962.0	E980.4
Para–aminophenol derivatives	965.4	E850.4	E935.4	E950.0	E962.0	E980.0
Para–aminosalicylic acid (derivatives)	961.8	E857	E931.8	E950.4	E962.0	E980.4
Paracetaldehyde (medicinal)	967.2	E852.1	E937.2	E950.2	E962.0	E980.2
Paracetamol	965.4	E850.4	E935.4	E950.0	E962.0	E980.0
Paracodin	965.09	E850.2	E935.2	E950.0	E962.0	E980.0
Paradione	966.0	E855.0	E936.0	E950.4	E962.0	E980.4
Paraffin(s) (wax)	981	E862.3	—	E950.9	E962.1	E980.9

Substance	Poisoning	Accident	Therapeutic Use	Suicide Attempt	Assault	Undetermined
liquid (medicinal)	973.2	E858.4	E943.2	E950.4	E962.0	E980.4
nonmedicinal (oil)	981	E962.1	—	E950.9	E962.1	E980.9
Paraldehyde (medicinal)	967.2	E852.1	E937.2	E950.2	E962.0	E980.2
Paramethadione	966.0	E855.0	E936.0	E950.4	E962.0	E980.4
Paramethasone	962.0	E858.0	E932.0	E950.4	E962.0	E980.4
Paraquat	989.4	E863.5	—	E950.6	E962.1	E980.7
Parasympatholytics	971.1	E855.4	E941.1	E950.4	E962.0	E980.4
Parasympathomimetics	971.0	E855.3	E941.0	E950.4	E962.0	E980.4
Parathion	989.3	E863.1	—	E950.6	E962.1	E980.7
Parathormone	962.6	E858.0	E932.6	E950.4	E962.0	E980.4
Parathyroid (derivatives)	962.6	E858.0	E932.6	E950.4	E962.0	E980.4
Paratyphoid vaccine	978.1	E858.8	E948.1	E950.4	E962.0	E980.4
Paredrine	971.2	E855.5	E941.2	E950.4	E962.0	E980.4
Paregoric	965.00	E850.2	E935.2	E950.0	E962.0	E980.0
Pargyline	972.3	E858.3	E942.3	E950.4	E962.0	E980.4
Paris green	985.1	E866.3	—	E950.8	E962.1	E980.8
insecticide	985.1	E863.4	—	E950.8	E962.1	E980.8
Parnate	969.0	E854.0	E939.0	E950.3	E962.0	E980.3
Paromomycin	960.8	E856	E930.8	E950.4	E962.0	E980.4
Paroxypropione	963.1	E858.1	E933.1	E950.4	E962.0	E980.4
Parzone	965.09	E850.2	E935.2	E950.0	E962.0	E980.0
PAS	961.8	E857	E931.8	E950.4	E962.0	E980.4
PCBs	981	E862.3	—	E950.9	E961.1	E980.9
PCP (pentachlorophenol)	989.4	E863.6	—	E950.6	E962.1	E980.7
herbicide	989.4	E863.5	—	E950.6	E962.1	E980.7
insecticide	989.4	E863.4	—	E950.6	E962.1	E980.7
phencyclidine	968.3	E855.1	E938.3	E950.4	E962.0	E980.4
Peach kernel oil (emulsion)	973.2	E858.4	E943.2	E950.4	E962.0	E980.4
Peanut oil (emulsion) NEC	973.2	E858.4	E943.2	E950.4	E962.0	E980.4
topical	976.3	E858.7	E946.3	E950.4	E962.0	E980.4
Pearly Gates (morning glory seeds)	969.6	E854.1	E939.6	E950.3	E962.0	E980.3
Pecazine	969.1	E853.0	E939.1	E950.3	E962.0	E980.3
Pecilocin	960.1	E856	E930.1	E950.4	E962.0	E980.4
Pectin (with kaolin) NEC	973.5	E858.4	E943.5	E950.4	E962.0	E980.4
Pelletierine tannate	961.6	E857	E931.6	E950.4	E962.0	E980.4
Pemoline	969.7	E854.2	E939.7	E950.3	E962.0	E980.3
Pempidine	972.3	E858.3	E942.3	E950.4	E962.0	E980.4
Penamecillin	960.0	E856	E930.0	E950.4	E962.0	E980.4
Penethamate hydriodide	960.0	E856	E930.0	E950.4	E962.0	E980.4
Penicillamine	963.8	E858.1	E933.8	E950.4	E962.0	E980.4
Penicillin (any type)	960.0	E856	E930.0	E950.4	E962.0	E980.4
Penicillinase	963.4	E858.1	E933.4	E950.4	E962.0	E980.4
Pentachlorophenol (fungicide)	989.4	E863.6	—	E950.6	E962.1	E980.7
herbicide	989.4	E863.5	—	E950.6	E962.1	E980.7
insecticide	989.4	E863.4	—	E950.6	E962.1	E980.7
Pentaerythritol	972.4	E858.3	E942.4	E950.4	E962.0	E980.4
chloral	967.1	E852.0	E937.1	E950.2	E962.0	E980.2
tetranitrate NEC	972.4	E858.3	E942.4	E950.4	E962.0	E980.4
Pentagastrin	977.8	E858.8	E947.8	E950.4	E962.0	E980.4
Pentalin	982.3	E862.4	—	E950.9	E962.1	E980.9
Pentamethonium (bromide)	972.3	E858.3	E942.3	E950.4	E962.0	E980.4
Pentamidine	961.5	E857	E931.5	E950.4	E962.0	E980.4
Pentanol	980.8	E860.8	—	E950.9	E962.1	E980.9
Pentaquine	961.4	E857	E931.4	E950.4	E962.0	E980.4
Pentazocine	965.8	E850.8	E935.8	E950.0	E962.0	E980.0
Penthienate	971.1	E855.4	E941.1	E950.4	E962.0	E980.4
Pentobarbital, pentobarbitone (sodium)	967.0	E851	E937.0	E950.1	E962.0	E980.1

Substance	Poisoning	External Cause (E-Code)				
		Accident	Therapeutic Use	Suicide Attempt	Assault	Undetermined
Pentolinium (tartrate)	972.3	E858.3	E942.3	E950.4	E962.0	E980.4
Pentothal	968.3	E855.1	E938.3	E950.4	E962.0	E980.4
Pentylenetetrazol	970.0	E854.3	E940.0	E950.4	E962.0	E980.4
Pentylsalicylamide	961.8	E857	E931.8	E950.4	E962.0	E980.4
Pepsin	973.4	E858.4	E943.4	E950.4	E962.0	E980.4
Peptavlon	977.8	E858.8	E947.8	E950.4	E962.0	E980.4
Percaine (spinal)	968.7	E855.2	E938.7	E950.4	E962.0	E980.4
topical (surface)	968.5	E855.2	E938.5	E950.4	E962.0	E980.4
Perchloroethylene (vapor)	982.3	E862.4	—	E950.9	E962.1	E980.9
medicinal	961.6	E857	E931.6	E950.4	E962.0	E980.4
Percodan	965.09	E850.2	E935.2	E950.0	E962.0	E980.0
Percogesic	965.09	E850.2	E935.2	E950.0	E962.0	E980.0
Percorten	962.0	E858.0	E932.0	E950.4	E962.0	E980.4
Pergonal	962.4	E858.0	E932.4	E950.4	E962.0	E980.4
Perhexiline	972.4	E858.3	E942.4	E950.4	E962.0	E980.4
Periactin	963.0	E858.1	E933.0	E950.4	E962.0	E980.4
Periclor	967.1	E852.0	E937.1	E950.2	E962.0	E980.2
Pericyazine	969.1	E853.0	E939.1	E950.3	E962.0	E980.3
Peritrate	972.4	E858.3	E942.4	E950.4	E962.0	E980.4
Permanganates NEC	983.9	E864.3	—	E950.7	E962.1	E980.6
potassium (topical)	976.0	E858.7	E946.0	E950.4	E962.0	E980.4
Pernocton	967.0	E851	E937.0	E950.1	E962.0	E980.1
Pernoston	967.0	E851	E937.0	E950.1	E962.0	E980.1
Peronin(e)	965.09	E850.2	E935.2	E950.0	E962.0	E980.0
Perphenazine	969.1	E853.0	E939.1	E950.3	E962.0	E980.3
Pertofrane	969.0	E854	E939.0	E950.3	E962.0	E980.3
Pertussis						
immune serum (human)	964.6	E858.2	E934.6	E950.4	E962.0	E980.4
vaccine (with diphtheria toxoid) (with tetanus toxoid)	978.6	E858.8	E948.6	E950.4	E962.0	E980.4
Peruvian balsam	976.8	E858.7	E946.8	E950.4	E962.0	E980.4
Pesticides (dust) (fumes) (vapor)	989.4	E863.4	—	E950.6	E962.1	E980.7
arsenic	985.1	E863.4	—	E950.8	E962.1	E980.8
chlorinated	989.2	E863.0	—	E950.6	E962.1	E980.7
cyanide	989.0	E863.4	—	E950.6	E962.1	E980.7
kerosene	981	E863.4	—	E950.6	E962.1	E980.7
mixture (of compounds)	989.4	E863.3	—	E950.6	E962.1	E980.7
naphthalene	983.0	E863.4	—	E950.7	E962.1	E980.6
organochlorine (compounds)	989.2	E863.0	—	E950.6	E962.1	E980.7
petroleum (distillate) (products) NEC	981	E863.4	—	E950.6	E962.1	E980.7
specified ingredient NEC	989.4	E863.4	—	E950.6	E962.1	E980.7
strychnine	989.1	E863.4	—	E950.6	E962.1	E980.7
thallium	985.8	E863.7	—	E950.6	E962.1	E980.7
Pethidine (hydrochloride)	965.09	E850.2	E935.2	E950.0	E962.0	E980.0
Petrichloral	967.1	E852.0	E937.1	E950.2	E962.0	E980.2
Petrol	981	E862.1	—	E950.9	E962.1	E980.9
vapor	987.1	E869.8	—	E952.8	E962.2	E982.8
Petrolatum (jelly) (ointment)	976.3	E858.7	E946.3	E950.4	E962.0	E980.4
hydrophilic	976.3	E858.7	E946.3	E950.4	E962.0	E980.4
liquid	973.2	E858.4	E943.2	E950.4	E962.0	E980.4
topical	976.3	E858.7	E946.3	E950.4	E962.0	E980.4
nonmedicinal	981	E862.1	—	E950.9	E962.1	E980.9
Petroleum (cleaners) (fuels) (products) NEC	981	E862.1	—	E950.9	E962.1	E980.9
benzin(e) — *see* Ligroin						
ether — *see* Ligroin						

Substance	Poisoning	Accident	Therapeutic Use	Suicide Attempt	Assault	Undetermined
jelly — *see* Petrolatum						
naphtha — *see* Ligroin						
pesticide	981	E863.4	—	E950.6	E962.1	E980.7
solids	981	E862.3	—	E950.9	E962.1	E980.9
solvents	981	E862.0	—	E950.9	E962.1	E980.9
vapor	987.1	E869.8	—	E952.8	E962.2	E982.8
Peyote	969.6	E854.1	E939.6	E950.3	E962.0	E980.3
Phanodorm, phanodorn	967.0	E851	E937.0	E950.1	E962.0	E980.1
Phanquinone, phanquone	961.5	E857	E931.5	E950.4	E962.0	E980.4
Pharmaceutical excipient or adjunct	977.4	E858.8	E947.4	E950.4	E962.0	E980.4
Phenacemide	966.3	E855.0	E936.3	E950.4	E962.0	E980.4
Phenacetin	965.4	E850.4	E935.4	E950.0	E962.0	E980.0
Phenadoxone	965.09	E850.2	E935.2	E950.0	E962.0	E980.0
Phenaglycodol	969.5	E853.8	E939.5	E950.3	E962.0	E980.3
Phenantoin	966.1	E855.0	E936.1	E950.4	E962.0	E980.4
Phenaphthazine reagent	977.8	E858.8	E947.8	E950.4	E962.0	E980.4
Phenazocine	965.09	E850.2	E935.2	E950.0	E962.0	E980.0
Phenazone	965.5	E850.5	E935.5	E950.0	E962.0	E980.0
Phenazopyridine	976.1	E858.7	E946.1	E950.4	E962.0	E980.4
Phenbenicillin	960.0	E856	E930.0	E950.4	E962.0	E980.4
Phenbutrazate	977.0	E858.8	E947.0	E950.4	E962.0	E980.4
Phencyclidine	968.3	E855.1	E938.3	E950.4	E962.0	E980.4
Phendimetrazine	977.0	E858.8	E947.0	E950.4	E962.0	E980.4
Phenelzine	969.0	E854.0	E939.0	E950.3	E962.0	E980.3
Phenergan	967.8	E852.8	E937.8	E950.2	E962.0	E980.2
Phenethicillin (potassium)	960.0	E856	E930.0	E950.4	E962.0	E980.4
Phenetsal	965.1	E850.3	E935.3	E950.0	E962.0	E980.0
Pheneturide	966.3	E855.0	E936.3	E950.4	E962.0	E980.4
Phenformin	962.3	E858.0	E932.3	E950.4	E962.0	E980.4
Phenglutarimide	971.1	E855.4	E941.1	E950.4	E962.0	E980.4
Phenicarbazide	965.8	E850.8	E935.8	E950.0	E962.0	E980.0
Phenindamine (tartrate)	963.0	E858.1	E933.0	E950.4	E962.0	E980.4
Phenindione	964.2	E858.2	E934.2	E950.4	E962.0	E980.4
Pheniprazine	969.0	E854.0	E939.0	E950.3	E962.0	E980.3
Pheniramine (maleate)	963.0	E858.1	E933.0	E950.4	E962.0	E980.4
Phenmetrazine	977.0	E858.8	E947.0	E950.4	E962.0	E980.4
Phenobal	967.0	E851	E937.0	E950.1	E962.0	E980.1
Phenobarbital	967.0	E851	E937.0	E950.1	E962.0	E980.1
Phenobarbitone	967.0	E851	E937.0	E950.1	E962.0	E980.1
Phenoctide	976.0	E858.7	E946.0	E950.4	E962.0	E980.4
Phenol (derivatives) NEC	983.0	E864.0	—	E950.7	E962.1	E980.6
disinfectant	983.0	E864.0	—	E950.7	E962.1	E980.6
pesticide	989.4	E863.4	—	E950.6	E962.1	E980.7
red	977.8	E858.8	E947.8	E950.4	E962.0	E980.4
Phenolphthalein	973.1	E858.4	E943.1	E950.4	E962.0	E980.4
Phenolsulfonphthalein	977.8	E858.8	E947.8	E950.4	E962.0	E980.4
Phenomorphan	965.09	E850.2	E935.2	E950.0	E962.0	E980.0
Phenonyl	967.0	E851	E937.0	E950.1	E962.0	E980.1
Phenoperidine	965.09	E850.2	E935.2	E950.0	E962.0	E980.0
Phenoquin	974.7	E858.5	E944.7	E950.4	E962.0	E980.4
Phenothiazines (tranquilizers) NEC	969.1	E853.0	E939.1	E950.3	E962.0	E980.3
insecticide	989.3	E863.4	—	E950.6	E962.1	E980.7
Phenoxybenzamine	971.3	E855.6	E941.3	E950.4	E962.0	E980.4
Phenoxymethyl penicillin	960.0	E856	E930.0	E950.4	E962.0	E980.4
Phenprocoumon	964.2	E858.2	E934.2	E950.4	E962.0	E980.4
Phensuximide	966.2	E855.0	E936.2	E950.4	E962.0	E980.4
Phentermine	977.0	E858.8	E947.0	E950.4	E962.0	E980.4

Substance	Poisoning	External Cause (E-Code)				
		Accident	Therapeutic Use	Suicide Attempt	Assault	Undetermined
Phentolamine	971.3	E855.6	E941.3	E950.4	E962.0	E980.4
Phenyl						
butazone	965.5	E850.5	E935.5	E950.0	E962.0	E980.0
enediamine	983.0	E864.0	—	E950.7	E962.1	E980.6
hydrazine	983.0	E864.0	—	E950.7	E962.1	E980.6
antineoplastic	963.1	E858.1	E933.1	E950.4	E962.0	E980.4
mercuric compounds — *see* Mercury						
salicylate	976.3	E858.7	E946.3	E950.4	E962.0	E980.4
Phenylephrin	971.2	E855.5	E941.2	E950.4	E962.0	E980.4
Phenylethybiguanide	962.3	E858.0	E932.3	E950.4	E962.0	E980.4
Phenylpropanolamine	971.2	E855.5	E941.2	E950.4	E962.0	E980.4
Phenylsulfthion	989.3	E863.1	—	E950.6	E962.1	E980.7
Phenyramidol, phenyramidon	965.7	E850.7	E935.7	E950.0	E962.0	E980.0
Phenytoin	966.1	E855.0	E936.1	E950.4	E962.0	E980.4
pHisoHex	976.2	E858.7	E946.2	E950.4	E962.0	E980.4
Pholcodine	965.09	E850.2	E935.2	E950.0	E962.0	E980.0
Phorate	989.3	E863.1	—	E950.6	E962.1	E980.7
Phosdrin	989.3	E863.1	—	E950.6	E962.1	E980.7
Phosgene (gas)	987.8	E869.8	—	E952.8	E962.2	E982.8
Phosphate (tricresyl)	989.89	E866.8	—	E950.9	E962.1	E980.9
organic	989.3	E863.1	—	E950.6	E962.1	E980.7
solvent	982.8	E862.4	—	E950.9	E926.1	E980.9
Phosphine	987.8	E869.8	—	E952.8	E962.2	E982.8
fumigant	987.8	E863.8	—	E950.6	E962.2	E980.7
Phospholine	971.0	E855.3	E941.0	E950.4	E962.0	E980.4
Phosphoric acid	983.1	E864.1	—	E950.7	E962.1	E980.6
Phosphorus (compounds) NEC	983.9	E864.3	—	E950.7	E962.1	E980.6
rodenticide	983.9	E863.7	—	E950.7	E962.1	E980.6
Phthalimidogluarimide	967.8	E852.8	E937.8	E950.2	E962.0	E980.2
Phthalylsulfathiazole	961.0	E857	E931.0	E950.4	E962.0	E980.4
Phylloquinone	964.3	E858.2	E934.3	E950.4	E962.0	E980.4
Physeptone	965.02	E850.1	E935.1	E950.0	E962.0	E980.0
Physostigma venenosum	988.2	E865.4	—	E950.9	E962.1	E980.9
Physostigmine	971.0	E855.3	E941.0	E950.4	E962.0	E980.4
Phytolacca decandra	988.2	E865.4	—	E950.9	E962.1	E980.9
Phytomenadione	964.3	E858.2	E934.3	E950.4	E962.0	E980.4
Phytonadione	964.3	E858.2	E934.3	E950.4	E962.0	E980.4
Picric (acid)	983.0	E864.0	—	E950.7	E962.1	E980.6
Picrotoxin	970.0	E854.3	E940.0	E950.4	E962.0	E980.4
Pilocarpine	971.0	E855.3	E941.0	E950.4	E962.0	E980.4
Pilocarpus (jaborandi) extract	971.0	E855.3	E941.0	E950.4	E962.0	E980.4
Pimaricin	960.1	E856	E930.1	E950.4	E962.0	E980.4
Piminodine	965.09	E850.2	E935.2	E950.0	E962.0	E980.0
Pine oil, pinesol (disinfectant)	983.9	E861.4	—	E950.7	E962.1	E980.6
Pinkroot	961.6	E857	E931.6	E950.4	E962.0	E980.4
Pipadone	965.09	E850.2	E935.2	E950.0	E962.0	E980.0
Pipamazine	963.0	E858.1	E933.0	E950.4	E962.0	E980.4
Pipazethate	975.4	E858.6	E945.4	E950.4	E962.0	E980.4
Pipenzolate	971.1	E855.4	E941.1	E950.4	E962.0	E980.4
Piperacetazine	969.1	E853.0	E939.1	E950.3	E962.0	E980.3
Piperazine NEC	961.6	E857	E931.6	E950.4	E962.0	E980.4
estrone sulfate	962.2	E858.0	E932.2	E950.4	E962.0	E980.4
Piper cubeba	988.2	E865.4	—	E950.9	E962.1	E980.9
Piperidione	975.4	E858.6	E945.4	E950.4	E962.0	E980.4
Piperidolate	971.1	E855.4	E941.1	E950.4	E962.0	E980.4
Piperocaine	968.9	E855.2	E938.9	E950.4	E962.0	E980.4
infiltration (subcutaneous)	968.5	E855.2	E938.5	E950.4	E962.0	E980.4

Substance	Poisoning	External Cause (E-Code)				
		Accident	Therapeutic Use	Suicide Attempt	Assault	Undetermined
nerve block (peripheral) (plexus)	968.6	E855.2	E938.6	E950.4	E962.0	E980.4
topical (surface)	968.5	E855.2	E938.5	E950.4	E962.0	E980.4
Pipobroman	963.1	E858.1	E933.1	E950.4	E962.0	E980.4
Pipradrol	970.8	E854.3	E940.8	E950.4	E962.0	E980.4
Piscidia (bark) (erythrina)	965.7	E850.7	E935.7	E950.0	E962.0	E980.0
Pitch	983.0	E864.0	—	E950.7	E962.1	E980.6
Pitkin's solution	968.7	E855.2	E938.7	E950.4	E962.0	E980.4
Pitocin	975.0	E858.6	E945.0	E950.4	E962.0	E980.4
Pitressin (tannate)	962.5	E858.0	E932.5	E950.4	E962.0	E980.4
Pituitary extracts (posterior)	962.5	E858.0	E932.5	E950.4	E962.0	E980.4
anterior	962.4	E858.0	E932.4	E950.4	E962.0	E980.4
Pituitrin	962.5	E858.0	E932.5	E950.4	E962.0	E980.4
Placental extract	962.9	E858.0	E932.9	E950.4	E962.0	E980.4
Placidyl	967.8	E852.8	E937.8	E950.2	E962.0	E980.2
Plague vaccine	978.3	E858.8	E948.3	E950.4	E962.0	E980.4
Plant foods or fertilizers NEC	989.89	E866.5	—	E950.9	E962.1	E980.9
mixed with herbicides	989.4	E863.5	—	E950.6	E962.1	E980.7
Plants, noxious, used as food	988.2	E865.9	—	E950.9	E962.1	E980.9
berries and seeds	988.2	E865.3	—	E950.9	E962.1	E980.9
specified type NEC	988.2	E865.4	—	E950.9	E962.1	E980.9
Plasma (blood)	964.7	E858.2	E934.7	E950.4	E962.0	E980.4
expanders	964.8	E858.2	E934.8	E950.4	E962.0	E980.4
Plasmanate	964.7	E858.2	E934.7	E950.4	E962.0	E980.4
Plegicil	969.1	E853.0	E939.1	E950.3	E962.0	E980.3
Podophyllin	976.4	E858.7	E946.4	E950.4	E962.0	E980.4
Podophyllum resin	976.4	E858.7	E946.4	E950.4	E962.0	E980.4
Poison NEC	989.9	E866.9	—	E950.9	E962.1	E980.9
Poisonous berries	988.2	E865.3	—	E950.9	E962.1	E980.9
Pokeweed (any part)	988.2	E865.4	—	E950.9	E962.1	E980.9
Poldine	971.1	E855.4	E941.1	E950.4	E962.0	E980.4
Poliomyelitis vaccine	979.5	E858.8	E949.5	E950.4	E962.0	E980.4
Poliovirus vaccine	979.5	E858.8	E949.5	E950.4	E962.0	E980.4
Polish (car) (floor) (furniture) (metal) (silver)	989.89	E861.2	—	E950.9	E962.1	E980.9
abrasive	989.89	E861.3	—	E950.9	E962.1	E980.9
porcelain	989.89	E861.3	—	E950.9	E962.1	E980.9
Poloxalkol	973.2	E858.4	E943.2	E950.4	E962.0	E980.4
Polyaminostyrene resins	974.5	E858.5	E944.5	E950.4	E962.0	E980.4
Polychlorinated biphenyl—*see* PCBs						
Polycycline	960.4	E856	E930.4	E950.4	E962.0	E980.4
Polyester resin hardener	982.8	E862.4	—	E950.9	E962.1	E980.9
fumes	987.8	E869.8	—	E952.8	E962.2	E982.8
Polyestradiol (phosphate)	962.2	E858.0	E932.2	E950.4	E962.0	E980.4
Polyethanolamine alkyl sulfate	976.2	E858.7	E946.2	E950.4	E962.0	E980.4
Polyethylene glycol	976.3	E858.7	E946.3	E950.4	E962.0	E980.4
Polyferose	964.0	E858.2	E934.0	E950.4	E962.0	E980.4
Polymyxin B	960.8	E856	E930.8	E950.4	E962.0	E980.4
ENT agent	976.6	E858.7	E946.6	E950.4	E962.0	E980.4
ophthalmic preparation	976.5	E858.7	E946.5	E950.4	E962.0	E980.4
topical NEC	976.0	E858.7	E946.0	E950.4	E962.0	E980.4
Polynoxylin(e)	976.0	E858.7	E946.0	E950.4	E962.0	E980.4
Polyoxymethyleneurea	976.0	E858.7	E946.0	E950.4	E962.0	E980.4
Polytetrafluoroethylene (inhaled)	987.8	E869.8	—	E952.8	E962.2	E982.8
Polythiazide	974.3	E858.5	E944.3	E950.4	E962.0	E980.4
Polyvinylpyrrolidone	964.8	E858.2	E934.8	E950.4	E962.0	E980.4
Pontocaine (hydrochloride) (infiltration) (topical)	968.5	E855.2	E938.5	E950.4	E962.0	E980.4

Substance	Poisoning	External Cause (E-Code)				
		Accident	Therapeutic Use	Suicide Attempt	Assault	Undetermined
nerve block (peripheral) (plexus)	968.6	E855.2	E938.6	E950.4	E962.0	E980.4
spinal	968.7	E855.2	E938.7	E950.4	E962.0	E980.4
Pot	969.6	E854.1	E939.6	E950.3	E962.0	E980.3
Potash (caustic)	983.2	E864.2	—	E950.7	E962.1	E980.6
Potassic saline injection (lactated)	974.5	E858.5	E944.5	E950.4	E962.0	E980.4
Potassium (salts) NEC	974.5	E858.5	E944.5	E950.4	E962.0	E980.4
aminosalicylate	961.8	E857	E931.8	E950.4	E962.0	E980.4
arsenite (solution)	985.1	E866.3	—	E950.8	E962.1	E980.8
bichromate	983.9	E864.3	—	E950.7	E962.1	E980.6
bisulfate	983.9	E864.3	—	E950.7	E962.1	E980.6
bromide (medicinal) NEC	967.3	E852.2	E937.3	E950.2	E962.0	E980.2
carbonate	983.2	E864.2	—	E950.7	E962.1	E980.6
chlorate NEC	983.9	E864.3	—	E950.7	E962.1	E980.6
cyanide — *see* Cyanide						
hydroxide	983.2	E864.2	—	E950.7	E962.1	E980.6
iodide (expectorant) NEC	975.5	E858.6	E945.5	E950.4	E962.0	E980.4
nitrate	989.89	E866.8	—	E950.9	E962.1	E980.9
oxalate	983.9	E864.3	—	E950.7	E962.1	E980.6
perchlorate NEC	977.8	E858.8	E947.8	E950.4	E962.0	E980.4
antithyroid	962.8	E858.0	E932.8	E950.4	E962.0	E980.4
permanganate	976.0	E858.7	E946.0	E950.4	E962.0	E980.4
nonmedicinal	983.9	E864.3	—	E950.7	E962.1	E980.6
Povidone–iodine (anti–infective) NEC	976.0	E858.7	E946.0	E950.4	E962.0	E980.4
Practolol	972.0	E858.3	E942.0	E950.4	E962.0	E980.4
Pralidoxime (chloride)	977.2	E858.8	E947.2	E950.4	E962.0	E980.4
Pramoxine	968.5	E855.2	E938.5	E950.4	E962.0	E980.4
Prazosin	972.6	E858.3	E942.6	E950.4	E962.0	E980.4
Prednisolone	962.0	E858.0	E932.0	E950.4	E962.0	E980.4
ENT agent	976.6	E858.7	E946.6	E950.4	E962.0	E980.4
ophthalmic preparation	976.5	E858.7	E946.5	E950.4	E962.0	E980.4
topical NEC	976.0	E858.7	E946.0	E950.4	E962.0	E980.4
Prednisone	962.0	E858.0	E932.0	E950.4	E962.0	E980.4
Pregnanediol	962.2	E858.0	E932.2	E950.4	E962.0	E980.4
Pregneninolone	962.2	E858.0	E932.2	E950.4	E962.0	E980.4
Preludin	977.0	E858.8	E947.0	E950.4	E962.0	E980.4
Premarin	962.2	E858.0	E932.2	E950.4	E962.0	E980.4
Prenylamine	972.4	E858.3	E942.4	E950.4	E962.0	E980.4
Preparation H	976.8	E858.7	E946.8	E950.4	E962.0	E980.4
Preservatives	989.89	E866.8	—	E950.9	E962.1	E980.9
Pride of China	988.2	E865.3	—	E950.9	E962.1	E980.9
Prilocaine	968.9	E855.2	E938.9	E950.4	E962.0	E980.4
infiltration (subcutaneous)	968.5	E855.2	E938.5	E950.4	E962.0	E980.4
nerve block (peripheral) (plexus)	968.6	E855.2	E938.6	E950.4	E962.0	E980.4
Primaquine	961.4	E857	E931.4	E950.4	E962.0	E980.4
Primidone	966.3	E855.0	E936.3	E950.4	E962.0	E980.4
Primula (veris)	988.2	E865.4	—	E950.9	E962.1	E980.9
Prinadol	965.09	E850.2	E935.2	E950.0	E962.0	E980.0
Priscol, Priscoline	971.3	E855.6	E941.3	E950.4	E962.0	E980.4
Privet	988.2	E865.4	—	E950.9	E962.1	E980.9
Privine	971.2	E855.5	E941.2	E950.4	E962.0	E980.4
Pro–Banthine	971.1	E855.4	E941.1	E950.4	E962.0	E980.4
Probarbital	967.0	E851	E937.0	E950.1	E962.0	E980.1
Probenecid	974.7	E858.5	E944.7	E950.4	E962.0	E980.4
Procainamide (hydrochloride)	972.0	E858.3	E942.0	E950.4	E962.0	E980.4
Procaine (hydrochloride) (infiltration) (topical)	968.5	E855.2	E938.5	E950.4	E962.0	E980.4
nerve block (peripheral) (plexus)	968.6	E855.2	E938.6	E950.4	E962.0	E980.4

Substance	Poisoning	External Cause (E-Code)				
		Accident	Therapeutic Use	Suicide Attempt	Assault	Undetermined
penicillin G	960.0	E856	E930.0	E950.4	E962.0	E980.4
spinal	968.7	E855.2	E938.7	E950.4	E962.0	E980.4
Procalmidol	969.5	E853.8	E939.5	E950.3	E962.0	E980.3
Procarbazine	963.1	E858.1	E933.1	E950.4	E962.0	E980.4
Prochlorperazine	969.1	E853.0	E939.1	E950.3	E962.0	E980.3
Procyclidine	966.4	E855.0	E936.4	E950.4	E962.0	E980.4
Producer gas	986	E868.8	—	E952.1	E962.2	E982.1
Profenamine	966.4	E855.0	E936.4	E950.4	E962.0	E980.4
Profenil	975.1	E858.6	E945.1	E950.4	E962.0	E980.4
Progesterones	962.2	E858.0	E932.2	E950.4	E962.0	E980.4
Progestin	962.2	E858.0	E932.2	E950.4	E962.0	E980.4
Progestogens (with estrogens)	962.2	E858.0	E932.2	E950.4	E962.0	E980.4
Progestone	962.2	E858.0	E932.2	E950.4	E962.0	E980.4
Proguanil	961.4	E857	E931.4	E950.4	E962.0	E980.4
Prolactin	962.4	E858.0	E932.4	E950.4	E962.0	E980.4
Proloid	962.7	E858.0	E932.7	E950.4	E962.0	E980.4
Proluton	962.2	E858.0	E932.2	E950.4	E962.0	E980.4
Promacetin	961.8	E857	E931.8	E950.4	E962.0	E980.4
Promazine	969.1	E853.0	E939.1	E950.3	E962.0	E980.3
Promedol	965.09	E850.2	E935.2	E950.0	E962.0	E980.0
Promethazine	967.8	E852.8	E937.8	E950.2	E962.0	E980.2
Promin	961.8	E857	E931.8	E950.4	E962.0	E980.4
Pronestyl (hydrochloride)	972.0	E858.3	E942.0	E950.4	E962.0	E980.4
Pronetalol, pronethalol	972.0	E858.3	E942.0	E950.4	E962.0	E980.4
Prontosil	961.0	E857	E931.0	E950.4	E962.0	E980.4
Propamidine isethionate	961.5	E857	E931.5	E950.4	E962.0	E980.4
Propanal (medicinal)	967.8	E852.8	E937.8	E950.2	E962.0	E980.2
Propane (gas) (distributed in mobile container)	987.0	E868.0	—	E951.1	E962.2	E981.1
distributed through pipes	987.0	E867	—	E951.0	E962.2	E981.0
incomplete combustion of – *see* Carbon monoxide, Propane						
Propanidid	968.3	E855.1	E938.3	E950.4	E962.0	E980.4
Propanol	980.3	E860.4	—	E950.9	E962.1	E980.9
Propantheline	971.1	E855.4	E941.1	E950.4	E962.0	E980.4
Proparacaine	968.5	E855.2	E938.5	E950.4	E962.0	E980.4
Propatyl nitrate	972.4	E858.3	E942.4	E950.4	E962.0	E980.4
Propicillin	960.0	E856	E930.0	E950.4	E962.0	E980.4
Propiolactone (vapor)	987.8	E869.8	—	E952.8	E962.2	E982.8
Propiomazine	967.8	E852.8	E937.8	E950.2	E962.0	E980.2
Propionaldehyde (medicinal)	967.8	E852.8	E937.8	E950.2	E962.0	E980.2
Propionate compound	976.0	E858.7	E946.0	E950.4	E962.0	E980.4
Propion gel	976.0	E858.7	E946.0	E950.4	E962.0	E980.4
Propitocaine	968.9	E855.2	E938.9	E950.4	E962.0	E980.4
infiltration (subcutaneous)	968.5	E855.2	E938.5	E950.4	E962.0	E980.4
nerve block (peripheral) (plexus)	968.6	E855.2	E938.6	E950.4	E962.0	E980.4
Propoxur	989.3	E863.2	—	E950.6	E962.1	E980.7
Propoxycaine	968.9	E855.2	E938.9	E950.4	E962.0	E980.4
infiltration (subcutaneous)	968.5	E855.2	E938.5	E950.4	E962.0	E980.4
nerve block (peripheral) (plexus)	968.6	E855.2	E938.6	E950.4	E962.0	E980.4
topical (surface)	968.5	E855.2	E938.5	E950.4	E962.0	E980.4
Propoxyphene (hydrochloride)	965.8	E850.8	E935.8	E950.0	E962.0	E980.0
Propranolol	972.0	E858.3	E942.0	E950.4	E962.0	E980.4
Propyl						
alcohol	980.3	E860.4	—	E950.9	E962.1	E980.9
carbinol	980.3	E860.4	—	E950.9	E962.1	E980.9
hexadrine	971.2	E855.5	E941.2	E950.4	E962.0	E980.4

Substance	Poisoning	External Cause (E-Code)				
		Accident	Therapeutic Use	Suicide Attempt	Assault	Undetermined
iodone	977.8	E858.8	E947.8	E950.4	E962.0	E980.4
thiouracil	962.8	E858.0	E932.8	E950.4	E962.0	E980.4
Propylene	987.1	E869.8	—	E952.8	E962.2	E982.8
Propylparaben (ophthalmic)	976.5	E858.7	E946.5	E950.4	E962.0	E980.4
Proscillaridin	972.1	E858.3	E942.1	E950.4	E962.0	E980.4
Prostaglandins	975.0	E858.6	E945.0	E950.4	E962.0	E980.4
Prostigmin	971.0	E855.3	E941.0	E950.4	E962.0	E980.4
Protamine (sulfate)	964.5	E858.2	E934.5	E950.4	E962.0	E980.4
zinc insulin	962.3	E858.0	E932.3	E950.4	E962.0	E980.4
Protectants (topical)	976.3	E858.7	E946.3	E950.4	E962.0	E980.4
Protein hydrolysate	974.5	E858.5	E944.5	E950.4	E962.0	E980.4
Prothiaden—*see* Dothiepin hydrochloride						
Prothionamide	961.8	E857	E931.8	E950.4	E962.0	E980.4
Prothipendyl	969.5	E853.8	E939.5	E950.3	E962.0	E980.3
Protokylol	971.2	E855.5	E941.2	E950.4	E962.0	E980.4
Protopam	977.2	E858.8	E947.2	E950.4	E962.0	E980.4
Protoveratrine(s) (A) (B)	972.6	E858.3	E942.6	E950.4	E962.0	E980.4
Protriptyline	969.0	E854.0	E939.0	E950.3	E962.0	E980.3
Provera	962.2	E858.0	E932.2	E950.4	E962.0	E980.4
Provitamin A	963.5	E858.1	E933.5	E950.4	E962.0	E980.4
Proxymetacaine	968.5	E855.2	E938.5	E950.4	E962.0	E980.4
Proxyphylline	975.1	E858.6	E945.1	E950.4	E962.0	E980.4
Prozac—*see* Fluoxetine hydrochloride						
Prunus						
laurocerasus	988.2	E865.4	—	E950.9	E962.1	E980.9
virginiana	988.2	E865.4	—	E950.9	E962.1	E980.9
Prussic acid	989.0	E866.8	—	E950.9	E962.1	E980.9
vapor	987.7	E869.8	—	E952.8	E962.2	E982.8
Pseudoephedrine	971.2	E855.5	E941.2	E950.4	E962.0	E980.4
Psilocin	969.6	E854.1	E939.6	E950.3	E962.0	E980.3
Psilocybin	969.6	E854.1	E939.6	E950.3	E962.0	E980.3
PSP	977.8	E858.8	E947.8	E950.4	E962.0	E980.4
Psychedelic agents	969.6	E854.1	E939.6	E950.3	E962.0	E980.3
Psychodysleptics	969.6	E854.1	E939.6	E950.3	E962.0	E980.3
Psychostimulants	969.7	E854.2	E939.7	E950.3	E962.0	E980.3
Psychotherapeutic agents	969.9	E855.9	E939.9	E950.3	E962.0	E980.3
antidepressants	969.0	E854.0	E939.0	E950.3	E962.0	E980.3
specified NEC	969.8	E855.8	E939.8	E950.3	E962.0	E980.3
tranquilizers NEC	969.5	E853.9	E939.5	E950.3	E962.0	E980.3
Psychotomimetic agents	969.6	E854.1	E939.6	E950.3	E962.0	E980.3
Psychotropic agents	969.9	E854.8	E939.9	E950.3	E962.0	E980.3
specified NEC	969.8	E854.8	E939.8	E950.3	E962.0	E980.3
Psyllium	973.3	E858.4	E943.3	E950.4	E962.0	E980.4
Pteroylglutamic acid	964.1	E858.2	E934.1	E950.4	E962.0	E980.4
Pteroyltriglutamate	963.1	E858.1	E933.1	E950.4	E962.0	E980.4
PTFE	987.8	E869.8	—	E952.8	E962.2	E982.8
Pulsatilla	988.2	E865.4	—	E950.9	E962.1	E980.9
Purex (bleach)	983.9	E864.3	—	E950.7	E962.1	E980.6
Purine diuretics	974.1	E858.5	E944.1	E950.4	E962.0	E980.4
Purinethol	963.1	E858.1	E933.1	E950.4	E962.0	E980.4
PVP	964.8	E858.2	E934.8	E950.4	E962.0	E980.4
Pyrabital	965.7	E850.7	E935.7	E950.0	E962.0	E980.0
Pyramidon	965.5	E850.5	E935.5	E950.0	E962.0	E980.0
Pyrantel (pamoate)	961.6	E857	E931.6	E950.4	E962.0	E980.4
Pyrathiazine	963.0	E858.1	E933.0	E950.4	E962.0	E980.4
Pyrazinamide	961.8	E857	E931.8	E950.4	E962.0	E980.4
Pyrazinoic acid (amide)	961.8	E857	E931.8	E950.4	E962.0	E980.4

Substance	Poisoning	External Cause (E-Code)				
		Accident	Therapeutic Use	Suicide Attempt	Assault	Undetermined
Pyrazole (derivatives)	965.5	E850.5	E935.5	E950.0	E962.0	E980.0
Pyrazolone (analgesics)	965.5	E850.5	E935.5	E950.0	E962.0	E980.0
Pyrethrins, pyrethrum	989.4	E863.4	—	E950.6	E962.1	E980.7
Pyribenzamine	963.0	E858.1	E933.0	E950.4	E962.0	E980.4
Pyridine (liquid) (vapor)	982.0	E862.4	—	E950.9	E962.1	E980.9
aldoxime chloride	977.2	E858.8	E947.2	E950.4	E962.0	E980.4
Pyridium	976.1	E858.7	E946.1	E950.4	E962.0	E980.4
Pyridostigmine	971.0	E855.3	E941.0	E950.4	E962.0	E980.4
Pyridoxine	963.5	E858.1	E933.5	E950.4	E962.0	E980.4
Pyrilamine	963.0	E858.1	E933.0	E950.4	E962.0	E980.4
Pyrimethamine	961.4	E857	E931.4	E950.4	E962.0	E980.4
Pyrogallic acid	983.0	E864.0	—	E950.7	E962.1	E980.6
Pyroxylin	976.3	E858.7	E946.3	E950.4	E962.0	E980.4
Pyrrobutamine	963.0	E858.1	E933.0	E950.4	E962.0	E980.4
Pyrrocaine	968.5	E855.2	E938.5	E950.4	E962.0	E980.4
Pyrvinium (pamoate)	961.6	E857	E931.6	E950.4	E962.0	E980.4
PZI	962.3	E858.0	E932.3	E950.4	E962.0	E980.4
Quaalude	967.4	E852.3	E937.4	E950.2	E962.0	E980.2
Quaternary ammonium derivatives	971.1	E855.4	E941.1	E950.4	E962.0	E980.4
Quicklime	983.2	E864.2	—	E950.7	E962.1	E980.6
Quinacrine	961.3	E857	E931.3	E950.4	E962.0	E980.4
Quinaglute	972.0	E858.3	E942.0	E950.4	E962.0	E980.4
Quinalbarbitone	967.0	E851	E937.0	E950.1	E962.0	E980.1
Quinestradiol	962.2	E858.0	E932.2	E950.4	E962.0	E980.4
Quinethazone	974.3	E858.5	E944.3	E950.4	E962.0	E980.4
Quinidine (gluconate) (polygalacturonate)						
(salts) (sulfate)	972.0	E858.3	E942.0	E950.4	E962.0	E980.4
Quinine	961.4	E857	E931.4	E950.4	E962.0	E980.4
Quiniobine	961.3	E857	E931.3	E950.4	E962.0	E980.4
Quinolines	961.3	E857	E931.3	E950.4	E962.0	E980.4
Quotane	968.5	E855.2	E938.5	E950.4	E962.0	E980.4
Rabies						
immune globulin (human)	964.6	E858.2	E934.6	E950.4	E962.0	E980.4
vaccine	979.1	E858.8	E949.1	E950.4	E962.0	E980.4
Racemoramide	965.09	E850.2	E935.2	E950.0	E962.0	E980.0
Racemorphan	965.09	E850.2	E935.2	E950.0	E962.0	E980.0
Radiator alcohol	980.1	E860.2	—	E950.9	E962.1	E980.9
Radio–opaque (drugs) (materials)	977.8	E858.8	E947.8	E950.4	E962.0	E980.4
Ranunculus	988.2	E865.4	—	E950.9	E962.1	E980.9
Rat poison	989.4	E863.7	—	E950.6	E962.1	E980.7
Rattlesnake (venom)	989.5	E905.0	—	E950.9	E962.1	E980.9
Raudixin	972.6	E858.3	E942.6	E950.4	E962.0	E980.4
Rautensin	972.6	E858.3	E942.6	E950.4	E962.0	E980.4
Rautina	972.6	E858.3	E942.6	E950.4	E962.0	E980.4
Rautotal	972.6	E858.3	E942.6	E950.4	E962.0	E980.4
Rauwiloid	972.6	E858.3	E942.6	E950.4	E962.0	E980.4
Rauwoldin	972.6	E858.3	E942.6	E950.4	E962.0	E980.4
Rauwolfia (alkaloids)	972.6	E858.3	E942.6	E950.4	E962.0	E980.4
Realgar	985.1	E866.3	—	E950.8	E962.1	E980.8
Red cells, packed	964.7	E858.2	E934.7	E950.4	E962.0	E980.4
Reducing agents, industrial NEC	983.9	E864.3	—	E950.7	E962.1	E980.6
Refrigerant gas (freon)	987.4	E869.2	—	E952.8	E962.2	E982.8
not freon	987.9	E869.9	—	E952.9	E962.2	E982.9
Regroton	974.4	E858.5	E944.4	E950.4	E962.0	E980.4
Rela	968.0	E855.1	E938.0	E950.4	E962.0	E980.4
Relaxants, skeletal muscle (autonomic)	975.2	E858.6	E945.2	E950.4	E962.0	E980.4
central nervous system	968.0	E855.1	E938.0	E950.4	E962.0	E980.4

Substance	Poisoning	External Cause (E-Code)				
		Accident	Therapeutic Use	Suicide Attempt	Assault	Undetermined
Renese	974.3	E858.5	E944.3	E950.4	E962.0	E980.4
Renografin	977.8	E858.8	E947.8	E950.4	E962.0	E980.4
Replacement solutions	974.5	E858.5	E944.5	E950.4	E962.0	E980.4
Rescinnamine	972.6	E858.3	E942.6	E950.4	E962.0	E980.4
Reserpine	972.6	E858.3	E942.6	E950.4	E962.0	E980.4
Resorcin, resorcinol	976.4	E858.7	E946.4	E950.4	E962.0	E980.4
Respaire	975.5	E858.6	E945.5	E950.4	E962.0	E980.4
Respiratory agents NEC	975.8	E858.6	E945.8	E950.4	E962.0	E980.4
Retinoic acid	976.8	E858.7	E946.8	E950.4	E962.0	E980.4
Retinol	963.5	E858.1	E933.5	E950.4	E962.0	E980.4
Rh$_0$ (D) immune globulin (human)	964.6	E858.2	E934.6	E950.4	E962.0	E980.4
Rhodine	965.1	E850.3	E935.3	E950.0	E962.0	E980.0
RhoGAM	964.6	E858.2	E934.6	E950.4	E962.0	E980.4
Riboflavin	963.5	E858.1	E933.5	E950.4	E962.0	E980.4
Ricin	989.89	E866.8	—	E950.9	E962.1	E980.9
Ricinus communis	988.2	E865.3	—	E950.9	E962.1	E980.9
Rickettsial vaccine NEC	979.6	E858.8	E949.6	E950.4	E962.0	E980.4
with viral and bacterial vaccine	979.7	E858.8	E949.7	E950.4	E962.0	E980.4
Rifampin	960.6	E856	E930.6	E950.4	E962.0	E980.4
Rimifon	961.8	E857	E931.8	E950.4	E962.0	E980.4
Ringer's injection (lactated)	974.5	E858.5	E944.5	E950.4	E962.0	E980.4
Ristocetin	960.8	E856	E930.8	E950.4	E962.0	E980.4
Ritalin	969.7	E854.2	E939.7	E950.3	E962.0	E980.3
Roach killers — *see* Pesticides						
Rocky Mountain spotted fever vaccine	979.6	E858.8	E949.6	E950.4	E962.0	E980.4
Rodenticides	989.4	E863.7	—	E950.6	E962.1	E980.7
Rolaids	973.0	E858.4	E943.0	E950.4	E962.0	E980.4
Rolitetracycline	960.4	E856	E930.4	E950.4	E962.0	E980.4
Romilar	975.4	E858.6	E945.4	E950.4	E962.0	E980.4
Rose water ointment	976.3	E858.7	E946.3	E950.4	E962.0	E980.4
Rotenone	989.4	E863.7	—	E950.6	E962.1	E980.7
Rotoxamine	963.0	E858.1	E933.0	E950.4	E962.0	E980.4
Rough–on–rats	989.4	E863.7	—	E950.6	E962.1	E980.7
Rubbing alcohol	980.2	E860.3	—	E950.9	E962.1	E980.9
Rubella virus vaccine	979.4	E858.8	E949.4	E950.4	E962.0	E980.4
Rubelogen	979.4	E858.8	E949.4	E950.4	E962.0	E980.4
Rubeovax	979.4	E858.8	E949.4	E950.4	E962.0	E980.4
Rubidomycin	960.7	E856	E930.7	E950.4	E962.0	E980.4
Rue	988.2	E865.4	—	E950.9	E962.1	E980.9
Ruta	988.2	E865.4	—	E950.9	E962.1	E980.9
Sabadilla (medicinal)	976.0	E858.7	E946.0	E950.4	E962.0	E980.4
pesticide	989.4	E863.4	—	E950.6	E962.1	E980.7
Sabin oral vaccine	979.5	E858.8	E949.5	E950.4	E962.0	E980.4
Saccharated iron oxide	964.0	E858.2	E934.0	E950.4	E962.0	E980.4
Saccharin	974.5	E858.5	E944.5	E950.4	E962.0	E980.4
Safflower oil	972.2	E858.3	E942.2	E950.4	E962.0	E980.4
Salbutamol sulfate	975.7	E858.6	E945.7	E950.4	E962.0	E980.4
Salicylamide	965.1	E850.3	E935.3	E950.0	E962.0	E980.0
Salicylate(s)	965.1	E850.3	E935.3	E950.0	E962.0	E980.0
methyl	976.3	E858.7	E946.3	E950.4	E962.0	E980.4
theobromine calcium	974.1	E858.5	E944.1	E950.4	E962.0	E980.4
Salicylazosulfapyridine	961.0	E857	E931.0	E950.4	E962.0	E980.4
Salicylhydroxamic acid	976.0	E858.7	E946.0	E950.4	E962.0	E980.4
Salicylic acid (keratolytic) NEC	976.4	E858.7	E946.4	E950.4	E962.0	E980.4
congeners	965.1	E850.3	E935.3	E950.0	E962.0	E980.0
salts	965.1	E850.3	E935.3	E950.0	E962.0	E980.0
Saliniazid	961.8	E857	E931.8	E950.4	E962.0	E980.4

Substance	Poisoning	Accident	Therapeutic Use	Suicide Attempt	Assault	Undetermined
Salol	976.3	E858.7	E946.3	E950.4	E962.0	E980.4
Salt (substitute) NEC	974.5	E858.5	E944.5	E950.4	E962.0	E980.4
Saluretics	974.3	E858.5	E944.3	E950.4	E962.0	E980.4
Saluron	974.3	E858.5	E944.3	E950.4	E962.0	E980.4
Salvarsan 606 (neosilver) (silver)	961.1	E857	E931.1	E950.4	E962.0	E980.4
Sambucus canadensis	988.2	E865.4	—	E950.9	E962.1	E980.9
berry	988.2	E865.3	—	E950.9	E962.1	E980.9
Sandril	972.6	E858.3	E942.6	E950.4	E962.0	E980.4
Sanguinaria canadensis	988.2	E865.4	—	E950.9	E962.1	E980.9
Saniflush (cleaner)	983.9	E861.3	—	E950.7	E962.1	E980.6
Santonin	961.6	E857	E931.6	E950.4	E962.0	E980.4
Santyl	976.8	E858.7	E946.8	E950.4	E962.0	E980.4
Sarkomycin	960.7	E856	E930.7	E950.4	E962.0	E980.4
Saroten	969.0	E854.0	E939.0	E950.3	E962.0	E980.3
Saturnine – *see* Lead						
Savin (oil)	976.4	E858.7	E946.4	E950.4	E962.0	E980.4
Scammony	973.1	E858.4	E943.1	E950.4	E962.0	E980.4
Scarlet red	976.8	E858.7	E946.8	E950.4	E962.0	E980.4
Scheele's green	985.1	E866.3	—	E950.8	E962.1	E980.8
insecticide	985.1	E863.4	—	E950.8	E962.1	E980.8
Schradan	989.3	E863.1	—	E950.6	E962.1	E980.7
Schweinfurt (h) green	985.1	E866.3	—	E950.8	E962.1	E980.8
insecticide	985.1	E863.4	—	E950.8	E962.1	E980.8
Scilla — *see* Squill						
Sclerosing agents	972.7	E858.3	E942.7	E950.4	E962.0	E980.4
Scopolamine	971.1	E855.4	E941.1	E950.4	E962.0	E980.4
Scouring powder	989.89	E861.3	—	E950.9	E962.1	E980.9
Sea						
anemone (sting)	989.5	E905.6	—	E950.9	E962.1	E980.9
cucumber (sting)	989.5	E905.6	—	E950.9	E962.1	E980.9
snake (bite) (venom)	989.5	E905.0	—	E950.9	E962.1	E980.9
urchin spine (puncture)	989.5	E905.6	—	E950.9	E962.1	E980.9
Secbutabarbital	967.0	E851	E937.0	E950.1	E962.0	E980.1
Secbutabaritone	967.0	E851	E937.0	E950.1	E962.0	E980.1
Secobarbital	967.0	E851	E937.0	E950.1	E962.0	E980.1
Seconal	967.0	E851	E937.0	E950.1	E962.0	E980.1
Secretin	977.8	E858.8	E947.8	E950.4	E962.0	E980.4
Sedatives, nonbarbiturate	967.9	E852.9	E937.9	E950.2	E962.0	E980.2
specified NEC	967.8	E852.8	E937.8	E950.2	E962.0	E980.2
Sedormid	967.8	E852.8	E937.8	E950.2	E962.0	E980.2
Seed (plant)	988.2	E865.3	—	E950.9	E962.1	E980.9
disinfectant or dressing	989.89	E866.5	—	E950.9	E962.1	E980.9
Selenium (fumes) NEC	985.8	E866.4	—	E950.9	E962.1	E980.9
disulfide or sulfide	976.4	E858.7	E946.4	E950.4	E962.0	E980.4
Selsun	976.4	E858.7	E946.4	E950.4	E962.0	E980.4
Senna	973.1	E858.4	E943.1	E950.4	E962.0	E980.4
Septisol	976.2	E858.7	E946.2	E950.4	E962.0	E980.4
Serax	969.4	E853.2	E939.4	E950.3	E962.0	E980.3
Serenesil	967.8	E852.8	E937.8	E950.2	E962.0	E980.2
Serenium (hydrochloride)	961.9	E857	E931.9	E950.4	E962.0	E980.4
Serepax—*see* Oxazepam						
Sernyl	968.3	E855.1	E938.3	E950.4	E962.0	E980.4
Serotonin	977.8	E858.8	E947.8	E950.4	E962.0	E980.4
Serpasil	972.6	E858.3	E942.6	E950.4	E962.0	E980.4
Sewer gas	987.8	E869.8	—	E952.8	E962.2	E982.8
Shampoo	989.6	E861.0	—	E950.9	E962.1	E980.9
Shellfish, nonbacterial or noxious	988.0	E865.1	—	E950.9	E962.1	E980.9

Substance	Poisoning	Accident	Therapeutic Use	Suicide Attempt	Assault	Undetermined
			External Cause (E-Code)			
Silicones NEC	989.83	E866.8	E947.8	E950.9	E962.1	E980.9
Silvadene	976.0	E858.7	E946.0	E950.4	E962.0	E980.4
Silver (compound) (medicinal) NEC	976.0	E858.7	E946.0	E950.4	E962.0	E980.4
anti–infectives	976.0	E858.7	E946.0	E950.4	E962.0	E980.4
arsphenamine	961.1	E857	E931.1	E950.4	E962.0	E980.4
nitrate	976.0	E858.7	E946.0	E950.4	E962.0	E980.4
ophthalmic preparation	976.5	E858.7	E946.5	E950.4	E962.0	E980.4
toughened (keratolytic)	976.4	E858.7	E946.4	E950.4	E962.0	E980.4
nonmedicinal (dust)	985.8	E866.4	—	E950.9	E962.1	E980.9
protein (mild) (strong)	976.0	E858.7	E946.0	E950.4	E962.0	E980.4
salvarsan	961.1	E857	E931.1	E950.4	E962.0	E980.4
Simethicone	973.8	E858.4	E943.8	E950.4	E962.0	E980.4
Sinequan	969.0	E854.0	E939.0	E950.3	E962.0	E980.3
Singoserp	972.6	E858.3	E942.6	E950.4	E962.0	E980.4
Sintrom	964.2	E858.2	E934.2	E950.4	E962.0	E980.4
Sitosterols	972.2	E858.3	E942.2	E950.4	E962.0	E980.4
Skeletal muscle relaxants	975.2	E858.6	E945.2	E950.4	E962.0	E980.4
Skin						
agents (external)	976.9	E858.7	E946.9	E950.4	E962.0	E980.4
specified NEC	976.8	E858.7	E946.8	E950.4	E962.0	E980.4
test antigen	977.8	E858.8	E947.8	E950.4	E962.0	E980.4
Sleep–eze	963.0	E858.1	E933.0	E950.4	E962.0	E980.4
Sleeping draught (drug) (pill) (tablet)	967.9	E852.9	E937.9	E950.2	E962.0	E980.2
Smallpox vaccine	979.0	E858.8	E949.0	E950.4	E962.0	E980.4
Smelter fumes NEC	985.9	E866.4	—	E950.9	E962.1	E980.9
Smog	987.3	E869.1	—	E952.8	E962.2	E982.8
Smoke NEC	987.9	E869.9	—	E952.9	E962.2	E982.9
Smooth muscle relaxant	975.1	E858.6	E945.1	E950.4	E962.0	E980.4
Snail killer	989.4	E863.4	—	E950.6	E962.1	E980.7
Snake (bite) (venom)	989.5	E905.0	—	E950.9	E962.1	E980.9
Snuff	989.89	E866.8	—	E950.9	E962.1	E980.9
Soap (powder) (product)	989.6	E861.1	—	E950.9	E962.1	E980.9
medicinal, soft	976.2	E858.7	E946.2	E950.4	E962.0	E980.4
Soda (caustic)	983.2	E864.2	—	E950.7	E962.1	E980.6
bicarb	963.3	E858.1	E933.3	E950.4	E962.0	E980.4
chlorinated — *see* Sodium, hypochlorite						
Sodium						
acetosulfone	961.8	E857	E931.8	E950.4	E962.0	E980.4
acetrizoate	977.8	E858.8	E947.8	E950.4	E962.0	E980.4
amytal	967.0	E851	E937.0	E950.1	E962.0	E980.1
arsenate — *see* Arsenic						
bicarbonate	963.3	E858.1	E933.3	E950.4	E962.0	E980.4
bichromate	983.9	E864.3	—	E950.7	E962.1	E980.6
biphosphate	963.2	E858.1	E933.2	E950.4	E962.0	E980.4
bisulfate	983.9	E864.3	—	E950.7	E962.1	E980.6
borate (cleanser)	989.6	E861.3	—	E950.9	E962.1	E980.9
bromide NEC	967.3	E852.2	E937.3	E950.2	E962.0	E980.2
cacodylate (nonmedicinal) NEC	978.8	E858.8	E948.8	E950.4	E962.0	E980.4
anti–infective	961.1	E857	E931.1	E950.4	E962.0	E980.4
herbicide	989.4	E863.5	—	E950.6	E962.1	E980.7
calcium edetate	963.8	E858.1	E933.8	E950.4	E962.0	E980.4
carbonate NEC	983.2	E864.2	—	E950.7	E962.1	E980.6
chlorate NEC	983.9	E864.3	—	E950.7	E962.1	E980.6
herbicide	983.9	E863.5	—	E950.7	E962.1	E980.6
chloride NEC	974.5	E858.5	E944.5	E950.4	E962.0	E980.4
chromate	983.9	E864.3	—	E950.7	E962.1	E980.6
citrate	963.3	E858.1	E933.3	E950.4	E962.0	E980.4

Substance	Poisoning	External Cause (E-Code)				
		Accident	Therapeutic Use	Suicide Attempt	Assault	Undetermined
cyanide — *see* Cyanide(s)						
cyclamate	974.5	E858.5	E944.5	E950.4	E962.0	E980.4
diatrizoate	977.8	E858.8	E947.8	E950.4	E962.0	E980.4
dibunate	975.4	E858.6	E945.4	E950.4	E962.0	E980.4
dioctyl sulfosuccinate	973.2	E858.4	E943.2	E950.4	E962.0	E980.4
edetate	963.8	E858.1	E933.8	E950.4	E962.0	E980.4
ethacrynate	974.4	E858.5	E944.4	E950.4	E962.0	E980.4
fluoracetate (dust) (rodenticide)	989.4	E863.7	—	E950.6	E962.1	E980.7
fluoride — *see* Fluoride(s)						
free salt	974.5	E858.5	E944.5	E950.4	E962.0	E980.4
glucosulfone	961.8	E857	E931.8	E950.4	E962.0	E980.4
hydroxide	983.2	E864.2	—	E950.7	E962.1	E980.6
hypochlorite (bleach) NEC	983.9	E864.3	—	E950.7	E962.1	E980.6
disinfectant	983.9	E861.4	—	E950.7	E962.1	E980.6
medicinal (anti–infective) (external)	976.0	E858.7	E946.0	E950.4	E962.0	E980.4
vapor	987.8	E869.8	—	E952.8	E962.2	E982.8
hyposulfite	976.0	E858.7	E946.0	E950.4	E962.0	E980.4
indigotindisulfonate	977.8	E858.8	E947.8	E950.4	E962.0	E980.4
iodide	977.8	E858.8	E947.8	E950.4	E962.0	E980.4
iothalamate	977.8	E858.8	E947.8	E950.4	E962.0	E980.4
iron edetate	964.0	E858.2	E934.0	E950.4	E962.0	E980.4
lactate	963.3	E858.1	E933.3	E950.4	E962.0	E980.4
lauryl sulfate	976.2	E858.7	E946.2	E950.4	E962.0	E980.4
L–triiodothyronine	962.7	E858.0	E932.7	E950.4	E962.0	E980.4
metrizoate	977.8	E858.8	E947.8	E950.4	E962.0	E980.4
monofluoracetate (dust) (rodenticide)	989.4	E863.7	—	E950.6	E962.1	E980.7
morrhuate	972.7	E858.3	E942.7	E950.4	E962.0	E980.4
nafcillin	960.0	E856	E930.0	E950.4	E962.0	E980.4
nitrate (oxidizing agent)	983.9	E864.3	—	E950.7	E962.1	E980.6
nitrite (medicinal)	972.4	E858.3	E942.4	E950.4	E962.0	E980.4
nitroferricyanide	972.6	E858.3	E942.6	E950.4	E962.0	E980.4
nitroprusside	972.6	E858.3	E942.6	E950.4	E962.0	E980.4
para–aminohippurate	977.8	E858.8	E947.8	E950.4	E962.0	E980.4
perborate (non-medicinal) NEC	989.89	E866.8	—	E950.9	E962.1	E980.9
medicinal	976.6	E858.7	E946.6	E950.4	E962.0	E980.4
soap	989.6	E861.1	—	E950.9	E962.1	E980.9
percarbonate — *see* Sodium, perborate						
phosphate	973.3	E858.4	E943.3	E950.4	E962.0	E980.4
polystyrene sulfonate	974.5	E858.5	E944.5	E950.4	E962.0	E980.4
propionate	976.0	E858.7	E946.0	E950.4	E962.0	E980.4
psylliate	972.7	E858.3	E942.7	E950.4	E962.0	E980.4
removing resins	974.5	E858.5	E944.5	E950.4	E962.0	E980.4
salicylate	965.1	E850.3	E935.3	E950.0	E962.0	E980.0
sulfate	973.3	E858.4	E943.3	E950.4	E962.0	E980.4
sulfoxone	961.8	E857	E931.8	E950.4	E962.0	E980.4
tetradecyl sulfate	972.7	E858.3	E942.7	E950.4	E962.0	E980.4
thiopental	968.3	E855.1	E938.3	E950.4	E962.0	E980.4
thiosalicylate	965.1	E850.3	E935.3	E950.0	E962.0	E980.0
thiosulfate	976.0	E858.7	E946.0	E950.4	E962.0	E980.4
tolbutamide	977.8	E858.8	E947.8	E950.4	E962.0	E980.4
tyropanoate	977.8	E858.8	E947.8	E950.4	E962.0	E980.4
valproate	966.3	E855.0	E936.3	E950.4	E962.0	E980.4
Solanine	977.8	E858.8	E947.8	E950.4	E962.0	E980.4
Solanum dulcamara	988.2	E865.4	—	E950.9	E962.1	E980.9
Solapsone	961.8	E857	E931.8	E950.4	E962.0	E980.4
Solasulfone	961.8	E857	E931.8	E950.4	E962.0	E980.4
Soldering fluid	983.1	E864.1	—	E950.7	E962.1	E980.6

Substance	Poisoning	External Cause (E-Code)				
		Accident	Therapeutic Use	Suicide Attempt	Assault	Undetermined
Solid substance	989.9	E866.9	—	E950.9	E962.1	E980.9
specified NEC	989.9	E866.8	—	E950.9	E962.1	E980.9
Solvents, industrial	982.8	E862.9	—	E950.9	E962.1	E980.9
naphtha	981	E862.0	—	E950.9	E962.1	E980.9
petroleum	981	E862.0	—	E950.9	E962.1	E980.9
specified NEC	982.8	E862.4	—	E950.9	E962.1	E980.9
Soma	968.0	E855.1	E938.0	E950.4	E962.0	E980.4
Somatotropin	962.4	E858.0	E932.4	E950.4	E962.0	E980.4
Sominex	963.0	E858.1	E933.0	E950.4	E962.0	E980.4
Somnos	967.1	E852.0	E937.1	E950.2	E962.0	E980.2
Somonal	967.0	E851	E937.0	E950.1	E962.0	E980.1
Soneryl	967.0	E851	E937.0	E950.1	E962.0	E980.1
Soothing syrup	977.9	E858.9	E947.9	E950.5	E962.0	E980.5
Sopor	967.4	E852.3	E937.4	E950.2	E962.0	E980.2
Soporific drug	967.9	E852.9	E937.9	E950.2	E962.0	E980.2
specified type NEC	967.8	E852.8	E937.8	E950.2	E962.0	E980.2
Sorbitol NEC	977.4	E858.8	E947.4	E950.4	E962.0	E980.4
Sotradecol	972.7	E858.3	E942.7	E950.4	E962.0	E980.4
Spacoline	975.1	E858.6	E945.1	E950.4	E962.0	E980.4
Spanish fly	976.8	E858.7	E946.8	E950.4	E962.0	E980.4
Sparine	969.1	E853.0	E939.1	E950.3	E962.0	E980.3
Sparteine	975.0	E858.6	E945.0	E950.4	E962.0	E980.4
Spasmolytics	975.1	E858.6	E945.1	E950.4	E962.0	E980.4
anticholinergics	971.1	E855.4	E941.1	E950.4	E962.0	E980.4
Spectinomycin	960.8	E856	E930.8	E950.4	E962.0	E980.4
Speed	969.7	E854.2	E939.7	E950.3	E962.0	E980.3
Spermicides	976.8	E858.7	E946.8	E950.4	E962.0	E980.4
Spider (bite) (venom)	989.5	E905.1	—	E950.9	E962.1	E980.9
antivenin	979.9	E858.8	E949.9	E950.4	E962.0	E980.4
Spigelia (root)	961.6	E857	E931.6	E950.4	E962.0	E980.4
Spiperone	969.2	E853.1	E939.2	E950.3	E962.0	E980.3
Spiramycin	960.3	E856	E930.3	E950.4	E962.0	E980.4
Spirilene	969.5	E853.8	E939.5	E950.3	E962.0	E980.3
Spirit(s) (neutral) NEC	980.0	E860.1	—	E950.9	E962.1	E980.9
beverage	980.0	E860.0	—	E950.9	E962.1	E980.9
industrial	980.9	E860.9	—	E950.9	E962.1	E980.9
mineral	981	E862.0	—	E950.9	E962.1	E980.9
of salt — *see* Hydrochloric acid						
surgical	980.9	E860.9	—	E950.9	E962.1	E980.9
Spironolactone	974.4	E858.5	E944.4	E950.4	E962.0	E980.4
Sponge, absorbable (gelatin)	964.5	E858.2	E934.5	E950.4	E962.0	E980.4
Sporostacin	976.0	E858.7	E946.0	E950.4	E962.0	E980.4
Sprays (aerosol)	989.89	E866.8	—	E950.9	E962.1	E980.9
cosmetic	989.89	E866.7	—	E950.9	E962.1	E980.9
medicinal NEC	977.9	E858.9	E947.9	E950.5	E962.0	E980.5
pesticides — *see* Pesticides						
specified content — *see* substance specified						
Spurge flax	988.2	E865.4	—	E950.9	E962.1	E980.9
Spurges	988.2	E865.4	—	E950.9	E962.1	E980.9
Squill (expectorant) NEC	975.5	E858.6	E945.5	E950.4	E962.0	E980.4
rat poison	989.4	E863.7	—	E950.6	E962.1	E980.7
Squirting cucumber (cathartic)	973.1	E858.4	E943.1	E950.4	E962.0	E980.4
Stains	989.89	E866.8	—	E950.9	E962.1	E980.9
Stannous — *see also* Tin						
fluoride	976.7	E858.7	E946.7	E950.4	E962.0	E980.4
Stanolone	962.1	E858.0	E932.1	E950.4	E962.0	E980.4

Substance	Poisoning	External Cause (E-Code)				
		Accident	Therapeutic Use	Suicide Attempt	Assault	Undetermined
Stanozolol	962.1	E853.0	E932.1	E950.4	E962.0	E980.4
Staphisagria or stavesacre (pediculicide)	976.0	E858.7	E946.0	E950.4	E962.0	E980.4
Stelazine	969.1	E853.0	E939.1	E950.3	E962.0	E980.3
Stemetil	969.1	E853.0	E939.1	E950.3	E962.0	E980.3
Sterculia (cathartic) (gum)	973.3	E858.4	E943.3	E950.4	E962.0	E980.4
Sternutator gas	987.8	E869.8	—	E952.8	E962.2	E982.8
Steroids NEC	962.0	E858.0	E932.0	E950.4	E962.0	E980.4
ENT agent	976.6	E858.7	E946.6	E950.4	E962.0	E980.4
ophthalmic preparation	976.5	E858.7	E946.5	E950.4	E962.0	E980.4
topical NEC	976.0	E858.7	E946.0	E950.4	E962.0	E980.4
Stibine	985.8	E866.4	—	E950.9	E962.1	E980.9
Stibophen	961.2	E857	E931.2	E950.4	E962.0	E980.4
Stilbamide, stilbamidine	961.5	E857	E931.5	E950.4	E962.0	E980.4
Stilbestrol	962.2	E858.0	E932.2	E950.4	E962.0	E980.4
Stimulants (central nervous system)	970.9	E854.3	E940.9	E950.4	E962.0	E980.4
analeptics	970.0	E854.3	E940.0	E950.4	E962.0	E980.4
opiate antagonist	970.1	E854.3	E940.1	E950.4	E962.0	E980.4
psychotherapeutic NEC	969.0	E854.0	E939.0	E950.3	E962.0	E980.3
specified NEC	970.8	E854.3	E940.8	E950.4	E962.0	E980.4
Storage batteries (acid) (cells)	983.1	E864.1	—	E950.7	E962.1	E980.6
Stovaine	968.9	E855.2	E938.9	E950.4	E962.0	E980.4
infiltration (subcutaneous)	968.5	E855.2	E938.5	E950.4	E962.0	E980.4
nerve block (peripheral) (plexus)	968.6	E855.2	E938.6	E950.5	E962.0	E980.4
spinal	968.7	E855.2	E938.7	E950.4	E962.0	E980.4
topical (surface)	968.5	E855.2	E938.5	E950.4	E962.0	E980.4
Stovarsal	961.1	E857	E931.1	E950.4	E962.0	E980.4
Stove gas — *see* Gas, utility						
Stoxil	976.5	E858.7	E946.5	E950.4	E962.0	E980.4
STP	969.6	E854.1	E939.6	E950.3	E962.0	E980.3
Stramonium (medicinal) NEC	971.1	E855.4	E941.1	E950.4	E962.0	E980.4
natural state	988.2	E865.4	—	E950.9	E962.1	E980.9
Streptodornase	964.4	E858.2	E934.4	E950.4	E962.0	E980.4
Streptoduocin	960.6	E856	E930.6	E950.4	E962.0	E980.4
Streptokinase	964.4	E858.2	E934.4	E950.4	E962.0	E980.4
Streptomycin	960.6	E856	E930.6	E950.4	E962.0	E980.4
Streptozocin	960.7	E856	E930.7	E950.4	E962.0	E980.4
Stripper (paint) (solvent)	982.8	E862.9	—	E950.9	E962.1	E980.9
Strobane	989.2	E863.0	—	E950.6	E962.1	E980.7
Strophanthin	972.1	E858.3	E942.1	E950.4	E962.0	E980.4
Strophanthus hispidus or kombe	988.2	E865.4	—	E950.9	E962.1	E980.9
Strychnine (rodenticide) (salts)	989.1	E863.7	—	E950.6	E962.1	E980.7
medicinal NEC	970.8	E854.3	E940.8	E950.4	E962.0	E980.4
Strychnos (ignatii) — *see* Strychnine						
Styramate	968.0	E855.1	E938.0	E950.4	E962.0	E980.4
Styrene	983.0	E864.0	—	E950.7	E962.1	E980.6
Succinimide (anticonvulsant)	966.2	E855.0	E936.2	E950.4	E962.0	E980.4
mercuric — *see* Mercury						
Succinylcholine	975.2	E858.6	E945.2	E950.4	E962.0	E980.4
Succinylsulfathiazole	961.0	E857	E931.0	E950.4	E962.0	E980.4
Sucrose	974.5	E858.5	E944.5	E950.4	E962.0	E980.4
Sulfacetamide	961.0	E857	E931.0	E950.4	E962.0	E980.4
ophthalmic preparation	976.5	E858.7	E946.5	E950.4	E962.0	E980.4
Sulfachlorpyridazine	961.0	E857	E931.0	E950.4	E962.0	E980.4
Sulfacytine	961.0	E857	E931.0	E950.4	E962.0	E980.4
Sulfadiazine	961.0	E857	E931.0	E950.4	E962.0	E980.4
silver (topical)	976.0	E858.7	E946.0	E950.4	E962.0	E980.4
Sulfadimethoxine	961.0	E857	E931.0	E950.4	E962.0	E980.4

Substance	Poisoning	Accident	External Cause (E-Code) Therapeutic Use	Suicide Attempt	Assault	Undetermined
Sulfadimidine	961.0	E857	E931.0	E950.4	E962.0	E980.4
Sulfaethidole	961.0	E857	E931.0	E950.4	E962.0	E980.4
Sulfafurazole	961.0	E857	E931.0	E950.4	E962.0	E980.4
Sulfaguanidine	961.0	E857	E931.0	E950.4	E962.0	E980.4
Sulfamerazine	961.0	E857	E931.0	E950.4	E962.0	E980.4
Sulfameter	961.0	E857	E931.0	E950.4	E962.0	E980.4
Sulfamethizole	961.0	E857	E931.0	E950.4	E962.0	E980.4
Sulfamethoxazole	961.0	E857	E931.0	E950.4	E962.0	E980.4
Sulfamethoxydiazine	961.0	E857	E931.0	E950.4	E962.0	E980.4
Sulfamethoxypyridazine	961.0	E857	E931.0	E950.4	E962.0	E980.4
Sulfamethylthiazole	961.0	E857	E931.0	E950.4	E962.0	E980.4
Sulfamylon	976.0	E858.7	E946.0	E950.4	E962.0	E980.4
Sulfan blue (diagnostic dye)	977.8	E858.8	E947.8	E950.4	E962.0	E980.4
Sulfanilamide	961.0	E857	E931.0	E950.4	E962.0	E980.4
Sulfanilylguanidine	961.0	E857	E931.0	E950.4	E962.0	E980.4
Sulfaphenazole	961.0	E857	E931.0	E950.4	E962.0	E980.4
Sulfaphenylthiazole	961.0	E857	E931.0	E950.4	E962.0	E980.4
Sulfaproxyline	961.0	E857	E931.0	E950.4	E962.0	E980.4
Sulfapyridine	961.0	E857	E931.0	E950.4	E962.0	E980.4
Sulfapyrimidine	961.0	E857	E931.0	E950.4	E962.0	E980.4
Sulfarsphenamine	961.1	E857	E931.1	E950.4	E962.0	E980.4
Sulfasalazine	961.0	E857	E931.0	E950.4	E962.0	E980.4
Sulfasomizole	961.0	E857	E931.0	E950.4	E962.0	E980.4
Sulfasuxidine	961.0	E857	E931.0	E950.4	E962.0	E980.4
Sulfinpyrazone	974.7	E858.5	E944.7	E950.4	E962.0	E980.4
Sulfisoxazole	961.0	E857	E931.0	E950.4	E962.0	E980.4
ophthalmic preparation	976.5	E858.7	E946.5	E950.4	E962.0	E980.4
Sulfomyxin	960.8	E856	E930.8	E950.4	E962.0	E980.4
Sulfonal	967.8	E852.8	E937.8	E950.2	E962.0	E980.2
Sulfonamides (mixtures)	961.0	E857	E931.0	E950.4	E962.0	E980.4
Sulfones	961.8	E857	E931.8	E950.4	E962.0	E980.4
Sulfonethylmethane	967.8	E852.8	E937.8	E950.2	E962.0	E980.2
Sulfonmethane	967.8	E852.8	E937.8	E950.2	E962.0	E980.2
Sulfonphthal, sulfonphthol	977.8	E858.8	E947.8	E950.4	E962.0	E980.4
Sulfonylurea derivatives, oral	962.3	E858.0	E932.3	E950.4	E962.0	E980.4
Sulfoxone	961.8	E857	E931.8	E950.4	E962.0	E980.4
Sulfur, sulfureted, sulfuric, sulfurous, sulfuryl (compounds) NEC	989.89	E866.8	—	E950.9	E962.1	E980.9
acid	983.1	E864.1	—	E950.7	E962.1	E980.6
dioxide	987.3	E869.1	—	E952.8	E962.2	E982.8
ether — *see* Ether(s)						
hydrogen	987.8	E869.8	—	E952.8	E962.2	E982.8
medicinal (keratolytic) (ointment) NEC	976.4	E858.7	E946.4	E950.4	E962.0	E980.4
pesticide (vapor)	989.4	E863.4	—	E950.6	E962.1	E980.7
vapor NEC	987.8	E869.8	—	E952.8	E962.2	E982.8
Sulkowitch's reagent	977.8	E858.8	E947.8	E950.4	E962.0	E980.4
Sulph — *see also* Sulf–						
Sulphadione	961.8	E857	E931.8	E950.4	E962.0	E980.4
Sulthiame, sultiame	966.3	E855.0	E936.3	E950.4	E962.0	E980.4
Superinone	975.5	E858.6	E945.5	E950.4	E962.0	E980.4
Suramin	961.5	E857	E931.5	E950.4	E962.0	E980.4
Surfacaine	968.5	E855.2	E938.5	E950.4	E962.0	E980.4
Surital	968.3	E855.1	E938.3	E950.4	E962.0	E980.4
Sutilains	976.8	E858.7	E946.8	E950.4	E962.0	E980.4
Suxamethoniam (bromide) (chloride) (iodide)	975.2	E858.6	E945.2	E950.4	E962.0	E980.4
Suxethonium (bromide)	975.2	E858.6	E945.2	E950.4	E962.0	E980.4

Substance	Poisoning	External Cause (E-Code)				
		Accident	Therapeutic Use	Suicide Attempt	Assault	Undetermined
Sweet oil (birch)	976.3	E858.7	E946.3	E950.4	E962.0	E980.4
Sym–dichloroethyl ether	982.3	E862.4	—	E950.9	E962.1	E980.9
Sympatholytics	971.3	E855.6	E941.3	E950.4	E962.0	E980.4
Sympathomimetics	971.2	E855.5	E941.2	E950.4	E962.0	E980.4
Synalar	976.0	E858.7	E946.0	E950.4	E962.0	E980.4
Synthroid	962.7	E858.0	E932.7	E950.4	E962.0	E980.4
Syntocinon	975.0	E858.6	E945.0	E950.4	E962.0	E950.4
Syrosingopine	972.6	E858.3	E942.6	E950.4	E962.0	E980.4
Systemic agents (primarily)	963.9	E858.1	E933.9	E950.4	E962.0	E980.4
specified NEC	963.8	E858.1	E933.8	E950.4	E962.0	E980.4
Tablets (see also specified substance)	977.9	E858.9	E947.9	E950.5	E962.0	E980.5
Tace	962.2	E858.0	E932.2	E950.4	E962.0	E980.4
Tacrine	971.0	E855.3	E941.0	E950.4	E962.0	E980.4
Talbutal	967.0	E851	E937.0	E950.1	E962.0	E980.1
Talc	976.3	E858.7	E946.3	E950.4	E962.0	E980.4
Talcum	976.3	E858.7	E946.3	E950.4	E962.0	E980.4
Tandearil, tanderil	965.5	E850.5	E935.5	E950.0	E962.0	E980.0
Tannic acid	983.1	E864.1	—	E950.7	E962.1	E980.6
medicinal (astringent)	976.2	E858.7	E946.2	E950.4	E962.0	E980.4
Tannin — *see* Tannic acid						
Tansy	988.2	E865.4	—	E950.9	E962.1	E980.9
TAO	960.3	E856	E930.3	E950.4	E962.0	E980.4
Tapazole	962.8	E858.0	E932.8	E950.4	E962.0	E980.4
Tar NEC	983.0	E864.0	—	E950.7	E962.1	E980.6
camphor — *see* Naphthalene						
fumes	987.8	E869.8	—	E952.8	E962.2	E982.8
Taractan	969.3	E853.8	E939.3	E950.3	E962.0	E980.3
Tarantula (venomous)	989.5	E905.1	—	E950.9	E962.1	E980.9
Tartar emetic (anti–infective)	961.2	E857	E931.2	E950.4	E962.0	E980.4
Tartaric acid	983.1	E864.1	—	E950.7	E962.1	E980.6
Tartrated antimony (anti–infective)	961.2	E857	E931.2	E950.4	E962.0	E980.4
TCA — *see* Trichloroacetic acid						
TDI	983.0	E864.0	—	E950.7	E962.1	E980.6
vapor	987.8	E869.8	—	E952.8	E962.2	E982.8
Tear gas	987.5	E869.3	—	E952.8	E962.2	E982.8
Teclothiazide	974.3	E858.5	E944.3	E950.4	E962.0	E980.4
Tegretol	966.3	E855.0	E936.3	E950.4	E962.0	E980.4
Telepaque	977.8	E858.8	E947.8	E950.4	E962.0	E980.4
Tellurium	985.8	E866.4	—	E950.9	E962.1	E980.9
fumes	985.8	E866.4	—	E950.9	E962.1	E980.9
TEM	963.1	E858.1	E933.1	E950.4	E962.0	E980.4
Temazepan—*see* Benzodiazepines						
TEPA	963.1	E858.1	E933.1	E950.4	E962.0	E980.4
TEPP	989.3	E863.1	—	E950.6	E962.1	E980.7
Terbutaline	971.2	E855.5	E941.2	E950.4	E962.0	E980.4
Teroxalene	961.6	E857	E931.6	E950.4	E962.0	E980.4
Terpin hydrate	975.5	E858.6	E945.5	E950.4	E962.0	E980.4
Terramycin	960.4	E856	E930.4	E950.4	E962.0	E980.4
Tessalon	975.4	E858.6	E945.4	E950.4	E962.0	E980.4
Testosterone	962.1	E858.0	E932.1	E950.4	E962.0	E980.4
Tetanus (vaccine)	978.4	E858.8	E948.4	E950.4	E962.0	E980.4
antitoxin	979.9	E858.8	E949.9	E950.4	E962.0	E980.4
immune globulin (human)	964.6	E858.2	E934.6	E950.4	E962.0	E980.4
toxoid	978.4	E858.8	E948.4	E950.4	E962.0	E980.4
with diphtheria toxoid	978.9	E858.8	E948.9	E950.4	E962.0	E980.4
with pertussis	978.6	E858.8	E948.6	E950.4	E962.0	E980.4
Tetrabenazine	969.5	E853.8	E939.5	E950.3	E962.0	E980.3

Substance	Poisoning	Accident	Therapeutic Use	Suicide Attempt	Assault	Undetermined
			External Cause (E-Code)			
Tetracaine (infiltration) (topical)	968.5	E855.2	E938.5	E950.4	E962.0	E980.4
nerve block (peripheral) (plexus)	968.6	E855.2	E938.6	E950.4	E962.0	E980.4
spinal	968.7	E855.2	E938.7	E950.4	E962.0	E980.4
Tetrachlorethylene—*see* Tetrachloroethylene						
Tetrachlormethiazide	974.3	E858.5	E944.3	E950.4	E962.0	E980.4
Tetrachloroethane (liquid) (vapor)	982.3	E862.4	—	E950.9	E962.1	E980.9
paint or varnish	982.3	E861.6	—	E950.9	E962.1	E980.9
Tetrachloroethylene (liquid) (vapor)	982.3	E862.4	—	E950.9	E962.1	E980.9
medicinal	961.6	E857	E931.6	E950.4	E962.0	E980.4
Tetrachloromethane — *see* Carbon, tetrachloride						
Tetracycline	960.4	E856	E930.4	E950.4	E962.0	E980.4
ophthalmic preparation	976.5	E858.7	E946.5	E950.4	E962.0	E980.4
topical NEC	976.0	E858.7	E946.0	E950.4	E962.0	E980.4
Tetraethylammonium chloride	972.3	E858.3	E942.3	E950.4	E962.0	E980.4
Tetraethyl lead (antiknock compound)	984.1	E862.1	—	E950.9	E962.1	E980.9
Tetraethyl pyrophosphate	989.3	E863.1	—	E950.6	E962.1	E980.7
Tetraethylthiuram disulfide	977.3	E858.8	E947.3	E950.4	E962.0	E980.4
Tetrahydroaminoacridine	971.0	E855.3	E941.0	E950.4	E962.0	E980.4
Tetrahydrocannabinol	969.6	E854.1	E939.6	E950.3	E962.0	E980.3
Tetrahydronaphthalene	982.0	E862.4	—	E950.9	E962.1	E980.9
Tetrahydrozoline	971.2	E855.5	E941.2	E950.4	E962.0	E980.4
Tetralin	982.0	E862.4	—	E950.9	E962.1	E980.9
Tetramethylthiuram (disulfide) NEC	989.4	E863.6	—	E950.6	E962.1	E980.7
medicinal	976.2	E858.7	E946.2	E950.4	E962.0	E980.4
Tetronal	967.8	E852.8	E937.8	E950.2	E962.0	E980.2
Tetryl	983.0	E864.0	—	E950.7	E962.1	E980.6
Thalidomide	967.8	E852.8	E937.8	E950.2	E962.0	E980.2
Thallium (compounds) (dust) NEC	985.8	E866.4	—	E950.9	E962.1	E980.9
pesticide (rodenticide)	985.8	E863.7	—	E950.6	E962.1	E980.7
THC	969.6	E854.1	E939.6	E950.3	E962.0	E980.3
Thebacon	965.09	E850.2	E935.2	E950.0	E962.0	E980.0
Thebaine	965.09	E850.2	E935.2	E950.0	E962.0	E980.0
Theobromine (calcium salicylate)	974.1	E858.5	E944.1	E950.4	E962.0	E980.4
Theophylline (diuretic)	974.1	E858.5	E944.1	E950.4	E962.0	E980.4
ethylenediamine	975.7	E858.6	E945.7	E950.4	E962.0	E980.4
Thiabendazole	961.6	E857	E931.6	E950.4	E962.0	E980.4
Thialbarbital, thialbarbitone	968.3	E855.1	E938.3	E950.4	E962.0	E980.4
Thiamine	963.5	E858.1	E933.5	E950.4	E962.0	E980.4
Thiamylal (sodium)	968.3	E855.1	E938.3	E950.4	E962.0	E980.4
Thiazesim	969.0	E854.0	E939.0	E950.3	E962.0	E980.3
Thiazides (diuretics)	974.3	E858.5	E944.3	E950.4	E962.0	E980.4
Thiethylperazine	963.0	E858.1	E933.0	E950.4	E962.0	E980.4
Thimerosal (topical)	976.0	E858.7	E946.0	E950.4	E962.0	E980.4
ophthalmic preparation	976.5	E858.7	E946.5	E950.4	E962.0	E980.4
Thioacetazone	961.8	E857	E931.8	E950.4	E962.0	E980.4
Thiobarbiturates	968.3	E855.1	E938.3	E950.4	E962.0	E980.4
Thiobismol	961.2	E857	E931.2	E950.4	E962.0	E980.4
Thiocarbamide	962.8	E858.0	E932.8	E950.4	E962.0	E980.4
Thiocarbarsone	961.1	E857	E931.1	E950.4	E962.0	E980.4
Thiocarlide	961.8	E857	E931.8	E950.4	E962.0	E980.4
Thioguanine	963.1	E858.1	E933.1	E950.4	E962.0	E980.4
Thiomercaptomerin	974.0	E858.5	E944.0	E950.4	E962.0	E980.4
Thiomerin	974.0	E858.5	E944.0	E950.4	E962.0	E980.4
Thiopental, thiopentone (sodium)	968.3	E855.1	E938.3	E950.4	E962.0	E980.4
Thiopropazate	969.1	E853.0	E939.1	E950.3	E962.0	E980.3
Thioproperazine	969.1	E853.0	E939.1	E950.3	E962.0	E980.3

Substance	Poisoning	Accident	Therapeutic Use	Suicide Attempt	Assault	Undetermined
Thioridazine	969.1	E853.0	E939.1	E950.3	E962.0	E980.3
Thio–TEPA, thiotepa	963.1	E858.1	E933.1	E950.4	E962.0	E980.4
Thiothixene	969.3	E853.8	E939.3	E950.3	E962.0	E980.3
Thiouracil	962.8	E858.0	E932.8	E950.4	E962.0	E980.4
Thiourea	962.8	E858.0	E932.8	E950.4	E962.0	E980.4
Thiphenamil	971.1	E855.4	E941.1	E950.4	E962.0	E980.4
Thiram NEC	989.4	E863.6	—	E950.6	E962.1	E980.7
medicinal	976.2	E858.7	E946.2	E950.4	E962.0	E980.4
Thonzylamine	963.0	E858.1	E933.0	E950.4	E962.0	E980.4
Thorazine	969.1	E853.0	E939.1	E950.3	E962.0	E980.3
Thornapple	988.2	E865.4	—	E950.9	E962.1	E980.9
Throat preparation (lozenges) NEC	976.6	E858.7	E946.6	E950.4	E962.0	E980.4
Thrombin	964.5	E858.2	E934.5	E950.4	E962.0	E980.4
Thrombolysin	964.4	E858.2	E934.4	E950.4	E962.0	E980.4
Thymol	983.0	E864.0	—	E950.7	E962.1	E980.6
Thymus extract	962.9	E858.0	E932.9	E950.4	E962.0	E980.4
Thyroglobulin	962.7	E858.0	E932.7	E950.4	E962.0	E980.4
Thyroid (derivatives) (extract)	962.7	E858.0	E932.7	E950.4	E962.0	E980.4
Thyrolar	962.7	E858.0	E932.7	E950.4	E962.0	E980.4
Thyrothrophin, thyrotropin	977.8	E858.8	E947.8	E950.4	E962.0	E980.4
Thyroxin(e)	962.7	E858.0	E932.7	E950.4	E962.0	E980.4
Tigan	963.0	E858.1	E933.0	E950.4	E962.0	E980.4
Tigloidine	968.0	E855.1	E938.0	E950.4	E962.0	E980.4
Tin (chloride) (dust) (oxide) NEC	985.8	E866.4	—	E950.9	E962.1	E980.9
anti–infectives	961.2	E857	E931.2	E950.4	E962.0	E980.4
Tinactin	976.0	E858.7	E946.0	E950.4	E962.0	E980.4
Tincture, iodine — *see* Iodine						
Tindal	969.1	E853.0	E939.1	E950.3	E962.0	E980.3
Titanium (compounds) (vapor)	985.8	E866.4	—	E950.9	E962.1	E980.9
ointment	976.3	E858.7	E946.3	E950.4	E962.0	E980.4
Titroid	962.7	E858.0	E932.7	E950.4	E962.0	E980.4
TMTD — *see* Tetramethylthiuram disulfide						
TNT	989.89	E866.8	—	E950.9	E962.1	E980.9
fumes	987.8	E869.8	—	E952.8	E962.2	E982.8
Toadstool	988.1	E865.5	—	E950.9	E962.1	E980.9
Tobacco NEC	989.84	E866.8	—	E950.9	E962.1	E980.9
Indian	988.2	E865.4	—	E950.9	E962.1	E980.9
smoke, second-hand	987.8	E869.4	—	—	—	—
Tocopherol	963.5	E858.1	E933.5	E950.4	E962.0	E980.4
Tocosamine	975.0	E858.6	E945.0	E950.4	E962.0	E980.4
Tofranil	969.0	E854.0	E939.0	E950.3	E962.0	E980.3
Toilet deodorizer	989.8	E866.8	—	E950.9	E962.1	E980.9
Tolazamide	962.3	E858.0	E932.3	E950.4	E962.0	E980.4
Tolazoline	971.3	E855.6	E941.3	E950.4	E962.0	E980.4
Tolbutamide	962.3	E858.0	E932.3	E950.4	E962.0	E980.4
sodium	977.8	E858.8	E947.8	E950.4	E962.0	E980.4
Tolmetin	965.69	E850.6	E935.6	E950.0	E962.0	E980.0
Tolnaftate	976.0	E858.7	E946.0	E950.4	E962.0	E980.4
Tolpropamine	976.1	E858.7	E946.1	E950.4	E962.0	E980.4
Tolserol	968.0	E855.1	E938.0	E950.4	E962.0	E980.4
Toluene (liquid) (vapor)	982.0	E862.4	—	E950.9	E962.1	E980.9
diisocyanate	983.0	E864.0	—	E950.7	E962.1	E980.6
Toluidine	983.0	E864.0	—	E950.7	E962.1	E980.6
vapor	987.8	E869.8	—	E952.8	E962.2	E982.8
Toluol (liquid) (vapor)	982.0	E862.4	—	E950.9	E962.1	E980.9
Tolylene–2,4–diisocyanate	983.0	E864.0	—	E950.7	E962.1	E980.6
Tonics, cardiac	972.1	E858.3	E942.1	E950.4	E962.0	E980.4

Substance	Poisoning	External Cause (E-Code)				
		Accident	Therapeutic Use	Suicide Attempt	Assault	Undetermined
Toxaphene (dust) (spray)	989.2	E863.0	—	E950.6	E962.1	E980.7
Toxoids NEC	978.8	E858.8	E948.8	E950.4	E962.0	E980.4
Tractor fuel NEC	981	E862.1	—	E950.9	E962.1	E980.9
Tragacanth	973.3	E858.4	E943.3	E950.4	E962.0	E980.4
Tramazoline	971.2	E855.5	E941.2	E950.4	E962.0	E980.4
Tranquilizers	969.5	E853.9	E939.5	E950.3	E962.0	E980.3
benzodiazepine–based	969.4	E853.2	E939.4	E950.3	E962.0	E980.3
butyrophenone–based	969.2	E853.1	E939.2	E950.3	E962.0	E980.3
major NEC	969.3	E853.8	E939.3	E950.3	E962.0	E980.3
phenothiazine–based	969.1	E853.0	E939.1	E950.3	E962.0	E980.3
specified NEC	969.5	E853.8	E939.5	E950.3	E962.0	E980.3
Trantoin	961.9	E857	E931.9	E950.4	E962.0	E980.4
Tranxene	969.4	E853.2	E939.4	E950.3	E962.0	E980.3
Tranylcypromine (sulfate)	969.0	E854.0	E939.0	E950.3	E962.0	E980.3
Trasentine	975.1	E858.6	E945.1	E950.4	E962.0	E980.4
Travert	974.5	E858.5	E944.5	E950.4	E962.0	E980.4
Trecator	961.8	E857	E931.8	E950.4	E962.0	E980.4
Tretinoin	976.8	E858.7	E946.8	E950.4	E962.0	E980.4
Triacetin	976.0	E858.7	E946.0	E950.4	E962.0	E980.4
Triacetyloleandomycin	960.3	E856	E930.3	E950.4	E962.0	E980.4
Triamcinolone	962.0	E858.0	E932.0	E950.4	E962.0	E980.4
ENT agent	976.6	E858.7	E946.6	E950.4	E962.0	E980.4
ophthalmic preparation	976.5	E858.7	E946.5	E950.4	E962.0	E980.4
topical NEC	976.0	E858.7	E946.0	E950.4	E962.0	E980.4
Triamterene	974.4	E858.5	E944.4	E950.4	E962.0	E980.4
Triaziquone	963.1	E858.1	E933.1	E950.4	E962.0	E980.4
Tribromacetaldehyde	967.3	E852.2	E937.3	E950.2	E962.0	E980.2
Tribromoethanol	968.2	E855.1	E938.2	E950.4	E962.0	E980.4
Tribromomethane	967.3	E852.2	E937.3	E950.2	E962.0	E980.2
Trichlorethane	982.3	E862.4	—	E950.9	E962.1	E980.9
Trichlormethiazide	974.3	E858.5	E944.3	E950.4	E962.0	E980.4
Trichloroacetic acid	983.1	E864.1	—	E950.7	E962.1	E980.6
medicinal (keratolytic)	976.4	E858.7	E946.4	E950.4	E962.0	E980.4
Trichloroethanol	967.1	E852.0	E937.1	E950.2	E962.0	E980.2
Trichloroethylene (liquid) (vapor)	982.3	E862.4	—	E950.9	E962.1	E980.9
anesthetic (gas)	968.2	E855.1	E938.2	E950.4	E962.0	E980.4
Trichloroethyl phosphate	967.1	E852.0	E937.1	E950.2	E962.0	E980.2
Trichlorofluoromethane NEC	987.4	E869.2	—	E952.8	E962.2	E982.8
Trichlorotriethylamine	963.1	E858.1	E933.1	E950.4	E962.0	E980.4
Trichomonacides NEC	961.5	E857	E931.5	E950.4	E962.0	E980.4
Trichomycin	960.1	E856	E930.1	E950.4	E962.0	E980.4
Triclofos	967.1	E852.0	E937.1	E950.2	E962.0	E980.2
Tricresyl phosphate	989.89	E866.8	—	E950.9	E962.1	E980.9
solvent	982.8	E862.4	—	E950.9	E962.1	E980.9
Tricyclamol	966.4	E855.0	E936.4	E950.4	E962.0	E980.4
Tridesilon	976.0	E858.7	E946.0	E950.4	E962.0	E980.4
Tridihexethyl	971.1	E855.4	E941.1	E950.4	E962.0	E980.4
Tridione	966.0	E855.0	E936.0	E950.4	E962.0	E980.4
Triethanolamine NEC	983.2	E864.2	—	E950.7	E962.1	E980.6
detergent	983.2	E861.0	—	E950.7	E962.1	E980.6
trinitrate	972.4	E858.3	E942.4	E950.4	E962.0	E980.4
Triethanomelamine	963.1	E858.1	E933.1	E950.4	E962.0	E980.4
Triethylene melamine	963.1	E858.1	E933.1	E950.4	E962.0	E980.4
Triethylenephosphoramide	963.1	E858.1	E933.1	E950.4	E962.0	E980.4
Triethylenethiophosphoramide	963.1	E858.1	E933.1	E950.4	E962.0	E980.4
Trifluoperazine	969.1	E853.0	E939.1	E950.3	E962.0	E980.3
Trifluperidol	969.2	E853.1	E939.2	E950.3	E962.0	E980.3

Substance	Poisoning	External Cause (E-Code)				
		Accident	Therapeutic Use	Suicide Attempt	Assault	Undetermined
Triflupromazine	969.1	E853.0	E939.1	E950.3	E962.0	E980.3
Trihexyphenidyl	971.1	E855.4	E941.1	E950.4	E962.0	E980.4
Triiodothyronine	962.7	E858.0	E932.7	E950.4	E962.0	E980.4
Trilene	968.2	E855.1	E938.2	E950.4	E962.0	E980.4
Trimeprazine	963.0	E858.1	E933.0	E950.4	E962.0	E980.4
Trimetazidine	972.4	E858.3	E942.4	E950.4	E962.0	E980.4
Trimethadione	966.0	E855.0	E936.0	E950.4	E962.0	E980.4
Trimethaphan	972.3	E858.3	E942.3	E950.4	E962.0	E980.4
Trimethidinium	972.3	E858.3	E942.3	E950.4	E962.0	E980.4
Trimethobenzamide	963.0	E858.1	E933.0	E950.4	E962.0	E980.4
Trimethylcarbinol	980.8	E860.8	—	E950.9	E962.1	E980.9
Trimethylpsoralen	976.3	E858.7	E946.3	E950.4	E962.0	E980.4
Trimeton	963.0	E858.1	E933.0	E950.4	E962.0	E980.4
Trimipramine	969.0	E854.0	E939.0	E950.3	E962.0	E980.3
Trimustine	963.1	E858.1	E933.1	E950.4	E962.0	E980.4
Trinitrin	972.4	E858.3	E942.4	E950.4	E962.0	E980.4
Trinitrophenol	983.0	E864.0	—	E950.7	E962.1	E980.6
Trinitrotoluene	989.89	E866.8	—	E950.9	E962.1	E980.9
fumes	987.8	E869.8	—	E952.8	E962.2	E982.8
Trional	967.8	E852.8	E937.8	E950.2	E962.0	E980.2
Trioxide of arsenic — *see* Arsenic						
Trioxsalen	976.3	E858.7	E946.3	E950.4	E962.0	E980.4
Tripelennamine	963.0	E858.1	E933.0	E950.4	E962.0	E980.4
Triperidol	969.2	E853.1	E939.2	E950.3	E962.0	E980.3
Triprolidine	963.0	E858.1	E933.0	E950.4	E962.0	E980.4
Trisoralen	976.3	E858.7	E946.3	E950.4	E962.0	E980.4
Troleandomycin	960.3	E856	E930.3	E950.4	E962.0	E980.4
Trolnitrate (phosphate)	972.4	E858.3	E942.4	E950.4	E962.0	E980.4
Trometamol	963.3	E858.1	E933.3	E950.4	E962.0	E980.4
Tromethamine	963.3	E858.1	E933.3	E950.4	E962.0	E980.4
Tronothane	968.5	E855.2	E938.5	E950.4	E962.0	E980.4
Tropicamide	971.1	E855.4	E941.1	E950.4	E962.0	E980.4
Troxidone	966.0	E855.0	E936.0	E950.4	E962.0	E980.4
Tryparsamide	961.1	E857	E931.1	E950.4	E962.0	E980.4
Trypsin	963.4	E858.1	E933.4	E950.4	E962.0	E980.4
Tryptizol	969.0	E854.0	E939.0	E950.3	E962.0	E980.3
Tuaminoheptane	971.2	E855.5	E941.2	E950.4	E962.0	E980.4
Tuberculin (old)	977.8	E858.8	E947.8	E950.4	E962.0	E980.4
Tubocurare	975.2	E858.6	E945.2	E950.4	E962.0	E980.4
Tubocurarine	975.2	E858.6	E945.2	E950.4	E962.0	E980.4
Turkish green	969.6	E854.1	E939.6	E950.3	E962.0	E980.3
Turpentine (spirits of) (liquid) (vapor)	982.8	E862.4	—	E950.9	E962.1	E980.9
Tybamate	969.5	E853.8	E939.5	E950.3	E962.0	E980.3
Tyloxapol	975.5	E858.6	E945.5	E950.4	E962.0	E980.4
Tymazoline	971.2	E855.5	E941.2	E950.4	E962.0	E980.4
Typhoid vaccine	978.1	E858.8	E948.1	E950.4	E962.0	E980.4
Typhus vaccine	979.2	E858.8	E949.2	E950.4	E962.0	E980.4
Tyrothricin	976.0	E858.7	E946.0	E950.4	E962.0	E980.4
ENT agent	976.6	E858.7	E946.6	E950.4	E962.0	E980.4
ophthalmic preparation	976.5	E858.7	E946.5	E950.4	E962.0	E980.4
Undecenoic acid	976.0	E858.7	E946.0	E950.4	E962.0	E980.4
Undecylenic acid	976.0	E858.7	E946.0	E950.4	E962.0	E980.4
Unna's boot	976.3	E858.7	E946.3	E950.4	E962.0	E980.4
Uracil mustard	963.1	E858.1	E933.1	E950.4	E962.0	E980.4
Uramustine	963.1	E858.1	E933.1	E950.4	E962.0	E980.4
Urari	975.2	E858.6	E945.2	E950.4	E962.0	E980.4
Urea	974.4	E858.5	E944.4	E950.4	E962.0	E980.4

Substance	Poisoning	Accident	Therapeutic Use	Suicide Attempt	Assault	Undetermined
topical	976.8	E858.7	E946.8	E950.4	E962.0	E980.4
Urethan(e) (antineoplastic)	963.1	E858.1	E933.1	E950.4	E962.0	E980.4
Urginea (maritima) (scilla) — *see* Squill						
Uric acid metabolism agents NEC	974.7	E858.5	E944.7	E950.4	E962.0	E980.4
Urokinase	964.4	E858.2	E934.4	E950.4	E962.0	E980.4
Urokon	977.8	E858.8	E947.8	E950.4	E962.0	E980.4
Urotropin	961.9	E857	E931.9	E950.4	E962.0	E980.4
Urtica	988.2	E865.4	—	E950.9	E962.1	E980.9
Utility gas — *see* Gas, utility						
Vaccine NEC	979.9	E858.8	E949.9	E950.4	E962.0	E980.4
bacterial NEC	978.8	E858.8	E948.8	E950.4	E962.0	E980.4
with						
other bacterial component	978.9	E858.8	E948.9	E950.4	E962.0	E980.4
pertussis component	978.6	E858.8	E948.6	E950.4	E962.0	E980.4
viral–rickettsial component	979.7	E858.8	E949.7	E950.4	E962.0	E980.4
mixed NEC	978.9	E858.8	E948.9	E950.4	E962.0	E980.4
BCG	978.0	E858.8	E948.0	E950.4	E962.0	E980.4
cholera	978.2	E858.8	E948.2	E950.4	E962.0	E980.4
diphtheria	978.5	E858.8	E948.5	E950.4	E962.0	E980.4
influenza	979.6	E858.8	E949.6	E950.4	E962.0	E980.4
measles	979.4	E858.8	E949.4	E950.4	E962.0	E980.4
meningococcal	978.8	E858.8	E948.8	E950.4	E962.0	E980.4
mumps	979.6	E858.8	E949.6	E950.4	E962.0	E980.4
paratyphoid	978.1	E858.8	E948.1	E950.4	E962.0	E980.4
pertussis (with diphtheria toxoid) (with tetanus toxoid)	978.6	E858.8	E948.6	E950.4	E962.0	E980.4
plague	978.3	E858.8	E948.3	E950.4	E962.0	E980.4
poliomyelitis	979.5	E858.8	E949.5	E950.4	E962.0	E980.4
poliovirus	979.5	E858.8	E949.5	E950.4	E962.0	E980.4
rabies	979.1	E858.8	E949.1	E950.4	E962.0	E980.4
rickettsial NEC	979.6	E858.8	E949.6	E950.4	E962.0	E980.4
with						
bacterial component	979.7	E858.8	E949.7	E950.4	E962.0	E980.4
pertussis component	978.6	E858.8	E948.6	E950.4	E962.0	E980.4
viral component	979.7	E858.8	E949.7	E950.4	E962.0	E980.4
Rocky mountain spotted fever	979.6	E858.8	E949.6	E950.4	E962.0	E980.4
rotavirus	979.6	E858.8	E949.6	E950.4	E962.0	E980.4
rubella virus	979.4	E858.8	E949.4	E950.4	E962.0	E980.4
sabin oral	979.5	E858.8	E949.5	E950.4	E962.0	E980.4
smallpox	979.0	E858.8	E949.0	E950.4	E962.0	E980.4
tetanus	978.4	E858.8	E948.4	E950.4	E962.0	E980.4
typhoid	978.1	E858.8	E948.1	E950.4	E962.0	E980.4
typhus	979.2	E858.8	E949.2	E950.4	E962.0	E980.4
viral NEC	979.6	E858.8	E949.6	E950.4	E962.0	E980.4
with						
bacterial component	979.7	E858.8	E949.7	E950.4	E962.0	E980.4
pertussis component	978.6	E858.8	E948.6	E950.4	E962.0	E980.4
rickettsial component	979.7	E858.8	E949.7	E950.4	E962.0	E980.4
yellow fever	979.3	E858.8	E949.3	E950.4	E962.0	E980.4
Vaccinia immune globulin (human)	964.6	E858.2	E934.6	E950.4	E962.0	E980.4
Vaginal contraceptives	976.8	E858.7	E946.8	E950.4	E962.0	E980.4
Valethamate	971.1	E855.4	E941.1	E950.4	E962.0	E980.4
Valisone	976.0	E858.7	E946.0	E950.4	E962.0	E980.4
Valium	969.4	E853.2	E939.4	E950.3	E962.0	E980.3
Valmid	967.8	E852.8	E937.8	E950.2	E962.0	E980.2
Vanadium	985.8	E866.4	—	E950.9	E962.1	E980.9
Vancomycin	960.8	E856	E930.8	E950.4	E962.0	E980.4

Substance	Poisoning	External Cause (E-Code)				
		Accident	Therapeutic Use	Suicide Attempt	Assault	Undetermined
Vapor (*see also* Gas)	987.9	E869.9	—	E952.9	E962.2	E982.9
kiln (carbon monoxide)	986	E868.8	—	E952.1	E962.2	E982.1
lead — *see* Lead						
specified source NEC (*see also*						
specific substance)	987.8	E869.8	—	E952.8	E962.2	E982.8
Varidase	964.4	E858.2	E934.4	E950.4	E962.0	E980.4
Varnish	989.89	E861.6	—	E950.9	E962.1	E980.9
cleaner	982.8	E862.9	—	E950.9	E962.1	E980.9
Vaseline	976.3	E858.7	E946.3	E950.4	E962.0	E980.4
Vasodilan	972.5	E858.3	E942.5	E950.4	E962.0	E980.4
Vasodilators NEC	972.5	E858.3	E942.5	E950.4	E962.0	E980.0
coronary	972.4	E858.3	E942.4	E950.4	E962.0	E980.4
Vasopressin	962.5	E858.0	E932.5	E950.4	E962.0	E980.4
Vasopressor drugs	962.5	E858.0	E932.5	E950.4	E962.0	E980.4
Venom, venomous (bite) (sting)	989.5	E905.9	—	E950.9	E962.1	E980.9
arthropod NEC	989.5	E905.5	—	E950.9	E962.1	E980.9
bee	989.5	E905.3	—	E950.9	E962.1	E980.9
centipede	989.5	E905.4	—	E950.9	E962.1	E980.9
hornet	989.5	E905.3	—	E950.9	E962.1	E980.9
lizard	989.5	E905.0	—	E950.9	E962.1	E980.9
marine animals or plants	989.5	E905.6	—	E950.9	E962.1	E980.9
millipede (topical)	989.5	E905.4	—	E950.9	E962.1	E980.9
plant NEC	989.5	E905.7	—	E950.9	E962.1	E980.9
marine	989.5	E905.6	—	E950.9	E962.1	E980.9
scorpion	989.5	E905.2	—	E950.9	E962.1	E980.9
snake	989.5	E905.0	—	E950.9	E962.1	E980.9
specified NEC	989.5	E905.8	—	E950.9	E962.1	E980.9
spider	989.5	E905.1	—	E950.9	E962.1	E980.9
wasp	989.5	E905.3	—	E950.9	E962.1	E980.9
Ventolin—*see* Salbutamol sulfate						
Veramon	967.0	E851	E937.0	E950.1	E962.0	E980.1
Veratrum						
album	988.2	E865.4	—	E950.9	E962.1	E980.9
alkaloids	972.6	E858.3	E942.6	E950.4	E962.0	E980.4
viride	988.2	E865.4	—	E950.9	E962.1	E980.9
Verdigris (*see also* Copper)	985.8	E866.4	—	E950.9	E962.1	E980.9
Veronal	967.0	E851	E937.0	E950.1	E962.0	E980.1
Veroxil	961.6	E857	E931.6	E950.4	E962.0	E980.4
Versidyne	965.7	E850.7	E935.7	E950.0	E962.0	E980.0
Viagra	972.5	E858.3	E942.5	E950.4	E962.0	E980.4
Vienna						
green	985.1	E866.3	—	E950.8	E962.1	E980.8
insecticide	985.1	E863.4	—	E950.6	E962.1	E980.7
red	989.89	E866.8	—	E950.9	E962.1	E980.9
pharmaceutical dye	977.4	E858.8	E947.4	E950.4	E962.0	E980.4
Vinbarbital, vinbarbitone	967.0	E851	E937.0	E950.1	E962.0	E980.1
Vinblastine	963.1	E858.1	E933.1	E950.4	E962.0	E980.4
Vincristine	963.1	E858.1	E933.1	E950.4	E962.0	E980.4
Vinesthene, vinethene	968.2	E855.1	E938.2	E950.4	E962.0	E980.4
Vinyl						
bital	967.0	E851	E937.0	E950.1	E962.0	E980.1
ether	968.2	E855.1	E938.2	E950.4	E962.0	E980.4
Vioform	961.3	E857	E931.3	E950.4	E962.0	E980.4
topical	976.0	E858.7	E946.0	E950.4	E962.0	E980.4
Viomycin	960.6	E856	E930.6	E950.4	E962.0	E980.4
Viosterol	963.5	E858.1	E933.5	E950.4	E962.0	E980.4
Viper (venom)	989.5	E905.0	—	E950.9	E962.1	E980.9

Substance	Poisoning	External Cause (E-Code)				
		Accident	Therapeutic Use	Suicide Attempt	Assault	Undetermined
Viprynium (embonate)	961.6	E857	E931.6	E950.4	E962.0	E980.4
Virugon	961.7	E857	E931.7	E950.4	E962.0	E980.4
Visine	976.5	E858.7	E946.5	E950.4	E962.0	E980.4
Vitamins NEC	963.5	E858.1	E933.5	E950.4	E962.0	E980.4
B_{12}	964.1	E858.2	E934.1	E950.4	E962.0	E980.4
hematopoietic	964.1	E858.2	E934.1	E950.4	E962.0	E980.4
K	964.3	E858.2	E934.3	E950.4	E962.0	E980.4
Vleminckx's solution	976.4	E858.7	E946.4	E950.4	E962.0	E980.4
Voltaren—*see* Diclofenac sodium						
Warfarin (potassium) (sodium)	964.2	E858.2	E934.2	E950.4	E962.0	E980.4
rodenticide	989.4	E863.7	—	E950.6	E962.1	E980.7
Wasp (sting)	989.5	E905.3	—	E950.9	E962.1	E980.9
Water						
balance agents NEC	974.5	E858.5	E944.5	E950.4	E962.0	E980.4
gas	987.1	E868.1	—	E951.8	E962.2	E981.8
incomplete combustion of — *see* Carbon, monoxide, fuel, utility						
hemlock	988.2	E865.4	—	E950.9	E962.1	E980.9
moccasin (venom)	989.5	E905.0	—	E950.9	E962.1	E980.9
Wax (paraffin) (petroleum)	981	E862.3	—	E950.9	E962.1	E980.9
automobile	989.89	E861.2	—	E950.9	E962.1	E980.9
floor	981	E862.0	—	E950.9	E962.1	E980.9
Weed killers NEC	989.4	E863.5	—	E950.6	E962.1	E980.7
Welldorm	967.1	E852.0	E937.1	E950.2	E962.0	E980.2
White						
arsenic — *see* Arsenic						
hellebore	988.2	E865.4	—	E950.9	E962.1	E980.9
lotion (keratolytic)	976.4	E858.7	E946.4	E950.4	E962.0	E980.4
spirit	981	E862.0	—	E950.9	E962.1	E980.9
Whitewashes	989.89	E861.6	—	E950.9	E962.1	E980.9
Whole blood	964.7	E858.2	E934.7	E950.4	E962.0	E980.4
Wild						
black cherry	988.2	E865.4	—	E950.9	E962.1	E980.9
poisonous plants NEC	988.2	E865.4	—	E950.9	E962.1	E980.9
Window cleaning fluid	989.89	E861.3	—	E950.9	E962.1	E980.9
Wintergreen (oil)	976.3	E858.7	E946.3	E950.4	E962.0	E980.4
Witch hazel	976.2	E858.7	E946.2	E950.4	E962.0	E980.4
Wood						
alcohol	980.1	E860.2	—	E950.9	E962.1	E980.9
spirit	980.1	E860.2	—	E950.9	E962.1	E980.9
Woorali	975.2	E858.6	E945.2	E950.4	E962.0	E980.4
Wormseed, American	961.6	E857	E931.6	E950.4	E962.0	E980.4
Xanthine diuretics	974.1	E858.5	E944.1	E950.4	E962.0	E980.4
Xanthocillin	960.0	E856	E930.0	E950.4	E962.0	E980.4
Xanthotoxin	976.3	E858.7	E946.3	E950.4	E962.0	E980.4
Xylene (liquid) (vapor)	982.0	E862.4	—	E950.9	E962.1	E980.9
Xylocaine (infiltration) (topical)	968.5	E855.2	E938.5	E950.4	E962.0	E980.4
nerve block (peripheral) (plexus)	968.6	E855.2	E938.6	E950.4	E962.0	E980.4
spinal	968.7	E855.2	E938.7	E950.4	E962.0	E980.4
Xylol (liquid) (vapor)	982.0	E862.4	—	E950.9	E962.1	E980.9
Xylometazoline	971.2	E855.5	E941.2	E950.4	E962.0	E980.4
Yellow						
fever vaccine	979.3	E858.8	E949.3	E950.4	E962.0	E980.4
jasmine	988.2	E865.4	—	E950.9	E962.1	E980.9
Yew	988.2	E865.4	—	E950.9	E962.1	E980.9
Zactane	965.7	E850.7	E935.7	E950.0	E962.0	E980.0
Zaroxolyn	974.3	E858.5	E944.3	E950.4	E962.0	E980.4

Substance	Poisoning	External Cause (E-Code)				
		Accident	Therapeutic Use	Suicide Attempt	Assault	Undetermined
Zephiran (topical)	976.0	E858.7	E946.0	E950.4	E962.0	E980.4
ophthalmic preparation	976.5	E858.7	E946.5	E950.4	E962.0	E980.4
Zerone	980.1	E860.2	—	E950.9	E962.1	E980.9
Zinc (compounds) (fumes) (salts) (vapor) NEC	985.8	E866.4	—	E950.9	E962.1	E980.9
anti–infectives	976.0	E858.7	E946.0	E950.4	E962.0	E980.4
antivaricose	972.7	E858.3	E942.7	E950.4	E962.0	E980.4
bacitracin	976.0	E858.7	E946.0	E950.4	E962.0	E980.4
chloride	976.2	E858.7	E946.2	E950.4	E962.0	E980.4
gelatin	976.3	E858.7	E946.3	E950.4	E962.0	E980.4
oxide	976.3	E858.7	E946.3	E950.4	E962.0	E980.4
peroxide	976.0	E858.7	E946.0	E950.4	E962.0	E980.4
pesticides	985.8	E863.4	—	E950.6	E962.1	E980.7
phosphide (rodenticide)	985.8	E863.7	—	E950.6	E962.1	E980.7
stearate	976.3	E858.7	E946.3	E950.4	E962.0	E980.4
sulfate (antivaricose)	972.7	E858.3	E942.7	E950.4	E962.0	E980.4
ENT agent	976.6	E858.7	E946.6	E950.4	E962.0	E980.4
ophthalmic solution	976.5	E858.7	E946.5	E950.4	E962.0	E980.4
topical NEC	976.0	E858.7	E946.0	E950.4	E962.0	E980.4
undecylenate	976.0	E858.7	E946.0	E950.4	E962.0	E980.4
Zoxazolamine	968.0	E855.1	E938.0	E950.4	E962.0	E980.4
Zygadenus (venenosus)	988.2	E865.4	—	E950.9	E962.1	E980.9

Substance	Poisoning	External Cause (E-Code)				
		Accident	Therapeutic Use	Suicide Attempt	Assault	Undetermined

SECTION 3

ALPHABETIC INDEX TO EXTERNAL CAUSES
OF INJURY AND POISONING (E CODE)

This section contains the index to the codes which classify environmental events, circumstances, and other conditions as the cause of injury and other adverse effects. Where a code from the section Supplementary Classification of External Causes of Injury and Poisoning (E800-E998) is applicable, it is intended that the E code shall be used in addition to a code form the main body of the classification, Chapters 1-17.

The alphabetic index to the E codes is organized by main terms which describe the *accident, circumstance, event,* or specific *agent* which caused the injury or other adverse effect.

> *Note—Transport accidents (E800-E848) include accidents involving:*
> *aircraft and space craft (E840-E845)*
> *watercraft (E830-E838)*
> *motor vehicle (E810-E825)*
> *railway (E800-E807)*
> *other road vehicles (E826-E829)*
>
> *For definitions and examples related to transport accidents—see Volume 1, pages 571-585.*
>
> *The fourth-digit subdivisions for use with categories E800-E848 to identify the injured person are found on pages 1447-1451.*
>
> *For identifying the place in which an accident or poisoning occurred (circumstances classifiable to categories E850-E869 and E880-E928)— see the listing in this section under "Accident, occurring."*

See the Table of Drugs and Chemicals (Section 2 of this volume) for identifying the specific agent involved in drug overdose or a wrong substance given or taken in error, and for intoxication or poisoning by a drug or other chemical substance.

The specific adverse effect, reaction, or localized toxic effect to a correct drug or substance properly administered in therapeutic or prophylactic dosage should be classified according to the nature of the adverse effect (e.g.: allergy, dermatitis, tachycardia) listed in Section 1 of this volume.

A

Abandonment
  causing exposure to weather conditions—*see*
    Exposure
  child, with intent to injure or kill E968.4
  helpless person, infant, newborn E904.0
  with intent to injure or kill E968.4
Abortion, criminal, injury to child E968.8
Abuse, (alleged) (suspected)
  adult
    by
      child E967.4
      ex-partner E967.3
      ex-spouse E967.3
      father E967.0
      grandchild E967.7
      grandparent E967.6
      mother E967.2
      non-related caregiver E967.8
      other relative E967.7
      other specified person(s) E967.1
      partner E967.3
      sibling E967.5
      spouse E967.3
      stepfather E967.0
      stepmother E967.2
      unspecified person E967.9
  child
    by
      boyfriend of parent or guardian E967.0
      child E967.4
      father E967.0
      female partner of parent or guardian
        E967.2
      girlfriend of parent or guardian E967.2
      grandchild E967.7
      grandparent E967.6
      male partner of parent or guardian E967.0
      mother E967.2
      non-related caregiver E967.8
      other relative E967.7
      other specified person(s) E967.1
      sibling E967.5
      stepfather E967.0
      stepmother E967.2
      unspecified person E967.9
Accident (to) E928.9
  aircraft (in transit) (powered) E841
    at landing, take-off E840
    due to, caused by cataclysm—*see*
      categories E908, E909
    late effect of E929.1
    unpowered (*see also* Collision, aircraft,
      unpowered) E842
    while alighting, boarding E843
  amphibious vehicle
    on
      land—*see* Accident, motor vehicle
      water—*see* Accident, watercraft
  animal, ridden NEC E828
  animal-drawn vehicle NEC E827
  balloon (*see also* Collision, aircraft,
    unpowered) E842
  caused by, due to
    abrasive wheel (metalworking) E919.3
    animal NEC E906.9
      being ridden (in sport or transport) E828
    avalanche NEC E909.2
    band saw E919.4
    bench saw E919.4

Accident—*continued*
  bore, earth-drilling or mining (land)
    (seabed) E919.1
  bulldozer E919.7
  cataclysmic
    earth surface movement or eruption E909.9
    storm E908.9
  chain
    hoist E919.2
      agricultural operations E919.0
      mining operations E919.1
    saw E920.1
  circular saw E919.4
  cold (excessive) (*see also* Cold, exposure
    to) E901.9
  combine E919.0
  conflagration—*see* Conflagration
  corrosive liquid, substance NEC E924.1
  cotton gin E919.8
  crane E919.2
    agricultural operations E919.0
    mining operations E919.1
  cutting or piercing instrument (*see also*
    Cut) E920.9
  dairy equipment E919.8
  derrick E919.2
    agricultural operations E919.0
    mining operations E919.1
  drill E920.1
    earth (land) (seabed) E919.1
    hand (powered) E920.1
      not powered E920.4
    metalworking E919.3
    woodworking E919.4
  earth(-)
    drilling machine E919.1
    moving machine E919.7
    scraping machine E919.7
  electric
    current (*see also* Electric shock) E925.9
    motor—*see also* Accident, machine, by
      type of machine
      current (of)—*see* Electric shock
  elevator (building) (grain) E919.2
    agricultural operations E919.0
    mining operations E919.1
  environmental factors NEC E928.9
  excavating machine E919.7
  explosive material (*see also* Explosion)
    E923.9
  farm machine E919.0
  fire, flames—*see also* Fire
    conflagration—*see* Conflagration
  firearm missile—*see* Shooting
  forging (metalworking) machine E919.3
  forklift (truck) E919.2
    agricultural operations E919.0
    mining operations E919.1
  gas turbine E919.5
  harvester E919.0
  hay derrick, mower, or rake E919.0
  heat (excessive) (*see also* Heat) E900.9
  hoist (*see also* Accident, caused by, due
    to, lift) E919.2
    chain—*see* Accident, caused by, due to,
      chain
    shaft E919.1

Assault—*continued*
  explosive(s) E965.9
    bomb (*see also* Assault, bomb) E965.8
    dynamite E965.8
  fight (hand) (fists) (foot) E960.0
    with weapon E968.9
      blunt or thrown E968.2
      cutting or piercing E966
      firearm—*see* Shooting, homicide
  fire E968.0
  firearm(s)—*see* Shooting, homicide
  garrotting E963
  gunshot (wound)—*see* Shooting, homicide
  hanging E963
  injury NEC E968.9
  knife E966
  late effect of E969
  ligature E963
  poisoning E962.9
    drugs or medicinals E962.0
    gas(es) or vapors, except drugs and
        medicinals E962.2
    solid or liquid substances, except drugs
        and medicinals E962.1
  puncture, any part of body E966
  pushing
    before moving object, train, vehicle
        E968.5
    from high place E968.1
  rape E960.1
  scalding E968.3
  shooting—*see* Shooting, homicide
  sodomy E960.1
  stab, any part of body E966
  strangulation E963
  submersion E964
  suffocation E963
  transport vehicle E968.5
  violence NEC E968.9
  vitriol E961
    swallowed E962.1
  weapon E968.9
    blunt or thrown E968.2
    cutting or piercing E966
    firearm—*see* Shooting, homicide
  wound E968.9
    cutting E966
    gunshot—*see* Shooting, homicide
    knife E966
    piercing E966
    puncture E966
    stab E966
Attack by animal NEC E906.9
Avalanche E909.2
  falling on or hitting
    motor vehicle (in motion) (on public
        highway) E909.2
    railway train E909.2
Aviators' disease E902.1

B

**Barotitis, barodontalgia, barosinusitis,
    barotrauma** (otitic) (sinus)—*see* Effects of,
    air pressure
Battered
  baby or child (syndrome)—*see* Abuse, child;
      category E967
  person other than baby or child—*see* Assault

Bayonet wound (*see also* Cut, by bayonet)
    E920.3
  in
    legal intervention E974
    war operations E995
Bean in nose E912
Bed set on fire NEC E898.0
Beheading (by guillotine)
  homicide E966
  legal execution E978
Bending, injury in E927
Bends E902.0
Bite
  animal (nonvenomous) NEC E906.5
    venomous NEC E905.9
  arthropod (nonvenomous) NEC E906.4
    venomous—*see* Sting
  black widow spider E905.1
  cat E906.3
  centipede E905.4
  cobra E905.0
  copperhead snake E905.0
  coral snake E905.0
  dog E906.0
  fer de lance E905.0
  gila monster E905.0
  human being
    accidental E928.3
    assault E968.7
  insect (nonvenomous) E906.4
    venomous—*see* Sting
  krait E905.0
  late effect of—*see* Late effect
  lizard E906.2
    venomous E905.0
  mamba E905.0
  marine animal
    nonvenomous E906.3
      snake E906.2
    venomous E905.6
      snake E905.0
  millipede E906.4
    venomous E905.4
  moray eel E906.3
  rat E906.1
  rattlesnake E905.0
  rodent, except rat E906.3
  serpent—*see* Bite, snake
  shark E906.3
  snake (venomous) E905.0
    nonvenomous E906.2
    sea E905.0
  spider E905.1
    nonvenomous E906.4
  tarantula (venomous) E905.1
  venomous NEC E905.9
    by specific animal—*see* category E905
  viper E905.0
  water moccasin E905.0
Blast (air) in war operations E993
  from nuclear explosion E996
  underwater E992
Blizzard E908.3
Blow E928.9
  by law-enforcing agent, police (on duty) E975
    with blunt object (baton) (nightstick)
        (stave) (truncheon) E973
Blowing up (*see also* Explosion) E923.9
Brawl (hand) (fists) (foot) E960.0

Breakage (accidental)
  cable of cable car not on rails E847
  ladder (causing fall) E881.0
  part (any) of
    animal-drawn vehicle E827
    ladder (causing fall) E881.0
    motor vehicle
      in motion (on public highway) E818
        not on public highway E825
      nonmotor road vehicle, except
        animal-drawn vehicle or pedal cycle
        E829
      off-road type motor vehicle (not on
        public highway) NEC E821
      on public highway E818
      pedal cycle E826
      scaffolding (causing fall) E881.1
      snow vehicle, motor-driven (not on public
        highway) E820
      on public highway E818
    vehicle NEC—*see* Accident, vehicle
Broken
  glass, injury by E920.8
  power line (causing electric shock) E925.1
Bumping against, into (accidentally)
  object (moving) (projected) (stationary) E917.9
    with fall E888
    caused by crowd (with fall) E917.1
    in
      running water E917.2
      sports E917.0
  person(s) E917.9
    with fall E886.9
      in sports E886.0
    as, or caused by, a crowd (with fall)
      E917.1
      in sports E917.0
      with fall E886.0
Burning, burns (accidental) (by) (from) (on)
  E899
  acid (any kind) E924.1
    swallowed—*see* Table of drugs and
      chemicals
  bedclothes (*see also* Fire, specified NEC)
    E898.0
  blowlamp (*see also* Fire, specified NEC)
    E898.1
  blowtorch (*see also* Fire, specified NEC)
    E898.1
  boat, ship, watercraft—*see* categories E830,
    E831, E837
  bonfire (controlled) E897
    uncontrolled E892
  candle (*see also* Fire, specified NEC) E898.1
  caustic liquid, substance E924.1
    swallowed—*see* Table of drugs and
      chemicals
  chemical E924.1
    from swallowing caustic, corrosive
      substance—*see* Table of drugs and
      chemicals
    in war operations E997.2
  cigar(s) or cigarette(s) (*see also* Fire,
    specified NEC) E898.1
  clothes, clothing, nightdress—*see* Ignition,
    clothes
    with conflagration—*see* Conflagration
  conflagration—*see* Conflagration
  corrosive liquid, substance E924.1
    swallowed—*see* Table of drugs and
      chemicals

Burning, burns—*continued*
  electric current (*see also* Electric shock)
    E925.9
  fire, flames (*see also* Fire) E899
  flare, Verey pistol E922.8
  heat
    from appliance (electrical) E924.8
    in local application or packing during
      medical or surgical procedure E873.5
  homicide (attempt) (*see also* Assault, burning)
    E968.0
  hot
    liquid E924.0
      caustic or corrosive E924.1
    object (not producing fire or flames)
      E924.8
    substance E924.9
      caustic or corrosive E924.1
      liquid (metal) NEC E924.0
      specified type NEC E924.8
    tap water E924.2
  ignition—*see also* Ignition
    clothes, clothing, nightdress—*see also*
      Ignition, clothes
      with conflagration—*see* Conflagration
    highly inflammable material (benzine)
      (fat) (gasoline) (kerosine) (paraffin)
      (petrol) E894
  inflicted by other person
    stated as
      homicidal, intentional (*see also* Assault,
        burning) E968.0
      undetermined whether accidental or
        intentional (*see also* Burn, stated as
        undetermined whether accidental or
        intentional) E988.1
  internal, from swallowed caustic, corrosive
    liquid, substance—*see* Table of drugs and
    chemicals
  in war operations (from fire-producing device
    or conventional weapon) E990.9
    from nuclear explosion E996
    petrol bomb E990.0
  lamp (*see also* Fire, specified NEC) E898.1
  late effect of NEC E929.4
  lighter (cigar) (cigarette) (*see also* Fire,
    specified NEC) E898.1
  lightning E907
  liquid (boiling) (hot) (molten) E924.0
    caustic, corrosive (external) E924.1
      swallowed—*see* Table of drugs and
        chemicals
  local application of externally applied
    substance in medical or surgical care
    E873.5
  machinery—*see* Accident, machine
  matches (*see also* Fire, specified NEC) E898.1
  medicament, externally applied E873.5
  metal, molten E924.0
  object (hot) E924.8
    producing fire or flames—*see* Fire
  oven (electric) (gas) E924.8
  pipe (smoking) (*see also* Fire, specified NEC)
    E898.1
  radiation—*see* Radiation
  railway engine, locomotive, train (*see also*
    Explosion, railway engine) E803
  self-inflicted (unspecified whether accidental
    or intentional) E988.1
    caustic or corrosive substance NEC
      E988.7

Burning, burns—*continued*
   stated as intentional, purposeful E958.1
     caustic or corrosive substance NEC E958.7
   stated as undetermined whether accidental or
     intentional E988.1
     caustic or corrosive substance NEC
      E988.7
   steam E924.0
     pipe E924.8
   substance (hot) E924.9
     boiling or molten E924.0
     caustic, corrosive (external) E924.1
       swallowed—*see* Table of drugs and
        chemicals
   suicidal (attempt) NEC E958.1
     caustic substance E958.7
     late effect of E959
   therapeutic misadventure
     overdose of radiation E873.2
   torch, welding (*see also* Fire, specified NEC)
     E898.1
   trash fire (*see also* Burning, bonfire) E897
   vapor E924.0
   vitriol E924.1
   x-rays E926.3
     in medical, surgical procedure—*see*
      Misadventure, failure, in dosage,
      radiation
Butted by animal E906.8

C

Cachexia, lead or saturnine E866.0
   from pesticide NEC (*see also* Table of drugs
     and chemicals) E863.4
Caisson disease E902.2
Capital punishment (any means) E978
Car sickness E903
Casualty (not due to war) NEC E928.9
   war (*see also* War operations) E995
Cat
   bite E906.3
   scratch E906.8
Cataclysmic (any injury)
   earth surface movement or eruption E909.9
     specified type NEC E909.8
   storm or flood resulting from storm E908.9
     specified type NEC E909.8
Catching fire —*see* Ignition
Caught
   between
     objects (moving) (stationary and moving)
      E918
     and machinery—*see* Accident, machine
   by cable car, not on rails E847
   in
     machinery (moving parts of)—*see*
      Accident, machine
     object E918
Cave-in (causing asphyxia, suffocation (by
   pressure)) (*see also* Suffocation, due to,
   cave-in) E913.3
   with injury other than asphyxia or suffocation
     E916
     with asphyxia or suffocation (*see also*
      Suffocation, due to, cave-in) E913.3
   struck or crushed by E916
     with asphyxia or suffocation (*see also*
      Suffocation, due to, cave-in) E913.3

Change(s) in air pressure—*see also* Effects of,
   air pressure
   sudden, in aircraft (ascent) (descent) (causing
     aeroneurosis or aviators' disease) E902.1
Chilblains E901.0
   due to manmade conditions E901.1
Choking (on) (any object except food or
   vomitus) E912
   apple E911
   bone E911
   food, any type (regurgitated) E911
   mucus or phlegm E912
   seed E911
Civil insurrection —*see* War operations
Cloudburst E908.8
Cold, exposure to (accidental) (excessive)
   (extreme) (place) E901.9
   causing chilblains or immersion foot E901.0
   due to
     manmade conditions E901.1
     specified cause NEC E901.8
     weather (conditions) E901.0
   late effect of NEC E929.5
   self-inflicted (undetermined whether
     accidental or intentional) E988.3
     suicidal E958.3
   suicide E958.3
Colic, lead, painters', or saturnine —*see*
   category E866
Collapse
   building E916
     burning E891.8
      private E890.8
   dam E909.3
   due to heat—*see* Heat
   machinery—*see* Accident, machine
   man-made structure E909.3
   postoperative NEC E878.9
   structure, burning NEC E891.8
Collision (accidental)

<table><tr><td>

Note—In the case of collisions between different types of vehicles, persons and objects, priority in classification is in the following order:

   Aircraft
   Watercraft
   Motor vehicle
   Railway vehicle
   Pedal Cycle
   Animal-drawn vehicle
   Animal being ridden
   Streetcar or other nonmotor road vehicle
   Other vehicle
   Pedestrian or person using pedestrian
     conveyance
   Object (except where falling from or set in
     motion by vehicle etc. listed above)

In the listing below, the combinations are listed only under the vehicle etc. having priority. For definitions, see Volume 1, page 477.

</td></tr></table>

   aircraft (with object or vehicle) (fixed)
     (movable) (moving) E841
     with
      person (while landing, taking off) (without
       accident to aircraft) E844
      powered (in transit) (with unpowered
       aircraft) E841
       while landing, taking off E840
      unpowered E842

Collision—*continued*
    another pedal cycle E826
    nonmotor road vehicle E826
    object (fallen) (fixed) (movable) (moving)
        not falling from or set in motion by
        aircraft, motor vehicle, or railway train
        NEC E826
    pedestrian (conveyance) E826
    person (using pedestrian conveyance) E826
    street car E826
  pedestrian(s) (conveyance) E917.9
    with fall E886.9
    in sports E886.0
    and
      crowd, human stampede (with fall) E917.1
      machinery—*see* Accident, machine
      object (fallen) (moving) (projected)
        (stationary) not falling from or set in
        motion by any vehicle classifiable to
        E800-E848 E917.9
      with fall E888
      caused by a crowd E917.1
      in
        running water E917.2
          with drowning or submersion—*see*
            Submersion
        sports E917.0
      vehicle, nonmotor, nonroad E848
    in
      running water E917.2
        with drowning or submersion—*see*
          Submersion
      sports E917.0
        with fall E886.0
  person(s) (using pedestrian conveyance) (*see*
    also Collision, pedestrian) E917.9
  railway (rolling stock) (train) (vehicle) (with
    (subsequent) derailment, explosion, fall or
    fire) E800
    with antecedent derailment E802
    and
      animal (carrying person) (herded)
        (unattended) E801
      another railway train or vehicle E800
      buffers E801
      fallen tree on railway E801
      farm machinery, nonmotor (in transport)
        (stationary) E801
      gates E801
      nonmotor vehicle E801
      object (fallen) (fixed) (movable) (moving)
        not falling from, set in motion by,
        aircraft or motor vehicle NEC E801
      pedal cycle E801
      pedestrian (conveyance) E805
      person (using pedestrian conveyance) E805
      platform E801
      rock on railway E801
      street car E801
  snow vehicle, motor-driven (not on public
    highway) E820
    and
      animal (being ridden) (-drawn vehicle)
        E820
      another off-road motor vehicle E820
      other motor vehicle, not on public
        highway E820
      other object or vehicle NEC, fixed or
        movable, not set in motion by aircraft
        or motor vehicle on highway E820
      pedal cycle E820

Collision—*continued*
    pedestrian (conveyance) E820
    railway train E820
  on public highway—*see* Collision, motor
    vehicle
  street car(s) E829
    and
      animal, herded, not being ridden,
        unattended E829
      nonmotor road vehicle NEC E829
      object (fallen) (fixed) (movable) (moving)
        not falling from or set in motion by
        aircraft, animal-drawn vehicle, animal
        being ridden, motor vehicle, pedal
        cycle, or railway train E829
      pedestrian (conveyance) E829
      person (using pedestrian conveyance) E829
  vehicle
    animal-drawn—*see* Collision,
      animal-drawn vehicle
    motor—*see* Collision, motor vehicle
    nonmotor
      nonroad E848
      and
        another nonmotor, nonroad vehicle
          E848
        object (fallen) (fixed) (movable)
          (moving) not falling from or set in
          motion by aircraft, animal-drawn
          vehicle, animal being ridden,
          motor vehicle, nonmotor road
          vehicle, pedal cycle, railway train,
          or streetcar E848
      road, except animal being ridden,
        animal-drawn vehicle, or pedal cycle
        E829
        and
          animal, herded, not being ridden,
            unattended E829
          another nonmotor road vehicle, except
            animal being ridden, animal-drawn
            vehicle, or pedal cycle E829
          object (fallen) (fixed) (movable)
            (moving) not falling from or set in
            motion by, aircraft, animal-drawn
            vehicle, animal being ridden,
            motor vehicle, pedal cycle, or
            railway train E829
          pedestrian (conveyance) E829
          person (using pedestrian conveyance)
            E829
          vehicle, nonmotor, nonroad E829
  watercraft E838
    and
      person swimming or water skiing E838
    causing
      drowning, submersion E830
      injury except drowning, submersion E831
Combustion, spontaneous —*see* Ignition
Complication of medical or surgical
    procedure or treatment
  as an abnormal reaction—*see* Reaction,
    abnormal
  delayed, without mention of
    misadventure—*see* Reaction, abnormal
  due to misadventure—*see* Misadventure
Compression
  divers' squeeze E902.2
  trachea by
    food E911
    foreign body, except food E912

Conflagration
building or structure, except private dwelling
(barn) (church) (convalescent or
residential home) (factory) (farm
outbuilding) (hospital) (hotel) (institution)
(educational) (dormitory) (residential)
(school) (shop) (store) (theatre) E891.9
with or causing (injury due to)
accident or injury NEC E891.9
specified circumstance NEC E891.8
burns, burning E891.3
carbon monoxide E891.2
fumes E891.2
polyvinylchloride (PVC) or similar
material E891.1
smoke E891.2
causing explosion E891.0
not in building or structure E892
private dwelling (apartment) (boarding house)
(camping place) (caravan) (farmhouse)
(home (private)) (house) (lodging house)
(private garage) (rooming house)
(tenement) E890.9
with or causing (injury due to)
accident or injury NEC E890.9
specified circumstance NEC E890.8
burns, burning E890.3
carbon monoxide E890.2
fumes E890.2
polyvinylchloride (PVC) or similar
material E890.1
smoke E890.2
causing explosion E890.0
Contact with
dry ice E901.1
liquid air, hydrogen, nitrogen E901.1
Cramp(s)
Heat—*see* Heat
swimmers (*see also* category E910) E910.2
not in recreation or sport E910.3
Cranking (car) (truck) (bus) (engine), injury
by E917.9
Crash
aircraft (in transit) (powered) E841
at landing, take-off E840
in war operations E994
on runway NEC E840
stated as
homicidal E968.8
suicidal E958.6
undetermined whether accidental or
intentional E988.6
unpowered E842
glider E842
motor vehicle—*see also* Accident, motor
vehicle
homicidal E968.5
suicidal E958.5
undetermined whether accidental or
intentional E988.5
Crushed (accidentally) E928.9
between
boat(s), ship(s), watercraft (and dock or
pier) (without accident to watercraft)
E838
after accident to, or collision, watercraft
E831
objects (moving) (stationary and moving)
E918

Crushed—*continued*
by
avalanche NEC E909.2
boat, ship, watercraft after accident to,
collision, watercraft E831
cave-in E916
with asphyxiation or suffocation (*see also*
Suffocation, due to, cave-in) E913.3
crowd, human stampede E917.1
falling
aircraft (*see also* Accident, aircraft) E841
in war operations E994
earth, material E916
with asphyxiation or suffocation (*see
also* Suffocation, due to, cave-in)
E913.3
object E916
on ship, watercraft E838
while loading, unloading watercraft E838
landslide NEC E909.2
lifeboat after abandoning ship E831
machinery—*see* Accident, machine
railway rolling stock, train, vehicle (part
of) E805
street car E829
vehicle NEC—*see* Accident, vehicle NEC
in
machinery—*see* Accident, machine
object E918
transport accident—*see* categories
E800-E848
late effect of NEC E929.9
Cut, cutting (any part of body) (accidental)
E920.9
by
arrow E920.8
axe E920.4
bayonet (*see also* Bayonet wound) E920.3
blender E920.2
broken glass E920.8
can opener E920.4
powered E920.2
chisel E920.4
circular saw E919.4
cutting or piercing instrument—*see also*
category E920
late effect of E929.8
dagger E920.3
dart E920.8
drill—*see* Accident, caused by drill
edge of stiff paper E920.8
electric
beater E920.2
fan E920.2
knife E920.2
mixer E920.2
fork E920.4
garden fork E920.4
hand saw or tool (not powered) E920.4
powered E920.1
hedge clipper E920.4
powered E920.1
hoe E920.4
ice pick E920.4
knife E920.3
electric E920.2
lathe turnings E920.8
lawn mower E920.4
powered E920.0
riding E919.8
machine—*see* Accident, machine

Effect(s)...—*continued*
   residence or prolonged visit (causing
     conditions classifiable to E902.0)
     E902.0
   due to
     diving E902.2
     specified cause NEC E902.8
   in aircraft E902.1
   cold, excessive (exposure to) (*see also* Cold,
     exposure to) E901.9
   heat (excessive) (*see also* Heat) E900.9
   hot
     place—*see* Heat
     weather E900.0
   insulation—*see* Heat
   late—*see* Late effect of
   motion E903
   nuclear explosion or weapon in war
     operations (blast) (fireball) (heat)
     (radiation) (direct) (secondary) E996
   radiation—*see* Radiation
   travel E903

Electric shock, electrocution (accidental)
   (from exposed wire, faulty appliance, high
   voltage cable, live rail, open socket) (by)
   (in) E925.9
   appliance or wiring
     domestic E925.0
     factory E925.2
     farm (building) E925.8
       house E925.0
     home E925.0
     industrial (conductor) (control apparatus)
       (transformer) E925.2
     outdoors E925.8
     public building E925.8
     residential institution E925.8
     school E925.8
     specified place NEC E925.8
   caused by other person
     stated as
       intentional, homicidal E968.8
       undetermined whether accidental or
         intentional E988.4
   electric power generating plant, distribution
     station E925.1
   homicidal (attempt) E968.8
   legal execution E978
   lightning E907
   machinery E925.9
     domestic E925.0
     factory E925.2
     farm E925.8
     home E925.0
   misadventure in medical or surgical procedure
     in electroshock therapy E873.4
   self-inflicted (undetermined whether
     accidental or intentional) E988.4
     stated as intentional E958.4
   stated as undetermined whether accidental or
     intentional E988.4
   suicidal (attempt) E958.4
   transmission line E925.1

Electrocution —*see* Electric shock

Embolism
   air (traumatic) NEC—*see* Air, embolism

Encephalitis
   lead or saturnine E866.0
     from pesticide NEC E863.4

Entanglement
   in
     bedclothes, causing suffocation E913.0
     wheel of pedal cycle E826

Entry of foreign body, material, any —*see*
   Foreign body

Execution, legal (any method) E978

Exhaustion
   cold—*see* Cold, exposure to
   due to excessive exertion E927
   heat—*see* Heat

Explosion (accidental) (in) (of) (on) E923.9
   acetylene E923.2
   aerosol can E921.8
   aircraft (in transit) (powered) E841
     at landing, take-off E840
     in war operations E994
     unpowered E842
   air tank (compressed) (in machinery) E921.1
   anesthetic gas in operating theatre E923.2
   automobile tire NEC E921.8
     causing transport accident—*see* categories
       E810-E825
   blasting (cap) (materials) E923.1
   boiler (machinery), not on transport vehicle
     E921.0
     steamship—*see* Explosion, watercraft
   bomb E923.8
     in war operations E993
       after cessation of hostilities E998
       atom, hydrogen or nuclear E996
       injury by fragments from E991.9
         antipersonnel bomb E991.3
   butane E923.2
   caused by
     other person
       stated as
         intentional, homicidal—*see* Assault,
           explosive
         undetermined whether accidental or
           homicidal E985.5
   coal gas E923.2
   detonator E923.1
   dynamite E923.1
   explosive (material) NEC E923.9
     gas(es) E923.2
     missile E923.8
       in war operations E993
         injury by fragments from E991.9
           antipersonnel bomb E991.3
     used in blasting operations E923.1
   fire-damp E923.2
   fireworks E923.0
   gas E923.2
     cylinder (in machinery) E921.1
     pressure tank (in machinery) E921.1
   gasoline (fumes) (tank) not in moving motor
     vehicle E923.2
   grain store (military) (munitions) E923.8
   grenade E923.8
     in war operations E993
       injury by fragments from E991.9
   homicide (attempt)—*see* Assault, explosive
   hot water heater, tank (in machinery) E921.0
   in mine (of explosive gases) NEC E923.2
   late effect of NEC E929.8
   machinery—*see also* Accident, machine
     pressure vessel—*see* Explosion, pressure
       vessel
   methane E923.2

Fire —*continued*
  prairie (uncontrolled) E892
  self-inflicted (unspecified whether accidental
    or intentional) E988.1
    stated as intentional, purposeful E958.1
  specified NEC E898.1
    with
      conflagration—*see* Conflagration
      ignition (of)
        clothing—*see* Ignition, clothes
        highly inflammable material (benzine)
          (fat) (gasoline) (kerosene) (paraffin)
          (petrol) E894
  started by other person
    stated as
      with intent to injure or kill E968.0
      undetermined whether or not with intent
        to injure or kill E988.1
  suicide (attempted) E958.1
    late effect of E959
  tunnel (uncontrolled) E892
Fireball effects from nuclear explosion in war
  operations E996
Fireworks (explosion) E923.0
Flash burns from explosion (*see also*
  Explosion) E923.9
Flood (any injury) (resulting from storm)
  E908.2
  caused by collapse of dam or manmade
    structure E909.3
Forced landing (aircraft) E840
Foreign body, object or material (entrance
  into (accidental))
  air passage (causing injury) E915
    with asphyxia, obstruction, suffocation
      E912
      food or vomitus E911
    nose (with asphyxia, obstruction,
      suffocation) E912
    causing injury without asphyxia,
      obstruction, suffocation E915
  alimentary canal (causing injury) (with
    obstruction) E915
    with asphyxia, obstruction respiratory
      passage, suffocation E912
      food E911
    mouth E915
      with asphyxia, obstruction, suffocation
        E912
      food E911
    pharynx E915
      with asphyxia, obstruction, suffocation
        E912
      food E911
  aspiration (with asphyxia, obstruction
    respiratory passage, suffocation) E912
  causing injury without asphyxia,
    obstruction respiratory passage,
    suffocation E915
    food (regurgitated) (vomited) E911
      causing injury without asphyxia,
        obstruction respiratory passage,
        suffocation E915
    mucus (not of newborn) E912
    phlegm E912
  bladder (causing injury or obstruction) E915
  bronchus, bronchi—*see* Foreign body, air
    passages
  conjunctival sac E914
  digestive system—*see* Foreign body,
    alimentary canal

Foreign body, object or material—*continued*
  ear (causing injury or obstruction) E915
  esophagus (causing injury or obstruction) (*see*
    also Foreign body, alimentary canal) E915
  eye (any part) E914
  eyelid E914
  hairball (stomach) (with obstruction) E915
  ingestion—*see* Foreign body, alimentary canal
  inhalation—*see* Foreign body, aspiration
  intestine (causing injury or obstruction) E915
  iris E914
  lacrimal apparatus E914
  larynx—*see* Foreign body, air passage
  late effect of NEC E929.8
  lung—*see* Foreign body, air passage
  mouth—*see* Foreign body, alimentary canal,
    mouth
  nasal passage—*see* Foreign body, air passage,
    nose
  nose—*see* Foreign body, air passage, nose
  ocular muscle E914
  operation wound (left in)—*see* Misadventure,
    foreign object
  orbit E914
  pharynx—*see* Foreign body, alimentary canal,
    pharynx
  rectum (causing injury or obstruction) E915
  stomach (hairball) (causing injury or
    obstruction) E915
  tear ducts or glands E914
  trachea—*see* Foreign body, air passage
  urethra (causing injury or obstruction) E915
  vagina (causing injury or obstruction) E915
Found dead, injured
  from exposure (to)—*see* Exposure
  on
    public highway E819
    railway right of way E807
Fracture (circumstances unknown or
  unspecified) E887
  due to specified external means—*see* manner
    of accident
  late effect of NEC E929.3
  occurring in water transport NEC E835
Freezing —*see* Cold, exposure to
Frostbite E901.0
  due to manmade conditions E901.1
Frozen —*see* Cold, exposure to

G

Garrotting, homicidal (attempted) E963
Gored E906.8
Gunshot wound (*see also* Shooting) E922.9

H

Hailstones, injury by E904.3
Hairball (stomach) (with obstruction) E915
Hanged himself (*see also* Hanging,
  self-inflicted) E983.0
Hang gliding E842
Hanging (accidental) E913.8
  caused by other person
    in accidental circumstances E913.8
    stated as
      intentional, homicidal E963
      undetermined whether accidental or
        intentional E983.0

Hit, hitting—*continued*
  snow vehicle, motor-driven (not on public highway) E820
    on public highway E814
  street car E829
  vehicle NEC—*see* Accident, vehicle NEC
Homicide, homicidal (attempt) (justifiable) (*see also* Assault) E968.9
Hot
  liquid, object, substance, accident caused by—*see also* Accident, caused by, hot, by type of substance
    late effect of E929.8
  place, effects—*see* Heat
  weather, effects E900.0
Humidity, causing problem E904.3
Hunger E904.1
  resulting from
    abandonment or neglect E904.0
    transport accident—*see* categories E800-E848
Hurricane (any injury) E908.0
Hypobarism, hypobaropathy —*see* Effects of, air pressure
Hypothermia —*see* Cold, exposure to

I

Ictus
  caloris—*see* Heat
  solaris E900.0
Ignition (accidental)
  anesthetic gas in operating theatre E923.2
  bedclothes
    with
      conflagration—*see* Conflagration
      ignition (of)
        clothing—*see* Ignition, clothes
        highly inflammable material (benzine) (fat) (gasoline) (kerosene) (paraffin) (petrol) E894
  benzine E894
  clothes, clothing (from controlled fire) (in building) E893.9
    with conflagration—*see* Conflagration
    from
      bonfire E893.2
      highly inflammable material E894
      sources or material as listed in E893.8
      trash fire E893.2
      uncontrolled fire—*see* Conflagration
    in
      private dwelling E893.0
      specified building or structure, except private dwelling E893.1
    not in building or structure E893.2
  explosive material—*see* Explosion
  fat E894
  gasoline E894
  kerosene E894
  material
    explosive—*see* Explosion
    highly inflammable E894
      with conflagration—*see* Conflagration
      with explosion E923.2
  nightdress—*see* Ignition, clothes
  paraffin E894
  petrol E894
Immersion —*see* Submersion
Implantation of quills of porcupine E906.8

Inanition (from) E904.9
  hunger—*see* Lack of, food
  resulting from homicidal intent E968.4
  thirst—*see* Lack of, water
Inattention after, at birth E904.0
  homicidal, infanticidal intent E968.4
Infanticide (*see also* Assault)
Ingestion
  foreign body (causing injury) (with obstruction)—*see* Foreign body, alimentary canal
  poisonous substance NEC—*see* Table of drugs and chemicals
Inhalation
  excessively cold substance, manmade E901.1
  foreign body—*see* Foreign body, aspiration
  liquid air, hydrogen, nitrogen E901.1
  mucus, not of newborn (with asphyxia, obstruction respiratory passage, suffocation) E912
  phlegm (with asphyxia, obstruction respiratory passage, suffocation) E912
  poisonous gas—*see* Table of drugs and chemicals
  smoke from, due to
    fire —*see* Fire
    tobacco, second-hand E869.4
  vomitus (with asphyxia, obstruction respiratory passage, suffocation) E911
Injury, injured (accidental(ly)) NEC E928.9
  by, caused by, from
    air rifle (B-B gun) E922.4
    animal (not being ridden) NEC E906.9
      being ridden (in sport or transport) E828
    assault (*see also* Assault) E968.9
    avalanche E909.2
    bayonet (*see also* Bayonet wound) E920.3
    being thrown against some part of, or object in
      motor vehicle (in motion) (on public highway) E818
        not on public highway E825
      nonmotor road vehicle NEC E829
      off-road motor vehicle NEC E821
      railway train E806
      snow vehicle, motor-driven E820
      street car E829
    bending E927
    bite, human E928.3
    broken glass E920.8
    bullet—*see* Shooting
    cave-in (*see also* Suffocation, due to, cave-in) E913.3
      without asphyxiation or suffocation E916
    cloudburst E908.8
    cutting or piercing instrument (*see also* Cut) E920.9
    cyclone E908.1
    earth surface movement or eruption E909.9
    earthquake E909.0
    electric current (*see also* Electric shock) E925.9
    explosion (*see also* Explosion) E923.9
    fire—*see* Fire
    flare, Very pistol E922.8
    flood E908.2
    foreign body—*see* Foreign body
    hailstones E904.3
    hurricane E908.0
    landslide E909.2

Injury, injured—*continued*
  law-enforcing agent, police, in course of
     legal intervention—*see* Legal
     intervention
  lightning E907
  live rail or live wire—*see* Electric shock
  machinery—*see also* Accident, machine
    aircraft, without accident to aircraft E844
    boat, ship, watercraft (deck) (engine
       room) (galley) (laundry) (loading) E836
  missile
    explosive E923.8
    firearm—*see* Shooting
    in war operations—*see* War operations,
      missile
  moving part of motor vehicle (in motion)
    (on public highway) E818
    not on public highway, nontraffic accident
     E825
    while alighting, boarding, entering,
      leaving—*see* Fall, from, motor vehicle,
      while alighting, boarding
  nail E920.8
  needle (sewing) E920.4
    hypodermic E920.5
  noise E928.1
  object
    fallen on
      motor vehicle (in motion) (on public
        highway) E818
      not on public highway E825
    falling—*see* Hit by, object, falling
  radiation—*see* Radiation
  railway rolling stock, train, vehicle (part
    of) E805
    door or window E806
  rotating propeller, aircraft E844
  rough landing of off-road type motor
    vehicle (after leaving ground or rough
    terrain) E821
    snow vehicle E820
  saber (*see also* Wound, saber) E920.3
  shot—*see* Shooting
  sound waves E928.1
  splinter or sliver, wood E920.8
  storm E908.9
  straining E927
  street car (door) E829
  suicide (attempt) E958.9
  sword E920.3
  third rail—*see* Electric shock
  thunderbolt E907
  tidal wave E909.4
    caused by storm E908.0
  tornado E908.1
  torrential rain E908.2
  twisting E927
  vehicle NEC—*see* Accident, vehicle NEC
  vibration E928.2
  volcanic eruption E909.1
  weapon burst, in war operations E993
  weightlessness (in spacecraft, real or
    simulated) E928.0
  wood splinter or sliver E920.8
  due to
    civil insurrection—*see* War operations
      occurring after cessation of hostilities E998
    war operations—*see* War operations
      occurring after cessation of hostilities
      E998
  homicidal (*see also* Assault) E968.9

Injury, injured—*continued*
  in, on
    civil insurrection—*see* War operations
    fight E960.0
    parachute descent (voluntary) (without
      accident to aircraft) E844
      with accident to aircraft—*see* categories
        E840-E842
    public highway E819
    railway right of way E807
    war operations—*see* War operations
  inflicted (by)
    in course of arrest (attempted),
      suppression of disturbance,
      maintenance of order, by
      law-enforcing agents—*see* Legal
      intervention
    law-enforcing agent (on duty)—*see* Legal
      intervention
    other person
      stated as
        accidental E928.9
        homicidal, intentional—*see* Assault
        undetermined whether accidental or
          intentional—*see* Injury, stated as
          undetermined
    police (on duty)—*see* Legal intervention
  late effect of E929.9
  purposely (inflicted) by other person(s)—*see*
    Assault
  self-inflicted (unspecified whether accidental
    or intentional) E988.9
    stated as
      accidental E928.9
      intentionally, purposely E958.9
  specified cause NEC E928.8
  stated as
    undetermined whether accidentally or
      purposely inflicted (by) E988.9
    cut (any part of body) E986
    cutting or piercing instrument (classifiable
      to E920) E986
    drowning E984
    explosive(s) (missile) E985.5
    falling from high place E987.9
      manmade structure, except residential
        E987.1
      natural site E987.2
      residential premises E987.0
    hanging E983.0
    knife E986
    late effect of E989
    puncture (any part of body) E986
    shooting—*see* Shooting, stated as
      undetermined whether accidental or
      intentional
    specified means NEC E988.8
    stab (any part of body) E986
    strangulation—*see* Suffocation, stated as
      undetermined whether accidental or
      intentional
    submersion E984
    suffocation—*see* Suffocation, stated as
      undetermined whether accidental or
      intentional
  to child due to criminal abortion E968.8
Insufficient nourishment —*see also* Lack of,
  food
  homicidal intent E968.4
Insulation, effects —*see* Heat

Interruption of respiration by
food lodged in esophagus E911
foreign body, except food, in esophagus E912
Intervention, legal —*see* Legal intervention
Intoxication, drug or poison —*see* Table of
drugs and chemicals
Irradiation —*see* Radiation

J

Jammed (accidentally)
between objects (moving) (stationary and
moving) E918
in object E918
Jumped or fell from high place, so stated
—*see* Jumping, from, high place, stated as
in undetermined circumstances
Jumping
before train, vehicle or other moving object
(unspecified whether accidental or
intentional) E988.0
stated as
intentional, purposeful E958.0
suicidal (attempt) E958.0
from
aircraft
by parachute (voluntarily) (without
accident to aircraft) E844
due to accident to aircraft—*see* categories
E840-E842
boat, ship, watercraft (into water)
after accident to, fire on, watercraft E830
and subsequently struck by (part of)
boat E831
burning, crushed, sinking E830
and subsequently struck by (part of)
boat E831
voluntarily, without accident (to boat) with
injury other than drowning or
submersion E883.0
building
burning E891.8
private E890.8
cable car (not on rails) E847
on rails E829
high place
in accidental circumstances or in
sport—*see* categories E880-E884
stated as
with intent to injure self E957.9
man-made structures NEC E957.1
natural sites E957.2
residential premises E957.0
in undetermined circumstances E987.9
man-made structures NEC E987.1
natural sites E987.2
residential premises E987.0
suicidal (attempt) E957.9
man-made structures NEC E957.1
natural sites E957.1
residential premises E957.0
motor vehicle (in motion) (on public
highway)—*see* Fall, from, motor
vehicle
nonmotor road vehicle NEC E829
street car E829
structure, burning NEC E891.8

Jumping—*continued*
into water
with injury other than drowning or
submersion E883.0
drowning or submersion—*see* Submersion
from, off, watercraft—*see* Jumping, from,
boat
Justifiable homicide —*see* Assault

K

Kicked by
animal E906.8
person(s) (accidentally) E917.9
with intent to injure or kill E960.0
as, or caused by a crowd (with fall)
E917.1
in fight E960.0
in sports (with fall) E917.0
Kicking against
object (moving) (projected) (stationary) E917.9
in sports E917.0
person—*see* Striking against, person
Killed, killing (accidentally) NEC (*see also*
Injury) E928.9
in
action—*see* War operations
brawl, fight (hand) (fists) (foot) E960.0
by weapon—*see also* Assault
cutting, piercing E966
firearm—*see* Shooting, homicide
self
stated as
accident E928.9
suicide—*see* Suicide
unspecified whether accidental or suicidal
E988.9
Knocked down (accidentally) (by) NEC E928.9
animal (not being ridden) E906.8
being ridden (in sport or transport) E828
blast from explosion (*see also* Explosion)
E923.9
crowd, human stampede E917.1
late effect of—*see* Late effect
person (accidentally) E917.9
in brawl, fight E960.0
in sports E917.0
transport vehicle—*see* vehicle involved under
Hit by
while boxing E917.0

L

Laceration NEC E928.9
Lack of
air (refrigerator or closed place), suffocation
by E913.2
care (helpless person) (infant) (newborn)
E904.0
homicidal intent E968.4
food except as result of transport accident
E904.1
helpless person, infant, newborn due to
abandonment or neglect E904.0
water except as result of transport accident
E904.2
helpless person, infant, newborn due to
abandonment or neglect E904.0

M

Misadventures—*continued*
  performance of inappropriate operation E876.5
  puncture—*see* Misadventure, cut
  specified type NEC E876.8
    failure
      suture or ligature during surgical operation
        E876.2
      to introduce or to remove tube or
        instrument E876.4
        foreign object left in body E871.9
    infusion of wrong fluid E876.1
    performance of inappropriate operation
      E876.5
    transfusion of mismatched blood E876.0
    wrong
      fluid in infusion E876.1
      placement of endotracheal tube during
        anesthetic procedure E876.3
  transfusion—*see also* Misadventure, by
      specific type, transfusion
    excessive amount of blood E873.0
    mismatched blood E876.0
  wrong
    drug given in error—*see* Table of drugs
      and chemicals
    fluid in infusion E876.1
    placement of endotracheal tube during
      anesthetic procedure E876.3
Motion (effects) E903
  sickness E903
Mountain sickness E902.0
**Mucus aspiration or inhalation, not of
  newborn** (with asphyxia, obstruction
    respiratory passage, suffocation) E912
Mudslide of cataclysmic nature E909.2
Murder (attempt) (*see also* Assault) E968.9

N

Nail, injury by E920.8
Needlestick (sewing needle) E920.4
  hypodermic E920.5
Neglect —*see also* Privation
  criminal E968.4
  homicidal intent E968.4
Noise (causing injury) (pollution) E928.1

O

Object
  falling
    from, in, on, hitting
      aircraft E844
        due to accident to aircraft—*see*
          categories E840-E842
      machinery—*see also* Accident, machine
        not in operation E916
      motor vehicle (in motion) (on public
        highway) E818
        not on public highway E825
        stationary E916
      nonmotor road vehicle NEC E829
      pedal cycle E826
      person E916
      railway rolling stock, train, vehicle E806
      street car E829
      watercraft E838
        due to accident to watercraft E831

Object—*continued*
  set in motion by
    accidental explosion of pressure
      vessel—*see* category E921
    firearm—*see* category E922
    machine(ry)—*see* Accident, machine
    transport vehicle—*see* categories
      E800-E848
  thrown from, in, on, towards
    aircraft E844
    cable car (not on rails) E847
      on rails E829
    motor vehicle (in motion) (on public
      highway) E818
      not on public highway E825
    nonmotor road vehicle NEC E829
    pedal cycle E826
    street car E829
    vehicle NEC—*see* Accident, vehicle NEC
Obstruction
  air passages, larynx, respiratory passages
    by
      external means NEC—*see* Suffocation
      food, any type (regurgitated) (vomited)
        E911
      material or object, except food E912
      mucus E912
      phlegm E912
      vomitus E911
  digestive tract, except mouth or pharynx
    by
      food, any type E915
      foreign body (any) E915
  esophagus
    food E911
    foreign body, except food E912
    without asphyxia or obstruction of
      respiratory passage E915
  mouth or pharynx
    by
      food, any type E911
      material or object, except food E912
  respiration—*see* Obstruction, air passages
Oil in eye E914
Overdose
  anesthetic (drug)—*see* Table of drugs and
    chemicals
  drug—*see* Table of drugs and chemicals
Overexertion (lifting) (pulling) (pushing) E927
Overexposure (accidental) (to)
  cold (*see also* Cold, exposure to) E901.9
    due to manmade conditions E901.1
  heat (*see also* Heat) E900.9
  radiation—*see* Radiation
  radioactivity—*see* Radiation
  sun, except sunburn E900.0
  weather—*see* Exposure
  wind—*see* Exposure
Overheated (*see also* Heat) E900.9
Overlaid E913.0
Overturning (accidental)
  animal-drawn vehicle E827
  boat, ship, watercraft
    causing
      drowning, submersion E830
      injury except drowning, submersion E831
  machinery—*see* Accident, machine
  motor vehicle (*see also* Loss of control,
    motor vehicle) E816
    with antecedent collision on public
      highway—*see* Collision, motor vehicle

Radiation—*continued*
  inadvertent exposure of patient (receiving test
    or therapy) E873.3
  infrared (heaters and lamps) E926.1
    excessive heat E900.1
  ionized, ionizing (particles, artificially
    accelerated) E926.8
    electromagnetic E926.3
  isotopes, radioactive—*see* Radiation,
    radioactive isotopes
  laser(s) E926.4
    in war operations E997.0
    misadventure in medical care—*see*
      Misadventure, failure, in dosage,
      radiation
  late effect of NEC E929.8
    excessive heat from—*see* Heat
  light sources (visible) (ultraviolet) E926.2
  misadventure in medical or surgical
    procedure—*see* Misadventure, failure, in
    dosage, radiation
  overdose (in medical or surgical procedure)
    E873.2
  radar E926.0
  radioactive isotopes E926.5
    atomic power plant malfunction E926.5
      in water transport E838
    misadventure in medical or surgical
      treatment—*see* Misadventure, failure,
      in dosage, radiation
  radiobiologicals—*see* Radiation, radioactive
    isotopes
    radiofrequency E926.0
  radiopharmaceuticals—*see* Radiation,
    radioactive isotopes
  radium NEC E926.9
  sun E926.2
    excessive heat from E900.0
  welding arc or torch E926.2
    excessive heat from E900.1
  x-rays (hard) (soft) E926.3
    misadventure in medical or surgical
      treatment—*see* Misadventure, failure,
      in dosage, radiation
Rape E960.1
Reaction —abnormal to or following(medical
  or surgical procedure) E879.9
  amputation (of limbs) E878.5
  anastomosis (arteriovenous) (blood vessel)
    (gastrojejunal) (skin) (tendon) (natural,
    artificial material, tissue) E878.2
    external stoma, creation of E878.3
  aspiration (of fluid) E879.4
    tissue E879.8
  biopsy E879.8
  blood
    sampling E879.7
    transfusion
      procedure E879.8
  bypass—*see* Reaction, abnormal, anastomosis
  catheterization
    cardiac E879.0
    urinary E879.6
  colostomy E878.3
  cystostomy E878.3
  dialysis (kidney) E879.1
  drugs or biologicals—*see* Table of drugs and
    chemicals
  duodenostomy E878.3
  electroshock therapy E879.3
  formation of external stoma E878.3

Reaction—*continued*
  gastrostomy E878.3
  graft—*see* Reaction, abnormal, anastomosis
  hypothermia E879.8
  implant, implantation (of)
    artificial
      internal device (cardiac pacemaker)
        (electrodes in brain) (heart valve
        prosthesis) (orthopedic) E878.1
      material or tissue (for anastomosis or
        bypass) E878.2
        with creation of external stoma E878.3
    natural tissues (for anastomosis or
      bypass) E878.2
      as transplantion—*see* Reaction, abnormal,
      transplant
      with creation of external stoma E878.3
  infusion
    procedure E879.8
  injection
    procedure E879.8
  insertion of gastric or duodenal sound E879.5
  insulin-shock therapy E879.3
  lumbar puncture E879.4
  perfusion E879.1
  procedures other than surgical operation (*see*
    also Reaction, abnormal, by specific type
    of procedure) E879.9
    specified procedure NEC E879.8
  radiological procedure or therapy E879.2
  removal of organ (partial) (total) NEC E878.6
    with
      anastomosis, bypass or graft E878.2
      formation of external stoma E878.3
      implant of artificial internal device E878.1
      transplant(ation)
        partial organ E878.4
        whole organ E878.0
  sampling
    blood E879.7
    fluid NEC E879.4
    tissue E879.8
  shock therapy E879.3
  surgical operation (*see also* Reaction,
    abnormal, by specified type of operation)
    E878.9
    restorative NEC E878.4
      with
        anastomosis, bypass or graft E878.2
        formation of external stoma E878.3
        implant(ation)—*see* Reaction, abnormal,
        implant
        transplant(ation)—*see* Reaction,
        abnormal, transplant
    specified operation NEC E878.8
  thoracentesis E879.4
  transfusion
    procedure E879.8
  transplant, transplantation (heart) (kidney)
    (liver) E878.0
    partial organ E878.4
  ureterostomy E878.3
  vaccination E879.8
Reduction in
  atmospheric pressure—*see also* Effects of, air
    pressure
    while surfacing from
      deep water diving causing caisson or
        divers' disease, palsy or paralysis
        E902.2
      underground E902.8

Residual (effect)—*see* Late effect
Rock falling on or hitting (accidentally)
  motor vehicle (in motion) (on public
    highway) E818
    not on public highway E825
  nonmotor road vehicle NEC E829
  pedal cycle E826
  person E916
  railway rolling stock, train, vehicle E806
Running off, away
  animal (being ridden) (in sport or transport)
    E828
    not being ridden E906.8
  animal-drawn vehicle E827
  rails, railway (*see also* Derailment) E802
  roadway
    motor vehicle (without antecedent
      collision) E816
      nontraffic accident E825
        with antecedent collision—*see* Collision,
          motor vehicle, not on public highway
    with
      antecedent collision—*see* Collision motor
        vehicle
      subsequent collision
        involving any object, person or vehicle
          not on public highway E816
          on public highway E811
    nonmotor road vehicle NEC E829
    pedal cycle E826
Run over (accidentally) (by)
  animal (not being ridden) E906.8
    being ridden (in sport or transport) E828
  animal-drawn vehicle E827
  machinery—*see* Accident, machine
  motor vehicle (on public highway)—*see* Hit
    by, motor vehicle
  nonmotor road vehicle NEC E829
  railway train E805
  street car E829
  vehicle NEC E848

S

Saturnism E866.0
  from insecticide NEC E863.4
Scald, scalding (accidental) (by) (from) (in)
  E924.0
  acid—*see* Scald, caustic
  boiling tap water E924.2
  caustic or corrosive liquid, substance E924.1
    swallowed—*see* Table of drugs and
      chemicals
  homicide (attempt)—*see* Assault, burning
  inflicted by other person
    stated as
      intentional or homicidal E968.3
      undetermined whether accidental or
        intentional E988.2
  late effect of NEC E929.8
  liquid (boiling) (hot) E924.0
  local application of externally applied
    substance in medical or surgical care
    E873.5
  molten metal E924.0
  self-inflicted (unspecified whether accidental
    or intentional) E988.2
    stated as intentional, purposeful E958.2
  stated as undetermined whether accidental or
    intentional E988.2

Scald, scalding—*continued*
  steam E924.0
  tap water (boiling) E924.2
  transport accident—*see* categories E800-E848
  vapor E924.0
Scratch, cat E906.8
Sea
  sickness E903
Self-mutilation —*see* Suicide
Shock
  anaphylactic (*see also* Table of drugs and
    chemicals) E947.9
    due to
      bite (venomous)—*see* Bite, venomous NEC
      sting—*see* Sting
  electric (*see also* Electric shock) E925.9
  from electric appliance or current (*see also*
    Electric shock) E925.9
Shooting, shot (accidental(ly)) E922.9
  air gun E922.4
  BB gun E922.4
  hand gun (pistol) (revolver) E922.0
  himself (*see also* Shooting, self-inflicted)
    E985.4
    hand gun (pistol) (revolver) E985.0
    military firearm, except hand gun E985.3
      hand gun (pistol) (revolver) E985.0
    rifle (hunting) E985.2
      military E985.3
    shotgun (automatic) E985.1
    specified firearm NEC E985.4
    Verey pistol E985.4
  homicide (attempt) E965.4
    air gun E968.6
    BB gun E968.6
    hand gun (pistol) (revolver) E965.0
    military firearm, except hand gun E965.3
      hand gun (pistol) (revolver) E965.0
    rifle (hunting) E965.2
      military E965.3
    shotgun (automatic) E965.1
    specified firearm NEC E965.4
    Verey pistol E965.4
  inflicted by other person
    in accidental circumstances E922.9
      hand gun (pistol) (revolver) E922.0
      military firearm, except hand gun E922.3
        hand gun (pistol) (revolver) E922.0
      rifle (hunting) E922.2
        military E922.3
      shotgun (automatic) E922.1
      specified firearm NEC E922.8
      Verey pistol E922.8
    stated as
      intentional, homicidal E965.4
        hand gun (pistol) (revolver) E965.0
        military firearm, except hand gun E965.3
          hand gun (pistol) (revolver) E965.0
        rifle (hunting) E965.2
          military E965.3
        shotgun (automatic) E965.1
        specified firearm E965.4
        Verey pistol E965.4
      undetermined whether accidental or
        intentional E985.4
      air gun E985.6
      BB gun E985.6
      hand gun (pistol) (revolver) E985.0
      military firearm, except hand gun E985.3
        hand gun (pistol) (revolver) E985.0
      rifle (hunting) E985.2

T

Tackle in sport E886.0
Thermic fever E900.9
Thermoplegia E900.9
Thirst —*see also* Lack of water
  resulting from accident connected with
      transport—*see* categories E800-E848
Thrown (accidentally)
  against object in or part of vehicle
    by motion of vehicle
      aircraft E844
      boat, ship, watercraft E838
      motor vehicle (on public highway) E818
        not on public highway E825
        off-road type (not on public highway)
            E821
          on public highway E818
          snow vehicle E820
            on public highway E818
      nonmotor road vehicle NEC E829
      railway rolling stock, train, vehicle E806
      street car E829
  from
    animal (being ridden) (in sport or
        transport) E828
    high place, homicide (attempt) E968.1
    machinery—*see* Accident, machine
    vehicle NEC—*see* Accident, vehicle NEC
  off—*see* Thrown, from
  overboard (by motion of boat, ship,
      watercraft) E832
    by accident to boat, ship, watercraft E830
Thunderbolt NEC E907
Tidal wave (any injury) E909.4
  caused by storm E908.0
Took
  overdose of drug—*see* Table of drugs and
      chemicals
  poison—*see* Table of drugs and chemicals
Tornado (any injury) E908.1
Torrential rain (any injury) E908.2
Traffic accident NEC E819
Trampled by animal E906.8
  being ridden (in sport or transport) E828
Trapped (accidentally)
  between
    objects (moving) (stationary and moving)
        E918
  by
    door of
      elevator E918
      motor vehicle (on public highway) (while
          alighting, boarding)—*see* Fall, from,
          motor vehicle, while alighting
      railway train (underground) E806
      street car E829
      subway train E806
  in object E918
Travel (effects) E903
  sickness E903
Tree
  falling on or hitting E916
    motor vehicle (in motion) (on public
        highway) E818
      not on public highway E825
    nonmotor road vehicle NEC E829
    pedal cycle E826
    person E916
    railway rolling stock, train, vehicle E806
    street car E829

Trench foot E901.0
Tripping over animal, carpet, curb, rug, or
    small object (with fall) E885.9
  without fall—*see* Striking against, object
Tsunami E909.4
Twisting, injury in E927

V

Violence, nonaccidental (*see also* Assault)
    E968.9
Volcanic eruption (any injury) E909.1
Vomitus in air passages (with asphyxia,
    obstruction or suffocation) E911

W

War operations (during hostilities) (injury)
    (by) (in) E995
  after cessation of hostilities, injury due to
      E998
  air blast E993
  aircraft burned, destroyed, exploded, shot
      down E994
  asphyxia from
    chemical E997.2
    fire, conflagration (caused by
        fire-producing device or conventional
        weapon) E990.9
      from nuclear explosion E996
      petrol bomb E990.0
    fumes E997.2
    gas E997.2
  battle wound NEC E995
  bayonet E995
  biological warfare agents E997.1
  blast (air) (effects) E993
    from nuclear explosion E996
    underwater E992
  bomb (mortar) (explosion) E993
    after cessation of hostilities E998
    fragments, injury by E991.9
      antipersonnel E991.3
  bullet(s) (from carbine, machine gun, pistol,
      rifle, shotgun) E991.2
    rubber E991.0
  burn from
    chemical E997.2
    fire, conflagration (caused by
        fire-producing device or conventional
        weapon) E990.9
      from nuclear explosion E996
      petrol bomb E990.0
    gas E997.2
  burning aircraft E994
  chemical E997.2
  chlorine E997.2
  conventional warfare, specified form NEC
      E995
  crushing by falling aircraft E994
  depth charge E992
  destruction of aircraft E994
  disability as sequela one year or more after
      injury E999
  drowning E995
  effect (direct) (secondary) nuclear weapon
      E996
  explosion (artillery shell) (breech block)
      (cannon shell) E993

RAILWAY ACCIDENTS (E800–E807)

The following fourth–digit subdivisions are for use with categories E800–E807 to identify the injured person.

.0 Railway employee

Any person who by virtue of his employment in connection with a railway, whether by the railway company or not, is at increased risk of involvement in a railway accident, such as:

catering staff on train	postal staff on train
driver	railway fireman
guard	shunter
porter	sleeping car attendant

.1 Passenger on railway

Any authorized person traveling on a train, except a railway employee

Excludes: intending passenger waiting at station (.8)
unauthorized rider on railway vehicle (.8)

.2 Pedestrian

See definition (r), Vol. 1, page 479

.3 Pedal cyclist

See definition (p), Vol. 1, page 479

.8 Other specified person

Intending passenger waiting at station

Unauthorized rider on railway vehicle

.9 Unspecified person

MOTOR VEHICLE TRAFFIC AND NONTRAFFIC ACCIDENTS
(E810–825)

The following fourth–digit subdivisions are for use with categories E810–E819 and E820–E825 to identify the injured person:

.0 Driver of motor vehicle other than motorcycle

See definition (l), Vol. 1, page 479

.1 Passenger in motor vehicle other than motorcycle

See definition (l), Vol. 1, page 479

.2 Motorcyclist

See definition (l), Vol. 1, page 479

.3 Passenger on motorcycle

See definition (l), Vol. 1, page 479

.4 Occupant of streetcar

.5 Rider of animal; occupant of animal–drawn vehicle

.6 Pedal cyclist

See definition (p), Vol. 1, page 479

.7 Pedestrian

See definition (r), Vol. 1, page 479

.8 Other specified person

Occupant of vehicle other than above

Person in railway train involved in accident

Unauthorized rider of motor vehicle

.9 Unspecified person

OTHER ROAD VEHICLE ACCIDENTS (E826–E829)

(animal–drawn vehicle, streetcar, pedal cycle, and other nonmotor road vehicle accidents)

The following fourth–digit subdivisions are for use with categories E826–E829 to identify the injured person:

.0 Pedestrian

    See definition (r), Vol. 1, page 479

.1 Pedal cyclist (does not apply to codes E827, E828, E829)

    See definition (p), Vol. 1, page 479

.2 Rider of animal (does not apply to code E829)

.3 Occupant of animal–drawn vehicle (does not apply to codes E828, E829)

.4 Occupant of streetcar

.8 Other specified person

.9 Unspecified person

WATER TRANSPORT ACCIDENTS (E830–E838)

The following fourth–digit subdivisions are for use with categories E830–E838 to identify the injured person:

.0 Occupant of small boat, unpowered

.1 Occupant of small boat, powered

See definition (t), Vol. 1, page 479

Excludes: water skier (.4)

.2 Occupant of other watercraft — crew

Persons:

engaged in operation of watercraft

providing passenger services [cabin attendants, ship's physician, catering personnel]

working on ship during voyage in other capacity [musician in band, operators of shops and beauty parlors]

.3 Occupant of other watercraft — other than crew

Passenger

Occupant of lifeboat, other than crew, after abandoning ship

.4 Water skier

.5 Swimmer

.6 Dockers, stevedores

Longshoreman employed on the dock in loading and unloading ships

.8 Other specified person

Immigration and custom officials on board ship

Person:

accompanying passenger or member of crew

visiting boat

Pilot (guiding ship into port)

.9 Unspecified person

AIR AND SPACE TRANSPORT ACCIDENTS (E840–E845)

The following fourth–digit subdivisions are for use with categories E840–E845 to identify the injured person:

.0 Occupant of spacecraft

.1 Occupant of military aircraft, any

Crew	in military aircraft [air force] [army]
Passenger (civilian) (military)	[national guard] [navy]
Troops	

> *Excludes:* occupants of aircraft operated under jurisdiction of police departments (.5) parachutist (.7).

.2 Crew of commercial aircraft (powered) in surface to surface transport

.3 Other occupant of commercial aircraft (powered) in surface to surface transport

Flight personnel:

> not part of crew
> on familiarization flight

Passenger on aircraft (powered) NOS

.4 Occupant of commercial aircraft (powered) in surface to air transport

Occupant [crew] [passenger] of aircraft (powered) engaged in activities, such as:

> aerial spraying (crops) (fire retardants)
> air drops of emergency supplies
> air drops of parachutists, except from military craft
> crop dusting
> lowering of construction material [bridge or telephone pole]
> sky writing

.5 Occupant of other powered aircraft

Occupant [crew] [passenger] of aircraft (powered) engaged in activities, such as:

> aerobatic flying
> aircraft racing
> rescue operation
> storm surveillance
> traffic surveillance

Occupant of private plane NOS

.6 Occupant of unpowered aircraft, except parachutist

Occupant of aircraft classifiable to E842

.7 Parachutist (military) (other)

Person making voluntary descent

> *Excludes:* person making descent after accident to aircraft (.1–.6)

.8 Ground crew, airline employee

Persons employed at airfields (civil) (military) or launching pads, not occupants of aircraft

.9 Other person

007.5	**Cyclosporiasis** New code
079.4	**Human papillomavirus** Revised code
082.4	**Ehrlichiosis** New sub-category
082.40	**Ehrlichiosis, unspecified** New code
082.41	**Ehrlichiosis chafeensis (E. chafeensis)** New code
082.49	**Other ehrlichiosis** New code
222.2	**Prostate** Exclusion terms revised
250.8	**Diabetes with other specified manifestations** Description added; "Use additional code" added
256.2	**Postablative ovarian failure** Exclusion term added
256.3	**Other ovarian failure** Exclusion term added
269.8	**Other nutritional deficiency** Exclusion term revised, added
285.2	**Anemia in chronic illness** New sub-category
285.21	**Anemia in end-stage renal disease** New code
285.22	**Anemia in neoplastic disease** New code
285.29	**Anemia of other chronic illness** New code
290	**Senile and presenile organic psychotic conditions** Exclusion term revised
290.1	**Presenile dementia** Exclusion term revised
294.10	**Dementia in conditions classified elsewhere without behavioral disturbance** New code
294.11	**Dementia in conditions classified elsewhere with behavioral disturbance** New code
306.4	**Gastrointestinal** Exclusion term revised
316	**Psychic factors associated with disease classified elsewhere** "Use additional code" revised
372.81	**Conjunctivochalasis** New code
372.89	**Other disorders of conjunctiva** New code
440.23	**Atherosclerosis of the extremities with ulceration** "Use additional code" added
459.81	**Venous (peripheral) insufficiency, unspecified** "Use additional code" revised
466.0	**Acute bronchitis** Exclusion terms added
477.1	**Due to food** New code
491.21	**With acute exacerbation** Description added
493	**Asthma** Fifth digit subclassification added
494.0	**Bronchiectasis without acute exacerbation** New code
494.1	**Bronchiectasis with acute exacerbation** New code
496	**Chronic airway obstruction, not elsewhere classified** Exclusion term revised
511.8	**Other specified forms of effusion, except tuberculosis** Exclusion term revised
558.3	**Allergic gastroenteritis and colitis** New code
558.9	**Other and unspecified noninfectious gastroenteritis and colitis** Description revised
564.1	**Irritable bowel syndrome** Revised code; description revised
596.51	**Hypertonicity of bladder** Description added
600	**Hyperplasia of prostate** Description deleted; exclusion term deleted
600.0	**Hypertrophy (benign) of prostate** New code
600.1	**Nodular prostate** New code
600.2	**Benign localized hyperplasia of prostate** New code
600.3	**Cyst of prostate** New code
600.9	**Hyperplasia of prostate, unspecified** New code
627	**Menopausal and postmenopausal disorders** Exclusion term added
645	**Late pregnancy** Revised code; description revised
645.1	**Post term pregnancy** New code
645.2	**Prolonged pregnancy** New code
646.8	**Other specified complications of pregnancy** Description added
656.3	**Fetal distress** Exclusion term deleted
663.5	**Vasa previa** Description deleted
663.8	**Other umbilical cord complications** Description added

692.75   **Disseminated superficial actinic porokeratosis (DSAP)**
New code

706.3   **Seborrhea**
Exclusion term revised

707.1   **Ulcer of lower limb, except decubitus**
Exclusion deleted; "Code first" added

707.10   **Ulcer of lower limb, unspecified**
New code

707.11   **Ulcer of thigh**
New code

707.12   **Ulcer of calf**
New code

707.13   **Ulcer of ankle**
New code

707.14   **Ulcer of heel and midfoot**
New code

707.15   **Ulcer of other part of foot**
New code

707.19   **Ulcer of other part of lower limb**
New code

723.8   **Other syndromes affecting cervical region**
Description added

727.83   **Plica syndrome**
New code

781.9   **Other symptoms involving nervous and musculoskeletal systems**
Description deleted

781.91   **Loss of height**
New code

781.92   **Abnormal posture**
New code

781.99   **Other symptoms involving nervous and musculoskeletal systems**
New code

783.2   **Abnormal loss of weight and underweight**
Revised code

783.21   **Loss of weight**
New code

783.22   **Underweight**
New code

783.4   **Lack of expected normal physiological development in childhood**
Revised code; description deleted; exclusion terms added

783.40   **Lack of normal physiological development, unspecified**
New code

783.41   **Failure to thrive**
New code

783.42   **Delayed milestones**
New code

783.43   **Short stature**
New code

783.7   **Adult failure to thrive**
New code

786.07   **Wheezing**
Exclusion term revised

790.0   **Abnormality of red blood cells**
Description deleted

790.01   **Precipitous drop in hematocrit**
New code

790.09   **Other abnormality of red blood cells**
New code

792.5   **Cloudy (hemodialysis) (peritoneal) dialysis effluent**
New code

795   **Nonspecific abnormal histological and immunological findings**
Exclusion term revised

795.3   **Nonspecific positive culture findings**
Exclusion term revised

840.4   **Rotator cuff (capsule)**
Exclusion term added

988   **Toxic effect of noxious substances eaten as food**
Exclusion term revised

995.3   **Allergy, unspecified**
Exclusion term revised

995.7   **Other adverse food reactions, not elsewhere classified**
New code

996.87   **Intestine**
New code

996.89   **Other specified transplanted organ**
Description deleted

V12.2   **Endocrine, metabolic, and immunity disorders**
Exclusion term revised

V13.7   **Perinatal problems**
Exclusion term added

V15.0   **Allergy, other than to medicinal agents**
Exclusion term added

V15.01   **Allergy to peanuts**
New code

V15.02   **Allergy to milk products**
New code

V15.03   **Allergy to eggs**
New code

V15.04   **Allergy to seafood**
New code

V15.05   **Allergy to other foods**
New code

V15.06   **Allergy to insects**
New code

V15.07   **Allergy to latex**
New code

V15.08   **Allergy to radiographic dye**
New code

V15.09   **Other allergy, other than to medicinal agents**
New code

V21.3   **Low birth weight status**
New sub-category

V21.30   **Low birth weight status, unspecified**
New code

V21.31   **Low birth weight status, less than 500 grams**
New code

V21.32   **Low birth weight status, 500-999 grams**
New code

V21.33	**Low birth weight status, 1000-1499 grams** New code
V21.34	**Low birth weight status, 1500-1999 grams** New code
V21.35	**Low birth weight status, 2000-2500 grams** New code
V25.8	**Other specified contraceptive management** Exclusion terms added
V26.2	**Investigation and testing** Description terms deleted
V26.21	**Fertility testing** New code
V26.22	**Aftercare following sterilization reversal** New code
V26.29	**Other investigation and testing** New code
V26.3	**Genetic counseling and testing** Revised code; exclusion term added
V42.84	**Intestines** New code
V45.74	**Other parts of urinary tract** New code
V45.75	**Stomach** New code
V45.76	**Lung** New code
V45.77	**Genital organs** New code
V45.78	**Eye** New code
V45.79	**Other acquired absence of organ** New code
V49	**Other conditions influencing health status** Revised code
V49.8	**Other specified conditions influencing health status** Revised code
V49.81	**Postmenopausal status (age-related) (natural)** New code
V49.89	**Other specified conditions influencing health status** New code
V56.3	**Encounter for adequacy testing for dialysis** New sub-category
V56.31	**Encounter for adequacy testing for hemodialysis** New code
V56.32	**Encounter for adequacy testing for peritoneal dialysis** New code
V58.4	**Other aftercare following surgery** Exclusion term added
V58.83	**Encounter for therapeutic drug monitoring** New code

V67.00	**Following surgery, unspecified** New code
V67.01	**Follow-up vaginal pap smear** New code
V67.09	**Following other surgery** New code
V71.81	**Abuse and neglect** New code
V71.89	**Other specified suspected conditions** New code
V72.3	**Gynecological examination** Description revised; "Use additional code" added
V76.46	**Ovary** New code
V76.47	**Vagina** New code
V76.49	**Other sites** Revised code
V76.5	**Intestine** New sub-category
V76.50	**Intestine, unspecified** New code
V76.51	**Colon** New code
V76.52	**Small intestine** New code
V76.81	**Nervous system** New code
V78.89	**Other neoplasm** New code
V77.91	**Screening for lipoid disorders** New code
V77.99	**Other and unspecified endocrine, nutritional, metabolic and immunity disorders** New code
V82.81	**Osteoporosis** New code
V82.89	**Other specified conditions** New code
E825	**Other motor vehicle nontraffic accident of other and unspecified nature** Exclusion term revised
E880.1	**Fall on or from sidewalk curb** Exclusion term revised
E885	**Fall on same level from slipping, tripping, or stumbling** Description deleted
E885.1	**Fall from roller skates** New code
E885.2	**Fall from skateboard** New code
E885.3	**Fall from skis** New code
E885.4	**Fall from snowboard** New code
E885.9	**Fall from other slipping, tripping, or stumbling** New code
E906	**Other injury caused by animals** Exclusion term revised

E917 **Striking against or struck accidentally by objects or persons**
Exclusion term revised

E919 **Accidents caused by machinery**
Exclusion term revised

E928.3 **Human bite**
New code

E967 **Perpetrator of child and adult abuse**
Revised code; "Note" added

E967.0 **By father, stepfather, or boyfriend**
Revised code; description added

E967.2 **By mother, stepmother, or girlfriend**
Revised code; description added

E967.3 **By spouse or partner**
Description revised

E968.7 **Human bite**
New code

E968.8 **Other specified means**
Description deleted

1457

PROCEDURES: TABULAR LIST
AND
ALPHABETIC INDEX
VOLUME 3

1.   OPERATIONS ON THE NERVOUS SYSTEM (01-05)

01   Incision and excision of skull, brain, and cerebral meninges

01.0   Cranial puncture

01.01   Cisternal puncture
Cisternal tap
| *Excludes:* | pneumocisternogram (87.02) |

01.02   Ventriculopuncture through previously implanted catheter
Puncture of ventricular shunt tubing

01.09   Other cranial puncture
Aspiration of
  subarachnoid space
  subdural space
Cranial aspiration NOS
Puncture of anterior fontanel
Subdural tap (through fontanel)

01.1   Diagnostic procedures on skull, brain, and cerebral meninges

01.11   Closed [percutaneous] [needle] biopsy of cerebral meninges
Burr hole approach

01.12   Open biopsy of cerebral meninges

01.13   Closed [percutaneous] [needle] biopsy of brain
Burr hole approach
Stereotactic method

01.14   Open biopsy of brain

01.15   Biopsy of skull

01.18   Other diagnostic procedures on brain and cerebral meninges
| *Excludes:* | cerebral: |

  arteriography (88.41)
  thermography (88.81)
contrast radiogram of brain (87.01-87.02)
echoencephalogram (88.71)
electroencephalogram (89.14)
microscopic examination of specimen from nervous system and of
  spinal fluid (90.01-90.09)
neurologic examination (89.13)
phlebography of head and neck (88.61)
pneumoencephalogram (87.01)
radioisotope scan:
  cerebral (92.11)
  head NEC (92.12)
tomography of head:
  C.A.T. scan (87.03)
  other (87.04)

01.19   Other diagnostic procedures on skull
| *Excludes:* | transillumination of skull (89.16) |
| | x-ray of skull (87.17) |

01.2   Craniotomy and craniectomy
Excludes:	decompression of skull fracture (02.02)
	exploration of orbit (16.01-16.09)
	that as operative approach—omit code

01.21   Incision and drainage of cranial sinus

01.22   Removal of intracranial neurostimulator
| *Excludes:* | removal with synchronous replacement (02.93) |

01.23   Reopening of craniotomy site

01.24 Other craniotomy
  Cranial:
    decompression
    exploration
    trephination
  Craniotomy NOS
  Craniotomy with removal of:
    epidural abscess
    extradural hematoma
    foreign body of skull

  | *Excludes:* | *removal of foreign body with incision into brain (01.39)* |

01.25 Other craniectomy
  Debridement of skull NOS
  Sequestrectomy of skull

  | *Excludes:* | *debridement of compound fracture of skull (02.02)* |
  | | *strip craniectomy (02.01)* |

01.3 Incision of brain and cerebral meninges

01.31 Incision of cerebral meninges
  Drainage of:
    intracranial hygroma
    subarachnoid abscess (cerebral)
    subdural empyema

01.32 Lobotomy and tractotomy
  Division of:
    brain tissue
    cerebral tracts
  Percutaneous (radio frequency) cingulotomy

01.39 Other incision of brain
  Amygdalohippocampotomy
  Drainage of intracerebral hematoma
  Incision of brain NOS

  | *Excludes:* | *division of cortical adhesions (02.91)* |

01.4 Operations on thalamus and globus pallidus

01.41 Operations on thalamus
  Chemothalamectomy
  Thalamotomy

01.42 Operations on globus pallidus
  Pallidoansectomy
  Pallidotomy

01.5 Other excision or destruction of brain and meninges

01.51 Excision of lesion or tissue of cerebral meninges
  Decortication
  Resection   } of (cerebral) meninges
  Stripping of subdural
    membrane

  | *Excludes:* | *biopsy of cerebral meninges (01.11-01.12)* |

01.52 Hemispherectomy

01.53 Lobectomy of brain

▲ **01.59 Other excision or destruction of lesion or tissue of brain**
  Curettage of brain
  Debridement of brain
  Marsupialization of brain cyst
  Transtemporal (mastoid) excision of brain tumor

  | *Excludes:* | *biopsy of brain (01.13-01.14)* |
  | | *that by stereotactic radiosurgery (92.30-92.39)* |

01.6 Excision of lesion of skull
  Removal of granulation tissue of cranium

  | *Excludes:* | *biopsy of skull (01.15)* |
  | | *sequestrectomy (01.25)* |

02 Other operations on skull, brain, and cerebral meninges

● Code new
to this edition

▲ Revision of
existing code

④ ⑤ Fourth or fifth
digit required

02.0 Cranioplasty

> | Excludes: | that with synchronous repair of encephalocele (02.12)

02.01 Opening of cranial suture
Linear craniectomy
Strip craniectomy

02.02 Elevation of skull fracture fragments
Debridement of compound fracture of skull
Decompression of skull fracture
Reduction of skull fracture
Code also any synchronous debridement of brain (01.59)

> | Excludes: | debridement of skull NOS (01.25)
> removal of granulation tissue of cranium (01.6)

02.03 Formation of cranial bone flap
Repair of skull with flap

02.04 Bone graft to skull
Pericranial graft (autogenous) (heterogenous)

02.05 Insertion of skull plate
Replacement of skull plate

02.06 Other cranial osteoplasty
Repair of skull NOS
Revision of bone flap of skull

02.07 Removal of skull plate

> | Excludes: | removal with synchronous
> replacement (02.05)

02.1 Repair of cerebral meninges

> | Excludes: | marsupialization of cerebral lesion (01.59)

02.11 Simple suture of dura mater of brain

02.12 Other repair of cerebral meninges
Closure of fistula of cerebrospinal fluid
Dural graft
Repair of encephalocele including synchronous cranioplasty
Repair of meninges NOS
Subdural patch

02.13 Ligation of meningeal vessel
Ligation of:
longitudinal sinus
middle meningeal artery

02.14 Choroid plexectomy
Cauterization of choroid plexus

02.2 Ventriculostomy
Anastomosis of ventricle to:
cervical subarachnoid space
cisterna magna
Insertion of Holter valve
Ventriculocisternal intubation

02.3 Extracranial ventricular shunt
Includes: that with insertion of valve

02.31 Ventricular shunt to structure in head and neck
Ventricle to nasopharynx shunt
Ventriculomastoid anastomosis

02.32 Ventricular shunt to circulatory system
Ventriculoatrial anastomosis
Ventriculocaval shunt

02.33 Ventricular shunt to thoracic cavity
Ventriculopleural anastomosis

02.34 Ventricular shunt to abdominal cavity and organs
Ventriculocholecystostomy
Ventriculoperitoneostomy

02.35 Ventricular shunt to urinary system
Ventricle to ureter shunt

Valid O.R. procedure   Non-O.R. procedure   Nonspecific O.R. procedure   Noncovered O.R. procedure

02.39 Other operations to establish drainage of ventricle
Ventricle to bone marrow shunt
Ventricular shunt to extracranial site NEC

02.4 Revision, removal, and irrigation of ventricular shunt

Excludes: *revision of distal catheter of ventricular shunt (54.95)*

02.41 Irrigation of ventricular shunt

02.42 Replacement of ventricular shunt
Reinsertion of Holter valve
Replacement of ventricular catheter
Revision of ventriculoperitoneal shunt at ventricular site

02.43 Removal of ventricular shunt

02.9 Other operations on skull, brain, and cerebral meninges

Excludes: *operations on:*
pineal gland (07.17, 07.51-07.59)
pituitary gland [hypophysis] (07.13-07.15, 07.61-07.79)

02.91 Lysis of cortical adhesions

02.92 Repair of brain

02.93 Implantation of intracranial neurostimulator
Implantation, insertion, placement, or replacement of intracranial:
brain pacemaker [neuropacemaker]
depth electrodes
electroencephalographic receiver
epidural pegs
foramen ovale electrodes
intracranial electrostimulator
subdural grids
subdural strips

02.94 Insertion or replacement of skull tongs or halo traction device

02.95 Removal of skull tongs or halo traction device

02.96 Insertion of sphenoidal electrodes

02.99 Other

Excludes: *chemical shock therapy (94.24)*
electroshock therapy:
subconvulsive (94.26)
other (94.27)

03 Operations on spinal cord and spinal canal structures

03.0 Exploration and decompression of spinal canal structures

03.01 Removal of foreign body from spinal canal

03.02 Reopening of laminectomy site

03.09 Other exploration and decompression of spinal canal
Decompression:
laminectomy
laminotomy
Exploration of spinal nerve root
Foraminotomy

Excludes: *drainage of spinal fluid by anastomosis (03.71-03.79)*
laminectomy with excision of intervertebral disc (80.51)
spinal tap (03.31)
that as operative approach—omit code

03.1 Division of intraspinal nerve root
Rhizotomy

03.2 Chordotomy

03.21 Percutaneous chordotomy
Stereotactic chordotomy

03.29 Other chordotomy
Chordotomy NOS
Tractotomy (one-stage) (two-stage) of spinal cord
Transection of spinal cord tracts

03.3 Diagnostic procedures on spinal cord and spinal canal structures

● Code new
to this edition

▲ Revision of
existing code

④ ⑤ Fourth or fifth
digit required

03.31 Spinal tap
Lumbar puncture for removal of dye

> *Excludes:* *lumbar puncture for injection of dye [myelogram] (87.21)*

03.32 Biopsy of spinal cord or spinal meninges

03.39 Other diagnostic procedures on spinal cord and spinal canal structures

> *Excludes:* *microscopic examination of specimen from nervous system or of spinal fluid (90.01-90.09)*
> *x-ray of spine (87.21-87.29)*

03.4 Excision or destruction of lesion of spinal cord or spinal meninges
Curettage
Debridement
Marsupialization of cyst } of spinal cord or spinal meninges
Resection

> *Excludes:* *biopsy of spinal cord or meninges (03.32)*

03.5 Plastic operations on spinal cord structures

03.51 Repair of spinal meningocele
Repair of meningocele NOS

03.52 Repair of spinal myelomeningocele

03.53 Repair of vertebral fracture
Elevation of spinal bone fragments
Reduction of fracture of vertebrae
Removal of bony spicules from spinal canal

03.59 Other repair and plastic operations on spinal cord structures
Repair of:
diastematomyelia
spina bifida NOS
spinal cord NOS
spinal meninges NOS
vertebral arch defect

03.6 Lysis of adhesions of spinal cord and nerve roots

03.7 Shunt of spinal theca
Includes: that with valve

03.71 Spinal subarachnoid-peritoneal shunt

03.72 Spinal subarachnoid-ureteral shunt

03.79 Other shunt of spinal theca
Lumbar-subarachnoid shunt NOS
Pleurothecal anastomosis
Salpingothecal anastomosis

03.8 Injection of destructive agent into spinal canal

03.9 Other operations on spinal cord and spinal canal structures

03.90 Insertion of catheter into spinal canal for infusion of therapeutic or palliative substances
Insertion of catheter into epidural, subarachnoid, or subdural space of spine with intermittent or continuous infusion of drug (with creation of any reservoir)

> *Code also any implantation of infusion pump (86.06)*

03.91 Injection of anesthetic into spinal canal for analgesia

> *Excludes:* *that for operative anesthesia—omit code*

03.92 Injection of other agent into spinal canal
Intrathecal injection of steroid
Subarachnoid perfusion of refrigerated saline

> *Excludes:* *injection of:*
> *contrast material for myelogram (87.21)*
> *destructive agent into spinal canal (03.8)*

03.93 Insertion or replacement of spinal neurostimulator

03.94 Removal of spinal neurostimulator

03.95 Spinal blood patch

03.96 Percutaneous denervation of facet

03.97 Revision of spinal thecal shunt

03.98 Removal of spinal thecal shunt

	Valid O.R. procedure		Non-O.R. procedure		Nonspecific O.R. procedure		Noncovered O.R. procedure

03.99 Other

04 **Operations on cranial and peripheral nerves**

04.0 **Incision, division, and excision of cranial and peripheral nerves**

Excludes: opticociliary neurectomy (12.79)
sympathetic ganglionectomy (05.21-05.29)

04.01 **Excision of acoustic neuroma**
That by craniotomy

Excludes: that by stereotactic radiosurgery (92.3)

04.02 **Division of trigeminal nerve**
Retrogasserian neurotomy

04.03 **Division or crushing of other cranial and peripheral nerves**

Excludes: that of:
glossopharyngeal nerve (29.92)
laryngeal nerve (31.91)
nerves to adrenal glands (07.42)
phrenic nerve for collapse of lung (33.31)
vagus nerve (44.00-44.03)

04.04 **Other incision of cranial and peripheral nerves**

04.05 **Gasserian ganglionectomy**

04.06 **Other cranial or peripheral ganglionectomy**

Excludes: sympathetic ganglionectomy (05.21-05.29)

04.07 **Other excision or avulsion of cranial and peripheral nerves**
Curettage
Debridement } of peripheral nerve
Resection
Excision of peripheral neuroma [Morton's]

Excludes: biopsy of cranial or peripheral nerve (04.11-04.12)

04.1 **Diagnostic procedures on peripheral nervous system**

04.11 **Closed [percutaneous] [needle] biopsy of cranial or peripheral nerve or ganglion**

04.12 **Open biopsy of cranial or peripheral nerve or ganglion**

04.19 **Other diagnostic procedures on cranial and peripheral nerves and ganglia**

Excludes: microscopic examination of specimen from nervous system
(90.01-90.09)
neurologic examination (89.13)

04.2 **Destruction of cranial and peripheral nerves**
Destruction of cranial or peripheral nerves by:
cryoanalgesia
injection of neurolytic agent
radiofrequency

04.3 **Suture of cranial and peripheral nerves**

04.4 **Lysis of adhesions and decompression of cranial and peripheral nerves**

04.41 **Decompression of trigeminal nerve root**

04.42 **Other cranial nerve decompression**

04.43 **Release of carpal tunnel**

04.44 **Release of tarsal tunnel**

04.49 **Other peripheral nerve or ganglion decompression or lysis of adhesions**
Peripheral nerve neurolysis NOS

04.5 **Cranial or peripheral nerve graft**

04.6 **Transposition of cranial and peripheral nerves**
Nerve transplantation

04.7 **Other cranial or peripheral neuroplasty**

04.71 **Hypoglossal-facial anastomosis**

04.72 **Accessory-facial anastomosis**

04.73 **Accessory-hypoglossal anastomosis**

04.74 **Other anastomosis of cranial or peripheral nerve**

04.75 **Revision of previous repair of cranial and peripheral nerves**

● Code new
to this edition

▲ Revision of
existing code

④ ⑤ Fourth or fifth
digit required

04.76 Repair of old traumatic injury of cranial and peripheral nerves

04.79 Other neuroplasty

04.8 Injection into peripheral nerve

> *Excludes:* destruction of nerve (by injection of neurolytic agent) (04.2)

04.80 Peripheral nerve injection, not otherwise specified

04.81 Injection of anesthetic into peripheral nerve for analgesia

> *Excludes:* that for operative anesthesia—omit code

04.89 Injection of other agent, except neurolytic

> *Excludes:* injection of neurolytic agent (04.2)

04.9 Other operations on cranial and peripheral nerves

04.91 Neurectasis

04.92 Implantation or replacement of peripheral neurostimulator

04.93 Removal of peripheral neurostimulator

04.99 Other

05 Operations on sympathetic nerves or ganglia

> *Excludes:* paracervical uterine denervation (69.3)

05.0 Division of sympathetic nerve or ganglion

> *Excludes:* that of nerves to adrenal glands (07.42)

05.1 Diagnostic procedures on sympathetic nerves or ganglia

05.11 Biopsy of sympathetic nerve or ganglion

05.19 Other diagnostic procedures on sympathetic nerves or ganglia

05.2 Sympathectomy

05.21 Sphenopalatine ganglionectomy

05.22 Cervical sympathectomy

05.23 Lumber sympathectomy

05.25 Periarterial sympathectomy

05.24 Presacral sympathectomy

05.29 Other sympathectomy and ganglionectomy
Excision or avulsion of sympathetic nerve NOS
Sympathetic ganglionectomy NOS

> *Excludes:* biopsy of sympathetic nerve or ganglion (05.11)
> opticociliary neurectomy (12.79)
> periarterial sympathectomy (05.25)
> tympanosympathectomy (20.91)

05.3 Injection into sympathetic nerve or ganglion

> *Excludes:* injection of ciliary sympathetic ganglion (12.79)

05.31 Injection of anesthetic into sympathetic nerve for analgesia

05.32 Injection of neurolytic agent into sympathetic nerve

05.39 Other injection into sympathetic nerve or ganglion

05.8 Other operations on sympathetic nerves or ganglion

05.81 Repair of sympathetic nerve or ganglion

05.89 Other

05.9 Other operations on nervous system

● Code new
to this edition

▲ Revision of
existing code

④ ⑤ Fourth or fifth
digit required

2.   OPERATIONS ON THE ENDOCRINE SYSTEM (06-07)

06   Operations on thyroid and parathyroid glands
Includes: incidental resection of hyoid bone

06.0   Incision of thyroid field

> *Excludes:*   *division of isthmus (06.91)*

06.01   Aspiration of thyroid field
Percutaneous or needle drainage of thyroid field

> *Excludes:*   *aspiration biopsy of thyroid (06.11)*
> *drainage by incision (06.09)*
> *postoperative aspiration of field (06.02)*

06.02   Reopening of wound of thyroid field
Reopening of wound of thyroid field for:
control of (postoperative) hemorrhage
examination
exploration
removal of hematoma

06.09   Other incision of thyroid field
Drainage of hematoma
Drainage of thyroglossal tract
Exploration:
   neck
   thyroid (field)
Removal of foreign body
Thyroidotomy NOS
} by incision

> *Excludes:*   *postoperative exploration (06.02)*
> *removal of hematoma by aspiration (06.01)*

06.1   Diagnostic procedures on thyroid and parathyroid glands

06.11   Closed [percutaneous] [needle] biopsy of thyroid gland
Aspiration biopsy of thyroid

06.12   Open biopsy of thyroid gland

06.13   Biopsy of parathyroid gland

06.19   Other diagnostic procedures on thyroid and parathyroid glands

> *Excludes:*   *radioisotope scan of:*
> *parathyroid (92.13)*
> *thyroid (92.01)*
> *soft tissue x-ray of thyroid field (87.09)*

06.2   Unilateral thyroid lobectomy
Complete removal of one lobe of thyroid (with removal of isthmus or portion of other lobe)
Hemithyroidectomy

> *Excludes:*   *partial substernal thyroidectomy (06.51)*

06.3   Other partial thyroidectomy

06.31   Excision of lesion of thyroid

> *Excludes:*   *biopsy of thyroid (06.11-06.12)*

06.39   Other
Isthmectomy
Partial thyroidectomy NOS

> *Excludes:*   *partial substernal thyroidectomy (06.51)*

06.4   Complete thyroidectomy

> *Excludes:*   *complete substernal thyroidectomy (06.52)*
> *that with laryngectomy (30.3-30.4)*

06.5   Substernal thyroidectomy

06.50   Substernal thyroidectomy, not otherwise specified

06.51   Partial substernal thyroidectomy

06.52   Complete substernal thyroidectomy

06.6 Excision of lingual thyroid
Excision of thyroid by:
  submental route
  transoral route

06.7 Excision of thyroglossal duct or tract

06.8 Parathyroidectomy

06.81 Complete parathyroidectomy

06.89 Other parathyroidectomy
Parathyroidectomy NOS
Partial parathyroidectomy

| *Excludes:* | *biopsy of parathyroid (06.13)* |

06.9 Other operations on thyroid (region) and parathyroid

06.91 Division of thyroid isthmus
Transection of thyroid isthmus

06.92 Ligation of thyroid vessels

06.93 Suture of thyroid gland

06.94 Thyroid tissue reimplantation
Autotransplantation of thyroid tissue

06.95 Parathyroid tissue reimplantation
Autotransplantation of parathyroid tissue

06.98 Other operations on thyroid glands

06.99 Other operations on parathyroid glands

07 Operations on other endocrine glands
Includes: operations on:
  adrenal glands
  pineal gland
  pituitary gland
  thymus

| *Excludes:* | *operations on:* |

  aortic and carotid bodies (39.8)
  ovaries (65.0-65.99)
  pancreas (52.01-52.99)
  testes (62.0-62.99)

07.0 Exploration of adrenal field

| *Excludes:* | *incision of adrenal (gland) (07.41)* |

07.00 Exploration of adrenal field, not otherwise specified

07.01 Unilateral exploration of adrenal field

07.02 Bilateral exploration of adrenal field

07.1 Diagnostic procedures on adrenal glands, pituitary gland, pineal gland, and thymus

07.11 Closed [percutaneous] [needle] biopsy of adrenal gland

07.12 Open biopsy of adrenal gland

07.13 Biopsy of pituitary gland, transfrontal approach

07.14 Biopsy of pituitary gland, transsphenoidal approach

07.15 Biopsy of pituitary gland, unspecified approach

07.16 Biopsy of thymus

07.17 Biopsy of pineal gland

07.19 Other diagnostic procedures on adrenal glands, pituitary gland, pineal gland, and thymus

| *Excludes:* | *microscopic examination of specimen from endocrine gland (90.11-90.19)* |
| | *radioisotope scan of pituitary gland (92.11)* |

07.2 Partial adrenalectomy

07.21 Excision of lesion of adrenal gland

| *Excludes:* | *biopsy of adrenal gland (07.11-07.12)* |

07.22 Unilateral adrenalectomy
Adrenalectomy NOS

| *Excludes:* | *excision of remaining adrenal gland (07.3)* |

● Code new
  to this edition   ▲ Revision of
  existing code   ④ ⑤ Fourth or fifth
  digit required

07.29 Other partial adrenalectomy
Partial adrenalectomy NOS

07.3 Bilateral adrenalectomy
Excision of remaining adrenal gland
Excludes: bilateral partial adrenalectomy (07.29)

07.4 Other operations on adrenal glands, nerves, and vessels

07.41 Incision of adrenal gland
Adrenalotomy (with drainage)

07.42 Division of nerves to adrenal glands

07.43 Ligation of adrenal vessels

07.44 Repair of adrenal gland

07.45 Reimplantation of adrenal tissue
Autotransplantation of adrenal tissue

07.49 Other

07.5 Operations on pineal gland

07.51 Exploration of pineal field
Excludes: that with incision of pineal gland (07.52)

07.52 Incision of pineal gland

07.53 Partial excision of pineal gland
Excludes: biopsy of pineal gland (07.17)

07.54 Total excision of pineal gland
Pinealectomy (complete) (total)

07.59 Other operations on pineal gland

07.6 Hypophysectomy

07.61 Partial excision of pituitary gland, transfrontal approach
Cryohypophysectomy,
   partial
Division of hypophyseal
   stalk
Excision of lesion of   } transfrontal approach
   pituitary [hypophysis]
Hypophysectomy, subtotal
Infundibulectomy,
   hypophyseal
Excludes: biopsy of pituitary gland, transfrontal approach (07.13)

07.62 Partial excision of pituitary gland, transsphenoidal approach
Excludes: biopsy of pituitary gland, transsphenoidal approach (07.14)

07.63 Partial excision of pituitary gland, unspecified approach
Excludes: biopsy of pituitary gland NOS (07.15)

07.64 Total excision of pituitary gland, transfrontal approach
Ablation of pituitary by
   implantation (stron-   } transfrontal approach
   tium-yttrium) (Y)
Cryohypophysectomy,
   complete

07.65 Total excision of pituitary gland, transsphenoidal approach

07.68 Total excision of pituitary gland, other specified approach

07.69 Total excision of pituitary gland, unspecified approach
Hypophysectomy NOS
Pituitectomy NOS

07.7 Other operations on hypophysis

07.71 Exploration of pituitary fossa
Excludes: exploration with incision of pituitary gland (07.72)

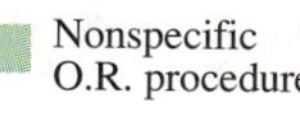

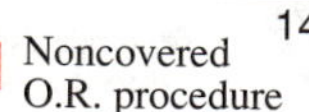

Noncovered
O.R. procedure

07.72 Incision of pituitary gland
Aspiration of:
 craniobuccal pouch
 craniopharyngioma
 hypophysis
 pituitary gland
 Rathke's pouch

07.79 Other
Insertion of pack into sella turcica

07.8 Thymectomy

07.80 Thymectomy, not otherwise specified

07.81 Partial excision of thymus
| Excludes: | biopsy of thymus (07.16)

07.82 Total excision of thymus

07.9 Other operations on thymus

07.91 Exploration of thymus field
| Excludes: | exploration with incision of thymus (07.92)

07.92 Incision of thymus

07.93 Repair of thymus

07.94 Transplantation of thymus

07.99 Other
Thymopexy

● Code new to this edition ▲ Revision of existing code ④ ⑤ Fourth or fifth digit required

3.   OPERATIONS ON THE EYE (08-16)

08   Operations on eyelids
Includes: operations on the eyebrow

08.0   Incision of eyelid

08.01   Incision of lid margin

08.02   Severing of blepharorrhaphy

08.09   Other incision of eyelid

08.1   Diagnostic procedures on eyelid

08.11   Biopsy of eyelid

08.19   Other diagnostic procedures on eyelid

08.2   Excision or destruction of lesion or tissue of eyelid
Code also any synchronous reconstruction (08.61-08.74)

| *Excludes:* | *biopsy of eyelid (08.11)* |

08.20   Removal of lesion of eyelid, not otherwise specified
Removal of meibomian gland NOS

08.21   Excision of chalazion

08.22   Excision of other minor lesion of eyelid
Excision of:
verruca
wart

08.23   Excision of major lesion of eyelid, partial-thickness
Excision involving one-fourth or more of lid margin, partial-thickness

08.24   Excision of major lesion of eyelid, full-thickness
Excision involving one-fourth or more of lid margin, full-thickness
Wedge resection of eyelid

08.25   Destruction of lesion of eyelid

08.3   Repair of blepharoptosis and lid retraction

08.31   Repair of blepharoptosis by frontalis muscle technique with suture

08.32   Repair of blepharoptosis by frontalis muscle technique with fascial sling

08.33   Repair of blepharoptosis by resection or advancement of levator muscle or aponeurosis

08.34   Repair of blepharoptosis by other levator muscle techniques

08.35   Repair of blepharoptosis by tarsal technique

08.36   Repair of blepharoptosis by other techniques
Correction of eyelid ptosis NOS
Orbicularis oculi muscle sling for correction of blepharoptosis

08.37   Reduction of overcorrection of ptosis

08.38   Correction of lid retraction

08.4   Repair of entropion or ectropion

08.41   Repair of entropion or ectropion by thermocauterization

08.42   Repair of entropion or ectropion by suture technique

08.43   Repair of entropion or ectropion with wedge resection

08.44   Repair of entropion or ectropion with lid reconstruction

08.49   Other repair of entropion or ectropion

08.5   Other adjustment of lid position

08.51   Canthotomy
Enlargement of palpebral fissure

08.52   Blepharorrhaphy
Canthorrhaphy
Tarsorrhaphy

08.59   Other
Canthoplasty NOS
Repair of epicanthal fold

08.6   Reconstruction of eyelid with flaps or grafts

| *Excludes:* | *that associated with repair of entropion and ectropion (08.44)* |

08.61 Reconstruction of eyelid with skin flap or graft

08.62 Reconstruction of eyelid with mucous membrane flap or graft

08.63 Reconstruction of eyelid with hair follicle graft

08.64 Reconstruction of eyelid with tarsoconjunctival flap
Transfer of tarsoconjunctival flap from opposing lid

08.69 Other reconstruction of eyelid with flap or graft

08.7 Other reconstruction of eyelid

Excludes: *that associated with repair of entropion and ectropion (08.44)*

08.70 Reconstruction of eyelid, not otherwise specified

08.71 Reconstruction of eyelid involving lid margin, partial-thickness

08.72 Other reconstruction of eyelid, partial-thickness

08.73 Reconstruction of eyelid involving lid margin, full-thickness

08.74 Other reconstruction of eyelid, full-thickness

08.8 Other repair of eyelid

08.81 Linear repair of laceration of eyelid or eyebrow

08.82 Repair of laceration involving lid margin, partial-thickness

08.83 Other repair of laceration of eyelid, partial-thickness

08.84 Repair of laceration involving lid margin, full-thickness

08.85 Other repair of laceration of eyelid, full-thickness

08.86 Lower eyelid rhytidectomy

08.87 Upper eyelid rhytidectomy

08.89 Other eyelid repair

08.9 Other operations on eyelids

08.91 Electrosurgical epilation of eyelid

08.92 Cryosurgical epilation of eyelid

08.93 Other epilation of eyelid

08.99 Other

09 Operations on lacrimal system

09.0 Incision of lacrimal gland
Incision of lacrimal cyst (with drainage)

09.1 Diagnostic procedures on lacrimal system

09.11 Biopsy of lacrimal gland

09.12 Biopsy of lacrimal sac

09.19 Other diagnostic procedures on lacrimal system

Excludes: *contrast dacryocystogram (87.05)*
soft tissue x-ray of nasolacrimal duct (87.09)

09.2 Excision of lesion or tissue of lacrimal gland

09.20 Excision of lacrimal gland, not otherwise specified

09.21 Excision of lesion of lacrimal gland

Excludes: *biopsy of lacrimal gland (09.11)*

09.22 Other partial dacryoadenectomy

Excludes: *biopsy of lacrimal gland (09.11)*

09.23 Total dacryoadenectomy

09.3 Other operations on lacrimal gland

09.4 Manipulation of lacrimal passage
Includes: removal of calculus
that with dilation

Excludes: *contrast dacryocystogram (87.05)*

09.41 Probing of lacrimal punctum

09.42 Probing of lacrimal canaliculi

09.43 Probing of nasolacrimal duct

Excludes: *that with insertion of tube or stent (09.44)*

   ● Code new
to this edition   ▲ Revision of
existing code   ④ ⑤ Fourth or fifth
digit required

09.44 **Intubation of nasolacrimal duct**
Insertion of stent into nasolacrimal duct

09.49 **Other manipulation of lacrimal passage**

09.5 **Incision of lacrimal sac and passages**

09.51 **Incision of lacrimal punctum**

09.52 **Incision of lacrimal canaliculi**

09.53 **Incision of lacrimal sac**

09.59 **Other incision of lacrimal passages**
Incision (and drainage) of nasolacrimal duct NOS

09.6 **Excision of lacrimal sac and passage**
  Excludes: *biopsy of lacrimal sac (09.12)*

09.7 **Repair of canaliculus and punctum**
  Excludes: *repair of eyelid (08.81-08.89)*

09.71 **Correction of everted punctum**

09.72 **Other repair of punctum**

09.73 **Repair of canaliculus**

09.8 **Fistulization of lacrimal tract to nasal cavity**

09.81 **Dacryocystorhinostomy [DCR]**

09.82 **Conjunctivocystorhinostomy**
Conjunctivodacryocystorhinostomy [CDCR]
  Excludes: *that with insertion of tube or stent (09.83)*

09.83 **Conjunctivorhinostomy with insertion of tube or stent**

09.9 **Other operations on lacrimal system**

09.91 **Obliteration of lacrimal punctum**

09.99 **Other**

10 **Operations on conjunctiva**

10.0 **Removal of embedded foreign body from conjunctiva by incision**
  Excludes: *removal of:*
  embedded foreign body without incision (98.22)
  superficial foreign body (98.21)

10.1 **Other incision of conjunctiva**

10.2 **Diagnostic procedures on conjunctiva**

10.21 **Biopsy of conjunctiva**

10.29 **Other diagnostic procedures on conjunctiva**

10.3 **Excision or destruction of lesion or tissue of conjunctiva**

10.31 **Excision of lesion or tissue of conjunctiva**
Excision of ring of conjunctiva around cornea
  Excludes: *biopsy of conjunctiva (10.21)*

10.32 **Destruction of lesion of conjunctiva**
  Excludes: *excision of lesion (10.31)*
  thermocauterization for entropion (08.41)

10.33 **Other destructive procedures on conjunctiva**
Removal of trachoma follicles

10.4 **Conjunctivoplasty**

10.41 **Repair of symblepharon with free graft**

10.42 **Reconstruction of conjunctival cul-de-sac with free graft**
  Excludes: *revision of enucleation socket with graft (16.63)*

10.43 **Other reconstruction of conjunctival cul-de-sac**
  Excludes: *revision of enucleation socket (16.64)*

10.44 **Other free graft to conjunctiva**

10.49 **Other conjunctivoplasty**
  Excludes: *repair of cornea with conjunctival flap (11.53)*

10.5 Lysis of adhesions of conjunctiva and eyelid
Division of symblepharon (with insertion of conformer)

10.6 Repair of laceration of conjunctiva
Excludes: that with repair of sclera (12.81)

10.9 Other operations on conjunctiva

    10.91 Subconjunctival injection

    10.99 Other

11 Operations on cornea

11.0 Magnetic removal of embedded foreign body from cornea
Excludes: that with incision (11.1)

11.1 Incision of cornea
Incision of cornea for removal of foreign body

11.2 Diagnostic procedures on cornea

    11.21 Scraping of cornea for smear or culture

    11.22 Biopsy of cornea

    11.29 Other diagnostic procedures on cornea

11.3 Excision of pterygium

    11.31 Transposition of pterygium

    11.32 Excision of pterygium with corneal graft

    11.39 Other excision of pterygium

11.4 Excision or destruction of tissue or other lesion of cornea

    11.41 Mechanical removal of corneal epithelium
    That by chemocauterization
    Excludes: that for smear or culture (11.21)

    11.42 Thermocauterization of corneal lesion

    11.43 Cryotherapy of corneal lesion

    11.49 Other removal or destruction of corneal lesion
    Excision of cornea NOS
    Excludes: biopsy of cornea (11.22)

11.5 Repair of cornea

    11.51 Suture of corneal laceration

    11.52 Repair of postoperative wound dehiscence of cornea

    11.53 Repair of corneal laceration or wound with conjunctival flop

    11.59 Other repair of cornea

11.6 Corneal transplant
Excludes: excision of pterygium with corneal graft (11.32)

    11.60 Corneal transplant, not otherwise specified
    Keratoplasty NOS

    11.61 Lamellar keratoplasty with autograft

    11.62 Other lamellar keratoplasty

    11.63 Penetrating keratoplasty with autograft
    Perforating keratoplasty with autograft

    11.64 Other penetrating keratoplasty
    Perforating keratoplasty (with homograft)

    11.69 Other corneal transplant

11.7 Other reconstructive and refractive surgery on cornea

    11.71 Keratomileusis

    11.72 Keratophakia

    11.73 Keratoprosthesis

    11.74 Thermokeratoplasty

    11.75 Radial keratotomy

    11.76 Epikeratophakia

    11.79 Other

● Code new to this edition   ▲ Revision of existing code   ④ ⑤ Fourth or fifth digit required

11.9 Other operations on cornea

    11.91 Tattooing of cornea

    11.92 Removal of artificial implant from cornea

    11.99 Other

12 Operation on iris, ciliary body, sclera, and anterior chamber

    Excludes: operations on cornea (11.0-11.99)

12.0 Removal of intraocular foreign body from anterior segment of eye

    12.00 Removal of intraocular foreign body from anterior segment of eye, not otherwise specified

    12.01 Removal of intraocular foreign body from anterior segment of eye with use of magnet

    12.02 Removal of intraocular foreign body from anterior segment of eye without use of magnet

12.1 Iridotomy and simple iridectomy

    Excludes: iridectomy associated with:
        cataract extraction (13.11-13.69)
        removal of lesion (12.41-12.42)
        scleral fistulization (12.61-12.69)

    12.11 Iridotomy with transfixion

    12.12 Other iridotomy
        Corectomy
        Discission of iris
        Iridotomy NOS

    12.13 Excision of prolapsed iris

    12.14 Other iridectomy
        iridectomy (basal) (peripheral) (total)

12.2 Diagnostic procedures on iris, ciliary body, sclera, and anterior chamber

    12.21 Diagnostic aspiration of anterior chamber of eye

    12.22 Biopsy of iris

    12.29 Other diagnostic procedures on iris, ciliary body, sclera, and anterior chamber

12.3 Iridoplasty and coreoplasty

    12.31 Lysis of goniosynechiae
        Lysis of goniosynechiae by injection of air or liquid

    12.32 Lysis of other anterior synechiae
        Lysis of anterior synechiae:
          NOS
          by injection of air or liquid

    12.33 Lysis of posterior synechiae
        Lysis of iris adhesions NOS

    12.34 Lysis of corneovitreal adhesions

    12.35 Coreoplasty
        Needling of pupillary membrane

    12.39 Other iridoplasty

12.4 Excision or destruction of lesion of iris and ciliary body

    12.40 Removal of lesion of anterior segment of eye, not otherwise specified

    12.41 Destruction of lesion of iris, nonexcisional
        Destruction of lesion of iris by:
          cauterization
          cryotherapy
          photocoagulation

    12.42 Excision of lesion of iris
        Excludes: biopsy of iris (12.22)

    12.43 Destruction of lesion of ciliary body, nonexcisional

    12.44 Excision of lesion of ciliary body

12.5 Facilitation of intraocular circulation

    12.51 Goniopuncture without goniotomy

    12.52 Goniotomy without goniopuncture

12.53 Goniotomy with goniopuncture

12.54 Trabeculotomy ab externo

12.55 Cyclodialysis

12.59 Other facilitation of intraocular circulation

12.6 Scleral fistulization

> *Excludes:* exploratory sclerotomy (12.89)

12.61 Trephination of sclera with iridectomy

12.62 Thermocauterization of sclera with iridectomy

12.63 Iridencleisis and iridotasis

12.64 Trabeculectomy ab externo

12.65 Other scleral fistulization with iridectomy

12.66 Postoperative revision of scleral fistulization procedure
Revision of filtering bleb

> *Excludes:* repair of fistula (12.82)

12.69 Other fistulizing procedure

12.7 Other procedures for relief of elevated intraocular pressure

12.71 Cyclodiathermy

12.72 Cyclocryotherapy

12.73 Cyclophotocoagulation

12.74 Diminution of ciliary body, not otherwise specified

12.79 Other glaucoma procedures

12.8 Operations on sclera

> *Excludes:* those associated with:
> retinal reattachment (14.41-14.59)
> scleral fistulization (12.61-12.69)

12.81 Suture of laceration of sclera
Suture of sclera with synchronous repair of conjunctiva

12.82 Repair of scleral fistula

> *Excludes:* postoperative revision of scleral fistulization procedure (12.66)

12.83 Revision of operative wound of anterior segment, not elsewhere classified

> *Excludes:* postoperative revision of scleral fistulization procedure (12.66)

12.84 Excision or destruction of lesion of sclera

12.85 Repair of scleral staphyloma with graft

12.86 Other repair of scleral staphyloma

12.87 Scleral reinforcement with graft

12.88 Other scleral reinforcement

12.89 Other operations on sclera
Exploratory sclerotomy

12.9 Other operations on iris, ciliary body, and anterior chamber

12.91 Therapeutic evacuation of anterior chamber
Paracentesis of anterior chamber

> *Excludes:* diagnostic aspiration (12.21)

12.92 Injection into anterior chamber
Injection of:
air
liquid } into anterior chamber
medication

12.93 Removal or destruction of epithelial downgrowth from anterior chamber

> *Excludes:* that with iridectomy (12.41-12.42)

12.97 Other operations on iris

12.98 Other operations on ciliary body

12.99 Other operations on anterior chamber

● Code new to this edition   ▲ Revision of existing code   ④ ⑤ Fourth or fifth digit required

13   **Operations on lens**

     13.0   **Removal of foreign body from lens**

         Excludes: *removal of pseudophakos (13.8)*

         13.00   **Removal of foreign body from lens, not otherwise specified**

         13.01   **Removal of foreign body from lens with use of magnet**

         13.02   **Removal of foreign body from lens without use of magnet**

     13.1   **Intracapsular extraction of lens**

         Code also any synchronous insertion of pseudophakos (13.71)

         13.11   **Intracapsular extraction of lens by temporal inferior route**

         13.19   **Other intracapsular extraction of lens**
            Cataract extraction NOS
            Cryoextraction of lens
            Erysiphake extraction of cataract
            Extraction of lens NOS

     13.2   **Extracapsular extraction of lens by linear extraction technique**

     13.3   **Extracapsular extraction of lens by simple aspiration (and irrigation) technique**
         Irrigation of traumatic cataract

     13.4   **Extracapsular extraction of lens by fragmentation and aspiration technique**

         13.41   **Phacoemulsification and aspiration of cataract**

         13.42   **Mechanical phacofragmentation and aspiration of cataract by posterior route**
            Code also any synchronous vitrectomy (14.74)

         13.43   **Mechanical phacofragmentation and other aspiration of cataract**

     13.5   **Other extracapsular extraction of lens**

         Code also any synchronous insertion of pseudophakos (13.71)

         13.51   **Extracapsular extraction of lens by temporal inferior route**

         13.59   **Other extracapsular extraction of lens**

     13.6   **Other cataract extraction**

         Code also any synchronous insertion of pseudophakos (13.71)

         13.64   **Discission of secondary membrane [after cataract)**

         13.65   **Excision of secondary membrane [after cataract)**
            Capsulectomy

         13.66   **Mechanical fragmentation of secondary membrane [after cataract]**

         13.69   **Other cataract extraction**

     13.7   **Insertion of prosthetic lens [pseudophakos]**

         13.70   **Insertion of pseudophakos, not otherwise specified**

         13.71   **Insertion of intraocular lens prosthesis at time of cataract extraction, one-stage**
            Code also synchronous extraction of cataract (13.11-13.69)

         13.72   **Secondary insertion of intraocular lens prosthesis**

     13.8   **Removal of implanted lens**
         Removal of pseudophakos

     13.9   **Other operations on lens**

14   **Operations on retina, choroid, vitreous, and posterior chamber**

     14.0   **Removal of foreign body from posterior segment of eye**

         Excludes: *removal of surgically implanted material (14.6)*

         14.00   **Removal of foreign body from posterior segment of eye, not otherwise specified**

         14.01   **Removal of foreign body from posterior segment of eye with use of magnet**

         14.02   **Removal of foreign body from posterior segment of eye without use of magnet**

     14.1   **Diagnostic procedures on retina, choroid, vitreous, and posterior chamber**

         14.11   **Diagnostic aspiration of vitreous**

         14.19   **Other diagnostic procedures on retina, choroid, vitreous, and posterior chamber**

   Valid O.R. procedure   Non-O.R. procedure   Nonspecific O.R. procedure   Noncovered O.R. procedure

14.2 **Destruction of lesion of retina and choroid**
Includes: destruction of chorioretinopathy or isolated chorioretinal lesion

> Excludes: that for repair of retina (14.31-14.59)

14.21 **Destruction of chorioretinal lesion by diathermy**

14.22 **Destruction of chorioretinal lesion by cryotherapy**

14.23 **Destruction of chorioretinal lesion by xenon arc photocoagulation**

14.24 **Destruction of chorioretinal lesion by laser photocoagulation**

14.25 **Destruction of chorioretinal lesion by photocoagulation of unspecified type**

14.26 **Destruction of chorioretinal lesion by radiation therapy**

14.27 **Destruction of chorioretinal lesion by implantation of radiation source**

14.29 **Other destruction of chorioretinal lesion**
Destruction of lesion of retina and choroid NOS

14.3 **Repair of retinal tear**
Includes: repair of retinal defect

> Excludes: repair of retinal detachment (14.41-14.59)

14.31 **Repair of retinal tear by diathermy**

14.32 **Repair of retinal tear by cryotherapy**

14.33 **Repair of retinal tear by xenon arc photocoagulation**

14.34 **Repair of retinal tear by laser photocoagulation**

14.35 **Repair of retinal tear by photocoagulation of unspecified type**

14.39 **Other repair of retinal tear**

14.4 **Repair of retinal detachment with sclera buckling and implant**

14.41 **Scleral buckling with implant**

14.49 **Other scleral buckling**
Scleral buckling with:
air tamponade
resection of sclera
vitrectomy

14.5 **Other repair of retinal detachment**
Includes: that with drainage

14.51 **Repair of retinal detachment with diathermy**

14.52 **Repair of retinal detachment with cryotherapy**

14.53 **Repair of retinal detachment with xenon arc photocoagulation**

14.54 **Repair of retinal detachment with laser photocoagulation**

14.55 **Repair of retinal detachment with photocoagulation of unspecified type**

14.59 **Other**

14.6 **Removal of surgically implanted material from posterior segment of eye**

14.7 **Operations on vitreous**

14.71 **Removal of vitreous, anterior approach**
Open sky technique
Removal of vitreous, anterior approach (with replacement)

14.72 **Other removal of vitreous**
Aspiration of vitreous by posterior sclerotomy

14.73 **Mechanical vitrectomy by anterior approach**

14.74 **Other mechanical vitrectomy**

14.75 **Injection of vitreous substitute**

> Excludes: that associated with removal (14.71-14.72)

14.79 **Other operations on vitreous**

14.9 **Other operations on retina, choroid, and posterior chamber**

15 **Operations on extraocular muscles**

15.0 **Diagnostic procedures on extraocular muscles or tendons**

15.01 **Biopsy of extraocular muscle or tendon**

15.09 **Other diagnostic procedures on extraocular muscles and tendons**

● Code new
to this edition   ▲ Revision of
existing code   ④ ⑤ Fourth or fifth
digit required

15.1 Operations on one extraocular muscle involving temporary detachment from globe

    15.11 Recession of one extraocular muscle

    15.12 Advancement of one extraocular muscle

    15.13 Resection of one extraocular muscle

    15.19 Other operations on one extraocular muscle involving temporary detachment from globe

        Excludes: *transposition of muscle (15.5)*

15.2 Other operations on one extraocular muscle

    15.21 Lengthening procedure on one extraocular muscle

    15.22 Shortening procedure on one extraocular muscle

    15.29 Other

15.3 Operations on two or more extraocular muscles involving temporary detachment from globe, one or both eyes

15.4 Other operations on two or more extraocular muscles, one or both eyes

15.5 Transposition of extraocular muscles

    Excludes: *that for correction of ptosis (08.31-08.36)*

15.6 Revision of extraocular muscle surgery

15.7 Repair of injury of extraocular muscle
Freeing of entrapped extraocular muscle
Lysis of adhesions of extraocular muscle
Repair of laceration of extraocular muscle, tendon, or Tenon's capsule

15.9 Other operations on extraocular muscles and tendon

16 Operations on orbit and eyeball

    Excludes: *reduction of fracture of orbit (76.78-76.79)*

16.0 Orbitotomy

    16.01 Orbitotomy with bone flap
    Orbitotomy with lateral approach

    16.02 Orbitotomy with insertion of orbital implant

        Excludes: *that with bone flap (16.01)*

    16.09 Other orbitotomy

16.1 Removal of penetrating foreign body from eye, not otherwise specified

    Excludes: *removal of nonpenetrating foreign body (98.21)*

16.2 Diagnostic procedures on orbit and eyeball

    16.21 Ophthalmoscopy

    16.22 Diagnostic aspiration of orbit

    16.23 Biopsy of eyeball and orbit

    16.29 Other diagnostic procedures on orbit and eyeball

        Excludes: *examination of form and structure of eye (95.11-95.16)*
        general and subjective eye examination (95.01-95.09)
        microscopic examination of specimen from eye (90.21-90.29)
        objective functional tests of eye (95.21-95.26)
        ocular thermography (88.82)
        tonometry (89.11)
        X-ray of orbit (87.14, 87.16)

16.3 Evisceration of eyeball

    16.31 Removal of ocular contents with synchronous implant into scleral shell

    16.39 Other evisceration of eyeball

16.4 Enucleation of eyeball

    16.41 Enucleation of eyeball with synchronous implant into Tenon's capsule with attachment of muscles
    Integrated implant of eyeball

    16.42 Enucleation of eyeball with other synchronous implant

    16.49 Other enucleation of eyeball
    Removal of eyeball NOS

16.5 Exenteration of orbital contents

16.51 Exenteration of orbit with removal of adjacent structures
Radical orbitomaxillectomy

16.52 Exenteration of orbit with therapeutic removal of orbital bone

16.59 Other exenteration of orbit
Evisceration of orbit NOS
Exenteration of orbit with temporalis muscle transplant

16.6 Secondary procedures after removal of eyeball

> *Excludes:* *that with synchronous:*
> *enucleation of eyeball (16.41-1642)*
> *evisceration of eyeball (16.31)*

16.61 Secondary insertion of ocular implant

16.62 Revision and reinsertion of ocular implant

16.63 Revision of enucleation socket with graft

16.64 Other revision of enucleation socket

16.65 Secondary graft to exenteration cavity

16.66 Other revision of exenteration cavity

16.69 Other secondary procedures after removal of eyeball

16.7 Removal of ocular or orbital implant

16.71 Removal of ocular implant

16.72 Removal of orbital implant

16.8 Repair of injury of eyeball and orbit

16.81 Repair of wound of orbit

> *Excludes:* *reduction of orbital fracture (76.78-76.79)*
> *repair of extraocular muscles (15.7)*

16.82 Repair of rupture of eyeball
Repair of multiple structures of eye

> *Excludes:* *repair of laceration of:*
> *cornea (11.51-11.59)*
> *sclera (12.81)*

16.89 Other repair of injury of eyeball or orbit

16.9 Other operations on orbit and eyeball

> *Excludes:* *irrigation of eye (96.51)*
> *prescription and fitting of low vision aids (95.31-95.33)*
> *removal of:*
> *eye prosthesis NEC (97.31)*
> *nonpenetrating foreign body from eye without incision (98.21)*

16.91 Retrobulbar injection of therapeutic agent

> *Excludes:* *injection of radiographic contrast material (87.14)*
> *opticociliary injection (12.79)*

16.92 Excision of lesion of orbit

> *Excludes:* *biopsy of orbit (16.23)*

16.93 Excision of lesion of eye, unspecified structure

> *Excludes:* *biopsy of eye NOS (16.23)*

16.98 Other operations on orbit

16.99 Other operations on eyeball

   ● Code new
to this edition   ▲ Revision of
existing code   ④ ⑤ Fourth or fifth
digit required

4.   OPERATIONS ON THE EAR (18-20)

18   Operations on external ear
Includes: operations on:
external auditory canal
skin and cartilage of:
auricle
meatus

18.0   Incision of external ear
Excludes: *removal of intraluminal foreign body (98.11)*

18.01   Piercing of ear lobe
Piercing of pinna

18.02   Incision of external auditory canal

18.09   Other incision of external ear

18.1   Diagnostic procedures on external ear

18.11   Otoscopy

18.12   Biopsy of external ear

18.19   Other diagnostic procedures on external ear
Excludes: *microscopic examination of specimen from ear (90.31-90.39)*

18.2   Excision or destruction of lesion of external ear

18.21   Excision of preauricular sinus
Radical excision of preauricular sinus or cyst
Excludes: *excision of preauricular remnant [appendage] (18.29)*

18.29   Excision or destruction of other lesion of external ear
Cauterization
Coagulation
Cryosurgery
Curettage   } of external car
Electrocoagulation
Enucleation
Excision of:
exostosis of external auditory canal
preauricular remnant [appendage]
Partial excision of ear
Excludes: *biopsy of external ear (18.12)*
radical excision of lesion (18.31)
removal of cerumen (96.52)

18.3   Other excision of external ear
Excludes: *biopsy of external ear (18.12)*

18.31   Radical excision of lesion of external ear
Excludes: *radical excision of preauricular sinus (18.21)*

18.39   Other
Amputation of external ear
Excludes: *excision of lesion (18.21-18.29, 18.31)*

18.4   Suture of laceration of external ear

18.5   Surgical correction of prominent ear
Ear:
pinning
setback

18.6   Reconstruction of external auditory canal
Canaloplasty of external auditory meatus
Construction [reconstruction] of external meatus of ear:
osseous portion
skin-lined portion (with skin graft)

18.7   Other plastic repair of external ear

18.71   Construction of auricle of ear
Prosthetic appliance for absent ear
Reconstruction:
auricle
ear

18.72 **Reattachment of amputated ear**

18.79 **Other plastic repair of external ear**
Otoplasty NOS
Postauricular skin graft
Repair of lop ear

18.9 **Other operations on external ear**
> *Excludes:* *irrigation of ear (96.52)*
> *packing of external auditory canal (96.11)*
> *removal of:*
> *cerumen (96.52)*
> *foreign body (without incision) (98.11)*

19 Reconstructive operations on middle ear

19.0 **Stapes mobilization**
Division, otosclerotic: Remobilization of stapes
  material   Stapediolysis
  process   Transcrural stapes mobilization
> *Excludes:* *that with synchronous stapedectomy (19.11-19.19)*

19.1 **Stapedectomy**
> *Excludes:* *revision of previous stapedectomy (19.21-19.29)*
> *stapes mobilization only (19.0)*

19.11 **Stapedectomy with incus replacement**
Stapedectomy with incus:
  homograft
  prosthesis

19.19 **Other stapedectomy**

19.2 **Revision of stapedectomy**

19.21 **Revision of stapedectomy with incus replacement**

19.29 **Other revision of stapedectomy**

19.3 **Other operations on ossicular chain**
Incudectomy NOS
Ossiculectomy NOS
Reconstruction of ossicles, second stage

19.4 **Myringoplasty**
Epitympanic, type I
Myringoplasty by:
  cauterization
  graft
Tympanoplasty (type I)

19.5 **Other tympanoplasty**

19.52 **Type II tympanoplasty**
Closure of perforation with graft against incus or malleus

19.53 **Type III tympanoplasty**
Graft placed in contact with mobile and intact stapes

19.54 **Type IV tympanoplasty**
Mobile footplate left exposed with air pocket between round window and graft

19.55 **Type V tympanoplasty**
Fenestra in horizontal semicircular canal covered by graft

19.6 **Revision of tympanoplasty**

19.9 **Other repair of middle ear**
Closure of mastoid fistula
Mastoid myoplasty
Obliteration of tympanomastoid cavity

20 Other operations on middle and inner ear

20.0 **Myringotomy**

20.01 **Myringotomy with insertion of tube**
Myringostomy

20.09 **Other myringotomy**
Aspiration of middle ear NOS

20.1 **Removal of tympanostomy tube**

20.2 **Incision of mastoid and middle ear**

● Code new
  to this edition   ▲ Revision of
  existing code   ④ ⑤ Fourth or fifth
  digit required

20.21 **Incision of mastoid**

20.22 **Incision of petrous pyramid air cells**

20.23 **Incision of middle ear**
Atticotomy
Division of tympanum
Lysis of adhesions of middle ear

> *Excludes:*   *divisions of otosclerotic process (19.0)*
> *stapediolysis (19.0)*
> *that with stapedectomy (19.11-19.19)*

20.3   **Diagnostic procedures on middle and inner ear**

20.31   **Electrocochleography**

20.32   **Biopsy of middle and inner ear**

20.39   **Other diagnostic procedures on middle and inner ear**

> *Excludes:*   *auditory and vestibular function tests (89.13, 95.41-95.49)*
> *microscopic examination of specimen from ear (90.31-90.39)*

20.4   **Mastoidectomy**
Code also any:
skin graft (18.79)
tympanoplasty (19.4-19.55)

> *Excludes:*   *that with implantation of cochlear prosthetic device (20.96-20.98)*

20.41   **Simple mastoidectomy**

20.42   **Radical mastoidectomy**

20.49   **Other mastoidectomy**
Atticoantrotomy
Mastoidectomy:
NOS
modified radical

20.5   **Other excision of middle ear**

> *Excludes:*   *that with synchronous mastoidectomy (20.41-20.49)*

20.51   **Excision of lesion of middle ear**

> *Excludes:*   *biopsy of middle ear (20.32)*

20.59   **Other**
Apicectomy of petrous pyramid
Tympanectomy

20.6   **Fenestration of inner ear**

20.61   **Fenestration of inner ear(initial)**
Fenestration of:
labyrinth
semicircular canals   with graft (skin) (vein)
vestibule

> *Excludes:*   *that with tympanoplasty type V (19.55)*

20.62   **Revision of fenestration of inner ear**

20.7   **Incision, excision, and destruction of inner ear**

20.71   **Endolymphatic shunt**

20.72   **Injection into inner ear**
Destruction by injection (alcohol):
inner ear
semicircular canals
vestibule

20.79   **Other incision, excision and destruction of inner ear**
Decompression of labyrinth
Drainage of inner ear
Fistulization:
endolymphatic sac
labyrinth
Incision of endolymphatic sac
Labyrinthectomy (transtympanic)
Opening of bony labyrinth
Perilymphatic tap

> *Excludes:*   *biopsy of inner ear (20.32)*

Valid O.R. procedure   Non-O.R. procedure   Nonspecific O.R. procedure   Noncovered O.R. procedure

20.8 **Operations on Eustachian tube**
 Catheterization
 Inflation
 Injection (Teflon paste)
 Insufflation (boric acid-salicylic acid) } of Eustachian tube
 Intubation
 Politzerization

20.9 **Other operations on inner and middle ear**

20.91 **Tympanosympathectomy**

20.92 **Revision of mastoidectomy**

20.93 **Repair of oval and round windows**
 Closure of fistula:
  oval window
  perilymph
  round window

20.94 **Injection of tympanum**

20.95 **Implantation of electromagnetic bearing device**
 Bone conduction hearing device

 | *Excludes:* | *cochlear prosthetic device (20.96-20.98)*

20.96 **Implantation or replacement of cochlear prosthetic device, not otherwise specified**
 Implantation of receiver (within skull) and insertion of electrode(s) in the cochlea
 Includes: mastoidectomy

 | *Excludes:* | *electromagnetic hearing device (20.95)*

20.97 **Implantation or replacement of cochlear prosthetic device, single channel**
 Implantation of receiver (within skull) and insertion of electrode in the cochlea
 Includes: mastoidectomy

 | *Excludes:* | *electromagnetic hearing device (20.95)*

20.98 **Implantation or replacement of cochlear prosthetic device, multiple channel**
 Implantation of receiver (within skull) and insertion of electrodes in the cochlea
 Includes: mastoidectomy

 | *Excludes:* | *electromagnetic hearing device (20.95)*

20.99 **Other operations on middle and inner ear**
 Repair or removal of cochlear prosthetic device (receiver) (electrode)

 | *Excludes:* | *adjustment (external components) of cochlear prosthetic device (95.49)*
      fitting of hearing aid (95.48)

● Code new to this edition ▲ Revision of existing code ④ ⑤ Fourth or fifth digit required

5.   OPERATIONS ON THE NOSE, MOUTH, AND PHARYNX (21-29)

21   Operation on nose
Includes: operations on:
bone
skin   } of nose

21.0   Control of epistaxis

21.00   Control of epistaxis, not otherwise specified

21.01   Control of epistaxis by anterior nasal packing

21.02   Control of epistaxis by posterior (and anterior) packing

21.03   Control of epistaxis by cauterization (and packing)

21.04   Control of epistaxis by ligation of ethmoidal arteries

21.05   Control of epistaxis by (transantral) ligation of the maxillary artery

21.06   Control of epistaxis by ligation of the external carotid artery

21.07   Control of epistaxis by excision of nasal mucosa and skin grafting on septum and lateral nasal wall

21.09   Control of epistaxis by other means

21.1   Incision of nose
Chondrotomy
Incision of skin of nose
Nasal septotomy

21.2   Diagnostic procedures on nose

21.21   Rhinoscopy

21.22   Biopsy of nose

21.29   Other diagnostic procedures on nose

> *Excludes:*   *microscopic examination of specimen from nose (90.31-90.39)*
> *nasal:*
> *function study (89.12)*
> *x-ray (87.16)*
> *rhinomanometry (89.12)*

21.3   Local excision or destruction of lesion of nose

> *Excludes:*   *biopsy of nose (21.22)*
> *nasal fistulectomy (21.82)*

21.30   Excision or destruction of nose, not otherwise specified

21.31   Local excision or destruction of intranasal lesion
Nasal polypectomy

21.32   Local excision or destruction of other lesion of nose

21.4   Resection of nose
Amputation of nose

21.5   Submucous resection of nasal septum

21.6   Turbinectomy

21.61   Turbinectomy by diathermy or cryosurgery

21.62   Fracture of the turbinates

21.69   Other turbinectomy

> *Excludes:*   *turbinectomy associated with sinusectomy (22.31-22.39, 22.42.*
> *22.60-22.64)*

21.7   Reduction of nasal fracture

21.71   Closed reduction of nasal fracture

21.72   Open reduction of nasal fracture

21.8   Repair and plastic operations on the nose

21.81   Suture of laceration of nose

21.82   Closure of nasal fistula
Nasolabial
Nasopharyngeal   } fistulectomy
Oronasal

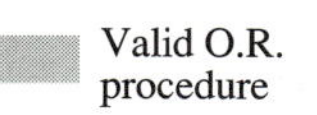
Valid O.R.
procedure

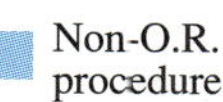
Non-O.R.
procedure

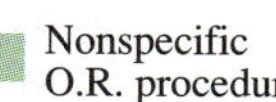
Nonspecific
O.R. procedure

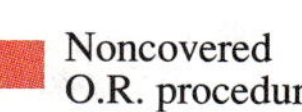
Noncovered
O.R. procedure

21.83 Total nasal reconstruction
Reconstruction of nose with:
  arm flap
  forehead flap

21.84 Revision rhinoplasty
Rhinoseptoplasty
Twisted nose rhinoplasty

21.85 Augmentation rhinoplasty
Augmentation rhinoplasty with:
  graft
  synthetic implant

21.86 Limited rhinoplasty
Plastic repair of nasolabial flaps
Tip rhinoplasty

21.87 Other rhinoplasty
Rhinoplasty NOS

21.88 Other septoplasty
Crushing of nasal septum
Repair of septal perforation

Excludes:	*septoplasty associated with submucous resection of septum (21.5)*

21.89 Other repair and plastic operations on nose
Reattachment of amputated nose

21.9 Other operations on nose

21.91 Lysis of adhesions of nose
Posterior nasal scrub

21.99 Other

Excludes:	*dilation of frontonasal duct (96.21)*
	irrigation of nasal passages (96.53)
	removal of:
	intraluminal foreign body without incision (98.12)
	nasal packing (97.32)
	replacement of nasal packing (97.21)

22 Operations on nasal sinuses

22.0 Aspiration and lavage of nasal sinus

22.00 Aspiration and lavage of nasal sinus, not otherwise specified

22.01 Puncture of nasal sinus for aspiration or lavage

22.02 Aspiration or lavage of nasal sinus through natural ostium

22.1 Diagnostic procedures on nasal sinus

22.11 Closed [endoscopic] [needle] biopsy of nasal sinus

22.12 Open biopsy of nasal sinus

22.19 Other diagnostic procedures on nasal sinuses
Endoscopy without biopsy

Excludes:	*transillumination of sinus (89.35)*
	x-ray of sinus (87.15-87.16)

22.2 Intranasal antrotomy

Excludes:	*antrotomy with external approach (22.31-22.39)*

22.3 External maxillary antrotomy

22.31 Radical maxillary antrotomy
Removal of lining membrane of maxillary sinus using Caldwell-Luc approach

22.39 Other external maxillary antrotomy
Exploration of maxillary antrum with Caldwell-Luc approach

22.4 Frontal sinusotomy and sinusectomy

22.41 Frontal sinusotomy

22.42 Frontal sinusectomy
Excision of lesion of frontal sinus
Obliteration of frontal sinus (with fat)

Excludes:	*biopsy of nasal sinus (22.11-22.12)*

22.5 Other nasal sinusotomy

● Code new
to this edition

▲ Revision of
existing code

④ ⑤ Fourth or fifth
digit required

22.50   **Sinusotomy, not otherwise specified**

22.51   **Ethmoidotomy**

22.52   **Sphenoidotomy**

22.53   **Incision of multiple nasal sinuses**

22.6   **Other nasal sinusectomy**
Includes: that with incidental turbinectomy

> *Excludes:*   *biopsy of nasal sinus (22.11-22.12)*

22.60   **Sinusectomy, not otherwise specified**

22.61   **Excision of lesion of maxillary sinus with Caldwell-Luc approach**

22.62   **Excision of lesion of maxillary sinus with other approach**

22.63   **Ethmoidectomy**

22.64   **Sphenoidectomy**

22.7   **Repair of nasal sinus**

22.71   **Closure of nasal sinus fist**
Repair of oro-antral fistula

22.79   **Other repair of nasal sinus**
Reconstruction of frontonasal duct
Repair of bone of accessory sinus

22.9   **Other operations on nasal sinuses**
Exteriorization of maxillary sinus
Fistulization of sinus

> *Excludes:*   *dilation of frontonasal duct (96.21)*

23   **Removal and restoration of teeth**

23.0   **Forceps extraction of tooth**

23.01   **Extraction of deciduous tooth**

23.09   **Extraction of other tooth**
Extraction of tooth NOS

23.1   **Surgical removal of tooth**

23.11   **Removal of residual root**

23.19   **Other surgical extraction of tooth**
Odontectomy NOS
Removal of impacted tooth
Tooth extraction with elevation of mucoperiosteal flap

23.2   **Restoration of tooth by filling**

23.3   **Restoration of tooth by inlay**

23.4   **Other dental restoration**

23.41   **Application of crown**

23.42   **Insertion of fixed bridge**

23.43   **Insertion of removable bridge**

23.49   **Other**

23.5   **Implantation of tooth**

23.6   **Prosthetic dental implant**
Endosseous dental implant

23.7   **Apicoectomy and root canal therapy**

23.70   **Root canal not otherwise specified**

23.71   **Root canal therapy with irrigation**

23.72   **Root canal therapy with apicoectomy**

23.73   **Apicoectomy**

24   **Other operations on teeth, gums, and alveoli**

24.0   **Incision of gum or alveolar bone**
Apical alveolotomy

24.1   **Diagnostic procedures on teeth, gums, and alveoli**

24.11   **Biopsy of gum**

24.12   **Biopsy of alveoli**

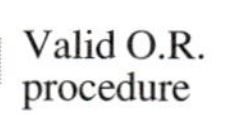 Valid O.R. procedure

 Non-O.R. procedure

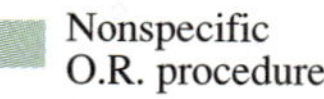 Nonspecific O.R. procedure

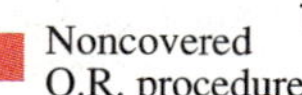 Noncovered O.R. procedure

24.19 Other diagnostic procedures on teeth, gums, and alveoli

> *Excludes:* *dental:*
> *examination (89.31)*
> *x-ray:*
> *full-mouth (87.11)*
> *other (87.12)*
> *microscopic examination of dental specimen (90.81-90.89)*

24.2 Gingivoplasty
Gingivoplasty with bone or soft tissue graft

24.3 Other operations on gum

24.31 Excision of lesion or tissue of gum

> *Excludes:* *biopsy of gum (24.11)*
> *excision of odontogenic lesion (24.4)*

24.32 Suture of laceration of gum

24.39 Other

24.4 Excision of dental lesion of jaw
Excision of odontogenic lesion

24.5 Alveoloplasty
Alveolectomy (interradicular) (intraseptal) (radical) (simple) (with graft or implant)

> *Excludes:* *biopsy of alveolus (24.12)*
> *en bloc resection of alveolar process and palate (27.32)*

24.6 Exposure of tooth

24.7 Application of orthodontic appliance
Application, insertion, or fitting of:
arch bars
orthodontic obturator
orthodontic wiring
periodontal splint

> *Excludes:* *nonorthodontic dental wiring (93.55)*

24.8 Other orthodontic operation
Closure of diastema (alveolar) (dental)
Occlusal adjustment
Removal of arch bars
Repair of dental arch

> *Excludes:* *removal of nonorthodontic wiring (97.33)*

24.9 Other dental operations

24.91 Extension or deepening of buccolabial or lingual sulcus

24.99 Other

> *Excludes:* *dental:*
> *debridement (96.54)*
> *examination (89.31)*
> *prophylaxis (96.54)*
> *scaling and polishing (96.54)*
> *wiring (93.55)*
> *fitting of dental appliance [denture] (99.97)*
> *microscopic examination of dental specimen (90.81-90.89)*
> *removal of dental:*
> *packing (97.34)*
> *prosthesis (97.35)*
> *wiring (97.33)*
> *replacement of dental packing (97.22)*

25 Operations on tongue

25.0 Diagnostic procedures on tongue

25.01 Closed [needle] biopsy of tongue

25.02 Open biopsy of tongue
Wedge biopsy

25.09 Other diagnostic procedures on tongue

● Code new
to this edition   ▲ Revision of
existing code   ④ ⑤ Fourth or fifth
digit required

25.1 Excision or destruction of lesion or tissue of tongue

> *Excludes:* *biopsy of tongue (25.01-25.02)*
> *frenumectomy:*
> *labial (27.41)*
> *lingual (25.92)*

25.2 Partial glossectomy

25.3 Complete glossectomy
Glossectomy NOS
Code also any neck dissection (40.40-40.42)

25.4 Radical glossectomy
Code also any:
neck dissection (40.40-40.42)
tracheostomy (31.1-31.29)

25.5 Repair of tongue and glossoplasty

25.51 Suture of laceration of tongue

25.59 Other repair and plastic operations on tongue
Fascial sling of tongue
Fusion of tongue (to lip)
Graft of mucosa or skin to tongue

> *Excludes:* *lysis of adhesions of tongue (25.93)*

25.9 Other operations on tongue

25.91 Lingual frenotomy

> *Excludes:* *labial frenotomy (27.91)*

25.92 Lingual frenectomy

> *Excludes:* *labial frenectomy (27.41)*

25.93 Lysis of adhesions of tongue

25.94 Other glossotomy

25.99 Other

26 Operations on salivary glands and ducts
Includes: operations on:
lesser salivary
parotid } gland and duct
sublingual
submaxillary

Code also any neck dissection (40.40-40.42)

26.0 Incision of salivary gland or duct

26.1 Diagnostic procedures on salivary glands and ducts

26.11 Closed [needle] biopsy of salivary gland or duct

26.12 Open biopsy of salivary gland or duct

26.19 Other diagnostic procedures on salivary glands and ducts

> *Excludes:* *x-ray of salivary gland (87.09)*

26.2 Excision of lesion of salivary gland

26.21 Marsupialization of salivary gland cyst

26.29 Other excision of salivary gland lesion

> *Excludes:* *biopsy of salivary gland (26.11-26.12)*
> *salivary fistulectomy (26.42)*

26.3 Sialoadenectomy

26.30 Sialoadenectomy, not otherwise specified

26.31 Partial sialoadenectomy

26.32 Complete sialoadenectomy
En bloc excision of salivary gland lesion
Radical sialoadenectomy

26.4 Repair of salivary gland or duct

26.41 Suture of laceration of salivary gland

26.42 Closure of salivary fistula

Valid O.R. procedure   Non-O.R. procedure   Nonspecific O.R. procedure   Noncovered O.R. procedure

26.49 **Other repair and plastic operations on salivary gland or duct**
Fistulization of salivary gland
Plastic repair of salivary gland or duct NOS
Transplantation of salivary duct opening

26.9 **Other operations on salivary gland or duct**

26.91 **Probing of salivary duct**

26.99 **Other**

27 **Other operations on mouth and face**
Includes: operations on:
lips
palate
soft tissue of face and mouth, except tongue and gingiva

| Excludes | *operations on:*
gingiva (24.0-24.99)
tongue (25.01-25.99)

27.0 **Drainage of face and floor of mouth**
Drainage of:
facial region (abscess)
fascial compartment of face
Ludwig's angina

Excludes: *drainage of thyroglossal tract (06.09)*

27.1 **Incision of palate**

27.2 **Diagnostic procedures on oral cavity**

27.21 **Biopsy of bony palate**

27.22 **Biopsy of uvula and soft palate**

27.23 **Biopsy of lip**

27.24 **Biopsy of mouth, unspecified structure**

27.29 **Other diagnostic procedures on oral cavity**

Excludes: *soft tissue x-ray (87.09)*

27.3 **Excision of lesion or tissue of bony palate**

27.31 **Local excision or destruction of lesion or tissue of bony palate**
Local excision or destruction of palate by:
cautery
chemotherapy
cryotherapy

Excludes: *biopsy of bony palate (27.21)*

27.32 **Wide excision or destruction of lesion or tissue of bony palate**
En bloc resection of alveolar process and palate

27.4 **Excision of other parts of mouth**

27.41 **Labial frenectomy**

Excludes: *division of labial frenum (27.91)*

27.42 **Wide excision of lesion of lip**

27.43 **Other excision of lesion or tissue of lip**

27.49 **Other excision of mouth**

Excludes: *biopsy of mouth NOS (27.24)*
excision of lesion of:
palate (27.31-27.32)
tongue (25.1)
uvula (27.72)
fistulectomy of mouth (27.53)
frenectomy of:
lip (27.41)
tongue (25.92)

27.5 **Plastic repair of mouth**

Excludes: *palatoplasty (27.61-27.69)*

27.51 **Suture of laceration of lip**

27.52 **Suture of laceration of other part of mouth**

● Code new to this edition   ▲ Revision of existing code   ④ ⑤ Fourth or fifth digit required

27.53 Closure of fistula of mouth

> *Excludes:* *fistulectomy:*
>> *nasolabial (21.82)*
>> *oro-antral (22.71)*
>> *oronasal (21.82)*

27.54 Repair of cleft lip

27.55 Full-thickness skin graft to lip and mouth

27.56 Other skin graft to lip and mouth

27.57 Attachment of pedicle or flap graft to lip and mouth

27.59 Other plastic repair of mouth

27.6 Palatoplasty

27.61 Suture of laceration of palate

27.62 Correction of cleft palate
Correction of cleft palate by push-back operation

> *Excludes:* *revision of cleft palate repair (27.63)*

27.63 Revision of cleft palate repair
Secondary:
  attachment of pharyngeal flap
  lengthening of palate

27.69 Other plastic repair of palate

> *Excludes:* *fistulectomy of mouth (27.53)*

27.7 Operations on uvula

27.71 Incision of uvula

27.72 Excision of uvula

> *Excludes:* *biopsy of uvula (27.22)*

27.73 Repair of uvula

> *Excludes:* *that with synchronous cleft palate repair (27.62)*
>> *uranostaphylorrhaphy (27.62)*

27.79 Other operations on uvula

27.9 Other operations on mouth and face

27.91 Labial frenotomy
Division of labial frenum

> *Excludes:* *lingual frenotomy (25.91)*

27.92 Incision of mouth, unspecified structure

> *Excludes:* *incision of:*
>> *gum (24.0)*
>> *palate (27.1)*
>> *salivary gland or duct (26.0)*
>> *tongue (25.94)*
>> *uvula (27.71)*

27.99 Other operations on oral cavity
Graft of buccal sulcus

> *Excludes:* *removal of:*
>> *intraluminal foreign body (98.01)*
>> *penetrating foreign body from mouth without incision (98.22)*

28 Operations on tonsils and adenoids

28.0 Incision and drainage of tonsil and peritonsillar structures
Drainage (oral) (transcervical) of:
  parapharyngeal
  peritonsillar ⎫
  retropharyngeal ⎬ abscess
  tonsillar ⎭

28.1 Diagnostic procedures on tonsils and adenoids

28.11 Biopsy of tonsils and adenoids

28.19 Other diagnostic procedures on tonsils and adenoids

> *Excludes:* *soft tissue x-ray (87.09)*

Valid O.R. procedure	Non-O.R. procedure	Nonspecific O.R. procedure	Noncovered O.R. procedure

28.2   **Tonsillectomy without adenoidectomy**

28.3   **Tonsillectomy with adenoidectomy**

28.4   **Excision of tonsil tag**

28.5   **Excision of lingual tonsil**

28.6   **Adenoidectomy without tonsillectomy**
Excision of adenoid tag

28.7   **Control of hemorrhage after tonsillectomy and adenoidectomy**

28.9   **Other operations on tonsils and adenoids**

    28.91   **Removal of foreign body from tonsil and adenoid by incision**
        Excludes: *that without incision (98.13)*

    28.92   **Excision of lesion of tonsil and adenoid**
        Excludes: *biopsy of tonsil and adenoid (28.11)*

    28.99   **Other**

29   **Operation on pharynx**
Includes: operations on:
      hypopharynx
      nasopharynx
      oropharynx
      pharyngeal pouch
      pyriform sinus

29.0   **Pharyngotomy**
Drainage of pharyngeal bursa
    Excludes: *incision and drainage of retropharyngeal abscess (28.0)*
               removal of foreign body (without incision) (98.13)

29.1   **Diagnostic procedures on pharynx**

    29.11   **Pharyngoscopy**

    29.12   **Pharyngeal biopsy**
       Biopsy of supraglottic mass

    29.19   **Other diagnostic procedures on pharynx**
        Excludes: *x-ray of nasopharynx:*
             contrast (87.06)
             other (87.09)

29.2   **Excision of branchial cleft cyst or vestige**
    Excludes: *branchial cleft fistulectomy (29.52)*

29.3   **Excision or destruction of lesion or tissue of pharynx**

    29.31   **Cricopharyngeal myotomy**
        Excludes   *that with pharyngeal diverticulectomy (29.32)*

    29.32   **Pharyngeal diverticulectomy**

    29.33   **Pharyngectomy (partial)**
        Excludes   *laryngopharyngectomy (30.3)*

    29.39   **Other excision or destruction of lesion or tissue of pharynx**

29.4   **Plastic operation on pharynx**
Correction of nasopharyngeal atresia
    Excludes: *pharyngoplasty associated with cleft palate repair (27.62-27.63)*

29.5   **Other repair of pharynx**

    29.51   **Suture of laceration of pharynx**

    29.52   **Closure of branchial cleft fistula**

    29.53   **Closure of other fistula of pharynx**
       Pharyngoesophageal fistulectomy

    29.54   **Lysis of pharyngeal adhesions**

    29.59   **Other**

29.9   **Other operations on pharynx**

    29.91   **Dilation of pharynx**
       Dilation of nasopharynx

    29.92   **Division of glossopharyngeal nerve**

● Code new to this edition   ▲ Revision of existing code   ④ ⑤ Fourth or fifth digit required

29.99 **Other**

> *Excludes:* insertion of radium into pharynx and nasopharynx (92.27)
> removal of intraluminal foreign body (98.13)

	Valid O.R. procedure		Non-O.R. procedure		Nonspecific O.R. procedure		Noncovered O.R. procedure

● Code new
to this edition

▲ Revision of
existing code

④ ⑤ Fourth or fifth
digit required

6.   OPERATIONS ON THE RESPIRATORY SYSTEM (30-34)

30   Excision of larynx

30.0   Excision or destruction of lesion or tissue of larynx

30.01   Marsupialization of laryngeal cyst

30.09   Other excision or destruction of lesion or tissue of larynx
Stripping of vocal cords

> *Excludes:* *biopsy of larynx (31.43)*
> *laryngeal fistulectomy (31.62)*
> *laryngotracheal fistulectomy (31.62)*

30.1   Hemilaryngectomy

30.2   Other partial laryngectomy

30.21   Epiglottidectomy

30.22   Vocal cordectomy
Excision of vocal cords

30.29   Other partial laryngectomy
Excision of laryngeal cartilage

30.3   Complete laryngectomy
Block dissection of larynx (with thyroidectomy) (with synchronous tracheostomy)
Laryngopharyngectomy

> *Excludes:* *that with radical neck dissection (30.4)*

30.4   Radical laryngectomy
Complete [total] laryngectomy with radical neck dissection (with thyroidectomy) (with synchronous tracheostomy)

31   Other operations on larynx and trachea

31.0   Injection of larynx
Injection of inert material into larynx or vocal cords

31.1   Temporary tracheostomy
Tracheotomy for assistance in breathing

31.2   Permanent tracheostomy

31.21   Mediastinal tracheostomy

31.29   Other permanent tracheostomy

> *Excludes:* *that with laryngectomy (30.3-30.4)*

31.3   Other incision of larynx or trachea

> *Excludes:* *that for assistance in breathing (31.1-31.29)*

31.4   Diagnostic procedures on larynx and trachea

31.41   Tracheoscopy through artificial stoma

> *Excludes:* *that with biopsy (31.43-31.44)*

31.42   Laryngoscopy and other tracheoscopy

> *Excludes:* *that with biopsy (31.43-31.44)*

31.43   Closed [endoscopic] biopsy of larynx

31.44   Closed [endoscopic] biopsy of trachea

31.45   Open biopsy of larynx or trachea

31.48   Other diagnostic procedures on larynx

> *Excludes:* *contrast laryngogram (87.07)*
> *microscopic examination of specimen from larynx (90.31-90.39)*
> *soft tissue x-ray of larynx NEC (87.09)*

31.49   Other diagnostic procedures on trachea

> *Excludes:* *microscopic examination of specimen from trachea (90.41-90.49)*
> *x-ray of trachea (87.49)*

31.5   Local excision or destruction of lesion or tissue of trachea

> *Excludes:* *biopsy of trachea (31.44-31.45)*
> *laryngotracheal fistulectomy (31.62)*
> *tracheoesophageal fistulectomy (31.73)*

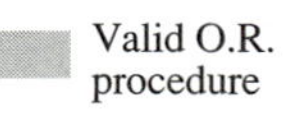 Valid O.R. procedure

 Non-O.R. procedure

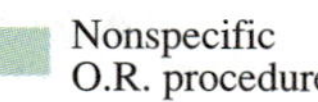 Nonspecific O.R. procedure

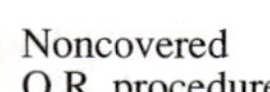 Noncovered O.R. procedure

31.6   **Repair of larynx**

31.61   **Suture of laceration of larynx**

31.62   **Closure of fistula of larynx**
Laryngotracheal fistulectomy
Take-down of laryngostomy

31.63   **Revision of laryngostomy**

31.64   **Repair of laryngeal fracture**

31.69   **Other repair of larynx**
Arytenoidopexy
Graft of larynx
Transposition of vocal cords
> *Excludes:*   construction of artificial larynx (31.75)

31.7   **Repair and plastic operations on trachea**

31.71   **Suture of laceration of trachea**

31.72   **Closure of external fistula of trachea**
Closure of tracheotomy

31.73   **Closure of other fistula of trachea**
Tracheoesophageal fistulectomy
> *Excludes:*   laryngotracheal fistulectomy (31.62)

31.74   **Revision of tracheostomy**

31.75   **Reconstruction of trachea and construction of artificial larynx**
Tracheoplasty with artificial larynx

31.79   **Other repair and plastic operations on trachea**

31.9   **Other operations on larynx and trachea**

31.91   **Division of laryngeal nerve**

31.92   **Lysis of adhesions of trachea or larynx**

31.93   **Replacement of laryngeal or tracheal stent**

31.94   **Injection of locally-acting therapeutic substance into trachea**

31.95   **Tracheoesophageal fistulization**

31.98   **Other operations on larynx**
Dilation
Division of congenital web   } of larynx
Removal of keel or stent
> *Excludes:*   removal of intraluminal foreign body from larynx without incision
> (98.14)

31.99   **Other operations on trachea**
> *Excludes:*   removal of:
> intraluminal foreign body from trachea without incision (98.15)
> tracheostomy tube (97.37)
> replacement of tracheostomy tube (97.23)
> tracheostomy toilette (96.35)

32   **Excision of lung and bronchus**
Includes: rib resection
sternotomy
sternum-splitting incision   } as operative approach
thoracotomy

Code also any synchronous bronchoplasty (33.48)

32.0   **Local excision or destruction of lesion or tissue of bronchus**
> *Excludes:*   biopsy of bronchus (33.24-33.25)
> bronchial fistulectomy (33.42)

32.01   **Endoscopic excision or destruction of lesion or tissue of bronchus**

32.09   **Other local excision or destruction of lesion or tissue of bronchus**
> *Excludes:*   that by endoscopic approach (32.01)

32.1   **Other excision of bronchus**
Resection (wide sleeve) of bronchus
> *Excludes:*   radical dissection [excision] of bronchus (32.6)

   ● Code new
to this edition
  ▲ Revision of
existing code
  ④ ⑤ Fourth or fifth
digit required

32.2 **Local excision or destruction of lesion or tissue of lung**

> **32.21** **Plication of emphysematous bleb**

> **32.22** **Lung volume reduction surgery**

> **32.28** **Endoscopic excision or destruction of lesion or tissue of lung**
>
>> *Excludes:* *biopsy of lung (33.26-33.27)*

> **32.29** **Other local excision or destruction of lesion or tissue of lung**
>> Resection of lung:
>>> NOS
>>> wedge
>>
>> *Excludes:* *biopsy of lung (33.26-33.27)*
>>> *that by endoscopic approach (32.28)*
>>> *wide excision of lesion of lung (32.3)*

32.3 **Segmental resection of lung**
> Partial lobectomy

32.4 **Lobectomy of lung**
> Lobectomy with segmental resection of adjacent lobes of lung
>
> *Excludes:* *that with radical dissection [excision] of thoracic structures (32.6)*

32.5 **Complete pneumonectomy**
> Excision of lung NOS
> Pneumonectomy (with mediastinal dissection)

32.6 **Radical dissection of thoracic structures**
> Block [en bloc] dissection of bronchus, lobe of lung, brachial plexus, intercostal structure, ribs (transverse process), and sympathetic nerves

32.9 **Other excision of lung**
> *Excludes:* *biopsy of lung and bronchus (33.24-33.27)*
>> *pulmonary decortication (34.51)*

33 **Other operations on lung and bronchus**
> Includes: rib resection
> sternotomy
> sternum-splitting incision   } as operative approach
> thoracotomy

33.0 **Incision of bronchus**

33.1 **Incision of lung**
> *Excludes:* *puncture of lung (33.93)*

33.2 **Diagnostic procedures on lung and bronchus**

> **33.21** **Bronchoscopy through artificial stoma**
>> *Excludes:* *that with biopsy (33.24, 33.27)*

> **33.22** **Fiber-optic bronchoscopy**
>> *Excludes:* *that with biopsy (33.24. 33.27)*

> **33.23** **Other bronchoscopy**
>> *Excludes:* *that for:*
>>> *aspiration (96.05)*
>>> *biopsy (33.24, 33.27)*

> **33.24** **Closed [endoscopic] biopsy of bronchus**
>> Bronchoscopy (fiberoptic) (rigid) with:
>>> brush biopsy of "lung"
>>> brushing or washing for specimen collection
>>> excision (bite) biopsy
>>
>> *Excludes:* *closed biopsy of lung, other than brush biopsy of "lung" (33.26, 33.27)*

> **33.25** **Open biopsy of bronchus**
>> *Excludes:* *open biopsy of lung (33.28)*

> **33.26** **Closed [percutaneous] [needle] biopsy of lung**
>> *Excludes:* *endoscopic biopsy of lung (33.27)*

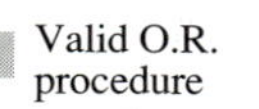 Valid O.R. procedure

 Non-O.R. procedure

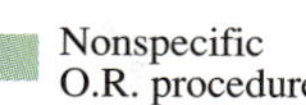 Nonspecific O.R. procedure

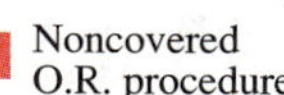 Noncovered O.R. procedure

33.27 Closed endoscopic biopsy of lung
Fiberoptic (flexible) bronchoscopy with fluoroscopic guidance with biopsy
Transbronchial lung biopsy

> *Excludes:* *brush biopsy of "lung" (33.24)*
> *percutaneous biopsy of lung (33.26)*

33.28 Open biopsy of lung

33.29 Other diagnostic procedures on lung and bronchus

> *Excludes:* *contrast bronchogram:*
> *endotracheal (87.31)*
> *other (87.32)*
> *lung scan (92.15)*
> *magnetic resonance imaging (88.92)*
> *microscopic examination of specimen from bronchus or lung*
> *(90.41-90.49)*
> *routine chest x-ray (87.44)*
> *ultrasonography of lung (88.73)*
> *vital capacity determination (89.37)*
> *x-ray of bronchus or lung NOS (87.49)*

33.3 Surgical collapse of lung

33.31 Destruction of phrenic nerve for collapse of lung

33.32 Artificial pneumothorax for collapse of lung
Thoracotomy for collapse of lung

33.33 Pneumoperitoneum for collapse of lung

33.34 Thoracoplasty

33.39 Other surgical collapse of lung
Collapse of lung NOS

33.4 Repair and plastic operation on lung and bronchus

33.41 Suture of laceration of bronchus

33.42 Closure of bronchial fistula
Closure of bronchostomy
Fistulectomy:
    bronchocutaneous
    bronchoesophageal
    bronchovisceral

> *Excludes:* *closure of fistula:*
> *bronchomediastinal (34.73)*
> *bronchopleural (34.73)*
> *bronchopleuromediastinal (34.73)*

33.43 Closure of laceration of lung

33.48 Other repair and plastic operation on bronchus

33.49 Other repair ad plastic operations on lung

> *Excludes:* *closure of pleural fistula (34.73)*

33.5 Lung transplant

Code also cardiopulmonary bypass [extracorporeal circulation] [heart-lung machine]
39.61

> *Excludes:* *Combined heart-lung transplantation (33.6)*

33.50 Lung transplantation, not otherwise specified

33.51 Unilateral lung transplantation

33.52 Bilateral lung transplantation
Double-lung transplantation
En bloc transplantation

33.6 Combined heart-lung transplantation

Code also cardiopulmonary bypass [extracorporeal circulation] [heart-lung machine]
(39.61)

33.9 Other operations on lung and bronchus

33.91 Bronchial dilation

33.92 Ligation of bronchus

33.93 Puncture of lung

> *Excludes:* *needle biopsy (33.26)*

● Code new
to this edition   ▲ Revision of
existing code   ④ ⑤ Fourth or fifth
digit required

33.98 **Other operations on bronchus**

Excludes: *bronchial lavage (96.56)*
removal of intraluminal foreign body from bronchus without incision (98.15)

33.99 **Other operations on lung**

Excludes: *other continuous mechanical ventilation (96.70-96.72)*
respiratory therapy (93.90-93.99)

34 **Operations on chest wall, pleura, mediastinum, and diaphragm**

Excludes: *operations on breast (85.0-85.99)*

34.0 **Incision of chest wall and pleura**

Excludes: *that as operative approach—omit code*

34.01 **Incision of chest wall**
Extrapleural drainage

Excludes: *incision of pleura (34.09)*

34.02 **Exploratory thoracotomy**

34.03 **Reopening of recent thoracotomy site**

34.04 **Insertion of intercostal catheter for drainage**
Chest tube
Closed chest drainage
Revision of intercostal catheter (chest tube) (with lysis of adhesions)

34.05 **Creation of pleuroperitoneal shunt**

34.09 **Other incision of pleura**
Creation of pleural window for drainage
Intercostal stab
Open chest drainage

Excludes: *thoracoscopy (34.21)*
thoracotomy for collapse of lung (33.32)

34.1 **Incision of mediastinum**

Excludes: *mediastinoscopy (34.22)*
mediastinotomy associated with pneumonectomy (32.5)

34.2 **Diagnostic procedures on chest wall, pleura, mediastinum, and diaphragm**

34.21 **Transpleural thoracoscopy**

34.22 **Mediastinoscopy**

Code also any lymph node biopsy (40.11)

34.23 **Biopsy of chest wall**

34.24 **Pleural biopsy**

34.25 **Closed [percutaneous] [needle] biopsy of mediastinum**

34.26 **Open biopsy of mediastinum**

34.27 **Biopsy of diaphragm**

34.28 **Other diagnostic procedures on chest wall, pleura, and diaphragm**

Excludes: *angiocardiography (88.50-88.58)*
aortography (88.42)
arteriography of:
intrathoracic vessels NEC (88.44)
pulmonary arteries (88.43)
microscopic examination of specimen from chest wall. pleura, and diaphragm (90.41-90.49)
phlebography of:
intrathoracic vessels NEC (88.63)
pulmonary veins (88.62)
radiological examinations of thorax:
C.A.T. scan (87.41)
diaphragmatic x-ray (87.49)
intrathoracic lymphangiogram (87.34)
routine chest x-ray (87.44)
sinogram of chest wall (87.38)
soft tissue x-ray of chest wall NEC (87.39)
tomogram of thorax NEC (87. 42)
ultrasonography of thorax (88.73)

	Valid O.R. procedure		Non-O.R. procedure		Nonspecific O.R. procedure		Noncovered O.R. procedure

34.29 Other diagnostic procedures on mediastinum

> *Excludes:* *mediastinal:*
> *pneumogram (87.33)*
> *x-ray NEC (87.49)*

34.3 Excision or destruction of lesion or tissue of mediastinum

> *Excludes:* *biopsy or mediastinum (34.25-34.26)*
> *mediastinal fistulectomy (34.73)*

34.4 Excision or destruction of lesion of chest wall
Excision of lesion of chest wall NOS (with excision of ribs)

> *Excludes:* *biopsy of chest wall (34.23)*
> *costectomy not incidental to thoracic procedure (77. 91)*
> *excision of lesion of:*
> *breast (85.20-85.25)*
> *cartilage (80.89)*
> *skin (86.2-86.3)*
> *fistulectomy (34. 73)*

34.5 Pleurectomy

34.51 Decortication of lung

34.59 Other excision of pleura
Excision of pleural lesion

> *Excludes:* *biopsy of pleura (34.24)*
> *pleural fistulectomy (34.73)*

34.6 Scarification of pleura
Pleurosclerosis

> *Excludes:* *injection of sclerosing agent (34.92)*

34.7 Repair of chest wall

34.71 Suture of laceration of chest wall

> *Excludes:* *suture of skin and subcutaneous tissue alone (86.59)*

34.72 Closure of thoracostomy

34.73 Closure of other fistula of thorax
Closure of:
bronchopleural ⎫
bronchopleurocutaneous ⎬ fistula
bronchopleuromediastinal ⎭

34.74 Repair of pectus deformity
Repair of:
pectus carinatum ⎫
pectus excavatum ⎬ (with implant)

34.79 Other repair of chest wall
Repair of chest wall NOS

34.8 Operations on diaphragm

34.81 Excision of lesion or tissue of diaphragm

> *Excludes:* *biopsy of diaphragm (34.27)*

34.82 Suture of laceration of diaphragm

34.83 Closure of fistula of diaphragm
Thoracicoabdominal ⎫
Thoracicogastric ⎬ fistulectomy
Thoracicointestinal ⎭

34.84 Other repair of diaphragm

> *Excludes:* *repair of diaphragmatic hernia (53.7-53.82)*

34.85 Implantation of diaphragmatic pacemaker

34.89 Other operations on diaphragm

34.9 Other operations on thorax

34.91 Thoracentesis

● Code new to this edition   ▲ Revision of existing code   ④ ⑤ Fourth or fifth digit required

34.92 Injection into thoracic cavity
Chemical pleurodesis
Injection of cytotoxic agent or tetracycline
Requires additional code for any cancer chemotherapeutic substance (99.25)

> | Excludes: | *that for collapse of lung (33.32)*

34.93 Repair of pleura

34.99 Other

> | Excludes: | *removal of:*
> > *mediastinal drain (97.42)*
> > *sutures (97.43)*
> > *thoracotomy tube (97.41)*

Valid O.R. procedure   Non-O.R. procedure   Nonspecific O.R. procedure   Noncovered O.R. procedure

● Code new
to this edition

▲ Revision of
existing code

④ ⑤ Fourth or fifth
digit required

7.   OPERATIONS ON THE CARDIOVASCULAR SYSTEM (35-39)

35   Operations on valves and septa of heart
Includes: sternotomy (median)
                      (transverse)
              thoracotomy   } as operative approach

Code also cardiopulmonary bypass [extracorporeal circulation] [heart-lung machine] (39.61)

35.0   Closed heart valvotomy

Excludes: *percutaneous (balloon) valvuloplasty (35.96)*

35.00   Closed heart valvotomy, unspecified valve

35.01   Closed heart valvotomy, aortic valve

35.02   Closed heart valvotomy, mitral valve

35.03   Closed heart valvotomy, pulmonary valve

35.04   Closed heart valvotomy, tricuspid valve

35.1   Open heart valvuloplasty without replacement
Includes: open heart valvotomy

Excludes: *that associated with repair of:*
endocardial cushion defect (35.54, 35.63, 35.73)
percutaneous (balloon) valvuloplasty (35.96)
valvular defect associated with atrial and ventricular septal defects (35.54, 35.63, 35.73)

Code also cardiopulmonary bypass, if performed [extracorporeal circulation] [heart-lung machine] (39.61)

35.10   Open heart valvuloplasty without replacement, unspecified valve

35.11   Open heart valvuloplasty of aortic valve without replacement

35.12   Open heart valvuloplasty of mitral valve without replacement

35.13   Open heart valvuloplasty of pulmonary valve without replacement

35.14   Open heart valvuloplasty of tricuspid valve without replacement

35.2   Replacement of heart valve
Includes: excision of heart valve with replacement

Code also cardiopulmonary bypass [extracorporeal circulation] [heart-lung machine] (39.61)

Excludes: *that associated with repair of:*
endocardial cushion defect (35.54, 35.63, 35.73)
valvular defect associated with atrial and ventricular septal defects (35.54, 35.63, 35.73)

35.20   Replacement of unspecified heart valve
Repair of unspecified heart valve with tissue graft or prosthetic implant

35.21   Replacement of aortic valve with tissue graft
Repair of aortic valve with tissue graft (autograft) (heterograft) (homograft)

35.22   Other replacement of aortic valve
Repair of aortic valve with replacement:
   NOS
   prosthetic (partial) (synthetic) (total)

35.23   Replacement of mitral valve with tissue graft
Repair of mitral valve with tissue graft (autograft) (heterograft) (homograft)

35.24   Other replacement of mitral valve
Repair of mitral valve with replacement:
   NOS
   prosthetic (partial) (synthetic) (total)

35.25   Replacement of pulmonary valve with tissue graft
Repair of pulmonary valve with tissue graft (autograft) (heterograft) (homograft)

35.26   Other replacement of pulmonary valve
Repair of pulmonary valve with replacement:
   NOS
   prosthetic (partial) (synthetic) (total)

35.27   Replacement of tricuspid valve with tissue graft
Repair of tricuspid valve with tissue graft (autograft) (heterograft) (homograft)

35.28 **Other replacement of tricuspid valve**
Repair of tricuspid valve with replacement:
NOS
prosthetic (partial) (synthetic) (total)

35.3 **Operations on structures adjacent to heart valves**

*Code also cardiopulmonary bypass [extracorporeal circulation] [heart-lung machine]
(39.61)*

35.31 **Operations on papillary muscle**
Division
Reattachment } of papillary muscle
Repair

35.32 **Operations on chordae tendineae**
Division
Repair } of chordae tendineae

35.33 **Annuloplasty**
Plication of annulus

35.34 **Infundibulectomy**
Right ventricular infundibulectomy

35.35 **Operations on trabeculae carneae cordis**
Division
Excision } of trabeculae carneae cordis
Excision of aortic subvalvular ring

35.39 **Operations on other structures adjacent to valves of heart**
Repair of sinus of Valsalva (aneurysm)

35.4 **Production of septal defect in heart**

35.41 **Enlargement of existing atrial septal defect**
Rashkind procedure
Septostomy (atrial) (balloon)

35.42 **Creation of septal defect in heart**
Blalock-Hanlon operation

35.5 **Repair of atrial and ventricular septa with prosthesis**
Includes: repair of septa with synthetic implant of patch

*Code also cardiopulmonary bypass [extracorporeal circulation] [heart-lung machine)
(39.61)*

35.50 **Repair of unspecified septal defect of heart with prosthesis**

Excludes:	*that associated with repair of:*
	endocardial cushion defect (35.54)
	septal defect associated with valvular defect (35.54)

35.51 **Repair of atrial septal defect with prosthesis, open technique**
Atrioseptoplasty
Correction of atrial septal
defect
Repair: } with prosthesis
foramen ovale (patent)
ostium secundum defect

Excludes:	*that associated with repair of:*
	atrial septal defect associated with valvular and ventricular septal defects (35.54)
	endocardial cushion defect (35.54)

35.52 **Repair of atrial septal defect with prosthesis, closed technique**
Insertion of atrial septal umbrella [King-Mills]

35.53 **Repair of ventricular septal defect with prosthesis**
Correction of ventricular
septal defect } with prosthesis
Repair of supracristal defect

Excludes:	*that associated with repair of:*
	endocardial cushion defect (35.54)
	ventricular defect associated with valvular and atrial septal defects (35.54)

35.54 **Repair of endocardial cushion defect with prosthesis**
Repair:

● Code new
to this edition

▲ Revision of
existing code

④ ⑤ Fourth or fifth
digit required

atrioventricular canal
ostium primum defect
valvular defect associated
with Atrial and
ventricular Septal defects
} with prosthesis (grafted to septa)

> *Excludes:* *repair of isolated:*
> *atrial septal defect (35.51-35.52)*
> *valvular defect (35.20, 35.22, 35.24, 35.26. 35.28)*
> *ventricular septal defect (35.53)*

35.6 Repair of atrial and ventricular septa with tissue graft

Code also cardiopulmonary bypass [extracorporeal circulation] [heart-lung machine] (39.61)

35.60 Repair of unspecified septal defect of heart with tissue graft

> *Excludes:* *that associated with repair of:*
> *endocardial cushion defect (35.63)*
> *septal defect associated with valvular, defect (33.63)*

35.61 Repair of atrial septal defect with tissue graft

Atrioseptoplasty
Correction of atrial septal
defect
Repair:
foramen ovale (patent)
ostium secundum defect
} with tissue graft

> *Excludes:* *that associated with repair of:*
> *atrial septal defect associated with valvular and ventricular septal*
> *defects (35.63)*
> *endocardial cushion defect (35.63)*

35.62 Repair of ventricular septal defect with tissue graft

Correction of ventricular
septal defect
Repair of supracristal defect
} with tissue graft

> *Excludes:* *that associated with repair of:*
> *endocardial cushion defect (35.63)*
> *ventricular defect associated with valvular and atrial septal defects*
> *(35.63)*

35.63 Repair of endocardial cushion defect with tissue graft

Repair of:
atrioventricular canal
ostium primum defect
valvular defect associated with
atrial and ventricular septal
defects
} with tissue graft

> *Excludes:* *repair of isolated*
> *atrial septal defect (35.61)*
> *valvular defect (35.20-35.21. 35.23, 35.25. 35.27)*
> *ventricular, septal defect (35.62)*

35.7 Other and unspecified repair of atrial and ventricular septa

Code also cardiopulmonary bypass [extracorporeal circulation] [heart-lung machine] (39.61)

35.70 Other and unspecified repair of unspecified septal defect of heart

Repair of septal defect NOS

> *Excludes:* *that associated with repair of:*
> *endocardial cushion defect (35.73)*
> *septal defect associated with valvular defect (35.73)*

35.71 Other and unspecified repair of atrial septal defect

Repair NOS:
atrial septum
foramen ovale (patent)
ostium secundum defect

> *Excludes:* *that associated with repair of:*
> *atrial septal defect associated with valvular and ventricular septal*
> *defects (35.73)*
> *endocardial cushion defect (35.73)*

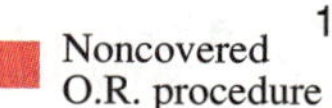

Noncovered
O.R. procedure

35.72 Other and unspecified repair of ventricular septal defect
Repair NOS:
   supracristal defect
   ventricular septum

> | Excludes: | *that associated with repair of:*
> *endocardial cushion defect (35.73)*
> *ventricular septal defect associated with valvular and atrial septal*
> *defects (35.73)*

35.73 Other and unspecified repair of endocardial cushion defect
Repair NOS:
   atrioventricular canal
   ostium primum defect
   valvular defect associated with atrial and ventricular septal defects

> | Excludes: | *repair of isolated:*
> *atrial septal defect (35.71)*
> *valvular defect (35.20, 35.22, 35.24, 35.26, 35.28)*
> *ventricular septal defect (35.72)*

35.8 Total repair of certain congenital cardiac anomalies
Note: For partial repair of defect [e.g. repair of atrial septal defect in tetralogy of Fallot]—
code to specific procedure

35.81 Total repair of tetralogy of Fallot
One-stage total correction of tetralogy of Fallot with or without:
   commissurotomy of pulmonary valve
   infundibulectomy
   outflow tract prosthesis
   patch graft of outflow tract
   prosthetic tube for pulmonary artery
   repair of ventricular septal defect (with prosthesis)
   take-down of previous systemic-pulmonary artery anastomosis

35.82 Total repair of total anomalous pulmonary venous connection
One-stage total correction of total anomalous pulmonary venous connection with or
   without:
   anastomosis between (horizontal) common pulmonary trunk and posterior wall of
      left atrium (side-to-side)
   enlargement of foramen ovale
   incision [excision] of common wall between posterior left atrium and coronary si-
      nus and roofing of resultant defect with patch graft (synthetic)
   ligation of venous connection (descending anomalous vein) (to left innominate
      vein) (to superior vena cava)
   repair of atrial septal defect (with prosthesis)

35.83 Total repair of truncus arteriosus
One-stage total correction of truncus arteriosus with or without:
   construction (with aortic homograft) (with prosthesis) of a pulmonary artery
      placed from right ventricle to arteries supplying the lung
   ligation of connections between aorta and pulmonary artery
   repair of ventricular septal defect (with prosthesis)

35.84 Total correction of transposition of great vessels, not elsewhere classified
Arterial switch operation [Jatene]
Total correction of transposition of great arteries at the arterial level by switching
   the great arteries, including the left or both coronary arteries, implanted in the
   wall of the pulmonary artery

> | Excludes: | *baffle operation [Mustard] [Senning] (35.91)*
> *creation of shunt between right ventricle and pulmonary artery*
> *[Rastelli] (35.92)*

35.9 Other operations on valves and septa of heart
Code also cardiopulmonary bypass, if performed [extracorporeal circulation] [heart-lung
machine) (39.61)

35.91 Interatrial transposition of venous return
Baffle:
   atrial
   interatrial
Mustard's operation
Resection of atrial septum and insertion of patch to direct systemic venous return to
   tricuspid valve and pulmonary venous return to mitral valve

● Code new
to this edition
   ▲ Revision of
existing code
   ④ ⑤ Fourth or fifth
digit required

35.92 Creation of conduit between right ventricle and pulmonary artery
Creation of shunt between right ventricle and (distal) pulmonary artery

Excludes: *that associated with total repair of truncus arteriosus (35.83)*

35.93 Creation of conduit between left ventricle and aorta
Creation of apicoaortic shunt
Shunt between apex of left ventricle and aorta

35.94 Creation of conduit between atrium and pulmonary artery
Fontan procedure

35.95 Revision of corrective procedure on heart
Replacement of prosthetic heart valve poppet
Resuture or prosthesis of:
  septum
  valve

Excludes: *complete revision—code to specific procedure*
replacement of prosthesis or graft of:
septum (35.50-35.63)
valve (35.20-35.28)

35.96 Percutaneous valvuloplasty
Percutaneous balloon valvuloplasty

35.98 Other operations on septa of heart

35.99 Other operations on valves of heart

36 Operations on vessels of heart
Includes: sternotomy (median)
                    (transverse)
                thoracotomy   as operative approach

Code also any injection or infusion of platelet inhibitor (99.20)

Code also cardiopulmonary bypass, if performed [extracorporeal circulation] [heart-lung machine] (39.61)

36.0   Removal of coronary artery obstruction and insertion of stent(s)

36.01   Single vessel percutaneous transluminal coronary angioplasty [PTCA] or coronary atherectomy without mention of thrombolytic agent
Code also any insertion of coronary stent(s) (36.06)
Balloon angioplasty of coronary artery
Coronary atherectomy
Percutaneous coronary angioplasty NOS
PTCA NOS

Excludes: *multiple vessel percutaneous transluminal coronary angioplasty [PTCA] or coronary atherectomy performed during the same operation (36.05)*

36.02   Single vessel percutaneous transluminal coronary angioplasty [PTCA] or coronary atherectomy with mention of thrombolytic agent
Code also any insertion of coronary stent(s) 36.06
Balloon angioplasty of coronary artery with infusion of thrombolytic agent [streptokinase]
Coronary Atherectomy

Excludes: *multiple vessel percutaneous transluminal coronary angioplasty [PTCA] or coronary atherectomy performed during the same operation (36.05)*
single vessel [PTCA] or coronary atherectomy without mention of thrombolytic agent (36.01)

36.03   Open chest coronary artery angioplasty
Code also any insertion of coronary stent(s) 36.06
Coronary (artery):
  endarterectomy (with patch graft)
  thromboendarterectomy (with patch graft)
Open surgery for direct relief of coronary artery obstruction

Excludes: *that with coronary artery bypass graft (36.10-36.19)*

Valid O.R. procedure   Non-O.R. procedure   Nonspecific O.R. procedure   Noncovered O.R. procedure

36.04 Intracoronary artery thrombolytic infusion
That by direct coronary artery injection, infusion, or catheterization
    enzyme infusion
    platelet inhibitor

> *Excludes:*   *infusion of platelet inhibitor (99.20)*
> *infusion of thrombolytic agent (99.10)*

36.05 Multiple vessel percutaneous transluminal coronary angioplasty [PTCA] or coronary atherectomy performed during the same operation, with or without mention of thrombolytic agent
Balloon angioplasty of multiple coronary arteries
Coronary Atherectomy

Code also any intracoronary artery thrombolytic infusion (36.04)

Code also any insertion of coronary artery stent(s) (36.06)

> *Excludes:*   *single vessel PTCA or coronary atherectomy without mention of*
> *thrombolytic agent (36.01)*
> *with mention of thrombolytic agent (36.02)*

36.06 Insertion of coronary artery stent(s)
Stent graft

Code also any open chest coronary artery angioplasty (36.03)

Code also any percutaneous transluminal coronary angioplasty [PTCA] or
coronary atherectomy (36.01, 36.02, 36.05)

36.09 Other removal of coronary artery obstruction
Coronary angioplasty NOS

> *Excludes:*   *that by open angioplasty (36.03)*
> *that by percutaneous transluminal coronary angioplasty [PTCA] or*
> *coronary atherectomy (36.01-36.02, 36.05)*

36.1 Bypass anastomosis for heart revascularization

Code also cardiopulmonary bypass [extracorporeal circulation] [heart-lung machine]
(39.61)

36.10 Aortocoronary bypass for heart revascularization, not otherwise specified
Direct revascularization:
    cardiac
    coronary   } with catheter stent, prosthesis, or vein graft
    heart muscle
    myocardial
Heart revascularization NOS

36.11 Aortocoronary bypass of one coronary artery

36.12 Aortocoronary bypass of two coronary arteries

36.13 Aortocoronary bypass of three coronary arteries

36.14 Aortocoronary bypass of four or more coronary arteries

36.15 Single internal mammary-coronary artery bypass
Anastomosis (single):
    mammary artery to coronary artery
    thoracic artery to coronary artery

36.16 Double internal mammary-coronary artery bypass
Anastomosis, double:
    mammary artery to coronary artery
    thoracic artery to coronary artery

36.17 Abdominal - coronary artery bypass
Anastomosis:
    gastroepiploic artery to coronary artery

36.19 Other bypass anastomosis for heart revascularization

36.2 Heart revascularization by arterial implant
Implantation of:
    aortic branches [ascending aortic branches] into heart muscle
    blood vessels into myocardium
    internal mammary artery [internal thoracic artery] into:
        heart muscle
        myocardium
        ventricle
        ventricular wall
Indirect heart revascularization NOS

    ● Code new   ▲ Revision of   ④ ⑤ Fourth or fifth
       to this edition   existing code   digit required

36.3 Other heart revascularization

36.31 Open chest transmyocardial revascularization

36.32 Other transmyocardial revascularization
Percutaneous transmyocardial revasculariztion
Thoracoscopic transmyocardial revascularization

36.39 Other heart revascularization
Abrasion of epicardium
Cardio-omentopexy
Intrapericardial poudrage
Myocardial graft:
mediastinal fat
omentum
pectoral muscles

36.9 Other operations on vessels of heart
Code also cardiopulmonary bypass [extracorporeal circulation] [heart-lung machine]
(39.61)

36.91 Repair of aneurysm of coronary vessel

36.99 Other operations on vessel of heart
Exploration
Incision } of coronary artery
Ligation
Repair of arteriovenous fistula

37 Other operations on heart and pericardium
Code also any injection or infusion of platelet inhibitor (99.20)

37.0 Pericardiocentesis

37.1 Cardiotomy and pericardiotomy
Code also cardiopulmonary bypass [extracorporeal circulation] [heart-lung machine]
(39.61)

37.10 Incision of heart, not otherwise specified
Cardiolysis NOS

37.11 Cardiotomy
Incision of:
atrium
endocardium
myocardium
ventricle

37.12 Pericardiotomy
Pericardial window operation
Pericardiolysis
Pericardiotomy

37.2 Diagnostic procedures on heart and pericardium

37.21 Right heart cardiac catheterization
Cardiac catheterization NOS

Excludes: *that with catheterization of left heart (37.23)*

37.22 Left heart cardiac catheterization

Excludes: *that with catheterization of right heart (37.23)*

37.23 Combined right and left heart cardiac catheterization

37.24 Biopsy of pericardium

37.25 Biopsy of heart

37.26 Cardiac electrophysiologic stimulation and recording studies
Electrophysiologic studies (EPS)
Programmed electrical stimulation
Code also any concomitant procedure

Excludes: *His bundle recording (37.29)*

37.27 Cardiac mapping
Code also any concomitant procedure

Excludes: *electrocardiogram (89.52)*
His bundle recording (37.29)

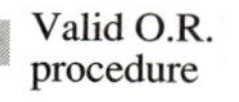

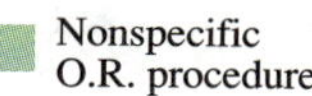

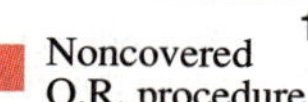

37.29   Other diagnostic procedures on heart and pericardium

> | *Excludes:* | *angiocardiography (88.50-88.58)* |
> | --- | --- |
> | | *cardiac function tests (89.41-89.69)* |
> | | *cardiovascular radioisotopic scan and function study (92.05)* |
> | | *coronary arteriography (88.55-88.57)* |
> | | *diagnostic pericardiocentesis (37.0)* |
> | | *diagnostic ultrasound of heart (88.72)* |
> | | *x-ray of heart (87.49)* |

37.3   Pericardiectomy and excision of lesion of heart

Code also cardiopulmonary bypass [extracorporeal circulation] [heart-lung machine] (39.61)

37.31   Pericardiectomy
Excision of:
  adhesions of pericardium
  constricting scar of: epicardium
                            pericardium

37.32   Excision of aneurysm of heart
Repair of aneurysm of heart

37.33   Excision or destruction of other lesion or tissue of heart

> | *Excludes:* | *catheter ablation of lesion or tissues of heart (37.34)* |
> | --- | --- |

37.34   Catheter ablation of lesion or tissue of heart
Cryoablation
Electrocurrent   } of lesion or tissues of heart
Resection

37.35   Partial ventriculectomy
Ventricular reduction surgery
Ventricular remodeling

Code also any synchronous:
  mitral valve repair (35.02, 35.12)
  mitral valve replacement (35.23-35.24)

37.4   Repair of heart and pericardium

37.5   Heart transplantation

> | *Excludes:* | *combined heart-lung transplantation (33.6)* |
> | --- | --- |

37.6   Implantation of heart assist system

37.61   Implant of pulsation balloon

37.62   Implant of other heart assist system
Insertion of:
  centrifugal pump
  heart assist system, not specified as pulsatile
  heart assist system, NOS
  heart pump

37.63   Replacement and repair of heart assist system

37.64   Removal of heart assist system

> | *Excludes:* | *that with replacement of implant (37.63)* |
> | --- | --- |

37.65   Implant of an external, pulsatile heart assist system
Note: Device not implantable (outside the body but connected to heart) with external circulation and pump

> | *Excludes:* | *implant of pulsation balloon (37.61)* |
> | --- | --- |

37.66   Implant of an implantable, pulsatile heart assist system
Note: Device directly connected to the heart and implanted in the upper left quadrant of peritoneal cavity
Transportable, implantable heart assist system

> | *Excludes:* | *Implant of pulsation balloon (37.61)* |
> | --- | --- |

37.67   Implantation of cardiomyostimulation system
Note: Two-step open procedure consisting of transfer of one end of the latissimus dorsi muscle; wrapping it around the heart; rib resection; implantation of epicardial cardiac pacing leads into the right ventricle; tunneling and pocket creation for the cardiomyostimulator.

37.7   Insertion, revision, replacement, and removal of pacemaker leads; insertion of temporary pacemaker system; or revision of pocket

Code also any insertion and replacement of pacemaker device (37.80-37.87)

     ● Code new
to this edition   ▲ Revision of
existing code   ④ ⑤ Fourth or fifth
digit required

37.70   **Initial insertion of lead [electrode], not otherwise specified**

> *Excludes:*   *insertion of temporary transvenous pacemaker system (37.78)*
> *replacement of atrial and/or ventricular lead(s) (37.76)*

37.71   **Initial insertion of transvenous lead [electrode] into ventricle**

> *Excludes:*   *insertion of temporary transvenous pacemaker system (37.78)*
> *replacement of atrial and/or ventricular lead(s) (37.76)*

37.72   **Initial insertion of transvenous leads [electrodes] into atrium and ventricle**

> *Excludes:*   *insertion of temporary transvenous pacemaker system (37.78)*
> *replacement of atrial and/or ventricular lead(s) (37.76)*

37.73   **Initial insertion of transvenous lead [electrode] into atrium**

> *Excludes:*   *insertion of temporary transvenous pacemaker system (37.78)*
> *replacement of atrial and/or ventricular lead(s) (37.76)*

37.74   **Insertion or replacement of epicardial lead [electrode] into epicardium**
Insertion or replacement of epicardial lead by:
    sternotomy
    thoracotomy

> *Excludes:*   *replacement of atrial and/or ventricular lead(s) (37.76)*

37.75   **Revision of lead [electrode]**
Repair of electrode [removal with re-insertion]
Repositioning of lead [electrode]
Revision of lead NOS

> *Excludes:*   *repositioning of temporary transvenous pacemaker system—omit code*

37.76   **Replacement of transvenous atrial and/or ventricular lead(s) [electrode]**
Removal or abandonment of existing transvenous or epicardial lead(s) with
    transvenous lead(s) replacement

> *Excludes:*   *replacement of epicardial lead [electrode] (37.74)*

37.77   **Removal of lead(s) [electrode] without replacement**
Removal:
    epicardial lead (transthoracic approach)
    transvenous lead(s)

> *Excludes:*   *removal of temporary transvenous pacemaker system—omit code*
> *that with replacement of:*
>   *atrial and/or ventricular lead(s) [electrode] (37.76)*
>   *epicardial lead [electrode] (37.74)*

37.78   **Insertion of temporary transvenous pacemaker system**

> *Excludes:*   *intraoperative cardiac pacemaker (39.64)*

37.79   **Revision or relocation of pacemaker pocket**
Debridement and reforming pocket (skin and subcutaneous tissue)
Relocation of pocket [creation of new pocket]

37.8   **Insertion, replacement, removal and revision of pacemaker device**
Code also any lead insertion, lead replacement, lead removal and/or lead revision (37.70-37.77)

37.80   **Insertion of permanent pacemaker, initial or replacement, type of device not specified**

37.81   **Initial insertion of single-chamber device, not specified as rate responsive**

> *Excludes:*   *replacement of existing pacemaker device (37.85-37.87)*

37.82   **Initial insertion of a single-chamber device, rate responsive**
Rate responsive to physiologic stimuli other than atrial rate

> *Excludes:*   *replacement of existing pacemaker device (37.85-37.87)*

37.83   **Initial insertion of dual-chamber device**
Atrial ventricular sequential device

> *Excludes:*   *replacement of existing pacemaker device (37.85-37.87)*

37.85   **Replacement of any type pacemaker device with single-chamber device, not specified as rate responsive**

37.86   **Replacement of any type pacemaker device with single-chamber device, rate responsive**
Rate responsive to physiologic stimuli other than atrial rate

Valid O.R. procedure   Non-O.R. procedure   Nonspecific O.R. procedure   Noncovered O.R. procedure

37.87 **Replacement of any type pacemaker device with dual-chamber device**
Atrial ventricular sequential device

37.89 **Revision or removal of pacemaker device**
Repair of pacemaker device

> *Excludes:* *removal of temporary transvenous pacemaker system—omit code*
> *replacement of existing pacemaker device (37.85-37.87)*

37.9 **Other operations on heart and pericardium**

37.91 **Open chest cardiac massage**

> *Excludes:* *closed chest cardiac massage (99.63)*

37.92 **Injection of therapeutic substance into heart**

37.93 **Injection of therapeutic substance into pericardium**

37.94 **Implantation or replacement of automatic cardioverter/defibrillator, total system [AICD]**
Implantation of defibrillator with leads (epicardial patches), formation of pocket (abdominal fascia) (subcutaneous), any transvenous leads, intraoperative procedures for evaluation of lead signals, and obtaining defibrillator thresholds measurements
Techniques:
    lateral thoracotomy
    medial sternotomy
    subxiphoid procedure

Code also extracorporeal circulation, if performed (39.61)

Code also any concomitant procedure [e.g., coronary bypass) (36.00-36.19)

37.95 **Implantation of automatic cardioverter/defibrillator lead(s) only**

37.96 **Implantation of automatic cardioverter/defibrillator pulse generator only**

37.97 **Replacement of automatic cardioverter/defibrillator lead(s) only**

37.98 **Replacement of automatic cardioverter/defibrillator pulse generator only**

37.99 **Other**
Removal of cardioverter/defibrillator pulse generator only without replacement
Repositioning of lead(s) (sensing) (pacing)[electrode]
Repositioning of pulse generator
Revision of cardioverter/defibrillator (automatic) pocket

> *Excludes:* *cardiac retraining (93.36)*
> *conversion of cardiac rhythm (99.60-99.69)*

38 **Incision, excision, and occlusion of vessels**

Code also cardiopulmonary bypass [extracorporeal circulation] [heart-lung machine] (39.61)

> *Excludes:* *that of coronary vessels (36.01-36.99)*

The following fourth-digit subclassification is for use with appropriate categories in sections 38.0, 38.1, 38.3, 38.5, 38.6, 38.8 and 38.9, which are marked with a symbol ④ to identify the site. Valid fourth digits are in [brackets] under each code.

0 unspecified site
1 intracranial vessels
    Cerebral (anterior) (middle)
    Circle of Willis
    Posterior communicating artery
2 other vessels of head and neck
    Carotid artery (common) (external) (internal)
    Jugular vein (external) (internal)
3 upper limb vessels
    Axillary   Radial
    Brachial   Ulnar
4 aorta
5 other thoracic vessels
    Innominate   Subclavian
    Pulmonary (artery) (vein)   Vena cava, superior
6 abdominal arteries
    Celiac   Mesenteric
    Gastric   Renal
    Hepatic   Splenic
    Iliac   Umbilical

> *Excludes:* *abdominal aorta (4)*

    ● Code new   ▲ Revision of   ④ ⑤ Fourth or fifth
        to this edition   existing code   digit required

7 abdominal veins

Iliac	Splenic
Portal	Vena cava(inferior)
Renal	

8 lower limb arteries
Femoral (common) (superficial)
Popliteal
Tibial

9 lower limb veins

Femoral	Saphenous
Popliteal	Tibial

④ **38.0** **Incision of vessels**
[0-9] Embolectomy
Thrombectomy

> *Excludes:* *puncture or catheterization of any:*
> *artery (38.91, 38.98)*
> *vein (38.92-38.95, 38.99)*

④ **38.1** **Endarterectomy**
[0-6,8] Endarterectomy with:
embolectomy
patch graft
temporary bypass during procedure
thrombectomy

38.2 **Diagnostic procedures on blood vessels**

38.21 **Biopsy of blood vessel**

38.22 **Percutaneous angioscopy**

> *Excludes:* *angioscopy of eye (95.12)*

38.29 **Other diagnostic procedures on blood vessels**

> *Excludes:* *blood vessel thermography (88.86)*
> *circulatory monitoring (89.61-89.69)*
> *contrast:*
> *angiocardiography (88.50-88.58)*
> *arteriography (88.40-88.49)*
> *phlebography (88.60-88.67)*
> *impedance phlebography (88.68)*
> *peripheral vascular ultrasonography (88.77)*
> *plethysmogram (89.58)*

④ **38.3** **Resection of vessel with anastomosis**
[0-9] Angiectomy
Excision of:
aneurysm (arteriovenous) } with anastomosis
blood vessel (lesion)

④ **38.4** **Resection of vessel with replacement**
[0-9] Angiectomy
Excision of
aneurysm (arteriovenous) or } with replacement
blood vessel (lesion)

> *Excludes:* *endovascular repair of aneurysm (39.71-39.79)*

Requires the use of one of the following fourth-digit subclassifications to identify site:
0 unspecified site
1 intracranial vessels
Cerebral (anterior) (middle)
Circle of Willis
Posterior communicating artery
2 other vessels of head and neck
Carotid artery (common) (external) (internal)
Jugular vein (external) (internal)
3 upper limb vessels

Axillary	Radial
Brachial	Ulnar

4 aorta, abdominal
Code also any thoracic vessel involvement (thoracoabdominal procedure) (38.45)

Valid O.R. procedure	Non-O.R. procedure	Nonspecific O.R. procedure	Noncovered O.R. procedure

5 thoracic vessel
Aorta (thoracic)   Subclavian
Innominate   Vena cava (superior)
Pulmonary (artery) (vein)
Code also any abdominal aorta involvement (thoracoabdominal procedure) (38.44)
6 abdominal arteries
Celiac   Mesenteric
Gastric   Renal
Hepatic   Splenic
Iliac   Umbilical

| Excludes: | *abdominal aorta (4)* |

7 abdominal veins
Iliac   Splenic
Portal   Vena cava (inferior)
Renal
8 lower limb arteries
Femoral (common) (superficial)
Tibial
9 lower limb veins
Femoral   Saphenous
Popliteal   Tibial

④ **38.5** **Ligation and stripping of varicose veins**
[0-3,5,7,9]

Excludes:	*ligation of varices:*
	esophageal (42.91)
	gastric (44.91)

④ **38.6** **Other excision of vessels**
[0-9]   Excision of blood vessel (lesion) NOS

Excludes:	*excision of vessel for aortocoronary bypass (36.10-36.14)*
	excision with:
	anastomosis (38.30-38.39)
	graft replacement (38.40-38.49)
	implant (38.40-38.49)

38.7 **Interruption of vena cava**
Insertion of implant or sieve in vena cava
Ligation of vena cava (inferior) (superior)
Plication of vena cava

④ **38.8** **Other surgical occlusion of vessels**
[0-9]   Clamping
Division
Ligation   } of blood vessel
Occlusion

Excludes:	*adrenal vessels (07.43)*
	esophageal varices (42.91)
	gastric or duodenal vessel for ulcer (44.40-44.49)
	gastric varices (44.91)
	meningeal vessel (02.13)
	percutaneous transcatheter infusion embolization (99.29)
	spermatic vein for varicocele (63.1)
	surgical occlusion of vena cava (38.7)
	that for chemoembolization (99.25)
	that for control of (postoperative) hemorrhage:
	anus (49.95)
	bladder (57.93)
	following vascular procedure (39.41)
	nose (21.00-21.09)
	prostate (60.94)
	tonsil (28.7)
	thyroid vessel (06.92)

38.9 **Puncture of vessel**

| Excludes: | *that for circulatory monitoring (89.61-89.69)* |

38.91 **Arterial catheterization**

38.92 **Umbilical vein catheterization**

● Code new   ▲ Revision of   ④ ⑤ Fourth or fifth
to this edition   existing code   digit required

38.93 Venous catheterization, not elsewhere classified

> *Excludes:* *that for cardiac catheterization (37.21-37.23)*
> *that for renal dialysis (38.95)*

38.94 Venous cutdown

38.95 Venous catheterization for renal dialysis

> *Excludes:* *insertion of totally implantable vascular access device [VAD] 86.07*

38.98 Other puncture of artery

> *Excludes:* *that for:*
> *coronary arteriography (88.55-88.57)*
> *arteriography (88.40-88.49)*

38.99 Other puncture of vein

Phlebotomy

> *Excludes:* *that for:*
> *angiography (88.60-88.69)*
> *extracorporeal circulation (39.61, 50.92)*
> *injection or infusion of:*
> *sclerosing solution (39.92)*
> *therapeutic or prophylactic substance (99.11-99.29)*
> *perfusion (39.96-39.97)*
> *phlebography (88.60-88.69)*
> *transfusion (99.01-99.09)*

39 Other operations on vessels

> *Excludes:* *those on coronary vessels (36.0-36.99)*

39.0 Systemic to pulmonary artery shunt

Descending aorta-pulmonary artery
Left to right   } anastomosis (graft)
Subclavian-pulmonary

Code also cardiopulmonary bypass [extracorporeal circulation] [heart-lung machine] (39.61)

39.1 Intra-abdominal venous shunt

Anastomosis:
mesocaval
portacaval
portal vein to inferior vena cava
splenic and renal veins
transjugular intrahepatic portosystemic shunt (TIPS)

> *Excludes:* *peritoneovenous shunt (54.94)*

39.2 Other shunt or vascular bypass

39.21 Caval-pulmonary artery anastomosis

Code also cardiopulmonary bypass (39.61)

39.22 Aorta-subclavian-carotid bypass

Bypass (arterial):
aorta to carotid and brachial
aorta to subclavian and carotid
carotid to subclavian

39.23 Other intrathoracic vascular shunt or bypass

Intrathoracic (arterial) bypass graft NOS

> *Excludes:* *coronary artery bypass (36.10-36.19)*

39.24 Aorta-renal bypass

39.25 Aorta-iliac-femoral bypass

Bypass:
aortofemoral
aortoiliac
aortoiliac to popliteal
aortopopliteal
iliofemoral [iliac-femoral]

Valid O.R. procedure	Non-O.R. procedure	Nonspecific O.R. procedure	Noncovered O.R. procedure

39.26 **Other intra-abdominal vascular shunt or bypass**
Bypass:
aortoceliac
aortic-superior mesenteric
common hepatic-common iliac-renal
Intra-abdominal arterial bypass graft NOS

Excludes: *peritoneovenous shunt (54.94)*

39.27 **Arteriovenostomy for renal dialysis**
Anastomosis for renal dialysis
Formation of (peripheral) arteriovenous fistula for renal (kidney] dialysis
Code also any renal dialysis (39.95)

39.28 **Extracranial-intracranial (EC-IC) vascular bypass**

39.29 **Other (peripheral) vascular shunt or bypass**
Bypass (graft):
axillary-brachial
axillary-femoral [axillofemoral] (superficial)
brachial
femoral-femoral
femoroperoneal
femoropopliteal (arteries)
femorotibial (anterior) (posterior)
popliteal
vascular NOS

Excludes: *peritoneovenous shunt (54.94)*

39.3 **Suture of vessel**
Repair of laceration of blood vessel

Excludes: *any other vascular puncture closure device—omit code*
suture of aneurysm (39.52)
that for control of hemorrhage (postoperative):
anus (49.95)
bladder (57.93)
following vascular procedure (39.41)
nose (21.00-21.09)
prostate (60.94)
tonsil (28.7)

39.30 **Suture of unspecified blood vessel**

39.31 **Suture of artery**

39.32 **Suture of vein**

39.4 **Revision of vascular procedure**

39.41 **Control of hemorrhage following vascular surgery**

Excludes: *that for control of hemorrhage (postoperative):*
anus (49.95)
bladder (57.93)
nose (21.00-21.09)
prostate (60.94)
tonsil (28.7)

39.42 **Revision of arteriovenous shunt for renal dialysis**
Conversion of renal dialysis:
end-to-end anastomosis to end-to-side
end-to-side anastomosis to end-to-end
vessel-to-vessel cannula to arteriovenous shunt
Removal of old arteriovenous shunt and creation of new shunt

Excludes: *replacement of vessel-to-vessel cannula (39.94)*

39.43 **Removal of arteriovenous shunt for renal dialysis**

Excludes: *that with replacement [revision] of shunt (39.42)*

39.49 **Other revision of vascular procedure**
Declotting (graft)
Revision of:
anastomosis of blood vessel
vascular procedure (previous)

● Code new
to this edition   ▲ Revision of
existing code   ④ ⑤ Fourth or fifth
digit required

39.5 **Other repair of vessels**

39.50 **Angioplasty or atherectomy of non-coronary vessel**
Percutaneous transluminal angioplasty (PTA) of non-coronary vessel:
Head and neck arteries:
basilar
carotid
vertebral
Lower extremity vessels
Mesenteric artery
Renal artery
Upper extremity vessels

Code also any injection or infusion of thrombolytic agent (99.10)
Code also any insertion of non-coronary stent(s) or stent graft(s) (39.90)

39.51 **Clipping of aneurysm**

| *Excludes:* | *clipping of arteriovenous fistula (39.53)* |

39.52 **Other repair of aneurysm**
Repair of aneurysm by:
coagulation
electrocoagulation
filipuncture
methyl methacrylate
suture
wiring
wrapping

| *Excludes:* | *endovascular repair of aneurysm (39.71-39.79)* |

re-entry operation (aorta) (39.54)
that with:
graft replacement (38.40-38.49)
resection (38.30-38.49, 38.60-38.69)

39.53 **Repair of arteriovenous fistula**
Embolization of carotid cavernous fistula
Repair of arteriovenous fistula by:
clipping
coagulation
ligation and division

| *Excludes:* | *repair of arteriovenous shunt for renal dialysis (39.42)* |

that with:
graft replacement (38.40-38.49)
resection (38.30-38.49, 38.60-38.69)

39.54 **Re-entry operation (aorta)**
Fenestration of dissecting aneurysm of thoracic aorta

Code also cardiopulmonary bypass [extracorporeal circulation] [heart-lung machine] (39.61)

39.55 **Reimplantation of aberrant renal vessel**

39.56 **Repair of blood vessel with tissue patch graft**

| *Excludes:* | *that with resection (38.40-38.49)* |

39.57 **Repair of blood vessel with synthetic patch graft**

| *Excludes:* | *that with resection (38.40-38.49)* |

39.58 **Repair of blood vessel with unspecified type of patch graft**

| *Excludes:* | *that with resection (38.40-38.49)* |

39.59 **Other repair of vessel**
Aorticopulmonary window operation
Arterioplasty NOS
Construction of venous valves (peripheral)
Plication of vein (peripheral)
Reimplantation of artery

Code also cardiopulmonary bypass [extracorporeal circulation] [heart-lung machine) (39.61)

| *Excludes:* | *interruption of the vena cava (38.7)* |

reimplantation of renal artery (39.55)
that with:
graft (39.56-39.58)
resection (38.30-38.49, 38.60-38.69)

Valid O.R. procedure   Non-O.R. procedure   Nonspecific O.R. procedure   Noncovered O.R. procedure

39.6　Extracorporeal circulation and procedures auxiliary to heart surgery

　　39.61　Extracorporeal circulation auxiliary to open heart surgery
　　　　Artificial heart and lung
　　　　Cardiopulmonary bypass
　　　　Pump oxygenator

　　　　| Excludes: | *extracorporeal hepatic assistance (50.92)*
　　　　　　extracorporeal membrane oxygenation [ECMO] (39.65)
　　　　　　hemodialysis (39.95)
　　　　　　percutaneous cardiopulmonary bypass (39.66)

　　39.62　Hypothermia (systemic) incidental to open heart surgery

　　39.63　Cardioplegia
　　　　Arrest:
　　　　　anoxic
　　　　　circulatory

　　39.64　Intraoperative cardiac pacemaker
　　　　Temporary pacemaker used during and immediately following cardiac surgery

　　39.65　Extracorporeal membrane oxygenation (ECMO)

　　　　| Excludes: | *extracorporeal circulation auxiliary to open heart surgery (39.61)*
　　　　　　percutaneous cardiopulmonary bypass (39.66)

　　39.66　Percutaneous cardiopulmonary bypass
　　　　Closed chest

　　　　| Excludes: | *extracorporeal circulation auxiliary to open heart surgery (39.61)*
　　　　　　extracorporeal hepatic assistance (50.92)
　　　　　　extracorporeal membrane oxygenation [ECMO] (39.65)
　　　　　　hemodialysis (39.95)

● **39.7　Endovascular repair of vessel**
　　　Endoluminal repair

　　　| Excludes: | *angioplasty or atherectomy of non-coronary vessel (39.50)*
　　　　　insertion of non-coronary stent or stents (39.90)
　　　　　other repair of aneurysm (39.52)
　　　　　resection of abdominal aorta with replacement (38.44)
　　　　　resection of lower limb arteries with replacement (38.48)
　　　　　resection of thoracic aorta with replacement (38.45)
　　　　　resection of upper limb vessels with replacement (38.43)

　● **39.71　Endovascular implantation of graft in abdominal aorta**
　　　　Endovascular repair of abdominal aortic aneurysm with graft
　　　　Stent graft(s)

　● **39.79　Other endovascular graft repair of aneurysm**
　　　　Implantation of graft in:
　　　　　lower extremity artery(s):
　　　　　　celiac
　　　　　　femoral
　　　　　　hepatic
　　　　　　iliac
　　　　　　mesenteric
　　　　　　popliteal
　　　　　　renal
　　　　　　splenic
　　　　　　tibial
　　　　　　thoracic aorta
　　　　　upper extremity artery(s):
　　　　　　axillary
　　　　　　brachial
　　　　　　brachiocephalic
　　　　　　carotid
　　　　　　radial
　　　　　　ulnar
　　　　Stent graft(s)

39.8　Operations on carotid body and other vascular bodies
　　　Chemodectomy　　　　　Glomectomy, carotid
　　　Denervation of:　　　　Implantation into carotid body:
　　　　aortic body　　　　　　electronic stimulator
　　　　carotid body　　　　　　pacemaker

　　　| Excludes: | *excision of glomus jugulare (20.51)*

39.9　Other operations on vessels

　● Code new　　　　　▲ Revision of　　　　④ ⑤ Fourth or fifth
　　to this edition　　　　existing code　　　　digit required

39.90 **Insertion of non-coronary artery stent or stents**
Endovascular recanalization techniques
Stent graft(s)

Code also any non-coronary angioplasty or atherectomy (39.50)

Excludes: *that for aneurysm repair (39.71-39.79)*

39.91 **Freeing of vessel**
Dissection and freeing of adherent tissue:
   artery-vein-nerve bundle
   vascular bundle

39.92 **Injection of sclerosing agent into vein**

Excludes: *injection:*
     esophageal varices (42.33)
     hemorrhoids (49.42)

39.93 **Insertion of vessel-to-vessel cannula**
Formation of:
   arteriovenous:
     fistula   } by external cannula
     shunt

Code also any renal dialysis (39.95)

39.94 **Replacement of vessel-to-vessel cannula**
Revision of vessel-to-vessel cannula

39.95 **Hemodialysis**
Artificial kidney   Hemofiltration
Hemodiafiltration   Renal dialysis

Excludes: *peritoneal dialysis (54.98)*

39.96 **Total body perfusion**

Code also substance perfused (99.21-99.29)

39.97 **Other perfusion**
Perfusion NOS
Perfusion, local [regional] of:
   carotid artery
   coronary artery
   head
   lower limb
   neck
   upper limb

Code also substance perfused (99.21-99.29)

Excludes: *perfusion of:*
     kidney (55.95)
     large intestine (46.96)
     liver (50.93)
     small intestine (46.95)

39.98 **Control of hemorrhage, not otherwise specified**
Angiotripsy
Control of postoperative hemorrhage NOS
Venotripsy

Excludes: *control of hemorrhage (postoperative):*
     anus (49.95)
     bladder (57.93)
     following vascular procedure (39.41)
     nose (21.00-21.09)
     prostate (60.94)
     tonsil (28.7)
    that by:
     ligation (38.80-38.89)
     suture (39.30-39.32)

39.99 **Other operations on vessels**

Excludes: *injection or infusion of therapeutic or prophylactic substance*
    (99.11-99.29)
   transfusion of blood and blood components (99.01-99.09)

● Code new
to this edition

▲ Revision of
existing code

④ ⑤ Fourth or fifth
digit required

8.   OPERATIONS ON THE HEMIC AND LYMPHATIC SYSTEM (40-41)

40   Operations on lymphatic system

40.0   Incision of lymphatic structures

40.1   Diagnostic procedures on lymphatic structures

40.11   Biopsy of lymphatic structure

40.19   Other diagnostic procedures on lymphatic structures

> *Excludes:*   *lymphangiogram*
> *abdominal (88.04)*
> *cervical (87.08)*
> *intrathoracic (87.34)*
> *lower limb (88.36)*
> *upper limb (88.34)*
> *microscopic examination of specimen (90.71-90.79)*
> *radioisotope scan (92.16)*
> *thermography (88.89)*

40.2   Simple excision of lymphatic structure

> *Excludes:*   *biopsy of lymphatic structure (40.11)*

40.21   Excision of deep cervical lymph node

40.22   Excision of internal mammary lymph node

40.23   Excision of axillary lymph node

40.24   Excision of inguinal lymph mode

40.29   Simple excision of other lymphatic structure
Excision of:
cystic hygroma
lymphangioma
Simple lymphadenectomy

40.3   Regional lymph node excision
Extended regional lymph node excision
Regional lymph node excision with excision of lymphatic drainage area including skin,
subcutaneous tissue, and fat

40.4   Radical excision of cervical lymph nodes
Resection of cervical lymph nodes down to muscle and deep fascia

> *Excludes:*   *that associated with radical laryngectomy (30.4)*

40.40   Radical neck dissection, not otherwise specified

40.41   Radical neck dissection, unilateral

40.42   Radical neck dissection, bilateral

40.5   Radical excision of other lymph nodes

> *Excludes:*   *that associated with radical mastectomy (85.45-85.48)*

40.50   Radical excision of lymph nodes, not otherwise specified
Radical (lymph) node dissection NOS

40.51   Radical excision of axillary lymph nodes

40.52   Radical excision of periaortic lymph nodes

40.53   Radical excision of iliac lymph nodes

40.54   Radical groin dissection

40.59   Radical excision of other lymph nodes

> *Excludes:*   *radical neck dissection (40.40-40.42)*

40.6   Operations on thoracic duct

40.61   Cannulation of thoracic duct

40.62   Fistulization of thoracic duct

40.63   Closure of fistula of thoracic duct

40.64   Ligation of thoracic duct

40.69   Other operations on thoracic duct

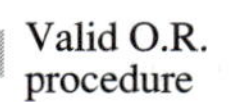 Valid O.R. procedure    Non-O.R. procedure   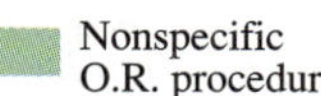 Nonspecific O.R. procedure   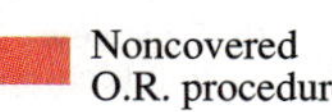 Noncovered O.R. procedure

40.9 **Other operations on lymphatic structures**
Anastomosis
Dilation
Ligation
Obliteration } of peripheral lymphatics
Reconstruction
Repair
Transplantation
Correction of lymphedema of limb, NOS

| *Excludes:* | *reduction of elephantiasis of scrotum (61.3)* |

41 **Operations on bone marrow and spleen**

41.0 **Bone marrow or hematopoietic stem cell transplant**

| *Excludes:* | *aspiration of bone marrow from donor (41.91)* |

41.00 **Bone marrow transplant, not otherwise specified**

▲ **41.01** **Autologous bone marrow transplant without purging**

| *Excludes:* | *that with purging (41.09)* |

41.02 **Allogeneic bone marrow transplant with purging**
Allograft of bone marrow with in vitro removal (purging) of T-cells

41.03 **Allogeneic bone marrow transplant without purging**
Allograft of bone marrow NOS

▲ **41.04** **Autologous hematopoietic stem cell transplant without purging**

| *Excludes:* | *that with purging (41.07)* |

▲ **41.05** **Allogeneic hematopoietic stem cell transplant without purging**

| *Excludes:* | *that with purging (41.08)* |

41.06 **Cord blood stem cell transplant**

● **41.07** **Autologous hematopoietic stem cell transplant with purging**
Cell depletion

● **41.08** **Allogeneic hematopoietic stem cell transplant with purging**
Cell depletion

● **41.09** **Autologous bone marrow transplant with purging**
With extracorporeal purging of malignant cells from marrow
Cell depletion

41.1 **Puncture of spleen**

| *Excludes:* | *aspiration biopsy of spleen (41.32)* |

41.2 **Splenotomy**

41.3 **Diagnostic procedures on bone marrow and spleen**

41.31 **Biopsy of bone marrow**

41.32 **Closed [aspiration] [percutaneous] biopsy of spleen**
Needle biopsy of spleen

41.33 **Open biopsy of spleen**

41.38 **Other diagnostic procedures on bone marrow**

| *Excludes:* | *microscopic examination of specimen from bone marrow (90.61-90.69)* |
| | *radioisotope scan (92.05)* |

41.39 **Other diagnostic procedures on spleen**

| *Excludes:* | *microscopic examination of specimen from spleen (90.61-90.69)* |
| | *radioisotope scan (92.05)* |

41.4 **Excision or destruction of lesion or tissue of spleen**

| *Excludes:* | *excision of accessory spleen (41.93)* |

41.41 **Marsupialization of splenic cyst**

41.42 **Excision of lesion or tissue of spleen**

| *Excludes:* | *biopsy of spleen (41.32-41.33)* |

41.43 **Partial splenectomy**

41.5 **Total splenectomy**
Splenectomy NOS

41.9 **Other operations on spleen and bone marrow**

● Code new
to this edition

▲ Revision of
existing code

④ ⑤ Fourth or fifth
digit required

41.91 **Aspiration of bone marrow from donor for transplant**

$\boxed{Excludes:}$ *biopsy of bone marrow (41.31)*

41.92 **Injection into bone marrow**

$\boxed{Excludes:}$ *bone marrow transplant (41.00-41.03)*

41.93 **Excision of accessory spleen**

41.94 **Transplantation of spleen**

41.95 **Repair and plastic operations on spleen**

41.98 **Other operations on bone marrow**

41.99 **Other operations on spleen**

Valid O.R. procedure	Non-O.R. procedure	Nonspecific O.R. procedure	Noncovered O.R. procedure

● Code new
to this edition

▲ Revision of
existing code

④ ⑤ Fourth or fifth
digit required

9. OPERATIONS ON THE DIGESTIVE SYSTEM (42-54)

42 Operations on esophagus

42.0 Esophagotomy

42.01 Incision of esophageal web

42.09 Other incision of esophagus
Esophagotomy NOS

Excludes:	esophagomyotomy (42.7)
	esophagostomy (42.10-42.19)

42.1 Esophagostomy

42.10 Esophagostomy, not otherwise specified

42.11 Cervical esophagostomy

42.12 Exteriorization of esophageal pouch

42.19 Other external fistulization of esophagus
Thoracic esophagostomy

Code also any resection (42.40-42.42)

42.2 Diagnostic procedures on esophagus

42.21 Operative esophagoscopy by incision

42.22 Esophagoscopy through artificial stoma

Excludes: *that with biopsy (42.24)*

42.23 Other esophagoscopy

Excludes: *that with biopsy (42.24)*

42.24 Closed [endoscopic] biopsy of esophagus
Brushing or washing for specimen collection
Esophagoscopy with biopsy
Suction biopsy of the esophagus

Excludes: *esophagogastroduodenoscopy [EGD] with closed biopsy (45.16)*

42.25 Open biopsy of esophagus

42.29 Other diagnostic procedures on esophagus

Excludes:	*barium swallow (87.61)*
	esophageal manometry (89.32)
	microscopic examination of specimen from esophagus (90.81-90.89)

42.3 Local excision or destruction of lesion or tissue of esophagus

42.31 Local excision of esophageal diverticulum

42.32 Local excision of other lesion or tissue of esophagus

Excludes:	*biopsy of esophagus (42.24-42.25)*
	esophageal fistulectomy (42.84)

42.33 Endoscopic excision or destruction of lesion or tissue of esophagus
Ablation of esophageal
   neoplasm
Control of esophageal
   bleeding
Esophageal polypectomy } by endoscopic approach
Esophageal varices
Injection of esophageal
   varices

Excludes:	*biopsy of esophagus (42.24-42.25)*
	fistulectomy (42.84)
	open ligation of esophageal varices (42.91)

42.39 Other destruction of lesion or tissue of esophagus

Excludes: *that by endoscopic approach (42.33)*

42.4 Excision of esophagus

Excludes: *esophagogastrectomy NOS (43.99)*

42.40 Esophagectomy, not otherwise specified

42.41 Partial esophagectomy

Code also any synchronous:
anastomosis other than end-to-end (42.51-42.69)

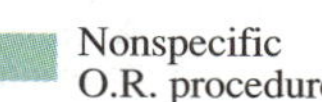

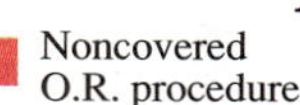

Noncovered
O.R. procedure

esophagostomy (42.10-42.19)
gastrostomy (43.11-43.19)

42.42 Total esophagectomy

Code also any synchronous:
gastrostomy (43.11-43.19)
interposition or anastomosis other than end-to-end (42.51-42.69)

Excludes: *esophagogastrectomy (43.99)*

42.5 Intrathoracic anastomosis of esophagus

Code also any synchronous:
esophagectomy (42.40-42.42)
gastrostomy (43.1)

42.51 Intrathoracic esophagoesophagostomy

42.52 Intrathoracic esophagogastrostomy

42.53 Intrathoracic esophageal anastomosis with interposition of small bowel

42.54 Other intrathoracic esophagoenterostomy
Anastomosis of esophagus to intestinal segment NOS

42.55 Intrathoracic esophageal anastomosis with interposition of colon

42.56 Other intrathoracic esophagocolostomy
Esophagocolostomy NOS

42.58 Intrathoracic esophageal anastomosis with other interposition
Construction of artificial esophagus
Retrosternal formation of reversed gastric tube

42.59 Other intrathoracic anastomosis of esophagus

42.6 Antesternal anastomosis of esophagus

Code also any synchronous:
esophagectomy (42.40-42.42)
gastrostomy (43.1)

42.61 Antesternal esophagoesophagostomy

42.62 Antesternal esophagogastrostomy

42.63 Antesternal esophageal anastomosis with interposition of small bowel

42.64 Other antesternal esophagoenterostomy
Antethoracic:
esophagoenterostomy
esophagoileostomy
esophagojejunostomy

42.65 Antesternal esophageal anastomosis with interposition of colon

42.66 Other antesternal esophagocolostomy
Antethoracic esophagocolostomy

42.68 Other antesternal esophageal anastomosis with interposition

42.69 Other antesternal anastomosis of esophagus

42.7 Esophagomyotomy

42.8 Other repair of esophagus

42.81 Insertion of permanent tube into esophagus

42.82 Suture of laceration of esophagus

42.83 Closure of esophagostomy

42.84 Repair of esophageal fistula, not elsewhere classified

Excludes: *repair of fistula:*
bronchoesophageal (33.42)
esophagopleurocutaneous (34.73)
pharyngoesophageal (29.53)
tracheoesophageal (31.73)

42.85 Repair of esophageal stricture

42.86 Production of subcutaneous tunnel without esophageal anastomosis

● Code new
to this edition

▲ Revision of
existing code

④ ⑤ Fourth or fifth
digit required

42.87 Other graft of esophagus

> *Excludes:* antesternal esophageal anastomosis with interposition of:
> colon (42.65)
> small bowel (42.63)
> antesternal esophageal anastomosis with other interposition (42.68)
> intrathoracic esophageal anastomosis with interposition of:
> colon (42.55)
> small bowel (42.53)
> intrathoracic esophageal anastomosis with other interposition (42.58)

42.89 Other repair of esophagus

42.9 Other operations on esophagus

42.91 Ligation of esophageal varices

> *Excludes:* that by endoscopic approach (42.33)

42.92 Dilation of esophagus
Dilation of cardiac sphincter

> *Excludes:* intubation of esophagus (96.03, 96.06-96.08)

42.99 Other

> *Excludes:* insertion of Sengstaken tube (96.06)
> intubation of esophagus (96.03, 96.06-96.08)
> removal of intraluminal foreign body from esophagus without incision
> (98.02)
> tamponade of esophagus (96.06)

43 Incision and excision of stomach

43.0 Gastrotomy

> *Excludes:* gastrostomy (43.11-43.19)
> that for control of hemorrhage (44.49)

43.1 Gastrostomy

43.11 Percutaneous [endoscopic] gastrostomy [PEG]
Percutaneous transabdominal gastrostomy

43.19 Other gastrostomy

> *Excludes:* percutaneous [endoscopic] gastrostomy [PEG] (43.11)

43.3 Pyloromyotomy

43.4 Local excision or destruction of lesion or tissue of stomach

43.41 Endoscopic excision or destruction of lesion or tissue of stomach
Gastric polypectomy by endoscopic approach
Gastric varices by endoscopic approach

> *Excludes:* biopsy of stomach (44.14-44.15)
> control of hemorrhage (44.43)
> open ligation of gastric varices (44.91)

43.42 Local excision of other lesion or tissue of stomach

> *Excludes:* biopsy of stomach (44.14-44.15)
> gastric fistulectomy (44.62-44.63)
> partial gastrectomy (43.5-43.89)

43.49 Other destruction of lesion or tissue of stomach

> *Excludes:* that by endoscopic approach (43.41)

43.5 Partial gastrectomy with anastomosis to esophagus
Proximal gastrectomy

43.6 Partial gastrectomy with anastomosis to duodenum
Billroth I operation
Distal gastrectomy
Gastropylorectomy

43.7 Partial gastrectomy with anastomosis to jejunum
Billroth II operation

43.8 Other partial gastrectomy

43.81 Partial gastrectomy with jejunal transposition
Henley jejunal transposition operation
Code also any synchronous intestinal resection (45.51)

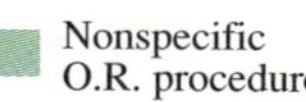

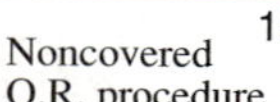

Nonspecific
O.R. procedure

Noncovered
O.R. procedure

43.89 **Other**
Partial gastrectomy with bypass gastrogastrostomy
Sleeve resection of stomach

43.9 **Total gastrectomy**

43.91 **Total gastrectomy with intestinal interposition**

43.99 **Other total gastrectomy**
Complete gastroduodenectomy
Esophagoduodenostomy with complete gastrectomy
Esophagogastrectomy NOS
Esophagojejunostomy with complete gastrectomy
Radical gastrectomy

44 **Other operations on stomach**

44.0 **Vagotomy**

44.00 **Vagotomy, not otherwise specified**
Division of vagus nerve NOS

44.01 **Truncal vagotomy**

44.02 **Highly selective vagotomy**
Parietal cell vagotomy
Selective proximal vagotomy

44.03 **Other selective vagotomy**

44.1 **Diagnostic procedures on stomach**

44.11 **Transabdominal gastroscopy**
Intraoperative gastroscopy

> *Excludes:* *that with biopsy (44.14)*

44.12 **Gastroscopy through artificial stoma**

> *Excludes:* *that with biopsy (44.14)*

44.13 **Other gastroscopy**

> *Excludes:* *that with biopsy (44.14)*

44.14 **Closed [endoscopic] biopsy of stomach**
Brushing or washing for specimen collection

> *Excludes:* *esophagogastroduodenoscopy [EGD] with closed biopsy (45.16)*

44.15 **Open biopsy of stomach**

44.19 **Other diagnostic procedures on stomach**

> *Excludes:* *gastric lavage (96.33)*
> *microscopic examination of specimen from stomach (90.81-90.89)*
> *upper GI series (87.62)*

44.2 **Pyloroplasty**

44.21 **Dilation of pylorus by incision**

44.22 **Endoscopic dilation of pylorus**
Dilation with balloon endoscope
Endoscopic dilation of gastrojejunostomy site

44.29 **Other pyloroplasty**
Pyloroplasty NOS
Revision of pylorus

44.3 **Gastroenterostomy without gastrectomy**

44.31 **High gastric bypass**
Printen and Mason gastric bypass

44.39 **Other gastroenterostomy**
Bypass:
gastroduodenostomy
gastroenterostomy
gastrogastrostomy
Gastrojejunostomy without gastrectomy NOS

44.4 **Control of hemorrhage and suture of ulcer of stomach or duodenum**

44.40 **Suture of peptic ulcer, not otherwise specified**

44.41 **Suture of gastric ulcer site**

> *Excludes:* *ligation of gastric varices (44.91)*

44.42 **Suture of duodenal ulcer site**

● Code new
to this edition

▲ Revision of
existing code

④ ⑤ Fourth or fifth
digit required

44.43 Endoscopic control of gastric or duodenal bleeding

44.44 Transcatheter embolization for gastric or duodenal bleeding

> *Excludes:* *surgical occlusion of abdominal vessels (38.86-38.87)*

44.49 Other control of hemorrhage of stomach or duodenum
That with gastrotomy

44.5 Revision of gastric anastomosis
Closure of:
gastric anastomosis
gastroduodenostomy
gastrojejunostomy
Pantaloon operation

44.6 Other repair of stomach

44.61 Suture of laceration of stomach

> *Excludes:* *that of ulcer site(44.41)*

44.62 Closure of gastrostomy

44.63 Closure of other gastric fistula
Closure of:
gastrocolic fistula
gastrojejunocolic fistula

44.64 Gastropexy

44.65 Esophagogastroplasty
Belsey operation
Esophagus and stomach cardioplasty

44.66 Other procedures for creation of esophagogastric sphincteric competence
Fundoplication
Gastric cardioplasty
Nissen's fundoplication
Restoration of cardio-esophageal angle

44.69 Other
Inversion of gastric diverticulum
Repair of stomach NOS

44.9 Other operations on stomach

44.91 Ligation of gastric varices

> *Excludes:* *that by endoscopic approach (43.41)*

44.92 Intraoperative manipulation of stomach
Reduction of gastric volvulus

44.93 Insertion of gastric bubble [balloon]

44.94 Removal of gastric bubble [balloon]

44.99 Other

> *Excludes:* *change of gastrostomy tube (97.02)*
> *dilation of cardiac sphincter (42.92)*
> *gastric:*
> *cooling (96.31)*
> *freezing (96.32)*
> *gavage (96.35)*
> *hypothermia (96.31)*
> *lavage (96.33)*
> *insertion of nasogastric tube (96.07)*
> *irrigation of gastrostomy (96.36)*
> *irrigation of nasogastric tube (96.34)*
> *removal of:*
> *gastrostomy tube (97.51)*
> *intraluminal foreign body from stomach without incision (98.03)*
> *replacement of:*
> *gastrostomy tube (97.02)*
> *(naso-)gastric tube (97.01)*

45 Incision, excision, and anastomosis of intestine

45.0 Enterotomy

> *Excludes:* *duodenocholedochotomy (51.41-51.42, 51.51)*
> *that for destruction of lesion (45.30-45.34)*
> *that of exteriorized intestine (46.14, 46.24, 46.31)*

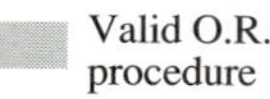

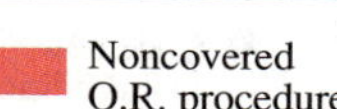

45.00 **Incision of intestine, not otherwise specified**

45.01 **Incision of duodenum**

45.02 **Other incision of small intestine**

45.03 **incision of large intestine**

> Excludes: proctotomy (48.0)

45.1 **Diagnostic procedures on small intestine**

Code also any laparotomy (54.11-54.19)

45.11 **Transabdominal endoscopy of small intestine**
Intraoperative endoscopy of small intestine

> Excludes: that with biopsy (45.14)

45.12 **Endoscopy of small intestine through artificial stoma**

> Excludes: that with biopsy (45.14)

45.13 **Other endoscopy of small intestine**
Esophagogastroduodenoscopy [EGD]

> Excludes: that with biopsy (45.14, 45.16)

45.14 **Closed [endoscopic] biopsy of small intestine**
Brushing or washing for specimen collection

> Excludes: esophagogastroduodenoscopy [EGD] with closed biopsy (45.16)

45.15 **Open biopsy of small intestine**

45.16 **Esophagogastroduodenoscopy [EGD] with closed biopsy**
Biopsy of one or more sites involving esophagus, stomach, and/or duodenum

45.19 **Other diagnostic procedures on small intestine**

> Excludes: microscopic examination of specimen from small intestine (90.91-90.99)
> radioisotope scan (92.04)
> ultrasonography (88.74)
> x-ray (87.61-87.69)

45.2 **Diagnostic procedures on large intestine**

Code also any laparotomy (54.11-54.19)

45.21 **Transabdominal endoscopy of large intestine**
Intraoperative endoscopy of large intestine

> Excludes: that with biopsy (45.25)

45.22 **Endoscopy of large intestine through artificial stoma**

> Excludes: that with biopsy (45.25)

45.23 **Colonoscopy**
Flexible fiberoptic colonoscopy

> Excludes: endoscopy of large intestine through artificial stoma (45.22)
> flexible sigmoidoscopy (45.24)
> rigid proctosigmoidoscopy (48.23)
> transabdominal endoscopy of large intestine (45.21)

45.24 **Flexible sigmoidoscopy**
Endoscopy of descending colon

> Excludes: rigid proctosigmoidoscopy (48.23)

45.25 **Closed [endoscopic] biopsy of large intestine**
Biopsy, closed, of unspecified intestinal site
Brushing or washing for specimen collection
Colonoscopy with biopsy

> Excludes: proctosigmoidoscopy with biopsy (48.24)

45.26 **Open biopsy of large intestine**

45.27 **Intestinal biopsy, site unspecified**

45.28 **Other diagnostic procedures on large intestine**

45.29 **Other diagnostic procedures on intestine, site unspecified**

> Excludes: microscopic examination of specimen (90.91-90.99)
> scan and radioisotope function study (92.04)
> ultrasonography (88.74)
> x-ray (87.61-87.69)

● Code new to this edition   ▲ Revision of existing code   ④ ⑤ Fourth or fifth digit required

45.3   Local excision or destruction of lesion or tissue of small intestine

    45.30   Endoscopic excision or destruction of lesion of duodenum

        Excludes: *biopsy of duodenum (45.14-45.15)*
           control of hemorrhage (44.43)
           fistulectomy (46.72)

    45.31   Other local excision of lesion of duodenum

        Excludes: *biopsy of duodenum (45.14-45.15)*
           fistulectomy (46.72)
           multiple segmental resection (45.61)
           that by endoscopic approach (45.30)

    45.32   Other destruction of lesion of duodenum

        Excludes: *that by endoscopic approach (45.30)*

    45.33   Local excision of lesion or tissue of small intestine, except duodenum
        Excision of redundant mucosa of ileostomy

        Excludes: *biopsy of small intestine (45.14-45.15)*
           fistulectomy (46.74)
           multiple segmental resection (45.61)

    45.34   Other destruction of lesion of small intestine, except duodenum

45.4   Local excision or destruction of lesion or tissue of large intestine

    45.41   Excision of lesion or tissue of large intestine
        Excision of redundant mucosa of colostomy

        Excludes: *biopsy of large intestine (45.25-45.27)*
           endoscopic polypectomy of large intestine (45.42)
           fistulectomy (46.76)
           multiple segmental resection (45.71)
           that by endoscopic approach (45.42-45.43)

    45.42   Endoscopic polypectomy of large intestine

        Excludes: *that by open approach (45.41)*

    45.43   Endoscopic destruction of other lesion or tissue of large intestine
        Endoscopic ablation of tumor of large intestine
        Endoscopic control of colonic bleeding

        Excludes: *endoscopic polypectomy of large intestine (45.42)*

    45.49   Other destruction of lesion of large intestine

        Excludes: *that by endoscopic approach (45.43)*

45.5   Isolation of intestinal segment

    Code also any synchronous:
      anastomosis other than end-to-end (45.90-45.94)
      enterostomy (46.10-46.39)

    45.50   Isolation of intestinal segment not otherwise specified
        Isolation of intestinal pedicle flap
        Reversal of intestinal segment

    45.51   Isolation of segment of small intestine
        Isolation of ileal loop
        Resection of small intestine for interposition

    45.52   Isolation of segment of large intestine
        Resection of colon for interposition

45.6   Other excision of small intestine

    Code also any synchronous:
      anastomosis other than end-to-end (45.90-45.93, 45.95)
      colostomy (46.10-46.13)
      enterostomy (46.10-46.39)

    Excludes: *cecectomy (45.72)*
           enterocolectomy (45.79)
           gastroduodenectomy (43.6-43.99)
           ileocolectomy (45.73)
           pancreatoduodenectomy (52.51-52.7)

    45.61   Multiple segmental resection of small intestine
        Segmental resection for multiple traumatic lesions of small intestine

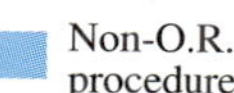
Valid O.R. procedure

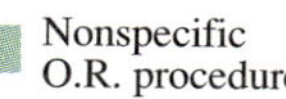
Non-O.R. procedure

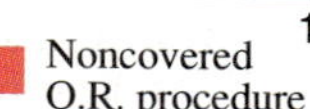
Nonspecific O.R. procedure

Noncovered O.R. procedure

45.62 Other partial resection of small intestine
Duodenectomy   Jejunectomy
Ileectomy

> *Excludes:* *duodenectomy with synchronous pancreatectomy (52.51-52.7)*
> *resection of cecum and terminal ileum (45.72)*

45.63 Total removal of small intestine

45.7 Partial excision of large intestine

Code also any synchronous:
anastomosis other than end-to-end (45.92-45.94)
enterostomy (46.10-46.39)

45.71 Multiple segmental resection of large intestine
Segmental resection for multiple traumatic lesions of large intestine

45.72 Cecectomy
Resection of cecum and terminal ileum

45.73 Right hemicolectomy
Ileocolectomy
Right radical colectomy

45.74 Resection of transverse colon

45.75 Left hemicolectomy

> *Excludes:* *proctosigmoidectomy (48.41-48.69)*
> *second stage Mikulicz operation (46.04)*

45.76 Sigmoidectomy

45.79 Other partial excision of large intestine
Enterocolectomy NEC

45.8 Total intra-abdominal colectomy
Excision of cecum, colon, and sigmoid

> *Excludes:* *coloproctectomy (48.41-48.69)*

45.9 Intestinal anastomosis

Code also any synchronous resection (45.31-45.8, 48.41-48.69)

> *Excludes:* *end-to-end anastomosis – omit code*

45.90 Intestinal anastomosis, not otherwise specified

45.91 Small-to-small intestinal anastomosis

45.92 Anastomosis of small intestine to rectal stump
Hampton procedure

45.93 Other small-to-large intestinal anastomosis

45.94 Large-to-large intestinal anastomosis

> *Excludes:* *rectorectostomy (48.74)*

45.95 Anastomosis to anus
Formation of endorectal ileal pouch (J-pouch) (H-pouch) (S-pouch) with
anastomosis of small intestine to anus

46 Other operations on intestine

46.0 Exteriorization of intestine
Includes: loop enterostomy
multiple stage resection of intestine

46.01 Exteriorization of small intestine
Loop ileostomy

46.02 Resection of exteriorized segment of small intestine

46.03 Exteriorization of large intestine
Exteriorization of intestine NOS
First stage Mikulicz exteriorization of intestine
Loop colostomy

46.04 Resection of exteriorized segment of large intestine
Resection of exteriorized segment of intestine NOS
Second stage Mikulicz operation

● Code new
to this edition

▲ Revision of
existing code

④ ⑤ Fourth or fifth
digit required

46.1   Colostomy

Code also any synchronous resection (45.49, 45.71-45.79, 45.8)

> *Excludes:*   *loop colostomy (46.03)*
> *that with abdominoperineal resection of rectum (48.5)*
> *that with synchronous anterior rectal resection (48.62)*

46.10   Colostomy, not otherwise specified

46.11   Temporary colostomy

46.13   Other permanent colostomy

46.14   Delayed opening of colostomy

46.2   Ileostomy

Code also any synchronous resection (45.34, 45.61-45.63)

> *Excludes:*   *loop ileostomy (46.01)*

46.20   Ileostomy, not otherwise specified

46.21   Temporary ileostomy

46.22   Continent ileostomy

46.23   Other permanent ileostomy

46.24   Delayed opening of ileostomy

46.3   Other enterostomy

Code also any synchronous resection (45.61-45.8)

46.31   Delayed opening of other enterostomy

46.32   Percutaneous [endoscopic] jejunostomy [PEJ]
Endoscopic conversion of gastrostomy to jejunostomy

46.39   Other
Duodenostomy
Feeding enterostomy

46.4   Revision of intestinal stoma

46.40   Revision of intestinal stoma, not otherwise specified
Plastic enlargement of intestinal stoma
Reconstruction of stoma of intestine
Release of scar tissue of intestinal stoma

> *Excludes:*   *excision of redundant mucosa (45.41)*

46.41   Revision of stoma of small intestine

> *Excludes:*   *excision of redundant mucosa (45.33)*

46.42   Repair of pericolostomy hernia

46.43   Other revision of stoma of large intestine

> *Excludes:*   *excision of redundant mucosa (45.41)*

46.5   Closure of intestinal stoma

Code also any synchronous resection (45.34, 45.49, 45.61-45.8)

46.50   Closure of intestinal stoma, not otherwise specified

46.51   Closure of stoma of small intestine

46.52   Closure of stoma of large intestine
Closure or take-down of:
  cecostomy
  colostomy
  sigmoidostomy

46.6   Fixation of intestine

46.60   Fixation of intestine, not otherwise specified
Fixation of intestine to abdominal wall

46.61   Fixation of small intestine to abdominal wall
Ileopexy

46.62   Other fixation of small intestine
Noble plication of small intestine
Plication of jejunum

46.63   Fixation of large intestine to abdominal wall
Cecocoloplicopexy
Sigmoidopexy (Moschowitz)

Valid O.R. procedure	Non-O.R. procedure	Nonspecific O.R. procedure	Noncovered O.R. procedure

46.64 **Other fixation of large intestine**
Cecofixation
Colofixation

46.7 **Other repair of intestine**

> *Excludes:* *closure of:*
> *ulcer of duodenum (44.42)*
> *vesicoenteric fistula (57.83)*

46.71 **Suture of laceration of duodenum**

46.72 **Closure of fistula of duodenum**

46.73 **Suture of laceration of small intestine, except duodenum**

46.74 **Closure of fistula of small intestine, except duodenum**

> *Excludes:* *closure of:*
> *artificial stoma (46.51)*
> *vaginal fistula (70.74)*
> *repair of gastrojejunocolic fistula (44.63)*

46.75 **Suture of laceration of large intestine**

46.76 **Closure of fistula of large intestine**

> *Excludes:* *closure of:*
> *gastrocolic fistula (44.63)*
> *rectal fistula (48.73)*
> *sigmoidovesical fistula (57.83)*
> *stoma (46.52)*
> *vaginal fistula (70.72-70.73)*
> *vesicocolic fistula (57.83)*
> *vesicosigmoidovaginal fistula (57.83)*

46.79 **Other repair of intestine**

46.8 **Dilation and manipulation of intestine**

46.80 **Intra-abdominal manipulation of intestine, not otherwise specified**
Correction of intestinal malrotation
Reduction of:
   intestinal torsion
   intestinal volvulus
   intussusception

> *Excludes:* *reduction of intussusception with:*
> *fluoroscopy (96.29)*
> *ionizing radiation enema (96.29)*
> *ultrasonography guidance (96.29)*

46.81 **Intra-abdominal manipulation of small intestine**

46.82 **Intra-abdominal manipulation of large intestine**

46.85 **Dilation of intestine**
Dilation (balloon) of duodenum
Dilation (balloon) of jejunum
Endoscopic dilation (balloon) of large intestine
That through rectum or colostomy

46.9 **Other operations on intestines**

46.91 **Myotomy of sigmoid colon**

46.92 **Myotomy of other parts of colon**

46.93 **Revision of anastomosis of small intestine**

46.94 **Revision of anastomosis of large intestine**

46.95 **Local perfusion of small intestine**
Code also substance perfused (99.21-99.29)

46.96 **Local perfusion of large intestine**
Code also substance perfused (99.21-99.29)

● **46.97** **Transplant of intestine**

● Code new
to this edition

▲ Revision of
existing code

④ ⑤ Fourth or fifth
digit required

46.99 **Other**
Ileoentectropy

> *Excludes:* *diagnostic procedures on intestine (45.11-45.29)*
> *dilation of enterostomy stoma (96.24)*
> *intestinal intubation (96.08)*
> *removal of:*
> *intraluminal foreign body from intestine without incision (98.04)*
> *intraluminal foreign body from small intestine without incision (98.03)*
> *tube from large intestine (97.53)*
> *tube from small intestine (97.52)*
> *replacement of:*
> *large intestine tube or enterostomy device (97.04)*
> *small intestine tube or enterostomy device (97.03)*

47 Operations on appendix
Includes: appendiceal stump

47.0 Appendectomy

> *Excludes:* *incidental appendectomy, so described (47.11, 47.19)*

47.01 **Laparoscopic appendectomy**

47.09 **Other appendectomy**

47.1 Incidental appendectomy

47.11 **Laparoscopic incidental appendectomy**

47.19 **Other incidental appendectomy**

47.2 **Drainage of appendiceal abscess**

> *Excludes:* *that with appendectomy (47.0)*

47.9 Other operations on appendix

47.91 **Appendicostomy**

47.92 **Closure of appendiceal fistula**

47.99 **Other**
Anastomosis of appendix

> *Excludes:* *diagnostic procedures on appendix (45.21-45.29)*

48 Operations on rectum, rectosigmoid, and perirectal tissue

48.0 **Proctotomy**
Decompression of imperforate anus
Panas' operation [linear proctotomy]

> *Excludes:* *incision of perirectal tissue (48.81)*

48.1 **Proctostomy**

48.2 **Diagnostic procedures on rectum, rectosigmoid, and perirectal tissue**

48.21 **Transabdominal proctosigmoidoscopy**
Intraoperative proctosigmoidoscopy

> *Excludes:* *that with biopsy (48.24)*

48.22 **Proctosigmoidoscopy through artificial stoma**

> *Excludes:* *that with biopsy (48.24)*

48.23 **Rigid proctosigmoidoscopy**

> *Excludes:* *flexible sigmoidoscopy (45.24)*

48.24 **Closed [endoscopic] biopsy of rectum**
Brushing or washing for specimen collection
Proctosigmoidoscopy with biopsy

48.25 **Open biopsy of rectum**

48.26 **Biopsy of perirectal tissue**

48.29 **Other diagnostic procedures on rectum, rectosigmoid and perirectal tissue**

> *Excludes:* *digital examination of rectum (89.34)*
> *lower GI series (87.64)*
> *microscopic examination of specimen from rectum (90.91-90.99)*

48.3 **Local excision or destruction of lesion or tissue of rectum**

48.31 **Radical electrocoagulation of rectal lesion or tissue**

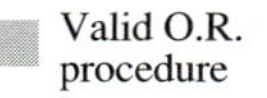

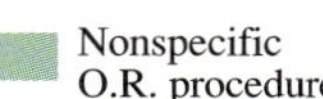

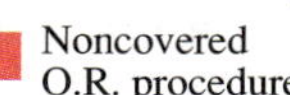

48.32 **Other electrocoagulation of rectal lesion or tissue**

48.33 **Destruction of rectal lesion or tissue by laser**

48.34 **Destruction of rectal lesion or tissue by cryosurgery**

48.35 **Local excision of rectal lesion or tissue**

> *Excludes:*   *biopsy of rectum (48.24-48.25)*
> *[endoscopic] polypectomy of rectum (48.36)*
> *excision of perirectal tissue (48.82)*
> *hemorrhoidectomy (49.46)*
> *rectal fistulectomy (48.73)*

48.36 **[Endoscopic] polypectomy of rectum**

48.4 **Pull-through resection of rectum**

Code also any synchronous anastomosis other than end-to-end (45.90, 45.92-45.95)

48.41 **Soave submucosal resection of rectum**
Endorectal pull-through operation

48.49 **Other pull-through resection of rectum**
Abdominoperineal pull-through
Altemeier operation
Swenson proctectomy

> *Excludes:*   *Duhamel abdominoperineal pull-through (48.65)*

48.5 **Abdominoperineal resection of rectum**
Combined abdominoendorectal resection
Complete proctectomy
Includes: with synchronous colostomy

Code also any synchronous anastomosis other than end-to-end (45.90, 45.92-45.95)

> *Excludes:*   *Duhamel abdominoperineal pull-through (48.65)*
> *that as part of pelvic exenteration (68.8)*

48.6 **Other resection of rectum**

Code also any synchronous anastomosis other than end-to-end (45.90, 45.92-45.95)

48.61 **Transsacral rectosigmoidectomy**

48.62 **Anterior resection of rectum with synchronous colostomy**

48.63 **Other anterior resection of rectum**

> *Excludes:*   *that with synchronous colostomy (48.62)*

48.64 **Posterior resection of rectum**

48.65 **Duhamel resection of rectum**
Duhamel abdominoperineal pull-through

48.69 **Other**
Partial proctectomy
Rectal resection NOS

48.7 **Repair of rectum**

> *Excludes:*   *repair of:*
> *current obstetric laceration (75.62)*
> *vaginal rectocele (70.50, 70.52)*

48.71 **Suture of laceration of rectum**

48.72 **Closure of proctostomy**

48.73 **Closure of other rectal fistula**

> *Excludes:*   *fistulectomy:*
> *perirectal (48.93)*
> *rectourethral (58.43)*
> *rectovaginal (70.73)*
> *rectovesical (57.83)*
> *rectovesicovaginal (57.83)*

48.74 **Rectorectostomy**
Rectal anastomosis NOS

48.75 **Abdominal proctopexy**
Frickman procedure
Ripstein repair of rectal prolapse

● Code new
to this edition   ▲ Revision of
existing code   ④ ⑤ Fourth or fifth
digit required

48.76 Other proctopexy
Delorme repair of prolapsed rectum
Proctosigmoidopexy
Puborectalis sling operation
Excludes: *manual reduction of rectal prolapse (96.26)*

48.79 Other repair of rectum
Repair of old obstetric laceration of rectum
Excludes: *anastomosis to:*
large intestine (45.94)
small intestine (45.92-45.93)
repair of:
current obstetrical laceration (75.62)
vaginal rectocele (70.50, 70.52)

48.8 Incision or excision of perirectal tissue or lesion
Includes: pelvirectal tissue
rectovaginal septum

48.81 Incision of perirectal tissue
Incision of rectovaginal septum

48.82 Excision of perirectal tissue
Excludes: *perirectal biopsy (48.26)*
perirectofistulectomy (48.93)
rectal fistulectomy (48.73)

48.9 Other operations on rectum and perirectal tissue

48.91 Incision of rectal stricture

48.92 Anorectal myectomy

48.93 Repair of perirectal fistula
Excludes: *that opening into rectum (48.73)*

48.99 Other
Excludes: *digital examination of rectum (89.34)*
dilation of rectum (96.22)
insertion of rectal tube (96.09)
irrigation of rectum (96.38-96.39)
manual reduction of rectal prolapse (96.26)
proctoclysis (96.37)
rectal massage (99.93)
rectal packing (96.19)
removal of:
impacted feces (96.38)
intraluminal foreign body from rectum without incision (98.05)
rectal packing (97.59)
transanal enema (96.39)

49 Operations on anus

49.0 Incision or excision of perianal tissue

49.01 Incision of perianal abscess

49.02 Other incision of perianal tissue
Undercutting of perianal tissue
Excludes: *anal fistulotomy (49.11)*

49.03 Excision of perianal skin tags

49.04 Other excision of perianal tissue
Excludes: *anal fistulectomy (49.12)*
biopsy of perianal tissue (49.22)

49.1 Incision or excision of anal fistula
Excludes: *closure of anal fistula (49.73)*

49.11 Anal fistulotomy

49.12 Anal fistulectomy

49.2 Diagnostic procedures on anus and perianal tissue

49.21 Anoscopy

49.22 Biopsy of perianal tissue

49.23 Biopsy of anus

Valid O.R.
procedure

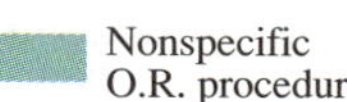
Non-O.R.
procedure

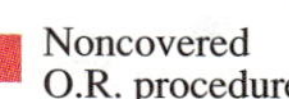
Nonspecific
O.R. procedure

Noncovered
O.R. procedure

49.29 Other diagnostic procedures on anus and perianal tissue

> *Excludes:* *microscopic examination of specimen from anus (90.91-90.99)*

49.3 Local excision or destruction of other lesion or tissue of anus
Anal cryptotomy
Cauterization of lesion of anus

> *Excludes:* *biopsy of anus (49.23)*
> *control of (postoperative) hemorrhage of anus (49.95)*
> *hemorrhoidectomy (49.46)*

49.31 Endoscopic excision or destruction of lesion or tissue of anus

49.39 Other local excision or destruction of lesion or tissue of anus

> *Excludes:* *that by endoscopic approach (49.31)*

49.4 Procedures on hemorrhoids

49.41 Reduction of hemorrhoids

49.42 Injection of hemorrhoids

49.43 Cauterization of hemorrhoids
Clamp and cautery of hemorrhoids

49.44 Destruction of hemorrhoids by cryotherapy

49.45 Ligation of hemorrhoids

49.46 Excision of hemorrhoids
Hemorrhoidectomy NOS

49.47 Evacuation of thrombosed hemorrhoids

49.49 Other procedures on hemorrhoids
Lord procedure

49.5 Division of anal sphincter

49.51 Left lateral anal sphincterotomy

49.52 Posterior anal sphincterotomy

49.59 Other anal sphincterotomy
Division of sphincter NOS

49.6 Excision of anus

49.7 Repair of anus

> *Excludes:* *repair of current obstetric laceration (75.62)*

49.71 Suture of laceration of anus

49.72 Anal cerclage

49.73 Closure of anal fistula

> *Excludes:* *excision of anal fistula (49.12)*

49.74 Gracilis muscle transplant for anal incontinence

49.79 Other repair of anal sphincter
Repair of old obstetric laceration of anus

> *Excludes:* *anoplasty with synchronous*
> *hemorrhoidectomy (49.46)*
> *repair of current obstetric laceration (75.62)*

49.9 Other operations on anus

> *Excludes:* *dilation of anus (sphincter) (96.23)*

49.91 Incision of anal septum

49.92 Insertion of subcutaneous electrical anal stimulator

49.93 Other incision of anus
Removal of:
  foreign body from anus with incision
  seton from anus

> *Excludes:* *anal fistulotomy (49.11)*
> *removal of intraluminal foreign body without incision (98.05)*

49.94 Reduction of anal prolapse

> *Excludes:* *manual reduction of rectal prolapse (96.26)*

49.95 Control of (postoperative) hemorrhage of anus

49.99 Other

● Code new to this edition   ▲ Revision of existing code   ④ ⑤ Fourth or fifth digit required

50   Operations on liver

50.0   Hepatotomy
Incision of abscess of liver
Removal of gallstones from liver
Stromeyer-Little operation

50.1   Diagnostic procedures on liver

50.11   Closed (percutaneous) [needle] biopsy of liver
Diagnostic aspiration of liver

50.12   Open biopsy of liver
Wedge biopsy

50.19   Other diagnostic procedures on liver

Excludes: *liver scan and radioisotope function study (92.02)*
microscopic examination of specimen from liver (91.01-91.09)

50.2   Local excision or destruction of liver tissue or lesion

50.21   Marsupialization of lesion of liver

50.22   Partial hepatectomy
Wedge resection of liver

Excludes: *biopsy of liver, (50.11-50.12)*
hepatic lobectomy (50.3)

50.29   Other destruction of lesion of liver
Cauterization
Enucleation   of hepatic lesion
Evacuation

Excludes: *percutaneous aspiration of lesion (50.91)*

50.3   Lobectomy of liver
Total hepatic lobectomy with partial excision of other lobe

50.4   Total hepatectomy

50.5   Liver transplant

50.51   Auxiliary liver transplant
Auxiliary hepatic transplantation leaving patient's own liver in situ

50.59   Other transplant of liver

50.6   Repair of liver

50.61   Closure of laceration of liver

50.69   Other repair of liver
Hepatopexy

50.9   Other operations on liver

Excludes: *lysis of adhesions (54.5)*

50.91   Percutaneous aspiration of liver

Excludes: *percutaneous biopsy (50.11)*

50.92   Extracorporeal hepatic assistance

50.93   Localized perfusion of liver

50.94   Other injection of therapeutic substance into liver

50.99   Other

51   Operations on gallbladder and biliary tract
Includes: operations on:
ampulla of Vater
common bile duct
cystic duct
hepatic duct
intrahepatic bile duct
sphincter of Oddi

51.0   Cholecystotomy and cholecystostomy

51.01   Percutaneous aspiration of gallbladder

Excludes: *needle biopsy (51.12)*

51.02   Trocar cholecystostomy

51.03   Other cholecystostomy

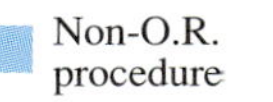

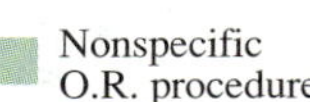

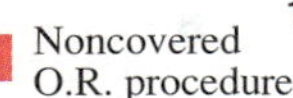

51.04   Other cholecystotomy
Cholelithotomy NOS

51.1   Diagnostic procedures on biliary tract

> *Excludes:*   *that for endoscopic procedures classifiable to 51.64, 51.84-51.88, 52.14, 52.21, 52.93-52.94, 52.97-52.98*

51.10   Endoscopic retrograde cholangiopancreatography [ERCP]

> *Excludes:*   *endoscopic retrograde:*
> *cholangiography [ERC] (51.11)*
> *pancreatography [ERP] (52.13)*

51.11   Endoscopic retrograde cholangiography [ERC]

> *Excludes:*   *endoscopic retrograde:*
> *cholangiopancreatography [ERCP] (51.10)*
> *pancreatography [ERP] (52.13)*

51.12   Percutaneous biopsy of gallbladder or bile ducts
Needle biopsy of gallbladder

51.13   Open biopsy of gallbladder or bile ducts

51.14   Other closed [endoscopic] biopsy of biliary duct or sphincter of Oddi
Brushing or washing for specimen collection
Closed biopsy of biliary duct or sphincter of Oddi by procedures classifiable to 51.10-51.11, 52.13

51.15   Pressure measurement of sphincter of Oddi
Pressure measurement of sphincter by procedures classifiable to 51.10-51.11, 52.13

51.19   Other diagnostic procedures on biliary tract

> *Excludes:*   *biliary tract x-ray (87.51-87.59)*
> *microscopic examination of specimen from biliary tract (91.01-91.09)*

51.2   Cholecystectomy

51.21   Other partial cholecystectomy
Revision of prior cholecystectomy

> *Excludes:*   *that by laparoscope (51.24)*

51.22   Cholecystectomy

> *Excludes:*   *laparoscopic cholecystectomy (51.23)*

51.23   Laparoscopic cholecystectomy
That by laser

51.24   Laparoscopic partial cholecystectomy

51.3   Anastomosis of gallbladder or bile duct

> *Excludes:*   *resection with end-to-end anastomosis (51.61-51.69)*

51.31   Anastomosis of gallbladder to hepatic ducts

51.32   Anastomosis of gallbladder to intestine

51.33   Anastomosis of gallbladder to pancreas

51.34   Anastomosis of gallbladder to stomach

51.35   Other gallbladder anastomosis
Gallbladder anastomosis NOS

51.36   Choledochoenterostomy

51.37   Anastomosis of hepatic duct to gastrointestinal tract

51.39   Other bile duct anastomosis
Anastomosis of bile duct NOS
Anastomosis of unspecified bile duct to:
intestine
liver
pancreas
stomach

51.4   Incision of bile duct for relief of obstruction

51.41   Common duct exploration for removal of calculus

> *Excludes:*   *percutaneous extraction (51.96)*

51.42   Common duct exploration for relief of other obstruction

51.43   Insertion of choledochohepatic tube for decompression
Hepatocholedochostomy

● Code new
to this edition   ▲ Revision of
existing code   ④ ⑤ Fourth or fifth
digit required

51.49 **Incision of other bile ducts for relief of obstruction**

51.5 **Other incision of bile duct**

> *Excludes:* *that for relief of obstruction (51.41-51.49)*

51.51 **Exploration of common duct**
Incision of common bile duct

51.59 **Incision of other bile duct**

51.6 **Local excision or destruction of lesion or tissue of biliary ducts and sphincter of Oddi**
Code also anastomosis other than end-to-end (51.31, 51.36-51.39)

> *Excludes:* *biopsy of bile duct (51.12-51.13)*

51.61 **Excision of cystic duct remnant**

51.62 **Excision of ampulla of Vater (with reimplantation of common duct)**

51.63 **Other excision of common duct**
Choledochectomy

> *Excludes:* *fistulectomy (51.72)*

51.64 **Endoscopic excision or destruction of lesion of biliary ducts or sphincter of Oddi**
Excision or destruction of lesion of biliary duct by procedures classifiable to
51.10-51.11, 52.13

51.69 **Excision of other bile duct**
Excision of lesion of bile duct NOS

> *Excludes:* *fistulectomy (51.79)*

51.7 **Repair of bile ducts**

51.71 **Simple suture of common bile duct**

51.72 **Choledochoplasty**
Repair of fistula of common bile duct

51.79 **Repair of other bile ducts**
Closure of artificial opening of bile duct NOS
Suture of bile duct NOS

> *Excludes:* *operative removal of prosthetic device (51.95)*

51.8 **Other operations on biliary ducts and sphincter of Oddi**

51.81 **Dilation of sphincter of Oddi**
Dilation of ampulla of Vater

> *Excludes:* *that by endoscopic approach (51.84)*

51.82 **Pancreatic sphincterotomy**
Incision of pancreatic sphincter
Transduodenal ampullary sphincterotomy

> *Excludes:* *that by endoscopic approach (51.85)*

51.83 **Pancreatic sphincteroplasty**

51.84 **Endoscopic dilation of ampulla and biliary duct**
Dilation of ampulla and biliary duct by procedures classifiable to 51.10-51.11, 52.13

51.85 **Endoscopic sphincterotomy and papillotomy**
Sphincterotomy and papillotomy by procedures classifiable to 51.10-51.11, 52.13

51.86 **Endoscopic insertion of nasobiliary drainage tube**
Insertion of nasobiliary tube by procedures classifiable to 51.10-51.11, 52.13

51.87 **Endoscopic insertion of stent (tube) into bile duct**
Endoprosthesis of bile duct
Insertion of stent into bile duct by procedures classifiable to 51.10-51.11, 52.13

> *Excludes:* *nasobiliary drainage tube (51.86)*
> *replacement of stent (tube) (97.05)*

51.88 **Endoscopic removal of stone(s) from biliary tract**
Laparoscopic removal of stone(s) from biliary tract
Removal of biliary tract stone(s) by procedures classifiable to 51.10-51.11, 52.13

> *Excludes:* *percutaneous extraction of common duct stones (51.96)*

51.89 **Other operations on sphincter of Oddi**

51.9 **Other operations on biliary tract**

51.91 **Repair of laceration of gallbladder**

51.92 **Closure of cholecystostomy**

Valid O.R. procedure	Non-O.R. procedure	Nonspecific O.R. procedure	Noncovered O.R. procedure

51.93 Closure of other biliary fistula
Cholecystogastroenteric fistulectomy

51.94 Revision of anastomosis of biliary tract

51.95 Removal of prosthetic device from bile duct

Excludes: *nonoperative removal (97.55)*

51.96 Percutaneous extraction of common duct stones

51.98 Other percutaneous procedures on biliary tract
Percutaneous biliary endoscopy via existing T-tube or other tract for:
    dilation of biliary duct stricture
    exploration (postoperative)
    removal of stone(s) except common duct stone
Percutaneous transhepatic biliary drainage

Excludes: *percutaneous aspiration of gallbladder (51.01)*
percutaneous biopsy and/or collection of specimen by brushing or
    washing (51.12)
percutaneous removal of common duct stone(s) (51.96)

51.99 Other
Insertion or replacement of biliary tract prosthesis

Excludes: *biopsy of gallbladder (51.12-51.13)*
irrigation of cholecystostomy and other biliary tube (96.41)
lysis of peritoneal adhesions (54.5)
nonoperative removal of:
    cholecystostomy tube (97.54)
    tube from biliary tract or liver (97.55)

52 Operations on pancreas
Includes: operations on pancreatic duct

52.0 Pancreatotomy

52.01 Drainage of pancreatic cyst by catheter

52.09 Other pancreatotomy
Pancreatolithotomy

Excludes: *drainage by anastomosis (52.4, 52.96)*
incision of pancreatic sphincter (51.82)
marsupialization of cyst (52.3)

52.1 Diagnostic procedures on pancreas

52.11 Closed [aspiration] [needle] [percutaneous] biopsy of pancreas

52.12 Open biopsy of pancreas

52.13 Endoscopic retrograde pancreatography [EPR]

Excludes: *endoscopic retrograde:*
    cholangiography [ERC] (51.11)
    cholangiopancreatography [ERCP] (51.10)
    that for procedures classifiable to 51.14-51.15, 51.64, 51.84-51.88,
      52.14, 52.21, 52.92-52.94, 52.97-52.98

52.14 Closed [endoscopic] biopsy of pancreatic duct
Closed biopsy of pancreatic duct by procedures classifiable to 51.10-51.11, 52.13

52.19 Other diagnostic procedure on pancreas

Excludes: *contrast pancreatogram (87.66)*
endoscopic retrograde pancreatography [ERP] (52.13))
microscopic examination of specimen from pancreas (91.01-91.09)

52.2 Local excision or destruction of pancreas and pancreatic duct

Excludes: *biopsy of pancreas (52.11-52.12, 52.14)*
pancreatic fistulectomy (52.95)

52.21 Endoscopic excision or destruction of lesion or tissue of pancreatic duct
Excision or destruction of lesion or tissue of pancreatic duct by procedures
    classifiable to 51.10-51.11, 52.13

52.22 Other excision or destruction of lesion or tissue of pancreas or pancreatic duct

52.3 Marsupialization of pancreatic cyst

Excludes: *drainage of cyst by catheter (52.01)*

● Code new
to this edition
    ▲ Revision of
existing code
    ④ ⑤ Fourth or fifth
digit required

52.4 **Internal drainage of pancreatic cyst**
Pancreaticocystoduodenostomy
Pancreaticocystogastrostomy
Pancreaticocystojejunostomy

52.5 **Partial pancreatectomy**

> *Excludes:* pancreatic fistulectomy (52.95)

52.51 **Proximal pancreatectomy**
Excision of head of pancreas (with part of body)
Proximal pancreatectomy with synchronous duodenectomy

52.52 **Distal pancreatectomy**
Excision of tail of pancreas (with part of body)

52.53 **Radical subtotal pancreatectomy**

52.59 **Other partial pancreatectomy**

52.6 **Total pancreatectomy**
Pancreatectomy with synchronous duodenectomy

52.7 **Radical pancreaticoduodenectomy**
One-stage pancreaticoduodenal resection with choledochojejunal anastomosis,
pancreaticojejunal anastomosis, and gastrojejunostomy
Two-stage pancreaticoduodenal resection (first stage) (second stage)
Radical resection of the pancreas
Whipple procedure

> *Excludes:* radical subtotal pancreatectomy (52.53)

52.8 **Transplant of pancreas**

52.80 **Pancreatic transplant, not otherwise specified**

52.81 **Reimplantation of pancreatic tissue**

52.82 **Homotransplant of pancreas**

52.83 **Heterotransplant of pancreas**

52.84 **Autotransplantation of cells of Islets of Langerhans**
Homotransplantation of islet cells of pancreas

52.85 **Allotransplantation of cells of Islets of Langerhans**
Heterotransplantation of islet cells of pancreas

52.86 **Transplantation of cells of Islets of Langerhans, not otherwise specified**

52.9 **Other operations on pancreas**

52.92 **Cannulation of pancreatic duct**

> *Excludes:* that by endoscopic approach (52.93)

52.93 **Endoscopic insertion of stent (tube) into pancreatic duct**
Insertion of cannula or stent into pancreatic duct by procedures classifiable to
51.10-51.11, 52.13

> *Excludes:* endoscopic insertion of nasopancreatic drainage tube (52.97)
> replacement of stent (tube) (97.05)

52.94 **Endoscopic removal of stone(s) from pancreatic duct**
Removal of stone(s) from pancreatic duct by procedures classifiable to 51.10-51.11,
52.13

52.95 **Other repair of pancreas**
Fistulectomy
Simple suture } of pancreas

52.96 **Anastomosis of pancreas**
Anastomosis of pancreas (duct) to:
  intestine
  jejunum
  stomach

> *Excludes:* anastomosis to:
> bile duct (51.39)
> gallbladder (51.33)

52.97 **Endoscopic insertion of nasopancreatic drainage tube**
Insertion of nasopancreatic drainage tube by procedures classifiable to 51.10-51.11,
52.13

> *Excludes:* drainage of pancreatic cyst by catheter (52.01)
> replacement of stent (tube) (97.05)

52.98 **Endoscopic dilation of pancreatic duct**
Dilation of Wirsung's duct by procedures classifiable to 51.10-51.11,52.13

52.99 **Other**
Dilation of pancreatic
[Wirsung's] duct
Repair of pancreatic — by open approach
[Wirsung's] duct

Excludes: *irrigation of pancreatic tube (96.42)*
removal of pancreatic tube (97.56)

53 **Repair of hernia**
Includes: hernioplasty
herniorrhaphy
herniotomy

Excludes: *manual reduction of hernia (96.27)*

53.0 **Unilateral repair of inguinal hernia**

53.00 **Unilateral repair of inguinal hernia, not otherwise specified**
Inguinal herniorrhaphy NOS

53.01 **Repair of direct inguinal hernia**

53.02 **Repair of indirect inguinal hernia**

53.03 **Repair of direct inguinal hernia with graft or prosthesis**

53.04 **Repair of indirect inguinal hernia with graft or prosthesis**

53.05 **Repair of inguinal hernia with graft or prosthesis, not otherwise specified**

53.1 **Bilateral repair of inguinal hernia**

53.10 **Bilateral repair of inguinal hernia, not otherwise specified**

53.11 **Bilateral repair of direct inguinal hernia**

53.12 **Bilateral repair of indirect inguinal hernia**

53.13 **Bilateral repair of inguinal hernia, one direct and one indirect**

53.14 **Bilateral repair of direct inguinal hernia with graft or prosthesis**

53.15 **Bilateral repair of indirect inguinal hernia with graft or prosthesis**

53.16 **Bilateral repair of inguinal hernia, one direct and one indirect, with graft or prosthesis**

53.17 **Bilateral inguinal hernia repair with graft or prosthesis, not otherwise specified**

53.2 **Unilateral repair of femoral hernia**

53.21 **Unilateral repair of femoral hernia with graft or prosthesis**

53.29 **Other unilateral femoral herniorrhaphy**

53.3 **Bilateral repair of femoral hernia**

53.31 **Bilateral repair of femoral hernia with graft or prosthesis**

53.39 **Other bilateral femoral herniorrhaphy**

53.4 **Repair of umbilical hernia**

Excludes: *repair of gastroschisis (54.71)*

53.41 **Repair of umbilical hernia with prosthesis**

53.49 **Other umbilical herniorrhaphy**

53.5 **Repair of other hernia of anterior abdominal wall (without graft or prosthesis)**

53.51 **Incisional hernia repair**

53.59 **Repair of other hernia of anterior abdominal wall**
Repair of hernia:
epigastric
hypogastric
spigelian
ventral

53.6 **Repair of other hernia of anterior abdominal wall with graft or prosthesis**

53.61 **Incisional hernia repair with prosthesis**

53.69 **Repair of other hernia of anterior abdominal wall with prosthesis**

53.7 **Repair of diaphragmatic hernia, abdominal approach**

53.8 **Repair of diaphragmatic hernia, thoracic approach**

● Code new
to this edition

▲ Revision of
existing code

④ ⑤ Fourth or fifth
digit required

53.80 **Repair of diaphragmatic hernia with thoracic approach, not otherwise specified**
Thoracoabdominal repair of diaphragmatic hernia

53.81 **Plication of the diaphragm**

53.82 **Repair of parasternal hernia**

53.9 **Other hernia repair**
Repair of hernia:
   ischiatic   omental
   ischiorectal   retroperitoneal
   lumbar   sciatic
   obturator

> *Excludes:* *relief of strangulated hernia with exteriorization of intestine (46.01, 46.03)*
> *repair of pericolostomy hernia (46.42)*
> *repair of vaginal enterocele (70.92)*

54 **Other operations on abdominal region**
Includes: operations on:
      epigastric region   male pelvic cavity
      flank   mesentery
      groin region   omentum
      hypochondrium   peritoneum
      inguinal region   retroperitoneal tissue space
      loin region

> *Excludes:* *female pelvic cavity (69.01- 70.92)*
> *hernia repair (53.00-53.9)*
> *obliteration of cul-de-sac (70.92)*
> *retroperitoneal tissue dissection (59.00-59.09)*
> *skin and subcutaneous tissue of abdominal wall (86.01-86.99)*

54.0 **Incision of abdominal wall**
Drainage of:
   abdominal wall
   extraperitoneal abscess
   retroperitoneal abscess

> *Excludes:* *incision of peritoneum (54.95)*
> *laparotomy (54.11-54.19)*

54.1 **Laparotomy**

54.11 **Exploratory laparotomy**

> *Excludes:* *exploration incidental to intra-abdominal surgery—omit code*

54.12 **Reopening of recent laparotomy site**
Reopening of recent laparotomy site for:
   control of hemorrhage
   exploration
   incision of hematoma

54.19 **Other laparotomy**
Drainage of intraperitoneal abscess or hematoma

> *Excludes:* *culdocentesis (70.0)*
> *drainage of appendiceal abscess (47.2)*
> *exploration incidental to intra-abdominal surgery—omit code*
> *Ladd operation (54.95)*
> *percutaneous drainage of abdomen (54.91)*
> *removal of foreign body (54.92)*

54.2 **Diagnostic procedures of abdominal region**

54.21 **Laparoscopy**
Peritoneoscopy

> *Excludes:* *laparoscopic cholecystectomy (51.23)*
> *that incidental to destruction of fallopian tubes (66.21-66.29)*

54.22 **Biopsy or abdominal wall or umbilicus**

54.23 **Biopsy of peritoneum**
Biopsy of:
   mesentery
   omentum
   peritoneal implant

> *Excludes:* *closed biopsy of:*
> *omentum (54.24)*
> *peritoneum (54.24)*

Valid O.R. procedure	Non-O.R. procedure	Nonspecific O.R. procedure	Noncovered O.R. procedure

54.24 Closed [percutaneous] [needle] biopsy of intra-abdominal mass
Closed biopsy of:
 omentum
 peritoneal implant
 peritoneum

> *Excludes:* *that of:*
> *fallopian tube (66.11)*
> *ovary (65.11)*
> *uterine ligaments (68.15)*
> *uterus (68.16)*

54.25 Peritoneal lavage
Diagnostic peritoneal lavage

> *Excludes:* *peritoneal dialysis (54.98)*

54.29 Other diagnostic procedures on abdominal region

> *Excludes:* *abdominal lymphangiogram (88.04)*
> *abdominal x-ray NEC (88.19)*
> *angiocardiography of venae cavae (88.51)*
> *C.A.T. scan of abdomen (88.01)*
> *contrast x-ray of abdominal cavity (88.11-88.15)*
> *intra-abdominal arteriography NEC (88.47)*
> *microscopic examination of peritoneal and retroperitoneal specimen*
> *(91.11-91.19)*
> *phlebography of:*
> *intra-abdominal vessels NEC (88.65)*
> *portal venous system (88.64)*
> *sinogram of abdominal wall (88.03)*
> *soft tissue x-ray of abdominal wall NEC (88.09)*
> *tomography of abdomen NEC(88.02)*
> *ultrasonography of abdomen and retroperitoneum (88.76)*

54.3 Excision or destruction of lesion or tissue of abdominal wall or umbilicus
Debridement of abdominal wall
Omphalectomy

> *Excludes:* *biopsy of abdominal wall or umbilicus (54.22)*
> *size reduction operation (86.83)*
> *that of skin of abdominal wall (86.22, 86.26, 86.3)*

54.4 Excision or destruction of peritoneal tissue
Excision of:
 appendices epiploicae
 falciform ligament
 gastrocolic ligament
 lesion of:
  mesentery
  omentum
  peritoneum
 presacral lesion NOS
 retroperitoneal lesion NOS

> *Excludes:* *biopsy of peritoneum (54.23)*
> *endometrectomy of cul-de-sac (70.32)*

54.5 Lysis of peritoneal adhesions
Freeing of adhesions of:
 biliary tract
 intestines
 liver
 pelvic peritoneum
 peritoneum
 spleen
 uterus

> *Excludes:* *lysis of adhesions of:*
> *bladder (59.11)*
> *fallopian tube and ovary (65.81, 65.89)*
> *kidney (59.02)*
> *ureter (59.01-59.02)*

54.51 Laparoscopic lysis of peritoneal adhesions

54.59 Other lysis of peritoneal adhesions

● Code new
to this edition

▲ Revision of
existing code

④ ⑤ Fourth or fifth
digit required

54.6 Suture of abdominal wall and peritoneum

54.61 **Reclosure of postoperative disruption of abdominal wall**

54.62 **Delayed closure of granulating abdomen wound**
Tertiary subcutaneous wound closure

54.63 **Other suture of abdominal wall**
Suture of laceration of abdominal wall

Excludes: *closure of operative wound—omit code*

54.64 **Suture of peritoneum**
Secondary suture of peritoneum

Excludes: *closure of operative wound—omit code*

54.7 Other repair of abdominal wall and peritoneum

54.71 **Repair of gastroschisis**

54.72 **Other repair of abdominal wall**

54.73 **Other repair of peritoneum**
Suture of gastrocolic ligament

54.74 **Other repair of omentum**
Epiplorrhaphy
Graft of omentum
Omentopexy
Reduction of torsion of omentum

Excludes: *cardio-omentopexy (36.39)*

54.75 **Other repair of mesentery**
Mesenteric plication
Mesenteropexy

54.9 Other operations of abdominal region

Excludes: *removal of ectopic pregnancy (69.11, 74.3)*

54.91 **Percutaneous abdominal drainage**
Paracentesis

Excludes: *creation of cutaneoperitoneal fistula (54.93)*

54.92 **Removal of foreign body from peritoneal cavity**

54.93 **Creation of cutaneoperitoneal fistula**

54.94 **Creation of peritoneovascular shunt**
Peritoneovenous shunt

54.95 **Incision of peritoneum**
Ladd operation
Revision of distal catheter of ventricular shunt
Revision of ventriculoperitoneal shunt at peritoneal site

Excludes: *that incidental to laparotomy (54.11-54.19)*

54.96 **Injection of air into peritoneal cavity**
Pneumoperitoneum

Excludes: *that for:*
collapse of lung (33.33)
radiography (88.12-88.13, 88.15)

54.97 **Injection of locally-acting therapeutic substance into peritoneal cavity**

Excludes: *peritoneal dialysis (54.98)*

54.98 **Peritoneal dialysis**

Excludes: *peritoneal lavage (diagnostic) (54.25)*

54.99 **Other**

Excludes: *removal of:*
abdominal wall sutures (97.83)
peritoneal drainage device (97.82)
retroperitoneal drainage device (97.81)

	Valid O.R. procedure		Non-O.R. procedure		Nonspecific O.R. procedure		Noncovered O.R. procedure

10. OPERATIONS ON THE URINARY SYSTEM (55-59)

55 Operations on kidney

Includes: operations on renal pelvis

Excludes: *perirenal tissue (59.00-59.09, 59.21-59.29, 59.91-59.92)*

55.0 Nephrotomy and nephrostomy

Excludes: *drainage by:*
anastomosis (55.86)
aspiration (55.92)
incision of kidney pelvis (55.11-55.12)

55.01 Nephrotomy

Evacuation of renal cyst
Exploration of kidney
Nephrolithotomy

55.02 Nephrostomy

55.03 Percutaneous nephrostomy without fragmentation

Nephrostolithotomy, percutaneous (nephroscopic)
Percutaneous removal of kidney stone(s) by:
basket extraction
forceps extraction (nephroscopic)
Pyelostolithotomy, percutaneous (nephroscopic)
With placement of catheter down ureter

Excludes: *percutaneous removal by fragmentation (55.04)*
repeat nephroscopic removal during current episode (55.92)

55.04 Percutaneous nephrostomy with fragmentation

Percutaneous nephrostomy with disruption of kidney stone by ultrasonic energy and
extraction (suction) through endoscope
With placement of catheter down ureter
With fluoroscopic guidance

Excludes: *repeat fragmentation during current episode (59.95)*

55.1 Pyelotomy and pyelostomy

Excludes: *drainage by anastomosis (55.86)*
percutaneous pyelostolithotomy (55.03)
removal of calculus without incision (56.0)

55.11 Pyelotomy

Exploration of renal pelvis
Pyelolithotomy

55.12 Pyelostomy

Insertion of drainage tube into renal pelvis

55.2 Diagnostic procedures on kidney

55.21 Nephroscopy

55.22 Pyeloscopy

55.23 Closed [percutaneous] [needle] biopsy of kidney

Endoscopic biopsy via existing nephrostomy, nephrotomy, pyelostomy, or
pyelotomy

55.24 Open biopsy of kidney

55.29 Other diagnostic procedures on kidney

Excludes: *microscopic examination of specimen from kidney (91.21-91.29)*
pyelogram:
intravenous (87.73)
percutaneous (87.75)
retrograde (87.74)
radioisotope scan (92.03)
renal arteriography (88.45)
tomography:
C.A.T. scan (87.71)
other (87.72)

55.3 Local excision or destruction of lesion or tissue of kidney

55.31 Marsupialization of kidney lesion

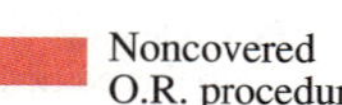

55.39 **Other local destruction or excision of renal lesion or tissue**
Obliteration of calyceal diverticulum

> *Excludes:* *biopsy of kidney (55.23-55.24)*
> *partial nephrectomy (55.4)*
> *percutaneous aspiration of kidney (55.92)*
> *wedge resection of kidney (55.4)*

55.4 **Partial nephrectomy**
Calycectomy
Wedge resection of kidney

Code also any synchronous resection of ureter (56.40-56.42)

55.5 **Complete nephrectomy**

Code also any synchronous excision of:
bladder segment (57.6)
lymph nodes (40.3, 40.52-40.59)

55.51 **Nephroureterectomy**
Nephroureterectomy with bladder cuff
Total nephrectomy (unilateral)

> *Excludes:* *removal of transplanted kidney (55.53)*

55.52 **Nephrectomy of remaining kidney**
Removal of solitary kidney

> *Excludes:* *removal of transplanted kidney (55.53)*

55.53 **Removal of transplanted or rejected kidney**

55.54 **Bilateral nephrectomy**

> *Excludes:* *complete nephrectomy NOS (55.51)*

55.6 **Transplant of kidney**

55.61 **Renal autotransplantation**

55.69 **Other kidney transplantation**

55.7 **Nephropexy**
Fixation or suspension of movable [floating] kidney

55.8 **Other repair of kidney**

55.81 **Suture of laceration of kidney**

55.82 **Closure of nephrostomy and pyelostomy**

55.83 **Closure of other fistula of kidney**

55.84 **Reduction of torsion of renal pedicle**

55.85 **Symphysiotomy for horseshoe kidney**

55.86 **Anastomosis of kidney**
Nephropyeloureterostomy
Pyeloureterovesical anastomosis
Ureterocalyceal anastomosis

> *Excludes:* *nephrocystanastomosis NOS (56.73)*

55.87 **Correction of ureteropelvic junction**

55.89 **Other**

55.9 **Other operations on kidney**

> *Excludes:* *lysis of perirenal adhesions (59.02)*

55.91 **Decapsulation of kidney**
Capsulectomy ⎫
Decortication ⎭ of kidney

55.92 **Percutaneous aspiration of kidney (pelvis)**
Aspiration of renal cyst
Renipuncture

> *Excludes:* *percutaneous biopsy of kidney (55.23)*

55.93 **Replacement of nephrostomy tube**

55.94 **Replacement of pyelostomy tube**

55.95 **Local perfusion of kidney**

55.96 **Other Injection of therapeutic substance into kidney**
Injection into renal cyst

 ● Code new to this edition   ▲ Revision of existing code   ④ ⑤ Fourth or fifth digit required

55.97 Implantation or replacement of mechanical kidney

55.98 Removal of mechanical kidney

55.99 Other

> *Excludes:* *removal of pyelostomy or nephrostomy tube (97.61)*

56 Operations on ureter

56.0 Transurethral removal of obstruction from ureter and renal pelvis

Removal of:
  blood clot
  calculus   } from ureter or renal pelvis without incision
  foreign body

> *Excludes:* *manipulation without removal of obstruction (59.8)*
> *that by incision (55.11, 56.2)*
> *transurethral insertion of ureteral stent for passage of calculus (59.8)*

56.1 Ureteral meatotomy

56.2 Ureterotomy

Incision of ureter for:
  drainage
  exploration
  removal of calculus

> *Excludes:* *cutting of ureterovesical orifice (56.1)*
> *removal of calculus without incision (56.0)*
> *transurethral insertion of ureteral stent for passage of calculus (59.8)*
> *urinary diversion (56.51-56.79)*

56.3 Diagnostic procedures on ureter

56.31 Ureteroscopy

56.32 Closed percutaneous biopsy of ureter

> *Excludes:* *endoscopic biopsy of ureter (56.33)*

56.33 Closed endoscopic biopsy of ureter

Cystourethroscopy with ureteral biopsy
Transurethral biopsy of ureter
Ureteral endoscopy with biopsy through ureterotomy
Ureteroscopy with biopsy

> *Excludes:* *percutaneous biopsy of ureter (56.32)*

56.34 Open biopsy of ureter

56.35 Endoscopy (cystoscopy) (looposcopy) of ileal conduit

56.39 Other diagnostic procedures on ureter

> *Excludes:* *microscopic examination of specimen from ureter (91.21-91.29)*

56.4 Ureterectomy

Code also anastomosis other than end-to-end (56.51-56.79)

> *Excludes:* *fistulectomy (56.84)*
> *nephroureterectomy (55.51-55.54)*

56.40 Ureterectomy, not otherwise specified

56.41 Partial ureterectomy

Excision of lesion of ureter
Shortening of ureter with reimplantation

> *Excludes:* *biopsy of ureter (56.32-56.34)*

56.42 Total ureterectomy

56.5 Cutaneous uretero-ileostomy

56.51 Formation of cutaneous uretero-ileostomy

Construction of ileal conduit
External ureteral ileostomy
Formation of open ileal bladder
Ileal loop operation
Ileoureterostomy (Bricker's) (ileal bladder)
Transplantation of ureter into ileum with external diversion

> *Excludes:* *closed ileal bladder (57.87)*
> *replacement of ureteral defect by ileal segment (56.89)*

56.52 Revision of cutaneous uretero-ileostomy

56.6 Other external urinary diversion

56.61 Formation of other cutaneous ureterostomy
Anastomosis of ureter to skin
Ureterostomy NOS

56.62 Revision of other cutaneous ureterostomy
Revision of ureterostomy stoma
| Excludes: | *nonoperative removal of ureterostomy tube (97.62)* |

56.7 Other anastomosis or bypass of ureter
| Excludes: | *ureteropyelostomy (55.86)* |

56.71 Urinary diversion to intestine
Anastomosis of ureter to intestine
Internal urinary diversion NOS
Code also any synchronous colostomy (46.10-46.13)
| Excludes: | *external ureteral ileostomy (56.51)* |

56.72 Revision of ureterointestinal anastomosis
| Excludes: | *revision of external ureteral ileostomy (56.52)* |

56.73 Nephrocystanastomosis, not otherwise specified

56.74 Ureteroneocystostomy
Replacement of ureter with bladder flap
Ureterovesical anastomosis

56.75 Transureteroureterostomy
| Excludes: | *ureteroureterostomy associated with partial resection (56.41)* |

56.79 Other

56.8 Repair of ureter

56.81 Lysis of intraluminal adhesions of ureter
| Excludes: | *lysis of periureteral adhesions (59.01-59.02)* |
| | *ureterolysis (59.01-59.02)* |

56.82 Suture of laceration of ureter

56.83 Closure of ureterostomy

56.84 Closure of other fistula of ureter

56.85 Ureteropexy

56.86 Removal of ligature from ureter

56.89 Other repair of ureter
Graft of ureter
Replacement of ureter with ileal segment implanted into bladder
Ureteroplication

56.9 Other operations on ureter

56.91 Dilation of ureteral meatus

56.92 Implantation of electronic ureteral stimulator

56.93 Replacement of electronic ureteral stimulator

56.94 Removal of electronic ureteral stimulator
| Excludes: | *that with synchronous replacement (56.93)* |

56.95 Ligation of ureter

56.99 Other
| Excludes: | *removal of ureterostomy tube and ureteral catheter (97.62)* |
| | *ureteral catheterization (59.8)* |

57 Operations on urinary bladder
| Excludes: | *perivesical tissue (59.11-59.29, 59.91-59.92)* |
| | *ureterovesical orifice (56.0-56.99)* |

   ● Code new to this edition   ▲ Revision of existing code   ④ ⑤ Fourth or fifth digit required

57.0 **Transurethral clearance of bladder**
Drainage of bladder without incision
Removal of:
    blood clots
    calculus   } from bladder without incision
    foreign body

    | *Excludes:* | *that by incision (57.19)* |

57.1 **Cystotomy and cystostomy**

    | *Excludes:* | *cystotomy and cystostomy as operative approach—omit code* |

    57.11 **Percutaneous aspiration of bladder**

    57.12 **Lysis of intraluminal adhesion with incision into bladder**

        | *Excludes:* | *transurethral lysis of intraluminal adhesions (57.41)* |

    57.17 **Percutaneous cystostomy**
        Closed cystostomy
        Percutaneous suprapubic cystostomy

        | *Excludes:* | *removal of cystostomy tube (97.63)* |
        | | *replacement of cystostomy tube (59.94)* |

    57.18 **Other suprapubic cystostomy**

        | *Excludes* | *percutaneous cystostomy (57.17)* |
        | | *removal of cystostomy tube (97.63)* |
        | | *replacement of cystostomy tube (59.94)* |

    57.19 **Other cystotomy**
        Cystolithotomy

        | *Excludes:* | *percutaneous cystostomy (57.17)* |
        | | *suprapubic cystostomy (57.18)* |

57.2 **Vesicostomy**

    | *Excludes:* | *percutaneous cystostomy (57.17)* |
    | | *suprapubic cystostomy (57.18)* |

    57.21 **Vesicostomy**
        Creation of permanent opening from bladder to skin using a bladder flap

    57.22 **Revision or closure of vesicostomy**

        | *Excludes:* | *closure of cystostomy (57.82)* |

57.3 **Diagnostic procedures on bladder**

    57.31 **Cystoscopy through artificial stoma**

    57.32 **Other cystoscopy**
        Transurethral cystoscopy

        | *Excludes:* | *cystourethroscopy with ureteral biopsy (56.33)* |
        | | *retrograde pyelogram (87.74)* |
        | | *that for control of hemorrhage (postoperative):* |
        | | *bladder (57.93)* |
        | | *prostate (60.94)* |

    57.33 **Closed [transurethral] biopsy of bladder**

    57.34 **Open biopsy of bladder**

    57.39 **Other diagnostic procedures on bladder**

        | *Excludes:* | *cystogram NEC (87.77)* |
        | | *microscopic examination of specimen from bladder (91.31-91.39)* |
        | | *retrograde cystourethrogram (87.76)* |
        | | *therapeutic distention of bladder (96.25)* |

57.4 **Transurethral excision or destruction of bladder tissue**

    57.41 **Transurethral lysis of intraluminal adhesions**

    57.49 **Other transurethral excision or destruction of lesion or tissue of bladder**
        Endoscopic resection of bladder lesion

        | *Excludes:* | *transurethral biopsy of bladder (57.33)* |
        | | *transurethral fistulectomy (57.83-57.84)* |

57.5 **Other excision or destruction of bladder tissue**

    | *Excludes:* | *that with transurethral approach (57.41-57.49)* |

| Valid O.R. procedure | Non-O.R. procedure | Nonspecific O.R. procedure | Noncovered O.R. procedure |

57.51 **Excision of urachus**
Excision of urachal sinus of bladder

> *Excludes:* *excision of urachal cyst of abdominal wall (54.3)*

57.59 **Open excision or destruction of other lesion or tissue of bladder**
Endometrectomy of bladder
Suprapubic excision of bladder lesion

> *Excludes:* *biopsy of bladder (57.33-57.34)*
> *fistulectomy of bladder (57.83-57.84)*

57.6 **Partial cystectomy**
Excision of bladder dome
Trigonectomy
Wedge resection of bladder

57.7 **Total cystectomy**
Includes: total cystectomy with urethrectomy

57.71 **Radical cystectomy**
Pelvic exenteration in male
Removal of bladder, prostate, seminal vesicles, and fat
Removal of bladder, urethra, and fat in a female

Code also any:
lymph node dissection (40.3, 40.5)
urinary diversion (56.51-56.79)

> *Excludes:* *that as part of pelvic exenteration in female (68.8)*

57.79 **Other total cystectomy**

57.8 **Other repair of urinary bladder**

> *Excludes:* *repair of:*
> *current obstetric laceration (75.61)*
> *cystocele (70.50-70.51)*
> *that for stress incontinence (59.3-59.79)*

57.81 **Suture of laceration of bladder**

57.82 **Closure of cystostomy**

57.83 **Repair of fistula involving bladder and intestine**
Rectovesicovaginal ⎫
Vesicosigmoidovaginal ⎬ fistulectomy

57.84 **Repair of other fistula of bladder**
Cervicovesical ⎫
Urethroperineovesical ⎪
Uterovesical ⎬ fistulectomy
Vaginovesical ⎭

> *Excludes:* *vesicoureterovaginal fistulectomy (56.84)*

57.85 **Cystourethroplasty and plastic repair of bladder neck**
Plication of sphincter of urinary bladder
V-Y plasty of bladder neck

57.86 **Repair of bladder exstrophy**

57.87 **Reconstruction of urinary bladder**
Anastomosis of bladder with isolated segment of ileum
Augmentation of bladder
Replacement of bladder with ileum or sigmoid [closed ileal bladder]

Code also resection of intestine (45.50-45.52)

57.88 **Other anastomosis of bladder**
Anastomosis of bladder to intestine NOS
Cystocolic anastomosis

> *Excludes:* *formation of closed ileal bladder (5787)*

57.89 **Other repair of bladder**
Bladder suspension, not elsewhere classified
Cystopexy NOS
Repair of old obstetric laceration of bladder

> *Excludes:* *repair of current obstetric laceration (75.61)*

57.9 **Other operations on bladder**

57.91 **Sphincterotomy of bladder**
Division of bladder neck

● Code new
to this edition

▲ Revision of
existing code

④ ⑤ Fourth or fifth
digit required

57.92 Dilation of bladder neck

57.93 Control of (postoperative) hemorrhage of bladder

57.94 Insertion of indwelling urinary catheter

57.95 Replacement of indwelling urinary catheter

57.96 Implantation of electronic bladder stimulator

57.97 Replacement of electronic bladder stimulator

57.98 Removal of electronic bladder stimulator

> *Excludes:*   *that with synchronous replacement (57.97)*

57.99 Other

> *Excludes:*   *irrigation of:*
> *cystostomy (96.47)*
> *other indwelling urinary catheter (96.48)*
> *lysis of external adhesions (59.11)*
> *removal of:*
> *cystostomy tube (97.63)*
> *other urinary drainage device (97.64)*
> *therapeutic distention of bladder (96.25)*

58 **Operations on urethra**
Includes: operations on:
bulbourethral gland [Cowper's gland]
periurethral tissue

58.0 **Urethrotomy**
Excision of urethral septum
Formation of urethrovaginal fistula
Perineal urethrostomy
Removal of calculus from urethra by incision

> *Excludes:*   *drainage of bulbourethral gland or periurethral tissue (58.91)*
> *internal urethral meatotomy (58.5)*
> *removal of urethral calculus without incision (58.6)*

58.1 **Urethral meatotomy**

> *Excludes:*   *internal urethral meatotomy (58.5)*

58.2 Diagnostic procedures on urethra

58.21 Perineal urethroscopy

58.22 Other urethroscopy

58.23 Biopsy of urethra

58.24 Biopsy of periurethral tissue

58.29 Other diagnostic procedures on urethra and periurethral tissue

> *Excludes:*   *microscopic examination of specimen from urethra (91.31-91.39)*
> *retrograde cystourethrogram (87.76)*
> *urethral pressure profile (89.25)*
> *urethral sphincter electromyogram (89.23)*

58.3 Excision or destruction of lesion or tissue of urethra

> *Excludes:*   *biopsy of urethra (58.23)*
> *excision of bulbourethral gland (58.92)*
> *fistulectomy (58.43)*
> *urethrectomy as part of:*
> *complete cystectomy (57.79)*
> *pelvic evisceration (68.8)*
> *radical cystectomy (57.71)*

58.31 Endoscopic excision or destruction of lesion or tissue of urethra
Fulguration of urethral lesion

58.39 Other local excision or destruction of lesion or tissue of urethra
Excision of:
congenital valve
lesion   } of urethra
stricture
Urethrectomy

> *Excludes:*   *that by endoscopic approach (58.31)*

Valid O.R. procedure   Non-O.R. procedure   Nonspecific O.R. procedure   Noncovered O.R. procedure

58.4   Repair of urethra

> | *Excludes:* | repair of current obstetric laceration (75.61)

58.41   Suture of laceration of urethra

58.42   Closure of urethrostomy

58.43   Closure of other fistula of urethra

> | *Excludes:* | repair of urethroperineovesical fistula (57.84)

58.44   Reanastomosis of urethra
Anastomosis of urethra

58.45   Repair of hypospadias or epispadias

58.46   Other reconstruction of urethra
Urethral construction

58.47   Urethral meatoplasty

58.49   Other repair of urethra
Benenenti rotation of bulbous urethra
Repair of old obstetric laceration of urethra
Urethral plication

> | *Excludes:* | repair of:
>   current obstetric laceration (75.61)
>   urethrocele (70.50-70.51)

58.5   Release of urethral stricture
Cutting of urethra] sphincter
Internal urethral meatotomy
Urethrolysis

58.6   Dilation of urethra
Dilation of urethrovesical junction
Passage of sounds through urethra
Removal of calculus from urethra without incision

> | *Excludes:* | urethral calibration (89.29)

58.9   Other operations on urethra and periurethral tissue

58.91   Incision of periurethral tissue
Drainage of bulbourethral gland

58.92   Excision of periurethral tissue

> | *Excludes:* | biopsy of periurethral tissue (58.24)
>   lysis of periurethral adhesions (59.11-59.12)

58.93   Implantation of artificial urinary sphincter [AUS]
Placement of inflatable:
    bladder sphincter
    urethral sphincter
Removal with replacement of sphincter device [AUS]
With pump and/or reservoir

58.99   Other
Removal of inflatable urinary sphincter without replacement
Repair of inflatable sphincter pump and/or reservoir
Surgical correction of hydraulic pressure of inflatable sphincter device

> | *Excludes:* | removal of:
>   intraluminal foreign body from urethra without incision (98.19)
>   urethral stent (97.65)

59   Other operations on urinary tract

59.0   Dissection of retroperitoneal tissue

59.00   Retroperitoneal dissection, not otherwise specified

59.02   Other lysis of perirenal or periureteral adhesions

> | *Excludes:* | that by laparoscope (59.03)

59.03   Laparoscopic lysis of perirenal or periureteral adhesions

59.09   Other incision of perirenal or periureteral tissue
Exploration of perinephric area
Incision of perirenal abscess

59.1   Incision of perivesical tissue

59.11   Other lysis of perivesical adhesions

    ● Code new   ▲ Revision of   ④ ⑤ Fourth or fifth
to this edition   existing code   digit required

59.12 Laparoscopic lysis of perivesical adhesions

59.19 Other incision of perivesical tissue
Exploration of perivesical tissue
Incision of hematoma of space of Retzius
Retropubic exploration

59.2 Diagnostic procedures on perirenal and perivesical tissue

59.21 Biopsy of perirenal or perivesical tissue

59.29 Other diagnostic procedures on perirenal tissue, perivesical tissue, and retroperitoneum

> *Excludes:* *microscopic examination of specimen from:*
> *perirenal tissue (91.21-91.29)*
> *perivesical tissue (91.31-91.39)*
> *retroperitoneum NEC (91.11-91.19)*
> *retroperitoneal x-ray (88.14-88.16)*

59.3 Plication of urethrovesical junction
Kelly-Kennedy operation on urethra
Kelly-Stoeckel urethral plication

59.4 Suprapubic sling operation
Goebel-Frangenheim-Stoeckel urethrovesical suspension
Millin-Read urethrovesical suspension
Oxford operation for urinary incontinence
Urethrocystopexy by suprapubic suspension

59.5 Retropubic urethral suspension
Burch procedure
Marshall-Marchetti-Krantz operation
Suture of periurethral tissue to symphysis pubis
Urethral suspension NOS

59.6 Paraurethral suspension
Pereyra paraurethral suspension
Periurethral suspension

59.7 Other repair of urinary stress incontinence

59.71 Levator muscle operation for urethrovesical suspension
Cystourethropexy with levator muscle sling
Gracilis muscle transplant for urethrovesical suspension
Pubococcygeal sling

59.72 Injection of implant into urethra and/or bladder neck
Collagen implant
Endoscopic injection of implant
Fat implant
Polytef implant

59.79 Other
Anterior urethropexy
Augmentation urethroplasty
Repair of stress incontinence NOS
Tudor "rabbit ear" urethropexy

59.8 Ureteral catheterization
Drainage of kidney by catheter
Insertion of ureteral stent
Ureterovesical orifice dilation

Code also any synchronous ureterotomy (56.2)

> *Excludes:* *that for:*
> *retrograde pyelogram (87.74)*
> *transurethral removal of calculus or clot from ureter and renal pelvis (56.0)*

59.9 Other operations on urinary system

> *Excludes:* *nonoperative removal of therapeutic device (97.61-97.69)*

59.91 Excision of perirenal or perivesical tissue

> *Excludes:* *biopsy of perirenal or perivesical tissue (59.21)*

59.92 Other operations on perirenal or perivesical tissue

59.93 **Replacement of ureterostomy tube**
Change of ureterostomy tube
Reinsertion of ureterostomy tube

> | Excludes: | nonoperative removal of ureterostomy
> tube (97.62)

59.94 **Replacement of cystostomy tube**

> | Excludes: | nonoperative removal of cystostomy tube (97.63)

59.95 **Ultrasonic fragmentation of urinary stones**
Shattered urinary stones

> | Excludes: | percutaneous nephrostomy with fragmentation (55.04)
> shockwave disintegration (98.51)

59.99 **Other**

> | Excludes: | instillation of medication into urinary tract (96.49)
> irrigation of urinary tract (96.45-96.48)

● Code new
to this edition

▲ Revision of
existing code

④ ⑤ Fourth or fifth
digit required

11. OPERATIONS ON THE MALE GENITAL ORGANS (60-64)

60 Operations on prostate and seminal vesicles
Includes: operations on periprostatic tissue

Excludes: *that associated with radical cystectomy (57.71)*

60.0 Incision of prostate
Drainage of prostatic abscess
Prostatolithotomy

Excludes: *drainage of periprostatic tissue only (60.81)*

60.1 Diagnostic procedures on prostate and seminal vesicles

60.11 Closed [percutaneous] [needle] biopsy of prostate
Approach:
transrectal
transurethral
Punch biopsy

60.12 Open biopsy of prostate

60.13 Closed [percutaneous] biopsy of seminal vesicles
Needle biopsy of seminal vesicles

60.14 Open biopsy of seminal vesicles

60.15 Biopsy of periprostatic tissue

60.18 Other diagnostic procedures on prostate and periprostatic tissue

Excludes: *microscopic examination of specimen from prostate (91.31-91.39)*
x-ray of prostate (87.92)

60.19 Other diagnostic procedures on seminal vesicles

Excludes: *microscopic examination of specimen from seminal vesicles*
(91.31-91.39)
x-ray:
contrast seminal vesiculogram (87.91)
other (87.92)

60.2 Transurethral prostatectomy

Excludes: *local excision of lesion of prostate (60.61)*

60.21 Transurethral (ultrasound) guided laser induced prostatectomy (TULIP)
Ablation (contact) (noncontact) by laser

60.29 Other transurethral prostatectomy
Excision of median bar by transurethral approach
Transurethral electrovaporization of prostate (TEVAP)
Transurethral enucleative procedure
Transurethral prostatectomy NOS
Transurethral resection of prostate (TURP)

60.3 Suprapubic prostatectomy
Transvesical prostatectomy

Excludes: *local excision of lesion of prostate (60.61)*
radical prostatectomy (60.5)

60.4 Retropubic prostatectomy

Excludes: *local excision of lesion of prostate (60.61)*
radical prostatectomy (60.5)

60.5 Radical prostatectomy
Prostatovesiculectomy
Radical prostatectomy by any approach

Excludes: *cystoprostatectomy (57.71)*

60.6 Other prostatectomy

60.61 Local excision of lesion of prostate
Excision of prostatic lesion by any approach

Excludes: *biopsy of prostate (60.11-60 12)*

Valid O.R. procedure   Non-O.R. procedure   Nonspecific O.R. procedure   Noncovered O.R. procedure

60.62 Perineal prostatectomy
Cryoablation of prostate
Cryoprostatectomy
Cryosurgery of prostate
Radical cryosurgical ablation of prostate (RCSA)

> *Excludes:* *local excision of lesion of prostate (60.61)*

60.69 Other

60.7 Operations on seminal vesicles

60.71 Percutaneous aspiration of seminal vesicle

> *Excludes:* *needle biopsy of seminal vesicle (60.13)*

60.72 Incision of seminal vesicle

60.73 Excision of seminal vesicle
Excision of Mullerian duct cyst
Spermatocystectomy

> *Excludes:* *biopsy of seminal vesicle (60.13-60.14)*
> *prostatovesiculectomy (60.5)*

60.79 Other operations on seminal vesicles

60.8 Incision or excision of periprostatic tissue

60.81 Incision of periprostatic tissue
Drainage of periprostatic abscess

60.82 Excision of periprostatic tissue
Excision of lesion of periprostatic tissue

> *Excludes:* *biopsy of periprostatic tissue (60.15)*

60.9 Other operations on prostate

60.91 Percutaneous aspiration of prostate

> *Excludes:* *needle biopsy of prostate (60.11)*

60.92 Injection into prostate

60.93 Repair of prostate

60.94 Control of (postoperative) hemorrhage of prostate
Coagulation of prostatic bed
Cystoscopy for control of prostate hemorrhage

60.95 Transurethral balloon dilation of the prostatic urethra

● **60.96 Transurethral destruction of prostate tissue by microwave thermotherapy**
Transurethral microwave thermotherapy (TUMT) of prostate

> *Excludes:* *Prostatectomy:*
> *other (60.61-60.69)*
> *radical (60.5)*
> *retropubic (60.4)*
> *suprapubic (60.3)*
> *transurethral (60.21-60.29)*

● **60.97 Other transurethral destruction of prostate tissue by other thermotherapy**
Radiofrequency thermotherapy
Transurethral needle ablation (TUNA) of prostate

> *Excludes:* *Prostatectomy:*
> *other (60.61-60.69)*
> *radical (60.5)*
> *retropubic (60.4)*
> *suprapubic (60.3)*
> *transurethral (60.21-60.29)*

60.99 Other

> *Excludes:* *prostatic massage (99.94)*

61 Operations on scrotum and tunica vaginalis

61.0 Incision and drainage of scrotum and tunica vaginalis

> *Excludes:* *percutaneous aspiration of hydrocele (61.91)*

61.1 Diagnostic procedures on scrotum and tunica vaginalis

61.11 Biopsy of scrotum or tunica vaginalis

61.19 Other diagnostic procedures on scrotum and tunica vaginalis

---

   ● Code new
to this edition   ▲ Revision of
existing code   ④ ⑤ Fourth or fifth
digit required

61.2 **Excision of hydrocele (of tunica vaginalis)**
Bottle repair of hydrocele of tunica vaginalis

> *Excludes:* *percutaneous aspiration of hydrocele (61.91)*

61.3 **Excision or destruction of lesion or tissue of scrotum**
Fulguration of lesion
Reduction of elephantiasis } of scrotum
Partial scrotectomy

> *Excludes:* *biopsy of scrotum (61.11)*
> *scrotal fistulectomy (61.42)*

61.4 **Repair of scrotum and tunica vaginalis**

> **61.41** **Suture of laceration of scrotum and tunica vaginalis**

> **61.42** **Repair of scrotal fistula**

> **61.49** **Other repair of scrotum and tunica vaginalis**
> Reconstruction with rotational or pedicle flaps

61.9 **Other operations on scrotum and tunica vaginalis**

> **61.91** **Percutaneous aspiration of tunics vaginalis**
> Aspiration of hydrocele of tunica vaginalis

> **61.92** **Excision of lesion of tunica vaginalis other than hydrocele**
> Excision of hematocele of tunica vaginalis

> **61.99** **Other**

> > *Excludes:* *removal of foreign body from scrotum without incision (98.24)*

62 **Operations on testes**

62.0 **Incision of testis**

62.1 **Diagnostic procedures on testes**

> **62.11** **Closed [percutaneous] [needle] biopsy of testis**

> **62.12** **Open biopsy or testis**

> **62.19** **Other diagnostic procedures on testes**

62.2 **Excision or destruction of testicular lesion**
Excision of appendix testis
Excision of cyst of Morgagni in the male

> *Excludes:* *biopsy of testis (62.11-62.12)*

62.3 **Unilateral orchiectomy**
Orchidectomy (with epididymectomy) NOS

62.4 **Bilateral orchiectomy**
Male castration
Radical bilateral orchiectomy (with epididymectomy)
Code also any synchronous lymph node dissection (40.3, 40.5)

> **62.41** **Removal of both testes at same operative episode**
> Bilateral orchidectomy NOS

> **62.42** **Removal of remaining testis**
> Removal of solitary testis

62.5 **Orchiopexy**
Mobilization and replacement of testis in scrotum
Orchiopexy with detorsion of testis
Torek (-Bevan) operation (orchidopexy) (first stage) (second stage)
Transplantation to and fixation of testis in scrotum

62.6 **Repair of testes**

> *Excludes:* *reduction of torsion (63.52)*

> **62.61** **Suture of laceration of testis**

> **62.69** **Other repair of testis**
> Testicular graft

62.7 **Insertion of testicular prosthesis**

62.9 **Other operations on testis**

> **62.91** **Aspiration of testis**

> > *Excludes:* *percutaneous biopsy of testis (62.11)*

> **62.92** **Injection of therapeutic substance into testis**

> **62.99** **Other**

	Valid O.R. procedure		Non-O.R. procedure		Nonspecific O.R. procedure		Noncovered O.R. procedure

63   Operations on spermatic cord, epididymis, and vas deferens

     63.0   Diagnostic procedures on spermatic cord, epididymis and vas deferens

        63.01   Biopsy of spermatic cord, epididymis, or vas deferens

        63.09   Other diagnostic procedures on spermatic cord, epididymis, and vas deferens

          Excludes: *contrast epididymogram (87.93)*
                    contrast vasogram (87.94)
                    other x-ray of epididymis and vas deferens (87.95)

     63.1   Excision of varicocele and hydrocele of spermatic cord
        High ligation of spermatic vein
        Hydrocelectomy of canal of Nuck

     63.2   Excision of cyst of epididymis
        Spermatocelectomy

     63.3   Excision of other lesion or tissue of spermatic cord and epididymis
        Excision of appendix epididymis

        Excludes: *biopsy of spermatic cord or epididymis (63.01)*

     63.4   Epididymectomy

        Excludes: *that synchronous with orchiectomy (62.3-62.42)*

     63.5   Repair of spermatic cord and epididymis

        63.51   Suture of laceration of spermatic cord and epididymis

        63.52   Reduction of torsion of testis or spermatic cord

          Excludes: *that associated with orchiopexy (62.5)*

        63.53   Transplantation of spermatic cord

        63.59   Other repair of spermatic cord and epididymis

     63.6   Vasotomy
        Vasostomy

     63.7   Vasectomy and ligation of vas deferens

        63.70   Male sterilization procedure not otherwise specified

        63.71   Ligation of vas deferens
           Crushing of vas deferens
           Division of vas deferens

        63.72   Ligation of spermatic cord

        63.73   Vasectomy

     63.8   Repair of vas deferens and epididymis

        63.81   Suture of laceration of vas deferens and epididymis

        63.82   Reconstruction of surgically divided vas deferens

        63.83   Epididymovasostomy

        63.84   Removal of ligature from vas deferens

        63.85   Removal of valve from vas deferens

        63.89   Other repair of vas deferens and epididymis

     63.9   Other operations on spermatic cord, epididymis and vas deferens

        63.91   Aspiration of spermatocele

        63.92   Epididymotomy

        63.93   Incision of spermatic cord

        63.94   Lysis of adhesions of spermatic cord

        63.95   Insertion of valve in vas deferens

        63.99   Other

64   Operations on penis
     Includes: operations on:
          corpora cavernosa
          glans penis
          prepuce

     64.0   Circumcision

     64.1   Diagnostic procedures on the penis

        64.11   Biopsy of penis

        64.19   Other diagnostic procedures on penis

● Code new to this edition   ▲ Revision of existing code   ④ ⑤ Fourth or fifth digit required

64.2 **Local excision or destruction of lesion of penis**

> *Excludes:* biopsy of penis (64.11)

64.3 **Amputation of penis**

64.4 **Repair and plastic operation on penis**

64.41 **Suture of laceration of penis**

64.42 **Release of chordee**

64.43 **Construction of penis**

64.44 **Reconstruction of penis**

64.45 **Replantation of penis**
Reattachment of amputated penis

64.49 **Other repair of penis**

> *Excludes:* repair of epispadias and hypospadias (58.45)

64.5 **Operations for sex transformation, not otherwise classified.**

64.9 **Other operations on male genital organs**

64.91 **Dorsal or lateral slit of prepuce**

64.92 **Incision of penis**

64.93 **Division of penile adhesions**

64.94 **Fitting of external prosthesis of penis**
Penile prosthesis NOS

64.95 **insertion or replacement of non-inflatable penile prosthesis**
Insertion of semi-rigid rod prosthesis into shaft of penis

> *Excludes:* external penile prosthesis (64.94)
> inflatable penile prosthesis (64.97)
> plastic repair, penis (64.43-64.49)
> that associated with:
>   construction (64.43)
>   reconstruction (64.44)

64.96 **Removal of internal prosthesis of penis**
Removal without replacement of non-inflatable or inflatable penile prosthesis

64.97 **Insertion or replacement or inflatable penile prosthesis**
Insertion of cylinders into shaft of penis and placement of pump and reservoir

> *Excludes:* external penile prosthesis (64.94)
> non-inflatable penile prosthesis (64.95)
> plastic repair, penis (64.43-64.49)

64.98 **Other operations on penis**
Corpora cavernosa-corpus spongiosum shunt
Corpora-saphenous shunt
Irrigation of corpus cavernosum

> *Excludes:* removal of foreign body:
>   intraluminal (98.19)
>   without incision (98.24)
> stretching of foreskin (99.95)

64.99 **Other**

> *Excludes:* collection of sperm for artificial insemination (99.96)

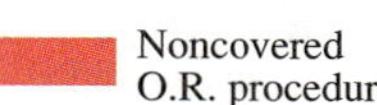

Noncovered
O.R. procedure

● Code new
to this edition

▲ Revision of
existing code

④ ⑤ Fourth or fifth
digit required

12. OPERATIONS ON THE FEMALE GENITAL ORGANS (65-71)

65 Operations on ovary

65.0 Oophorotomy
Salpingo-oophorotomy

65.01 Laparoscopic oophorotomy

65.09 Other oophorotomy

65.1 Diagnostic procedures on ovaries

65.11 Aspiration biopsy of ovary

65.12 Other biopsy of ovary

65.13 Laparoscopic biopsy of ovary

65.14 Other laparoscopic diagnostic procedures on ovaries

65.19 Other diagnostic procedure on ovaries

> *Excludes:* *microscopic examination of specimen from ovary (91.41-91-49)*

65.2 Local excision or destruction of ovarian lesion or tissue

65.21 Marsupialization of ovarian cyst

> *Excludes:* *that by laparoscope (65.23)*

65.22 Wedge resection of ovary

> *Excludes:* *that by laparoscope (65.24)*

65.23 Laparoscopic marsupialization of ovarian cyst

65.24 Laparoscopic wedge resection of ovary

65.25 Other laparoscopic local excision or destruction of ovary

65.29 Other local excision or destruction of ovary
Bisection
Cauterization } of ovary
Partial excision

> *Excludes:* *biopsy of ovary (65.11-65.13)*
> *that by laparoscope (65.25)*

65.3 Unilateral oophorectomy

65.31 Laparoscopic unilateral oophorectomy

65.39 Other unilateral oophorectomy

> *Excludes:* *that by laparoscope (65.31)*

65.4 Unilateral salpingo-oophorectomy

65.41 Laparoscopic unilateral salpingo-oophorectomy

65.49 Other unilateral salpingo-oophorectomy

65.5 Bilateral oophorectomy

65.51 Other removal of both ovaries at same operative episode
Female castration

> *Excludes:* *that by laparoscope (65.53)*

65.52 Other removal of remaining ovary
Removal of solitary ovary

> *Excludes:* *that by laparoscope (65.54)*

65.53 Laparoscopic removal of both ovaries at same operative episode

65.54 Laparoscopic removal of remaining ovary

65.6 Bilateral salpingo-oophorectomy

65.61 Other removal of both ovaries and tubes at same operative episode

> *Excludes:* *that by laparoscope (65.63)*

65.62 Other removal of remaining ovary and tube
Removal of solitary ovary and tube

> *Excludes:* *that by laparoscope (65.64)*

65.63 Laparoscopic removal of both ovaries and tubes at same operative episode

65.64 Laparoscopic removal of remaining ovary and tube

| Valid O.R. procedure | Non-O.R. procedure | Nonspecific O.R. procedure | Noncovered O.R. procedure |

65.7 **Repair of ovary**

Excludes: *salpingo-oophorostomy (66.72)*

65.71 **Other simple suture of ovary**

Excludes: *that by laparoscope (65.74)*

65.72 **Other reimplantation of ovary**

Excludes: *that by laparoscope (65.75)*

65.73 **Other salpingo-oophoroplasty**

Excludes: *that by laparoscope (65.76)*

65.74 **Laparoscopic simple suture of ovary**

65.75 **Laparoscopic reimplantation of ovary**

65.76 **Laparoscopic salpingo-oophoroplasty**

65.79 **Other repair of ovary**
Oophoropexy

65.8 **Lysis of adhesions of ovary and fallopian tube**

65.81 **Laparoscopic lysis of adhesions of ovary and fallopian tube**

65.89 **Other lysis of adhesions of ovary and fallopian tube**

Excludes: *that by laparoscope (65.81)*

65.9 **Other operations on ovary**

65.91 **Aspiration of ovary**

Excludes: *aspiration biopsy of ovary (65.11)*

65.92 **Transplantation of ovary**

Excludes: *reimplantation of ovary (65.72, 65.75)*

65.93 **Manual rupture of ovarian cyst**

65.94 **Ovarian denervation**

65.95 **Release of torsion of ovary**

65.99 **Other**

66 **Operations on fallopian tubes**

66.0 **Salpingotomy and salpingostomy**

66.01 **Salpingotomy**

66.02 **Salpingostomy**

66.1 **Diagnostic procedures on fallopian tubes**

66.11 **Biopsy of fallopian tube**

66.19 **Other diagnostic procedures on fallopian tubes**

Excludes: *microscopic examination of specimen from fallopian tubes*
(91.41-91.49)
radiography of fallopian tubes (87.82-87.83, 87.85)
Rubin's test (66.8)

66.2 **Bilateral endoscopic destruction or occlusion of fallopian tubes**
Includes: bilateral endoscopic destruction or occlusion of fallopian tubes by:
culdoscopy
endoscopy
hysteroscopy
laparoscopy
peritoneoscopy
endoscopic destruction of solitary fallopian tube

66.21 **Bilateral endoscopic ligation and crushing of fallopian tubes**

66.22 **Bilateral endoscopic ligation and division of fallopian tubes**

66.29 **Other bilateral endoscopic destruction or occlusion of fallopian tubes**

66.3 **Other bilateral destruction or occlusion of fallopian tubes**
Includes: destruction of solitary fallopian tube

Excludes: *endoscopic destruction or occlusion of fallopian tubes (66.21-66.29)*

66.31 **Other bilateral ligation and crushing of fallopian tubes**

66.32 **Other bilateral ligation and division of fallopian tubes**
Pomeroy operation

● Code new
to this edition

▲ Revision of
existing code

④ ⑤ Fourth or fifth
digit required

66.39 **Other bilateral destruction or occlusion of fallopian tubes**
Female sterilization operation NOS

66.4 **Total unilateral salpingectomy**

66.5 **Total bilateral salpingectomy**

Excludes: *bilateral partial salpingectomy for sterilization (66.39)*
that with oophorectomy (65.61-65.64)

66.51 **Removal of both fallopian tubes at same operative episode**

66.52 **Removal of remaining fallopian tube**
Removal of solitary fallopian tube

66.6 **Other salpingectomy**
Includes: salpingectomy by:
cauterization
coagulation
electrocoagulation
excision

Excludes: *fistulectomy (66.73)*

66.61 **Excision or destruction of lesion of fallopian tube**

Excludes: *biopsy of fallopian tube (66.11)*

66.62 **Salpingectomy with removal of tubal pregnancy**
Code also any synchronous oophorectomy (65.31, 65.39)

66.63 **Bilateral partial salpingectomy, not otherwise specified**

66.69 **Other partial salpingectomy**

66.7 **Repair of fallopian tube**

66.71 **Simple suture of fallopian tube**

66.72 **Salpingo-oophorostomy**

66.73 **Salpingo-salpingostomy**

66.74 **Salpingo-uterostomy**

66.79 **Other repair of fallopian tube**
Graft of fallopian tube
Reopening of divided fallopian tube
Salpingoplasty

66.8 **Insufflation of fallopian tube**
Insufflation of fallopian tube with:
air
dye
gas
saline
Rubin's test

Excludes: *insufflation of therapeutic agent (66.95)*
that for hysterosalpingography (87.82-87.83)

66.9 **Other operations on fallopian tubes**

66.91 **Aspiration of fallopian tube**

66.92 **Unilateral destruction or occlusion of fallopian tube**

Excludes: *that of solitary tube (66.21-66.39)*

66.93 **Implantation or replacement of prosthesis of fallopian tube**

66.94 **Removal of prosthesis of fallopian tube**

66.95 **Insufflation of therapeutic agent into fallopian tubes**

66.96 **Dilation of fallopian tube**

66.97 **Burying of fimbriae in uterine wall**

66.99 **Other**

Excludes: *lysis of adhesions of ovary and tube (65.81, 65.89)*

67 **Operations on cervix**

67.0 **Dilation of cervical canal**

Excludes: *dilation and curettage (69.01-69.09)*
that for induction of labor (73.1)

67.1 **Diagnostic procedures on cervix**

	Valid O.R. procedure		Non-O.R. procedure		Nonspecific O.R. procedure		Noncovered O.R. procedure

67.11 Endocervical biopsy

> *Excludes:* conization of cervix (67.2)

67.12 Other cervical biopsy
Punch biopsy of cervix NOS

> *Excludes:* conization of cervix (67.2)

67.19 Other diagnostic procedures on cervix

> *Excludes:* microscopic examination of specimen from cervix (91.41-91.49)

67.2 Conization of cervix

> *Excludes:* that by:
> cryosurgery (67.33)
> electrosurgery (67.32)

67.3 Other excision or destruction of lesion or tissue of cervix

67.31 Marsupialization of cervical cyst

67.32 Destruction of lesion of cervix by cauterization
Electroconization of cervix
LEEP (loop electrosurgical excision procedure)
LLETZ (large loop excision of the transformation zone)

67.33 Destruction of lesion of cervix by cryosurgery
Cryoconization of cervix

67.39 Other excision or destruction of lesion or tissue of cervix

> *Excludes:* biopsy of cervix (67.11-67.12)
> cervical fistulectomy (67.62)
> conization of cervix (67.2)

67.4 Amputation of cervix
Cervicectomy with synchronous colporrhaphy

67.5 Repair of internal cervical os
Cerclage of isthmus uteri
Shirodkar operation

67.6 Other repair of cervix

> *Excludes:* repair of current obstetric laceration (75.51)

67.61 Suture of laceration of cervix

67.62 Repair of fistula of cervix
Cervicosigmoidal fistulectomy

> *Excludes:* fistulectomy:
> cervicovesical (57.84)
> ureterocervical (56.84)
> vesicocervicovaginal (57.84)

67.69 Other repair of cervix
Repair of old obstetric laceration of cervix

68 Other incision and excision of uterus

68.0 Hysterotomy
Hysterotomy with removal of hydatidiform mole

> *Excludes:* hysterotomy for termination of pregnancy (74.91)

68.1 Diagnostic procedures on uterus and supporting structures

68.11 Digital examination of uterus

> *Excludes:* pelvic examination, so described (89.26)
> postpartal manual exploration of uterine cavity (75.7)

68.12 Hysteroscopy

> *Excludes:* that with biopsy (68.16)

68.13 Open biopsy of uterus

> *Excludes:* closed biopsy of uterus (68.16)

68.14 Open biopsy of uterine ligaments

> *Excludes:* closed biopsy of uterine ligaments (68.15)

68.15 Closed biopsy of uterine ligaments
Endoscopic (laparoscopy) biopsy of uterine adnexa, except ovary and fallopian tube

---

● Code new
to this edition

▲ Revision of
existing code

④ ⑤ Fourth or fifth
digit required

68.16 Closed biopsy of uterus
Endoscopic (laparoscopy) (hysteroscopy) biopsy of uterus

Excludes: *open biopsy of uterus (68.13)*

68.19 Other diagnostic procedures on uterus and supporting structures

Excludes: *diagnostic:*
aspiration curettage (69.59)
dilation and curettage (69.09)
microscopic examination of specimen from uterus (91.41-91.49)
pelvic examination (89.26)
radioisotope scan of:
placenta (92.17)
uterus (92.19)
ultrasonography of uterus (88.78-88.79)
x-ray of uterus (87.81-87.89)

68.2 Excision or destruction of lesion or tissue of uterus

68.21 Division of endometrial synechiae
Lysis of intraluminal uterine adhesions

68.22 Incision or excision of congenital septum of uterus

68.23 Endometrial ablation
Dilation and curettage
Hysteroscopic endometrial ablation

68.29 Other excision or destruction of lesion of uterus
Uterine myomectomy

Excludes: *biopsy of uterus (68.13)*
uterine fistulectomy (69.42)

68.3 Subtotal abdominal hysterectomy
Supracervical hysterectomy

68.4 Total abdominal hysterectomy
Hysterectomy:
extended

Code also any synchronous removal of tubes and ovaries (65.3-65.6)

68.5 Vaginal hysterectomy

Code also any synchronous:
removal of tubes and ovaries (65.31-65.64)
repair of cystocele or rectocele (70.50-70.52)
repair of pelvic floor (70.79)

68.51 Laparoscopically assisted vaginal hysterectomy (LAVH)

68.59 Other vaginal hysterectomy

Excludes: *laparoscopically assisted vaginal hysterectomy (LAVH) (68.51)*
radical vaginal hysterectomy (68.7)

68.6 Radical abdominal hysterectomy
Modified radical hysterectomy
Wertheim's operation

Code also any synchronous:
lymph gland dissection (40.3, 40.5)
removal of tubes and ovaries (65.61-65.64)

Excludes: *pelvic evisceration (68.8)*

68.7 Radical vaginal hysterectomy
Schauta operation

Code also any synchronous:
lymph gland dissection (40.3, 40.5)
removal of tubes and ovaries (65.61-65.64)

68.8 Pelvic evisceration
Removal of ovaries, tubes, uterus, vagina, bladder and urethra (with removal of sigmoid colon and rectum)

Code also any synchronous:
colostomy (46.12-46.13)
lymph gland dissection (40.3, 40.5)
urinary diversion (56.51-56.79)

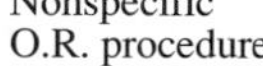

Valid O.R.
procedure

Non-O.R.
procedure

Nonspecific
O.R. procedure

Noncovered
O.R. procedure

68.9 **Other and unspecified hysterectomy**
Hysterectomy NOS

> Excludes: *abdominal hysterectomy, any approach (68.3, 68.4, 68.6)*
> *vaginal hysterectomy, any approach (68.51, 68.59, 68.7)*

69 **Other operations on uterus and supporting structures**

69.0 **Dilation and curettage of uterus**

> Excludes: *aspiration curettage of uterus (69.51-69.59)*

69.01 **Dilation and curettage for termination of pregnancy**

69.02 **Dilation and curettage following delivery or abortion**

69.09 **Other dilation and curettage**
Diagnostic D and C

69.1 **Excision or destruction of lesion or tissue of uterus and supporting structures**

69.19 **Other excision or destruction of uterus and supporting structures**

> Excludes: *biopsy of uterine ligament (68.14)*

69.2 **Repair of uterine supporting structures**

69.21 **Interposition operation**
Watkins procedure

69.22 **Other uterine suspension**
Hysteropexy
Manchester operation
Plication of uterine ligament

69.23 **Vaginal repair of chronic inversion of uterus**

69.29 **Other repair of uterus and supporting structures**

69.3 **Paracervical uterine denervation**

69.4 **Uterine repair**

> Excludes: *repair of current obstetric laceration (75.50-75.52)*

69.41 **Suture of laceration of uterus**

69.42 **Closure of fistula of uterus**

> Excludes: *uterovesical fistulectomy (57.84)*

69.49 **Other repair of uterus**
Repair of old obstetric laceration of uterus

69.5 **Aspiration curettage of uterus**

> Excludes: *menstrual extraction (69.6)*

69.51 **Aspiration curettage of uterus for termination of pregnancy**
Therapeutic abortion NOS

69.52 **Aspiration curettage following delivery or abortion**

69.59 **Other aspiration curettage of uterus**

69.6 **Menstrual extraction or regulation**

69.7 **Insertion of intrauterine contraceptive device**

69.9 **Other operations on uterus, cervix, and supporting structures**

> Excludes: *obstetric dilation or incision of cervix (73.1, 73.93)*

69.91 **Insertion of therapeutic device into uterus**

> Excludes: *insertion of:*
> *intrauterine contraceptive device (69.7)*
> *laminaria (69.93)*
> *obstetric insertion of bag, bougie, or pack (73.1)*

69.92 **Artificial insemination**

69.93 **Insertion of laminaria**

69.94 **Manual replacement of inverted uterus**

> Excludes: *that in immediate postpartal period (75.94)*

69.95 **Incision of cervix**

> Excludes: *that to assist delivery (73.93)*

69.96 **Removal of cerclage material from cervix**

● Code new
to this edition

▲ Revision of
existing code

④ ⑤ Fourth or fifth
digit required

69.97 **Removal of other penetrating foreign body from cervix**

> *Excludes:* removal of intraluminal foreign body
> from cervix (98.16)

69.98 **Other operations on supporting structures of uterus**

> *Excludes:* biopsy of uterine ligament (68.14)

69.99 **Other operations on cervix and uterus**

> *Excludes:* removal of:
> foreign body (98.16)
> intrauterine contraceptive device (97.71)
> obstetric bag, bougie, or pack (97.72)
> packing (97.72)

70 **Operations on vagina and cul-de-sac**

70.0 **Culdocentesis**

70.1 **Incision of vagina and cul-de-sac**

70.11 **Hymenotomy**

70.12 **Culdotomy**

70.13 **Lysis of intraluminal adhesion of vagina**

70.14 **Other vaginotomy**
Division of vaginal septum
Drainage of hematoma of vaginal cuff

70.2 **Diagnostic procedures on vagina and cul-de-sac**

70.21 **Vaginoscopy**

70.22 **Culdoscopy**

70.23 **Biopsy of cul-de-sac**

70.24 **Vaginal biopsy**

70.29 **Other diagnostic procedures on vagina and cul-de-sac**

70.3 **Local excision or destruction of vagina and cul-de-sac**

70.31 **Hymenectomy**

70.32 **Excision or destruction of lesion of cul-de-sac**
Endometrectomy of cul-de-sac

> *Excludes:* biopsy of cul-de-sac (70.23)

70.33 **Excision or destruction of lesion of vagina**

> *Excludes:* biopsy of vagina (70.24)
> vaginal fistulectomy (70.72-70.75)

70.4 **Obliteration and total excision of vagina**
Vaginectomy

> *Excludes:* obliteration of vaginal vault (70.8)

70.5 **Repair of cystocele and rectocele**

70.50 **Repair of cystocele and rectocele**

70.51 **Repair of cystocele**
Anterior colporrhaphy (with urethrocele repair)

70.52 **Repair of rectocele**
Posterior colporrhaphy

70.6 **Vaginal construction and reconstruction**

70.61 **Vaginal construction**

70.62 **Vaginal reconstruction**

70.7 **Other repair of vagina**

> *Excludes:* lysis of intraluminal adhesions (70.13)
> repair of current obstetric laceration (75.69)
> that associated with cervical amputation (67.4)

70.71 **Suture of laceration of vagina**

70.72 **Repair of colovaginal fistula**

70.73 **Repair of rectovaginal fistula**

70.74 **Repair of other vaginoenteric fistula**

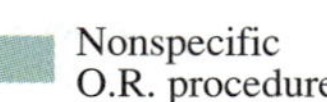

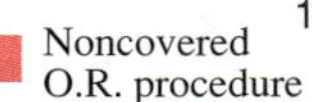

Noncovered
O.R. procedure

70.75 Repair of other fistula of vagina

| Excludes: | *repair of fistula:*
rectovesicovaginal (57.83)
ureterovaginal (56.84)
urethrovaginal (58.43)
uterovaginal (69.42)
vesicocervicovaginal (57.84)
vesicosigmoidovaginal (57.83)
vesicoureterovaginal (56.84)
vesicovaginal (57.84)

70.76 Hymenorrhaphy

70.77 Vaginal suspension and fixation

70.79 Other repair of vagina
Colpoperineoplasty
Repair of old obstetric laceration of vagina

70.8 Obliteration of vaginal vault
LeFort operation

70.9 Other operations on vagina and cul-de-sac

70.91 Other operations on vagina

| Excludes: | *insertion of:*
diaphragm (96.17)
mold (96.15)
pack (96.14)
pessary (96.18)
suppository (96.49)
removal of:
diaphragm (97.73)
foreign body (98.17)
pack (97.75)
pessary (97.74)
replacement of:
diaphragm (97.24)
pack (97.26)
pessary (97.25)
vaginal dilation (96.16)
vaginal douche (96.44)

70.92 Other operations on cul-de-sac
Obliteration of cul-de-sac
Repair of vaginal enterocele

71 Operations on vulva and perineum

71.0 Incision of vulva and perineum

71.01 Lysis of vulvar adhesions

71.09 Other incision of vulva and perineum
Enlargement of introitus NOS

| Excludes: | *removal of foreign body without*
incision (98.23)

71.1 Diagnostic procedures on vulva

71.11 Biopsy of vulva

71.19 Other diagnostic procedures on vulva

71.2 Operations on Bartholin's gland

71.21 Percutaneous aspiration of Bartholin's gland (cyst)

71.22 Incision of Bartholin's gland (cyst)

71.23 Marsupialization of Bartholin's gland (cyst)

71.24 Excision or other destruction of Bartholin's gland (cyst)

71.29 Other operations on Bartholin's gland

71.3 Other local excision or destruction of vulva and perineum
Division of Skene's gland

| Excludes: | *biopsy of vulva (71.11)*
vulvar fistulectomy (71.72)

● Code new
to this edition

▲ Revision of
existing code

④ ⑤ Fourth or fifth
digit required

71.4 **Operations on clitoris**
Amputation of clitoris
Clitoridotomy
Female circumcision

71.5 **Radical vulvectomy**
Code also any synchronous lymph gland dissection (40.3, 40.5)

71.6 **Other vulvectomy**

71.61 **Unilateral vulvectomy**

71.62 **Bilateral vulvectomy**
Vulvectomy NOS

71.7 **Repair of vulva and perineum**

[*Excludes:*] *repair of current obstetric laceration (75.69)*

71.71 **Suture of laceration of vulva or perineum**

71.72 **Repair of fistula of vulva or perineum**

[*Excludes:*] *repair of fistula:*
urethroperineal (58.43)
urethroperineovesical (57.84)
vaginoperineal (70.75)

71.79 **Other repair of vulva and perineum**
Repair of old obstetric laceration of vulva or perineum

71.8 **Other operations on vulva**

[*Excludes:*] *removal of:*
foreign body without incision (98.23)
packing (97.75)
replacement of packing (97.26)

71.9 **Other operations on female genital organs**

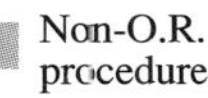
Valid O.R.
procedure

Non-O.R.
procedure

Nonspecific
O.R. procedure

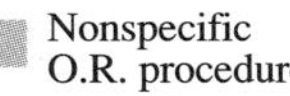
Noncovered
O.R. procedure

● Code new
to this edition

▲ Revision of
existing code

④ ⑤ Fourth or fifth
digit required

13. OBSTETRICAL PROCEDURES (72-75)

72 Forceps, vacuum, and breech delivery

72.0 Low forceps operation
Outlet forceps operation

72.1 Low forceps operation with episiotomy
Outlet forceps operation with episiotomy

72.2 Mid forceps operation

72.21 Mid forceps operation with episiotomy

72.29 Other mid forceps operation

72.3 High forceps operation

72.31 High forceps operation with episiotomy

72.39 Other high forceps operation

72.4 Forceps rotation of fetal head
DeLee maneuver
Key-in-lock rotation
Kielland rotation
Scanzoni's maneuver
Code also any associated forceps extraction (72.0-72.39)

72.5 Breech extraction

72.51 Partial breech extraction with forceps to aftercoming head

72.52 Other partial breech extraction

72.53 Total breech extraction with forceps to aftercoming head

72.54 Other total breech extraction

72.6 Forceps application to aftercoming head
Piper forceps operation

Excludes:	*partial breech extraction with forceps to aftercoming head (72.51)*
	total breech extraction with forceps to aftercoming head (72.53)

72.7 Vacuum extraction
Includes: Malström's extraction

72.71 Vacuum extraction with episiotomy

72.79 Other vacuum extraction

72.8 Other specified instrumental delivery

72.9 Unspecified instrumental delivery

73 Other procedures inducing or assisting delivery

73.0 Artificial rupture of membranes

73.01 Induction of labor by artificial rupture of membranes
Surgical induction NOS

Excludes:	*artificial rupture of membranes after onset of labor (73.09)*

73.09 Other artificial rupture of membranes
Artificial rupture of membranes at time of delivery

73.1 Other surgical induction of labor
Induction by cervical dilation

Excludes:	*injection for abortion (75.0)*
	insertion of suppository for abortion (96.49)

73.2 Internal and combined version and extraction

73.21 Internal and combined version without extraction
Version NOS

73.22 Internal and combined version with extraction

73.3 Failed forceps
Application of forceps without delivery
Trial forceps

73.4 Medical induction of labor

Excludes:	*medication to augment active labor—omit code*

73.5 Manually assisted delivery

73.51 Manual rotation of fetal head

	Valid O.R. procedure		Non-O.R. procedure		Nonspecific O.R. procedure		Noncovered O.R. procedure

73.59 Other manually assisted delivery
Assisted spontaneous delivery
Crede maneuver

73.6 Episiotomy
Episioproctotomy
Episiotomy with subsequent episiorrhaphy

> | Excludes: | *that with:*
> *high forceps (72.31)*
> *low forceps (72.1)*
> *mid forceps (72.21)*
> *outlet forceps (72.1)*
> *vacuum extraction (72.71)*

73.8 Operations on fetus to facilitate delivery
Clavicotomy on fetus
Destruction of fetus
Needling of hydrocephalic head

73.9 Other operations assisting delivery

73.91 External version

73.92 Replacement of prolapsed umbilical cord

73.93 Incision of cervix to assist delivery
Dührssen's incisions

73.94 Pubiotomy to assist delivery
Obstetrical symphysiotomy

73.99 Other

> | Excludes: | *dilation of cervix obstetrical, to induce labor (73.1)*
> *insertion of bag or bougie to induce labor (73.1)*
> *removal of cerclage material (69.96)*

74 Cesarean section and removal of fetus
Code also any synchronous:
hysterectomy (68.3-68.4, 68.6, 68.8)
myomectomy (68.29)
sterilization (66.31-66.39, 66.63)

74.0 Classical cesarean section
Transperitoneal classical cesarean section

74.1 Low cervical cesarean section
Lower uterine segment cesarean section

74.2 Extraperitoneal cesarean section
Supravesical cesarean section

74.3 Removal of extratubal ectopic pregnancy
Removal of:
ectopic abdominal pregnancy
fetus from peritoneal or extraperitoneal cavity following uterine or tubal rupture

> | Excludes: | *that by salpingostomy (66.02)*
> *that by salpingotomy (66.01)*
> *that with synchronous salpingectomy (66.62)*

74.4 Cesarean section of other specified type
Peritoneal exclusion cesarean section
Transperitoneal cesarean section NOS
Vaginal cesarean section

74.9 Cesarian section of unspecified type

74.91 Hysterotomy to terminate pregnancy
Therapeutic abortion by hysterotomy

74.99 Other cesarean section of unspecified type
Cesarean section NOS
Obstetrical abdominouterotomy
Obstetrical hysterotomy

● Code new
to this edition

▲ Revision of
existing code

④ ⑤ Fourth or fifth
digit required

75   **Other obstetric operations**

    75.0   **Intra-amniotic injection for abortion**
Injection of:
    prostaglandin
    saline   } for induction of abortion
Termination of pregnancy by intrauterine injection
> *Excludes:* *insertion of prostaglandin suppository for abortion (96.49)*

    75.1   **Diagnostic amniocentesis**

    75.2   **Intrauterine transfusion**
Exchange transfusion in utero
Insertion of catheter into abdomen of fetus for transfusion
> *Code also any hysterotomy approach (68.0)*

    75.3   **Other Intrauterine operations on fetus and amnion**
> *Code also any hysterotomy approach (68.0)*

        75.31 **Amnioscopy**
Fetoscopy
Laparoamnioscopy

        75.32 **Fetal EKG (scalp)**

        75.33 **Fetal blood sampling and biopsy**

        75.34 **Fetal monitoring not otherwise specified**

        75.35 **Other diagnostic procedures on fetus and amnion**
Intrauterine pressure determination
> *Excludes:* *amniocentesis (75.1)*
> *diagnostic procedures on gravid uterus*
> *and placenta (87.81, 88.46, 88.78, 92.17)*

        75.36 **Correction of fetal defect**

        75.37 **Amnioinfusion**
> *Code also* injection of antibiotic (99.21)

    75.4   **Manual removal of retained placenta**
> *Excludes:* *aspiration curettage (69.52)*
> *dilation and curettage (69.02)*

    75.5   **Repair of current obstetric laceration of uterus**

        75.50 **Repair of current obstetric laceration of uterus not otherwise specified**

        75.51 **Repair of current obstetric laceration of cervix**

        75.52 **Repair of current obstetric laceration of corpus uteri**

    75.6   **Repair of other current obstetric laceration**

        75.61 **Repair of current obstetric laceration of bladder and urethra**

        75.62 **Repair of current obstetric laceration of rectum and sphincter ani**

        75.69 **Repair of other current obstetric laceration**
Episioperineorrhaphy
Repair of:
  pelvic floor
  perineum
  vagina
  vulva
Secondary repair of episiotomy
> *Excludes:* *repair of routine episiotomy (73.6)*

    75.7   **Manual exploration of uterine cavity, postpartum**

    75.8   **Obstetric tamponade of uterus or vagina**
> *Excludes:* *antepartum tamponade (73.1)*

    75.9   **Other obstetric operations**

        75.91 **Evacuation of obstetrical incision hematoma of perineum**
Evacuation of hematoma of:
  episiotomy
  perineorrhaphy

        75.92 **Evacuation of other hematoma of vulva or vagina**

Valid O.R. procedure   Non-O.R. procedure   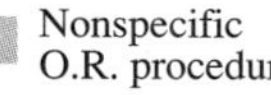 Nonspecific O.R. procedure   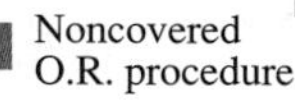 Noncovered O.R. procedure

75.93 **Surgical correction of inverted uterus**
Spintelli operation

Excludes: *vaginal repair of chronic inversion of uterus (69.23)*

75.94 **Manual replacement of inverted uterus**

75.99 **Other**

● Code new
to this edition

▲ Revision of
existing code

④ ⑤ Fourth or fifth
digit required

14. OPERATIONS ON THE MUSCULOSKELETAL SYSTEM (76-84)

76 Operations on facial bones and joints

> *Excludes:* *accessory sinuses (22.00-22.9)*
> *nasal bones (21.00-21.99)*
> *skull (01.01-02.99)*

76.0 Incision of facial bone without division

76.01 Sequestrectomy of facial bone
Removal of necrotic bone chip from facial bone

76.09 Other incision of facial bone
Reopening of osteotomy site of facial bone

> *Excludes:* *osteotomy associated with orthognathic surgery (76.61-76.69)*
> *removal of internal fixation device (76.97)*

76.1 Diagnostic procedures on facial bones and joints

76.11 Biopsy of facial bone

76.19 Other diagnostic procedures on facial bones and joints

> *Excludes:* *contrast arthrogram of temporomandibular joint (87.13)*
> *other x-ray (87.11-87.12 87.14-87.16)*

76.2 Local excision or destruction of lesion of facial bone

> *Excludes:* *biopsy of facial bone (76.11)*
> *excision of odontogenic lesion (24.4)*

76.3 Partial ostectomy of facial bone

76.31 Partial mandibulectomy
Hemimandibulectomy

> *Excludes:* *that associated with temporomandibular arthroplasty (76.5)*

76.39 Partial ostectomy of other facial bone
Hemimaxillectomy (with bone graft or prosthesis)

76.4 Excision and reconstruction of facial bones

76.41 Total mandibulectomy with synchronous reconstruction

76.42 Other total mandibulectomy

76.43 Other reconstruction of mandible

> *Excludes:* *genioplasty (76.67-76.68)*
> *that with synchronous total mandibulectomy (76.41)*

76.44 Total ostectomy of other facial bone with synchronous reconstruction

76.45 Other total ostectomy of other facial bone

76.46 Other reconstruction of other facial bone

> *Excludes:* *that with synchronous total ostectomy (76.44)*

76.5 Temporomandibular arthroplasty

76.6 Other facial bone repair and orthognathic surgery

Code also any synchronous:
bone graft (76.91)
synthetic implant (76.92)

> *Excludes:* *reconstruction of facial bones (76.41-76.46)*

76.61 Closed osteoplasty [osteotomy] of mandibular ramus
Gigli saw osteotomy

76.62 Open osteoplasty [osteotomy] of mandibular ramus

76.63 Osteoplasty [osteotomy] of body of mandible

76.64 Other orthognathic surgery on mandible
Mandibular osteoplasty NOS
Segmental or subapical osteotomy

76.65 Segmental osteoplasty [osteotomy] of maxilla
Maxillary osteoplasty NOS

76.66 Total osteoplasty [osteotomy] of maxilla

76.67 Reduction genioplasty
Reduction mentoplasty

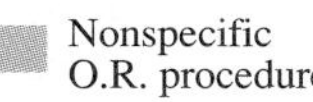

Valid O.R. procedure Non-O.R. procedure Nonspecific O.R. procedure Noncovered O.R. procedure

76.68 Augmentation genioplasty
Mentoplasty:
NOS
with graft or implant

76.69 Other facial bone repair
Osteoplasty of facial bone NOS

76.7 Reduction of facial fracture
Includes: internal fixation

Code also any synchronous:
bone graft (76.91)
synthetic implant (76.92)

Excludes: *that of nasal bones (21.71-21.72)*

76.70 Reduction of facial fracture, not otherwise specified

76.71 Closed reduction of malar and zygomatic fracture

76.72 Open reduction of malar and zygomatic fracture

76.73 Closed reduction of maxillary fracture

76.74 Open reduction of maxillary fracture

76.75 Closed reduction of mandibular fracture

76.76 Open reduction of mandibular fracture

76.77 Open reduction of alveolar fracture
Reduction of alveolar fracture with stabilization of teeth

76.78 Other closed reduction of facial fracture
Closed reduction of orbital fracture

Excludes: *nasal bone (21.71)*

76.79 Other open reduction of facial fracture
Open reduction of orbit rim or wall

Excludes: *nasal bone (21.72)*

76.9 Other operations on facial bones and joints

76.91 Bone graft to facial bone
Autogenous
Bone bank   } graft to facial bone
Heterogenous

76.92 Insertion of synthetic implant in facial bone
Alloplastic implant to facial bone

76.93 Closed reduction of temporomandibular dislocation

76.94 Open reduction of temporomandibular dislocation

76.95 Other manipulation of temporomandibular joint

76.96 Injection of therapeutic substance into temporomandibular joint

76.97 Removal of internal fixation device from facial bone

Excludes: *removal of:*
dental wiring (97.33)
external mandibular fixation device NEC (97.36)

76.99 Other

77 Incision, excision, and division of other bones

Excludes· *laminectomy for decompression (03.09)*
operations on:
accessory sinuses (22.00-22.9)
ear ossicles (19.0-19.55)
facial bones (76.01-76.99)
joint structures (80.00-81.99)
mastoid (19.9-20.99)
nasal bones (21.00-21.99)
skull (01.01-02.99)

      ● Code new   ▲ Revision of   ④ ⑤ Fourth or fifth
to this edition   existing code   digit required

The following fourth-digit subclassification is for use with appropriate categories in section 77, marked with a symbol to identify the site. Valid fourth-digit categories are in [brackets] under each code.

    0 unspecified site
    1 scapula, clavicle, and thorax [ribs and sternum]
    2 humerus
    3 radius and ulna
    4 carpals and metacarpals
    5 femur
    6 patella
    7 tibia and fibula
    8 tarsals and metatarsals
    9 other
        Pelvic bones
        Phalanges (of foot) (of hand)
        Vertebrae

④ **77.0** **Sequestrectomy**
[0-9]

④ **77.1** **Other incision of bone without division**
[0-9] Reopening of osteotomy site

> *Excludes:*   *aspiration of bone marrow (41.31,41.91)*
>   *removal of internal fixation device (78.60-78.69)*

④ **77.2** **Wedge osteotomy**
[0-9]

> *Excludes:*   *that for hallux valgus (77.51)*

④ **77.3** **Other division of bone**
[0-9] Osteoarthrotomy

> *Excludes:*   *clavicotomy of fetus (73.8)*
>   *laminotomy or incision of vertebra (03.01-03.09)*
>   *pubiotomy to assist delivery (73.94)*
>   *sternotomy incidental to thoracic operation—omit code*

④ **77.4** **Biopsy of bone**
[0-9]

77.5 **Excision and repair of bunion and other toe deformities**

77.51 **Bunionectomy with soft tissue correction and osteotomy of the first metatarsal**

77.52 **Bunionectomy with soft tissue correction and arthrodesis**

77.53 **Other bunionectomy with soft tissue correction**

77.54 **Excision or correction of bunionette**
    That with osteotomy

77.56 **Repair of hammer toe**
    Fusion
    Phalangectomy (partial)   } of hammer toe
    Filleting

77.57 **Repair of claw toe**
    Fusion
    Phalangectomy (partial)
    Capsulotomy   } of claw toe
    Tendon lengthening

77.58 **Other excision, fusion, and repair of toes**
    Cockup toe repair
    Overlapping toe repair
    That with use of prosthetic materials

77.59 **Other bunionectomy**
    Resection of hallux valgus joint with insertion of prosthesis

④ **77.6** **Local excision of lesion or tissue of bone**
[0-9]
> *Excludes:*   *biopsy of bone (77.40-77.49)*
>
>   *debridement of compound fracture (79.60-79.69)*

④ **77.7** **Excision of bone for graft**
[0-9]

---

④ **77.8** **Other partial ostectomy**
[0-9] Condylectomy

| *Excludes:* | *amputation (84.00-84.19,84.91)* |

arthrectomy (80.90-80.99)
excision of bone ends associated with:
arthrodesis (81.00-81.29)
arthroplasty (81.51-81.59, 81.71-81.81, 81.84)
excision of cartilage (80.5-80.6, 80.80-80.99)
excision of head of femur with synchronous replacement (81.51-81.53)
hemilaminectomy (03.01-03.09)
laminectomy (03.01-03.09)
ostectomy for hallux valgus (77.51-77.59)
partial amputation:
finger (84.01)
thumb (84.02)
toe (84.11)
resection of ribs incidental to thoracic operation—omit code
that incidental to other operation—omit code

④ **77.9** **Total ostectomy**
[0-9]

| *Excludes:* | *amputation of limb (84.00-84.19, 84.91)* |

that incidental to other operation—omit code

78 **Other operations on bones, except facial bones**

| *Excludes:* | *operations on:* |

accessory sinuses (22.00-22.9)
facial bones (76.01-76.99)
joint structures (80.00-81.99)
nasal bones (21.00-21.99)
skull (01.01-02.99)

The following fourth-digit subclassification is for use with Categories in section 78 to identify the site. Valid fourth-digit categories are in [brackets] under each code.

0 unspecified site
1 scapula, clavicle, and thorax (ribs and sternum]
2 humerus
3 radius and ulna
4 carpals and metacarpals
5 femur
6 patella
7 tibia and fibulas
8 tarsals and metatarsals
9 other
  Pelvic bones
  Phalanges (of foot) (of hand)
  Vertebrae

④ **78.0** **Bone graft**
[0-9] Bone:
  bank graft
  graft (autogenous) (heterogenous)
That with debridement of bone graft site (removal of sclerosed, fibrous, or necrotic bone or tissue)
Transplantation of bone
Code also any excision of bone for graft (77.70-77.79)

| *Excludes:* | *that for bone lengthening (78.30-78.39)* |

④ **78.1** **Application of external fixation device**
[0-9] Minifixator with insertion of pins/wires/screws into bone

| *Excludes:* | *other immobilization, pressure, and attention to wound (93.51-93.59)* |

④ **78.2** **Limb shortening procedures**
[0,2-5,7-9] Epiphyseal stapling
  Open epiphysiodesis
  Percutaneous epiphysiodesis
  Resection/osteotomy

④ **78.3** **Limb lengthening procedures**
[0,2-5,7-9] Bone graft with or without internal fixation devices or osteotomy
  Distraction technique with or without corticotomy/osteotomy
  Code also any application of an external fixation device (78.10-78.19)

  ● Code new to this edition   ▲ Revision of existing code   ④ ⑤ Fourth or fifth digit required

④ **78.4** **Other repair or plastic operations on bone**
[0-9]   Other operation on bone NEC
           Repair of malunion or nonunion fracture NEC

> *Excludes:* *application of external fixation device (78.10-78.19)*
> *limb lengthening procedures (78.30-78.39)*
> *limb shortening procedures (78.20-78.29)*
> *osteotomy (77.3)*
> *reconstruction of thumb (82.61-82.69)*
> *repair of pectus deformity (34.74)*
> *repair with bone graft (78.00-78.09)*

④ **78.5** **Internal fixation of bone without fracture reduction**
[0-9]   Internal fixation of bone (prophylactic)
           Reinsertion of internal fixation device
           Revision of displaced or broken fixation device

> *Excludes:* *arthroplasty and arthrodesis (81.00-81.85)*
> *bone graft (78.00-78.09)*
> *limb shortening procedures (78.20-78.29)*
> *that for fracture reduction (79.10-79.19, 79.30-79.59)*

④ **78.6** **Removal of implanted devices from bone**
[0-9]   External fixator device (invasive)
           Internal fixation device
           Removal of bone growth stimulator (invasive)

> *Excludes:* *removal of cast, splint, and traction device (Kirschner wire) (Steinmann pin)*
> *(97.88)*
> *removal of skull tongs or halo traction device (02.95)*

④ **78.7** **Osteoclasis**
[0-9]

④ **78.8** **Diagnostic procedures on bone, not elsewhere classified**
[0-9]
> *Excludes:* *biopsy of bone (77.40-77.49)*
>
> *magnetic resonance imaging (88.94)*
> *microscopic examination of specimen from*
> *bone (91.51-91.59)*
> *radioisotope scan (92.14)*
> *skeletal x-ray (87.21-87.29, 87.43, 88.21-88.33)*
> *thermography (88.83)*

④ **78.9** **Insertion of bone growth stimulator**
(0-9)   Insertion of:
             bone stimulator (electrical) to aid bone healing
             osteogenic electrodes for bone growth stimulation
             totally implanted device (invasive)

> *Excludes:* *non-invasive (transcutaneous) (surface) stimulator (99.86)*

79 **Reduction of fracture and dislocation**
        Includes: application of cast or splint
                     reduction with insertion of traction device (Kirschner wire) (Steinmann pin)

Code also any application of external fixation device (78.10-78.19)

> *Excludes:* *external fixation alone for immobilization of fracture (93.51-93.56,93.59)*
> *internal fixation without reduction of fracture (78.50-78.59)*
> *operations on:*
>   *facial bones (76.70-76.79)*
>   *nasal bones (21.71-21.72)*
>   *orbit (76.78-76.79)*
>   *skull (02.02)*
>   *vertebrae (03.53)*
> *removal of cast or splint (97.88)*
> *replacement of cast or splint (97.11-97.14)*
> *traction alone for reduction of fracture (93.41-93.46)*

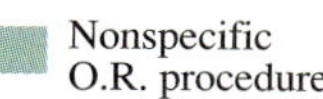

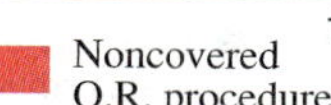

Noncovered
O.R. procedure

The following fourth-digit subclassification is for use with appropriate categories in section 79, marked with a symbol to identify the site. Valid fourth-digit codes are in [brackets] under each code.

  0 unspecified site
  1 humerus
  2 radius and ulna
    Arm NOS
  3 carpals and metacarpals
    Hand NOS
  4 phalanges of hand
  5 femur
  6 tibia and fibula
    Leg NOS
  7 tarsals and metatarsals
    Foot NOS
  8 phalanges of foot
  9 other specified bone

④ **79.0** **Closed reduction of fracture without internal fixation**
[0-9] | *Excludes:* | *that for separation of epiphysis (79.40-79.49)*

④ **79.1** **Closed reduction of fracture with internal fixation**
[0-9] | *Excludes:* | *that for separation of epiphysis (79.40-79.49)*

④ **79.2** **Open reduction of fracture without internal fixation**
[0-9] | *Excludes:* | *that for separation of epiphysis (79.50-79.59)*

④ **79.3** **Open reduction of fracture with internal fixation**
[0-9] | *Excludes:* | *that for separation of epiphysis (79.50-79.59)*

④ **79.4** **Closed reduction of separated epiphysis**
[0-2,5,6,9] Reduction with or without internal fixation

④ **79.5** **Open reduction of separated epiphysis**
[0-2,5,6,9] Reduction with or without internal fixation

④ **79.6** **Debridement of open fracture site**
[0-9]   Debridement of compound fracture

79.7 **Closed reduction of dislocation**
  Includes: closed reduction (with external traction device)
  | *Excludes:* | *closed reduction of dislocation of temporomandibular joint (76.93)*

  79.70 **Closed reduction of dislocation of unspecified site**

  79.71 **Closed reduction of dislocation of shoulder**

  79.72 **Closed reduction of dislocation of elbow**

  79.73 **Closed reduction of dislocation of wrist**

  79.74 **Closed reduction of dislocation of hand and finger**

  79.75 **Closed reduction of dislocation of hip**

  79.76 **Closed reduction of dislocation of knee**

  79.77 **Closed reduction of dislocation of ankle**

  79.78 **Closed reduction of dislocation of foot and toe**

  79.79 **Closed reduction of dislocation of other specified sites**

79.8 **Open reduction of dislocation**
  Includes: open reduction (with internal and external fixation devices)
  | *Excludes:* | *open reduction of dislocation of temporomandibular joint (76.94)*

  79.80 **Open reduction of dislocation of unspecified site**

  79.81 **Open reduction of dislocation of shoulder**

  79.82 **Open reduction of dislocation of elbow**

  79.83 **Open reduction of dislocation of wrist**

  79.84 **Open reduction of dislocation of hand and finger**

  79.85 **Open reduction of dislocation of hip**

  79.86 **Open reduction of dislocation of knee**

  79.87 **Open reduction of dislocation of ankle**

  79.88 **Open reduction of dislocation of foot and toe**

  ● Code new
    to this edition
  ▲ Revision of
    existing code
  ④ ⑤ Fourth or fifth
    digit required

79.89 Open reduction or dislocation of other specified sites

④ **79.9** **Unspecified operation on bone injury**
[0-9]

80 **Incision and excision of joint structures**
Includes: operations on:
capsule of joint
cartilage
condyle
ligament
meniscus
synovial membrane

Excludes: *cartilage of:*
ear (18.01-18.9)
nose (21.00-21.99)
temporomandibular joint (76.01-76.99)

The following fourth-digit subclassification is for use with appropriate categories in section 80, that
are marked with a symbol to identify the site:
0 **unspecified site**
1 **shoulder**
2 **elbow**
3 **wrist**
4 **hand and finger**
5 **hip**
6 **knee**
7 **ankle**
8 **foot and toe**
9 **other specified sites**
Spine

④ **80.0** **Arthrotomy for removal of prosthesis**
Includes: cement spacer

④ **80.1** **Other arthrotomy**
Arthrostomy

Excludes: *that for:*
arthrography (88.32)
arthroscopy (80.20-80.29)
injection of drug (81.92)
operative approach—omit code

④ **80.2** **Arthroscopy**

④ **80.3** **Biopsy of joint structure**
Aspiration biopsy

④ **80.4** **Division of joint capsule, ligament, or cartilage**
Goldner clubfoot release
Heyman-Herndon(-Strong) correction of metatarsus varus
Release of:
adherent or constrictive joint capsule
joint
ligament

Excludes: *symphysiotomy to assist delivery (73.94)*
that for:
carpal tunnel syndrome (04.43)
tarsal tunnel syndrome (04.44)

80.5 **Excision or destruction of intervertebral disc**

80.50 **Excision or destruction of intervertebral disc, unspecified**
Unspecified as to excision or destruction

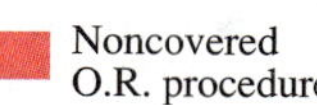

80.51 Excision of intervertebral disc
Diskectomy
Levels:
  cervical
  lumbar (lumbosacral)
  thoracic
Removal of herniated nucleus pulposus
That by laminotomy or hemilaminectomy
That with decompression of spinal nerve root at same level
Requires additional code for any concomitant decompression of spinal nerve root at
  different level from excision site
Code also any concurrent spinal fusion (81.00-81.09)

> *Excludes:*   *intervertebral chemonucleolysis (80.52)*
> *laminectomy for exploration of intraspinal canal (03.09)*
> *laminotomy for decompression of spinal nerve root only (03.09)*

80.52 Intervertebral chemonucleolysis
Injection of proteolytic enzyme into intervertebral space (chymopapain)
With aspiration of disc fragments
With diskography

> *Excludes:*   *injection of anesthetic substance (03.91)*
> *injection of other substances (03.92)*

80.59 Other destruction of intervertebral disc
Destruction NEC
That by laser

80.6 Excision of semilunar cartilage of knee
Excision of meniscus of knee

④ **80.7 Synovectomy**
Complete or partial resection of synovial membrane

> *Excludes:*   *excision of Baker's cyst (83.39)*

④ **80.8 Other local excision or destruction of lesion of joint**

④ **80.9 Other excision of joint**

> *Excludes:*   *cheilectomy of joint (77.80-77.89)*
> *excision of bone ends (77.80-77.89)*

81 Repair and plastic operations on joint structures

81.0 Spinal fusion
Includes: arthrodesis of spine with:
      bone graft
      internal fixation

81.00 Spinal fusion, not otherwise specified

81.01 Atlas-axis spinal fusion
Craniocervical fusion
C1-C2 fusion   } by anterior transoral or posterior technique
Occiput-C2 fusion

> *Excludes:*   *that for pseudoarthrosis (81.09)*

81.02 Other cervical fusion, anterior technique
Arthrodesis of C2 level or below:
  anterior (interbody) technique
  anterolateral technique

> *Excludes:*   *that for pseudarthrosis (81.09)*

81.03 Other cervical fusion, posterior technique
Arthrodesis of C2 level or below:
  posterior (interbody) technique
  posterolateral technique

> *Excludes:*   *that for pseudarthrosis (81.09)*

81.04 Dorsal and dorsolumbar fusion, anterior technique
Arthrodesis of thoracic or thoracolumbar region:
  anterior (interbody) technique
  anterolateral technique

> *Excludes:*   *that for pseudarthrosis (81.09)*

  ● Code new   ▲ Revision of   ④ ⑤ Fourth or fifth
    to this edition   existing code   digit required

81.05 Dorsal and dorsolumbar fusion, posterior technique
Arthrodesis of thoracic or thoracolumbar region:
    posterior (interbody) technique
    posterolateral technique
> *Excludes:*   *that for pseudarthrosis (81.09)*

81.06 Lumbar and lumbosacral fusion, anterior technique
Arthrodesis of lumbar or lumbosacral region:
    anterior (interbody) technique
    anterolateral technique
> *Excludes:*   *that for pseudarthrosis (81.09)*

81.07 Lumbar and lumbosacral fusion, lateral transverse process technique
> *Excludes:*   *that for pseudarthrosis (81.09)*

81.08 Lumbar and lumbosacral fusion, posterior technique
Arthrodesis of lumbar or lumbosacral region:
    posterior (interbody) technique
    posterolateral technique

81.09 Refusion of spine, any level or technique
Correction of pseudarthrosis of spine

81.1 Arthrodesis of foot and ankle
Includes: arthrodesis of foot and ankle with:
    bone graft
    external fixation device

81.11 Ankle fusion
Tibiotalar fusion

81.12 Triple arthrodesis
Talus to calcaneus and calcaneus to cuboid and navicular

81.13 Subtalar fusion

81.14 Midtarsal fusion

81.15 Tarsometatarsal fusion

81.16 Metatarsophalangeal fusion

81.17 Other fusion of foot

81.2 Arthrodesis of other joint
Includes: arthrodesis with:
    bone graft
    external fixation device
    excision of bone ends and compression

81.20 Arthrodesis of unspecified joint

81.21 Arthrodesis of hip

81.22 Arthrodesis of knee

81.23 Arthrodesis of shoulder

81.24 Arthrodesis of elbow

81.25 Carporadial fusion

81.26 Metacarpocarpal fusion

81.27 Metacarpophalangeal fusion

81.28 Interphalangeal fusion

81.29 Arthrodesis of other specified joints

81.4 Other repair of joint of lower extremity
Includes: arthroplasty of lower extremity with:
    external traction or fixation
    graft of bone chips or cartilage
    internal fixation device

81.40 Repair of hip, not elsewhere classified

81.42 Five-in-one repair of knee
Medial meniscectomy, medial collateral ligament repair, vastus medialis
    advancement, semitendinosus advancement, and pes anserinus transfer

81.43 Triad knee repair
Medial meniscectomy with repair of the anterior cruciate ligament and the medial
    collateral ligament
O'Donoghue procedure

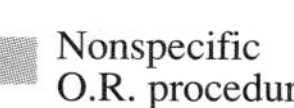 Valid O.R. procedure   Non-O.R. procedure   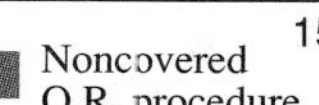 Nonspecific O.R. procedure   Noncovered O.R. procedure

81.44 Patellar stabilization
  Roux-Goldthwait operation for recurrent dislocation of patella

81.45 Other repair of the cruciate ligaments

81.46 Other repair of the collateral ligaments

81.47 Other repair of knee

81.49 Other repair of ankle

81.5 Joint replacement of lower extremity
  Includes: arthroplasty of lower extremity with:
    external traction or fixation
    graft of bone (chips) or cartilage
    internal fixation device or prosthesis
   removal of cement spacer

81.51 Total hip replacement
  Replacement of both femoral head and acetabulum by prosthesis
  Total reconstruction of hip

81.52 Partial hip replacement
  Bipolar endoprosthesis

81.53 Revision of hip replacement
  Partial
  Total

81.54 Total knee replacement
  Bicompartmental
  Tricompartmental
  Unicompartmental (hemijoint)

81.55 Revision of knee replacement

  Excludes: *arthrodesis of knee (81.22)*

81.56 Total ankle replacement

81.57 Replacement of joint of foot and toe

81.59 Revision of joint replacement of lower extremity, not elsewhere classified

81.7 Arthroplasty and repair of hand, fingers, and wrist
  Includes: arthroplasty of hand and finger with:
    external traction or fixation
    graft of bone (chips) or cartilage
    internal fixation device or prosthesis

  Excludes: *operations on muscle, tendon, and fascia of hand (82.01-82.99)*

81.71 Arthroplasty of metacarpophalangeal and interphalangeal joint with implant

81.72 Arthroplasty of metacarpophalangeal and interphalangeal joint without implant

81.73 Total wrist replacement

81.74 Arthroplasty of carpocarpal or carpometacarpal joint with implant

81.75 Arthroplasty of carpocarpal or carpometacarpal joint without implant

81.79 Other repair of hand, fingers, and wrist

81.8 Arthroplasty and repair of shoulder and elbow
  Includes: arthroplasty of upper limb NEC with:
    external traction or fixation
    graft of bone (chips) or cartilage
    internal fixation device or prosthesis

81.80 Total shoulder replacement

81.81 Partial shoulder replacement

81.82 Repair of recurrent dislocation of shoulder

81.83 Other repair of shoulder
  Revision of arthroplasty of shoulder

81.84 Total elbow replacement

81.85 Other repair of elbow

  ● Code new ▲ Revision of ④ ⑤ Fourth or fifth
    to this edition   existing code   digit required

81.9 Other operations on joint structures

81.91 Arthrocentesis
Joint aspiration

> *Excludes:* that for:
> arthrography (88.32)
> biopsy of joint structure (80.30-80.39)
> injection of drug (81.92)

81.92 Injection of therapeutic substance into joint or ligament

81.93 Suture of capsule or ligament of upper extremity

> *Excludes:* that associated with arthroplasty (81.71-81.75, 81.80-81.81, 81.84)

81.94 Suture of capsule or ligament of ankle and foot

> *Excludes:* that associated with arthroplasty (81.56-81.59)

81.95 Suture of capsule or ligament of other lower extremity

> *Excludes:* that associated with arthroplasty (81.51-81.55, 81.59)

81.96 Other repair of joint

81.97 Revision of joint replacement of upper extremity
partial
total
Includes: removal of cement spacer

81.98 Other diagnostic procedures on joint structures

> *Excludes:* arthroscopy (80.20-80.29)
> biopsy of joint structure (80.30-80.39)
> microscopic examination of specimen from joint (91.51-91.59)
> thermography (88.83)
> x-ray (87.21-87.29, 88.21-88.33)

81.99 Other

82 Operations on muscle, tendon, and fascia of hand
Includes: operations on:
aponeurosis
synovial membrane (tendon sheath)
tendon sheath

82.0 Incision of muscle, tendon, fascia, and bursa of hand

82.01 Exploration of tendon sheath of hand
Incision of
Removal of rice bodies in } tendon sheath of hand

> *Excludes:* division of tendon (82.11)

82.02 Myotomy of hand

> *Excludes:* myotomy for division (82.19)

82.03 Bursotomy of hand

82.04 Incision and drainage of palmar or thenar space

82.09 Other incision of soft tissue of hand

> *Excludes:* incision of skin and subcutaneous tissue alone (86.01-86.09)

82.1 Division of muscle, tendon, and fascia of hand

82.11 Tenotomy of hand
Division of tendon of hand

82.12 Fasciotomy of hand
Division of fascia of hand

82.19 Other division of soft tissue of hand
Division of muscle of hand

82.2 Excision of lesion of muscle, tendon, and fascia of hand

82.21 Excision of lesion of tendon sheath of hand
Ganglionectomy of tendon sheath (wrist)

82.22 Excision of lesion of muscle of hand

82.29 Excision of other lesion of soft tissue of hand

> *Excludes:* excision of lesion of skin and subcutaneous tissue (86.21-86.3)

Valid O.R. procedure   Non-O.R. procedure   Nonspecific O.R. procedure   Bilateral procedure

82.3 **Other excision of soft tissue of hand**

Code also any skin graft (86.61-86.62, 86.73)

> Excludes: excision of skin and subcutaneous tissue (86.21-86.3)

82.31 **Bursectomy of hand**

82.32 **Excision of tendon of hand for graft**

82.33 **Other tenonectomy of hand**
Tenosynovectomy of hand

> Excludes: excision of lesion of:
> tendon (82.29)
> sheath (82.21)

82.34 **Excision of muscle or fascia of hand for graft**

82.35 **Other fasciectomy of hand**
Release of Dupuytren's contracture

> Excludes: excision of lesion of fascia (82.29)

82.36 **Other myectomy of hand**

> Excludes: excision of lesion of muscle (82.22)

82.39 **Other excision of soft tissue of hand**

> Excludes: excision of skin (86.21-86.3)
> excision of soft tissue lesion (82.29)

82.4 **Suture of muscle, tendon, and fascia of hand**

82.41 **Suture of tendon sheath of hand**

82.42 **Delayed suture of flexor tendon of hand**

82.43 **Delayed suture of other tendon of hand**

82.44 **Other suture of flexor tendon of hand**

> Excludes: delayed suture of flexor tendon of hand (82.42)

82.45 **Other suture of other tendon of hand**

> Excludes: delayed suture of other tendon of hand (82.43)

82.46 **Suture of muscle or fascia of hand**

82.5 **Transplantation of muscle and tendon of hand**

82.51 **Advancement of tendon of hand**

82.52 **Recession of tendon of hand**

82.53 **Reattachment of tendon of hand**

82.54 **Reattachment of muscle of hand**

82.55 **Other change in hand muscle or tendon length**

82.56 **Other hand tendon transfer or transplantation**

> Excludes: pollicization of thumb (82.61)
> transfer of finger, except thumb (82.81)

82.57 **Other hand tendon transposition**

82.58 **Other hand muscle transfer or transplantation**

82.59 **Other hand muscle transposition**

82.6 **Reconstruction of thumb**
Includes: digital transfer to act as thumb
Code also any amputation for digital transfer (84.01, 84.11)

82.61 **Pollicization operation carrying over nerves and blood supply**

82.69 **Other reconstruction of thumb**
"Cocked-hat" procedure [skin flap and bone]
Grafts:
bone
skin (pedicle)   } to thumb

82.7 **Plastic operation on hand with graft or implant**

82.71 **Tendon pulley reconstruction**
Reconstruction for opponensplasty

82.72 **Plastic operation on hand with graft of muscle or fascia**

● Code new
to this edition

▲ Revision of
existing code

④ ⑤ Fourth or fifth
digit required

82.79 Plastic operation on hand with other graft or implant
Tendon graft to hand

82.8 Other plastic operations on hand

82.81 Transfer of finger, except thumb

Excludes: *pollicization of thumb (82.61)*

82.82 Repair of cleft hand

82.83 Repair of macrodactyly

82.84 Repair of mallet finger

82.85 Other tenodesis of hand
Tendon fixation of hand NOS

82.86 Other tenoplasty of hand
Myotenoplasty of hand

82.89 Other plastic operations on hand
Plication of fascia
Repair of fascial hernia

Excludes: *that with graft or implant (82.71-82.79)*

82.9 Other operations on muscle, tendon, and fascia of hand

Excludes: *diagnostic procedures on soft tissue of hand (83.21-83.29)*

82.91 Lysis of adhesions of hand
Freeing of adhesions of fascia, muscle, and tendon of hand

Excludes: *decompression of carpal tunnel (04.43)*
that by stretching or manipulation only (93.26)

82.92 Aspiration of bursa of hand

82.93 Aspiration of other soft tissue of hand

Excludes: *skin and subcutaneous tissue (86.01)*

82.94 Injection of therapeutic substance into bursa of hand

82.95 Injection of therapeutic substance into tendon of hand

82.96 Other injection of locally-acting therapeutic substance into soft tissue of hand

Excludes: *subcutaneous or intramuscular injection (99.11-99.29)*

82.99 Other operations on muscle, tendon, and fascia of hand

83 Operations on muscle, tendon, fascia, and bursa, except hand
Includes: operations on:
aponeurosis
synovial membrane of bursa and tendon sheaths
tendon sheaths

Excludes: *diaphragm (34.81-34.89)*
hand (82.01-82.99)
muscles of eye (15.01-15.9).

83.0 Incision of muscle, tendon, fascia, and bursa

83.01 Exploration of tendon sheath
Incision of tendon sheath
Removal of rice bodies from tendon sheath

83.02 Myotomy

Excludes: *cricopharyngeal myotomy (29.31)*

83.03 Bursotomy
Removal of calcareous deposit of bursa

Excludes: *aspiration of bursa (percutaneous) (83.94)*

83.09 Other incision of soft tissue
Incision of fascia

Excludes: *incision of skin and subcutaneous tissue alone (86.01-86.09)*

83.1 Division of muscle, tendon, and fascia

83.11 Achillotenotomy

83.12 Adductor tenotomy of hip

Valid O.R. procedure   Non-O.R. procedure   Nonspecific O.R. procedure   Noncovered O.R. procedure

83.13 **Other tenotomy**
Aponeurotomy
Division of tendon
Tendon release
Tendon transection
Tenotomy for thoracic outlet decompression

83.14 **Fasciotomy**
Division of fascia
Division of iliotibial band
Fascia stripping
Release of Volkmann's contracture by fasciotomy

83.19 **Other division of soft tissue**
Division of muscle
Muscle release
Myotomy for thoracic outlet decompression
Myotomy with division
Scalenotomy
Transection of muscle

83.2 **Diagnostic procedures on muscle, tendon, fascia, and bursa, including that of hand**

83.21 **Biopsy of soft tissue**

> *Excludes:* *biopsy of chest wall (34.23)*
> *biopsy of skin and subcutaneous tissue (86.11)*

83.29 **Other diagnostic procedures on muscle, tendon, fascia, and bursa, including that of hand**

> *Excludes:* *microscopic examination of specimen (91.51-91.59)*
> *soft tissue x-ray (87.09, 87.38-87.39, 88.09, 88.35, 88.37)*
> *thermography of muscle (88.84)*

83.3 **Excision of lesion of muscle, tendon, fascia, and bursa**

> *Excludes:* *biopsy of soft tissue (83.21)*

83.31 **Excision of lesion of tendon sheath**
Excision of ganglion of tendon sheath, except of hand

83.32 **Excision of lesion of muscle**
Excision of:
heterotopic bone
muscle scar for release of Volkmann's contracture
myositis ossificans

83.39 **Excision of lesion of other soft tissue**
Excision of Baker's cyst

> *Excludes:* *bursectomy (83.5)*
> *excision of lesion of skin and subcutaneous tissue (86.3)*
> *synovectomy (80.70-80.79)*

83.4 **Other excision of muscle, tendon, and fascia**

83.41 **Excision of tendon for graft**

83.42 **Other tenonectomy**
Excision of:
aponeurosis
tendon sheath
Tenosynovectomy

83.43 **Excision of muscle or fascia for graft**

83.44 **Other fasciectomy**

83.45 **Other myectomy**
Debridement of muscle NOS
Scalenectomy

83.49 **Other excision of soft tissue**

83.5 **Bursectomy**

83.6 **Suture of muscle, tendon, and fascia**

83.61 **Suture of tendon sheath**

83.62 **Delayed suture of tendon**

83.63 **Rotator cuff repair**

● Code new
to this edition

▲ Revision of
existing code

④ ⑤ Fourth or fifth
digit required

83.64 **Other suture of tendon**
Achillorrhaphy
Aponeurorrhaphy

| Excludes: | delayed suture of tendon (83.62)

83.65 **Other suture of muscle or fascia**
Repair of diastasis recti

83.7 **Reconstruction of muscle and tendon**

| Excludes: | reconstruction of muscle and tendon associated with arthroplasty

83.71 **Advancement of tendon**

83.72 **Recession of tendon**

83.73 **Reattachment of tendon**

83.74 **Reattachment of muscle**

83.75 **Tendon transfer or transplantation**

83.76 **Other tendon transposition**

83.77 **Muscle transfer or transplantation**
Release of Volkmann's contracture by muscle transplantation

83.79 **Other muscle transposition**

83.8 **Other plastic operations on muscle, tendon, and fascia**

| Excludes: | plastic operations on muscle, tendon, and fascia associated with arthroplasty

83.81 **Tendon graft**

83.82 **Graft of muscle or fascia**

83.83 **Tendon pulley reconstruction**

83.84 **Release of clubfoot, not elsewhere classified**
Evans operation on clubfoot

83.85 **Other change in muscle or tendon length**
Hamstring lengthening
Heel cord shortening
Plastic achillotenotomy
Tendon plication

83.86 **Quadricepsplasty**

83.87 **Other plastic operations on muscle**
Musculoplasty
Myoplasty

83.88 **Other plastic operations on tendon**
Myotenoplasty
Tendon fixation
Tenodesis
Tenoplasty

83.89 **Other plastic operations on fascia**
Fascia lengthening
Fascioplasty
Plication of fascia

83.9 **Other operations on muscle, tendon, fascia, and bursa**

| Excludes: | nonoperative:
manipulation (93.25-93.29)
stretching (93.27-93.29)

83.91 **Lysis of adhesions of muscle, tendon, fascia,and bursa**

| Excludes: | that for tarsal tunnel syndrome (04.44)

83.92 **Insertion or replacement of skeletal muscle stimulator**
Implantation, insertion, placement, or replacement of skeletal muscle:
electrodes
stimulator

83.93 **Removal of skeletal muscle stimulator**

83.94 **Aspiration of bursa**

83.95 **Aspiration of other soft tissue**

| Excludes: | that of skin and subcutaneous tissue (86.01)

83.96 **Injection of therapeutic substance into bursa**

Valid O.R. procedure   Non-O.R. procedure   Nonspecific O.R. procedure   Noncovered O.R. procedure

83.97 Injection of therapeutic substance into tendon

83.98 Injection of locally-acting therapeutic substance into other soft tissue

> *Excludes:* *subcutaneous or intramuscular injection (99.11-99.29)*

83.99 **Other operations on muscle, tendon, fascia and bursa**
Suture of bursa

84 **Other procedures on musculoskeletal system**

84.0 **Amputation of upper limb**

> *Excludes:* *revision of amputation stump (84.3)*

84.00 **Upper limb amputation, not otherwise specified**
Closed flap amputation
Kineplastic amputation
Open or guillotine
   amputation   } of upper limb NOS
Revision of current
   traumatic amputation

84.01 **Amputation and disarticulation of finger**

> *Excludes:* *ligation of supernumerary finger (86.26)*

84.02 **Amputation and disarticulation of thumb**

84.03 **Amputation through hand**
Amputation through carpals

84.04 **Disarticulation of wrist**

84.05 **Amputation through forearm**
Forearm amputation

84.06 **Disarticulation of elbow**

84.07 **Amputation through humerus**
Upper arm amputation

84.08 **Disarticulation of shoulder**

84.09 **Interthoracoscapular amputation**
Forequarter amputation

84.1 **Amputation of lower limb**

> *Excludes:* *revision of amputation stump (84.3)*

84.10 **Lower limb amputation, not otherwise specified**
Closed flap amputation
Kineplastic amputation
Open or guillotine
   amputation   } of lower limb NOS
Revision of current
   traumatic amputation

84.11 **Amputation of toe**
Amputation through metatarsophalangeal joint
Disarticulation of toe
Metatarsal head amputation
Ray amputation of foot (disarticulation of the metatarsal head of the toe extending
   across the forefoot just proximal to the metatarsophalangeal crease)

> *Excludes:* *ligation of supernumerary toe (86.26)*

84.12 **Amputation through foot**
Amputation of forefoot
Amputation through middle of foot
Chopart's amputation
Midtarsal amputation
Transmetatarsal amputation (amputation of the forefoot, including all the toes)

> *Excludes:* *ray amputation of foot (84.11)*

84.13 **Disarticulation of ankle**

84.14 **Amputation of ankle through malleoli of tibia and fibula**

84.15 **Other amputation below knee**
Amputation of leg through tibia and fibula NOS

  ● Code new
to this edition ▲ Revision of
existing code ④ ⑤ Fourth or fifth
digit required

84.16 **Disarticulation of knee**
Batch, Spitler, and McFaddin amputation
Mazet amputation
S.P. Roger's amputation

84.17 **Amputation above knee**
Amputation of leg through femur
Amputation of thigh
Conversion of below-knee amputation into above-knee amputation
Supracondylar above-knee amputation

84.18 **Disarticulation of hip**

84.19 **Abdominopelvic amputation**
Hemipelvectomy
Hindquarter amputation

84.2 **Reattachment of extremity**

84.21 **Thumb reattachment**

84.22 **Finger reattachment**

84.23 **Forearm, wrist, or hand reattachment**

84.24 **Upper arm reattachment**
Reattachment or arm NOS

84.25 **Toe reattachment**

84.26 **Foot reattachment**

84.27 **Lower leg or ankle reattachment**
Reattachment of leg NOS

84.28 **Thigh reattachment**

84.29 **Other reattachment**

84.3 **Revision of amputation stump**
Reamputation
Secondary closure } of stump
Trimming

> *Excludes:* *revision of current traumatic amputation [revision by further amputation of current injury] (84.00-84.19, 84.91)*

84.4 **Implantation or fitting of prosthetic limb device**

84.40 **Implantation or fitting of prosthetic limb device not otherwise specified**

84.41 **Fitting of prosthesis of upper arm and shoulder**

84.42 **Fitting of prosthesis of lower arm and hand**

84.43 **Fitting of prosthesis of arm, not otherwise specified**

84.44 **Implantation of prosthetic device of arm**

84.45 **Fitting of prosthesis above knee**

84.46 **Fitting of prosthesis below knee**

84.47 **Fitting of prosthesis of leg, not otherwise specified**

84.48 **Implantation of prosthetic device of leg**

84.9 **Other operations on musculoskeletal system**

> *Excludes:* *nonoperative manipulation (93.25-93.29)*

84.91 **Amputation, not otherwise specified**

84.92 **Separation of equal conjoined twins**

84.93 **Separation of unequal conjoined twins**
Separation of conjoined twins NOS

84.99 **Other**

Valid O.R. procedure	Non-O.R. procedure	Nonspecific O.R. procedure	Noncovered O.R. procedure

● Code new
to this edition

▲ Revision of
existing code

④ ⑤ Fourth or fifth
digit required

15. OPERATIONS ON THE INTEGUMENTARY SYSTEM (85-86)

85 Operations on the breast

Includes: operations on the skin and subcutaneous tissue of:
breast
previous mastectomy site } female or male
revision of previous mastectomy site

85.0 Mastotomy
Incision of breast (skin)
Mammotomy

Excludes: aspiration of breast (85.91)
removal of implant (85.94)

85.1 Diagnostic procedures on breast

85.11 Closed [percutaneous] [needle] biopsy of breast

85.12 Open biopsy of breast

85.19 Other diagnostic procedures on breast

Excludes: mammary ductogram (87.35)
mammography NEC (87.37)
manual examination (89.36)
microscopic examination of specimen (91.61-91.69)
thermography (88.85)
ultrasonography (88.73)
xerography (87.36)

85.2 Excision or destruction of breast tissue

Excludes: mastectomy (85.41-85.48)
reduction mammoplasty (85.31-85.32)

85.20 Excision or destruction of breast tissue, not otherwise specified

85.21 Local excision of lesion of breast
Lumpectomy
Removal of area of fibrosis from breast

Excludes: biopsy of breast (85.11-8.5.12)

85.22 Resection of quadrant of breast

85.23 Subtotal mastectomy

Excludes: quadrant resection (85.22)

85.24 Excision of ectopic breast tissue
Excision of accessory nipple

85.25 Excision of nipple

Excludes: excision of accessory nipple (85.24)

85.3 Reduction mammoplasty and subcutaneous mammectomy

85.31 Unilateral reduction mammoplasty
Unilateral:
amputative mammoplasty
size reduction mammoplasty

85.32 Bilateral reduction mammoplasty
Amputative mammoplasty
Reduction mammoplasty (for gynecomastia)

85.33 Unilateral subcutaneous mammectomy with synchronous implant

Excludes: that without synchronous implant (85.34)

85.34 Other unilateral subcutaneous mammectomy
Removal of breast tissue with preservation of skin and nipple
Subcutaneous mammectomy NOS

85.35 Bilateral subcutaneous mammectomy with synchronous implant

Excludes: that without synchronous implant (85.36)

85.36 Other bilateral subcutaneous mammectomy

Valid O.R. procedure	Non-O.R. procedure	Nonspecific O.R. procedure	Noncovered O.R. procedure

85.4 **Mastectomy**

85.41 **Unilateral simple mastectomy**
Mastectomy:
 NOS
 complete

85.42 **Bilateral simple mastectomy**
Bilateral complete mastectomy

85.43 **Unilateral extended simple mastectomy**
Extended simple mastectomy NOS
Modified radical mastectomy
Simple mastectomy with excision of regional lymph nodes

85.44 **Bilateral extended simple mastectomy**

85.45 **Unilateral radical mastectomy**
Excision of breast, pectoral muscles, and regional
 lymph nodes [axillary, clavicular, supraclavicular]
Radical mastectomy NOS

85.46 **Bilateral radical mastectomy**

85.47 **Unilateral extended radical mastectomy**
Excision of breast, muscles, and lymph nodes [axillary, clavicular, supraclavicular,
 internal mammary, and mediastinal]
Extended radical mastectomy NOS

85.48 **Bilateral extended radical mastectomy**

85.5 **Augmentation mammoplasty**

| *Excludes:* | *that associated with subcutaneous mammectomy (85.33, 85.35)* |

85.50 **Augmentation mammoplasty, not otherwise specified**

85.51 **Unilateral injection into breast for augmentation**

85.52 **Bilateral injection into breast for augmentation**
Injection into breast for augmentation NOS

85.53 **Unilateral breast implant**

85.54 **Bilateral breast implant**
Breast implant NOS

85.6 **Mastopexy**

85.7 **Total reconstruction of breast**

85.8 **Other repair and plastic operations on breast**

| *Excludes:* | *that for:* |

   augmentation (85.50-85.54)
   reconstruction (85.7)
   reduction (85.31-85.32)

85.81 **Suture of laceration of breast**

85.82 **Split-thickness graft to breast**

85.83 **Full-thickness graft to breast**

85.84 **Pedicle graft to breast**

85.85 **Muscle flap graft to breast**

85.86 **Transposition of nipple**

85.87 **Other repair or reconstruction of nipple**

85.89 **Other mammoplasty**

85.9 **Other operations on the breast**

85.91 **Aspiration of breast**

| *Excludes:* | *percutaneous biopsy of breast (85.11)* |

85.92 **Injection of therapeutic agent into breast**

| *Excludes:* | *that for augmentation of breast (85.51-85.52)* |

85.93 **Revision of implant of breast**

85.94 **Removal of implant of breast**

85.95 **Insertion of breast tissue expander**
Insertion (soft tissue) of tissue expander (one or more) under muscle or platysma to
 develop skin flaps for donor use

85.96 **Removal of breast tissue expander(s)**

● Code new
to this edition

▲ Revision of
existing code

④ ⑤ Fourth or fifth
digit required

85.99 Other

86 **Operations on skin and subcutaneous tissue**
Includes: operations on:
  hair follicles
  male perineum
  nails
  sebaceous glands
  subcutaneous fat pads
  sudoriferous glands
  superficial fossae

Excludes: *those on skin of:*
  anus (49.01-49.99)
  breast (mastectomy site) (85.0-85.99)
  ear (18.01-18.9)
  eyebrow (08.01-08.99)
  eyelid (08.01-08.99)
  female perineum (71.01-71.9)
  lips (27.0-27.99)
  nose (21.00-21.99)
  penis (64.0-64.99)
  scrotum (61.0-61.99)
  vulva (71.01-71.9)

86.0 **Incision of skin and subcutaneous tissue**

86.01 **Aspiration of skin and subcutaneous tissue**
Aspiration of:
  abscess
  hematoma   } of nail, skin, or subcutaneous tissue
  seroma

86.02 **Injection or tattooing of skin lesion or defect**
Injection   } of filling material
Insertion
Pigmenting of skin

86.03 **Incision of pilonidal sinus or cyst**

Excludes: *marsupialization (86.21)*

86.04 **Other incision with drainage of skin and subcutaneous tissue**

Excludes: *drainage of:*
  fascial compartments of face and mouth (27.0)
  palmar or thenar space (82.04)
  pilonidal sinus or cyst (86.03)

86.05 **Incision with removal of foreign body from skin and subcutaneous tissue**
Removal of loop recorder
Removal of tissue expander(s) from skin or soft tissue other than breast tissue

Excludes: *removal of foreign body without incision (98.20-98.29)*

86.06 **Insertion of totally implantable infusion pump**

Code also any associated catheterization

Excludes: *insertion of totally implantable vascular access device (86.07)*

86.07 **Insertion of totally implantable vascular access device [VAD]**
Totally implanted port

Excludes: *insertion of totally implantable infusion pump (86.06)*

86.09 **Other incision of skin and subcutaneous tissue**
Creation of loop recorder pocket, new site and insertion/relocation of device
Creation of pocket for implantable, patient-activated cardiac event recorder and
  insertion/relocation of device
Creation of thalamic stimulator pulse generator pocket, new site
Escharotomy
Exploration:
  sinus tract, skin
  superficial fossa
Undercutting of hair follicle

Excludes: *that of cardiac pacemaker pocket, new site (37.79)*
  that of fascial compartments of face and mouth (27.0)

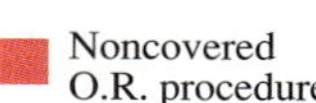

Valid O.R. procedure   Non-O.R. procedure   Nonspecific O.R. procedure   Noncovered O.R. procedure

86.1 Diagnostic procedures on skin and subcutaneous tissue

    86.11 Biopsy of skin and subcutaneous tissue

    86.19 Other diagnostic procedures on skin and subcutaneous tissue

        | Excludes: | *microscopic examination of specimen from skin and subcutaneous tissue (91.61-91.79)* |

86.2 Excision or destruction of lesion or tissue of skin and subcutaneous tissue

    86.21 Excision of pilonidal cyst or sinus
        Marsupialization of cyst

        | Excludes: | *incision of pilonidal cyst or sinus (86.03)* |

    86.22 Excisional debridement of wound, infection, or burn
        Removal by excision of:
          devitalized tissue
          necrosis
          slough

        | Excludes: | *debridement of:* |

          abdominal all (wound) (54.3)
          bone (77.60-77.69)
          muscle (83.45) of hand (82.36)
          nail (bed) (fold) (86.27)
          nonexcisional debridement of wound, infection, or burn (86.28)
          open fracture site (79.60-79.69)
          pedicle or flap graft (86.75)

    86.23 Removal of nail, nailbed, or nail fold

    86.24 Chemosurgery of skin
        Chemical peel of skin

    86.25 Dermabrasion
        That with laser

        | Excludes: | *dermabrasion of wound to remove embedded debris (86.28)* |

    86.26 Ligation of dermal appendage

        | Excludes: | *excision of preauricular appendage (18.29)* |

    86.27 Debridement of nail, nail bed, or nail fold
        Removal of:
          necrosis
          slough

        | Excludes: | *removal of nail, nail bed, or nail fold (86.23)* |

    86.28 Nonexcisional debridement of wound, infection, or burn
        Debridement NOS
        Removal of devitalized tissue, necrosis, and slough by such methods as:
          brushing
          irrigation (under pressure)
          scrubbing
          washing

86.3 Other local excision or destruction of lesion or tissue of skin and subcutaneous tissue
    Destruction of skin by:
      cauterization
      cryosurgery
      fulguration
      laser beam
    That with Z-plasty

    | Excludes: | *adipectomy (86.83)* |

      biopsy of skin (86.11)
      wide or radical excision of skin (86.4)
      Z-plasty without excision (86.84)

86.4 Radical excision of skin lesion
    Wide excision of skin lesion involving underlying or adjacent structure
    Code also any lymph node dissection (40.3-40.5)

▲ **86.5 Suture or other closure of skin and subcutaneous tissue**

    86.51 Replantation of scalp

● Code new to this edition   ▲ Revision of existing code   ④ ⑤ Fourth or fifth digit required

▲ **86.59** **Closure of skin and subcutaneous tissue of other sites**
Adhesives (surgical) (tissue)
Staples
Sutures

Excludes: *application of adhesive strips (butterfly)—omit code*

86.6 **Free skin graft**
Includes: excision of skin for autogenous graft

Excludes: *construction or reconstruction of:*
penis (64.43-64.44)
trachea (31.75)
vagina (70.61-70.62)

86.60 **Free skin graft, not otherwise specified**

86.61 **Full-thickness skin graft to hand**

Excludes: *heterograft (86.65)*
homograft (86.66)

86.62 **Other skin graft to hand**

Excludes: *heterograft (86.65)*
homograft (86.66)

86.63 **Full-thickness skin graft to other sites**

Excludes: *heterograft (86.65)*
homograft (86.66)

86.64 **Hair transplant**

Excludes: *hair follicle transplant to eyebrow or eyelash (08.63)*

86.65 **Heterograft to skin**
Pigskin graft
Porcine graft

86.66 **Homograft to skin**
Graft to skin of:
amnionic membrane
skin
} from donor

86.67 **Dermal regenerative graft**
Artificial skin, NOS
Creation of "neodermis"
Decellularized allodermis
Integumentary matrix implants
Prosthetic implant of dermal layer of skin
Regenerate dermal layer of skin

Excludes: *heterograft to skin (86.65)*
homograft to skin (86.66)

86.69 **Other skin graft to other sites**

Excludes: *heterograft (86.65)*
homograft (86.66)

86.7 **Pedicle grafts or flaps**

Excludes: *construction or reconstruction of:*
penis (64.43-64.44)
trachea (31.75)
vagina (70.61-70.62)

86.70 **Pedicle or flap graft, not otherwise specified**

86.71 **Cutting and preparation of pedicle grafts or flaps**
Elevation of pedicle from its bed
Flap design and raising
Partial cutting of pedicle or tube
Pedicle delay

Excludes: *pollicization or digital transfer (82.61, 82.81)*
revision of pedicle (86.75)

86.72 **Advancement of pedicle graft**

86.73 **Attachment of pedicle or flap graft to hand**

Excludes: *pollicization or digital transfer (82.61, 82.81)*

Valid O.R. procedure Non-O.R. procedure Nonspecific O.R. procedure Noncovered O.R. procedure

86.74 **Attachment of pedicle or flap graft to other sites**
Attachment by: Attachment by:
  advanced flap   rotating flap
  double pedicled flap   sliding flop
  pedicle graft   tube graft

86.75 **Revision of pedicle or flap graft**
Debridement
Defatting } of pedicle or flap graft

86.8 **Other repair and reconstruction of skin and subcutaneous tissue**

86.81 **Repair for facial weakness**

86.82 **Facial rhytidectomy**
Face lift

Excludes: *rhytidectomy of eyelid (08.86-08.87)*

86.83 **Size reduction plastic operation**
Liposuction
Reduction of adipose tissue of:
  abdominal wall (pendulous)
  arms (batwing)
  buttock
  thighs (trochanteric lipomatosis)

Excludes: *breast (85.31-85.32)*

86.84 **Relaxation of scar or web contracture of skin**
Z-plasty of skin

Excludes: *Z-plasty with excision of lesion (86.3)*

86.85 **Correction of syndactyly**

86.86 **Onychoplasty**

86.89 **Other repair and reconstruction of skin and subcutaneous tissue**

Excludes: *mentoplasty (76.67-76.68)*

86.9 **Other operations on skin and subcutaneous tissue**

86.91 **Excision of skin for graft**
Excision of skin with closure of donor site

Excludes: *that with graft at same operative episode (86.60-86.69)*

86.92 **Electrolysis and other epilation of skin**

Excludes: *epilation of eyelid (08.91-08.93)*

86.93 **Insertion of tissue expander**
Insertion (subcutaneous) (soft tissue) of expander (one or more) in scalp (subgaleal
  space), face, neck, trunk except breast, and upper and lower extremities for
  development of skin flaps for donor use

Excludes: *flap graft preparation (86.71)*
    tissue expander, breast (85.95)

86.99 **Other**

Excludes: *removal of sutures from:*
  abdomen (97.83)
  head and neck (97.38)
  thorax (97.43)
  trunk NEC (97.84)
wound catheter:
  irrigation (96.58)
  replacement (97.15)

● Code new
to this edition
    ▲ Revision of
existing code
    ④ ⑤ Fourth or fifth
digit required

16. MISCELLANEOUS DIAGNOSTIC AND THERAPEUTIC PROCEDURES (87-99)

87 Diagnostic Radiology

87.0 Soft tissue x-ray of face, head, and neck

> Excludes: *angiography (88.40-88.68)*

87.01 Pneumoencephalogram

87.02 Other contrast radiogram of brain and skull
Pneumocisternogram
Pneumoventriculogram
Posterior fossa myelogram

87.03 Computerized axial tomography of bead
C.A.T. scan of head

87.04 Other tomography of bead

87.05 Contrast dacryocystogram

87.06 Contrast radiogram of nasopharynx

87.07 Contrast laryngogram

87.08 Cervical lymphangiogram

87.09 Other soft tissue x-ray of face, head, and neck
Noncontrast x-ray of:
  adenoid
  larynx
  nasolacrimal duct
  nasopharynx
  salivary gland
  thyroid region
  uvula

> Excludes: *x-ray study of eye (95.14)*

87.1 Other x-ray of face, head, and neck

> Excludes: *angiography (88.40-88.68)*

87.11 Full-mouth x-ray of teeth

87.12 Other dental x-ray
Orthodontic cephalogram or cephalometrics
Panorex examination of mandible
Root canal x-ray

87.13 Temporomandibular contrast arthrogram

87.14 Contrast radiogram of orbit

87.15 Contrast radiogram of sinus

87.16 Other x-ray of facial bones
X-ray of:
  frontal area
  mandible
  maxilla
  nasal sinuses
  nose
  orbit
  supraorbital area
  symphysis menti
  zygomaticomaxillary complex

87.17 Other x-ray of skull
Lateral projection
Sagittal projection   } of skull
Tangential projection

87.2 X-ray of spine

87.21 Contrast myelogram

87.22 Other x-ray of cervical spine

87.23 Other x-ray of thoracic spine

87.24 Other x-ray of lumbosacral spine
Sacrococcygeal x-ray

87.29 Other x-ray of spine
Spinal x-ray NOS

Valid O.R. procedure	Non-O.R. procedure	Nonspecific O.R. procedure	Noncovered O.R. procedure

87.3   Soft tissue x-ray of thorax

> Excludes: *angiocardiography (88.50-88.58)*
> *angiography (88.40-88.68)*

87.31   Endotracheal bronchogram

87.32   Other contrast bronchogram
Transcricoid bronchogram

87.33   Mediastinal pneumogram

87.34   Intrathoracic lymphangiogram

87.35   Contrast radiogram of mammary ducts

87.36   Xerography of breast

87.37   Other mammography

87.38   Sinogram of chest wall
Fistulogram of chest wall

87.39   Other soft tissue x-ray of chest wall

87.4   Other x-ray of thorax

> Excludes: *angiocardiography (88.50-88.58)*
> *angiography (88.40-88.68)*

87.41   Computerized axial tomography of thorax
C.A.T. scan
Crystal linea scan of x-ray
    beam
Electronic substraction   } of thorax
Photoelectric response
Tomography with use of
    computer, x-rays, and
    camera

87.42   Other tomography of thorax
Cardiac tomogram

87.43   X-ray of ribs, sternum, and clavicle
Examination for:
    cervical rib
    fracture

87.44   Routine chest x-ray, so described
X-ray of chest NOS

87.49   Other chest x-ray
X-ray of:
    bronchus NOS
    diaphragm NOS
    heart NOS
    lung NOS
    mediastinum NOS
    trachea NOS

87.5   Biliary tract x-ray

87.51   Percutaneous hepatic cholangiogram

87.52   Intravenous cholangiogram

87.53   Intraoperative cholangiogram

87.54   Other cholangiogram

87.59   Other biliary tract x-ray
Cholecystogram

87.6   Other x-ray of digestive system

87.61   Barium swallow

87.62   Upper GI series

87.63   Small bowel series

87.64   Lower GI series

87.65   Other x-ray of intestine

87.66   Contrast pancreatogram

87.69   Other digestive tract x-ray

87.7   X-ray of urinary system

> Excludes: *angiography of renal vessels (88.45, 88.65)*

   ● Code new   ▲ Revision of   ④ ⑤ Fourth or fifth
      to this edition   existing code   digit required

87.71 Computerized axial tomography of kidney
C.A.T. scan of kidney

87.72 Other nephrotomogram

87.73 Intravenous pyelogram
Diuretic infusion pyelogram

87.74 Retrograde pyelogram

87.75 Percutaneous pyelogram

87.76 Retrograde cystourethrogram

87.77 Other cystogram

87.78 Ileal conduitogram

87.79 Other x-ray of the urinary system
KUB x-ray

87.8 X-ray of female genital organs

87.81 X-ray of gravid uterus
Intrauterine cephalometry by x-ray

87.82 Gas contrast hysterosalpingogram

87.83 Opaque dye contrast hysterosalpingogram

87.84 Percutaneous hysterogram

87.85 Other x-ray of fallopian tubes and uterus

87.89 Other x-ray of female genital organs

87.9 X-ray of male genital organs

87.91 Contrast seminal vesiculogram

87.92 Other x-ray of prostate and seminal vesicles

87.93 Contrast epididymogram

87.94 Contrast vasogram

87.95 Other x-ray of epididymis and vas deferens

87.99 Other x-ray of male genital organs

88 Other diagnostic radiology and related techniques

88.0 Soft tissue x-ray of abdomen

Excludes:	angiography (88.40-88.68)

88.01 Computerized axial tomography of abdomen
C.A.T. scan of abdomen

Excludes:	C.A.T. scan of kidney (87.71)

88.02 Other abdomen tomography

Excludes:	nephrotomogram (87.72)

88.03 Sinogram of abdominal wall
Fistulogram of abdominal wall

88.04 Abdominal lymphangiogram

88.09 Other soft tissue x-ray of abdominal wall

88.1 Other x-ray of abdomen

88.11 Pelvic opaque dye contrast radiography

88.12 Pelvic gas contrast radiography
Pelvic pneumoperitoneum

88.13 Other peritoneal pneumogram

88.14 Retroperitoneal fistulogram

88.15 Retroperitoneal pneumogram

88.16 Other retroperitoneal x-ray

88.19 Other x-ray of abdomen
Flat plate of abdomen

88.2 Skeletal x-ray of extremities and pelvis

Excludes:	contrast radiogram of joint (88.32)

88.21 Skeletal x-ray of shoulder and upper arm

88.22 Skeletal x-ray of elbow and forearm

88.23 Skeletal x-ray of wrist and hand

	Valid O.R. procedure		Non-O.R. procedure		Nonspecific O.R. procedure		Noncovered O.R. procedure

88.24 Skeletal x-ray of upper limb, not otherwise specified

88.25 Pelvimetry

88.26 Other skeletal x-ray of pelvis and hip

88.27 Skeletal x-ray of thigh, knee, and lower leg

88.28 Skeletal x-ray of ankle and foot

88.29 Skeletal x-ray of lower limb, not otherwise specified

88.3 Other x-ray

88.31 Skeletal series
X-ray of whole skeleton

88.32 Contrast arthrogram
> *Excludes:* *that of temporomandibular joint (87.13)*

88.33 Other skeletal x-ray
> *Excludes:* *skeletal x-ray of:*
> *extremities and pelvis (88.21-88.29)*
> *face, head, and neck (87.11-87.17)*
> *spine (87.21-87.29)*
> *thorax (87.43)*

88.34 Lymphangiogram of upper limb

88.35 Other soft tissue x-ray of upper limb

88.36 Lymphangiogram of lower limb

88.37 Other soft tissue x-ray of lower limb
> *Excludes:* *femoral angiography (88.48, 88.66)*

88.38 Other computerized axial tomography
C.A.T. scan NOS
> *Excludes:* *C.A.T. scan of:*
> *abdomen (88.01)*
> *head (87.03)*
> *kidney (87.71)*
> *thorax (87.41)*

88.39 X-ray, other and unspecified

88.4 Arteriography using contrast material
Includes: angiography of arteries
arterial puncture for injection of contrast material
radiography of arteries (by fluoroscopy)
retrograde arteriography

Note: The fourth-digit subclassification identifies the site to be viewed, not the site of injection.

> *Excludes:* *arteriography using:*
> *radioisotopes or radionuclides (92.01-92.19)*
> *ultrasound (88.71-88.79)*
> *fluorescein angiography of eye (95.12)*

88.40 Arteriography using contrast material, unspecified site

88.41 Arteriography of cerebral arteries
Angiography of:
basilar artery
carotid (internal)
posterior cerebral circulation
vertebral artery

88.42 Aortography
Arteriography of aorta and aortic arch

88.43 Arteriography of pulmonary arteries

88.44 Arteriography of other intrathoracic vessels
> *Excludes:* *angiocardiography (88.50-88.58)*
> *arteriography of coronary arteries (88.55-88.57)*

88.45 Arteriography of renal arteries

88.46 Arteriography of placenta
Placentogram using contrast material

88.47 Arteriography of other intra-abdominal arteries

88.48 Arteriography of femoral and other lower extremity arteries

● Code new
to this edition

▲ Revision of
existing code

④ ⑤ Fourth or fifth
digit required

88.49   **Arteriography of other specified sites**

88.5   **Angiocardiography using contrast material**

    Includes: arterial puncture and insertion of arterial catheter for injection of contrast material
           cineangiocardiography
           selective angiocardiography

Code also synchronous cardiac catheterization (37.21-37.23)

    Excludes: *angiography of pulmonary vessels (88.43, 88.62)*

88.50   **Angiocardiography, not otherwise specified**

88.51   **Angiocardiography of venae cavae**
    Interior vena cavography
    Phlebography of vena cava (inferior) (superior)

88.52   **Angiocardiography of right heart structures**
    Angiocardiography of:
      pulmonary valve
      right atrium
      right ventricle (outflow tract)

    Excludes: *that combined with left heart angiocardiography (88.54)*

88.53   **Angiocardiography of left heart structures**
    Angiocardiography of:
      aortic valve
      left atrium
      left ventricle (outflow tract)

    Excludes: *that combined with right heart angiocardiography (88.54)*

88.54   **Combined right and left heart angiocardiography**

88.55   **Coronary arteriography using a single catheter**
    Coronary arteriography by Sones technique
    Direct selective coronary arteriography using a single catheter

88.56   **Coronary arteriography using two catheters**
    Coronary arteriography by:
      Judkins technique
      Ricketts and Abrams technique
    Direct selective coronary arteriography using two catheters

88.57   **Other and unspecified coronary arteriography**
    Coronary arteriography NOS

88.58   **Negative-contrast cardiac roentgenography**
    Cardiac roentgenography with injection of carbon dioxide

88.6   **Phlebography**

    Includes: angiography of veins
           radiography of veins (by fluoroscopy)
           retrograde phlebography
           venipuncture for injection of contrast material
           venography using contrast material

    Note: The fourth-digit subclassification (88.60-88.67) identifies the site to be viewed, not the site of injection.

    Excludes: *angiography using:*
        radioisotopes or radionuclides (92.01-92.19)
        ultrasound (88.71-88.79)
      fluorescein angiography of eye (95.12)

88.60   **Phlebography using contrast material, unspecified site**

88.61   **Phlebography of veins of head and neck using contrast material**

88.62   **Phlebography of pulmonary veins using contrast material**

88.63   **Phlebography of other intrathoracic veins using contrast material**

88.64   **Phlebography of the portal venous system using contrast material**
    Splenoportogram (by splenic arteriography)

88.65   **Phlebography of other intra-abdominal veins using contrast material**

88.66   **Phlebography of femoral and other lower extremity veins using contrast material**

88.67   **Phlebography of other specified sites using contrast material**

88.68   **Impedance phlebography**

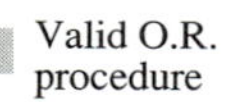
Valid O.R. procedure

Non-O.R. procedure

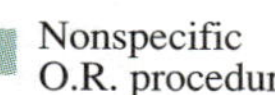
Nonspecific O.R. procedure

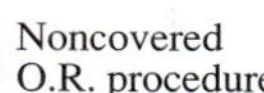
Noncovered O.R. procedure

88.7 **Diagnostic ultrasound**
Includes: echography
ultrasonic angiography
ultrasonography

88.71 **Diagnostic ultrasound of head and neck**
Determination of midline shift of brain
Echoencephalography
|Excludes:| eye (95.13)

88.72 **Diagnostic ultrasound of heart**
Echocardiography
Intravascular ultrasound of heart

88.73 **Diagnostic ultrasound of other sites of thorax**
Aortic arch
Breast   } ultrasonography
Lung

88.74 **Diagnostic ultrasound of digestive system**

88.75 **Diagnostic ultrasound of urinary system**

88.76 **Diagnostic ultrasound of abdomen and retroperitoneum**

88.77 **Diagnostic ultrasound of peripheral vascular system**
Deep vein thrombosis ultrasonic scanning

88.78 **Diagnostic ultrasound of gravid uterus**
Intrauterine cephalometry:
echo
ultrasonic
Placental localization by ultrasound

88.79 **Other diagnostic ultrasound**
Ultrasonography of:
multiple sites
nongravid uterus
total body

88.8   **Thermography**

88.81 **Cerebral thermography**

88.82 **Ocular thermography**

88.83 **Bone thermography**
Osteoarticular thermography

88.84 **Muscle thermography**

88.85 **Breast thermography**

88.86 **Blood vessel thermography**
Deep vein thermography

88.89 **Thermography of other sites**
Lymph gland thermography
Thermography NOS

88.9   **Other diagnostic imaging**

88.90 **Diagnostic imaging, not elsewhere classified**

88.91 **Magnetic resonance imaging of brain and brain stem**

88.92 **Magnetic resonance imaging of chest and myocardium**
For evaluation of hilar and mediastinal lymphadenopathy

88.93 **Magnetic resonance imaging of spinal canal**
Levels:
cervical
lumbar (lumbosacral)
thoracic
Spinal cord
Spine

88.94 **Magnetic resonance imaging of musculoskeletal**
Bone marrow blood supply
Extremities (upper) (lower)

88.95 **Magnetic resonance imaging of pelvis, prostate, and bladder**

88.97 **Magnetic resonance imaging of other and unspecified sites**
abdomen   neck
face   eye orbit

   ● Code new   ▲ Revision of   ④ ⑤ Fourth or fifth
to this edition   existing code   digit required

88.98 **Bone mineral density studies**
Dual photon absorptiometry
Quantitative computed tomography (CT) studies
Radiographic densitometry
Single photon absorptiometry

89 **Interview, evaluation, consultation, and examination**

89.0 **Diagnostic interview, consultation, and evaluation**

    Excludes: *psychiatric diagnostic interview (94.11-94.19)*

89.01 **Interview and evaluation, described as brief**
Abbreviated history and evaluation

89.02 **Interview and evaluation, described as limited**
Interval history and evaluation

89.03 **Interview and evaluation, described as comprehensive**
History and evaluation of new problem

89.04 **Other interview and evaluation**

89.05 **Diagnostic interview and evaluation, not otherwise specified**

89.06 **Consultation, described as limited**
Consultation on a single organ system

89.07 **Consultation, described as comprehensive**

89.08 **Other consultation**

89.09 **Consultation, not otherwise specified**

89.1 **Anatomic and physiologic measurements and manual examinations—nervous system and sense organs**

    Excludes: *ear examination (95.41-95.49)*
           eye examination (95.01-95.26)
           the listed procedures when done as part of a general physical examination (89.7)

89.10 **Intracarotid amobarbital test**
Wada test

89.11 **Tonometry**

89.12 **Nasal function study**
Rhinomanometry

89.13 **Neurologic examination**

89.14 **Electroencephalogram**

    Excludes: *that with polysomnogram (89.17)*

89.15 **Other nonoperative neurologic function tests**

89.16 **Transillumination of newborn skull**

89.17 **Polysomnogram**
Sleep recording

89.18 **Other sleep disorder function tests**
Multiple sloop latency test [MSLT]

89.19 **Video and radio-telemetered electroencephalographic monitoring**
Radiographic
Video   } EEG monitoring

89.2 **Anatomic and physiologic measurements and manual examinations—genitourinary system**

    Excludes: *the listed procedures when done as part of a general physical examination (89.7)*

89.21 **Urinary manometry**
Manometry through:
   indwelling urethral catheter
   nephrostomy
   pyelostomy
   ureterostomy

89.22 **Cystometrogram**

89.23 **Urethral sphincter electromyogram**

89.24 **Uroflowmetry [UFR]**

89.25 **Urethral pressure profile [UPP]**

Valid O.R. procedure   Non-O.R. procedure   Nonspecific O.R. procedure   Noncovered O.R. procedure

89.26 Gynecological examination
Pelvic examination

89.29 Other nonoperative genitourinary system measurements
Bioassay of urine
Renal clearance
Urine chemistry

89.3 Other anatomic and physiologic measurements and manual examinations

> | *Excludes:* | *the listed procedures when done as part of a general physical examination (89.7)*

89.31 Dental examination
Oral mucosal survey
Periodontal survey

89.32 Esophageal manometry

89.33 Digital examination of enterostomy stoma
Digital examination of colostomy stoma

89.34 Digital examination of rectum

89.35 Transillumination of nasal sinuses

89.36 Manual examination of breast

89.37 Vital capacity determination

89.38 Other nonoperative respiratory measurements
Plethysmography for measurement of respiratory function
Thoracic impedance plethysmography

89.39 Other nonoperative measurements and examinations
Basal metabolic rate [BMR]
14 C-Urea breath test
Gastric:
  analysis
  function NEC

> | *Excludes:* | *body measurements (93.07)*
> *cardiac tests (89.41-89.69)*
> *fundus photography (95.11)*
> *limb length measurement (93.06)*

89.4 Cardiac stress tests and pacemaker checks

89.41 Cardiovascular stress test using treadmill

89.42 Masters' two-step stress test

89.43 Cardiovascular stress test using bicycle ergometer

89.44 Other cardiovascular stress test
Thallium stress test with or without transesophageal pacing

89.45 Artificial pacemaker rate check
Artificial pacemaker function check NOS

89.46 Artificial pacemaker artifact wave form check

89.47 Artificial pacemaker electrode impedance check

89.48 Artificial pacemaker voltage or amperage threshold check

89.5 Other nonoperative cardiac and vascular diagnostic procedures

> | *Excludes:* | *fetal EKG (75.32)*

89.50 Ambulatory cardiac monitoring
Analog devices [Holter-type]

89.51 Rhythm electrocardiogram
Rhythm EKG (with one to three leads)

89.52 Electrocardiogram
ECG NOS
EKG (with 12 or more leads)

89.53 Vectorcardiogram (with ECG)

89.54 Electrographic monitoring
Telemetry

> | *Excludes:* | *ambulatory cardiac monitoring (89.50)*
> *electrographic monitoring during surgery—omit code*

89.55 Phonocardiogram with ECG lead

● Code new
to this edition

▲ Revision of
existing code

④ ⑤ Fourth or fifth
digit required

89.56 Carotid pulse tracing with ECG lead
> *Excludes:* oculoplethysmography (89.58)

89.57 Apexcardiogram (with ECG lead)

89.58 Plethysmogram
> *Excludes:* plethysmography (for):
> measurement of respiratory function (89.38)
> thoracic impedance (89.38)

89.59 Other nonoperative cardiac and vascular measurements

89.6 Circulatory monitoring
> *Excludes:* electrocardiographic monitoring during surgery—omit code

89.61 Systemic arterial pressure monitoring

89.62 Central venous pressure monitoring

89.63 Pulmonary artery pressure monitoring
> *Excludes:* pulmonary artery wedge monitoring (89.64)

89.64 Pulmonary artery wedge monitoring
Pulmonary capillary wedge [PCW] monitoring
Swan-Ganz catheterization

89.65 Measurement of systemic arterial blood gases

89.66 Measurement of mixed venous blood gases

89.67 Monitoring of cardiac output by oxygen consumption technique
Fick method

89.68 Monitoring of cardiac output by other technique
Cardiac output monitor by thermodilution indicator

89.69 Monitoring of coronary blood flow
Coronary blood flow monitoring by coincidence counting technique

89.7 General physical examination

89.8 Autopsy

90 Microscopic examination—I
The following fourth-digit subclassification is for use with categories in section 90 to identify type of examination:
> **1 bacterial smear**
> **2 culture**
> **3 culture and sensitivity**
> **4 parasitology**
> **5 toxicology**
> **6 cell block and Papanicolaou smear**
> **9 other microscopic examination**

④ **90.0 Microscopic examination of specimen from nervous system and of spinal fluid**

④ **90.1 Microscopic examination of specimen from endocrine gland, not elsewhere classified**

④ **90.2 Microscopic examination of specimen from eye**

④ **90.3 Microscopic examination of specimen from ear, nose, throat, and larynx**

④ **90.4 Microscopic examination of specimen from trachea, bronchus, pleura, lung, and other thoracic specimen, and of sputum**

④ **90.5 Microscopic examination of blood**

④ **90.6 Microscopic examination of specimen from spleen and of bone marrow**

④ **90.7 Microscopic examination of specimen from lymph node and of lymph**

④ **90.8 Microscopic examination of specimen from upper gastrointestinal tract and of vomitus**

④ **90.9 Microscopic examination of specimen from lower gastrointestinal tract and of stool**

91 Microscopic examination—II
The following fourth-digit subclassification is for use with categories in section 91 to identify type of examination:
> **1 bacterial smear**
> **2 culture**
> **3 culture and sensitivity**
> **4 parasitology**
> **5 toxicology**
> **6 cell block and Papanicolaou smear**
> **9 other microscopic examination**

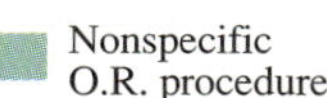
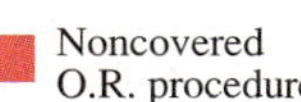

Valid O.R. procedure   Non-O.R. procedure   Nonspecific O.R. procedure   Noncovered O.R. procedure

④ **91.0** **Microscopic examination of specimen from liver, biliary trace and pancreas**

④ **91.1** **Microscopic examination of peritoneal and retroperitoneal specimen**

④ **91.2** **Microscopic examination of specimen from kidney, ureter, perirenal and periureteral tissue**

④ **91.3** **Microscopic examination of specimen from bladder, urethra, prostate, seminal vesicle, perivesical tissue, and of urine and semen**

④ **91.4** **Microscopic examination of specimen from female genital tract**
   Amnionic sac
   Fetus

④ **91.5** **Microscopic examination of specimen from musculoskeletal system and of joint fluid**
   Microscopic examination of:

bone	ligament
bursa	muscle
cartilage	synovial membrane
fascia	tendon

④ **91.6** **Microscopic examination of specimen from skin and other integument**
   Microscopic examination of:
   hair
   nails
   skin

   | Excludes: | mucous membrane—code to organ site that of operative wound (91.70-91.79) |

④ **91.7** **Microscopic examination of specimen from operative wound**

④ **91.8** **Microscopic examination of specimen from other site**

④ **91.9** **Microscopic examination of specimen from unspecified site**

92 **Nuclear Medicine**

 92.0 **Radioisotope scan and function study**

   92.01 **Thyroid scan and radioisotope function studies**
      Iodine-131 uptake
      Protein-bound iodine
      Radio-iodine uptake

   92.02 **Liver scan and radioisotope function study**

   92.03 **Renal scan and radioisotope function study**
      Renal clearance study

   92.04 **Gastrointestinal scan and radioisotope function study**
      Radio-cobalt B_{12} Schilling test
      Radio-iodinated triolein study

   92.05 **Cardiovascular and hematopoietic scan and radioisotope function study**
      Bone marrow
      Cardiac output
      Circulation time   } scan or function study
      Radionuclide cardiac
         ventriculogram
      Spleen

   92.09 **Other radioisotope function studies**

 92.1 **Other radioisotope scan**

   92.11 **Cerebral scan**
      Pituitary

   92.12 **Scan of other sites of head**

   | Excludes: | eye (95.16) |

   92.13 **Parathyroid scan**

   92.14 **Bone scan**

   92.15 **Pulmonary scan**

   92.16 **Scan of lymphatic system**

   92.17 **Placental scan**

   92.18 **Total body scan**

   92.19 **Scan of other sites**

   ● Code new to this edition   ▲ Revision of existing code   ④ ⑤ Fourth or fifth digit required

92.2   Therapeutic radiology and nuclear medicine

> *Excludes:*   *that for:*
> *ablation of pituitary gland (07.64-07.69)*
> *destruction of chorioretinal lesion (14.26-14.27)*

92.21   Superficial radiation
Contact radiation [up to 150 KVP]

92.22   Orthovoltage radiation
Deep radiation [200-300 KVP]

92.23   Radioisotopic teleradiotherapy
Teleradiotherapy using:
    cobalt-60
    iodine-125
    radioactive cesium

92.24   Teleradiotherapy using photons
Megavoltage NOS
Supervoltage NOS
Use of:
    Betatron
    linear accelerator

92.25   Teleradiotherapy using electrons
Beta particles

92.26   Teleradiotherapy of other particulate radiation
Neutrons   Protons NOS

92.27   Implantation or insertion of radioactive elements
Code also incision of site

92.28   Injection or instillation of radioisotopes
Intracavitary
Intravenous   } injection or instillation

92.29   Other radiotherapeutic procedure

92.3   Stereotactic radiosurgery

> *Excludes:*   *stereotactic biopsy*

Code also stereotactic head frame application (93.59)

92.30   Stereotactic radiosurgery, not otherwise specified

92.31   Single source photon radiosurgery
High energy x-rays
Linear accelerator (LINAC)

92.32   Multi-source photon radiosurgery
Cobalt 60 radiation
Gamma irradiation

92.33   Particulate radiosurgery
Particle beam radiation (cyclotron)
Proton accelerator

92.39   Stereotactic radiosurgery, not elsewhere classified

93   Physical therapy, respiratory therapy, rehabilitation, and related procedures

93.0   Diagnostic physical therapy

93.01   Functional evaluation

93.02   Orthotic evaluation

93.03   Prosthetic evaluation

93.04   Manual testing of muscle function

93.05   Range of motion testing

93.06   Measurement of limb length

93.07   Body measurement
Girth measurement
Measurement of skull circumference

93.08   Electromyography

> *Excludes:*   *eye EMG (95.25)*
> *that with polysomnogram (89.17)*
> *urethral sphincter EMG (89.23)*

93.09   Other diagnostic physical therapy procedure

Valid O.R. procedure   Non-O.R. procedure   Nonspecific O.R. procedure   Noncovered O.R. procedure

93.1 Physical therapy exercises

    93.11 Assisting exercise

        Excludes: *assisted exercise in pool (93.31)*

    93.12 Other active musculoskeletal exercise

    93.13 Resistive exercise

    93.14 Training in joint movements

    93.15 Mobilization of spine

    93.16 Mobilization of other joints

        Excludes: *manipulation of temporomandibular joint (76.95)*

    93.17 Other passive musculoskeletal exercise

    93.18 Breathing exercise

    93.19 Exercise, not elsewhere classified

93.2 Other physical therapy musculoskeletal manipulation

    93.21 Manual and mechanical traction

        Excludes: *skeletal traction (93.43-93.44)*
                  skin traction (93.45-93.46)
                  spinal traction (93.41-93.42)

    93.22 Ambulation and gait training

    93.23 Fitting of orthotic device

    93.24 Training in use of prosthetic or orthotic device
        Training in crutch walking

    93.25 Forced extension of limb

    93.26 Manual rupture of joint adhesions

    93.27 Stretching of muscle or tendon

    93.28 Stretching of fascia

    93.29 Other forcible correction of deformity

93.3 Other physical therapy therapeutic procedures

    93.31 Assisted exercise in pool

    93.32 Whirlpool treatment

    93.33 Other hydrotherapy

    93.34 Diathermy

    93.35 Other heat therapy
        Acupuncture with smouldering moxa
        Hot packs
        Hyperthermia NEC
        Infrared irradiation
        Moxibustion
        Paraffin bath

        Excludes: *hyperthermia for treatment of cancer (99.85)*

    93.36 Cardiac retraining

    93.37 Prenatal training
        Training for natural childbirth

    93.38 Combined physical therapy without mention of the components

    93.39 Other physical therapy

93.4 Skeletal traction and other traction

    93.41 Spinal traction using skull device
        Traction using:
          caliper tongs
          Crutchfield tongs
          halo device
          Vinke tongs

        Excludes: *insertion of tongs or halo traction device (02.94)*

    93.42 Other spinal traction
        Cotrel's traction

        Excludes: *cervical collar (93.52)*

    93.43 Intermittent skeletal traction

● Code new to this edition   ▲ Revision of existing code   ④ ⑤ Fourth or fifth digit required

93.44 Other skeletal traction
Bryant's
Dunlop's
Lyman Smith } traction
Russell's

93.45 Thomas' splint traction

93.46 Other skin traction of limbs
Adhesive tape traction
Boot traction
Buck's traction
Gallows traction

93.5 Other immobilization, pressure, and attention to wound

> *Excludes:* *wound cleansing (96.58-96.59)*

93.51 Application of plaster jacket

> *Excludes:* *Minerva jacket (93.52)*

93.52 Application of neck support
Application of:
  cervical collar
  Minerva jacket
  molded neck support

93.53 Application of other cast

93.54 Application of splint
Plaster splint   Tray splint

> *Excludes:* *periodontal splint (24.7)*

93.55 Dental wiring

> *Excludes:* *that for orthodontia (24.7)*

93.56 Application of pressure dressing
Application of:
  Gibney bandage
  Robert Jones' bandage
  Shanz dressing

93.57 Application of other wound dressing

93.58 Application of pressure trousers
Application of:
  anti-shock trousers
  MAST trousers
  vasopneumatic device

93.59 Other immobilization, pressure, and attention to wound
Elastic stockings
Electronic gaiter
Intermittent pressure device
Oxygenation of wound (hyperbaric)
Stereotactic head frame application
Velpeau dressing

93.6 Osteopathic manipulative treatment

93.61 Osteopathic manipulative treatment for general mobilization
General articulatory treatment

93.62 Osteopathic manipulative treatment using high-velocity low-amplitude forces
Thrusting forces

93.63 Osteopathic manipulative treatment using low-velocity high-amplitude forces
Springing forces

93.64 Osteopathic manipulative treatment using isotonic, isometric forces

93.65 Osteopathic manipulative treatment using indirect forces

93.66 Osteopathic manipulative treatment to move tissue fluids
Lymphatic pump

93.67 Other specified osteopathic manipulative treatment

93.7 Speech and reading rehabilitation and rehabilitation of the blind

93.71 Dyslexia training

93.72 Dysphasia training

93.73 Esophageal speech training

Valid O.R. procedure	Non-O.R. procedure	Nonspecific O.R. procedure	Noncovered O.R. procedure

93.74 Speech defect training

93.75 Other speech training and therapy

93.76 Training in use of lead dog for the blind

93.77 Training in braille or Moon

93.78 Other rehabilitation for the blind

93.8 Other rehabilitation therapy

93.81 Recreation therapy
Diversional therapy
Play therapy
| *Excludes:* | *play psychotherapy (94.36)*

93.82 Educational therapy
Education of bed-bound children
Special schooling for the handicapped

93.83 Occupational therapy
Daily living activities therapy
| *Excludes:* | *training in activities of daily living for the blind (93.78)*

93.84 Music therapy

93.85 Vocational rehabilitation
Sheltered employment
Vocational:
    assessment
    retraining
    training

93.89 Rehabilitation, not elsewhere classified

93.9 Respiratory therapy
| *Excludes:* | *insertion of airway (96.01-96.05)*
    other continuous mechanical ventilation (96.70-96.72)

93.90 Continuous positive airway pressure [CPAP]

93.91 Intermittent positive pressure breathing [IPPB]

93.93 Nonmechanical methods of resuscitation
Artificial respiration
Manual resuscitation
Mouth-to-mouth resuscitation

93.94 Respiratory medication administered by nebulizer
Mist therapy

93.95 Hyperbaric oxygenation
| *Excludes:* | *oxygenation of wound (93.59)*

93.96 Other oxygen enrichment
Catalytic oxygen therapy
Cytoreductive effect
Oxygenators
Oxygen therapy
| *Excludes:* | *oxygenation of wound (93.59)*

93.97 Decompression chamber

93.98 Other control of atmospheric pressure and composition
Antigen-free air conditioning
Helium therapy

93.99 Other respiratory procedures
Continuous negative pressure ventilation [CNP]
Postural drainage

94 Procedures related to the psyche

94.0 Psychologic evaluation and testing

94.01 Administration of intelligence test
Administration of:
    Stanford-Binet
    Wechsler Adult Intelligence Scale
    Wechsler Intelligence Scale for Children

  ● Code new
to this edition   ▲ Revision of
existing code   ④ ⑤ Fourth or fifth
digit required

94.02 Administration of psychologic test
Administration of:
Bender Visual - Motor Gestalt Test
Benton Visual Retention Test
Minnesota Multiphasic Personality Inventory
Wechsler Memory Scale

94.03 Character analysis

94.08 Other psychologic evaluation and testing

94.09 Psychologic mental status determination, not otherwise specified

94.1 Psychiatric interviews, consultations, and evaluations

94.11 Psychiatric mental status determination
Clinical psychiatric mental status determination
Evaluation for criminal responsibility
Evaluation for testimentary capacity
Medicolegal mental status determination
Mental status determination NOS

94.12 Routine psychiatric visit, not otherwise specified

94.13 Psychiatric commitment evaluation
Pre-commitment interview

94.19 Other psychiatric interview and evaluation
Follow-up psychiatric interview NOS

94.2 Psychiatric somatotherapy

94.21 Narcoanalysis
Narcosynthesis

94.22 Lithium therapy

94.23 Neuroleptic therapy

94.24 Chemical shock therapy

94.25 Other psychiatric drug therapy

94.26 Subconvulsive electroshock therapy

94.27 Other electroshock therapy
Electroconvulsive therapy (ECT)
EST

94.29 Other psychiatric somatotherapy

94.3 Individual psychotherapy

94.31 Psychoanalysis

94.32 Hypnotherapy
Hypnodrome
Hypnosis

94.33 Behavior therapy
Aversion therapy
Behavior modification
Desensitization therapy
Extinction therapy
Relaxation training
Token economy

94.34 Individual therapy for psychosexual dysfunction

> *Excludes:* *that performed in group setting (94.41)*

94.35 Crisis intervention

94.36 Play psychotherapy

94.37 Exploratory verbal psychotherapy

94.38 Supportive verbal psychotherapy

94.39 Other individual psychotherapy
Biofeedback

94.4 Psychotherapy and counselling

94.41 Group therapy for psychosexual dysfunction

94.42 Family therapy

94.43 Psychodrama

94.44 Other group therapy

94.45 Drug addiction counselling

Valid O.R. procedure   Non-O.R. procedure   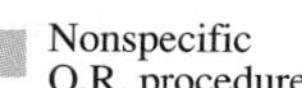 Nonspecific O.R. procedure   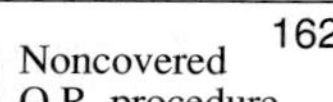 Noncovered O.R. procedure

94.46 **Alcoholism counselling**

94.49 **Other counselling**

94.5 **Referral for psychologic rehabilitation**

94.51 **Referral for psychotherapy**

94.52 **Referral for psychiatric aftercare**
That in:
halfway house
outpatient (clinic) facility

94.53 **Referral for alcoholism rehabilitation**

94.54 **Referral for drug addiction rehabilitation**

94.55 **Referral for vocational rehabilitation**

94.59 **Referral for other psychologic rehabilitation**

94.6 **Alcohol and drug rehabilitation and detoxification**

94.61 **Alcohol rehabilitation**

94.62 **Alcohol detoxification**

94.63 **Alcohol rehabilitation and detoxification**

94.64 **Drug rehabilitation**

94.65 **Drug detoxification**

94.66 **Drug rehabilitation and detoxification**

94.67 **Combined alcohol and drug rehabilitation**

94.68 **Combined alcohol and drug detoxification**

94.69 **Combined alcohol and drug rehabilitation and detoxification**

95 **Ophthalmologic and otologic diagnosis and treatment**

95.0 **General and subjective eye examination**

95.01 **Limited eye examination**
Eye examination with prescription of spectacles

95.02 **Comprehensive eye examination**
Eye examination covering all aspects of the visual system

95.03 **Extended ophthalmologic work-up**
Examination (for):
glaucoma
neuro-ophthalmology
retinal disease

95.04 **Eye examination under anesthesia**
Code also type of examination

95.05 **Visual field study**

95.06 **Color vision study**

95.07 **Dark adaptation study**

95.09 **Eye examination, not otherwise specified**
Vision check NOS

95.1 **Examinations of form and structure of eye**

95.11 **Fundus photography**

95.12 **Fluorescein angiography or angioscopy of eye**

95.13 **Ultrasound study of eye**

95.14 **X-ray study of eye**

95.15 **Ocular motility study**

95.16 **P^{32} and other tracer studies of eye**

95.2 **Objective functional tests of eye**

Excludes: *that with polysomnogram (89.17)*

95.21 **Electroretinogram [ERG]**

95.22 **Electro-oculogram [EOG]**

95.23 **Visual evoked potential [VEP]**

95.24 **Electronystagmogram [ENG]**

95.25 **Electromyogram of eye [EMG]**

95.26 **Tonography, provocative tests, and other glaucoma testing**

● Code new
to this edition

▲ Revision of
existing code

④ ⑤ Fourth or fifth
digit required

95.3 Special vision services

95.31 Fitting and dispensing of spectacles

95.32 Prescription, fitting, and dispensing of contact lens

95.33 Dispensing of other low vision aids

95.34 Ocular prosthetics

95.35 Orthoptic training

95.36 Ophthalmologic counselling and instruction
Counselling in:
adaptation to visual loss
use of low vision aids

95.4 Nonoperative procedures related to hearing

95.41 Audiometry
Békésy 5-tone audiometry
Impedance audiometry
Stapedial reflex response
Subjective audiometry
Tympanogram

95.42 Clinical test of hearing
Tuning fork test
Whispered speech test

95.43 Audiological evaluation
Audiological evaluation by:
Barany noise machine
blindfold test
delayed feedback
masking
Weber lateralization

95.44 Clinical vestibular function tests
Thermal test of vestibular function

95.45 Rotation tests
Barany chair

95.46 Other auditory and vestibular function tests

95.47 Hearing examination, not otherwise specified

95.48 Fitting of hearing aid

> *Excludes:* *implantation of electromagnetic hearing device (20.95)*

95.49 Other nonoperative procedures related to hearing
Adjustment (external components) of cochlear prosthetic device

96 Nonoperative intubation and irrigation

96.0 Nonoperative intubation of gastrointestinal and respiratory tracts

96.01 Insertion of nasopharyngeal airway

96.02 Insertion of oropharyngeal airway

96.03 Insertion of esophageal obturator airway

96.04 Insertion of endotracheal tube

96.05 Other intubation of respiratory tract

96.06 Insertion of Sengstaken tube
Esophageal tamponade

96.07 Insertion of other (naso-)gastric tube
Intubation for decompression

> *Excludes:* *that for enteral infusion of nutritional substances (96.6)*

96.08 Insertion of (naso-)intestinal tube
Miller-Abbott tube (for decompression)

96.09 Insertion of rectal tube
Replacement of rectal tube

96.1 Other nonoperative insertion

> *Excludes:* *nasolacrimal intubation (09.44)*

96.11 Packing of external auditory canal

96.14 Vaginal packing

96.15 Insertion of vaginal mold

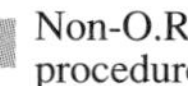
Valid O.R.
procedure

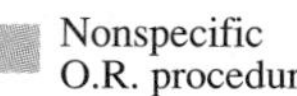
Non-O.R.
procedure

Nonspecific
O.R. procedure

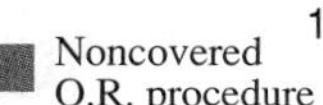
Noncovered
O.R. procedure

96.16 Other vaginal dilation

96.17 Insertion of vaginal diaphragm

96.18 Insertion of other vaginal pessary

96.19 Rectal packing

96.2 Nonoperative dilation and manipulation

96.21 Dilation of frontonasal duct

96.22 Dilation of rectum

96.23 Dilation of anal sphincter

96.24 Dilation and manipulation of enterostomy stoma

96.25 Therapeutic distention of bladder
Intermittent distention of bladder

96.26 Manual reduction of rectal prolapse

96.27 Manual reduction of hernia

96.28 Manual reduction of enterostomy prolapse

96.29 Reduction with intussusception of alimentary tract
With:
Fluoroscopy
Ionizing radiation enema
Ultrasonography guidance
Hydrostatic reduction
Pneumantic reduction

> *Excludes:* *intra-abdominal manipulation of intestine, not otherwise specified (46.80)*

96.3 Nonoperative alimentary tract irrigation, cleaning, and local instillation

96.31 Gastric cooling
Gastric hypothermia

96.32 Gastric freezing

96.33 Gastric lavage

96.34 Other irrigation of (naso-)gastric tube

96.35 Gastric gavage

96.36 Irrigation of gastrostomy or enterostomy

96.37 Proctoclysis

96.38 Removal of impacted feces
Removal of impaction:
by flushing
manually

96.39 Other transanal enema
Rectal irrigation

> *Excludes:* *reduction of intussusception of alimentary tract by ionizing radiation enema (96.29)*

96.4 Nonoperative irrigation, cleaning, and local instillation of other digestive and genitourinary organs

96.41 Irrigation of cholecystostomy and other biliary tube

96.42 Irrigation of pancreatic tube

96.43 Digestive tract instillation, except gastric gavage

96.44 Vaginal douche

96.45 Irrigation of nephrostomy and pyelostomy

96.46 Irrigation of ureterostomy and ureteral catheter

96.47 Irrigation of cystostomy

96.48 Irrigation of other indwelling urinary catheter

96.49 Other genitourinary instillation
Insertion of prostaglandin suppository

96.5 Other nonoperative irrigation and cleaning

96.51 Irrigation of eye
Irrigation of cornea

> *Excludes:* *irrigation with removal of foreign body (98.21)*

  ● Code new to this edition   ▲ Revision of existing code   ④ ⑤ Fourth or fifth digit required

96.52 Irrigation of ear
Irrigation with removal of cerumen

96.53 Irrigation of nasal passages

96.54 Dental scaling, polishing, and debridement
Dental prophylaxis
Plaque removal

96.55 Tracheostomy toilette

96.56 Other lavage of bronchus and trachea

96.57 Irrigation of vascular catheter

96.58 Irrigation of wound catheter

96.59 Other irrigation of wound
Wound cleaning NOS

> Excludes: *debridement (86.22, 86.27-86.28)*

96.6 Enteral infusion of concentrated nutritional substances

96.7 Other continuous mechanical ventilation
Includes: Endotracheal respiratory assistance
Intermittent mandatory ventilation [IMV]
Positive end expiratory pressure [PEEP]
Pressure support ventilation [PSV]
That by tracheostomy
Weaning of an intubated (endotracheal tube) patient

> Excludes: *bi-level airway pressure (93.90)*
> *continuous negative pressure ventilation [CNP] (iron lung) (cuirass) (93.99)*
> *continuous positive airway pressure [CPAP] (93.90)*
> *intermittent positive pressure breathing [IPPB] (93.91)*
> *that by face mask (93.90-93.99)*
> *that by nasal cannula (93.90-93.99)*
> *that by nasal catheter (93.90-93.99)*

Code also any associated:
endotracheal tube insertion (96.04)
tracheostomy (31.1-31.29)

Note: Endotracheal Intubation
To calculate the number of hours (duration) of continuous mechanical ventilation during a hospitalization, begin the count from the start of the (endotracheal) intubation. The duration ends with (endotracheal) extubation.

If the patient is intubated prior to admission, begin counting the duration from the time of admission. If a patient is transferred (discharged) while intubated, the duration would end at the time of transfer (discharge).

For patients who begin on (endotracheal) intubation and subsequently have a tracheostomy performed for mechanical ventilation, the duration begins with the (endotracheal) intubation and ends when the mechanical ventilation is turned off (after the weaning period).

Tracheostomy
To calculate the number of hours of continuous mechanical ventilation during a hospitalization, begin counting the duration when mechanical ventilation is started. The duration ends when the mechanical ventilator is turned off (after the weaning period).

If a patient has received a tracheostomy prior to admission and is on mechanical ventilation at the time of admission, begin counting the duration from the time of admission. If a patient is transferred (discharged) while still on mechanical ventilation via tracheostomy, the duration would end at the time of the transfer (discharge).

96.70 Continuous mechanical ventilation of unspecified duration
Mechanical ventilation NOS

96.71 Continuous mechanical ventilation for less than 96 consecutive hours

96.72 Continuous mechanical ventilation for 96 consecutive hours or more

97 Replacement and removal of therapeutic appliances

97.0 Nonoperative replacement of gastrointestinal appliance

97.01 Replacement of (naso-)gastric or esophagostomy tube

97.02 Replacement of gastrostomy tube

97.03 Replacement of tube or enterostomy device of small intestine

97.04 Replacement of tube or enterostomy device of large intestine

 Valid O.R. procedure

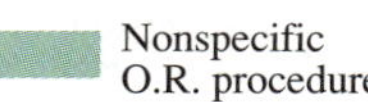 Nonspecific O.R. procedure

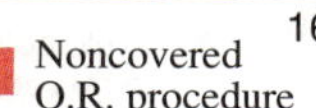 Noncovered O.R. procedure

Non-O.R. procedure

97.05 Replacement of stent (tube) in biliary or pancreatic duct

97.1 Nonoperative replacement of musculoskeletal and integumentary system appliance

97.11 Replacement of cast on upper limb

97.12 Replacement of cast on lower limb

97.13 Replacement of other cast

97.14 Replacement of other device for musculoskeletal immobilization

97.15 Replacement of wound catheter

97.16 Replacement of wound packing or drain

> *Excludes:* *repacking of:*
> *dental wound (97.22)*
> *vulvar wound (97.26)*

97.2 Other nonoperative replacement

97.21 Replacement of nasal packing

97.22 Replacement of dental packing

97.23 Replacement of tracheostomy tube

97.24 Replacement and refitting of vaginal diaphragm

97.25 Replacement of other vaginal pessary

97.26 Replacement of vaginal or vulvar packing or drain

97.29 Other nonoperative replacements

97.3 Nonoperative removal of therapeutic device from head and neck

97.31 Removal of eye prosthesis

> *Excludes:* *removal of ocular implant (16.71)*
> *removal of orbital implant (16.72)*

97.32 Removal of nasal packing

97.33 Removal of dental wiring

97.34 Removal of dental packing

97.35 Removal of dental prosthesis

97.36 Removal of other external mandibular fixation device

97.37 Removal of tracheostomy tube

97.38 Removal of sutures from head and neck

97.39 Removal of other therapeutic device from head and neck

> *Excludes:* *removal of skull tongs (02.94)*

97.4 Nonoperative removal of therapeutic device from thorax

97.41 Removal of thoracotomy tube or pleural cavity drain

97.42 Removal of mediastinal drain

97.43 Removal of sutures from thorax

97.49 Removal of other device from thorax

97.5 Nonoperative removal of therapeutic device from digestive system

97.51 Removal of gastrostomy tube

97.52 Removal of tube from small intestine

97.53 Removal of tube from large intestine or appendix

97.54 Removal of cholecystostomy tube

97.55 Removal of T-tube, other bile duct tube, or liver tube

97.56 Removal of pancreatic tube or drain

97.59 Removal of other device from digestive system
Removal of rectal packing

97.6 Nonoperative removal of therapeutic device from urinary system

97.61 Removal of pyelostomy and nephrostomy tube

97.62 Removal of ureterostomy tube and ureteral catheter

97.63 Removal of cystostomy tube

97.64 Removal of other urinary drainage device
Removal of indwelling urinary catheter

97.65 Removal of urethral stent

● Code new
to this edition   ▲ Revision of
existing code   ④ ⑤ Fourth or fifth
digit required

97.69 Removal of other device from urinary system

97.7 **Nonoperative removal of therapeutic device from genital system**

97.71 Removal of intrauterine contraceptive device

97.72 Removal of intrauterine pack

97.73 Removal of vaginal diaphragm

97.74 Removal of other vaginal pessary

97.75 Removal of vaginal or vulva packing

97.79 Removal of other device from genital tract
Removal of sutures

97.8 **Other nonoperative removal of therapeutic device**

97.81 Removal of retroperitoneal drainage device

97.82 Removal of peritoneal drainage device

97.83 Removal of abdominal wall sutures

97.84 Removal of sutures from trunk, not elsewhere classified

97.85 Removal of packing from trunk, not elsewhere classified

97.86 Removal of other device from abdomen

97.87 Removal of other device from trunk

97.88 Removal of external immobilization device
Removal of:
brace
cast
splint

97.89 Removal of other therapeutic device

98 **Nonoperative removal of foreign body or calculus**

98.0 **Removal of intraluminal foreign body from digestive system without incision**

| Excludes: | *removal of therapeutic device (97.51-97.59)* |

98.01 Removal of intraluminal foreign body from mouth without incision

98.02 Removal of intraluminal foreign body from esophagus without incision

98.03 Removal of intraluminal foreign body from stomach and small intestine without incision

98.04 Removal of intraluminal foreign body from large intestine without incision

98.05 Removal of intraluminal foreign body from rectum and anus without incision

98.1 **Removal of intraluminal foreign body from other sites without incision**

| Excludes: | *removal of therapeutic device (97.31-97.49, 97.61-97.89)* |

98.11 Removal of intraluminal foreign body from ear without incision

98.12 Removal of intraluminal foreign body from nose without incision

98.13 Removal of intraluminal foreign body from pharynx without incision

98.14 Removal of intraluminal foreign body from larynx without incision

98.15 Removal of intraluminal foreign body from trachea and bronchus without incision

98.16 Removal of intraluminal foreign body from uterus without incision

| Excludes: | *removal of intrauterine contraceptive device (97.71)* |

98.17 Removal of intraluminal foreign body from vagina without incision

98.18 Removal of intraluminal foreign body from artificial stoma without incision

98.19 Removal of intraluminal foreign body from urethra without incision

98.2 **Removal of other foreign body without incision**

| Excludes: | *removal of intraluminal foreign body (98.01-98.19)* |

98.20 Removal of foreign body, not otherwise specified

98.21 Removal of superficial foreign body from eye without incision

98.22 Removal of other foreign body without incision from head and neck
Removal of embedded foreign body from eyelid or conjunctiva without incision

98.23 Removal of foreign body from vulva without incision

98.24 Removal of foreign body from scrotum or penis without incision

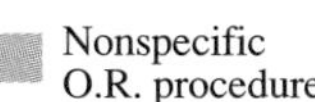

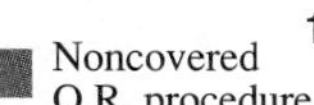

98.25 Removal of other foreign body without incision from trunk except scrotum, penis, or vulva

98.26 Removal of foreign body from hand without incision

98.27 Removal of foreign body without incision from upper limb, except hand

98.28 Removal of foreign body from foot without incision

98.29 Removal of foreign body without incision from lower limb, except foot

98.5 **Extracorporeal shockwave lithotripsy [ESWL]**
Lithotriptor tank procedure
Disintegration of stones by extracorporeal induced shockwaves
That with insertion of stent

98.51 Extracorporeal shockwave lithotripsy [ESWL] of the kidney, ureter and/or bladder

98.52 Extracorporeal shockwave lithotripsy [ESWL] of the gallbladder and/or bile duct

98.59 Extracorporeal shockwave lithotripsy of other sites

99 Other nonoperative procedures

99.0 **Transfusion of blood and blood components**
Use additional code for that done via catheter or cutdown (38.92-38.94)

99.00 **Perioperative autologous transfusion of whole blood or blood components**
Intraoperative blood collection
Postoperative blood collection
Salvage

99.01 **Exchange transfusion**
Transfusion:
exsanguination
replacement

99.02 **Transfusion of previously collected autologous blood**
Blood component

99.03 **Other transfusion of whole blood**
Transfusion:
NOS
blood NOS
hemodilution

99.04 **Transfusion of packed cells**

99.05 **Transfusion of platelets**
Transfusion of thrombocytes

99.06 **Transfusion of coagulation factors**
Transfusion of antihemophilic factor

99.07 **Transfusion of other serum**
Transfusion of plasma

> *Excludes:* injection [transfusion] of:
> antivenin (99.16)
> gamma globulin (99.14)

99.08 **Transfusion of blood expander**
Transfusion of Dextran

99.09 **Transfusion of other substance**
Transfusion of:
blood surrogate
granulocytes

> *Excludes:* transplantation [transfusion] of bone marrow (41.0)

99.1 **Injection or Infusion of therapeutic or prophylactic substance**
Includes: injection or infusion given:
hypodermically
intramuscularly   } acting locally or systemically
intravenously

● Code new to this edition   ▲ Revision of existing code   ④ ⑤ Fourth or fifth digit required

99.10 Injection or infusion of thromboblytic agent
Streptokinase
Tissue plasminogen activator (TPA)
Urokinase

> *Excludes:*   *aspirin—omit code*
> *GP IIB/IIIa platelet inhibitors (99.20)*
> *heparin (99.19)*
> *single vessel percutaneous transluminal coronary angioplasty [PTCA]*
> *or coronary atherectomy with mention of thrombolytic agent*
> *(36.02)*
> *warfarin—omit code*

99.11 Injection of Rh immune globulin
Injection of:
Anti-D (Rhesus) globulin
RhoGAM

99.12 Immunization for allergy
Desensitization

99.13 Immunization for autoimmune disease

99.14 Injection of gamma globulin
Injection of immune sera

99.15 Parenteral infusion of concentrated nutritional substances
Hyperalimentation
Peripheral parenteral nutrition [PPN]
Total parenteral nutrition [TPN)

99.16 Injection of antidote
Injection of:
antivenin
heavy metal antagonist

99.17 Injection of insulin

99.18 Injection or infusion of electrolytes

99.19 Injection of anticoagulant

99.2   Injection or infusion of other therapeutic or prophylactic substance
Includes: injection or infusion given:
hypodermically
intramuscularly   } acting locally or systemically
intravenously

Use additional code for:
injection (into):
breast (85.92)
bursa (82.94, 83.96)
intraperitoneal (cavity) (54.97)
intrathecal (03.92)
joint (76.96, 81.92)
kidney (55.96)
liver (50.94)
orbit (16.91)
other sites—see Alphabetic Index
perfusion:
NOS (39.97)
intestine (46.95, 46.96)
kidney (55.95)
liver (50.93)
total body (39.96)

99.20 Injection or infusion of platelet inhibitor
Glycoprotein IIB/IIIa inhibitor
GP IIB/IIIa inhibitor
GP IIB-IIIa inhibitor

> *Excludes:*   *infusion of heparin (99.19)*
> *injection or infusion of thrombolytic agent (99.10)*

99.21 Injection of antibiotic

99.22 Injection of other anti-infective

99.23 Injection of steroid
Injection of cortisone
Subdermal implantation of progesterone

99.24 Injection of other hormone

	Valid O.R. procedure		Non-O.R. procedure		Nonspecific O.R. procedure		Noncovered O.R. procedure

99.25 Injection or infusion of cancer chemotherapeutic substance
Chemoembolization
Injection or infusion of antineoplastic agent

> | *Excludes:* | *immunotherapy, antineoplastic (99.28)* |
> | | *injection or infusion of biological response modifier [BRM] as an* |
> | | *antineoplastic agent (99.28)* |
> | | *injection of radioisotopes (92.28)* |

99.26 Injection of tranquilizer

99.27 Iontophoresis

99.28 Injection or infusion of biological response modifier [BRM] as an antineoplastic agent
Immunotherapy, antineoplastic
Tumor vaccine

99.29 Injection or infusion of other therapeutic or prophylactic substance

> | *Excludes:* | *administration of neuroprotective agent (99.75)* |
> | | *immunization (99.31-99.59)* |
> | | *injection of sclerosing agent into:* |
> | | *esophageal varices (42.33)* |
> | | *hemorrhoids (49.42)* |
> | | *veins (39.92)* |
> | | *injection or infusion of platelet inhibitor (99.20)* |
> | | *injection or infusion of thrombolytic agent (99.10)* |

99.3 Prophylactic vaccination and inoculation against certain bacterial diseases

99.31 Vaccination against cholera

99.32 Vaccination against typhoid and paratyphoid fever
Administration of TAB vaccine

99.33 Vaccination against tuberculosis
Administration of BCG vaccine

99.34 Vaccination against plague

99.35 Vaccination against tularemia

99.36 Administration of diphtheria toxoid

> | *Excludes:* | *administration of:* |
> | | *diphtheria antitoxin (99.58)* |
> | | *diphtheria-tetanus-pertussis combined (99.39)* |

99.37 Vaccination against pertussis

> | *Excludes:* | *administration of diphtheria-tetanus-pertussis, combined (99.39)* |

99.38 Administration of tetanus toxoid

> | *Excludes:* | *administration of:* |
> | | *diphtheria-tetanus-pertussis combined (99.39)* |
> | | *tetanus antitoxin (99.56)* |

99.39 Administration of diphtheria-tetanus-pertussis, combined

99.4 Prophylactic vaccination and inoculation against certain viral diseases

99.41 Administration of poliomyelitis vaccine

99.42 Vaccination against smallpox

99.43 Vaccination against yellow fever

99.44 Vaccination against rabies

99.45 Vaccination against measles

> | *Excludes:* | *administration of measles-mumps-rubella vaccine (99.48)* |

99.46 Vaccination against mumps

> | *Excludes:* | *administration of measles-mumps-rubella vaccine (99.48)* |

99.47 Vaccination against rubella

> | *Excludes:* | *administration of measles-mumps-rubella vaccine (99.48)* |

99.48 Administration of measles-mumps-rubella vaccine

99.5 Other vaccination and inoculation

99.51 Prophylactic vaccination against the common cold

99.52 Prophylactic vaccination against influenza

99.53 Prophylactic vaccination against arthropod-borne viral encephalitis

● Code new to this edition   ▲ Revision of existing code   ④ ⑤ Fourth or fifth digit required

99.54   **Prophylactic vaccination against other arthropod-borne viral diseases**

99.55   **Prophylactic administration of vaccine against other disease**
Vaccination against:
  anthrax
  brucellosis
  Rocky Mountain spotted fever
  Staphylococcus
  Streptococcus
  typhus

99.56   **Administration of tetanus antitoxin**

99.57   **Administration of botulism antitoxin**

99.58   **Administration of other antitoxins**
Administration of:
  diphtheria antitoxin
  gas gangrene antitoxin
  scarlet fever antitoxin

99.59   **Other vaccination and inoculation**
Vaccination NOS

> | *Excludes:* | *injection of:*
> *gamma globulin (99.14)*
> *Rh immune globulin (99.11)*
> *immunization for:*
> *allergy (99.12)*
> *autoimmune disease (99.13)*

99.6   **Conversion of cardiac rhythm**

> | *Excludes:* | *open chest cardiac:*
> *electric stimulation (37.91)*
> *massage (37.91)*

99.60   **Cardiopulmonary resuscitation, not otherwise specified**

99.61   **Atrial cardioversion**

99.62   **Other electric countershock of heart**
Cardioversion:
  NOS
  external
Conversion to sinus rhythm
Defibrillation
External electrode stimulation

99.63   **Closed chest cardiac massage**
Cardiac massage NOS
Manual external cardiac massage

99.64   **Carotid sinus stimulation**

99.69   **Other conversion of cardiac rhythm**

▲ **99.7**   **Therapeutic apheresis or other injection, administration, or infusion of other therapeutic or prophylactic substance**

99.71   **Therapeutic plasmapheresis**

99.72   **Therapeutic leukopheresis**
Therapeutic leukocytapheresis

99.73   **Therapeutic erythrocytapheresis**
Therapeutic erythropheresis

99.74   **Therapeutic plateletpheresis**

● **99.75**   **Administration of neuroprotective agent**

99.79   **Other**
Apheresis (harvest) of stem cells

99.8   **Miscellaneous physical procedures**

99.81   **Hypothermia (central) (local)**

> | *Excludes:* | *gastric cooling (96.31)*
> *gastric freezing (96.32)*
> *that incidental to open heart surgery (39.62)*

99.82   **Ultraviolet light therapy**
Actinotherapy

99.83 Other phototherapy
Phototherapy of the newborn

> | *Excludes:* | *extracorporeal photochemotherapy (99.88)*
> *photocoagulation of retinal lesion (14.23-14.25, 14.33-14.35,*
> *14.53-14.55)*

99.84 Isolation
Isolation after contact with infectious disease
Protection of individual from his surroundings
Protection of surroundings from individual

99.85 Hyperthermia for treatment of cancer
Hyperthermia (adjunct therapy) induced by microwave, ultrasound, low energy
radiofrequency, probes (interstitial), or other means in the treatment of cancer

Code also any concurrent chemotherapy or radiation therapy

99.86 Non-invasive placement of bone growth stimulator
Transcutaneous (surface) placement of pads or patches for stimulation to aid bone
healing

> | *Excludes:* | *insertion of invasive or semi-invasive bone growth stimulators (device)*
> *(percutaneous electrodes) (78.90-78.99)*

99.88 Therapeutic photopheresis
Extracorporeal photochemotherapy
Extracorporeal photopheresis

> | *Excludes:* | *other phototherapy (99.83)*
> *ultraviolet light therapy (99.82)*

99.9 Other miscellaneous procedures

99.91 Acupuncture for anesthesia

99.92 Other acupuncture

> | *Excludes:* | *that with smouldering moxa (93.35)*

99.93 Rectal massage (for levator spasm)

99.94 Prostatic massage

99.95 Stretching of foreskin

99.96 Collection of sperm for artificial insemination

99.97 Fitting of denture

99.98 Extraction of milk from lactating breast

99.99 Other

● Code new
to this edition

▲ Revision of
existing code

④ ⑤ Fourth or fifth
digit required

A

Abbe operation
construction of vagina 70.61
intestinal anastomosis—*see* Anastomosis intestine
Abciximab, infusion 99.20
Abdominocentesis 54.91
Abdominohysterectomy 68.4
Abdominoplasty 86.83
Abdominoscopy 54.21
Abdominouterotomy 68.0
obstetrical 74.99
Abduction, arytenoid 31.69
Ablation
biliary ducts (lesion) by ERCP 51.64
endometrial (hysteroscopic) 68.23
inner ear (cryosurgery) (ultrasound) 20.79
by injection 20.72
lesion
esophagus 42.39
endoscopic 42.33
heart (ventricular) 37.33
by cardiac catheter 37.34
intestine
large 45.49
endoscopic 45.43
large intestine 45.49
endoscopic 45.43
pituitary 07.69
by
Cobalt-60 92.32
implantation (strontium-yttrium) (Y) NEC
07.68
transfrontal approach 07.64
transphenoidal approach 07.65
proton beam (Bragg peak) 92.33
prostate
by
cryoablation 60.62
laser, transurethral 60.21
radical cryosurgical ablation (RCSA) 60.62
radiofrequency thermotherapy 60.97
transurethral needle ablation (TUNA) 60.97
Abortion, therapeutic 69.51
by
aspiration curettage 69.51
dilation and curettage 69.01
hysterectomy—*see* Hysterectomy
hysterotomy 74.91
insertion
laminaria 69.93
prostaglandin suppository 96.49
intra-amniotic injection (saline) 75.0
Abrasion
corneal epithelium 11.41
for smear or culture 11.21
epicardial surface 36.39
pleural 34.6
skin 86.25
Abscission, cornea 11.49
Absorptiometry
photon (dual) (single) 88.98
Aburel operation (intra-amniotic injection for abortion) 75.0
Accouchement forcé 73.99
Acetabulectomy 77.85
Acetabuloplasty NEC 81.40
with prosthetic implant 81.52
Achillorrhaphy 83.64
delayed 83.62

Achillotenotomy 83.11
plastic 83.85
Achillotomy 83.11
plastic 83.85
Acid peel, skin 86.24
Acromionectomy 77.81
Acromioplasty 81.83
for recurrent dislocation of shoulder 81.82
partial replacement 81.81
total replacement 81.80
Actinotherapy 99.82
Activities of daily living (ADL)
therapy 93.83
training for the blind 93.78
Acupuncture 99.92
with smouldering moxa 93.35
for anesthesia 99.91
Adams operation
advancement of round ligament 69.22
crushing of nasal septum 21.88
excision of palmar fascia 82.35
Adenectomy —*see also* Excision, by site
prostate NEC 60.69
retropubic 60.4
Adenoidectomy (without tonsillectomy) 28.6
with tonsillectomy 28.3
Adhesiolysis —*see also* Lysis, adhesions
for collapse of lung 33.39
middle ear 20.23
Adipectomy 86.83
Adjustment
cardiac pacemaker program
(reprogramming)—*omit code*
cochlear prosthetic device (external components) 95.49
dental 99.97
occlusal 24.8
spectacles 95.31
Administration (of)—*see also* Injection
antitoxins NEC 99.58
botulism 99.57
diphtheria 99.58
gas gangrene 99.58
scarlet fever 99.58
tetanus 99.56
Bender Visual-Motor Gestalt test 94.02
Benton Visual Retention test 94.02.
intelligence test or scale (Stanford-Binet)
(Wechsler) (adult) (children) 94.01
Minnesota Multiphasic Personality Inventory
(MMPI) 94.02
MMPI (Minnesota Multiphasic Personality
Inventory) 94.02
neuroprotective agent 99.75
psychologic test 94.02
Stanford-Binet test 94.01
toxoid
diphtheria 99.36
with tetanus and pertussis, combined (DTP)
99.39
tetanus 99.38
with diphtheria and pertussis, combined
(DTP) 99.39
vaccine—*see also* Vaccination
BCG 99.33
measles-mumps-rubella (MMR) 99.48
poliomyelitis 99.41
TAB 99.32

Amputation—*continued*
  penis (circle) (complete) (flap) (partial) (radical)
    64.3
  Pirogoff's (ankle amputation through malleoli
    of tibia and fibula) 84.14
  ray
    finger 84.01
    foot 84.11
    toe (metatarsal head) 84.11
  root (tooth) (apex) 23.73
    with root canal therapy 23.72
  shoulder (disarticulation) 84.08
  Sorondo-Ferré (hindquarter) 84.19
  S.P. Rogers (knee disarticulation) 84.16
  supracondylar, above-knee 84.17
  supramalleolar, foot 84.14
  Syme's (ankle amputation through malleoli of
    tibia and fibula) 84.14
  thigh 84.17
  thumb 84.02
  toe (through metatarsophalangeal joint) 84.11
  transcarpal 84.03
  transmetatarsal 84.12
  upper limb NEC (*see also* Amputation, arm)
    84.00
  wrist (disarticulation) 84.04
Amygdalohippocampotomy 01.39
Amygdalotomy 01.39
Analysis
  character 94.03
  gastric 89.39
  psychologic 94.31
  transactional
    group 94.44
    individual 94.39
Anastomosis
  abdominal artery to coronary artery 36.17
  accessory-facial nerve 04.72
  accessory-hypoglossal nerve 04.73
  anus (with formation of endorectal ileal pouch)
    45.95
  aorta (descending)—pulmonary (artery) 39.0
  aorta-renal artery 39.24
  aorta-subclavian artery 39.22
  aortoceliac 39.26
  aorto(ilio)femoral 39.25
  aortomesenteric 39.26
  appendix 47.99
  arteriovenous NEC 39.29
    for renal dialysis 39.27
  artery (suture of distal to proximal end) 39.31
    with
      bypass graft 39.29
        extracranial-intracranial [EC-IC] 39.28
      excision or resection of vessel—*see*
        Arteriectomy, with anastomosis, by site
      revision 39.49
  bile ducts 51.39
  bladder NEC 57.88
    with
      isolated segment of intestine 57.87 *[45.50]*
        colon (sigmoid) 57.87 *[45.52]*
        ileum 57.87 *[45.51]*
        open loop of ileum 57.87 *[45.51]*
      to intestine 57.88
        ileum 57.87 *[45.51]*
  bowel—(*see also* Anastomosis, intestine) 45.90
  bronchotracheal 33.48
  bronchus 33.48
  carotid-subclavian artery 39.22
  caval-mesenteric vein 39.1

Anastomosis—*continued*
  caval-pulmonary artery 39.21
  cervicoesophageal 42.59
  colohypopharyngeal (intrathoracic) 42.55
    antesternal or antethoracic 42.65
  common bile duct 51.39
  common pulmonary trunk and left atrium
    (posterior wall) 35.82
  cystic bile duct 51.39
  cystocolic 57.88
  epididymis to vas deferens 63.83
  esophagocolic (intrathoracic) NEC 42.56
    with interposition 42.55
    antesternal or antethoracic NEC 42.66
      with interposition 42.65
  esophagocologastric (intrathoracic) 42.55
    antesternal or antethoracic 42.65
  esophagoduodenal (intrathoracic) NEC 42.54
    with interposition 42.53
  esophagoenteric (intrathoracic) NEC *see also*
    Anastomosis, esophagus to intestinal
    segment) 42.54
    antesternal or antethoracic NEC (*see also*
      Anastomosis, esophagus, antesternal, to
      intestinal segment) 42.64
  esophagoesophageal (intrathoracic) 42.51
    antesternal or antethoracic 42.61
  esophagogastric (intrathoracic) 42.52
    antesternal or antethoracic 42.62
  esophagus (intrapleural) (intrathoracic)
    (retrosternal) NEC 42.59
    with
      gastrectomy (partial) 43.5
        complete or total 43.99
      interposition (of) NEC 42.58
        colon 42.55
        jejunum 42.53
        small bowel 42.53
    antesternal or antethoracic NEC 42.69
      with
        interposition (of) NEC 42.68
          colon 42.65
          jejunal loop 42.63
          small bowel 42.63
        rubber tube 42.68
    to intestinal segment NEC 42.64
      with interposition 42.68
      colon NEC 42.66
        with interposition 42.65
      small bowel NEC 42.64
        with interposition 42.63
    to intestinal segment (intrathoracic) NEC
      42.54
      with interposition 42.58
      antesternal or antethoracic NEC 42.64
        with interposition 42.68
      colon (intrathoracic) NEC 42.56
        with interposition 42.55
        antesternal or antethoracic 42.66
          with interposition 42.65
      small bowel NEC 42.54
        with interposition 42.53
        antesternal or antethoracic 42.64
          with interposition 42.63
  facial-accessory nerve 04.72
  facial-hypoglossal nerve 04.71
  fallopian tube 66.73
    by reanastomosis 66.79
  gallbladder 51.35
    to
      hepatic ducts 51.31

B

Bacterial smear —*see* Examination, microscopic
Baffes operation (interatrial transposition of
venous return) 35.91
Baffle, atrial or interatrial 35.91
Balanoplasty 64.49
Baldy-Webster operation (uterine suspension)
69.22
Ballistocardiography 89.59
Balloon
angioplasty—*see* Angioplasty, balloon
dilation of pylorus 44.22
pump, intra-aortic 37.61
systostomy (atrial) 35.41
valvuloplasty, percutaneous 35.96
Ball operation
herniorrhaphy—*see* Repair, hernia, inguinal
undercutting 49.02
Bandage 93.57
elastic 93.56
Banding, pulmonary artery 38.85
Bankhart operation (capsular repair into
glenoid, for shoulder dislocation) 81.82
Bardenheurer operation (ligation of innominate
artery) 38.85
Barium swallow 87.61
Barkan operation (goniotomy) 12.52
with goniopuncture 12.53
Barr operation (transfer of tibialis posterior
tendon) 83.75
Barsky operation (closure of cleft hand) 82.82
Basal metabolic rate 89.39
Basiotripsy 73.8
Bassett operation (vulvectomy with inguinal
lymph node dissection) 71.5 *[40.3]*
Bassini operation —*see* Repair, hernia, inguinal
Batch-Spittler-McFaddin operation (knee
disarticulation) 84.16
Batista operation (partial ventriculectomy)
(ventricular reduction) (ventricular
remodeling) 37.35
Beck operation
aorta-coronary sinus shunt 36.39
epicardial poudrage 36.39
Beck-Jianu operation (permanent gastrostomy)
43.19
Behavior modification 94.33
Bell-Beuttner operation (subtotal abdominal
hysterectomy) 68.3
Belsey operation (esophagogastric sphincter)
44.65
Benenenti operation (rotation of bulbous
urethra) 58.49
Berke operation (levator resection of eyelid)
08.33
Bicuspidization of heart valve 35.10
aortic 35.11
mitral 35.12
Bicycle dynamometer 93.01
Biesenberger operation (size reduction of
breast, bilateral) 85.32
unilateral 85.31
Bifurcation, bone (*see also* Osteotomy) 77.30
Bigelow operation (litholapaxy) 57.0
Bililite therapy (ultraviolet) 99.82
Billroth I operation (partial gastrectomy with
gastroduodenostomy) 43.6
Billroth II operation (partial gastrectomy with
gastrojejunostomy) 43.7
Binnie operation (hepatopexy) 50.69

Biofeedback, psychotherapy 94.39
Biopsy
abdominal wall 54.22
adenoid 28.11
adrenal gland NEC 07.11
closed 07.11
open 07.12
percutaneous (aspiration) (needle) 07.11
alveolus 24.12
anus 49.23
appendix 45.26
artery (any site) 38.21
aspiration—*see* Biopsy, by site
bile ducts 51.14
closed (endoscopic) 51.14
open 51.13
percutaneous (needle) 51.12
bladder 57.33
closed 57.33
open 57.34
transurethral 57.33
blood vessel (any site) 38.21
bone 77.40
carpal, metacarpal 77.44
clavicle 77.41
facial 76.11
femur 77.45
fibula 77.47
humerus 77.42
marrow 41.31
patella 77.46
pelvic 77.49
phalanges (foot) (hand) 77.49
radius 77.43
scapula 77.41
specified site NEC 77.49
tarsal, metatarsal 77.48
thorax (ribs) (sternum) 77.41
tibia 77.47
ulna 77.43
vertebrae 77.49
bowel—*see* Biopsy, intestine
brain NEC 01.13
closed 01.13
open 01.14
percutaneous (needle) 01.13
breast 85.11
blind 85.11
closed 85.11
open 85.12
percutaneous (needle) (Vimm-Silverman)
85.11
bronchus NEC 33.24
brush 33.24
closed (endoscopic) 33.24
washings 33.24
open 33.25
bursa 83.21
cardioesophageal (junction) 44.14
closed (endoscopic) 44.14
open 44.15
cecum 45.25
brush 45.25
closed (endoscopic) 45.25
open 45.26
cerebral meninges NEC 01.11
closed 01.11
open 01.12

C

D

1670

E

F

Face lift 86.82
Facetectomy 77.89
Facilitation, Intraocular circulation NEC 12.59
Failed (trial) forceps 73.3
Family
  counselling (medical) (social) 94.49
  therapy 94.42
Farabeuf operation (ischiopubiotomy) 77.39
Fasanella-Servatt operation
  (blepharoptosis repair) 08.35
Fasciaplasty —*see* Fascioplasty
Fascia sling operation —*see* Operation, sling
Fasciectomy 83.44
  for graft 83.43
    hand 82.34
  hand 82.35
    for graft 82.34
  palmar (release of Dupuytren's contracture)
    82.35
Fasciodesis 83.89
  hand 82.89
Fascioplasty (*see also* Repair, fascia) 83.89
  hand (*see also* Repair, fascia, hand) 82.89
Fasciorrhaphy —*see* Suture, fascia
Fasciotomy 83.14
  Dupuytren's 82.12
    with excision 82.35
  Dwyer 83.14
  hand 82.12
  Ober-Yount 83.14
  orbital (*see also* Orbitotomy) 16.09
  palmar (release of Dupuytren's
    contracture) 82.12
    with excision 82.35
Fenestration
  aneurysm (dissecting), thoracic aorta 39.54
  aortic aneurysm 39.54
  cardiac valve 35.10
  chest wall 34.01
  ear
    inner (with graft) 20.61
      revision 20.62
    tympanic 19.55
  labyrinth (with graft) 20.61
  Lempert's (endaural) 19.9
  operation (aorta) 39.54
  oval window, ear canal 19.55
  palate 27.1
  pericardium 37.12
  semicircular canals (with graft) 20.61
  stapes foot plate (with vein graft) 19.19
    with incus replacement 19.11
  tympanic membrane 19.55
  vestibule (with graft) 20.61
Ferguson operation (hernia repair) 53.00
Fetography 87.81
Fetoscopy 75.31
Fiberoscopy —*see* Endoscopy, by site
Fibroidectomy, uterine 68.29
Fick operation (perforation of foot plate) 19.0
Filipuncture (aneurysm) (cerebral) 39.52
Filleting
  hammer toe 77.56
  pancreas 52.3
Filling, tooth (amalgam) (plastic) (silicate) 23.2
  root canal (*see also* Therapy, root canal) 23.70

Fimbriectomy (*see also* Salpingectomy, partial)
  66.69
  Uchida (with tubal ligation) 66.32
Finney operation (pyloroplasty) 44.29
Fissurectomy, anal 49.39
  endoscopic 49.31
  skin (subcutaneous tissue) 49.04
Fistulectomy —*see also* Closure, fistula, by site
  abdominothoracic 34.83
  abdominouterine 69.42
  anus 49.12
  appendix 47.92
  bile duct 51.79
  biliary tract NEC 51.79
  bladder (transurethral approach) 57.84
  bone (*see also* Excision, lesion, bone) 77.60
  branchial cleft 29.52
  bronchocutaneous 33.42
  bronchoesophageal 33.42
  bronchomediastinal 34.73
  bronchopleural 34.73
  bronchopleurocutaneous 34.73
  bronchopleuromediastinal 34.73
  bronchovisceral 33.42
  cervicosigmoidal 67.62
  cholecystogastroenteric 51.93
  cornea 11.49
  diaphragm 34.83
  enterouterine 69.42
  esophagopleurocutaneous 34.73
  esophagus NEC 42.84
  fallopian tube 66.73
  gallbladder 51.93
  gastric NEC 44.63
  hepatic duct 51.79
  hepatopleural 34.73
  hepatopulmonary 34.73
  intestine
    large 46.76
    small 46.74
  intestinouterine 69.42
  joint (*see also* Excision, lesion, joint) 80.80
  lacrimal
    gland 09.21
    sac 09.6
  laryngotracheal 31.62
  larynx 31.62
  mediastinocutaneous 34.73
  mouth NEC 27.53
  nasal 21.82
    sinus 22.71
  nasolabial 21.82
  nasopharyngeal 21.82
  oroantral 22.71
  oronasal 21.82
  pancreas 52.95
  perineorectal 71.72
  perineosigmoidal 71.72
  perirectal, not opening into rectum 48.93
  pharyngoesophageal 29.53
  pharynx NEC 29.53
  pleura 34.73
  rectolabial 71.72
  rectourethral 58.43
  rectouterine 69.42
  rectovaginal 70.73
  rectovesical 57.83
  rectovulvar 71.72

G

H

I

Incision—*continued*
submaxillary 86.09
  with drainage 86.04
submental space 27.0
subphrenic space 54.19
supraclavicular fossa 86.09
  with drainage 86.04
sweat glands, skin 86.04
temporal pouches 27.0
tendon (sheath) 83.01
  with division 83.13
    hand 82.11
    hand 82.01
      with division 82.11
testis 62.0
thenar space 82.04
thymus 07.92
thyroid (field) (gland) NEC 06.09
  postoperative 06.02
tongue NEC 25.94
  for tongue tic 25.91
tonsil 28.0
trachea NEC 31.3
tunica vaginalis 61.0
umbilicus 54.0
urachal cyst 54.0
ureter 56.2
urethra 58.0
uterus (corpus) 68.0
  cervix 69.95
  for termination of pregnancy 74.91
  septum (congenital) 68.22
uvula 27.71
vagina (cull) (septum) (stenosis) 70.14
  for
    incisional hematoma (episiotomy) 75.91
    obstetrical hematoma NEC 75.92
    pelvic abscess 70.12
vas deferens 63.6
vein 38.00
  abdominal 38.07
  head and neck NEC 38.02
  intracranial NEC 38.01
  lower limb 38.09
  thoracic NEC 38.05
  upper limb 38.03
vertebral column 03.09
vulva 71.09
  obstetrical 75.92
web, esophageal 42.01
Incudectomy NEC 19.3
with
  stapedectomy (*see also* Stapedectomy) 19.19
  tympanoplasty—*see* Tympanoplasty
Incudopexy 19.19
Incudostapediopexy 19.19
with incus replacement 19.11
Indentation, sclera, for buckling (*see also*
  Buckling, scleral) 14.49
Indicator dilution flow measurement 89.68
Induction
abortion
  by
    D and C 69.01
    insertion of prostaglandin suppository 96.49
    intra-amniotic injection (prostaglandin)
      (saline) 75.0
labor
  medical 73.4
  surgical 73.01
    intra- and extra-amniotic injection 73.1
    stripping of membranes 73.1

Inflation
belt wrap 93.99
Eustachian tube 20.8
fallopian tube 66.8
  with injection of therapeutic agent 66.95
Infolding sclera, for buckling (*see also*
  Buckling, scleral) 14.49
Infraction, turbinates (nasal) 21.62
Infundibulectomy
hypophyseal (*see also* Hypophysectomy,
  partial) 07.63
ventricle (heart) (right) 35.34
  in total repair of tetralogy of Fallot 35.81
Infusion, (intra-arterial) (intravenous)
Abciximab 99.20
antineoplastic agent (chemotherapeutic) 99.25
  biological response modifier [BRM] 99.28
biological response modifier [BRM],
  antineoplastic agent 99.28
cancer chemotherapy agent NEC 99.25
electrolytes 99.18
enzymes, thrombolytic (streptokinase) (tissue
  plasminogen activator) (TPA) (urokinase)
  direct coronary artery 36.04
  intravenous 99.10
Eptifibatide 99.20
GP IIB/IIIa inhibitor 99.20
hormone substance NEC 99.24
neuroprotective agent 99.75
nimodipine 99.75
nutritional substance (*see* Nutrition)
platelet inhibitor
  direct coronary artery 36.04
  intravenous 99.20
prophylactic substance NEC 99.29
reteplase 99.10
therapeutic substance NEC 99.29
thrombolytic agent (enzyme) (streptokinase)
  99.10
  with percutaneous transluminal angioplasty
    coronary (single vessel) 36.02
      multiple vessels 36.05
    non-coronary vessel(s) 39.50
    specified site NEC 39.50
  direct intracoronary artery 36.04
tirofiban (HCl) 99.20
vaccine
  tumor 99.28
Injection (into) (hypodermically)
  (intramuscularly) (intravenously) (acting
  locally or systemically)
Actinomycin D, for cancer chemotherapy 99.25
alcohol
  nerve—*see* Injection, nerve
  spinal 03.8
anterior chamber, eye (air) (liquid) (medication)
  12.92
antibiotic 99.21
anticoagulant 99.19
anti-D (Rhesus) globulin 99.11
antidote NEC 99.16
anti-infective NEC 99.22
antineoplastic agent (chemotherapeutic) NEC
  99.25
  biological response modifier [BRM] 99.28
antivenin 99.16
BCG
  for chemotherapy 99.25
  vaccine 99.33
biological response modifier [BRM],
  antineoplastic agent 99.28

1712

J-K

L

Labbe operation (gastrotomy) 43.0
Labiectomy (bilateral) 71.62
  unilateral 71.61
Labyrinthectomy (transtympanic) 20.79
Labyrinthotomy (transtympanic) 20.79
Ladd operation (mobilization of intestine) 54.95
Lagrange operation (iridosclerectomy) 12.65
Lambrinudi operation (triple arthrodesis) 81.12
Laminectomy (decompression) (for exploration)
  03.09
  as operative approach—*omit code*
  with
    excision of herniated intervertebral disc
      (nucleus pulposus) 80.51
    excision of other intraspinal lesion (tumor)
      03.4
  reopening of site 03.02
Laminography —*see* Radiography
Laminotomy (decompression) (for exploration)
  03.09
  as operative approach—*omit code*
  reopening of site 03.02
Langenbeck operation (cleft palate repair) 27.62
Laparoamnioscopy 75.31
Laparorrhaphy 54.63
Laparoscopy 54.21
  with
    biopsy (intra-abdominal) 54.24
      uterine ligaments 68.15
      uterus 68.16
    destruction of fallopian tubes—*see*
      Destruction, fallopian tube
Laparotomy NEC 54.19
  as operative approach—*omit code*
  exploratory (pelvic) 54.11
  reopening of recent operative site (for control of
    hemorrhage) (for exploration) (for incision
    of hematoma) 54.12
Laparotrachelotomy 74.1
Lapidus operation (bunionectomy with
  metatarsal osteotomy) 77.51
Larry operation (shoulder disarticulation) 84.08
Laryngectomy
  with radical neck dissection (with synchronous
    thyroidectomy) (with synchronous
    tracheostomy) 30.4
  complete (with partial laryngectomy) (with
    synchronous tracheostomy) 30.3
    with radical neck dissection (with
      synchronous thyroidectomy) (with
      synchronous tracheostomy) 30.4
  frontolateral partial (extended) 30.29
  glottosupraglottic partial 30.29
  lateral partial 30.29
  partial (frontolateral) (glottosupraglottic)
    (lateral) (submucous) (supraglottic)
    (vertical) 30.29
  radical (with synchronous thyroidectomy) (with
    synchronous tracheostomy) 30.4
  submucous (partial) 30.29
  supraglottic partial 30.29
  total (with partial pharyngectomy) (with
    synchronous tracheostomy) 30.3
    with radical neck dissection (with
      synchronous thyroidectomy) (with
      synchronous tracheostomy) 30.4
  vertical partial 30.29
  wide field 30.3

Laryngocentesis 31.3
Laryngoesophagectomy 30.4
Laryngofissure 30.29
Laryngogram 87.09
  contrast 87.07
Laryngopharyngectomy (with synchronous
  tracheostomy) 30.3
  radical (with synchronous thyroidectomy) 30.4
Laryngopharyngoesophagectomy (with
  synchronous tracheostomy) 30.3
  with radical neck dissection (with synchronous
    thyroidectomy) 30.4
Laryngoplasty 31.69
Laryngorrhaphy 31.61
Laryngoscopy (suspension) (through artificial
  stoma) 31.42
Laryngostomy (permanent) 31.29
  revision 31.63
  temporary (emergency) 31.1
Laryngotomy 31.3
Laryngotracheobronchoscopy 33.23
  with biopsy 33.24
Laryngotracheoscopy 31.42
Laryngotracheostomy (permanent) 31.29
  temporary (emergency) 31.1
Laryngotracheotomy (temporary) 31.1
  permanent 31.29
Laser —*see also* Coagulation, Destruction, *and*
  Photocoagulation by site
  angioplasty, percutaneous transluminal 39.59
    coronary—*see* angioplasty, coronary
Lash operation (internal cervical os repair) 67.5
Latzko operation
  cesarean section 74.2
  colpocleisis 70.4
Lavage
  antral 22.00
  bronchus NEC 96.56
  endotracheal 96.56
  gastric 96.33
  nasal sinus(es) 22.00
    by puncture 22.01
    through natural ostium 22.02
  peritoneal (diagnostic) 54.25
  trachea NEC 96.56
Leadbetter operation (urethral reconstruction)
  58.46
Leadbetter-Politano operation
  (ureteroneocystostomy) 56.74
LEEP (loop elecrosurgical excision procedure)
  of cervix 67.32
Le Fort operation (colpocleisis) 70.8
LeMesurier operation (cleft lip repair) 27.54
Lengthening
  bone (with bone graft) 78.30
    femur 78.35
    for reconstruction of thumb 82.69
    specified site NEC (*see also category* 78.3)
      78.39
    tibia 78.37
    ulna 78.33
  extraocular muscle NEC 15.21
    multiple (two or more muscles) 15.4
  fascia 83.89
    hand 82.89
  hamstring NEC 83.85
  heel cord 83.85

Ligation—*continued*
    head and neck NEC 38.52
    intracranial NEC 38.51
    lower limb 38.59
    stomach 44.91
    thoracic NEC 38.55
    upper limb 38.53
  vena cava, inferior 38.7
  venous connection between anomalous
      vein to
    left innominate vein 35.82
    superior vena cava 35.82
  wart 86.26
Light coagulation *see* Photocoagulation
Lindholm operation (repair of ruptured tendon)
    83.88
Lingulectomy, lung 32.3
Linton operation (varicose vein) 38.59
Lipectomy (subcutaneous tissue) (abdominal)
    (submental) 86.83
Liposuction 86.83
Lip reading training 95.49
Lip shave 27.43
Lisfranc operation
  foot amputation 84.12
  shoulder disarticulation 84.08
Litholapaxy, bladder 57.0
  by incision 57.19
Lithotomy
  bile passage 51.49
  bladder (urinary) 57.19
  common duct 51.41
    percutaneous 51.96
  gallbladder 51.04
  hepatic duct 51.49
  kidney 55.01
    percutaneous 55.03
  ureter 56.2
Lithotripsy
  bile duct NEC 51.49
    extracorporeal shockwave (ESWL) 98.52
  bladder 57.0
    extracorporeal shockwave (ESWL) 98.51
    with ultrasonic fragmentation 57.0 *[59.95]*
  extracorporeal shockwave (ESWL) NEC 98.59
    bile duct 98.52
    bladder (urinary) 98.51
    gallbladder 98.52
    kidney 98.51
    Kock pouch 98.51
    renal pelvis 98.51
    specified site NEC 98.59
    ureter 98.51
  gallbladder NEC 51.04
    endoscopic 51.88
    extracorporeal shockwave (ESWL) 98.52
  kidney 56.0
    extracorporeal shock wave (EWSL) 98.51
    percutaneous nephrostomy with fragmentation
        (laser) (ultrasound) 55.04
  renal pelvis 56.0
    extracorporeal shock wave (EWSL) 98.51
    percutaneous nephrostomy with fragmentation
        (laser) (ultrasound) 55.04
  ureter 56.0
    extracorporeal shockwave (ESWL) 98.51
Littlewood operation (forequarter amputation)
    84.09
LLETZ (large loop excision of the
    transformation zone) of cervix 67.32
Lloyd-Davies operation (abdominoperineal
    resection) 48.5

Lobectomy
  brain 01.53
    partial 01.59
  liver (with partial excision of adjacent lobes)
      50.3
  lung (complete) 32.4
    partial 32.3
    segmental (with resection of adjacent lobes)
        32.4
  thyroid (total) (unilateral) (with removal of
      isthmus) (with removal of portion of
      remaining lobe) 06.2
    partial (*see also* Thyroidectomy, partial) 06.39
    substernal 06.51
    subtotal (*see also* Thyroidectomy, partial)
        06.39
Lobotomy, brain 01.32
Localization, placenta 88.78
  by RISA injection 92.17
Longmire operation (bile duct anastomosis)
    51.39
Loop ileal stoma (*see also* Ileostomy) 46.01
Loopogram 87.78
Looposcopy (ileal conduit) 56.35
Lord operation
  dilation of anal canal for hemorrhoids 49.49
  hemorrhoidectomy 49.49
  orchidopexy 62.5
Lower GI series (x-ray) 87.64
Lucas and Murray operation (knee arthrodesis
    with place) 81.22
Lumpectomy
  breast 85.21
  specified site—*see* Excision, lesion, by site
Lymphadenectomy (simple) (*see also* Excision,
    lymph, node) 40.29
Lymphadenotomy 40.0
Lymphangiectomy (radical) (*see also* Excision,
    lymph, node, by site, radical) 40.50
Lymphangiogram
  abdominal 88.04
  cervical 87.08
  intrathoracic 87.34
  lower limb 88.36
  pelvic 88.04
  upper limb 88.34
Lymphangioplasty 40.9
Lymphangiorrhaphy 40.9
Lymphangiotomy 40.0
Lymphaticostomy 40.9
  thoracic duct 40.62
Lysis
  adhesions
    abdominal 54.59
      laparoscopic 54.51
    appendiceal 54.59
      laparoscopic 54.51
    artery-vein-nerve bundle 39.91
    biliary tract 54.59
      laparoscopic 54.51
    bladder (neck) (intraluminal) 57.12
      external 59.11
        laparoscopic 59.12
      transurethral 57.41
    blood vessels 39.91
    bone—*see category* 78.4
    bursa 83.91
      by stretching or manipulation 93.28
      hand 82.91
    cartilage of joint 93.26
    chest wall 33.99

M

N

Nailing, intramedullary—*see* Reduction, fracture
   with internal fixation
Narcoanalysis 94.21
Narcosynthesis 94.21
Narrowing, palpebral fissure 08.51
Nasopharyngogram 87.09
   contrast 87.06
Necropsy 89.8
Needleoscopy (fetus) 75.31
Needling
   Bartholin's gland (cyst) 71.21
   cataract (secondary) 13.64
   fallopian tube 66.91
   hydrocephalic head 73.8
   lens (capsule) 13.2
   pupillary membrane (iris) 12.35
Nephrectomy (complete) (total) (unilateral) 55.51
   bilateral 55.54
   partial (wedge) 55.4
   remaining or solitary kidney 55.52
   removal transplanted kidney 55.53
Nephrocolopexy 55.7
Nephrocystanastomosis NEC 56.73
Nephrolithotomy 55.01
Nephrolysis 59.02
   laparoscopic 59.03
Nephropexy 55.7
Nephroplasty 55.89
Nephropyeloplasty 55.87
Nephropyeloureterostomy 55.86
Nephrorrhaphy 55.81
Nephroscopy 55.21
Nephrostolithotomy, percutaneous 55.03
Nephrostomy (with drainage tube) 55.02
   closure 55.82
   percutaneous 55.03
     with fragmentation (ultrasound) 55.04
Nephrotomogram, nephrotomography NEC
   87.72
Nephrotomy 55.01
Nephroureterectomy (with bladder cuff) 55.51
Nephroureterocystectomy 55.51 *[57.79]*
Nerve block (cranial) (peripheral) NEC (*see also*
   Block, by site) 04.81
Neurectasis (cranial) (peripheral) 04.91
Neurectomy (cranial) (infraorbital) (occipital)
   (peripheral) (spinal) NEC 04.07
   gastric (vagus) (*see also* Vagotomy) 44.00
   opticociliary 12.79
   paracervical 05.22
   presacral 05.24
   retrogasserian 04.07
   sympathetic—*see* Sympathectomy
   trigeminal 04.07
   tympanic 20.91
Neurexeresis NEC 04.07
Neuroanastomosis (cranial) (peripheral) NEC
   04.74
   accessory-facial 04.72
   accessory-hypoglossal 04.73
   hypoglossal-facial 04.71

Neurolysis (peripheral nerve) NEC 04.49
   carpal tunnel 04.43
   cranial nerve NEC 04.42
   spinal (cord) (nerve roots) 03.6
   tarsal tunnel 04.44
   trigeminal nerve 04.41
Neuroplasty (cranial) (peripheral) NEC 04.79
   of old injury (delayed repair) 04.76
   revision 04.75
Neurorrhaphy (cranial) (peripheral) 04.3
Neurotomy (cranial) (peripheral) (spinal) NEC
   04.04
   acoustic 04.01
   glossopharyngeal 29.92
   lacrimal branch 05.0
   retrogasserian 04.02
   sympathetic 05.0
   vestibular 04.01
Neurotripsy (peripheral) NEC 04.03
   trigeminal 04.02
Nicola operation (tenodesis for recurrent
   dislocation of shoulder) 81.82
Nimodipine, infusion 99.75
Nissen operation (fundoplication of stomach)
   44.66
Noble operation (plication of small intestine)
   46.62
Norman Miller operation (vaginopexy) 70.77
Norton operation (extraperitoneal cesarean
   section) 74.2
Nuclear magnetic resonance imaging
   —*see* Imaging, magnetic resonance
Nutrition, concentration substances
   enteral infusion (of) 96.6
   parenteral, total 99.15
     peripheral 99.15

O

Operation—*continued*
salivary gland or duct NEC 26.99
Salter (innominate osteotomy) 77.39
Sauer-Bacon (abdominoperineal resection) 48.5
Schanz (femoral osteotomy) 77.35
Schauta (Amreich) (radical vaginal
   hysterectomy) 68.7
Schede (thoracoplasty) 33.34
Scheie
  cautery of sclera 12.62
  sclerostomy 12.62
Schlatter (total gastrectomy) 43.99
Schroeder (endocervical excision) 67.39
Schuchardt (nonobstetrical episiotomy) 71.09
Schwartze (simple mastoidectomy) 20.41
sclera NEC 12.89
Scott
  intestinal bypass for obesity 45.93
  jejunocolostomy (bypass) 45.93
scrotum NEC 61.99
Seddon-Brooks (transfer of pectoralis major
   tendon) 83.75
Semb (apicolysis of lung) 33.39
seminal vesicle NEC 60.79
Senning (correction of transposition of great
   vessels) 35.91
Sever (division of soft tissue of arm) 83.19
Sewell (heart) 36.2
sex transformation NEC 64.5
Sharrard (iliopsoas muscle transfer) 83.77
shelf (hip arthroplasty) 81.40
Shirodkar (encirclement suture, cervix) 67.5
sigmoid NEC 46.99
Silver (bunionectomy) 77.59
Sistrunk (excision of thyroglossal cyst) 06.7
Skene's gland NEC 71.8
skin NEC 86.99
skull NEC 02.99
sling
  eyelid
    fascia lata, palpebral 08.36
    frontalis fascial 08.32
    levator muscle 08.33
    orbicularis muscle 08.36
    palpebrae ligament, fascia lata 08.36
    tarsus muscle 08.35
  fascial (fascia lata)
    eye 08.32
    for facial weakness (trigeminal nerve
     paralysis) 86.81
    palpebral ligament 08.36
    tongue 25.59
  tongue (fascial) 25.59
  urethra (suprapubic) 59.4
   retropubic 59.5
  urethrovesical 59.5
Slocum (pes anserinus transfer) 81.47
Sluder (tonsillectomy) 28.2
Smith (open osteotomy of mandible) 76.62
Smith-Peterson (radiocarpal arthrodesis) 81.25
Smithwick (sympathectomy) 05.29
Soave (endorectal pull-through) 48.41
soft tissue NEC 83.99
  hand 82.99
Sonneberg (inferior maxillary neurectomy)
   04.07
Sorondo-Ferré (hindquarter amputation) 84.19
Soutter (iliac crest fasciotomy) 83.14
Spalding-Richardson (uterine suspension) 69.22
spermatic cord NEC 63.99
sphincter of Oddi NEC 51.89

Operation—*continued*
spinal (canal) (cord) (structures) NEC 03.99
Spinelli (correction of inverted uterus) 75.93
Spivack (permanent gastrostomy) 43.19
spleen NEC 41.99
S.P. Rogers (knee disarticulation) 84.16
Ssabanejew-Frank (permanent gastrostomy)
   43.19
Stacke (simple mastoidectomy) 20.41
Stallard (conjunctivocystorhinostomy) 09.82
  with insertion of tube or stent 09.83
Stamm (Kader) (temporary gastrostomy) 43.19
Steinberg 44.5
Steindler
  fascia stripping (for cavus deformity) 83.14
  flexorplasty (elbow) 83.77
  muscle transfer 83.77
sterilization NEC
  female (*see also* specific operation) 66.39
  mate (*see also* Ligation, vas deferens) 63.70
Stewart (renal plication with pyeloplasty) 55.87
stomach NEC 44.99
Stone (anoplasty) 49.79
Strassman (metroplasty) 69.49
  metroplasty (Jones modification) 69.49
  uterus 68.22
Strayer (gastrocnemius recession) 83.72
stress incontinence—*see* Repair, stress
  incontinence
Stromeyer-Little (hepatotomy) 50.0
Strong (unbridling of celiac artery axis) 39.91
Sturmdorf (conization of cervix) 67.2
subcutaneous tissue NEC 86.99
sublingual gland or duct NEC 26.99
submaxillary gland or duct NEC 26.99
Summerskill (dacryocystorhinostomy by
   intubation) 09.81
Surmay (jejunostomy) 46.39
Swenson
  bladder reconstruction 57.87
  proctectomy 48.49
Swinney (urethral reconstruction) 58.46
Syme
  ankle amputation through malleoli of tibia and
   fibula 84.14
  urethrotomy, external 58.0
sympathetic nerve NEC 05.89
Taarnhoj (trigeminal nerve root decompression)
   04.41
Tack (sacculotomy) 20.79
Talma-Morison (omentopexy) 54.74
Tanner (devascularization of stomach) 44.99
TAPVC NEC 35.82
tarsus NEC 08.99
  muscle sling 08.35
tendon NEC 83.99
  extraocular NEC 15.9
  hand NEC 82.99
testis NEC 62.99
tetralogy of Fallot
  partial repair—*see specific procedure*
  total (one-stage) 35.81
Thal (repair of esophageal stricture) 42.85
thalamus (stereotactic) 01.41
Thiersch
  anus 49.79
  skin graft 86.69
   hand 86.62
Thompson
  cleft lip repair 27.54
  correction of lymphedema 40.9

Orbitotomy (anterior) (frontal) (temporofrontal)
   (transfrontal) NEC 16.09
  with
    bone flap 16.01
    insertion of implant 16.02
  Kroenlein (lateral) 16.01
  lateral 16.01
Orchidectomy (with epididymectomy)
   (unilateral) 62.3
  bilateral (radical) 62.41
  remaining or solitary testis 62.42
Orchidopexy 62.5
Orchidoplasty 62.69
Orchidorrhaphy 62.61
Orchidotomy 62.0
Orchiectomy (with epididymectomy) (unilateral)
   62.3
  bilateral (radical) 62.41
  remaining or solitary testis 62.42
Orchiopexy 62.5
Orchioplasty 62.69
Orthoroentgenography —*see* Radiography
Oscar Miller operation (midtarsal arthrodesis)
   81.14
Osmond-Clark operation (soft tissue release
   with peroneus brevis tendon transfer) 83.75
Ossiculectomy NEC 19.3
  with
    stapedectomy (*see also* Stapedectomy) 19.19
    stapes mobilization 19.0
    tympanoplasty 19.53
     revision 19.6
Ossiculotomy NEC 19.3
Ostectomy (partial), except facial—*see also*
   category 77.8
  facial NEC 76.39
   total 76.45
    with reconstruction 76.44
  first metatarsal head—*see* Bunionectomy
  for graft (autograft) (homograft)—*see also*
   category 77.7
   mandible 76.31
    total 76.42
     with reconstruction 76.41
  total, except facial—*see also category* 77.9
   facial NEC 76.45
    with reconstruction 76.44
   mandible 76.42
    with reconstruction 76.41
Osteoarthrotomy (*see also* Osteotomy) 77.30
Osteoclasis 78.70
  carpal, metacarpal 78.74
  clavicle 78.71
  ear 20.79
  femur 78.75
  fibula 78.77
  humerus 78.72
  patella 78.76
  pelvic 78.79
  phalanges (foot) (hand) 78.79
  radius 78.73
  scapula 78.71
  specified site NEC 78.79
  tarsal, metatarsal 78.78
  thorax (ribs) (sternum) 78.71
  tibia 78.77
  ulna 78.73
  vertebrae 78.79
Osteolysis —*see category* 78.4
Osteopathic manipulation (*see also*
  Manipulation, osteopathic) 93.67

Osteoplasty NEC—*see category* 78.4
  with bone graft—*see* Graft, bone
  for
    bone lengthening—*see* Lengthening, bone
    bone shortening—*see* Shortening, bone
    repair of malunion or nonunion of
      fracture—*see* Repair, fracture, malunion
     or nonunion
  carpal, metacarpal 78.44
  clavicle 78.41
  cranium NEC 02.06
   with
    flap (bone) 02.03
    graft (bone) 02.04
  facial bone NEC 76.69
  femur 78.45
  fibula 78.47
  humerus 78.42
  mandible, mandibular NEC 76.64
   body 76.63
   ramus (open) 76.62
    closed 76.61
  maxilla (segmental) 76.65
   total 76.66
  nasal bones 21.89
  patella 78.46
  pelvic 78.49
  phalanges (foot) (hand) 78.49
  radius 78.43
  scapula 78.41
  skull NEC 02.06
   with
    flap (bone) 02.03
    graft (bone) 02.04
  specified site NEC 78.49
  tarsal, metatarsal 78.48
  thorax (ribs) (sternum) 78.41
  tibia 78.47
  ulna 78.43
  vertebrae 78.49
Osteorrhaphy (*see also* Osteoplasty) 78.40
Osteosynthesis (fracture) —*see* Reduction,
  fracture
Osteotomy (adduction) (angulation) (block)
   (derotational) (displacement) (partial)
   (rotational) 77.30
  carpals, metacarpals 77.34
   wedge 77.24
  clavicle 77.31
   wedge 77.21
  facial bone NEC 76.69
  femur 77.35
   wedge 77.25
  fibula 77.37
   wedge 77.27
  humerus 77.32
   wedge 77.22
  mandible (segmental) (subapical) 76.64
   angle (open) 76.62
    closed 76.61
   body 76.63
   Gigli saw 76.61
   ramus (open) 76.62
    closed 76.61
  maxilla (segmental) 76.65
   total 76.66
  metatarsal 77.38
   wedge 77.28
    for hallux valgus repair 77.51
  patella 77.36
   wedge 77.26

Osteotomy—*continued*
  pelvic 77.39
    wedge 77.29
  phalanges (foot) (hand) 77.39
    for repair of
      bunion—*see* Bunionectomy
      bunionette 77.54
      hallux valgus—*see* Bunionectomy
    wedge 77.29
      for repair of
        bunion—*see* Bunionectomy
        bunionette 77.54
        hallux valgus—*see* Bunionectomy
  radius 77.33
    wedge 77.23
  scapula 77.31
    wedge 77.21
  specified site NEC 77.39
    wedge 77.29
  tarsal 77.38
    wedge 77.28
  thorax (ribs) (sternum) 77.31
    wedge 77.21
  tibia 77.37
    wedge 77.27
  toe 77.39
    for repair of
      bunion—*see* Bunionectomy
      bunionette 77.54
      hallux valgus—*see* Bunionectomy
    wedge 77.29
      for repair of
        bunion—*see* bunionectomy
        bunionette 77.54
        hallux valgus—*see* Bunionectomy
  ulna 77.33
    wedge 77.23
  vertebrae 77.39
    wedge 77.29
Otonecrectomy (inner ear) 20.79
Otoplasty (external) 18.79
  auditory canal or meatus 18.6
  auricle 18.79
  cartilage 18.79
    reconstruction 18.71
  prominent or protruding 18.5
Otoscopy 18.11
Outfolding, sclera, for buckling (*see also*
    Buckling, scleral) 14.49
Outfracture, turbinates (nasal) 21.62
Output and clearance, circulatory 92.05
Overdistension, bladder (therapeutic) 96.25
Overlapping, sclera, for buckling (*see also*
    Buckling, scleral) 14.49
Oversewing
  pleural bleb 32.21
  ulcer crater (peptic) 44.40
    duodenum 44.42
    stomach 44.41
Oxford operation (for urinary incontinence) 59.4
Oxygenation 93.96
  extracorporeal membrane (ECMO) 39.65
  hyperbaric 93.95
    wound 93.59
Oxygen therapy (catalytic) (pump) 93.96
  hyperbaric 93.95

P

Pacemaker
  cardiac—*see also* Insertion, pacemaker, cardiac
    intraoperative (temporary) 39.64
    temporary (during and immediately following
      cardiac surgery) 39.64
Packing —*see also* Insertion, pack
  auditory canal 96.11
  nose, for epistaxis (anterior) 21.01
    posterior (and anterior) 21.02
  rectal 96.19
  sella turcica 07.79
  vaginal 96.14
Palatoplasty 27.69
  for cleft palate 27.62
    secondary or subsequent 27.63
Palatorrhaphy 27.61
  for cleft palate 27.62
Pallidectomy 01.42
Pallidoansotomy 01.42
Pallidotomy 01.42
Panas operation (linear proctotomy) 48.0
Pancoast operation (division of trigeminal nerve
  at foramen ovale) 04.02
Pancreatectomy (total) (with synchronous
    duodenectomy) 52.6
  partial NEC 52.59
    distal (tail) (with part of body) 52.52
    proximal (head) (with part of body) (with
      synchronous duodenectomy) 52.51
    radical 52.53
      subtotal 52.53
    radical 52.7
      subtotal 52.53
Pancreaticocystoduodenostomy 52.4
Pancreaticocystoenterostomy 52.4
Pancreaticocystogastrostomy 52.4
Pancreaticocystojejunostomy 52.4
Pancreaticoduodenectomy (total) 52.6
  partial NEC 52.59
    proximal 52.51
    radical subtotal 52.53
  radical (one-stage) (two-stage) 52.7
    subtotal 52.53
Pancreaticoduodenostomy 52.96
Pancreaticoenterostomy 52.96
Pancreaticogastrostomy 52.96
Pancreaticoileostomy 52.96
Pancreaticojejunostomy 52.96
Pancreatoduodenectomy (total) 52.6
  partial NEC 52.59
  radical (one-stage) (two-stage) 52.7
    subtotal 52.53
Pancreatogram 87.66
  endoscopic retrograde (ERP) 52.13
Pancreatolithotomy 52.09
  endoscopic 52.94
Pancreatotomy 52.09
Pancreatolithotomy 52.09
  endoscopic 52.94
Panendoscopy 57.32
  specified site, other than bladder—*see*
    Endoscopy, by site
  through artificial stoma 57.31
Panhysterectomy (abdominal) 68.4
  vaginal 68.59
    laparoscopically assisted (LAVH) 68.51
Panniculectomy 86.83
Panniculotomy 86.83

Pantaloon operation (revision of gastric
    anastomosis) 44.5
Papillectomy, anal 49.39
  endoscopic 49.31
Papillotomy (pancreas) 51.82
  endoscopic 51.85
Paquin operation (ureteroneocystostomy) 56.74
Paracentesis
  abdominal (percutaneous) 54.91
  anterior chamber, eye 12.91
  bladder 57.11
  cornea 12.91
  eye (anterior chamber) 12.91
  thoracic, thoracis 34.91
  tympanum 20.09
    with intubation 20.01
Parasitology *see* Examination, microscopic
Parathyroidectomy (partial) (subtotal) NEC
    06.89
  complete 06.81
  ectopic 06.89
  global removal 06.81
  mediastinal 06.89
  total 06.81
Parenteral nutrition, total 99.15
  peripheral 99.15
Parotidectomy 26.30
  complete 26.32
  partial 26.31
  radical 26.32
Partsch operation (marsupialization of dental
    cyst) 24.4
Passage —*see* Insertion and Intubation
Passage of sounds, urethra 58.6
Patch
  blood, spinal (epidural) 03.95
  graft—*see* Graft
  spinal, blood (epidural) 03.95
  subdural, brain 02.12
Patellapexy 78.46
Patellaplasty NEC 78.46
Patellectomy 77.96
  partial 77.86
Pattee operation (auditory canal) 18.6
Pectenotomy (*see also* Sphincterotomy, anal)
    49.59
Pedicle flap —*see* Graft, skin, pedicle
Peet operation (splanchnic resection) 05.29
PEG (percutaneous endoscopic gastrostomy)
    43.11
PEJ (percutaneous endoscopic jejunostomy)
    46.32
Pelvectomy, kidney (partial) 55.4
Pelvimetry 88.25
  gynecological 89.26
Pelviolithotomy 55.11
Pelvioplasty, kidney 55.87
Pelviostomy 55.12
  closure 55.82
Pelviotomy 77.39
  to assist delivery 73.94
Pelvi-ureteroplasty 55.87
Pemberton operation
  osteotomy of ilium 77.39
  rectum (mobilization and fixation for prolapse
    repair) 48.76
Penectomy 64.3

Pneumocentesis 33.93
Pneumocisternogram 87.02
Pneumoencephalogram 87.01
Pneumogram, pneumography
extraperitoneal 88.15
mediastinal 87.33
orbit 87.14
pelvic 88.13
peritoneum NEC 88.13
presacral 88.15
retroperitoneum 88.15
Pneumogynecography 87.82
Pneumomediastinography 87.33
Pneumonectomy (complete) (extended) (radical)
(standard) (total) (with mediastinal dissection)
32.5
partial
complete excision, one lobe 32.4
resection (wedge), one lobe 32.3
Pneumonolysis (for collapse of lung) 33.39
Pneumonotomy (with exploration) 33.1
Pneumoperitoneum (surgically-induced) 54.96
for collapse of lung 33.33
pelvic 88.12
Pneumothorax (artificial) (surgical) 33.32
intrapleural 33.32
Pneumoventriculogram 87.02
Politano-Leadbetter operation
(ureteroneocystostomy) 56.74
Politzerization, Eustachian tube 20.8
Pollicization (with carry over of nerves and
blood supply) 82.61
Polya operation (gastrectomy) 43.7
Polypectomy —*see also* Excision, lesion, by site
esophageal 42.32
endoscopic 42.33
gastric (endoscopic) 43.41
large intestine (colon) 45.42
nasal 21.31
rectum (endoscopic) 48.36
Polysomnogram 89.17
Pomeroy operation (ligation and division of
fallopian tubes) 66.32
Poncet operation
lengthening of Achilles tendon 83.85
urethrostomy, perineal 58.0
Porro operation (cesarean section) 74.99
Positrocephalogram 92.11
Positron emission tomography (PET) —*see*
Scan, radioisotope
Postmortem examination 89.8
Potts-Smith operation (descending aorta-left
pulmonary artery anastomosis) 39.0
Poudrage
intrapericardial 36.39
pleural 34.6
PPN (peripheral parenteral nutrition) 99.15
Preparation (cutting), pedicle (flap) graft 86.71
Preputiotomy 64.91
Prescription for glasses 95.31
Pressure support
ventilation [PSV]—*see* category 96.7
Printen and Mason operation (high gastric
bypass) 44.31
Probing
canaliculus, lacrimal (with irrigation) 09.42
lacrimal
canaliculi 09.42
punctum (with irrigation) 09.41
nasolacrimal duct (with irrigation) 09.43
with insertion of tube or stent 09.44

Probing—*continued*
salivary duct (for dilation of duct) (for removal
of calculus) 26.91
with incision 26.0
Procedure —*see also* specific procedure
diagnostic NEC
abdomen (region) 54.29
adenoid 28.19
adrenal gland 07.19
alveolus 24.19
amnion 75.35
anterior chamber, eye 12.29
anus 49.29
appendix 45.28
biliary tract 51.19
bladder 57.39
blood vessel (any site) 38.29
bone 78.80
carpal, metacarpal 78.84
clavicle 78.81
facial 76.19
femur 78.85
fibula 78.87
humerus 78.82
marrow 41.38
patella 78.86
pelvic 78.89
phalanges (foot) (hand) 78.89
radius 78.83
scapula 78.81
specified site NEC 78.89
tarsal, metatarsal 78.88
thorax (ribs) (sternum) 78.81
tibia 78.87
ulna 78.83
vertebrae 78.89
brain 01.18
breast 85.19
bronchus 33.29
buccal 27.24
bursa 83.29
canthus 08.19
cecum 45.28
cerebral meninges 01.18
cervix 67.19
chest wall 34.28
choroid 14.19
ciliary body 12.29
clitoris 71.19
colon 45.28
conjunctiva 10.29
cornea 11.29
cul-de-sac 70.29
dental 24.19
diaphragm 34.28
duodenum 45.19
ear
external 18.19
inner and middle 20.39
epididymis 63.09
esophagus 42.29
Eustachian tube 20.39
extraocular muscle or tendon 15.09
eye 16.29
anterior chamber 12.29
posterior chamber 14.19
eyeball 16.29
eyelid 08.19
fallopian tube 66.19
fascia (any site) 83.29
fetus 75.35

Pyloroplasty (Finney) (Heineke-Mikulicz) 44.29
   dilation, endoscopic 44.22
     by incision 44.21
   not elsewhere classified 44.29
   revision 44.29
Pylorostomy —*see* Gastrostomy

Pyloroplasty (Finney) (Heineke-Mikulicz) 44.29
   dilation, endoscopic 44.22
     by incision 44.21
   not elsewhere classified 44.29
   revision 44.29
Pylorostomy —*see* Gastrostomy

Q-R

 Removal

Removal—*continued*
  canthus 98.22
    by incision 08.51
  cerebral meninges 01.31
  cervix (intraluminal) NEC 98.16
    penetrating 69.97
  choroid (by incision) 14.00
    with use of magnet 14.01
    without use of magnet 14.02
  ciliary body (by incision) 12.00
    with use of magnet 12.01
    without use of magnet 12.02
  conjunctiva (by magnet) 98.22
    by incision 10.0
  cornea 98.21
    by incision 11.1
    by magnet 11.0
  duodenum 98.03
    by incision 45.01
  ear (intraluminal) 98.11
    with incision 18.09
  epididymis 63.92
  esophagus (intraluminal) 98.02
    by incision 42.09
  extrapleural (by incision) 34.01
  eye, eyeball (by magnet) 98.21
    anterior segment (by incision) 12.00
      with use of magnet 12.01
      without use of magnet 12.02
    posterior segment (by incision) 14.00
      with use of magnet 14.01
      without use of magnet 14.02
      superficial 98.21
  eyelid 98.22
    by incision 08.09
  fallopian tube
    by salpingostomy 66.02
    by salpingotomy 66.01
  fascia 83.09
    hand 82.09
  foot 98.28
  gall bladder 51.04
  groin region (abdominal wall) (inguinal) 54.0
  gum 98.22
    by incision 24.0
  hand 98.26
  head and neck NEC 98.22
  heart 37.11
  internal fixation, device—*see* Removal,
    fixation device, internal
  intestine
    by incision 45.00
    large (intraluminal) 98.04
      by incision 45.03
    small (intraluminal) 98.03
      by incision 45.02
  intraocular (by incision) 12.00
    with use of magnet 12.01
    without use of magnet 12.02
  iris (by incision) 12.00
    with use of magnet 12.01
    without use of magnet 12.02
  joint structure (*see also* Arthrotomy) 80.10
  kidney (transurethral) (by endoscopy) 56.0
    by incision 55.01
    pelvis (transurethral) 56.0
      by incision 55.11
  labia 98.23
    by incision 71.09
  lacrimal
    canaliculi 09.42

Removal—*continued*
    by incision 09.52
    gland 09.3
      by incision 09.0
    passage(s) 09.49
      by incision 09.59
    punctum 09.41
      by incision 09.51
    sac 09.49
      by incision 09.53
  large intestine (intraluminal) 98.04
    by incision 45.03
  larynx (intraluminal) 98.14
    by incision 31.3
  lens 13.00
    by incision 13.02
    with use of magnet 13.01
  liver 50.0
  lower limb, except foot 98.29
    foot 98.28
  lung 33.1
  mediastinum 34.1
  meninges (cerebral) 01.31
    spinal 03.01
  mouth (intraluminal) 98.01
    by incision 27.92
  muscle 83.02
    hand 82.02
  nasal sinus 22.50
    antrum 22.2
      with Caldwell-Luc approach 22.39
    ethmoid 22.51
    frontal 22.41
    maxillary 22.2
      with Caldwell-Luc approach 22.39
    sphenoid 22.52
  nerve (cranial) (peripheral) NEC 04.04
    root 03.01
  nose (intraluminal) 98.12
    by incision 21.1
  oral cavity (intraluminal) 98.01
    by incision 27.92
  orbit (by magnet) 98.21
    by incision 16.1
  palate (penetrating) 98.22
    by incision 27.1
  pancreas 52.09
  penis 98.24
    by incision 64.92
  pericardium 37.12
  perineum (female) 98.23
    by incision 71.09
    male 98.25
      by incision 86.05
  perirenal tissue 59.09
  peritoneal cavity 54.92
  perivesical tissue 59.19
  pharynx (intraluminal) 98.13
    by pharyngotomy 29.0
  pleura (by incision) 34.09
  popliteal space 98.29
    by incision 86.05
  rectum (intraluminal) 98.05
    by incision 48.0
  renal pelvis (transurethral) 56.0
    by incision 56.1
  retina (by incision) 14.00
    with use of magnet 14.01
    without use of magnet 14.02
  retroperitoneum 54.92
  sclera (by incision) 12.00

Repair—*continued*

          with prosthesis or graft 53.16
      bilateral 53.11
          with prosthesis or graft 53.14
      indirect (unilateral) 53.02
          with prosthesis or graft 53.04
          and direct (unilateral) 53.01
              with prosthesis or graft 53.03
              bilateral 53.13
                  with prosthesis or graft 53.16
          bilateral 53.12
              with prosthesis or graft 53.15
    internal 53.9
    ischiatic 53.9
    ischiorectal 53.9
    lumbar 53.9
    manual 96.27
    obturator 53.9
    omental 53.9
    paraesophageal 53.7
    parahiatal 53.7
    paraileostomy 46.41
    parasternal 53.82
    paraumbilical 53.49
      with prosthesis 53.41
    pericolostomy 46.42
    perineal (enterocele) 53.9
    preperitoneal 53.29
    pudendal 53.9
    retroperitoneal 53.9
    sciatic 53.9
    scrotal—*see* Repair, hernia, inguinal
    spigelian 53.59
      with prosthesis or graft 53.69
    umbilical 53.49
      with prosthesis 53.41
    uveal 12.39
    ventral 53.59
      incisional 53.51
        with prosthesis or graft 53.61
  hydrocele
    round ligament 69.19
    spermatic cord 63.1
    tunica vaginalis 61.2
  hymen 70.76
  hypospadias 58.45
  ileostomy 46.41
  ingrown toenail 86.23
  intestine, intestinal NEC 46.79
    fistula—*see* Closure, fistula, intestine
    laceration
      large intestine 46.75
      small intestine NEC 46.73
    stoma—*see* Repair, stoma
  inverted uterus NEC 69.29
    manual
      nonobstetric 69.94
      obstetric 75.94
    obstetrical
      manual 75.94
      surgical 75.93
    vaginal approach 69.23
  iris (rupture) NEC 12.39
  jejunostomy 46.41
  joint (capsule) (cartilage) NEC (*see also*
      Arthroplasty) 81.96
  kidney NEC 55.89
  knee (joint) NEC 81.47
    collateral ligaments 81.46
    cruciate ligaments 81.45
    five-in-one 81.42

Repair—*continued*

  triad 81.43
  labia—*see* Repair, vulva
  laceration—*see* Suture, by site
  lacrimal system NEC 09.99
    canaliculus 09.73
    punctum 09.72
      for eversion 09.71
  laryngostomy 31.62
  laryngotracheal cleft 31.69
  larynx 31.69
    fracture 31.64
    laceration 31.61
  leads (cardiac) NEC 37.75
  ligament (*see also* Arthroplasty) 81.96
    broad 69.29
    collateral, knee NEC 81.46
    cruciate, knee NEC 81.45
    round 69.29
    uterine 69.29
  lip NEC 27.59
    cleft 27.54
    laceration (by suture) 27.51
  liver NEC 50.69
    laceration 50.61
  lop ear 18.79
  lung NEC 33.49
  lymphatic (channel) (peripheral) NEC 40.9
    duct, left (thoracic) NEC 40.69
  macrodactyly 82.83
  mallet finger 82.84
  mandibular ridge 76.64
  mastoid (antrum) (cavity) 19.9
  meninges (cerebral) NEC 02.12
    spinal NEC 03.59
        meningocele 03.51
        myelomeningocele 03.52
  meningocele (spinal) 03.51
    cranial 02.12
  mesentery 54.75
  mouth NEC 27.59
    laceration NEC 27.52
  muscle NEC 83.87
    by
        graft or implant (fascia) (muscle) 83.82
          hand 82.72
          tendon 83.81
            hand 82.79
        suture (direct) 83.65
          hand 82.46
        transfer or transplantation (muscle) 83.77
          hand 82.58
    hand 82.89
      by
          graft or implant NEC 82.79
            fascia 82.72
          suture (direct) 82.46
          transfer or transplantation (muscle) 82.58
  musculotendinous cuff, shoulder 83.63
  myelomeningocele 03.52
  nasal
    septum (perforation) NEC 21.88
    sinus NEC 22.79
      fistula 22.71
  nasolabial flaps (plastic) 21.86
  nasopharyngeal atresia 29.4
  nerve (cranial) (peripheral) NEC 04.79
    old injury 04.76
    revision 04.75
    sympathetic 05.81
  nipple NEC 85.87

S

Switch, switching
  coronary arteries 35.84
  great arteries, total 35.84
Syme operation
  ankle amputation through malleoli of tibia and
     fibula 84.14
  urethrotomy, external 58.0
Sympathectomy NEC 05.29
  cervical 05.22
  cervicothoracic 05.22
  lumbar 05.23
  periarterial 05.25
  presacral 05.24
  renal 05.29
  thoracolumbar 05.23
  tympanum 20.91
Sympatheticotripsy 05.0
Symphysiotomy 77.39
  assisting delivery (obstetrical) 73.94
  kidney (horseshoe) 55.85
Symphysis, pleural 34.6
Synchondrotomy (*see also* Division, cartilage)
    80.40
Syndactylization 86.89
Syndesmotomy (*see also* Division, ligament)
    80.40
Synechiotomy
  endometrium 68.21
  iris (posterior) 12.33
    anterior 12.32
Synovectomy (joint) (complete) (partial) 80.70
  ankle 80.77
  elbow 80.72
  foot and toe 80.78
  hand and finger 80.74
  hip 80.75
  knee 80.76
  shoulder 80.71
  specified site NEC 80.79
  spine 80.79
  tendon sheath 83.42
    hand 82.33
  wrist 80.73
Syringing
  lacrimal duct or sac 09.43
  nasolacrimal duct 09.43
    with
      dilation 09.43
      insertion of tube or stent 09.44

T

Taarnhoj operation (trigeminal nerve root
  decompression) 04.41
Tack operation (sacculotomy) 20.79
Take-down
  anastomosis
    arterial 39.49
    blood vessel 39.49
    gastric, gastrointestinal 44.5
    intestine 46.93
    stomach 44.5
    vascular 39.49
    ventricular 02.43
  arterial bypass 39.49
  arteriovenous shunt 39.43
    with creation of new shunt 39.42
  cecostomy 46.52
  colostomy 46.52
  duodenostomy 46.51
  enterostomy 46.50
  esophagostomy 42.83
  gastroduodenostomy 44.5
  gastrojejunostomy 44.5
  ileostomy 46.51
  intestinal stoma 46.50
    large 46.52
    small 46.51
  jejunoileal bypass 46.93
  jejunostomy 46.51
  laryngostomy 31.62
  sigmoidostomy 46.52
  stoma
    bile duct 51.79
    bladder 57.82
    bronchus 33.42
    common duct 51.72
    esophagus 42.83
    gall bladder 51.92
    hepatic duct 51.79
    intestine 46.50
      large 46.52
      small 46.51
    kidney 55.82
    larynx 31.62
    rectum 48.72
    stomach 44.62
    thorax 34.72
    trachea 31.72
    ureter 56.83
    urethra 58.42
  systemic-pulmonary artery anastomosis 39.49
    in total repair of tetralogy of Fallot 35.81
  tracheostomy 31.72
  vascular anastomosis or bypass 39.49
  ventricular shunt (cerebral) 02.43
Talectomy 77.98
Talma-Morison operation (omentcpexy) 54.74
Tamponade
  esophageal 96.06
  intrauterine (nonobstetric) 69.91
    after delivery or abortion 75.8
    antepartum 73.1
  vagina 96.14
    after delivery or abortion 75.8
    antepartum 73.1
Tanner operation (devascularization of
  stomach) 44.99

Tap
  abdomen 54.91
  chest 34.91
  cisternal 01.01
  crania] 01.09
  joint 81.91
  lumbar (diagnostic) (removal of dye) 03.31
  perilymphatic 20.79
  spinal (diagnostic) 03.31
  subdural (through fontanel) 01.09
  thorax 34.91
Tarsectomy 08.20
  de Grandmont 08.35
Tarsoplasty (*see also* Reconstruction, eyelid)
  08.70
Tarsorrhaphy (lateral) 08.52
  division or severing 08.02
Tattooing
  cornea 11.91
  skin 86.02
Tautening, eyelid for entropion 08.42
Telemetry (cardiac) 89.54
Teleradiotherapy
  beta particles 92.25
  Betatron 92.24
  cobalt-60 92.23
  electrons 92.25
  iodine-125 92.23
  linear accelerator 92.24
  neutrons 92.26
  particulate radiation NEC 92.26
  photons 92.24
  protons 92.26
  radioactive cesium 92.23
  radioisotopes NEC 92.23
Temperature gradient study (*see also*
  Thermography) 88.89
Temperament assessment 94.02
Tendinoplasty —*see* Repair, tendon
Tendinosuture (immediate) (primary) (*see also*
  Suture, tendon) 83.64
  hand (*see also* Suture, tendon, hand) 82.45
Tendolysis 83.91
  hand 82.91
Tendoplasty *see* Repair, tendon
Tenectomy 83.39
  eye 15.13
    levator palpebrae 08.33
    multiple (two or more tendons) 15.3
  hand 82.29
  levator palpebrae 08.33
  tendon sheath 83.31
    hand 82.21
Tenodesis (tendon fixation to skeletal
  attachment) 83.88
  Fowler 82.85
  hand 82.85
Tenolysis 83.91
  hand 82.91
Tenomyoplasty (*see also* Repair, tendon) 83.88
  hand (*see also* Repair, tendon, hand) 82.86
Tenomyotomy —*see* Tenonectomy
Tenonectomy 83.42
  for graft 83.41
    hand 82.32
  hand 82.33
    for graft 82.32
Tenontomyoplasty —*see* Repair, tendon
Tenontoplasty —*see* Repair, tendon

                                    Transfusion

U

V

Vaccination (prophylactic) (against) 99.59
  anthrax 99.55
  brucellosis 99.55
  cholera 99.31
  common cold 99.51
  disease NEC 99.55
    arthropod-borne viral NEC 99.54
  encephalitis, arthropod-borne viral 99.53
  German measles 99.47
  hydrophobia 99.44
  infectious parotitis 99.46
  influenza 99.52
  measles 99.45
  mumps 99.46
  paratyphoid fever 99.32
  pertussis 99.37
  plague 99.34
  poliomyelitis 99.41
  rabies 99.44
  Rocky Mountain spotted fever 99.55
  rubella 99.47
  rubeola 99.45
  smallpox 99.42
  Staphylococcus 99.55
  Streptococcus 99.55
  tuberculosis 99.33
  tularemia 99.35
  typhoid 99.32
  typhus 99.55
  tumor 99.28
  undulant fever 99.55
  yellow fever 99.43
Vacuum extraction, fetal head 72.79
  with episiotomy 72.71
Vagectomy (subdiaphragmatic) (*see also*
  Vagotomy) 44.00
Vaginal douche 96.44
Vaginectomy 70.4
Vaginofixation 70.77
Vaginoperineotomy 70.14
Vaginoplasty 70.79
Vaginorrhaphy 70.71
  obstetrical 75.69
Vaginoscopy 70.21
Vaginotomy 70.14
  for
    culdocentesis 70.0
    pelvic abscess 70.12
Vagotomy (gastric) 44.00
  parietal cell 44.02
  selective NEC 44.03
    highly 44.02
    Holle's 44.02
    proximal 44.02
  truncal 44.01
Valvotomy —*see* Valvulotomy
Valvulectomy, heart —*see* Valvuloplasty, heart
Valvuloplasty
  heart (open heart technique) (without valve
    replacement) 35.10
    with prosthesis or tissue graft—*see*
      Replacement, heart, valve, by site
    aortic valve 35.11
      percutaneous (balloon) 35.96
    combined with repair of atrial and ventricular
      septal defects—*see* Repair, endocardial
      cushion defect
    mitral valve 35.12

Valvuloplasty—*continued*
    percutaneous (balloon) 35.96
    pulmonary valve 35.13
      in total repair of tetralogy of Fallot 35.81
      percutaneous (balloon) 35.96
    tricuspid valve 35.14
Valvulotomy
  heart (closed heart technique) (transatrial)
    (transventricular) 35.00
    aortic valve 35.01
    mitral valve 35.02
    open heart technique—*see* Valvuloplasty,
      heart
    pulmonary valve 35.03
      in total repair of tetralogy of Fallot 35.81
    tricuspid valve 35.04
Varicocelectomy, spermatic cord 63.1
Varicotomy, peripheral vessels (lower limb)
  38.59
  upper limb 38.53
Vascular closure, percutaneous puncture—*omit
  code*
Vascularization —*see* Revascularization
Vasectomy (complete) (partial) 63.73
Vasogram 87.94
Vasoligation 63.71
  gastric 38.86
Vasorrhaphy 63.81
Vasostomy 63.6
Vasotomy 63.6
Vasotripsy 63.71
Vasovasostomy 63.82
Vectorcardiogram (VCG) (with ECG) 89.53
Venectomy —*see* Phlebectomy
Venipuncture NEC 38.99
  for injection of contrast material—*see*
    Phlebography
Venography —*see* Phlebography
Venorrhaphy 39.32
Venotomy 38.00
  abdominal 38.07
  head and neck NEC 38.02
  intracranial NEC 38.01
  lower limb 38.09
  thoracic NEC 38.05
  upper limb 38.03
Venotripsy 39.98
Venovenostomy 39.29
Ventilation
  bi-level airway pressure 93.90
  continuous positive airway pressure [CPAP]
    93.90
  endotracheal respiratory assistance—*see*
    category 96.7
  intermittent positive airway pressure breathing
    [IPPB] 93.91
  mechanical
    endotracheal respiratory assistance—*see*
      category 96.7
    intermittent mandatory ventilation
      [IMV]—*see category* 96.7
    other continuous (unspecified duration) 96.70
      for less than 96 consecutive hours 96.71
      for 96 consecutive hours or more 96.72
    positive and expiratory pressure [PEEP]—*see*
      category 96.7
    pressure support ventilation [PSV]—*see*
      category 96.7
  negative pressure (continuous) [CNP] 93.99

W

SUMMARY OF ADDITIONS, DELETIONS AND REVISIONS TO VOLUME 3

01.59 Other excision or destruction of lesion or tissue of brain
Exclusion term revised

38.4 Resection of vessel with replacement
Exclusion term added

38.8 Other surgical occlusion of vessels
Exclusion term added

39.52 Other repair of aneurysm
Exclusion term added

39.7 Endovascular repair of vessel
New sub-category

39.71 Endovascular implantation of graft in abdominal aorta
New code

39.79 Other endovascular graft repair of aneurysm
New code

39.90 Insertion of non-coronary artery stent or stents
Exclusion term added

41.01 Autologous bone marrow transplant without purging
Code revised; inclusion terms deleted; exclusion term added

41.04 Autologous hematopoietic stem cell transplant without purging
Code revised; exclusion term added

41.05 Allogeneic hematopoietic stem cell transplant without purging
Code revised; exclusion term added

41.07 Autologous hematopoietic stem cell transplant with purging
New code

41.08 Allogeneic hematopoietic stem cell transplant with purging
New code

41.09 Autologous bone marrow transplant with purging
New code

46.97 Transplant of intestine
New code

54.19 Other laparotomy
Exclusion term added

54.24 Closed [percutaneous] [needle] biopsy of intra-abdominal mass
Inclusion term added

57.39 Other diagnostic procedures on bladder
Exclusion term added

60.96 Transurethral destruction of prostate tissue by microwave thermotherapy
New code

60.97 Other transurethral destruction of prostate tissue by other thermotherapy
New code

78.5 Internal fixation of bone without fracture reduction
Exclusion term revised

83.92 Insertion or replacement of skeletal muscle stimulator
Inclusion term added

84.11 Amputation of toe
Inclusion terms added

84.12 Amputation through foot
Inclusion term revised; exclusion term added

86.05 Incision with removal of foreign body from skin and subcutaneous tissue
Inclusion term added

86.09 Other incision of skin and subcutaneous tissue
Inclusion terms added

86.5 Suture or other closure of skin and subcutaneous tissue
Sub-category revised

86.59 Closure of skin and subcutaneous tissue of other sites
Code revised; inclusion terms added; exclusion term added

88.72 Diagnostic ultrasound of heart
Inclusion term added

99.10 Injection or infusion of thrombolytic agent
Exclusion term revised

99.20 Injection or infusion of platelet inhibitor
Exclusion term revised

99.29 Injection or infusion of other therapeutic or prophylactic substance
Exclusion term added

99.7 Therapeutic apheresis or other injection, administration, or infusion of other therapeutic or prophylactic substance
Sub-category revised

99.75 Administration of neuroprotective agent
New code

1792